W9-AXZ-253

King's Cross Station
KING'S CROSS
ST. PANCRAS
St. Pancras Station
Pentonville Rd.
ANGEL
City Rd.
Shepherdess Walk
East Rd.
Hoxton St.
Hackney Rd.
Lever St.
Old St.
OLD ST.
Gt. Eastern St.
Shoreditch High St.
Commercial St.
Woburn Pl.
Pancras Rd.
Midland Rd.
Gray's Inn Rd.
King's Cross Rd.
St. John's St.
Goswell Rd.
Bath Row
City Rd.
Bunhill Row
RUSSEL SQ.
BLOOMSBURY
CLERKENWELL
University College London
Montague Pl.
British Museum
Southampton Row
Theobalds Rd.
CHANCERY LANE
Clerkenwell Rd.
FARRINGDON
Aldersgate
BARBICAN
Beech St.
Barbican Centre
Chiswell St.
MOORGATE
Liverpool St. Station
LIVERPOOL ST.
Rosebery Ave.
Farringdon Rd.
Smithfield Market
London Wall
Moorgate
Houndsditch
ALDGATE
New Oxford St.
TOTTENHAM COURT RD.
HOLBORN
Lincoln's Inn Field
Royal Courts of Justice
High Holborn
Bloomsbury Way
Chancery Ln.
Holborn Viaduct
Newgate St.
Old Bailey
CITY OF LONDON
Bank of England
ST. PAUL'S
St. Paul's
Cheapside Poultry
Threadneedle
Cornhill
Leadenhall St.
Bishopsgate
Gracechurch St.
COVENT GARDEN
TOTTENHAM COURT RD.
Drury Ln.
Kingsway
Fleet St.
Ludgate Hill
Queen Victoria
BANK
Lombard St.
Fenchurch St. Station
TOWER HILL
LEICESTER SQ.
COVENT GARDEN
ALDWYCH
STRAND
TEMPLE
BLACKFRIARS
Queen Victoria St.
MANSION HOUSE
Cannon St.
CANNON ST.
MONUMENT
Eastcheap
National Gallery
Charing Cross Station
CHARING CROSS
EMBANKMENT
Lancaster Pl.
Waterloo Bridge
Victoria Embankment
Blackfriars Station
Blackfriars Bridge
Millennium Bridge
Southwark Bridge
Cannon St. Station
London Bridge
Upper Thames St.
The Tower of London
Tower Bridge
Hungerford Footbridge
National Theatre
Tate Modern
Globe Theatre
River Thames
WESTMINSTER
Big Ben
Houses of Parliament
Westminster Abbey
Westminster Br.
York Rd.
Stamford St.
SOUTHWARK
WATERLOO
Waterloo Station
LAMBETH NORTH
Southwark St.
Union St.
SOUTH BANK
BOROUGH
LONDON BRIDGE
London Bridge Station
Tooley St.
Long Ln.
Tower Bridge Rd.
Abbey St.
Horseferry Rd.
Tate Britain
Lambeth Bridge
LAMBETH
Lambeth Palace Rd.
Lambeth Rd.
Bridge Rd.
Borough Rd.
Imperial War Museum
ELEPHANT & CASTLE
London Rd.
New Kent Rd.
Harper Rd.
Great Dover St.
Tabard St.
Willow Walk
Old Kent Rd.
Albert Embankment
Black Prince Rd.
Kennington Rd.
Walworth Rd.
Rodney Pl.
Flint St.
East St.
New Kent Rd.
Regency St.
Vauxhall Bridge
VAUXHALL
Vauxhall Station
Kennington Ln.
KENNINGTON
Manor Pl.
Braganza St.
Crampton St.
Portland St.
Albany Rd.
Thurlow Rd.
South Lambeth Rd.
Wandsworth Rd.
Fentiman Rd.
The Oval
OVAL
Clapham Rd.
Brixton Rd.
Yassall Rd.
Camberwell New Rd.
John Ruskin St.
Camberwell Rd.
N

0   500 yards
0   500 meters

London Overview

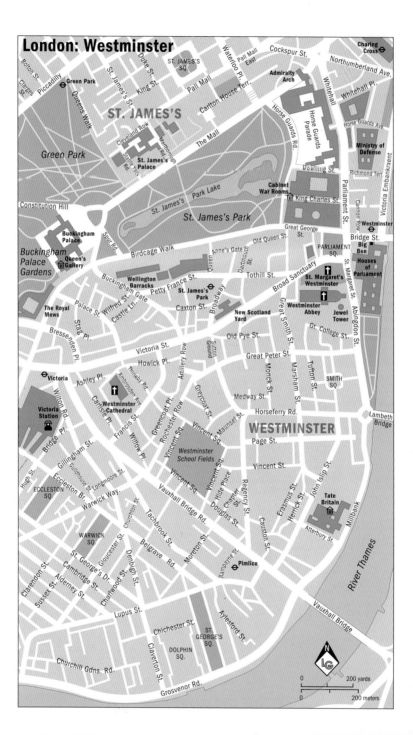

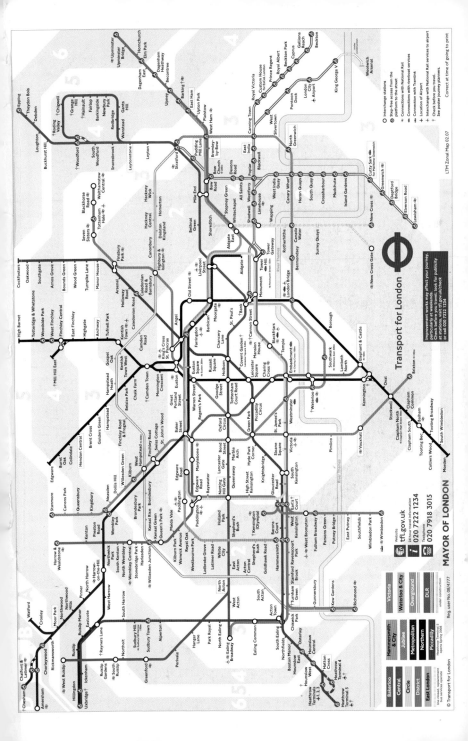

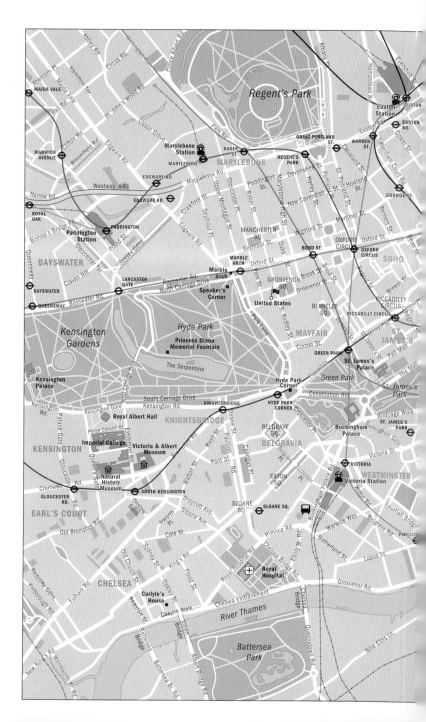

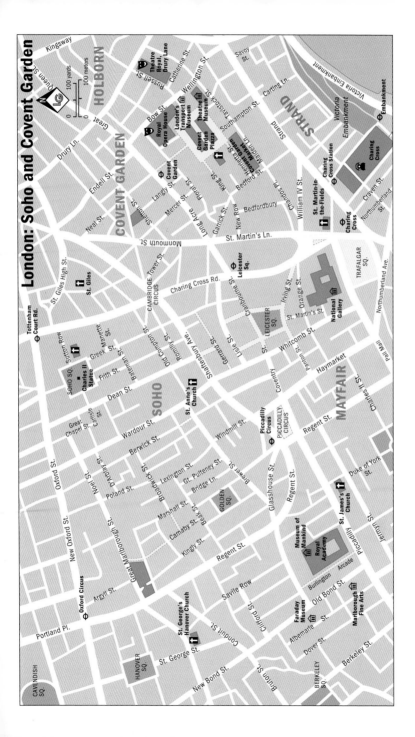

London: Soho and Covent Garden

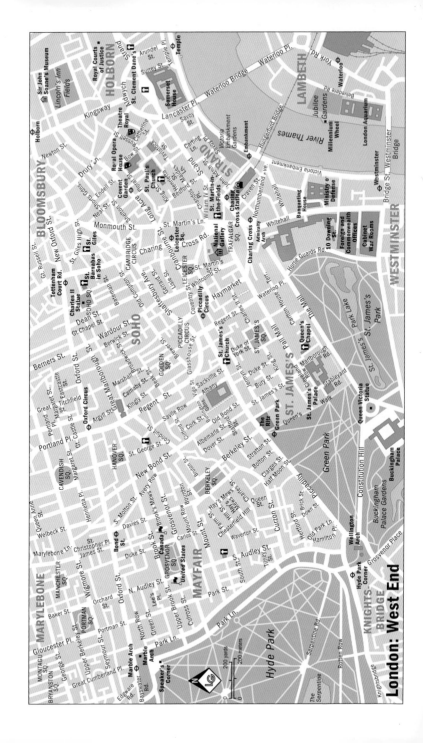

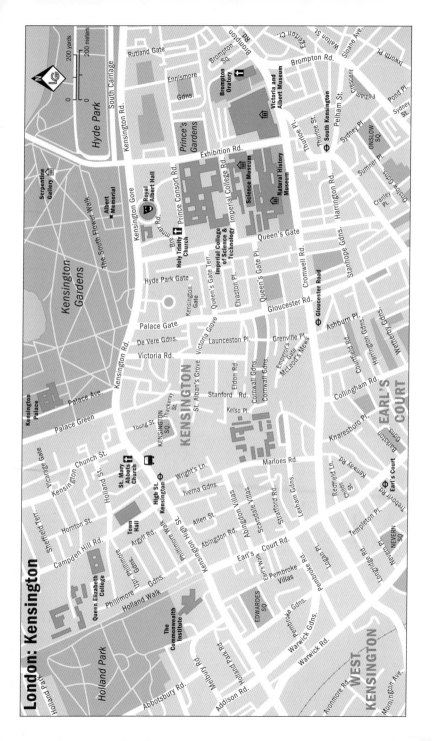

London: Kensington

London: Notting Hill and Bayswater

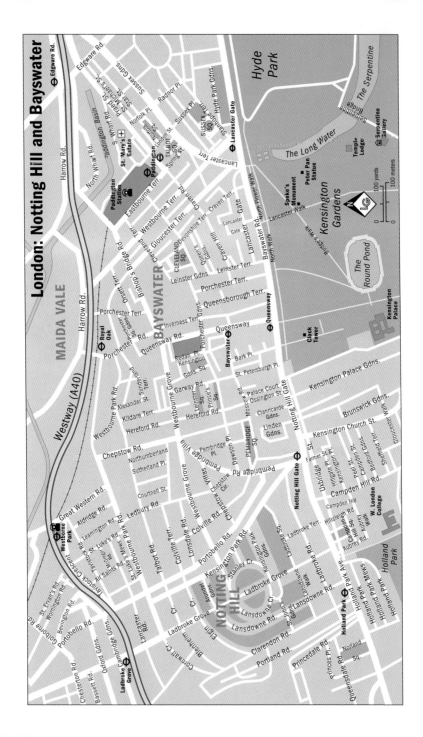

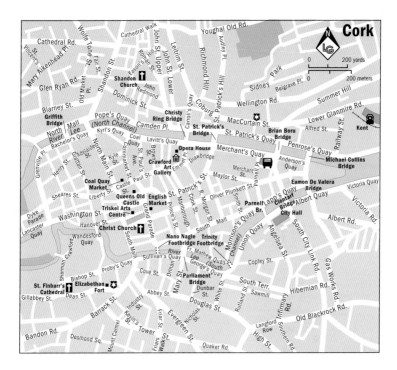

Cork

N LG

0   200 yards

0   200 meters

Cathedral Walk   Youghal Old Rd.

Cathedral Rd.

St. Vincent's St.

Wolfe Tone St.

John St. Upper

John St. Lower

Leitrim St.

Richmond Hill

Patrick's Hill

Audley Pl.

Richmond Hill

Sidney   Park

Belgrave Pl.

Summer Hill

Mary Aikenhead Pl.

Glen Ryan Rd.

Shandon St.

Old Market Pl.

John Redmond

Shandon Church

Dominick St.

Coburg

Wellington Rd.

Lower Glanmire Rd.

Alfred St.

Railway St.

Kent

Blarney St.

Griffith Bridge

Pope's Quay (North Channel)

Christy Ring Bridge

Camden Pl.

Carroll's Quay

MacCurtain St.

St. Patrick's Bridge

Brian Boru Bridge

St. Patrick's Quay

Penrose's Quay

Michael Collins Bridge

North Mall

River Lee

Bachelor's Quay

Kyrl's Quay

Lavitt's Quay

Merchant's Quay

Anderson's Quay

Grenville Pl.

Henry St.

Grattan St.

Adelaide St.

North Main St.

Kyle St.

Coal Quay

St. Paul's Ave.

Browning St.

Emmet Pl.

Opera House

Crawford Art Gallery

Drawbridge

Merchant's Quay

Coal Quay Market

Castle St.

Paul St.

Queens Old Castle

Triskel Arts Centre

English Market

Cornmarket St.

St. Patrick's St.

Oliver Plunkett St.

Lapp's Quay

Eamon De Valera Bridge

Clontarf Bridge

Albert Quay

Victoria Quay

Sheares St.

Liberty St.

Grand Parade

Prince's St.

Cook St.

Morgan St.

Marlborough

Parnell Br.

City Hall

Albert Rd.

Dyke Parade

Washington St.

Hanover St.

Christ Church

South Mall

Morrison's Quay

Union Quay

Anglesea St.

South City Link Rd.

Lancaster Quay

Wandesford Quay

South Main

Nano Nagle Footbridge

Trinity Footbridge

Fr. Mathew Quay

Lee

George's Quay

South

Copley St.

Gas Works Rd.

Sharman Crawford St.

Bishop St.

Proby's Quay

Cove St.

Sullivan's Quay

Mary St.

Drinan St.

South (Channel)

St. Finbarr's Cathedral

Elizabethan Fort

Parliament Bridge

Dunbar St.

South Terr.

Hibernian Rd.

Gillabbey St.

Dean St.

Abbey St.

Sawmill

Rutland St.

Infirmary Rd.

Old Blackrock Rd.

Bandon Rd.

Barrack St.

Industry St.

Kev'n St.

Friar St.

Friars Walk

Evergreen St.

Douglas St.

High St.

Langford Row

Southern Rd.

Desmond Sq.

Mount Carmel

Quaker Rd.

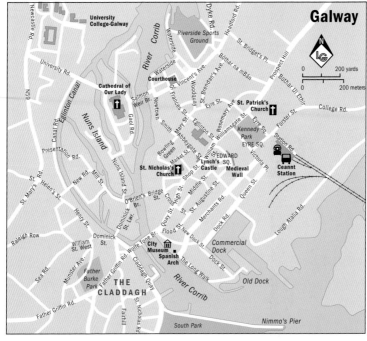

Galway

N LG

0   200 yards

0   200 meters

Newcastle Rd.

University College-Galway

River Corrib

Waterside

Dyke Rd.

Riverside Sports Ground

Headford Rd.

St. Bridger's Pl.

Prospect Hill

Bothar Ui Eithir

University Rd.

N59

Eglinton Canal

Canal Rd.

Nuns Island

Cathedral of Our Lady

Courthouse

Salmon Weir Br.

Gaol Rd.

Newtown Smith

Waterside

St. Vincent's Ave.

Frances St.

St. Brendan's Ave.

Bothar na mBán

Eyre St.

St. Patrick's Church

Forster St.

College Rd.

Presentation Rd.

Nuns Island Rd.

Bowling Green

Mary St.

Abbeygate St.

Eglinton St.

Williamsgate St.

Rosemary Ave.

Kennedy Park

EYRE SQ.

Station Rd.

Ceannt Station

St. Mary's Rd.

St. Helen's St.

New Rd.

Mill St.

St. Nicholas's Church

Lynch's Castle

Market St.

Shop St.

High St.

St. EDWARD SQ.

Medieval Wall

Victoria St.

Queen St.

Lough Atalia Rd.

Raleigh Row

Henry St.

O'Brien's Bridge Br.

Dominick St. Lwr.

Cross St.

Middle St.

St. Augustine St.

Merchants Rd.

Dock St.

Commercial Dock

William St. West

Dominick St.

Wolfe Tone Br.

Griffin Rd.

Quay St.

Flood St.

New Dock St.

Dock St.

Sea Rd.

Munster Ave.

Father Burke Park

Father Griffin Rd.

City Museum

Spanish Arch

Claddagh Quay

The Long Walk

Old Dock

THE CLADDAGH

Father Griffin Rd.

Faithill

St. Nicholas Rd.

River Corrib

South Park

Nimmo's Pier

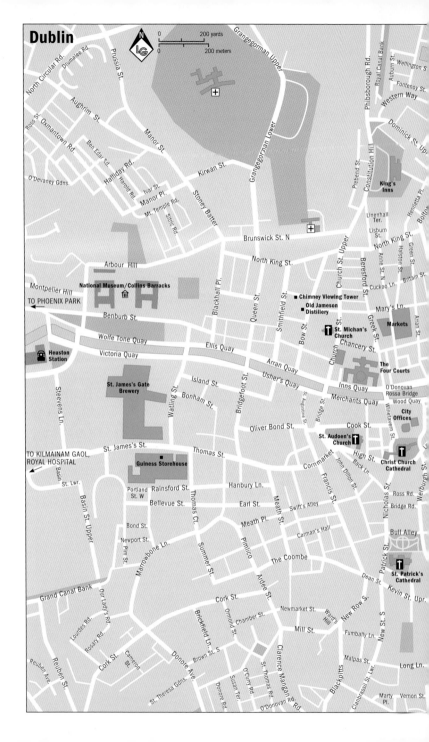

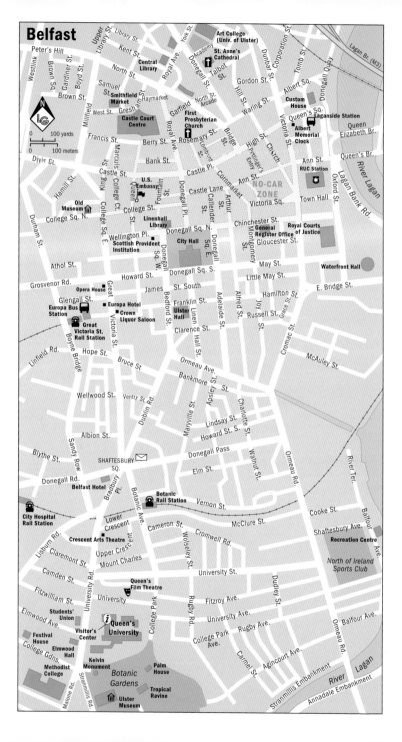

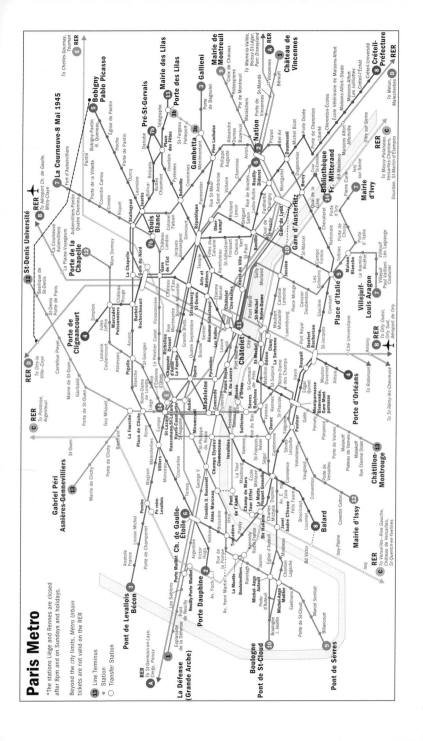

Paris: Overview and Arrondissements

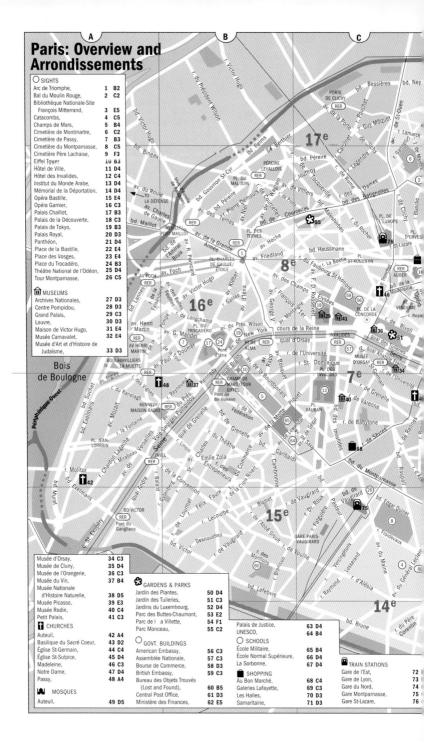

SIGHTS

Arc de Triomphe,	1 B2
Bal du Moulin Rouge,	2 C2
Bibliothèque Nationale-Site François Mitterrand,	3 E5
Catacombs,	4 C5
Champs de Mars,	5 B4
Cimetière de Montmartre,	6 C2
Cimetière de Passy,	7 B3
Cimetière de Montparnasse,	8 C5
Cimetière Père Lachaise,	9 F3
Eiffel Tower	10 B3
Hôtel de Ville,	11 D4
Hôtel des Invalides,	12 C4
Institut du Monde Arabe,	13 D4
Mémorial de la Déportation,	14 D4
Opéra Bastille,	15 E4
Opéra Garnier,	16 C3
Palais Chaillot,	17 B3
Palais de la Découverte,	18 C3
Palais de Tokyo,	19 B3
Palais Royal,	20 D3
Panthéon,	21 D4
Place de la Bastille,	22 E4
Place des Vosges,	23 E4
Place du Trocadéro,	24 B3
Théâtre National de l'Odéon,	25 D4
Tour Montparnasse,	26 C5

MUSEUMS

Archives Nationales,	27 D3
Centre Pompidou,	28 D3
Grand Palais,	29 C3
Louvre,	30 D3
Maison de Victor Hugo,	31 E4
Musée Carnavalet,	32 E4
Musée d'Art et d'Histoire de Judaisme,	33 D3
Musée d'Orsay,	34 C3
Musée de Cluny,	35 D4
Musée de l'Orangerie,	36 C3
Musée du Vin,	37 B4
Musée Nationale d'Histoire Naturelle,	38 D5
Musée Picasso,	39 E3
Musée Rodin,	40 C4
Petit Palais,	41 C3

CHURCHES

Auteuil,	42 A4
Basilique du Sacré Coeur,	43 D2
Église St-Germain,	44 C4
Église St-Sulpice,	45 D4
Madeleine,	46 C3
Notre Dame,	47 D4
Passy,	48 A4

MOSQUES

Auteuil,	49 D5

GARDENS & PARKS

Jardin des Plantes,	50 D4
Jardin des Tuileries,	51 C3
Jardins du Luxembourg,	52 D4
Parc des Buttes-Chaumont,	53 E2
Parc de l a Villette,	54 F1
Parc Monceau,	55 C2

GOVT. BUILDINGS

American Embassy,	56 C3
Assemblée Nationale,	57 C3
Bourse de Commerce,	58 D3
British Embassy,	59 C3
Bureau des Objets Trouvés (Lost and Found),	60 B5
Central Post Office,	61 D3
Ministère des Finances,	62 E5
Palais de Justice,	63 D4
UNESCO,	64 B4

SCHOOLS

École Militaire,	65 B4
École Normal Supérieure,	66 D4
La Sorbonne,	67 D4

SHOPPING

Au Bon Marché,	68 C4
Galeries Lafayette,	69 C3
Les Halles,	70 D3
Samaritaine,	71 D3

TRAIN STATIONS

Gare de l'Est,	72
Gare de Lyon,	73
Gare du Nord,	74
Gare Montparnasse,	75
Gare St-Lazare,	76

Bois de Boulogne

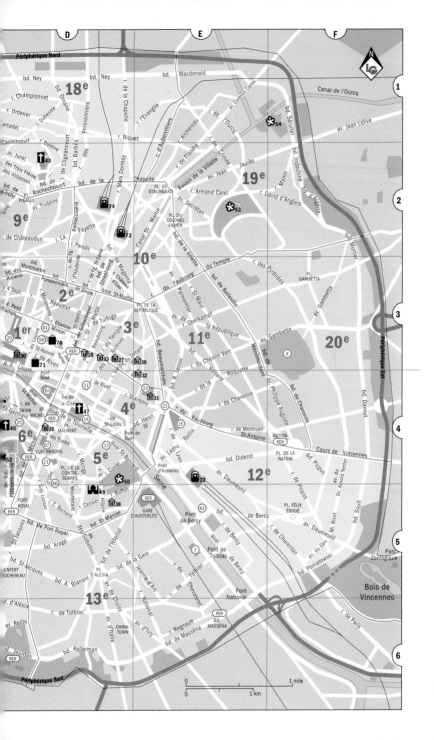

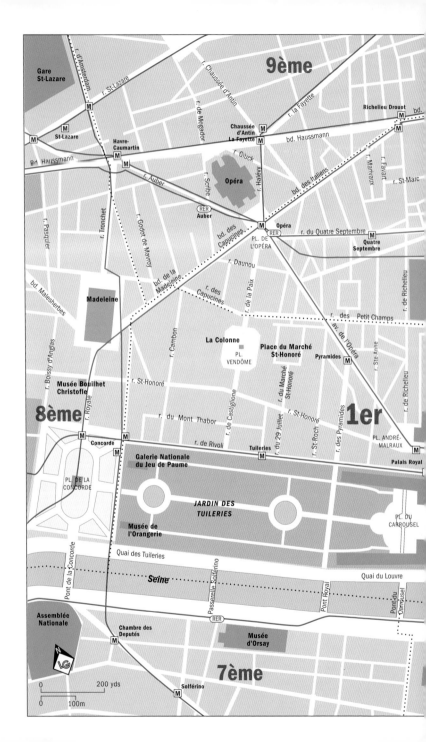

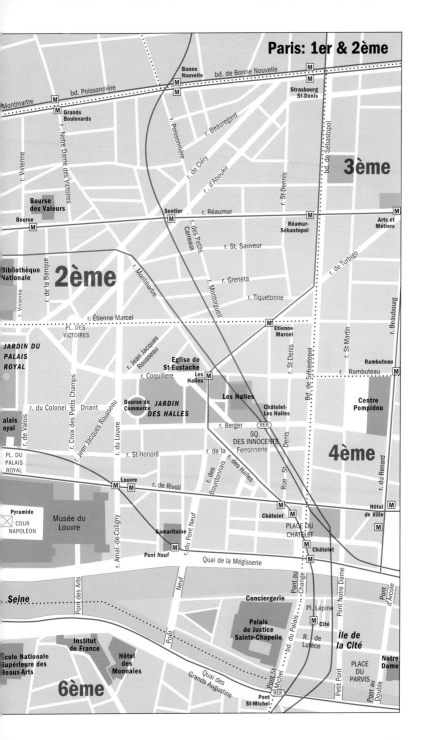

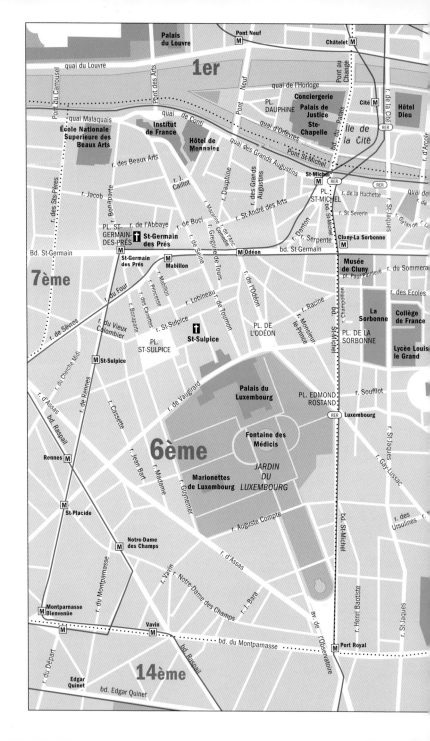

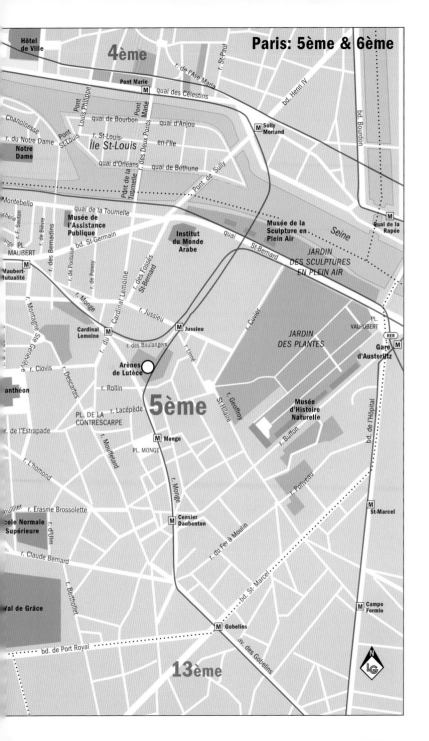

Hôtel de Ville

4ème

r. de St-Paul

r. de l'Ave Maria

Pont Marie
M
quai des Célestins

bd. Henri IV

quai de Bourbon

Pont Louis Philippe

Pont Marie

quai d'Anjou

M **Sully Morland**

bd. Bourdon

Chanoinesse

Pont St-Louis

r. St-Louis- **Île St-Louis**

r. du Notre Dame

Notre Dame

en-l'Île

quai d'Orléans

r. des Deux Ponts

quai de Béthune

Pont de la Tournelle

Pont de Sully

Montebello

cherie

r. F. Sauton

ange

quai de la Tournelle

r. de Bièvre

Musée de l'Assistance Publique

bd. St-Germain

Musée de la Sculpture en Plein Air

Seine

M **Quai de la Rapée**

PL. **MAUBERT**

r. des Bernardins

r. de Pontoise

r. de Poissy

r. des Fossés St-Bernard

Institut du Monde Arabe

quai

quai St-Bernard

JARDIN DES SCULPTURES EN PLEIN AIR

M **Maubert-Mutualité**

r. Cardinal Lemoine

r. Monge

r. Jussieu

M **Jussieu**

r. Cuvier

PL. **VALHUBERT**

RER

M

Cardinal Lemoine
M

r. du Cardinal Lemoine

r. des Boulangers

r. Linné

JARDIN DES PLANTES

Gare d'Austerlitz

r. Montagne Ste Geneviève

r. Clovis

r. Descartes

Arènes de Lutèce
○

r. Rollin

5ème

r. Geoffroy

St-Hilaire

Musée d'Histoire Naturelle

bd. de l'Hôpital

anthéon

PL. DE LA **CONTRESCARPE**

r. Lacépède

r. Mouffetard

r. de l'Estrapade

M **Monge**

PL. MONGE

r. Buffon

r. L'homond

r. Monge

r. Poliveau

uillier

r. Erasme Brossolette

r. d'Ulm

M **Censier Daubenton**

M **St-Marcel**

cole Normale Supérieure

r. Claude Bernard

r. du Fer à Moulin

r. Berthollet

al de Grâce

bd. St-Marcel

M **Campo Formio**

M **Gobelins**

bd. de Port Royal

av. des Gobelins

13ème

N

LG

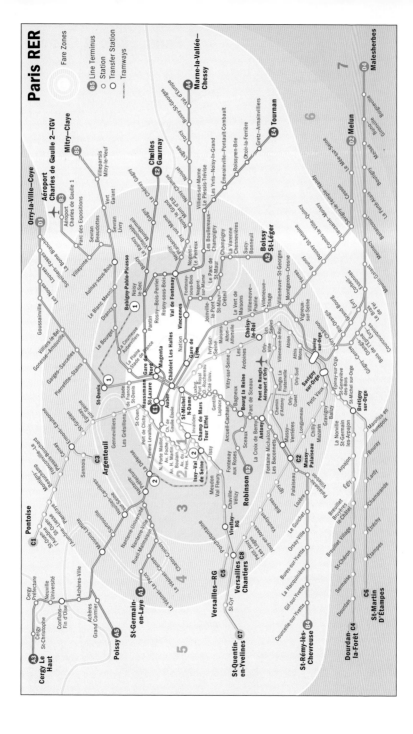

Paris RER

Berlin Transit

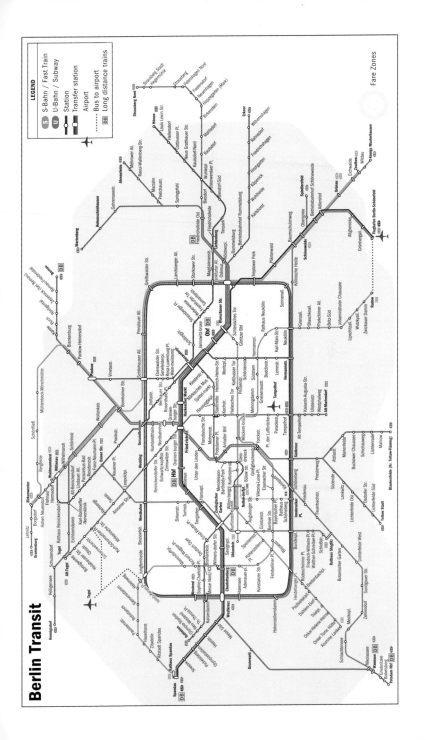

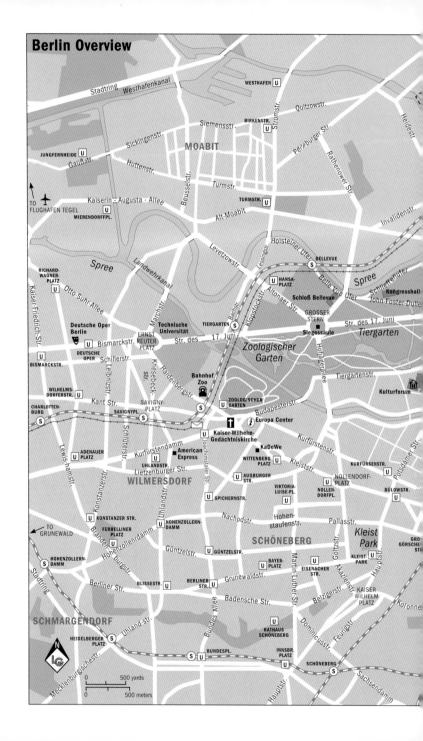

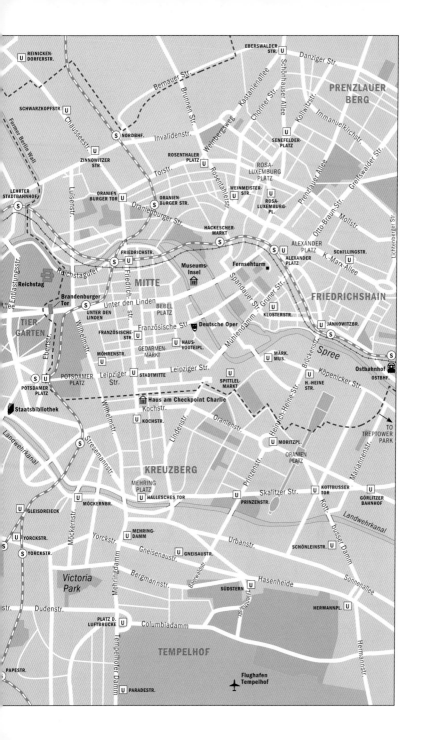

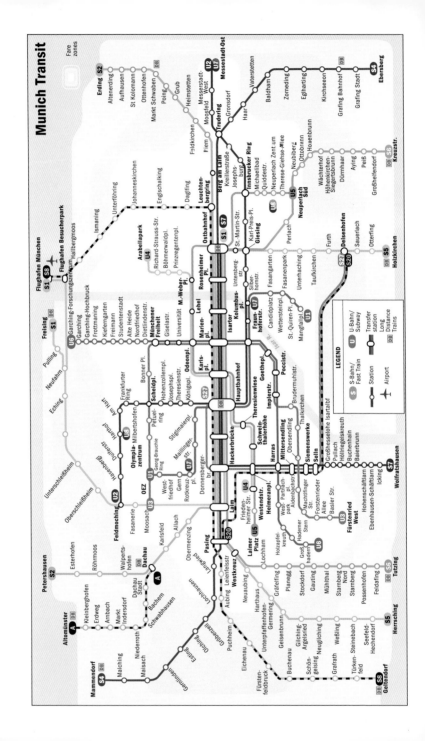

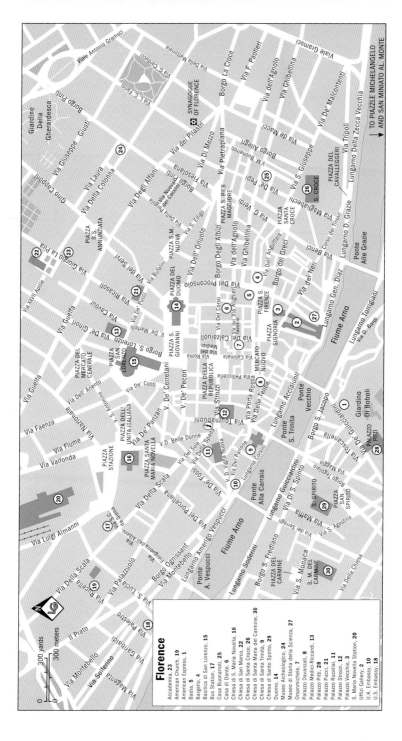

Florence

Accademia, **23**
American Church, **19**
American Express, **1**
Badia, **5**
Bargello, **4**
Basilica di San Lorenzo, **15**
Bus Station, **17**
Casa Buonarroti, **25**
Casa di Dante, **6**
Chiesa di S. Maria Novella, **16**
Chiesa di San Marco, **22**
Chiesa di Santa Croce, **26**
Chiesa di Santa Maria del Carmine, **30**
Chiesa di Santa Trinita, **9**
Chiesa di Santo Spirito, **29**
Duomo, **14**
Museo Archeologico, **24**
Museo di Storia della Scienza, **27**
Orsanmichele, **7**
Palazzo Davanzati, **8**
Palazzo Medici-Riccardi, **13**
Palazzo Pitti, **28**
Palazzo Pucci, **21**
Palazzo Rucellai, **11**
Palazzo Strozzi, **12**
Palazzo Vecchio, **3**
S. Maria Novella Station, **20**
Uffizi Gallery, **2**
U.K. Embassy, **10**
U.S. Embassy, **18**

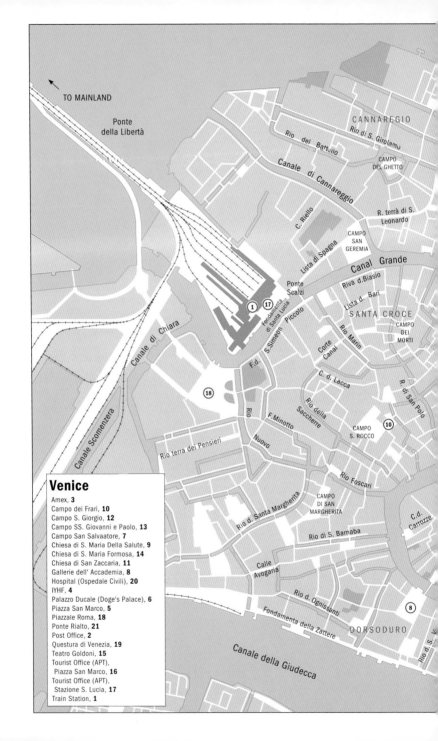

TO MAINLAND

Ponte
della Libertà

CANNAREGIO

Rio di S. Girolamo

Rio del Battello

CAMPO
DEL GHETTO

Canale di Cannaregio

C. Riello

R. terrà di S.
Leonardo

CAMPO
SAN
GEREMIA

Lista di Spagna

Canal Grande

Ponte
Scalzi

Riva d.Biasio

Lista d. Bari

Fondamenta
di Santa Lucia

F.d. S.Simeon Piccolo

SANTA CROCE

CAMPO
DEI
MORTI

Canale di Chiara

Corte
Canal

Rio Marin

C. d. Lacca

R. di San Polo

Rio della
Saccherre

Rio
Nuovo

F.Minotto

CAMPO
S. ROCCO

Rio terra dei Pensieri

Rio Foscari

Canale Scomenzera

CAMPO
DI SAN
MARGHERITA

Rio d. Santa Margherita

C.d.
Carrozze

Rio di S. Barnaba

Calle
Avogaria

Rio d. Ognissanti

Fondamenta della Zattere

DORSODURO

Rio d. S. V

Canale della Giudecca

Venice

Amex, **3**
Campo dei Frari, **10**
Campo S. Giorgio, **12**
Campo SS. Giovanni e Paolo, **13**
Campo San Salvaatore, **7**
Chiesa di S. Maria Della Salute, **9**
Chiesa di S. Maria Formosa, **14**
Chiesa di San Zaccaria, **11**
Gallerie dell' Accademia, **8**
Hospital (Ospedale Civili), **20**
IYHF, **4**
Palazzo Ducale (Doge's Palace), **6**
Piazza San Marco, **5**
Piazzale Roma, **18**
Ponte Rialto, **21**
Post Office, **2**
Questura di Venezia, **19**
Teatro Goldoni, **15**
Tourist Office (APT),
 Piazza San Marco, **16**
Tourist Office (APT),
 Stazione S. Lucia, **17**
Train Station, **1**

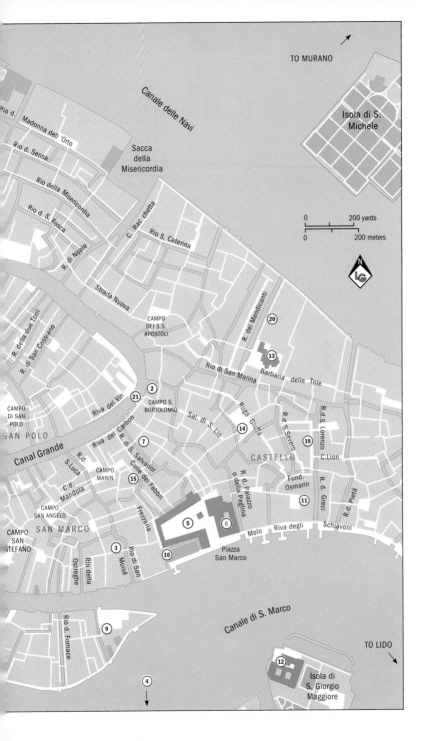

TO MURANO

Isola di S. Michele

Canale delle Navi

Rio d.
Madonna dell 'Orto

Rio d. Sensa

Rio della Misericordia

Rio d. S. Fosca

Sacca
della
Misericordia

R.' di Noale

C. Racchetta

Rio S. Caterina

Strada Nuova

R. della due Torri

R. d. San Cassiano

R.' di Noale

CAMPO
DEI S.S.
APOSTOLI

R. dei Mendicanti

20

13

Rio di San Marina

Barbaria delle Tole

2

21

Riva del Vin

CAMPO S.
BORTOLOMIO

Sal. di S. Lio

Ruga Giuffa

R. d. S. Severo

R. d. S. Lorenzo

CAMPO
DI SAN
POLO

SAN POLO

Canal Grande

Riva del Carbon

R. d. S. Salvador

7

14

CASTELLO

C. Lion

19

R. d.
S. Luca

CAMPO
MANIN

Calle dei Fabbri

15

R. d. Palazzo
o della Paglina

Fond.
Osmarin

R. d. Greci

R. di Pietà

C. d.
Mandola

CAMPO
SAN ANGELO

Frezzaria

11

CAMPO
SAN
STEFANO

SAN MARCO

3

Rio di San
Moisè

5

6

Molo   Riva degli   Schiavoni

Ostreghe

Rio della

16

Piazza
San Marco

9

Rio d. Fornace

Canale di S. Marco

TO LIDO

4

12

Isola di
S. Giorgio
Maggiore

0   200 yards

0   200 meters

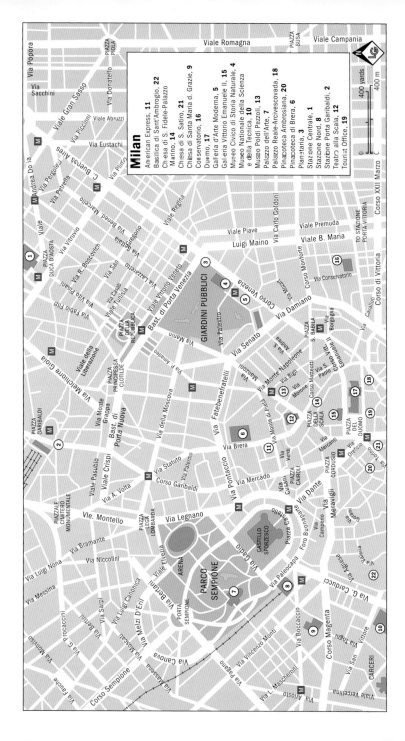

Milan

American Express, **11**
Basilica di Sant'Ambrogio, **22**
Chiesa di S. Fidele-Palazzo Marino, **14**
Chiesa di S. Satiro, **21**
Chiesa di Santa Maria d. Grazie, **9**
Conservatorio, **16**
Duomo, **17**
Galleria d'Arte Moderna, **5**
Galleria Vittorio Emanuele II, **15**
Museo Civico di Storia Naturale, **4**
Museo Nazionale della Scienza e della Tecnica, **10**
Museo Poldi Pezzoli, **13**
Palazzo dell'Arte, **7**
Palazzo Reale-Arcivescovada, **18**
Pinacoteca Ambrosiana, **20**
Pinacoteca di Brera, **6**
Planetaria, **3**
Stazione Centrale, **1**
Stazione Nord, **8**
Stazione Porta Garibaldi, **2**
Teatro alla Scala, **12**
Tourist Office, **19**

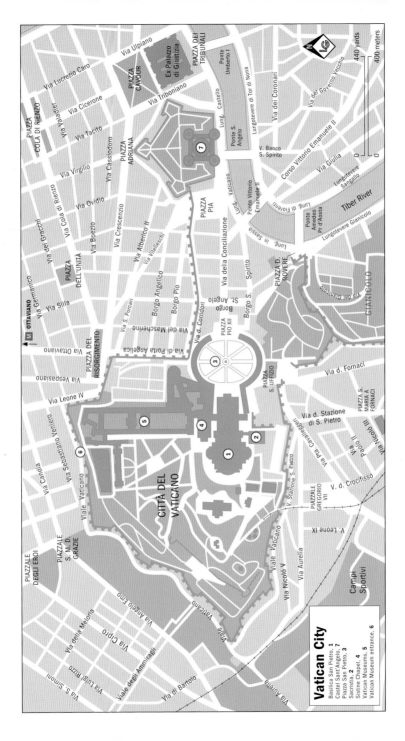

Vatican City

Basilica San Pietro, **1**
Castel Sant'Angelo, **7**
Piazza San Pietro, **3**
Sacristia, **2**
Sistine Chapel, **4**
Vatican Museums, **5**
Vatican Museum entrance, **6**

440 yards

400 meters

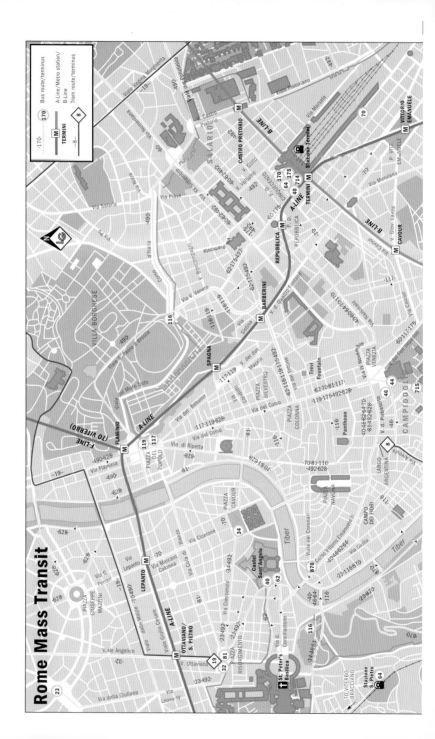

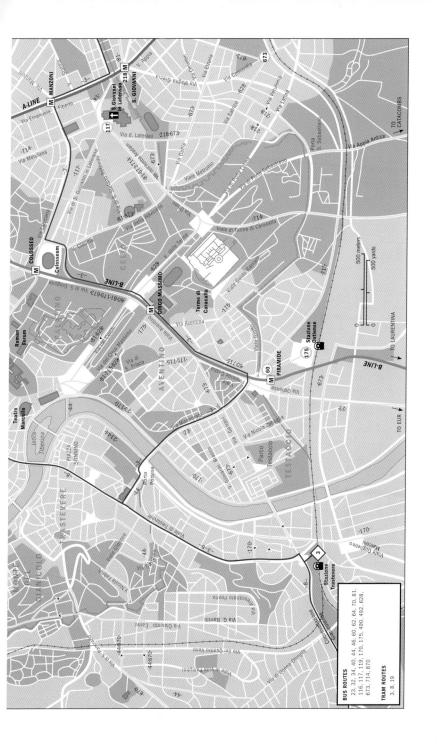

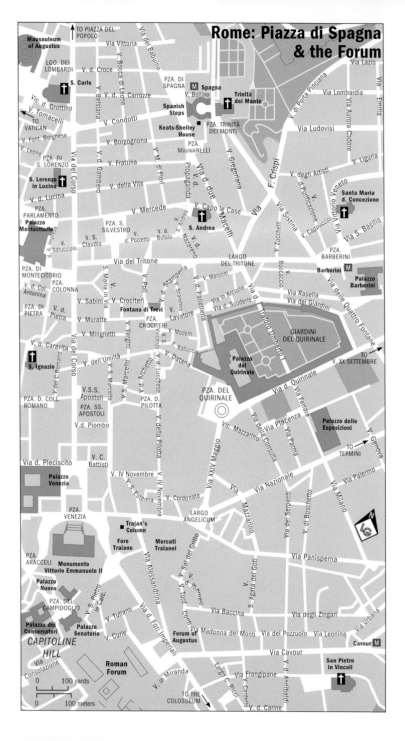

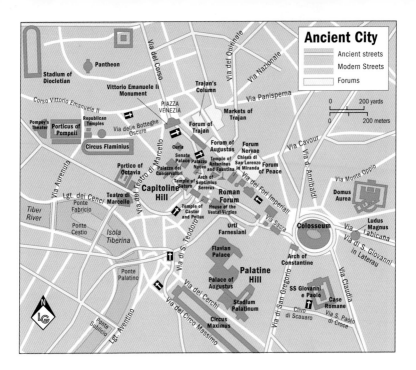

Ancient City

- Ancient streets
- Modern Streets
- Forums

| 0 | 200 yards |
| 0 | 200 meters |

Stadium of Diocletian
Pantheon
Via del Corso
Via del Quirinale
Via Nazionale
Vittorio Emanuele II Monument
Trajan's Column
Via Panisperna
Corso Vittorio Emanuele II
PIAZZA VENEZIA
Markets of Trajan
Via Cavour
Pompey's Theater
Porticus of Pompeii
Republican Temples
Via delle Botteghe Oscure
Forum of Trajan
Circus Flaminius
Curia
Senate Palace Palazzo Nuovo
Forum of Augustus
Forum Nervae
Temple of Antoninus and Faustina
Chiesa di San Lorenzo in Miranda
Forum of Peace
Via d. Annibaldi
Portico of Octavia
Palazzo dei Conservatori
Temple of Saturn
Arch of Septimius Severus
Via dei Fori Imperiali
Via Monte Oppio
Via Aurelia
Lgt. dei Cenci
Ponte Fabricio
Teatro di Marcello
Capitoline Hill
Temple of Castor and Pollux
House of the Vestal Virgins
Roman Forum
Domus Aurea
Tiber River
Ponte Cestio
Isola Tiberina
Via di S. Teodoro
Orti Farnesiani
Via Sacra
Colosseum
Via Labicana
Ludus Magnus
Via di S. Giovanni in Laterau
Ponte Palatino
Flavian Palace
Palatine Hill
Arch of Constantine
Via Claudia
Via di San Gregorio
SS Giovanni e Paolo
Case Romane
Ponte Subliclo
Lgt. Aventino
Via dei Cerchi
Palace of Augustus
Stadium Palatinum
Circus Maximus
Via dei Circo Massimo
Clivo di Scauaro
Via S. Paolo di Croce

LG

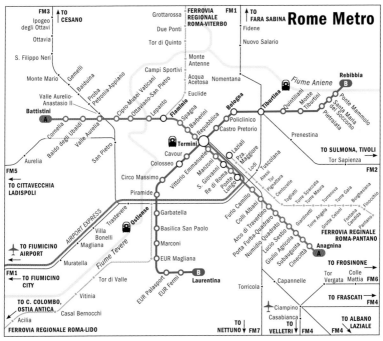

Rome Metro

FM3
Ipogeo degli Ottavi
TO CESANO
Grottarossa
FERROVIA REGIONALE ROMA-VITERBO
FM1
TO FARA SABINA
Ottavia
Due Ponti
Fidene
S. Filippo Neri
Tor di Quinto
Nuovo Salario
Monte Antenne
Campi Sportivi
Monte Mario
Gemelli
Balduina
Acqua Acetosa
Nomentana
Fiume Aniene
Rebibbia
Valle Aurelio-Anastasio II
Proba Petronia-Appiano
Cipro-Musei Vaticani
Euclide
B
Battistini
A
Ottaviano-San Pietro
Lepanto
Flaminio
Spagna
Barberini
Repubblica
Bologna
Tiburtina
Quintiliani
Monte Tiburtini
Ponte Mammolo
Santa Maria del Soccorso
Pietralata
Cornelia
Baldo degli Ubaldi
Valle Aurelia
San Pietro
Policlinico
Castro Pretorio
Prenestina
Aurelia
Termini
Cavour
Vittorio Emanuele
Manzoni
S. Giovanni
Re di Roma
Pza Ldiali
Pza Maggiore
Lodi
TO SULMONA, TIVOLI
Tor Sapienza
FM5
TO CITTAVECCHIA LADISPOLI
Colosseo
Circo Massimo
Ponte Lungo
Tuscolana
Alessi
Tor Pignattara
FM2
Piramide
AIRPORT EXPRESS
Garbatella
Furio Camillo
Centocelle
Togliatti
Torre Spaccata
Giardinetti
Torre Maura
Torrenova
Torre Gaia
Borghesiana
Trastevere
Ostense
Villa Bonelli
Magliana
Basilica San Paolo
Colli Albani
Arco di Travertino
Porta Furba-Quadraro
Torre Angela
Grotte Celoni
Giardini
Fontana Candida
Finocchio
Pantano
FERROVIA REGIONALE ROMA-PANTANO
TO FIUMICINO AIRPORT
Muratella
Fiume Tevere
Marconi
Numidio Quadrato
Lucio Sestio
Giulio Agricola
Subaugusta
Cinecittà
Anagnina
A
FM1
TO FIUMICINO CITY
Tor di Valle
EUR Magliana
EUR Palasport
EUR Fermi
Laurentina
B
Torricola
Capannelle
TO FROSINONE
Tor Vergata
Colle Mattia
FM6
Vitinia
TO C. COLOMBO, OSTIA ANTICA
Casal Bernocchi
Acilia
FERROVIA REGIONALE ROMA-LIDO
Ciampino
Casabianca
TO NETTUNO
FM7
TO VELLETRI
FM4
FM4
TO FRASCATI
FM4
TO ALBANO LAZIALE

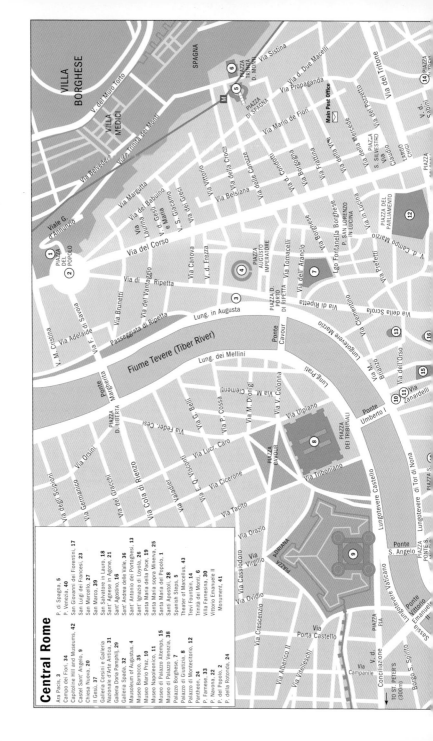

Central Rome

Ara Pacis, **3**
Campo dei Fiori, **34**
Capitoline Hill and Museums, **42**
Castel Sant' Angelo, **9**
Chiesa Nuova, **20**
Il Gesù, **37**
Galleria Corsini e Galleria
Nazionale d'Arte Antica, **31**
Galleria Doria Pamphilj, **29**
Galleria Spada, **32**
Mausoleum of Augustus, **4**
Museo Barrocco, **35**
Museo Mario Praz, **10**
Museo Napoleonico, **11**
Museo di Palazzo Altemps, **15**
Museo di Palazzo Venezia, **38**
Palazzo Borghese, **7**
Palazzo di Giustizia, **8**
Palazzo di Montecitorio, **12**
Pantheon, **24**
P. Farnese, **33**
P. Navona, **22**
P. del Popolo, **2**
P. della Rotonda, **24**

P. di Spagna, **5**
P. Venezia, **40**
San Giovanni dei Fiorentini, **17**
San Luigi dei Francesi, **23**
San Marcello, **27**
San Marco, **39**
San Salvatore in Lauro, **18**
Sant' Agnese in Agone, **21**
Sant' Agostino, **16**
Sant' Andrea delle Valle, **36**
Sant' Antonio dei Portoghesi, **13**
Sant' Ignazio di Loyola, **26**
Santa Maria della Pace, **19**
Santa Maria sopra Minerva, **25**
Santa Maria del Popolo, **1**
Santi Apostoli, **28**
Spanish Steps, **5**
Theater of Marcellus, **43**
Trevi Fountain, **14**
Trinità dei Monti, **6**
Villa Farnesina, **30**
Vittorio Emanuele II
Monument, **41**

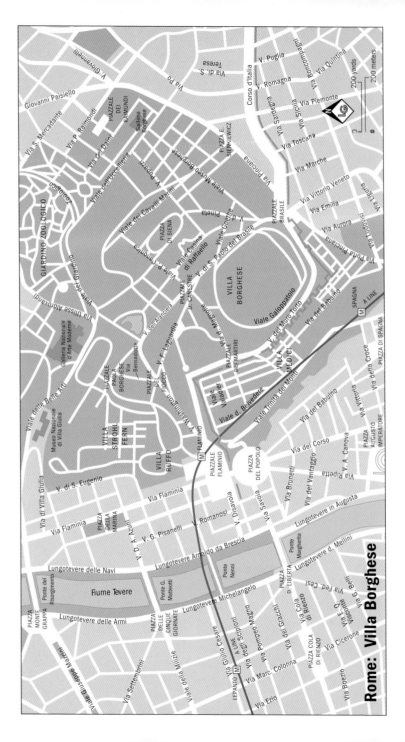

Rome: Villa Borghese

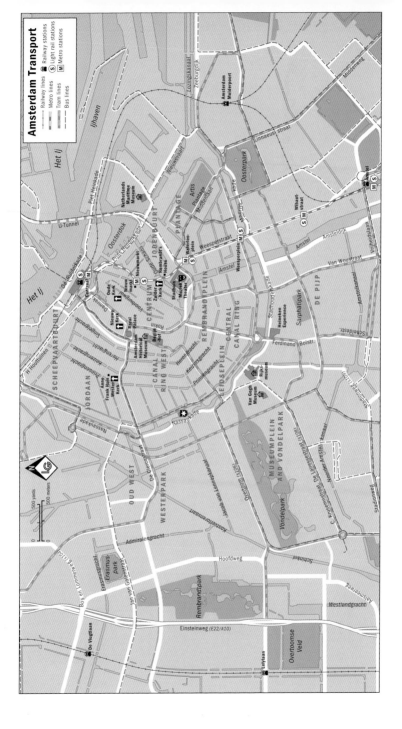

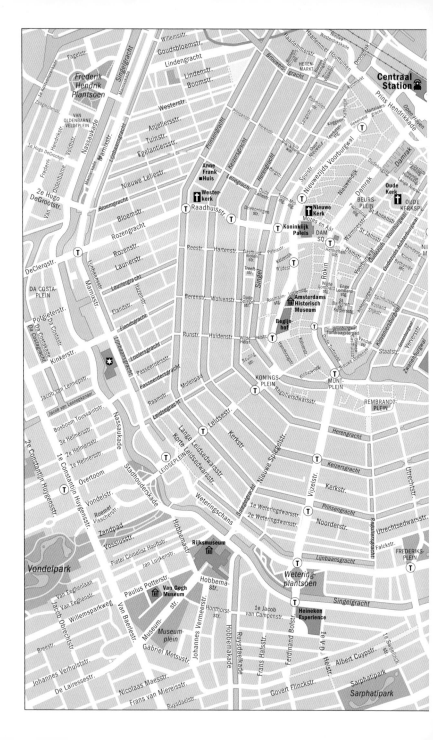

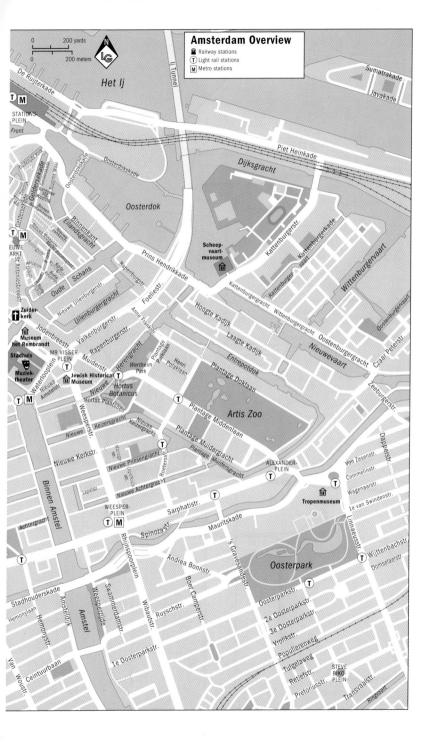

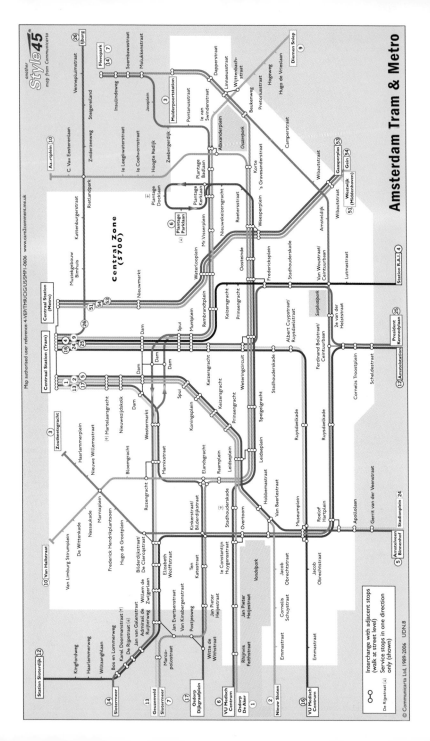

Amsterdam Tram & Metro

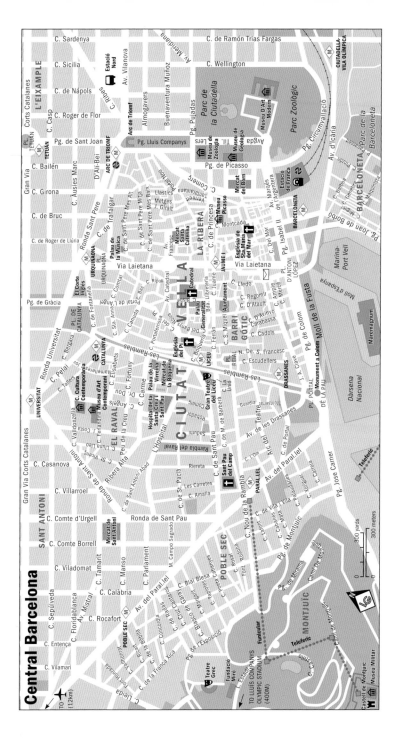

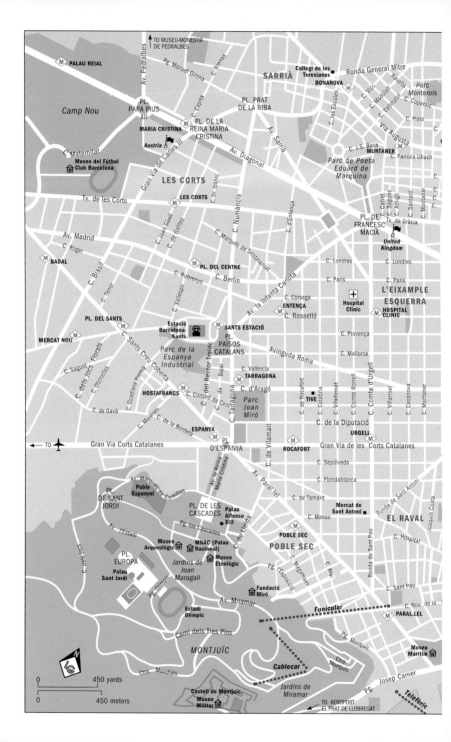

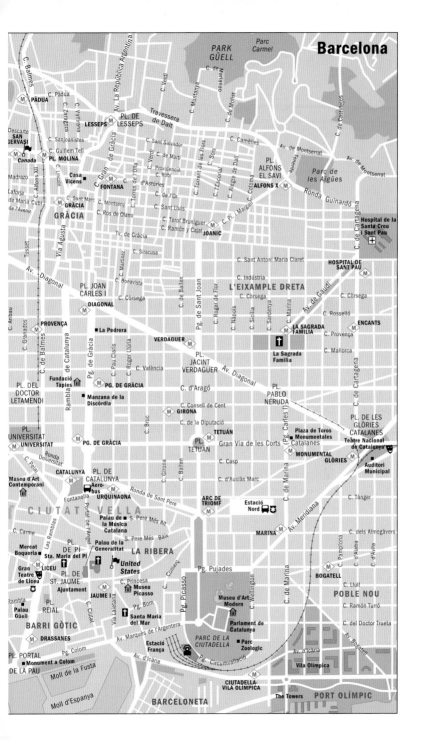

Barcelona Metro

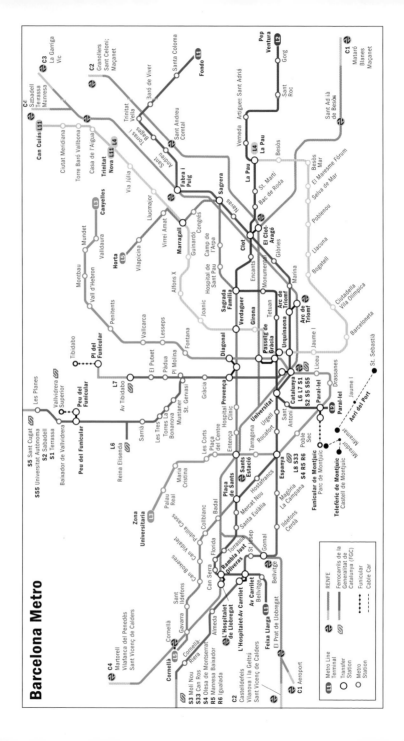

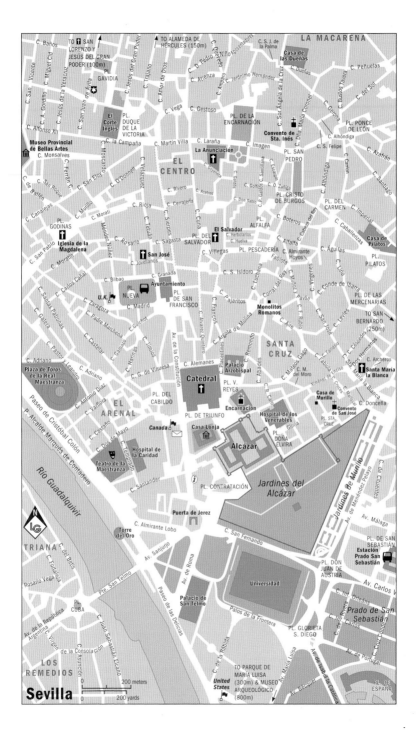

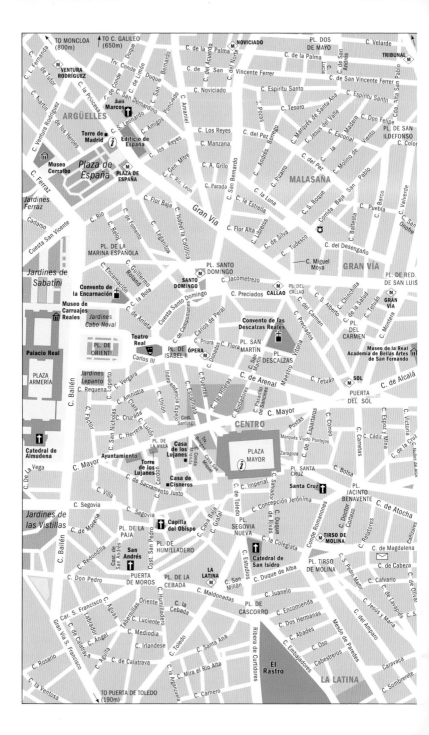

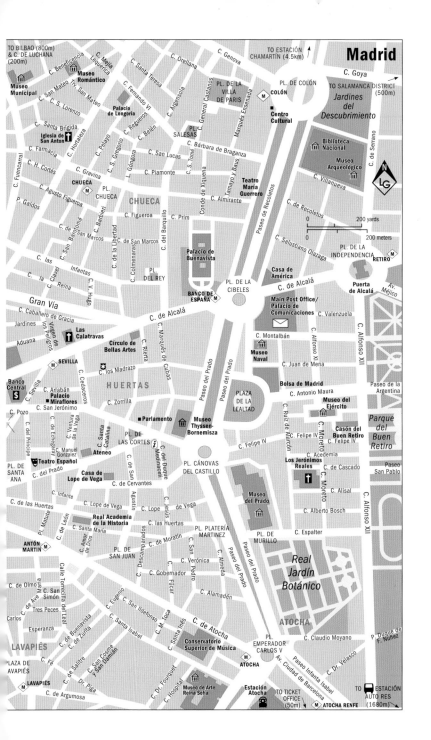

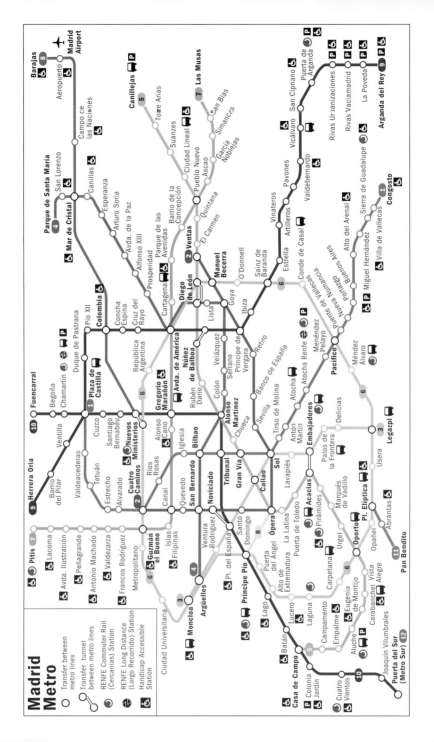

Madrid
Metro

○ Transfer between metro lines

Transfer tunnel between metro lines

◎ RENFE Commuter Rail (Cercanías) Station

◉ RENFE Long Distance (Largo Recorrido) Station

♿ Handicap Accessible Station

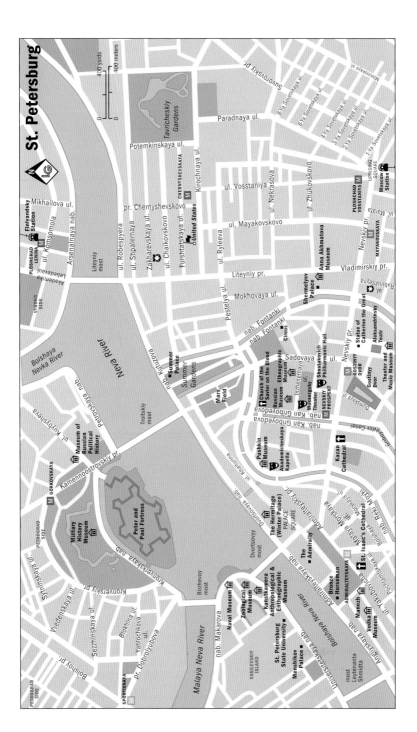

St. Petersburg

0   400 yards
0   400 meters

PETROGRAD SIDE

VYBORG SIDE

PLOSHCHAD LENINA Ⓜ Finlyandsky Station

Mikhailova ul.

ul. Komsomola

Akademika Lebedeva ul.

Arsenalnaya nab.

Liteyniy most

Bolshaya Nevka River

Neva River

Museum of Russian Political History

Ⓜ GORKOVSKAYA

Kamennoostrovskiy pr.

ul. Kuybisheva

Petrogradskaya nab.

Troitskiy most

PETROGRAD SIDE

Shpalernaya ul.

Sezzhinskaya ul.

Blokhina ul.

Yablochkova ul.

pr. Dobrolyubova

Boishoy pr.

Ⓜ SPORTIVNAYA

Peter and Paul Fortress

Military History Museum

Kronverkskiy pr.

Kronverkskaya nab.

Dvortsovaya nab.

Birzhevoy most

nab. Makarova

Malaya Neva River

VASILEVSKIY ISLAND

Naval Museum

Zoological Museum

Kunstkamera Anthropological & Ethnographic Museum

St. Petersburg State University

Menshikov Palace

Universitetskaya nab.

Bolshaya Neva River

most Leytenanta Shmidta

Angliyskaya nab.

Summer Palace

Summer Gardens

nab. Kutuzova

Mars Field

Church of the Savior on the Blood

Russian Museum

Ethnographic Museum

Inzhenernaya ul.

Pushkin Museum

Akademicheskaya Kapella

ul. Malajma

nab. Kan. Griboyedova

Kazan Cathedral

Griboedov Canal

The Hermitage (Winter Palace)

PALACE SQUARE

The Admiralty

ADMIRALTEYSKAYA Ⓜ

Bronze Horseman

Manezh

Vodka Museum

St. Isaac's Cathedral

Malaya Morskaya ul.

Bolshaya Morskaya ul.

Admiralteyskaya nab.

nab. reki Moyki

Voznesenskiy pr.

ul. Dekabristov

Shestheninskaya ul.

nab. Fontanki

nab. Fontanki

Circus

Sheremetev Palace

Anna Akhmatova Museum

Vladimirskiy pr.

Sadovaya ul.

Mussorgsky Theater

Shostakovich Philharmonic Hall

NEVSKIY PROSPEKT Ⓜ

Nevskiy pr.

Ⓜ GOSTINIY DVOR

Gostiny Dvor

Sadovaya Ⓜ

Statue of Catherine the Great

Aleksandrinsky Teatr

Theater and Music Museum

ul. Rubinshteyna

Pestelya ul.

Mokhovaya ul.

Liteyniy pr.

ul. Ryleeva

ul. Mayakovskovo

Furshtatskaya ul.

United States

ul. Chaikovskovo

Zakharevskaya ul.

pr. Chernyshevskovo

ul. Shpalernaya

ul. Robespyera

CHERNYSHEVSKAYA Ⓜ

Kirochnaya ul.

ul. Vosstaniya

ul. Nekrasova

ul. Zhukovskovo

Nevskiy pr.

MAYAKOVSKAYA Ⓜ

ul. Marata

PLOSHCHAD VOSSTANIYA Ⓜ

UPRISING SQUARE

Moscow Station

Potemkinskaya ul.

Tavricheskiy Gardens

Paradnaya ul.

Suvorovskiy pr.

8-Ya Sovetskaya ul.

7-Ya Sovetskaya ul.

6-Ya Sovetskaya ul.

5-Ya Sovetskaya ul.

4-Ya Sovetskaya ul.

3-Ya Sovetskaya ul.

2-Ya Sovetskaya ul.

1-Ya Sovetskaya ul.

Mitninskaya ul.

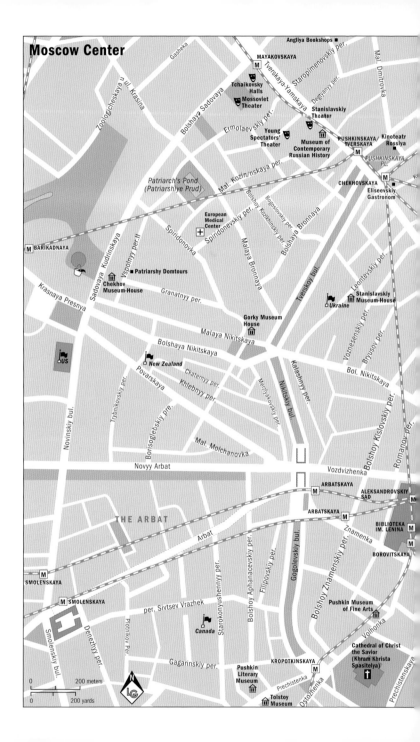

Moscow Center

Angliya Bookshops ■

MAYAKOVSKAYA Ⓜ

Gasheka

Zoologicheskaya u. ш. Krasina

Tverskaya-Yamskaya

Staropimenovskiy per.

Mal. Dmitrovka

Bolshaya Sadovaya

Tchaikovsky Halls

Mossoviet Theater

Ermolaevskiy per.

Degtyarny per.

Stanislavskiy Theater

Young Spectators' Theater

Museum of Contemporary Russian History

PUSHKINSKAYA/ TVERSKAYA Ⓜ

Kinoteatr Rossiya

PUSHKINSKAYA PL.

Patriarch's Pond (Patriarshiye Prud)

Mal. Kozinskaya per.

Bogoslovskiy per.

Bolshoy Kozikhinskiy per.

CHEKHOVSKAYA Ⓜ

Eliseevskiy Gastronom

European Medical Center ✚

Spiridonevskiy per.

Spiridonovka

Malaya Bronnaya

Bolshaya Bronnaya

BARIKADNAYA Ⓜ

Vspolnyy per. II

Sadovaya Kudrinskaya

Krasnaya Presnya

Chekhov Museum-House

■ Patriarshy Domtours

Granatnyy per.

Tverskoy bul.

Ukraine

Stanislavskiy Museum-House

Leontevskiy per.

Voznesenskiy per.

Bryusov per.

Gorky Museum House

Malaya Nikitskaya

Bolshaya Nikitskaya

Bol. Nikitskaya

US

New Zealand

Ckaternyy per.

Povarskaya

Khlebnyy per.

Kalashnyy per.

Nikitskiy bul.

Merzlyakovskiy per.

Bolshoy Kislovskiy per.

Romanov per.

Trubnikovskiy per.

Borisoglebskiy pre.

Mal. Molchanovka

Novinskiy bul.

Novyy Arbat

Vozdvizhenka

ARBATSKAYA Ⓜ

ALEKSANDROVSKIY SAD

Ⓜ

THE ARBAT

Arbat

ARBATSKAYA Ⓜ

BIBLIOTEKA IM. LENINA Ⓜ

Znamenka

Ⓜ

BOROVITSKAYA Ⓜ

SMOLENSKAYA Ⓜ

per. Sivtsev Vrazhek

Bolshoy Aphanacevskiy per.

Filippovskiy per.

Gogolevskiy bul.

Bolshoy Znamenskiy per.

SMOLENSKAYA Ⓜ

Plotnikov Per.

Starokonyushennyy per.

Canada

Pushkin Museum of Fine Arts

Smolenskiy bul.

Denezhny per.

Gagarinskiy per.

Pushkin Literary Museum

KROPOTKINSKAYA Ⓜ

Prechistenka

Cathedral of Christ the Savior (Khram Khrista Spasitelya)

Volhonka

Ostozhenka

Prechistenka

Tolstoy Museum

0   200 meters

0   200 yards

N
LG

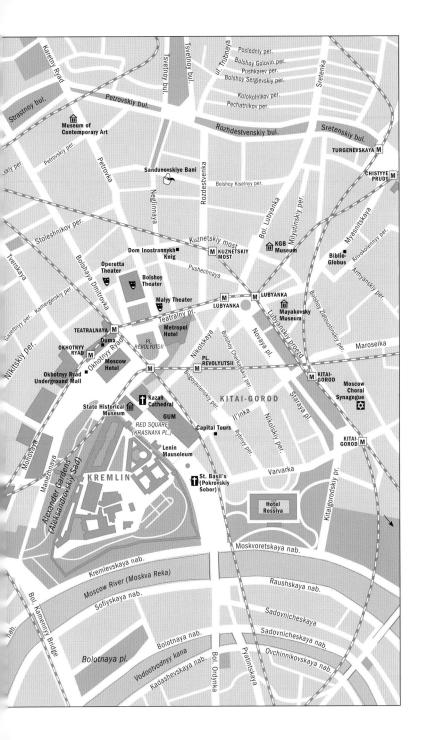

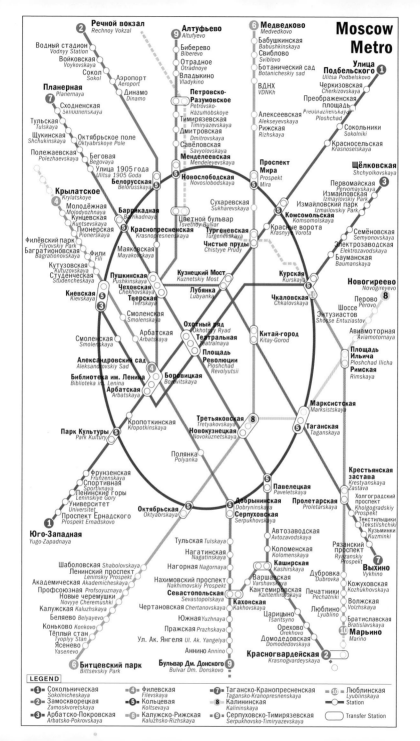

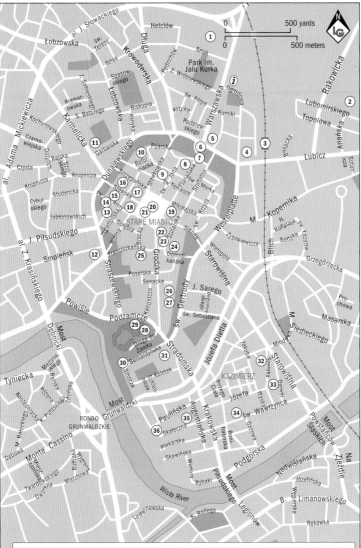

Central Kraków

Akademia Ekonomiczna, **2**
Almatur Office, **22**
Barbican, **6**
Bernardine Church, **31**
Bus Station, **4**
Carmelite Church, **11**
Cartoon Gallery, **9**
Collegium Maius, **14**
Corpus Christi Church, **34**
Czartoryski Art Museum, **8**
Dominican Church, **24**

Dragon Statue, **30**
Filharmonia, **12**
Franciscan Church, **25**
Grunwald Memorial, **5**
History Museum of Kraków, **17**
Jewish Cemetery, **32**
Jewish Museum, **33**
Kraków Główny Station, **3**
Monastery of the
  Reformed Franciscans, **10**
Pauline Church, **36**
Police Station, **18**
Politechnika Krakowska, **1**

St. Andrew's Church, **27**
St. Anne's Church, **15**
St. Catherine's Church, **35**
St. Florian's Gate, **7**
St. Mary's Church, **19**
St. Peter and Paul Church, **26**
Stary Teatr (Old Theater), **16**
Sukiennice (Cloth Hall), **20**
Town Hall, **21**
United States Embassy, **23**
University Museum, **13**
Wawel Castle, **28**
Wawel Cathedral, **29**

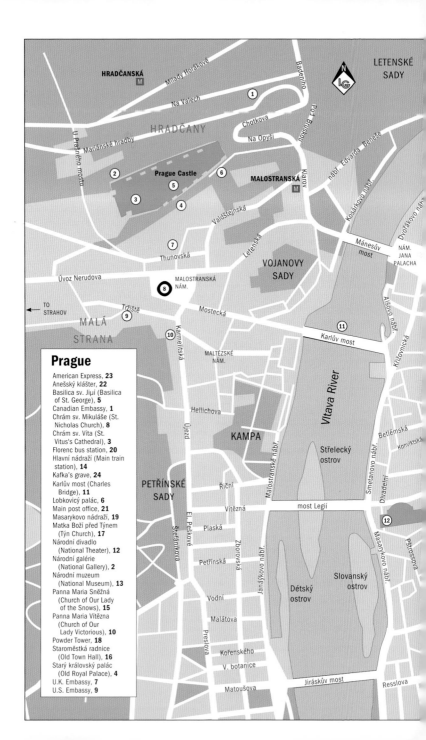

Prague

American Express, **23**
Anešský klášter, **22**
Basilica sv. Jiµí (Basilica of St. George), **5**
Canadian Embassy, **1**
Chrám sv. Mikuláše (St. Nicholas Church), **8**
Chrám sv. Víta (St. Vitus's Cathedral), **3**
Florenc bus station, **20**
Hlavní nádraží (Main train station), **14**
Kafka's grave, **24**
Karlův most (Charles Bridge), **11**
Lobkovicý palác, **6**
Main post office, **21**
Masarykovo nádraží, **19**
Matka Boží před Týnem (Týn Church), **17**
Národní divadlo (National Theater), **12**
Národní galérie (National Gallery), **2**
Národní muzeum (National Museum), **13**
Panna Maria Sněžná (Church of Our Lady of the Snows), **15**
Panna Maria Vítězna (Church of Our Lady Victorious), **10**
Powder Tower, **18**
Staroměstská radnice (Old Town Hall), **16**
Starý královský palác (Old Royal Palace), **4**
U.K. Embassy, **7**
U.S. Embassy, **9**

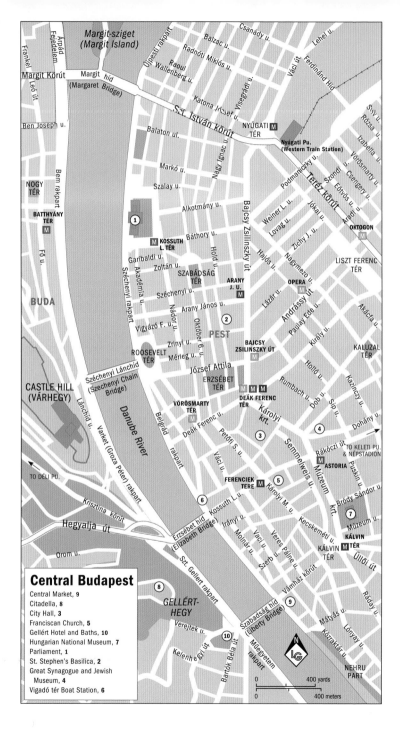

Margit-sziget
(Margit Island)

Csanády u.

Balzac u.

Lehel u.

Vác u.

Újpesti rakpart

Radnóti Miklós u.

Ferdinánd Híd

Raoul
Wallenberg u.

Frankel

Árpád
Fejedelem

Leó út

Margit Körút

Margit híd
(Margaret Bridge)

Katona József u.

Visegrádi u.

Ben Joseph u.

Szt. István Körút

NYÚGATI TÉR M

Balaton ul.

Nagy Ignác u.

Szent
(Western Train Station)

Nyúgati Pu.
(Western Train Station)

Bem rakpart

NOGY
TÉR

Markó u.

Podmaniczky u.

Szondi u.

Teréz Körút

Rózsa u.

Szív u.

Izabella u.

Vörösmarty u.

BATTHYÁNY
TÉR M

Szalay u.

Alkotmány u.

Weiner L. u.

Eötvös u.

Csengery u.

Eötvös u.

OKTOGON M

①

Lovag u.

Jókai u.

Zichy J. u.

Nagymező u.

Aradi u.

Fő u.

KOSSUTH
L. TÉR M

Báthory u.

Hajós u.

Garibaldi u.

Zoltán u.

Bajcsy Zsilinszky út

Hold u.

LISZT FERENC
TÉR

Széchenyi rakpart

Akadémia u.

SZABÁDSÁG
TÉR

Széchenyi u.

ARANY
J. U. M

OPERA M

Andrássy út

Akácfa u.

BUDA

Nádor u.

Arany János u.

②

Lázár u.

Paulay Ede u.

Vigyázó F. u.

Október 6 u.

PEST

BAJCSY
ZSILINSZKY ÚT M

Király u.

KALUZAL
TÉR

Zrinyi u.

ROOSEVELT
TÉR

Mérleg u.

József Attila

Holló u.

Kazinczy u.

Széchenyi Lánchíd
(Szechenyi Chain
Bridge)

ERZSÉBET
TÉR

Rumbach u.

Dob u.

Síp u.

Dohány u.

CASTLE HILL
(VÁRHEGY)

Lánchíd u.

Varket (Groza Péter) rakpart

VÖRÖSMARTY
TÉR

DEÁK FERENC
TÉR M M M

Károlyi
krt.

TO KELETI PU.
& NÉPSTADION

③

Semmelweis u.

Rákóczi út

Puskin u.

Bródy Sándor u.

Deák Ferenc u.

Petőfi S. u.

Danube River

Belgrád rakpart

Váci u.

ASTORIA M

Múzeum krt.

⑦

TO DÉLI PU.

Krisztina körút

Hegyalja út

FERENCIEK
TERE M

Károlyi M. u.

Kecskeméti u.

MÚZEUM
KÁLVIN
TÉR

⑥

Kossuth L.u.

④

⑤

KÁLVIN
TÉR M

Orom u.

Erzsébet híd
(Elizabeth Bridge)

Irányi u.

Molnár u.

Váci u.

Veres Pálne u.

Szerb u.

Vámház körút

Üllői út

Ráday u.

⑧

GELLÉRT-
HEGY

Szt. Gellert rakpart

Szabadság híd
(Liberty Bridge)

Mátyás u.

Lónyay u.

Vámház körút

Mūegyetem
rakpart

Verejtek u.

⑨

Közraktár u.

Kelenhegyi út

⑩

Bartók Béla út

N

LG

NEHRU
PÁRT

Central Budapest

Central Market, **9**
Citadella, **8**
City Hall, **3**
Franciscan Church, **5**
Gellért Hotel and Baths, **10**
Hungarian National Museum, **7**
Parliament, **1**
St. Stephen's Basilica, **2**
Great Synagogue and Jewish
  Museum, **4**
Vigadó tér Boat Station, **6**

0   400 yards

0   400 meters

LET'S GO

■ PAGES PACKED WITH ESSENTIAL INFORMATION

"Value-packed, unbeatable, accurate, and comprehensive."

—The Los Angeles Times

"The guides are aimed not only at young budget travelers but at the independent traveler; a sort of streetwise cookbook for traveling alone."

—The New York Times

"Unbeatable; good sight-seeing advice; up-to-date info on restaurants, hotels, and inns; a commitment to money-saving travel; and a wry style that brightens nearly every page."

—The Washington Post

■ THE BEST TRAVEL BARGAINS IN YOUR BUDGET

"All the dirt, dirt cheap."

—People

"Let's Go follows the creed that you don't have to toss your life's savings to the wind to travel—unless you want to."

—The Salt Lake Tribune

■ REAL ADVICE FOR REAL EXPERIENCES

"The writers seem to have experienced every rooster-packed bus and lunar-surfaced mattress about which they write."

—The New York Times

"[Let's Go's] devoted updaters really walk the walk (and thumb the ride, and trek the trail). Learn how to fish, haggle, find work—anywhere."

—Food & Wine

"A world-wise traveling companion—always ready with friendly advice and helpful hints, all sprinkled with a bit of wit."

—The Philadelphia Inquirer

■ A GUIDE WITH A SPIRIT AND A SOCIAL CONSCIENCE

"Lighthearted and sophisticated, informative and fun to read. [Let's Go] helps the novice traveler navigate like a knowledgeable old hand."

—Atlanta Journal-Constitution

"The serious mission at the book's core reveals itself in exhortations to respect the culture and the environment—and, if possible, to visit as a volunteer, a student, or a teacher rather than a tourist."

—San Francisco Chronicle

LET'S GO PUBLICATIONS

TRAVEL GUIDES

Australia 9th edition
Austria & Switzerland 12th edition
Brazil 1st edition
Britain 2008
California 10th edition
Central America 9th edition
Chile 2nd edition
China 5th edition
Costa Rica 3rd edition
Eastern Europe 13th edition
Ecuador 1st edition
Egypt 2nd edition
Europe 2008
France 2008
Germany 13th edition
Greece 9th edition
Hawaii 4th edition
India & Nepal 8th edition
Ireland 13th edition
Israel 4th edition
Italy 2008
Japan 1st edition
Mexico 22nd edition
New Zealand 8th edition
Peru 1st edition
Puerto Rico 3rd edition
Southeast Asia 9th edition
Spain & Portugal 2008
Thailand 3rd edition
USA 24th edition
Vietnam 2nd edition
Western Europe 2008

ROADTRIP GUIDE

Roadtripping USA 2nd edition

ADVENTURE GUIDES

Alaska 1st edition
Pacific Northwest 1st edition
Southwest USA 3rd edition

CITY GUIDES

Amsterdam 5th edition
Barcelona 3rd edition
Boston 4th edition
London 16th edition
New York City 16th edition
Paris 14th edition
Rome 12th edition
San Francisco 4th edition
Washington, D.C. 13th edition

POCKET CITY GUIDES

Amsterdam
Berlin
Boston
Chicago
London
New York City
Paris
San Francisco
Venice
Washington, D.C.

LET'S GO

EUROPE

2008

INÉS PACHECO EDITOR

ASSOCIATE EDITORS

LAUREN CARUSO   **CAROLINE CORBITT**
BRIANNA GOODALE   **JAKE SEGAL**
NICHOLAS TRAVERSE

RESEARCHER-WRITERS

JULIAN ARNI   **DANIEL NORMANDIN**
DAVID PALTIEL   **JOANNA PARGA**
VALENTINE QUADRAT   **RAVI RAMCHANDANI**

THOMAS MACDONALD BARRON MAP EDITOR
RACHEL NOLAN MANAGING EDITOR

ST. MARTIN'S PRESS ❧ NEW YORK

HELPING LET'S GO. If you want to share your discoveries, suggestions, or corrections, please drop us a line. We read every piece of correspondence, whether a postcard, a 10-page email, or a coconut. **Address mail to:**

> **Let's Go: Europe**
> **67 Mount Auburn St.**
> **Cambridge, MA 02138**
> **USA**

Visit Let's Go at **http://www.letsgo.com,** or send email to:

> **feedback@letsgo.com**
> **Subject: "Let's Go: Europe"**

In addition to the invaluable travel advice our readers share with us, many are kind enough to offer their services as researchers or editors. Unfortunately, our charter enables us to employ only currently enrolled Harvard students.

Maps by David Lindroth copyright © 2008 by St. Martin's Press.

Distributed outside the USA and Canada by Macmillan.

ISBN-13: 978-0-312-37448-8
ISBN-10: 0-312-37448-8
First edition
10 9 8 7 6 5 4 3 2 1

Let's Go: Europe is written by Let's Go Publications, 67 Mount Auburn St., Cambridge, MA 02138, USA.

HOW TO USE THIS BOOK

It all started with a ◥. With one fiery breath from his fearsome jowls, the great continent that is ◩**Europe** was born. Yes, dear reader, there are many mysteries in this Old World. That is why you have come to us. We will be your Virgil, teaching you the art of budget travel. We will guide you through Genoa's labyrinthine *vicoli* and Vilnius's breakaway artists' republic. We will be a less-than-comfortable pillow on long train rides. First bit of wisdom: Europe is awesome. From old-school Parisian cafes to unexplored limestone karsts on Croatia's Dalmatian Coast, this continent—like a Turkish bazaar—has it. And our gritty, dutiful researchers have fanned out to Irish shoals and Russian *stolis*, between Norway's herring pickling factories and Austria's posh ski towns, to bring you this: the freshest, most comprehensive budget travel guide ever produced. Here's how to use it:

COVERING THE BASICS. The first chapter is **Discover** (p. 1). Read it before you go. Its purpose is to help you find the best this chunk o' earth has to offer. If you like people telling you what to do (or just want some ideas), check out this chapter's **suggested itineraries.** The **Essentials** (p. 13) section gets down to the nitty-gritty, detailing the info you'll need to get around and stay safe on your journey. The **Transportation** (p. 43) section will help you get to and around Europe, while the **Beyond Tourism** (p. 56) chapter suggests ways to work and vounteer your way across the Continent. Then we get to the meat of the book: 33 jam-packed **country chapters,** organized alphabetically. The **Appendix** (p. 1057) has a weather chart for major cities and a handy dandy phrasebook with nine languages to help you say "I'm lost," land a bed, or find your way to a bathroom no matter where you are.

TRANSPORTATION INFO. Because you've told *Let's Go* you're traveling on budget airlines, we've created a new transportation format to help you navigate getting to where you really want to go from that random town an hour away: **Let's Go To...**, listed at the end of some major cities (for instance, Let's Go to Milan: Bergamo). We've also collected info on bus, ferry, and train routes; these range from rock-solid Spanish AVE schedules to, well, any transportation in Romania.

RANKINGS AND FEATURES. Our researchers list establishment in order of value from best to worst, with absolute favorites denoted by the *Let's Go* thumbpick ◪. Since the lowest price does not always mean the best value, we've incorporated a system of price ranges (❶-❺) for food and accommodations. Tipboxes come in a variety of flavors: warnings (◨), helpful hints and resources (◧), insider deals (◪), cheap finds (◩), and then a smattering of stuff you should know (◪, ◪, ◪).

AWESOMENESS. From ☎ codes to avoiding scams, from the best borscht to the boldest brews, we'll guide you through the souvenir-cluttered jungle of old-school Europa to the most authentic food, craziest nightlife, and most mind-bendingly beautiful landscapes around. Start in Brussels, in Stockholm, in Bucharest. Open this bad boy up, and choose your own adventure.

A NOTE TO OUR READERS. The information for this book was gathered by *Let's Go* researchers from May through August of 2007. Each listing is based on one researcher's opinion, formed during his or her visit at a particular time. Those traveling at other times may have different experiences since prices, dates, hours, and conditions are always subject to change. You are urged to check the facts presented in this book beforehand to avoid inconvenience and surprises.

CONTENTS

Europe

N

300 miles
300 kilometers

Reykjavík **ICELAND**

Faroe Islands

Shetland Islands

Bergen

Orkney Islands

NORTHERN IRELAND

SCOTLAND

North Sea

Glasgow
Edinburgh

D E N

Belfast

IRELAND

GREAT BRITAIN

Dublin

A T L A N T I C
O C E A N

WALES
Cardiff

ENGLAND

NETHERLANDS

Amsterdam

London

G E R

Brussels
BELGIUM

Frankfurt

Nantes

Paris

LUXEMBOURG

FRANCE

LIECHTENSTEIN

Zurich

Bay of Biscay

SWITZERLAND Bern

Santiago de Compostela

Bordeaux

Lyon

Milan

Marseille Nice Florence

PORTUGAL

Madrid

ANDORRA

MONACO

Corsica (Fr.)

Lisbon

SPAIN

Barcelona

Seville

Valencia

Sardinia (It.)

Granada

Balearic Islands (Sp.)

Tangier **GIBRALTAR**

Mediterranean Sea

Fez

Rabat **MOROCCO**

ALGERIA Algiers

TUNISIA

XIV

ABOUT LET'S GO

NOT YOUR PARENTS' TRAVEL GUIDE

At Let's Go, we see every trip as the chance of a lifetime. If your dream is to grab a machete and forge through the jungles of Costa Rica, we can take you there. If you'd rather bask in the Riviera sun at a beachside cafe, we'll set you a table. We write for readers who know that there's more to travel than sharing double deckers with tourists and who believe that travel can change both themselves and the world—whether they plan to spend six days in Mexico City or six months in Europe. We'll show you just how far your money can go, and prove that the greatest limitation on your adventures is not your wallet, but your imagination.

BEYOND THE TOURIST EXPERIENCE

To help you gain a deeper connection with the places you travel, our fearless researchers scour the globe to give you the heads-up on both world-renowned and off-the-beaten-track attractions, sights, and destinations. They engage with the local culture only to emerge with the freshest insights on everything from local festivals to regional cuisine. We've also opened our pages to respected writers and scholars to hear their takes on the countries and regions we cover, and asked travelers who have worked, studied, or volunteered abroad to contribute first-person accounts of their experiences. In addition, we increased our coverage of responsible travel and expanded each guide's Beyond Tourism chapter to share more ideas about how to give back while on the road.

FORTY-EIGHT YEARS OF WISDOM

Let's Go got its start in 1960, when a group of creative and well-traveled students compiled their experience and advice into a 20-page mimeographed pamphlet, which they gave to travelers on charter flights to Europe. Four and a half decades later, we've expanded to cover six continents and all kinds of travel—while retaining our founders' adventurous attitude toward the world. Laced with witty prose and total candor, our guides are still researched and written entirely by students on shoestring budgets, experienced travelers who know that train strikes, stolen luggage, food poisoning, and marriage proposals are all part of a day's work.

THE LET'S GO COMMUNITY

More than just a travel guide company, Let's Go is a community. Our small staff comes together because of our shared passion for travel and our desire to help other travelers see the world the way it was meant to be seen. We love it when our readers become part of the Let's Go community as well—when you travel, drop us a postcard (67 Mt. Auburn St., Cambridge, MA 02138, USA), send us an e-mail (feedback@letsgo.com), or post on our forum (http://www.letsgo.com/connect/forum) to tell us about your adventures and discoveries.

For more information, visit us online: www.letsgo.com.

RESEARCHER-WRITERS

Julian Arni
Belgium, Denmark, and Luxembourg

This Brazil native sauntered through unpredictable weather, conquered tricky transportation schedules, and even soldiered on through sickness. Not letting total technological meltdown or booked-solid accommodations get him down, he persevered through it all, producing clear and concise copy. Julian kept his cool, took his time, and enjoyed Europe. This backpacking veteran will be staying abroad next semester to see more of the world.

Daniel Normandin
Switzerland and Germany

Clad in his new Swiss jeans, Dan tackled the bewitched Black Forest, a cloud-covered Matterhorn, multiple chocolate museums, and the seductive Lorelei maiden. Along the way, he paraglided above Interlaken and got up-close-and-personal with Charlemagne. Disdaining gaudy tourist traps, Dan found many new local spots. His pun-filled and well-crafted prose, as well as his consistently cheerful attitude, kept his editors very happy.

David Paltiel
Austria, Germany, and Liechtenstein

After kickin' it with the kangaroos for *LG: Australia* last year, David outwitted a dying laptop, a runaway wheelchair, and Austrian escalators this summer. He paraded through salt mines in Hallstatt, swung from cable cars in Malbun, and philosophized in Vienna. This map macdaddy won his editors' admiration with nose-to-the-grindstone dedication and attention to detail, but still made time to mingle with Bavarian monks and call home daily.

Joanna Parga
Iceland and Norway

It's tough traveling in the north, with indecipherable bus schedules and menacing *huldufolk*. There's also the polar bear issue. Despite challenges, Jo toured the region like an all-star with a keen eye for sights, filling her copy with the scoop on that Icelandic lake you can't miss or that glacier that just isn't that cool. She scaled Norway's peaks, sailed the fjords, and even caught a few drunken mine stories in Svalbard after a day of dog sledding. Jealous yet?

Valentine Quadrat
Finland and Sweden

Val emerged from her journey through Finland and Sweden as a master reindeer lassoer and ice sculptor. As if that weren't impressive enough, she was also an expert researcher. She cruised through the region, working continuously and earning the admiration of fellow travelers and hostel proprietors. We eagerly awaited her pristine copy with legendary tales of midnight sun hikes in Sweden and office hours with Santa Claus in Finland.

Ravi Ramchandani
London, Netherlands, and Germany

The word "savior" comes to mind. With skill and dedication, Ravi traveled across Western Europe, working for four different Let's Go books. He skirted hipsters and pub grub in the Soho night scene and braved the world's largest flower trading floor, before arcing across the *Deutsche* heartland into beerhalls and *Schnitzel* stands. Rushing through the Nieuwe Zijd or relaxing in Hanover's palatial gardens, Ravi was unshakable. He was—and is—the man.

REGIONAL EDITORS AND RESEARCHER-WRITERS

CONTRIBUTING WRITERS

Leanna Boychenko *Excavating in Athens*
Leanna Boychenko majored in Classics at Harvard College. She was the Associate Editor of *Let's Go: Greece 2005* and the Editor of *Let's Go: New Zealand*, 7th ed.

Simon Schama *Britain: A Ruinous State*
Simon Schama is University Professor of Art History at Columbia University. His most recent book is *Rough Crossings: Britain, the Slaves, and the American Revolution* (Ecco, May 2006).

Clem Wood *A Dead Language Lives*
Clem Wood will graduate from Harvard in the spring of 2008 with an A.B. in Classics and plans to return to Italy in the future for further adventures and studies.

Jane Yager *Berlin*
Jane Yager is a Let's Go alum living in Berlin. She was a Researcher-Writer for *Let's Go: Europe*, 11th ed. and *Let's Go: Thailand*, 3rd ed., and the Editor of *Let's Go: Eastern Europe*, 12th ed.

Editor
Inés Pacheco
Associate Editors
Lauren Caruso, Caroline Corbitt, Brianna Goodale, Jake Segal, Nicholas Traverse
Managing Editor
Rachel Nolan
Map Editor
Thomas MacDonald Barron
Typesetter
Teresa Elsey

ACKNOWLEDGMENTS

TEAM EUROPE THANKS: ⬛Our RWs. ◧EEUR for sick summer jams, friendship, and general hilarity. ⬛RaNo for followership, jorts, and something serious. ⬛Tom for being dreamy and making life easy. ⬛Vicki for teaching us to tame Frame. The ⬛crunch teams: snap crackle pop! You rock. The fine folks at Post, for 216 boxes of HBO. Calina for being a podmate. ⬛Silvia for mad skillz. Mmm Denly's ❷. No thanks to Mississippi or Widener Circulation. ⬛Boom!

INÉS THANKS: L, C, B, J, and N: I could not have asked for a funnier, more dedicated, or generally balla team. RaNo, for everything. S&J, for leading the way. Ingrid & Co. for the Europod. My Ma Go family, for support, late-nights, drinks, and caffeine. Serge, for helping me up. 6Ex for MTV and Esopus. Sam, Jana, Clarie, I owe you my meninges. Stephen, for always. Mama, Papa, and Belly, for Paris.

LAUREN THANKS: Inés for leading with style. RaNo for glorious MEdits. Bri for nicknames like lucky Lauren. Caroline for slicing and dicing. Jake for answering my questions. Nick for keeping it real. Tom for hours of map party fun. ITA for jokes. IRE for putting up with me. Jeff for walks to work. And Scoow, my travel buddy, for being my Shmiku. Thanks MDMJMLPT. ⬛For Joanna and her family.

CAROLINE THANKS: Inés, for back pats and making every day fun; Bri, for conversations and chick flicks; Jake, for niceness and irreverence; Lauren, for sly jokes and good humor; Nick, for being a fantastic neighbor; Rachel, for being crazy brilliant; Dan, who it was a pleasure to get to know; Portugal, for the laughs; EEUR, Tom, and Team S&P; Mom, Dad, and my friends, for your love and support.

BRI THANKS: Inés for the ABCs and bidding high; RaNo for worldy insight; Jake for an Acton home and pick-up soccer; Nick for Santa's workshop and Nick-names; Caroline for Dawson's Creek and Diet Coke; Lauren for Denly's and patience; GCE, FRA, & Mapland; David for an easy job; DGs for Th ice cream; Coop for Su picnics; the IPFA for breaking-in Boston; Mom, Dad, and Cort for showing me the world⬛.

JAKE THANKS: iners, for alphabetizing and potato; bri, for beasting; machete, for unexpectedness; nick, trip to santa's kingdom?; tornado, see you at denly's; Rizzle B. McNizzle, for witticisms; the fam, for resweek dins and fam fun; ⬛cec, for everything ever, and then some; ⬛; the lemon song; dan, for hilarity and late-night kengriffs; coop, for lovin' (and dinners). albert, we always knew you'd go wrong.

NICK THANKS: To team awesome: Inés, Bri-Bri, Caroline, Lauren, Jake, I've never had more fun working. Much <3. RaNo, for choosing my future career. See you in Svalbard. Pat, Jen, and team Britain: YOLO! Tom: woo woo! Jo and Val, for the best Scandinavia coverage yet. EEUR, for Ra-ra-rasputin. Eva, for everything, and putting up with my hours. Dad, Ben, Hannah, and my friends for the love. To the *huldufolk:* I can see you, you bastards. Denly's ❷. Santa: time to go back to the Pole.

RACHEL THANKS: Inés for making my job easy. Caroline, Nick, Bri, Lauren, and Jake: hone your rifle skills for Svalbard 2008. The MEs for a great year. Amy for supplying the world's best editing buddy. Mom, dad, grandma, and Laura—as always.

TOM THANKS: Inés, Caroline, Nick, Bri, Jessica, and Jake for being the best EUR team in recent memory. Sheena and fake sheena for solid companionship, and 2008 ME team for always holding it down. Mum, Dad, Kay, Jamil, and Mia for all the love.

PRICE RANGES
EUROPE

1 2 3 4 5

Our researchers list establishments in order of value from best to worst; our favorites are denoted by the Let's Go thumbs-up (👍). Since the best value is not always the cheapest price, however, we have also incorporated a system of price ranges, based on a rough expectation of what you will spend. For **accommodations,** we base our range on the cheapest price for which a single traveler can stay for one night. For **restaurants** and other dining establishments, we estimate the average amount a traveler will spend. The table below tells you what you will *typically* find in Europe at the corresponding price range; keep in mind that no system can allow for every individual establishment's quirks.

ACCOMMODATIONS	WHAT YOU'RE *LIKELY* TO FIND
1	Camping; most dorm rooms, such as HI or other hostels or university dorm rooms. Expect bunk beds and a communal bath; you may have to provide or rent towels and sheets.
2	Upper-end hostels or small hotels. You may have a private bathroom, or there may be a sink in your room and communal shower in the hall.
3	A small room with a private bath. Should have decent amenities, such as phone and TV. Breakfast may be included in the price of the room.
4	Similar to 3, but may have more amenities or be in a more touristed area.
5	Large hotels or upscale chains. If it's a 5 and it doesn't have the perks you want, you've paid too much.

FOOD	WHAT YOU'RE *LIKELY* TO FIND
1	Mostly street-corner stands, falafel and shawarma huts, or fast-food joints. Most of the Dutch snack food, including *tostis* and *broodjes*. Desserts like *stropwafels* and *pannekoeken*. Soups and simple noodle dishes in minimalist surroundings. You may have the option of sitting down or getting take-out.
2	Sandwiches, appetizers at a bar, or low-priced entrees and *tapas*. Ethnic eateries and pan-Asian noodle houses. Takeout is less frequent; generally a sit-down meal, sometimes with servers, but only slightly more upscale decor.
3	Mid-priced entrees, seafood and exotic pasta dishes. More upscale ethnic eateries. Tip'll bump you up a couple dollars, since you will have a waiter.
4	A somewhat fancy restaurant or a steakhouse. Either way, you'll have a special knife. Few restaurants in this range have a dress code, but some may look down on T-shirts and jeans.
5	Food with foreign names and a decent wine list. Slacks and dress shirts may be expected. Don't order PB&J.

DISCOVER EUROPE

For many, the Continent's draw is familiar imagery. Aspiring writers still spin romances in Parisian garrets; a glass of sangria at twilight on the Plaza Mayor tastes as sweet as ever; and iconic treasures, from the onion domes of St. Basil's cathedral to the behemoth slabs of Stonehenge, inspire no small awe. Yet against this ancient backdrop, a freshly costumed continent takes the stage. As the European Union grew from a small clique of nations trading coal and steel to a 27-member commonwealth with a parliament and a central bank, Eastern and Western Europe find themselves more closely connected than ever before. Ease of travel between the two make it seem like the Continent is simultaneously shrinking and expanding. As a result, travelers can easily determine on their own the must-see destinations of 21st-century Europe.

While Prague and Barcelona may have been the hot spots a few years ago, emerging cities like Kraków and Stockholm are poised to inherit the tourist money train. Newly minted cultural meccas like Bilbao's Guggenheim and London's Tate Modern have joined the ranks of timeless galleries like the Louvre and the Hermitage, while a constant influx of students and DJs keep Europe's nightlife dependably hot. Whether it's Dublin's pubs, Lyon's upscale bistros, Sweden's frozen north country, or Croatia's dazzling beaches that call to you, *Let's Go: Europe 2008* will help keep you informed and on-budget.

TACKLING EUROPE

Anyone who tells you that there is any one "best way" to see Europe should be politely ignored. This book is designed to facilitate all varieties of travel, from a few days in Paris to a breathless continent-wide summer sprint to a leisurely year (or two) abroad. This chapter is made up of tools to help you create your own itinerary: **themed categories** let you know where to find your museums, your mountains, and your madhouses, while **suggested itineraries** outline various paths across Europe. Look to chapter introductions for country-specific itineraries and for more detailed information.

WHEN TO GO

While summer sees the most tourist traffic in Europe, the best mix of value and accessibility comes in late spring and early fall. To the delight of skiing and ice-climbing enthusiasts, traveling during the low season (mid-Sept. to June) brings cheaper airfares and accommodations, in addition to freedom from hordes of fannypack toting tourists. On the flip side, many attractions, hostels, and tourist offices close in the winter, and in some rural areas local transportation dwindles or shuts down altogether. Most of Europe's best **festivals** (p. 5) also take place in summer. For more advice on the best time to visit, see the **Weather Chart** on p. 1069 and the **Essentials** section at the beginning of each chapter.

WHAT TO DO

🏛 MUSEUMS

Europe has kept millennia worth of artistic masterpieces close to home in strongholds like the Louvre, the Prado, and the Vatican Museums. European museums do not merely house art, however. They also have exhibits on erotica, leprosy, marijuana, marzipan, puppets, secret police, and spirits both literal and figurative—in short, whatever can captioned. A trip across Europe qualifies as little more than a stopover without an afternoon spent among some of its paintings and artifacts—whether they include the pinnacles of Western culture, or more morbid or risqué fare.

THE CLASSY	THE SASSY
BRITAIN: THE BRITISH MUSEUM (p. 133). Holding world artifacts like Egypt's Rosetta Stone or Iran's Oxus Treasure, the British Museum contains almost nothing British at all.	**DENMARK: LOUISIANA MUSEUM OF MODERN ART** (p. 263). This well-rounded museum's name honors the three wives of the estate's original owner—all of them were named Louisa.
BRITAIN: TATE MODERN (p. 132). Organized thematically, this former power station turned modern art powerhouse is as much a work of art as any of the pieces in its galleries.	**GERMANY: SCHOKOLADENMUSEUM** (p. 423). This chocolate museum, detailing the chocolate-making process, has gold fountains that spurt out samples and can only be described as magical.
FRANCE: THE LOUVRE (p. 323). Six million visitors come each year to see 35,000 works of art, including Da Vinci's surprisingly small painting of art's most famous face, the *Mona Lisa*.	**HUNGARY: SZAMOS MARZIPAN MUSEUM** (p. 510). Only one statuette on display at this museum is not composed of marzipan: an 80kg white chocolate effigy of Michael Jackson.
GERMANY: GEMÄLDEGALERIE (p. 405). With over 1000 works from 1200 to 1800 by the likes of Bruegel and Raphael, it's no wonder this is one of the most visited museums in Germany.	**ICELAND: PHALLOLOGICAL MUSEUM** (p. 535). With specimens from over 90 species, this museum—a mix of science and humor—is all about penises. We'll leave the puns up to you.
GREECE: NATIONAL ARCHAEOLOGICAL MUSEUM (p. 467). Athens itself may be museum enough for some, but this building collects what's too small to be seen with a placard on the street.	**ITALY: PALERMO CATACOMBS** (p. 660). The withered faces and mostly empty eye sockets of 8000 posing corpses gaze enviously at living spectators in Europe's creepiest underground tomb.
ITALY: VATICAN MUSEUMS (p. 597). Look for the *School of Athens* here; the painting crowns a mindblowing amount of Renaissance and other art, including the incredible Raphael Rooms.	**THE NETHERLANDS: CANNABIS COLLEGE** (p. 714). Cannabis College is just like college, except there are no libraries, no lectures, no studying, no liquor, no dorms, and no full-time students.
THE NETHERLANDS: RIJKSMUSEUM (p. 715). Renovations shouldn't deter visitors who come to see the pinnacles of the Dutch Golden Age, including Rembrandts and Vermeers, that line the walls.	**NORWAY: VIGELANDPARKEN** (p. 740). Not quite a museum, but with enough art to be one, this park contains over 200 of Gustav Vigeland's controversial sculptures. Each depicts a stage of human life.
POLAND: NATIONAL MUSEUM (p. 796). In the vaults of a former Franciscan monastery, Gdańsk's National Museum has a large collection of 16th- to 20th-century art and furniture.	**PORTUGAL: OCEANÁRIO** (p. 810). Europe's largest oceanarium, with interactive exhibits exploring the four major oceans, allows visitors to get within a meter of sea otters and penguins.
SLOVAKIA: PRIMACIÁLNY PALÁC (p. 873). This pink- and gold "Primate's Palace" was built in the 1700s for Hungarian religious leaders (not monkeys) and is now home to Bratislava's mayor.	**SPAIN: TEATRE-MUSEU DALÍ** (p. 946). Dali's final resting place has works like *Napoleon's Nose Transformed into a Pregnant Woman Strolling Her Shadow with Melancholic amongst Original Ruins*.
SPAIN: MUSEO DEL PRADO (p. 903). It's an art-lover's heaven to see hell, as painted by Hieronymus Bosch. Velázquez's famous 10½ by 9 ft. painting of *Las Meninas* is as luminous as it is tall.	**SWITZERLAND: VERKEHRSHAUS DER SCHWEIZ** (p. 1012). The Swiss Transport Museum, with an IMAX theater and a wide array of cool contraptions, isn't nearly as dorky as its name implies.

⚏ ARCHITECTURE

European history lives on in the tiled roofs and soaring arches of the Continent's architecture. Royal lines from the early Welsh dynasties and Greek ruling families to the Bourbons, Habsburgs, and Romanovs have all been outlasted by the emblems of their magnificence—castles, palaces, and châteaux. Monarchs were careless of expense, and jealous of each other; Louis XIV's palace at Versailles (p. 331), which has become a byword for opulence, whet the ambition of rival monarchs and spurred the construction of rival domiciles. No expense was spared for God, either, as the many splendid cathedrals, monasteries, synagogues, temples, and mosques rising skyward from their cityscapes attest. Córdoba's Mezquita (p. 914 and Budapest's Great Synagogue (p. 507) are among the finest of their kind, while Chartres's Cathédrale de Notre Dame (p. 332) and Cologne's Dom (p. 423) are pinnacles—pun intended—of the Gothic style.

ROYAL REAL ESTATE	SACRED SITES
◼ **AUSTRIA: SCHLOß SCHÖNBRUNN** (p. 74). If the palace isn't impressive enough, check out the classical gardens that extend behind for four times the length of the structure.	◼ **BRITAIN: WESTMINSTER ABBEY** (p. 124). Royal weddings and coronations take place in the sanctuary; nearby, poets and politicians from the earliest kings to Winston Churchill rest in peace.
◼ **BRITAIN: BUCKINGHAM PALACE** (p. 124). Britain's royal family has lived in Buckingham Palace since 1832, guarded by everybody's favorite stoic, puffy-hatted guards.	◼ **FRANCE: CHARTRES CATHEDRAL** (p. 332). The world's finest example of early Gothic architecture has intact stained-glass windows from the 12th century and a crypt from the 9th.
◼ **DENMARK: EGESKOV SLOT** (p. 266). This idyllic castle seems to be floating in a lake. Its moat seems straight out of a fairy tale, with imaginative gardens and hedge mazes to match.	◼ **GERMANY: KÖLNER DOM** (p. 423). With a 44m ceiling and 1350 sq. m of stained glass illuminating the interior with particolored sunlight, Cologne's cathedral is Germany's greatest.
◼ **FRANCE: VERSAILLES** (p. 331). Once home to the entire French court, the lavish palace, manicured gardens, and hall of mirrors epitomize Pre-Revolutionary France's regal extravagance.	◼ **HUNGARY: THE GREAT SYNAGOGUE** (p. 507). Europe's largest synagogue can hold 3000. Inscribed leaves of a metal tree in the courtyard commemorate the victims of the Holocaust.
◼ **GERMANY: NEUSCHWANSTEIN** (p. 447). A waterfall, an artificial grotto, a byzantine throne room, and a Wagnerian opera hall deck out the inspiration for Disney's Cinderella Castle.	◼ **ITALY: SISTINE CHAPEL** (p. 595). Each fresco on its famous ceiling depicts a scene from *Genesis*. Michaelangelo painted himself as a flayed human skin hanging between heaven in hell.
◼ **ITALY: PALAZZO DUCALE** (p. 607). The home of the Venetian *Doge* (mayor) could pass as a city unto itself, complete with on-site prisons that miscreants once entered via the Bridge of Sighs.	◼ **RUSSIA: ST. BASIL'S CATHEDRAL** (p. 851). Commissioned by Ivan the Terrible to celebrate his victory over the Tatars, today its colorful, onion-shaped domes are instantly recognizable.
◼ **LUXEMBOURG: CHÂTEAU DE VIANDEN** (p. 697). Though its displays of armor, furniture, and tapestries are run-of-the-mill, the expansive views from the hills make the castle a must-see.	◼ **SPAIN: MEZQUITA** (p. 914). Córdoba's Mezquita, one of the most important Islamic monuments in the West, is supported by 850 pink and blue marble and alabaster columns.
◼ **PORTUGAL: QUINTA DA REGALEIRA** (p. 813). An eccentric millionaire owner turned this stunning palace into a fantasy land in the early 20th century, complete with "Dantesque" caves below.	◼ **SPAIN: SAGRADA FAMILIA** (p. 941). Though it looks like it's already melting, Antoni Gaudí's cathedral isn't even finished. The world's most visited construction site, it should be done in 2026.
◼ **SPAIN: THE ALHAMBRA** (p. 925). The Spanish say, *"Si mueres sin ver la Alhambra, no has vivido."* ("If you die without seeing the Alhambra, you have not lived.") We agree.	◼ **TURKEY: AYA SOFIA** (p. 1041). The gold-leafed mosaic dome of Byzantine emperor Justinian's masterful cathedral-turned-mosque appears to be floating on a bed of luminescent pearls.
◼ **SWEDEN: KUNGLIGA SLOTTET (p. 969)**. Still the official residence of the Swedish royal family, the Kungliga Slottet (Royal Palace) recently hosted lavish festivities for the Crown Princess's 30th birthday.	◼ **UKRAINE: KYIV-CAVE MONASTERY** (p. 1053). Kyiv's oldest holy site houses the Refectory Church, the 12th-century Holy Trinity Gate Church, and caves where monks lie mummified.

⚠ OUTDOORS

Granted, it may not be what you came for. Europe's museums and ruins tend be a stronger draw than its mountains and rivers. But for any traveler, budget or otherwise, solo or companioned, expert or neophyte, an excursion to the outdoors can round off (or salvage, as the case may be) any journey. Fjords, volcanoes, valleys, gorges, and plateaus mark the spots where the Earth's plates collide. Waters of innumerable shades of blue wash up on uninhabited shores of black-, white-, and red-sand beaches. Mountains, whether sprawling with trees or culminating in ice, continue to challenge mankind and dwarf the manmade—just as they did when civilization began.

CRUISING...	...FOR A BRUISING?
AUSTRIA: THE HOHE TAUERN NATIONAL PARK (p. 84). Filled with glaciers, mountains, lakes, and endangered species, Europe's largest park offers mountain paths once trod by Celts and Romans.	**AUSTRIA: INNSBRUCK** (p. 85). The free Club Innsbruck membership is one of the best deals in Western Europe for avid skiers. When skiing becomes old hat, adventurers opt for paragliding.
BRITAIN: LAKE DISTRICT NATIONAL PARK (p. 165). Four million sheep have cast their votes for the loveliest park in England—an equal number of summertime tourists seem to agree.	**FRANCE: MONT BLANC** (p. 355). The tallest mountain in Europe (4807m), Mont Blanc has vertigo-inducing slopes and is a haven for international bikers, hikers, snowboarders, and skiers.
CROATIA: THE DALMATIAN COAST (p. 216). Touted as the new French Riviera, the Dalmatian Coast has some of the cleanest and clearest waters in the Mediterranean.	**GERMANY: DER SCHWARZWALD** (p. 435). The eerie darkness pervading this tangled evergreen, once the inspiration for the Brothers Grimm, lures hikers and skiers instead of red-caped little girls.
DENMARK: ÆRØSKØBING (p. 267). Economic stagnation and recent conservation efforts have successfully fossilized the 19th-century lifestyle and charm of this tiny island town.	**ITALY: CINQUE TERRE** (p. 613). An outdoorsman's paradise, the hiking trails of Cinque Terre have opportunities for cliff diving, horseback riding, and kayaking between villages.
ESTONIA: HIIUMAA (p. 280). The Soviets unwittingly preserved rare species on this island by restricting access for 50 years. The Säärtirp peninsula's promontory is especially beautiful.	**NORWAY: FJÆRLAND** (p. 753). At the base of the Jostedalsbreen glacier, Fjærland provides a perfect rest from serious, year-round hiking and camping through Norway's fjords.
FRANCE: D-DAY BEACHES (p. 340). The heroism of the Allied forces is tastefully preserved on the beaches near Bayeux, where thousands of soldiers were killed or wounded over 60 years ago.	**NORWAY: SVALBARD ARCHIPELAGO** (p. 764). The northernmost town in the world also happens to be the badassmost. Rifle skills are a must for solo trekking, but dog sledding is open to all.
GREECE: MYRTOS BEACH (p. 482). Myrtos's snowy white pebbles, lucent waters, and location against the cliffs make it one of the most heart-stirring beaches in all of Europe.	**PORTUGAL: SAGRES** (p. 820). Once considered the edge of the world, the windy town of Sagres now plays host to more windsurfers than it does to would-be navigators.
ICELAND: THERMAL POOLS (p. 527). Iceland may be expensive, but freeloaders can find naturally occuring "hot pot" outside of Reykjavík. Each thermal pool maintains its distinct character.	**SLOVAKIA: THE TATRA MOUNTAINS** (p. 874). Part of the Carpathian range and spanning the border between Slovakia and Poland, the Tatras make a great, if extremely demanding, hiking destination.
IRELAND: KILLARNEY NATIONAL PARK (p. 556). Glacial activity during the Ice Age shaped Ireland's best park, which has pristine lakes, forested mountains, and an elusive herd of 850 red deer.	**SPAIN: PAMPLONA** (p. 947). While not outdoorsy in the traditional sense, the Running of the Bulls in Pamplona attracts runners and adrenaline junkies from all over the world.
THE NETHERLANDS: HOGE VELUWE NATIONAL PARK (p. 727). Wild boars and red deer inhabit the 13,500 acres of forestry, while the park's museum houses works by Picasso and van Gogh.	**SWITZERLAND: INTERLAKEN** (p. 1003). Thanks to its mild climate and pristine landscape, Interlaken is Europe's adventure sports capital, with every adrenaline-inducing opportunity imaginable.

❀ FESTIVALS

COUNTRIES	APR. – JUNE	JULY – AUG.	SEPT. – MAR.
AUSTRIA AND SWITZERLAND	Vienna Festwochen (early May to mid-June)	Salzburger Festspiele (late July-Aug.)	Escalade (Geneva; Dec. 12-14) Fasnacht (Basel; Feb. 11-13)
BELGIUM	Festival of Fairground Arts (Wallonie; late May)	Gentse Feesten (Ghent; mid- to late July)	International French Language Film Festival (Namur; late Sept.)
BRITAIN AND IRELAND	Bloomsday (Dublin; June 16) Wimbledon (London; late June-early July)	Fringe Festival (Edinburgh; Aug.) Edinburgh Int'l Festival (mid-Aug. to early Sept.)	Matchmaking Festival (Lisdoonvarna; Sept.) St. Patrick's Day (Mar. 17)
CZECH REPUBLIC	Prague Spring Festival (May-June)	Int'l Film Festival (Karlovy Vary; July)	Int'l Organ Festival (Olomouc; Sept.)
FRANCE	Cannes Film Festival (May 14-25)	Festival d'Avignon (July-Aug.) Bastille Day (July 14)	Carnevale (Nice, Nantes; Jan. 25-Feb. 5)
GERMANY	May Day (Berlin; May 1) Christopher St. Day (late June)	Rhine in Flames Festival (various locations in the Rhine Valley; throughout summer)	Oktoberfest (Munich; Sept. 20-Oct. 5) Fasching (Munich; Feb. 1-5)
HUNGARY	Danube Festival (Budapest; June)	Golden Shell Folklore (Siófok; June) Sziget Rock Festival (Budapest; Aug.)	Éger Vintage Days (Sept.) Festival of Wine Songs (Pécs; Sept.)
ITALY	Maggio Musicale (Florence; May to mid-June)	Il Palio (Siena; July 2 and Aug. 16) Umbria Jazz Festival (July)	Carnevale (late Feb.) Scoppio del Carro (Florence; Easter Su)
THE NETHERLANDS	Queen's Day (Apr. 30) Holland Festival (June)	Gay Pride Parade (Aug.)	Flower Parade (Aalsmeer; early Sept.) Cannabis Cup (Amsterdam; Nov.)
PORTUGAL	Burning of the Ribbons (Coimbra; early May)	Lisbon Beer Festival (July)	Carnaval (early Mar.) Semana Santa (Mar. 14-Mar. 23)
SCANDINAVIA	Midsummer (June 19-25) Festspillene (Bergen; late May-early June)	Savonlinna Opera Festival (July) Quart Music Festival (Kristiansand; early July)	Helsinki Festival (late Aug.-early Sept.) Tromsø Film Festival (mid-Jan.)
SPAIN	Feria de Abril (Sevilla; mid-April)	San Fermines (Pamplona; early to mid-July)	Las Fallas (Valencia; Mar.) Carnaval (Mar.)

SUGGESTED ITINERARIES

THE GRAND TOUR OF EUROPE

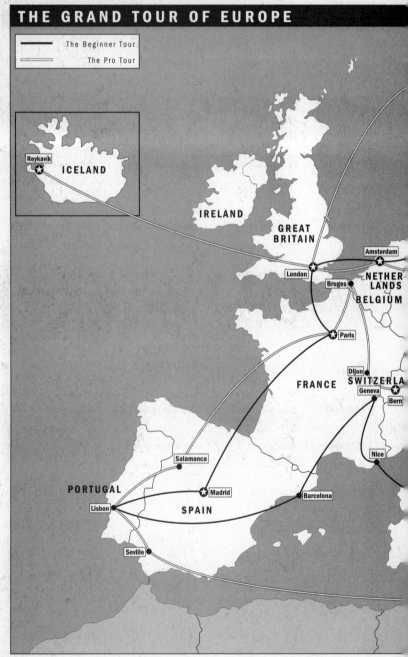

DISCOVER EUROPE

The Beginner Tour
The Pro Tour

ICELAND
Reykavik

IRELAND

GREAT
BRITAIN

London
Bruges
Amsterdam
NETHER-
LANDS
BELGIUM

Paris

Dijon
SWITZERLA
Geneva
Bern

FRANCE

Nice

Salamanca

PORTUGAL

Madrid
Barcelona

Lisbon
SPAIN

Seville

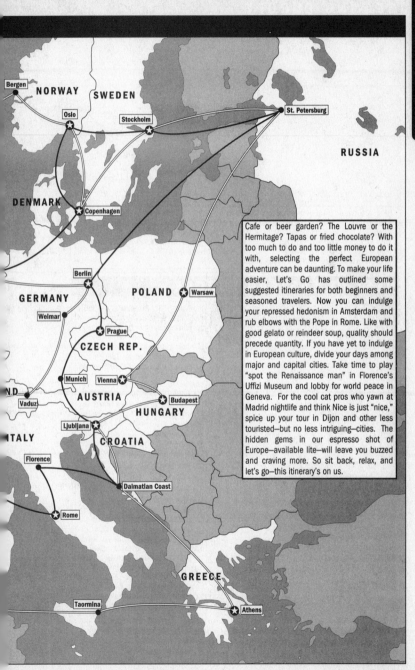

Cafe or beer garden? The Louvre or the Hermitage? Tapas or fried chocolate? With too much to do and too little money to do it with, selecting the perfect European adventure can be daunting. To make your life easier, Let's Go has outlined some suggested itineraries for both beginners and seasoned travelers. Now you can indulge your repressed hedonism in Amsterdam and rub elbows with the Pope in Rome. Like with good gelato or reindeer soup, quality should precede quantity. If you have yet to indulge in European culture, divide your days among major and capital cities. Take time to play "spot the Renaissance man" in Florence's Uffizi Museum and lobby for world peace in Geneva. For the cool cat pros who yawn at Madrid nightlife and think Nice is just "nice," spice up your tour in Dijon and other less touristed—but no less intriguing—cities. The hidden gems in our espresso shot of Europe—available lite—will leave you buzzed and craving more. So sit back, relax, and let's go—this itinerary's on us.

SEA-ING EUROPE

Begin your trip on the shores of Portugal, soaking in the views from the cliffs, the sun on the beach, and the drinks at the bars. Move on to Spain, stopping first in **Seville** (p. 915), home to some of Europe's best tapas and flamenco. Make your way through the country to **Barcelona** (p. 932), where lively nightlife is matched by the fantastic Modernisme architecture. When Spain's endless energy has worn you out, head to the **French** (p. 373) and **Italian Riviera** (p. 610) for some beach-bumming before returning to your high-paced tourist lifestyle.

BEST OF EASTERN EUROPE

Start off in **St. Petersburg** (p. 855), Peter the Great's lavish and utterly paradoxical city-on-a-marsh. Next, head to **Tallinn** (p. 275), where the steeples and beer gardens of the Gothic Raekoja Plats are punctuated by 18th century gardens. Make your pilgrimage to the world's only Frank Zappa statue in **Vilnius** (p. 682), then check out **Warsaw's** (p. 772) exuberant nightlife and cutting-edge arts scene. Head next to **Kraków** (p. 780), Poland's darling. No good tour would be complete without **Prague's** (p. 229) cobblestone streets, Baroque buildings, and all-night clubs. Take a train to **Lviv** (p. 1054), the cultural and patriotic center of Ukraine before checking out **Bratislava's** (p. 870) sophisticated artistic culture. Find your way to the underground club scene in **Budapest** (p. 499), Eastern Europe's "it" destination—then take a soothing mud bath to get rid of your hangover. Hit up the hot rocks on **Brač** island (p. 220) and **Hvar** (p. 219) as you travel down the Dalmatian coast to **Dubrovnik** (p. 221). After lounging on the beach, make like a Sultan in **İstanbul's** (p. 1032) Topkapi Palace and haggle through the city's Grand Bazaar before bar hopping through Sultanahmet. Then walk to Asia.

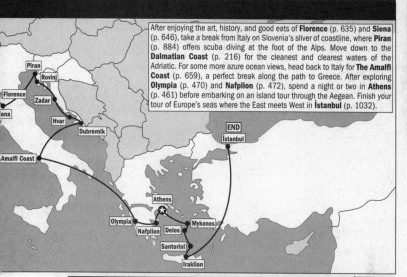

After enjoying the art, history, and good eats of **Florence** (p. 635) and **Siena** (p. 646), take a break from Italy on Slovenia's sliver of coastline, where **Piran** (p. 884) offers scuba diving at the foot of the Alps. Move down to the **Dalmatian Coast** (p. 216) for the cleanest and clearest waters of the Adriatic. For some more azure ocean views, head back to Italy for **The Amalfi Coast** (p. 659), a perfect break along the path to Greece. After exploring **Olympia** (p. 470) and **Nafplion** (p. 472), spend a night or two in **Athens** (p. 461) before embarking on an island tour through the Aegean. Finish your tour of Europe's seas where the East meets West in **İstanbul** (p. 1032).

BEST OF SCANDINAVIA

Start your trip in **Reykjavík** (p. 522) and daytrip through Iceland's natural sights, such as the jagged lava fields of **Þingvellir National Park** (p. 529) and the volatile terrain of **Gulfoss and Geysir** (p. 529). Move on to Denmark's capital, **Copenhagen** (p. 253), and hit up **Odense** (p. 265), Hans Christian Andersen's hometown, en route to laid-back **Århus** (p. 267). Cutting back through Copenhagen, hop over to **Malmö** (p. 979), Sweden's most diverse city. Travel north to **Gothenburg** (p. 983) before arriving in **Oslo** (p. 735). After enjoying a whale burger, head to **Bergen** (p. 746), a gateway to the sexy **Western Fjords** (p. 745). Hang out with the students of **Uppsala** (p. 975) on your way to **Stockholm** (p. 964). Cruise across the Baltic to **Helsinki** (p. 286) and wrap things up in **Turku** (p. 294), Finland's oldest city.

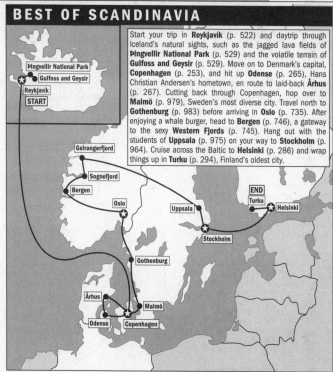

THE MIDDLE GROUND

Enjoy the beer gardens of **Tallinn** (p. 275) before moving on to **Rīga** (p. 669) for a night at the opera and a morning in the clubs. Continue south to Lithuania's influential capital, **Vilnius** (p. 682). In **Warsaw** (p. 112), exuberant nightlife and a cutting-edge arts scene contrast with an all-too-evident past. Explore the sights by day and the clubs by night in **Kraków** (p. 780) and **Prague** (p. 229). Don't let the increased tourist traffic keep you away from **Český Krumlov** (p. 244). Then, forget Amsterdam and Paris in **Vienna** (p. 67), Europe's true coffeehouse capital. For goulash, prehistoric labyrinths, and soothing baths head to **Budapest** (p. 499). Leave the city for the **Dalmatian Coast** (p. 216), finishing your tour of Europe's "Middle Ground" lounging on the Adriatic in **Dubrovnik** (p. 221).

CHANNEL JUMPING

Start your tour in the Emerald Isle's capital, **Dublin** (p. 542). Move on to the scenic **Ring of Kerry** (p. 557) and north to **Galway** (p. 561), Ireland's leading musical city. Hop over to **Belfast** (p. 566), and step (now safely) into the heart of The Troubles. Head to Great Britain, stopping in the jewel of Scotland, **Edinburgh** (p. 174). Leave the urban hustle behind to tour the **Lake District** (p. 165) before continuing south to **Liverpool** (p. 158), one of the EU's 2008 Cultural Capitals, and **Manchester** (p. 157). Take a breather from all things modern—hang out with grazing sheep in **The Cotswolds** (p. 152) and soak in **Bath's** (p. 144) springs. A trip to England wouldn't be complete without experiencing **Oxford's** (p. 148) binge studying and diligent drinking. Make **London** (p. 116) your final stop in England and swim down to France, landing at Dieppe. After a few days in **Paris** (p. 308), stay in the **Loire Valley** (p. 332) for spectacular cathedrals and manors. Wrap up your Anglo-centric tour with **Brittany** (p. 335), the Celtic side of France.

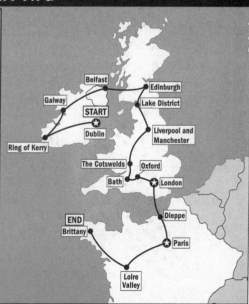

THE ULTIMATE PUB CRAWL

It's not called **Publin** (p. 542) for nothing. Start your debaucherous journey in this pub-filled city, before moving on to party with the best and brightest in **Oxford** (p. 148). After spending a few nights in **London** (p. 116), hop over to **Amsterdam** (p. 703), for its infamous coffee shops and the best GLBT nightlife in Europe. Preview Germany's party scene in **Cologne** (p. 420) on your way to **Sopot** (p. 798) and **Warsaw** (p. 772), where you'll find everything from cafes to clubs and sprawling beer gardens. Head down to **Eger's** (p. 512) Valley of Beautiful Women, full of attractive wine cellars ranging from loud to low-key. After you've had your share of wine, switch back to beer in **Prague** (p. 229), before hitting up the Pilsner Urquell Brewery in **Plzeň** (p. 243). Head back to Germany for **Munich** (p. 436), the city that brought the world Oktoberfest and the beer garden. Hang out with students in the university towns of **Zürich** (p. 1006) and **Grenoble** (p. 354) en route to sleepless Spain. See the sun come up in **Barcelona** (p. 932) and **Salamanca** (p. 909) before finishing your Ultimate Pub Crawl in **Lagos** (p. 819).

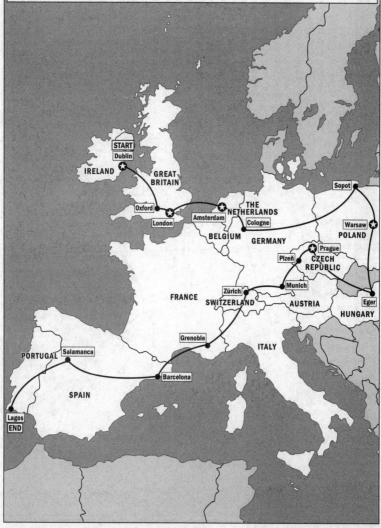

THE TREE-HUGGER'S TOUR

If you want to save the world one European town at a time, start outside of Málaga, at **Ecoforest** (p. 893), a vegan and raw food commune dedicated to teaching visitors about ecologically sustainable lifestyles. When you've had enough vegetables, head to France's beautiful Hautes-Alpes region, where you can repair and restore historic châteaux with the **Club du Vieux Manoir** (p. 308). If châteaux aren't old enough for you, work alongside archaeologists from the **Gruppi Archeologici** (p. 578) in Pisa. After sifting through ruins in Italy, help the **Archelon Sea Turtle Protection Society** (p. 461) study and protect hatchlings on Zakynthos. **The Bergwald Projekt** (p. 1000) in Austria's Hohe Tauern National Park offers a variety of conservation projects in one of Western Europe's most beautiful landscapes. Though Dresden is better known for its thriving nightlife, it's also the base for Germany's branch of **World-Wide Opportunities on Organic Farms** (p. 389). End your trip in Ireland's Donegal County, where the **Sustainable Land Use Co.** (p. 542) offers opportunities to assist with organic farming, forestry, habitat maintenance, and wildlife. For more info on environmental opportunities and nature conservation across Europe, check out our **Beyond Tourism** chapter (p. 56) and the country-specific organizations and programs listed in the beginning of each country chapter.

Zakynthos

Dresden

Hohe Tauern National Park

Pisa

Hautes-Alpes

Donegal County
END

START
Málaga

ESSENTIALS

PLANNING YOUR TRIP

BEFORE YOU GO

Passport (p. 13). Required for all non-EU citizens traveling in Europe.

Visa (p. 14). Not required for citizens of Australia, Canada, Ireland, New Zealand, the UK, and the US for stays shorter than 90 days in a 6-month period in most European countries.

Work Permit (p. 14). Required for all non-EU citizens planning to work in any European country.

Vaccinations (p. 24). Visitors to Europe should be up to date on vaccines, especially for diphtheria, hepatitis A, hepatitis B, and mumps. Visitors to Eastern Europe should also be vaccinated for measles, rabies, and typhoid.

EMBASSIES AND CONSULATES

CONSULAR SERVICES

Information about European consular services abroad and foreign consular services in Europe is located in individual country chapters; it can also be found at **www.embassiesabroad.com, www.embassyworld.com,** and **www.tyzo.com/planning/embassies.html.**

TOURIST OFFICES

Information about national tourist boards in Europe is located in individual country chapters; it can also be found at **www.towd.com.**

DOCUMENTS AND FORMALITIES

PASSPORTS

REQUIREMENTS. Citizens of Australia, Canada, Ireland, New Zealand, the UK, and the US need valid passports to enter European countries and to re-enter their home countries. Most countries do not allow entrance if the holder's passport expires within six months. Returning home with an expired passport is illegal and may result in a fine.

NEW PASSPORTS. Citizens of Australia, Canada, Ireland, New Zealand, the UK, and the US can apply for a passport at any passport office and most post offices and courts of law. New passport or renewal applications must be filed at least two months before the departure date, though most passport offices offer rush services for a very steep fee. Be warned that even "rushed" passports can take up to two weeks to arrive. Citizens living abroad who need a passport or renewal should contact the nearest passport office or consulate of their home country.

PASSPORT MAINTENANCE. Photocopy the page of your passport with your photo, as well as your visas, traveler's check serial numbers, and any other important documents. Carry one set of copies in a safe place, apart from the

ONE EUROPE. European unity has come a long way since 1958, when the European Economic Community (EEC) was created to promote European solidarity and cooperation. Since then, the EEC has become the European Union (EU), a mighty political, legal, and economic institution. On May 1, 2004, 10 South, Central, and Eastern European countries—Cyprus, the Czech Republic, Estonia, Hungary, Latvia, Lithuania, Malta, Poland, Slovakia, and Slovenia— were admitted to the EU, joining 15 other member states: Austria, Belgium, Denmark, Finland, France, Germany, Greece, Ireland, Italy, Luxembourg, the Netherlands, Portugal, Spain, Sweden, and the UK.

What does this have to do with the average non-EU tourist? The EU's policy of **freedom of movement** means that border controls between the first 15 member states (not including Ireland and the UK, but including Norway and Iceland) have been abolished, and visa policies have been harmonized. Under this treaty, formally known as the **Schengen Agreement,** you're still required to carry a passport (or government-issued ID card for EU citizens) when crossing an internal border, but once you've been admitted into one country, you're free to travel to other participating states. On June 5, 2005, Switzerland ratified the treaty, and will become fully participant by 2007. The 10 newest member states of the EU are anticipated to implement the policy after 2006. Ireland and the UK have also formed a **common travel area,** abolishing passport controls between the UK and the Republic of Ireland. For more important consequences of the EU for travelers, see The Euro (p. 17) and Customs in the EU (p. 15).

originals, and leave another set at home. Consulates also recommend that you carry an expired passport or an official copy of your birth certificate in a part of your baggage separate from other documents.

If you lose your passport, immediately notify the local police and the nearest embassy or consulate of your home government. To expedite its replacement, you must show ID and proof of citizenship. It also helps to know all information previously recorded in the passport. In some cases, a replacement may take weeks to process, and it may be valid only for a limited time. Any visas stamped in your old passport will be irretrievably lost. In an emergency, ask for immediate temporary traveling papers that will permit you to re-enter your home country.

VISAS, INVITATIONS, AND WORK PERMITS

VISAS. As of August 2007, citizens of Australia, Canada, Ireland, New Zealand, the UK, or the US did not need a visa to visit the following countries for fewer than 90 days: Austria, Belgium, Britain, Croatia, the Czech Republic, Denmark, Estonia, Finland, France, Germany, Greece, Hungary, Iceland, Ireland, Italy, Latvia, Liechtenstein, Luxembourg, the Netherlands, Norway, Poland, Portugal, the Slovakia, Slovenia, Spain, Sweden, and Switzerland. For travelers planning to spend more than 90 days in any European country, visas cost US$35-200 and typically allow you six months in that country. Visas can usually be purchased at a consulate or at **www.itseasypassport.com/services/visas/visas.htm.**

Double-check entrance requirements at the nearest embassy or consulate of **your destination** for up-to-date info before departure. US citizens can also consult http://travel.state.gov/foreignentryreqs.html.

WORK PERMITS. Admission as a visitor does not include the right to work, which is authorized only by a work permit. Entering a country in Europe to study typically requires a special study visa, though many study-abroad programs are able to subsidize it. For more info, see **Beyond Tourism,** p. 56.

IDENTIFICATION

When you travel, always carry at least two forms of identification on your person, including a photo ID; a passport and a driver's license or birth certificate is usually adequate. Never carry all of your IDs together; split them up in case of theft or loss, and keep photocopies of all of them in your luggage and at home.

STUDENT, TEACHER, AND YOUTH IDENTIFICATION. The **International Student Identity Card (ISIC),** the most widely accepted form of student ID, provides discounts on some sights, accommodations, food, and transportation; access to a 24hr. emergency helpline; and insurance benefits for US cardholders (see **Insurance,** p. 24). Applicants must be full-time secondary or post-secondary school students. Because of the proliferation of fake ISICs, some services (particularly airlines) require additional proof of student identity.

The **International Teacher Identity Card (ITIC)** offers teachers the same insurance coverage as the ISIC and similar but limited discounts. For travelers who are under 26 years old but are not students, the **International Youth Travel Card (IYTC)** also offers many of the same benefits as the ISIC.

Each of these identity cards costs US$22. ISICs and ITICs are valid until the new year unless purchased between September and December, in which case they are valid until the beginning of the following new year. IYTCs are valid for one year from the date of issue. To learn more about ISICs, ITICs, and IYTCs, see www.myisic.com. Many travel agencies issue the cards; for more info, see the **International Student Travel Confederation (ISTC)** website (www.istc.org).

The **International Student Exchange Card (ISE Card)** is a similar identification card available to students, faculty, and youths aged 12 to 26. The card provides discounts, medical benefits, access to a 24hr. emergency helpline, and the ability to purchase student airfares. An ISE Card costs US$25; for more info, call in the US ☎800-255-8000, or visit www.isecard.com.

CUSTOMS

When you enter a European country, you must declare certain items from abroad and pay a duty on the value of those articles if they exceed a set allowance. Note that goods purchased at **duty-free** shops are not exempt from duty or sales tax; "duty-free" merely means that you need not pay a tax in the country of purchase. Duty-free allowances were abolished for travel between EU member states, but still exist for those arriving from outside the EU. Upon returning home, you must likewise declare all articles acquired abroad and pay a duty on the value of articles in excess of your home country's allowance. In order to expedite your return, make a list of any valuables brought from home and register them with customs before traveling abroad, and be sure to keep receipts for all goods acquired abroad.

 CUSTOMS IN THE EU. In addition to the freedom of movement of people within the EU (p. 14), travelers in the 15 original EU member countries (Austria, Belgium, Denmark, Finland, France, Germany, Greece, Ireland, Italy, Luxembourg, the Netherlands, Portugal, Spain, Sweden, and the UK) can also take advantage of the freedom of movement of goods. This means that there are no customs controls at internal EU borders (i.e., you can take the blue customs channel at the airport), and travelers are free to transport whatever legal substances they like as long as it is for their own personal (non-commercial) use— up to 800 cigarettes, 10L of spirits, 90L of wine (including up to 60L of sparkling wine), and 110L of beer. Duty-free allowances were abolished on June 30, 1999 for travel between the original 15 EU member states; this now also applies to Cyprus and Malta. However, travelers between the EU and the rest of the world still get a duty-free allowance when passing through customs.

MONEY

CURRENCY AND EXCHANGE

The currency chart on the next page is based on August 2007 exchange rates between euro and Australian dollars (AUS$), Canadian dollars (CDN$), New Zealand dollars (NZ$), British pounds (UK£), and US dollars (US$). Check the currency converter on websites like www.xe.com or www.bloomberg.com, or a large newspaper, for the latest exchange rates.

As a general rule, it's cheaper to convert money in Europe than at home. While currency exchange will probably be available in your arrival airport, it's wise to bring enough currency to last for the first 24-72hr. of your trip.

EURO (€)		
AUS$1 = €0.62	€1 = AUS$1.61
CDN$1 = €0.69	€1 = CDN$1.45
NZ$1 = €0.55	€1 = NZ$1.80
UK£1 = €1.47	€1 = UK£0.68
US$1 = €0.73	€1 = US$1.38

When exchanging money abroad, try to go only to banks or official exchange establishments that have at most a 5% margin between their buy and sell prices. Because you lose money with every transaction, **convert large sums** (unless the currency is depreciating rapidly), but **no more than you'll need.**

If you use traveler's checks or bills, carry some in small denominations (the equivalent of US$50 or less) for times when you are forced to exchange money at disadvantageous rates, but bring a range of denominations, as charges may be levied per check cashed. Store your money in a variety of forms; ideally, at any given time you will be carrying some cash, some traveler's checks, and an ATM and/or credit card. All travelers should also consider carrying some US dollars (about US$50 worth), which are often preferred by local tellers.

CREDIT, ATM, AND DEBIT CARDS

Where they are accepted, credit cards often offer superior exchange rates—up to 5% better than the retail rate used by banks and other currency exchange establishments. Credit cards may also offer services such as insurance or emergency help, and are sometimes required when reserving hotel rooms or rental cars. **MasterCard** (a.k.a. **EuroCard** or **Access** in Europe) and **Visa** (a.k.a. **Carte Bleue** or **Barclaycard**) are the most widely accepted; **American Express** cards work at some ATMs and at AmEx offices and most major airports. A **debit card** can be used wherever its associated credit card company (usually MasterCard or Visa) is accepted, and the money is withdrawn directly from the holder's checking account. Debit cards also often function as ATM cards and can be used to withdraw cash from associated banks and ATMs throughout Europe. Ask your bank about obtaining one.

The use of ATM cards is widespread in Europe. Depending on the system that your home bank uses, you can most likely access your personal bank account from abroad. ATMs get the same wholesale exchange rate as credit cards, but there is often a limit on the amount of money you can withdraw per day (usually around US$500). There is typically also a surcharge of US$1-5 per withdrawal. The two major international money networks are **MasterCard/Maestro/Cirrus** (for ATM locations ☎ 800-424-7787; www.mastercard.com) and **Visa/PLUS** (for ATM locations ☎ 800-847-2911; www.visa.com).

PINS AND ATMS. To use a debit or credit card to withdraw money from a cash machine (ATM) in Europe, you must have a 4-digit **Personal Identification Number (PIN).** If your PIN is longer than 4 digits, ask your bank whether you can just use the first 4, or whether you'll need a new one. **Credit cards** don't usually come with PINs, so if you intend to hit up ATMs in Europe with a credit card to get cash advances, call your credit card company to request one before leaving. Travelers with alphabetic, rather than numerical, PINs may also be thrown off by the lack of letters on European cash machines. The following are the corresponding numbers to use: QZ=1; ABC=2; DEF=3; GHI=4; JKL=5; MNO=6; PRS=7; TUV=8; and WXY=9. Note that if you mistakenly punch the wrong code into the machine 3 times, it will swallow your card for good.

TRAVELER'S CHECKS

Traveler's checks are one of the safest and least troublesome means of carrying funds. American Express and Visa are the most recognized brands. Many banks and agencies sell them for a small commission. Check issuers provide refunds if the checks are lost or stolen, and many provide additional services, such as toll-free refund hotlines abroad, emergency message services, and assistance with lost and stolen credit cards or passports. Traveler's checks are readily accepted in most of Western Europe; in Eastern Europe, they will be accepted in most major cities. Ask about toll-free refund hotlines and the location of refund centers when purchasing checks, and always carry emergency cash.

 THE EURO. The official currency of 13 members of the European Union—Austria, Belgium, Finland, France, Germany, Greece, Ireland, Italy, Luxembourg, the Netherlands, Portugal, and Spain—is now the euro. Slovenia is set to join in 2007. The currency has some important—and positive—consequences for travelers hitting more than one euro-zone country. For one thing, money-changers across the euro-zone are obliged to exchange money at the official, fixed rate, and at no commission (though they may still charge a small service fee). Second, euro-denominated traveler's checks allow you to pay for goods and services across the euro-zone, again at the official rate and commission-free.

American Express: Checks available with commission at select banks, at all AmEx offices, and online (www.americanexpress.com; US residents only). Cardholders can also purchase checks by phone (☎800-528-4800). AmEx also offers the Travelers Cheque Card, a prepaid reloadable card. Cheques for Two can be signed by either of 2 people traveling together. For purchase locations or more info, contact AmEx's service: Australia ☎800 688 022, Canada 866-296-5198, US 800-221-7282, New Zealand 050 855 5358, UK 0800 587 6023.

Travelex: Thomas Cook MasterCard and Interpayment Visa traveler's checks available. For information about Thomas Cook MasterCard in Canada and the US call ☎800-223-7373, UK ☎0800 622 101; elsewhere, call UK collect 44 1733 318 950. For information about Interpayment Visa in Canada and the US 800-732-1322, in the UK 0800 515 884; elsewhere, call UK collect 44 1733 318 949. For more info, visit www.travelex.com.

Visa: Checks available (generally with commission) at banks worldwide. For the location of the nearest office, call the Visa Travelers Cheque Global Refund and Assistance Center: in the UK ☎0800 895 078, US 800-227-6811; elsewhere, call UK collect 44 2079 378 091. Visa also offers TravelMoney, a pre-paid debit card that can be reloaded

ESSENTIALS

online or by phone. For more info on Visa travel services, see http://usa.visa.com/personal/using_visa/travel_with_visa.html.

GETTING MONEY FROM HOME

The easiest and cheapest solution for running out of money while traveling is to have someone back home make a deposit to the bank account linked to your credit card or ATM card. Failing that, consider one of the options below. The online **International Money Transfer Consumer Guide** (http://international-money-transfer-consumer-guide.info) may also be of help.

WIRING MONEY

It is possible to arrange a **bank money transfer,** which means asking a bank back home to wire money to a bank in Europe. This is the cheapest way to transfer cash, but it's also the slowest, usually taking several days or more. Note that some banks may only release your funds in local currency, potentially sticking you with a poor exchange rate; inquire about this in advance. Money transfer services like **Western Union** are faster and more convenient than bank transfers, but also much pricier. Western Union has many locations worldwide. To find one, visit www.westernunion.com, or call: Australia ☎800 173 833, Canada and US 800-325-6000, UK 0800 833 833. To wire money using a credit card (Discover, MasterCard, or Visa), call in Canada and the US ☎800-225-5227, UK 0800 833 833. Money transfer services are also available to **American Express** cardholders and at selected **Thomas Cook** offices.

US STATE DEPARTMENT (US CITIZENS ONLY)

In serious emergencies only, the US State Department will forward money within hours to the nearest consular office. If you wish to use this service, you must contact the Overseas Citizens Service division of the US State Department (☎202-501-4444, toll-free 888-407-4747).

COSTS

The cost of your trip will vary depending on where you go, how you travel, and where you stay. The most significant expenses will probably be your round-trip (return) **airfare** to Europe (see **Getting to Europe: By Plane,** p. 46) and a **rail pass** or **bus pass** (see **Getting around Europe,** p. 46).

STAYING ON A BUDGET

Your daily budget will vary greatly from country to country. A bare-bones day in Europe would include camping or sleeping in hostels and buying food in supermarkets. A slightly more comfortable day would include sleeping in hostels or guesthouses and the occasional budget hotel, eating one meal per day at a restaurant, and going out at night. For a luxurious day, the sky's the limit. In any case, be sure to factor in emergency reserve funds (at least US$200) when planning how much money you'll need.

TIPS FOR SAVING MONEY

Some simple ways to save include searching out free entertainment, splitting accommodation and food costs with trustworthy fellow travelers, and buying food in grocery stores. Full- or multi-day local transportation passes can also save you valuable pocket change. Bring a **sleepsack** (p. 21) to save at hostels that charge for linens, and do your **laundry** in the sink (unless you're explicitly prohibited from doing so). Museums often have certain days when admission is free. If you are eligible, consider getting an ISIC or an IYTC; many sights and museums offer reduced admission to students and youths. Renting a bike is cheaper than renting a moped or scooter. Purchasing drinks at bars and clubs quickly becomes expensive; it's cheaper to buy alcohol at a supermarket and drink before going out. Remember, though, that while staying within your budget is important, don't do so at the expense of your health or a great travel experience.

TIPPING AND BARGAINING

In most European countries, a 5-10% gratuity is included in the food service bill. Additional tipping is not expected, but an extra 5-10% for good service is not unusual. Where gratuity is not included, 10-15% tips are standard and rounding up to the next unit of currency is common. Many countries have their own unique tipping practices with which you should familiarize yourself before visiting. In general, tipping in bars and pubs is unnecessary and money left on the bar may not make it into the bartender's hands. For other services such as taxis or hairdressers, a 10-15% tip is usually recommended. Watch other customers to gauge what is appropriate. Bargaining is useful in Greece, Turkey, and in outdoor markets across Europe. See individual country chapters for more specific information.

TAXES

The EU imposes a **value added tax (VAT)** on goods and services, usually included in the sticker price. Non-EU citizens visiting Europe may obtain a refund for taxes paid on retail goods, but not for taxes paid on services. As the VAT is 15-25%, it might be worthwhile to file for a refund. To do so, you must obtain Tax-Free Shopping Cheques, available from shops sporting the Europe Tax-Free Shopping logo, and save your receipts. Upon leaving the EU, present your goods, invoices, and passport to customs and have your checks stamped. Then, go to an ETS cash refund office on site or file for a refund once back home. Keep in mind that goods must be taken out of the country within three months of purchase, and that most countries require minimum purchase amounts per store to become eligible for a refund. See www.globalrefund.org for more info and downloads of relevant forms.

PACKING

Pack lightly. Lay out only what you absolutely need, then take half the clothes and twice the money. The Travelite FAQ (www.travelite.org) is a good resource for tips on traveling light. The online **Universal Packing List** (http://upl.codeq.info) will generate a customized list of suggested items based on your trip length, the expected climate, your planned activities, and other factors. If you plan to do a lot of hiking, also consult **The Great Outdoors**, p. 33.

TOP TEN WAYS TO SAVE IN EUROPE

1. Always ask about discounts. If **under 26,** you should rarely go a full day without being rewarded for your youth and inexperience.

2. Be aware that room prices tend to shoot up and transportation is a hassle on **festival dates** and during local holidays.

3. Consider purchasing the combination transportation and sights **discount passes** offered by many city tourist offices; they often pay for themselves many times over.

4. Get **out** of the city. A day hiking or beach-lounging provides relief for both you and your wallet.

5. Travel early; trains, buses, and ferries leaving early in the day or on weekdays (as opposed to weekends) are generally cheaper than those leaving at other times.

6. Don't expect to eat out every meal in Europe. **Street markets** are excellent places to find cheap fruits and vegetables, and most hostels have kitchens.

7. In major cities, make your base on the **outskirts** of the town, where food and beds tend to be both cheaper and less touristed.

8. Bring a **sleepsack** to avoid the occasional linens rental charge.

9. Clubbing is expensive enough without depending on overpriced mojitos; start the night off with ▨ **market-purchased booze.**

10. Be your own tour guide; sightseeing is best—and free—on your own with your **Let's Go.**

Luggage: If you plan to cover most of your itinerary by foot, a sturdy **frame backpack** is unbeatable. (For backpack basics, see p. 36.) Toting a **suitcase** or **trunk** is fine if you plan to live in 1 or 2 cities, but not a great idea if you plan to move around frequently. In addition to your main piece of luggage, a **daypack** (a small backpack or courier bag) is useful.

Clothing: No matter when you're traveling, it's a good idea to bring a warm jacket or wool sweater, a rain jacket (Gore-Tex® is both waterproof and breathable), sturdy shoes or hiking boots, and thick socks. Waterproof sandals are a must-have for grubby hostel showers. You may also want one outfit for going out, and maybe a nicer pair of shoes. If you plan to visit religious or cultural sites, remember to dress modestly.

 DISPOSABLES. If you're tight on space and plan to give your clothes a good workout, consider buying a pack of simple cotton undershirts. A pack of plain t-shirts is cheap and light, and you won't feel bad throwing them away when they get covered in backpacker grime.

Sleepsack: Some hostels require that you either provide your own linens or rent linens from them. Save cash by making your own sleepsack: fold a full-size sheet in half the long way, then sew it closed along the long side and one of the short sides.

Adapters and Converters: In Europe, electricity is 230V AC, enough to fry any 120V North American appliance. Americans and Canadians should buy an adapter (changes the shape of the plug; US$10-30) and a converter (changes the voltage; US$10-30); don't use an adapter without a converter unless appliance instructions explicitly state otherwise. Australians and New Zealanders, who use 230V at home, won't need a converter, but will need a set of adapters. For more on all things adaptable, check out http://kropla.com/electric.htm.

Toiletries: Toothbrushes, towels, soap, talcum powder (to keep feet dry), deodorant, razors, tampons, and condoms are available, but it may be difficult to find your preferred brand, so bring extras. Also, be sure to bring enough extra contact lenses and solution for your entire trip. Bring your glasses and a copy of your prescription, too, in case you need an emergency replacement. If you use heat disinfection, either switch temporarily to a chemical disinfection system (check first to make sure it's safe with your brand of lenses), or buy a converter to 220/240V.

 KEEP IT CLEAN. Multi-purpose liquid soaps will save space and keep you from smelling like last night's fish and chips. Dr. Bronner's® and Campsuds® both make soap that you can use as toothpaste, shampoo, laundry detergent, dishwashing liquid, and more. Plus, they're biodegradable.

First Aid: For a basic first-aid kit, pack bandages, a pain reliever, antibiotic cream, a thermometer, a pocket knife, tweezers, moleskin, decongestant, motion-sickness remedy, diarrhea or upset-stomach medication (Pepto Bismol® or Imodium®), an antihistamine, sunscreen, insect repellent, and burn ointment. If you will be in remote regions of less-developed Eastern European countries, consider a syringe for emergencies (get an explanatory letter from your doctor). Leave all sharp objects in your checked luggage.

Film: Digital cameras can be a more economical option and less of a hassle than regular cameras, just be sure to bring along a large enough **memory card** and extra (or rechargeable) **batteries.** Less serious photographers may want to bring a disposable camera or two. Despite disclaimers, airport security X-rays can fog film, so buy a **lead-lined** pouch at a camera store or ask security to hand-inspect it. Always pack film in your carry-on luggage, as higher-intensity X-rays are used on checked luggage.

Other Useful Items: For safety, bring a **money belt** and a small **padlock.** Basic **outdoors equipment** (water bottle, compass, waterproof matches, pocketknife, sunglasses, sunscreen, hat) may also prove useful. Make quick repairs with a needle and thread; also consider electrical tape for patching tears. To do laundry by hand, bring detergent, a small rubber ball to stop up the sink, and string for a makeshift clothesline. Extra **plastic bags** are crucial for storing food, dirty shoes, and wet clothes, and for keeping liquids from exploding all over your clothes. Other items include an umbrella, a battery-powered **alarm clock,** safety pins, rubber bands, a flashlight, a utility pocketknife, earplugs, garbage bags, and a small calculator. A **mobile phone** can be a lifesaver on the road; see p. 28 for information on acquiring one that will work at your destination.

Important Documents: Don't forget your passport, traveler's checks, ATM and/or credit cards, adequate ID, and photocopies of all of the aforementioned. Other documents you may wish to have include: hostelling membership card (p. 31); a driver's license (p. 15); travel insurance forms (p. 24); an ISIC (p. 15); a rail or bus pass (p. 46).

SAFETY AND HEALTH

GENERAL ADVICE

In any type of crisis, the most important thing to do is **stay calm.** Your country's embassy abroad is usually your best resource when things go wrong; registering with that embassy upon arrival in the country is often a good idea.

DRUGS AND ALCOHOL. Drug and alcohol laws vary widely throughout Europe. In the Netherlands "soft" drugs are available on the open market, while in much of Eastern Europe drug possession may lead to a heavy prison sentence. If you carry

prescription drugs, carry both a copy of the prescriptions themselves and a note from a doctor, especially at border crossings. **Public drunkenness** is culturally unacceptable and against the law in many countries; it can also jeopardize your safety.

TERRORISM AND CIVIL UNREST. In the wake of September 11 and the war in Iraq, be vigilant near Western embassies and be wary of crowds and demonstrations. Keep an eye on the news, pay attention to travel warnings, and comply with security measures. Overall, risks of civil unrest tend to be localized and rarely directed toward tourists.

TRAVEL ADVISORIES. The following government offices provide travel information and advisories by telephone, by fax, or via the web:

Australian Department of Foreign Affairs and Trade: ☎612 6261 1111; www.dfat.gov.au.

Canadian Department of Foreign Affairs and International Trade (DFAIT): Call ☎800-267-8376; www.dfait-maeci.gc.ca. Call for their free booklet, *Bon Voyage...But.*

New Zealand Ministry of Foreign Affairs: ☎044 398 000; www.mfat.govt.nz.

United Kingdom Foreign and Commonwealth Office: ☎020 7008 1500; www.fco.gov.uk.

US Department of State: ☎888-407-4747; http://travel.state.gov. Visit the website for the booklet *A Safe Trip Abroad.*

PERSONAL SAFETY

EXPLORING AND TRAVELING

To avoid unwanted attention, try to blend in as much as possible. Respecting local customs (in many cases, dressing more conservatively than you would at home) may placate would-be hecklers. Familiarize yourself with your surroundings before setting out, and carry yourself with confidence. Check maps in shops and restaurants rather than on the street. If you are traveling alone, be sure someone at home knows your itinerary, and never tell anyone you meet that you're by yourself. When walking at night, stick to busy, well-lit streets and avoid dark alleyways. If you ever feel uncomfortable, leave the area as quickly and directly as you can.

There is no sure-fire way to avoid all the threatening situations you might encounter while traveling, but a good **self-defense course** will give you concrete ways to react to unwanted advances. **Impact, Prepare,** and **Model Mugging** can refer you to local self-defense courses in Australia, Canada, Switzerland and the US.

If you are using a **car,** learn local driving signals and wear a seatbelt. For long drives in desolate areas, invest in a cellular phone and a roadside assistance program (p. 52). **Sleeping in your car** is very dangerous, and it's also illegal in many countries. For info on the perils of **hitchhiking,** see p. 55.

POSSESSIONS AND VALUABLES

Never leave your belongings unattended; crime occurs in even the most safe-looking hostel or hotel. Bring your own padlock for hostel lockers, and don't ever store valuables in a locker. Be particularly careful on **buses** and **trains;** horror stories abound about determined thieves who wait for travelers to fall asleep. Carry your bag or purse in front of you where you can see it. When traveling with others, sleep in alternate shifts. When alone, use good judgment in selecting a train compartment: never stay in an empty one, and use a lock to secure your pack to the luggage rack. Use extra caution if traveling at night or on overnight trains. Try to sleep on top bunks with your luggage stored above you (if not in bed with you), and keep important documents and other valuables on you at all times.

There are a few steps you can take to minimize the financial risk associated with traveling. First, **bring as little with you as possible.** Second, buy a few combination **padlocks** to secure your belongings either in your pack or in a hostel or train station locker. Third, **carry as little cash as possible.** Keep your traveler's checks and ATM/credit cards in a **money belt**— not a "fanny pack"—along with your passport and ID cards. Fourth, **keep a small cash reserve separate from your primary stash.** This should be about US$50 (US$ or euro are best) sewn into or stored in the depths of your pack, along with photocopies of your passport, your birth certificate, and other important documents.

In large cities **con artists** often work in groups and may involve children. Beware of certain classics: sob stories that require money, rolls of bills "found" on the street, mustard spilled (or saliva spit) onto your shoulder to distract you while they snatch your bag. **Never let your passport and your bags out of your sight.** Hostel workers will sometimes stand station arrival points to try to recruit tired and disoriented travelers to their hostel; never believe strangers who tell you that theirs is the only hostel open. Beware of **pickpockets** in crowds, especially on public transportation. Also, be alert in public telephone booths: If you must say your calling card number, do so very quietly; if you punch it in, make sure no one can look over your shoulder.

If you will be traveling with electronic devices, such as a laptop computer or a PDA, check whether your homeowner's insurance covers loss, theft, or damage when you travel. If not, you might consider purchasing a low-cost separate insurance policy. **Safeware** (☎ 800-800-1492; www.safeware.com) specializes in covering computers. State rates vary, but average US$200 for global coverage up to $4000.

PRE-DEPARTURE HEALTH

In your **passport,** write the names of any people you wish to be contacted in case of a medical emergency, and list any allergies or medical conditions. Matching a prescription to a foreign equivalent is not always easy, safe, or possible, so if you take prescription drugs, consider carrying up-to-date prescriptions or a statement from your doctor stating the medication's trade name, manufacturer, chemical name, and dosage. While traveling, be sure to keep all medication with you in your carry-on luggage. For tips on packing a **first-aid kit** and other health essentials, see p. 25.

INSURANCE

Travel insurance covers four basic areas: medical/health problems, property loss, trip cancellation/interruption, and emergency evacuation. Though regular insurance policies may well extend to travel-related accidents, you may consider purchasing separate travel insurance if the cost of potential trip cancellation, interruption, or emergency medical evacuation is greater than you can absorb. Prices for independent travel insurance generally run about US$50 per week for full coverage, while trip cancellation/interruption may be purchased separately at a rate of US$3-5 per day depending on length of stay.

Medical insurance (especially university policies) often covers costs incurred abroad; check with your provider. **Australians** traveling in Finland, Ireland, Italy, the Netherlands, Sweden, or the UK are entitled to many of the services that they would receive at home as part of the Reciprocal Health Care Agreement. **Homeowners' insurance** often covers theft during travel and loss of travel documents (passport, plane ticket, rail pass, etc.) up to US$500. **ISIC** and **ITIC** (p. 15) provide basic insurance benefits to US cardholders (see www.isicus.com for details). Cardholders have access to a toll-free 24hr. helpline for medical, legal, and financial emergencies. **American Express** (☎800-338-1670) grants most cardholders automatic collision and theft insurance on car rentals made with the card

USEFUL ORGANIZATIONS AND PUBLICATIONS

The American **Center for Disease Control and Prevention** (**CDC;** ☎877-FYI-TRIP; www.cdc.gov/travel) maintains an international travelers' hotline and an informative website. Consult the appropriate government agency of your home country for consular information sheets on health, entry requirements, and other issues for various countries (see the listings in the box on **Travel Advisories**, p. 23). For quick information on health and other travel warnings, call the **Overseas Citizens Services** (M-F 8am-8pm from US ☎888-407-4747, from overseas 202-501-4444), or contact a passport agency, embassy, or consulate abroad. For information on medical evacuation services and travel insurance firms, see the US government's website at http://travel.state.gov/travel/abroad_health.html or the **British Foreign and Commonwealth Office** (www.fco.gov.uk). For general health information, contact the **American Red Cross** (☎202-303-4498; www.redcross.org).

STAYING HEALTHY

Common sense is the simplest prescription for health. Drink water to prevent dehydration and constipation, and wear sturdy, broken-in shoes and clean socks.

For food- and water-borne diseases, prevention is the best cure: be sure your food is properly cooked and that the water you drink is clean. Tap water and fruits and vegetables with the peel on should be safe in most of Europe, especially in Western Europe. In some parts of Southern and Eastern Europe (in particular Moscow and St. Petersburg), avoid tap water and peel fruits and vegetables (including ice cubes and anything washed in tap water, like salad). Watch out for food from markets or street vendors. Buy bottled water, or purify your own water by bringing it to a rolling boil or treating it with **iodine tablets;** note, that some parasites such as *Giardia* have iodine-resistant exteriors, so boiling is more reliable.

 COMING IN HANDY. A small bottle of liquid hand cleanser, a stash of moist towelettes, or even a package of baby wipes can keep your hands and face germ-free and refreshed on the road. The hand cleanser should have an alcohol content of at least 70% to be effective.

Heat exhaustion and dehydration: Heat exhaustion leads to nausea, excessive thirst, headaches, and dizziness. Avoid it by drinking plenty of fluids, eating salty foods (e.g., crackers), abstaining from dehydrating beverages (e.g., alcohol and caffeine), and wearing sunscreen. Continuous heat stress can eventually lead to heatstroke, characterized by a rising temperature, severe headache, delirium and cessation of sweating. Victims should be cooled off with wet towels and taken to a doctor.

Sunburn: Always wear sunscreen (SPF 30 or higher) when spending time outdoors. If you get sunburned, drink more fluids than usual and apply an aloe-based lotion. Severe sunburns can lead to sun poisoning, a condition that can cause fever, chills, nausea, and vomiting. Sun poisoning should always be treated by a doctor.

Hypothermia: A rapid drop in body temperature is the clearest sign of overexposure to cold. Victims may also shiver, feel exhausted, have poor coordination, slur their speech, hallucinate, or suffer amnesia. *Do not let hypothermia victims fall asleep.* To avoid hypothermia, keep dry, wear layers, and stay out of the wind.

Tick-borne encephalitis: A viral infection of the central nervous system transmitted during the summer by tick bites (primarily in wooded areas) or by consumption of unpasteurized dairy products. Tick-borne encephalitis can occur across Europe.

Cholera: An intestinal disease caused by bacteria in contaminated food. Symptoms include diarrhea, dehydration, vomiting, and muscle cramps. If left untreated, cholera can be lethal within hours. Antibiotics are available, but the most important treatment is rehydration. Occurs in Moldova, the former Soviet Union, and Ukraine.

Giardiasis: Transmitted through parasites and acquired by drinking untreated water from streams or lakes. Symptoms include diarrhea, cramps, bloating, fatigue, weight loss, and nausea. If untreated, it can lead to severe dehydration. Giardiasis occurs worldwide.

Traveler's diarrhea: Results from drinking fecally contaminated water or eating uncooked and undercooked foods. Symptoms include nausea, bloating, and urgency. Try quick-energy, non-sugary foods with protein and carbohydrates to keep your strength up. Over-the-counter anti-diarrheals (e.g., Imodium) may counteract the problem. The most dangerous side effect is dehydration; drink 8 oz. of water with ½ tsp. of sugar or honey and a pinch of salt, try uncaffeinated soft drinks, or eat salted crackers. If you develop a fever or your symptoms don't go away after 4-5 days, consult a doctor.

Sexually transmitted infections (STIs): Gonorrhea, chlamydia, genital warts, syphilis, herpes, HPV, and other STIs are easier to catch than HIV and can be just as serious. Though condoms may protect you from some STIs, oral or even tactile contact can lead to transmission. If you think you may have contracted an STI, see a doctor immediately.

OTHER HEALTH CONCERNS

MEDICAL CARE ON THE ROAD. While healthcare systems in Western Europe tend to be quite accessible and of high quality, medical care varies greatly across Eastern and Southern Europe. Major cities such as Prague have English-speaking medical centers or hospitals for foreigners. In general, medical service in these

regions is not up to Western standards; though basic supplies are usually there, specialized treatment is not. Tourist offices may have names of local doctors who speak English. In the event of a medical emergency, contact your embassy for aid and recommendations. All EU citizens can receive free or reduced-cost first aid and emergency services by presenting a **European Health Insurance Card.**

If you're concerned about obtaining medical assistance while traveling, you may wish to employ special support services. The *MedPass* from **GlobalCare, Inc.,** (US ☎800-860-1111; www.globalcare.net), provides 24hr. international medical assistance and medical evacuation resources. The **International Association for Medical Assistance to Travelers** (**IAMAT;** US ☎716-754-4883, Canada 519-836-0102; www.iamat.org) has free membership, lists English-speaking doctors worldwide, and offers info on immunization requirements and sanitation. If your regular **Insurance** policy does not cover travel, you may wish to purchase additional coverage (see p. 24). Those with medical conditions (such as diabetes, allergies to antibiotics, epilepsy, or heart conditions) may want to obtain a **MedicAlert** (☎888-633-4298, outside US ☎209-668-3333; www.medicalert.org) membership (US$40 per year), which includes a stainless steel ID tag and a 24hr. collect-call number.

WOMEN'S HEALTH. Women traveling in unsanitary conditions are vulnerable to **urinary tract infections** (including bladder and kidneys). Over-the-counter medicines can sometimes alleviate symptoms, but if they persist, see a doctor. Vaginal **yeast infections** may flare up in hot and humid climates. Wearing loosely fitting trousers or a skirt and cotton underwear will help, as will over-the-counter remedies. Bring supplies from home if you are prone to infection, as it may be difficult to find the brands you prefer on the road. **Tampons, pads,** and **contraceptive devices** are widely available in most of Western Europe, but they can be hard to find in areas of Eastern Europe—bring supplies with you. **Abortion** laws also vary from country to country. In much of Western Europe, abortion is legal during at least the first 10-12 weeks of pregnancy, but it remains illegal in Ireland, Monaco, Spain, Poland, and Portugal, except in extreme circumstances. Portugal revised its strict laws in summer 2007 and legalized abortion for the first 10 weeks of pregnancy.

KEEPING IN TOUCH

BY EMAIL AND INTERNET

Email is popular and easily accessible in most of Europe. Though in some places it's possible to forge a remote link with your home server, in most cases this is a much slower (and more expensive) option than taking advantage of free **web-based email accounts** (e.g., www.gmail.com or www.hotmail.com). **Internet cafes** and the occasional free Internet terminal at a public library or university are listed in the **Practical Information** sections of major cities, and hostels frequently offer Internet access. For lists of additional cybercafes in Europe, check www.cybercaptive.com or www.cybercafe.com.

Increasingly, travelers find that taking their **laptops** on the road with them can be convenient for staying connected. Laptop users can call an Internet service provider via a modem using long-distance phone cards specifically intended for such calls. Another option is **Voice over Internet Protocol (VoIP).** A particularly popular VoIP provider, **Skype,** allows users to contact other users for free, and to call landlines and cell phones for an additional fee. Some Internet cafes allow travelers to connect their laptops, and those with wireless-enabled computers may be able to take advantage of an increasing number of Internet "hot spots," where they can get online for free or for a small fee. For info on insuring your laptop, see p. 24.

WARY WI-FI. Wireless hot spots make Internet access possible in public and remote places. Unfortunately, they also pose **security risks.** Hot spots are public, open networks that use unencrypted, unsecured connections. They are susceptible to hacks and "packet sniffing"—ways of stealing passwords and other private information. To prevent problems, disable ad hoc mode, turn off file sharing, turn off network discovery, encrypt your e-mail, turn on your firewall, beware of phony networks, and watch for over-the-shoulder creeps. Ask the establishment whose Wi-Fi you're using for the name of the network so you know you're on the right one. If you are in the vicinity and do not plan to access the Internet, turn off your Wi-Fi adapter.

BY TELEPHONE

CALLING HOME FROM EUROPE

You can usually make **direct international calls** from pay phones, but if you aren't using a phone card, you will need to feed the machine regularly. **Prepaid phone cards are a common and relatively inexpensive means of calling abroad.** Each one comes with a Personal Identification Number (PIN) and a toll-free access number. You call the access number and then follow the directions for dialing your PIN. To purchase prepaid phone cards, check online for the best rates; **www.callingcards.com is a good place to start. Online providers generally send your access number and PIN via email, with no actual "card" involved.** You can also call home with prepaid phone cards purchased in Europe (see **Calling Within Europe,** p. 29). Keep in mind that phone cards can be very country-specific, so buying an international phone card once you arrive will probably save you a headache.

PLACING INTERNATIONAL CALLS. All international dialing prefixes and country codes for Europe are shown in a chart on the **Inside Back Cover** of this book. To place international calls, dial:
1. The **international dialing prefix.** To call from **Australia,** dial 0011; **Canada** or the **US,** 011; **Ireland, New Zealand,** or the **UK,** 00.
2. The **country code** of the country you want to call. To call **Australia,** dial 61; **Canada** or the **US,** 1; **Ireland,** 353; **New Zealand,** 64; the **UK,** 44.
3. The **city/area code.** *Let's Go* lists the city/area codes for cities and towns in Europe opposite the city or town name, next to a ☎. If the 1st digit is a zero (e.g., 020 for London), omit it when calling from abroad (e.g., dial 20 from Canada to reach London).
4. The **local number.**

Another option is to purchase a **calling card,** linked to a major national telecommunications service in your home country. Calls are billed collect or to your account. To obtain a calling card, contact the appropriate company listed below. Where available, there are often advantages to purchasing calling cards online, including better rates and immediate access to your account. Companies that offer calling cards include: **AT&T Direct** (US ☎800-364-9292; www.att.com); **Canada Direct** (☎800-561-8868; www.infocanadadirect.com); **MCI WorldPhone** (US ☎800-777-5000; consumer.mci.com); **Telecom New Zealand Direct** (www.telecom.co.nz); **Telstra Australia** (☎1800 676 638; www.telstra.com). To call home with a calling card, contact the local operator for your service provider by dialing the appropriate toll-free access number. Placing a **collect call** through an international operator can be expensive, but may be necessary in case of an emergency. You can frequently call collect without even possessing a company's calling card just by calling its access number and following the instructions. *Let's Go* lists access numbers in the Essentials sections of each chapter.

CALLING WITHIN EUROPE

The simplest way to call within a country is to use a public pay phone. However, much of Europe has switched to a **prepaid phone card** system, and in some countries you may have a hard time finding coin-operated phones. **Prepaid phone cards** (available at newspaper kiosks and tobacco stores), which carry a certain amount of phone time depending on the card's denomination, usually save time and money in the long run. The phone will tell you how much time, in units, you have left on your card. Another kind of prepaid phone card comes with a PIN and a toll-free access number. Instead of inserting the card into the phone, you call the access number and follow the directions on the card. These cards can be used to make international as well as domestic calls. Phone rates typically tend to be highest in the morning, lower in the evening, and lowest on Sunday and late at night.

MOBILE PHONES

Cell phones are an increasingly popular option for travelers calling within Europe. In addition to greater convenience and safety, mobile phones often provide an economical alternative to expensive landline calls. Virtually all of Western Europe has excellent coverage, and the use of the **Global System for Mobiles (GSM)** allows one phone to function in multiple countries. To make and receive calls in Europe, you need a **GSM-compatible phone** and a **subscriber identity module (SIM) card,** a country-specific, thumbnail-sized chip that gives you a local phone number and plugs you into the local network. Many SIM cards are **prepaid,** meaning that they come with calling time included and you don't need to sign up for a monthly service plan. Incoming calls are free. When you use up the prepaid time, you can buy additional cards or vouchers (usually available at convenience stores) to "top up" your phone. For more info on GSM phones, check out www.orange.co.uk, www.roadpost.com, www.planetomni.com, www.telestial.com, or www.virginmobile.com. Companies like **Cellular Abroad** (www.cellularabroad.com) rent cell phones that work in a variety of destinations around the world, providing a simpler option than picking up a phone in-country.

GSM PHONES. Just having a GSM phone doesn't mean you're necessarily good to go when you travel abroad. The majority of GSM phones sold in the United States operate on a different **frequency** (1900) than international phones (900/1800) and will not work abroad. Tri-band phones work on all three frequencies (900/1800/1900) and will operate through most of the world. Additionally, some GSM phones are **SIM-locked** and will only accept SIM cards from a single carrier. You'll need a **SIM-unlocked** phone to use a SIM card from a local carrier when you travel.

TIME DIFFERENCES

All of Europe falls within 3hr. of Greenwich Mean Time (GMT). For more info, consult the time zone chart on the **Inside Back Cover.** GMT is 5hr. ahead of New York time, 8hr. ahead of Vancouver and San Francisco time, 10hr. behind Sydney time, and 12hr. behind Auckland time. Iceland is the only country in Europe to ignore Daylight Saving Time; fall and spring switchover times vary in countries that do observe Daylight Saving. For more info, visit www.worldtimeserver.com.

BY MAIL

SENDING MAIL HOME FROM EUROPE

Airmail is the best way to send mail home from Europe. From Western Europe to North America, delivery time averages about seven days. **Aerogrammes,** printed sheets that fold into envelopes and travel via airmail, are available at post offices and are the cheapest types of mail. Write "airmail" or *"par avion"* (or *por avión, mit Luftpost, via aerea,* etc.) on the front. **Surface mail** is by far the cheapest and slowest way to send mail. It takes one to two months to cross the Atlantic and one to three to cross the Pacific—good for heavy items you won't need for a while, such as souvenirs that you've acquired along the way. Check the **Essentials** section of each chapter for country-specific postal info.

SENDING MAIL TO EUROPE

To ensure timely delivery, mark envelopes "airmail" in both English and the local language. In addition to standard postage systems, **Federal Express** (Australia ☎ 13 26 10, Canada and the US 800-463-3339, Ireland 1800 535 800, New Zealand 0800 733 339, the UK 08456 070 809; www.fedex.com) handles express mail services from most countries to Europe.

There are several ways to arrange pick-up of letters sent to you while you are abroad. Mail can be sent via **Poste Restante** (General Delivery; *Lista de Correos, Fermo Posta, Postlagernde Briefe,* etc.) to almost any city or town in Europe with a post office, though it can be unreliable in Eastern Europe. See individual country chapters for more info on addressing *Poste Restante* letters. The mail will go to a special desk in a town's central post office, unless you specify a post office by street address or postal code. It's best to use the largest post office, since mail may be sent there regardless. It's usually safer and quicker, though more expensive, to send mail express or registered. Bring your passport for pick-up; there may be a small fee. If the clerks insist that there is nothing for you, ask them to check under your first name as well. *Let's Go* lists post offices in the **Practical Information** section for each city and most towns.

American Express's travel offices throughout the world offer a free **Client Letter Service** (mail held up to 30 days and forwarded upon request) for cardholders who contact them in advance. Some offices provide these services to non-cardholders (especially AmEx Travelers Cheque holders), but call ahead to make sure. *Let's Go* lists AmEx locations for most large cities in **Practical Information** sections; for a complete list, call ☎ 800-528-4800 or visit www.americanexpress.com/travel.

ACCOMMODATIONS

HOSTELS

Many hostels are laid out dorm-style, often with large single-sex rooms and bunk beds, although private rooms that sleep two to four are becoming more common. They sometimes have kitchens and utensils for your use, bike or moped rentals, storage areas, transportation to airports, breakfast and other meals, laundry facilities, and Internet access. There can be drawbacks: some hostels close during certain daytime "lockout" hours, have a curfew, don't accept reservations, impose a maximum stay, or—less frequently—require that you do chores. In Western and Eastern Europe, a dorm bed in a hostel will average around US$15-30 and US$5-20, respectively, and a private room around US$30-50 and US$20.

A HOSTELER'S BILL OF RIGHTS. There are certain standard features that we do not include in our hostel listings. Unless we state otherwise, you can expect that every hostel has free hot showers, no lockout, no curfew, some system of secure luggage storage, and no key deposit.

HOSTELLING INTERNATIONAL (HI)

Joining the youth hostel association in your own country (listed below) automatically grants you membership privileges in **Hostelling International (HI)**, a federation of national hostelling associations. Non-HI members may be allowed to stay in some hostels, but will have to pay extra. HI hostels are scattered throughout Europe and are typically less expensive than private hostels. HI's umbrella organization's website (www.hihostel.com), which lists the web addresses and phone numbers of all national associations, can be a great place to begin researching hostelling in a specific region. Other comprehensive hostelling websites include www.hostels.com and www.hostelplanet.com.

Most HI hostels also honor **guest memberships**—you'll get a blank card with space for six validation stamps. Each night you'll pay a nonmember supplement (one-sixth the membership fee) and earn one guest stamp; get six stamps and you're a member. In some countries you may need to remind the hostel reception. A new membership benefit is the **FreeNites** program, which allows hostelers to gain points toward free rooms. Most student travel agencies (see p. 43) sell HI cards, as do all of the national hostelling organizations listed below. All prices listed below are valid for **one-year memberships** unless otherwise noted.

Australian Youth Hostels Association (AYHA), 422 Kent St., Sydney, NSW 200 (☎02 9261 1111; www.yha.com.au). AUS$52, under 18 AUS$19.

Hostelling International-Canada (HI-C), 205 Catherine St. Ste. 400, Ottawa, ON K2P 1C3 (☎613-237-7884; www.hihostels.ca). CDN$35, under 18 free.

An Óige (Irish Youth Hostel Association), 61 Mountjoy St., Dublin 7 (☎830 4555; www.irelandyha.org). EUR€20, under 18 EUR€10.

Hostelling International Northern Ireland (HINI), 22-32 Donegall Rd., Belfast BT12 5JN (☎02890 32 47 33; www.hini.org.uk). UK£15, under 25 UK£10.

Scottish Youth Hostels Association (SYHA), 7 Glebe Cres., Stirling FK8 2JA (☎01786 89 14 00; www.syha.org.uk). UK£8, under 18 £4.

Youth Hostels Association (England and Wales), Trevelyan House, Dimple Rd., Matlock, Derbyshire DE4 3YH (☎08707 708 868; www.yha.org.uk). UK£16, under 26 UK£10.

Hostelling International-USA, 8401 Colesville Rd., Ste. 600, Silver Spring, MD 20910 (☎301-495-1240; www.hiayh.org). US$28, under 18 free.

BOOKING HOSTELS ONLINE. One of the easiest ways to ensure you've got a bed for the night is by reserving online. Click to the **Hostelworld** booking engine through **www.letsgo.com,** and you'll have access to bargain accommodations from Argentina to Zimbabwe with no added commission.

HOTELS, GUESTHOUSES, AND PENSIONS

In Western Europe, **hotel singles** cost about US$30 (€23) per night, doubles US$40 (€30) while Eastern European hotels run lower, around US$20 (€15) and US$30 (€23). You'll typically share a hall bathroom; a private bathroom and hot showers may cost extra. Some hotels offer full or half pension (all meals or no lunch).

Smaller **guesthouses** and **pensions** are often cheaper than hotels. If you make **reservations** in writing, note your night of arrival and the number of nights you plan to stay. After sending you a confirmation, the hotel may request payment for the first night. Often it's easiest to make reservations over the phone with a credit card.

OTHER TYPES OF ACCOMMODATIONS

YMCAS AND YWCA

Young Men's Christian Association (YMCA) and **Young Women's Christian Association (YWCA)** lodgings are usually cheaper than a hotel but more expensive than a hostel. Not all locations offer lodging; those that do are often located in urban downtowns. Many YMCAs accept women and families; some will not lodge those under 18 without parental permission. **World Alliance of YMCAs,** 12 Clos Belmont, 1208 Geneva, SWI (☎41 22 849 5100; www.ymca.int), has more info and a register of Western European YMCAs with housing options.

> **YMCA of the USA,** 101 North Wacker Dr., Chicago, IL 60606 (☎800-872-9622; www.ymca.net). Provides a listing of the nearly 1000 Ys across the US and Canada, as well as info on prices and services.
>
> **European Alliance of YMCAs,** Na Porici 12, CZ-110 30 Prague 1, Czech Republic (☎420 22 487 20 20; www.ymcaeurope.com). Maintains listings of European Ys.

BED & BREAKFASTS (B&BS)

For a cozy alternative to impersonal hotel rooms, **B&Bs** (private homes with rooms available to travelers) range from acceptable to sublime. Rooms in B&Bs generally

cost about €35 for a single and €70 for a double in Europe. Any number of websites provide listings for B&Bs. Check out **InnFinder** (www.inncrawler.com), **InnSite** (www.innsite.com), **BedandBreakfast.com** (www.bedandbreakfast.com), or **Pamela Lanier's Bed & Breakfast Guide Online** (www.lanierbb.com).

PRIVATE ROOMS

In much of Eastern Europe, due to a lack of budget travel infrastructure, the only accommodations in a backpacker's price range are rooms in **private houses** or **apartments.** Owners seek out tourists at the train or bus stations; tourist offices are also a source for finding a room. In larger towns there are agencies that book private rooms. If renting directly from the owner, feel free to negotiate prices, and don't agree to anything before seeing the room. This practice is illegal in some areas; check **local laws** before renting and always exercise caution when doing so.

UNIVERSITY DORMS

Many **colleges** and **universities** open their residence halls to travelers when school is not in session; some do so even during term-time. Getting a room may take a couple of phone calls and require advanced planning, but rates tend to be low and many offer free local calls and Internet. Where available, university dorms are listed in the **Accommodations** section of each city.

HOME EXCHANGES AND HOSPITALITY CLUBS

Home exchange offers the traveler various types of homes (houses, apartments, condominiums, villas, even castles), plus the opportunity to live like a native and to cut down on accommodation fees. For more info, contact **HomeExchange.com Inc.,** P.O. Box 787, Hermosa Beach, CA 90254, USA (☎310 798 3864 or toll free 800-877-8723; www.homeexchange.com), **or Intervac International Home Exchange** (www.intervac.com; see site for phone listings by country).

  Hospitality clubs link their members with individuals or families abroad who are willing to host travelers for free or for a small fee to promote cultural exchange and general good karma. In exchange, members usually must be willing to host travelers in their own homes; a small membership fee may also be required. **The Hospitality Club** (www.hospitalityclub.org) is a good place to start. **Servas** (www.servas.org) is an established, more formal, peace-based organization, and requires a fee and an interview to join. As always, use common sense when planning to stay with or host someone you do not know.

LONG-TERM ACCOMMODATIONS

Travelers planning to stay in Europe for extended periods of time may find it most cost-effective to rent an **apartment.** Rent varies widely by region, season, and quality. Besides the rent itself, prospective tenants usually are also required to front a security deposit (usually one month's rent) and the last month's rent. Generally, for stays shorter than three months, it is more feasible to **sublet** than lease your own apartment. Sublets are also more likely to be furnished. Out of session, it may be possible to arrange to sublet rooms from university students on summer break. It is far easier to find an apartment once you have arrived at your destination than to attempt to use the Internet or phone from home. By staying in a hostel for your first week or so, you can make local contacts and, more importantly, check out your new digs before you commit.

CAMPING

With Europe's vast terrain encompassing beaches, mountains and plains, camping always has a new adventure to offer. Furthermore, you can explore nature for

ESSENTIALS

prices refreshingly easy on the wallet. Most towns have several campgrounds within walking distance, occasionally offering a cheap shuttle service to reach them. Even the most rudimentary **campings** (campgrounds) provide showers and laundry facilities, though almost all forbid campfires. In addition to tent camping, others opt to drive RVs across Europe. Campgrounds usually charge a flat fee per person (around €4-6) plus a few euro extra for electricity, tents, cars, or running water. Most larger campgrounds also operate on-site general stores or cafes perfect for a quick, cheap bite. In some countries, it is illegal to pitch your tent or park your RV overnight along the road; look for designated camping areas within national parks, recognized campgrounds, or ask landowners permission before setting up residency on private property. In Sweden, Finland, and Norway, the right of public access permits travelers to tent one night in Scandinavia's forests and wilderness for free; for more info, see the Essentials Section of each country.

If campgrounds become your go-to accommodation, consider buying an **International Camping Carnet** (**ICC**, US$45). Available through the association of Family Campers and RVers (☎800-245-9755; www.fcrv.org), the card entitles holders to discounts at some campgrounds and may save travelers from having to leave their passport as a deposit. National tourist offices offer more info on country-specific camping. Also check out **Interhike** (www.interhike.com) which lists campgrounds by region. First-time campers may want to peruse **KarmaBum Cafe** (www.karmabum.com) for suggested itineraries, packing lists, blogs, and camping recipes. For more info on European outdoor activities, see **The Great Outdoors,** below.

THE GREAT OUTDOORS

Camping can be a great way to see Europe on the cheap. There are organized **campgrounds** outside most cities. Showers, bathrooms, and a small restaurant or store are common; some sites have more elaborate facilities. Prices are low, usually US$5-15 per person plus additional charges for tents and cars. While camping is a cheaper option than hosteling, the cost of transportation to and from campgrounds can add up. Some parks and public grounds allow **free camping**, but check local laws. Many areas have additional park-specific rules. The **Great Outdoor Recreation Pages** (www.gorp.com) provides excellent general info.

USEFUL RESOURCES

A variety of publishing companies offer hiking guidebooks to meet the educational needs of the novice or the expert. For information about biking, camping, and hiking, write or call the publishers listed below to receive a free catalog. Campers heading to Europe should consider buying an **International Camping Carnet.** Similar to a hostel membership card, it's required at a few campgrounds and provides discounts at others. It is available in North America from the **Family Campers and RVers Association** (www.fcrv.org) and in the UK from **The Caravan Club** (see below).

 LEAVE NO TRACE. Let's Go encourages travelers to embrace the "Leave No Trace" ethic, minimizing their impact on natural environments. Trekkers should set up camp on durable surfaces, use cookstoves instead of campfires, bury human waste away from water supplies, bag trash and carry it out with them, and respect wildlife and natural objects. For more detailed information, contact the **Leave No Trace Center for Outdoor Ethics,** P.O. Box 997, Boulder, CO 80306 (☎800-332-4100 or 303-442-8222; www.lnt.org).

Automobile Association, Contact Centre, Carr Ellison House, William Armstrong Dr., Newcastle-upon-Tyne NE4 7YA, UK (☎08706 000 371; www.theaa.com). Publishes

Caravan and Camping Europe and *Britain & Ireland* (UK£10) as well as road atlases for Europe as a whole and for Britain, France, Germany, Ireland, Italy, and Spain.

The Caravan Club, East Grinstead House, East Grinstead, West Sussex RH19 1UA, UK (☎01342 326 944; www.caravanclub.co.uk). For UK£35, members get access to campgrounds, insurance services, equipment discounts, maps, and a magazine.

Sierra Club Books, 85 2nd St., 2nd fl., San Francisco, CA 94105, USA (☎415-977-5500; www.sierraclub.org). Publishes general resource books on hiking and camping.

The Mountaineers Books, 1001 SW Klickitat Way, Ste. 201, Seattle, WA 98134, USA (☎206-223-6303; www.mountaineersbooks.org). Over 600 titles on hiking, biking, mountaineering, natural history, and conservation.

WILDERNESS SAFETY

Staying **warm, dry,** and **well hydrated** are the keys to a happy and safe wilderness experience. Before any hike, prepare yourself for an emergency by packing a first-aid kit, a reflector, a whistle, high-energy food, extra water, raingear, a hat, mittens, and several **extra pairs of socks.** For warmth, wear wool or insulating synthetic materials designed for the outdoors. Cotton is a bad choice as it takes a ridiculously long time to dry and loses its insulating effect when wet.

Check **weather forecasts** often and pay attention to the skies when hiking, as weather patterns can change suddenly, especially in mountainous areas. Always let someone—a friend, your hostel staff, a park ranger, or a local hiking organization—know when and where you are going. Know your physical limits and do not attempt a hike beyond your ability.

CAMPING AND HIKING EQUIPMENT

WHAT TO BUY

Good camping equipment is both sturdy and light. North American suppliers tend to offer the most competitive prices.

Sleeping Bags: Most sleeping bags are rated by season; "summer" means 30-40°F (around 0°C) at night; "four-season" or "winter" often means below 0°F (-17°C). Bags are made of **down** (warm and light, but expensive, and miserable when wet) or of **synthetic** material (heavy, durable, and warm when wet). Prices range US$50-250 for a summer synthetic and US$200-300 for a good down winter bag. **Sleeping bag pads** include foam pads (US$10-30), air mattresses (US$15-50), and self-inflating mats (US$30-120). Bring a **stuff sack** to store your bag and keep it dry.

Tents: The best tents are free-standing (with their own frames and suspension systems), set up quickly, and only require staking in high winds. Low-profile dome tents are the best all-around. 2-person tents start at US$100, 4-person tents US$160. Make sure your tent has a rain fly and seal its seams with waterproofer. Other useful accessories include a **battery-operated lantern,** a plastic **groundcloth,** and a nylon **tarp.**

Backpacks: Internal-frame packs mold to your back, keep a lower center of gravity, and flex to allow you to hike difficult trails, while **external-frame packs** are more comfortable for long hikes over even terrain, as they carry weight higher and distribute it more evenly. Make sure your pack has a hip-belt to transfer weight to your legs. Any serious backpacking requires a pack of at least 4000 cu. in. (16,000cc), plus 500 cu. in. for sleeping bags in internal-frame packs. Sturdy backpacks cost anywhere from US$125 to 420—your pack is an area where it doesn't pay to economize. On your hunt for the perfect pack, fill up each prospective model with something heavy, strap it on, and walk around the store to get a sense of how the model distributes weight. Either buy a **rain cover** (US$10-20) or store your belongings in plastic bags inside your pack.

Boots: Be sure to wear hiking boots with good **ankle support.** They should fit snugly and comfortably over 1-2 pairs of **wool socks** and a pair of thin **liner socks.** Break in boots over several weeks before you go to spare yourself from blisters.

Other Necessities: Synthetic layers, like those made of polypropylene or polyester, and a pile jacket will keep you warm even when wet. A **space blanket** (US$5-15) will help you to retain body heat, and doubles as a groundcloth. Plastic **water bottles** are vital; look for shatter- and leak-resistant models. Carry **water-purification tablets** for when you can't boil water. Virtually every organized campground in Europe forbids fires or the gathering of firewood, so you'll need a **camp stove** (the classic Coleman starts at US$50) and a propane-filled **fuel bottle** to operate it. Also bring a **first-aid kit, pocket-knife, insect repellent,** and **waterproof matches** or a **lighter.**

WHERE TO BUY IT

The online and mail-order companies listed below offer lower prices than many retail stores. A visit to a local camping or outdoors store will give you a good sense of the look and weight of certain items before you buy.

Campmor, 28 Parkway, P.O. Box 700, Upper Saddle River, NJ 07458, USA (☎800-525-4784; www.campmor.com).

Cotswold Outdoor, Unit 11 Kemble Business Park, Crudwell, Malmesbury Wiltshire SN16 9SH, UK (☎08704 427 755; www.cotswoldoutdoor.com).

Discount Camping, 833 Main North Rd., Pooraka, SA 5095, Australia (☎08 8262 3399; www.discountcamping.com.au).

ORGANIZED ADVENTURE TRIPS

Organized adventure tours offer another way of exploring the wild. Activities include hiking, biking, skiing, canoeing, kayaking, rafting, climbing, photo safaris, and archaeological digs. Organizations that specialize in camping and outdoor equipment like REI and EMS (see above) are also a good source for info. **Specialty Travel Index** lists organized tour opportunities throughout Europe (from the US ☎888-624-4030, from elsewhere 415-455-1643; www.specialtytravel.com.)

SPECIFIC CONCERNS

SUSTAINABLE TRAVEL

As the number of travelers on the road rises, the detrimental effect they can have on natural environments becomes an increasing concern. With this in mind, Let's Go promotes the philosophy of **sustainable travel.** Through sensitivity to issues of ecology and sustainability, today's travelers can be a powerful force in preserving as well as restoring the places they visit.

Ecotourism, a rising trend in sustainable travel, focuses on the conservation of natural habitats and their use in building up an economy without exploitation or overdevelopment. Travelers can make a difference by doing research in advance and by supporting organizations and establishments that pay attention to their impact on their natural surroundings and that strive to be environmentally friendly. **International Friends of Nature** (www.nfi.at) has info about sustainable travel options in Europe. For more info, see **Beyond Tourism,** p. 56.

ECOTOURISM RESOURCES. For more info on environmentally responsible tourism, contact one of the organizations below:

Conservation International, 2011 Crystal Dr., Ste. 500, Arlington, VA 22202, USA (☎800-406-2306 or 703-341-2400; www.conservation.org).

Green Globe, Green Globe vof, Verbenalaan 1, 2111 ZL Aerdenhout, The Netherlands (☎31 23 544 0306; www.greenglobe.com).

International Ecotourism Society, 1333 H St. NW, Ste. 300E, Washington, D.C. 20005, USA (☎202-347-9203; www.ecotourism.org).

United Nations Environment Program, 39-43 Quai André Citroën, 75739 Paris Cedex 15, France (☎33 1 44 37 14 50; www.uneptie.org/pc/tourism).

RESPONSIBLE TRAVEL

The impact of tourist money on the destinations you visit should not be underestimated. The choices you make during your trip can have potent effects on local communities—for better or for worse. Travelers who care about the destinations they explore should become aware of the social, cultural, and political implications of the choices they make when they travel. Simple decisions such as buying local products instead of globally available ones, paying fair prices for products or services, and attempting to say a few words in the local language can have a strong, positive effect on the community.

Community-based tourism aims to channel tourist money into the local economy by emphasizing tours and cultural programs run by members of the host community that benefit disadvantaged groups. This type of tourism also benefits the tourists themselves, as it often takes them beyond the traditional tours of the region. The *Ethical Travel Guide* (UK£13), a project of **Tourism Concern** (☎+44 020 7133 3330; www.tourismconcern.org.uk), is an excellent resource for information on community-based travel with a directory of 300 establishments in 60 countries.

TRAVELING ALONE

Benefits to traveling alone include independence and a greater opportunity to connect with locals. However, solo travelers are more vulnerable to harassment and street theft. If traveling alone, look confident, try not to stand out as a tourist, and be careful in deserted or crowded areas. Avoid poorly lit areas. If questioned, never admit that you are traveling alone. In Eastern Europe, be particularly careful about train travel; some travelers find it safer to ride in more crowded compartments and to avoid traveling at night. Maintain regular contact with someone at home who knows your itinerary, and always research your destination before traveling. For more tips, pick up *Traveling Solo* by Eleanor Berman (Globe Pequot Press, US$18), visit www.travelaloneandloveit.com, or subscribe to **Connecting: Solo Travel Network,** 689 Park Rd., Unit 6, Gibsons, BC V0N 1V7, Canada (☎604-886-9099; www.cstn.org; membership US$30-48).

WOMEN TRAVELERS

Women traveling on their own face some additional safety concerns, but it's easy to be adventurous without taking undue risks. If you are concerned, consider staying in hostels that offer single rooms that lock from the inside or rooms for women only. Stick to centrally located accommodations and avoid solitary late-night treks or metro rides. Always carry extra money for a phone call, bus, or taxi. **Hitchhiking** is never safe for lone women, or even for two women traveling together. Look as if you know where you're going, and approach older women or couples for directions if you're lost or uncomfortable. Generally, the less you look like a tourist, the better off you'll be. Dress modestly, especially in rural areas. Wearing a conspicuous **wedding band** sometimes helps prevent unwanted advances.

Your best answer to verbal harassment is no answer at all; feigning deafness, pretending you don't understand the language, or staring straight ahead will usually do the trick. The extremely persistent can sometimes be dissuaded by a firm, loud "Go away!" in the appropriate language. Seek out a police officer or a passerby if you are being harassed. Memorize the emergency numbers in places you visit, and consider carrying a whistle on your keychain. A self-defense course will both prepare you for a potential attack and raise your level of awareness (see **Self Defense**, p. 24).

GLBT TRAVELERS

Attitudes toward gay, lesbian, bisexual, and transgendered (GLBT) travelers are particular to each region in Europe. On the whole, countries in Northern and Western Europe tend to be queer-friendly, while Eastern Europe harbors enclaves of tolerance in cities amid stretches of cultural conservatism. Countries like Romania that outlawed homosexuality as recently as 2002 are becoming more liberal today, and can be considered viable destinations for GLBT travelers. **Out and About** (www.planetout.com) has a newsletter and website addressing gay travel concerns. The online newspaper **365gay.com** (www.365gay.com/travel/travelchannel.htm) has a travel section, while the French-language site **netgai.com** (http://netgai.com/international/Europe) includes links to country-specific resources.

Gay's the Word, 66 Marchmont St., London WC1N 1AB, UK (☎020 72 78 76 54; http://freespace.virgin.net/gays.theword). The largest gay and lesbian bookshop in the UK, with both fiction and non-fiction titles. Mail-order service available.

Giovanni's Room, 345 S. 12th St., Philadelphia, PA 19107, USA (☎215-923-2960; www.queerbooks.com). An international lesbian and gay bookstore with mail-order service (carries some of the publications listed below).

International Lesbian and Gay Association (ILGA), Avenue des Villas 34, 1060 Brussels, BEL (☎32 25 02 24 71; www.ilga.org). Provides political information, such as homosexuality laws of individual countries.

ADDITIONAL RESOURCES.

Spartacus International Gay Guide 2006. Bruno Gmunder Verlag and Briand Bedford (US$33).

The Damron Men's Travel Guide 2006. Gina M. Gatta, Damron Co. (US$20).

The Gay Vacation Guide: The Best Trips and How to Plan Them. Mark Chesnut, Kensington Books (US$15).

TRAVELERS WITH DISABILITIES

European countries vary in accessibility to travelers with disabilities. Some tourist boards, particularly in Western and Northern Europe, provide directories on the accessibility of various accommodations and transportation services. If these services are not available, contact establishments directly. Be sure to inform airlines and hostels of any pertinent disabilities when making reservations; some time may be needed to prepare special accommodations. **Guide dog owners** should inquire as to the quarantine policies of each destination country.

Rail is the most convenient form of travel for disabled travelers in Europe: many stations have ramps, and some trains have wheelchair lifts, special seating areas, and special toilets. All Eurostar, some InterCity (IC), and some EuroCity (EC) trains are wheelchair-accessible. CityNightLine trains, French TGV (high speed), and Conrail trains feature special compartments. In general, the countries with the most **wheelchair-accessible rail networks** are: Denmark (IC and Lyn trains), France (TGVs and other long-distance trains), Germany (ICE, EC, IC, and IR trains), Ireland (most major trains), Italy (EC and IC trains), the Netherlands (most trains), Sweden (X2000s, most IC and IR trains), and Switzerland (all IC, most EC, and some regional trains). Austria, Poland, and the UK offer accessibility on selected routes. Bulgaria, the Czech Republic, Greece, Hungary, Slovakia, and Spain's rail systems have limited wheelchair accessibility. For those who wish to rent cars, some major **car rental** agencies (e.g., Hertz) offer hand-controlled vehicles.

USEFUL ORGANIZATIONS

Access Abroad, www.umabroad.umn.edu/access. A website devoted to making study abroad available to students with disabilities. The site is maintained by Disability Services, University of Minnesota, 230 Heller Hall, 271 19th Ave. S., Minneapolis, MN 55455, USA (☎612-626-7379).

Accessible Journeys, 35 W. Sellers Ave., Ridley Park, PA 19078, USA (☎800-846-4537; www.disabilitytravel.com). Designs tours for wheelchair users and slow walkers. The site has tips and forums for all travelers.

Flying Wheels, 143 W. Bridge St., P.O. Box 382, Owatonna, MN 55060, USA (☎507-451-5005; www.flyingwheelstravel.com). Specializes in escorted trips to Europe for people with physical disabilities; plans custom trips worldwide.

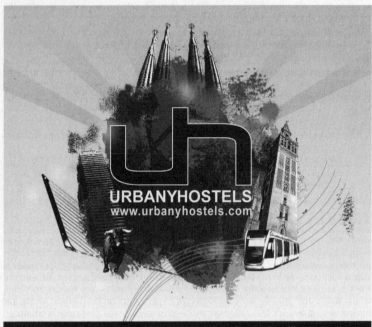

The Guided Tour, Inc., 7900 Old York Rd., Ste. 114B, Elkins Park, PA 19027, USA (☎800-783-5841; www.guidedtour.com). Organizes travel programs for persons with developmental and physical challenges in Ireland, Italy, Spain, and the UK.

Society for Accessible Travel and Hospitality (SATH), 347 5th Ave., Ste. 610, New York, NY 10016, USA (☎212-447-7284; www.sath.org). An advocacy group that publishes free online travel information and the travel magazine *Open World* (annual subscription US$13, free for members). Annual membership US$45, students and seniors US$30.

MINORITY TRAVELERS

In general, minority travelers will find a high level of tolerance in large cities; small towns and the countryside are less predictable. The increasingly mainstream reality of anti-immigrant sentiments means that travelers of African or Arab descent (regardless of their citizenship) may be the object of unwarranted assumptions and even hostility. The September 11 terrorist attacks on the United States and the July 7 attacks on the London Tube corresponded with an upsurge in anti-Muslim sentiments in Europe, while anti-Semitism also remains a very real problem in many countries, especially in France, Austria, and much of Eastern Europe. Discrimination is particularly forceful against Roma (gypsies) throughout much of Eastern Europe. Jews, Muslims, and other minority travelers should keep an eye out for skinheads, who have been linked to racist violence in Central and Eastern Europe, and elsewhere. **The European Monitoring Centre on Racism and Xenophobia,** Rahlgasse 3, 1060 Vienna, AUT (☎43 15 80 30; http://eumc.eu.int), publishes a wealth of country-specific statistics and reports. Travelers can consult **United for Intercultural Action,** Postbus 413, 1000 AK, Amsterdam, NTH (☎31 20 6834778; www.unitedagainstracism.org), for a list of over 500 country-specific organizations that work against racism and discrimination.

DIETARY CONCERNS

Vegetarians will find no shortage of meat-free dining options throughout most of Northern and Western Europe, although **vegans** may have a trickier time away from urban centers, where eggs and dairy can dominate traditional cuisine. The cuisine of Eastern Europe still tends to be heavy on meat and gravy, although major cities often boast surprisingly inventive vegetarian and ethnic fare.

The travel section of The Vegetarian Resource Group's website, at www.vrg.org/travel, has a comprehensive list of organizations and websites that are geared toward helping vegetarians and vegans traveling abroad. The website for the **European Vegetarian Union (EVU),** at www.europeanvegetarian.org, includes links to organizations in 26 European countries. For more info, consult *The Vegetarian Traveler: Where to Stay if You're Vegetarian, Vegan, Environmentally Sensitive,* by Jed and Susan Civic (Larson Publications; US$16), *Vegetarian Europe,* by Alex Bourke (Vegetarian Guides; US$17), and the indispensable, multilingual *Vegan Passport* (The Vegan Society; US$5), along with the websites www.vegdining.com, www.happycow.net, and www.vegetariansabroad.com.

Those looking to keep **kosher** will find abundant dining options across Europe; contact synagogues in larger cities for information, or consult www.kashrut.com/travel/Europe for country-specific resources. Hebrew College Online also offers a searchable database of kosher restaurants at www.shamash.org/kosher. Another good resource is the *Jewish Travel Guide,* edited by Michael Zaidner (Vallentine Mitchell; US$18). Travelers looking for **halal** groceries and restaurants will have the most success in France and Eastern European nations with substantial Muslim populations; consult www.zabihah.com for establishment reviews. **Keep in mind that** if you are strict in your observance, you may have to prepare your own food.

OTHER RESOURCES

TRAVEL PUBLISHERS AND BOOKSTORES

The Globe Corner Bookstore, 90 Mt. Auburn St., Cambridge, MA 02138 (☎617-492-6277; www.globecorner.com). The Globe Corner sponsors an Adventure Travel Lecture Series and carries a vast selection of guides and maps to every imaginable destination. Online catalog includes atlases and monthly staff picks of outstanding travel writing.

Hippocrene Books, 171 Madison Ave., New York, NY 10016 (☎718-454-2366; www.hippocrenebooks.com), publishes foreign-language dictionaries and learning guides, along with ethnic cookbooks and a smattering of guidebooks.

WORLD WIDE WEB

Almost every aspect of budget travel is accessible via the web. In 10min. at the keyboard, you can make a hostel reservation, get advice on travel hot spots from other intrepid travelers, or find out how much a train ride from Geneva to Nice costs. Listed here are some regional and travel-related sites to start off your surfing; other relevant websites are listed throughout the book. Because website turnover is high, use search engines (e.g., www.google.com) to strike out on your own.

WWW.LETSGO.COM. Our website features extensive content from our guides; a community forum where travelers can connect with each other, ask questions or advice, and share stories and tips; and expanded resources to help you plan your trip. Visit us to browse by destination and find information about ordering our titles!

Backpacker's Ultimate Guide: www.bugeurope.com. Tips on packing, transportation, and where to go. Also tons of country-specific travel information.

BootsnAll.com: www.bootsnall.com. Numerous resources for independent travelers, from planning your trip to reporting on it when you get back.

How to See the World: www.artoftravel.com. A compendium of great travel tips, from cheap flights to self defense to interacting with local culture.

Travel Intelligence: www.travelintelligence.net. A large collection of travel writing by distinguished travel writers.

Travel Library: www.travel-library.com. A fantastic set of links for general information and personal travelogues.

World Hum: www.worldhum.com. An independently produced collection of "travel dispatches from a shrinking planet."

INFORMATION ABOUT EUROPE

BBC News: http://news.bbc.co.uk/europe. The latest coverage from one of Europe's most reputable sources for English-language news, for free.

CIA World Factbook: www.odci.gov/cia/publications/factbook/index.html. Tons of vital statistics on countries' geography, government, economy, and people.

EUROPA: http://europa.eu.int/index_en.htm. English-language gateway to the European Union, featuring news articles and a citizen's guide to EU institutions.

TRANSPORTATION

GETTING TO EUROPE

BY PLANE

When it comes to airfare, a little effort can save you a bundle. Tickets sold by consolidators, couriers, and standby seating are good deals, but last-minute specials, airfare wars, and charter flights often beat these fares. The key is to hunt around, be flexible, and ask about discounts. Students, seniors, and those under 26 should never pay full price for a ticket.

AIRFARES

Airfares to Europe peak between mid-June and early September; holidays are also expensive. The cheapest times to travel are November to mid-December and January to March. Midweek (M-Th morning) round-trip flights run US$50-100 cheaper than weekend flights, but they are generally more crowded and less likely to permit frequent-flier upgrades. Not fixing a return date ("open return") or arriving in and departing from different cities ("open jaw") can be pricier than buying a round-trip. Flights between Europe's capitals or regional hubs (Amsterdam, London, Paris, Prague, Warsaw, Zürich) tend to be cheaper than to more rural areas.

If your European destinations are part of a more extensive globe-hop, consider a round-the-world (RTW) ticket. Tickets usually include at least five stops and are valid for about a year; prices range US$1200-5000. Try **Northwest Airlines/ KLM** (☎800-225-2525; www.nwa.com) or **Star Alliance** (www.staralliance.com), a consortium of 16 airlines including United.

BUDGET AND STUDENT TRAVEL AGENCIES

While agents specializing in flights to **Europe** can make your life easy, they may not spend the time to find you the lowest possible fare—they get paid on commission. Travelers holding **ISICs** and **IYTCs** (p. 15) qualify for big discounts from student travel agencies. Most flights from budget agencies are on major airlines, but in peak season some may sell seats on less reliable chartered aircrafts.

STA Travel, 5900 Wilshire Blvd., Ste. 900, Los Angeles, CA 90036, USA (24hr. reservations and info ☎800-781-4040; www.statravel.com). A student and youth travel organization with over 150 offices worldwide, including US offices in many college towns. Ticket booking, travel insurance, rail passes, and more..

Travel CUTS (Canadian Universities Travel Services Limited), 187 College St., Toronto, ON M5T 1P7, Canada (☎888-592-2887; www.travelcuts.com). Offices across Canada and the US including Los Angeles, New York, Seattle, and San Francisco.

USIT, 19-21 Aston Quay, Dublin 2, Ireland (☎01 602 1904; www.usit.ie), Ireland's leading student/budget travel agency has 20 offices throughout Northern Ireland and the Republic of Ireland. Offers programs to work, study, and volunteer worldwide.

COMMERCIAL AIRLINES

Commercial airlines' lowest regular offer is the **APEX** (Advance Purchase Excursion) fare, which provides confirmed reservations and allows "open-jaw" tickets.

FLIGHT PLANNING ON THE INTERNET. The Internet may be the budget traveler's dream when it comes to finding and booking bargain fares, but the array of options can be overwhelming. Many airline sites offer special last-minute deals online, though some require membership log-ins or email subscriptions. Try www.airfrance.com, www.britishairways.com, www.icelandair.com, and www.lufthansa.de. **STA** (www.sta.com) and **StudentUniverse** (www.studentuniverse.com) provide quotes on student tickets, while **Expedia** (www.expedia.com), **Orbitz** (www.orbltz.com), and **Travelocity** (www.travelocity.com) offer full travel services. **Priceline** (www.priceline.com) lets you specify a price, and obligates you to buy any ticket that meets or beats it; **Hotwire** (www.hotwire.com) offers bargain fares but won't reveal the airline or flight times until you buy. Other sites that compile deals include www.bestfares.com, www.flights.com, www.lowestfare.com, www.onetravel.com, and www.travelzoo.com. There are tools available to sift through multiple offers; **Booking Buddy** (www.bookingbuddy.com), **SideStep** (www.sidestep.com), and **Kayak** (www.kayak.com) let you enter your trip information once and search multiple sites. Spain-based **eDreams** (www.edreams.com) is convenient to book budget flights within Europe.

Generally, reservations must be made seven to 21 days ahead of departure, with seven- to 14-day minimum stay and 90-day maximum stay restrictions. These fares carry hefty cancellation and change penalties (fees rise in summer). Reserve peak-season APEX fares early. Use **Expedia** or **Travelocity** to get an idea of the lowest published fares, then use the resources listed here to try to beat those fares. Low-season fares should be appreciably cheaper than the **high-season** ones listed here.

TRAVELING FROM NORTH AMERICA

Basic round-trip fares to **Europe** range from roughly US$200-1200: to **Frankfurt,** US$350-750; **London,** US$250-550; **Paris,** US$300-700. Standard commercial carriers like **American** (☎800-433-7300; www.aa.com), **United** (☎800-538-2929; www.ual.com), and **Northwest** (☎800-225-2525; www.nwa.com) will probably offer the most convenient flights, but they may not be the cheapest. Check **Lufthansa** (☎800-399-5838; www.lufthansa.com), **British Airways** (☎800-247-9297; www.britishairways.com), **Air France** (☎800-237-2747; www.airfrance.us), and **Alitalia** (☎800-223-5730; www.alitaliausa.com) for cheap tickets from destinations throughout the US to all over Europe. You might find an even better deal on one of the following airlines, if any of their limited departure points is convenient for you.

Icelandair: ☎800-223-5500; www.icelandair.com. Stopovers in Iceland for no extra cost on most flights. New York to Frankfurt Apr.-Aug. US$700; Sept.-Oct. US$500; Dec.-Mar. US$400. For last-minute offers, subscribe to their "Lucky Fares" email list.

Finnair: ☎800-950-5000; www.finnair.com. Cheap round-trips from New York, San Francisco, and Toronto to Helsinki; connections throughout Europe. New York to Helsinki June-Sept. US$1050; Oct.-May US$670-770.

TRAVELING FROM THE UK AND IRELAND

Because of the many carriers flying from the British Isles to the continent, we only include discount airlines or those with cheap specials here. The **Air Travel Advisory Bureau** in London (www.atab.co.uk) provides referrals to travel agencies and consolidators that offer discounted airfares. **Cheapflights** (www.cheapflights.co.uk) publishes bargains. For more info on budget airlines like Ryanair, see p. 47.

Aer Lingus: Ireland ☎08 18 36 50 00; www.aerlingus.com. Round-trip tickets from Cork, Dublin, and Shannon to destinations across Europe (€15-300).

bmibaby: UK ☎08 712 240 224; www.bmibaby.com. Departures from throughout the UK to destinations across Europe. Fares from UK£25.

TRAVELING FROM AUSTRALIA AND NEW ZEALAND

Air New Zealand: New Zealand ☎0800 73 70 00; www.airnz.co.nz. Auckland to London.

Qantas Air: Australia ☎13 13 13, New Zealand 800 00 14 00 14; www.qantas.com.au. Flights from Australia to London for around AUS$2000.

Singapore Air: Australia ☎13 10 11, New Zealand 0800 808 909; www.singaporeair.com. Flies from Adelaide, Auckland, Brisbane, Christchurch, Melbourne, Perth, Sydney, and Wellington to Western Europe.

Thai Airways: Australia ☎13 00 65 19 60, New Zealand 09 377 3886; www.thai-air.com. Major cities in Australia and New Zealand to Frankfurt, and London.

AIR COURIER FLIGHTS

Those who travel light should consider courier flights. Couriers help transport cargo on international flights by using their checked luggage space for freight. Generally, couriers are limited to carry-ons and must deal with complex flight restrictions. Most flights are round-trip only, with short fixed-length stays (usually one week) and a limit of a one ticket per issue. Most of these flights also operate only out of major gateway cities. Round-trip courier fares from the US to Europe run about US$200-500. Most flights leave from L.A., Miami, New York, or San Francisco in the US; and from Montreal, Toronto, or Vancouver in Canada. Generally, you must be over 18 (in some cases 21). In summer, the most popular destinations require an advance reservation. Super-discounted fares are common for "last-minute" flights (3-14 days ahead).

Air Courier Association, 1767A Denver West Blvd., Golden, CO 80401, USA (☎800-461-8556; www.aircourier.org). Departure cities throughout Canada and the US to **Western Europe** (US$150-650). 1-year membership US$39, plus some monthly fees.

International Association of Air Travel Couriers (IAATC; www.courier.org). Courier and consolidator fares from North America to Europe. 1-year membership US$45.

Courier Travel (www.couriertravel.org). Searchable online database. 6 departure points in the US to various European destinations. Membership US$40 per household.

STANDBY FLIGHTS

Traveling standby requires considerable flexibility in arrival and departure dates and cities. Companies dealing in standby flights sell vouchers, along with the promise to get you to your destination (or near it) within a certain window of time (typically 1-5 days). You call in before your specific window of time to hear your flight options and the probability that you will be able to board each flight. You can then decide which flights you want to try to make, show up at the right airport at the appropriate time, present your voucher, and board if space is available. Vouchers can usually be bought for both one-way and round-trip travel. You may receive a refund only if every available flight within your date range is full; if you opt not to take an available (but less convenient) flight, you can only get credit toward future travel. Read agreements carefully, as tricky fine print abounds. To check on a company's service record in the US, contact the **Better Business Bureau** (☎703-276-0100; www.bbb.org). It is difficult to receive refunds, and clients' vouchers will not be honored when an airline fails to receive payment in time.

TICKET CONSOLIDATORS

Ticket consolidators, also known as **"bucket shops,"** buy unsold tickets in bulk from commercial airlines and sell them at discounted rates. Look for tiny ads in the Sunday travel section of any major newspaper; call quickly, as availability is extremely limited. Not all bucket shops are reliable, so insist on a receipt that gives full details of flight restrictions, refund policies, and tickets, and pay by credit card (in spite of the 2-5% fee). For more info, see www.travel-library.com/air-travel/consolidators.html.

GETTING AROUND EUROPE

GOING MY WAY, SAILOR? In Europe, fares are listed as either **single** (one-way) or **return** (round-trip). "Period returns" require you to return within a specific number of days; "day return" means you must return on the same day. Round-trip fares on trains and buses in Europe are simply twice the one-way fare. Unless stated otherwise, Let's Go always lists single fares.

BY PLANE

A number of European airlines offer discount coupon packets. Most are only available as add-ons for transatlantic passengers, but some are stand-alone offers. Most must be purchased before departure. **Europe by Air's** *FlightPass* allows non-EU residents to country-hop to over 150 European cities for US$99 or $129 per flight, plus tax. (☎888-321-4737; www.europebyair.com.) **Iberia's** *Europass* allows passengers flying from the US to Spain to add a minimum of two additional destinations in Europe for $139 per trip. (US ☎800-772-4642; www.iberia.com.)

BY TRAIN

Trains in Europe are generally comfortable, convenient, and reasonably fast, although quality varies by country. Second-class compartments, which seat two to six, are great places to meet fellow travelers. However, trains can be unsafe, especially in Eastern Europe. For safety tips, see p. 22. For long trips, make sure you are on the correct car, as trains sometimes split at crossroads. Towns listed in parentheses on European train schedules require a switch at the town listed immediately before the parentheses.

You can either buy a **rail pass,** which allows you unlimited travel within a particular region for a given period of time, or rely on buying individual **point-to-point** tickets as you go. Almost all countries give students or youths (usually defined as anyone under 26) direct discounts on regular domestic rail tickets, and many also sell a student or youth card that provides 20-50% off all fares for up to a year.

RESERVATIONS. While seat reservations are required only for selected trains (usually on major lines), you are not guaranteed a seat without one (usually US$5-30). You should strongly consider reserving in advance during peak holiday and tourist seasons (at the very latest, a few hours ahead). You will also have to purchase a **supplement** (US$10-50) or special fare for high-speed or high-quality trains such as Spain's AVE, Switzerland's Cisalpino, Finland's Pendolino, Italy's ETR500 and Pendolino, Germany's ICE, and certain French TGVs. InterRail holders must

BEFORE YOU BOOK. The emergence of no-frills airlines has made hop-scotching around Europe by air increasingly affordable. Many budget airlines save money by flying out of smaller, regional airports. A flight billed as Paris to Barcelona might in fact be from Beauvais (80km north of Paris) to Girona (104km northeast of Barcelona). For a more detailed list of these airlines by country, check out www.whichbudget.com.

easyJet: UK ☎0871 244 2366; www.easyjet.com. 72 destinations in Belgium, Czech Republic, Denmark, Estonia, France, Germany, Greece, Hungary, Italy, Latvia, the Netherlands, Poland, Portugal, Slovakia, Slovenia, Spain, Switzerland, and the UK.

Ryanair: Ireland ☎0818 303 030, UK 0871 246 00 00; www.ryanair.com. Serves 120 destinations in Austria, Belgium, the Czech Republic, France, Germany, Ireland, Italy, Latvia, the Netherlands, Poland, Portugal, Scandinavia, Spain, and the UK.

SkyEurope: UK ☎0905 7222 747; www.skyeurope.com. 39 destinations in 19 countries around Central and Eastern Europe, including the Czech Republic and Slovakia.

Sterling: Denmark ☎70 10 84 84, UK ☎870 787 8038. The first Scandinavian-based budget airline. Connects Denmark, Norway, and Sweden to 33 cities across Europe.

Wizz Air: Hungary ☎01 470 9499, Poland ☎ 22 351 9499; www.wizzair.com. 47 destinations in Belgium, Bulgaria, Croatia, France, Germany, Greece, Hungary, Ireland, Italy, the Netherlands, Norway, Poland, Romania, Slovenia, Spain, Sweden, and the UK.

You'll have to buy shuttle tickets to reach the airports of many of these airlines, and add an hour or so to your travel time. After round-trip shuttle tickets and fees for checked luggage or other services that might come standard on other airlines, that €0.01 sale fare can suddenly jump to €20-100. Prices vary dramatically; shop around, book months ahead, pack light, and stay flexible to nab the best fares.

TRANSPORTATION

also purchase supplements (US$3-20) for trains like EuroCity, InterCity, and many TGVs; supplements are often unnecessary for Eurail Pass and Europass holders.

OVERNIGHT TRAINS. On night trains, you won't waste valuable daylight hours traveling and you can avoid the hassle and expense of staying at a hotel. However, the main drawbacks include discomfort, sleepless nights, and the lack of scenery. The risk of theft also increases dramatically at night, particularly in Eastern Europe. **Sleeping accommodations** on trains differ from country to country. **Couchettes** (berths) typically have four to six seats per compartment (supplement about US$10-50 per person); **sleepers** (beds) in private sleeping cars offer more privacy and comfort, but are considerably more expensive (supplement US$40-150). If you are using a rail pass valid only for a restricted number of days, inspect train schedules to maximize the use of your pass: an overnight train or boat journey often uses up only one of your travel days if it departs after 7pm.

SHOULD YOU BUY A RAIL PASS? Rail passes were designed to allow you to jump on any train in Europe, go wherever you want whenever you want, and change your plans at will. In practice, it's not so simple. You still must stand in line to validate your pass, pay for supplements, and fork over cash for seat and couchette reservations. More importantly, rail passes don't always pay off. Estimate the point-to-point cost of each leg of your journey; add them up and compare the total with the cost of a rail pass. If you are planning to spend a great deal time on trains, a rail pass will probably be worth it. But especially if you are under 26, point-to-point tickets may be cheaper.

In Scandinavia, where distances are long and rail prices are high, a **Scanrail pass** is often your best bet. A rail pass won't always pay for itself in the Balkans, Belgium, Eastern Europe, Greece, Iceland, Ireland, Italy, Luxembourg, the Netherlands, Portugal, or Spain, where train fares are reasonable, distances short, or buses preferable. If, however, the total cost of your trips nears the price of the pass, the convenience of avoiding ticket lines may be worth the difference.

MULTINATIONAL RAIL PASSES

EURAIL PASSES. Eurail is valid in most of Western Europe: Austria, Belgium, Denmark, Finland, France, Germany, Greece, Italy, Luxembourg, the Netherlands, Norway, Portugal, the Republic of Ireland, Spain, Sweden, and Switzerland. It is **not valid** in the UK. **Eurail Global Passes,** valid for a number of consecutive days, are best for those planning on spending extensive time on trains every few days. Other types of global passes are valid for any 10 or 15 (not necessarily consecutive) days within a two-month period, and are more cost-effective for those traveling longer distances less frequently. **Eurail Pass Saver** provides first-class travel for travelers in groups of two to five (prices are per person). **Eurail Pass Youth** provides parallel second-class perks for those under 26. Passholders receive a timetable for major routes and a map with details on bike rental, car rental, hotel, and museum discounts. Passholders also often receive reduced fares or free passage on many boat, bus, and private railroad lines. The **Eurail Select Pass** is a slimmed-down version of the Eurail Pass: it allows five to 15 days of unlimited travel in any two-month period within three, four, or five bordering European countries. **Eurail Select Passes** (for individuals) and **Eurail Select Pass Saver** (for people traveling in groups of two to five) range from US$429/365 per person (5 days) to US$949/805 (15 days). The **Eurail Select Pass Youth** (second-class), for those ages 12-25, costs US$279-619. You are entitled to the same **freebies** afforded by the Eurail Pass, but only when they are within or between countries that you have purchased.

PICKY PASSES. In **Eastern Europe,** finding a pass is complicated. Global passes aren't accepted anywhere in Eastern Europe except Hungary and Romania; Select passes apply to Bulgaria, Croatia, and Slovenia, as well as Hungary and Romania; and **Regional passes** are available for all of those countries, with the exception of Bulgaria and the additions of the Czech Republic and Poland.

SHOPPING AROUND FOR A EURAIL. Eurail Passes can be bought only by non-Europeans from non-European distributors. These passes must be sold at uniform prices determined by the EU. However, some travel agents tack on a US$10 handling fee, and others offer certain bonuses with purchase, so shop around. Also, remember that pass prices rise annually, so if you're planning to travel early in the year, you can save cash by purchasing before January 1 (you have 3 months from the purchase date to validate your pass in Europe). It's best to buy a Eurail before leaving; only a few places in major cities sell them, and at a marked-up price. You can get a replacement for a lost pass only if you have purchased insurance on it under the **Pass Security Plan** (US$14). Eurail Passes are available through travel agents, student travel agencies like **STA** (p. 43), and **Rail Europe** (Canada ☎800-361-7245, US 877-257-2887; www.raileurope.com). It is also possible to buy directly from **Eurail's** website, www.eurail.com. Shipping is free to North America, Australia, New Zealand, and Canada.

OTHER MULTINATIONAL PASSES. If you have lived for at least six months in one of the European countries where **InterRail Passes** are valid, they are an economical option. The InterRail Pass allows travel within 30 European countries (excluding the passholder's country of residence). The **Global Pass** is valid for a given number of days (not necessarily consecutive) within a 10 day to one-month period. (5 days within 10 days, adult 1st class €329, adult 2nd class €249, youth €159; 10 days within 22 days €489/359/239; 1 month continuous €809/599/399. The **One Country Pass** limits travel within to one country (€33 for 3 days). Passholders receive free admission to many museums, as well as **discounts** on accommodations, food, and many ferries to Ireland, Scandinavia, and the rest of Europe. Passes are available at www.interrailnet.com, as well as from travel agents, at major train stations throughout Europe, and through online vendors (www.railpassdirect.co.uk).

DOMESTIC RAIL PASSES

If you are planning to spend a significant amount of time within one country or region, a national pass—valid on all rail lines of a country's rail company—may be more cost-effective than a multinational pass. Many national passes are limited and don't provide the free or discounted travel on private railways and ferries that Eurail does. Some of these passes can be bought only in Europe, some only outside Europe; check with a rail pass agent or with national tourist offices.

NATIONAL RAIL PASSES. The domestic analogs of the Eurail pass, national rail passes are valid either for a given number of consecutive days or for a specific number of days within a given time period. Usually, they must be purchased before you leave. Though they will usually save travelers some money, the passes may actually be a more expensive alternative to point-to-point tickets, particularly in Eastern Europe. For more info, check out www.raileurope.com/us/rail/passes/single_country_index.htm.

RAIL-AND-DRIVE PASSES. In addition to rail passes, many countries (as well as Eurail) offer rail-and-drive passes, which combine car rental with rail travel—a good option for travelers who wish both to visit cities accessible by rail and to travel in the surrounding areas. Prices range US$300-2400. Children under 11 cost US$102-500, and adding more days costs US$72-105 per day (see **By Car**, p. 50).

FURTHER READING & RESOURCES ON TRAIN TRAVEL.

Info on rail travel and rail passes: www.raileurope.com or www.eurail.com.

Point-to-point fares and schedules: www.raileurope.com/us/rail/fares_schedules/index.htm. Allows you to calculate whether buying a rail pass would save you money.

Railsaver: www.railpass.com/new. Uses your itinerary to calculate the best rail pass for your trip.

European Railway Server: www.railfaneurope.net. Links to rail servers throughout Europe.

Thomas Cook European Timetable, updated monthly, covers all major and most minor train routes in Europe. Buy directly from Thomas Cook (www.thomascooktimetables.com).

BY BUS

In some cases, buses prove a better option than train travel. In Britain and Hungary, the bus and train systems are on par; in the Baltics, Greece, Ireland, Spain, and Portugal, bus networks are more extensive, efficient, and often more comfortable; in Iceland and parts of northern Scandinavia, bus service is the only ground transportation available. In the rest of Europe, bus travel is more of a gamble. Scattered offerings from private companies are often cheap, but sometimes unreliable. Amsterdam, Athens, London, Munich, and Oslo are centers for lines that offer long-distance rides across Europe. **International bus passes** allow unlimited travel on a hop-on, hop-off basis between major European cities, often at cheaper prices than rail passes.

Eurolines, offices in 19 countries (UK ☎ 15 82 40 45 11; www.eurolines.co.uk or www.eurolines.com). The largest operator of Europe-wide coach services. Unlimited 15-day (high season €329, under 26 €279; low season €199/169) or 30-day (high season €439/359; low season €299/229) travel passes offer unlimited transit among 40 major European cities. Discount passes €29 or €39.

Busabout, 258 Vauxhall Bridge Rd., London, SW1V 1BS, UK (☎ 020 7950 1661; www.busabout.com). Offers 4 interconnecting bus circuits. 1 loop US$579; 2 loops US$890; 3 loops US$1319. Flexipass with 6 stops $475; additional stops $59. Also sells discounted international SIM cards (US$9; from US$0.29 per min.)

BY CAR

Cars offer speed, freedom, access to the countryside, and an escape from the town-to-town mentality of trains. Although a single traveler won't save by renting a car, four usually will. If you can't decide between train and car travel, you may benefit from a combination of the two; RailEurope and other rail pass vendors offer rail-and-drive packages. Fly-and-drive packages are also often available from travel agents or airline/rental agency partnerships. Before setting off, know the laws of the countries in which you'll be driving (e.g., both seat belts and headlights must be on at all times in **Scandinavia,** and remember to keep left in **Ireland and the UK**). For an informal primer on European road signs and conventions, check out www.travlang.com/signs. The **Association for Safe International Road Travel (ASIRT)** can provide more specific information about road conditions (☎ 301-983-5252; www.asirt.org). ASIRT considers road travel (by car or bus) to be relatively **safe** in Denmark, Ireland, the Netherlands, Norway, Sweden, Switzerland, and the UK, and relatively **unsafe** in Turkey and many parts of Eastern Europe. Western Europeans use **unleaded gas** almost exclusively, but it's not available in many gas stations in Eastern Europe.

RENTING A CAR

Cars can be rented from a US-based firm (Alamo, Avis, Budget, or Hertz) with European offices, from a European-based company with local representatives (Europcar), or from a tour operator (Auto Europe, Europe By Car, or Kemwel Holiday Autos) that will arrange a rental for you from a European company. Multinationals offer greater flexibility, but tour operators often strike better deals. Ask airlines about special fly-and-drive packages; you may get up to a week of free or discounted rental. See **Costs and Insurance,** p. 50, for more info. Minimum age requirements vary but tend to fall in the range of 21-25, with some as low as 18. There may be an additional insurance fee for drivers under 25. At most agencies, to rent a car, you'll need a driver's license from home with proof that you've had it for a year or an International Driving Permit (p. 52). Car rental in Europe is available through the following agencies:

Auto Europe (Canada and the US ☎ 888-223-5555; www.autoeurope.com).

Budget (Australia ☎ 1300 36 28 48, Canada ☎ 800-268-8900, New Zealand ☎ 0800 283 438, UK 87 01 56 56 56, US 800-527-0700; www.budgetrentacar.com).

Europcar International (UK ☎ 18 70 607 5000; www.europcar.com).

Hertz (Canada and the US 800-654-3001; www.hertz.com).

COSTS AND INSURANCE

Expect to pay US$200-600 per week, plus tax (5-25%), for a tiny car with a manual transmission; automatics can double or triple the price. Larger vehicles and 4WD will also raise prices. Reserve and pay in advance if at all possible. It is less expensive to reserve a car from the US than from Europe. Rates are generally lowest in Belgium, Germany, the Netherlands, and the UK, higher in Ireland and Italy, and highest in Scandinavia and Eastern Europe. Some companies charge fees for traveling into Eastern Europe. National chains often allow one-way rentals, with pickup in one city and drop-off in another. There is usually a minimum hire period and sometimes an extra drop-off charge of several hundred dollars.

Many rental packages offer unlimited kilometers, while others offer a fixed distance per day with a per-kilometer surcharge after that. Be sure to ask whether the price includes **insurance** against theft and collision. Remember that if you are driving a conventional vehicle on an **unpaved road** in a rental car, you are almost never covered by insurance. Always check if prices quoted include tax and collision insurance; some credit cards provide insurance, allowing their customers to decline the collision damage waiver. Ask about discounts and check the terms of insurance, particularly the size of the deductible. Beware that cars rented on an **American Express** or **Visa/MasterCard Gold or Platinum** credit cards in Europe might not carry the automatic insurance that they would in some other countries. Check with your credit card company. Insurance plans almost always come with an **excess** (or deductible) for conventional vehicles; excess is usually higher for younger drivers and for 4WD. This provision means you pay for all damages up to the specified sum, unless they are the fault of another vehicle. The excess you will be quoted applies to collisions with other vehicles; other collisions ("single-vehicle collisions") will cost you even more. The excess can often be reduced or waived for an additional charge. Remember to return the car with a **full tank** of gas to avoid high fuel charges. Gas prices are generally highest in Scandinavia. Throughout Europe, fuel tends to be cheaper in cities than in outlying areas.

LEASING A CAR

Leasing can be cheaper than renting, especially for more than 17 days. It is often the only option for those aged 18 to 21. The cheapest leases are agreements to buy the car and then sell it back to the manufacturer at a prearranged price. Leases generally include insurance coverage and are not taxed. The most affordable ones usually originate in Belgium, France, or Germany. Expect to pay US$1000-2000 for 60 days. **Renault Eurodrive** leases new cars in a tax-free "all-inclusive" package to qualifying non-EU citizens (Australia ☎9299 33 44, Canada 450-461-1149, New Zealand 0800 807 778, US 212-730-0676; www.renault-eurodrive.com).

BUYING A CAR

If you're brave and know what you're doing, buying a used car or van in Europe and selling it just before you leave can provide the cheapest wheels for long trips. Check with consulates for import-export laws concerning used vehicles, registration, and safety and emission standards.

ON THE ROAD

Road conditions and **regional hazards** are variable throughout Europe. Steep, curvy mountain roads may be closed in winter. Road conditions in Eastern Europe are often poor as a result of maintenance issues and inadequately enforced traffic laws; many travelers prefer public transportation. Western European roads are generally excellent, but each area has its own dangers. In Scandinavia, for example, drivers should be on the lookout for moose and elk; on the Autobahn, the threat may come from cars speeding by at 150kph. In this book, region-specific hazards are listed in country introductions. Carry emergency equipment with you

TRANSPORTATION

(see **Driving Precautions,** below) and know what to do in case of a breakdown. Car rental companies will often have phone numbers for emergency services.

 DRIVING PRECAUTIONS. When traveling in summer, bring substantial amounts of **water** (5L per person per day) for drinking and for the radiator. For long drives to unpopulated areas, register with police before beginning the trip, and again upon arrival at the destination. Check with the local automobile club for details. Make sure tires are in good repair and have enough air, and get good maps. A **compass** and a **car manual** can also be very useful. Always carry a **spare tire** and **jack, jumper cables, extra oil, flares,** a **flashlight** (torch), and **heavy blankets** (in case your car breaks down at night or in winter). A **cell phone** may help in an emergency. If you don't know how to change a tire, learn, especially if you're traveling in deserted areas. Blowouts on dirt roads are very common. If the car breaks down, stay with your car to wait for help.

DRIVING PERMITS AND CAR INSURANCE

INTERNATIONAL DRIVING PERMIT (IDP). To drive a car in **Europe**, you must **be over 18 and** have an International Driving Permit (IDP), though certain countries (such as the UK) allow travelers to drive with a valid American or Canadian license for a limited number of months. It may be a good idea to get an IDP anyway, in case you're in a situation (e.g., you get in an accident or become stranded in a small town) **where the police do not know English; information on the IDP is printed in 11 languages, including French, German, Italian, Portuguese, Russian, Spanish, and Swedish.** Your IDP, valid for one year, must be issued in your home country before you depart. An application for an IDP usually requires a photo, a current license, an additional form of identification, and a fee of around US$20. To apply, contact your country's automobile association (i.e., the AAA in the US or the CAA in Canada). Be wary of buying IDPs from unauthorized online vendors.

CAR INSURANCE. If you rent, lease, or borrow a car, you will need an International Insurance Certificate, or Green Card, to certify that you have liability insurance and that it applies abroad. Green Cards can be obtained at car rental agencies, car dealerships (for those leasing cars), some travel agents, and some border crossings. Rental agencies may require you to purchase theft insurance in countries they consider to have a high risk of auto theft.

BY CHUNNEL FROM THE UK

Traversing 27 mi. under the sea, the Chunnel is undoubtedly the fastest, most convenient, and least scenic route from England to France.

BY TRAIN. Eurostar, Eurostar House, Waterloo Station, London SE1 8SE (UK ☎08 705 186 186; www.eurostar.com) runs frequent trains between London and the continent. Ten to 28 trains per day run to 100 destinations including Paris (4hr., US$75-400, 2nd class), Disneyland Paris, Brussels, Lille, and Calais. Book online, at major rail stations in the UK, or at the office above.

BY BUS. Eurolines provides bus-ferry combinations (see p. 50).

BY CAR. Eurotunnel, Customer relations, P.O. Box 2000, Folkestone, Kent CT18 8XY (UK ☎08 705 353 535; www.eurotunnel.co.uk) shuttles cars and passengers between Kent and Nord-Pas-de-Calais. Return fares for vehicle and all passengers range from UK£223-253 with car. Same-day return costs UK£19-34, two- to five-day return for a car UK£123-183. Book online or via phone. Travelers with cars can also look into sea crossings by ferry (see below).

BY BOAT

Most long-distance ferries are quite comfortable; the cheapest ticket typically includes a reclining chair or couchette. Fares jump sharply in July and August. Ask for discounts; ISIC holders can often get student fares, and Eurail Pass holders get reductions and sometimes free trips. You'll occasionally have to pay a port tax (around US$10). The fares below are **one-way** for **adult foot passengers** unless otherwise noted. Though standard round-trip fares are usually twice the one-way fare, **fixed-period returns** (usually within 5 days) may be cheaper. Ferries run **year-round** unless otherwise noted. Bringing a **bike** costs up to US$15 in high season.

FERRIES FROM BRITAIN AND IRELAND

Ferries are frequent and dependable. The main route across the English Channel from Britain to France is Dover-Calais. The main ferry port on England's southern coast is Portsmouth, with connections to France and Spain. Ferries also cross the Irish Sea, connecting Northern Ireland with Scotland and England, and the Republic of Ireland with Wales. See the directory at www.seaview.co.uk/ferries.html.

Brittany Ferries: UK ☎08709 076 103, France ☎825 828 828, Spain ☎942 360 611; www.brittany-ferries.com. **Cork** to **Roscoff, FRA** (14hr.); **Plymouth** to **Roscoff, FRA** (6hr.) and **Santander, SPA** (18hr.); **Poole** to **Cherbourg, FRA** (4¼hr.); **Portsmouth** to **St-Malo** (10¾hr.) and **Caen, FRA** (5¾hr.).

DFDS Seaways: UK ☎0871 522 9955; www.dfdsseaways.co.uk. **Harwich** to **Cuxhaven** (19½hr.) and **Esbjerg, DEN** (18hr.); **Newcastle** to **Amsterdam, NTH** (16hr.), **Kristiansand, NOR** (18¼hr.), and **Gothenburg, SWE** (26hr.).

Irish Ferries: Nothern Ireland ☎353 818 300 400; Republic of Ireland ☎08 18 30 04 00, Great Britain ☎87 05 17 17 17; www.irishferries.ie. **Rosslare** to **Pembroke** (3¾hr.) and **Cherbourg** or **Roscoff, FRA** (18hr.). **Holyhead** to **Dublin, IRE** (2-3hr.).

P&O Ferries: UK ☎08 705 980 333; www.posl.com. **Dover** to **Calais, FRA** (1¼hr., 25 per day, UK £10-20); **Hull** to **Rotterdam, NTH** (10hr.) and **Zeebrugge, BEL** (12½hr.).

FERRIES IN SCANDINAVIA

Ferries run to many North Sea destinations. Those content with deck passage rarely need to book ahead. Baltic Sea ferries sail between Poland and Scandinavia.

Color Line: Norway ☎0810 00 811; www.colorline.com. Ferries run from 6 cities and towns in Norway to **Frederikshavn** and **Hirtshal, DEN** (€24-80); **Strömsand, SWE** (€9-22); **Kiel, GER** (€98-108). Car packages from €137. Student discounts available.

Tallinksilja Line: Finland ☎09 180 41, Sweden ☎08 22 21 40; www.tallinksilja.com. Connects **Helsinki** and **Turku** to Sweden (€18-116) and **Stockholm, SWE** to **Tallinn, EST** (€20-33); **Rostock, GER** (€91-133); **Riga, LAT** (€22-32). Eurail passes accepted.

Viking Line: Finland ☎0600 415 77, Sweden ☎0452 40 00; www.vikingline.fi. Ferries run between **Helsinki** and **Turku, FIN** to destinations in Estonia and Sweden. Su-Th cruises min. age 18, F-Sa 21. One-way €33-59. Eurail discounts available.

MEDITERRANEAN AND AEGEAN FERRIES

Mediterranean ferries may be the most glamorous, but they can also be the most turbulent. Ferries run from Spain to Morocco, from Italy to Tunisia, and from France to both Morocco and Tunisia. Reservations are recommended, especially in July and August. Schedules are erratic, with varying prices for similar routes. Shop around, and beware of small companies that don't take reservations. Ferries traverse the Adriatic from Ancona, ITA to Split, CRO and from Bari, ITA to Dubrovnik, CRO. They also cross the Aegean, from Ancona, ITA to Patras, GCE and from Bari, ITA to Igoumenitsa and Patras, GCE. **Eurail** is valid on certain fer-

ries between Brindisi, ITA and Corfu, Igoumenitsa, and Patras, GCE. Many ferry companies operate on these routes; see specific country chapters for more info.

BY MOPED AND MOTORCYCLE

Motorized bikes and **mopeds** don't use much gas, can be put on trains and ferries, and are a good compromise between costly car travel and the limited range of bicycles. However, they're uncomfortable for long distances, dangerous in the rain, and unpredictable on rough roads. Always wear a helmet, and never ride with a backpack. If you've never ridden a moped before, a twisting Alpine road is not the place to start. Expect to pay about US$20-35 per day; try auto repair shops, and remember to bargain. **Motorcycles** are more expensive and normally require a license, but are better for long distances. Before renting, ask if the price includes tax and insurance, or you may be hit with an unexpected fee. Avoid handing your passport over as a deposit; if you have an accident or mechanical failure you may not get it back until you cover all repairs. Pay ahead of time instead.

BY THUMB

 Let's Go strongly urges you to consider the risks before you choose to hitch. We do not recommend hitchhiking, and none of the information presented here is intended to do so.

No one should hitch without careful consideration of the risks involved. Hitching means entrusting your life to a unknown person and risking theft, assault, sexual harassment, and unsafe driving. However, some travelers report that hitchhiking in Europe allows them to meet locals and travel in areas where public transportation is sketchy. **Britain** and **Ireland** are probably the easiest places in Western Europe to get a lift. Hitching in **Scandinavia** is slow but steady. Long-distance hitching in the developed countries of northwestern Europe demands close attention to expressway junctions, rest stop locations, and destination signs. Hitching in southern Europe is generally mediocre. In some Eastern European countries, the line between hitching and taking a taxi is virtually nonexistent. Hitchhiking at night can be particularly dangerous; experienced hitchers stand in well-lit places. For women traveling alone or even two women traveling together, hitching is simply too dangerous. A man and a woman are a safer combination, two men will have a harder time, and three will go nowhere. Experienced hitchers pick a spot outside of built-up areas, where drivers can stop, return to the road without causing an accident, and have time to look over potential passengers as they approach. Hitching (or even standing) on super-highways is usually illegal: one may only thumb at rest stops or at the entrance ramps to highways. Finally, success often depends on appearance. Most Western European countries have ride services that pair drivers with riders; fees vary according to destination. **Eurostop** (www.taxistop.be/index_ils.htm), Taxistop's ride service, is one of the largest in Europe. Also try **Allostop** in France (French-language website www.allostop.net) and **Verband der Deutschen Mitfahrzentralen** in Germany (German-language website www.mitfahrzentrale.de). Not all organizations screen drivers and riders; ask ahead.

BEYOND TOURISM

A PHILOSOPHY FOR TRAVELERS

BEYOND TOURISM HIGHLIGHTS

NURTURE endangered griffon vultures on the Cres Island in **Croatia** (p. 210).

RESTORE castles in **France** (p. 57) and **Germany** (p. 389).

POLITICK as an intern at NATO in **Belgium** (p. 95).

IMMERSE yourself in film production in the **Czech Republic** (p. 228).

As a tourist, you are always a foreigner. While hostel-hopping and sightseeing can be fun, you may want to consider going beyond tourism. Experiencing a foreign place through studying, volunteering, or working can help reduce that stranger-in-a-strange-land feeling. With this Beyond Tourism chapter, *Let's Go* hopes to promote a better understanding of Europe and to provide suggestions for those who want more than a photo album out of their travels. The "Giving Back" sidebar feature (p. 218, p. 382) also highlights regional Beyond Tourism opportunities.

As a **volunteer** in Europe, you can participate in projects either on a short-term basis or as the main component of your trip. Later in this chapter, we recommend organizations that can help you find opportunities that best suit your interests, whether you're looking to get involved for a day or a year. **Studying** at a college or in a language program is another option. Those who choose to study in Europe often find the immersion in an educational environment to be much more rewarding than the backpacker trail alone. Many travelers also structure their trips by the **work** available to them along the way, ranging from odd jobs on-the-go to full-time, long-term stints in cities. The availability and legality of temporary work varies widely across Europe. If you are interested in working your way across the Continent, we recommend picking up *Let's Go* city and country guides.

VOLUNTEERING

 WHY PAY MONEY TO VOLUNTEER? Many volunteers are surprised to learn that some organizations require large fees or "donations." While this may seem ridiculous, such fees often keep the organization afloat, in addition to covering airfare, room, board, and administrative expenses for the volunteers. (Other organizations must rely on private donations and government subsidies.) If you're concerned about how a program spends its fees, request an annual report or finance account. A reputable organization won't refuse to inform you of how volunteer money is spent. Pay-to-volunteer programs might be a good idea for young travelers who are looking for more support and structure (such as pre-arranged transportation and housing), or anyone who would rather not deal with the uncertainty implicit in creating a volunteer experience from scratch.

Volunteering can be a powerful and fulfilling experience, especially when combined with the thrill of traveling in a new place. Whether your passion is for ecological, political, or social work, Europe can channel your energies. Most people who volunteer in Europe do so on a short-term basis at organizations that make use of drop-in or once-a-week volunteers. The best way to find opportunities that match your interests and schedule may be to check with local or national volunteer centers. Those looking for longer, more intensive volunteer experiences usually choose to go through a parent organization that takes care of logistical details and often provides a group environment and support system—for a fee. There are two main types of organizations—religious and secular—although there are rarely restrictions on participation in either.

ONLINE DIRECTORIES: VOLUNTEERING

www.alliance-network.org. Umbrella website that brings together various international service organizations.

www.idealist.org. Provides extensive listings of service opportunities.

www.worldvolunteerweb.org. Lists organizations and events around the world.

COMMUNITY DEVELOPMENT

If working closely with locals and helping in a hands-on fashion appeals to you, check out community development options. Many returning travelers report that working among locals was one of their most rewarding experiences.

Global Volunteers, 375 E. Little Canada Rd., St. Paul, MN 55109, USA (☎800-487-1074; www.globalvolunteers.org). A variety of 1- to 3-week volunteer programs throughout Europe. Fees range US$50-3000, including room and board but not airfare.

Habitat for Humanity, 121 Habitat St., Americus, GA 31709, USA (☎229-924-6935; www.habitat.org). A Christian non-profit organization coordinating 9- to 14-day service trips in Britain, Germany, Greece, Hungary, Ireland, the Netherlands, Poland, Portugal, and Switzerland. Participants aid local families in constructing future homes. Program costs fluctuate around US$1300-2200.

Service Civil International Voluntary Service (SCI-IVS), 5505 Walnut Level Rd., Crozet, VA 22932, USA (☎206-350-6585; www.sci-ivs.org). Arranges placement in 2- to 3-week outdoor service camps, or "workcamps," or 3-month teaching opportunities throughout Europe. 18+. Registration fee US$195, including room and board.

CONSERVATION

As more people realize that long-cherished habitats and structures are in danger, diverse programs have stepped in to aid the concerned in lending a hand.

Club du Vieux Manoir, Ancienne Abbaye du Moncel, 60700 Pontpoint, FRA (☎33 03 44 72 33 98; http://cvmclubduvieuxmanoir.free.fr). Offers year-long and summer programs restoring castles and churches throughout France. €15 annual membership and insurance fee. Costs €14 per day, including food and tent.

Earthwatch Institute, 3 Clock Tower Pl., Ste. 100, P.O. Box 75, Maynard, MA, 01754, USA (☎800-776-0188; www.earthwatch.org). Arranges 2-day to 3-week programs promoting the conservation of natural resources. Fees vary based on program location and duration. Costs range US$400-4000, including room and board but not airfare.

The National Trust, P.O. Box 39, Warrington, WA5 7WD, UK (☎44 0870 458 4000; www.nationaltrust.org.uk/volunteers). Arranges numerous volunteer opportunities, including Working Holidays. From £60 per week, including room and board.

World-Wide Opportunities on Organic Farms (WWOOF), WWOOF Administrator, Moss Peteral, Brampton CA8 7HY, England, UK (www.wwoof.org). Arranges volunteer work with organic and eco-conscious farms around the world. You become a member of WWOOF in the country in which you plan to work; prices vary by country.

BEYOND TOURISM

HUMANITARIAN AND SOCIAL SERVICES

Europe's complex, war-torn history has provided many opportunities to help rebuild. Numerous peace programs often prove to be fulfilling for those interested in humanitarian work.

Brethren Volunteer Service (BVS), 1451 Dundee Ave., Elgin, IL 60120, USA (☎800-323-8039; www.brethrenvolunteerservice.org). Peace and social justice based programs in European countries. Min. 2yr. commitment, must be 21 to serve overseas. US$75 background check fee; additional US$500 fee for international volunteers.

Simon Wiesenthal Center, 1399 South Roxbury Dr., Los Angeles, CA 90035, USA (☎800-900-9036; www.wiesenthal.org). Fights anti-Semitism and Holocaust denial throughout Europe. Small, variable donation required for membership.

Volunteers for Peace, 1034 Tiffany Rd., Belmont, VT 05730, USA (☎802-259-2759; www.vfp.org). Arranges placement in camps throughout Europe. US$30 membership required for registration. Programs average US$250-500 for 2-3 weeks.

STUDYING

VISA INFORMATION. Different countries have different requirements for study-abroad students. Ask the local consulate for info about acquiring a visa. Generally, applicants must be able to provide a passport, proof of enrollment, insurance, and financial support before their visa can be issued.

Study-abroad programs range from basic language or culture courses to college-level classes. To choose a program best fitting your needs, research as much as possible before making your decision. Determine costs and duration, as well as what kind of students participate and what accommodations are provided.

In programs that have large groups of students who speak the same language, there is a trade-off. You may feel more comfortable, but you will not have the same opportunity to practice a foreign language or to befriend other international students. For accommodations, dorm life provides a better opportunity to mingle with fellow students, but there is less of a chance to experience the local scene. If you live with a family, there is a potential to build lifelong friendships and to experience day-to-day life in more depth, but familial conditions can vary greatly.

UNIVERSITIES

Most university-level programs, conducted in the local language, offer cultural and linguistic enrichment opportunities. Those relatively fluent in a foreign language may find it cheaper to enroll directly in a university abroad, although getting college credit may be more difficult. Search www.studyabroad.com for various semester-abroad programs that meet your criteria, including your desired location and focus of study. Where applicable, we note region specific programs. See Beyond Tourism listings in individual chapters. The following resources can help place students in university programs abroad or have their own European branch.

ONLINE DIRECTORIES: STUDY-ABROAD

These websites are good resources for finding programs that cater to your particular interests. Each has links to various study-abroad programs broken down by a variety of criteria, including desired location and focus of study.

www.petersons.com/stdyabrd/sasector.html Lists summer and term-time study-abroad programs at accredited institutions that usually offer cross credits.

www.studyabroad.com A great starting point for finding college- or high-school-level programs in foreign languages or specific academic subjects. Also includes info for teaching and volunteering opportunities.

AMERICAN PROGRAMS

The following is a list of organizations that can either help place students in university programs abroad or that have their own branch in Europe.

American Institute for Foreign Study, College Division, River Plaza, 9 W. Broad St., Stamford, CT 06902, USA (☎800-727-2437; www.aifsabroad.com). Organizes programs for high school and college study in universities in Austria, Britain, the Czech Republic, France, Hungary, Ireland, Italy, Russia, and Spain. Summer programs US$5200-6500; Semester-long programs US$11,000-16,000. Scholarships available.

American Field Service (AFS), 71 West 23rd St., 17th fl., New York, NY, 10010 (☎212-807-8686; www.afs.org), has branches in over 50 countries. Summer-, semester-, and year-long homestay exchange programs for high-school students and graduating seniors. Some locations include Austria, Belgium, the Czech Republic, Denmark, Finland, Hungary, Iceland, Latvia, Norway, Russia, Slovakia, Sweden and Turkey. Community service programs are also offered to those 18+.

Council on International Educational Exchange (CIEE), 7 Custom House St., 3rd fl., Portland, ME, 04101, USA (☎800-407-8839; www.ciee.org/study). Sponsors work, volunteer, academic, and internship programs in Belgium, Britain, the Czech Republic, France, Hungary, Ireland, Italy, the Netherlands, Spain and Turkey for around US$10,000 per semester. Also offers volunteer opportunities. US$30 application fee.

Cultural Experiences Abroad (CEA), 1400 E. Southern Ave., Ste. B-108, Tempe, AZ 85282 (☎800-266-4441; www.gowithcea.com). Operates programs in Britain, the Czech Republic, France, Germany, Ireland, Italy, Poland, Russia, and Spain for undergraduates studying in Canada and the US. Costs range from US$3695 for a summer course to US$29,995 for the academic year.

Institute for the International Education of Students (IES), 33 N. LaSalle St., 15th fl., Chicago, IL 60602 (☎800-995-2300; www.iesabroad.org). Offers year-, semester-, and summer-long study abroad programs across Western Europe, as well as a special European Union (EU) program based in Germany for college students. US$13,000-18,000 per semester. US$50 application fee.

International Association for the Exchange of Students for Technical Experience (IAESTE), 10400 Little Patuxent Pkwy. Ste. 250, Columbia, MD 21044, USA (☎410-997-3068; www.iaeste.org). Offers 8- to 12-week internships in Europe for college students who have completed 2 years study in a particular trade.

School for International Training, College Semester Abroad, Kipling Rd., P.O. Box 676, Brattleboro, VT 05302, USA (☎888-272-7881 or 802-258-7751; www.sit.edu/studyabroad). Semester-long programs in Europe cost around US$12,900-16,000. Also runs **The Experiment in International Living** (☎800-345-2929; fax 802-258-3428; www.usexperiment.org), 3- to 5-week summer programs that offer high school students cross-cultural homestays, community service, ecological adventure, and language training in Europe for US$1900-5000.

Youth for Understanding International Exchange (YFU), (☎800-833-6243; www.yfu-usa.org). Places US high school students and recent graduates with host families throughout Europe. Summer-, semester-, and year-long programs: US$5595-20,000. US$75 application fee plus US$500 deposit.

LANGUAGE SCHOOLS

Language schools can be independently-run international or local organizations as well as divisions of foreign universities. They rarely offer college credit. They are a good alternative to university study for a deeper focus on the language or a slightly less rigorous courseload. Some worthwhile programs include:

Eurocentres, Seestr. 247, CH-8038 Zürich, SWI (☎41 1 485 50 40; www.eurocentres.com). Language programs for beginning to advanced students with homestays in Britain, France, Germany, Ireland, Italy, Spain, and Switzerland.

Language Immersion Institute, SCB 106, State University of New York at New Paltz, 1 Hawk Dr., New Paltz, NY 12561, USA (☎845-257-3500; www.newpaltz.edu/lii). 2-week summer language courses and some overseas courses in French, German, Greek, Hungarian, Italian, Polish, Portugese, Spanish, and Swedish. Around US$1000 for a 2-week course, not including accommodations.

Sprachcaffe Languages Plus, 413 Ontario St., Toronto, ON M5A 2V9, CAN (☎888-526-4758; www.sprachcaffe.com). Language classes in France, Germany, Italy, the Netherlands, and Spain for US$200-600 per week. Homestays available. Also offers French and Spanish language and travel programs for teenagers.

WORKING

As with volunteering, work opportunities tend to fall into two categories: long-term jobs that allow travelers to integrate into a community, or short-term jobs to finance the next leg of their travels. In Europe, people who want to work long-term might find success where their language skills are in demand, such as in teaching or working with tourists. Employment opportunities for those who want short-term work may be more limited and are generally contingent upon the economic needs of the city or region. In addition to local papers, international English-language newspapers, such as the *International Herald Tribune* (www.iht.com), often list job opportunities in their classified sections. If applicable, travelers should also consult federally run employment offices. Note that working abroad often requires a special work visa; see the box below for info about obtaining one.

VISA INFORMATION. EU Citizens: The EU's 2004 and 2007 enlargements led the 15 previous member states (EU-15) to fear that waves of Eastern European immigrants would flood their labor markets. This fear caused some members of the union to institute a transition period of up to 7 years during which citizens of the new EU countries may still need a visa or permit to work. EU-15 citizens generally have the right to work in the pre-enlargement countries for up to 3 months without a visa; longer-term employment usually requires a work permit. By law, all EU-15 citizens are given equal consideration for jobs not directly related to national security.

Everyone else: Getting a work visa in Europe is difficult for non-EU citizens. Different countries have different laws for employing foreigners; ask at your local embassy for specific info. The process is invariably time-consuming and frustrating. Having a job lined up before braving the bureaucratic gauntlet can speed up the process, as employers can perform much of the administrative leg-work.

LONG-TERM WORK

If you're planning to spend more than three months working in Europe, search for a job well in advance. International placement agencies are often the easiest way to find employment abroad, especially for those interested in teaching English. Although they are often only available to college students, **internships** are a good way to segue into working abroad; although they are often un- or underpaid, many say the experience is well worth it. Be wary of advertisements for companies claiming to be able get you a job abroad for a fee—often the same listings are available online or in newspapers. Some organizations include:

Escapeartist.com (http://jobs.escapeartist.com). International employers post directly to this website; various European jobs advertised.

International Cooperative Education, 15 Spiros Way, Menlo Park, CA, 94025, USA (☎650-323-4944; www.icemenlo.com). Finds summer jobs in Belgium, Britain, Germany, and Switzerland. $200 application fee and a $600 placement fee.

StepStone (www.stepstone.com, branches across Europe listed at www.stepstone.com/EN/Company/Locations). Database covering international employment in Austria, Belgium, Britain, Denmark, France, Germany, Italy, the Netherlands, Norway, Portugal, and Sweden. Several search options and a constantly updated list of openings.

BEYOND TOURISM

TEACHING ENGLISH

Teaching jobs abroad are rarely well-paid, although some elite private American schools offer competitive salaries. Volunteering as a teacher in lieu of getting paid is a popular option; even then, teachers often receive some sort of a daily stipend to help with living expenses. In almost all cases, you must have at least a bachelor's degree to be a full-fledged teacher, although college undergraduates can often get summer positions teaching or tutoring. The difficulty of finding teaching jobs varies by country; EU countries often give EU applicants priority. Many schools require teachers to have a **Teaching English as a Foreign Language (TEFL)** certificate. Not having this certification does not necessarily exclude you from finding a teaching job, but certified teachers often find higher-paying positions. Native English speakers working in private schools are most often hired for English-immersion classrooms where the local language is not spoken. Those teaching in poorer public schools are more likely to be working in both English and the native tongue. Placement agencies or university programs are the best resources for finding jobs. The alternative is to contact schools directly or to try your luck once you get there. The best time to look for the latter is several weeks before the school year starts. The following organizations are helpful in placing teachers in Europe:

International Schools Services (ISS), 15 Roszel Rd., P.O. Box 5910, Princeton, NJ 08543, USA (☎609-452-0990; www.iss.edu). Hires teachers for more than 200 international and American schools around the world; candidates should have 2 years teaching experience and/or teacher certification. 2-year commitment expected.

Teaching English as a Foreign Language (TEFL), TEFL Professional Network Ltd., 72 Pentyla Baglan Rd., Port Talbot, SA12 8AD, UK (www.tefl.com). Maintains the most extensive database of openings throughout Europe. Offers job training and certification.

AU PAIR WORK

Au pairs are typically women (although sometimes men), aged 18-27, who work as live-in nannies, caring for children and doing light housework in foreign countries in exchange for room, board, and a small spending allowance or stipend. One job perk is that you get to know the country without the high expense of travel. Drawbacks, however, can include mediocre pay and long hours. Au pairs in Europe typically work 25-40hr. per week and receive US$300-450 per month. Much of the au pair experience depends on the family with whom you are placed. The agencies below are a good starting point for looking for employment.

Childcare International, Ltd., Trafalgar House, Grenville Pl., London NW7 3SA (☎44 020 8906 3116; www.childint.co.uk). Offers au pair and nanny placement.

InterExchange, 161 6th Ave., New York, NY, 10013, USA (☎212-924-0446; www.inter-exchange.org). Au pair, internship, and short-term work placement in France, Germany, the Netherlands, and Spain. US$495-600 placement fee.

Sunny AuPairs (☎44 020 8144 1635, in US 503-616-3026; www.sunnyaupairs.com). Online, worldwide database connecting au pairs with families. Free registration. No placement fee.

SHORT-TERM WORK

Traveling for long periods of time can be hard on the finances. Therefore, many travelers try their hand at odd jobs for a few weeks at a time to help pay for another month or two of touring. The legality of short-term work varies by country. Contact the consulate of the country you'll be traveling in for more info. Another popular option is to work several hours a day at a hostel in exchange for free or discounted room and/or board. Most often, these short-term jobs are found by word of mouth, or by expressing interest to the owner of a hostel or restaurant. *Let's Go* lists temporary jobs of this nature whenever possible; check out the practical info section of larger cities.

FURTHER READING ON BEYOND TOURISM.

Alternatives to the Peace Corps: A Guide of Global Volunteer Opportunities, by Paul Backhurst. Food First Books, 2005 (US$12).

The Back Door Guide to Short-Term Job Adventures: Internships, Summer Jobs, Seasonal Work, Volunteer Vacations, and Transitions Abroad, by Michael Landes. Ten Speed Press, 2005 (US$22).

Green Volunteers: The World Guide to Voluntary Work in Nature Conservation, ed. Fabio Ausenda. Universe, 2007 (US$15).

How to Get a Job in Europe, by Cheryl Matherly and Robert Sanborn. Planning Communications, 2003 (US$23).

How to Live Your Dream of Volunteering Overseas, by Joseph Collins, Stefano DeZerega, and Zahara Heckscher. Penguin Books, 2002 (US$20).

International Job Finder: Where the Jobs Are Worldwide, by Daniel Lauber and Kraig Rice. Planning Communications, 2002 (US$20).

Live and Work Abroad: A Guide for Modern Nomads, by Huw Francis and Michelyne Callan. Vacation-Work Publications, 2001 (US$16).

Overseas Summer Jobs 2002. Peterson's Guides and Vacation Work, 2002 (US$18).

Volunteer Vacations: Short-Term Adventures That Will Benefit You and Others, by Doug Cutchins, Anne Geissinger, and Bill McMillon. Chicago Review Press, 2006 (US$18).

Work Abroad: The Complete Guide to Finding a Job Overseas, by Clayton Hubbs. Transitions Abroad Publishing, 2002 (US$16).

Work Your Way Around the World, by Susan Griffith. Vacation-Work Publications, 2007 (US$22).

AUSTRIA (ÖSTERREICH)

With Vienna's high culture and the Alps's high mountains, Austria offers different extremes of beauty. Many of the world's most famous composers and thinkers, including Mozart and Freud, called Austria home. Today, its small villages brim with locally brewed beer, jagged peaks draw hikers and skiers, and magnificent palaces, museums, and concerts are omnipresent. Stroll along the blue Danube River or relax in a Viennese coffeehouse and listen for a strain of the waltz.

 DISCOVER AUSTRIA: SUGGESTED ITINERARIES

THREE DAYS Spend all three days in **Vienna** (p. 67), the Imperial headquarters. From the stately **Stephansdom** to the majestic **Hofburg Palace,** Vienna's many attractions will leave you with enough sensory stimulation to last until your next trip.

ONE WEEK Begin in **Kitzbühel** (1 day; p. 89) to take advantage of its hiking and skiing opportunities. Stop in **Salzburg** (2 days; p. 78) to see the home of Mozart and the Salzburger Festspiele (p. 77). Move on to the Salzkammergut region to spelunk in the **Dachstein Ice Caves** (1 day; p. 84). End your trip by basking in the glory of **Vienna** (3 days).

TWO WEEKS Start in **Innsbruck,** where museums and mountains meet (2 days; p. 85), then swing by **Zell am See** and the Krimml Waterfalls (1 day; p. 84). Spend another two days wandering **Hohe Tauern National Park** (p. 84), visiting the Pasterze Glacier and Großglockner Hochalpenstraße. Next, tour **Hallstatt** and its nearby ice caves (2 days; p. 82). Follow your ears to **Salzburg** (2 days), then head to **Graz** (1 day; p. 89) for its throbbing nightlife. Finally, make your way to **Vienna** for a grand finale of romance, waltzes, and coffeehouse culture (4 days).

ESSENTIALS

FACTS AND FIGURES

Official Name: Republic of Austria.
Capital: Vienna.
Major Cities: Graz, Innsbruck, Salzburg.
Population: 8,200,000.
Land Area: 82,400.
Time Zone: GMT +1.

Language: German.
Religions: Roman Catholic 74%, Protestant 5%, Muslim 4%, Other/None 17%.
Adjusted Gross of the 1965 film version of *The Sound of Music***:** $937,093,200.

WHEN TO GO

Between November and March, prices in western Austria double and travelers need reservations months in advance. The situation reverses in the summer, when the eastern half of the country fills with tourists. Accommodations are cheaper and less crowded in the shoulder seasons (May-June and Sept.-Oct.). Cultural opportunities also vary with the seasons: the Vienna State Opera, like many other theaters, has no shows in July or August, while the Vienna Boys' Choir only performs April-June and September-October.

DOCUMENTS AND FORMALITIES

EMBASSIES. Foreign embassies in Austria are in Vienna (p. 67). Austrian embassies abroad include: **Australia,** 12 Talbot St., Forrest, Canberra, ACT, 2603

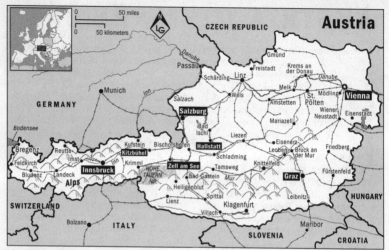

(☎02 6295 1533; www.austriaemb.org.au); **Canada,** 445 Wilbrod St., Ottawa, ON, K1N 6M7 (☎613-789-1444; www.austro.org); **Ireland,** 15 Ailesbury Ct., 93 Ailesbury Rd., Dublin, 4 (☎01 269 45 77); **New Zealand,** Level 2, Willbank House, 57 Willis St., Wellington, 6001 (☎04 499 63 93); **UK,** 18 Belgrave Mews West, London, SW1X 8HU (☎020 7344 3250; www.bmaa.gv.at/london); **US,** 3524 International Ct., NW, Washington, D.C., 20008 (☎202-895-6700; www.austria.org).

VISA AND ENTRY INFORMATION. EU citizens do not need a visa. Citizens of Australia, Canada, New Zealand, and the US do not need a visa for stays of up to 90 days, beginning upon entry into any of the countries in the EU's freedom-of-movement zone. For more info, see p. 14. For stays longer than 90 days, all non-EU citizens need visas, available at Austrian embassies. For American citizens, visas are $82 but free of charge for students studying abroad.

TOURIST SERVICES AND MONEY

EMERGENCY	Ambulance: ☎144. Police: ☎133. Fire: ☎122.

TOURIST OFFICES. For general info, contact the **Austrian National Tourist Office,** Margaretenstr. 1, A-1040 Vienna (☎158 86 60; www.austria.info). All tourist offices are marked by signs with a green "i"; most brochures are available in English.

MONEY. The **euro (€)** has replaced the **schilling** as the unit of currency in Austria. For more info, see p. 17. As a general rule, it's cheaper to exchange money in Austria than at home. Railroad stations, airports, hotels, and most travel agencies offer exchange services, as do banks. If you stay in hostels and prepare most of your own food, expect to spend €30-60 per day. Accommodations start at about €12 and a basic sit-down meal usually costs around €8. Menus will say whether service is included (*Preise inklusive* or *Bedienung inklusiv*); if it is, a tip is not expected. If not, 10% will do. Austrian restaurants expect you to seat yourself, and servers will not bring the bill until you ask them to do so. Say *"Zahlen bitte"* (TSAHL-en BIT-uh) to settle your accounts, and give tips directly to the server. Don't expect to bargain except at street markets.

Austria has a 20% **value added tax (VAT)**, a sales tax applied to most purchased goods. The prices given in *Let's Go* include VAT. In an airport upon exiting the EU, non-EU citizens can claim a refund on the tax paid for goods purchased at participating stores. In order to qualify for a refund in a store, you must spend at least €75; make sure to ask for a refund form when you pay. For more info on qualifying for a VAT refund, see p. 19.

BUSINESS HOURS. Businesses are generally open M-Th 8am-6pm, F 8am-3pm. Government offices are open M-F 9am-3pm, and most shops M-F 9am-6pm, Sa 9am-5pm. Banks are open M-F 8am-4pm, but smaller ones may close for lunch.

TRANSPORTATION

BY PLANE. Vienna's **Schwechat-Flughafen (VIE)** is the main international airport. From London, **Ryanair** (☎3531 249 7791; www.ryanair.com) flies to Salzburg and Graz. Innsbruck also has an airport. For more info on flying to Austria, see p. 43.

BY TRAIN. The **Österreichische Bundesbahn** (**ÖBB;** www.oebb.at), Austria's state railroad, operates an efficient system with comfortable, fast trains. **Eurail** and **InterRail** passes are valid in Austria but do not guarantee a seat without a reservation. The **Austrian Railpass** allows three to eight days of travel within a 15-day period on all rail lines. It also entitles holders to 40% off bike rentals at train stations (2nd-class US$107; each additional day US$15).

BY BUS. The Austrian bus system consists mainly of **PostBuses,** which cover areas inaccessible by train for comparably high prices. Buy tickets at the station or on board. For info, call ☎43 17 11 01 from abroad or ☎0810 222 333 within Austria.

BY CAR. Driving is a convenient way to see the more isolated parts of Austria, but gas is costly, an international license is required, and some small towns prohibit cars. The roads are well maintained and well marked, and Austrian drivers are quite careful. **Mitfahrzentralen** (ride-share services) in larger cities pair drivers with riders for a small fee. Riders then negotiate fares with the drivers. Be aware that not all organizations screen their drivers or riders; ask ahead.

BY BIKE. Bicycles are a great way to travel, as Austria's smooth country roads are usually safe. Many train stations rent bikes, returnable at any participating station.

KEEPING IN TOUCH

PHONE CODES	**Country code: 43. International dialing prefix:** 00 (for Vienna, dial 00 431). For more info on how to place international calls, see **Inside Back Cover.**

EMAIL AND THE INTERNET. It's easy to find Internet cafes (€2-6 per hr.) in Austria, especially in larger cities. In small towns, however, cafes are less frequent and may charge more. Ask a hostel or tourist office receptionist for suggestions.

TELEPHONES. Wherever possible, use a calling card for international phone calls, as long-distance rates for national phone services are often exorbitant. Prepaid phone cards and major credit cards can be used for direct international calls but are still less cost-efficient. For info on mobile phones, see p. 29. The most popular companies are A1, One, and T-mobile. Direct-dial access numbers for calling out of Austria include: **AT&T Direct** (☎0800 200 288); **British Telecom** (☎0800 200 209);

AUSTRIA

Canada Direct (☎0800 200 217); **MCI WorldPhone** (☎0800 999 762); **Sprint** (☎0800 200 236); **Telecom New Zealand** (☎0800 200 222); **Telstra Australia** (☎0800 200 202).

MAIL. Letters take one or two days within Austria. Airmail (€1.25) to North America takes four to seven days, and up to nine days to Australia and New Zealand. Mark all letters and packages *"mit Flugpost"* (airmail). Aerogrammes are the cheapest option. To receive mail in Austria, have mail delivered **Poste Restante.** Mail will go to the main post office unless you specify a subsidiary by street address. Address mail to be held according to the following example: LAST NAME, First name, *Postlagernde Briefe*, Postal code City, AUSTRIA.

ACCOMMODATIONS AND CAMPING

AUSTRIA	❶	❷	❸	❹	❺
ACCOMMODATIONS	under €16	€16-26	€27-34	€35-55	over €55

Always ask if your lodging provides a **guest card** *(Gästekarte)*, which grants discounts on activities, museums, and public transportation. The **Österreichischer Jugendherbergsverband-Hauptverband (ÖJH)** runs the over 80 **HI hostels** in Austria. Because of the rigorous standards of the national organization, these are usually very clean and orderly. Most charge €18-25 per night for dorms, with a €3-5 HI discount. **Independent hostels** vary in quality, but often have more personality and foster a lively backpacking culture. Slightly more expensive **Pensionen** are similar to American and British B&Bs. In small to mid-sized towns, singles will cost about €20-30, but expect to pay twice as much in big cities. **Hotels** are expensive (singles over €35; doubles over €48). Cheaper options have *"Gasthof," "Gästehaus,"* or *"Pension-Garni"* in the name. Renting a **Privatzimmer** (room in a family home) is an inexpensive option. Contact the tourist office about rooms (€16-30). **Camping** in Austria is less about getting out into nature than having a cheap place to sleep; most sites are large plots glutted with RVs and are open in summer only. Prices run €10-15 per tent site and €5-8 per extra person. In the high Alps, hikers and mountaineers can retire to the well-maintained system of **Hütten** (mountain huts) where traditional Austrian fare and a good night's rest await them. Reserve ahead.

HIKING AND SKIING. Almost every town has hiking trails in its vicinity; consult the local tourist office. Trails are marked with either a red-white-red marker (only sturdy boots and hiking poles necessary) or a blue-white-blue marker (mountaineering equipment needed). Because of snow, most mountain hiking trails and mountain huts are open only from late June to early September. Western Austria is one of the world's best skiing regions; the areas around Innsbruck and Kitzbühel are full of runs. High season runs from November to March.

FOOD AND DRINK

AUSTRIA	❶	❷	❸	❹	❺
FOOD AND DRINK	under €5	€5-10	€11-16	€17-25	over €25

Loaded with fat, salt, and cholesterol, traditional Austrian cuisine is bad for your skin, your heart, and your figure—enjoy! *Wienerschnitzel* is a breaded meat cutlet (usually veal or pork) fried in butter. Natives nurse their sweet tooths with *Sacher Torte* (a rich chocolate cake layered with marmalade) and *Linzer Torte* (a light yellow cake with currant jam). Austrian beers are outstanding—try Stiegl, a Salzburg brew; Zipfer, from Upper Austria; and Styrian Gösser.

EAT YOUR VEGGIES. Vegetarians should look on the menu for *Spätzle* (noodles), *Eierschwammerl* (yellow mushrooms), or anything with "*Vegi*" in it.

HOLIDAYS AND FESTIVALS

Holidays: Just about everything closes on public holidays, so plan accordingly. New Year's Day (Jan. 1); Epiphany (Jan. 6); Good Friday (Mar. 21); Easter (Mar. 23-24); Labor Day (May 1); Ascension (May 1); Corpus Christi (May 22); Assumption (Aug. 15); Austrian National Day (Oct. 26); All Saints' Day (Nov. 1); Immaculate Conception (Dec. 8); Christmas (Dec. 25); Boxing Day (Dec. 26).

Festivals: Vienna celebrates Fasching (Carnival) from New Year's until the start of Lent. Austria's most famous summer music festivals are the Wiener Festwochen (early May to mid-June; www.festwochen.at) and the Salzburger Festspiele (late July-late Aug.).

BEYOND TOURISM

Austria caters more to tourism than volunteerism; there are only limited opportunities to give back, so your best bet is to find them through a placement service. Opportunities for short-term work abound at hotels, ski resorts, and farms. For more info on opportunities across Europe, see **Beyond Tourism**, p. 56.

Actilingua Academy, Glorietteg. 8, A-1130 Vienna (☎431 877 6701; www.actilingua.com). Study German in Vienna (from €419) for 2 to 4 weeks.

Concordia, Heversham House, 2nd fl., 20-22 Boundary Rd., East Sussex, BN2 3HJ, UK (☎012 7342 2218; www.concordia-iye.org.uk). British volunteer organization that directs community projects in Austria, which have previously included renovating historic buildings and parks and directing a youth drama project.

VIENNA (WIEN)   ☎01

War, marriage, and Habsburg maneuvering transformed Vienna (pop. 1,800,000) from a Roman camp along the Danube into Europe's political linchpin. Beethoven and Mozart made Vienna an everlasting arbiter of high culture. With dozens of coffeehouses and museums, Vienna radiates artistic, intellectual energy. On any given afternoon, cafes turn the sidewalks into a sea of umbrellas while bars and clubs pulse with experimental techno and indie rock until dawn.

INTERCITY TRANSPORTATION

Flights: The **Wien-Schwechat Flughafen (VIE;** ☎700 70), 18km from the city center, is home to **Austrian Airlines** (☎517 89; www.aua.com). The cheapest way to reach the city, the S-Bahn (☎65 17 17) stops at **Wien Mitte** (30min., 2-3 per hr., €3). The Vienna Airport Lines **bus** (☎930 00 23 00) takes 20min. to reach Südbahnhof and 40min. to Westbahnhof (2 per hr.; €6, round-trip €11). The **City Airport Train** (**CAT;** ☎252 50; www.cityairporttrain.com) takes only 16min. to reach Wien Mitte (2 per hr. 6:05am-11:35pm; purchased online €8, round-trip €15; from a ticket machine €9, round-trip €16; on board €10; Eurail not valid.)

Trains: Vienna has 2 train stations with international departures. Call ☎05 17 17 or check www.oebb.at for more info. Most ticket counters and machines take AmEx/MC/V.

Westbahnhof, XV, Mariahilferstr. 132. Info counter open daily 7:30am-9pm. Trains go to: **Amsterdam, NTH** (12hr., 4 per day, €135); **Berlin, GER** (9-11hr., 1 per 2hr., €100-130); **Budapest, HUN** (3hr., 17 per day, €36); **Hamburg, GER** (9-12hr., 6 per day, €80); **Innsbruck** (4½-5hr., 7

AUSTRIA

Vienna

▲▲ ACCOMMODATIONS

Camping Neue Donau,	1 F2
Hostel Ruthensteiner,	2 A5
Pension Hargita,	3 B5
Pension Kraml,	4 B5
Westend City Hostel,	5 A5
Wien Süd,	6 A6
Wombats "T e Base",	7 A5
Wombats "The Lounge",	8 A5

🍴 FOOD

Centimeter,	9 C3
Yak and Yeti,	10 B5

Ⓤ3 U-Bahn ⓈS-Bahn

TO ▲ (2km)

Engerthstr.

Vorgartenstr.

Ⓤ1 **VORGARTENSTR.**

■ Pedal Power
Ausstellungsstr.

II

**PRATERSTERN-
WIEN NORD**

Bahnhof
Wien-Nord

Franzensbrstr.

Nordbahnstr.

Heinestr.

Nordwestbahnstr.

Rauscherstr.

Taborstr.

Große Stadtgut.

Novarag.

Nestroyg.

Rotensterng.

NESTROYPL. Ⓤ1

Taborstr.

SCHWEDENPL. Ⓤ1 Ⓤ4

Lilienbrunng. Ⓤ1 Ⓤ4

Handelskai

Engerthstr.

TRAISENG. Ⓢ

Dresdnerstr.

Marchfeldstr.

F.-ENGELS-PL.

Stromstr.

Pappenheimg.

Jägerstr.

Wallensteinstr.

Obere Augarten-Str.

Augarten

Wasag.

Leopoldsgasse

Obere Donau-Str

Obere Donaustr.

Franz Josefs Kai

SCHOTTENRING
Ⓤ2 Ⓤ4

Neutorg.

Börseg.

Tiefer Graben

Wipplingerstr.

Klosterneuburgerstr.

Brigittenauer Lände

Donaukanal

Heiligenstädterstr.

Spittelauer Lände

SPITTELAU
Ⓤ4 Ⓤ6 Ⓢ

Althanstr.

FRIEDENSBRÜCKE
Ⓤ4

Obere Donaustr.

Roßauer Lände

Rößerg.

Rotenlöweng.

Glasröstr.

Seeg.

**ROßAUER
LÄNDE** Ⓤ4

Müllnerg.

Pramerg.

Grünentorg.

Berg.

Liechtenstr.

Schlickg.

Türkenstr.

Beeth.

Porzellang.

Wasag.

Servitong.

Berggasse

Kolingasse

Hörlg.

**SCHOTTENTOR
UNIVERSITÄT** Ⓤ2

Universität
Wien

Dr.-Karl-Lueger-Ring

Dr.-Karl-Renner-Ring

Hardtg.

Billrothstr.

XIX

Döblinger Hauptstr.

**NUßDORFERSTR.
VOLKSOPER** Ⓤ6

Döblinger Gürtel

Franz-Josefs
Bahnhof Ⓤ4 Ⓤ6 Ⓢ

Liechtensteinstr.

Nußdorferstr.

Liechten-
stein-
Park

Alserbachstr.

Boltzmanng.

Währingerstr.

Spitalg.

IX

Liechtensteinstr.

Sobieskig.

Sechschimm.g.

■ Volksoper

W. Exner-G.

Sensengasse

Lazarettg.

Spitalg.

Landesge-
richtsstr.

Gymnasiumstr.

**WÄHRINGERSTR.
VOLKSOPER** Ⓤ6

Währinger Gürtel

Schopenhauerstr.

**Allgemeines
Krankenhaus**

Borschkeg.

Alserstr.

Lazarettg.

Alser str.

Laudong.

XVIII

**MICHELBEUERN
ALLG. KRANKENHAUS** Ⓤ6

Martinstr.

**MICHELBEUERN
ALLG. KRANKENHAUS** Ⓤ6

Hernalser-Haupt-Str. **ALSERSTR.** Ⓤ6

Alserstr.

Kinderspitalg.

Skodag.

Albertpl.

Benno-
pl.

Florianig.

Krottenbachstr.

Peter-Jordan-Str.

**Türkenschanz-
Park**

XVIII

Gentzg.

Staudig.

Kreuzg.

Antong.

Schuhmanng.

TO ⑫ (2km)

Schelhammerg.

Scheibenbergstr.

TO ⑩
(2.5km) Ottakringerstr.

Brunnenmarkt

Hernalser Gürtel

Payerg.

XVI

XVII

WINE TAVERNS
10er Marie, **11 A3**
Buschenschank
Heinrich Nierscher, **12 A2**

BARS
Chelsea, **13 A4**
Mango, **14 C5**

MUSEUMS
Kunst Huas Wien, **15 E4**
Österreichische Galerie:
Oberes Belvedere, **16 D5**
Österreichische Galerie:
Unteres Belvedere, **17 E5**
Freud Museum, **18 C3**

AUSTRIA

per day, €54); **Munich, GER** (5hr., 10 per day, €72); **Paris, FRA** (14-24hr., 2 per day, €70-160); **Salzburg** (2½-3hr., 1 per hr., €43); **Zürich, SWI** (9hr., 3 per day, €88).

Südbahnhof, X, Wiener Gürtel 1a. Info counter open daily 7am-8pm. Trains go south and east to: **Graz** (2½hr., 1 per hr., €30); **Kraków, POL** (7hr., 4 per day, €46); **Prague, CZR** (4-5hr., 8 per day, €44); **Rome, ITA** (13-18hr., 6 per day, €75-100); **Venice, ITA** (7-11hr., 6 per day, €50-70).

Buses: Buses here are rarely cheaper than trains; compare prices before buying a ticket. **Postbus** (☎517 17; www.postbus.at) provides regional service. **Eurolines** (☎798 29 00; www.eurolines.at) connects international departures. Buses leave from Erdberg, Floridsdorf, Heiligenstadt, Hütteldorf, Kagran, Reumannpl., and Wien Mitte/Landstr.

✈ ORIENTATION

Vienna is divided into 23 **Bezirke** (districts). The first is **Innenstadt** (city center), defined by the **Ringstraße** (ring road) on three sides and the Danube Canal on the fourth. At the center of the Innenstadt lies **Stephansplatz** and much of the pedestrian district. The best way to reach Innenstadt is to take the U-bahn to Stephanspl. (U1, U3) or **Karlsplatz** (U1, U2, U4); **Schwedenplatz** (U1, U4) is close to the city's nightlife. Tram lines 1 and 2 circle the Innenstadt on the Ringstr., with line 2 heading clockwise and 1 counterclockwise.

The Ringstraße consists of different segments, such as Opernring or Kärntner Ring. Many of Vienna's major attractions are in District I and around the Ringstr. Districts II-IX spread out from the city center following the Ring's clockwise traffic. The remaining districts expand from yet another ring road, the **Gürtel** (Belt), which also has many segments, including Margaretengürtel, Neubaugürtel, and Währinger Gürtel. Like Vienna's street signs, *Let's Go* indicates the district number in Roman or Arabic numerals before the street and number.

▣ LOCAL TRANSPORTATION

Public Transportation: Wiener Linien (☎790 91 00; www.wienerlinien.at.) The **U-Bahn** (subway), **Straßenbahn** (tram), **S-Bahn** (elevated tram), and **bus** lines operate on a 1-ticket system, so you can transfer between types of transportation without buying a new ticket. Purchase tickets at a counter, machine, on board, or at a tobacco shop. A **single fare** (€1.70 in advance, €2.20 on board) lets you travel to any destination in the city and switch from bus to U-bahn to tram to S-bahn in any order, provided your travel is uninterrupted. Other ticket options include a **1-day pass** (€5.70), **1-day "shopping" pass** (M-Sa 8am-8pm, €4.60), **3-day rover ticket** (€13.60), **7-day pass** (€14; valid M 9am to the next M 9am), and an **8-day pass** (€28; valid any 8 days; can be split between several people travelling together, but must be validated for each person). The **Vorteilscard** (Vienna Card; €19) allows for 72hr. of travel and discounts at museums and sights. To avoid a €60 fine from plainclothes inspectors, **validate your ticket** by punching it in the machine. Tickets do not need to be restamped when switching trains. Regular trams and subway cars do not run midnight-5am. **Night buses** run 2 per hr., 12:30-4:30am, along most routes; "N" signs designate night bus stops. A night bus schedule and discount passes are available from Wiener Linien information offices (open M-F 6:30am-6:30pm, Sa-Su 8:30am-4pm) in the Karlspl., Stephahnspl., Westbahnhof, and some other U-Bahn stations, as well as at the tourist office (p.71).

Taxis: ☎313 00, 401 00, 601 60, or 814 00. Stands at Südbahnhof, Karlspl. in the city center, Westbahnhof, and by the Bermuda Dreieck. Accredited taxis have yellow-and-black signs on the roof. Base rate M-Sa €2.80, €0.20 per 0.2km; base rate Su 11pm-6am €3; holidays slightly more expensive. €2 surcharge for calling a taxi.

Car Rental: Hertz (☎700 73 26 61), at the airport. Open M-F 7am-11:30pm, Sa 8am-8pm, Su 7am-11:30pm. **Europcar** (☎700 73 26 99), at the airport. Open M-F 7:30am-11pm, Sa 8am-7pm, Su 7am-11pm.

Bike Rental: Citybike (www.citybikeien.at) has automated rental stations at 50 locations. €2 per day, €1 per 1st 2hr., then €4 per hr. thereafter. MC/V.

🔁 PRACTICAL INFORMATION

Main Tourist Office: I, Albertinapl. on the corner of Maysederg. (☎245 55; www.vienna.info). Follow Operng. up 1 block from the Opera House. Books rooms for a €2.90 fee. Open daily 9am-7pm.

Embassies and Consulates: Australia, IV, Mattiellistr. 2-4 (☎50 67 40). Open M-F 8:30am-4:30pm. **Canada,** I, Laurenzerberg 2 (☎531 38 30 00) M-F 8:30am-12:30pm and 1:30-3:30pm. **Ireland,** I, Rotenturmstr. 16-18, 5th fl. (☎715 42 46). Open M-F 9:30-11am and 1:30-4pm. **New Zealand,** III, Salesianerg. 15 (☎318 85 05). **UK,** III, Jaurèesg. 10 (☎716 13 53 33, after hours for UK nationals in emergencies only 0676 569 40 12). Open M-F 9:15am-12:30pm and 2-3:30pm. **US,** X, Boltzmanng. 16 (☎31 33 90). Open M-F 8-11:30am. 24hr. emergency services.

American Express Travel Agency: I, Kärntnerstr. 21-23 (☎51 51 10), between Himmelpfortg. and Weinburgg. Cashes travelers checks (€5 min. commission for up to €250, then 2%). Open M-F 9am-5:30pm, Sa 9am-1pm.

Luggage Storage: Lockers available at all train stations. €2-3.50 per 24hr.

GLBT Resources: Pick up the *Vienna Gay Guide* (www.gaynet.at/guide), *Coxx*, or *Xtra* from any tourist office or gay bar, cafe, or club. **Rosa Lila Tip,** VI, Linke Wienzeile 102 (lesbians ☎586 51 50, gay men 585 43 43; www.villa.at), is a knowledgeable resource and social center. Take the U4 to Pilgramg. Open M, W, F 5-8pm.

Emergency: ☎141.

24hr. Pharmacy: ☎15 50. Consulates have lists of English-speaking doctors.

Hospital: Allgemeines Krankenhaus, IX, Währinger Gürtel 18-20 (☎40 40 00).

Post Office: Hauptpostamt, I, Fleischmarkt 19 (☎0577 677 10 10). Open daily 6am-10pm. Branches throughout the city and at the train stations; look for yellow signs with a trumpet logo. **Postal Codes:** A-1010 (1st district) through A-1230 (23rd district).

🏠 🏕 ACCOMMODATIONS AND CAMPING

🏨 **Hostel Ruthensteiner,** XV, Robert-Hamerlingg. 24 (☎893 42 02; www.hostelruthensteiner.com). Knowledgeable staff, spotless rooms, kitchen, and a secluded courtyard. Breakfast €2.50. Linens €2. Internet €2 per 40min. Key deposit €10. Reception 24hr. 32-bed summer dorm €13; 8-bed dorms €15; singles €30; doubles €48, with bath €54; quads €68/76. AmEx/MC/V; €0.40-0.80 per day surcharge. ❶

🏨 **Wombats City Hostel,** (☎897 23 36; www.wombats-hostels.com) has 2 separate locations. **"The Lounge"** (XV, Mariahilferstr. 137). Leather couches add a modern touch to its college dorm flavor. **"The Base"** (XV, Grang. 6). Farther from the train station, this hostel compensates with guided tours, nightly English-language movies, and a pub. Breakfast €4. Internet €2 per hr. Laundry €5. Dorms €21; doubles €50. MC/V. ❷

Westend City Hostel, VI, Fügerg. 3 (☎597 67 29; www.westendhostel.at), near Westbahnhof. A rose-filled courtyard and plain dorms provide respite. Breakfast included. Internet €6 per hr. Reception 24hr. Check-out 10:30am. Lockout 10:30am-2pm. Open mid-Mar. to Nov. Dorms €18-21; singles €50-63; doubles €60-78. Cash only. ❷

Camping Neue Donau, XXII, Am Kleehäufel 119 (☎202 40 10; www.campingwien.at/nd). U1: Kaisermühlen. Take the Schüttaustr. exit, then bus #91a to Kleehäufel. 4km from the city center, adjacent to (but not on) Neue Donau beaches. Boat and bike available. Kitchen, showers, and supermarket. Laundry €4.50. Reception 8am-12:30pm and 3-6:15pm. Open Easter-Sept. €6-7 per person, €10-12 per tent. AmEx/MC/V. ❶

Pension Hargita, VII, Andreasg. 1 (☎526 19 28; www.hargita.at). U3: Zieglerg. Hungarian decorations and hardwood floors accompany blue-and-white furniture. Breakfast €5. Reception 8am-midnight. Singles €38, with shower €45, with bath €55; doubles €52/58/66; triples with shower €73, with bath €80. MC/V. ❹

Pension Kraml, VI, Brauerg. 5 (☎587 85 88; www.pensionkraml.at). U3: Zieglerg. Plush rooms in rich red and a lounge with cable TV. Breakfast included. Reception 24hr. Singles €30; doubles €50, with shower €60, with bath €70; triples €70/80. 3- to 5-person apartment with bath €95-125. Cash only. ❸

Wien Süd, XXIII, Breitenfurter. Str. 269 (☎867 36 49; www.campingwien.at/ws). U6: Philadelphiabrücke, and bus #62A to Wien Süd. 27 sq. km of woods and fields, a cafe, playground, and supermarket comprise this former imperial park. Laundry €5. Reception 8am-8pm. Open May-Sept. €6-7 per person, €10-12 per tent. AmEx/MC/V. ❶

◖ FOOD

Restaurants that call themselves *Stüberl* ("little sitting room") or advertise *Schmankerl* serve Viennese fare. Innenstadt restaurants are expensive. The neighborhood north of the university, where Universitätsstr. and Währingerstr. meet (U2: Schottentor), is more budget-friendly. Affordable cafes and restaurants also line **Burggasse** (District VII) and surround the Rechte and Linke Wienzeile near Naschmarkt (U4: Kettenbrückeng). The **Naschmarkt** hosts the city's biggest market of fresh (if pricey) produce. (Stands open M-F 6am-6:30pm, Sa 6am-2pm.) The **Brunnenmarkt** (XVI, U6: Josefstädterstr.) has Turkish flair. A **kosher** supermarket is at II, Hollandstr. 10. (☎216 96 75. Open M-Th 8:30am-6:30pm, F 8am-2pm.)

▨ **Trzesniewski,** I, Dorotheerg. 1 (☎512 32 91), 3 blocks down on the left side of the Graben. Once Kafka's favorite, this establishment has served open-faced mini-sandwiches (€0.90) for over 100 years. Open M-F 8:30am-7:30pm, Sa 9am-5pm. Cash only. ❶

▨ **Centimeter,** IX, Liechtensteinstr. 42 (☎470 06 06; www.centimeter.at). Tram D to Bauernfeldpl. Huge portions of greasy Austrian fare (€6-7) and open-faced sandwiches (€0.15 per cm). Open M-F 10am-midnight, Sa-Su 11am-midnight. AmEx/MC/V. ❶

Yak and Yeti, VI, Hofmühlg. 21 (☎595 54 52; www.yakundyeti.at). U3: Zieglerg. This Himalayan restaurant serves ethnic specialties. *Momos* (Nepalese dumplings) €10-11. Lunch buffet €6.50. Entrees €7-13. Open May-Sept. M-Sa 11:30am-10:30pm; Oct.-Apr. M-F 11:30am-2:30pm and 6-10:30pm, Sa 11:30am-10:30pm. Cash only. ❸

Smutny, I, Elisabethstr. 8 (☎587 13 56; www.smutny.com), U6: Karlspl. A traditional Viennese restaurant serving *Wiener Schnitzel* (€14) and *Fiakergulash* (goulash with beef, egg, potato, and sausage; €11). M-F lunch *Menü* (soup and entree) €8, Sa-Su includes dessert €10. M-F daily special €5. Open daily 10am-midnight. AmEx/MC/V. ❷

Inigo, I, Bäckerstr. 18 (☎512 74 51; www.inigo.at). Founded by a Jesuit priest, Inigo hires the long-term unemployed as cooks. Hearty entrees (€8-10) come with a salad. Vegetarian options. Open M-Sa 9:30am-midnight, Su 10am-4pm. AmEx/MC/V. ❷

Pizza Bizi, I, Rotenturmstr. 4 (☎513 37 05), 1 block from Stephanspl. One of Vienna's best deals. Big pizza slices €3. Pasta €6. Open daily 10:30am-11:30pm. Cash only. ❷

Amerlingbeisl, VII, Stiftg. 8 (☎526 16 60). U3: Neubaug. Serves Mediterranean-influenced buffet entrees (€7-12). Vegetarian options. Breakfast until 3pm €4-8. Sa-Su brunch 9am-3pm €10. Open daily 9am-2am. Kitchen open until 1am. AmEx/MC/V. ❷

☕ COFFEEHOUSES

For years these establishments have been artists' and writers' havens: Freud, Herzl, and Kafka indulged their caffeine cravings sitting in a Viennese cafe. An important dictate of coffeehouse etiquette is to linger; the *Herr Ober* (waiter) will serve you, then leave you to sip your *Mélange* (half coffee, half steamed milk), and cogitate. When you're ready to leave, ask to pay *("Zahlen bitte")*.

▧ **Kleines Café,** I, Franziskanerpl. 3. Escape from the busy pedestrian streets with a *Mélange* (€3) and conversation on a leather couch, or by the fountain in the square. Sandwiches €3-5. Open daily 10am-2am. Cash only.

▧ **Café Central,** I, Herreng. 14 (☎533 37 63; www.palaisevents.at), at the corner of Strauchg. With green-gold arches and live music (M-Sa 3pm-9pm, Su 10am-6pm), this luxurious coffeehouse deserves its status as mecca of the cafe world. *Mélange* €3.50. Open M-Sa 7:30am-10pm, Su 10am-10pm. AmEx/MC/V.

Café Hawelka, I, Dorotheerg. 6 (☎512 82 30). A Viennese institution since 1939, this cafe has a long history as an artisan's meeting place. *Mélange* €3.20. *Buchteln* (cake with plum marmalade) €3. Open M, W-Sa 8am-2am, Su 10am-2am. Cash only.

Demel, I, Kohlmarkt 14 (☎535 17 10). 5min. from the Stephansdom, down Graben. Vienna's most lavish *konditorei* (confectioner), Demel once served the imperial court. Fresh chocolate made daily. *Mélange* €3.80. Open daily 10am-7pm. AmEx/MC/V.

🍷 WINE TAVERNS (HEURIGEN)

Heurigen serve wine and savory Austrian delicacies, often outdoors. Tourist buses head to the most famous region, **Grinzing,** in District XIX; you'll find better atmosphere in the hills of **Sievering, Neustift am Walde** (both in District XIX), and **Neuwaldegg** (in XVII). True *Heuriger* devotees make the trip to **Gumpoldskirchen.** Enjoy a glass of *Heuriger* (€2.20) in the country kitchen or backyard of ▧**Buschenschank Heinrich Nierscher,** XIX, Strehlg. 21. Take U6 to Währingerstr., then tram #41 to the last stop, and bus #41A to Plötzleinsfriedhof (the 2nd stop), or walk up Pötzleinsdorfer Str. which becomes Khevenhüller Str. and go right on Strehlg. (☎440 21 46. Open M, Th-Su 3pm-midnight. Cash only.) To reach **10er Marie,** XVI, Ottakringerstr. 222-224, take U3 to Ottakring, turn left on Thaliastr., then right onto

ON THE MENU

COFFEE CULTURE

Vienna is the world's coffee capital, but for those used to *mocha lattes* or half-caff lite soys, understanding the jumble of German words on the *Kaffeehaus* menu can be daunting. Here's a cheatsheet for deciphering the menu:

A **Mokka** or a **Schwarzer** is strong, pure black espresso and nothing more. The **Kleiner Brauner** ("small brown") lightens the espresso with milk or cream, while the **Verlängerter** lowers the stakes yet again with weaker coffee. The quintessential Viennese cafe drink, a **Mélange** melds black espresso with steamed milk, sometimes capping it with a dollop of whipped cream. The **Kapuziner** ("the monk") also consists of espresso with gently foamed milk but is more commonly known by its Italian name, "cappuccino." The **Einspanner** is a strong black coffee heaped with whipped cream and sometimes a dash of chocolate shavings. **Eiskaffee,** or hot coffee with vanilla ice cream, is a refreshing jolt on hot summer days.

Vienna's specialty coffee drinks combine espresso with a variety of liqueurs for caffeine with a punch. Some cafes serve the **Maria-Theresia,** with orange liqueur, or the **Pharisär,** with rum and sugar. Other liqueurs include **Marillen** (apricot) and **Kirsche** (cherry). Or, for a protein boost, try the milk-less mocha **Kaisermelange,** stirred with brandy and an egg yolk. Be prepared to shell out €6-7 for an indulgent delight.

Johannes-Krawarik. Locals relax in the yellow house's large garden. (☎489 46 47. 0.25L of wine €2. Open M-Sa 3pm-midnight. MC/V.)

SIGHTS

A stroll in District I, the social and geographical center, is a feast for the senses. Cafe tables spill into the streets and musicians attract onlookers as Romanesque arches, Jugendstil apartments, and the modern **Haas Haus** look on. Some of Vienna's most famous modern architecture is outside the Ring, where 20th-century designers found space to build. This area is also home to a number of Baroque palaces and parks that were once beyond the city limits.

STEPHANSDOM AND GRABEN. In the heart of the city, massive **Stephansdom** is one of Vienna's most treasured symbols. For a view of the old city, take the elevator up the North Tower or climb the South Tower's 343 steps. *(☎515 52 35 26. North Tower open daily Apr.-June and Sept.-Oct. 8:30am-5:30pm; Nov.-Mar. 8:30am-5pm; July-Aug. 9am-5pm. South Tower open daily 9am-5:30pm. North Tower €4. South Tower €3.)* Downstairs, skeletons of plague victims fill the **catacombs.** The **Gruft** (vault) stores urns containing the Habsburgs' innards. *(Tours daily 2 per hr. €4.)* From Stephanspl., follow Graben for Jugendstil architecture, including Otto Wagner's red-marble **Grabenhof** and the underground public toilets designed by **Adolf Loos.**

HOFBURG PALACE. A medieval castle expanded over 800 years, this imperial palace was the Habsburgs' home until 1918. It now contains the President's office and a few small museums. *(☎525 24 ext. 69 03; www.khm.at. U3: Herreng. Open Tu-W and F-Su 10am-6pm, Th 10am-9pm. €10, students €7.50. Open M, W-Su 10am-6pm.)*

HOHER MARKT AND STADTTEMPEL. Hoher Markt's biggest draw is the 1914 **Ankeruhr** (clock), whose figures—from Marcus Aurelius to Maria Theresa—rotate past the Viennese coat of arms. *(1 figure per hr. All figures appear at noon.)* Hidden on Ruprechtspl. is the **Stadttempel,** Vienna's only synagogue to escape Kristallnacht. *(Seitenstetteng. 4. Mandatory tours M and Th at 11:30am, 2pm. €2, students €1.)*

SCHLOß SCHÖNBRUNN. Schönbrunn began as a humble hunting lodge, but Maria Theresa's ambition transformed it into a splendid palace. The **Imperial Tour** passes through the **Hall of Mirrors,** where six-year-old Mozart played. The longer **Grand Tour** also visits Maria Theresa's exquisite 18th-century rooms, including the ornate **Millions Room.** *(Schönbrunnerstr. 47. U4: Schönbrunn. ☎811 13 239; www.schoenbrunn.at. Open daily July-Aug. 8:30am-6pm; Apr.-June and Sept.-Oct. 8:30am-5pm; Nov.-Mar. 8:30am-4:30pm. Imperial Tour 22 rooms; 35min.; €10, students €9. Grand Tour 40 rooms; 50min.; €13/12. Includes English-language audio tour.)* Equally impressive, the well-manicured **gardens** behind Schönbrunn contain a **labyrinth.** *(Park open daily 6am-dusk. Labyrinth open daily July-Aug. 9am-7pm; Apr.-June and Sept. 9am-6pm; Oct. 9am-5pm; Nov. 9am-3:30pm. Park free. Labyrinth €2.90, students €2.40.)*

AM HOF AND FREYUNG. Having served as a medieval jousting square, Am Hof now houses the **Kirche am Hof** (Church of the Nine Choirs of Angels) and **Collalto Palace,** where Mozart gave his first public performance. Medieval fugitives once took asylum in the **Schottenstift** (Monastery of the Scots), west of Am Hof, giving rise to the square's name *Freyung*, or "sanctuary." Today, the annual **Christkindl market** fills the plaza with baked goods and holiday cheer (Dec. 1-24).

KARLSKIRCHE. In Karlspl., **Karlskirche** (the Church of St. Borromeo) is an eclectic masterpiece. Under restoration in 2007, it incorporates Baroque, Neoclassical, and Trajan-inspired elements. Save your money, as the church may be best viewed from the outside. *(IV, Kreuzherreng. 1. U1, 2, or 4 to Karlspl. ☎504 61 87. Open M-Sa 9am-12:30pm and 1-7pm, Su 1-7pm. €6, students €4.)*

Vienna Ring

● FOOD
Amerlingbeisl, 18
Inigo, 4
Pizza Bizi, 3
Smutny, 20
Trzesniewski, 8

🏛 MUSEUMS
Albertina, 15
Jüdische Museum, 9
Haus der Musik, 17
Kunsthalle Wien, 19
Kunsthistorisches Museum, 16
Leopold Museum, 21
MAK, 7
Museum Moderner Kunst, 14

🍴 BARS
Chelsea, 12
Das Möbel, 13

☕ COFFEEHOUSES
Café Central, 2
Café Hawelka, 6
Demel, 5
Kleines Café, 10

NIGHTLIFE
Flex, 1
Volksgarten Disco, 11

AUSTRIA

300 yards
300 meters

ZENTRALFRIEDHOF. The Viennese describe the Central Cemetery, with over 2.5 million graves, as half the size of Geneva but twice as lively. **Tor II** (Gate 2) contains the tombs of Beethoven, Brahms, Schubert, Strauss, and an honorary monument to Mozart, whose true resting place is an unmarked grave in the **Cemetery of St. Marx,** III, Leberstr. 6-8. **Tor I** (Gate 1) holds the old **Jewish Cemetery.** *(XI, Simmeringer Hauptstr. 234. Tram #71 from Schwarzenbergpl. or Simmering. ☎ 760 410. Open daily May-Aug. 7am-8pm; Apr. and Sept. 7am-7pm; Mar. and Oct. 7am-6pm; Nov.-Feb. 8am-5pm. Free.)*

PARKS AND GARDENS. The **Stadtpark** (City Park) was the first municipal park outside the former city walls. *(U4: Stadtpark.)* Clockwise up the Ring, the greenhouses of **Burggarten** (Palace Garden) were reserved for the imperial family until 1918. *(☎ 533 85 70. Open Apr.-Oct. M-F 10am-4:45pm, Sa-Su 10am-6:15pm; Nov.-Mar. M-Sa 10am-3:45pm.)* In 1775, Kaiser Josef II gave **Augarten,** Vienna's oldest public park, a Baroque face-lift and opened it to the public. *(Tram #31 from Schottenring or tram N to Obere Augartenstr. Open sunrise to sunset.)*

🏛 MUSEUMS

With a museum around almost every corner, Vienna could exhaust any zealous visitor. The **Vienna Card** (€19), available at the tourist office, large U-bahn stops, and most hostels, entitles holders to museum and transit discounts for 72hr.

🖼 **ÖSTERREICHISCHE GALERIE (AUSTRIAN GALLERY).** The grounds of **Schloß Belvedere** houses two museums. Home to Klimt's *The Kiss*, the **Oberes Belvedere** has a great collection of 19th- and 20th-century art. *(III, Prinz-Eugen-Str. 27. Tram D from Schwarzenbergpl. to Schloß Belvedere. €10, students €6.)* The **Unteres Belvedere** contains the Museum of Baroque Art and the Museum of Medieval Art. *(Unteres Belvedere, III, Rennweg 6. Tram #71 from Schwarzenbergpl. to Unteres Belvedere. €8, students €5. Both Belvederes ☎ 795 570. Open daily 10am-6pm. Combo ticket €13, students €9.)*

🖼 **KUNST HAUS WIEN.** Artist-environmentalist Friedenreich Hundertwasser built this museum without straight lines—even the floor bends. Arboreal "tree tenants" grow from the windowsills and the top floor. *(III, Untere Weißgerberstr. 13. U1 or 4 to Schwedenpl., then tram N to Radetzkypl. Take Löweng. to Kriegler-G. and then left on Untere Weißgerberstr. ☎ 712 0491; www.kunsthauswien.at. Open daily 10am-7pm. Each exhibit €9, both €12; students €7/9. M €4.50/6, except holidays.)*

🖼 **ÖSTERREICHISCHES MUSEUM FÜR ANGEWANDTE KUNST (MAK).** This intimate and eclectic museum is dedicated to design, examining Thonet bentwood chairs' smooth curves, Venetian glass's intricacies, and modern architecture's steel heights. *(I, Stubenring 5. U3: Stubentor. ☎ 711 360; www.mak.at. Open Tu 10am-midnight, W-Su 10am-6pm. €7.90, students €5.50. Sa and holidays free.)*

HAUS DER MUSIK. At the **Haus de Musik,** science meets music. Relax in the prenatal listening room, learn about famous Viennese composers, and have a go at conducting an orchestra. *(I, Seilerstätte 30, near the opera house. ☎ 51 64 80; www.hdm.at. Open daily 10am-10pm. €10, students €8.50. ½-price Tu after 5pm.)*

KUNSTHISTORISCHES MUSEUM (MUSEUM OF FINE ARTS). One of the world's largest art collections features Italian paintings, Classical art, and an Egyptian burial chamber. The main building contains works by the Venetian and Flemish masters and across the street, in the Neue Burg wing of the Hofburg Palace, the **Ephesos Museum** exhibits findings from excavations in Turkey. The **Sammlung alter Musikinstrumente** includes Beethoven's harpsichord and Mozart's piano. *(U2: Muse-*

umsquartier. Across from the Burgring and Heldenpl., to the right of Maria Theresienpl. ☎525 24 41; *www.khm.at. Main building open Tu-W, F-Su 10am-6pm, Th 10am-9pm; Ephesos and Sammlung open M, W-Su 10am-6pm. €10, students €7.50. English-language audio tour €3.)*

ALBERTINA MUSEUM. First an Augustinian monastery, then part of Hofburg Palace, this Museum now houses the Collection of Graphic Arts. The *Prunkräume* (state rooms) display some of Albrecht Dürer's finest prints. *(I, Albertinapl. 1.* ☎534 835 40; *www.albertina.at. Open M-Tu and Th-Su 10am-6pm, W 10am-9pm. €9, students €7.)*

MUSEUMSQUARTIER. Central Europe's largest collection of modern art, the **Museum Moderner Kunst (MUMOK)** highlights Classical Modernism, Fluxus, Pop Art, Photo Realism, and Viennese Actionism. *(Open M-W and F-Su 10am-6pm, Th 10am-9pm. €9, students €7.)* The **Leopold Museum** has the world's largest Schiele collection. *(Open M-W and F-Su 10am-6pm, Th 10am-9pm. €9, students €6.)*

🎵 🎭 ENTERTAINMENT AND NIGHTLIFE

Many of classical music's greats composed, lived, and performed in Vienna. Today, Vienna hosts many budget performances, though prices rise in summer. **Staatsoper,** I, Opernring 2, Vienna's premier opera performs almost nightly September through June. (☎514 442 250; www.wiener-staatsoper.at. €2-254.) The **Wiener Sängerknaben** (Vienna Boys' Choir) sings at 9:15am mass every Sunday mid-September to late June. (U3: Herreng. ☎533 99 27. Seats €5-29. Standing room free.) The **Bundestheaterkasse,** I, Hanuschg. 3, sells tickets for the Staatsoper, the Volksoper, and the Burgtheater. (☎514 44 78 80. Open June to mid-Aug. M-F 10am-2pm; mid-Aug. to June M-F 8am-6pm, Sa-Su 9am-noon; Sa during Advent 9am-5pm.)

Vienna hosts an array of important festivals. The **Wiener Festwochen** (early May to mid-June) has a diverse program of concerts, exhibits, and plays. (☎58 92 20; www.festwochen.or.at.) In May, over 4000 people attend **Lifeball,** Europe's largest AIDS charity event and Vienna's biggest gay celebration. (☎595 56 77; www.lifeball.org. €75-135). The Staatsoper and Volkstheater host the **Jazzfest Wien** (☎503 56 47; www.viennajazz.org) during the first weeks of July. The city-wide film festival, **Viennale** (www.viennale.at), kicks off in mid-October.

> **EURO CUP 2008.** The **2008 European Football Championship** (June 7-29) will be held in Austria and Switzerland. Vienna, Innsbruck, Klagenfurt, and Salzburg will host matches. Expect crowds and unrestrained merrymaking. Visit www.uefa.com for more info. For venues in Switzerland, see p. 1014.

With one of the world's highest bar-to-cobblestone ratios, Vienna is the place to party. Take U1 or 4 to Schwedenpl. to reach the club-packed **Bermuda Dreieck** (Bermuda Triangle). Afterwards, head down **Rotenturmstraße** toward Stephansdom. Outside the Ring, the streets off **Burggasse** and **Stiftgasse** in District VII and the **university quarter** in Districts XIII and IX have outdoor courtyards and hip bars. Viennese nightlife starts late, often after 11pm. For listings, pick up *Falter* (€2.60).

Das Möbel, VII, Burgg. 10. (☎524 94 97; www.das-moebel.at). U2 or 3: Volkstheater. An artsy crowd chats amid metal couches and Swiss-army tables, all available for sale. Don't leave without seeing the bathroom. Internet free for 1st 15min., €0.90 per 15min. thereafter. Open daily 10am-1am. Cash only.

Chelsea, VIII, Lerchenfeldergürtel 29-31. (☎407 93 09; www.chelsea.co.at), under the U-Bahn. U6: Thaliastr. or Josefstädterstr. International bands rock this underground club twice a week. Sa-Su DJs spin techno-pop. 0.5L beer €3.30. Cover €6-12 for band performances. Happy hour 4-5pm. Open M-Sa 6pm-4am, Su 4pm-3am. Cash only.

Flex, I, Donaulände (☎533 75 25; www.flex.at), near the Schottenring U-Bahn station (U2 or U4) by the Danube. Dance, grab a beer or bring your own, and sit by the river with everyone else. DJs start spinning electronic, house, reggae, ska or techno at 11pm. Beer €4. Cover €2-10, free 3:30-4am. Open daily 8pm-4am. Cash only.

Volksgarten Disco, I, Burgring 1 (☎532 42 41; www.volksgarten.at). U2: Volkstheater. One of Vienna's trendiest clubs. M tango. Th alternative. F hip-hop. Sa house. Cover €5-10. Open June-Aug. M 8pm-2am, Th 8pm-4am, F 11pm-6am, Sa 9pm-6am; Sept.-May M 8pm-2am, Th 8pm-4am, F 11pm-6am, Sa 11pm-6am. MC/V; min. €70.

Mango, VI, Laimgrubeng. 3 (☎587 44 48; www.mangobar.at). U2: Museumsquartier. Mango draws gay men with its casual climate, golden walls, and pop music. Mixed drinks €6.50. Open daily 9pm-4am. Cash only.

▓ LET'S GO TO VIENNA: BRATISLAVA, SLK   ☎(0)2

Home to the **M.R. Štefánik International Airport** (BTS; ☎48 57 11 11; www.letiskobratislava.sk), Bratislava (pop. 500,000) often serves as a gateway to Western Europe. In addition to domestic flights from Slovakia, budget airlines **SkyEurope** (☎48 50 11 11; www.skyeurope.com) and **Ryanair** (www.ryanair.com; see **Transportation,** p. 47) run **shuttle buses** to and from Vienna (1-1¼hr., 7-8 per day, 363Sk). Vienna-bound **trains** (☎20 29 11 11; www.zsr.sk) depart from **Bratislava Hlavná Stanica,** at the end of Predstaniˉné nám. (1hr., 1 per hr., round-trip 283Sk). **Buses** make a similar journey, leaving from Mlynské nivy 31 (1½hr., 1 per hr., 400Sk). Another option is to sail to Vienna (1¾hr., 2 per day, 150Sk) with **Lodná osobná doprava,** Fajnorovo nábr. 2 (☎52 93 22 26; www.lod.sk; open daily 8:30am-5:30pm). For overnight accommodations, food listings, and more info on Bratislava, see p. 870.

SALZBURGER LAND AND HOHE TAUERN REGION

Salzburger Land's precious white gold, *Salz* (salt), first drew settlers more than three thousand years ago. Modern visitors instead seek out Salzkammergut's lakes and hills, with Salzburg and Hallstatt among the more enticing getaways.

SALZBURG   ☎0662

Graced with Baroque wonders, Salzburg was Austria's ecclesiastical center in the 17th and 18th centuries. The birthplace of Mozart, its rich musical culture lives on today, in everything from high concert halls to public square folk performances.

▐ TRANSPORTATION

Trains leave from **Hauptbahnhof,** in Südtirolerpl. (☎05 17 17) for: Graz (4hr., 1 per hr. 8am-6:30pm, €40); Innsbruck (2hr., 11 per day, €34); Munich, GER (2-3hr., 30 per day, €27); Vienna (3½hr., 26 per day, €44); Zürich, SWI (6hr., 7 per day, €73). **Buses** depart from the depot in front of the train station. Single tickets (€1.80) available at automatic machines or from the drivers. Books of 5 tickets (€8), day passes (€4.20), and week passes (€11) are available at machines. Punch your ticket when you board or risk a €36 fine. Buses stop running 10:30-11:30pm.

✈ ▐ ORIENTATION AND PRACTICAL INFORMATION

Three hills and the **Salzach River** delineate Salzburg, located just a few kilometers from the German border. The **Neustadt** is north of the river, and the beautiful **Alts-**

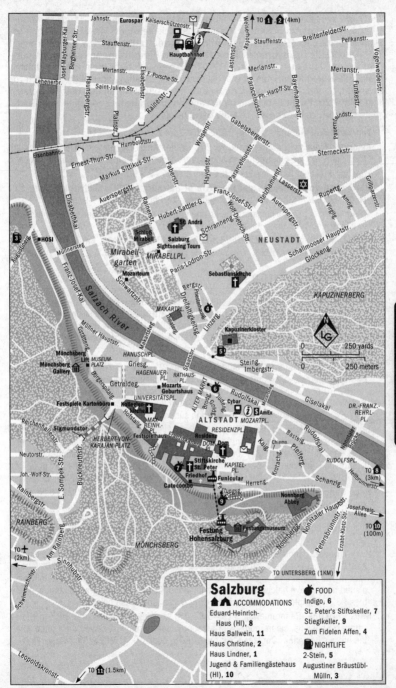

AUSTRIA

Salzburg

🏠🏠 ACCOMMODATIONS

Eduard-Heinrich-
Haus (HI), **8**
Haus Ballwein, **11**
Haus Christine, **2**
Haus Lindner, **1**
Jugend & Familiengästehaus
(HI), **10**

🍎 FOOD

Indigo, **6**
St. Peter's Stiftskeller, **7**
Stieglkeller, **9**
Zum Fidelen Affen, **4**

🎵 NIGHTLIFE

2-Stein, **5**
Augustiner Bräustübl-
Mülln, **3**

tadt squeezes between the southern bank and the **Mönchsberg** hill. The *Hauptbahnhof* is on the northern side of town beyond the Neustadt; bus #1 connects it to **Hanuschplatz,** the *Altstadt's* main public transportation hub, by the river near Griesg. and the Staatsbrücke. Buses #3, 5, and 6 run from the Hauptbahnof to Rathaus and Mozartsteg, also in the *Altstadt.* Neustadt hubs include **Mirabellplatz, Makartplatz,** and **Mozartsteg,** the pedestrian bridge leading across the Salzach to Mozartpl. To reach the *Altstadt* on foot, turn left out of the station onto Rainerstr. and follow it straight under the tunnel and on to Mirabellpl.; continue to Makartplatz and turn right to cross the **Makartsteg** bridge.

Tourist Office: Mozartpl. 5 (☎ 88 98 73 30). Open daily 9am-6pm.

American Express: Mozartpl. 5 (☎ 80 80). Cashes AmEx cheques (free for cheques in US dollars; €5 fee otherwise) and books tours. Open M-F 9am-5:30pm, Sa 9am-noon.

Luggage Storage: 24hr. lockers at the train station €2-3.50.

GLBT Resources: Homosexual Initiative of Salzburg (HOSI), Müllner Hauptstr. 11 (☎ 43 59 27; www.hosi.or.at). Open sporadically. Phone staffed F 7-9pm.

Pharmacies: 3 pharmacies rotate being open 24hr.; ask for a calendar at any pharmacy or check the list on the door of a closed one.

Post Office: At the train station (☎ 88 30 30). Open M-F 7am-6pm, Sa 8am-2pm, Su 1-6pm. **Postal Code:** A-5020.

▐ ACCOMMODATIONS

Within the city itself, budget hotels are few. Try looking for accommodations outside Salzburg still accessible by public transportation. For the best deal, check out *Privatzimmer* (rooms in a family home), usually located on the city's outskirts. Reservations are recommended, especially in summer. For a complete list of *Privatzimmer* and booking help, see the tourist office.

Eduard-Heinrich-Haus (HI), Eduard-Heinrich-Str. 2 (☎ 62 59 76; www.hostel-ehh.at). Spacious rooms overlook the garden and forest. Breakfast included. Laundry €6. Internet €2.60 per 20min. Key deposit €20 or ID. Reception 7-10am and 5pm-midnight. Dorms €18; singles €27, with bath €31; doubles €41/47; triples €47/55; quads €62/78. €3 HI discount. Reserve ahead in summer. AmEx/MC/V. ❶

Jugend & Familiengästehaus (HI), Josef-Preis-Allee 18 (☎ 84 26 700; www.jfgh.at). Take bus #5 (dir.: Birkensiedlung) to Justizgebäude, close to the *Altstadt*. School children pack this hostel in May and June. Poorly ventilated dorms. Breakfast included. Laundry €3. Internet €3 per 40min. Reception 7am-12:30am. Dorms €21; doubles €47-€62. €1.50 HI discount. €3 discount for 2 or more nights. AmEx/MC/V. ❷

Haus Ballwein, Moosstr. 69a (☎ 82 40 29; www.privatvermieter.com/haus-ballwein), south of the city. Take a bus to Makartpl., then south-bound bus #21 to Gsengerweg. Rooms with colorful curtains and wood paneling. Bike rental €5 per day. Breakfast included. Singles €25, with shower €35; doubles €48/50-55; triples with bath €75; 4-person apartment €80. Cash only. ❷

Haus Lindner, Panoramaweg 5 (☎ 45 66 81; www.haus-lindner.at), north of the city in Kasern Berg. Take the S2 train to Salzburg Kasern (6min.; 2 per hr.; €1.60, Eurail valid). Walk uphill on Bergstr. and turn left on Panormaweg. Some of the tastefully furnished rooms have balconies. Breakfast included. Call for pickup from the station. Doubles €32-36; triples €48, with shower €56; quads €56. Cash only. ❷

Haus Christine, Panoramaweg 3 (☎ 45 67 73; www.haus-christine.org), next to Haus Lindner. Spacious, clean rooms with a country motif. Breakfast served on a patio with the block's best view. Doubles €36; triples €48; quads €64. MC/V; 5% charge. ❶

🍴 FOOD

Beer gardens and pastry-shop patios make Salzburg a great place for outdoor dining. Local specialties include *Salzburger nockerl* (egg whites, sugar, and raspberry filling baked into three mounds that represent Salzburg's hills) and world-famous *Mozartkugel* (hazelnuts coated in pistachio marzipan, nougat, and chocolate). **Open-air markets** are in Universitätspl. (Open M-F 6am-7pm, Sa 6am-1pm.)

Indigo, Rudolfskai 8 (☎84 34 80), left of the Staatsbrücke when facing the *Altstadt*. This tiny corner eatery draws locals with its delicious salads (€1.20 per 100g), Asian noodles (€5), and sushi (€4.50-5). Open June-Aug. M-W 10am-10pm, Th-Sa 10am-midnight; Sept.-May M-Sa 10am-10pm. Cash only. ❶

Zum Fidelen Affen, Priesterhausg. 8 (☎87 73 61), off Linzerg. Hearty Austrian fare keeps patrons coming back to Zum Fidelen Affen ("The Faithful Ape"). Try the Monkey Steak (roasted pork with bacon, mushrooms, and tomatoes; €10). Vegetarian options. Open M-Sa 5pm-midnight. AmEx/MC/V. ❷

St. Peter's Stiftskeller, St-Peter-Bezirk 1-4 (☎84 12 68), next to St. Peter's Monastery. Central Europe's oldest restaurant, established in AD 803. The innovative entrees (€10-23) are anything but archaic. Open M-F 11am-midnight. AmEx/MC/V. ❸

Stieglkeller, Festungsg. 10 (☎84 26 81). A short walk from the bottom of the Festungsbahn. A Salzburg favorite since 1492. Seating for 1600, outside or indoors. Bratwurst with sauerkraut and potatoes €7.60. Open daily May-Sept. 10:30am-11pm. MC/V. ❸

👁 SIGHTS

FESTUNG HOHENSALZBURG. Built between 1077 and 1681 by ruling archbishops, the Hohensalzburg Fortress looms over Salzburg from atop Mönchsberg. It is Europe's largest completely preserved castle—partly because it was never successfully attacked. The **Festungsmuseum** inside the fortress has side-by-side histories of the fortress and Salzburg. An audio tour (30min., 4 per hr.) leads visitors up the **watch-tower** for an unmatched panorama of the city and to an organ nicknamed the "Bull of Salzburg" for its off-key snorting. (☎8424 3011. *Take the trail or the Festungsbahn funicular up to the fortress from Festungsg. Funicular May-Aug. 9am-10pm; Sept. 9am-9pm; Oct-Apr. 9am-5pm. Open daily July-Aug. 9am-7pm; Sept. and May-June 9am-6pm; Oct.-Apr. 9am-5pm. Last museum entry 30min. before closing. €10; includes round-trip funicular ride.*)

MOZARTS GEBURTSHAUS. Mozart's overtouristed birthplace holds a collection of the child genius's belongings, including his first violin and keyboard instruments. Arrive before 11am to avoid the crowd. (☎84 43 13. *Getreideg. 9. Open daily July-Aug. 9am-7pm; Sept.-June 9am-6pm. Last entry 30min. before closing. €6, students €5.*)

STIFTSKIRCHE, CATACOMBS, AND THE DOM. The **Monastery of St. Peter** rests against the Mönchsberg cliffs. **Stiftskirche St. Peter,** a church within the monastery, features a marble portal from 1244. In the 18th century, the building was remodeled in Rococo style. (☎844 5760. *Open daily 9am-12:15pm and 2:30-6:30pm.*) To the right of the church's entrance is the monastery's **Friedhof** (cemetery). The entrance to the **catacombs** is on the far right, against the Mönchsberg. (*Monastery open May-Sept. Tu-Su 10:30am-5pm; Oct.-Apr. W-Th 10:30am-3:30pm, F-Su 10:30am-4pm. €1, students €0.60. Cemetery open Apr.-Sept. 6:30am-7:30pm; Oct.-Mar. 6:30am-6pm. Free.*) The exit at the other end of the cemetery leads to the immense Baroque **Dom** (cathedral), where Mozart was christened in 1756 and later worked as concertmaster and court organist. The square in front of the cathedral, **Domplatz**, features a statue of the Virgin Mary and figures representing the Church, the Devil, Faith, and Wisdom.

RESIDENZ. Home to Salzburg princes, this palace once boasted 180 rooms of Baroque, Classical and Renaissance art. Most of the building is now used by the University of Salzburg, but the second floor staterooms—the **Prunkräume**—still contain their original ornate furnishing. *(☎804 226 90. Residenzpl. 1. Open daily 10am-5pm. Last entry 4:30pm. €5.20, students €4.20; includes audio tour.)*

MIRABELL PALACE AND GARDENS. Mirabellpl. holds the **Schloß Mirabell,** which the Archbishop Wolf Dietrich built for his mistress and their 15 children in 1606. *(Open daily 7am-9pm. Free.)* Behind the palace, the **Mirabellgarten,** a well-maintained maze of flower beds and fountains, contains **Zauberflötenhäuschen** ("The Magic Flute Little House") where Mozart purportedly composed *The Magic Flute*.

🎵 ENTERTAINMENT

During the **Salzburger Festspiele** (July-Aug.), operas, plays, films, concerts, and tourists overrun every public space; expect room prices to rise and plan ahead. The **Festspiele Kartenbüro** (ticket office) and **Direkt Verkauf** (daily box office), Karajanpl. 11, have info and tickets for *Festspiele* events. (☎804 5500; www.salzburg-festival.at. Open mid-Mar. to June M-F 9:30am-3pm, through the end of *Festspiele* daily 9:30am-6pm. Tickets €15-360.) In other months, head to a concert organized by the **Mozarteum**. Their **Mozartwoche**, a week-long celebration of Mozart, occurs at the end of January. (Jan. 25-Feb. 5. ☎87 31 54; www.mozarteum.at.) The **Dom** has a concert program in July, August, and early October. (☎88 46 23 45. €20, students €7.) From May to September, the Mirabell Gardens hosts **outdoor performances** including concerts, folk singing, and dancing. The tourist office has leaflets on scheduled events. **Mozartplatz** and **Kapitelplatz** are popular stops for street musicians and school bands. For more info, visit www.salzburg-festivals.com.

🍺 BARS AND BEER GARDENS

Salzburg's pubs and *Biergärten* (beer gardens) cluster along the **Salzach River.** More boisterous revelers stick to **Rudolfskai,** between Staatsbrücke and Mozartsteg. Along **Chiemseegasse** and around **Anton-Neumayr-Platz,** throw back a few drinks in a reserved *Beisl* (pub). Refined bars with middle-aged patrons line **Steingasse** and **Giselakai** on the other side of the river. No longer a monastery, ⊠**Augustiner Bräustübl-Mülln,** Augustinerg. 4, has turned out home-brewed beer since 1621. Follow the long halls to the end to reach the *Biergärten*. (☎43 12 46. Beer 0.3L €2.10, 0.5L €2.60. Open M-F 3-11pm, Sa-Su 2:30-11pm; last call 10:30pm. Cash only.) **2-Stein**, Giselakai 9, is the go-to place for Salzburg's GLBT scence. (☎87 71 79. Mixed drinks from €5. Open M-W and Su, 6pm-4am, Th-Sa 6pm-5am. MC/V.)

HALLSTATT ☎06134

Easily the Salzkammergut's most striking, touristed lakeside village, tiny Hallstatt (pop. 960) teeters on the Hallstattersee's banks. The town's salt-rich earth has helped preserve its archaeological treasures—so extensive that one era in Celtic studies (800-400 BC) is dubbed "the Hallstatt era." Back when Rome was still a village, the "white gold" from the salt mines made Hallstatt a world-famous settlement. Above Hallstatt, the 2500-year-old **Salzbergwerk** is the world's oldest salt mine. Zip down a wooden mining slide to an eerie lake deep inside the mountain on the 1hr. guided tour. Ride the **Salzbergbahn funicular** (open daily 9am until 1hr. after last tour; one-way €8.50, with Salzbergbahn €5.10. Round-trip €8.50/5.10) or follow the footpath from town 1hr. to reach Salzbergwerk. (☎200 24 00; www.salzwelten.at. €16, students €9.30; with funicular €21/13. English-language tours June 4 per hr. 9am-3pm; July-Sept. 14 4 per hr. 9am-4pm; Apr. 26-May and Sept. 15-Oct. 26 1 per 2hr. 9am-3pm.) Hallstatt is also the site of an immense, well-preserved Iron Age archaeological find. The tourist office has English-language **hiking** guides (free) suggesting 50 day hikes and 10 multi-day traverses. The easy **Waldbachstrub Waterfall hike** (1¾-2hr. round-trip) follows a glacial stream up to a waterfall. From the bus stop, follow the brown Malerweg signs near the supermarket until you reach a gazebo (about 30min.), which marks the trail's beginning. At the bridge before the waterfall, the path branches off to the left up to the **Gletschergarten,** a series of small glacial-stream waterfalls and polished rocks. The more difficult **Gangsteig** trail (look to the right just before the falls for a slippery stairway carved into a cliff), requires sturdy shoes. Hikers will have to derive pleasure from the trek itself—there is no rewarding view at the end.

To reach **Gästehaus Zur Mühle ❶,** Kirchenweg 36, from the tourist office, walk uphill and head for a short tunnel at the upper right corner of the square; it's at the end of the tunnel by the waterfall. (☎48 13. Linens €3. Reception 11am-2pm and 4-10pm. Dorms €12. MC/V.) Enjoy the lake view from the beachside lawn at **Frühstückspension Sarstein ❷,** Gosamühlstr. 83. From the ferry, turn right on Seestr. and walk 10min. (☎82 17; www.pension-sarstein.com. Breakfast included. Showers €1 per 10min. Doubles €44-50, with bath €60-66; quads for 3 or more days €60-80. Reserve ahead in summer. Cash only.) **Camping Klausner-Höll ❶,** Lahnstr. 201, lies at the trail head of valley hikes. To get there, turn right out of the tourist office and follow Seestr. for 10min. From the bus stop, turn left on Lahnstr. (☎83 22; www.campingwelt.com/klausner-hoell. Kitchen available. Laundry €6. Reception 8am-noon and 4-8pm. Lockout daily noon-3pm and 10pm-7:30am. Open Apr. 15-Oct. 15. €7 per person, €11 per tent sites. Discounts Apr. 15-June and Sept.-Oct. 15. AmEx/MC/V.) The cheapest eats are at **Konsum** supermarket, Kernmagazinpl. 8, across from the bus stop, where the butcher prepares sandwiches on request. (☎82 26. Open M-F 7:30am-noon and 3-6pm, Sa 7:30am-noon. Cash only.)

Trains leave Hallstatt for Salzburg (2½hr., 1 per hr., €21) via Attnang-Puchheim and Graz (3hr., 1 per

HOW DO YOU SOLVE A PROBLEM LIKE MARILLE?

By baking a strudel 50m long, of course.

During the *Alles Marille* ("Everything Apricot") festival in Krems, the fuzzy fruit appears in every form imaginable, from apricot schnapps to apricot ice cream to apricot dumplings to apricot spritzer. The *pièce de résistance,* however, is Café Hagmann's 50m long *Marillenstrudel,* which stretches down Taglisher Markt street. Everyone in town can get a piece of the action from this perpetual pastry, laden with fluffy apricot cream and sugared almonds (€3 per 30min. tasting). A traditionally dressed folk band serenades the town with Austrian favorites from under an awning festooned with apricot balloons, while revelers sun themselves and imbibe all things apricot. All of Krems turns out for the fun—including the mayor himself—creating the closest thing to traffic the town gets. To top it all off, Saturday ends with a huge party down by the *Schiffstation,* where the *Marillen* schnapps and punch flow like milk and honey. So as you bike, drive, or walk along the Danube and see the trees laden with their precious golden goods, drop into Krems and indulge with the locals in a lavish fruit fest.

July 17-20, 2008. ☎*2732 82676. For more info, check www.allesmarille.at.*

2hr., €31) via Stainach-Irdning. **Postbus** #150 runs from Salzburg to Hallstatt (30min., 1 per hr. 7am-6pm, €3.40) via Bad Ischl (1½hr., 1 per hr., €10). **Local buses** to neighboring towns leave from **Lahn**, at the far end of town. A **ferry**, synced with the train schedule, runs between Hallstatt and the train station across the lake (€2). The **tourist office** is at Seestr. 169. (☎82 08. Open July-Aug. M-F 9am-noon and 2-5pm, Nov.-May M-F 9am-noon.) **Postal Code:** A-4830.

▶ DAYTRIP FROM HALLSTATT: DACHSTEIN ICE CAVES. Above Obertraun, across the lake from Hallstatt, the famed **Rieseneishöhle** (Giant Ice Cave) is part of the largest system of ice caves in the world. The Rieseneishöhle and mammoth **Mammuthöhle** rock caves are up on the mountain near the *Schönbergalm* cable car station. Mandatory German-language tours run 2 per hr.; groups are assigned at the top station of the Schönbergalm. (☎84 00; www.dachsteinhoehlen.at. *Both caves open daily May to mid-Sept. 9am-4pm. Each cave €24; both €29; includes round-trip ride on Schönbergalm.*) **Koppenbrüllerhöhle,** a giant spring, is located in the valley below. (*Take a bus to Koppenbrullerhohle and walk 15min., or walk 45min. along a wooded path from the base of the Schönbergalm. Open June-July. Tours 2 per 3hr. €7.70.*) The cave temperatures are near freezing, so bring warm clothes. **Buses** from Hallstatt go to Obertraun Dachsteinseilbahn (15min., 1 per 1-2hr., €1.60).

ZELL AM SEE   ☎06542

Surrounded by a ring of snow-capped mountains cradling a turquoise lake, Zell am See (pop. 9700) lures visitors craving the outdoors. The **Schmittenhöhebahn** cable car leads to many hikes. (Lift runs daily 2 per hr. Up €16, down €12, round-trip €20. Guest card discounts available.) To reach the lift, walk 20min. up Schmittenstr. or take PostBus #661 (5min., 1 per 1-2hr., €2). The moderately strenuous **Pinzgauer Spaziergang,** marked "Alpenvereinsweg" #19 or 719, begins at the top of the Schmittenhöhebahn and levels off high in the Kitzbüheler Alps. Most hikers devote an entire day to it, taking a side path to one of the valley towns west of Zell, where buses return to Zell am See. For a faster-paced experience, **Outdo,** Schmittenstr. 8 (☎701 65; www.outdoadventures.com) leads a variety of trips.

Ask at your hostel or hotel for a free **guest card,** which provides discounts throughout Zell. **⬛Haus der Jugend (HI) ❷,** Seespitzstr. 13, with a lakeside terrace, brings luxury to budget housing. From the station, take the exit facing the lake ("Zum See"), turn right on the lakeside footpath, and left on Seespitzstr. (☎571 85; www.jungehotels.at/seespitzstrasse. Breakfast included. Internet €1 per 12min. Reception 7:30-10am and 4-10pm. Dorms €18-22; doubles with bath €44. AmEx/MC/V.) **Ristorante Giuseppe ❷,** Kircheng. 1, serves personal pizzas (€6-10) and pasta (€7-11). From the station, walk right on Bahnhofstr. past the church. (☎723 730; www.ristorante-giuseppe.at. Open daily 11:30am-11:30pm. MC/V; €40 min.)

Leaving the station at the intersection of Bahnhofstr. and Salzmannstr., **trains** run to: Innsbruck (1½-2hr., 1 per hr., €24); Kitzbühel (45min., 1 per 2hr., €10); Vienna (5hr., €47) via Salzburg (1hr., 1 per hr., €13). **Buses** leave the station on Postpl. for Franz-Josefs-Höhe (#651; mid-June to mid-Sept. 2 per day, €11) and Salzburg (2hr., 1 per 2hr., €11). Buy tickets on board or at the kiosk. (☎54 44. Open M-F 7:45am-1:45pm.) The **tourist office** is at Brucker Bundesstr. 1a. (☎770; www.europasportregion.info. Open June-Sept. and Nov.-Apr. M-F 9am-6pm, Sa 9am-noon and 2-6pm, Su 10am-noon; May and Oct. M-F 9am-6pm, Sa 9am-noon.) For **mountain rescue,** call ☎140. **Postal Code:** A-5700.

HOHE TAUERN NATIONAL PARK

The enormous Hohe Tauern range, part of the Austrian Central Alps and forming central Europe's largest nature reserve, encompasses 246 glaciers and 304 mountains. Preservation is the park's primary goal, so large campgrounds and recreation areas are illegal. *Experiencing Nature: Walking Destinations*, available at park centers and most tourist offices, describes 54 different hikes of varying difficulties. At the center of the park lies **Franz-Josefs-Höhe**, the most visited section, and the **Pasterze Glacier,** which hovers above the town of Heiligenblut.

▛ TRANSPORTATION. Hohe Tauern National Park sits at the meeting point of the Kärnten, Salzburger Land, and Tyrol provinces. The park center is best reached by the highway, ▟**Großglockner Hochalpenstraße** (open May to mid-June and mid-Sept. to Nov. 6am-8:30pm; mid-June to mid-Sept. 5am-10pm). As the zigzagging road climbs higher, it passes Alpine meadows, glacial waterfalls, jagged peaks, and plunging valleys. **PostBus** #651 goes from Zell am See to Franz-Josefs-Höhe (1½-2½hr., 2 per day, €11). Snow chains are required in snow. (Car toll €28.)

▟ FRANZ-JOSEFS-HÖHE. Numerous buses, cars, and motorcycles climb the Großglockner Hochalpenstraße to this tourist mecca above the edge of the **Pasterze Glacier.** Once out of the parking area, the Panoramaweg offers a great view of **Großglockner** (3798m). On the ridge above the info center, the **Swarovski Observation Tower** provides free telescope use. (Open daily 10am-4pm.) **Buses** from Franz-Josefs-Höhe travel to **Heiligenblut** (30min., 3-9 per day, €4), the closest town. The **National Park office** is across the street. (☎04824 27 00. Open daily late June-Sept. 10am-5pm.) To reach the **Jugendgästehaus (HI) ❷**, Hof 36, take the path down from the wall behind the bus stop parking lot. (☎04824 22 59; www.hiyou.at. Breakfast included. Reception daily July-Aug. 7-11am and 5-10pm; Sept.-June 7-10am and 5-9pm. Lockout 10am-4pm. Dorms €21; singles €26; doubles €44. €3 HI discount.)

▟ HIKING. Pick up a free hiking map from the National Park or tourist office. A topographic map (€10-15) is necessary for prolonged hikes. From the Franz-Josefs-Höhe parking lot, the initially steep **Pasterze Gletscherweg** (3hr.) descends to the edge of the retracting Pasterze Glacier before continuing through the valley and around the Stausee Margaritze to the **Glocknerhaus Alpine Center;** stay on the well-marked path. A free shuttle bus runs between Franz-Josefs-Höhe and Glocknerhaus. Ask the Glocknerhaus staff to call for it. Many hikes in the Großglockner area start at Heiligenblut, from the Retschitzbrücke parking area outside of town via Gemeindestr. The easy **Gößnitzfall-Kachlmoor** trail (round-trip 2hr.) leads through the Kachlmoor swamp to the Gößnitz Waterfalls at the head of the Gößnitz Valley. The rewarding but long **Gößnitztal-Langtalseen** hike (round-trip 10-12hr.) continues through Alpine pastures. Spend the night in the **Elberfelder Hütte ❶**. (Floor space €11; beds €21.) In the morning, pass three gleaming lakes before heading back to Heiligenblut via the Wirtsbauer Alm.

TYROL (TIROL)

Tyrol's soaring peaks challenge hikers with their celestial scale. Craggy summits in the northeast and south cradle the pristine Ötzal and Zillertal valleys while the mighty Hohe Tauern mountain range marches across eastern Tyrol.

INNSBRUCK   ☎0512

After hosting the 1964 and 1976 winter Olympics, the mountain city of Innsbruck (pop. 118,000) rocketed to international recognition. Colorful architecture and relics from the Habsburg Empire pepper the tiny cobblestone streets of the *Altstadt* (Old Town), while the nearby Tyrolean Alps await skiers and hikers.

AUSTRIA

⊟ 🔖 TRANSPORTATION AND PRACTICAL INFORMATION

Trains: Hauptbahnhof, Südtirolerpl. (☎517 17). To: **Graz** (6hr., 2 per day, €48); **Salzburg** (2½hr., 1 per hr., €34); **Vienna** (5-6hr., 1 per hr., €54); **Munich, GER** (2hr., 1 per hr., €35); **Zürich, SWI** (4hr., 8 per day, €48).

Public Transportation: The **IVB** Office, Stainerstr. 2 (☎530 7500; www.ivb.at), off Marktgraben, has bus schedules and route maps. Open M-F 7:30am-6pm. Single fare €1.70, 24hr. pass €3.80, week €12. Discounts for students under 20. Most buses stop around 11:30pm; 4 **Nachtbus** lines run 1 per hr. midnight-5am; most pass Maria-Theresien-Str., the train station, and Landesmuseum. IVB's **Sightseer** bus is the easiest way to visit Innsbruck's far-flung attractions. Single fare €2.80, round-trip €4.40, day pass €8.80. May-Oct. 2 per hr. 9am-6:30pm; Nov.-Apr. 1 per hr. 10am-6pm. Tickets for all buses and trams can be bought on board, at a kiosk, or from the tourist office.

Bike Rental: Neuner Radsport, Maximilianstr. 23 (☎56 15 01). Mountain bikes €16 per ½-day, €20 per day. Open M-F 9am-6pm, Sa 9am-noon.

Tourist Office: Innsbruck Tourist Office, Burggraben 3 (☎598 50; www.innsbruck.info), off Museumstr. Sells the **Innsbruck Card,** with unlimited public transport and entry to most sights (1-day €24, 2-day €29, 3-day €34). Maps €1. Open daily 9am-6pm.

Mountain Rescue: ☎140.

Post Office: Maximilianstr. 2 (☎0577 677 6010). Open M-F 7am-9pm, Sa 7am-3pm, Su 10am-7:30pm. **Postal Code:** A-6010.

⛺ ACCOMMODATIONS

Options for budget accommodations are limited in June, when some hostels close, although student dorms open to travelers in July and August. Request a free **Club Innsbruck** card from your hotel or hostel for discounts on hiking, skiing, and tours.

Hostel Fritz Prior-Schwedenhaus (HI), Rennweg 17b (☎58 58 14). From the station, take bus #4 to Handelsakademie, continue to the end and cross Rennweg. By the river, this hostel has comfortable rooms with bath. Breakfast 7-8am €5. Linen €1.50. Laundry €5.40. Reception 7-9am and 5-10:30pm. Lockout 9am-5pm. Open July-Aug. Dorms €13; singles €23; doubles €38; triples €49. Cash only. ❶

Gasthof Innbrücke, Innstr. 1 (☎28 19 34). From the *Altstadt,* cross the Innbrücke. This 582-year-old inn has a bar and restaurant. Breakfast included. Reserve ahead. Singles €31, with shower €39; doubles €50/67. MC/V. ❸

Jugendherberge Innsbruck (HI), Reichenauer Str. 147 (☎34 61 79; www.youth-hostel-innsbruck.at). From the train station, take tram #3 to Museumstr. and bus O to Jugendherberge. This former Olympic athlete housing turned hostel has clean rooms. Bike rental €11 per day. Breakfast included. Laundry €3.30. Internet €1 per 10min. Reception July-Aug. 7am-1pm and 3-11pm; Sept.-June 7am-1pm and 5-11pm. Dorms €16-21 1st night, €14-16 thereafter; singles €33; doubles €50. Cash only. ❷

🍴 FOOD

The *Altstadt* cafes on Maria-Theresien-Str. are good but overpriced. **M-Preis** supermarket is at Maximilianstr. 3 (☎580 5110; open M-F 7:30am-7pm, Sa 7:30am-5pm) and inside the train station (☎58 07 30; open daily 6am-9pm).

Theresienbräu, Maria-Theresien-Str. 51-53 (☎58 75 80). Built around giant copper brewing kettles. Try the golden brown house lager (0.5L €3.10) or Tyrolean specialties (€6-7). Open M-W 10am-1am, Th-Sa 10am-2am, Su 10am-midnight. MC/V. ❷

Noi Original Thaiküche, Kaiserjägerstr. 1 (☎58 97 77). This tiny Thai kitchen packs a powerful punch with its spicy soups (€5-16) and noodles (€7-10). Lunch specials €8-9. Open M-F 11:30am-2:30pm and 6-11pm, Sa 6-11pm. Cash only. ❷

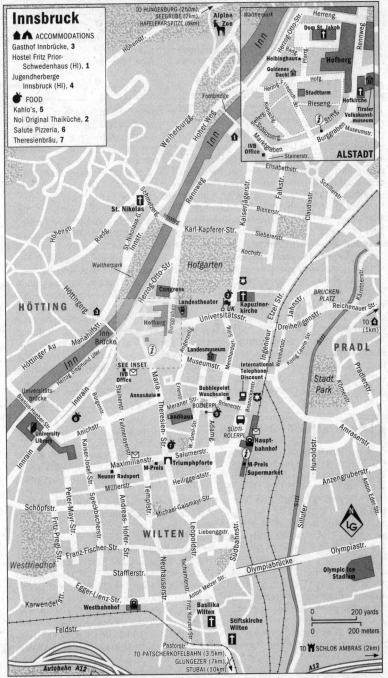

Innsbruck

ACCOMMODATIONS

Gasthof Innbrücke, **3**
Hostel Fritz Prior-
  Schwedenhaus (HI), **1**
Jugendherberge
  Innsbruck (HI), **4**

FOOD

Kahlo's, **5**
Noi Original Thaiküche, **2**
Salute Pizzeria, **6**
Theresienbräu, **7**

TO HUNGERBURG (250m),
SEEGRUBE (2km),
HAFELEKARSPITZE (5km)

Alpine Zoo

ALSTADT

Walterpark

Herreng.
Dom St. Jakob
Hofburg
Helbinghaus
Goldenes Dachl
Stadtturm
Rieseng.
Hofkirche
Tiroler
Volkskunst-
museum
Burggraben
Museumstr.

Herzog-Otto-Str.
Badg.
Pfarrg.
Hofg.
Herzog-F.-Leopold-Str.
Kiebachg.
Seilerg.
Schlosserg.
Marktgraben
Stainerstr.

Rennweg

Inn

IVB Office

Höhenstr.
Weiherburgg.
Hoher Weg
Footbridge
Inn

St. Nikolas
Schmelzerg.
Innstieg
St.-Nikolaus-G.
Innstr.
Riedg.
Höhenstr.
Höttingerg.

HÖTTING

Waltherpark

Herzog-Otto-Str.
Congress
Landestheater
Hofburg
Burggraben
Universitätsstr.
Seilerg.
Meinhardstr.
Sillg.

Karl-Kapferer-Str.
Kaiserjägerstr.
Bienerstr.
Sieberstr.
Kochstr.

Hofgarten

Kapuziner-
kirche
UK

Elisabethstr.
Falkstr.
Schillerstr.
Claudiastr.

Ingenieur
Etzel Str.
Jahnstr.
Weinhartstr.

BRUCKEN-
PLATZ
Reichenauer Str.
Kärntnerstr.

TO (1km)

PRADL

Dreiheiligenstr.
König Laurin Str.

Stadt
Park

Pradlerstr.
Kornstr.

Amraserstr.

Anzengruberstr.
Anton Eder Str.

Mariahilfstr.
Inn-
Brücke
Innrain
Bürgerstr.
Herzog Siegmund Ufer
SEE INSET
IVB Office
Annasäule
Maria-
Theresien-
Str.
Meraner Str.
Erlerstr.
BOZNERPL.
Adamg.
Anich-Str.

Universitäts-
brücke
Blasius-Hueber-Str.
University
Library
Kaiser-Josef-Str.
Anichstr.
Müllerstr.
Fallmerayerstr.
Salurnerstr.
Maximilianstr.
M-Preis
Triumphpforte
Neuner Radsport
Heiliggeiststr.

Landesmuseum
Museumstr.
Bubblepoint
Waschsalon
Brixnerstr.
Landhaus
Kahlo's
SÜDTI-
ROLERPL.
Haupt-
bahnhof
International
Telephone
Discount
Brunecker Str.

M-Preis
Supermarket

Sillufer
Sill
Hunoldstr.

Schöpfstr.
Peter-Mayr-Str.
Fritz-Pregl-Str.
Franz-Fischer-Str.
Speckbacherstr.
Andreas-Hofer-Str.
Templstr.
Michael-Gaismayr-Str.
Leopoldstr.
Neuhauserstr.
Tschamlerstr.

WILTEN

Liebenggstr.
Südbahnstr.
Anton Melzer Str.

Olympiastr.

Olympiabrücke
Olympic Ice
Stadium

Westfriedhof
Stafflerstr.
Egger-Lienz-Str.
Karwendelstr.
Feldstr.

Westbahnhof
Basilika
Wilten
Stiftskirche
Wilten

Pastorstr.
Fritz Konzert Str.

TO PATSCHERKOFELBAHN (3.5km),
GLUNGEZER (7km),
STUBAI (10km)

Autobahn A12

A12

0   200 yards
0   200 meters

TO SCHLOß AMBRAS (2km)

Salute Pizzeria, Innrain 35 (☎ 58 58 18). Students come for good, cheap pizza (€3.20-8.20). Pasta €4.70-7.10. Open daily 11am-midnight. Cash only. ❶

Kahlo's, Boznerpl. 6 (☎ 567 330; www.kahlos.com), serves spicy Mexican fare in a setting filled with cacti, strings of chilis, and Kahlo's famous unibrow paintings. Enchiladas and burritos €9-12. Fajitas €12-15. Open daily 11:30am-11pm. AmEx/MC/V. ❷

🔆 SIGHTS

The greens and pinks of Innsbruck's *Altstadt* stand out brilliantly against the surrounding mountains' earth tones. The Old Town centers around the **Goldenes Dachl** (Golden Roof), Herzog-Friedrich-Str. 15. The 16th-century gold-shingled balcony honors Maximilian I, Innsbruck's favorite Habsburg emperor. The nearby **Helblinghaus** is graced with pale-green floral detail and intricate stucco work. Church domes and shopping boutiques line Innsbruck's most distinctive street, **Maria-Theresien-Straße,** which runs south from the edge of the *Altstadt*. At its far end stands the **Triumphpforte** (Triumphal Arch), built in 1765 after the betrothal of Emperor Leopold II. In the middle, the **Annasäule** (Anna Column) commemorates the Tyroleans' 1703 victory over the Bavarians. Built from pink-and-white marble, **Dom St. Jakob,** 1 block behind the *Goldenes Dachl*, illustrates High Baroque ornamentation. Its prized possession is the small altar painting of *Our Lady of Succor* by Lukas Cranach the Elder. (Open Apr.-Sept. M-Sa 8am-7:30pm, Su 12:30-7:30pm; Oct.-Mar. M-Sa 10am-6:30pm, Su 12:30-6:30pm. Free. Mass M-Sa 9:30am, Su 10, 11:30am.) In front of the Dom, **Hofburg,** the imperial palace, originally built in 1460, was completely remodeled under Maria Theresa. (Rennweg 1. ☎ 58 71 86. www.hofburg-innsbruck.at. Open daily 9am-5pm. Last entry 4:30pm. €5.50, students €4. English-language guidebook €1.80.) Accessible by Sightseer bus or tram #3 and a short 15min. walk uphill, **🔆Schloß Ambras** transformed from hunting lodge into elegant castle during Ferdinand II's reign. While the faces in the **Habsburg Portrait Gallery** may start to look identical, giant stuffed sharks and paintings of the incredibly hirsute Petrus and Madleine Gonzalez in the **Kunst- und Wunderkammer** (Cabinet of Curiosities) are guaranteed to stand out. (Schloß 20. ☎ 0525 24 4802; www.khm.at/ambras. Open daily Aug. 10am-7pm; Sept.-Oct. and Dec.-July 10am-5pm. May-Oct. €8, students €6; Dec.-Apr. €4.50/3.)

🥾🎿 HIKING AND SKIING

A **🔆Club Innsbruck** membership (free; see **Accommodations,** p. 86) lets you in on one of Austria's best deals. The club's popular **hiking** program around Innsbruck and its surrounding villages provides free guides, transportation, and equipment. Moderate 3-5hr. group hikes from Innsbruck meet in front of the Congress Center (early June to early Oct. daily 9am; return around 4-5pm). Free 1hr. nighttime **lantern hikes** to Heiligwaßer near Igls leave Tuesday at 7:45pm and culminate in a hut party with traditional Austrian song and dance. For the early birds, the club also offers Friday **sunrise hikes** to Rangger Köpfl. leaving at 4:50am; reserve ahead. For self-guided hikes, take the J bus to **Patscherkofel Seilbahnen** (20min.). The lift provides access to moderately difficult 1½-5hr. hikes near the 2246m bald summit of the Patscherkofel. (Open July-Aug. 9am-5pm; June and Sept. M-F 9am-4:30pm, Sa-Su 9am-5pm. €11, round-trip €17.) For more challenging climbs, ride the lifts up to the **Nordkette** mountains. Take the J bus to Hungerburg and catch the cable car to Seegrube (1905m) or continue on to Hafelekarspitze (2334m). Both stops lead to several hiking paths along jagged ridges and around rocky peaks, but be prepared: they are neither easy nor well-marked. (☎ 29 33 44. Hungerburg to Seegrube €11, under 20 €9; to Hafelekar €12/10; Seegrube to Hafelekar €2.70/2.20)

To view Innsbruck from above, Mountain Fly offers a €95 tandem **paragliding** package, including transport and equipment (☎ 0664 282 8968).

For Club-led **ski excursions,** take the complimentary ski shuttle (schedules at the tourist office) to any cable car. The **Innsbruck Gletscher Ski Pass** (available at the tourist office) is valid for all 60 lifts in the region (with Club Innsbruck membership: 3-day €90, 6-day €155). Individual lift passes are available for Nordpark-See-grube (☎ 29 33 44; www.nordpark.com), Patscherkofel (☎ 598 50; www.patscherkofelbahnen.at), and Glungezer (☎ 0552 378 321; www.glungezer-bahn.at; €21). One day of skiing on **Stubai glacier** costs about €35. Stubai is also the only slope for summer skiing; packages (bus, lift, and rental) start at €50.

KITZBÜHEL   ☎ 05356

During ski season, everyone in Kitzbühel is merely catching his breath before the next run; the town's ski area, the **Ski Circus,** is home to the most venerable downhill course in the world—the legendary **Hahnenkamm.** A one-day **ski pass** (€34-39) or a three- or six-day summer **vacation pass** (€38/52) include all lifts and the buses that connect them; purchase either at any lift. In summer, tourists meander along one of the 87 **hiking trails** that snake up the mountains; trail maps are free at the tourist office. Down comforters ensure a cozy night at noisy **Pension Hörl ❷**, Joseph-Pirchlstr. 60. From Hotel Kaiser, turn left onto Joseph-Pirchlstr. (☎ 631 44. Breakfast included. €23-30 per person. Cash only.) **Huberbräu-Stüberl ❷**, Vorderstadt 18, has a variety of *Schnitzel* (€6.80-14) and *Tirolean Gröstl* (€6.50). (☎ 65 677. Open mid-June to mid-May M-Sa 8am-midnight, Su 9am-midnight. Cash only.) **Trains** leave from the *Hauptbahnhof* for Innsbruck (1hr., 1 per 2hr., €14) and Vienna (6hr., €50) via Salzburg (2½hr., 1 per day, €24). The **tourist office** is at Hinterstadt 18, near the Rathaus. (☎ 777; www.kitzbuehel.com. Open July-Aug. and Dec. 26 to mid-Mar. M-F 8:30am-6pm, Sa 9am-6pm, Su 10am-6pm; Nov.-Dec. 25 and mid-Mar. to June M-F 8:30am-12:30pm and 2:30-6pm, Sa 9am-1pm.) Pension and hotels offer free **guest cards,** entitling holders to English-language city tours (Tu 10am), guided hikes (June-Oct. M-F 8:45am), and equipment rental discounts. **Postal Code:** A-6370.

STYRIA (STEIERMARK)

Many of southern Austria's folk traditions live on in the emerald hills and sloping pastures of Styria, where even the largest city—Graz—remains calm and relatively untouristed. Its vineyards draw tourists from across Europe.

GRAZ   ☎ 0316

Graz, Austria's second-largest city (pop. 290,000), is also the nation's best-kept secret. The *Altstadt* (Old Town) has an unhurried Mediterranean feel, picturesque red-tiled roofs, and Baroque domes. To the left of the tourist office, the **Landeszeughaus** (Provincial Armory), Herreng. 16, details the history of Ottoman attacks on the arsenal and has enough spears, muskets, and armor to outfit 28,000 mercenaries. (☎ 80 17 98 10. Open Apr.-Oct. M-W and F-Su 10am-6pm, Th noon-8pm; Nov.-Mar. Tu-Su 10am-3pm.) North of Hauptpl., the wooded **Schloßberg** (Castle Mountain) rises above Graz. Climb the zigzagging stone steps of the **Kriegsteig,** built by Russian prisoners during WWI, to the city's emblem, the **Uhrturm** (clock tower), for sweeping views of Graz and the vast Styrian plain. The newest addition to the riverscape, the mussel shell-shaped **Murinsel** in the center of the river, houses a chic cafe, open-air theater, and playground. The **Opernhaus,** Franz-Josef-Pl. 10, at Opernring and Burgg., stages high-quality performances.

Most accommodations are pricey and far from the center, but efficient local transport at least provides an easy commute. To reach the family-oriented **Jugendgästehaus Graz (HI) ❷**, Idlhofg. 74, from the station, cross the street, head right on Eggenberger Gürtel, turn left on Josef-Huber-G., then take the first right; the hostel complex is your right. Buses #31, 32, and 33 run from Jakominipl. Be cautious in the neighborhood, especially at night. (☎ 708 3210; www.jfgh.at. Breakfast included. Laundry €4. Internet €1.50 per 20min. Reception 7am-11pm. Curfew 1am; night-key deposit €20. Dorms €24; singles €40; doubles €66. €1.10 HI discount. MC/V.) On **Hauptplatz,** concession stands sell sandwiches and *Wurst* (€2-3). Situated in the shadow of Schloßberg, **Alte Münze ❷**, Schloßbergpl. 8, serves Styrian specialties. (☎82 91 51. Entrees €7-15, vegetarian €7-12. Open mid-Mar. to Dec. Tu-Sa 8am-11:30pm; June-Sept. Tu-Sa 8am-11:30pm, Su 11am-10pm. Cash only.) The hub of after-hours activity is the so-called **Bermuda Triangle,** an area of the old city behind Hauptpl. and bordered by Mehlpl., Färberg., and Prokopig.

Trains run to: Innsbruck (6-7hr., 7 per day, €48); Munich, GER (6¼hr., 3 per day, €72); Salzburg (4¼hr., 1 per 2hr., €43); Vienna (2½hr., 1 per hr., €30); Zürich, SWI (10hr., 3 per day, €83). To reach the city center take tram #1, 3, 6, or 7 (€1.70, day pass €3.70). By foot, exit right from the train station, then turn left onto Annenstr. Follow it to the main bridge and cross to reach **Hauptplatz.** Five minutes away is **Jakominiplatz,** the public transportation system's hub. **Herrengasse,** a pedestrian street lined with cafes and boutiques, connects the two squares. The **tourist office** is at Herreng. 16. (☎807 50; www.graztourismus.at. July-Aug. M-F 10am-7pm, Sa-Su 10am-6pm; Apr.-June, Sept.-Oct., and Dec. M-Sa 10am-6pm, Su 10am-4pm; Jan.-Mar. and Nov. M-F 10am-5pm, Sa-Su 10am-4pm.) **Postal Code:** A-8010.

BELGIUM
(BELGIQUE, BELGIË)

 Surrounded by France, Germany, and the Netherlands, Belgium is a convergence of different cultures. Appropriately, the small country attracts an array of travellers: chocoholics, Europhiles, and art-lovers all come together to worship in Belgium. Sweet-toothed foreigners flock to Brussels, the home of filled chocolate, to nibble confections from one of 2000 cocoa-oriented specialty shops and to brush shoulders with diplomats en route to European Union and NATO headquarters. In Flanders, Gothic towers surround cobblestone squares, while visitors below admire Old Masters' canvases and guzzle monk-brewed ale. Wallonie has less tourist infrastructure, but the caves of the Lesse Valley and the forested hills of the Ardennes compensate with their stunning natural beauty.

 DISCOVER BELGIUM: SUGGESTED ITINERARY

Plan for at least two days in **Brussels** (p. 95), the capital whose **Grand-Place** Victor Hugo called "the most beautiful square in the world." Head north to the elegant boulevards of **Antwerp** (p. 105) and historic **Ghent** (p. 106), then go west to the winding streets and canals of romantic **Bruges** (p. 101). Visit **Liège** (p. 108), a university town and transit hub, or take your time exploring the leafy Ardennes, using **Namur** (p. 109) as a base for hikes into Belgium's rural south.

ESSENTIALS

FACTS AND FIGURES

Official Name: Kingdom of Belgium.

Capital: Brussels.

Major Cities: Antwerp, Ghent, Liège.

Population: 10,392,000.

Land Area: 30,500 sq. km.

Time Zone: GMT +1.

Languages: Dutch (60%), French (40%).

Religions: Roman Catholic (75%), Protestant (25%).

French Fries: Invented in Belgium during the 18th century, despite what the name suggests. Served with mayonnaise.

Varieties of beer: Over 500. Bottoms up!

WHEN TO GO

May, June, and September are the best months to visit Belgium, with temperatures around 18-22°C (64-72°F) in Brussels and Antwerp, and approximately 6°C (10°F) higher in Liège and Ghent. July and August tend to be rainy and hotter. Winters are cool, with temperatures of 2-7°C (36-45°F), somewhat colder in the Ardennes.

DOCUMENTS AND FORMALITIES

EMBASSIES AND CONSULATES. Foreign embassies in Belgium are in Brussels. Belgian embassies abroad include: **Australia and New Zealand,** 19 Arkana St., Yarralumla, ACT 2600 (☎02 62 73 25 02; www.diplomatie.be/canberra); **Canada,**

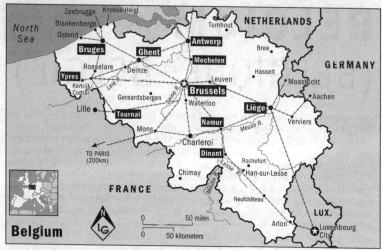

Belgium

360 Albert St., Ste. 820, Ottawa, ON, K1R 7X7 (☎613-236-7267; www.diplomatie.be/ottawa); **Ireland,** 2 Shrewsbury Rd., Ballsbridge, Dublin, 4 (☎01 205 71 00; www.diplomatie.be/dublin); **UK,** 17 Grosvenor Crescent, London, SW1X 7EE (☎020 7470 3700; www.diplomatie.be/london); **US,** 3330 Garfield St., NW, Washington, D.C., 20008 (☎202-333-6900; www.diplobel.us).

VISA AND ENTRY INFORMATION. EU citizens do not need a visa. Citizens of Australia, Canada, New Zealand, and the US do not need a visa for stays of up to 90 days, beginning upon entry into any of the countries in the EU's freedom-of-movement zone. For more info, see p. 14. For stays longer than 90 days, all non-EU citizens need visas (around US$85), available at Belgian consulates. Visit www.diplobel.us. For US citizens, visas are usually issued a few weeks after application submission.

TOURIST SERVICES AND MONEY

EMERGENCY	Ambulance: ☎100. Fire: ☎100. Police: ☎101.

TOURIST OFFICES. Bureaux de Tourisme, marked by green-and-white or blue signs labeled "i," are supplemented by **Infor Jeunes/Info-Jeugd,** info centers that help people find work and secure accommodations in Wallonie and Flanders, respectively. The **Belgian Tourist Information Center (BBB),** Grasmarkt 63, Brussels (☎025 04 03 90), has national tourist info. The weekly English-language *Bulletin* (www.thebulletin.be; €2.80 at newsstands) includes cultural events, movie listings, and news.

MONEY. The **euro (€)** has replaced the Belgian **franc** as the unit of currency in Belgium. For more info, see p. 16. **ATMs** generally offer the best exchange rates. A bare-bones day in Belgium might cost €35, while a more comfortable day runs about €50-65. Tipping is not common, though rounding up is. Restaurant bills usually include a service charge, although outstanding service warrants an extra 5-10% tip. Give bathroom attendants €0.25 and movie and theater attendants €0.50.

Belgium has a 21% **value added tax (VAT),** a sales tax applied to most goods and services. Restaurant and taxi prices usually include VAT; at restaurants, this may be listed as *service comprise* or *incluse.* The prices given in *Let's Go* include

VAT. In the airport upon exiting the EU, non-EU citizens can claim a refund on the tax paid for goods bought at participating stores. In order to qualify for a refund, you must spend at least €125 on a single item; make sure to ask for a refund form when you pay. For more info on qualifying for a VAT refund, see p. 19.

BUSINESS HOURS. Banks are generally open Monday through Friday 9am-4pm but often close for lunch midday. **Stores** are open Monday through Saturday 10am-5pm or 6pm; stores sometimes close on Mondays, but may be open Sundays in summer. Most **sights** are open Sundays but closed Mondays; in Bruges and Tournai, museums close Tuesdays or Wednesdays.

TRANSPORTATION

BY PLANE. Most international flights land at **Brussels International Airport (BRU;** ☎27 53 87 98; www.brusselsairport.be), located roughly 20min. away from Brussels. Budget airlines, like **Ryanair** and **easyJet,** fly out of **Brussels South Charleroi Airport (CRL;** ☎71 25 12 11; www.charleroi-airport.com), approximately 1hr. south of Brussels, and Brussels International Airport. The Belgian national airline, **Brussels Airlines** (☎070 35 11 11, US ☎516-740-5200, UK ☎087 0735 2345; www.brusselsairlines.com), flies into Brussels from most major European cities. For more info on traveling by plane around Europe, see p. 43.

BY TRAIN AND BUS. The extensive and reliable **Belgian Rail** (www.b-rail.be) network traverses the country. **Eurail** is valid in Belgium. A **Benelux Tourrail Pass** (US$207, under 26 US$158) allows five days of unlimited train travel in a one-month period in Belgium, the Netherlands, and Luxembourg. Travelers with time to explore Belgium's nooks and crannies might consider the **Rail Pass** (€69) or **Go Pass** (under 26 only; €45), both of which allow 10 single trips within the country over a one-year period and can be transferred among travelers. Because trains are widely available, **buses** are used primarily for local transport. Single tickets are €1.50, and cheaper when bought in packs.

BY FERRY. P&O Ferries (☎070 70 77 71, UK ☎087 0598 03 33; www.poferries.com) from **Hull, BRI** to **Zeebrugge,** north of Bruges (12½hr., 7pm, from €150).

BY CAR, BIKE, AND THUMB. Belgium honors drivers' licenses from Australia, Canada, the EU, and the US. **New Zealanders** must contact the New Zealand Automobile Association (☎0800 822 422; www.aa.co.nz) for an International Driving Permit. **Speed limits** are 120kph on motorways, 90kph on main roads, and 50kph elsewhere. **Biking** is popular, and many roads in Flanders have bike lanes. Wallonie has started to convert old railroad beds into bike paths. Hitchhiking is illegal and uncommon in Belgium. Let's Go does not recommend hitchhiking.

KEEPING IN TOUCH

PHONE CODES	**Country code: 32. International dialing prefix:** 00. For more info on how to place international calls, see **Inside Back Cover.**

EMAIL AND THE INTERNET. There are cyber cafes in all of the larger towns and cities in Belgium. Expect to pay €2-3 per 30min. In smaller towns, Internet is generally available in hostels for €5-6 per hr.

TELEPHONE. Most pay phones require a **phone card** (from €5), available at post offices, supermarkets, and newsstands. Whenever possible, use a calling card for international phone calls, as long-distance rates for national phone services are

BELGIUM

often very high. Calls are cheapest 6:30pm-8am and weekends. Mobile phones are an increasingly popular and economical option. Major mobile carriers include **Vodafone, Base,** and **Mobistar.** When dialing within a city, the city code must still be dialed. For operator assistance within Belgium, dial ☎ 12 07; for international, dial ☎ 12 04 (€0.25). Direct-dial access numbers for calling out of Belgium include: **AT&T** (☎ 0800 100 10); **British Telecom** (☎ 0800 100 24); **Canada Direct** (☎ 0800 100 19); **Telecom New Zealand** (☎ 0800 100 64); **Telstra Australia** (☎ 0800 100 61).

MAIL. Most post offices are open Monday to Friday 9am-5pm, with a midday break. Sent within Belgium, a postcard or letter (up to 50g) costs €0.46 for non-priority and €0.52 for priority. Within the EU, costs are €0.70/0.80, and for the rest of the world €0.75/0.90. Additional info is available at www.post.be.

ACCOMMODATIONS AND CAMPING

BELGIUM	❶	❷	❸	❹	❺
ACCOMMODATIONS	under €10	€10-20	€21-30	€31-40	over €40

Hotels in Belgium are fairly expensive, with rock-bottom singles from €30 and doubles from €40-45. Belgium's 31 **HI youth hostels** are run by the Flemish Youth Hostel Federation (www.vjh.be) in Flanders and Les Auberges de Jeunesses (www.laj.be) in Wallonie. Expect to pay around €18 per night, including linen, for modern, basic hostels. **Private hostels** cost about the same but are usually nicer, although some charge separately for linen. Most receptionists speak some English. Reservations are a good idea, particularly in summer and on weekends. **Campgrounds** charge about €4 per night, and are common in Wallonie but not in Flanders. An **International Camping Card** is not needed in Belgium.

FOOD AND DRINK

BELGIUM	❶	❷	❸	❹	❺
FOOD	under €5	€5-8	€9-12	€13-18	over €18

Belgian cuisine, acclaimed but expensive, fuses French and German styles. An evening meal may cost as much as a night's accommodations. Fresh seafood appears in *moules* or *mosselen* (steamed mussels) and *moules frites* (steamed mussels with french fries), the national dishes, which are often tasty and reasonably affordable (€14-20). *Frites* (french fries) are ubiquitous and budget-friendly; Belgians eat them dipped in mayonnaise. Look for *friekots* ("french fry shacks") in Belgian towns. Belgian **beer** is a source of national pride, its consumption a national pastime. More varieties—over 500, ranging from ordinary pilsners (€1) to Trappist ales (€3) brewed by monks—are produced here than in any other country. Leave room for chocolate **pralines** from Leonidas or Neuhaus and Belgian **waffles** (*gaufres*), sold on the street and in cafes.

HOLIDAYS AND FESTIVALS

Holidays: New Year's Day (Jan. 1); Epiphany (Jan. 6); Good Friday (Mar. 21); Easter (Mar. 23-24); Ascension (May 1); Labor Day (May 1); Pentecost (May 11-12); Corpus Christi (May 22); Flemish Community Day (July 11); National Day (July 21); Assumption (Aug. 15); French Community Day (Sept. 27); All Saints' Day (Nov. 1); Armistice Day (Nov. 11); Christmas (Dec. 25-26).

Festivals: Ghent hosts Gentse Feesten (July 19-28; www.gentsefeesten.be), which brings *al fresco* theater, puppet performances, the 10 Days Off (www.10daysoff.be) dance festival, and free music and food to the city's streets. Antwerp runs films, circuses, plays, and concerts in its Zomer van Antwerpen festival (mid-July to mid-August; www.zva.be). Bruges's Cactus Festival (mid-July; www.cactusfestival.be) draws alt-pop and hip-hop acts for a weekend with nearby camping available. Eastern Belgium's Puk-kelpop (mid-Aug.; www.pukkelpop.be) is a festival for the alternative music set.

BEYOND TOURISM

Volunteer *(benévolat)* and work opportunities in Belgium focus on its strong international offerings, especially in Brussels, which is home to both NATO and the EU. Private-sector short- and long-term employment is listed at www.jobs-in-europe.net. A selection of public-sector job and volunteer opportunities is listed below. For more info on opportunities across Europe, see **Beyond Tourism**, p. 56.

Amnesty International, r. Berckmans 9, 1060 Brussels (☎02 538 8177; www.amnesty-international.be). One of the world's foremost human rights organizations has offices in Brussels. Paid positions and volunteer work available.

The International School of Brussels, Kattenberg-Botisfort 19, Brussels (☎02 661 42 11; www.isb.be). The ISB hires teachers for positions lasting more than 1yr. Must have permission to work in Belgium.

North Atlantic Treaty Organization (NATO), bd. Leopold III, 1110 Brussels (www.nato.int). Current students and recent graduates (within 1yr.) who are nationals of a NATO member state and fluent in 1 official NATO language (English or French), with a working knowledge of the other, can apply for 6-month internships. Requirements and application details available at www.nato.int/structur/interns/index.html. Application deadlines are far ahead of start dates.

BRUSSELS (BRUXELLES, BRUSSEL) ☎02

The headquarters of NATO and the European Union, Brussels (pop. 1,200,000) is often identified by its population of officials. Yet these civil servants aren't the only ones who speak for Belgium's capital; beneath the drone of parliamentary procedure bustles the spirited clamor of local life.

▐ TRANSPORTATION

Flights: Brussels Airport (BRU; ☎753 42 21, specific flight info 090 07 00 00, €0.45 per min.; www.brusselsairport.be) is 14km from the city and accessible by train. **South Charleroi Airport (CRL;** ☎71 25 12 11; www.charleroi-airport.com) is 46km outside the city, between Brussels and Charleroi, and services a number of European airlines, including **Ryanair.** From the airport, **Bus A** runs to the Charleroi-SUDT train station where you can catch another train to Brussels (€11). There is also a bus service which goes from the airport to Brussels's Gare du Midi (1hr., buy tickets on board).

Trains: (☎555 2555; www.sncb.be). All international trains stop at **Gare du Midi;** most also stop at **Gare Centrale** or **Gare du Nord.** Trains run to: **Amsterdam, NTH** (3hr.; €32, under 26 €24); **Antwerp** (45min., €6.10); **Bruges** (45min., €12); **Cologne, GER** (2¾hr.; €41, under 26 €29); **Liège** (1hr. €13); **Luxembourg City, LUX** (1¾hr., €28.80); **Paris, FRA** (1½hr., €54). **Eurostar** goes to **London, BRI** (2¾hr., €79-224), with Eurail or Benelux pass from €75, under 26 from €60.

Public Transportation: The **Société des Transports Intercommunaux Bruxellois (STIB;** ☎090 01 03 10, €0.45 per min.; www.stib.irisnet.be) runs the **Métro (M), buses,** and **trams** daily 5:30am-12:30am. 1hr. ticket €1.50, 1-day pass €4, 3-day pass €9, 5 trips €7, 10 trips €11.

HOLD THAT STUB. Always hold on to your receipt or ticket stub to avoid steep fines on public transportation; although enforcement appears rather lax, authorities may conduct spot checks and charge you a fine for not validating.

ORIENTATION AND PRACTICAL INFORMATION

Most major attractions are clustered around **Grand-Place**, between the **Bourse** (Stock Market) to the west and the **Parc de Bruxelles** to the east. One **Métro** line circles the city and another bisects it, while efficient **trams** run north-south. Signs list street names in both French and Flemish; *Let's Go* lists all addresses in French.

Tourist Office: The **Brussels International Tourism and Congress (BITC;** ☎513 8940; www.brures.com). M: Bourse. On Grand-Place in the Town Hall, BITC is the official tourist office. It books accommodations in the city for no charge and sells the **Brussels Card,** which provides free public transport and access to 30 museums for 1, 2, or 3 days (€20/28/33). Open Easter-Dec. daily 9am-6pm; Jan.-Easter M-Sa 9am-6pm.

Embassies and Consulates: Australia, 6-8 r. Guimard (☎286 0500; www.austemb.be). **Canada,** 2 av. Tervuren (☎741 0611; www.international.gc.ca/brussels). **Ireland,** 50 r. Wiertz (☎235 6676). **New Zealand,** 1 sq. de Meeus (☎512 1040). **UK,** 85 r. d'Arlon (☎287 6211; www.british-embassy.be). **US,** 27 bd. du Régent (☎508 2111; www.brussels.usembassy.gov).

Currency Exchange: Travelex, 4 Grand-Place (☎513 2845). Open M-F 10am-5pm, Sa 10am-7pm, Su 10am-4pm.

GLBT Resources: The tourist office offers the *Safer Guide* to gay nightlife.

Laundromat: Wash Club, 68 r. du Marché au Charbon. M: Bourse. Wash €3.50 per 8kg, €7 per 18kg. Open daily 7am-10pm, or take your laundry to 71 van Arteveldestraat and pick it up after a few hours (☎478 23 18 30).

Pharmacy: Neos-Bourse Pharmacie, 61 bd. Anspach at r. du Marché aux Poulets (☎218 0640). M: Bourse. Open M-Sa 8:30am-6:30pm.

Medical Services: St. Luc's, 10 av. Hippocrate (☎764 1111), convenient to Grand-Place. **Clinique St Etienne Kliniek,** 100 r. du Meridien (☎ 225 9111).

Internet Access: Axen, 179 r. Royale, is located 1 block from the Centre Van Gogh Hostel. Open daily 9am-midnight. €1.50 per hr.

Post Office: Corner of bd. Anspach and r. des Augustins (☎226 9700; www.laposte.be). M: De Brouckère. Open M-F 8am-7pm, Sa 10:30am-6:30pm. Poste Restante available.

ACCOMMODATIONS

Lodging can be difficult to find, especially on weekends in summer. Overall, accommodations are well-kept and centrally located. The BITC (see **Practical Information,** p. 96) books rooms for no fee, sometimes at discounts up to 50%.

Sleep Well, 23 r. du Damier (☎218 5050; www.sleepwell.be). M: Rogier. Choose hotel-like "Star" service or hostel-like "non-Star" service. Lockout for non-Star 11am-3pm. Non-star dorms €17-28; singles €29; doubles €52; triples €69. Star singles €40; doubles €58. €4 discount after 1st night for all non-Star rooms except singles. MC/V. ❷

Centre Vincent Van Gogh (CHAB), 8 r. Traversière (☎217 0158; www.chab.be). M: Botanique. Spartan rooms are countered with a kitchen, courtyard, and sunroom with pool table. Ages 18 to 35 only. Breakfast included. Linens €3.80. Laundry €4.50. Internet €1 per 15min. Reception 24hr. Lockout 10am-2pm. Dorms €18-21; singles €33; doubles €42; triples €68. Prices reduced by €4 after 1st night. AmEx/MC/V. ❷

Les Auberges de Jeunesse "Jacques Brel" (HI), 30 r. de la Sablonnière (☎218 0187). M: Botanique. Spacious rooms surround a courtyard with a picturesque fountain. Breakfast and linens included. Bring lock for storage. Laundry €8. Free Internet 7pm-midnight. Reception 8am-1am. Lockout noon-3pm. Dorms €19-21; singles €34; doubles €52; triples and quads €63-84. €3 HI discount. MC/V. ❷

Hotel des Eperonniers, 1 r. des Eperonniers (☎513 5366). M: Gare Centrale. Choose basic singles or spacious studios for up to 6 people, right near Grand-Place. Breakfast €3.75. Reception 7am-midnight. Singles €27-57; doubles €45-73. AmEx/MC/V. ❹

🍴 FOOD

Brussels has earned its reputation as one of the culinary capitals of Europe, although the city's restaurants are often more suited to the five-star port-wine-reduction set than to the budget traveler. Inexpensive eateries cluster outside **Grand-Place.** Vendors along **Rue du Marché aux Fromages** to the south hawk cheap Greek and Middle Eastern food until late at night, while maîtres d' along **Rue des Bouchers** noisily promote their shellfish and paella.

🍴 't Spinnekopke, 1 pl. du Jardin aux Fleurs (☎511 8695). M: Bourse. Locals "inside the spider's head" savor the authentically Belgian menu. Cozy, yet elegant setting. Entrees €15-25. Open M-F noon-3pm, 6pm-midnight, Sa 6pm-midnight. AmEx/MC/V. ❺

🍴 Poechenellekelder, 5 r. du Chêne (☎511 9262). If the ongoing trickle of water from *Manneken Pis* makes your throat parched, head across the street for a drink amid hanging marionettes. Beer (€3.20-4) is supplemented by a limited menu of *tartines* (open-faced sandwiches; €4-7) and *pâté* (€8). Open Tu-Su 11am-2am. Cash only. ❸

Hémisphères, 65 r. de l'Ecuyer (☎513 9370; www.hemispheres-resto.be). This restaurant, art gallery, and "intercultural space" serves Middle Eastern, Indian, and Asian fare. Couscous with veggies or meat (€11-15). Entrees €7-15. Concerts 1 Sa per month. Open M-F noon-3pm and 6:30-10:30pm, Sa 6:30pm-midnight. MC/V. ❹

Mokafe, in Galeries Royals St. Hubert (☎511 7870). Give your feet a rest and pause at this coffee shop while watching others walk by. Crepes (€2.80-5.60), waffles (€2.80-4.90), salads, and omelettes are among the light fare offered. Indoor and outdoor seating. Open daily 8am-11pm. ❷

Maison Antoine, 1 pl. Jourdan. M: Schuman. After 58 years frying, the Maison makes the best *frites* (€1.90-2.10) in town—and they only improve with a side of flavored mayo (€0.50). Open Su-Th 11:30am-1am, F-Sa 11:30am-2am. ❶

ON THE MENU

LETTIN' GO OF THE EGGO

At the base of the budget tourist's food pyramid in Belgium lies an auspicious dietary group: the waffle (*gaufre* in French, *wafel* in Dutch). There are two type of Belgian waffles, both made on such particular waffle irons that they can not be made well elsewhere.

Brussels waffles are flat and more or less rectangular. They're light and airy, and bear some resemblance to ones eaten in the US (the kind served at diner brunches, not the ones that emerge from the freezer, pop out of the toaster, and beg to be drowned in high fructose corn syrup). Belgian recipes tend to use beaten egg whites and yeast as leavening agents, which give them their light, crisp texture. **De Lièges** waffles, ubiquitous on Belgian streets, are generally smaller, sweeter, and denser than their counterparts, and have a crunchy caramelized-sugar crust.

Pause at a cafe for a Brussels waffle, and savor it with a knife and fork. Approach a street vendor for a hand-held Liège waffle and continue to wander (in search of your next waffle?). Both can be topped with chocolate, fruit, or ice cream, or dusted with powdered sugar. Waffles generally cost about €1.50, though prices mount with the toppings.

Since you can't visit Belgium without sampling its waffles, you might as well indulge.

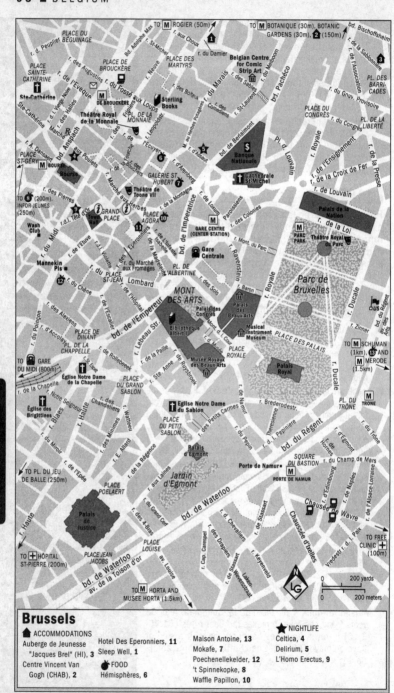

BELGIUM

Brussels

ACCOMMODATIONS

Auberge de Jeunesse "Jacques Brel" (HI), **3**

Centre Vincent Van Gogh (CHAB), **2**

Hotel Des Eperonniers, **11**

Sleep Well, **1**

FOOD

Hémisphères, **6**

Maison Antoine, **13**

Mokafe, **7**

Poechenellekelder, **12**

't Spinnekopke, **8**

Waffle Papillon, **10**

NIGHTLIFE

Celtica, **4**

Delirium, **5**

L'Homo Erectus, **9**

Waffle Papillon, Pl. Agora. Of Brussels's abundant waffle stands, this one is distinctive. Gorge on waffles topped with homemade ice cream (€1.50-5.50) or choose to add chocolate, whipped cream, strawberries, or bananas (€1.50-4.20). Cash only. ➊

🔘 SIGHTS

GRAND-PLACE AND ENVIRONS. Three blocks behind the town hall, on the corner of r. de l'Étuve and r. du Chêne, is Brussels's most giggled-at sight, the **Mannekin Pis,** a tiny fountain shaped like a boy who seems to be peeing continuously. Legend claims it commemorates a young Belgian who defused a bomb destined for the Grand-Place. In reality, the fountain was installed to supply the neighborhood with water during the reign of Albert and Isabelle. Locals have created hundreds of outfits for him, each with a strategically placed hole. To even the gender gap, a statue of a squatting girl *(Jeanneken)* now pees down an ally off r. des Bouchers. Victor Hugo once called the statued and gilded Grand-Place "the most beautiful square in the world." During the day, be sure to visit **La Maison du Roi** (King's House), now the city museum whose most riveting exhibit is the collection of clothes worn by *Mannekin Pis*, and the town hall where 40min. guided tours reveal over-the-top decorations and an impressive collection of paintings. *(La Maison du Roi ☎279 4350. Open Tu-Su 10am-5pm. €3. Town Hall ☎548 0445. English-language tours Tu-W 3:15pm, Su 10:45am and 12:15pm; arrive early. €3, students €2.50.)* You'll find a brief introduction to Belgium's famed beers at the **Belgian Brewer's Museum.** *(10 Grand-Place. 2 buildings left of the town hall. ☎511 4987; www.beerparadise.be. Open daily 10am-5pm. €5, includes 1 beer.)* Nearby, the **Museum of Cocoa and Chocolate** tells of Belgium's other renowned edible export. Cacao fruits grow on display and the smell of chocolate permeates the air. *(11 r. de la Tête d'Or. ☎514 2048; www.mucc.be. Open July-Aug. and holidays daily 10am-4:30pm; Sept.-June Tu-Su 10am-4:30pm. €5, students €4.)* In the skylit **Galeries Royals St-Hubert** arcade, one block behind Grand-Place, a long covered walkway is lined with shops whose wares range from haute couture to marzipan frogs. Just north of Gare Centrale, the **Cathédrale St-Michel et Ste-Gudule** hosts royal affairs under its soaring ribbed vaults. At times, music—pipe organ or carillon—serenade visitors. *(Pl. Ste-Gudule. Open M-F 7am-6pm, Sa-Su 8:30am-6pm. Free.)*

MONT DES ARTS. The 🔲**Musées Royaux des Beaux-Arts** encompass the **Musée d'Art Ancien,** the **Musée d'Art Moderne,** several contemporary exhibits, and the **Musée Magritte,** opening in 2008. Together, the museums steward a huge collection of Belgian art, including Bruegel's famous *Landscape with the Fall of Icarus* and pieces by Rubens and Brussels native René Magritte. Other masterpieces on display include David's *Death of Marat* and paintings by Delacroix, Gauguin, Seurat, and van Gogh. The great hall itself is a work of architectural beauty; the panoramic view of Brussels from the fourth floor of the 19th-century wing alone justifies the admission fee. *(3 r. de la Régence. M: Parc. ☎508 3211; www.fine-arts-museum.be. Open Tu-Su 10am-5pm. Some wings close noon-2pm. €9, students €3.50. 1st W of each month 1-5pm free. Audio tour €2.50.)* The **Musical Instrument Museum (MIM)** houses over 1500 instruments; stand in front of one and your headphones automatically play a sample of its music. *(2 r. Montagne de la Cour. ☎545 0130; www.mim.fgov.be. Open Tu-F 9:30am-4:45pm, Sa-Su 10am-5pm. €5, students €4. 1st W of each month 1-5pm free.)*

BELGIAN CENTER FOR COMIC STRIP ART. Comic strips *(les BD)* are serious business in Belgium. Today, a restored warehouse designed by famous architect Victor Horta pays tribute to what Belgians call the Ninth Art. Amusing displays document comic strip history, the museum library makes thousands of books available to scholarly researchers, and Tintin and the Smurfs make several appearances. *(☎214 0140. R. des Sables. M: Rogier. Open Tu-Su 10am-6pm, students with ISIC €6.)*

BELGIUM

OTHER SIGHTS. The eerily illuminated Treasure Room and the Greco-Roman collection are the main attractions at the enormous Musées Royaux d'Art et d'Histoire, set in a beautiful park, while the Gothic Room and the Chinese draw-loom exhibits are quirkily enjoyable. *(10 Parc du Cinquantenaire. ☎ 741 7211. M: Mérode. Open Tu-F 9:30am-5pm, Sa-Su 10am-5pm. Ticket office closes at 4pm. €5, students €4. 1st W of each month 1-5pm free.)* The out-of-the-way **Musée Horta,** home of 20th-century master architect Victor Horta, gracefully applies his Art Nouveau style to a domestic setting. *(25 r. Américaine. M: Horta. Take a right out of the stop, walk 7min. uphill on ch. de Waterloo, then turn left onto ch. de Charleroi and right onto r. Américaine. ☎ 543 0490; www.hortamuseum.be. Open Tu-Su 2-5:30pm. €7, students €3.50.)*

🎵 🎭 ENTERTAINMENT AND NIGHTLIFE

The weekly *What's On,* available free at the tourist office, contains extensive info on cultural events. The **Théâtre Royal de la Monnaie,** on pl. de la Monnaie, is renowned for its opera and ballet. (M: De Brouckère. ☎ 229 1200, box office 70 23 39; www.lamonnaie.be. Tickets from €8, ½-price tickets go on sale 20min. prior to the event.) The **Théâtre Royal de Toone VII,** 21 Petite r. des Bouchers, stages marionette performances. (☎ 513 5486; www.toone.be. F 8:30pm, Sa 4pm and 8:30pm, occasionally Tu-Th. €10, students €7.) **Nova,** 3 r. d'Arenberg, screens foreign and independent films. (☎ 511 2477; www.nova-cinema.com. €5, students €3.50.)

On summer nights, performances and live concerts on Grand-Place and the Bourse bring the streets to life. The *All the Fun* pamphlet, available at the tourist office, lists the newest clubs and bars. On **Place St-Géry,** outdoor patios are jammed with a laid-back crowd of students and backpackers. Choose from 2000 beers at ▓**Delirium,** 4A impasse de la Fidélité. (☎ 251 4434. Open daily 10am-4am.) **Celtica,** 55 r. aux Poulets, might have the world's longest Happy hour: throbbing techno accompanies €1 and €2 drafts 1pm-midnight. The bar downstairs is more relaxed, but a DJ spins at the upstairs disco. (☎ 514 3253. Bar open daily 1pm-late. Disco open Th-Sa 10pm.) **L'Homo Erectus,** 57 r. des Pierres, is a popular GLBT option. (☎ 514 7493; www.lhomoerectus.com. Open daily 3pm-3am.)

🏛 DAYTRIP FROM BRUSSELS: MECHELEN (MALINES)

The residents of Mechelen (pop. 78,000) are nicknamed the "Moon Extinguishers" for once mistaking fog and a red moon for a fire in the tower of **St-Rombouts Tower and Cathedral.** Today, the cathedral's tower holds two 49-bell carillons and is home to the world's foremost bell-ringing school. In summer, you can hear recitals from anywhere in Grote Markt on Monday and Saturday at 11:30am and Sunday at 3pm. To reach St-Rombouts from Centraal station, walk down Hendrick Consciencestr. to the pedestrian Grote Markt. *(Cathedral open daily Easter-Oct. 8:30am-5:30pm; Nov.-Easter 8:30am-4:30pm.* ▓ *Tours Easter-Sept. Sa-Su 2:15pm, July-Aug. daily 2:15pm. €5.)* Nearby, the 15th-century **St. John's Church** boasts Rubens's *The Adoration of the Magi.* From the Grote Markt, walk down Fr. de Merodestr. and turn left onto St-Janstr. *(Open Tu-Su Easter-Oct. 1:30-5:30pm; Nov.-Easter 1:30-4:30pm.)* To reach the ▓**Jewish Museum of Deportation and Resistance,** 153 Goswin de Stassartstr., follow Wollemarkt from behind St-Rombouts until it becomes Goswin de Stassart; it's on your left when the streets end at the canal, in 18th-century barracks once used to hold Jews en route to Auschwitz-Birkenau. *(☎ 29 06 60. Open Su-Th 10am-5pm, F 10am-1pm. Free.)* **Trains** run to Antwerp (20min., 4 per hr., €3.70) and Brussels (20min., 4-5 per hr., €3.70). The **tourist office,** 2-6 Hallestr., is in the Grote Markt. *(☎ 070 22 28 00; www.inenuitmechelen.be. Open Apr.-Sept. M 9:30am-7pm, Tu-F 9:30am-5:30pm, Sa-Su 10am-4:30pm; Oct.-Mar. M-F 9:30am-4:30pm, Sa-Su 10:30am-3:30pm.)*

FLANDERS (VLAANDEREN)

BRUGES (BRUGGE) ☎50

Bruges (pop. 116,000) is arguably Belgium's most romantic city. Canals carve their way through rows of stone houses and cobblestone streets en route to the breath-taking Gothic Markt. The city remains one of the best-preserved examples of Northern Renaissance architecture. Don't let the swarms of tourists deter you from visiting—a trip to Belgium is incomplete without a stop in Bruges.

⌐ TRANSPORTATION

Trains leave from the **Stationsplein,** a 15min. walk south of the city. (Open daily 4:30am-11pm. Info desk open daily 8am-7pm.) Trains head to: Antwerp (1¾hr., 2 per hr., €13); Brussels (1hr., 1-3 per hr., €12); Ghent (20min., 3 per hr., €5.40); Knokke (30min., 2 per hr., €3); Ostend (15min., 3 per hr., €3.30).

⚡ ⁊ ORIENTATION AND PRACTICAL INFORMATION

Bruges is enclosed by a circular canal, with the train station, **Stationsplein,** just beyond its southern extreme. The historic district is entirely accessible on foot, while bikes are popular for countryside visits. The dizzying **Belfort** looms high over the center of town, presiding over the handsome **Markt.** The windmill-lined **Kruis-vestraat** and serene **Minnewater Park** are the most beautiful spots in Bruges.

 WATCH THAT BIKE! In Bruges, as in many Flemish cities, bike lanes are marked in red. To forestall cyclists' ire, pedestrians should avoid these areas.

Tourist Office: In and Uit, 't Zand 34 (☎44 46 46; www.brugge.be). From the train station, head left to 't Zand and walk for 10min.; it's in the red concert hall. (Open M-W and F-Su 10am-6pm, Th 10am-8pm). Branch at the train station. (Open Apr.-Sept. Tu-Su 10am-1pm and 2-6pm; Oct.-Mar. Tu-Sa 9:30am-noon and 1-5pm).

Tours: 5 companies offer 30min. **boat tours** of Bruges's canals. Vessels glide by otherwise inaccessible city corners (Mar.-Nov., 2-4 per hr., €6); inquire at tourist office. **QuasiMundo Tours** has 3 different **bike tours** of Bruges and the countryside (3-4hr.). Tours depart daily at 10am and 7pm from Bruges, 1pm from the countryside. (☎33 07 75; www.quasimundo.com. Tours Mar.-Oct. €20, under 26 €18; includes free drink.)

Currency Exchange: Goffin, Steenstraat 2, is near the Markt, and charges no commission on cash exchange (☎34 04 71. Open M-Sa 9am-5:30pm).

Luggage Storage: At the train station. €2.60-3.60.

Laundromat: Belfort, Ezelstr. 51. Wash €3-6, dry €1. Open daily 7am-10pm.

Bike Rental: At the train station (☎30 23 28). Passport required. €6.50 per day.

Police: Hauwerstr. 7 (☎44 89 30).

BELGIUM

Hospitals: A. Z. St-Jan (☎45 21 11; not to be confused with Oud St-Janshospitaal, a museum). **St-Lucas** (☎36 91 11). **St-Franciscus Xaveriuskliniek** (☎47 04 70).

Internet Access: Teleboutique Brugge, Predikherenstr. 48, is one of the cheaper options. €2 per hour. Open daily 10am-10pm. Cash only.

Post Office: Markt 5. Open M and W-F 9am-6pm, Sa 9:30am-12:30pm.

■ ACCOMMODATIONS

▨ **Snuffel Backpacker Hostel,** Ezelstr. 47-49 (☎33 31 33; www.snuffel.be). Take bus #3 or 13 (€1.30) from the station to the stop after Markt, then take the 1st left. Staff leads free walking tours every other day. The bar's Happy hour is so cheap, even locals frequent it (9-10pm, beer €1). Bike rental €6 per day. Breakfast €3. Lockers available. Linens included. Internet €2 per hr.; free Wi-Fi. Key deposit €5. Reception 7:30am-midnight. Dorms €14; doubles €36; quads €60-64. AmEx/MC/V. ❷

Passage, Dweersstr. 26 (☎34 02 32; www.passagebruges.com). Old-world, refined hostel-hotel-cafe in an ideal location. Safes available. Breakfast €5; included in private rooms. Internet €4 per hr. Reception 9am-midnight. Open mid-Feb. to mid-Jan. Dorms €14; singles €25-45; doubles €45-60; triples and quads €75-90. AmEx/MC/V. ❷

Hotel Lybeer, Korte Vuldersstr. 31 (☎33 43 55; www.hostellybeer.com). Charming and well situated. Breakfast and linens included. Free Internet. Reception 7:30am-11pm. Dorms €14-24; singles €23-38; doubles €43-65; triples €70-80. AmEx/MC/V. ❸

Bauhaus International Youth Hostel and Hotel, Langestr. 133-137 (☎34 10 93; www.bauhaus.be). Take bus #6 or 16 from the station; ask to stop at the hostel. A giant candelabra and popular bar lead the way to airy rooms. Bike rental €9 per day. Breakfast and linens included. Lockers €1.50. Internet €3 per hr. Reception 8am-midnight. Dorms €14-15; singles from €26; doubles from €40; triples from €57. AmEx/MC/V. ❷

Charlie Rockets, Hoogstr. 19 (☎33 06 60; www.charlierockets.com). Americans might feel at home at this wannabe Charlie Rockets in a converted movie theatre, equipped with pool tables, darts, and, of course, 50s decor. Breakfast €3. Lockers €3. Linens included. Internet €2 per 20min. Dorms €16. MC/V. ❷

▮ FOOD

Inexpensive restaurants can be hard to find in Bruges. Seafood lovers should splurge at least once on the city's famous *mosselen* (mussels; €15-22) found at the **Vismarkt,** near the Burg. (Open Tu-Sa 8am-1pm.) Grab groceries at **Delhaize Proxy,** Noordzandstr. 4, near the Markt. (Open M-Sa 9am-7pm.)

Grand Kaffee de Passage, Dweersstr. 26-28 (☎34 02 32). Next to the Passage hostel. Traditional Belgian cuisine in a candlelit setting. Try the excellent Flemish stew (€11). Open daily 6-11pm. Closed from mid-Jan. to mid-Feb. AmEx/MC/V. ❸

Du Phare, Sasplein 2 (☎34 35 90; www.duphare.be). From the Burg, walk down Hoogstr. and turn left at the canal onto Verversdijk, crossing to the right side at the second bridge. Follow the canal for 20min. to Sasplein. Bus #4 stops right outside. This jazz and blues bistro serves international fare (€11-20). Open M and W 11:30am-2:30pm and 7pm-midnight, Tu and F-Sa 11:30am-2:30pm and 6:30pm-midnight, Su 11:30am-midnight. Reservations recommended F-Sa. AmEx/MC/V. ❸

Hobbit, Kemelstr. 8-10 (☎33 55 20; www.hobbitgrill.be). Order filling meats and pastas from clever newsprint menus. Entrees €7-11. Open daily 6pm-1am. AmEx/MC/V. ❷

De Belegde Boterham, Kleine St-Amandsstr. 5 (☎34 91 31). Health-conscious spot serves sandwiches (€7-8) and innovative salads (€11) in its chic interior or on endearingly mismatched tables outside. Open M-Sa noon-4pm. Cash only. ❷

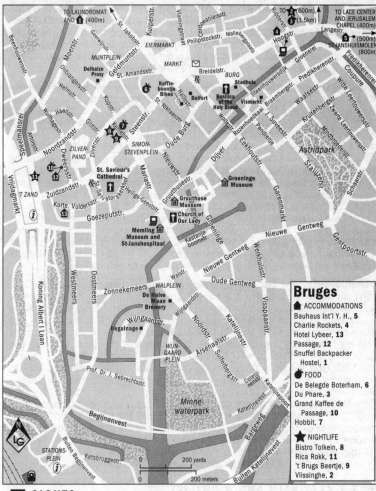

Bruges

ACCOMMODATIONS
Bauhaus Int'l Y. H., 5
Charlie Rockets, 4
Hotel Lybeer, 13
Passage, 12
Snuffel Backpacker
Hostel, 1

FOOD
De Belegde Boterham, 6
Du Phare, 3
Grand Kaffee de
Passage, 10
Hobbit, 7

NIGHTLIFE
Bistro Tolkein, 8
Rica Rokk, 11
't Brugs Beertje, 9
Vlissinghe, 2

BELGIUM

👁 SIGHTS

Filled with Gothic and neo-Gothic buildings and crisscrossed by canals, picturesque Bruges is best experienced on foot. Avoid visiting Bruges on Mondays, when
museums are closed. If you plan to visit many museums, consider a cost-saving
combination ticket (€15, includes admission to 5 museums).

MARKT AND BURG. The medieval **Belfort** (belfry) looms over the Markt; climb its
366 steep steps for a phenomenal view. *(Belfort open Tu-Su 9:30am-5pm. Last entry
4:15pm. €5. Bell concerts mid-June to Sept. M, W, and Sa 9pm, Su 2:15pm; Oct. to mid-June W
and Sa-Su 2:15pm.)* Behind the Markt, the Burg is dominated by the finely detailed
facade of the **Stadhuis** (Town Hall). Inside, wander through the gilded **Gothic Hall,**
where residents of Bruges still get married. *(☎44 81 10. Open Tu-Su 9:30am-4:30pm.
€2.50, under 26 €1.50. Audio tour included.)* This ticket will also get you into **Liberty of**

Bruges Museum, which contains an ornate fireplace. *(Open M-Sa 9:30am-12:30pm and 1:30-5pm).* Tucked away in a corner of the Burg next to the Stadhuis, the **Basilica of the Holy Blood** supposedly holds the blood of Christ in a spectacularly ornate sanctuary upstairs; its disappointing museum has paintings and clerical garments. *(Basilica open daily Apr.-Sept. 9:30-noon and 2-6pm; Oct.-Mar. 10am-noon and 2-4pm; closed W afternoon. Holy Relic can be viewed at 11am and 2-4pm. Museum €1.50.)*

MUSEUMS. From the Burg, follow Wollestr. left and then head right on Dijver and walk through the garden to reach the **Groeninge Museum;** its highlights are works by Jan van Eyck and Hans Memling. *(Dijver 12. ☎ 44 87. Open Tu-Su 9:30am-5pm. €8, under 26 €6. Audio tour included.)* Formerly a palace, the nearby **Gruuthuse Museum** houses a large collection of intricate 16th- and 17th-century tapestries. *(Dijver 17. ☎ 44 87 62. Open Tu-Su 9:30am-5pm. €6, students €4. Audio tour included.)* Continue on Dijver as it becomes Gruuthusestr. and walk under the stone archway to enter the **Memling Museum,** in Oud St-Janshospitaal, a pretty brick building that was a hospital in medieval times. The museum reconstructs everyday life in the hospital and has several paintings by its namesake, Hans Memling. *(Mariastr. 38. ☎ 44 87 71. Open Tu-Su 9:30am-5pm, ticket office closes 4:30pm. €8, under 26 €5. Audio tour included.)* To get to the **Lace Center,** Peperstr. 3A, walk down Hoogstr. from the Burg. Take a left onto Molenmeers after the canal. The center shares a gate with the **Jerusalem Chapel.** Lace-making demonstrations by wrinkled octogenarians are surprisingly fun to watch. *(☎ 33 00 72; www.kantcentrum.com. Open M-F 10am-noon and 2-6pm, Sa 10am-noon and 2-5pm. €2.50, under 26 €1.50 for both Lace Center and Chapel.)*

OTHER SIGHTS. The 14th-century **Church of Our Lady,** at Mariastr. and Gruuthusestr., contains Michelangelo's *Madonna and Child.* *(Open Tu-F 9:30am-5pm, Sa 9:30am-4:45pm, Su 12:30-5pm; last entry 4:30pm. Church free. Tomb viewing €2.50, students €1.50. Ticket for the tomb included in Gruuthuse Museum ticket.)* Beer aficionados will enjoy the samples at 150-year-old **De Halve Maan,** a beer museum and brewery. *(Welplein 26. ☎ 33 26 97; www.halvemaan.be. 45min. tours Apr.-Sept. 1 per hr. M-F 11am-4pm, Sa-Su 11am-5pm; Oct.-Mar. tours M-F 11am and 3pm, Sa-Su 1 per hr. 11am-4pm. €5, includes beer.)* For God-sanctioned fun, wander the grounds of the **Beguinage,** home to nuns who share their tree-covered yard with passersby. The Beguine's house displays furnishings typical of medieval Flemish households. *(From Simon Stevinplein, follow Mariastr., and turn right on Wijngaardstr.; at the canal, turn right and cross the footbridge. ☎ 33 00 11. Open Mar.-Nov. daily 10am-noon and 1:45-5pm; gate open 6:30am-6:30pm. Garden free; house €2, under 26 €1.)* Walk along the river to see the windmills; to enter, go down to 235-year-old windmill **St-Janshuismolen,** which still gives occasional flour-grinding demonstrations in summer when the wind is right. *(☎ 33 00 44. Open May-Sept. daily 9:30am-12:30pm and 1:30-5pm. €2, under 26 €1.)*

▓▒ ▐ FESTIVALS AND NIGHTLIFE

Bruges plays host to the **Cactusfestival** (☎ 33 20 14; www.cactusfestival.be. €25 per day, €63 for 3 days), a series of alt-pop and hip-hop concerts the first full weekend in July. The city also sponsors **Klinkers,** an open-air music and film series that's free to the public during July and August (☎ 33 20 14; www.klinkers-brugge.be). At **'t Brugs Beertje,** Kemelstr. 5, off Steenstr., sample some of the 250 varieties of beer. (☎ 33 96 16. Open Su-M and Th 4pm-12:30am, F-Sa 4pm-2am.) Next door, the candlelit **Bistro Tolkien,** Kemelstr. 9, pours fruity *jenever* (€2), a flavored Dutch gin. (☎ 34 24 21. Entrees €6-16. Open M and W-Sa noon-2pm and 6pm-11pm.) For a quieter night, try Bruges's oldest pub, **Vlissinghe,** Blekersstr. 2, established in 1515. From the Burg, take Hoogstr. and turn left onto Verversdijk immediately before the canal. Cross the second bridge onto Blekersstr. (☎ 34 37 37. Open W-Sa 11am-midnight, Su 11am-7pm.) Steer clear of the tourist clubs behind the Markt. Belgian students tend to prefer the dance floor of **Rica Rokk,** 't Zand 6, where shots are €3 and a meter of beer starts at €19. (☎33 24 34; www.maricarokk.com. Open daily 9:30am-5am.) The tourist office has a list of **GLBT establishments.**

 THE LONG ARM OF THE LAW. If you're wobbling back to your hostel with a bellyful of beer, think twice before yielding to nature's call en route. Police will fine you up to €152 if they catch you urinating in public. Keep €0.30 handy for public toilets, although many of these stalls close at 8pm.

ANTWERP (ANTWERPEN, ANVERS)   ☎03

While Antwerp (pop. 455,000) used to be known for its avant-garde fashion and jet-setting party hoppers, the hipster scene has since calmed. Antwerp's main prome-nades, **De Keyserlei** and the **Meir,** draw crowds to their elegant department stores and chic boutiques. On the western edge of the shopping area, the **Cathedral of Our Lady,** Groenpl. 21, holds Rubens's *Descent from the Cross.* (www.dekathe-draal.be. Open M-F 10am-5pm, Sa 10am-3pm, Su 1-4pm. Tours 1-3 per day. €2.) Take in the busy exterior of the nearby **Stadhuis** (city hall), then hop on tram #11 (dir.:Eksterlaar) to see the wildly opulent mansions that line **Cogels Osylei.** A stroll by the Schelde River leads to the 13th-century **Steen Castle,** Steenplein 1, which houses the extensive collections of the **National Maritime Museum.** (☎201 9340. Museum open Tu-Su 10am-5pm. €4.) The **Museum Voor Schone Kunsten** (KMSKA; Royal Museum of Fine Arts), Leopold De Waelpl. 1-9, possesses one of the world's finest collections of Flemish paintings. From Centraal, take tram #12 or 24 and get off at Verbondstr. (☎238 7809; www.kmska.be. Open Tu-Sa 10am-5pm, Su 10am-6pm. €6, under 19 free.) The **RubensHuis,** Wapper 9, off the Meir, was home to Baroque artist Peter Paul Rubens, and its intact rooms are filled with his works, including *The Annunciation.* (☎201 1555. Open Tu-Su 10am-4:45pm. €6, under 26 €4.) The **Diamant Museum,** Kon. Astridplein 19-23, chronicles Antwerp's historic importance in the diamond industry through interesting audiovisual displays. (☎202 4890. Open M-Tu and Th-Su 10am-5:30pm. €6, students €4.)

The well-worn **New International Youth Hotel ❷,** Provinciestr. 256, is a 15min. walk from Centraal Station, on the corner of De Boeystr. and Provinciestr. Turn left out of the station onto Pelikaanstr., which becomes Simonsstr.; turn left on Plantin en Moretus, walk under the bridge, then turn right onto Provinciestr. (☎230 0522. Breakfast included. Reception 8am-midnight. Dorms €19-21, under 26 with sleeping bag €15; singles €34; doubles €49-61; triples €70-79. MC/V.) Take the metro to Groenpl. to reach **Guesthouse 26 ❺,** Pelgrimsstr. 26, in the heart of the city. Inventive decor keeps guests returning, even as prices rise. (☎289 3995; www.guesthouse26.be. Breakfast included. Reserve ahead. Singles €55-75; doubles €65-85. AmEx/MC/V.) **Da Giovanni ❷,** Jan Blomstr. 8, just off Groenpl., serves hearty pizzas (€5-16) and tries to bring Italy to Belgium. (☎226 7450; www.dagiovanni.be. Open daily 11am-midnight. 20% student discount. AmEx/MC/V.) More than 400 reli-gious figurines accompany your meal at **'t Elfde Gebod ❹,** Torfburg 10. (☎289 3466. Entrees €8-20. Open daily noon-2am. Kitchen open noon-10:30pm. MC/V.) Get gro-ceries at the **Super GB** supermarket in the Grand Shopping Bazaar. (Open M-Th and Sa 8:30am-8pm, F 8:30am-9pm. MC/V.) The palatial club **Café d'Anvers,** Verversrui 15, north of Grote Markt in the red-light district, features popular DJs and caters to a younger crowd. (☎226 3870; www.cafe-d-anvers.com. Open F-Sa 11pm-7am.) Bars behind the cathedral and in the trendy neighborhood around the Royal Museum of Fine Arts offer an alternative to the club scene. For daily live jazz, hole up in the loft of **De Muze,** Melkmarkt 15, or sip Grimbergen Abbey beer at one of the tables out-side. (Open daily 11am-4am.) Step into the 15th-century cellars for a candlelit dinner at **Pelgrom,** Pelgrimstr. 15, before sampling the local *elixir d'Anvers* (a strong herbal liqueur; €5) doled out by bartenders in traditional dress. (☎234 0809. Open daily noon-late.) Gay nightlife clusters around **Van Schoonhovenstraat,** just north of Centraal Station. Head to the **Gay and Lesbian Center,** Dambruggestr. 204, for more info.

Antwerp has two train stations: **Berchem,** which handles most international traffic, and **Centraal,** the domestic station. Centraal's soaring arches make it a tourist destination in its own right. **Trains** go from Berchem to Amsterdam, NTH (2hr., 1 per hr., €21-29); Brussels (45min., 4 per hr., €6.10); and Rotterdam, NTH (1hr., 1 per hr., €13-18). Lockers are available in Centraal. The **tourist office** is downstairs in Centraal. To get to the Grote Markt from Berchem, take tram #8 (€1.20, €1.50 on board) to Groenpl. From Centraal take tram #2 (dir.: Linkeroever) or walk down Meir, the main pedestrian thoroughfare, to Groenpl. (☎232 0103. Open M-Sa 9am-5:45pm, Su 9am-4:45pm. €5.) **Postal Code:** 2000.

GHENT (GENT)   ☎09

Once the heart of Flanders's textile industry, modern Ghent (pop. 228,000) still celebrates the memory of its medieval greatness and its more recent industrial past. The Gentse Feesten brings performers, carnival rides, and flowing *jenever* (flavored gin) to the city center. (July 12-21 2008. ☎269 4600; www.gentsefeesten.be.) The **Lele canal** runs through the city and wraps around the **Gravensteen** (Castle of Counts), St-Veerlepl. 11, a partially restored medieval fortress. (☎225 9306. Open daily Apr.-Sept. 9am-6pm; Oct.-Mar. 9am-5pm. €6, under 26 €1.20.) From Gravensteen, head down Geldmunt, make a right on Lange Steenst., and then a right into the historical **Partershol** quarter, a network of 16th- to 18th-century houses. Stroll down along the **Graslei,** a medieval street along the water, on the way to **St-Michielshelling,** lined with handsome guild houses. St-Michielshelling affords the best view of the Ghent's steepled skyline. Facing the bridge with Graslei behind you, find **St-Niklaaskerk,** where rich, medieval merchants worshipped. (☎225 3700. Open M 2:30-5pm, Tu-Su 10am-5pm. Free.) On the left, on Limburgstr., ▨**St-Baafskathedraal** holds Hubert and Jan van Eyck's many-paneled *Adoration of the Mystic Lamb* and Rubens's *St. Bavo's Entrance into the Monastery of Ghent.* (Cathedral and crypt open daily Apr.-Oct. 8:30am-6pm; Nov.-Mar. 8:30am-5pm. *Mystic Lamb* exhibit open Apr.-Oct. M-Sa 9:30am-5pm, Su 1-5pm; Nov.-Mar. M-Sa 10:30am-4pm, Su 1-4pm. Cathedral and crypt free. *Mystic Lamb* exhibit €3.) **Stedelijk Museum voor Actuele Kunst (SMAK),** in Citadel Park, a 30min. walk from the tourist office, rotates its collection of modern art. (☎221 1703; www.smak.be. Open Tu-Su 10am-6pm. €5, students €3.80.)

To reach **De Draecke (HI) ❷,** St-Widostr. 11, from the station, take tram #1 (€1.20, €1.50 on board) to Gravensteen (15min.). Facing the castle, head left over the canal, then right on Gewad and right on St-Widostr. (☎233 7050; www.vjh.be. Breakfast and linens included. Internet €2 per 30min. Reception 7:30am-11pm. Dorms €20; doubles €50. €3 HI discount. AmEx/MC/V.) To get to **Camping Blaarmeersen ❶,** Zuiderlaan 12, take bus #9 from St-Pietersstation toward Mariakerke and get off at Europabrug (Watersportbaan); cross the street and hop on bus #38 or 39 to Blaarmeersen. Take the first street on the left to its end. (☎266 8160. Laundry available. Open Mar. to mid-Oct. €4.50 per person, €4.50 per tent; low season €3.50/3.50.) **St-Pietersnieuwstraat,** by the university, has inexpensive kebab and pita joints that stay open late. **Magazijn ❷,** Penitentenstr. 24, has filling fare (€8.50-16) and vegetarian options. (☎234 0708. Kitchen open Tu-F noon-2pm and 6-11pm, Sa 6-11pm. Bar open until late. Cash only.) For groceries, stop by the **Contact GB** at Hoogpoort 42. (☎225 0592. Open M-Sa 8:30am-6pm. MC/V.)

Korenmarkt and **Vrijdagmarkt** are filled with restaurants and pubs. One popular haunt is the dimly lit **Charlatan,** Vlasmarkt 6, which features a nightly DJ. (☎224 2457; www.charlatan.be. Live bands Th and Su. Open Tu-Su 7pm-late.) To sit down and have a drink, try **K27,** in the Vrijdag Markt at the corner of Baudelost. (Beer €2-3. Mixed drinks €5. Open M-F noon-late, Sa 2pm-late.) For GLBT nightlife, consult Use-It's Ghent Gay Map or head to the **Foyer Casa Rosa,** Kammerstr. 22/Belfortstr. 39, an info center and bar. (☎269 2812; www.casarosa.be. Bar open M-F 3pm-1am, Sa-Su 3pm-2am; info center open M 6-9pm, W 3-9pm, Sa 3-6pm.)

Trains run from St-Pietersstation (accessible by tram #1) to Antwerp (50min., 2 per hr., €11), Bruges (25min., 3 per hr., €8), and Brussels (35min., 5 per hr., €7.40). The **tourist office,** Botermarkt 17A, is in the crypt of the belfry. (☎266 5232; www.visitgent.be. Open daily Apr.-Oct. 9:30am-6:30pm; Nov.-Mar. 9:30am-4:30pm. Tours Nov.-Apr. daily 2:30pm; buy tickets by 2pm. €7.) At the tourist office and most museums, you can buy a pass for 15 museums and monuments in Ghent (€12.50). ☒**Use-It,** St-Pietersnieuwstr. 21, has quirky maps and free **Internet.** (☎324 3906; www.use-it.be. Open M-F 1-6pm.) **Postal Code:** 9000.

YPRES (IEPER)   ☎57

Famous for its fields filled with poppies and lined with tombstones of fallen soldiers, Ypres (pop. 35,000) and its environs continue to bear witness to the city's significant role in WWI. Once a medieval textile center, Ypres was completely destroyed by four years of combat, but was impressively—and defiantly— rebuilt as a near-perfect replica of its former self. Today, the town is surrounded by over 150 **British cemeteries** and filled with memorial sites. The ☒**In Flanders Field Museum,** Grote Markt 34, documents the gruesome history of the Great War. (☎23 92 20; www.inflandersfields.be. Open Apr.-Sept. daily 10am-6pm, last entry 5pm; Oct.-Mar. Tu-Su 10am-5pm. €7.50. MC/V.) Behind the museum is **St. Martin's Cathedral,** rebuilt using pre-war plans and furnished with a rose window given to Belgium by the British military. (☎20 80 04. Open daily 9am-noon and 2-6pm. Free.) Cross the street in front of St. Martin's and head right to reach **St. George's Memorial Church,** Elverdingsestr. 1 (☎21 56 85). Each brass plaque and kneeling pillow in the church commemorates a particular military group. (Open daily Apr.-Oct. 9:30am-8pm; Nov.-Mar. 9:30am-4pm. Free.) Across the Markt, the names of 54,896 of the 100,000 British soldiers whose bodies were never found are inscribed on the somber **Menin Gate.** Every night at 8pm, the **Last Post** bugle ceremony honors those who defended Ypres (www.lastpost.be). With Menin Gate behind you, go right and take the **Rose Coombs Walk** to visit nearby **Ramparts Cemetery,** where white tombstones line the river. The battlefields are a long walk from town; **car tours** are the way to go. **Salient Tours,** Meenestr. 5 (☎21 46 57; www.salienttours.com; tours 10am and 2:30pm; €28-35) offers English-language tours. A thriftier option is to **bike** the 3-4km journey to the first cemetery or to make a daytrip out of the nearly 40km ride necessary to see them all.

B&Bs are the cheapest lodgings in Ypres, and though there are many, call ahead to ask about availability. **B&B Zonneweelde ❸,** Masscheleinlann 18, has TVs in every room and is not far from Grote Markt. (☎20 27 23. Singles €25; doubles €50; triples €75.) The huts at **Camping Jeugdstadion ❶,** Bolwaerkstr. 1, are less refined. (☎21 72 82; www.jeugdstadion.be. Bike rental €10 per day. Reception Mar. to mid-Nov. 8am-noon and 4-7:30pm. €3 per person, €1.50 per tent site. 4-bed huts with kitchenette €32.) Restaurants line the Grote Markt; the crowded **Taverne Central Tea Room ❸,** Grote Markt 12, is a safe bet. (Entrees €6-15. Open daily 9am-10pm. AmEx/MC/V.) Free chocolate samples are handed out in the square and are espe-

BELGIUM

cially rich at **Vandaele,** Grote Markt 9. (☎20 03 87. Open Tu-Su 9:30am-7pm. MC/V.) Groceries are at **Super GB,** Vandepeereboompl. 15. (☎20 29 35. Open M-Th and Sa 8:30am-7pm, F 8:30am-8pm.) **Trains** run to Bruges (2hr., 1 per hr., €11), Brussels (1¾hr., 1 per hr., €15), and Ghent (1¼hr., 1 per hr., €9.50). The **tourist office,** Grote Markt 34, is inside Cloth Hall. (☎23 92 20; www.ieper.be. Open Apr.-Sept. M-Sa 9am-6pm, Su 10am-6pm; Oct.-Mar. daily 9am-5pm.) **Postal Code:** 8900.

WALLONIE

LIÈGE (LUIK)   ☎04

Liège (lee-AJH; pop. 200,000), the largest city in Wallonie, is often dismissed as a mere transportation hub for eastbound travelers, but its cutting-edge art scene and night-owl student hangouts temper the city's industrial character. The **Coeur Historique** is a quaint area knotted with cobblestone streets. By the river, you'll find the **Musée de L'Art Wallon,** 86 Féronstrée, a collection of Belgian art dating back to the Renaissance. (☎221 9231. Open Tu-Sa 1-6pm, Su 11am-4:30pm. €3.80, students €2.50.) Turn onto r. de Bueren and climb the steps of the **Montagne de Bueren** for an expansive view of the city. From Féronstrée, turn left onto r. Léopold and right onto r. de la Cathédrale; after 10min. you will reach the Gothic naves and sparkling gold treasure of the **Cathédrale de St-Paul.** (☎232 6131. Cathedral open daily 8am-5pm. Treasure room open Tu-Su 2-5pm. Tour 3pm. Cathedral free. Treasure room €4, students €2.50.) In between the banks of the river, a large island makes up the working-class neighborhood of Outremeuse and is home to the ▧**Musée d'Art Moderne et d'Art Contemporain (MAMAC),** 3 Parc de la Boverie, which showcases minor works by Gauguin, Chagall, Rodin, and one piece each by Monet and Picasso. The museum's beautiful building and lovely surrounding park are across the river and to the right from the Coeur Historique and St. Paul's (20min.). Take bus #17 (€1.30) to reach MAMAC from the station. (☎343 0403; www.mamac.be. Open Tu-Sa 1-6pm, Su 11am-4:30pm. €3.80, students €2.50.) To reach the convenient and modern **Auberge Georges Simenon de Jeunesse de Liège (HI) ❷,** 2 r. Georges Simenon, walk across the Pont des Arches from the Coeur Historique, or take bus #4 and ask to get off at Auberge Simenon. (☎344 5689. Breakfast and linens included. Internet €0.60 per 15min. Reception 7:30am-1am. Lockout 10am-3pm. Dorms €20; singles €32; doubles €48. €3 HI discount. MC/V.) **Newave à la Passerelle ❷,** 13 bd. Saucy, serves big *panini* (€3.20-3.50) and couscous (€6-16) to a hungry crowd. (☎341 1566. Open Tu-Su noon-10pm. Cash only.) Pick up groceries a block from the hostel at **Colruyt,** r. Gaston Grégoire. (Open M-F 9am-8pm, Sa 9am-7pm.) **Trains** run to Brussels (1hr., 2-5 per hr., €13). The **tourist office,** 92 Féronstrée, is just a couple doors down from the Musée de L'Art Wallon. (☎221 9221; www.liege.be. Open M-F 9am-5pm, Sa 10am-4:30pm, Su 10am-2:30pm.) Across the Pont des Arches from the hostel, **Cyberman,** 48 r. Léopold, has **Internet** access. (☎87 60 56 95. Open daily 10am-11pm. €1 per hr.)

TOURNAI (DOORNIK)   ☎069

The first city liberated from the Nazis by Allied forces, Tournai (pop. 68,000) was once the capital of Gaul. The city's most spectacular sight is the world's only five-steepled cathedral, 800-year-old **Cathédrale Notre-Dame.** A 1999 tornado left the landmark in need of renovations, and though half of the building is inaccessible, visitors are still welcome. (Open daily June-Oct. 9:15am-noon and 2-6pm; Nov.-May 9:15am-noon and 2-5pm. Free.) Climb the 257 steps of the nearby **belfry,** the oldest in Belgium, for a stunning view. (Open Mar.-Oct. Tu-Sa 10am-1pm and 2-5:30pm, Su 11am-

1pm and 2-6:30pm; Nov.-Feb. Tu-Sa 10am-noon and 2-5pm, Su 2-5pm. €2, under 20 €1.) Two blocks away, next to the hostel, Victor Horta's **Musée des Beaux-Arts**, Enclos St-Martin, houses a small collection of Belgian and Dutch art. (Open Apr.-Oct. M and W-Su 9:30am-12:30pm and 2-5:30pm; Nov.-Mar. M and W-Sa 10am-noon and 2-5pm, Su 2-5pm. €3, first Su of each month free.) To reach the convenient **Auberge de Jeunesse (HI) ❷**, 64 r. St-Martin, continue up the hill from the tourist office. (☎21 61 36; www.laj.be. Breakfast and linens included. Reception 8am-noon and 5-10pm; varies in low season. Reserve ahead. Open Feb.-Nov. Dorms €18-20; singles €33; doubles €49. €3 HI discount. MC/V.) Grab a bite at **En Cas de Faim ❸**, 50 r. des Chapeliers, by the belfry. (☎56 04 84. Entrees €6-13. Open M-Th noon-2:30pm, F-Sa noon-2:30pm and 7-9:30pm. AmEx/MC/V.) **Trains** leave from pl. Crombez to Brussels (1hr., 1 per hr., €11) and Namur (2hr., 1 per hr., €15). The **tourist office** is at 14 Vieux Marché aux Poteries. (☎22 20 45; www.tournai.be. Open Apr.-Sept. M-F 8:30am-6pm, Sa 9:30am-noon and 2-5pm, Su 10am-noon and 2:30-6pm; Oct.-Mar. M-F 8:30am-5:30pm, Sa 10am-noon and 2-5pm, Su 2:30-6pm.) **Postal Code:** 7500.

NAMUR   ☎081

Namur, capital of Wallonie (pop. 110,000), is a gateway for **hiking, biking, caving,** and **kayaking** in Belgium's mountainous regions. In September, Namur hosts a multicultural crowd at the **International French Language Film Festival** (☎24 12 36; www.fiff.be). The town's foreboding **citadel** (☎65 45 00; www.citadelle.namur.be) remained an active Belgian military base until 1978. To get there take bus #3 (1 per hr., dir.: Citadel). The free *Storming the Citadel!*, at the tourist office, lists five historical walking tours (1-1¾hr.). Trails thread through the surrounding **Parc de Champeau.** Flocks of geese dally near the homey ◪ **Auberge Félicien Rops (HI) ❷**, 8 av. Félicien Rops. Take bus # 4, 17, 30 or 31 from the train station. (☎22 36 88; www.laj.be. Breakfast and linens included. Kitchen available. Laundry €6.50. Free Internet. Reception 8am-11pm. Lockout 10am-4pm. Dorms €18-20. €3 HI discount. MC/V.) To reach the **tourist office,** on the Sq. de l'Europe Unie, turn left out of the train station onto r. de la Gare. (☎24 64 49; www.namurtourisme.be. Open daily 9:30am-6pm.) Rent bikes at **La Maison des Cyclistes**, 2B pl. de la Station. (☎81 38 48. Open M-W and F 10am-1pm and 2-4pm. €4 per hr., €9 per day.) **Trains** link Namur to Brussels (1hr., 2 per hr., €7.40) and Dinant (30min., 1 per hr., €4).

DINANT   ☎082

Razed by the German army in 1914, Dinant (pop. 13,000) has reinvented itself as a tourist destination. Descend into the beautiful depths of the **Grotte Merveilleuse,** 142 rte. de Phillipeville, 600m from the train station, for a witty 50min. tour of the cave's limestone formations. Bring a jacket to avoid underground chills. (☎22 22 10; www.dinantourism.com. Open July-Aug. daily 10am-6pm; Apr.-June and Sept.-Oct. daily 11am-5pm; Dec.-Mar. Sa-Su 1-4pm. Tours 1 per hr., usually in English. €6.) Rooms in Dinant tend to be pricey, so try accommodations in nearby towns. **Café Leffe ❸**, 2 r. Sax, named after the famous beer originally brewed in an abbey in Dinant, is past the bridge from the tourist office, on the left (☎22 23 72; www.leffe.be. Entrees €7-13. Open daily 11am-11pm. MC/V.) Get set up to **kayak** at **Anseremme.** (☎22 43 97; www.lessekayaks.be. Kayaks €17-26.) To get to the **tourist office** from the train station, turn right, take the first left, and another immediate left by the river. (☎22 28 70; www.dinant-tourisme.be. Open M-F 8:30am-6pm, Sa 9:30am-5pm, Su 10am-4:30pm; low season reduced hours.) Rent bikes at **Raid Mountain-Bike,** 15 r. du Vélodrome (☎21 35 35. €16-20 per day). **Trains** run to Brussels (1½hr., 1 per hr., €12) and Namur (30min., 1 per hr., €4).

GREAT BRITAIN

 Having colonized two-fifths of the globe, spearheaded the Industrial Revolution, and won almost every foreign war in its history, Britain seems intent on making the world forget its tiny size. It's hard to believe that the rolling farms of the south and the rugged cliffs of the north are only a day's train ride apart. Though the sun may have set on the British Empire, a colonial legacy survives in multicultural urban centers and a dynamic arts and theater scene. Brits now eat kebabs and curry as often as they do scones, and dance clubs in post-industrial settings draw as much attention as elegant country inns.

 DISCOVER BRITAIN: SUGGESTED ITINERARIES

THREE DAYS. Spend it all in **London** (p. 116), the city of tea, royalty, and James Bond. After a stroll through **Hyde Park,** head to **Buckingham Palace** for the changing of the guard. Check out the renowned collections of the **British Museum** and the **Tate Modern.** Stop at famed **Westminster Abbey** and catch a play at Shakespeare's **Globe Theatre** before grabbing a drink in the **East End.**

ONE WEEK. Begin, of course, in **London** (3 days), then visit academia at the colleges of **Oxford** (1 day; p. 148). Travel to Scotland to spend a day in the museums and galleries of **Glasgow** (1 day; p. 182) and finish off with pubs and parties in lively **Edinburgh** (2 days; p. 174).

THREE WEEKS. Start in **London** (4 days), to explore the museums, theaters, and clubs. Tour the college greens in **Cambridge** (2 days; p. 154) and **Oxford** (2 days), then amble through the rolling hills of the **Cotswolds** (1 day; p. 152). Don't miss Shakespeare's hometown, **Stratford-upon-Avon** (1 day; p. 151), or that of The Beatles, **Liverpool** (1 day; p. 158). Head to **Manchester** for its nightlife (1 day; p. 157) before moving on to **Glasgow** (1 day) and nearby **Loch Lomond** (1 day; p. 185). Energetic **Edinburgh** (4 days) will keep you busy, especially during festival season. Finally, enjoy the beautiful **Lake District** (2 days; p. 165) and historic **York** (1 day; p. 161).

ESSENTIALS

FACTS AND FIGURES

Official Name: United Kingdom of Great Britain and Northern Ireland.

Capital: London.

Major Cities: Cardiff, Edinburgh, Glasgow, Liverpool, Manchester.

Population: 60,776,000.

Land Area: 244,800 sq. km.

Time Zone: GMT.

Language: English; also Welsh and Scottish Gaelic.

Religions: Christian: Protestant and Catholic (72%), Muslim (3%).

Harry Potter Books Sold: More than the populations of Britain, France, Germany, and Italy combined: 325,000,000.

WHEN TO GO

It's wise to plan around the high season (June-Aug.). Spring and fall are better times to visit; the weather is still reasonable and flights are cheaper, though there

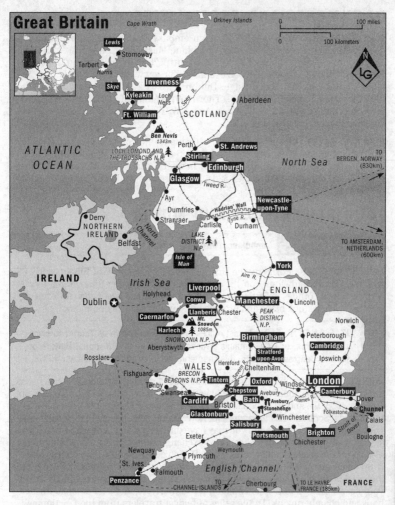

Great Britain

Cape Wrath • Orkney Islands

0 — 100 miles
0 — 100 kilometers

N
LG

Lewis
Stornoway
Tarbert
Harris
Skye
Kyleakin
Inverness
Loch Ness
Spey R.
Aberdeen
Ft. William
SCOTLAND
Ben Nevis 1343m
Perth
St. Andrews
LOCH LOMOND AND THE TROSSACHS N.P.
Stirling
ATLANTIC OCEAN
Glasgow
Edinburgh
Tweed R.
North Sea
TO BERGEN, NORWAY (830km)
Ayr
Dumfries
Hadrian' Wall
Newcastle-upon-Tyne
Stranraer
Carlisle
Tyne R.
Durham
Derry
NORTHERN IRELAND
North Channel
LAKE DISTRICT N.P.
TO AMSTERDAM, NETHERLANDS (600km)
Belfast
Isle of Man
Aire R.
York
IRELAND
Irish Sea
Liverpool
ENGLAND
Holyhead
Conwy
Manchester
Lincoln
Dublin
Caernarfon
Llanberis
Chester
PEAK DISTRICT N.P.
Mt. Snowdon 1085m
Norwich
Harlech
SNOWDONIA N.P.
Birmingham
Peterborough
Aberystwyth
Cambridge
Stratford-upon-Avon
Ipswich
WALES
Hereford R.
Severn R.
BRECON BEACONS N.P.
Cheltenham
Fishguard
Tenby
Tintern
Oxford
Windsor
London
Swansea
Chepstow
Avebury
Canterbury
Cardiff
Bath
Thames R.
Dover
Bristol
Stonehenge
Folkestone
Chunnel
Glastonbury
Winchester
Calais
Salisbury
Brighton
Strait of Dover
Boulogne
Exeter
Portsmouth
Chichester
Newquay
Weymouth
St. Ives
Plymouth
Penzance
Falmouth
English Channel
FRANCE
Rosslare
TO CHANNEL ISLANDS
Cherbourg
TO LE HAVRE, FRANCE (185km)

may be less transportation to rural areas. If you plan to visit the cities and stick to museums and theaters, the low season (Nov.-Mar.) is most economical. Keep in mind, however, that sights and accommodations often close or have reduced hours. In Scotland, summer light lasts almost until midnight, but in winter, the sun may set as early as 3:45pm. Regardless of when you go, it will rain—always.

IT'S ALL BRITISH TO ME. The United Kingdom is a political union of England, Northern Ireland, Scotland, and Wales. This is also referred to as Britain, not to be confused with the island of Great Britain, which only includes England, Scotland, and Wales. *Let's Go* uses United Kingdom and Britain interchangeably. This chapter covers Great Britain. For Northern Ireland, see p. 565.

DOCUMENTS AND FORMALITIES

EMBASSIES AND CONSULATES. Foreign embassies in Britain are in London (p. p. 116). British embassies abroad include: **Australia,** Commonwealth Ave., Yarralumla, ACT 2600 (☎02 62 70 66 66; http://bhc.britaus.net); **Canada,** 80 Elgin St., Ottawa, ON, K1P 5K7 (☎613-237-1530; www.britainincanada.org); **Ireland,** 29 Merrion Rd., Ballsbridge, Dublin, 4 (☎01 205 3700; www.britishembassy.ie); **New Zealand,** 44 Hill St., Thorndon, Wellington, 6011 (☎04 924 2888; www.britain.org.nz); **US,** 3100 Mass. Ave. NW, Washington, D.C., 20008 (☎900-255-6685; www.britainusa.com).

VISA AND ENTRY INFORMATION. EU citizens do not need a visa. Citizens of Australia, Canada, New Zealand, and the US do not need a visa for stays of up to 6 months. Students planning to study in the UK for six months or more must obtain a student visa (around US$90). For more info, call your British embassy or visit www.ukvisas.gov.uk.

TOURIST SERVICES AND MONEY

EMERGENCY Ambulance, Fire, and Police: ☎999.

TOURIST OFFICES. Formerly the British Tourist Authority, **Visit Britain** (☎020 88 46 90 00; www.visitbritain.com) is an umbrella organization for regional tourist boards. Tourist offices in Britain are listed under **Practical Information** for each city and town. They stock maps and provide info on sights and accommodations.

TIP **IT'S JUST A TIC.** Tourist offices in Britain are known as **Tourist Information Centres,** or **TICs.** Britain's National Parks also have **National Park Information Centres,** or **NPICs.** This chapter refers to all offices as TICs and NPICs.

MONEY. The British unit of currency is the **pound sterling (£),** plural pounds sterling. One pound is equal to 100 pence, with standard denominations of 1p, 2p, 5p, 10p, 20p, 50p, £1, and £2 in coins, and £5, £10, £20, and £50 in notes. Quid is slang for pounds. Scotland has its own bank notes, which can be used interchangeably with English currency, though you may have difficulty using Scottish £1 notes outside Scotland. As a rule, it's cheaper to exchange money in Britain than at home. **ATMs** offer the best exchange rates. Many British department stores, such as Marks & Spencer, also offer excellent exchange services. **Tips** in restaurants are often included in the bill, sometimes as a "service charge." If gratuity is not included, tip your server 12%. A 10% tip is common for taxi drivers, and £1-3 is usual for bellhops and chambermaids. To the relief of budget travelers from the US, tipping is not expected at pubs and bars in Britain. Aside from open-air markets, don't expect to bargain. For more info on money in Europe, see p. 16.

The UK has a 17.5% **value added tax (VAT),** a sales tax applied to everything but food, books, medicine, and children's clothing. The tax is **included** in the amount indicated on the price tag. The prices stated in *Let's Go* include VAT. In the airport upon exiting the EU, non-EU citizens can claim a refund on the tax paid for goods purchased at participating stores. You can obtain refunds only for goods you take out of the country. Participating shops display a "Tax-Free Shopping" sign. They may have a purchase minimum of £50-100 before they offer refunds, and the complex procedure is probably only worthwhile for large purchases. To apply for a refund, fill out the form that you are given in the shop and present it with the goods and receipts at customs upon departure—look for the Tax-Free Refund

Desk at the airport. At peak times, this process can take an hour. You must leave the UK within three months of your purchase to claim a refund, and you must apply for the refund before leaving. For more info on qualifying for a VAT refund, see p. 19. For VAT info specific to the UK, visit http://customs.hmrc.gov.uk.

BRITISH POUND (£)		
	AUS$1 = £0.420	£1 = AUS$2.38
	CDN$1 = £0.466	£1 = CDN$2.15
	EUR€1 = £0.674	£1 = EUR€1.48
	NZ$1 = £0.375	£1 = NZ$2.66
	US$1 = £0.492	£1 = US$2.03

TRANSPORTATION

BY PLANE. Most international flights land at London's **Heathrow** (**LHR**; ☎0870 000 0123; www.heathrowairport.com) or **Gatwick** (**WSX**; ☎0870 000 2468; www.gatwickairport.com) airports; **Manchester (MAN)** and **Edinburgh (EDI)** also have international airports. Budget airlines, like **Ryanair** and **easyJet,** fly out of many locales, including **Stansted Airport** and **Luton Airport** (see *Let's Go to London,* p. 140). The British national airline, **British Airways** (☎0870 850 9850, US 800-247-9297; www.britishairways.com), offers discounted youth fares for those younger than 24. For more info on plane travel in Europe, see p. 43.

BY TRAIN. Britain's main carrier is **National Rail Enquiries** (☎08457 484 950). The country's train network is extensive, criss-crossing the length and breadth of the island. Prices and schedules often change; find up-to-date information from National Rail Enquiries website (www.nationalrail.co.uk/planmyjourney) or **Network Rail** (www.networkrail.co.uk; schedules only). **Eurostar** trains run to Britain from the Continent through the **Chunnel** (p. 52). The **BritRail Pass,** sold only outside Britain, allows unlimited travel in England, Scotland, and Wales (www.britrail.net). In Canada and the US, contact **Rail Europe** (Canada ☎800-361-7245, US 888-382-7245; www.raileurope.com). **Eurail passes are not valid in Britain.** Rail discount cards (£20), available at rail stations and through travel agents, grant 33% off most point-to-point fares and are available to those ages 16-25 or over 60, full-time students, and families. In general, traveling by train costs more than by bus. For more info on traveling by train around Europe, see p. 46.

BY BUS. The British distinguish between **buses,** which cover short routes, and **coaches,** which cover long distances; *Let's Go* refers to both as buses. **National Express** (☎08705 808 080; www.nationalexpress.com) is the main operator of long-distance bus service in Britain, while **Scottish Citylink** (☎08705 505 050; www.citylink.co.uk) has the most extensive coverage in Scotland. The **Brit Xplorer Pass** offers unlimited travel on National Express buses (7-day £79, 14-day £139, 28-day £219). **NX2** cards (£10), available online for ages 16-26, reduce fares by up to 30%. For those who plan far ahead, the cheapest rides are National Express's **funfares,** available only online (limited number of seats on buses out of London from £1).

BY CAR. To drive, you must be 18 and have a valid license from your home country; to rent, you must be over 21. Britain is covered by a high-speed system of **motorways** (M-roads) that connect London to other major cities. Visitors may not be accustomed to **driving on the left,** and automatic transmission is rare in rental cars. Roads are generally well maintained, but **gasoline** (petrol) prices are high. In London, driving is restricted during weekday working hours, with charges imposed in certain congestion zones; parking can be similarly nightmarish.

BY FERRY. Several ferry lines provide service between Britain and the Continent. Ask for discounts; ISIC holders can sometimes get student fares, and Eurail pass-holders are eligible for reductions and free trips. **Seaview Ferries** (www.seaview.co.uk/ferries.html) has a directory of UK ferries. In summer, it's a good idea to book ahead. For more info on boats to Ireland and the Continent, see p. 53.

BY BIKE AND BY FOOT. Much of the British countryside is well suited to **biking.** Many cities and villages have rental shops and route maps. Large-scale **Ordnance Survey** maps, often available at TICs, detail the extensive system of long-distance **hiking** paths. TICs and NPICs can provide extra information about routes.

BY THUMB. Hitchhiking or standing on M-roads is illegal. Despite this, hitchhiking is fairly common in rural parts of Scotland and Wales (England is tougher) where public transportation is spotty. Let's Go does not recommend hitchhiking.

KEEPING IN TOUCH

PHONE CODES	**Country code: 44. International dialing prefix:** 00. Within Britain, dial city code + local number, even when dialing inside the city. For more info on how to place international calls, see **Inside Back Cover.**

EMAIL AND THE INTERNET. Internet access is ubiquitous in big cities, common in towns, and sparse in rural areas. **Internet cafes** or public terminals can be found almost everywhere; they usually cost £2-6 per hour. For more info, see www.cybercafes.com. Public **libraries** usually have free or inexpensive Internet access, but you might have to wait or reserve ahead.

TELEPHONE. Most public pay phones in Britain are run by **British Telecom (BT).** Public phones charge at least 30p and don't accept 1, 2, or 5p coins. A BT Charge-card bills calls to your credit card, but most pay phones now have readers where you can swipe credit cards directly (generally AmEx/MC/V). The number for the operator in Britain is ☎100, the international operator ☎155. Whenever possible, use a calling card for international phone calls, as long-distance rates for national phone services are often very high. Mobile phones are an increasingly popular and economical option. Major mobile carriers include **T-Mobile, Vodafone,** and **O₂.** Direct-dial access numbers for calling out of Britain include: **AT&T Direct** (☎0800 89 0011); **British Telecom** (☎0800 14 41 44); **Canada Direct** (☎0800 096 0634 or 0800 559 3141); **Telecom New Zealand Direct** (☎0800 8900 64); **Telstra Australia** (☎0800 856 6161). For more info on calling home from Europe, see p. 28.

MAIL. Royal Mail has tried to standardize their rates around the world. To check shipment costs, use the Postal Calculator at www.royalmail.com. From Britain, it costs £0.24 to send a postcard domestically, £0.48 within Europe, and £0.54 to the rest of the world. Airmail letters up to 20g cost £0.24 domestically, £0.48 within Europe, and £0.78 elsewhere. Remember to write "Par Avión—Airmail" on the top left corner of your envelope or stop by any post office to get a free airmail label. Letters sent via Airmail should be delivered within three working days to European destinations and five working days worldwide. To receive mail in the UK, have mail delivered **Poste Restante.** Mail will go to the main post office unless you specify a subsidiary by street address. Address mail to be held according to the following example: First Name, Last Name, Poste Restante, post office address, Postal Code, UK. Bring a passport to pick up your mail; there may be a small fee.

ACCOMMODATIONS AND CAMPING

BRITAIN	❶	❷	❸	❹	❺
ACCOMMODATIONS	under £15	£15-20	£21-30	£31-40	over £40

Hostelling International (HI) hostels are prevalent throughout Britain. They are run by the **Youth Hostels Association of England and Wales (YHA;** ☎0870 770 8868; www.yha.org.uk), the **Scottish Youth Hostels Association (SYHA;** ☎01786 89 14 00; www.syha.org.uk), and the **Hostelling International Northern Ireland (HINI;** ☎28 9032 4733; www.hini.org.uk). Dorms cost around £11 in rural areas, £14 in larger cities, and £15-25 in London. You can book **B&Bs** by calling directly, or by asking the local TIC to help you. TICs usually charge a flat fee of £1-5 plus 10% deposit, deductible from the amount you pay the B&B proprietor. **Campgrounds** tend to be privately owned and cost £3-10 per person per night. It is illegal to camp in national parks.

FOOD AND DRINK

BRITAIN	❶	❷	❸	❹	❺
FOOD	under £6	£6-10	£11-15	£16-20	over £20

A pillar of traditional British fare, the cholesterol-filled, meat-anchored **English breakfast** is still served in most B&Bs across the country. **Beans on toast** or toast smothered in **Marmite** (the most acquired of tastes—a salty, brown spread made from yeast) are breakfast staples. The best native dishes for lunch or dinner are **roasts**—beef, lamb, and Wiltshire hams—and **Yorkshire pudding,** a type of popover drizzled with meat juices. Despite their intriguing names, **bangers and mash** and **bubble and squeak** are just sausages and potatoes and cabbage and potatoes, respectively. Pubs serve savory meat pies like **Cornish pasties** (PASS-tees) or **ploughman's lunches** consisting of bread, cheese, and pickles. **Fish and chips** (french fries) are traditionally drowned in malt vinegar and salt. **Crisps,** or potato chips, come in an astonishing variety, with flavors like prawn cocktail. Britons make their **desserts** (often called "puddings" or "afters") exceedingly sweet and gloopy. Sponges, trifles, tarts, and the ill-named spotted dick (spongy currant cake) will satiate the sweetest tooth. To escape English food, try Chinese, Greek, or Indian cuisine. British "tea" refers to both a drink, served strong and milky, and to a social ritual. A **high tea** might include cooked meats, salad, sandwiches, and pastries, while the oft-stereotyped **afternoon tea** comes with finger sandwiches, scones with jam and clotted cream (a sinful cross between whipped cream and butter), and small cakes. **Cream tea,** a specialty of Cornwall and Devon, includes scones or crumpets, jam, and clotted cream.

HOLIDAYS AND FESTIVALS

Holidays: New Year's Day (Jan. 1); Epiphany (Jan. 6); Good Friday (Mar. 21); Easter (Mar. 23-24); Ascension (May 1); May Day (May 1); Pentecost (May 11-12); Corpus Christi (May 22); Bank Holidays (May 26 and Aug. 25); Assumption (Aug. 15); All Saints' Day (Nov. 1); Christmas (Dec. 25); Boxing Day (Dec. 26).

Festivals: Scotland's New Year's Eve celebration, Hogmanay, takes over the streets in Edinburgh and Glasgow. The National Eisteddfod of Wales (Aug. 2-9) has brought Welsh writers, musicians, and artists together since 1176. One of the largest music and theater festivals in the world is the Edinburgh International Festival (Aug. 8-31); also highly recommended is the Edinburgh Fringe Festival (Aug.). Manchester's Gay

Village hosts Manchester Pride (www.manchesterpride.com) in August, and London throws a huge street party at the Notting Hill Carnival (Aug. 24-25). Bonfires and fireworks abound on England's Guy Fawkes Day (Nov. 5) in celebration of a conspirator's failed attempt to destroy the Houses of Parliament in 1605.

BEYOND TOURISM

There are many opportunities for **volunteering, studying,** and **working** in Britain. As a volunteer, you can participate projects ranging from archaeological digs to lobbying for social change. Explore your academic passions at the country's prestigious institutions or pursue an independent research project. Paid work opportunities include Parliament internships and teaching, among others. For more info on opportunities across Europe, see **Beyond Tourism,** p. 56.

The National Trust, National Trust Central Volunteering Team, The National Trust, Heelis, Kemble Dr., Swindon SN2 2NA (☎0870 609 5383; www.nationaltrust.org.uk/volunteering). Arranges numerous volunteer opportunities, including working holidays.

The Teacher Recruitment Company, Pennineway Offices (1), 87-89 Saffron Hill, London EC1N 8QU (☎0845 833 1934; www.teachers.eu.com). International recruitment agency lists positions and provides information on jobs in the UK.

University of Oxford, College Admissions Office, Wellington Sq., Oxford OX1 2JD (☎0186 528 8000; www.ox.ac.uk). Large range of summer programs (£900-4000) and year-long courses (£8880-11,840).

ENGLAND

A land where the stately once prevailed, England is now a youthful, hip, and forward-looking nation on the cutting edge of art, music, and film. But traditionalists can rest easy; for all the moving and shaking in large cities, just around the corner scores of ancient towns, opulent castles, and comforting cups of tea still abound.

LONDON ☎020

London offers visitors an array of choices: Leonardo at the National Gallery or Hirst at the Tate Modern; Rossini at the Royal Opera or *Les Misérables* at the Queen's—you could spend your entire stay just deciding what to do. London is often described as a conglomeration of evolving villages. Thanks to each area's feisty independence, the London "buzz" is continually on the move.

✈ INTERCITY TRANSPORTATION

Flights: Heathrow (LON; ☎08700 000 123) is London's main airport. The **Piccadilly Line** heads from the airport to central London (1hr., every 5min., £4-10). **Heathrow Connect** runs to Paddington (20min., 2 per hr., £10), as does the more expensive **Heathrow Express** (15min.; 4 per hr.; £14.50, round-trip £27). From **Gatwick Airport (LGW;** ☎08700 002 468), the **Gatwick Express** heads to Victoria (30min.; 4 per hr.; £13, round-trip £24). See **Let's Go to London** (p. 140) for info on budget airline hubs.

Trains: London has 8 major train stations: **Charing Cross** (southern England); **Euston** (the northwest); **King's Cross** (the northeast); **Liverpool Street** (East Anglia); **Paddington** (Wales); **St. Pancras** (the Midlands and the northwest); **Victoria** (the south); **Waterloo** (the south, the southwest, and the Continent). All stations are linked by the subway, a.k.a. the Underground or Tube (⊖). Itineraries involving a change of stations in London usually include a cross-town transfer by Tube. Get info at the station ticket office or from the **National Rail Enquiries Line** (☎08457 484 950; www.britrail.com).

Buses: Long-distance **coaches** (buses) arrive in London at **Victoria Coach Station,** 164 Buckingham Palace Rd. ⊖Victoria. National Express (☎08705 808 080; www.nationalexpress.com) is the largest operator of intercity services.

⚡ ORIENTATION

The **West End,** stretching east from Park Lane to Kingsway and south from Oxford St. to the River Thames, is the heart of London. In this area you'll find aristocratic **Mayfair,** the shopping streets near **Oxford Circus,** the clubs of **Soho,** and the boutiques of **Covent Garden.** Heading east of the West End, you'll pass legalistic **Holborn** before hitting the ancient **City of London** ("the City"), the site of the original Roman settlement and home to Tower Bridge and the Tower of London. The City's eastern border bounds the ethnically diverse, working-class **East End.**

Westminster encompasses the grandeur of **Trafalgar Square** and extends south along the Thames; this is the location of both royal and political London, with the Houses of Parliament, Buckingham Palace, and Westminster Abbey. Farther west lies rich, snooty **Chelsea.** Across the river, the **South Bank** has an incredible variety of entertainment and museums. To the south, **Brixton** is one of the hottest nightlife spots in town, besides touristy Leicester Square and Piccadilly Circus. The huge expanse of **Hyde Park** lies west of the West End; along its southern border are chic **Knightsbridge** and posh **Kensington.** North of Hyde Park is the media-infested **Notting Hill** and the B&B- and hostel-filled **Bayswater.** Bayswater, Mayfair, and **Marylebone** meet at Marble Arch, on Hyde Park's northeast corner; from there, Marylebone stretches west to meet academic **Bloomsbury,** north of Soho and Holborn. **Camden Town, Islington, Hampstead,** and **Highgate** lie to the north of Bloomsbury and the City. A good street atlas is essential. **▓London A to Z** (£6) is available at newsstands and bookstores.

🄴 LOCAL TRANSPORTATION

Public Transportation: Run by **Transport for London (TfL;** 24hr. info ☎7222 1234; www.thetube.com). The **Underground** (a.k.a. the **Tube)** is divided into 6 concentric zones; fares depend on the number of zones crossed. Buy your ticket before you board and pass it through automatic gates at both ends of your journey. Runs approximately 5:30am-midnight. See color Tube map in the opening pages. **Buses** are divided into 4 zones. Zones 1-3 are identical to the Tube zones. Buses run 5:30am-midnight, after which a network of **Night Buses,** prefixed by "N," take over. Fares £1. **Travelcard** valid on all TfL services. 1-day Travelcard from £6.20 (Zones 1-2).

Licensed Taxicabs: An illuminated "taxi" sign on the roof of a black cab signals availability. Tip 10%. For pickup (min. £2 charge), call **Taxi One-Number** (☎08718 718 710).

Minicabs: Private cars. Cheaper but less reliable—stick to a reputable company. **London Radio Cars** (☎8905 0000; www.londonradiocars.com) offers 24hr. pickup.

🄷 PRACTICAL INFORMATION

Tourist Information Centre: Britain Visitor Centre, 1 Regent St. (www.visitbritain.com), ⊖Piccadilly Circus. Open M 9:30am-6:30pm, Tu-F 9am-6:30pm, Sa-Su 10am-4pm. **London Information Centre,** 1 Leicester Pl. (☎7930 6769; www.londoninformationcentre.com) ⊖Leicester Sq. Open M-F 8am-midnight, Sa-Su 9am-6pm.

Central London

● SIGHTS

Sight		
Apsley House,	1	C4
Barbican Hall,	2	E3
British Library,	3	D2
British Museum,	4	D3
Buckingham Palace,	5	C4
Cabinet War Rooms,	6	D4
Chelsea Physic Garden,	7	C5
Chinatown,	8	D4
Courtauld Institute,	9	D4
The Houses of Parliament,	10	D4
Kensington Palace,	11	B4
London Eye,	12	D4
Marble Arch,	13	C3
Millennium Bridge,	14	E4
Monument,	15	F4
Museum of London,	16	E3
National Gallery,	17	D4
National Portrait Gallery,	18	D4
Natural History Museum,	19	B5
Royal Courts of Justice,	20	E3
The Royal Hospital,	21	C5
The Royal Mews,	22	C4
St. Martin-in-the-Fields,	23	D4
St. Mary-le-Bow,	24	E3
St. Pancras Chambers,	25	D2
St. Paul's Cathedral,	26	E2
Science Museum,	27	B5

BRITAIN

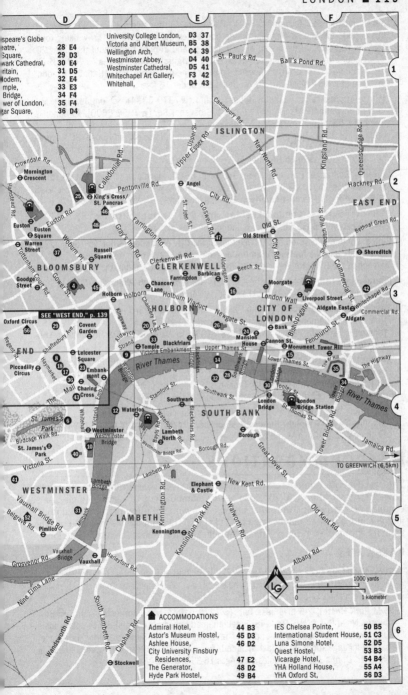

speare's | | |
eatre, | **28** | **E4**
Square, | **29** | **D3**
wark Cathedral, | **30** | **E4**
ritain, | **31** | **D5**
Modern, | **32** | **E4**
mple, | **33** | **E3**
Bridge, | **34** | **F4**
wer of London, | **35** | **F4**
tar Square, | **36** | **D4**

University College London, **D3 37**
Victoria and Albert Museum, **B5 38**
Wellington Arch, **C4 39**
Westminster Abbey, **D4 40**
Westminster Cathedral, **D5 41**
Whitechapel Art Gallery, **F3 42**
Whitehall, **D4 43**

ACCOMMODATIONS

Admiral Hotel,	44 B3	IES Chelsea Pointe,	50 B5
Astor's Museum Hostel,	45 D3	International Student House,	51 C3
Ashlee House,	46 D2	Luna Simone Hotel,	52 D5
City University Finsbury		Quest Hostel,	53 B3
Residences,	47 E2	Vicarage Hotel,	54 B4
The Generator,	48 D2	YHA Holland House,	55 A4
Hyde Park Hostel,	49 B4	YHA Oxford St,	56 D3

BRITAIN

Tours: The **Big Bus Company,** 35-37 Grosvenor Gardens (☎7233 7797; www.big-bus.co.uk). ⊖Victoria. Multiple routes and buses every 5-15min. 1hr. walking tours and Thames cruise. Buses start at central office and at hubs throughout the city. £20. £2 discount for online purchase. AmEx/MC/V. **Original London Walks** (☎7624 3978, recorded info 7624 9255; www.walks.com) has themed walks, from "Haunted London" to "Slice of India." Most 2hr. £6, students £5, under 16 free.

Embassies: Australia, Australia House, Strand (☎7379 4334). ⊖Temple. Open M-F 9am-5pm. **Canada,** MacDonald House, 1 Grosvenor Sq. (☎7258 6600). ⊖Bond St. Open M-F 9am-5pm. **Ireland,** 17 Grosvenor Pl. (☎7235 2171). ⊖Hyde Park Corner. Open M-F 9:30am-1pm and 2:15-5pm. **New Zealand,** New Zealand House, 80 Haymarket (☎7930 8422). ⊖Piccadilly Circus. Open M-F 9am-5pm. **US,** 24 Grosvenor Sq. (☎7499 9000). ⊖Bond St. Open M-F 8:30am-5:30pm.

Currency Exchange: Banks, such as **Barclays, HSBC, Lloyd's,** and **National Westminster** (NatWest) have the best rates. Branches open M-F 9:30am-4:30pm. Call ☎0895 456 6524 for the nearest **American Express** location.

GLBT Resources: London Lesbian and Gay Switchboard (☎7837 7324; www.queery.org.uk). 24hr. helpline and information service.

Police: London is covered by 2 police forces: the **City of London Police** (☎7601 2222) for the City and the **Metropolitan Police** (☎7230 1212) for the rest. At least 1 station in each of the 32 boroughs is open 24hr. Call ☎7230 1212 to find the nearest station.

Pharmacies: Late-night and 24hr. chemists are rare. **Zafash Pharmacy,** 233-235 Old Brompton Rd. (☎7373 2798), ⊖Earl's Ct., is 24hr.

Hospitals: Charing Cross, Fulham Palace Rd. (☎8846 1234), entrance on St. Dunstan's Rd., ⊖Hammersmith. **Royal Free,** Pond St. (☎7794 0500), ⊖Belsize Park. **St. Thomas's,** Lambeth Palace Rd. (☎7188 7188), ⊖Waterloo. **University College London Hospital,** Grafton Way (☎0845 155 500), ⊖Warren St.

Internet Access: Don't pay more than £2 per hr. Try the ubiquitous **easyInternet** (☎7241 9000; www.easyeverything.com) at: 9-16 Tottenham Ct. Rd. (⊖Tottenham Ct. Rd.); 456/459 Strand (⊖Charing Cross); 358 Oxford St. (⊖Bond St.); 160-166 Kensington High St. (⊖High St. Kensington). Prices around £1.60 per hr. but may vary.

Post Office: When sending mail to London, be sure to include the full postal code. The largest office is the **Trafalgar Square Post Office,** 24-28 William IV St. (☎7484 9305), ⊖Charing Cross. Open M and W-F 8:30am-6:30pm, Tu 9:15am-6:30pm, Sa 9am-5:30pm.

⌐ ACCOMMODATIONS

The best deals are student residence halls, which rent rooms in summer and sometimes Easter vacations. "B&B" includes accommodations of varying quality, personality, and price. Be aware that in-room showers are often prefabricated units jammed into a corner. Linens are included at all YHAs, but towels are not; buy one from reception ($4). YHAs sell discount tickets to theaters and major attractions.

BAYSWATER

Quest Hostel, 45 Queensborough Terr. (☎7229 7782; www.astorhostels.com). ⊖Bayswater. Night Bus #N15, 94, 148. A chummy staff keeps co-ed dorms spotless. Continental breakfast included. Internet £1 per hr. Dorms £18-23; doubles £30. MC/V. ❶

Hyde Park Hostel, 2-6 Inverness Terr. (☎7229 5101; www.astorhostels.com). ⊖Bayswater. Night Bus #N15, 94, 148. Jungle-themed basement bar and dance space hosts DJs and parties (open W-Th and Su 7pm-2am, F-Sa 7pm-3am). Laundry, TV lounge, secure luggage room. Breakfast included. Reception 24hr. Reserve 2 weeks ahead in summer. Dorms £11-18; doubles £25. Ages 16-35 only. MC/V. ❶

Admiral Hotel, 143 Sussex Gardens (☎7723 7309; www.admiral-hotel.com). ⊖Paddington. Night Bus #N15, 94, 148. Recently redecorated rooms with bath, hair dryer, satellite TV, and kettle. English breakfast included. Free Wi-Fi. Singles £40-50; doubles £58-75; triples £75-90; quads £88-110; quints £100-130. MC/V. ❸

BLOOMSBURY

Many B&Bs and hostels are on busy roads, so be wary of noise levels. The area becomes seedier closer to King's Cross.

▨**The Generator,** Compton Pl. (☎7388 7666; www.generatorhostels.com), off 37 Tavistock Pl. ⊖Russell Sq. or King's Cross St. Pancras. Night Bus #N19, 35, 38, 41, 55, 91, 243. The ultimate party hostel. 18+. Breakfast included. Internet 50p per 10min. Reserve 1 week ahead for Sa-Su. Online booking. Credit card required with reservation. 12- to 14-bed dorms M-W and Su £13, Th-Sa £18; singles £30/35; doubles with 2 twin beds £40/44; triples £54/60; quads £60/68. Discounts for long stays. Under 18 not allowed unless part of a family group. MC/V. ❶

▨**Ashlee House,** 261-265 Gray's Inn Rd. (☎7833 9400; www.ashleehouse.co.uk). ⊖King's Cross St. Pancras. Night Bus #N10, 63, 73, 91, 390. A friendly budget accommodation fit for the most discerning of backpackers. Private rooms include table, sink, and kettle. Breakfast and linens included; towels £1. Internet £1 per hr. Apr.-Oct. dorms £9-20; singles £37; doubles £50. MC/V. ❶

Astor's Museum Hostel, 27 Montague St. (☎7580 5360; www.astorhotels.com). ⊖Tottenham Court Rd., Russell Sq., or Goodge St. Night Bus #N19, 35, 38, 41, 55, 91, 243. Plain but friendly. Under-35 only. English breakfast and linens included. Reserve ahead. Dorms £19-23; doubles £66. AmEx/MC/V. ❷

KENSINGTON AND EARL'S COURT

▨**YHA Holland House,** Holland Walk (☎7937 0748; www.hihostels.com). ⊖High St. Kensington or Holland Park. Night Bus #N27, 94, 148. 17th-century mansion with TV room, laundry, and kitchen. Breakfast included. Internet 50p per 7min. Reception 24hr. Reserve 2-3 weeks ahead in summer, although there are frequent last-minute vacancies. Dorms £22, under 18 £17. £3 discount with student ID. AmEx/MC/V. ❶

Vicarage Hotel, 10 Vicarage Gate (☎7229 4030; www.londonvicaragehotel.com). ⊖High St. Kensington. Night Bus #N27, 28, 31, 52. Immaculately maintained Victorian house. All rooms have wood furnishings, kettle, and hair dryer. Rooms with private bath have TV. Full English breakfast included. Reserve 2 months ahead with 1 night's deposit; personal checks accepted with at least 2 months notice. Singles £50, with private bathroom £85; doubles £85/110; triples £105/140; quads £112/155. MC/V. ❸

OTHER NEIGHBORHOODS

▨**YHA Oxford Street (HI),** 14 Noel St. (☎7734 1618; www.yha.org.uk), in the West End. ⊖Oxford Circus. More than 10 Night Buses run along Oxford St., including #N7, 8, and 207. Small, clean, sunny rooms with limited facilities but an unbeatable location for nightlife. Towels £3.50. Internet and Wi-Fi available. 3- to 4-bed dorms £25, under 18 £21; 2-bed dorms £27. Oct.-Mar. £24/19/26. MC/V. ❶

City University Finsbury Residences, 15 Bastwick St. (☎7040 8811; www.city.ac.uk/ems/accomm/fins.html), in Clerkenwell. ⊖Barbican. Night Bus #N35 and 55 stop at the corner of Old St. and Goswell Rd. Open June to early Sept. Singles £21. ❷

Luna Simone Hotel, 47-49 Belgrave Rd. (☎7834 5897; www.lunasimonehotel.com), in Westminster. ⊖Victoria or Pimlico. Night Bus #N2, 24, 36. Overachieving staff and lovely rooms. Breakfast included. Free Internet. Reserve at least 3 weeks ahead. Singles £40, with bath £60; doubles with bath £90; triples with bath £110; quads with bath £130. 10-20% discount in low season. MC/V. ❸

IES Chelsea Pointe (☎7808 9200; www.iesreshall.com), in Chelsea, on the corner of Manresa Rd. and King's Rd.; entrance on Manresa Rd. ⊖Sloane Sq., then Bus #11, 19, 22, 319; ⊖South Kensington, then Bus #49. Night Bus #N11, 19, 22. Unheard-of prices in Soho. 20 rooms wheelchair-accessible. Reserve ahead. Singles £285 per week; doubles £375 per week. AmEx/MC/V. ❸

International Student House, 229 Great Portland St. (☎7631 8310; www.ish.org.uk), in Marylebone. ⊖Great Portland St. Night Bus #N18. Most rooms have sink and fridge; some have bath. Bar, cafeteria, and fitness center £6 per day. Continental breakfast included except for dorms (£2.30); English breakfast £3. Internet £2 per hr. Key deposit £20. Dorms £12; singles £34; doubles £52; triples £62; quads £76. 10% discount on singles, doubles, and triples with ISIC. MC/V. ❶

◖◗ FOOD

Any restaurant charging under £10 for a main course is relatively inexpensive; add drinks and service and you're nudging £15. It *is* possible to eat cheaply—and well—in London. For the best, cheapest **ethnic restaurants,** head to the source: **Whitechapel** for Bangladeshi *baltis*, **Chinatown** for dim sum, **South Kensington** for French pastries, **Edgware Road** for shawarma. The cheapest places to get your own ingredients are **street markets** (see **Shopping,** p. 137). To get all your food under one roof, try supermarket chains **Tesco, Safeway, Sainsbury's,** or **Marks & Spencer.**

BAYSWATER

▩ **Levantine,** 26 London St. (☎7262 1111; www.levant.co.uk). ⊖Paddington. Lebanese restaurant with loads of vegetarian options, nightly belly-dancing, and *shisha* (hookah). Lunch *menu* £7 noon-5:30pm. Open daily noon-12:30am. MC/V. ❷

La Bottega del Gelato, 127 Bayswater Rd. (☎7243 2443). ⊖Queensway. Serves handmade, creamy gelato. 1-3 scoops £2-4. Open daily 11am-10pm. ❶

BLOOMSBURY

▩ **ICCo (Italiano Coffee Company),** 46 Goodge St. (☎7580 9688). ⊖Goodge St. To-die-for thin-crust 30cm pizzas for only £3. Pasta from £2. Sandwiches and baguettes ½-price after 4pm. Pizzas available after noon. Open daily 7am-11pm. AmEx/MC/V. ❶

Navarro's Tapas Bar, 67 Charlotte St. (☎7637 7713; www.navarros.co.uk). ⊖Goodge St. Authentic tapas £3.50-11; 2-3 per person is plenty. Min. £7.50 per person. Open M-F noon-3pm and 6-10pm, Sa 6-10pm. AmEx/MC/V. ❸

CHELSEA

▩ **Buona Sera,** at the Jam, 289a King's Rd. (☎7352 8827). ⊖Sloane Sq., then Bus #19 or 319. The "bunk" tables here are stacked on top of each other; ascend a ladder for pasta, fish, and steak entrees (£7-12). Open M 6pm-midnight, Tu-F noon-3pm and 6pm-midnight, Sa-Su noon-midnight. Reservations recommended F-Sa. AmEx/MC/V. ❸

Chelsea Bun, 9a Limerston St. (☎7352 3635). ⊖Sloane Sq., then bus #11 or 22. Spirited and casual. Extensive vegetarian and vegan options. Sandwiches, pasta, and burgers £2.80-8. Early-bird specials M-F 7am-noon (£2.20-3.20). Sandwiches (£2.80-7) and breakfast (from £4) served until 6pm. Min. £3.50 per person during lunch, £5.50 dinner. Open M-Sa 7am-midnight, Su 9am-7pm. MC/V. ❸

THE CITY OF LONDON

Cafe Spice Namaste, 16 Prescot St. (☎7488 9242; www.cafespice.co.uk). ⊖Tower Hill or DLR: Tower Gateway. The menu helpfully explains each Goan and Parsee specialty. Meat entrees are pricey (from £15), but vegetarian meals (from £4.75) are affordable. Open M-F noon-3pm and 6:15-10:30pm, Sa 6:30-10:30pm. AmEx/MC/V. ❸

Futures, 8 Botolph Alley (☎7623 4529; www.futures-vta.net), between Botolph and Lovat Ln. ⊖Monument. London's workforce beseiges this tiny takeaway joint during the lunch hour. Vegetarian soups, salads, and entrees (£2.20-5.20) change weekly. Open M-F 8-10am and 11:30am-2:30pm. ❶

CLERKENWELL AND HOLBORN

▩ **Anexo,** 61 Turnmill St. (☎7250 3401; www.anexo.co.uk). ⊖Farringdon. This funky Spanish restaurant and bar serves up Iberian dishes, including authentic paella (£7.50-9). Happy hour M-Sa 5-7pm. Open M-F 10am-11pm, Sa 6-11:30pm, Su 4:30-11pm. Bar open 11am-2am. AmEx/MC/V. ❷

▩ **Bleeding Heart Tavern,** corner of Greville St. and Bleeding Heart Yard (☎7242 2056; www.bleedingheart.co.uk). ⊖Farringdon. Highlights include the roast suckling pig with delicately spiced apple slices (£12). Open M-F 7-10:30am, noon-2:30pm, 6-10:30pm. Upstairs pub open M-F 11:30am-11pm. AmEx/MC/V. ❸

EAST LONDON

▩ **Café 1001,** Dray Walk (☎7247 9679; www.cafe1001.co.uk). ⊖Aldgate East. Off Brick Ln. Twentysomethings lounge in the smoky, spacious upstairs and numerous outdoor tables. Fresh cakes (£2 per slice), pre-made salads (£3), sandwiches (£2.50), and outdoor barbecue, weather permitting. Nightly DJs or bands 7pm-close. Open M-W and Su 7am-11:30pm, Th-Sa 7pm-midnight. ❶

Yelo, 8-9 Hoxton Sq. (☎7729 4626; www.yelothai.com). ⊖Old St. Hip and comfortable. Industrial lighting, exposed brick, and house music shake things up. For a more formal affair, call to book a "proper" table downstairs. Pad thai, curry, and stir-fry £5. Take-out and delivery available. Open daily noon-3pm and 6-11pm. ❶

MARYLEBONE AND REGENT'S PARK

Mandalay, 444 Edgware Rd. (☎7258 3696). ⊖Edgware Rd. Burmese entrees with good vegetarian items (£4-7.90). Lunch specials are great deals. Open M-Sa noon-2:30pm and 6-10:30pm. Dinner reservations recommended. AmEx/MC/V. ❶

Patogh, 8 Crawford Pl. (☎7262 4015). ⊖Edgware Rd. This charming Persian hole-in-the-wall serves large portions of sesame-seed flatbread (£2) and freshly prepared starters (£2.50-6). Take-out available. Open daily noon-midnight. Cash only. ❷

NORTH LONDON

Gallipoli, 102 Upper St. (☎7359 0630; www.gallipolicafe.com), **Gallipoli Again,** 120 Upper St. (☎7359 1578), **Gallipoli Bazaar,** 107 Upper St. (☎7226 5333). ⊖Angel. Lebanese, North African, and Turkish deliciousness. 2-course lunch £7. Open M-Th 10:30am-11pm, F-Sa 10:30am-midnight. Reservations recommended F-Sa. MC/V. ❷

La Crêperie de Hampstead, 77 Hampstead High St. (www.hampsteadcreperie.com), metal stand on the side of the King William IV. ⊖Hampstead. A local fixture. French-speaking cooks take your order and leave you to anticipate your crepe (£3-4). Open M-Th 11:45am-11pm, F-Su 11:45am-11:30pm. Cash only. ❶

THE WEST END

▩ **Masala Zone,** 9 Marshall St. (☎7287 9966; www.realindianfood.com). ⊖Oxford Circus. South Indian favorites (£6-8), in addition to small bowls of "street food" (£3.40-5.50), and large *thali* (sampler platters; £7.50-12). Open M-F noon-2:45pm and 5:30-11pm, Sa 12:30-11pm, Su 12:30-3:30pm and 6-10:30pm. MC/V. ❷

▩ **Rock and Sole Plaice,** 47 Endell St. (☎7836 3785). ⊖Covent Garden. Self-proclaimed "master fryer" (qualifications unclear) delivers fish and chips for £9-11. Samosas (£4.50). Open M-Sa 11:30am-11:30pm, Su 11:30am-10 pm. MC/V. ❷

OTHER NEIGHBORHOODS

🖼 **George's Portobello Fish Bar,** 329 Portobello Rd. (☎8969 7895), in Notting Hill. ⊖Ladbroke Grove. George opened up here in 1961, and the fish and chips (from £7) are as good as ever. Another specialty is the barbecue ribs (£7), whose secret recipe is closely guarded. Open M-F 11am-midnight, Sa 11am-9pm, Su noon-9:30pm. ❷

Jenny Lo's Teahouse, 14 Eccleston St. (☎7259 0399), in Knightsbridge. ⊖Victoria. The small modern cafe bustles on weekdays, but the delicious *cha shao* (pork noodle soup; £6.50) and the broad selection of Asian noodles, from Vietnamese to Beijing style (£6.50-8), make eating here worth the wait. Vegetarian options. Takeaway and delivery available (min. £5). Open M-F noon-3pm and 6-10pm, Sa 6-10pm. Cash only. ❷

Cantina del Ponte, 36c Shad Thames, Butlers Wharf (☎7403 5403), in the South Bank. ⊖Tower Hill or London Bridge. 2-course Lunch *menu* £10, 3-course £14 (available M-F noon-3pm). Pizzas from £5. Entrees from £8.50. Wheelchair-accessible. Open M-Sa noon-3pm and 6-10:45pm, Su noon-3pm and 6-9:45pm. AmEx/MC/V. ❸

👁 SIGHTS

WESTMINSTER

The City of Westminster, now a borough of London, has been the seat of British power for over a thousand years. William the Conqueror was crowned in Westminster Abbey on Christmas Day, AD 1066, and his successors built the Palace of Westminster that today houses Parliament.

🖼**WESTMINSTER ABBEY.** Founded as a Benedictine monastery, Westminster Abbey has evolved into a house of kings and queens both living and dead. Almost nothing remains of St. Edward's Abbey: Henry III's 13th-century Gothic reworking created most of the grand structure you see today. A door off the east cloister leads to the **Chapter House,** the original meeting place of the House of Commons. Just north of the Abbey, **St. Margaret's Church** enjoys a peculiar status: as a part of the Royal Peculiar, it is not under the jurisdiction of the diocese of England nor the archbishop of Canterbury. Since 1614, it's been the official worshiping place of the House of Commons. *(Parliament Sq. Access Old Monastery, cloister, and garden from Dean's Yard, behind the Abbey. ⊖Westminster. Abbey ☎7654 4900, Chapter House 7222 5152; www.westminster-abbey.org. No photography. Abbey open M-Tu and Th-F 9:30am-3:45pm, W 9:30am-7pm, Sa 9:30am-1:45pm, Su open for services only. Museum open daily 10:30am-4pm. Partially wheelchair-accessible. Abbey and museum £10, students and children 11-17 £7, families of 4 £24. Services free. 1½hr. tours £5 Apr.-Oct. M-F 10, 10:30, 11am, 2, 2:30pm, Sa 10, 10:30, 11am; Oct.-Mar. M-F 10:30, 11am, 2, 2:30pm, Sa 10:30, 11am. Audio tours £4 available M-F 9:30am-3pm, Sa 9:30am-1pm. AmEx/MC/V.)*

BUCKINGHAM PALACE. The Palace is open to visitors from the very end of July to the end of September every year. Don't expect to find any insights into the Queen's personal life—the **State Rooms** are the only rooms on view, and they are used only for formal occasions. "God Save the Queen" is the rallying cry at the **Queens Gallery,** dedicated to jaw-droppingly valuable items from the Royal Collection. Detached from the palace and tour, the **Royal Mews** acts as a museum, stable, riding school, and working carriage house. The main attraction is the Queen's collection of coaches, including the Cinderella-like "Glass Coach" used to carry royal brides, including Diana, to their weddings, and the State Coaches of Australia, Ireland, and Scotland. Another highlight is the four-ton **Gold State Coach,** which can occasionally be seen wheeling around the streets in the early morning on practice runs for major events. To witness the Palace without the cost, attend a session of

Changing of the Guard. Show up well before 11:30am and stand in front of the Palace in view of the morning guards, or use the steps of the Victoria Memorial as a vantage point. *(At the end of the Mall, between Westminster, Belgravia, and Mayfair. ⊖St. James's Park, Victoria, Green Park, or Hyde Park Corner. ☎ 7766 7324; www.the-royal-collection.com. Palace open late July to late Sept. daily 9:30am-6:30pm, last admission 4:15pm. £15, students £14, children 6-17 £8.50, under 5 free, families of 5 £70. Advance booking recommended; required for disabled visitors. Queens Gallery open daily 10am-5:30pm, last admission 4:30pm. Wheelchair-accessible. £8, students £7, families £22. Royal Mews open late July to late Sept. daily 10am-5pm, last admission 4:15pm; Mar.-July and late Sept. to late Oct. M-Th and Sa-Su 11am–4pm, last admission 3:15pm. Wheelchair-accessible. £7, seniors £6, children under 17 £4.50, families £19. Changing of the Guard Apr. to late July daily, Aug.-Mar. every other day, excepting the Queen's absence, inclement weather, or pressing state functions. Free.)*

THE HOUSES OF PARLIAMENT. The Palace of Westminster has been home to both the House of Lords and the House of Commons (together known as Parliament) since the 11th century, when Edward the Confessor established his court here. Standing guard on the northern side of the building, the **Clock Tower** is famously nicknamed **Big Ben,** after the robustly proportioned Benjamin Hall—a former Commissioner of Works. "Big Ben" actually refers only to the 14-ton bell that hangs inside the tower. **Victoria Tower,** at the south end of the palace building, contains copies of every Act of Parliament since 1497. Sir Charles Barry rebuilt the tower in the 1850s after it burned down in 1834; his design won an anonymous competition, and his symbol, the portcullis, still remains the official symbol of the Houses of Parliament. A flag flying from the top indicates that Parliament is in session. When the Queen is in the building, a special royal banner is flown instead of the Union flag. *(Parliament Sq., in Westminster. Queue for both Houses forms at St. Stephen's entrance, between Old and New Palace Yards. ⊖Westminster. ☎ 08709 063 773; www.parliament.uk/visiting/visiting.cfm. UK residents can contact their MPs for tours year-round, generally M-W mornings and F. Foreign visitors may tour Aug.-Sept. Book at Abingdon Green ticket office (open mid-July) across from Palace of Westminster. Open Aug. M-Tu and F-Sa 9:15am-4:30pm, W-Th 1:15-4:30pm; Sept. M and F-Sa 9:15am-4:30pm, Tu-Th 1:15-4:30pm. 75min. tours depart every few min. £12, students £8, families of 4 £30. MC/V.)*

PARLIAMENTARY PROCEDURE. Arrive early in the afternoon to minimize waiting, which often exceeds 2hr. Keep in mind that the wait for Lords is generally shorter than the wait for Commons. To sit in on Parliament's "question time" (40min.; M-W 2:30pm, Th-F 11am) apply for tickets several weeks in advance through your embassy in London.

ST. JAMES'S PARK AND GREEN PARK. The streets leading up to Buckingham Palace are flanked by two sprawling expanses of greenery: St. James's Park and Green Park. In the middle of St. James's Park is the **St. James's Park Lake**—the lake and the surrounding grassy area are a waterfowl preserve. Across the Mall, the Green Park is the creation of Charles II, connecting Westminster and St. James. *(The Mall. ⊖St. James's Park or Green Park. Open daily 5am-midnight. Lawn chairs available, weather permitting, Mar.-Oct. 10am-6pm; June-Aug. 10am-10pm £2 for 2hr., student deal £30 for the season. Last rental 2hr. before close. Summer walks in the park some M 1-2pm, including tour of Guard's Palace and Victoria Tower Gardens. Book in advance by calling ☎ 7930 1793.)*

WESTMINSTER CATHEDRAL. Following Henry VIII's divorce from the Catholic Church, London's Catholic community remained without a cathedral until 1884, when the Church purchased a derelict prison on a former monastery site. The Neo-Byzantine building looks somewhat like a fortress and is now one of London's

BRITAIN

great religious landmarks. An elevator, well worth the fee, carries visitors up the 273 ft. bell tower for a view of Westminster, the river, and Kensington. *(Cathedral Piazza, off Victoria St.* ❸*Victoria.* ☎*7798 9055; www.westminstercathedral.org.uk. Open daily 8am-7pm. Free; suggested donation £2. Bell tower open daily 9:30am-12:30pm and 1-5pm.)*

WHITEHALL. Whitehall refers to the stretch of road connecting Trafalgar Sq. with **Parliament Square.** Toward the north end of Whitehall, **Great Scotland Yard** marks the former headquarters of the Metropolitan Police. Nearer Parliament Sq., guarded gates mark the entrance to **Downing Street.** In 1735, No. 10 was made the official residence of the First Lord of the Treasury, a position that soon became permanently identified with the Prime Minister. The Chancellor of the Exchequer traditionally resides at No. 11 and the Parliamentary Chief Whip at No. 12. When Tony Blair's family was too big for No. 10, he switched with Gordon Brown, a move that proved convenient when Brown was appointed Prime Minister in 2007. The street is closed to visitors, but if you wait, you may see the PM going to or coming from work. *(Between Trafalgar Sq. and Parliament Sq.* ❸*Westminster, Embankment, or Charing Cross.)*

THE CITY OF LONDON

▧ ST. PAUL'S CATHEDRAL. Christopher Wren's masterpiece is the 5th cathedral to occupy this site. After three designs were rejected by the bishops, Wren, with Charles II's support, started building—he had persuaded the king to let him make "necessary alterations" as work progressed, and the building that emerged in 1708 bore little resemblance to what Charles II had approved. The **Nave** can seat 2500 worshippers. The tombs, including those of Nelson, Wellington, and Florence Nightingale, are downstairs in the **crypt.** Christopher Wren lies beneath the epitaph *"Lector, si monumentum requiris circumspice"* ("Reader, if you seek his monument, look around"). To see the inside of the second-tallest freestanding **dome** in Europe (after St. Peter's in the Vatican), climb the 259 steps to the **Whispering Gallery.** From here, 119 more steps lead to the **Stone Gallery,** on the outer base of the dome, and it's another 152 to the summit's **Golden Gallery.** *(St. Paul's Churchyard.* ❸*St. Paul's.* ☎*7246 8350; www.stpauls.co.uk. Open M-Sa 8:30am-4pm; last admission 3:45pm. Dome and galleries open M-Sa 9:30am-4pm. Open for worship daily 7:15am-6pm. Partially wheelchair-accessible. Admission £9.50, students £8.50, children 7-16 £3.50; worshippers free. Group of 10 or more 50p discount per ticket. "Supertour" M-F 11, 11:30am, 1:30, 2pm; £3, students £2.50, children 7-16 £1; English only. Audio tour available in many languages daily 9am-3:30pm; £3.50, students £3.)*

ST. PAUL'S FOR POCKET CHANGE. To gain access to the Cathedral's nave for free, attend an Evensong service (45min., M-Sa 5pm). Arrive at 4:50pm to be admitted to seats in the quire.

THE TOWER OF LONDON. The turrets and towers of this multi-functional block—serving as palace, prison, royal mint, and living museum over the past 900 years—played integral role in England's history. Most travelers join one of the animated and theatrical **▧Yeoman Warders' Tours.** Queen Anne Boleyn passed through Traitor's Gate just before her death, but entering the Tower is no longer as perilous. St. Thomas's Tower begins the self-guided tour of the Medieval Palace. At the end of the **Wall Walk**—a series of eight towers—is **Martin Tower,** home to a collection of retired crowns (without the gemstones that have been recycled into the current models). The crown jewels are held in the Jewel House. With the exception of the Coronation Spoon, everything dates from after 1660, since Cromwell melted down the original booty. The centerpiece of the fortress is White Tower, which begins with the first-floor **▧Chapel of St. John the Evangelist.** Outside, Tower Green is a lovely grassy area—not so lovely, though, for those once executed there. *(Tower Hill, next to Tower Bridge. ⊖Tower Hill or DLR: Tower Gateway. ☎0870 751 5175, ticket sales 0870 756 6060; www.hrp.org.uk. Open Mar.-Oct. M 10am-6pm, Tu-Sa 9am-6pm, Su 10am-6pm; last entry 5pm; Nov.-Feb. closes daily at 5pm. Tower Green open only by Yeoman tours, after 4:30pm, or for daily services. Admission £16, students £13, 5-15 £9.50, under 5 free, families of 5 £45. Tickets sold at Tube stations; buy ahead to avoid long queues. Yeoman Warders' Tours meet near entrance; 1hr., 2 per hr. Audio tours £3.50, students £2.50.)*

TOWER BRIDGE. Not to be mistaken for its plainer sibling, **London Bridge,** Tower Bridge is in all the London-based movies. Historians and technophiles will appreciate the **Tower Bridge Exhibition,** which combines 140 ft. glass-enclosed walkways with videos of the bridge's history. *(Entrance to the Tower Bridge Exhibition is through the upriver side of the North Tower. ⊖Tower Hill or London Bridge. ☎7403 3761, for lifting schedule 7940 3984; www.towerbridge.org.uk. Open daily Apr.-Sept. 10am-6:30pm; Oct.-Mar. 9:30am-6pm. Last entry 1hr. before closing. Wheelchair-accessible. £6, students £5, 5-16 £3.)*

THE SOUTH BANK

▧ SHAKESPEARE'S GLOBE THEATRE. This incarnation of the Globe is faithful to the original. The first Globe burned down in 1613 after a 14-year run as the Bard's playhouse. Today's reconstruction had its first full season in 1997 and is the cornerstone of the International Shakespeare Globe Centre. For more info on performances, see p. 136. *(Bankside, close to the pier. ⊖Southwark or London Bridge. ☎7902 1400; www.shakespeares-globe.org. Open daily Apr.-Sept. 9am-noon and 12:30-5pm; Oct.-Apr. 10am-5pm. Wheelchair-accessible. £9, students £8, chil 5-15 £7, families of 5 £20.)*

SOUTHWARK CATHEDRAL. In the rear of the 1400-year-old nave, there are four smaller chapels; the northernmost Chapel of St. Andrew is specifically dedicated to those with HIV/AIDS. Near the center, the **archaeological gallery** is actually an excavation of a first-century Roman road. *(Montague Close. ⊖London Bridge. ☎7367 6700; www.southwark.anglican.org/cathedral. Open M-F 8am-6pm, Sa-Su 9am-6pm. Wheelchair-accessible. Admission free, suggested donation £4. Groups should book ahead; discounts available. Audio tours £5; students £4, children 5-15 £2.50. Photography £2; video £5.)*

LONDON EYE. Also known as the Millennium Wheel, at 135m the British Airways London Eye is the biggest observational wheel in the world. The ellipsoidal glass "pods" give uninterrupted views throughout each 30min. revolution. *(Jubilee Gardens, between County Hall and the Festival Hall. ⊖Waterloo. ☎087 990 8883; www.ba-london-eye.com. Open daily Oct.-May 10am-8pm, June-Sept. 10am-9pm. Wheelchair-accessible. Buy tickets at the corner of County Hall before joining the queue at the Eye. Advance booking recommended, but check the weather. £15, students £11, children under 16 £7.25.)*

 THE REAL DEAL. While the **London Eye** does offer magnificent views (particularly at night), the queues are long, and it's expensive. For equally impressive sights in a quieter atmosphere, head to **Hampstead Heath** (p. 117).

BLOOMSBURY AND MARYLEBONE

Marylebone's most famous resident (and address) never existed. 221b Baker St. was the fictional home to Sherlock Holmes, but 221 Baker St. is actually the headquarters of the Abbey National Bank. Bloomsbury's intellectual reputation was bolstered in the early 20th century when Gordon Sq. resounded with the philosophizing of the **Bloomsbury Group,** a set of intellectuals including John Maynard Keynes, Bertrand Russell, Lytton Strachey, and Virginia Woolf.

Time: 8-9hr.

Distance: 2½ mi. (4km)

When To Go: Start early morning.

Start: ⊖Tower Hill

Finish: ⊖Westminster

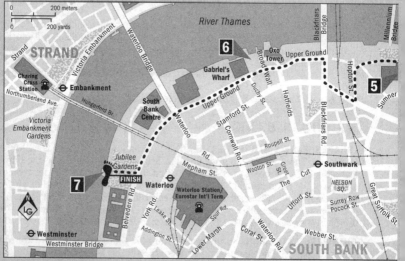

THE MILLENNIUM MILE

A stroll along the South Bank is a trip through history and back again. Across the river you will pass the timeless monuments of London's past, like the Tower of London and St. Paul's Cathedral, while next to you the round glass sphere of City Hall and the converted power facility of the Tate provide a stark, modern contrast. Whether it's a search for Shakespeare and Picasso that brings you to the South Bank, or just a hankering for a nice walk, you will find yourself rewarded.

1. TOWER OF LONDON. Begin your trek to the Tower **early** to avoid the crowds. Tours given by the Yeomen Warders meet every 1½hr. near the entrance. Listen as they expertly recount tales of royal conspiracy, treason, and murder. See the **White Tower,** once a fortress and residence of kings. Shiver at the executioner's stone on the tower green and pay your respects at the Chapel of St. Peter ad Vinculum, holding the remains of three queens. First, get the dirt on the gemstones at **Martin Tower,** then wait in line to see the **Crown Jewels.** The jewels include such glittering lovelies as the First Star of Africa, the largest cut diamond in the world (p. 148). Time: 2hr.

2. TOWER BRIDGE. An engineering wonder that puts its plainer sibling, the London Bridge, to shame. Marvel at its beauty, but skip the Tower Bridge Experience tour. Better yet, call in advance to inquire what times the Tower drawbridge is lifted (p. 150). Time: no need to stop walking; take in the mechanics as you head to the next sight.

3. DESIGN MUSEUM. On Butler's Wharf, let the Design Museum introduce you to the latest innovations in contemporary design. See what's to come in the forward-looking Review Gallery or hone in on individual designers and products in the Temporary Gallery (see p. 199). From the museum, walk along the **Queen's Walk.** To your left you will find the **HMS Belfast,** which was launched in 1938 and led the landing for D-Day, 1944 (p. 160). Time: 1hr.

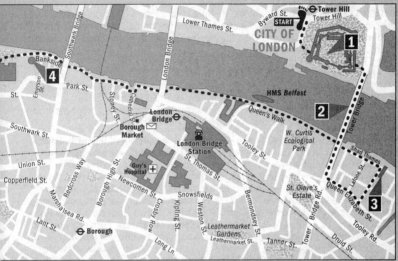

4. SHAKESPEARE'S GLOBE THEATRE. "I hope to see London once ere I die," says Shakespeare's Davy in *Henry IV*. In time, he may see it from the beautiful recreation of The Bard's most famous theater. Excellent exhibits demonstrate how Shakespearean actors dressed and the secrets of stage effects, and tell of the painstaking process of rebuilding of the theater almost 400 years after the original burned down (p. 127). You might be able to catch a matinee performance if you time your visit right. Call in advance for tour and show times. Time: 1hr. for tour; 3hr. for performance.

5. TATE MODERN. It's hard to imagine anything casting a shadow over the Globe Theatre, but the massive former Bankside Power Station does just that. One of the world's premier Modern art museums, the Tate promises a new spin on well-known favorites and works by emerging British artists. Be sure to catch one of the informative docent tours and don't forget to check out the rotating installation in the Turbine Room (p. 132). Time: 2hr.

6. GABRIEL'S WHARF. Check out the cafes, bars, and boutiques of colorful **Gabriel's Wharf.** If you missed the top floor of the Tate Modern, go to the public viewing gallery on the 8th fl. of the **OXO Tower Wharf.** On your way to the London Eye, stop by the **South Bank Centre.** Established as a primary cultural center in 1951, it now exhibits a range of music from Philharmonic extravaganzas to low-key jazz. You may even catch one of the free lunchtime or afternoon events. Call in advance for dates and times. Time: 1½hr. for schmoozing and dinner.

7. LONDON EYE. The London Eye has firmly established itself as one of London's top attractions, popular with locals and tourists alike. The Eye offers amazing 360° views from its glass pods; you may be able to see all of London lit up at sunset. Book in advance to minimize queue time (p. 127). Time: 1hr.

■**REGENT'S PARK.** This is perhaps London's most attractive and popular park, with landscapes from football-scarred fields to Italian-style formal plantings. It's all very different from John Nash's vision of wealthy villas and exclusive gardens; fortunately for us common folk, Parliament intervened in 1811 and guaranteed the space would remain open to all. (➍*Baker St., Regent's Park, Great Portland St., or Camden Town.* ☎*7486 7905, police 7706 7272; www.royalparks.org. Open daily 5am-dusk. Free.)*

BRITISH LIBRARY. Criticized during its long construction by traditionalists for being too modern and by modernists for being too traditional, the completed British Library building is unequivocally impressive. The heart of the library is underground, with 12 million books on 322km of shelving. The brick building aboveground is home to reading rooms and an ■**exhibition gallery.** (*96 Euston Rd.* ➍*Euston Sq. or King's Cross St. Pancras.* ☎*7412 7332; www.bl.uk. Open M 9:30am-6pm, Tu 9:30am-8pm, W-F 9:30am-6pm, Sa 9:30am-5pm, Su 11am-5pm. Tours of public areas M, W, F 3pm; Sa 10:30am and 3pm. Tours including one of the reading rooms Su and bank holidays 11:30am and 3pm. Wheelchair-accessible. To use reading rooms, bring 2 forms of ID, 1 with a signature and 1 with a home address. Free. Tours £8, students £7. Audio tours £4, students £3.)*

OTHER BLOOMSBURY SIGHTS. A co-founder and key advisor of **University College London**—the first in Britain to ignore race, creed, and politics in admissions and, later, the first to allow women to sit for degrees—social philosopher Jeremy Bentham still watches over his old haunts; his body has sat on display in the South Cloister since 1850, wax head and all. (*Main entrance on Gower St. South Cloister entrance through the courtyard.* ➍*Euston.* ☎*7679 2000; www.ucl.ac.uk. Quadrangle gates close at midnight; access to Jeremy Bentham ends at 6pm. Wheelchair-accessible. Free.)* Next to the British Library are the soaring Gothic spires of **St. Pancras Chambers.** Formerly housing the Midland Grand Hotel, today the gorgeous red brick building is a hollow shell being developed as apartments and a five-star hotel. (*Euston Rd. just west of the King's Cross St. Pancras Tube station.* ➍*King's Cross St. Pancras.)*

CLERKENWELL AND HOLBORN

Although mostly off limits to tourists, Clerkenwell is full of lovely buildings. The **Clerkenwell Historic Trail** passes many of them. Maps are available at **3 Things Coffee Room.** (53 Clerkenwell Close. ➍Farringdon. ☎7125 37438. Open daily 8am-8pm.)

■**THE TEMPLE.** South of Fleet St., the land upon which this compound rests belonged to the Knights Templar in the 13th century. The only remnant of that time is the round **Temple Church.** (☎*7353 3470. Hours vary depending on the week's services and are posted outside the door of the church for the coming week. Organ recitals W 1:15-1:45pm; no services Aug.-Sept.)* According to Shakespeare's *Henry VI*, the red and white flowers that served as emblems in the Wars of the Roses were plucked in **Middle Temple Garden,** south of the hall. (*Open May-Sept. M-F noon-3pm.)*

ROYAL COURTS OF JUSTICE. Straddling the official division between the City of Westminster and the City of London, this neo-Gothic structure encloses courtrooms and the Great Hall (home to Europe's largest mosaic floor) amid elaborate passageways. All courtrooms are open to the public during trials. (*Where the Strand becomes Fleet St.; rear entrance on Carey St.* ➍*Temple or Chancery Ln.* ☎*7947 6000, tours 7947 7684. Open M-F 9am-4:30pm; cases are heard 10:30am-1pm and 2-4pm. Wheelchair-accessible. Be prepared to go through a security checkpoint with metal detector. Free. Tours £6.)*

KENSINGTON AND EARL'S COURT

Nobody took much notice of Kensington before 1689, when the newly crowned William III and Mary II moved into Kensington Palace. In 1851, the Great Exhibition brought in enough money to finance museums and colleges. Now that the neighborhood is home to expensive stores like Harrods and Harvey Nichols, it's hard to imagine the days when the area was known for taverns and highwaymen.

HYDE PARK AND KENSINGTON GARDENS. Surrounded by London's wealthiest neighborhoods, Hyde Park has served as the model for city parks around the world, including Central Park in New York and Paris's Bois de Boulogne. **Kensington Gardens**, contiguous with Hyde Park and originally part of it, was created in the late 17th century when William and Mary set up house in Kensington Palace. *(Framed by Kensington Rd., Knightsbridge, Park Ln., and Bayswater Rd. ⊖Queensway, Lancaster Gate, Marble Arch, Hyde Park Corner, or High St. Kensington. ☎7298 2100; www.royalparks.org.uk. Park open daily 6am-dusk. Admission free.)* In the middle of the park is the **Serpentine,** officially known as the "Long Water West of the Serpentine Bridge." Dog-paddling tourists, rowers, and pedal boaters have made it London's busiest swimming hole. Nowhere near the water, the **Serpentine Gallery** holds contemporary art, and is free and open to the public from 10am-6pm daily. *(⊖Hyde Park Corner. ☎7262 1330. Open daily Apr.-Sept. 10am-5pm or later in good weather. £4 per person for 30min., £6 per hr.; children £1.50/2.50. Deposit may be required for large groups. Swimming at the Lido, south shore; ☎7706 3422. Open daily June-early Sept. 10am-5:30pm. Lockers and sun lounges available. £3.50, £2.80 after 4pm, students £2.50/1.60, children 80p/60p, families £8. Gallery open daily 10am-5pm. Free.)* At the northeast corner of the park, near **Marble Arch,** you can see free speech in action as proselytizers, politicos, and flat-out crazies dispense wisdom to bemused tourists at **Speaker's Corner** on Sundays, the only place in London where demonstrators can assemble without a permit.

KENSINGTON PALACE. Remodeled by Christopher Wren for William and Mary, parts of the palace are still a royal residence. Diana lived here until her death. The **Royal Ceremonial Dress Collection** features 19th-century court costumes along with the Queen's demure evening gowns and some of Diana's sexier numbers. *(Western edge of Kensington Gardens; enter through the park. ⊖High St. Kensington, Notting Hill Gate, or Queensway. ☎7937 9561; www.royalresidences.com. Open daily 10am-6pm, last entry 1hr. earlier. Wheelchair-accessible. £12, students £10, children 5-15 £6, families of 5 no more than 2 people over 15 £33. Combo passes with Tower of London or Hampton Court available. MC/V.)*

KNIGHTSBRIDGE AND BELGRAVIA

APSLEY HOUSE AND WELLINGTON ARCH. Apsley House, with the convenient address of "No. 1, London," was bought in 1817 by the Duke of Wellington. On display is his outstanding art collection, much of it given by grateful European royalty following the Battle of Waterloo. *(Hyde Park Corner. ⊖Hyde Park Corner. ☎7499 5676; www.english-heritage.org.uk/london. Open Apr.-Oct. Tu-Su 10am-5pm; Nov.-Mar. Tu-Su 10am-4pm. Wheelchair-accessible. £5.30, students £4, children 5-18 £2.70. Joint ticket with Wellington Arch £6.90/5.20/3.50. Audio tour free. MC/V.)* Across from Apsley House, the **Wellington Arch** was dedicated to the Duke in 1838. Later, to the horror of its architect, a huge statue of the Duke was placed on top. *(Hyde Park Corner. ⊖Hyde Park Corner. ☎7930 2726; www.english-heritage.org.uk/london. Open W-Su Apr.-Oct. 10am-5pm, Nov.-Mar. 10am-4pm. Wheelchair-accessible. £3.20, students with ISIC £2.40, children 5-16 £1.60. Joint tickets with Apsley House available. MC/V.)*

THE WEST END

TRAFALGAR SQUARE. The square is named in commemoration of the defeat of Napoleon's navy at Trafalgar, considered England's greatest naval victory. It has traditionally been a site for public rallies and protests. Towering over the square is the 51m granite **Nelson's Column,** which used to be one of the world's tallest displays of pigeon droppings. Now, thanks to a deep-clean sponsored by the mayor, this monument to hero Lord Nelson sparkles once again. *(⊖Charing Cross.)*

BRITAIN

ST. MARTIN-IN-THE-FIELDS. The 4th church to stand here, James Gibbs's 1726 creation is instantly recognizable: the rectangular portico building supporting a soaring steeple made it the model for countless Georgian churches America. Handel and Mozart both performed here, and the church hosts frequent concerts. In order to support the cost of keeping the church open, a surprisingly extensive and delicious cafe, book shop, and art gallery dwell in the Crypt. *(St. Martin's Ln., north-east corner of Trafalgar Sq.; crypt entrance on Duncannon St.* ⊖*Leicester Sq. or Charing Cross.* ☎ *7766 1100; www.smitf.org. Call or visit website for hours and further information.)*

SOHO. Soho is one of London's most diverse areas. **Old Compton Street** is the center of London's GLBT culture. In the 1950s, Hong Kong immigrants began moving to the blocks just north of Leicester Sq., near **Gerrard Street** and grittier **Lisle Street,** now **Chinatown.** Gaudy, brash, and world-famous, **Piccadilly Circus** is made up of four of the West End's major arteries (Piccadilly, Regent St., Shaftesbury Ave., and the Haymarket). In the middle of all the glitz stands Gilbert's famous **Statue of Eros.** *(*⊖*Piccadilly Circus.)* Lined with tour buses, overpriced clubs, fast-food restaurants, and generic cafes, **Leicester Square** is one spot Londoners go out of their way to avoid. *(*⊖*Piccadilly Circus or Leicester Sq.)* A calm in the storm, **Soho Square** is a scruffy, green patch popular with picnickers. Its removed location makes it more hospitable than Leicester. *(*⊖*Tottenham Court Rd. Park open daily 10am-dusk.)*

🏛 MUSEUMS AND GALLERIES

Centuries spent as the capital of an empire, together with a decidedly English penchant for collecting, have given London a spectacular set of museums. Art lovers, history buffs, and amateur ethnologists won't know which way to turn. And there's even better news for museum lovers: since 2002, admission to all major collections is free indefinitely in celebration of the Queen's Golden Jubilee.

MAJOR COLLECTIONS

▨**TATE MODERN.** Sir Giles Gilbert Scott's mammoth building, formerly the Bankside power station, houses the second half of the national collection (the earlier set is held in the National Gallery). The Tate Modern is probably the most popular museum in London, as well as one of the most famous modern art museums in the world. The collection is enormous while gallery space is limited—works rotate frequently. If you are dying to see a particular piece, head to the museum's computer station on the 5th floor to browse the entire collection. *(Main entrance on Bankside, on the South Bank; 2nd entrance on Queen's Walk.* ⊖*Southwark or Blackfriars. From the Southwark tube, turn left up Union, then left on Great Suffolk, then left on Holland.* ☎ *7887 8000; www.tate.org.uk. Open M-Th and Su 10am-6pm, F-Sa 10am-10pm. Free; special exhibits can be up to £10. Free tours meet on the gallery concourses: Level 3 at 11am and noon, Level 5 at 2 and 3pm. 5 types of audio tours include highlights, collection tour, architecture tour, children's tour, and the visually impaired tour; £2. Free talks M-F 1pm; meet at the concourse on the appropriate level. Wheelchair-accessible on Holland St.)*

▨**NATIONAL GALLERY.** The National Gallery was founded by an Act of Parliament in 1824, with 38 pictures displayed in a townhouse; over the years its grown to hold an enormous collection. Numerous additions have been made, the most recent (and controversial) being the massive modern Sainsbury Wing—Prince Charles described it as "a monstrous carbuncle on the face of a much-loved and elegant friend." The Sainsbury Wing holds almost all of the museum's large exhibitions as well as restaurants and lecture halls. If pressed for time, head to **Art Start** in the Sainsbury Wing, where you can design and print out a personalized tour of the paintings you want to see. Themed audio guides and family routes also available from the information desk. *(Main entrance Portico Entrance on north side of Trafalgar Sq. ⊖Charing Cross or Leicester Sq. ☎ 7747 2885; www.nationalgallery.org.uk. Wheelchair-accessible at Sainsbury Wing on Pall Mall East, Orange St., and Getty Entrance. Open M-Tu and Th-Su 10am-6pm, W 10am-9pm. Special exhibitions in the Sainsbury Wing occasionally open until 10pm. Free; some temporary exhibitions £5-10, seniors £4-8, students and children ages 12-18 £2-5. 1hr. tours start at Sainsbury Wing information desk. Tours M-F and Su 11:30am and 2:30pm, Sa 11:30am, 12:30, 2:30, 3:30pm. Audio tours free, suggested donation £4. AmEx/MC/V for ticketed events.)*

■ **NATIONAL PORTRAIT GALLERY.** The Who's Who of Britain began in 1856 and has grown to be the place to see Britain's freshest artwork along with centuries-old portraiture. It was recently bolstered by the sleek Ondaatje Wing. New facilities include an IT Gallery, with computers to search for pictures and print out a personalized tour, and a third-floor restaurant offering an aerial view of London—although the inflated prices (meals around £15) will limit most visitors to coffee. To see the paintings in historical order, take the escalator in the Ondaatje Wing to the top floor. The Tudor Gallery is especially impressive, but the paintings done since 1990 are also worth a visit. *(St. Martin's Pl., at the start of Charing Cross Rd., Trafalgar Sq. ⊖Leicester Sq. or Charing Cross. ☎ 7312 2463; www.npg.org.uk. Wheelchair-accessible on Orange St. Open M-W and Sa-Su 10am-6pm, Th-F 10am-9pm. Free; some special exhibitions free, others up to £6. Audio tours £2. Lectures Tu 3pm free, but popular events require tickets, from the information desk. Evening talks Th 7pm free-£3. Live music F 6:30pm free.)*

BRITISH MUSEUM. With 50,000 items from all corners of the globe, the magnificent collection is expansive and, although a bit difficult to navigate, definitely worth seeing. Most people don't even make it past the main floor, but they should—the galleries upstairs and downstairs are some of the best. Must sees include the Rosetta stone, which was the key in deciphering ancient Egyptian hieroglyphs, and the ancient mummies. *(Great Russell St. ⊖Tottenham Court Rd., Russell Sq., or Holborn. ☎ 7323 8299; www.thebritishmuseum.ac.uk. Great Court open Su-W 9am-6pm, Th-Sa 9am-11pm (9pm in winter); galleries open daily 10am-5:30pm, selected galleries open Th-F 10am-8:30pm. Free 30-40min. tours daily starting at 11am from the Enlightenment Desk. Tours daily 10:30am, 1, 3pm; £8, students £5; book ahead. Wheelchair-accessible. Free; £3 suggested donation. Temporary exhibitions around £5, students £3.50. Audio tours £3.50, family audio tours for 2 adults and up to 3 children £10. MC/V.)*

VICTORIA AND ALBERT MUSEUM. As the largest museum of decorative (and not-so-decorative) arts and design in the world, the V&A has over nine and a half miles of corridors open to the public, and is twice the size of the British Museum. It displays "the fine and applied arts of all countries, all styles, all periods." Unlike the British Museum, the V&A's documentation is consistently excellent. Interactive displays, hi-tech touch points, and engaging activities ensure that the goodies won't get boring. Some of the most interesting areas of the museum are the Glass Gallery, the Japanese and Korean areas with suits of armor and kimonos, and the Indian Gallery. Themed itineraries (£5) available at the desk can help streamline your visit, and **Family Trail** cards suggest kid-friendly routes through the museum. *(Main entrance on Cromwell Rd., wheelchair-accessible entrance on Exhibition Rd. ⊖South Kensington. ☎ 7942 2000; www.vam.ac.uk. Open M-Th and Sa-Su 10am-5:45pm, F 10am-10pm. Wheelchair-accessible. Free tours meet at rear of main entrance. Introductory tours daily 10:30, 11:30am, 1:30, 3:30pm, plus W 4:30pm. British gallery tours daily 12:30, 2:30pm. Talks and events meet at rear of main entrance. Free gallery talks Th 1pm and Su 3pm, 45-60min. Admission free; additional charge for some special exhibits.)*

TATE BRITAIN. Tate Britain is the foremost collection on British art from 1500 to the present, including pieces from foreign artists working in Britain and Brits working abroad. There are four Tate Galleries in England; this is the original Tate, opened in 1897 to house Sir Henry Tate's collection of "modern" British art and later expanded to include a gift from famed British painter J.M.W. Turner. Turner's donation of 282 oils and 19,000 watercolors can make the museum feel like one big tribute to the man. The annual and always controversial **Turner Prize** for contemporary visual art is still given here. Four contemporary British artists are nominated for the £40,000 prize; their short-listed works go on show from late October through late January. The Modern British Art Gallery, featuring works by Vanessa Bell and Francis Bacon, is also worth a look. (*Millbank, near Vauxhall Bridge, in Westminster. ⊖Pimlico. Information ☎ 7887 8008, M-F exhibition booking 7887 8888; www.tate.org.uk. Open daily 10am-5:50pm, last admission 5pm. Wheelchair-accessible via Clore Wing. Free; special exhibitions £7-11. Audio tours free. Free tours. Regular events include "Painting of the Month Lectures" (15min.) M 1:15pm and Sa 2:30pm; occasional "Friday Lectures" F 1pm.*)

OTHER MUSEUMS AND GALLERIES

▨ **Courtauld Institute,** Somerset House, Strand, Clerkenwell and Holborn (☎ 7420 9400; www.courtauld.ac.uk). ⊖Charing Cross. Small, outstanding collection. 14th- to 20th-century abstractions, focusing on Impressionism. Cézanne's *The Card Players*, Manet's *A Bar at the Follies Bergères*, and van Gogh's *Self Portrait with Bandaged Ear*. Open daily 10am-6pm. £6.50, students £6. Free M 10am-2pm.

▨ **Cabinet War Rooms,** Clive Steps, Westminster (☎ 7930 6961; www.iwm.org.uk). ⊖Westminster. Churchill and his strategists lived and worked underground here from 1939 to 1945. Highlights include the room with the top-secret transatlantic hotline—the official story was that it was Churchill's personal toilet. Open daily 9:30am-6pm. £10, students £8. MC/V.

British Library Galleries, 96 Euston Rd. (☎ 7412 7332; www.bl.uk). ⊖King's Cross. A stunning display of texts from the 2nd-century *Unknown Gospel* to The Beatles' hand-scrawled lyrics. Other highlights include Joyce's handwritten *Finnegan's Wake*, and pages from da Vinci's notebooks. Open M and W-F 9:30am-6pm, Tu 9:30am-8pm, Sa 9:30am-5pm, Su 11am-5pm. Wheelchair-accessible. Free. Audio tours £4, students £2.50.

Science Museum, Exhibition Rd., Kensington (☎ 08708 704 868; www.sciencemuseum.org.uk.). ⊖South Kensington. A mix of state-of-the-art interactive displays and priceless historical artifacts, encompassing all forms of technology. Daily demonstrations and workshops in the basement galleries and IMAX theater. Open daily 10am-6pm. Free.

Natural History Museum, on Cromwell Rd., Kensington (☎ 7942 5000; www.nhm.ac.uk). ⊖South Kensington. The Natural History Museum is home to an array of minerals and stuffed animals. Highlights include a suspended blue whale and the colossal dinosaur gallery. Open M-Sa 10am-5:50pm, Su 11am-5:50pm. Free.

Museum of London, London Wall, The City of London (☎ 0870 444 3851; www.museumoflondon.org.uk). ⊖Barbican. Enter through the Barbican. The collection traces the history of London from its foundations to the present day, cleverly incorporating adjacent ruins. Open M-Sa 10am-5:50pm, Su noon-5:50pm. Free.

Whitechapel Art Gallery, Whitechapel High St. (☎ 7522 7888; www.whitechapel.org). ⊖Aldgate East. At the forefront of the East End's art scene, Whitechapel hosts excellent, often controversial, shows of contemporary art. Th nights bring music, poetry readings, and film screenings. Open Tu-W and F-Su 11am-6pm, Th 11am-9pm. Wheelchair-accessible. Gallery may close between installations; call ahead. Free.

🎵 ENTERTAINMENT

Although West End ticket prices are sky high and the quality of some shows questionable, the city that brought the world Shakespeare, the Sex Pistols, and Andrew Lloyd Webber still retains its originality and theatrical edge.

CINEMA

Leicester Square holds premieres a day before movies hit the city's chains. The dominant cinema chain is **Odeon** (☎08712 241 999; www.odeon.co.uk). Tickets to West End cinemas cost ₤9-13; weekday matinees are cheaper. For less mainstream offerings, try the ⬛**Electric Cinema**, 191 Portobello Rd., for the combination of baroque stage splendor and the buzzing effects of a big screen. Try to get a luxury armchair or two-seat sofa. (⊖Ladbroke Grove. ☎ 7908 9696; www.the-electric.co.uk. Front 3 rows M ₤5, Tu-Su ₤10; regular tickets M ₤7.50, Tu-Su ₤13; 2-seat sofa M ₤20, Tu-Su ₤30. Double bills Su 2pm ₤5-20. Wheelchair-accessible. Box office open M-Sa 9am-8:30pm, Su 10am-8:30pm. MC/V.) **Riverside Studios**, Crisp Rd., shows a wide range of excellent foreign and classic films. (⊖Hammersmith. ☎8237 1111; www.riversidestudios.co.uk. ₤6.50, students ₤5.50.) The **National Film Theatre (NFT)** screens a wide array of films—six movies hit the three screens every evening at around 6pm (South Bank, underneath Waterloo Bridge. ⊖Waterloo, Embankment, or Temple. ☎7928 3232; www.bfi.org.uk/nft. ₤7.50, students ₤5.70.)

COMEDY

Summertime visitors should note that London empties of comedians in **August**, when most head to Edinburgh for the annual festivals (p. 181). **July** brings comedians trying out material; check *TimeOut* or a newspaper. ⬛**Comedy Store**, 1a Oxendon St., is the UK's top comedy club and sower of the seeds that gave rise to *Ab Fab*, *Whose Line is it Anyway?*, and *Blackadder*. (⊖Piccadilly Circus. ☎7839 6642, tickets 08700 602 340; www.thecomedystore.biz. Tu "Cutting Edge" (current events-based satire), W and Su Comedy Store Players improv, Th-Sa standup. Shows daily 8pm, plus F-Sa midnight. 18+. Tu "Cutting Edge," W and Su Comedy Store Players improv, Th-Sa standup. Shows Su-Th 8pm, F-Sa 8pm and midnight. 18+. Tu-W, F midnight, Su ₤13, students ₤8. Th-F early show and Sa ₤15. Box office open Tu-Th and Su 6:30-9:30pm, F-Sa 6:30pm-1:30am. M hours vary. AmEx/MC/V.) North London's **Canal Cafe Theatre**, Delamere Terr., above the Bridge House pub, is one of the few venues to specialize in sketch, as opposed to stand-up. (⊖Warwick Ave. ☎7289 6054; www.canalcafetheatre.com Shows W-Sa 7:30, 9:30pm; ₤5, students ₤4. Newsrevue ₤9, students ₤7. ₤1 membership included in price.)

MUSIC

CLASSICAL

Barbican Hall, Silk St. (☎0845 1216827; www.barbican.org.uk), in City of London. ⊖Barbican or Moorgate. A multi-function venue, the hall is home to a library, theater, and art gallery. The resident **London Symphony Orchestra** plays here; the hall also hosts concerts by international orchestras, jazz artists, and world-class musicians. Call ahead for tickets, especially for popular events. The online and phone box office sometimes have good last-minute options. Orchestra tickets £10-35. AmEx/MC/V.

English National Opera, London Coliseum, St. Martin's Ln. (☎7632 8300; www.eno.org), in Covent Garden. ⊖Charing Cross or Leicester Sq. All performances in English. Box office open M-Sa 10am-8pm. Discounted tickets available 3hr. before show; balcony (£8-10), upper circle (£10), or dress circle (£20). Call to verify daily availability; however, tickets are usually available. Wheelchair-accessible. AmEx/MC/V.

Holland Park Theatre, Holland Park (box office ☎08452 309 769; www.operahollandpark.com), in Kensington and Earl's Court. ⊖High St. Kensington or Holland Park. Outdoor performance space in the ruins of Holland House. Performances June-early Aug. Tu-Sa 7:30pm. Box office in the Old Stable Block; open late Mar.-early Aug. M-Sa 10am-6pm or 30min. after curtain. Tickets £21, £38 (£35 for students during select performances), and £43. Special allocation of tickets for wheelchair users. MC/V.

BRITAIN

JAZZ

■ **Spitz,** 109 Commercial St. (☎ 7392 9032; www.spitz.co.uk), in East London. ❍Liverpool St. Fresh range of music, from klezmer and jazz to rap. Profits to charity. Cover free to £15. Open M-W 10:30am-midnight, Th-Sa 10:30am-1am, Su 4-10:30pm. MC/V.

■ **Jazz Café,** 5 Parkway (☎ 7344 0044; www.jazzcafe.co.uk), in North London. ❍Camden Town. Shows can be pricey, but with a top roster of jazz, hip-hop, funk, and Latin performers (9pm, £15-30). DJs spin F-Sa after shows to 2am. Wheelchair-accessible. Cover F-Sa after show £11, with flyer £6. Open daily 7pm-2am. AmEx/MC/V.

Ronnie Scott's, 47 Frith St. (☎ 7439 0747; www.ronniescotts.co.uk), in **Soho.** ❍Tottenham Court Rd. or Leicester Sq. London's oldest and most famous jazz club, having hosted everyone from Dizzy Gillespie to Jimi Hendrix. Table reservations essential for big-name acts; limited unreserved standing room. If it's sold out, try coming back at the end of the main act's first set. Box office open M-F 11am-6pm, Sa noon-6pm. Club open M-Sa 6pm-3am, Su 6pm-midnight. Tickets generally £26. AmEx/MC/V.

POP AND ROCK

■ **The Water Rats,** 328 Grays Inn Rd., in Bloomsbury. (☎ 7837 7269; www.plummusic.com for the music gigs). ❍King's Cross St. Pancras. Cafe by day, stomping ground for top new talent by night (from 8pm). Crowd varies with the music. Cover £5-6, with band flyer £4-5. Music M-Sa 8pm-late; headliner 9:45pm. AmEx/MC/V; min. £7.

Carling Academy, Brixton, 211 Stockwell Rd. (☎ 7771 3000, tickets 0870 771 2000; www.brixton-academy.co.uk), in South London. ❍Brixton. Named *TimeOut's* "Live Venue of the Year" in 2004, and was *NME's* "Best Live Venue" in 2005. Order tickets online, by phone, or go to the Carling Academy, Islington box office. (16 Parkfield Street, Islington. Open M-Sa noon-4pm.) Tickets generally £5-30. AmEx/MC/V.

London Astoria (LA1), 157 Charing Cross Rd. (☎ 7434 9592, 24hr. tickets 0870 060 3777; www.londonastoria.com), in Soho. ❍Tottenham Ct. Rd. Formerly a pickle factory and strip club, this 2000-person venue now caters to rock fans and gay clubbers. M and Th-Sa G-A-Y club nights. Box office open M-F 10am-6pm, Sa 10am-5pm. MC/V.

THEATER

London's West End is dominated by musicals and plays that run for years, if not decades. For a list of shows and discount tickets, head to the **tkts** booth in Leicester Sq. (❍Leicester Sq. www.tkts.co.uk. Most shows £20-30; up to £2.50 booking fee per ticket. Open M-Sa 10am-7pm, Su noon-3pm. MC/V.)

REPERTORY

■ **Shakespeare's Globe Theatre,** 21 New Globe Walk (☎ 7401 9919; www.shakespeares-globe.org), in South Bank. ❍London Bridge. Stages plays by Shakespeare and his contemporaries. Choose from 3 covered tiers of wooden benches or brave the elements as a "groundling." Wheelchair-accessible. Performances mid-May to early Oct. Tu-Sa 7:30pm, Su 6:30pm; June-Sept. also Tu-Sa 2pm, Su 1pm. Box office open M-Sa 10am-6pm, 8pm on performance days. Seats from £12, students from £10; standing £5.

National Theatre, South Bank (☎ 7452 3400, box office 7452 3000; www.nationaltheatre.org.uk), in South Bank. ❍Waterloo. Laurence Olivier founded the National Theatre in 1976, and it has been at the forefront of British theater ever since. Wheelchair-accessible. Box office open M-Sa 10am-7:45pm. Complicated pricing scheme; contact box office for details. Tickets typically start at £10. AmEx/MC/V.

"OFF-WEST END"

▨ **The Almeida,** Almeida St. (☎7359 4404; www.almeida.co.uk), North London. ❺Angel or Highbury and Islington. Top fringe theater in London. Wheelchair-accessible. Shows M-F 7:30pm, Sa 3 and 7:30pm. Tickets from £10. Student tickets available. MC/V.

Donmar Warehouse, 41 Earlham St. (☎08700 606 624; www.donmarwarehouse.com), in Covent Garden. ❺Covent Garden. Artistic director Sam Mendes transformed this gritty space into one of the best theaters in England. Tickets £13-29; student standby 30min. before curtain, £12 (when available); £7.50 standing-room tickets available day of, once performance sells out. Box office open M-Sa 10am-7:30pm. AmEx/MC/V.

Royal Academy of Dramatic Arts (RADA), 62-64 Gower St. (☎7636 7076; www.rada.org), entrance on Malet St.; in Bloomsbury. ❺Goodge St. Britain's most famous drama school has 3 on-site theaters. £3-10, students £2-8. Regular events during the academic year include plays, music, and readings M-Th 7 or 7:30pm (some free, others up to £4). Box office open M-F 10am-6pm, on performance days 10am-7:30pm. AmEx/MC/V.

▣ SHOPPING

London has long been considered one of the fashion capitals of the world. Unfortunately, the city features as many underwhelming chain stores as it does one-of-a-kind boutiques. The truly budget-conscious should forget buying altogether and stick to window-shopping in **Knightsbridge** and on **Regent Street.** Vintage shopping in **Notting Hill** is also a viable alternative; steer clear of **Oxford Street,** where so-called vintage clothing was probably made in 2002 and marked up 200%.

DEPARTMENT STORES

Harrods, 87-135 Brompton Rd. (☎7730 1234; www.harrods.com), in Knightsbridge and Belgravia. ❺Knightsbridge. The only thing bigger than the store is the mark-up on the goods—no wonder only tourists and oil sheikhs actually shop here. Wheelchair-accessible. Open M-Sa 10am-8pm, Su noon-6pm. AmEx/MC/V.

Harvey Nichols, 109-125 Knightsbridge (☎7235 5000; www.harveynichols.com), in Knightsbridge. ❺Knightsbridge. Rue St-Honoré and Fifth Ave. rolled into 5 fl. of fashion. Wheelchair-accessible. Open M-Sa 10am-8pm, Su noon-6pm. AmEx/MC/V.

Fortnum & Mason, 181 Piccadilly (☎7734 8040; www.fortnumandmason.co.uk), in the West End. ❺Green Park or Piccadilly Circus. Gourmet department store. Open M-Sa 10am-6:30pm, Su noon-6pm (food hall and patio restaurant only). AmEx/MC/V.

STREET MARKETS

Portobello Road Markets includes foods, antiques, secondhand clothing, and jewelry. To see it all, come Friday or Saturday when everything is sure to be open. (❺Notting Hill Gate; also Westbourne Park and Ladroke Grove. Stalls set own hours. Generally open Th 8am-1pm, F 9am-5pm, and Sa 6:30am-5pm.) ▨**Camden Passage Market** is more for looking than for buying—London's premier antique shops line these charming alleys. (Islington High St., in North London. ❺Angel. Turn right from the Tube; it's the alley that starts behind "The Mall" antiques gallery on Upper St. Open W 7:30am-6pm, Sa 9am-6pm; some stores open daily, but W is the best day to go.) Its overrun sibling **Camden Markets** (☎7969 1500) mostly includes cheap clubbing gear and tourist trinkets; avoid the canal areas. The best bet is to stick with the **Stables Market,** farthest north from the Tube station. (❺Camden Town. Make a sharp right out of the Tube station to reach Camden High St., where most of the markets start. Many stores open daily 9:30am-6pm; Stables open F-Su.) Colorful, noisy **Brixton Market** has London's best selection of Afro-Caribbean fruits, veggies, spices, and fish. (Along Electric Ave., Pope's Rd., and Brixton Station Rd., and inside markets in Granville Arcade and Market Row; in South London. ⊖Brixton. Open M-Tu and Th-Sa 7am-7pm, W 7am-3:30pm.) Formerly a wholesale vegetable market, **▧Spitalfields** has become the best of the East End markets. On Sundays, the food shares space with rows of clothing by 25-30 independent local designers. (Commercial St., in East London. ⊖Shoreditch (during rush hour), Liverpool St., or Aldgate East. Crafts market open M-F 11am-3:30pm, Su 10am-5pm. Antiques market open Th 9am-5pm. Organic market open F and Su 10am-5pm.) **Petticoat Lane Market,** located on Petticoat Ln., off of Commercial St., it sells everything from clothes to crafts, and is open M 8am-2pm and Tu-F 9am-4pm. Crowds can be overwhelming; head to the **Sunday (Up) Market** for similar items in a calmer environment. (☎7770 6100; www.bricklanemarket.com. Housed in a portion of the old Truman Brewery just off Hanbury St., in East London. ⊖Shoreditch or Aldgate East. Open Su 10am-5pm.)

▧ NIGHTLIFE

First-time visitors may initially head directly to the **West End,** drawn by the flashy lights and pumping music of Leicester Sq. Be warned, though, that nightlife here is not the definitive voice of Londoners; for a more authentic experience, head to the **East End** or **Brixton.** Soho's **Old Compton Street,** though, is still the center of GLBT nightlife. Before heading out for the evening, make sure to plan **Night Bus** travel. Listings open past 11pm include local Night Bus routes. Night Buses in the West End are ubiquitous—head to Trafalgar Sq., Oxford St., or Piccadilly Circus.

PUBS

▧ **Fitzroy Tavern,** 16 Charlotte St. (☎7580 3714), in Bloomsbury. ⊖Goodge St. A perfect pub for sunny days and sipping beer on the street outside, this place attracts artists, writers, locals, and students in droves. W 8:30pm comedy night (£5). Open M-Sa 11am-11pm, Su noon-10:30pm. MC/V.

The Jerusalem Tavern, 55 Britton St. (☎7490 4281; www.stpetersbrewery.co.uk), in Clerkenwell. ⊖Farringdon. A broad selection of ales (£2.40), including grapefruit, cinnamon, and apple, rewards the adventuresome. Open M-F 11am-11pm. AmEx/MC/V.

Ye Olde Cheshire Cheese, Wine Office Court. (☎7353 6170; www.yeoldecheshirecheese.com), in Holborn. By 145 Fleet St., not to be confused with The Cheshire Cheese on the other side of Fleet St. Entrance in alleyway. ⊖Blackfriars or St. Paul's. Dating from 1667, the Cheese was once a haunt of Samuel Johnson, Charles Dickens, Mark Twain, and Theodore Roosevelt. Open M-Sa 11am-11pm, Su noon-6pm. Cellar Bar open M-Th noon-2:30pm and 5:30-11pm, F noon-2:30pm. Chop Room open M-F noon-9:30pm, Sa noon-2:30pm and 6-9:30pm, Su noon-5pm. Johnson Room open M-F noon-2:30pm and 7-9:30pm. AmEx/MC/V.

BARS

▧ **Lab,** 12 Old Compton St. (☎7437 7820; www.lab-townhouse.com), in the West End. ⊖Leicester Sq. or Tottenham Court Rd. With restrooms for "bitches" and "bastards," the only thing this cocktail bar takes seriously is its stellar drink menu. DJs spin house and funk from 8pm nightly. Open M-Sa 4pm-midnight, Su 4-10:30pm. AmEx/MC/V.

Bar Kick, 127 Shoreditch High St. (☎7739 8700), in East London. ⊖Old St. The dozens of flags on the ceiling add even more international flavor to the European-style food and music. Wheelchair-accessible. Open M-W noon-11pm, Th-Sa noon-midnight, Su noon-7pm. Kitchen open M-F noon-3:30pm and 6-10pm, Sa-Su all day. AmEx/MC/V.

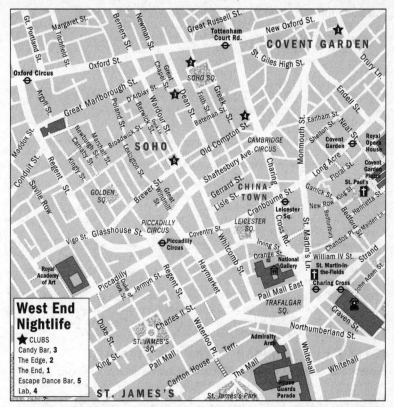

West End Nightlife

★ CLUBS
Candy Bar, **3**
The Edge, **2**
The End, **1**
Escape Dance Bar, **5**
Lab, **4**

Vibe Bar, 91-95 Brick Ln. (☎7247 3479; www.vibe-bar.co.uk), in East London. ⊖Aldgate East or Liverpool St. Night Bus: hub at Liverpool St. Station. Dance to hip-hop, soul, acoustic, and jazz. Pint £3. DJs spin M-Sa from 7pm, Su from 6pm. Cover F-Sa after 8pm £3.50. Open Su-Th 11am-11:30pm, F-Sa 11am-1am. Cash only; ATM in bar.

CLUBS

▨ **Ministry of Sound,** 103 Gaunt St. (☎7378 6528; www.ministryofsound.co.uk), in the South Bank. ⊖Elephant and Castle; take the exit for South Bank University. Night Bus #N35, 133, 343. Mecca for serious clubbers worldwide. Dress code casual, but famously unsmiling door staff make it prudent to err on the side of smartness. Cover F £12, Sa £15.

The End, 16a West Central St. (☎7419 9199; www.endclub.com), in the West End. ⊖Tottenham Ct. Rd. Cutting edge clubbers' Eden; theme nights online. Wheelchair-accessible. Cover M £6; W £5-6; Th £6-8; F £10-13; Sa £16. Open M 10pm-3am, W 10:30pm-3am, Th-F 10pm-4am, Sa 6pm-7am. AmEx/MC/V.

Fabric, 77a Charterhouse St. (☎7336 8898; www.fabriclondon.com), in Clerkenwell. ⊖Farringdon. Night Bus #242. This club is deep underground with 5 bars, 3 rooms. F "Fabriclive"; Su "DTPM Polysexual Night" (☎7749 1199; www.blue-cube.net). Wheelchair-accessible. Get there before 11pm on Saturday to avoid lines. Cover F £12; Sa after 11pm £15. Open F 9:30pm-5am, Sa 10pm-7am, Su 10pm-5am. AmEx/MC/V.

Notting Hill Arts Club, 21 Notting Hill Gate (☎ 7598 5226; www.nottinghill-artsclub.com), in Notting Hill. ⊖Notting Hill Gate. Night Bus #N94, 148, 207, 390. Unlabeled and unmarked (but right next to the Tex-Mex Tapas Bar). Not touristy and very chill. Later in the night 1-in, 1-out policy. Cover Th-Sa after 8pm £5-7. Open M-F 6pm-2am, Sa 4pm-2am, Su 4pm-1am. MC/V.

GLBT NIGHTLIFE

Many venues have Gay and Lesbian nights on a rotating basis. Check **TimeOut** and look for flyers/magazines floating around Soho: **The Pink Paper** (free from news-agents) and **Boyz** (www.boyz.co.uk; free in gay bars and clubs).

▨ **The Edge,** 11 Soho Sq. (☎ 7439 1313; www.edge.uk.com), in the West End. ⊖Oxford Circus or Tottenham Court Rd. A chill, friendly gay and lesbian drinking spot. Piano bar Tu-Sa, DJs and dancing Th-Sa. Cover Th-Sa after 10pm £2. Open M-Sa noon-1am, Su noon-11pm. MC/V.

▨ **The Black Cap,** 171 Camden High St. (☎ 7428 2721; www.theblackcap.com), in North London. ⊖Camden Town. North London's most popular gay bar and cabaret is always buzzing. Mixed crowd. Cover for downstairs M-Th and Su before 11pm £2, 11pm-close £3; F-Sa before 11pm £3, 11pm-close £4. Open M-Th noon-2am, F-Sa noon-3am, Su noon-1am. Kitchen open noon-10pm.

Escape Dance Bar, 10A Brewer St. (☎ 7731 2626; www.kudosgroup.com), in the West End. ⊖Leicester Sq. Dance to the latest pop hits in an enjoyably cramped space. A video DJ plays tunes with big, bright screens from 8pm to 3am daily. Open Tu-Sa 4pm-3am. AmEx/MC/V.

Candy Bar, 4 Carlisle St. (☎ 7494 4041; www.thecandybar.co.uk), in the West End. ⊖Tottenham Court Rd. or Oxford Circus. This drinking spot is the place for lesbian entertainment. Stripteases, DJs, and popular dance nights. W karaoke. Cover F-Sa after 9pm £5. Open M-Th 5-10:30pm, F-Sa 3pm-2am, Su 3-10:30pm. MC/V.

⚄ LET'S GO TO LONDON: LUTON AND STANSTED

London Luton Airport (LTN; ☎ 1582 405 100; www.london-luton.co.uk), 50km north of London, is a budget airline hub for **easyJet, Ryanair,** and **Wizz Air.** First Capital Connect (☎ 0845 026 4700; www.firstcapitalconnect.co.uk) and Midland Mainline (☎ 0870 010 1296; www.midlandmainline.com) run **trains** between London King's Cross and Luton (30min.-1hr., 3-4 per hr., £10-20). Easybus (www.easybus.co.uk) and National Express (☎ 08705 808 080; www.nationalexpress.com) operate **buses** between London Victoria and Luton (1¼hr., 2-3 per hr., from £2).

London Stansted Airport (STN; ☎ 0870 000 0303; www.stanstedairport.com), 48km northeast of London, is the main hub for **Ryanair** and also serves **easyJet** and **Wizz Air.** The Stansted Express (☎ 0845 600 7245; www.website.com) train shuttles between London Liverpool and Stansted (45min., 4 per hr., £15-24). Easybus runs buses between London Baker St. and Stansted and National Express runs from London Victoria (1hr., 3-6 per hr., from £2).

⚄ DAYTRIP FROM LONDON

▨ **ROYAL BOTANICAL GARDENS, KEW.** In the summer of 2003, UNESCO announced the Royal Botanical Gardens as a World Heritage site—a privilege shared by many of the historic sights in London. The three conservatories are at the center of the collection. The steamy Victorian Palm House boasts *Enceph-alartos Altensteinii*, "The Oldest Pot Plant In The World"; while the Princess of Wales Conservatory houses 10 different climate zones, from rainforest to desert, including two devoted entirely to orchids. Low-season visitors will not be disappointed—the Woodland Glade is renowned for displays of autumn color. Close to the Thames in the northern part of the gardens, newly renovated Kew Palace is a modest red-brick affair used by royalty on Garden visits, and which is now open to the public for the first time in 200 years. Seventeenth-century medicinal plants flourish in the stunning Queen's Garden. *(Kew, on the south bank of the Thames. Main entrance and Visitors Center are at Victoria Gate, nearest the Tube. Go up the white stairs that go above the station tracks, and walk straight down the road. ⊖Kew Gardens (zone 3). ☎8332 5000; www.kew.org. Open Apr.-Aug. M-F 9:30am-6:30pm, Sa-Su 9:30am-7:30pm; Sept.-Oct. daily 9:30am-6pm; Nov.-Jan. daily 9:30am-4:15pm. Last admission 30min. before close. Glasshouses close Apr.-Oct. 5:30pm; Nov.-Feb. 3:45pm. £13, students £11, children under 17 free; 45min. before close £11. Free 1hr. walking tours daily 11am and 2pm start at Victoria Gate Visitors Center. "Explorer" hop-on, hop-off shuttle makes 40min. rounds of the gardens; 1st shuttle daily 11am, last 4pm; £3.50, children under 17 £1. Free 1hr. "Discovery Bus" tours for mobility-impaired daily 11am and 2pm; booking required; free.)*

SOUTHERN ENGLAND

History and myth shroud Southern England. Cornwall, the alleged birthplace of King Arthur, was the last stronghold of the Celts in England, but traces of even older Neolithic communities linger in the stone circles their builders left behind. In WWII, German bombings uncovered long-buried evidence of an invasion by Caesar, whose Romans dotted the countryside with settlements. William the Conqueror left his mark in the form of awe-inspiring castles and cathedrals. Apart from this pomp and circumstance is another, less palpable, presence: the voices of British literati still seem to echo above the sprawling pastures and seaside cliffs.

CANTERBURY   ☎01227

Archbishop Thomas Becket met his demise at ◪**Canterbury Cathedral** in 1170 after an irate Henry II asked, "Will no one rid me of this troublesome priest?" Later, in his famed *Canterbury Tales*, Chaucer caricatured the pilgrims who traveled the road from London to England's most famous execution site. (☎762 862; www.canterbury-cathedral.org. Cathedral open Easter-Sept. M-Sa 9am-6:30pm, Su 12:30-2:30pm and 4:30-5:30pm; Oct.-Easter M-Sa 9am-5pm, Su 12:30-2:30pm and 4:30-5:30pm. 1¼hr. tours M-Sa 3 per day; check nave or welcome center for times. Evensong M-F 5:30pm, Sa-Su 3:15pm. £6.50, students £5. Tours £4/3. 40min. audio tour £3.50/2.50.) The skeletons of arches and crumbling walls are all that remain of **Saint Augustine's Abbey,** outside the city wall near the cathedral. St. Augustine is buried under a humble pile of rocks. (☎767 345. Open Apr.-Sept. daily 10am-6pm; Oct.-Mar. W-Su 10am-4pm. £4, students £3.) England's first Franciscan friary, **Greyfriars,** 6A Stour St., has quiet riverside gardens. (☎462 395. Open Easter-Sept. M-Sa 2-4pm. Free.) **The Canterbury Tales,** on St. Margaret's St., recreates Chaucer's medieval England with audio narration, ambient lighting and wax characters. The smell isn't the guy next you—the facility pipes in "authentic" stenches. (☎479 227; www.canterburytales.org.uk. Open daily July-Aug. 9:30am-5pm; Mar.-June and Sept.-Oct. 10am-5pm; Nov.-Feb. 10am-4:30pm. £7.30, students £6.30.)

    B&Bs are around **High Street** and on **New Dover Road.** Ten minutes from the city center, **Kipps Independent Hostel ❶,** 40 Nunnery Fields, is a century-old townhouse with modern amenities. (☎786 121. Kitchen available. Laundry £3. Internet £2 per hr. If there are no vacancies, ask to set up a tent in the garden. Key deposit £10. Dorms £14; singles £19; doubles £33. MC/V.) Share sizzling steak fajitas (£22) and grab your own margarita (£6) at **Cafe des Amis du Mexique ❷,** St. Dunstan's St., home to inspired Mexican dishes in a funky cantina setting. (☎464 390. Entrees £5-10. Open M-Sa noon-10:30pm, Su noon-9:30pm. AmEx/MC/V.) **Coffee & Corks,** 13 Palace St., is a cafe-bar with a cool, bohemian feel. (☎457 707. Tea £1.50. Mixed

BRITAIN

drinks £4. Bottles of wine £10. Free Wi-Fi. Open daily noon-midnight. MC/V.) **Trains** run from East Station, off Castle St., to London Victoria (1¾hr., 2 per hr., £20) and Cambridge (3hr., 2 per hr., £33). Trains from West Station, Station Rd. W, off St. Dunstan's St., go to Central London (1½hr., 1 per hr., £17) and Brighton (3hr., 3 per hr., £16). National Express (☎08705 808 080) **buses** run from St. George's Ln. to London (2hr., 2 per hr., £14). The **TIC** is in the Buttermarket, 12-13 Sun St. (☎378 100; www.visitcanterbury.co.uk. Open Easter-Christmas M-Sa 9:30am-5pm, Su 10am-4pm; Christmas-Easter M-Sa 10am-4pm.) **Postal Code:** CT1 2BA.

BRIGHTON ☎01273

Brighton (pop. 250,000) has been one of Britain's largest seaside resorts for the last three centuries. King George IV came to the city in 1783 and enjoyed the anything-goes atmosphere so much that he made it his headquarters for debauchery (the Royal Pavilion). The rumpus continues, and today, Brighton is still the unrivaled home of the "dirty weekend," sparkling with a tawdry luster all its own. The extravagant **Royal Pavilion,** on Pavilion Parade, next to Old Steine, is a touch of the Far East in the heart of England with Taj Mahal-style architecture. (☎292 880. Open daily Apr.-Sept. 9:30am-5:45pm; Oct.-Mar. 10am-5:15pm. Tours daily 11:30am and 2:30pm; £1.60. Pavilion £6, students £4.30.) Around the corner on Church St. stands the **Brighton Museum and Art Gallery,** showcasing Art Nouveau and Art Deco pieces, and an exhibit that thoroughly explains the phrase "dirty weekend." (☎292 882. Open Tu 10am-7pm, W-Sa 10am-5pm, Su 2-5pm. Free.) Before heading to the **beach** and piers, visit the novelty shops and cafes of the **North Laines,** off Trafalgar St.

West of West Pier along King's Rd. Arches, ▧**Baggies Backpackers ❶,** 33 Oriental Pl., is a social hostel where parties on "Baggies Beach" are common. Book ahead, especially on weekends. (☎733 740. Co-ed bathrooms. Dorms £13; 1 double £35. Cash only.) **Food for Friends ❷,** 17a-18a Prince Albert St., serves a decadent after-noon tea (£5.50). Entrees (£8-11) draw on Indian and East Asian cuisines. (☎202 310. Open M-Th and Su noon-10pm, F-Sa noon-10:30pm. AmEx/MC/V.) Buy grocer-ies at **Somerfield,** 6 St. James's St. (☎570 363. Open M-Sa 8am-10pm, Su 11am-5pm.)

▧**Fortune of War,** 157 King's Rd. Arches, is a beachfront bar shaped like a 19th-century ship hull. (☎205 065. Pints £3.10. Open daily noon until they feel like clos-ing.) Most **clubs** are open Monday through Saturday 9pm-2am; after close, the party moves to the shore. **Audio,** 10 Marine Parade, is the city's nightlife fixture, with two floors of debauchery and a mix of music. (☎606 906; www.audiobrigh-ton.com. Cover M-Th £3-4, F £5, Sa £7. Open M-Sa 10pm-2am.) **The Beach,** 171-181 King's Rd. Arches, is packed with weekenders dancing to a mix of hits. (☎722 272. Cover £10, students £8. Open M and W-Th 10pm-2am, F-Sa 10pm-3am.) **Charles St.,** 8-9 Marine Parade, is a gay-friendly club with live DJs spinning dance tracks. The anything-goes atmosphere is conducive to anything-goes dancing. (☎624 091. Cover M £1.50, Th £3, Sa £5-8. Open M 10:30pm-2am, Th-Sa 10:30pm-3am.) **Trains** (☎08457 484 950) go from the northern end of Queen's Rd. to London Victoria (1hr., 2 per hr., £19) and Portsmouth (1½hr., 2 per hr., £14). National Express (☎08705 808 080) **buses** leave from Preston Park for London Victoria (2-2½hr., 1 per hr., £9.30). The **TIC** is at Royal Pavilion Shop, 4-5 Pavilion Buildings. (☎09067 112 255; www.visitbrighton.com. Open June-Sept. M-F 9am-5pm, Sa 10am-5pm, Su 10am-4pm; Oct.-May M-F 9:30am-5pm, Sa 10am-5pm.) **Postal Code:** BN1 1BA.

PORTSMOUTH ☎02392

Sailing enthusiasts and history buffs will wet themselves at this waterfront destina-tion, a famous naval port since Henry V set sail for France in 1415. Portsmouth's Vic-torian seaside setting and its 900-year history of prostitutes, drunkards, and cursing sailors give the city a compelling, gritty history. Portsmouth sprawls along the coast for miles—**Portsmouth, Old Portsmouth** (near the Portsmouth and Southsea train station and Commercial Rd.), and the resort community of **Southsea** (stretching to the east) can seem like entirely different cities. Armchair admirals will want to plunge head-first into the ⬛**Portsmouth Historic Dockyard,** in the Naval Yard, which houses some of Britain's most storied ships: Henry VIII's *Mary Rose,* Nelson's HMS *Victory,* and the HMS *Warrior.* The entrance is next to the TIC on The Hard. (Ships open daily Apr.-Oct. 10am-5:30pm; Nov.-Mar. 10am-5pm. Last entry 1hr. before closing. Each ship £10. Combo ticket £16.) The ⬛**D-Day Museum,** on Clarence Esplanade in Southsea, has life-size dioramas of the 1944 invasion. (☎9282 7261. Open daily Apr.-Sept. 10am-5:30pm; Oct.-Mar. 10am-5pm. £6, students £3.60.)

Moderately priced **B&Bs** (around £25) clutter Southsea, 2.5km southeast of The Hard along the coast. Take any Southsea bus from Commercial Rd. and get off at the Strand for the **Portsmouth and Southsea Backpackers Lodge ❶,** 4 Florence Rd. This hostel attracts a pan-European crowd with satellite TV, and grocery counter. (☎832 495. Kitchen available. Laundry £2. Internet £2 per hr. Dorms £13; doubles £30, with bath £34. Cash only.) **Britannia Guest House ❸,** 48 Granada Rd., has spotless rooms decorated with the owner's art. (☎814 234. Breakfast included. Singles £25; doubles £45-50. MC/V.) **Agora Cafe-Bar and Restaurant ❷,** 9 Clarendon Rd., serves English breakfasts (£3-5), light fare by day, and Turkish and Greek cuisine (£7-10) by night. (☎822 617. Open daily 9am-4pm and 5:30-11:30pm. Student discount. MC/V; £10 min.) Pubs near **The Hard** have galley fare and grog, while those on **Albert Road** cater to students. **Trains** (☎08457 484 950) run from Commercial Rd., in the city center, to London Waterloo (1¾hr., 4 per hr., £23) and Salisbury (1hr., 1 per hr., £13). National Express **buses** run from the Hard Interchange, next to Harbour Station, to London Victoria (2½hr., 1 per hr., £21) and Salisbury (1½hr., 1 per day, £8.30). The **TIC** is on The Hard. (☎826 722; www.visitportsmouth.co.uk. Open daily Apr.-Sept. 9:30am-5:45pm; Oct.-Mar. 9:30am-5:15pm.) **Postal Code:** PO1 1AA.

SALISBURY   ☎01722

Salisbury (pop. 37,000) centers on 13th-century ⬛**Salisbury Cathedral.** Its spire was the tallest in medieval England, and the bases of its marble pillars bend inward under 6400 tons of stone. If you hear a cracking sound, you should probably run as far away as possible. (☎555 120. Open June-Aug. M-Sa 7:15am-8pm, Su 7:15am-6:15pm; Sept.-May daily 7:15am-6:15pm. Call ahead. Suggested donation £4, students £3.50. Cathedral tours free. Roof and tower tours £4.50, students £3.50.) A well-preserved copy of the **Magna Carta** rests in the nearby **Chapter House.** (Open June-Aug. M-Sa 9:30am-5:30pm, Su noon-5:30pm; Sept.-May daily 9:30am-5:30pm. Free.) The **YHA Salisbury (HI) ❷,** Milford Hill House, on Milford Hill, offers basic, comfortable dorms. (☎327 572. Breakfast included. Laundry £3. Internet £4.20 per hr. Reserve ahead. Dorms £18, under 18 £14. MC/V.) At ⬛**Harper's "Upstairs Restaurant" ❷,** 6-7 Ox Rd., Market Sq., inventive international and English dishes (£7-10) make hearty meals. (☎333 118. Early Bird 2-course special before 8pm £7.50. Open M-F noon-2pm and 6-9:30pm, Sa noon-2pm and 6-10pm, Su 6-9pm; Oct.-May closed Su. AmEx/MC/V.) **Trains** run from South Western Rd., west of town across the River Avon, to London Waterloo (1½hr., 2 per hr., £27), Portsmouth (1½hr., 2 per hr., £13), and Winchester (1hr., 2 per hr., £12). National Express **buses** (☎08705 808 080) depart from 8 Endless St. and go to London (3hr., 3 per day, £14). Wilts and Dorset buses (☎336 855) run to Bath (X4; 1 per hr., £4.20) and Winchester (#68; 1¾hr., 8 per day, £4.50). An **Explorer** ticket is good for one day of travel on Wilts and Dorset buses (£6.50). The **TIC** is on Fish Row, in back of the Guildhall in Market Sq. (☎334 956; www.visitsalisbury.com. Open June-Sept. M-Sa 9:30am-6pm, Su 10:30am-4:30pm; Oct.-May M-Sa 9:30am-5pm.) **Postal Code:** SP1 1AB.

BRITAIN

▶ DAYTRIP FROM SALISBURY: STONEHENGE AND AVEBURY. A ring of colossal stones amid swaying grass and indifferent sheep, Stonehenge has been battered for millennia by winds whipping at 80km per hour and visited by legions of people for over 5000 years. The monument, which has retained its present shape since about 1500 BC, was once a complete circle of 6.5m tall stones weighing up to 45 tons each. Though the construction of Stonehenge has been attributed to builders as diverse as Merlin and extraterrestrials, the more plausible explanation—Neolithic builders using still unknown methods—is perhaps the most astonishing of all. Admission to Stonehenge includes a 30min. audio tour. The effect may be more haunting than the rocks themselves—a bizarre march of tourists who stop suddenly to silently devote their attention to black handsets. Ropes confine the throngs to a path around the outside of the monument. From the roadside or from Amesbury Hill, 2km up the A303, you can get a free, if distant, view of the stones. There are also many walks and trails that pass by; ask at the Salisbury TIC. (☎ *01980 624 715. Open daily June-Aug. 9am-7pm; mid-Mar. to May and Sept. to mid-Oct. 9:30am-6pm; mid-Oct. to mid-Mar. 9:30am-4pm. £6, students £4.40.)*

> **RUIN YOUR DAY.** Early risers can see Stonehenge, Avebury, and Old Sarum, an ancient settlement, in one day. Head to Stonehenge on the 8:45 or 9:45am bus (buy the Explorer ticket; see above), then catch the 11:10am or 12:20pm bus to Amesbury and transfer to an Avebury bus. Take the 2 or 3pm bus back from Avebury and stop off in Old Sarum before you reach Salisbury.

A wonder for the world: why is **Avebury's** stone circle, larger and older than its favored cousin Stonehenge, often so lonely during the day? Avebury gives an up-close and largely untouristed view of its 98 stones, dated to 2500 BC and standing in a circle with a 300m diameter. Wilts and Dorset **buses** (☎ 336 855) run daily service from the Salisbury train station and bus station (#3, 5, and 6; 30min.-2hr.; round-trip £4-8). The first bus leaves Salisbury at 9:45am, and the last leaves Stonehenge at 4:05pm. Check a schedule before you leave; intervals between drop-offs and pickups are at least 1hr. Wilts and Dorset also runs a **tour** bus from Salisbury (3 per day, £7.50-15). The closest lodgings are in **Salisbury** (see above).

BATH   ☎ 01225

Perhaps the world's first tourist town, Bath (pop. 90,000) has been a must-see for travelers since AD 43, when the Romans built an elaborate complex of baths to house the town's curative waters. For 400 years, the Romans harnessed Bath's bubbling springs, where nearly 1,000,000L of 47°C (115°F) water flow every day. The **Roman Baths Museum,** Stall St., shows the complexity of Roman architecture and engineering, which included central heating and internal plumbing. (☎ 447 785; www.romanbaths.co.uk. Open daily July-Aug. 9am-9pm; Sept.-Oct. and Mar.-June 9am-6pm; Nov.-Feb. 9:30am-5:30pm. £11, students £8.50. Joint ticket with Museum of Costume £13/11. Audio tour included.) Next to the baths, the towering **Bath Abbey** meets masons George and William Vertue's oath to build "the goodliest vault in all England and France." (☎ 422 462; www.bathabbey.org. Open Apr.-Oct. M-Sa 9am-6:30pm, Su 8am-6pm; Nov.-Mar. M-Sa 9am-4pm, Su between services. Requested donation £2.50.) Walk up Gay St. to **The Circus,** a classic Georgian block where painter Thomas Gainsborough and 18th-century prime minister William Pitt lived. Near The Circus, the **Museum of Costume,** on Bennett St., has a dazzling parade of 400 years of fashions, from 17th-century silver tissue garments to J. Lo's racy Versace jungle-print ensemble. (☎ 477 785; www.museumofcostume.co.uk. Open daily Mar.-Oct. 11am-6pm; Nov.-Feb. 11am-5pm. £6.50, students £5.50.)

Bath Backpackers ❶, 13 Pierrepont St., is a laid-back backpackers' lair with a TV lounge and "dungeon" bar. (☎446 787; www.hostels.co.uk/bath. Kitchen available. Internet £2 per hr., free Wi-Fi. Luggage storage £2 per bag. Reception 8am-11pm. Check-out 10:30am. Reserve ahead in summer. Dorms £15; doubles £35; triples £53. MC/V.) **St. Christopher's Inn ❷**, 16 Green St., has clean rooms and a downstairs pub. (☎481 444; www.st-christophers.co.uk. Internet £3 per hr. Dorms £14-22. Discount for online booking. MC/V.) Try the exotic vegetarian dishes, or the superb chocolate fudge cake at **Demuths Restaurant ❸**, 2 N. Parade Passage. (☎446 059; www.demuths.co.uk. Entrees £11-16. *Prix-fixe* lunch £8. Open M-F and Su 10am-5pm and 6-10pm, Sa 9:30am-5:30pm and 6-11pm. Reserve ahead in summer. MC/V.) **Trains** leave Dorchester St. for: Birmingham (2hr., 1 per hr., £33); Bristol (15min., 3 per hr., £6); London Paddington (1½hr., 2 per hr., £46); London Waterloo (2½hr., 2 per day, £34). National Express **buses** (☎08705 808 080) go from Manvers St. to London (3½hr., 1 per 1½hr., £17) and Oxford (2¼hr., 1 per day, £9.20). The train and bus stations are near the south end of Manvers St. Walk toward the town center and turn left on York St. for the **TIC**, in Abbey Chambers. (☎08704 446 442; www.visitbath.co.uk. Open May-Sept. M-Sa 9:30am-6pm, Su 10am-4pm; Oct.-Apr. M-Sa 9:30am-5pm, Su 10am-4pm.) **Postal Code:** BA1 1AJ.

GLASTONBURY

☎01458

The reputed birthplace of Christianity in England, an Arthurian hot spot, and home to England's biggest summer music festival, Glastonbury (pop. 8800) is a quirky intersection of mysticism and pop culture. Legend holds that Joseph of Arimathea founded ▨**Glastonbury Abbey,** on Magdalene St., in AD 63. Though the abbey was destroyed during the English Reformation, the colossal pile of ruins and accompanying museum evoke the abbey's original grandeur. (☎832 267; www.glastonbury-abbey.com. Open daily June-Aug. 9am-6pm; Sept.-Nov. and Mar.-May 9:30am-dusk; Dec.-Feb. 10am-dusk. £4.50, students £4.) For Arthurians, **Glastonbury Tor** is a must-see. The 160m tower offers great views and is supposedly where King Arthur sleeps until his country needs him. To reach the Tor between April and October, take the bus from St. Dunstan's Car Park (£2), or turn right at the top of High St. onto Lambrook, which becomes Chilkwell St.; turn left on Wellhouse Ln. and follow the public footpath up the hill, looking out for cow dung. (Open year-round. Free.) The annual ▨**Glastonbury Festival** is the biggest and best of Britain's summer music festivals. The week-long concert series (June 27-29, 2008) and has featured top bands, with recent headliners including The Killers, The Who, and Radiohead. (Tickets ☎834 596; www.glastonburyfestivals.co.uk.)

Glastonbury Backpackers ❶, 4 Market Pl., at the corner of Magdalene and High St., has spacious rooms and a bar. (☎833 353; www.glastonburybackpackers.com. Kitchen available. Internet £5 per hr. Reception until 11pm. Check-in 4pm. Check-out 11:30am. Dorms £14; doubles £34. MC/V.) **Heritage Fine Foods,** 32-34 High St., stocks groceries. (☎831 003. Open M-W 7am-9pm, Th-Sa 9am-10pm, Su 8am-9pm.) First Badgerline **buses** (☎08706 082 608, fare info 08456 064 446) go from town hall to Bristol (#375 or 376; 1hr., £5.10). Travel to Yeovil on #376 (1hr., 1 per hr.) to connect to points south, including Lyme Regis and Dorchester. From the bus stop, turn right on High St. for the **TIC**, the Tribunal, 9 High St. (☎832 954; www.glastonburytic.co.uk. Open Apr.-Sept. M-Th and Su 10am-5pm, F-Sa 10am-5:30pm; Oct.-Mar. M-Th and Su 10am-4pm, F-Sa 10am-4:30pm.) **Postal Code:** BA6 9HG.

CHANNEL ISLANDS

Jersey, Guernsey, and seven smaller islands constitute the Channel Islands. Situated 128km south of England and 64km west of France, the islands offer a mix of cultures and a touch of expensive elegance.

■ **FERRIES.** Condor high-speed **ferries** (☎01202 207 216; www.condorferries.com) run one early and one late ferry per day from Poole and Weymouth, as well as St-Malo, FRA, docking at St. Peter Port, Guernsey (2hr.), and Elizabeth Harbor at St. Helier, Jersey (3½-3¾hr.). The season and tides affect frequency and ticket prices. Call ☎0845 124 2003 or visit the website for schedules. ISIC holders are eligible for a 20% discount; ask before purchasing a ticket. Daytrips can be the most affordable, with round-trip tickets to Jersey and Guernsey from £25.

■ **JERSEY.** The largest Channel Island, Jersey is notorious for its landscape-altering tides and its budget-altering high prices. Avoid the latter by avoiding the trendy port of **Saint Helier** and escaping to the island's countryside, where you'll experience the region's beguiling blend of British sensibility and French *joie de vivre*. The 13th-century ■**Mont Orgueil Castle** on Gorey Pier was built in the 13th century to protect the island from the French. The top of the castle yields spectacular views. (☎01534 853 292. Open daily Apr.-Oct. 10am-6pm; Nov.-Mar. 10am-dusk. Last entry 1hr. before closing. £9, students £8.20.) Across from Liberation Sq. by St. Helier Marina, the **Maritime Museum** contains a nautical hodgepodge of exhibits on the surrounding seas. (☎01534 811 043. Open daily Apr.-Oct. 10am-5pm; Nov.-Mar. 10am-4pm. £6.50, students £5.70.) In October, Jersey hosts **Tennerfest**, challenging local restaurants to come up with the best £10 menu. Check www.jersey.com for more on festivals throughout the year. To reach the island's only hostel, **YHA Jersey ❸,** Haut de la Garenne, La Rue de la Pouclée et des Quatre Chemins, St. Martin, take bus #3A from St. Helier (20min., 1 per hr.), get off before Ransoms Garden Centre, and walk 180m; after 5:45pm take #1 to Gorey (last bus 11pm), walk up the hill, cross the road, and turn left up the larger hill. (☎0870 770 6130. Breakfast included. Reception 7-10am and 5-11pm. Open Feb.-Nov. daily; Dec.-Jan. F-Sa. Dorms £22, under 18 £15. MC/V.) Jersey offers a range of restaurants with fare from Asian to seafood. Visit **Beach House ❷,** Gorey Pier, for ample people-watching. (☎01534 859 902. Open M 11am-6pm, Tu-Su 12:30-3:30pm and 6:30-9:30pm. Kitchen open until 30min. before closing. MC/V.) Connex **buses** leave from the Weighbridge Terminal in St. Helier and travel all over the island. (☎01534 877 772; www.mybus.je. £1-1.60.) Island Explore offers a hop-on, hop-off **tour** service from Weighbridge. (☎01534 876 418. M-F and Su. 1-day Explorer ticket £7.50, 3-day £18, 5-day £23.) From the harbor, follow the pedestrian signs along the pier toward the **TIC** at Liberation Sq. (☎01534 448 800; www.jersey.com. Open M-Sa 8:30am-5:30pm, Su 8:30am-2:15pm; winter hours vary.)

THE REAL DEAL. Though part of the UK, Jersey and Guernsey are essentially self-governing states. The British pound is the official currency, but ATMs dish out Jersey or Guernsey pounds. These local pounds are on par with their British counterparts, but are not accepted outside the Channel Islands; you will have to exchange them upon returning to the mainland. Toward the end of your stay in the islands, make sure to ask local merchants to give you change in British pounds. Also keep in mind that your mobile phone carrier may think you are in France (or not recognize you at all) and charge accordingly.

■ **GUERNSEY.** Smaller than Jersey in size but not in charm, Guernsey flaunts its French roots—cultural fusion is evident in its architecture, cuisine, and locals's speech. Pull yourself away from Guernsey's wildflowers and beaches long enough to tour ■**Hauteville House,** St. Peter Port. The house remains virtually unaltered since Victor Hugo lived here and penned *Les Misérables* during his exile from France. Hauteville is full of hidden inscriptions and mantles built by Hugo from recycled furniture. (☎01481 721 911. Open May to early Oct. M-Sa 10am-4pm; Apr. M-Sa noon-4pm. £4, students £2, under 20 free.) For lodgings near town with views of Sark and Herm Island, try **St. George's Guest House ❹**, St. George's Esplanade, St. Peter Port. (☎01481 721 027. Breakfast included. £33-35. MC/V.) **Christies ❸**, Le Pollet, has an airy French bistro serving local seafood salads and sandwiches, and a more expensive restaurant in back. (☎01481 726 624. Lunch entrees £4.50-15. Open daily noon-2:30pm and 6-10:30pm. MC/V.) Island Coachways (☎01481 720 210; www.buses.gg) **buses** operate throughout the island and offer **tours** from May to September; call the office for fares and info. Routes #7 and 7a circle the coast (1 per hr., £0.60). To reach the **TIC** on North Esplanade, take a left at the end of the ferry landing at St. Julian's pier. *Naturally Guernsey* is a helpful guide to the island. (☎01481 723 552; www.visitguernsey.com. Open in summer M-Sa 9am-6pm, Su 9am-1pm; in winter M-F 9am-5pm, Sa 9am-4pm.)

THE CORNISH COAST

With cliffsides stretching out into the Atlantic, Cornwall's terrain doesn't feel English. Years ago, the Celts fled westward in the face of Saxon conquest. Today, the migration to Cornwall continues in the form of artists, surfers, and vacationers. Though the Cornish language is no longer spoken, the area remains protective of its distinctive past and its ubiquitous pasties, the region's famous pie.

TIP **THAT'S EMBARRASSING.** Cornwall's famous pasties (PAH-stees) are pie-like pastries usually filled with diced meat and vegetables. Not to be confused with the pasties (PAY-stees) you might find in a lingerie shop.

PENZANCE. Once a model pirate town, it appears Disney has since moved all the pirates to the Caribbean. The only ones here are in murals or made of wax. What Penzance lacks in swashbucklers it makes up for in galleries, quirky stores, and sunsets. A former Benedictine monastery, **St. Michael's Mount**, on a hill that becomes an island at high tide, marks the spot where some believe St. Michael appeared in AD 495. The views from the top are worth the 30-story climb. (☎01736 710 507, ferry and tide info 01736 710 265. Open Apr.-Oct. M-F and Su 10:30am-5:30pm; Nov.-Mar. by tour only, appointment necessary. Last entry 4:45pm. £6.40; with private garden £9.40.) Penzance contains an impressive number of art galleries; pick up the *Cornwall Galleries Guide* (£1) at the TIC. Walk 20min. from the train or bus station, or take First bus #5 or 6 from the bus station to the Pirate Pub and walk 10min. up Castle Horneck Rd. to reach the spacious dorms at **YHA Penzance (HI) ❶**, Castle Horneck, an 18th-century mansion. (☎01736 362 666. Internet £0.07 per min. Lockout 10am-noon. Dorms £16, under 18 £13; doubles £35. Tent sites £7. MC/V.) **Admiral Benbow,** 46 Chapel St., is the town's liveliest pub and is decorated with trinkets from shipwrecks. (☎01736 363 448. Pints £2.20. Open M-Sa 11am-11pm, Su noon-10:30pm.) **Trains** leave Wharf Rd., at the head of Albert Pier, for London (5½hr., 7 per day, £69) and Newquay (3hr., 8 per day, £7). **Buses** also leave Wharf Rd. for London (8½hr., 7 per day, £36). The **TIC** is between the train and bus stations on Station Rd. (☎01736 362 207; www.penwith.gov.uk. Open May-Sept. M-F 9am-5pm, Sa 10am-4pm, Su 9am-2pm; Oct.-Apr. M-F 9am-5pm, Sa 10am-1pm.)

EAST ANGLIA AND THE MIDLANDS

The rich farmland and watery flats of East Anglia stretch northeast from London, cloaking the counties of Cambridgeshire, Norfolk, Suffolk, and parts of Essex. Mention of The Midlands inevitably evokes grim urban images, but there is a unique heritage and quiet grandeur to this smokestacked landscape. Even Birmingham, the region's much-maligned center, has its saving graces, among them a lively nightlife scene and the Cadbury chocolate empire.

OXFORD ☎ 01865

Sprawling college grounds and 12th-century spires mark this Holy Grail of British academia. Nearly a millennium of scholarship at Oxford (pop. 145,000) has included the education of world leaders, including 25 British prime ministers. Despite the tourist crowds, Oxford has an irrepressible grandeur and pockets of tranquility: the basement room of Blackwell's Bookshop, the galleries of the Ashmolean, and the perfectly maintained quadrangles of the university's 39 colleges.

🖪🛤 TRANSPORTATION AND PRACTICAL INFORMATION. Trains (☎ 08457 484 950) run from Botley Rd., down Park End, to: Birmingham (1¼hr., 2 per hr., £20); Glasgow (5-7hr., 1 per hr., £70); London Paddington (1hr., 2-4 per hr., £10-19); Manchester (3hr., 1-2 per hr., £21-42). Stagecoach **buses** (☎ 772 250; www.stagecoachbus.com) run to: Cambridge (3hr., 2 per hr., £6); London (1¾hr.; 3-5 per hr.; £12, students £10). National Express (☎ 08705 808 080) runs to: Birmingham (1½hr., 5 per day, £15); Cambridge (3hr., 2 per hr., £9); Stratford-upon-Avon (1hr., 2 per day, £9). Oxford Bus Company (☎ 785 400; www.oxfordbus.co.uk) runs to: London (1¾hr.; 3-5 per hr.; £12, students £10); Gatwick (2hr, 1 per hr. 8am-9pm, £20); Heathrow (1¼hr., 3 per hr., £15). The **TIC** is at 15-16 Broad St. (☎ 726 871; www.visitoxford.org. Open M-Sa 9:30am-5pm; Easter-June and Aug.-Oct. also Su 10am-3:30pm; June-July also Su 10am-4pm.) **Internet** is available at **Oxford Central Library,** Queen St. near the Westgate Shopping Center. (☎ 815 549. Open M-Th 9:15am-7pm, F-Sa 9:15am-5pm. Free.) **Postal Code:** OX1 1ZZ.

🖪🏠 ACCOMMODATIONS AND FOOD. Book at least a week ahead in summer, especially for singles. If it's late, call the **Oxford Association of Hotels and Guest Houses** (East Oxford ☎ 721 561, West Oxford 862 138, North Oxford 244 691, South Oxford 244 268). Oxford's newest hostel, 🖪**Central Backpackers ❷,** 13 Park End St., has spacious rooms and a rooftop terrace perfect for barbecues. (☎ 242 288. Kitchen available. Free luggage storage. Free Internet. Reception 8am-11pm. Check-out 11am. 4-bed dorms £18; 6-bed female or 8-bed mixed dorms £16; 12-bed dorms £14. MC/V.) Turn right from the train station to reach the **YHA Oxford (HI) ❷,** 2a Botley Rd., which features quiet rooms and a kitchen. (☎ 727 275. Full English breakfast included. Lockers £1. Laundry £3. Internet £4.20 per hr. 4- and 6-bed dorms £21, under 18 £16; doubles £46. £3 student discount. MC/V.) The **Oxford Backpackers Hostel ❶,** 9a Hythe Bridge St., between the bus and train stations, fosters a lively social scene with an inexpensive bar, pool table, and constant music. (☎ 721 761. Laundry £2.50. Internet £2 per hr. Dorms £14; quads £64. MC/V.)

Look for after-hours **kebab vans,** usually at Broad, High, Queen, and St. Aldate's St. Students and residents gather at 🖪**The Alternative Tuck Shop ❶,** 24 Holywell St., for their famous panini and a slew of delicious made-to-order sandwiches, all for under £3. (☎ 792 054. Open daily 8:30am-6pm. Cash only.) For a delectable meal made with local ingredients, head to **Vaults and Garden ❷,** Radcliffe Square, under St. Mary's Church. (☎ 279 112. Open daily 9am-5:30pm. Cash only.) **Kazbar ❶,** 25-27 Cowley Rd., is a Mediterranean tapas bar with Spanish-style decor. (☎ 202 920. Tapas £2.20-4.75. Free tapas with drink M-F 4-7pm. Open M-F 4-11pm, Sa-Su noon-midnight. AmEx/MC/V.) Try **Gloucester Green Market,** behind the bus station (open W 8am-3:30pm) or the **Covered Market** between Market St. and Carfax for fresh produce and deli goods (open M-Sa 7am-8pm, Su 11am-5pm). Pick up groceries at the **Sainsbury's** in Westgate Shopping Center. (Open M-Sa 7am-8pm, Su 11am-5pm.)

🖪 SIGHTS. The TIC sells maps (£1.25) and the *Welcome to Oxford* guide (£1), which lists the visiting hours of Oxford's **colleges.** Don't bother trying to sneak in after hours. Even after you hide your pack and copy of *Let's Go,* bouncers, affec-

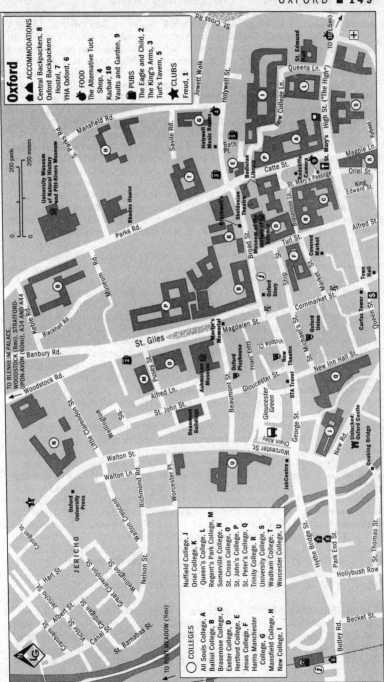

Oxford

▲▲ ACCOMMODATIONS
Central Backpackers, 8
Oxford Backpackers
Hostel, 7
YHA Oxford, 6

☛ FOOD
The Alternative Tuck
Shop, 4
Kazbar, 10
Vaults and Garden, 9

☛ PUBS
The Eagle and Child, 2
The King's Arms, 3
Turf's Tavern, 5

★ CLUBS
Freud, 1

○ COLLEGES
All Souls College, A
Balliol College, B
Brasenose College, C
Exeter College, D
Hertford College, E
Jesus College, F
Harris Manchester
College, G
Mansfield College, H
New College, I

Nuffield College, J
Oriel College, K
Queen's College, L
Regent's Park College, M
Somerville College, N
St. Cross College, O
St. John's College, P
St. Peter's College, Q
Trinity College, R
University College, S
Wadham College, T
Worcester College, U

TO BLENHEIM PALACE/
WOODSTOCK (8mi), STRATFORD-
UPON-AVON (60mi), A34 AND A44

TO PORT MEADOW (¾mi)

University Museum
of Natural History
and Pitt-Rivers Museum

BRITAIN

tionately known as "bulldogs," will squint and kick you out. Just down St. Aldate's St. from Carfax, **Christ Church College** has Oxford's grandest quad and most distinguished alumni, including 13 past prime ministers. The dining hall and Tom Quad are also shooting locations for the *Harry Potter* movies. The **Christ Church Chapel** is the university's cathedral. It was here that the Rev. Charles Dodgson (better known as Lewis Carroll) first met Alice Liddell, the dean's daughter; the White Rabbit is immortalized in the hall's stained glass. **Tom Quad** takes its name from Great Tom, the seven-ton bell in Tom Tower that has faithfully rung 101 strokes at 9:05pm (the original undergraduate curfew) every evening since 1682. (☎286 573; www.chch.ox.ac.uk. Open M-Sa 9am-5:30pm, Su 1-5:30pm. Chapel services M-F 6pm; Su 8, 10, 11:15am, 6pm. £4.70, students £3.70.) J.R.R. Tolkien lectured at **Morton College,** Merton St., whose library houses the first printed Welsh Bible. Nearby **St. Alban's Quad** has some of the university's best gargoyles. (☎276 310; www.merton.ox.ac.uk. Open M-F 2-4pm, Sa-Su 10am-4pm. Free.) Soot-blackened **University College,** High St., was built in 1249 and vies with Merton for the title of oldest, claiming Alfred the Great as its founder. Bill Clinton spent his Rhodes scholar days here. (☎276 602; www.univ.ox.ac.uk. Open to tours only.) South of Oriel, **Corpus Christi College,** the smallest of Oxford's colleges, surrounds a sundialed quad. The garden gate was built for visits between Charles I and his queen, who lived nearby during the Civil Wars. (☎276 700; www.ccc.ox.ac.uk. Open daily 1:30-4:30pm.) The prestigious **All Souls College,** at the corner of High and Cattle St., admits only the best scholars and stores only the best wine in its cellar. (☎279 379; www.all-souls.ox.ac.uk. Open Sept.-July M-F 2-4pm. Free.) At **Queen's College,** High St., a boar's head graces the table at Christmas to honor a student who, attacked by a boar on the outskirts of Oxford, choked the animal to death with a volume of Aristotle. (☎279 120; www.queens.ox.ac.uk. Open to tours only.) With extensive grounds, flower-edged quads, and a deer park, **Magdalen College** (MAUD-lin), on High St. near the Cherwell, is considered Oxford's handsomest. Oscar Wilde is among the distinguished alumni. (☎276 000; www.magd.ox.ac.uk. Open daily Oct.-Mar. 1pm-dusk; Apr.-June 1-6pm; July-Sept. noon-6pm. £3, students £2.)

Opened in 1684, the grand **Ashmolean Museum,** Beaumont St., was Britain's first public museum and still holds one of the country's finest collections, with works by da Vinci, Michelangelo, and van Gogh. The museum is undergoing renovations until 2009, but continues to show an exhibit of 200 artifacts from its galleries. (☎278 000. Open Tu-Sa 10am-5pm, Su noon-5pm; in summer open Th until 7pm. Free. Tours £2.) **Bodleian Library,** Broad St., is Oxford's main reading and research library with over five million books and 50,000 manuscripts. It receives a copy of every book printed in Great Britain, but no one has ever been allowed to check one out. (☎277 000; www.bodley.ox.ac.uk. Library open M-F 9am-10pm, Sa 9am-1pm; summer M-F 9am-7pm, Sa 9am-1pm. Tours leave from the Divinity School in the main quad M-Sa 2-4 per day. Tours £4, audio tour £2.) A teenage Christopher Wren designed the **Sheldonian Theatre,** next door on Broad St. Graduation ceremonies, conducted in Latin, take place in the theatre, as do opera performances. (☎277 299. Open M-Sa 10am-12:30pm and 2-4:30pm; in winter until 3:30pm; in July and Aug. also Su 11am-4pm. £2, students £1.) With 10km of bookshelves, **Blackwell's Bookstore,** 53 Broad St., is Oxford's largest bookshop and is famous for letting patrons read undisturbed. (☎792 792. Open M and W-Sa 9am-6pm, Tu 9:30am-6pm, Su 11am-5pm.)

⚅⚅ ENTERTAINMENT AND NIGHTLIFE. **Punting** on the River Thames, known in Oxford as the "Isis," or on the River Cherwell (CHAR-wul), is a traditional pastime. Punters propel their small wooden vessels using a tall pole and oar. **Magdalen Bridge Boathouse,** just under Magdalen Bridge, rents boats. (☎202 643. Open daily Mar.-Oct. 10am-dusk. £12 per hr.; £30 deposit and ID required. Checks and cash only.) Bring wine for a floating toast. Music and drama at Oxford are cherished arts. *This Month in Oxford* and *Daily Information* (www.dailyinfo.co.uk), both available at the TIC for free, list upcoming events. **Pubs** outnumber colleges in Oxford. Many are so small that a single band of students will squeeze out other patrons. Luckily, there's usually another place just around the corner, so be ready to crawl. **⚑Turf's Tavern,** 4 Bath Pl., off Holywell St., is a 13th-century student pub tucked in an alley off an alley. (☎243 235. Open M-Sa 11am-11pm, Su noon-10:30pm. Kitchen closes 7:30pm. AmEx/MC/V.) Merry masses head to the back rooms at **The King's Arms,** 40 Holywell St., considered to be Oxford's unofficial student union. (☎242 369. Open M-Sa 10:30am-11pm, Su 10:30am-10:30pm. MC/V.) *The Hobbit* and *The Chronicles of Narnia* were first read aloud at **The Eagle and Child,** 49 St. Giles, the favored haunt of their authors, J.R.R. Tolkien and C.S. Lewis. (☎302 925. Open M-Sa 11am-11pm, Su noon-10:30pm. Kitchen closes M-F 10pm, Sa-Su 9pm.) After Happy hour, head to clubs at **Walton Street** or **Cowley Road.** In a former church, **Freud,** 119 Walton St., is a cafe by day and cocktail bar by night. (☎311 171. Open Su-Tu 11am-midnight, W 11am-1am, Th-Sa 11am-2am. MC/V.)

STRATFORD-UPON-AVON   ☎01789

Shakespeare was born here, and this fluke of fate has made Stratford-upon-Avon a major stop on the tourist superhighway. Proprietors tout the dozen-odd properties linked, however remotely, to the Bard and his extended family. Stratford's Will-centered sights are best seen before 11am, when daytrippers arrive, or after 4pm, when crowds disperse. Fans can buy the **All Five Houses** ticket for admission to all official Shakespeare properties: Anne Hathaway's Cottage, Mary Arden's House, Hall's Croft, New Place and Nash's House, and Shakespeare's Birthplace. (Tickets available at all houses. £14, students £12.) The **Three In-Town Houses** pass covers the latter three sights. (£11, students £9.) **Shakespeare's Birthplace,** on Henley St., is part period re-creation and part exhibit of Shakespeare's life and works. (☎201 822. Open in summer M-Sa 9am-5pm, Su 9:30am-5pm; mid-season daily 10am-5pm; winter M-Sa 10am-4pm, Su 10:30am-4pm. £7, students £5.50.) **New Place,** on Chapel St., was Stratford's finest home when Shakespeare bought it in 1597; now only the foundation remains. View it from **Nash's House,** on Chapel St., which belonged to the first husband of Shakespeare's granddaughter. Pay homage to the Bard's **grave** in the **Holy Trinity Church,** Trinity St. (☎266 316. Open Apr.-Sept. M-Sa 8:30am-6pm, Su noon-5pm; Mar. and Oct. M-Sa 9am-5pm, Su noon-5pm; Nov.-Feb. M-Sa 9am-4pm, Su noon-5pm. Last entry 20min. before close. Requested donation £1.) The **⚑Royal Shakespeare Company** sells well over one million tickets each year. The **Royal Shakespeare Theatre** and the **Swan Theatre,** the RSC's more intimate neighbor, are currently undergoing a £100 million renovation and will re-open in 2010. The company will continue to perform shows down the road at **The Courtyard Theatre.** Visitors can get backstage tours and a glimpse at the high-tech stage to be installed at the Royal Shakespeare Theatre. Tickets are sold through the box office in the foyer of the Courtyard Theatre. (☎0870 800 1110; www.rsc.org.uk. Open M and W-Sa 9:30am-8pm, Tu 10am-8pm. Tickets £5-40. Students and those under 25 receive half-price tickets for M-W evening performances in advance, otherwise by availability on performance days. Standby tickets in summer £15; winter £12. Disabled travelers should call ahead to advise the box office of their needs; some performances feature sign language interpretation or audio description.)

B&Bs line **Evesham Place, Evesham Road, Grove Road,** and **Shipston Road,** but reservations are a must. **⚑Carlton Guest House ❸,** 22 Evesham Pl., has spacious rooms and spectacular service. (☎293 548. Singles £20-26; doubles £40-52; triples £60-78. Cash only.) Locals rave about classy yet cozy **The Oppo ❸,** 13 Sheep St. (☎269 980. Entrees from £9. Open daily for lunch noon-2pm; dinner M-Th 5:30-9:30pm, F-Sa 5-

11pm, and Su 6-9:30pm. MC/V.) A **Somerfield** supermarket is in Town Sq. (☎292 604. Open M-W 8am-7pm, Th-Sa 8am-8pm, Su 10am-4pm.) RSC actors make appearances at ◧**Dirty Duck Pub,** 66 Waterside. (☎297 312. Open M-Sa 11am-11pm, Su noon-10:30pm.) **Trains** (☎08457 484 950) arrive at Station Rd., off Alcester Rd., and run to: Birmingham (1hr., 2 per hr., £6); London Paddington (2¼hr., 2 per hr., £42). National Express (☎08705 808 080) **buses** go to: London (3hr., 5 per day, £17); Oxford (1hr., 2 per day, £9.50). Local Stratford Blue bus #X20 stops at Wood and Bridge St., and goes to Birmingham (1¼hr., 1 per hr., £4). The **TIC** is at Bridgefoot, across Warwick Rd. (☎0870 160 7930. Open Apr.-Oct. M-Sa 9am-5:30pm, Su 10am-4pm; Nov.-Mar. M-Sa 9am-5pm.) **Internet** is at **Cyber Junction,** 28 Greenhill St. (☎263 400. £4 per hr. Open M-F 10am-6pm, Sa 10:30am-5:30pm.) **Postal Code:** CV37 6PU.

THE COTSWOLDS

The Cotswolds have deviated little from their etymological roots: "Cotswolds" means "sheep enclosures in rolling hillsides." Despite the sleepy moniker, the Cotswolds are filled with rich history and traditions like cheese-rolling that reach back to Roman and Saxon times.

■▊ **TRANSPORTATION AND PRACTICAL INFORMATION.** Public transit to and in the Cotswolds is scarce; planning ahead is a must. Useful gateway cities are Bath, Bristol, Cheltenham, Oxford, and Stratford-upon-Avon. **Moreton-in-Marsh,** one of the larger villages, runs **trains** to London (1½hr., 1 per 1-2hr., £30) via Oxford (30min., £10). It's easier to reach the Cotswolds by **bus.** The Cheltenham **TIC,** 77 The Promenade (☎522 878), offers *Getting There* (free), which has detailed bus info. *Explore the Cotswolds by Public Transport* (free), available at village TICs, has bus frequency and routes. Pulham's Coaches #801 (☎01451 820 369) runs from Cheltenham to Moreton-in-Marsh (1hr., M-Sa 7 per day, £1.75) via Bourton-on-the-Water (35min., £1.65) and Stow-on-the-Wold (50min., £1.75).

For a comprehensive look at the region, try the **Cotswold Discovery Tour,** a full-day bus tour that starts in Bath and visits five of the most scenic and touristed villages. (☎09067 112 000; www.madmax.abel.co.uk. Apr.-Oct. Tu, Th, Su 9am-5:15pm. £25.) Local roads are ideal for **biking,** the best way to explore the Cotswolds. Rent bikes at **The Toy Shop,** High St. in Moreton-in-Marsh, where you can also find maps and route suggestions. (☎01608 650 756. £12 per ½-day, £14 per day. Open M, W-Sa 9am-1pm and 2-5pm.) Visitors can also see the Cotswolds as the English have for centuries by treading the paths from village to village. The **Cotswold Way,** spanning 160km from Bath to Chipping Camden, can be done in a week and passes through pasturelands and the ruins of ancient settlements. The **National Trails Office** (☎01865 810 224) has details on this and other trails. Town TICs offer helpful walking and cycling guides and the free *Cotswold Events* booklet, which lists music festivals, antique markets, cheese-rolling events, and woolsack races.

WINCHCOMBE, STOW-ON-THE-WOLD, AND BOURTON-ON-THE-WATER. Ten kilometers north of Cheltenham on A46, 15th-century **Sudeley Castle** crowns the town of **Winchcombe.** Today, the castle is home of Lord and Lady Ashcombe and has pristine gardens and exhibits on Tudor life. (☎01242 602 308; www.sudeley-castle.co.uk. Open daily Mar.-Oct. 11am-5pm. £7.20, students £6.20.) The Winch-combe **TIC** is on High St., next to Town Hall. (☎01242 602 925. Open Apr.-Oct. M-Sa 10am-5pm, Su 10am-4pm; Nov.-Mar. Sa-Su 10am-4pm.) **Stow-on-the-Wold** is the self-proclaimed "Heart of the Cotswolds" and home to many inns and taverns. The **YHA hostel (HI) ❷,** next to the TIC in The Square, offers rooms with village views and bath. (☎01451 830 497. Laundry available. Reception 8-10am and 5-10pm. Lockout

10am-5pm. Curfew 11pm. Reserve 1 month ahead. Dorms £18, under 18 £15. £3 HI discount. MC/V.) A **Tesco** supermarket is on Fosse Way. (Open M-F 6am-midnight, Sa 6am-10pm, Su 10am-4pm.) The **TIC** is in Hollis House on The Square. (☎01451 831 082. Open Easter-Oct. M-Sa 9:30am-5:30pm; Nov.-Easter M-Sa 9:30am-4:30pm.) **Bourton-on-the-water** is acclaimed as the Cotswolds' most beautiful village. The footbridge-straddled River Windrush runs along the main street, giving the town the moniker "Venice of the Cotswolds." The region is home to many trailheads, including those for the **Oxford, Warden's, Heart of England, Windrush,** and **Gloucestershire Ways.** The **Cotswold Perfumery,** Victoria St., offers a factory tour and a make-your-own perfume course, but a mere visit to the shop is an olfactory experience. (☎01451 820 698; www.cotswold-perfumery.co.uk. Open M-Sa 9:30am-5pm, Su 10:30am-5pm. £5, students £3.50. Call ahead for a tour; usually 1-2 per day.)

BIRMINGHAM   ☎0121

Second to London in population, Birmingham (pop. 1,000,000) has a long-standing reputation as a grim, industrial metropolis. To counter this bleak stereotype, the city has revitalized its central district with a visitor magnet: **shopping**—and lots of it. The epic **Bullring,** Europe's largest retail establishment, is the foundation of Birmingham's material-world makeover. Recognizable by the wavy, scaled Selfridges department store, the center has more than 140 shops and cafes. (☎632 1500; www.bullring.co.uk. Open M-F 9:30am-8pm, Sa 9am-8pm, Su 11am-5pm.) Twelve minutes south of town by rail or bus lies ◪**Cadbury World,** a cavity-inducing celebration of the famed chocolate empire. Take a train from New St. to Bournville, or bus #84 from the city center. (☎451 4159. Open Mar.-Oct. daily 10am-3pm; Nov.-Feb. Tu-Th and Sa-Su 10am-3pm. Reserve ahead. £12.50, students £10.) The **Birmingham International Jazz Festival** brings over 200 performers to town during the first two weeks of July. (☎454 7020; www.birminghamjazzfestival.com.)

    Hagley Road has several budget B&Bs—the farther away from downtown, the lower the prices (and standards). Take bus #9, 109, 126, or 139 from Colomore Row to Hagley Rd. Near the bus stop, **Birmingham Central Backpackers ❷,** 58 Coventry St., is a recently renovated pub now sporting tidy dorm rooms. The bar also stocks plenty of snacks and simple dinner items. (☎643 0033; www.birmingham-backpackers.com. Breakfast included. Laundry and Internet available for a small donation to the Oxfam International charity. Beds from £16. AmEx/MC/V.) Slightly farther out, **The Merry Maid ❷,** 263 Moseley Rd., offers standard dorm-style rooms. (☎440 6126; www.birminghambackpackers.com. Beds from £16. MC/V.) **Canalside Cafe ❶,** 35 Worcester Bar, serves baguettes and hearty specials. (☎441 9862. Most sandwiches £3-5. Open daily 9am-5pm, with occasional evening openings. Cash only.) **Broad Street,** with trendy cafe-bars and clubs, gets rowdy on weekends; as always, exercise caution at night. Pick up the bimonthly *What's On* for Birmingham's latest hot spots. ◪**The Yardbird,** Paradise Pl., is an alternative to the club scene. No dress code, no cover, no pretense. DJs spin beats on Friday, with live music on Saturdays. (☎212 2524. Open M-W and Su 11am-midnight, Th-Sa 11am-2am.) A GLBT-friendly scene centers around **Lower Essex Street.**

    Transit routes between London, central Wales, southwest England, and points north converge in Birmingham. **Trains** run from New St. Station (☎08457 484 950) to: Liverpool Lime St. (1½hr., 1 per hr., £20); London Euston (1½hr., 2 per hr., £28); Manchester Piccadilly (2hr., 2 per hr., £19); Oxford (1¼hr., 1 per hr., £19). National Express **buses** (☎08705 808 080) go from Digbeth Station to: Cardiff (1½hr., 4 per day, £20); Liverpool (1hr., 5 per day, £13); London Heathrow (3hr., 1 per hr., £14); Manchester (2½hr., 1 per 2hr., £11). The **TIC** is at The Rotune, 150 New St. (☎202 5099; www.beinbirmingham.com. Branch at the junction of New and Corporation St. Open M-Sa 9:30am-5:30pm, Su 10:30am-4:30pm.) **Postal Code:** B2 4TU.

CAMBRIDGE
☎ **01223**

Unlike museum-oriented, metropolitan Oxford, Cambridge is a town for students before tourists. It was here that Newton's gravity, Watson and Crick's model of DNA, Byron and Milton's poetry, and Milne's Winnie the Pooh were born. No longer the exclusive academy of upper-class sons, the university feeds the minds of female, international, and state-school pupils alike. At exams' end, Cambridge explodes in Pimm's-soaked glee, and May Week is a swirl of parties and balls.

█▐ TRANSPORTATION AND PRACTICAL INFORMATION. Trains (☎ 08457 484 950) run from Station Rd. to London King's Cross (45min., 3 per hr., £18) and Ely (20min., 3 per hr., round-trip £3.50). National Express **buses** (☎ 08705 808 080) run from Drummer St. Station to London Victoria (3hr., 1 per hr., £10). Stagecoach Express buses (☎ 01604 676 060) go to Oxford (3hr., 1 per hr., from £6.50). **Bicycles** are the main mode of transportation in Cambridge. Rent at **Mike's Bikes**, 28 Mill Rd. (☎ 312 591. £10 per day plus £35 deposit. Open M-Sa 9am-6pm, Su 10am-4pm. MC/V.) The **TIC**, south of Market Sq. on Wheeler St., sells the Cambridge Visitors Card (£2.50), which gives city-wide discounts. (☎ 09065 862 526; www.visitcambridge.org. Open Easter-Oct. M-F 10am-5:30pm, Sa 10-5pm, Su 11am-4pm; Nov.-Easter M-F 10am-5:30pm, Sa 10am-5pm.) **Postal Code:** CB2 3AA.

▐▐ ACCOMMODATIONS AND FOOD. John Maynard Keynes, who studied and taught at Cambridge, tells us that low supply and high demand usually means one thing: high prices. **B&Bs** are around **Portugal Street** and **Tenison Road** outside downtown. Book ahead in summer and check the guide to accommodations (£0.50) at the TIC. **YHA Cambridge (HI) ❷**, 97 Tenison Rd., close to the train station, is relaxed and welcoming, with TV lounges and a well-equipped kitchen. (☎ 354 601. Breakfast included. Lockers £1. Laundry £3. Internet £0.50 per 7min. Reception 24hr. Dorms £19, under 18 £15. MC/V.) **Tension Towers Guest House ❹**, 148 Tension Rd., two blocks from the train station, has freshly baked muffins and impeccable rooms. (☎ 363 924; www.cambridgecitytenisontowers.com. Singles £35; doubles £55. Cash only.) South of town, **Hills Road** and **Mill Road** are full of popular budget restaurants. **█Clown's ❶**, 54 King St., serves huge portions (£2.50-6.50) of pasta and dessert. (☎ 355 711. Set menu with drink, salad, small pasta, and cake £6.50. Open M-Sa 8am-midnight, Su 8am-11pm. Cash only.) **CB1 ❶**, 32 Mill Rd., is a decidedly chill coffee shop. (☎ 576 306. Free Wi-Fi. Coffee £1-1.50. Open M-F 8am-8pm, Sa-Su 10am-8pm. Cash only.) **Dojo's Noodle Bar ❶**, 1-2 Mill Rd., whips up enormous plates of Asian noodles for less than £7. (☎ 363 471; www.dojonoodlebar.co.uk. Open M-Th noon-2:30pm and 5:30-11pm, F noon-4pm and 5:30-11pm, Sa-Su noon-11pm. MC/V.) **Market Square** has pyramids of fruits and vegetables. (Open M-Sa 9:30am-4:30pm.) Students buy their Pimm's and baguettes at **Sainsbury's**, 44 Sidney St. (☎ 366 891. Open M-Sa 8am-10pm, Su 11am-5pm.)

◙ SIGHTS. Cambridge packs some of England's most breathtaking architecture into three square kilometers. Soaring **King's College Chapel** and St. John's **Bridge of Sighs** are sightseeing staples, while more obscure college courts veil largely undiscovered gardens and courtyards. The **University of Cambridge** has three eight-week terms: Michaelmas (Oct.-Dec.), Lent (Jan.-Mar.), and Easter (Apr.-June). Many of its colleges close to sightseers during Easter term, and virtually all are closed during exams (mid-May to mid-June); your best bet is to call ahead for hours. Porters (bowler-wearing former servicemen) guard the gates. Travelers who look like undergrads (no backpack, camera, or Cambridge sweatshirt) can often wander freely through the grounds after hours. The fastest way to blow your cover is to trample the sacred grass of the courtyards, a privilege reserved for the elite.

If you only have time for a few colleges, visit Trinity, King's, St. John's, and Queens's. Sir Isaac Newton originally measured the speed of sound by timing the

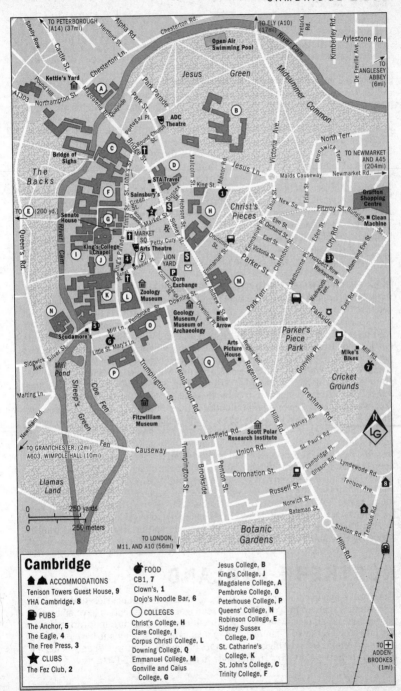

Cambridge

ACCOMMODATIONS
Tenison Towers Guest House, 9
YHA Cambridge, 8

PUBS
The Anchor, 5
The Eagle, 4
The Free Press, 3

CLUBS
The Fez Club, 2

FOOD
CB1, 7
Clown's, 1
Dojo's Noodle Bar, 6

COLLEGES
Christ's College, H
Clare College, I
Corpus Christi College, L
Downing College, Q
Emmanuel College, M
Gonville and Caius
College, G

Jesus College, B
King's College, J
Magdalene College, A
Pembroke College, O
Peterhouse College, P
Queens' College, N
Robinson College, E
Sidney Sussex
College, D
St. Catharine's
College, K
St. John's College, C
Trinity College, F

BRITAIN

echo in the cloisters along the north side of the Great Court at **Trinity College,** on Trinity St. Also the alma mater of Vladimir Nabokov, Ernest Rutherford, and Alfred Lord Tennyson, Trinity houses the stunning **Wren Library,** with A. A. Milne's handwritten manuscript of *Winnie the Pooh* and the original copy of Newton's *Principia*. (☎338 400. Chapel and courtyard open daily 10am-5pm. Library open M-F noon-2pm. Easter-Oct. £2.20, students £1.30; Nov.-Easter free.) **King's College,** south of Trinity on King's Parade, is E. M. Forster and Salman Rushdie's alma mater. Peter Paul Reubens's *Adoration of the Magi* hangs behind the altar of its Gothic chapel. (☎331 100. Open M-Sa 9:30am-5pm, Su 10am-5pm. Tours arranged through the TIC. £4.50, students £3.) Established in 1511 by Henry VIII's mother, **St. John's College,** on St. John's St., is one of seven colleges founded by women. It boasts the 12th-century School of Pythagoras, thought to be the oldest complete building in Cambridge, a replica of the Bridge of Sighs, and the longest room in the city—the Fellows' Room in Second Court spans 28m. (☎338 600. Open daily 10am-5:30pm. £2.50, students £1.50.) **Queens' College,** Silver St., has the only unaltered Tudor courtyard in Cambridge. Despite rumors to the contrary, its Mathematical Bridge is supported by screws and bolts, not just by mathematical principle. (☎335 511. Open Mar.-Oct. M-F 10am-5pm, Sa-Su 9:30am-5pm. £1.30.) A break from academia, the 🅜**Fitzwilliam Museum,** on Trumpington St., displays Egyptian, Greek, and Asian treasures as well as works by Brueghel, Monet, and Reubens. (☎332 900. Open Tu-Sa 10am-5pm, Su noon-5pm. Suggested donation £3.)

🎭🎵 **ENTERTAINMENT AND NIGHTLIFE. May Week** is in June—you would think those bright Cambridge students could understand a calendar. An elaborate celebration of the end of the term, the week is crammed with concerts, plays, and balls followed by recuperative riverside breakfasts and 5am punting. 🅜**Punting** (p. 150) on the River Cam is a favorite pastime in Cambridge. Beware of punt-bombers: jumping from bridges into the river alongside a punt, thereby tipping its occupants into the Cam, has evolved into an art form. Touristy? Maybe, but it's still a blast. **Scudamore's,** Silver St. Bridge, rents boats. (☎359 750; www.scudamores.com. M-F £14 per hr. plus £70 deposit, Sa-Su £16 per hr. MC/V.) **King Street** has a diverse collection of pubs. **The Anchor,** Silver St., is a crowded undergrad watering hole. Savor a pint outdoors and scoff at colliding amateur punters. (☎353 554. Open M-Sa 10am-11pm, Su 11am-10:30pm. Food served M-Sa noon-9:30pm, Su noon-9pm.) Popular with locals, **The Free Press,** Prospect Row, has no pool table, no cell phones, and no loud music—just good beer and conversation. (☎368 337. Open M-F noon-2:30pm and 6-11pm, Sa noon-3pm and 6-11pm, Su noon-3pm and 7-10:30pm.) When Watson and Crick ran into **The Eagle,** 8 Benet St., to announce their discovery of DNA, the barmaid insisted they settle their 4-shilling tab before she'd serve them. Cambridge's oldest pub also has a Royal Airforce room, where WWII pilots stood on each other's shoulders to burn their initials into the ceiling. (☎505 020. Open M-Sa 11am-11pm, Su noon-10:30pm.) **The Fez Club,** 15 Market Passage, draws students to its Moroccan setting with Latin and trance. (Cover £2-8. M and W students ½-price. Open daily 9pm-3am.)

NORTHERN ENGLAND

The north's major cities grew out of the wool and coal industries, and bear the 19th-century scars to prove it, but their reinvigorated city centers have embraced post-industrial hipness with fresh youth culture. The region's innovative music and arts scenes are world-famous: Liverpool and Manchester alone have produced four of *Q Magazine*'s 10 biggest rock stars of the 20th century. When you need a break from frenetic urbanity, find respite in the Peak or Lake District.

MANCHESTER   ☎ 0161

Teeming with electronic beats and post-industrial glitz, Manchester (pop. 430,000) has risen from factory soot to savor a reputation as one of England's hippest spots. In 1996, the IRA bombed the city center, sparking urban renewal that has given Manchester a sleek modern look. The city is a hive of activity, from the shopping districts and museums to the wild nightlife and preeminent football team.

◪◪ TRANSPORTATION AND PRACTICAL INFORMATION. Flights arrive at **Manchester International Airport (MAN;** ☎ 489 3000). **Trains** leave Piccadilly Station on London Rd., for: Birmingham (1¾hr., 1 per hr., £23); Edinburgh (4hr., 5 per day, £45); Liverpool (50min., 2 per hr., £9); London Euston (2½-3hr., 1 per hr., £59); York (40min., 2 per hr., £18). Trains from Victoria Station on Victoria St. go to Liverpool (50min., 2 per hr., £9). National Express **buses** (☎ 08705 808 080) go from Chorlton St. to Liverpool (1hr., 1 per hr., £6) and London (4-6hr., 1 per hr., £22). Nearly 50 local bus routes stop at Piccadilly Gardens (1-day bus pass £3.30); route maps are available at the TIC. **Manchester Visitor Centre** is in the Town Hall Extension on Lloyd St. (☎ 234 3157; www.visitmanchester.com. Open M-Sa 10am-5:30pm, Su 10:30am-4:30pm.) Free **Internet** is available at **Central Library,** St. Peter's Sq. (☎ 234 1900. Open M-Th 9am-8pm, F-Sa 9am-5pm.) **Postal Code:** M2 1BB.

◪◪ ACCOMMODATIONS AND FOOD. Browse *Where to Stay* (free at the TIC) for listings. Book ahead in summer. **Hilton Chambers ❷,** 15 Hilton St., has a helpful staff and large, clean rooms, topped off with a grill-equipped roof deck. (☎ 236 4414; www.hattersgroup.com. Laundry £5. Free Wi-Fi. Reception 24hr. Dorms £15-21; doubles £28-35. MC/V.) Around the corner, **The Hatters Tourist Hostel ❷,** 50 Newton St., housed in a renovated hat factory, has clean but crowded rooms and friendly service. (☎ 236 9500; www.hattersgroup.com. Breakfast included. Laundry £1.50. Reception 24hr. Dorms £14-18; doubles £45; triples £60. MC/V.) Take the metro to G-Mex Station or bus #33 (dir.: Wigan) from Piccadilly Gardens to Deansgate to reach the spacious **YHA Manchester (HI) ❸,** Potato Wharf, Castlefield. (☎ 0870 770 5950; www.yhamanchester.org.uk. Breakfast included. Laundry £1.50. Internet £0.70 per min. Reception 24hr. Dorms £21; doubles £45. MC/V.)

Restaurants in **Chinatown** can be pricey, but most offer a reasonable, multicourse "Businessman's Lunch" (M-F noon-2pm; £4-8). Better yet, visit **Curry Mile,** a stretch of affordable Asian restaurants on Wilmslow Rd. For delicious food with unique character, stop at ◪**Trof ❷,** 2a Landcross Rd, a bohemian cafe, bar, and restaurant. Wash down a bacon and brie sandwich (£4.25) with one of 45 international beers. (☎ 224 0476; www.trof.co.uk. Open daily 9am-midnight. MC/V.) **Soup Kitchen ❶,** 31-33 Spear St., serves homemade soups and pies. Arrive early—the soups of the day are usually gone by 2pm. (☎ 236 5100; www.soup-kitchen.co.uk. Lunch special £4. Open M-F 9am-4pm. Cash only.) **Tampopo Noodle House ❷,** 16 Albert Sq., is a Manchester favorite, serving noodles from Indonesia, Japan, Malaysia, Thailand, and Vietnam. (☎ 819 1966; www.tampopo.co.uk. Noodles £6-11. Open daily noon-11pm. AmEx/MC/V.) Pick up groceries at **Tesco,** 58-66 Market St. (☎ 911 9400. Open M-F 6am-midnight, Sa 6am-10pm, Su 11am-5pm.)

◪◪ SIGHTS AND ENTERTAINMENT. The ◪**Manchester Art Gallery,** Nicholas St., has interactive exhibits (try to make a painting burp) and an art restoration gallery. The pre-Raphaelite collection is impressive. (☎ 235 8888. Open Tu-Su and bank holidays 10am-5pm. Free.) Don't miss the exploration of modern urban culture and art at the **Urbis** museum, Cathedral Gardens. The awe-inspiring museum is itself a sculpture, covered in 2200 plates of glass beneath a copper roof. (☎ 605 8200; www.urbis.org.uk. Open Tu-Su 10am-6pm. Free.) The **Museum of Science and**

Industry, Liverpool Rd., in Castlefield, displays working looms and steam engines in an illustration of Britain's industrialization. (☎832 2244. Open daily 10am-5pm. Free. Special exhibits £3-5.) The **John Rylands Library,** 150 Deansgate, keeps rare books. Its most famous holding is the St. John Fragment, a piece of New Testament writing from the 2nd century. (☎275 3764; www.library.manchester.ac.uk. Open M and W-Sa 10am-5m, Tu and Su noon-5pm. Free.) Loved and reviled in equal proportion, Manchester United is one of England's top football teams. From Old Trafford Metrolink stop, follow the signs up Warwick Rd. to the **Manchester United Museum and Tour Centre,** Sir Matt Busby Way, at the Old Trafford football stadium. Memorabilia from the club's 1878 inception to its recent trophy-hogging success may just convert you into a fanatic. (☎0870 442 1994. Open daily 9:30am-5pm. Tours 6 per hr. except on match days. Reserve ahead. £9.)

Streets in the **Northern Quarter** are dimly lit at night. If you're crossing from Piccadilly to Swan St. or Great Ancoats St., use Oldham St., where the neon-lit clubs provide reassurance. There's no shame in short taxi trips at night.

☒ NIGHTLIFE. At night, many of Manchester's lunchtime spots turn into preclub drinking venues or become clubs themselves. At **Thirsty Scholar,** off Oxford St., the students crowd into a small, dark bar underneath a railroad bridge. On weekend nights, the thud of overhead trains is drowned out by the music of local DJs. (☎236 6071. M and Th acoustic nights. F-Su DJ. Open M-Th 11am-2am, F-Sa 11am-2:30am, Su 11am-1am.) **The Temple,** 100 Great Bridgewater, makes for a one-of-a-kind experience, serving German beer in a Victorian public-toilet-turned-pub. (☎278 1610. Open daily 1pm-1am.) Centered around **Oldham Street,** the **Northern Quarter** is the city's outlet for live music. Partiers head to **Oxford Street** for late-night clubbing. Gay and lesbian clubbers should check out the **Gay Village,** northeast of Princess St. **Queer,** 4 Canal St., has huge booths and flatscreen TVs. (☎228 1360; www.queer-manchester.com. Open M-Sa 11am-2am, Su 11am-12:30am.)

LIVERPOOL ☎0151

Many Brits still scoff at once-industrial Liverpool, but Scousers—as Liverpudlians are colloquially known, in reference to a local stew dish—have watched their metropolis undergo a cultural face-lift, trading in working-class grit for offbeat vitality. Several free museums, two deified football teams, and top-notch nightlife helped earn the city the title of **European Capital of Culture 2008,** along with Stavanger, NOR (p. 744). Oh, yeah—some fuss is made over The Beatles.

☒ TICKET TO RIDE. Trains (☎08457 484 950) leave Lime St. Station for: Birmingham (1¾hr., M-Sa 1 per hr., £28); London Euston (3hr., 1 per hr., £60); Manchester Piccadilly (1hr., 2-4 per hr., £8.50). National Express **buses** (☎08705 808 080) run from Norton St. Station to: Birmingham (3hr., 4 per day, £14); London (4½-5½hr., 2 per hr., £22); Manchester (1hr., 1-3 per hr., £6). The Isle of Man Steam Packet Company (☎08705 523 523; www.steam-packet.com) runs **ferries** from Princess Dock to the Isle of Man. P&O Irish Ferry service (☎870 2424 777; www.poirishsea.com) runs to Dublin, IRE. The **TIC,** 08 Pl., has the free, handy *Visitor Guide to Liverpool, Merseyside, and England's Northwest.* (☎233 2008; www.visitliverpool.com. Open M and W-Sa 9am-6pm, Tu 10am-6pm, Su 11am-4pm.) Expert guide Phil Hughes runs personalized 3-4hr. Beatles tours from Strawberry Fields and Eleanor Rigby's grave (☎228 4565; £13). Surf the **Internet** for free or peruse a model of the city at the Central **Library** on William Brown St. (☎233 5817. Open M-F 9am-6pm, Sa 9am-5pm, Su noon-4pm.) **Postal Code:** L1 1AA.

GOLDEN SLUMBERS AND STRAWBERRY FIELDS FOREVER. Budget hotels are around **Lord Nelson Street,** next to the train station, and **Mount Pleasant,** one block from Brownlow Hill. **Embassie Backpackers ❷,** 1 Falkner Sq., is a first-rate hostel. (☎707 1089; www.embassie.com. Free laundry. Free Internet. Reception 24hr. Dorms £15 first night, £14 thereafter. Cash only.) A former Victorian warehouse, **International Inn ❷,** 4 South Hunter St., is clean and fun, with an adjoining Internet cafe. (☎709 8135; www.internationalinn.co.uk. Free coffee, tea, and toast. Internet £3 per hr. Dorms Su-Th £15, F-Sa £20; doubles £36/45. AmEx/MC/V.) **YHA Liverpool (HI) ❷,** 25 Tabley St., off The Wapping, is a tidy place with Beatles-themed rooms. (☎0870 7705 924. Kitchen available. Breakfast included. Dorms from £18, under 18 £16. Members only. MC/V.) Trendy cafes and budget-friendly kebab stands line **Bold** and **Hardman Streets.** Many of the fast-food joints on **Berry** and **Leece Streets** stay open late. At **Tabac ❶,** 126 Bold St., sleek, trendy decor belies affordable food. Sandwiches (from £3.50) on freshly baked bread are served all day. (☎709 9502. Breakfast from £2. Dinner specials £5.50-8. Open M-F 9am-11pm, Sa 9am-midnight, Su 10am-11pm. MC/V.) The **Granary Sandwich Bar ❶,** Drury Lane, has outrageously low prices. (☎236 0509. Open M-F 7:30am-2:30pm. Cash only.) **Hole in the Wall ❶,** 37 School Ln., offers barms (sandwiches) and quiches from £4 for eat-in or take-out. (☎709 7733. Open M-Sa 10am-4:30pm. Cash only.) Pick up groceries at the **Tesco Metro** in Clayton Sq., across from St. John's Shopping Centre. (Open M-F 6am-midnight, Sa 6am-10pm, Su 11am-5pm.)

MAGICAL MYSTERY TOUR. The TIC's **Beatles Map** (£3) leads visitors through the city's Beatles-themed sights including **Strawberry Fields** and **Penny Lane.** At Albert Dock, **The Beatles Story** traces the rise and fall of the band through Hamburg, the Cavern Club, and a pseudo-shrine to John's legacy of love. (☎709 1963; www.beatlesstory.com. Open daily 10am-6pm. £10, students £7.) The Liverpool branch of the **Tate Gallery,** also on Albert Dock, contains a collection of 19th- and 20th-century art. (☎702 7400; www.tate.org.uk/liverpool. Open Tu-Su 10am-5:50pm. Suggested donation £2. Special exhibits £5, students £4.) The **Walker Art Gallery** focuses on British artists, from the 1700s to today. (☎709 1963; www.thewalker.org.uk. Open daily 10am-5pm. Free.) Completed in 1978, the Anglican **Liverpool Cathedral,** on Upper Duke St., boasts the highest Gothic arches and the heaviest bells in the world. Climb the tower for a view that extends to Wales. (☎709 6271; www.liverpoolcathedral.org.uk. Cathedral open daily 8am-6pm. Tower open daily Mar.-Sept. 11am-5pm; Oct.-Feb. 11am-4pm. Cathedral free, tower £4.25.) Neon-blue stained glass casts a glow over the controversially modern interior of the **Metropolitan Cathedral of Christ the King,** on Mt. Pleasant. (☎709 9222. Open in summer M-Sa 8am-6pm, Su 8am-5pm; reduced hours in winter. Free.) The **Liverpool** and **Everton football clubs**—intense rivals—offer tours of their grounds. Bus #26 runs from the city center to Liverpool F.C.'s Anfield; bus #19 from the city center to Everton's Goodison Park. (Liverpool ☎260 6677; tour £10, students £6. Everton 330 2277; tour £8.50, students £5. Reserve ahead.)

A HARD DAY'S NIGHT. *Liverpool Echo* (£0.35), sold daily by street vendors, has up-to-date nightlife information. The **Ropewalks** area—especially **Matthew, Church,** and **Bold Streets**—overflows with clubbers on weekends. Fabulous **Society,** 64 Duke St., draws decadent crowds and posh VIPs to its steamy dance floor. (☎707 3575. Cover F and Su £5, Sa £10. Open F 10:30pm-2am, Sa 10:30pm-4am, Su 10:30pm-1am.) The **Cavern Club,** 10 Matthew St., where the Fab Four gained prominence, draws live bands, who hope history will repeat itself. (☎236 9091. Cover £2 on DJ nights, varies for live bands. Pub open M-Sa from 11am, Su noon-11:30pm.

BRITAIN

Club open M-Tu 11am-6pm, W-Sa 11am-2am, Su noon-12:30am.) **BaaBar,** 43-45 Fleet St., draws a youthful crowd and offers 35 varieties of shots ($1) with nightly specials. (☎708 8673. Open M-Th 5pm-2am, F-Sa 5pm-3am, Su 5pm-1am. MC/V.)

PEAK DISTRICT NATIONAL PARK

The Peak District isn't home to any true mountains, but its 1400 sq. km offer a bit of almost everything else. Surrounded by industrial giants Manchester, Nottingham, and Sheffield, the Peak District is a sanctuary of deep gullies, green pastures, and rocky hillsides, with picturesque villages and historic manors set against some of Britain's best scenery. Transportation is easiest in the south and near outlying cities, but hikers should head north for a more isolated escape.

▐▐ TRANSPORTATION AND PRACTICAL INFORMATION. The invaluable *Peak District Timetables* ($0.80), available at TICs, has accommodation and **bike** rental info, maps, and transit routes. Two **train** lines (☎08457 48 49 50) start in Manchester and enter the park at New Mills. One stops at Buxton, near the park's edge (1hr., 1 per hr., $6.70). The other crosses the park via Edale (50min., 12 per day, $7.70), Hope, and Hathersage (both 1hr., 12 per day, $7.85), ending in Sheffield (1½hr., 1 per hr., $12.90). **Buses** make a noble effort to connect scattered Peak towns; **Traveline** (☎0870 608 2608; www.traveline.org.uk) is a vital resource. **Transpeak** makes the 3hr. journey between Buxton, Bakewell, and Matlock (continuing to Manchester in one direction and Nottingham in the other), stopping at towns along the way (15 per day). Bus #173 runs from Bakewell to Castleton (1hr., 3-4 per day). Bus #200 runs from Castleton to Edale (20min., M-F 3 per day). The **Derbyshire Wayfarer** ticket, available at Manchester train stations and **NPICs,** allows one day of unlimited train and bus travel through Peak District as far north as Sheffield and as far south as Derby ($8, students $4). The NPICs at Bakewell, Buxton, Castleton, and Edale offer walking guides. **YHA Hostels ❶** operates 15 locations in the park (reserve ahead; dorms $13-16). For Buxton, Castleton, and Edale, see below. For the park's **YHA Camping Barns (HI) ❶,** book at the **YHA Camping Barns Department,** Trevelyan House, Dimple Rd., Matlock, Derbyshire, DE4 3YH. (☎0870 770 8868; $6 per person.) The park has three **Cycle Hire Centres** ($14 per day); *Cycle Derbyshire* (free), available at NPICs, includes hours, locations, and a trail map.

BAKEWELL AND EDALE. The town of Bakewell, 50km southeast of Manchester, is the best base for exploring the region. Several scenic walks through the **White Peaks** begin nearby. **The Garden Room ❹,** 1 Park Rd., is a 5min. walk from the town center. (☎81 42 99. Singles $45. Cash only.) A **Midlands Co-op** sells groceries at the corner of Granby Rd. and Market St. (Open M-Sa 8am-10pm, Su 10am-4pm.) Bakewell's **NPIC** is in Old Market Hall, on Bridge St. (☎0870 444 7275. Open daily Mar.-Oct. 9:30am-5:30pm; Nov.-Feb. 10am-5pm.) The northern Dark Peak area contains some of the wildest, most rugged hill country in England, including the spectacular peat marshes around Edale. For details on shorter **trails** nearby, check out the National Park Authority's *8 Walks Around Edale* ($1.40). Edale itself offers little more than a church, cafe, pub, school, and the nearby **YHA Edale (HI) ❶,** Rowland Cote. (☎0870 770 5808. Dorms $15, under 18 $11. MC/V.)

CASTLETON. Castleton's main attraction is ▉**Treak Cliff Cavern** and its purple seams of Blue John, a unique semi-precious mineral. (☎01433 62 05 71; www.blue-johnstone.com. Open daily Mar.-Oct. 10am-4:20pm; Nov.-Feb. 10am-3:20pm. 40min. tours 2-4 per hr. $6.80, students and YHA members $5.80.) The **NPIC** is on Buxton Rd. (☎01629 81 65 58. Open daily Easter-Oct. 9:30am-5:30pm; Nov.-Easter

10am-5pm.) **YHA Castleton (HI) ❷** is in the heart of town. It may be unavailable in July and August, when it hosts children's camps. (☎0870 770 5758. Kitchen available. Reserve 2-3 weeks ahead. Open Feb.-Dec. Dorms £14, under 18 £10. MC/V.)

BUXTON. A main hub for Peak travel, the spa town of Buxton, highly reminiscent of Bath, is a picture of Georgian elegance. Just outside town in the Buxton Country Park is spectacular **Poole's Cavern,** a cave that has drawn tourists for centuries; legend has it that Mary, Queen of Scots, once visited. (☎01298 269 78; www.poolescavern.co.uk. Open daily Mar.-Oct. 10am-5pm. 45min. tours every 30min. £6.75, students £5.50. Dress warmly.) The **TIC** is in The Crescent, a large Georgian-style building at the center of town. (☎01298 251 06; www.visitbuxton.com. Open daily Mar.-Oct. 9:30am-5pm; Nov.-Feb. 10am-4pm.) **Roseleigh Hotel ❸,** Broad Walk overlooking Pavilion Gardens, has a library with travel and adventure books; the hosts are former tour guides. (☎01298 249 04; www.roseleighhotel.co.uk. £31-33 per person. MC/V.) **Co-op,** Spring Gardens, sells groceries (☎278 44; open daily 8am-11pm). **The Slopes Bar ❶,** also on Spring Gardens, serves light meals in a swanky bistro setting. (☎01298 238 04. Open 9:30am-midnight; hot food served noon-5pm. MC/V.)

YORK
☎01904

With a history rife with conflict, York (pop. 137,000) is known as the "most haunted city in the world." Despite the lore—or because of it—the city remains one of England's top destinations. Once impenetrable to outsiders, the crumbling medieval walls of York are now defenseless against hordes of travelers. Brandishing cameras in place of swords, visitors come to ogle Britain's largest Gothic cathedral and down a pint at one of the city's many pubs.

█ ▉ TRANSPORTATION AND PRACTICAL INFORMATION. Trains (☎08457 484 950) leave Station Rd. for: Edinburgh (2½hr., 2 per hr., £67); London King's Cross (2hr., 2 per hr., £74); Manchester Piccadilly (1½hr., 3 per hr., £18); Newcastle (1hr., 4 per hr., £21). National Express **buses** (☎08705 808 080) depart from 20 Rougier St.; the train station; Exhibition Sq.; the train station; Piccadilly, and the Stonebow for: Edinburgh (6hr., 1 per day, £31); London (5½hr., 15 per day, £23); and Manchester (3hr., 15 per day, £12). Take Station Rd. to Museum St., cross the bridge, and go left on St. Leonard's Pl. for the **TIC,** Exhibition Sq. (☎550 099; www.visityork.org. Open Apr.-Oct. M-Sa 9am-6pm, Su 10am-5pm; Nov.-Mar. M-Sa 9am-5pm, Su 10am-4pm.) **York Central Library,** Museum St., has **Internet** (☎655 631. £2 per hr.). **Postal Code:** YO1 8DA.

▉ ▉ ACCOMMODATIONS AND FOOD. B&Bs (from £30) are outside the city walls and scattered along **Blossom, Bootham,** and **Clifton Streets,** and **Bishopthorpe Road.** Reserve weeks ahead in summer. ▉**Foss Bank Guest House ❸,** 16 Huntington Rd., has elegant, bright rooms with Wi-Fi, and a guest lounge. (☎635 548. Singles £29; doubles £60. Cash only.) **YHA York International ❷,** Water End, Clifton, 3km from the train station, has clean rooms, a bar (beer £2), and restaurant. Follow the river path "Dame Judi Dench" off Water End. (☎653 147. Kitchen available. Breakfast included. Dorms £20, under 18 £15; singles £28; doubles £52-55. AmEx/MC/V.)

At ▉**El Piano ❶,** 15 Grape Ln., Mexican flavors infuse veggie dishes (£3-6) in a laid-back dining room. (☎610 676. Open M-Sa 10am-midnight, Su noon-5pm. MC/V.) Part the crowds and find a seat on the patio of **Oscar's Wine Bar and Bistro ❷,** 8 Little Stonegate, for epic portions. (☎652 002. Meals £6-8. Happy hour M 4-11pm, Tu-F 5-7pm, Su 4-10:30pm. Open M-Sa 11:30am-11pm, Su noon-10:30pm. MC/V). **Victor J's Artbar ❶,** 1 Finkle St., serves huge sandwiches and burgers in a

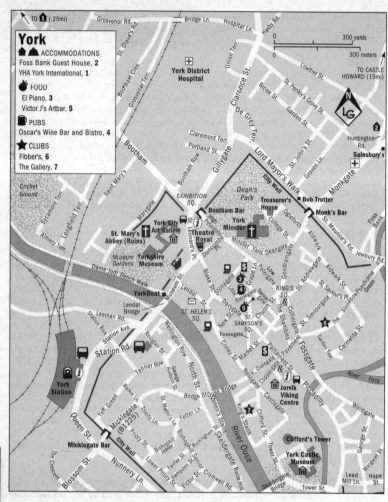

York

🏠🏕 ACCOMMODATIONS
Foss Bank Guest House, **2**
YHA York International, **1**

🍖 FOOD
El Piano, **3**
Victor J's Artbar, **5**

🍺 PUBS
Oscar's Wine Bar and Bistro, **4**

⭐ CLUBS
Fibber's, **6**
The Gallery, **7**

casual bistro. (☎ 541 771. Open M-W 10am-midnight, Th-Sa 10am-1am, Su 11am-6pm. MC/V.) Try sausages (£2) and burgers (£2) from stands in **Saint Sampson's Square.** For authentic York grub, visit one of the city's pubs, or find cheap eats at the many Indian restaurants outside the city gates. Greengrocers have peddled for centuries at **Newgate Market** between Parliament St. and the Shambles. (Open Apr.-Dec. M-Sa 9am-5pm, Su 9am-4:30pm; Jan.-Mar. M-Sa 9am-5pm.)

🔲 **SIGHTS.** A 4km walk along the **medieval walls** is the best introduction to York. Beware the tourist stampede, which only wanes in the morning and just before the walls and gates close at dusk. The **Association of Voluntary Guides** (☎ 621 756) offers free 2hr. **walking tours** at 10:15am, 2:15, and 6:45pm in summer and 10:15am in winter. 🏛**York Minster** is the largest Gothic cathedral outside of Italy. It's estimated that half of the medieval stained glass in England lines this cathedral's walls. The

Great East Window depicts the beginning and end of the world in over 100 scenes. See if you can spot Archbishop Thomas Lamplugh's statue. (☎557 216; www.york-minster.org. Open daily 7am-6:30pm. Evensong M-Sa 5pm, Su 4pm. Combined ticket with Undercroft, Treasury, and Crypt £7.50; students £4.50. Free 1hr. tours when volunteers are available, daily Apr.-Sept. 9:30am-3:30pm; Oct.-Mar. 10am-2pm. £5.50) Other cathedral sights include the **Chapter House,** which displays grotesque medieval carvings of everything from demons to a three-faced woman. Look for the Virgin Mary on the right upon entering, a small carving that went unnoticed by Cromwell's idol-smashing thugs. (Open daily 9am-6pm. Free.) The **Central Tower** offers city views. Ascents are permitted during a 5min. period every half hour. (Open daily Apr.-Sept. 9:30am-6pm; Oct.-Mar. 10am-4pm. £4.)

York Castle Museum, between Tower St. and Piccadilly, is arguably Britain's premier museum of daily life. Rooms include Kirkgate, a reconstructed Victorian shopping street, and Half Moon Court, its Edwardian counterpart. (☎687 687; www.yorkcastlemuseum.org.uk. Open daily 9:30am-5pm. £6.50, students £5.) **Clifford's Tower,** Tower St., is one of the last remaining pieces of **York Castle** and a chilling reminder of the worst outbreak of anti-Jewish violence in English history. In 1190, Christian merchants tried to erase their debts to Jewish bankers by annihilating York's Jewish community. One hundred fifty Jews took refuge in the tower where, faced with the prospect of starvation or butchery, they committed mass suicide. (☎646 940. Open daily Apr.-Sept. 10am-6pm; Oct. 10am-5pm; Nov.-Mar. 10am-4pm. £3, students £2.30.) The **Yorkshire Museum** houses Roman, Anglo-Saxon, and Viking artifacts, as well as the Middleham Jewel (c. 1450), an opulent sapphire set in gold. The haunting ruins of **St. Mary's Abbey,** once the most influential Benedictine monastery in northern England, are nearby. (Enter from Museum St. or Marygate. ☎687 687; www.yorkshiremuseum.org.uk. Open daily 10am-5pm. £5, students £4, families £14. Gardens and ruins free.)

🔟🔣 **ENTERTAINMENT AND NIGHTLIFE.** The Minster and area churches host a series of **summer concerts,** including the **York Early Music Festival.** (☎658 338; www.ncem.co.uk. Mid-July.) The *What's On* guide, available at the TIC, publishes info on current cultural events. In the evening, barbershop quartets fill **King's Square** and **Stonegate** along with jugglers and magicians. There are more **pubs** in York than gargoyles on the Minster's wall. York's dressy club, **The Gallery,** 12 Clifford St., has two hot dance floors and six bars. (☎647 947. Cover £3.50-10. Open Su-Th 10pm-2am, F-Sa 10pm-3am.) Hear up-and-coming bands nightly at **Fibber's,** Stonebow House, the Stonebow, followed by DJs after 10:30pm. (☎651 250; www.fibbers.co.uk. Cover £5, students £3 before 11:30pm. Live music 8-10:30pm.)

NEWCASTLE-UPON-TYNE   ☎0191

The largest city in the northeast, Newcastle (pop. 278,000) has shed its image as a faded capital of industry. The ▧**BALTIC Centre for Contemporary Art,** housed in a renovated grain warehouse, showcases a cutting-edge collection. (☎478 1810; www.balticmill.com. Open Su-Tu and Th-Sa 10am-6pm, W 10am-8pm. Free.) The BALTIC Centre is one of a trio of new buildings on the river, including the Norman Foster designed steel-and-glass **Sage Gateshead,** a complex of concert halls, and the **Gateshead Millennium Bridge,** a pedestrian and bicycle bridge that, in an impressive engineering feat, swivels upward once or twice per day to allow ships to pass. **Castle Garth Keep,** at the foot of St. Nicholas St., is all that remains of the 12th-century New Castle complex. The city did not get its name from the New Castle—it actually derives its name from a castle that existed over 100 years earlier. (☎232 7938. Open daily Apr.-Sept. 9:30am-5:30pm; Oct.-Mar. 9:30am-4:30pm. £1.50, students £0.50.) Theater buffs can treat themselves to an evening at the **Theatre Royal,** 100 Grey St.,

A REALLY COLD WAR

Despite the perpetual and divisive intra-Continental conflicts of the 20th century, Europe has unified. Today, Icelanders and Greeks and everyone in between live in economic and political cooperation. Everyone, that is, except for the citizens of Russia and of the small English village of Berwick-upon-Tweed.

Due to an unfortunate accident of semantics, Berwick-upon-Tweed has been at war with Russia for 153 years. In a 1502 treaty, Berwick was described as being "of" the Kingdom of England, rather than "in" it; Berwick received special mention in every ensuing royal proclamation. Nothing came of this inconvenience until 1853, when Queen Victoria signed a declaration of war on Russia, in the name of "Victoria, Queen of Great Britain, Ireland, Berwick-upon-Tweed, and the British Dominions beyond the sea." In the peace treaty ending the war, no mention of Berwick appeared.

Sources vary on what happened next. Some say the matter was cleared up by Tsarist Russia in 1914. Others assert a Soviet official signed a peace treaty in 1966 with the mayor of Berwick, who then said, "please tell the Russian people that they can sleep peacefully in their beds." Either way, no official documents have surfaced that can resolve the debate. Berwick, for its part, appears to have no intention of backing down.

northern England's premier stage. (☎0870 905 5060; www.theatreroyal.co.uk. Student tickets half-price on performance day when not sold out.)

Book ahead for accommodations during the weekend, when stag- and hen-night parties fill budget options. **Albatross Backpackers ❷**, 51 Grainger St., has modern facilities, 2min. from the train station and adjacent to major nightlife. (☎233 1330; www.albatrossnewcastle.com. Reception 24hr. 2- to 10-bed dorms £17-23. MC/V.) **Pani's Cafe ❷**, 61 High Bridge St., serves Italian dishes (£5-10) amid a boisterous vibe. (☎232 4366; www.paniscafe.com. Open M-Sa 10am-10pm. MC/V.) Pick up groceries at the **Safeway** on Clayton St. (☎261 2805. Open M-Sa 8am-7pm, Su 11am-5pm.) Home of the nectar known as brown ale, Newcastle has a legendary party scene. *The Crack* (free at record stores) is the best source for nightlife listings. Rowdy **Bigg Market** has England's highest concentration of pubs, while neighboring **Quayside** attracts herds to its clubs. Catch live bands nightly at **The Cluney**, 36 Lime St., Newcastle's premier underground music venue. (☎230 4474. Open daily 11am-late, food served until 9pm.) A state-of-the-art sound system keeps things pumping through the wee hours at **Digital**, Time Square. Saturday night's "Shindig" attracts Britain's top DJs. (☎261 9755. Cover £3-12. Open M-Tu and Th 10:30pm-2:30am, F-Sa 10:30pm-4am.) Newcastle's **Pink Triangle** of gay bars and clubs is west of the Centre for Life along Westmoreland Rd., St. James Blvd. and Marlborough Cres. No matter what your plans are, finish the night Newcastle-style with a kebab and extra chili sauce. **Trains** leave from Central Station for Edinburgh (1½hr., £40) and London King's Cross (3hr., 2 per hr., £103.) National Express **buses** (☎08705 80 80 80) leave St. James Blvd. for Edinburgh (3hr., 4 per day, £15) and London (7hr., 4 per day, £27). The **TIC** is at 27 Market St. in the Central Arcade. (☎277 8000. Open M-F 9:30am-5:30pm, Sa 9am-5:30pm.) **Postal Code:** NE1 7AB.

HADRIAN'S WALL

In AD 122, Roman Emperor Hadrian ordered the construction of a wall to guard Britannia's border, hoping to prevent those uncouth blue-tattooed barbarians to the north from infiltrating his empire. The wall is Britain's most important Roman monument, stretching 117km from Carlisle in the west to Newcastle in the east. West from Newcastle or north from Hexham, the **Chesters** cavalry fort is along the wall near Chollerford. The well-preserved bath house remains show how seriously the Romans took hygiene. (☎01434 681 379. Open daily

Apr.-Sept. 9:30am-6pm; Oct. 10am-5pm; Nov.-Mar. 10am-4pm. £3.80, students £3.) Continuing west, **Housesteads**, on a scenic ridge 1km from the road, has one of the best-preserved wall sections. (☎01434 344 363. Open daily Apr.-Sept. 10am-6pm; Oct. 10am-5pm; Nov.-Mar. 10am-4pm. £3.80, students £3.) Just 1.5km from Once Brewed Hostel (see below), archaeologists unearth artifacts daily at ▧**Vindolanda** fort and settlement. An on-site museum displays finds from the area. (☎01434 344 277; www.vindolanda.com. Open daily Apr.-Sept. 10am-6pm; mid-Feb. to Mar. and Oct. to mid-Nov. 10am-5pm. £5, students £4.10; combo ticket with Roman Army Museum £6.50/5.50.) Built from stones "borrowed" from the wall, the **Roman Army Museum** is at Carvoran, 1.5km northeast of Greenhead Hostel (see below) and five stops from Vindolanda on the AD122. (☎01697 747 485. Open daily Apr.-Sept. 10am-6pm; Feb.-Mar. and Oct.-Nov. 10am-5pm. Last entry 30min. before close. £4, students £3.50.)

Birdoswald Roman Fort, 25km east of Carlisle, offers views of walls, turrets, and milecastles. (☎01697 747 602. Open daily Apr.-Sept. 10am-5:30pm; Mar. and Oct. 10am-4pm. Museum and wall £3.80, students £3.) West of Carlisle, on the cliffs of Maryport, the **Senhouse Museum** houses Britain's oldest antiquarian collection, with exhibits on Roman warfare. (☎01900 816 168; www.senhousemuseum.co.uk. Open July-Oct. daily 10am-5pm; Apr.-June Tu and Th-Su 10am-5pm; Nov.-Mar. F-Su 10:30am-4pm. £2.50.) **Hadrian's Wall National Trail** is a 135km route from coast to coast. Guides and information are at TICs. **Hadrian's Cycleway** provides access to all the wall's main attractions following minor roads and bike paths.

Carlisle and Hexham have many **B&Bs** and make good bases for daytrips to the wall. Two hostels lie along the Hadrian's Wall Bus route. **YHA Greenhead ❷**, 26km east of Carlisle near the Greenhead bus stop, is in a converted chapel near the wall. (☎08707 705 842. Breakfast £4. Reception 8-10am and 5-10pm. Curfew 11pm. Dorms £13, under 18 £9.50. MC/V.) The AD122 stops at the **YHA Once Brewed ❷**, Military Rd., Bardon Mill, 1km from the wall. (☎08707 705 980. Breakfast £4. Laundry £1. Internet £2.50 per 30min. at the pub next door. Reception 8-10am and 2-10pm. Open Feb.-Nov. Dorms £15, under 18 £10. MC/V.) Although traveling by **car** is the easiest option, ▧**Hadrian's Wall Bus AD122** (who knew public transportation had a sense of humor?) provides reliable service, occasionally with a guide on board. The bus runs between Carlisle and Newcastle, stopping at historical sights. Buy the **DayRover** ticket, available from TICs and bus drivers, to get the most out of AD122. (2¼hr., Apr.-Oct. 7-8 per day, £7.) **Bus** #685 runs between Newcastle and Carlisle via Greenhead, Hexham, and other wall towns (2hr., 1 per hr.). **Trains** (☎08457 484 950) run between Carlisle and Newcastle (1½hr., 1 per hr., £11). Stations are roughly 2½km from the wall. The Hexham **TIC** is at the bottom of the hill from the abbey on Hallgate Rd., and the **NPIC** is in Once Brewed, on Military Rd. (☎01434 344 396. Open Apr.-Oct. daily 9:30am-5pm; Nov.-Mar. Sa-Su 10am-3pm.) Pick up the free and invaluable **Hadrian's Wall Bus AD122 Bus & Rail Timetables**, available from any area TIC or bus. For general info, call the **Hadrian's Wall Information Line** (☎01434 322 002; www.hadrians-wall.org).

LAKE DISTRICT NATIONAL PARK

Blessed with some of the most stunning scenery in England, the Lake District owes its beauty to a thorough glacier-gouging during the Ice Age. The district's jagged peaks and glassy lakes form a giant playground for bikers, boaters, and hikers, who in summer nearly equal sheep in number—and with four million sheep, that's quite a feat. Yet there's always some lonely hill or quiet cove where you will seem the sole visitor. Use the villages of Ambleside, Grasmere, Keswick, and Windermere as bases for exploring the region's hills—the farther west you go from A591, the more countryside you'll have to yourself.

🕮 TRANSPORTATION AND PRACTICAL INFORMATION. Trains (☎08457 484 950) run from Oxenholme, the primary gateway for the lakes, to: Birmingham (2hr., 1 per hr., £47); Edinburgh (2hr., 5-10 per day, £33); London Euston (3½hr., 7-9 per day, £108); Manchester Piccadilly (1½hr., 4-10 per day, £20). Trains also run from Windermere to Oxenholme (20min., 1 per hr., £3.50), and Manchester Piccadilly (1¾hr., 1-5 per day, £20). National Express **buses** (☎08705 808 080) arrive in Windermere from Birmingham (4½hr., 1 per day, £31) and London (8hr., 1 per day, £29), continuing north through Ambleside and Grasmere to Keswick. Stagecoach in Cumbria (☎0870 608 2608) is the region's primary bus service; *The Lakesrider* timetable (free) is at TICs and on buses. An **Explorer ticket** offers unlimited travel on all area Stagecoach buses (1-day £9; 4-day £19; 7-day £28). YHA Ambleside offers a **minibus** service (☎015394 323 04) between hostels (2 per day, £2.50) and service from the Windermere train station to hostels in Windermere and Ambleside (7 per day, 1st ride free, £2 thereafter). The **NPIC** is in **Brockhole**, halfway between Windermere and Ambleside. (☎015394 466 01; www.lake-district.gov.uk. Open Apr.-Oct. daily 10am-5pm.) Though B&Bs line every street in every town and there's a hostel around every bend, lodgings fill up in summer; reserve ahead.

WINDERMERE AND BOWNESS. Windermere and its sidekick Bowness-on-Windermere fill with vacationers in summer, when sailboats swarm the lake. The short climb to **Orrest Head** (round-trip 2.5km) is moderately difficult, but offers one of the best views in the Lake District. It begins opposite the TIC on the other side of A591. In Windermere, **Lake District Backpackers ❶** is a hostel well-suited to independent travelers—they won't coddle you, but they'll give you a warm bed. (☎015394 463 74; www.lakedistrictbackpackers.co.uk. Dorms £10-13. MC/V.) To get to the spacious **YHA Windermere (HI) ❶**, Bridge Ln., 3.2km north of Windermere off A591, catch the YHA shuttle from the train station. This hostel offers panoramic views of the lake and rents **bikes.** (☎015394 435 43. Breakfast, packed lunch, and dinner available with advance notice for £3.50-5.50 per meal. Internet £5 per hr. Open Feb.-Nov. daily; early Dec. F-Sa only. Dorms £13-16, under 18 £9-11.) **Windermere Lake Cruises** (☎015394 433 60), at the northern end of Bowness Pier, sends boats to Waterhead Pier in Ambleside (30min., round-trip £7.50) and south to Lakeside (40min., round-trip £7.80). Lakeland Experience **bus** #599 (3 per hr., £1.60) runs to Bowness pier from the train station in Windermere. The **TIC** is near the train station. (☎015394 464 99. Open Easter-Aug. M-Sa 9am-5:30pm, Su 10am-5pm.) The local **NPIC**, on Glebe Rd., is beside Bowness Pier. (☎015394 428 95. Open daily Apr.-Oct. 9.30am-5.30pm; Nov.-Mar. 10am-4pm.)

AMBLESIDE. Set in a valley 1.5km north of Lake Windermere, Ambleside is an attractive village with convenient access to the southern lakes. **Hiking** trails extend in all directions. The top of **Loughrigg**, a moderately difficult climb (round-trip 11km), has splendid views of high fells. The **Stockghyll Force** waterfall is an easy 1.5km from town. Lakeslink bus #555 stops in front of ◪**YHA Ambleside (HI) ❷**, 1.5km south of Ambleside and 5km north of Windermere, a former hotel with great food, refurbished rooms, and swimming. (☎015394 323 04. Bike rental £1.50 per hr. Internet £5 per hr. Dorms £20, under 18 £15.) Pick up fruits and veggies at **Granny Smith's** in Market Pl. (☎015394 331 45. Open M-F 8am-5pm, Sa 8am-6pm, Su 9am-4pm. Cash only.) **Bus** #555 (☎015394 322 31) leaves from Kelsick Rd. for Grasmere, Keswick, and Windermere (1 per hr., £2-6.50). The **TIC** is in the Central Building on Market Cross. (☎015394 325 82. Open daily 9am-5pm.)

GRASMERE. The peace that William Wordsworth enjoyed in the village of Grasmere is still palpable on quiet mornings. Guides provide 30min. tours of the early 17th-century **Dove Cottage**, 10min. from the center of town, where the poet lived from 1799 to 1808. The cottage is almost exactly as he left it. Next door is the outstanding **Wordsworth Museum.** (☎015394 355 44. Both open daily mid-Feb. to mid-Jan. 9:30am-5pm. Cottage and museum £6.40, students and HI members £5. Museum only £5.) The 10km **Wordsworth Walk** circumnavigates the two lakes of the Rothay River, passing the cottage, the poet's **grave** in St. Oswald's church-yard, and **Rydal Mount,** where he lived until his death in 1850. (Rydal ☎015394 330 02. Open Mar.-Oct. daily 9:30am-5pm; Nov. and Feb. M and W-Su 10am-4pm. £5, students £3.75.) **YHA Butharlyp Howe (HI) ❷,** on Easedale Rd., is a large Victo-rian house. (☎015394 353 16. Free Internet. Dorms £16, under 18 £11. MC/V.) The famous gingerbread at ◼**Sarah Nelson's Grasmere Gingerbread Shop ❶,** in Church Cottage, outside St. Oswald's Church, is a bargain at £0.33 per piece. (☎015934 354 28; www.grasmeregingerbread.co.uk. Open Easter-Sept. M-Sa 9:15am-5:30pm, Su 12:30-5:30pm; Oct.-Easter M-Sa 9:30am-4:30pm, Su 12:30-5:30pm.) **Bus** #555 stops in Grasmere every hour on its way south to Ambleside or north to Keswick.

KESWICK. Between Skiddaw peak and the northern edge of Lake Derwentwater, Keswick (KEZ-ick) is a tourist mecca for the region. A standout 6km dayhike from Keswick culminates with the eerily striking **Castlerigg Stone Circle,** a 5000-year-old Neolithic henge. Another short walk leads to the scenic **Friar's Crag,** on the shore of Derwentwater, and **Castlehead,** a viewpoint encompassing the town, lakes, and peaks beyond. Both walks are fairly easy, with only a few strenuous spurts. The riverside ◼**YHA Keswick (HI) ❷** has modern facilities near the town center. (☎0870 770 5894. Breakfast included. Dorms £20, under 10 £15. MC/V.) The **NPIC** is in Moot Hall, Market Sq. (☎017687 726 45. Open Apr.-Oct. daily 9:30am-5:30pm.)

ISLE OF MAN   ☎01624

Wherever you go on this Irish Sea islet, you'll come across an emblem: three legs joined together like the spokes of a wheel. It's the Three Legs of Man, the symbol of Manx pride and independence. Its accompanying motto translates to "Which-ever Way You Throw Me, I Stand." This speaks to the predicament of the island over the last few millennia, during which it's been thrown around between English, Scots, and Vikings. Today, Man controls its own affairs while remaining a crown possession, although it is technically not part of the UK or the EU.

⊠ GETTING THERE

Ronaldsway Airport (IOM; ☎821 600; www.gov.im/airport) is 16km southwest of Douglas on the coast road. Buses #1, 1C, 2A, and 2 connect to Douglas (25min., 1-3 per hr.), while others stop at points around the island. British Airways (☎0845 773 3377; www.britishairways.com), British European (☎01232 824 354; www.flybe.com), Manx2 (☎0870 242 2226; www.manx2.com), and Euromanx (☎0870 787 7879; www.euromanx.com) **fly** to the Isle. **Ferries** dock at the Sea Ter-minal at the southern end of Douglas, where North Quay and the Promenade meet near the bus station. The Isle of Man Steam Packet Company (☎661 661 or 08705 523 523; www.steam-packet.com) runs to Belfast (2¾hr., 2 per week), Dublin, IRE (3hr.; Jun.-Aug. 2 per week, Sept.-May 1-2 per month), Heysham, Lancashire (3½hr., 2 per day), and Liverpool (2½hr., 1-4 per day). Fares are highest in summer and on weekends (£15-32, round-trip £30-64). Book online for cheaper fares.

DOUGLAS

The Isle's capital and largest city, Douglas (pop. 27,000), a useful gateway for Isle exploration, sprawls along the eastern side of Man. The city's broad promenade bordered with pastel-colored rowhouses gives it the feeling of a Victorian resort.

BRITAIN

TRANSPORTATION. Isle of Man Transport (☎662 525; www.iombusand-rail.info) runs public **buses** and **trains.** The **Travel Shop,** on Lord St. next to the bus station, has bus maps and schedules. (☎663 366. Open M 8am-12:30pm and 1:30-5:45pm, Tu-F 8am-5:45pm, Sa 8am-12:30pm and 1:30-3:30pm.) The Travel Shop and the Douglas TIC sell **Island Explorer Tickets,** which provide unlimited travel on most buses, trains, and horse trams (1-day £12, 3-day £24, 5-day £35). **Protours,** Summer Hill, buses travelers from Douglas for ½ and full-day Isle tours. (☎676 105. W and Su 8:30am. £11-18). The island's small size makes it easy to navigate by **bike.** Try Eurocycles for rentals. (☎624 909. £15 per day. ID deposit. Open M-Sa 9am-5pm.)

⚡ ORIENTATION AND PRACTICAL INFORMATION. Douglas stretches 3km along the shore, from **Douglas Head** to the **Electric Railway** terminal. Douglas Head is separated from town by the **River Douglas.** Ferry and bus terminals lie just north of the river. The **Promenade** curves from the ferry terminal to the Electric Railway terminal along the beach, dividing the coastline from the shopping district with a line of Victorian rowhouses. Shops and cafes line **The Strand,** a pedestrian thoroughfare that begins near the bus station and runs parallel to the Promenade, turning into Castle St. and ending at a taxi queue near the Gaiety Theatre. The **TIC** is in the Sea Terminal Building just outside the ferry departure lounge. (☎686 766; www.visitis-leofman.com. Open Easter-Sept. M-Sa 8am-7pm, Su 9am-3pm; Oct.-Easter M-F 9:15am-5:30pm.) **Internet** is at Feegan's Lounge, 8 Victoria St. (☎619 786; www.fee-gan.com; £1 per 20min.; open M-Sa 8:30am-6pm). **Postal Code:** IM1 2EA.

> **YOU DA (ISLE OF) MAN.** The Isle of Man sets itself apart from other lesser isles. The island has its own Manx language (a cousin of Irish and Scottish Gaelic), tailless Manx cat, multi-horned Manx Loghtan sheep, and a local delicacy—kipper (herring smoked over oak chips).

Manx currency is equivalent in value to British pounds, but it's not accepted outside the Isle. If you use an ATM on the island, it will likely give you Manx currency. Notes and coins from England, Scotland, and Northern Ireland can be used in Man. Some Manx shops accept euro—look for signs. When preparing to leave, you will generally be successful asking for your change in UK tender. Post offices and newsstands sell Manx Telecom **phonecards.** Mobile phone users on plans from elsewhere in Britain will likely incur surcharges. The Isle shares Britain's **international dialing code,** ☎44. In an **emergency,** dial ☎999 or 112. It's wise to rely on phone cards and landlines for a short stay, although more long-term visitors should probably invest in a **Manx prepay SIM card,** available at the shop on Victoria St. in Douglas for £15. These allow access to the only official service, **Manx Pronto.**

⬛ ACCOMMODATIONS AND FOOD. Douglas is awash with **B&Bs** and **hotels.** For TT weeks, they fill a year ahead and raise their rates. The **Devonian Hotel ❷,** 4 Sherwood Terr., on Broadway, is a Victorian-style townhouse just off the Promenade. (☎674 676; www.thedevonian.co.uk. All rooms have TV. Breakfast included. Singles £25-28; doubles from £44. Cash only.) Next door, **Athol House Hotel ❸,** 3 Sherwood Terr. on Broadway, features elegant rooms with bath and TV. (☎629 356; www.atholhouse.net. From £26. Cash only.) TICs list 11 **campgrounds ❶.**

Grill and chip shops line **Duke, Strand,** and **Castle Streets,** while many hotels along the **Promenade** have elegant restaurants. **Copperfield's Olde Tea Shoppe and Restaurant ❸,** 24 Castle St., holds Viking Feasts and Edwardian Extravaganzas, and serves classically British fare. (☎613 650. Open in summer M-F 11am-8pm, Sa 11am-6pm; winter M-Sa 10am-4pm. MC/V, with a £0.50 charge.) Guinness posters and traditional music at **Brendann O'Donnell's ❶,** 16-18 Strand St., remind patrons of the Man's proximity to Ireland. (☎621 566. Open M-Th and Su noon-11pm, F-Sa noon-midnight. Cash only.) The **Food For Less** grocery is on Chester St., behind The Strand. (Open M-W and Sa 8am-8pm, Th-F 8am-9pm, Su 9am-6pm.)

◨◨ **SIGHTS AND HIKING.** From the shopping district, signs point to the Chester St. parking garage next to Food For Less; an elevator ride to the 8th-floor roof leads to a footbridge to the **Manx Museum**. The museum covers the geology and history of Man, with the artistic side displayed at the **Manx National Gallery of Art**. Don't miss exhibits about the island's days as a Victorian getaway, when it was unofficially known as the Isle of Woman due to its attractive seasonal population. (☎648 000. Open M-Sa 10am-5pm. Free.) The museum and gallery are part of the island-wide **Story of Mann,** a collection of museums and exhibits focused on island heritage, including sites in Ballasalla, the former capital Castletown, Peel, and Ramsey. A **Heritage Pass** (£11), available at all museums, grants admission to any four sites, which otherwise cost £3.30-5.50. (☎648 000; www.storyofmann.com).

Raad ny Foillan (Road of the Gull) is a 135km path around the island marked with blue seagull signs. The spectacular ◪**Port Erin to Castletown Route** (20km) offers the best of the island's beaches, cliffs, surf, and wildlife. **Bayr ny Skeddan** (The Herring Road), once used by Manx fishermen, covers the less thrilling 23km land route between Peel in the west and Castletown in the east. Appropriately, signs with herring pictures mark the trail. It overlaps the **Millennium Way**, which runs 45km from Castletown to Ramsey along the 14th-century Royal Highway, ending 1½km from Ramsey's Parliament Sq. *Walks on the Isle of Man* (free), available at the TIC, gives a cursory description of 11 walks. Free pamphlets also list dozens of routes. Eleven **campsites,** listed at the TIC, dot the isle.

▨▨ **FESTIVALS AND NIGHTLIFE.** TICs stock a calendar of events; ask for *What's On the Isle of Man* or check out www.isleofman.com or www.visitisle-ofman.com. During the two weeks from late May to early June, Man turns into a motorcycle mecca for the **Tourist Trophy (TT) Races** as the population doubles and 10,000 bikes flood the island (www.iomtt.com). The races were first held on Man in 1907 because restrictions on vehicle speed were less severe (read: nonexistent) on the island than on mainland Britain. The circuit consists of 60km of hairpin turns that top racers navigate at speeds over 120 mph. The **World Tin Bath Championships,** a race across the harbor in tin tubs in August, and a **Darts Festival** in March invite Manx natives and visitors alike to revel in idiosyncrasy.

Pubs in Douglas are numerous and boisterous, especially during the TT Races. Pass through the subway-like turnstile at **Quids Inn,** on the Promenade, where drinks cost £1-1.50. Prepare to drink standing up on weekends. (☎611 769. Hours vary.) Most of the **clubs** in Douglas are 21+ and some have free entrance until 10 or 11pm, with a £2-5 cover thereafter. Relax at **Colours,** on Central Promenade, in the Hilton. A spacious sports bar gives way to live cover bands and dance music as the night goes on. (☎662 662. Open daily noon-3:30am. £5 cover after 10pm).

▧ **DAYTRIP FROM DOUGLAS: PEEL.** Long ago, this "cradle of Manx heritage" played host to the Vikings. The Quayside maintains a rough-and-tumble sailor's edge (and holds a miniature Viking longhouse), while ◪ruins across the harbor are set against western sunsets. The most prominent relics are the stone towers of **Peel Castle,** which share the skyline of **St. Patrick's Isle** with the stone arches of **St. German's Cathedral** and the an excavated Viking tomb. The audio tour, included in the admission price, informs visitors about the history of the ruins. The site is on a cliff overlooking Peel, accessible by pedestrian causeway from the Quay. *(Open daily Easter-Oct. 10am-5pm. Last entry 1hr. before close. £3.30, children £1.70.)* **Moore's Tra-**

ditional Curers, Mill Rd., is supposedly the only kipper factory of its kind left in the world. Informal tours let visitors watch kippering in action and even climb up the interior of one of the smoking chimneys. Free kipper samples are available. (☎843 622; www.manxkippers.com. Shop open M-Sa 10am-5pm. Tours Apr.-Oct. M-Sa 3:30pm. £2, children free.) Outside of Peel at Ballacraine Farm, **Ballacraine Quad Bike Trails** leads 1½hr. trail rides, including training and refreshments. (☎801 219. £40 per person.) **Buses** (☎062 525) arrive and depart across the street from the Town Hall on Derby Rd., going to Douglas (#4, 4B, 5A, 6, 6B, X5; 35min.; 1-2 per hr.; £2) and Port Erin (#8; 55min., M-Sa 4 per day, £2). The **TIC** is a window in the Town Hall, Derby Rd (☎842 341. Open M-Th 8:45am-4:45pm, F 8:45am-4:30pm.) **Postal Code:** IM5 1AA.

WALES (CYMRU)

If many of the nearly three million Welsh people had a choice, they would float away from the English. Ever since England solidified control over Wales with the murder of Prince Llywelyn ap Gruffydd in 1282, Wales has attempted to assert its national identity. The country clings steadfastly to its Celtic heritage, and the Welsh language endures in conversation, commerce, and literature. As mines faltered in the mid-20th century, Wales turned from heavy industry to tourism. Travelers today come for dramatic beaches, castles, cliffs, and mountains.

CARDIFF (CAERDYDD)   ☎029

Cardiff calls itself "Europe's Youngest Capital" and seems eager to meet the title, with a metropolitan renaissance alongside rich history. Next to traditional monuments are landmarks of a different tenor: a new riverside stadium and cosmopolitan dining and entertainment venues. At the same time, local pride, shown in the red dragons on flags and in windows, remains as strong as ever.

▐▐ **TRANSPORTATION AND PRACTICAL INFORMATION. Trains** (☎08457 484 950) leave Central Station, Central Sq., for: Bath (1-1½hr., 1-3 per hr., £14); Birmingham (2hr., 2 per hr., £32); Edinburgh (7-7½hr., 3 per day, £100); London Paddington (2hr., 2 per hr., £53). National Express **buses** (☎08705 808 080) leave from Wood St. for Birmingham (2¼hr., 8 per day, £21), London (3½hr., 9 per day, £20), and Manchester (6hr., 8 per day, £39). Pick up a free *Wales Bus, Rail, and Tourist Map and Guide* at the TIC. Cardiff Bus (Bws Caerdydd), St. David's House, Wood St. (☎2066 6444), runs green and orange city buses in Cardiff and surrounding areas. (Service ends M-Sa 11:20pm, Su 11pm. £1-1.60, week pass £13.) The **TIC** is at Old Library, The Hayes. (☎2022 7281; www.visit-cardiff.info. Open M-Sa 9:30am-6pm, Su 10am-4pm.) The public **library,** on Bute St. just past the rail bridge, offers free **Internet** in 30min. slots. (☎2038 2116. Open M-W and F 9am-6pm, Th 9am-7pm, Sa 9am-5:30pm.) **Postal Code:** CF10 2SJ.

▐▐ **ACCOMMODATIONS AND FOOD.** Budget lodgings are hard to find in Cardiff. The cheapest B&Bs (from £20) are on the outskirts of the city. ◪**Cardiff International Backpacker ❷,** 98 Neville St., is a backpacker's dream, with Happy hours (Su-Th 7-9pm) and a rooftop patio with hammocks. (☎2034 5577; www.cardiffbackpacker.com. Breakfast included. Internet £2 per hr. Su-Th curfew 2:30am. Dorms £18; singles £24; doubles £38; triples £48. Credit card required for reservations. MC/V.) **Acorn Camping and Caravaning ❶,** near Rosedew Farm, Ham Ln. South, Llantwit Major, is 1hr. by bus X91 from Central Station and a 15min. walk from the Ham Ln. stop. (☎01446 794 024. £3.80 per person; £6.80 per tent site,

£9 per 2 tent sites. Electricity £3. AmEx/MC/V.) **Pancake House ❶**, Old Brewery Quarter, serves specialty crepes, such as bacon, avocado, and sour cream (£3.80), at low prices. (☎644 954. Open M-Th 10am-10pm, F 10am-11pm, Sa 9am-11pm, Su 9am-10pm. AmEx/MC/V.) Scavenge the stalls of **Central Market**, between St. Mary St. and Trinity St., for groceries. (Open daily 10am-4pm.) **Caroline Street** is a surefire post-club hot spot, with curried or fried goodies at shops that stay open until 3 or 4am.

◖◗ SIGHTS AND NIGHTLIFE. From a Roman legionary outpost to a Norman keep, medieval stronghold, and finally a Victorian neo-Gothic curiosity, extravagant **⬛Cardiff Castle**, Castle St., has seen some drastic changes in its 2000-year existence. (☎2087 8100. Open daily Mar.-Oct. 9:30am-6pm; Nov.-Feb. 9:30am-5pm. £7.50, students £6.) The **Civic Centre**, in Cathays Park, includes Alexandra Gardens, City Hall, and the **National Museum and Gallery**. The museum's exhibits range from a room of Celtic crosses to a walk-through display of Wales's indigenous flora and fauna. (☎2039 7951. Open Tu-Su 10am-5pm. Free.)

After 11pm, many of Cardiff's downtown pubs stop serving alcohol and the action migrates to nearby clubs, most located on or around **St. Mary Street**. For nightlife info, check the free *Buzz* guide or the *Itchy Cardiff Guide* (£3.50), available at the TIC. Three worlds collide at **Clwb Ifor Bach**, 11 Womanby St. The ground floor plays cheesy pop, especially on Wednesday student nights, the middle floor bar has softer music, and the top rocks out to live bands or trance. Cover is £3-4, but up to £10 for popular bands. (☎232 199; www.clwb.net. Drink specials nightly. Open Su-W until 2am, Th-Sa until 3 am. Call ahead for opening hours.) **Club X**, 35 Charles St., attracts a mixed gay and straight crowd with techno, live bands, and a beer garden. The club keeps the latest hours in Cardiff. (☎400 876; www.club-x-cardiff.co.uk. Cover £3-7. Open W 9pm-4am, F-Sa 10pm-6am.)

◪ DAYTRIP FROM CARDIFF: CAERPHILLY CASTLE. ⬛**Caerphilly Castle**, 13km north of Cardiff, may be easy to navigate today, but 13th-century warriors had to contend with pivoting drawbridges, trebuchets, crossbows, and catapults (replicas of which are now displayed) when attacking this stronghold, the most technologically advanced castle of its time. Take the train (20min., M-Sa 2 per hr., £3.30) or bus #26 from Central Station. *(☎2088 3143. Open June-Sept. daily 9:30am-6pm; Apr.-May daily 9:30am-5pm; Oct.-Mar. M-Sa 9:30am-4pm, Su 11am-4pm. £3.50, students £3.)*

WYE VALLEY

William Wordsworth mused on the tranquility and pastoral majesty of the once-troubled Welsh-English border territory around Wye Valley. As the *Afon Gwy* (Wye River) winds through the surrounding abbeys, castles, farms, and trails, much of the landscape seems untouched by human hands and the passage of time.

▤ TRANSPORTATION. Chepstow is the best entrance to the valley. From Chepstow, **trains** (☎08457 484 950; www.nationalrail.com) go to Cardiff (40min., 1-2 per hr., £6). National Express (☎08705 808 080; www.nationalexpress.com) **buses** go to Cardiff (50min., 13 per day, £4.60) and London (2½hr., 7 per day, £20). TICs offer the free *Monmouthshire Local Transport Guide* and *Discover the Wye Valley by Foot and by Bus* (£0.50). **Hiking** is a great way to explore the region. The 220km **Wye Valley Walk** treks north from Chepstow, through Hay-on-Wye, and on to Prestatyn. **Offa's Dyke Path** has 285km of hiking and biking paths along the Welsh-English border. For info, call the Offa's Dyke Association (☎01547 528 753).

CHEPSTOW AND TINTERN. Flowers spring from the ruins of Chepstow's **Castell Casgwent**, Britain's oldest dateable stone castle (c. 1070), which offers stunning views of the Wye from its tower walls. (☎ 01291 624 065. Open daily 9:30am-6pm. £3.50, students £3.) The **First Hurdle Guest House ❹**, 9-10 Upper Church St., has comfortable rooms near the castle. (☎ 01291 622 189. Singles £40; doubles £60. AmEx/MC/V; £1.50 charge.) Pick up groceries at **Tesco** on Station Rd. (Open M 8am-midnight, Tu-F 24hr., Sa midnight-10pm, Su 10am-4pm.) **Trains** arrive on Station Rd.; buses stop in front of Somerfield supermarket. Buy tickets at **The Travel House,** 9 Moor St. (☎ 01291 623 031. Open M-Sa 9am-5:30pm.) The **TIC** is on Bridge St. (☎ 623 772; www.chepstow.co.uk. Open daily Apr.-Oct. 10am-5:30pm; Nov.-Mar. 10am-3:30pm.) **Postal Code:** NP16 5DA.

Eight kilometers north of Chepstow on A466, the Gothic arches of ▨**Tintern Abbey** "connect the landscape with the quiet of the sky," as described by Wordsworth. (☎ 01291 689 251. Open June-Sept. daily 9:30am-6pm; Apr.-May and Oct. daily 9:30am-5pm; Nov.-Mar. M-Sa 9:30am-4pm, Su 11am-4pm. £3.50, students £3. 45min. audio tour £1.) A 3km hike along **Monk's Trail** leads to **Devil's Pulpit,** from which Satan is said to have tempted the monks as they worked in the fields. **YHA St. Briavel's Castle (HI) ❶**, 6km northeast of Tintern across the English border, occupies a 13th-century fortress. While a unique experience—it was formerly King John's hunting lodge—it's somewhat remote, and should only be booked by those prepared for a 3km uphill hike. From A466 (bus #69 from Chepstow; ask to be let off at Bigsweir Bridge) or Offa's Dyke, follow signs from the edge of the bridge. (☎ 01594 530 272. Lockout 10am-5pm. Curfew 11:30pm. Dorms from £17. MC/V.) Campers can use the **field ❶** next to the old train station (£2). Try **The Moon and Sixpence ❷**, on High St., for classic pub grub with great views of the Wye. (☎ 01291 689 284. Kitchen open noon-2:30pm and 6:30-9:30pm. Open daily noon-11pm.)

SNOWDONIA NATIONAL PARK

Amid Edward I's impressive 13th-century manmade battlements in Northern Wales lies the 2175 sq. km natural fortress of Snowdonia National Park. The region's craggy peaks, the highest in England and Wales, yield diverse terrain— pristine blue lakes dot rolling grasslands, while slate cliffs slope into wooded hills.

◨▨ TRANSPORTATION AND PRACTICAL INFORMATION. Trains (☎ 08457 484 950) stop at larger towns on the park's outskirts, including Conwy (p. 173). The Conwy Valley Line runs across the park from Llandudno through Betws-y-Coed to Blaenau Ffestiniog (1hr., 2-7 per day). There, it connects with the Ffestiniog Railway, which runs through the mountains to Porthmadog, meeting the Cambrian Coaster line to Llanberis and Aberystwyth. **Buses** run to the park interior from Conwy and Caernarfon; consult the *Gwynedd Public Transport Maps and Timetables* and *Conwy Public Transport Information*, free in all regional **TICs.** The **NPIC** is in Penrhyndeudraeth, Gwynedd (☎ 01766 770 274; www.eryri-npa.gov.uk or www.gwynedd.gov.uk).

▨ HIKING. The highest peak in England and Wales, **Mount Snowdon** (1085m) is the park's most popular destination. Its Welsh name is *Yr Wyddfa* (the burial place)—local lore holds that Rhita Gawr, a giant cloaked with the beards of the kings he slaughtered, is buried here. Six paths of varying difficulty wind their way up Snowdon; pick up *Ordnance Survey Landranger Map #115* (£6.50) and *Outdoor Leisure Map #17* (£7.50), as well as individual trail guides, at TICs and NPICs. No matter how beautiful the weather is below, it will be cold, wet, and unpredictable high up—dress accordingly. Contact **Mountaincall Snowdonia** (☎ 09068 500 449) for local forecasts and ground conditions or visit an NPIC.

HARLECH. Harlech Castle is part of the "iron ring" of fortresses built by Edward I to quell Welsh troublemakers, but it later served as the insurrection headquarters of Welsh rebel Owain Glyndŵr. (☎01766 780 552. Open June-Sept. daily 9:30am-6pm; Apr.-May and Oct. daily 9:30am-5pm; Nov.-Mar. M-Sa 9:30am-4pm, Su 11am-4pm. £3.50, students £3.) Enjoy spacious rooms and castle views at ⊠Arundel ❷, Stryd Fawr. Call ahead for a ride. (☎01766 780 637. £16. Cash only.) **The Weary Walker's Cafe ❶**, on Stryd Fawr near the bus stop, has sandwiches for £2-3. (☎01766 780 751. Open in summer daily 9:30am-5pm; low season 10:30am-4pm. Cash only.) Harlech lies midway on the Cambrian Coaster line; Arriva Cymru **train** T5 (☎08457 484 950) arrives from and runs to Porthmadog (20min., 3-9 per day, £2.40) and connects to other towns on the Llyn Peninsula. The **Day Ranger** pass allows unlimited travel on the Coaster line for one day (£7, children £3.50, families £14). The **TIC** and **NPIC** are on Stryd Fawr. (☎01766 780 658. Open daily Easter-Oct. 9:30am-12:30pm and 1:30-5:30pm.) **Postal Code:** LL46 2YA.

CAERNARFON. Edward I started building ⊠Caernarfon Castle (car-NAR-von) in 1283 to contain and intimidate the rebellious Welsh, but ran out of money before he could finish it. The castle is nonetheless an architectural feat; its walls withstood a rebel siege in 1404 with only 28 defenders. (☎01286 677 617. Open June-Sept. daily 9:30am-6pm; Apr.-May and Oct. daily 9:30am-5pm; Nov.-Mar. M-Sa 9:30am-4pm, Su 11am-4pm. £4.90, students £4.50.) **Totter's Hostel ❶**, 2 High St., has spacious rooms and terrific owners. (☎01286 672 963; www.totters.co.uk. Dorms £14. MC/V.) Charming **Hole-in-the-Wall Street** has cafes and restaurants. Arriva Cymru (☎08706 082 608) **buses** #5 and 5X leave the city center at Penllyn for Conwy (1¾hr., 1-3 per hr.). KMP (☎870 880) #88 goes to Llanberis (25min.; 1-2 per hr.; £1.50, £2). National Express buses (☎08705 808 080) run to London (9hr., 1 per day, £28). The **TIC** is on Castle St. (☎01286 672 232. Open Apr.-Oct. daily 9:30am-4:30pm; Nov.-Mar. M-Sa 9:30am-4:30pm.) **Postal Code:** LL55 2ND.

CONWY. The central attraction of this tourist mecca is the imposing, 13th-century ⊠Conwy Castle and its impressive **town walls.** Try to get on "celebrity" guide Neville Hortop's tour; his ferocious approach to history is very entertaining. (☎01492 592 358. Open June-Sept. daily 9:30am-6pm; Apr.-May and Oct. daily 9:30am-5pm; Nov.-Mar. M-Sa 9:30am-4pm, Su 11am-4pm. £4.50, students £4. Tours £1.) Enjoy comfortable rooms (some with quay views) at ⊠Swan Cottage ❷, 18 Berry St., a B&B in a renovated 16th-century building near the town center. (☎01492 596 840; myweb.tiscali.co.uk/swancottage. Singles £25; doubles £45. Cash only.) **Pen-y-Bryn Tea Rooms ❶**, on High St., offers Welsh tea (£4.50) and 16th-century timbered nooks. (☎01492 596 445. Sandwiches from £3.50. Open M-F 10am-5pm, Sa-Su 10am-5:30pm. Cash only.) Arriva Cymru **buses** (☎08706 082 608) #5 and 5X stop in Conwy on their way to Caernarfon from Llandudno (1¼hr., 2-4 per hr., £5). The **TIC** is at the castle entrance. (☎01492 592 248. Open daily June-Sept. 9:30am-6pm; May and Oct.-Nov. 9:30am-5pm; Dec.-Apr. 9:30am-4pm.) **Postal Code:** LL32 8H7.

SCOTLAND

Half the size of England with only one-tenth of its population, Scotland has open spaces and natural splendor unrivaled by its southern neighbor. The craggy, heathered Highlands and the mists of the Hebrides elicit awe, while farmlands and fishing villages harbor a gentler beauty. Scotland at its best is a world apart from the rest of the UK, and its people revel in a culture all their own. The Scots defended their independence for hundreds of years before reluctantly joining England in 1707. While the kilts, bagpipes, and souvenir clan paraphernalia of the big cities may grow tiresome, a visit to Scotland's less touristed areas will allow you to rub elbows with the inheritors of many cherished traditions: a B&B owner speaking Gaelic to her children, a crofter cutting peat, or a fisherman setting out in his skiff.

▧ GETTING TO SCOTLAND

Buses from London (8-12hr.) are generally the cheapest option. National Express (☎08705 808 080; www.nationalexpress.com) connects England and Scotland via Edinburgh and Glasgow. **Trains** are faster but more expensive. From London, GNER runs trains (☎08457 225 225; www.gner.co.uk) to Edinburgh and Glasgow (4½-6hr., £27-100). Book online for discounts. **British Airways** (☎0870 8509 850; www.ba.com) sells round-trip England-to-Scotland tickets from £85. **easyJet** (☎08706 000 000; www.easyjet.com) flies to Edinburgh and Glasgow from London Gatwick, Luton, and Stansted. The fares are web-only; book far ahead and fly for as little as £5. **Ryanair** (☎08712 460 000; www.ryanair.com) flies to Edinburgh and to Glasgow Prestwick (1hr. from the city) from Dublin and London.

▛ TRANSPORTATION

In the **Lowlands** (south of Stirling and north of the Borders), train and bus connections are frequent. In the **Highlands,** Scotrail and GNER **trains** snake slowly on a few routes, bypassing the northwest almost entirely. Many stations are unstaffed—buy tickets on board. A great money-saver is the **Freedom of Scotland Travelpass,** which allows unlimited train travel and transportation on most **Caledonian MacBrayne** ("CalMac") ferries, with discounts on other ferry lines. Purchase the pass before traveling to Britain at any BritRail distributor (p. 113). **Buses** tend to be the best way to travel. **Traveline Scotland** has the best information on all routes and services (☎0871 200 2233; www.travelinescotland.com). Scottish Citylink (☎08705 505 050) runs most intercity routes. **Postbuses** (Royal Mail customer service ☎08457 740 740) are a British phenomenon. Red mail vans pick up passengers and mail once or twice a day in the most remote parts of the country, typically charging £2-5 (and sometimes nothing). Many travelers believe them to be a reliable way to get around the Highlands. **HAGGIS** (☎0131 558 3738; www.haggisadventures.com) and **MacBackpackers** (☎01315 589 900; www.macbackpackers.com) cater to the young and adventurous, with many tours departing from Edinburgh. Both run hop-on, hop-off excursions that let you travel at your own pace.

EDINBURGH   ☎0131

A city of elegant stone amid rolling hills and ancient volcanoes, Edinburgh (ED-in-bur-ra; pop. 500,000) is the jewel of Scotland. Since David I granted it *burgh* (town) status in 1130, it has been a hotbed for forward-thinking artists and intellectuals. The tradition lives on today as new clubs emerge beneath its medieval spires. In August, Edinburgh becomes a mecca for the arts, drawing talent and crowds to its wild International and Fringe Festivals.

▛ TRANSPORTATION

Flights: Edinburgh International Airport (EDI; ☎0870 040 0007) is 11km west of the city. Lothian **Airlink** (☎555 6363) shuttles between the airport and Waverley Bridge (25min.; 4-6 per hr., 1 per hr. after midnight; £3, round-trip £5; children £2/3.)

Trains: Waverley Station (☎08457 484 950), between Princes St., Market St., and Waverley Bridge. Trains to: **Aberdeen** (2½hr.; M-Sa 1 per hr., Su 8 per day; £34); **Glasgow** (1hr., 4 per hr., £10); **Inverness** (3½hr., 1 per 2hr., £32); **London King's Cross** (4¾hr., 1 per hr., £103); **Stirling** (50min., 2 per hr., £6.10).

Buses: Edinburgh Bus Station, St. Andrew Sq. Open daily 6am-midnight. Ticket office open daily 8am-8pm. National Express (☎08705 808 080) to **London** (10hr., 4 per day, £21). Scottish Citylink (☎08705 505 050) to: **Aberdeen** (4hr., 1 per hr., £18), **Glasgow** (1hr., 2-4 per hr., £4), and **Inverness** (4½hr., 8-10 per day, £17). A bus-ferry route goes to **Belfast** (2 per day, £20) and **Dublin, IRE** (1 per day, £27).

Public Transportation: Lothian buses (☎555 6363; www.lothianbuses.com) provide most services. Exact change required (£1 flat fare, children £0.60). **Daysaver** ticket (£2.30, children £2) available from any driver. **Night buses** cover select routes after midnight (£2). **First Edinburgh** (☎0870 872 7271) also operates locally. **Traveline** (☎0870 608 2608) has information on all area public transport.

Bike Rental: Biketrax, 11 Lochrin Pl. (☎228 6633; www.biketrax.co.uk). Mountain bikes £12 per ½-day, £16 per day. Open M-Sa 9:30am-5:30pm, Su noon-5pm.

◼⚡ ❷ ORIENTATION AND PRACTICAL INFORMATION

Edinburgh is a perfect city for walking. **Princes Street** is the main thoroughfare in **New Town,** the northern section of the city. From there you can view the impressive stone facade of the towering **Old Town** to the south. The **Royal Mile** (Castle Hill, Lawnmarket, High St., and Canongate) is the major road in the Old Town and connects **Edinburgh Castle** in the west to the **Palace of Holyroodhouse** in the east. **North Bridge, Waverley Bridge,** and **The Mound** connect Old and New Town. Two kilometers northeast, **Leith** is the city's seaport on the Firth of Forth.

Tourist Information Centre: Waverley Market, 3 Princes St. (☎0845 225 5121), on the north side of Waverley Station. Books rooms for £3 plus 10% deposit; sells bus, museum, theater, and tour tickets. Open July-Aug. M-Sa 9am-8pm, Su 10am-8pm; May-June and Sept. M-Sa 9am-7pm, Su 10am-7pm; Apr. and Oct. M-Sa 9am-6pm, Su 10am-6pm; Nov.-Mar. M-Sa 9am-5pm, Su 10am-5pm.

GLBT Services: Edinburgh Lesbian, Gay, and Bisexual Centre, 58a-60 Broughton St. (☎478 7069), inside Sala Cafe-Bar, or visit **Gay Edinburgh** at www.visitscotland.com.

Police: Headquarters at Fettes Ave. (☎311 3901; www.lbp.police.uk).

Hospital: Royal Infirmary, 51 Little France Cr. (☎536 1000, emergencies 536 6000).

Internet Access: Free at the **Central Library** (☎242 8000) on George IV Bridge. Open M-Th 10am-8pm, F 10am-5pm, Sa 9am-1pm. **easyInternet Cafe,** 58 Rose St. (☎220 3577), inside Caffe Nero. £2 per hr. Open M-Sa 7am-10pm, Su 9am-10pm.

Post Office: (☎556 9546.) In the St. James Centre beside the bus station. Open M-Sa 9am-5:30pm. **Postal Code:** EH1 3SR.

▶ ACCOMMODATIONS

Edinburgh's accommodations cater to every kind of traveler. Hostels and hotels are the only city-center options, while B&Bs and guesthouses begin on the periphery. It's a good idea to reserve ahead in summer, and essential to be well ahead of the game at New Year's and during festival season (late July-early Sept.).

▩ Budget Backpackers, 37-39 Cowgate (☎226 2351; www.budgetbackpackers.co.uk). A modern inner city hostel, renowned for its pub crawls (M-Sa). Spacious 2- to 12-bed rooms; women-only dorms available. Free daily city tour. Breakfast £2. Lockers free.

TOP TEN WAYS TO CLOG YOUR ARTERIES

Edinburgh is famous for its fried foods. Here are the greasiest options:

10. Deep-Fried Cheeseburger: Patty and cheese are deep fried, then placed on the bun and enjoyed as usual.

9. Deep-Fried Sausage: Tastes a bit like a corn dog. looks a bit like—well, never mind.

8. Deep-Fried Haggis: The traditional Scottish favorite. Improved upon? Opinions differ.

7. Deep-Fried Steak: This is no filet mignon. Think deep fried burger, minus the bun.

6. Deep-Fried Skittles: How do they not lose the Skittles through the holes in the bottom of the fryer? More importantly, who was the first person who thought, "Hey, these Skittles are good. You know what would make them even better? Dousing them in a pan of hot lard."

5. Deep-Fried Pizza: With your choice of toppings.

4. Deep-Fried Black Pudding: The only way to improve upon a sausage made from pig's blood is to throw it in a deep fat fryer.

3. Deep-Fried White Pudding: Like black pudding, but white.

2. Deep-Fried Mars Bar: ▨

1. Deep-Fried Hospitality: Many chip shops will deep fry anything you want, if you bring it to the shop and ask nicely. Be creative!

Internet £0.15 per 30min. Reception 24hr. Ages 18+ only. Rooms £9-24. MC/V. ❶

▨ **Globetrotter Inn,** 46 Marine Dr. (☎336 1030; www.globetrotterinns.com). 15min. from Waverley train station and Edinburgh International Airport. This hostel feels like a world of its own on large grounds next to the Firth of Forth. An hourly shuttle service runs to and from the city, though a bar, gym, hot tub, shop, and TV room make it tempting to stay put. Curtained bunks offer maximum privacy. Light breakfast included. Lockers free. Key card access. Dorms £9.50-19; doubles with bath £23. MC/V. ❶

Castle Rock Hostel, 15 Johnston Terr. (☎225 9666). Just steps from the castle, this friendly hostel has a party atmosphere and a top-notch cinema room. Nightly movies. Ask about their haircut offer: £10 with a free shot of vodka. 8- to 16-bed dorms £13-15; doubles and triples £15-17. AmEx/MC/V. ❷

Royal Mile Backpackers, 105 High St. (☎557 6120). A well-kept hostel with a community aura. As a branch of Scotland's Top Hostels, guests have access to Mac-Backpackers Tours of Scotland, run by the same branch. Amenities, such as free Wi-Fi, at nearby High St. Hostel. 8-bed dorms £13-15. AmEx/MC/V. ❶

◖ FOOD

Scotland's capital features an exceptionally wide range of cuisines and restaurants. For a traditional taste of the country, Edinburgh offers everything from haggis to creative "modern Scottish." Many pubs offer student and hosteler discounts in the early evening. Take-out shops on **South Clerk Street, Leith Street,** and **Lothian Road** have reasonably priced Chinese and Indian food. Buy groceries at **Sainsbury's,** 9-10 St. Andrew Sq. (☎225 8400. Open M-Sa 7am-10pm, Su 10am-8pm.)

▨ **The City Cafe,** 19 Blair St. (☎220 0125), right off the Royal Mile behind the Tron Kirk. This popular Edinburgh institution is a cafe by day and a flashy pre-club by night. Try the herb chicken and avocado melt (£6) or their incredible milkshakes. Street-side seating ideal for people-watching. Happy hour daily 5-8pm. Open daily 11am-1am; during festival 11am-3am. Kitchen open M-Th 11am-11pm, F-Su 11am-10pm. MC/V. ❷

▨ **The Mosque Kitchen,** 50 Potterrow. In the courtyard of Edinburgh's central mosque, a jumble of mismatched chairs and long tables make up an outdoor cafeteria. Popular with students. Their heaping plates of curry (£3) are unbeatable. Open M-Th and Sa-Su noon-7pm; F noon-1pm and 1:45-7pm. Cash only. ❶

The Elephant House, 21 George IV Bridge (☎220 5355). Harry Potter and Hogwarts were conceived here on hastily scribbled napkins. A perfect place to chill, chat, or start a best-selling book series. Teas, coffees, and the best shortbread in the universe. Selections from scrumptious pastries (£1.25) to sandwiches, panini, and pizzas (from £5.30). Turns into a sit-down restaurant with live music Th 8pm. Great views of the castle. Happy hour daily 8-9pm. Open daily 8am-11pm. MC/V. ❶

Sadivino, 52 West Richmond St. (☎667 7719). This friendly sidewalk cafe fills up during lunch. Everything from panini to more substantial Italian fare is under £4. Most entrees £3. Open M-F 11am-6pm, Sa noon-6pm. Cash only. ❶

Henderson's Salad Table, 94 Hanover St. (☎225 2131). The founding member of Edinburgh's vegetarian scene, Henderson's has dished up seriously good salads (£4) for as long as anyone can remember. Feel healthy while drunk: the wine bar offers a range of organic and vegan beers, spirits, and wines. Open M-Su 7:30am-10:30pm. MC/V. ❶

⊙ SIGHTS

Among the array of tours touting themselves as "the original," ◪**Edinburgh Literary Pub Tour** is the best. Led by professional actors, this 2hr. crash course in Scottish literature meets outside the Beehive Inn on Grassmarket. (☎226 6665; www.edinburghliterarypubtour.co.uk. Tours June-Sept. daily 7:30pm; Mar.-May and Oct. Th-Su 7:30pm; Nov.-Feb. F 7:30pm. £7, students £6. Discount for online booking.)

THE OLD TOWN AND THE ROYAL MILE

Edinburgh's medieval center, the fascinating Royal Mile, defines the Old Town. Once lined with narrow shopfronts and slums towering a dozen stories high, this famous strip is now a playground for hostelers and locals alike, buzzing with bars, attractions, and the inevitable cheesy souvenir shops.

◪**EDINBURGH CASTLE.** Dominating the Edinburgh skyline from atop a thankfully extinct volcano, Edinburgh Castle is a testament to the city's past strategic importance. Today's castle is the product of centuries of rebuilding, the most recent additions hailing from the 1920s. The **One O'Clock Gun** fires Monday through Saturday. *(You can't miss it.* ☎225 9846; www.historic-scotland.gov.uk. Open daily Apr.-Oct. 9:30am-6pm; Nov.-Mar. 9:30am-5pm. £11, students £9; includes guided tour.)

CASTLE HILL AND LAWNMARKET AREA. The Scotch Whisky Experience at the **Scotch Whisky Heritage Centre** provides a Disney-style tour through the "history and mystery" of Scotland's most famous export. *(354 Castle Hill.* ☎220 0441. Open daily June-Sept. 9:45am-5:30pm; Oct.-May 10am-5pm. £9, students £7. Tours 4 per hr.) Staffed with knowledgeable guides, **Gladstone's Land** (c. 1617) is the oldest surviving house on the Royal Mile. *(477B Lawnmarket.* ☎226 5856. Open daily July-Aug. 10am-7pm; Apr.-June and Sept.-Oct. 10am-5pm. £5, students £4.) Nearby, **Lady Stair's House** contains the **Writer's Museum,** featuring memorabilia of three of Scotland's greatest literary figures: Robert Burns, Sir Walter Scott, and Robert Louis Stevenson. *(Lawnmarket.* ☎529 4901. Open M-Sa 10am-5pm; during Festival daily 2-5pm. Free.)

HIGH STREET AND CANONGATE AREA. At the ◪**High Kirk of St. Giles** (St. Giles Cathedral), Scotland's principal church, John Knox delivered the fiery Presbyterian sermons that drove Catholic Mary, Queen of Scots, into exile. Most of today's structure was built in the 15th century, but parts date as far back as 1126. The Kirk hosts free concerts throughout the year. *(Where Lawnmarket becomes High St.* ☎225 9442; www.stgilescathedral.org.uk. Suggested donation £1.) The **Canongate Kirk,** on the hill at the end of the Royal Mile, is the resting place of Adam Smith; royals worshiped here when in residence. *(Both kirks open daily M-Sa 9am-5pm, Su 1-5pm.)*

Edinburgh

FOOD
The City Cafe, 1 D3
The Elephant House, 2 D3
Henderson's Salad Table, 3 C1
Mosque Kitchen, 4 D4
Sadivino, 5 E4

PUBS
The Globe, 6 E3
The Outhouse, 7 E1
The Three Sisters, 8 D3
The Tron, 9 D3

CLUBS
Bongo Club, 10 F3
Cabaret-Voltaire, 11 D3
Ego, 12 E1
Po Na Na, 13 C1

ACCOMMODATIONS
Budget Backpackers, 14 D3
Castle Rock Hostel, 15 C3
Globetrotter Inn, 16 A1
Royal Mile Backpackers, 17 E3

MUSEUMS
John Knox House, 18 D3
Museum of Childhood, 19 D3
Museum of Edinburgh, 20 F3
Royal Museum, 21 D4
National Gallery, 22 C2
National Portrait Gallery, 23 D1
People's Story Museum, 24 F3
Royal Academy, 25 C2
Surgeon's Hall Museum, 26 E4
Writer's Museum, 27 D3

SIGHTS
City Observatory, 28 F2
Edinburgh Castle, 29 B3
Georgian House, 30 A1
Greyfriars Tolbooth, 31 D4
Holyrood Abbey, 32 G3
National Monument, 33 F2
Nelson Monument, 34 F2
New Scottish Parliament Building, 35 G3
Our Dynamic Earth, 36 G3
Palace of Holyroodhouse, 37 G3
Scottish Poetry Library, 38 F3
Walter Scott Monument, 39 D2

BRITAIN

THE PALACE OF HOLYROODHOUSE. This Stewart palace, at the base of the Royal Mile beside Holyrood Park, is Queen Elizabeth II's Scottish residence. Only parts of the interior are open to the public. The ruins of **Holyrood Abbey** sit on the grounds, built by David I in 1128 and ransacked during the Reformation. Most of the ruins date from the 13th century. The **Queen's Gallery,** in a renovated 17th-century schoolhouse near the palace entrance, displays pieces from the royal art collection. (☎556 5100. Open Apr.-Sept. daily 9:30am-6pm; Nov.-Mar. M-Sa 9:30am-4:30pm. Last entry 1hr. before closing. No entry while royals are in residence, often June-July. Palace £9.50, students and seniors £8.50, under 17 £5.50, families £25, under 5 free. Queen's Gallery £5.50/5/3.50/14. Joint ticket £13/12/7.50/33.50. Audio tour free.)

OTHER SIGHTS IN THE OLD TOWN. South of the George IV Bridge on Chambers St., the ▨**Museum of Scotland** houses Scottish artifacts. Check out the working **Corliss Steam Engine** and the **Maiden,** Edinburgh's pre-French-Revolution guillotine. The nearby **Royal Museum** has a mix of European art and ancient Roman and Egyptian artifacts. (☎247 4422; www.nms.ac.uk. Both museums open daily 10am-5pm. Free.) Across the street, a statue of Greyfriar's pooch marks the entrance to the 17th-century **Highland Kirk,** ringed by a haunted churchyard. (Off Candlemaker Row. ☎225 1900. Open Apr.-Oct. M-F 10:30am-4:30pm, Sa 10:30am-2:30pm; Nov.-Mar. Th 1:30-3:30pm. Free.)

THE NEW TOWN

Don't be fooled by the name. Edinburgh's New Town, a masterpiece of Georgian design, has few buildings younger than a century or two old. James Craig, a 23-year-old architect, won the city-planning contest in 1767; his rectangular grid of three parallel streets (**Queen, George,** and **Princes**) linking two large squares (**Charlotte** and **St. Andrew**) reflects the Scottish Enlightenment's love of order.

▨ **ROYAL YACHT BRITANNIA.** Northeast of the city center floats the Royal Yacht *Britannia.* Used by monarchs from 1953 to 1997, *Britannia* sailed around the world on state visits and royal holidays before settling in Edinburgh for permanent retirement. (Entrance on the Ocean Terminal's 3rd fl. Take bus #22 from Princes St. or #35 from the Royal Mile to Ocean Terminal; £1. ☎555 5566; www.royalyachtbritannia.co.uk. Open daily Mar.-Oct. 9:30am-4pm; Nov.-Feb. 10am-4:30pm. £9, students £7. Audio tour free.)

THE WALTER SCOTT MONUMENT AND THE GEORGIAN HOUSE. The ▨**Walter Scott Monument** is a "steeple without a church"; climb to the top for views of Princes St., the castle, and the surrounding city. (Princes St. between The Mound and Waverley Bridge. ☎529 4068. Open Apr.-Sept. M-Sa 9am-6pm, Su 10am-6pm; Oct.-Mar. M-Sa 9am-3pm, Su 10am-3pm. £2.50.) **Georgian House** gives a fair picture of how Edinburgh's elite lived 200 years ago. (7 Charlotte Sq. ☎226 3318. Open daily July-Aug. 10am-7pm; Apr.-June and Sept.-Oct. 10am-5pm; Mar. and Nov. 11am-3pm. £5, students £4.)

THE NATIONAL GALLERIES. Edinburgh's National Galleries of Scotland form an elite group, with excellent collections housed in stately buildings connected by a free shuttle (1 per 45min.) The flagship is the superb ▨**National Gallery of Scotland,** on The Mound, which has works by Renaissance, Romantic, and Impressionist masters. Don't miss the octagonal room with Poussin's entire *Seven Sacraments.* The **Scottish National Portrait Gallery,** 1 Queen St., north of St. Andrew Sq., features the faces of famous men and women who have shaped Scotland's history. The gallery also hosts contemporary art exhibits. Take the free bus #13 from George St., or walk to the **Scottish National Gallery of Modern Art,** 75 Belford Rd., west of town, to see works by Braque, Matisse, and Picasso. The landscaping out front uses dirt and greenery to represent the concept of chaos theory. The **Dean Gallery,** 73 Belford Rd., is dedicated to Dadaist and Surrealist art. (☎624 6200; www.nationalgalleries.org. All open daily 10am-5pm; during Festival 10am-6pm. Free.)

GARDENS AND PARKS

Off the eastern end of the Royal Mile, the oasis of **Holyrood Park** is a natural wilderness. ◧**Arthur's Seat** is the park's highest point; the walk to the summit takes about 45min. Located in the city center and offering great views of the Old Town and the castle, the **Princes Street Gardens** are on the site of the drained Nor'Loch, where Edinburghers used to drown accused witches. On summer days, it seems all of Edinburgh eats lunch here. The **Royal Botanic Gardens** are north of the city center. Tours go across the grounds and through greenhouses. *(Inverleith Row. Take bus #23 or 27 from Hanover St. ☎552 7171. Open daily Apr.-Sept. 10am-7pm; Mar. and Oct. 10am-6pm; Nov.-Feb. 10am-4pm. Parks free. Greenhouses £3.50, students £3, children £1, families £8.)*

🎵 ENTERTAINMENT

The summer sees a joyful string of events—music in the gardens, plays and films, and *ceilidhs* (KAY-lee; traditional Scottish dances). In winter, shorter days and the crush of students promote nightlife shenanigans. For up-to-date info on what's going on, check out *The List* (£2.50), available from newsstands. The **Festival Theatre,** 13-29 Nicholson St., stages ballet and opera, while the **King's Theatre,** 2 Leven St., hosts comedy, drama, musicals, and opera. (☎529 6000. Box office open M-Sa 10am-6pm. Tickets £5-55.) **The Stand Comedy Club,** 5 York Pl., has nightly acts. (☎558 7272. Tickets £1-10.) The **Filmhouse,** 88 Lothian Rd., shows arthouse, European, and Hollywood cinema. (☎228 2688. Tickets £3.50-5.50.) Edinburgh has a vibrant live music scene. Enjoy live jazz at **Henry's Jazz Cellar,** 8 Morrison St. (☎538 7385. £5. Open daily 8pm-3am.) **Whistle Binkie's,** 4-6 South Bridge, off High St., is a subterranean pub with live bands every night. (☎557 5114. Open daily until 3am.) **The Royal Oak,** 1 Infirmary St., hosts live traditional music nightly at 7pm. (☎557 2976. Tickets £3. Open M-F 10am-2am, Sa 11am-2am, Su 12:30pm-2am.)

🎭🎦 NIGHTLIFE

PUBS

Students and backpackers gather nightly in the Old Town. Pubs on the Royal Mile attract a mixed crowd, while casual pub-goers move to live music on **Grassmarket, Candlemaker Row,** and **Victoria Street.** Historic pubs New Town line **Rose Street,** parallel to Princes St. Depending on where you are, you'll hear last call sometime between 11pm and 1am or 3am during festival season.

🍺 **The Tron,** 9 Hunter Sq. (☎226 0931), behind the Tron Kirk. Friendly student bar. Downstairs is a mix of alcoves and pool tables. Frequent live music. Burger and a pint £4.50. W night £1 pints can't be beat. Open M-Sa noon-1am, Su 12:30pm-1am; during Festival daily 8:30am-3am. Kitchen open M-Sa noon-9pm, Su 12:30-9pm.

The Outhouse, 12a Broughton St. (☎557 6668). Hidden up an alley off Broughton St., this bar is well worth seeking out. More stylish than your average pub but just as cheap, with one of the best beer gardens in the city. Open daily 11am-1am.

The Globe, 13 Niddry St. (☎557 4670). This hole-in-the-wall is recommended up and down the Royal Mile. DJs, international sports, karaoke, and quiz nights. Open M-F 4pm-1am, Sa noon-1am, Su 12:30pm-1am; during Festival until 3am.

The Three Sisters, 139 Cowgate (☎622 6801). Loads of space for dancing, drinking, and lounging with 3 bars (Irish, Gothic, and American). Beer garden and barbecue. Open daily 9am-1am. Kitchen open M-F 9am-9pm, Sa-Su 9am-8pm.

CLUBS

Club venues are constantly closing down and reopening under new management; consult *The List* for updated info. Many clubs are around the historically disreputable **Cowgate**, downhill from and parallel to the Royal Mile. Most venues close at 3am, 5am during the Festival. The Broughton St. area of the New Town (better known as the **Broughton Triangle**) is the center of Edinburgh's gay community.

🔲 **Cabaret-Voltaire**, 36-38 Blair St. (☎220 6176; www.thecabaretvoltaire.com). With a wide range of art, dance, and live music, this club throws a great party. M cheap drinks. W huge 'We Are Electric' party. Cover up to £12. Open daily 10pm-3am.

Bongo Club, 14 New St. (☎558 7604). Students and backpackers flock to the popular Messenger (reggae) and Headspin (funk) nights, each 1 Sa per month. Cover up to £7. Cafe by day has free Internet. Open Su-W 10am-midnight, Th-Sa 10am-3am.

Po Na Na, 43B Frederick St. (☎226 2224), below Cafe Rouge. Moroccan-themed with velvet couches, parachute ceilings, and eclectic music. Cover £3-6. Open Su-M and Th 11pm-3am, F-Sa 10pm-3am.

Ego, 14 Picardy Pl. (☎478 7434; www.clubego.co.uk). Not strictly a GLBT club, but hosts several gay nights within its elegantly paneled interior. Open Su-W 10pm-1am, Th-Sa 11pm-3am; check *The List* for gay night dates. Cover £3-10.

✳ FESTIVALS

In August, Edinburgh is *the* place to be in Europe. What's referred to as "the Festival" actually encompasses several events. For more info, check out www.edinburghfestivals.co.uk. The **Edinburgh International Festival** (www.eif.co.uk; Aug. 8-31), the largest of them all, features a kaleidoscopic program of art, dance, drama, and music. Tickets (£7-58, students £3.50-29) are sold beginning in April, but a limited number of £5 tickets are available 1hr. before every event. Bookings can be made by mail, phone, fax, web, or in person at **The HUB** (☎473 2000), Edinburgh's Festival center, on Castle hill. A less formal 🔲**Fringe Festival** (www.edfringe.com; Aug. 3-25) has grown around the established festival. Anyone who can afford the small registration fee can perform, guaranteeing many great to not-so-good independent acts and an absolutely wild month. Pick up a free copy of *The Fringe Programme*, distributed throughout the city, for a complete listing of events. The **Edinburgh Jazz and Blues Festival** is in late July. (www.jazzmusic.co.uk. Tickets on sale in June.) The fun doesn't stop in winter. 🔲**Hogmanay** is a New Year's Eve festival with a week of events (www.edinburghshogmanay.org).

▶ DAYTRIP FROM EDINBURGH: ST. ANDREWS

If you love golf, play golf, or think that you might ever want to play golf, this is your town. The game originated here centuries ago and its presence is still felt at yearly tournaments on its courses. Mary, Queen of Scots supposedly played at the **Old Course** just days after her husband was murdered. Nonmembers must present a handicap certificate or letter of introduction from a golf club. Reserve at least a year ahead, enter your name into a near-impossible lottery by 2pm the day before you hope to play, or get in line before dawn by the caddie master's hut as a single. (☎01334 466 666. Apr.-Oct. £80-120 per round; Nov.-Mar. £56.) The lovely budget option is the nine-hole **Balgove Course** (£10). Next to the Old Course on Bruce Embankment, the **British Golf Museum** covers the origins of the game for dedicated fans. (☎01334 460 046. Open Mar.-Oct. M-Sa 9:30am-5:30pm, Su 10am-5pm; Nov.-Mar. daily 10am-4pm. £5.25, students £4.25.) The ruins of **St. Andrews Castle** hold medieval siege tunnels and dungeons. (☎01334 477 196. Open daily Apr.-Sept. 9:30am-6:30pm; Oct.-Mar.

BRITAIN

9:30am-4:30pm. £5.) Founded in 1410, **St. Andrews University,** between North St. and The Scores, maintains a well-heeled student body (including recent alumnus Prince William). Tours go through placid quads and include tales of the school's many traditions, from polar bear swims to commencement quirks. (☎01334 462 *245. Buy tickets from the Admissions Reception, Butts Wynd, beside St. Salvator's Chapel Tower on North St. 1hr. £5.50, students £4.50. Tours mid-June to Aug. M-F 11am and 2:30pm.)* **Trains** (☎08457 484 950) stop 8km away in Leuchars, where buses #94 and 06 depart for St. Andrews (£1.85). **Buses** (☎01383 621 249) run from City Rd. to Edinburgh (#X60; 2hr., M-Sa 1-2 per hr., £7). To get from the bus station to the **TIC,** 70 Market St., turn right on City Rd. and take the first left. Ask for the free *St. Andrews Town Map and Guide.* (☎01334 472 021. *Open July-Sept. M-Sa 9:30am-7pm, Su 9:30am-5pm; Apr.-June M-Sa 9:30am-5:30pm, Su 11am-4pm; Oct.-Mar. M-Sa 9:30am-5pm.)*

GLASGOW   ☎0141

Glasgow (pop. 580,000), Scotland's largest city, has reinvented itself many times and retains the mark of each transformation. Stately architecture recalls Queen Victoria's reign, while cranes littering the River Clyde bear witness to its past as an industrial hub. By day, world-class museums give Glasgow a thriving energy, but the city truly comes alive at night, fueled by its football-crazed locals.

🖥️📶 TRANSPORTATION AND PRACTICAL INFORMATION. Flights land at **Glasgow International Airport** (**GLA;** ☎08700 400 0008; www.baa.co.uk/glasgow). Citylink bus #905 connects to Buchanan Station (25min., 6 per hr., £3.30). From **Glasgow Prestwick International Airport** (**PIK;** ☎08712 230 700; www.gpia.co.uk), 52km away, express bus #X99 runs to Buchanan Station (50min., 1 per hr., £7) and trains leave for Central Station (30min.; 2 per hr.; £5.20, with Ryanair receipt £2.60). **Trains** run from Central Station, Gordon St. (U: St. Enoch), to: London King's Cross (6hr., 1 per hr., £91); Manchester (4hr., 1 per hr., £40). From Queen St. Station, George Sq. (U: Buchanan St.), trains go to: Aberdeen (2½hr., M-Sa 1 per hr., Su 7 per day, £34); Edinburgh (50min., 4 per hr., £8.20); Inverness (3¼hr., 4-7 per day, £34). Bus #88 (£0.50) connects the two stations, but it's only a 10min. walk. Scottish Citylink (☎08705 505 050; www.citylink.co.uk) **buses** leave Buchanan Station, on Killermont St., for Aberdeen (4hr., 1 per hr., £18), Edinburgh (1¼hr., 4 per hr., £4.20), and Inverness (3½hr., 1 per hr., £18). National Express (☎08705 808 080) travels to London (8½hr., 3 per day, £18). Local transport includes the **Underground (U)** subway line (☎08457 484 950; www.spt.co.uk. M-Sa 6:30am-11pm, Su 11am-5:30pm; prices vary depending on final stop). A **Discovery Ticket** (£1.90) allows one day of unlimited travel on the U (valid M-Sa after 9:30am, Su all day). The **TIC** is at 11 George Sq. (☎204 4400; www.seeglasgow.com. U: Buchanan St. Open July-Aug. M-Sa 9am-8pm, Su 10am-6pm; June and Sept. M-Sa 9am-7pm, Su 10am-6pm; Oct.-May M-Sa 9am-6pm.) Surf the **Internet** at **EasyInternet Cafe,** 57-61 Vincent St. (☎222 2365. £1 per 30min. Open daily 7am-10:45pm.) **Postal Code:** G2 5QX.

🏠🍴 ACCOMMODATIONS AND FOOD. Reserve ahead for B&Bs and hostels, especially in summer. B&Bs are along either side of **Argyle Street,** near the university, and near **Renfrew Street.** The former residence of a nobleman, ▓**SYHA Glasgow (HI) ❶,** 7-8 Park Terr., is now the best hostel in town. (☎332 3004. U: St. George's Cross. Laundry available. Basement coffeehouse offers Internet £1 per hr. and light eats. June-Sept. dorms £16, under 18 £12. Oct.-May rates vary, from £12. MC/V.) Conveniently located **Alamo Guest House ❸,** 46 Gray St., has a family feel and newly refurbished rooms. (☎339 2395; www.alamoguesthouse.com. Breakfast included. Free Wi-Fi. Singles from £26; doubles from £48. MC/V.) The **Euro Hostel Glasgow ❷,** at the corner of Clyde St. and Jamaica St., features quiet, clean rooms, and a bar, all near some of Glasgow's hippest clubs. (☎222 2828; www.euro-hos-

Glasgow

▲ ACCOMMODATIONS

Alamo Guest House,	1	A1
Euro Hostel Glasgow,	2	C2
SYHA Glasgow,	3	B1

🏛 MUSEUMS

Gallery of Modern Art,	4	E3
Hunterian Museum and Art Gallery,		
Kelvingrove Art Gallery and Museum,	5	
McLellan Galleries,	6	BR
Provand's Lordship,	7	D2
St. Mungo Museum,	8	G3
	12	G3

🍴 FOOD

Grassroots Cafe,	13	C1
Wee Curry Shop,	14	D2
Willow Tea Rooms,	15	D2

🍺 PUBS

Babbity Bowster,	16	F3
Uisge Beatha,	17	B1

★ CLUBS

The Buff Club,	18	D2
The Polo Lounge,	18	F3

● SIGHTS AND SERVICES

Buchanan Galleries,	19	E2
Centre for Contemporary Arts,	20	D2
City Chambers,	21	F3
City Hall/Ticket Centre,	22	F3
Glasgow LGBT Centre,	23	F4
Glasgow School of Art,	24	D2
Glasgow Film Theater,	25	D2
Market Square,	26	F3
Princes Sq. Shopping Centre,	27	E3
Royal Concert Hall,	28	E2
St. Enoch Shopping Ctr.,	29	E3
Somerfield Supermarket,	30	E4
Thomas Cook,	31	E3
Tron Theatre,	32	F4
STA Travel	33	F3

tels.com. U: St. Enoch. Breakfast included. Laundry £2. Free Wi-Fi. Computer access £1 per 15min. Wheelchair-accessible. Dorms £15; singles £40. MC/V.)

Glasgow is often called the curry capital of Britain, and for good reason. The city's West End brims with kebab and curry joints, and fusion cuisine is all the rage. **Byres Road** and tiny, parallel **Ashton Lane** overflow with affordable, trendy cafes. The ◪**Willow Tea Rooms** ❷, 217 Sauchiehall St., upstairs from Henderson Jewellers, are a cozy Glasgow landmark. (☎ 332 0521; www.willowtearooms.co.uk. U: Buchanan St. Tea £2 per pot. 3-course high tea £11. Salads and sandwiches £4-7. Open M-Sa 9am-5pm, Su 11am-4:45pm. MC/V.) Find Glasgow's best vegetarian food and creative organic dishes at the happening **Grassroots Cafe** ❷, 97 St. George's Rd. (☎ 333 0534. U: St. George's Cross. Handmade pastas from £6.80. Open daily 10am-9:45pm. AmEx/MC/V.) **The Wee Curry Shop** ❶, 7 Buccleuch St., is the best deal in a town full of pakora and poori. (☎ 353 0777. U: Cowcaddens. Entrees £5.80-10. Seats 25; reservations are a must. Open M-Sa noon-2:30pm and 5:30-10:30pm. Cash only. Branch at 23 Ashton Ln. ☎ 357 5280. U: Hillhead. MC/V.)

◪ **SIGHTS.** Glasgow is a budget traveler's paradise, with many free cathedrals and museums. *The List* (www.list.co.uk; £2.50), available at newsstands, is an essential review of exhibitions, music, and nightlife. Your first stop should be the Gothic ◪**Glasgow Cathedral,** Castle St., the only full-scale cathedral spared by the 16th-century Scottish Reformation. (☎ 552 6891. Open Apr.-Sept. M-Sa 9:30am-6pm, Su 1-5pm; Oct.-Mar. M-Sa 9:30am-4pm, Su 1-4pm. Organ recitals and concerts July-Aug. Tu 7:30pm, £7. Ask for free personal tours.) Behind the cathedral is the **Necropolis,** where tombstones lie aslant. Climb to the top of the hill for city views. (Open 24hr. Free.) **St. Mungo Museum of Religious Life and Art,** 2 Castle St., surveys religions from Islam to Yoruba, and displays Dalí's *Christ of St. John's Cross*. (☎ 553 2557. Open M-Th and Sa 10am-5pm, F and Su 11am-5pm. Free.)

In the West End, wooded **Kelvingrove Park** lies on the banks of the River Kelvin. In the southwestern corner of the park, at Argyle and Sauchiehall St., the magnificent **Kelvingrove Art Gallery and Museum** features works by van Gogh, Monet, and Rembrandt. (☎ 276 9599; www.glasgowmuseums.com. U: Kelvinhall. Open M-Th and Sa 10am-5pm, F and Su 11am-5pm. Free.) Farther west are the Gothic edifices of the **University of Glasgow.** The main building is on University Ave., which runs into Byres Rd. On campus, stop by the **Hunterian Museum,** home to the Blackstone chair, used until 1858, where all students sat for oral examinations while timed by an overhead hourglass. The ◪**Hunterian Art Gallery,** across the street, displays a large Whistler collection and a variety of Rembrandts and Pissaros. (☎ 330 4221; www.hunterian.gla.ac.uk. U: Hillhead. Both open M-Sa 9:30am-5pm. Free.) Take bus #45, 47, 48, or 57 from Jamaica St. (15min., £1.20) to reach the famous ◪**Burrell Collection,** in Pollok Country Park. Once the private stash of ship magnate William Burrell, the collection includes works by Cézanne and Degas, medieval tapestries, and fine china. (☎ 287 2550. Open M-Th and Sa 10am-5pm, F and Su 11am-5pm. Tours daily 11am and 2pm. Free.) Also in the park is the less spectacular **Pollok House,** a Victorian mansion with a small collection of paintings, some by El Greco and Goya. (☎ 616 6410. Open daily 10am-5pm. £5, students £3.80. Nov.-Mar. free.)

◪▣ **ENTERTAINMENT AND NIGHTLIFE.** The infamous **Byres Road** pub crawl slithers past the University area, running from Tennant's Bar toward the River Clyde. For Scottish grub and ambience, you can't beat ◪**Babbity Bowster,** 16-18 Blackfriars St. (☎ 552 5055. Entrees £4-8. Open M-Sa 11am-midnight, Su 10am-midnight. MC/V.) **Uisge Beatha** (ISH-ker VAH), 232 Woodlands Rd., is Gaelic for "water of life," a.k.a. whisky in Scotland—choose from over 100 varieties. (☎564 1596. U: Kelvinbridge. Whisky from £2. Open M-Sa noon-midnight, Su 12:30pm-midnight.) ◼The Buff Club, 142 Bath Ln., with a pub and two dance floors, is *the* after-hours club scene in Glasgow. (☎248 1777; www.thebuffclub.com. Cover £3-6, free with receipt from local bar; ask at the door for details. Open M-Th and Su 11pm-3am, F-Sa 10:30pm-3am.) The Polo Lounge, 58 Wilson St., is Glasgow's largest gay and lesbian club. (☎553 1221. Cover £5. Open M-Th 5pm-1am, F-Sa 5pm-3am.)

◪ DAYTRIP FROM GLASGOW: LOCH LOMOND. Immortalized by a famous ballad, the Loch Lomond's wilderness continues to awe visitors. Britain's largest loch has some 38 islands. Given their proximity to Glasgow, parts of these bonnie banks can get crowded, especially in summer when daytrippers pour into Balloch, the area's largest town. Hikers adore the West Highland Way, which snakes along the eastern side of the loch and stretches north 150km from Milngavie to Fort William. The *West Highland Way* guide (£15) includes maps for the route. The Loch Lomond Shores visitor complex and shopping mall in Balloch includes an aquarium, a NPIC, a TIC, and bike and canoe rentals. (☎01389 722 406. Open daily June-Sept. 10am-6pm; Oct.-May 10am-5pm.) Departing from Loch Lomond Shores and the Balloch TIC on the River Leven, Sweeney's Cruises provides excellent 1hr. introductions to the area. (☎01389 752 376; www.sweeneyscruises.com. 1 per hr. 10:30am-4:30pm. £5.50, children £3, families £19.50.) The ◼SYHA Loch Lomond (HI) ❷, 3km north of town, is in a 19th-century mansion. Looking for an adrenaline rush after a day of hiking? Ask for the haunted room. From the train station, follow the main road west for 1km, turn right at the roundabout, continue 2.5km, and follow signs to the hostel. Citylink buses to Oban and Campbelltown stop right outside, as do buses #305 and 306 from Balloch. (☎01389 850 226. Internet £5 per hr. Open Mar.-Oct. Dorms £15, under 18 £11. MC/V.) Trains (☎08457 484 950) leave Balloch Rd. for Glasgow (45min., 2 per hr., £3.80). Scottish Citylink (☎08705 505 050) buses also serve Glasgow (45min., 7 per day, £4.30). The TIC, Balloch Rd., is in the Old Station Building. (☎01389 753 533. Open daily July-Aug. 9:30am-6pm; June 9:30am-5:30pm; Sept. 10am-5:30pm; May 10am-5pm.)

STIRLING   ☎01786

It was once said that "he who controls Stirling controls Scotland." The third point of a strategic triangle completed by Glasgow and Edinburgh, Stirling has historically presided over north-south travel in the region. ◼Stirling Castle is decorated with prim gardens that belie its turbulent history. Argyll's Lodging, a 17th-century mansion below the castle, is considered one of the most important surviving Renaissance mansions in Scotland. (☎450 000. Castle and Lodging open daily Apr.-Oct. 9:30am-6pm; Nov.-Mar. 9:30am-5pm. Castle £9, students £7. Lodging £4, students £3; free with castle admission. Free castle 30min. guided tours.) At the 1297 Battle of Stirling Bridge, William Wallace (of *Braveheart* fame) overpowered the English army, enabling Robert the Bruce to finally overthrow the English at Bannockburn, 3km south of town. (Take bus #51 or 52 from Murray Pl. in Stirling. Visitor's Center open Mar.-Oct. daily 10am-4pm. Battlefield open year-round.)

A fun vibe prevails in the vivaciously decorated rooms of ◼ Willy Wallace Hostel ❶, 77 Murray Pl., near the train station. (☎446 773. Internet £1 per hr. Dorms £10-14. MC/V.) Cisco's ❶, 70 Port St., serves every sandwich combination (£1.35-4) under the sun. (☎445 900. Open M-Sa 10am-4pm. MC/V.) The Greengrocer, 81 Port St., has fresh produce. (☎479 159. Open M-Sa 9am-5:30pm.) Trains (☎08457 484

BRITAIN

950) run from Goosecroft Rd. to: Aberdeen (2hr.; M-Sa 1 per hr., Su 6 per day; £35); Edinburgh (50min., 2 per hr., £6.20); Glasgow (40min., 1-3 per hr., £5.90); Inverness (3hr., 3-4 per day, £54); London King's Cross (5½hr., 1 per day, £124). Scottish Citylink **buses** (☎0870 505 050) also leave from Goosecroft Rd. and run to: Edinburgh (1¼hr., 1 per hr., £4.30); Fort William (2¾hr., 1 per day, £16); Glasgow (40min., 1 per hr., £4.30); Inverness via Perth (3¾hr., 4-6 per day, £16). The **TIC** is at 41 Dumbarton Rd. (☎475 019. Open M-Sa 9am-7pm, Su 10am-4pm; reduced hours low season.) **Postal Code:** FK8 2BP.

THE TROSSACHS   ☎01877

The most accessible tract of Scotland's wilderness, the mountains and misty lochs of the Trossachs (from Scottish Gaelic for "bristly country") are popular for their moderate hikes and unbeatable beauty. The Trossachs and Loch Lomond constitute Scotland's first national park, established in 2002, where the highlands meet the lowlands. You'll find long bike routes winding through dense forest, peaceful loch-side walks, and some of Scotland's more manageable peaks.

▐ **TRANSPORTATION.** Access to the Trossachs is easiest from Stirling. First **buses** (☎01324 613 777) connect to the region's two main towns, running from Stirling to Aberfoyle (#11; 45min., 4 per day, £2.50) and Callander (#59; 45min., 12 per day, £3). Scottish Citylink also runs a bus from Edinburgh to Callander (1¾hr., 1 per day, £9.60) via Stirling. In summer, the useful Trossachs Trundler (☎01786 442 707) **ferries** between Aberfoyle, Callander, and the Trossachs Pier at Loch Katrine; one daily trip begins and ends in Stirling. (July-Sept. M-Th 4 per day; Day Rover £5, students £4, children £1.75; including travel from Stirling £8/6/2.50.)

CALLANDER. Along the quiet River Teith, Callander is a good base for exploring the Trossachs. Dominating the horizon, **Ben Ledi** (880m) provides a strenuous but manageable trek. A trail up the mountain (9km) begins just north of town along A84. A number of excellent walks depart from Callander itself. **The Crags** (10km) heads up through the woods to the ridge above town, while the popular walk to **Bracklinn Falls** (8km) wanders through a picturesque glen. **Cyclists** can join the **Lowland Highland Trail,** which runs north to Strathyre along an old railway line. Passing through the forest and beside Loch Lubnaig, a side-track from the route runs to **Balquhidder,** where Rob Roy, Scotland's legendary patriot, and his family find peace under a stone which reads, "MacGregor Despite Them"—an act of defiance since his surname, MacGregor, had been banned by King James VI of Scotland in 1603. Callander's **Rob Roy and Trossachs Visitor Centre,** Main St., is a combination **TIC** and exhibit on the 17th-century hero. (☎330 342. Open daily June-Sept. 10am-6pm; Mar.-May and Oct. 10am-5pm; Nov.-Feb. 11am-4pm. Exhibit £3.60, students £2.40.) Walkers should grab the *Callander Walks and Fort Trails* pamphlet; cyclists can consult *Rides around the Trossachs* (both £2). Rent bikes at **Cycle Hire Callander,** Ancaster Sq., beside the TIC. (☎331 052. £7 per ½-day, £10 per day. Open daily 9am-6pm. MC/V.) The hidden gem of the region's lodgings is ▓**Trossachs Backpackers ❷,** Invertrossachs Rd., 0.8km south of Callander. The owners will often pick up guests from Callander. (For hostel ☎331 200, for bike rental 331 100. Bikes £13 per day, £8 per ½-day. Breakfast included. Laundry included. Dorms £15. MC/V.)

ABERFOYLE AND LOCH KATRINE. Aberfoyle, another springboard into the wild, is at the heart of the **Queen Elizabeth Forest Park,** established in 1953 to celebrate her Majesty's coronation. The park covers a vast territory from the shore of Loch Lomond to the slopes of the Strathyre Mountains. For more info on **trails,** visit the **Trossachs Discovery Centre** in town. (☎382 352. Open July-Aug. daily 9:30am-6pm; Apr.-June and Sept.-Oct. daily 10am-5pm; Nov.-Mar. Sa-Su 10am-5pm.) Keep an eye out for visiting foxes at **Corrie Glen B&B ❺**, Manse Rd. (☎382 427. Open Mar.-Nov. Singles from £30; doubles from £50. Cash only.)

The A821, named the **Trossachs Trail,** winds through the heart of the Trossachs between Aberfoyle and Callander. This scenic drive passes near majestic Loch Katrine, the Trossachs' original attraction and the setting of Sir Walter Scott's "The Lady of the Lake." The **SS Sir Walter Scott** cruises the loch from Trossachs Pier, stopping at Stronachlachar, on the northwestern bank. (☎376 316. Apr.-Oct. M-Tu and Th-Su 11am, 1:45, 3:15pm; W 1:45 and 3:15pm. 45min. tour £6.50; 1hr. tour £7.50.) At the pier, rent bikes from **Katrinewheelz.** (☎376 284. £14 per day.) For a daytrip, take the ferry to Stronachlachar and then walk or ride back along the 22km wooded shore road to the pier. Above the loch hulks **Ben A'an** (460m), a reasonable 3km ascent that begins from a parking lot 1.5km along A821.

INVERNESS AND LOCH NESS   ☎01463

The only city in the Highlands, Inverness has an appealing mix of Highland hospitality and urban hustle. Split by the River Ness, the city is a base for exploring the region. Its amenities and proximity to Loch Ness ensure a constant stream of tourists in summer. **◪Loch Ness,** 8km south of Inverness, draws crowds captivated by tales of its legendary inhabitant. In AD 565, St. Columba repelled a savage sea beast as it attacked a monk. Whether prehistoric leftover, giant sea snake, or product of a saintly imagination, the monster and its lair remain a mystery. The easiest way to see the loch is with a tour group, departing from the Inverness TIC. **Jacobite Cruises,** Tomnahurich Bridge, Glenurquhart Rd., whisk you around on coach or boat trips. (☎233 999; www.jacobite.co.uk. £9-20, includes admission to Urquhart Castle. Student discounts available.) South on A82 sits the ruined **Urquhart Castle** (URK-hart), one of the largest in Scotland before it was blown up in 1692 to prevent Jacobite occupation. Today it's a popular viewing area for hopeful Nessie watchers. (☎450 551. Open Apr.-Sept. daily 9:30am-6:30pm; Oct.-Mar. M-Sa 9:30am-4:30pm. £6.50, students £5.) Made famous by its role in Shakespeare's *Macbeth,* **Cawdor Castle** is the stuff of fairy tales, complete with humorous placards describing the castle's sights. Take Highland Country bus #7 (30min., 1 per hr., £5), leaving from the Inverness post office at 14-16 Queensgate. (☎01667 404 401; www.cawdorcastle.com. Open May-Oct. daily 10am-5pm. £7, students £6.) Riverside **◪Inverness Student Hotel ❶**, 8 Culduthel Rd., is a sociable hangout with quiet rooms. (☎236 556. Breakfast £2. Laundry £2.50. Internet £0.80 per 30min., £1 per hr. Dorms £12-14. MC/V.) Behind the bus station, the **Inverness Tourist Hostel ❶**, 34 Rose St., has swank leather couches and TV. (☎241 962. Dorms £11-14. MC/V). **Hootananny,** 67 Church St., is a feisty bar complete with Scottish song and dance and a mouth-watering, if slightly out of place, Thai restaurant downstairs (entrees £5-6). Groove to live bands in the club upstairs. (☎233 651; www.hootananny.com. Restaurant open daily noon-1am. Club open W-Th 8pm-1am, F-Sa 8pm-3am. MC/V.) Try the Thai soup (£3) or cakes (£2) at the **Lemon Tree ❶**, 18 Inglis St. (☎241 114. Open M-Sa 8:30am-5:30pm. Cash only.) **Trains** (☎08457 484 950) run from Academy St. in Inverness's Station Sq. to: Edinburgh (3½hr., 8 per day, £37); Glasgow (3½hr., 8 per day, £37); Kyle of Lochalsh (2½hr., 4 per day, £16.50); London (8-11hr., 1 per day, £133). **Buses** run from Farraline Park, off Academy St., to: Edinburgh (4½hr., 1 per hr., £20.20); Glasgow (4hr., 1 per hr., £20.20); Kyle of Lochalsh

BRITAIN

(2hr., 2 per day, £15); London (13hr., 1 per day, £39). The **TIC** is at Castle Wynd; from the stations, turn left on Academy St., right on Union St., and left on Church St. (☎234 353. Internet £1 per 20min., £2.50 per hr. Open mid-June to Aug. M-Sa 9am-6pm, Su 9:30am-4pm; Sept. to mid-June M-Sa 9am-5pm, Su 10am-4pm.)

FORT WILLIAM AND BEN NEVIS   ☎01397

In 1654, General Monck founded Fort William among Britain's highest peaks to keep out "savage clans and roving barbarians." His scheme backfired: today, thousands of Highlands-bound hikers invade Fort William, a base for exploring some of Scotland's impressive wilderness. Just outside of town, beautiful **Glen Nevis** runs southeast into Britain's tallest mountain. **Ben Nevis** (1343m) offers a challenging but manageable hike. One trail starts at the **Glen Nevis Visitor Centre**, where hikers stock up on maps and useful advice. (☎705 922. Open Easter-Oct. daily 9am-5pm.) The ascent (13km; 6-8hr. round-trip) is difficult more in its length than in its terrain, but harsh conditions near the summit can be treacherous for the unprepared. Bring plenty of water and warm, waterproof clothes, and be sure to inform someone of your route. The ◪**West Coast Railway's** Jacobite steam train rose to stardom as the Hogwarts Express in the *Harry Potter* films. The route, connecting Fort William and Mallaig, passes some of Scotland's finest scenery. (☎01463 239 026; www.westcoastrailway.co.uk. 2hr.; Runs June and Sept.-Oct. M-F; July-Aug. M-F and Su. Departs Fort William at 10:20am. £20, round-trip £27.)

Lodgings fill quickly in summer. From the train station, turn left on Belford Rd. and right on Alma Rd., bear left at the fork, and vault into a top bunk at ◪**Fort William Backpackers ❶**, 6 Alma Rd., a fun, welcoming hostel with facilities geared toward hikers. (☎700 711; www.scotlandstophostels.com. Breakfast £2. Laundry £2.50. Internet £1 per 20min. Reception 7-11am and 5-11pm. Curfew 2am. AmEx/MC/V.) Before hitting the trails, pick up a packed lunch (£3) at the **Nevis Bakery ❶**, 49 High St., across from the TIC. (☎704 101. Open M-F 8am-5pm, Sa 8am-4pm. Cash only.) Buy groceries at **Tesco**, at the north end of High St. (☎902 400. Open M-Sa 8am-9pm, Su 9:30am-6pm.) Follow the sounds of merriment down an underground alleyway to **Maryburgh Inn,** 26 High St., a popular local pub. (Open M-W and Su 9am-midnight, F-Sa 9am-1am. Karaoke Th, F, and Sa nights.) **Trains** (☎08457 484 950) depart from the station north of High St. for Glasgow Queen St. (3¾hr., 2-3 per day, £20). The train runs to London Euston (12hr., 1 per day, £99). **Buses** arrive next to Morrison's grocery store by the train station. Scottish Citylink (☎08705 505 050) travels to: Edinburgh (4hr., 3 per day, £21), Glasgow (3hr., 4 per day, £15), and Inverness (2hr., 7-8 per day, £9.20). The **TIC** is in Cameron Sq. (☎703 781. Open July-Aug. M-Sa 9am-7pm, Su 9:30am-5pm; Sept.-Oct. and Apr.-June M-Sa 9am-6pm, Su 10am-4pm; Nov.-Mar. M-Sa 9am-5pm.) **Internet** (30min., free) is available at the **Fort William Library,** High St., across from Nevisport (open M and Th 10am-8pm, Tu and F 10am-6pm, W and Sa 10am-1pm). **Postal Code:** PH33 6AR.

ISLE OF SKYE

Mountains extend into the clouds on the Isle of Skye, whose hills, peninsulas, and seaside walks hold many secrets for the savvy traveler. Small towns provide glimpses into highland culture and Gaelic tradition. Because visitors tend to stick to major roads, many of Skye's most unique landscapes lay undisturbed, a far cry from the island's revived castles and their summer crowds.

⌐ TRANSPORTATION. Skye Bridge links Kyleakin, on the island, to mainland Kyle of Lochalsh. Pedestrians can take the bridge's 2.5km **footpath** or the **shuttle bus** (1 per hr., £0.70). **Trains** (☎08457 484 950) run from Kyle to Inverness (2½hr., 2-4 per day, £16). Scottish Citylink **buses** #915 and 917 travel to Fort William (2hr., 3 per day, £12), Glasgow (6hr., 3 per day, £22), and Inverness (2hr., 3 per day, £12). Buses on Skye are infrequent and expensive; grab the handy *Public Transport Map: The Highlands, Orkney, Shetland and Western Isles* at any TIC. From Portree, Highland Country **buses** run to most island sights (M-Sa 3-8 per day).

▨ TROTTERNISH PENINSULA. Many cliffs, waterfalls, and ancient standing stones on Trotternish remain virtually untouched. A steep hike (1hr. round-trip) leads to the **Old Man of Storr,** a 165 ft. basalt stone at the top of the highest peak in Trotternish (2358 ft.), located north of Portree on the A855. Start your ascent at the car park. North of Staffin, a footpath leads through the **Quirang** rocks, some of the world's most striking geological formations (3hr. round-trip). Nearby **Staffin Bay** has Jurassic fossils and pottery remains from more recent settlers. South of Staffin, **Kilt Rock** has pleated lava columns above a rocky base crumbling into the sea. Climb to the top of nearby **Mealt Falls** (300 ft.) for the best view of the formation. Take the Staffin bus from Portree and ask to be let off. (☎552 212. Internet access £1 per 30min. Dorms £12.50. Camping £6 per person. Cash only.

KYLE OF LOCHALSH AND KYLEAKIN. Kyle of Lochalsh ("Kyle" for short) and Kyleakin (Ky-LOCK-in) serve as hubs for travelers to and from the isle. ▨**Mac-Backpackers Skye Trekker Tour,** departing Skye Backpackers hostel in Kyleakin, offers a one-day tour emphasizing the mystical, historical side of the island. (☎01599 534 510; www.macbackpackers.com. Weekly departure Sa 7:30am. £18.) Several kilometers east of Kyle near Dornie, **Eilean Donan Castle** is the restored 13th-century seat of the MacKensie family, and offers one of the country's best castle tours. (☎01599 555 202; www.eileandonancastle.com. Open Apr.-Oct. daily 10am-5:30pm. £5, students £4.) The laid-back staff and humorously themed rooms at Kyleakin's **Skye Backpackers ❶** create a social starting point for any trip to Skye. (☎01599 534 510; www.skyebackpackers.com. Laundry £2.50. Internet £0.80 per 30min. Curfew M-Th and Su 12:30am, F-Sa 1:30am. Dorms £11-14. AmEx/MC/V.) **Cu'chulainn's ❶** offers upscale Kyle seafood in its beer garden. (☎01599 534 492. Open M-Sa 11am-12:45am. Kitchen open 11am-8pm. MC/V.) In Kyleakin, **Saucy Mary's,** named after a Norse seductress, packs in pints, crowds, and occasional live music. (Open M-Th 5pm-midnight, F 5pm-1am, Sa 5-11:30pm, Su 5-11pm.) The **TIC** is by the pier in Kyle. (Open May-Oct. M-F 9:30am-5pm, Sa-Su 10am-4pm.) The **Kyle Library** has free **Internet.** (☎01599 534 146. Open Tu 12:30-3:30pm and 4:30-8pm.)

PORTREE. The island's festive harbor capital is a hub for culture and transportation. Off A850, **Dunvegan Castle,** seat of the MacLoed clan, is the longest-inhabited Scottish castle, occupied since the 13th century. Highland Country bus #56 (M-Sa 2 per day) runs from Portree to the castle. (☎01470 521 206; www.dunvegancastle.com. Open daily mid-Mar. to Oct. 10am-5:30pm; Nov. to mid-Mar. 11am-4pm. £7, students £6. Gardens only £5/3.50.) The **Portree Independent Hostel ❶,** in the center of town, has many amenities, including a well-stocked kitchen. (☎01478 613 737. Dorms £12-13. MC/V.) Scottish Citylink and Highland Country **buses** travel from Somerled Sq. to Kyle and Kyleakin (5-10 per day). To reach the **TIC,** Bayfield Rd., from the square, face the Bank of Scotland, turn left down the lane, and left again onto Bridge Rd. (☎01478 612 137.

Open July-Aug. M-Sa 9am-6pm, Su 10am-4pm; Sept.-Oct. and Apr.-June M-F 9am-5pm, Su 10am-4pm; Nov.-Mar. M-Sa 9am-4pm.)

ISLE OF LEWIS (LEODHAS)   ☎01851

Fantastic hiking, biking, surfing, and historic sites attract travelers to Lewis, the most populous of the Outer Hebridean Islands. The small city of **Stornoway** (pop. 5600) adds a splash of urban life to the otherwise rural island. Many of Lewis's natural and historical attractions line its west coast along A858 and are accessible by the W2 bus from Stornoway (M-Sa 4-6 per day in either direction). Alternatively, travel with **Out and About Tours** (☎612 288; personalized group tours from £67 per ½-day, £102 per day) in the untouched moorland and half-cut fields of peat. Second only to Stonehenge in grandeur and less overrun with tourists, the gargantuan ▧**Callanish Stones** are 22km west of Stornoway on A858. Archaeologists have dated the formation to 2000 BC and believe that prehistoric people used Callanish and two nearby circles to track the movements of the heavens. Lewis is also home to crashing waves and consistent surf. Warm currents and long daylight hours draw **surfers** to the popular **Dalmor Beach,** near the village of **Dalbeg,** which has hosted several competitions (take the W2 bus from Stornoway).

The immaculate ▧**Heb Hostel ❷**, 25 Kenneth St., offers exceptional facilities. (☎709 889. Internet £1 per 30min. £15 per person. Cash only.) Feast on classic dishes in the green-curtained glow of the ▧**Thai Cafe ❷**, 27 Church St., which serves mouth-watering entrees (£4-6) by candlelight. (☎701 811. Open M-Sa noon-2:30pm and 5-11pm. MC/V.) Buy groceries at the **Co-op** on Cromwell St. (☎702 703. Open M-Sa 8am-8pm.) CalMac **ferries** sail to Ullapool (2¾hr.; M-Sa 2-3 per day; £15, 5-day round-trip £26; car £73/125). **Lewis Car Rentals** is at 52 Bayhead St. (☎703 760. 21+. £25-45 per day. Open M-Sa 9am-6pm. AmEx/MC/V.) Rent bikes at **Alex Dan's Cycle Centre,** 67 Kenneth St. (☎704 025. £12 per day, £38 per week. Open M-Sa 9am-6pm.) Western Isles **buses** depart from Stornoway's Beach St. station; pick up a free *Lewis and Harris Bus Timetable* for destinations. Be aware that the only things running on Sundays are planes and churchgoers late for services. The **TIC** is at 26 Cromwell St. From the ferry terminal, turn left onto South Beach, then right on Cromwell St. (☎703 088. Open Apr.-Oct. daily 9am-6pm and 8-9pm; Nov.-Mar. M-F 9am-5pm.) **Internet** is free at the **Stornoway Library.** (☎708 631. Open M-W and Sa 10am-5pm, Th-F 10am-6pm.) **Postal Code:** HS1 2AA.

a ruinous state

The British thrive on ruin. The delight in the physical remnants of the past, shared by all classes and passed from generation to generation, is one of those cultural tics which makes Britain truly singular among nations. This desire to commune with times long gone, to wax wistful about the ambitions of ages past brought low by history's pratfalls, is as British as milky tea and cow parsley in country lanes.

It's possible to experience the great British romance of ruins at many of the most celebrated piles of stones. The shell of **Tintern Abbey**, near the River Avon, marks the spot where Wordsworth made introspection a national poetic pastime. But the danger of sampling the obvious sites is, of course, the buzzing business of the present—so many tourist coaches, so much bad ice

"Head to the lesser known and commune with bumblebees and fellow pilgrims."

cream, so many postcards. Better to head to the lesser known and commune with bumblebees and the occasional wandering fellow pilgrim.

Go, for instance, to Northamptonshire to see what's left of **Lyveden New Bield,** the late 16th-century oratory of the Anglo-Catholic Thomas Tresham and a ruin almost as soon as it was constructed. The oratory was supposed to be a place where the Elizabethan gentleman, who tried to be loyal to both his Queen and his Church, could practice his devotions safe from the prying eyes of Protestant authorities. Tresham ran out of money and time to finish the structure, and was jailed for failing to pay the recusancy fines imposed for not subscribing to the official church. The entire building was left exposed to the elements, and visitors must now wade through knee-high meadowland to see the delicate frieze of the stations of the cross that adorns its exterior walls.

However, most of the ruins in Britain are the work of sudden disaster rather than the slow crumblings of time. **Corfe Castle** in Dorset bears the charred scars of Oliver Cromwell's besieging army during the Second Civil War of 1647-1648. And some of the imposing Iron Age "brochs" of **Orkney** and **Shetland** look as brutal as they do because at some point they failed to hold back the oncoming waves of invaders and local rivals. Stunning, sandstone-red **Lindisfarne,** on the Northumbrian shore, was twice ravaged, first by Vikings who sacked the place and slaughtered the monks. The monastery was hit again during the Protestant Reformation, when it was predictably emptied of its community and treasures. Equally sudden was the end of the spectacular **Binham Priory** in southern Norfolk. The enforcers of the Reformation under Henry VIII and Edward VI turned what had been one of the most palatial Benedictine foundations into a sparse parish church. Miraculously, the Reformation's erasure of the painted screen separating the nave from the choir have themselves become ruins, peeling away to reveal some of the most astonishing church paintings that survived from the world of Roman Catholic England.

Some of the most commanding ruins are also the most modern. A little way from the center of Dublin stands Kilmainham Gaol, a working prison until 1924. Now a historical museum, the Gaol reveals the complications of crime and punishment in nationalist Ireland. The exterior is just standard-issue prison. But the interior is a cathedral of incarceration; simultaneously shocking and operatically grand, with its iron staircase and rat-hole cells where ancient pallets and fragments of anonymous rags gather grime. The effect is as powerful as it is challenging, but this is how ruins are supposed to get you. Not with a cheap rush of sentiment, much less a pang of nostalgia, but with the tender inspection of ancient scars, which linger to remind us of the resilience and redeeming vulnerability of the human condition.

Simon Schama is University Professor of Art History at Columbia University. He writes for The New Yorker and was the writer and host of the BBC's History of Britain. His most recent book is Rough Crossings: Britain, the Slaves, and the American Revolution (Ecco, May 2006).

BULGARIA (Бъ лгариЯ)

From the pine-covered slopes of the Rila, Pirin, and Rodopi Mountains to the beaches of the Black Sea, Bulgaria is blessed with a countryside rich in natural resources. The history of the Bulgarian people, however, is not as serene as the landscape: crumbling Greco-Thracian ruins and Soviet-style high-rises attest to centuries of turmoil and political struggle. Though Bulgaria's flagging economy and dual-pricing system for foreigners can dampen the mood, travelers willing to make the trek to the beautiful Black Sea Coast, cosmopolitan Sofia, and picturesque villages will be greatly rewarded. And until the country succumbs to globalization, you can bet that Bulgaria will remain happily free of crowds.

DISCOVER BULGARIA: SUGGESTED ITINERARIES

THREE DAYS. Two days are probably enough to take in **Sofia's** (p. 197) museums, cathedrals, and cafes. Going to the **Rila Monastery** (1 day; p. 202) is often easier said than done, but the gorgeous atmosphere and environs are worth it.

ONE WEEK. If two days among the stunning ruins of **Veliko Tarnovo** (p. 203) aren't enough, bus down to **Plovdiv** (2 days; p. 202) for more Roman remains before heading to the **Rila Monastery** (1 day). End in bustling **Sofia** (2 days).

ESSENTIALS

FACTS AND FIGURES

Official Name: Republic of Bulgaria.
Capital: Sofia.
Major Cities: Plovdiv, Varna, Burgas.
Population: 7,323,000.

Official Language: Bulgarian.
International Ranking on IQ Tests: 2.
Expected Sunflower Exports in 2007: 900,000 tons.

WHEN TO GO

Bulgaria's temperate climate makes it easy to catch good weather. Spring (Apr.-May) is pleasant and has a bevy of festivals and events. Summer (June-Sept.) isn't too hot, making it perfect for hiking and beachgoing—expect crowds on the Black Sea Coast and at campgrounds. Skiing is best from December until April.

DOCUMENTS AND FORMALITIES

EMBASSIES AND CONSULATES. Foreign embassies are in Sofia (p. 199). Bulgarian embassies abroad include: **Australia,** 33 Cultoa Circuit, O'Malley, Canberra, ACT 2600 (☎62 86 97 11; www.bulgaria.org.au); **Canada,** 325 Stewart St., Ottawa, ON, K1N 6K5 (☎613-789-3215; www.bgembassy.ca); **Ireland,** 22 Burlington Rd., Dublin, 4 (☎16 60 32 93; www.bulgaria.bg/europe/dublin); **UK,** 186-188 Queensgate, London, SW7 5HL (☎20 75 84 94 00; www.bulgaria.embassyhomepage.com); **US,** 1621 22nd St., NW, Washington, D.C., 20008 (☎202-387-0174; www.bulgaria-embassy.org).

VISA AND ENTRY INFORMATION. Citizens of Australia, Canada, Ireland, New Zealand, the UK, and the US do not need a **visa** for stays of up to 90 days within a six-month period. In all cases, however, passports are required and must be valid for six months beyond the date of departure; proof of medical insurance for the

ENTRANCE REQUIREMENTS.
Passport: Required for all travelers; must be valid for 6 months after end of stay.
Visa: Not required for citizens of Australia, Canada, Ireland, New Zealand, the UK, and the US for stays of up to 90 days.
Letter of Invitation: Not required.
Inoculations: Recommended up-to-date on DTaP (diphtheria, tetanus, and pertussis), Hepatitis A, Hepatitis B, MMR (measles, mumps, and rubella), rabies, polio booster, and typhoid.
Work Permit: Required of all foreigners planning to work in Bulgaria.
International Driving Permit: Required of all those planning to drive.

duration of the stay is also required. Travelers should consult the Bulgarian embassy in their country of origin to apply for a long-term visa. For US citizens, a single-entry visa costs US$60, a multiple-entry visa costs US$145; both entail an additional US$25 processing fee. Visas must be obtained before arrival; it is not possible to apply for an extended visa within Bulgaria. If staying in a private residence, **register your visa** with police within 48hr. of entering Bulgaria; hotels and hostels will do this for you. Keep the registration with your passport and make sure you re-register every time you change accommodation. A Bulgarian **border crossing** can take several hours. The border crossing into Turkey is particularly difficult. Try to enter from Romania at Ruse or Durankulac.

TOURIST SERVICES AND MONEY

EMERGENCY	Ambulance: ☎ 150. Fire: ☎ 160. Police: ☎ 166.

TOURIST OFFICES. Tourist offices and local travel agencies—when they can be found—are knowledgeable and helpful with reserving private rooms. The most common foreign languages spoken by staff are English, German, and Russian. In smaller cities, tourist agencies are either privately owned or nonexistent. Big hotels offer a good alternative; they often have an English-speaking receptionist and **maps.**

MONEY. The Bulgarian unit of currency is the **lev** (lv), plural leva. One lev is equal to 100 stotinki (singular stontinka), with standard denominations of 1, 2, 5, 10, 20, and 50 stotinki in coins and 1, 2, 5, 10, 20, and 50lv in notes. US dollars and euro are sometimes accepted. The government struggles to control **inflation,** which has increased in recent years to around 6.5%. Private banks and exchange bureaus change money, but bank rates are more reliable. It is illegal to exchange currency on the street. **Traveler's checks** can only be cashed at banks. As identity theft rings sometimes target ATMs, travelers should use machines located inside banks and check for evidence of tampering. **Credit cards** are rarely accepted, especially in the countryside. Beware officially sanctioned **tourist overcharging;** some museums and theaters will charge foreigners double or more.

BULGARIAN LEVA (LV)		
AUS$1 = 1.16LV	1LV = AUS$0.87	
CDN$1 = 1.36LV	1LV = CDN$0.73	
EUR€1 = 1.96LV	1LV = EUR€0.51	
NZ$1 = 1.01LV	1LV = NZ$0.99	
UK£1 = 2.87LV	1LV = UK£0.35	
US$1 = 1.45LV	1LV = US$0.69	

HEALTH AND SAFETY

While basic **medical supplies** are available in Bulgarian hospitals, specialized treatment is not. Emergency care is better in Sofia than in the rest of the country, but it's best to **avoid hospitals** entirely. Although travelers are required to carry proof of insurance, most doctors expect cash payment. In case of extreme emergency, air evacuation costs about US$50,000. There is typically a night-duty pharmacy in larger towns. Tampons are widely available, and foreign brands of condoms (*prezervatifs*) are safer than local ones. Public **bathrooms** ("Ж" for women, "М" for men) are often holes in the ground; pack toilet paper and hand sanitizer and expect to pay 0.05-0.20lv. Don't buy bottles of **alcohol** from street vendors, and be careful with homemade liquor. Keep an eye out for petty **street crime,** especially pickpocketing and purse snatching. Also be wary of people posing as government officials; ask them to show ID and, if necessary, to escort you to a police station. Before buying drinks for strangers, always ask to see a menu to verify the price and then clarify exactly what you want. The price might otherwise prove astronomical; some travelers report that bartenders will use force to assure payment of bills as high as several thousand dollars. Taxi drivers often attempt to overcharge unsuspecting tourists; be sure to take only marked taxis and ensure that the meter is on for the entire ride. Nightclubs in large cities are often associated with organized crime—avoid fights. It's generally safe for **women** to travel alone, but it's always safer to have at least one travel companion. Women should wear skirts and blouses to avoid unwanted attention, as Bulgarian women tend to dress quite formally. Darker-skinned travelers may be mistaken for **Roma** (gypsies), the target of Bulgarian **racial discrimination.** While hate crimes are rare, those of foreign ethnicities may receive stares. Acceptance of homosexuality is slow in coming; it is prudent to avoid public displays of affection. For more info about gay and lesbian clubs and resources, check out www.queer_bulgaria.org or www.bulgayria.com.

TRANSPORTATION

BY PLANE. All flights to Sofia (SOF) connect through Western European cities. Though tickets to the capital may run over US$1500 during the summer months, budget airline **Wizz Air** offers cheap flights from London, Paris, and Frankfurt through Budapest, HUN (☎029 603 888; www.wizzair.com). Travelers might also fly into a nearby hub—Athens, Bucharest, or İstanbul—and take a bus to Sofia.

BY TRAIN. Bulgarian trains run to Greece, Hungary, Romania, and Turkey and are the best form of transportation in the north. **Rila** is the main international company; find international timetables at www.bdz-rila.com. Neither the **Eurail Pass** nor the **Eastpass** is accepted in Bulgaria. The train system is comprehensive but slow, crowded, and smoke-filled. Purse-slashing and theft have been reported. There are three types of trains: express *(ekspres)*, fast *(burz)*, and slow *(putnicheski)*. Avoid *putnicheski*—they stop at anything that looks inhabited, even if only by goats. Arrive well ahead if you want a seat. Station markings are irregular and often only in Cyrillic; know when you're reaching your destination, bring a map, and ask for help. *Purva klasa* (first class) is identical to *vtora* (second), and not worth the extra money.

BY BUS. Buses are better for travel in eastern and western Bulgaria and are often faster than trains, though they are less frequent and less comfortable. Buses head north from Ruse, to İstanbul, TUR from anywhere on the Black Sea Coast, and from Blagoevgrad to Greece. For long distances, **Group Travel** and **Etap** have buses with A/C and bathrooms. Some have set departure times; others leave when full.

BY FERRY, BY TAXI, AND BY CAR. Ferries from Varna make trips to İstanbul, TUR and Odessa, UKR. Yellow **taxis** are everywhere in cities. Refuse to pay in dollars and insist on a ride *sus apparata* (with meter); ask the distance and price per kilometer. Don't try to bargain. Some taxi drivers rig the meters to charge more. Tipping taxi drivers usually means rounding up to the nearest lev or half-lev. Some Black Sea towns can only be reached by car. Renting is cheapest from a local agency, which will charge less than the €15-60 that larger companies do. Driving in Bulgaria is quite dangerous; a road system in disrepair, aggressive driving habits, and a high number of old-model cars contribute to a high fatality rate. Rocks and landslides pose a threat in mountainous areas. Those driving should be aware that a police officer cannot enforce fines on the spot, but only issue tickets.

BY BIKE AND BY THUMB. Motoroads (www.motoroads.com) and travel agencies offer bike tours. Stay alert when bicycling in cities, as Bulgarian drivers disregard traffic signals. Although **hitchhiking** is rare in Bulgaria, it is almost always free. While those who hitchhike say it is generally safe, Let's Go does not recommend it.

KEEPING IN TOUCH

PHONE CODES	**Country code: 359. International dialing prefix:** 00. For more information on how to place international calls, see **Inside Back Cover.**

EMAIL AND INTERNET. Internet cafes can be found throughout urban centers and are often open 24hr. Internet access costs approximately 1-3lv per hr.

TELEPHONE. Making international **telephone** calls from Bulgaria can be a challenge. Pay phones are ludicrously expensive; opt for phone offices instead. If you must make an **international call** from a pay phone with a card, purchase the 400 unit card (22lv). Units run out quickly on international calls, so talk fast or have multiple cards ready. There are two brands: **BulFon** (orange) and **Mobika** (blue), which work only at telephones of the same brand; BulFon is more prevalent. To **call collect,** dial ☎01 23 for an international operator. The Bulgarian phrase for collect call is *obazhdane na smetka na abonata.* For **local calls,** pay phones do not accept coins, so it's best to buy a phone card (see above). You can also call from the post office, where a clerk assigns you a booth, a meter records your bill, and you pay when finished. International access codes include: **AT&T Direct** (☎800 0010); **British Telecom Payphones** (☎800 99 44); **Canada Direct** (☎800 1359; service not available from payphones); **MCI** (☎800 0001); and **Sprint** (☎800 1010).

MAIL. "Свъздушна поща" on letters indicates **airmail.** Though it is far more reliable than ground transport, it is sometimes difficult to convince postal workers to let you pay extra to have letters sent airmail. Sending a letter or postcard abroad costs 1.40lv; a Bulgarian return address is required. Packages must be unwrapped for inspection. Mail can be received general delivery through **Poste Restante,** though the service is unreliable. Address envelope as follows: first name, LAST NAME, POSTE RESTANTE, писма до поискване централна поща, post office address (optional), city, Postal Code, България (Bulgaria).

LANGUAGE. Bulgarian is a South Slavic language written in the Cyrillic alphabet. Though a few words are borrowed from Turkish and Greek, most are similar to Russian and its relatives. English is most commonly spoken by young people in cities and tourist areas. Russian is often understood and is spoken by virtually everyone over the age of 35. The Bulgarian alphabet is much the same as Russian (see **Cyrillic Alphabet** p. 1057), except that "щ" is pronounced "sht" and "ъ" is "ŭ" (like the "u" in bug).

> **YES AND NO.** Bulgarians shake their heads from side to side to indicate "yes" and up and down to indicate "no," the exact opposite of Brits and Yanks. For the uncoordinated, it's easier to just hold your head still and say *da* or *neh*.

ACCOMMODATIONS AND CAMPING

BULGARIA	❶	❷	❸	❹	❺
ACCOMMODATIONS	under 25lv	25-35lv	36-49lv	50-70lv	over 70lv

Bulgarian **hotels** are classed on a star system and licensed by the Government Committee on Tourism; rooms in one-star hotels are nearly identical to rooms in two- and three-star hotels, but have no private baths. All accommodations provide linens and towels. Expect to pay US$25-35. Beware that foreigners are often charged double of what locals pay. **Hostels** can be found in most major cities and run US$10-18 per bed. For a complete list of hostels in Bulgaria, see www.hostels.com/en/bg.html. **Private rooms,** which can be found in any small town, are cheap (US$6-12) and usually have all the amenities of a good hotel. Outside major towns, most **campgrounds** provide spartan bungalows and tent space. Call ahead in summer to reserve bungalows.

FOOD AND DRINK

BULGARIA	❶	❷	❸	❹	❺
FOOD	under 5lv	5-9lv	10-14lv	15-18lv	over 18lv

Kiosks sell *kebabcheta* (sausage burgers), sandwiches, pizzas, and *banitsa sus sirene* (feta-cheese-filled pastries). *Kavarma*, meat with onions, spices, and egg is slightly more expensive than *skara* (grills). **Vegetarians** should request *jadene bez meso* (JA-de-ne bez meh-SO) for meals without meat. **Kosher** diners would be wise to order vegetarian meals, as pork often works itself into main dishes. Bulgaria is known for its cheese and yogurt. *Ayran* (yogurt with water and ice) and *boza* (similar to beer, but sweet and thicker) are popular drinks that complement breakfast. Melnik produces famous red **wine,** while the northeast is known for its excellent white wines. On the Black Sea Coast, Albenu is a good sparkling wine. Bulgarians begin meals with *rakiya* (grape or plum brandy). Good Bulgarian **beers** include Kamenitza and Zagorka. The drinking age is 18.

HOLIDAYS AND FESTIVALS

Holidays: New Year's Day (Jan. 1); Liberation Day (Mar. 3); Orthodox Easter (Apr. 27, 2008); Labor Day (May 1); St. George's Day (May 6); Education and Culture Day/Day of Slavic Heritage (St. Cyril and Methodius Day; May 24); Festival of the Roses (June 5, 2008); Day of Union (Sept. 6); Independence Day (Sept. 22).

Festivals: Christmas and New Year's are marked by the two related Bulgarian customs of *koledouvane* and *souvakari.* On Christmas, groups of people go from house to house and perform *koledouvane,* or caroling, while holding oak sticks called *koledarkas.* Baba Marta (Spring Festival; Mar. 1) celebrates the beginning of spring.

BEYOND TOURISM

For more info on opportunities across Europe, see **Beyond Tourism,** p. 56.

American University in Bulgaria, Blagoevgrad 2700, Bulgaria (☎359 73 88 82 18; www.aubg.bg). University based on the American liberal arts model.

Cadip, 111-1271 Howe Street, Vancouver, British Columbia V6Z 1R3, Canada (☎1-604-628-7400; www.cadip.org). Runs work camps of volunteers who assist with orphan childcare. Program and membership fee min. US$270. Travel costs not included.

SOFIA (СОФИЯ)   ☎02

Far from the concrete Soviet grayscape you might expect, Sofia (pop. 1,100,000) is a city of magnificent domed cathedrals and grand old buildings, set against the backdrop of Mt. Vitosha. Although the city lacks the old-world feel of Prague or Vienna, it is remarkably diverse. Skateboarders listen to American rock music in front of the Soviet Army monument, while worshippers pass each other near the central square on their way to a synagogue, mosque, or cathedral. Sofia is a manifestation of the Bulgarian mentality, both aware of its complex past, and moving quickly, if a bit unsurely, to join the West.

▐ TRANSPORTATION

Flights: Airport Sofia (International info ☎937 2211; www.sofia-airport.bg) is a 5km hike from the center. Bus #84 is to the right exiting international arrivals. Tickets (0.70lv). The bus runs from the airport to Eagle Bridge (Орлов Мост; Orlov Most), near Sofia University. If you take a taxi, make sure to go with **OK Supertrans** (☎973 2121); others will overcharge you. Fare should run about 5-10lv to the center.

Trains: Tsentralna Gara (Централна Гара; Central Train Station), Knyaginya Mariya Luiza (Княгиня Мария Луиза; ☎931 1111), a 1.6km walk north from pl. Sveta Nedelya past the department store TSUM (ЦУМ) and the mosque. Trams #1 and 7 run between pl. Sveta Nedelya and the station; #9 and 12 head down Khristo Botev (Христо Ботев) and bul. Vitosha (Витоша). To: **Plovdiv** (14 per day, 6.70lv), **Varna** (6 per day, 19lv), and **Veliko Turnovo** (6 per day, 12lv). International tickets available at the **Rila Travel Bureau** (☎932 3346; open daily 7am-11pm) desk on the 1st fl., to the left of the main entrance. **Branch** at Gurko 5 (Гурко), off pl. Sveta Nedelya (☎987 0777; open M-F 7am-7:30pm, Sa 7am-6:30pm). Destinations include: **Bucharest, ROM** (2 per day,

Sofia

🔺 ACCOMMODATIONS
Apartment, 5
Art Hostel, 4
Hostel Sofia, 1
🍴 FOOD
Divaka, 3
Pod Lipite, 7
🍸 NIGHTLIFE
Hambara, 6
My Mojito, 2

36lv); **Budapest, HUN** via Bucharest (1 per day, 105lv; sleeper car only), and **İstanbul, TUR** (1 per day, 52lv; sleeping car only); **Thessaloniki, GCE** (2 per day, 25lv).

Buses: Private buses leave from either the **Central Bus Station** (Централна Автоара; Tsentralna Avtogara; ☎090 021 000; www.centralbusstation-sofia.com), Maria Luiza 100 (Мария Луиза), down the street from the train station; or the parking lot across from the train station, the **Trafik-Market** (☎981 2979). Pricier than trains, private buses are faster and more comfortable. International bus companies are across the train station entrance, domestic buses are more likely to leave from the bus station.

Public Transportation: Trams, trolleys, and **buses** cost 0.70lv per ride, 6lv for 10 rides, day pass 3lv, month pass 37lv. Buy tickets from the driver (single rides only; 0.10lv extra) or at kiosks with "билети" (bileti) signs in the window; exact change only. Validate in the machines on board to avoid a 5lv fine. If you put your backpack on a seat, you may be required to buy a 2nd ticket, or pay a 7lv fine for an "unticketed passenger." This policy is observed much more stringently on routes to and from the airport. All transportation runs daily 5:30am-11pm; after 9pm, service becomes less frequent.

Taxis: Some travelers relate horror stories about local taxi companies, but **OK Supertrans** (ОК Супертранс; ☎973 2121) remains a reliable option. Always make sure the company's name and phone number are on the side of the car. Many drivers don't speak English, so learn to pronounce Bulgarian names for places and directions. 0.50-0.60lv per km; slightly more expensive 10pm-6am.

✈ ⊡ ORIENTATION AND PRACTICAL INFORMATION

Sv. Nedelya Church is the locus of the city center, **ploshtad Sveta Nedelya** (Света Неделя). **Bulevard Knyaginya Mariya Luiza** (Княгиня Мария Луиза) connects pl. Sveta Nedelya to the train station. Trams #1 and 7 run from the train station through pl. Sveta Nedelya to **bul. Vitosha** (Витоша), one of the main thoroughfares. Bul. Vitosha links pl. Sveta Nedelya to **ploshtad Bulgaria** and the concrete **Natsionalen Dvorets na Kulturata** (Национален Дворец на Културата; NDK, National Palace of Culture). Historic **bulevard Tsar Osvoboditel** (Цар Освободител; Tsar the Liberator) runs by the Presidency building on the north, starting at **ploshtad Nezavisimost** (Независимост). Bul. Tsar Osvoboditel leads to the former **Royal Palace**, the **Parliament** building, and **Sofia University**. The free *Insider's Guide* and *In Your Pocket Sofia* are indispensable. *The Program* (Програмата; Programata; www.programata.bg) is a weekly city guide. The print version is in Bulgarian; look online for the English version.

Tourist Office: Tourist Information Center, pl. Sveta Nedelya 1 (☎933 5826; www.bulgariatravel.org), next to Happy Bar and Grill. The English-speaking staff answers questions about Sofia and Bulgaria and hand out free maps and English-language publications about Sofia. Open M-F 9am-6pm. **Odysseia-In/Zig Zag Holidays,** bul. Stamboliyski 20-B (Стамболийски; ☎980 5102; www.zigzagbg.com). Arranges tour packages, including homestays in Bulgarian villages, tours, trips to Rila Monastery, and outdoor excursions. They also create individualized tours upon request. Consultation 5lv per session; individualized tours from €30; commission on accommodations booking 10%. Open in high season daily 8:30am-7:30pm; in low season open M-F. MC/V.

Embassies: Australia, Trakiya 37 (Тракия; ☎946 1334). Consulate only. **Canada,** Moskovska 9 (Московска; ☎969 9710; consular@canada-bg.org). **UK,** Moskovska 9 (☎933 9222; www.british-embassy.bg). Open M-Th 9am-noon and 2-4pm, F 9am-noon. **Ireland,** Bacho Kiro 26-28 (Бачо Киро; ☎985 3425; info@embassyofireland.org). Citizens of **New Zealand** should contact the UK embassy. **US,** Kozyak 16 (Козяк; ☎937 5100; www.usembassy.bg). Open M-F 9am-noon, 2-4pm.

Luggage Storage: Downstairs at the central train station. 2lv per piece. Claim bags 30min. before departure. Open daily 6am-11pm.

24hr. Pharmacies: Apteka Sv. Nedelya (Аптека Св. Неделя), pl. Sv. Nedelya 5 (☎950 5026; www.apteka.bg), on bul. Stamboliyski. MC/V.

Medical Services: State-owned hospitals offer free 24hr. emergency aid to all; note that staff may not all speak English. For dog bites or emergency tetanus shots (10lv), go to **First City Hospital** (Първа Градска Болница; Purva Gradska Bolnitsa), bul. Patriarkh Evtimiy 37 (Патриарх Евтимий; ☎988 3631).

Telephones: Telephone Center, General Gurko 4 (Гурко; ☎980 1010). Go right out of the post office on Vasil Levski (Васил Левски) and then left on Gurko. Local calls 0.09lv, international calls from 0.36lv per min.**Internet** 0.80lv per hr., 1.40lv per 2hr., 2lv per 3hr. Fastest connections in town.

Internet: Stargate, Pozitano 20 (Позитано), near Hostel Sofia. 1.20lv per hr. Open 24hr. Cash Only. Also at **Telephone Center** (see above).

Post Office: General Gurko 6 (Гурко; ☎949 6446; www.bgpost.bg). **Poste Restante** at window #12 in the 2nd hall; look for the signs in English. Money transfers at window #4 in the 1st hall. Open M-Sa 7am-8:30pm, Su 8am-1pm. **Postal Code: 1000.**

⌂ ⊡ ACCOMMODATIONS AND FOOD

Hotels are rarely worth the exorbitant prices; hostels or private rooms are the best option. ◪**Hostel Sofia ❶**, Pozitano 16 (Позитано), has a great location and a homey feel. Though sociable, it's still quieter than some of the city's other, more party-oriented lodgings. From pl. Sv. Nedelya, walk down bul. Vitosha and turn right on Pozitano. (☎989 8582; www.hostelsofia.com. Common room with TV and DVD. Breakfast included. Laundry 5lv. Free Internet. Reception 24hr. 8-11 bed dorms €10 for 1st and 2nd nights, €9 thereafter. 10% discount per night Nov.-May. Cash only.) **Art-Hostel ❶**, Angel Kunchev 21A (Ангел Кънчев), draws an international crowd that stays up late at the bar and garden. From pl. Sv. Nedelya, walk down Vitosha and turn left on William Gladstone. Walk 2 blocks and turn right on Angel Kunchev. (☎987 0545; www.art-hostel.com. Kitchen, bar, and tea room. Breakfast included. Laundry 5lv. Free Internet. Reception 24hr. 6- to 10-bed dorms June-Aug. €10 for 1st to 3rd nights, €9 thereafter; Sept.-May €8/7. Cash only.)

Cheap meals are easy to find. Across bul. Mariya Luiza from TSUM are two large **markets,** the Women's Bazaar, and Central Hall. Facing McDonald's in pl. Slaveikov, take the left side-street and continue right at the fork to 🔣**Divaka ❷**, ul. William Gladstone 54, for huge salads and sizzling veggie and meat dishes. The restaurant is so popular, you might have to share a table with strangers. (☎989 9543. English menu available. Beer 1.10lv. Entrees 3-12lv. Open 24hr. Cash only.) **Pod Lipite** (Подъ Липите) **❷**, Elin Pelin 1 (Елин Пелин), serves Bulgarian cuisine in a recreation of a rustic tavern. Walk down Graf Ignatiyev (Граф Игнатиев), which becomes bul. Dragan Tsankov (Драган Цанков) when it hits the park; continue for a long time until you reach Elin Pelin. (☎866 5053. English menu. Beer from 1.10lv. Wine from 19lv per bottle. Entrees 3.30-17lv. Vegetarian options. Outdoor terrace. Call ahead. Open daily noon-1am. Cash only.)

👁 SIGHTS

🔣**BOYANA CHURCH** (БОЯНСКА ЦЪРКВА; BOYANSKA TSURKVA). In the woods of the Boyana suburb, this UNESCO World Heritage site boasts some of the most striking religious artwork in the country. The tiny red-brick church houses two layers of religious murals painted by unknown medieval masters. The church is in a little park with such a striking sense of tranquility that Queen Eleanor broke royal protocol and asked to be buried on the grounds. (☎959 0939. *Take bus #64 from Khladilnika (Хладилника), or a taxi from the center for 4-5lv. Open daily Nov.-Mar. 9am-5:30pm; Apr.-Oct. 9:30am-6pm; free M after 3pm. 10lv, students 5lv. Tour in English 5lv. English pamphlet 5lv. Combined ticket with the National History Museum12lv.)*

| **NATIONAL HISTORY MUSEUM.** Opulent residence of former Bulgarian dictator Todor Zhivkov, the fortress-like Natural History Museum, (Национален Исторически Музей; Natsionalen Istoricheski Muzey) is communist architecture at its most imposing. Standing in a sprawling park at the base of Vitosha mountain, the museum traces the evolution of Bulgarian culture from prehistoric times to the present. A new exhibit on the top floor now pays homage to the roles of minority ethnicities and religions in Bulgarian life. *(Residence Boyana, Palace 1. Take minibus #21, trolley #2, or bus #63 or 111 from the center, or tram #5 from Makedonya to Boyana. Even then, it's about a 15min. walk; it's best to just hire a taxi, 5lv. ☎955 4280; www.historymuseum.org. Open daily Nov.-Mar. 9am-5:30pm, Apr.-Oct. 9:30am-6pm. 10lv, students 5lv. Combined ticket with Boyana Church 12lv. Cash only.)*

CHURCHES. The huge gold- and green-domed Byzantine-style **St. Alexander Nevsky Cathedral** (Св. Александър Невски; Sv. Aleksandur Nevski) dominates the Sofia skyline. Housing over 400 frescoes by Russian and Bulgarian artists, it is the grandest edifice in all of Sofia. In a separate entrance to the left of the church, the **crypt** contains the National Art Gallery's spectacular array of painted icons and religious artifacts. *(In the center of pl. Aleksandur Nevski. English-language captions. Open daily 7am-7pm; crypt open Tu-Su 10am-6pm. Cathedral free. Crypt 4lv, students 2lv.)* The 1913 **St. Nicholas**

Russian Church (Св. Николай; Sv. Nikolai) was built to appease a Russian diplomat unwilling to worship in Bulgarian churches. In the crypt, the Russian Orthodox come to write prayers. *(On bul. Tsar Osvoboditel near pl. Sveta Nedelya. Open daily 7:45am-6:30pm. Liturgy W-Su 9am, W also 5pm, Sa also 5:30pm. Free.)*

SYNAGOGUE OF SOFIA (СОФИЙСКА СИНАГОГА; SOFIYSKA SINAGOGA). Built upon a foundation of Jewish gravestones, Sofia's only synagogue opened for services in 1909 as the largest Sephardic synagogue in the Balkans, and one of the largest in Europe. It boasts a vast interior decorated with a star-spangled dome, marble columns, and the largest chandelier in Bulgaria. Recent renovations repaired damage done by a stray Allied bomb from WWII, which miraculously didn't explode. A museum upstairs outlines the history of Jews in Bulgaria. *(Ekzarkh Yosif 16. ☎983 5085; www.sophiasynagogue.com. English-language captions. Open daily 8:30am-4pm. Services daily 8am, also Sa 10am. Museum open M-F 8:30am-12:30pm, 1-3:30pm. Museum 2lv, students 1lv. Synagogue 2lv/1lv; includes English-language pamphlet.)*

BANYA BOSHI MOSQUE (БАНЯ БОШИ). Constructed in 1576 during the Ottoman occupation, this mosque escaped the fate suffered by the 26 other mosques in Sofia shut down or destroyed during the communist era. The mosque's name derives from the old Turkish bath upon which it is built. The red brick building with minaret still intact has a sumptuous interior of red and blue floral tiled walls and a ceiling inscribed in golden calligraphy. *(Across from Central Hall, on Mariya Luiza (Мария Луиза). Open daily 3:30am-11:30pm. Entrance is free, but tourists are allowed to enter only when prayer is not underway. Shoe removal required at door. Females must wear mosque-provided robe with hood to cover knees, shoulders, and head.)*

NATIONAL ART GALLERY. Displaying Bulgaria's most prized traditional and contemporary art in a palatial setting, the National Gallery (Национална Художествена Галерия; Natsionalna Khudozhestvena Galeriya) showcases an array of exhibits, predominantly paintings from the 19th and 20th centuries, beginning with the National Revival movement. *(In the Royal Palace on bul. Tsar Osvoboditel. English captions. ☎980 0093. Open W and F-Su 10am-6pm, Tu and Th 10am-7pm. 4lv, students 2lv. Guided tours in English for groups of 5 or more 20lv, for fewer than five 15lv.)*

NATIONAL PALACE OF CULTURE. This monolith of black glass and white paneling was erected by the Communist government in 1981 to celebrate the country's 1300th birthday. It dominates the surrounding park, which is filled with a jumble of both communist statues and newer anti-communist memorials. The Palace of Culture (Национален Дворец на Културата; Natsionalen Dvorets na Kulturata) houses a number of restaurants, cinemas (screening both local and recent American movies), and concert halls. Its 12 halls host everything from conferences to chamber music to rock concerts. *(From pl. Sv. Nedelya, take bul. Vitosha to bul. Patriarkh Evtimiy (Патриарх Евтимий) and enter the park. The Palace is at Pl. Bulgaria 1. ☎916 6369; www.ndk.bg. Ticket office open M-Sa 9am-7pm. Cinema downstairs; ☎951 5101; 4-10lv.)*

🎵🎭 ENTERTAINMENT AND NIGHTLIFE

To get the latest events and nightlife listings, buy the English-language newspaper, the *Sofia Echo* (2.40lv) from a kiosk. For more info, consult the **"Program"** (Програмата) Cyrillic guide, or visit www.programata.bg for the English version. Sofia's week-long **Beer Fest** takes place in late summer. Each night, different bands light up the crowd with traditional Bulgarian music, as well as pop and jazz. Fish and chips (1.50lv) complement beer (0.80lv). The event takes place in Alexander Batemberg. Half a dozen theaters line **Rakovski** (Раковски). From the town center, a left on Rakovski leads to the columns of the **National Opera and Ballet** (Национална Опера и Балет; Natsionalna Opera i Balet), Vrabcha 1. (Врабча; ☎987 1366;

www.operasofia.com. Performances most days 6 or 7pm. Box office open M-F 9:30am-6:30pm, Sa-Su 10:30am-6pm. Closed July-Aug. Tickets 5-15lv. Cash only.)

At night, Sofians fill the outdoor bars along **bulevard Vitosha** (Витоша) and the cafes around the **National Palace of Culture.** For the younger set, nightlife centers around **Sofia University,** at the intersection of **Vasil Levski** (Васил Левски) and **Tsar Osvoboditel** (Цар Освободител). ⚑**Apartment,** Neofit Rilski 68 (Неофит Рилски), is a chill hangout that achieves the practically impossible: artsiness that iseffort less. A DJ table remains open to enterprising guests. (☎08 86 65 50 93; www.apartment.org. Foreign films most nights at 10:30pm. Free Wi-Fi. Fresh squeezed juice 3lv. Beer from 1.50lv. No cover. Open daily noon-2am. Cash only.) At **My Mojito,** Ivan Vazov 12 (Иван Вазов), students mix with young professionals. (☎08 89 52 90 01. Cover F-Sa men 5lv. Beer from 2.80lv. Mixed drinks from 4.80lv. Open daily 9:00pm-5am. Cash only.) Hidden away at 6-ti Septemvri 22 (6-ти Септември), **Hambara** (The Barn) is a former Communist newspaper office turned tavern. (W, Sa live music. Beer 3lv. Open 8pm-4am. Cash only.)

▚ DAYTRIPS FROM SOFIA

RILA MONASTERY. Holy Ivan of Rila built the 10th-century Rila Monastery (Рилски Манастир; Rilski Manastir), the largest and most famous in Bulgaria, as a refuge from worldly temptation. The **Nativity Church** is decorated with 1200 brilliantly colored frescoes. Modest clothing is necessary, especially for women. *(Monastery open daily approximately 7am-9pm.)* The **museum** in the monastery houses the intricate ⚑**wooden cross** that took 12 years to carve (with a needle) and left its creator, the monk Rafail, blind. *(Open daily 8:15am-4pm. 8lv, students 4lv. English lecture 20lv.)* Signs throughout the monastery show hiking routes in nearby **Rila National Park;** Cyrillic/English maps of the paths (7lv) are sold in the **Manas-tirski Padarutsi** (Манастирски Падарьци) shop.

Inquire at room #170 in the monastery about staying in a spartan but heated **monastic cell ❶.** *(☎070 54 22 08. Reception open from 2pm. 2-3 beds per room, single-sex. Doors lock at 10pm; ring the bell after that. Rooms 20lv.)* Behind the monastery are restaurants, cafes, and a mini-market. To get to the monastery, take **tram** #5 from pl. Sv. Nedelya to Ovcha Kupel Station (Овча Къпел) and take the **bus** to Rila Town (2hr., 6:25am and 10:20am, 5lv). From there, catch a bus to the monastery (30min., 3 per day, 1.50lv). A bus goes back from Rila to Sofia at 3pm (7lv).

KOPRIVSHTITSA. Todor Kableshkov's 1876 "letter of blood," urging rebellion against Ottoman rule, incited the **April Uprising** and ultimately the **War of Liberation** in this little village in the Sredna Gora mountains. Today, Koprivshtitsa (Копри-вщица; pop. 2600), is an enchanting village of stone cottages and winding streets. Many homes have verandas and famously delicate woodwork, and six have been turned into **museums;** buy tickets at the houses or the souvenir shop next to the tourist office. *(Open W-Su 9:30am-5:30pm. Each 2lv, students 1lv; combo ticket 5lv/2lv.)* **Trains** run to Plovdiv (3-4hr., 3 per day, 4.50lv) and Sofia (2hr., 5 per day, 5.80lv). Private **buses** also run to Plovdiv (2½hr., 1 per day, 5lv) and Sofia (2hr., 4 per day, 6lv). Backtrack along the river to the main square to reach the **tourist office.** *(☎071 842 191; www.koprivshtitsa.info. Open daily 10am-7pm.)*

PLOVDIV (ПЛОВДИВ)   ☎032

Churches, galleries, Roman ruins, and 19th-century National Revival structures pack picturesque Plovdiv (pop. 350,000). The city's historical and cultural treasures are concentrated among the **Trimontium** (three hills) of **Starlya Grad** (Стария Град; Old Town). To reach the 2nd-century ⚑**Roman amphitheater** (Античен

Теат]p; Antichen Teatur) from pl. Tsentralen (Централен), take a right off Knyaz Aleksandr (Княз Александр) on Suborna (Съборна), then go right up the steps along Mitropolit Paisii. Dating from the early Roman occupation, this marble masterpiece now hosts concerts and shows, such as the **Verdi Opera Festival** in June and July (☎63 23 48; 8-20lv) and the **Festival of the Arts** in late summer. (Amphitheater open daily 9am-7pm. 3lv.) Follow Knyaz Alekzsandr to pl. Dzhu-maya (Джумая) to see the remains of an ancient Roman **stadium**. (Free.) At the end of ul. Suborna on Dr. Chomakov 2, the **Museum of Ethnography** (Етнографски Музей; Etnografski Muzey) exhibits artifacts such as *kukerski maski*, masks used to scare away evil spirits. (☎62 56 54. Open Tu, Th, Sa-Su 9am-noon and 2-5pm; W and F 9am-noon. 4lv, students 2lv. Cash only.)

■**Hiker's Hostel ❶**, ul. Suborna 59 (Съборна), offers free Internet and big break-fasts. The staff organizes daytrips. (☎359 885 194 553; www.hikers-hostel.org/ pd. Free pickup. Kitchen available. Laundry 4lv. Reserve ahead. Reception 24hr. Dorms 20lv. Cash only.) **Trains** run to Burgas (5hr., 4 per day, 11lv), Sofia (2½-3hr., 15 per day, 6.70lv), and Varna (6-7hr., 3 per day, 14lv). Buy international tickets at **Rila**, bul. Khristo Botev 31A. (Христj Ъоттв. ☎64 31 20. Open M-F 8am-7:30pm, Sa 8am-2pm. Cash only.) **Buses** to Sofia (2hr., 1-3 per hr., 10lv) leave from the Yug (Юг) station, bul. Khristo Botev 47 (☎62 69 37), opposite the train station. Check email at **Speed**, Knyaz Aleksandr 12. (Княз Александр. 1lv per hr. Open 24hr.) The municipal **tourist information center** is at pl. Tsentralen 1. (☎65 67 94; tic@plo-vdiv.bg. Open daily 9am-7pm.) **Postal Code:** 4000.

▶ **DAYTRIP FROM PLOVDIV: BACHKOVO MONASTERY.** In the Rodopi moun-tains 28km south of Plovdiv lies Bulgaria's second-largest monastery, **Bachkovo Monastery** (<ачковски Манастир; Bachkovski Manastir; ☎03 32 72 77). Built in 1083, the main church holds the **Icon of the Virgin Mary and Child** (Вкона Света <огородица; Ikona Sveta Bogoroditsa), which is said to have miraculous healing powers. *(Open daily 8am-8pm. Free.)* **Hiking** paths lie uphill from the monastery. The Smolyan **bus** (30min., 1-2 per hr., 4lv) leaves from platform #1 at the Rodolpi station in Plovdiv; ask to go to Bachkovo. *(Kassa open 5:30am-8pm.)*

VELIKO TURNOVO (ВЕЛИКО ТЪРНОВО)   ☎062

Veliko Turnovo (pop. 66,000), on the steep hills above the Yantra River, has watched over Bulgaria for more than 5000 years. The city's residents led the 1185 national uprising against Byzantine rule, and its revolutionaries wrote the coun-try's first constitution in 1879. The ruins of the ■**Tsarevets** (Царевец), a fortress that was the main citadel and Second Bulgarian Kingdom's center of power (1185-1393), span a hillside outside the city. (Open daily 8am-7pm, *kassa* closes 6pm. 4lv, students 2lv.) Once inside, climb uphill to the **Church of the Ascension** (Църква Възнесениегосподне; Tsurkva Vuzneseniyegospodne), which was restored in honor of the country's 1300th anniversary in 1981. Cobblestone **Rakovski** (Раковски) street is a great place to browse traditional Bulgarian crafts. For a foray into mod-ern Bulgarian history, go down Nezavisimost (Независимост), and turn right at ul. Ivan Vazov (Иван Вазов) to reach the **National Revival Museum** (Музей на Възраждането; Muzey na Vuzrazhdaneto). The museum building housed Bulgaria's first parliament and now contains a copy of its first constitution. (☎62 98 21. Open M and W-Su 9am-6pm. 4lv, students 2lv.) On summer evenings when there is suffi-cient tourist demand, there is a ■**sound and light show** above Tsarevets Hill. (20min., 9:45pm, 15lv.) The **International Folklore Festival** takes place in late July or early August and features folk dance and music.

■**Hiker's Hostel ❶** is at Rezervoarska 91 (Резервоарска). From Stambolov (Стамболов), turn left on Rakovski (Раковски), left into the small square, go straight, and take the small street uphill. (☎889 691 661; www.hikers-hostel.org/vt. Breakfast included. Free Internet. Dorms 20lv; doubles 26lv. Cash only.) ETAP sends **buses** to Sofia (3hr., 13 per day, 40lv) and Varna (3hr., 10 per day, 40lv). Bus #10 (1lv) leaves from the main square in Veliko Turnovo for Gorna Oryakhovitsa (Горна Оряховица), the train station. **Trains** go to Burgas (6hr., 7 per day, 11lv), Sofia (5hr., 8 per day, 14lv), and Varna (4-5hr., 5 per day, 12lv). **Navigator Internet Club** (Навигатор), Nezavisimost 3 (Независимост), is open 24hr. (☎67 02 88. 0.49-0.79lv per hr. Cash only.) The **tourist office** is at bul. Hristo Botev 5. (Христj Ботв. ☎62 21 48. Open M-F 9am-6pm.) **Postal Code:** 5000.

BLACK SEA COAST (ЧЕРНО МОРЕ)

Bulgaria's premier vacation spot, the Black Sea Coast is laden with secluded bays and pricey resorts. Still, ancient fishing villages are just a step off the beaten path.

VARNA (ВАРНА)   ☎052

Expansive beaches, a Mediterranean climate, open-air nightlife, and frequent summer festivals draw visitors to Varna (pop. 312,000). From the train station, go right on bul. Primorski (Приморски) to reach the town ▨beaches and seaside gardens. The ▨Archaeological Museum (Fh[tjkjubxtcrb Veptq; Arheologicheski Muzey), bul. Maria Luiza 41, in the park on Maria Luiza, has the world's oldest gold artifacts, dating from over 6000 years ago. (☎68 10 30; www.amvarna.com. Open in high season Tu-Su 10am-6pm; low season Tu-Sa 10am-5pm. 8lv, students 2lv.) On San Stefano in the city's old quarter, **Grütska Makhala** (Гръцка Махала), visit the well-preserved ruins of the **Roman Thermal Baths** (Римски Терми; Rimski Termi. ☎60 00 59. Open in high season Tu-Su 10am-5pm; in low season Tu-Sa 10am-5pm. 4lv, students 2lv.) The **Ethnographic Museum,** str. Panagjurishte 22, portrays the traditional Bulgarian lifestyle. (☎63 05 88. Open in high season Tu-Su 10am-5pm; in low season M-Sa 10am-5pm.) Varna's cultural events include the **International Jazz Festival** in August (☎65 91 67; www.vsjf.com) and the **Varna Summer Festival** (☎60 35 04 or ☎65 91 59; www.varnasummerfest.org), a music, theater, and folk festival in late June-late July. For schedules and tickets, check the **Festival and Congress Center,** bul. Primorski, which is also the location of **Love is Folly,** a film festival in September. (☎60 84 45. Box office open daily 10am-9pm.)

▨**Gregory's Backpackers Hostel ❶,** str. Fenix 82, in Zvezditsa 10km from Varna, has a bar and a swimming pool. (☎37 99 09; www.hostelvarna.com. Free pickup. Breakfast included. Laundry 12lv. Internet 1.40lv per hr. Reserve ahead. Open Apr.-Oct. Dorms 20lv. Cash only.) Nightlife is centered on the beach in **Primorski Park,** which features a strip of **outdoor discos** along **Krabrezhna Aleya.** Near the commercial harbor, **trains** depart for Plovdiv (6-7hr., 2 per day, 14lv) and Sofia (9-11hr., 6 per day, 19lv). **Buses** leave from ul. Vladislav Varenchik (Владислав Варенчик). ETAP buses go to Sofia (6hr., 11 per day, 22lv) via Veliko Tŭrnovo (3hr., 11lv) while Victory buses go to Burgas (2hr., 2 per day, 10lv). The **tourist office** is on bul. Knyaz Boris I, near the Masala Palace Hotel. **Astra Tour,** near track #6 at the train station, finds private singles for 16-24lv and doubles for 25-40lv. (☎60 58 61; astratur@yahoo.com. Open May-Oct. daily 6am-9pm.) Access the **Internet** at **Bitex.com,** str. Zamenhof 1, 3rd fl., off pl. Nezavisimost. (☎63 17 65. 1lv per hr., 2lv 9am-2pm, 3lv midnight-8am. Open 24hr.) **Postal Code:** 9000.

CROATIA (HRVATSKA)

 With attractions ranging from the sun-drenched beaches and cliffs around Dubrovnik to the dense forests around Plitvice, Croatia's wonders never cease. And, like so many treasures, Croatia has been fought over many times, often finding itself in the middle of dangerous political divides deadly ethnic tensions. It was only after the devastating 1991-1995 ethnic war that Croatia achieved full independence for the first time in 800 years. That said, while some marked-off areas still contain land mines, the biggest threats currently facing travelers to Croatia are the ever-rising prices and tides of tourists who clog the ferryways. Still, this friendly, fun-loving, and upbeat country demands to be seen at any cost.

 DISCOVER CROATIA: SUGGESTED ITINERARIES

THREE DAYS. Spend a day poking around the bizarre architecture of **Split** (p. 218) before ferrying down the coast to the beach paradise of either **Hvar** or **Brac** islands (1 day; p. 219). Then make your way to former war-zone—and what some consider Eastern Europe's most beautiful city—**Dubrovnik** (1 day; p. 221).

BEST OF CROATIA, ONE WEEK. Enjoy the East-meets-West feel of **Zagreb** (1 day; p. 210) and head to **Zadar** (1 day; p. 216) with a few hours' stop in gorgeous **Plitvice National Park** (p. 214). Next, ferry to tree-lined **Korčula** (1 day; p. 220) before **Hvar** and **Brac** (2 days). End your journey in **Dubrovnik** (2 days).

ESSENTIALS

FACTS AND FIGURES

Official Name: Republic of Croatia.
Capital: Zagreb.
Major Cities: Dubrovnik, Split.
Population: 4,493,000.

Time Zone: GMT + 1.
Language: Croatian.
Religions: Roman Catholic (88%).
Population Growth Rate: -0.035%.

WHEN TO GO

Croatia's best weather lasts from May to September, and crowds typically show up along the Adriatic coast in July and August. If you go in late August or September, you'll find fewer crowds, lower prices, and an abundance of fruits such as figs and grapes. Late autumn is wine season. While April and October may be too cool for camping, the weather is usually nice along the coast, and private rooms are plentiful and inexpensive. You can swim in the sea from mid-June to late September.

DOCUMENTS AND FORMALITIES

EMBASSIES AND CONSULATES. Foreign embassies in Croatia are in Zagreb (p. 210). Embassies abroad include: **Australia,** 14 Jindalee Crescent, O'Malley ACT 2606, Canberra (☎262 866 988; croemb@dynamite.com.au); **Canada,** 229 Chapel Street, Ottawa, ON K1N 7Y6 (☎613-562-7820; www.croatiaemb.net); **Ireland,** Adelaide Chambers, Peter St., Dublin, 8 (☎01 476 7181; croatianembassy@eircom.net); **New Zealand,** 291 Lincoln Rd., Henderson (☎9 836 5581; cro-consulate@xtra.co.nz), mail to: P.O. Box 83-200, Edmonton, Auckland; **UK,** 21 Conway Street, London, W1P 5HL. (☎020 7387 2022; http://croatia.embassyhomepage.com); **US,** 2343 Massachusetts Ave., NW, Washington, D.C. 20008 (☎202-588-5899; http://www.croatiaemb.org)

Croatia

VISA AND ENTRY INFORMATION. Citizens of Australia, Canada, the EU, New Zealand, and the US do not need a visa for stays of up to 90 days. Visas cost US$26 (single-entry), US$33 (double-entry), and US$52 (multiple-entry). Apply for a visa at your nearest Croatian embassy or consulate at least one month before planned arrival. All visitors must **register with the police** within 48hr. of arrival—hotels, campsites, and accommodation agencies should automatically register you, but those staying with friends or in private rooms must do so themselves to avoid fines or expulsion. To register, go to room 103 on the 2nd floor of the central police station at Petrinjska 30, Zagreb. (☎456 3623, after hours 456 3111. Bring your passport and use form #14. Open M-F 8am-4pm.) Police may check foreigners' passports at any time and place. There is no entry fee. The easiest way of entering or exiting Croatia is by bus or train between Zagreb and a neighboring capital.

ENTRANCE REQUIREMENTS.
Passport: Required for all travelers.
Visa: see above.
Letter of Invitation: Not required for citizens of Australia, Canada, the EU, Ireland, New Zealand, the UK, and the US.
Inoculations: Recommended up-to-date on DTaP (diphtheria, tetanus, and pertussis), Hepatitis A, Hepatitis B, MMR, polio booster, rabies, and typhoid.
Work Permit: Required for all foreigners planning to work in Croatia.
International Driving Permit: Required for all those planning to drive in Croatia.

TOURIST SERVICES AND MONEY

EMERGENCY	Ambulance: ☎94. Fire: ☎93. Police: ☎92. General Emergency: ☎112.

TOURIST OFFICES. Even the smallest towns have a branch of the excellent, resourceful **state-run tourist board** *(turistička zajednica)*. Their staff speak English and give out **free maps** and booklets. Private agencies *(turistička/ putnička agencija)*, such as the ubiquitous **Atlas,** handle private accommodations. Local outfits are cheaper.

MONEY. The Croatian unit of currency is the **kuna** (kn), plural kunas. One kuna is equal to 100 lipa. Inflation hovers around 2.6%, so prices should stay relatively constant in the near future. Croatia became an official candidate for European Union membership in 2004, with admission projected for the end of the decade; travelers may occasionally find prices listed in euro (€), especially in heavily touristed areas like the Istrian Peninsula. Most tourist offices, hostels, and transportation stations **exchange currency** and **traveler's checks;** banks have the best rates. Some establishments charge a 1.5% commission to exchange traveler's checks. Most banks give MasterCard and Visa cash advances, and **credit cards** (especially American Express, MasterCard, and Visa) are widely accepted. Common banks include Zagrebačka Banka, Privredna Banka, and Splitska Banka. **ATMs** are everywhere.

CROATIAN KUNA (KN)		
AUS$1 = 4.44KN	1KN = AUS$0.23	
CDN$1 = 5.07KN	1KN = CDN$0.20	
EUR€1 = 7.39KN	1KN = EUR€0.14	
NZ$1 = 3.89KN	1KN = NZ$0.26	
UK£1 = 10.94KN	1KN = UK£0.09	
US$1 = 5.91KN	1KN = US$0.17	

Expect to spend anywhere from 300 to 470kn per day. Travel in Croatia is becoming more costly, with the bare minimum for accommodations, food, and transport costing 240kn. **Tipping** is not expected, although it is appropriate to round up when paying; in some cases, the establishment will do it for you—check your change. Fancy restaurants often add a hefty service charge. **Bargaining** is reserved for informal transactions, such as hiring a boat for a day or renting a private room directly from an owner. Posted prices should usually be followed.

HEALTH AND SAFETY

Medical facilities in Croatia include public hospitals and clinics and private medical practitioners and pharmacies. Due to disparities in funding, private clinics and pharmacies tend to be better supplied. Both public and private facilities may demand cash payment for services, and most do not usually accept credit cards.
Pharmacies sell Western products, including tampons, sanitary napkins *(sanitami ulosci)*, and condoms *(prezervativ)*. UK citizens receive free medical care with a valid passport. Tap water is chlorinated; though it is relatively safe, it may cause mild abdominal discomfort. Croatia's crime rate is relatively low, but travelers should beware of pickpockets. Travel to the former conflict areas of **Slavonia** and **Krajina** remains dangerous due to **unexploded landmines,** which are not expected to be cleared until at least 2010. In 2005, a tourist was injured by a mine on the island of Vis, which inspectors had previously declared safe. Do not stray from known safe areas, and consult www.hcr.hr for detailed info. **Women** should go out in public with a companion to ward off unwanted attention. Although incidents of hate crime in Croatia are rare, **minority** travelers may experience stares. **Disabled travel-**

ers should contact Savez Organizacija Invalida Hrvatske (☎ 1 4829 394), in Zagreb, as cobblestones and a lack of ramps render it a more difficult area. Although **homosexuality** is slowly becoming accepted, discretion is recommended.

TRANSPORTATION

BY PLANE AND TRAIN. Croatia Airlines flies to and from many cities, including Frankfurt, London, Paris, Zagreb, Dubrovnik, and Split. Budget airlines like Ryanair fly to Zadar and Pula. Trains (www.hznet.hr) are slow everywhere and nonexistent south of Split. Trains (www.hznet.hr) run to Zagreb from **Budapest, HUN; Ljubljana, SLV; Venice, ITA;** and **Vienna, AUT,** and continue on to other Croatian destinations. *Odlazak* means departures, *dolazak* means arrivals.

BY BUS. Buses run faster and farther than trains at comparable or slightly higher prices and are the easiest way to get to many destinations, especially south of Split. Major companies include Croatiabus (www.croatiabus.hr), Autotrans Croatia (www.autotrans.hr) and Austobusni Promet Varaždin (www.ap.hr). The website of the main bus terminal in Zagreb (Austobusni Kolodvor Zagreb; www.akz.hr) provides info on timetables, although unfortunately not in English.

BY CAR AND BY TAXI. Anyone over 18 can rent a car in larger cities, but parking and gas are expensive. Rural roads are in bad condition, and those traveling through the Krajina region and other conflict areas should be cautious of off-road landmines. Taxis are reliable and run on meter.

BY BOAT. The Jadrolinija ferry company (www.jadrolinija.hr) sails the Rijeka-Split-Dubrovnik route, stopping at islands on the way. Ferries also go to Ancona, ITA from Split and Zadar and to Bari, ITA from Split and Dubrovnik. Though slower than buses and trains, ferries are more comfortable. A basic ticket only grants a place on the deck. Cheap beds sell out fast, so buy tickets in advance.

BY BIKE AND BY THUMB. Moped and **bike rentals** are an option in resort or urban areas. **Hitchhiking** is relatively uncommon and is not recommended by Let's Go.

KEEPING IN TOUCH

PHONE CODES	**Country code: 385. International dialing prefix:** 00. For more info on how to place international calls, see **Inside Back Cover.**

EMAIL AND INTERNET. Most towns, no matter how small, have at least one **Internet** cafe. Connections on the islands are slower and less reliable than those on the mainland. Internet usage typically costs 20kn per hour.

TELEPHONE. Post offices usually have **public phones;** pay after you talk. All phones on the street require a country-specific phone card *(telekarta)*, sold at newsstands and post offices for 15-100kn. A Global Card allows calls for as cheap as 0.99kn per minute and provides the best international rates. For the **international operator,** dial ☎ 901. Croatia has two **cell phone** networks, T-Mobile and VIP. If you bring or buy a phone compatible with the GSM 900/1800 network, SIM cards are widely available. Pressing the "L" button will cause the phone instructions to switch into English.

MAIL. The Croatian Postal Service is reliable. Mail from the US arrives within a week. Post office workers are generally helpful to foreigners. A postcard or letter to the US typically costs 3.50kn. *Avionski* and *zrakoplovom* both mean "airmail." Mail addressed to **Poste Restante** will be held for up to 30 days at the receiving post office. Address envelopes: First name LAST NAME, POSTE RESTANTE, Pt. Republike 28, post office address, Postal Code, city, CROATIA.

LANGUAGE. Croats speak **Croatian,** a South Slavic language written in the Latin alphabet. The language has fairly recently become differentiated from Serbo-Croatian. Only a few expressions differ from Serbian, but be careful not to use the Serbian ones in Croatia—you'll make few friends. **German** and **Italian** are common second languages among adults. Most Croatians under 30 speak some **English.** For a phrasebook and glossary, see **Appendix: Croatian,** p. 1058.

ACCOMMODATIONS AND CAMPING

CROATIA	❶	❷	❸	❹	❺
ACCOMMODATIONS	under 150Kn	150-250Kn	251-350Kn	351-450Kn	over 450Kn

For info on Croatia's youth hostels (in Krk, Pula, Punat, Šibenik, Veli Losinj, Zadar, and Zagreb), contact the **Croatian Youth Hostel Association,** Savska 5/1, 10000 Zagreb (☎1 482 9294; www.hfhs.hr/home.php?lang=en). **Hotels** in Croatia can be expensive. If you opt for a hotel, call a few days ahead, especially in the summer along the coast. Those looking to stay in either hostels or hotels in the July-August tourist season should book early, as rooms fill up quickly. Apart from hostels, **private rooms** are the major budget option for accommodations. Look for *sobe* signs, especially near transportation stations. English is rarely spoken by room owners. All accommodations are subject to a tourist tax of 5-10kn (one reason the police require foreigners to register). Croatia is also one of the top **camping** destinations in Europe—33% of travelers stay in campgrounds. Facilities are usually comfortable, and prices are among the cheapest along the Mediterranean. Camping outside of designated areas is illegal. For more info, contact the **Croatian Camping Union,** 8. Marta 1, P.O. Box 143, HR-52440 Poreč (☎52 45 13 24; www.camping.hr).

FOOD AND DRINK

CROATIA	❶	❷	❸	❹	❺
FOOD	under 30Kn	30-60Kn	61-90Kn	91-150Kn	over 150Kn

Croatian cuisine is defined by the country's varied geography. In continental Croatia in and to the east of Zagreb, heavy meals featuring meat and creamy sauces dominate. *Purica s mlincima* (turkey with pasta) is the regional dish near Zagreb. Also popular are *burek,* a layered pie made with meat or cheese, and the spicy Slavonian *kulen,* considered one of the world's best **sausages.** *Pašticada* (slow-cooked meat) is also excellent. On the coast, textures and flavors change with the presence of **seafood** and Italian influence. Don't miss out on *lignje* (squid) or *Dalmatinski pršut* (Dalmatian smoked ham). The **oysters** from Ston Bay have received a number of awards at international competitions. If your budget does not allow for such treats, *slane sardele* (salted sardines) are a tasty substitute. **Vegetarian** and **kosher** eating are difficult in Croatia, but not impossible. In both cases, pizza and bakeries are safe and ubiquitous options. Mix red wine with tap water to get the popular *bevanda,* and white wine with carbonated water to get *gemišt. Šljivovica* is a plum brandy found in many small towns. *Karlovačko* and *Ožujsko* are the two most popular beers.

HOLIDAYS AND FESTIVALS

Holidays: New Year's Day (Jan. 1); Epiphany (Jan. 6); Easter Sunday and Monday Easter Sunday (March 23-4, 2008; April 12-3, 2009); May Day (May 1); Anti-Fascist Struggle Day (June 22); National Thanksgiving Day (Aug. 5); Independence Day (Oct. 8).

Festivals: In June, Zagreb holds the catch-all festival Cest Is D'Best ("The Streets are the Best"). Open-air concerts and theatrical performances make the Dubrovnik Summer Festival (*Dubrovački Ljetni;* from early July to late Aug.) the event of the summer. From July to Aug., Korčula (p. 220) unsheathes the Festival of Sword Dances (*Festival Viteških Igara*) with performances of sword dances all over the island. Zagreb's International Puppet Festival is from late Aug. to early Sept.

BEYOND TOURISM

Coalition for Work With Psychotrauma and Peace, M. Drzica 12, 32000 Vukovar, Croatia (☎385 32 45 09 91; www.cwwpp.org). Work in education and health care related to long-term conflict stress in Croatia.

Learning Enterprises, 2227 20th St. #304, NW, Washington, D.C. 20009, USA (☎001 20 23 09 34 53; www.learningenterprises.org). 6-week summer programs place first-time English teachers in rural Croatia, Hungary, Romania, and Slovakia. No-fee program includes orientation and room and board with a host family.

Eco-Centre Caput Insulae-Bell, Beli 4, 51559 Beli, Cres Island, Croatia (☎/fax 385 51 84 05 25; www.caput-insulae.com). Protect the natural and historical heritage of Cres. Bring 3 friends and get 1 week of accommodations. 2 week min. volunteer period.

ZAGREB ☎01

Too often treated as little more than a stopover en route to the Adriatic coast, Croatia's capital and largest city (pop. 779,000) possesses all the grand architecture, wide boulevards, and sprawling parks of a major European city. In the old city center, smartly-dressed Zagrebčani outnumber visitors as both enjoy the sights and smells of outdoor cafes, flower markets, and fresh fruit stands. With its welcoming, English-speaking inhabitants, growing economy, impressive cultural offerings, and unspoiled surroundings, Zagreb is an enjoyable, laid-back, and worthwhile alternative to the sun-splattered coast.

⬛🔢 TRANSPORTATION AND PRACTICAL INFORMATION. Trains leave the **Glavni Kolodvor,** Trg Kralja Tomislava 12 (☎060 333 444, international info 378 2583; www.hznet.hr.; AmEx/MC/V) for: Ljubljana (2 hr.; 8 per day; 100kn, round-trip 130kn), Rijeka (4-6hr., 3 per day, 105kn); Split (6-9hr., 5 per day, 155kn); Budapest, HUN (7¼hr., 3 per day, 225kn); Venice, ITA (6hr., 1 per day, 320kn); Vienna, AUT (6½hr., 2 per day, 355kn); Zurich, SWI (14hr., 1 per day, 647kn). There are no trains to Dubrovnik. For travel within Croatia, buses, leaving from the **Autobusni Kolodvor,** Drziceva bb (☎060 313 333; information and reservations from abroad ☎611 2789; www.akz.hr, click on "Vozni red") are often more efficient than trains. They leave for: Dubrovnik (11hr., 9 per day, 190-230kn); Plitvice (2½hr., 15 per day, 65-83kn); Pula (4½hr., 15 per day, 140-195kn); Rijeka (3½hr., 15 per day, 130kn); Split (7-9hr., every hour 155kn); Varaždin (1¾hr., 1 per hr., 70kn); Frankfurt, GER (15hr., 1 per day, 685kn); Ljubljana, SLN (2½hr., 1 per day, 100kn); Vienna, AUT (8hr., 2 per day, 250kn). Large backpacks cost 7kn extra. Buy tickets on either side of the ticket area. Luggage storage can be found in the **garderoba** up the staircase to the right of the main hall (1.20kn per hr.). Restrooms (3kn) are upstairs in the waiting lounge.

The **Tourist Information Center (TIC),** Trg Jelačića 11, gives out free **maps** and pamphlets *Zagreb Info A-Z, Zagreb in Your Pocket,* and *Events and Performances.* (☎481 4051; www.zagreb-touristinfo.hr.) They also sell a **Zagreb Card** which covers all bus and tram rides and provides discounts in restaurants and museums. (☎481 4052; www.zagrebcard.fivestars.hr. Valid for 1 or 3 days; 60/90kn.) Get online at **Ch@rlie's,** Gajeva 4a (☎488 0233), through the courtyard and on the right, where you will find a English-speaking staff, great connections, and printing and scanning. (Open M-Sa 8am-10pm, Su 11am-9pm. 16kn per hr.) **Postal Code:** 10000.

CROATIA

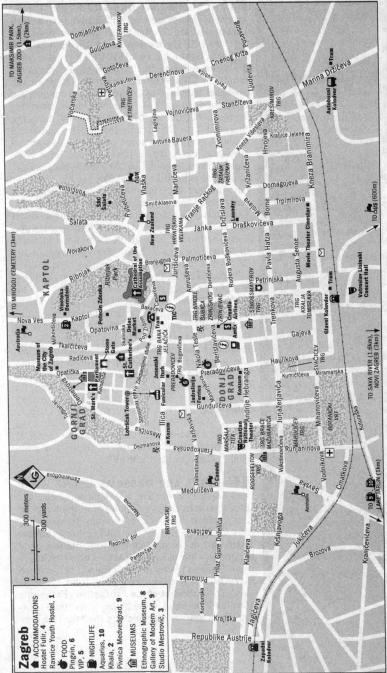

Zagreb

ACCOMMODATIONS
Hostel Fulir, 4
Ravnice Youth Hostel, 1

FOOD
Pingvin, 6
VIP, 5

NIGHTLIFE
Aquarius, 10
Khala, 2
Pivnica Medvedgrad, 9

MUSEUMS
Ethnographic Museum, 8
Gallery of Modern Art, 9
Studio Meštrović, 3

CROATIA COMES OUT

In October 2005, Croatians opened several of the country's major newspapers to read, under the heading "We don't want to hide anymore," the names of over 1200 countrymen and women going public with their homosexuality. Though no last names were published, the names were folllowed by age, specific sexual orientation, and the invitation to "Reconsider your prejudice."

In a country where 88% of the population declares itself Roman Catholic, homosexuality continues to be a major taboo, and despite the 2003 law recognizing gay civil unions, discrimination and severe intolerance remain common. The first 200-person Gay Pride of the Balkans march was held in Zagreb in 2002. It was not received well. After police left the parade, many of the marchers were badly beaten by angry religious protesters. Still, gay rights groups like *Iskorak* (Step Forward) have been challenging the nation's conservatism one step at a time in spite of violent anti-gay protests.

Because of lingering homophobia, Croatia's recent government-sponsored coming out is more than symbolic: it is truly an act of courage.

The group Queer Zagreb sponsors an annual GLBT festival, featuring movies, visual art, dance, and discussions about being gay in Croatia (www.queerzagreb.com).

ACCOMMODATIONS AND FOOD. Cheap accommodations are scarce in Zagreb, even as budget travelers are becoming more common. When hostels are full, try a **private room** through **Evistas,** Augusta Šenoe 28. (☎483 9554. Open M-F 9am-1:30pm and 3-8pm, Sa 9:30am-5pm.) Rooms in the family-run **Ravnice Youth Hostel ❶**, 1 Ravnice 38d, are clean, with brightly colored tie-dyed curtains and hardwood floors. Take tram #11 or 12 from Trg Jelačica, #4 from the train station, or #7 from the bus station to Dubrava or Dubec. The unmarked Ravnice stop is two stops past football stadium "Dinamo;" two traffic lights later, look for a white sign marked "hostel." (☎233 2325; www.ravnice-youth-hostel.hr. Bike rental 8kn per hr., 60kn per day. Laundry 40kn. Internet 16kn per hr. Reception daily 9am-10pm. Check-out noon. Dorms 125kn. Cash only.) The incredibly social, laid-back **Hostel Fulir ❶**, in a neighborhood packed with bars, is a perfect location for partygoers. Communal kitchen, linen, and lockers included. Free Internet. (☎483 0882; www.fulir-hostel.com. 145kn per night. MC/V.)

To find **VIP ❶**, Prereadovicev Trg 5 (☎152 8696), head to the western side of the square and look for the "KinoZagreb" sign and red umbrellas. This music-filled restaurant offers tasty and inexpensive Italian fare with great people-watching in the middle of the flower market. (Sandwiches 15kn. Pizza 25-32kn. Pasta and lasagna 25-40kn. Internet 15kn per hr.) The courtyard sandwich shop **Pingvin ❶** (Penguin), Teslina 7, is a local favorite. Grilled sandwich and drink combos are 16-23kn. (Open M-Sa 24hr., Su 5am-noon. Cash only.) The largest open-air market, **Dolac,** is behind Trg Jelačića in *Gornji Grad* (Upper Town), along Pod Zidom. (Open M-Sa 6am-3pm, Su 6am-1pm.) **Konzum** supermarket is at the corner of Preradovićeva and Hebrangova. (Open M-F 7am-8pm, Sa 7am-3pm. AmEx/MC/V.)

SIGHTS AND MUSEUMS. Zagreb is best seen on foot. From Trg b. Josipa Jelačića, take Ilica, then turn right on Tomiceva to the funicular (3kn), which gives access to many sights on the hills of *Gornji Grad*. The 13th-century **Lotrščak Tower,** part of the original city wall, offers a great panoramic view of Zagreb. (At the corner of Strossmayerovo and Dverce, right at the top of the funicular. Open May-Sept. 11am-8pm. 10kn, students 5kn.) The **Cathedral of the Assumption** (Katredrala Marijina Uznesnja), known simply as "the Cathedral," has graced Zagreb since the late 11th cen-

CROATIA

tury, and has seen no end of additions and renovations since. (Kaptol 1. Open daily 10am-5pm. Services M-Sa 7, 8, 9am; Su 7, 8, 9, 10, 11:30am. Free.) **Mirogoj Cemetery,** Croatia's largest, just north of the Cathedral, contains 12 cream-colored towers, a garden with cypress trees, and touching epitaphs that tell the troubled history of the region. (Take the 106 "Mirogoj" bus from Kaptol in front of the Cathedral; 8min., 4 per hr. Open M-F 6am-8pm, Su 7:30am-6pm. Free. No photography.) The **Stone Gate,** once one of the four gateways to the city, remains as a site where passersby stop to pray.

The ▓**Ethnographic Museum** (Etnografski Muzej), Mažuranićev Trg 14, across the street from the Mimara, displays artifacts from 19th- and 20th-century Croatian voyages to Africa, Asia, and South America, as well as a mix of traditional costumes and etchings of local architecture. (☎482 6220; www.etnografski-muzej.hr. English-language captions. Open Tu-Th 10am-6pm, F-Su 10am-1pm. 15kn, students and over 60 10kn, Th free. Cash only.) **Studio Mestrovič,** Mletačka 8, behind St. Mark's, is in the former home and studio of Ivan Mestrovič, Croatia's most celebrated sculptor. His intensely dramatic portraits are displayed in a beautiful building. (☎485 1123. Open Tu-F 10am-6pm, Sa-Su 10am-2pm. 20kn, students 10kn. Cash only.) The **Gallery of Modern Art (Moderna Galerija),** Herbrangova 1, has exhibits of Croatia's best art. (☎492 2368. Open Tu-F 10am-6pm, Sa-Su 10am-1pm. Prices vary by exhibition. Cash only.)

▓▓ **FESTIVALS AND NIGHTLIFE.** In the beginning of June, streets burst with performances for the annual Zagreb street festival **Cest is d'Best** ("The Streets are the Best"), and the **Eurokaz Avant-Garde Theaters Festival.** In late July, Zagreb holds the **International Folklore Festival,** the premier gathering of European folk dancers and singing groups. The huge **International Puppet Festival** occurs in early September. Every year, mid-December is filled with the colorful **Christmas Fair.** For up-to-date, detailed info and schedules, check out www.zagreb-touristinfo.hr.

With a variety of clubs at **Lake Jarun** and many relaxed sidewalk cafes and bars on lovely **Tkalcićeva,** Zagreb has an exceptional nightlife scene, which intensifies in summer when the city's youth pours into the streets. Dance and swim at the lakeside cafe-club, ▓**Aquarius,** on Lake Jarun. Take tram #17 to Srednjaci, the third unmarked stop after Studenski dom S. Radić (15min.). Cross the street, and when you reach the lake (15min.), turn left and continue along the boardwalk; Aquarius is the last building. (☎364 0231. Cafe open daily 9am-9pm. Club open Tu-Su 10pm-4am. Cover 30kn. Cash only.) **Khala,** Nova Ves 17, is a surprisingly affordable lounge and wine bar. (☎486 0647. Open M-Th 8am-1am, F-Su 8am-4am. Cash only.) Microbrewery and local favorite **Pivnica Medvedgrad,** Savska 56, has the cheapest beer in town. (1L Beer 18kn. Open M-Sa 10am-midnight, Su noon-midnight.)

▓**DAYTRIP FROM ZAGREB:** ▓**TRAKOŠĆAN CASTLE.** The white walls of Trakošćan rise high above the surrounding forests and rolling hills. Built as a defense tower in the 13th century, it passed in 1584 to the Drašković nobility, who enlarged and refurbished it, retaining the castle until WWII. Today, stately family portraits, elaborate tapestries, Rococo furniture, mounted antlers, and collections of firearms and armor from the 15th to 19th century are on display in the castle's preserved interior. Aside from its detailed woodwork and different colored rooms, the castle evokes a fairytale world, with knight's armor mixed in with the surreal paintings of Julijana Erdödy, the first woman in Croatia to achieve the title of an academic painter. Leave time to wander around the quiet lake and to hike through the oak and hornbeam hills, if only to escape the crowds of Croatian schoolchildren. The restaurant at the bottom of the hill is expensive, so bring a sandwich.

PLITVICE LAKES NATIONAL PARK

Though it's a trek from either Zagreb or Zadar, **Plitvice Lakes National Park** (Nacionalni Park Plitvička Jezera) is definitely worth the transportation hassle. Some 30,000 sq. km of forested hills, dappled with 16 lakes and hundreds of waterfalls, make this one of Croatia's most spectacular sights. Declared a national park in 1949, Plitvice was added to the UNESCO World Heritage list in 1979 for the unique evolution of its lakes and waterfalls, which formed through the interaction of water and petrified vegetation. There are eight main trails, lettered A-K, around the lake, all of different lengths and difficulties; none is particularly demanding, although C has the best views. A system of wooden paths hovering just above the iridescent turquoise surface of the lakes winds around the many waterfalls.

> The takeover of Plitvice Lakes National Park by the Serbs in 1991 marked the beginning of Croatia's bloody war for independence. Throughout the 1991-95 conflict, the Serbs holding the area planted landmines in the ground. Both the park's premises and surrounding area have been officially cleared of mines, and the last mine-related accident dates back to 2002. Never wander into the woods or stray from the trail for any reason.

Free shuttles drive around the lakes every (3 per hr.), and a boat goes across Jezero Kozjak, the largest. (2-3 per hr., 9:30am-6:30pm.) At the entrance, local women sell delicious **strudels:** bread-cakes stuffed with cheese, apples, or cherries (15kn). Often, unfortunately, the lake is crowded; if you want to enjoy the peace of the lakes by yourself, go early in the morning or late in the afternoon and keep away from the shortest trails. Most tourists circulate around the four lower lakes (Donja Jezera) to get a shot of Plitvice's famous 78m waterfall, **Veliki Slap.** The hidden falls of the 12 upper lakes, **Gornja Jezera,** make for a more relaxed walk. A private accommodation service across from tourist center #1 helps find rooms. (☎75 12 80. Open daily June-Sept. 7am-8pm. Singles 150kn; doubles 200-300kn.)

Buses run to: Rijeka (3hr., 1 per day, 120kn); Split (3½hr., 9 per day, 150kn); Zadar (2½hr., 6-7 per day., 72kn); Zagreb (2½hr., 1 per hr., 70kn). Most bus drivers let passengers off at the park's main entrance. Tourist offices offer maps and exchange currency for a 1.5% commission at each of the three entrances. (☎75 20 15; www.np-plitvicka-jezera.hr. Park open daily July-Aug. 7am-8pm; May-June 7am-7pm. Apr.-Oct. 110kn, students 55kn; Nov.-Mar. 70kn/40kn. Tour guide 700kn, min. 4hr. for groups only. MC/V.) To get to the main info center, walk toward the pedestrian overpass; crossing the road can be dangerous. Though no luggage storage is officially provided, they may let you keep your bags at the info center.

NORTHERN COAST

Croatia's Northern coast is surrounded by cold, crystal-clear waters, and covered in wild forests and low coastal hills. Part of Italy until WWII, this region mixes Italian culture with Croatian sensibilities.

THE NAKED TRUTH. Wondering about those FKK signs on the beach? FKK is a German acronym for *Freikörperkultur,* or "free body culture": they indicate that there's a nude beach nearby. Check for the sign before dropping your drawers—skinny-dipping on non-nude beaches isn't generally accepted.

PULA (POLA)   ☎052

Pula (pop. 62,000), the largest city on the Istrian Peninsula and a chaotic transportation hub, is Istria's unofficial capital. Its relatively unimpressive beaches don't make up for the ever-expanding residential complexes that cover the city. Home to some of the best-preserved Roman ruins in Croatia, Pula has a giant white-stone ▧ **Amphitheater,** the second-largest in the world, which is often used as a concert venue. To get there from the bus station, take a left on Istarska. (Open daily 8am-9pm. 20kn, students 10kn.) From there, walk down to the water and along the port to reach the **Forum** and **Temple of Augustus** (Augustov hram), finished in AD 1, and then climb up the narrow streets of the Old Town to the peaceful **Franciscan Monastery,** the **Fort** (hosting the **Historical Museum of Istria;** 30kn, students 15kn), the ancient **Roman Theater,** and the **Arch of the Sergians** (Slavoluk obitelji Sergii), a stone structure dating from 29 BC. To reach the private coves of Pula's **beaches,** buy a bus ticket (10kn) from newsstands and take bus #1 to the Stója campground.

Arenaturist, Splitska 1, inside Hotel Riviera, arranges accommodations throughout Pula with no fee, and has a friendly, English-speaking staff. (☎529 400; www.arenaturist.hr. Open M-Sa 8am-8pm; also Su 8am-1pm in high season. Accommodations €31-83.) To reach the **Omladinski Hostel (HI) ❶,** Zaljev Valsaline 4, take bus #2 or 3 (dir.: Veruda; 10kn) from the station. Get off at the first stop on Veruda and follow the HI sign; take a left off the road and walk 5min. down the hill. (☎391 133; www.hfhs.hr. Breakfast included. Reception daily 8am-10pm. Reservations recommended. Dorms July-Aug. 100kn; Sept. and June 84kn; Oct. and May 79kn; Nov. and Apr. 74kn. Camping July-Aug. 65kn; Sept.-June 40kn. 4-person private condos also available, complete with bathrooms. HI nonmembers 10kn extra per night. Tax 4.50-7kn.) **Pizzeria Jupiter ❶,** Castropola 42 (☎214 333), with its log benches hidden in warm yellow alcoves, is the perfect spot for a bite before amphitheater concerts. Walk behind the bus station along Carrarina, past the Archaeological Museum and then curve to the left up the ramp; it's on the left. (Pizza 20-39kn.Open M-F 9am-11pm, Sa-Su 1-11pm. AmEx.)

Trains (☎541 783) run from Kolodvorska 5 to Ljubljana, SLV (7½hr., 2 per day, 127kn), and Zagreb (7hr., 3 per day, 148kn). **Buses** (☎502 997), a much more convenient option, run from Trg Istarske Brigade to Dubrovnik (15hr., 1 per day, 477kn); Zagreb (5-6hr., 15 per day, 155kn); Trieste, ITA (3hr., 5 per day, 88-112kn). The **tourist office** is at Forum 3 (☎212 987; www.pulainfo.hr). **Postal Code:** 52100.

ROVINJ   ☎052

Purported to be one of the healthiest places in the world due to its mild climate and cool waters, Rovinj (ro-VEEN; pop. 14,000) was the favorite summer resort of Austro-Hungarian emperors. Today's vacationers still bask in this Mediterranean jewel's unspoiled beauty. Rovinj is the most Italian of Istria's towns: everybody here either is or speaks Italian and all streets have names and signs in both languages. Eighteenth-century **Saint Euphemia's Church** (Crkva Sv. Eufemije) houses the remains of St. Euphemia, the 15-year-old martyr who was killed by circus lions in AD 800. Inside, stairs lead to the ▧**bell tower** (61m), with views of the city and coast. In summer, there are classical music performances on the lawn. (Open M-Sa 10am-6pm. Services M-Sa 7pm, Su 10:30am and 7pm. Free. Bell tower 10kn.)

Rovinj's best beaches are on **Sv. Katarina Island** and ▧**Red Island** (Crveni Otok), two small islands right in front of town. The first has a huge resort and crowds, while the second is a haven for snorkelers and nude sunbathers. To get there, take the ferry from the dock at the center of town to Sv. Katarina (15kn) and Crveni Otok (40kn). At night, head through the arch in the main square and follow the signs up Grisia toward the church at the top of the hill, where members of an artist colony display their work. Across the street from the bus station is **Natale,** Carducci 4, a travel agency which arranges private rooms in and around the center commission-free. (☎813 365; www.rovinj.com. Open July-Aug. M-Sa 7:30am-9:30pm, Su 8am-9:30pm; Sept.-June M-Sa 7:30am-8pm, Su 8am-noon. Singles €14-18; doubles €20-26; apartments €32-57.) **Camping Polari ❶,** 2.5km east of town, has a supermarket, several bars, and a new pool. To get there, take one of the frequent buses (6min., 9kn) from the station. (☎801 501. July-Aug. 100kn per person; June 85kn per person.) Popular **Stella di Mare ❷**, Santa Croce 4, offers great deals on huge pizzas. (☎528 8883. Pizzas and pastas 30-45kn. Seafood 45-120kn. Open daily 10am-11pm. AmEx/MC/V.) Near the church, **▨Valentino Bar**, Santa Croce 28 (☎830 683), has elegant white tables right on the water.

To reach the **tourist office**, walk along the water past the main square, to Pino Budičin 12. (☎811 566; www.tzgrovinj.hr. Open daily mid-June to Sept. 8am-9pm; Oct. to mid-June 8am-4pm.) Rovinj is best explored on bike trails. Bike rental (60kn per day) is available at **Bike Planet**, Trg na Lokvi 3, which also has maps. (☎813 396. 60kn per day. Open M-F 7:30am-12:30pm and 5-8pm, Sa 8:30am-1pm.) Boats, tied along the dock, offer slightly overpriced 1½hr. **excursions** (€10) and one-day boat trips to Venice, ITA (380-480kn). With no train station, Rovinj sends **buses** to Pula (45min., 20 per day, 29kn); Zagreb (5-6hr., 9 per day, 165kn); Ljubljana, SLV (5hr., 1 per day, 146kn). The bus station has luggage storage. (☎811 453. 10kn per day; 15 kn per day for items over 30kg.) **Postal Code:** 52210.

CRES   ☎051

Though most visitors spend the duration of their stay in Cres Town and on the beaches nearby, Cres island (pop. 3300) has a wealth of undiscovered beauties, from tiny villages with less than a dozen inhabitants to idyllic, totally isolated beaches. Explore the island by car, rent a bike and try out the numerous nature trails, or discover the intricate coast by boat, available at the marina for 500kn per day, or 400kn per half-day (☎33 22 22). Smaller towns, like the amazing 4000-year-old settlement **▨Lubenice**, above the unforgiving rocky coastline on one of the highest peaks of the island, are worth exploring. A 1hr. hike down from town leads to a pristine beach; on clear mornings, you can see the Italian coast across the Adriatic. In July, classical concerts are held in the town's old chapel. For those arriving in late July or August, reserve a couple months ahead. The beachfront **▨Camp Kovacine ❶**, 1km north of Cres Town, hosts most of the island's visitors, with its popular beach and peaceful pine covering. Besides the usual amenities, the camp also has a nudist section (indicated by the yellow FKK sign), as does the nearby beach. (☎57 31 50; www.campkovacine.com. €5-10 per person, €4-8 per tent site; 4-person bungalow €40-110. Additional cleaning charge of €15 for stays of less than 3 nights. AmEx/MC/V.) Next to the camp, **Hotel Kimen ❷**, Varozina 25, is an old-fashioned place to stay in a tranquil park. (☎57 11 61; www.hotel-kimen.com. Breakfast included. Singles €24-42, other rooms €20-35.) **Feral ❷**, Palada 2, serves delicious salads along with pasta and fish. (Entrees 30-60kn. Open 9am-11pm.) Getting to Cres can be complicated. **Ferries** run from Rijeka (1hr., 1 per day, 30kn) to Cres Town and from Brestova, Istria, to Porozina, at the northern tip of the island (30min.; 12 per day; 13kn per person, 60kn per car). **Buses** go directly from Cres Town to Losinj, the next island, stopping in several smaller towns along the way (1¼hr., 6-8 per day, 40kn). The **tourist office** is in Cres Town, Cons 10 (☎57 15 35; www.tzg-cres.hr). **Postal Code:** 51557.

DALMATIAN COAST

Touted as the new French Riviera, the Dalmatian Coast offers a seascape of unfathomable beauty set against a backdrop of dramatic mountains. With more than 1100 islands, Dalmatia not only is Croatia's largest archipelago, but also has the cleanest and clearest waters in the Mediterranean.

ZADAR   ☎023

Zadar (pop. 77,000), crushed in both WWII and the recent Balkan war, is now beautifully rejuvenated. Though its modern neighborhoods might not impress those entering the city, in the *Stari Grad* (Old Town) time seems to have stopped long before both conflicts. The area's history is so well preserved that Roman ruins serve as city benches. With the Kornati Islands just a boat ride away, and plenty of boutiques and cafes, Zadar is the quintessential Dalmatian city. On the southern dock of the Old Town, concrete steps into the water are actually part of a 70m long ◨**Sea Organ,** which plays notes at random as the seawater rushes in, resulting in continual melody. In the ancient Forum in the center of the peninsula, the Byzantine **St. Donat's Church** (Crkva Sv. Donata), a rare circular church, sits atop the ruins of an ancient Roman temple. (Open daily 9am-7:30pm. 10kn.)

At the entrance to the Old Town, coming from Obala Kralja Tomislava, **Miatours** ❷, on Vrata Sv. Krševana, books private rooms and transportation to nearby islands. (☎25 44 00; www.miatours.hr. Open July-Aug. 8am-8pm; Sept.-June 8am-2:30pm. Doubles 200-300kn. AmEx/MC/V.) ◨**Trattoria Canzona** ❷, Stomorica 8, is always packed with young Zadarians, as are many of the similar restaurants in this rocking corner of town. (☎21 20 81. Entrees 30-70kn. Open M-Sa 10am-11pm, Su noon-11pm. Cash only.) There is also a small **supermarket** between Borelli and Madijevaca. (Open M-Sa 6:30am-9pm, Su 7am-noon.)

Buses (☎21 15 55) run from Ante Starevica 1 to: Dubrovnik (8hr., 8 per day, 157-220kn); Pula (7hr., 3 per day, 190kn); Rijeka (4½hr., 12 per day, 125-160kn); Split (3¼hr., 2 per hr., 90-110kn); Zagreb (3½hr., 2 per hr., 105-130kn); Trieste, ITA (7hr., 2 per day, 170kn). **Luggage storage** is available at the bus station. (1.20kn per hr. Open 6am-10pm.) Both the train and bus stations are a 20min. walk from town, but trains are less convenient. To get to the Old Town, go through the pedestrian underpass and on to Zrinsko-Frankopanska to the water and turn left. At the **Kopnena Vrata** (Main Gate) of the Old Town, turn on Široka, the main street. The **tourist office,** M. Klaića bb, in the far corner of Narodni trg, has free maps and an English-speaking staff. (☎31 61 66; tzg-zadar@zd.tel.hr. Open daily 8am-midnight; low season 8am-8pm.) There is **Internet** on Varoska 3. (☎31 12 65. 30kn per hr. Open daily 10am-11pm.) **Postal Code:** 23000.

PAKLENICA NATIONAL PARK

The 400m-high cliffs of Paklenica, near Zadar, make the national park a favorite stop for climbers, who compete annually in the **Big Wall Speed Climbing** competition on May 1st. But while Paklenica is best known for climbing, it's only one feature of the amazing topography of the park. Chalky karsts jump out of tall forests, and abundant fauna—over 80 species of butterfly, along with peregrine falcons and sparrowhawks—make the deep gorges and meadows of Paklenica worth a visit. **Mala** and **Vela Paklenica** are popular cliffs to climb, while underground explorers prefer the half-submerged caves, the largest of which, **Manića Paklenica,** runs for 200m inside the mountain range. **Anića Kuk** (712m) is the most popular peak for hikers and climbers. All climbing routes are outfitted with spits and petons, except the "Psycho Killer" route, which should be attempted only by expert climbers. For a panoramic view out to the islands, try **Velika Golić** (1285m); passing through limestone ridges and farms bordered by drystone walls, the walk itself is a hard but rewarding 4-5hr. ascent.

Two campsites are available in the park. **Camping Paklenica** ❶, Dr. Franje Tudjman, is on the beach and has excellent facilities. (☎320 9062. Open Apr.-Oct. 54kn per adult, 80kn per site.) The cheaper **National Park Camping** ❶, Dr. Franje Tudjman, is also beach-accessible, but does not accept reservations. (☎36 91 55. Open Apr.-Oct. 30kn per adult, 35kn per site.) Outside of camping, private rooms are undoubtedly the cheapest option. The **Stari Grad Tourist Office** (☎36 92 55) helps book rooms (150-300kn). There are several **huts** along the ridges, but be sure to book ahead in summer. There's a **supermarket** near the park entry; otherwise, head to the **Lugarnica** ❶ hut for a range of grilled options. (Open daily in the summer.)

To reach Paklenica, take the Rijeka-Zadar **bus.** Facing **Hotel Alan,** walk to your right for 300m up the dirt road to the park entrance. The **Park Office** provides a map with the entrance fee (30kn per day, 60kn per 3 days, 90kn per 5 days). For serious hikes, fork out the 15-25kn for a more detailed map. (☎36 92 02; www.paklenica.hr. Open Apr.-Oct. M-F 8am-3pm.)

GIVING BACK

DEFENDING THE DOLPHINS

Human tourists aren't the only ones who flock to the Adriatic waters off Veli Losinj; in recent years, a large pod of around 120 bottlenose dolphins have become permanent residents. Fortunately, you won't find the Losinj harbors teeming with tour boats offering travelers a chance to swim with these sleek creatures.

Instead, Blue World, a marine research and conservation organization has established itself in the port, and has made protecting the dolphins' natural habitat its primary mission.

Co-operating with local excursion companies to avoid interference with ongoing research, Blue World's workers have been given a unique dolphin-watching opportunity. These opportunities are in turn open to anyone who wishes to join a minimum 12-day volunteer course in Rovenska Bay. Volunteers help with collecting and logging data and doing preliminary analysis. When the weather prevents researchers from taking to the waters, volunteers get to listen to lectures by experts in the field of marine biology.

For those who wish to aid Blue World but cannot volunteer for the minimum period, the organization accepts donations as part of its adopt-a-dolphin program. All funds go directly towards the organization's non profit activties. Check out the website www.blueworld.com for more details.

SPLIT   ☎021

With many activities and nightlife, this city by the sea is more a cultural center than a beach resort. The *Stari Grad* (Old Town), wedged between a mountain range and a palm-lined waterfront, sprawls inside and around a luxurious open-air **palace**, where the Roman emperor Diocletian used to summer when not persecuting Christians. Here, centuries of history have left their trace, making the city a fascinating labyrinth of perfectly preserved Roman monuments, medieval streets with laundry hanging from the windows, and modern bars with huge TV screens showing soccer matches. The city's **cellars** are near the palace entrance, at the beginning of pedestrian street Obala hrvatskog narodnog preporoda; lose your way in this haunting maze of imperial statues, modern art exhibits, and the cool relief of underground Split. (Open M-F 9am-9pm, Sa-Su 9am-6pm. 8kn.)

Through the cellars and up the stairs is the open-air **peristyle**, a roofless, round building that leads to the Catholic **cathedral**, the world's oldest. Ironically, it was once Diocletian's mausoleum, and is now opulently decorated in an elaborate combination of styles. The treasury inside is replete with gold and silver. The view from the adjoining ▓**Bell Tower of St. Dominus** (Zvonik sv. Duje; 60m) is incredible, but watch your head when climbing up. (Cathedral and tower open 7am-noon and 5-7pm. 5kn each.) A 25min. walk along the waterfront, the ▓**Mestrović Gallery** (Galerija Ivana Meštrovića), Šetaliste Ivana Meštrovića 46, houses the splendid bronze, stone, and wood works of Croatia's most celebrated sculptor in a gorgeous villa facing the sea. To get there from the center of town, walk right facing the water, pass the marina, and follow the road up the hill; the gallery is right after the Archaeological Museum. (☎34 08 00. Open May-Sept. Tu-Sa 9am-9pm, Su noon-9pm; Oct.-Apr. Tu-Sa 9am-4pm, Su 10am-3pm. 20kn, students 10kn.) At night, locals swim at the hip **Bacvice beach**, near a strip of waterfront bars.

The small **Daluma Travel Agency**, Obala kneza domagoja 1, near the train station, books private rooms, exchanges currency, and organizes excursions. (☎33 84 84; www.daluma.hr. Open July-Aug. M-F 8am-9pm, Sa 8am-8pm, Su 8am-1pm; Sept.-June M-F 8am-8pm, Sa 8am-1pm.) **Al's Place ●**, Kruziceva 10, is the first hostel in Split, outside the right corner of the palace. There are only 12 beds, which are usually full; reserve ahead. (☎09 89 18 29 23; www.hostel-split.com. June-Aug. 150kn; Sept.-May 100kn. Cash only.) In the Old Town there are plenty of snack bars and restaurants, as well as kiosks with filling pizzas (slices 6-8kn) and *bureks* (10kn); you can also stock up on fruit and vegetables at the crowded **market** on the road between

Obala Riva and the bus and ferry terminal. The best cafes are lined up on palm-lined Obala Riva, and at night they turn into popular bars. ■**St. Riva,** right in the center, has side-street swing-couches and a narrow balcony packed with partying youth. Hidden on a narrow line of steps, ■**Puls** is a great bar with low tables, cushions directly on the pavement, and occasional live jazz. To get there from Obala Riva, enter Trg brace Radic, turn right at the corner snack bar, and continue straight. (Open M-F 7am-midnight, Sa 7am-1am, Su 4pm-midnight.)

Buses (☎32 73 27; www.ak-split.hr) run to: Dubrovnik (4¼hr.; 19 per day; 90-130kn, round-trip 160-195kn); Rijeka (7½hr., 13 per day, 270kn); Zadar (3¼hr., 2 per hr., 100kn); Zagreb (5hr., 2 per hr., 185kn); Ljubljana, SLV (11hr., 1 per day, 280kn). **Ferries** (☎33 83 33) depart from the dock right across from the bus station to: Supetar, Brač Island (45min., 10-14 per day, 28kn) and *Stari Grad*, Hvar Island (1hr., 3 per day, 38kn). Ferries also leave the international harbor to Ancona, ITA (10hr., 4 per wk., 330kn) and Bari, ITA (25hr., 3 per week, 330kn). Deciphering the ferry schedules distributed at the **Jadrolinija** office can be a bit nerve-wracking, so ask for help from the busy assistants. (Open daily 4:15am-8:30pm.) The **tourist office** is at Obala HNP 12. (☎34 72 71; www.turistbiro-split.hr. Open July-Aug. M-F 8am-9pm, Sa 8am-10pm, Su 8am-1pm; Sept.-June M-F 8am-9pm, Sa 8am-10pm.) Those who stay in town for more than three days are entitled to a free **SplitCard** that gets big discounts for sightseeing, shopping, and sleeping. Bring a hostel receipt to any tourist office to prove your stay; otherwise purchase one for 60kn. **Postal Code:** 21000.

HVAR ISLAND   ☎021

The thin, 88km Hvar Island (pop. 11,000) grants its visitors mind-blowing views of mainland mountains and nearby islands from its own rugged, lavender-covered hills. Hvar is a prime destination for classy tourists, with an increasing number of wealthy Americans and a consequent rise in prices. **Hvar Town** maintains its easy-going village feel, even as the latest American pop hits play from buses' radios and souvenir shops. Many other destinations reachable by car or a rented boat remain virtually untouched by tourists. The island is packed in July and August. From mid-May to mid-October, the **Hvar Summer Festival** brings outdoor classical music and drama performances to the island's Franciscan monastery. **Trg Svetog Stjepana,** directly below the bus station by the waterfront, is the main square. From there, facing the sea, take a left to reach the **tourist office** and ferry terminal. To the right, stairs lead to the 13th-century Venetian ■**Fortica.** The climb is short (20min.) but steep; avoid climbing in the heat and bring water. Once there, you can relax at the restaurant, count the islands in front of Hvar, or—legend has it—watch the fairies that dance here at night. Nearby, the **Hellish Islands** (Pakleni Otoci), which include **Palmižana** beach, with sparse sand, and **Jerolim,** with many sunbathers, provide relief from the crowds. (Taxi boats 2 per hr. 10am-6:30pm; 30-40kn.)

Lodging rates in Hvar are not backpacker-friendly; for the cheapest rooms, try haggling with the owners of *sobes* (private rooms). Expect to pay 100-150kn. The **Green Lizard Hostel ❶,** Lučića bb, offers spotless dorms, as well as private doubles for reasonable rates. Reserve ahead. (☎74 25 60; www.greenlizard.hr. July-Aug. dorms 135-150kn.) **Luna ❷,** on a side street up the steps to the fortress, has a gorgeous "moon" terrace. (☎74 86 95. Entrees 50-120kn. Cover 8kn. Open daily noon-3pm and 6pm-midnight.) At the end of Riva past the Jadrolinija office, waterfront ■**Carpe Diem** has low sofas, a hip crowd, and live DJs playing from inside the Roman stone walls. (☎74 23 69; www.carpe-diem-hvar.com. Juices and shakes 28-38kn. Sandwiches 48kn. Mixed drinks 55-68kn. Open daily 9am-2am.)

Ferries run to Split (2hr., 3-7 per day, 38kn) and Vela Luka, Korčula (3hr., 1 per day, 22kn). Faster private **catamarans** go directly to Korčula Town (2hr., 1 per day,

33kn) and Split (1 per day, 32kn) from Hvar Town. **Buses** connect Old Town to Hvar Town (25min., 7 per day, 17kn); from the marina, walk through Trg Sv. Stjepana, bearing left of the church. **Jadrolinija,** Riva bb, on the left tip of the waterfront, sells ferry tickets for Stari Grad. (☎74 11 32. Open M-Sa 5:30am-1pm and 3-8pm; Su 8-9am, noon-1pm, and 3-4pm.) The **tourist office,** Trg Sv. Stjepana 16, has island maps (20kn) and bus schedules. (☎74 10 59; www.tzhvar.hr. Open July-Aug. M-Sa 8am-1pm and 5 0pm, Su 9am-noon; Sept.-June 8am-2pm. **Postal Code:** 21450.

BRAČ ISLAND: BOL   ☎021

Central Dalmatia's largest island, Brač (pop. 13,000) is an ocean-lover's paradise. Most visitors come here for **Zlatni rat,** a beautiful and crowded peninsula of white-pebble beach surrounded by emerald waters and big waves. If you prefer the "deserted island" environment, head for the less explored, calmer beaches to the east of town. Bol is also pleasant, small enough to cross in 10min., and equipped with its fair share of ice cream parlors, exchange offices, and plenty of tiny chapels. The 1475 **Dominican Monastery,** on the eastern tip of Bol, displays Tintoretto's altar painting *Madonna with Child.* (Open daily 10am-noon and 5-7pm. 10kn.) There are five **campsites** around Bol; most of them lie on the road into the western part of town. The largest is **Kito ❶**, Bračka cesta bb.(☎63 55 51. kamp_kito@inet.hr. Open May-Sept. 60kn per person, tent and tax included.)

The **ferry** from Split docks at Supetar (1hr., 12-16 per day, 25kn), the island's largest town. (Open daily 4:15am-8:30pm and 12:45-1:30am. AmEx/MC/V.) From there, take a **bus** to Bol (1hr., 9 per day, last bus M-Sa 7pm, Su 6pm; 24kn). The buses (1 per hr.) don't always coordinate with the ferries' arrivals; if you don't want to wait, you can take a slightly overpriced **taxi van** to Bol. (35min., 400kn, max. 7 people). Otherwise, kill the wait at the beach across the street. With your back to the water from the bus station in Bol, walk right to reach the **tourist office,** Porad bolskich pomorca bb, on the far side of the marina. (☎63 56 38; www.bol.hr. Open M-Sa 8:30am-2pm and 5-9pm, Su 9am-1pm.) **Postal Code:** 21420.

KORČULA   ☎020

Within sight of the mainland, the slender cypresses of Korčula mark Marco Polo's birthplace, where sacred monuments date back to the time of the Apostles. **Marko Polo's house** is in a tower in the Old Town. (Open daily 9:30am-1:30pm and 4:30-8pm. 10kn.) Though now turned into a biweekly tourist attraction, the **Festival of Sword Dances** is a millennia-old tradition in which local dancers come to reproduce the story of the White Prince and Black Prince fighting over a kidnapped princess. The sword fight is spectacular; go on July 29th for the real (not touristy) thing. (www.moreska.hr. 90kn; tickets available at travel agencies.)

Ⓜ︎Marko Polo ❷, Biline 5, is a helpful travel agency that books rooms. (☎71 54 00; www.korcula.com. Reserve ahead. Singles 150-200kn; doubles 200-280kn. 30% more for stays under 3 nights. Open daily 8am-9pm.) The **Happy House (Korčula Backpacker) ❶,** Hrvatske Bratske Zajednice 6, is a colorful, party hostel, with clean, comfortable co-ed rooms. The common room turns into pub at night, with music, cheap beer, and international snacks for 20kn. (☎09 89 97 63 53; booking@korculabackpacker.com. Shuttle service to Dubrovnik 90kn. Mountain biking and fishing daytrips 300kn. Ages 18-35 only. Dorms 90kn. Cash only.) Camping is available at **Autocamp Kalac ❶,** with a sandy beach and nice views of the mainland across the water. A bus (10min., 1 per hr., 13kn) runs to the camp from the station. (☎71 11 82. Reception daily 7am-10pm. 40kn per person, 35kn per tent. Tourist tax 7.50kn.) **Fresh ❶,** right next to the bus station, specializes in healthy wraps (22-25kn) and smoothies. Find some beach reading from Fresh's English-language book exchange. (☎09 18 96 75 09; www.igotfresh.com. Open daily 9am-2am. Cash only.) The eatery **Adio Mare ❷**, Marka Pola 2, serves authentic local fare. (☎71 12 53. Entrees 40-90kn. Open M-Sa 5:30pm-midnight, Su 6pm-midnight.)

Buses (Obala Korčulanskih Brodograditelja) board ferries to the mainland and head to Dubrovnik (3½hr., 1 per day, 85kn) and Zagreb (11-13hr., 1 per day, 210kn). On the island, they run to Lumbarda (9 per day, 13kn), Pupnat (8 per day, 40kn), and Vela Luka (5 per day, 30kn). Ticket and info office is open Monday through Saturday 6am-8pm and Sunday 2-8pm. The **Jadrolinija** office sells ferry tickets. (☎71 54 10. Open M-F 5:30am-7pm, Sa-Su 7:30am-7:30pm. AmEx/MC/V.) Ferries run to Dubrovnik (3½hr., 5 per week, 79kn) from both sides of Korčula Town; make sure to check where yours leaves. **Postal Code:** 20260.

DUBROVNIK   ☎020

Lord Byron considered Dubrovnik (du-BROV-nik; pop. 43,800) "the pearl of the Adriatic," and George Bernard Shaw knew it as "Paradise on Earth." Although it's tough to live up to such adulation, a stroll through the torch-lit winding lanes of the *Stari Grad* (Old Town) and a sunset look into the sea from the city walls certainly justify Dubrovnik's reputation as one of Croatia's top destinations.

◨◪ TRANSPORTATION AND PRACTICAL INFORMATION. Jadrolinija **ferries** (☎41 80 00; www.jadrolinija.hr) depart opposite Obala S. Radica 40 for: Korčula (3½hr., 5 per week, 79kn); Rijeka (22hr., 2 per week, 233kn); Split (8hr., 4 per day, 115 kn); and Bari, ITA (9hr., 5 per week, 97kn). The **Jadrolinija** office is across the dock. (Open M-Tu and Th 8am-8pm, W and F 8am-8pm and 9-11pm, Sa 8am-2pm and 7-8pm, Su 8-10am and 7-8:30pm.) **Buses** (☎35 70 88) run from Vukovarska, behind the new port, to: Rijeka (12hr., 4 per day, 415kn); Split (4½hr., 1 per hr., 132kn); Zagreb (11hr., 8 per day, 234kn); Trieste, ITA (15hr., 1 per day, 370kn). There's **luggage storage** at the station (open daily 5am-10:30pm; 15kn per bag). To reach the Old Town, face away from the station and turn left on Ante Starčevića; follow it 25min. uphill to the **Pile Gate.** All local buses except #5, 7, and 8 go to the Pile Gate (8kn at kiosks, 10kn on board). Walk 50m away from the Old Town's entrance to reach the **tourist office,** Ante Starčevića 7, for free maps and cheap **Internet.** (☎42 75 91. Internet 8am-10pm 10kn per 15min. Office open daily 8am-9pm.) The **post office,** Široka 8, in the Stari Grad, has ATMs, public telephones, and offers Western Union services. (☎32 34 27. Open M-F 7:30am-9pm, Sa 10am-5pm.) **Postal Code:** 20108.

◪◨ ACCOMMODATIONS AND FOOD. A private room tends to be the cheapest and most comfortable option for two; arrange one through any of the indistinguishable agencies, or bargain with locals at the station (doubles should go for 100-150kn per person). Take bus #6 from *Stari Grad* or #7 from the ferry and bus terminal, get off two stops past the Lapad post office, cross the street, climb the steps uphill on Mostarska, and turn left at Dubravkina to reach **▨Apartmani Burum ❶,** Dubravkina 16, in Babin Kuk. This popular guesthouse is comfortable, and the owner is known to drive guests around town for a small price. (☎43 54 67; www.burum-accommodation.com. Kitchen available. Pickup available. 100-150kn per person. Cash only.) **Begović Boarding House ❶,** Primorska 17, offers spacious doubles and apartments in a cozy villa with satellite TVs, a social terrace shaded by fig trees, and a pleasant family feel. Call ahead and the owner will pick you up. (☎43 51 91; bega_dbk@yahoo.com. Reserve ahead July-Aug. Singles 150-200kn; doubles 200-240kn; triples 180-300kn. Cash only.) **▨Lokarda Peskarija ❷,** Na Ponti

CROATIA

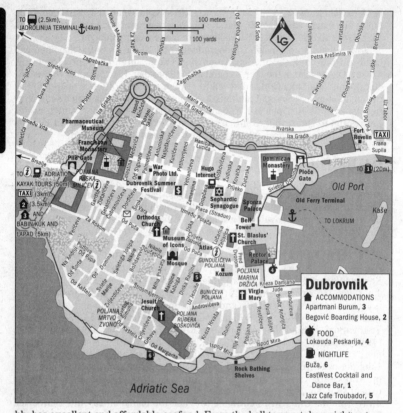

Dubrovnik

🏠 ACCOMMODATIONS
Apartmani Burum, **3**
Begović Boarding House, **2**

🍎 FOOD
Lokauda Peskarija, **4**

🍸 NIGHTLIFE
Buža, **6**
EastWest Cocktail and
  Dance Bar, **1**
Jazz Cafe Troubador, **5**

bb, has excellent and affordable seafood. From the bell tower, take a right out on Pred Dvorum and the first left out of the city walls. (☎32 47 50. Seafood 35-60kn. Open daily 8am-3am.) Exchange books, savor smoothies, and nosh on wraps at **Fresh ❷,** on Vetranićeva. (Wraps 25kn. Smoothies 20kn. Open daily 8am-2am.)

> ❗ Make sure to ask for a receipt when you pay for a private room. Without a receipt, your stay won't be registered and the accommodation will be illegal.

🔆 **SIGHTS.** The Old Town is packed with churches, museums, monasteries, palaces, and fortresses. The entrance to the 2km limestone 🏰**city wall** *(gradske zidine)* lies just inside the Pile Gate on the left, with a second entrance at the other end of town. Go at dusk to be dazzled by the sunset. (Open daily 8am-7:30pm. 50kn, students 20kn. Audio tour 40kn.) The 14th-century **Franciscan Monastery** (Franjevački samostan), next to the city wall entrance on Placa, houses the oldest pharmacy in Europe (est. 1317) and an elegant courtyard. (Open daily 9am-6pm. 20kn, students 13kn.) The **Cathedral of the Assumption of the Virgin Mary** (Riznica Katedrale), Kneza Damjana Jude 1, is built on the site of a Romanesque cathedral and a 7th-century Byzantine cathedral. Its treasury houses the "Diapers of Jesus," along with a host of golden reliquaries. (Cathedral open daily 6:30am-

8pm; treasury open daily 8am-8pm. Cathedral free, treasury 10kn.) The 19th-century **Serbian Orthodox Church** (Pravoslavna Crkva) and its **Museum of Icons** (Muzej Ikona), Od Puča 8, stand as a symbol of Dubrovnik's tolerance together with the small, but intricate **synagogue** and **mosque**. (Museum open M-Sa 10am-2pm; 10kn. Synagogue open May-Oct. M-F 9am-8pm; 15kn. Mosque open daily 10am-1pm and 8-9pm. Free.) Classical performances are held in many churches during summer.

■ BEACHES. Outside the fortifications of the Old Town are a number of **rock shelves** good for sunning and swimming. To reach a pristine but overcrowded **pebble beach** from the Placa's end, turn left on Svetog Dominika, bear right after the footbridge, and continue on Frana Supila. Descend the stairs by the post office. For a surreal seaside swim, take a dip in the cove at the foot of the old **Hotel Libertas.** Once Dubrovnik's most luxurious hotel, the building was damaged during WWII and then abandoned; new construction, though, has taken away from its post-apocalyptic appeal. Local kids carelessly dive into the sea from 6 ft. rocks, but this isn't the smartest idea: the water often is much shallower than it looks. Ferries run daily from the Old Port (20min., 2 per hr., 35kn return) to the nearby island of **Lokrum,** which has a beach with great cliff jumping. More modest travelers can stroll (fully clothed) through the **nature preserve** to a smaller section of rock shelves on the other side of the island.

As tempting as it may be to stroll through the hills above Dubrovnik or wander the unpaved paths on Lopud, both may still be laced with **landmines.** Stick to paved paths and beaches.

■ FESTIVALS AND NIGHTLIFE. Dubrovnik becomes a party scene and cultural mecca from mid-July to mid-August during the **Dubrovnik Summer Festival** (Dubrovački Ljetni Festival). The **festival office** on Placa has schedules and tickets. (☎ 42 88 64; www.dubrovnik-festival.hr. Open daily during the festival 8:30am-9pm, tickets 9am-2pm and 3-7pm. 50-300kn.) By night Dubrovnik's crowds gravitate to bars in *Stari Grad* and cafes on Buničeva Poljana, where live bands and street performers turn up in summer. From the open-air market, climb the stairs toward the monastery, veer left, and follow the signs marked "Cool Drinks and (truly) the Most Beautiful View" along Od Margarite to **Buža,** Crijevićeva 9. Above the bright blue Adriatic, this laid-back watering hole on the city's rocks is the best place to enjoy spectacular sunsets and a midnight swim. (Beer 17-22kn. Mixed drinks 30kn. Open daily 9am-2am.) Enjoy occasional belly dancing at the classy but unpretentious **Jazz Cafe Troubador,** Buničeva 2. (Beer 18-40kn. Wine 20-40kn. Open daily 9am-2am.) At **EastWest Cocktail and Dance Bar,** Frana Supila bb, a dressed-to-impress clientele reclines on white leather sofas and plush beds on the beach. (Beer 12-30kn. Mixed drinks 40-100kn. Thai massage 200kn per 30min., 300kn for 1hr. Open daily 8am-4am.)

CZECH REPUBLIC
(ČESKÁ REPUBLIKA)

From the days of the Holy Roman Empire to reign of the USSR, the Czech people have stood at a crossroads of international affairs. Unlike many of their neighbors, however, the citizens of this small, landlocked country have rarely resisted as armies marched across their borders, often choosing to protest with words instead of weapons. As a result, Czech towns are among the best-preserved and most beautiful in Europe. Today, the Czechs face a different kind of invasion, as tourists sweep in to savor the magnificent capital, the baroque architecture, and some of the world's best beer.

DISCOVER CZECH REPUBLIC: SUGGESTED ITINERARIES

THREE DAYS. Voyage to the capital, **Prague** (p. 229). Stroll across the **Charles Bridge** to see **Prague Castle,** leave to explore areas like **Josefov,** and have some beer.

ONE WEEK. Keep exploring **Prague** (5 days; p. 229). Relax at the **Petřín Hill Gardens** and visit the **Troja** château. Then head to **Český Krumlov** (2 days; p. 244) for hiking, biking, and an ancient castle.

BEST OF CZECH REPUBLIC, 3 WEEKS. Begin with 2 weeks in **Prague,** including a daytrip to the **Terezín** concentration camp (p. 240). Then spend 4 days in UNESCO-protected **Český Krumlov** (p. 244) getting to know the bike trails and floating down the **Vltava River** in an inner tube. Check out the weird **Revolving Theater** while you're at it. Wrap things up with 3 days in **Olomouc** (p. 246), stronghold of old-fashioned Moravian culture.

ESSENTIALS

FACTS AND FIGURES

Official Name: Czech Republic.
Capital: Prague.
Major Cities: Brno, Olomouc, Plzeň.
Population: 10,229,000.
Time Zone: GMT +1.

Language: Czech.
Religions: Atheist (49%) Roman Catholic (27%), Protestant (2%).
Beer Consumption Per Capita: 161 liters per year (largest in the world).

WHEN TO GO

The Czech Republic is the most touristed country in Eastern Europe, and Prague in particular is overrun. To beat the crowds, you may want to avoid the high season (June-Aug.), though the weather is most pleasant then. A good compromise is to go in late spring or early fall.

DOCUMENTS AND FORMALITIES

EMBASSIES AND CONSULATES. Foreign embassies to the Czech Republic are in Prague (p. 230). Czech consulates and embassies abroad include: **Australia,** 8 Culoga Circuit, O'Malley, Canberra, ACT 2606 (☎02 62 90 13 86; www.mzv.cz/canberra); **Canada,** 251 Cooper St., Ottawa, ON K2P 0G2 (☎613-562-3875;

www.embassy.mzv.cz/Ottawa); **Ireland,** 57 Northumberland Rd., Ballsbridge, Dublin 4 (☎016 681 135; www.embassy.msz.cz/Dublin); **New Zealand,** Level 3, BMW Mini Centre, 11-15 Great South Road and corner of Margot Street, Newmarket, Auckland. (☎9 522 8736; auckland@honorary.mvz.cz); **UK,** 6-30 Kensington Palace Gardens, Kensington, London W8 4QY (☎020 72 43 11 15; www.mzv.cz/london); **US,** 3900 Spring of Freedom St., NW, Washington, D.C. 20008 (☎202-274-9100; www.mzv.cz/washington).

VISA AND ENTRY INFORMATION. Citizens of Australia, Canada, New Zealand and the US do not need a visa for stays of up to 90 days; UK citizens do not need visas for stays of up to 180 days. Visas for extended stays are available at embassies or consulates. One cannot obtain a Czech visa at the border. Processing takes 14 days when the visa is submitted by mail, seven when submitted in person.

ENTRANCE REQUIREMENTS.

Passport: Required of all travelers. Must be valid for 90 days after end of stay.

Letter of Invitation: Not required of citizens of Australia, Canada, Ireland, New Zealand, the UK, and the US.

Inoculations: Recommended up-to-date on DTap (diphtheria, tetanus, and pertussis) Hepatitis A, Hepatitis B, MMR (measles, mumps and rubella), polio booster, rabies, and typhoid.

Work Permit: Required of all foreigners planning to work in the Czech Republic.

International Driving Permit: Required of foreigners. For EU citizens, a national driver's license is sufficient.

TOURIST SERVICES AND MONEY

EMERGENCY Ambulance: ☎155. Fire: ☎150. Police: ☎158.

TOURIST OFFICES. Municipal **tourist offices** in major cities provide info on sights and events, distribute lists of hostels and hotels, and often book rooms. **Tourist Infomration Centrum** is state-run. Be aware that in Prague these offices are often crowded and may be staffed by disgruntled employees. **CKM,** a national student tourist agency, books hostels and issues ISICs and HI cards. Most bookstores sell a national hiking map collection, *Soubor turistických map*, with an English key.

MONEY. The Czech unit of currency is the **koruna** (Kč; crown), plural koruny. The government postponed its slated 2009 conversion to the euro and 2012 has been suggested as the earliest date. **Inflation** is around 2%. Relative to the rest of Eastern Europe, the Czech Republic's inflation rate is quite stable. Banks offer good exchange rates; **Komerční banka** is a common bank chain. **ATMs** are everywhere and offer the best exchange rates. Bargaining is usually acceptable, especially in heavily touristed areas, though less so in formal indoor shops.

CZECH (Kč)		
AUS$1 = 16.34Kč		10Kč = AUS$0.61
CDN$1 = 19.33Kč		10Kč = CDN$0.52
EUR€1 = 27.33Kč		10Kč = EUR€0.36
NZ$1 = 14.26Kč		10Kč = NZ$0.70
UK£1 = 40.74Kč		10Kč = UK£0.25
US$1 = 20.56Kč		10Kč = US$0.49

HEALTH AND SAFETY

Medical facilities, especially in Prague, are of high quality, and sometimes employ English-speaking doctors. They often require cash payment, but some may accept credit cards. Travelers are urged to check with their insurance companies to see if they will cover emergency medical expenses. **Pharmacies** are *Lekarna*, and the most common chain is Droxi; they and supermarkets carry international brands of *náplast* (bandages), *tampóny* (tampons), and *kondomy* (condoms). The Czech Republic has quite a low level of violent crime, but **petty crime** has increased with the influx of tourism, it is especially common in big cities, on public transportation, and near sites known to be touristy, such as main squares in Prague. Tourists should be alert and avoid carrying large bags. **Women** traveling alone should not experience many problems, but should exercise caution while riding public transportation, especially after dark. Hate crimes are rare in the Czech Republic, but **minorities** might experience some discrimination. This is especially true for travelers with darker skin. Travelers with **disabilities** might encounter trouble with the Czech Republic's accessibility, but there is a strong movement to make Prague's transportation system more wheelchair-friendly. Gay nightlife is taking off in Prague, and the country recently legalized registered partnerships for same-sex couples. Though tolerance is increasing, **GLBT travelers** are advised to avoid public displays of affection, especially outside Prague.

TRANSPORTATION

BY PLANE. Most major European carriers, including **Air Canada, Air France, American Airlines, British Airways, CSA, Delta, KLM, Lufthansa,** and **SAS** fly into Prague. Direct flights are quite expensive; travelers might consider flying to a Western European capital and taking a train or discount airline into Prague.

BY TRAIN. The easiest and cheapest way to travel between cities in the Czech Republic is by **train. Eurail** is accepted in the Czech Republic. The fastest international trains are *EuroCity* and *InterCity* (*expresní;* marked in blue on schedules). *Rychlík* trains are fast domestic trains (*zrychlený vlak;* marked in red on schedules). Avoid slow *osobni* trains, marked in white. *Odjezdy* (departures) are printed on yellow posters, *příjezdy* (arrivals) on white. Seat reservations (*mistenka*, 10Kč) are recommended on express and international trains.

BY BUS. Czech **buses** are often quicker and cheaper than trains in the countryside. **CSAD** runs national and interntational bus lines (www.ticketsbti.csad.cz), and many European companies operate international service. Consult the timetables or buy a bus schedule (25Kč) from kiosks.

BY CAR AND BY TAXI. Roads are generally well-kept, but side-roads can be dangerous, and the number of fatal car accidents is increasing in the Czech Republic. **Roadside assistance** is usually available. To drive in the Czech Republic, an **International Driver's Permit** is required. **Taxis** are a safe way to travel, though many overcharge you. Negotiate the fare beforehand and make sure the meter is running during the ride. Phoning a taxi service is generally more affordable than flagging down a cab on the street. Let's Go does not recommend **hitchhiking.**

KEEPING IN TOUCH

PHONE CODES	**Country code:** 420. **International dialing prefix:** 00. For more information on how to place international calls, see **Inside Back Cover.**

EMAIL AND THE INTERNET. Internet access is readily available throughout the Czech Republic. Internet cafes offer fast connections for about 1-2Kč per minute.

TELEPHONE. Card-operated phones (175Kč per 50 units; 320Kč per 100 units) are simpler to use and easier to find than coin phones. You can purchase phone cards (telefonní karta) at most tábaks and trafika (convenience stores). To make domestic calls, dial the entire number. City codes no longer exist in the Czech Republic, and dialing zero is not necessary. To make an international call to the Czech Republic, dial the country code followed by the entire phone number. Calls run 8Kč per minute to Australia, Canada, the UK, or the US; and 12Kč per minute to New Zealand. Dial ☎1181 for English info, 0800 12 34 56 for the international operator. International access codes include: **AT&T** (☎00 800 222 55288); **British Telecom** (☎00 420); **Canada Direct** (☎800 001 115); **MCI** (☎800 001 112); **Sprint** (☎800 001 187); and **Telstra Australia** (☎800 001 161).

MAIL. The postal system is reliable and efficient, though finding English-speaking postal employees can be a challenge. A postcard to the US costs 12Kč, to Europe 9Kč. To send airmail, stress that you want your package to go on a plane (letecky). Go to the customs office to send packages heavier than 2kg abroad. **Poste Restante** is generally available. Address envelopes as follows: First Name LAST NAME, POSTE RESTANTE, post office address, Postal Code, city, CZECH REPUBLIC.

LANGUAGE. Czech is a West Slavic language, closely related to Slovak and Polish. English is widely understood among young people, and German can be useful, especially in South Bohemia. In eastern regions, you're more likely to encounter Polish. Russian was taught to all school children under communism, the language is not always welcome. For a phrasebook, see **Appendix: Czech,** p. 1058.

ACCOMMODATIONS AND CAMPING

CZECH REPUBLIC	❶	❷	❸	❹	❺
ACCOMMODATIONS	under 320Kč	320-500Kč	501-800Kč	801-1200Kč	over 1200Kč

Hostels and **university dorms** are the cheapest options in July and August; two- to four-bed dorms cost 250-400Kč. Hostels are generally clean and safe throughout the country, though are often rare in areas with few students. **Pensions** are the next most affordable option at 600-800Kč. **Hotels** (from 1000Kč) tend to be more luxurious and expensive. From June to September, reserve at least a week ahead in Prague, Český Krumlov, and Brno. **Private homes** are not nearly as popular (or as cheap) as in the rest of Eastern Europe. Scan train stations for *Zimmer frei* signs. As quality varies, don't pay in advance. There are many **campgrounds** scattered throughout the country; most are open only from mid-May to September.

FOOD AND DRINK

CZECH REPUBLIC	❶	❷	❸	❹	❺
FOOD	under 80Kč	80-110Kč	111-150Kč	151-200Kč	over 200Kč

Loving Czech cuisine starts with learning to pronounce *knedlíky* (KNED-lee-kee). These thick, wheat- or potato-based loaves of dough, feebly known in English as dumplings, are a staple. Meat, however, lies at the heart of almost all main dishes; the **national meal** (known as *vepřo-knedlo-zelo*) is *vepřové* (roast pork), *knedlíky*, and *zelí* (sauerkraut), frequently served with cabbage. If you're in a hurry, grab *párky* (frankfurters) or *sýr* (cheese) at a food stand. **Vegetarian** restaurants serving *bez masa* (meatless) specialties are uncommon outside Prague; traditional restaurants serve few options beyond *smaženy sýr* (fried cheese) and *saláty* (salads), and even these may contain meat products. Eating **kosher** is feasible, but beware—pork may sneak unnoticed into many dishes. *Jablkový závin* (apple strudel) and *ovocné knedlíky* (fruit dumplings) are favorite sweets, but the most beloved is *koláč*—a tart filled with poppy seeds or sweet cheese. *Vinárnas* (wine bars) serve Moravian wines and a variety of spirits, including *slivovice* (plum brandy) and *becherovka* (herbal bitter), the **national drink.** World-class local brews like *Plzeňský Prazdroj* (Pilsner Urquell), *Budvar*, and *Krušovice* dominate the drinking scene.

HOLIDAYS AND FESTIVALS

Holidays: New Year's Day (Jan. 1); Easter Holiday (Mar. 24, 2008; Apr. 13, 2009); May Day/Labor Day (May 1); Liberation Day (May 8); Saints Cyril and Methodius Day (July 5); Jan Hus Day (July 6); St. Wencesclas Day (Sept. 28); Independence Day (Oct. 28); Struggle for Freedom and Democracy Day (Nov. 17); Christmas (Dec. 24-26).

Festivals: The Czech Republic hosts a number of internationally renowned festivals. If you are planning to attend, reserve tickets well in advance. In June, the Five-Petaled Rose Festival, a medieval festival in Český Krumlov (p. 244) features music, dance, and a jousting tournament. Masopust, the Moravian version of Mardi Gras, is celebrated in villages across the country from Epiphany to Ash Wednesday (Jan.-Mar.).

BEYOND TOURISM

For more info on opportunities across Europe, see **Beyond Tourism,** p. 56.

INEX—Association of Voluntary Service, Senovážné nám. 24, 116 47 Praha 1, Czech Republic (☎420 234 621 527; www.inexsda.cz/eng). Ecological and historical preservation efforts, as well as construction projects, in the Czech Republic.

The Prague Center for Further Education and Professional Development, Pštrossova 19, Nové Město, 110 00 Praha 1, Czech Republic (☎420 257 534 013; www.filmstudies.cz). Teaches courses on art, filmmaking, and design in Prague.

University of West Bohemia, Univerzitní 8, 306 14 Plzeň (☎420 377 631 111; www.zcu.cz). International university centrally located in a student-friendly brewery city.

PRAGUE (PRAHA)

Home to stately Prague Castle and Old Town Square's pastel facades, Prague (pop. 1,200,000) retains small-town charm despite its size. In the 14th century, Holy Roman Emperor Charles IV refurbished Prague with stone bridges and lavish palaces visible today. Since the 1989 lifting of the Iron Curtain, outsiders have flooded the Czech capital. In summer, most locals leave for the countryside when foreigner-to-resident ratio soars above nine-to-one. Despite rising prices and a hypertouristed *Staré Město* (Old Town), Prague still commands awe from its visitors.

⊡ INTERCITY TRANSPORTATION

Flights: Ruzyně Airport (PRG; ☎220 111 111), 20km northwest of the city. Take bus #119 to Metro A: Dejvická (12Kč, luggage 6Kč per bag); buy tickets from kiosks or machines. **Airport buses** run by **Cedaz** (☎220 114 296; 20-45min., 2 per hr.) collect travelers from nám. Republiky (120Kč) and Dejvická Metro stops (90Kč). **Taxis** to the airport are expensive (700-900Kč); try to settle on a price before departing.

Trains: (☎221 111 122, international 224 615 249; www.vlak.cz). Prague has 4 main terminals. **Hlavní nádraží** (☎224 615 786; Metro C: Hlavní nádraží) and **Nádraží Holešovice** (☎224 624 632; Metro C: Nádraží Holešovice) are the largest and cover most international service. Domestic trains leave **Masarykovo nádraží** (☎840 112 113; Metro B: nám. Republiky) and from **Smíchovské nádraží** (☎972 226 150; Metro B: Smíchovské nádraží). International trains run to: **Berlin, GER** (5hr., 6 per day, 1400Kč); **Bratislava, SLK** (4½-5½hr., 6 per day, 600Kč); **Budapest, HUN** (7-9hr., 5 per day, 1400Kč); **Kraków, POL** (7-8hr., 3 per day, 900Kč); **Moscow, RUS** (31hr., 1 per day, 3000Kč); **Munich, GER** (7hr., 3 per day, 1650Kč); **Vienna, AUT** (4½hr., 7 per day, 1000Kč); **Warsaw, POL** (9½hr., 2 per day, 1290Kč).

Buses: (☎900 144 444; www.vlak-bus.cz.) State-run **ČSAD** (☎257 319 016) has several terminals. The biggest is **Florenc**, Křižíkova 4 (☎900 149 044; Metro B or C: Florenc). Info office open daily 6am-9pm. To: **Berlin, GER** (7hr., 2 per day, 900Kč); **Budapest, HUN** (8hr., 3 per day, 1600Kč); **Paris, FRA** (15hr., 2 per day, 2200Kč); **Sofia, BUL** (24hr., 2 per day, 1600Kč); **Vienna, AUT** (5hr., 1 per day, 600Kč). 10% ISIC discount. **Tourbus** office (☎224 218 680; www.eurolines.cz), at the terminal, sells **Eurolines** and airport bus tickets. Open M-F 7am-7pm, Sa 8am-7pm, Su 9am-7pm.

⊞ ORIENTATION

Shouldering the river **Vltava**, greater Prague is a mess of suburbs and maze-like streets. All destinations of interest to travelers are in the compact downtown. The Vltava runs south to north through central Prague, separating **Staré Město** (Old Town) and **Nové Město** (New Town) from **Malá Strana** (Lesser Side). On the right bank, **Staroměstské náměstí** (Old Town Square) is Prague's focal point. From the square, the elegant **Pařížská ulice** (Paris Street) leads north into **Josefov,** the old Jewish quarter. South of Staré Město, the more modern **Nové Město** houses **Václavské náměstí** (Wenceslas Square), the city's commercial core. West of Staroměstské nám., **Karlův Most** (Charles Bridge) spans the Vltava, connecting Staré Město with **Malostranské náměstí** (Lesser Town Square). **Pražský Hrad** (Prague Castle) overlooks Malostranské nám. from **Hradčany** hill. The train station and bus station lie northeast of Václavské nám. To reach Staroměstské nám., take Metro A line to Staroměstská and follow Kaprova away from the river.

CZECH REPUBLIC

▣ LOCAL TRANSPORTATION

Public Transportation: Buy interchangeable tickets for the **bus, Metro,** and **tram** at newsstands, *tabák* kiosks, machines in stations, or the DP (*Dopravní podnik;* transport authority) kiosks. Validate tickets in machines above escalators to avoid fines issued by plainclothes inspectors who roam transport lines. 3 **Metro** lines run daily 5am-midnight: A is green on maps, B yellow, C red. **Night trams** #51-58 and **buses** #502-514 and 601 run after the last Metro and cover the same areas as day trams and buses (2 per hr. 12:30am-4:30am); look for dark blue signs with white letters at bus stops. 8Kč tickets are good for a 15min. ride or 4 stops. 12Kč tickets are valid for 1hr., with transfers, for all travel in the same direction. Large bags and baby carriages 6Kč. DP offices (☎296 191 817; www.dpp.cz; open daily 7am-9pm), in the Muzeum stop on Metro A and C lines, sells **multi-day passes** (1-day 80Kč, 3-day 220Kč, 1-week 280Kč).

Taxis: **City Taxi** (☎257 257 257) and **AAA** (☎140 14). 30Kč base, 22Kč per km, 4Kč per min. waiting. Hail a cab anywhere but call ahead to avoid getting ripped off.

> **TIP** **GOING THE DISTANCE.** To avoid taxi scams, always ask in advance for a receipt *(Prosím, dejte mi paragon)* with distance traveled and price paid.

◪ PRACTICAL INFORMATION

Tourist Offices: Green "i"s mark tourist offices. **Pražská Informační Služba** (PIS; Prague Information Service; ☎12 444; www.pis.cz) is in the Staroměstské Radnice (Old Town Hall). Open Apr.-Oct. M 11am-6pm, Tu-Su 9am-6pm; Nov.-Mar. M 11am-5pm, Tu-Su 9am-5pm. Branches at Na příkopě 20 and Hlavní nádraží. Open in summer M-F 9am-7pm, Sa-Su 9am-5pm; winter M-F 9am-6pm, Sa 9am-3pm. Branch in the tower by the Malá Strana side of the Charles Bridge. Open Apr.-Oct. daily 10am-6pm.

Budget Travel: CKM, Mánesova 77 (☎222 721 595; www.ckm-praha.cz). Metro A: Jiřího z Poděbrad. Sells budget airline tickets to those under 26. Also books accommodations in Prague from 300Kč. Open M-Th 10am-6pm, F 10am-4pm. **GTS,** Ve smečkách 27 (☎222 119 700; www.gtsint.cz). Metro A or C: Muzeum. Offers student discounts on airline tickets (225-2500Kč in Europe). Open M-F 8am-10pm, Sa 10am-4pm.

Embassies and Consulates: Australia, Klimentská 10, 6th fl. (☎296 578 350; www.embassy.gov.au/cz.html; open M-Th 8:30am-5pm, F 8:30am-2pm) and **New Zealand,** Dykova 19 (☎222 514 672) have consulates, but citizens should contact the UK embassy in an emergency. **Canada,** Muchova 6 (☎272 101 800; www.canada.cz). Open M-F 8:30am-12:30pm and 1:30-4:30pm. Consular section open only in the morning. **Ireland,** Tržiště 13 (☎257 530 061; irishembassy@iol.cz). Metro A: Malostranská. Open M-F 9:30am-12:30pm and 2:30-4:30pm. **UK,** Thunovská 14 (☎257 402 111; prague@fco.gov.uk). Metro A: Malostranská. Open M-Th 9am-noon. **US,** Tržiště 15 (☎257 530 663, after-hours 257 022 000; www.usembassy.cz). Metro A: Malostranská. Open M-F 8am-4:30pm. Consular section open M-F 8:30-11:30am.

Currency Exchange: Exchange counters are everywhere but rates vary wildly. The counters in the train station have high rates. Never change money on the street. **Chequepoints** are plentiful and open late, but can charge large commissions. **Komerční banka,** Na příkopě 33 (☎222 432 111), buys notes and checks for 2% commission. Open M-W 9am-6pm, Th-F 9am-5pm. A 24hr. **Citibank** is at Rytířska 24.

American Express/Interchange: Václavské nám. 56 (☎222 800 224). Metro A or C: Muzeum. AmEx **ATM** outside. **Western Union** services available. MC/V **cash advances** (3% commission). Western Union services available. Open daily 9am-7pm.

Luggage Storage: Lockers in train and bus stations take 2 5Kč coins. For storage over 24hr., use the luggage offices to the left in the basement of Hlavní nádraží. 20Kč per

CZECH REPUBLIC

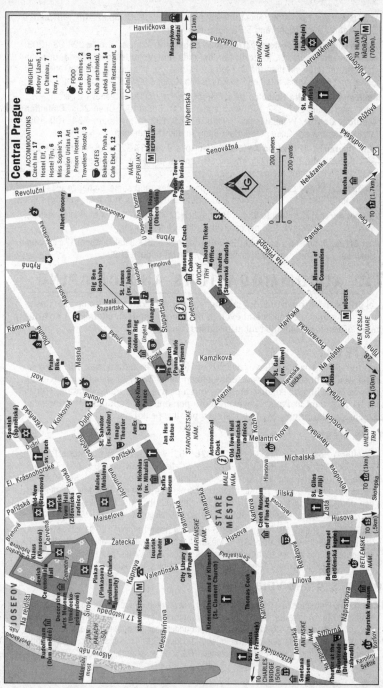

Central Prague

▲ ACCOMMODATIONS
Czech Inn, 17
Hostel Elf, 9
Hostel Týn, 6
Miss Sophie's, 16
Pension Unitas Art
Prison Hostel, 15
Travellers' Hostel, 3

☕ CAFES
Bakeshop Praha, 4
Cafe Ebel, 8, 12

♪ NIGHTLIFE
Karlovy Lázně, 11
Le Chateau, 7
Roxy, 1

🍴 FOOD
Cafe Bambus, 2
Country Life, 10
Klub architektů, 13
Lehká Hlava, 14
Yami Restaurant, 5

day, bags over 15kg 40Kč. Fine for forgotten lock code 30Kč. Open 24hr. with breaks 5:30-6am, 11-11:30am, and 5:30-6pm.

English-Language Bookstore: 🔲**The Globe Bookstore,** Pštrossova 6 (☎224 934 203; www.globebookstore.cz). Metro B: Národní třída. Exit Metro left on Spálená, take the 1st right on Ostrovní, then the 3rd left on Pštrossova. Wide variety of new and used books and periodicals. Internet 1.50Kč per min. Open daily 9:30am-midnight.

Medical Services: Na Homolce (Hospital for Foreigners), Roentgenova 2 (☎257 271 111, after hours 257 272 146; www.homolka.cz). Bus #167. Open 24hr. **Canadian Medical Center,** Velesavínská 1 (☎235 360 133, after hours 724 300 301; www.cmc.praha.cz). Open M,W,F 8am-6pm, Tu and Th 8am-8pm.

24hr. Pharmacy: U Lékárna Anděla, Štefánikova 6 (☎257 320 918, after hours 257 324 686). Metro B: Anděl.For after-hours service, press the button marked "Pohoto-vost" to the left of the main door.

Telephones: Phone cards sold at kiosks, post offices, and some exchange establish-ments for 200Kč and 300Kč. Coins also accepted (local calls from 4Kč per min.).

Internet Access: 🔲**Bohemia Bagel,** Masná 2 (☎224 812 560; www.bohemiabagel.cz), Metro A: Staroměstská. 2Kč per min. Open daily 7am-midnight,

Post Office: Jindřišská 14 (☎221 131 445). Metro A or B: Můstek. Internet 1Kč per min. Open daily 2am-midnight. Tellers close 7pm. **Postal Code:** 11000.

🏠 🏕 ACCOMMODATIONS AND CAMPING

Hotel prices are through the roof in Prague, and hostel rates are on the rise. Reser-vations are a must at hotels and even at the nicer hostels in summer. A growing number of Prague residents rent affordable rooms.

HOSTELS

If you tote a backpack in Hlavní nádraží or Holešovice stations, you will likely be approached by hostel runners offering cheap beds. Many of these are university dorms vacated June to August, and they often provide free transportation, conve-nient for late-night arrivals. However, more personal, well-appointed options can be had at similiar prices. Staff at hostels typically speak English.

STARÉ MĚSTO

Travellers' Hostel, Dlouhá 33 (☎224 826 662; www.travellers.cz). Metro B: nám. Republiky. Branches at Husova 3, Josefská, Střelecký Ostrov, and U Lanové Dráhy 3. Social atmosphere. Smallish dorms. Same building as the Roxy (p. 240). Breakfast and linens included. Laundry 150Kč. Internet 1Kč per min. Reserve ahead in summer. 10-bed dorm 380Kč; 6-bed dorms 450Kč; singles 1120Kč, with bath 1300Kč; doubles 650/750Kč; apartments 2400-3500Kč. 40Kč ISIC discount. AmEx/D/MC/V. ❷

Hostel Týn, Týnská 19 (☎224 828 519; www.hostel-tyn.web2001.cz). Metro A: Staroměstská. In the heart of Staré Město, Avoids the extremes of overcrowding and boredom: dorms are small, but the crowd is social. Soft beds. Clean facilities. In-room lockers. Check-out 10am. 5-bed dorms 400Kč; doubles 1100Kč. 200Kč deposit. ❷

NOVÉ MĚSTO AND VINOHRADY

🔲 **Czech Inn,** Francouzská 76 (☎267 267 600; www.czech-inn.com). Metro A: nám. Míru. From the Metro, take tram #4, 22, or 23 to Krymská and walk uphill. This ultra-modern, fashionable hostel sets sky-high standards for budget accommodations. Breakfast 120Kč. Internet 50Kč per hr. Reserve 2 weeks ahead. Dorms 390-450Kč; singles 1200Kč; dou-bles 1400Kč. Private room prices increase 200Kč on weekends. AmEx/MC/V. ❷

Miss Sophie's, Melounová 3 (☎296 303 532; www.missophies.com). Metro C: IP Pavlova. Take 1st left from subway platform, then follow Katerinská to 1st right onto Melounová. For the stylish budget traveler, a brick cellar lounge and artistic dorm decor make up for the bathroom shortage. Free Internet. Reception 24hr. High season dorms 400-490Kč; singles 1590Kč; doubles 1790Kč; triples 2100Kč; apartments 1990-3390Kč. Low season 350/1200/1500/1700/1400-1900Kč. AmEx/MC/V. ❷

Hostel Elf, Husitská 11 (☎222 540 963; www.hostelelf.com). Metro B: Florenc. From the Metro, take bus #207 to U Památníku; the hostel is through the wooden gate. Despite noisy train tracks nearby, this graffiti-covered hostel is always packed. The party continues past dawn in the downstairs lounge. Breakfast included. Free Internet. 9-bed dorms 340Kč; singles 800Kč, with baths 1000Kč; doubles 900/1200Kč. ❷

Pension Unitas Art Prison Hostel, Bartolomějská 9 (☎224 221 802; www.unitas.cz). Metro B: Národní třída. Cross Národní třída, head up Na Perštýně, and turn left on Bartolomějská. This former 🅰Communist prison is now a clean and colorful hostel, with small spotless rooms. Superb breakfast buffet included. Reception 24hr. Check-out 10am. Apr.-Oct. dorms 440Kč; singles 1350Kč; doubles 1700Kč; triples 2100Kč; quads 2360Kč. Nov.-Mar. 350/890/980/1380/1700Kč. 7th night free. MC/V. ❷

OUTSIDE THE CENTER

🏠 **Sir Toby's,** Dělnická 24 (☎283 870 635; www.sirtobys.com). Metro C: Nádraží Holešovice. From the Metro, take the tram to Dělnická, walk to the corner of Dělnická, and turn left. Beautiful, classy hostel with a huge, fully equipped kitchen. Free Wi-Fi. Dorms 350-420Kč; singles 1000Kč; doubles 2900Kč. MC/V. ❷

🏠 **Hostel Boathouse,** Lodnická 1 (☎241 770 051; www.hostelboathouse.com). Take tram #3, 17,or 52 from Karlovo nam. south toward Sídliště. Get off at Černý Kůň (20min.), go down the ramp to the left, and follow the yellow signs. Social atmosphere, caring staff, and home-cooked meals. Breakfast included. Dorms from 420Kč. ❶

Welcome Hostel at Strahov Complex, Vaníčkova 7 (☎224 320 202; www.bed.cz). By an enormous stadium, Strahov is 10 concrete blocks of blue high-rise dormitories. Rooms are basic but clean and only 10min. by foot from Prague Castle. Not luxurious but sufficient. Open July-Sept. Singles 400Kč; doubles 500Kč. 10% ISIC discount. ❶

OTHER ACCOMMODATIONS

Budget hotels are scarce, and generally the better hostel options offer more bang for your buck. Lower rates at hotels are often available if you call ahead. Campgrounds can be found on the Vltava Islands as well as on the outskirts of Prague. Bungalows must be reserved ahead, but tent sites are generally available without prior notice. Tourist offices sell a guide to sites near the city (20Kč).

Dům U Krále Jiřího (Hotel King George), Liliová 10 (☎222 220 925; www.kinggeorge.cz). Metro A: Staroměstská. Elegant rooms with private bath. Breakfast included. Reception 7am-11pm. Singles 2250Kč; doubles 3550Kč; triples 4950Kč; apartments 3550-7500Kč. Prices fall by 500-900Kč Jan.-Feb. and Nov.-Dec. ❺

Pension Museum, Mezibranská 15 (☎296 325 186; www.pension-museum.cz). Metro C: Muzeum. This ultra-modern B&B near Wenceslas Sq is well worth the splurge. Beautiful courtyard leads to elegant rooms with TVs and spacious baths. Reserve 1-2 months ahead. Apr.-Dec. singles 2460Kč; doubles 2920Kč; apartments 3000-6000Kč. Jan.-Mar. 1580/1970/2000-5000Kč. AmEx/MC/V. ❺

Camp Sokol Troja, Trojská 171 (☎233 542 908), north of the center in the Troja district. From Metro C: Nádraží Holešovice, take bus #112 and ask for Kazanka. Similar places line the road. Clean facilities. July-Aug. and Dec. tent sites 120Kč per person, 90-150Kč per tent site. Singles 330Kč; doubles 660Kč. Low season reduced rates. ❶

CZECH REPUBLIC

🖸 FOOD

The nearer you are to the city center, the more you'll pay. You will be charged for everything the waiter brings to the table; check your bill carefully. **Tesco,** Národní třída 26, has groceries. (Open M-F 7am-10pm, Sa 8am-8pm, Su 9am-8pm.) Look for the **daily market** in Staré Město. After a night out, grab a *párek v rohlíku* (hot dog) or a *smažený sýr* (fried cheese sandwich) from a Václavské nám. vendor.

RESTAURANTS

STARÉ MĚSTO

🖾 **Klub architektů,** Betlémské nám. 169/5A (☎224 401 214). Metro B: Národní třída. A 12th-century cellar with 21st-century ambience. Veggie options 70-150Kč. Meat entrees 160-320Kč. Open daily 11:30am-midnight. AmEx/MC/V. ❸

Lehká Hlava (Clear Head), Boršov 2 (☎222 220 665; www.lehkahlava.cz). Metro A: Staroměstská. Cooks up vegetarian and vegan cuisine that even devout carnivores will enjoy. Try the eggplant quesadilla with guacamole (110Kč). Entrees 80-160Kč. Open M-F 11:30am-11:30pm; Sa and Su noon-11:30pm. Kitchen closed 2:30pm-5pm. Only cold food after 10pm. Cash only. ❷

Country Life, Melantrichova 15 (☎224 213 366; www.countrylife.cz). Metro A: Staroměstská. 3 fresh vegetarian buffets—hot, cold, and salad bar—are a welcome respite from meat-heavy Czech cuisine. Buffet 20-50Kč per 100g. Soup 20Kč. Juices from 20Kč. Open M-Th 9am-8:30pm, F 8:30am-5pm, Su 11am-8:30pm. Cash only. ❷

Yami Restaurant, Masná 3 (☎222 312 756) Metro A: Staroměstská. A wide variety of Japanese dishes in a relaxed, Zen dining room. The courtyard out back holds 4 coveted tables behind a screen where diners devour Yami's fusion rolls (196-320Kč per 8pc.). Entrees 120-260Kč. Sushi 55-320Kč. Open daily noon-11pm. MC/V. ❸

Cafe Bambus, Benediktská 12 (☎224 828 110; www.cafebambus.com). Metro B: nám. Republiky. Patrons nosh on Thai and Indian dishes (around 130Kč) and Czech *palančinky* (crepes; 55-75Kč). Beer from 42Kč. Good variety of alcoholic and non-alcoholic drinks. Open M-F 9am-2am, Sa 11am-2am, Su 11am-midnight. AmEx/MC/V. ❷

NOVÉ MĚSTO

🖾 **Radost FX,** Bělehradská 120 (☎224 254 776; www.radostfx.cz). Metro C: I.P. Pavlova. A stylish dance club and late-night cafe with an imaginative menu and great vegetarian food. Entrees 120-195Kč. Brunch Sa-Su 50-200Kč. Open daily 9am-late. ❸

Universal, V jirchářích 6 (☎224 934 416). Metro B: Národní třída. Asian, French, and Mediterranean cuisines served in an eclectically decorated dining room. Huge, fresh salads 131-195Kč. Entrees 150-300Kč. Su brunch buffet 185-205Kč. Open M-Sa 11:30am-1am, Su 11am-midnight. MC/V; min. 500Kč. ❸

Ultramarin Grill, Ostrovní 32 (☎224 932 249; www.ultramarin.cz). Metro B: Národní třída. Classy decor without the prices to match. American dishes as well as Thai-inspired steak, duck, and lamb entrees 130-350Kč. Salads 100-180Kč. Open daily 10am-11pm. AmEx/MC/V. ❸

Velryba (The Whale), Opatovická 24. Metro B: Národní třída. Cross the tram tracks and follow Ostrovní, then go left onto Opatovická. Relaxed Italian/Czech restaurant with art gallery downstairs. Entrees 62-145Kč. Open daily 11am-midnight. MC/V. ❷

MALÁ STRANA

Bar bar, Všehrdova 17 (☎257 313 246; www.barbar.cz). Metro A: Malostranská. From Malostranské nám., go down Karmelitská and left on Všehrdova. Reggae-inspired basement cafe with affordable international menu. Lunch noon-2pm 100Kč. Entrees 98-175Kč. Beer from 28Kč. Open Su-Th noon-midnight, F-Sa noon-2am. MC/V. ❷

U Tři Černých Ruží, Zámecká 5 (☎257 530 019; www.u3cr.com). Metro A: Malostranská. At the foot of the New Castle steps. Quirky restaurant and bar. Large portions and pints at low prices. Entrees 80-250Kč. Beer 25Kč. Open daily 11am-midnight. ❷

CAFES AND TEAHOUSES

▨ **Cafe Rybka,** Opatovická 7. Metro B: Národní třída. Congenial corner cafe with a sea motif, fantastic coffee, and a tiny bookstore. Espresso 25Kč. Tea 22Kč. Open daily 9:15am-10pm. Cash only.

▨ **Cafe Ebel,** Řetězová 9 (☎603 441 434; www.ebelcoffee.cz). Metro A or B: Staroměstská. Ebel's espresso (40-50Kč) is blended in-house by people who clearly know what they're doing. Small selection of sandwiches and pastries. English spoken. Branch at Týnská 2. Both open M-F 8am-8pm, Sa-Su 8:30am-8pm. AmEx/MC/V.

Kavárna Medúza, Belgická 17. Metro A: nám. Míru. Walk down Rumunská and turn left at Belgická. Local clientele by day, hipsters by night. Coffee 19-30Kč. Crepes 52-70Kč. Open M-F 10am-1am, Sa-Su noon-1am. MC/V.

U zeleného čaje, Nerudova 19 (☎225 730 027). Metro A: Malostranská. From Malostranské nám., go down Nerudova. This adorable shop at the foot of Prague Castle takes tea to new heights. Serves up several alcohol-infused teas. Tea 35-75Kč. Open daily 11am-10pm. Cash only.

◎ SIGHTS

Escape the crowds that flock to Prague's downtown sights by venturing away from **Staroměstské náměstí,** the **Charles Bridge,** and **Václavské náměstí.** There are plenty of attractions for visitors hidden in the old Jewish quarter of **Josefov,** the hills of **Vyšehrad,** and the streets of **Malá Strana.**

STARÉ MĚSTO (OLD TOWN)

Navigating the 1000-year-old **Staré Město** (Old Town)—a jumble of narrow streets and alleys—can be difficult. Once the sun sets, the ancient labyrinth comes alive with the city's youth, who enliven its many bars and jazz clubs.

CHARLES BRIDGE. Thronged with tourists and the hawkers who feed on them, the Charles Bridge (Karlův Most) is Prague's most treasured landmarks. The defense towers on each side offer splendid views. Five stars and a cross mark the spot where, according to legend, St. Jan Nepomuck was tossed over the side of the bridge for concealing the queen's extramarital secrets from a suspicious King Wenceslas IV in the 14th century. *(Metro A: Malostranská or Staroměstská.)*

OLD TOWN SQUARE. Staroměstské náměstí (Old Town Square) is the heart of Staré Město, surrounded by eight magnificent towers. *(Metro A: Staroměstská; Metro A or B: Můstek.)* Composed of several different architectural styles, the **Staroměstské Radnice** (Old Town Hall) has been missing a piece of its front facade since the Nazis partially demolished it in the final days of WWII. Crowds gather on the hour to watch the **astronomical clock** chime as skeletal Death empties his hourglass and a procession of apostles marches by. *(Exhibition hall open in summer M 10am-7pm, Tu-F 9am-7pm, Sa-Su 9am-6pm. Clock tower open daily 10am-6pm; enter through 3rd fl. of Old Town Hall. Exhibition hall 20Kč, students 10Kč. Clock tower 60/40Kč.)* The spires of **Týn Church** (Chrám Matky Boží před Týnem) rise above a mass of baroque homes. Buried inside is astronomer Tycho Brahe, whose overindulgence at Emperor Rudolf's lavish dinner party in 1601 may have cost him his life. Since it was deemed improper to leave the table unless the emperor himself did so, Tycho had to remain in his chair until his bladder burst. He died 11 days later, though scholars believe mercury poisoning may have been the culprit. *(Open M-F 9am-noon and 1-2pm. Mass July-*

Aug. W-F 6pm, Sa 8am, Su 11am, 12:30 and 9pm; Sept.-June W-F 6pm, Sa 8am, Su 11am and 9pm. Free.) The bronze statue of 15th-century theologian **Jan Hus,** the country's most famous martyr, stands in the middle of the square. Barely a surface in **St. James's Church** (kostel sv. Jakuba) remains un-figured, un-marbleized, or unpained. But keep your hands to yourself—legend has it that 500 years ago a thief tried to pilfer a gem from the Virgin Mary of Suffering, whereupon the figure sprang to life and yanked off his arm. *(Metro B: Staroměstská. Un Malá Štupartská, behind Týn Church. Open M-Sa 10am-noon and 2-3:45pm. Mass Su 8, 9, and 10:30am.)*

NOVÉ MĚSTO (NEW TOWN)

Established in 1348 by Charles IV, Nové Město has become Prague's commercial center. The Franciscan Gardens offer a calm oasis from the bustling businesses.

WENCESLAS SQUARE. More a commercial boulevard than a square, **Václavské náměstí** (Wenceslas Square) owes its name to the statue of 10th-century Czech ruler and patron **Saint Wenceslas** (Václav) that stands in front of the National Museum. At his feet in solemn prayer kneel smaller statues of the country's other patron saints: St. Agnes, St. Adalbert (Vojtěch), St. Ludmila, and St. Prokop. The sculptor, Josef Václav Myslbek, took 25 years to complete the statue. The inscription under St. Wenceslas reads, "Do not let us and our descendants perish." *(Metro A or B: Můstek or Metro A or C: Muzeum.)*

FRANCISCAN GARDEN AND VELVET REVOLUTION MEMORIAL. Franciscan monks somehow manage to preserve this serene **rose garden** in the heart of Prague's commercial district. *(Metro A or B: Můstek. Enter through the arch to the left of Jungmannova and Národní, behind the statue. Open daily mid-Apr. to mid-Sept. 7am-10pm; mid-Sept. to mid-Oct. 7am-8pm; mid-Oct. to mid-Apr. 8am-7pm. Free.)* Down the street on Národní, a **plaque** under the arcades and across from the Black Theatre memorializes the hundreds of citizens beaten by police in a 1989 protest. A subsequent wave of protests led to the collapse of communism in Czechoslovakia during the Velvet Revolution.

DANCING HOUSE. American architect Frank Gehry (of Guggenheim-Bilbao fame) built the gently swaying **Tančící dům** (Dancing House) at the corner of Resslova and Rašínovo nábřeží. Since its 1996 unveiling, it has been called an eyesore by some and a shining example of postmodern design by others. *(Metro B: Karlovo nám. As you walk down Resslova toward the river, the building is on the left.)*

JOSEFOV

Josefov, Central Europe's oldest Jewish settlement, lies north of Staroměstské nám., along Maiselova. In 1180, Prague's citizens built a 4m wall around the area. The closed neighborhood bred exotic tales, many of which centered around **Rabbi Loew ben Bezalel** (1512-1609) and his legendary **golem**—a mud creature that supposedly came to life to protect Prague's Jews. The city's Jews remained clustered in Josefov until WWII, when the Nazis sent the residents to death camps. Ironically, Hitler's decision to create a "museum of an extinct race" sparked the preservation of Josefov's cemetery and synagogues.

SYNAGOGUES. The **Maiselova synagoga** (Maisel Synagogue) displays artifacts from the Jewish Museum's collections, only returned to the community in 1994. *(On Maiselova, between Široká and Jáchymova.)* Turn left on Široká to reach the **Pinkasova** (Pinkas Synagogue). Drawings by children interred at the Terezín camp are upstairs. Some 80,000 names line the walls downstairs, a sobering requiem for Czech Jews persecuted in the Holocaust. Backtrack along Široká and go left on Maiselova to reach Europe's oldest operating synagogue, the 700-year-old **Staronová** (Old-New Synagogue), still the religious center of Prague's Jewish community. Up Široká at Dušní, the **Španělská** (Spanish Synagogue) has an ornate Moorish interior and was first in adopting the 1830s Reform movement. *(Metro A: Staroměstská. Men must cover their heads; kippot free. Synagogues open M-F and Su Apr.- Oct. 9am-6pm; Nov.-Mar. 9am-4:30pm. Closed Jewish holidays. Admission to all synagogues except Staronová 290Kč, students 190Kč. Staronová 200/140Kč.)*

OLD JEWISH CEMETERY. Filled with thousands of broken headstones, the Old Jewish Cemetery (Starý židovský hřbitov) stretches between the Pinkas Synagogue and the Ceremonial Hall. Between the 14th and 18th centuries, the graves were dug in layers. The clustering tombstones visible today formed as older stones rose from beneath newer graves. Rabbi Loew is buried by the wall opposite the entrance. *(At the corner of Široká and Žatecká.)*

MALÁ STRANA

Criminals and counter-revolutionaries' hangout for nearly a century, the cobblestone streets of Malá Strana have become prized real estate. In **Malostranské Náměstí,** the towering dome of the Baroque **St. Nicholas's Cathedral** (Chrám sv. Mikuláše) is one of Prague's most prominent landmarks. Mozart played the organ here when he visited Prague, and the cathedral now hosts nightly classical music concerts. *(Metro A: Malostranská. Follow Letenská to Malostranské nám. ☎ 257 534 215. Open daily 8:30am-4:45pm. 50Kč, students 25Kč. Concerts 390/290Kč.)* Along Letenská, a wooden gate opens into the **Wallenstein Garden** (Valdštejnská zahrada). With a beautifully tended stretch of green and a bronze Venus fountain, this is one of the city's best-kept secrets. *(Letenská 10. Metro A: Malostranská. Open Apr.-Oct. daily 10am-6pm. Free.)* The **Church of Our Lady Victorious** (Kostel Panny Marie Vítězné) contains the famous wax statue of the **Infant Jesus of Prague,** said to bestow miracles on the faithful. *(Follow Letecká through Malostranské nám. and continue onto Karmelitská. ☎ 257 533 646. Open daily 8:30am-7pm. Catholic mass Su noon. Free.)* ▓**Petřín Gardens and View Tower,** on the hill beside Malá Strana, provide a tranquil retreat with spectacular views. Climb the steep, serene footpath, or take the funicular from above the intersection of Vítězná and Újezd. *(Look for Lanovka Dráha signs. Funicular 4-6 per hr. 9am-11pm, 20Kč. Tower open daily 10am-10pm. Tower 50Kč, students 40Kč.)*

PRAGUE CASTLE (PRAŽSKÝ HRAD)

Prague Castle, one of the world's biggest castles, has been the seat of the Czech government for over 1000 years. Since the first Bohemian royal family established their residence here in the 9th century, the castle has housed Holy Roman Emperors, the Communist Czechoslovak government, and now the Czech Republic's president. In the **Royal Gardens** (Královská zahrada), the **Singing Fountain** spouts its harp-like tune before the **Royal Summer Palace.** *(Trams #22 or 23 to Pražský Hrad and go down U Prašného Mostu. ☎ 224 373 368; www.hrad.cz. Castle open daily Apr.-Oct. 9am-5pm; Nov.-Mar. 9am-4pm. Royal Garden open Apr.-Oct. 24hr. Ticket office opposite St. Vitus's Cathedral, inside castle walls. Tickets valid for 2 days at all sites. 350Kč, students 175Kč.)*

ST. VITUS'S CATHEDRAL. Inside the castle walls stands the beautiful Gothic St. Vitus's Cathedral (Katedrála sv. Víta), which was completed in 1929, after 600 years of construction. To the right of the high altar stands the silver **tomb of St. Jan Nepomuck.** In the main church, precious stones and paintings telling the saint's story line the walls of **St. Wenceslas's Chapel** (Svatováclavská kaple). Climb the 287 steps of the **Great South Tower** for an excellent view, or descend underground to the **Royal Crypt** (Královská hrobka), which holds the tomb of Charles IV.

OLD ROYAL PALACE. The Old Royal Palace (Starý královský palác), to the right of the cathedral, is one of the Czech's few castles where visitors can wander largely unattended. The lengthy **Vladislav Hall** once hosted jousting competitions.

Upstairs in the **Chancellery of Bohemia,** a Protestant assembly found two Catholic governors guilty of religious persecution and threw them out the window during the 1618 Second Defenestration of Prague. The men landed in a pile of manure and survived, but the event contributed to the beginning of the Thirty Years' War.

ST. GEORGE'S BASILICA AND ENVIRONS. Across the courtyard from the Old Royal Palace stands St. George's Basilica (Bazilika sv. Jiří), where the skeleton of St. Ludmila is on display. The convent next door houses the **National Gallery of Bohemian Art,** which displays pieces ranging from Gothic to Baroque. *(Open Tu-Su 10am-6pm. 100Kč, students 50Kč.)* To the right of the Basilica, follow Jiřská halfway down and take a right on tiny **Golden Lane** (Zlatá ulička), where alchemists once tried to perfect their art. Franz Kafka had his workspace at #22.

OUTER PRAGUE

In the beautiful neighborhood of Troja, French architect J. B. Mathey's 17th-century **château** overlooks the Vltava. The building has a terraced garden, oval staircase, and a collection of 19th-century Czech artwork. *(Metro C: Nádraží Holešovice, take bus #112 to Zoologická Zahrada. Open Apr.-Oct. Tu-Su 10am-6pm; Nov.-Mar. Sa-Su 10am-5pm. 100Kč, students 50Kč.)* For wilder pursuits, venture next door to the **Prague Zoo.** *(Open daily 9am-7pm. Apr.-Sept. 80Kč, students 50Kč; Oct.-Mar. 50/30Kč.)* Guided by a divine dream to build a monastery atop a bubbling stream, King Boleslav II and St. Adalbert founded **Břevnov Monastery,** Bohemia's oldest, in AD 993. To the right of **St. Margaret's Church** (Bazilika sv. Markéty), the stream leads to a pond. *(Metro A: Malostranská. Take tram #22 to Břevnovský klášter. Church open for mass M-Sa 7am and 6pm, Su 7:30, 9am, and 6pm. Tours Sa-Su 10am, 2, 4pm. 50Kč, students 30Kč.)*

🏛 MUSEUMS

🖼**MUCHA MUSEUM.** The museum is devoted to the work of Alfons Mucha, the Czech's most celebrated artist. Mucha, an Art Nouveau pioneer, gained fame for his poster series of "la divine" Sarah Bernhardt. *(Panská 7. Metro A or B: Můstek. Walk up Václavské nám. toward the St. Wenceslas statue. Go left on Jindřišská and left again on Panská.* ☎ *221 451 333; www.mucha.cz. Open daily 10am-6pm. 120Kč, students 60Kč.)*

🖼**FRANZ KAFKA MUSEUM.** This fantastic multimedia exhibit of Kafka memorabilia uses photographs and original letters to bring visitors back to 19th-century Prague, as experienced by the renowned author. *(Cihelná 2b. Metro A: Malostranská. Go down Klárov toward the river, turn right on U. Luzické Semináré and left on Cilhená.* ☎ *221 451 333; www.kafkamuseum.cz. Open daily 10am-6pm. 120Kč, students 60Kč.)*

CITY GALLERY PRAGUE. With seven locations throughout greater Prague, the City Gallery (Galerie Hlavního Města Prahy) offers a variety of permanent and rotating collections. The **House of the Golden Ring** has an especially massive permanent collection of 19th- and 20th-century Czech art. *(Týnská 6. Metro A: Staroměstská. Behind and to the left of Týn Church.* ☎ *222 327 677; www.citygalleryprague.cz. Open Tu-Su 10am-6pm. Museum 70Kč; top 3 fl. 60Kč, students 30Kč; 1st Tu of each month free.)*

MUSEUM OF ▨COMMUNISM. This gallery tries to expose the flaws of the Communist system that oppressed the Czech people from 1948 to 1989. Nowhere will you find more pitchforks or propaganda. *(Na Příkopě 10. Metro A: Můstek.* ☎ *224 212 966; www.museumofcommunism.com. Open daily 8am-9pm. 180Kč, students 140Kč.)*

🎵 ENTERTAINMENT

To find info on Prague's concerts and performances, consult *The Prague Post*, *Threshold*, *Do města-Downtown*, or *The Pill* (all free at many cafes and restaurants). Most performances start at 7pm and offer standby tickets 30min. before curtain. Between mid-May and early June, the **Prague Spring Festival** (May 7-15, 2008) draws musicians from around the world. June brings all things avant-garde with the **Prague Fringe Festival** (☎224 935 183; www.praguefringe.com), featuring dancers, comedians, performance artists, and—everyone's favorite—mimes. For tickets to the city's shows, try **Bohemia Ticket International,** Malé nám. 13, next to Čedok. (☎224 227 832; www.ticketsbti.cz. Open M-F 9am-5pm, Sa 9am-1pm.)

HIGH CULTURE, LOW BUDGET. Prague's state-run theaters often hold a group of seats in the higher balconies until the day of the performance before selling them at reduced prices. By visiting your venue of choice the morning of a performance, you can often score tickets for as little as 50Kč.

The majority of Prague's theaters close in July and August, but the selection is extensive during the rest of the year. The **National Theater** (Národní divadlo), Národní 2/4, stages ballet, drama, and opera. (☎224 901 487; www.narodni-divadlo.cz. Metro B: Národní třída. Box office open Sept.-June daily 10am-8pm and 45min. before performances. Tickets 30-1000Kč.) Every performance at the **Image Theatre,** Pařížská 4, is silent, conveying the message through dance, pantomime, and creative use of black light. (☎222 314 448; www.blacktheatreprague.cz. Performances daily 8pm. Box office open daily 9am-8pm.) The **Marionette Theater** (Říše loutek), Žatecká 1, stages a hilarious version of *Don Giovanni*, now in its 15th season. (☎224 819 322. Metro A: Staroměstská. Performances June-July M-Tu and Th-Su 8pm. Box office open daily 10am-8pm. 490-600Kč, students 390-590Kč.)

🎵 NIGHTLIFE

With some of the world's best beer on tap, it's no surprise that pubs and beer halls are Prague's most popular nighttime hangouts. Tourists overrun the city center, so authentic pub experiences are largely restricted to the suburbs and outlying Metro stops. Although clubs are everywhere, Prague isn't a prime dancing town—locals prefer the many jazz and rock hangouts scattered throughout the city.

BARS

Vinárna U Sudu, Vodičkova 10 (☎222 237 207). Metro A or B: Můstek. Cross Václavské nám. to Vodičkova and follow the curve left. A labyrinth of cavernous cellars. 1L red wine 125Kč. Open M-Th 8am-3am, F-Sa 8am-4am, Su 8am-2am. MC/V.

Vinárna Vinečko, Lodynská 135/2 (☎222 511 035). Metro A: Nám. Miru. Head west on Rumunská and turn left on Lodynská. A classy wine bar in the heart of the Vinohrady district brimming with thirsty locals and expats. 0.2L wine 26-34Kč, bottle 64-92Kč. Open M-F 11am-midnight, Sa-Su 2pm-midnight. MC/V.

Le Chateau, Jakubská 2 (☎222 316 328). From Metro B: nám. Republiky, walk through the Powder Tower to Celetná, then take a right on Templová. Seductive red walls and a youthful clientele keep this place overflowing onto the street until dawn. Open M-Th noon-3am, F noon-6am, Sa 4pm-6am, Su 4pm-2am.

Jo's Bar and Garáž, Malostranské nám. 7. Metro A: Malostranská. Foosball, darts, card games, and a dance floor downstairs and American bar food upstairs—burgers, burritos, nachos, and steaks (60-295Kč). Beer from 31Kč. Long Island iced tea 115Kč. Open M-Th 11am-8pm, Sa-Su 11am-2am. AmEx/MC/V.

CLUBS AND DISCOS

Radost FX, Bělehradská 120 (☎224 254 776; www.radostfx.cz). Metro C: IP Pavlova. Radost is the best of Prague nightlife, playing only the hippest music from internationally renowned DJs. The spacious, ventilated chill-out room is perfect for taking a break from the dance floor. Creative drinks (Frozen Sex with an Alien; 140Kč) will expand your clubbing horizons. Cover from 100Kč. Open M-Sa 10pm-5am.

Karlovy Lázně, Novotného lávka 1, next to the Charles Bridge. Popularly known as "Five Floors," this tourist magnet boasts 5 levels of sweaty, themed dance floors. Cover 120Kč, 50Kč before 10pm and after 4am. Open daily 9pm-5am.

Roxy, Dlouhá 33. Metro B: Nám. Republiky. Same building as the Travellers' Hostel (p. 232). Hip, youthful studio and club with experimental DJs and theme nights. Beer 35Kč. Cover Tu and Th-Sa 100-350Kč. Open daily 10pm-late.

Mecca, U Průhonu 3 (☎283 870 522; www.mecca.cz). Metro C: Nádraží Holešovice. The place for Prague's beautiful celebrities, Mecca offers a packed house, with industrial-chic decoration. House music and some techno. Live DJs nightly. Open 9pm-late.

U Malého Glena II, Karmelitská 23 (☎257 531 717; www.malyglen.cz), near Prague Castle. Basement bar with nightly live music including blues, jazz, and salsa. Call ahead for weekend tables. Beer 35Kč. Entrees 95-130Kč. Shows at 9:30pm, F-Sa 10pm-1:30am. Cover 100-150Kč. Open daily 8pm-2am. AmEx/MC/V.

GLBT NIGHTLIFE

All of the places below distribute *Amigo* (90Kč; www.amigo.cz), the most thorough English-language guide to gay life in the Czech Republic. Check www.praguegayguide.net or www.praguesaints.cz for a list of attractions and resources.

The Saints, Polská 32 (☎332 250 326; www.praguesaints.cz). Metro A: Jiřího z Poděbrad. This small, comfy club welcomes GLBT visitors and organizes the GLBT community. Foreign and local crowd. Free Wi-Fi. Beer from 22Kč. Open daily 7pm-4am.

Friends, Bartolomejská 11 (☎224 236 272; www.friends-prague.cz). Metro B: Národní třída. From the station, turn right, head down Na Perštýně, and take a left on Bartolomejská. Rotating schedule features music videos, parties, and theme nights. Women and straight customers welcome, but rare. Beer from 30Kč. Open daily 6pm-5am.

Valentino, Vinohradská ul. 40 (☎222 513 491; www.club-valentino.cz). Metro A or C: Muzeum. The Czech's largest gay club draws crowds to its 4 bars and 3 levels. House music dominates the packed and sweaty dance floors, although rotating DJs spice it up. Chill downstairs or at the outside tables. No cover. Open daily 11am-late.

▶ DAYTRIPS FROM PRAGUE

TEREZÍN (THERESIENSTADT). In 1941, when the Nazis opened a concentration camp at Terezín, their propaganda films touted the area as a resort. In reality, over 30,000 Jews died there, while another 85,000 were transported to camps farther east. The **Ghetto Museum,** left of the bus stop, places Terezín in the wider context of WWII. Across the river, the **Small Fortress** was used as a Gestapo prison. *(Bus from Prague's Florenc station to the Terezín LT stop. 1hr., 70Kč. Museum and barracks open daily Apr.-Oct. 9am-6pm; Nov.-Mar. 9am-5:30pm. Fortress open daily Apr.-Oct. 8am-6pm; Nov.-Mar. 8am-4:30pm. Tour included in admission price for groups larger than 10; reserve ahead. Museum, bar-*

racks, and fortress 180Kč, students 140Kč.) Outside the walls lie the incredibly moving **cemetery** and **crematorium**. Men should cover their heads before entering. *(Open Su-F Apr.-Sept. 10am-5pm; Nov.-Mar. 10am-4pm. Free.)* Since WWII, Terezín has been repopulated to about half its former size. Families live in the former barracks, and supermarkets occupy old Nazi offices. The **tourist office**, nám. ČSA 179, is near the bus stop. *(☎416 782 616; www.terezin.cz. Open M-Th 8am-5pm, F 8am-1:30pm, Su 9am-3pm.)*

ČESKÝ RÁJ NATIONAL PRESERVE. The sandstone pillars and gorges of **Prachovské skály** (Prachovské rocks) offer climbs and hikes with stunning views. Highlights include the **Pelíšek** rock pond and the ruins of the 14th-century **Pařez** castle. A network of **trails** cross the 588 acres of the park; green, blue, and yellow signs guide hikers to sights, while triangles indicate scenic vistas. Red signs mark the "Golden Trail," which connects Prachovské skály to **Hrubá Skála** (Rough Rock), a rock town surrounding a castle. From the castle, the trail leads up to the remains of **Valdštejnský Hrad** (Wallenstein Castle). The red and blue trails are open to cyclists, but only the blue trail is suited for biking. *(Buses run from Prague's Florenc station to Jičín. From there, buses go to Prachovské skály and other spots in Český Ráj. Buses can be unpredictable; you can walk along a 6km trail from Motel Rumcajs, Konwva 331, to the Preserve.)*

WEST AND SOUTH BOHEMIA

West Bohemia overflows with curative springs; over the centuries, emperors and intellectuals alike have soaked in the waters of Karlovy Vary (*Carlsbad* in German). Visitors seeking good beer head to the Pilsner Urquell brewery in Plzeň or the Budvar brewery in České Budějovice. Brooks, hills, and ruins mark rustic South Bohemia's landscape, making it a favorite among Czech cyclists and hikers.

KARLOVY VARY ☎ 353

The hot springs and enormous spas of Karlovy Vary (pop. 55,000) have drawn legendary Europeans including J.S. Bach, Sigmund Freud, Karl Marx, and Peter the Great. Today, the most frequent visitors are wealthy elderly Germans and Russians who sip from jugs filled with the therapeutic spring waters. Movie stars and fans also journey to the town for its International Film Festival each July.

THE LOCAL STORY

BONE-CHILLING CHAPEL

In and around Prague, you'll find churches made of stone, brick, iron, glass—and one of bones. Kutná Hora, a small, picturesque village 1hr. from Prague, is infamous for its ossuary, a chapel filled with artistic and religious creations made entirely from parts of human skeletons. The village earned its fame from silver mining in the 14th century. Its morbid side only came out when its graveyard gained a reputation as a sacred place to bury plague victims. Since the cemetery was overflowing with corpses, the Cistercian Order built a chapel to house the extra remains. In a fit of creativity (or possibly insanity), one monk began designing flowers from pelvises and crania. He never finished the ossuary, but the artist František Rint eventually completed the project in 1870, decorating the chapel from floor to ceiling with the bones of over 40,000 people.

Trains run from Hlavní nádraži in Prague to Kutná Hora (1½hr., 1 per hr., round-trip 196Kč). The ossuary is a 1km walk from the station. Turn right out of the station, then take a left, and go left again on the highway. Continue for 500m and go right at the church; the ossuary is at the end of the road. Open daily Apr.-Sept. 8am-6pm; Oct. 9am-noon and 1-5pm; Nov.-Mar. 9am-noon and 1-4pm. 40Kč, students 20Kč. Cameras 30Kč, video cameras 60Kč.

CZECH REPUBLIC

▐▐ TRANSPORTATION AND PRACTICAL INFORMATION. Buses, much more convenient than trains, run from Dolní nádraží, on Západní (☎504 516), to Plzeň (1¾hr., 10 per day, 92Kč) and Prague (2¼hr., 20 per day, 120Kč). To reach the town center from the station, turn left and take the left fork of the pedestrian underpass toward Lázně. Turn right at the next fork, follow the sign for the super-market, and go up the stairs to reach T.G. Masaryka, which runs parallel to the main thoroughfare, Dr. Davida Bechera. **Centrum Taxi,** Zeyerova 9 (☎223 236), offers 24hr. service. **Infocentrum,** Lázeňská 1, next to the Mill Colonnade, has free Internet, books rooms (from 450Kč), and sells theater tickets (250-500Kč) and maps. (☎224 097; www.karlovyvary.cz. Open Jan.-Oct. M-F 9am-7pm, Sa-Su 10am-6pm; Nov.-Dec. M-F 9am-5pm, Sa-Su 10am-5pm.) Another branch is in the bus station (☎232 838). The **post office,** T.G. Masaryka 1, has **Western Union** and **Poste Restante.** (Open M-F 7:30am-7pm, Sa 8am-1pm, Su 8am-noon.) **Postal Code:** 36001.

▐▐ ACCOMMODATIONS AND FOOD. When it comes to lodging, **Quest Hostel and Apartments ❷,** Moravská 42, is a winner, offering apartment-like rooms with spacious bathrooms and kitchens. Guests get a 10% discount at the bar. Take bus #2, go past the market, down a hill, and then continue straight ahead uphill on Moravská. (☎239 071; www.hostel-karlovy-vary.cz. Breakfast included. 4- to 6-bed dorms 450Kč; doubles 500Kč.) Next to the post office, **Pension Romania ❹,** Zahradní 49, has rooms overlooking the Teplá River. (☎222 822. Breakfast included. Singles 900Kč; students 715Kč; doubles 1480-1630Kč; triples 1900Kč. Oct.-Mar. reduced rates.) Karlovy Vary is known for its sweet *oplatky* (spa wafers; from 5Kč). In a town geared mainly to the old and the wealthy, **E&T Bar ❷,** Zeyerova 3, is a haven of quality Czech food at reasonable prices, with pleasant terrace seating. (☎226 022. Salads and entrees 60-210Kč. Open M-Sa 9am-2am, Su 10am-2am.) Travelers looking for variety can spice up their meal at **Mañana ❷,** Na Vyhlídce 52, next to the bus stop, a restaurant serving heaping plates of Mexican cuisine. (☎226 407. Salads and entrees 70-220Kč. Open daily 10am-10pm. MC/V.)

▐▐ SIGHTS AND ENTERTAINMENT. The **spa district,** with springs, baths, and colonnades, starts at **Alžbětiny Lázně 5** (Elizabeth Bath 5), Smetanovy Sady 1, across from the post office. The spa offers water-based treatments including thermal baths (355Kč), massages (360-600Kč), and lymph drainage (180Kč). Reserve a few days ahead. (☎222 536; www.spa5.cz. Pool and sauna open M-F 7:30am-6pm, Sa-Su 8:30am-6pm. Treatments M-F 7am-3pm. Pool 90Kč. MC/V.) Follow the Teplá River to **Bath 3,** Mlýnské nábř 5, which offers massages for 550Kč. (☎225 641. Treatments daily 7-11:30am and noon-3pm. Pool 100Kč.) Next door, the **Mlýnská kolonáda** (Mill Colonnade) hosts free concerts in the summer. Farther down is **Zawojski House,** Tržiště 9, an ornate Art Nouveau building that now houses Živnostenská Banka. Two doors down, **Vřídlo pramen** (Sprudel Spring), inside **Vřídelní kolonáda** (Sprudel Colonnade), is Karlovy Vary's hottest and highest-shooting spring, spouting 30L of water each second. (Open daily 6am-7pm.)

Follow Stará Louka to find signs for the funicular, which takes passengers up 127m to the **Diana Observatory** and its panoramic view of the city. (Funicular 4 per hr. June-Sept. 9am-7pm; Apr.-May and Oct. 9am-6pm; Feb.-Mar. and Nov.-Dec. 9am-4pm. Tower open daily 9am-7pm. Funicular 36Kč, round-trip 60Kč. Tower 10Kč.) *Promenáda,* a monthly booklet with schedules and other info, is available for free at kiosks around town. It includes details on the popular **International Film Festival,** which screens independent films usually in the first week of July. **Rotes Berlin,** Jaltská 7, off Dr. Davida Bechera, attracts Karlovy Vary's youth with cheap beer and live music. (Beer from 20Kč. Open M-F noon-midnight, Sa-Su 3pm-2am.)

DAYTRIP FROM KARLOVY VARY: PLZEŇ.

Recent attempts to clean up Plzeň (pop. 175,000) have left its buildings and gardens looking, well, clean. But it's the world-famous beer, not the architecture, which lures so many visitors. A beer-lover's perfect day begins at legendary **Pilsner Urquell Brewery** (Měšťanský Pivovar Plzeňský Prazdroj), where knowledgeable guides lead groups to the cellars for samples. The entrance to the complex is across the Radbuza River from Staré Město, where Pražská becomes Prazdroje u. Cross the street and take the overpass. (☎377 062 888. Brewery open daily 8am-4pm. 70min. tours daily June-Aug. 12:30 and 2pm; Sept.-May 12:30pm. Tours 140Kč, students 70Kč. Brewery tap open M-Th and Sa 11am-10pm, F 11am-11pm, Su 11am-9pm.) Plzeň is also home to the world's third-largest ◪**synagogue,** built in the Neoclassical style but with onion domes. Closed from 1973 to 1988, the synagogue is now a museum; the marble halls house photography exhibits. From the southern end of nám. Republiky, go down Prešovská to Sady Pětatřicátníků and turn left; the synagogue is on the right. (Open Su-F Apr.-Sept. 10am-6pm; Oct. 10am-5pm; Nov. 10am-4pm. 50Kč, students 30Kč.) Just when you think you've had enough of beer halls, ◪**U Salzmannů Restaurace ❸**, Pražská 8 (☎235 855), redeems their existence. Opened in 1637, the restaurant specializes in the old Czech standbys, though some are modified in new ways. The goulash (Plzeňsky Guláš; 129Kč) is sure to satiate even the most ravenous traveler. (Giant Pilsner Urquell 25Kč. Fries 24Kč. Open M-Th and Sa-Su 11am-11pm, F 11am-midnight. MC/V.) **Buses** leave from Husova 58 for Karlovy Vary (1¾hr., 16 per day, 70-80Kč) and Prague (2½hr., 16 per day, 65-80Kč). To reach nám. Republiky, turn left on Husova, which becomes Smetanovy Sady, and turn left on Bedřicha Smetany, or take tram #2 (12Kč). The **tourist office,** nám. Republiky 41, books rooms (from 190Kč) and sells phone cards (150-350Kč). (☎378 035 330; www.icpilsen.cz. Open Apr.-Sept. daily 9am-7pm; Oct.-Mar. M-F 10am-5pm, Sa-Su 10am-3:30pm.) **Postal Code:** 30101.

ČESKÉ BUDĚJOVICE   ☎38

České Budějovice (pop. 100,000), also known as Budweis, inspired the namesake pale American brew, which bears little resemblance to the thoroughly enjoyable, malty local Budvar. Animosity lingers between Anheuser-Busch and the **Budvar Brewery,** Karoliny Světlé 4. From the center, take bus #2 toward Borek, Točna. (Tours for groups of 8 or more by reservation M-F 9am-6pm, Sa 9am-5pm, Su 9am-4pm. 100Kč, students 50Kč.) **Staré Město** centers on the main square, **Náměstí Přemysla Otakara II,**

THE LOCAL STORY

BREW HA-HA

Tourists befuddled by visiting the Czech factory of the allegedly all-American Budweiser aren't alone in their confusion. In fact, they've stumbled upon one of the world's longest standing legal battles: who has the right to use the Budweiser name on their product.

The American version, first bottled under the name in 1876, reminded its brewer, Adolphus Busch, of the lagers from his German homeland; he therefore gave his beer a distinctly German name. While the Czech version received the name in 1895, the beer had been brewed in Budějovice since the 14th century. Initially, the identically titled beers did not compete with one another. But the increasing popularity of both products has led to heated court battles across the globe. The Czech version, banned in the United States by a 1939 agreement, has won out in much of the rest of the world. In Germany, Budweiser Budvar has rights to the name and Anheuser-Busch must sell its products under a different name. In the U.K., both companies have been permitted to hawk their products under the Budweiser name, leading to quite a bit of confusion. Needless to say, while in the Czech Republic, there is nary an American Budweiser in the land—and asking for it will not endear you to Czechs.

which is surrounded by colorful Renaissance and Baroque buildings. **Jihočeské Motocylově Museum,** Piaristická nám., houses the private antiques collection of a motorcycle fanatic. (40Kč, students 20Kč.) To reach **AT Penzion ❸,** Dukelská 15, from Nám. Otakara II, turn right on Dr. Stejskala. At the first intersection, turn left and follow Široká, veering right on Dukelská; AT Penzion is on the left. The rooms have private bath, TV, and fridge. (☎731 2529. Breakfast 50Kč. Reception 24hr. Singles 500Kč; doubles 800Kč.) At **Restaurace Kněžská ❷,** Kněžsk 1, locals chat at plain tables. The "Jagersteak" (sirloin, cream, and mushrooms; 249Kč) is a worthy splurge. (☎635 8829. Entrees 25-249Kč. Open M-Th 10am-11pm, F 10am-midnight, Sa 11am-midnight. Cash only.) **Trains** (☎785 4490) leave from Nádražní 12 for: Brno (4½hr., 5 per day, 274Kč); Český Krumlov (50min., 9 per day, 46Kč); Plzeň (2hr., 9 per day, 162Kč); Prague (2½hr., 13 per day, 204Kč). **Buses** (☎635 4444) run to Brno (4½hr., 6 per day, 220Kč), Český Krumlov (50min., 22 per day, 28Kč), and Prague (2½hr., 10 per day, 120-144Kč). To reach the town center from the train station, turn right on Nádražní, take a left at the first crosswalk, and follow Lannova třída, which becomes Kanovnická. The **tourist office** is at nám. Otakara II 2. (☎680 1413; www.c-budejovice.cz. Open M-F 8:30am-6pm, Sa 8:30am-5pm, Su 10am-noon and 12:30-4pm.) **Postal Code:** 37001.

ČESKÝ KRUMLOV   ☎ 38

This once-hidden gem of the Czech Republic has been discovered—some might say besieged—by tourists escaping Prague's overcrowded attractions. Yet Český Krumlov won't disappoint. The majestic **Zamek** (Castle) has been home to a succession of Bohemian and Bavarian nobles since the 1200s. Follow Radniční across the river to the entrance on Latrán. Climb the 162 steps of the tower for a fabulous view. (☎380 704 721. Castle open Tu-Su June-Aug. 9am-noon and 1-6pm; Apr.-May and Sept.-Oct. 9am-noon and 1-5pm. Last tour 1hr. before closing. Tower open daily June-Aug. 9am-5:30pm; Apr.-May and Sept.-Oct. 9am-4:30pm. Castle tour 160Kč, students 80Kč. Tower 35Kč.) The castle gardens host the popular **Revolving South Bohemia Theater,** where operas and plays are performed in summer. (Gardens open daily May-Sept. 8am-7pm; Apr. and Oct. 8am-5pm. Free. Shows begin 8:30-9:30pm. Tickets 200-900Kč; available at the tourist office. Reserve ahead.)

The laid-back ◪**Krumlov House ❶,** Rooseveltova 68, is run by an American expat couple. To get there from the bus station, walk out of the square on Horní. Turn left on Rooseveltova after the lights, then follow the signs. (☎071 1935; www.krumlovhostel.com. Apr.-Oct. 14 dorms 300Kč; doubles 375Kč; with bath 400Kč; suites 450Kč. Oct. 15-Mar. dorms 250Kč; doubles 300Kč; with bath 350Kč; suites 400Kč.) ◪**Hostel 99 ❷,** Věžní 99, has a free keg every Wednesday night, endearing itself to the rowdy, fun-loving crowd. From nám. Svornosti, take Radniční, which becomes Latrán; turn right on Věžní at the red-and-yellow gate. (☎071 2812; www.hostel99.com. Dorms 300-390Kč; doubles 700Kč.) Tiny **Hostel Merlin ❶,** Kájovská 59, on the right before the bridge, has cheerful yellow rooms. (☎606 256 145; www.hostelmerlin.com. Free Internet. Reception 11am-8pm. One bed in shared double 250Kč; doubles 500Kč, with bath 660Kč.) Just off Radniční, ◪**Laibon ❶,** Parkán 105, serves excellent vegetarian cuisine and has a nice terrace. (Entrees 30-150Kč. Open daily 11am-11pm. Cash only.) **Egon Schiele** (1890-1918) lived in Český Krumlov until residents ran him out for painting the burghers' daughters in the nude. The ◪**Egon Schiele Art Center,** Široká 70-72, displays Schiele's works alongside those of other 20th-century Baltic artists. (☎070 4011; www.schieleartcentrum.cz. Open daily 10am-6pm. 180Kč, students 145Kč.) The busy nighttime spot **Cikánská Jizba** (Gypsy Bar), Dlouhá 31, offers Roma cuisine (80-180Kč), cheap beer (18Kč), and live music. (☎071 7585. Open daily 3-11pm.)

Most hostels provide free **inner tubes** so guests can ride down the Vltava River and admire the castle. **VLTAVA**, Kájovská 62, rents equipment or provides package trips for **rafting** down the river, and rents **bikes** as well. (☎071 1978; www.ckvltava.cz. Bike rental 320Kč per day. Open daily 9am-5pm.) Go horseback riding at **Jezdecký klub Slupenec**, Slupenec 1. Follow Horní to the highway, take the second left on Křížová, and follow the red trail to Slupenec. (☎071 1052; www.jk-slupenec.cz. Open Tu-Su 9am-6pm. 250Kč per hr.) **Trains** run from Nádrazní 31 (☎755 1111), 2km uphill from the center, to **České Budějovice** (1hr., 8 per day, 46Kč) and **Prague** (2½hr., 5 per day, 224Kč). A bus runs from the station to the center of town (5Kč). To get to the main square, **Náměstí Svornosti**, take the path behind the terminal to the right of stops #20-25. Go downhill at Kaplická, cross the highway, and head to Horní, to the square. The **tourist office**, Nám. Svornosti 2, books rooms and provides info for visitors. (☎071 1183; www.ckrumlov.cz/infocentrum. Open Apr.-Oct. M-Sa 9am-1pm and 2-7pm.) **Postal Code:** 38101.

MORAVIA

The valleys and peaks of Moravia make up the easternmost third of the Czech Republic. Home to the country's two leading universities, the region is the birthplace of Tomáš G. Masaryk, first president of the former Czechoslovakia, psychoanalyst Sigmund Freud, and geneticist Johann Gregor Mendel. In addition to producing famous names, Moravia is renowned for producing the nation's finest wines and the Moravian Spice Cookie, the world's thinnest dessert.

BRNO

The two thin spires of St. Peter's Cathedral dominate the skyline of Brno (pop. 388,000), the second largest city in the Czech Republic and an international marketplace since the 13th century. Today, global corporations compete with family-owned produce stands, and ancient churches soften the glare of casinos and clubs.

▐▜ TRANSPORTATION AND PRACTICAL INFORMATION. Trains (☎542 214 803) go to: Prague (3-4hr., 22 per day, 355Kč); Bratislava, SLK (2hr., 12 per day, 200Kč); Budapest, HUN (4hr., 5 per day, 970Kč); Vienna, AUT (1½hr., 5 per day, 540Kč). **Buses** (☎543 217 733) leave from the corner of Zvonařka and Plotní for Prague (2½hr., 36 per day, 140Kč) and Vienna, AUT (2½hr., 2 per day, 200Kč). Student Agency buses (☎542 4242) run to Prague (40 per day, 100-145Kč) from down the road from the train station. From the station, cross the tram tracks, walk left, then head right on Masarykova to reach **Náměstí Svobody** (Freedom Square), the center of the city. The **tourist office**, Radnická 8, is inside the town hall. From Nám. Svobody, take Masarykova and turn right on Průchodní. (☎542 211 090; www.ticbrno.cz. Open M-F 8:30am-6pm, Sa-Su 9am-5:30pm.) **Postal Code:** 60100.

▐▐ ACCOMMODATIONS AND FOOD. From the train station, cross the tram tracks, turn right, then take a left up the stairs. At the top, turn right and follow Novobranská to the centrally located ◪**Hotel Astorka ❸**, Novobranská 3. (☎542 592 111. Open July-Sept. Singles 580Kč; doubles 1160Kč; triples 1740Kč. 50% student discount. AmEx/MC/V.) **Travellers' Hostel ❶**, Jánská 22, sets up rock-hard dorm beds in the sterile classrooms of a secondary school in summer. Follow the directions to Hotel Astorka, continue down Novobranská, and bear left on Jánská. (☎542 213 573. Breakfast 15Kč. Beer 15Kč. Free Internet. Dorms 290Kč. MC/V.) From Masarykova, turn left and walk down Orlí to reach the all-organic vegetarian buffet at ⬛Rebio ❶, Orlí 26. (☎542 211 130. Entrees 19Kč per 100g. Open M-F 8am-7pm, Sa 10am-3pm. Cash only.) A suit of armor guards the door and the kitchen prepares meat-heavy Czech feasts at **Dávně Časy** ❸, Starobrněnská 20, off Zelný trh. (Entrees 70-400Kč. Open daily 11am-11pm. AmEx/V.)

◨⬛ **SIGHTS AND NIGHTLIFE.** ⬛**Špilberk Castle** (Hrad Špilberk) earned a reputation as the cruelest prison in Habsburg Europe. Today the castle is a museum, and its former solitary cells house Baroque art. From Nám. Svobody, take Zámečnická and go right on Panenská; after Husova, head uphill. (www.spilberk.cz. Open July-Aug. daily 9am-6pm; May-June and Sept. Tu-Su 9am-6pm; Apr. and Oct. Tu-Su 9am-5pm; Nov.-Mar. W-Su 10am-5pm. 100Kč, students 50Kč.) Standing atop the city's skyline, the **Peter and Paul Cathedral** was allegedly saved from the Swedish siege of 1645 by the clever townspeople. The attacking general promised to retreat if his army didn't capture the city by noon; when the townsfolk learned of his claim, they struck the noon bells one hour early and the Swedes slunk away. The bells have been striking noon at 11am ever since. (On Petrov Hill. Climb Petrska from Zelný trh. Cathedral open M-Sa 8:15am-6:15pm. Su 7am-6pm. Chapel, tower, and crypt open M-Sa 11am-6pm, Su 1-6pm. Cathedral and chapel free. Tower 25Kč, students 20Kč. Crypt 25/10Kč.) Down Masarykova on the left is the **Capuchin Monastery Crypt** (Hrobka Kapucínského kláštera), where 18th-century monks developed a burial technique to allow bodies to dry naturally. One hundred bodies attest to its effectiveness. (Open June-Aug. daily 9am-5pm; Sept.-Oct. M-F 9am-5pm, Sa-Su 9am-4pm; Apr.-May Tu-Su 9am-4pm. 40Kč, students 20Kč.) The **Mendelianum,** Mendlovo nám. 1A, documents the life and work of Johann Gregor Mendel, who discovered inherited genotypes while raising peas in a Brno monastery, founding the study of genetics. (Open May-Oct. daily 10am-6pm; Nov.-Apr. W-Su 10am-6pm. 80Kč, students 40Kč.) In summer, posters announce upcoming **raves.** After performances in the attached **Merry Goose Theater,** artsy crowds gather at **Divadelní hospoda Veselá husa,** Zelný trh. 9. (Open M-F 11am-1am, Sa-Su 3pm-1am.) **Klub Flëda,** Štefánikova 24, hosts concerts and live DJs. Take tram #26 up Štefánikova to Hrncirska; Flëda is on the right. (www.fleda.cz. Open daily 2pm-midnight.) The free guide *Metropolis* lists upcoming events.

OLOMOUC   ☎585

Formerly the capital of Moravia, the inviting university town of Olomouc (pop. 103,000) resembles Prague as it was before the city was totally overwhelmed by tourists. Baroque architecture lines the paths in the town center, locals stroll outdoors during the day, and students keep the clubs thumping until dawn. Every May, the town plays host to the second-largest Oktoberfest celebration in Europe. The 1378 **radnice** (town hall) and its clock tower dominate the town center. The tourist office arranges trips up the tower (daily 11am and 3pm; 15Kč). An amusing **astronomical clock** is set in the town hall's north side. In 1955, Communist clockmakers replaced the attractive mechanical saints with archetypes of "the people." Today, the masses still strike noon with their ⬛**hammers and sickles.** The 35m black-and-gold **Trinity Column** (Sloup Nejsvětější Trojice), the dolphin-shaped **Arion Fountain,** and the 750-year-old **St. Wenceslas Cathedral** (Metropolitní Kostel sv. Václava) surround the square. (Cahtedral open Tu and Th-Sa 9am-5pm, W 9am-4pm, Su 11am-5pm. Donations requested.)

The small ▓**Poet's Corner Hostel ❶**, Sokolská 1, feels more like home than a hostel, with owners who cheerfully offer guidance on the town's attractions. Eclectic decoration and comfy beds make it hard to leave. From the train station, take tram #4, 5, 6, or 7 to Nám. Hridinů and walk north toward the Red Dome. Turn right on Sokolská; the hostel is on the 4th floor through the door on the left. (☎ 777 570 730; www.hostelolomouc.com. Laundry 100Kč. 7-bed dorms July-Aug. 300Kč; doubles 800Kč; triples 1100Kč.) ▓**Hanácká Hospoda ❶**, Dolní nám. 38, is packed with locals devouring excellent Czech fare. (☎ 777 721 171. Entrees 45-199Kč. Open daily 10am-midnight. AmEx/MC/V.) Kick back with a bottle of the cheapest beer in Old Town at **Vertigo**, Universitni 6, Olomouc's most popular student club. (Beer from 15Kč. Open daily 5pm-2am.) Those seeking a drunken workout should head to **9A Bar and Boulder**, Premyscorcu 9A, which tempts its lively patrons to scale its very own rock climbing wall in the back. It's probably better to stop earlier in the night before those *pivos* affect your coordination. (Open M-F 3pm-late; Sa-Su 5pm-late.) **Trains** (☎ 584 722 175) leave from Jeremenkova 23 for Brno (1½hr., 5 per day, 120Kč) and Prague (3½hr., 19 per day, 294Kč). **Buses** (☎ 585 313 917) leave from Rolsberská 66 for Brno (1½hr., 10 per day, 75-85Kč) and Prague (4½hr., 4 per day, 240-275Kč). From the stations, take the pedestrian path under Jeremenkova, then tram #4 or 5 to the center. The **tourist office**, Horní nám., in the town hall, gives out maps and books rooms. (☎ 685 513 385; www.olomoucko.cz. Open daily Mar.-Nov. 9am-7pm; Dec.-Feb. 9am-5pm.) **Internet u Dominika**, Slovenská 12, has many terminals. (☎ 777 181 857. 60Kč per hr. Open M-F 9am-9pm, Sa-Su 10am-9pm.) **Postal Code:** 77127.

DENMARK (DANMARK)

Straddling the border between Scandinavia and continental Europe, Denmark packs majestic castles, pristine beaches, and thriving nightlife onto the compact Jutland peninsula and its network of islands. Vibrant Copenhagen boasts the busy pedestrian thoroughfare of Strøget and the world's tallest carousel in Tivoli Gardens, while beyond the city, fairytale lovers can tour Hans Christian Andersen's home in rural Odense. In spite of the nation's historically homogenous population, its Viking past has given way to a dynamic multicultural society that draws in visitors as it turns out Legos and Skagen watches.

 DISCOVER DENMARK: SUGGESTED ITINERARIES

3 DAYS. Start off in the capital of **Copenhagen** (p. 253), soaking up some sun on a **bike tour** (p. 258) of the city or waiting out showers in the medieval ruins beneath **Christianborg Slot.** Channel the Bard at Kronborg Slot in **Helsingør** (p. 262), where the real-life Hamlet slept.

BEST OF DENMARK, 12 DAYS. Begin your journey in **Copenhagen** (3 days), then castle-hop to Frederiksborg Slot in nearby **Hillerød** (1 day; p. 262). The best way to explore the beautiful beaches, farm-lands, and forests of **Bornholm** (2 days; p. 264) is to bike around the island. After returning to the mainland, head west to **Odense** (1 day; p. 265) for celebrations of Hans Christian Andersen's birth. Discover the museums and nightlife of little-known **Århus** (2 days; p. 267) before indulging your inner child at Legoland in **Billund** (1 day; p. 268). Finish your journey at the northern tip of Jutland, where the yellow houses of **Skagen** (2 days; p. 270) look out on the Baltic Sea.

ESSENTIALS

FACTS AND FIGURES

Official Name: Kingdom of Denmark.

Capital: Copenhagen.

Major Cities: Aalborg, Århus, Odense.

Population: 5,468,000.

Land Area: 42,400 sq. km.

Time Zone: GMT +1.

Languages: Danish. Pockets of Faroese, Greenlandic, and German. English is nearly universal as a second language.

Tallest Lego Tower: Constructed in 2003 at Billund's Legoland (p. 268); 27.22m.

WHEN TO GO

Denmark is best between May and September, when days are usually sunny and temperatures average 10-16°C (50-61°F). Winter temperatures average 0°C (32°F). Although temperate for its northern location, Denmark can turn rainy or cool at a moment's notice; pack a sweater and an umbrella, even in summer.

DOCUMENTS AND FORMALITIES

EMBASSIES AND CONSULATES. All foreign embassies are in Copenhagen (p. 255). Danish embassies abroad include: **Australia,** Gold Fields House, Level 14, 1 Alfred St., Circular Quay, Sydney, NSW, 2000 (☎02 92 47 22 24; www.gksydney.um.dk/en); **Canada,** 47 Clarence St., Ste. 450, Ottawa, ON, K1N 9K1 (☎613-562-

1811; www.ambottawa.um.dk/en); **Ireland,** Harcourt Road, 7th floor, Block E, Iveagh Court, Dublin 2 (☎01 475 6404; www.ambdublin.um.dk/en); **New Zealand,** Forsyth Barr House, Level 7, 45 Johnston Street, P.O. Box 10-874, Wellington, 6036 (☎04 471 0520; www.danishconsulatesnz.org.nz); **UK,** 55 Sloane St., London, SW1X 9SR (☎020 73 33 02 00; www.amblondon.um.dk/en); **US,** 3200 Whitehaven St., NW, Washington, D.C., 20008 (☎202-234-4300; www.denmarkemb.org).

VISA AND ENTRY INFORMATION. EU citizens do not need a visa. Citizens of Australia, Canada, New Zealand, and the US do not need a visa for stays of up to 90 days, beginning upon entry into any of the countries in the EU's freedom-of-movement zone. For more info, see p. 14. For stays longer than 90 days, non-EU citizens need a residence and/or work permit. More info is available at www.um.dk/en.

TOURIST SERVICES AND MONEY

EMERGENCY	Ambulance, Fire, and Police: ☎112.

TOURIST OFFICES. The Danish Tourist Board has offices in most cities throughout the country, with its main office in Copenhagen at Islands Brygge 43 (☎3288 9900; www.visitdenmark.dt.dk). The website offers a wealth of info as well as an online booking tool for accommodations.

MONEY. The Danish unit of currency is the **krone (kr)**, plural **kroner**. One krone is equal to 100 **øre**. The easiest way to get cash is from ATMs; cash cards are widely accepted, and many machines give advances on credit cards. Money and traveler's checks can be exchanged at most banks for a fee of 30kr. Denmark has a high cost of living, which it passes along to visitors; expect to pay 100-150kr for a hostel bed, 450-800kr for a hotel room, 80-130kr for a day's groceries, and 50-90kr for a cheap restaurant meal. A bare-bones day might cost 250-350kr, and a slightly more comfortable one 400-600kr. There are no hard and fast rules for tipping. In general, service at restaurants is included in the bill, but it's always polite to round up to the nearest 10kr, and to leave an additional 10-20kr for good service.

Denmark has a 25% **value added tax** (VAT), a sales tax applied to most goods and services. The prices given in *Let's Go* include VAT. In the airport upon exiting the EU, non-EU citizens can claim a refund on the tax paid for goods purchased at participating stores. In order to qualify for a refund in a store, you must spend at least 300kr; make sure to ask for a refund form when you pay. For more info on qualifying for a VAT refund, see p. 19.

KRONER (KR)		
AUS$1 = 4.41KR	10KR = AUS$2.27	
CDN$1 = 5.22KR	10KR = CDN$1.92	
EUR€1 = 7.44KR	10KR = EUR€1.34	
NZ$1 = 3.83KR	10KR = NZ$2.61	
UK£1 = 10.93KR	10KR = UK£0.91	
US$1 = 5.52KR	10KR = US$1.81	

BUSINESS HOURS. Shops are normally open Monday to Thursday from about 9 or 10am to 6pm and Friday until 7 or 8pm; they are always open Saturday mornings and in Copenhagen, they stay open all day Saturday. Regular banking hours are Monday to Wednesday and Friday 10am-4pm, Thursday 10am-6pm.

TRANSPORTATION

BY PLANE. International flights arrive at **Kastrup Airport** in Copenhagen (**CPH**; ☎3231 3231; www.cph.dk). Flights from Europe also arrive at **Billund Airport**, outside Århus (**BLL**; ☎7650 5050; www.billund-airport.dk). Smaller airports in Århus and Esbjerg serve as hubs for budget airline **Ryanair** (☎353 12 49 77 91; www.ryanair.com). **SAS** (**Scandinavian Airlines**; Denmark ☎70 10 20 00, UK 0870 60 72 77 27, US 800-221-2350; www.scandinavian.net), the national airline company, offers youth discounts to some destinations.

BY TRAIN AND BY BUS. The state-run rail line in Denmark is **DSB**; their helpful route planner is online at www.rejseplanen.dk. **Eurail** is valid on all state-run routes. The **Scanrail pass** (p. 47) is good for rail travel through Denmark, Finland, Norway, and Sweden, as well as many discounted ferry and bus rides. Remote towns are typically served by buses from the nearest train station. **Buses** are reliable and can be less expensive than trains.

RAIL SAVINGS. Scanrail passes purchased outside Scandinavia may be cheaper, depending on the exchange rate, and they are also more flexible. Travelers who purchase passes within Scandinavia can only use three travel days in the country of purchase. Check www.scanrail.com for more info.

BY FERRY. Several companies operate ferries to and from Denmark. **Scandlines** (☎33 15 15 15; www.scandlines.dk) arrives from Germany and Sweden and also operates many domestic routes. **Color Line** (Norway ☎47 81 00 08 11; www.color-line.com) runs ferries between Denmark and Norway. **DFDS Seaways** (UK ☎08715 229 955; www.dfdsseaways.co.uk) sails from Harwich, BRI to Esbjerg and from Copenhagen to Oslo, NOR. For more info, check www.aferry.to/ferry-to-denmark-ferries.htm. Tourist offices help sort out the dozens of smaller ferries that serve Denmark's outlying islands. For more info on connections from Bornholm to Sweden, see p. 264; for connections from Jutland to Norway and Sweden, see p. 269.

BY CAR. Denmark's only toll roads are the **Storebæltsbro** (Great Belt Bridge; 205kr) and the **Øresund bridge** (245kr). Speed limits are 50kph (30mph) in urban areas, 80kph (50mph) on highways, and 110-130kph (65-80mph) on motorways. **Gas** averages 9-11kr per liter. Watch out for bikes, which have the right-of-way. High parking prices and numerous one-way streets make driving something of a nightmare in cities. For more info on driving, contact the **Forenede Danske Motorejere,** Firskovvej 32, Box 500, 2800 Kgs. Lyngby (☎70 13 30 40; www.fdm.dk).

BY BIKE AND BY THUMB. With its flat terrain and well-marked bike routes, Denmark is a cyclist's dream. You can rent bikes (50-80kr per day) from designated shops as well as some tourist offices and train stations. The **Dansk Cyklist Forbund** (☎3332 3121; www.dcf.dk) provides info about cycling in Denmark and investing in long-term rentals. Pick up *Bikes and Trains* at any train station for info on bringing your bike on a train, which can cost up to 50kr. **Hitchhiking** on motorways is illegal and uncommon. Let's Go does not recommend hitchhiking.

KEEPING IN TOUCH

PHONE CODES	**Country code: 45. International dialing prefix:** 00. For more info on how to place international calls, see **Inside Back Cover.**

EMAIL AND THE INTERNET. In Copenhagen and other cities, you can generally find at least one Internet cafe; expect to pay 20-40kr per hr. DSB, the national railroad, maintains Internet cafes in some stations as well. In smaller towns, access at public libraries is free, although you typically have to reserve a slot in advance.

TELEPHONE. Pay phones accept both coins and phone cards, available at post offices or kiosks in 100kr denominations. Mobile phones (p. 29) are a popular and economical alternative. For domestic directory info, dial ☎118; for international info, dial ☎113. International direct dial numbers include: **AT&T Direct** (☎8001 0010); **Canada Direct** (☎8001 0011); **MCI WorldPhone** (☎8001 0022); **Sprint** (☎8001 0877); **Telecom New Zealand** (☎8001 0064); **Telstra Australia** (☎8001 0061).

MAIL. Mailing a postcard or letter to Australia, Canada, New Zealand, or the US costs 8kr; to elsewhere in Europe costs 7kr. Domestic mail costs 4.50kr.

ACCOMMODATIONS AND CAMPING

DENMARK	❶	❷	❸	❹	❺
ACCOMMODATIONS	under 100kr	100-160kr	161-220kr	221-350kr	over 350kr

Denmark's hotels are uniformly expensive, so **youth hostels** *(vandrehjem)* tend to be mobbed by budget travelers of all ages. HI-affiliated **Danhostels** are the most common, and are often the only option in smaller towns. Facilities are clean, spacious, and comfortable, often attracting families as well as backpackers. Eco-conscious tourists can choose from one of the six Danhostels that have earned a **Green Key** (www.green-key.org) for their environmentally friendly practices. Room rates vary according to season and location; dorms range from 100 to 200kr per night, with a 35kr HI discount. Linens cost 40-60kr; sleeping bags are not permitted. Reserve ahead, especially in summer and near beaches. Danhostel check-in times are usually a non-negotiable 3-4hr. window. For more info, contact the Danish Youth Hostel Association (☎3331 3612; www.danhostel.dk). **Independent hostels,** found mostly in cities and larger towns, draw a younger crowd and tend to be more sociable, although their facilities are rarely as nice as those in Danhostels. Most tourist offices book rooms in private homes (150-250kr).

Denmark's 496 **campgrounds** (about 60kr per person) range from one star (toilets and drinking water) to three stars (showers and laundry) to five stars (swimming, restaurants, and stoves). Info is available at **DK-Camp** (☎7571 2962; www.dk-camp.dk). You'll need a **Camping Card Scandinavia** (125kr for 1yr. membership; available at www.camping.se; allow at least 3 weeks for delivery), valid across Scandinavia and sold at campgrounds as well as through the Danish Youth Hostel Association. Campsites affiliated with hostels generally do not require a card. If you plan to camp for only a night, you can buy a 24hr. pass (20kr). The **Danish Camping Council** *(Campingradet)*, Mosedalvej 15, 2500 Valby (☎39 27 88 44; www.campingraadet.dk) sells passes and the *Camping Denmark* handbook (95kr). Sleeping in train stations, in parks, or on public property is illegal.

FOOD AND DRINK

DENMARK	❶	❷	❸	❹	❺
FOOD	under 40kr	40-70kr	71-100kr	101-150kr	over 150kr

A "danish" in Denmark is a *wienerbrød* (Viennese bread), found in bakeries along-side other flaky treats. Traditionally, Danes have favored open-faced sandwiches called *smørrebrød* for a more substantial meal, although today these delicacies are rarely found in restaurants. Herring is served in various forms, usually pickled or raw with onions or curry mayonnaise. For cheap eats, look for lunch specials *(dagens ret)* and all-you-can-eat buffets. National beers include Carlsberg and Tuborg; bottled brews tend to be cheaper than drafts. A popular alcohol is *snaps* (or *aquavit*), a clear liquor flavored with fiery spices, usually served chilled and unmixed. Many vegetarian *(vegetarret)* options are the result of Indian and Mediterranean influences, and salads and veggies *(grønsager)* can be found on most menus. Expect to pay around 120kr for a sit-down meal at a restaurant, while cheaper eats can be found in cafes and ethnic takeaways for 40-80kr.

HOLIDAYS AND FESTIVALS

Holidays: New Year's Day (Jan. 1); Easter (Mar. 23); Queen's Birthday (Apr. 16); Worker's Day (May 1); Whit Sunday and Monday (May 11-12); Constitution Day (June 5); Midsummer's Eve (June 23); Christmas (Dec. 24-26).

Festivals: In February before the start of Lent, Danish children assault candy-filled barrels with birch branches on *Fastelavn* (Shrovetide), while adults take to the streets for carnivals. Guitar solos ring out over Roskilde during the Roskilde Festival (July 3-6), just before Copenhagen and Århus kick off their annual jazz festivals in mid- to late July.

BEYOND TOURISM

For short-term employment in Denmark, check www.jobs-in-europe.net. See **Beyond Tourism,** p. 56, for opportunities throughout Europe.

The American-Scandinavian Foundation (AMSCAN), 58 Park Ave., New York, NY, 10016, USA (☎212-879-9779; www.amscan.org/jobs/index.html). Volunteer and job opportunities throughout Scandinavia. Limited number of fellowships for study in Denmark available to Americans.

Vi Hjælper Hinanden (VHH), Aasenv. 35, 9881 Bindslev, DEN, c/o Inga Nielsen (☎98 93 86 07; www.wwoof.dk). For 50kr, the Danish branch of World-Wide Opportunities on Organic Farms (WWOOF) provides a list of farmers currently accepting volunteers.

COPENHAGEN (KØBENHAVN)   ☎33, 35

The center of Europe's oldest monarchy, Copenhagen (pop. 1,800,000) embodies a laid-back spirit. The Strøget, the city's famed pedestrian thoroughfare, now bustles with Middle Eastern restaurants and cybercafes, and neon signs glimmer next to angels in the architecture. The up-and-coming districts of Vesterbro and Nørrebro reverberate with some of Europe's wildest nightlife, while the hippie paradise of Christiania swings to a more downbeat vibe.

⌐ TRANSPORTATION

Flights: Kastrup Airport (CPH; ☎3231 3231; www.cph.dk). **Trains** connect the airport to København H (13min., 6 per hr., 29kr or 2 clips). Ryanair flies into nearby **Sturup Airport** in Malmö, SWE **(MMX;** ☎40 613 1000; www.sturup.com) at low rates.

Trains: København H (Hovedbanegården or Central Station; domestic travel ☎7013 1415, international 7013 1416; www.dsb.dk). Trains run to: **Berlin, GER** (8hr., 9 per day, 803kr); **Hamburg, GER** (5hr., 5 per day, 537kr); **Malmö, SWE** (25min., every 20min., 71kr); **Oslo, NOR** (8hr., 2 per day, 821kr); **Stockholm, SWE** (5hr., 1 per 1-2hr., 1040kr). For international trips, fares depend on seat availability and can drop to as low as 50% of the quotes listed above; ▒ **book at least 2 weeks in advance.**

Public Transportation: Copenhagen has an extensive public transportation system. **Buses** (☎3613 1415; www.hur.dk) run daily 5:30am-12:30am; maps are available on any bus. **S-togs** (subways and suburban trains; ☎3314 1701) run M-Sa 5am-12:30am, Su 6am-12:30am. The **metro** (☎7015 1615; www.m.dk) is small but efficient. All 3 types of public transportation operate on a zone system. To travel any distance, a 2-zone **ticket** is required (19kr; additional zones 9.50kr), which covers most of Copenhagen. For extended stays, the best deal is the **rabatkort** (rebate card; 120kr), available from supermarkets, corner stores, and kiosks, which offers 10 2-zone tickets at a discount. The **24hr. pass** (120kr), available at train stations, grants unlimited bus and train transport in the Northern Zealand region, as does the **Copenhagen Card** (see **Orientation and Practical Information,** p. 255). **Night buses,** marked with an "N," run 12:30-5:30am on limited routes and charge double fare; they accept the 24hr. pass.

 TAKE A RIDE. Tickets on the S-togs are covered by Eurail, ScanRail, and Inter Rail passes. So ride away!

Taxis: Københavns Taxa (☎3535 3535) and **Hovedstadens Taxi** (☎3877 7777) charge a base fare of 35kr for arranged pickups and 23kr otherwise, plus 10kr per km during the day and 13kr at night. From København H to Kastrup Airport costs around 200kr.

Bike Rental: City Bike (www.bycyklen.dk/engelsk) lends bikes mid-Apr. to Nov. from 110 racks all over the city for a 20kr deposit. Anyone can return your bike and claim your deposit, so keep an eye on it. **Københavns Cyklebørs,** Gothersg. 157 (☎3314 0717; www.cykelborsen.dk) rents bikes for 60kr per day, 270kr per week; 200kr deposit. Open M-F 8:30am-5:30pm, Sa 10am-1:30pm. MC/V.

DENMARK

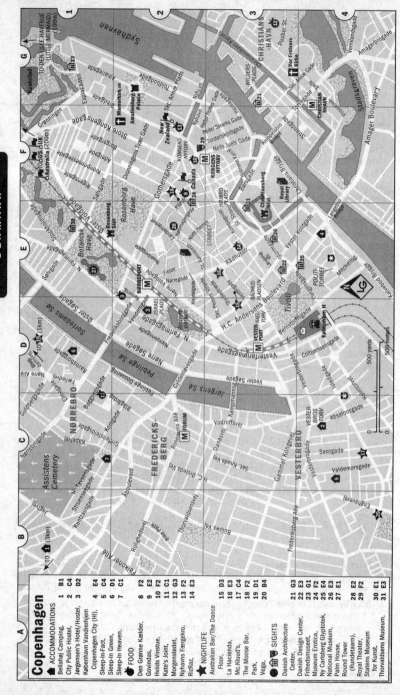

Copenhagen

▲ ACCOMMODATIONS

Bellahøj Camping,	1 B1
City Public Hostel,	2 C4
Jørgensen's Hotel/Hostel,	3 D2
København Vandrerhjem	
Copenhagen City (HI),	4 E4
Sleep-In-Fact,	5 C4
Sleep-In Green,	6 D1
Sleep-In Heaven,	7 C1

● FOOD

Den Grønne Kælder,	8 F2
Govindas,	9 E2
Hvids Vinstue,	10 F2
Kate's Joint,	11 C1
Morgenstedet,	12 G3
Nyhavns Færgekro,	13 F2
RizRaz,	14 E3

★ NIGHTLIFE

Australian Bar/The Dance	
Floor,	15 D3
La Hacienda,	16 E3
Mc.Kluud's,	17 C4
The Moose Bar,	18 F2
Park,	19 D1
Vega,	20 B4

● ▥ SIGHTS

Danish Architecture	
Center,	21 G3
Danish Design Center,	22 E3
Frihedsmuseet,	23 G1
Museum Erotica,	24 F2
Ny Carlsberg Glyptotek,	25 E4
National Museum,	26 E3
Palm House,	27 E1
Round Tower	
(Rundetaarn),	28 E2
Royal Theater,	29 F2
Statens Museum	
for Kunst,	30 E1
Thorvaldsens Museum,	31 E3

▓ 7 ORIENTATION AND PRACTICAL INFORMATION

Copenhagen lies on the east coast of the island of **Zealand** (Sjælland), across the Øresund Sound from Malmö, Sweden. The 28km **Øresund Bridge**, which opened July 1, 2000, established the first "fixed link" between the two countries. Copenhagen's main train station, København H, lies near the city center. Just north of the station, **Vesterbrogade** passes **Tivoli** and **Rådhuspladsen,** the main square, then cuts through the city center as **Strøget** (STROY-yet), the world's longest pedestrian thoroughfare. As it heads east, Strøget goes through a series of names: **Frederiksberggade, Nygade, Vimmelskaftet, Amagertorv,** and **Østergade.** The city center is bordered to the west by five **lakes,** outside of which are the less touristed communities of **Vesterbro, Nørrebro,** and **Østerbro.** Vesterbro and Nørrebro are home to many of the region's immigrants, while some of Copenhagen's highest-income residents live on the wide streets of Østerbro.

Tourist Offices: Copenhagen Right Now, Vesterbrog. 4A (☎7022 2442; www.visitcopenhagen.com). From København H, cross Vesterbrog. toward the Axelrod building. Open July-Aug. M-Sa 9am-8pm, Su 10am-6pm; May-June M-Sa 9am-6pm; Sept.-Apr. M-F 9am-4pm, Sa 9am-2pm. Sells the **Copenhagen Card** (1-day 199kr; 3-day 429kr), which grants free or discounted admission to most sights and unlimited travel throughout Northern Zealand; however, cardholders will need to keep up an almost manic pace to justify the cost. █**Use It,** Rådhusstr. 13 (☎3373 0620; www.useit.dk), has indispensable info and services for budget travelers. Offers *Playtime,* a comprehensive budget guide to the city. Provides daytime luggage storage, has free **Internet** (max. 20min.), holds mail, and finds lodgings for no charge. Open mid-June to mid-Sept. daily 9am-7pm; mid-Sept. to mid-June M-W 11am-4pm, Th 11am-6pm, F 11am-2pm.

Budget Travel: STA Travel, Fiolstr. 18 (☎3314 1501). Open M-Th 9:30am-5:30pm, F 10am-5:30pm. **Kilroy Travels,** Skinderg. 28 (☎7015 4015). Open M-F 10am-5:30pm, Sa 10am-2pm. **Wasteels Rejser,** Skoubog. 6 (☎3314 4633). Open M-F 9am-5pm.

Embassies and Consulates: Australia, Dampfærgev. 26, 2nd fl. (☎7026 3676). **Canada,** Kristen Bernikowsg. 1 (☎3348 3200). **Ireland,** Østbaneg. 21 (☎3542 3233). **New Zealand,** Store Strandst. 21, 2nd fl. (☎3337 7702). **UK,** Kastelsv. 36-40 (☎3544 5200). **US,** Dag Hammarskjölds Allé 24 (☎3341 7100).

Currency Exchange: Forex, in København H. 20kr commission for cash exchanges, 10kr per traveler's check. Open daily 8am-9pm.

Luggage Storage: Free at **Use It** (see above) and most hostels.

Laundromats: Look for **Vascomat** and **Møntvask** chains. Locations at Borgerg. 2, Vendersg. 13, and Istedg. 45. Wash and dry each 40-50kr. Most open daily 7am-9pm. At the █**Laundromat Café,** Elmeg. 15 (☎3535 2672), bus 3A or 80N, you can pick up a used book, check email on the free Wi-Fi, or enjoy a meal while you wait for your laundry. Brunch 68-110kr. Wash 32kr, dry 1kr per min. Open M-Th 8am-midnight, F-Sa 8am-2am, Su 10am-midnight. MC/V.

GLBT Resources: Landsforeningen for Bøsser og Lesbiske (LBL), Teglgårdstr. 13 (☎3313 1948; www.lbl.dk). Open M-F noon-2:30pm and 3-4:30pm. The monthly *Out and About,* which lists nightlife options, is available at gay clubs and the tourist office. Other resources include www.copenhagen-gay-life.dk and www.gayguide.dk.

Police: ☎3325 1448. Headquarters at Halmtorvet 20.

24hr. Pharmacy: Steno Apotek, Vesterbrog. 6C (☎3314 8266), across from the Banegårdspl. exit of København H. Ring the bell at night. Cash only.

Medical Services: Doctors on Call (☎7027 5757). Emergency rooms at **Amager Hospital,** Italiensv. 1 (☎3234 3234), **Frederiksberg Hospital,** Nordre Fasanv. 57 (☎3816 3816), and **Bispebjerg Hospital,** Bispebjerg Bakke 23 (☎3531 3531).

DENMARK

Internet Access: Free at **Use It** and **Copenhagen Hovedbibliotek** (Central Library), Krystalg. 15 (☎3373 6060). Coffee shop on 1st fl. Open M-F 10am-7pm, Sa 10am-2pm. **Boomtown,** Axeltorv. 1-3 (☎3332 1032; www.boomtown.net), across from the Tivoli entrance. 30kr per hr. Open 24hr.

English-Language Bookstore: Arnold Busck International Boghandel, Købmagerg. 49 (☎3373 3500; www.arnoldbusck.dk). Open M 10am-6pm, Tu-Th 9:30am-6pm, F 9:30am-7pm, Sa 10am-4pm. MC/V.

Post Office: In København H. Open M-F 8am-9pm, Sa-Su 10am-4pm. Address mail to be held as follows: LAST NAME First name, Post Denmark, Hovedbanegårdens Posthus, Hovedbanegården, 1570 Copenhagen V, DENMARK. **Use It** also holds mail for 2 months. Address mail to be held as follows: First name LAST NAME, *Poste Restante*, Use It, Rådhusstr. 13, 1466 Copenhagen K, DENMARK.

🏠🏕 ACCOMMODATIONS AND CAMPING

Comfortable and inexpensive accommodations can be hard to find near the city center, but pedestrian-friendly streets and the great public transportation system ensure that travelers are never far from the action. Many hostels are also dynamic social worlds unto themselves. Reserve well ahead in summer.

■ **Sleep-In Heaven,** Struenseeg. 7 (☎3535 4648; www.sleepinheaven.com), in Nørrebro. M: Forum. Take bus #250S from the airport or from København H. (dir.: Buddinge; every 10-20min.) to H.C. Ørsteds V. Take your 1st right on Kapelvej, then take a left into the alley just after Kapelvej 44. Guests chat around the pool table or on the outdoor patio. Breakfast 40kr. Linens for dorms 40kr. Free Wi-Fi. Reception 24hr. Under age 35 only. Dorms 130-160kr; doubles 500kr; triples 600kr. AmEx/MC/V; 5% surcharge. ❷

■ **City Public Hostel,** Absalonsg. 8 (☎3331 2070; www.city-public-hostel.dk), in Vesterbro. Popular hostel with huge co-ed dorms, close to sights and nightlife. Breakfast 20-30kr. Linens 35kr, towel 5kr, pillow 10kr. Internet 10kr per 20min.; free Wi-Fi. Reception 24hr. Check-out 10am. Open May-Aug. Dorms 110-140kr. Cash only. ❷

Sleep-In Green, Ravnsborgg. 18, Baghuset (☎3537 7777). M: Nørreport. Eco-friendly hostel. Breakfast 40kr. Linens included; pillow 10kr, blanket 20kr. Free Internet. Reception 24hr. Lockout noon-4pm. Open June-Oct. 10. 30-bed dorms 120kr. Cash only. ❶

Jørgensen's Hostel/Hotel Jørgensen, Rømersg. 11 (☎3313 8186; www.hoteljoergensen.dk). M: Nørreport. The hostel is in the basement of the hotel and offers cozy rooms in a convenient location. Breakfast included. Linens 30kr. Max. 5-night stay. Dorm lockout 11am-3pm. Dorms under age 35 only. 6- to 14-bed dorms 150kr; singles 500-600kr; doubles 600-725kr. Cash only for dorms; AmEx/MC/V for private rooms. ❷

København Vandrerhjem Copenhagen City (HI), H.C. Andersens Bvd. 50 (☎3311 8585; www.danhostel.dk/copenhagencity). This 15-story hostel provides sleek accommodations just 5min. from the city center. Bike rental 100kr per day. Breakfast 50kr. Linens 60kr. Internet 39kr per hr. Reception 24hr. Check-in 2-5pm. Reserve ahead. Dorms 165-200kr; private rooms 555-695kr. 35kr HI discount. AmEx/MC/V. ❷

Sleep-In-Fact, Valdemarsg. 14 (☎3379 6779; www.sleep-in-fact.dk), in Vesterbro. Spacious, modern factory-turned-hostel. Bike rental 50kr per day. Breakfast included. Linens 30kr. Internet 20kr per 30min. Reception 7am-noon and 3pm-3am. Lockout noon-3pm. Curfew 3am. Open July-Aug. 10- to 30-bed dorms 100-120kr. Cash only. ❷

Bellahøj Camping, Hvidkildev. 66 (☎3810 1150; www.bellahoj-camping.dk). Take bus #2A from København H. (dir.: Tingbjerg; 15min., 6-12 per hr.) all the way to Hulgårdsv. Backtrack from there and turn left on Hulgårdsv., stay left of the church, and then make another left. Basic campground 5km from the city center. Reception 24hr. Open June-Aug. Tent sites 65kr. Electricity 25kr. Showers included. Cash only. ❶

FOOD

Good, inexpensive food is plentiful in central Copenhagen. **Strøget** is lined with all-you-can-eat pizza, pasta, and Indian buffets. Around **Kongens Nytorv,** elegant cafes serve filling *smørrebrød* (open-faced sandwiches) and herring meals. **Open-air markets** provide fresh fruits and veggies; a popular one is at **Israel Plads** near Nørreport Station. (Open M-Th 9am-5:30pm, F 9am-6:30pm, Sa 9am-3pm. Cash only.) Greengrocers line the main streets in **Vesterbro** and **Nørrebro,** and **Fakta** and **Netto** supermarkets are common around Nørrebro (M: Nørreport).

▨ **Morgenstedet,** Langgaden, Bådsmandsstr. 43 (☎3295 7770; www.morgenstedet.dk), in Christiania. Walk down Pusher St. and take a left at the end, leaving Cafe Nemoland to your right. Then take a right up the concrete ramp at the bike shop and left before the bathrooms; it will be on your right. This unassuming restaurant serves cheap organic meals. Soup 45kr. Entrees 60kr, with salad 70kr. Open Tu-Su noon-9pm. Cash only. ❷

▨ **RizRaz,** Kompagnistr. 20 (☎3315 0575). M: Kongens Nytorv. Also at Store Kannikestr. 19 (☎3332 3345). Vegetarian buffet with Mediterranean and Middle Eastern specials. Lunch buffet 69kr. Dinner 79kr. Open daily 11:30am-midnight. AmEx/MC/V. ❸

Den Grønne Kælder, Pilestr. 48 (☎3393 0140). M: Kongens Nytorv. Vegetarian and vegan dining in a cozy basement cafe. Takeout available. Sandwiches 40kr. Lunch 65kr. Dinner 95kr. Open M-Sa 11am-10pm. Cash only. ❷

Nyhavns Færgekro, Nyhavn 5 (☎3315 1588; www.nyhavnsfaergekro.dk). M: Kongens Nytorv. Upscale cafe along the canal with lunch bargains. Try 10 styles of herring at the all-you-can-eat lunch buffet (109kr) or pick just one (45kr). Dinners from 164kr. Kitchen open daily 11:30am-11:30pm. Lunch served daily 11:30am-5pm. MC/V. ❹

Govindas, Nørre Farimagsg. 82 (☎3333 7444). M: Nørreport. Hare Krishnas serve vegetarian and vegan fare. Not much atmosphere, but great deals. All-you-can-eat lunch buffet 55kr, dinner buffet 75kr. Open M-F noon-9pm, Sa 1-7pm. Cash only. ❷

Kate's Joint, Blågårdsg. 12 (☎3537 4496), in Nørrebro. Bus: 5A. Rotating menu of pan-Asian cuisine with African and Middle Eastern influences. Entrees 62-90kr. Stir-fry, tofu, other appetizers 50-69kr. Open daily 5:30-10:30pm. MC/V. ❷

Hviids Vinstue, Kongens Nytorv 19 (☎3315 1064). M: Kongens Nytorv. Copenhagen's oldest pub. Lunch special includes 3 varieties of *smørrebrød* and a Danish beer. Open M-Th 10am-1am, F-Sa 10am-2am, Su 10am-10pm. AmEx/MC/V. ❷

◉ SIGHTS

Flat Copenhagen lends itself to exploration by **bike** (p. 258). **Walking tours** are detailed in *Playtime* (available at **Use It,** p. 255). Window-shop down pedestrian **Strøget** until you reach Kongens Nytorv; opposite is the picturesque **Nyhavn,** where Hans Christian Andersen penned his first fairy tale. On a clear day, take the 6.4km walk along the five **lakes** on the western border of the city center. Wednesday is the best day to visit museums; most are free and some have extended hours.

CITY CENTER. Near the train station, ▨**Tivoli Gardens,** the famous 19th-century amusement park, features old-fashioned and new rides, shimmering fountains, and a world-class **Commedia dell'arte** variety show. **Tivoli Illuminations,** an evocative light show, is staged on Tivoli Lake each night 30min. before closing. (☎3315 1001; www.tivoligardens.com. Open mid-June to mid-Aug. Su-Th 11am-midnight, F-Sa 11am-12:30am; mid-Aug. to mid-June reduced hours. Admission 79kr. Rides 10-60kr. Admission with unlimited rides 279kr. AmEx/MC/V.) Across the street, the beautiful **Ny Carlsberg Glyptotek** is home to an excellent collection of Impressionist and Danish art. Tickets for free guided tours go quickly. (Dantes Pl. 7. ☎3341 8141. Open Tu-Su 10am-

DENMARK

TIME: 4hr. With visits to Rosenborg Slot and Christiansborg Slot, 6hr.

DISTANCE: About 6km.

SEASON: Year-round, although Rosenborg Slot has reduced hours Nov.-Apr.

A BIKING TOUR OF COPENHAGEN

The *Copenhagen Post* estimates that there may be more bikes than Danes in Denmark, and the city of Copenhagen leads the way as one of Europe's most bike-friendly capitals this side of Amsterdam. Rentals from **City Bike** (p. 253) are the most convenient way to go, although their rules require that you only ride the bikes in the city center. The eastern banks of the five western lakes are fair game, but if you cross over to the other side of the lakes, you'll face a 1000kr fine.

When biking through the city, you should avoid pedestrian thoroughfares like Strøget, unless you're in the mood for slaloming around strolling couples and scampering children. If you want to ride out into the countryside, ask your hostel about rental bikes. You can take your bike onto an S-tog for 10kr. In Denmark you are legally required to use lights when riding at night, and police are not shy about handing out 400kr fines to enforce this law. Helmets are strongly recommended, but not mandatory.

This tour starts and ends at the **Rådhus.** Begin by carefully making your way down busy Hans Christian Andersens Boulevard.

1. BOTANISK HAVE. Take a right onto Nørre Voldg. and follow it until you see the gates leading into the University of Copenhagen's lush **Botanical Gardens** (p. 261). Wander along paths lined with more than 13,000 species of plants, or hone in on the **Palm House** to view its extravagant orchids, cycads, and other tropical rarities.

2. STATENS MUSEUM FOR KUNST AND ROSENBORG SLOT. Turn left out of the gardens onto Øster Voldg. At the intersection with Sølvg., you'll see the gates of the **Statens Museum for Kunst** (State Museum of Fine Arts; p. 261) to the north and the spires of **Rosenborg Slot** (p. 261) to the south. The latter served as the 16th-century summer house of King Christian IV, and the royal family took refuge here in 1801 when the British navy was shelling Copenhagen. Lock up your bike and pop inside for a look at the Sculpture Street in the museum or Denmark's crown jewels in the Slot's treasury.

3. ROUND TOWER. Backtrack down Øster Voldg. and turn left onto Gothersg. Make a right onto Landemærket and then hop off again to scale the heights of the **Round Tower** (p. 260), a one-time royal observatory that still affords a sweeping view of the city.

4. AMALIENBORG PALACE. Head back up to Gothersg. and turn right. Pass by **Kongens Nytorv,** the 1670 "new square" that turns into a skating rink each winter, and take a left onto Bredg. Keep your eyes peeled for the gilded dome of the **Marmorkirken** (Marble Church; p. 260) on your left, and then turn right to enter the octagonal plaza of **Amalienborg Palace** (p. 260), a set of four Rococo mansions that the queen and her family call home.

5. NYHAVN. Continue on through the plaza, turn right on Toldbodg., and then right before the bridge onto Nyhavn. Part of the city's old waterfront, Nyhavn was known for centuries as a seedy strip for sailors to find grog, women, and a tattoo artist sober enough to wield a firm needle. Over the past 30 years, Copenhagen has embarked on a clean-up campaign, and today you're more likely to find an upscale deli serving *smørrebrod* than a tumbledown soup kitchen. Whenever a scrap of sunshine can be found, the good people of Copenhagen are soaking it up along the wharf, joined by Swedes from Malmö in search of cheap Danish beer.

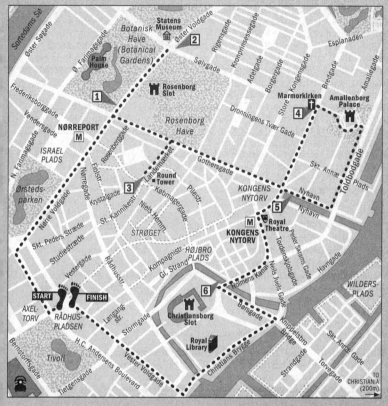

6. CHRISTIANBORG SLOT. Walk your bike through Kongens Nytorv, and then thread your way between the **Royal Theater** (p. 261) and the metro station down Neils Juels G. Turn right onto Holmens Kanal and cross the bridge to reach **Christiansborg Slot** (p. 260), seat of the Danish Parliament. Look for the 103m tower; it's difficult to miss. If you arrive before 3:30pm, try to catch a tour of the **Royal Reception Rooms,** or head down into the ruins of the four previous castles underneath the present-day building. The first castle was demolished to make way for a larger one, the next two burned down in fires, and the Hanseatic League dismantled the fourth castle stone by stone after they captured the city in 1369.

7. SLIDING INTO HOME. You're in the home stretch. Head east toward the **Knippelsbro Bridge** and **Christiania** (p. 260), taking in the industrial skyline before lugging your bike down the steps to Christians Brygge below. Turn right and bike along the canal. Keep watch for the Black Diamond annex of the **Royal Library,** built in 1996 from black marble imported from Zimbabwe. Make a quick stop to check your email at one of the two free terminals inside. Make a right onto Vester Voldg. and coast back up to the Rådhus. You've earned the right to call it a day.

4pm. 40kr. Su free. Tours mid-June to Aug. W 2pm. MC/V.) Nearby, the **Danish Design Center** showcases trends in Danish fashion and lifestyles. The Flow Market exhibition downstairs lets visitors purchase items. *(H.C. Andersens Bvd. 27. ☎3369 3369; www.ddc.dk. Open M-Tu and Th-F 10am-5pm, W 10am-9pm, Sa-Su 11am-4pm. 50kr, students 25kr. W after 5pm free. AmEx/MC/V.)* To reach the ◙**National Museum** from H.C. Andersens Bvd., turn onto Stormg., take a right on Vester Volg., and go left on Ny Vesterg. Its vast collections include several large rune stones, examples of ancient Viking art, and the fabulous permanent ethnographic exhibit, "People of the Earth." *(Ny Vesterg. 10. ☎3313 4411; www.natmus.dk. Open Tu-Su 10am-5pm. Free.)*

Christiansborg Slot, the home of Parliament *(Folketing)* and the royal reception rooms, displays vivid modernist tapestries that were designed by Bjørn Nørgård and presented to the Queen on her 50th birthday. Visitors can tour the subterranean ruins underneath the Slot. *(Prins Jørgens Gård 1. ☎3392 6494; www.ses.dk/christrainsborg. Ruins open May-Sept. daily 10am-4pm; Oct.-Apr. Tu-Su 10am-4pm. Call ☎3392 6492 for English-language castle tours, May-Sept. daily 11am, 1, 3pm; Oct.-Apr. Tu, Th, and Sa-Su 3pm. Ruins 40kr, students 30kr. Castle tour 60/50kr.)* Nearby, the **Thorvaldsens Museum** has colorfully painted rooms with works by Danish sculptor Bertel Thorvaldsen, including some original plaster models. Head upstairs to see the collection of Etruscan and Egyptian artifacts. *(Bertel Thorvaldsens Pl. 2. ☎3332 1532; www.thorvaldsensmuseum.dk. Open Tu-Su 10am-5pm. 20kr. W free.)* Sixteenth-century astronomer Tycho Brahe once observed the stars from the top of the **Round Tower** (Rundetaarn), which provides a sweeping view of the city. *(Købmagerg. 52A. ☎3373 0373; www.rundetaarn.dk. Open June to mid-Aug. M-Sa 10am-8pm, Su noon-8pm; Sept. to mid-Oct. and Apr.-May M-Sa 10am-5pm, Su noon-5pm; mid-Oct. to Mar. M and Th-Sa 10am-5pm, Tu-W 10am-5pm and 7-10pm, Su noon-5pm. 25kr. AmEx/MC/V.)* Down the street, the **Museum Erotica** celebrates all things carnal; the videos from the Porn Room can be purchased at the front desk. *(Købmagerg. 24. ☎3312 0311; www.museumerotica.dk. Open May-Sept. daily 10am-11pm; Oct.-Apr. Su-Th 11am-8pm, F-Sa 11am-10pm. 109kr with guidebook. AmEx/MC/V.)*

CHRISTIANSHAVN. In 1971, a few dozen flower children established the "free city" of **Christiania** in an abandoned Christianshavn fort. Today, the thousand-odd residents continue the tradition of artistic expression and unconventionality. Vendors sell clothing and jewelry, while spots like **Woodstock Cafe** and **Cafe Nemoland** have cheap beer and diverse crowds. Recent government crackdowns have driven **Pusher Street's** once open drug trade underground, and arrests for possession have become commonplace. A large sign warns passersby not to take pictures on Pusher St. *(Main entrance on Prinsesseg. Take bus #66 from København H.)* **Vor Frelsers Kirke** (Our Savior's Church) has recently reopened its gold-accented interior to the public. *(Sankt Annæg. 9. M: Christianshavn or bus #66. Turn left onto Prinsesseg. ☎3257 2798; www.vorfrelserskirke.dk. Spire ☎3254 1573. Church free. Spire 20kr. Cash only.)* The **Danish Architecture Center** hosts elegantly presented exhibits. *(Strandg. 27B. ☎3257 1930; www.dac.dk. Open daily 10am-5pm. 40kr, students 25kr. MC/V.)*

FREDERIKSTADEN. Northeast of the city center, Edvard Eriksen's tiny **Little Mermaid** (Lille Havfrue) statue at the mouth of the harbor honors Hans Christian Andersen's beloved tale. *(S-tog: Østerport. Turn left out of the station, go left on Folke Bernadottes Allé, bear right on the path bordering the canal, go left up the stairs, and then head right along the street.)* Head back along the canal and turn left across the moat to reach **Kastellet,** a rampart-enclosed 17th-century fortress that's now a park. *(Open daily 6am-10pm.)* On the other side of Kastellet, the **Frihedsmuseet** (Museum of Danish Resistance) documents the German occupation of 1940-1945, when the Danes helped over 7000 Jews escape to Sweden. *(At Churchillparken. ☎3313 7714. Open May-Sept. Tu-Su 10am-5pm; Oct.-Apr. Tu-Su 10am-3pm. English-language tours July-Sept. Tu and Th 11am. Free.)* Walk south down Amalieng. to reach **Amalienborg Palace,** a complex of four enormous mansions that serve as the winter residences of the royal family. Several apartments are open to the public, including the studies of 19th-century Danish kings. The changing of the guard takes place at noon on the vast plaza. (☎3312 0808; www.rosenborgslot.dk. Open May-Oct. daily 10am-4pm; Nov.-Apr. Tu-Su 11am-4pm. 50kr, students 30kr. Combined ticket with Rosenborg Slot 80kr. MC/V.) The imposing 19th-century **Marmorkirken** (Marble Church), opposite the palace, features an ornate interior under Europe's third-largest dome. (Fredriksg. 4. ☎3315 0144; www.marmorkirken.dk. Open M-Tu and Th 10am-5pm, W 10am-6pm, F-Sa noon-5pm. English-language tours to the top of the dome mid-June to Aug. daily 1 and 3pm; Oct. to mid-June Sa-Su 1 and 3pm. Church free. Tours 25kr. Cash only.)

The **Statens Museum for Kunst** (State Museum of Fine Arts) displays an eclectic collection of Danish and international art in two buildings linked by a glass-roof gallery. (Sølvg. 48-50. S-tog: Nørreport. Walk up Øster Voldg. ☎3374 8494; www.smk.dk. Open Tu and Th-Su 10am-5pm, W 10am-8pm. English-language tours July-Aug. Sa-Su 2pm. Permanent collection free. Special exhibits 50kr, students 30kr. W free. AmEx/MC/V.) Opposite the museum, the Baroque **Rosenborg Slot,** built by King Christian IV in the 17th century as a summer residence, shows off the crown jewels and the opulent **Unicorn Throne,** which legend holds is constructed from unicorn horns. (Øster Voldg. 4A. M: Nørreport. ☎3315 3286; www.rosenborgslot.dk. Open June-Aug. daily 11am-5pm; May and Sept. daily 10am-4pm; Oct. daily 11am-3pm; Nov.-Apr. Tu-Su 11am-2pm. 50kr, students 40kr. AmEx/MC/V.) About 13,000 plant species thrive in the ▨**Botanisk Have** (Botanical Gardens); tropical and subtropical plants mingle happily in the iron-and-glass **Palm House.** (Gardens open May-Sept. daily 8:30am-6pm; Oct.-Apr. Tu-Su 8:30am-4pm. Palm House open May-Dec. daily 10am-3pm; Jan.-Apr. Tu-Su 10am-3pm. Free.)

♫ ※ ENTERTAINMENT AND FESTIVALS

For info on events, consult *Copenhagen This Week* or ask at Use It (see p. 255). The **Royal Theater** is home to the world-famous Royal Danish Ballet. The box office, August Bournonville Pass. 1, is just off the Konges Nytorv metro and sells same-day half-price tickets. (☎3369 6969. Open M-Sa 10am-6pm.) The **Tivoli ticket office,** Vesterbrog. 3, has half-price tickets for the city's other theaters. (☎3315 1012. Open daily mid-Apr. to mid-Sept. 11am-8pm; mid-Sept. to mid-Apr. 9am-5pm.) Tickets are also available online at www.billetnet.dk. Relaxed **Kulkaféen,** Teglgårdsstr. 5, is a great place to see live performers and listen to stand-up comedy. (☎3332 1777. Cover up to 50kr. Open M 11am-midnight, Tu-Sa 11am-2am. MC/V.) In late March and early April, international and domestic releases compete for Danish distribution deals at the **Nat-Film Festival** (☎3312 0005; www.natfilm.dk). During the world-class ▨**Copenhagen Jazz Festival** (early July 2008; ☎3393 2013; www.festival.jazz.dk), the city teems with free outdoor concerts. Throughout July and August, **Zulu Sommerbio** (Summer Cinema; www.zulu.dk) holds free screenings in parks and squares across the city. Movies are shown in their original languages with Danish subtitles.

☒ NIGHTLIFE

In Copenhagen, weekends begin on Wednesday, and clubs pulse with activity late enough to serve breakfast with their martinis. On Thursdays, many bars and clubs have cheaper drinks and reduced covers. The streets of the city center, as well as those of **Nørrebro** and **Vesterbro,** are lined with hip, crowded bars. Look for fancier options along Nyhavn, where laid-back Danes bring their own beer and sit on the pier; open containers are legal within the city limits. Unless otherwise noted, all bars and clubs are 18+. Copenhagen has a thriving gay and lesbian scene; check out *Playtime* or *Out and About* for listings.

DENMARK

The areas behind København H, the central train station, can be unsafe, especially at night. Explore with caution, and bring a friend.

Vega, Enghavev. 40 (☎3326 0954; www.vega.dk), in Vesterbro. Bus: 80N, 84N. Copenhagen's largest nightclub, 2 concert venues, and a popular bar. Come before 1am to avoid paying cover and party all night with the glitterati. Bar 18+; club 20+. Club cover 60kr after 1am. Bar open F-Sa 7pm-5am. Club open F-Sa 11pm-5am. MC/V.

The Moose Bar, Sværtev. 5 (☎3391 4291). M: Kongens Nytorv. Rowdy local spirit dominates in this popular bar, famous for its cheap beer and its jukebox playing classic rock hits. Beer 24kr, 2 for 32kr. 2 mixed drinks 30-35kr. Reduced prices Tu, Th, and Sa 9pm-close. Open M and Su 1pm-3am, Tu-F 1pm-6am. AmEx/MC/V.

The Australian Bar, Vesterg. 10 (☎2024 1411). M: Nørreport. This bar boasts cheap drinks, a smoke machine, and a dance-club playlist. Beer 20kr. Mixed drinks 30kr. Reduced prices Th. Cover 40kr. Open Su-W 4pm-2am, Th-Sa 4pm-5am. MC/V.

Park, Østerbrog. 79 (☎3525 1661; www.park.dk). Bus 85N. Far from the center, this club has a live music hall, lavish lounges, and a rooftop patio. Beer 45kr. Dress to impress. F 20+, Sa 22+. Cover Th-Sa 50-70kr. Restaurant open Tu-Sa 11am-10pm. Club open Su-Tu 11am-midnight, W 11am-2am, Th-Sa 11am-5am. AmEx/MC/V.

Mc.Kluud's, Istedg. 126 (☎3331 6383; www.mckluud.dk), in Vesterbro. Bus: 10, 84N. Artists and students come to sample the cheap beer at this Wild West bar inspired by the American TV show *McCloud*. Beer 15-17kr. Open daily 2pm-2am. Cash only.

La Hacienda/The Dance Floor, Gammel Torv 8 (☎3311 7478; www.la-hacienda.dk). M: Nørreport. Choose between **La Hacienda,** a laid-back lounge playing soul and hip hop, and **The Dance Floor,** a 2-story trance-driven club. Cover for men 150kr, women 130kr, 75kr before midnight; includes 1 champagne and 1 beer. Open F 11pm-8am, Sa 11pm-10am. AmEx/MC/V.

DAYTRIPS FROM COPENHAGEN

Copenhagen's **S-togs** and other regional lines can whisk travelers away from the urban din to castles, countryside scenery, museums, and well-trodden beaches. It's significantly cheaper and more flexible for travelers to buy cards and stamp them with clips rather than purchasing one-way tickets.

HILLERØD. Hillerød is home to **Frederiksborg Slot,** one of Denmark's most impressive castles. Close to 90 rooms are open to the public, including the Chapel, the Rose Room, the Great Hall, and the Baroque gardens. From the train station, cross the street onto Vibekev. and continue straight along the path until you can follow the signs; at the Torvet (main plaza), walk to the pond and bear left, following its perimeter to reach the castle entrance. *(Hillerød is at the end of S-tog lines A and E. 40min., 6 per hr., 67kr or 4 clips. ☎4826 0439; www.frederiksborgmuseet.dk. Gardens open May-Aug. daily 10am-9pm; Sept.-Apr. reduced hours. Castle open daily Apr.-Oct. 10am-5pm; Nov.-Mar. 11am-3pm. Gardens free. Castle 60kr, students 50kr. AmEx/MC/V.)*

TIP **STOP THAT TRAIN!** In much of Denmark, especially rural areas, trains do not stop at every station on the line. Be sure to check at the ticket counter to find out which train to take, and ask whether you need to sit in a particular car.

HELSINGØR. Helsingør sits at a strategic entrance to the Baltic Sea, just 5km from Sweden. Originally built to levy taxes on passing ships, the majestic 16th-century **Kronborg Slot** is better known as **Elsinore,** the setting for Shakespeare's *Hamlet*. A statue of Viking chief Holger Danske sleeps in the dank, forbidding **dungeon;** legend holds that he will awake to defend Denmark in its darkest hour. (☎4921 3078; www.kronborg.dk. Book tours ahead. Open May-Sept. daily 10:30am-5pm; Apr. and Oct. Tu-Su 11am-4pm; Nov.-Mar. Tu-Su 11am-3pm. 85kr. AmEx/MC/V.) In early August, the **Hamlet Sommer Festival** (www.hamletsommer.dk) brings Hamlet's ghost back to life in a series of performances in the castle's commons. The **tourist office**, Havnepl. 3, is in the Kulturhus, across from the station. (☎4921 1333; www.visithelsingor.dk. Open July M-F 10am-5pm, Sa 10am-2pm; Aug. to June M-F 10am-4pm, Sa 10am-1pm. Helsingør is at the end of the northern train line from Malmö, SWE via Copenhagen. 1hr., 3 per hr., 67kr or 4 clips.)

HUMLEBÆK AND RUNGSTED. The █Louisiana Museum of Modern Art, 13 Gl. Strandv., in Humlebæk, honors the three wives (all named Louisa) of the estate's original owner. It rounds out its permanent collection—including works by Lichtenstein, Picasso, and Warhol—with several major exhibits each year. Landscape architects have lavished attention on the seaside sculpture garden and the sloping lake garden. From the Humlebæk station, follow signs for 10min. or catch bus #388. (From Copenhagen, take a Helsingør-bound train. 45min., 3 per hr., 63kr or 4 clips. ☎4919 0719; www.louisiana.dk. Open M-Tu and Th-Su 10am-5pm, W 10am-10pm. 80kr, students with ISIC 70kr. AmEx/MC/V.) Near the water in Rungsted stands the house where Karen Blixen wrote her autobiographical 1937 novel Out of Africa under the pseudonym Isak Dinesen. The **Karen Blixen Museum**, Rungsted Strandv. 111, provides a chronicle of the author's life. The grounds are home to 40 species of birds. Follow the street leading out of the train station and turn right on Rungstedv., then right again on Rungsted Strandv., or take bus #388. (From Copenhagen, take a Nivå-bound train. 30min., 3 per hr., 67kr or 4 clips. ☎4557 1057. Open May-Sept. Tu-Su 10am-5pm; Oct.-Apr. W-F 1-4pm, Sa-Su 11am-4pm. 45kr. AmEx/MC/V.)

MØN ☎55

Hans Christian Andersen once called the isle of Møn the most beautiful spot in Denmark. The sheer white **Møns Klint** (Chalk Cliffs), which plunge straight into calm blue waters, can be viewed from the rocky beaches below or the densely forested hiking trails above. The **Liselund Slot** (Doll Castle) looks more like a country house than a castle. The main attraction is the surrounding park, with peacocks and thatched-roof farmhouses. Walking away from the castle, you'll reach a path that becomes a █hiking trail, which snakes 3km through a lush forest before arriving at the cliffs. Buses to Møn arrive in **Stege**, the island's largest town, across the island from the castle and cliffs. From Stege, take bus #52 to Busene (1 per 1-2hr., 13kr) and walk 10min. to the cliffs. Between mid-June and late August, bus #632 runs from Stege to the parking lots at the cliffs (30min., 3 per day, 13kr). Another way to see Møn is by renting a **bike** in Klintholm Havn, the last stop on bus #52.

Orchids line the trail of the 143m **Aborrebjerg** (Bass Mountain) near the island's youth hostel, lakeside **Møns Klint Vandrerhjem (HI) ❷**, Langebjergv. 1. Between late June and mid-August, take bus #632 from Stege to the campground stop, then continue in the direction of the bus and take the first right. In low season, take bus #52 to Magleby and walk left 2.5km down the road. (☎81 20 30. Breakfast 50kr. Linens 45kr. Laundry 30kr. Reception 8-10:30am and 4-7pm. Open May-Sept. Dorms 185kr; singles and doubles 335-370kr. 35kr HI discount. MC/V; 5% surcharge.) **Stege Camping ❶**, Flacksvej 5, is just a 5min. walk from the Stege bus stop. (☎81 84 04. Reception 9am-10pm. Open May to mid-Oct. 50kr per tent site. Hot water 20kr. Cash only.) To get to Møn, take the **train** from Copenhagen to Vordingborg (1½hr., 108kr), then bus #62 to Stege (45min., 39kr). The info center, **Feriepartner Møn**, Storeg. 2, is next to the Stege bus stop. (☎86 04 00; www.feriepartnermoen.dk. Open M-F 9:30am-5pm, Sa 9am-6pm.)

ROSKILDE ☎46

Once the capital of the Danish Empire, Roskilde (pop. 53,000) is an easy daytrip from Copenhagen. Each summer, music fans arrive in droves to hear performances by artists such as The Who and Red Hot Chili Peppers at the ■**Roskilde Music Festival** (July 3-6, 2008; www.roskilde-festival.dk), northern Europe's largest outdoor concert. Stunning sarcophagi hold the remains of Danish royalty in the red-brick church, **Roskilde Domkirke,** off the Stændertorvet. Head left out of the train station, go right on Herseg., and left onto Alg. (☎35 16 24; www.roskilde-domkirke.dk. Open Apr.-Sept. M-Sa 9am-5pm, Su 12:30-5pm; Oct.-Mar. Tu-Sa 10am-4pm, Su 12:30-4pm. English-language tours mid-June to mid-Aug. M-F 11am and 2pm, Sa-Su 2pm depending on church services. 25kr, students 15kr. Tours 20kr.) On the harbor, the ■**Viking Ship Museum,** Vindeboder 12, displays five ships unearthed from the Roskilde Fjord. The museum includes a shipyard where volunteers build vessels using Viking methods. Some of the ships are available for sailing. (☎30 02 53; www.vikingeskibsmuseet.dk. Open daily 10am-5pm. May-Sept. 80kr, students 70kr; Oct.-Apr. 50/40kr. AmEx/MC/V.) The harborside **Roskilde Vandrerhjem (HI) ❸,** Vindeboder 7, has bright rooms. (☎35 21 84; www.danhostel.dk/roskilde. Breakfast 45kr. Linens 45kr. Reception 7am-10pm. Dorms 185kr. 35kr HI discount. AmEx/MC/V.) Restaurants line **Algade** and **Skomagergade** in the town center. **Memos ❶,** Jernbanegade 8, serves pita sandwiches (25-35kr) and has an **Internet** cafe (15kr per hr.) downstairs. (☎32 70 76. Open M-Th 11am-8pm, F-Sa 11am-4am.) **Trains** depart for Copenhagen (25-30min., 4 per hr., 66kr) and Odense (1¼hr., 3 per hr., 181kr). The **tourist office** is at Gullandsstr. 15. Walk through the Stændertorvet with the Domkirke on your right, turn left on Allehelgensgade, and follow the signs. (☎31 65 65. Open late June-late Aug. M-F 10am-5pm, Sa 10am-1pm; low season reduced hours.)

BORNHOLM

Residents of the island of Bornholm like to say that when Scandinavia was created, God saved the best piece for last and dropped it into the Baltic Sea. After a day or two in Bornholm, you might be inclined to agree. The undulating farmlands of the south are ideal for bikers, while nature lovers will favor the dramatic, rocky landscape of the north. The central forest is one of the largest in Denmark, and the sandiest beaches are at Dueodde, on the island's southern tip.

▣ TRANSPORTATION. The cheapest way to get to Bornholm from Copenhagen is by a **bus** and **ferry** combination. Bornholmerbussen #866 leaves from København H for Ystad, SWE, where passengers can transfer to the ferry. (☎4468 4400. 3hr., 5 per day, 225kr.) A **train** and **ferry** combo runs from Copenhagen to Rønne by way of Ystad. (Train ☎7013 1415; www.dsb.dk; 1¼hr., 5-6 per day. Ferry ☎5695 1866; www.bornholmferries.dk; 80min. Combination 200-251kr.) A discount "red ticket" (224kr, low season 150kr) for the ferry is available online a week in advance, but the combo ticket is cheaper for travelers coming from Copenhagen. Overnight ferries from Køge (S-tog: A+, E, Ex), south of Copenhagen, leave at 11:30pm and arrive in Rønne at 6:30am (244kr, 281kr for a bed).

Bornholm has an efficient BAT **local bus** service; buses run less frequently on weekends. (☎5695 2121. 36-45kr, bikes 22kr; 24hr. pass 140kr.) Bus #7 makes a circuit of the coastline, heading from Rønne to Hammershus and stopping at most of the island's towns and attractions along the way. Bus #3 from Rønne passes by Østerlars Church on its way to Gudhjem, where the ferry departs for Christiansø, a small island to the north of Bornholm. There are well-marked **bike** paths between all the major towns; pick up a guide (40kr) at Rønne's tourist office. The ride from Rønne to either Sandvig in the north or Dueodde in the southeast is about 30km.

RØNNE. Rønne (pop. 14,000), on Bornholm's southwestern coast, is the principal port of entry. **Rønne Vandrerhjem (HI) ❷,** Arsenalv. 12, is in a peaceful, wooded area. From the ferry, head toward the tourist office and turn right on Munch Petersens V. Bear left up the hill on Zahrtmannsv., follow it to the left at the top of the hill, and turn right at the roundabout onto Søndre Allé; Arsenalv. is 100m up on the right. (☎5695 1340; www.danhostel-roenne.dk. Breakfast 45kr. Linens 50kr. Wash 30kr, dry 50kr. Reception 8am-noon and 4-5pm. Open Apr.-Oct. Dorms 185kr; singles 370kr. 35kr HI discount. Cash only.) **Galløkken Camping ❶,** Strandvejen 4, is 15min. south of the town center, near the beach. Follow directions to the hostel, but continue down Søndre Allé until it becomes Strandvejen; the campground is on the right. (☎5695 2320; www.gallokken.dk. Bike rental 60kr per day. Reception 8am-noon and 5-7pm. Open May-Aug. 64kr per tent site. Electricity 25kr. Scandinavian Camping Card required; available for purchase at reception, 100kr. MC/V; 5% surcharge.) **Sam's Corner ❷,** St. Torv 2, is a basic burger and pizza joint with low prices (45-75kr) and large portions. (☎5695 1523. Open daily in summer 10am-10pm; in winter 10am-9pm. Cash only.) Get groceries at **Kvickly,** opposite the tourist office. (☎5695 1777. Open mid-June to Aug. daily 9am-8pm; Sept. to mid-June M-F 9am-8pm, Sa 9am-5pm, Su 10am-4pm. Cash only.) The **tourist office** is at Ndr. Kystv. 3. Turn right out of the ferry terminal, pass the BAT bus terminal, and cross toward the gas station; look for the green flag. (☎5695 9500. Open mid-June to mid-Aug. daily 9am-5pm; mid-Aug. to mid-June reduced hours. MC/V.)

ALLINGE AND SANDVIG. These seaside villages are excellent starting points for hikes and bike rides through Bornholm's northern coast. Many trails originate in Sandvig. The rocky area around **Hammeren,** northwest of the town, is a beautiful 2hr. walk that can be covered only on foot. Just outside Sandvig is the lakeside **Sandvig Vandrerhjem (HI) ❷,** Hammershusv. 94. Get off the bus one stop past Sandvig Gl. Station and follow the signs. (☎5648 0362. Breakfast 45kr. Linens 50kr. Laundry 40kr. Reception 9-10am and 4-6pm. Open May-Sept. Dorms 150kr; singles 275kr; doubles 400kr. 35kr HI discount. Cash only.) **Riccos ❷,** Strandg. 8, in Sandvig, is a pleasant cafe in a private home near the sea and has free **Internet.** (☎5648 0314. Open daily 7am-10pm. MC/V.) The **tourist office** is at Kirkeg. 4 in Allinge. (☎5648 0001. Open June-Aug. M-F 10am-4pm, Sa 10am-1pm; Oct.-May M-F 11am-4pm.) Rent **bikes** at the **Sandvig Cykeludlejning,** Strandvejen 121. (☎2145 6013. Open May-Sept. M-F 9am-3:30pm, Sa 9am-1pm, Su 10am-1pm. 60kr per day. Cash only.)

FUNEN (FYN)

Nestled between Zealand to the east and the Jutland Peninsula to the west, the island of Funen attracts cyclists and fairytale fans. Isolated in the time of golden son Hans Christian Andersen, this once-remote breadbasket has since been connected to Zealand by the magnificent Storebæltsbro bridge and tunnel.

ODENSE
☎63, 65, 66

The legacy of Hans Christian Andersen draws most tourists to Odense (OH-densuh; pop. 200,000), Denmark's third-largest city. While fairy tales still reign supreme in the writer's hometown, a thriving nightlife and music scene also make Odense a destination for the young and trendy.

◪ ◪ TRANSPORTATION AND PRACTICAL INFORMATION. Trains run to Copenhagen (1½hr., 2 per hr., 214kr). **Buses** depart from behind the train station. The **tourist office,** in the Rådhuset, offers free **Internet** and bike maps. Turn left out of

D E N M A R K

the train station, make a right on Thomas Thriges G. at the second light, then go right on Vesterg. (☎66 12 75 20; www.visitodense.com. Open July-Aug. M-F 9:30am-6pm, Sa 10am-3pm, Su 11am-2pm; Sept. to mid-June M-F 9:30am-4:30pm, Sa 10am-1pm.) The library in the station also has free Internet. (☎65 51 44 21. Open Apr.-Sept. M-Th 10am-7pm, F 10am-4pm, Sa 10am-2pm; low season extended hours.) Rent **bikes** at **City Cyklor,** Vesterbro 27. Continue down Vesterg. from the tourist office for 10min.; it will be on the right. (☎66 13 97 83. 99kr per day, with 750kr deposit. Open M-F 10am-5:30pm, Sa 10am-1pm.) **Postal Code:** 5000.

▐▛ ▐▟ ACCOMMODATIONS AND FOOD. **Danhostel Odense City (HI)** ❸, next to the train station, has excellent facilities. (☎63 11 04 25; www.cityhostel.dk. Breakfast 50kr. Linens 60kr. Laundry 45kr. Internet 10kr per 15min. Reception 8am-noon and 4-8pm. Dorms 185kr; singles 400kr; doubles 550kr; triples 585kr; quads 617kr. 35kr HI discount. MC/V; 4% surcharge.) To reach **DCU-Camping Odense** ❷, Odensev. 102, take bus #21-24 (dir.: Højby; 14kr) 4km from town. (☎66 11 47 02; www.camping-odense.dk. Reception mid-June to mid-Aug. 7:30am-noon and 2-10pm; low season 7:30am-noon and 4-10pm. 108kr per tent site; low season 86kr. 4-person cabin with stove 390kr. Electricity 25-30kr. AmEx/MC/V.) **Vestergade,** a long pedestrian street, has ethnic restaurants and cafes. Don't overlook the alleys off Vesterg., including **Brandts Passage,** filled with hip cafes, and the more low-key **Vintapperstræde.** Get groceries at **Aktiv Super,** Nørreg. 63, at the corner of Nørreg. and Skulkenborgg. (☎66 12 85 59. Open M-F 9am-7pm, Sa 9am-4pm. Cash only.)

▐▛ ▐▟ SIGHTS AND NIGHTLIFE. At **Hans Christian Andersen Hus,** Bangs Boder 29, visitors can learn about the author's eccentricities and see the home where he grew up. Enjoy free performances of his timeless stories in a mix of Danish, English, and German. From the tourist office, walk right on Vesterg., turn left on Thomas Thriges G., and go right on Hans Jensens Str. (☎65 51 46 01; www.museum.odense.dk. Open June-Aug. daily 9am-6pm; Sept.-May Tu-Su 10am-4pm. 60kr. Summer performances 11am, 1, 3pm.) Music wafts through the halls of the **Carl Nielsen Museum,** Claus Bergs G. 11, which depicts the life of the Danish composer. (Open Th-F 4-8pm, Su noon-4pm. 25kr.) Down Vesterg., near the tourist office, **St. Knud's Cathedral** has a magnificent triptych by Claus Berg. Inside, view the skeleton of St. Knud, murdered at the altar of the church that previously stood on the site. (☎66 12 03 92. Open daily Apr.-Oct. 10am-5pm; low season 10am-4pm.)

On weekend evenings, the area around Vesterg. is packed with people of all ages drinking and listening to live bands. After 11pm, the club and bar scene takes over. *What's On?,* available at the tourist office, provides nightlife info. **Crazy Daisy,** Klingenberg 14, Skt. Knuds Kirkestr. just past Radhuspl., has six bars on three floors. (☎66 14 67 88. Cover 50kr. Open F-Sa 11pm-6am.) A young crowd moves to the beats of Odense's best DJs at **Boogie Dance Cafe,** Norreg. 21. (☎66 14 00 39. Cover Th 20kr; F-Sa 40kr after midnight. Open Tu-Sa 10:30pm-5:30am. MC/V.)

▐▟ DAYTRIP FROM ODENSE: KVÆRNDRUP. ◾**Egeskov Slot,** 25min. south of Odense in Kværndrup, is a magnificent castle that appears to float on the lake. The grounds include imaginative gardens, hedge mazes, and small museums. (☎62 27 10 16. *Castle open July M-Tu and Th-Su 10am-7pm, W 10am-11pm; May-June and Aug.-Sept. daily 10am-5pm. Grounds open daily July 10am-8pm; June and Aug. 10am-6pm; May and Sept. 10am-5pm. Grounds, mazes, and museums 110kr; with castle 165kr. MC/V.)* Take the Svendborg-bound **train** (25min., 51kr) that leaves 35min. past the hour from Odense. In Kværndrup, turn right out of the station and walk up to Bøjdenv., where you can catch **bus** #920 (1 per hr., 16kr), or turn right and walk 20min. to the castle. From mid-June to mid-August, you can take FynBus #801 from Odense directly to the castle (1hr., 3-8 per day, 44kr).

🏝 ÆRØ ☎ 62

The wheat fields, harbors, and hamlets of Ærø (EH-ruh), a small island off the southern coast of Funen, use modern technology to preserve an earlier era of Danish history. Almost 80% of the island is powered by renewable energy sources, keeping the air pristine. The town of **Ærøskøbing** (pop. 3900) serves as a gateway to the island. Hollyhocks and half-timbered houses line the cobblestone streets, and one-lane roads and picturesque windmills lure vacationing Danes into exploring the rest of the island by bicycle. Several **trains** running from Odense to Svendborg are timed to meet the ferry to Ærøskøbing. (2hr., 5-6 per day, 153kr. Cash only.) On the island, **bus** #990 travels among the towns of Ærøskøbing, Marstal, and Søby (23kr, day pass 75kr). Ærøskøbing's **tourist office,** Havnen 4, has **Internet** for 25kr per 15min. (☎52 13 00; www.arre.dk. Open M-F 10am-2pm.) **Postal Code:** 5970.

JUTLAND (JYLLAND)

Jutland's sandy beaches and historic houses complement its sleek wind turbines and contemporary art. Vikings once journeyed to the trading centers on the western half of the peninsula, but now the coast attracts windsurfers in search of prime waves. Cyclers and canoers enjoy the vast open spaces of the central lakes region, while the cities of Århus and Aalborg have emerged as cultural havens in the east.

ÅRHUS ☎ 86-89

Pedestrian walkways wind through the impressive museums, crowded nightclubs, and well-developed art scene of Århus (OR-hoos; pop. 280,000), Denmark's second-largest city. Copenhagen may draw more tourists, but Århus tempers urban sophistication with a dose of Jutland practicality.

🖿🖬 TRANSPORTATION AND PRACTICAL INFORMATION. Flights arrive at Århus airport (**AAR;** ☎8775 7000), 45km from the city center. **Airport buses** leave from the front of the main terminal building for Århus (45min., 85kr). Some budget airlines fly also fly to **Billund** (p. 268). **Trains** run to Aalborg (1½hr., 2 per hr., 153kr), Copenhagen (3hr., 2 per hr., 302kr), and Frederikshavn (2¾hr., 1 per hr., 199kr). **Buses** leave from outside the train station. From May to October, **free bikes** are available to borrow from stands across the city with a 20kr deposit. **MM Cykler Værksted,** Mejlg. 41, rents bikes for 85kr per day. (☎8619 2927. Open M-F 9am-5pm.) To get to the **tourist office,** Banegårdspl. 20, head left after exiting the train station. The office sells the **24hr. Tourist Ticket** (55kr), which offers unlimited use of the city's extensive bus system. The **Århus pass** (1-day 119kr, 2-day 149kr, 1-week 206kr) includes admission to most museums and sights as well as unlimited public transit. (☎87 31 50 10; www.visitaarhus.com. Open mid-June to early Sept. M-F 9:30am-6pm, Sa 9:30am-5pm, Su 9:30am-1pm; low season reduced hours.) The main public **library,** Mølleg. 1 in Mølleparken, offers free **Internet.** (☎89 40 92 55. Open May-Sept. M-Th 10am-7pm, F 10am-5pm, Sa 10am-2pm; Oct.-Apr. M-Th 10am-8pm, F 10am-6pm, Sa-Su 10am-3pm.) **Postal Code:** 8000.

🖿🖸 ACCOMMODATIONS AND FOOD. The popular 🌑**Århus City Sleep-In ❷,** Havneg. 20, is near the city's nightlife. From the train station, turn right and follow Ny Banegårdsg., passing Europalads, then turn left onto Havneg. when the street forks in front of the train tracks. (☎86 19 20 55; www.citysleep-in.dk. Breakfast 48-55kr. Linens 48kr, 50kr deposit. Laundry 30kr. Internet 20kr per hr. Key deposit 50kr. Reception 24hr. Dorms 120-125kr; doubles 380-460kr. MC/V; 5% surcharge.) The quieter **Århus Vanderhjem (HI) ❶,** Marienlundsv. 10, is 5min. north of the city in a park near one of Århus's nicest beaches. Take bus #1, 6, 9, or 16 to Marienlunds. (☎86 21 21 20; www.aarhus-danhostel.dk. Breakfast 50kr. Linens 45kr. Free Wi-Fi. Reception Apr.-Oct. 8am-noon and 4-8pm, Nov.-Mar. 8am-noon and 4-7pm. Dorms 175kr; private rooms 483kr. 35kr HI discount. MC/V; 2.3% surcharge.) Ethnic restaurants and pizzerias line **Skolegade**, which becomes Mejlg. Get traditional Danish food at **Pinden's Restaurant ❷**, Skoleg. 29. (☎8612 1102. Entrees 42-86kr. Open daily 11:30am-9pm. AmEx/MC/V.) Get groceries at **Netto,** in St. Knuds Torv; take Ryeseg. from the station and turn right into the square across from the church. (☎8612 3112. Open M-Th 5-10pm, F-Sa noon-10pm. Cash only.)

🎲🎭 **SIGHTS AND ENTERTAINMENT.** The exceptional ⬛**Århus Kunstmuseum (ARoS),** Aros Allé 2, off Vester Allé, features eight levels of galleries that hold multimedia exhibits and modern art. Highlights include Ron Mueck's *Boy*, a colossal 5m statue of a crouching boy. (☎87 30 66 00; www.aros.dk. Open Tu and Th 10am-5pm, W 10am-10pm. 90kr, students 75kr.) The nation's tallest cathedral, **Århus Domkirke,** Skoleg. 17, is near the harbor. (☎86 20 54 00; www.aarhus-domkirke.dk. Open May-Sept. M-Sa 9:30am-4pm, Oct.-Apr. M-Sa 10am-3pm. Free.) At ⬛**Den Gamle By,** Viborgvej 2, actors bring to life a medieval village with authentic houses transported from all over Denmark. (☎86 12 31 88; www.dengamleby.dk. Open daily mid-June to mid-Sept. 9am-6pm; low season reduced hours.) The **Moesgård Museum of Prehistory,** Moesgård Allé 20, 15min. south of town, features the mummified **Grauballe Man.** Take bus #6 from the train station to the end. (☎89 42 11 00; www.moesmus.dk. Open Apr.-Sept. daily 10am-5pm; Oct.-Mar. Tu-Su 10am-4pm. 45kr, students 35kr. AmEx/MC/V.) The 3km ⬛**Prehistoric Trail** behind the museum reconstructs Danish forests from different ages and leads to a popular **beach.** In summer, bus #19 returns from the beach to the train station.

Every year in mid-July, Århus hosts its acclaimed **International Jazz Festival** (www.jazzfest.dk). The **Århus Festuge** (☎89 40 91 91; www.aarhusfestuge.dk), a rollicking celebration of theater, dance, and music, is held from late August through early September. ⬛**The Social Club,** Klosterg. 34, has three bars on two levels with loud music. (☎85 19 42 50; www.socialclub.dk. Beer and liquor 20kr. Cover after 2am Th 20kr; F-Sa 40kr. 11pm-midnight entrance only with student ID; one free beer and no cover. Open Th-Sa 11pm-6am.) **Train,** Tolbodg. 6, has reinvented a dockside warehouse as a club and concert hall. (☎86 13 47 22; www.train.dk. Concerts all ages, club 23+. Club open F-Sa 11pm-late.)

⬛ LET'S GO TO LEGOLAND: BILLUND   ☎ 75, 76

Budget airlines like **Iceland Express, Ryanair,** and **Sterling** serve **Billund's airport (BLL; ☎76 50 50 50).** Buses leave the airport for Århus (1½hr., 8-9 per day, 180kr) and Legoland (10min., 1-2 per hr.).

Tourists are drawn to Billund not just for its airport. The city is home to ⬛**Legoland,** an amusement park with sprawling Lego sculptures made from over 50 million of the candy-colored blocks. The **Power Builder** ride will convert any skeptic. (☎75 33 13 33; www.legoland.com. Open daily Apr.-Oct. 10am-6pm with extended hours during the summer; check website for detailed schedule. Day pass 229kr. Free 30min. before rides close.) If not flying, take the **train** from Århus to Vejle (45min., 1 per hr., 88kr), then **bus** #244 (dir.: Grinsted; 46kr).

RIBE   ☎ 75, 76

Denmark's oldest settlement, Ribe (pop. 18,000) is a well-preserved medieval town near Jutland's west coast. The tower of the 12th-century **Domkirke** (Cathedral) offers a sweeping view of the town. (☎75 42 06 19. Open July to mid-Aug. M-Sa 10am-5:30pm, Su noon-5:30pm; May-June and mid-Aug. to Sept. M-Sa 10am-5pm,

Su noon-5pm; low season reduced hours. 12kr.) Near the **Torvet** (Main Square), the **Old Town Hall**, on Von Støckens Pl., houses a former debtors' prison where artifacts of Ribe's medieval "justice" system are displayed. (☎76 88 11 22. Open June-Aug. daily 1-3pm; May and Sept. M-F 1-3pm. 15kr.) A singing **☒night watchman** leads entertaining walking tours, beginning in the Torvet. (40min. June-Aug. 8 and 10pm; May and Sept. 10pm. Free.) The no-frills **Ribe Vandrerhjem (HI) ❷**, Sct. Pedersg. 16, has a knowledgeable staff that relates tidbits of Ribe's history. From the station, cross the parking lot, bear right, walk to the end of Sct. Nicolajg., then turn right on Saltg. and immediately left. (☎75 42 06 20; www.danhostel-ribe.dk. Breakfast 50kr. Linens 50kr. Laundry 45kr. Internet 10kr per 15min. Reception 8am-noon and 4-6pm. Check-in 4-6pm. Open Feb.-Nov. Dorms 135-185kr; singles 320-535kr; doubles 350-535kr. 35kr HI discount. AmEx/MC/V.) **Overdammen**, which begins at the Torvet, has inexpensive cafes and pizzerias. **Trains** go to Århus (3½hr., 1 per 1-2hr., 218kr) via Fredricia. The **tourist office** is at Torvet 3. From the train station, walk down Dagmarsg. (☎75 42 15 00; www.visitribe.dk. Open July-Aug. M-F 9am-6pm, Sa 10am-5pm, Su 10am-2pm; June and Sept. M-F 9am-5pm, Sa 10am-1pm; Jan.-May and Oct.-Dec. M-F 9:30am-4:30pm, Sa 10am-1pm.)

AALBORG   ☎96, 98, 99

A laid-back haven for university students by day, Aalborg (OLE-borg; pop. 162,000) heats up at night. At the corner of Alg. and Molleg., an elevator descends from outside the Salling Department Store to the half-excavated ruins of a **Franciscan friary**. (☎96 31 04 10. Open Tu-Su 10am-5pm; elevator closes at 4:30pm. Elevator 20kr per 2-3 people, up to 250kg.) North of town, the solemn grounds of **Lindholm Høje**, Vendilav. 11, hold 700 ancient Viking graves and a museum of artifacts. Take bus #2C, which departs near the tourist office. (☎99 31 74 40; www.nordjyllandshistoriskemuseum.dk. Grounds open 24hr. Museum open Apr.-Oct. daily 10am-5pm; Nov.-Mar. Tu 10am-4pm, Su 11am-4pm. English-language tours in July W 2pm. Grounds free. Museum 30kr, students 15kr. MC/V.) After a day of dusty antiquarianism, head to **Jomfru Ane Gade**, a pedestrian strip of bars and clubs that's packed with students. For an even wilder time, hit up Aalborg the last weekend in May for **Karneval i Aalborg** (May 17-24, 2008; www.karnevaliaalborg.dk), when the city celebrates spring with Northern Europe's largest carnival.

Cozy private cabins double as dorms at **Aalborg Vandrerhjem and Camping (HI) ❸**, Skydebanev. 50. Take bus #13 (dir.: Fjordparken, 2 per hr.) to the end of the line. (☎98 11 60 44. Breakfast 50kr. Linens 36kr. Laundry 35kr. Free Internet. Reception mid-June to mid-Aug. 8am-11pm; low season 8am-noon and 4-9pm. Reserve ahead in summer. Dorms 195kr; singles 325-525kr; doubles 385-555kr. 35kr HI discount. 70-82kr per tent site. Camping electricity 28kr. MC/V; 4% surcharge.) **Føtex supermarket**, Slotsg. 8-14, is just past Boomtown on Nytorv. (☎99 32 90 00. Open M-F 9am-8pm, Sa 8am-5pm. Cash only.) **Trains** run to Århus (1½hr., 1 per hr., 153kr) and Copenhagen (5hr., 2 per hr., 338kr). To find the **tourist office**, Østeråg. 8, head out of the train station, cross JFK Pl., and turn left on Boulevarden, which becomes Østeråg. (☎99 30 60 90; www.visitaalborg.com. Open July M-F 9am-5:30pm, Sa 10am-4pm; late June and Aug. M-F 9am-5:30pm, Sa 10am-1pm; Sept. to mid-June M-F 9am-4:30pm, Sa 10am-1pm.)

FREDERIKSHAVN   ☎96, 98, 99

Since its days as a fishing village and naval base, Frederikshavn (fred-riks-HOW-n; pop. 35,000) has evolved into a transportation hub for Scandinavian ferry lines. **Stena Line** ferries (☎96 20 02 00; www.stenaline.com) leave for Gothenburg, SWE (3¼hr.; from 160kr, 30% Scanrail discount) and Oslo, NOR (8½hr.; from 180kr, 50% Scanrail discount). **Color Line** (☎99 56 19 77; www.colorline.com) sails to Larvik,

NOR (6¼hr., from 120kr). To get from the station to the **Frederikshavn Vandrerhjem (HI) ❷**, Buhlsv. 6, walk right on Skipperg. for 10min., turn left onto Nørreg., and take a right on Buhlsv. (☎98 42 14 75; www.danhostel.dk/frederikshavn. Breakfast 50kr. Linens 45kr. Laundry 40kr. Reception 8am-noon and 4-8pm. Dorms 120kr; singles 285kr; doubles 440kr. 35kr HI discount. Cash only.) Restaurants and shops cluster along **Søndergade** and **Havnegade; Rådhus Allé** has several grocery stores. To get to the commercial area from the train station, turn left and cross Skipperg. A church, the Frederikshavn Kirke, with a huge anchor on its front lawn, will be on the left. Walk up one block to Danmarksg., the main pedestrian thoroughfare, and turn left. Danmarksg. becomes Sønderg. and intersects with Havneg.

SKAGEN
☎98

Located on Denmark's northernmost tip, Skagen (SKAY-en; pop. 10,000) is bordered by long stretches of white sand dunes that descend to ice-blue water. Bright "Skagen yellow" houses topped by red-tiled roofs welcome fishermen home from sea. The **Skagens Museum,** Brøndumsv. 4, features 19th- and 20th-century works by local artists. From the train station, walk left down Sct. Laurentii V. and turn right on Brøndumsv. (☎44 64 44; www.skagensmuseum.dk. Open Apr.-Sept. Tu.-Su. 10am-5pm; Oct.-Mar. W-Su 10am-3pm. 70kr.) At nearby **Grenen,** the currents of the North and Baltic Seas collide in striking rhythm, but swimming is strictly off-limits because of life-threatening tides. Take the bus from the Skagen station (15kr; last return 7:30pm) or walk 5km down Fyrv. About 13km south of Skagen is the enormous ⬛**Råberg Mile** (ROH-bayrg MEE-leh), a sand dune formed by a 16th-century storm. The dune resembles a vast moonscape and migrates 15m east each year. Take bus #99 or the train from Skagen to Hulsig, then walk 4km down Kandestedv. Each July, the town welcomes Irish fiddlers and Scandinavian troubadours for the ⬛**Skagen Folk Music Festival** (☎44 40 94; www.skagenfestival.dk; early July).

Reserve ahead at the popular **Skagen Ny Vandrerhjem ❸**, Rolighedsv. 2. From the station, turn right on Chr. X's V., which becomes Frederikshavnv., then go left on Rolighedsv. (☎44 22 00; www.danhostelnord.dk/skagen. Breakfast 50kr. Linens 50kr. Reception 9am-noon and 4-6pm. Open Feb.-Nov. Dorms 185kr; singles 335-535kr; doubles 385-635kr. 35kr HI discount. Cash only.) To reach the campgrounds at **Poul Eeg Camping ❶**, Batterivej 21, turn left out of the train station, walk 3km straight down Sct. Laurentii V., and go left on Batterivej. (☎44 14 70. Bike rental 60kr per day. Tent sites 67-78kr. Cash only.) Turn right out of the station onto Sct. Laurentii V. to get to an area of restaurants near **Havnevej.** In the town center, **Orchid Thai Restaurant ❶**, Sct. Laurentii V. 60, offers authentic, cheap, and filling lunch boxes for 35kr. (☎44 60 44. Open daily 11am-10pm. MC/V.) Pick up picnic supplies at **Super Brugsen,** Sct. Laurentii V. 28. (☎44 17 00. Open daily 9am-10pm.)

Trains run from Skagen to Frederikshavn (40min., 1 per hr., 48kr). Despite the wind, **biking** is the best way to experience the region. Rent bikes at **Cykelhandler,** Kappelborgv. 23; from the station, turn right onto Sct. Laurentii V., right on to Havnev., and right again. (☎44 25 28. 20kr per hr., 60kr per day. Open M-F 8am-5:30pm, Sa 9:30am-noon. Cash only.) The **tourist office** is in the station. (☎44 13 77; www.skagen-tourist.dk. Open July M-Sa 9am-6pm, Su 10am-4pm; June and Aug. M-Sa 9am-5pm, Su 10am-2pm; low season reduced hours.)

ESTONIA (EESTI)

Eager to sever its Soviet bonds, Estonia has been quick to revive its historical and cultural ties to its Nordic neighbors, while Finnish tourism and investment help to revitalize the nation. The wealth that has reinvigorated Tallinn, however, belies the poverty that still predominates outside of Estonia's big cities, as well as the discontent of its ethnically Russian minority, uneasy with Estonia's increasingly European leanings. Still, having overcome successive centuries of domination by the Danes, Swedes, and Russians, most Estonians are now proud to take their place as members of modern Europe.

 DISCOVER ESTONIA: SUGGESTED ITINERARIES

THREE DAYS. Spend a day exploring the streets and sights of Old Town **Tallinn** (p. 275)–don't miss the Museum of Occupations. On your second day, head outside the old city walls to **Kumu** (p. 278), Estonia's main art museum, before heading down to **Pärnu** (p. 278). Spend your third day in there lying on the beaches and exploring the town by bike.

ONE WEEK. Begin in the south by enjoying the uniqueness of **Tartu** (2 days; p. 279). Then move west to **Pärnu** (1 day), and its Museum of New Art. Next, head out to the island of **Saaremaa** (2 days; p. 280). Rent a bicycle and take in the unspoiled beauty of the region, including meteorite craters and far-flung peninsulas. Spend your last 2 days in **Tallinn.**

ESSENTIALS

FACTS AND FIGURES

Official Name: Republic of Estonia.
Capital: Tallinn (pop. 409,516).
Major Cities: Pärnu, Tartu.
Population: 1,316,000

Time Zone: GMT + 2.
Language: Estonian.
Words with many vowels: tööööööbik (nightingale or workaholic); hauaöööudused (horrors of the night in the grave).

WHEN TO GO

The best time to visit is in late spring (Apr.-May) and summer (June to early Sept.). Temperatures reach highs of 30°C (86°F) in July and August. Although winters can be cold, with limited daylight hours, Estonia offers an abundance of skiing and skating. Beware, however, that the warm summer weather draws in the tourist crowds, which overrun Tallinn and the beaches.

DOCUMENTS AND FORMALITIES

EMBASSIES AND CONSULATES. Foreign embassies to Estonia are in **Tallinn** (p. 277). Embassies and consulates abroad include: **Australia,** 86 Louisa Rd., Birchgrove, NSW 2041 (☎2 9810 7468; eestikon@ozemail.com.au); **Canada,** 260 Dalhousie St., Ste. 210, Ottawa, ON K1N 7E4 (☎613-789-4222; www.estemb.ca); **UK,** 16 Hyde Park Gate, London SW7 5DG (☎020 7589 3428; www.estonia.gov.uk); **US,** 2131 Massachusetts Ave., NW, Washington, D.C. 20008 (☎202-588-0101; www.estemb.org).

ENTRANCE REQUIREMENTS.
Passport: Required for all travelers.
Visa: Not required for citizens of EU countries, Australia, Canada, New Zealand, the US, and assorted other countries for stays under 90 days.
Letter of Invitation: Not required.
Inoculations: Recommended up-to-date on DTaP (diphtheria, tetanus, and pertussis), Hepatitis A, Hepatitis B, MMR (measles, mumps, and rubella), polio booster, tick-borne encephalitis, and typhoid.
Work Permit: Required of all those planning to work in Estonia.
International Driving Permit: Required of all those planning to drive.

TOURIST SERVICES AND MONEY

TOURIST OFFICES. Offices of the **Estonian Tourist Board,** marked with a white "i" on a green background, are in most towns and sell maps and offer advice about accommodations and services. They keep extended hours in summer months, except on national holidays June 23-24 and August 20, when they're open from 10am to 3pm.

MONEY. At the time of publication, the Estonian unit of currency is the **kroon (EEK),** plural krooni, which is divided into 100 **senti.** Since its 2004 accession to the EU, however, Estonia has followed the path of economic integration and intends to switch to the **euro** on January 1, 2008. Currently, the best foreign currencies to bring to Estonia are the euro and US dollar; travelers should stay attuned to economic developments over the coming months. Annual inflation averages 4.1%, although this has been decreasing over the last decade. Common banks in Estonia are **Hansabank,** which offers the most services, including **Western Union** transfers, exchanging **currency** and **travelers checks.** Hansabank also generally offers the best rates. **SEB Banks** are also very common. **ATMs** are available everywhere, and offer acceptable exchange rates. **Tipping** is common; 10% is expected in restaurants. **Bargaining** is appropriate only at outdoor markets; written prices should be treated as fixed.

ESTONIAN KROONI (EEK)		
AUS$1 = 9.08EEK		10EEK = AUS$1.10
CDN$1 = 10.98EEK		10EEK = CDN$0.91
EUR€1 = 15.65EEK		10EEK = EUR€0.64
NZ$1 = 7.64EEK		10EEK = NZ$1.31
UK£1 = 22.75EEK		10EEK = UK£0.44
US$1 = 12.06EEK		10EEK = US$0.83

HEALTH AND SAFETY

Medical services for foreigners are few and far between, and usually require cash payments. There are two kinds of **pharmacies** *(apteek);* some stock prescription medication, but most are chains that stock everything. Public **toilets** *(tasuline),* marked with an "N" or a triangle pointing up for women and "M" or a triangle pointing down for men, usually cost 3EEK. While Tallinn's tap water is generally safe to drink, **bottled water** is necessary in the rest of the country. Petty **crime** is rare, though pickpocketing is common in Tallinn's Old Town, especially along Viru St. **Women** should not have a problem traveling alone, but may want to dress modestly. **Minorities** in Estonia are rare; they receive stares but generally experience little discrimination. For English-language help in an emergency, contact your embassy. **Homosexuality** is generally treated with curiosity rather than suspicion.

EMERGENCY **Police:** ☎ 110. **Ambulance** and **Fire:** ☎ 112.

TRANSPORTATION

BY PLANE, TRAIN, AND FERRY. Several international airlines offer flights to Tallinn, the site of Estonia's major international airport; try **SAS** or **AirBaltic,** or consider the budget airline **easyJet** (p. 47). Some travelers find it easier to fly into the larger international airport in **Riga, Latvia,** from which some regions in southern Estonia can be reached as or more easily than from Tallinn itself. **Trains** in Estonia are mainly used for hauling freight. If you are traveling from Russia or another Baltic state, you may consider taking a **ferry,** but expect more red tape when crossing the border. Tallinksilja serves the entire Baltic Sea region (www.tallinksilja.com/en/). Ferries also connect with **Finland, Germany,** and **Sweden.**

BY BUS. **Euroline** (www.eurolines.ee) and **Ecoline** (www.ecoline.net) **buses** run to Estonia from international cities. Domestic buses (www.bussireisid.ee) are cheaper and more efficient than trains, though service can be infrequent between smaller cities. Taking buses on the islands can be especially frustrating. From September to late June, students receive half-price bus tickets.

BY CAR, BIKE, AND THUMB. If entering Estonia by car, avoid routes through Kaliningrad and Belarus: both require visas. Although road conditions are steadily improving, the availability of **roadside assistance** remains poor. Check out the Estonian National Road Administration (www.mnt.ee). **Taxis** (about 7EEK per km) are generally a safe. Bicycling is common in Estonia. Those who want to **hitchhike** just stretch out an open hand. Let's Go does not recommend hitchhiking.

KEEPING IN TOUCH

PHONE CODES	**Country code: 372. International dialing prefix:** 800. For more info on international calls, see **Inside Back Cover.**

EMAIL AND INTERNET. Although **Internet** cafes are not as common as you might expect, Wi-Fi is widespread. Free Wi-Fi is available throughout Tallinn; check **www.wifi.ee** for more info or look for the wifi.ee sign.

TELEPHONE. Public telephones, which are very common at bus stations and shopping malls, require magnetic cards, available at any kiosk. These come in 20, 50,

100 EEK denominations. International calls are expensive, usually costing around US$0.80 per minute. **Tele 2** cards offer the best rates. International access codes include: **AT&T** (☎0 800 12 001), **Canada Direct** (☎0 800 12 011), and **MCI** (☎0 800 12 122). If you bring a GSM mobile phone, SIM cards (around US$1) offer a convenient and sometimes cheap way to keep in touch. Tallinn, unlike other Estonian cities, has no city code; to call Tallinn from outside Estonia, dial Estonia's country code (372) and then the number. To call any city besides Tallinn from outside the country, dial the country code, the city code, and the number. The 0 before each city code need only be dialed when placing calls within Estonia.

MAIL. Estonia's state-run **postal system** is reliable, and mail from Estonia generally arrives in the US or Canada within 5-9 days. Most postal workers speak good English. Mail can be received general delivery through Poste Restante to Tallinn, Pärnu and Tartu. Address envelopes as follows: First name, LAST NAME, POSTE RESTANTE, post office address, 0001 (Postal Code) Tallinn (city), ESTONIA.

LANGUAGE. Estonian is a Finno-Ugric language, closely related to Finnish. Knowledge of English is widespread among Estonians, especially those of the younger generations. Many also know Finnish or Swedish, but German is more common among the older set and in resort towns. Russian was once mandatory, but Estonians in secluded areas are likely to have forgotten much of it.

ACCOMMODATIONS AND CAMPING

ESTONIA	❶	❷	❸	❹	❺
ACCOMMODATIONS	under 200EEK	200-400EEK	401-550EEK	551-600EEK	over 600EEK

Each tourist office has accommodations listings for its town and can often arrange a bed for visitors. There is little distinction between **hotels, hostels,** and **guesthouses;** some upscale hotels still have hall toilets and showers. The word *võõrastemaja* (guesthouse) in a place's name usually implies that it's less expensive. Many hotels provide laundry services for an extra charge. Some hostels are part of hotels, so be sure to ask for the cheaper rooms. **Homestays** are common and inexpensive. For info on HI hostels around Estonia, contact the **Estonian Youth Hostel Association,** Narva Mantee 16-25, 10121 Tallinn (☎372 6461 455; www.baltichostels.net). **Camping** is the best way to experience Estonia's islands; doing so outside of designated areas, however, is illegal and a threat to wildlife. Farm stays provide a great peek into local life. For more info visit Rural Tourism (www.maaturism.ee), or search for a variety of accommodations at www.visitestonia.com.

FOOD AND DRINK

ESTONIA	❶	❷	❸	❹	❺
FOOD	under 50EEK	50-80EEK	81-100EEK	101-140EEK	over 140EEK

Most cheap Estonian food is fried and doused with **sour cream.** Local specialties include *schnitzel* (breaded, fried pork fillet), *seljanka* (meat stew), *pelmenid* (dumplings), and smoked fish. Bread is usually dark and dense; a loaf of *Hiiumaa leib* easily weighs a kilo. Pancakes with cheese curd and berries are a delicious dessert. The national beer *Saku* and the darker *Saku Tume* are acquired tastes. Local beer, like Kuressaare's *Saaremaa*, is of inconsistent quality. *Värska*, a brand of carbonated mineral water, is particularly salty. It is difficult to keep a vegetarian or kosher diet in Estonia; buying your own groceries may be your best bet.

HOLIDAYS AND FESTIVALS

Holidays: New Year's Day (Jan. 1); Independence Day (Feb. 24); Good Friday (March 21, 2008; April 10, 2009); Easter Sunday (March 23, 2008; April 12, 2009); Labor Day (May 1); Pentecost (May 11, 2008; May 31, 2009); Victory Day (June 23); Jaanipäev (June 23-24); Restoration of Independence (Aug. 20).

Festivals: Tallinn's Beersummer (p. 278), held in early July, is the kind of celebration its name leads you to expect. Tallinn also hosts the Dark Nights Film Festival in December, featuring student and animation subfestivals in addition to showcasing international films. Pärnu's mid-June Estonian Country Dance Festival culminates in a line dance the length of a city street. Check an updated list of cultural events is at www.kultuuriinfo.ee.

BEYOND TOURISM

For more information on opportunities across Europe, see **Beyond Tourism**, p. 56.

Earthwatch, 3 Clocktower Pl., Ste. 100, P.O. Box 75, Maynard, MA 01754 USA (☎1-800-776-0188 or 1-978-461-0081; www.earthwatch.org). Arranges 1- to 3-week programs to promote conservation of natural resources. Programs average US$2000.

Youth for Understanding USA (YFU), 6400 Goldsboro Rd., Ste. 100, Bethesda, MD 20817, USA (☎1-866-493-8872; www.yfu.org). Places US high school students for a year, semester, or summer. US$75 application fee plus $500 enrollment deposit.

TALLINN   ☎0

Crisp sea air gusts over the medieval buildings and spires of Tallinn (pop. 401,000), the self-proclaimed "Heart of Northern Europe." Unfortunately, wall-to-wall tourists and vendors in "historical dress" often give the cobblestone streets of Old Town a theme-park feel. Visitors willing to venture beyond the compact center will be delighted by quirky cafes, lush parks, and the glorious seaside promenade.

ESTONIA

▐▀ TRANSPORTATION

Trains: Toompuiestee 35 (☎615 86 10; www.evr.ee). Trams #1 and 2 run between the station and the Mere pst., just south of the town center. To **Pärnu** (2½hr., 2 per day, 60EEK); **Tartu** (3-4hr., 4 per day, 80-130EEK); **Moscow, RUS** (14½hr.; 1 per day; 568EEK, sleeper car 898EEK).

Buses: Lastekodu 46 (☎680 0900), 1.5km southeast of *Vanalinn*. Trams #2 and 4 run on Tartu mnt. between Hotel Viru and the station. Buy tickets at the station (10EEK) or from the driver (15EEK). **Eurolines** (www.eurolines.ee) runs to **Rīga, LAT** (5-6hr., 9 per day, 200-250EEK), **St. Petersburg, RUS** (8-10½hr., 6 per day, 190-270EEK), and **Vilnius, LIT** (10½hr., 4 per day, 430EEK). 10% ISIC discount.

Ferries: At the end of Sadama (☎631 8550). Ferries cross to **Helsinki, FIN** (1½-3½hr., 47 per day, 350-755EEK). ▨ **Mainedd** travel agency, Raekoja pl. 18 (☎644 4744; mainedd@hot.ee), books ferry tickets with no commission. Student rates available. Open M-F 9:30am-5:30pm. MC/V.

Public Transportation: Buses, trams, minibuses, and **trolleys** run 6am-midnight. Buy tickets from kiosks (10EEK) or from drivers (15EEK). 10-ticket booklet 80EEK. Tickets valid on all but minibuses. Validate tickets in metal boxes onboard or face a 600EEK fine. 1hr., 2hr., and 1-day tickets are available from kiosks (15/20/45EEK). Cash only.

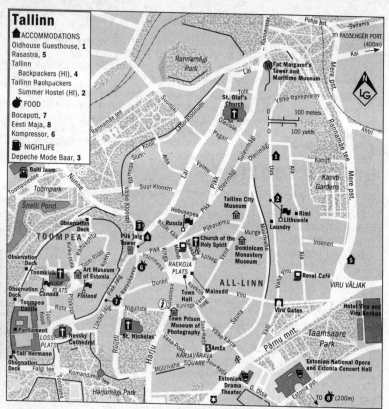

Tallinn

🏠 ACCOMMODATIONS
Oldhouse Guesthouse, **1**
Rasastra, **5**
Tallinn
  Backpackers (HI), **4**
Tallinn Backpackers
  Summer Hostel (HI), **2**

🍎 FOOD
Bocapott, **7**
Eesti Maja, **8**
Kompressor, **6**

🎵 NIGHTLIFE
Depeche Mode Baar, **3**

Taxi: Rate per km should be posted on your taxi's window. Call ahead and order a car to avoid a "waiting fee." **Klubi Takso** (☎142 00), 35EEK plus 7.50EEK per km. **Silver Takso** (☎152 22) 35EEK plus 7.50EEK per km. **Linnatakso** (☎644 2442), 7EEK per km, can provide taxis for disabled passengers. Another option Mar.-Oct. is a bicycle taxi (Velotaxi; ☎508 8810), which operate in *Vanalinn* and costs 35EEK per passenger.

✈ 🚉 ORIENTATION AND PRACTICAL INFORMATION

Even locals lose their way along the winding medieval streets of Tallinn's **Vanalinn** (Old Town), an egg-shaped maze ringed by five main streets: **Rannamäe tee, Mere puistee, Pärnu mantee, Kaarli puistee,** and **Toompuiestee.** *Vanalinn* has two sections: **All-linn** (Lower Town) and **Toompea,** a rocky, fortified hill west of *All-linn.* Only about 50% of the wall that once encircled *Vanalinn* is intact, but the best entrance is still through the 15th-century **Viru Gate,** across from Hotel Viru, Tallinn's central landmark (unless you come from the ferry terminal, in which case it's best to go through the Great Coastal Gate, **Surr Rannavärav,** to the north). **Viru,** the main thoroughfare, leads directly to **Raekoja plats** (Town Hall Square), in the center of town.

Tourist Office: Kullassepa 4/Niguliste 2 (☎645 7777; www.tourism.tallinn.ee). Open July-Aug. M-F 9am-8pm, Sa-Su 10am-6pm; May-June M-F 9am-7pm, Sa-Su 10am-5pm; Sept. M-F 9am-6pm, Sa-Su 10am-5pm; Oct.-Apr. M-F 9am-5pm, Sa 10am-3pm.

Embassies: For more info, contact the Estonian Foreign Ministry (www.vm.ee). **Canada,** Toom-kooli 13 (☎627 3311; tallinn@canada.ee). Open M, W, F 9am-noon. **Ireland,** Vene 2 (☎681 1888; embassytallinn@eircom.net). Open M-F 10am-1pm and 2-3:30pm. **UK,** Wismari 6 (☎667 4700; www.britishembassy.ee). Open M-F 10am-noon and 2-4:30pm. **US,** Kentmanni 20 (☎668 8100, emergency 509 2129; www.usemb.ee). Open M-F 9am-noon and 2-5pm. **Australian** citizens should contact the embassy in Stockholm, SWE. Citizens of **New Zealand** should contact the embassy in The Hague, NTH.

Currency Exchange: Banks have better rates than hotels and private exchange bureaus. Try **Eesti Uhispank,** Pärnu mnt. 12 (☎640 3614). Open M-F 9am-6pm, Sa 10am-3pm. There are **ATMs** throughout the city.

American Express: Suur-Karja 15 (☎626 6335; www.estravel.ee). Books hotels and tours, sells airline, ferry, and rail tickets, and provides visa services. Open June-Aug. M-F 9am-6pm, Sa 10am-5pm; Sept.-May M-F 9am-6pm, Sa 10am-3pm.

Pharmacy: Tönismae Apteek, Töniamagi 5 (☎644 2282). Open 24hr.

Laundry: Keemilin Pubastus, Uus 9. Full service 20EEK per kg. Open M-F 9am-6pm, Sa 10am-4pm. Cash only.

Internet Access: Metro, Viru valjak 4 (☎610 1519), in the bus station below Viru keskus. 15EEK per 15min.; 35EEK per hr., students 15EEK. Open M-F 7am-11pm, Sa-Su 10am-11pm. MC/V; min. 50EEK. **Central Library,** Estonia pst. 8, 2nd fl. (☎683 0902). Free if you call ahead. Open M-F 11am-7pm, Sa 10am-5pm.

Post Office: Narva mnt. 1 (☎661 6616), opposite Hotel Viru. **Poste Restante** in basement. Open Tu-F 7:30am-8pm, Sa 8am-6pm. **Postal Code: 10101.**

ACCOMMODATIONS AND FOOD

Hostels fill up fast, so reserve ahead. ◪**Rasastra** ❷, Mere pst. 4, 2nd fl., finds private rooms in Tallinn, Rīga, and Vilnius. (☎661 6291; www.bedbreakfast.ee. Open M-Sa 9:30am-6pm, Su 9:30am-5pm. Singles 300EEK; doubles 500EEK; triples 650EEK. Cash only.) ▩ **Oldhouse Guesthouse** ❸, Uus 22 (☎641 1464; www.oldhouse.ee). Oldhouse maintains three properties along Uus and boasts the cleanest, most comfortable rooms in town. (Fully equipped kitchen. Breakfast included. Free Wi-Fi. 8-bed dorms 250EEK; singles 450-550EEK; doubles 650EEK. 10% ISIC discount, or for stays over 3 nights. Cash only.) **Tallinn Backpackers (HI)** ❷, Lai 10, and the smaller **Tallinn Backpackers Summer Hostel** ❷, Uus 14, offer some of the city's most sociable settings. Tallinn Backpackers offers a large common room with a TV for nightly movies and a foosball table—perfect for mingling with fellow travelers. (☎644 0298; www.tallinnbackpackers.com. Free Internet and Wi-Fi. Fully equipped kitchen. Linens 25EEK. 8-bed dorms 225EEK. MC/V.) Summer Hostel only has room for 10 people and fills up quickly. (☎517 1337; www.balticbackpackers.com. Linens 25EEK. Internet 5EEK per 15min. Dorms 225EEK, members 200EEK. MC/V.)

The secret is out about ◪**Kompressor** ❶, Rataskaevu 3. This is the best place in town for Estonian pancakes, offering giant portions with fish, meat, and veggie fillings. (Pancakes 45-80EEK. Kitchen open daily noon-10pm, longer on weekends; bar open late. Cash only.) **Eesti Maja** ❷, A. Lauteri 1, has favorites like *sült* (jellied pig legs; 80EEK), and its own history magazine. (www.eestimaja.ee. M-F 11am-3pm all-you-can-eat buffet 95EEK. Entrees 45-195EEK. Open daily 11am-11pm. MC/V.) **Bocapott** ❶, Pikk Jalg 9, serves crepes, sandwiches, and savory pies on dishes made in the adjoining ceramics studio. (www.bogapott.ee. Sandwiches 22EEK; crepes 40EEK; pies 10EEK. Open daily 10am-7pm. MC/V.)

👁 SIGHTS

ALL-LINN (LOWER TOWN). Head up Viru to reach **Raekoja plats,** where beer flows and local troupes perform throughout the summer. Tallinn's **town hall,** Europe's oldest, is right on the square. The museum inside details daily life in medieval Tallinn. Next door is a tower with one of the world's tallest toilets (77m), built so guards could relieve themselves without descending. (Town hall open July-Aug. M-Sa 10am-4pm; 35EEK. Tower open June-Aug. daily 11am-6pm; 25EEK. Cash only.) Take Mündi from the square, turn right on Pühavaimu, and then right on Vene to reach **Katariinan Käytävä,** an alley lined with galleries and cafes. At the north end of All-linn, the tower of **St. Olaf's Church** offers such a great view of the Old Town that the KGB used it as an observation post. (Lai 50. Open daily Apr.-Oct. 10am-6pm. Services M and F 6:30pm, Su 10am and noon. Church free. Tower 30EEK, students 15EEK. Cash only.)

TOOMPEA. Toompea's **Lossi plats** (Castle Sq.) is dominated by the onion domes of the Russian Orthodox **Alexander Nevsky Cathedral.** (From Raekoja pl., head down Kullassepa, right on Niguliste, and uphill on Lühike jalg. Open daily 8am-6:30pm. Services 9am.) **Dome Church,** the oldest in Estonia, towers over the hill. Over 300 barons are buried just inches below the floor; their intricately carved, wooden family crests line the walls of the church. Walk south on Toompea from Lossi pl. to the **Museum of Occupation and of the Fight for Freedom,** which documents Estonia's repression by the Germans and Soviets. (Open Tu-Su 11am-6pm. 10EEK, students 5EEK. Cash only.)

KADRIORG. In Kadriorg Park is Peter the Great's **⬛Kadriorg Palace,** whose sumptuous grand hall is a stunning example of Baroque architecture and houses a lovely art collection. The grounds also house the **Mikkel Museum,** with similar work, and the **Peter the Great House Museum** in his former temporary residence which holds many of the tsar's original furnishings, as well as an imprint of his extremely large hand. (Mäekalda 2. Palace open May-Sept. Tu-W and F-Su 10am-5pm, Th 10am-9pm; Oct.-Apr. W-Su 10am-5pm. Mikkel Museum open May-Sept. W and F-Su 10am-9pm; Oct.-Apr. W-Su 10am-5pm. House Museum open mid-May to Sept. W-Su 10:30am-5pm. Palace 45EEK, students 35EEK. Mikkel Museum 25/10 EEK. House Museum 15/10EEK. MC/V.) At the opposite end of the park from the tram stop is the main branch of the ⬛**Art Museum of Estonia.** (Weizenbergi 34. www.ekm.ee. Open May-Sept. Tu-Su 11am-6pm, Oct-Apr. W-Su 11am-6pm. Contemporary art 30EEK, permanent exhibition 55EEK, combined ticket 75EEK. Free admission once a month; see website for specific dates. MC/V.)

🎵 🎭 ENTERTAINMENT AND NIGHTLIFE

Pick up a free copy of *Tallinn This Week* at the tourist office. The **Estonia Concert Hall** and the **Estonian National Opera** (Rahvusooper Estonia) are both at Estonia pst. 4. (Concert hall ☎614 7760; www.concert.ee. Opera ☎683 1260; www.opera.ee. Concert hall box office open M-F noon-7pm, Sa noon-5pm, Su 1hr. before curtain. Opera box office open daily 11am-7pm. Tickets 60-400EEK. MC/V.) Celebrate the power of barley early July at **Beersummer** (www.ollesummer.ee). In the midst of December, the international **Dark Nights Film Festival** (www.poff.ee) showcases cinematic talent. ⬛**Depeche Mode Baar,** Nomme 4, plays all Depeche Mode, all day long and serves mixed drinks (40-80EEK) named after their songs. (www.edmfk.ee/dmbaar. 0.5L beer 45EEK. Open daily noon-4am. Cash only.)

PÄRNU

☎44

Famous for its mud baths, beaches, and festivals, Pärnu (pop. 45,000) is the summer capital of Estonia. Soak up some culture at Pärnu's **Museum of New Art,** Esplanaadi 10, which features a statue of Lenin with an amputated right hand as well as local contemporary art. (☎307 72. Open daily 9am-9pm. 25EEK, students 15EEK. MC/V.) Check out the ⬛Estonian Lithograph Center (Eesti Litograafiakeskus), Kuninga 17, to see printmakers at work. (☎55 60 46 31; www.hot.ee/litokeskus. Hours vary.) Hostel Lõuna ❷, Lõuna 2, has comfortable rooms with clean shared baths and a large kitchen. (☎443 0943; www.eliisabet.ee/hostel. Reception 24hr. Dorms 250-300EEK; doubles 500-900EEK; triples 750-900EEK.) It is wise to make restaurant reservations ahead in summer. Kadri Kohvik ❷, Nikolai 12, around the corner from the TIC, is a popular cafeteria serving filling fish and meat dishes. (☎442 9782. Entrees 30-70EEK. Open M-F 7:30am-9pm, Sa-Su 9am-5pm.) Head to Veerev Olu (The Rolling Beer), Uus 3A, for live rock and folk Saturday 9:30pm-1am. (☎53 40 31 49. Beer 20EEK 0.5L. Food 35-80EEK. Su-Th 11am-midnight, F-Sa 11am-1am. MC/V.) Eurolines buses (☎442 7841) go from Ringi 3 to Tallinn (2hr., 2 per hr., 100-110EEK), Tartu (2½hr., 21 per day, 120-135EEK), and Rīga, LAT (3½hr., 6-8 per day, 180-210EEK)—beware, they only accept cash. City Bike, based in the beachside Rannahotell, will deliver a bicycle to you anywhere in Pärnu. (☎56 60 80 90; www.citybike.ee. 120EEK per ½-day., 150EEK per day. MC/V.) The tourist office, Rüütli 16, books rooms for a 25EEK fee and hands out free maps. (☎730 00; www.parnu.ee. Open mid-May to mid-Sept. M-F 9am-6pm, Sa 9am-4pm, Su 10am-3pm; mid-Sept. to mid-May M-F 9am-5pm. Cash only.) Postal Code: 80010.

TARTU   ☎7

The vibrant college town of Tartu (pop. 100,000) is home to Tartu University (Tartu Ülikool). In Raekoja plats (Town Hall Square), the building that has the ⬛Tartu Art Museum (Tartu Kunstimuuseum) leans a little to the left—just like the student population. (Open W-Su 11am-6pm. 25EEK, students 10EEK. Ground floor 12/5EEK. F free. Cash only.) In the attic of the university's main building is the student lock-up (kartser), which was used to detain rule-breaking students; their drawings and inscriptions are still visible. (Open M-F 11am-5pm. 5EEK. Cash only.) The university dorms at ⬛Hostel Raatuse ❷, Raatuse 22, are more luxurious than rooms in many hotels. (☎740 9958; www.kyla.ee. Free Wi-Fi. Singles 300EEK; doubles 500EEK. MC/V.) At attic lounge Maailm, Rüütli 12, you can enjoy drinks or ice-cream shakes (25EEK). (☎742 9099; www.klubi-maailm.ee. 21+ after 9pm. Open M-Sa noon-1am, Su noon-10pm. MC/V.) Wilde Irish Pub, Vallikraavi 4, is a raucous nighttime pub with karaoke on Tuesdays at

IN RECENT NEWS

CYBERWARS

On April 29, 2007, the very same night that Tallinn erupted in violent protest over the removal of a bronze Soviet WWII memorial, a mysterious wave of data began to flow through Estonia's websites. This junk data, initially merely a mall nuisance, increased dramatically in volume over several days, flooding key government and financial websites. In Estonia, where voting, banking, bill payment, and filing taxes are all conducted over the Internet, business came to a sudden halt. By the time the worst was over, Parliament had been without email for days, and several major banks were forced to shut down.

Estonian officials accused the Russian government of secretly orchestrating the attacks, and investigators found detailed instructions on how to send junk data to Estonian websites on Russian language forums and chat groups. The attack spiked dramatically on May 9th, or Victory Day, the Russian holiday marking the Soviet Union's defeat of Nazi Germany and the start of their occupation of the Baltic countries.

Nevertheless, Internet's sheer scale and anonymity makes identifying the hackers' true identity virtually impossible. Estonia's relationship with Russia is the most strained of the Baltic countries, the political and social tensions only strengthened in the wake of 2007's first ever large-scale cyber-attack.

9pm. (Entrees 50-195EEK. Open M-Tu noon-midnight, W-Th noon-1am, F-Sa noon-2am. Su 1pm-midnight. MC/V.) **Buses** (☎47 72 27) leave from Turu 2, 300m southeast of Raekoja pl., for: Pärnu (2½hr., 20 per day, 110EEK), Tallinn (2-3hr., 46 per day, 130-140EEK) and Rīga, LAT (5hr., 1 per day, 170-200EEK). **Trains** (☎615 6851), generally less reliable than buses, go from the intersection of Kuperjanovi and Vaksali to Tallinn (2½-3½hr., 3 per day, 85EEK). The **tourist office**, Raekoja pl. 14, offers free **Internet**. (☎44 21 11; www.visittartu.com. Open mid-Sept. to mid-May M-F 9am-6pm, Sa 10am-5pm, Su 10am-3pm; late Sept.-early May M-F 9am-5pm, Sa-Su 10am-3pm.) *Raekoja plats*, the town hall square, offers free Wi-Fi. **Postal Code:** 51001.

ESTONIAN ISLANDS

🏝 SAAREMAA
☎45

Kuressaare (pop. 16,000) is the largest town on Saaremaa. The local accent and folklore distinguish it from the mainland, although tourists seem to outnumber locals in summer months. Head south from Raekoja pl. (Town Hall Sq.) along Lossi to reach ◼**Bishopric Castle** (Piiskopilinnus). Inside, hidden staircases and lion statues share space with the **Saaremaa Museum,** which chronicles the island's history. (Open May-Aug. daily 10am-7pm; Sept.-Apr. W-Su 11am-6pm. 50EEK, students 25EEK. Cash only.) **SYG Hostel ❶,** Kingu 6, is your best bet for clean budget rooms. (☎455 4388. Breakfast 40EEK. Free Internet. Reception 24hr. Open June-Aug. Dorms 110-130EEK; singles 255EEK; doubles 300-350EEK; quads 480-580EEK. MC/V.) Grab traditional Estonian pancakes (16-33EEK), hotpots (45-61EEK), or non-traditional Estonian pizza (40-61EEK) at **Pannkoogikohvik ❶,** Kohtu 1. (☎453 3575. Open M-Th 9am-midnight, F-Sa 9am-2am, Su 10am-midnight. MC/V.) Direct **buses** (☎453 1661) leave from Pihtla tee 2, at the corner with Tallinna, for Pärnu (3hr., 3-5 per day, 180-194EEK) and Tallinn (4-5hr., 9-11 per day, 190-200EEK.) The **tourist office,** Tallinna 2, in the town hall, offers free **Internet** and arranges private rooms. (☎453 3120; www.saaremaa.ee. Open May to mid-Sept. M-F 9am-7pm, Sa 9am-5pm, Su 10am-3pm; mid-Sept. to Apr. M-F 9am-5pm.)

🏝 HIIUMAA
☎46

By restricting access to Hiiumaa (pop. 11,000) for 50 years, the Soviets unwittingly preserved the island's rare wildlife and scenery. Creek-laced **Kärdla** (pop. 4000) is Hiiumaa's biggest town. To explore the sights along the coast, rent a **bike** (150EEK per day) from **Priit Tikka,** which will deliver anywhere on the island (☎56 60 63 77; www.hot.ee/jalgrattalaenutus. Cash only.) Bike west from Kärdla toward Kõrgessaare to the chilling **Hill of Crosses** (Ristimägi; 6km). About 2km past that, a right turn leads to the cast-iron **Tahkuna Lighthouse** (11km). Back on the main road, turn right again toward Kõrgessaare; continue 20km past the town to reach the impressive 16th-century **Kõpu Lighthouse.** (25EEK, students 15EEK. Cash only.) Local **buses** (3-4 per day, 14EEK) run to the town of Kaina, an ideal base for exploring the island of **Kassari,** attached to Hiiumaa by a land bridge. From Kaina, biking either east or west on highway 83 will lead you to the 15km loop that runs through Kassari. On Kassari's southern tip is the ◼**Sääretirp** peninsula, where pine and juniper bushes give way to a windswept rocky promontory.

Eesti Posti Hostel ❶, Posti 13, has comfy beds and clean baths. (☎53 31 18 60. Call for check-in. May-Sept. 255EEK per person; Oct.-Apr. 200EEK. Cash only.) In the town square, **Arteesia Kohvik ❶**, Keskväljak 5, is a local haunt. (Entrees 30-85EEK. Open M-Th 9am-11pm, F-Sa 11am-midnight, Su 11am-10pm. MC/V.) Direct **buses** run from Sadama 13 (☎463 2077), north of Kärdla's main square, Keskväljak, to Tallinn (4½hr.; 2-3 per day; 160EEK, 15% ISIC discount; cash only). Once on Hiiumaa, you can get to Saaremaa via public transportation, but it's difficult to find transportation in the opposite direction, or from the ferry terminal on Saaremaa to town. The **tourist office**, Hiiu 1, in Keskväljak, passes out vital free maps and bus schedules and sells ◪**The Lighthouse Tour** (25EEK), a guide to sights with local legends. (☎462 2232; www.hiiumaa.ce. Open May to mid-Sept. M-F 9am-6pm, Sa-Su 10am-3pm; mid-Sept. to Apr. M-F 9am-5pm. Cash only.) The **cultural center**, Rookopli 18, has free **Internet,** and the town center has free Wi-Fi.

FINLAND (SUOMI)

Caught in a territorial tug-of-war between Sweden and Russia since the 1400s, Finland finally secured autonomy in 1917 and never looked back, successfully defending its independence through both World Wars. Tarja Halonen, Finland's first female president, presides over the home of Nokia cell phones and host of the annual World Sauna Championships. The country's lakes and boreal forest entice hikers while southern cities draw architecture students and art gurus. Finland—outside of stylish Helsinki—is more affordable than its Scandinavian neighbors.

 DISCOVER FINLAND: SUGGESTED ITINERARY

Start off in **Helsinki** (p. 286) by ambling along the tree-lined *Esplanadi* and checking out some of the city's grade-A museums. Leave time to bike down the Pellinge archipelago south of **Porvoo** (p. 293). Out west, the venerable **Turku** (p. 294) is worth a look, but **Tampere** (p. 296) is the rising star of Finnish cities, with a lively music scene and museums in the shells of factories. Picnic on the islands of **Savonlinna** (p. 298) and daytrip out to the transcendent Retretti Art Center. From here, head back to Helsinki or embark on the trek north to **Rovaniemi** (p. 301), where you can launch a foray into the wilds of Finnish Lapland.

ESSENTIALS

FACTS AND FIGURES

Official Name: Republic of Finland.

Capital: Helsinki.

Major Cities: Oulu, Tampere, Turku.

Population: 5,238,000.

Land Area: 338,000 sq. km.

Time Zone: GMT +2.

Languages: Finnish, Swedish.

Religions: Evangelical Lutheran (84%).

National Celebrity: Father Christmas, or Santa Claus, rumored to live in a northern province (p. 301).

WHEN TO GO

The long days of Finnish summer are a tourist's dream, while the two-month polar night *(kaamos)* in the country's northern regions draws winter-sports fanatics. Ski season starts in early February, continuing well into March and April. Reindeer and snowmobile safaris along with glimpses of the rare *aurora borealis* reward travelers willing to brave winter temperatures, which regularly drop to -20°C (-4°F). Summer tourists, celebrating Midsummer *(Juhannus)* festivities (June 21-22), can expect average temperatures of 20-25°C (68-77°F).

DOCUMENTS AND FORMALITIES

EMBASSIES AND CONSULATES. Foreign embassies in Finland are in Helsinki (p. 288). Finnish embassies abroad include: **Australia** and **New Zealand,** 12 Darwin Ave., Yarralumla, ACT, 2600 (☎26 273 38 00; www.finland.org.au); **Canada,** 55 Metcalfe St., Ste. 850, Ottawa, ON, K1P 6L5 (☎613-288-2233; www.finland.ca/en); **Ireland,** Russell House, Stokes Pl., St. Stephen's Green, Dublin, 2 (☎01 478 1344; www.finland.ie/en); **UK,** 38 Chesham Pl., London, SW1X 8HW (☎020 78 38 62 00; www.finemb.org.uk/en); **US,** 3301 Massachusetts Ave., NW, Washington, D.C., 20008 (☎202-298-5800; www.finland.org).

VISA AND ENTRY INFORMATION. EU citizens do not need a visa. Citizens of Australia, Canada, New Zealand, and the US do not need a visa for stays of up to 90 days, beginning upon entry into any of the countries in the EU's freedom-of-movement zone. For more info, see p. 14. For stays longer than 90 days, all non-EU citizens need Schengen visas (around US$41), available at Finnish embassies and online at www.finland.org/en. Application processing takes about two weeks.

TOURIST SERVICES AND MONEY

EMERGENCY	Ambulance, Police, and Fire: ☎112.

TOURIST OFFICES. The **Finnish Tourist Board** (☎010 60 58 000; www.visitfinland.com) maintains an official online travel guide, which customizes its travel information and advice by home country.

MONEY. In 2002, the **euro (€)** replaced the markka as the unit of currency in Finland. For more info, see p. 17. Banks exchange currency for a €2-5 commission, though **Forex** offices and **ATMs** offer the best exchange rates. Food from grocery stores runs €10-17 per day; meals cost around €8 for lunch and €12 for dinner. Although restaurant bills include a service charge, leaving small change for particularly good service is becoming more common. For other services, tips are not expected. Finland has a 22% **value added tax (VAT)**, a sales tax applied to services and imports. The nation has a reduced VAT of 17% for food products and 8% for public transportation, books, and medicines. The prices given in *Let's Go* include VAT. In the airport upon exiting the EU, non-EU citizens can claim a refund on the tax paid for goods purchased at participating stores. In order to qualify for a refund in a store, you must spend at least €40; make sure to ask for a refund form when you pay. For more info on qualifying for a VAT refund, see p. 19.

TRANSPORTATION

BY PLANE. Several airlines fly into Helsinki from Australia, Europe, and North America. **Finnair** (Finland ☎0600 140 140, UK 087 0241 4411, US 800-950-5000; www.finnair.com) flies from 120 international cities and also covers the domestic market. The airline offers special youth rates—inquire before purchasing. **AirÅland** (www.airaland.com) flies to Stockholm, SWE and the Åland Isles. **Ryanair** (☎353 12 49 77 91; www.ryanair.com) flies to **Tampere-Pirkkala Airport (TMP).**

BY TRAIN. The national rail company is **VR Ltd., Finnish Railways** (☎0600 41 902; www.vr.fi). Finnish rail is efficient and prices are high; seat reservations are required on Pendolino and recommended on InterCity trains (€6.40-12.60). **Eurail** is valid in Finland. A **Finnrailpass,**

Finland

available only to non-natives, allows for three (€126), five (€168), or ten travel days (€227) in a one-month period. The **Scanrail pass**, purchased abroad, is good for rail travel through Denmark, Finland, Norway, and Sweden, as well as discounted ferry and bus rides. Scanrail passes purchased outside Scandinavia arc more flexible than Scanrail passes purchased once you arrive, and may be less expensive depending on the exchange rate. Check www.scanrail.com for more info on where to purchase passes at home. See p. 46 for more info. A Finnrail or Scanrail pass is often the best bet for longer trips; only students with Finnish IDs receive discounted fares for trains in Finland.

SAY WHAT? Travelers should note that some town names take a modified form on train and bus schedules. "To Helsinki" is written *Helsinkiin,* while "from Helsinki" is *Helsingistä.*

BY BUS. Buses are the only way to reach some smaller towns and points beyond the Arctic Circle. **Oy Matkahuolto Ab** (☎09 682 701; www.matkahuolto.fi) coordinates bus service. ISIC holders can buy a **sticker** (€6) for their **Matkahuolto Student Identity Card,** which is free and obtainable from Matkahuoloto service outlets, agents, and VR (previously Suomen Valtion Rautatiet) ticket offices. The sticker gives students a 50% discount on one-way tickets purchased ahead for routes exceeding 80km. **Rail passes** are valid on buses when trains are not in service.

BY FERRY. Viking Line (Finland ☎09 123 51, Sweden 08 452 4000; www.vikingline.fi) and **Tallinksilja** (Finland ☎09 180 41, Sweden 08 666 33 30; www.tallinksilja.fi) sail from Stockholm, SWE to Helsinki, Mariehamn, and Turku. On Viking ferries, **Scanrail** holders get 50% off. Travelers with both a **Eurail Pass** and a train ticket receive free passenger fare (mention this discount when booking). Viking's "early bird" discounts provide 15-50% off on ferry fares when booking trips within Finland or Sweden at least 30 days ahead. On Tallinksilja, both Scan- and Eurailers ride for free or at lower rates, depending on the route and ticket type.

BY CAR. Finland honors foreign driver's licenses issued in the US, EU, and EEA countries for up to one year for drivers aged 18 years or older. **Speed limits** are 120kph on expressways, 30-40kph in densely populated areas, and 80-100kph on most major roads. Headlights must be used at all times. Finnish law requires all cars be winterized with snow tires from December 1 to March 3. Be wary of reindeer at night. For more info on car rental and driving in Europe, see p. 50.

BY BIKE AND BY THUMB. Finland has a well-developed network of **cycling** paths. **Fillari GT** route maps are available at bookstores (€10-16). Check www.visitfinland.com/cycling for pre-trip route planning. **Hitchhiking** is uncommon in Finland and illegal on highways. Let's Go does not recommend hitchiking.

KEEPING IN TOUCH

PHONE CODES

Country code: 358. International dialing prefix: 00. For more info on how to place international calls, see **Inside Back Cover.**

EMAIL AND THE INTERNET. Internet cafes in Helsinki are relatively scarce compared to other European capitals, and in smaller towns they are virtually nonexistent. However, many **tourist offices** and **public libraries** offer short (15-30min.) slots of free Internet, and there is some free Wi-Fi access in Helsinki.

TELEPHONE. To make a long-distance call within Finland, dial 0 and then the number. **Pay phones** are rare but dependable. **Mobile phones** are extremely popular in the nation that gave the world Nokia, and prepaid mobile phone cards can be used to make international calls (cheapest 10pm-8am). For more info on mobile phones, see p. 29. For operator assistance, dial ☎118; for help with international calls, dial ☎92020. International direct dial numbers include: **AT&T Direct** (☎0800 1100 15); **Canada Direct** (☎0800 1100 11); **Telecom New Zealand** (☎0800 1106 40).

MAIL. Finnish mail service is efficient. Postcards and letters under 50g cost €0.70 within Finland, €1 to the EU, and €1.40 to other destinations. International letters under 20g cost €0.70. Check www.posti.fi/english/index.html for more prices and mailing restrictions. To receive mail in Finland, have mail delivered **Poste Restante.** Mail will go to the main post office unless you specify a subsidiary by street address. Address mail to be held according to the following example: First name, Last Name, Poste Restante, post office address, city, FINLAND.

LANGUAGES. Finnish is spoken by most of the population (92%), although children learn both Swedish and Finnish from the seventh grade. Three dialects of Sámi are also spoken by an ethnic minority in northern Finland. English is also widely spoken, with two-thirds of Finns reporting that they can speak at least some English; city-dwellers and those under 35 are generally the most proficient. For basic Finnish words and phrases, see **Phrasebook: Finnish,** p. 1059.

ACCOMMODATIONS AND CAMPING

FINLAND	❶	❷	❸	❹	❺
ACCOMMODATIONS	under €15	€15-28	€29-50	€51-75	over €75

Finland has over 100 **youth hostels** (*retkeilymaja*; RET-kay-loo-MAH-yah), although only half of them are open year-round. The **Finnish Youth Hostel Association** (Suomen Retkeilymajajärjestö; ☎09 565 7150; www.srmnet.org) is Finland's HI affiliate. Prices are generally around €23 per person for a dorm room, with a €2.50 HI discount. Most have laundry facilities and a kitchen; some have saunas and rent bikes or skis. **Hotels** are generally expensive (over €50 per night); *kesähotelli* (summer hotels) are usually student lodgings vacated from June to August, and cost about €25 per night. **Camping** is common; seventy of them are open year-round (tent sites €10-25 per night; small cottages from €40). The **Camping Card Scandinavia** (€6) qualifies cardholders for discounts and includes limited accident insurance. For a guide or to purchase the Camping Card, contact the **Finnish Camping Site Association** (☎09 477 407 40; www.camping.fi. Allow 3 weeks for delivery of the card.). Finland's **right of public access** (*jokamiehenoikeudet*) allows travelers to temporarily camp for free in the countryside, as long as they stay a reasonable distance (about 150m) from private homes. See p. 33 for more info.

FOOD AND DRINK

FINLAND	❶	❷	❸	❹	❺
FOOD	under €8	€8-15	€16-20	€21-30	over €30

Kebab and pizza joints are cheap and popular, but the local **Kauppatori** markets and **Kauppahalli** food courts are more likely to serve recognizably Finnish fare. Traditional diet slants toward breads and sausages. In summer, however, menus feature freshly caught trout, perch, pike, and herring; a new wave of five-star chefs in Helsinki are pairing French and Mediterranean ingredients with the bounty of local fisheries. To Santa's displeasure, bowls of reindeer stew are a staple of Lapland, while Kuopio is known for its pillowy rye pastries. Try the strawberries in summer—Finland is the top European producer. A surprising number of adults drink milk with meals, followed by interminable pots of coffee. You must be 18 to purchase beer and wine, 20 for liquor; the minimum age in bars is usually 18, but can go up to 25. Alcohol stronger than light beer must be bought at state-run **Alko** liquor stores, open weekdays until at least 6pm and Saturdays until at least 4pm.

HOLIDAYS AND FESTIVALS

Holidays: New Year's Day (Jan. 1); Epiphany (Jan. 6); Good Friday (Mar. 21); Easter (Mar. 23-24); May Day (May 1); Ascension (May 1); Pentecost (May 11-12); Corpus Christi (May 22); Midsummer (June 21-22); Assumption (Aug. 15); All Saints' Day (Nov. 1); Independence Day (Dec. 6); Christmas (Dec. 25); Boxing Day (Dec. 26).

Festivals: Flags fly high and *kokko* (bonfires) blaze on Midsummer's Eve (June 21), when the Finnish desert their cities for seaside cabins. July is the festival high season in Finland, with gays and lesbians celebrating Helsinki Pride, Turku's youth taking to the mosh pits of Ruisrock, and Pori's residents launching their eclectic Jazz Festival. Savonlinna's Opera Festival continues into early August, while the Helsinki Festival, Oulu's Music Video Festival, and Lahti's Sibelius Festival close out the summer. Check out www.festivals.fi for more info.

BEYOND TOURISM

It is relatively difficult for foreigners to secure full-time employment in Finland, but travelers may be able to obtain summer work. Check the **CIMO** website (see below) or www.jobs-in-europe.net for information on work placement. The organizations below coordinate limited work and volunteer opportunities. For more info on opportunities across Europe, see **Beyond Tourism**, p. 56.

The American-Scandinavian Foundation (AMSCAN), 58 Park Ave., New York, NY 10016, USA (☎212-879-9779; www.amscan.org/jobs/index.html). Volunteer and job opportunities throughout Scandinavia. Limited number of fellowships for study in Finland available to Americans.

Centre for International Mobility (CIMO), Säästöpankinranta 2A, P.O. Box 343, 00531 Helsinki (☎2069 05 01; http://finland.cimo.fi). Provides information on youth exchange programs, technical and agricultural internships, and study abroad. CIMO also organizes **European Voluntary Service** programs (http://europa.eu.int/comm/youth/program/guide/action2_en.html) for EU citizens, who can spend a fully funded year doing service in another EU country. EVS opportunities are largely in social work.

HELSINKI (HELSINGFORS)   ☎09

With all the appeal of a big city but none of the grime, Helsinki's (pop. 560,000) broad avenues, grand architecture, and parks make it a showcase Northern Europe. A hub of the design world, the city also distinguishes itself with multicultural flair and youthful energy mingling with old-world charm.

▐ TRANSPORTATION

Flights: Helsinki-Vantaa Airport (**HEL**; ☎0200 146 36; www.ilmailulaitos.fi). **Bus #615** runs from airport Platform 1B and the train station. (40min., 1-6 per hr.; from the airport M-F 5:30am-1am, Sa-Su 6am-1am; to the airport M-F 4:50am-1:20am, Sa-Su 5:20am-1:20am. €3.60. Cash only.) A **Finnair bus** runs from airport Platform 1A and the Finnair building next to the train station (☎0600 140 140; www.finnair.com. 35min., 1-3 per hr.; from the airport 6am-1am; to the airport 5am-midnight. €5.20. AmEx/MC/V.)

Trains: (☎030 072 0900, English-language info 231 999 02; www.vr.fi.) To: **Moscow, RUS** (14hr., 3 per day, €97); **Rovaniemi** (10-13hr., 5-8 per day, €76); **St. Petersburg, RUS** (5½hr., 2 per day, €56); **Tampere** (2hr., 8-12 per day, €26); **Turku** (2hr., 12 per day, €23-34). See p. 840 for **entrance requirements** to Russia.

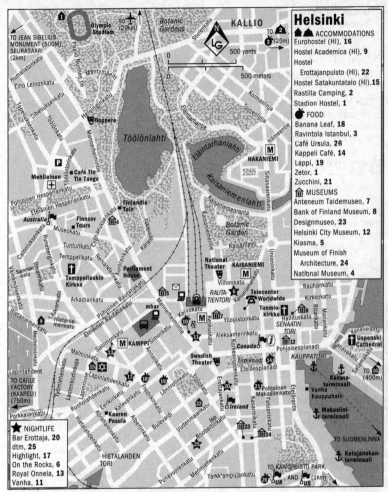

Helsinki

▲▲ ACCOMMODATIONS
Eurohostel (HI), **16**
Hostel Academica (HI), **9**
Hostel
  Erottajanpuisto (HI), **22**
Hostel Satakuntatalo (HI),**15**
Rastilla Camping, **2**
Stadion Hostel, **1**

● FOOD
Banana Leaf, **18**
Ravintola Istanbul, **3**
Café Ursula, **26**
Kappeli Café, **14**
Lappi, **19**
Zetor, **1**
Zucchini, **21**

🏛 MUSEUMS
Anteneum Taidemuseo, **7**
Bank of Finland Museum, **8**
Designmuseo, **23**
Helsinki City Museum, **12**
Kiasma, **5**
Museum of Finish
  Architecture, **24**
National Museum, **4**

★ NIGHTLIFE
Bar Erottaja, **20**
dtm, **25**
Highlight, **17**
On the Rocks, **6**
Royal Onnela, **13**
Vanha, **11**

FINLAND

Buses: Leave the Kamppi shopping center, Narinkka 3 (☎0200 4000; www.matkahuolto.fi). From the train station, take Postik. past the statue of Mannerheim. Cross Mannerheimintie onto Salomonk. Station will be on your left. To **Lahti** (1½-3hr., 1-6 per hr., €19), **Tampere** (2½hr., 1 per hr., €22), and **Turku** (2½hr., 2 per hr., €25).

Ferries: Viking Line, Lönnrotink. 2 (☎12 351; www.vikingline.fi), sails to **Stockholm, SWE** (16hr., 5:30pm, from €48) and **Tallinn, EST** (4hr., 12:30pm, €21). Tram #2 or bus #13 to Katajanokka terminal. **Tallinksilja,** Erottajank. 19 (☎228 311; www.tallinksilja.com), sails to **Tallinn, EST** (2-3½hr.; May to mid-Aug. 6-7 per day, mid-Aug. to Apr. 3-5 per day; from €22). Take bus #15 to West terminal. For more info on Scandinavian ferries, see p. 53.

Local Transportation: (☎310 1071; www.hkl.fi). **Buses, trams,** and the **metro** run 5:30am-11pm; major bus and tram lines, including tram #3T, run until 1:30am. **Night buses,** marked with "N," run F-Sa after 2am (€3.50). Single-fare tram €1.80; with 1hr. transfers to buses, trams, and the metro €2.20. **HKL Palvelupiste** (City Transport

Office) is in the Rautatientori metro, below the train station. Open mid-June to July M-Th 7:30am-6pm, F 7:30am-5pm, Sa 10am-3pm; Aug. to mid-June M-Th 7:30am-7pm, F 7:30am-5pm, Sa 10am-3pm. Sells the **tourist ticket** (as does the tourist office), a good investment for unlimited access to buses, trams, the metro, and trains. 1-day €6, 3-day €12, 5-day €18. AmEx/MC/V.

Taxis: Taxi Centre Helsinki (☎0100 0700). Special airport fares with **Yellow Line** (☎0600 555 555). Reserve 1 day ahead, before 6pm. 30-55min. €22. AmEx/MC/V.

Bike Rental: From mid-June to Aug., the city provides over 300 ■ **free, lime-green bikes** at major destinations throughout the city; it can be tricky to track one down, but when you do, deposit a €2 coin in the lock and then retrieve your deposit upon "returning" the bike to any location. Free cycling maps of the city are available at the tourist office.

◧ 🛈 ORIENTATION AND PRACTICAL INFORMATION

Water surrounds Helsinki in every direction, with many beaches and lakeside parks. The city's main street, **Mannerheimintie,** passes between the bus and train stations on its way south to the city center, ending at the **Esplanadi.** This tree-lined promenade leads east to **Kauppatori** (Market Square) and the beautiful South Harbor. Northeast of the city center lies **Kallio,** the bohemian district. Both Finnish and Swedish are used on all street signs and maps; *Let's Go* uses the Finnish names.

Tourist Offices: Pohjoisesplanadi 19 (☎3101 3300; www.visithelsinki.fi). Free **Internet** and **Wi-Fi.** Open May-Sept. M-F 9am-8pm, Sa-Su 9am-6pm; Oct.-Apr. M-F 9am-6pm, Sa-Su 10am-4pm. Representatives in green vests roam the city center in summer to distribute maps and answer questions. **Helsinki Card,** sold at the **Tour Shop** (☎2288 1500; www.helsinkiexpert.fi.) in the tourist office, provides unlimited local transportation and free or discounted tours and admission, though cardholders have to keep up a blistering pace to make the card worth it. 1-day €33, 2-day €43, 3-day €53. Open June-Aug. M-F 9am-7pm, Sa-Su 9am-5pm; Sept.-May M-F 9am-5pm, Sa 10am-4pm. AmEx/MC/V.) **Finnsov Tours,** Museok. 15 (☎436 6961; www.finnsov.info) arranges trips to Russia and expedites the visa process. Open M-F 8:30am-5pm. AmEx/MC/V.

Embassies: Canada, Pohjoisesplanadi 25B (☎228 530; www.canada.fi). Open June-Aug. M-Th 8am-noon and 1-4:30pm, F 8am-1:30pm; Sept.-May M-F 8:30am-noon and 1-4:30pm. **Ireland,** Erottajank. 7A (☎646 006; helsinki@dfa.ie). Open M-F 9am-5pm. **UK,** Itäinen Puistotie 17 (☎2286 5100; www.britishembassy.gov.uk/finland). Open late June-late Aug. M-F 8:30am-3pm; late Aug. to late June M-F 9am-5pm. Citizens of **Australia** and **New Zealand** should contact the UK embassy. **US,** Itäinen Puistotie 14A (☎616 250; www.usembassy.fi). Open M-F 8:30am-5pm.

Luggage Storage: Lockers in the train station €2-3 per day. The Kiasma museum (p. 292) provides free same day storage even if you don't pay admission.

GBLT Resources: Seta Ry, Mannerheimintie 170A 4, 5th fl. (☎681 2580; www.seta.fi). Tram #10. A national organization with info on gay services in the country and a trans support center. Copies of *Gay Guide Helsinki* are at the tourist office.

Laundromat: Café Tin Tin Tango, Töölöntorink. 7 (☎2709 0972; www.tintintango.info), a combination bar, cafe, laundromat, and sauna. Wash €3.50, dry €1.80, detergent €1. Sandwiches €5-8. Open M-Th 7am-midnight, F 7am-2am, Sa 9am-2am, Su 10am-2am. AmEx/MC/V.

Police: ☎100 22. **24hr. Medical Hotline:** ☎100 23.

24hr. Pharmacy: Yliopiston Apteekki, Mannerheimintie 96 (☎0203 202 00).

Hospital: 24hr. clinic **Mehiläinen,** Pohjoinen Hesperiankatu 17 (☎010 414 4444).

Telephone: Telecenter Worldwide, Vuorik. 8 (☎670 612; www.woodgong.com), offers reasonable rates to call most countries. Open M-F 10am-9pm, Sa 11am-7pm, Su noon-7pm. Australia €0.16 per min., UK €0.20, US €0.21. MC/V.

Internet Access: Library 10, Elielinaukio 2G (☎3108 5000), upstairs in the main post office building. Free Wi-Fi, free 30min. slots of Internet, up to 2hr. with reservation. Open M-Th 10am-8pm, F-Su noon-6pm. Many cafes provide free Internet and Wi-Fi. Visit www.hel.fi/en/wlan or check the tourist office for locations.

Post Office: Elielinaukio 2F (☎2007 1000). Open M-F 7am-9pm, Sa-Su 10am-6pm. **Postal Code:** 00100.

🏠🏕 ACCOMMODATIONS AND CAMPING

🏠 **Hostel Erottajanpuisto (HI),** Uudenmaank. 9 (☎642 169; www.erottajanpuisto.com). Well-kept rooms in a central location. Breakfast €5. Lockers €1. Laundry €7. Free Internet and Wi-Fi. Reception 24hr. Summer dorms €24; singles €46; doubles €63. Low season singles €48; doubles €64. €2.50 HI discount. AmEx/MC/V. ❷

Hostel Satakuntatalo (HI), Lapinrinne 1A (☎6958 5232; www.sodexho.fi/satakunta). M: Kamppi. Spacious, well-equipped rooms near the city center. Breakfast, sauna, and towels included. Lockers €2. Linens €5. Laundry €5.50. Free Internet and Wi-Fi; cables not included. Reception 24hr. Open June-Aug. Dorms €20; singles from €36; doubles from €54; triples from €75; quads from €86. €2.50 HI discount. AmEx/MC/V. ❷

Hostel Academica (HI), Hietaniemenk. 14 (☎1311 4334; www.hostelacademica.fi). M: Kamppi. Turn right onto Runebergink. and left after crossing the bridge. University housing becomes a hostel in summer. Rooms have kitchenettes and private bath. Morning sauna, swim, linens, and towels included. Internet €2 per 30min.; Wi-Fi €2 per hr., €5 per day. Reception 24hr. Open June-Aug. Dorms €22; singles €40-53; doubles €60-67. €2.50 HI discount. AmEx/MC/V. ❷

Eurohostel (HI), Linnank. 9 (☎622 0470; www.eurohostel.fi), near Katajanokka ferry terminal. Bright rooms, cafe, and free morning sauna. Breakfast €6.50. Linens and towels included. Laundry €1. Internet €2 per 15min.; Wi-Fi €5 per day. Reception 24hr. Singles €39-43; doubles €47-54; triples €70-80. €2.50 HI discount. AmEx/MC/V. ❸

Stadion Hostel (HI), Pohj. Stadiontie 4B (☎477 8480; www.stadionhostel.com). Tram #3 or 7A to Auroran Sairaala and walk down Pohj. Cheap rooms and an active social scene. Breakfast €6. Linens €4, with towels €5. Laundry €2.50. Free Internet and Wi-Fi. Reception June to mid-Sept. 24hr.; mid-Sept. to May 7am-3am. Lockout noon-4pm. Dorms €17; singles €35; doubles €44. €2.50 HI discount. AmEx/MC/V. ❷

Rastila Camping, Karavaanik. 4 (☎3107 8517; www.hel.fi/rastila). M: Rastila. Change trains at Itäkeskus. A large campground 12km from the city next to a public beach. Kitchen, showers, and electricity each €4.50-7. Reception mid-May to mid-Sept. 24hr.; mid-Sept. to mid-May daily 8am-10pm. €5 per person; €10 per tent site in summer, €6 in winter; Cabins €38-64. Hostel (HI) open mid-June to July. Dorms €19. MC/V. ❶

🍴 FOOD

Restaurants and cafes are easy to find on Esplanadi and the streets branching off **Mannerheimintie** and **Uudenmaankatu.** Cheaper options surround the **Hietalahti** flea market at the southern end of Bulevardi. A large **supermarket** is under the train station. (Open M-Sa 7am-10pm, Su 10am-10pm.) Helsinki has many budget restaurants that serve ethnic food. Get lunch at the open-air market **Kauppatori,** where stalls sell freshly cooked fish and local produce; a meal from one of the cafes will cost about €5-8. (Open June-Aug. M-Sa 6:30am-6pm; Sept.-May M-F 7am-5pm.)

🍴 **Zetor,** Mannerheimintie 3-5 (☎666 966; www.zetor.net), in the mall opposite the train station. Cheeky menu, cheekier farm-inspired decor, a trademark tractor, and ridiculously good Finnish food. Homemade beer €5. Entrees €12-28. Attached bar 22+. Open Su-M 3pm-1am, Tu 3pm-3am, W-F 3pm-4am, Sa 11am-4am. AmEx/MC/V. ❷

Kappeli Café, Eteläesplanadi 1 (☎766 3880; www.kappeli.fi). This cafe has served the bohemian and the elite since 1867. Salads and sandwiches €8-9. Open May to mid-Sept. M-Th 9am-midnight, F-Sa 9am-2am, Su 9am-11pm; mid-Sept. to Apr. M-Sa 10am-midnight, Su 10am-11pm. Kitchen closes 1hr. before closing. AmEx/MC/V. ❶

Café Ursula, Ehrenströmintie 3 (☎652 817; www.ursula.fi). This upscale cafe also has delicious budget options and an idyllic setting on the Baltic Sea. Sandwiches €5-6. Salad bar €11. Entrees €9-18. Open daily in summer 9am-midnight; spring and fall 9am-10pm; winter 9am-8pm. AmEx/MC/V. ❷

Zucchini, Fabianink. 4 (☎622 2907), south of the tourist office. Popular vegetarian and vegan fare with organic produce. Open M-F 11am-4pm. Closed July. AmEx/MC/V. ❷

Banana Leaf, Fredrikink. 49 (☎605 167; www.malesia.net/bananaleaf). Delicious Malaysian and Thai food in a serene setting. Ask the server to add some spice to your dish—Finns take their Asian food bland. Lunch buffet €8. Entrees €9-20. Open M-F 11am-11pm, Sa-Su noon-3pm. AmEx/MC/V. ❷

Lappi, Annank. 22 (☎645 550; www.lappires.com). Tourists splurge on specialties like reindeer, lingonberries, and Arctic char amid smoky smells, wood, and fur. Entrees from €16. Reserve ahead. Open in summer daily 5-10:30pm; winter M-F noon-10:30pm, Sa-Su 1-10:30pm. AmEx/MC/V. ❸

🄖 SIGHTS

Helsinki's Neoclassical buildings and new forms reflect Finnish architect Alvar Aalto's joke: "Architecture is our form of expression because our language is so impossible." Helsinki's Art Nouveau (*Jugendstil*) and Modernist structures are home to a dynamic design community. Much of the layout and architecture of the old center, however, is the brainchild of German Carl Engel, who modeled his design after St. Petersburg. Older buildings are adorned with humorous statues, so keep an eye out. Most sights are in the city's compact center, making it ideal for walking tours; pick up *See Helsinki on Foot* from the tourist office for routes. Trams #3B and 3T loop around the major sights in 1hr., providing a cheap alternative to tour buses. Helsinki has many parks, including **Kaivopuisto** in the south, **Töölönlahti** in the north, and **Esplanadi** and **Tähtitorninvuori** in the center of town.

■**SUOMENLINNA.** This 18th-century military fortification, spanning five islands, was built by Sweden to stave off Russia. The fortress's dark passageways are an adventure to explore. The **Suomenlinna Museum** details the history of the fortress and its accompanying fleet. (☎4050 9691; www.suomenlinna.fi. Museum open daily May-Aug. 10am-6pm; Sept.-Apr. 11am-4pm. €5, students €4. 30min. film 2 per hr. AmEx/MC/V.) The islands also feature the world's only combination church and **lighthouse** and Finland's only remaining WWII **submarine,** the Vesikko. (Church ☎709 2665. Usually open May-Aug. W-F noon-4pm. Submarine ☎1814 6238. Open mid-May to Aug. 11am-6pm. €4, students €2. Cash only. Fortress tours leave from the museum June-Aug. daily 11am and 2pm; Sept.-May Sa-Su 1:30pm. Summer €6, winter €6.50, including admission to the Ehrensvard Museum, the Commander's residence. AmEx/MC/V.) The **Toy Museum,** on the main island, has extensive exhibits on toys from the 19th century to today. A note of caution: some of the dolls look downright creepy. (☎668 417. Open July daily 11am-6pm; May-June and Aug. daily 11am-5pm; early Sept. daily 11am-4pm; Apr. Sa-Su 11am-4pm. €5, students €4. MC/V.) Southern island's smooth rocks are popular with sunbathers and swimmers. (City Transport ferries depart from Market St.; 15min., 1-3 per hr., round-trip €3.80. Combo ticket for museums and submarine €6, students €3. Cash only.)

SENAATIN TORI (SENATE SQUARE). The square and its gleaming white ▓**Tuomiokirkko** (Dome Church) showcase Carl Engel's architecture and exemplify the splendor of Finland's 19th-century Russian period. The church's stunning marble reliefs house an interior so elegantly simple that every gilded detail becomes magnified. *(Unioninkatu 29. ☎2340 6120. Free organ recitals W at noon in July. Church open June-Aug. M-Sa 9am-6pm, Su noon-8pm; Sept.-May M-Sa 9am-6pm, Su noon-6pm.)* Just south of Senate Sq., the **Helsinki City Museum** chronicles the city's 450-year history. The City Museum also has exhibits throughout Helsinki; pick up a list at the museum or at the tourist office. *(Sofiank. 4. ☎3103 6631. Open M-F 9am-5pm, Sa-Su 11am-5pm. Each exhibit €4, students €2. Th free. MC/V.)* The red-brick ▓**Uspenski Orthodox Cathedral** (Uspenskinkatedraadi), the largest Orthodox church in Northern and Western Europe, evokes images of Russia with its ornate interior and 13 golden cupolas. *(☎634 267. Open M and W-F 9:30am-4pm, Tu 9:30am-6pm, Sa 9:30am-2pm, Su noon-3pm. Closed M in winter.)*

ESPLANADI AND MANNERHEIMINTIE. A boulevard dotted with statues and fountains, Esplanadi is a great place to people-watch. The **Designmuseo** presents the work of designers like Aalto and Eliel Saarinen alongside creations by young artists and first-rate temporary exhibits. *(Korkeavuorenk. 23. ☎622 0540; www.designmuseum.fi. Open June-Aug. daily 11am-6pm; Sept.-May Tu 11am-8pm, W-Su 11am-6pm. €7, students €3. AmEx/MC/V.)* One block away, the small **Museum of Finnish Architecture** has temporary displays on the history and future of building design. *(Kasarmik. 24. ☎8567 5100; www.mfa.fi. Open Tu-Su 10am-4pm, W 10am-8pm. €3.50, students €1.70. Free W. AmEx/MC/V.)* At the end of Esplanadi, turn right onto Mannerheimintie and right again onto Kaivok. past the train station for the **Ateneum Art Museum** (Ateneum Taidemuseo), Finland's largest, with comprehensive exhibits on Finnish art. *(Kaivok. 2, opposite the train station. ☎1733 6401; www.ateneum.fi. Open Tu and F 9am-6pm, W-Th 9am-8pm, Sa-Su 11am-5pm. €6, students €4; €8/6.50 during temporary exhibits, W free 5-8pm. AmEx/MC/V.)* Continue on Mannerheimintie to ▓**Kiasma** (Museum of Contemporary Art), a warehouse that features top-flight modern art and calibrates the width of its doors to Fibonacci's golden ratio. The first floor and outdoor exhibits are often free. *(Mannerheiminaukio 2. ☎1733 6501; www.kiasma.fi. Open Tu 9am-5pm, W-Su 10am-8:30pm. €6, students €4, F free 5-8:30pm. AmEx/MC/V.)* Farther down the road is the grand **Parliament House,** Mannerheimintie 30. *(☎432 2027. Only accessible by 1hr. tours to the Session Hall, Hall of State, and the Parliament cafeteria July and Aug. M-F*

AALTO'S HELSINKI

Finlandia Hall may be architect Alvar Aalto's most recognizable gift to Helsinki, but a number of his other Modernist creations give a sense of his aesthetic breadth.

1 Rautatalo (Iron House), Keskusk. 3. The stark facade conceals an airy atrium meant to recall an Italian *piazza*, one of Aalto's favorite motifs.

2 Academic Bookstore, Pohjoisesplanadi 39. Finland's largest bookstore named its upstairs cafe after the architect who designed the copper and marble building in 1969.

3 Savoy Restaurant, Eteläesplanadi 14. The €40 entrees are too pricey for the budget traveler, but the decor is all Aalto's work—right down to the trademark vases.

4 Stora Enso Headquarters, Kanavak. 1. This ultramodern "sugar cube" overlooks the South Harbor and provides a provocative contrast to the two churches that flank it.

11am and 1pm, Sa 11am and 12:30pm, Su noon and 1:30pm. Free.) Nearby is Saarinen's **National Museum of Finland** (Suomen Kansallismuseo), featuring a 1928 ceiling fresco by Gallen-Kallela and many exhibits on Finnish history. (Mannerheimintie 34. ☎40 501; www.kansallismuseo.fi. Open Tu-W 11am-8pm, Th-Su 11am-6pm. €6, students €4, under 18 free, Tu 5:30-8pm free. AmEx/MC/V.) Head back to the city center down Mannerheimintie, turn right on Arkadiank., and right again on Fredrikink. to reach the heavily touristed **Temppeliaukio Kirkko.** This striking church is hewn out of a hill of rock with only the domed roof visible from the outside. (Lutherink. 3. ☎494 698. English-language services Su 2pm. Usually open M-Tu and Th 10am-8pm, W and F 10am-6pm, Sa 10am-noon, Su 11:45am-1:45pm and 3:30-6pm; winter M-Th 10am-5pm.)

OTHER SIGHTS. The University of Helsinki's **Botanic Garden** is north of Senate Sq. along Unionink. (Unionink. 44. Take trams #3B/3T or 6 to Kaisaniemi. ☎1912 4455. Garden open M-F 7am-8pm, Sa-Su 9am-8pm. Free. Greenhouses open Tu-Su Apr.-Sept. 10am-5pm; Oct.-Mar. 10am-3pm. €4.20, students €2.20. MC/V.) The 72m high **Olympic Stadium Tower,** Paavo Nurmentie 1, built for the 1952 Summer Games, offers a fine view of the city. (☎436 6010. Open M-F 9am-8pm, Sa-Su 9am-4pm. €2, students €1. AmEx/MC/V.) In an industrial area west of the city center, the **Cable Factory** (Kaapeli) houses three museums, dozens of studios and galleries, and various performance areas. The **Finnish Museum of Photography** (www.fmp.fi) has provocative displays, the **Hotel and Restaurant Museum** (www.hotellijaravintolamuseo.fi) offers a history of menus and minibars, and the **Theater Museum** (www.teatterimuseo.fi) contains set models and costume designs from the National Theater. (Tallbergink. 1. M: Ruoholahti. After exiting, walk 5 blocks down Itämerenk. Museums are in the G entrance. ☎020 796 1670; www.kaapelite-hdas.fi. Open Tu-Su 11am-6pm. Theater Museum closed in July. Photography Museum €6, students €4; Hotel and Restaurant Museum €2/1; Theater Museum €5.50/2.50. MC/V.) Near the Western Harbor, the crowded **Jean Sibelius Monument** pays homage to one of the 20th century's great composers. (On Mechelinink. in Sibelius Park. Take bus #24, dir.: Seurasaari to Rasjasaarentie; the monument will be behind you.)

🎵 ENTERTAINMENT

Helsinki's parks are always animated. A **concert series** enlivens the Esplanadi park all summer Monday through Friday at 4pm. Highlights of the program are **Jazz Espa** in July, and **Ethno Espa** showcasing international music (www.kulttuuri.hel.fi/espanlava). In fall and winter, the Espa stage is used as an exhibition for young artists. Late June's **Helsinki Pride** (www.helsinkipride.fi) is Finland's largest GLBT event. The **Helsinki Festival** (www.helsinkifestival.fi), toward the end of August, wraps up the summer with cultural events ranging from music and theater to film and visual arts. At the end of September, **Helsinki Design Week** (www.helsinkidesignweek.fi) reinforces the city's image as a style capital, while the **Love and Anarchy Film Festival** (www.hiff.fi) features works from across the globe. Throughout summer, concerts rock **Kaivopuisto** (on the corner of Puistok. and Ehrenstromintie, in the southern part of town) and **Hietaniemi Beach** (down Hesperiank. on the western shore). Check out the ■**Nordic Oddity** pamphlet series, with insider advice on sights, bars, and activities. For high culture, try the Helsinki Philharmonic and Radio Symphony Orchestra, the National Opera, or the National Theater. **Lippupiste** and **Lippupalvelu,** Aleksanterink. 52 (☎0600 900 900), in the Stockmann department store, sell tickets for most big venues (AmEx/MC/V).

🍸 NIGHTLIFE

Bars and beer terraces fill up in late afternoon; most clubs don't get going until midnight and stay crazy until 4am. Bars and clubs line **Mannerheimintie, Uudenmaankatu,** and **Iso Roobertinkatu.** East of the train station, nightlife centers around

Yliopistonkatu and **Kaisaniemenkatu**, while in bohemian Kallio, the bars around **Fleminginkatu** have some of the cheapest beer in the city. A popular night activity is heavy-metal karaoke; check out Wednesday and Sunday at **Hevimesta**, Hallitusk. 3.

Royal Onnela, Fredrikink. 46 (☎020 7759 460; www.ravintolaonnela.fi). The biggest nightclub in Scandinavia has a room for most music tastes, from Finnish pop to disco and 80s/90s hits. Beer €4.50; €1 W, Th, Su. Mixed drinks €7. M-Sa 22+, Su 20+. Cover F-Sa €7. Club open M and W-Su 10pm-3:30am. Lapland Poro Bar M and W-Su 6pm-4am. Karaoke bar M and W-Su 8pm-2:30pm, Tu 8pm-3:30am. AmEx/MC/V.

On the Rocks, Mikonk. 15 (☎612 2030; www.ontherocks.fi). This legendary rock bar and club offers Finnish bands for cheap. Beer €4.80. Tu-Th live music. 23+. Cover Tu-Th free-€12; F-Sa €7. Open daily in summer noon-4am; winter 4pm-4am. AmEx/D/MC/V.

Bar Erottaja, Erottajank. 13-17 (☎611 196). This art-student hangout is usually packed with people engaged in conversation over music. Beer €4.50. F-Sa DJ. 22+ after 6pm. Open M 2pm-1am, Tu 2pm-2am, W-Sa 2pm-3am, Su 6pm-3am. AmEx/D/MC/V.

Vanha, Mannerheimintie 3 (☎1311 4368; www.vanha.fi). A student crowd gathers here for club nights (F-Sa). Check website for performance schedule. Beer €4.50. Cover €5. Open F-Sa 10pm-4am. AmEx/MC/V.

Highlight, Fredrikink. 42 (☎050 409 0079). A dance club for the young and fit. Beer €4. 10pm-midnight beer, cider, and shots €2. 18+. Cover after 11pm €5. Open F-Sa 10pm-4am. AmEx/D/MC/V.

dtm, Iso Roobertink. 28 (☎676 314; www.dtm.fi). This popular gay club draws a mixed crowd to 2 stories of everything from foam parties to drag shows. Beer €4.60. Lesbian nights on occasional F or Sa. 22+ after 10pm. Cover Sa €5, special events €5-10. Happy hour M-Sa 9am-4pm. Open M-Sa 9am-4am, Su noon-4am. AmEx/MC/V.

⚡ OUTDOOR ACTIVITIES

Just north of the train station lie the two city lakes, **Töölönlahti** and **Eläintarhanlahti.** Take an afternoon walk on the winding paths around them. Northwest of the Sibelius Monument across a bridge, the island of **Seurasaari** offers retreat from the city. It is also home to an **open-air museum** of farmsteads and churches transplanted from around Finland. On Midsummer's Eve, tall *kokko* (bonfires) are set ablaze during a drunken party. *(Take bus #24 from Erottaja to the last stop. The island is always open for hiking. Museum ☎4050 9660. Open June-Aug. M-Tu and Th-Su 11am-5pm, W 11am-7pm; late May and early Sept. M-F 9am-3pm, Sa-Su 11am-5pm. Tours June 15 to Aug. 15 daily 3pm. €5, students €4. MC/V.)* Many islands south of the city feature **public beaches** that are accessible by ferry, including a nude beach on Pihljasaari Island. Beyond Espoo to the west is the **Nuuksio National Park,** where flying squirrels are more common than anywhere else in Finland. *(☎0205 64 4790; www.outdoors.fi/ nuuksionp. Take the train to Espoo station and bus #85 from there to Nuuksionpää.)*

⚡ DAYTRIPS FROM HELSINKI

PORVOO. Porvoo (pop. 47,000) is along **Old King Road,** 50km east of Helsinki. In 1809, Tsar Alexander I granted Finland autonomy at the whitewashed **cathedral** in Porvoo's Old Town. Unfortunately, the cathedral fell victim to arson attack in May 2006; all that can be seen now is the spire above the scaffolding. Pick up a walking tour map from the tourist office, or join the guide that leaves from Town Hall Sq. from late June to mid-August (weekdays at 2pm; €6). A free guided walking tour leaves from the harbor on Saturdays. The house of Finland's national poet **Johan Ludvig Runeberg,** Aleksanterink. 3, looks just as it did when he called it home in the mid-1800s. The works of his son, sculptor Walter Runeberg, are on display across the street. (☎019 581 330. *Open May-Aug. daily 10am-4pm; Sept.-Apr. W-Su 10am-4pm. For both €5, students €2 Cash only.*) The **Historical Museum,** in the 1764 Town Hall in Old Market Sq., features local artists like Impressionist painter Albert Edelfelt and has an eccentric array of artifacts. (☎019 574 7500. *Open May-Aug. M-Sa 10am-4pm, Su 11am-4pm; Sept.-Apr. W-Su noon-4pm. €5. MC/V.*) Charming, if overpriced, cafes line the streets of Old Town. Many sell Runeberg cakes, which the poet enjoyed, for about €3. Recipes vary, but essentially it's a small round cake with almonds and cinnamon topped off with raspberry jam and a squeeze of icing. Bottom line: delicious. **Porvoo Pyörätalo,** Mannerheimink. 12 (☎019 585 104), rents **bikes** to visitors heading as far south as Pellinki (30km). **Buses** run from Helsinki (1hr., 4 per hr., €9-12). The **tourist office,** Rihkamak. 4, has free **Internet** and helps book rooms. (☎019 520 2316; www.porvoo.fi. *Open mid-June to Aug. M-F 9am-6pm, Sa-Su 10am-4pm; Sept. to mid-June reduced hours.*) **Postal Code:** 06100.

LAHTI. World-class winter sports facilities make Lahti (pop. 100,000) a popular destination for snow-lovers. The **Ski Museum** has ski-jump and slalom simulators, a rifle range, and exhibits on the city's winter sports history. (☎038 144 523. *Open M-F 10am-5pm, Sa-Su 11am-5pm. €5, students €3. MC/V.*) Towering 200m above the museum, the tallest of three **ski jumps,** accessible by a chairlift/elevator combo, offers excellent views of the city. (*Open in summer daily 10am-5pm. €5, students €3; with Ski Museum €8/€5.*) The cross-country **ski trails** (100km) from the sports complex are great for summer hiking; the tourist office has info on the **Ilvesvaellus Trail,** a 30min. bus ride northwest. In Kariniemi Park, the **Musical Fountains** combine water and music daily at 1 and 6pm in summer, 7pm in spring and fall. At the harbor, Sibelius Hall holds the **Sibelius Festival** in September, with performances of many of the composer's works. **Trains** head to Helsinki (1-1½hr., 1 per hr., from €13), Savonlinna (3-3½hr., 5-6 per day, from €40), and Tampere (2hr., 1 per 1-2hr., from €24). The **tourist office,** Rautatienk. 22, has free **Internet** and rents **bikes** for €15 per day. (☎0207 281 750; www.lahtitravel.fi. *Open M-Th 9am-5pm, F 9am-4pm; also open mid-July to mid-Aug. Sa 10am-2pm. AmEx/MC/V.*) Free **Wi-Fi** is available in the city center, just north of the train station. **Postal Code:** 15110.

TURKU (ÅBO)   ☎02

Finland's oldest city, Turku (pop. 175,000), has grown weatherbeaten with the passing of 775 years. It was the focal point of Swedish and Russian power struggles, the seat of Finnish governance and religion until 1812, and then the victim of the worst fire in Scandinavian history in 1827. Despite its difficult past, Turku has rebuilt itself into a cultural and academic center that continues to endure.

🖃📷 TRANSPORTATION AND PRACTICAL INFORMATION. Trains run to Helsinki (2hr., 1 per hr., €23-30) and Tampere (2hr., 1 per 1-2hr., €21-23). Viking Line **ferries** sail to Stockholm, SWE (10hr., 2 per day, €14-30; AmEx/MC/V), as do Tallinksilja Line ferries (12hr., daily 6:30pm, from €20; MC/V). To get to the ferry terminal, catch bus #1 from the Kauppatori (€2.50) or walk to the end of Linnank. A bus day pass costs €5.50. The **tourist office,** Aurak. 4, rents bikes (€12), offers **Internet** (€0.04 per min.) and sells the **TurkuCard** (24hr. €21; 48hr. €28), which provides free entry to the city's museums and buses, as well as other discounts. (☎262 7444; www.turkutouring.fi. *Open Apr.-Sept. M-F 8:30am-6pm, Sa-Su 9am-4pm; Oct.-Mar. M-F 8:30am-6pm, Sa-Su 10am-3pm. AmEx/MC/V.*) There are unstaffed—and usually crowded—**cybercafes** at Hämeenk. 12 and Mariank. 2. (*Open M-F 9am-9pm, Sa-Su 10am-9pm. €0.04 per min. Coins only.*) Many cafes in the city center offer free **Wi-Fi,** as does the university campus to the east. **Postal Code:** 20100.

ⁿⁱ▢ ACCOMMODATIONS AND FOOD. To get to the spacious, riverside ◪**Hostel Turku (HI) ❷**, Linnank. 39, from the station, walk west on Ratapihank., turn left on Puistok., and go right at the river. (☎ 262 7680; www.turku.fi/hostelturku. Bike rental €5 per 4hr., €10 per day, €10 deposit. Breakfast €4.50. Linens €4.70. Laundry €2 per hr. Internet €1 per 20min. Reception 6-10am and 3pm-midnight. Check-in 3-9pm. Dorms curfew 2am. Reserve 1 month ahead in high season. Dorms €16; singles €36; doubles €65; quads €58. €2.50 HI discount. MC/V.) **Interpoint Hostel ❶**, Vähä Hämeenk. 12A, offers what may well be the cheapest beds in Finland. (☎ 231 4011. Open mid-July to mid-Aug. Breakfast €2.50. Linens €0.50. Laundry €1.50. Reception 8-11am and 5-10pm. Lockout 11am-5pm. Dorms €8.50; singles €20; doubles €30; quads €40. Cash only.) For peaceful, well-kept rooms try the nun-run **Bridgettine Convent Guesthouse ❸**, Ursinink. 15A, at Puutarhak. (☎ 250 1910; www.kolumbus.fi/birgitta/turku. Breakfast included. Reception 8am-9pm. Singles €45; doubles €65; triples €90. Cash only.)

Produce fills the outdoor **Kauppatori** (open M-Sa in summer 7am-2pm; winter 7am-7pm) and indoor **Kauppahalli** (open M-F 7am-5:30pm, Sa 7am-2pm) on Eerikink. Sokos, next to the Kauppatori, has a **supermarket**. (Open M-F 9am-9pm, Sa 9am-6pm. MC/V.) Cheap eats line **Humalistonkatu**. Locals pack **Kerttu ❷**, Läntinen Pitkäk. 35, where they feast on Jallupulla meatballs (€9.20) and other fare while surfing free Wi-Fi or doing laundry (€2.50 per 2hr.). Kerttu is a bar by night. (☎ 250 6990; www.kerttu.fi. Open M-F 10:30am-3pm; Kitchen closes 2pm.) The boat-restaurant **Kasvisravintola Keidas ❷**, Itäinen Rantak. 61, serves vegetarian food (€5-8.50). Walk 20min. along the river, or take bus #3, 14, 15, or 55 from the Kauppatori. (☎ 535 3018; www.kasviskeidas.com. Open M-F 11am-4pm. MC/V.)

◪ⁿ SIGHTS AND ENTERTAINMENT. Over a decade ago, during construction on a museum in a tobacco tycoon's riverside mansion, workers discovered a medieval city block beneath the house. Today, at the ◪**Aboa Vetus and Ars Nova Museums**, Itäinen Rantak. 4-6, visitors can stroll through the ruins and view the accompanying modern art collection. The building is a sight in itself and houses the **Aula Cafe ❶**, which serves sandwiches (€4) and other snacks. (☎ 250 0552; www.aboavetusarsnova.fi. Open Apr. to mid-Sept. daily 11am-7pm; late Sept.-Mar. Tu-Su 11am-7pm. Tours July-Aug. 11:30am. €8, students €7. AmEx/MC/V.) The medieval **Turku Cathedral**, Tuomiokirkkotori 20, is the spiritual center of Finland's Lutheran Church. Finnish public radio has broadcast the cathedral's noontime bells since 1944. (☎ 261 7100; www.turunseurakunnat.fi. Open daily mid-Apr. to mid-Sept. 9am-8pm; mid-Sept. to mid-Apr. 9am-7pm. Evening concerts June-Aug. Tu 8pm. English services Su 4pm. Free.) Around the corner, the **Sibelius Museum**, Piispank. 17, presents the life of Finland's most famous composer. Over 300 instruments, from organs to African whistles, are also displayed. (☎ 215 4494; www.sibeliusmuseum.abo.fi. Open Tu and Th-Su 11am-4pm, W 11am-4pm and 6-8pm. 1hr. concerts in summer, fall, and spring W 7pm. Museum €3, students €1. Concerts €7/3. MC/V.) The 700-year-old **Turun Linna** (Turku Castle), Linnank. 80, 3km from the town center, has a historical museum with medieval artifacts. Catch bus #1 (€2) from Market Sq. or walk to the end of Linnank. (☎ 262 0300. Open mid-Apr. to mid-Sept. daily 10am-6pm; mid-Sept. to mid-Apr. Tu-F and Su 10am-3pm, Sa 10am-5pm. €7, students €3.50. Tours in summer 12:10, 2:10, 4:10pm; €2. MC/V.)

The end of June brings the **Medieval Market** to town, while power chords rock Ruissalo Island at July's **Ruisrock** festival (www.ruisrock.fi). In August, the annual **Turku Music Festival** (www.turkumusicfestival.fi) brings a range of artists to nontraditional venues throughout the city. Turku is known throughout Finland for its laid-back pubs and breweries. In summer, Turku's nightlife centers around the river, where Finns and tourists crowd boats docked by the banks to dance and

FINLAND

drink. Pull up a stool at the old apothecary, **Pub Uusi Apteekki**, Kaskenk. 1, across the Auran bridge from the center. (☎250 2595; www.uusiapteekki.fi. 20+. Open daily 10am-3am. MC/V.) **Koulu**, Eerikink. 18, Finland's largest brewery restaurant and a former girls' school, offers its own beers, along with wine and popular blueberry cider. (☎274 5757; www.panimoravintolakoulu.fi. Beer €3-5.20. Cider €4-4.20. F-Sa 22+. Open M-Th and Su 10am-2am, F-Sa 10am-3am. AmEx/MC/V.)

DAYTRIPS FROM TURKU: RAUMA AND PORI. Farther north on the Baltic Coast, **Rauma** (pop. 36,000) is known for the well-preserved wooden buildings that make up the **Old Town**, a UNESCO World Heritage Site. **Tours** begin at the frescoed **Church of the Holy Cross**, which shed its past as a Franciscan monastery to become a Lutheran chapel, making it a poster child for the Reformation. The Old Town has four **museums**: two art museums and two devoted to the cultural and maritime history of the town. All can be seen with a combo ticket (€4; individual museums €2). Many islands in Rauma's **archipelago** are great for hiking. Try the trails on **Kuuskajaskari**, a former fortress. *(Ferries 30min., in summer 1-3 per day, €8. MC/V.)* The **Finnish Rock Festival** (www.rmj.fi; late June) throws the biggest midsummer party in Finland. Late August brings the **Blue Sea Film Festival** (www.blueseafilmfestival.com), which shows the best domestic films of the year. **Buses** head to Turku (1½-2hr., 1 per hr., €11). To reach the **tourist office**, Valtak. 2, follow the street by the supermarket. *(☎8378 7731; www.visitrauma.fi. Free Wi-Fi. Open mid-June to Aug. M-F 8am-6pm, Sa 10am-2pm, Su 11am-2pm; Sept. to mid-June M-F 8am-4pm.)*

Each July, crowds mob elegant **Pori** (pop. 76,000) for the renowned **Pori Jazz Festival.** *(☎626 2200; www.porijazz.fi. July 12-20, 2008. Tickets from €10; some concerts free. AmEx/MC/V.)* The **Pori Art Museum**, on the corner of Etelärantak. and Raatihuonek, has modern art exhibits. *(☎621 1080; www.poriartmuseum.fi. Open Tu and Th-Su 11am-6pm, W 11am-8pm. €5, students €2.50. MC/V.)* In a graveyard west of the town center on Maantiek., the **Juselius Mausoleum** is adorned with frescoes originally painted by native Akseli Gallén-Kallela—later redone by his son after a fire. *(☎623 8746. Open daily May-Aug. noon-3pm. Free.)* Bus #2 (30min. €4.20) leads northwest to **Yyteri Beach**, home to windsurfers and cross-country skiers. Loll in the sand with a Karhu beer, brewed in Pori. **Trains** go to Helsinki (3-3½hr., 5-6 per day, €37). **Buses** run to Tampere (2hr., 4 per day, €17) and Turku (2hr., 6-7 per day, €18). The **tourist office,** Yrjönk. 17, offers 15min. of free **Internet** and books rooms. *(☎621 7900; www.pori.fi. Open June to mid-Aug. M-F 9am-6pm, Sa 10am-3pm; mid-Aug. to May M-F 9am-4:30pm.)*

TAMPERE
☎03

A striking example of successful urban renewal, the city of Tampere (pop. 205,000) has converted its old brick factories into innovative museums and beautified waterways once clogged with paddle wheels and turbines. As telecommunications and information technology edged out textile and metal plants, an attractive city has emerged to give Turku a run for its money as Finland's second capital.

TRANSPORTATION AND PRACTICAL INFORMATION. Trains go to Helsinki (1½-2hr., 2 per hr., €26-31), Oulu (4-5hr., 8 per day, €53-60), and Turku (2hr., 1 per 1-2hr., €21). Most city **buses** (€2) run through the main square on Hämeenk. Ryanair (☎353 12 49 77 91; www.ryanair.com) **flies** to **Tampere-Pirkkala Airport (TMP).** The **tourist office** is at Verkatehtaank. 2. From the train station, walk four blocks up Hämeenk.; turn left before the bridge. (☎5656 6800; www.tampere.fi/tourism. Open June-Aug. M-F 9am-8pm, Sa-Su 10am-5pm; Sept. M-F 9am-5pm, Su 10am-5pm; Oct.-May M-F 9am-4pm.) The **library**, Pirkank. 2, has 1-2hr. of free **Internet**. (☎5656 4015. Open June to mid-Aug. M-F 9:30am-7pm, Sa 9:30am-3pm; late Aug.-May M-F 9:30am-8pm, Sa 9:30am-3pm.) **Postal Code:** 33100.

┌╔┐ ACCOMMODATIONS AND FOOD. Newly renovated **Hostel Sofia (HI) ❷**, Tuomiokirkonk. 12A, has comfy dorms. (☎254 4020. Breakfast M-F €6.50. Linens and towels included. Free Wi-Fi. Reception 8-10am and 4-11pm. Dorms €22-23; singles €40; doubles €58. €2.50 HI discount. MC/V.) **Hostel Tampere (HI) ❷**, Pirkank. 10, has larger, but older, rooms. (☎222 9460; www.hosteltampere.com. Breakfast €4.50. Reception May-Aug. M-Th 6:30am-11:30pm, F-Sa 24hr., Su midnight-9:30pm; Sept.-Apr. M-Sa 6:30am-10:30pm, Su 6:30am-2:30pm. Dorms €21; singles €40-43; doubles €56; triples €71. €2.50 HI discount. MC/V.) Bus #1 (€2) goes to **Camping Härmälä ❶**, Leirintäk. 8, where tightly packed cabins sit on the shore of Lake Pyhäjärvi. (☎265 1355; www.lomaliitto.fi. Open May-late Aug. €2-4 per person, €10-12 per tent site. Cabins €30-69. Electricity €5. MC/V.)

Restaurants line **Hämeenkatu** and **Aleksanterinkatu.** The city's oldest pizzeria, **Napoli ❶**, Aleksanterink. 31, serves 100 varieties in a casual yet classy setting. (☎223 8887. Pizza €8-13. Open M-Th 11am-11pm, F 11am-midnight, Sa noon-midnight, Su 1-11pm. MC/V.) Next to the Finlayson food court, **Plevna Panimoravintola ❷**, Itäinenk. 8, serves microbrews in a a converted weaving mill. (☎260 1200; www.plevna.fi. Entrees €8-16. Beer €4.50-6. Open M 11am-11pm, Tu-Th 11am-1am, F-Sa 11am-2am, Su noon-11pm. MC/V.) The gastronomically bold can try *mustamakkara*, black blood sausage (from €1) at Tampere's vast market hall, **Kauppahalli,** Hämeenk. 19. (Open M-F 8am-6pm, Sa 8am-3pm.)

◙ SIGHTS. The delightfully haphazard **Vapriikki Museum Center,** Veturiaukio 4, has collections that run the gamut from shoe history to Finnish hockey. (☎5656 6966; www.tampere.fi/english/vapriikki. Open Tu and Th-Su 10am-6pm, W 11am-8pm; June-Aug also open M 10am-6pm. €5, students €1. Special exhibitions €6-8, students €2-3, including museum admission. AmEx/MC/V.) The **Finlayson Complex,** named for Scottish cotton magnate James Finlayson, houses the **Media Museum Rupriikki,** with exhibits on the history of mass communications and news. (☎5656 6411; www.tampere.fi/mediamuseo/english. Open Tu-Su 10am-6pm. €5, students €1; temporary exhibits €4/1; combo ticket €5/2. AmEx/MC/V.) The complex also houses the world's oldest **Spy Museum,** Satakunnank. 18, where you can unleash your inner James Bond. (☎212 3007; www.vakoilumuseo.fi. Open June-Aug. M-Sa 10am-6pm, Su 10am-4pm; Sept.-May M-F noon-6pm, Sa-Su 11am-5pm. Agent test €4. Museum €7, students €5.50. Cash only.) The frescoes on the **Tuomiokirkko,** Tuomiokirkonk. 3 (open daily 9am-6pm), are matched in beauty only by the vaulted wooden ceiling of the **Aleksanterinkirkko,** on Pyynikin kirkkopuisto. (Open daily June-Aug. 10am-5pm; Sept.-May 11am-3pm.) At Tampere's western edge, the **Pyynikki Observation Tower** offers views of the city and the surrounding nature preserve. Enjoy a traditional *munkki*, a doughnut-like pastry (€1.20), at its cafe. (☎212 3247. Open daily 9am-8pm. €1. Cash only.) The city's northern lakefront is home to **Särkänniemi** theme park. An aquarium, a dolphinarium, a planetarium, and rides round out the attractions. (☎0207 130 212; www.sarkanniemi.fi. "Adventure Key" grants admission to all attractions, including rides, for €29. Each attraction or ride €5. Hours vary; check website. MC/V.) Off the southern shore is **Viikinsaari Island,** a popular spot for picnics, short hikes, and relaxing on the beach. Ferries depart from Laukontori harbor (20min.; Tu-Su 1 per hr.; €7, students €6).

▨▨ FESTIVALS AND NIGHTLIFE. Tampere's **Short Film Festival** draws entries from around the globe (www.tamperefilmfestival.fi; Mar. 5-9, 2008). Mid-July's **Tammerfest** (www.tammerfest.net) fills the city with music, while August's **International Theater Festival** puts on Finnish works (www.teaterikesa.fi). **Hämeenkatu, Aleksanterinkatu, Itsenäisyydenkatu,** and the surrounding streets bustle with energy at night. ▧**Cafe Europa,** Aleksanterink. 29, serves drinks in a bohemian lounge. (☎223 5526; www.caf-

FINLAND

eeuropa.net. Beer €4. Cider €4.30. ISIC discounts. Open Su-Tu noon-1am, W-Th noon-2am, F-Sa noon-3am. AmEx/MC/V.) Finland's oldest gay bar, **Mixei,** Itsenäisyydenk. 7-9, fills up late. (☎222 0364; www.mixei.com. Beer €4. Karaoke Th 9pm. 18+. Happy hour 8-10pm. Cover F-Sa €5-7 after 10pm. Open Tu-Th 8pm-2am, F-Sa 8pm-4am. MC/V.)

SAVONLINNA   ☎015

The captivating town of Savonlinna (pop. 28,000) spans three islands in the heart of Finland's lake region, a popular summer destination. The town draws 60,000 people for July's month-long **Opera Festival,** which features stunning performances in **Olavinlinna Castle.** (www.operafestival.fi. Tickets, from €32, can be booked up to a year ahead.) The castle was built in 1475 to reinforce the eastern border against the tsars. A 50min. English-language tour, included in festival ticket prices, takes you into rooms closed to general visitors. There are also three small museums with exhibits on the castle's history and ecclesiastical artifacts. (☎531 164. Open daily June to mid-Aug. 10am-5pm; mid-Aug. to May 10am-3pm. Tour departs on the hour. €5, students €3.50. MC/V.) Near the castle, on Riihisaari, the **Provincial Museum** explores the history of the region, focusing on the shipping industry. While you're there, creep around the well-preserved museum ships moored at the island. (☎571 4712. Museum open June and Aug.-May Tu-Su 11am-5pm; July-Aug daily 11am-7:30pm. Ships open mid-May to Sept. 2. €5, students €3. Cash only.) The secluded northern island **Sulosaari** has several walking trails. From the *Kauppatori,* go under the train tracks, cross the footbridge, go through the parking lot, and cross the next bridge; look for the "no cars" sign to the right of the building. Make time for a daytrip to the ■**Retretti Art Center,** where caves have contemporary art pieces that play off subterranean illumination, shadows, and water reflections. (☎775 2200; www.retretti.fi. Open daily July 10am-6pm; June and Aug. 10am-5pm. €15, students €9. AmEx/MC/V.) Trains (4-5 per day, €3.50) make the 20min. trip from Savolinna. Walk along the breathtaking **Punkaharju Ridge** to reach **Lusto** (Finnish Forest Museum), which details the environmental history of the area. (☎345 100; www.lusto.fi. Open daily June-Aug. 10am-7pm; Sept.-May reduced hours. 1hr. tour departs July-Aug. daily 3pm. €7, students €6. MC/V.)

Summer Hotel Vuorilinna (HI) ❸, on Kylpylaitoksentie near the casino, has well-equipped student apartments. From the Kauppatori, walk under the tracks and cross the bridge. (☎739 5494; www.spahotelcasino.fi. Linens and laundry included. Free Internet and Wi-Fi. Reception 7am-11pm. Open June-Aug.; call ahead for specific dates. Dorms €30; singles €55-65; doubles €65-75. €2.50 HI discount. AmEx/MC/V.) Bus #3 (€2.50) runs to **Vuohimäki Camping ❶,** on the Lake Pihlajavesi shore. (☎537 353. Bike rental €10 per day. Laundry €2. Reception and cafe open M-Th 8am-10pm, F-Sa 8am-11pm, Su 8am-9pm. Open June-Aug. Tent sites €10-12. 4- and 6-person cabins with bath June and late Aug. €74-82; July-early Aug. €76-89. Electricity €5. Showers €4. MC/V.) The **Kauppatori** market sells local produce and pastries. (Open June M-F 6am-4pm, Sa 6am-3pm; July M-F 6am-8pm, Sa 6am-4pm, Su 9am-4pm; Aug.-May M-F 7am-3pm, Sa 7am-2pm.) **Huvila,** Puisok. 4, offers beer brewed on-site. It has a **B&B ❹** that's a good budget option in low season. (☎555 0555. Beer €3.50-5.50. Pub and concerts 18+. Open June-Aug. M-Sa noon-2am, Su noon-midnight; Sept.-May reduced hours. Doubles June to mid-Aug. €120; late-Aug. to May €75. AmEx/MC/V.)

Trains run to Helsinki (5-6hr., 3-5 per day, from €50). The **Savonlinna-Kauppatori** stop is in the center of town; **Savonlinna Station** is closer to the bus station and campground. Neither station is staffed. To get to town from the main station, walk straight out, cross the street, and continue on Olavink. The **tourist office,** Puistok. 1, across the bridge from the market, offers Internet and luggage storage for no fee. (☎517 510; www.savonlinnatravel.com. Open mid- to late June M-F 9am-6pm; late June to late July M-F 9am-8pm; late July-Aug. daily 9am-6pm; Sept. to mid-June M-F 9am-5pm. AmEx/MC/V.) **Postal Code:** 57100.

KUOPIO
☎017

Eastern Finland's largest city, Kuopio (pop. 91,000) lies in the Kallavesi lake district. The archbishop of the Finnish Orthodox Church lives here, and the ◪**Orthodox Church Museum,** 10min. from town at Karjalank. 1, showcases a collection of stunning textiles and icons. (☎206 100 266; www.ort.fi/kirkkomuseo. Open May-Aug. Tu-Su 10am-4pm; Sept.-Apr. M-F noon-3pm, Sa-Su noon-5pm. €5, students €3. Cash only.) The **Kuopio Museum,** Kauppak. 23, which holds both the Natural and Cultural History Museums, delights with its life-size mammoth reconstruction. In summer 2008, the museum will hold an exhibition on the 1808-09 Finnish War with Russia. (☎182 603; www.kuopionmuseo.fi. Open Tu and Th-F 10am-5pm, W 10am-7pm, Sa-Su 11am-5pm. €5, students €3. Cash only.) The 2km hike uphill to ◪**Puijo Tower** culminates in a view of Kuopio, Lake Kallavesi, and the coniferous forests beyond. From the Kauppatori, walk toward the train station on Puijonk., cross the tracks and the highway on your left, and continue uphill, following signs for "Puijon Torni." (☎255 5253; www.puijo.com. Open June M-Sa 9am-11pm, Su 9am-9pm; July-Aug. M-Sa 9am-11pm; Sept. M-Sa 11am-10pm, Su 11am-6pm; Oct.-May Tu-Sa 11am-10pm. €4, students €3.50. AmEx/MC/V.) In mid-June, the **Kuopio Dance Festival** (www.kuopiodancefestival.fi) draws crowds to its performances, and lures wannabe Baryshnikovs with dance lessons for all. (Adult classes from €60. MC/V.) Happy winos toast to a different country every year at the early July **Kuopio International Wine Festival** (www.kuopiowinefestival.fi).

> **⬛TIP** **BUG OFF!** Mosquito-killing is a sport in Finland (see Eternal Glory, p. 300), but if going on a rampage doesn't appeal, carry a large supply of bug spray when heading into northern forests. You'll thank us once you get there. Supposedly, some of the mosquitoes are as big as horses. You heard it here first.

Embrace your inner schoolmarm at the **Virkkula Youth Hostel ❷,** Asemak. 3, which offers bare-bones dorms in an old-fashioned schoolhouse. (☎040 418 2178. Communal showers. Linens and towels €6. Internet €1 for 1st 30min., €0.50 per 30min. thereafter. Reception 24hr. Open June-July. Dorms €15. Cash only.) Rooms at **Rautatie Guest House ❸,** Asemak. 1, have their own TVs; pricier rooms have baths. Reception is in the Asemagrilli restaurant in the train station. (☎580 0569. Breakfast and linens included. Reception M-F and Su 7:30am-8pm, Sa 7:30am-6pm. Singles €40-50; doubles €60-80; triples €100; quads €125. AmEx/MC/V.) The town center has many affordable eateries. **Muikkuravintola Sampo ❷,** Kauppak. 13, draws praise for its take on *muikku*, a small local whitefish. (☎261 4677. Entrees €9-12. Open M-Sa 11am-midnight, Su noon-midnight. AmEx/MC/V.) There's fresh produce at the **Kauppatori** market in the center of town and inside the **Kauppahalli** market hall, where you can also get a taste of the local specialty, *kalakukko* fish-and-pork pie, for €2 in the first shop on your left. (www.kuopionkauppahalli.net. Kauppatori open M-Sa 8am-4pm. Kauppahalli open M-F 8am-5pm, Sa 8am-3pm.)

Trains go to Helsinki (4-5hr., 5-10 per day, from €51) and Oulu (4½hr., 3-5 per day, from €40). To get to the **tourist office,** Haapaniemenk. 17, from the station, go right on Asemak. and left on Haapaniemenk. It sells the **Kuopio Card** (€12), which pays for itself after 2-3 sights. (☎182 584; www.kuopioinfo.fi. Open July M-F 9:30am-5pm, Sa 9:30am-3pm; June and Aug. M-F 9:30am-5pm; Sept.-May M-F 9:30am-4:30pm. AmEx/MC/V.) **Internet** is free (Drop-in 30min., reserved slots 1hr.) at branches of the Kuopio library. (☎182 319; www.kuopio.fi/kirjasto. Open Sept.-May M-F 10am-7pm, Sa 10am-3pm; June-Aug. M-F 10am-7pm.) **Postal Code:** 70100.

ETERNAL GLORY

If Oulu's Air Guitar tournament or the Ant Hill event (who can sit naked on an ant hill the longest) don't sate your competitive appetite, fear not. Finland has world championships in:

Wife Carrying: Inspired by the 19th century practice of stealing wives from neighboring villages. Brave the 253.5m obstacle course, but be careful: a wife dropping infraction leads to a 15sec. penalty (and likely a night on the couch). Prize: Wife's weight in beer. (www.sonkajarvi.fi. July 5, 2008. Sonkajärvi)

Sauna Endurance: Compete on the cusp of death or injury. The temperature starts at a mild 110°C (230°F) and rises every 30sec. The winner is the last person sitting upright who can walk out unassisted. Prize: A one week vacation to a different type of sauna: Morocco. (www.saunaheinola.com. Aug., 2008. Heinola)

Mobile Phone Throwing: Finland has the most cell phones per capita in the world. Might as well throw some. Prize: A new phone. (www.savonlinnafestivals.com. Aug. 2008, Savonlinna)

Mosquito-Killing: Henri Pellonpää is the world record holder, with 21 kills in 5min. in 1995. The government worries that the event will disrupt the balance of nature, but it doesn't seem like a scarcity of mosquitos will ever be possible in Finland. Squash away. Prize: Mosquitoes will fear you. (Summer 2008. Pelkosenniemi)

OULU ☎08

Most travelers pass by Oulu (pop. 129,000), a relaxed university town. Unless you are in for late August and early September's **Oulu Music Video Festival** (www.omvf.net), there is little reason for a long stay. The associated **Air Guitar World Championships** (www.airguitarworldchampionships.com) brings national champions and other wannabes together to compete for eternal glory. For a brief diversion between trains, stroll through **Ainola Park.** The north corner borders Finland's longest Salmon ladder. Turn right from the train station, then left down Asemak., and right on Kirkkok. Down Nahkurinpl., the **Science Center Tietomaa,** Nahkatehtaank. 6, attracts crowds with interactive exhibits, IMAX, and a tower. (☎5584 1340; www.tietomaa.fi. Open July daily 10am-7pm; May-June daily 10am-6pm; Aug.-Apr. M-F 10am-4pm, Sa-Su 10am-6pm. €13, students €10. MC/V.) The scenic nearby island of **Pikisaari** draws picnickers; take the footbridge at the end of Kaarlenväylä. Free guided city **tours** depart from City Hall, Kirkkok. 2a (late June to mid-Aug.; walking tour W 6-8pm, bus tour Sa 1-3pm).

Cheap rooms are rare in Oulu. The **Oppimestari Summer Hotel (HI) ❸,** Nahkatehtaank. 3, provides well-furnished rooms with kitchenettes. (☎884 8527; www.merikoski.fi/oppimestari. Breakfast €6. Linens and laundry included. Free Internet and Wi-Fi. Open mid-June to July. Reception 24hr. Dorms €29; singles €40; doubles €58. €2.50 HI discount. AmEx/MC/V.) Bus #17 (€2.60) goes to **Nallikari Camping ❶,** Hietasaari, located on the water. (☎5586 1350; www.nallikaricamping.fi. Open year-round. €4 per person, €8-10 per tent site. 4-person cabins €30-34. Electricity €4. Showers included. AmEx/MC/V.) Cheap food, on the other hand, is easy to find; the streets are lined with pizzerias. The harborside **Kauppatori,** at the end of Kauppurienk., sells produce and is flanked by yuppie cafes. (Open M-F 8am-6pm, Sa 8am-3pm.) Nightlife centers on the marketplace square in front of **Kauppatori** and the terraces lining **Otto Karhin Park** and **Kappurienkatu.**

Trains head south to Helsinki (6-7hr., 9-10 per day, €64-70) and north to Rovaniemi (2½hr., 6-7 per day, from €28). To reach the **tourist office,** Uusik. 26, which has free **Internet,** take Hallitusk. and turn left at the park. (☎5584 1330; www.oulutourism.fi. Open M-F mid-June to Aug. 9am-4pm; Sept. to mid-June 9am-4pm.) Two blocks left of the train station, **Taitonetti Ky,** Rautatienkatu 16, has **Internet.** (☎530 2000. €1 per 15min. Open M-Th noon-6pm, F-Sa noon-8pm. MC/V.) Free **Wi-Fi** is available in some Oulu public areas; check www.panoulu.net. **Postal Code:** 90100.

ROVANIEMI

☎016

Just south of the Arctic Circle, Rovaniemi (pop. 58,000) is the capital of Finnish Lapland and a gateway to the northern wilderness. After retreating German troops burned the city to the ground in October 1944, architect Alvar Aalto stepped in with the **Reindeer Antler Plan**, a reconstruction scheme using rivers and existing highways to rebuild the settlement in the shape of a reindeer's head. Not all of Aalto's plan was executed, but you can sort of see it in a modern map of Rovaniemi with east facing up. The **Arktikum**, housed in a glass corridor at Pohjoisranta 4, has a cache of info on the Arctic and the history of Lapland's people and landscapes. (☎322 3260; www.arktikum.fi. Open daily mid-June to mid-Aug. 9am-7pm; mid-Aug. to mid-June reduced hours. €10, students €8. AmEx/MC/V.) To dash your childhood dreams of Christmas once and for all, head to **Santa Claus Village,** 8km north of Rovaniemi, where enterprising Father Christmas holds daily office hours while his elf crew mans an empire of gift shops (to fund present manufacturing, of course). It's unclear why Santa lives in a gift shop in northern Finland and who maintains the North Pole workshop while he hangs out here. After discussing such concerns with Jolly St. Nick, cross the white Arctic Circle line, which runs through the center of the village. Take bus #8 (30min.; €3.20, round-trip €5.80) from the train station or the city center to Arctic Circle. (☎356 2096; www.santaclausvillage.info. Open daily May-Aug. 9am-6pm; Sept.-Nov. and Jan.-Apr. 9am-5pm; Dec. 9am-7pm. Closed for "Santa naptime" 11am-noon and 3-4pm.)

Hostel Rudolf (HI) ❷, Koskik. 41, has well-furnished rooms with bath. Turn left out of the tourist office, walk two blocks, then go left on Koskik. for the hostel and right for reception. (☎321 321; www.rudolf.fi. Reception 24hr. at the Clarion Hotel Santa Claus, Korkalonk. 29. Breakfast €8 at hotel. Apr. to mid-Nov. dorms €25; singles €37. Mid-Nov. to Mar. €37/48. €2.50 HI discount. AmEx/MC/V.) **Koskikatu** is lined with cafes, bars, and a **K** supermarket. (Open M-F 8am-9pm, Sa 8am-6pm. MC/V.) Finnish "monster band" Lordi runs **Lordi's Rocktaurant ❷,** Koskik. 25, good for buffet eats (€9-10) and brushing shoulders with zombies. (☎050 433 9811; www.rocktaurant.com. Buffet M-F and Sa 11am-6pm. Open M-F 11am-10pm, Sa noon-10pm. MC/V.) **Trains** run to Helsinki (10hr., 4-5 per day, €78) via Oulu (2½hr., €30) and Kuopio (8hr., 3-4 per day, from €55). **Buses** go to northern Finland and to Nordkapp, NOR (11hr., 1 per day, €114). The **tourist office,** Rovak. 21, books Lapland wilderness safaris (€22-122); turn right out of the train station or walk straight from the bus station toward the yellow building marked "Posti." Walk under the highway, then bear left to reach the sidewalk. Follow it two blocks to Rovak., then turn left and walk three blocks. (☎346 270; www.rovaniemi.fi. Internet €2 per 15min. Open June-Aug. M-F 8am-6pm, Sa-Su 10am-4pm; Sept.-Nov. and Jan.-May M-F 8am-5pm; Dec. M-F 8am-5pm, Sa-Su 10am-2pm. AmEx/MC/V.) The **library,** Jorma Eton tie 6, an Aalto design, has free **Internet.** (20min. drop-in; 1hr. with reservation) Open in summer M-Th 11am-7pm, F 11am-5pm, Sa 11am-3pm; winter M-Th 11am-8pm, F 11am-5pm, Sa 11am-4pm.) **Postal Code:** 96200.

FRANCE

With its lavish châteaux, lavender fields, medieval streets, and sidewalk cafes, France conjures up any number of postcard-ready scenes. To the proud French, it is only natural that outsiders flock to their history-steeped and art-rich homeland. Although France may no longer manipulate world events, the vineyards of Bordeaux, the museums of Paris, the beaches of the Riviera, and many other attractions draw more tourists than any other nation in the world. Centuries-old farms and churches share the landscape with inventive, modern architecture; street posters advertise jazz festivals as well as Baroque concerts. The country's rich culinary tradition rounds out a culture that cannot be sent home on a four-by-six.

 DISCOVER FRANCE: SUGGESTED ITINERARIES

3 DAYS. Don't even think of leaving **Paris,** the City of Light (p. 308). Explore the shops and cafes of the **Latin Quarter,** then cross the Seine to reach **Île de la Cité** to admire **Sainte Chapelle** and the **Cathédrale de Notre Dame.** Visit the wacky **Centre National d'Art et de Culture Georges Pompidou** before swinging through **Marais** for food and fun. The next day, stroll down the **Champs-Elysées,** starting at the **Arc de Triomphe,** meander through the **Jardin des Tuileries,** and over to the **Musée d'Orsay.** See part of the **Louvre** the next morning, then spend the afternoon at **Versailles.**

1 WEEK. After 3 days in **Paris,** go to **Tours** (1 day; p. 334), a great base for exploring the châteaux of the **Loire Valley** (1 day; p. 358). Head to **Rennes** for medieval sights and modern nightlife (1 day; p. 335), then to the dazzling island of **Mont-St-Michel** (1 day; p. 341).

BEST OF FRANCE, 3 WEEKS. Begin with 3 days in **Paris,** with a daytrip to the royal residences at **Versailles.** Whirl through the **Loire Valley** (2 days) before traveling to the wine country of **Bordeaux** (1 day; p. 359). Check out the rose-colored architecture of **Toulouse** (1 day; p. 362) and the medieval walls of **Carcassonne** (1 day; p. 364) before sailing through **Avignon** (p. 370), **Aix-en-Provence** (p. 370), and **Nîmes** (p. 372) in sunny Provence (3 days). Let loose in **Marseille** (2 days; p. 365), and bask in the glitter of the Riviera in **Nice** (2 days; p. 373). Then show off your tan in the Alps as you travel to **Lyon** (2 days; p. 357) and **Chamonix** (1 day; p. 355). Spice it up with a mustard tour in **Dijon** (1 day; p. 344), and finish your trip with some German flavor in **Strasbourg** (1 day; p. 345), where trains will whisk you away to your next European adventure.

ESSENTIALS

WHEN TO GO

In July, Paris starts to shrink; by August it is devoid of Parisians, animated only by tourists and the pickpockets who love them. The French Riviera fills with Anglophones from June to September, when French natives flee to other parts of the country. Early summer and fall are the best times to visit Paris—the city has warmed up but not completely emptied out. The north and west have cool winters and mild summers, while the center and east have a more temperate climate. From December through April, the Alps provide some of the world's best skiing, while the Pyrénées offer a calmer, if less climatically dependable, alternative.

DOCUMENTS AND FORMALITIES

FACTS AND FIGURES

Official Name: French Republic.

Capital: Paris.

Major Cities: Lyon, Marseille, Nice.

Population: 60,880,000.

Land Area: 547,000 sq. km.

Time Zone: GMT+1.

Language: French.

Religion: Roman Catholic (88%), Muslim (9%), Protestant (2%), Jewish (1%).

Number of Cheese Varieties: over 500.

EMBASSIES AND CONSULATES. Foreign embassies in France are in Paris (p. 310). French embassies abroad include: **Australia,** 6 Perth Ave., Yarralumla, Canberra, ACT 2600 (☎02 62 16 01 00; www.ambafrance-au.org); **Canada,** 42 Sussex Dr., Ottawa, ON, K1M 2C9 (☎613-789-1795; www.ambafrance-ca.org); **Ireland,** 36 Ailesbury Rd., Ballsbridge, Dublin, 4 (☎00 353 1 227 5000; www.ambafrance.ie); **New Zealand,** 34-42 Manners St., Wellington (☎64 384 25 55; www.ambafrance-nz.org); **UK,** 58 Knightsbridge, London, SW1X 7JT (☎44 207 073 1000; www.ambafrance-uk.org); **US,** 4101 Reservoir Rd., NW, Washington, D.C., 20007 (☎202-944-6195; www.ambafrance-us.org).

VISA AND ENTRY INFORMATION. EU citizens do not need a visa. Citizens of Australia, Canada, New Zealand, and the US do not need a visa for stays of up to 90 days, beginning upon entry into any of the countries in the EU's freedom-of-movement zone. For more info, see p. 17. For stays longer than 90 days, all non-EU citizens need Schengen visas (around US$81), available at French consulates and online at www.consulfrance-washington.org.

TOURIST SERVICES AND MONEY

EMERGENCY	Ambulance: ☎ 15. Fire: ☎ 18. Police: ☎ 17. General Emergency: ☎ 112.

TOURIST OFFICES. The **French Government Tourist Office** (**FGTO;** www.franceguide.com), also known as **Maison de la France,** runs tourist offices (called *syndicats d'initiative* or *offices de tourisme*) and offers tourist services. In smaller towns, the **mairie** (town hall) may also distribute maps and pamphlets, help travelers find accommodations, and suggest sights and excursions.

MONEY. The **euro (€)** has replaced the **franc** as France's unit of currency. For more info, see p. 17. As a general rule, it's cheaper to exchange money in France than at home. Be prepared to spend at least €20-40 per day and much more in Paris. **Tips** are usually included in restaurant and cafe meal prices and in drink prices at bars and clubs; ask or look for the phrase *service compris* on the menu. If service is not included, tip 15-20%. Even with an included tip, it's polite to leave a *pourboire* of up to 5% at a bar, bistro, cafe, or restaurant. Workers such as concierges may expect at least a €1.50 tip for services beyond the call of duty. Taxi drivers expect 10-15% of the metered fare. It's customary to tip tour guides and bus drivers €2-3.

France has a 19.6% **value added tax** (**VAT; TVA** in French), a sales tax applied to a wide range of goods and services. The prices included in *Let's Go* include VAT. In the airport upon exiting the EU, non-EU citizens can claim a refund on the tax paid for goods purchased at participating stores. In order to qualify for a refund in a store, you must spend at least €175; make sure to ask for a refund form when you pay. For more info on qualifying for a VAT refund, see p. 19.

FEATURED ITINERARY: WINE-TASTING IN FRANCE

Start your tour in **Paris** (p. 308), and preview some of France's most distinctive vintages at **La Belle Hortense,** an egghead wine bar in the Marais. Then set out for **Reims** (p. 342), where the folks at **Champagne Pommery** offer tours of cellars that hold magnums of the bubbly stuff. Spend a night in **Epernay** (p. 343), and saunter down the avenue de Champagne for wine tastings at blue-blood **Moët & Chandon** and the more populist **Mercier.** Then head for **Strasbourg** (p. 345), the northernmost point on Alsace's legendary **Route du Vin** (p. 346). Frequent trains will whisk you south to touristy **Colmar** (p. 347), the site of a ten-day wine festival or ride to **Dijon**—just to the south lies **Beaune** (p. 344), surrounded by the **Côte de Beaune** vineyards. Don't pass up a visit to **Patriarche Père et Fils,** where a tour of the byzantine cellars includes tasting 13 regional wines. Then dart back to Paris, or extend your itinerary to explore the **Médoc** region around **Bordeaux** (p. 359) and the vineyards at **Sélestat** (p. 346).

TRANSPORTATION

BY PLANE. Most transatlantic flights to Paris land at **Roissy-Charles de Gaulle** (**CDG;** ☎ 01 48 62 22 80). Many continental and charter flights use **Orly** (**ORY;** ☎ 01 49 75 15 15). **Aéroports de Paris** (www.aeroportsdeparis.fr) has info about both airports.

Paris Beauvais Tillé (BVA; ☎38 92 68 20 66; www.aeroportbeauvais.com) caters to budget travelers, servicing discount airlines like **Ryanair (☎38 92 68 20 73; www.ryanair.com)**. For more info on flying to France, see p. 43. Once in France, most people prefer alternative travel modes unless heading to Corsica (p. 381).

BY TRAIN. The French national railway company, **SNCF (☎08 36 35 35 35; www.sncf.fr)**, manages one of Europe's most efficient rail networks. Among the fastest in the world, **TGV (www.tgv.com)** trains (high-speed, or *train à grande vitesse*) now link many major cities in France, as well as some other European destinations, including Brussels, Geneva, Lausanne, and Zürich. **Rapide** trains are slower. Local **Express** trains are, strangely enough, the slowest option. French trains offer discounts of 25-50% on tickets for travelers under 26 with the **Carte 12-25** (€52; good for 1yr.). Locate the **guichets** (ticket counters), the **quais** (platforms), and the **voies** (tracks), and you will be ready to roll. Terminals can be divided into **banlieue** (suburb) and the bigger **grandes lignes** (intercity trains). While only select trains require a reservation, you are not guaranteed a seat without one (usually US$5-30). Reserve ahead during peak holiday and tourist seasons.

 VALIDATE = GREAT. Be sure to validate *(composter)* your ticket before boarding. Orange validation boxes can be found in every train station.

If you're planning to spend a good deal of time on trains, a rail pass might be worthwhile, but in many cases—especially if you're under 26—point-to-point tickets may be cheaper. **Eurail** is valid in France. **Eurail Passes,** valid for a given number of consecutive days, are best for long distances travel. **Flexipasses,** valid for any 10 or 15 (not necessarily consecutive) days within a two-month period, are more cost-effective for those traveling longer distances less frequently. **Youth Passes** and **Youth Flexipasses** provide the same second-class perks for those under 26. It is best to purchase a pass before going to France. For prices and more info, contact **DER Travel Services (☎800-782-2424; www.der.com)**, student travel agencies, or **Rail Europe** (Canada ☎800-361-7245, US 877-257-2887; www.raileurope.com).

BY BUS. Within France, long-distance buses are a secondary transportation choice, as service is relatively infrequent. However, in some regions buses are indispensable for reaching out-of-the-way towns. Bus services operated by **SNCF** accept rail passes. *Gare routière* is French for "bus station."

BY FERRY. Ferries across the English Channel *(La Manche)* link France to England and Ireland. The shortest and most popular route is between Dover, BRI and Calais (1-1½hr.) and is run by **P&O Stena Line (☎0870 598 0333; www.poferries.com)** and **SeaFrance (☎0871 663 2546; www.seafrance.com)**. **Norfolkline (☎44 0870 870 1020; www.norfolkline-ferries.com)** provides an alternative route from Dover, BRI to Dunkerque (1¾hr.). **Brittany Ferries** (France ☎0825 82 88 28, UK 0870 9 076 103; www.brittany-ferries.com) travels from Portsmouth to Caen (4¾-6¾hr.), Cherbourg (4hr.) and St-Malo (7¾-11¾hr.). For more info on English Channel ferries, see p. 53. For info on ferries to Corsica, see p. 381.

BY CAR. Drivers in France visiting for fewer than 90 days must be 18 years old and carry either an **International Driving Permit (IDP)** or a valid EU-issued or American driving license. You need to also have the vehicle's registration, national plate, and current insurance certificate on hand; French car rental agencies provide necessary documents. Agencies require renters to be 20 and most charge those aged 21-24 an additional insurance fee (€20-25 per day). If you don't know how to drive stick, you may have to pay a hefty premium for a car with automatic transmission. French law requires that both drivers and passengers wear seat belts. The almost 1,000,000km of French roads are usually in great condition, due in part to expensive tolls paid by travelers. Check www.francetourism.com/practicalinfo for more info on domestic travel and car rentals.

FRANCE

BY BIKE AND BY THUMB. Of Europeans, the French alone may love cycling more than football. Bicycles usually rent for €8-19 per day. Hitchhiking is illegal on French highways, although some people describe the French's ready willingness to lend a ride. Let's Go does not recommend hitchhiking.

KEEPING IN TOUCH

PHONE CODES	**Country code: 33. International dialing prefix:** 00. When calling within a city, dial 0 + city code + local number. For more info on how to place international calls, see **Inside Back Cover.**

EMAIL AND THE INTERNET. Internet access is readily available throughout France. Only the smallest villages lack Internet cafes, and in larger towns Internet cafes are well equipped and widespread, though often pricey. In addition to the locations suggested here, check out www.cybercaptive.com for more options. McDonald's almost always offers free Wi-Fi.

TELEPHONE. Whenever possible, use a calling card for international phone calls, as long-distance rates for national phone services are often very high. Publicly owned **France Télécom** pay phones charge less than their privately owned counterparts. They accept stylish **Télécartes** (phonecards), available in 50-unit (€7.50) and 120-unit (€15) denominations at newspaper kiosks and *tabacs*. Mobile phones are an increasingly popular and economical option. Major mobile carrieres include Orange, Bouyges Telecom, and SFR. *Décro-chez* means pick up; you'll then be asked to **patientez** (wait) to insert your card; at *numérotez* or *composez*, you can dial. The number for general info is ☎ 12; for an international operator, call ☎ 00 33 11. International direct dial numbers include: **AT&T Direct** ☎ 0 800 99 00 11; **Canada Direct** ☎ 0 800 99 00 16 or 99 02 16; **MCI WorldPhone** ☎ 0 800 99 00 19; **Telecom New Zealand** ☎ 0 800 90 42 80; **Telstra Australia** ☎ 0 800 99 00 61.

MAIL. Send mail from **La Poste** offices throughout France (www.laposte.net. Open M-F 9am-7pm, Sa 9am-noon). Airmail between France and North America takes five to 10 days; writing "prioritaire" on the envelope should ensure delivery in four to five days at no extra charge. To send a 20g airmail letter or postcard within France or from France to another EU destination costs around €0.50, to a non-EU European country €0.75, and to Australia, Canada, New Zealand, or the US €0.90. To receive mail in France, have mail delivered **Poste Restante.** Mail will go to the main post office unless you specify a subsidiary by street address. Address mail to be held according to the following example: Last name First name, *Poste Restante*, city, France. Bring a passport to pick up your mail; there may be a small fee.

LANGUAGE AND POLITESSE. Even if your French is near-perfect, waiters and salespeople who detect the slightest accent will often respond in English. If your language skills are good, continue to speak in French; more often than not, the person will revert to French. The French put a premium on pleasantries. Always say *"bonjour Madame/Monsieur"* when you come into a business, restaurant, or hotel, and *"au revoir"* upon leaving. If you bump into someone on the street, always say *"pardon."* When meeting someone for the first time, a handshake is appropriate. However, friends and acquaintances greet each other with a kiss on each cheek. For some useful French, see **Phrasebook: French** (p. 1060).

ACCOMMODATIONS AND CAMPING

FRANCE	❶	❷	❸	❹	❺
ACCOMMODATIONS	under €15	€15-27	€28-38	€39-55	over €55

The French Hostelling International (HI) affiliate, **Fédération Unie des Auberges de Jeunesse (FUAJ; ☎** 01 44 89 87 27; www.fuaj.org), runs 160 hostels within France. A hostel dorm bed averages €10-15. Some hostels accept reservations through the **International Booking Network** (www.hostelbooking.com). Two or more people traveling together can save money by staying in cheap hotels rather than hostels. The French government employs a four-star hotel rating system. *Gîtes d'étapes* are accommodations for cyclists, hikers, and other amblers in less-populated areas. After 3000 years of settlement, true French wilderness is hard to find. It's illegal to camp in most public spaces, including national parks. Instead, look for organized **campings** (campgrounds), replete with vacationing families and programmed fun.

FOOD AND DRINK

FRANCE	❶	❷	❸	❹	❺
FOOD	under €7	€7-12	€13-18	€19-33	over €33

French chefs cook for one of the world's most finicky clienteles. The largest meal of the day is **le déjeuner** (lunch). A complete French meal includes an **apéritif** (drink), **entrée** (appetizer), **plat** (main course), salad, cheese, dessert, fruit, coffee, and **digestif** (after-dinner drink). The French drink wine with virtually every meal; *boisson comprise* entitles you to a free drink with your food. France's legal drinking age is 16. Most restaurants offer a **menu à prix fixe** (fixed-price meal) that costs less than ordering *à la carte*. The *formule* is a cheaper, two-course version for the hurried luncher. Between lunch and dinner cravings can be satisfied at *brasseries* or *crêperies*, the middle ground between cafes and restaurants. *Service compris* means the tip is included in **l'addition** (the check). It's easy to get a satisfying dinner for under €10 with staples such as bread, cheese, chocolate, pâté, and wine. For a picnic, buy fresh produce at a **marché** (outdoor market), then hop between specialty shops. Start with a **boulangerie** (bakery) for bread, proceed to a **charcuterie** (butcher) for meats, and then **pâtisserie** (pastry shop), and **confiserie** (candy shop) to satisfy a sweet tooth. When choosing a cafe, remember that major boulevards provide more expensive venues than smaller places on side streets. Prices are also cheaper at the **comptoir** (counter) than in the **salle** (seating area). For supermarket shopping, look for the chains **Carrefour, Casino,** and **Monoprix.**

HOLIDAYS AND FESTIVALS

Holidays: New Year's Day (Jan. 1); Good Friday (Mar. 21); Easter (Mar. 23-24); Labor Day (May 1); Ascension Day (May 1); Victory Day (May 8); Pentecost (May 11-12); Whit Monday (May 12); Bastille Day (July 14); Assumption (Aug. 15); All Saints' Day (Nov. 1); Armistice Day (Nov. 11); Christmas (Dec. 25-26).

Festivals: Many cities celebrate a pre-Lenten *Carnaval*—for over-the-top festivities, head to Nice (Jan. 25-Feb. 5). The Cannes Film Festival (May 14-25; www.festival-cannes.com) caters to the rich and famous. The Tour de France will start in Brittany (p.335), the 1st time in more than 40 years (begins July 5; www.letour.fr). The Festival d'Avignon (July-Aug.; www.festival-avignon.com) is famous for its theater productions.

FRANCE

BEYOND TOURISM

As the most visited nation in the world, France benefits economically from the tourism industry. Yet the country's popularity has adversely affected some French communities and their natural life. Throw off the *touriste* stigma and advocate for immigrant communities, restore a crumbling chateau, or educate others about the importance of environmental issues while exploring France. For more info on opportunities across Europe, see **Beyond Tourism,** p. 56.

Care France, CAP 19, 13 r. Georges Auric, 75019 Paris (☎01 53 19 89 89; www.care-france.org). An international organization providing volunteer opportunities, from combating AIDS to promoting education.

Club du Vieux Manoir, Ancienne Abbaye du Moncel, 60700 Pontpoint (☎03 44 72 33 98; cvmclubduvieuxmanoir.free.fr). Year-long and summer work restoring castles and churches. €14 membership and insurance fee; €12.50 per day, plus food and tent.

International Partnership for Service-Learning and Leadership, 815 Second Ave., Ste. 315, New York, NY 10017, USA (☎212-986-0989; www.ipsl.org). Matches volunteers with host families, provides intensive French classes, and requires 10-15hr. per week for a year, semester, or summer. Ages 18-30. Based in Montpellier. Costs range US$7200-US$23,600.

Jeunesse et Reconstruction, 10 r. de Trévise, 75009 Paris (☎01 47 70 75 69; www.volontariat.org). Database of volunteer opportunities for young people (ages 15+) in preservation and historical reconstruction.

PARIS

☎01

Paris (pah-ree; pop. 2,153,600), a cultural and commercial center for over 2000 years, draws millions of visitors each year, from students who come to study at the Sorbonne to tourists who wonder why the French ignore so many consonants. The City of Light, Paris is a source of inspiration unrivaled in beauty. Art emanates from its world-class museums and history from every Roman ruin, medieval street, Renaissance hotel, and 19th-century boulevard. A vibrant political center, Paris blends the spirit of revolution with a reverence for tradition, devoting as much energy to preserving conventions as it does to shattering them.

✈ INTERCITY TRANSPORTATION

Flights: Some budget airlines fly into **Aéroport de Paris Beauvais Tillé (BVA)** about 1hr. outside of Paris (p. 304). **Aéroport Roissy-Charles de Gaulle (CDG, Roissy;** ☎3950; www.adp.fr), 23km from Paris, serves transatlantic flights. 24hr. English-speaking info center. The **RER B** (one of the Parisian commuter rail lines) runs to central Paris from Terminals 1 and 2. (30-45min.; €8.20, under 18 €5.80). **Aéroport d'Orly (ORY;** ☎49 75 15 15), 18km south of Paris, has chartered and continental flights.

Trains: Paris has 6 major train stations: **Gare d'Austerlitz** (to the Loire Valley, southwestern France, Portugal, and Spain); **Gare de l'Est** (to Austria, eastern France, Czech Republic, southern Germany, Hungary, Luxembourg, and Switzerland); **Gare de Lyon** (to southern and southeastern France, Greece, Italy, and Switzerland); **Gare du Nord** (to Belgium, Britain, Eastern Europe, northern France, northern Germany, the Netherlands, and Scandinavia); **Gare Montparnasse** (to Brittany and southwestern France via TGV); **Gare St-Lazare** (to Normandy). All are accessible by Metro.

Buses: Gare Routière Internationale du Paris-Gallieni, 28 av. du Général de Gaulle, outside Paris. Ⓜ Gallieni. **Eurolines** (☎49 72 57 80, €0.34 per min.; www.eurolines.fr) sells tickets to most destinations in France and bordering countries.

FRANCE

⚜ ORIENTATION

The **Seine River** (SEHN) flows from east to west through Paris with two islands, **Ile de la Cité** and **Ile St-Louis,** situated in the city's geographical center. The Seine splits Paris in half: the **Rive Gauche** (REEV go-sh; Left Bank) to the south and the **Rive Droite** (REEV dwaht; Right Bank) to the north. Modern Paris is divided into **20 arrondissements** (districts) that spiral clockwise outward from the center of the city. Each *arrondissement* is referred to by its number (e.g. the Third, the Sixteenth). Sometimes it is helpful to orient yourself around central Paris's major monuments: on *Rive Gauche*, the Jardin du Luxembourg lies in the southeast; the Eiffel Tower, stands in the southwest; moving clockwise and crossing the Seine to *Rive Droite*, the Champs Elysées and Arc de Triomphe occupy the northwest and the Sacre-Coeur stands high in the northeast. *Let's Go: Europe* splits Paris into four sections according to geographical grouping of *arrondissements*: the city center (1er, 2ème, 3ème, and 4ème); Left Bank East (5ème, 6ème, and 13ème); Left Bank West (7ème, 14ème, and 15ème); Right Bank East (10ème, 11ème, 12ème, 18ème, 19ème, and 20ème); Right Bank West (8ème, 9ème, 16ème, and 17ème).

🚇 LOCAL TRANSPORTATION

Public Transportation: The **Métro** (Ⓜ) runs 5:30am-1:20am. Lines are numbered and are generally referred to by their number and final destinations; connections are called *correspondances.* Single-fare tickets within the city cost €1.40; carnet of 10 €10.90. Buy extras for when ticket booths are closed (after 10pm) and hold onto your ticket until you exit. The **RER (Réseau Express Régional),** the commuter train to the suburbs,

> The following stations can be dangerous at night: Anvers, Barbès-Rochechouart, Château d'Eau, Châtelet, Châtelet-Les-Halles, Gare de l'Est, Gare du Nord, and Pigalle. If concerned, take a taxi, or sit near the driver on a *Noctilien* bus.

serves as an express subway within central Paris. **Keep your ticket:** changing to and getting off the RER requires sticking your validated ticket into a turnstile. Watch the signboards next to the RER tracks and check that your stop is lit up before riding. **Buses** use the same €1.40 tickets (validate in the machine by the driver). Buses run 7am-8:30pm, *Autobus de Nuit* until 1:30am, and *Noctambus* 1 per hr. 12:30-5:30am at stops marked with a blue "N" inside a white circle, with a red star on the upper right-hand side. The **Mobilis** pass covers the Métro, RER, and buses (€5.50 for a 1-day pass in Zones 1 and 2). A **Carte Orange** weekly pass *(carte orange hebdomadaire)* costs €16 and expires on Su; photo required. Refer to the front of the book for **color maps.**

Taxis: Taxis Bleus (☎08 25 16 24 24). Taxis take 3 passengers (4th €2-3 surcharge). *Tarif A,* daily 7am-7pm (€0.62 per km). *Tarif B,* M-Sa 7pm-7am, Su 24hr., and from the airports and immediate suburbs (€1.06 per km). *Tarif C,* from the airports 7pm-7am (€1.24 per km). €2 base fee and min. €5 charge. It is customary to tip 15%.

Bike Rental: Paris-Vélo, 2 r. de Fer-à-Moulin, 5ème (☎43 37 59 22). Ⓜ Censier-Daubenton. €14 per day. Open Apr.-Sept. M-Sa 10am-7pm, Su 10am-2pm and 5-7pm; Oct.-Mar. M-Sa 10am-6pm, Su 10am-2pm and 5-7pm.

🛈 PRACTICAL INFORMATION

Tourist Office: Bureau Pyramides, 25 r. des Pyramides, 1er (☎08 92 68 30 00). Ⓜ Pyramides. Open June-Oct. daily 9am-7pm; Nov.-May M-Sa 10am-7pm, Su 11am-7pm. **Bureau Gare de Lyon,** 20 bd. Diderot, 12ème (☎08 92 68 30 00). Ⓜ Gare de

GAY OLD TIME

Boasting a substantial GLBT population and the first openly gay mayor of a major European city, Paris is bursting at the seams with queer-friendly entertainment and resources. Most notably, the City of Light participates in a campaign of marches across France to celebrate and raise awareness for queer communities. The highlight of Paris is its annual **Gay Pride Festival**, held on the last Saturday of June.

Nearly all of Paris's vibrant queer communities turn out for this exuberant parade. The festive din can be heard from several Metro stops away; attendance is only partially optional if you're within the city limits, but that's for the best. A fabulous Carnaval scene greets visitors as they reach the festival. Drag queens in feathered costumes pose daintily next to scantily clad dancers bumping, grinding, and shimmying on floats.

This might be the only time the Communist Party, the Socialist Party, and the UMP (Sarkozy's right-wing party) root for the same cause. A sense of organized chaos ensues as the crowds and floats wiggle and bob from Montparnasse to the Bastille, dancing, chanting, and waving banners. While there is a hint of political consciousness, it hardly distracts from the parade's glittery, muscled, and celebratory mood.

Gay Pride Paris (p. 167), last weekend in June (www.gaypride.fr).

Lyon. Open M-Sa 8am-6pm. **Montmartre Tourist Office,** 21 pl. du Tertre, 18ème (☎42 62 21 21). Ⓜ Anvers. Open daily 10am-7pm.

Embassies: Australia, 4 r Jean-Rey, 15ème (☎40 59 33 00; www.france.embassy.gov.au). Open M-F 9am-5pm. **Canada,** 35 av. Montaigne, 8ème (☎44 43 29 00; www.international.gc.ca/canada-europa/france). Open daily 9am-noon and 2-5pm. **Ireland,** 12 av. Foch, 16ème (☎44 17 67 00; www.embassyofireland-paris.netfirms.com). Open M-F 9:30am-noon. **New Zealand,** 7ter r. Léonard de Vinci, 16ème (☎45 01 43 43; www.nzembassy.com/france). Open July-Aug. M-Th 9am-1pm and 2-4:30pm, F 9am-2pm; Sept.-June M-Th 9am-1pm and 2-5:30pm, F 9am-1pm and 2-4pm. **UK,** 18bis r. d'Anjou, 8ème (☎44 51 31 02; www.amb-grandebretagne.fr). Open M-F 9:30am-12:30pm and 2:30-4:30pm. **US,** 2 av. Gabriel, 8ème (☎43 12 22 22; www.amb-usa.fr). Open M-F 9am-12:30pm.

GLBT Resources: Centre Gai et Lesbien, 3 r. Keller, 11ème (☎43 57 21 47). Ⓜ Ledru-Rollin or Bastille. Open M-F 4-8pm.

Crisis Lines: Rape, SOS Viol (☎08 00 05 95 95). Open M-F 10am-7pm. **SOS Help!** (☎46 21 46 46). Confidential English-speaking crisis hotline. Open daily 3-11pm.

Hospitals: American Hospital of Paris, 63 bd. Hugo, Neuilly (☎46 41 25 25). Ⓜ Port Maillot, then bus #82 to the end of the line. **Hôpital Franco-Britannique de Paris** (Hertford British Hospital), 3 r. Barbès, in the Levallois-Perret suburb (☎46 39 22 22). Ⓜ Anatole France. Some English-speaking doctors.

Post Office: Poste du Louvre, 52 r. du Louvre, 1er (☎40 28 20 40). Ⓜ Louvre. Open 24hr. *Poste Restante* available. **Postal Codes:** 750xx, where "xx" is the *arrondissement* (e.g., 75003 for any address in the 3ème).

ACCOMMODATIONS

Parisian accommodations are expensive. Expect to pay at least €20 for a hostel dorm-style bed and €28 for a hotel single. Hostels are a better option for single travelers, whereas staying in a hotel is more economical for groups. Paris's hostels skip many standard restrictions (e.g., curfews) and may have flexible maximum stays. In cheaper hotels, few rooms have private baths. Rooms fill quickly after morning check-out; arrive early or reserve ahead. Most hostels and *foyers* include the **taxe de séjour** (€0.10-2 per person per day) in listed prices.

CITY CENTER

▣ **Hôtel des Jeunes,** 4ème (MIJE; ☎42 74 23 45; www.mije.com). Books beds in 3 small hostels in beautiful Marais residences recognized as historical monuments. No smoking. Breakfast, private shower, and linens included. Internet €6 per hr. €0.50 connection fee. Lockers €1 deposit. Max. 7-night stay. Reception 7am-1am. Check-in noon. Lockout noon-3pm. Curfew 1am. Quiet hours after 10pm. Dorms €28; singles €43; doubles €66; triples €87; quads €108. MIJE membership required (€2.50). Cash only. ❸

Maubuisson, 12 r. des Barres, Ⓜ Hôtel de Ville or Pont Marie, is a half-timbered former girls' convent on a silent street by the St-Gervais monastery. Accommodates more individuals than groups.

Le Fourcy, 6 r. de Fourcy, Ⓜ St-Paul or Pont Marie, surrounds a large, social courtyard–think Tuileries in miniature–ideal for outdoor picnicking. Le Fourcy's restaurant offers a main course with drink (€9, lunch only) and a 3-course "hosteler special" (€11).

Le Fauconnier, 11 r. de Fourcy, Ⓜ St-Paul or Pont Marie. Ivy-covered, sun-drenched building just steps away from the Seine and Île St-Louis.

Centre International de Paris (BVJ): Paris Louvre, 20 r. Jean-Jacques Rousseau, 1er (☎53 00 90 90; www.bvjhotel.com). Ⓜ Louvre or Palais-Royal. Bright, dorm-style rooms. Guests must be ages 18-35. Breakfast included. Lockers €2. Internet €6 per hr. Reception 24hr. Reserve ahead. Dorms €27, doubles €29. Cash only. ❷

Hôtel Tiquetonne, 6 r. Tiquetonne, 2ème (☎42 36 94 58). Ⓜ Etienne-Marcel. Small, simple rooms a stone's throw from the sex shops on r. St-Denis and the r. Montorgueil market. Elevator. Breakfast €6. Showers €6. Closed Aug. and late Dec. Reserve ahead. Singles €30, with shower €40; doubles €50. AmEx/MC/V. ❷

LEFT BANK EAST

▨ **Young and Happy (Y&H) Hostel,** 80 r. Mouffetard, 5ème (☎47 07 47 07; www.youngandhappy.fr). Ⓜ Monge. A funky, friendly hostel. Laid-back staff and clean (if basic) rooms. Kitchen. Breakfast included. Linens €3 with €5 deposit, towels €1. Internet €4 per hr. Lockout 11am-4pm. Apr.-Dec. dorms €23; doubles €52. Jan.-Mar. €21/24. ❷

▨ **Hôtel Stella,** 41 r. Monsieur-le-Prince, 6ème (☎40 51 00 25; http://site.voila.fr/hotel-stella). Ⓜ Odéon. Centuries-old woodwork takes the exposed-beam look to a whole new level. Huge rooms with high ceilings, some with pianos. Reserve ahead. Singles €35-45; doubles €55-65; triples €75-85; quads €85-95. ❸

Hôtel Marignan, 13 r. du Sommerard, 5ème (☎43 54 63 81; www.hotel-marignan.com). Ⓜ Maubert-Mutualité. Clean, freshly decorated rooms. English-speaking owner combines hotel privacy with hostel-like friendliness. Kitchen. Breakfast and laundry included. Hall showers open until 10:45pm. Internet. Reserve ahead. Singles €45-60; doubles €55-85; triples €75-110; quads €85-135; quints €90-150. Cash only. ❹

Hôtel Esmeralda, 4 r. St-Julien-le-Pauvre, 5ème (☎43 54 19 20). Ⓜ St-Michel. Antique wallpaper, ceiling beams, and red velvet create a Victorian ambience. The location is outstanding—less than a block from the Seine, and within earshot of Notre Dame's bells. Breakfast €6. Singles €35, with bath €65; doubles €85-120; triples €110. ❸

LEFT BANK WEST

▨ **Hôtel Montebello,** 18 r. Pierre Leroux, 7ème (☎47 34 41 18; hmontebello@aol.com). Ⓜ Vaneau. Sparsely furnished, clean rooms with a helpful English-speaking staff. A bit far from the 7ème's sights, but unbeatable rates for the neighborhood. Breakfast €4. Reserve ahead. Singles €25-42; doubles €40-49. Extra bed €10. Cash only. ❸

Aloha Hostel, 1 r. Borromée, 15ème (☎42 73 03 03; www.aloha.fr). Ⓜ Volontaires. Colorful hostel fills with international backpackers sharing travel tips over drinks at its cafe. No outside alcohol allowed. Breakfast included. Safe deposit boxes. Linens €3. Towels €3. Internet €2 per 30min.; free Wi-Fi. Reception 7am-2am. Lockout 11am-5pm. Curfew 2am. Reserve ahead. Apr.-Oct. dorms €25; doubles €50. Nov.-Mar. €19/46. ❷

Hôtel Eiffel Rive Gauche, 6 r. du Gros Caillou, 7ème (☎45 51 24 56; www.hotel-eiffel.com). Ⓜ École Militaire. On a quiet street, this family-run hotel is refreshingly open and filled with light. Rooms have cable TV, Internet jacks, and full bath; some have Eiffel

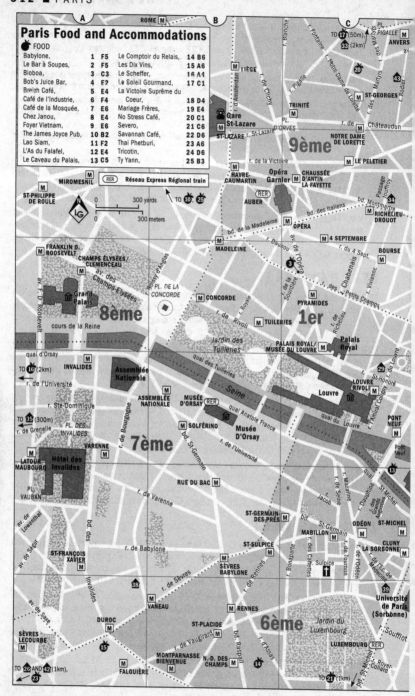

Paris Food and Accommodations

🍴 FOOD

Babylone,	1 F5	Le Comptoir du Relais,	14 B6
Le Bar à Soupes,	2 F5	Les Dix Vins,	15 A6
Bioboa,	3 C3	Le Scheffer,	16 A4
Bob's Juice Bar,	4 F2	Le Soleil Gourmand,	17 C1
Breizh Café,	5 E4	La Victoire Suprême du	
Café de l'Industrie,	6 F4	Coeur,	18 D4
Café de la Mosquée,	7 E6	Mariage Frères,	19 E4
Chez Janou,	8 E4	No Stress Café,	20 C1
Foyer Vietnam,	9 E6	Severo,	21 C6
The James Joyce Pub,	10 B2	Savannah Café,	22 D6
Lao Siam,	11 F2	Thai Phetburi,	23 A6
L'As du Falafel,	12 E4	Tricotin,	24 D6
Le Caveau du Palais,	13 C5	Ty Yann,	25 B3

RER — Réseau Express Régional train

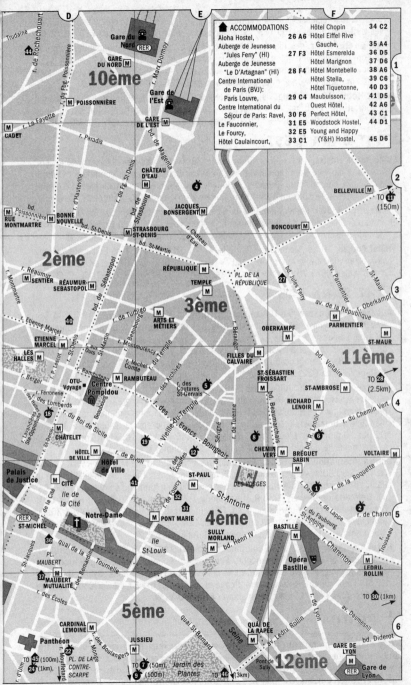

ACCOMMODATIONS

Aloha Hostel,	26 A6
Auberge de Jeunesse "Jules Ferry" (HI)	27 F3
Auberge de Jeunesse "Le D'Artagnan" (HI)	28 F4
Centre International de Paris (BVJ): Paris Louvre,	29 C4
Centre International du Séjour de Paris: Ravel,	30 F6
Le Fauconnier,	31 E5
Le Fourcy,	32 E5
Hôtel Caulaincourt,	33 C1
Hôtel Chopin	34 C2
Hôtel Eiffel Rive Gauche,	35 A4
Hôtel Esmerelda	36 D5
Hôtel Marignon	37 D6
Hôtel Montebello	38 A6
Hôtel Stella,	39 C6
Hôtel Tiquetonne,	40 D3
Maubuisson,	41 D5
Ouest Hôtel,	42 A6
Perfect Hôtel,	43 C1
Woodstock Hostel,	44 D1
Young and Happy (Y&H) Hostel,	45 D6

FRANCE

Tower views. Breakfast €10. Safe deposit box €3. Singles €75-115; doubles €75-125; triples €95-145; quads €105-175. Rates fluctuate with demand. Extra bed €10. MC/V. ❺

Hôtel de Blois, 5 r. des Plantes, 14ème (☎45 40 99 48; www.hoteldeblois.com). Ⓜ Mouton-Duvernet. One of the best deals in Paris. Lushly carpeted rooms have hair dryer, phone, and TV. Laundromat and public pool nearby. Breakfast €6.30. Reserve ahead. Singles or doubles with shower €60-65, with bath €65-82. AmEx/MC/V. ❹

Ouest Hôtel, 27 r. de Gergovie, 14ème (☎45 42 64 99). Ⓜ Pernety. A modest hotel decorated in 70s bling. Owner keeps a lending library with books left by previous guests. Breakfast €5. Showers €5. Doubles €22-28, with shower €37-39. MC/V. ❷

RIGHT BANK WEST

▓ **Woodstock Hostel,** 48 r. Rodier, 9ème (☎48 78 87 76; www.woodstock.fr). Ⓜ Anvers. A VW bug hanging from the ceiling and a case of Beatles-worship contribute to Woodstock's fun, can-do spirit. Breakfast included. Linens €3. Towels €1. Internet €4 per hr. Max. 2-week stay. Lockout 11am-3pm. Curfew 2am. Dorms €22; doubles €50. ❷

Perfect Hôtel, 39 r. Rodier, 9ème (☎42 81 18 86; www.paris-hostel.biz). Ⓜ Anvers. Lives up to its name with hotel-quality rooms at hostel prices, some with balconies. Breakfast included. Reserve ahead. Singles €44, with toilet €60; doubles €50/60. MC/V. ❷

Hôtel Chopin, 10 bd. Montmartre, 9ème (☎47 70 58 10). Ⓜ Grands Boulevards. Mostly new, clean rooms with fan, phone, and TV by request. Breakfast €7. Reserve 2-3 months ahead. Singles €61-76; doubles with shower or bath €81-92; triples €109. MC/V. ❺

RIGHT BANK EAST

Auberge de Jeunesse "Le D'Artagnan" (HI), 80 r. Vitruve, 20ème (☎40 32 34 56; www.hihostels.com). Ⓜ Porte de Bagnolet. Well-lit, generously sized rooms. Breakfast 7-11am. Lockers €2 per day. Linens included. Towel €3. Laundry €4. Internet €4 per hr. Restaurant, bar, and small cinema (free films, nightly at 6:30pm). Max. 8-night stay. Reception 8am-1am. Lockout noon-3pm. Reservations required. 9-bed dorms €20; 3-, 4-, 5-bed dorms €22; 2-bed dorm €26. Children under 10 ½-price, under 5 free. ❷

Auberge de Jeunesse "Jules Ferry" (HI), 8 bd. Jules Ferry, 11ème (☎43 57 55 60; auberge@micronet.fr). Ⓜ République. A party atmosphere in a great location next to a park and pl. de la République. 100 beds. Modern, clean rooms with mirrors, sinks, and tiled floors. Breakfast, linens, and showers included. Lockers €2. Laundry €5. Internet €1 per 10min. Max. 1-week stay. Reception 24hr. Lockout 10:30am-2pm. Arrive 8-11am to ensure a room. 4- to 6-bed dorms €21; doubles €42. MC/V. ❷

Centre International du Séjour de Paris: CISP "Ravel," 6 av. Maurice Ravel, 12ème (☎44 75 60 00; www.cisp.asso.fr). Ⓜ Porte de Vincennes. The price makes the hike to Paris's main attractions worth it. Large, clean rooms with bath and an outdoor pool (€3-4). Cafeteria open daily 7:30-9:30am, noon-1:30pm, and 7-10:30pm; meals €11. Breakfast, linens, and towels included. Free Internet. Reception 24hr. Curfew 1:30am; arrange with the night guard to be let in later. Reserve ahead. 8-bed dorms €19; 2- to 4-bed dorms €25; singles €37; doubles €54. AmEx/MC/V. ❷

Hôtel Caulaincourt, 2 sq. Caulaincourt, 18ème (☎46 06 46 06; www.caulaincourt.com). Ⓜ Lamarck-Caulaincourt. Formerly artists' studios, the simple rooms, all with phone and TV, have wonderful views of Montmartre and the Paris skyline. Breakfast €5.50. Free Internet. Reserve 1 month ahead. Singles €25, with shower €50, with bath €60; doubles €63-76; triples with shower €89. MC/V. ❸

◪ FOOD

When in doubt, spend your money on food in Paris. Skip the museum, sleep in the dingy hotel, but ▓**eat well.** Eating in the City of Light remains as exciting today as it was when Sun King Louis XIV made feasts an everyday occurrence. Beyond traditional French cuisine, the city has delicious international dishes. *Bon Appetit!*

RESTAURANTS

CITY CENTER

Chez Janou, 2 r. Roger Verlomme (☎42 72 28 41). Ⓜ Chemin-Vert. Hidden in a quiet section of the 3ème, this bistro is lauded for its inexpensive, gourmet food. Shady terrace is superb for summer dining. *Plats* €15. Open daily noon-3pm and 7pm-midnight. Reserve ahead, as this local favorite is packed every night of the week. Cash only. ❷

Bioboa, 3 r. Danielle Casanova, 1er (☎42 61 17 67). Ⓜ Pyramides. Cheap, delicious, organic lunches in a bright, trendy setting. Prepared foods available. Panini with *chèvre* and grilled veggies €7. Fruit smoothies €5-7. Open daily 11am-6pm. MC/V. ❶

Breizh Café, 109 r. Vieille du Temple, 4ème (☎42 72 13 77; www.breizhcafe.com). Ⓜ St-Sebastien. While Parisian crepes aren't hard to find, inexpensive, inventive crepes made with the highest quality ingredients (raw milk, cheese, and organic veggies) are rare. Crepe with potatoes, herring, *crème fraiche*, and caviar €10.50. Wide selection of regional ciders and Breton beers €3.50. Open M and W-Su noon-11:30pm. MC/V. ❷

La Victoire Suprême du Coeur, 41 r. des Bourdonnais, 1er (☎40 41 93 95). Ⓜ Châtelet. Vegetarian and vegan dishes like *escalope de seitan à la sauce champignon* (scallops in mushroom sauce; €14) highlight a health-conscious menu. One of the area's best lunches. *Menu* €13. Open M-F 11:45am-10pm, Sa noon-10pm. AmEx/MC/V. ❸

Le Caveau du Palais, 19 pl. Dauphine, 1er (☎43 26 04 28). Ⓜ Cité. Serves up hearty French fare under timbered ceilings. Well-heeled locals crowd the terrace in the summertime. The pricey meat dishes are worth the splurge. Entrees €17-50. Desserts €8-9. Reserve ahead. Open daily 12:15-2:30pm and 7:15-10:30pm. AmEx/MC/V. ❹

L'As du Falafel, 34 r. des Rosiers, 4ème (☎48 87 63 60). Ⓜ St-Paul. Recommended by Lenny Kravitz, this always-packed kosher falafel stand and restaurant rocks the falafel world. Wash down their incredible falafel special (€6.50, takeout €4) with a glass of the house lemonade (€4). Open M-Th and Su 11am-midnight, F 11am-6pm. MC/V. ❶

LEFT BANK EAST

Le Comptoir du Relais, 9 carrefour de l'Odeon, 6ème (☎44 27 07 97). Ⓜ Odeon. With no weak link on its menu, this locals-heavy, hyper-crowded bistro loves all things meat. Try *foie gras* on toast (€11) or beef stew with noodles, onions, and refreshing hints of lemon (€16). Open M-F noon-6pm and 8:30-10pm, Sa-Su noon-10pm. Reserve ahead for dinner M-Th, reservations not accepted F-Su. MC/V. ❹

Foyer Vietnam, 80 r. Monge, 5ème (☎45 35 32 54). Ⓜ Place Monge. This local favorite serves big portions without big prices. Start the 2-course lunch *menu* (€7 with student ID) with the tasty phô before trying the *porc au caramel*. Other dishes include duck with bananas (€9) and lychees in syrup (€3). Open M-Sa noon-2pm and 7-10pm. ❶

Café de la Mosquée, 39 r. Geoffroy-St-Hilaire, 5ème (☎43 31 38 20). Ⓜ Censier-Daubenton. In the Mosquée de Paris. With fountains, white marble floors, and an outdoor terrace, this cafe deserves a visit. Persian mint tea €2.50. *Maghrebain* pastries €2.50. Couscous €9-25. Open daily 9am-11pm. MC/V. ❷

Tricotin, 15 av. de Choisy, 13ème (☎45 84 74 44). Ⓜ Porte de Choisy. 6 chefs prepare delicious food from Cambodia, Thailand, and Vietnam, including *vapeur* (dim sum) options like steamed shrimp ravioli (€3.50). Open daily 9:30am-11:30pm. MC/V. ❶

Savannah Café, 27 r. Descartes, 5ème (☎43 29 45 77). Ⓜ Cardinal Lemoine. This cheerful restaurant serves Lebanese food including eggplant caviar, taboule, and a selection of pasta dishes. *Plats* €13-15. Open M-Sa 7-11pm. MC/V. ❸

LEFT BANK WEST

Thai Phetburi, 31 bd. de Grenelle, 15ème (☎40 58 14 88; www.phetburi-paris.com). Ⓜ Bir-Hakeim. Try the award-winning *tom yam koung* (shrimp soup with lemongrass; €7.30). Vegetarian options. Open M-Sa noon-2:45pm and 7-11pm. AmEx/MC/V. ❷

FRANCE

Le Dix Vins, 57 r. Falguière, 15ème (☎43 20 91 77). ⓜ Pasteur. This intimate bistro has a *menu* (€20-24) that, while not exactly cheap, offers a classic meal with a *nouvelle cuisine* twist. Open M-F noon-2:30pm and 8-11pm. MC/V. ❹

Severo, 8 r. des Plantes, 14ème (☎45 40 40 91). ⓜ Mouton Duvernet. Its out-of-the-way location is a blessing: a *New York Times* shout-out hasn't altered its local following. While worthwhile to splurge on fine cuts here, a delicious, inexpensive meal is possible. Entrees with *frites* €14-29. Open M-F noon-2:30pm and 7:30-10:30pm. MC/V. ❸

RIGHT BANK WEST

■ **Ty Yann,** 10 r. de Constantinople, 8ème (☎40 08 00 17). ⓜ Europe. The chef-owner, M. Yann, prepares outstanding, inexpensive *galettes* (€7-10) and crepes (€6-7). Takeout discount 15%. Open M-F noon-2:30pm and 7-10:30pm, Sa 7-10:30pm. MC/V. ❷

No Stress Café, 2 pl. Gustave Toudouze, 9ème (☎48 78 00 27). ⓜ St-Georges. A French crowd comes for American-sized salads: giant piles of veggies and well sea-soned meats (€13-16). Onion rings with spicy sauce €5. Vegetarian options. W-Sa massages 9pm-2am. Su brunch noon-3:30pm. Open Tu-Su 11am-2am. MC/V. ❸

The James Joyce Pub, 71 bd. Gouvion St-Cyr, 17ème (☎44 09 70 32). ⓜ Porte Maillot (exit at Palais de Congrès). Stained-glass windows depicting Joyce's novels brighten the upstairs restaurant and downstairs bar, both of which serve as informal tourist offices for Anglophone expats. Traditional Irish meals from €9.50. Free "Funky Maps" listing English-speaking bars and pubs in Paris. F nights live Irish rock music at 9:30pm, except in summer. Open daily 11am-2am. Kitchen open noon-9pm. AmEx/MC/V. ❷

Le Scheffer, 22 r. Scheffer, 16ème (☎47 27 81 11). ⓜ Trocadero. From the sounds of clattering pans to the red-checkered tablecloths, Le Scheffer is an unpretentious bas-tion of traditional French cuisine and a local favorite. Lunchtime service can be slow. Appetizers €6-7.50. *Steak tartare* (raw ground beef with mustard, capers, and other ingredients) €14. Open M-Sa 10:30am-11pm. ❸

RIGHT BANK EAST

■ **Lao Siam,** 49 r. de Belleville, 19ème (☎40 40 09 68). ⓜ Belleville. Even before your food arrives, you'll be impressed by this Chinese and Thai favorite. A unique Thai-dried calamari salad (€7) makes for a light preamble to the *poulet royal au curry* (€9) or *filet du poisson* with "hip-hop" sauce (€9). Wash it down with a *citron pressé* (lemonade; €3) and finish it off with kumquats (€3). Open daily noon-3pm and 7-11pm. MC/V. ❶

■ **Le Bar à Soupes,** 33 r. Charonne, 11ème (☎43 57 53 79; www.lebarasoupes.com). ⓜ Bastille. Featuring—you guessed it—big bowls of tasty soup (€5.50). The €10 lunch *menu* comes with a roll, salad, or cheese plate, soup, and wine or coffee. Try gooey *gateau chocolat* (€3) for dessert. Open M-Sa noon-3pm, 6:30-11pm. MC/V. ❶

 SAVE YOUR WALLET, HAVE A PICNIC. As a major tourist attraction, Montmartre has inevitably high prices. Save a couple euro by avoiding its touristy cafes, and picnic over Paris. Buy a *croque monsieur* or ham sandwich *à emporter*, and eat on the church's steps.

Bob's Juice Bar, 15 r. Lucien-Sampaix, 10ème (☎06 82 63 72 74; www.bobsjuice-bar.com). ⓜ Jacques Bonsergent. This vegetarian eatery serves freshly made juices (€3-4.50), pancakes (€2), salads, sandwiches, and soups. A large communal table gives it a social character, and the cool indie tunes add style points. Over a dozen *for-mules* (€5-9). Open Tu-F 7:30am-6pm, Sa-Su 7:30am-4pm. Cash only. ❶

Babylone, 21 r. Daval, 11ème (☎47 00 55 02). ⓜ Bastille. In an area full of cheap sand-wich shops and crepe stands, this *Shawarma* and falafel spot stands out. Flickering neon sign and a checkered tile floor exude a 50s diner vibe. Falafel €4. *Shawarma* €5. Falafel and *Shawarma* sandwich €5. Open M 10am-7pm, Tu-Sa 10am-12:30am. Cash only. ❶

Le Soleil Gourmand, 10 r. Ravignan, 18ème (☎ 42 51 00 50). Ⓜ Abbesses. Local favorite serves light *Provençale* fare in a cheerful, half-underground dining room. Try the *bricks* (grilled stuffed filo dough; €11) or the 5-cheese *tartes* with salad (€11). Vegetarian options like the *assiette sud* (grilled and marinated vegetables; €13). Open daily 12:30-2:30pm and 7:30-11pm. ❷

SALONS DU THÉ (TEA ROOMS)

◪ Café de l'Industrie, 15-17 r. St-Sabin, 12ème (☎ 47 00 13 53). Ⓜ Breguet-Sabin. Frequented by funky 20-somethings, l'Industrie may be the only Parisian restaurant to straddle a street. Diverse menu includes tagliatelle with pesto (€10). Coffee €3. *Vin chaud* (warm wine) €5. Popular brunch Sa-Su €18. Open daily 10am-2am. MC/V. ❸

Mariage Frères, 30 r. du Bourg-Tibourg, 4ème (☎ 42 72 28 11). Ⓜ Hôtel-de-Ville. Started by 2 brothers who found British tea shoddy, this salon offers 500 varieties of tea (€7-15). Also at 13 r. des Grands Augustins, 6ème (☎ 40 51 82 50) and at 260 r. du Faubourg St-Honoré, 8ème (☎ 46 22 18 54). Open daily 10:30am-7:30pm; lunch M-Sa noon-3pm; afternoon tea 3-6:30pm; Su brunch 12:30-6:30pm. AmEx/MC/V. ❹

SPECIALTY SHOPS AND MARKETS

Food shops, particularly *boulangeries* (bakeries) and *pâtisseries* (pastry shops), are on virtually every street in Paris. Your gustatory experiences, particularly with bread or pastries, will vary depending on how recently your food has left the oven.

◪ Amorino, 47 r. St-Louis-en-l'Île, 4ème (☎ 44 07 48 08). Ⓜ Pont Marie. With over 20 *gelati* and *sorbetti* flavors, Amorino serves amazing concoctions in more generous portions than its better known neighborhood rivals. Cone €3-5.50. Cup €3-8.50. ❶

Gusto Italia, 199 r. de Grenelle, 7ème (☎ 45 55 00 43). Ⓜ École Militaire. This unassuming spot sells a small selection of cheeses, meats, and wines. Authentic Italian lasagna or pizza big enough to share €11. Lunch served daily noon-3pm. ❷

Berthillon, 31 r. St-Louis-en-l'Île, 4ème (☎ 43 54 31 61). Ⓜ Cité or Pont Marie. Berthillon plays up its own celebrity so well—it's reputed to have Paris's best ice cream—you may trick yourself into believing your tiny scoop was worth €2. 1 scoop €2; double €3; triple €4. Open Sept. to mid-July W-Su 10am-8pm. Closed 2 weeks in Feb. and Apr. ❶

Saxe-Breteuil Outdoor Market, 15ème. Ⓜ Ségur. Saxe-Breteuil backs up its impeccable style with an incredible selection of cheese, produce, and seafood, including even a falafel stand. A wine vendor often hands out samples of the day's stock if you ask nicely. Try to arrive before noon when vendors run low on produce. Open Sa 7am-3pm.

Davoli, 32 r. Cler, 7ème (☎ 45 51 23 41). Ⓜ École Militaire. Gourmet paradise Davoli is a closet-sized food-market with a celebrity pedigree. Perfect for budget travelers caught in a rich neighborhood, Davoli has baked goods, cheeses, meats, cheeses, and prepared foods sure to be a hit. Try their *escargots de bourgogne* (€8.20 per dozen).

Belleville Outdoor Market, 20ème. Ⓜ Belleville. Produce, spices, sneakers, belts, and everything else you can think of squeezed onto bd. de Belleville. Not for the faint of heart; vendors behind the tables bellow at anyone who walks by. Strong Middle Eastern influence. Look out for pickpockets. Open Tu and F 7:30am-2:30pm.

◉ SIGHTS

While it would take weeks to see every garden, monument, and museum in Paris, the city's size makes sightseeing easy and enjoyable. In a few hours, you can walk from the Bastille to the Eiffel Tower, passing most monuments along the way. A solid day of wandering will show you how close the medieval Notre Dame is to the modern Centre Pompidou and the funky Latin Quarter to the royal Louvre.

FRANCE

CITY CENTER

In the 3rd century BC, Paris consisted only of the **Île de la Cité,** inhabited by the Parisii, a Gallic tribe of merchants and fishermen. Today, all distance-points in France are measured from *kilomètre zéro*, a sundial in front of Notre Dame. On the far west side of the island is the **Pont Neuf** (New Bridge), actually Paris's oldest bridge in Paris—and now the city's most popular make-out spot. (ⓂPont Neuf.) To the east of Île de la Cité is the tiny **Île Saint-Louis.** Rue Saint-Louis-en-l'Île rolls down the center, and is a welcome distraction from busy Parisian life. There's a wealth of ice cream parlors, upscale shops, and boutique hotels, but not much to see. (ⓂPont Marie.) On right bank, the **Marais** is home to some of Paris's best falafel (p. 315), museums, bars, as well as much of Paris's Orthodox Jewish community. At the end of **rue des Francs-Bourgeois** sits the magnificent **place des Vosges,** Paris's oldest public square. Victor Hugo lived at no. 6. (ⓂChemin Vert or St-Paul.)

CATHÉDRALE DE NOTRE DAME DE PARIS. This 12th- to 14th-century cathedral, begun under Bishop Maurice de Sully, is one of the world's most famous and beautiful examples of medieval architecture. After the Revolution, the building fell into disrepair—it was even used to shelter livestock—until Victor Hugo's 1831 novel *Notre Dame de Paris* (a.k.a. *The Hunchback of Notre Dame*) inspired citizens to lobby for the cathedral's restoration. The apocalyptic facade and seemingly weightless walls—effects produced by Gothic engineering and optical illusions—are inspiring even for the most church-weary. The cathedral's biggest draws are its enormous stained-glass rose windows that dominate the transept's northern and southern ends. The best time to view the Cathedral is late at night, when you can see the full facade without mobs blocking the view. (ⓂCité. ☎42 34 56 10. *Cathedral open daily 7:45am-7pm. Towers open July-Aug. M-F 10am-6:30pm, Sa-Su 10am-11pm; Apr.-June and Sept. daily 10am-6:30pm; Oct.-Mar. daily 10am-5:30pm. English-language tours W-Th noon, Sa 2:30pm; free. Cathedral and towers €7.50, 18-25 €5, under 18 free.*)

STE-CHAPELLE, CONCIERGERIE, AND PALAIS DE JUSTICE. The **Palais de la Cité** contains three vastly different buildings. ◨**Ste-Chapelle** remains the foremost example of flamboyant Gothic architecture and a tribute to the craft of medieval stained glass. Around the corner is the **Conciergerie,** one of Paris's most famous prisons; Marie-Antoinette and Robespierre were incarcerated here during the Revolution. (*6 bd. du Palais.* Ⓜ Cité. ☎53 40 60 93. *Open daily Mar.-Oct. 9:30am-6pm; Nov.-Feb. 9am-5pm. Last entry 30min. before closing. €7.50, seniors and 18-25 €4.80, under 18 free. Combo ticket with Conciergerie €9.50/7/free.*) Built after the great fire of 1776, the **Palais de Justice** houses France's district courts. (*4 bd. du Palais.* Ⓜ Cité. ☎44 32 51 51. *Courtrooms open M-F 9am-noon and 1:30-end of last trial. Free.*)

MÉMORIAL DE LA DÉPORTATION. Commemorating the 200,000 French victims of Nazi concentration camps, the museum includes a tunnel lined with 200,000 quartz pebbles that reflects the Jewish custom of placing stones on graves. (Ⓜ Cité. *At the very tip of the island on pl. de l'Île de France. Open daily Apr.-Sept. 10am-noon and 2-7pm; Oct.-Mar. 10am-noon and 2-5pm. Last entry 10min. before closing. Free.*)

HÔTEL DE VILLE. Paris's grandiose city hall dominates a large square filled with fountains and *Belle Époque* lampposts. The present edifice is a 19th-century replica of the original medieval structure, a meeting hall for the cartel that controlled traffic on the Seine. (*29 r. de Rivoli.* Ⓜ Hôtel-de-Ville. ☎42 76 43 43. *Open M-F 9am-6pm.*)

LEFT BANK EAST

The **Latin Quarter,** named for the prestigious universities that taught in Latin until 1798, has its soul in the ever-vibrant student population. Since the student riots in May 1968, many artists and intellectuals have migrated to the cheaper outer *arrondissements*, and the *haute bourgeoisie* have moved in. The 5*ème* still presents the city's most diverse array of bookstores, cinemas, and jazz clubs.

Designer shops and edgy art galleries are found around **St-Germain-des-Prés** in the 6*ème*. Farther east, the residential 13*ème* doesn't have much to attract typical tourists, but its diverse neighborhoods offer an authentic view of Parisian life.

■ **JARDIN DU LUXEMBOURG.** Parisians sunbathers flock to these formal gardens. A Roman residential area, the site of a medieval monastery, and later home to 17th-century French royalty, the gardens were liberated during the Revolution. *(6ème. ⓜ Odéon or RER: Luxembourg. Main entrance on bd. St-Michel. Open daily dawn-dusk.)*

ODÉON. The **Cour du Commerce St-André** is one of the 6*ème*'s most picturesque walking areas, with cobblestone streets and centuries-old cafes (including **Le Procope**). Just south of bd. St-Germain, the **Carrefour de l'Odéon,** a favorite Parisian hangout, has more bistros and cafes. *(ⓜ Odéon.)*

ÉGLISE ST-GERMAIN-DES-PRÉS. Paris's oldest standing church, Église de St-Germain-des-Prés was the centerpiece of the Abbey of St-Germain-des-Prés, the crux of Catholic intellectual life until the 18th century. Worn away by fire and a saltpetre explosion, the abbey's exterior looks appropriately world-weary. Its interior frescoes depict the life of Jesus in maroon, green, and gold. *(3 pl. St-Germain-des-Prés. ⓜ St-Germain-des-Prés. ☎ 55 42 81 18. Open daily 8am-7:45pm. Info office open M 2:30-6:45pm, Tu-F 10:30am-noon and 2:30-6:45pm, Sa 3-6:45pm.)*

LA SORBONNE. One of Europe's oldest universities, the Sorbonne was founded in 1253 by Robert de Sorbon as a dormitory for 16 theology students. Bookstores and cafes fill nearby **place de la Sorbonne,** off bd. St-Michel. The **Chapelle de la Sorbonne**, which usually houses temporary exhibits on arts and letters, is undergoing renovations through 2009. *(45-47 r. des Écoles. ⓜ Cluny-La Sorbonne or RER: Luxembourg.)*

PANTHÉON. The Pantheon, on the Left Bank's highest point, celebrates great French thinkers. In its crypt lie the tombs of Marie and Pierre Curie, Victor Hugo, Jean Jaurès, Rousseau, Voltaire, and Émile Zola. On the main level, **Foucault's Pendulum** confirms the rotation of the earth. *(Pl. du Panthéon. ⓜ or RER: Cardinal Lemoine. ☎ 44 32 18 04. Open daily Apr.-Sept. 10am-6:30pm; Oct.-Mar. 10am-6pm. Last entry 45min. before closing. €8, 18-25 €5, under 18 and Oct.-Mar. 1st Su of month free.)*

RUE MOUFFETARD. South of pl. de la Contrescarpe, r. Mouffetard plays host to one of Paris's busiest **street markets,** drawing a mix of Parisians and visitors. The stretch of r. Mouffetard past pl. de la Contrescarpe and onto r. Descartes and r. de la Montagne Ste-Geneviève is the quintessential Latin Quarter stroll. *(ⓜ Cardinal Lemoine, Pl. Monge, or Censier Daubenton.)*

MOSQUÉE DE PARIS. The **Institut Musulman** houses the Persian gardens, elaborate minaret, and shady porticoes of the Mosquée de Paris, a mosque constructed in 1920 by French architects to honor North African countries' role in WWI. Travelers can relax in the Turkish baths at the exquisite *hammam* or sip mint tea in the cafe. *(39 r. St-Hilaire. ⓜ Censier Daubenton. ☎ 43 31 38 20; www.la-mosquee.com. Open daily 10am-noon and 2-5:30pm. Tour €3, students €2. Hammam open for men Tu 2-9pm, Su 10am-9pm; women M, W-Th, Sa 10am-9pm, F 2-9pm. €15.)*

JARDIN DES PLANTES. Opened in 1640 to grow medicinal plants for King Louis XIII, the garden now features rosaries, science museums, and a zoo. *(ⓜ Gare d'Austerlitz, Jussieu, or Censier-Daubenton. ☎ 40 79 37 94. Jardin and rosarie open daily in summer 7:30am-8pm; winter 8am-5:30pm. Free. Zoo open daily Apr.-Sept. 10am-6pm; Oct.-Mar. 10am-5:30pm. Last entry 30min. before closing. €6, students €4.)*

BIBLIOTHÈQUE NATIONALE DE FRANCE: SITE FRANÇOIS MITTERRAND. The complex that many Parisians refer to as "the ugliest building ever built" is the result of the last and most expensive of Mitterrand's *Grands Projets.* Its L-shaped towers of Dominique Perrault's controversial design resemble open books. Its uncrowded, rotating art exhibits are a welcome break from the packed sights in the center of the city. Avoid going around opening hours, especially during university exam season, when students line up around the block to get a desk. *(Q. F. Mauriac.* ☎ *53 79 59 79; www.bnf.fr.* Ⓜ *Q. de la Gare or Bibliothèque François Mitterand. Reception M 2-7pm, Tu-Sa 9am-7pm, Su 1-7pm; closed Su Sept. 16+. €3.50. MC/V.)*

QUARTIER DE LA BUTTE-AUX-CAILLES. Historically a working-class neighborhood, the old-fashioned *Butte-aux-Cailles* (Quail Knoll) Quarter now attracts trend-setters, artists, and intellectuals. Funky new restaurants and galleries have cropped up in recent years. **Rue de la Butte-aux-Cailles** and **rue des Cinq Diamants** share duties as the quartier's main drags. *(*Ⓜ *Corvisart.)*

LEFT BANK WEST

■**EIFFEL TOWER.** Gustave Eiffel wrote of his tower: "France is the only country in the world with a 300m flagpole." Designed in 1889, the Eiffel Tower was conceived as a modern engineering monument that would surpass the Egyptian pyramids in size and notoriety but critics dubbed it a "metal asparagus." Writer Guy de Maupassant ate lunch every day at its ground-floor restaurant—the only place in Paris, he claimed, from which he couldn't see the offensive thing. Nevertheless, when it was inaugurated in March 1889 as the centerpiece of the World's Fair, the tower earned Parisians' love: nearly two million people ascended it during the fair. Some still criticize its glut of tourists, trinkets, and vagrants, but don't believe the anti-hype—the tower is a wonder worth seeing. *(*Ⓜ *Bir-Hakeim or Trocadéro.* ☎ *44 11 23 23; www.tour-eiffel.fr. Open daily mid-June to Aug. 9am-midnight; Sept. to mid-June 9:30am-11pm; stairs 9:30am-6pm. Last access to top 30min. before closing. Elevator to 1st fl. €5, under 12 €3, to 2nd fl. €8/5, to top €12/7. Stairs to 1st and 2nd fl. €4. Under 3 free.)*

CHAMPS DE MARS. The Champs de Mars, a tree-lined expanse stretching from the École Militaire to the Eiffel Tower, is named, appropriately enough, after the Roman god of war. Close to the *7ème*'s monuments and museums, the field was a drill ground for the École Militaire during Napoleon's reign. Today, despite frolicking children and a monument to international peace, the Champs can't quite hold a candle to Paris's many spectacular public parks and gardens. *(*Ⓜ *La Motte Picquet-Grenelle or École Militaire. From the av. de la Motte-Picquet, walk toward École Militaire.)*

INVALIDES. The gold-leaf dome of the **Hôtel des Invalides,** built by Napoleon as a hospital for crippled and ill soldiers, shines at the center of the *7ème*. The grassy **Esplanade des Invalides** runs from the *hôtel* to the **Pont Alexandre III,** a bridge with gilded lampposts and a view of Invalides and the Seine. Housed inside the Invalides complex, the **Musée de l'Armée** and **Musée de l'Ordre de la Libération,** documenting the Free France movement under General de Gaulle, are worth a look. Invalides's real star, the ■**Musée des Plans-Reliefs** features enormous, detailed models of French fortresses and towns, all made around 1700. **Napoleon's tomb** is also here, resting in the **Église St-Louis.** *(127 r. de Grenelle.* Ⓜ *Invalides. Enter from pl. des Invalides or pl. Vauban and av. de Tourville. Open daily Apr.-Sept. 10am-6pm; Oct.-Mar. 10am-5pm.)*

CATACOMBS. Originally excavated to provide stone for building Paris, the Catacombs were converted into a mass grave in 1785 when the stench of the city's public cemeteries became unbearable. Built twice as far underground as the Metro, Paris's "municipal ossuary" now has dozens of winding tunnels and hundreds of thousands of bones. *(1 av. du Colonel Henri Rol-Tanguy.* Ⓜ *Denfert-Rochereau. Exit to pl. Denfert-Rochereau and cross av. du Colonel Henri Roi-Tanguy.* ☎ *43 22 47 63. 45min. tours. Open Tu-Su 10am-4pm. €7, over 60 €5.50, 14-26 €3.50, under 14 free. MC/V; min. €15.)*

BOULEVARD DU MONTPARNASSE. In the early 20th century, avant-garde artists like Chagall, Duchamp, Léger, and Modigliani moved to Montparnasse. Soviet exiles Lenin and Trotsky talked strategy over cognac in cafes like **Le Dôme, Le Sélect,** and **La Coupole.** After WWI, Montparnasse attracted American expats like Calder, Hemingway, and Henry Miller. Chain restaurants and tourists crowd the now heavily commercialized street. Classic cafes (pricey **La Coupole,** for example) still hold their own, providing a wonderful place to sip coffee, read Apollinaire, and daydream away. (Ⓜ *Montparnasse-Bienvenüe or Vavin.*)

■ **PARC ANDRÉ CITROËN.** Landscapers Alain Provost and Gilles Clémenthe created the futuristic Parc André Citroën in the 1990s. Hot-air balloon rides launch from the central garden and offer terrific views of Paris. (Ⓜ *Javelor Balard.* ☎ *44 26 20 00; www.aeroparis.com. Park open 24hr. Balloon rides M-F 7am-9:30pm, Sa-Su 9am-9:30pm. Sa-Su and holidays 10min. rides €12, 12-17 €10, 3-11 €6, under 3 free; M-F €10/9/5/free.*)

RIGHT BANK WEST

OPÉRA GARNIER. The exterior of the Opéra Garnier—with its newly restored multi-colored marble facade, sculpted golden goddesses, and ornate columns and friezes—is as impressive as it is kitschy. It's no wonder that Oscar Wilde once swore he saw an angel floating on the sidewalk. Inside, Chagall's whimsical ceiling design contrasts with the gold and red that dominate the theater. For shows, see **Entertainment,** p. 325. (Ⓜ *Opéra.* ☎ *08 92 89 90 90; www.operadeparis.fr. Concert hall and museum open daily mid-July to Aug. 10am-5:30pm; Sept. to mid-July 10am-4:30pm. Concert hall closed during rehearsals; call ahead. €8, students and under 25 €4. English-language tours daily 11:30am and 2:30pm; €12, seniors €10, students €9, under 10 €6.*)

PLACE DE LA CONCORDE. Paris's most infamous public square, built between 1757 and 1777, is the eastern terminus of the Champs-Élysées at its intersection with the Jardin des Tuileries. During the Reign of Terror, it became known as the **place de la Révolution,** site of the guillotine that severed the heads of 1343 aristocrats, including Louis XVI, Marie Antoinette, and Robespierre. In 1830, the square was renamed *concorde* (peace) and the 3200-year-old **Obélisque de Luxor,** given to Charles X by the Viceroy of Egypt, replaced the guillotine. (Ⓜ *Concorde.*)

■ **ARC DE TRIOMPHE AND THE CHAMPS-ÉLYSÉES.** Napoleon commissioned the **Arc,** at the western end of the Champs-Elysées, in 1806 to honor his Grande Armée. In 1940, Parisians were brought to tears by the sight of Nazis goose-stepping through the Arc. At the end of the German occupation, a sympathetic Allied army made sure that a French general would be the first to drive under the arch. The terrace at the top has a fabulous view. The **Tomb of the Unknown Soldier** has been under the Arc since November 11, 1920 while an eternal flame has been burning since 1921. The center of Parisian opulence in the early 20th century, the **Champs-Élysées** has since undergone a bizarre kind of democratization. Shops along the avenue now range from designer fashion to low-budget tchotchkes, but while it may be an inelegant spectacle, the Champs offers some of the city's best people-watching. (*Pl. Charles de Gaulle.* Ⓜ *Charles-de-Gaulle-Étoile.* ☎ *43 80 31 31. Open daily Apr.-Sept. 10am-11pm; Oct.-Mar. 10am-10:30pm. €8, 18-25 €5, under 18 free.*)

TROCADÉRO. In the 1820s, the Duc d'Angoulême built a memorial to his victory in Spain at Trocadéro. For the 1937 World's Fair, Jacques Carlu created the **Palais de Chaillot,** which features two white stone wings and an imposing, austere veranda. The terrace, flanked by two theaters, offers brilliant views of the Eiffel Tower. Be wary of pickpockets and traffic, however, as you gaze upward. (Ⓜ *Trocadéro.*)

BOIS DE BOULOGNE. By day, this 2000-acre park, with several gardens, stadiums, and two lakes, is a popular picnicking, jogging, and bike-riding spot. By night, the *bois* becomes a bazaar of crime, drugs, and prostitution. (*On the western edge of the 16ème.* Ⓜ *Porte Maillot, Sablons, Pont de Neuilly, or Porte Dauphine or Porte d'Auteil.*)

■ **LA DÉFENSE.** Outside the city limits, west of the 16*ème*, the skyscrapers and modern architecture of La Défense make up Paris's newest (unofficial) *arrondissement*, a playground for many of Paris's biggest corporations. Its centerpiece is hard to miss: the **Grande Arche de la Défense** stretches 35 stories into the air and is shaped like a hollow cube. The roof of this unconventional office covers one hectare—Notre Dame could nestle in its concave core. *(1 parvis de la Défense, 92040 Paris-La Défense. Ⓜ or RER: La Défense. ☎49 07 27 57; www.paris.org/Monuments/ Defense. Open daily 9am-8pm. Winter reduced hours. €8, students and under 18 €6.)*

RIGHT BANK EAST

PLACE DE LA BASTILLE. This busy intersection was once home to the famous Bastille Prison, stormed on July 14, 1789, sparking the French Revolution. Two days later, the National Assembly ordered the prison demolished, but the ground plan of the prison's turrets remains embedded in the road near r. Saint-Antoine. At the center of the square is a monument of the winged Mercury holding a torch of freedom, symbolizing France's movement towards democracy. *(Ⓜ Bastille.)*

OPÉRA DE LA BASTILLE. One of Mitterrand's *Grands Projets*, the Opéra opened in 1989 to loud protests over its unattractive design. It has been described as a huge toilet because of its resemblance to the city's coin-operated *pissoirs*. Not striking a completely sour note, the opera has helped renew local interest in the arts. *(130 r. de Lyon. Ⓜ Bastille. Look for the words "Billeterie" on the building. ☎08 92 89 90 90; www.opera-de-paris.fr. Open daily 10am-6pm. Last entry 30min. before closing. 1hr. French-language tours usually 2 per day; call ahead; English-language tours for groups of 10 or more. €12, students and under 25 €9, under 10 €6.)*

BAL DU MOULIN ROUGE. Along bd. de Clichy and bd. de Rochechouart, you'll find many Belle Époque cabarets and nightclubs, including the Bal du Moulin Rouge, immortalized by Toulouse-Lautrec's paintings, Offenbach's music, and Baz Luhrmann's 2001 Hollywood blockbuster. The crowd consists of tourists out for an evening of sequins, tassels, and skin. The revues are still risqué, but the real shock is the price of admission. *(82 bd. de Clichy. Ⓜ Blanche. ☎53 09 82 82; www.moulin-rouge.com. Shows daily 7, 9, 11pm. Tickets €89-175; includes champagne.)*

▨BASILIQUE DU SACRÉ-COEUR. This ethereal basilica, with its signature white onion domes, was commissioned to atone for France's war crimes in the Franco-Prussian War. During WWII, 13 bombs were dropped on Paris, all near the structure, but miraculously no one was killed. This inspired fervent devotion, making Sacré-Coeur an even holier site. *(35 r. du Chevalier-de-la-Barre. Ⓜ Anvers or Abbesses. ☎53 41 89 00. Open daily 6am-11pm. Wheelchair-accessible. Free. Dome open daily 9am-6pm. €5.)*

▨CIMITIÈRE PÈRE LACHAISE. This cemetery holds the remains of such famous Frenchmen as Balzac, Bernhardt, Colette, David, Delacroix, Piaf, La Fontaine, Haussmann, Molière, Proust, and Seurat within its peaceful paths and elaborate sarcophagi. Foreigners buried here include Chopin, Modigliani, Gertrude Stein, and Oscar Wilde, though the most frequently visited grave is that of Jim Morrison. French Leftists make a ceremonial pilgrimage to the **Mur des Fédérés** (Wall of the Federals), where 147 *communards* were executed in 1871. *(16 r. du Repos. 20ème. Ⓜ Père Lachaise. ☎55 25 82 10. Open Mar.-Oct. M-F 8am-6pm, Sa 8:30am-6pm, Su and holidays 9am-6pm; Nov.-Feb. M-F 8am-5:30pm, Sa 8:30am-5:30pm, Su and holidays 9am-5:30pm. Last entry 15min. before closing. Free. Call ☎40 71 75 60 for tour times and fares.)*

PARC DES BUTTES-CHAUMONT. In the south of the 19*ème*, Parc des Buttes-Chaumont is a mix of man-made topography and transplanted vegetation; previously a lime quarry and gallows, Napoleon III commissioned Baron Haussman to redesign the space in 1862. Today's visitors walk the winding paths surrounded by lush greenery and dynamic—sometimes exhausting—hills, enjoying a great view of the *quartier* from the Roman temple atop cave-filled cliffs. *(Ⓜ Buttes-Chaumont or Botzaris. Open daily May-Sept. 7am-10:15pm; Oct.-May 7am-8:15pm. Some gates close early.)*

🏛 MUSEUMS

No visitor should miss Paris's museums, which are universally considered to be among the world's best. Cost-effective for visiting more than three museums or sights daily, the **Carte Musées et Monuments** offers admission to 65 museums in greater Paris. It is available at major museums, tourist office kiosks, and many Metro stations. A pass for one day is €15, for three days €30, for five days €45. Students with art or art history ID can get into art museums free. Most museums, including the **Musée d'Orsay,** are closed on Mondays.

▨ MUSÉE D'ORSAY. If only the *Académiciens* who turned the Impressionists away from the Louvre could see the Musée d'Orsay. Now considered master-pieces, these "rejects" are well worth the pilgrimage to this mecca of modernity. The collection, installed in a former railway station, includes painting, sculpture, decorative arts, and photography from 1848 until WWI. On the ground floor, Classical and Proto-Impressionist works are on display, including Manet's *Olympia,* a painting that caused scandal when it was unveiled in 1865. Other highlights include Monet's *Poppies,* Renoir's *Bal au moulin de la Galette,* Dégas's *La classe de danse,* and paintings by Cézanne, Gauguin, Seurat, and Van Gogh. The top floor offers one of the most comprehensive collections of Impressionist and Post-Impressionist art in the world. In addition, the exterior and interior balconies offer supreme views of the Seine and the jungle of sculptures below. Don't miss Rodin's imperious *Honoré de Balzac,* or Pompon's adorably big-footed *Ours Blanc. (62 r. de Lille, 7ème. Ⓜ Solférino, RER: Musée d'Orsay. Visitor's entrance on the square off 1 r. de la Légion d'Honneur. ☎40 49 48 14; www.musee-orsay.fr. Wheelchair-accessible. Open mid-June to mid-Sept. Tu-W and F-Sa 9:30am-6pm, last ticket sales 5pm; Th 10am-9:45pm, last ticket sales 9:15pm; Su 9am-6pm. Mid-Sept. to mid-June Tu-W and F-Su 9:30am-6pm, Th 10am-9:45pm. Bookstore open Tu-W and F-Su 9:30am-6:30pm, Th 10am-9:30pm. €7.50, Th after 8pm, Tu-W and F-Sa after 4:15pm, and Su €6, 18-25 €5, under 18 free. English-language tours 1hr. Tu-Sa 11:30am and 2:30pm, call ahead to confirm; €6.50/5/free. AmEx/MC/V.)*

> **⬡TIP⬡ CROWDLESS CULTURE.** Orsay's undeniably amazing collection draws massive crowds, marring an otherwise enjoyable museum. A Sunday morning or Thursday evening visit will avoid the tourist throngs and calm the inner artist.

▨ MUSÉE DU LOUVRE. No visitor has ever allotted enough time to consider every display at the Louvre, namely because it would take weeks to read every caption of the over 30,000 items in the museum. Its masterpieces include Hammurabi's Code, Jacques-Louis David's *The Oath of the Horatii* and *The Coronation of Napoleon,* Delacroix's *Liberty Leading the People,* Vermeer's *Lacemaker,* da Vinci's *Mona Lisa,* the classical Winged Victory of Samothrace, and the Venus de Milo. Enter through I. M. Pei's glass Pyramid in the Cour Napoléon, or skip the line by entering directly from the Métro. The Louvre is organized into three different wings: Denon, Richelieu, and Sully. Each is divided according to the artwork's date, national origin, and medium. *(1er. Ⓜ Palais-Royal/Musée du Louvre. ☎40 20 53 17; www.louvre.fr. Open M, Th, Sa 9am-6pm, W and F 9am-10pm. Last entry 45min. before closing. €9, W and F after 6pm €6, under 18, under 26 F after 6pm, and 1st Su of month free. MC/V.)*

▨ CENTRE POMPIDOU. This inside-out building has inspired debate since its 1977 opening. Whatever its aesthetic merits, the exterior's chaotic colored piping provides an appropriate shell for the Fauvist, Cubist, Pop, and Conceptual works inside. The **Musée National d'Art Moderne** is the Centre Pompidou's main attraction. *(Pl. Georges-Pompidou, r. Beaubourg, 4ème. Ⓜ Rambuteau or Hôtel-de-Ville. ☎44 78 12 33; www.centrepompidou.fr. Centre open M and W-Su 11am-9:50pm. Museum open M and W-Su 11am-8:50pm, last ticket sales 8pm. €10, under 26 €8, under 18 and 1st Su of month free.)*

FRANCE

■ **MUSÉE RODIN.** The 18th-century Hôtel Biron holds hundreds of sculptures by Auguste Rodin. Bring a book and relax amid the gestures of bending flowers and flexing sculptures. *(79 r. de Varenne, 7ème. ⓜ Varenne. ☎ 44 18 61 10; www.musee-rodin.fr. Open Tu-Su Apr.-Sept. 9:30am-5:45pm; Oct.-Mar. 9:30am-4:45pm. Last entry 30min. before closing. Ground floor and gardens wheelchair-accessible. €6, 18-25 €4, under 18 and first Su of the month free; special exhibits €7/5/free. Audio tour €4 for permanent or temporary exhibits; combo ticket €6. Touch tours for the blind available, call ☎ 44 18 61 24. MC/V.)*

■ **MUSÉE JACQUEMART-ANDRÉ.** The 19th-century mansion of Nélie Jacquemart and her husband contains a world-class collection of Renaissance art, including *Madonna and Child* by Botticelli and *St. George and the Dragon* by Ucello. *(158 bd. Haussmann, 8ème. ⓜ Miromesnil. ☎ 45 62 11 59. Open daily 10am-6pm. Last entry 30min. before closing. €9.50, students and 7-17 €7, under 7 free. 1 free youth ticket with every 3 purchased by the same family. Audio tour included. AmEx/MC/V; min. €10.)*

■ **MUSÉE DE CLUNY.** The Musée de Cluny, housed in a monastery built atop Roman baths, holds one of the world's finest collections of medieval art. Works include ■**La Dame et La Licorne** (The Lady and the Unicorn), a striking 15th-century tapestry series. *(6 pl. Paul Painlevé, 5ème. ⓜ Cluny-La Sorbonne. ☎ 53 73 78 00. Open M and W-Sa 9:15am-5:45pm. €7.50, 18-25 and 1st Su of each month €5.50, under 18 free.)*

■ **EXPLORA SCIENCE MUSEUM.** Dedicated to bringing science to young people, the Explora Science Museum is the star attraction of La Villette, in the complex's Cité des Sciences et de l'Industrie. The building's impressive, futuristic architecture only hints at the close to 300 exhibits waiting inside. *(30 av. Corentin-Cariou, 19ème. ⓜ Porte de la Villette. ☎ 40 05 80 00; www.cite-sciences.fr. Open Tu-Sa 10am-6pm, Su 10am-7pm. Last entry Tu-Sa 5:30pm, Su 6pm. €8, under 25 or families of 5+ €6, under 7 free.)*

MUSÉE PICASSO. When Picasso died in 1973, his family paid the French inheritance tax in artwork. The French government put this collection, which includes work from his Cubist, Surrealist, and Neoclassical years, on display in 1985 in the 17th-century Hôtel Salé. *(5 r. de Thorigny, 3ème. ⓜ Chemin Vert. ☎ 42 71 25 21; www.musee-picasso.fr. Open M and W-Su Apr.-Sept. 9:30am-6pm; Oct.-Mar. 9:30am-5:30pm. Last entry 45min. before closing. €7.70, 18-25 €5.70, under 18 and 1st Su of each month free.)*

INSTITUT DU MONDE ARABE (IMA). Housing 3rd- through 18th-century Arabesque art, the IMA building was designed to look like the ships that carried North African immigrants to France. Its southern face is comprised of ■**240 mechanical portals** which automatically open and close depending on how much light is needed to illuminate the interior. *(1 r. des Fossés St-Bernard, 5ème. ⓜ Jussieu. ☎ 40 51 38 38; www.imarabe.org. Open Tu-Su 10am-6pm. €5, under 26 €4, under 12 free.)*

MUSÉE CARNAVALET. Housed in Mme. de Sévigné's 16th-century *hôtel particulier*, this museum presents rooms and rooms of historical objects and curiosities from Paris's origins through the present day. *(23 r. de Sévigné, 3ème. ⓜ Chemin Vert. ☎ 44 59 58 58. Open Tu-Su 10am-6pm. Last entry 5pm. Free.)*

MAISON DE BALZAC. Honoré de Balzac hid from bill collectors in this three-story hillside *maison*, his home from 1840-1847. Here in this tranquil retreat, he wrote a substantial part of *La Comédie Humaine;* today's visitors can see his original manuscripts, along with his beautifully embroidered chair and desk at which he purportedly wrote and edited for 17hr. a day. *(47 r. Raynouard, 16ème. ⓜ Passy. Walk up the hill and turn left onto r. Raynouard. ☎ 55 74 41 80; www.paris.fr/musees/balzac. Open Tu-Su 10am-6pm. Last entry 30min. before closing. Free. Tours €4.50, students and seniors €4.)*

PALAIS DE TOKYO. Recently refurbished, this large warehouse contains the **site création contemporaine,** exhibiting today's hottest (and most controversial) art, as well as the ■**Musée d'Art Moderne de la Ville de Paris.** The museum's

FRANCE

unrushed atmosphere and spacious architecture provide a welcome relief from the maelstrom of the Louvre and Musée d'Orsay. (☎53 67 40 00; www.mam.paris.fr. Open Tu and Th-Su 10am-6pm, W 10am-10pm. Permanent collections free; call ahead for temporary exhibit prices.) The Palais is outfitted to host prominent avant-garde sculptures, video displays, and multimedia installations. Exhibits change every two or three months; be on the lookout for each exhibit's *vernissage* (premiere party) for free entrance and refreshments. (11 av. du Président Wilson, 16ème. Ⓜ Iéna. ☎47 23 38 86; www.palaisdetokyo.com. Open Tu-Su noon-midnight. Wheelchair-accessible. €6, students under 26 €4.50.)

MUSÉE D'ART ET D'HISTOIRE DU JUDAÏSME. Housed in the **Hôtel de St-Aignan,** once a tenement populated by Jews fleeing Eastern Europe, this museum displays a history of Jews in Europe, France, and North Africa. The collection includes extensive and interesting relics from the end of the 19th-century Dreyfus affair, in which Captain Alfred Dreyfus, a French Jew, was wrongfully accused of treason. (71 r. de Temple, 3ème. Ⓜ Rambuteau. ☎53 01 86 60; www.mahj.org. Open M-F 11am-6pm, Su 10am-7pm. Last entry 30min. before closing. €7, 18-26 €4.50, under 18 free. MC/V; min. €12.)

MUSÉE D'HISTOIRE NATURELLE. The Jardin des Plantes is home to the three-part Natural History museum, comprised of the modern **Grande Galerie de l'Evolution,** the **Musée de Minéralogie,** and the ghastly ▧**Galeries de Paléontologie et d'Anatomie Comparée.** (57 r. Cuvier, 5ème. Ⓜ Gare d'Austerlitz or Jussieu. ☎40 79 32 16; www.mnhn.fr. Grande Galerie de l'Evolution open M and W-Su 10am-6pm. €8, 4-14 and students under 26 €6. Musée de Minéralogie and Galeries de Paléontologie et d'Anatomie Comparée open Apr.-Sept. M and W-F 10am-5pm, Sa-Su 10am-6pm; Oct.-Mar. M,W-Su 10am-5pm. Each museum €6, students €4. Weekend pass for the 3 museums €20, students €15.)

🎭 ENTERTAINMENT

Pick up one of the weekly bibles of Parisian entertainment, *Pariscope* (includes English-language section; €0.40) and *Figaroscope* (€1), at newsstands or *tabacs*. For concert listings, check the free magazine *Paris Selection*, available at tourist offices. Popular, free concerts are often held in churches and parks, especially during summer festivals; arrive early. FNAC (p. 327) sells concert tickets.

OPERA AND THEATER

La Comédie Française, pl. Collette, 1er (☎44 58 15 15; www.comedie-francaise.fr). Ⓜ Palais-Royal. Founded by Molière, this is the granddaddy of all French theaters. Expect slapstick farce. Tickets €11-35. Rush tickets available 1hr. before show. AmEx/MC/V.

Opéra Garnier, pl. de l'Opéra, 9ème (☎08 92 89 90 90; www.operadeparis.fr). Ⓜ Opéra. Beautiful building (p. 321) hosts ballet, operas, and symphonies. Tickets usually available 2 weeks before shows. Box office open M-Sa 10am-6:30pm. Rush tickets on sale 1hr. before showtime. Tickets €5-200. AmEx/MC/V.

Opéra Comique, 5 r. Favart, 2ème (☎42 44 45 46; www.opera-comique.com). Ⓜ Richelieu-Drouot. Operas on a lighter scale. June 2008 shows include *Porgy and Bess.* Box office open M-Sa 9am-9pm. Tickets €6-95.

Opéra de la Bastille, pl. de la Bastille, 12ème (☎08 92 89 90 90; www.operadeparis.fr). Ⓜ Bastille. Opera and ballet with a modern spin. Subtitles in French. Tickets can be purchased mail, phone (M-Th 9am-6pm, Sa 9am-1pm), online, or in person (M-Sa 10:30am-6:30pm). Rush tickets for students under 25 and over 65 15min. before show. For wheelchair access or those with hearing/sight disabilities, call 2 weeks ahead (☎40 01 18 50). Tickets €5-160. AmEx/MC/V.

FROLICSOME FIREMEN

You know Bastille Day is approaching when two things occur: French flags go up around the city, and all Parisians escape to the countryside. The weekend is the most extravagant and fun of the year, but expats find themselves enjoying the festivities with a large proportion of other tourists. Despite the prevalence of the English language, Bastille "Day" provides an action-packed weekend of fun. For a truly unusual patriotic experience, be sure not to miss **Les Saupeurs Pompiers.**

Paris celebrates the night of July 13th and 14th with huge parties in fire stations called "Fireman's Balls." Makes sense, *n'est-ce pas? Les Saupeurs Pompiers* open the courtyards of their *caserne* (stations) to the public for a night of flowing alcohol, loud music, and, yes, firemen. Doors open at around 9pm, depending on the station, and lines can be very long with waits up to an hour. Show up early or late for shorter queues. The parties go until 4am, but time flies as you dance, drink, and are entertained by shows—not all G-rated—put on by the *pompiers.* Entrance is free and drinks are cheap, usually €2-5.

For more festival info, see p. 307. Check online at www.pompier-sparis.fr for a list of participating stations and addresses.

JAZZ AND CABARET

☒ **Le Baiser Salé,** 58 r. des Lombards, 1er (☎42 33 37 71; www.lebaisersale.com). Ⓜ Châtelet. African, Antillean, and Cuban music featured with funk and modern jazz. Beer €7-12. Mixed drinks €9. Month-long African music festival in July. Jazz concerts 10pm-2:30am. Cover €12-18. Happy hour 5-8:30pm. Open daily 5pm-6am. AmEx/MC/V.

Au Duc des Lombards, 42 r. des Lombards, 1er (☎42 33 22 88; www.ducdeslombards.fr). Ⓜ Châtelet. One of France's premier jazz spots. Newly renovated for 2008. Cover €19-23; in advance students €12, couples €30. Beer €7-10. Mixed drinks €10. Music 10pm-1:30am. Open M-Sa 5pm-2am. MC/V.

Au Lapin Agile, 22 r. des Saules, 18ème (☎46 06 85 87). Ⓜ Lamarck-Coulaincourt. Apollinaire, Picasso, Renoir, and Verlaine hung out here during Montmartre's heyday; now mostly tourists crowd in for comical poems and songs. Drinks €6-7. Shows Tu-Su 9pm-2am. €24, includes 1 drink; students M-F and Su €17.

CINEMA

Paris has many theaters, particularly in the Latin Quarter and on the Champs-Elysées. The big theater chains—**Gaumont** and **UGC**—offer discounts for five visits or more. Most cinemas offer family, senior, student, and matinee discounts. On Monday and Wednesday, prices drop by about €1.50. Check *Pariscope* or *l'Officiel des Spectacles* for schedules, prices, and reviews. English-language films in V.O. are shown in English; screenings in V.F. are dubbed into French. ☒**Accattone,** 20. r. Cujas, 5ème, sets the standard for art-house ambience with a carefully selected line-up. (☎46 33 86 86. Ⓜ Luxembourg. All films in V.O. €7, students €6.) Nearby, **Les Trois Luxembourg,** 67 r. Monsieur-le-Prince, 6ème, screens classic, foreign, and independent films in V.O. (☎46 33 97 77. €7, students and seniors €6.)

🗂 SHOPPING

In a city where Hermès scarves function as slings and department store history stretches back to the 19th century, shopping is nothing less than an art form and as diverse as the city itself, from the wild club wear sold near r. Etienne-Marcel to the off-the-beaten path boutiques in the **18ème** or the **Marais.** The great **soldes** (sales) of the year begin after New Year's and at the very end of June, with the best prices at the beginning of February and the end of July. If at any time of year you see the word *braderie* (clearance) in a store window, enter without hesitation.

The multi-level, ultra-hip **Colette,** 213 r. St-Honoré, 1*er,* has an extremely wide range of prices for its accessories, clothes, and gadgets. It's a destination for too-cool-for-school kids with extra cash as well as tried and true fashionistas. (Ⓜ Pyramides ☎55 35 33 90; www.colette.fr. Open M-Sa 11am-7pm. AmEx/MC/V.) At the **Abbey Bookshop,** 29 r. de la Parcheminerie, 5*ème,* Canadian ex-pat Brian occasionally gives out cups of the best coffee in Paris free, complete with a dollop of maple syrup. (Ⓜ St-Michel or Cluny. ☎46 33 16 24; www.abbeybookshop.net. Open M-Sa 10am-7pm, sometimes later.) **FNAC,** the big Kahuna of Parisian media chains, has 9 branches in the city, including on the Champs-Élysées and in the mall in the Forum Les Halles. Purchase tickets to nearly any show in Paris at the ticket desk. (Fédération Nationale des Achats et Cadres; www.fnac.com. Most open M-Sa 10am-7:30 or 8pm. Champs-Élysées branch closes midnight. MC/V.)

Paris's department stores are as much sights as they are shopping destinations, especially in December, when the stores go all out to decorate their windows. The chaotic ✠**Galeries Lafayette,** 40 bd. Haussmann, 9ème, has a domed, stained-glass ceiling, and a cafeteria with amazing views of the city. (Ⓜ Chaussée d'Antin. ☎42 82 34 56. Open M-W and F-Sa 9:30am-7:30pm, Th 9:30am-9pm. AmEx/V.) Paris's oldest department store, **Le Bon Marché,** 24 r. de Sèvres, has it all. Don't be fooled by its name. Though bon marché means cheap, this is Paris's most expensive department store. More budget-friendly luxuries can be found across the street in its food annex, ✠**La Grande Épicerie de Paris.** (Ⓜ Sèvres-Babylone. ☎44 39 80 00. Store open M-W and F 9:30am-7pm, Th 10am-9pm, Sa 9:30am-8pm. La Grande Epicerie open M-Sa 8:30am-9pm. AmEx/MC/V.)

▓ NIGHTLIFE

In the **5ème** and **6ème,** bars draw French and foreign students, while Paris's young and hip, queer and straight swarm the **Marais,** the center of the city's GLBT life. Great neighborhood spots are springing up in the Left Bank's outlying areas, particularly in the **13ème** and **14ème.** A slightly older crowd congregates around **Les Halles,** while the outer *arrondissements* cater to locals. The **Bastille,** another central party area, is more suited to pounding vodka shots than sipping Bordeaux.

TIP   **PILLOW TALK.** The French often mock English-speakers for their unwitting sexual references. Here are a couple of common expressions to avoid:

Je suis excité(e) might be an attempt to express excitement at a new museum or film but actually means "I am sexually aroused."

Je suis plein(e) may seem to translate to "I am full (of food)," but for a girl, this means "I have been sexually satisfied."

Oh my God! This English expression may seem harmless, but in French, *godde* means vibrator, so what you're really saying is "Oh my vibrator!"

Clubbing in Paris is less about hip DJs' beats than about dressing up and getting in. Drinks are expensive and clubbers consume little beyond the first round. Many clubs accept reservations, so come early to assure entry on busy nights. Bouncers like tourists because they generally spend more money, so speaking English might actually give you an edge. Parisian GLBT life centers around the **Marais.**

CAFES AND BARS

▓ **buddha-bar,** 8 r. Boissy d'Anglas, 8*ème* (☎53 05 90 00; www.buddha-bar.com). Ⓜ Madeleine or Concorde. The legendary buddha-bar has to be the most glamorous drinking hole in the world (Madonna drops by when she's in town). Beer €8-9. Wine €10-12. Open M-F noon-3pm and 6pm-2am, Sa-Su 6pm-2am.

Paris Nightlife

● DANCE CLUBS
Batofar, **24**
Folies Pigalle, **2**
Raidd Bar, **14**
Rex Club, **5**
Wax, **17**

🎷 JAZZ CLUBS
Au Lapin Agile, **1**
Le Baiser Salé, **11**
Au Duc des Lombards, **12**

FRANCE

bd. des Batignolles
VILLIERS
ROME
LIÈGE
r. d'Amsterdam
r. de Clichy
r. Blanche
r. Fontaine
TO 1 N (800m)
2
PL. PIGALLE
ANVERS
PL. MARTYRS
r. de Douai

EUROPE
PL. DE L'EUROPE
r. de Rome
Gare St-Lazare
ST-LAZARE
r. du Rocher
ST-AUGUSTIN
bd. Hausmann
r. La Boétie
PL. ST-AUGUSTIN
HAVRE-CAUMARTIN
r. Tronchet

r. Pigalle
r. Notre-Dame-de-Lorette
TRINITÉ
r. de Châteaudun
ST-GEORGES
NOTRE DAME DE LORETTE
PL. D'ORVES
r. St-Lazare
r. de la Victoire
9ème
LE PELETIER
CHAUSSÉE D'ANTIN LA FAYETTE
AUBER
Opéra Garnier
bd. Montmartre
RICHELIEU DROUOT
RUE MONTMARTRE

MIROMESNIL
ST-PHILIPPE DE ROULE
8ème
r. du Faubourg St-Honoré
FRANKLIN D. ROOSEVELT
CHAMPS ÉLYSÉES CLEMENCEAU
av. des Champs Élysées
av. F. D.-Roosevelt
Grand Palais
PL. DE LA CONCORDE
r. Boissy d'Anglas
CONCORDE
MADELEINE
bd. de la Madeleine
OPÉRA
4 SEPTEMBRE
r. Daunou
av. de l'Opéra
r. du 4 Sept.
BOURSE
r. Vivienne
PYRAMIDES
r. des Petits Champs
1er
r. de Richelieu
TUILERIES
r. de Rivoli

cours de la Reine
quai d'Orsay
INVALIDES
r. de l'Université
Assemblée Nationale
r. Ste-Dominique
ASSEMBLÉE NATIONALE
Jardin des Tuileries
quai des Tuileries
Seine
MUSÉE D'ORSAY
Musée D'Orsay
quai Anatole France
r. de l'Université
SOLFÉRINO
PALAIS ROYAL/ MUSÉE DU LOUVRE
Palais Royal
Louvre
quai du Louvre
LOUVRE RIVOLI
r. St-Honoré
r. Amiral Coligny
PONT NEUF
Pont Neuf
PL. DAUPHINE

r. de Grenelle
PL. DES INVALIDES
r. de Bourgogne
7ème
bd. St-Germain
VARENNE
LATOUR MAUBOURG
Hôtel des Invalides
PL. VAUBAN
r. de Varenne
RUE DU BAC
r. du Bac
ST GERMAIN DES PRÉS
bd. St-Germain
r. de Seine
r. Jacob
r. Mazarine
r. Dauphine
ODÉON
CLUNY LA SORBONNE
r. de l'Éc. de Médecine

av. de Lowenthal
av. de Ségur
ST-FRANÇOIS XAVIER
bd. des Invalides
r. de Babylone
r. de Sèvres
SÈVRES BABYLONE
ST-SULPICE
r. du Four
r. Bonaparte
r. des Canettes
St. Sulpice
r. de Rennes
Université de Pàris (Sorbonne)
r. de Tournon
r. de l'Odéon

SÈVRES LECOURBE
FALGUIÈRE
VANEAU
DUROC
r. de Vaugirard
MONTPARNASSE BIENVENUE
ST-PLACIDE
RENNES
bd. Raspail
6ème
r. d'Assas
Jardin du Luxembourg
LUXEMBOURG
r. Royer-Collard
r. St-Michel

N
0   300 yards
0   300 meters
TO 🎷 (1.2km)
N.-D. DES CHAMPS
TO 🎷 (800m)

av. Trudaine

Gare du Nord

GARE DU NORD
RER
M

r. de Rochechouart

r. du Fbg. Poissonnière

r. Marx Dormoy

10ème

M POISSONNIÈRE

Gare de l'Est

GARE DE L'EST
M

CADET
M

r. La Fayette

r. Paradis

r. des Petites Ecuries

r. de Fg. St-Denis

CHÂTEAU D'EAU
M

bd. de Magenta

↑ TO ★ (1km)

TO ★ (800m)

BELLEVILLE
M

bd. Poissonnière

r. d'Hauteville

bd. de Strasbourg

r. Château d'eau

JACQUES BONSERGENT
M

BONCOURT
M

5

BONNE NOUVELLE
M

bd. St-Denis

STRASBOURG ST-DENIS
M

bd. St-Martin

2ème

r. Réaumur

RÉPUBLIQUE
M

PL. DE LA RÉPUBLIQUE

bd. Jules Ferry

av. Parmentier

r. St-Maur

SENTIER
M

RÉAUMUR-SEBASTOPOL
M

TEMPLE
M

3ème

av. de la République

r. de Oberkampf

r. Etienne Marcel

bd. de Sébastopol

r. de Turbigo

ARTS ET MÉTIERS
M

r. Béranger

OBERKAMPF
M

PARMENTIER
M

ST-MAUR
M

8

ETIENNE MARCEL
M

r. Beaubourg

r. Montmorency

Le Michel le Comte

r. du Temple

FILLES DU CALVAIRE
M

bd. Voltaire

11ème

LES HALLES
M

St-Denis

r. P. Lescot

r. aux Ours

r. St-Martin

RAMBUTEAU
M

r. des Archives

ST-SÉBASTIEN FROISSART
M

ST-AMBROSE
M

r. Berger

Rambuteau

Centre Pompidou

r. des Coutures St-Gervais

bd. Beaumarchais

RICHARD LENOIR
M

r. du Chemin Vert

Le Rivoli

r. Ferronnerie

des Lombards

r. du Roi de Sicile

r. des Francs-Bourgeois

r. de Sévigné

r. de Turenne

CHEMIN VERT
M

Lavandières Ste-Opportune

CHÂTELET
M

14

15

BRÉGUET SABIN
M

r. du Chemin Vert

Palais de Justice
M

CITÉ
M

r. de Rivoli

16

Hôtel de Ville

r. Vieille-du-Temple

ST-PAUL
M

PL. DES VOSGES

17

r. de la Roquette

FRANCE

Ile de la Cité

r. de Fourcy

r. des Ecouffes

r. St-Antoine

r. de Lappe

r. de Charonne

M RER
ST-MICHEL

de la Cité

Notre-Dame

r. du Faubourg - St-Antoine

r. de Lappe

Trousseau

PL. MAUBERT

Ile St-Louis

SULLY MORLAND
M

bd. Henri IV

BASTILLE
M

r. Charenton

LEDRU-ROLLIN
M

r. St-Jacques

quai de la Tournelle

Opéra Bastille
19

MAUBERT MUTUALITÉ
M

r. des Bernardins

r. des Ecoles

Seine

r. de Lyon

av. Daumesnil

5ème

quai St-Bernard

QUAI DE LA RAPÉE
M

GARE DE LYON
M

CARDINAL LEMOINE
M

r. des Boulange

JUSSIEU
M

r. Lédru Rollin

Gare de Lyon
RER

Panthéon

PL. DE LA CONTRE-SCARPE

r. Mouffetard

Jardin des Plantes

12ème

r. d'Ulm

(1km)

TO ★ (1km)

Pont de Sully

TO 24 (1.5km)

▓ **Le 10 Bar,** 10 r. de l'Odéon, 6ème (☎ 43 26 66 83). ⓜ Odéon. A classic student hang-out, where the city's youth indulge in philosophical and political discussion. Jukebox plays everything from Édith Piaf to Aretha Franklin. Open daily 6pm-2am.

▓ **Le Club des Poètes,** 30 r. de Bourgogne, 7ème (☎ 47 05 06 03; www.poesie.net). ⓜ Varenne. In 1961, Jean-Pierre Rosnay started "making poetry contagious and inevitable—*vive la poésie!*" His son has inherited the tradition; a restaurant by day, Le Club des Poètes is transformed Tu, F, and Sa nights at 10pm. Drinks €7.50. Open Sept.-July Tu-Sa noon-3pm and 8pm-1am. Kitchen open Tu-Sa noon-3pm and 8-10pm. MC/V.

▓ **Chez Georges,** 11 r. des Canettes, 6ème (☎ 43 26 79 15). ⓜ Mabillon. Upstairs, Chez Georges is a small wine bar with a diverse crowd; downstairs, it's a smoky, candlelit cellar packed with students drinking and dancing. Beer €3.50-4. Wine €1.50-4. Upstairs open Sept.-July Tu-Sa noon-2am. Cellar open Sept.-July Tu-Sa 10pm-2am.

Café Flèche d'Or, 102bis r. de Bagnolet, 20ème (☎ 44 64 01 02; www.flechedor.fr). ⓜ Alexandre Dumas. In an old train station, this bar/cafe/performance space serves internationally-inspired dishes like the "New York" (bacon cheddar cheeseburger; €15). Nightly entertainment. *Menus* €12-15. Kitchen open 8pm-midnight. MC/V.

La Belle Hortense, 31 r. Vieille du Temple, 4ème (☎ 48 04 71 60). ⓜ St-Paul. This wine bar has books lining the walls, wannabe philosophers lining its couches, and mellow music to go with the merlot. Frequent readings, signings, lectures. and discussions. Coffee €1.30-2. Wine from €4 per glass, €8 per bottle. Open daily 5pm-2am. MC/V.

Le Café Noir, 65 r. Montmartre, 2ème (☎ 40 39 07 36). ⓜ Sentier. With a leopard-skin bike in the window and bartenders leaping onto the bar to perform comedy, one of Paris's least predictable bars mixes locals and Anglophones. Beer €3-4. Open M-F 8am-2am, Sa 4pm-2am. MC/V.

L'Entrepôt, 7-9 r. Francis de Pressensé, 14ème (☎ 45 40 07 50; www.lentrepot.fr). ⓜ Pernety. Offers a quadruple combo: a 3-screen independent cinema; a restaurant with a garden patio; an art gallery; and a bar with jazz, Latin, and world music. Open M-Sa 11am-1am or later, Su 11am-midnight. Kitchen open daily noon-3pm and 8-11pm.

Café Chéri(e), 44 bd. de la Villette, 19ème (☎ 42 02 02 05). ⓜ Belleville. With cheap drinks and attractive artsy patrons, this is quickly becoming one of the 19ème's hottest spots. Beer from €3; comes with potato chips. Creative mixed drink menu. Nightly DJ at 10pm. Open daily 8am-2am.

La Folie en Tête, 33 r. de la Butte-aux-Cailles, 13ème (☎ 45 80 65 99). ⓜ Corvisart. Exotic instruments line the walls of this beaten-up neighborhood hangout. Sept.-June Sa night concerts, usually Afro-Caribbean music (€8). Beer €3. *Ti* punch €5.50. Happy hour 6-8pm. Open M-Sa 6pm-2am; last call 1:30am. MC/V.

Le Pop In, 105 r. Amelot, 11ème (48 05 56 11). ⓜ St-Sebastien Froissart. Both neighborhood bar and rock club, this crowded spot is a favorite among Paris's carefully bedraggled youth and Anglophone study abroaders. Nightly concerts in their tiny basement. Plays pop and rock. Beer €2.50-5. Open Tu-Su 6:30pm-1:30am.

L'Academie de la Bière, 88 bis bd. Port Royal, 5ème (☎ 43 54 66 65; www.academie-biere.com). RER: Port Royal. 12 beers on tap and over 300 bottled. Beer €6.50-8.50. Happy hour daily 3:30-7:30pm. Open M-Th 10am-2am, F-Sa 10am-3am.

Folies Pigalle, 11 pl. Pigalle, 9ème (☎ 48 78 55 25; www.folies-pigalle.com). ⓜ Pigalle. The largest, wildest club in the sleazy Pigalle *quartier*—not for the faint of heart. A former strip joint, the Folies is popular with both GLBT and straight clubbers. 1st M of each month *Soirées Transsexuelles.* Open M-Th and Su midnight-dawn, F-Sa midnight-noon. Drinks €10. Cover €20; includes 1 drink. AmEx/MC/V.

Smoke Bar, 29 r. Delambre, 14ème (☎ 43 20 61 73). ⓜ Vavin. Local bar with cheap drinks (€3-7) that undercut Paris prices. Open M-F noon-2am. Sa 6pm-2am. MC/V.

Experience Europe by Eurail!

It's not just the Best Way to See Europe, it's also the cleanest, greenest and smartest

enjoy *experience* *explore*

If you believe the journey's as important as the destination then rail's clearly the best way to experience the real Europe. Fast, sleek trains get you where you want to go when you want to go and - mile for mile - do less damage to the environment than cars or planes. Even better, you don't have to navigate unfamiliar roads, pay for gas (it's not cheap in Europe!) or find parking - leaving you more time and money to spend simply enjoying your travel.

Eurail has created a range of passes to suit every conceivable itinerary and budget. So whether you want to discover the whole continent, or focus on just one or two countries, you'll find Eurail the smartest way to do Europe, all around.

Welcome to Europe by Eurail!

 *The best way to see Europe*

Otel.com

Are you aiming for a budget vacation **?**

DO NOT DISTURB

GLBT NIGHTLIFE

▨ **Raidd Bar,** 23 r. du Temple, 3ème. Ⓜ Hôtel de Ville. The hippest GLBT club in the Marais and perhaps Paris, with the most muscular bartenders. Watch performers strip for the clients in a glass shower cubicle built into the wall (yes, they take it all off at 11pm, midnight, 1, and 2am). Beer €4. Tu disco night, W 80s and house and Su 90s.

▨ **Le Champmeslé,** 4 r. Chabanais, 2ème (☎42 96 85 20). Ⓜ Pyramides. This lesbian bar is Paris's oldest and most famous; everyone is welcome. Beer €4-5. Mixed drinks €8. Th cabaret show 10pm. Free drink on your birthday. Open M-Sa 3pm-dawn.

Oh Fada!, 35 r. Ste-Croix de la Bretonnerie, 4ème (☎40 29 44 40) Ⓜ Hotel de Ville. The Marais' most likeable GLBT spot. Mostly gay men, but women and straight men welcome. Beer €4-6. Open M-W, Su 5pm-2am, Th-Sa 5pm-4am.

Banana Café, 13 r. de la Ferronerie, 1er (☎42 33 35 31; www.bananacafeparis.com). Ⓜ Châtelet. This *très branché* (way cool) evening arena is the 1er's most popular GLBT bar and draws a very mixed group. Drinks €4-9. Th-Sa Go-Go Boys. Happy hour 6-9pm. Cover F-Sa €10; includes 1 drink. Open daily 5:30pm-6am. AmEx/MC/V.

DANCE CLUBS

Batofar, facing 11 q. François-Mauriac, 13ème (☎53 60 17 42). Ⓜ Q. de la Gare. This 45m long, 520t barge/bar/club has made it big with the electronic music crowd. Live artists and DJs daily. Su "Electronic brunch." Cover €8-15; usually includes 1 drink. Open M-Th 11pm-6am, F-Su 11pm-dawn; hours may vary. MC/V.

Rex Club, 5 bd. Poissonnière, 2ème (☎42 36 10 96; www.rexclub.com). Ⓜ Bonne-Nouvelle. Club very selective about international DJs who spin house, jungle, and techno. Drinks €8-10. Cover up to €13. Open W-Th 11:30pm-6am, F-Sa midnight-6am.

Wax, 15 r. Daval, 11ème (☎48 05 88 33). Ⓜ Bastille. In a concrete bunker with retro couches, this mod bar/club gets crowded at night. Beer €5.50-7. Mixed drinks €9.50. W, Su disco/funk, Th R&B, F-Sa house. Open daily 9pm-dawn. MC/V; min. €15.

▣ DAYTRIPS FROM PARIS

▨**VERSAILLES.** Louis XIV, the Sun King, built and held court at Versailles's extraordinary palace, 12km west of Paris. The château embodies the Old Regime's extravagance, especially in the newly renovated **Hall of Mirrors.** Arrive as soon as the château opens to avoid large crowds. The line to buy tickets is to the left of the courtyard, while the line to get into the château is to the right; skip the former line by buying a day pass at the Versailles **tourist office,** 2bis av. de Paris, or skip the latter line by buying a combo guided tour and entrance ticket to the right of the château ticket office. (☎30 83 78 00. *Château open Tu-Su Apr.-Oct. 9am-6:30pm; Nov.-Mar. 9am-5:30pm. Gardens open daily Apr.-Oct. 7:30am-8:30pm, Nov.-Mar. 8am-6pm. Day pass including entrance to château, gardens, and Trianons €20, during Grandes Eaux €25, under 18 free. Château only €14, 2½hr. before closing €10, under 18 free. Gardens Apr.-Sept. Sa-Su €7, students and under 18 €6, M-F free; Oct.-Mar. daily free. 1½hr. guided tour and château €22, under 18 €6. Audio tour €6.)* A **shuttle** (round-trip €6, 11-18 €4.50) runs through the gardens to Louis XIV's pink marble hideaway, the **Grand Trianon,** and Marie-Antoinette's **Petit Trianon,** including her pseudo-peasant **Hameau,** or hamlet. (*Grand Trianon open daily Apr.-Oct. noon-6:30pm, Nov.-Mar. noon-5:30pm. Petit Trianon open daily Apr.-Oct. noon-6pm. Marie-Antoinette's gardens open Apr.-Oct. noon-7:30pm, Nov.-Mar. 9am-5:30pm. All three €9, after 4pm €5, under 18 free.)* Take the **RER C5 train** from Ⓜ Invalides to Versailles Rive Gauche (30-40min., 4 per hr., round-trip €5.60).

■ **CHARTRES.** Chartres's phenomenal cathedral is one of the most beautiful surviving creations of the Middle Ages. Arguably the finest example of early Gothic architecture in Europe, the cathedral retains nearly all of its original 12th- and 13th-century stained-glass windows, featuring the "Chartres blue." Climb the spiral staircase to the 16th-century Flamboyant Gothic left tower, **Tour Jehan-de-Beauce,** built 300 years after the rest of the cathedral. (☎ 02 37 21 75 02; www.diocese-chartres.com/cathedrale. Open daily 8:30am-7:30pm. Tower open May-Aug. M-Sa 9:30am-12:30pm and 2-6pm, Su 2-6pm; Sept.-Apr. M-Sa 9:30am-12:30pm and 2-5pm, Su 2-5pm. Last entry 30min. before closing. Cathedral free. Tower €7, 18-25 €5. Nov.-May 1st Su of month free.) Trains run from Paris's Gare Montparnasse (1¼hr., 1 per hr., round-trip €26).

LOIRE VALLEY (VAL DE LOIRE)

The Loire, France's longest river, meanders toward the Atlantic through a valley containing vineyards that produce some of the nation's best wines. It's hardly surprising that a string of French (and English) kings chose to live in opulent châteaux by these waters rather than in the commotion of their capital cities.

▐ TRANSPORTATION

Faced with widespread grandeur, many travelers plan overly ambitious itineraries—two châteaux per day is a reasonable goal. The city of **Tours** (p.334) is the region's best **rail** hub. However, train schedules are inconvenient, and many châteaux aren't accessible by train. **Biking** is the best way to explore the region. Many stations distribute the invaluable *Châteaux pour Train et Vélo* booklet.

ORLÉANS   ☎ 02 38

A gateway from into the Loire, Orléans (pop. 113,000) cherishes its historical connection to **Joan of Arc,** who marched triumphantly past the **rue de Bourgogne** in 1429 after liberating the city from a seven-month British siege. Most of Orléans's highlights are near **place Ste-Croix.** With towering buttresses and stained-glass windows that depict Joan's story, the ▐**Cathédrale Sainte-Croix,** pl. Ste-Croix, is Orléans's crown jewel. (Open daily July-Aug. 9:15am-7pm; Sept.-June reduced hours.) The **Hôtel Groslot d'Orléans,** pl. de l'Étape, left of the Musée des Beaux Arts, contains Joan of Arc memorabilia and the final resting place of François II, who died in disgrace in 1560. (☎ 79 22 30; hotelgroslot@ville-orleans.fr. Open July-Sept. Su-F 9am-7pm, Sa 5-8pm; Oct.-June Su-F 10am-noon and 2-6pm.) The same family has owned the ▐**Hôtel de L'Abeille ❹,** 64 r. Alsace-Lorraine, since 1919. Thirty-one comfortable rooms with antique furniture are worth the price. (☎ 53 54 87; www.hoteldelabeille.com. Breakfast €7, in bed €8. Singles with shower €42-52, with bath €59; doubles €45-58/89; triples €59/89; quads €75. AmEx/MC/V.) **Rue de Bourgogne** and **rue Ste-Catherine** have cheap buffets and a lively bar scene at night. At ▐**Mijana ❸,** 175 r. de Bourgogne, a Lebanese couple prepares gourmet cuisine, including vegetarian options. (☎ 62 02 02; www.mijanaresto.com. Falafel €7. *Plats* from €12. Open M-Sa noon-1:30pm and 7-10pm. AmEx/MC/V.) **Trains** leave from the Gare d'Orléans on pl. Albert I for Blois (30min., 15 per day, €10), Paris (1¼hr., 1 per hr., €17), and Tours (1½hr., 2 per hr., €16). The **tourist office** is at 2 pl. de l'Étape. (☎ 24 05 05; www.tourisme-orleans.com. Open daily July-Aug. 9:30am-7pm; June 9:30am-1pm and 2-6:30pm; Sept-Apr. reduced hours.) **Postal Code:** 45000.

BLOIS   ☎ 02 54

Awash in regal history, Blois (pop. 50,000) is one of the Loire's most popular cities. Once home to monarchs Louis XII and François I, Blois's gold-trimmed ▐**Château** was the Versailles of the late 15th and early 16th centuries. Housed within are well-preserved collections and historical museums. Tthe **Musée des Beaux-Arts** features a gallery of 16th- to 19th-century portraits, and the **Musée Lapidaire** exhibits sculptures from nearby châteaux. (☎90 33 33. Open daily Apr.-Sept. 9am-6:30pm; Jan.-Mar. and Oct.-Dec. 9am-noon and 2-5:30pm. €7, students under 25 €5.) Bars and bakeries on **rue des Trois Marchands** tempt those en route to the 12th-century **Abbaye St-Laumer**, also called **l'Église St-Nicolas**. (Open daily 9am-6:30pm. Su mass 9:30am.) Five hundred years of expansions to **Cathédrale St-Louis**, endowed it with an eclectic mix of styles. (Open daily 7:30am-6pm.) A spectacular view from the ▨**Jardin de l'Evêché**, behind the cathedral, runs past the rooftops and winding alleys of the old quarter, stretching along the Loire. ▨**Hôtel du Bellay ❷**, 12 r. des Minimes, 2min. above the city center, offers comfortable rooms with colorful decor. (☎78 23 62; http://hoteldubellay.free.fr. Breakfast €5. Reserve ahead. Singles and doubles €25, with toilet €27, with shower €28, with bath €37; triples or quads €54-62. MC/V.) Fragrant *pâtisseries* entice visitors on **rue Denis Papin**, while **rue St-Lubin, place Poids du Roi**, and **place de la Résistance** offer more dining options. At night, the château's *"Son et Lumiere"* light show brightens Blois. The **Velvet Jazz Lounge**, 15 r. Haute, an abbey-turned-bar, has occasional live jazz and a medieval flavor. (☎78 36 32. Beer €3. Mixed drinks €7-8. Open Tu-Su 3pm-2am).

Trains leave pl. de la Gare for Orléans (30-50min., 14 per day, €9), Paris (1¾hr., 8 per day, €23), and Tours (40min., 8-13 per day, €8.75). Transports Loir-et-Cher (TLC; ☎58 55 44; www.TLCinfo.net) send **buses** from the station to nearby châteaux (35min., May 15-Sept. 2-3 per day; €11.25, students €9). Rent a **bike** from **Bike in Blois**, 8 r. Henri Drussy near pl. de la Résistance. (☎56 07 73; www.location-develos.com. 1st day €14, discount thereafter. Open M-Sa 9:15am-1pm and 3-6:30pm, Su 10:30am-1pm and 3-6:15pm. Cash only.) The **tourist office** is on pl. du Château. (☎90 41 41; www.bloispaysdechambord.com. Open Apr.-Sept. M-Sa 9am-7pm, Su 10am-7pm; Oct.-Mar. reduced hours.) **Postal Code:** 41000.

▶ DAYTRIPS FROM BLOIS

CHAMBORD. Built between 1519 and 1545 to satisfy François I's egomania, **Chambord** is one of the largest, most extravagant of the Loire châteaux. With 426 rooms, 365 chimneys, and 77 staircases, the castle could accommodate up to 10,000 people. To cement his claim, François stamped 200 of his trademark stone salamanders throughout the hunting lodge, which also features a double-helix staircase thought to be designed by Leonardo da Vinci. (☎*50 40 00. Open daily Apr.-June 9am-6:15pm; July-Aug. 9am-7:30pm; Sept.-Mar. reduced hours. €10, 18-25 €7, under 17 free.*) Take the TLC **bus** from Blois or **bike** south from Blois for 2-3km until St-Gervais-la-Forêt, then turn left on D33 (1hr.).

CHEVERNY. With a tumultuous past, this castle has been privately owned since 1634 by the Hurault family, who served as financiers and officers to the French kings. The château's magnificent furnishings include royal portraits, tapestries, and vases. Fans of Hergé's *Tintin* books may recognize Cheverny's Renaissance facade as the inspiration for Marlinspike, Captain Haddock's mansion. The kennels hold 120 mixed English-Poitevin hunting hounds whose impressive dinner manners can be observed daily at 5pm. (☎*79 96 29. Open daily July-Aug. 9:15am-6:45pm; Apr.-June and Sept. 9:15am-6:15pm; Oct.-Mar. reduced hours. €7, students €5.*) Cheverny, 45min. south of Blois by bike, is on the TLC bus route.

AMBOISE ☎02 47

Parapets of the 15th-century château that six French kings called home guard Amboise (pop. 12,000). In the **Logis du Roi**—where the kidnapping of the Dauphin king was plotted—intricate 16th-century Gothic chairs stand over 2m tall to prevent attacks from behind. The jewel of the grounds is the **Chapelle St-Hubert**, the final resting place of **Leonardo da Vinci.** (☎57 00 98. Open daily July-Aug. 9am-6:30pm; Sept.-June reduced hours. €9, students €7.) Da Vinci spent his last three years at **Clos Lucé,** 400m farther north. One of the manor's main attractions is a collection of 40 machines realized from da Vinci's designs, including the world's first machine gun. (☎57 00 73. Open daily July-Aug. 9am-8pm; Apr.-June and Sept.-Oct. 9am-7pm; Nov.-Dec. 9am-6pm; Jan. 10am-5pm. €12, students €10. Sept.-June €9/7.) The **Centre International de Séjour Charles Péguy (HI)** ❶, sits on Île d'Oran, an island in the Loire. Follow r. Jules Ferry from the station, cross the first bridge on your left, and head downhill to the right. (☎30 60 90; www.mjcamboise.fr. Breakfast €3. Linens €3. Reception M-F 10am-noon and 2-8pm. Dorms €12. Cash only.) Try the local favorite **Chez Hippeau** ❸, 1 r. François 1er, for delicious regional treats. The staff will happily guide you through the menu options. (☎57 26 30. *Menu* €15-24. Large salads €7-15. Open daily noon-3:30pm and 7-10:30pm. MC/V.) **Trains** leave 1 r. Jules-Ferry for: Blois (20min., 10 per day, €6); Orléans (1hr., 2 per 3hr., €13); Paris (2¼hr., 1 per hr., €26); Tours (20min., 24 per day, €5). To reach the **tourist office,** take a left from the station and follow r. Jules-Ferry, taking a right at the end of the street, crossing the first bridge to your left, and passing the Île d'Or. Turn right after crossing the second bridge; the office is in a circular building on q. du Général de Gaulle. (☎57 09 28; www.amboise-valde-loire.com. Open M-Sa 9am-1pm and 2-6pm; hours may vary). **Postal Code:** 37400.

TOURS ☎02 47

Tours (pop. 137,000) has the bars and shops of a modern metropolis, but ancient buildings, cathedrals, and towers loom behind its store-lined streets. Home to 30,000 students, numerous restaurants, and a booming nightlife, Balzac's birthplace is a comfortable base for château-hopping. The **Cathédrale St-Gatien,** off r. Lavoisier, first built in the AD 4th century, combines Romanesque columns, Gothic carvings, and two Renaissance spires into an intricate facade. (Cathedral open daily 9am-7pm. Cloister open May-Sept. M-Sa 9:30am-12:30pm and 2-6pm; Oct.-Mar. Th-Sa 9:30am-12:30pm and 2-5pm. Cathedral free. Cloister €3, under 18 and art students free.) Jutting up from modern commercial streets, the **Tour de l'Horloge** and **Tour de Charlemagne,** on r. Descartes, stand as testimony to the impressive proportions of the old basilique, destroyed after the 1789 Revolution. The **Nouvelle Basilique St-Martin** is an ornate church designed by Victor Laloux, architect of Paris's Musée d'Orsay (p. 323) and Tours's train station. (Open daily 8am-8pm. Mass daily 11am.) **Musée des Compagnons,** 8 r. Nationale, showcases the masterpieces of France's best craftsmen and explains the decade-long traditional training of the *Compagnonage*. (☎21 62 20. €4.90, students and seniors €2.90, under 12 free. Open M and W-Su mid-Sept. to mid-June 9am-noon and 2-6pm; mid-June to mid-Oct. 9am-12:30pm and 2-6pm).

The **Association Jeunesse et Habitat** ❷, 16 r. Bernard Palissy, houses backpackers, students, and workers in spacious rooms. When exiting the tourist office, turn right on r. Bernard Palissy. (☎60 51 51. Free Internet. Singles with shower €18; doubles with bath €26.) Try **place Plumereau** and **rue Colbert** for cafes and restaurants. Cheese-lovers converge for the delicious selection at ■**La Souris Gourmande** ❷, 100 r. Colbert. (☎47 04 80. Fondue €13-14, min. 2 people. Crepes and omelettes €8-9. Open Tu-Sa noon-2pm and 7-10:30pm. MC/V.) At night, **place Plumereau** blossoms with energetic bars. The friendly staff and quirky interior at **Au Temps des Rois,** 3 pl. Plumereau, make it popular among a mixed crowd. (☎05 04 51. Beer €2.50-5. Open daily 8:30am-2am. AmEx/MC/V.) **Trains** leave pl. du Général Leclerc for Bordeaux (2½hr., 1 per hr., €44) and Paris (3hr., 14 per day, €29; TGV 1hr., 1 per hr., €53). To reach the **tourist office,** 78-82 r. Bernard Palissy, from the station, walk through pl. du Général Leclerc. Across the street, the office's neon sign will be in plain sight. (☎70 37 37; www.ligeris.com. Open mid-Apr. to mid-Oct. M-Sa 8:30am-7pm, Su 10am-12:30pm and 2:30-5pm; mid-Oct. to mid-Apr. M-Sa 9am-12:30pm and 1:30-6pm, Su 10am-1pm.) **Postal Code:** 37000.

⚡ DAYTRIPS FROM TOURS

CHENONCEAU. Nicknamed the *château des dames* (castle of the ladies), Chenonceau owes its beauty to the series of women who designed it: first Katherine Bohier, the wife of a 16th-century tax collector; then Henri II's lover, Diane de Poitiers; and Henri's widowed wife, Catherine de Médici. The part of the château bridging the Cher River marked the border between occupied and Vichy France during WWII. (☎ 23 90 07. *Open daily mid-Mar. to mid-Sept. 9am-7pm; mid-Sept. to mid-Mar. reduced hours. €9, students €7.50.*) **Trains** from Tours stop at the station in front of the castle (30min., 8 per day, €5.70). Fil Vert **buses** also run from Amboise (25min., M-Sa 2 per day, €1.50) and Tours (1hr., M-Sa 2 per day, €1.50).

AZAY-LE-RIDEAU. Atop an island in the Indre, Azay-le-Rideau stands on an earlier fortress' ruins. Seized by Francois I in the 16th century, the castle still bears his royal insignia: cruelness salamanders slinking above external doors. Away's furniture and the Italian second-floor staircase reflect the Renaissance style while Gothic influence appears in the *grand sale*, or grand drawing room. (☎ 45 45 04. *Open daily July-Aug. 9:30am-7pm; Apr.-June and Sept. 9:30am-6pm; Oct.-Mar. 9:30am-12:30pm and 2-5:30pm. Last entry 45min. before closing. Light show daily early July 9:45pm; mid-July to mid-Aug. 10pm. Chateau €8, show €9, both €12; 18-25 €4.80/5/7, under 18 free. Gardens €3. Guided tour €4, students €3; audio tour €4.*) **Trains** run from Tours to the town of Away-led-Roadie (25min., 3-9 per day, €5). **Buses** run from Tours train station to the tourist office (50min., 3 per day, €6).

BRITTANY (BRETAGNE)

Despite superficially French *centre-villes*, châteaux, and *crêperies*, Brittany reveres its pre-Roman Celtic roots. After 800 years of Breton settlement, the province became part of France in 1491 when the duke's daughter married two successive French kings. Black-and-white *Breizh* (Breton) flags still decorate buildings, however, and the Celtic language *Brezhoneg* remains on street signs.

RENNES   ☎02 99

The cultural capital of Brittany, Rennes (pop. 212,000) flourishes from September to June. Ethnic eateries, colorful nightspots, and crowds of university students liven the cobblestone streets and half-timbered houses of the *vieille ville*.

⚡ TRANSPORTATION AND PRACTICAL INFORMATION. Trains leave pl. de la Gare for: Caen (3hr., 4 per day, €30); Paris (2hr., 1 per hr., €53-65); St-Malo (1hr., 15 per day, €12); Tours (3hr., 4 per day, €37) via Le Mans. **Buses** go from 16 pl. de la Gare to Mont-St-Michel (1½hr., 4 per day, €10). Local buses run Monday through Saturday 5:15am-12:30am and Sunday 7:25am-midnight. The **metro** line uses the same ticket (€1.10, day pass €4, *carnet* of 10 €10). The **tourist office** is at 11 r. St-Yves. (☎67 11 11; www.tourisme-rennes.com. Open July-Aug. M-Sa 9am-7pm, Su 11am-1pm and 2-6pm; Sept.-June reduced hours.) **Postal Code:** 35000.

⚡ ACCOMMODATIONS AND FOOD. The **Auberge de Jeunesse (HI) ❶**, 10-12 Canal St-Martin, has simple dorms and a cafeteria. Take the metro (dir.: Kennedy) to Ste-Anne. Follow r. de St-Malo downhill onto r. St-Martin; the hostel is on the right after the bridge. (☎33 22 33; rennes@fuaj.org. Breakfast and linens included. Reception 7am-11pm. Dorms €16. MC/V.) **Hôtel Maréchal Joffre ❷**, 6 r. Maréchal Joffre, has small, quiet rooms above a tiny lunch counter in the town center. (☎79 37 74. Breakfast €5. Reception M-Sa 24hr., Su midnight-1pm and 8pm-midnight. Singles €25-34; doubles €25-38; triples €40-44. AmEx/MC/V.) **Rue St-Malo** has many ethnic restaurants, while the *vieille ville* contains traditional *brasseries*. **Place Ste-Anne** has cheap kebab stands. 🔲**Le St-Germain des Champs (Restaurant Végétarien-Biologique)** ❸, 12 r. du Vau St-Germain, serves organic, vegetarian *plats* for €10. (☎79 25 52. *Menus* €14-18. Open M-Sa noon-2:30pm. MC/V.)

🔳🎭 **SIGHTS AND ENTERTAINMENT.** Medieval architecture peppers the *vieille ville*, particularly **rue de la Psalette** and **rue St-Guillaume.** At the end of r. St-Guillaume, turn left onto r. de la Monnaie to see the **Cathédrale St-Pierre,** a 19th-century church with a Neoclassical facade and gilded interior. Hidden in a side chapel, an intricate, carved altarpiece depicts the life of the Virgin Mary. (Open daily 9:30am-noon and 3-6pm.) The **Musée des Beaux-Arts,** 20 q. Émile Zola, houses Baroque and Breton masterpieces but few famous works. (☎02 23 62 17 45; www.mbar.org. Open Tu 10am-6pm, W-Su 10am-noon and 2-6pm. €5, students €3, under 18 free.) Across the river, up r. Gambetta, the 🔲**Jardin du Thabor** is one of France's most beautiful gardens and hosts frequent concerts. (☎28 56 62. Open daily June-Aug. 7:30am-8:30pm; Sept.-June 7:30am-6:30pm.) With enough bars for a city twice its size and clubs that draw students from beyond Paris, Rennes is a partygoer's dream. Look for action around place Ste-Anne, **place St-Michel,** and **place de Lices.** The young and beautiful pack two floors and four bars at **Le Zing,** 5 pl. des Lices. (☎79 64 60. Mixed drinks €8-9. Open daily 3pm-3am. MC/V.) In a former prison, **Delicatessen,** 7 impasse Rallier du Baty, near pl. St-Michel, has swapped jailhouse bars for heavy beats. (Drinks €6-10. Cover €5-15. Open Tu-Sa midnight-5am.)

ST-MALO   ☎02 99

St-Malo (pop. 52,000) merges the best of northern France: cultural festivals, imposing ramparts, and sandy beaches. East of the walled city, **Grande Plage de Sillon** is the town's largest, longest beach. The slightly more sheltered **Plage de Bon Secours** lies to the west and features the curious (and free) **Piscine de Bon Secours,** three cement walls that hold in a deep pool of water even when the tide recedes. The best view of St-Malo is from the **château's** watchtower, part of the **Musée d'Histoire.** (☎40 71 57. Open Apr.-Sept. daily 10am-12:30pm and 2-6pm; Oct.-Mar. reduced hours. €5, students €3.) All entrances to the city have stairs leading to the old **ramparts;** the view from the north side reveals a sea speckled with islands, including the **Grand Bé**—where French author **Chateaubriand** is buried—and the **Fort National,** both of which can be reached on foot at low tide. The **Centre Patrick Varangot (HI)** ❶, 37 av. du Révérend Père Umbricht, has 242 beds near the beach. From the train station, take bus #5 (dir.: Croix Désilles) or 10 (dir.: Cancale). By foot from the station (30min.), turn right and go straight at the roundabout onto av. de Moka. Turn right on av. Pasteur, which becomes av. du Révérend Père Umbricht. (☎40 29 80; www.centrevarangot.com. Breakfast and linens included. Laundry €4. Free Internet and Wi-Fi. Reception daily 8am-11pm. Dorms €15-19; singles €25-29. MC/V.) The best eateries lie farther from the *vieille ville*. For gluttonous scoops of *gelato*, head to 🔲**Le Sanchez** ❶, 9 r. de la Vieille Boucherie at pl. du Pilori. (☎56 67 17. 1 scoop €2, 2 scoops €3. Super Sanchez 3-scoop sundae; €4.80. Open mid-June to mid-Sept. daily 8:30am-midnight; mid-Sept. to mid-June reduced hours. MC/V; min. €15.) **Trains** run from Sean Coquelin to Dinan (1hr., 4 per day, €8), Paris (5hr., 10 per day, €57-72), and Rennes (1hr., 7-15 per day, €12). From the station, cross bd. de la République and follow av. Louis Martin to esplanade St-Vincent for the **tourist office.** (☎56 64 48. Open July-Aug. M-Sa 9am-7:30pm, Su 10am-6pm; Sept.-June reduced hours.) **Postal Code:** 35400.

DINAN   ☎02 96

Perhaps the best-preserved medieval town in Brittany, Dinan (pop. 11,000) has cobblestone streets lined with 15th-century houses. On its ramparts, the 13th-century **Porte du Guichet** is the original entrance to the **Château de Dinan.** Once a military stronghold, ducal residence, and prison, its two towers are now a museum. The **donjon** (keep) displays local art and artifacts, while the 15th-century **Tour de Coëtquen**'s basement stores funerary sculptures. (Open June-Sept. daily 10am-6:30pm; Oct.-May reduced hours. €4.25, 12-18 €1.70.) To reach the **Auberge de Jeunesse (HI) ❶,** in Vallée de la Fontaine-des-Eaux, turn left from the station, cross the tracks, then turn right and head downhill for 2km before turning right again for another 2km. (☎39 10 83; dinan@fuaj.org. Breakfast €3.50. Linens included. Free Internet. Reception July-Aug. 8am-noon and 5-9pm; Sept.-June 9am-noon and 5-8pm. Dorms €12. HI members only. MC/V.) Bars, *brasseries,* and *crêperies* sit along **rue de la Cordonnerie** and **place des Merciers.** From pl. du 11 Novembre 1918, **trains** run to Paris (3hr., 6 per day, €59) and Rennes (1hr., 8 per day, €13). The **tourist office** is at 9 r. du Château. (☎87 69 76. Open July-Aug. M-Sa 9am-7pm, Su 10am-12:30pm and 2:30-6pm; Sept.-June reduced hours.) **Postal Code:** 22100.

QUIMPER   ☎02 98

With a central waterway crisscrossed by flower-adorned footbridges, Quimper (kam-pair; pop. 63,000) has irrepressible charm to fuel its fierce Breton pride. At **Faïenceries de Quimper HB-Henriot,** r. Haute, guides lead visitors through the studios of the town's renowned earthenware. (☎90 09 36; www.hb-henriot.com. Open July-Aug. M-Sa 9:30-11:45am and 2-5:15pm; Sept.-June M-F 9:30-11:15am and 2-4:15pm. Mandatory English- or French-language tours every 45min. €4, 8-14 €2, under 8 free.) The twin windowed spires of the **Cathédrale St-Corentin,** built between the 13th and 15th centuries, rise over the Old Town. Inside the light-filled, colorful church, a bent choir supposedly mimics the angle of Jesus's head drooping from the cross. (Open May-Oct. daily 8:30am-noon and 1:30-6:30pm; Nov.-Apr. M-Sa 9am-noon and 1:30-6pm, Su 1:30-6pm. Hours may vary.)

To reach **Camping Municipal ❶,** 4 av. des Oiseaux, take bus #1 (dir.: Kermoysan; last bus 7:30pm) from pl. de la Résistance to Chaptal; the campground will be up the street on the left. (☎ 55 61 09; camping-municipal@quimper.fr. Reception June-Sept. M 1-7pm; Tu, Th 8-11am and 3-8pm; W 9am-noon; F 9-11am and 3-8pm; Sa 8am-noon and 3-8pm; Su 9-11am. Oct.-May M-Tu, Th 9-11:30am and 3:30-7:30pm; F 9:30-10:30am and 3:30-7:30pm; Sa 9:30-11:30am and 4:30-6:30pm. €4 per adult, €2 per child under 7, €1 per tent, €1.70 per car, €1.50 per RV. Electricity €2.90.) **Les Halles market,** on r. St-François off r. Kéréon, has cheese, meat, produce, and seafood. (Open daily 9am-7pm; hours may vary.) At night, head to the cafes near the cathedral, or to **An Poitín Still,** 2 av. de la Liberation by the train station. (F live Irish music 10pm. Beer €2-5. Open M-Sa 3pm-1am, Su 5pm-1am. AmEx/MC/V.) **Trains** go from av. de la Gare to Rennes (2½hr., 14 per day, €30-36). From the train station, go right onto av. de la Gare and follow it, with the river on your right, as it becomes bd. Dupleix and leads to pl. de la Résistance. The **tourist office,** 7 r. de la Déesse, is on the left. (☎53 04 05; www.quimper-tourisme.com. Open July-Aug. M-Sa 9am-7pm, Su 10am-1pm and 3-5:45pm; Sept.-June reduced hours.) **Postal Code:** 29000.

NANTES   ☎02 40

With broad boulevards, relaxing public parks, and great bistros, Nantes (pop. 280,000) knows how to take life easy. The massive **Château des Ducs de Bretagne,** built to safeguard Breton independence in the late 15th century, now houses several exhibits detailing regional history. Look for elaborate grafitti carved into its walls by former prisoners. (Open mid-May to mid-Sept. 9:30am-7pm; mid-Sept. to mid-May 10am-6pm. Grounds free. Exhibits each €5, 18-26 €3; both €8/4.80.) Gothic vaults soar 39m in the **Cathédrale St-Pierre.** A complete restoration of the interior has undone the ravages of time, though it could not salvage the stained glass shattered during WWII. (Open daily Apr.-Oct. 8am-7pm, Nov.-Mar. 8am-6pm.) The **Musée des Beaux-Arts,** 10 r. Georges Clemenceau, features a wide range of European masterpieces, as well as temporary exhibits on contemporary French art. (☎02

THE LOCAL STORY

PARDON ME, ST-ROMAIN

Every year since 1156, on Ascension Day, a prisoner is brought before Rouen's parliament. Without a judge, jury, or trial, he is set free. By this annual act of mercy, Rouen celebrates the most famous miracle of its patron saint, St-Romain: his defeat of a dragon aided by a convict.

While serving as Bishop of Rouen in the 7th century, St-Romain lived a life of quiet piety; it was not until well after his death in 641 that his fame as a dragon-slayer began to spread. When the saint's remains were moved within Rouen's walls in the 10th century, they were interred in a flood-prone part of town that subsequently stopped flooding. With this new miracle attributed to St-Romain, the old legend of his run-in with a river dragon recaptured popular imagination.

As the story goes, one day a dragon emerged from the Seine and sent a flood over Rouen. St-Romain tried to recruit villagers to stop the beast, but only one man—a prisoner—answered his plea. The two entered the dragon's cave, St-Romain made the sign of the cross, and the beast collapsed.

To honor their legendary patron saint and the lone convict who aided him, the people of Rouen began to annually pardon a prisoner. Improbable as it may seem, this millennium-old tradition continues to this day.

51 17 45 00. Open M, W, F-Su 10am-6pm, Th 10am-8pm. €3.50, students €2, under 18, Th 6-8pm, and 1st Su of each month free; €2 daily after 4:30pm.)

A 15min. walk from the train station, **Auberge de Jeunesse "La Manu" (HI) ❶**, 2 pl. de la Manu, once a tobacco factory, has an industrial feel. (☎29 29 20; nanteslamanu@fuaj.org. Breakfast and linens included. Internet €1 per 40min. Reception daily July-Aug. 8am-noon and 4-11pm; Sept.-June 8am-noon and 5-11pm. Lockout July-Aug. 10am-4pm; Sept.-June 10am-5pm. Open Jan. to mid-Dec. 3- to 6-bed dorms €16. HI members only. MC/V.) Plenty of reasonably priced eateries—from crepe stands to sit-down venues—are between **place du Bouffay** and **place du Pilori**. One of France's most beautiful bistros, **◪La Cigale ❸**, 4 pl. Graslin, has exquisite food and excellent service. (☎02 51 84 94 94; www.lacigale.com. *Plats* €10-25. 2-course lunch *menus* €13-24; 3-course dinner *menus* €17-27. Open daily 7:30am-12:30am. AmEx/MC/V.) **Quartier St-Croix**, near pl. du Bouffay, has countless bars and cafes. **Trains** leave from 27 bd. de Stalingrad for Bordeaux (4hr., 5 per day, €42), Paris (2-4hr., 1 per hr., €54-69), and Rennes (1¾hr., 7-15 per day, €21). The **tourist office** is at 3 cours Olivier de Clisson. (☎08 92 46 40 44; www.nantes-tourisme.com. Open M-W and F-Sa 10am-6pm, Tu 10:30am-6pm.) **Postal Code:** 44000.

NORMANDY (NORMANDIE)

Rainy Normandy is a land of cathedrals, fields, and fishing villages. Invasions have twice secured the region's place in military history: in 1066, William of Normandy conquered England; on D-Day, June 6, 1944, Allied armies returned the favor, liberating France from Normandy's beaches.

ROUEN   ☎02 35

Madame Bovary—literature's most famous desperate housewife—may have criticized Rouen (pop. 106,000), but Flaubert's hometown is no provincial hamlet. Historically important as Normandy's capital and the city where Joan of Arc burned at the stake in 1431, modern Rouen buzzes with urban energy. The most famous of its "hundred spires" belong to the **◪Cathédrale de Notre-Dame,** pl. de la Cathédrale. The central spire, standing at 151m, is France's tallest. Art lovers may also recognize the cathedral's facade from Monet's celebrated studies of light. (Open Apr.-Oct. M 2-7pm, Tu-Sa 7:30am-7pm, Su 8am-6pm; Nov.-Mar. M 2-7pm, Tu-Sa 7:30am-noon and 2-6pm, Su 8am-6pm.) The **Musée Flaubert et d'Histoire de la Médicine,** 51 r. de Lecat, down r. de Crosne from pl. de Vieux-Marché, houses a large collection of bizarre paraphernalia on the history of medicine and the disparate themes of Flaubert, who was raised on its premises. (☎15 59 95; www.chu-rouen.fr. Open Tu 10am-6pm, W-Sa 10am-noon and 2-6pm. €3, 18-25 €1.50, under 18 free.)

Hotel des Arcades ❸, 52 r. de Carmes, is down the street from Notre-Dame. (☎70 10 30; www.hotel-des-arcades.fr. Breakfast €6.50. Singles €29-36, with shower €40-46; doubles €30-37/41-47; triples with shower €53. AmEx/MC/V.) Cheap eateries surround **place du Vieux-Marché** and **Gros Horloge.** Near l'Abbatiale St-Ouen, **Chez Wam ❶,** 67 r. de la République, serves *kebab-frites* (gyros with fries; €3-4) ideal for picnics in the nearby **Jardins de l'Hôtel de Ville.** (☎15 97 51. Open daily 11am-2am. AmEx/MC/V.) **Trains** leave r. Jeanne d'Arc for Lille (3hr., 3 per day, €29) and Paris (1½hr., 1 per hr., €19). The **tourist office** is at 25 pl. de la Cathédrale. (☎02 32 08 32 40; www.rouentourisme.com. Open May-Sept. M-Sa 9am-7pm, Su 9:30am-12:30pm and 2-6pm; Oct.-Apr. M-Sa 9:30am-6:30pm.) **Postal Code:** 76000.

CAEN   ☎02 31

Although Allied bombing leveled most of its buildings during WWII, Caen (pop. 114,000) has successfully rebuilt itself into an university town. Its strength and endurance would make even its infamous founder, William the Conqueror, proud.

⌨ � TRANSPORTATION AND PRACTICAL INFORMATION. Trains run to: Paris (2¼hr., 11 per day, €28); Rennes (3hr., 2 per day, €30); Rouen (1½hr., 9 per day, €21); Tours (3hr., 3 per day, €31). Bus Verts **buses** (☎08 10 21 42 14) cover the beaches and the rest of Normandy. Twisto, operating local buses and **trams,** has comprehensive schedules at its office on 15 r. de Gêole. (☎15 55 55; www.twisto.fr; €1.20, *carnet* of 10 €10.) The **tourist office** is in pl. St-Pierre. (☎27 14 14; www.caen.fr/tourisme. Open July-Aug. M-Sa 9am-7pm, Su 10am-1pm and 2-5pm; Mar.-June and Sept. M-Sa 9:30am-6:30pm, Su 10am-1pm; Oct.-Feb. M-Sa 9:30am-1pm and 2-6pm, Su 10am-1pm.) **Postal Code:** 14000.

🛏🍴 ACCOMMODATIONS AND FOOD. In the center of town, **Hôtel de la Paix ❷,** 14 r. Neuve-St-Jean, off av. du 6 Juin, is close to the château and offers simple, clean rooms with a firm bed and TV. (☎86 18 99. Breakfast €5. Reception 24hr. Singles €26, with shower €29, with bath €32; doubles €29/35/37; triples €37/43/45; quads with shower €53. Extra bed €8. AmEx/MC/V.) Ethnic restaurants, *brasseries*, and *crêperies* lie near the château and around **Place Courtonne.**

🎭🎵 SIGHTS AND NIGHTLIFE. Caen's biggest (and priciest) draw is the **▧Mémorial de Caen,** which powerfully, tastefully, and creatively explores WWII, from the "failure of peace" to modern prospects for global harmony. Take bus #2 dir: Mémorial/La Folie to Mémorial. (☎06 06 44; www.memorial-caen.fr. Open mid-Feb. to mid-Nov. daily 9am-7pm; mid-Nov. to mid-Feb. Tu-Su 9:30am-6pm. €17-18; students, seniors, and 10-18 €15-16; under 10 free. Prices vary by season.) The ruins of William the Conqueror's enormous **château,** whose ramparts are open for visiting (free), sprawl above the center of town. The **Musée de Normandie,** within the château grounds on the left, traces the cultural evolution of people living on Norman soil. (☎30 47 60; www.musee-de-normandie.caen.fr. Open June-Sept. daily 9:30am-6pm; Oct.-May M and W-Su 9:30am-6pm. Free.) The **Musée des Beaux-Arts de Caen,** inside the château to the right, houses European works from the 16th century to the present. (☎30 47 70; www.ville-caen.fr/mba. Open M and W-Su 9:30am-6pm. Free.) At night, Caen's busy streets turn boisterous; well-attended bars and clubs populate the area around **rue de Bras, rue des Croisiers,** and **rue St-Pierre.** Begin your quest by checking out the medieval decor of **Vertigo,** 14 r. Ecuyère, just past the intersection with r. St-Pierre. (☎85 43 12. Drinks €2.20-3. Open M-Sa 10am-1am.) Later, head over to lively **Le Semaphore,** 44 r. le Bras, whose loud music, neon lights, and sleek leather bar stools set the mood. (☎39 08 57. Beer €2.20-3.50. Mixed drinks €3-4.50. Happy hour 7-9pm. Open M-Sa 7pm-4am. MC/V.)

BAYEUX   ☎ 02 31

Relatively unharmed by WWII, beautiful Bayeux (pop. 15,000) is an ideal base for exploring nearby D-Day beaches. Visitors should not miss the 900-year-old ◼**Tapisserie Bayeux,** depicting William the Conqueror's invasion of England. The 70m tapestry is displayed in the **Centre Guillaume le Conquérant,** on r. de Nesmond. (Open daily May-Aug. 9am-7pm; mid-Mar. to Apr. and Sept.-Oct. 9am-6:30pm; Nov. to mid-Mar. 9:30am-12:30pm and 2-6pm. €7.70, students €3.80.) Close by, **Cathédrale Notre-Dame** was the tapestry's original home. (Open daily July-Sept. 8:30am-7pm; Oct.-Dec. 8:30am-6pm; Jan.-Mar. 9am-5pm; Apr.-June 8am-6pm. French-language tours of the Old Town, including access to the labyrinth and treasury 5 tours per day July-Aug., €4.) The **Musée de la Bataille de Normandie,** bd. Fabian Ware, recounts the D-Day landing and subsequent 76-day struggle for northern France. (☎51 46 90. Open daily May-Sept. 9:30am-6:30pm; Oct.-Apr. 10am-12:30pm and 2-6pm. English-language film about every 2hr. €6.50, students €3.80.) **Le Maupassant ❸,** 19 r. St-Martin, in the center of town, has cheerful, clean rooms above a *brasserie*. (☎92 28 53; h.lemaupassant@orange.fr. Breakfast €6. Singles €29; doubles with shower €40; quads with bath €69. Extra bed €10. MC/V.) Get groceries at **Marché Plus,** down the street from the tourist office on r. St-Jean. (Open M-Sa 7am-9pm, Su 8:30am-12:30pm.)

   Trains leave pl. de la Gare for Caen (20min., 11 per day, €5) and Paris (2½hr., 7 per day, €31). To reach the **tourist office,** r. St-Jean, turn left on bd. Sadi-Carnot, go right at the roundabout, bear right up r. Larcher past the cathedral, then turn right on r. St-Jean. (☎51 28 28; www.bayeux-bessin-tourism.com. Open July-Aug. M-Sa 9am-7pm, Su 9am-1pm and 2-6pm; Sept.-June reduced hours.) **Postal Code:** 14400.

◼ DAYTRIPS FROM BAYEUX

D-DAY BEACHES. On June 6, 1944, more than a hundred thousand Allied soldiers invaded Normandy's beaches, leading to France's liberation and the downfall of Nazi Europe. Today, reminders of that devastating battle can be seen in the somber gravestones, remnants of German bunkers, and pockmarked landscapes. Elite Army Rangers scaled 30m cliffs under heavy fire at the ◼**Pointe du Hoc,** between **Utah** and **Omaha Beaches,** to capture a strongly fortified German naval battery. Having achieved their objective, they held the battery against counter attacks for two full days past their anticipated relief. Of the division's 225 men, only 90 survived. Often referred to as "bloody Omaha," Omaha Beach, east of the Pointe du Hoc, is the most famous D-Day beach. On June 6, Allied bombings missed the German positions due to fog, while the German bunkers inflicted an 85% casualty rate on the first waves of Americans; ultimately, over 800 soldiers died on the beach. The 9387 graves at the **American Cemetery** stretch throughout expansive grounds on the cliffs overlooking the beach. *(Open daily 9am-6pm.)* To Omaha's east and just west of **Gold Beach** is **Arromanches,** a small town where the ruins of the Allies' temporary **Port Winston** lie in a giant semicircle off the coast. The **Arromanches 360°** **Cinéma** combines images of modern Normandy and 1944 D-Day. *(Open daily June-Aug. 9:40am-6:40pm; Sept.-May reduced hours. €4, students €3.50.)*

   Reaching the beaches can be difficult without a car. Some sites are accessible by **Bus Verts** from Caen on lines #1, 3, and 4 and from Bayeux on lines #70 and 74; more buses run in July-Aug., including a D-Day line from Bayeux and Caen to Omaha Beach (€1.50-10, 1-day pass €12.) **Normandy Sightseeing Tours,** based in Bayeux, runs half-day and full-day guided tours with English-speaking guides.

(☎51 70 52; www.normandywebguide.com. Reservations required. ½-day tour €40-45, students €35-40; full-day tour €75/65. Pickup at train station, pl. du Québec, or your hotel. MC/V.) **Vélos Location,** 5 r. Larcher, in Bayeux, rents bikes. (☎92 89 16. €10 per ½-day, €15 per day, €90 per week. Passport deposit required.)

MONT-ST-MICHEL
☎02 33

Once regarded as a paradise, the fortified island of Mont-St-Michel is a medieval wonder. Stone and half-timbering enclose the town's narrow main street, which leads steeply up to the **abbey's** twisting stairs. Adjacent to the abbey church is **La Merveille** (the Marvel), a 13th-century Gothic monastery supported by four crypts. (Open daily May-Aug. 9am-7pm; Sept.-Apr. 9:30am-6pm. €8, 18-25 €5.) Hotels on Mont-St-Michel are expensive, starting at €50 per night. Pontorson, 9km away by bus, has **Camping Haliotis ❶,** chemin des Soupirs and r. du Général Patton, a mini-resort offering cabins as well as campsites. (☎68 11 59; www.camping.haliotis-mont-saint-michel.com. Breakfast €5. Laundry €5. Reception 7:30am-10pm. Open Apr.-Nov. €4.50-6 per adult, €2-3.50 per child, €5-7 per tent and car or RV; cabins from €25. Electricity €3. MC/V.) Courriers Bretons (☎02 99 19 70 70), runs **buses** from Mont-St-Michel to Rennes (1¼hr., 2-3 per week, €2.50). The **tourist office** is to the left of the entrance. (☎60 14 30; www.ot-mont-saintmichel.com. Open July-Aug. daily 9am-7pm; Sept. and Apr.-June M-Sa 9am-12:30pm and 2-6:30pm, Su 9am-noon and 2-6pm; Oct.-Mar. reduced hours.) **Postal Code:** 50170.

> ❗ **DON'T BE CAUGHT ADRIFT.** Those hoping to see the Mont illuminated at night should plan ahead. Evening transportation off the island doesn't exist, and walking across the 1km of sand during low tide is extremely dangerous.

FLANDERS AND PAS DE CALAIS

Every day, thousands of tourists pass through the channel ports of the Côte d'Opale on their way to Britain, yet few manage more than a quick glimpse at the surrounding regions, leaving Flanders, Picardy, and the coastal Pas de Calais undiscovered. When fleeing the ferry ports, don't miss the area's hidden gems.

LILLE
☎03 20

A long-time international hub with rich Flemish ancestry and the best nightlife in the north, Lille (pop. 220,000) has abandoned its industrial days to become a stylish metropolis. The **Palais des Beaux-Arts,** on pl. de la République (M: République), has the second-largest art collection in France, with a comprehensive exhibit of 15th- to 20th-century French and Flemish masterpieces. (Open M 2-6pm, W-Su 10am-6pm. €10, students €7.) With artwork displayed around an indoor pool, the aptly named **La Piscine,** 23 r. de L'Espérance (M: Gare Jean Lebas), has creative exhibits and a collection that includes works from the 19th and 20th centuries. (Open Tu-Th 11am-6pm, F 11am-8pm, Sa-Su 1-6pm. €3.50, F students free.) Dating from the 15th century, the **Vieille Bourse** (Old Stock Exchange), pl. Général de Gaulle, is now home to regular book markets. (Open Tu-Su 9:30am-7:30pm.)

To reach the affable **Auberge de Jeunesse (HI) ❶,** 12 r. Malpart, circle left around the train station, then turn right onto r. du Molinel, left onto r. de Paris, and right onto r. Malpart. (☎57 08 94; lille@fuaj.org. Breakfast and linens included. Reception 24hr. Lockout 11am-3pm. Open late Jan. to mid-Dec. 3- to 6-bed dorms €20. €3 HI discount. MC/V.) The garden-themed **La Pâte Brisée ❷,** 65 r. de la Monnaie, in *ville* Lille, has seating on a quiet street. (☎74 29 00. *Menus* €8-18. Open M-F noon-10:30pm, Sa-Su noon-11pm. MC/V.) At night, students swarm **rue Solférino** and **rue Masséna's** pubs, while *vieux* Lille has a trendier bar scene.

Trains leave from Gare Lille Flandres, on pl. de la Gare (M: Gare Lille Flandres), for Paris (1hr., 20 per day, €37-50) and Brussels, BEL (1¾hr., 1-3 per day, €18-24). Gare Lille Europe, on r. Le Corbusier (M: Gare Lille Europe), sends Eurostar trains to Brussels, BEL (40min., 15 per day, €18-24) and London, BRI (1¾hr., 15 per day, €110-175) and TGVs to Paris (1¼hr., 6 per day, €37-50). Eurolines **buses** (☎78 18 88) also leave there for: Amsterdam, NTH (5hr., 2 per day, round-trip €47), Brussels, BEL (1½hr., 3 per day, round-trip €22), and London, BRI (5½hr., 2 per day, round-trip €61). From Gare Lille Flandres, walk straight down r. Faidherbe and turn left through pl. du Théâtre and pl. Général de Gaulle; turn right at the Théâtre du Nord. Offering bus, bike, Segway, and mobile phone tours, the **tourist office,** pl. Rihour (M: Rihour), is inside the Palais Rihour. (☎21 94 21; www.lilletourism.com. Open M-Sa 9:30am-6:30pm, Su 10am-noon and 2-5pm.) **Postal Code:** 59000.

CALAIS
☎03 21

Calais (pop. 80,000) is a relaxing Channel port where people speak English as often as French. Rodin's famous sculpture **The Burghers of Calais** stands in front of the Hôtel de Ville, at bd. Jacquard and r. Royale, though most visitors come for Calais's wide, sandy ▓**beaches.** ▓**Centre Européen de Séjour/Auberge de Jeunesse (HI) ❶,** av. Maréchal Delattre de Tassigny, less than a block from the beach, offers a bar and library. (☎34 70 20; www.auberge-jeunesse-calais.com. Singles €26; doubles €21. €3 HI discount. AmEx/MC/V.) Open-air morning **markets** are on pl. Crèvecoeur (Th and Sa) and pl. d'Armes (W and Sa). For more info on **ferries** to Dover, BRI, see p. 53. During the day, free **buses** connect the ferry terminal and Gare Calais-Ville on bd. Jacquard, where **trains** leave for Boulogne (30min., 11 per day, €8), Lille (1¼hr., 16 per day, €16), and Paris (3¼hr., 6 per day, €30-60). To reach the **tourist office,** 12 bd. Clemenceau, turn left from the station and cross the bridge; it's on the right. (☎96 62 40; www.ot-calais.fr. Open June-Aug. M-Sa 10am-1pm and Su 10am-1pm and 2-6:30pm; Sept.-May 10am-1pm.) **Postal Code:** 62100.

CHAMPAGNE AND BURGUNDY

Legend has it that when Dom Perignon first tasted champagne, he exclaimed, "Come quickly! I am drinking stars!" Few modern-day visitors need further convincing as they flock to the wine cellars in Reims and Epernay, where champagne is produced from regional grapes according to a rigorous, time-honored method. To the east, Burgundy's abbeys and cathedrals bear witness to the Middle Ages religious fervor. Today, the region draws epicureans with its fine wines and delectable dishes like *coq au vin* and *bœuf bourguignon*.

REIMS
☎03 26

From the 26 monarchs crowned in its cathedral to the bubbling champagne of its famed *caves* (cellars), everything Reims (pop. 191,000) touches turns to gold. The ▓**Cathédrale de Notre-Dame,** built with golden limestone from the medieval city walls, features stained-glass windows by Marc Chagall and an impressive royal history. (☎47 55 34. Open daily 7:30am-7:30pm. Free. English-language audio tour €5.) The adjacent **Palais du Tau,** 2 pl. du Cardinal Luçon, houses original statues from the cathedral's facade alongside 16th-century tapestries. (☎47 81 79. Open May-Aug. Tu-Su 9:30am-6:30pm; Sept.-Apr. 9:30am-12:30pm and 2-5:30pm. €6.50, 18-25 €4.50, under 18 free.) ▓**Champagne Pommery,** 5 pl. du Général Gouraud, gives the best tours of Reims's champagne *caves*. Its 75,000L *tonneau* (vat) is one of the largest in the world; it, along with the *maison's* modern art exhibits, can be viewed in the lobby free of charge. (☎61 62 56; www.pommery.com. Tours by reservation only €10-17.) The small schoolroom where Germany surrendered to the Allies during WWII is now the **Museé de la Reddition,** 12 r. Franklin Roosevelt. (☎47

84 19. Open M and W-Su 10am-noon and 2-6pm, Tu 2-6pm. €3, students free; includes Musée-Abbaye St-Rémi, Foujita Chapel, Musée de Beaux-Arts, and the planetarium.) In July, Reims kicks off the **Flâneries Musicales d'Eté**, with over 80 concerts in six weeks. (☎77 45 12. Tickets free-€12, students free-€10.)

The **⚜Centre International de Séjour (HI) ❶**, chaussée Bocquaine, has clean rooms next to a park. (☎40 52 60. Breakfast €4. Reception 24hr. Dorms €19, with bath €22; singles €28/41; doubles €21/28; triples with shower €22. €3 HI discount. MC/V.) Bars, cafes, and restaurants crowd **place Drouet d'Erlon**, Reims's choice nightspot. **Trains** leave bd. Joffre for Epernay (20min., 11 per day, €5) and Paris (1½hr., 11 per day, €21). To reach the **tourist office**, 2 r. Guillaume de Machault, follow the right curve of the roundabout to pl. Drouet d'Erlon, turn left on r. de Vesle, and right on r. du Trésor; the office is before the cathedral. (☎77 45 00; www.reims-tourisme.com. Open mid-Apr. to mid-Oct. M-Sa 9am-7pm, Su 10am-6pm; mid-Oct. to mid-Apr. M-Sa 9am-6pm, Su 11am-6pm.) **Postal Code:** 51100.

EPERNAY   ☎03 26

Champagne's showcase town, Epernay (pop. 26,000) is lavish and seductive. Palatial mansions, lush gardens, and swanky champagne companies distinguish **avenue de Champagne**. Here you'll find **⚜Moët & Chandon**, 20 av. de Champagne, producers of the king of all champagnes: **Dom Perignon**. (☎51 20 20; www.moet.com. Open daily 9:30-11:30am and 2-4:30pm. Tours €11-23, 10-18 €6.70, under 10 free; includes tastings for those 18+.) **Mercier**, 70 av. de Champagne, 10min. away, produces the self-proclaimed "most popular champagne in France." Tours in roller-coaster-style cars tell the story of its founder, Eugène Mercier. (☎51 22 22. Open mid-Mar. to mid-Nov. daily 9:30-11:30am and 2-4:30pm; mid-Nov. to mid-Dec. and mid-Feb. to mid-Mar. M and Th-Su 9:30-11:30am and 2-4:30pm. 30min. tour €7-15.)

Budget hotels are rare in Epernay, but **⚜Hôtel St-Pierre ❷**, 1 r. Jeanne d'Arc, offers spacious rooms at unbeatable prices. (☎54 40 80. Breakfast €6. Reception 7am-10pm. Singles €21, with shower €30; doubles €24/36. MC/V.) Ethnic food, as well as pricier champagne-soaked cuisine, line **rue Gambetta**. Bakeries and delis dot the area around **place des Arcades** and **place Hugues Plomb**. From Cours de la Gare, **trains** go to Paris (1¼hr., 18 per day, €19) and Strasbourg (3½hr., 3 per day, €40). From the station, walk straight through pl. Mendès France, go one block up r. Gambetta to pl. de la République, and turn left on av. de Champagne to reach the **tourist office**, 7 av. de Champagne. (☎53 33 00; www.ot-epernay.fr. Open Easter to mid-Oct. M-Sa 9:30am-12:30pm and 1:30-7pm, Su 11am-4pm; mid-Oct. to Easter M-Sa 9:30am-12:30pm and 1:30-5:30pm.) **Postal Code:** 51200.

TROYES   ☎03 25

Although the city layout resembles a champagne cork, little else links Troyes (pop. 60,000) with its grape-crazy northern neighbors. Troyes features Gothic churches, 16th-century mansions, and numerous museums that complement its social scene. Flying buttresses and ornate detail mark the enormous, Gothic **⚜Cathédrale St-Pierre et St-Paul**, pl. St-Pierre, on r. Clemençeau. Its stained glass, in the unique Troyes style, has survived several fires, bombings, and other disasters. (Open Tu-Sa 10am-1pm and 2-6pm, Su 10am-noon and 2-5pm. Free.) The **Musée d'Art Moderne**, next door on pl. St-Pierre, houses over 2000 works by French artists. (☎76 26 80. Open Tu-Su 10am-1pm and 2-6pm. €5; students, under 18, and 1st Su of each month free.) The fresh-water **Grands Lacs** dot the Forêt d'Orient region around Troyes. The **Comité Départemental du Tourisme de l'Aube**, 34 q. Dampierre, provides info on outdoor activities. (☎42 50 00. Open M-F 9:30am-12:30pm and 1:30-6pm.)

⚜Les Comtes de Champagne ❸, 56 r. de la Monnaie, is in a 16th-century mansion with large rooms. (☎73 11 70; www.comtesdechampagne.com. Reception 7am-10pm. Singles from €32; doubles from €38; triples from €61; quads from €67. AmEx/MC/V.) *Crêperies* and inexpensive eateries lie near **rue Champeaux**, in *quar-*

tier St-Jean, and on **rue Général Saussier,** in *quartier* Vauluisant. **Aux Crieurs de Vin ❷,** 4-6 pl. Jean Jaurès, compensates for a tiny menu of *plats* with an elaborate selection of wines. (☎40 01 01. Open Tu-Sa noon-2pm and 7:30-10pm. MC/V.) Lining Champeaux and **rue Molé** near **place Alexandre Israël,** cafes and taverns draw locals on warm nights. **Trains** run from av. Maréchal Joffre to Paris (1½hr., 16 per day, €22.) The **tourist office,** 16 bd. Carnot, is one block from the station. (☎82 62 70; www.ot-troyes.fr. Open Nov.-Mar. M-Sa 9am-12:30pm and 2-6:30pm, Su 10am 1pm; Apr.-Oct. M-Sa 9am-12:30pm and 2-6:30pm.) **Postal Code:** 10000.

DIJON   ☎03 80

Dijon (pop. 150,000) isn't just about the mustard. The capital of Burgundy, once home to dukes who wielded a power greater than the French monarchy, counters its historic grandeur with a modern irreverence. The diverse ◪**Musée des Beaux-Arts** occupies the east wing of the colossal **Palais des Ducs de Bourgogne,** on pl. de la Libération, at the center of the *vieille ville*. (☎74 52 70. Open M and W-Su May-Oct. 9:30am-6pm; Nov.-Apr. 10am-5pm. Free. Temporary exhibits €2, students €1.) Built in only 20 years, the **Église Notre-Dame,** pl. Notre Dame, is one of France's most famous churches. Its 11th-century statue of the Black Virgin is credited with liberating the city on two occasions: in 1513 from a Swiss siege and in 1944 from the German occupation. (☎41 86 76; www.notre-dame-dijon.net.) The brightly tiled towers of **Cathédrale St-Bénigne,** on pl. St-Bénigne, are visible from anywhere in town. Inside, the church features a spooky, circular crypt. (☎30 39 33. Open daily 9am-7pm. Crypt €1.) Dijon's **Estivade** (☎74 53 33; tickets under €8) brings dance, music, and theater to the city throughout July. In late summer, the weeklong **Fêtes de la Vigne** and **Folkloriades Internationales** (☎30 37 95; www.fetesdelavigne.com; tickets €10-46) celebrate the grape harvest with dance and music from around the world. ◪**Hotel Le Jacquemart ❸,** 32 r. Verrerie, offers tidy rooms. (☎60 09 60. Breakfast €6. Reception 24hr. Singles €29-53; doubles €32-63. AmEx/MC/V.) **Rue Amiral Boussin** has charming cafes, while reasonably priced restaurants line **rue Berbisey, rue Monge, rue Musette,** and **place Émile Zola.** From cours de la Gare, **trains** run to Lyon (2hr., 14 per day, €25), Nice (6-8hr., 6 per day, €88), and Paris (1¾-3hr., 15 per day, €52). The **tourist office,** in pl. Darcy, is down av. Maréchal Foch from the station. (☎08 92 70 05 58; www.dijon-tourism.com. Open daily May to mid-Oct. 9am-7pm; mid-Oct. to Apr. 10am-6pm.) **Postal Code:** 21000.

BEAUNE   ☎03 80

Wine has poured out of well-touristed Beaune (pop. 23,000), just south of Dijon, for centuries. Surrounded by the famous Côte de Beaune vineyards, the town is packed with middle-aged American tourists and wineries offering free *dégustations* (tastings). The largest of the *caves* (cellars), a 5km labyrinth of corridors with over four million bottles, belongs to **Patriarche Père et Fils,** 5-7 r. du Collège. (☎24 53 78. Open daily 9:30-11:30am and 2-5:30pm. €10; all proceeds to charity.) Oenophiles thirsty for knowledge can learn more about Côte wine-making at the **Musée du Vin,** r. d'Enfer, off pl. Général Leclerc. (☎22 08 19. Open Apr.-Nov. daily 9:30am-6pm; Dec.-Mar. W-Su 9:30am-5pm. €5.40, students €3.50.) Beaune is also home to the ◪**Hôtel-Dieu,** 2 r. de l'Hôtel-Dieu, one of France's architectural icons. A hospital built in 1443 to help the city's poor recover from the famine following the Hundred Years' War, the building is now a museum. (☎24 45 00. Open daily late Mar. to mid-Nov. 9am-7:30pm; mid-Nov. to late Mar. 9-11:30am and 2-6:30pm. Last entry 1hr. before closing. €5.60, students €4.80.) **Hôtel le Foch ❷,** 24 bd. Foch, across the ramparts from the train station, has bright blue rooms with large windows. (☎24 05 65. Singles and doubles €25, with shower €33-38; triples €45; quads €48. MC/V.) Cheap accommodations are hard to come by in Beaune, so staying in Dijon (p.344) may be a better option. **Relais de la Madeleine ❷**, 44 pl. Madeleine, features large portions of specialties like duck *pâté* with pistachio, peppered trout, and a wonderful *mousse au chocolat*—all of which can be sampled in a four-course €16 *menu*. (☎22 07 47. *Menus* from €13. Open M-Tu and F-Su noon-2pm and 7-10pm, Th noon-2pm. AmEx/MC/V.) Rent a bike at **Bourgogne Randonées**, 7 av. du 8 Septembre, near the station, and follow their route to the *caves*. (☎22 06 03. €4 per hr., €17 per day, €32 per 2 days, €90 per week. Credit card deposit required. Open M-Sa 9am-noon and 1:30-7pm, Su 10am-noon and 2-7pm. MC/V.) **Trains** go to Dijon (20-35min., 26 per day, €7-9), Lyon (1½-2hr., 10 per day, €21), and Paris (2-2½hr., 14 per day, €45-55). The **tourist office** is at 1 r. de l'Hôtel-Dieu. (☎26 21 30; www.ot-beaune.fr. Open late June to late Sept. M-Sa 9am-7pm, Su 9am-6pm; late Sept. to late June reduced hours.) **Postal Code:** 21200.

ALSACE-LORRAINE AND FRANCHE-COMTÉ

Influenced by its tumultuous past, the region's fascinating blend of French and German surfaces in the local dialects, cuisine, and architecture. Alsatian towns display half-timbered Bavarian houses, while Lorraine's wheat fields are interspersed with elegant cities. The Jura mountains in Franche-Comté offer some of France's finest cross-country skiing in winter and challenging hiking and biking trails in summer.

STRASBOURG   ☎03 88

On the Franco-German border, Strasbourg (pop. 270,000) is a city with true international character. The tower of the Gothic **■Cathédrale de Strasbourg** stretches 142m skyward; young Goethe scaled its 332 steps regularly to cure his fear of heights. Inside the cathedral, the **Horloge Astronomique** demonstrates 16th-century Swiss clockmaking wizardry daily at 12:30pm, and the **Pilier des Anges** (Angels' Pillar) depicts the Last Judgment. (Cathedral open M-Sa 7-11:40am and 12:40-7pm, Su 12:45-6pm. Tower open daily July-Aug. 8:30am-7pm; Apr.-June and Sept. 9am-6pm; Mar. and Oct. 9am-5:30pm; Nov.-Feb. 9am-4:30pm. Clock tickets for sale at the northern entrance to the cathedral; €1. Tower €4.40, students €2.20.) **Palais Rohan**, 2 pl. du Château, houses three small but excellent museums: the **Musée des Beaux-Arts**, the **Musée des Arts Décoratifs**, and the **Musée Archéologique**. (All open M and W-Su 10am-6pm. €4 each, students €2; free 1st Su of every month.)

High-quality, inexpensive hotels are all over the city, especially around the train station. Wherever you stay, reserve ahead, particularly in summer. The **Centre International d'Accueil de Strasbourg (CIARUS) ❷**, 7 r. Finkmatt, has a friendly staff and bright rooms complete with bath. From the train station, take r. du Maire-Kuss to the canal, turn left, and follow q. St-Jean. Turn left on r. Finkmatt. (☎15 27 88; www.ciarus.com. Breakfast included; other meals €5-7. Free Wi-Fi. When parliament is in session 6- to 8-bed dorms €24; 3- to 4-bed dorms €28; 2-bed dorms €31; singles €47; family rooms €24 per person. When parliament is out of session €21/€25/€28/€44/€21. MC/V.) The scenic **■La Petite France** neighborhood, especially along r. des Dentelles, is full of informal *winstubs* with Alsatian specialties such as *choucroute garnie* (spiced sauerkraut with meats). **■Bar Exils**, 28 r. de l'Ail, has leather couches and over 40 beers from €2. (☎35 52 70. Open M-F noon-4am, Sa-Su 2pm-4am. MC/V; min. €6.) Rock all night at **Le Tribord,** Ponts Couverts, a lively gay and lesbian club in a small boat. From pl. du Quartier Blanc, make a right onto the footpath by the canal in front of the Hotel du Département, and follow it to the waterside. (☎36 22 90. Beer from €3. Mixed drinks from €4. Open Th-Sa 10pm-4am). **Trains** go to: Frankfurt, GER (2-4hr., 13 per day, €52); Luxembourg, LUX (2-

3hr., 10 per day, €33); Paris (4hr., 24 per day, €47; TGV 2½hr., €63); Zürich, SWI (3hr., 4 per day, €40-47). The main **tourist office** is at 17 pl. de la Cathédrale. (☎52 28 28; www.ot-strasbourg.fr. Open daily 9am-7pm.) **Postal Code:** 67000.

 BIG BUCKS FOR BIGWIGS. Strasbourg's prices rise during EU plenary sessions. To take in the city's sights without breaking the bank, avoid visiting (in 2008) Jan. 14-17, Feb. 18-21, Mar. 10-13, Apr. 21-24, May 19-22, June 16-19, July 7-10, Sept. 1-4 and 22-25, Oct. 20-23, Nov. 17-20, and Dec. 15-18.

LA ROUTE DU VIN

The vineyards of Alsace flourish along the foothills of the Vosges from Strasbourg to Mulhouse—a region known as the *Route du Vin*. The Romans were the first to ferment Alsatian grapes, and today Alsatians sell over 150 million bottles annually. Consider staying in **Colmar** (p. 347) or **Sélestat** (p. 346), and daytripping to the smaller (and pricier) towns. The best source of info on regional *caves* is the **Centre d'Information du Vin d'Alsace**, 12 av. de la Foire aux Vins, at the Maison du Vin d'Alsace in Colmar. (☎03 89 20 16 20. Open M-F 9am-noon and 2-5pm.)

⌐ TRANSPORTATION

Buses, the most inexpensive option, run frequently from Colmar to surrounding towns, though smaller northern towns prove difficult to reach. **Car rental** from Strasbourg or Colmar expensively resolves transportation problems. Despite well marked trails and turn-offs, only those with stamina should **bike** the lengthy and often hilly roads from Colmar. **Trains** connect Sélestat, Molsheim, Barr, Colmar, and Mulhouse. Minimal sidewalks make country roads difficult to walk along.

SÉLESTAT ☎03 88

Sélestat (pop. 17,500), between Colmar and Strasbourg, is an oft-overlooked haven of good wines. Founded in 1452 and considered one of Alsace's greatest treasures, the ▓**Bibliothèque Humaniste,** 1 r. de la Bibliothèque, contains a collection of illuminated manuscripts and handwritten books produced during Sélestat's 15th-century Humanist heyday. (Open July-Aug. M and W-F 9am-noon and 2-6pm, Sa 9am-noon and 2-5pm, Su 2-5pm; Sept.-June M-F 9am-noon and 2-6pm, Sa 9am-noon. €4, students €3.) Nearby, on r. du Sel, the **Maison du Pain** reveals the history of breadmaking from 12,500 BC to the present. Take history into your own hands; a workshop in the ground-floor *pâtisserie* allows visitors to twist and bake their own pretzels. (Open Dec. daily 10am-7pm; Jan. and Mar.-Nov. Tu-F 9:30am-12:30pm and 2-6pm, Sa 9am-12:30pm and 2-6pm, Su 9am-12:30pm and 2:30-6pm. Closed Dec. 25-Jan. 7 and mid-Jan to Feb. €5, students €4.)

Hôtel des l'Ill ❸, 13 r. des Bateliers, has 15 cheerfully colored rooms with shower and TV. (☎92 91 09. Breakfast €5. Reception 7am-9pm. Check-out 10am. Singles €30; doubles €40; triples €50. AmEx/MC/V.) A local favorite, **JP Kamm ❶,** 15 r. des Clefs, has outdoor dining and a large selection of mouthwatering desserts. (☎92 11 04. Pizzas and quiches €3.50-4.70. Ice cream from €4.60; takeout orders cheaper. Open Tu and Th-F 8am-7pm, W 8:30am-7pm, Sa 8am-6pm, Su 8am-1pm. MC/V; min. €8.) From pl. de la Gare, **trains** run to Colmar (15min., 38 per day, €4) and Strasbourg (30min., 54 per day, €7). The **tourist office,** bd. Général Leclerc, in the Commanderie St-Jean, rents **bikes** (€13 per day). (☎58 87 20; www.selestat-tourisme.com. Open July-Aug. M-Sa 9:30am-12:30pm and 1:30-6:45pm, Su 10:30am-3pm; Sept.-June reduced hours.) **Postal Code:** 67600.

COLMAR
☎ 03 89

Colmar (pop. 68,000) is a great base for exploring smaller Route towns. The **Musée Unterlinden**, 1 r. d'Unterlinden, has a collection ranging from Romanesque to Renaissance, including Grünewald's *Issenheim altarpiece*, an Alsatian treasure. (Open May.-Oct. daily 9am-6pm; Nov.-Apr. W-M 9am-noon and 2-5pm. €7, students €5. MC/V; min. €8.) The **Église des Dominicains**, pl. des Dominicains, is a bare-bones showroom for Colmar's other masterpiece, Schongauer's *Virgin in the Rose Bower*. (Open June-Oct. Su-Th 10am-1pm and 3-6pm, F-Sa 10am-6pm; Apr.-May and Nov.-Dec. daily 10am-1pm and 3-6pm. €1.50, students €1.) The 10-day **Foire aux Vins d'Alsace**, the region's largest wine fair, offers concerts, free tastings, and exhibits. (☎ 03 90 50 50 50; www.foire-colmar.com. Mid-Aug. 11:30am-1:30pm €1, 1:30pm-5pm €3, after 5pm €5. Concerts €20-43.) To reach **Auberge de Jeunesse (HI) ❶**, 2 r. Pasteur, take bus #4 (dir.: Europe) to Pont Rouge. (☎ 80 57 39. Breakfast €4. Linens €4. Reception Nov. to mid-Dec. and mid-Jan. to Feb. 7-10am and 5-11pm; Apr.-Sept. 7-10am and 5pm-10:30pm. Lockout 10am-5pm. Curfew midnight, in winter 11pm. Open mid-Jan. to mid-Dec. Dorms €12; singles €17; doubles €26. €3 HI discount. MC/V.) A **Monoprix** supermarket is on pl. Unterlinden. (Open M-Sa 8am-8pm. AmEx/MC/V.) **Trains** depart pl. de la Gare for Lyon (4½-5½hr., 9 per day, €42), Paris (5¼hr., 2 per day, €52), and Strasbourg (30min., 12 per day, €10). The **tourist office** is at 4 r. d'Unterlinden. (☎ 20 68 92; www.ot-colmar.fr. Open July-Aug. M-Sa 9am-7pm, Su 10am-1pm; Sept.-June reduced hours.) **Postal Code:** 68000.

NANCY
☎ 03 83

Nancy (pop. 106,000), the city that spawned the Art Nouveau "Nancy School" in 1901, is modern Lorraine's artistic and intellectual heart. The works on display at the ▉**Musée de L'École de Nancy**, 36-38 r. du Sergent Blandan, reject straight lines, instead using organic forms to recreate aspects of the natural landscape. Take bus #122 (dir.: Villers Clairlieu) or 123 (dir.: Vandoeuvre Cheminots) to Painlevé. (☎ 40 14 86; www.ecole-de-nancy.com. Open W-Su 10:30am-6pm. €6, students €4. W students free. €8 pass to all museums.) The recently renovated ▉**place Stanislas** houses three Neoclassical pavilions, including **place de la Carrière**, a former jousting ground that Stanislas Leszczynski—Duke of Lorraine from 1737 to 1766—refurbished with Baroque architecture, angel sculptures, and wrought-iron ornaments. The collection in the **Musée des Beaux-Arts**, 3 pl. Stanislas, features works dating from the 14th century to the present, including gems by Delacroix, Monet, Picasso, Rodin, and stunning glass work by Daum. (☎ 85 30 72. Open M, W-Su 10am-6pm. €6, students €4. W students free.)

Don't let the shabby exterior of **Hôtel de L'Académie ❷**, 7 r. des Michottes, deter you; it has large, clean rooms in a convenient location. (☎ 35 52 31. Breakfast €3.50. Reception 7am-11pm. Singles €20-28; doubles €28-39. AmEx/MC/V.) Immerse yourself (or your bread) in the cheesy delights of ▉**Le Bouche à Oreille ❷**, 42 r. des Carmes. (☎ 35 17 17. Fondues €14-15. Lunch *menu* €11. Dinner *menu* €17. Open M, Sa 7-10:30pm, Tu-F noon-1:30pm and 7-10:30pm. AmEx/MC/V.) Restaurants also line **rue des Maréchaux, place Lafayette**, and **place St-Epvre**. Grab a drink along **rue Stanislas, Grand Rue**, or at **Blitz**, 76 r. St-Julien. (Beer from €2.20. Mixed drinks from €5. Open M 5:30pm-2am, Tu-Sa 2pm-2am. AmEx/MC/V; min. €7.) **Trains** depart from the station at 3 pl. Thiers for Paris (3½ hr., 27 per day, €42-50) and Strasbourg (1¼hr., 20 per day, €23). The new **TGV Est line** also connects Nancy to Paris (1½hr.). To reach the **tourist office**, head through pl. Thiers, turn left on r. Mazagran, pass through a stone archway on the right, and continue straight. (☎ 35 22 41; www.ot-nancy.fr. Open Apr.-Oct. M-Sa 9am-7pm, Su 10am-5pm; Nov.-Mar. M-Sa 9am-6pm, Su 10am-1pm.) **Postal Code:** 54000.

BESANÇON   ☎03 81

Bounded by the Doubs River on three sides and a steep bluff on the fourth, Besançon (pop. 123,000) hosts a slew of world-class museums and an active student population. Julius Caesar conquered the city in 58 BC, unaware that Vauban's 17th-century enormous **citadelle**, at the end of r. des Fusilles de la Résistance, would one day make Besançon impenetrable. More daunting than pretty, Besançon's mountaintop fortresses require an intense uphill climb to reach but reward visitors with emotionally moving displays. Within the *citadelle*, the ▓**Musée de la Résistance et de la Déportation** chronicles the Nazi rise to power and the events of WWII from a French perspective. (☎87 83 33; www.citadelle.com. Open daily July-Aug. 9am-7pm, Sept.-June reduced hours. In summer €7.80, students €6.50; in winter €7.20/6.) The ticking **Musée du Temps,** 96 Grand Rue, exhibits its clocks from Galileo's era to the present day. (☎87 81 53. Open Tu-Sa 9:15am-noon and 2-6pm, Su 10am-6pm. Tu-F €5, Sa €2.50, Su and students free.)

To reach the **Foyer Mixte de Jeunes Travailleurs (HI) ❷**, 48 r. des Cras, take a left from the train station onto r. de la Viotte, turn right on r. de l'Industrie, and right on r. de Belfort. Take bus #5 or night line A (dir.: Orchamps, 3-5 per hr., €1.05) to Les Oiseaux. The hostel offers clean rooms with private baths and free Internet in the lobby. (☎40 32 00. Breakfast included. Open Apr.-Sept. Singles €23, 2nd night €18. AmEx/MC/V.) **Rue Claude-Pouillet** and **rue des Granges** have the cheapest dining options and the best nightlife. **Au Gourmand ❷**, 5 r. Megevand, serves hearty meat and potato dishes. (☎81 40 56. Entrees €6-8. Open Tu-F 11:30am-1:45pm and 6:45-8:30pm, Sa 6:45-8:30pm. Reserve ahead. MC/V.)

Trains (☎08 36 35 35 35) leave av. de la Paix for Dijon (1hr., 34 per day, €13), Paris (2½hr., 9 per day, €49), and Strasbourg (3hr., 9 per day, €30). Monts Jura **buses**, with an office in the train station (☎08 25 00 22 44), go to Pontarlier (1hr., 8 per day, €7.50). From the station, walk downhill; follow av. de la Paix as it turns into av. Maréchal Foch and continue to the left as it becomes av. de l'Helvétie. The **tourist office,** 2 pl. de la 1ère Armée Française, will be in the park on the right. (☎80 92 55; www.besancon-tourisme.com. Open June-Sept. M 10am-7pm, Tu-Sa 9:30am-7pm, Su 10am-5pm; Oct.-May reduced hours.) **Postal Code:** 25000.

PONTARLIER AND THE HAUT-JURA MOUNTAINS   ☎03 81

The sedate town of Pontarlier (pop. 18,400) is a good base for exploring the oft-overlooked Haut-Jura Mountains. The Jura are best known for **cross-country skiing;** nine trails cover every skill level. (Day pass available at the Le Larmont and Le Malmaison trails; €6, under 17 €3.50.) Le Larmont is the closest **Alpine ski** area (☎46 55 20). In summer, **fishing, hiking,** and **mountain biking** are popular. There's a mountain bike departure point to the north off r. Pompée, and another to the south, about 2km west of Forges. Hikers can choose between the **GR5**, an international 262km trail accessible from Le Larmont, and the **GR6**, which leads to a narrow valley and dramatic château. To get to **Camping du Larmont ❶**, on r. du Tolombief, from the station, turn right onto Rocade Georges Pompidou, cross the river, and bear left on r. de l'Industrie. Take the first right onto av. de Neuchâtel and follow the signs. (☎46 23 33; www.camping-pontarlier.fr. Reception July-Aug. daily 8am-10pm, Sept.-June M-Sa 9am-noon and 5-8pm, Su 9am-noon. July-Aug. €3.20 per adult, €2 per child, €7.50 per tent and car; Sept.-June €3.20/2/6.50. 2-person chalets July-Aug. €60 per day, €405 per week; Sept.-June €53/315. Extra person €5 per night. 6 person max. Electricity Sept.-June €6; July-Aug. €4. MC/V.) Monts Jura **buses** (☎39 88 80) run to Besançon (1hr., 5 per day, €8). The **tourist office** is at 14bis r. de la Gare. (☎46 48 33; www.pontarlier.org. Open July-Aug. M-Sa 9am-7pm, Su 10am-noon; Sept.-June M-Sa 9am-12:30pm and 1:30-6pm.) **Postal Code:** 25300.

RHÔNE-ALPES AND MASSIF CENTRAL

Natural architecture is the Alps' real attraction. The curves of the Chartreuse Valley rise to rugged crags in the Vercors range and crescendo at Europe's highest peak, Mont Blanc (4807m). From bases like Chamonix, winter skiers enjoy some of the world's most challenging slopes. In summer, hikers take over the mountains, seeking pristine vistas and clear air. As a rule, the farther into the mountains you want to go, the harder it is to get there, especially outside of ski season.

LYON ☎04 78

Ultra-modern, ultra-friendly Lyon (pop. 453,000) elicits cries of "Forget Paris!" from backpackers. Its location—at the confluence of the Rhône and Saône rivers and along an Italian road—earned Lyon (then Lugdunum) its place as Roman Gaul's capital. The city continues to be a major transportation and trading hub today, also known for its financial center, Renaissance quarter, and fantastic restaurants. If the way to your heart is through your stomach, Lyon will have you at *"bon appetit."*

▐ TRANSPORTATION

Flights: Aéroport Lyon-Saint-Exupéry (☎08 26 80 08 26). **Satobuses/Navette Aéroport** (☎72 68 72 17) **shuttles** to Gare de la Part-Dieu, Gare de Perrache, and subway stops Grange-Blanche, Jean Macé, and Mermoz Pinel (every 20min., €8.60). **Air France**, 10 q. Jules Courmont, 2ème (☎08 20 32 08 20), has 10 daily flights to Paris's Orly and Charles de Gaulle airports (from €118). Open M-Sa 9am-6pm.

Trains: The **TGV**, which stops at the airport, is cheaper than daily flights to Paris. Trains passing through Lyon stop at **Gare de la Part-Dieu**, 5 pl. Béraudier (M: Part-Dieu), on the Rhône's east bank. Info desk open daily 5am-12:45am. Ticket window open M-Th and Sa 5:15am-11pm, F and Su 5:15am-midnight. Trains terminating in Lyon continue to **Gare de Perrache**, pl. Carnot (M: Perrache). Open daily 4:45am-12:30am. Ticket window open M 5am-10pm, Tu-Sa 5:30am-10pm, Su 7am-10pm. SNCF trains leave both stations for: **Dijon** (2hr., 1 per hr., €26); **Grenoble** (1½hr., 1 per hr., €18); **Marseille** (1½hr., 1 per hr., €44); **Nice** (6hr., 3 per day, €62); **Paris** (2hr., 17 per day, €60); **Strasbourg** (5½hr., 6 per day, €49); **Geneva, SWI** (4hr., 6 per day, €23). The **SNCF Boutique** is at 2 pl. Bellecour. Open M-F 9am-6:45pm, Sa 10am-6:30pm.

Buses: On the Gare de Perrache's lowest level and at Gorge de Loup in the 9ème. (☎72 61 72 61) It's almost always cheaper, faster, and simpler to take the train. Domestic companies include **Philibert** (☎72 75 06 06). **Eurolines** (☎72 56 95 30; www.eurolines.fr) travels out of France; office on the main floor of Perrache open M-Sa 9am-9pm.

Local Transportation: TCL (☎08 20 42 70 00; www.tcl.fr) has info offices at both bus stations and all major metro stops. Pocket maps available from any TCL branch. The efficient **métro** system runs 5am-12:20am, as do **buses** and **trams**. Tickets valid for all forms of mass transport. Tickets €1.50, *carnet* of 10 €13; student discount includes 10 passes valid for 1 month €10.80. Pass valid 1hr. in 1 dir., connections included. The *Ticket Liberté* day pass (€4.40) allows for unlimited use of mass transit.

✸▮ ORIENTATION AND PRACTICAL INFORMATION

Lyon is divided into nine **arrondissements** (districts). The 1er, 2ème, and 4ème lie on the **presqu'île** (peninsula), which juts toward the **Saône** River to the west and the **Rhône** to the east. Starting in the south, the 2ème (the *centre-ville*) includes the **Gare de Perrache** and **place Bellecour**. The nocturnal **Terreaux** neighborhood, with its sidewalk cafes and student-packed bars, makes up the 1*er*. Farther north, the *presqu'île* widens into the 4*ème* and the famous **Croix-Rousse**. The main pedestrian roads on the *presqu'île* are **rue de la République** and **rue Victor Hugo**.

> **Tourist Office:** In the **Pavilion**, pl. Bellecour, 2*ème* (☎04 72 77 69 69; www.lyon-france.com). M: Bellecour. **Lyon City Card** grants unlimited public transport and entry to museums, tours, and river boat cruises. 1-day pass €19; 2-day €29; 3-day €39. Open June-Sept. M-Sa 9:30am-6:30pm, Su 10am-5:30pm; Oct.-May reduced hours. MC/V.

> **Police:** 47 r. de la Charité (☎42 26 56). M: Perrache.

> **Hospital:** Hôpital Hôtel-Dieu, 1 pl. de l'Hôpital, 2*ème*, near q. du Rhône. City hospital line ☎08 20 69.

> **Post Office:** pl. Antonin Poncet, 2*ème* (☎04 72 40 65 22), near pl. Bellecour. **Postal Code:** 69001-69009; last digit indicates *arrondissement*.

■ ACCOMMODATIONS

September is Lyon's busiest month; it's easier and cheaper to find a place in summer but still wise to reserve ahead. A room less than €30 is rare. Low-end hotels are east of **place Carnot**. There are inexpensive options north of **place des Terraux**. Watch out for budget-breaking accommodations in *vieux* Lyon.

> ▨ **Auberge de Jeunesse (HI),** 41-45 montée du Chemin Neuf, 5*ème* (☎15 05 50). M: Vieux Lyon. A grassy terrace and bar draw international backpackers. Breakfast and linens included. Laundry €5. Internet €5 per hr. Max. 6-night stay. Reception 24hr. Reserve ahead. Dorms €17. HI members only. MC/V. ❶

> ▨ **Hôtel Iris,** 36 r. de l'Arbre Sec, 1*er* (☎39 93 80; www.hoteliris.freesurf.fr). M: Hôtel de Ville. This convent-turned-hotel has a tranquil feel in a prime location. Creatively decorated rooms reveal its owner's artistic eye. Breakfast €6. Reception 8am-8:30pm. Reserve ahead in summer. Singles and doubles €40-42, with bath €48-50. MC/V. ❸

> **Hôtel d'Ainay,** 14 r. des Remparts d'Ainay, 2*ème* (☎42 43 42). M: Ampère-Victor Hugo. Offers spacious rooms with private bath in a great location. Breakfast €5. Reception 24hr. Singles €27, with shower €42; doubles €32/48. Extra bed €8. MC/V. ❸

◗ FOOD

The galaxy of Michelin stars adorning Lyon's restaurants confirms its status as the gastronomic capital of France. It's difficult to go wrong when it comes to cuisine here, though most dinner *menus* don't dip below €16. Equally appealing alternatives can be found on **rue St-Jean, rue des Marronniers,** and **rue Mercière** for less during lunchtime. Ethnic restaurants center near **rue de la République.** There are **markets** on the quais of the Rhône and Saône (open Tu-Su 8am-1pm).

> ▨ **Le Sud,** 11 pl. Antonin Poncet, 2*ème* (☎04 72 77 80 00). M: Bellecour. Mediterranean fare in a casual dining room. Seafood from €15. *Menus* €19-22. Open daily noon-2:30pm and 7-11pm, F-Sa noon-2:30pm and 7pm-midnight. AmEx/MC/V. ❹

> ▨ **Chez Mounier,** 3 r. des Marronniers, 2*ème* (☎37 79 26). M: Bellecour. Despite small portions, a friendly staff and great prices make this restaurant a good choice. 4-course *menus* €11-20. Open Tu-Sa noon-2pm and 7-11pm, Su noon-1:30pm. MC/V. ❸

> **Chabert et Fils,** 11 r. des Marronniers, 2*ème* (☎37 01 94). M: Bellecour. A well-loved *bouchon*, 1 of 4 run by the same family. *Museau de bœuf* (cow tongue) is one of many unique *lyonnais* concoctions on the €18 *menu*. Lunch *menus* €8-13. Dinner *menus* €18-34. Open daily noon-2pm and 7-11pm, F-Sa until 11:30pm. MC/V. ❸

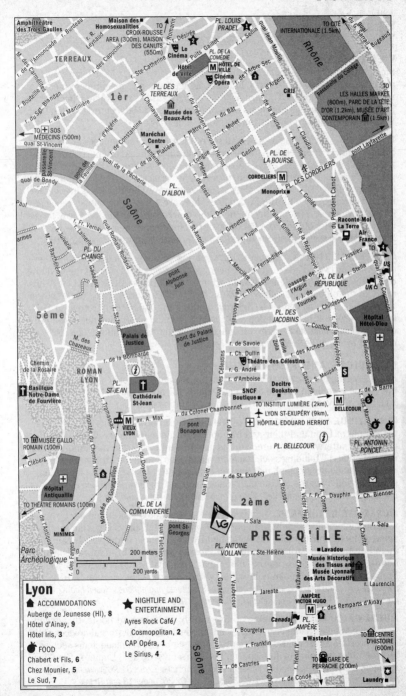

FRANCE

👁 SIGHTS

VIEUX LYON

Stacked against the Saône at the foot of the Fourvière hill, *vieux* Lyon's narrow streets are home to lively cafes, hidden passageways, and magnificent medieval and Renaissance homes. The striking *hôtels particuliers*, with their delicate carvings and ornate turrets, sprang up between the 15th and 18th centuries when Lyon was the center of Europe's silk and printing industries.

TRABOULES. The distinguishing features of *vieux* Lyon townhouses are their **traboules,** tunnels connecting parallel streets through a maze of courtyards, often with vaulted ceilings and exquisite spiral staircases. Although their original purpose is debated, the *traboules* were often used to transport silk safely from looms to storage rooms. During WWII, the passageways proved invaluable as info-gathering and escape routes for the Resistance. Many are open to the public, especially in the morning. A 2hr. tour beginning at the tourist office is the ideal way to see them. The tourist office has a list of open *traboules* and their addresses. *(English-language tours in summer every few days at 2:30pm; in winter hours vary. €9, students €5.)*

CATHÉDRALE ST-JEAN. The cathedral's soaring columns dominate the southern end of *Vieux* Lyon. Paris might have been worth a Mass, but Lyon got the wedding cake; it was here that Henri IV met and married Maria de Médici in 1600. While many of the older stained-glass windows depict Bible stories, some of the newer geometric ones replaced those destroyed during the Nazis' hasty retreat in 1944. Inside, every hour between noon and 4pm, mechanical angels pop out of the 14th-century ⬛astronomical clock in a reenactment of the Annunciation. *(Open M-F 8am-noon and 2-7:30pm, Sa-Su 8am-noon and 2-7pm. Free.)*

FOURVIÈRE AND ROMAN LYON

Fourvière Hill, the nucleus of **Roman Lyon,** towers above the old city and is accessible via the rose-lined **Chemin de la Rosaire** and, for non-walkers, **la ficelle** (funicular), which leaves from the *vieux* Lyon Metro station.

⬛ **BASILIQUE NOTRE-DAME DE FOURVIÈRE.** During the Franco-Prussian War, the people of Lyon and their archbishop prayed fervently to the Virgin Mary for protection; afterward, they erected this magnificent basilica in her honor. Locals maintain that the building's octagonal turrets makes it look like *"un éléphant renversé"* (upside-down elephant). Inside, colorful mosaics depict the life of Mary and other religious scenes, such as Joan of Arc at Orléans. *(Behind the esplanade at the top of the hill. Chapel open daily 7am-7pm. Basilica open daily 8am-7pm.)*

MUSÉE DES BEAUX-ARTS. This converted palace takes visitors on a whirlwind tour through diverse exhibits: an archaeological wing displays Egyptian sarcophagi and Roman busts while distinguished Dutch, French, and Spanish paintings including works by Monet, Renoir, and Picasso line the third-floor walls. Other highlights include a fascinating Islamic art display and an unbelievably large French, Greek, and Roman coin collection. *(20 pl. des Terreaux. ☎04 72 10 17 40; www.mairie-lyon.fr. Open M and W-Su 10am-6pm. Sculptures and antiques closed noon-2:15pm; paintings closed 1-2:15pm. €6, under 26 €4, students free. MC/V.)*

MUSÉE GALLO-ROMAIN. Taking up five mostly underground floors, this expansive, fascinating museum is also highly educational. History buffs and novices alike will appreciate a vast collection of mosaics and statues, and unique items such as a bronze tablet inscribed with a speech by Lyon's favorite son, Emperor Claudius. Artifacts are mostly labeled in English and French. *(☎72 38 81 90; www.musees-gallo-romains.com. Open Tu-Su 10am-6pm. €3.80, students €2.30; under 18 and Th free.)*

LA CROIX-ROUSSE AND THE SILK INDUSTRY

Though mass silk manufacturing is based elsewhere today, Lyon is proud of its historical dominance of the industry in Europe. The city's Croix-Rousse district, a steep, uphill walk from pl. Terreaux, houses the vestiges of its silk-weaving days; Lyon's few remaining silk workers still create delicate handiwork, reconstructing and replicating rare patterns for museum and château displays.

■ **LA MAISON DES CANUTS.** The silk industry lives on at this Croix-Rousse workshop, which provides the best intro to Lyon's *canuts* (silk weavers). The weavers specialize in two methods of embroidery—both impossible to automate—and still use 19th-century looms. Scarves cost €32 or more, but silk enthusiasts can purchase a handkerchief for €9. *(10-12 r. d'Ivry, 4ème. ☎28 62 04. Open Tu-Sa 10am-6:30pm. €5, students €2.50, under 12 free. English-language tours daily at 11am and 3:30pm.)*

MUSÉE HISTORIQUE DES TISSUS. Clothing and textile fanatics will enjoy the rows of extravagant 18th-century dresses and 4000-year-old Egyptian tunics displayed here. Other highlights include scraps of Byzantine cloth and silk wall-hangings resembling stained glass. The neighboring **Musée des Arts Décoratifs,** housed in an 18th-century *hôtel* has rooms showcasing clocks, furniture, painted plates, and silverware from the Renaissance to the present. *(34 r. de la Charité, 2ème. M: Ampère Victor Hugo. ☎38 42 00. Tissus open Tu-Su 10am-5:30pm. Arts Décoratifs open Tu-Su 10am-noon and 2-5:30pm. €5, students €3.50, under 18 free; includes both museums.)*

EAST OF THE RHÔNE AND MODERN LYON

Lyon's newest train station and monstrous space-age mall form the core of the ultra-modern Part-Dieu district. Locals call the commercial **Tour du Crédit Lyonnais** *"le Crayon"* for its unintentional resemblance to a giant pencil standing on end. Next to it, the shell-shaped **Auditorium Maurice Ravel** hosts major cultural events.

CENTRE D'HISTOIRE DE LA RÉSISTANCE ET DE LA DÉPORTATION. Housed in a building where Nazis tortured detainees during the Occupation, the museum presents documents, photos, and films about Lyon's role in the Resistance. Audio tours lead visitors through displays of heartbreaking letters and inspiring biographies. *(14 av. Berthelot, 7ème. M: Jean Macé. ☎72 23 11. Open W-F 9am-5:30pm, Sa-Su 9:30am-6pm. €4, students €2, under 18 free; includes audio tour in 3 languages.)*

MUSÉE D'ART CONTEMPORAIN. This extensive mecca of modern art, video, and high-tech installations resides in the futuristic **Cité International de Lyon,** a supermodern complex with shops, theaters, and Interpol's world headquarters. All of its exhibits are temporary—even the walls are rebuilt for each display. *(Q. Charles de Gaulle, next to Parc de la Tête d'Or, 6ème. Take bus #4 from M: Foch. ☎04 72 69 17 17; www.moca-lyon.org. Open W-Su noon-7pm. €5, students €2, under 18 free.)*

◙ NIGHTLIFE

Nightlife in Lyon is fast and furious. The best late-night spots are **riverboat dance clubs** docked by the Rhône's east bank. Students buzz in and out of tiny, intimate bars on **rue Ste-Catherine** (1er) before hitting up the clubs. For a more mellow (and expensive) evening, head to the **jazz and piano bars** off **rue Mercerie.** *Lyon Libertin* (€2) lists hot nightlife venues. For tips on gay nightlife, pick up *Le Petit Paumé.*

■ **Ayers Rock Café,** 2 r. Désirée, 1er (☎08 20 32 02 03). M: Hôtel de Ville. This Aussie bar is a cacophony of loud rock music and wild bartenders drumming on the hanging lights for twentysomethings. Bouncers can be selective. Open daily 9pm-3am. Next door and with the same owners, slightly more chic **Cosmopolitan,** 4 r. Désirée (☎08 20 32 02 03) serves New York-themed drinks. Both bars shots €3; mixed drinks from €7. Tu student nights; happy hour 8pm-3am. Open M-Sa 8pm-3am. MC/V.

Le Sirius, across from 4 q. Augagneur, 3*ème* (☎71 78 71; www.lesirius.com). M: Guillo-
tière. A young, international crowd packs the lower-level dance floor and bar of this cargo ship-
themed riverboat. Open Tu-Sa 6pm-3am.

CAP Opéra, 2 pl. Louis Pradel, 1*er*. A popular gay pub, with red lights to match the
Opéra next door. A mellow early evening crowd spills onto the lively stairs outside as
night descends. Occasional *soirées à thème*. Open daily 9am-3am. Cash only.

GRENOBLE   ☎04 76

Young scholars from all corners of the globe including sizable North and West
African populations meet in Grenoble (pop. 168,000), a dynamic city whose surrounding snow-capped peaks are cherished by both athletes and aesthetes.

▐▌ TRANSPORTATION AND PRACTICAL INFORMATION. Trains leave pl. de
la Gare for: Lyon (1½hr., 30 per day, €18); Marseille (4-5½hr., 15 per day, €37);
Nice (5-6½hr., 5 per day, €57); Paris (3hr., 9 per day, €70). **Buses** leave from left of
the train station for Geneva, SWI (3hr., 1 per day, €26). The **tourist office** is at 14 r.
de la République. (☎42 41 41; www.grenoble-isere.info. Open M-Sa 9am-6:30pm,
Su 10am-1pm and 2-5pm.) **Postal Code:** 38000.

▐▌ ACCOMMODATIONS AND FOOD. From the tourist office, follow pl. Ste-
Claire to pl. Notre-Dame and take r. du Vieux Temple on the right to reach ▨**Le Foyer
de l'Étudiante ❶,** 4 r. Ste-Ursule, which serves as a student dorm during most of the
year, but opens its large, modern rooms to co-ed travelers from June to August. (☎42
00 84. Laundry €2.20. Free Wi-Fi. Singles €15; doubles €24.) *Grenoblaise* restaurants
cater to locals around **place de Gordes,** while Italian eateries and cheap pizzerias line
quai Perrière across the river. *Pâtisseries* and North African joints center around **rue
Chenoise** and **rue Lionne,** between the pedestrian area and river. Cafes and smaller
bistros cluster around **place Notre-Dame** and **place St-André,** in the *vieille ville*. **Tête à
l'Envers ❸,** 12 r. Chenoise, serves international cuisine. (☎51 13 42. *Plat du jour* €11.
Dessert platter €10. Guess 5 of the 6 exotic flavors on the dessert platter for a free coffee or *digestif*. Open Tu-F noon-3pm and 7:30pm-1am, Sa 7:30pm-1am. MC/V.)

▐▌ SIGHTS AND ENTERTAINMENT. Téléphériques (cable cars) depart from
q. Stéphane-Jay every 10min. for the 16th-century **Bastille,** a fort perched 475m
above the city. (Open July-Aug. M 11am-12:15am, Tu-Su 9:15am-12:15am; Sept.-
June reduced hours. €4, students €3.30; round-trip €5.80/4.70.) After enjoying
the view, you can walk down **Parc Guy Pape,** through the fortress's other end, to
the **Jardin des Dauphins** (1hr.). Cross Pont St-Laurent and go up Montée Chalem-
ont to reach the **Musée Dauphinois,** 30 r. Maurice Gignoux, which has exhibits on
the history of skiing. (Open M and W-Su June-Sept. 10am-7pm; Oct.-May 10am-
6pm. Free.) The ▨**Musée de Grenoble,** 5 pl. de Lavelette, houses one of France's
most prestigious art collections. (☎63 44 44; www.museedegrenoble.fr. Open
daily 10am-6:30pm. €5, students €2.) Grenoble's biggest and most developed
ski areas are to the east in **Oisans;** the **Alpe d'Huez** has 250km of trails. (Tourist
office ☎11 44 44, ski area 80 30 30.) The **Belledonne** region, northeast of Grenoble, has a lower elevation and lower prices; its most popular ski area is **Cham-
rousse.** (Tourist office ☎89 92 65. Lift tickets €26 per day, €149 per week.)
Grenoble's funky night scene can be found between **place St-André** and **place
Notre-Dame.** International students and twentysomethings mix it up at **Le
Couche-Tard,** 1 r. du Palais. (Mixed drinks €2.50. Happy hour M-W 7-11pm, Th-Sa
7-9pm. Open M-Sa 7pm-2am. AmEx/MC/V.)

ANNECY
☎ 04 50

With cobblestone streets, romantic canals, and a turreted castle, Annecy (pop. 53,000), the "Venice of the Alps," seems more like a fairy tale than a modern city. A 13th-century château in the *vieille ville*, the **Palais de l'Isle** served as a prison for WWII Resistance fighters. (☎33 87 30. Open June-Sept. daily 10:30am-6pm; Oct.-May M, W-Su 10am-noon and 2-5pm. €3.30, students €1.) Award-winning floral displays in the **Jardin de l'Europe** are Annecy's pride and joy. In summer, its **lake** is a popular windsurfing and kayaking spot, particularly along the **plage d'Albigny.** Annecy's Alpine forests have excellent hiking and biking trails. One of the best hikes begins within walking distance of the *vieille ville* at the **Basilique de la Visitation,** while a scenic 30km *piste cyclable* (bike route) hugs the lake's eastern shore.

Reach the clean █**Auberge de Jeunesse "La Grande Jeanne" (HI) ❷**, rte. de Semnoz, via the *ligne d'été* bus in summer (dir.: Semnoz; €1) from the train station, or take bus #6 (dir.: Marquisats) from the station to Hôtel de Police, turn right on av. du Tresum, and follow signs to Semnoz. (☎45 33 19; annecy@fuaj.org. Breakfast and linens included. Internet €2 per 20min. Reception 7am-11pm. Open mid-Jan. to Nov. 4- and 5-bed dorms with showers €18. MC/V.) **Place Ste-Claire** has morning **markets** (Tu, F, Su 8am-noon) and some of the city's most charming restaurants. At **La Bastille ❸**, 4 q. des Vieilles Prisons, sample *savoyard* specialties from its canalside terrace. (☎45 09 37. *Plats* €9-14. *Menus* €14-19. Open M-F 11am--2:30pm and 6-10:30pm, Sa-Su 11am-2:30pm and 6-11pm. MC/V.) **Trains** run from pl. de la Gare to: Chamonix (2½hr., 7 per day, €20); Grenoble (€1½hr., 8 per day, €16); Lyon (2½hr., 8 per day, €22); Nice (7-9hr., 6 per day, €86); Paris (4hr., 7 per day, €85). Autocars Frossard **buses** (☎45 73 90) leave from next to the station for Geneva, SWI (1¼hr., 2-3 per day, €10). From the train station, walk one block down r. de la Gare, turn left onto r. Vaugelas for four blocks, and enter the Bonlieu shopping mall to reach the **tourist office,** 1 r. Jean Jaurès, in pl. de la Libération. (☎45 00 33; www.lac-annecy.com. Open June-Aug. M-Sa 9am-6:30pm, Su 9am-12:30pm and 1:45-6:30pm; Sept. to mid-Oct. and Mar.-May daily 9am-12:30pm and 1:45-6pm; late Oct.-Feb. M-Sa 9am-12:30pm and 1:45-6pm.) **Postal Code:** 74000.

CHAMONIX
☎ 04 50

The site of the first Winter Olympics in 1924 and home to Europe's highest peak (**Mont Blanc;** 4807m), Chamonix (pop. 10,000) draws outdoor enthusiasts from around the world. Whether you're climbing its mountains or skiing down them, be cautious—steep grades and potential avalanches make the slopes challenging and dangerous. The pricey █**Aiguille du Midi téléphérique** (cable car) offers a knuckle-whitening ascent over snowy forests and cliffs to a needlepoint peak, revealing a fantastic panorama from 3842m. (☎08 92 68 00 67. Round-trip €37.) Bring your passport to continue via gondola to **Helbronner, ITA** for views of three countries, the **Matterhorn** and Mont Blanc. (Open May-Sept. Round-trip €54; includes Aiguille du Midi.) To the south of Chamonix, **Le Tour-Col de Balme** (☎54 00 58; day pass €37), above the village of **Le Tour,** draws beginners and intermediate **skiers,** while **Les Grands Montets** (☎54 00 71; day pass €37), to the north, is the *grande dame* of Chamonix skiing, with advanced terrain and **snowboarding** facilities. Chamonix has 350km of **hiking;** the tourist office has a map (€4) with departure points and estimated duration of all trails, though some are accessible only by cable car.

Chamonix's *gîtes* (mountain hostels) are cheap, but fill up fast; call ahead. From the train station, walk down av. Michel Croz and turn onto r. du Docteur Paccard for **Gîte le Vagabond ❶**, 365 av. Ravanel le Rouge, where a young group of Brits provide bunk rooms with stone walls and a popular bar. (☎53 15 43; www.gitevagabond.com. Climbing wall. Breakfast €5. Linens €5. Free Wi-Fi. Dorms €15. Credit card deposit. MC/V.)

FRANCE

LOST IN TRANSLATION

Hollywood movies and American TV may have captivated an enthusiastic French market, but there's often little rhyme or reason regulating the translation of their titles:

Lolita in Spite of Myself (*Mean Girls*): Nabokov and Lindsay Lohan: the perfect pop culture union.

The Counter Attack of the Blondes (*Legally Blond*): Perhaps a little aggressive for a movie about Reese Witherspoon and handbags?

Sexy Dance (*Step Up*): If broken toenails and tortured soles (souls?) define your foot fetish, then sure, poor players stumbling over pirouettes is erotic.

The Little Champions (*Mighty Ducks*): From the Flying V to the quack chant, doesn't the *canard* hold this movie together?

Rambo (*Rambo*): Some words just transcend linguistic and cultural lines.

The Man who would Murmur at the Ears of Horses (*The Horse Whisperer*): Just in case there was any ambiguity in the original title.

A Day with No End (*Groundhog Day*): If you don't get the Groundhog Day reference, this is going to be a long movie.

Lost in Translation (*Lost in Translation*): Apparently this one wasn't.

–Vinnie Chiappini

Restaurants and nightlife center around **Rue du Docteur Paccard** and **Rue des Moulins**. Leaving from pl. de la Gare, **trains** (☎35 36) usually connect through St-Gervais to: Annecy (1½hr., 8 per day, €13); Lyon (3½hr., 7 per day, €29); Paris (5-8hr., 6 per day, €75-95); Geneva, SWI (4½hr., 2 per day, €51). Société Alpes Transports **buses** (☎53 01 15) leave the train station for Geneva, SWI (1½hr., 1-5 per day, €35). Local buses (€1.50) connect to ski slopes and hiking trails. From the station, follow av. Michel Croz, turn left on r. du Dr. Paccard, and take the first right to reach the **tourist office**, 85 pl. du Triangle de l'Amitié. (☎53 00 24; www.chamonix.com. Free Wi-Fi. Open daily 8:30am-7pm.) **Postal Code:** 74400.

LE MONT-DORE ☎04 73

Le Mont-Dore ("luh mohn dohr"; pop. 1700), sits besides a dormant volcano. Only 3.5km from town, Le Puy de Sancy, the Massif's highest peak, is a skiing and hiking mecca. First channeled by Romans, Le Mont-Dore's *thermes* (hot springs) have attracted visitors for centuries. The **Établissement Thermal,** 1 pl. du Panthéon. Today, entertains *curistses* with a French-language tour of the *thermes*, providing a free *douche nasale gazeuse*, a blast of carbon and helium that effectively ▨clears sinuses. (☎65 05 10. Tours late Apr.-late Oct. M-Sa 4 per day; €4.)

Over 650km of trails lace the region's dormant volcanic mountains. Those planning a multi-day hike should consult the tourist office and leave an itinerary with the **peloton de montagne** (mountain police; ☎65 04 06), r. des Chasseurs or Puy de Sancy's base. Little more than dirt paths, some trails may be unmarked. Be sure to check weather reports-mist in the valley often signifies hail or snow in the peaks. For all the views without all the exertion, the **téléphérique** runs from the base by the hostel to a station below the Puy de Sancy; a 10min. climb up wooden stairs leads to the summit. (☎08 20 82 09 48. 5 per hr. €6, children €5; round-trip €8/6. MC/V.) The **funicular** departs from near the tourist office to Salon des Capucins, a rocky outcropping above town. (3 per hr. €4, under 10 €3; round-trip €5/4. MC/V.) The funicular and *téléphérique* can be used as launching points for many hikes. A few hundred meters to the right of *téléphérique* #2, the path up **Puy de Sancy** (round-trip 6.2km, 3hr., 555m vertical) culminates in a spectacular 360° view. Hikers should be careful, though, as the trail borders steep drop offs. The hike to ▨**La Grande Cascade** (round-trip 4km, 1½hr., 222m ascent) starts from the center of town and ends above the area's largest falls (30m).

Skiers and **snowboarders** encounter smaller crowds than elsewhere in France. A network of ski trails covers much of the Massif du Sancy; skiers can also venture down the other side of the valley into ritzy Super-Besse. **Ski-rental shops** fill the main village (rental packages about €10-26 per day; lift tickets €19 per ½-day, €24 per day). Call the central cross-country resort (☎21 54 32) or ask at the tourist office for info on **cross-country skiing** trails.

Hôtel Artense ❷, 19 av. de la Libération, near the tourist office, has clean, comfortable rooms. (☎65 03 43; www.artense-hotel.com. Breakfast €5. Reception 8am-7pm. Open Dec.-Oct. Singles and doubles €20-40; triples with bath €40-45; quads €43-53. MC/V.) The most convenient of the town's four campsites is **Des Crouzets ❶,** av. des Crouzets, across from the train station. (☎65 21 60. Reception M-Sa 9am-noon and 3-6:30pm, Su 9:30am-noon and 4-6pm. Open mid-Dec. to mid.-Oct. €3 per person, €3.10 per tent. Electricity €4.) Le Mont-Dore restaurants take a back seat to outdoor pursuits. Streetside shops between **place de la Republique** and **place du Panthéon** offer regional specialities. Many restaurants are affiliated with a hotel and give discounts to guests. **Trains** and SNCF **buses** (☎65 00 02) run from pl. de la Gare to Paris (6hr., 2 per day, €57). The **tourist office** is on av. de la Libération, near the ice-skating rink. (☎65 20 21. Open July-Aug. M-Sa 9am-7pm, Su 10am-noon and 2-6pm; Sept.-June reduced hours.) **Postal Code:** 63240.

DORDOGNE AND LIMOUSIN

A lack of large population centers, waterfronts and well-known attractions has kept this region from the fame it deserves. The Dordogne river cuts through the region's rolling hillsides, creating a spectacular backdrop for the many castles and hilltop cities. In nearby Périgord, green countryside is splashed with yellow sunflowers, chalky limestone cliffs, and ducks paddling down shady rivers.

BOURGES
☎02 48

Once the capital of France, Bourges (pop. 75,000) attracts visitors with its flamboyant Gothic architecture, half-timbered houses, and shop-filled medieval streets. Bourges's wealth originated in 1433, when **Jacques Cœur,** Charles VII's financier, chose the city as the site for his palatial home. During the long French-language tour, you'll see more of the unfurnished **Palais Jacques Coeur,** 10bis r. Jacques Cœur, than Cœur ever did, since he was imprisoned for embezzlement before its completion. (Open July-Aug. 9:30am-noon and 2-7pm; Sept.-June reduced hours. €6.50, 18-25 €4.50, under 18 free.) Ask at the tourist office about excursions to 13 other châteaux along the **Route Jacques Cœur;** most are accessible only by car or bike. **Cathedral St-Étienne's** complex stained-glass scenes, tremendous size, and infinitely intricate facade make it Bourges's most impressive sight. (Open M-Sa Apr.-Sept. 8:30am-7:15pm; Oct.-Mar. 9am-5:45pm. Closed Su morning for mass. Free. Crypt and tower €6.50, students €4.50.) To get from the station to the well-kept **Auberge de Jeunesse (HI) ❶,** 22 r. Henri Sellier, bear right on r. du Commerce onto r. des Arènes, which becomes r. Fernault; and cross to r. René Ménard, then turn left onto r. Henri Sellier. (☎24 58 09. HI members only. Breakfast €3.50. Reception 8-10am and 6-10pm. Dorms €13. Cash only.) **Place Gordaine** and **rue des Beaux-Arts** are lined with cheap eateries. **Trains** leave from pl. du Général Leclerc (☎08 92 35 35 35) for Paris (2hr., 8 per day, €28) and Tours (1½hr., 4 per day, €20). From the station, follow av. H. Laudier as it turns into av. Jean Jaurès; bear left on r. du Commerce, which becomes r. Moyenne and leads to the **tourist office,** 21 r. Victor Hugo. (☎23 02 60. Open Apr.-Sept. M-Sa 9am-7pm, Su 10am-6pm; Oct.-Mar. reduced hours.) **Postal Code:** 18000.

FRANCE

PÉRIGUEUX   ☎ 05 53

Périgord's capital, Périgueux (pop. 65,000) rests on the hills high above the Isle River. Rich with tradition and gourmet cuisine, Périgueux's old quarters preserve architecture from medieval and Gallo-Roman times. Périgueux's **Cathédrale St-Front**, the largest cathedral in southwestern France, is a massive Greek cross crowned by five immense Byzantine cupolas next to a belfry. The interior features beautiful chandeliers, an impressive organ, and a spectacular wooden altarpiece. (Open daily 8am-noon and 2:30-7pm.) Just down r. St-Front, the **Musée du Périgord**, 22 cours Tourny, houses one of France's most important collections of prehistoric artifacts, including a set of 2m mammoth tusks. (☎06 40 70. Open Apr.-Sept. M and W-F 10:30am-5:30pm, Sa-Su 1-6pm; Oct.-Mar. M and W-F 10am-5pm. €4, students €2, under 18 free.) The ▧**Musée Gallo-Romain**, r. Claude Bertrand, has a walkway over the excavated ruins of the Domus de Vésone, once the home of a wealthy Roman merchant. (☎05 65 60. Open July 5-Sept. 2 daily 10am-7pm; Apr.-July 4 and Sept. 3-Nov. 11 Tu-Su 10am-12:30pm and 2-6pm; Nov. 12-Jan. 6 and Feb. 7-Mar. Tu-Su 10am-12:30pm and 2-5:30pm. €5.70, under 12 €3.70. French-language tours daily July-Aug. €1. English-language audio tour €1.) Across from the train station, the welcoming owners of **Les Charentes ❷**, 16 r. Denis Papin, offer clean rooms and plenty of info about Périgord. (☎53 37 13. Breakfast €5. Reception 7am-10pm. Open early Jan.-late Dec. Reserve ahead in summer. Singles with shower €25, with TV €30, with toilet €35; doubles €30/35/40. Extra person €5. AmEx/MC/V.) **Les Barris ❹**, 2 r. Pierre Magne, a comfortable riverside hotel close to the center of town, commands spectacular views of the cathedral and *vieille ville*. (☎53 04 05; www.hoteldesbarris.com. Breakfast €6. Wi-Fi available. Singles €44; doubles €49; triples €54; quads €59; quints €64. MC/V.) ▧**Au Bien Bon ❷**, 15 r. de l'Aubergerie, serves regional specialties. (☎09 69 91. *Plats* €9-14. Lunch *menus* €10-14. Open M noon-1:30pm, Tu-F noon-1:30pm and 7:30-9:30pm, Sa 7:30-9:30pm. MC/V.) **Trains** leave r. Denis Papin for: Bordeaux (1½hr., 12 per day, €18); Lyon (6-8hr., 2 per day, €51); Paris (4-6hr., 13 per day, €57); Toulouse (4hr., 12 per day, €32-44). The **tourist office** is at 26 pl. Francheville. From the train station, turn right on r. Denis Papin, bear left on r. des Mobiles-de-Coulmierts, which becomes r. du Président Wilson, and take the next right after the Monoprix; the office will be on the left. (☎53 10 63; www.tourisme-perigueux.fr. Open June-Sept. M-Sa 9am-6pm, Su 10am-1pm and 2-6pm; Oct.-May M-Sa 9am-1pm and 2-6pm.) **Postal Code:** 24000.

SARLAT   ☎ 05 53

Sarlat (pop. 11,000), best used as a base for exploring the **Caves of Lascaux** and the Dordogne Valley (see below), also merits attention for its gorgeous medieval *centre-ville*. Accommodations have become quite expensive since the town's only hostel closed. The best option is to book a room at one of the nearby *chambres d'hôtes* (rooms €25-50; visit the tourist office for a complete list) or rough it overnight at a nearby campsite. The campground **Maisonneuve ❶**, 11km from Sarlat, provides an exceptional base from which to explore Castlenaud, Chateau des Millandes, Domme, and La Roque Gageac. (☎29 51 29; www.campingmaisonneuve.com. Reception 9am-8pm. Open Apr.-Oct. and July-Aug. €5.30 per adult, €3.60 per child under 7, €7.20 per tent and vehicle. 10-bed *gîte* €10 per person. Electricity €3.60. 10-30% discount Sept.-Oct. and Apr.-June. MC/V.) Next to Maisonneuve, **MultiTravel** bike rentals makes countryside excursions even easier. The strings of sausages hanging from the ceiling of ▧**Chez le Gaulois ❷**, 3 r. Tourny, near the tourist office, hint at the restaurant's emphasis on generous portions of excellent cuts of meat. (☎59 50 64. *Plats* €9.50-11. Open July-Aug. daily noon-2pm and 7-10pm; Sept.-June Tu-Sa 11:30am-2:30pm and 6:30-9:30pm. V.) **Trains** go from av. de la Gare to Bordeaux (2½hr., 5-8 per day, €23) and

Périgueux (3hr., 3 per day, €14). Trans-Périgord **buses** run from pl. Pasteur to Périgueux (1½hr., 1 per day, €9). The **tourist office** is off r. Tourny in the *centre-ville*. (☎31 45 45; www.sarlat-tourisme.com. Open July-Aug. M-Sa 9am-7pm, Su 10am-noon and 2-6pm; Sept.-June reduced hours.) **Postal Code:** 24200.

THE VÉZÈRES VALLEY   ☎05 53

Arguably the most spectacular cave paintings ever discovered line the **Caves of Lascaux**, "the Sistine Chapel of prehistory," near the town of **Montignac**, 25km north of Sarlat. Uncovered in 1940 by four teenagers, the caves were closed to the public in 1963 when algae and mineral deposits—nourished by visitors' breathing—threatened to ruin the paintings. **Lascaux II** replicates the original cave exactly. Although the Lascaux II drawings lack ancient mystery, the new caves—replete with paintings of 5m bulls, horses, and bison—inspire a wonder all their own. The ticket office (☎51 96 23) shares a building with Montignac's **tourist office** (☎51 82 60), on pl. Bertrand-de-Born. (Ticket office open 9am until sold out. Reserve 1 week ahead. €8.) The **train** station nearest Montignac is at Le Lardin, 10km away. From there, you can call a **taxi** (☎50 86 61). During the academic year, CFTA (☎05 55 59 01 48) runs **buses** from Périgueux and Sarlat; call or check the stations for times and prices. Numerous **campgrounds** dot the Vézères Valley near Montignac; the tourist office has a complete list. At the **Grotte de Font-de-Gaume**, 1km east of **Les Eyzies-de-Tayac** on D47, 15,000-year-old friezes are still open for viewing. (☎06 86 00; www.leseyzies.com/grottes-ornees. Open mid-May to mid-Sept. Su-F 9:30am-5:30pm; mid-Sept. to mid-May daily 9:30am-12:30pm and 2-5:30pm. English-language tours 1hr. Reserve 2-4 weeks ahead. €7, 18-25 €5.) Rooms tend to be expensive—consider staying in **Périgueux** (p.358) or check out quiet ▨**Demaison Chambre d'Hôte ❷**, rte. de Sarlat, 3min. outside of Les Eyzies-de-Tayac. From the train station, follow signs to Sarlat; the house is past the laundromat on the right. (☎06 91 43. Breakfast €5. Reserve ahead. Singles and doubles €25-36; triples and quads €48. Cash only.) The Les Eyzies-de-Tayac **tourist office** is on pl. de la Mairie. (☎06 97 05; www.leseyzies.com. Open July-Aug. M-Sa 9am-7pm, Su 10am-noon and 2-6pm; Sept. and Apr.-June M-Sa 9am-noon and 2-6pm, Su 10am-noon and 2-5pm; Oct.-Mar. M-Sa 9am-noon and 2-6pm.) From Les Eyzies, **trains** go to Paris (4-6hr., 4 per day, €59), Périgueux (30min., 6 per day, €7), and Sarlat (1hr., 2 per day, €8).

AQUITAINE AND PAYS BASQUE

At the geographical edge of both France and Spain, Aquitaine (AH-kee-tenn) and the Pays Basque (PAY-ee bahss-kuh) are diverse in landscape and culture. In Aquitaine, sprawling vineyards abound and in Pays Basque, closer to the Spanish border, the clinking of cowbells mixes with the scent of seafood. When locals aren't out enjoying the beach or mountain trails, they're relishing the regional cuisine.

BORDEAUX   ☎05 56

Though its name is synonymous with wine, the city of Bordeaux ("bohr-doh;" pop. 235,000) has more to offer than most lushes would expect. Punks and tourists and everyone in between gather on the elegant streets of the shop- and café-filled city center, while in the surrounding countryside, the vineyards and festivals of St-Emilion, Médoc, Sauternes, and Graves draw international renown. The city is filled with history, drenched in culture, and animated with student nightlife.

🖪 🖬 TRANSPORTATION AND PRACTICAL INFORMATION. Trains leave Gare St-Jean, r. Charles Domercq, for: Lyon (8-10hr., 7 per day, €61-154); Marseille (6-7hr., 10 per day, €73); Nice (9-12hr., 2 per day, €105); Paris (3hr., 15-25 per day,

€55); Toulouse (2-3hr., 10 per day, €32). From the train station, take tramway line C to pl. Quinconces (€1.30) and cross the street to reach the **tourist office**, 12 cours du 30 juillet, which arranges winery tours. (☎00 66 00; www.bordeaux-tourisme.com. Open July-Aug. M-Sa 9am-7:30pm, Su 9:30am-6:30pm; May-June and Sept.-Oct. M-Sa 9am-7pm, Su 9:30am-6:30pm; Nov.-Apr. M-Sa 9am-6:30pm, Su 9:45am-4:30pm.) **Postal Code:** 33000.

ACCOMMODATIONS AND FOOD. Backpacker-friendly ▨**Hôtel Studio ❷**, 26 r. Huguerie, has tiny, relatively clean rooms with bath, phone, and TV. (☎48 00 14; www.hotel-bordeaux.com. Breakfast €5. Reserve ahead. Singles €19-28; doubles €25-35. AmEx/MC/V.) Shiny metal and bright colors characterize rooms at the popular **Auberge de Jeunesse Barbey (HI) ❷**, 22 cours Barbey, four blocks from the Gare St-Jean in the run-down red light district. Travelers, especially those alone, should exercise caution at night. (☎33 00 70. Breakfast and linens included. Free Internet. Max. 3-night stay. Lockout 10am-4pm. Curfew 2am. Dorms €21. MC/V.)

The Bordelais's flair for food rivals their vineyard expertise. **Rue St-Remi** and **place St-Pierre** have regional specialties: *foie gras*, oysters, and *lamproie à la bordelaise* (eel braised in red wine). ▨**L'Ombrière ❸**, 14 pl. du Parlement, offers perfectly prepared French cuisine in one of the city's most beautiful squares. (☎44 82 86. *Menu* €15-20. Open daily noon-2pm and 7-11pm. MC/V.) Overload on cow decor in tiny **La Fromentine ❷**, 4 r. du Pas St-Georges, near pl. du Parlement, serving imaginatively-named *galettes* for €6-8. (☎79 24 10. 3-course *menu* €10-15. Open M-F noon-2pm and 7-10pm, Sa 7-10pm. MC/V.) Choose from over 30 French staples at **Cassolette Café ❷**, 20 pl. de la Victoire. (☎92 94 96; www.cassolette-cafe.com. *Menu* €10-12. Open daily noon-midnight. MC/V.)

SIGHTS AND ENTERTAINMENT. Nearly nine centuries after its consecration, the **Cathédrale St-André**, in pl. Pey-Berland, sits at the heart of Gothic Bordeaux. Its bell tower, the **Tour Pey-Berland**, rises 66m. (Cathedral open M 2-7pm, Tu-F 7:30am-6pm, Sa 9am-7pm, Su 9am-6pm. Tower open June-Sept. daily 10am-1:15pm and 2-6pm; Oct.-May Tu-Su 10am-12:30pm and 2-5:30pm. €5, 18-25 and seniors €3.50, under 18 with an adult free.) For the best cityscape of Bordeaux, look down from the 114m bell tower of the **Église St-Michel**. (Open June-Sept. daily 2-7pm. €2.50, under 12 free.) Back at ground level, a lively flea market sells anything from Syrian *narguilas* (hookahs) to African specialties (open daily 9am-1pm). Note that this area, like around the train station, should not be frequented alone at night. On pl. de Quinconces, the elaborate **Monument aux Girondins** commemorates guillotined Revolutionary leaders from towns bordering the Gironde. Bordeaux's opera house, the **Grand Théâtre,** conceals a breathtaking interior behind its Neoclassical facade and houses concerts, operas, and plays in fall and winter. (☎00 85 95; www.opera-bordeaux.com. Tours M-Sa 11am-6pm. Concert tickets from €8. Opera tickets up to €80. 50% discount for students and under 26.)

Bordeaux has a varied, student nightlife. For an overview, check out the free *Clubs and Concerts* brochure at the tourist office. Students and visitors pack the bars in year-round hot spots **Place de la Victoire, Place Gambetta**, and **Place Camille Julian.** Popular but cheesy **El Bodegon**, on pl. de la Victoire, draws students with cheap drinks, theme nights, and weekend giveaways. (Beer €2.80. Happy hour 6-8pm. Open M-Sa 7am-2am, Su 2pm-2am.) Decorated with flashing lights and mirrors, the fashionable gay bar **BHV**, 4 r. de l'Hôtel de Ville, is almost always full. (Beer €3.50. W theme night. Open daily 6pm-2am.)

BIARRITZ
☎05 59

Once a playground for 19th-century aristocrats, Biarritz (pop. 29,000) can still make a dent in your wallet. Luckily, its sparkling beaches are free for rich and budget travelers alike. At **Grande Plage,** thousands of bodies soak up the summer sun or surf the waves. **Plage Miramar,** just to the north, is less crowded. Facing away from Plage

Miramar, turn left along av. de l'Impératrice to reach **Pont St-Martin** for a fantastic view. The **⚑Auberge de Jeunesse (HI) ❷**, 8 r. de Chiquito de Cambo, has a welcoming staff and a lakefront location. (☎41 76 00; aubergejeune.biarritz@wanadoo.fr. Internet €3 per hr. Reception 8:30am-12:30pm and 6-10pm. Dorms €18. AmEx/MC/V.) **Rue Mazagran** and **rue du Port Vieux** have cheap, filling crepes and sandwiches. Budget airline **Ryanair** (☎08 92 23 23 75; www.ryanair.com) flies daily from Biarritz's **Aéroport de Parme**, 7 espl. de l'Europe (**BIQ;** ☎43 83 83), to Dublin, IRE, Frankfurt, GER, London, BRI, and Shannon, IRE for €32-170. **Trains** leave from Biarritz-la-Négresse (☎50 83 07), 3km from town, for Bayonne (10min.; 29 per day; €2.50, TGV €4), Bordeaux (2hr.; 14 per day; €29, TGV €26), and Paris (5hr., 12 TGV per day, €79). Local bus #2 (dir.: Sainsontan) and 9 (dir.: La Barre or St-Madeleine) run from the train station to the city center and tourist office Monday through Saturday (3 per hr., €1.20). On Sundays, bus B (dir.: Sainsontan) travels the same route (2 per hr., €1.20). To reach Biarritz on foot, keep left as you walk out of the train station. Continue on allée du Moura, which becomes av. du Président Kennedy, then turn left onto av. du Maréchal Foch the *centre-ville* (30min.). The **tourist office** is on pl. d'Ixelles. (☎22 37 10; www.biarritz.fr. Open July-Aug. daily 8am-8pm; Sept.-June M-F 9am-6pm, Sa-Su 10am-5pm.) **Postal Code:** 64200.

BAYONNE   ☎05 59

In Bayonne (pop. 42,000), France's self-proclaimed chocolate capital, visitors wander along the banks of the narrow Nive river and admire the small bridges, petite streets, and colorful shutters before heading to the nearest chocolaterie. The **⚑Musée Bonnat**, 5 r. Jacques Laffitte, showcases works by Degas, van Dyck, Goya, Rembrandt, Reubens, and Bayonnais painter Léon Bonnat. (Open May-Oct. Su-M and W-Sa 10am-6:30pm; July-Aug. Th-Tu 10am-6:30pm, W 10am-9:30pm; Nov.-Apr. daily 10am-12:30pm and 2-6pm. €6, students €3; Sept.-June free 1st Su of the month and July-Aug. free W 6:30-9:30pm.) Starting the first Wednesday in August, locals let loose during the **Fêtes Traditionnelles** (Aug. 6-10; www.fetes-de-bayonne.com).

The **⚑Hôtel Paris-Madrid ❷**, pl. de la Gare, has clean rooms and knowledgeable, English-speaking proprietors. (☎55 13 98. Breakfast €4. Reception Sept.-June daily 6:15am-1am; Oct.-May M-Sa 6:15am-1am, Su 6:15am-noon and 6pm-1am. Singles €19, with shower €27, with bath €34-49; doubles €24/28/34-49; triples and quads with bath €49-59. MC/V.) A **Monoprix** supermarket is at 8 r. Orbe. (Open M-Sa 8:30am-8pm.) **Trains** depart from pl. de la Gare for: Biarritz (10min.; 36 per day; €2.20, TGV €4); Bordeaux (2hr., 28 per day, €28); Paris (5hr., 10 TGV per day, €81); San Sebastián, SPA, via Hendaye (30min., 15 per day, €8); Toulouse (4hr., 5 per day, €37). Local STAB **buses** (☎59 04 61) depart from the Hôtel de Ville for Biarritz (buses #1, 2, and 6 run M-Sa 6:30am-8pm, lines A and B run Su 6:30am-7pm. €1.50). From the train station, take the middle fork onto pl. de la République, veer right over pont St-Esprit, pass through pl. Réduit, cross pont Mayou, and turn right on r. Bernède, which becomes av. Bonnat. The **tourist office,** pl. des Basques, is on the left. (☎42 64 64; www.bayonne-tourisme.com. Open July-Aug. M-Sa 9am-7pm, Su 10am-1pm; Sept.-June M-F 9am-6:30pm, Sa 10am-6pm.) **Postal Code:** 64100.

PARC NATIONAL DES PYRÉNÉES

Punctuated by sulfurous springs and unattainable peaks, the Pyrénées change dramatically with the seasons, never failing to impress visitors. To get a full sense of the mountains' breadth, hikers should experience both the lush French and barren Spanish sides of the Pyrénées (a 4- to 5-day round-trip hike from Cauterets).

CAUTERETS   ☎05 62

Nestled in a narrow valley on the edge of the **Parc National des Pyrénées Occidentales** (p.362)is tiny, sleepy Cauterets (pop. 1300). Cauterets's sulfuric *thermes* (hot springs) have long been instruments of healing. **Thermes de César,** av. du Docteur

Domer, still offers spring treatments today. (☎92 51 60. Open June-Sept. M-Sa 5-8pm; Sept.-June M-Sa 4-8pm and some Su. Hours may vary.) Most visitors come to Cauterets to ski and hike. **Hotel le Chantilly ❸,** 10 r. de la Raillère, one street away from the center of town, is owned by a charming Irish couple. (☎92 52 77; www.hotel-cauterets.com. Open late Dec. to Oct. Reception 7am-10pm. Breakfast €6. July-Sept. singles and doubles €34, with shower €38; triples from €42. Oct.-June singles and doubles €30, with shower €34; triples from €38. MC/V.) SNCF **buses** run from pl. de la Gare to Paris (2-3hr., 15 per day, €39-46) and Tours (1hr., 10 per day, €16) via Lourdes (1hr., 8 per day, €6.50). The **tourist office** is in pl. Foch. (☎92 50 50; www.cauterets.com. Open July-Aug. M-Sa 9am-12:30pm and 2-7pm, Su 9am-noon and 3-6pm; Sept.-June reduced hours.) **Postal Code:**65110.

◪ OUTDOOR ACTIVITIES

The **Parc National des Pyrénées Occidentales** shelters hundreds of endangered species in its snow-capped mountains and lush valleys. Touch base with the friendly **Parc National Office,** Maison du Parc, pl. de la Gare, in Cauterets, before braving the park's **ski** paths or 14 **hiking** trails. (☎92 52 56; www.parc-pyrenees.com. Open July-Aug. M-F 9:30am-noon and 2:30-7pm; Sept.-June M-F 9:30am-noon and 3-6pm. Maps €7-9.) Appropriate for a variety of skill levels, the trails begin and end in Cauterets. From there, the **GR10** (a.k.a. **circuit de Gavarnie**), which intersects most other hikes in the area, winds through Luz-St-Saveur, over the mountain, and then on to Gavarnie, another day's trek up the valley. One of the most spectacular trails follows the GR10 past the turquoise **Lac de Gaube** to the end of the glacial valley (2hr. past the *lac*), where you can spend the night at the **Refuge des Oulettes ❶.** (☎92 62 97. Open June-Sept. Dorms €19.) Other *gîtes* (shelters) in the park, usually located in towns along the GR10, cost about €11 per night.

LANGUEDOC-ROUSSILLON

With reasonable prices all over, Languedoc-Roussillon provides a great opportunity for travelers to see the south of France on a budget. Though it has been part of France since the 12th century, Languedoc preserves its rebellious spirit and its *joie de vivre* shows up in impromptu street performances and large neighborhood parties. Between the Mediterranean coast and the peaks of the Pyrénées, Roussillon inspired Matisse and Picasso and now attracts a mix of sunbathers and backpackers. The region was historically part of Catalunya, not France, and many inhabitants of Roussillon identify more with Barcelona than with Paris.

TOULOUSE ☎05 61

Vibrant, zany Toulouse (pop. 390,000) is known as *la ville en rose* (the pink city). It's the place to visit when all French towns begin to look alike. Family-owned art galleries, a diverse music scene, and independent theaters make Toulouse a university town that graduating students don't want to leave. With many museums and concert halls, France's fourth-largest city is the southwest's cultural capital.

◪◪ TRANSPORTATION AND PRACTICAL INFORMATION. Trains leave Gare
Matabiau, 64 bd. Pierre Sémard, for: Bordeaux (2-3hr., 14 per day, €33); Lyon (4½hr., 7 per day, €70); Marseille (4hr., 12 per day, €50); Paris (6hr., 12 per day, €90). The ticket office is open daily 7am-9:10pm. Eurolines, 68-70 bd. Pierre Sémard, sends **buses** to major European cities. (☎26 40 04; www.eurolines.fr. Open M-F 9:30am-12:30pm and 2-6:30pm, Sa 9:30am-12:30pm and 2-5pm.) To get

from the station to the **tourist office,** r. Lafayette, in pl. Charles de Gaulle, head straight down r. de Bayard. Veer left around pl. Jeanne d'Arc and continue on r. d'Alsace-Lorraine; the office is on the right. (☎ 11 02 22; www.ot-toulouse.fr. Open June-Sept. M-Sa 9am-7pm, Su 10:30am-12:30pm and 2-5:15pm; Oct.-May M-Sa 9am-6pm, Su 10:30am-12:30pm and 2-5pm.) **Postal Code:** 31000.

▐█ ACCOMMODATIONS AND FOOD. A member of the French League of Youth Hostels, ▰**Residence Jolimont ❶,** 2 av. Yves Brunaud, doubles as a long-term *résidence sociale* for 18- to 25-year-olds. Ping-pong tables, billiards, and a basketball court bring excitement to large, plain double rooms. (☎ 05 34 30 42 80; www.residence-jolimont.com. Breakfast M-F €2. Dinner daily €8. Linens included. Reception 24hr. Doubles €16. HI member discount €1. AmEx/MC/V.) Take bus #59 (dir.: Fenouillet) from pl. Jeanne d'Arc to camp at **Pont de Rupé ❶,** 21 ch. du Pont de Rupé, at av. des États-Unis along N20 north. (☎ 70 07 35. €13 for 2 adults and a tent, €2.80 per additional person. MC/V.) Cheap eateries on **rue du Taur,** in the student quarter, serve meals for €5.50-10. Markets (open Tu-Su 6am-1pm) line **place des Carmes, place Victor Hugo,** and **place Saint-Cyprien.** Neighborhood favorite **Jour de Fête ❷,** 43 r. du Taur, is a relaxed *brasserie* with tastes as creative as the local art decorating its brick walls. (☎ 23 36 48. *Plat du jour* €7. Open daily noon-midnight. Cash only.) Part restaurant, art gallery, and theater, **La Faim des Haricots ❸,** r. du Puits Vert, between pl. Capitole and the student quarter, is a vegetarian's heaven. *Menus* (€10-13) let you pick up to five choices from the unlimited salad, *tarte*, soup, and dessert bars. (☎ 22 49 25. Open M-W noon-2:30pm, Th-Sa noon-2:30pm and 7-10:30pm. MC/V.)

◪▐ SIGHTS AND NIGHTLIFE. The **Capitole,** a brick palace next door to the tourist office, is Toulouse's most prominent monument. The building was once home to the bourgeois *capitouls* (unofficial city magistrates) in the 12th century. (Open daily 9am-7pm. Free.) Rue du Taur leads to the **Basilique St-Sernin,** the longest Romanesque structure in the world. Its **crypt** houses holy relics from the time of Charlemagne. (☎ 21 80 45. Church open July-Sept. daily 8:30am-6:30pm; Oct.-June daily 8:30-noon and 2-6pm. Crypt open July-Sept. M-Sa 10am-5pm, Su 11:30am-5pm; Oct.-June M-Sa 10-11:30am and 2:30-5pm, Su 11:30-5pm. €2.) The 13th-century southern Gothic **Jacobin church,** 69 r. Pargaminières, entrance on r. Lakanal, houses the remains of St. Thomas Aquinas in an elevated tomb. (☎ 22 21 92; www.jacobins.mairie-toulouse.fr. Open daily 9am-7pm.) Just across the river, **Les Abbatoirs,** 76 allées Charles-de-Fitte, previously an old slaughterhouse, presents intermittent exhibits by up-and-coming artists. (☎ 51 10 60. Open Tu-Su 11am-7pm. €6, students €3.) The restored **Hôtel d'Assézat,** at pl. d'Assézat on r. de Metz, displays the **Fondation Bemberg,** a modest collection of Bonnards, Gauguins, and Pissarros. From mid-March to mid-June 2008, the museum will host an exhibit of distinguished monochromatic painting, featuring Rubens, Boucher, and Doré, among others. (☎ 12 06 89. Open Th 10am-12:30pm, Tu-W and F-Su 10am-12:30pm and 1:30-6pm. €4.60, students €2.75.) Toulouse has something to please almost any nocturnal whim, although nightlife generally caters to the students. Numerous cafes flank **place St-Georges, place St-Pierre,** and **place Capitole,** and late-night bars line **rue de la Colombette** and **rue des Filatiers.** For cheap drinks and a rambunctious atmosphere, try **Café Populaire,** 9 r. de la Colombette. (☎ 63 07 00. 13 glasses of beer €20, M 9:30pm-12:45am €13. Happy hour 7:30-8:30pm. Every 13th of the month beer €1. Open M-F 11am-2am, Sa 2pm-4am. Cash only.) The best dancing is at the spacious, touristy two-story **Bodega-Bodega,** 1 r. Gabriel Péri, just off bd. Lazare Carnot. (Beer €3. Mixed drinks €6. Tapas €5-10. Th-Sa cover €6 after 11:30pm. Open M-F and Su 7pm-2am, Sa 7pm-6am. AmEx/MC/V.)

CARCASSONNE   ☎04 68

Walking over the drawbridge and through the stone portals into Carcassonne's La Cité (pop. 46,000) is like stepping into a fairy tale; the first-century ramparts still seem to resound with the clang of armor. However, the only battles raging today are between camera-wielding visitors vying for space on the narrow streets. Built as a palace in the 12th century, the **Château Comtal,** 1 r. Viollet-le-Duc, became a citadel after the 1226 royal takeover. (☎11 70 77. 45min. English-, French-, and Spanish-language tours. Open daily Apr.-Sept. 10am-6:30pm; Oct.-Mar. 9:30am-5pm. €7.50, under 25 €4.80.) In the summer, Agglo'Bus runs **shuttles** from the bus stop across the canal from the train station to the citadel gates (☎47 82 22. Daily mid-June to mid-Sept. 9:30am-noon and 1:30-7:30pm, 4 per hr., round-trip €1.50). Converted into a fortress after the city was razed during the Hundred Years' War, the Gothic **Cathédrale St-Michel,** r. Voltaire, in the Bastide St-Louis, still has fortifications on its southern side. (Open M-Sa 7am-noon and 2-7pm, Su 9am-1pm.) Nestled in an alley in the heart of *La Cité*, the **⊠Auberge de Jeunesse (HI) ❷**, r. de Vicomte Trencavel, offers affordable comfort. (☎25 23 16; carcassonne@fuaj.org. Breakfast included. Laundry €5. Internet €3 per hr. Reception 24hr. Lockout 10am-3pm. Reservations recommended. Dorms €20; €3 HI discount. MC/V.) **⊠Maison de la Blanquette de Limoux 3,** pl. Marcou, is the best place to enjoy *cassoulet* (€11-13), a white bean stew. (☎71 66 09. 3-course menu, including *apéritif, cassoulet,* and wine €14. Open July-Aug. daily 9am-midnight; Apr.-June and Sept. to mid-Nov. Th-M 9am-midnight and Tu 9am-5pm; closed Nov. 15-Apr. 1. MC/V). Save room for crepes and other desserts offered around **place Marcou.** While Carcassonne has effervescent nightlife during the year, the city quickly falls asleep in summer when most of the regulars go to the beach. Nonetheless, several bars on **place Verdun,** in the lower city, stay open past midnight. **Le Bar à Vins,** 6 r. du Plô, where wine bar meets beer garden, remains popular and crowded in summer. (☎47 38 38. Beer €2.80-5. Wine €2 per glass. Open Feb.-Nov. daily 9am-2am; hours may vary Mar.-May and Oct. MC/V.)

    Trains (☎71 79 14) depart behind Jardin A. Chenier for: Marseille (3hr., 4 per day, €42); Nice (6hr., 4 per day, €63); Nîmes (2hr., 10 per day, €28); Toulouse (1hr., 10 per day, €13). Shops, hotels, the cathedral, and the train station are in the **Bastide St-Louis,** once known as the *basse-ville* (lower city). From the station, walk down av. de Maréchal Joffre, which becomes r. Clemençeau; after pl. Carnot, turn left on r. de Verdun to reach the **tourist office,** 28 r. de Verdun. (☎10 24 30; www.carcassonne-tourisme.com. Open July-Aug. daily 9am-7pm; Sept.-June M-Sa 9am-6pm, Su 9am-1pm.) **Postal Code:** 11000.

MONTPELLIER   ☎04 67

Occasional live music brings each street corner to life in Montpellier (pop. 225,000), southern France's most lighthearted city. The gigantic, beautifully renovated **⊠Musée Fabre,** 39 bd. Bonne Nouvelle, holds one of the largest collections of 17th- to 19th-century paintings outside Paris, with works by Delacroix, Ingres, and Poussin. The museum will host a temporary Courbet exhibit in winter 2007 and spring 2008. (☎14 83 00. Open Tu, Th-F, and Su 10am-6pm, W 1-9pm, Sa 11am-6pm. €6, with temporary exhibits €7; students €4/5.) Bd. Henri IV leads to the **Jardin des Plantes,** France's first botanical garden. (☎63 43 22. Open Tu-Su June-Sept. noon-8pm; Oct.-Mar. noon-6pm. Free.) The friendly owner of **Hôtel des Etuves ❷**, 24 r. des Etuves, keeps 13 plain, comfortable rooms with bath. (☎60 78 19; www.hoteldesetuves.fr. Breakfast €5. Reception M-Sa 6:30am-11pm, Su 7am-noon and 6-11pm. Reserve 1 week ahead. Singles €23, with TV €33; doubles €37; singles and doubles with bath €42. Cash only.) Standard French cuisine dominates Montpellier's *vieille ville*, while a number of Indian and Lebanese restaurants are on **rue des Écoles Laïques.** Behind the Crédit Lyonnaise on pl. de la Comédie, **Crêperie le Kreisker ❶**, 3 passage Bruyas, serves 80 different crepes (€1.90-6.60) topped with everything from buttered bananas to snails. (☎60 82 50. Open M-Sa 11:30am-3pm and 6:30-11pm. AmEx/MC/V.) At dusk, **rue de la Loge** fills with vendors, musicians, and stilt-walkers. The liveliest bars are in **place Jean-Jaurès.** Just off pl. de la Comédie, **Cubanito Cafe,** 13 r. de Verdun overflows with twentysomethings who salsa to Latin beats (M and Su) and hip-hop (Tu-Sa) in the back. (☎92 65 82. Mixed drinks €5. Open daily July-Aug. noon-2am; Sept.-June noon-1am. AmEx/MC/V.) Prominent gay nightlife centers around **place du Marché aux Fleurs.**

Trains leave pl. Auguste Gibert (☎08 92 35 35 35) for: Avignon (1 hr., 13 per day, €14); Marseille (2hr., 11 per day, €26); Nice (4hr., 2 per day, €48); Paris (3½hr., 12 per day, €93); Toulouse (2½hr., 13 per day, €33). The **tourist office** is at 30 allée Jean de Lattre de Tassigny. (☎60 60 60; www.ot-montpellier.fr. Open July-Sept. M-F 9am-7:30pm, Sa 10am-6pm, Su 9:30am-1pm and 2:30-6pm; Oct.-June M-F 9am-6:30pm, Sa 10am-6pm, Su 10am-1pm and 2-5pm.) **Postal Code:** 34000.

PROVENCE

If Paris boasts world-class paintings, it's only because Provence inspired them. Fierce mistral winds cut through olive groves in the north, while pink flamingoes, black bulls, and unicorn-like white horses gallop freely in the marshy south. From the Roman arena and cobblestone elegance of Arles to Cézanne's lingering footsteps in Aix-en-Provence, Provence provides a taste of *La Vie en Rose.*

MARSEILLE ☎04 91

Dubbed "the meeting place of the entire world" by Alexandre Dumas, Marseille (pop. 800,000) is a jumble of color and commotion. The vibrant hues of West African fabrics, the sounds of Arabic music, and the smells of North African cuisine punctuate a walk down its sidestreets. A true immigrant city, Marseille offers visitors a taste of multiple Mediterranean cultures, some long gone.

▐ TRANSPORTATION

Flights: Aéroport Marseille-Provence (MRS; ☎04 42 14 14 14; www.marseille.aeroport.fr). Flights to: **Corsica, Lyon** and **Paris.** Shuttle buses run to Gare St-Charles (3 per hr.; €8.50). Taxis from the *centre-ville* to airport cost €40-50.

Trains: Gare St-Charles, pl. Victor Hugo (☎08 92 35 35 35). To **Lyon** (1½hr., 21 per day, €55), **Nice** (2¾hr., 21 per day, €31), and **Paris** (3hr., 18 per day, €94).

Buses: Gare Routière, pl. Victor Hugo, near the train station. M: Gare St-Charles. To **Aix-en-Provence** (2-6 per hr. 9-11:30pm; €4.60), **Cannes** (2¼-3hr., 4 per day, €18-25), and **Nice** (2¾hr., 1 per day, €18-26). Ticket windows open M-F 6:15am-7:30pm, Sa 6:30am-6:30pm, Su 7:30am-noon and 12:45-6pm.

Ferries: SNCM, 61 bd. des Dames (☎08 25 88 80 88; www.sncm.fr). To **Corsica** (11½hr.; €35-53, students €20-40) and **Sardinia, ITA** (14½hr., €59-69/50-65). Open M-F 8am-6pm, Sa 8:30am-noon and 2-5:30pm. Prices higher June-Sept.

Local Transportation: RTM, 6 r. des Fabres (☎91 92 10; www.rtm.fr). Tickets sold at bus and metro stations (€1.70; day pass €4.50; 5- to 10-ride Carte Liberté €6-12). **Metro** runs M-Th 5am-9pm, F-Su 5am-12:30am.

Taxis: Marseille Taxi (☎02 20 20). 24hr. €20-30 to hostels from Gare St-Charles.

▟ ▞ ORIENTATION AND PRACTICAL INFORMATION

Marseille is divided along major streets into 16 *quartiers* (neighborhoods). **La Canebière,** the main artery, funnels into the **vieux port** (Old Port) to the west and

Marseille

🏠 **ACCOMMODATIONS**
Hôtel Montgrand, **11**
Hôtel Relax, **7**
Le Vertigo, **1**

🍎 **FOOD**
Au Falafel, **9**
Ivoire Restaurant, **4**
La Kahena, **3**
Le Sud du Haut, **8**

⭐ **NIGHTLIFE AND ENTERTAINMENT**
Dan Racing, **6**
New Can-Can, **2**
Poulpason, **5**
Trolleybus, **10**

TO SNCM FERRIES (50m)

TO Ⓜ JOLIETTE (50m)

quai de la Joliette

av. Robert Schuman

r. Jean-François Lecas

r. de la République

r. Moisson

r. Triggance

La Vieille Charité

r. de l'Observance

LE PANIER

r. Marchetti

Cathédrale la Major

r. de l'Evêché

r. de Petit Puits

r. de Lorette

r. du Panier

quai de la Tourette

r. des Repenties

r. du Refuge

r. des Moulins

Montée des Accoules

r. St-Pons

av. Vaudoyer

r. Caisserie

r. du lacydon

MEDITERRANEAN SEA

SQ. PROTIS

r. de la Loge

quai du Port

av. de St-Jean

⚓

← TO HARBOR ISLANDS (2km)

Mémorial des Camps de La Mort

Fort St-Jean

Vieux Port

Tunnel du Vieux Port

Jardin du Pharo

Bas Fort St-Nicolas

Théâtre National de Marseille

r. du Chantier

🔟

r. Nueve Ste-Catherine

r. des Tyans

r. de la Croix

bd. Charles Livon

r. de Suez

av. Pasteur

r. de Georges Charras

r. Papety

r. César Aleman

r. des Catalans

Fort St-Nicolas

Fort d'Entrecosteaux

Rompe St-Maurice

SQ. L. AUDEBERT

r. Robert

r. Sainte

Abbaye St-Victor

bd. de la Corderie

Tunnel

av. de la Corse

r. des Lices

r. Abbé d'Assy

promenade de la corniche du Président J. F. Kennedy

r. du Cpt. Dessemond

LE PHARO

r. Cimas

PL. DU QUATRE SEPTEMBRE

r. du Rempart

r. Candolle

TO BEACHES (1.5km), VALLON DES AUFFES (2km)

r. Sanatan

r. Paul Codaccioni

r. de Chateaubriand

r. Saveur Tobelem

r. Georges Charras

r. du Coteau

r. d'Endoume

bd. Tellene

r. Vaurenargues

r. Guidicelli

r. d'Endoume

Bd. M. Thomas

Montée du Valentir

0 ____ 500 meters
0 ____ 500 yards

FRANCE

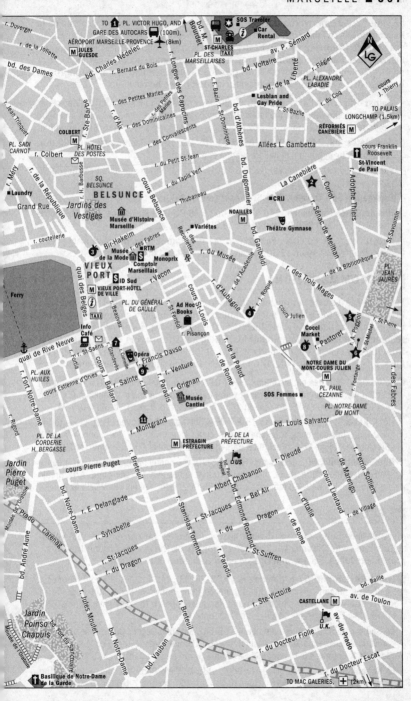

FRANCE

becomes urban sprawl to the east. North of the *vieux port* and west of **rue de la République** lies **Le Panier,** the city's oldest neighborhood. Surrounding La Canebière are several *Maghreb,* or North African and Arabic communities, including the market-filled **Belsunce quartier.** The area around **rue Curiol** should be avoided late at night. Marseille's quick metro lines provide limited service. The more thorough bus system is complex—a map from the tourist office helps a lot.

Tourist Office: 4 la Canebière (☎13 89 00; www.marseille-tourisme.com) M: Vieux Port. Sells **Marseille City Pass** (includes RTM day pass, city tours, ferry to Île d'If, and entry to 14 museums; €20 for 1 day, €27 for 2 days). Open M-Sa 9am-7pm, Su 10am-5pm.

Consulates: UK, 24 av. du Prado (☎15 72 10). **US,** 12 bd. Paul Peytral (☎54 92 00). Both open by appointment M-F 9am-noon and 2-4pm.

Police: 2 r. du Antoine Becker (☎39 80 00). Also in the train station on esplanade St-Charles (☎04 96 13 01 88).

Emergency: SOS Traveler, Gare St-Charles (☎62 12 80).

Hospital: Hôpital Timone, 246 r. St-Pierre (☎38 00 00). M: Timone. **SOS Médecins** (☎52 91 52) and **SOS Dentist** (☎85 39 39). Doctors on call.

Post Office: 1 pl. Hôtel des Postes (☎15 47 00). **Currency exchange** at main branch only. Open M-F 9:30am-12:30pm and 1:30-6pm. **Postal Code:** 13001.

ACCOMMODATIONS

Marseille has a range of housing options, from pricey hotels scattered throughout the *vieux port* to Belsunce's less reputable but temptingly cheap lodgings. Listings here prioritize safety and location. The tourist office also provides a list of recommended safe accommodations. The quiet HI hostel is inconveniently far from the city center—particularly in light of infrequent bus service and early curfews. Most places fill up quickly on weekends and in summer; reserve ahead.

Le Vertigo, 42 r. des petites Maries (☎91 07 11; www.hotelvertigo.fr), 100m from train station. Vertigo combines the best of youth hostel and small hotel. Breakfast €5. Internet €2 per hr.; free Wi-Fi. Reception 24hr. Dorms €24; doubles €50-60. MC/V. ❷

Hôtel Relax, 4 r. Corneille (☎33 15 87; www.hotelrelax.fr). M: Vieux Port. Close to the *vieux port,* this charming hotel offers small, clean rooms with A/C, bath, phone, and TV. Breakfast €6. Free Wi-Fi. Reception 6am-midnight. Doubles €50-55. AmEx/MC/V. ❷

Hôtel Montgrand, 50 r. Montgrand (☎00 35 20; www.hotel-montgrand-marseille.com). M: Estragin-Préfecture. Quiet, recently renovated rooms near the *vieux port.* A/C. Breakfast €5. Singles €42-49; family-size rooms €54-62. Extra person €8. MC/V. ❸

FOOD

Marseille's restaurants are as diverse as its inhabitants. African eateries and kebab stands line **cours St-Louis,** while outdoor cafes pack the streets around the *vieux port.* **Cours Julien** has a wonderful, eclectic collection of restaurants.

Ivoire Restaurant, 57 r. d'Aubagne (☎33 75 33). M: Noailles. Patrons come for authentic African cuisine and helpful advice from its owner, Mama Africa. *Maffé* (a meat dish with peanut sauce; €8) and *jus de gingembre* (a spicy ginger drink; €3). *Plats* €8-11. Open daily 11am-2am. Cash only. ❷

Le Sud du Haut, 80 cours Julien (☎92 66 64). M: Cours Julien. Outdoor seating, and *provençal* cuisine make for a leisurely meal. **Lunch formule** (*plat,* coffee, and dessert) €11. Entrees €8-11. Open M-Sa noon-2:30pm and 8-10:30pm. MC/V. ❸

La Kahena, 2 r. de la République (☎90 61 93). M: Vieux Port. Has speedy service and tasty couscous dishes (€9-15). Open daily noon-2:30pm and 7-10:30pm. MC/V. ❸

Au Falafel, 5 r. Lulli (☎ 54 08 55). M: Vieux Port. Visit this Israeli eatery for its soft pitas. *Shawarma* €10-16. Open M-Th and Su noon-midnight, F noon-4pm. AmEx/MC/V. ❸

SIGHTS

Revealing active African and Arabic communities amid Roman ruins and 17th-century forts, a walk through the city's streets tops any sights-oriented itinerary. Unless otherwise noted, all museums below keep the same hours: June-Sept. Tu-Su 11am-6pm; Oct.-May Tu-Su 10am-5pm. For more info, check www.museum-paca.org.

■BASILIQUE DE NOTRE DAME DE LA GARDE. A stunning view of the city, surrounding mountains, and island-studded bay make this a must-see. During the WWII liberation, the Resistance fought to regain the basilica. Towering above the city, the church's statue of Madonna is regarded by many as the symbol of Marseille. *(Bus #60, dir.: Notre Dame. ☎ 13 40 80. Open daily in summer 7am-8pm; in winter 7am-7pm. Free.)*

HARBOR ISLANDS. Resembling a sandcastle, the **Château d'If** guards the city from its rocky perch outside the harbor. Its dungeon, immortalized in Dumas's *Count of Monte Cristo*, once held a number of hapless Huguenots. The nearby **Île Frioul** was only marginally successful in isolating plague victims when a 1720 outbreak killed 40,000 citizens. Small shops, restaurants, and popular swimming inlets make the islands a convenient escapes from the city. *(Boats leave q. des Belges for both islands. Round-trip 1hr.; 1 island €10, both €15. Château €5, 18-25 €4, under 18 with an adult free.)*

ABBAYE ST-VICTOR. Fortified against pirates and Saracen invaders, this medieval abbey's ■**crypt** is one of Europe's oldest Christian sites. Its 5th-century construction brought Christianity to the pagan *Marseillais*. The abbey hosts an annual concert festival from September to December. *(On r. Sainte at the end of q. de Rive Neuve. ☎ 04 96 11 22 60, festival info 05 84 48. Open daily 9am-7pm. Crypt €2. Festival tickets €13-32.)*

MUSÉE CANTINI. This museum chronicles the region's 20th-century artistic successes, with Cubist, Fauvist, and Surrealist painters, including Matisse and Signac. *(19 r. Grignan. M: Estragin-Préfecture. ☎ 54 77 75. €2, students €1, over 65 and under 10 free.)*

PALAIS LONGCHAMP. Constructed in 1838 to honor the completion of a canal which brought fresh water to the plague-ridden city, the complex now houses a museum, observatory, and park. The **Musée de l'Histoire Naturelle** holds temporary exhibits on subjects like dinosaurs, milk, and human speech. *(M: Cinq Avenues Longchamps. ☎ 14 59 50. Open Tu-Su 10am-5pm. €3, students €1.50, seniors and under 10 free.)*

MÉMORIAL DES CAMPS DE LA MORT. Located in a blockhouse built by the Germans during their occupation, this museum's exhibits recall WWII death camps and the 1943 deportation of thousands of Jews from the *vieux port*. Unsettling quotes and a collection of ashes are on display. *(Q. de la Tourette. M: Vieux Port. ☎ 90 73 15. Open Tu-Su June-Aug. 11am-6pm; Sept.-May 10am-5pm. Free.)*

OTHER SIGHTS. The **Musée de la Mode's** rotating exhibits feature international clothing from various eras. *(Espace Mode Méditerranée, 11 La Canebière. M: Vieux Port-Hôtel de Ville. ☎ 04 96 17 06 00. €3, students €2, seniors free.)* Bus #83 (dir.: Rond-Point du Prado) goes from the *vieux port* to **public beaches.** Get off the bus just after it rounds the David statue (20-30min.).

NIGHTLIFE

Late-night restaurants and nightclubs center around **place Thiers,** near the *vieux port*. Tourists should exercise caution at night, especially in Panier and Belsunce, and near the Opera on the *vieux port*. Night buses are scarce and the metro closes early (Su-Th 9pm, F-Sa 12:30am).

Trolleybus, 24 q. de Rive Neuve. M: Vieux Port. In an old warehouse with separate pop-rock, soul-funk-salsa, and techno rooms. Prize-winning DJs. Drinks €4-8. Cover Sa €10; includes 1 drink. Open July-Aug. W-Sa 11pm-6am; Sept.-June Th-Sa 11pm-6am. MC/V.

Dan Racing, 17 r. André Poggiol. M: Cours Julien. Let out your inner rock star on W night jam sessions; instruments provided. Drinks €2-5. Open W-Sa 9pm-2am.

New Can-Can, 3 r. Sénac de Meilhan. M: Noailles. A perpetual party for the city's GLBT community. Drinks €9. Cover F €10-15. Open daily 11pm-dawn. AmEx/MC/V.

Poulpason, 2 r. André Poggioli. M: Cours Julien. DJs spin funk, hip hop, jazz, reggae, and electro-house while a giant octopus stretches out from the wall. Drinks €3-5. Cover on specially featured DJ nights €3-10. Open M-Sa 10pm-2am. MC/V.

AIX-EN-PROVENCE
☎04 42

Famous for festivals, fountains, and former residents Paul Cézanne and Émile Zola, Aix-en-Provence ("X"; pop. 170,000) caters to tourists without being ruined by them. The **chemin de Cézanne,** 9 av. Paul Cézanne, features a 2hr. self-guided tour that leads to the artist's birthplace and favorite cafes. (Open daily July-Aug. 10am-6pm; Apr.-June and Sept. 10am-noon and 2-6pm; Oct.-Mar. 10am-noon and 2-5pm. €6, students €2.) The **Fondation Vasarely,** av. Marcel Pagnol, in nearby Jas-de-Bouffan, is a must-see for Op-Art fans. (Open Apr.-Oct. M-Sa 10am-6pm; Nov.-Mar. Tu-Sa 10am-6pm. €7, students €4.) A mix of Baroque, Gothic, and Romanesque, the **Cathédrale St-Sauveur,** r. Gaston de Saporta, fell victim to misplaced violence during the Revolution; angry *Aixois* mistook the apostle statues for statues of royalty and chopped off their heads. Though recapitated in the 19th century, the statues remain sans neck. (Open daily 8am-noon and 2-6pm.) In June and July, celebrities descend on Aix for the **Festival d'Aix-en-Provence,** a series of opera and orchestral performances. (☎16 11 70; www.festival-aix.com. Tickets from €8.)

Aix has few cheap hotels; July travelers should reserve rooms in March. **Hôtel Paul ❸,** 10 av. Pasteur, has relatively cheap, clean rooms. (☎23 23 89; hotel.paul@wanadoo.fr. Breakfast €5. Check-in before 6pm. Singles and doubles with bath €40-€50; triples €62; quads €72. Cash only.) To camp at **Arc-en-Ciel ❶,** on rte. de Nice, take bus #3 from La Rotonde to Trois Sautets. (☎26 14 28. Reception 8:30-11am and 3-8pm. €7 per person, €6 per tent. Electricity €4.) Charming restaurants pack **rue Verrerie** and the roads north of **cours Mirabeau.** Bars and clubs line **Rue Verrerie,** off r. des Cordiliers. **IPN,** 42 cours Sextius, hosts international students in a cave-like bar. (Open Tu-Sa 6pm-4am.)

Trains go from the station on av. Victor Hugo to Marseille (45min., 27 per day, €7), Nice (3-4hr., 25 per day, €35), and Paris (TGV 3hr., 10 per day, €77-131). **Buses** (☎08 91 02 40 25) leave av. de l'Europe for Marseille (30min., 6 per hr., €5). From the train station, follow av. Victor Hugo, bearing left at the fork, until it feeds into La Rotonde. On the left is the **tourist office,** 2 pl. du Général de Gaulle. (☎16 11 61; www.aixenprovencetourism.com. Open July-Aug. M-Sa 8:30am-9pm, Su 10am-8pm; Sept.-June M-Sa 8:30am-8pm, Su 10am-1pm and 2-6pm.) **Postal Code:** 13100.

AVIGNON
☎04 90

For three weeks in July, Avignon (pop. 90,000) hosts Europe's most prestigious theater festival. The ▧**Festival d'Avignon** holds theatrical performances in at least 30 venues, from factories to cloisters to palaces. (☎14 14 14; www.festival-avignon.com. Reservations accepted from mid-June. Tickets free-€45, under 25 50% dicount.) The **Festival OFF,** also in July, is more experimental and almost as well established. (☎25 24 30; www.avignon-off.org. Tickets under €16. €10 Carte OFF grants holders a 30% discount.) The golden ▧**Palais des Papes,** the largest Gothic palace in Europe, is a reminder of the city's brief stint as the center of the Catholic

Church. Although revolutionary looting stripped the interior of its lavish furnishings and fires erased its medieval murals, its vast chambers and few remaining frescoes are still remarkable. (☎27 50 00. Open daily Aug. 9am-9pm; July and Sept. 9am-8pm; Oct. and Apr.-June 9am-7pm; Nov.-Mar. 9:30am-5:45pm. €9.50.) A French children's song about its 12th-century bridge, **Pont St-Bénézet,** has further immortalized Avignon. Despite its supposedly divinely ordained location, the bridge has suffered from warfare and the once-turbulent Rhône and now extends only partway across the river. (☎27 51 16. €3.50; in summer €4. Free audio tour. Open daily Aug. 9am-9pm; July and Sept. 9am-8pm; Apr.-June and Oct. 9am-7pm; Nov.-Mar. 9:30am-5:45pm.) Farther downstream, **Pont Daladier** makes it all the way across, offering free views of the broken bridge and the Palais.

Avignon's accommodations fill up three to four months before festival season; reserve ahead or stay in Arles (see below) or Nîmes (p.372). Rooms with lots of amenities make **Hôtel Mignon ❸,** 12 r. Joseph Vernet, a good deal despite its small, inconvenient bathrooms. (☎82 17 30; www.hotel-mignon.com. Breakfast included. Free Internet and in-room Wi-Fi. Reception 7am-11pm. Singles €38-€49, during festival €45-62; doubles €55-60/62-73; triples €66/80; quads €86/100. AmEx/MC/V.) Sleep for cheap at **Camping du Pont d'Avignon ❶,** 10 chemin de la Barthelasse, while enjoying its jacuzzi, laundry facilities, pool, restaurant, hot showers, supermarket, and tennis and volleyball courts. (☎80 63 50; www.camping-avignon.com. Internet €4 per hr. Reception July-Aug. 8am-10pm; Sept. and June 8:30am-8pm; Oct. and Mar.-May 8:30am-6:30pm. Open Mar.-Oct. 1-person tent site €15; 2-person €22; extra person €5.10. Electricity €2.60-3.10. MC/V.) Restaurants group on **rue des Teinturiers.** For basic French fare with some Lebanese and Indian touches, try **Citron Pressé ❷,** 38 r. Carreterie. (☎86 09 29. 3-course *menu* with wine €12. *Plats* €3-7. Open M-Th noon-2:30pm, F-Sa noon-2pm and 7:30pm-11:30pm; during festival daily noon-2am. Cash only.) During the July theater festival, free theatrical performances spill into the streets at night, and many eateries stay open until 2 or 3am. **Place des Corps Saints** has a few bars that remain busy year-round.

Trains (☎27 81 89) run from bd. St-Roch to: Arles (20min., 1-2 per hr., €9); Lyon (2hr., 7 per day, €31); Marseille (1¼hr., 1 per hr., €28); Nîmes (30min., 14 per day, €9); Paris (TGV 3-4hr., 13 per day, €97). Exit the train station and turn right for **buses,** which go to Arles (1½hr., 5 per day, €8) and Marseille (2hr., 1 per day, €19). Walk straight through porte de la République to reach the **tourist office,** 41 cours Jean Jaurès. (☎04 32 74 32 74; www.avignon-tourisme.com. Open July M-Sa 9am-7pm, Su 10am-5pm; Apr.-June and Aug.-Oct. M-Sa 9am-5pm, Su 10am-5pm; Nov.-Mar. M-F 9am-6pm, Sa 9am-5pm, Su 10am-noon.) **Postal Code:** 84000.

ARLES
☎04 90

All roads in Arles (pop. 35,000), once the capital of Roman Gaul, seem to meet at the great Roman arena. Built in the AD first century to seat 20,000 spectators, **Les Arènes** is still used for bullfights. (☎49 36 86. Open daily May-Sept. 9am-6pm; Oct. and Mar.-Apr. 9am-5:30pm; Nov.-Feb. 10am-4pm.) The **Musée de l'Arles Antique,** on av. de la 1er D. F. L., 10min. walk from the town center, recreates the city's Roman past. (Open daily Apr.-Oct. 9am-7pm; Nov.-Mar. 10am-5pm. €6, students €4.) The **Musée Réattu,** 10 r. du Grand Prieuré, houses 57 Arles-inspired Picasso drawings. (Open daily July-Sept. 10am-7pm; Mar.-June and Oct. 10am-12:30pm and 2-6pm; Nov.-Feb. 1-6pm. €4, students €3; during photography festival €6/4.50.) The annual three-week-long **Fête d'Arles,** beginning on summer solstice, brings traditional costumes, *Provençal* dancing, and bullfights to town. Once every three years, during the **Fête des Gardians** (May 1), the city elects the Queen of Arles and her six ladies, who represent Arles at local and international events. The next election will occur in 2008. At the annual ⊠**Rencontres Internationales de la Photographie,** in July, undiscovered photographers court potential agents while established artists hold nightly slide shows (€8-12). When the five-day festival crowd departs, the exhibits are left behind until mid-September (€3.50 per exhibit; all exhibits €28, students €22, under 16 free). For info, contact **Rencontres d'Arles,** 10 rond-point des Arènes (☎96 76 06; www.rencontres-arles.com). If you plan to stay in Arles during the photography festival, reserve a room at least two months ahead.

To get from the train station to the **Auberge de Jeunesse (HI)** ❶, 20 av. Maréchal Foch, walk along bd. Émile Zola, then turn left on av. du Maréchal Foch. Comfortable single-sex dorms await. (☎96 18 25. Breakfast and linens included. Reception 7-10am and 5-11pm. Lockout 10am-5pm. Curfew in summer midnight, winter 11pm. 8-bed dorms €15. MC/V.) Cafes on **place Voltaire** have simple, cheap fare. **Trains** leave av. P. Talabot for: Avignon (20min., 12-20 per day, €7); Marseille (50min., 18-27 per day, €15); Montpellier (1hr., 5-8 per day, €16); Nîmes (20min., 8-11 per day, €10). **Buses** depart near the train station and from bd. Georges Clemenceau for Nîmes (1hr., 4 per day, €6). To get to the **tourist office,** esplanade Charles de Gaulle, turn left outside the train station. Veer clockwise around the roundabout, then go left after the Monoprix onto bd. Émile Courbes. Take a right by the city tower onto bd. des Lices. (☎18 41 20; www.arlestourisme.com. Open daily Apr.-Sept. 9am-6:45pm; Oct.-Mar. 9am-4:45pm.) **Postal Code:** 13200.

NÎMES
☎04 66

Southern France flocks to Nîmes (pop. 135,000) for its *férias,* celebrations including bullfights and flamenco dancing (mid-Sept. and May 7-12, 2008). Every Thursday night in summer, art and musical performances fill the squares of the Old Town. **Les Arènes** is a well-preserved first-century **Roman amphitheater** that still holds bullfights and concerts. (☎21 82 56. Open daily June-Aug. 9am-7pm; Mar.-May and Sept.-Oct. 9am-6pm; Nov.-Feb. 9:30am-5pm. Closed during *férias* or concerts; call ahead. €8, students €6.) North of the arena stands the **Maison Carrée,** a rectangular temple built in the first century BC. Today, visitors can enjoy a 3D film retracing the town's Roman past. (Open daily June-Aug. 9am-7:30pm; Apr.-May and Sept. 10am-7pm; Mar. and Oct. 10am-6:30pm; Jan.-Feb. and Nov.-Dec. 10am-1pm and 2-5pm. Film screening 2 per hr. €4.50, students €3.60.) Across the square, the **Carrée d'Art** displays traveling contemporary art exhibits. (Open Tu-Su 10am-6pm. Last entry at 5:30pm. €5, students €3.70.) Near the mouth of the canals enjoy the **Jardins de la Fontaine's** spacious grounds, *pétanque* (similar to *bocce* and lawn bowling) courts, and **Tour Magne,** the ruins of a Roman tower. (Garden open daily mid.-Mar. to mid-Oct. 7:30am-10pm; mid-Oct. to mid-Mar. 7:30am-6:30pm. Tower open daily June-Aug. 9:30am-7pm; Apr.-May and Sept. 9:30am-6:30pm; Mar. and Oct. 9:30am-1pm and 2-4:30pm. Garden free. Tower €2.70, students €2.30.)

To get to the ⊠**Auberge de Jeunesse (HI)** ❶, 257 ch. de l'Auberge de Jeunesse, take bus I (dir.: Alès) from the train station to Stade, rte. d'Alès and follow the signs. With a jovial staff and courtyard garden, this hostel is worth the 45min. trek from the train station. (☎68 03 20. Breakfast €3.40. Internet €1 per 15min; free Wi-Fi. Reception 7:30am-1am. Open Mar.-Sept. Dorms €15. Camping €9. €3 HI discount. MC/V.) For groceries, head to the **Monoprix,** 3 bd. Admiral Courbet, near Esplanade Charles de Gaulle. (Open M-Sa 8:30am-8:30pm, Su 9am-noon. AmEx/MC/V.) **Trains** go from bd. Talabot to: Arles (25min., 8 per day, €10); Marseille (1¼hr., 9 per day, €22); Montpellier (30min., 31-46 per day, €8); Toulouse (3hr., 17 per day, €38). **Buses** (☎29 52 00) depart from behind the train station for Avignon (1½hr., 3-5 per day, €8.30). The **tourist office,** is at 6 r. Auguste. (☎58 38 00; www.ot-nimes.fr. Open July-Aug. M-W and F 8:30am-8pm, Th 8:30am-9pm, Sa 9am-7pm, Su 10am-6pm; Sept.-June reduced hours.) **Postal Codes:** 30000; 30900.

FRENCH RIVIERA (CÔTE D'AZUR)

Between Marseille and the Italian border, sun-drenched beaches and warm Mediterranean waters combine to form the fabled playground of the rich and famous. Chagall, F. Scott Fitzgerald, Matisse, Picasso, and Renoir all flocked to the coast in its heyday. Now, the Riviera is a curious combination of high-rolling millionaires and low-budget tourists. In May, high society makes its yearly pilgrimage to the Cannes Film Festival and the Monte-Carlo Grand Prix, while Nice's February *Carnaval* and summer jazz festivals draw budget travelers.

NICE ☎04 93

Classy, colorful Nice ("NIECE"; pop. 340,000) is the Riviera's unofficial capital. Its non-stop nightlife, top-notch museums, and packed beaches are tourist magnets. During February **Carnaval,** visitors and *Niçois* alike ring in spring with costumes and revelry. When visiting Nice, prepare to have more fun than you'll remember.

TRANSPORTATION

Flights: Aéroport Nice-Côte d'Azur (**NCE;** ☎08 20 42 33 33). **Air France,** 10 av. de Verdun (☎08 02 80 28 02). To: **Bastia, Corsica** (€116; under 25, over 60, and couples €59) and **Paris** (€93/50).

Trains: Gare SNCF Nice-Ville, av. Thiers (☎14 82 12). Open daily 5am-12:30am. To: **Cannes** (40min., 3 per hr., €5.60); **Marseille** (2½hr., 16 per day, €27); **Monaco** (15min., 2-6 per hr., €3.10); **Paris** (5½hr., 9 per day, €94).

Buses: 5 bd. Jean Jaurès (☎85 61 81). Info booth open M-F 8:30am-5:30pm, Sa 9am-4pm. To **Cannes** (2hr., 2-3 per hr., €6) and **Monaco** (1hr., 3-6 per hr., €1.30).

Ferries: Corsica Ferries (☎04 92 00 42 93; www.corsicaferries.com). Bus #1 or 2 (dir.: Port) from pl. Masséna. To **Corsica** (€20-40, bikes €10, cars €40-57). MC/V.

Public Transportation: Ligne d'Azur, 10 av. Félix Faure (☎93 13 53 13; www.lignedazur.com), near pl. Leclerc. Buses run daily 7am-8pm. Tickets €1.30, 1-day pass €4, 8-ticket *carnet* €8.30, 5-day pass €13, 1-week pass €17. Purchase tickets and day passes on board the bus; *carnet,* 5-day, and 1-week passes from the office. **Noctambus** (night service) runs 4 routes daily 9:10pm-1:10am.

Bike and Scooter Rental: Holiday Bikes, 34 av. Auber (☎16 01 62; nice@holidaybikes.com), near the train station. Bikes €16 per day, €70 per week; €230 deposit. Scooters €35/175; €500 deposit. Open M-Sa 9am-6:30pm. AmEx/MC/V.

FRANCE

ORIENTATION AND PRACTICAL INFORMATION

Avenue Jean Médecin, on the left as you exit the train station, and **boulevard Gambetta,** on the right, run directly to the beach. **Place Masséna** is 10min. down av. Jean Médecin. On the coast, **promenade des Anglais** is a people-watcher's paradise. To the southeast, past av. Jean Médecin and toward the bus station, is **vieux Nice.** Women should not walk alone after dark, and everyone should exercise caution at night, around the train station, in *vieux* Nice, and on promenade des Anglais.

Tourist Office: av. Thiers (☎08 92 70 74 07; www.nicetourisme.com), next to the train station. The free *Le Pitchoun* (www.pitchoun.com) offers insight on local venues. Open June-Sept. M-Sa 8am-8pm, Su 10am-5pm; Oct.-May M-Sa 8am-7pm, Su 9am-6pm.

Consulates: Canada, 10 r. Lamartine (☎92 93 22; cancons.nce@club-internet.fr). Open M-F 9am-noon. **US,** 7 av. Gustave V (☎88 89 55). Open M-F 9-11:30am and 1:30-4:30pm.

FRANCE

Nice

ACCOMMODATIONS
Les Camélias (HI), 3
Hôtel Belle Meunière, 1
Hôtel Petit Trianon, 4

FOOD
Acchiardo, 10
Lou Pilha Leva, 5
La Merenda, 7
Le Restaurant
d'Angleterre, 2

**NIGHTLIFE AND
ENTERTAINMENT**
Blue Moon, 12
Le Klub, 6
Tapas la Movida, 9
Thor, 11
Wayne's, 8

TO CATHÉDRALE ORTHODOXE RUSSE ST-NICHOLAS (550m)
TO MUSÉE DES BEAUX-ARTS (25m)
TO AÉROPORT NICE-CÔTE D'AZUR (4km)

TO MUSÉE NATIONAL MESSAGE BIBLIQUE MARC CHAGALL (200m), MUSÉE MATISSE (1km)

Gare Nice-Ville
Office Provençal
Holliday Bikes
Nicea
Travelex
r. de Belgique
Alonso
Royal Com
Lavomatique
Paganini
Monoprix
FNAC
Basilique Notre-Dame
Centre Commercial Nice Étoile
The Cat's Whiskers
J.Canada
r. Lamartine
Hôpital St-Roch
Musée d'Art Moderne et d'Art Contemporain
Théâtre Nationale de Nice
Gare Routière
CRIJ
Ligne d'Azur
Flamme et Fumée
Espace Masséna
MASSÉNA
Cyber Internet
Air France
Travelex
Paradis
Espace Chaud
OTU Travel
Air France
Hôtel de Ville
Palais de Justice
PALAIS
Opéra de Nice
VIEUX NICE
Palais Lascaris
Église St-Jacques
Théâtre du Cours
St-Martin
Hôtel Négresco
Galion Plage
Ruhl Plage
promenade des Anglais

PL. J. TOJA
PL. ST-FRANÇOIS
PL. WILSON
PL. MASSÉNA
PL. DU PALAIS

av. St-Jean-Baptiste
bd. Risso
bd. Carabacel
bd. Carabacel
av. Maréchal Foch
av. Notre Dame
av. Jean-Médecin
av. Jean-Médecin
bd. Dubouchage
r. de l'Hôtel des Postes
r. Gubernatis
r. Blacas
r. Pastorelli
r. Chauvin
r. Gustave Deloye
r. Gioffredo
r. Delille
r. Edr Berl
r. Derly
r. Giofrredo
r. Pierre Dévoluy
r. Biscarra
r. Gaiilean
r. Sottalion
av. Jean-Médecin
r. de Russie
r. d'Angleterre
r. d'Italie
r. Paganini
r. Déroulède
r. Rossini
r. Durante
av. Georges Clémenceau
av. Auber
av. Thiers
r. Gounod
r. Berlioz
r. Verdi
r. Victor Hugo
bd. Victor Hugo
r. Grimaldi
r. Macarani
r. Alphonse Karr
r. de la Liberté
r. Dr. Barety
r. du Congrès
r. du Maréchal Joffre
r. de la Buffa
r. Meyerbeer
r. de France
r. de Rivoli
passage Cronstadt
passage Merlanzone
bd. Gambetta
Jardin Alsace-Lorraine
r. Massenet
av. des Phocéens
av. de Verdun
r. Masséna
r. de la Préfecture
cours Saleya
Cité du Parc
Jardin Albert J.
r. de France

Police: 1 av. Maréchal Foch (☎04 92 17 22 22), opposite end from bd. Jean Médecin.

Hospital: St-Roch, 5 r. Pierre Dévoluy (☎04 92 03 33 75).

Post Office: 23 av. Thiers (☎82 65 22), near the station. Open M-F 8am-7pm, Sa 8am-noon. **Postal Code:** 06033.

ACCOMMODATIONS

Make reservations before visiting Nice; it can be hard to find beds, particularly in summer. Most budget accommodations are near the train station or *vieux* Nice. Those by the station are newer but more remote; the surrounding neighborhood has a deservedly rough reputation, so exercise caution at night. Hotels closer to *vieux* Nice are more convenient but less modern.

■ **Hôtel Belle Meunière,** 21 av. Durante (☎88 66 15), opposite the train station. Relaxed backpers fill 4- to 5-bed co-ed dorms in a former mansion. Showers €2. Laundry from €5.50. Reception 7:30am-midnight. Dorms €15, with shower €20; 2-person apartment, min. 3-night stay, €36; doubles €50; triples €60; quads €80. MC/V. ❷

Auberge de Jeunesse Les Camélias (HI), 3 r. Spitalieri (☎62 15 54; nice-camelias@fuaj.org), behind the Centre Commercial Nice Étoile. A new hostel with clean rooms. Breakfast included. Laundry €6. Internet €5 per hr. Reception 24hr. Lockout 11am-3pm. Dorms €20. MC/V. ❷

Hôtel Petit Trianon, 11 r. Paradis (☎87 50 46; hotel.nice.lepetittrianon@wanadoo.fr). The caring owner looks after guests in 8 comfortable rooms off pl. Masséna. Breakfast €5. Free beach towel loan. Laundry €10 per 5kg. Free Internet and Wi-Fi. Reserve ahead. Mid-June to mid-Sept. singles €30, with bath €35; doubles €40-42/50-53; triples €60-75; quads €76-96. Mid.-Sept. to mid-June prices €2-5 less. MC/V. ❸

FOOD

Mediterranean spices flavor *Niçois* cuisine. Try crusty *pan bagnat,* a round loaf of bread topped with tuna, sardines, vegetables, and olive oil, or *socca,* a thin, olive-oil-flavored chickpea bread. Famous *salade niçoise* combines tuna, olives, eggs, potatoes, tomatoes, and a spicy mustard dressing. The eateries along promenade des Anglais and av. Masséna are expensive and unremarkable. Save your euro for olives, cheese, and produce from the **markets** at **cours Saleya** and **avenue Maché de la Libération** (both open Tu-Su 7am-1pm). **Avenue Jean-Médecin** features reasonable *brasseries,* panini vendors, and kebab stands.

■ **La Merenda,** 4 r. de la Terrasse. Behind a stained-glass exterior and a beaded curtain, this intimate restaurant serves some of the best regional dishes in the city. Seatings at 7 and 9pm only; reserve in person in the morning for dinner. *Plats* €11-16. Open M-F noon-1:30pm and 7-9pm. Cash only. ❷

■ **Lou Pilha Leva,** 10-13 r. du Collet (☎13 99 08), in *vieux* Nice. At lunch and dinnertime, the line of locals and tourists hungry for cheap *Niçois* fare extends around the corner. Open daily 8am-midnight. Cash only. ❶

Acchiardo, 38 r. Droite (☎85 51 16), in *vieux* Nice. Long, crowded, family-style tables fill with simple but appetizing French and Italian dishes served up by a quick, dedicated staff. Open M-F July 7-10pm; Sept.-June noon-1:30pm and 7-10pm. Cash only. ❶

Le Restaurant d'Angleterre, 25 r. d'Angleterre (☎88 64 49), near the train station. Frequented by a loyal crowd of locals who come for traditional French favorites. The €14 *menu* includes salad, *plat,* side dish, dessert, and *digestif.* Open Tu-Sa 11:45am-2pm and 6:45-9:55pm, Su 11:45am-2pm. AmEx/MC/V. ❸

👁 SIGHTS

One look at Nice's waves and you may be tempted to spend your entire stay stretched out on the sand. As the city with the second-most museums in France, however, Nice offers more than azure waters and topless sunbathers.

◼ MUSÉE NATIONAL MESSAGE BIBLIQUE MARC CHAGALL. Chagall founded this extraordinary museum to showcase an assortment of biblically themed pieces that he gave to the French state in 1966. Twelve of these colorful canvases illustrate the first two books of the Old Testament. The museum also includes an auditorium with stained-glass panels depicting the creation story. The auditorium hosts concerts; ask at the entrance for program info. (*Av. du Dr. Ménard. Walk 15min. north of the station, or take bus #15, dir.: Rimiez, to Musée Chagall. ☎53 87 20; www.musee-chagall.fr. Open M and W-Su July-Sept. 10am-6pm; Oct.-June 10am-5pm. €6.70, students 18-25 €5.20, under 18 and 1st and 3rd Su of each month free. MC/V.*)

◼ MUSÉE MATISSE. Henri Matisse visited Nice in 1916 and never left. His 17th-century Genoese villa, this museum contains a small collection of paintings and a dazzling exhibit of Matisse's three-dimensional work, including dozens of cut paper tableaux. (*164 av. des Arènes de Cimiez. Bus #15, 17, 20, 22, or 25 to Arènes. Free bus between Musée Chagall and Musée Matisse. ☎81 08 08; www.musee-matisse-nice.org. Open M and W-Su 10am-6pm. €4, students €1.50, 1st and 3rd Su of each month free. MC/V.*)

MUSÉE D'ART MODERNE ET D'ART CONTEMPORAIN. A glass facade welcomes visitors to exhibits of French New Realists and American pop artists like Lichtenstein and Warhol while minimalist galleries enshrine avant-garde pieces. (*Promenade des Arts, at the intersection of av. St-Jean Baptiste and Traverse Garibaldi. Bus #5, dir.: St-Charles, to Musée Promenade des Arts. ☎62 61 62; www.mamac-nice.org. Open Tu-Su 10am-6pm. €7, 1st and 3rd Su of each month free. Cash only.*)

MUSÉE DES BEAUX-ARTS JULES CHARET. The former villa of Ukraine's Princess Kotschoubey has been converted into a celebration of French and Italian painting. Raoul Dufy, a local Fauvist painter, celebrated his city's spontaneity with sensational pictures of the town at rest and at play. (*33 av. Baumettes. Bus #38 to Musée Chéret or #12 to Grosso. ☎04 92 15 28 28; www.musee-beaux-arts-nice.org. Open Tu-Su 10am-6pm. €4, students €2.50, under 18 and 1st and 3rd Su of each month free.*)

CATHÉDRALE ORTHODOXE RUSSE ST-NICOLAS. Also known as the **Église Russe,** the cathedral was commissioned by Empress Marie Feodorovna in memory of her husband, Tsar Nicholas Alexandrovich, who died in Nice in 1865. Soon after its 1912 dedication, the cathedral's gold interior became a haven for exiled Russian nobles. (*17 bd. du Tzarewitch, off bd. Gambetta. ☎96 88 02. Open M-Sa 9am-noon and 2:30-6pm, Su 2:30-5:30pm. Closed during mass. €2.50, students €2.*)

LE CHÂTEAU. At the eastern end of promenade des Anglais, Le Château—the remains of an 11th-century fort—marks the city's birthplace. The château itself was destroyed by Louis XIV in 1706, but it still provides a spectacular ◼**view** of Nice and the sparkling Baie des Anges. In summer, an outdoor theater hosts orchestral and vocal musicians. (*☎85 62 33. Park open daily June-Aug. 9am-8pm; Sept. 10am-7pm; Oct.-Mar. 8am-6pm; Apr.-May 8am-7pm. Free walk to the top. Elevator daily June-Aug. 9am-8pm; Apr.-May and Sept. 10am-7pm; Oct.-Mar. 10am-6pm. €0.70, round-trip €1.*)

JARDIN ALBERT I. The city's oldest park, Jardin Albert I, below pl. Masséna, has plenty of benches, fountains, and palm trees. The outdoor **Théâtre de Verdure** presents concerts in summer. Contact the tourist office for info. Unfortunately, the park is one of Nice's most dangerous spots after dark. Tourists should avoid crossing the park at night. (*Between av. Verdun and bd. Jean Jaurès, off promenade des Anglais. Box office open daily 10:30am-noon and 3:30-6:30pm. MC/V.*)

OTHER SIGHTS. Named by the rich English community that commissioned it, the **promenade des Anglais,** a palm-lined seaside boulevard, is filled with ice-cream eating tourists and jogging locals. **Hôtel Négresco** presents the best of *Belle Époque* luxury with coffered ceilings, crystal chandeliers, and a large collection of valuable artwork. The seashore between bd. Gambetta and the Opéra alternates **private beaches** with crowded **public strands,** but a large section west of bd. Gambetta is public. Many travelers are surprised to find that stretches of rock—not soft sand—line the Baie des Anges; bring your beach mat.

♫ 🎭 ENTERTAINMENT AND NIGHTLIFE

Nice's **Jazz Festival,** at the Parc et Arènes de Cimiez, attracts world-famous performers. (mid-July; ☎08 20 80 04 00; www.nicejazzfest.com. €33.) The ⚑**Carnaval** gives Rio a run for its money with three weeks of confetti, fireworks, parades, and parties. (Feb. 16-Mar. 2, 2008. ☎04 92 14 46 46; www.nicecarnaval.com.)

Bars and nightclubs around **rue Masséna** and **Vieux Nice** pulsate with dance and jazz but have a strict dress code. Many clubs will turn revelers away for wearing shorts, sandals, or baseball caps. To experience Nice's nightlife without spending a euro, head down to the **promenade des Anglais,** where street performers, musicians, and pedestrians fill the beach and boardwalk. Hard to find, student-produced French-language *Le Pitchoun* provides the lowdown on trendy bars and clubs (free; www.lepitchoun.com). Exercise caution after dark; men have a reputation for harassing lone women on the promenade, in the Jardin Albert I, and near the train station, while the beach sometimes becomes a gathering place for prostitutes and thugs. Travelers should walk in groups if possible, and take only prominent, well-lit avenues when returning to their accommodations.

⚑ **Blue Moon,** 26 q. Lunel (☎26 54 79). Hip fashionistas flash their threads before a backdrop of white vinyl stools and bare tile walls. Cover €15. Open Th-Sa midnight-5am.

Thor, 32 cours Saleya (☎62 49 90). Svelte bartenders pour pints for a young clientele in Viking-horn-shaped glasses at this faux-Scandinavian pub. Daily live rock bands 10pm-2:30am. Happy hour 6-9pm; pints €5. Open daily 6pm-2:30am. MC/V.

Wayne's, 15 r. de la Préfecture (☎13 46 99; www.waynes.fr). A laid-back crowd drinks at tables while a rowdier crew finds its way to the darker dance floor. Pints €6.10. Su karaoke. Happy hour noon-9pm; all drinks €3.50. Open daily noon-2am.

Le Klub, 6 r. Halévy (☎16 87 26). Nice's most popular gay klub attracts a large krew of men and women to its sleek lounge and active dance floor. Mixed drinks €6-10. Cover €11-14; includes 1 drink. Open W-Su midnight-5am. AmEx/MC/V.

Tapas la Movida, 3 r. de l'Abbaye (☎62 27 46). This hole-in-the-wall bar attracts a young, crowd. Figure out how to crawl home before attempting the *bar-o-mètre* (a meter-long box of shots; €15). M-F live reggae, rock, and ska (€2). F-Sa DJ and theme parties. Open July-Aug. daily 9pm-12:30am; Sept.-June M-Sa 9pm-12:30am. Cash only.

MONACO AND MONTE-CARLO ☎04 93

In 1297, François Grimaldi of Genoa established his family as Monaco's rulers, staging a coup aided by several henchmen disguised as *monaco* (Italian for monk). The tiny principality has since jealously guarded its independence. Monaco (pop. 7100) proves its wealth with ubiquitous surveillance cameras, high-speed luxury cars, multi-million-dollar yachts, and Monte-Carlo's famous casino.

| **CALLING TO AND FROM MONACO** | Monaco's country code is 377. To call Monaco from France, dial 00377, then the eight-digit Monaco number. To call France from Monaco, dial 0033 and drop the first zero of the French number. |

FRENCH 101:
A CRASH COURSE

Traveling through France, you will undoubtedly encounter familiar words on signs and menus. Though these cognates will appear to help in your struggle to comprehend *le monde francophone*, beware! Some can also lead you astray. Here are some *faux amis* (false cognates; literally, "false friends") to watch out for:

Blesser has nothing to do with spirituality (or sneezing). It means **to hurt,** not to bless.

Pain is anything but misery for the French: it's their word for **bread.**

Bras is not a supportive undergarment, it's an **arm.**

Rage is not just regular anger, it's **rabies.**

Rabais, it follows, is not the disease you can catch from a dog, but a **discount.**

A *sale* is not an event with a lot of *rabais;* it means **dirty.**

Draguer means **to hit on,** not to drag, unless you encounter an overly aggressive flirt.

Balancer is **to swing,** not to steady oneself.

A *peste* is slightly more serious than a bothersome creature. It is a **plague.**

Puéril is not grave danger, just **childhood.**

Preservatif is not something found in packaged food, but it can be found in other packages, so to speak. This is the French word for **condom.**

Crayon means **pencil,** not

TRANSPORTATION AND PRACTICAL INFORMATION. Trains run from **Gare SNCF**, pl. Ste-Dêvote, to Antibes (1hr., 2 per hr., €7), Cannes (1¼hr., 2 per hr., €8), and Nice (25min., 2 per hr., €4). **Buses** (☎85 64 44) leave bd. des Moulins and av. Princesse Alice for Nice (45min., 4 per hr., €1.30). Atop the enormous **Rocher de Monaco** (Rock of Monaco), **Monaco-Ville**—the city's historical and legislative heart—is home to the Palais Princier, the Cathédrale de Monaco, and narrow pedestrian avenues. **La Condamine** quarter, Monaco's port, sits below Monaco-Ville, with a morning market, spirited bars, and lots of traffic. Monaco's famous glitz is concentrated in **Monte-Carlo**, whose casino draws international visitors. Bus #4 links the Ste-Dêvote train station to the casino; buy tickets on board (€1.50, *carnet* of 4 €3.60). The **tourist office** is at 2A bd. des Moulins. (☎04 92 16 61 16. Open M-Sa 9am-7pm, Su and holidays 10am-noon.) **Postal Code:** MC 98000 Monaco.

ACCOMMODATIONS AND FOOD. Rather than stay in expensive Monaco, the nearby town of **Beausoleil, France,** a 10min. walk from the casino, offers budget accommodations. Modest rooms at **Hôtel Diana ❸**, 17 bd. du Général Leclerc, come with A/C and TV. (☎78 47 58; www.monte-carlo.mc/hotel-diana-beausoleil. Singles €40-48; doubles €35-65; triples €67-70. AmEx/MC/V.) Not surprisingly, Monaco has little in the way of cheap fare. Try the narrow streets behind the **place du Palais** for affordable sit-down meals, or fill a picnic basket at the **market** on pl. d'Armes at the end of av. Prince Pierre. (Open daily 6am-1pm.) The merry **Café Costa Rica ❷**, 40 bd. des Moulins, serves *bruschetta*, salads, and other Italian staples. (☎25 44 45. Pasta €8-11. Tea and crepes after 3pm. Open Sept.-June daily 8am-7pm; July and late Aug. M-F 8am-7:30pm, Sa-Su 8am-3pm. Closed Aug. 1-15. V.)

SIGHTS AND ENTERTAINMENT. At the notorious ■**Monte-Carlo Casino**, pl. du Casino, Richard Burton wooed Elizabeth Taylor and Mata Hari shot a Russian spy. Optimists tempt fate at blackjack, roulette (daily from noon), and slot machines (July-Aug. daily from noon; Sept.-June M-F from 2pm, Sa-Su from noon). French games like *chemin de fer* and *trente et quarante* begin at noon in the more exclusive **salons privés.** (Cover €10. Coat and tie required.) Next door, the more relaxed **Café de Paris** opens at 10am and has no cover. All casinos have **dress codes** at night (no shorts, sneakers, sandals, or jeans). Guards are strict about the age requirement (18+); bring a passport as proof. On a cliff by the sea, the **Palais Princier** is the occasional home of Monaco's tabloid-darling royal family. Visitors curious for a glimpse of royal life can tour the small but lavish palace. (Open daily June-Sept. 9:30am-6pm; Oct. 10am-5pm. €6, students €3.) The nearby **Cathédrale de Monaco**, at pl. St-Martin, is the burial site for 35 generations of the Grimaldi family and was the venue for Prince Rainier and Grace Kelly's 1956 wedding. Princess Grace lies behind the altar in a tomb marked with her Latinized name, "Patritia Gracia," with Prince Rainier buried on her right. (Open daily Mar.-Oct. 8am-7pm; Nov.-Feb. 8am-6pm. Mass Sa 6pm, Su 10:30am. Free.) The **Private Collection of Antique Cars of His Serene Highness Prince Rainier III**, on les Terraces de Fontvieille, showcases 100 of the sexiest cars ever made. (Open daily 10am-6pm. €6, students €3.)

Monaco's nightlife offers fashionistas a chance to see and be seen. Speckled with cheaper venues, **La Condamine**, near the port, caters to a young clientele while glitzy trust-funders frequent pricier spots near the casino. Vintage decor, video games, and the latest pop and techno beats draws young, international masses to **Stars N' Bars**, 6 q. Antoine 1er. (☎04 97 97 95 95; www.starsnbars.com. Open June-Sept. daily 11am-3am; Oct.-May Tu-Su 11am-3am.)

ANTIBES   ☎04 93

Blessed with beautiful beaches and a charming *vieille ville*, Antibes (pop. 80,000) is less touristy than Nice and more relaxed than St-Tropez. It provides much needed middle ground on the glitterati-controlled coast. The ▓**Musée Picasso**, in the Château Grimaldi on pl. Mariejol, which displays works by the former Antibes resident and his contemporaries, is closed for renovations through early 2008. The two main public beaches in Antibes, **plage du Pontell** and neighboring **plage de la Salls**, are crowded all summer. Cleaner and slightly more secluded, the rocky beaches on **Cap d'Antibes** have white cliffs and blue water perfect for snorkeling.

For the cheapest accommodations in Antibes, grab a bunk with a rowdy crowd of yacht-hands at **The Crew House ❷**, 1 av. St-Roch. From the train station, walk down av. de la Libération; just after the roundabout, make a right onto av. St-Roch. (☎04 92 90 49 39; workstation_fr@yahoo.com. Internet €4.80 per hr. Reception M-F 9am-7pm, Sa-Su 10am-6pm. Dorms Apr.-Oct. €20; Nov.-Mar. €15. MC/V.) A variety of restaurants set up outdoor tables along **boulevard d'Aguillon**, behind the *vieux port*. For cheaper eats, you're better off at **place Nationale**, a few blocks away. The **Marché Provençal**, on cours Masséna, is one of the best fresh produce markets on the Côte

crayon, and *gomme* is not for chewing, unless you like the taste of rubber—it is an **eraser.**

An *extincteur* is not some sort of bazooka. It is a **fire extinguisher.**

Fesses is not a colloquial term for "coming clean"; it means **buttocks.**

As is not another way to say *fesses* or even an insult. This is a French compliment, meaning **ace** or **champion.**

Ranger is neither a woodsman nor a mighty morpher. This means **to tidy up.**

A *smoking* has little to do with tobacco (or any other substance). It is a **tuxedo** or **dinner suit.**

Raisins are juicy **grapes,** not the dried-up snack food. Try *raisins-secs* instead.

Prunes are plums. *Pruneaus* are the dried fruit.

Tampons are stamps (for documents), not the feminine care item. If you are looking for those, ask for a *tampon hygiénique* or *napkins*. To wipe your mouth, you would do better with a *serviette*.

The *patron* is the **boss**, not the customer.

A *glacier* does translate literally, meaning glacier, but you are more likely to see it around town on signs for **ice cream vendors;** *glace* does not mean glass, but a frozen summer treat.

If the French language seems full of deception, think again. *Deception* in French actually means **disappointment.**

—*Jack Pararas*

d'Azur. (Open Tu-Su 6am-1pm.) Boutiques generally remain open until midnight, cafes until 2am, discotheques until 5am, and bars past dawn.

Come summer, the neighboring town **Juan-les-Pins** is synonymous with hot nightlife. **Pam Pam Rhumerie,** 137 bd. Wilson, a Brazilian sit-down bar, turns wild when bikinied showgirls take the stage at 9:30pm to dance and down flaming drinks. (☎61 11 05. Open daily mid-Mar. to early Nov. 2pm-5am.) In **Whisky à Gogo,** 5 r. Jacques Leonetti, water-filled columns lit with black lights frame a young, dancing crowd. (Cover €16, students €8; includes 1 drink. Open July-Aug. daily midnight-5am; Apr.-June and Sept.-Oct. Th-Sa midnight-5am.) Take a **bus** (10min., 2 per hr., €1) or **train** (5min., 1-2 per hr., €1.20) from Antibes or walk along bd. Wilson to reach Juan-les-Pins. Although touristy, the **petit train** (☎06 03 35 61 35) leaves r. de la République and serves as both a guided tour of Antibes and a means of transportation to Juan-les-Pins. (30min.; 1 per hr. July-Aug. 10am-11pm, May-Oct. 10am-7pm. Round-trip €8, 3-10 €3.50. Buy tickets on board. Cash only.)

Trains leave pl. Pierre Semard in Antibes, off av. Robert Soleau, for Cannes (15min., 23 per day, €2.30), Marseille (2¼hr., 12 per day, €25), and Nice (15min., 25 per day, €3.60). RCA **buses** leave pl. de Gaulle for Cannes (20min.) and Nice (45min.). All buses depart every 20min. and cost €1.30. From the train station, turn right on av. Robert Soleau and follow the signs to the **tourist office,** 11 pl. de Gaulle. (☎04 97 23 11 11; www.antibesjuanlespins.com. Open July-Aug. daily 9am-7pm; Sept.-June M-F 9am-12:30pm and 1:30-5pm.) **Postal Code:** 06600.

CANNES ☎04 93

Stars compete for camera time at Cannes's annual, world-famous—and invite only—■**Festival International du Film** (May 14-25, 2008). During the rest of the year, Cannes (pop. 67,000) rolls up the red carpet—save its most famous one, still at the Palais for your tacky photographic pleasure—and becomes the most accessible of all the Riviera's glam towns. A palm-lined boardwalk, sandy beaches, and numerous boutiques draw the wealthy as well as the young. Of the town's three **casinos,** the least exclusive is **Le Casino Croisette,** 1 Lucien Barrière, next to the Palais des Festivals. (No shorts, jeans, or T-shirts. Jackets required for men. 18+. Cover €10. Open daily 10am-4am; table games 8pm-4am.)

Hostels are 10-20min. farther from the beach than other lodgings, but are the cheapest options. **Hotel Mimont ❸,** 39 r. de Mimont, two streets behind the train station, off bd. de la , is Cannes's best budget hotel. English-speaking owners maintain basic, clean rooms two streets behind the train station. (☎39 51 64; canneshotelmimont65@wanadoo.fr. Free Wi-Fi. Singles €34-40; doubles €40-47; triples €58. Prices about 15% higher July-Aug. Ask about *Let's Go* discounts. AmEx/MC/V.) Run by a young, English-speaking couple, **Hostel Les Iris ❷,** 77 bd. Carnot, was converted from an old hotel into a bright hostel with sturdy bunks and a Mexican-themed terrace restaurant. (☎68 30 20; www.iris-solola.com. Dorms €23. AmEx/MC/V.) The pedestrian zone around **rue Meynadier** has inexpensive restaurants. A great alternative to the expense of gambling and posh clubs, cafes and bars near the waterfront stay open all night. Nightlife thrives around **rue Dr. G. Monod.** Try ■**Morrison's,** 10 r. Teisseire, for casual company in a literary-themed pub. (☎04 92 98 16 17. Beer from €5. Happy hour 5-8pm. Open daily 5pm-2am. MC/V.) **Trains** depart from 1 r. Jean Jaurès for: Antibes (15min., €2.30); Marseille (2hr., €24); Monaco (1hr., €7.50); Nice (40min., €5.50); St-Raphaël (25min., €5.70). **Buses** leave from the pl. de l'Hôtel de Ville (☎48 70 30) for Nice (1½hr., 3 per hr., €6). The **tourist office** is at 1 bd. de la Croisette. (☎39 24 53; www.cannes.fr. Open July-Aug. daily 9am-8pm; Sept.-June M-F 9am-7pm.) **Postal Code:** 06400.

ST-TROPEZ ☎04 94

Hollywood stars, corporate giants, and curious backpackers congregate on the spotless streets of St-Tropez (pop. 5400), where the glitz and glamor of the Riviera shines brightest. The young, beautiful, and restless flock to this "Jewel of the Riviera" to flaunt tans and designer clothing on notorious **beaches** and in posh night-clubs. The best beaches are difficult to reach without a car, but a **navette municipale** (shuttle) leaves pl. des Lices for secluded **Les Salins** and **plage Tahiti** (Capon-Pinet stop), the first of the famous **plages des Pampelonne.** (M-Sa 5 per day, €1.) Take a break from the sun at the **Musée de l'Annonciade,** pl. Grammont, which showcases Fauvist and neo-Impressionist paintings. (Open M and W-Su June-Sept. 10am-noon and 2-6pm; Oct.-May 10am-1pm and 4-7pm. €4.60, students €2.30.)

Budget hotels do not exist in St-Tropez. **Camping** is the cheapest option, but is only available outside the city. Prices remain shockingly high, especially in July and August. To reach **Les Prairies de la Mer ❸,** a social campground on the beach, take a *bateau vert* (☎49 29 39) from the *vieux port* to Port Grimaud (Apr.-early Oct., 5min., 1 per hr., round-trip €11). Bowling, supermarkets, and tennis courts are available. (☎79 09 09; www.riviera-villages.com. Bike rental €7 per day. Open early Apr.-early Oct. July to mid-Aug. €6 per person, €42 per tent; Apr.-June and late Aug. €5/25; Sept. to mid-Oct. €5/18-25. Free electricity. MC/V.) For a cheap meal, stop by the snack stands and cafes near **place des Lices,** the center of St-Tropez's wild nightlife. Shell out €25,000 for a bottle of Cristal at **Les Caves du Roy,** av. Paul Signac, in the **Hotel Byblos,** or if things look shaky on the trust-fund front, settle for a €25 gin and tonic. (☎56 68 00. Open July-Aug. daily 11pm-5am; June and Sept. F-Sa 11:30pm-4am. AmEx/MC/V.)

Take a Sodetrav **bus** (☎97 88 51) from av. Général Leclerc to St-Raphaël (2hr., 10-14 per day, €10), where you can connect to **trains** serving Cannes (25min., 2 per hr., €6), Marseille (1¾hr., 1 per hr., €24), and Nice (1hr., 2 per hr., €9.80). **Ferries** (☎95 17 46; www.tmr-saintraphael.com), at the *vieux port,* also serve St-Tropez from St-Raphaël (1hr., 4-5 per day, €12). St-Tropez's **tourist office** is on q. Jean Jaurès. (☎97 45 21. Open daily July-Sept. 9:30am-8pm; Sept.-Oct. and mid-Mar. to June 9:30am-12:30pm and 2-7pm; early Nov. to mid-Mar. 9:30am-12:30pm and 2-6pm.) **Postal Code:** 83990.

▓CORSICA (LA CORSE)   ☎04 95

Bathed in turquoise Mediterranean waters, Corsica (COHR-sih-kuh; pop. 279,000) was dubbed *Kallysté* (the most beautiful) by the Greeks. Fiercely defensive of its identity, Corsica has long resisted foreign rule. The island guarded its culture during centuries of invasions by Phoenicia, Carthage, Rome, Pisa, and Genoa. Natives remain divided over the issue of national allegiance, often rejecting the French language in favor of Corse. Most visitors come for Corsica's unspoiled landscapes, easily accessible from major towns. Nearly one-third of the island is a protected nature reserve, and over 100 summits pierce its sunny sky—it only rains 55 days of the year. An unbroken coastlines draws kayakers, windsurfers, and sunbathers.

▐ TRANSPORTATION

Air France and **Compagnie Corse Méditerranée (CCM)** fly to Ajaccio and Bastia from Marseille (€88, students €71); Nice (€85/68); and Paris (€112/109). In Ajaccio, the Air France/CCM office is at 3 bd. du Roi Jérôme (☎08 20 82 08 20). **Ferries** between the mainland and Corsica aren't always cheaper than planes. Hydrofoils (3½hr.) run from Nice, while overnight ferries from Marseille take nearly 10hr. The Société National Maritime Corse Méditerranée (SNCM; ☎08 91 70 18 01; www.sncm.fr) sends ferries from Marseille (€40-58, under 25 €25-45) and Nice (€35-47/20-35) to Ajaccio and Bastia. Corsica Ferries (☎08 25 09 50 95; www.corsicaferries.com) has similar destinations and prices. SAREMAR (☎73 00 96) and Moby Lines (☎073 00 29) go from Santa Teresa, ITA to Bonifacio (2-5 per day, €14-15, cars €26-52). Moby Lines (€16-28) and Corisca Ferries (€16-32) cross from Genoa, ITA and Livorno, ITA to Bastia. Corsican **train** service is limited to destinations north of Ajaccio and

HELPING THROUGH HUMOR

At the age of 26, Michel Colucci adopted the name Coluche and—like so many before him with only one appellation—embarked on a career in entertainment. Sure enough, the man with the razor-sharp political wit quickly became one of France's most beloved comedians. He ran for president in 1981—"I'll quit politics when politicians quit comedy"—but dropped out of the race when polls showed that he actually had a chance of winning. Before a motorcycle accident ended his life in 1986, Coluche founded the charity **Restos du Coeur** (restaurants of the heart), leaving a permanent mark on France.

Restos du Coeur comprises a network of soup kitchens and other volunteer activities. Their emphasis on fostering personal relationships between those who volunteer and those who receive aid, as well as on good humor—would a comedian have it any other way?—has set them apart as a uniquely positive force of goodwill. Volunteers can work the kitchens, provide face-to-face companionship, or help combat illiteracy, but they have to be able to do it for a few months.

Paris office: 4 cité d'Hauteville (☎ 53 24 98 00; www.restosducoeur.org). Meals distributed daily in different regions of the city.

doesn't accept rail passes. Eurocorse Voyages **buses** (☎21 06 30) serve the whole island. **Hiking** is the best way to explore Corsica's mountainous interior. The difficult GR20, a 12- to 15-day, 180km trail, spans from Calenzana to Conca. The **Parc Naturel Régional de la Corse**, 2 Sargent Casalonga, Ajaccio, has a guide to *gîtes d'étape* (rest houses) and maps. (☎51 79 00; www.parc-naturel-corse.com.)

AJACCIO (AIACCIU)

Napoleon must have insisted on the best from the very beginning: the little dictator couldn't have picked a better place to call home. Brimming with more energy than most Corsican towns, Ajaccio (pop. 60,000) has excellent museums and summer nightlife to complement its white-sand beaches. Inside the ▨**Musée Fesch,** 50-52 r. Cardinal Fesch, cavernous rooms hold an impressive collection of 14th- to 19th-century Italian paintings gathered by Napoleon's uncle. Also within the complex is the **Chapelle Impériale,** the final resting place of most of the Bonaparte family, though Napoleon himself is buried in Paris. (Open July-Aug. M 2-6pm, Tu-Th 10:30am-6pm, F 2-9:30pm, Sa-Su 10:30am-6pm; Sept.-June reduced hours. Museum €5.35, students €3.80. Chapel €1.50/0.75.) Although Ajaccio has many hotels, rates soar and vacancies plummet from June through August. The welcoming ▨**Pension de Famille Tina Morelli ❹,** 1 r. Major Lambroschini, fills up quickly. (☎21 16 97. Breakfast included. Singles €50, with half-pension €72; doubles €70/124. Cash only.) Though Ajaccio has no shortage of restaurants, your best option is the **morning market** on pl. du Marché. (Open Tu-Su 8am-1pm.) Pizzerias, bakeries, and one-stop panini shops can be found on **rue Cardinal Fesch;** at night, patios on the festive dock offer affordable seafood and pizza. **Boulevard Pascal Rossini,** near the casino, is home to Ajaccio's busiest strip of bars. TCA bus #8 (€4.50) shuttles passengers from the bus station at q. l'Herminier to **Aéroport Campo dell'Oro (AJA; ☎**23 56 56), where flights serve Lyon, Marseille, Nice, and Paris. **Trains** (☎23 11 03) leave pl. de la Gare for Bastia (3-4hr., 4 per day, €24). Eurocorse Voyages **buses** (☎21 06 30) go to Bastia (3hr., 2 per day, €18) and Bonifacio (3hr., 2 per day, €21). The **tourist office** is at 3 bd. du Roi Jérôme. (☎51 53 03; www.ajaccio-tourisme.com. Open July-Aug. M-Sa 8am-8:30pm, Su 9am-1pm and 4-7pm; Sept.-June reduced hours.) **Postal Code:** 20000.

BASTIA

Bastia (pop. 40,000), Corsica's second-largest city, is one of the island's most trampled gateways, with connections to the French mainland and more remote villages. **Terra Nova,** its enormous 14th-century citadel, is impressively intact, with ramparts reaching downhill toward the *vieux port*, dwarfing nearby shops. The tiny **Eco-Musée**, in the citadel's old powder magazine (ammunition storehouse), contains a detailed replica of a traditional Corsican village. (Open Apr.-Oct. M-Sa 9am-noon and 2-6pm. €4, students €3.) On the other side of the *vieux port*, the 17th-century **Église St-Jean Baptiste**, pl. de l'Hôtel de Ville, is Corisca's largest church. Its gilded walls and ornate altars were constructed with funds raised by local fishermen. While there're no true budget hotels in Bastia, **Hôtel Posta Vecchia ❹**, 8 r. Posta-Vecchia, has a few small rooms that remain reasonably priced during high season (☎32 32 38; www.hotel-postavecchia.com. Breakfast €6. July-Sept. singles €45, doubles €55-90, triples €90-100; Oct.-Feb. €40/53-75/80-86; Mar.-June €40/45-70/70-80. AmEx/MC/V.) To reach **Camping Les Orangers ❶**, take bus #4 from the tourist office to Licciola-Miomo. (☎33 24 09. Open May to mid-Oct. €5 per person, €3 per tent, €2.60 per car. Electricity €3.50.) Inexpensive cafes crowd **place St-Nicolas**. Though Bastia nightlife is less dynamic than in other Corsican towns, young people find their way to **Port de Plaisance de Toga**. Shuttle buses (30min., €8) leave from the *préfecture*, across from the train station, for the **Bastia-Poretta Airport** (**BIA**; ☎54 54 54). Flights go to Marseille, Nice, and Paris. **Trains** (☎32 80 61) run from pl. de la Gare to Ajaccio (4hr., 3-5 per day, €24). Eurocorse **buses** (☎21 06 31) leave from rte. du Nouveau Port for Ajaccio (3hr., 1-2 per day, €20). The **tourist office** is in pl. St-Nicolas. (☎54 20 40; www.bastia-tourisme.com. Open daily July-Aug. 8am-8pm; Sept.-June 8:30am-noon and 2-6pm.) **Postal Code:** 20200.

BONIFACIO (BONIFAZIU)

At the southern tip of Corsica, the stone ramparts of Bonifacio (pop. 2660), atop 70m limestone cliffs, present an imposing visage to miles of empty turquoise sea. Bonifacio's fantastic **boat tours** reveal multicolored cliffs, coves, and stalactite-filled grottoes. Ferries also run to the pristine sands of **Îles Lavezzi**, a nature reserve with beautiful reefs perfect for **scuba diving**. Book tours with **Les Vedettes**. (☎06 86 34 00 49. Grottes-Falaises-Calanques tour 2 per hr. 9am-6:30pm; €17. Îles Lavezzi tour 5 departures per day, last return 5:30pm; €25. Cash only.) To explore the *haute-ville*, head up the steep, broad steps of the **montée Rastello**, located halfway down the port, from where excellent views of the hazy cliffs to the east can be seen. Continue up montée St-Roch to the lookout at **Porte des Gênes**, a drawbridge built by invaders, then walk to the **Poste du Gouvernail** at the southern tip of the *haute-ville*, where an underground tunnel leads to grottoes carved out by Italians and Germans during WWII. **Camping** is the best option when prices soar in August. (☎73 02 96. Open Apr. to mid-Oct. €6.10 per person, €2.40 per tent, €2.40 per car. Electricity free. Laundry €5. Cash only.) A **SPAR** supermarket is on rte. de Santa Manza, near the port. (Open daily July-Aug. 8am-8:30pm; Sept.-June reduced hours.) The main **tourist office** is at the corner of av. de Gaulle and r. F. Scamaroni. (☎73 11 88. Open July-Aug. daily 9am-8pm; May-June and Sept. daily 10am-7pm; Oct.-Apr. M-F 9am-noon and 2-6pm.) **Postal Code:** 20169.

FRANCE

GERMANY
(DEUTSCHLAND)

 Encounters with history are unavoidable on visits to Germany, as changes in outlook, policy, and culture are manifest in the country's architecture, landscape, and customs. Streamlined glass skyscrapers rise from former concrete wastelands; towns crop up from fields and forests, interspersed with medieval castles and industrial structures. World-class music rings out from sophisticated city centers, while a grittier youth culture flourishes in quite different neighborhoods. Such divisions echo the entrenched Cold War separation between East and West. Today, nearly 20 years after the fall of the Berlin Wall, Germans have fashioned a new identity for themselves. Visitors will find flowing beer and wondrous sights from the darkest corners of the Black Forest to the shores of the Baltic Sea.

DISCOVER GERMANY: SUGGESTED ITINERARIES

THREE DAYS. Enjoy 2 days in **Berlin** (p. 389): stroll along **Unter den Linden** and the **Ku'damm**, gape at the **Brandenburger Tor** and the **Reichstag**, and explore the **Tiergarten.** Walk along the **East Side Gallery** and visit **Checkpoint Charlie** for a history of the Berlin Wall, then pass an afternoon at **Schloß Sanssouci** (p. 411). Overnight it to **Munich** (p. 436) for a Stein-themed last day.

ONE WEEK. After scrambling through **Berlin** (3 days), head north to racy **Hamburg** (1 day; p. 412). Take in the cathedral of **Cologne** (1 day; p. 420) before slowing down in the bucolic **Lorelei Cliffs** (1 day; p. 430). End your trip Bavarian-style with the beer gardens, castles, and cathedrals of **Munich** (1 day).

THREE WEEKS. Begin in **Berlin** (3 days). Party in **Hamburg** (2 days), then zip to **Cologne** (1 day) and the former West German capital, **Bonn** (1 day; p. 424). Contrast the Roman ruins at **Trier** (1 day; p. 428) with glitzy **Frankfurt** (1 day; p. 425), then visit Germany's oldest university in **Heidelberg** (2 days; p. 431). Lose your way in the fairy-tale **Black Forest** (2 days; p. 435), before finding it again in **Munich** (2 days). Marvel at **Neuschwanstein** (1 day; p. 447) and see the beauty of the **Romantic Road** (2 days; p. 446). Get cultured in Goethe's **Weimar** (1 day; p. 448)—then dramatize your learnings in Faust's cellar in **Leipzig** (1 day; p. 454). End your trip in the reconstructed splendor of **Dresden** (1 day; p. 450).

ESSENTIALS

WHEN TO GO

Germany's climate is temperate. The cloudy, mild months of May, June, and September are the best time to go, as there are fewer tourists and the weather is pleasant. In July, Germans head en masse to summer spots. Winter sports gear up from November to April; ski season takes place from mid-December to March.

FACTS AND FIGURES

Official Name: Federal Republic of Germany.

Capital: Berlin.

Major Cities: Cologne, Frankfurt, Hamburg, Munich.

Population: 82,401,000.

Land Area: 349,200 sq. km.

Time Zone: GMT +1.

Religions: Protestant (34%), Roman Catholic (34%), Muslim (2%).

Percentage of European Beer Production: 26.5%.

Beer Consumed Annually: 9,200,000hL.

Per Capita: 111.6L (a whole lot of beer).

DOCUMENTS AND FORMALITIES

EMBASSIES. All foreign embassies are in Berlin (p. 389). German embassies abroad include: **Australia,** 119 Empire Circuit, Yarralumla, Canberra, ACT 2600 (☎02 6270 1911; www.germanembassy.org.au); **Canada,** 1 Waverly St., Ottawa, ON, K2P OT8 (☎613-232-1101; www.ottawa.diplo.de); **Ireland,** 31 Trimleston Ave., Booterstown, Blackrock, Co. Dublin (☎01 269 3011; www.dublin.diplo.de); **New Zealand,** 90-92 Hobson St., Thorndon, Wellington 6001 (☎04 473 6063; www.wellington.diplo.de); **UK,** 23 Belgrave Sq., London, SW1X 8PZ (☎020 7824 1300; www.london.diplo.de); **US,** 4645 Reservoir Rd. NW, Washington, D.C., 20007 (☎202-298-4000; www.germany-info.org).

VISA AND ENTRY INFORMATION. EU citizens do not need a visa. Citizens of Australia, Canada, New Zealand, and the US do not need a visa for stays of up to 90 days, beginning upon entry into any of the countries in the EU's freedom-of-movement zone. For more info, see p. 13. For stays longer than 90 days, all non-EU citizens need visas (around €100), available at Germany consulates.

TOURIST SERVICES AND MONEY

EMERGENCY **Ambulance** and **Fire:** ☎112. **Police:** ☎110.

TOURIST OFFICES. The **National Tourist Board** website (www.germany-tourism.de) links to regional info and provides dates of national and local festivals. Every city in Germany has a tourist office, usually near the *Hauptbahnhof* (main train station) or *Marktplatz* (central square). All are marked by a sign with a thick lowercase "*i,*" and many book rooms for a small fee.

MONEY. The **euro (€)** has replaced the **Deutschmark (DM)** as the unit of currency in Germany. For more info, see p. 16. As a general rule, it's cheaper to exchange money in Germany than at home. Costs for those who stay in hostels and prepare their own food may range anywhere from €25-50 per person per day. **Tipping** is not practiced as liberally in Germany as elsewhere—most natives just round up €1. Tips are handed directly to the server with payment of the bill—if you don't want any change, say "*Das stimmt so*" (das SHTIMMT zo; "so it stands"). Germans rarely bargain except at flea markets. Germany has a 19% **value added tax (VAT),** a sales tax applied to most goods and services. The prices given in *Let's Go* include VAT. In the airport upon exiting the EU, non-EU citizens can claim a refund on the tax paid for goods purchased at participating stores. In order to qualify for a refund in a store, you must spend at least €25; make sure to ask for a refund form when you pay. For more info on qualifying for a VAT refund, see p. 19.

BUSINESS HOURS. Offices and stores are open from 9am-6pm, Monday through Friday, often closing for an hour lunch break. Stores may be open on

GERMANY

Saturday in cities or shopping centers. Banks are also open from approximately 9am-6pm, and close briefly in the late afternoon but may stay open late on Thursday nights. Many museums are closed on Monday.

TRANSPORTATION

BY PLANE. Most international flights land at **Frankfurt Airport** (**FRA;** ☎ 069 6900; www.airportcity-frankfurt.com); **Berlin (BML), Munich (MUC),** and **Hamburg (HAM)** also have international airports. **Lufthansa,** the national airline, is not always the best-priced option. Often it is cheaper to travel domestically by plane than by train; check out **Air Berlin** (www.airberlin.com), among other options.

BY TRAIN. The **Deutsche Bahn** (**DB;** www.bahn.de) network is Europe's best—and one of its most expensive. Luckily, all trains have clean and comfy second-class compartments, and there are a wide variety of train lines to choose from. **Regional-Bahn (RB)** trains include rail networks between neighboring cities and connects to **RegionalExpress (RE)** lines. **InterRegioExpress (IRE)** trains, covering larger networks between cities, are speedy and comfortable. **S-Bahn** trains run locally within large cities and high density areas. Some S-Bahn stops also service speedy **StadtExpress (SE)** trains, which directly connects city centers. **EuroCity (EC)** and **InterCity (IC)** trains zoom between major cities every 1-2hr. **InterCityExpress (ICE)** trains approach the luxury and kinetics of airplanes, barreling along the tracks at speeds up to 300kph, and service international destinations including Austria, Belgium, the Netherlands, and Switzerland. For overnight travel, choose between the first-class **DB Autozug** or cheaper **DB Nachtzug** lines.

Eurail is valid in Germany. The **German Rail Pass** allows unlimited travel for four to 10 days within a one-month period, including Basel, SWI and Salzburg, AUT. Non-EU citizens can purchase German Rail Passes at select major train stations in Germany (5- or 10-day passes only) or through travel agents (2nd class 4-day pass €169, 10-day €289; under 26 €139/199). A **Schönes-Wochenende-Ticket** (€33) gives up to five people unlimited travel on any of the slower trains (RE or RB) from 12:01am Saturday or Sunday until 3am the next day; single travelers often find larger groups who will share their ticket.

BY BUS. Bus service runs from the local **ZOB** *(Zentralomnibusbahnhof)*, usually close to the main train station. Buses are usually slightly more expensive than trains. Rail passes are not valid on buses except for a few run by Deutsche Bahn.

BY CAR AND BY BIKE. Given generally excellent road conditions, Germans drive fast. The rumors are true: the *Autobahn* does not have a speed limit, only a recommendation of 130kph (80 mph). Watch for signs indicating the right-of-way (usually a yellow triangle). Signs with an "A" denote the *Autobahn;* signs bearing a "B" accompany secondary highways, which typically have a 100kph (60mph) speed limit. In cities and towns, speed limits hover around 30-60kph (20-35 mph). For a small fee, **Mitfahrzentralen,** and their women-only counterparts, **Frauenmitfahrzentralen,** agencies pair up drivers and riders, who then negotiate trip payment between themselves. Seat belts are mandatory, and police strictly enforce driving laws. Germany has designated lanes for **bicycles.** *Germany by Bike*, by Nadine Slavinski (Mountaineers Books, 1994), details 20 tours throughout Germany.

BY THUMB. Hitchhiking or even standing on the Autobahn is illegal. In some parts of Germany, hitchhiking does occur. Let's Go does not recommend hitchhiking.

KEEPING IN TOUCH

PHONE CODES	**Country code: 49. International dialing prefix: 00.** For more info on how to place international calls, see **Inside Back Cover.**

EMAIL AND THE INTERNET. Almost all German cities, as well as a surprising number of smaller towns, have at least one Internet cafe with web access for about €2-10 per hour. Wi-Fi is often available in bigger cities; in Berlin's new Sony Center (p. 400), the Wi-Fi is completely, blissfully free. Some German universities have Internet in their libraries intended for student use.

TELEPHONE. Most public phones will accept only a phone card *(Telefonkarte)*, available at post offices, kiosks, and some Deutsche Bahn counters. **Mobile phones** are an increasingly popular and economical alternative (p. 29). Phone numbers have no standard length. Direct-dial access numbers for calling out of Germany include: **AT&T USADirect** (☎0800 225 5288); **Canada Direct** (☎0800 888

0014); **MCI WorldPhone** (☎0800 888 8000); **Telecom New Zealand** (☎0800 080 0064); and **Telstra Australia** (☎0800 080 0061); most of these services require a calling card or credit card. For more info, see p. 28.

MAIL. Airmail (*Luftpost* or *par avion*) usually takes three to six days to Ireland and the UK, four to 10 days to Australia and North America. *Let's Go* lists addresses for mail to be held **Poste Restante** (*Postlagernde Briefe*) in the **Practical Information** sections of big cities. Mail will go to the main post office unless you specify a subsidiary by street address. Address mail to be held as follows: First name Last name, *Postlagernde Briefe*, Postal code, City, GERMANY.

ACCOMMODATIONS AND CAMPING

GERMANY	❶	❷	❸	❹	❺
ACCOMMODATIONS	under €15	€15-25	€26-33	€34-50	over €50

Germany currently has more than 600 **youth hostels**—more than any other nation. Official hostels in Germany are overseen by **DJH** (*Deutsches Jugendherberg-swerk*), Bismarckstr. 8, D 32756 Detmold, Germany (☎05231 740 10; www.jugendherberge.de). A growing number of **Jugendgästehäuser** (youth guest-houses) have more facilities than hostels and attract slightly older guests. DJH publishes *Jugendherbergen in Deutschland*, a guide to federated German hostels. Most charge €15-25 for dorms. The cheapest **hotel-style** accommodations are places with *Pension, Gasthof,* or *Gästehaus* in the name. Hotel rooms start at €20 for singles and €30 for doubles; in large cities, expect to pay nearly twice as much. *Frühstück* (breakfast) is almost always available, if not included. The best bet for a cheap bed is often a **Privatzimmer** (room in a family home), where a basic knowledge of German is very helpful. Prices can be as low as €15 per person. Reservations are made through the local tourist office or through a *Zimmervermittlung* (private booking office), sometimes for a small fee. Over 2500 **campsites** dot the German landscape. Bathrooms, a restaurant or store, and showers generally accompany a campground's well-maintained facilities. Camping costs €3-12 per tent site and €4-6 per extra person, with additional charges for tent and vehicle rental. Blue signs with a black tent on a white background indicate official sites.

 CHILDREN, CHILDREN, EVERYWHERE. Schools in Germany often take students on week-long trips at the end of May and throughout June. As a result, hostels tend to be booked on weekdays—make reservations early!

FOOD AND DRINK

GERMANY	❶	❷	❸	❹	❺
FOOD AND DRINK	under €4	€4-8	€9-12	€13-20	over €20

A typical breakfast (*Frühstück*) consists of coffee or tea with rolls (*Brötchen*), **cold sausage** (*Wurst*), and **cheese** (*Käse*). Germans' main meal, lunch (*Mittagessen*), includes soup, broiled sausage or roasted meat, potatoes or dumplings, and a salad or vegetable. Dinner (*Abendessen* or *Abendbrot*) is a reprise of breakfast, with beer in place of coffee and a wider selection of meats and cheeses. Many older Germans indulge in a daily ritual of coffee and cake (*Kaffee und Kuchen*) at 3 or 4pm. To eat cheaply, stick to a restaurant's daily menu (*Tagesmenü*), buy food in supermarkets, or head to a **university cafeteria** (*Mensa*). Fast-food stands (*Imbiß*) also offer cheap, often foreign eats—try a *Döner* kebab. The average German beer is maltier and more "bread-like" than Czech or American beers; a common nickname for German brew is liquid bread (*flüßiges Brot*).

HOLIDAYS AND FESTIVALS

Holidays: New Year's Day (Jan. 1); Epiphany (Jan. 6); Good Friday (Mar. 21); Easter (Mar. 23-24); Ascension (May 1); Pentecost (May 11-12); Corpus Christi (May 22); Assumption (Aug. 15); German Unity Day (Oct. 3); All Saints' Day (Nov. 1); Christmas (Dec. 25-26).

Festivals: Check out the pre-Lenten bacchanalia during *Fasching* in Munich and *Karneval* in Cologne. (Feb. 1-5); international film in the Berlinale Film Festival (Feb. 7-17; p. 407); gay pride parades on Christopher Street Day in major cities (early June; p. 410); vanishing kegs during Oktoberfest in Munich (Sept. 20-Oct. 5; p. 443); and the Christmas Market in Nuremberg (Nov. 28-Dec. 24).

BEYOND TOURISM

Germany's volunteering opportunities often involve environmental preservation—working on farms or in forests and educating people on conservation—though civil service and community building prospects still exist, especially in eastern Germany. For more info on opportunities across Europe, see **Beyond Tourism**, p. 56

World-Wide Opportunities on Organic Farms (WWOOF), Postfach 210259, 01263 Dresden, Germany (www.wwoof.de). €18 membership in WWOOF gives you room and board at a variety of organic farms in Germany in exchange for chores.

Open Houses Network, Goethepl. 9B, D-99423 Weimar (☎03 643 502 390; www.openhouses.de). A group dedicated to restoring and sharing public space (mostly in Eastern Germany), providing lodging in return for work.

BERLIN   ☎030

Berlin is bigger than Paris, up later than New York, and wilder than Amsterdam. Dizzying and electric, this city of 3.4 million has an increasingly diverse population, and it can be hard to keep track of which *Bezirk* (neighborhood) is currently the trendiest. Traces of the past century's Nazi and Communist regimes remain etched in residents' minds, and a psychological division between East and West Germany—the problem dubbed *Mauer im Kopf* ("wall in the head")—still exists nearly two decades after the Berlin Wall's destruction. Restless and contradictory, Germany's capital shows no signs of slowing down its self-reinvention, and the Berlin of next year may be radically different from the Berlin of today.

◼ INTERCITY TRANSPORTATION

Flights: The city is now transitioning from 3 airports to 1 (Flughafen Schönefeld will become the Berlin-Brandenburg International Airport), but at least until 2011, **Flughafen Tegel (TXL)** will remain West Berlin's main international airport. For info on all 3 of Berlin's airports, call ☎0180 500 0186 (www.berlin-airport.de). Take express bus #X9 from Bahnhof Zoo, bus #109 from Jakob-Kaiser-Pl. on U7, bus #128 from Kurt-Schumacher-Pl. on U6, or bus TXL from Potsdamer Pl. or Bahnhof Zoo. **Flughafen Schönefeld (BER),** southeast of Berlin, is used for intercontinental flights and travel to developing countries. Take S9 or 45 to Flughafen Berlin Schönefeld, or ride the Schönefeld Express train (2 per hr. through most major S-Bahn stations). **Flughafen Tempelhof (THF)** is slated to close October 31, 2008, but remains open until then for European flights. Take U6 to Pl. der Luftbrücke.

Trains: Berlin's massive new **Hauptbahnhof,** which opened in time for the 2006 World Cup, is the city's major transit hub, with some international and domestic trains continuing to **Ostbahnhof** in the East. Hauptbahnhof currently connects only to the S-Bahn,

GERMANY

Berlin Overview

Stadtring · **Westhafenkanal** · WESTHAFEN Ⓤ

Quitzowstr. · Heidestr.

Siemensstr. · BIRKENSTR. Ⓤ · Stromstr. · Perleberger Str. · Rathenower Str.

MOABIT

JUNGFERNHEIDE Ⓤ · Sickingenstr. · Gaußstr. · Hüttenstr. · Beusselstr. · Turmstr. · Invalidenstr.

TO ✈ FLUGHAFEN TEGEL · Kaiserin- Augusta- Allee · TURMSTR. Ⓤ · Alt-Moabit

MIERENDORFFPL. Ⓤ · Alt-Moabit

Spree

CHARLOTTENBURG & SCHÖNEBERG, SEE MAP p. 402

Levetzowstr. · BELLEVUE Ⓢ · **Spree**

RICHARD-WAGNER- PL. Ⓤ · Otto-Suhr-Allee · Wilmersdorfer Str. · Landwehrkanal · HANSA-PL. · Altonaér Str.

Kaiser-Friedrich-Str. · Marchstr. · **Technische Universität** · TIERGARTEN Ⓢ · GROSSER STERN · Str. des 17. Juni · **Tiergarten**

Deutsche Oper Ⓤ · Bismarckstr. · ERNST-REUTER-PL. · Str. des 17. Juni · Siegessäule · Hofjägerallee

TO ZOB (4km) · DEUTSCHE OPER Ⓤ · **Zoologischer Garten**

BISMARCKSTR. Ⓤ · Schillerstr. · Leibnizstr. · Knesebeckstr. · Hardenbergstr. · **Bahnhof Zoo** · Kulturforum 🏛

WILMERS-DORFER STR. Ⓤ · Kant Str. · SAVIGNY-PL. · ZOOLOGISCHER GARTEN Ⓤ · Budapesterstr.

CHARLOTTEN-BURG Ⓢ · SAVIGNYPL. Ⓢ · ⓘ Ⓢ · ✉ · ✝ Europa Center · Kurfürstenstr. · Einemstr. · Potsdamer Str.

CHARLOTTENBURG · Schlüterstr. · Kaiser-Wilhelm-Gedächtniskirche · Joachimstaler Str.

Lewishamstr. · ADENAUER PL. Ⓤ · Kurfürstendamm · UHLANDSTR. Ⓤ · Ⓢ **American Express** · WITTENBERG Ⓤ · Kleiststr. · NOLLENDORF-PL. Ⓤ · KURFÜRSTENR. Ⓤ

Kurfürstendamm · Konstanzerstr. · Lietzenburger Str. · AUGSBURGER STR. Ⓤ · VIKTORIA-LUISE PL. · NOLLEN-DORFPL. Ⓤ · BÜLOWSTR. Ⓤ

WILMERS-DORF · Uhlandstr. Ⓤ · SPICHERNSTR. Ⓤ

KONSTANZER STR. Ⓤ · HOHENZOLLERN-DAMM Ⓤ · Nachodstr. · Hohenstaufenstr. · Pallasstr. · **Kleistpark**

TO GRUNEWALD · FEHRBELLINER PL. Ⓤ · Brandenburgische Str. · Hohenzollerndamm · Güntzelstr. · GÜNTZELSTR. Ⓤ · **SCHÖNEBERG** · Goltzstr. · KLEIST-PARK Ⓤ · Hauptstr.

Stadtring Ⓢ · HOHENZOLLERNDAMM · Berliner Str. · BLISSESTR. Ⓤ · BERLINER STR. Ⓤ · Grunewaldstr. · BAYER. PL. Ⓤ · Martin-Luther-Str. · EISENACHER STR. Ⓤ · Mazierstr. · KAISER WILHELM PL.

SCHMARGENDORF · Uhland-Str. · Badensche Str. · Dominicusstr.

HEIDELBERGER PL. Ⓢ · Mecklenburgischestr. · Bundes Allee · RATHAUS SCHÖNEBERG Ⓤ · Feurigstr.

Ⓢ Ⓤ BUNDESPL. · INNSBR. PL. Ⓤ · Hauptstr. · SCHÖNEBERG Ⓢ Sachsendamm

0 — 1 mile
0 — 1 kilometer

GERMANY

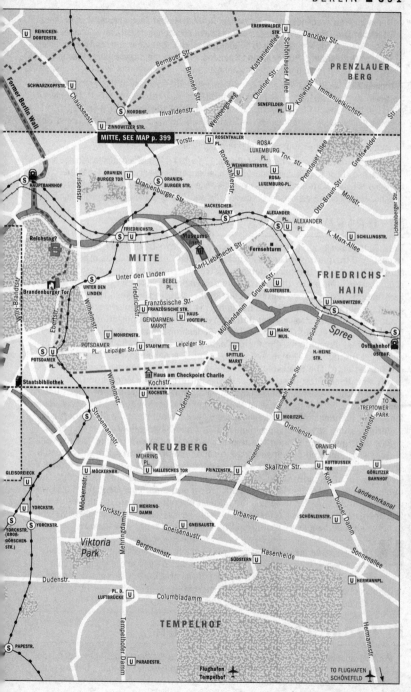

MITTE, SEE MAP p. 399

MITTE, SEE MAP p. 399

but a U55 line is scheduled to open in late 2007. **Bahnhof Zoologischer Garten** (a.k.a. **Bahnhof Zoo**), formerly the West's main station, now connects only to regional destinations. Many trains also connect to **Schönefeld** airport. A number of U- and S-Bahn lines stop at **Oranienburg, Potsdam,** and **Spandau.** Trains in the Brandenburg regional transit system tend to stop at all major stations, as well as Alexanderpl. and Friedrichstr.

Buses: ZOB (☎301 03 80), the "central" bus station, is actually at the western edge of town, by the Funkturm near Kaiserdamm. U2 to Kaiserdamm or S41/42 to Messe Nord/ICC. Open M-F 6am-9pm, Sa-Su 6am-3pm. **Gullivers,** at ZOB (☎311 0211; www.gullivers.de), Hardenbergpl. 14 (☎0800 48 55 48 37), and **Berlin Linien Bus** (030 851 9331, www.berlinlinienbus.de) often have good deals on bus fares. Open in summer daily 8am-9:30pm; in winter reduced hours.

Mitfahrzentralen: Citynetz, Joachimstaler Str. 17 (☎194 44), has a computerized ride-share database. U9 or 15 to Kurfürstendamm. To **Hamburg** or **Hanover** (€18) and **Frankfurt** (€31). Open M-F 9am-8pm, Sa-Su 10am-6pm. Other ride share bulletins at www.mitfahrzentrale.de and www.mitfahrgelegenheit.de. Check *030, Tip,* and *Zitty* for addresses and phone numbers.

✦ ORIENTATION

Berlin's landmarks include the **Spree River,** which flows through the city from west to east, and the narrower **Landwehrkanal Canal** that dumps into the Spree from the south. The vast central park, **Tiergarten,** stretches between the waterways. Two radio towers loom above the city: the pointed **Funkturm,** in the west, and the globed **Fernsehturm,** rising above **Alexanderplatz** in the east. In the west, the major thoroughfare **Kurfürstendamm** (a.k.a. Ku'damm) is lined with department stores and leads to the **Bahnhof Zoologischer Garten,** West Berlin's transportation hub. Nearby is the elegant wreck of the **Kaiser-Wilhelm Gedächtniskirche,** as well as one of Berlin's few real skyscrapers, the **EuropaCenter.** Tree-lined **Straße des 17. Juni** runs east-west through the Tiergarten, ending at the **Brandenburger Tor,** the park's eastern border gate. The **Reichstag** (Parliament) is north of the gate; several blocks south, **Potsdamer Platz** bustles beneath the glittering Sony Center and the headquarters of the Deutsche Bahn. Heading east, Straße des 17. Juni becomes **Unter den Linden** and travels past most of Berlin's imperial architecture. In the east, **Karl-Marx-Allee, Prenzlauer Allee,** and **Schönhauser Allee** fan out from the Alexanderplatz.

Berlin's short streets change names often; addresses often climb higher and higher and then wrap around to the other side of the street, placing the highest- and lowest-numbered buildings across from one another. Berlin is rightly considered a collection of towns, not a homogeneous city; each neighborhood has a strong sense of its individual history. **Mitte** is currently its commercial heart. The neighboring eastern districts of **Friedrichshain** and **Prenzlauer Berg** are the city's most youthful, while Kreuzberg is the outpost of counterculture in the west. **Charlottenburg** in the west has a more staid, upscale character, while **Schöneberg** is right in between **Kreuzberg** and Charlottenburg, both in geography and in spirit.

Berlin is by far the most tolerant city in Germany, with thriving minority communities. However, minorities, gays, and lesbians should exercise caution in the outlying eastern suburbs, especially at night. If you see people wearing dark combat boots (especially with white laces)—a potential sign of neo-Nazis—exercise caution but do not panic, and avoid drawing attention to yourself.

▐ LOCAL TRANSPORTATION

Public Transportation: The **BVG** (www.bvg.de) is one of the most efficient transportation systems in the world; the extensive **Bus, Straßenbahn** (streetcar or tram), **U-Bahn** (subway), and **S-Bahn** (surface rail) networks will get you to your destination quickly. The city is divided into 3 transit zones. **Zone A** encompasses central Berlin, including Flughafen Tempelhof. The rest of Berlin is in **Zone B; Zone C** consists of the outlying areas, including Potsdam and Oranienburg. An AB ticket is the best deal, as you can buy extension tickets for the outlying areas. A **one-way ticket** (Einzelfahrausweis) is good for 2hr. after validation. Zones AB €2.10, BC €2.40, ABC €2.70. Under 6 free with an adult; children under 14 pay a reduced fare. Within the validation period, the ticket may be used on any S-Bahn, U-Bahn, bus, or tram.

Night Transport: U- and S-Bahn lines generally don't run M-F 1-4am. On F-Sa nights, all trains except for the U4, S45, and S85 continue but less frequently. An extensive system of approximately 70 **night buses** runs 2-3 per hr. and tends to follow major transit lines; pick up the free Nachtliniennetz map at a Fahrscheine und Mehr office. The letter N precedes night bus numbers. Trams continue to run at night.

Taxis: ☎080 02 63 00 00. Call at least 15min. ahead. Trips within the city cost up to €21. Request a *Kurzstrecke* to travel up to 2km in any direction for a flat €3 fee.

Car Rental: Most companies have counters at the airports and around Bahnhof Zoo, Friedrichstr., and Ostbahnhof stations. Offices are also in EuropaCenter, with entrances at Budapester Str. 39-41. Rates around €65 for a car. 19+. **Hertz** (☎261 10 53). Open M-F 7am-8pm, Sa 8am-4pm, Su 9am-1pm.

LIFE (OR, UH, DEATH) IN THE FAST LANE. When you're walking on Berlin's sidewalks, make sure you don't step onto a bike path. Lanes usually run through the middle of walkways and are marked by subtle, reddish lanes. Bikers usually don't tolerate wandering tourists well, so stay clear.

Bike Rental: Fahrradstation, Dorotheenstr. 30 (☎20 45 45 00; www.fahrradstation.de), near the Friedrichstr. S-Bahn station. Turn in at the parking lot next to STA. €15 per day. Open in summer daily 8am-8pm; winter M-F 8am-7pm, Sa 10am-3pm. Less central **Orange Bikes,** Kollwitzstr. 35, is a youth community project. Bikes €2.50 per 3hr., €5 per day. Open M-F 2:30-7pm, Sa 10am-7pm. **Deutsche Bahn Call-A-Bike** (☎0700 522 5522; www.callabike.de) operates all over the city. After signing up (€5), call to unlock a bike. €0.07 per min.; up to €15 per day. €60 per week.

⚅ PRACTICAL INFORMATION

Tourist Offices: Euraide (www.euraide.com), in the *Hauptbahnhof*. Sells phone cards, rail- and walking-tour tickets. Open June-Oct. daily 8am-noon and 1-6pm; Nov.-May M-F 8am-noon and 1-4:45pm. **Berlin Tourismus Marketing (BTM),** in the EuropaCenter, on Budapester Str., in Charlottenburg. Reserves rooms (€3). Open M-Sa 10am-7pm, Su 10am-6pm. Branches at Brandenburger Tor and Alexanderpl. Fernsehturm.

City Tours: The guides at ▓**Terry Brewer's Best of Berlin** (www.brewersberlintours.com) are legendary for their vast knowledge and engaging personalities. 8hr. tours (€12) and shorter free tours leave daily at 10:30am from in front of the Bandy Brooks shop on Friedrichstr. (S5, 7, 9, or 75 or U6 to Friedrichstr.). **Berliner Unterwelten** (www.berliner-unterwelten.de) earns praise for their Berlin Underground tours, which explore the spaces underneath the city (1½hr., 1-2 per day, €9). English-language tours leave from Brunnenstr. 108a (U or S to Gesundbrunnen); check website for tour times.

Boat Tours: The city's canal system makes boat tours a popular option. **Reederei Heinz Riedel,** Planufer 78, Kreuzberg (☎693 4646; U8 Schönleinstr.). Tours €7-16. Open Mar.-Sept. M-F 6am-9pm, Sa 8am-6pm, Su 10am-3pm; Oct.-Feb. M-F 8am-4pm.

Embassies and Consulates: Australia, Mitte, Wallstr. 76-79 (☎880 0880; www.australian-embassy.de). U2: Märkisches Museum. Open M-Th 8:30am-5pm, F 8:30am-4:15pm. **Canada,** Mitte, Leipziger Pl. 17 (☎20 31 20; www.canada.de). S1, 2 or U2: Potsdamer Pl. Open M-F 8:30am-12:30pm and 1:30-5pm. **Ireland,** Mitte, Friedrichstr. 200 (☎22 07 20; www.botschaft-irland.de). U2 or 6: Stadtmitte. Open M-F 9:30am-

12:30pm and 2:30-4:45pm. **New Zealand,** Mitte, Friedrichstr. 60 (☎20 62 10; www.nzembassy.com). U2 or 6: Stadtmitte. Open M-Th 9am-1pm and 2-5:30pm, F 9am-1pm and 2-4:30pm. **UK,** Mitte, Wilhelmstr. 70-71 (☎20 45 70; www.britische-botschaft.de). S1-3, 5, 7, 9, 25, or 75, or U6: Friedrichstr. Open M-F 9am-5:30pm. **US,** Clayalle 170 (☎832 9233; fax 83 05 12 15). U1: Oskar-Helene-Heim. After a long dobate over the security of proposed locations, the US Embassy will move to a spot next to the Brandenburg Gate by 2008. Open M-F 8:30am-noon. Telephone advice available M-F 2-4pm; after hours, call ☎830 50 for emergency advice.

American Express: Main Office, Bayreuther Str. 37-38 (☎21 47 62 92). U1 or 2 to Wittenbergpl. Holds mail and offers banking services. No commission for cashing American Express Travelers Cheques. Expect long lines F-Sa. Open M-F 9am-7pm, Sa 10am-2pm. Branch at Friedrichstr. 172 (☎204 5572). U6 to Französische Str.

Luggage Storage: In **DB Gepack Center,** in the *Hauptbahnhof.* €3 for up to 3 bags. In **Bahnhof Zoo.** Lockers €3-5 per day. Max 72hr. Open daily 6:15am-10:30pm. Lockers, accessible 24hr., also at **Ostbahnhof** and **Alexanderpl.,** as well as the bus station.

English-language Bookstores: Marga Schöler Bücherstube, Knesebeckstr. 33 (☎881 1112), at Mommsenstr., between Savignypl. and the Ku'damm. S5, 7, 9, or 75 to Savignypl. Off-beat, contemporary English reading material. Open M-W 9:30am-7pm, Th-F 9:30am-8pm, Sa 9:30am-4pm.

Crisis Lines: American Hotline (☎0177 814 1510). **Berliner Behindertenverband,** Jägerstr. 63D (☎204 3847), has advice for the disabled. Open M-F 8am-4pm. **Frauenkrisentelefon** (☎611 0333) is a women's crisis line. Open M, W noon-2pm, Th 2-4pm.

Pharmacies: *Apotheken* (pharmacies) list a rotating schedule of 24hr. service.

Medical Services: The American and British embassies list English-speaking doctors. **Emergency doctor:** ☎31 00 31. **Emergency dentist:** ☎89 00 43 33. Both 24hr.

Post Offices: Joachimstaler Str. 7 (☎88 70 86 11), down Joachimstaler Str. from Bahnhof Zoo and near the Kantstr. intersection. Open M-Sa 9am-8pm. Branches: **Tegel Airport,** open M-F 8am-6pm, Sa 8am-noon; **Ostbahnhof,** open M-F 8am-8pm, Sa-Su 10am-6pm. **Postal Code:** 10706.

⚑ ACCOMMODATIONS

Longer stays are most conveniently arranged through one of Berlin's many **Mitwohnzentrale,** which can set up house-sitting gigs or sublets (from €250 per month). **Home Company Mitwohnzentrale,** Joachimstaler Str. 17, has a useful placement website. (☎194 45; www.homecompany.de. U9 or 15 to Ku'damm. Open M-Th 9am-6pm, F 9am-5pm, Sa 11am-2pm. MC/V.)

MITTE

🏨 **BaxPax Downtown Hostel/Hotel,** Ziegelstr. 28 (☎251 5202; www.baxpax-downtown.de). S1, 2, or 25 to Oranienburger Str. or U6 to Oranienburger Tor. Has a young, party-happy crowd and bright, spotless rooms. Wheelchair-accessible. Breakfast €5. Laundry €5-8. Internet €3 per hr.; Wi-Fi €1.50 per hr. K-Studio €13; dorms €16-21; singles €30-45; doubles €59-88; triples €66; quads €88. MC/V. ❷

🏨 **CityStay Hostel,** Rosenstr. 16 (☎23 62 40 31; www.citystay.de). S5, 7, 9, or 75 to Hackescher Markt or U2, 5, or 8 to Alexanderpl. Central location, but it's still on a quiet side street. Individual showers and organic breakfast made to order. All-night bar serves dinner 6-10pm. Breakfast €4. Linens €2.50. Laundry €5. Internet €3 per hr.; free Wi-Fi. Dorms €17-21; singles €34-45; doubles €50-64; quads €84. Cash only. ❷

Circus, Weinbergsweg 1A (☎28 39 14 33; www.circus-berlin.de). U8 to Rosenthaler Pl. Clean, modern, and well run. Wheelchair-accessible. Breakfast €2-5. Internet €0.50 per 10min; free Wi-Fi. Reception and bar 24hr. Dorms €17-19; singles €33, with shower €45; doubles €50; triples €63; apartments with balcony €77. MC/V. ❷

TIERGARTEN

Jugendherberge Berlin International (HI), Kluckstr. 3 (☎257 998 08; www.jh-berlin-international.de). U1 to Kurfürstenstr. Berlin's only HI hostel has a summer-camp feel but features a big-screen TV, table tennis, and large common room. Bike rental €10 per day. Breakfast included; other meals €5. Internet €3 per hr. Reception and cafe 24hr. Dorms €24, under 27 €21; doubles €28/24. Backyard camping €16. MC/V. ❷

CHARLOTTENBURG

Berolina Backpacker, Stuttgarter Pl. 17 (☎32 70 90 72; www.berolinabackpacker.de). S3, 5, 7, 9, or 75 to Charlottenburg. Quiet hostel with an ivy-laced facade has print art in its bunk-free dorms and daisies on the breakfast table. The quiet residential surroundings and proximity to the S-Bahn make up for its removed location. Breakfast €6. Reception 24hr. Check-out 11am. May-Sept. dorms €14-17; singles €35; doubles €46; triples €48. Nov.-Apr. €4 discount. AmEx/MC/V. ❶

Jugendgästehaus am Zoo, Hardenbergstr. 9A (☎312 9410; www.jgh-zoo.de), opposite the Technical University Mensa. U2 Ernst-Reuter-Platz or U to Zoo. Simple rooms on the 4th fl. of *Jugendstil* building. Reception 24hr. Check-out 10am. Lockout 10am-2pm. Dorms €21; singles €29; doubles €49. Under 27 €3 discount. Cash only. ❷

Frauenhotel Artemisia, Brandenburgische Str. 18 (☎873 8905; www.frauenhotel-berlin.de). U7 to Konstanzer Str. Women-only hotel with terrace features work by Berlin-based female artists in its rooms. Breakfast included. Reception 9am-10pm. Free Wi-Fi. Singles €54, with bath €64-74; doubles €78/98-108. Extra bed €20. AmEx/MC/V. ❺

SCHÖNEBERG AND WILMERSDORF

Jugendhotel Berlincity, Crellestr. 22 (☎78 70 21 30; www.jugendhotel-berlin.de). U7 to Kleistpark. Airy, stylish common rooms cause this small hotel to fill up fast; reserve ahead. Breakfast included. Singles €35-40, with bath €45-55; doubles €55-65/60-79; triples €84/99; quads €108/118. Discounted rates for extended stays. MC/V. ❹

Meininger City Hostel, Meininger Str. 10 (☎0800 634 6464, from abroad 666 361 00; www.meininger-hostels.de). U4 or bus #146 to *Rathaus* Schöneberg. 1 branch of a Berlin hostel chain, Meininger has formulaic splashy colors and unfailing cleanliness. Bar and beer garden compensate for less-than-ideal location. Breakfast included. Linens deposit €5. Internet €3 per hr. Reception 24hr. Dorms €14-16; singles €31; doubles €41; quads €68. 10% Let's Go discount on 1st night. MC/V. ❶

KREUZBERG

Bax Pax, Skalitzer Str. 104 (☎69 51 83 22; www.baxpax.de). U1 or 15 to Görlitzer Bahnhof. Offers a pool table, shared balcony for BBQs, and a low-key common area. Each room has a different country theme; the Germany room (#3) features a bed inside a VW Bug. Linens €3. Internet €3 per hr. Reception 24hr. Dorms €16; singles €30; doubles €46; triples €60. Nov.-Feb €1-2 discount. AmEx/MC/V. ❷

Hostel X Berger, Schlesische Str. 22 (☎695 1863; www.hostelxberger.com). U1 to Schlesisches Tor or night bus #N65 to Taborstr. Opened in 2006, this hostel is in one of Kreuzberg's most up-and-coming areas. Spacious, plain dorms off brightly-painted hallways. Women-only dorms available. Linens €2. Free Internet. Reception 24hr. Dorms €12-16; singles €26; doubles €36; triples €48; quads €56. Cash only. ❶

FRIEDRICHSHAIN

Globetrotter Hostel Odyssee, Grünberger Str. 23 (☎29 00 00 81; www.globetrotterhostel.de). U1 to Warschauer Str. or U5 to Frankfurter Tor. Gothic statues and candlelit tables give the lobby a funky feel, while the tattooed staff keep everything spotless. Bar open until dawn. Breakfast €3. Linens deposit €3. Internet €0.50 per 10min.; free Wi-

Fi. Reception 24hr. Check-in 4pm. Check-out noon. Reserve ahead. Dorms €14-22; singles €36-39; doubles €54-57; triples €66; quads €80. MC/V. ❶

Schlafmeile, Weichselstr. 25 (☎965 14676; www.schlafmeile.de). S to Ostbahnhof and then bus 240 to Boxhagener/Holteistr., or S to Ostkreuz. Beside a park in a residential neighborhood. This family business adds the personal touch missing from slicker Mitte hostels. Attached cafe serves Kiwi food. Wheelchair-accessible. Kitchen facilities. Linens included. Internet €1 per hr. Dorms €14-20; doubles €39-57; apartment with kitchen €120. Discounts for longer stays. Cash only. ❶

PRENZLAUER BERG

▨ **East Seven,** Schwedter Str. 7 (☎93 62 22 40; www.eastseven.de). U2 to Senefelderpl. Hip hostel on a quiet street in Prenzlauer Berg. From its classy decor to the Italian coffee served at breakfast, East 7 is unbeatable. Stag and hen party groups banned. Free tours. Linens €3. Laundry €4. Internet €1.50 per hr.; free Wi-Fi. Dorms €15-17; singles €35; doubles €48; triples €63; quads €76. Low season reduced rates. MC/V. ❷

Lette'm Sleep Hostel, Lettestr. 7 (☎44 73 36 23; www.backpackers.de). U2 to Eberswalder Str. The big kitchen with its comfy red couches is the social nexus of this homey 48-bed hostel. Beer garden in the back. Wheelchair-accessible. Linens included. Free Internet. Dorms €17-20; doubles €49; new apartments with bath €68. Low season reduced rates. 10% discount for stays over 3 nights. AmEx/MC/V. ❷

🍴 FOOD

Berlin's cuisine is quite diverse thanks to its Middle Eastern and Southeast Asian populations. Seasonal highlights include the beloved *Spargel* (white asparagus) in early summer, Pfifferling mushrooms in late summer, and *Federweiße* (young wine) in September. Perhaps the dearest culinary tradition is breakfast; Germans love to wake up late over a *Milchkaffee* (bowl of coffee with foamed milk) and a sprawling brunch buffet. Vendors of Currywurst or Bratwurst supply a quick bite, or find a 24hr. Turkish *Imbiß* (snack food stand) to satisfy a midnight craving.

MITTE

Gorki Park, Weinbergsweg 25 (☎448 7286; www.gorki-park.de). U8 to Rosenthaler Pl. Nobody does borscht, *bliny, wareniki,* or *pelmeni* like this feisty little Russian cafe. Outdoor seating. Entrees €4-10. Open M-Sa 9:30am-2am, Su 10am-2am. Cash only. ❷

Dolores, Rosa-Luxembourg-Str. 7. U or S to Alexanderplatz. Simple, tasty, and affordable. The ingredients at this California-style burrito bar are as fresh as the cherry-and-lime color scheme and the only authentic guacamole in Berlin. Vegetarian-friendly. Burritos €3.60-4.70. Open M-F 10am-9pm, Sa 12:30pm-late. Cash only. ❶

Beth Cafe, Tucholskystr. 40 (☎281 3135), off Auguststr. S1, 2, or 25 to Oranienburger Str. Come for the tranquil garden seating in a historic *Hinterhof*. Kosher and vegetarian options available. Entrees €6-11. Cake slices €1.70. Open in summer Su-Th 11am-10pm, F 11am-5pm; in winter Su-Th 11am-10pm, F 11am-3pm. AmEx/MC. ❷

CHARLOTTENBURG

Schwarzes Cafe, Kantstr. 148 (☎313 8038). S3, 5, 7, 9, or 75 to Savignypl. Labyrinthine institution of bohemian Berlin is both loud and romantic, with candlelit tables and a 24hr. breakfast menu (€5-8). Open 24hr. except Tu closed 3-11am. Cash only. ❷

Orchidee Sushi Restaurant, Stuttgarter Pl. 13 (☎31 99 74 67; www.restaurantorchidee.de). S to Charlottenburg. Though it touts its sushi, this pan-Asian cafe serves outstanding Vietnamese cuisine. Lunch special 11am-5pm; ½-price sushi or free appetizer with €5-11 entree. Open M-Sa 11am-midnight, Su 3pm-midnight. Cash only. ❸

Witty's, Wittenbergplatz, facing KaDeWe. U to Wittenbergplatz. Perhaps Berlin's best *Imbiß*. An organic beer accompanies the Pommes's organic potatoes and the Curry-wurst's organic meat well. Open daily 11am-1am. Cash only. ❶

SCHÖNEBERG

▨ **Cafe Bilderbuch,** Akazienstr. 28 (☎78 70 60 57; www.cafe-bilderbuch.de). U7 to Eisen-acher Str. Relax in the Venetian library or the airy courtyard of the "Picturebook Cafe." Known for daily breakfasts named after fairy tales (€7-8), the menu comes with a monthly literature magazine. Open M-Th 9am-1am, F-Sa 9am-2am, Su 10am-1am. Kitchen open M-Sa 9am-11pm, Su 10am-11pm. Cash only. ❷

▨ **Cafe Berio,** Maaßenstr. 7 (☎216 1946; www.cafe-berio.de). U1, 2, 3, or 4 to Nollendor-fpl. Always packed with locals, this subtly retro 2-fl. Viennese-style cafe tempts passers-bys with its unbeatable breakfast menu (€4-9). Open daily 8am-1am. Cash only. ❷

Die Feinbäckerei, Vorbergstr. 2 (☎81 49 42 40; www.feinbaeck.de). U7 to Kleistpark or Eisenacher. Neighborhood bistro has unassuming Swabian fare. Amazing *Spätzle* (noo-dles; €7). Lunch special M-F 10am-5pm €5. Open daily noon-midnight. Cash only. ❷

KREUZBERG

Café V, Lausitzer Pl. 12 (☎612 4505). U1 to Görlitzer Bahnhof. Vegan and fish entrees served in the romantic interior of Berlin's oldest vegetarian cafe. Top-of-the-line German and Middle Eastern entrees (€6-8). Open daily 10am-2am. Cash only. ❸

Pagode, Bergmannstr. 88 (☎691 2640). U7 to Gneisenaustr. One of Berlin's best Thai restaurants, Pagode is staffed by Thai women who churn out excellent curries and soups in record time. The ground floor can look crowded, but there's extra basement seating beside a giant aquarium. Entrees €4-9. Open daily noon-midnight. Cash only. ❷

FRIEDRICHSHAIN AND PRENZLAUER BERG

I Due Forni, Schönhauser Allee 12 (44 01 73 33). Locals swear by the stone-oven pizza at this hilltop pizzeria run by Italian rocker dudes. Long summer waits are eased by lively graffiti on the walls. Pizzas €5.40-8.50; if you're feeling adventurous, try the one featuring *Pferdefleisch* (horse meat). Open daily noon-1am. Cash only. ❷

Babel, Kastanienallee 33 (☎44 03 13 18). U2 to Eberswalder Str. Locals and tourists obsessed with Babel's falafel (€3-5) keep this neighborhood Middle Eastern joint busy at all hours. Open daily 11am-midnight. Cash only. ❷

Prater Biergarten, Kastanienallee 7-9 (☎448 5688; www.pratergarten.de). U2 to Eber-swalder Str. Berlin's oldest beer garden is a summertime institution. Heaping plates of old-school German food. Bratwurst €2. Entrees €5.70-15. Beer €2.20-3.10. Open in good weather Apr.-Sept. M-Sa 6pm-late, Su noon-late. Cash only. ❶

Asian Deli, Lychener Str. 28 (☎44 04 89 20). U2 to Eberswalder Str. A neighborhood crowd scarfs down Malaysian, Thai, and Vietnamese standards at this Helmholzkiez cafe. Entrees €4-7. Outdoor seating. Open daily 11:30am-midnight. Cash only. ❷

◉ SIGHTS

Most of central Berlin's major sights lie along the route of **bus #100,** which runs every 5min. from Bahnhof Zoo to Prenzlauer Berg. It passes the **Siegessäule** (p. 398), **Brandenburger Tor** (p. 398) and **Unter den Linden,** the **Berliner Dom** (p. 400), and **Alexanderplatz** (p. 400). Remnants of the **Berlin Wall** still survive in only a few places: in **Potsdamer Platz** (p. 400); near the **Haus Am Checkpoint Charlie** (p. 403); in **Prenzlauer Berg,** next to the sobering **Documentation Center** (p. 404); and in altered form at the **East Side Gallery** (p. 403) in Friedrichshain.

MITTE

Mitte was once the heart of Berlin, but the wall split it down the middle, and much of it languished in disrepair under the GDR. The wave of revitalization that swept Berlin after the collapse of communism came to Mitte first. It's becoming ever harder to find war wrecks squeezed in among the glittering modern buildings, swank galleries, and stores so hyper-hip that they only sell one thing, like messenger bags, acid-tone sweaters, or rugs with words on them.

UNTER DEN LINDEN

One of Europe's best-known boulevards, Unter den Linden was the spine of imperial Berlin. During the Cold War it was known as the "Idiot's Mile" because it was often all that visitors to the East saw, and it gave them little idea of what the city was like. Beginning in Pariser Pl. in front of Brandenburger Tor, the street extends east through Bebelpl. and the Lustgarten, punctuated by dramatic squares. *(S1, 2, or 25 to Unter den Linden. Bus #100 runs the length of the boulevard; 10-15 per hr.)*

■**BRANDENBURGER TOR.** Built as a tribute to 18th century peace, this gate at the heart of Pariser Pl. came to symbolize the city's division: facing the Berlin Wall, it became a barricaded gateway to nowhere. After serving as the memorable backdrop for the fall of the Berlin Wall, the gate is now the most powerful emblem of reunited Germany. Visitors can reflect in the **Room of Silence** at the northern end.

RUSSIAN EMBASSY. One of the most striking buildings along Unter den Linden is the Stalinist-style 1950s edifice that once demonstrated the Soviet Union's might. Berlin's largest embassy, it covers almost an entire city block. It draws visitors who gaze from behind a cast-iron fence and speculate on the rumor that there's a swimming pool inside with a mosaic of Lenin on the bottom. *(Unter den Linden 55.)*

BEBELPLATZ. In this square on May 10, 1933, Nazi students burned nearly 20,000 books by communist, Jewish, and pacifist authors including Heinrich Heine and Sigmund Freud, both of Jewish descent. Today, a small window in the ground reveals empty bookcases beneath and a quote from Heine: "Wherever they burn books, eventually they will burn people too." On the western side of Bebelpl., the building with a curved facade is the **Alte Bibliothek;** once the royal library, it's now home to the law faculty of Humboldt-Universität. On the eastern side is the **Deutsche Staatsoper,** one of Berlin's three opera houses, fully rebuilt after the war based on the original sketches. The blue dome at the end of the square belongs to **St.-Hedwigs-Kathedrale,** the first Catholic church built in Berlin after the Reformation. Modeled on the Roman Pantheon and completed in 1773, it was destroyed by Allied bombers in 1943. The church was rebuilt in the 1950s in a more modern style. *(Open M-Sa 10am-5pm, Su 1-5pm. Organ concerts W 3pm. Cathedral free.)*

TIERGARTEN

Once a hunting ground for Prussian monarchs, the lush Tiergarten (Animal Park) is now the eye of Berlin's metropolitan storm. From Bahnhof Zoo to the Brandenburger Tor, the vast landscaped park is frequented by bikers, joggers, and more than a few nude sunbathers. Straße des 17. Juni bisects the park from west to east. Near S-Bahnhof Tiergarten, is the open-air gas lantern museum (Gaslaternen Freilichtmuseum), which takes on a magical quality at dusk.

■**THE REICHSTAG.** Today home to the *Bundestag,* Germany's governing body, the Reichstag was central to one of the most critical moments in history. When it mysteriously burned down in 1933, Hitler declared a state of emergency and seized power. Today, a glass dome offers visitors 360° views of the city as they climb the spiral staircase inside. Go before 8am or after 8pm to avoid long lines. *(☎ 22 73 21 52; www.bundestag.de. Open daily 8am-midnight; last entrance 10pm. Free.)*

SIEGESSÄULE. Above the Tiergarten, this column commemorates Prussia's 1870 victory over France. The goddess of victory on the top is made of melted French

Berlin Mitte

400 yards

400 meters

GERMANY

Invaliden Park

HAUPTBAHNHOF

Heidestr.

Alt-Moabit

Willy Brandt-str.

Paul-Löbe Allee

PL. DER REPUBLIK

Reichstag

Scheidemannstr.

Straße des 17. Juni

Tiergarten

Bellevuealle

KEMPERPL.

Sony Center

POTSDAMER PL.

Kulturforum

Sigismundstr.

Potsdamerstr.

TO SCHÖNEBERG

TO CHARLOTTENBURG

Dorotheen Städtischer Friedhof

VOR DEM NEUEN TOR

Chausseestr.

Luisenstr.

Schumannstr.

Reinhardtstr.

Albrechtstr.

Marienstr.

ORANIENBURGER TOR

Torstr.

Linienstr.

Gormannstr.

Rosenthaler Str.

Gipsstr.

Sophienstr.

Gr. Hamburger Str.

Krausnickstr.

ROSENTHALER PL.

WEINMEISTERSTR.

Alte Schönhauser Str.

M-Beer-Str.

Münz-Str.

Prenzlauer Berg

Prenzlauer Allee

Am-Friedrichshain Volkspark

Friedrichshain

Friedenstr.

Mollstr.

Otto-Braun-Str.

ROSA-LUXEMBURG-PL.

SCHILLINGSTR.

Karl-Marx-Allee

Neue Blumenstr.

Lichtenberger Str.

STRAUSBERGER PL.

Singerstr.

Andreasstr.

TO KREUZBERG

Spree

JANNOWITZBR.

Holzmarktstr.

Brückenstr.

Köpenicker Str.

Heinrich-Heine-Str.

MICHAEL-KIRCHPL.

Michaelkirchstr.

Sebastianstr.

Alte Jakobstr.

Waldeckpark

Axel-Springer-Str.

Former Berlin Wall

Zimmerstr.

Kochstr.

Niederkirchnerstr.

Stresemannstr.

Former Berlin Wall

Ebertstr.

Wilhelmstr.

Voßstr.

Mohrenstr.

Leipziger Str.

Kronenstr.

Französische Str.

Unter den Linden

Charlottenstr.

Friedrichstr.

Markgrafenstr.

GENDARMEN-MARKT

HAUSVOGTEIPL.

SPITTELMARKT

Gertraudenstr.

NIKOLAIVIERTEL

KLOSTERSTR.

Klosterstr.

Stralauer Str.

Breite Str.

Spree

Fischerinsel

MÄRK. MUS.

H.-HEINE-STR.

ALEXANDERPL.

HACKESCHER MARKT

Monbijou

Museums-insel

Zeughaus

SCHLOßPL.

Spandauer Str.

Karl-Liebknecht-Str.

Dirckenstr.

Alexanderstr.

Alexander Pl.

Mühlendamm

STADTMITTE

FRANZ. STR.

FRIEDRICHSTR.

ORANIENBURGER STR.

Tucholskystr.

Johannisstr.

Ziegelstr.

Universitätsstr.

Georgenstr.

Dorotheenstr.

Am Kupfergraben

Am Weidendamm

Schiffbauerdamm

Reichstagufer

PARISER PL.

UNTER DEN LINDEN

Behrenstr.

Mauerstr.

Glinkastr.

Jäger-str.

Tauben-str.

Leipziger Str.

Schützenstr.

Krausenstr.

Oberwallstr.

Niederwallstr.

Werderscher Markt

MARX-ENGELS-FORUM

Rosenstr.

An der Spandauer Brücke

An der Rosenthaler Str.

Augustst.

Linienstr.

Torstr.

Gormannstr.

Gontardstr.

MOHRENSTR.

POTSDAMER PL.

cannons. Climb the 285 steps for a panoramic view. *(Großer Stern. Bus #100 or 187 to Großer Stern or S5, 7, or 9 to Tiergarten. Walk 5min. down Straße des 17. Juni. Accessible via the stairs at the West corners around the traffic circle. ☎391 2961. Open Apr.-Nov. M-F 9:30am-6:30pm, Sa-Su 9:30am-7pm; Dec.-Mar. M-F 10am-5pm, Sa-Su 10am-5:30pm. €3, students €2.)*

POTSDAMER PLATZ. Originally designed to allow the rapid mobilization of troops under Friedrich Wilhelm I, Potsdamer Pl. now strives to reclaim its former role as Berlin's commercial center. During the 1990s, the city sunk a fortune into rebuilding what was mostly an empty lot, and the resulting style has met mixed reviews. Though most of the new office space is empty, the central complex includes Berlin's Film Museum, the towering headquarters of the Deutsche Bahn, and the glitzy ▓**Sony Center,** where travelers can watch a movie, enjoy free Wi-Fi, or window-shop under a retractable steel-and-glass roof. *(U2, S1, 2, or 25 to Potsdamer Pl.)*

GENDARMENMARKT. Several blocks south of Unter den Linden, this gorgeous square was considered the French Quarter in the 18th century, when it became the main settlement for Protestant Huguenots fleeing persecution by "Sun King" Louis XIV. During the last week of June and the first week of July, the square transforms into a stage for classical concerts. *(U6 to Französische Str. or U2 or 6 to Stadtmitte.)*

MUSEUMSINSEL AND ALEXANDERPLATZ

After crossing the Spree, Unter den Linden becomes Karl-Liebknecht-Str. and cuts through the Museumsinsel (Museum Island), home to five major museums and the **Berliner Dom.** Karl-Liebknecht-Str. then continues onward to Alexanderpl. Take S3, 5, 7, 9, or 75 to Hackescher Markt, or bus #100 to Lustgarten.

BERLINER DOM. Berlin's most recognizable landmark, this multi-domed cathedral proves that Protestants can be as dramatic as Catholics. Built during the reign of Kaiser Wilhelm II, the Dom suffered damage in a 1944 air raid and only recently emerged from three decades of restoration. Inside, keep an eye out for the likenesses of Protestant luminaries Calvin, Luther, and Zwingli, or enjoy the glorious view of Berlin from the tower. In the crypt, check out the nearly 100 Hohenzollern sarcophagi. *(Open M-Sa 9am-8pm, Su noon-8pm, closed during services 6:30-7:30pm. Free organ recitals W-F 3pm. Frequent concerts in summer; buy tickets in the church or call ☎20 26 91 36. Combined admission to crypt, Dom, galleries, and tower €5, students €3.)*

FERNSEHTURM. Berlin's tallest structure (368m), this bizarre TV tower was built to prove East Germany's technological capabilities—even though Swedish engineers helped construct it. The Swedes left a controversial surprise known as the "Papsts Rache" (Pope's Revenge): a crucifix appears when the sun hits the dome, defying the GDR's attempt to rid the city of religious symbols. An elevator whisks tourists up to a magnificent view from the spherical node 203m above the city. *(☎242 3333. Open daily Mar.-Oct. 9am-11pm; Nov.-Feb. 10am-midnight. €8.50, under 16 €4.)*

ALEXANDERPLATZ. This plaza formed the heart of Berlin in the Weimar era, but it is now overwhelmed by construction and overgrown grass. Socialist relics like the 1950s-style Weltzeituhr, a clock showing the time around the former communist world, share space with capitalist add-ons like the department store **Kaufhof.**

SCHEUNENVIERTEL. Northwest of Alexanderpl. is the Scheunenviertel, once the center of Berlin's Orthodox Jewish community. Prior to WWII, Berlin didn't have ghettos; assimilated Jews lived in Western Berlin, while Orthodox Jews from Eastern Europe settled here. The district shows a few traces of Jewish life back to the 13th century but is now known mainly for its street prostitutes and touristy Indian restaurants. *(S1, 2, or 25 to Oranienburger Str. or U6 to Oranienburger Tor.)*

NEUE SYNAGOGE. This synagogue was used for worship until 1940, when the Nazis occupied it and used it for storage. Amazingly, the building survived *Kristallnacht* (Night of the Broken Glass)—even though the SS torched it, a local police chief managed to bluff his way past SS officers and order that the fire be extinguished. The building no longer holds services; instead, it houses small exhibits on the history of Berlin's Jews. *(Oranienburger Str. 29. ☎88 02 83 00. Open May-Aug. Su-M 10am-8pm, Tu-Th 10am-6pm, F 10am-5pm; Sept.-Apr. M-Th and Su 10am-6pm, F 10am-2pm. A series of security checks is required to enter. €3, students €2.)*

CHARLOTTENBURG

Originally a separate town huddled around Friedrich I's imperial palace, Charlottenburg is now home to one of Berlin's main shopping streets, the Ku'damm. The area's sights can be expensive; budget travelers come mostly to explore the attractions near Bahnhof Zoo.

AROUND BAHNHOF ZOO. Former West Berlin centered on Bahnhof Zoo, the station that inspired U2's "Zoo TV" tour. Nearby, peepshows mingle with department stores. The **Zoologischer Garten,** one of the world's largest and oldest zoos, gained international attention in 2007 as the home of celebrity polar bear **Knut.** Now that the fuss has subsided, there's more room to take in the zoo's open-air habitats and collection of endangered species. At the second entrance across from Europa-Center is the **Elefantentor,** a pagoda of pachyderms. *(Budapester Str. 34. Open daily May-Sept. 9am-6:30pm; Mar.-Apr. 9am-5:30pm; Oct.-Feb. 9am-5pm. €11, students €8.)*

KAISER-WILHELM-GEDÄCHTNISKIRCHE. Nicknamed *hohler Zahn* ("the hollow tooth"), this shattered church has been left in its jagged state as a reminder of WWII. The church houses an exhibit of photos, but the exterior is most impressive by night. In summer, Berlin's salesmen, street performers, and youth gather in front to hang out, hawk their wares, and play bagpipes and sitars. *(☎218 5023. www.gedaechtniskirche.com. Church open daily 9am-7pm. Exhibit open M-Sa 10am-4pm.)*

SCHLOß CHARLOTTENBURG. This monumental Baroque palace occupies a park in northern Charlottenburg and contains more 18th-century French paintings than any other location outside of France. Its pristine grounds include: the beautifully furnished **Altes Schloß;** the **Belvedere,** which houses the royal family's porcelain collection; the marbled receiving rooms of the **Neuer Flügel,** the **Neuer Pavillon,** and the palace **Mausoleum.** Leave time to stroll the **Schloßgarten** behind the main buildings, a paradise of footbridges, fountains, and small lakes. *(Bus #145 from Bahnhof Zoo to Luisenpl./Schloß Charlottenburg or U2 to Sophie-Charlotte Pl. Walk 10-15min. up Schlosstr. ☎320 92 75. Altes Schloß open Tu-F 9am-5pm, Sa-Su 10am-5pm. Mandatory German-language tour €8, students €5; upper floor €2/1.50. Neuer Flügel open Tu-F 10am-6pm, Sa-Su 11am-6pm. €5/4. Neuer Pavillon open Tu-Su 10am-5pm. €2/1.50. Mausoleum open Apr.-Oct. Tu-Su 10am-noon and 1-5pm. €1. Belvedere open Apr.-Oct. Tu-Su 10am-5pm; Nov.-Mar. Tu-F noon-4pm, Sa-Su noon-5pm. €2/1.50. Schloßgarten open Tu-Su 6am-10pm. Free. Combo ticket includes admission to everything except the Altes Schloß €9/7.)*

SCHÖNEBERG

South of the Ku'damm, Schöneberg is a residential district notable for its laid-back cafes and good restaurants. In spirit as well as geography, it lies between posh Charlottenburg to the west and funky Kreuzberg to the east. In **Nollendorfplatz,** the nexus of Berlin's gay community, rainbow flags drape even the military store.

GRUNEWALD. In summer, this 745-acre birch forest—the dog-walking turf of many a Berliner—provides a retreat from the chaos of the city. About 1km into the forest, on the edge of the Grunewaldsee, the **Jagdschloß,** a restored 16th-century royal hunting lodge, houses paintings by Cranach, Graff, and other German artists. *(Am Grunewaldsee 29. U3 or 7 to Fehrbelliner Pl., or S45 or 46 to Hohenzollerndamm, then bus #115, dir.: Neuruppiner Str., to Pücklerstr. ☎813 3597. Open May 15-Oct. 15 Tu-Su 10am-5pm; Oct.-16-May 14 Sa-Su tours at 11am, 1, 3pm. €2, students €1.50; with tour €3/2.50.)*

GERMANY

GERMANY

Charlottenburg and Schöneberg

Spandauer Damm
TO SPANDAU
Schloßstr.
Schustehrus-park
Kaiser-Friedrich-Str.
Fritschestr.
Zillestr.
GIERKE-PL.
RICHARD-WAGNER-PL.
Richard-Wagner-Str.
Otto-Suhr-Allee
Deutsche Oper
DEUTSCHE OPER
Krumme Str.
Schillerstr.
Goethestr.
Pestalozzistr.
Krumme Str.
Wilmersdorfer Str.
Windscheidstr.
Suarezstr.
Wilmersdorfer Str.
Leonhardtstr.
CHARLOTTENBURG
SOPHIE-CHARLOTTE-PL.
SOPHIE-CHAR.-PL.
BISMARCKSTR.
SHAKESPEARE-PL.
ERNST-REUTER-PL.
DEUTSCHE OPER
Goethe Park
Goslarer
Kaiser-Friedrich-Str.
Pestalozzistr.
Kantstr.
Lewishamstr.
STUTTGARTER PL.
CHARLOTTENBURG
Stuttgarter Pl.
WILMERSDORFER STR.
Friedrich-Str.
Holtzen-dorffstr.
Droysenstr.
FUNKTURM (1km)
AMTSGERICHT.
Lehniner Pl.
LEHNINER PL.
ADENAUERPL.
ADENAUERPL.
Brandenburgische Str.
WILMERSDORF
Konstanzer Str.
Pariser Str.
OLIVAER PL.
GEORGE-GROSZ-PL.
Joachim-Friedrich-Str.
Hochmeister Platz
Westfälische Str.
Paulsborner Str.
WÜRTTEMBERG
Württemberg.
FEHR-BELLINER-PL.
Brandenburgische Str.

Landwehrkanal
Spree
Salzufer
Einsteinufer
Marchstr.
Franklinstr.
Technische Universität
Straße des 17 Juni
HANSA-PL.
HANSAPL.
TIERGARTEN
Bachstr.
Flotowstr.
Großer Weg
Altonaer Str.
Handelallee
Klopstockstr.
Levetzowstr.
Lessingstr.
Spreeweg
Spreeweg
BELLEVUE
Schloßpark
Bellevue
Bellevue
John-Foster-Dulles-Allee
TO MITTE &
PRENZLAUER BERG
BRANDENBURGER TOR
FRIEDRICHSHAIN
Tiergarten
Straße des 17 Juni
GROSSER STERN
Hofjägerallee
Neuer See
Großer Weg
Tiergartenstr.
Stauffenbergstr.
Reichpietschufer
Klingelhöferstr.
Schöneberger Ufer
Schöneberger Str.
Potsdamer Str.
TO KREUZBERG
Pohlstr.
LÜTZOW-PL.
Lützowstr.
Lützowufer
Einemstr.
Derfflingerstr.
Genthiner Str.
Magdeburger Pl.
Kurfürstenstr.
Budapester Str.
Schillstr.
Martin-Luther-Str.
Kleiststr.
Kurfürstenstr.
An der Urania
KurFürstenstraße
Tauentzienstr.
Wittenbergpl.
WITTENBERGPL.
Aquarium
Zoologischer Garten
Elefantentor
Europa Center
Budapester Str.
BREITSCHEID-PL.
KaDeWe
Augsburger Str.
AUGSBURGER STR.
Ansbacher Str.
Ranke-str.
Nürnberger Str.
Joachimstaler Str.
Kantstr.
Hardenbergstr.
ZOOLOGISCHER GARTEN
HARDENBERG-PL.
Fasanenstr.
Kantstr.
STEINPL.
SAVIGNY-PL.
Uhlandstr.
UHLANDSTR.
Grolmanstr.
Kneseseck-str.
Bleibtreustr.
Wieland-str.
Niebuhrstr.
Mommsenstr.
Leibnizstr.
SAVIGNYPL.
Lietzenburger Str.
Bundesallee
Fasanenstr.
Düsseldorfer Str.
Pariser Str.
Weimarer Str.
Meierottostr.
Ludwigkirchstr.
LUDWIGKIRCHPL.
Geisbergstr.
SPICHERNSTR.
TO
Bundesallee
Hohenzollerndamm
Lietzenburger Str.
Kurfürstendamm

SCHÖNEBERG
Kurfürstenstr.
Kurfürststr.
NOLLENDORFPL.
NOLLEN-DORFPL.
Maaßenstr.
Gleditschstr.
Goltzstr.
Nollendorfstr.
Winterfeldtstr.
VIKTORIA-LUISE-PL.
VIKTORIA-LUISE-PL.
Motzstr.
Eisenacher Str.
Martin-Luther-Str.
Frobenstr.
Bülowstr.
BÜLOWSTR.
Dennewitzpl.
DENNEWITZPL.
Nelly-Sachs-Park
Potsdamer Str.
Kurfürstenstr.
KURFÜRSTENSTR.

Straße des 17 Juni
Hardenbergstr.

400 yards
400 meters
0

KREUZBERG

Kreuzberg was once the most countercultural place in West Germany, home to artists, draft dodgers, and Turkish guest workers. Most of the punk *Hausbesetzer* (squatters) who long occupied the area are gone now, following 1980s government evictions, but the district retains its distinctive spirit. Protests are still frequent and intense; the most prominent is an annual demonstration on Labor Day that nearly always escalates into rioting. The eastern half of the district, Kreuzberg 36, is the center of Berlin's Turkish population and fashionable nightlife (around Schlesische Str.), while Kreuzberg 61 to the west is more ritzy.

HAUS AM CHECKPOINT CHARLIE. A strange mix of eastern sincerity and glossy western salesmanship, Checkpoint Charlie documents the history of the Berlin Wall and the dramatic escapes that once centered there. The museum showcases artwork, newspaper clippings, and photographs of the Wall, as well as a collection of contraptions used to get over, under, or through it. Out on the street, the checkpoint itself is overshadowed by staged photos of two soldiers, one American and one Russian, each symbolically keeping watch. *(Friedrichstr. 43-45. U6 to Kochstr. ☎253 7250; www.mauer-museum.de. Museum open daily 9am-10pm. German-language films with English subtitles 1 per 2hr. €9.50, students €5.50. Audio tour €3.)*

FRIEDRICHSHAIN AND LICHTENBERG

As Berlin's legendary alternative scene follows low rents eastward, **Friedrichshain** is becoming the hallowed ground of the unpretentiously hip. Not extensively renovated since reunification, the district retains old pre-fab apartments and large stretches of the Wall. Outdoor cafes and a crowd of twentysomethings fill **Simon-Dach-Straße.** The grungier area around **Rigärstraße** is one of the alternative scene's strongholds, home to squatter bars, makeshift clubs, and loitering punks.

EAST SIDE GALLERY. The longest remaining portion of the Wall, this 1.3km stretch of cement slabs and asbestos also serves as the world's largest open-air art gallery, unsupervised and open at all hours. The murals are from an international group of artists who gathered here in 1989 to celebrate the end of the city's division. It was expected that the wall would be destroyed soon after, but in 2000, with this portion still standing, many of the artists reconvened to repaint their work, covering others' scrawlings. Unfortunately, the new paintings are being rapidly eclipsed by graffiti. Keep in mind that this art project is in no way meant to show

Charlottenburg and Schöneberg

🏠 ACCOMMODATIONS
Berolina Backpacker, **7**
Frauenhotel Artemisia, **19**
Jugendgästehaus am Zoo, **4**
Jugendhotel Berlincity, **22**
Meininger City Hostel, **14**

🍴 FOOD
Cafe Berio, **17**
Cafe Bilderbuch, **16**
Die Feinbäckerei, **20**
Orchidee Sushi
  Restaurant, **8**
Schwarzes Cafe, **12**
Witty's, **13**

🍸 BARS AND ★ NIGHTLIFE
Mister Hu, **21**
Quasimodo, **9**
Slumberland, **15**

● SIGHTS
Bahnhof Zoologischer
  Garten, **5**
Elefantententor, **10**
Grunewald, **18**
Kaiser-Wilhelm-
  Gedächtiskirche, **11**
Siegessäule, **3**

🏛 MUSEUMS
Bauhaus-Archiv Museum Für
  Gemäldegalerie, **6**
Museum Berggruen, **2**
Schloß Charlottenburg, **1**

GERMANY

what the wall actually looked like during GDR times—only on the western side was it graffitied. *(Along Mühlenstr. Take U1 or 15 or S3, 5-7, 9, or 75 to Warschauer Str. or S5, 7, 9, or 75 to Ostbahnhof and walk back toward the river. www.eastsidegallery.com.)*

> **↰ NO DANCING IN THIS REVOLUTION.** Let's Go uses GDR to refer to the German Democratic Republic, more commonly known as former East Germany. InGerman, it's DDR, for **Deutsche Demokratische Republik.**

FORSCHUNGS- UND GEDENKSTÄTTE NORMANNENSTRAßE. The Lichtenberg suburb harbors the most feared building of the GDR regime: the headquarters of the **secret police** (*Staatssicherheit*, or *Stasi*). During the Cold War, the Stasi kept dossiers on six million East Germans. Spy aficionados will enjoy the exhibits of the Stasi's many varieties of bugging devices. Communist kitsch also has strong presence here. *(Ruschestr. 103, Haus 1. U5 to Magdalenenstr. From the station, walk up Ruschestr. and take the 1st right into the complex of buildings. Haus #1 is straight ahead; a sign on Ruschestr. marks the turn. ☎ 553 6854; www.stasimuseum.de. Exhibits in German. Helpful English-language info booklet €3. Open M-F 11am-6pm, Sa-Su 2-6pm. €3.50, students €2.50.)*

PRENZLAUER BERG

Everything in Prenzlauer Berg used to be something else. Brunches unfold in former butcher shops, furniture exhibits bring domestic grace to a former power plant, and kids cavort in breweries-turned-nightclubs. Reputed to have the highest birth rate in Europe, Prenzlauer Berg is perhaps most striking for—no joke—the sheer number of fashionably dressed babies swarming its parks and sidewalks.

▨ DOKUMENTATIONSZENTRUM BERLINER MAUER. Nowhere else is the full structure of the Wall—two concrete barriers separated by the open **Todesstreife** (death strip)—preserved as it is here. The center assembles film clips, historic photos, and sound bites from the Wall's history in order to display it as authentically as possible. Ascend the spiral staircases for the full, desolate effect. *(Bernauer Str. 111. ☎ 464 1030; www.berliner-mauer-dokumentationszentrum.de. U8 to Bernauer Str. Open Tu-Su Apr.-Oct. 10am-6pm; Nov.-Mar. 10am-5pm. Free.)*

🏛 MUSEUMS

Over 170 museums with collections from every epoch in history makes Berlin one of the world's top museum cities. The *Berlin Programm* (€1.60) lists them all.

SMB MUSEUMS

Staatliche Museen zu Berlin (SMB) runs over 20 museums in four major areas of Berlin—the **Museumsinsel, Tiergarten-Kulturforum, Charlottenburg,** and **Dahlem**—and elsewhere in Mitte and the Tiergarten. All museums sell single-admission tickets (€8, students €4) and the three-day card (Drei-Tage-Karte; €15, students €7). Admission is free the first Sunday of every month and on Thursdays after 6pm. Unless otherwise noted, all SMB museums are open Tuesday through Sunday 10am-6pm and Thursday 10am-10pm. All offer free English-language audio tours.

MUSEUMSINSEL (MUSEUM ISLAND)

Germany's greatest cultural treasures reside in five separate museums, separated from the rest of Mitte by two arms of the Spree. The **Neues Museum** is undergoing renovation and scheduled to reopen in late 2008. *(S3, 5, 7, 9, or 75 to Hackescher Markt or bus #100 to Lustgarten. ☎ 20 90 55 55.)*

▨ PERGAMONMUSEUM. One of the great ancient history museums, with almost an entire reconstructed ancient city. Named for the Turkish city from which the huge **Altar of Zeus** (180 BC) was taken, the museum's collection of artifacts from the ancient Near East includes the colossal blue **Ishtar Gate of Babylon** (575 BC) and the Roman **Market Gate of Miletus**. *(Bodestr. 1-3.* ☎ *20 90 55 77.* €*10, students* €*5.)*

ALTE NATIONALGALERIE (OLD NATIONAL GALLERY). This museum of 19th-century art reopened after extensive renovations. The gallery presents everything from German Realism to French Impressionism; Manet, Monet, Degas, and Renoir are just a few names in an all-star cast. Enjoy a drink at the outdoor Sage Bar under the columns overlooking the water. *(Lustgarten.* ☎ *20 90 58 01.)*

TIERGARTEN-KULTURFORUM

Fine-arts students and local aficionados favor Tiergarten-Kulturforum, a museum complex at the end of the Tiergarten near the Staatsbibliothek and Potsdamer Pl. *(Take S1, 2, or 25, or U2 to Potsdamer Pl. Look for Matthäikirchpl. on the right.* ☎ *20 90 55 55.)*

▧ **GEMÄLDEGALERIE.** One of Germany's best-known museums, the Gemäldegalerie displays over 1000 masterpieces by Dutch, Flemish, German, and Italian masters from the 13th to 18th centuries, including works by Botticelli, Dürer, Raphael, Rembrandt, Titian, and Vermeer. *(Stauffenbergstr. 40.* ☎ *266 2951. Open Tu, W-Su 10am-6pm, Th 10am-10pm.* €*8, students* €*4, Tu 6-10pm free.)*

▧ **HAMBURGER BAHNHOF/MUSEUM FÜR GEGENWART.** North of the Tiergarten, Berlin's foremost contemporary art collection occupies 10,000 sq. m of this former train station. Its artist roster includes Beuys, Kiefer, and Warhol. The museum hosts outrageous sculptures and attention-grabbing temporary exhibits. *(Invalidenstr. 50-51. S3, 5, 7, 9, or 75 to Hauptbahnhof, or U6 to Zinnowitzer Str.* ☎ *39 78 34 11. Open Tu-F 10am-6pm, Sa 11am-8pm, Su 11am-6pm.* €*8, students* €*4, Th 2-6pm free.)*

CHARLOTTENBURG

Many excellent museums surround **Schloß Charlottenburg**. Take bus #145 from Bahnhof Zoo to Luisenpl./Schloß Charlottenburg, or take U2 to Sophie-Charlotte-Pl. and walk 10-15min. up the tree-lined Schloßstr.

MUSEUM BERGGRUEN. Subtitled "Picasso and His Time," the three-story Museum Berggruen explores the work of the groundbreaking 20th-century artist and the movements that sprung up around him. Picasso's influences, which include African masks and late paintings by Matisse, occupy the bottom floor. On the top floor are the elongated sculptures of Giacometti and paintings by Klee. *(Schlosstr. 1.* ☎ *32 69 58 11. Open Tu-Su 10am-6pm.* €*6, students* €*3.)*

DAHLEM

▧ **ETHNOLOGISCHES MUSEUM.** It's worth the trek to Dahlem to see the ancient Central American stonework and boats from the South Pacific, among many other stunning exhibits displayed in the **Ethnologisches Museum**. In the same building, the smaller Museum für Indische Kunst (Museum of Indian Art) has ornate shrines and murals. The Museum für Ostasiatisches Kunst (Museum of East Asian Art) houses extremely long tapestries. *(U3 to Dahlem-Dorf; follow the "Museen" signs.* ☎ *830 1438. Open Tu-F 10am-6pm, Sa-Su 11am-6pm. Th 2-6pm free. 3-day ticket* €*15.)*

INDEPENDENT (NON-SMB) MUSEUMS

JÜDISCHES MUSEUM BERLIN. Daniel Libeskind designed this museum so that no facing walls run parallel. Jagged hallways end in windows overlooking "the void." Wander through the labyrinthine **Garden of Exile** or shut yourself in the **Holocaust Tower**, a room nearly devoid of light and sound. End with the incredibly exhaustive exhibit on the last millennium of German Jewish history. *(Lindenstr. 9-14. U6 to Kochstr., or U1, 6, or 15 to Hallesches Tor.* ☎ *308 785 681; www.jmberlin.de. Open M 10am-10pm, Tu-Su 10am-8pm.* €*5, students* €*2.50. Special exhibits* €*4.)*

FILMMUSEUM BERLIN. This interactive new museum chronicles German film's development, with a focus on older films and multimedia exhibits devoted to superstars including Leni Riefenstahl and Marlene Dietrich. *(Potsdamer Str. 2, 3rd and 4th fl. of the Sony Center. S1, 2, 25 or U2 to Potsdamer Pl. ☎ 300 9030; www.filmmuseum-berlin.de. Open Tu-W and F-Su 10am-6pm, Th 10am-8pm. €6, students €4, children €2.50.)*

DEUTSCHE GUGGENHEIM BERLIN. In a renovated building across from the Deutsche Staatsbibliothek, the Deutsche Bank and the Guggenheim Foundation's joint venture is relatively small, featuring exhibits on modern and contemporary art. *(Unter den Linden 13-15. S1, 2, or 25 to Unter den Linden. ☎ 202 0930; www.deutsche-guggenheim.de. Open M-W and F-Su 11am-8pm, Th 11am-10pm. €4, students €3, M free.)*

KUNST-WERKE BERLIN. Under the direction of Mitte art luminary Klaus Biesen-bach, this former margarine factory houses artists' studios, rotating modern exhib-its, and a garden cafe in a glass cube. *(Auguststr. 69. U6 to Oranienburger Tor. ☎ 243 4590; www.kw-berlin.de. Open Tu-W and F-Su noon-7pm, Th noon-9pm. €6, students €4.)*

🎵 ENTERTAINMENT

Berlin has one of the world's most vibrant cultural scenes. Posters advertising everything from Chinese film to West African music plaster the city. Despite recent cutbacks, the city still generously subsidizes its art scene, and tickets are usually reasonably priced. Most theaters and concert halls offer up to 50% off for students who buy at the *Abendkasse* (evening box office), which opens 1hr. before shows. Other ticket outlets charge 15-18% commissions and do not offer student discounts. The **KaDeWe** (p. 407) has a ticket counter. (☎217 7754. Open M-F 10am-8pm, Sa 10am-4pm.) Most theaters and operas close from mid-July to late August. The monthly pamphlets *Konzerte und Theater in Berlin und Brandenburg* (free) and *Berlin Programm* (€1.75) list concerts, film, and theater info, as do the biweekly *030, Kultur!news, Tip*, and *Zitty*.

CONCERTS, DANCE, AND OPERA

Berlin reaches its musical zenith in September, during the **Berliner Festwochen**, which draws the world's best orchestras and soloists. The **Berliner Jazztage** in November features top jazz musicians. For tickets (which sell out months ahead) and more info on both festivals, call **Berliner Festspiele** (☎25 48 90; www.berlin-erfestspiele.de). In mid-July, the **Bachtage** feature an intense week of classical music, while every Saturday night in August the **Sommer Festspiele** turns the Ku'damm into a multi-faceted concert hall with folk, punk, and steel-drum groups competing for attention. The programs for many theaters and opera houses are listed on posters in U-Bahn stations. Tickets for the *Philharmonie* and the *Oper* are nearly impossible to get without writing months ahead; you can try standing outside before performances with a sign saying *"Suche Karte"* (seeking ticket)—people often try to sell tickets at the last moment, usually at outrageous prices.

🎭 **Berliner Philharmoniker**, Herbert Von Karajanstr. 1 (☎25 48 81 32; www.berlin-philhar-monic.com). Take S1, 2, or 25 or U2 to Potsdamer Pl. It may look bizarre, but this yel-low building, designed by Scharoun in 1963, is acoustically perfect: every audience member hears the music exactly as it is meant to sound. The Berliner Philharmoniker, led by Sir Simon Rattle, is one of the world's finest orchestras. It is practically impossi-ble to get a seat; check 1hr. before concert time, write at least 8 weeks ahead, or check their website. Open mid-Sept. to mid-June. Box office open M-F 3-6pm, Sa-Su 11am-2pm. Standing room from €7, seats from €13. AmEx/MC/V.

THEATER

Theater listings can be found on the yellow and blue posters in most U-Bahn sta-tions and in the monthly pamphlets listed above. In addition to the world's best German-language theater, Berlin also has a strong English-language scene; look for listings in *Zitty* or *Tip* that say *"in englischer Sprache"* (in English). A number of privately run companies called Off-Theaters also occasionally feature English-language plays. As with concert halls, virtually all theaters are closed in July and August, indicated by the words *Theaterferien* or *Sommerpause*.

Deutsches Theater, Schumannstr. 13A (☎28 44 12 25; www.deutsches-theater.berlin.net). U6 or S1, 2, 5, 7, 9, 25, or 75 to Friedrichstr. Even former West Berliners admits it: the one-time East German state theater is Germany's best. Made great by Max Reinhardt 100 years ago, it now produces innovative takes on classics and newer works from Büchner to Ibsen. The **Kammerspiel** (☎28 44 12 26) stages smaller, provocative productions. Box office for both open M-Sa 11am-6:30pm, Su 3-6:30pm. Tickets for Deutsches Theater €5-43, for Kammerspiel €12-30; students €8. AmEx/MC/V.

FILM
On any given night you can choose from over 150 different films. O.F. next to a movie listing means original version; O.m.U. means original version with German subtitles. Mondays through Wednesdays are *Kinotage* days at most theaters, with reduced prices. In summer, *Freiluftkino* (open-air cinemas) show movies in the city's parks; winter brings the international **Berlinale** film festival (Feb. 7-17, 2008).

Arsenal, in the Filmhaus, Potsdamer Pl. (☎26 95 51 00). U2 or S1, 2, or 25 to Potsdamer Pl. Run by the Berlinale's founders, Arsenal showcases an eccentric program of cult favorites, indie films, and international classics. Frequent appearances by guest directors make the theater popular with Berlin filmmakers. €7, students €5.

◘ SHOPPING

The high temple of consumerism is the dazzling, pricey seven-story **KaDeWe department store** on Wittenbergpl. at Tauentzienstr. 21-24, continental Europe's largest department store. The name is a German abbreviation of *Kaufhaus des Westens* (Department Store of the West; ☎212 10. Open M-F 10am-8pm, Sa 9:30am-8pm.) The sidewalks of the 3-kilometer-long **Kurfürstendamm,** near Bahnhof Zoo, contain a branch of every mega-chain you can name. Near Hackescher Markt and Alte Schönhauser Str., the art galleries of Mitte give way to clothing galleries with high price tags. The flea market on Str. des 17. Juni has a good selection but still high prices. (Take S5, 7, 9, or 75 to Tiergarten; open Sa-Su 11am-5pm.) **Winterfeldtplatz,** near Nollendorfpl., overflows with food, flowers, and people crooning Bob Dylan tunes over acoustic guitars. (Open W and Sa 8am-1pm.) On Sundays a massive second-hand market takes over Prenzlauer Berg's **Mauerpark.**

◪ NIGHTLIFE

Berlin's nightlife is absolute madness. Bars typically open around 6pm and get going around midnight, just as clubs begin opening their doors. The bar scene winds down anywhere between 1 and 6am; meanwhile, clubs fill up and don't empty until well after dawn, when they pass the baton to after-parties and 24hr. cafes. Between 1 and 4am, take advantage of the **night buses** and **U-Bahn** 9 and 12, which run all night on Friday and Saturday. Info about bands and dance venues can be found in the pamphlets *Tip* (€2.50) and *Zitty* (€2.30), available at newsstands, or in *030* (free), distributed in bars, cafes, and hostels.

Berlin's most touristed bar scene sprawls down pricey, packed **Hackescher Markt** and **Oranienburger Straße** in Mitte. Prices fall only slightly around yuppie **Kollwitzplatz** and **Kastanienallee** in Prenzlauer Berg, but areas around Schönhauser Allee and **Danziger Straße** still harbor a somewhat edgier scene. Bars line Simon-Dach-Straße, **Gabriel-Max-Straße,** and **Schlesiche Straße.** Businessmen and middle-aged tourists drink at bars along the Ku'damm. Gay nightlife centers on Nollendorfplatz, in the west, and lesbian nightlife has its stronghold in Kreuzberg.

I EAT BEATS FOR BREAKFAST

So proclaims the T-shirt of the boy bopping arhythmically in front of me at Maria am Bahnhof, a hot spot in the Friedrichshain club scene. Yes, I am at a techno concert—my first—and am trying to learn the particularities of dancing to something that has neither lyrics nor a recognizable melody (not that I can dance under any circumstances, to be fair).

More difficult, even, than learning the nuances of moving to electronic music is knowing what its various sub-categories even mean. As I researched Berlin, I would frequently learn that a club played, say, "drum 'n' bass" on Fridays and "electro" on Saturdays. I would give a confident nod and record this information while secretly having no idea what these terms meant, my own taste being generally confined to faux-obscure indie pop. So for those who are looking to test the waters of Berlin nightlife but are equally clueless about its fiendish electronic music culture, I can offer some info, if not some dance moves:

Drum 'n' Bass—Also called "dnb," this form is mostly a product of British rave culture. The quick drum beats and complex bass lines are the most prominent sonic elements. Influenced by hip-hop, it is usually mid-tempo and can involve samples or synthesized bass lines.

BARS AND CLUBS

MITTE

💽 **Weekend,** Alexanderpl. 5 (www.week-end-berlin.de), on the 12th fl. of the building with the neon "Sharp" sign. A touch on the posh side, with a fashionable crowd, Weekend is a must-see for its panoramic rooftop terrace; watch the sun rise over the block-housing of East Berlin. Wheelchair-accessible. Cover €6-10. Open Th-Sa 11pm-late. Cash only.

💽 **Cafe Moskau,** Karl-Marx-Allee 34. U5 to Schillingstr. The varied spaces tucked into this steel-and-glass GDR edifice play host to events from hip-hop and electronic nights to fashion shows. Also home to the too-cool-for-a-name bar known by its address, KMA 36. Beer €3. Su gay night. Cover €7-13. Open Sa 11pm-6am, Su 10pm-5am. Cash only.

2BE-Club, Ziegelstr. 23 (☎89 06 84 10; www.2be-club.de). U6 to Oranienburger Tor. Hip-hop and occasional reggae in a huge space with 2 dance floors. Cover €7.50-8; Sa until midnight women free. Open F-Sa and sometimes W 11pm-late. Cash only.

Kaffee Burger, Torstr. 60 (☎28 04 64 95; www.kaffee-burger.de). U2 to Rosa-Luxemburg-Pl. A true Berlin institution, this worn-in and comfortable bar/club has cheap drinks and a tinge of GDR-era retro. Th live bands 10pm. Cover Su-Th €1, F-Sa €2-6. Open Su-Th 7pm-late, F 8pm-late, Sa 9pm-late. Cash only.

CHARLOTTENBURG (SAVIGNYPLATZ)

Quasimodo, Kantstr. 12A (www.quasimodo.de). U2 or S5, 7, 9, or 75 to Zoologischer Garten. Beneath a cafe, this cozy venue showcases mostly jazz with occasional R&B and soul. Concert tickets available from 5pm at the cafe upstairs or through the Kant-Kasse ticket service (☎313 4554). Concerts 11pm. Cover €8-20. Call or check website for schedules. Reserve ahead for cheaper tickets. Open daily noon-late. Cash only.

SCHÖNEBERG

Slumberland, Goltzstr. 24 (☎216 5349). U1, 2, 3, or 4, to Nollendorfpl. Quirky, pink space with African art, palm trees, a sand floor and tantalizing mixed drinks encourages jamming to the reggae music. Open Su-F 6pm-late, Sa 11am-late. Cash only.

Mister Hu, Goltzstr. 39 (☎217 2111; www.misterhu-berlin.de). U1, 2, 3, or 4 to Nollendorfpl. This bar made of rocky tiles serves creative drinks that the relaxed crowd enjoys indoor or out on the sidewalk patio. Happy hour M-Sa 5-8pm, Su 6pm-2am; mixed drinks €4.50. Open Su-Th 6pm-2am, F-Sa 6pm-4am. Cash only.

KREUZBERG

Club der Visionaere, Am Flutgraben 1 (☎69 51 89 44; www.clubdervisionaere.de). U1 to Schlesisches Tor or night bus #N65 to Heckmannufer. From the many languages drifting through the air to the people settled on ground-cushions, canal-side Club der Visionaere gives off a backpacker vibe. Drift on a raft attached to the terrace. DJ spins house inside. Beer €3. Open M-F 4pm-late, Sa-Su noon-late. Cash only.

Watergate, Falckensteinstr. 49 (☎61 28 03 96; www.water-gate.de). U1 to Schlesisches Tor. Hugging the river, this stylish 2 fl. club has windows opening onto the water with spectacular views of the Oberbaumbrücke. Features different DJs on each floor, mostly spinning electronic and house. Often packed, with a energetic, sophisticated crowd. €6-10 cover. Open W, F-Sa 11pm-late, occasionally open Tu and Th. Cash only.

S036, Oranienstr. 190 (☎61 40 13 06; www.S036.de). U1 to Görlitzer Bahnhof or night bus #N29 to Heinrichpl. A staple of Berlin's club scene, with a punk feel. Named for the local postal code, the club has a dark, massive dance floor and a stage for concerts (€7-25). Diverse array of music. Cover €4-8. Cash only.

Heinz Minki, Vor dem Schlesischen Tor 3 (☎695 337 66; www.heinzminki.de). U1 to Schlesisches Tor or night bus #N65 to Heckmannufer. A beer garden sandwiched between two canals. Patrons pound down beers (0.5L €3.10) at long tables under hanging colored lights, surrounded by trees and shrubs. Gourmet pizza €2.60. Open daily in summer noon-late; in winter reduced hours. Cash only.

FRIEDRICHSHAIN

Rosi's, Revaler Str. 29 (www.rosis-berlin.de). U/S to Warshauerstr. An unpretentious warren of bars, clubs, and outdoor lounges strung across a former industrial space. Art markets and exhibitions round out the roster of DJs and live bands. There's something for everyone, from pubbers to clubbers to people who just want to lie around on couches. Nightly music runs the gamut from indie to drum-and-bass to reggae. Open Th-Sa 8pm-late, Su 2pm-late. Occasional daytime events. Cash only.

PRENZLAUER BERG

Intersoup, Schliemannstr. 31 (☎23 27 30 45; www.intersoup.de). U2 to Eberswalder Str. This bar eschews big-name drink brands and popular music in favor of worn 70s furniture, soup specials (€4.50-5), and retro floral wallpaper. Downstairs, the small club **Undersoup** has live music (most W and Sa), karaoke Th, films, and even puppet theater (M-Tu). DJs most nights. Club cover max. €3. Open daily 4pm-late. Cash only.

Electro - Shorthand for "electro funk." This brand of electronic hip-hop, sometimes traced all the way back to German stalwarts Kraftwerk, relies heavily on drum machines, synthetic bass lines, and elaborate sonic reverberations. It often takes on futuristic themes. Lyrics are digitially remastered in order to make the voices sound mechanical.

House - A form of electronic dance music in which the 4/4 beat is heavily accentuated by the drum. It tends to have a Latin influence and often tries to approximate the experience of live music, sampling everything from pop to jazz. Although the drum accents vary in their placement, the uptempo beat structure stays relatively consistent.

Techno - Techno employs computerized sequences that layer different rhythms and syncopations. Generally more melodic than its counterparts, it tends to use exclusively inorganic sounds.

Trance - Using the high degree of repetition common to melodic song structures, trance often builds up a steady crescendo using recurring synthesizer phrases. A bass drum catches the down beats while minor scales add variety. Occasionally, though not often, vocal layers are added to the mix.

—Amelia Atlas

Morgenrot, Kastanienallee 85. U2 to Eberswalder Str. With candy-print wallpaper and funky art, Morgenrot is the last outpost of punk spirit on an increasingly upscale street. Frosty vodka shots €4. Vegetarian brunch Th-Su 11am-4pm, €3-7. *Volksküche* dinner Tu €2. Open Tu-Th 10am-1am, F 10am-3am, Sa 11am-3am, Su 11am-1am. Cash only.

TREPTOW

■ **Insel,** Alt-Treptow 6 (☎20 91 49 90; www.insel-berlin.net). S4, 6, 8, or 9 to Treptower Park, then bus #265 or N65 from Puschkinallee to Rathaus Treptow. Enter through the park at the corner of Alt-Treptow. Located on an island in the Spree River, the club is a winding 3-story tower crammed with gyrating bodies, and an open-air movie theater. Cover Th-Sa €4-6. Open F-Sa from 10 or 11pm-late, some W 7pm-late. Cafe open in summer daily 2pm-late; winter Th 2-7pm, Sa-Su 2pm-late. Cash only.

GLBT NIGHTLIFE

Berlin is one of Europe's most gay-friendly cities. **Akazienstraße, Goltzstraße, Schöneberg,** and **Winterfeldtstraße** have mixed bars and cafes, while the **"Bermuda Triangle"** of Eisenacherstr., Fuggerstr., and Motzstr. is more exclusively gay. *Gay-yellowpages, Sergej,* and *Siegessäule* have GLBT entertainment listings. **Mann-o-Meter,** Bülowstr. 106, at the corner of Else-Lasker-Schüler-Str., provides counseling, info on gay nightlife. (☎216 8008; www.mann-o-meter.de. Open M-F 5-10pm, Sa-Su 4-10pm.) **Spinnboden-Lesbenarchiv,** Anklamer Str. 38, has hip lesbian offerings, including exhibits, films, and other cultural info. Take U8 to Bernauer Str. (☎448 5848. Open W and F 2-7pm.) The **Christopher Street Day (CSD)** parade, a 6hr. street party with ecstatic, champagne-soaked floats, draws over 250,000 participants annually in June. Nollendorfpl. hosts the **Lesbisch-schwules Stadtfest** (Lesbian-Gay City Fair) the weekend before the parade.

■ **Das Haus B,** Warschauer Pl. 18 (☎296 0800; www.dashausb.de). U1 or S3, 5-7, 9, or 75 to Warschauer Str. East Berlin's most famous disco in the GDR era is still a color-saturated haven for dancers, spinning techno, Top 40, and German Schlager to a mixed crowd. Cover €2-6. Open W 10pm-5am, F-Sa 10pm-7am. Cash only.

Hafen, Motzstr. 19 (www.hafen-berlin.de). U1-4 to Nollendorfpl. The owners of "Harbor" created its nautical decor. A fashionable—mostly gay male—crowd in summer. 1st M of each month English-language pub quiz 10pm. Open daily 8pm-late. Cash only.

Rose's, Oranienstr. 187 (☎615 6570). U1 or U8 to Kottbusser Tor or U1 to Görlitzer Bahnhof. Marked only by a sign over the door reading "Bar." A friendly, mixed clientele packs this claustrophobic party spot at all hours. The campy dark-red interior is filled with hearts, glowing lips, furry ceilings, feathers, and glitter. Vodka tonic €5 and absolutely "no fucking cocktails." Open daily 10pm-6am. Cash only.

SchwuZ, Mehringdamm 61 (☎629 0880; www.schwuz.de). U6 or 7 to Mehringdamm. Enter through Sundström. An underground lair lined with pipes and disco lights. Boisterous disco features 2 small dance floors and a lounge area with its own DJ. Music varies but usually pop. Cover €5 before midnight, €6 after. Open F-Sa 11pm-late. Cash only.

◪ DAYTRIPS FROM BERLIN

KZ SACHENHAUSEN. Located just north of Berlin, the small town of Oranienburg was the setting for the Nazi concentration camp Sachsenhausen, where over 100,000 Jews, communists, intellectuals, Roma (gypsies), and homosexuals were killed between 1936 and 1945. **Gedenkstätte Sachsenhausen,** Str. der Nationen 22, a memorial preserving the camp remains, includes some of the original barracks, the cell block where "dangerous" prisoners were tortured, and a pathology wing where Nazis experimented on inmates. The chilling remnants of **Station Z,** the extermination block, stand beside a mass grave that holds the ashes of victims. A stone monolith commemorating the camp's victims stands guard over the grounds and museums. To get there, take S1 (dir.: Oranienburg) to the end (40min.), then either use the infrequent bus service on lines #804 and 821 to Gedenkstätte or take a 15-20min. walk from the station. Follow the signs, turn right on Bernauer Str., left on Str. der Einheit, and right on Str. der Nationen. (☎ 033 012 000; www.stiftung-bg.de. Open daily Mar. 15-Oct. 14 8:30am-6pm; Oct. 15-Mar. 14 8:30am-4:30pm. Museums closed M. Free. Audio tour €3.)

POTSDAM. Satisfy cravings for imperial splendor in nearby Potsdam, the glittering city of Friedrich II (the Great). Best seen by bike or tour, Potsdam's attractions are spread out. On the S-Bahn platform at the station, ▇**Potsdam Per Pedales** rents bikes. (☎ 748 0057; www.potsdam-per-pedales.de. Open May-Sept. daily 9:30am-7pm.) The **tourist office** is at Brandenburger Str. 3. (☎ 508 8838. Tours Apr.-Oct. Tu-Su at 11am €26. Open Apr.-Oct. M-F 9am-6pm, Sa-Su 9:30am-4pm; Nov.-Mar. M-F 10am-6pm, Sa-Su 10am-2pm.) Spread over 600 acres, ▇**Park Sanssouci** is testimony to the size of Friedrich's treasury and the diversity of his aesthetic. (Open daily May-Oct. 8am-5pm; Nov.-Feb. 9am-4pm.) **Schloß Sanssouci**, the park's main attraction, was Friedrich's answer to Versailles. German-language tours leave every 20min.; the final tour at 5pm usually sells out hours earlier. Also in the park, the **Bildergalerie** displays works by Caravaggio, van Dyck, and Rubens. (☎ 0331 969 4181. Open mid-May to mid-Oct. Tu-Su 10am-5pm.) The stunning **Sizilianischer Garten** is at the opposite end of the park from the largest of the four castles, the 200-chambered **Neues Palais**. (Open M-Th and Sa-Su Apr.-Oct. 9am-5pm; Nov.-Mar. 9am-4pm. €6, students €5. Summer tours €1.) Potsdam's second park, the **Neuer Garten**, contains several royal residences.

NORTHERN GERMANY

Schleswig-Holstein, Germany's gateway to Scandinavia, gains its livelihood from the trade generated at its port towns. In Lower Saxony, cities begin to rise from the coastal plains, straddling rivers or sprawling through the countryside. The huge, less idyllic Hamburg is notoriously rich and radical, while the small city of Hanover charms visitors with its orderly English gardens and flourishing culture.

LÜBECK   ☎ 0451

Lübeck (pop. 215,000), a UNESCO World Cultural Heritage Site, is easily Schleswig-Holstein's most beautiful city. Massive medieval churches and winding alleys feature architecture of every style including medieval and renaissance—you'd never guess it was mostly razed in WWII. In its heyday, Lübeck controlled Northern European trade; today the city is a merchant of marzipan and Dückstein beer, as well as a gateway to the Baltics. Between the station and the *Altstadt* stands the massive **Holstentor**, one of Lübeck's four 15th-century defensive gates and the city's symbol. Its small museum focuses on the city's history. (Open Apr.-Sept. daily 10am-5pm; Oct.-Mar. Tu-Su 10am-5pm. €5, students and seniors €3, families €9.) The twin brick towers of the **Marienkirche**, a church that houses the world's largest mechanical organ, dominate the skyline. (☎ 39 77 01 80. Open daily in summer 10am-6pm; winter 10am-4pm. Suggested donation €2. €4, students €3.) Next to Marienkirche sits Lübeck's **Rathaus** (town hall), whose oldest portions date back to the 13th century. For a sweeping view of the spire-studded *Altstadt*, take the elevator to the top of **Petrikirche**. (☎ 39 77 30. Church open Tu-Su 11am-4pm. Tower open daily Apr.-Oct. 9am-7pm, Nov.-Mar. 10am-7pm. Church suggested donation €2. Tower €3, students €2.) The **Theaterfigurenmuseum**, Kolk 14, displays 1200 holdings from the world's largest private puppet collection—over 40,000. (☎ 786 26. Open daily 10am-6pm. €4, students €3, children €2.)

To reach ▇**Rucksack Hotel ❶**, Kanalstr. 70, take bus #1, 11, 21, or 31 to Katharineum and turn right at the church onto Glockengießerstr and continue until you reach the water. This popular hostel is a member of a collective of eco-friendly shops in a former glass factory. (☎70 68 92; www.rucksackhotel-lue-beck.de. Breakfast €3. Linens €3. Reception 10am-1pm and 5-9pm. 6- to 8-bed dorms €13; doubles €34, with bath €40; quads €60/68. Cash only.) Stop by the famous confectionery ▓I.G. Niederegger Marzipan Café ❶, Breitestr. 89, for marzipan, a delicious treat made of almonds, rosewater, and sugar. Lübeck's specialty is created in the shape of fruit, fish, and even the town gate. (☎530 1126. Open M-F 9am-7pm, Sa 9am-6pm, Su 10am-6pm. AmEx/MC/V.) **Trains** run to Berlin (2½hr., 1 per hr., €49-71) and Hamburg (50min., 1 per hr., €15). The **tourist office** is at Holstentorpl. 1. (☎88 22 33. Open June-Sept. M-F 9:30am-7pm, Sa 10am-3pm Su 10am-2pm; Jan.-May and Oct.-Nov. M-F 9:30am-6pm, Sa 10am-3pm; Dec. M-F 9:30am-6pm, Sa 10am-3pm.) The **Happy Day Card** provides unlimited access to public transportation and museum discounts. **Postal Code:** 23552.

HAMBURG   ☎040

Germany's largest port city and the second largest in Europe, Hamburg (pop. 1,800,000) radiates an inimitable recklessness. Riots and restorations defined the post-WWII landscape. Today, Hamburg is a haven for contemporary artists, intellectuals, and partygoers who live it up in Germany's self-declared "capital of lust."

▛ TRANSPORTATION

Trains: The **Hauptbahnhof** has connections every hr. to: **Berlin** (1½hr., €62); **Copenhagen, DEN** (5hr., €78); **Frankfurt** (3½hr., €98); **Hanover** (1½hr., €38); **Munich** (6hr., €119). **DB Reisezentrum** ticket office open M-F 5:30am-10pm, Sa-Su 7am-10pm. The **Dammtor** train station is near the university; **Harburg** station is south of the Elbe; **Altona** station is to the west of the city; and **Bergedorf** is to the southeast. **Lockers** (€2.50-5 per day, €7.50-15 per 3 days) are available at stations.

Buses: The **ZOB** is on Steintorpl. across from the *Hauptbahnhof*, just past the Museum für Kunst und Gewerbe. Open Su-Th 5am-10pm, F-Sa 5am-midnight. **Autokraft** (☎280 8660) runs to **Berlin** (3¼hr., 10-12 per day, €25). **Gulliver's** (☎280 048 35) runs to **Paris, FRA** (12hr., 1 per day, €66). Student discounts available.

Public Transportation: HVV operates an efficient U-Bahn, S-Bahn, and bus network. One-way tickets within the downtown area cost €2.60; prices vary with distance and network. 1-day pass €6, after 9am or Sa-Su €5.10; 3-day pass €15. Buy tickets at *Automaten* (machines), or consider buying a **Hamburg Card** (p. 414).

Bike Rental: Fahrradstation Dammtor/Rothebaum, Schlüterstr. 11 (☎41 46 82 77), rents bikes for just €3 per day. Open M-F 9am-6:30pm. **Fahrradladen St. Georg,** Schmilinskystr. 6 (☎24 39 08), is off Lange Reihe toward the Außenalster. €8 per day, €56 per week with €50 deposit. Open M-F 10am-7pm, Sa 10am-1pm.

✳▐ ORIENTATION AND PRACTICAL INFORMATION

Hamburg's city center sits between the **Elbe River** and two lakes, **Außenalster** and **Binnenalster.** Bisecting the downtown, the **Alsterfleet** canal separates the *Altstadt* on the eastern bank from the *Neustadt* on the west. Most major sights lie between the **St. Pauli Landungsbrücken** port area in the west and the *Hauptbahnhof* in the east. **Mönckebergstraße** and **Spitalerstraße,** Hamburg's most famous shopping streets, run all the way to **Rathausmarkt.** North of downtown, the **university** dominates the **Dammtor** area and sustains an animated community of students and intellectuals. To the west of the university, the **Schanzenviertel** is a politically active community home to artists, squatters, and a sizable Turkish population. At the south end of town, an entirely different atmosphere reigns in **St. Pauli,** where the raucous **Fischmarkt** (fish market) is surpassed only by the wilder **Reeperbahn,** home to Hamburg's best discos and its infamous sex trade.

GERMANY

Hamburg

ACCOMMODATIONS
Instant Sleep, 3
Jugendherberge auf dem
Stintfang (HI), 14
Schanzenstern Altona, 12
Schanzenstern Übernachtungs-
und Gasthaus, 5

FOOD
Oma's Apotheke, 4
La Sepia, 6
Mensa, 2
Schanzenstern, 7
Unter den Linden, 9

NIGHTLIFE
Fabrik, 8
G-Bar, 10
Große Freiheit 36/
Kaiserkeller, 13
Logo, 1
Meanie
Bar/ Molotow, 11

Tourist Offices: The **Hauptbahnhof** office, in the Wandelhalle near the Kirchenallee exit (☎30 05 12 01; www.hamburg-tourism.de), books rooms for €4. Open M-Sa 8am-9pm, Su 10am-6pm. The **St. Pauli Landungsbrücken** office, between piers 4 and 5 (☎30 05 12 03), is less crowded. Both sell the **Hamburg Card,** which provides unlimited access to public transportation, and discounts to museums. 1-day card €8, 3-day €18, 5-day €33. The **Group Card** provides the same benefits for up to 5 people. 1-day €12, 3-day €30, 5-day €51.

Consulates: Canada, Ballindamm 35 (☎460 0270). S- or U-Bahn to Jungfernstieg; between Alstertor and Bergstr. Open M-F 9:30am-12:30pm. **Ireland,** Feldbrunnenstr. 43 (☎44 18 61 13). U1 to Hallerstr. Open M-F 9am-1pm. **New Zealand,** Domstr. 19, Zürich-Haus, Cout C, 3rd fl. (☎442 5550). U1 to Messberg. Open M-Th 9am-1pm and 2-5:30pm, F 9am-1pm and 2-4:30pm.

GLBT Resources: The neighborhood of St. Georg is the center of the gay community. Pick up the free *Hinnerk* magazine and *Friends: The Gay Map* from **Cafe Gnosa** or from the tourist office. Organizations include **Hein und Fiete,** Pulverteich 21 (☎24 03 33). Walk down Steindamm away from the *Hauptbahnhof,* turn right on Pulverteich; it's a building with a rainbow flag. Open M-F 4-9pm, Sa 4-7pm.

Post Office: At the Kirchenallee exit of the *Hauptbahnhof.* Open M-F 8am-6pm, Sa 8:30am-12:30pm. **Postal Code:** 20099.

ACCOMMODATIONS

Hamburg's dynamic **Schanzenviertel** area, filled with students, working-class Turks, and left-wing dissenters, houses two of the best backpacker hostels in the city. Small, relatively cheap pensions line **Steindamm** and the area around the *Hauptbahnhof,* although the area's prostitutes and wannabe mafiosi detract from its charm. **Lange Reihe** has equivalent lodging options in a cleaner neighborhood. More expensive accommodations line the **Binnenalster** and eastern **Außenalster.**

■ **Schanzenstern Übernachtungs- und Gasthaus,** Bartelsstr. 12 (☎439 8441; www.schanzenstern.de). S21 or 31, or U3 to "Sternschanze." Near St. Pauli, bright, clean, and comfortable rooms in a renovated pen factory, most with bath. Wheelchair-accessible. Breakfast €4.30-6.30. Reception 7am-1:30am. Reserve ahead. Dorms €19; singles €38; doubles €53; triples €63; quads €77; quints €95. Cash only. ❷

■ **Instant Sleep,** Max-Brauer-Allee 277 (☎43 18 23 10; www.instantsleep.de). S21 or 31 or U3 to "Sternschanze." Helpful, bilingual staff—as well as an improvised library and communal kitchen—contribute to a family feel at this backpacker hostel. Close to the S-Bahn, making it convenient and sometimes noisy. Lockers €5 deposit. Linens €2. Internet €1 per 30min. Reception 8am-2am. Check-out 11am. Dorms €16; singles €30; doubles €23 per person; triples €21 per person. Cash only. ❷

Jugendherberge auf dem Stintfang (HI), Alfred-Wegener-Weg 5 (☎31 34 88). S1, S3, or U3 to Landungsbrücke. The hostel is above the Landungsbrücke station—look for stairs on the left side. Newly renovated and expanded, this huge hostel has an incredible view of the harbor. Bunks, checkered curtains, and views of the nearby woods contribute to a camp feel. Breakfast and linens included. Reception 24hr. Check-out 10am. Lockout 10am-1pm. Dorms €23-25, under 27 €19-21. HI members only, although membership can be purchased at the hostel for €3.10 per night. MC/V. ❷

Schanzenstern Altona, Kleiner Rainstr. 24-26 (☎39 91 91 91; www.schanzenstern-altona.de). As nice as its Schanzenviertel counterpart with brightly colored walls and rooms with bath. Close to the Altona station. Wheelchair-accessible. Dorms €19; singles €43; doubles €58-68; triples €73; quads €83. Cash only. ❷

FOOD

Seafood is common in the port city of Hamburg. In Schanzenviertel, avant-garde cafes and Turkish falafel stands entice hungry passersby. **Schulterblatt, Susannen-straße,** and **Schanzenstraße** are home to funky cafes and restaurants, while cheaper establishments crowd in the **university** area, especially along **Rentzelstraße, Grindel-hof,** and **Grindelallee.** In **Altona,** the pedestrian zone approaching the train station is packed with food stands and produce shops. The Portuguese community gives its take on seafood in the area between the Michaelskirche and the river.

La Sepia, Schulterblatt 36 (☎432 2484; www.lasepia.de). This Portuguese-Spanish restaurant serves some of the city's most reasonably priced seafood. For your pocketbook's sake, come for lunch (11am-5pm), when €5 gets you a big plate of grilled tuna with sauteed and scalloped carrots and potatoes, a basket of fresh bread, and a bowl of soup. Lunch €3.50-6. Dinner €7.50-22. Open daily noon-3am. AmEx/MC/V. ❷

Schanzenstern, Bartelsstr. 12 (☎43 29 04 09; www.schanzenstern.de). Organic masterpieces are served in the Schanzenstern Übernachtungs und Gasthaus hostel. Breakfast €4.30-9.40. Lunch €4-11.50. Daily lunch special €6.20. Dinner €8-12.50. Open M 3pm-1am, Tu-Sa 10:30am-1am, Su 11am-midnight. Cash only. ❷

Unter den Linden, Juliusstr. 16 (☎43 81 40). Read free German papers over *Milchkaffee* (coffee with foamed milk; €3-4), breakfast (€5-8), or salad and pasta (€4-7) underneath, as the name suggests, linden trees. Open daily 10am-1am. Cash only. ❷

Oma's Apotheke, Schanzenstr. 87 (☎43 66 20). Old-style ambience and large portions, popular with students. German, Italian, and American cuisine. *Schnitzel* €7.50. Hamburger with 1lb. fries €6.60. Open Su-Th 9am-1am, F-Sa 9am-2am. Cash only. ❷

Mensa, Von-Melle-Park 5 (☎41 90 22 02). S21 or 31 to Dammtor, then bus #4 or 5 to Staatsbibliothek (1 stop). Cafeteria food and listings of university events. Meals €2.50-4, student €1.60-3.40. Open M-Th 10am-4pm, F 10am-3:30pm. Cash only. ❶

🔄 SIGHTS

ALTSTADT

GROßE MICHAELSKIRCHE. The 18th-century Michaelskirche is the symbol of Hamburg, and with good reason. Named for the Archangel Michael, who stands guard over the main entrance, the church was destroyed successively by lightning, accidents, and Allied bombs. It was finally rebuilt after the Cold War, and restored in 1996. Its fate, essentially, has kept in tandem with the city's. A panoramic view of Hamburg awaits those who climb the 462 stairs of the spire (or those who opt for the elevator). In the crypt, a multimedia presentation on the history of the church screens on weekends. *(U-Bahn to Baumwall, S-Bahn to Stadthausbrücke. ☎37 67 81 00. Church open daily 9am-8pm. Crypt open June-Oct. daily 11am-4:30pm; Nov.-May Sa-Su 11am-4:30pm. Screenings M-Sa 1 per hr. 12:30-3:30pm, Su 2 per hr. 11:30am-3:30pm. Church suggested donation €2. Crypt €1.50. Screenings €2.50. Tower €3.)*

RATHAUS. Built between 1886 and 1897, intricate mahogany carvings and two-ton chandeliers make the city's town hall—home to the city and state governments—one of the *Altstadt*'s most impressive buildings. In front, the **Rathausmarkt** hosts festivities from demonstrations to medieval fairs. *(☎428 312 470. M-Th 10:15am-3:15pm, F-Su 10:15am-1:15pm. Building open daily 8am-6pm. €1.50, under 14 €0.50.)*

NIKOLAIKIRCHE. The spire of this neo-Gothic ruin, bombed in 1943, has been preserved as a memorial for victims of war and persecution. *(U3 to Rödingsmarkt. Open daily Nov.-Mar. 10:30am-5:30pm; Apr.-May and Sept.-Oct. 10am-7pm; June-Aug. M-Th and Su 9:30am-8pm, F-Sa 9:30am-8pm, F-Sa 9:30am-10pm. Tower €3, students €1.50, children €1.)*

MÖNCKEBERGSTRAßE. Two spires punctuate Hamburg's shopping zone, which stretches from the *Rathaus* to the *Hauptbahnhof.* Next to the *Rathaus,* **St. Petrikirche** is Hamburg's oldest church, dating back to 1195. *(☎325 7400. Open M-Tu and Th-F 10am-4:30pm, W 10am-7pm, Sa 10am-5pm, Su 9am-9pm.)* The other spire belongs to

St. Jakobikirche, which is known for its 17th-century Arp-Schnittger organ. (☎ *303 7370. Open M-Sa 10am-5pm.*) The buildings along **Trostbrücke** sport copper models of clipper ships on their spires, testiments to Hamburg's sea-trade wealth.

BEYOND THE ALTSTADT

PLANTEN UN BLOMEN. West of the Außenalster, this huge expanse of manicured flower beds and trees includes Europe's largest Japanese garden, complete with a teahouse built in Japan. (*S21 or 31 to Dammtor. www.plantenunblomen.hamburg.de. Open May-Sept. daily 7am-11pm, Oct.-Apr. 7am-8pm. Free.*) In summer, performers in the outdoor **Musikpavillon** range from Irish step-dancers to Hamburg's police choir. (*May-Sept. Most performances 3pm. See garden website for details.*) At night, opt for the **Wasserlichtkonzerte,** with a choreographed play of fountains and underwater lights. (*May-Aug. daily 10pm; Sept. 9pm.*) To the north, the tree-lined paths bordering the two **Alster lakes** provide refuge from city crowds.

ST. PAULI LANDUNGSBRÜCKEN. International ships light up the harbor at night. Look for the 426m **Elbtunnel,** completed in 1911 and still active. (*Behind Pier 6 in the building with the copper cupola. Free for pedestrians.*) At the **Fischmarkt,** vendors hawk fish, produce, and other goods. (*S1, S3, or U3 to Landungsbrücken or S1 or S3 to Königstr. or Reeperbahn. Open Su Apr.-Oct. 5-10am; Nov.-Mar. 7-10am.*)

KZ NEUENGAMME. An idyllic agricultural village east of Hamburg provided the backdrop for the Neuengamme concentration camp, where Nazis killed 55,000 prisoners through slave labor. In 1989, the Hamburg Senate built a memorial on the site. A mile-long path begins at the **Haus des Gedenkens,** a memorial building containing banners inscribed with the names and death dates of the victims. The path leads to the former **Prisoners' Block,** which contains a detailed exhibit on the history of the camp, including the recorded testimony of survivors in English, French, German, and Russian. (*Jean-Doldier-Weg 39. S21 to Bergedorf, then bus #227 or 327, about 1hr. from city. Buses runs from Bergedorf M-Sa 3-4 per hr., Su 1 per hr. ☎ 428 131 500; www.kz-gedenkstaette-neuengamme.de. Museum and memorial open May-Sept. M-F 9:30am-4pm, Sa-Su noon-7pm; Oct.-Mar. daily noon-5pm. Path open 24hr.*)

GEDENKSTÄTTE BULLENHUSER DAMM UND ROSENGARTEN. Surrounded by warehouses, this schoolhouse is a memorial to 20 Jewish children who were subjected to medical experimentation while in Auschwitz and murdered by the SS in an attempt to destroy evidence only hours before Allied troops arrived. Visitors are invited to plant a rose for the children in the flower garden behind the school, where memorial plaques line the fence. (*Bullenhuser Damm 92. S21 to Rothenburgsort. Follow the signs to Bullenhuser Damm along Ausschläger Bildeich to the intersection with Grossmannstr.; the garden is on the far left; the school is 200m farther. ☎ 428 131 500. Rose garden open 24hr. Exhibit open Su 10am-5pm, Th 2-8pm. Free.*)

 MUSEUMS

The **Hamburg Card** provides discounted access to all museums except the Deichtorhallen and the Hafen Basar. *Museumswelt Hamburg*, a free newspaper available at tourist offices, lists events. Most museums are closed on Monday.

HAMBURGER KUNSTHALLE. This sprawling fine-arts museum presents the Old Masters and special exhibits, including a large number of Impressionist works by the likes of Degas, Monet, and Renoir, in the oldest building. In the connected four-level **Galerie der Gegenwart,** contemporary art mixes with temporarary and permanent exhibits. (*Glockengießerwall 1. Turn right from the Spitalerstr. City exit of the Hauptbahnhof and cross the street. ☎ 428 131 200; www.hamburger.kunsthalle.de. Open Tu-W and F-Su 10am-6pm, Th 10am-9pm. €8.50, students €5, families €14.*)

MUSEUM FÜR KUNST UND GEWERBE. Handicrafts, china, and furnishings from all corners of the earth fill this arts and crafts museum. Check out the **Hall of Mirrors**, a reconstruction of a room in the home of a Hamburg banker. *(Steintorpl. 1., 1 block south of the Hauptbahnhof. ☎428 542 732; www.mkg-hamburg.de. Open Tu-W and F-Su 10am-6pm, Th 10am-9pm. €8, students, Hamburg Card holders, and seniors €5, under 18 free.)*

HARRY'S HAMBURGER HAFEN BASAR. After sailing the world and collecting many oddities, Harry dropped anchor and set up this cavernous museum displaying various statues, idols, masks, and gourds; everything except the shrunken heads and the stuffed leopard is for sale. *(Balduinstr. 18. S1 or S3 to Reeperbahn or U3 to St. Pauli. ☎31 24 82; www.hafenbasar.de. Open Tu-Su noon-6pm. €2.50, 6-12 €1.50.)*

♫ 🎧 ENTERTAINMENT AND NIGHTLIFE

The **Staatsoper,** Große Theaterstr. 36, houses one of the best **opera** companies in Germany; the associated **ballet** is one of the nation's best. (U2 to Gänsemarkt. ☎35 68 68. Open M-Sa 10am-6:30pm and 1½hr. before performances.) **Orchestras** include the Philharmonie, the Norddeutscher Rundfunk Symphony, and Hamburg Symphonia, which all perform at the **Musikhalle** on Johannes-Brahms-Pl. (U2 to Gänsemarkt. ☎34 69 20; www.musikhalle-hamburg.de. Box office open M-F 10am-4pm.) Live music also prospers in Hamburg. Superb traditional jazz swings at the **Indra** (Große Freiheit 64). Early on Sundays, musicians talented and otherwise play at the **Fischmarkt.** The **West Port Jazz Festival** runs in mid-July; for info, call the *Konzertkasse* (ticket office; ☎32 87 38 54).

Hamburg's nightlife scene heats up in the **Schanzenviertel** and **St. Pauli** areas. The infamous **Reeperbahn** runs through the heart of St. Pauli; lined with sex shops, strip joints, and peep shows, it's also home to the city's best bars and clubs. Though the Reeperbahn is generally safe, women may want to avoid adjacent streets. Parallel to the Reeperbahn lies **Herbertstraße,** Hamburg's official prostitution strip, where licensed sex entrepeneurs flaunt their flesh. Herbertstr. is open only to those over the age of 18. Students head north to the streets of the Schanzenviertel, where cafes create an atmosphere more leftist than lustful. The **St. Georg** district, near Berliner Tor and along Lange Reihe, is the center of Hamburg's **gay scene.** In general, clubs open and close late, with some techno and trance clubs remaining open all night. *Szene* (€3), available at newsstands, lists events.

🏆 **Große Freiheit 36/Kaiserkeller,** Große Freiheit 36 (☎317 7780). Everyone from Ziggy Marley to Prince to Matchbox 20 has performed on the big stage and dance floor upstairs. Live music or DJs usually 10pm-4am. F-Sa club nights cover €3-6. Concerts usually at 7pm; €10-30, with higher prices for bigger names. Often free until 11pm.

Fabrik, Barnerstr. 36 (☎39 10 70; www.fabrik.de). From Altona station, head toward Offenser Hauptstr. and go right on Bahrenfelderstr. This former weapons factory now cranks out raging beats. Cover for live music €5-30. Every 2nd Sa of the month, "Gay Factory" attracts a mixed crowd. Live DJ 10pm most Sa; cover €7-8. Cash only.

Meanie Bar/Molotow, Spielbudenpl. 5 (☎31 08 45; www.molotowclub.com), parallel to the Reeperbahn. The Molotow, in the basement of the retro Meanie Bar, has 70s decor and alternative music, great bands, and good dancers. The bar upstairs has a more relaxed atmosphere. Meanie Bar open daily from 9pm. No cover. Molotow cover for club nights and other events €3-4; live bands €8-15. Open from 8pm when there are concerts, and from 11pm F-Sa for disco. Cash only.

Logo, Grindelallee 5 (☎36 26 22; www.logohamburg.de). U-Bahn to Stephanspl., or S21 or 31 to Dammtor. Educates the college crowd with its live folk, hip-hop, rock, and samba. Cover €5-15. Live music from 9pm. Cash only.

G-Bar, Lange Reihe 81 (☎28 00 46 90). Young male waiters could be models at this clean-cut gay bar. Beer €2-3. Mixed drinks €5-7. Open daily 7pm-2am. Cash only.

HANOVER (HANNOVER)   ☎0511

Despite its relatively small size, the city of Hanover (pop. 515,000) has the art, culture, and landscape to rival any European city. Hanover's highlights are the three bountiful ■**Herrenhausen gardens.** The largest, **Großer Garten,** features geometrically pruned shrubbery and is also home to the **Große Fontäne,** one of Europe's highest-shooting fountains. To get there from the train station, walk to the far end of the lower shop level and take the U4 or 5 to Herrenhauser Garten. (Fountain spurts Apr.-Oct. M-F 11am-noon and 3-5pm, Sa-Su 11am-noon and 2-5pm. Garden open daily Apr. 9am-7pm; May-Aug. 9am-8pm; Sept. 9am-7pm; early Oct. 9am-6pm. Entrance €4, including admission to *Berggarten*. Concerts and performances June-Aug.; ☎16 84 12 22 for schedule.) On the outskirts of the *Altstadt* stands the **Neues Rathaus;** take the elevator up the tower for a lovely view year-round or ascend to the dome on a summer evening. (Open May-Sept. M-F 9am-6pm, Sa-Su 10am-6pm. Free. Elevator M-F 9:30am-6pm, Sa-Su 10am-6pm. €2.50, students €2.) Nearby, the ■**Sprengel Museum,** Kurt-Schwitters-Pl., hosts some of the 20th century's greatest art, including works by Kandinsky, Leger, and Picasso. (Open Tu 10am-8pm, W-Su 10am-6pm. €7, students €4.) On Leibnizufer, North of Friederikenplatz, is the **Sculpture Mile,** a 1.5km stretch of sculpture and art exhibits.

■ **Hotel Flora ❹,** Heinrichstr. 36, is located in the center of town 10min. from the station. Take the back exit and continue straight ahead onto Berliner Allee, cross the street, then turn left onto Heinrichstr, a quiet street close to the *Hauptbanhof*. Rooms come with carpeting, framed Monet prints, and TVs. (☎38 39 10; www.hotel-flora-hannover.de. Breakfast included. Reception 8am-8pm. Singles €37-49, doubles €64-75, triples €84-96. Dogs €7.50. AmEx/MC/V.) **Hollandische Kakaostube ❶,** Standehausstr. 2-3, features a dozen different award-winning hot chocolates (€3.70) and a gorgeous assortment of cakes. Try the *Mohrenkof*, a merengue filled with hazelnuts and enrobed in chocolate (€2.10). The classy gold-accented dining room features old-world elegance. (☎30 41 00. Open M-F 9am-7:30pm and Sa 8:30am-6pm. Cash only.)

Trains leave at least every hour for: Berlin (2hr., €45-56); Frankfurt (3hr., €75); Hamburg (1½hr., €38); Munich (4½hr., €110); Amsterdam, NTH (4½-5hr., €60-80). The **tourist office** is at Ernst-August-Pl. 8. (☎12 34 51 11) and sells the **Hannover Card** (1-day €9; 3-day €15; up to 5 people €17/29), which covers transportation costs and reduces museum and sightseeing tour prices. **Postal Code:** 30159.

CENTRAL AND WESTERN GERMANY

Niedersachsen (Lower Saxony), which stretches from the North Sea to the hills of central Germany, comprises agricultural plains and foggy marshland. Just south, North Rhine-Westphalia—the most economically powerful area in Germany—is so densely populated that it's nearly impossible to travel through the countryside without glimpsing the next hamlet, metropolis, or village ahead.

DÜSSELDORF   ☎0211

Düsseldorf (pop. 571,000), the nation's *"Hautstadt"*—a pun on the German *"Hauptstadt"* (capital)—is a stately metropolis with an *Altstadt* (Old Town) that features stellar nightlife and pricey shopping. In addition to glitz and glamour, Düsseldorf has an internationally recognized art school and top-notch museums.

⚡ TRANSPORTATION AND PRACTICAL INFORMATION. Trains run to: **Amsterdam, NTH** (2hr., 1 per 2hr., €32-42); **Berlin** (4½hr., 1-2 per hr., €94-96); **Frankfurt** (2hr., 2 per hr., €45-70); **Hamburg** (4hr., 1-2 per hr., €68-80); **Munich** (5-6hr., 2 per hr., €93-121). Düsseldorf's S-Bahn is integrated into the regional **VRR** *(Verkehrsverbund Rhein-Ruhr)* system, which links most nearby cities and is the cheapest way to get to Cologne. On the **public transportation** system, single tickets cost €1.10-2.10. *Tagestickets* (€11-18) allow up to five people to travel for 24hr. on any line. The **tourist office,** Immermannstr. 65, is to the right of the train station. (☎172 0228. Open M-F 9:30am-6:30pm, Sa 9am-2pm.) **Postal Code:** 40210.

⚡❖ ACCOMMODATIONS AND FOOD. Düsseldorf's hotels and hostels often double their prices during trade fairs, which take place from August to April. Close to the center of town, **▨Backpackers Düsseldorf ❷,** Fürstenwall 180, has carpeted floors, colorful beds, and a common room equipped with leather sofas, a TV, and a DVD player. Take bus #725 (dir.: Hafen/Lausward) from the station, and get off at Kirchpl. (☎302 0848; www.backpackers-duesseldorf.de. Kitchen available. Breakfast, lockers, linens, and towel included. Free Internet and Wi-Fi. Reception 8am-9pm. Reserve ahead in summer F-Sa. Dorms €22. MC/V.) The modern **Jugendgästehaus Düsseldorf (HI) ❷,** Düsseldorfer Str. 1, is just over the Rheinkniebrücke from the Altstadt. Take U70 or 74-77 to Luegpl.; then walk 500m down Kaiser-Wilhelm-Ring, or get off at Belsenpl., and take bus #835 or 836 to the Jugendherberge stop. (☎55 73 10; www.duesseldorf-jugendherberge.de. Breakfast included. Reception 7am-1am. Curfew 1am. Dorms €26; singles €42; doubles €60; quads €93. €3.10 HI discount. Cash only.) To reach **Campingplatz Unterbachersee ❶,** Kleiner Torfbruch 31, take any S-Bahn to Düsseldorf Geresheim, then bus #735 (dir.: Stamesberg) to Seeweg. (☎899 2038. Open Apr.-Oct. €5 per person, €10 per tent. Cash only.) For a cheap meal, the *Altstadt* can't be beat. An outlet of the Czech brewery **Pilsner Urquell ❷,** Grabenstr. 6, specializes in Eastern European fare. (☎868 1411. Entrees €5-13. Beer €2.50-4.10. Open M-Sa 11am-1pm, Su 4pm-midnight. MC/V.) **Rewe** supermarket is in Carlspl. in the *Altstadt.* (Open M-Sa 7am-8pm.)

◎ SIGHTS. Königsallee ("the Kö"), outside the *Altstadt,* embodies wealthy Düsseldorf. To reach the Kö from the train station, walk 10min. down Graf-Adolf-Str. Midway up the street is the marble-and-copper **Kö-Galerie.** Better deals in non-designer stores can be found along Flingerstr. in the *Altstadt.* To get to the Baroque **Schloß Benrath,** Benrather Schloßallee 104, in the suburbs of Düsseldorf, take tram #701. The Schloß was originally built as a pleasure palace and hunting grounds for Elector Karl Theodor. (☎899 3832; www.schloss-benrath.de. Open Tu-Su mid-Apr. to Oct. 10am-6pm; Nov. to mid-Apr. 11am-5pm. Tours 1 per hr. €5, students €4.) At the upper end of the Kö is the **Hofgarten,** Germany's oldest public park. To its west, the **K20 Kunstsammlung Nordrhein-Westfalen,** Grabbepl. 5, has various works by Expressionists, Surrealists, and former Düsseldorf resident Paul Klee. (U70 or 75-79 to Heinrich-Heine-Allee, and walk two blocks north. ☎838 1130; www.kunstsammlung.de. Open Tu-F 10am-6pm, Sa-Su 11am-6pm. €7, students €4.50.) To the north at Ehrenhof 4-5, the works of the **museum kunst palast** emphasize the Düsseldorf school; there's also an extensive collection of glass artwork. (U74-77 to Kulturzentrum Ehrenhof/Tonhalle and follow the signs. ☎899 2460; www.museum-kunst-palast.de. Open Tu-Su 11am-6pm. €6, students €4.50.)

◎ NIGHTLIFE. It's said that Düsseldorf's 500 pubs make up the longest bar in the world. By nightfall, it's nearly impossible to see where one pub ends and the next begins in the packed *Altstadt.* The newsletter *Prinz* (€3) gives tips on the entertainment scene; some youth hostels have it for free. The spacious **Oberbayern,**

Bolkerstr. 37, draws a young crowd to its flashy, frenetic dance floor and mellow bar. (☎854 9070; www.oberbayern-duesseldorf.de. Mixed drinks €2-4.50. Open W-Su 7pm-5am. Cash only.) **Zur Uel,** Ratinger Str. 16, is a restaurant by day and a rowdy German pub by night. (☎32 53 69. Beer €2-3. Open Su-Th 9am-2am, F-Sa 9am-3am. MC/V.) Sleek clubs, such as the half-lounge, half-disco **Nachtresidenz,** Bahnstr. 13-15, are located farther from the *Altstadt.* (☎136 5755; www.nachtresidenz.de. 21+. Open F-Sa 10pm-5am. Cash only.) **GLBT nightlife** clusters along Bismarckstr., at the intersection with Charlottenstr. *Facolte* (€2), a gay and lesbian nightlife magazine, is available at most newsstands in the city.

AACHEN   ☎0241

Easygoing Aachen (pop. 246,000), Germany's westernmost city, was once "Roma secunda," the capital of Charlemagne's enormous Frankish empire in the 8th century. The legacy of the medieval superstar is ubiquitous—even local pharmacies use him as their namesake. For a glimpse of Aachen's former splendor, visit the three-tiered dome, octagonal interior, and blue-gold mosaics of the 🖾**Dom,** in the city center. Charlemagne's remains are housed in the ornate reliquary behind the altar. (Open M-Sa 7am-7pm, Su 1-7pm, except during services.) Around the corner is the **Schatzkammer,** Klosterpl. 2, considered the most important ecclesiastical treasury north of the Alps. A silver bust of Charlemagne containing the emperor's skull is just one of several priceless artifacts. (☎47 70 91 27. Open M 10am-1pm, Tu-W and F-Su 10am-6pm, Th 10am-9pm. €4, students €3.) Aachen's earliest settlers were scared off by the natural springs that run through the area, believing that they came from hell. The Romans were indifferent to satanic connections and constructed the city's first **mineral baths,** now the luxurious **Carolus Thermen,** Passstr. 79. Take bus #51 from the Normaluhr bus stop on Theaterst. to Carolus Thermen. (☎18 27 40; www.carolus-thermen.de. 2½hr. soak €10, with sauna €20; day-long soak €15, sauna €29. Open daily 9am-11pm. Cash only.)

Hotel Cortis ❸, Krefelderstr. 52, is an intimate B&B with cable TV in each room. Take bus #34 (dir.: Kohlscheid Banhof) from the Normaluhr bus stop to Carolus Thermen, then take bus #51 to Rolandstr. Turn left on Krefelderstr. (☎997 4110; www.hotel-cortis.de. Breakfast included. Singles €30; doubles €53-58, with bath €62. MC/V.) **Euroregionales Jugendgästehaus (HI) ❷,** Maria-Theresia-Allee 260, has clean, bright rooms 20min. from the city center. Take bus #2 (dir.: Preusswald) from the Misereor bus stop to Ronheide. (☎71 10 10; aachen.jugendherberge.de. Breakfast included. Curfew 1am. Dorms €25; singles €39; doubles €61. €3.10 HI discount. MC/V.) **Sausalitos ❸,** Markt 47, is a popular Mexican restaurant with a huge cocktail bar. (☎234 9200; www.sausolitos.de. Entrees €6-14. Open Su-Th noon-1am, F-Sa noon-2am. Cash only.) The **pedestrian zone** and **Pontstraße,** off Marktpl., have a number of restaurants that are easy on the wallet. **Trains** go to Brussels, BEL (2hr., 1 per hr., €25-30), Cologne (1hr., 2 per hr., €13-19), and Paris, FRA (3hr., 6-7 per day, €126). The **tourist office** is on Friedrich-Wilhelm-Pl. in the Atrium Elisenbrunnen. (☎180 2960. Open M-F 9am-6pm, Sa 9am-2pm, Su 10am-2pm; Closed Su Christmas-Easter.) **Postal Code:** 52062.

COLOGNE (KÖLN)   ☎0221

Although 90% of inner historic Cologne (pop. 968,000) crumbled to the ground during WWII, the magnificent Gothic *Dom* amazingly survived 14 bombings and remains one of Germany's main attractions. Today, the city is the largest in North Rhine-Westphalia, offering first-rate museums, theaters, and nightlife.

▄▀ TRANSPORTATION

Flights: Planes depart from **Köln-Bonn Flughafen (CGN).** Flight info ☎022 03 40 40 01 02; www.koeln-bonn-airport.de. Airport shuttle S13 leaves the train station M-F 3-6 per hr., Sa-Su 2 per hr. Shuttle to **Berlin** 24 per day 6:30am-8:30pm.

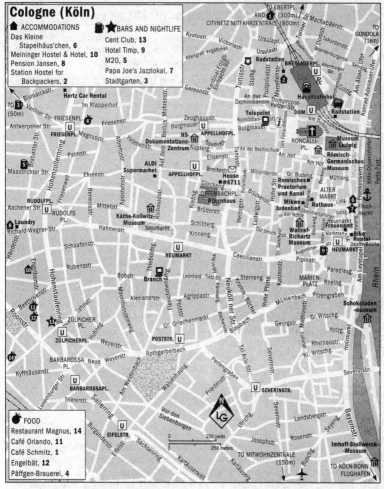

Cologne (Köln)

ACCOMMODATIONS
Das Kleine
  Stapelhäus'chen, **6**
Meininger Hostel & Hotel, **10**
Pension Jansen, **8**
Station Hostel for
  Backpackers, **2**

BARS AND NIGHTLIFE
Cent Club, **13**
Hotel Timp, **9**
M20, **5**
Papa Joe's Jazzlokal, **7**
Stadtgarten, **3**

FOOD
Restaurant Magnus, **14**
Café Orlando, **11**
Café Schmitz, **1**
Engelbät, **12**
Päffgen-Brauerei, **4**

Trains: Cologne's **Hauptbahnhof** is one of Germany's rail hubs. Trains leave for **Berlin** (4-5hr., 1-2 per hr., €82-100); **Düsseldorf** (30min., 5-6 per hr., €10-17); **Frankfurt** (1¼-2hr., 2-3 per hr., €42-60); **Hamburg** (4hr., 1-2 per hr., €70-84); **Munich** (4½-5hr., 1-2 per hr., €90-120); **Amsterdam, NTH** (2½-3½hr., 1 per 2hr., €42-55); **Paris, FRA** (4hr., 5-6 per day, €87-120).

Ride Share: Citynetz Mitfahrzentrale, Krefelderst. 21 (☎ 194 44). Turn left from the back of the train station, left at the intersection onto Eigelstein, then another left on Weidengasse, which becomes Krefelderst. Open M-F 9am-8pm, Sa-Su 10am-6pm.

Public Transportation: KVB offices have free maps of the S- and U-Bahn, bus, and streetcar lines; branch downstairs in the Hauptbahnhof. Major terminals include the **Hauptbahnhof, Neumarkt,** and **Appellhofplatz.** Single-ride tickets €1.40-2.30, depending on distance. Day pass €6.40. The Minigruppen-Ticket (from €9.50) allows up to 5 people to ride M-F 9am-midnight and all day Sa-Su. Week tickets €14-20.

Bike Rental: Radstation, in Breslauerpl. behind the *Hauptbahnhof.* (☎ 139 7190). €5 per 3hr., €10 per day, €20 per 3 days, €40 per week. Open M-F 5:30am-10:30pm, Sa 6:30am-8pm, Su 8am-8pm.

▣ ❔ ORIENTATION AND PRACTICAL INFORMATION

Cologne extends across the Rhine, but the city center and nearly all sights are located on the western side. The *Altstadt* splits into **Altstadt-Nord,** near the **Hauptbahnhof,** and **Altstadt-Süd,** just south of the **Severinsbrücke** bridge.

Tourist Office: KölnTourismus, Unter Fettenhennen 19 (☎22 13 04 10; www.koelntourismus.de), across from the main entrance to the *Dom* books rooms for a €3 fee and sells the **Welcome Card** (€9), which provides a day's worth of free public transportation and museum discounts. Open daily M-Sa 9am-8pm, Su 10am-5pm.

Post Office: At the corner of Breitestr. and Tunisstr. in the WDR-Arkaden shopping gallery. Open M-F 9am-7pm, Sa 9am-2pm. **Postal Code:** 50667.

▚ ACCOMMODATIONS

Conventions fill hotels in spring and fall, and Cologne's hostels often sell out. If you're staying over a weekend in summer, reserve at least two weeks ahead.

▨ **Station Hostel for Backpackers,** Marzellenstr. 44-56 (☎912 5301; www.hostel-cologne.de). Large dorms without bunks and an ideal location attract crowds of backpackers. Breakfast price varies. Free Wi-Fi. Reception 24hr. 4- to 6-bed dorms €17-21; singles €30-37; doubles €45-52; triples €72. Cash only. ❷

▨ **Meininger City Hostel & Hotel,** Engelbertst. 33-35 (☎92 40 90; www.meininger-hostels.de). U1, 7, 12, 15, 16, or 18 to Rudolfpl. A bar and lounge as well as proximity to Rudolpl. and Zülpicherpl. nightlife keep things hopping. Breakfast included. Reception 24hr. Dorms €17-24; singles €43-49; doubles €58-68; triples €72-81. Cash only. ❷

Pension Jansen, Richard-Wagner-Str. 18 (☎25 18 75; www.pensionjansen.de). U1, 6, 7, 15, 17, or 19 to Rudolfpl. Family-run with beautiful, high-ceilinged rooms and colorful walls. Breakfast included. Singles €30-42; doubles €62. Cash only. ❸

Das Kleine Stapelhäus'chen, Fischmarkt 1-3 (☎272 7777; www.koeln-altstadt.de/stapelhaeuschen). An old-fashioned, richly decorated inn overlooking the Rhine. Breakfast included. Singles €39-51, with bath €53-85; doubles €67-90/90-148. MC/V. ❹

▣ FOOD

The *Kölner* diet includes *Rievekoochen* (fried potato dunked in applesauce) and the city's trademark smooth *Kölsch* beer. Cheap restaurants converge on **Zülpicherstraße** to the southeast and **Eigelstein** and **Weidengasse** in the Turkish district. Ethnic restaurants line the perimeter of the *Altstadt,* particularly from **Hohenzollernring** to **Hohenstaufenring.** German eateries surround **Domplatz.** An open-air market on Wilhelmspl. fills the Nippes neighborhood. (Open M-Sa 8am-1pm.)

▨ **Päffgen-Brauerei,** Friesenstr. 64. Take U3-5, 12, 16, or 18 to Friesenpl. A local favorite since 1883. *Kölsch* (€1.40) is brewed on the premises, consumed in cavernous halls and in the 600-seat beer garden, and refilled until you put your coaster on top of your glass. Entrees €7-15. Open daily 10am-12:30am. Cash only. ❸

▨ **Café Orlando,** Engelbertstr. 7 (☎23 75 23; www.cafeorlando.de). U8 or 9 to "Zülpicher Pl." Free Wi-Fi and an assortment of newspapers create a Sunday morning ambience any time of day. Complete breakfasts (€4-6), omelettes (€6-8), pasta (€5-7), and mixed drinks (€4-5) draw a devoted student following. Open daily 9am-11pm. Cash only. ❷

Restaurant Magnus, Zülpicherstr. 48 (☎24 14 69). Take U8, 9, 12, 15, 16, or 18 to Zülpicher Pl. Locals flock to this crowded cafe for funky tunes, artfully prepared meals (mostly Italian; from €4), and many vegetarian options (€5-8). Open M-Th 8am-3am, F-Sa 8am-4am, Su 8am-1am. Cash only. ❷

Café Schmitz, Hansaring 98. (☎ 139 7733). Features a large bar and an extensive breakfast menu (€3-7). Try the Nutella-rich Sweet Sue breakfast (€5.80). Open daily from 9am-11:30pm. Cash only. ❶

Engelbät, Engelbertst. 7. (☎ 24 69 14). U8 or 9 to Zülpicher Pl. The best place for plentiful crepes, vegetarian and otherwise (€4-7.50). Breakfast (€1.50-3.50) served daily until 3pm. Open daily 11am-midnight. Cash only. ❶

👁 SIGHTS

▨ **DOM.** Germany's greatest cathedral, the *Dom*, is a perfect realization of High Gothic style. Built over the course of six centuries, it was finally finished in 1880 and miraculously escaped destruction during WWII. Today, its colossal spires define the skyline of Cologne. A chapel on the inside right houses a 15th-century **triptych** depicting the city's five patron saints. Behind the altar in the center of the choir is the **Shrine of the Magi,** which allegedly holds the remains of the Three Kings and was once a pilgrimage site. Before exiting the choir, stop in the **Chapel of the Cross** to admire the 10th-century **Gero crucifix,** which is the oldest intact sculpture of a crucified Christ. It takes about 15min. to scale the 509 steps of the **Südturm** (south tower). *(Cathedral open daily 6am-7:30pm. 45min. English-language tours M-Sa 10:30am and 2:30pm, Su 2:30pm. Tower open daily May-Sept. 9am-6pm; Nov.-Feb. 9am-4pm; Mar.-Apr. and Oct. 9am-5pm. Cathedral free. Tour €4, children €2. Tower €2, students €1.)*

MUSEUMS. Gourmands head straight for the ▨ **Schokoladenmuseum,** which is best described as Willy Wonka's factory made real. It presents every step of chocolate production, from the rainforests to the gold fountain that spurts streams of free samples. *(Rheinauhafen 1A, near the Severinsbrücke. ☎ 931 8880; www.schokoladenmuseum.de. From the train station, head for the Rhine, and walk to the right along the river; go under the Deutzer Brücke, and take the 1st footbridge. Open Tu-F 10am-6pm, Sa-Su 11am-7pm. €6.50, students €4.)* Masterpieces from the Middle Ages to the Post-Impressionist period are gathered in the **Wallraf-Richartz Museum.** *(Martinstr. 39. From the Heumarkt, take Gürzenichtstr. 1 block to Martinstr. ☎ 276 94; www.museenkoeln.de/wrm. Open Tu 10am-8pm, W-F 10am-6pm, Sa-Su 11am-6pm. €5.80, students €3.30.)* The collection of the **Museum Ludwig** focuses on 20th-century and contemporary art. *(Bischofsgartenstr. 1, behind the Römisch-Germanisches Museum. ☎ 22 12 61 65. Open Tu-Su 10am-6pm, 1st F of each month 10am-10pm. €7.50, students €5.50.)* The **Römisch-Germanisches Museum** displays a large array of artifacts documenting the daily lives of Romans in ancient Colonia. *(Roncallipl. 4, beside the Dom. Open Tu-Su, W 10am-8pm. €4.50, students €2.70.)*

HOUSE #4711. The fabled **Eau de Cologne,** once prescribed as a drinkable curative, earned the town worldwide recognition. Today, the house of its origin, labeled #4711 by a Napoleonic system that abolished street names, is a boutique where a fountain flows with the scented water. Visit the gallery upstairs for a history of the fragrance. *(On Glockeng. near the intersection with Tunisstr. From Hohe Str., turn right on Brückenstr., which becomes Glockeng. Open M-F 9am-7pm, Sa 9am-6pm. Free.)*

🎵 🎭 ENTERTAINMENT AND NIGHTLIFE

Cologne explodes in celebration during ▨ **Karneval** (late Jan. to early Feb. 2008), a week-long pre-Lenten festival made up of 50 neighborhood processions. **Weiberfastnacht** (Jan. 31, 2008) is the first major to-do: the mayor mounts the platform at Alter Markt and surrenders leadership to the city's women, who then hunt down their husbands at work and chop off their ties. For more info, pick up the Karneval booklet at the tourist office. For summer visitors, Cologne offers the huge **C/O Pop Festival** in mid-August, a multi-day event that draws some 200 electronic and independent musicians for 40 shows. (www.c-o-pop.de. €49.)

GERMANY

Roman mosaics dating back to the 3rd century record the wild excesses of the city's early residents; they've toned it down only a bit since. The monthly *Kölner* (€1), sold at newsstands, lists clubs, parties, and concerts. The closer to the Rhine or *Dom* you venture, the faster your wallet will empty. After dark in **Hohenzollernring,** crowds of people move from theaters to clubs and finally to cafes in the early morning. The area around **Zülpicherpl.** is a favorite of students and the best option for an affordable good time. Radiating westward from Friesenpl., the **Belgisches Viertel** (Belgian Quarter) has slightly more expensive bars and cafes. Gay nightlife thrives in Cologne, centering on the **Bermuda-Dreieck** (Bermuda Triangle), around Rudolfpl., and also in the area running up Matthiasstr. to Mühlenbach, Hohe Pforte, Marienpl., and the Heumarkt neighborhood by **Deutzer Brücke.** The **Cologne Pride** festival (late June to early July), centered in Rudolfpl., culminates in the massive **Christopher Street Day Parade,** which draws up to a million visitors.

■ **Papa Joe's Jazzlokal,** Buttermarkt 37 (☎257 7931). Papa Joe has a legendary reputation for providing good jazz and good times. Add your business card or expired ID to the collage that adorns the bar. *Kölsch* (€3.60) in 0.4L glasses, not the usual 0.2L. Live jazz M-Sa 10:30pm-12:30am. Open daily 7pm-1am, F-Sa 7pm-3am. Cash only.

■ **Hotel Timp,** Heumarkt 25 (☎258 1409; www.timp.de). Across from the U-Bahn stop. Gay and straight crowds come here for the glitter-filled cabarets. Drag shows daily 1-4am. No cover. 1st drink Su-Th €8, F-Sa €13. Open daily 11am-late. AmEx/MC/V.

Cent Club, Hohenstaufenring 25-27 (www.centclub.de). Near Zülpicher Pl. This student disco features more dance (R&B, pop, dance classics) than talk and low-priced drinks. Shots €0.50. Beer €1-2. Mixed drinks €3. Cover W-Sa €5. Open M-Sa 9pm-late.

M20, Maastrichterstr. 20 (☎51 96 66; www.m20-koeln.de). U1, 6, or 7 to Rudolfpl. DJs deliver some of the city's best drum 'n' bass and punk to a local crowd. Beer €1.50-3.20. Open Su-Th 10pm-2am, F-Sa 10pm-4am. Cash only.

Stadtgarten, Venloerstr. 40 (☎95 29 94 33). Take U3, 5, 6, or 12 to Friesenpl. An outdoor beer garden and 2 indoor clubs. Downstairs hosts parties playing everything from soul to techno, while the upper concert hall is renowned for its jazz recordings and performances. Cover €5-8. Open M-Th 9pm-1am, F-Sa 9pm-3am. Cash only.

BONN ☎0228

As First Chancellor Konrad Adenauer's residence, Bonn (pop. 305,000) served as the West German capital—and was derided as *"Hauptdorf,"* or "capital village." The *Bundestag* moved to Berlin in 1999, but Bonn remains a center of international diplomacy. ■**Beethovenhaus,** Bonng. 20, Ludwig van Beethoven's birthplace, houses a great collection of the composer's personal effects, from his first viola to his primitive hearing aids—even some of his hair. The Digital Archives Studio offers recordings and scores of all of his works. (☎981 7525; www.beethovenhaus-bonn.de. Open Apr.-Oct. M-Sa 10am-6pm, Su 11am-6pm; Nov.-Mar. M-Sa 10am-5pm, Su 11am-5pm. €5, students €4.) A huge 18th-century palace now serves as the center of **Friedrich-Wilhelms-Universität.** Five museums line the *Museumsmeile* near the banks of the Rhine, though they're not within walking distance; take U16, 63, 66, 67, 68 to the Heussallee/Museumsmeile stop. Around 7,000 interactive exhibits examine post-WWII Germany at the ■**Haus der Geschichte,** Willy-Brandt-Allee 14. (☎916 50. Open Tu-Su 9am-7pm. Free.) One block away, the immense **Kunstmuseum Bonn,** Friedrich-Ebert-Allee 2, has a superb collection of 20th-century German art. (☎77 62 60. Open Tu and Th-Su 11am-6pm, W 11am-9pm. €5, students €3.) *Schnüss* (€1), sold at newsstands, has club and concert listings.

■**Deutsches Haus ❸,** Kasernenstr. 19-21, on a residential street within walking distance of the *Altstadt*, has a decadent included breakfast. (☎63 37 77; info@hotel-deutscheshaus.net. Reception 7am-11pm. Singles €32, with bath €55-70; doubles €65-77; triples €66-99. AmEx/MC/V.) For the spacious but distant **Jugendherberge Bonn (HI) ❷,** Haager Weg 42, take bus #621 (dir.: Ippendorf Altenheim) to Jugendgästehaus. (☎28 99 70; bonn@jugendherberge.de. Reception 7am-1am. Breakfast and linens included. Laundry €4. Curfew 1am. Dorms €26; singles €42; doubles €64. MC/V.) The **market** on Münsterpl. teems with haggling vendors. (Open M-Sa 8am-6pm.) Take a break from meaty German specialties at **Cassius-Garten ❷**, Maximilianstr. 28D, across from the train station. This veggie bar serves 50 kinds of salad, pasta, and whole-grain baked goods, all for €1.50 per 100g. (☎65 24 29; www.cassiusgarten.de. Open M-F 11am-8pm.) **⬛The Jazz Galerie**, Oxfordstr. 24, is a popular, mostly jazz-less bar and disco. (☎63 93 24. Cover Th €5, F-Sa €8; includes 1 drink. Open Tu and Th 9pm-3am, F-Sa 10pm-5am. Cash only.) **Trains** go to Berlin (5hr., 4 per day, €87-100) and Cologne (30min., 4-5 per hr., €9-15). The **tourist office** is at Windeckstr. 1, off Münsterpl. (☎77 50 00; www.bonn.de. Open M-F 9am-6:30pm, Sa 9am-4pm, Su 10am-2pm.) **Postal Code:** 53111.

KASSEL   ☎0561

Grandiose monuments and sweeping green vistas surround Kassel (pop. 194,000). The city's **⬛Wilhelmshöhe** park is famed throughout Germany. To reach the park, take tram #1 from Banhof Wilhelmshöhe (dir.: Wilhelmshöhe) to the last stop. Inside, **Schloß Wilhelmshöhe** is a dressed-down version of the Residenz in Würzburg. Wilhelm IX built **Schloß Löwenburg** in the 18th century with stones deliberately missing so it would resemble a medieval castle—he was obsessed with the year 1495 and imagined himself a knight. (☎31 68 02. Open Mar.-Oct. Tu-Su 10am-5pm; Nov.-Feb. 10am-4pm. Required tours 1 per hr.; €3.50, students €2.50.) Park paths lead to the statue of **Herkules**, Kassel's emblem, where visitors can climb onto the pedestal. (Pedestal open mid-Mar. to mid-Nov. Tu-Su 10am-5pm. €2, students €1.25.) The **Brüder-Grimm-Museum**, Schöne Aussicht 2 in the city itself, displays a handwritten copy of The Brothers Grimm's *Children's and Household Tales.* (☎787 2033; www.grimms.de. Open daily 10am-5pm. €1.50.)

To reach the flower-filled **Jugendherberge und Bildungsstätte Kassel (HI) ❷**, Schenkendorfstr. 18, take streetcar #4 from the Wilhelmshöhe station to Querallee, then turn left on Querallee, which becomes Schenkendorfstr. (☎77 64 55; www.djh-hessen.de/jh/kassel. Breakfast included. Internet €2 per hr., €15 per day. Linens €3. Reception 8am-11:30pm. Curfew 12:30am. Floor mattresses €15; dorms €23; singles €33; doubles €38. €3.10 HI discount. Cash only.) The cozy, peaceful **Hotel Garni Kö78 ❸**, Kölnische Str. 78, has a lovely garden in back, as well as cable TV and phones. (☎716 14; www.koe78.de. Breakfast included. Reception 6am-10pm. Singles €34, with toilet €43-48; doubles €53/64-78. Prices rise about €5 in summer. AmEx/MC/V.) **Friedrich-Ebert-Straße,** the upper part of **Wilhelmshöher Allee,** and the area around **Königsplatz** all have supermarkets, takeout stands, and cafes among clothing stores. **⬛Limerick ❷**, Wilhelmshöher Allee 116, has a pan-European menu boasting 237 entrees and appetizers. The pizza list (over 60 total, €3-8) is broken down into meat, vegetarian, poultry, and seafood categories. The 25 beers on tap (€2-3) attract loyal crowds to its spacious dining room and garden. (☎77 66 49; www.restaurant-limerick.de. Open M-Sa 11am-1am, Su 11am-11pm. Cash only.) Kassel has two **train** stations, *Bahnhof* Wilhelmshöhe and the *Hauptbahnhof,* but most trains stop only at Wilhelmshöhe. Trains run to: Berlin (3hr., 2 per hr., €78); Düsseldorf (3hr., 1 per 2hr., €44-80); Frankfurt (2hr., 3-4 per hr., €35-45); Hamburg (2½hr., 3 per hr., €65); Munich (4hr., 2-3 per hr., €89). The **tourist office**, in Bahnhof Wilhelmshöhe, books rooms for a €4 fee. (☎70 77 07; www.kassel-tourist.de. Open M-Sa 9am-6pm.) **Postal Code:** 34117.

FRANKFURT AM MAIN   ☎069

International offices, shiny skyscrapers, and expensive cars can be found at every intersection in Frankfurt (pop. 660,000), nicknamed "Mainhattan" for its location on the Main River and its glitzy vitality. Both people and money are constantly in motion in this transport hub, which is also home to the central bank of the EU.

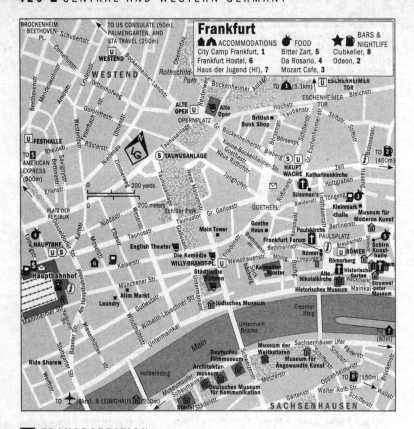

Frankfurt

ACCOMMODATIONS
City Camp Frankfurt, **1**
Frankfurt Hostel, **6**
Haus der Jugend (HI), **7**

FOOD
Bitter Zart, **5**
Da Rosario, **4**
Mozart Cafe, **3**

BARS & NIGHTLIFE
Clubkeller, **8**
Odeon, **2**

⌐ TRANSPORTATION

Flights: The busy **Flughafen Rhein-Main** (☎01805 37 24 36) is connected to the *Haupt-bahnhof* by S-Bahn trains S8 and 9 (2-3 per hr.). Buy tickets (€3.55) from the green machines marked *Fahrkarten* before boarding. Taxis to the city center cost around €20.

Trains: Trains run from the **Hauptbahnhof** to: **Amsterdam, NTH** (4hr., 1 per 2hr., €150); **Berlin** (4hr., 2 per hr., €87-104); **Cologne** (1½hr., 1 per hr., €38-60); **Hamburg** (3½-5hr., 1 per hr., €78-98); **Munich** (3hr., 1 per hr., €64-81). Call ☎01805 19 41 95 for schedules, reservations, and info.

Public Transportation: Frankfurt's public transportation system runs daily 4am-1:30am. Single-ride tickets (€2) are valid for 1hr. in 1 dir. **Eurail** is valid only on S-Bahn trains. The **Tageskarte** (day pass; €5.40) provides unlimited transportation on the S-Bahn, U-Bahn, streetcars, and buses, and can be purchased from machines in any station (€5.40). Ticketless passengers can be fined €40.

Ride share: Stuttgarter Str. 12 (☎23 64 44). Take a right on Baseler Str. at the side exit of the *Hauptbahnhof* (track 1) and walk 2 blocks. Arranges rides to **Berlin** (€30), **Munich** (€23), and elsewhere. Open M-F 6:30am-9pm, Sa 8am-9pm, Su 9am-8pm.

Taxis: ☎23 00 01, ☎23 00 33, or ☎25 00 01. €1.50-1.75 per km.

Bike Rental: Deutsche Bahn (DB) runs the citywide service **Call a Bike** (☎0700 05 22 55 22; www.callabike.de). Bikes marked with the red DB logo can be found throughout the city. To rent one, call the service hotline. €0.10 per min., €15 per day.

✈ 🛈 ORIENTATION AND PRACTICAL INFORMATION

Frankfurt's *Hauptbahnhof* opens onto the city's red-light district; from the station, the *Altstadt* is a 20min. walk down Kaiserstr. or Münchenerstr. The tourist heavy **Römerberg** square is just north of the Main River, while the city's commercial center lies farther north along **Zeil**. Cafes and services cluster near the university in **Bockenheim** (U6 or 7 to Bockenheimer Warte). Across the river, the **Sachsenhausen** area draws pub-crawlers and museum-goers (U1, 2, or 3 to Schweizer Pl.).

Tourist Office: in the *Hauptbahnhof* (☎21 23 88 00; www.frankfurt-tourismus.de). Books rooms for a €3 fee; free if you call ahead. Sells the **Frankfurt Card** (1-day €8, 2-day €12), which allows unlimited use of public transportation and provides discounts on many sights. Open M-F 8am-9pm, Sa-Su and holidays 9am-6pm. **Branch** in Römerberg square (open M-F 9:30am-5:30pm, Sa-Su 10am-4pm).

Laundromat: Miele Wash World, Moselstr. 17; walk straight on Kaiserstr. from the Hauptbanhof and turn right after one block. Wash €4, dry €1 per 15min.

Post Office: Goethe Pl. Walk 10min. down Taunusstr. from the *Hauptbahnhof,* or take the U- or S-Bahn to Hauptwache and walk south to the square. Open M-F 9:30am-7pm, Sa 9am-2pm. **Postal Code:** 60313.

🏠 🏕 ACCOMMODATIONS AND CAMPING

Deals are rare and trade fairs make rooms scarce; reserve at least 2-3 weeks ahead. The **Westend/University** area has a few cheap options.

▨ **Frankfurt Hostel,** Kaiserstr. 74 (☎247 5130; info@frankfurt-hostel.com). Near the *Hauptbahnhof* (and red-light district), this social hostel organizes free city tours and F "club crawls." Luggage storage and laundry included. Internet €1 per hr. Dorms €18-22; singles €50; doubles €60; triples €66. Higher rates during trade fairs. MC/V. ❷

Haus der Jugend (HI), Deutschherrnufer 12 (☎610 0150; www.jugendherberge-frankfurt.de). Bus #46 (dir.: Mühlberg) from the station to Frankensteiner Pl., or take tram #16 (dir.: Offenbach Stadtgrenze) to *Lokalbahnhof* and walk back up Dreicherstr., turning left on Deutschherrnufer. Great location along the Main, in front of Sachsenhausen's pubs and cafes. Some private baths. Breakfast and linens included. Check-in 1pm. Check-out 9:30am. Curfew 2am. Dorms from €25, under 27 €20; singles €39/43; doubles €56-68/66-76. €3.10 HI discount. MC/V. ❷

City Camp Frankfurt, An der Sandelmühle 35B (☎57 03 32; www.city-camp-frankfurt.de). U1-3: Heddernheim. Take a left at the Kleingartnerverein sign and continue until you reach the Sandelmühle sign. Cross the stream, turn left, and follow signs to the campground. Reception Mar.-Oct. 9am-1pm and 4-8pm; Nov.-Feb. 4-8pm. €6 per person, €3.50 per tent. Showers €1 per 4min. Cash only. ❶

🍴 FOOD

The most reasonably priced meals can be found near the university in **Bockenheim,** and many **Sachsenhausen** pubs serve food at decent prices. Just blocks from the HI hostel is a well-stocked **Rewe** supermarket, Dreieichstr. 56. (Open M-Sa 8am-10pm.) ▨**Kleinmarkthalle,** on Haseng. between Berlinerstr. and Töngesg., is a three-story warehouse with bakeries, butchers, and fruit, nuts, cheese, and vegetable stands. (Open M-F 8am-6pm, Sa 8am-4pm.)

- ▨ **Mozart Cafe,** Töngesg. 23-25 (☎29 19 54). Lauded by locals, this cafe serves famously huge breakfasts (€5-12) and a wide selection of pastas (€7.20-8), salads (€9.50-11.50), and desserts (€3-6). Open daily 8am-9pm. MC/V. ❷
- **Da Rosario,** Ottostr. 17 (☎24 24 81 82). Go left out of the *Hauptbahnhof*, take the first left on Poststr., and go right on Ottostr. This small pizzeria is endearingly hectic. Pizzas from €4. Open M-F 11:30am-3pm and 6-11:30pm, Sa-Su 3-11:30pm. Cash only. ❷
- **Bitter Zart,** Domstr. 5 (☎94 94 28 46). This famous sweets shop sells some of the best chocolates and *gelee früchte* (from €3.80 per 100g) in the city. The hot chocolate (€7.90-15) suits any season. Open M-F 10am-7pm, Sa 10am-4pm. Cash only. ❷

◔ SIGHTS

Allied bombing in 1944 destroyed everything but the cathedral, so Frankfurt's historic splendor survives mostly in memories and reconstructed monuments. If you plan on touring the city's museums, consider buying a **Frankfurt Card** (p. 427).

▨ **STÄDEL.** The *Städel's* impressive collection comprises seven centuries of art, including notable works by Old Masters, Impressionists, and Modernists. *(Schaumainkai 63, between Dürerstr. and Holbeinstr. ☎605 0980; www.staedelmuseum.de. Open Tu and F-Su 10am-6pm, W-Th 10am-9pm. €10, students €8, under 12 and last Sa of each month free. English-language audio tour €4, students €3.)*

▨ **MUSEUM FÜR MODERNE KUNST.** Dubbed "slice of cake," this triangular building displays European and American art from the 1960s to the present, including works by Lichtenstein, Johns, and emerging talents. *(Domstr. 10. ☎21 23 04 47; www.mmk-frankfurt.de. Open Tu and Th-Su 10am-5pm, W 10am-8pm. €6, students €3.)*

RÖMERBERG. Buried between modern structures, this square comprises most of the city's *Altstadt;* its reconstructed half-timbered homes appear on most postcards. Across from Römerberg, **Paulskirche** (St. Paul's Church), the birthplace of Germany's 19th-century attempt at constitutional government, memorializes the trials of German democracy and displays an acclaimed mural. *(☎21 23 85 26. Open daily 10am-5pm. Free.)* Emperors were once crowned in the sandstone **Dom,** the lone survivor of WWII bombings. *(Church open M-Th and Sa-Su 9am-noon and 2:30-6pm. Museum open Tu-F 10am-5pm and Sa-Su 11am-5pm. Church free. Museum €2, students €1.)*

◔ NIGHTLIFE

Although out of the way, **Odeon,** Seilerstr. 34, in a medieval villa has a unique allure. *(☎28 50 55. M hip-hop, Th student night, F 27+, Sa Wild Card. M and Th-F drinks ½-price 10pm-midnight. Cover €5, Th students €3. Open M-Sa 10pm-late. Cash only.)* **Clubkeller,** Textorstr. 26, attracts a fun-loving clientele to its small bar with diverse theme nights and cheap €3-4 beer. *(☎66 37 26 97; www.clubkeller.com. Cover €3. Open M-Sa 9pm-late. Cash only.)*

SOUTHWESTERN GERMANY

The Rhine and Mosel River Valleys are filled with much to be seen and drunk. Along river banks, medieval castles loom over vineyards. Farther south, modern cities fade slowly into the beautiful hinterlands of the Black Forest.

TRIER ☎0651

The oldest town in Germany, Trier (pop. 100,000) has weathered more than two millennia in the western end of the Mosel Valley. An inscription at Trier's **Hauptmarkt** (Main Market) reads: "Trier stood one thousand and three hundred years before Rome." Founded by the Gallo-Celtic Treveri tribe and seized by the Romans during the reign of Augustus, Trier reached its zenith in the early 4th century, when it served as the capital of the Western Roman Empire and was a major center of Christianity in Europe. Today, Trier hums with students pondering life's questions in the tradition of the town's most famous son, **Karl Marx**.

The most famous of the city's Roman monuments is the massive 2nd-century ▨**Porta Nigra** (Black Gate), which travelers can climb for a view of Trier. (Open daily Apr.-Sept. 9am-6pm; Oct. and Mar. 9am-5pm; Nov.-Feb. 9am-4pm. €2.10, students €1.60.) The enormous **Dom** nearby shelters the **Tunica Christi** (Holy Robe of Christ) and the tombs of archbishops. Amazingly, the original 4th-century church was four times larger. The adjoining **Church of Our Lady** adds some Gothic flair to the complex. (Both open daily Apr.-Oct. 6:30am-6pm; Nov.-Mar. 6:30am-5:30pm. Free.) The 4th-century **Basilika,** originally Emperor Constantine's throne room, is the largest single surviving room from antiquity. (Open Easter-Oct. M-Sa 10am-6pm, Su noon-6pm; Nov.-Easter Tu-Sa 11am-noon and 3-4pm, Su noon-1pm. Free.) Near the southeast corner of the city walls are the 4th-century **Kaiserthermen** (Emperor's Baths), with underground passages that once served as Roman sewers. A 10min. walk uphill along Olewiger Str. leads to the **amphitheater.** (Baths and amphitheater open daily Apr.-Sept. 9am-6pm; Oct. and Mar. 9am-5pm; Nov.-Feb. 9am-4pm. Both €2.10, students €1.60.)

With its large, comfortable beds and prime location near all the major sights, the joint hostel and guest house **Warsberger Hof ❶,** Dietrichstr. 42, is the best deal in town. Head straight through the Porta Nigra down Simeonst. to the Hauptmarkt, then turn right on Dietrichstr. (☎97 52 50; www.warsberger-hof.de. Dorms €19; singles €23-27; doubles €45; triples €65. Reception 8am-11pm. Check-in 2:30pm. Reserve ahead. MC/V.) **Jugendgästehaus Trier (HI) ❷,** An der Jugendherberge 4, is far from town, but its riverside location is ideal for promenades. Take buses #12 or 87 from the train station to Zurlaubenerufer, then walk 10min. downstream. (☎14 66 20; www.diejugendherbergen.de. Breakfast included. Laundry €5. Dorms €18; doubles €47. €3.10 HI discount. MC/V.) Moderately priced restaurants line the pedestrian path along the river between the youth hostel and the Kaiser-Wilhelm-Brücke. **Astarix ❷,** Karl-Marx-Str. 11, attracts a young crowd with generous portions of pasta and pizza. Walk down Brückenstr. toward the river. (Salads €3-6.50. Pasta and pizza €2.50-5. Open daily 1am-11pm.) **Plus** supermarket, Brotstr. 54, is near the Hauptmarkt. (Open M-F 8:30am-8pm, Sa 8:30am-6pm.)

Trains run to Koblenz (1½hr., 1-2 per hr., €18-22) and Luxembourg City, LUX (45min., 1 per hr., €13-17). From the station, walk down Theodor-Haus-Allee, and turn left under the Porta Nigra to reach the **tourist office.** (☎97 80 80; www.trier.de/tourismus. Open May-Oct. M-Th 9am-6pm, F-Sa 9am-7pm, Su 10am-5pm; Mar.-Apr. and Nov.-Dec M-Sa 9am-6pm, Su 10am-3pm; Jan.-Feb. M-Sa 10am-5pm, Su 10am-1pm. 2hr. English-language city tour Sa 1:30pm; 1hr. German- and English-language coach tour daily 1pm. Both tours €7, students €6.) Pick up a **Trier Card** for free intracity bus fare and discounts on sites over a three-day period (€9, students €6.50). **Postal Code:** 54290.

RHINE VALLEY (RHEINTAL)

The Rhine River carves its way through the 80km stretch of the Rhine Valley, flowing north from Mainz to Bonn. According to German folklore, this region of medieval castles and jagged cliffs is enchanted.

▣ TRANSPORTATION

Two different **train** lines traverse the Rhine Valley, one on each bank; the line on the western side stays closer to the water and has better views. It's often tricky to switch banks, as train and ferry schedules don't always match up. **Boats** are the best way to see the sights; the **Köln-Düsseldorfer (KD) Line** and **Bingen Rüdesheim Line** cover the Mainz-Koblenz stretch three to four times per day in summer (€20-40).

GERMANY

MAINZ ☎ 06131

The pastel-colored buildings in the *Altstadt* (Old Town) of Mainz (pop. 190,000) contain many bookstores, one reminder among many that this was the birthplace and home of famed printer Johannes Gutenberg. The advent of movable type in AD 1455 is immortalized at the **Gutenberg-Museum,** Liebfrauenpl. 5, across from the Dom, which has a replica of Gutenberg's original press. (Open Tu-Sa 9am-5pm, Su 11am-3pm. €5, students €3.) The **Martinsdom** is a colossal sandstone 10th-century cathedral. (☎25 34 12. Open Mar.-Oct. M-F 9am-6:30pm, Sa 9am-4pm, Su 1-2:45pm and 4-6:30pm; Nov.-Feb. M-F 9am-5pm, Sa 9am-4pm, Su 12:45-3pm and 4-5pm. Free.) On a hill south of the *Dom*, the Gothic **Stephanskirche** on Stephansberg is inlaid with stunning stained-glass windows by Russian exile Marc Chagall. (Open M-F 10am-noon and 2-5pm, Sa 2-5pm. Free.)

To reach the plain, comfortable rooms and downstairs bistro of the **Jugendgästehaus (HI) ❷,** Otto-Brunfels-Schneise 4, take bus #62 (dir.: Weisenau) or 63 (dir.: Laubenheim) to Viktorstift/Jugendherberge, and follow the signs. (☎853 32; www.diejugendherbergen.de. Breakfast included. Reception 7:30am-9:30pm. 4- to 6-bed dorms €18; doubles €47. MC/V.) **Der Eisgrub-Bräu ❷,** Weißlileng. 1A, on the edge of the *Altstadt*, offers breakfast and lunch buffets (€3.50/5.30) as well as house beer in its cellar-like interior. (Open Su-Th 9am-1pm, F-Sa 9am-2pm. MC/V.) **Trains** run to Cologne (1¾hr., 2-3 per hr., €27-50); Frankfurt (40min., 4 per hr., €10-15); Hamburg (6hr., 1 per hr., €84-100). KD **ferries** (☎23 28 00; www.k-d.com) depart from the wharfs on the other side of the *Rathaus* (City Hall). To reach the **tourist office,** in Brückenturm from the station, walk straight down Schottstr., turn right onto Kaiserstr., and continue straight until you reach Ludwigstr.; turn left and follow the green signs beginning at the cathedral. (☎28 62 10; www.info-mainz.de/tourist. Open M-F 9am-6pm, Sa 10:30am-2pm. 2hr. English-language tours May-Oct. W and F-Sa 2pm; Nov.-Apr. Sa 2pm. €5.) **Postal Code:** 55001.

BACHARACH ☎ 06473

Bacharach (Altar of Bacchus; pop. 2000) lives up to its wine-god namesake, with *Weinkeller* (wine cellars) tucked between every other house. Try some of the Rhine's best wines (from €2) and cheeses (€3-7) at **Die Weinstube,** Oberstr. 63. (Open M-F from 1pm, Sa-Su from noon. Cash only.) On the path to the hostel is the 14th-century **Wernerkapelle,** the remains of a red sandstone chapel that took 140 years to build but only hours to destroy during the 1689 Palatinate War of Succession. At the height of hostel greatness, **❸Jugendherberge Stahleck (HI) ❷** is in a converted 12th-century castle with a panoramic view of the Rhine Valley. The steep 15min. hike to the hostel is worth every step. Make a right out of the station, turn left at the stairs between the tourist office and the Peterskirche, and follow signs up the hill. (☎12 66; www.diejugendherbergen.de. Breakfast included. Reception 7:30am-7:30pm. Curfew 10pm. Reserve ahead. Dorms €17; doubles €45. MC/V.) A friendly couple serves three-course meals of regional fare (€6-11) at **❸Café Restaurant Rusticana ❷,** Oberstr. 40A. (☎17 41. Open May-Oct. daily noon-9pm. Cash only.) **Trains** run to Koblenz (40min., 2-3 per hr., €7.90) and Mainz (40min., 2-3 per hr., €7.20). The **tourist office** is at Oberstr. 45. (☎91 93 03. Open Apr.-Oct. M-F 9am-5pm, Sa-Su 10am-3pm; Nov.-Mar. M-F 9am-noon.) **Postal Code:** 55422.

LORELEI (LORELEY) CLIFFS AND CASTLES ☎ 067

The mythological Lorelei maiden once lured sailors to their deaths on the cliffs of the Rhine. Tiny **St. Goarshausen** and larger **St. Goar,** towns on either side of the Rhine, host the spectacular **Rhein in Flammen** (Rhine Ablaze) fireworks celebration in mid-September. St. Goarshausen, on the east bank, provides access by foot to a statue of the Lorelei and the cliffs. Directly above the town, the dark **Burg Katz** (Cat Castle) eternally stalks its prey, the smaller **Burg Maus** (Mouse Castle) downstream. While the castles are mostly closed to visitors, Burg Maus offers daily falconry demonstrations at 11am and 2:30pm from May to early October. (Face the river, turn right, and follow the signs. ☎71 76 69. €6.50, children €5.50.)

The family-oriented **Loreley-Jugendherberge (HI) ❶** sits directly beneath Burg Rheinfels. Follow the signs from St. Goar's main street. (☎413 88. Breakfast included. Reception 7-9am and 5-10pm. Dorms €14; doubles €35. MC/V.) **Trains** run from St. Goarshausen to Koblenz (30min., 2 per hr., €6) and Mainz (1½hr., 2 per hr., €10.60) and from St. Goar to Koblenz (30min. 2 per hr., €6) and Mainz (1hr., 2 per hr., €9.60). The Loreley VI **ferry** connects St. Goarshausen and St. Goar (M-F 6am-11pm, Sa-Su 8am-11pm. €1.30). For St. Goarhausen's **tourist office,** Bahnhofstr. 8, make a left out of the train station. (☎71 91 00; www.loreley-touristik.de. Open M-F 9am-1pm and 2-5pm, Sa 10am-noon.) St. Goar's **tourist office,** Heerstr. 86, is a 5min. walk from the ferry dock. (☎413 83; www.st-goar.de. Open M-F 9am-12:30pm and 1:30-6pm, Sa 10am-noon.) **Postal Code:** 56329.

KOBLENZ   ☎0261

A menacing fortress high above the city of Koblenz (pop. 107,000) overlooks the confluence of two of Germany's major rivers, the Rhine and the Mosel. Koblenz has long been a strategic hot spot; in the two millennia since its birth, the city has hosted every empire seeking to conquer Europe. Koblenz centers around the **Deutsches Eck** (German Corner), at the intersection of the rivers. The **Mahnmal der Deutschen Einheit** (Monument to German Unity) is a tribute to Kaiser Wilhelm I. The **Ludwig Museum,** Danziger Freiheit 1, features mostly contemporary French art. (☎30 40 40; www.ludwigmuseum.org. Open Tu-Sa 10:30am-5pm, Su 11am-6pm. €2.50, students €1.50.) Head across the river to the **Festung Ehrenbreitstein,** the fortress at the city's highest point, which contains numerous museums (€1.10).

Jugendherberge Koblenz (HI) ❷, a hostel in the fortress, has spacious dorms and views of the rivers. Take bus #8 or 9 from the bus station to Ehrenbreitstein. From there, walk left along the main road for 100m, take the path to your right, and climb up the hill for 20min. (☎97 28 70; www.diejugendherbergen.de. Breakfast included. Reception 7:15am-10pm. Curfew midnight. Dorms €17; doubles €45. €3.10 HI discount. MC/V.) At Markitst. 8 near the *Altstadt,* **Cafe Extra Blatt ❶** serves cheap pizza (€4-10), pasta (€6-7), and salads (€2.50-7) to a young crowd. (Open M-F 8am-midnight; Sa-Su 9am-1am. Cash only.) **Trains** run to: Bonn (30min., 2-3 per hr., €9-15); Cologne (1½hr., 2 per hr., €16-21); Frankfurt (1½hr., 1 per hr., €20-24); Mainz (1hr., 2-3 per hr., €15-19); Trier (1½hr., 1 per hr., €18-22). Across from the station is the **tourist office,** Bahnhofpl. 17. (☎100 4399. Open May-Oct. daily 9am-7pm; Nov.-Apr. M-F 9am-6pm.) **Postal Code:** 65068.

HEIDELBERG   ☎06221

Heidelberg (pop. 142,000) has been one of Germany's top attractions ever since the Romantics waxed poetic about its crumbling castle and beautiful setting above the Neckar River. Today, legions of visitors fill the length of *Hauptstraße*, where postcards sell like hotcakes and every sign is posted in four languages. Fortunately, Heidelberg maintains university town charm in spite of the crowds.

▐▌ TRANSPORTATION AND PRACTICAL INFORMATION

Trains run to Frankfurt (1¼hr., 1-2 per hr., €14-24), Hamburg (7hr., 1 per hr., €87-101), and Stuttgart (1¼hr., 1-2 per hr., €18-33). Within Heidelberg, single-ride **bus** tickets cost around €2 and day passes €5. **Rhein-Neckar-Fahrgastschifffahrt** (☎201 81; www.rnf-schifffahrt.de), in front of the *Kongresshaus,* runs **ferries** all over Germany. Heidelberg's attractions lie mostly in the eastern part of the city, along the south bank of the Neckar. From the train station, take any bus or streetcar to Bismarckpl., then walk east down **Hauptstraße,** the city's main thoroughfare, to the *Altstadt.* The **tourist office** is in front of the station. (☎138 8121. Open Apr.-Oct. M-

Sa 9am-7pm, Su 10am-6pm; Nov.-Mar. M-Sa 9am-6pm.) The office sells the **Heidelberg Card,** which includes unlimited public transit and admission to most sights. (1-day card €10, 2-day €14, 4-day €20.) **Postal Code:** 69115.

ACCOMMODATIONS AND FOOD

In summer, reserve accommodations ahead. ▓**Pension Jeske ❸,** Mittelbadg. 2, offers the area's friendliest lodgings, with a perfect location next to the Marktpl. Take bus #33 (dir.: Ziegelhausen) to Rathaus/Bergbahn. (☎237 33; www.pension-jeske-heidelberg.de. Reception 11am-1pm and 5-7pm. Singles €25, with bath €35; doubles €40/60; triples €60/75; quints with bath €100. Cash only.) For the **Jugendherberge (HI) ❷,** Tiergartenstr. 5, take bus #32 from the *Hauptbahnhof* to Chirurgische Klinik, then take bus #31 to Jugendherberge. Next to one of Europe's largest zoos, this hostel also teems with wild species, including *Schoolchildus germanus*, and features a discotheque in its basement. (☎65 11 90. Breakfast included. Reception until 2am. Reserve ahead. Dorms €24, under 27 €21; singles €29; doubles €34. MC/V.) For camping on the banks of the Neckar, go to **Halde ❶.** Take bus #35 (dir.: Neckargmünd) to Orthopädisches Klinik, cross the river, turn right, and walk for 20min. (☎062 23 21 11. Reception 8-11:30am and 4-8pm. Open mid-Apr to late-Oct. €5 per person, €3 per tent or RV, €2 per car. Cabins €13. Electricity €2 per night. Showers €0.50 per 5min. Cash only.)

Restaurants near Hauptstr. are expensive; historic student pubs outside the center are cheaper. **Hemingway's Bar-Café-Meeting Point ❷,** Fahrtg. 1, serves food on a shaded patio near the Neckar. (☎16 50 331. Entrees €5-12. Open daily 9am-11pm. Cash only.) Near Untere Str. in the *Altstadt,* **Sylvie ❷,** Steing. 11, serves affordable Italian specialties and regional salads for €6-12. (☎65 90 90. Open Su-Th 11am-1am, F-Sa 11am-2am. Cash only.)

SIGHTS

▓**HEIDELBERGER SCHLOß.** Every summer, hordes of tourists lay siege to **Heidelberg Castle,** one of Germany's top attractions. The 14th-century castle has been destroyed twice by war (1622 and 1693) and once by lightning (1764), leaving it with a unique, battered beauty. The cool, musty wine cellar houses the **Großes Faß;** with a 221,726L capacity, it is the largest wine barrel ever used. The castle **gardens** offer great views of the city below; they're always open, so trek up at night to enjoy the city's lights. (☎53 84 21. Castle grounds open daily 8am-6pm; last entry 5:30pm. English-language audio tour €3.50. English-language tours 1 per hr. M-F 11:15am-4:15pm, Sa-Su 10:15am-4:15pm; €4, students €2. Schloß, Großes Faß, and Pharmaceutical Museum €3, students €1.50.) Reach the castle by the uphill path (10min.) from the Kornmarkt or by the **Bergbahn,** one of Germany's oldest cable cars. (Take bus #33, dir.: Köpfel, to Rathaus/Bergbahn. Cable cars leave from the parking lot next to the bus stop daily Mar.-Oct. 6 per hr. 9am-8pm; Nov.-Feb. 3 per hr. 9am-6pm. Round-trip €5.)

UNIVERSITÄT. Heidelberg is home to Germany's oldest (est. 1386) and most prestigious university, which launched the field of sociology. The oldest remaining buildings border the stone lion fountain of the Universitätspl. The **Museum der Universität Heidelberg** traces the institution's tumultuous history; in the same building is the **Alte Aula,** the school's oldest auditorium. (Grabeng. 1. ☎54 21 52.) Before 1914, students were exempt from prosecution by civil authorities due to a code of academic freedom. View the irreverent, colorful graffiti of guilty students in the ▓**Studentkarzer** jail. (Augustinerg. 2. ☎54 35 54. Museum, auditorium, and jail open Apr.-Sept. Tu-Su 10am-6pm; Oct.-Mar. Tu-Sa 10am-4pm. €3, students €2.50.)

Heidelberg

ACCOMMODATIONS
Camping Haide, **1**
Jugendherberge (HI), **2**
Pension Jeske, **7**

FOOD & DRINK
Hemingway's, **4**
Sylvie, **5**

BARS & NIGHTLIFE
Destille, **6**
Schwimmbad Musikclub, **3**

GERMANY

TO Karlstor (5km)
Wehrsteig
Am Hackteufel
TO KÖNIGSTUHL (300m)
Molkenkur
Molkenkurweg
BERGBAHN
Apothekenmuseum
Heidelberger Schloß
SEE INSET BOTTOM!
Schloßbergtunnel
Schlossberg
Zwingerstr.
Zwingerstr.
Seminarstr.

Ziegelhäuser Landstr.
NECKARMÜNZ. PL.
Rathaus
MARKT-PL.
Hercules Fountain
KARLS-PL.
Steingas.
Haspelg.
Heilig.-Kirche
Haus Zum Ritter
Brückentor
Untere Str.
UNIVERSITÄTS-PL.
Grabeng.
PETERSKIRCHE
Univ. Bibliothek

Schlangenweg
TO HEILIGENBERG (2km)
Philosophenweg
Philosophen Gärtchen
Neckar
Neckarstaden
Karl-Theodor-Br. (Alte Brücke)
Marstallstr.
Sandg.
Theaterstr.
Schiffg.
Kurpfälzisches Museum
Friedrichstr.
Langniedstr.
Plöck
Märzg.

Philosophenweg
Brückenkopfstr.
Neuenheimer Landstr.
Kongresshaus
Ziegelg.
Bootsverleih Simon
Brunneng.
Akademiestr.
Hauptstr.
Plöck
Friedrich-Ebert-Anlage
Gaisbergtunnel

Brückenkopfstr.
Uferstraße
Neckarstaden
Fahtg.
Sofienstr.
Bismarckstr.
BISMARCK-PL.
ADENAUERPL.
Gaisbergstr.

NEUENHEIM
Ladenburger Str.
Uferstr.
Theodor-Heuss-Brücke
Brückenstr.
Schurmanstr.
Thibautstr.
Bergheimer Str.
Poststr.
Alnatura
Kurfürstenanlage
Bahnhofstr.
Bunsenstr.
Rohrbacherstr.
Hausserstr.
Goethestr.
Landhausstr.
Blumenstr.
Kaiserstr.

Jahnstr.
Posseltstr.
Uferstr.
Ernst-Walz-Brücke
Berlinerstr.
TO (1km) & (1.5km)
Neckar
Vangerowstr.
Bergheimer Str.
Alte Eppelheimer Str.
Mittermeierstr.
Römerstr.
RÖMER-KREIS
Römerstr.
Ringstr.
Kurfürsten-Anlage
SCHÖPL.
Hauptbahnhof
Piccadilly English Books

Inset:
Brückentor
MARKT-PL.
Steingas.
Haspelg.
Hauptstr.
Kornmarkt
Rathaus
Hercules Fountain
City Markt
Heilig.-Kirche
Haus Zum Ritter
Laundry
Kettengasse
Bike Rental
Untere Str.
Lauerstr.
Gr. Mantelg.
STA Travel
Alte Universität
UNIVERSITÄTS-PL.
Grabeng.
Seminarstr.
Marstallstr.
BERGBAHN
Obere Fauler Pelz

N

400 yards
400 meters

UNIVERSITY POLITICS

The University of Heidelberg, Germany's oldest, has proudly held to its democratic traditions and autonomy from local authorities for centuries. So it came as a shock to many when the spread of Nazism in the early 1930s managed to engulf even this vanguard of independent thought.

Spurred by the influence of a few far-right-wing professors—most notably Philipp Lenard, head of the physics department, Nobel Prize winner, and vehement anti-Semite who once criticized the theory of relativity as "Jewish physics"—the university expelled all "undesirables" from its faculty. This included both Jews and many liberal thinkers. The Weimar Republic era had been one of educational freedom in Heidelberg; now, Nazi propaganda was expounded in the lecture halls. The sign in Universitätsplatz that read "To the Living Spirit" soon proclaimed, "To the German Spirit." Most dramatically, forced labor was used to construct Thingstätte, a huge amphitheatre on top of Heiligenberg hill across the Neckar River. Built on an ancient Celtic site, it was used to profess Nazi ideology to the local masses.

Today, the amphitheater is abandoned, hollow, and decrepit. But it remains Heidelberg's most tangible memory of a period so dark that it managed to corrupt one of Germany's leading educational institutions.

PHILOSOPHENWEG. On the opposite side of the Neckar from the *Altstadt*, the steep Philosophenweg (Philosopher's Path) offers unbeatable views of the city. Famed thinkers Goethe, Ludwig Feuerbach, and Ernst Jünger once strolled here. Follow signs to the top of **Heiligenberg** (Holy Mountain), where you'll find the ruins of the 9th-century **St. Michael Basilika,** the 11th-century **Stefanskloster,** and **Thingstätte,** an amphitheater built by the Nazis using forced labor. *(To get to the path, use the steep, stone-walled footpath 10m west of the Karl-Theodor-Brücke.)*

ALTSTADT. At the center of the *Altstadt* is the cobblestoned **Marktplatz,** where alleged witches and heretics were burned at the stake in the 15th century. Two of Heidelberg's oldest structures border the square. The 14th-century **Heiliggeistkirche** (Church of the Holy Spirit) is now used for Protestant worship; its tower offers great views of the city and mountains. *(Open M-Sa 11am-5pm, Su 1-5pm. Church free. Tower €1.)* The 16th-century inn **Haus Zum Ritter** is opposite the church. East of the Marktplatz, the **Kornmarkt** offers great views of the looming castle above. The twin domes of the **Brückentor** loom over the 18th-century *Alte Brücke.*

🌿 🍺 FESTIVALS AND NIGHTLIFE

The **Schlossbeleuchtung** (castle lighting) occurs on the first Saturday in June, the second Saturday in July, and the first Saturday in September. The ceremony begins after nightfall with the "burning" of the castle, which commemorates the three times it was ravaged by fire. Meanwhile, fireworks are set off over the *Altstadt* from the Alte Brücke. Head to Neuenheim or the Philosophenweg across the river for the best views. Heidelberg's traditional **Christmas Market** runs daily from November 24 to December 22 in the Kornmarkt, Marktpl., and Universitätspl.

Most popular nightspots fan out from the Marktpl. On the Neckar side of the Heiliggeistkirche, **Untere Straße** has the densest collection of bars in the city. Revelers fill the narrow way until 1 or 2am. **Steingasse,** off Marktpl. toward the Neckar, also attracts crowds, and Hauptstr. harbors a number of higher-end venues. **Schwimmbad Musikclub,** Tiergartenstr. 13, near the youth hostel, has four levels of live music, dancing, and movies—plus a pool. From the Jugendherberge bus stop, walk forward another 500m. (☎47 02 01; www.schwimmbad-musik-club.de. Open Th 9pm-3am, F-Sa 9pm-4am. Cover varies; students often free. Cash only.) A giant tree grows in the center of the forest-themed bar **Destille,** Unterstr. 16, which serves quirky shots. (☎228 08. Open Su-Th noon-2am, F-Sa noon-3am. Cash only.)

STUTTGART

☎ 0711

Daimler-Benz, Porsche, and a host of other corporate thoroughbreds keep Stuttgart (pop. 591,000) speeding along in the fast lane. The city's amazing **Mineralbäder** (mineral baths) are fueled by Western Europe's most active mineral springs. The health-care facility **Mineralbad Leuze,** Am Leuzebad 2-6, has indoor and outdoor thermal pools. Take U1, U2, or U14 to Mineralbäder. (☎ 216 4210. Open M-Th 6am-8pm, F-Sa 6am-9pm, Su 6am-5pm. Entrance to mineral baths €6.50, students €3.50. Day pass for thermal baths and sauna €14, students €11. Cash only.) The superb ◪**Staatsgalerie Stuttgart,** Konrad-Adenauer-Str. 30-32, displays Dalí, Kandinsky, and Picasso in its new wing, as well as paintings from the Middle Ages to the 19th century in its old wing. (☎ 47 04 00; www.staatsgalerie.de. Open Tu-W and F-Su 10am-6pm, Th 10am-9pm. €7, students €5.50, W free.) The sleek, modern **Mercedes-Benz Museum,** Mercedesstr. 100, is a must for car-lovers. Take S1 (dir.: Plochingen) to Gottlieb-Daimler-Stadion and follow the signs. (☎ 173 0000; www.mercedes-benz.com/museum. Open Tu-Su 9am-6pm. €8, students €4.)

An international clientele crashes in hip rooms with funky wall paintings at ◪**Alex 30 Hostel** ❷, Alexanderstr. 30. Take tram #15 (dir.: Ruhbank) to Olgaeck. (☎ 838 8950; www.alex30-hostel.de. Breakfast €6. Linens €3. Dorms €22; singles €34; doubles €54, with shower €64. MC/V.) The comfortable rooms at the hillside **Jugendherberge Stuttgart International (HI)** ❷, Haufmanstr. 27, have spectacular views of the city. Take tram #15 (dir.: Ruhbank) to Eugenspl., walk up the hill, and turn left on top of the second incline. (☎ 66 47 470; www.jugendherberge-stuttgart.de. Breakfast and linens included. Reception 24hr. Dorms €27-24; singles €32; doubles €37. €3.10 HI discount. Reduced rates for stays over one night. MC/V.) Look for mid-range restaurants in the pedestrian zone between Pfarrstr. and Charlottenstr. **San's Sandwich Bar** ❷, Eberhardstr. 47, serves sandwiches (€2.70-3.50) with plenty of vegetarian options; the brownies and muffins are heavenly. (☎ 410 1118; www.sans-stuttgart.de. Open M-F 8:30am-10pm, Sa 10am-7pm. Cash only.) Stuttgart's club scene doesn't pick up until after midnight, and when it does, **Eberhardstraße,** **Rotebühlplatz,** and **Theodor-Heuss-Straße** are the most popular areas. **Suite 212,** Theodor-Heuss-Str. 15, is a popular bar and lounge featuring DJs and video-mixing on weekends. (☎ 253 6113; www.suite212.org. Beer €2.50-3. Mixed drinks €6.50-8. Open Su-Th 11am-2am, F-Sa 11am-5am. Cash only.)

Trains run to: Berlin (6hr., 1 per hr., €118); Frankfurt (1½hr., 2 per hr., €36-52); Munich (2½hr., 2 per hr., €33-49); Paris, FRA (8hr., 6 per day, €120-150). The **tourist office,** Königstr. 1A, is across from the train station. (☎ 222 80. Open M-F 9am-8pm, Sa 9am-6pm, Su 11am-6pm.) **Postal Code:** 70173.

BLACK FOREST (SCHWARZWALD)

The eerie darkness of the Black Forest has inspired a host of German fairy tales, most notably Hansel and Gretel. Today, the trees lure hikers and skiers with their grim beauty. Visitors tend to favor exploring the area by bike or by car, as public transportation is sparse. Rail lines encircle the forest, but only two cut through. Bus service is more thorough, but slow and infrequent. The gateway to the forest is **Freiburg** (pop. 210,000). The city's centerpiece is its ◪**Münster,** a 13th- to 16th-century stone cathedral that amazes from every angle. (☎ 0761 298 59 63. Open M-Sa 9:30am-5pm, Su 1-5pm. Tower €1.50, students €1. Tours M-F 2-3pm, Sa-Su 2:30-3:30pm.) Tourists flock in summer to the tiny village of **Triberg** (pop. 5000) to see the world's two largest **cuckoo clocks** or hike to the **Gutacher Wasserfall,** the highest waterfall in Germany. (Park open 24hr.; admission 9am-7pm. €2.50, under 18 €2.)

CONSTANCE (KONSTANZ) ☎ 07531

Located on the **Bodensee** (Lake Constance) and ranking among Germany's most popular vacation spots, Constance (pop. 29,000) has river promenades and narrow streets that wind around beautiful Baroque and Renaissance facades. Since part of the city extends in neutral Switzerland, Constance emerged unscathed from Allied bombs during WWII. The **Münster** (Cathedral) in the town center features ancient religious relics and dark tunnels beneath its 76m Gothic spire. (Open M-F 10am-5pm, Sa-Su 12:30-5:30pm.) Wander down **Seestraße,** near the yacht harbor, or **Rheinsteig,** along the Rhine. Constance has several **public beaches;** all are free and open from May to September. Take bus #5 to **Freibad Horn,** which is the largest and most crowded beach and has a nude sunbathing section enclosed by hedges.

Reserve accommodations a month ahead in summer. In the center of town, **Pension Gretel ❸,** Zollernstr. 6-8, offers clean rooms at surprisingly low prices. (☎ 45 58 23; www.hotel-gretel.de. Breakfast included. Singles €45; doubles €60-78; triples €96; quads €120; extra bed €18. Nov.-Mar. around €10 discount per person. Cash only.) Fall asleep to lapping waves at **DKV-Campingplatz Brudehofer ❶,** Fohrenbühlweg 50. Take bus #1 to Staad and walk for 10min. with the lake to your left. The campground is on the waterfront. (☎ 313 88; www.campingkonstanz.de. Showers €1. Reception closed noon-2:30pm. €3.50 per person, €2 per child, €3.10-4.50 per tent, €2.60 per car, €7 per RV, €0.50 per bike. Cash only.) **Cafe Restaurant Antrik ❶,** on Hussenst. about 5 min. from the Münster cathedral, offers cheap yet bountiful meals (€4-7, beer/wine €2-3) in both its friendly downstairs area and in the slightly fancier cafe upstairs. Groceries are in the basement of the **Lago** shopping center on Augustinerpl. and Blätzlepl. by the train station. (☎ 12 31 58. Open M-F 9:30am-8pm, Sa 9:30am-7pm.) **Trains** run from Constance to most cities in southern Germany; a short hop to neighboring Kreuzlingen connects you to destinations in Switzerland. **BSB ferries** leave hourly for ports around the lake. Buy tickets on board or in the building behind the train station, Hafenstr. 6. (☎ 364 0389; www.bsb-online.com. Open Apr.-Oct. M-Th 8am-noon and 1-4pm, F 8am-noon and 1-5pm.) The **tourist office** is at Bahnhofspl. 13, to the right of the train station. (☎ 13 30 30; www.konstanz.de. Open Apr.-Oct. M-F 9am-6:30pm, Sa 9am-4pm, Su 10am-1pm; Nov.-Mar. M-F 9:30am-12:30pm and 2-6pm.) **Postal Code:** 78462.

BAVARIA (BAYERN)

Bavaria is the Germany of Teutonic myth and Wagnerian opera. From the Baroque cities along the Danube to mad King Ludwig's castles high in the Alps, the region attracts more tourists than any other part of the country.

MUNICH (MÜNCHEN) ☎ 089

Bavaria's capital and cultural center, Munich (pop. 1,300,000) is a sprawling, liberal metropolis where world-class museums, handsome parks, colossal architecture, and a genial population create a thriving city. *Müncheners* party zealously during **Fasching** (Mardi Gras; Jan. 7-Feb. 5, 2008), shop with abandon during the **Christkindlmarkt** (Christ Child Market; Dec. 1-23), and chug unfathomable quantities of beer during the legendary **Oktoberfest** (Sept. 20-Oct. 5, 2008).

▐ TRANSPORTATION

Flights: Flughafen München (MUC; ☎ 97 52 13 13). S1 and 8 run from the airport to the *Hauptbahnhof* and Marienpl. (40min., 3 per hr., €8 or 8 strips on the *Streifenkarte*). Buy a **Gesaskamtnetz** day pass that covers all zones (€10). The **Lufthansa** shuttle bus goes to the *Hauptbahnhof* (40min., 3 per hr., €10).

Trains: Munich's **Hauptbahnhof** (☎118 61) is the hub of southern Germany with connections to: **Berlin** (5¾-6½hr., 1-2 per hr., €105-119); **Cologne** (6hr., 2-4 per hr., €88-121); **Frankfurt** (3-4½hr., 1-2 per hr., €64-81); **Füssen** (2hr., 1 per hr., €21); **Hamburg** (5¾-6½hr., 1-2 per hr., €104-119); **Amsterdam, NTH** (7-11hr., 17 per day, €134-144); **Budapest, HUN** (7½-9½hr., 8 per day, €98); **Copenhagen, DEN** (11-15hr., 8 per day, €156); **Paris, FRA** (8-10hr., 9 per day, €124-152); **Prague, CZR** (6-8¼hr., 9 per day, €49-84); **Rome, ITA** (10-11hr., 5 per day, €126); **Salzburg, AUT** (1½-2hr., 2 per hr., €21-27); **Venice, ITA** (7-10hr., 6 per day, €92); **Vienna, AUT** (4¼-6hr., 1-2 per hr., €69-85); **Zürich, SWI** (4¼-5½hr., 20 per day, €50-102). Purchase a **Bayern-Ticket** (single €21, 2-5 people €27) for unlimited train transit M-Sa 9am-3am, Su midnight-3am the next day in Bavaria and to Salzburg. **EurAide**, in the station, sells tickets. **Reisezentrum** ticket counters at the station are open daily 7am-9:30pm.

Ride Share: Mitfahrzentrale, Lämmerstr. 6 (☎194 40; www.mifaz.de/muenchen). Arranges intercity rides with drivers going the same way. See **Transportation,** p. 387.

Public Transportation: MVV (☎41 42 43 44; www.mvv-muenchen.de) operates buses, trains, the S-Bahn (underground trains), and the U-Bahn (subway). Most run M-Th 5am-12:30am, F-Sa 5am-2am. S-Bahn trains go until 2 or 3am daily. Night buses and trams ("N") serve Munich's dedicated clubbers. Eurail, Inter Rail, and German rail passes valid on the S-Bahn but not on buses, trams, or the U-Bahn.

Tickets: Buy tickets at the blue vending machines and validate them in the blue boxes before entering the platform or risk a €40 fine.

Prices: Single-ride tickets €2.20 (valid 2hr.). **Kurzstrecke** (short-trip) tickets €1.10 (1hr. or 2 stops on the U- or S-Bahn, 4 stops on a tram or bus). A **Streifenkarte** (10-strip ticket; €10) can be used by more than 1 person. Cancel 2 strips per person for a normal ride, or 1 strip for a short trip; for rides beyond the city center, cancel 2 strips per zone. A **Single-Tageskarte** (single-day ticket; €5) for *Innenraum* (the city's central zone) is valid until 6am the next day; the **partner** day pass (€9) is valid for up to 5 people. **3-day** single pass €13; 5-person pass €21. The **XXL Ticket** (single €6.70, partner €12) gives day-long transit in Munich's 2 innermost zones, white and green. Single **Gesamtnetz** (day ticket for all zones) €10; 5-person pass €18.

Taxis: Taxi-München-Zentrale (☎216 10 or 194 10).

Bike Rental: Mike's Bike Tours, Bräuhausstr. 10 (☎25 54 39 87). €12 per 1st day; €9 per following day. 50% discount with tour (p. 439). After hours, call ☎0172 852 0660. Open daily mid.-Apr. to mid-Oct. 10am-8pm; Mar. to mid-Apr. and mid-Oct. to mid-Nov. 10:30am-1pm and 4:30-5:30pm.

✦ ORIENTATION

Downtown Munich is split into quadrants by thoroughfares running east-west and north-south. These intersect at Munich's central square, **Marienplatz,** and link the traffic rings at **Karlsplatz** (called Stachus by locals) in the west, **Isartorplatz** in the east, **Odeonsplatz** in the north, and **Sendlinger Tor** in the south. In the east beyond the Isartor, the Isar River flows north-south. The *Hauptbahnhof* is beyond Karlspl., to the west of the ring. To get to Marienpl. from the station, take any east-bound S-Bahn or use the main exit and make a right on Bahnhofpl., a left on Bayerstr. heading east through Karlspl., and continue straight. The **university** is to the north amid the **Schwabing** district's budget restaurants; to the east of Schwabing is the **English Garden** and to the west, **Olympiapark.** South of downtown is the **Glockenbachviertel,** filled with nightlife hot spots and gay bars. A seedy area with hotels and sex shops surrounds the *Hauptbahnhof.* Oktoberfest takes place on the large, open **Theresienwiese,** southeast of the train station on the U4 and 5 lines.

🔢 PRACTICAL INFORMATION

The most comprehensive list of services, events, and museums can be found in the English-language monthly *Munich Found,* available for free at the tourist office.

GERMANY

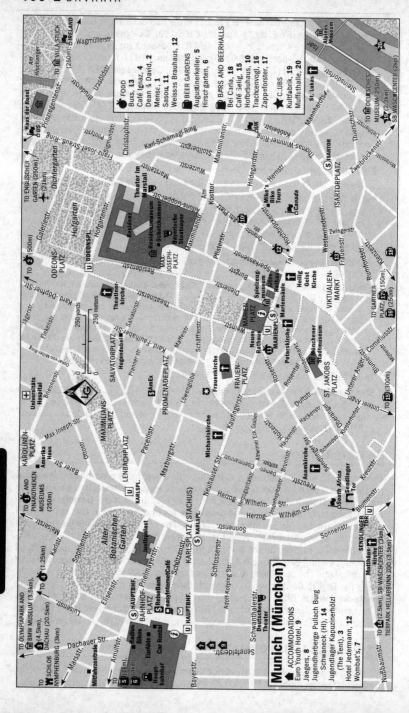

Munich (München)

♦ ACCOMMODATIONS
Euro Youth Hotel, **9**
Jaegers, **8**
Jugendherberge Pullach Burg
  Schwaneck (HI), **14**
Jugendlager Kapuzinerhölzl
  (The Tent), **3**
Hotel Jedermann, **12**
Wombat's, **7**

♣ FOOD
Buxs, **13**
Café Ignaz, **4**
Dean & David, **2**
Mensa, **1**
Sasou, **11**
Weisses Brauhaus, **12**

▤ BEER GARDENS
Augustinerkeller, **5**
Hirsch garten, **6**

▤ BARS AND BEERHALLS
Bei Carla, **18**
Café Selig, **15**
Hofbräuhaus, **10**
Trachenvogl, **16**
Zapp-förster, **17**

⊚ C-UBS
Kultfabrik, **19**
Muffathalle, **20**

Tourist Offices: Main office (☎23 39 65 55), on the front side of the *Hauptbahnhof*, next to the SB-Markt on Bahnhofpl. Books rooms for free with a 10-15% deposit, and sells English-language city maps (€0.30). Open M-Sa 9:30am-6:30pm, Su 10am-6pm. **Branch office**, on Marienpl. at the entrance to the Neues Rathaus tower, is open M-F 10am-8pm, Sa 10am-4pm and accepts MC/V. Books tickets for concerts and other events. **EurAide** (☎59 38 89), room #2 along track 11 of the *Hauptbahnhof*, books train tickets for free, English-language city tours, and explains public transportation. Pick up the free brochure *Inside Track*. Open June-Sept. M-Sa 7:45am-12:45pm and 2-6pm, Su 8am-noon; Oct.-May reduced hours.

Tours: **Mike's Bike Tours,** Bräuhausstr. 10 (☎25 54 39 87; www.mikesbike-tours.com). If you only have 1 day in Munich, take this tour. Starting from the Altes Rathaus on Marienpl., the 4hr., 6.5km city tour includes a *Biergarten* break. Tours leave daily mid-Apr. to Aug. 11:30am and 4pm; Sept. to mid-Nov. and Mar. to mid-Apr. 12:30pm. €24. Look for €6 coupons at youth hostels.

Consulates: Canada, Tal 29 (☎219 9570). Open M-F 9am-noon; 2-4pm by appointment only. **Ireland,** Dennigerstr. 15 (☎20 80 59 90). Open M-F 9am-noon. **UK,** Möhlstr. 5 (☎21 10 90). Open M-Th 8:30am-noon and 1-5pm, F 8:30am-noon and 1-3:30pm. **US,** Königinstr. 5 (☎288 80). Open M-F 1-4pm.

Currency Exchange: ReiseBank (☎551 0813), at the front of the *Hauptbahnhof*. Slightly cheaper than other banks. Open daily 7am-10pm.

Laundromat: SB Waschcenter, Lindwurmstr. 124. Wash €3.50, dry €0.60 per 10min. Soap €0.30. Open daily 7am-11pm. **Branch** at Untersbergstr. 8 (U2, 7, or 8 to Untersbergstraße) has free Wi-Fi.

Medical Emergency: ☎192 22.

Post Office: Bahnhofpl. In the yellow building opposite the *Hauptbahnhof* exit. Open M-F 7:30am-8pm, Sa 9am-4pm. **Postal Code:** 80335.

ACCOMMODATIONS AND CAMPING

Lodgings in Munich tend to be either seedy, expensive, or booked solid. In mid-summer and Oktoberfest, rooms are hard to find and prices jump 10% or more.

> **OH TO BE YOUNG AND BROKE.** HI-affiliated hostels in Bavaria usually do not admit guests over 26, except families or adults with young children.

■ **Euro Youth Hotel,** Senefelderstr. 5 (☎59 90 88 11; www.euro-youth-hotel.de). *Hauptbahnhof* to Bayerstr. The fun and colorful travelers' bar serves *Augustinerbräu* (€3) daily 6pm-4am, lending the laid-back hostel an energetic atmosphere at night. Happy hour 6-9pm; beer €2. Breakfast €4. Laundry €4.10. Internet €2 per hr.; free Wi-Fi. Reception 24hr. In summer dorms €20-24; singles €45; doubles €60, with breakfast, shower, and TV €75. In winter €10-13/45/60/75. Cheapest beds available online. MC/V. ❷

■ **Jugendlager Kapuzinerhölzl (The Tent),** In den Kirchen 30 (☎141 4300; www.the-tent.de). Tram #17 from the *Hauptbahnhof* (dir.: Amalienburgstr.) to Botanischer Garten (15min.). Join 250 "campers" under a huge tent on a wooden floor. Evening campfires. W morning free English- and German-language city tours. Kitchen and laundry available. Free lockers. Internet €2 per hr. Key deposit €25 or passport. Reception 24hr. Open June 15-Oct. 15. €8, includes breakfast, foam pad, and wool blankets; beds €11, linens not included; camping €6 per person, €6 per tent. Cash only. ❶

Wombat's, Senefelderstr. 1 (☎59 98 91 80; www.wombats.at/munich-hostel/index.php). Unique touches include a glass-enclosed garden and welcome drink. Breakfast €4. Internet €3 per hr. Reception 24hr. Dorms €24; private rooms €68. MC/V. ❷

Jaegers, Senefelderstr. 3 (☎55 52 81; www.jaegershostel.de). Modern, colorful hostel with a mellow lounge by day and a boisterous bar by night. Breakfast included. Internet

€1 per 20min.; free Wi-Fi. Laundry €4. Reception 24hr. 40-bed dorms €20; smaller dorms €23-25; singles €55; doubles with bath €79. Rates may vary. AmEx/MC/V. ❷

Jugendherberge Pullach Burg Schwaneck (HI), Burgweg 4-6 (☎74 48 66 70; www.burgschwaneck.de), in a castle 12km from city center. S7 (dir.: Wolfratshausen) to Pullach (20min.). From the train platform, turn right towards the football field, then cross the tracks and follow the signs down Margarethenstr. (10min.). Caters largely to an under-18 crowd. Bowling €25. Breakfast and linens included. Meals €4.30-4.80. Reception 7:30am-12:45pm and 1:30-5:30pm. Curfew 11:30pm. 10-bed dorms €17; 4- to 6-bed dorms €19; singles €28; doubles €50. MC/V. ❷

Hotel Jedermann, Bayerstr. 95 (☎54 32 40; www.hotel-jedermann.de). Take the *Haupt-bahnhof* to Bayerstr. or tram #19 (dir.: Freiham Süd) to Hermann-Lingg-Str. Family-owned hotel offers inviting common areas and beautiful rooms with TV. Breakfast included. Free Internet. Singles from €49; doubles from €67. Extra bed €15. MC/V. ❹

🍴 FOOD

For a typical Bavarian lunch, spread a *Brez'n* (pretzel) with *Leberwurst* (liver-wurst) or cheese. *Weißwürste* (white veal sausages) are a specialty. Don't eat the skin; slice them open instead. *Leberknödel* are tasty liver dumplings.

Off **Ludwigstraße**, the university district supplies students with inexpensive, fill-ing meals. Many reasonably priced restaurants and cafes cluster on **Schelling-straße, Amalienstraße**, and **Türkenstraße** (U3 or 6 to Universität). Munich is also the place where someone first connected the separate concepts of "beer" and "gar-den" to create **Biergärten** (beer garden; see below).

Dean & David, Schellingstr. 13 (☎33 09 83 18; www.deananddavid.com). U3 or U6 to Universität. Curries and fresh salads (from €3) in an airy, modern setting. Entrees €5-7. Free Wi-Fi. Open M-F 8am-9pm, Sa 10am-7pm. Cash only. ❷

Café Ignaz, Georgenstr. 67 (☎271 6093). U2 to Josephspl., then take Adelheidstr. 1 block north and turn right on Georgenstr. Dinners range from crepes to stir-fry dishes (€5-9) at this eco-friendly vegetarian cafe. Breakfast buffet M and W-F 8-11:30am (€7); lunch buffet M-F noon-2pm (€6.50); brunch buffet Sa-Su 9am-1:30pm (€8). Open M and W-F 8am-10pm, Tu 11am-10pm, Sa-Su 9am-10pm. AmEx. ❷

Weisses Bräuhaus, Tal 7 (☎290 1380). This 500-year-old tavern serves traditional Bavarian fare. Adventurous eaters can try *Münchener Voressen* (calf and pig lungs; €8). Entrees €10-20. Large daily specials menu. Open daily 8am-midnight. MC/V. ❹

Buxs, Frauenstr. 9 (☎291 9550). This vegetarian restaurant has artful pastas, salads, and soups. Self-serve, with a weight-based charge (€2.20 per 100g). Takeout avail-able. Open M-F 11am-6:45pm, Sa 11am-3pm. Cash only. ❷

Sasou, Marienpl. 28 (☎26 37 01; www.sasou.de). This pan-Asian restaurant attracts hordes of locals with its noodles, soups, and sushi. For a snack, stick to the finger food: fresh and lightly salted edamame €3.60. Open M-Sa 11am-10pm. Cash only. ❸

Mensa, Arcisstr. 17 (☎86 46 62 51; www.studentenwerk.mhn.de). U2 or U8 to König-spl. Students hit the ground fl. cafeteria for light meals (€0.70-2) or devour large por-tions of German "fare" (€2-4) at the Mensa upstairs. At least 1 vegetarian dish. To eat here, get a "Legic-Karte" in the library (€6 deposit); student ID required. Open M-Th 8am-4:30pm, F 8am-2:30pm; hours vary during vacations. Cash only. ❶

BEER GARDENS (BIERGÄRTEN)

Munich has six great labels: *Augustiner, Hacker-Pschorr, Hofbräu, Löwen-bräu, Paulaner*, and *Spaten-Franziskaner*. Most establishments have chosen sides and only serve one brewery's beer, in four varieties: *Helles* (light), *Dunkles* (dark), *Weißbier* (a cloudy blond wheat beer), and *Radler* ("biker's brew"; half beer, half lemon soda). To order a *Maß* (liter; €4-6), you need only say, *"Ein Bier, bitte."* Specify for only a *halb-Maß* (half-liter; €3-4) or a *Pils* (0.3L; €2-3).

GARDEN PARTY ETIQUETTE. Despite serving similar drinks, beer gardens and beer halls offer very different experiences. Munich *Biergärtens*, removed from the city center, often have outdoor patios on which patrons recline in the afternoon sun, surrounded by bright flowers and chirping birds. In contrast, beer halls tend to be noisier, more closely resembling a bar.

■ **Augustinerkeller**, Arnulfstr. 52 (☎59 43 93), at Zirkus-Krone-Str. S1-8 to Hackerbrücke. From the station, make a right on Arnulfstr. Founded in 1824, Augustiner is viewed by many as Munich's finest *Biergarten*, with enormous *Brez'n* and dim lighting beneath 100-year-old chestnut trees. Don't miss the delicious, sharp Augustiner beer (*Maß* €6.50). Open daily 10am-1am. Kitchen open 10am-10:30pm. AmEx/MC/V.

Hirschgarten, Hirschgarten 1 (☎17 25 91). Tram #17 (dir.: Amalienburgstr.) to Romanpl. Walk to the end of Guntherstr. Families come to Europe's largest *Biergarten* (seats 9000) for its carnival rides, grassy park, on-site deer, and flea market. Entrees €5-15. *Maß* €6. Open daily 9am-midnight. Kitchen open 9am-10pm. Cash only.

⚙ SIGHTS

■ **RESIDENZ.** Down the pedestrian zone from Odeonspl., the state rooms and apartments of the Residenz, home to the Wittelsbach dynasty from 1623 to 1918, represent Baroque, Neoclassical, and Rococo styles. Highlights of the **Residenzmuseum** include the painting-packed **Antiquarium**, the royal **family portraits**, and the **papal chambers.** The adjacent **Schatzkammer** (treasury) contains crowns, crucifixes, reliquaries, and swords. Out back, the **Hofgarten** shelters the temple of Diana. *(Max-Joseph-Pl. 3. U3-6 to Odeonspl. ☎29 06 71. Open daily Apr. to mid-Oct. 9am-6pm; mid-Oct. to Mar. 10am-4pm. Half of the Residenz is open in the morning until 1:30pm and the other half is open after 1:30pm. Each €6, students €5; both €9/8. Garden free. Free audio tour.)*

 Be wary when passing through Marienpl. With all the tourists looking upward at the Glockenspiel, pickpockets have a field day.

MARIENPLATZ. The **Mariensäule**, a 1683 monument to the Virgin Mary, commemorates Munich's survival of the Thirty Years' War. At the **Neues Rathaus**, the **Glockenspiel** chimes, pleasing tourists with jousting knights and dancing coopers. *(Daily in summer at 11am, noon, 3pm, 5pm; in winter 11am, noon, 3pm.)* At 9pm, a mechanical watchman marches out and the Guardian Angel escorts the *Münchner Kindl* (Munich Child) to bed. Adorning the **Altes Rathaus** tower, at the end of Marienpl., are all of Munich's coats of arms but one: the swastika emblem of the Nazi era.

PETERSKIRCHE AND FRAUENKIRCHE. Across from the Neues Rathaus, the 12th-century **Peterskirche** is the city's oldest parish church. Scale over 300 steps up the tower for a spectacular view. *(Open M-Tu and Th-Su 7:30am-7pm. Tower €1.50, students €1.)* From Marienpl., take Kaufingerstr. toward the *Hauptbahnhof* to the onion-domed towers of the 15th-century **Frauenkirche**—one of Munich's most notable landmarks and a city emblem. *(Frauenpl. 1. Open daily 7am-7pm. €3.50, students €1.50.)*

ENGLISCHER GARTEN. More expansive than New York's Central Park or London's Hyde Park, the Englischer Garten is Europe's largest metropolitan public park. The garden includes a Chinese pagoda, classic *Biergarten*, Greek temple, and Japanese tea house. FKK (*Frei Körper Kultur;* free body culture) on signs and park maps designates nude sunbathing areas. Daring *Müncheners* raft, surf, or swim the rapids of the Eisbach, which flows through the park.

SCHLOß NYMPHENBURG. After a decade of trying for an heir, Ludwig I celebrated his son's 1662 birth by building an elaborate summer playground north-

THE HIDDEN DEAL

PRICELESS ENTERTAINMENT

The **Olympia Stadium**, just 3km north of Munich's city center, hosts dozens of concerts every summer. While most charge admission, savvy Müncheners are unlikely to pay for 2hr. in a cramped stadium seat; they know that the sounds of big-name bands carry freely to the surrounding park, where 850,000 sq. m of beautifully manicured lawns encompass a swan-filled lake. On a typical concert night, half the city fills this sprawling park to listen in for free and relax under a summer sky.

Beer and Bratwurst are plentiful and the nearby fairground has games and delicious chocolate-covered bananas. In 2007 alone, the *Olympiazentrum* hosted classic acts like Aerosmith, Genesis, The Police, and Rod Stewart, along with pop star Gwen Stefani and jazz singers Michael Bublé and Norah Jones. To catch the eye candy behind the guitar, scope out *Olympiazentrum*'s occasional free concerts, including classical concerts nightly throughout most of August. Check www.theatron.de for more info.

Take U3 to "Olympiazentrum" and follow the crowds toward the stadium. ☎ 306 724 14; www.olympia-park-muenchen.de. Concerts usually start around 8pm.)

west of Munich. Modeled after Versailles, the palace's most unusual asset is its **Gallery of Beauties,** a collection of portraits of noblewomen and commoners whom the king fancied. See royal carriages, as well as portraits of Ludwig's favorite horses, in the **Marstallmuseum.** *(Tram #17, dir.. Amalienburgstr., to Schloß Nymphenburg. ☎ 17 90 80. Complex open daily Apr. to mid-Oct. 9am-6pm; mid-Oct. to Mar. 10am-4pm. Badenburg and Pagodenburg closed mid-Oct. to Mar. Schloß €5, students €4; audio tour €3. Manors each €2/1. Marstallmuseum €4/3. Entire complex €10/8; in winter €8/6.)*

🏛 MUSEUMS

Many of Munich's museums would require days to explore completely. All state-owned museums, including the three **Pinakotheken,** are €1 on Sunday.

■ **PINAKOTHEKEN.** Designed by *Münchener* Stephan Braunfels, the beautiful **Pinakothek der Moderne** is four museums in one. Subgalleries display architecture, design, drawings, and paintings by artists ranging from Picasso to contemporary masters. *(Barerstr. 40. U2 to Königspl or tram #27 to Pinakotheken. ☎ 23 80 53 60. Open Tu-W and Sa-Su 10am-5pm, Th-F 10am-8pm. €9.50, students €6. Audio guide €2.)*

■ **DEUTSCHES MUSEUM.** Even if you don't know (or care) how engines power a Boeing 747, the Deutsches Museum's over 50 departments on science and technology will keep you entertained and educated. Exhibits include one of the first telephones and a recreated subterranean labyrinth of mining tunnels. *(Museuminsel 1. S1-8 to Isartor or tram #18 to Deutsches Museum. ☎ 217 91; www.deutsches-museum.de. Open daily 9am-5pm. €9, students €3. English-language guidebook €4.)*

BMW MUSEUM. This driving museum displays past, present, and future BMW products. The main building is closed for renovation until spring 2008; in the meantime, the museum has a temporary home nearer to the Olympiaturm. *(Main building at Petuelring 130. U3 to Olympiazentrum, take the Olympiaturm exit, and walk a block up Lerchenauer Str.; the museum will be on your left. ☎ 38 22 56 52; www.bmw-museum.de. Open daily 10am-8pm. €2, students €1.50. Check website for post-renovation prices and hours.)*

🎵 ENTERTAINMENT

Munich deserves its reputation as a world-class cultural center. Sixty theaters are scattered throughout the city; venues range from dramatic classics at the **Residenztheater** and **Volkstheater** to comic opera at the **Staatstheater am Gärtnerplatz** to experimental works at the **Theater im Marstall**. Munich's numerous fringe theaters, cabaret stages, and art cinemas in **Schwabing** reveal its bohemian spirit. *Monatsprogramm* (€1.50) and *Munich Found* (free at the tourist office) list schedules for festivals, museums, and performances. In July, a magnificent **opera festival** arrives at the ▓**Bayerische Staatsoper** (Bavarian National Opera), Max-Joseph-Pl. 2. (☎21 85 01; www.bayerische.staatsoper.de. U3-6 to Odeonspl. or tram #19 to Nationaltheater.) Snag leftover tickets—if there are any—at the evening box office, Max-Joseph-Pl. 2, near the theater, for €10. (Opens 1hr. before curtain.) Standing-room tickets are half-price and can be purchased at any time. The daytime box office is at Marstallpl. 5. (☎21 85 19 20. Open M-F 10am-6pm, Sa 10am-1pm. No performances Aug. to mid-Sept.)

◗ NIGHTLIFE

BARS AND BEER HALLS

▓ **Zappeforster,** Corneliusstr. 16 (☎20 24 52 50). U. Students and twentysomething hipsters huddle around the tables on Gärtner Platz or bop along to the alternative beats in the no-frills interior. During the day, *Müncheners* lounge around on cushions and blankets for coffee and conversation. Beer 0.3L €2.50. Open daily 9am-1am. Cash only.

▓ **Trachtenvogl,** Reichenbachstr. 47 (☎201 5160; www.trachtenvogl.de). U1-2 or 7-8 to Frauenhofer. Enjoy 1 of their 32 types of hot chocolate—some with alcohol, of course—in a cozy living room with chic lamps. F live bands. Su chocolate fondue; reservations required. Happy hour daily 6-7pm; Astra beer €1.60. Jäger hour daily 9-10pm; Jägermeister drinks ½-price. Open Su-Th 10am-1am, F-Sa 10am-3am. Cash only.

Hofbräuhaus, Platzl 9 (☎290 1360), 2 blocks from Marienpl. Come for the full beer hall experience: this is as jolly, as festive, and as loud as it gets. Go in the early afternoon to avoid tourists. *Maß* €6.20. *Weißwürste* €4.20. Open daily 9am-midnight. Cash only.

Café Selig, Hans-Sachs Str. 3 (☎23 88 88 78; www.einfachselig.de). U1 or 2 to Frauenhofer Str. Join the diverse crowd (mixed by day, mostly gay Sa-Su and by night) at this unpretentious cafe and bar with homemade cakes, international coffees, and strudel (€5-7). Open M and W 9pm-1am, F 9am-3am, Sa-Su 9am-late. AmEx/MC/V.

Bei Carla, Buttermelcherstr. 9 (☎22 79 01). S1-8 to Isartor. Women in their 20s and 30s flock to this lesbian bar—one of Munich's best-kept secrets—for pleasant conversation and a round or 2 of darts. Open M-Sa 4pm-2am, Su 6pm-2am. Cash only.

CLUBS

▓ **Muffathalle,** Zellstr. 4 (☎45 87 50 10; www.muffathalle.de), in Haidhausen. Take S1-8 to Rosenheimerpl. and walk toward the river on Rosenheimer Str. for 2 blocks, or take tram #18 (dir.: St. Emmeram) to Deutsches Museum. This former power plant generates hiphop, jazz, spoken word, and techno. Features a non-traditional *Biergarten*. Cover from €5. Open M-Th 5pm-late, F-Su noon-late. Buy tickets online or through München Ticket.

Kultfabrik, Grafingerstr. 6 (☎49 00 90 70; www.kultfabrik.info). Take U5 or S1-8 to Ostbahnhof. With 23 clubs in 1 complex, Kultfabrik attracts dedicated partygoers for all-night revelry. The Russian-themed **Club Kalinka** is 1 of the more rowdy spots, popular with young locals and backpackers. Most doors open around 10pm and close late.

◪ OKTOBERFEST

Every fall, tourists make an unholy pilgrimage to Munich to drink and be merry in true Bavarian style. From the penultimate Saturday of September through early October (Sept. 20-Oct. 5, 2008), beer consumption prevails. The numbers for this festival have become truly mindboggling: participants chug five million liters of beer, but only on a full stomach of 200,000 *Würste*. What began in 1810 as a celebration of the wedding of Ludwig I has become the world's largest folk festival. Bavarian citizens met outside the city gates, for a week of horse racing on fields they named **Theresienwiese** in honor of Ludwig's bride (U4 or U5 to Theresienwiese). The bash was such fun that Munich's citizens have repeated the revelry (minus the horses) ever since. An agricultural show, inaugurated in 1811, is still held every three years. Festivities begin with the "Grand Entry of the *Oktoberfest* Landlords and Breweries," a **parade** ending at noon with the ceremonial drinking of the first keg, to the cry of *"O'zapft is!"* or "it's tapped!" by Munich's Lord Mayor. Other highlights include a costume and rifleman's parade and an open-air concert. Each of Munich's breweries set up tents in the Theresienwiese. Arrive by 4:30pm to get a table; you must have a seat to be served alcohol. Drinking hours are fairly short, from 9am to 10:30pm, depending on the day; fairground attractions and sideshows are open slightly later.

▓ DAYTRIPS FROM MUNICH: DACHAU

Arbeit Macht Frei (Work Will Set You Free) was the first message prisoners saw as they passed through the **Jourhaus** gate into Dachau, where over 206,000 "undesirables" were interned between 1933 and 1945. The Third Reich's first concentration camp, Dachau was primarily a work rather than a death camp like Auschwitz; knowing the Allies would not bomb prisoners, the SS reserved it for the construction of armaments. Restored in 1962, the crematorium, gates, and walls now form a memorial to the victims. *(Open Tu-Su 9am-5pm. Free.)* In former administrative buildings, the ▓**museum** examines pre-1930s anti-Semitism, the rise of Nazism, the establishment of the concentration camp system, and the lives of prisoners. A short film (22min., free) screens in English at 11:30am, 2, and 3:30pm. Displays in the **Bunker,** the former prison and torture chamber, chronicle prisoners' lives and SS guards' barbarism. A 2½hr. English-language tour covers the entire camp. *(May-Sept. Tu-F at 1:30pm, Sa-Su at noon and 1:30pm; Oct.-Apr. Th-Su at 1:30pm. €3.)* A brief orientation (30min.) gives an overview of the complex. *(May-Sept. Tu-F at 12:30pm, Sa-Su at 11am and 12:30pm; Oct.-Apr. Th-Su at 12:30pm. €1.50.)* Or, purchase the worthwhile audio tour (€3, students €2) for a self-tour of the camp. Food and beverages are not available at Dachau; pack your own. Take the S2 (dir.: Petershausen) to Dachau (20min.), then bus #726 (dir.: Saubachsiedlung) to KZ-Gedenkstätte (10min.); a €6.70 XXL day pass covers the trip.

PASSAU ☎ 0851

Baroque arches cast shadows across the cobblestone alleys of Passau (pop. 51,000), a two-millennium-old city at the confluence of the Danube, Ilz, and Inn rivers. Passau's crowning attraction is the Baroque **Stephansdom,** Dompl., where the world's largest church organ—accommodating up to five organists—looms. (Open daily in summer 6:30am-7pm; winter 6:30am-6pm. Church free. Organ concerts May-Oct. and Dec. 27-31 M-F noon and Th 7:30pm. €4, students €2; evening concerts €5-8/3-4.) Behind the cathedral, the **Residenz** is home to the **Domschatz,** an extravagant collection of tapestries and gold. Enter through the back of the Stephansdom, to the right of the altar. (☎39 33 74. Open May 2-Oct. M-Sa 10am-4pm. €2, students €1.) Various floods have left their high-water marks on the outer wall of the 13th-century Gothic **Rathaus** (town hall). A bus runs every 30min. 10am-5pm between the *Rathaus* and the former palace of the bishopric **Veste Oberhaus,** which now houses the **Kulturhistorisches** (Cultural History) **Museum.** (☎49 33 50; www.oberhausmuseum.de. Open mid-Apr. to mid-Nov. M-F 9am-5pm, Sa-Su 10am-6pm; mid-Nov. to mid-Mar. Tu-Su 9am-5pm. €5, students €4.)

    Fahrrad Pension ❶, Bahnhofstr. 33, has cheap beds over a bakery. (☎347 84; www.fahrrad-pension.com. 4-bed dorms €8; singles €18. Cash only.) Possibly the most oddly shaped hotel you'll ever stay in, the **Rotel Inn** ❸, Hauptbahnhof/Donauufer, is built like a sleeping man, with tiny rooms just wide enough to fit a bed. (☎951 60; www.rotel-inn.de. Breakfast €5. Reception 24hr. Dorms €20; singles €25; doubles €30. Cash only.) **Sensasian** ❷, Heuwinkel 9, between Ludwigstr. and Rindermarkt, dishes up pan-Asian cuisine with plenty of vegetarian options. (☎989 0152. Ramen €6-8. Open M-Sa 10am-11pm, Su 11am-11pm. Cash only.) There is an **open-air market** in the Dompl. (Tu and F mornings). The free German-language magazine *Pasta* lists the hottest nightlife venues. **Trains** depart for: Frankfurt (4¼hr., 1 per 2hr., €72); Munich (2¼-3hr., 1-2 per hr., €28-34); Nuremberg (2-4hr., 1 per hr., €31-38); Regensburg (1½-1¾hr., 1 per hr., €19). The **tourist office** is at Rathauspl. 3. (☎95 59 80. Open Easter to mid-Oct. M-F 8:30am-6pm, Sa-Su 9am-4pm; mid-Oct. to Easter M-Th 8:30am-5pm, F 8:30am-4pm.) **Postal Code:** 94032.

NUREMBERG (NÜRNBERG) ☎0911

Before it witnessed the fanaticism of Hitler's Nazi rallies, Nuremberg (pop. 491,000) hosted Imperial Diets (parliamentary meetings) in the first Reich. Today, the remnants of both regimes draw visitors to the city, which new generations have rechristened *Stadt der Menschenrechte* (City of Human Rights). Allied bombing destroyed most of old Nuremberg, but its castle and some other buildings have been reconstructed. The walled-in **Handwerkerhof** near the station is a tourist trap disguised as a history lesson; head up Königstr. for the real sights. Take a detour to the left for the pillared **Straße der Menschenrechte** (Avenue of Human Rights) as well as the glass **Germanisches Nationalmuseum,** Kartäuserg. 1, which chronicles German art since prehistoric times. (☎133 10. Open Tu-Su 10am-6pm, W 10am-9pm. Last entry 1hr. before closing. €6, students €4, W 6-9pm free.) Across the river is the **Hauptmarktplatz**, site of the annual **Christmas market** (Nov. 30-Dec. 24, 2007; Nov. 28-Dec. 24, 2008). Hidden in the fence of the **Schöner Brunnen** (Beautiful Fountain), in the Hauptmarkt, is a seamless, spinning golden ring, thought to bring good luck. Atop the hill, the **Kaiserburg** (Fortress of the Holy Roman Emperor) looms over Nuremberg. Climb the **Sinwellturm** for the best views of the city. (Open daily 9am-6pm. €6, students €5.) The ruins of **Reichsparteitagsgelände,** where the Nazi Party held Congress rallies, remind visitors of the city's darker history. On the far side of the lake is the **Zeppelintribüne,** the grandstand where Hitler addressed the masses. The Fascination and Terror exhibit, in the ▉**Kongresshalle** at the north end of the park, covers the Nazi era. (☎231 5666. Open M-F 9am-6pm, Sa-

Su 10am-6pm. €5, students €2.50; includes audio tour.) Tram #9 from the train station stops directly at Kongresshalle (Dokumentationszentrum stop). To reach the Zeppelintribüne, walk clockwise (10min.) around the lake.

Jugendgästehaus (HI) ❷, Burg 2, sits in a castle above the city. From the tourist office, follow Königstr. over the bridge to the Hauptmarkt, head diagonally across to the fountain, and continue up Burgstr. (☎230 9360. Reception 7am-1am. Curfew 1am. Dorms €20-21; singles €39; doubles €46. MC/V.) The quirkily-named rooms—like "Wrong Room" and "Right Room"—of **Lette'm Sleep ❷**, Frauentormauer 42, are near the train station. Take the first left after entering the *Altstadt* through Königpl. (☎992 8128. Linens €3. Free Internet. Reception 24hr. Dorms €16; singles €30; doubles €48-52. MC/V.) **Zum Gulden Stern ❷**, Zirkelschmiedg. 26, is the world's oldest *Bratwürst* kitchen. (☎205 9298. 6 for €7.80. Entrees €5-10. Open daily 11am-10pm. AmEx/MC/V.) **Super Markt Straub,** Hauptmarkt 12, is near the Frauenkirche. (Open M-Sa 8am-6pm.) Most of Nuremberg's nightlife is in the *Altstadt.* **Cine Città,** Gewerbemuseumspl. 3, U-Bahn to Wöhrder Wiese, packs 16 bars and cafes, 17 German-language cinemas, an IMAX theater, and a disco inside one complex. (☎20 66 60. Open Su-Th until 2am, F-Sa until 3am.) **Hirsch,** Vogelweiherstr. 66, has multiple bars and a *Biergärten* out front. (Take nightbus #5 to Vogelweiherstr. www.der-hirsch.de. Mixed drinks €5.50. M-Th frequent concerts. Cover €3-15. Open M-Th 8pm-2am, F-Sa 10pm-5am. Cash only.) **Cartoon,** An der Sparkasse 6, is a popular gay bar near Lorenzpl. (☎22 71 70. Shots €3.80. Mixed drinks €6-7. Open M-Th 11am-1am, F-Sa 11am-3am, Su 2pm-1am.)

Trains go to: Berlin (4.5hr., 1 per hr., €83); Frankfurt (2-3½hr., 2 per hr., €33-45); Munich (1½hr., 2-4 per hr., €29-45); Stuttgart (2¼-3hr., 1 per hr., €29-35). Walk through the tunnel from the train station to the *Altstadt* and take a right to reach the **tourist office,** Königstr. 93. (☎233 6132. Open M-Sa 9am-7pm.) A second office is in the Hauptmarkt. (Open M-Sa 9am-6pm.) **Postal Code:** 90402.

ROMANTIC ROAD

Castles, sunflowers, and vineyards checker the landscape between Würzburg and Füssen. Officially christened *Romantische Straße* in 1950, the Romantic Road is one of Germany's most traversed routes.

█ TRANSPORTATION

Train travel is the most flexible, economical way to visit the Romantic Road. **Deutsche Bahn** operates a bus route along the Romantic Road, shuttling tourists from Frankfurt to Munich (13¼hr., €99), stopping in Würzburg (2hr., €22), Rothenburg (4¾hr., €35), and Füssen (11¾hr., €80). A **Castle Road** route connects Rothenburg with Nuremburg (3hr., €14). Both buses run once a day in each direction. For reservations and more info, see www.romanticroadcoach.de. There is a 10% student and under 26 discount and a 60% Eurail and German Rail Pass discount.

A GOOD REASON TO SLEEP IN. Try to take trains after 9am so you can use the Bayern Ticket (€21), which offers unlimited travel within Bavaria and parts of Austria on weekdays between 9am and 3am the following day, and on weekends between midnight and 3am the following day. If you can find other travelers going your way, the €27 Bayern Ticket covers two to five people.

FÜSSEN ☎08362

Füssen ("feet") seems an apt name for a little town at the foot of the Romantic Road. Füssen's main attraction is its proximity to Ludwig's famed **Königsschlößer** (see below), best seen as a daytrip. Above the pedestrian district, the town's own **Hohes Schloß** (High Castle) features *trompe-l'oeil* windows in its inner courtyard.

(☎90 31 64. Open Tu-Su Apr.-Oct. 11am-4pm; Nov.-Mar. 2-4pm. €2.50, students €2.) Although Füssen's best accommodations are pensions, the tourist office keeps a list of *Privatzimmer* with vacant rooms. **Jugendherberge (HI) ❷**, Mariahilfer Str. 5, lies in a residential area 15min. from the town center. Turn right from the station and follow the railroad tracks. (☎77 54. Laundry €3.60. Reception daily Mar.-Sept. 7am-noon and 5-10pm; Oct. and Dec.-Apr. 5-10pm. Lockout 11pm-6:30am. Dorms €18. MC/V.) Bakeries, butcher shops, and *Imbiße* (snack bars) stand among the pricey cafes on **Reichenstraße,** particularly off the Luitpold Passage. **Trains** run to Augsburg (1¾hr., 1 per hr., €17) and Munich (2hr., 1 per hr., €21). To reach the **tourist office,** Kaiser-Maximilian-Pl. 1, from the train station, walk the length of Bahnhofstr. and head across the roundabout to the big yellow building on your left. (☎938 50; www.fuessen.de. Open June-Sept. M-F 9am-6pm, Sa 10am-2pm; Oct.-May M-F 9am-5pm, Sa 10am-noon.) **Postal Code:** 87629.

◪ DAYTRIP FROM FÜSSEN: ◪KÖNIGSSCHLÖßER. King Ludwig II, a frenzied visionary, built fantastic castles soaring into the alpine skies. In 1886, a band of nobles and bureaucrats deposed Ludwig, declared him insane, and imprisoned him; three days later, the king was mysteriously discovered dead in a lake. The fairy-tale castles that Ludwig created and the enigma of his death captivate tourists. The glitzy **Schloß Neuschwanstein** inspired Disney's Cinderella Castle and is one of Germany's iconic attractions. Its chambers include an artificial grotto and an immense Wagnerian opera hall. Hike 10min. to the **Marien-brücke,** a bridge that spans the gorge behind the castle. Climb the mountain on the other side of the bridge for enchantment minus the crowds. Ludwig spent his summers in the bright yellow **Schloß Hohenschwangau** across the valley. Don't miss the night-sky frescoes in the king's bedroom. Separate paths lead uphill to the castles. (☎08362 93 08 30. *Both castles open daily Apr.-Sept. 9am-6pm, ticket windows open 8am-5pm; Oct.-Mar. castles 10am-4pm, tickets 9am-3pm. Mandatory tours of each castle €9, students €8; 10 languages available. Combo ticket €17/15.)* From the Füssen train station, take **bus** #73 or 78, marked "Königsschlößer" (10min.; 1-2 per hr.; €1.70, round-trip €3.20). Tickets for both castles are sold at the **Ticket-Service Center,** about 100m uphill from the bus stop. Arrive before 10am to escape long lines.

ROTHENBURG OB DER TAUBER ☎09861

Possibly the only walled medieval city without a single modern building, Rothenburg (pop. 12,000) is *the* Romantic Road stop. After the Thirty Years' War, without money to modernize, the town remained unchanged for 250 years. Tourism later brought economic stability and a reason to preserve the medieval *Altstadt*. The English-language tour led by the **night watchman** gives an entertaining intro to Rothenburg history. (Starts at the *Rathaus* on Marktpl. Easter-Dec. 25 daily 8pm. €6, students €4.) A long climb up the stairs of the 60m **Rathaus Tower** leads to a panoramic view of the town. (Open Apr.-Oct. daily 9:30am-12:30pm and 1:30-5pm; Dec. daily noon-3pm; Nov. and Jan.-Mar. Sa-Su noon-3pm. €1.) According to local lore, during the Thirty Years' War, conquering Catholic general Johann Tilly offered to spare the town from destruction if any local could chug 3.25L (almost a gallon) of wine. Mayor Nusch successfully met the challenge, passed out for several days, then lived to a ripe old age. His saving **Meistertrunk** (Master Draught) is reenacted with fanfare each year (May 9-12, Sept. 7, Oct. 4 and 11, 2008).

For private rooms unregistered at the tourist office (€15-45), look for the *Zimmer frei* (free room) signs in restaurants and stores. The 500-year-old **◪Pension Raidel ❷**, Wengg. 3, will make you feel like you're sleeping in the past. (☎31 15; www.romanticroad.com/raidel. Breakfast included. Singles €24, with bath €39; doubles €45/59. Cash only.) **Zur Höll** ("To Hell") **❷**, Burgg. 8. Zur Höll serves sinfully good Franconian fare (€4-18) by candlelight. (☎42 29. Open daily 5pm-midnight. Cash only.) **Trains** run to Steinach (15min., 1 per hr., €1.80), which has transfers to Munich (€32). The **tourist office,** Marktpl. 2, offers 15min. of free **Internet.** (☎404 800. Open May-Oct. M-F 9am-noon and 1-6pm, Sa-Su 10am-3pm; Nov.-Apr. M-F 9am-noon and 1-5pm, Sa 10am-1pm.) **Postal Code:** 91541.

EASTERN GERMANY

Saxony *(Sachsen)* and Thuringia *(Thüringen)*, the most interesting regions in eastern Germany outside of Berlin, encompass Dresden, Leipzig, and Weimar. The architecture is defined by contrasts: castles surrounding Dresden attest to Saxony's one-time wealth, while boxy GDR-era buildings recall the socialist aesthetic.

WEIMAR   ☎03643

The writer Goethe once said of Weimar (pop. 62,000), "Where else can you find so much that is good in a place that is so small?" Indeed, Weimar's diverse cultural attractions, lustrous parks, and rich history make it a worthwhile destination. The **Goethehaus** and **Goethe-Nationalmuseum,** Frauenplan 1, preserve the chambers where the poet wrote, entertained guests, and, after a half-century in Weimar, died. (Open Apr.-Sept. Tu-F and Su 9am-6pm, Sa 9am-7pm; Oct. Tu-Su 9am-6pm; Nov.-Mar. Tu-Su 9am-4pm. €6.50, students €5. Museum €3/2.50.) The multi-talented Goethe landscaped the **Park an der Ilm,** Corona-Schöfer-Str., which contains his first Weimar residence, the **Gartenhaus.** (Open daily Apr.-Oct. 10am-6pm, Nov.-Mar. 10am-4pm. €3.50, students €2.50.) South of the town center is the **Historischer Friedhof** cemetery, where Goethe and Schiller both rest. (Cemetery open daily Mar.-Sept. 8am-9pm; Oct.-Feb. 8am-6pm. Tomb open daily Apr.-Oct. 10am-6pm; Nov.-Mar. 10am-4pm. Tomb €2.50, students €2.)

Relax in front of the piano at the **Hababusch Hostel ❶,** Geleitstr. 4, a bohemian hostel run by art students. The prices can't be beat. To get there, follow Geleitstr. from Goethepl. After a sharp right, you'll come to a statue on your left; the entrance is behind it. (☎85 07 37; www.hababusch.de. Linens €2.50. Key deposit €10. Reception 9am-9pm. Dorms €10; singles €20; doubles €30. Cash only.) **Jugendherberge Germania (HI) ❷,** Carl-August-Allee 13, is close to the train station but a 15min. walk from the city center. (☎85 04 90; www.djh-thueringen.de. Breakfast included. 1st night €24, under 27 €21; €22/19 thereafter. Cash only.) Enjoy one of the crepes at **⊠Crêperie du Palais ❷,** Am Palais 1, near Theaterpl. (Open daily M-F 10am-midnight. Cash only.) Both a cafe and a gallery, **ACC ❷,** Burgpl. 1-2, serves creative daily specials (€5-6.50), screens art films, and offers free Wi-Fi (Open daily May-Sept. 10am-1am; Oct.-Apr. 11am-1am. AmEx/MC/V.)

Trains run to Dresden (2hr., 1 per hr., €49), Frankfurt (3hr., 1 per hr., €51), and Leipzig (1hr., 1 per hr., €23). To reach **Goetheplatz,** a bus hub at the center of the Altstadt, from the station, follow Carl-August-Allee downhill to Karl-Liebknecht-Str., which leads into Goethepl. (15min.). The efficient **Weimar Information** is at Markt 10. (☎74 50. www.weimar.de. Open Apr.-Oct. M-Sa 9:30am-7pm, Su 9:30am-3pm; Nov.-Mar. M-F 9:30am-6pm, Sa-Su 9:30am-2pm.)

⚡ DAYTRIP FROM WEIMAR: BUCHENWALD. During WWII, the Buchenwald camp interred 250,000 prisoners, including communists, gypsies, homosexuals, and Jews. Although Buchenwald was not built as an extermination camp, over 50,000 died here from medical experimentation or harsh treatment by the SS. The **Buchenwald National Monument and Memorial** has two principal sites. The **KZ-Lager** is what remains of the camp; a large storehouse documents the history of Buchenwald (1937-1945) and of Nazism. Camp **archives** are open to anyone searching for records of family and friends between 1937 and 1945; schedule an appointment with the curator. *(Archives ☎43 01 54. Outdoor camp area open daily sunrise-sunset.)* Sadly, the suffering at Buchenwald did not end with liberation. Soviet authorities later used the site as an internment camp, **Special Camp No. 2.** The best way to reach the camp is by **bus #6** from Weimar's train station or from Goethepl. Check the schedule carefully; some #6 buses go to Ettersburg rather than Gedenkstätte Buchenwald. (20min.; 1-2 per hr.). The bus picks up at the KZ-Lager parking lot and at the road by the *Glockenturm* (bell tower). Be sure to watch the info center's video (30min.; 1 per hr.), which has English-language subtitles. (☎43 00; www.buchenwald.de. Open daily Apr.-Oct. 10am-6pm; Nov.-Mar. 10am-4pm.)

EISENACH   ☎03691

Eisenach (pop. 44,000) is best known as the home of the ▒**Wartburg Fortress,** which protected Martin Luther in 1521 after his excommunication. It was here, disguised as a bearded noble named *Junker* (Squire) Jörg, that Luther famously fought an apparition of the devil with an inkwell. The view from its southern tower is spectacular. (Open daily Mar.-Oct. 8:30am-5pm; Nov.-Feb. 9am-3:30pm. Mandatory tours €6.50, students €3.50. English-language tour 1:30pm.) Eisenach is also the birthplace of composer **Johann Sebastian Bach.** Local legend holds that Bach was born in 1685 in the **Bachhaus,** Frauenplan 21. Roughly every hr., a guide plays one of the museum's period instruments and provides historical context in German. (Open M-Sa 10am-12:30pm and 2-5pm, Su 11:30am-12:30pm and 2-5pm.) Up the street is the latticed **Lutherhaus,** Lutherpl. 8, where Luther lived during his school days. (Open daily 10am-5pm. €3, students €1.50.) The **Residenz Haus ❷,** Auf der Esplanade, offers nicely decorated, spacious rooms off an 18th-century tower. (☎21 41 33; www.residenzhaus-eisenach.de. Breakfast €6. Singles, doubles, and 4- and 6-person rooms €20 per person, students €15. Cash only.) **La Fontana ❶,** Georgenstr. 22, with a large fountain in front, is the best deal in town. (☎74 35 39. Pizza and pasta €3-4. Open Su-Th 11:30am-2:30pm and 5-11pm, F-Sa 11:30am-2:30pm and 5-11:30pm. Cash only.) **Trains** run to Weimar (1hr., 1 per hr., €13-21). The **tourist office** is at Markt 9. (☎792 30. Open Apr.-Oct. M-F 10am-6pm, Sa 10am-4pm, Su 10am-4pm; Nov.-Mar. M-F 10am-6pm, Sa 10am-4pm.) **Postal Code:** 99817.

WITTENBERG   ☎03491

Martin Luther began the Protestant Reformation here in 1517 when he nailed his 95 Theses to the door of the **Schloßkirche;** Wittenberg (pop. 48,000) has been fanatical about its native heretic ever since. The ▒**Lutherhalle,** Collegienstr. 54, chronicles the Reformation through letters, texts, art, and artifacts. (☎420

A MEMORABLE MUSEUM

Weimar's newest museum isn't one dedicated to a classical German author or a noteworthy Grand Duke. This museum features a plant.

The ginkgo tree—the beloved plant of the city's most noted residents, Johann Wolfgand von Goethe—was brought from Asia, where it had been used for centuries for its medicinal effects, in the 18th century. It was first cultivated in Europe in the Netherlands during the 1730s. It began to appear in Weimar in the early 1800s, most likely thanks to Goethe, who included a poem titled "Gingko Biloba" extolling the plant in his 1815 collection of poems, "East-West Divan." A short walk from Markt, behind the Prince's Palace on the Plaz de Demokratie, you can see the oldest Gingko tree in Weimar, planted in 1813.

The Gingko Museum, on Windischenstr., right off Markt, sells everything Ginko in the shop on its first floor. On the second floor, there are a few small exhibits dedicated to the plant, its unique character, its medicinal effects (one of which is to enhance memory), and its use in artistic expression.

Planet Weimar Gingko Museum and Gallery. Windischenstr. 1. ☎80 54 52; www.planet-weimar.de. Open M-F 10am-5pm. Sa-Su 10am-3:30pm.

3118. Open Apr.-Oct. daily 9am-6pm; Nov.-Mar. Tu-Su 10am-5pm. €5, students €3.) Down Schloßstr., the *Schloßkirche* allegedly holds Luther's body and a copy of the Theses. (Tower ☎40 25 85. Church open daily 10am-6pm. Tower open Easter-Oct. Tu-Su 10am-noon and 2-4pm. Church free. Tower €2, students €1.) The **Jugendherberge (HI) ❷,** Schloßstr. 14/15, is the white building next to the church. Find the incongruously glass entrance in the courtyard to the left after the main entrance. (☎40 32 55. Breakfast included. Linens €3.50. Reception 8am-10pm. Check-out 9:30am. Curfew 10pm. Dorms €20, under 27 €17. HI members only. MC/V.) People, potatoes, and a very strange ceiling converge at the **Wittenberger Kartoffelhaus,** Schloßstr. 2. (☎41 12 00. Entrees €3.50-13. Open daily 11am-1am. V.) **Trains** leave for Berlin (45min., 1 per hr., €21) and Leipzig (1hr., every 2hr., €10). The **tourist office** is at Schloßpl. 2. (☎49 86 10. Open Mar.-Oct. M-F 9am-6:30pm, Sa-Su 10am-4pm; Nov.-Feb. M-F 10am-4pm, Sa 10am-2pm, Su 11am-3pm.) **Postal Code:** 06886.

DRESDEN ☎0351

The buildings that form the skyline of Dresden's magnificent *Altstadt* look ancient, but most of them are newly reconstructed—the Allied firebombings in February 1945 that claimed over 40,000 lives also destroyed 75% of the city center. Serious reconstruction followed, and today, the city's Baroque architecture, world-class museums, and thriving *Neustadt* nightlife earn small Dresden (pop. 479,000) celebrity status and an esteemed stop on the path from Berlin to Prague.

▉ TRANSPORTATION

Flights: Dresden's **airport** (**DRS;** ☎881 3360; www.dresden-airport.de) is 9km from the city. S2 runs there from both train stations (13min. from *Neustadt,* 23min. from the *Hauptbahnhof;* 2 per hr. 4am-11:30pm; €1.80).

Trains: Nearly all trains stop at both the **Hauptbahnhof** in the *Altstadt* and **Bahnhof Dresden Neustadt** across the Elbe. Trains run to: **Berlin** (3hr., 1 per hr., €33-55); **Frankfurt am Main** (4½hr., 1 per hr., €80); **Leipzig** (1½hr., 1-2 per hr., €25); **Munich** (6hr., 1-2 per hr., €93); **Budapest, HUN** (11hr., 2 per day, €81); **Prague, CZR** (2½hr., 9 per day, €20). Tickets, also available from the machines in the station main hall, are cheaper at the *Reisezentrum* desk.

Public Transportation: Much of Dresden is accessible on foot, but **streetcars** cover the whole city. 1hr. ticket €1.80. Day pass €4.50. The €6 **Family Card,** good for 2 passengers until 4am, is probably the best deal. Weekly pass €17. Tickets are available from *Fahrkarte* dispensers at major stops and on streetcars. For info and maps, go to one of the **Service Punkt** stands in front of the *Hauptbahnhof* (open M-F 8am-7pm, Sa 8am-6pm, Su 9am-6pm) or at Postpl. (open M-F 8am-7pm, Sa 8am-6pm). Most major lines run 1 per hr. after midnight until 4am—look for the moon sign marked **Gute-Nacht-Linie.**

Taxis: ☎21 12 11 and 88 88 88 88.

Ride-Share: Mitfahrzentrale, Dr.-Friedrich-Wolf-Str. 2 (☎194 40; www.mf24.de). On Slesischen Pl., across from *Bahnhof Neustadt.* Open M-F 9am-8pm, Sa-Su 10am-2pm. Non-German speakers may require assistance from their hostels in order to book.

▉▉ ORIENTATION AND PRACTICAL INFORMATION

The **Elbe River** bisects Dresden 60km northwest of the Czech border, dividing the city into the **Altstadt** in the south (where the *Hauptbahnhof* is located) and the **Neustadt** in the north. Many of Dresden's attractions lie in the *Altstadt* between **Altmarkt** and the Elbe. Nightlife centers in the *Neustadt* to the north by **Albertplatz.**

Tourist Office: 2 main branches: Prager Str. 2A, near the *Hauptbahnhof* (open M-F 9:30am-6:30pm, Sa 9:30am-6pm), and Theaterpl. in the Schinkelwache, a small building directly in front of the Semper-Oper (open M-Th 10am-6pm, F 10am-7pm, Sa-Su

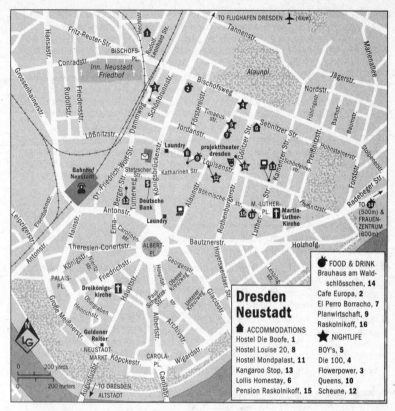

Dresden Neustadt

🏠 ACCOMMODATIONS
Hostel Die Boofe, 1
Hostel Louise 20, 8
Hostel Mondpalast, 11
Kangaroo Stop, 13
Lollis Homestay, 6
Pension Raskolnikoff, 15

🍎 FOOD & DRINK
Brauhaus am Wald-schlösschen, 14
Cafe Europa, 2
El Perro Borracho, 7
Planwirtschaft, 9
Raskolnikoff, 16

⭐ NIGHTLIFE
BOY's, 5
Die 100, 4
Flowerpower, 3
Queens, 10
Scheune, 12

10am-5pm). Call the city hotlines for general info (☎49 19 21 00), room reservations (☎49 19 22 22), and tours and advance tickets (☎49 19 22 33).

Currency Exchange: ReiseBank (☎471 2177), in the main hall of the *Hauptbahnhof*. €5 commission for cash; 1-1.5% commission to cash **traveler's checks.** Western Union money transfers. Open M-F 8am-7:30pm, Sa 9am-noon and 12:30-4pm, Su 9am-1pm.

ATMs: The **Deutsche Bank** and Sparkasse bank at the corner of Königsbrücker Str. and Stetzscherstr. have 24hr. ATMs, as do many central *Neustadt* and *Altstadt* banks.

Luggage Storage: At all train stations. Lockers €2-2.50 for 24hr.

Laundromat: Eco-Express, Königsbrücker Str. 2. Wash 6-11am €1.90, 11am-11pm €2.40. Dry €0.50 per 10min. Open M-Sa 6am-11pm. Also try **"Crazy" Waschsalon,** 6 Louisenstr. Wash €2.50-2.70. Dry €0.50 per 10min. Open M-Sa 7am-11pm.

24hr. Pharmacy: Notdienst signs outside most pharmacies list 24hr. pharmacies.

Post Office: The Hauptpostamt, Königsbrücker Str. 21/29 (☎819 1373), in the *Neustadt*. Open M-F 9am-7pm, Sa 10am-1pm. Branch in the *Altstadt* on Weberg. at the Altmarkt Galerie. Open daily 9:30am-9pm.

🏠 ACCOMMODATIONS

In Dresden's *Neustadt*, high-quality hostels with late check-out times neighbor countless clubs and bars. In the *Altstadt*, quieter hostels and pricier hotels are closer to the sights. Reservations are a good idea from April through November.

Hostel Mondpalast, Louisenstr. 77 (☎563 4050; www.mondpalast.de). Settle down in a comfy bed in large, clean rooms, some with TV, after a night hanging out in the lively bar downstairs. Bike rental €5 per 3hr., €7 per day. Breakfast €5. Linens €2. Internet €2 per hr. Reception 24hr. Dorms €14-17; singles €29-34, with bath €39-44; doubles €37-44/50-52; quads €74-78. AmEx/MC/V. ❶

Hostel Louise 20, Louisenstr. 20 (☎889 4894; www.louise20.de). Above the restaurant Planwirtschaft. Walk through a courtyard to this luxurious hostel, where a winding staircase leads up to modern rooms with wooden furniture. Breakfast €5. Linens €2.50. Reception 7am-11pm. Check-out noon. Dorms €16-17; singles €29-32; doubles €39-43; triples €51; quads €68; quints €80. Free linens with ISIC. MC/V. ❷

Lollis Homestay, Görlitzer Str. 34 (☎81 08 45 58; www.lollishome.de). This hostel reproduces the relaxed feel of a student flat, with free coffee, tea, and a book exchange. Old bikes available to borrow. Breakfast €3. Linens €2. Laundry €3. Internet €2.50 per hr. Dorms €13-16; singles €27-38; doubles €36-42; triples €48-57; quads €60-72. 10% ISIC discount. MC/V; €2.50 surcharge. ❶

FOOD

It's difficult to find anything in the Altstadt not targeting tourists; the cheapest eats are at the *Imbiß* stands along **Prager Straße** and around **Postplatz.**

Cafe Aha, Kreuzstr. 7 (☎496 0673; www.ladencafe.de), in the *Altstadt.* Always delicious, Cafe Aha introduces food from a different developing country each month. Vegetarian options. Entrees €5-11. Fair trade shop in the basement. Cafe open daily 10am-midnight. Kitchen open 10am-10:30pm. Cash only. ❷

Planwirtschaft, Louisenstr. 20 (☎801 3187; www.planwirtschaft.de). German dishes with ingredients fresh from local farms. Inventive soups, crisp salads (€4.30-8.40), and entrees (€7-11) from stuffed eggplant to fresh lake fish. Breakfast buffet (€8) until 3pm. Outdoor courtyard seating. Open Su-Th 9am-1am, F-Sa 9am-2am. MC/V. ❷

Brauhaus am Waldschlösschen, Am Brauhaus 8B (☎652 3900; www.waldschloesschen.de). Take tram #11 to Waldschlösschen or walk 25min. up Baunitzerstr. Beautiful views overlooking the Elbe complement the house brews (€1.90) and German entrees (€8-13). Open daily 11-1am. AmEx/MC/V. ❸

SIGHTS

Saxony's electors once ruled nearly all of central Europe from the banks of the majestic Elbe. Despite the *Altstadt*'s demolition in WWII and only partial reconstruction during Communist times, the area remains an impressive cultural center.

SEMPER-OPER. Dresden's opera house echoes the splendor of the Zwinger's (p. 453) north wing. Painstaking restoration has returned the building to its pre-war state. *(Theaterpl. 2. ☎491 1496. Tours usually M-Sa 2 per hr., but times vary each week; check at the entrance or the ticket office in the Schinkelwache building. €7, students €3.50.)*

DRESDENER SCHLOß. Once home to August the Strong, the Polish king who built most of the Dresden area's castles, this palace, re-opened in 2006, houses the **Grünes Gewölbe** (Green Vault). The vault dazzles with some of the finest metal and gem work in all of Europe including rare medieval chalices and lavish Baroque jewels. *(☎49 14 20 00. Open M and W-Su 10am-7pm. €8, students €2.50, €10 with audio tour.)*

FRAUENKIRCHE. The product of a 10-year reconstruction, the Frauenkirche re-opened on October 31, 2005, completing Dresden's skyline with its regal silhouette. Floods of tourists gaze at the circular ascending balconies, golden altar, and cupola. *(Neumarkt. ☎498 1131. Open M-F 10am-noon and 1-6pm, Sa-Su hours vary, check the small, white info center on Neumarkt for details. English-language audio tour €2.50.)*

🏛 MUSEUMS

After several years of renovations, Dresden's museums are once again ready to compete with the best in Europe. If you plan on visiting more than one in a day, consider a **Tageskarte** (€10, students €6), which grants one-day admission to the Schloß, most of the Zwinger, and more. The **Dresden City-Card** and **Dresden Regio-Card** (see **Practical Information**, p. 450) include museum admission. Info about all the museums is at www.skd-dresden.de. Most museums close on Mondays.

ZWINGER. Through the archway from the Semper-Oper, ■**Gemäldegalerie Alte Meister** has a first-rate collection of Italian and Dutch paintings from 1400 to 1800, including Cranach the Elder's *Adam and Eve*, Giorgione's *Sleeping Venus*, and Raphael's enchanting *Sistine Madonna*. (☎49 14 20 00. Open Tu-Su 10am-6pm. €6, students €3.50; includes entry to the Rüstkammer.) The **Rüstkammer** shows shiny but deadly toys from the court of the Wettin princes: ivory-inlaid guns, chain mail, and the armor of the Wettin toddlers. (☎491 46 82. Open Tu-Su 10am-6pm. €3, students €2.)

STADTMUSEUM. Artifacts of Dresden's early history, which begins in the 13th century, pale before the museum's 20th-century memorabilia, including a People's Gas Mask (*Volksgasmask*) and a 1902 replica firefighter with a helmet-sprinkler. (Wilsdruffer Str. 2. ☎65 64 80. Open Tu-Th and Sa-Su 10am-6pm, F noon-8pm. €3, students €2.)

🎵 ENTERTAINMENT

Dresden has long been a focal point of music, opera, and theater. Most theaters break from mid-July to early September, but open-air festivals bridge the gap. Outdoor movies screen along the Elbe during **Filmnächte am Elbufer** in July and August. (Office at Alaunstr. 62. ☎89 93 20. Movies show around 9pm. Tickets €6.) The **Zwinger** has classical concerts in summer at 6:30pm.

Sächsische Staatsoper (Semper-Oper), Theaterpl. 2 (☎491 1705; www.semper-oper.de). Some of the world's finest opera. Call ahead. Tickets €4.50-160. Box office at Schinkelwache open M-F 10am-6pm, Sa-Su 10am-4pm, and 1hr. before curtain.

Kulturpalast, Schloßstr. 2, in Altmarkt (☎486 1866; www.kulturpalast-dresden.de). Home to the **Dresdner Philharmonie** (☎486 6306; www.dresdnerphilharmonie.de) and a variety of performances. Open M and W-F 10am-6pm, Tu 10am-7pm, Su 10am-2pm.

🍺 NIGHTLIFE

It's as if the entire *Neustadt* spends the day anticipating nightfall. A decade ago, the area north of Albertpl. was a maze of gray streets and crumbling buildings; since then, an alternative community has thrived in bars on **Louisenstraße, Königs-brücker straße, Bischofsweg, Kamenzerstraße,** and **Albertplatz.** The German-language *Dresdener Kulturmagazin*, free at *Neustadt* hostels, describes every bar.

Scheune, Alaunstr. 36 (☎804 38; www.scheune.org). The granddaddy of the *Neustadt* scene, this huge bar and cafe is a starting point for hipsters. Entrees €4.50-10. Club opens 8pm and hosts a variety of events including live music. Cover €5-20. Cafe open M-Th 5pm-1am, F 5pm-2am, Sa 10am-2am, Su 10am-1am. Cash only.

Flowerpower, Eschenstr. 11 (☎804 9814; www.flower-power.de). Over-the-top decor from the 60s and 70s attracts a dedicated crowd of 20-somethings. M student night; discounts on beer and wine. Th Karaoke. F club night. Open daily 8pm-5am. Cash only.

Die 100, Alaunstr. 100 (☎801 3957). The candlelit interior and intimate stone court-yard of this laid-back, well-stocked wine cellar provide an escape from the social flurry elsewhere. Wine from €3 per glass. Open daily 5pm-3am. Cash only.

BOY's, Alaunstr. 80, beyond the Kunsthof Passage. A ½-clad devil mannequin guards the popular gay-friendly bar. Drinks €2-5. Open Tu-Th 8pm-3am, F-Su 8pm-5am. MC/V.

DAYTRIP FROM DRESDEN: MEIßEN

In 1710, the Saxon elector contracted a severe case of the "porcelain bug," and he turned the city's defunct castle into Europe's first porcelain factory. Tour the **Staatliche Porzellan-Manufaktur Meißen,** Talstr. 9, to observe the craftsmen in action or peruse finished products in the *Schauhalle.* The real fun is in the *Schauwerkstatt* (demonstration showroom), where porcelain artists paint petal-perfect flowers before your disbelieving eyes. *(☎0352 146 8208. Open daily May-Oct. 9am-6pm; Nov.-Apr. 9am-5pm. €8.50, students €4.50. English-language audio tour €3.)* Cutesy souvenir-lined alleyways snake up to the castle, cathedral, and beery eateries of **Albrechtsburg** (www.albrechtsburg-meissen.de). To get there from the train station, walk straight onto Bahnhofstr. and follow it over the Elbbrücke. Cross the bridge, continue straight to the Markt, and turn right onto Burgstr. Follow the signs up the hill, then look for a long staircase hugging a wall to your right; this will leads to the castle. *(Open daily Mar.-Oct. 10am-6pm; Nov.-Feb. 10am-5pm. Last entry 15min. before closing. €3.50, students €2.50. English-language audio tour €2.)* Next door looms the **Dom zu Meißen,** a Gothic cathedral featuring four 13th-century statues by the Naumburg Master, an amazing 13th-century stained-glass window, and a triptych by Cranach the Elder. *(Open daily Apr.-Oct. 9am-6pm; Nov.-Mar. 10am-4pm. €2.50, students €1.50.)* **Trains** run to Meißen from Dresden (40min., €5.10). The **tourist office,** Markt 3, across from Frauenkirche, finds private rooms. *(☎419 40. Open Apr.-Oct. M-F 10am-6pm, Sa-Su 10am-43pm; Nov.-Mar. M-F 10am-5pm, Sa 10am-3pm.)* **Postal Code:** 01662.

LEIPZIG ☎0341

In Leipzig (pop. 493,000), the city of music, it's hard to walk more than a few blocks without being serenaded by a classical quartet, wooed by a Spanish guitar, or riveted by choir music. Large enough to have a life outside its university, but small enough to feel the influence of its students, Leipzig boasts world-class museums and corners packed with cafes, cabarets, and second-hand stores.

TRANSPORTATION AND PRACTICAL INFORMATION. Leipzig lies on the Berlin-Munich line. **Trains** run to: Berlin (1½hr., 2 per hr., €39); Dresden (2hr., 2 per hr., €27); Frankfurt (3½hr., 1 per hr., €65); Munich (5hr., 1 per hr., €81). The **tourist office** is at Richard-Wagner-Str. 1. The **Leipzig Card** is good for free public transport and discounted museums (1-day until 4am, €9; 3-day €19. ☎710 4265. Open Mar.-Oct. M-F 9:30am-6pm, Sa 9:30am-4pm, Su 9:30am-3pm; Nov.-Feb. M-F 10am-6pm.) **Postal Code:** 04109.

ACCOMMODATIONS AND FOOD. To reach **Hostel Sleepy Lion ❶,** Käthe-Kollwitz-Str. 3, take streetcar #1 (dir.: Lausen) to Gottschedstr.; or, from the station, turn right and walk along Trondlinring, then left onto Goerdelering and continue straight onto Käthe-Kollwitz-Str. Run by young locals, it draws an international crowd with its spacious lounge, foosball table, and separate non-smoking area. (☎993 9480; www.hostel-leipzig.de. All rooms with bath. Bike rental €5 per day. Breakfast €3.50. Linens €2.50. Internet €2 per hr. Reception 24hr. Dorms €14-16; singles €30; doubles €42; quads €68. AmEx/MC/V.) **Central Globetrotter ❶,** Kurt-Schumacher-Str. 41, fills its spray-painted rooms with young backpackers. Take the west exit and turn right onto Kurt-Schumacher-Str. (☎149 8960; www.globetrotter-leipzig.de. Communal showers. Breakfast €4. Linens €2. Internet €2 per hr. Dorms €13-14; singles €24; doubles €36; quads €60. AmEx/MC/V.)

Imbiß stands, bistros, and bakeries line **Grimmaischestraße** in the Innenstadt. Outside the city center, cafes, bars, and *Döner* stands pack **Karl-Liebknecht-Straße** (streetcar #10 or 11 to Südpl.). The hip cafe **Bellini's** ❷, Barfußgäßchen 3-5, serves salads, and pasta (€3.80-11) in the heart of the Markt. (☎961 7681. Open daily noon-late. MC/V.) Designed in the imaginatively whimsical style of Friedrich Hundertwasser, **100-Wasser Cafe** ❸, Barfußg. 15, serves generous pastas and other dishes. (☎215 7927. Entrecs €5.50-13. Open daily 9am-2am. Cash only.)

⚅🎵 SIGHTS AND NIGHTLIFE. The heart of Leipzig is the **Marktplatz,** guarded by the slanted 16th-century **Altes Rathaus** (town hall). Head to the Rathaus and follow Thomasg. to the **Thomaskirche.** Bach spent his last 27 years here as cantor; his grave is by the altar. (☎960 2855. Open daily 9am-6pm. Free.) Behind the church is the **Johann-Sebastian-Bach-Museum,** Thomaskirchof 16, with exhibits on the composer's life, an annual Bach festival (June 13-22, 2008), and fall concerts. (Open daily 10am-5pm. €4, students €2. Free English-language audio tour.) Head back to Thomasg., turn left, then turn right on Dittrichring to reach the 🎵**Museum in der Runden Ecke,** Dittrichring 24, with blunt exhibits on the GDR-era *Stasi* (secret police). Ask in the office for a €0.50 English-language brochure. (☎961 2443; www.runde-ecke-leipzig.de. Open daily 10am-6pm. Free.) Leipzig's **Gewandhaus-Orchester,** Augustuspl. 8, has been a major orchestra since 1843. (☎127 0280. Open M-F 10am-6pm, Sa 10am-2pm, and 1hr. before curtain. Tickets €10-65.) The free magazines *Fritz* and *Blitz* have nightlife info, as does *Kreuzer* (€2 at newsstands). **Barfußgäßchen,** a street just off the Markt, is the place to see and be seen for the student and young professional crowd. Leipzig university students spent eight years excavating a series of medieval tunnels so they could get their groove on in the 🎵**Moritzbastei,** Universitätsstr. 9, a massive cave with bars, and dance floors under vaulted brick ceilings. (☎70 25 90. Cover W €4, students €2.50; Sa €4.50/3. Cafe open M-F 10am-midnight, Sa noon-midnight, Su 9am-midnight. Club open W 10am-6am, Sa noon-6am. Cash only.)

GREECE
(ÉΛΛΑς)

With sacred monasteries as mountainside fixtures, standard three hour siestas, and circle dancing and drinking until daybreak, Greece revels in its epic past. Renaissance men long before the Renaissance, the ancient Greeks sprung to prominence with their intellectual and athletic mastery. The Greek lifestyle is a mix of high speed and sun-inspired lounging.

 DISCOVER GREECE: SUGGESTED ITINERARIES

THREE DAYS. Spend it all in **Athens** (p. 461). Roam the **Acropolis,** gaze at treasures in the **National Archaeological Museum,** and pay homage at the **Parthenon.** Visit the ancient **Agora,** then take a trip down to **Poseidon's Temple** at Cape Sounion.

ONE WEEK. Begin your sojourn in **Athens** (3 days). Scope out sea turtles in **Zakynthos** (1 day; p. 483), then sprint to **Olympia** (1 day; p. 470) to see where the games began. Sail to **Corfu** (1 day; p. 481) and peer into Albania from atop Mt. Pantokrator. Lastly, soak up Byzantine history in **Thessaloniki** (1 day; p. 474).

BEST OF GREECE, THREE WEEKS. Explore **Athens** (4 days) before visiting the mansions of **Nafplion** (1 day; p. 472). Race west to **Olympia** (1 day) and take a ferry to the beaches of **Corfu** (2 days). Back on the mainland, wander **Thessaloniki** (2 days), then climb to the cliffside monasteries of **Meteora** (1 day; p. 480). Consult the gods at **Mount Olympus** (1 day; p. 478) and the Oracle of **Delphi** (1 day). On **Crete** (3 days; p. 489), hike Europe's largest gorge. Seek rest on **Santorini** (1 day; p. 488), debauchery on **Ios** (1 day; p. 487), and sun on **Mykonos** (1 day; p. 484).

ESSENTIALS

FACTS AND FIGURES

Official Name: Hellenic Republic.
Capital: Athens.
Major Cities: Thessaloniki, Patras.
Population: 10,688,000.
Land Area: 131,900 sq. km.

Time Zone: GMT +2.
Language: Greek.
Religion: Eastern Orthodox (98%).
Highest Peak: Mt. Olympus (2917m).
Length of National Anthem: 158 verses.

WHEN TO GO

July through August is high season; it is best to visit in May, early June, or September, when smaller crowds enjoy the gorgeous weather. Visiting during low season ensures lower prices, but many sights and accommodations have shorter hours or close altogether. Transportation runs less frequently, so plan accordingly.

Greece

DOCUMENTS AND FORMALITIES

EMBASSIES. Foreign embassies in Greece are in Athens (p. 461). Greek embassies abroad include: **Australia,** 9 Turrana St., Yarralumla, Canberra, ACT, 2600 (☎62 7330 11); **Canada,** 80 MacLaren St., Ottawa, ON, K2P 0K6 (☎613-238-6271; www.greekembassy.ca); **Ireland,** 1 Upper Pembroke St., Dublin, 2 (☎31 676 7254, ext. 5); **New Zealand,** 5-7 Willeston St., 10th fl., Wellington (☎4 473 7775, ext. 6); **UK,** 1a Holland Park, London, W11 3TP (☎020 72 21 64 67; www.greekembassy.org.uk); **US,** 2217 Massachusetts Ave., NW, Washington, D.C., 20008 (☎202-939-1300; www.greekembassy.org).

VISA AND ENTRY INFORMATION. EU citizens do not need a visa. Citizens of **Australia, Canada, New Zealand, and the US** do not need a visa for stays of up to 90 days, beginning upon entry into any of the countries in the EU's freedom-of-movement zone. For more info, see p. 14. For stays longer than 90 days, all non-EU citizens need Schengen visas, available at Greek embassies and online at www.greekembassy.org. Processing a tourist visa takes approximately 20 days.

TRANSPORTATION

BY PLANE. Most international flights land in Athens International Airport (**ATH**; ☎21035 30 000; www.aia.gr), though some also serve Corfu (**CFU**), Iraklion (**HER**),

Kos (**KSG**), and Thessaloniki (**SKG**). **Olympic Airlines,** 96 Syngrou Ave., Athens, 11741 (☎21092 691 11; www.olympicairlines.com), offers extensive domestic service. A 1hr. flight from Athens (€60-100) can get you to almost any Grecian island.

BY TRAIN. Greece is served by a number of international train routes that connect Athens and Thessaloniki to most European cities. Train service within Greece, however, is limited and sometimes uncomfortable. The new air-conditioned, inter-city express trains, while slightly more expensive and less frequent, are worth the price. **Eurail Passes** are valid on all Greek trains. **Hellenic Railways Organization** (OSE; ☎1110; www.osenet.gr) connects Athens to major Greek cities.

BY BUS. Few buses run directly from any European city to Greece, except for chartered tour buses. Domestic bus service is extensive and fares are cheap. **KTEL** (www.ktel.org) operates most domestic buses; always check with an official source about scheduled departures, as posted schedules are often outdated.

BY FERRY. Boats travel from Bari, ITA, to Corfu, Durres, Igoumenitsa, Patras, and Sami and from Ancona, ITA, to Corfu, Igoumenitsa, and Patras. Ferries also run from Greece to various points on the Turkish coast. There is frequent ferry service to the Greek islands, but schedules are irregular and incorrect info is common. Check schedules posted at the tourist office, at the port office, or at www.ferries.gr. Make reservations and arrive at least 1hr. before your departure time. In addition to conventional service, **Hellenic Seaways** (☎21041 99 000; www.hellenic-seaways.gr) provides high-speed vessels between the islands at twice the cost and speed of ferries. Student and children receive reduced fares; additionally, travelers buying tickets up to 15 days before intended departure date receive a 15% Early Booking Discount on ferries leaving Tuesday through Thursday.

BY CAR AND MOPED. You must be 18 to drive in Greece, and 21 to rent a car; some agencies require renters to be at least 23 or 25; most rental cars start at €35. Rental agencies may quote low daily rates that exclude the 18% tax and **collision damage waiver (CDW)** insurance. Foreign drivers must have an **International Driving Permit** and an **International Insurance Certificate**. The **Automobile and Touring Club of Greece (ELPA),** Messogion 395, Athens, 15343, provides help and offers reciprocal membership to members of foreign auto clubs like AAA. (☎21060 68 800, 24hr. emergency roadside assistance 104, infoline 174; www.elpa.gr.) Mopeds, while great for exploring, are extremely dangerous—wear a helmet.

TOURIST SERVICES AND MONEY

EMERGENCY	Ambulance: ☎166. Fire: ☎199. Police: ☎100. General Emergency: ☎112.

TOURIST OFFICES. Two national organizations oversee tourism in Greece: **Greek National Tourist Organization (GNTO;** known as the **EOT** in Greece) and the **tourist police** *(touristiki astinomia)*. The GNTO, Tsoha 7, Athens supplies general info about Grecian sights and accommodations. (☎2108 70 70 00; www.gnto.gr. Open M-F 8am-3pm.) In addition to the "Tourist Police" insignia decorating their uniforms, white belts, gloves, and cap bands help identify the tourist police. The **Tourist Police Service** and **General Police Directorate,** P. Kanellopoulou 4, Athens (☎2106 92 8510, 24hr. general emergency 171) deal with local and immediate problems concerning bus schedules, accommodations, and lost passports. Offices are open long hours and are willing to help, but their staff's English may be limited.

MONEY. The **euro (€)** has replaced the **Greek drachma** as the unit of currency in Greece. For more info, see p. 17. It's generally cheaper to change money in Greece than at home. When changing money in Greece, try to go to a bank (τράπεζα;

TRAH-peh-za) with at most a 5% margin between its buy and sell prices. A bare-bones day in Greece costs €40-60. A day with more comforts runs €55-75. While all restaurant prices include a 15% **gratuity**, tipping an additional 5-10% for the assistant waiters and busboys is considered good form. **Taxi** drivers do not expect tips although patrons generally round their fare up to the nearest euro. Generally, **bargaining** is expected for street wares and at other informal venues, but when in doubt, wait and watch to avoid offending merchants. Bargaining for cheaper *domatia* (rooms to let) and at small hotels, as well as for unmetered taxi rides is also common. For more info on money in Europe, see p. 16.

Greece has a 19% **value added tax (VAT)**, a sales tax applied to goods and services sold in mainland Greece and 13% VAT on the Aegean islands. Both are included in the listed price. The prices given in *Let's Go* include VAT. In the airport upon exiting the EU, non-EU citizens can claim a refund on the tax paid for goods purchased at participating stores. In order to qualify for a refund in a store, you must spend at least €120; make sure to ask for a refund form when you pay. For more info on qualifying for a VAT refund, see p. 19.

KEEPING IN TOUCH

PHONE CODES	**Country code: 30. International dialing prefix:** 00. For more info on how to place international calls, see **Inside Back Cover.**

EMAIL AND THE INTERNET. The availability of the Internet in Greece is rapidly expanding. In all big cities, most small cities and large towns, and on most islands, you'll be able to find Internet cafes. Expect to pay €2-6 per hr.

TELEPHONE. Whenever possible use a calling card for international phone calls, as long-distance rates for national phone services are often very high. Pay phones in Greece use prepaid phone cards, sold at *peripteros* (streetside kiosks) and OTE offices. Mobile phones are an increasingly popular, economical option. Major mobile carriers include **Q-Telecom, Telestet,** and **Vodaphone.** Direct-dial access numbers for calling out of Greece include: **AT&T Direct** (☎00 800 1311); **British Telecom** (☎00 800 4411); **Canada Direct** (☎00 800 1611); **Sprint** (☎00 800 1411); **NTL** (☎00 800 4422); **Telstra Australia** (☎00 800 6111). For more info on calling home from Europe, see p. 28.

MAIL. Airmail is the best way to send mail home from Greece. To send a letter (up to 20g) anywhere from Greece costs €0.65. To receive mail in Greece, have it delivered **Poste Restante.** Mail will go to the main post office unless you specify a subsidiary by street address. Address mail to be held as follows: First name LAST NAME, Town Post Office, Island, Greece, Postal Code, POSTE RESTANTE. Bring a passport to pick up your mail; there may be a small fee.

ACCOMMODATIONS AND CAMPING

GREECE	❶	❷	❸	❹	❺
ACCOMMODATIONS	under €17	€17-27	€28-37	€38-70	over €70

Local tourist offices usually have lists of inexpensive accommodations. A **hostel** bed averages €15-30. Those not endorsed by HI are usually still safe and reputable. In many areas, **domatia** are a good option; locals offering cheap lodging may approach you as you enter town, a common practice that is illegal. It's usually a better bet to go to an official tourist office. Prices vary; expect to pay €15-35 for a single and €25-45 for a double. Always see the room and negotiate with *domatia* owners before settling on a price; never pay more than you would to stay in a hotel. If in doubt, ask the tourist police; they may set you up with a room and conduct the negotiations themselves. **Hotel** prices are regulated, but proprietors may push you to take the most expensive room. Budget hotels start at €20 for singles and €30 for doubles. Check your bill carefully, and threaten to contact the tourist police if you think you're being cheated. Greece has plenty of official **campgrounds**, which cost €2-3 per tent plus €4-8 per person. Though common in summer, camping on public beaches—sometimes illegal—may not be the safest option.

FOOD AND DRINK

GREECE	❶	❷	❸	❹	❺
FOOD	under €5	€5-9	€10-15	€16-25	over €25

Penny-pinching carnivores will thank Zeus for lamb, chicken, or pork **souvlaki**, stuffed into a pita to make **gyros** (YEE-ros). Vegetarians can also find cheap eateries; options include **horiatiki** (Greek salad), savory pastries like **tiropita** (cheese pie) and **spanakopita** (spinach and feta pie). Frothy iced coffee milkshakes take the edge off the summer heat. **Ouzo** (a powerful licorice-flavored spirit) is served with **mezedes** (snacks of octopus, cheese, and sausage). Breakfast, served only in the early morning, is generally very simple: a piece of toast with **marmelada** or a pastry. Lunch, a hearty and leisurely meal, can begin as early as noon but is more likely eaten sometime between 2 and 5pm. Dinner is a drawn-out, relaxed affair served late. Greek restaurants are known as **tavernas** or **estiatorios;** a grill is a **psistaria.**

HOLIDAYS AND FESTIVALS

Holidays: Feast of St. Basil/New Year's Day (Jan. 1); Epiphany (Jan. 6); Clean Monday (Mar. 10); Independence Day (Mar. 25); St. George's Day (Apr. 23); Orthodox Good Friday (Apr. 25); Orthodox Easter (Apr. 27-28); Labor Day (May 1); Pentecost (May 11-12); Day of the Holy Spirit (June 16); Assumption (Aug. 15); Feast of St. Demetrius (Oct. 26); Okhi Day (Oct. 28); All Saints' Day (Nov. 1); Christmas (Dec. 25-26).

Festivals: Three weeks of Carnival feasting and dancing (Feb. 18-Mar. 10) precede Lenten fasting. April 23 is St. George's Day, when Greece honors the dragon-slaying knight with horse races, wrestling matches, and dances. The Feast of St. Demetrius (Oct. 26) is celebrated with particular enthusiasm in Thessaloniki.

BEYOND TOURISM

Doing more than just sightseeing on a trip to Greece is as easy (and as challenging) as offering some of one's own time. Though considered wealthy by international standards, Greece has an abundance of aid organizations to combat the nation's very real problems. From preserving storied remnants of the past to ensuring the survival of wildlife species in the future, plenty of opportunities exist to give back. For more info on opportunities across Europe, see **Beyond Tourism,** p. 56.

American School of Classical Studies at Athens (ASCSA), 54 Souidias St., GR-106 76 Athens (☎21072 36 313; www.ascsa.edu.gr). Provides study abroad opportunities in Greece for students interested in archaeology and the classics. US$2950-17,000 including tuition, room, and partial board.

Anglo-Hellenic Teacher Recruitment, 45 Kyprou St., 20100 Corinth (☎27410 53 511; www.anglo-hellenic.com). Provides TEFL training, employment, and support for English teachers in Greece.

Archelon Sea Turtle Protection Society, Solomou 57, Athens 10432 (☎/fax 21052 31 342; www.archelon.gr). Non-profit group devoted to studying and protecting sea turtles on the beaches of Zakynthos, Crete, and the Peloponnese. Opportunities for seasonal field work and year-round work at the rehabilitation center. €100 participation fee.

Conservation Volunteers Greece, Veranzerou 15, 10677 Athens (☎21038 25 506; www.cvgpeep.gr; phones answered M-F 9am-2pm). Offers 2- to 3-week summer programs in environmental and cultural conservation, as well as courses in leadership and First Aid. Participants must be over 18, under 30 and speak English. €120 participation fee.

Seaturtle Rescue Center, on the Third Marina, Glyfada (☎21089 82 600). Volunteer at Athens's only turtle hospital. Open daily 5-8pm. No participation fee.

ATHENS Αθήνα ☎210

An illustrious past invigorates Athens. The ghosts of antiquity peer down from its hilltops, instilling residents and visitors with a sense of the city's historic importance. Home to 6 million people—half of Greece's population—Athens is daring and modern; its patriotic citizens pushed their capital into the 21st century with massive clean-up and building projects before the 2004 Olympic Games. Creative international menus, hipster bars, and large warehouse performance spaces crowd Byzantine churches, traditional *tavernas*, and toppled columns.

◼ TRANSPORTATION

Flights: Eleftherios Venizelou (ATH; ☎353 0000; www.aia.gr). Greece's international airport operates as 1 massive yet navigable terminal. Arrivals are on the ground floor, departures on the 2nd. The **Suburban Rail** services the airport from the city center in 30min. 4 bus lines run to Athens, Piraeus, and Rafina. Budget airlines **SkyEurope** (www.skyeurope.com) and **Wizz Air** (www.wizzair.com) fly to Athens.

Trains: Hellenic Railways (OSE), Sina 6 (☎21036 24 402; www.ose.gr). **Larisis Train Station** (☎529 8837) serves northern Greece. Ticket office open daily 5am-midnight. Trolley #1 from El. Venizelou in Pl. Syndagma (5 per hr., €0.50) or the Metro to Sepolia. Trains go to **Thessaloniki** (7hr., 5 per day, €14; express 5½hr., 6 per day, €28).

Buses: Terminal A, Kifissou 100 (☎512 4910). Take blue bus #051 from the corner of Zinonos and Menandrou near Pl. Omonia (4 per hr., €0.50). Buses to: **Corfu** (10hr., 4 per day, €30); **Corinth** (1½hr., 2 per hr., €7); **Patras** (3hr., 2 per hr., €16; express 2½hr., 20 per day); **Thessaloniki** (6hr., 11 per day, €32). **Terminal B,** Liossion 260 (☎831 7153). Take blue bus #024 from Amalias, outside the National Gardens (45min., 3 per hr., €0.50). Buses to **Delphi** (3hr., 6 per day, €13).

Ferries: Most leave from the Piraeus port. Ferry schedule changes daily; check ahead at the tourist office, in the *Athens News,* or over the phone (☎14 40). Ferries sail directly to all major Greek islands except for the Sporades and Ionians. To Crete: **Hania** (11hr., €22); **Iraklion** (11hr., €24); **Rethymno** (11hr., €24). Others to: **Ios** (7½hr., €22); **Kos** (13½hr., €36); **Lesvos** (12hr., €26); **Mykonos** (6hr., €20); **Naxos** (6hr., €24); **Paros** (5hr., €24); **Patmos** (8hr., €30); **Rhodes** (14hr., €43); **Santorini** (9hr., €28). International ferries head to **Turkey** (€30).

Public Transportation: Yellow KTEL **buses** travel all around Attica from orange bus stops around the city. Other buses around Athens and its suburbs are blue and designated by 3-digit numbers. Electrical antennae distinguish **trolleys** from buses. Buy bus and trolley tickets at any street kiosk. Hold on to your ticket or face a €18-30 fine. A standard bus/trolley ticket costs €0.50. The modern Athens **metro** consists of 3 lines running 5am-midnight. The green **M1** line runs from northern Kifisia to Piraeus, the red **M2** from

A

B

C

TO (200m) 2

Filadelfias

TO

Khomatianou

Mamouri

Neof. Metaxa

Livaniou

M. Voda

Alkamenous

Smirnis

Akharnon

Ioulianou

Ferron

Enianos

Areos Park

TO MAROUSI (9km)

TO KIFISIA (13km)

Leoforos Alexandras

Filis

Aristotelous

Agiou Pavlou

Paleologou

Kritis

Sourmeli

Makednoias

Averof

3 Septemvriou

Inirou

Patission-28 Oktovriou

Mavromateon

Metsovou

Vas. Irakliou

Fotifa

Sitsis

Ioustianou

Psalla

Poulkerias

Strе

Hil

Deligianni

Iliou

Mezonos

Elefsinion

Favierou

Khiou

Kodratou

Victor Hugo

Karolou

METAXOURGIO M

PL. KARAISKAKI

OSE

METAXOURGIO

TO

Somieron

Magner

Marni

VATHI

PL. VATHIS

Solomou

Kapodistriou

Halkokondili

Veranzerou

Politeknniou

Polytechnic University/School of Fine Arts

Stournara

Tossitsa

Kountouriotou

EXARHIA

Boubulinas

Zaimi

Notara

Tsamadou

Trikoupi

Methonis

Zosimadon

Em. Benaki

Zoodokou Pigis

M. Themistokleous

M. Monomou

Rivera Garden Art Cinema

Valtetsiou

Daverleon

Benaki

Kaliodromiou

Eressou

Mavromihali

PL. EXARHIA

Galaxias

Café 4U

Kaningos

Tzortz

PL. KANINGOS

Glad. stonos

Gamveta

Fridou

Aristotelous

Satovriandou

Agiou Konstantinou

National Theater

Nikiforou

Vilare

Zinonos

Voulgari

Aghia

MoCafe

PL. OMONIA

OMONIA M

OMONIA

Har. Trikoupi

Ippokratous

Asklipiou

Sina

Solonos

Menandrou

Geraniou

Sokratous

Klisthenous

Efpolidos

Kratinou

Likourgou

Aiolou

Santaroza

Panepistimiou

Opera House

Diodou

Massalias

M. Alexandrou

Iassonon

Koinonu

Geteron

Keramikou

Kolokinthous

Agisilaou

P. Tsaldari

Sofokleous

Armodiou

Aristogitonos

KOTZIA

Pesmazoglou

Korai

National Library

Academy of Arts

PANEPISTIMIOU M

Sina

Vissarionos

Akademias-Rouzvelt

Pl. Eleftherias (Koumoundourou)

PL. THEATROU

Pireos

Evripidou

Sarri

Ag. Dimitriou

Ag. Anargiron

Palados

Protogenous

Voreou

Polikliti

Hrissospiliotissas

Aiolou

Athinas

Praxitelous

Romnu

Kapnikareas

Kolokotroni

Periklous

Chroma

Arcade Internet Café

Karageorgi Servias

Georgiou A

SYNDAGMA

Filellinon

Anerikis

Voukourestiou

El. Venizelou

Stadiou

Amalias

National Gardens

Keramikos

TO ELEFSIS (15km)

TO (50m)

Leoktidi

Konstantinoupolis

Ag. Assomati

Synagogue

PSIRI

Ermou

Flea Market

MONASTIRAKI M

MONASTIRAKI

Pandrossou

Mitropoleos

Bits 'n Bytes Internet

Dexipou

Cathedral Metropolis

Adrianou

Apollonos

Rendevous Internet Café

Ermou

Mitropoleos

Othonos

Syndagma

PL. Syndagma

Parliament Building

Xenofontos

Hephaesteion

Apostolou Pavlou

Iraclidhon

Amfiktionos

Agora

Pikilis

Vrisakiou

Roman Agora

Polignotou

Dioskouron

Kinstou

Lissiou

Pritaniou

PLAKA

Flessa

Laundromat

Nikodimou

Voulis

Skoufou

Nikis

Ipendou

Farmaki

Kidathineon

Adrianou

Diogenous

Navarhou Nikodimou

National Gardens

Zappeion

300 yards

300 meters

Acropolis

Temple of Athena Nike

Parthenon

Herod Atticus Odeum

Pnyx Hill

Dion. Areopagitou

Thrasilou

Makrigianni

MAKRIGIANI

ACROPOLIS M

Epimenidi

Lysikratous

Vironos

Temple of Zeus and Hadrian's Arch

Philapappos Hill

KOUKAKI

Rovertou

Gkalli

Kalisperi

Parthenonos

Kariatidon

Mitseon

Propileon

Erehthiou

Garivaldi

Zitrou

Syngrou

ACROPOLIS

TO VOULIAGMENI (11km)

To Sounio

TO PIRAEUS (10km)

TO GLYFADA (10km)

KINOSSARGEU

GREECE

Athens

ACCOMMODATIONS

Athens Backpackers,	**1 B6**
Hostel Aphrodite (HI),	**2 A1**
Hotel Cecil,	**3 B4**
Hotel Orion,	**4 C2**
Pagration Athens Youth Hostel,	**5 F6**
Phaedra Hotel,	**6 A4**
Student & Traveller's Inn,	**7 C5**

FOOD

Chroma,	**8 C4**
Mandras,	**9 A4**
Noodle Bar,	**10 C5**
O Barba Giannis,	**11 C2**

NIGHTLIFE

Bretto's,	**12 B6**
The Daily,	**13 E3**
Wunderbar,	**14 C2**

MUSEUMS

Acropolis Museum,	**15 B5**
Agora Museum,	**16 A5**
Benaki Museum of Islamic Art,	**17 A4**
Byzantine & Christian Museum,	**18 D4**
National Archaeolgical Museum,	**19 C1**
Oberlaender Museum,	**20 A4**
Popular Musical Instruments Museum,	**21 B5**

NEAPOLI

Lycavittos Theater

Lycavittos Hill

Chapel of St. George

St. Andrew's

Lycavittos Funicular

Doras Distria

M AMBELOKIPI

PL. DEXAMENI

KOLONAKI

PL. KOLONAKI

Evangelismos Hospital

EVANGELISMOS M

PL. RIGILIS

Vasilisis Sofias

Vasileos Konstantinou

Alsos Syngrou

Athens Conservatory

TRUMAN SQ.

Royal Palace

PANGRATI

Veropoulos

PL. STADIOU

PL. PLASTIRA

Panathenaic Stadium

Ardittos

TO NATIONAL CEMETERY (150m)

TO RAFINA (20km)

TO LAVRIO (30km)

Ev. Skholas

GREECE

Ag. Antonios to Ag. Dimitrios, the blue **M3** from Doukissis Plakentias to Monastiraki in central Athens. Buy tickets (€0.70) in any station.

Taxis: Companies include **Ikaros** (☎51 52 800); **Ermis** (☎41 15 200); **Kosmos** (☎1300). Base fare €0.85; €0.30 per km, midnight-5am €0.53 per km. €3 surcharge from airport, €0.80 surcharge for trips from bus and railway terminals, plus €0.30 for each piece of luggage over 10kg. Call for pickup (€1.50-2.50 extra).

Car Rental: Agencies on **Syngrou.** €35-50 for car with 100km mileage (includes tax and insurance); €200-350 per week. Prices higher in summer. Up to 50% student discount.

◀▶ ✎ ORIENTATION AND PRACTICAL INFORMATION

Most travelers hang around the **Acropolis** and **Agoras,** while guide-bearing foreigners pack central **Plaka.** Marked by the square and flea market, **Monastiraki** (Little Monastery) is a hectic, exciting neighborhood where packed *tavernas* and Psiri's trendy bars keep pedestrian traffic flowing late into the night. In the heart of Athens, **Syndagma** square is the transportation center. On the opposite side of Stadiou, **Omonia** square bursts with ethnic and ideological diversity. A short walk north on **Emmanuil Benaki** leads to the student-filled neighborhood of **Exarhia,** packed with thrift shops and record stores. The **Larissa** train station is to the northwest of town, while most museums are on **Vas Sofias** to the east. The neighborhood of **Kolonaki** is under Lycavittos Hill. Take the M1 (green) south to its end or bus #040 from Filellinon and Mitropoleos, in Syndagma (4 per hr.) to reach Athens's port city, **Piraeus.** The metro also travels east to several beaches. If you get lost, just look for Syndagma or the Acropolis, Athens's clearest reference points.

Tourist Office: Information Office, Amalias 26 (☎331 0392; www.gnto.gr). Open M-F 10am-6pm, Sa-Su 10am-3pm.

Budget Travel: STA Travel, Voulis 43 (☎21032 11 188). Open M-F 9am-5pm, Sa 10am-2pm. **Consolas Travel,** Aiolou 100 (☎21032 19 228), on the 9th fl. above the post office. Open M and Sa 9am-2pm, Tu-F 9am-5pm.

Bank: National Bank, Karageorgi Servias 2 (☎21033 40 500), in Pl. Syndagma. Open M-Th 8am-2:30pm, F 8am-2pm; open for **currency exchange** M-F 3:30-5pm, Sa 9am-2pm, Su 9am-1pm. Commission about 5%. 24hr. currency exchange at the airport, but commissions there are usually exorbitant.

Emergencies: Poison control ☎779 3777. **AIDS Help Line** ☎722 2222.

Tourist Police: Dimitrakopoulou 77 (☎171). English spoken. Open 24hr.

Pharmacies: Check *Athens News* for a current list of 24hr. pharmacies.

Hospitals: *Athens News* lists emergency hospitals. Free emergency health care for tourists. **Geniko Kratiko Nosokomio (Y. Gennimatas; Public State Hospital),** Mesogion 154 (☎777 8901). **Aeginitio,** Vas. Sofias 72 (☎722 0811) and Vas. Sofias 80 (☎777 0501), are closer to Athens's center. Near Kolonaki is the public hospital **Evangelismos,** Ypsilantou 45-47 (☎720 1000).

Internet Access: Athens has numerous Internet cafes. Expect to pay around €3 per hr. **Bits'n Bytes Internet,** Kapnikareas 19 (☎382 2545; www.bnb.gr), in Plaka. 9am-midnight €5 per hr., midnight-9am €3 per hr. Open 24hr. 2nd location in Exarhia, Akadamias 78 (☎522 7717). **Rendez-Vous Cafe,** Voulis 18 (☎322 3158), in Syndagma. €3 per hr.; min. €1. Open M-F 7:30am-9pm, Sa 7:30am-6pm.

Post Office: Syndagma (☎622 6253), on the corner of Mitropoleos. Open M-F 7:30am-2pm. **Postal Code:** 10300.

♖ ACCOMMODATIONS

Many budget accommodations exist in Athens, but prices generally increase toward the city center at Syndagma Square. The **Greek Youth Hostel Association,**

Damareos 75, in Pangrati, lists cheap hostels throughout Greece (☎751 9530; www.grhotels.com). The **Hellenic Chamber of Hotels,** Stadiou 24, in Syndagma, lists all hotels in Greece, but does not make reservations. Call for info in several languages. The office is on the 7th fl. to the left. (☎323 7193. Open M-F 8am-2pm.)

▨ **Athens Backpackers,** Makri 12 (☎922 4044; www.backpackers.gr), in Plaka. Near the metro and most Athenian sights, this popular place provides cold beer (€2) and a nightly party in summer atop their rooftop bar under the Acropolis. Free luggage storage and Wi-Fi. Laundry €5. 6- or 8-bed dorms €18-25. AmEx/MC/V. ●

▨ **Pagration Athens Youth Hostel,** Damareos 75 (☎751 9530; www.athens-yhostel.com), in Pangrati. From Omonia or Pl. Syndagma, take trolley #2 or 11 to Filolaou. Only the number 75 and a green door—no sign—mark this cheery, family-owned hostel. Large common spaces make up for the 20-25min. walk to the city center. TV lounge and full kitchen. Bring a sleeping bag to stay on the roof (€10). Hot showers €0.50. Linens included. Laundry €7. Quiet hours 2:30-5pm and 11:30pm-7am. Dorms €10-12. Low season reduced rates. Cash only. ●

Hostel Aphrodite (HI), Einardou 12 (☎881 0589; www.hostelaphrodite.com), in Omonia. Welcoming place with clean, basic rooms, and basement bar. Breakfast €4-5. Safe deposit box available. Free luggage storage. Laundry €8. Free Internet. 8-bed dorms €15; doubles €44; triples €57; quads €68. Low season reduced rates. Cash only. ●

Phaedra Hotel, Kodrou 3 (☎324 9737), in Plaka. The amiable family owners keep their 21 plain rooms spic and span. Bonus: the enormous rooftop garden offers a side view of the nearby Acropolis. Singles €50-60; doubles €60-70; triples €75-85. ❸

Hotel Cecil, Athinas 39 (☎321 7079), on the border of Psiri, 4 blocks from the Monastiraki metro. Wood-floored, high-ceilinged rooms with A/C, spotless, private baths, and TV. Roof bar with Acropolis view. Breakfast included. Free luggage storage. Singles €50-70; doubles €79-99; triples €120-140; quads €145. AmEx/MC/V. ❹

Hotel Orion, Em. Benaki 105 (☎330 2387; www.orion-dryades.com), in Exarhia. A 10min. walk up the hill on Em. Benaki. University students intent on experiencing Athens away from the tourist machine fill Orion. Offers fully furnished rooftop lounge, complete with kitchen, TV, and a clear view of the Acropolis. Breakfast €6. Laundry €3. Internet €2 per hr. Singles €25-30; doubles €45-55; triples €60-65. MC/V. ❷

Student's and Traveller's Inn, Kydatheneon 16 (☎324 4808; www.studenttravellersinn.com), in central Plaka. Clean hostel with 24hr. cyber cafe and garden bar (open daily until midnight). Breakfast €4-5.50. Free Wi-Fi. Reception 24hr. The "dungeon" (windowless, downstairs co-ed dorm) €12; co-ed dorms €25-27; doubles €55-65, with bath €60-70; triples €75-85; quads €88-100. V. ❷

◖ FOOD

Athens offers a mix of fast-food stands, open-air cafes, side-street *tavernas,* and intriguing restaurants. On the streets, vendors sell dried fruits and nuts or fresh coconut (€1-2), and you can find *spanakopita* (cheese and spinach pies) at any local bakery (€1.50-2). The area around **Syndagma** serves cheap food. Places in **Plaka** tend to advertise "authentic Greek for tourists." If you really want to eat like a local, head to the simple *tavernas* uphill on **Emmanuil Benaki** in Exarhia.

▨ **O Barba Giannis,** Em. Benaki 94 (☎382 4138), in Exarhia. With tall green doors, "Uncle John's" is informal—just how the Athenian students, CEOs, and artists who consider themselves regulars like it. Entrees €5-10. Open M-Sa noon-1:30am. Cash only. ❸

Chroma, Lekka 8 (☎331 7793), in Syndagma. Dine on leather couches and listen to lounge music in this modern cafe by day and bar by night. Entrees €6-14. Open Su-F 8am-2am, Sa 8am-10pm. Kitchen open Su-F 1pm-midnight, Sa 1pm-10pm. MC/V. ❸

Noodle Bar, Apollonos 11 (☎318 585), in Syndagma. Greek salads please even the feta-phobic. Lighter fare includes mango salad (€5) and Thai chicken coconut soup (€4.10). Open M-Sa 11am-midnight, Su 5:30pm-midnight. ❷

Mandras, Ag. Anargiron 8 (☎321 3765), at Taki. Live, modern Greek music plays for a young, buzzing crowd of locals in this attractive brick building in the heart of Psiri. *Pleurotous* (mushrooms grilled with oil and vinegar; €6.20) makes a great light meal. Spicy grilled chicken €9.20. Open daily 8am-4am. Music 2pm-4am. ❸

👁 SIGHTS

ACROPOLIS

The Acropolis has loomed over the heart of Athens since the 5th century BC. Although each Greek *polis* had an *acropolis* (high point), the buildings atop Athens's peak outshone their imitators and continue to awe visitors. Visit as early in the day as possible to avoid crowds and the broiling midday sun. *(Enter on Dionissiou Areopagitou or Theorias. ☎321 0219. Open daily in summer 8am-7:30pm; in winter 8am-2:30pm. Admission includes access to the Acropolis, the Agora, the Roman Agora, the Olympian Temple of Zeus, and the Theater of Dionysos, within a 48hr. period; purchase tickets at any of the sights. €12, students and EU seniors over 65 €6, under 19 free. Cash only.)*

▧ **PARTHENON.** The **Temple of Athena Parthenos** (Athena the Virgin), commonly known as the Parthenon, watches over Athens. Ancient Athenians saw their city as the capital of civilization; the **metopes** (scenes in the spaces above the columns) on the sides of the temple celebrate Athens's rise. The architect Iktinos integrated the Golden Mean, about a four-to-nine ratio, in every aspect of the temple.

▧ **ACROPOLIS MUSEUM.** Currently under extensive renovations that were supposed to have finished to before the 2004 Olympic games, the museum houses a superb collection of statues, including five of the original **Caryatids** that supported the southern side of the Erechtheion. The carvings of a lion devouring a bull and of a wrestling match between Herakles and a sea monster display the Ancient mastery of anatomical and emotional detail. Notice the empty space where room has been left for the British to return the missing Elgin marbles. *(Open during renovations daily 8am-7:30pm; low season reduced hours. No flash photography. Avoid going 10am-1pm.)*

TEMPLE OF ATHENA NIKE. Currently undergoing renovation, this tiny temple was first raised during the Peace of Nikias (421-415 BC), a respite from the Peloponnesian War. Ringed by eight miniature Ionic columns, it housed a winged statue of Nike, the goddess of victory. Athenians, afraid Nike might abandon them, clipped the statue's wings. The remains of the 5m thick **Cyclopean wall** that once circled the Acropolis now lie below the temple.

ERECHTHEION. Completed in 406 BC, just before Sparta defeated Athens in the Peloponnesian War, the Erechtheion lies to the left of the Parthenon, supported by copies of the famous Caryatids in the museum. The building is named after a snake-bodied hero, whom Poseidon speared during in a dispute over the city's patronage. When Poseidon struck a truce with Athena, he was allowed to share her temple—the eastern half is devoted to the goddess of wisdom and the western part to the god of the sea. The eastern porch contained an olive-wood statue of Athena meant to contrast with the Parthenon's dignified Doric columns.

OTHER SIGHTS

AGORA. The Agora served as Athens's marketplace, administrative center, and focus of daily life from the 6th century BC to the AD 6th century. Many of Athenian democracy's great debates were held here; Socrates, Aristotle, Demosthenes, Xenophon, and St. Paul all lectured in the Agora. The 415 BC **■Hephaesteion**, on a hill in the Agora's northwest corner, is Greece's best-preserved Classical temple, with friezes depicting Theseus's adventures. The **Stoa of Attalos**, an ancient shopping mall, was home to informal philosophers' gatherings. Reconstructed in the 1950s, it now houses the **Agora Museum.** *(Enter the Agora off Pl. Thission, from Adrianou, or as you descend from the Acropolis. ☎321 0185. Agora open daily 8am-7:30pm. Museum open Tu-Su 8am-7:20pm. €4, students and EU seniors €2, under 19 and with Acropolis ticket free.)*

ROMAN AGORA. Built between 19 and 11 BC with donations from Julius and Octavian Caesar, the Roman Agora was once a lively meeting place. The ruined columns of the two surviving *prophylae* (halls), a nearly intact entrance gate, and the **gate of Athena Archgetis** stand as testaments to what was once a lively meeting place. Also nearby are the *vespasianae* (public toilets), constructed in the AD first century, as well as a 1456 mosque. By far the most intriguing structure in the site is the well-preserved (and restored) **Tower of the Winds**, with reliefs of the eight winds on each side of the octagonal clock tower. A weathervane crowned the original stone structure, built in the first century BC by the astronomer Andronikos. Etched onto the walls are markings that allowed it to be used as a sundial from the outside and a water-clock from the inside. *(☎324 5220. Open daily 8am-7pm. €2; students €1; under 19, EU students, and with Acropolis ticket free.)*

TEMPLE OF ZEUS AND HADRIAN'S ARCH. On the edge of the National Gardens in Plaka, you can spot traces of the Temple of Zeus, the largest temple ever built in Greece. Shifts in power delayed the temple's complete until AD 131 under Roman emperor Hadrian, who added an arch to mark the boundary between the ancient city of Theseus and his new city. *(Vas. Olgas at Amalias. ☎922 6330. Open daily 8am-7pm. Temple €2, students €1, under 19 free. Arch free.)*

KERAMIKOS. A large cemetery built around the **Sacred Way**—the road to Eleusis—is Keramikos's primary attraction. A wide boulevard ran from there to the sanctuary of **Akademes,** home of Plato's school. The **Oberlaender Museum** displays funerary stones, pottery, and sculptures. *(Northwest of the Agora. From Syndagma, walk 1km toward Monastiraki on Ermou. ☎346 3552. Open M 11am-7:30pm, Tu-Su 8am-7:30pm. €2; students and EU seniors €1; under 19, EU students, and with Acropolis ticket free.)*

PANATHENAIC STADIUM. Also known as *Kallimarmaro* ("Pretty Marble"), the horseshoe-shaped Panathenaic Stadium is wedged between the National Gardens and Pangrati. The site of the first modern Olympic Games in 1896, the stadium seats over 60,000 and served as the finish line of the marathon and the venue for archery during the 2004 Summer Olympic Games. Be warned that visitors are no longer permitted to walk past the fence running along its open end. *(On Vas. Konstantinou. From Syndagma, walk down Amalias 10min. to Vas. Olgas, then follow it left. Or take trolley #2, 4, or 11 from Syndagma. Free.)*

🏛 MUSEUMS

■ NATIONAL ARCHAEOLOGICAL MUSEUM. Almost every artifact in this collection is a masterpiece. The museum's highlights include the so-called **Mask of Agamemnon,** excavated from the tomb of a king who lived at least three centuries before Agamemnon, as well as a female **Cycladic statue,** the largest, most intact such sculpture to have survived, topping 1.5m. *(Patission 44. Take trolley #2, 4, 5, 9, 11, 15, or 18 from the uphill side of Syndagma, or trolley #3 or 13 from the north side of Vas. Sofias. ☎821 7717. Open Apr.-Oct. Tu-Su 8:30am-3pm; Nov.-Mar. M 10:30am-5pm, Tu-Su 8:30am-3pm. €7, students and EU seniors €3, EU students and under 19 free. No flash photography.)*

■ **BENAKI MUSEUM OF ISLAMIC ART.** Built on the ruins of ancient Athenian fortifications, the building's glass windows, marble staircases, and white walls showcase a collection of brilliant tiles, metalwork, and tapestries documenting the history of the 12th- to 18th-century Islamic world. The exhibit includes an inlaid marble reception room brought from a 17th-century Cairo mansion and pottery with Kufic inscriptions. *(Ag. Asomaton 22, in Psiri. M: Thissou. ☎ 325 1311; www.benaki.gr. Open Tu and Th-Su 9am-3pm, W 9am-9pm. €5, students and seniors €2.50, W free.)*

BYZANTINE AND CHRISTIAN MUSEUM. Within its newly renovated interior, this well-organized museum documents the political, religious, and day-to-day aspects of life during the Byzantine Empire. Its collection of metalware, mosaics, sculpture, and painted icons presents Christianity in its earliest stages. *(Vas. Sofias 22. ☎ 721 1027. Open Tu-Su 8:30am-3pm. €4; students and seniors €2; EU students, under 18, disabled, families with 3 or more children, military, and classicists free.)*

POPULAR MUSICAL INSTRUMENTS MUSEUM. Showcasing instruments from the 18th, 19th, and 20th centuries, this interactive museum is no place for silent contemplation. Audio headsets reproduce the music of the *kementzes* (bottle-shaped lyres) and *tsambouras* (goatskin bagpipes) on display. *(Diogenous 1-2, in Plaka. ☎ 325 0198. Open Tu and Th-Su 10am-2pm, W noon-6pm. Free.)*

🎵 🎭 ENTERTAINMENT AND NIGHTLIFE

The weekly *Athens News* (€1) lists cultural events, as well as news and ferry info. Summertime performances are staged in **Lycavittos Theater** as part of the **Athens Festival** (May-Aug.; www.greekfestival.gr). Chic Athenians head to the seaside clubs in **Glyfada**, enjoying the breezy night air. **Psiri** is the bar district, just across the main square in Monastiraki. Get started on **Miaouli,** where young crowds gather after dark. For an alternative to bar hopping, follow the guitar-playing local teens and couples that pack **Pavlou** at night. This serene promenade around the Acropolis is Athens's most romantic spot after sunset.

■ **Bretto's,** Kydatheneon 41 (☎ 232 2110), between Farmaki and Afroditis in Plaka. Prepare for a delicious sensuous assault when entering this high-ceilinged, century-old wooden distillery. Glass of wine from €3. Cup of *ouzo* €3. Open daily 10am-3am.

The Daily, Xenokratous 47 (☎ 722 3430), under a covered trellis at the foot of Mt. Lycavittos. TVs show sports and locals mingle with the staff at this cozy cafe-bar. Outdoor seating in summer. Pints from €4. Mixed drinks €6-10. Open daily 8am-2am.

Wunderbar, Themistokleous 80 (☎ 381 8577), on Pl. Exarhia, plays pop and electronic music to relaxed martini-sippers. Late-night revelers lounge outside under large umbrellas. Beer €5-6. Mixed drinks €8-9. Open M-Th 9am-3am, F-Su 9am-sunrise.

THE PELOPONNESE Πελοπόννησος

Stretching its fingers into the Mediterranean, the Peloponnese transports its visitors to another time and place. The achievements of ancient civilizations dot the peninsula's landscape, as most of Greece's significant archaeological sites—including Olympia, Mycenae, Messini, Corinth, Mystras, and Epidavros—rest in this former home of King Pelops. Away from urban transportation hubs, serene villages welcome visitors to traditional Greece.

NEW CORINTH Κόρινθος   ☎ 27410

New Corinth (pop. 37,000) is a modern town exploding with automobile and pedestrian traffic, reprising its ancient role as a transportation hub and gateway to the Peleponnese. In ancient times, the port controlled maritime activity on both sides of the nearby isthmus bearing the same name. Today, numerous shops and restaurants bear witness to the large number of people passing through on their way to destinations across Southwestern Greece. Those with a day to spare can take a **bus** to **Ancient Corinth,** where prosperous Greek merchants once mingled with *hetairai,* clever courtesans in the service of Aphrodite. (☎31 207. Open daily 8am-7:30pm. Site map €2.50. Guidebooks €6. Site and museum €6, students €3, EU students and under 18 free. Free Nov. 1-Mar. 31 Su; last weekends of Apr., May, June, and Sept.; major holidays.) Buses leave from outside the bakery on Koliatsou and Kolokotroni (20min., 2 per hr., 6:10am-9:10pm; return buses leave hourly at half past the hr. €1.20). The remains of the dead Roman city stand with the older Greek ruins at the base of the **Acrocorinth Fortress,** against a scenic mountain and ocean backdrop. Take a taxi there from the village of Ancient Corinth and walk to the top for a spellbinding panorama of Corinthia. Make sure you have the taxi wait for you, however, as no return bus exists (taxi round-trip €15).

Recently renovated **Hotel Apollon ❹,** Damaskinou 2, on the corner a block away from the in-town train station, offers small but comfortable rooms with TV and A/C. (☎25 920. Breakfast €7. Internet €1 per hr. Reservations recommended. Singles €35; doubles €45; triples €50. Low season reduced rates.) **Kalamia Beach** provides the best restaurants and nightlife. Walk down Ent. Antistaseos away from the marina until **Notara.** Make a right on Notara and follow it to the end; the beachside establishments will be on your left. Corinth's in-town **train station** (☎22 522) is on Dimokratias, off Damaskinou, and services mainly the Pelopponese's larger towns. **Trains** go to: Diakopto (1¼hr., 5 per day, €3; express 1hr., 2 per day, €5), Kyparissia (5hr., 1 per day, €7; express 4hr., 2 per day, €8), and Pirgos (4½hr., 1 per day, €5; express: 3½hr., 2 per day, €6). Corinth's in-town station offers connector trains to a second train station, off Argous Ave., about 2km away from town (6 per day, free). From there, trains travel to Athens (1hr., 9 per day, €6) and Athens International Airport (1¼hr., 8 per day, €8). **Buses** leave from three different stations, going to Athens (Station A, 1½hr., every 30min., 5am-9pm, €7). The **tourist office** is at Ermou 51. (☎23 282. Open daily 8am-2pm.) **Postal Code:** 20100.

TIP **A FERRY HELPFUL HINT.** If the Greeks can't satiate your thirst for classical antiquity, hop on a Patras ferry bound for one of four Italian cities: Ancona (p. 651), Bari, Brindisi, or Venice (p. 619). Several ferries, all with different prices, make the trip, so check with multiple travel offices lining Othonoas Amalias to find the cheapest fares. **Superfast Ferries,** Oth. Amalias 12 (☎622 500; open daily 9am-9pm), accepts Eurail passes. Questions about departures from Patras should be directed to the Port Authority (☎341 002).

PATRAS Πάτρας ☎2610

Located on the northwestern tip of the Peloponnese, Patras (pop. 350,000) operates as the region's fundamental transportation hub. Charter tourism often skips the city, favoring other nearby islands. During ◼**Carnival** (Jan. 17-Feb. 21; ☎222 157; www.carnivalpatras.gr), however, Patras becomes one gigantic dance floor of costumed, inebriated people consumed by pre-Lenten madness. The biggest European festival of its kind revives ancient celebrations in honor of Dionysus—god of debauchery. Entirely covered in colorful frescoes, **Agios Andreas** is Greece's largest Orthodox cathedral. Follow the waterfront with the town to your left to get there. (Dress modestly. Open daily 7am-9pm.) Sweet black grapes are made into Mavrodaphne wine at the ◼**Achaïa Clauss Winery.** Take bus #7 (30min., €1.20) toward Seravali from the intersection of Kanakari and Gerokostopoulou. (☎368

276. Open daily 11am-3pm. English-language tours 1 per hr. Free.) Built on the ruins of an ancient acropolis and continuously in use from the AD 6th century through WWII, Patras's **fortress** is up the steps from the central Nikolaou. (☎990 691. Open Tu-Su 8:30am-3pm. Free.) Visible from the many pebble beaches, the recently completed **Rio-Antirio Bridge,** the world's longest cable-anchored suspension bridge, connects the Peloponnese to the mainland. Centrally located ■**Pension Nicos ❷,** Patreos 3, sparkles with marble and inlaid stone decor while offering comfortable, pristine rooms at affordable prices. (☎623 757. Reception 3rd fl. Curfew 4am. Singles €20; doubles €30, with bath €35; triples €40/45. MC/V.) Lounge on the deck of **Rooms to Let Spyros Vazouras ❸,** Tofalou 2, where roof-top ocean views complement brightly tiled rooms with A/C and TV. (☎452 152. Singles €30; doubles €40; extra bed €10.) For more Patras accommodations and info, browse www.patrasrooms.gr. Serving large portions, enthusiastic Boston-raised Greeks run the laid-back, cafeteria-style ■**Europa Center ❷,** on Amalias next to the tourist office. (Entrees €5-9. Internet €2 per hr. Open daily 7am-midnight. MC/V.)

Trains (☎639 108) leave from Amalias 47, right across the port, for Athens (4¼hr., 8 per day, €10-13) and Kalamata (5½hr., 4 per day, €5-10) via Pirgos (2hr., €3-6), where you can catch a train to Olympia. KTEL **buses** (☎623 886; www.ktel.org) leave from farther down on Amalias for: Athens (3hr., 2 per hr., €17); Ioannina (4hr., 2 per day, €20); Kalamata (3½hr., 2 per day, €20); Thessaloniki (7½hr., 4 per day, €38). **Ferries** go to Corfu (7hr., M-W and F-Su midnight, €30-33), Vathy on Ithaka (2-3½hr.; Su-F 12:30, 8:30pm, Sat 12:30pm; €15), and Sami on Kephalonia (3hr.; Su-F 12:30, 8:30pm; €15). Six major ferry lines also travel to Italy: Ancona (21hr.); Bari (16hr.); Brindisi (14hr.); Venice (30hr.). The **tourist office** on Amalias is 50m past the bus station. (☎461 740. Open daily 8am-10pm.) **Postal Code:** 26001.

OLYMPIA Ολυμπία   ☎26240

Every four years, ancient city-states would call a sacred truce and travel to Olympia for a pan-Hellenic assembly that showcased athletic ability and fostered peace and diplomacy. Modern Olympia, set among meadows and shaded by cypress and olive trees, is recognized as much for its pristine natural beauty as for its illustrious past. The ancient ■**Olympic Site,** whose central sanctuary was called the **Altis,** draws hordes of tourists. Toward the entrance lie the ruins of the **Temple of Zeus.** Once home to master sculptor Phidias's awe-inspiring Statue of Zeus, one of the Seven Wonders of the Ancient World, the 27m sanctuary was the largest temple completed on the Greek mainland before the Parthenon. The **Temple of Hera,** dating from the 7th century BC, is better preserved than Zeus's Temple; it sits to the left facing the hill, past the temples of Metroön and the Nymphaeum. Today, the **Olympic Flame** lighting ceremony takes place here before the symbol travels around the world to herald the Olympic Games' commencement. (Open June-Sept. daily 8am-7:30pm.) The ■**Archaeological Museum** has an impressive sculpture collection. (Open M 12:30-7:30pm, Tu-Su 8am-7:30pm. Temple and museum each €6, non-EU students €3, EU students free. Both €9/5/free.) Also onsite are the **Museum of the History of the Olympic Games** and the **Museum of the History of Excavations**. (Both museums open M 12:30-7:30pm, Tu-Su 8am-7:30pm. Free.)

The centrally located **Youth Hostel ❶,** Kondili 18, across from the main square, is a cheap place to meet international backpackers and has airy rooms with narrow balconies. (☎22 580. Linens €1. Limited hot showers. Check-out 10am. Lockout 10am-12:30pm. Curfew 10:45pm. Open Feb.-Dec. Dorms €10; doubles €25. Cash only.) Mini-markets, bakeries, and fast food restaurants line **Kondili,** while a walk toward the railroad station or up the hill leads to inexpensive *tavernas*. A filling meal is as Greek as it gets at **Vasilakis Restaurant ❷,** on the corner of Karamanli and Spiliopoulou. Take a right off Kohili before the Youth Hostel walking towards the ruins. (☎22 104. *Souvlaki* pita €1.50. Chicken and fries €10. Open daily 11:30am-midnight.) **Trains** leave the station in the lower part of town for Pirgos (25min., 5 per day, €0.70), as do **buses** (45min., 15 per day, €1.90). The Town Hall **info center**, at the right end of Kondili, before the turn to the sights, serves as a tourist office. (☎22 549; aolympia@otenet.gr. Open M-F 8am-3pm.) **Postal Code:** 27065.

SPARTA Σπάρτη ☎27310

Though the Spartans of antiquity purportedly threw babies off cliffs, they left little of their fierce legacy behind. Modern Spartans, no longer producing Greek hoplites, make olive oil. Barely worth exploring, a couple of stones and a grove of olive trees comprise the meager ruins at **Ancient Sparta,** a 1km walk north along Paleologou from the town center. Two blocks from the central *plateia* lies the city's **Archaeological Museum.** Opening into a garden of orange trees and headless statues, the museum displays votive masks, intricate mosaics, and lead figures resembling a toy army in addition to Grecian vases. (☎28 575. Open Tu-Su 8am-7:30pm. €2, students €1, EU students free.) Accommodations in Sparta rarely come cheap and few attractions exist to assuage an empty wallet. **Hotel Cecil ❸,** Paleologou 125, on the corner of Thermopylon, has ordinary, spotless rooms with A/C, bath, phone, and TV in a recently renovated building. (☎24 980. Reserve ahead. Singles €25-35; doubles €45-55; triples €55-65.) **Diethnes ❷,** on Paleologou, a few blocks to the right of the main intersection with Lykergous facing the *plateia*, serves tasty Greek food in an intimate garden with orange trees, turtles, and cats. Though it has a few vegetarian options (€5), the restaurant specializes in €7 lamb entrees. (☎28 636. Open 8am-midnight.) **Buses** from Sparta go to Athens (3½hr., 10 per day, €17) via Tripoli (1hr., €5), Corinth (2½hr., €12), and Monemvasia (2hr., 4 per day, €9). To reach the town center from the bus station, walk 10 blocks uphill on Lykourgou; the **tourist office** is on the third floor of the glass building in the *plateia*. (☎26 771. Open M-F 8am-2pm.) **Postal Code:** 23100.

▶ **DAYTRIP FROM SPARTA: MYSTRAS** ΜΥΣΤΡΆς. Once Byzantium's religious center and the locus of Constantinople's rule over the Peloponnese, Mystras, 6km from Sparta, is a well-preserved medieval town. The **Agia Sophia** church, where the city's royalty lies buried, and the **Agios Theodoros fresco** contribute to Mystras's timelessness. Don't miss the **Palace,** with its pointed arches and stone walls telling the region's history. Modest dress is required to visit the functioning **convent** and its beautifully decorated **Pantanassa Church.** (☎83 377. *Open daily Aug.-Sept. 8am-7:30pm; Oct.-*

BELOVED BACKGAMMON

Walk down a Greek side street or past a cafe, and chances are you'll see people playing backgammon. Among the younger generation, it's usually a solitary activity, but with elderly men the game invokes good-natured ribbing and tense competition.

Although quite similar to its American cousin, Greece's unofficial national board game has a few differences. The patterned board is called the *tavli* and three variations of the game are played, often in succession: *portes, plakoto,* and *fevga.* Many Greeks learn all three games as children. Most like western backgammon, *portes* means "door" in Greek and represents a slight variation from American rules. Two checkers placed side-by-side form a "door" or wall that stops opposing markers from being played there. *Plakoto*—perhaps the original Greek variation—derives from the verb *plakono* (to stack). In this version, opponents can place checkers on top of other markers. Finally, in *fevga* (to run), players race to their home quarters.

One of the reasons for the game's popularity is that it has been played in Greece for thousands of years. Archaeological evidence of old *tavli* suggests ancient Greeks played backgammon, potentially learning it from Mesopotamian Persians. It is no wonder, then, that the game is a beloved pastime.

July 8:30am-3pm. €5, students €3, EU students free.) **Buses** to Mystras leave from the station and from the corner of Lykourgou and Leonidou in Sparta for the ruins, returning 15min. later (20min., 4-9 per day, €2). **Taxis** go to Mystras from the corner of Paleologou and Lykourgou (€5).

▲MONEMVASIA Μονεμβασία   ☎27320

On a monolithic rock that seems to spring from the sea, the island of Monemvasia is a Grecian treasure. No cars or bikes are allowed within the Old Town's walls, so wandering around the flowered balconies and picturesque corners gives the feeling that time stopped in the Middle Ages. On the top of the rock, uphill from the *plateia* is **Agia Sofia**, a 12th-century basilica. From Agia Sofia, paths continue uphill toward the old **citadel**, whose ruins are visible from the New Town. In the *plateia*, along the shop-lined main street, is the **Archaeological Museum.** (Open M noon-7:30pm, Tu-Su 8am-5pm. Free.) To get to the Old Town, cross the bridge from New Monemvasia and follow the road as it curves up the hill. It's an easy 20min. walk, but the heat and crowd both increase as the day wears on. It's better to go in the early morning or late evening, when the setting sun gives the panorama breathtaking shades. A bus also shuttles people up and down the road and leaves from the bridge at the foot of the hill (2min., 4 per hr. 8am-midnight, €1).

Waterfront *domatia* along the New Town harbor are a budget traveler's best option. The rock walls and elegant interior of ■**Hotel Belissis ❸**, with beautiful rooms, A/C, fridge, private bath, and TV, feel like they belong in the Old Town. From the bus station, walk along the main road, Spartis, away from the bridge for less than 5min. It's on the left, across the street from the ocean. (☎61 217. Singles and doubles €30-50; 4-person 2-fl. apartment with kitchenette and two baths €60-80. Cash only.) With a unique ambience, dining in the Old Town is beautiful but expensive. On the main road to the right, just before the Archaeological Museum, is **Restaurant Matoula ❸**, which offers terrace seating and unobstructed views of the waters below. (☎61 660. Entrees €8-14. *Moussaka* €8. Open daily noon-midnight. MC/V.) For those on a tight budget, there are many cheap Greek fast-food eateries and bakeries. Backpackers often picnic on the beach in New Town, soaking up the same beautiful views for free. **Buses** leave from Spartis for Athens (1 per day, €26) and Sparta (2hr., €8.70). **Postal Code:** 23070.

NAFPLION Ναύπλιο   ☎27520

A tiny Venetian town surrounded on three sides by sky-blue waters, Nafplion is one of the Peloponnese's most beautiful—and most popular—tourist destinations. In July and August, the town plays host to more Americans and Italians than locals. After passing from the Venetians to Ottomans, Nafplion became Greece's first capital in 1821. The town's jewel is the 18th-century ■**Palamidi fortress,** with spectacular views of the town and gulf. Walk up the 999 steps from across the central plateia, right across from the bus station or take a taxi up the 3km road. (Open 8am-7pm. €4, students €2, EU students and under 18 free.) A small, pebbly beach, **Arvanitia,** is farther along Polizoidhou, past the Palamidi steps; if it's too crowded, follow the footpath to private coves, or take a taxi (€5) to sandy **Karathona** beach.

To reach **Bouboulinas,** the waterfront promenade, go left from the bus station and follow Syngrou to the harbor; the **Old Town** is on your left. If you are coming from Arvanitia, you can also walk the short **path** around the promontory, keeping the sea to your left and the town's walls to your right. Old Town accommodations are often expensive, but ■**Dimitris Bekas's Domatia ❷** is a great budget option. This small pension offers cozy rooms and a roof deck. The friendly manager steadfastly refuses to raise his prices during high season. From the bus station, walk right on Fotomara until you reach the small Catholic church, then turn right on

Zygomala, and left up the first set of stairs. (☎24 256. Reserve ahead July-Aug. Singles €22; doubles €28, with bath €30.) Considering its central location, ▓Ellas ❷, in Pl. Syndagm, has inexpensive Greek and Italian food. The cheerful staff serves people-watching patrons on the outdoor *plateia*. (☎27 278. Entrees €5-7. Open daily noon-4pm and 7-11pm. MC/V.) **Buses** (☎27 323) leave from Syngrou to: Athens (3hr., 1 per hr., €11.30); Epidavros (40min., 5 per day, €2.50); and Mycenae (45min., 3 per day, €2.50). The **tourist office** is at 25 Martiou, across from the bus station. (☎24 444. Open daily 9am-1pm and 4-8pm.) **Postal Code:** 21100.

▓ DAYTRIPS FROM NAFPLION

EPIDAVROS (Επίδαυρος). Like Olympia and Delphi, **Epidavros** was once both a town and a sanctuary—first to the ancient deity Maleatas and then to Apollo. Eventually, the energies of the sanctuary were directed toward the demigod Asclepius, the son of Apollo who caught Zeus's wrath (and even worse, his fatal thunderbolt) when the good doctor began to raise people from the dead. Under the patronage of **Asclepius,** Epidavros became famous across the ancient world as a center of medicine. Today, visitors can explore the **sanctuary,** which is undergoing heavy restoration, and visit an overcrowded and non-air-conditioned **museum** of ancient medical equipment and other artifacts. *(☎22 009. Sanctuary open daily June-Sept. 8am-7pm; Oct.-May 8am-5pm. Museum open June-Sept. M noon-7pm, Tu-Su 8am-7pm; Oct.-May M noon-5pm, Tu-Su 8am-5pm. Both open during festival F-Sa 8am-8pm. €6, students €3, EU students and under 19 free.)* The best-known structure at the site, however, is the splendidly preserved ▓**theater,** built in AD 2 and renowned for its extraordinary acoustics. When the theater is silent, you can hear a piece of paper being ripped on stage from any seat in the house, but the place is usually too packed to test it out. Fortunately for today's visitors, Greece's most famous ancient theater has come alive again after centuries of silence: during July and August it hosts the ▓**Epidavros Theater Festival,** with performances by international artists and modern interpretations of classical plays. The season program is available at the site as well as at the tourist info center in Athens (☎210 3272 000; performances begin at 9pm, tickets at the site's box office; www.hellenicfestival.gr; €10-100), the Athens Festival Box Office (☎210 3221 459), or Nafplion's bus station. KTEL **buses** go to Nafplion (4 per day, €4) and make a special trip on performance nights (7:30pm, €4), returning spectators to Nafplion 20min. after the performance ends. Buses also go to Athens (2hr., 2 per day, €7). The tourist office is near the theater. *(☎22 026. Open June-Aug. M-Th 9am-7pm, F-Su 9am-10pm.)*

MYCENAE (Μυκήνες). The center of the Greek world from 1600 to 1100 BC, **Mycenae** was ruled by the legendary Agamemnon, leader of the Greek forces in the Trojan War. Excavations of ancient Mycenae have continued since 1876, turning the spectacular hillside ruins into one of Greece's most visited sites. The imposing **Lion's Gate** into the ancient city has two lions carved in relief above the lintel and is estimated to weigh 20 tons. On top, a line of stones marks the perimeter of what used to be one of the ancient world's most illustrious palaces. At the far end of the city, between the palace and the **postern gate,** is the **underground cistern,** which guaranteed water during sieges and is still open for exploration; watch your step and bring a flashlight. Across from the entrance, a **museum** details the history of the town and its excavations. Mycenae's most famous *tholos* (a beehive-shaped tomb built into the side of a hill) is the **Tomb of Agamemnon** (a.k.a. the Treasury of Atreus), 400m downhill toward the town. *(Open daily June-Oct. 8am-7:30pm; Nov.-May 8am-3pm. €8, students €4, EU students and children free. Keep your ticket for the museum and tholos or pay twice.)* From Mycenae, **buses** go to Nafplion (45min., 3 per day, €2.30) via Argos (30min., €2). For connections to Athens and Corinth, walk 3km downhill to nearby Fihtio.

NORTHERN AND CENTRAL GREECE

Northern and central Greece offer an escape from tourist packed Athens, with fantastic hiking and Byzantine and Hellenistic heritage. Scattered across the region, traditional villages host diverse attractions: the depths of the Vikos Gorge, the heights of Mount Olympus, and the serenity of Meteora. Greece's heartland boasts some of the country's great cities, including Thessaloniki and Ioannina. Connected to its Balkan neighbors, the north is where multicultural Greece emerges.

THESSALONIKI Θεσσαλονίκη ☎ 2310

Thessaloniki (a.k.a. Salonica; pop. 1,083,000), the Balkans' trade center, has historically been one of the most diverse cities in Greece, and second in size only to Athens. The city is an energetic bazaar of cheap clothing shops and fashionable cafes, while its churches and mosques provide a material timeline of the region's restless past. Thessaloniki's current lack of tourism infrastructure and subway construction through 2012 may frustrate some travelers.

▐ TRANSPORTATION

Flights: Macedonia Airport (SKG; ☎ 985 000), 16km east of town. Take bus #78 from the KTEL station on Pl. Aristotelous (€0.60, 2 per hr.) or taxi (€15). **Olympic Airways,** Kountouriotou 3 (☎ 368 311; www.olympicairlines.com; open M-F 8am-4pm) and **Aegean Airlines,** 1 Nikis, off Venizelou, (☎ 239 225; www.aegeanair.com; open M-F 8am-3pm, Sa 8am-2pm) fly to: **Athens** (1hr., 24 per day, €80); **Corfu** (1hr., 5 per week, €65); **Hania** (1½hr., 4 per week, €130); **Ioannina** (35min., 4 per week, €55); **Iraklion** (1½hr., 1 per day, €115); **Lesvos** (1½hr., 1 per day, €93); **Rhodes** (2hr., 7 per week, €129).

Trains: To reach the **main terminal** (☎ 517 517), Monastiriou 28, in the western part of the city, take any bus down Egnatia (€0.60). Trains go to: **Athens** (7hr., 3 per day, €10; express 5hr., 4 per day, €25); **İstanbul, TUR** (14hr., 1 per day, €14); **Sofia, BUL** (7hr., 1 per day, €50); **Skopje, MAC** (4hr., 2 per day, €11). The **Travel Office** (☎ 11 10) has schedules.

Buses: Most **KTEL** buses leave from the central, dome-shaped **Macedonia Bus Station** 3km west of the city center (☎ 595 408). Bus #1 shuttles between the train and bus stations (6 per hr., €0.50). Bus #78 connects the bus station to the airport, passing through the waterfront corridor (2 per hr., €0.60). To: **Athens** (6hr., 8 per day, €24); **Corinth** (7½hr., 1 per day, €37); **Ioannina** (6½hr., 6 per day, €28); **Patras** (7½hr., 4 per day, €33). Schedules are subject to change.

Ferries: Buy tickets at **Karacharisis Travel and Shipping Agency,** Kountouriotou 8 (☎ 513 005). Open M-F 8:30am-8:30pm, Sa 8:30am-2:30pm. Ferries leave once per week for: **Iraklion** (21-24hr., €38) via **Skiathos** (5½hr., €19); **Mykonos** (13½hr., €42); **Mytilini** (14 hr., €35); **Naxos** (14hr., €39) via **Syros** (12hr., €38); **Santorini** (17-18hr., €41).

Local Transportation: Local buses run often throughout the city. Buy tickets at *periptera* (newsstands; €0.50) or on board (€0.60). **Taxis** (☎ 551 525) run down Egnatia, Mitropoleos, and Tsimiski with stands at Ag. Sophia and the intersection of Mitropoleos and Aristotelous. Rides should not exceed €4, though phone orders cost an extra €1.50.

◀ ▐ ORIENTATION AND PRACTICAL INFORMATION

Thessaloniki stretches along the Thermaic Gulf's northern shore from the iconic **White Tower** in the east to the prominent western **harbor.** Its rough grid layout makes it nearly impossible to get lost. Its most important arteries run parallel to the water. Closest to shore is **Nikis,** which goes from the harbor to the White Tower and is home to the city's main cafes. Farthest from shore is **Egnatia,** the city's busiest thoroughfare, a six-lane avenue; the Arch of Galerius stands at its intersection

Thessaloniki

▲ ACCOMMODATIONS
Hotel Atlantis, 9
Hotel Augustos, 8
Hotel Olympic, 7

♦ FOOD
Chatzi, 2
Delicatessen, 3
Healthy Advice, 1
Ouzeri Melathron, 6

■ NIGHTLIFE
Rodon, 4
Shark, 5

INTERNATIONAL
FAIRGROUNDS

MESSEGELANDE

Thermaic Gulf

300 yards

300 meters

0

0

GREECE

INTERNATIONAL FAIRGROUNDS / MESSEGELANDE

Archaeological
Museum

Ellinis
Cinema

Garden
Theater

Vassiliko

Kritiko Theater

White
Tower

Rotunda

Arch of
Galerius

Ag.
Panteleimon

Octaon
Building

Palace

Ag. Ioannis
Prodromos

Pilgrim's
Bureau

Museum of the
Macedonian
Struggle

Alpha
Odeon

OTE
Office

Panagia
Acheiropoietos

Hamam
bey

Yahudi
Hamami

Alaca
Imaret

Ag.
Nikolaos

Roman
Agora

Public
Market

Aegean
Airlines

City Bus Terminals

Jewish
Museum

Panagia
Chalkeon

Bey
Hamam

Bedesten

Musical
Instruments
Museum

LADADIKA

Ag.
Dimitriou

Profitis
Ilia

Monasteriote
Synagogue

Ag. Aikaterini

Karachrisis Travel
and Shipping Agency

Ag. Apostoloi

PL. DIMOKRATIAS
(VARDARI)

26 Oktovriou

Train
Station

TO PELLA
(38km)

TO DOME
(3 km), ANCIENT
VERGINA (30km)

with D. Gounari. Farther inland from Egnatia are **Agios Dimitriou** and the **Old Town.** The city's center, Aristotelous has numerous banks, businesses, and restaurants.

Tourist Offices: EOT, at the airport (www.eot.gr). Open daily 9am-9pm.

Banks: Banks with currency exchange and 24hr. **ATMs** line Tsimiski, including **Citibank,** Tsimiski 21 (☎373 300). Open M-Th 8am-2:30pm, F 8am-2pm.

Tourist Police: Dodekanissou 4, 5th fl. (☎554 871). Open daily 7:30am-10pm. For the **local police,** call ☎553 800. Police booths also at the train station.

Hospital: Acepa Hospital, Kiriakidi 1 (☎993 111). **Hippokratio Public Hospital,** Costantinos Polius 49 (☎892 000). On weekends and at night call ☎1434.

Internet Access: Behind the shopping complex housing the American Consulate, **E-Global,** Vas. Irakliou 40 (☎252 780; www.e-global.gr), is 1 block to the right. €2.20 per hr.; min. €1. Open 24hr. Another location at Egnatia 17 (☎968 404), 1 block east of the Arch of Galerius. **Meganet,** Pl. Navarinou 5 (☎2 50 331; www.meganet.gr), in the square by the ruins of Galerius's palace. Noon-midnight €2 per hr., midnight-noon €1 per hr. Open 24hr.

Post Office: Aristotelous 26, just below Egnatia. Open M-F 7:30am-8pm, Sa 7:30am-2pm, Su 9am-1:30pm. Send parcels at the branch on Eth. Aminis near the White Tower (☎227 604). Open M-F 7am-8pm. Both offer *Poste Restante.* **Postal Code:** 54101.

ACCOMMODATIONS

Budget options are available, but be prepared to get what you pay for. Thessaloniki's less expensive, slightly run-down hotels are along the western end of **Egnatia** between **Plateia Dimokratias** (500m east of the train station) and **Aristotelous.** Most face the chaotic road on one side and squalid back streets on the other. Hotels fill up quickly during Thessaloniki's high season, April through September.

Hotel Olympic, Egnatia 25 (☎566 870; fax 555 353). Simple, newly renovated rooms have A/C, bath, refrigerator, and TV. English-speaking staff eager to offer advice about Thessaloniki. Breakfast €5. Reception 24hr. Singles €40, doubles €50. €10 discount with *Let's Go* book Oct.-Aug. AmEx/MC/V. ❸

Hotel Augustos, El. Svoronou 4 (☎522 955; www.augustos.gr). Better kept than most in the same price range. Comfortable rooms with frescoed ceilings and wooden floors. Singles €20, with bath and A/C €30; doubles €25/38; triples €50. Cash only. ❷

Hotel Atlantis, Egnatia 14 (☎540 131; atlalej@otenet.gr). English-speaking management offers rooms with sinks and tiny balconies. Some newly renovated rooms with A/C. Singles €20, with bath €25; doubles €25/40; triples €30/45. Cash only. ❷

FOOD

The old city overflows with *tavernas* and restaurants providing sweeping views of the gulf, while in and around the lovely **Bit Bazaar,** you will find characteristic *ouzeries.* Thessaloniki's restaurants have a delightful custom of giving patrons free watermelon or sweets after a meal, but if you crave anything from dried fruits to apple-sized cherries, head to the bustling public **market,** right off Aristotelous.

Ouzeri Melathron, Karypi 21-34 (☎275 016; www.ouzoumelathron.gr). Student favorite for its great prices and pub atmosphere. Long, wittily subtitled menu features chicken, snails, lamb, octopus, and cheese tapas. Entrees €4-14. Free round of drinks with ISIC. Open M-F 1:30pm-1:30am, Sa-Su 1:30pm-2am. D/MC/V. ❷

Healthy Advice, Alex Svolou 54 (☎283 255). This Canadian-run joint serves fresh, Western-style sandwiches (€4-6). Salami straight from Italy, lean turkey and ham, and daily baked bread. English-, French-, and Arabic-speaking staff. Open daily 11:30am-2am. ❷

Delicatessen, Kouskoura 7 (☎236 367). Hands down most popular among locals for *souvlaki* (€2). Waitstaff speaks little English. Open daily 11:30am-3am. ❶

Chatzi, El. Venizelou 50 (☎279 058; www.chatzis.gr), now with 4 stores in town, has been acting as the city's Willy Wonka since 1908. For a less intense delight than their pure sugar and honey Greek sweets, try a one of their yogurts. The *kourkoumpinia* and *bak-lava* are orgasmic (€1.20 per 100g). Open Su-F 7am-3am, Sa 7am-4am. MC/V. ❶

🅖 SIGHTS

Reminders of Thessaloniki's Byzantine and Ottoman might pervade its streets. The **Roman Agora,** a 2nd-century odeon and covered market, still rests at the top of Aristo-telous. Its lower square once held eight *caryatids*, sculptures of women believed to have been magically petrified. (Open daily 8am-8pm. Free) Originally a temple honor-ing Jupiter, the **Rotunda** (now **Agios Georgios**) was erected by the Roman Caesar Gale-rius at the end of the AD 3rd century. It later became a church honoring martyred Christians, then a mosque under the Ottomans. (☎968 860. Open Tu-F 8am-7pm, Sa-Su 8:30am-3pm. Free.) At D. Gounari and Egnatia stands the striking ▓**Arch of Gale-rius,** known locally as just *Kamara* (Arch). Erected by Galerius to commemorate his victory over the Persians, it now serves as the main meeting spot for locals. Two blocks south of the arch in Pl. Navarino, a small section of the once 150 sq. km **Palace of Galerius** is open for viewing. The weathered mosaic floors and octagonal hall, believed to have housed Galerius's throne, are particularly nota-ble. The ▓**Archaeological Museum** features some of the area's most prized artifacts, including the Derveni krater and sculptures of Greek goddesses. (☎830 538. Open in summer M 1-7:30pm, Tu-Su 8am-7pm; winter reduced hours. €6, students and seniors €3, EU students and children free.) Its gruesome executions earned the **White Tower** the nickname "Bloody Tower," all that remains of a 15th-century Ottoman seawall. A walk to the top of Thessaloniki's most prominent landmark no longer means inevitable death, instead offering a marvelous view of the city and its shoreline. (Bus #3, 5, 6, 33, or 39. ☎267 832. Open Tu-Su 8:30am-3pm. €2, students free.)

🅢 NIGHTLIFE

Thessaloniki is a city that lives outside, with citizens patrolling its bars, board-walks, and cafes. The **Ladadika** district, a two-by-three-block rectangle of *tavernas* behind the port, was the city's red-light strip until the 80s, but has since trans-formed into a sea of dance clubs. The heart of the city's social life during the win-ter, it shuts down almost entirely in summer, when everyone moves to the open-air discos around the airport. **Rodon,** east of the city along the main highway about 200m after the turn to the airport, and **Shark,** Themistokli Sofouli and Argonavton 2, are the city's most expensive clubs. (Rodon ☎476 720. Cover €10; includes 1 drink. Open 11pm-7:30am. Shark ☎416 855. Mixed drinks €10. Open 9pm-4am.) As Thessaloniki's popular clubs change frequently, ask the locals for an update. The waterfront cafes and the **Aristotelous promenade** are always packed, as is the stu-dent-territory Bit Bazaar, a cobblestoned square of *ouzeries* and wine and tapas bars. For a unique experience, drink and dance to music on one of the three ▓**pirate boats** that leave from behind the White Tower for 30min. harbor tours.

🅓 DAYTRIP FROM THESSALONIKI: ANCIENT VERGINA

The tombs of Vergina (Βέργινα), final resting places of ancient Macedonian royalty, lie only 30km from Thessaloniki. Its principal sight, the ▓ **Great Tumulus,** is a manmade mound 12m tall and 110m wide. Visitors enter the dimly-lit "Cave of Wonders" to see its ornate burial treasures, brilliant frescoes, and the tombs of royalty in their original 4th-century BC placement. The tombs' unparalleled splendor has convinced archaeologists that they hold the bones of **Philip II** and **Alexander IV,** respectively the murdered father and son of **Alexander the Great.** The museum's atmosphere will send shivers down your spine. *(Open in summer M noon-7:30pm, Tu-Su 8am-7:30pm; in winter Tu-Su 8:30am-3pm. €8, non-EU students €4, EU students free.)* **Buses** run from Thessaloniki to Vergina's *platela* (25-30min., 1 per hr., €1.30) via Veria (1hr., 1 per hr., €6.10); follow the signs to reach the tombs.

MOUNT OLYMPUS Ολύμπος Όρος   ☎23520

Erupting out of the Thermaic Gulf, the formidable slopes of Mt. Olympus, Greece's highest peak, mesmerized the ancient Greeks, who believed it to be their pantheon's divine dwelling place. Today, a network of well-maintained **hiking** trails makes the summit accessible to anyone with sturdy legs. Mt. Olympus has eight peaks: Ag. Andonios (2817m), Kalogeros (2701m), Mytikas (2918m), Profitis Ilias (2803m), Skala (2866m), Skolio (2911m), Stefani (the Throne of Zeus; 2907m), and Toumba (2801m). The region became Greece's first national park in 1938. All means for challenging Olympus originate from **Litochoro Town** (pop. 6000, 500m). The easiest and most popular trail begins at **Prionia** (1100m), 18km from the village, and ascends 4km through a sheltered, forested ravine to ◙**Zolotas** refuge, also known as Refuge A or—to the Greeks—as Spilios Agapitos. At the Zolotas refuge, you'll find reliable resources for all aspects of hiking: updates on weather and trail conditions, advice on routes, and reservations for any of the **Greek Alpine Club (EOS)** refuges. With years of experience, the staff is happy to dispense info over the phone in English. (☎81 800. Curfew 10pm. Open mid-May to Oct. Camping €5; dorms €10.) After spending the night at Zolotas, you can ascend Olympus's summit the next day. Regrouping hikers may also stay the night in a mountaintop refuge, walking down to Diastavrosi (3-4hr.) the following morning. All trails are easy to follow, and most are marked with red and yellow blazes. Unless you're handy with crampons and an ice axe, make your ascent between May and October. Mytikas, the tallest peak, is accessible only with special equipment before June.

Relaxed Litochoro Town, at the foot of Olympus, is only a 5min. bus ride from the sea. On the last Sunday in June, the **Olympus Marathon** (June 29, 2008; www.olympus-marathon.com) gathers athletes and fans for a 44km run with the gods. To rest up before your big hike or race, head to **Hotel Park ❷,** Ag. Nikolaou 23, at the bottom of the hill after the park, which has large rooms with A/C, bath, fridge, phone, TV, and a few balconies. (☎81 252; hotelpark_litochoro@yahoo.gr. Breakfast €5. Reception 24hr. Singles €25; doubles €35; triples €45. Cash only.) For a meal with a view, try ◙**Gastrodromio En Olympo ❸,** off the *plateia* by the church. (☎21 300; www.gastrodomio.gr. Entrees €8-14. Open daily 10am-midnight. MC/V.) Those wisely seeking water and trail snacks for the arduous hike up Olympus should stay away from the expensive supermarkets above the *plateia* and head to **Arvanitides,** Perikliko Torba 14, at the end of Odos Ermi. (☎23520 21 195. Open 8am-9pm.) KTEL **buses** (☎81 271) leave from the Litochoro station, Ag. Nikolaou 20, opposite the tourist office, for Athens (5hr., 3 per day, €28), Plaka (15min., 1 per hr., €2), and Thessaloniki (1½hr., 16 per day, €8) via Katerini (30min., 1 per hr. €2). The **tourist office** is on Ag. Nikolaou by the park. (☎83 100. Open daily 7:30am-2:30pm.) **Postal Code:** 60200.

IOANNINA Ιωάννινα   ☎26510

The capital of Epirus, Ioannina (pop. 170,000) serves as the natural transportation hub for northern Greece. The city reached its height of fame after its 1788 capture by **Ali Pasha,** an Albanian-born visionary leader and womanizer. Legend has it that when Ali Pasha wasn't able to get the girl he wanted, he strangled all of his other lovers and threw their bodies into Ioannina's lake. The city is also the site of the **Frourio,** a monumental fortress built in the 14th century, where many of the city's residents live today. To reach the **Itş Kale** (inner citadel) from the Frourio's main entrance, veer left, and follow the signs. To the right along the wall are the remnants of Ali Pasha's **hamam** (baths). Catch a ferry from the waterfront (10min., 2 per hr. 7am-midnight, €2) for **Nisi** (the Island) to explore Byzantine monasteries and the **Ali Pasha Museum** (open daily 9am-9pm; €2). **Hotel Tourist ❸,** Kolleti 18, on the right a few blocks up G. Averof from the *kastro*, offers simple rooms with A/C, bath, and phone. (☎25 070. Singles €30; doubles €45; triples €70.) Portions are huge and prices reasonable at lakeside **Limni ❷.** (☎78 988. Entrees €5-8.) **Buses,** Zossimadon 4, depart from the main terminal to: Athens (6hr., 7 per day, €34); Kalambaka (2hr., 2 per day, €11); Thessaloniki (5hr., 4 per day, €27). For info, call ☎26 286. To reach the **tourist office,** walk down Dodonis; the office is immediately after the school. (☎46 662. Open M-F 7:30am-7:30pm.) **Postal Code:** 45110.

ZAGOROHORIA Ζαγοροχώρια ☎26530

Between the Albanian border and the North Pindos mountain range, a string of 46 *horia* (little hamlets) show few signs of interference from modern society. Home to **Vikos Gorge**—the world's deepest canyon—and **Vikos-Aoös National Park,** the region provides nature enthusiasts with plenty of hiking opportunities. Any trip should include a visit to the Zagori Information Center in the town of **Aspraggeli.** (☎22 241. Open daily 9am-6pm.) North of Vikos Gorge, the two **Papingo** villages, **Megalo** (Μεγάλο; large) and **Mikro** (Μικρό; small), have become vacation destinations for wealthy Greeks and serve as the starting point for some beautiful hikes.

◧ TRANSPORTATION. Buses go to Ioannina from the Papingos (1½hr., 2 per week, €5). Papingo visitors may consider hiking 3hr. to **Klidonia** to catch more frequent buses (1hr., 8 per day, €4). **Taxis** can take you to Ioannina or Konitsa (€35). The closest banks are in Kalpaki and Konitsa.

⚠ VIKOS GORGE Φοράγγι Βίκου. Vikos Gorge, whose walls are 900m deep and only 110m apart, is the steepest on earth. In spring, the gorge's river rushes along the 15km stretch of canyon floor. By summer, all that is left is the occasional puddle in the dry riverbed. People have walked through the gorge's ravine since the 12th century BC, when early settlers took shelter in its caves. Today, hikers follow the well-marked **O3 domestic trail** (red diamonds on white square backgrounds) section of the Greek National E4 route through the gorge. The path stretches from the village of Kipi in the south to Megalo Papingo at its northernmost tip, winding through Zagorohoria's center. The gorge can be accessed from Kipi, Monodendri, the Papngo villages, and Vikos Village.

⛺ HIKING AROUND THE PAPINGOS (Τα Πάπινγκα). An increase in tourism has raised Papingos's lodging prices. If **pensions** and **domatia** are full or high-season prices outrageous, backpackers may hike 3km to the **EOS Refuge ❶,** near Mt. Astraka. (☎26 553. 60-bed dorm €10.) Freelance camping is illegal. **◪Pension Koulis ❸,** has rooms reminiscent of an alpine ski lodge. Facing the town from where the cobblestoned road starts, take the first left after the church. The pension is on the corner of the next crossroads to the left. (☎41 115. Breakfast included. Reception 24hr. Singles €35; doubles €50; triples €65. MC/V.) In Mikro Papingo, take the left fork off the main road to find **Hotel Dias ❸,** whose rooms will make you forget you're on a budget. (☎41 257. Breakfast included. Reception 8am-11pm. Singles €35; doubles €60; triples €75; quads €90.) At **Tsoumanis Estiatorio ❷,** outside town on the road to Mikro Papingo, two brothers serve lamb from their father's flock and vegetables from their gardens. (☎42 108. Entrees €5-9. Open daily 11am-1am.)

Zagorohoria's most spectacular hikes begin in **Mikro Papingo**, from where visitors can climb **Mount Astraka** (2436m). Most ascents take about 4hr. and are appropriate for intermediate-level hikers. More advanced hikers climb 4½hr. to the pristine ◪**Drakolimni** (Dragon Lake; 2000m), an alpine pool filled with spotted newts. Both hikes can be paired with a stay in the **EOS Refuge** (1900m), on a nearby ridge. From the refuge, a path (3km, 1¼hr.) descends into the blossom-dotted valley, passes **Xeroloutsa**, a shallow alpine lake, and ends at Drakolimni. Multi-day treks deep into the Pindos are possible, using the EOS hut as a starting point. For easier hikes, the family-friendly **Papingo Natural Pools** are a great option. When the road curves right before ascending to Mikro Papingo from Megalo on the main road, you'll see a small bridge and a parking lot. Opposite the parking lot, the white-rock trail begins. The pools become warmer and cleaner as you climb but beware taking a dip—snakes have been known to inhabit lower pools.

METEORA Μετέωρα AND KALAMBAKA Καλαμπάκα ☎24320

The monastic community of Meteora lies atop a series of awe-inspiring pinnacles. Believed to be inhabited by hermits since the 11th century, these summits were picked as the location of a series of 21 frescoed Byzantine monasteries in the 14th century. Six monasteries remain in use and open to the public. Don't expect a hidden treasure—tour buses and sweaty faces are as common here as Byzantine icons, and the traditionally dressed monks drive Jeeps. For monastic silence impossible to experience during the day, visit the complex after hours, when the museums have closed. The largest, oldest, and most popular monastery, the ▨**Grand Meteora Monastery** houses a **folk museum** and the 16th-century **Church of the Transfiguration** whose collection includes early printed secular books by Aristotle and Plato and many monks' skulls. The complex's second largest monastery, **Varlaam**, is 800m down the road. If you take the right fork, you'll reach **Roussanou**, which was accessible only by rope ladder until 1897. (Modest dress required. Hours vary by season and monastery. Apr.-Sept. Grand Meteora open M and W-Su 9am-5pm; Varlaam open M-W and F-Su 9am-2pm and 3:15-5pm; Roussanou open M-Tu and Th-Su 9am-6pm. Each monastery €2.) Meteora is accessible from the Kalambaka bus station (15min., 2 per day, €1), or visitors can walk 45min. up the hill along the footpath found at the end of Vlachava.

Meteora and Kalambaka's rocky landscapes create a **climber's** paradise; for info, equipment rental, guided excursions, and lessons, contact the local **Climbing Association** (☎6972 567 582; kliolios@kalampaka.com). Room owners may approach you at the bus station offering lower prices for decent rooms; be aware that picking up people from the station is illegal here. In the Old Town, at the base of Meteora, ▨**Alsos House ❸**, Kanari 5, has rooms with A/C, balcony, bath, and gorgeous views. From the Town Hall and *plateia*, walk along Vlachava until it ends, then follow the signs. The owner sometimes hires students in summer in exchange for room and board. (☎24 097; www.alsoshouse.gr. Breakfast included. Free Internet and Wi-Fi. Free parking. Reserve ahead. Singles €30; doubles €40-50; triples €60; 2-room apartment with kitchen €70-80. 10% Let's Go or ISIC discount. AmEx/MC/V.) On the road up to Meteora, **Camping Vrachos Kastraki ❶** has 24hr. hot water, barbecues, a climbing wall, and free fridges and stoves, as well as a restaurant and mini-market. (☎23 134; www.campingmeteora.gr. €6; €3 per tent, €1 per car. MC/V.) Right in the center of town, ▨**Taverna Paramithy ❶** (Fairy Tale), Dimitriou 14, has cheap, delicious traditional Greek cuisine cooked on a wood-burning grill. (☎24 441. Entrees €4-8. Open daily 11am-midnight. Cash only.) **Trains** leave Kalambaka for Athens (5hr., 2 per day, €21). **Buses** depart Kalambaka for: Athens (5hr., 7 per day, €24); Ioannina (3hr., 2 per day, €11); Patras (5hr.; Tu, F, Su 1 per day; €25); Thessaloniki (3½hr., 4 per day, €11). The **Office of Public Services,** at the beginning of Vlachava, is the closest thing to a tourist office. (☎77 900. Open M-F 8am-8pm, Sa 8am-2pm.) **Postal Code:** 42200.

DELPHI Δέλφοι ☎22650

Troubled denizens of the ancient world journeyed to the stunning mountaintop of the ◙**Oracle of Delphi,** where the priestess of Apollo related the gods' cryptic prophecies. Leading up **Sacred Way** hillside are the remains of the legendary **Temple of Apollo,** followed by a perfectly preserved **theater** and a **stadium** that once hosted the holy **Delphic Games.** At the entrance to the site, the **archaeological museum** exhibits an extensive collection of artifacts found near the temple, including the **Sphinxes** (the oracle's guards). Head east from Delphi to reach the temple, but go early in the morning to avoid the nonstop flow of guided groups. (Temple open daily 7:30am-7:30pm. Museum open Tu-Su 7:30am-7:30pm. Each €6, both €9; students €3/5; EU students free.) For overnight stays, the recently renovated **Hotel Sibylla ❷,** Pavlou 9, offers wonderful views and private baths at the best prices in town. (☎82 335; www.sibylla-hotel.gr. No-commission currency exchange. Singles €20-24; doubles €26-30; triples €35-40. €2 *Let's Go* discount.) In July, Delphi springs to life with a series of musical and theatrical **performances** at its Cultural Center (☎210 331 2781; www.eccd.gr). From Delphi, **buses** go to Athens (3hr., 6 per day, €13). Delphi's **tourist office,** Pavlou 12 or Friderikis 11, is right up to the stairs next to the town hall. (☎82 900. Open M-F 8am-2:30pm.) **Postal Code:** 33054.

IONIAN ISLANDS Νησιά Του Ιόνιου

West of mainland Greece, the Ionian Islands entice travelers with their lush vegetation and turquoise waters. Never conquered by the Ottomans, the islands bear the marks of British, French, Russian, and Venetian occupants. Today, they are a favorite among Western Europeans and travelers seeking unconventional Greece.

▨CORFU Κέρκυρα ☎26610

Ever since Homer's Odysseus raved about Corfu's beauty, the surrounding seas have brought a constant stream of conquerors, colonists, and tourists. There is something for everyone in Corfu, with archaeological sights, beautiful beaches, and wild nightlife. **Corfu Town** (pop. 10,000) is a jumbled labyrinth of Venetian buildings. Discover the pleasures of colonialism at the English-built ◙**Mon Repos Estate,** which features lovely gardens and an exhibit depicting the island's archaeological treasures. (☎41 369. Estate open daily 8am-7pm. Museum open Tu-Su 8:30am-3pm. Estate free. Museum €3, EU students €2.) **Paleokastritsa beach,** with caves perfect for exploring, lies west of Corfu Town; take a KTEL bus to Paleokastritsa (45min., 2-7 per day, €2). Traditional villages encircle ◙**Mt. Pantokrator,** which offers a pretty sunset panorama and views into Albania and Italy.

Finding cheap accommodations in Corfu Town is virtually impossible. Plan to stay in a nearby village or book months ahead. The **Corfu Owners of Tourist Villas and Apartments Federation,** Polilas 2A, is more of a local service for hostel owners than a tourist office, but can be helpful in a crunch. (☎26 133; oitkcrf@otenet.gr. Open M-F 9am-3pm and 5-8pm.) KTEL **buses** run from Corfu Town to Ag. Gordios (45min., 3-6 per day, €1.90), home to an impressive beach and the backpacker's legend **Pink Palace Hotel ❷.** Patrons can partake in 24/7 bacchanalia: among the many excuses to drink and get naked at this quintessential party hostel are toga parties, the Booze Cruise, cliff diving (€15), and a kayak safari (€18). Lock up your valuables in the front desk's safety deposit box before enjoying the daily events. (☎53 103; www.thepinkpalace.com. Bus service to Athens; €49, round-trip €75. Scooter and kayak rentals €10 per day. Bar open 24hr. Breakfast, cafeteria-style dinner, and ferry pickup included. Laundry €9. Internet €2 per 35min. Dorms from €18; private rooms €25-30.) For more mellow digs, take bus #11 to nearby Pelekas (20min., 7 per day, €1), where the ▓**Pension Tellis and Brigitte ❷,** down the hill from the bus stop on the left side of the street, offers rooms with balconies and superb views. (☎94 326; martini@pelekas.com. Singles €20; doubles €30-40.)

Olympic and **Aegean Airlines** connect Corfu's **Ioannis Kapodistrias Airport** (**CFU** or **LGKR;** ☎39 040) to Athens (1hr., 2-3 per day, €120-150) and Thessaloniki (1hr., 3 per week, €70-100). **Ferries** run from Corfu Town to: Bari, ITA (10hr., 4 per week); Brindisi, ITA (8hr., 1-2 per day); Patras (8hr., 5 per week); Venice, ITA (24hr., 1 per day). Prices vary significantly. For more info, try any of the travel agencies that line the road to the port. **International Tours** (☎39 007) and **Ionian Cruises** (☎31 649), both across the street from the old port on El. Venizelou, book international ferries. Buy your ticket at least a day ahead and ask if it includes port tax. Green KTEL intercity **buses** depart from between I. Theotaki and the New Fortress for Athens (8hr., 3 per day, €38) and Thessaloniki (8hr., 2 per day, €36); prices include ferry. Blue municipal buses leave from Pl. San Rocco (€0.70-1). The **tourist office** is in Pl. San Rocco in a green kiosk. (☎20 733. Open daily 9am-2pm and 6-9pm.) **Postal Code:** 49100.

▓KEPHALONIA Κεφαλόνια ☎26710

With soaring mountains and subterranean lakes, Kephalonia (pop. 45,000) is a nature lover's paradise and deservedly popular. The bus schedules are erratic and the taxis very expensive, but armed with your own transportation, you can uncover picturesque villages on lush hillsides and cliff-cuddled beaches. **Argostoli** (pop. 8000), Kephalonia's capital, is a pastel-colored city that offers the easiest access to other points on the island. **St. Gerassimos ❷,** 6 Ag. Gerassimou Str., just off the waterfront road, is a family-run establishment offering seven rooms each equipped with A/C, balcony, private bath, and TV. (☎28 697. Open June-Sept. Rooms €20-45; prices negotiable.) People gravitate to **La Gondola ❷,** 21 Maiou, for its divine Italian dishes like *risotto sabbia d'oro* (€8.80) with pumpkin and shrimp. (Pizza €8.60-10. Pasta €5.60-11. Greek entrees €7-8.30. Wine from €8.50. Open daily 7pm-1am. MC/V.) The **tourist office,** near the ferry docks, opens irregularly. (☎23 364. Generally open July-Aug. daily 8am-2:30pm; Sept.-June M-F 8am-2:30pm.) **Internet** is available at **B.B.'s Club,** in the bottom right corner of the *plateia,* facing inland. (☎26 669. €2.50 per hr. Open daily 9am-2am.) **Ferries** from Argostoli go to Kyllini on the Peloponnese (30min., 1 per day, €13) and Lixouri, Kephalonia (20min., 2 per hr. until 10:30pm, €2).

On the northeastern coast, 24km from Argostoli, the hushed town of **Sami** is a major port and a great base from which to explore many nearby beaches. Two and four kilometers west, the striking **Melissani Lake** and **Drogarati Cave,** are respectively an underground pool of cold crystalline water and a large stalactite- and stalagmite-filled cavern. (Lake ☎26740 22 997; cave 26740 23 302. Lake open daily 9:30am-sunset; €6. Cave open 8:30am-sunset; €4.) **Fiskardo,** on the island's northern tip and one of its most beautiful towns, has Venetian architecture that escaped the devastating 1953 earthquake. Nearby ▓**Myrtos Beach,** 4km from the main-road turn off, is possibly the single best spot on the island, with brilliant white pebbles and clear blue water lapping against sheer cliffs. This popular beach offers wonderful swims, but beware of the strong underwater currents and keep close to shore. Argostoli presents the best accommodation options for visitors looking to explore

Sami and Fiskardo. **Buses** leave the Sami station on the left end of the waterfront for Argostoli (45min.; 4 per day M-Sa; €4). From the Fiskardo parking lot next to the church, uphill from town, buses leave for Argostoli (1½hr., 2 per day, €5) and Sami (1½hr., 2 per day, €4). **Postal Codes:** 28100 (Argostoli) and 28080 (Sami).

☙ITHAKA Ιθάκη   ☎26740

Discovering Ithaka means uncovering 6000 years of history and traversing Odysseus's homeland. Surprisingly not as touristy as its neighboring islands, Ithaka is relaxing beyond imagination and truly suspended in time. Small enough for streets to have no names, **Vathy,** Ithaka's alluring capital, wraps around a circular bay filled with fishing boats and yachts, with precipitous green hillsides nudging up against the water. Taxis to nearby villages are very expensive; it's best to rent a car or a scooter. **Sholi Omirou** (Homer's School) is one of three sites contending for recognition as **Odysseus's Palace.** From the village of **Stavros,** accessible by bus from Vathy (1hr., 2 per day, €2), follow the signs to a dirt road, which ends about 500m later in a footpath leading to the site. The **Cave of the Nymphs** is 2km outside Vathy on the road uphill to Stavros, though the site appears poorly maintained and deserted. The enchanting **Monastery of Panagia Katharon** perches on Ithaka's highest mountain, ☙**Mt. Neritos,** and has views of the surrounding islands and sea; take a moped or taxi (€25 round-trip) toward the town of Anoghi and follow the signs up the curvy road for about 20min. The monks ask visitors to close the front door and expect women to cover their legs while in the church. (Open sunrise-sunset. Free.) On the stunning white pebble beaches of ☙**Filiatro** and **Sarakiniko,** 3.5 and 2.5km out, respectively, rocky ridges steeply drop to the sea. From Vathy, walk to the end of town with the water on your left and turn uphill before the last houses. Another beautiful beach is by the tiny **Piso Aetos** port. Clean **Aktaion Domatia ❸,** across from the ferry dock on the far right side of the waterfront (facing inland), has rooms with A/C, bath, minifridge, and TV. (☎32 387. Summer singles €30; doubles €56. Negotiate for low-season discounts. Cash only.) For a light snack, stop by **Drakouli ❶,** an old white mansion-turned-cafe. Walk with the water to your left away from the Vathy *plateia* until you see the sea-fed pool. (☎33 435. Coffee €2-3.20. Ice cream €2 per scoop. Sandwiches €2-3.50. Open daily 9am-midnight. Cash only.) **Ferries** depart from Piso Aetos to Sami, Kephalonia (45min., 2 per day, €2.50) or from Vathy to Sami, Kephanlonia (1hr., 2 per day, €6) and Patras (3¾hr., 2 per day, €15). **Postal Code:** 28300.

☙ZAKYNTHOS Ζάκυνθος   ☎26950

Known as the greenest Ionian Island, Zakynthos is home to thousands of species of plants and flowers as well as a large *Caretta caretta* (loggerhead sea turtles) population. **Zakynthos Town** maintains a romantic, nostalgic air. Boats leave Zakynthos Town for many of the island's spectacular sights, including the glowing **Blue Caves** on the northeastern shore past Skinari. Southwest of the Blue Caves is ☙**Smuggler's Wreck.** A shipwrecked boat's remains has made the beach one of the most photographed in the world. **Keri Caves** and **Marathonisi.** Agencies giving tours of Zakynthos advertise along Lomvardou; most excursions leave around 9:30am, return at 5:30pm, and cost €16-25. For a more intimate travel experience, skip the huge cruise ships and hire a small fishing boat from the docks in northern villages. A 10min. walk down the beach (with the water on your right) will take you to the deserted sands of ☙**Kalamaki,** a turtle nesting site and protected **National Marine Park** (www.nmp-zak.org). At night, the turtles inhabit some of Zakynthos's most picturesque beaches, like **Gerakas,** on the island's southeastern tip.

  Athina Marouda Rooms for Rent ❶, on Tzoulati and Koutouzi, has simple, clean rooms with fans, large windows, and communal baths. (☎45 194. June-Sept. sin-

> The loggerhead turtles that share Zakynthos's shores with beachgoers are an **endangered species,** and their nesting ground should be respected. Let's Go encourages readers to embrace the "Leave No Trace" ethic (p. 35) when visiting the island's more secluded beaches.

gles €15; doubles €30. Oct.-May €10/20. Cash only.) Dining in the *plateias* and by the waterfront is a treat. **Village Inn ❸,** Lomvardou 20, at the right end of the waterfront before Pl. Solomou, offers no rooms and feels more like a bayou lounge than small town eatery but has tables facing the water. (☎26 991. Entrees €6-15. Th night live Greek music. Open daily 8am-midnight. MC/V.) Getting around the island can be frustrating—taxis can be terribly overpriced and tour operators may seem like glorified tourist baby-sitters. Dozens of places rent **scooters** (€15 per day), but driver's license requirements are strictly enforced. **Buses** go from the station, two blocks away from the water, to Laganas (20min., 15 per day, €1.20) and Kalamaki (20min., 12 per day, €1.20). Buses also board ferries to the mainland and continue to Athens (6hr., 5 per day, €23), Patras (3hr., 3 per day, €7), and Thessaloniki (10hr., Su-Th 1 per day, €43). **Postal Code:** 29100.

CYCLADES Κυκλάδες

Sun-drenched, winding stone streets, and trellis-covered *tavernas* define the Cycladic islands, but subtle quirks make each distinct. Orange and black sands coat Santorini's shoreline of Santorini, and celebrated archaeological sites testify to Delos's mythical and historical significance. Naxos and Paros offer travelers peaceful mountains and villages, while notorious party spots Ios and Mykonos uncork some of the world's wildest nightlife.

🏝 MYKONOS Μύκονος ☎22890

Coveted by 18th-century pirates, Mykonos still attracts revelers and gluttons. Although Mykonos is a fundamentally chic, sophisticates' playground, you don't have to break the bank to have a good time. Ambling down **Mykonos Town's** colorful alleyways at dawn or dusk, surrounded by tourist-friendly pelicans, is the cheapest, most exhilarating way to experience the island. Drinking and sunbathing are Mykonos's main forms of entertainment. While the island's beaches are nude, bathers' degree of bareness varies; in most places, people prefer to show off their designer bathing suits rather than their birthday suits. **Platis Yialos** and **Super Paradise** appeal to more brazen nudists, while **Elia** beach attracts a tamer crowd. The super-famous **Paradise** beach is so crowded with hungover Italians and overpriced sun beds that you can barely see its gorgeous water. Buses run south from Mykonos Town to Platis Yialos and Paradise (20min., 2 per hr., €1.20-1.50) and to Elia (30min., 8 per day, €1.10). The **Skandinavian Bar,** inland from the waterfront towards Little Venice, is a two-building party complex. (☎22 669. Beer €4-6. Mixed drinks from €8. Open daily 9pm-5am.) After drinking the night away, usher in a new day at 🏝**Cavo Paradiso,** on Paradise beach. Considered one of the world's top dance clubs, it hosts internationally renowned DJs and inebriated crowds. Take the bus to Paradise beach and follow the signs; it's a 10min. walk. (☎27 205. Drinks from €10. Cover €25, after 2am €40; includes 1 drink. Open daily 3-11am.)

Like everything else on Mykonos, accommodations are prohibitively expensive. Camping is the best budget option. The popular **Paradise Beach Camping ❶,** 6km from Mykonos Town, has decent facilities, plenty of services, and is just steps away from the beach. (☎22 129; www.paradisemykonos.com. Free pickup at port

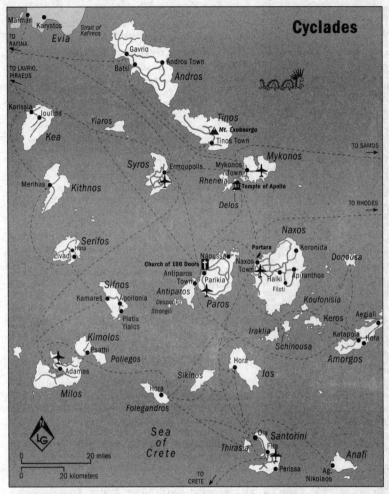

Cyclades

or airport. Safes available. Breakfast included. Internet €4.50 per hr. €5-10 per person, €2.50-4 per small tent, €4.50-7 per large tent; 1- to 2-person cabin €15-50. 3-person tent rental €8-18.) At **Hotel Philippi ④,** Kalogera 25, in Mykonos Town, rooms with A/C, bath, and fridge center around a bright garden. (☎22 294. Open Apr.-Oct. Singles €55-85; doubles €70-110; triples €84-132. AmEx/MC/V.) **Kalidonios ❸,** Dilou 1, off Kalogera, serves a range of Greek and Mediterranean dishes in a cozy, colorful interior. (☎27 606. Entrees €8-15. Open daily noon-12:30am. MC/V.) For a cheap meal, head to **Pasta Fresca ❶,** on Georgouli, near the Skandinavian Bar. Its streetside take-out window is a good place to grab the best gyros (€2) and chicken pitas (€2) that Mykonos has to offer. (☎22 563. Open daily 4pm-late.) **Ferries** run from the New Port, west of town, to Naxos (3hr., 1 per week, €9.50), Paros (3hr., 1 per day, €8.40), and Piraeus (6hr., 1 per day, €26). The **tourist police** are at the ferry landing. (☎22 482. Open daily 8am-9pm.) **Windmills Travel,** on Xenias,

GREECE

THE LOCAL STORY

PETROS: PELICAN OF MYSTERY

Every summer, tourist-paparazzi swarm Mykonos Town, attempting to get a photo of the area's biggest celebrity in action—taking a stroll by the windmills or enjoying a seafood dinner in Little Venice.

The town superstar is a pelican named "Petros." In his standard pose, the pink-and-white bird can be hard to pick out against the town's white buildings—at least until he blinks his beady black eyes and extends his heavy wings and slender neck. Though he is constantly surrounded by admirers, Petros's main concern is scoring free fish; if you feed him, be prepared to be followed and "asked" for more.

But Petros's obsessive fish habit, typical of most pelicans, is no mask for the fact that he's not really Petros after all. The first pelican known as "Petros" lived here for over 30 years after being stranded by a storm in the 1950s and adopted by locals. Since his death, any pelican in Mykonos gets the royal treatment; there are currently two to three regulars.

Petros (or possibly the Petroses) has been sighted all over the northwestern city. To catch a glimpse, wander around the Paraportiani churches and the surrounding tavernas. Some maintain Petros has a sweet tooth and hangs near Mykonos's bakery. Look for a crowd of tourists wielding cameras and one over-indulged, puffed-up pelican.

around the corner from South Station, has GLBT resources. (☎26 555; www.windmillstravel.com. Open daily 8am-10pm.) **Postal Code:** 84600.

🎫 DAYTRIP FROM MYKONOS: 🏛 DELOS Δήλος.

Delos was the ancient sacred center of the Cyclades. Though archaeological site covers the whole island, its highlights can be seen in 3hr. *(Open Tu-Su 8:30am-3pm. €5, students and EU seniors €3, EU students free.)* From the dock, head straight to the **Agora of the Competaliasts;** go in the same direction and turn left on the wide **Sacred Road** to reach the **Sanctuary of Apollo,** a group of temples that date from Mycenaean times to the 4th century BC. On the right is the biggest, most famous Delos structure, the **Temple of Apollo.** Continue 50m past the Sacred Road's end to the beautiful **Terrace of the Lions.** The museum, next to the cafeteria, contains an assortment of archaeological finds. *(Open Tu-Su 8:30am-3pm. €5, students and seniors €3.)* From the museum, a path leads to the summit of **Mount Kythnos** (112m), from which Zeus supposedly watched Apollo's birth. Temples dedicated to Egyptian gods, including the **Temple of Isis,** line the descent. Excursion **boats** (30min.; 4 per day; round-trip €13, with tour €30) leave for Delos from Mykonos Town's Old Port, past Little Venice. Buy tickets at Hellas or Blue Star Ferries on the waterfront.

🏛 PAROS Πάρος   ☎22840

Now a central transportation hub, Paros was once famed for its slabs of pure white marble, used for many of the ancient world's great statues and buildings. It's a favorite destination for families and older travelers, removed from the luxurious debauchery of Mykonos and the youth-filled streets of Ios. Behind the commercial surface of **Parikia,** Paros's port and largest city, flower-lined streets wind through archways to one of the world's most treasured Orthodox basilicas, the **Panagia Ekatontapiliani** (Church of Our Lady of 100 Doors). This white three-building complex is dedicated to St. Helen, mother of the Emperor Constantine, who reportedly had a vision of the True Cross here while traveling to the Holy Land. (Dress modestly. Open daily 7am-10pm. Mass M-Sa 7-7:30pm, Su 7-10am. Free.) About 8km north of town, **Naoussa** beach is the most popular and crowded destination on the island. On the opposite coast, 🏖**Aliki** beach is much quieter, but often windy. Turn left at the dock and take a right after the cemetery ruins to reach the well-kept, cottage-like **Rena Rooms ❷.** (☎22 220; www.cycladesnet.gr/rena. Free pickup and luggage storage. Reserve ahead. Singles €15-35; doubles €20-40; triples €30-55. 20% discount for *Let's Go* readers; discount if paid in cash. MC/V.) The funky

▓**Happy Green Cow** ❸, a block off the *plateia* behind the National Bank, serves tasty vegetarian dinners. (☎24 691. Entrees €12-15. Open Apr.-Nov. daily 7pm-midnight.) At the far end of the Old Town's waterfront, 5min. past the port and bus station, Paros' nightlife pulses late into the night. A central courtyard connects themed bar areas of **The Dubliner,** an Irish pub, **Down Under,** the Aussie bar, and the **Paros Rock Cafe,** with bright colors and the appropriate flags. Follow the spotlight and crowds to the end of the harbor. (☎Beer €3-5. Mixed drinks €5-6. Cover €3; includes 1 drink.) **Ferries** go to: Folegandros (5hr., 3 per week, €9); Ios (3hr., 5 per week, €13); Mykonos (5hr., 5 per week, €7); Naxos (1hr., 2 per day €7); Thessaloniki (19hr., 2 per week, €38). Ferry schedules fluctuate weekly; check with the budget travel office **Polos Tours** (☎22 092; www.polostours.gr), 50m to the right of the ferry dock gate, for departure times. The **tourist police** are on the *plateia* behind the telephone office. (☎21 673. Open M-F 7am-2:30pm.) **Postal Code:** 84400.

▓ NAXOS Νάξος ☎22850

Ancient Greeks believed Dionysus, the god of wine and revelry once lived on Naxos (pop. 20,000), the largest of the Cyclades. Olive groves, small villages, chalky ruins, silent monasteries, and unadulterated hikes fill its interior, while sandy beaches line its shores. **Naxos Town,** its capital, is a dense collection of labyrinthine streets, bustling *tavernas,* and tiny museums, crowned by the ▓**Kastro,** an inhabited Venetian fortress, tranquil despite the tourists. At the Kastro's entrance, the **Domus Della Rocca-Barozzi** (a.k.a. the Venetian Museum) exhibits photographs, books, and furniture belonging to a local aristocratic family still living there. (☎223 87; www.naxosisland.gr/VenetianMuseum. Open daily in high season 10am-3pm and 7-11pm; low season 10am-3pm and 7-10pm. €5, students €3. Nightly summer concerts at 9:15pm. €10; reserve ahead at the museum reception.) The **Archaeological Museum** occupies the former Collège Français, where Nikos Kazantzakis, author of *The Last Temptation of Christ* and *Zorba the Greek,* studied. (Open Tu-Su 8am-5pm. €3, students €2.) Accommodations in Naxos are available in private rooms and studios on the street between the town's center and the nearby Ag. Giorgios beach, or in campsites by the island's many beaches. Though most campgrounds vary little in price (generally €4-8 per person, €2-3 per tent), **Naxos Camping** ❶ is the closest to Naxos Town (2km) and only 150m from **Ag. Giorgios** beach. (☎235 00. Prices vary seasonally.) Nearby **Heavens Cafe Bar** ❷ serves scrumptious Belgian waffles with fresh fruit for €5. (☎227 47. Internet €3 per hr.; free Wi-Fi. Open daily 8am-2am.) **Ferries** go from Naxos Town to: Crete (7hr., 1 per week, €21); Ios (1hr., 1 per day, €10); Mykonos (3hr., 1 per day, €9); Paros (1hr., 4 per day, €8); Piraeus (6hr., 4 per day, €28); Rhodes (13hr., 1 per week, €25); Santorini (3hr., 3 per day, €13). A bus goes from the port to the beaches of Ag. Giorgios, Ag. Prokopios, Ag. Anna, and Plaka (2 per hr. 7:30am-2am, €1.20). **Buses** (☎222 91) also run from Naxos Town to ▓**Apiranthos,** a beautiful village with narrow, marble paths (1hr., 5 per day, €2.30). The Naxos town **tourist office** is next to the bus station. (☎229 93. Open daily 8am-11pm.) **Postal Code:** 84300.

▓ IOS Ίος ☎22860

Despite recent concerted efforts to tone down its party-animal reputation, Ios remains the Greek debauchery heaven—or hell. Life on the island revolves around its insane and non-stop party scene: breakfast is served at 2pm, drinking begins at 3pm, people don't go out before midnight, and revelers dance madly in the streets until well after dawn. The **port** of Gialos is at one end of the island's sole paved road. The town of **Hora** sits above it on a hill, but most visitors spend their days at **Mylopotas beach,** a 25min. walk downhill from Hora or a short bus ride from town (3-6 per hr., €1.20). Establishments on the beach offer snorkeling, water-skiing, and windsurfing during the day (€9-45). Sunning is typically followed—or accompanied—by drinking; the afternoon bars are no less crowded than the nighttime ones. Head up from the *plateia* to reach the **Slammer Bar** for tequila slammers (€3), then stop by **Disco 69** for some dirty dancing (beer €5; cover €6 midnight-4am). Get lost in the streetside ■**Red Bull** (beer €3) dance on the tables at **Sweet Irish Dream** (beer €3; cover €5 2:30-4:30am), or grind to techno at **Scorpion Disco,** the island's largest club (cover €7 2-4:30am, includes a mixed drink and shot). Most clubs close between 4 and 7am, when the drunkenness spills onto the streets. A few hours later, crowds begin to re-gather at the beach.

In addition to cheap dorms, ■**Francesco's ❶** offers stunning sunset harbor views from its terrace. Take the steps up the hill to the left in the *plateia* and then the first left at the Diesel shop. (☎91 223; www.francescos.net. Breakfast 9am-2pm €2.50-5. Internet €1 per 15min. Reception 9am-2pm and 6-10pm. Check-out 11am. Dorms €11-18; 2- to 4-person rooms with A/C and bath €15-28 per person.) Back in town, ■**Ali Baba's ❷,** next to Ios Gym, serves authentic Thai food. (☎91 558. Entrees €6-12. Open Mar.-Oct. daily 6pm-1am.) Off the main church's *plateia*, **Old Byron's ❸** is an intimate wine bar and bistro with creative renditions of Greek staples. (☎697 819 2212. Entrees €9-15. Reserve ahead. Open M-Sa 6-11:30pm, Su noon-11:30pm. MC/V.) Greek fast food and creperies pack the central *plateia*. **Ferries** go to: Naxos (1¾hr., 1-3 per day, €9); Paros (3hr., 1-3 per day, €10); Piraeus (8hr., 2-3 per day, €35); Santorini (1½hr., 3-5 per day, €7). **Postal Code:** 84001.

◪ SANTORINI Σαντορίνη   ☎22860

Whitewashed towns sitting delicately on cliffs, black-sand beaches, and deeply scarred hills make Santorini's landscape nearly as dramatic as the volcanic cataclysm that created it. Despite the overabundance of expensive boutiques and glitzy souvenirs in touristy **Fira** (pop. 2500), the island's capital, nothing can ruin the pleasure of wandering the town's cobbled streets or browsing its craft shops. At Santorini's northern tip, the town of **Oia** (*EE-ah;* pop. 700) is the best place in Greece to watch the sunset, though its fame draws crowds hours in advance. To catch a glimpse of the sun, and not of someone taking a picture of it, walk down the hill from the village and settle alone near the many windmills and pebbled walls. To get to Oia, take a bus from Fira (25min., 23 per day, €1.20). Although every establishment in Oia makes you pay for the spectacular views, a romantic stroll along the gleaming paths should not be missed.

Red Beach, as well as the impressive archaeological excavation site of the Minoan city **Akrotiri,** entirely preserved by lava but currently closed for repairs, lie on Santorini's southwestern edge. Buses run to Akrotiri from Fira (30min., 15 per day, €1.60). Buses also leave Fira for the black-sand beaches of **Kamari** (20min., 32 per day, €1.20), **Perissa** (30min., 32 per day, €1.90), and **Perivolos** (20min., 21 per day, €1.90). The bus stops before Perissa in Pyrgos; from there, you can ■hike (2¼hr.) across a rocky mountain path to the ruins of **Ancient Thira.** Stop after 1hr. on a paved road at **Profitis Ilias Monastery,** whose lofty location provides an island panorama. (Open M and W 4-5pm, Sa 4:30-8:30pm. Dress modestly. Free.) Close to Perissa's beach, ■**Youth Hostel Anna ❶** has colorful rooms and loads of backpackers hanging out on its streetside veranda. (☎82 182. Port pickup and drop-off included. Reception 9am-5pm and 7-10pm. Check-out 11:30am. Reserve ahead. June-Aug. 10-bed dorms €12; 4-bed dorms €15; doubles €50; triples €60. Sept.-May €6/8/22/30. MC/V.) At night, head to ■**Murphy's** in Fira, which claims to be Greece's first Irish pub. (Beer €5. Mixed drinks €6.50. Cover €5 after 10pm. Open Mar.-Oct. daily 11:30am-late.) **Olympic Airways** (☎22 493) and **Aegean Airways** (☎28 500) fly from Fira's airport to Athens (50min., 4-7 per day, €85-120) and Thessaloniki (1¼hr., 1-2 per day, €125). **Ferries** depart from Fira to: Crete (4hr., 4 per week,

€16); Ios (1hr., 1-3 per day, €7); Naxos (3hr., 1-2 per day, €16); Paros (4hr., 1-4 per day, €17); Piraeus (10hr., 2-3 per day, €33). Most ferries depart from Athinios Harbor. Frequent **buses** (25min., €1.70) with changing daily schedules connect to Fira, but most hostels and hotels offer shuttle service. Check bus and ferry schedules at any travel agency, and be aware that the self-proclaimed tourist offices at the port are actually for-profit agencies. **Postal Codes:** 84700 (Fira); 84702 (Oia).

⚑ CRETE Κρήτη

According to a Greek saying, a Cretan's first loyalty is to his island, his second to his country. Since 3000 BC, when Minoan civilization flourished on the island, Crete has maintained an identity distinct from the rest of Greece; pride in the island proves well-founded. Travelers will be drawn to Crete's warm hospitality, and enticing beaches, gorges, grottoes, monasteries, mosques, and villages.

IRAKLION Ηράκλειο   ☎ 2810

Iraklion (pop. 130,000), Crete's capital and primary port, may not be particularly pretty but its importance as a transportation hub makes it a necessary stop on the way to Crete's more scenic destinations. **Olympic Airways** and **Aegean Airlines** fly domestically from the **Heraklion International Airport: Kazantzakis (HER;** ☎397 800; www.hcaa-eleng.gr/irak.htm) to Athens (50min., 5-6 per day, €75-115), Rhodes (1hr., 1-2 per week, €100-110), and Thessaloniki (1¾hr., 2 per day, €105-130). Budget airline **Wizz Air** also flies from Iraklion to Budapest, HUN (1¼-3hr., 1 per week, €270) and Katowice, POL (3¾hr., 1 per week, €280). From Terminal A, between the old city walls and the harbor, **buses** leave for Agios Nikolaos (1½hr., 23 per day, €6.20) and Hania (3hr., 16 per day, €12) via Rethymno (1½hr., €6.50). Buses leave across from Terminal B for Phaistos (1½hr., 10 per day, €5.10). **Ferries** also go to: Mykonos (8½hr., 2 per week, €25); Naxos (8hr., 3 per week, €22); Paros (7hr., 4 per week, €25); Santorini (4hr., 3 per week, €16). Check for travel delays online at **Netc@fé,** 1878 4. (€1.50 per hr. Open M-Sa 8:30am-8:30pm.)

Soothe the burn of a missed flight with drinks or a borrowed book atop the quiet roof lounge at **Rent a Room Hellas ❶,** Handakos 24. Walk east along the waterfront and turn left onto Handakos. (☎288 851. Free luggage storage. Check-out 11am. Dorms €11; doubles €25-31; triples €42.) The **open-air market** on 1866, near Pl. Venizelou, sells cheese, meat, and produce. (Open M-Sa 8am-9pm.) **Ouzeri Tou Terzaki ❷,** Loch. Marineli 17, in the center of town, serves fresh Greek meals with complimentary *raki* liquor and fruit. (☎221 444. Entrees €5-8. Open M-Sa noon-midnight. MC/V.) Those looking to kill time between connections should check out the ⬛**Tomb of Nikos Kazantzakis,** on top of the city walls. Even visitors unfamiliar with his most famous novel, *Zorba the Greek*, should make the climb to catch a spectacular sunset over Mt. Ida. **Postal Code:** 71001.

KNOSSOS Κνωσός   ☎ 2810

⬛**Knossos,** Crete's most famous archaeological site, is a must-see. Excavations have revealed the remains of the largest, most complicated of Crete's **Minoan palaces.** It is difficult to differentiate between legend and fact at the palace of Knossos. Famous throughout history, the palace is the site of King Minos's machinations, the labyrinth with its monstrous son Minotaur, and the imprisonment—and winged escape—of Daedalus and Icarus. The first palace was built around 1700 BC, but was partially destroyed by fire around 1450 BC and subsequently forgotten. In the early 20th century, Sir Arthur Evans financed and supervised the excavations, restoring large parts of the palace. His work often crossed the line from preservation to tenuous interpretation, painting the palace's current form with controversy. Tourist crowds give the Minoan palace a Disneyland feel, but the sights are well worth navigating. Don't miss the **Queen's Bathroom,** where, over 3000 years ago, she took milk baths while gazing up at dolphin frescoes. Walking north from the royal quarters, you'll stumble across the grand **pithoi**—jars so big that, according to legend, Minos's son met a sticky demise by drowning in one filled with honey. (Open daily 8am-7.30pm. €6, students €3.) To reach Knossos from Iraklion, take **bus** #2 from Terminal A (20min., 2 per hr., €1.10).

HANIA Χάνια   ☎28210

Despite an avalanche of tourists, Hania (pop. 60,000), Crete's second largest city, still manages to remain low key. A day in Old Hania is easily spent people-watching from cafes or wandering along the waterfront. The **Venetian lighthouse** marks the entrance to the city's stunning architectural relic, the **Venetian Inner Harbor,** built by conquerors in the 13th century. The ruins of the fortress have sunset views over the open sea. The inlet has retained its original breakwater and Venetian arsenal, though the Nazis destroyed much of it during WWII. Nestled away on the northwestern tip of Crete, the heavenly ⊠**blue lagoon** of **Balos** is the island's uncontested best beach, where bright white sand, warm shallow water, and sky melt into one. The most popular excursion from Hania and Iraklion (p. 489) is the 5-6hr. hike down ⊠**Samaria Gorge** (Φράγγι της Σαμαριάς), a spectacular 18km ravine extending through the White Mountains. Sculpted by 14 million years of rainwater, the gorge is the longest in Europe. (Open daily May to mid-Oct. 6am-3pm. €5, under 15 free.) The trail starts at **Xyloskalo** and ends at **Agia Roumeli,** on the southern coast; take an early bus from Hania to Xyloskalo (1½hr., €6) for a day's worth of hiking.

The only backpacker-friendly accommodation in Hania is central **Eftihis Rooms ❶,** 2 Tsouderon. From the bus station, walk toward the harbor on Halidon and turn right on Skrydlof, which becomes Tsouderon. (☎46 829. A/C. Singles €15; doubles €20; triples €30. Cash only.) Fresh food is available at the covered municipal **market,** connecting new and old Hania, while touristy *tavernas* also line the town. Hania's nightlife buzzes along **Sourmelis Street,** in the heart of the old harbor.

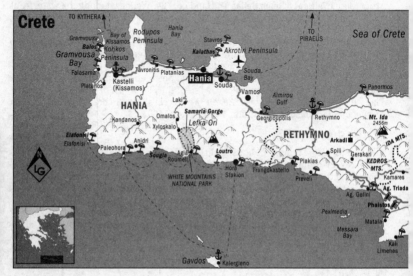

From the port of Souda, **ferries** go to Piraeus (9½hr.; 2 per day; €30). Buses connect from the port of Souda to Hania's municipal market on Zymvrakakidon (25min., €1). **Buses** (☎93 052) leave from the corner of Kidonias and Kelaidi for the airport (25min., 3 per day), Iraklion (2½hr., 18 per day, €12), and Rethymno (1hr., 19 per day, €6). **Taxis** to the airport cost €16-18. The **tourist office,** Kidonias 29, is next to the city hall. (☎36 155; www.chania.gr. Open M-F 8:30am-2:30pm; self-service M-F 8:30am-8pm, Sa 9am-2pm.) **Postal Code:** 73001.

EASTERN AEGEAN ISLANDS

Scattered along Turkey's coast, the islands of the **Dodecanese** are marked by a history of persistence in the face of countless invasions. The more isolated islands of the **Northeast Aegean** remain sheltered from creeping globalization. Cultural authenticity here is palpable—a traveler's welcome and reward.

🔂RHODES Ρόδος   ☎22410

The undisputed tourism capital of the Dodecanese, the island of Rhodes has retained its sense of serenity in the sandy beaches along its eastern coast, jagged cliffs skirting its western coast, and green mountains dotted with villages in its interior. Beautiful ancient artifacts, remnants from a rich past, carpet the island. Rhodes is best known for a sight that no longer exists—the 33m **Colossus,** which was once one of the Seven Wonders of the Ancient World. The pebbled streets of the Old Town, constructed by the Knights of St. John, lend **Rhodes Town** a medieval flair. At the top of the hill, a tall, square tower marks the entrance to the **Palace of the Grand Master,** which contains 300 rooms filled with intricate mosaic floorwork. (☎25 500. €6, students €3.) The beautiful halls and courtyards of the **Archaeological Museum,** which dominates the **Platela Argiokastrou,** shelter the exquisite first century BC statue of Aphrodite Bathing. (☎25 500. Open Tu-Su 8:30am-3pm. €3, students €2.) On Rhodes's western shore, the ruins of **Kamiros** offer a glimpse of an ancient chessboard-patterned city. Daily **buses** run out of Rhodes Town (☎40 037. €4, students €2.) North of Kamiros, the Valley of Butterflies, or **Petaloudes,** attracts Jersey moths and nature-enthusiasts

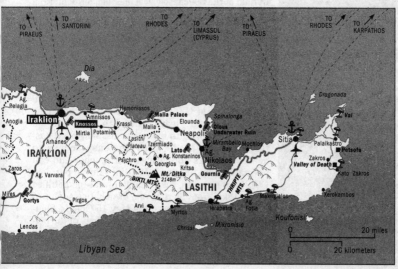

GREECE

ON THE MENU

THE IDIOT'S GUIDE TO DRINKING OUZO

When you go out for your first meal in Greece, don't be surprised, shocked, or flattered if your waiter rushes out before your entree arrives to present you with a shot glass of opaque liquor and the simple command, "Drink!" He's just assuming that you, like almost every Greek, want to cleanse your palate and ease your mind with some ouzo.

There's an art to enjoying the anise-flavored national drink, however, which is important to understand if you don't want to reveal yourself as a neophyte. First, don't go bottoms up. Good ouzo is around 40% alcohol by volume; it just isn't made to be chugged. It's invariably served with a glass of water for the purpose of mixing, which turns your shot milky-white. The key is to keep adding water as you drink to avoid dehydration and ill effects.

Second, snack on some *mezedes* while you take your ouzo. Nibbling on some cheese, a salad, or vegetables will temper the alcohol and prolong the experience. That's the point, after all: Greece's obsession with ouzo is not really focused on getting plastered on liquid licorice. Instead, it's about drinking lazily, relaxing in a *kafeneion*, and chatting with friends until the sun sets and dinner begins.

best **beaches** stretch along southern Kos to Kardamena and are accessible by bus (stops made by request). For a steamy daytrip, hop on a ferry to the neighboring island of **Nisyros** (1½hr., 1 per week, €7.50) and trek into the sulphur-lined craters of ▨**Mandraki Volcano.** In Kos Town, take the first right off Megalou Alexandrou to get to **Pension Alexis ❷**, Irodotou 9, a beloved travel institution run by a hospitable mother and son. (☎28 798. Breakfast €5. Laundry €5. Singles €25; doubles €30-33; triples €39-45; quads €48-50.) Generous portions characterize **Taverna Hellas ❷**, Psaron 7, down the street from Pension Alexis at the corner of Amerikis. (☎30 322. Open daily 10am-3pm and 5pm-midnight.) Most bars radiate out from **Nafkilrou**, circling **Place Iroön Politechniou** to continue along the beach. **Ferries** run to Kalymnos (1hr., 3 per week, €6), Piraeus (11-15hr., 1 per day, €44), and Rhodes (4hr., 1 per day, €14). The **tourist office** is at Vas. Georgiou B1. (☎24 460; www.hippocrates.gr. Open M-F 7:30am-3pm.) **Postal Code:** 85300.

▨ LESVOS Λέσβος   ☎ 22510

Olive groves, art colonies, and a petrified forest harmonize Lesvos, or Lesbos. Born on this island, the 7th-century lyrical poet Sappho garnered a large female following. Due to her much-debated homosexuality, the word "lesbian"—once describing a native islander—developed its modern connotation. Visitors can gaze upon **Sappho's statue** at **Mytilini**, the island's capital and central port city, or walk on preserved mosaic floors excavated from ancient Ag. Kyriaki at the ▨**Archaeological Museum,** 8 Noemvriou. (Open Tu-Su 8am-3pm. €3, students €2, EU students and under 18 free.) Only 4km south of Mytilini, the village of **Varia** is home to the **Musée Tériade,** which displays lithographs by Chagall, Matisse, Miró, and Picasso, and the **Theophilos Museum,** which features work by neo-Primitivist Theophilos Hadzimichali. (☎23 372. Musée Tériade open Tu-Su 9am-2pm and 5-8pm. Theophilos Museum open Tu-Su 10am-4pm. Each museum €2, students free.) Local buses (20min., 1 per hr.) leave Mytilini to Varia. Tell the driver you're going to the museums. **Molyvos,** a castle-crowned village, provides easy access to nearby **Eftalou's** hot springs and beaches and can be reached by bus from Mytilini (2hr., 5 per day, €6). Farther south, the 20-million-year-old **petrified forest,** 18km from Sigri, is one of only two such forests worldwide. (Open daily May 15-Oct. 14 8am-8pm; Oct. 15-May 14 8am-4pm. €2.) Many of the petrified artifacts have been moved to Sigri at the ▨**Natural History Museum of the Lesvos Petrified Forest.** (☎22530 54 434; www.petrifiedforest.gr. Open daily

8am-10pm. €5, students €2.50.) Doubles at Mytilini *domatia*—plentiful and well advertised—run €30-35 before July 15, and €35-50 during the high season. **Olympic and Aegean Airlines** fly out of the airport (**MJT; ☎**61 590), 6km south of Mytilini, for Athens (1hr., 6 per day, €50-150) and Rhodes (1hr., 5 per week, €58). **Ferries** go from Mytilini to Thessaloniki (13hr., 1 per week, €35). **Zoumboulis Tours** (☎37 755) sells tickets. **Postal Code:** 81100.

▓SAMOTHRAKI Σαμοθράκη ☎22510

Samothraki (Samothrace) was once a pilgrimage site for Thracians who worshipped Anatolian gods. When the first colonists arrived in the 10th century BC, they saw the same vista still viewable from the ferry dock today: grassy fields at the base of the Aegean's tallest peak, Fengari (1670m). From **Kamariotissa**, Samothraki's port town, it is easy to reach the **Sanctuary of the Great Gods at Paleopolis,** where the famous *Winged Victory of Samothrace*, now a centerpiece in the Louvre, was found in 1863. (Open daily 8:30am-8:30pm. €3, students €2, EU students free.) Above the sanctuary rest the remains of the ancient Samothraki. **Therma**, a charming one-road village, has natural hot springs and hosts the trailhead for the 4hr. climb up Fengari. Unmarked waterfalls near Therma are also a worthwhile trip; check with the locals for hikes suiting your schedule and abilities. **Kaviros Hotel ❷**, to the left of the grocery store in Therma, has well-lit rooms with A/C, TV, and fridges. (☎98 277. Singles and doubles €30-40 depending on season.) **Sinatisi ❷**, a few doors down from the national bank in Kamariotissa, is a local favorite for fresh fish. (☎41 308. Open daily noon-5pm and 7pm-1am.) **Ferries** dock on the southern edge of Kamariotissa and run to Lesvos (7hr.). **Postal Code:** 68002.

HUNGARY
(MAGYARORSZÁG)

A country as singular as its language, Hungary has much more to offer than a profusion of wine, goulash, and thermal spas. Hip, vibrant Budapest remains Hungary's ascendant social, economic, and political capital. Beyond the big-city rush are towns lined with cobblestone streets and wine valleys nestled in Hungary's northern hills; beach resorts and plains abound in the east. Though Hungary can be more expensive than some of its neighbors, you always get what you pay for.

 DISCOVER HUNGARY: SUGGESTED ITINERARIES

THREE DAYS. Three days is hardly enough time for **Budapest** (p. 499). Spend a day at the churches and museums of **Castle Hill** and an afternoon in the waters of the **Széchenyi Baths** before exploring the **City Park**. Get a lesson in Hungarian history at the **Parliament** before taking in the **Opera House.**

ONE WEEK. After four days in the capital, head up the Danube Bend to see the rustic side of Hungary in **Szentendre** (1 day; p. 510). Farther down the river, **Visegrad's** citadel looms over the town (1 day; p. 511). Next, explore **Eger** (1 day; p. 512) and sample the wines of the **Valley of the Beautiful Women.**

ESSENTIALS

WHEN TO GO

Spring is best, as flowers are in bloom throughout the countryside and the tourists haven't yet arrived in droves. July and August comprise Hungary's high season, which entails crowds, booked hostels, and sweltering summer weather; consider going before or after. Autumn is beautiful, with mild, cooler weather through October. Avoid going in January and February, as temperature average around freezing and many museums and tourists spots shut down or reduce their hours.

FACTS AND FIGURES

Official Name: Hungary.

Capital: Budapest.

Major Cities: Debrecen, Miskolc, Szeged.

Population: 9,957,000.

Time Zone: GMT + 1.

Language: Hungarian.

Religions: Roman Catholic (52%).

Number of McDonald's Restaurants: 76.

DOCUMENTS AND FORMALITIES

EMBASSIES AND CONSULATES. Foreign embassies to Hungary are in Budapest (see p. 502). Hungary's embassies and consulates abroad include: Australia, 17 Beale Crescent, Deakin, ACT 2600 (☎62 82 32 26; www.mata.com.au/~hungemb); Canada, 299 Waverley St., Ottawa, ON K2P 0V9 (☎613-230-2717; www.docuweb.ca/Hungary); Ireland, 2 Fitzwilliam Pl., Dublin 2 (☎661 2902; www.kum.hu/dublin); New Zealand, Consulate-General, 37 Abbott St., Wellington 6004 (☎973 7507; www.hungarianconsulate.co.nz); UK, 35 Eaton Pl., London SW1X 8BY (☎20 72 35 52 18; www.huemblon.org.uk); US, 3910 Shoemaker St., NW, Washington, D.C. 20008 (☎202-362-6730; www.hungaryembwas.org).

ENTRANCE REQUIREMENTS.
Passport: Required for all non-EU citizens.
Visa: See below.
Letter of Invitation: Not required.
Inoculations: Not required. Recommended up-to-date on DTaP (diphtheria, tetanus, and pertussis), hepatitis A, hepatitis B, MMR (measles, mumps, and rubella), polio booster, and typhoid.
Work Permit: Required for all foreigners planning to work in Hungary.
Driving Permit: International Driving Permits are recognized in Hungary, as are US and European driver's licenses with Hungarian translations attached.

VISA AND ENTRY INFORMATION. Citizens of Australia, Canada, Ireland, New Zealand, and the US can visit Hungary without visas for up to 90 days; UK citizens can visit without a visa for up to 180 days. Consult your embassy for longer stays. Passports must be valid for six months after the end of the trip. There is no fee for crossing a Hungarian border. In general, border officials are efficient; plan on 30min. crossing time.

TOURIST SERVICES AND MONEY

TOURIST OFFICES. Tourinform has branches in most cities and is a useful first-stop **tourist service.** Tourinform doesn't make accommodation reservations but will find vacancies, especially in university dorms and private *panzió*. Agencies also stock maps and provide local information; employees generally speak English and German. Most **IBUSZ** offices throughout the country book private rooms, exchange money, and sell train tickets, but they are generally better at assisting in travel plans than at providing info. Local agencies may be staffed only by Hungarian and German speakers, but they are often very helpful and offer useful tips.

MONEY. The national currency is the **forint (Ft).** One forint is divided into 100 fillérs, which have disappeared almost entirely from circulation. Hungary has a **Value Added Tax (VAT)** rate of 20%. **Inflation** hovers at a relatively stable 3.5%. Currency exchange machines are slow but offer good rates, though banks like **OTP Bank** and **Raiffensen** offer the best exchange rates for **traveler's checks.** Never

HUNGARIAN FORINTS (FT)	
AUS$1 = 158.49FT	1000FT = AUS$6.31
CDN$1 = 192.19FT	1000FT = CDN$5.20
EUR€1 = 270.26FT	1000FT = EUR€3.70
NZ$1 = 133.64FT	1000FT = NZ$7.48
UK£1 = 395.34FT	1000FT = UK£2.53
US$1 = 213.97FT	1000FT = US$4.67

change money on the street, as it is illegal, and avoid extended-hour exchange offices, which have poor rates. Watch for scams: the maximum legal commission for cash-to-cash exchange is 1%. 24-hr. **ATMS** are common. Major **credit cards** are accepted in many hotels and restaurants in large cities, but they're very rarely accepted in the countryside. Service is not usually included in restaurant bills and while **tipping** is not mandatory, it's generally appropriate to do so. Don't bother bargaining with cabbies, but make sure to set a price before getting in.

HEALTH AND SAFETY

In Budapest, **medical assistance** is easy to obtain and fairly inexpensive, but may not always be up to western standards. In an emergency, especially outside Budapest, one might be sent to Germany or Vienna. Most hospitals have English-speaking doctors on staff. **Tourist insurance** is useful—and necessary—for many medical services. In the event of an emergency, however, even non-insured foreigners are entitled to free medical services. **Tap water** is usually clean, but the water in Tokaj is poorly purified. **Bottled water** can be purchased at most food stores. **Public bathrooms** (*férfi* for men, *női* for women) vary in cleanliness: pack soap, a towel, and 30Ft for the attendant. Carry **toilet paper,** as many hostels do not provide it and public restrooms provide only a single square. Many **pharmacies** (*gyógyszertár*) stock Western brands, tampons (*betet*), and condoms (*ovszer*).

Violent **crime** is rare. Tourists, however, are targets for petty theft and pickpocketing. Check prices before getting in taxis or ordering food or drinks; cab drivers and servers may attempt to overcharge unsuspecting tourists. **Women** traveling alone in Hungary should take the usual precautions. **Minorities** are generally accepted, though dark-skinned travelers may encounter prejudice. In an emergency, your embassy will likely be more helpful than the **police.** Though Hungary is known for being open-minded, **GLBT** travelers may face serious discrimination, especially outside Budapest.

EMERGENCY	**Police:** ☎107. **Ambulance:** ☎104 **Fire:** ☎105. **General Emergency:** ☎112.

TRANSPORTATION

BY PLANE. Many international airlines fly to Budapest. The national airline, **Malév,** flies to Budapest's airport, **Esterhazy,** from London, New York and other major cities. Direct flights can be quite expensive, starting at around $1,500. Flying to another European hub and taking a connecting plane or train may be the cheapest option. Other European airlines that fly to Hungary include **Sky Europe** (www.skyeurope.com) and **WizzAir** (www.wizzair.com).

BY TRAIN. Budapest is connected by train to most European capitals. Several types of **Eurail passes** are valid in Hungary. Check schedules and fares at **www.elvira.hu.** *Személyvonat* trains have many local stops and are excruciatingly slow; *gyorsvonat* trains, listed in red on schedules, move much faster for the same price. Large towns are connected by blue express lines; these air-conditioned InterCity trains are the fastest. A *pótjegy* (seat reservation) is required on trains labeled "R," and violators face a hefty fine. The *peron* (platform) is rarely indicated until the train approaches the station and will sometimes be announced in Hungarian; look closely out the window as you approach a station. Many stations are not marked; ask the conductor what time the train will arrive (or simply point to your watch and say the town's name). Train reservations cost around US$5, and are recommended in summer and for night trains to get a sleeper compartment.

BY BUS AND BY FERRY. Buses tend to be efficient and well-priced, but generally not more so than trains. The major line is **Volanbusz,** a privately owned company. Purchase tickets on board, and arrive early for a seat. In larger cities, buy tickets at a kiosk, and punch them as you get on. Beware: plainclothes inspectors fine those caught without a ticket. A ferry runs down the Danube from Vienna and Bratislava to Budapest. For more info, contact **Utinform** (☎322 3600).

BY CAR AND BY TAXI. To **drive** in Hungary, carry your **International Driving Permit** and registration, and insurance papers. Car rental is available in most major cities but can be expensive. For 24hr. English assistance, contact the **Magyar Autóklub** (**MAK;** in Budapest, ☎345 1800). **Taxi** prices should not exceed the following: 6am-10pm base fare 200Ft per km, 60Ft per min. waiting; 10pm-6am 300/70Ft. Beware of taxi scams. Before getting in, check that the meter works and ask how much the ride will cost. Taxis ordered by phone are than those hailed on the street.

BY BIKE AND BY THUMB. Biking terrain varies. The northeast is topographically varied; the south is flat. **Bike** rental is sometimes difficult to find; tourist bureaus should have information on where and how to rent. Biking can be dangerous because bicyclists do not have the right of way and drivers are not careful. Though it is fairly common in Hungary, Let's Go does not recommend **hitchhiking.**

KEEPING IN TOUCH

PHONE CODES	**Country code: 36. International dialing prefix:** 00. For more info on how to place international calls, see **Inside Back Cover.**

EMAIL AND THE INTERNET. Internet is readily available in major cities. The Hungarian keyboard differs significantly from English-language keyboards. Look for free Internet access at hostels. Most Internet cafes charge 500-600Ft per hour.

TELEPHONE. For **intercity calls,** wait for the tone and dial slowly; "06" goes before the phone code. **International calls** require red or blue phones. The blue phones tend to end calls after 3-9min. Phones often require *telefonkártya* (phone cards). The best ones for international calls is **Barangolo.** International calls cost around 9Ft. Make direct calls from Budapest's phone office. International phone cards are sold by 2000Ft, and national cards are 800Ft. A 20Ft coin is required to start most calls. International access numbers include: **AT&T Direct** (☎06 800 01111); **Australia Direct** (☎06 800 06111); **BT Direct** (☎0800 89 0036); **Canada Direct** (☎06 800 01211); **MCI WorldPhone** (☎06 800 01411); **NZ Direct** (☎06 800 06411); and **Sprint** (☎06 800 01877). **Mobile phones** are common. Major vendors include Pannon GSM, T-Mobile, or Vodafone. Dialing a mobile from a public or private phone anywhere in Hungary is treated as a long distance call, requiring the entire 11-digit number.

MAIL. Hungarian mail is usually reliable; **airmail** *(légiposta)* takes one week to 10 days to the US and Europe. Mailing a letter costs about 36Ft domestically and 250Ft internationally.Those without permanent addresses can receive mail through **Poste Restante.** Use Global Priority mail, as it is reliable. Address envelopes: First name, LAST NAME, POSTE RESTANTE, Post office address, Postal Code, city, HUNGARY.

LANGUAGE. Hungarian, a Finno-Ugric language, is distantly related to Turkish, Estonian, and Finnish. After Hungarian and German, English is Hungary's third most commonly spoken language. Almost all young people know some English. *"Hello"* is often used as an informal greeting. Coincidentally, *"Szia!"* (sounds like "see ya!") is another greeting—friends will often cry, "Hello, see ya!" For a phrasebook and glossary, see **Appendix: Hungarian,** p.1062.

ACCOMMODATIONS AND CAMPING

HUNGARY	❶	❷	❸	❹	❺
ACCOMMODATIONS	under 2500Ft	2500-4000Ft	4000-7000Ft	7000-12,000Ft	over 12,000Ft

Tourism is developing rapidly, and rising prices make **hostels** attractive. Hostels are usually large enough to accommodate summer crowds. Many hostels can be booked through **Express** (in Budapest ☎266 3277), a student travel agency, or through local tourist offices. From June to August, many university dorms become hostels. These may be the cheapest options in smaller towns, as hostels are less common outside Budapest. Locations change annually; inquire at Tourinform and call ahead. **Guesthouses and pensions** *(panzió)* are more common than hotels in small towns. Singles are scarce, though some guesthouses have a singles rate for double rooms—it can be worth finding a roommate, as solo travelers must often pay for doubles. Check prices; agencies may try to rent you their most expensive rooms. **Private rooms** *(zimmer frei)* booked through tourist agencies are sometimes cheap. After staying a few nights, make arrangements directly with the owner to save your agency's 20-30% commission. Hungary has over 300 **campgrounds.** Most open from May to September. For more info, consult *Camping Hungary,* a booklet available in most tourist offices, or contact Tourinform in Budapest (see **Tourist Services and Money,** p. 503).

FOOD AND DRINK

HUNGARY	❶	❷	❸	❹	❺
FOOD	under 400Ft	400-800Ft	800-1300Ft	1300-2800Ft	over 2800Ft

Hungarian food is more flavorful than many of its Eastern European culinary counterparts, with many spicy meat dishes. **Paprika,** Hungary's chief agricultural export, colors most dishes red. In Hungarian restaurants *(vendéglő* or *étterem), halászlé,* a spicy fish stew, is a traditional starter. Or, try *gyümölcsleves,* a cold fruit soup with whipped cream. The Hungarian national dish is *bográcsgulyás,* a soup of beef, onions, green pepper, tomatoes, potatoes, dumplings, and plenty of paprika. *Borjúpaprikás* is veal with paprika and potato-dumpling pasta. For **Vegetarians** there is tasty *rántott sajt* (fried cheese) and *gombapörkölt* (mushroom stew). Delicious Hungarian fruits and vegetables abound in summer. Vegetarians should also look for *salata* (salad) and *sajt* (cheese), as these will be the only options in many small-town restaurants. Keeping kosher, on the other hand, is fairly difficult. Avoid American food like hot dogs which can cause food poisoning. The northeastern towns of Eger and Tokaj produce famous red and white **wines,** respectively. *Sör* (Hungarian **beer**) ranges from first-rate to acceptable. Lighter beers include *Dreher Pils, Szalon Sör,* and licensed versions of *Steffl, Gold Fassl,* and *Amstel.* Among the best-tasting *pálinka,* (brandy-like liquor) are *barackpálinka* (an apricot schnapps) and *körtepálinka* (pear brandy). *Unicum,* advertised as the national drink, is an **herbal liqueur** containing over 40 herbs; it was once used by the Habsburgs to cure digestive ailments.

HOLIDAYS AND FESTIVALS

Holidays: New Year's Day (Jan. 1); National Day (Mar. 15); Easter Holiday (Mar. 24, 2008; Apr. 13, 2009); Labor Day (May 1); Pentecost (May 11, 2008; May 31, 2009); Constitution Day (St. Stephen's Day, Aug. 20); Republic Day (Oct. 23); All Saints' Day (Nov. 1); Christmas (Dec. 25-26).

Festivals: Central Europe's largest rock festival, Sziget Festival, hits Budapest for a week in late July or early August, featuring rollicking crowds and international superstar acts. Eger's fabulous World Festival of Wine Songs celebration kicks off in late September, bringing together boisterous choruses and world-famous vintage wines.

BEYOND TOURISM

Central European University, Nador u. 9, Budapest 1051, Hungary (☎36 13 27 30 09; www.ceu.hu). Affiliated with the Open Society Institute-Budapest offers international students the opportunity to take graduate-level courses. Tuition US$9395 per semester, not including personal expenses. Financial aid available.

Hungarian Dance Academy, Columbus u. 87-89, Budapest H-1145, Hungary (☎36 12 73 34 34; www.mtf.hu). Summer dance programs for students ages 11-24.

Central European Teaching Program, 3800 NE 72nd Ave., Portland, OR 97213, USA (☎1-503-287-4977; www.ticon.net/~cetp). Places English teachers in state schools in Hungary and Romania for one semester (US$1700) or a full school year (US$2,250).

BUDAPEST ☎01

While other parts of Hungary maintain a slow pace, Budapest (pop. 1.9 million) has seized upon cosmopolitan chic with a vengeance, without giving up its old-time charms. Unlike in toyland Prague, the sights of Budapest spread throughout the energetic city, giving it a life independent of the growing crowds of tourists; Turkish thermal baths and Roman ruins mix seamlessly with modern buildings and a legendary night scene. The area that constitutes Budapest was once two entities: the pasture-ruled city of Pest and viticulture hills of Buda. In 1873, the two areas separated by the Danube were unified by a Habsburg initiative. Although the city was ravaged by WWII, Hungarians rebuilt it, and then weathered a Soviet invasion and 40 years of Communism. That resilient spirit resonates through the streets as the city reassumes its place as a major European capital.

▛ TRANSPORTATION

Flights: Ferihegy Airport (**BUD;** ☎296 9696). **Malév** (Hungarian Airlines; reservations ☎235 3888) flies to major cities. To the center, take **bus** #93 (20min., every 15min. 4:55am-11:20pm, 260Ft), then M3 to Kőbánya-Kispest (15min. to Deák tér, in downtown Budapest). **Airport Minibus** (☎296 8555) goes to hotels or hostels (2300Ft).

Trains: Major stations are **Keleti Pályaudvar, Nyugati Pályaudvar,** and **Déli Pályaudvar.** (International and domestic information ☎40 49 49 49.) Most international trains arrive at Keleti pu., but some from Prague go to Nyugati pu. For schedules, check www.elvira.hu. To: **Berlin, GER** (12-15hr.; 2 per day; 28,305Ft, reservation 765Ft); **Bucharest, ROM** (14hr., 5 per day, 19,482Ft); **Prague, CZR** (8hr., 4 per day, 11,700Ft); **Vienna, AUT** (3hr.; 17 per day; 3315Ft); **Warsaw, POL** (11hr.; 2 per day; 18,411Ft). The daily **Orient Express** stops on its way from **Paris, FRA** to **Istanbul, TUR.** Trains run to most major destinations in Hungary. Purchase tickets at an **International Ticket Office** (Keleti pu. open daily 8am-7pm; Nyugati pu. open M-Sa 5am-9pm; info desk 24hr.). Or try **MÁV Hungarian Railways,** VI, Andrássy út 35, with branches at all

HUNGARY

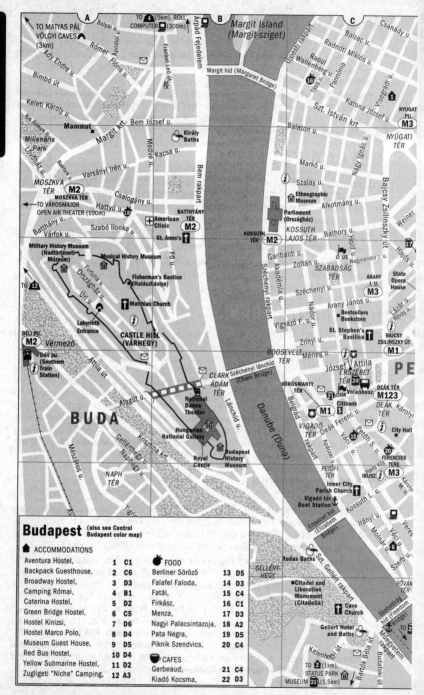

Budapest (also see Central Budapest color map)

■ ACCOMMODATIONS

Aventura Hostel,	1	C1
Backpack Guesthouse,	2	C6
Broadway Hostel,	3	D3
Camping Római,	4	B1
Caterina Hostel,	5	D2
Green Bridge Hostel,	6	C5
Hostel Kinizsi,	7	D6
Hostel Marco Polo,	8	D4
Museum Guest House,	9	D5
Red Bus Hostel,	10	D4
Yellow Submarine Hostel,	11	D2
Zugligeti "Niche" Camping,	12	A3

🍎 FOOD

Berliner Söröző	13	D5
Falafel Faloda,	14	D3
Fatál,	15	C4
Firkász,	16	C1
Menza,	17	D3
Nagyi Palacsintazoja,	18	A2
Pata Negra,	19	D5
Piknik Szendvics,	20	C4

☕ CAFES

Gerbeaud,	21	C4
Kiadó Kocsma,	22	D3

HUNGARY

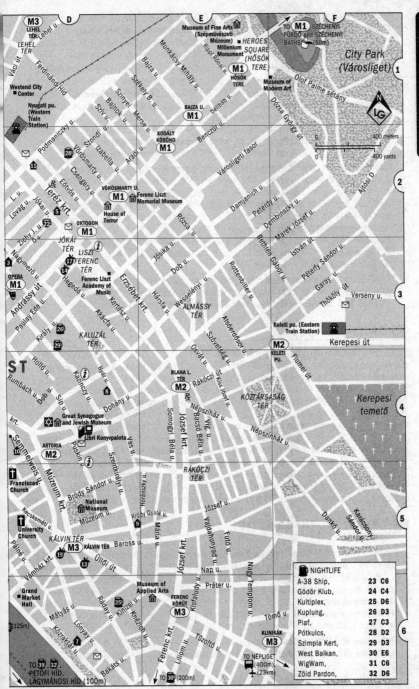

■ NIGHTLIFE	
A-38 Ship,	23 C6
Gödör Klub,	24 C4
Kultiplex,	25 D6
Kuplung,	26 D3
Piaf,	27 C3
Pótkulcs,	28 D2
Szimpla Kert,	29 D3
West Balkan,	30 E6
WigWam,	31 C6
Zöld Pardon,	32 D6

stations. (☎461 5500. Open Apr.-Sept. M-F 9am-6pm, Oct.-Mar. M-F 9am-5pm. Say *"diák"* for student or under 26 discounts.) The HÉV **commuter railway** station is at Batthyány tér, opposite Parliament. Trains head to **Szentendre** (45min., every 15min. 5am-9pm, 460Ft). Purchase tickets at the station for transport beyond the city limits.

Buses: Buses to international and some domestic destinations leave from the **Népliget** station, X, Ulloi u. 131. (M3: Népliget. ☎382 0888. Ticket window open M-F 6am-9pm, Sa-Su 6am-4pm.) To **Berlin, GER** (14½hr., 6 per week, 17,010Ft); **Prague, CZR** (8hr., 6 per week, 9810Ft); **Vienna, AUT** (3-3½hr., 5 per day, 2950Ft). Catch buses to destinations east of Budapest at the **Népstadion** station, XIV, Hungária körút 46-48. (M2: Népstadion. ☎252 4498. Open M-F 6am-6pm, Sa-Su 6am-4pm.) Buses to the Danube Bend and parts of the Uplands depart outside **Árpád híd** metro station on the M3 line. (☎329 1450. Cashier open 6am-8pm.) Check www.volanbusz.hu for schedules.

Public Transportation: Subways, buses, and **trams** are cheap and convenient. The **metro** has 3 lines: M1 (yellow), M2 (red), and M3 (blue). Night transit (É) buses run midnight-5am along major routes: #7É and 78É follow the M2 route; #6É follows the 4/6 tram line; #14É and 50É follow the M3 route. **Single-fare tickets** for public transport (one-way on 1 line; 230Ft, trams 160Ft) are sold in metro stations, in *Trafik* shops, and by sidewalk vendors. Punch them in the orange boxes at the gate of the metro or on buses and trams; punch a new ticket when you change lines, or face fines. One-way tickets are cheaper in blocks of 10 or 20. Day pass 1350Ft, 3-day 3100Ft, 1-week 3600Ft, 2-week 4800Ft, 1-month 7350Ft.

Taxis: Beware of scams; check for yellow license plates and meter. **Budataxi** (☎222 4444) charges less for rides requested by phone. Also reliable are **Főtaxi** (☎222 2222) and **6x6 Taxi** (☎466 6666). Base fare 300Ft, 350Ft per km, 70Ft per min. waiting.

ORIENTATION

Buda and Pest are separated by the **Danube River** (Duna), and the modern city preserves the distinctive character of each side. On the west bank, **Buda** has winding streets, beautiful vistas, a hilltop citadel, and the Castle District. Down the north slope of **Várhegy** (Castle Hill) is **Moszkva tér,** Buda's tram and local bus hub. On the east bank, **Pest,** the commercial center, is home to shopping boulevards, theaters, Parliament (Országház), and the Opera House. Metro lines converge in Pest at **Deák tér,** next to the main international bus terminal at **Erzsébet tér.** Two blocks west toward the river lies **Vörösmarty tér** and the pedestrian shopping zone **Váci utca.** Three main bridges join Budapest's halves: **Széchenyi Lánchíd** (Chain Bridge), **Erzsébet híd** (Elizabeth Bridge), and **Szabadság híd** (Freedom Bridge).

Budapest addresses begin with a Roman numeral representing one of the city's 23 **districts.** Central Buda is I; central Pest is V. A **map** is essential for navigating Budapest's confusing streets; pick one up at any tourist office or hostel.

PRACTICAL INFORMATION

Tourist Offices: All offices sell the **Budapest Card** (Budapest Kártya), which provides discounts, unlimited public transportation, and admission to most museums (2-day card 6450Ft, 3-day 7950Ft.). A great deal, except on Mondays when museums are closed. An excellent first stop in the city is **Tourinform,** V, Sütő u. 2 (☎438 8080; www.hungary.com). M1, 2, or 3: Deák tér. Off Deák tér behind McDonald's. Open daily 8am-8pm. **Vista Travel Center,** Andrássy út 1 (☎429 9751; incoming@vista.hu), arranges tours and accommodations. Open M-F 9am-6:30pm, Sa 9am-2:30pm.

Embassies and Consulates: Australia, XII, Királyhágó tér 8/9 (☎457 9777; www.australia.hu). M2: Déli pu., then bus #21 or tram #59 to Királyhágó tér. Open M-F 9am-noon. **Canada,** XII, Ganz u. 12-14 (☎392 3360). Open M-Th 8:30-10:30am and 2-3:30pm. **Ireland,** V, Szabadság tér 7 (☎302 9600), in Bank Center. M3: Arany János. Walk down Bank u. toward the river. Open M-F 9:30am-12:30pm and 2:30-4:30pm. **New Zealand,** VI, Nagymezo u. 50 (☎302 2484). M3: Nyugati pu. Open M-F 11am-4pm by appointment only. **UK,** V, Harmincad u. 6 (☎266 2888; www.britemb.hu), near the intersection with Vörösmarty tér. M1: Vörösmarty tér. Open M-F 9:30am-12:30pm and 2:30-4:30pm. **US,** V, Szabadság tér 12 (☎475 4164, after hours 475 4703; www.usembassy.hu). M2: Kossuth tér. Walk 2 blocks on Akadémia and turn on Zoltán. Open M-Th 1-4pm, F 9am-noon and 1-4pm.

Currency Exchange: Banks have the best rates. **Citibank,** V, Vörösmarty tér 4 (☎374 5000). M1: Vörösmarty tér. Cashes traveler's checks for no commission and provides MC/V cash advances. Bring your passport. Open M-Th 9am-5pm, F 9am-4pm.

Luggage Storage: Lockers at all 3 train stations. 150-600Ft.

English-Language Bookstore: Libri Könyvpalota, VII, Rákóczi u. 12 (☎267 4843). M2: Astoria. The best choice in the city; a multilevel bookstore, it has 1 fl. of up-to-date English titles. Open M-F 10am-7:30pm, Sa 10am-3pm. MC/V.

GLBT Hotline: GayGuide.net Budapest (☎06 30 93 23 334; www.budapest.gayguide.net). Posts an online guide and runs a hotline (daily 4-8pm) with info and reservations at GLBT-friendly lodgings. See also **GLBT Budapest,** p. 503.

Tourist Police: V, Sütő u. 2 (☎438 8080). M1, 2, or 3: Deák tér. Inside the Tourinform office. Open 24hr. Beware of people on the street pretending to be Tourist Police and demanding to see your passport.

Pharmacies: Look for green-and-white signs labeled *Apotheke, Gyógyszertár,* or *Pharmacie.* Minimal after-hours service fees apply. **II,** Frankel Leó út 22 (☎212 4406). AmEx/MC/V. **VI,** Teréz krt. 41 (☎311 4439). Open M-F 8am-8pm, Sa 8am-2pm. **VII,** Rákóczi út 39 (☎314 3695). Open M-F 7:30am-9pm, Sa 7:30am-2pm; no after-hours service.

Medical Services: Falck (SOS) KFT, II, Kapy út 49/b (☎275 1535). Ambulance service US$120. **American Clinic,** I, Hattyú u. 14 (☎224 9090; www.americanclinics.com). Open M 8:30am-7pm, Tu-W 10am-6pm, Th 11:30am-6pm, F 10am-6pm. 24hr. emergency ☎224 9090. The US embassy also maintains a list of English-speaking doctors.

Telephones: Phone cards are sold at kiosks and metro stations. 50-unit card 800Ft, 120-unit card 1800Ft. Domestic operator and info ☎198; international operator 190, info 199.

Internet Access: Cybercafes are everywhere, but they can be expensive and long waits are common. **Ami Internet Coffee,** V, Váci u. 40 (☎267 1644; www.amicoffee.hu). M3: Ferenciek tér. 200Ft per 15min., 700Ft per hr. Open daily 9am-2am.

Post Office: V, Városház u. 18 (☎318 4811). **Poste Restante** (Postán Mar) in office around the right side of the building. Open M-F 8am-8pm, Sa 8am-2pm. Branches at Nyugati pu.; VI, Teréz krt. 105/107; Keleti pu.; VIII, Baross tér 11/c; and elsewhere. Open M-F 7am-8pm, Sa 8am-2pm. **Postal Code:** Depends on the district—postal codes are 1XX2, where XX is the district number (1052 for post office listed above).

ACCOMMODATIONS AND CAMPING

Budapest's hostels are centers for the backpacker social scene, and their common rooms can be as exciting as most bars and clubs. Many hostels are run by the **Hungarian Youth Hostels Association (HI),** which operates from an office in Keleti pu. Representatives wearing Hostelling International shirts—and legions of competitors—accost travelers as they get off the train. Beware that they may provide inaccurate descriptions of other accommodations in order to sell their own. Private rooms are more expensive than hostels, but they do offer peace, quiet, and private showers. Arrive early, bring cash, and haggle. **Best Hotel Service,** V, Sütő u. 2, arranges apartment, hostel, and hotel reservations (6000Ft and up). Take M1, 2, or 3 to Deák tér. (☎318 4848; www.besthotelservice.hu. Open daily 8am-8pm.)

Backpack Guesthouse, XI, Takács Menyhért u. 33 (☎385 8946; www.backpackers.hu), 12min. from central Pest. From Keleti pu., take bus #7 or 7a toward Buda. Get off at Tétényi u., then backtrack and turn left to go under the bridge. Take another left on Hamzsabégi út and continue to the 3rd right. A common room stocked with movies and a slew of hammocks in an inner garden make this neighborhood house a quiet, earthy hideaway from the traffic of the city. The 49E night bus runs here after trams stop. Laundry 1500Ft. Free Internet. Reception 24hr. Mattress in gazebo 2500Ft; 7- to 11-bed dorms 3000Ft, 4- to 5-bed dorms 3500Ft; doubles 9000Ft. MC/V. ❷

Aventura Hostel, XIII, Visegrádi u. 12 (☎703 102 003; www.aventurahostel.com), in Pest. M3: Nyugati tér. Tasteful interior design and clean bathrooms. Provides info on special event and party listings around town. Breakfast included. Laundry 1500Ft. Free Internet. Reception 24hr. Dorms 3500-4500Ft; doubles 12,500Ft. Cash only. ❸

Yellow Submarine Hostel, VI, Podmaniczky u. 27, 1st floor (☎331 9896, www.yellow-submarinehostel.com). Take a left out of Nyugati pu. and another left at the first street; ring bell #33 on the first porch on the opposite side of the street. It's known as a party hostel, and rowdy crowds hang out in the common room. Large dorms with bunks and lockers. Doubles and triples in nearby apartments. Breakfast included for dorms. Laundry 1700Ft. Internet 10Ft per min. Check-out 10am. Dorms 3000Ft; singles 8000Ft; doubles 9600Ft; triples 11,100Ft; quads 14,800Ft. 10% HI discount. MC/V. ❷

Green Bridge Hostel, V, Molnár u. 22-24 (☎266 6922; greenbridge@freemail.hu), in Pest's central district. The unbeatable location, friendly staff, and free snacks. Free Internet. Reception 24hr. Reserve ahead. Dorms 3750-4500Ft. Cash only. ❸

Museum Guest House, VIII, Mikszáth Kálmán tér 4, 1st fl. (☎318 9508; museumgh@freemail.c3.hu), in Pest. M3: Kálvin tér. Convenient location, colorful rooms, and loft beds. English spoken. Free Internet. Reception 24hr. Check-out 11am. Reserve ahead. Dorms 3200Ft. Cash only. ❸

Broadway Hostel, VI, Ó u. 24-26 (☎688 1662; www.broadwayhostel.hu). M1: Opera. A new, luxurious alternative to the backpacking scene, with curtain partitions, fluffy comforters, and lockable closets. Inner courtyard with hammocks provides a laid-back hangout. Internet 250Ft per 30min. Reception 24hr. Check-out 10:30am. Dorms 3200-3300Ft; singles 5500Ft; doubles 9500Ft. Cash only. ❷

Red Bus Hostel, V, Semmelweis u. 14 (☎266 0136; www.redbusbudapest.hu). Newly renovated hardwood-floored rooms on a quiet street near the action of downtown Pest. A large common room provides a hangout for travelers. Kitchen available. Breakfast included. Free luggage storage. Laundry 1300Ft. Internet 10Ft per min. Reception 24hr. Check-out 10am. Dorms 3600Ft; singles and doubles 9500Ft; triples 11,350Ft. V. ❷

Caterina Hostel, III, Teréz krt. 30, apt. #28, ring code: #48 (☎269 5990; www.caterinahostel.hu). M1: Oktogon, or trams #4 or 6. Sunny, slick rooms with fresh wooden furniture. Fresh linens and in-room TVs. Transport to airport 2000Ft. English spoken. Laundry 1400Ft. Free Internet. Reception 24hr. Check-out 10am. Lockout 10am-1pm. Dorms with bunks 2500-3000Ft; private rooms 6800Ft. Cash only. ❷

Hostel Marco Polo, VII, Nyár u. 6 (☎413 2555; www.marcopolohostel.com). M2: Astoria or Blaha Lujza tér. Hotel-esque and more private than other hostels, as dorm bunks are in separate compartments blocked off by curtains. Courtyard patio and basement restaurant with bar open 24hr. Laundry 600Ft. Internet 250 per 30min. Reception 24hr. Reserve ahead July-Aug. Dorms 4400Ft; singles 15,400Ft; doubles 19,200Ft; triples 21,000Ft; quads 25,400Ft. 400Ft ISIC discount. Cash only. ❸

Hostel Kinizsi, IX, Kinizsi u. 2-6 (☎933 0660, www.kinizsi.uni-corvinus.hu). In an artsy district, a block from the Museum of Applied Arts. Large common room and adjoining cafe open late draw many the many backpackers out of their rooms to chat and mingle. 5500Ft shuttle service to airport. Check-out 10am. 5-bed dorm 3200Ft; triples 3400Ft; doubles 3600Ft. Open July-Aug. Cash only. ❶

Camping Római, III, Szentendrei út. 189 (☎388 7167). M2: Batthyány tér. Take HÉV to Római fürdő; walk 100m toward river. If you're looking to get away from the buzz of the city, this campground offers a huge complex with swimming pool, park, and nearby grocery store and restaurants. Laundry 800Ft. Tent sites 4400Ft per person; bungalows 3000Ft per person. Cars 4710Ft. Electricity included. 3% tourist tax. 10% HI discount. Reserve far ahead as campsites fill up quickly in the summer. ❸

Zugligeti "Niche" Camping, XII, Zugligeti út 101 (☎/fax 200 8346; www.camping-niche.hu). Take bus #158 from above Moszkva tér to Laszállóhely, the last stop. Communal showers. 1400Ft per person, 990Ft per tent, 1400Ft per large tent, 1050Ft per car, 2550Ft per caravan. Cash only. ❶

▟ HUNGARY?

Cafeterias with *"Önkiszolgáló Étterem"* signs serve cheap food (entrees 300-500Ft), and a neighborhood *kifőzés* (kiosk) or *vendéglő* (family-style restaurant) offers a real taste of Hungary. Corner markets, many with 24hr. windows, stock the basics. The ▧**Grand Market Hall,** IX, Fövam tér 1/3, next to Szabadság híd (M3: Kálvin tér), has two and a half acres of stalls, making it an attraction in itself. Ethnic restaurants inhabit the upper floors of **Mammut Plaza,** just outside the Moszkva tér metro in Buda, and **West End Plaza,** near the Nyugati metro in Pest.

RESTAURANTS

▧ **Fatál,** V, Váci u. 67 (☎266 2607), in Pest. M3: Ferenciek tér. Enormous portions of down-home, delicious Hungarian cuisine in a cool underground setting, off hustling Váci u. Entrees 590-2500Ft. Open daily 11:30am-2am. MC/V. ❷

▧ **Nagyi Palacsintazoja,** II, Hattyu u. 16 (☎201 5321), in Buda. M2: Moszkva tér. Tiny, mirror-covered eatery dishes out sweet and savory crepes (118-298Ft) piled with toppings like cheese, fruit, or chocolate sauce. Limited space. Open 24hr. ❶

Berliner Söröző, IX, Ráday u. 5 (☎217 6757; www.berliner.hu). An interesting mix of old-school Hungarian flavors and smooth Belgian drafts. Lively patio lets you enjoy warm summer nights and indulge in the chill atmosphere of Ráday utca. Beer 400Ft. Open M-Sa noon-1am. Cash only. ❸

Firkász, XIII, Tátra u. 18 (☎450 1118; www.firkaszetterem.hu). The most traditional Hungarian restaurant in the city, from its paprika-infused dishes to its delicately embroidered table cloths. Entrees 800Ft-3000Ft. Open daily noon-midnight. Cash only. ❸

Pata Negra, IX, Kávin tér 8 (www.patanegra.hu). This Spanish restaurant stands at the center of Kávin tér. Entrees (300Ft-1900Ft) are dirt cheap and daringly Latin. Tapas (300Ft-580Ft)Open M-Th and Su 11am-midnight, F-Sa noon-midnight. Cash only. ❶

Menza, Liszt Ferenc tér 2 (☎413 1482; www.menza.co.hu). Reminiscent of Communist-era *"menza,"* or canteens, this elegant eatery's decor offers a mix of 70s camp and modern chic. Menu boards list all manner of excellent Hungarian and international dishes on offer. Entrees 650-1790Ft. Open daily 10am-1am. AmEx/MC/V. ❷

Falafel Faloda, VI. Paulay Ede u. 53 (☎351 1243), in Pest. M1: Opera. Vegetarians come in droves for on-the-go falafel (20Ft) and the city's best salad bar. Salads 280-420Ft. Smoothies 290Ft-350Ft and a wide selection of teas 180Ft-220Ft. Open M-F 10am-8pm, Sa 10am-6pm. Cash only. ❶

Piknik Szendvics, V, Haris Köz 1 (☎318 3334; www.piknik-szendvics.hu), in Pest. M3: Ferenciek tér. Create a meal from inexpensive appetizer-sized open-faced sandwiches (120-290Ft). Open M-F 9am-6pm, Sa 9am-2pm. Cash only. ❶

REVISITING THE GYPSY FOLKTALE

Eastern Europe is home to an estimated seven to nine million gypsies, or Roma, making them the region's largest minority group. In Hungary, they account for 9-11% of the population. Roma are believed to have migrated from India, and they have been living in Europe for centuries, particularly in the Balkans. The scarf-clad gypsies have long been a staple character in Eastern European folk tales, stereotypically cast as colorful roving musician-types.

In reality, the Roma story is not so rosy—they have long been victims of extreme discrimination, with inadequate access to housing, jobs, public education, and healthcare. At its most extreme, this discrimination has taken the form of forced sterilization or racially motivated murders.

The plight of the Roma is beginning to generate a worldwide outcry. The first large-scale conference to address the situation was held in Budapest in 2003. Delegates from eight Eastern European countries and international NGOs joined forces to launch the "Decade of Roma Inclusion," beginning in 2005. It aims to "change the lives of Roma" across the region and reduce poverty and illiteracy. Recent news updates suggest that the Roma are slowly on the path to an improved socioeconomic status. (*See www.romadecade.com for info.*)

CAFES

Once the haunts of the literary, intellectual, and cultural elite—as well as political dissidents—Budapest's cafes boast mysterious histories and delicious pastries.

Kiadó Kocsma, VI, Jókai tér 3 (☎331 1955), in Pest, next to Cafe Alhambra. M1: Oktogon. Irresistibly playful atmosphere and tranquil, shady terrace, perfect for coffee (250Ft), tea (200Ft), or spirits (550-700Ft) as well as light, Hungarian-style snacks (390Ft-590Ft) or crazy twists on Hungarian entrees try the salami and mushroom gnocchi with mascarpone sauce (2490F). Open daily 5pm-2am. MC/V.

Gerbeaud, V, Vörösmarty tér 7 (☎429 9020; www.gerbeaud.hu). M1: Vörösmarty tér. Hungary's most famous cafe and dessert shop has served delicious, homemade layer cakes (680Ft) and ice cream (260Ft) since 1858. Large terrace. Go for the tradition, but beware that sweets here cost at least double the price of any other dessert shop, and you'll be surrounded by double the tourists. Open daily 9am-9pm. AmEx/MC/V.

◎ SIGHTS

In 1896, Hungary's millennial birthday bash prompted the construction of what are today Budapest's most prominent sights. Among the works commissioned by the Habsburgs were **Hősök tér** (Heroes' Square), **Szabadság híd** (Liberty Bridge), **Vajdahunyad Vár** (Vajdahunyad Castle), and continental Europe's first **metro** system. Slightly grayer for wear, war, and occupation, these monuments attest to the optimism of a capital on the verge of its Golden Age. See the sights, find your way around, and meet other travelers with **Absolute Walking and Biking Tours.** (☎211 8861; www.absolutetours.com. 3½hr. tours 4000Ft, students 3500ft. Specialized tours 4000-7000Ft.) **Boat tours** leave from Vigadó tér piers 6-7, near Elizabeth Bridge in Pest. The evening *Danube Legend* costs 4200Ft; its daytime counterpart, the *Duna Bella*, costs 3800Ft for 2hr.

BUDA

On the east bank of the Danube, Buda sprawls between the base of **Várhegy** (Castle Hill) and southern **Gellérthegy** and leads into the city's main residential areas. Older and more peaceful than Pest, Buda is filled with parks and lush hills.

CASTLE DISTRICT. Towering above the Danube on Várhegy, the Castle District has been razed three times in its 800-year history, most recently in 1945. With its winding, statue-filled streets, impressive views, and hodgepodge of architectural styles, the UNESCO-protected district now appears much as it did under the

Habsburg reign. The reconstructed **Buda Castle** (Vár) houses fine museums (p. 509). Bullet holes in the facade recall the 1956 uprising. *(M1, 2, or 3: Deák tér. From the metro, take bus #16 across the Danube. Or, from M2: Moszkva tér, walk up to the hill on Várfok u. "Becsi kapu" marks the castle entrance.)* Beneath Buda Castle, the ▓**Castle Labyrinths** (Budvári Labirinths) provide a spooky glimpse of the subterranean city. *(Úri u. 9. ☎212 0207; www.labirintus.com. Open daily 9:30am-7:30pm. 1500Ft, students 1200Ft.)*

MATTHIAS CHURCH. The colorful roof of Matthias Church (Mátyás templom) on Castle Hill is one of Budapest's most photographed sights. The church was converted into a mosque in 1541, then renovated again 145 years later when the Habsburgs defeated the Turks. Ascend the spiral steps to view the exhibits of the **Museum of Ecclesiastical Art.** *(I, Szentháromság tér 2. Open M-F 9am-5pm, Sa 9am-1:45pm, Su 1-5pm. High mass daily 7, 8:30am, 6pm; Su and holidays also 10am and noon. Church and museum 650Ft, students 450Ft.)*

GELLÉRT HILL. After the coronation of King Stephen, the first Christian Hungarian monarch, in AD 1001, the Pope sent Bishop Gellért to convert the Magyars. After those unconvinced by the bishop's message hurled him to his death from the summit of Budapest's principal hill, it was named Gellérthegy in his honor. The **Liberation Monument** (Szabadság Szobor), on the hilltop, honors Soviet soldiers who died ridding Hungary of Nazis. The adjoining **Citadel** was built as a symbol of Habsburg power after the foiled 1848 revolution; the view from there is especially stunning at night. At the base of the hill is **Gellért** (p. 509), Budapest's most famous Turkish bath. *(XI. Take tram #18 or 19 or bus #7 to Hotel Gellért; follow Szabó Verjték u. to Jubileumi Park, continuing on marked paths to the summit. Citadel 1200Ft.)*

PEST

Constructed in the 19th century, the winding streets of Pest now link cafes, corporations, and monuments. The crowded **Belváros** (Inner City) is based around **Vörösmarty tér** and the swarming pedestrian boulevard **Váci utca.**

▓**PARLIAMENT.** The palatial Gothic Parliament (Országház) stands 96m tall, a number that symbolizes the date of Hungary's millennial anniversary. The building was modeled after the UK's, right down to the facade and the riverside location. The **crown jewels** were moved from Hungary's National Museum to the Cupola Room here in 1999. *(M2: Kossuth tér. ☎441 4000. English-language tours M-F 10am, noon, 2, 2:30pm; Sa-Su 10am; arrive early. Min. 5 people. Ticket office at Gate X opens at 8am. Entrance with mandatory tour 2300Ft, students 1150Ft. Free with EU passport.)*

GREAT SYNAGOGUE. The largest synagogue in Europe and the second-largest in the world, Pest's Great Synagogue (Zsinagóga) was designed to hold 3000 worshippers. The enormous metal **Tree of Life,** a Holocaust memorial, sits in the garden above a mass grave for thousands of Jews killed near the end of the war. The Hebrew inscription reads: "Whose pain can be greater than mine?" and the Hungarian beneath pledges: "Let us remember." Each leaf bears the name of a family that perished. Next door, the **Jewish Museum** (Zsidó Múzeum) documents the storied past of Hungary's Jews. *(VII. At the corner of Dohány u. and Wesselényi u. M2: Astoria. Open May-Oct. M-Th 10am-5pm, F and Su 10am-2pm; Nov.-Apr. M-Th 10am-3pm, F and Su 10am-1pm. Services F 6pm. Admissions often start at 10:30am. Covered shoulders required. Tours M-Th 10:30am-3:30pm on the half-hour, F and Su 10:30, 11:30am, 12:30pm. Admission 1400Ft, students 750Ft. Tours 1900Ft/1600Ft.)*

ST. STEPHEN'S BASILICA (SZ. ISTVÁN BAZILIKA). Though seriously damaged in WWII, the neo-Renaissance facade of the city's largest church has been mostly restored. The **Panorama Tower** offers an amazing 360° view of the city. A curious attraction is St. Stephen's mummified right hand, one of Hungary's most revered religious relics; a 100Ft donation dropped in the box will illuminate it for 2min. *(V. M1, 2, or 3: Deák tér. Open May-Oct. M-Sa 9am-5pm; Nov.-Apr. M-Sa 10am-4pm. Mass M-Sa 7, 8am, 6pm; Su 8:30, 10am, noon, 6pm. Free. Tower open daily June-Aug. 9:30am-6pm; Sept.-Oct. 10am-5:30pm; Apr.-May 10am-4:30pm. 500Ft, students 400Ft.)*

ANDRÁSSY ÚT AND HEROES' SQUARE. Hungary's grandest boulevard, Andrássy út extends from Erzsébet tér northeast to Heroes' Square (Hősök tér). The **State Opera House** (Magyar Állami Operaház) is a vivid reminder of Budapest's Golden Age; its gilded interior glows on performance nights. Take a tour if you can't see an opera. *(Andrássy út 22. M1: Opera. ☎332 8197. 1hr. English-language tours daily 3 and 4pm. 2500Ft, students 1300Ft.)* At the Heroes' Sq. end of Andrássy út, the **Millennium Monument** (Millenniumi emlékmű) commemorates the nation's most prominent leaders.

CITY PARK (VÁROSLIGET). Budapest's park, located northeast of Heroes' Sq., is home to a zoo, a circus, an aging amusement park, and the lakeside **Vajdahunyad Castle.** The castle's collage of Baroque, Gothic, and Romanesque styles chronicles the history of Hungarian design. Outside the castle is the hooded statue of King Béla IV's **anonymous scribe,** who left the major record of medieval Hungary. Rent a **rowboat** or **ice skates** on the lake next to the castle. The park's main road is closed to automobiles on weekends. *(XIV. M1: Széchényi Fürdő. Zoo ☎343 3710. Open May-Aug. M-Th 9am-6:30pm, F-Su 9am-7pm; Mar. and Oct. M-Th 9am-5pm, F-Su 9am–5:30pm; Apr. and Sept. M-Th 9am-5:30pm, F-Su 9am-6pm; Nov.-Jan. daily. 9am-4pm. 1700Ft, students 1200Ft. Park ☎363 8310. Open July-Aug. daily 10am-8pm; May-June M-F 11am-7pm, Sa-Su 10am-8pm. 3100Ft, children 2100Ft weekdays; weekends 3500Ft, kids 2500Ft.)*

🏛 MUSEUMS

■**MUSEUM OF APPLIED ARTS (IPARMŰVÉSZETI MÚZEUM).** This collection of handcrafted pieces—including ceramics, furniture, metalwork, and Tiffany glass—deserves careful examination. Excellent temporary exhibits highlight specific crafts. Built for the 1896 millennium, the tiled Art Nouveau edifice is as intricate as the pieces within. *(IX. Üllői út 33-37. M3: Ferenc krt. ☎456 5100. Open Tu-Su 10am-6pm. Prices vary; usually around 1600Ft, students 800Ft. Tours usually 2300Ft/1150Ft.)*

■**HOUSE OF TERROR.** Both the Nazi and Soviet regimes housed prisoners in the basement of this building near Heroes' Sq. An acclaimed museum opened here in 2002 to document life under the two reigns of terror and memorialize the victims who were tortured and killed. *(VI. Andrássy Út 60. M1: Vörösmarty u. ☎374 2600; www.terrorhaza.hu. Open Tu-F 10am-6pm, Sa-Su 10am-7:30pm. 1500Ft, students 750Ft.)*

LUDWIG MUSEUM (LUDVIG MÚZEUM). Located on the outskirts of the city, the Ludwig Museum ("LuMu") displays cutting-edge Hungarian painting and sculpture. *(IX. Komor Marcell u. 1. Take tram #4 or 6 to Boráros tér, then take the HÉV commuter rail 1 stop to Lagymanyosi híd. ☎555 3444; www.ludwigmuseum.hu. Open Tu-Su 10am-8pm, last Sa. of the month 10am-10pm. Temporary exhibit 1200Ft, students 600Ft.)*

MUSEUM OF FINE ARTS (SZÉPMŰVÉSZETI MÚZEUM). A spectacular collection of European art is housed in this museum near Heroes' Sq. The El Greco room is not to be missed. *(M1: Hősök tér. ☎496 7100. Open Tu-Su 10am-6pm, ticket booth until 5pm. 2400Ft, students 1200Ft.)*

NATIONAL MUSEUM (NEMZETI MÚZEUM). An extensive exhibit on the second floor chronicles the history of Hungary from the founding of the state through the 20th century; the first floor is reserved for temporary exhibits. *(VIII. Múzeum krt. 14/ 16. M3: Kálvin tér. ☎338 2122; www.mng.hu. Open Tu-Su 10am-6pm. 600Ft.)*

STATUE PARK MUSEUM. After the collapse of Soviet rule, the open-air Statue Park Museum (Szoborpark Múzeum) was created in Buda, south of Gellérthegy, to display Soviet statues removed from Budapest's parks and squares. The indispensable English-language guidebook (1000Ft) explains the statues' histories. *(XXII. On the corner of Balatoni út and Szabadkai út. Take express bus #7 from Keleti pu. to Étele tér, then take the yellow Volán bus from terminal #7 bound for Diósd 15min., every 15min., and get off at the Szoborpark stop. ☎ 424 7500; www.szoborpark.hu. BudapestCards and 2-week passes for intercity transportation not taken. Open daily 10am-dusk. 600Ft, students 400Ft.)*

BUDA CASTLE. Buda Castle (p. 506) houses several museums. **Wings B-D** hold the huge **Hungarian National Gallery** (Magyar Nemzeti Galéria), a definitive collection of Hungarian painting and sculpture. Its treasures include works by Realist Mihály Munkácsy and Impressionist Paál Lászlo, and medieval gold altarpieces. *(☎ 375 7533. Open Tu-Su 10am-6pm. Free. Special exhibits 800Ft, students 400Ft.)* In **Wing E,** the **Budapest History Museum** (Budapesti Történeti Múzeum) displays a collection of recently unearthed medieval artifacts. *(I. Szent György tér 2. ☎ 225 7815. Open daily May-Sept. 10am-6pm; Nov.-Feb. 10am-4pm. 900Ft, students 450Ft.)*

🌸🎵 FESTIVALS AND ENTERTAINMENT

The **Budapest Spring Festival** (www.fesztivalvaros.hu), March 14-30 in 2008, showcases Hungary's premier musicians and actors. In August, Óbudai Island hosts the week-long **Sziget Festival** (www.sziget.hu), an open-air rock festival. *Budapest Program, Budapest Panorama, Pesti Est*, and *Budapest in Your Pocket* are the best English-language entertainment guides, available at tourist offices and hotels. The "Style" section of the *Budapest Sun* (www.budapestsun.com; 300Ft) has film reviews and a 10-day calendar. Prices are reasonable; check **Ticket Express Hungary,** Andrássy u. 18. *(☎ 312 0000; www.tex.hu. Open M-F 9:30am-6:30pm.)*

The ◙**State Opera House** (Magyar Állami Operaház), VI, Andrássy út 22 (p. 508), is one of Europe's leading performance centers. (M1: Opera. Box office ☎ 353 0170; www.opera.hu. Tickets 800-8700Ft. Box office open M-Sa 11am-7pm, Su 11am-1pm and 4-7pm. Closes at 5pm on non-performance days.) The **National Dance Theater** (Nemzetí Táncszínház), Szinház u. 1-3, on Castle Hill, hosts a variety of shows, but Hungarian folklore is the most popular. (☎ 201 4407, box office 375 8649; www.nemzetitancszinhaz.hu. Most shows 7pm. Tickets 1200-4000Ft. Box office open M-Th 10am-6pm, F 10am-5pm.) The lovely **Városmajor Open-Air Theater,** XII, Városmajor, in Buda, hosts musicals, operas, and ballets. (M1: Moszkva tér. ☎ 375 5922; www.szabadter.hu. Open June 27-Aug. 18. Box office open daily 2-6pm.)

Both travelers and locals head to Budapest's **thermal baths** to soak away the urban grime. In operation since 1565, the baths offer services from mud baths to massages. ◙**Széchenyi,** XIV, Állatkerti u. 11/14, is one of Europe's largest bath complexes. (M1: Hősök tér. ☎ 363 3210. Open May-Sept. daily 6am-7pm; Oct.-Apr. M-F 6am-7pm, Sa-Su 6am-5pm. 2400Ft; 400Ft returned if you leave within 2hr., 200Ft within 3hr.; **keep your receipt.** 15min. massage 2000Ft. Cash only.) The elegant **Gellért,** XI, Kelenhegyi út 4/6, has a rooftop sundeck and an outdoor wave pool. Take bus #7 or tram #47 or 49 to Hotel Gellért, at the base of Gellérthegy. (Open May-Sept. daily 6am-7pm; Oct.-Apr. M-F 6am-7pm, Sa-Su 6am-5pm. 3100Ft, with scaled refund. 15min. massage 2500Ft. MC/V.)

🅝 NIGHTLIFE

Relaxing garden "cafe-clubs," elegant after-hours scenes, and nightly "freakin'" fests make up Budapest's nightlife scene. Pubs and bars stay busy until at least 4am and more club-like venues are alive past 5am. Upscale cafes near Pest's **Ferencz Liszt tér** (M2: Oktogon) attract Budapest's hip residents in their 20s and 30s, while less apparent, sidestreets house a more relaxed setting.

◙ **West Balkan,** VIII, Futó u. 46 (☎ 371 1807; www.west-balkan.com), in Pest. M3: Ferenc körút. 3 bars, indoor dance floor, and a whimsical outdoor garden keep Budapest's alternative scene grooving. Beer 450Ft. Open daily 4pm-4am.

■ **Szimpla Kert,** VII, Kazinczy u. 14 (www.szimpla.hu). Graffiti designs on the walls, personal furniture, and colorful lighting give this garden/cafe/bar with movie screen and concert stage the most balanced and down-to-earth atmosphere in the city. Fresh crepes (100Ft) and a changing menu. Beer 250Ft. Open 10am-2am. Cash only.

Kultiplex, IX, Kinizsi u. 28 (☎219 0706; www.kulti.hu), in Pest. M3: Kálvin tér. With 2 bars, a cinema, a concert hall, and a courtyard, this hangout serves inexpensive beer (250Ft) and screens movies (250-500Ft). Cover usually 200Ft. Open daily 11am-5am.

A-38 Ship, XI (☎464 3940; www.a38.hu), anchored on the Buda side of the Danube, south of Petőfi Bridge. DJs spin on the decks of this revamped Ukrainian freighter. Beer 300Ft. Cover varies. Restaurant open daily 11am-midnight. DJ nights open 11am-4am.

Zöld Pardon, XI (www.zp.hu), on the Buda side of Petőfi Bridge. This giant open-air summer festival features a pool and 5 bars; 3 large screens project the crowd on the dance floor. Beer 250-400Ft. Cover 100Ft. Open Apr. 20-Sept. 16 daily 9am-6am.

Piaf, VI, Nagymező u. 25, in Pest. M1: Opera. Knock on the inconspicuous door at this popular lounge near the bus station. Cover 800Ft; includes 1 beer. Open Su-Th 10pm-6am, F-Sa 10pm-7am.

Pótkulcs, VII, Csengery u. 65/b. (☎269 1050; www.potkulcs.hu). No sign at the entrance, but look for the house number. Huge selection of drinks (try Honey Palinka; 450Ft) at this outdoor garden that serves Hungarian food until midnight—try the popular beef stew (1290Ft). Tu live Hungarian folk music. Open daily 5pm-2am. Cash only.

Kuplung, VI, Király u. 46 (www.kuplung.net). An old warehouse provides a huge, open hall with distinctive, one-of-a-kind furniture. Mixed crowd of locals in their late teens to 30s come to drink and listen to free concerts (3 per week). Check online for schedules of local bands. Open 6pm-late. Cash only.

Gödör Klub, V, Erzsébet Tér. (☎201 3868; www.godorklub.hu). Outside setting right at the middle of Elizabeth square makes you the center of attention at this nightclub that hosts jazz and rock concerts and other special events every night, beginning around 9pm. Check website for schedules. Shots 300Ft. Beer 400Ft. Open M-Sa 5pm-4am.

WigWam, XI, Fehérvári u. 202 (☎ 208 5569; www.wigwamrockclub.hu). Tram #47 from Moricz Zsigmond. Crowded with young locals and adventure-seeking travelers, this club is host to rock music weekends, karaoke, erotic shows, singing competitions, and wild foam parties. Open daily 9pm-5am. Cover varies. Cash only.

▮ NIGHTLIFE SCAM. There have been reports of a scam involving English-speaking Hungarian women who ask foreign men to buy them drinks. When the bill comes, accompanied by imposing men, it can be US$1000 per round. If victims claim to have no money, they are directed to an ATM in the bar. For a list of questionable establishments, check the US Embassy website at http://budapest.usembassy.gov/tourist_advisory.html. If you are taken in, call the police. You'll probably still have to pay, but get a receipt to file a complaint.

DAYTRIPS FROM BUDAPEST: THE DANUBE BEND

North of Budapest, the Danube sweeps in a dramatic arc called the **Dunakanyar** (Danube Bend), one of Hungary's most popular tourist attractions.

■ **SZENTENDRE.** The cobblestone streets of Szentendre (pop. 23,000) brim with upscale galleries and restaurants. Head up **Templomdomb** (Church Hill) in Fő tér for an amazing view from the 13th-century church. The **Czóbel Museum,** Templom tér 1, exhibits work by post-Impressionist artist Béla Czóbel, including his bikini-clad *Venus of Szentendre. (Open Tu-Su 10am-6pm. 500Ft, students 300Ft.)* The popular **Kovács Margit Museum,** Vastagh György u. 1, off Görög u., displays whimsical ceramics by the 20th-century Hungarian artist. *(Open daily Oct.-Feb. 9am-7pm; Mar.-Sept. 9am-5pm. 700Ft.)* The real "thriller" at the ▓**Szamos Marzipan Museum and Confectionery,** Dumtsa Jenő u. 12, is an 80kg white-chocolate statue of Michael Jackson. *(www.szamosmarcipan.hu. Open daily May-Oct. 10am-7pm; Nov.-Apr. 10am-6pm. 350Ft.)* The **Nemzeti Bormúzeum** (National Wine Museum), Bogdányi u. 10, exhibits wines from across Hungary. *(www.bor-kor.hu. Open daily 10am-10pm. Exhibit 200Ft, tasting and English-language tour 1800Ft.)*

HÉV **trains** go to Szentendre (45min., 3 per hr., 480Ft) from Budapest's Batthyány tér station. **Buses** run from Szentendre to Budapest's Árpád híd metro station (30min., 1-3 per hr., 280Ft), Esztergom (1½hr., 1 per hr., 660Ft), and Visegrád (45min., 1 per hr., 359Ft). The train and bus stations are 10min. from Fő tér; descend the stairs past the HÉV tracks and head through the underpass up Kossuth u. At the fork, bear right on Dumtsa Jenő u. **Tourinform,** Dumtsa Jenő u. 22, is between the center and the stations. *(☎026 31 79 65. Open mid-Mar. to Oct. daily 9:30am-1pm and 1:30-4:30pm; Nov. to mid-Mar. M-F 9:30am-1pm and 1:30-4:30pm.)*

VISEGRÁD. Host to the medieval royal court, Visegrád was devastated in 1702 when the Habsburgs destroyed its 13th-century **citadel.** The citadel, a former Roman outpost, provides a dramatic view of the Danube and surrounding hills. To reach it, head north on Fő út, go right on Salamontorony u., and follow the path. In the foothills above Fő út are the ruins of King Matthias's **Királyi Palota** (Royal Palace), once considered just a myth. Exhibits include a computerized reconstruction of the original palace. At the end of Salamontorony u., the **King Matthias Museum** inside **Alsóvár Salamon Torony** (Solomon's Tower) displays artifacts from the ruins. *(Palace open Tu-Su 9am-5pm. Museum open May-Oct. Tu-Su 9am-5pm. Free. 50min. English-language tours 9000Ft.)* The palace grounds relive their glory days with parades, jousting, and music during the mid-July **Viségrad Palace Games.** *(☎30 933 7749; www.palotajatekok.hu.)* **Buses** run to Visegrád from Budapest's Árpád híd metro station (1½hr., 30 per day, 500Ft). The **tourist office** is at Rév út 15. *(☎026 39 81 60; www.visegradtours.hu. Open Apr.-Oct. daily 8am-6pm; Nov.-Mar. M-F 10am-4pm.)*

ESZTERGOM. A millennium of religious history revolves around the **Basilica of Esztergom,** a hilltop cathedral now the seat of the Hungarian Catholic Church. Although pilgrims travel here to see the relics of saints, the ▓**cupola** has a stunning view of the Danube Bend. *(Open Mar.-Oct. Tu-Su 9am-4:30pm; Nov.-Dec. Tu-F 9am-4:30pm, Sa-Su 10am-3:30pm. Cupola 200Ft.)* The red marble **Bakócz Chapel,** to the left of the nave, is a Renaissance masterpiece. *(Open daily Mar.-Oct. 6:30am-6pm; Nov.-Dec. 7am-4pm. Free.)* *Trains go to Budapest (1½hr., 22 per day, 620Ft).* To reach the main square from the train station, turn left on Baross Gábor út and right on Kiss János Altábornagy út, which becomes Kossuth Lajos u. **Buses** run to Szentendre (1½hr., 1 per hr., 490Ft) and Visegrád (45min., 1 per hr., 320Ft). MAHART **boats** (☎484 4013; www.mahartpassnave.hu) leave the pier at Gőzhajó u. on Primas Sziget Island for Budapest (4hr., 3 per day, 1550Ft) and Visegrád (1½hr., 2 per day, 790Ft). **Grantours,** Széchenyi tér 25, at the edge of Rákóczi tér, sells maps (300-500Ft) and books rooms. *(☎033 41 70 52; grantour@mail.holop.hu. Open July-Aug. M-F 8am-6pm, Sa 9am-noon; Sept.-June M-F 8am-4pm.)*

PÉCS   ☎062

Pécs (PAYCH; pop. 180,000), at the foot of the Mecsek mountains, is an animated university town, rich in bookstores, museums, and sidewalk cafes. The atelier at the ▓**Zsolnay Museum,** Káptalan u. 4, exhibits the Zsolnay family's world-famous porcelains, crafted since the 19th century. There is also a reconstruction of the family's elegant residence. To get there, walk up Szepessy I. u. and turn left on Káptalan u. (☎514 040. Open daily 10am-6pm. 750Ft, students 400Ft; photography 300Ft.) Across the street, the **Vasarely Museum,** Káptalan u. 5, displays the works of Viktor Vasarely, a pioneer of Op-Art. (☎51 40 40, ext. 21. Open Apr.-Oct. Tu-Sa 10am-6pm, Su 10am-4pm. 600Ft, students 350Ft; photography 400Ft, video 800Ft.) In the same yard, the unusual **Mecksek Museum** reproduces a traditional mine in a 400m cellar. Staffed by actual mine workers, it impressively reproduces a mine's claustrophobic feel. (500Ft, students 300Ft.) At central Széchenyi tér stands the **Gázi Khasim Pasa Dzsámija** (Mosque of Ghazi Kassim), once a Turkish mosque built on the site of an even earlier church. Its modern fusion of Christian and Muslim traditions has made it a city emblem. (Open mid-Apr. to mid-Oct. M-Sa 10am-4pm, Su 12:30-4pm; mid-Oct. to mid-Apr. M-Sa 10am-noon, Su open for Mass only 9:30, 10:30, and 11:30am. Free.) Walk downhill from Széchenyi tér on Irgalmasok u. to Kossuth tér to find the 1869 **Synagogue.** Its intricate ceiling frescoes and stunning Ark of the Covenant give it a magical aura. Its entrance details the history of the Holocaust and names the 112 local children killed in concentration camps. (Yarmulkes provided; mandatory for men. Open Mar.-Oct. M-F and Su 10-11:30am and noon-1pm. 300Ft, students 200Ft.) Atop Pécs's hill on Dóm tér, is the 4th-century Romanesque **Cathedral,** whose towers are visible from anywhere in the city. (☎51 30 30. Open M-Sa 9am-5pm, Su 1-5pm. Mass M-Sa 6pm; Su 8, 9:30, 11am, and 6pm. 800Ft, students 400Ft.) Private rooms close to the town center are the best budget option. **Pollack Mihály Students' Hostel ❷,** Jokai u. 8, has small but comfortable dorm-like singles with clean shared baths. (☎51 36 50. Singles 2300Ft.) Take bus #21 from the main bus terminal or #43 from the train station and get off at 48-as tér, or walk 20min. up the hill to Rákóczi út. and turn right to reach **Janus Pannonius University ❶,** Universitas u. 2, behind McDonald's. (☎31 14 01. Reception 24hr. Check-out 9am. Open July-Sept. 3-bed dorms 1800Ft. Cash only.) Pécs's bars, cafes, and restaurants are among its biggest attractions. Chill with artists and students at ▓**Dante Cafe ❶,** Janus Pannonis u. 11, in a courtyard of the Csontváry Museum. (Beer 240-450Ft. Live jazz Sa-Su. Open May-Oct. Th-Su 10am-6pm.) Enjoy pastries or ice cream (130-270Ft) at **Mecsek ❶,** Hunyadi u. 20, corner of Hunyadi and Király. (☎31 54 44. Open daily 9am-10pm. Cash only.) **Cellarium Étterem ❸,** Hunyadi u. 2, is a prison-themed restaurant buried in a cellar. Here, you can live out your fantasy of eating Hungarian fare while being served by waiters in inmate costumes. The menu promises that the house champagne is "equal with a good foreplay on a table (instead of a bed)." (☎314 453. Entrees 950-4000Ft. Live Hungarian music on weekends. AmEx/MC/V.)

Trains run to: Budapest (3hr., 4 per day, 2220Ft). To reach the train station, just south of the historic district, take bus #30, 32, or 33 from town, or walk for about 20min. down Szabadsag or Irganasok. Be alert on Irgalmasok, which can feel unsafe at night. **Buses** go to Budapest (4½hr., 5 per day, 2450Ft) and Siófok (3hr., 3 per day, 255Ft). The bus station is 15min. from the old city; from the center take Irgalmasok and turn right on Nagy Lajos Kiraly (☎52 01 55). Local **bus** tickets cost 280Ft, but most places in the city are walkable. **TourInform** is at Széchenyi tér 9. (☎21 11 34. Open May-Oct. Sa-Su 9am-2pm; Nov.-Apr. M-F 8am-4pm.) There are **pharmacies** at Széchenyi tér. **Internet Cafe Kávézó,** Ferencesek 32, offers speedy connections (10Ft per min.). It is relatively easy to find English-speakers here; students are generally eager to help. **Postal Code:** 7621.

EGER   ☎036

In the 16th century, Eger (EGG-air; pop. 57,000) was the site of Captain István Dobó's legendary struggles against Ottoman conquest. In addition to its proud history, the town's claim to fame is its homemade wine. The spirited cellars of the ▓**Valley of the Beautiful Women** lure travelers from Budapest who seek the alleged strengthening powers of Egri Bikavér (Bull's Blood) wine.

❏❷ TRANSPORTATION AND PRACTICAL INFORMATION. Trains leave from the station on Vasút u. (☎31 42 64) for Budapest (2hr.; 21 per day, 4 direct; 1420Ft). Indirect trains run to Budapest via Füzesabony. Trains also go to: Aggtelek (3hr., 8 per day, 1420Ft); Debrecen (3hr., 12 per day, 1212Ft); Szeged (4½hr., 12 per day, 2670Ft); Szilvásvárad (1hr., 6 per day., 342Ft). **Buses** (☎51 77 77; www.agriavolan.hu) head from the station on Barkóczy u. to Budapest (2hr., 25-30 per day, 1520Ft). **City Taxi** (☎55 55 55) runs cabs. **Dobó tér,** the main square, is a 15min. walk from the train station. Head straight and turn right on Deák Ferenc út, right on Kossuth Lajos u., and left on Jókai u. To get to the center from the bus station, turn right on Barkóczy u. from terminal #10 and right again at Bródy u. Follow the stairs to the end of the street, turn right on Széchenyi u., and go left down Érsek u. **TourInform** is at Bajcsy-Zsilinszky u. 9. (☎51 77 15; www.ektf.hu/eger. Open M-F 9am-5pm, Sa 9am-1pm.) **Postal Code:** 3300.

❏❏ ACCOMMODATIONS AND FOOD. Private rooms are the best budget option; look for *"Zimmer frei"* or *"szòba eladò"* signs, particularly on Almagyar u. and Mekcsey István u. near the castle. **Eger Tourist ❷,** Bajcsy-Zsilinszky u. 9, next to TourInform, arranges private rooms that cost about 3000Ft. (☎51 70 00. Open M-F 9am-5pm.) Family-run ❏ **Lukács Vendéghaz ❸,** Bárány u. 10, next to Eger Castle, has a lush garden, an outdoor patio, and large, comfortable rooms. (☎/fax 41 15 67. Singles 3000Ft; doubles 5000Ft. Tourist tax 310Ft. Cash only.) Centrally located **Hotel Minaret ❹,** Knézich K. u. 4, features a gym, restaurant, and swimming pool. (☎41 02 33; www.hotelminaret.hu. All rooms with satellite TV. Singles 10,600Ft; doubles 18,500Ft; triples 24,400Ft; quads 28,900Ft. Prices about 2000Ft lower Nov.-Mar. AmEx/MC/V.) From the Valley of the Beautiful Women, follow signs to **Tulipan Camping ❶,** Szépasszonyvölgy. (☎410 530. Open mid-Apr. to mid-Oct. 24hr. Office open daily 8-10am and 7-8pm. 600Ft per person, 500 Ft per tent site. Cash only.) **Széchenyi utca** is lined with restaurants. In the Valley of the Beautiful Women, crowds fill the courtyard of **Kulacs Csárda Panzió ❸.** (☎31 13 75; www.kulacscsarda.hu. Entrees 950-2000Ft. Open daily noon-10pm. AmEx/MC/V.) Near Eger Castle, **Palacsintavár Étterem ❷,** Dobó u. 9, lures a steady stream of crepe-craving customers. (☎41 33 90. Crepes 640-1490Ft. Open daily noon-11pm. MC/V.) **Dobos Cukrászda ❶,** Széchenyi u. 6, serves mouth-watering desserts. (Ice cream 130Ft. Desserts 350-850Ft. Open daily 9:30am-10pm.)

THE HIDDEN DEAL

STAYIN' A-LAVA

A bustling town by day, Eger seems suspiciously quiet at night. That's because the real scene is underground—literally—as Eger continues to offer festive diversions in the form of clubs built into a series of lava tunnels.

Unknown to most visitors, an elaborate labyrinth lies below Eger, the carved remnants of the 120km bed of lava upon which the city was founded. Locals have converted three sections into nightclubs, invisible to the world above except for small, barely marked entrances.

One of the most popular is **Club Amazon,** on Pyrter 3, alongside Kossuth L. u, under the Eger Cathedral, where youths dance the night away in the jungle-like disco. Guest DJs give the place a dynamic vibe. *(☎596 3848. Open W 10pm-5am, Cover 500Ft, Sa 10pm-5am, Cover 800Ft. Every 2nd F 10pm-5am, select W in June students 400Ft.)*

Another popular spot is the Liget Dance Cafe, on Erksekkert, under Excalibur Restaurant in the Archbishop's Gardens. *(☎427 7547. Cover (cash only) 800Ft. Open F-Sa 10pm-5am. AmEx/MC/V.)* Clearly marked by spotlights, the club draws a younger crowd. **Hippolit Club and Restaurant,** Katona ter 2, is classier and more subdued with a secluded, candle-lit second-floor patio. *(☎411 031. Open Tu-Th 9pm-3am, F-Sa 9pm-5am.)*

HUNGARY

◐ ✿ **SIGHTS AND FESTIVALS.** To sample Eger's renowned vintage, wander through the web of wine cellars at the Valley of the Beautiful Women (Szépasszonyvölgy). Walk down Széchenyi u. with Eger Cathedral to your right, turn right on Kossuth Lajos u., and left when it dead-ends into Vörösmarty u. Take a right on Király u. and keep walking (25min.). Built into the hillside, the valley contains 200 cellars. Most consist of only a few tables with benches, but each has its own personality; some are hushed while others burst with Hungarian and Gypsy sing-alongs. (Open from 9am, closing times vary; July-Aug. some open until midnight. 0.1L taste 50-150Ft, 1L 350Ft.) In summer, **open-air baths** offer a break from the sweltering heat. (www.egertermal.hu. Open May-Sept. M-F 6am-7pm, Sa-Su 8am-7pm; Oct.-Apr. daily 9am-7pm. 1050Ft, students 900Ft., seniors 400Ft.) From late July to mid-August, Eger resonates with opera and early court music at the **Baroque Festival.**

◪ **DAYTRIP FROM EGER: BARADLA CAVES.** On the Slovak-Hungarian border, **Aggtelek National Park** is home to more than 1000 caves, including the ever-popular Baradla Cave. Knowledgeable guides lead 1km tours, beginning in an ancient cave where skeletons from the Neolithic period were found. Concerts, violin competitions, and wedding ceremonies are held in the music hall throughout the year; calendars of events are available at **TourInform** (☎50 30 00). Tours range from 1hr. basic (daily 10am, noon, 1, 3, 5pm; low season no 5pm tour; 4000Ft, students 2400Ft) to 5hr. guided hikes (6000/2400Ft). Arrange longer tours with Tour-Inform. The temperature is 10°C year-round, so bring a jacket. The caves can be visited as a daytrip from Eger, but you'll miss the return bus if you take a longer hike. The **bus** leaves Eger daily at 8:45am and arrives in Aggtelek at 11:25am, returning from the stop across the street at 3pm. From the bus, cross the street and go down the path to the caves; the park entrance is on the right. *(☎50 30 02; www.anp.hu. Open daily Apr.-Sept. 8am-6pm; Oct.-Mar. 8am-4pm.)*

GYŐR
☎096

In the unspoiled western region of Őrség, Győr (DYUR; pop. 130,000) overflows with monuments, museums, and 17th- and 18th-century architecture. Turn right out of the train station, take a left before the underpass, and cross the street to reach the pedestrian-only **Baross Gábor utca.** Walk uphill on Czuczor Gergely u., one street to the right of Baross Gábor u., and turn left at Gutenberg tér to reach the **Ark of the Covenant** statue (Frigylada szobov) and **Chapter Hill** (Káptalandomb). At the top of the hill is the **Episcopal Cathedral** (Székesegyház) with its **Weeping Madonna of Győr.** According to legend, the icon wept blood for persecuted Irish Catholics on St. Patrick's Day in 1697. The **Diocesan Library and Treasury** (Egyházmegyei Kincstár), Káptalandomb 26, in an alley off the cathedral square, displays 14th-century gold and silver. (Open Mar.-Oct. Tu-Su 10am-4pm. 700Ft, students 400Ft.) The **Imre Patkó collection,** Széchenyi tér 4, presents contemporary art; buy tickets in the Xántus Janos Museum next door and enter at Stelczera u. (Open Tu-Su 10am-6pm. 500Ft, students 300Ft.) Across the river is the huge **Rába Quelle water park,** Fürdő tér 1, supplied by thermal springs. From Bécsi Kapu tér, take the bridge over the small island and make the first right on the other side, then go right again on Cziráky tér. (www.gyortermal.hu. Open daily 9am-8pm. 3hr. ticket 1400Ft, students 1000Ft; full-day ticket 1600/1200Ft.)

In an alley off Bécsi Kapu tér, **⬛Katalin Kert ❹,** Sarkantyú köz 3, has huge, beautiful rooms with private baths. (☎54 20 88; katalinkert@axelero.hu. Singles 7100Ft; doubles 9900Ft. Tax 330Ft per person. Cash only.) **Matróz Restaurant ❷,** Dunakapu tér 3, off Jedlik Ányos u., serves succulent fish, pork, and turkey dishes. (Entrees 500-1350Ft. Open Su-Th 9am-10pm, F-Sa 9am-11pm.) **Tejivó ❶,** on Kisfaludy u. 30, is a local hot spot for good, cheap fast food. Try a bowl of rice in milk (tejberizs; 380Ft). (☎51 26 30. Entrees 180-900Ft. Open M-F 8am-5pm, Sa 8am-1pm.At night, dancing enthusiasts head to **Darius Music Club,** Czuszor u. 6, is popular among the locals for its changing scene and music, especially the "Latin Nights" with salsa dancing. (☎309 360 878. Beer 450Ft. Open M-W 9am-10pm, Th 9am-2am, F-Sa 9am-4am. Cash only.) For a more relaxing night, head to ⬛**Patio Belvárosi Kavéház,** Baross Gábor út 12, which serves beer (400-650Ft), wine, and gigantic ice cream sundaes. (Open M-Th 10am-10pm, F-Sa 10am-11pm, Su 2-9pm. Cash only.)

Trains run from Budapest (2½hr., 34 per day, 2040Ft) and Vienna, AUT (2hr., 13 per day, 5250Ft). **Buses** run to Budapest (2½hr., 1 per hr., 2040Ft). The train station is 3min. from the city center. An underpass linking the platforms also leads to the bus station, heading in the opposite direction from the town. The **TourInform kiosk,** Árpád u. 32, at the intersection with Baross Gábor u., arranges lodgings. (☎31 17 71. Open June-Aug. M-F 8am-8pm, Sa-Su 9am-6pm.) **Postal Code:** 9021.

▣ DAYTRIP FROM GYŐR: ARCHABBEY OF PANNONHALMA. Visible on a clear day from Győr, the hilltop Archabbey of Pannonhalma (Pannonhalmi Főapátság) has seen a millennium of destruction and rebuilding since its establishment by the Benedictine order in AD 996. It now houses a 360,000-volume library and a 13th-century basilica, and hosts organ concerts (1800Ft, students 900Ft). **TriCollis Tourist Office** is to the left of the entrance. *(☎57 01 91; www.bences.hu. Hungarian-language tour of abbey with English text 1 per hr. 1600Ft, students 800Ft. English-language tours June-Sept. daily 11:20am, 1:20, 3:20pm; Oct.-May Tu-Su 11:20am and 1:20pm. 2400/1500Ft.)* Tours of the on-site **winery** provide insight into traditional monastic viticulture. *(Tours daily June-Sept. 12:30, 2:30, 4:30pm; Oct.-Nov. and Apr.-May 11:30am, 1:30, 3:30pm; Dec.-Mar. 11:30am and 1:30pm. 750Ft, with tasting 1600Ft.)* From Győr, take the **bus** from platform #11 (45min., 7 per day, 380Ft). Ask for Pannonhalma vár and get off at the huge gates.

LAKE BALATON

A retreat since Roman times, warm Lake Balaton drew the European elite in the 19th century, but is now a budget paradise for German and Austrian students.

Storms roll in quickly—when the yellow lights on harbor buildings speed up to one revolution per second, one is approaching. Don't worry about a spoiled vacation, however; most storms last less than half an hour.

SIÓFOK. The density of tourist offices reflects Siófok's popularity with summer vacationers. The **Strand** is a series of lawns running to the shore; entry is free to some sections, and about 500Ft to others. The largest private **beach** lies to the right of town as you face the water. (800Ft, children 450Ft. Open M-F 8am-3am.) Bars and clubs line the lakefront. **Renegade Pub,** Petőfi sétány 3, is a crowded bar and dance club. (Open June-Aug. daily 8pm-4am.) Up-and-coming **Big Shot's Pub,** Fő út. 43, doubles as a restaurant and Internet cafe. (Pizzas 890-1200Ft. Beer 0.25L 320Ft, 0.4L 520Ft. Internet 290Ft per 15min. Open daily 11am-2am. MC/V.) Take a 25min. bus or train ride to Balatonszéplak felső to reach ⬛**Villa Benjamin Youth Hostel ❷,** Siófoki u. 9. (☎084 350 704. Free Internet. Singles 3000Ft; doubles 6000Ft; triples 9000Ft; 4- to 6-person apartments 14,000-21,000Ft; 8- to 10-person house 28,000-35,000Ft. Tax 300Ft. 10% HI discount. Cash only.) **Balaton Véndegló és Panzió ❷,** Kinizsi u. 3, is a conveniently located hotel and restaurant. (☎084 31 13 13. 2-person dorms 5000-7600Ft. MC/V.) **Trains** run to Budapest (2hr., 7 per day, 1250Ft). **Buses** head to Budapest (1½hr., 9 per day, 1480Ft) and Pécs (3hr., 4 per day, 2550Ft). **TourInform,** Fő út. at Szabadság tér, is in the water tower opposite the train station. (☎061 438 8080; www.tourinform.hu. Open mid-June to mid-Sept. M-Sa 8am-8pm, Sa-Su 9am-6pm; mid-Sept. to mid-June M-F 9am-4pm.)

KESZTHELY AND TIHANY. At the lake's western tip, **Keszthely** (KEST-hay), once the playground of the powerful Austro-Hungarian Festetics family, is home to thermal springs. The ◼Helikon Palace Museum (Helikon Kastélymúzeum) in the Festetics Palace is a storybook Baroque palace with a 90,000-volume library, extravagant chambers, an exotic arms collection, and a porcelain exhibit. From Fő tér, follow Kossuth Lajos u. toward Tourinform (see below) until it becomes Kastély u. (Open July-Aug. daily 9am-6pm., June Tu-Su 9am-5pm, Sept.-May Tu-Su 10am-5pm. 1500Ft, students 850Ft.) The **Strand,** on the coast to the right as you exit the train station, draws crowds with its giant slide, paddle boats, and volleyball nets. From the center, walk down Erzsébet Királyné u. as it curves right into Vörösmarty u., then cut through the park, crossing the train tracks on the other side to get to the beach. (Open mid-May to mid-Sept. daily 8:30am-7pm. 700Ft, children 500Ft. 6:30-7pm free.) **Central Kiss Máté Panzió ❸,** Katona J u. 27, has spacious rooms. (☎83 31 90 72. Singles 5000Ft; doubles 8000Ft; triples 12,000Ft.) **Castrum Camping ❶,** Móra Ferenc u. 48, offers large sites and tennis courts. (☎83 31 21 20. 1000Ft per person. July-Aug. 1000Ft per tent site; Sept.-June 550Ft.) **Donatello ❷,** Balaton u. 1/A, serves pizza and pasta in an open courtyard. Though the restaurant is named after the Teenage Mutant Ninja Turtle, the vittles are genuine Italian masterpieces. (☎83 31 59 89. Pasta 710-880Ft. Pizza 520-1440Ft. Open daily noon-11pm.) **Trains** run to Budapest (3hr.; 13 per day; 2780Ft, reservations 440Ft). **Buses** run from near the train station to Pécs (4hr., 5 per day, 2320Ft). From the station, take Mártirok u., ending in Kossuth Lajos u., and turn left to reach the main square, Fő tér. **Tourinform,** Kossuth Lajos u. 28, on the palace side of Fő tér, has free maps and checks for room availability. (☎83 31 41 44. Open July-Aug. M-F 9am-8pm, Sa-Su 9am-6pm; Sept.-June M-F 9am-5pm, Sa 9am-1pm.)

Scenic hikes, charming cottages, and panoramic views grace the **Tihany** Peninsula. Though slightly creepy, the fascinating **Dolls' Museum,** Visszhang u. 4, packs an impressive collection of 19th-century toys into two rooms. (Open daily 10am-6pm. 500Ft, students 400Ft.) The **Benedictine Abbey** (Bencés Apátság) draws over a million visitors annually with its luminous frescoes and gilded Baroque altars. (Open daily Mar.-Oct. 9am-6pm; last entry 5:30pm. 600Ft, students 300Ft.) The well-marked ◼green line trail runs past the **Hermit's Place** (Barátlakások), where the cells and chapel hollowed by 11th-century hermits are still visible. MAHART **ferries** run to Siófok (1-1¼hr.; 6-9 per day; 1020 Ft, students 765Ft). To reach the town from the ferry pier and neighboring **Strand,** walk underneath the elevated road and follow the Apátság signs up the steep hill to the abbey.

ICELAND (ÍSLAND)

Created when the European and North American continents collided, Iceland's landscape is uniquely warped and contorted, marked by active volcanoes and the tortoise-like crawl of advancing and retreating glaciers. Nature is the country's greatest attraction, and visitors can pick their way through sunken ice kettles (holes left by glaciers), bathe in natural hot springs, and bike through fishing villages or on mountainous dirt roads. An emphasis on natural farming has made Icelandic produce and meat sought-after exports and Icelandic dining a pleasure. Covered by more glaciers than the rest of continental Europe combined and highly dependent on and protective of its fishing industry, Iceland is quickly becoming one of Europe's hottest travel destinations and a leader in ecotourism.

ESSENTIALS

FACTS AND FIGURES

Official Name: Republic of Iceland.

Capital: Reykjavík.

Major Cities: Akureyri, Ísafjörður, Kópavogur, Hafnarfjörður.

Population: 302,000.

Time Zone: GMT.

Language: Icelandic.

Percentage of Arable Land: 0.07%.

Percentage of Export Earnings Provided by the Fishing Industry: 70%.

WHEN TO GO

Visitors should brave high-season crowds to enjoy all Iceland has to offer. June through August have the most accommodation and transportation options. The sky never gets quite dark in summer months, though the sun dips below the horizon for a few hours each night. July temperatures average around 11°C (52°F). December and January receive four or five hours of sunlight daily, but the nights are illuminated by the *aurora borealis*, the famous Northern Lights. Winter in Reykjavík averages 0°C (32°F), making transportation slower and less reliable.

 BURNING THE MIDNIGHT OIL. During summer, the sun never really sets over Iceland. While the near 24hr. sunlight makes for easy all-night partying, it can take its toll on visitors. Bring a sleeping mask and over-the-counter, non-habit-forming sleep aids, such as melatonin, to avoid sleepless nights.

DOCUMENTS AND FORMALITIES

EMBASSIES AND CONSULATES. Foreign embassies in Iceland are in Reykjavík. Icelandic embassies and consulates abroad include: **Australia,** 16 Hann St., Griffith, Canberra (☎262 95 68 19; benefitfarm@bigpond.com.au); **Canada,** 360 Albert St., Ste. 710, Ottawa, ON, K1R 7X7 (☎613-482-1944; www.iceland.org/ca); **Ireland,** Cavendish House, Smithfield, Dublin (☎1 872 9299; jgg@goregrimes.ie); **New Zealand,** Sanford Ltd., 22 Jellicoe St., Auckland (☎9 379 4720); **UK,** 2A Hans St., London, SW1X 0JE (☎020 72 59 39 99; www.iceland.org/uk); **US,** 1156 15th St. NW, Ste. 1200, Washington, D.C., 20005 (☎202-265-6653; www.iceland.org/us).

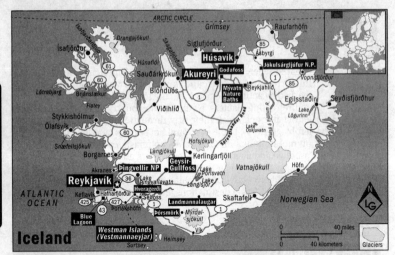

Iceland

VISA AND ENTRY INFORMATION. EU citizens do not need a visa. Citizens of Australia, Canada, New Zealand, and the US do not need a visa for stays of up to 90 days, beginning upon entry into any of the countries in the EU's freedom-of-movement zone. For more info, see p. 14. For stays longer than 90 days, all non-EU citizens need visas, available at embassies abroad; check www.utl.is/english/visas/apply to find the nearest to you.

TOURIST SERVICES AND MONEY

EMERGENCY	Ambulance, Fire, and Police: ☎ 112.

TOURIST OFFICES. Tourist offices in large towns have maps, brochures, and the all-important BSÍ bus schedule; check at hotel reception desks in smaller towns for local info. The **Icelandic Tourist Board** website is www.icetourist.is. **Destination Iceland** (☎ 585 4270; www.dice.is), which has offices in the Reykjavík bus terminal, has a helpful vacation planning website.

MONEY. Iceland's unit of currency is the **króna (ISK),** plural krónur. One króna is equal to 100 aurars, with standard denominations of 1, 5, 10, 50, and 100kr in coins, and 500, 1000, and 5000kr in notes. For currency exchange, **ATMs** are located throughout the larger cities. Banks are usually open M-F 9:15am-4pm. Major Icelandic banks, such as Landsbankinn, do not have sister banks in other countries that allow lower exchange fees. In general, there's no way around the high costs in Iceland. On average, a night in a hostel will cost 1700ISK, a guesthouse 3000-4000ISK, and a meal's worth of groceries 700-1200ISK. Restaurants include a service charge on the bill. **Tipping** further is unnecessary and even discouraged.

Iceland has a 24.5% **value added tax (VAT),** a sales tax on goods and services purchased within the European Economic Area (EEA: the EU plus Iceland, Liechtenstein, and Norway). The prices given in *Let's Go* include VAT. In the airport upon exiting the EEA, non-EEA citizens can claim a refund on the tax paid for goods at particpating stores. In order to qualify for a refund in a store, you must spend at least 4000ISK; make sure to ask for a refund form when you pay. For more info on qualifying for a VAT refund, see p. 19.

ICELANDIC KRÓNUR (ISK)	AUS$1 = 54.36ISK	100ISK = AUS$1.84
	CDN$1 = 64.31ISK	100ISK = CDN$1.56
	EUR€1 = 91.84ISK	100ISK = EUR€1.09
	NZ$1 = 47.42ISK	100ISK = NZ$2.11
	UK£1 = 135.01ISK	100ISK = UK£0.74
	US$1 = 68.16ISK	100ISK = US$1.47

TRANSPORTATION

BY PLANE. Icelandair (Iceland ☎505 0700, UK 0845 758 1111, US and Canada 800-223-5500; www.icelandair.net) flies to Reykjavík year-round from Europe and the US. They also provide free stopovers of up to seven days on flights to many European cities, and run a Lucky Fares email list with discounted flights. No-frills **Iceland Express** (Iceland ☎550 0600, UK 0870 240 5600; www.icelandexpress.com) flies to nine Western European countries on the cheap. Icelandair's domestic counterpart **Air Iceland** (☎570 3030; www.airiceland.is) flies from Reykjavík to most major towns in Iceland and Greenland.

 SOARING PRICES. To get the most for your money, consider traveling by plane instead of bus. Discount airfare is often just as expensive, or cheaper, than terrestrial tickets. Check with Air Iceland for more info.

BY BUS. Several bus lines are organized by **Bifreiðastöð Íslands** (**BSÍ;** www.bsi.is); buses can be cheaper and more scenic than flights, although they run infrequently in the low season. From mid-June to August, buses run daily on the **Ring Road (Rte. 1),** the highway that circles Iceland. Even then the going is slow; some stretches in the east are unpaved. The **Full Circle Passport** lets travelers circle the island at their own pace on the Ring Road (June-Aug.; 23,900ISK). However, it only allows travel in one direction, so travelers must move either clockwise or counter-clockwise around the country to get back to where they started. For an extra 12,000ISK, the pass provides access to the Westfjords in the extreme northwest. The **Omnibus Passport** is valid for periods of up to four weeks for unlimited travel on all scheduled bus routes, including non-Ring roads (1-week 26,900ISK, 2-week 42,000ISK, 3-week 50,000ISK; valid May 15-Sept. 15). Travelers, especially those arriving in groups of two or more, should note that the inflexibility of the Full Circle Passport and the high cost of the Omnibus Passport make it wise for those heading to rural areas to rent cars. Iceland has no intercity train service.

BY FERRY. The best way to see Iceland's gorgeous shoreline is on the **Norröna** ferry (☎570 8600; www.smyril-line.fo, website in Icelandic) that crosses the North Atlantic to Hanstholm, DEN; Tórshavn in the Faroe Islands; and Seyðisfjörður. (7 days; May 28-Sept. 2. 1-way sleeper cabin €350; low season €250; students under 26 25% discount.) From Tórshavn, you can either continue on to Bergen, NOR, or return to Seyðisfjörður. An **Eimskip Transport** liner leaves Reykjavík weekly (Mar.-Oct.) and takes five days to get to continental ports at Århus, DEN; Gothenburg, SWE; Hamburg, GER; and Rotterdam, NTH. (Reservations ☎585 4300; travel@dice.is. Fares from 33,030ISK. Bikes 3150ISK.)

BY CAR. Rental cars provide the most freedom for travelers and may even be the cheapest option for those who want to visit rural areas. Getting a car and touring Iceland's **Ring Road (Rte. 1),** which circles the entire island and passes many of the best destinations, is a popular way to explore the country. Book before you arrive for lower rates. Car rental *(bílaleiga)* companies charge 4000-8000ISK per day for a small car, and 10,000-25,000ISK for the **four-wheel-drive vehicles** that are imperative outside settled areas. On these routes, drivers should bring a container of extra gas, since some roads continue for 300km without a single gas station and strong headwinds can significantly affect the rate of fuel consumption. It is not uncommon for local drivers to **ford streams** in their vehicles; do not attempt this in a compact car, and cross in a convoy if possible. (24hr. reports on road conditions ☎800 6316, June-Aug. in English.) Drivers are required to wear seat belts and to keep their headlights on at all times. Iceland recognizes foreign driver's licenses, but you may need to purchase insurance for the rental vehicle (1500-3500ISK).

BY BIKE AND BY THUMB. Ferocious winds, driving rain, and gravel roads make long-distance cycling difficult. Hug the Ring Road if you prefer company; for less-traveled paths, branch out to the coastal roads that snake their way through the Eastfjords, or check **Cycling in Iceland** (http://home.wanadoo.nl/erens/icecycle.htm). Also check out the **Icelandic Mountain Bike Club,** Brekkustíg. 2, in Reykjavík, or drop by their clubhouse in the first Thursday night of each month after 8pm for some advice(☎562 0099; www.mmedia.is/~ifhk). Buses will carry bikes for a 500-900ISK fee, depending on the route. Hitchhikers try the roads in summer, but sparse traffic and harsh weather exacerbate the risks. Still, rides can be found with relative ease between Reykjavík and Akureyri; flagging down a ride is harder in the east and the south. Let's Go does not recommend hitchhiking.

KEEPING IN TOUCH

PHONE CODES	**Country code: 354. International dialing prefix:** 00. There are no city codes in Iceland. For more info on how to place international calls, see **Inside Back Cover.**

EMAIL AND INTERNET. Internet access is widespread in Iceland. In small towns get it for free in libraries; at cafes, Internet costs 200-300ISK per hour.

TELEPHONE. The state-owned telephone company, **Síminn,** usually has offices with post offices, where you can buy phone cards and get the best international call rates. Pay phones accept prepaid phone cards, credit cards (cheapest for calls to mobile phones), as well as 10ISK, 50ISK, and 100ISK coins. Iceland uses two different mobile phone networks: digital GSM phones service 98% of the country's population, but only a small fraction of its land area, so hikers, fishermen, and others who travel outside of settled areas rely on analog NMT phones. Prepaid GSM phone cards are available at gas stations and convenience stores. OG Vodafone generally offers the best prepaid rates. For operator assistance, dial ☎118; for international assistance, dial ☎1811. International direct dial numbers include: **AT&T Direct** (☎800 222 55 288); **British Telecom** (☎800 9044); **Canada Direct** (☎800 9010); **Telecom New Zealand** (☎800 9064).

MAIL. Mailing a letter or postcard (up to 20g) from Iceland costs from 60ISK within Iceland, from 70ISK to Europe, and from 80ISK outside of Europe. Post offices *(póstur)* are generally open Monday to Friday 9am-6pm in Reykjavík and 9am-4:30pm in the countryside. Check www.postur.is for additional info. To receive mail in Iceland, have mail delivered **Poste Restante.** Mail will go to the main post office unless you specify a subsidiary by street address. Address mail to be held according to the following example (Reykjavík): First name, Last Name, **Poste Restante,** ÍSLANDSPÓSTUR, Posthússtr. 5, 101 Reykjavík, ICELAND.

LANGUAGE. Icelandic is a Nordic language which developed in 9th-century Norway and came into its present form in 12th-century Iceland. Most Icelanders, especially those under 35, speak at least some English.

ACCOMMODATIONS AND CAMPING

ICELAND	❶	❷	❸	❹	❺
ACCOMMODATIONS	under 2000ISK	2000-3000ISK	3001-5000ISK	5001-10,000ISK	over 10,000ISK

Iceland's **HI youth hostels** are clean and reasonably priced at roughly 1800-2300ISK for nonmembers. HI members receive a 150-400ISK discount. Visit **Hostelling International Iceland,** Sundlaugarvegur 34, 105 Reykjavík (☎553 8110; www.hostel.is), for locations and pricing as well as for info on Iceland's seven eco-friendly **Green Hostels.** Expect to pay around 2100ISK for **sleeping-bag accommodations** (*svefn-pokapláss;* beds with no linens or blankets) and another 650ISK for linens. Guesthouses and **farmhouses** (☎570 2700; www.farmholidays.is) are a cheap, homey option outside cities. Many remote lodgings will pick up tourists in the nearest town for a small fee. Campers can choose among Iceland's 125 designated **campsites** (usually open June-August). Camping outside official sites isn't allowed. Official campsites range from grassy areas with cold-water taps to sumptuous facilities around Reykjavík; listings can be found at www.camping.is. Most charge around 600-800ISK, and many don't allow open flames (so be sure to bring a camp stove). Visit www.infoiceland.is/infoiceland/accommodation/camping for tips.

FOOD AND DRINK

ICELAND	❶	❷	❸	❹	❺
FOOD	under 500ISK	500-1000ISK	1001-1400ISK	1401-2000ISK	over 2000ISK

Iceland is currently in the middle of a culinary explosion. A history of food shortages led Iceland to value all that was pickled, dried, or smoked. But now, with more exotic methods and flavors introduced by a trickle of Asian immigrants in the past decade, not everything is simply boiled and salted. Fresh fish and gamey free-range lamb—staples of Icelandic cuisine—remain essentials of the diet. But they're being mixed in new and delicious ways with vitamin-rich vegetables grown in greenhouse towns (such as Hveragerði; p. 530) and a range of cheeses. Still, tradition is strong: **skyr,** a dairy product that tastes like a cross between yogurt and fresh cheese, and **hangikjot,** smoked lamb sandwiches, are more popular than ever. Food in Iceland is very expensive, and a cheap restaurant meal will cost at least 800ISK. Grocery stores are the way to go in virtually every town. Alcohol presents the same quandary: beer costs 500-600ISK for a large glass (½L, approx. 17 oz.) at pubs and cafes, while the price of hard liquor is even steeper. The country's national drink is **brennivín,** a schnapps made from potato, usually seasoned with caraway, and nicknamed "Black Death." Bootleggers in the countryside cook up batches of **landi,** a potent homemade moonshine, in protest against high liquor taxes. Let's Go does not recommend moonshine.

HOLIDAYS AND FESTIVALS

Holidays: New Year's Day (Jan. 1); Maundy Thursday (Mar. 20); Good Friday (Mar. 21); Easter (Mar. 23-24); *Sumardagurinn Fyrsti* (1st day of summer; Apr. 24); Labor Day (May 1); Ascension (May 1); Pentecost (May 11-12); National Day (June 17); Tradesman's Day (Aug. 4); Christmas (Dec. 25); Boxing Day (Dec. 26).

Festivals: The month-long Þorrablót festival (during Feb.) is a holdover from the midwinter feasts of past centuries. Icelanders eat *svið* (singed and boiled sheep's head), *hrútspungur* (pickled ram's testicles), and *hákarl* (shark meat that has been allowed to rot underground) in celebration of their heritage. "Beer Day," celebrated in bars and restaurants, celebrates the March 1st, 1989 lifting of a 75yr. prohibition.

ICELAND

Sumardagurinn Fyrsti marks the 1st day of summer with a carnival. The Reykjanes Peninsula celebrates *Sjómannadagur* (Seamen's Day) on June 4 with boat races and tug-of-war. During the 1st weekend in August, Icelanders head to the country for *Verslunarmannahelgi*, a weekend of barbecues, camping, and drinking.

BEYOND TOURISM

Travelers hoping to stay in Iceland may be able to secure summer work. Check www.jobs-in-europe.net for info on job placement. Ecotourism opportunities abound; organizations run tours on horseback, to hot springs, and up mountains. For more info on opportunities across Europe, see **Beyond Tourism**, p. 56.

Earthwatch Institute, 3 Clock Tower Pl., Ste. 100, Box 75, Maynard, MA, 01754 (Canada and the US ☎800-776-0188, the UK 44 18 65 31 88 38, Australia 03 96 82 68 28; www.earthwatch.org). For a hefty fee (€1650-2000), Earthwatch organizes volunteers, guided by scientists, to conduct geological fieldwork in the Icelandic glaciers. They also coordinate fundraising efforts to curtail the fee.

International Cultural Youth Exchange, Große Hamburger Str. 30, Berlin, GER (☎49 30 28 39 05 50; www.icye.org). ICYE brings together volunteers and host organizations on a variety of projects worldwide, including several in Iceland. ICYE also organizes European Voluntary Service programs (http://europa.eu.int/comm/youth/program/guide/action2_en.html) for EU citizens to serve for a fully funded year in another EU country.

Volunteers for Peace (☎802-259-2759; www.vfp.org). Runs 2800 "workcamps" throughout the world, including several in Iceland. $250 per 2- to 3-week workcamp, including room and board, plus $20 VFP membership fee.

REYKJAVÍK

Home to three-fifths of Icelanders, Reykjavík (pop. 190,000) is a modestly sized capital with an international clubbing reputation. Bold, modern architecture juts out above the blue waters of the Faxaflói Bay, and the city's refreshingly clear air complements the clean streets and well-kept gardens. The spring rain and the endless winter night force social life indoors, where many locals sip espresso while arguing over environmental policy in this hub of renewable energy.

TRANSPORTATION

Flights: International flights arrive at **Keflavík Airport (KEF),** 55km from Reykjavík. From the main exit, catch a **Flybus** (☎562 1011; www.flybus.is) to BSÍ Bus Terminal (40-50min.; 1200ISK, round-trip 2100ISK). Flybus also offers free minivan transport from the bus terminal to many hostels and hotels; check website for more info. A public bus to the city center runs from Gamla-Hringbraut stop across the street from the bus terminal (M-F 7am-midnight, Sa-Su 10am-midnight; 275ISK). Flybus service to the airport departs from BSÍ; most hostels and hotels can also arrange trips. Nearby **Reykjavík Airport (RKV)** is the departure point for domestic flights. Take bus #15 or Flybus from BSÍ.

Buses: Umferðarmiðstöð BSÍ (BSÍ Bus Terminal), Vatnsmýrarveg. 10 (☎562 1011; www.bsi.is), off Gamla-Hringbraut. Walk 15-20min. south along Tjörnin from the city center or take bus #14, 15, S1, or S3-S6 (2-3 per hr., 275ISK). Open daily May-Oct. 24hr.; Nov.-Apr. 5am-10pm.

Public Transportation: Bus service can be infrequent and roundabout; walking is often a speedier option. **Strætó** (☎540 2700; www.bus.is) operates yellow city buses (275ISK). **Lækjartorg,** on Lækjarg., is the main bus station for the city center. **Hlemmur,** 1km east of Lækjartorg where Hverfisg. meets Laugavegur, is another major terminal with more connections than Lækjartorg (open M-Sa 7am-11:30pm,

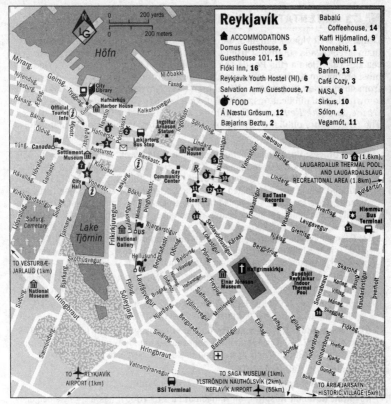

Reykjavík

ACCOMMODATIONS
Domus Guesthouse, **5**
Guesthouse 101, **15**
Flóki Inn, **16**
Reykjavík Youth Hostel (HI), **6**
Salvation Army Guesthouse, **7**

FOOD
Á Næstu Grösum, **12**
Bæjarins Beztu, **2**

Babalú
Coffeehouse, **14**
Kaffi Hljómalind, **9**
Nonnabiti, **1**

NIGHTLIFE
Barinn, **13**
Café Cozy, **3**
NASA, **8**
Sirkus, **10**
Sólon, **4**
Vegamót, **11**

Su 10am-11:30pm). Pick up a schedule at the terminal. Don't feel bad asking for navigational help at hostels and info desks—recent changes in the bus routes have confused even some drivers. Buy packages of 10 adult fares (2000ISK) or pay fare with coins; drivers do not give change. Ticket packages are sold at the terminal and at swimming pools. If you need to change buses, ask the driver of the 1st bus for *skiptimiði* (a free transfer ticket), valid for 1hr. after the fare has been paid. Most buses 2-3 per hr. M-Sa 7am-midnight, Su 10am-midnight.

Taxis: BSR (☎561 0000). 24hr. service. **Hreyfill** (☎588 5522; www.hreyfill.is/english). Also offers private tours for groups of 1-8, 7900-44,000ISK.

Car Rental: Berg, Bíldshöfða 10 (☎577 6050; www.bergcar.is). Under 100km from 4900ISK per day, unlimited km from 8850ISK per day; low season reduced rates. Pick-up available at Keflavík and Reykjavík Airports (2000ISK). **Hertz** (☎505 0600; www.hertz.is), at the Reykjavík Airport. From 6110ISK per day. Pickup available at Keflavík Airport (2300ISK). **Avis** (☎591 4000; www.avis.is) and **Budget** (☎562 6060; www.budget.is) have locations in Reykjavík. Fuel costs around 3000ISK per day.

Bike Rental: Reykjavík Youth Hostel campground (p. 525). 1700ISK per 6hr., 2000ISK per day. Helmet included. **Borgarhjól,** Hverfisgata 50, is closer to the city center, down the road from Culture House. (☎551 5653. Call for prices; fees change frequently.)

Hitchhiking: Many foreigners hitchhike outside of Reykjavík because of confusing bus routes, but it is never completely safe. Let's Go does not recommend hitchhiking.

■ ? ORIENTATION AND PRACTICAL INFORMATION

Lækjartorg is Reykjavík's main square and a good base for navigation. **Lækjargata**, a main street, leads southwest from Lækjartorg and becomes **Fríkirkjuvegur** when it reaches **Lake Tjörnin** (the Pond), the southern limit of the city center. Reykjavík's most prominent thoroughfare extends eastward from Lækjartorg, changing names from **Austurstræti** to **Bankastræti** and then to **Laugavegur**, as it is most commonly known. Helpful publications, including *What's On in Reykjavík*, *Reykjavík City Guide*, and *The Reykjavík Grapevine*, are available for free at tourist offices. The *Grapevine*, published by American expatriates, includes opinionated local news coverage and comprehensive listings of current music and arts events.

Tourist Offices: Upplýsingamiðstöð Ferðamanna í Reykjavík, Aðalstr. 2 (☎590 1550; www.visitreykjavik.is). Open June-Aug. daily 8:30am-7pm; Sept.-May M-Sa 9am-6pm, Su 10am-2pm. Sells the **Reykjavík Card** (1-day 1200ISK, 2-day 1700ISK, 3-day 2200ISK), which allows unlimited public transportation, free entry to some sights and thermal pools (p. 527), and limited Internet access at the tourist center. Several discount coupon books are also available at the center. **Kleif Tourist Information Center,** Bankastræti 2 (☎510 5700; www.kleif.is). Open June-Aug. daily 8am-9pm; Sept.-May. M-F 8am-6pm, Sa-Su 8am-4pm. **City Hall Information Center,** Vonarstræti 3 (☎563 2005), in the lobby of City Hall. Open M-F 8:20am-6:15pm, Sa-Su noon-4pm. Visit www.reykjavik.com for general info on sights around the city.

Embassies: Canada, Túng. 14 (☎575 6500). Open M-F 9am-noon. **UK,** Lauf. 31 (☎550 5100). Open M-F 9am-noon. **US,** Lauf. 21 (☎562 9100). Open M-F 9am-5pm.

Luggage Storage: At BSÍ Bus Terminal (☎580 5462), next to the ticket window. 400ISK for the 1st day, 200ISK per day thereafter. Open daily 7:30am-7pm.

GLBT Resources: Gay Community Center, Laugavegur 3, 4th fl. (☎552 7878; www.samtokin78.is). Open M and Th 1-5pm and 8-11pm, Tu-W and F 1-5pm; cafe open M and Th 8-11:30pm; library open M and Th 8-11pm. More info at www.gayice.is.

Police: Hverfisg. 113 (☎444 1000).

24hr. Pharmacy: Lyfja Lágmúla, Lágmúla 5 (☎533 2300).

Hospital: National Hospital, on Hringbraut (☎543 1000), has a 24hr. emergency department. Take bus #14, S1, or S3-S6 southeast from the city center.

Internet Access: Reykjavík Public Library, Tryggvag. 15 (☎563 1705), is the cheapest option. 200ISK per hr. Open M-Th 10am-7pm, F-Su 1-5pm. Cash only. **Snarrót,** Laugavegur 21 (☎551 8927). In the basement of Kaffi Hljómalind (p. 525), Snarrót is also a hub for local student activism. 300ISK per hr. Open M-F 9am-11pm, Sa-Su 10am-11pm. MC/V. **Ground Zero,** Vallarstr. 4 (☎562 7776). 300ISK per 30min., 500ISK per hr. Open M-F 11am-1am, Sa-Su noon-1am. AmEx/MC/V.

Post Office: Íslandspóstur, Pósthússtr. 5 (☎580 1121), at the intersection with Austurstr. Open M-F 9am-6:00pm. **Poste Restante** available.

⌂ ⋀ ACCOMMODATIONS AND CAMPING

Gistiheimili (guesthouses) offer sleeping-bag accommodations starting from 2500ISK (bed and pillow in a small room; add 300-600ISK for linens). Hotels cost at least 5500ISK. Call ahead for reservations, especially in summer.

▨ **Reykjavík Youth Hostel (HI),** Sundlaugarveg. 34 (☎553 8110). Bus #14 from Lækjarg. This popular, eco-friendly hostel is east of the city center, but it's adjacent to Reykjavík's largest thermal pool and has excellent facilities. The staff gives tips for exploring the city's less touristy sights. Breakfast 800ISK. Linens 600ISK. Laundry 350ISK. Internet 300ISK per 30min, 500ISK per hr. Reception 8am-midnight; ring bell after hours. Dorms 2050ISK, with HI discount 1700ISK; doubles 4100/3500ISK. ❷

Salvation Army Guesthouse, Kirkjustr. 2 (☎561 3203; www.guesthouse.is). Located near City Hall in the heart of Reykjavík, this bright yellow hostel is cozy with modest, but neat, accommodations. Its prime location makes it ideal for exploring the nightlife. Breakfast 700ISK. Laundry 800ISK. Sleeping-bag accommodations 2500ISK; singles 5500ISK; doubles 8000ISK. AmEx/MC/V. ❷

Domus Guesthouse, Hverfisgt. 45 (☎561 1200). Take bus #13, S1, or S3-S6 and get off across from the Regnboginn movie theater on Hverfisgötu. Close to the city center, the guesthouse offers spacious rooms with TVs and couches. All sleeping-bag accommodations are located across the street in a large room partitioned by curtains. Breakfast included with private rooms. Sleeping-bag accommodations 3900ISK; singles 9500ISK; doubles 11,300ISK. Reduced prices Oct.-Apr. MC/V. ❸

Flóki Inn, Flókag. 1 (☎552 1155; www.innsoficeland.is), a 15min. walk from the city center. A relaxing, intimate guesthouse with kettle, fridge, and TV in every room. Breakfast included. Reception 24hr. Check-in 2pm. Check-out 11am. Singles 8300ISK; doubles 10,900ISK. Extra bed 3700ISK. Reduced prices Oct.-May. AmEx/MC/V. ❹

Guesthouse 101, Laugavegur 101 (☎562 6101; www.iceland101.com), off Snorrabraut. This converted office building east of the city center has small, bright, modern rooms. Wheelchair-accessible. Breakfast included. Singles 7300ISK; doubles 9600ISK; triples 11,900ISK. 10% off with cash payment. Reduced prices in winter. MC/V. ❹

Reykjavík Youth Hostel Campsite (☎568 6944), next to the hostel. Helpful staff and a sociable character make this a good alternative to indoor facilities. Luggage storage 300ISK. Reception 24hr. Open mid-May to mid-Sept. Tent sites 800ISK. 4-person cabins 4500ISK. Showers. Electricity 400ISK. MC/V. ❶

◨ FOOD

An authentic Icelandic meal featuring *hákarl* (shark meat that has been allowed to rot underground), lamb, or puffin costs upwards of 1500ISK, but it's worth the splurge at least once. To maintain a leaner budget, head to the stands west of Lækjartorg, which hawk *pylsur* (lamb meat hot dogs) for around 200ISK. Ask for "the works," including *remoulade* (a spicy mayonnaise-based sauce). Pick up groceries at **Bónus,** Laugavegur 59. (☎562 8200. Open M-F noon-6:30pm, Sa 10am-8pm.) Other stores are on Austurstræti and Hverfisgata.

▨ Á Næstu Grösum, Laugavegur 20B (☎552 8410), entrance off Klapparstígur. The 1st all-vegetarian restaurant in Iceland uses only fresh, seasonal ingredients in creative ways. The airy dining room showcases the work of up-and-coming local artists. Soup (700ISK) comes with free refills. Small plate 550ISK; medium 850ISK; large 1250ISK. Open M-F 11:30am-10pm, Sa 1-10pm, Su 5-10pm. MC/V. ❷

▨ Babalú Coffeehouse, Skólavörðustigur 22A (☎552 2278). A perfect place to relax. Serves savory crepes (920ISK) and smaller, sweet crepes (500ISK). Enjoy a coffee (280ISK) on the patio. Free Wi-Fi. Open daily 11am-10pm. AmEx/MC/V. ❷

Kaffi Hljómalind, Laugavegur 21 (☎517 1980), east of the city center. Organic, vegetarian-friendly cafe serves big portions of soup, with free refill and bread (700ISK). Free Wi-Fi, vocal patrons, a box of toys, and large windows make this a great place for people-watching or passing the time before nightlife kicks into high gear. Live music (500ISK) or poetry reading W-F 8pm. Open M-Sa 9am-11pm, Su 11am-6pm. MC/V. ❷

Nonnabiti, Hafnarstr. 9 (☎551 2312), west of Lækjartorg. toward the main tourist office. This no-frills sandwich shop is good for cheap, satisfying meals. Burgers 440ISK. Hot sandwiches 610ISK. 100ISK discount on subs M-F 9:30am-1:30pm. Open Su-Th 9:30am-2am, F-Sa 8:30am-6:00am. MC/V. ❶

Bæjarins Beztu, corner of Tryggvag. and Pósthússtr. This tiny stand on the harbor serves the Icelandic hot dog (210ISK) by which all others are measured. The owner proudly displays a picture of Bill Clinton eating one of her franks. Weekend crowds head here to satisfy late-night cravings, often singing while they wait. Open until 12:30am, or until crowds dissipate—sometimes past 6am. MC/V. ❶

◉ SIGHTS

CITY CENTER. Reykjavík's **City Hall,** on the northern shore of **Lake Tjörnin,** houses an impressive three-dimensional model of Iceland that vividly renders the country's striking topography. *(Open in summer M-F 8am-7pm, Sa-Su 10-6pm; winter M-F 8am-7pm, Sa-Su noon-6pm. Free.)* Just beyond City Hall lies **Aðalstræti,** the oldest street in the city. The recently opened **871 +/- 2 Settlement Museum,** 16 Aðalstræti, features the preserved foundation of a Viking longhouse, with interactive displays and artifacts. By dating surrounding volcanic deposits, archaeologists theorize that the structure was built around AD 869-873. *(☎411 6370. Open daily 10am-5pm. 600ISK. AmEx/MC/V.)* Nearby is the oldest house in the city, **Fogetastofur,** Aðalstræti 10, built in 1762, which offers exhibits, pictures, and maps describing Reykjavík's growth since the 18th century. *(Museum open M-F 9am-6pm, Sa-Su noon-5pm. Free.)* The **Hafnarhús** (Harbor House) is the most eclectic of the three wings of the **Reykjavík Art Museum.** The museum, a renovated warehouse, holds a collection of paintings by Erro, Iceland's preeminent contemporary artist. *(Tryggvag. 17, off Aðalstr. ☎590 1201; www.listasafnreykjavikur.is. Open daily high season 10am-5pm; low season 1-4pm. 500ISK. Th free.)* Follow Tryggvag. to the intersection of Lækjarg. and Hverfisg. to see the **statue of Ingólfur Arnason,** Iceland's first settler, and revel in the view of the mountains to the north. The ◼Culture House has a detailed exhibit on Iceland's ancient history and mythology, including carefully preserved vellum manuscripts of the Eddas and Sagas. *(Hverfisg. 15. ☎545 1400. Open daily 11am-5pm. Free.)*

East of Lake Tjörnin, the **National Gallery of Iceland** presents highlights of contemporary Icelandic art. The toys and cushions on the bottom floor aren't part of an ultramodern exhibit; they're for the restless children of patrons. *(Frikirkjuveg. 7. ☎515 9600. Open Tu-Su 11am-5pm. Free.)* Continue eastward to the landmark **Hallgrímskirkja** church on Skólavörðustígur, designed by Guðjón Samúelsson to look like it formed from a volcanic eruption. *(☎510 1000. Open daily 9am-5pm. Elevator to the top 350ISK.)* Across from the church, the **Einar Jónsson Museum** on Njarðarg. exhibits 300 of the sculptor's imposing, allegorical works inspired by Iceland's Christian and pagan heritage. Don't miss the free sculpture garden in the back. *(☎561 3797; www.skulptur.is. Open June to mid-Sept. Tu-Su 2-5pm; mid-Sept.-May Sa-Su 2-5pm. 400ISK.)*

 DON'T GET FLEECED. Visiting Reykjavík isn't cheap. For deals on clothes, music, and jewelry, check out the **Sirkus** (flea market) on Laugavegur next to Kaffi Hljómalind (June-Aug. F-Sa). Cap it off with a discounted brew.

LAUGARDALUR. Sights cluster around Laugardalur, a large park east of the city center. The white dome of the ◼Ásmundarsafn (Ásmundur Sveinsson Sculpture Museum), on Sigtún, houses works spanning Sveinsson's career in a building the artist designed and lived in. The free sculpture garden around the museum features larger works, some of which are interactive pieces ideal for climbing. *(Take bus #14 to the Laugardalslaug thermal pools, turn left and walk down Reykjavegur to Sigtún. ☎553 2155. Open daily May-Sept. 10am-4pm; Oct.-Apr. 1-4pm. 500ISK, includes admission to Harbor House. Th free.)* Walking out of the museum, continue straight down Sigtún until it becomes Engjaveg. and proceed to the **Reykjavík Botanic Garden,** one of the few forested areas in Iceland. *(Skúlatún 2. ☎553 8870. Garden open 24hr. Greenhouse and pavilion open daily Apr.-Sept. 10am-10pm; Oct.-Mar. 10am-5pm. Free.)* Just outside the garden, opposite the pavilion and greenhouse, a free outdoor exhibit outlines the history of the **Washing Springs,** Reykjavík's geothermal square, where the women of the city once came to do their cooking and laundry. The city's largest thermal swimming pool, **Laugardalslaug** (see **Thermal Pools,** below), is also in the area.

OTHER SIGHTS. The **Saga Museum** rivals Madame Tussauds with its depiction of Icelandic history using life-size wax models. One figure shows a woman exposing her breast, an event that supposedly caused the entire army of Norway to retreat during a bygone battle. We don't get it either. *(Bus #18 south to Perlan.* ☎*511 1517; www.sagamuseum.is. Open Mar.-Oct. 10am-6pm; Nov.-Feb. noon-5pm. 800ISK, students 600ISK.)* The renovated ■**National Museum** has a more comprehensive overview of Iceland's past with audio/visuals and interactive exhibits that let you try on Icelandic garb. *(Suðurgt. 41. Bus #14, S1, or S3-S6 from Hlemmur station.* ☎*530 2200; www.natmus.is. Open May-Sept. 15 daily 10am-5pm; Sept 16-Apr. Tu-Su 11am-5pm. 600ISK, students 300ISK. W free.)* From the National Museum, take bus #12 to **Árbæjarsafn,** an open-air museum that chronicles the lives and architecture of past generations of Icelanders. Check www.reykjavikmuseum.is for summer weekend special events, like folk dances and Viking games. *(Kistuhylur 4.* ☎*577 1111. Open June-Aug. M 11am-4pm, Tu-F 10am-5pm, Sa-Su 10am-6pm. 600ISK. Low season tours M, W, F 1pm; call ahead.)*

ⓒ THERMAL POOLS

Reykjavík's thermal pools are all equipped with a hot pot (naturally occurring hot tub) and steam room or sauna, although each pool maintains a distinct character. Freeloaders should seek out the city beach and its free hot pot at Nauthólsvik. All pools listed below charge 350ISK admission, with 10 visits for 3000ISK.

Laugardalslaug, Laugardalslaug-Sundlaugarveg. 105 (☎411 5100). Take bus #14 from the city center; entrance is on the right, facing the parking lot. The city's largest thermal pool features indoor and outdoor facilities, a water slide, a children's slide, 4 hot pots, and a sauna. Swimsuit or towel rental 350ISK. Open Apr.-Sept. M-F 6:30am-10:30pm, Sa-Su 8am-10pm; Oct.-Mar. M-F 6:30am-10:30pm, Sa-Su 8am-8pm. MC/V.

Sundhöll Reykjavíkur, Barónsstígur 101 (☎551 4059). Take bus #14, 15 or 16. This centrally located pool has a smaller outdoor area than other pools, but is the only one with diving boards. Open M-F 6:30am-9:30pm, Sa-Su 8am-7pm. AmEx/MC/V.

Sundlaug Seltjarness, Suðurströnd 170 (☎561 1551). Take bus #11 from Hlemmur station to Sundlaug stop and follow the signs. Recently renovated, this is the only pool that offers salt-water hot pots. Facilities include a water slide, 2 hot pots, and a sauna. Swimsuit or towel rental 300ISK. Open M-F 7am-9pm, Sa-Su 8am-7pm. AmEx/MC/V.

Ylströndin Nauthólsvík. Take bus #16 south until the last stop, or take bus #18 to Perlan and hike down Öskuhlíð. Though the locals don't consider this a classic thermal pool, this remote city beach is worth the hard trek to soak in the hot pot in the midst of sea water and take in the view of Reykjavík's smaller fjords. Lockers 200ISK. Swimming free. Open May-Sept. daily 10am-8pm. Closed in rainy weather.

ⓢ HIKING

Reykjavík has a range of hikes for different experience levels. Take precaution when scaling heights—conditions on hilltops can be very different compared to weather at sea level. For easier hikes, take bus #18 to the Perlan stop by the Saga Museum to reach trails on the forested hill around Perlan, one of which features a working model of the Strokkur Geyser (see Gullfoss and Geysir, p. 529). At the southwest corner of the park is **Nauthólsvík** beach (see **Thermal Pools,** above) and a scenic trail around the airport that leads back to the city. If you get tired, catch bus #12 on Skeljanes back to the center. Pick up maps at the tourist office. If basking in the midnight sun on a black lava beach is what you've always dreamed of, visit the bird reserve ▨**Grótta** on the western tip of the peninsula. Take bus #11 out to Hofgarður and walk 15min. along the sea on Byggarðstangi. Although the Grótta itself is closed during nesting season (May-June), the bird-filled sky is still an amazing sight. Check out the lighthouse at the edge of the peninsula: high tides make it a temporary island. South of the city lies the **Heiðmörk Reserve**, a large park with picnic spots and beginner- to intermediate-hiking trails. Take bus S1 or S2 from Hlemmur to Hamraborg and transfer to bus #28. Ask the driver to let you off at Lake Elliðavatn; from there, walk 3-4km south to the reserve.

DOOR-TO-DOOR. Legs aching after a long hike? The BSÍ bus drivers will generally let you off anywhere along the route upon request. You can also flag buses down like taxis and they will often stop to pick you up.

Secluded and slow-paced **Viðey Island,** home to Viking structures and Iceland's second-oldest church, has been inhabited since the 10th century. The island features several sculpture exhibitions and the new, playfully postmodern "Blind Pavilion." Take the ferry from the Reykjavík harbor Miðbakki. (☎892 0098; www.ferja.is. Ferry departs daily at 1, 2, 3, 7, and 9pm; June 10-Aug. 12 also at 8:30am. Round-trip 750ISK.) Across the bay from Reykjavík looms **Mt. Esja,** which you can ascend via a well-maintained trail (2-3hr.). The trail is not difficult, but hikers should be prepared for rain, hail, or even a brief but powerful snow squall. Arrive early in the morning in order to make the buses there and back. Take bus #15 to Háholt and transfer to bus #27, exiting at Mógilsá. (Bus #27 runs once every 1-2hr.; consult SVR city bus schedule.)

▨ NIGHTLIFE

Despite being unnervingly quiet on weeknights, Reykjavík asserts its status as a wild party town each weekend. The city's thriving independent music scene centers at ▨**12 Tónar,** Skólavörðustígur 12, and **Bad Taste Records,** Laugavegur 59, in the basement of the Bónus supermarket. After taking in the concerts, Icelanders hit the bars and clubs until the wee hours. Most bars do not have cover charges, but bouncers tend to regulate who enters after 2am. Clubs have steep drink prices, so many locals drink at home or head to the *vínbuð* (liquor store) before going out. Don't bother showing up before 12:30am and plan to be out until 4 or 5am. Boisterous crowds tend to bar-hop around **Austurstræti, Tryggvagata,** and **Laugavegur.** The establishments listed below are 20+, unless otherwise noted.

▨ **Barinn,** Laugavegur 22 (☎578 7800). With 3 floors, this bar and club has a DJ every night playing a mix of 80s, classic R&B, and contemporary Icelandic beats for dancing. The top floor is the conversation room for those literally above it all. Beer 500ISK. Mixed drinks 700ISK. Open Su-Th 10am-1am, F-Sa 10am-5:30am. AmEx/MC/V.

Sirkus, Klapparstíg. 30 (☎551 1999). A plant-filled, well-lit patio and upstairs bungalow room contribute to a deliciously out-of-place atmosphere at this venue frequented by local underground artists. Beer 500ISK. Open Su-Th 2pm-1am, F-Sa 2pm-5am.

Sólon, Bankastr. 7A (☎562 3232). This trendy cafe morphs at night into a posh club bouncing with hip-hop, pop, and electronica. Cafe downstairs, large dance floor and bar upstairs. Try their famous drink, the black death, used to stave off the dark, cold winters (550ISK). Beer 500ISK. Th live music. Open M-Th 11am-1am, F-Sa 11am-5am.

Café Cozy, Austurstræti 3 (☎511 1033; cafecozy@simnet.is), near the tourist center. This quiet cafe serves traditional Icelandic fare (such as lamb soup) during the day, but at night it's one of the wildest clubs in Reykjavík. Gay-friendly. Attracts a mixed, energetic crowd. Expect to see dancing on the tables by 3am. Beer 600ISK. Mixed drinks 800ISK. F-Sa live DJ. Open Su-Th 11:00am-1am, F-Sa 10am-6am. AmEx/MC/V.

Vegamót, Vegamótarstíg. 4 (☎511 3040), off Laugavegur. Students and well-dressed urban professionals head to this posh bar to flaunt it and see others do the same. Beer 500ISK. Th-Sa live DJ. Open M-Th 11:30am-1am, F-Sa 11:30am-5am. MC/V.

NASA, Thorraldssenstr. 2 (☎511 1313; www.nasa.is), at Austurvollur Sq. The large central dance floor draws a varied crowd, depending on the evening's band. Beer 700ISK. F-Sa live bands. Cover 500-1500ISK. Open F-Sa 11am-last customer. MC/V.

🔳 DAYTRIPS FROM REYKJAVÍK

Iceland's main attractions are its natural wonders. ▧Iceland Excursions runs the popular "Golden Circle Classic" tour, which stops at Hveragerði, Kerið, Skálholt, Geysir, Gullfoss, and Þingvellir National Park. (☎540 1313; www.grayline.is. 9-10hr., 6600ISK.) **Highlanders** offers exciting, but pricey, off-road tours in jeeps that can traverse rivers, crags, and glaciers. (☎568 3030; www.hl.is. 10,600-17,500ISK.)

GULLFOSS AND GEYSIR. The glacial river Hvita plunges down 32m to create **Gullfoss** (Golden Falls). A dirt path passes along the falls, where many get soaked in the mist. The adjacent hill houses a small cafeteria and gift shop and affords a stunning view of the surrounding mountains, plains, and cliffs. On the horizon you can see the tip of Longjökull, a glacier the size of Hong Kong. The **Geysir** area, 10km down the road, is a teeming bed of hot springs in a barren landscape. The **Strokkur Geyser** (the Churn) erupts every 5min., spewing sulfurous water at heights up to 35m. Exercise caution around the thermal pools—more than one tourist has fallen into the nearby **Blesi pool** and been badly scalded. The excellent **museum** at the visitors center offers a multimedia show on the science behind these natural phenomena. The top portion of the museum is dedicated to Aðalbjörg Egilsdottur, who donated her collection of early 19th-century Icelandic artifacts, including a spinning wheel, stove, and saddle. (Museum 500ISK, students 400ISK. BSÍ runs a round-trip bus to Gulfoss and Geysir with Iceland Excursions, departing from the BSÍ Terminal in Reykjavík June-Aug. daily 1pm; 6hr., round-trip 5200ISK.)

ÞINGVELLIR NATIONAL PARK. The European and North American tectonic plates meet at Þingvellir National Park, a place of both geologic and cultural significance for Iceland. Stand in the chasm between the continents, but don't linger too long—the plates are moving apart at a rate of 2cm per year. Train your eyes on the dark lines in the sloping hills of the valley; these fault lines mirror the slow movement of the plates. The Öxará River, slicing through lava fields and jagged fissures, leads to the **Drekkingarhylur** (Drowning Pool), where adulterous women were once drowned, and to **Lake Þingvallavatn,** Iceland's largest lake. Not far from the Drekkingarhylur lies the site of the **Alþing** (ancient parliament), where for almost nine centuries, starting in AD 930, Icelanders gathered in the shadow of the **Lögberg** (Law Rock) to discuss matters of blood, money, and justice. Maps are available at the **Þingvellir Visitors Center.** (Info Center ☎482 2660. Open June-Aug. daily 9am-8pm; Apr.-May and Sept.-Oct. daily 9am-5pm; Nov.-Mar. Sa-Su 9am-5pm. BSÍ does not run buses to Þingvellir; the site can only be reached by taking a tour bus or driving.)

BLUE LAGOON. The southwest corner of the Reykjanes Peninsula harbors an oasis in the middle of a lava field: a vast pool of geothermally heated water. The lagoon has become a tourist magnet, but it's worth braving the crowds. The cloudy blue waters, rich in silica, minerals, and algae, are famous for their healing powers. Bathers who have their fill of wading through the 36-39°C (97-102°F) waters can indulge in a steam bath, a silica facial, or an in-water massage (1600ISK per

10min.). Stand under the waterfall for a free, all-natural shoulder massage. *(Buses run from BSÍ Bus Terminal in Reykjavík. 1hr., 6 per day 8:30am-8pm; round-trip 2200ISK, 3800 ISK with Blue Lagoon admission. ☎ 420 8800; www.bluelagoon.com. Open daily mid-May to Aug. 9am-9pm; Sept. to mid-May 10am-8pm. Towel rental 350ISK. Bathing suit rental 400ISK. Admission and locker 1800ISK, over 67 1200ISK, 12-15 900ISK, under 11 free. AmEx/MC/V.)*

HVERAGERÐI. Hveragerði (pop. 2000) sits on a volatile geothermal hotbed that occasionally shoots geysers through the floors of local houses—the basement leak to end all basement leaks. Geothermal energy from the geysers powers the town's numerous **greenhouses,** where locals grow cucumbers, bananas, and other exotic produce that would not normally survive in Iceland's cool climate. Most of the greenhouses do not run organized tours, but some owners will show you around upon request. **The Garden of Eden,** Austurmörk 25, which boasts a nursery and a low-fat ice cream parlor, is one of the few places in the town that caters to tourists. *(Across the street from the gas station where the bus stops. ☎ 483 4900; www.eden.smart.is. Open daily high season 9am-11pm; low season 9am-7pm.)* The **tourist office,** Sunnumörk 2, has info on guesthouses, campgrounds, and hiking routes in the surrounding area. *(Buses run from the BSÍ terminal in Reykjavík. 40min.; 5-6 times per day in high season. ☎ 483 4601. Open high season M-F 9am-5pm, Sa-Su noon-4pm; low season M-F 9am-4:30pm.)*

NESJAVELLIRI. This power plant provides Reykjavík with half of its hot water and electricity by capturing geothermal heat that escapes from the sultry meeting of the North American and European tectonic plates. Insulated pipes run 26km from Nesjavelliri to the capital city on rollers to avoid destruction by one of Iceland's frequent earthquakes. The geothermal energy hub is also fueled by three nearby volcanic systems. Free **tours** of the facilities are available and provide a detailed look at Iceland's latest strides in renewable energy. *(Only accessible by tour bus, such as the Iceland Excursions bus. ☎ 617 6786. Open June-Aug. M-Sa 9am-5pm; Sept.-May by request.)*

WESTMAN ISLANDS (VESTMANNAEYJAR)

The black cliffs of the Westman Islands (pop. 4500) are the most recent offerings of the volcanic fury that created Iceland. The archipelago is made up of 15 islands and many isolated rock pillars breaking through the waves—Heimaey is the only inhabited island with the town of Vestmannaeyjar.

◨◪ TRANSPORTATION AND PRACTICAL INFORMATION. It usually requires a full day of travel to reach the islands by bus and ferry from Reykjavík. Air Iceland runs **flights** to the Westman Islands from Reykjavík Airport. (☎ 481 3255; www.flugfelag.is. 20min., from 4400ISK. Discounts for 21 and under.) To get to Vestmannaeyjar from the airport, exit and take a left down the main road—a 20min. walk will put you in the center of town. The Herjólfur **ferry** departing from Þorlákshöfn is slower but cheaper than flying. (☎ 481 2800. 2¾-3hr.; departs daily noon and 7:30pm; returns daily 8:15am and 4pm. 1800ISK, with ISIC 900ISK; 10% discount on Internet tickets.) **Buses** go from BSÍ Station to the ferry 1hr. before departure (1200ISK). The **tourist office** is on Ráðhúströ, on the first floor of the Cultural Center. (☎ 481 3535; www.vestmannaeyjar.is. Open mid-May to mid-Sept. M-F 9am-5pm, Sa-Su 11am-4pm; mid-Sept. to mid-May M-F 9am-5pm.)

┏◖ ACCOMMODATIONS AND FOOD. Many islanders offer space in their homes as guesthouses, an affordable and cozy accommodation option. The centrally located **Guesthouse Hreiðrið ❷,** Faxastíg. 33, is just past the Volcanic Film Show theater on Heiðarveg. (☎ 481 1045; http://tourist.eyjar.is. Reception 24hr. in summer. Sleeping-bag accommodations 1900ISK; singles 3800ISK; doubles

5800ISK. Low season reduced rates. 10% ISIC discount. AmEx/MC/V.) **Guesthouse Erna ❷**, Kirkjubæjarbraut 14, has a homey feel with TV-equipped rooms. It's slightly east of the city center, but closer to the lava fields than other accommodations. (☎481 2112. Reception 24hr. Sleeping-bag accommodations 2000ISK; singles 4000ISK; doubles 6000ISK; triples 9000ISK. AmEx/MC/V.) **Guesthouse Sunnuhóll (HI) ❷**, Vestmannabraut 28B, has newly renovated rooms with ample space to stretch out after a hike. The reception desk is in Hotel Þórshamar, Vestaunrabraut 28, near the center of town. (☎481 2900; www.hotelvestmannaeyjar.is. Breakfast 900ISK. Linens 700ISK. Free Wi-Fi in the hotel. Sleeping-bag accommodations 2100ISK, with HI discount 1800ISK; singles 3400ISK. Low season reduced rates. AmEx/MC/V.) **Herjólfsdal Camping ❶**, 10min. west of town on Dalveg., sits at the bottom of one of the island's oldest craters. The site of the island's first settlement is next door, marked by models of the original inhabitants' stone and grass roof huts. (Campground ☎692 6952 or 481 1045. Free showers. 700ISK per tent site. MC/V.) Pick up groceries at **Krónan** on Strandaveg. (Open daily 11am-7pm.)

◉ ⚠ SIGHTS AND OUTDOOR ACTIVITIES. As recently as 1973, **Eldfell** (fire mountain) volcano tore through the northern section of Heimaey, spewing lava and ash and forcing Vestmannaeyjar's population to evacuate overnight. When the eruption ended five months later, many of the town's houses had been destroyed, and the island had grown by nearly 2 sq. km. Visitors can still feel the heat of the cooling lava—harnessing the energy provides some electricity and hot water. The 1973 eruption has also spurred the creation of many related attractions. **◪Pompei of the North,** a modern archeological site, unearths houses destroyed by Eldfell, offering a unique perspective on the magnitude of the disaster (www.pompeiofthenorth.com). **The Volcanic Film Show,** on Heiðarveg., runs a documentary about the eruption. (☎481 1045. 55min. shows daily mid-June to mid-Aug. 11am, 2, 3:30, 9pm; mid-Aug. to mid-Sept. 11am and 3:30pm. 600ISK, students 500ISK.) Across the street from the film show, the **Aquarium** and **Natural History Museum,** Heiðarveg. 12, feature exhibits on Westman's sea creatures, birds, and geology. A combined ticket (450ISK) grants access to both attractions, along with the **Folkmuseum,** in the cultural center on Ráðhúströ, and the medical museum at **Landlyst,** the second-oldest house in the city, next to the harbor and off Strandvegur. (Aquarium and Natural History Museum ☎418 1997; Folkmuseum 481 1194. All museums open May 15-Sept. 15 daily 11am-5pm; Sept. 16 to May 14 Sa-Su 3-5pm. 400ISK per site without museum key. AmEx/MC/V.) Landlyst is on the site of **Skansinn,** an ancient fortress used to guard against maurauding pirates in search of booty; only the foundations remain. The spot is now home to a medieval wooden church, donated by Norway to commemorate 1000 years of Christianity in Iceland.

Heimaey's 15 sq. km offer several spectacular hikes. **Cafe Kró,** Suðurgerdi 4, provides hiking advice, tour offers, Internet access, and caffeine to fuel the journey. (☎488 4884. Coffee 250-300ISK. Internet 200ISK per 30min or free with drink purchase. Open daily 9am-9pm. Boat and bus tours from 2900ISK.) On the western side of the island, the cliff's edge at Há is a scenic spot. A popular, longer hike (2hr. round-trip) along Ofanleitishamar on the western coast passes two puffin colonies (nesting in mid-Aug.) and a black beach, **Klauf,** where brave swimmers tackle the 12°C (54°F) water in summer. **Surtsey,** the world's youngest island at 44 years old, is in the distance. After a steep climb, the best view awaits on the top of **Heimaklettur,** the island's highest point. Neighboring Eldfell can be scaled (1½hr.). Temperatures reach 180°C (356°F) in the caldera. Hidden in the northeast corner of the lava bed is **Gaujulundur,** a small garden and elf village, complete with a miniature windmill (hint: some disbelievers can't see the elves). This spot is quiet and remote. Some consider it sacred and have built a miniature fence to protect the elves. To get there, walk east along Strandvegur into the lava bed. Stay on the side

SURVIVING ICELAND

You might have the sixth sense—and no, not the one involving Bruce Willis and dead people. The Icelandic sixth sense allows you to see *huldufolk* (hidden people), magical creatures that 80% of Icelanders believe exist. Some *huldufolk* are friendly, upstanding citizens. Others are up to no damn good. To help you get through your trip to Iceland, Let's Go offers a brief survival guide:

Elves: Apparently, some look like humans, which makes picking them out a total crapshoot. **Strategy:** No cause for alarm. They're harmless and live in their Westman Islands (p. 530) village.

Faeries: A deceptive bunch. The beautiful faeries are known to lure you with soft, plaintive music. Then, BOOM—they'll carry you off. **Strategy:** Earplugs, or just run if you hear soft, plaintive music.

Gnomes: Small and subterranean. **Strategy:** Nothing to fear. Icelandic roads are often built around their settlements. They're that respected.

Trolls: Bad news if you run into one of these nocturnal beasts. Some live in Dimmuborgir, near Mývatn (p. 534). **Strategy:** Although they're ugly, trolls fuss over hygiene. Get them dirty, mess with their hair, etc. The power plant at Nesjavelliri (p. 530), for example, maintains a shower for the trolls to enjoy so they don't meddle with Reykjavík's water supply. An A+ tactic.

of the road to leave room for passing cars and continue until you hit a fork in the road. Take the left fork and walk until you see a sign for the garden. The three-day **People's Feast** (Þjóðhátíð) draws a young crowd of 10,000-12,000 to the island on the first Monday in August for bonfires, drinking, and related shenanigans. Reserve transportation ahead. A smaller set of festivities during the first weekend of July celebrates the end of the Eldfell eruption.

LANDMANNALAUGAR AND ÞÓRSMÖRK

Wedged between two of southern Iceland's glaciers, Landmannalaugar and Þorsmörk are gateways to the diverse landscapes of the country, from jagged lava fields and mammoth volcanic craters to desert and pristine forests. With this natural splendor, the area is a popular jumping-off point for **hikers.** The demanding four-day, 54km trek between the two regions poses a number of challenges, among them variable weather conditions (trails open mid-June to Aug.). More manageable hikes include a 2hr. loop through Landmannalaugar's multi-colored volcanoes and bubbling hot springs, and the walk from Þórsmörk's glacial valley to the peak of **Valahnjukur,** which overlooks rivers and ash fields. **Ferðafélag Íslands** (Iceland Touring Association) offers guided hikes and general info on camping (☎568 2533; www.fi.is). Footsore travelers can soak away their aches and pains in Landmannalaugar's soothing **thermal brook.** Landmannalaugar has a **campsite ❶** and **lodge ❷** run by Ferðafélag Íslands. (Reserve online at www.fi.is/en. Open July-Sept. Camping 800ISK; mountain huts 2800ISK.) In Þórsmörk, **Húsadalur Þórsmörk ❷** provides hiking tips and simple accommodations. (☎580 5400; www.thorsmork.is. Breakfast 950ISK. Showers 300ISK. Open mid-Apr. to mid-Oct. Camping 600ISK; sleeping-bag accommodations 2000ISK; 5-person cabin with kitchen 7500ISK.) **Buses** run from the BSÍ terminal in Reykjavík to Landmannalaugar (4½hr., mid-June to mid-Sept. 2 per day, round-trip 9600ISK) and Þorsmork (3½hr., June to mid-Sept. 2 per day, round-trip 7800ISK).

AKUREYRI

Although Akureyri (ah-KOO-rare-ee) has only 16,000 inhabitants, it's still Iceland's second-largest city. A college town known for trendy hangouts, Akureyri also serves as an outpost for exploring the region's breathtaking highlands.

■■ **TRANSPORTATION AND PRACTICAL INFORMATION. Flights** arrive from Reykjavík daily at **Akureyri Airport (AEY),** 3km south of the city along Drottningarbraut, the seaside road. Reserve ahead or fly standby—you may get rates cheaper than bus fares. See p. 519 for more info. **Buses** run from the Trex bus station, Hafnarstraeæti 77, to Reykjavík (6hr., 2 per day, 7300ISK). Most **car rental** agencies are at the airport: **Avis** (☎820 4010; www.avis.is); **Budget** (☎660 0629; www.budget.is); **Hertz** (☎461 1005; www.hertz.is). **National Car Rental**, Tryggvabraut 12, is in town (☎461 6000; www.nationalcar.is). Most have 24hr. service, but not necessarily onsite. For **taxis,** try **BSÓ,** Strandgata. (☎461 1010. Open M-F 7am-2am, Sa-Su 24hr.)

Mountains and the harbor border Akureyri to the west, while the **Eyjafjörður** fjord lines the east. Within the city, follow **Hafnarstræti** to its end to reach Akureyri's main square, **Ráðhústorg.** Most major services, including **banks,** can be found around Ráðhústorg. The **police** station is at Þorunnarstræti 138 (☎464 7700). The **hospital,** Eyrarlandsvegur (☎463 0100), on the south side of the botanical gardens, has a 24hr. emergency department. The **tourist office,** Hafnarstr. 82, books tours, accommodations, and car rentals for a 50ISK fee. (☎550 0720; www.nordurland.is. Internet 300ISK per hr. Open late June-Aug. M-F 7:30am-5:30pm, Sa-Su 8am-5pm; Sept.-May M-F 8:30am-5pm. MC/V.) For **Internet,** walk from Ráðhústorg up Brekkugata to the **library,** Brekkugata 17, on the corner of Oddeyrargata. (☎460 1250. Open M-F 10am-7pm, Sa noon-5pm. 200ISK per hr.)

⌐C ACCOMMODATIONS AND FOOD. Akureyri's only hostel, ▓**Stórholt ❶,** Stórholt 1, draws an adventurous crowd of Arctic travelers to its quiet, comfy common spaces. Ask about discounts at local eateries and tourist attractions. Book early for their cabin guesthouses. (☎462 3657; www.akureyrihostel.com. Linens 600ISK. Laundry 600ISK. Reception June-Aug. 8am-10pm; Sept.-May 9am-8pm. Dorms 1800ISK; singles 3300ISK; doubles 5400ISK. 400-600ISK HI discount.) ▓**Guesthouse Sulur ❸,** Þórunnarstræti 93, is in a hilltop home just behind the main square. The guesthouse caters to students and feels like home with its fully-equipped kitchen and TV in every room. (☎863 1400. Free laundry and Wi-Fi. Reception 24hr. Check-in 10pm. Singles 3600ISK; doubles 5000ISK; triples 8400ISK.) The **Central Campsite ❶,** on a hill in the city center, is next to a thermal pool and overlooks the fjord. (☎462 3379. Tent sites 800ISK.)

Travelers staying at Stórholt hostel enjoy a 10% discount at **Café Konditori ❶,** Langholt (☎460 5920), attached to the cheapest supermarket in Akureyri, **Bónus.** Konditori offers cheap pastries (150ISK), pizza (295ISK), and coffee to go (170ISK) in a cafeteria-like setting. (☎466 3500. Cafe and grocery store open M-Th noon-6:30pm, F 10am-7:30pm, Sa 10am-6pm, Su noon-6pm. MC/V.) **Brynja ❶,** Aðalstræti 3, has the definitive Icelandic treat: frozen yogurt smothered in chocolate or caramel. (☎462 4478. Cones from 190ISK. Open M-F 9am-11pm, Sa-Su 10am-11pm. MC/V.) For other cheap food options, try the pedestrian alleys off Ráðhústorg.

◐▓ SIGHTS AND NIGHTLIFE. For a glimpse of late 19th-century life in Akureyri, walk down Aðalstr. and take a look at numbers 14 and 50, the city's oldest houses. Down the street, **Nonnahús,** Aðalstr. 54., focuses on famous Icelandic author Jón Sveinsson, whose children's book *Nonni and Manni* has been translated into over 30 languages. (☎462 3555. Open June-Sept. daily 10am-5pm; call ahead in low season. 350ISK. MC/V.) Up a nearby hill, **Akureyri Museum,** Aðalstr. 58, is marked by a garden at the entrance. The first floor chronicles Icelandic history while the basement focuses on Akureyri. (☎462 4162. Open June-Sept. 15 daily 10am-5pm; Sept. 16-May Sa 2-4pm. 500ISK, groups 400ISK. 650ISK combination pass with Nonnahús.) Organ music emanates from **Akureyrarkirkja,** við Eyrarlandsveg, the town's main church. The building looks similar to Reykjavík's Hallgrímskirkja—they were designed by the same architect, Guðjón Samúelsson. Note the stained glass windows above the altar, which were salvaged from Britain's Coventry Cathedral after the Blitz. (☎462 7700. Open M-F until

ICELAND

10pm, Sa-Su until 8:30pm. Free.) Tropical and subtropical plants fight off the sub-Arctic climate at the northernmost **botanical gardens** in the world, at Hrafnagilsstr. and Eyrarlandsveg. (Open June-Sept. M-F 8am-10pm, Sa-Su 9am-10pm. Free.) Travelers can hike to **Mount Súlur** (1144m) along a trail that starts 4km out of town. More challenging hikes requiring gear for glaciers include **Strýta** (1456m) and **Kerling** (1536m). Visit the tourist office for map maps (200-300ISK). The **Summer Arts Festival** (late June-late Aug.) includes history walks and theater.

Many streets in Akureyri are deserted at night, but lines of cars slowly circle one building in the town square in a tradition known as **Rúnturinn.** Adults and other locals find it tiresome, but it's popular amongst high schoolers for passing time and exchanging furtive glances from one windshield to another. Inside the circled central building, a well-dressed crowd spends hours people-watching at ◨**Café Amour.** Beer starts at 600ISK (try the locally brewed Thule), but look for deals on five bottles (1500ISK) during occasional Happy hours. Amour becomes a techno dance hall on the 2nd floor during weekends. (☎461 3030; www.cafeamour.is. Mixed drinks from 1000ISK. Open Su-Th 10am-1am, F-Sa 10am-4am. MC/V.) **Kaffi Akureyri,** Strandgt. 7, is a no-frills bar, with a crowd ranging from 20- to 60-year-olds. Knock down Opal licorice shots with locals for 400ISK. (☎461 3999; kaffiakureyri.is. 20+. Open Su-Th 2pm-1am, F-Sa 2pm-4am. AmEx/MC/V.)

MÝVATN AND GOÐAFOSS

Mývatn (MEE-va-ten), like Þingvellir National Park to the south, is a colliding point for the European and North American tectonic plates, creating a volatile volcanic environment prone to eruption every 200 years. The current landscape was shaped by 18th-century eruptions and, more recently, a nine-year eruption to the north from 1975 to 1984. The underground magma chambers have forged a landscape unlike any other in the world. The focal point of the area is enormous and pristine **Lake Mývatn,** a shallow body of water less than 4m deep, scarred by many small craters and surround by canyons, volcanoes, hot springs, and cooled lava sculpture gardens. Due to its shallowness, the lake is an ideal breeding ground for flies. Of note is the vicious **myvargur fly,** whose name roughly translates to "tiny aggressive wolf." While this might be paradise for an entomologist, ordinary travelers will be slightly annoyed. Bring a mosquito mask to enjoy the scenery.

The freshwater **Mývatn Nature Baths** are a 4km hike from **Reynihlíð,** a small town on Lake Mývatn 90km east of Akureyri. Facing the lake, with the Verslun supermarket to your back, turn left, walk past the info office, and take your first right on Rte. 1. Walk for 20min. until you reach the glass bath building, where you can enjoy relaxing in the blue waters, steam, and cleansing minerals. (☎464 4411; www.naturebaths.com. Open daily June-Aug. 9am-midnight; Sept.-May noon-10pm. 1400ISK. Towel or swimsuit rental 350ISK. MC/V.) Aside from the baths, Mývatn is home to many nature trails and remarkable volcanic formations. Stop by the Reynihlíð **information office,** Hraunvegur 8, next to the supermarket, to pick up a map. (☎464 4390; infomyvatn@est.is. Open daily mid-June to Aug. 9am-7pm; Sept. to mid-June 9am-5pm. Maps 150ISK.) **Hverfjall,** a massive, 2000-year-old volcanic crater, is just 3½km north of the info office and is clearly visible from town. The caves at **Grotagja,** farther north along a circle hike, feature hot water baths too warm for swimming. Continuing 1hr. north on the hike brings you through **Leirhnjúkur,** the newest black lava bed in the area, sliced by a steaming fissure that reveals the tectonic plate divide. **Dimmuborgir,** south of Hverfjall, is a forest of fantastic natural lava formations, the most famous being **kirkja,** which resembles a Gothic church. *Dimmuborgir* is Icelandic for "dark castles"—the lava structures often look like citadels, supposedly inhabited by trolls and goblins. To get to the Lake Mývatn region, catch a **bus** from Akureyri to Reynihlíð (daily mid-June to mid-Aug. 8:30am, 2300ISK). SBA buses run from Húsavík (45min., late June-Aug. 2-3 per day, 1600ISK). According to legend, Þorgeir, a 10th-century Icelandic lawmaker, flung statues of pagan gods into a waterfall in AD 1000 to celebrate Iceland's conversion to Christianity. **Goðafoss** (Waterfall of the Gods), 12m high, is set against a stunning backdrop, making it an ideal rest stop on the road from Akureyri to Mývatn. The waterfall is 50km from both Akureyri and Húsavík off Rte. 1, and difficult to reach without a **car**. The **bus** from Akureyri to Reynihlíð makes a stop in the region—ask if they can wait while you take a look at the falls.

The cheapest lodgings in Reynihlíð are clustered around the Verslun supermarket. **Guesthouse Elda ❹**, Helluhrauni 15, is conveniently located behind the market in a cozy home along Rte. 1. (☎464 4220. Min. 2-night stay. Singles 6000ISK; doubles 8200ISK; triples 11,600ISK.) The campgrounds at **Blarg ❶**, in front of the tourist office at Rte. 1 and Rte. 8, have superb lake vistas. Fully-stocked kitchen tent and showers available. The **Blarg Guesthouse ❹** is also onsite. (☎464 4240; ferdabjarg@simnet.is. Campground open mid-June to Aug. Campsites 750ISK; singles 5800ISK; doubles 8200ISK; triples 10,500ISK. AmEx/D/MC/V.) Pick up groceries or a snack for the trail at **Verslun**, at the bus stop in Reynihlíð.

HÚSAVÍK

Europe's premier whale-watching destination, Húsavík (WHO-saah-veek; pop. 2500) has attractions ranging from the natural to the bizarre. Erected in 1974, **The Icelandic Phallological Museum,** Héðinsbraut 3A, is hard to miss with the giant phallus that greets passersby. The collection includes the penises of over 90 species, from the 2mm hamster specimen to the sperm whale's 70kg behemoth. Don't miss the folklore section, which displays a merman penis and two different types of ghost's penises—yes, they are visible. See if you can spot the elusive elf member. There's no Homo sapiens display, but purportedly, donors have lined up to endow the museum posthumously. (☎561 6663; www.phallus.is. Open daily mid-May to mid-Sept. noon-6pm. 500ISK.) Farther down Héðinsbraut, the **Húsavík Whale Museum,** next to the harbor, examines whales in a somewhat different way with complete skeletons of different cetacean species whose enormous length is incredible to behold. Visitors can stand inside the lower jaw bone of a humpback whale or learn about Keiko, the star of the film *Free Willy*, who was captured near Iceland in 1979 and died in 2003 after a failed reintroduction to the wild. The museum's volunteer program draws students from abroad interested in working with ecotourism. (☎464 2520; www.icewhale.is. Open daily June-Aug. 9am-9pm; May and Sept. 10am-5pm. 600ISK, students 500ISK. MC/V.) **Safnahúsið,** Stórigarður 17, features natural history, folk, and maritime museums along with the city archives and an art gallery. (☎464 1860. Open June-Aug. daily 10am-6pm. 400ISK; includes a cup of coffee. Tours available in over 8 languages.) For whale-watching, book a 3hr. tour with **Gentle Giants** or **North Sailing.** (Gentle Giants ☎464 1500; www.gentlegiants.is. 3800ISK. MC/V. North Sailing ☎464 2350; www.north-sailing.is. 3900ISK. MC/V. Both run tours May-Sept.; call for hours.)

Guesthouse options are available along Baldursbrekka, the second street on the right when heading north from the bus stop along the main harbor road. **Emhild K. Olsen ❷**, Baldursbrekka 17, caters to backpackers with large rooms in the basement of a family's home and spectacular views of the water. (☎464 1618. Breakfast 900ISK; included with private rooms. Free laundry. Sleeping-bag accommodations 2000ISK; singles 3000ISK; doubles 5000ISK. Cash only.) A **campground ❶**, 2min. further down Rte. 85, offers free indoor showers and a small kitchen. (☎898 0036 or 898 8305. Open June-Aug. Laundry 300ISK. Campsite 850ISK. Electricity 400ISK.) **Salka Restaurant ❷**, on the harbor, is famous for its shrimp and salmon dishes (850-2050ISK). Relax with a beer upstairs on leather couches and take in the harbor view. (☎464 2551. Entrees from 850ISK. Pizzas from 1600ISK. Kitchen open daily 11:30am-10pm. Bar open June-Aug. M-Th until 11pm, year-round F-Sa until 3am. MC/V.) During the day, **Heimabakarí konditorí ❶**, Garðarsbraut 15, serves Icelandic treats such as *kleina* (54ISK), a donut-like snack, and *skúffukaka*, a type of chocolate cake. (☎464 2901. Open M-F 8am-6pm, Sa 10am-2pm. MC/V.)

Trex (☎587 6000; www.trex.is) **buses** run to Akureyri (1hr., 4 per day, 2100ISK) from the Esso gas station at Héðinsbraut 2, on the main street north of the harbor. SBA (☎550 0700; www.sba.is) has bus tours of the area. Buses leave the Shell at Héðinsbraut 6 for Reynihlíð on Lake Mývatn (45min., late June-Aug. 2-3 per day, 1600ISK). The **tourist office,** Garðarsbraut 7, is next door to the Kasko supermarket. (☎464 4300; www.markthing.is. Open June-Aug. M-F 10am-6pm, Sa-Su 10am-5pm.) **Internet** is available at the tourist office or at the **Húsavík Public Library** in Safnahúsið, Stórigarður 17. (☎464 1173. Open June-Aug. M-Th 10am-6pm, F 10am-5pm; Sept.-May M-Th 10am-7pm, F 10am-5pm, Sa 11am-3pm. 5ISK per min.)

JÖKULSÁRGLJÚFUR NATIONAL PARK

The Jökulsa á Fjöllum River flows into Jökulsárgljúfur National Park from the Vatnajökull glacier to the south, creating astounding waterfalls throughout the region. Jökulsárgljúfur is a trek from any transport hub, but the park's magnificent **Dettifoss** waterfall rewards travelers who sit through the trip. Dettifoss is the most powerful waterfall in Europe, and lush fauna surrounds its horseshoe-shaped torrent. Walk 1.4km upstream, past river beaches covered with dark lava sand, to reach **Sellfoss,** a smaller but still impressive waterfall. Jökulsárgljúfur's third major waterfall, **Hafragilsfoss,** is 2km downstream from Dettifoss. The Hafragilsfoss parking area has a majestic view of both the waterfall and the canyon below. A **rental car** (p. 532), preferably four-wheel-drive, is often the cheapest and easiest way to reach Jökulsárgljúfur. **Buses** can bring you to the park, but often leave little time to see the sights, unless you camp overnight. The cheapest bus tours are run by SBA (☎550 0700; www.sba.is), partnered with Reykjavík Excursions, and leave at varying times from Akureyri and Húsavík. Check with the local tourist offices to book a trip. (Tours from mid-June to Aug. 6500-12,000ISK.)

IRELAND

REPUBLIC OF IRELAND

The green, rolling hills of Ireland, dotted with Celtic crosses, medieval monasteries, and Norman castles, have long inspired poets and musicians, from Yeats to U2. Today, the Emerald Isle's jagged coastal cliffs and untouched mountain ranges balance the country's thriving urban centers. Dublin pays tribute to the virtues of fine brews and the legacy of resisting British rule, while Galway offers a vibrant arts scene. In the past few decades, the computing and tourism industries have raised Ireland out of the economic doldrums, and current living standards are among the highest in Western Europe. Despite fears for the decline of traditional culture, the Irish language lives on in secluded areas known as the *gaeltacht*, and village pubs still echo with reels and jigs.

DISCOVER IRELAND: SUGGESTED ITINERARIES

THREE DAYS. Spend it all in **Dublin** (p. 542). Wander through **Trinity College**, admire the ancient **Book of Kells**, and sample the whiskey at the **Old Jameson Distillery.** Take a day to visit the **National Museums,** stopping to relax on **St. Stephen's Green**, and get smart at the **James Joyce Cultural Centre.** Work your pubbing potential by night in **Temple Bar** and on **Grafton Street.**

ONE WEEK. After visiting the sights and pubs of **Dublin** (3 days), enjoy the natural wonders of **Killarney** (1 day; p. 556) and the **Ring of Kerry** (1 day; p. 557). Return to the urban scene in the cultural center of **Galway** (2 days; p. 561).

BEST OF IRELAND, THREE WEEKS. Explore **Dublin** (4 days), then head to **Sligo** (3 days; p. 564) and visit the surrounding lakes and mountains. Continue on to **Galway** (3 days) and the **Aran Islands** (1 day; p. 562). After taking in the views from the **Cliffs of Moher** (1 day; p. 560), tour the scenic **Ring of Kerry** (2 days). Spend time in beautiful **Killarney** (2 days; p. 556) and the southernmost **Schull Peninsula** (1 day; p. 555) before hitting the big city of **Cork** (2 days; p. 553). On the way back to Dublin, stop by the beaches and crystal factory in Ireland's oldest city, **Waterford** (1 day, p. 551).

ESSENTIALS

FACTS AND FIGURES

Official Name: Republic of Ireland.
Capital: Dublin.
Major Cities: Cork, Galway, Limerick.
Population: 4,109,000.

Time Zone: GMT.
Languages: English, Irish.
Longest Place Name in Ireland: Muckanaghederdauhaulia, in Galway County.

WHEN TO GO

Ireland has a cool, wet climate, with average temperatures ranging from around 4°C (39°F) in winter to 16°C (61°F) in summer. Don't be discouraged by cloudy, foggy mornings—the weather usually clears by noon. The southeastern coast is the driest and sunniest, while western Ireland is considerably wetter. December and January have short, wet days, but temperatures rarely drop below freezing.

DOCUMENTS AND FORMALITIES

EMBASSIES AND CONSULATES. Foreign embassies in Ireland are in Dublin (p. 542). Irish embassies abroad include: **Australia,** 20 Arkana St., Yarralumla, Canberra, ACT 2600 (☎06 273 3022; irishemb@cyberone.com.au); **Canada,** Ste. 1105, 130 Albert St., Ottawa, ON K1P 5G4 (☎613-233-6281; www.irishembassyottawa.com); **New Zealand,** Level 7, Citigroup Building, 23 Customs Street E., Auckland (☎09 977 2252; www.ireland.co.nz); **UK,** 17 Grosvenor Pl., London SW1X 7HR (☎020 72 35 21 71; www.ireland.embassyhomepage.com); **US,** 2234 Massachusetts Ave., NW, Washington, D.C., 20008 (☎202-462-3939; www.irelandemb.org).

VISA AND ENTRY INFORMATION. EU citizens do not need a visa. Citizens of Australia, Canada, New Zealand, and the US do not need a visa for stays of up to 90 days, beginning upon entry into any of the countries in the EU's freedom-of-movement zone. For more info see p. 14. For stays longer than 90 days, non-EU citizens must register with the **Garda National Immigration Bureau,** 13-14 Burgh Quay, Dublin, 2 (☎01 666 9100; www.garda.ie/angarda/gnib.html).

TOURIST SERVICES AND MONEY

EMERGENCY	Ambulance, Fire, and Police: ☎999. Emergency: ☎112.

TOURIST OFFICES. Bord Fáilte (Irish Tourist Board; ☎1850 23 03 30; www.ireland.ie) operates a nationwide network of offices. Most tourist offices book rooms for a small fee and a 10% deposit.

MONEY. The **euro (€)** has replaced the **Irish pound (£)** as the unit of currency in the Republic of Ireland. For more info, see p. 16. Northern Ireland uses the **pound sterling (£).** For more info, see p. 112. As a general rule, it is cheaper to exchange money in Ireland than at home. If you stay in hostels and prepare your own food, expect to spend about €30 per person per day; a slightly more comfortable day (sleeping in B&Bs, eating one meal per day at a restaurant, going out at night) would cost €60. Most people working in restaurants do not expect a tip, unless the restaurant is targeted exclusively toward tourists. In that case, consider leaving 10-15%. In most cases, people are happy if you simply round up the bill to the nearest euro.

Ireland has a 21% **value added tax (VAT),** a sales tax applied to most goods and services, excluding food, health services, and children's clothing. The prices listed in *Let's Go* include VAT. In the airport upon exiting the EU, non-EU citizens can claim a refund on the tax paid for goods purchased at participating stores. While there is no minimum purchase amount to qualify for a refund, purchases greater than €250 must be approved at the customs desk before the refund can be issued. For more info on qualifying for a VAT refund, see p. 19.

TRANSPORTATION

BY PLANE. A popular carrier to Ireland is national airline **Aer Lingus** (☎081 836 5000, US 800-474-7424; www.aerlingus.com), with direct flights to London, Paris, and the US. **Ryanair** (☎081 830 3030; www.ryanair.com) offers low fares from Cork, Dublin, and Shannon to destinations across Europe.

Ireland

Giant's Causeway
North Channel
TO STRANRAER CAIRNRYAN, SCOTLAND (75km)
Inishowen Peninsula
Ballycastle
Glens of Antrim
Cushendall
L. Foyle
Letterkenny
Derry/Londonderry
Cushendun
Larne
Glencolmcille
Ballymena
Donegal Town
L. Neagh
NORTHERN IRELAND
Belfast
Donegal Bay
Portadown
Sligo
Monaghan
Bangor
TO LIVERPOOL, ENGLAND (300km)
Achill I.
Carrick-on-Shannon
Clare I. Clew Bay
Boyne Valley
Inishturk
Westport
Inishbofin
L. Mask
Roscommon
Mullingar
Dublin
Irish Sea
Inishshark
Connemara NP
Cong
Howth Peninsula
Clifden
L. Corrib
L. Ree
Athlone
Dun Laoghaire
Galway
REPUBLIC OF IRELAND
Kildare
TO HOLYHEAD, WALES (120km)
Kilronan Galway Bay Ballyvaghan
ARAN ISLANDS
Doolin
L. Derg
Wicklow
Cliffs of Moher
Lisdoonvarna
Carlow
Arklow
ATLANTIC OCEAN
Ennis
Limerick
Kilkenny
Shannon R.
Cashel
Dingle Peninsula
Clonmel
Wexford
Rosslare Harbour
Dunquin Dingle Town
Tralee
Waterford
St. George's Channel
Slea Head
Ventry
Killarney
Blarney
Youghal
Cahersiveen
Macroom
Cork
TO FISHGUARD, WALES (120km), PEMBROKE, WALES (80km), ROSCOFF, FRANCE (80km)
Iveragh Peninsula
Sneem
Kinsale
Bantry
Beara Peninsula
Mizen Head Peninsula
Schull
Cape Clear Island
0 30 miles
0 30 kilometers
N
LG

Side margin: IRELAND

BY FERRY. Ferries run between Britain and Ireland many times per day. Fares for adults generally range from €15 to 30, with additional fees for cars. **Irish Ferries** (Ireland ☎01 850 366 222, UK 8705 17 17 17, US 772-563-2856; www.irishferries.com) and **Stena Line** (☎01 204 7777; www.stenaline.com) typically offer discounts to students, seniors, families, and youth traveling alone. Ferries run from Dublin to Holyhead, BRI; from Cork to Roscoff, FRA; and from Rosslare Harbour to Pembroke, Wales, Cherbourg, FRA, and Roscoff, FRA.

BY TRAIN. Iarnród Éireann (Irish Rail; ☎01 850 366 222; www.irishrail.ie) is useful for travel to urban areas. The **Eurail Global pass** is accepted in the Republic but not in Northern Ireland. The **BritRail** pass does not cover travel in the Republic or in Northern Ireland, but the **BritRail+Ireland** pass (€345-550) offers five or 10 days of travel in a one-month period as well as ferry service between Britain and Ireland.

BY BUS. Bus Éireann (☎01 836 6111; www.buseireann.ie), Ireland's national bus company, operates Expressway buses that link larger cities as well as local buses that serve the countryside and smaller towns. One-way fares between cities generally range €5-25; student discounts are available. Bus Éireann offers the **Irish Rover** pass, which also covers the Ulsterbus service in Northern Ireland (3 of 8 consecutive days €73, under 16 €42; 8 of 15 days €165/90; 15 of 30 days €245/133). The **Emerald Card,** also available through Bus Éireann, offers unlimited travel on Expressway and other buses, Ulsterbus, Northern Ireland Railways, and local services (8 of 15 consecutive days €236, under 16 €118; 15 of 30 days €406/202).

Bus Éireann works in conjunction with ferry services and the bus company **Eurolines** (www.eurolines.com) to connect Ireland with Britain and the Continent. Eurolines passes for unlimited travel between major cities range €199-439. Discounts are available in the low season and for people under 26 or over 60. A major route runs between Dublin and Victoria Station in London; other stops include Birmingham, Bristol, Cardiff, Glasgow, and Liverpool, with services to Cork, Derry/Londonderry, Galway, Limerick, Tralee, and Waterford, among others.

BY CAR. Drivers in Ireland use the **left side** of the road. **Gasoline** (petrol) prices are high. Be particularly cautious at roundabouts—give way to traffic from the right. **Dan Dooley** (☎062 53103, UK 0800 282 189, US 800-331-9301; www.dandooley.com) and **Enterprise** (☎1 800 227 800, UK 0870 350 3000, US 800-261-7331; www.enterprise.com) will rent to drivers between 21 and 24, though such drivers must pay an additional daily surcharge. Fares are €85-200 per week (plus VAT), including insurance and unlimited mileage. If you plan to drive a car in Ireland for longer than 90 days, you must have an **International Driving Permit (IDP).** If you rent, lease, or borrow a car, you will need a **green card** or an **International Insurance Certificate** to certify that you have liability insurance that applies abroad. It is always significantly less expensive to reserve a car from the US than from within Europe.

BY BIKE, FOOT, AND THUMB. Ireland's countryside is well suited to **biking,** as many roads are not heavily traveled. Single-digit "N" roads are more trafficked and should be avoided. Ireland's mountains, fields, and hills make **walking** and **hiking** arduous joys. Some locals caution against **hitchhiking** in County Dublin and the Midlands, where it is not very common. Let's Go does not recommend hitchhiking.

KEEPING IN TOUCH

PHONE CODES	**Country code: 353. International dialing prefix:** 00. For more info on how to place international calls, see **Inside Back Cover.**

EMAIL AND THE INTERNET. Internet access is available in most cafes, hostels, and libraries. One hour of web time costs about €3-6, though discounts are often available with an ISIC. Find listings of Internet cafes at www.cybercafes.com.

TELEPHONE. Whenever possible, use a calling card for international phone calls, as long-distance rates for national phone services are often very high. Mobile phones are an increasingly popular and economical option, and carriers Vodafone and O_2 offer the best service. Direct-dial access numbers for calling out of Ireland include: **AT&T Direct** (☎800 550 000); **British Telecom** (☎800 550 144); **Canada Direct** (☎800 555 001); **MCI WorldPhone** (☎800 55 10 01); **Telecom New Zealand Direct** (☎800 55 00 64); **Telstra Australia** (☎800 55 00 61).

MAIL. Letters up to 50g cost €0.48 within Ireland and €0.75 to international destinations. Airmail parcels take five to nine days between Ireland and North America. Dublin is the only place in the Republic with Postal Codes (p. 545). To receive mail in Ireland, have mail delivered **Poste Restante.** Mail will go to the main post office unless you specify a subsidiary by street address. Address mail to be held according to the following example: First name LAST NAME, *Poste Restante*, City, Ireland. Bring a passport to pick up your mail; there may be a small fee.

ACCOMMODATIONS AND CAMPING

IRELAND	❶	❷	❸	❹	❺
ACCOMMODATIONS	under €17	€17-26	€27-40	€41-56	over €56

A **hostel** bed will average €13-20. **An Óige** (an OYJ), the **HI** affiliate, operates 24 hostels countrywide. (☎01 830 4555; www.irelandyha.org. One-year membership €20, under 18 €10.) Many An Óige hostels are in remote areas or small villages and are designed to serve nature-seekers. They therefore do not offer the same social environment typical of other European hostels. Over 100 hostels in Ireland belong to **Independent Holiday Hostels** (**IHH;** ☎01 836 4700; www.hostels-ireland.com). Most IHH hostels have no lockout or curfew, accept all ages, require no membership card, and have a less institutional feel than their An Óige counterparts; all are Bord Fáilte-approved. In virtually every Irish town, **B&Bs** can provide a quiet, luxurious break from hostelling. Expect to pay €30-35 for singles and €45-60 for doubles. "Full Irish breakfasts" are often filling enough to last until dinner. **Camping** in Irish State Forests and National Parks is not allowed. Camping on public land is permissible only if there is no official campsite nearby. Sites cost €5-13. For more info, see www.camping-ireland.ie.

FOOD AND DRINK

IRELAND	❶	❷	❸	❹	❺
FOOD	under €6	€6-10	€11-15	€16-20	over €20

Food in Ireland can be expensive, but the basics are simple and filling. Find quick and greasy staples at **chippers** (fish and chips shops) and **takeaways**. Most pubs serve Irish stew, burgers, soup, and sandwiches. Cafes and restaurants have begun to offer more vegetarian options to complement the typical meat-based entrees. **Soda bread** is delicious, and Irish **cheddars** are addictive. **Guinness,** a rich, dark stout, is revered with a zeal usually reserved for the Holy Trinity. Known as "the dark stuff" or "the blonde in the black skirt," a proper pint has a head so thick that you can stand a match in it. **Irish whiskey,** which Queen Elizabeth once said was her only true Irish friend, is sweeter than its Scotch counterpart. "A big one" (a pint of Guinness) and "a small one" (a glass of whiskey) are often ordered alongside one another. Ordering at an Irish **pub** is not to be done willy-nilly. In a small group, one individual will usually approach the bar and buy a round of drinks for everyone. Once those drinks are downed, another individual will buy the next round. It's considered poor form to refuse someone's offer to buy you a drink. The legal age in Ireland to purchase alcohol is 18.

HOLIDAYS AND FESTIVALS

Holidays: New Year's Day (Jan. 1); St. Patrick's Day (Mar. 17); Good Friday and Easter Monday (Mar. 21 and Mar. 24); and Christmas (Dec. 25). There are 4 bank holidays in the Republic and Northern Ireland, which will be observed on May 5, Jun. 2, Aug. 4, and Aug. 27 in 2008. Northern Ireland also observes Orangemen's Day (July 12).

Festivals: All of Ireland goes green for St. Patrick's Day (Mar. 17). On Bloomsday (June 16), Dublin celebrates James Joyce's *Ulysses*. In mid-July, the Galway Arts Festival

IRELAND

offers theater, trad, rock, and film. Tralee crowns a lucky young lady "Rose of Tralee" at a festival in late August, and many return happy from the Lisdoonvarna Matchmaking Festival in the Burren in early September.

BEYOND TOURISM

To find opportunities that accommodate your interests and schedule, check with national agencies such as **Volunteering Ireland** (www.volunteeringireland.com). For more info on opportunities across Europe, see **Beyond Tourism**, p. 56.

L'Arche Ireland, "Seolta," Warrenhouse Rd., Baldoyle, Dublin, 13 (☎01 839 4356; www.larche.ie). Assistants can join residential communities in Cork, Dublin, or Kilkenny to live with, work with, and teach people with learning disabilities. Room, board, and small stipend provided. Commitment of 1-2yr. expected.

Sustainable Land Use Company, Doorian, Glenties, Co. Donegal (☎074 955 1286; www.donegalorganic.ie). Offers opportunities to assist with organic farming, forestry, habitat maintenance, and wildlife in the northern county of Donegal.

Focus Ireland, 9-12 High St., Dublin, 8 (☎01 881 5900; www.focusireland.ie). Advocacy and fundraising for the homeless in Dublin, Limerick, and Waterford.

DUBLIN   ☎01

In a country known for its rural landscapes, the international flavor and frenetic pace of Dublin stick out like the 120m spire in the city's heart. Ireland's capital since the Middle Ages, Dublin offers all the amenities of other world-class cities on a more manageable scale, with all buildings topping off at five stories. The city's musical, cultural, and drinkable attractions continue to draw droves of visitors.

TRANSPORTATION

Flights: Dublin Airport (DUB; ☎814 1111; www.dublinairport.com). Dublin **buses** #41, 41B, and 41C run from the airport to Eden Quay in the city center (40-45min., 6 per hr., €1.80). **Airlink shuttle** (☎703 3139) runs nonstop to Busáras Central Bus Station and O'Connell St. (30-35min., 4 per hr., €6), and to Heuston Station (50min., €6). A **taxi** to the city center costs roughly €20-25.

Trains: The **Irish Rail Travel Centre,** 35 Lower Abbey St. (www.irishrail.ie), sells train tickets. Open M-F 9am-5pm. Info ☎836 6222 daily 8:30am-6pm.

Pearse Station, Pearse St. (☎286 000), is a departure point for **Dublin Area Rapid Transit (DART)** trains serving the suburbs and coast (4-6 per hr., €2-6.70).

Connolly Station, Amiens St. (☎703 2359), north of the Liffey and close to Busáras. Bus #20B heads south of the river, and the DART runs to Tara Station on the south quay. Trains to **Belfast** (2hr., 5-8 per day, €50) and **Sligo** (3hr., 3-4 per day, €34).

Heuston Station (☎703 3299), south of Victoria Quay and west of the city center (a 25min. walk from Trinity College). Buses #78 and 79 run to the city center. Trains to: **Cork** (3hr., 9 per day, €67); **Galway** (2¾hr., 8 per day, €67); **Limerick** (2½hr., 9 per day, €55); **Waterford** (2½hr., 4-5 per day, €30).

Buses: Intercity buses to Dublin arrive at **Busáras Central Bus Station,** Store St. (☎836 6111), next to Connolly Station. Buses to: **Belfast** (3hr., 6-7 per day, €20); **Derry/Londonderry** (4¼hr., 4-5 per day, €28); **Donegal** (4¼hr., 4-5 per day, €25); **Galway** (3½hr., 15 per day, €17); **Limerick** (3½hr., 13 per day, €21); **Rosslare** (3hr., 13 per day, €21); **Sligo** (4hr., 4-6 per day, €27); **Tralee** (6hr., 6 per day, €34). ISIC discount.

Ferries: Ferries depart for **Holyhead, BRI** at the **Dublin Port** (☎855 2296), and bus #53 runs from the port to Busáras station (1 per hr., €1.40). **Stena Line** ferries leave for Holyhead at the **Dún Laoghaire** ferry terminal (☎204 7777; www.stena-line.ie); from there DART trains run to the city center. Dublin Bus runs buses timed to fit the ferry schedules (€2.50).

IRELAND

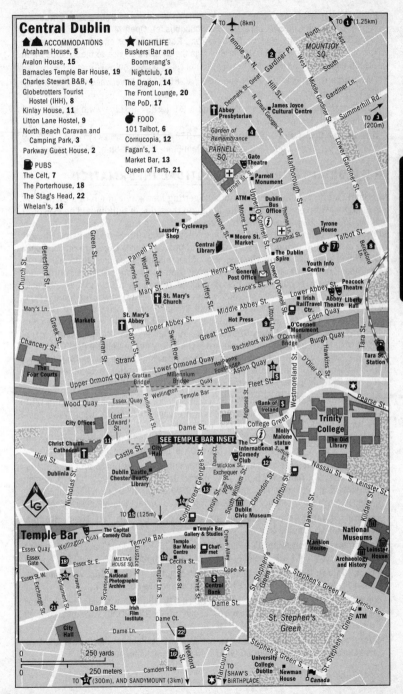

Central Dublin

ACCOMMODATIONS
Abraham House, **5**
Avalon House, **15**
Barnacles Temple Bar House, **19**
Charles Stewart B&B, **4**
Globetrotters Tourist
  Hostel (IHH), **8**
Kinlay House, **11**
Litton Lane Hostel, **9**
North Beach Caravan and
  Camping Park, **3**
Parkway Guest House, **2**

PUBS
The Celt, **7**
The Porterhouse, **18**
The Stag's Head, **22**
Whelan's, **16**

NIGHTLIFE
Buskers Bar and
  Boomerang's
  Nightclub, **10**
The Dragon, **14**
The Front Lounge, **20**
The PoD, **17**

FOOD
101 Talbot, **6**
Cornucopia, **12**
Fagan's, **1**
Market Bar, **13**
Queen of Tarts, **21**

Public Transportation: Info on local bus service available at **Dublin Bus Office,** 59 Upper O'Connell St. (☎873 4222; www.dublinbus.ie). Open M 8:30am-5:30pm, Tu-F 9am-5:30pm, Sa 9am-2pm, Su 9:30am-2pm. **Rambler** passes offer unlimited rides for a day (€6) or a week (€21). Dublin Bus runs the **NiteLink** service to the suburbs (M-Th 12:30 and 2am, F-Sa 3 per hr. 12:30-4:30am; €4-6; passes not valid).

Taxis: Blue Cabs (☎802 2222) and **ABC** (☎285 5444) have wheelchair-accessible cabs (call ahead). Available 24hr.

Car Rental: Budget, 151 Lower Drumcondra Rd. (☎837 9611; www.budget.ie), and at the airport. From €40 per day. 23+.

Bike Rental: Cycleways, 185-6 Parnell St. (☎873 4748; www.cycleways.com). €20 per day, €80 per week. Open M-W and F-Sa 10am-6pm, Th 10am-8pm, Su 11am-5pm.

◤◢ 7 ORIENTATION AND PRACTICAL INFORMATION

Although Dublin is refreshingly compact, getting lost is not much of a challenge. Street signs, when posted, are located high on the sides of buildings. The essential *Dublin Visitor Map* is available for free at the Dublin Bus Office and at the tourist office. The **Liffey River** divides Dublin's North and South Sides. Heuston Station and the more famous sights, posh stores, and upscale restaurants are on the **South Side,** while Connolly Station, the majority of hostels, and the bus station are on the **North Side.** The North Side is less expensive than the more touristed South Side, but it also has the reputation of being rougher, especially after dark. The streets running alongside the Liffey are called **quays** (pronounced "keys"); the name of the quay changes with every bridge. **O'Connell Street,** three blocks west of Busáras Central Bus Station, is the primary link between northern and southern Dublin. On the North Side, **Henry** and **Mary Streets** make up a pedestrian shopping zone, intersecting with O'Connell St. two blocks from the Liffey at the **General Post Office.** On the South Side, one block from the river, **Fleet Street** becomes **Temple Bar,** an area full of music centers and galleries. **Dame Street** runs parallel to Temple Bar and leads east to **Trinity College,** the nerve center of Dublin's cultural activity.

Tourist Office: Main Office, Suffolk St. (☎605 7700, international 0800 039 7000; www.visitdublin.com). Near Trinity College in a converted church. Open M-Sa 9am-5:30pm, Su 10:30am-3pm. July-Aug. open until 7pm. Reservation desks for buses and tour bookings close 30min. earlier. **Northern Ireland Tourist Board,** 16 Nassau St. (☎679 1977 or 1850 230 230). Open M-F 9:15am-5:30pm, Sa 10am-5pm.

Embassies: Australia, Fitzwilton House, Wilton Terr., 7th fl. (☎664 5300; www.australianembassy.ie); **Canada,** 65-68 St. Stephen's Green (☎417 4100); **UK,** 29 Merrion Rd. (☎205 3700; www.britishembassy.ie); **US,** 42 Elgin Rd. (☎668 8777; http://dublin.usembassy.gov). Citizens of **New Zealand** should contact their embassy in London.

Luggage Storage: Connolly Station. Lockers €4-6. Open daily 7am-10pm. **Busáras.** Lockers €6-10. Open 24hr.

Laundromat: Laundry Shop, 191 Parnell St. (☎872 3541). Full service €10; self-service €8.80. Detergent €1.10. Open M-F 9am-7pm, Sa 9am-6pm.

Police (Garda): Dublin Metro Headquarters, Harcourt St. (☎666 6666; www.garda.ie); Store St. Station (☎666 8000); Fitzgibbon St. Station (☎666 8400).

Hospitals: St. James's Hospital, James's St. (☎410 3000; www.stjames.ie). Take bus #123. **Mater Misericordiae Hospital,** Eccles St. (☎803 2000; www.mater.ie), off Lower Dorset St. Buses #3, 10, 11, 16, 22, and 121.

Internet Access: Free 50min. sessions and Wi-Fi are available to members at the **Central Library,** Henry and Moore St. (☎873 4333). Membership free with ID.

Post Office: General Post Office, O'Connell St. (☎705 7000). Open M-Sa 8am-8pm. Smaller post offices (Rathmines Post Office, 4 Upper Rathmines Rd.; Dun Laoghaire, Upper Georges St.) open M-Tu and Th-F 9am-6pm, W 9:30am-6pm. **Postal Codes:** The city is organized into regions numbered 1-18, 20, 22, and 24, with odd-numbered codes for areas north of the Liffey and even-numbered ones to the south. The numbers radiate out from the center of the city: North City Centre is 1, South City Centre 2. Dublin is the only city in the Republic with Postal Codes.

ACCOMMODATIONS

Some of Dublin's hostels tend toward the institutional. For travelers who plan to stay out late in Temple Bar, picking a hostel close by will make the stumble home much easier. B&Bs with a green shamrock sign out front are registered and approved by Bord Fáilte. On the North Side, B&Bs cluster along Upper and Lower Gardiner St., on Sheriff St., and near Parnell Sq.

■ **Avalon House (IHH),** 55 Aungier St. (☎475 0001; www.avalon-house.ie). Turn off Dame St. onto S. Great Georges St. and walk 5min. An entertainment mecca with air hockey, foosball, ping-pong, and video games. Breakfast included. Lockers €1 per day. Laundry €5. Free Internet and Wi-Fi. Check-in 2pm. Check-out 10am. Dorms €14-27; singles €30-39; doubles €66-74. 10% discount for 1st night's stay with ISIC. AmEx/MC/V. ❶

■ **Globetrotters Tourist Hostel (IHH),** 46-7 Lower Gardiner St. (☎873 5893). Right near Busáras station and perfect for late-night arrivals. Finely decorated common areas and exceptionally clean rooms. Breakfast included. Towels €1, €5 deposit. Free Internet, luggage storage, and parking. Reserve at least 1 month ahead in summer. Dorms €20-23; singles €60-66; doubles €104-110; triples €114-126; quads €127. ❸

Kinlay House (IHH), 2-12 Lord Edward St. (☎679 6644). Great location a few blocks from Temple Bar. Well-run hostel with views of Christ Church Cathedral. Breakfast included. Lockers €1, deposit €5. Laundry €8. Free Internet. 16- to 24-bed dorms €17-20; 4- to 6-bed €24-29; singles €44-56; doubles €29-33; triples €27-33. ❷

Parkway Guest House, 5 Gardiner Pl. (☎874 0469; www.parkway-guesthouse.com), 5min. walk from O'Connell St. B&B run by a cheery hurling veteran who offers advice on the city's restaurants and pubs. Singles €40; doubles €60-70, with bath €65-80. ❸

Charles Stewart B&B, 5-6 Parnell Sq. E (☎878 0350; www.charlesstewart.ie). Dark wood furniture and large windows create an air of old-fashioned elegance. TV room with leather armchairs. Luggage storage. Check-in 2:30pm. Check-out 10:30am. Singles €57-63; doubles €75-99; triples €120-130. Discounts for online booking. ❺

Abraham House, 82-3 Lower Gardiner St. (☎855 0600). Take a left off Lower Abbey St. Staff is dependable for service, advice, and a laugh. Large dorms with bath. Comfortable private bedrooms sleep up to 4 and have TVs. Light breakfast included. Free luggage storage. Security box €1 per day, €5 deposit. Free Wi-Fi. 20- and 10-bed dorms €10-29; 8- and 6-bed €18-25; 4-bed €23-33; private rooms €80. ❷

Barnacles Temple Bar House, 19 Temple Ln. (☎671 6277; www.barnacles.ie). Unbeatable location near Temple Bar. Very clean. Kitchen and TV lounge. Continental breakfast included. Luggage storage available. Internet €1 per 15min. Reception 24hr. Check-out 10:30am. Dorms €16-26; doubles €68-82. MC/V. ❷

Litton Lane Hostel, 2-4 Litton Ln. (☎872 8389; www.littonlane.hostel.com), off Bachelor's Walk. Former studio for the likes of U2, Van Morrison, and Sinéad O'Connor. Free luggage storage. Free Wi-Fi. Key deposit €1. Dorms €20-22; doubles €80. ❷

North Beach Caravan and Camping Park (☎843 7131; www.northbeach.ie), in Rush. Accessible by bus #33 from Eden Quay (45min., 25 per day), and by suburban rail. Open Apr.-Sept. €9 per person, €5 per child. Electricity €3. Showers €2. ❶

IRELAND

◘ FOOD

Fresh, cheap fixings are available at Dublin's many **open-air markets,** including the cozy market held on Sundays in Market Sq. in the heart of Temple Bar. On the North Side, Henry St., off O'Connell St., hosts a large market with fruit and flowers (M-Sa 7:30am-6pm). The **Epicurean Food Hall**, accessible from Lower Liffey St. and Middle Abbey St., offers fare from nearly every corner of the globe. (Most shops open M-W 9am-8pm, Th 9am-9pm, F-Su 9am-7pm.)

▧ **Queen of Tarts,** Dame St. (☎670 7499), across from Dublin Castle. This little shop offers scrumptious homemade pastries, cakes, soups, and sandwiches. Go early for the apple crumble before it sells out. Breakfast €4-8. Flaky chocolate and raspberry scones with fresh cream €3. Open M-F 7:30am-6pm, Sa 9am-6pm, Su 9:30am-6pm. ❷

▧ **Market Bar,** Fade St. (613 9094; www.tapas.ie). Right off South Great Georges after Lower Stephen St. Old sausage factory now serves tasty tapas. Classy, high-ceilinged house usually packed to gills for fish pie. Small tapas €7.50. Large tapas €11. Food served M-W noon-9:30pm, Th noon-10pm, F-Sa noon-10:30pm, Su 3pm-9:30pm. ❸

Cornucopia, 19 Wicklow St. (☎677 7583). If there's space, sit down in this cozy, popular spot for a delicious and filling meal (€11-12) or a cheaper but equally tasty salad smorgasbord (€3-8 for choice of 2, 4, or 6 salads). Open M-W and F-Sa 8:30am-8pm, Th 8:30am-9pm, Su noon-7pm. ❷

101 Talbot, 101 Talbot St. (☎874 5011), between Marlborough and Gardiner St. Excellent Italian-Mediterranean food aimed at theater-goers. Large windows look onto busy Talbot St. below. Menu changes often but always has vegetarian specialties. Reserve ahead. Early bird 5-8pm €21. Entrees €14-20. Open Tu-Sa 5-11pm. ❹

Fagan's, Lower Drumcondra R. (836 9491), just before Botanic Ave. Attractive indoor and outdoor seating meets gorgeous food to produce beautiful evening in friendly pub. Worth the trek from the city or a must-stop for anyone staying in the north. Carvery €11. Entrees €10-15. Food served daily 12:30-3pm and 4-9pm. ❸

◧ SIGHTS

Most of Dublin's sights lie less than 2km from **O'Connell Bridge.** The two-hour **Historical Walking Tour,** led by Trinity College graduates, stops at many of them. Meet at the College's main gate. (Info 17 St. Mary's Pl., ☎087 688 9412; www.historicalinsights.ie. Tours May-Sept. daily 11am and 3pm; Apr. and Oct. daily 11am; Nov.-Mar. F-Su 11am. €12, students €10.) You can hop on and off **City Tour** buses that stop at major sights with guides that sing along the way (24hr. pass €14).

TRINITY COLLEGE AND GRAFTON STREET. The British built **Trinity College** in 1592 as a Protestant seminary that would "civilize the Irish and cure them of Popery." The Catholic Church still deemed it a cardinal sin to attend Trinity until the 1960s, so until then it served as an Oxbridge safety school. Today, Trinity is one of Ireland's most prestigious universities and a not-to-be-missed stop on a tour of Dublin. *(Between Westmoreland and Grafton St., on the South Side. The main entrance fronts the roundabout now called College Green. ☎608 1724; www.tcd.ie. Grounds always open. Free.)* Trinity's **Old Library** holds a collection of ancient manuscripts including the renowned **Book of Kells.** Upstairs, the **Long Room** contains Ireland's oldest harp—the **Brian Ború Harp,** pictured on Irish coins—and one of the few remaining copies of the original **1916 Proclamation** of the Republic of Ireland. *(On the south side of Library Sq. ☎608 2320; www.tcd.ie/library. Open May-Sept. M-Sa 9:30am-5pm, Su 9:30am-4:30pm; Oct.-Apr. M-Sa 9:30am-5pm, Su noon-4:30pm. €8, students €7.)* The blocks south of College Green are off-limits to cars, making the area a pedestrian playground. Performers on Grafton St. keep crowds entertained, while stores happily collect their money.

KILDARE STREET. Just southeast of Trinity College, the museums on Kildare St. offer scientific and artistic wonders. The ⬛**Natural History Museum** displays fascinating examples of taxidermy, including enormous Irish deer skeletons. Though the museum closed in 2007 for lengthy renovations, it is sure to regain its beloved status when it finally reopens in 2009. The **National Gallery's** extensive collection includes canvases by Brueghel, Caravaggio, Goya, Rembrandt, and Vermeer. *(Merrion Sq. W. Open M-W and F-Sa 9:30am-5:30pm, Th 9:30am-8:30pm, Su noon-5:30pm. Free.)* **Leinster House,** the former home of the Duke of Leinster, today provides chambers for the **Irish Parliament.** The **National Museum of Archaeology and History,** Dublin's largest museum, has artifacts spanning the last two millennia, including the **Tara Brooch** and the bloody vest of nationalist **James Connolly.** *(Kildare St., next to Leinster House. ☎677 7444. Open Tu-Sa 10am-5pm, Su 2-5pm. Free.)*

TEMPLE BAR. West of Trinity College, between Dame St. and the Liffey, the cobblestone streets and central square of Temple Bar contain cafes, hotels, and some of Dublin's best pubs and clubs. The government-sponsored Temple Bar Properties spent over €40 million to build a fleet of arts-related attractions. **The Irish Film Institute** screens specialty and art-house films. *(6 Eustace St. ☎679 5744; www.irishfilm.ie. Open M-F 10am-6pm.)* Ireland's **National Photographic Archive** includes extensive historical collections and holds special exhibitions. *(Meeting House Sq. ☎603 0374; www.nli.ie. Open M-F 10am-5pm and Sa 10am-2pm.)* The **Temple Bar Music Centre** hosts shows by local and international performers. *(Curved St. ☎670 9202; www.tbmc.ie.)*

DAME STREET AND THE CATHEDRALS. King John built **Dublin Castle** in 1204, and for the next 700 years it would be the seat of British rule in Ireland. Since 1938, each president of Ireland has been inaugurated here. *(Dame St., at the intersection of Parliament and Castle St. Open M-F 10am-4:45pm, Sa-Su 2-4:45pm. €4.50, students €3.50. Grounds free.)* At the **Chester Beatty Library,** behind Dublin Castle, visitors can see the treasures bequeathed to Ireland by American mining magnate Alfred Chester Beatty. *(☎407 0750; www.cbl.ie. Open May-Sept. M-F 10am-5pm, Sa 11am-5pm, Su 1-5pm; Oct.-Apr. closed M. Free.)* Across from the castle sits the historic **Christ Church Cathedral.** Sitric Silkenbeard, King of the Dublin Norsemen, built a wooden church on the site around 1038; Strongbow rebuilt it in stone in 1169. Fragments of the ancient pillars are now scattered about like bleached bones. *(At the end of Dame St. Take bus #50 from Eden Quay or 78A from Aston Quay. ☎677 8099. Open daily 9:45am-5pm, except during services. €5, students €2.50.)* Deriving its name from an ancient Latin term for Dublin, ⬛**Dublinia** is an engaging three-story interactive exhibit recounting the city's history. Try on ancient armor, smell spices, and see rune stones. *(Across from Christ Church Cathedral. ☎679 4611; www.dublinia.ie. Open Apr.-Sept. daily 10am-5pm; Oct.-Mar. M-F 11am-4pm, Sa-Su 10am-4pm. Last entry 45min. before closing. €6.30, students €5.30.)* **St. Patrick's Cathedral,** Ireland's largest, dates to the 12th century, although Sir Benjamin Guinness remodeled much of it in 1864. Jonathan Swift spent his last years as Dean of St. Patrick's; his grave is marked on the floor of the south nave. *(Patrick St. ☎475 4817; www.stpatrickscathedral.ie. Open Mar.-Oct. daily 9am-6pm; Nov.-Feb. Sa 9am-5pm, Su 10am-3pm. €5, students €4.)*

GUINNESS BREWERY AND KILMAINHAM. Guinness brews its black magic at the St. James's Gate Brewery, right next door to the ⬛**Guinness Storehouse.** Walk through the quirky seven-story atrium containing Arthur Guinness's 9000-year lease on the original brewery. Then drink, thirsty traveler, drink. *(St. James's Gate. From Christ Church Cathedral, follow High St. west through its name changes: Cornmarket, Thomas, and St. James. Or, take bus #51B or 78A from Aston Quay or #123 from O'Connell St. Open daily July-Aug. 9:30am-8pm; Sept.-June 9am-5pm. €14, students over 18 €9.50.)* Almost all the rebels who fought in Ireland's struggle for independence from 1792 to 1921 spent time at **Kilmainham Gaol,** located 600m west of the Guinness Storehouse.

Guided tours of the jail wind through the eerie limestone corridors. *(Inchicore Rd. Take bus #51B, 51C, 78A, or 79 from Aston Quay. ☎453 5984. Tours 2 per hr. Open Apr.-Sept. daily 9:30am-5pm; Oct.-Mar. M-F 9:30am-4pm, Su 10am-5pm. €5.30, students €2.10.)*

O'CONNELL STREET AND PARNELL SQUARE. Once Europe's widest street, O'Connell St. on the North Side now holds the less prestigious distinction of being Dublin's biggest shopping thoroughfare. Statues of Irish leaders **Daniel O'Connell, Charles Parnell,** and **James Larkin** adorn the traffic islands. The city's rich literary heritage comes to life at the **Dublin Writers' Museum,** which displays rare editions, manuscripts, and memorabilia of Beckett, Joyce, Wilde, Yeats, and other famous Irish writers. *(18 Parnell Sq. N. ☎872 1302; www.writersmuseum.com. Open June-Aug. M-F 10am-6pm, Sa 10am-5pm, Su 11am-5pm; Sept.-May M-Sa 10am-5pm, Su 11am-5pm. €7, students €6.)* The **James Joyce Cultural Centre** features a wide range of Joyceana. Call for info on lectures, Bloomsday events, and walking tours. *(35 N. Great Georges St. ☎878 8547; www.jamesjoyce.ie. Open July-Aug. M-Sa 9:30am-5pm, Su 11am-5pm; Sept.-June M-Sa 9:30am-5pm, Su 12:30am-5pm. €5, students €4.)*

OTHER SIGHTS. Once a private estate, **St. Stephen's Green** was later bequeathed to the city by the Guinness clan. The 27-acre park on the South Side, at the end of Grafton St., hosts musical and theatrical productions in the summer. *(Open M-Sa 8am-dusk, Su 10am-dusk.)* The dry air in the nave of ⊠**St. Michan's Church** has preserved the corpses in the vaults; it was these seemingly living bodies that inspired Bram Stoker to write about the living dead in *Dracula.* The church, near Four Courts on Church St., boasts Dublin's earliest altar plates and an incredible organ from 1723. *(☎872 4154. Open Mar. 18-Oct. M-F 10am-12:45pm and 2-4:30pm, Sa 10am-12:45pm; Nov.-Mar. 16 M-F 12:30-3:30pm, Sa 10am-12:45pm. Church of Ireland services Su 10am. Crypt tours €3.50, students €3.)* At the **Old Jameson Distillery,** learn how science, grain, and tradition come together to create world-famous Irish whiskey. Everyone gets a free glass of the "water of life" at the end of the 30min. tour. *(Bow St. From O'Connell Bridge, at the foot of O'Connell St., walk down the quays to Four Courts and take a right on Church St. Follow the signs to the Distillery, which is down a cobblestone street on the left. Buses #68, 69, and 79 run from the city center to Merchant's Quay. ☎807 2355; www.jamesonwhiskey.com. Tours daily 1-2 per hr. 9:30am-5:30pm. €9.80, students €8.)*

🎵 ENTERTAINMENT

Whether you fancy poetry, punk, punchlines, or pubs, Dublin will entertain you. There's no true theater district, but smaller theater companies thrive off Dame St. and Temple Bar. Call ahead for tickets. Showtime is generally around 8pm. There's nothing funny about how fast Dublin's comedy scene is growing. Popular festivals, such as **Bulmers International Comedy Festival** (www.bulmerscomedy.ie), are making their way onto the calendar. The free *Event Guide*, available at the tourist office and Temple Bar restaurants, offers comprehensive entertainment listings.

⊠**Abbey Theatre,** 23-26 Lower Abbey St. (☎878 7222). Ireland's national theater was founded in 1904 by Yeats and Lady Gregory to promote Irish culture and modernist theater. Box office open M-Sa 10:30am-7pm. Tickets €15-30; Sa 2:30pm matinee €18, students and seniors with ID €14.

Peacock Theatre, 26 Lower Abbey St. (☎878 7222). The Abbey's experimental studio theater downstairs offers evening shows in addition to occasional lunchtime plays, concerts, and poetry. Tickets €20; Sa 2:30pm matinee €12.

The Capital Comedy Club, Wellington Quay (☎677 0616; www.capitalcomedyclub.com.), upstairs from Ha' Penny Bridge Inn. Intimate and engaging setting sure to give you an ab workout. The MC, an up-and-coming stand-up, keeps the laughter rolling between big and small comedians. Cover €7; students €5. Doors open W and Su 9pm; show starts 9:30pm.

The International Comedy Club, 23 Wicklow St. (☎677 9250; www.theinternational-comedyclub.com). Popular club packs punchlines. Improv M. Cover €10; students €8. Doors open Th-Sa 8:45pm; show starts 9:15pm.

📧 NIGHTLIFE

Begin your after-hours journey through Dublin's pubs and clubs at the gates of Trinity College, stumble onto Grafton St., teeter down Camden St., stagger onto South Great Georges St., and finally, crawl triumphantly into the Temple Bar area. Just don't expect to do any early sightseeing the next morning.

PUBLIN

James Joyce once proposed that a "good puzzle would be to cross Dublin without passing a pub." Decades later, pubs still dominate Dublin's scene, and they quickly fill up at the end of every day of the week. Pubs normally close at 11:30pm Sunday through Wednesday and 12:30am Thursday through Saturday, but an increasing number of establishments are staying open later.

■ **The Stag's Head,** 1 Dame Ct. (☎679 3701), in Temple Bar. Victorian pub with stained-glass windows, marble-topped tables, and a gigantic moose head suspended above the bar. Additional bars upstairs and downstairs for busy nights. Excellent pub grub. Pints €4.10. Entrees €5-11. Live music W-Sa 9:30pm-midnight. Open M-Th 10:30am-11:30pm, F-Sa 10:30am-12:30am, Su 11:30am-11pm. Kitchen open M-Sa until 4pm.

■ **The Porterhouse,** 16-18 Parliament St. (☎679 8847), in Temple Bar. A change in scenery and color; switch it up from the usual black stuff to this microbrewery's own popular Porterhouse Red. Live music every night. Pints €3.90. Open M-W 11:30am-11:30pm, Th-F 11:30am-2am, Sa 11:30am-2:30am, Su 11:30am-11pm. Pub grub until 9:30pm.

The Celt, 81-82 Talbot St. (☎878 8665), north of Trinity College. Tiny but mighty. Hosts some of the most energetic trad bands around and has cheaper pints than its southern counterparts. Pints €3.90. Trad M-Sa 9pm-close, Su 5-7pm and 9-11pm. Open M-Th 10:30am-11:30pm, F-Sa 10:30am-12:30am, Su 12:30-11pm.

Whelan's, 25 Wexford St. (☎478 0766), south of Temple Bar near St. Stephen's Green. Dark, busy pub with all-wood interior hosts big-name acts. The crowd depends on the music. Carvery lunch (starter, entree, dessert, and tea; €10) and entrees (€6-12) served noon-2pm. Live music nightly from 8:30pm; doors open 8pm. Cover €8-21. Open Su-W 10am-1:30am, Th-Sa 10:30am-2:30am.

CLUBLIN

Clubs generally open at 10:30 or 11pm, but things don't heat up until around midnight, after pubs start closing. Clubbing is an expensive way to end the night, as covers run €7-20 and mixed drinks cost €7-10. The gay nightclub scene is clustered in the "pink triangle" zone of Parliament and S. Great Georges St. Keep up to date by checking out *In Dublin* for gay-friendly pubs, restaurants, and clubs.

■ **The PoD,** 35 Harcourt St. (☎478 0225; www.pod.ie), corner of Hatch St., in an old train station. A stylishly futuristic orange interior in a club that's serious about its music. Upstairs is **The Red Box** (☎478 0225), a huge, separate club with a warehouse atmosphere, brain-crushing music, and a crowd at the bar so deep it seems designed to winnow out the weak. The more mellow **Crawdaddy** hosts musical gigs, including some international stars. Cover €10-20; Th students €5. Open until 3am on weekends.

■ **Buskers Bar and Boomerang's Nightclub,** Fleet St. (☎612 9246), in Temple Bar. 3 bars, modern decor, and sizzling music attract a student crowd. Pints €4.70. 21+. Cover W-Th €5, F €10, Sa €15. Bar open M-Sa 11:30am-2am, Su noon-1am. Downstairs nightclub open W-Sa 9pm-2:30am.

The Dragon, 64-65 S. Great Georges St. (☎478 1590), south of Temple Bar, a few doors down from The George. Largest gay club in Dublin packs a happening crowd on weekends. Huge bar, lounge, dance floor, and high blue-lit ceilings with fuzzy lamps. Pints from €4.70. 18+. Open M and Th-Sa 5pm-2:30am, Tu-W 5-11:30pm, Su 5-11pm.

The Front Lounge, 33-34 Parliament St. (☎670 4112). The red velvet seats of this gay-friendly bar are filled nightly by a young, trendy, and mixed crowd. Pints €4.40. Mixed drinks €8.50. Open M-Th noon-midnight, F-Sa 3pm-3am, Su 3pm-midnight.

▶ DAYTRIP FROM DUBLIN

MALAHIDE. An impressive cultural complex, housing several museums, **Malahide Castle** is more than just an 800-year-old blend of architectural styles surrounded by hectares of perfectly manicured parklands. The castle is full of 14th- through 19th-century furnishings and portraits. A live peacock welcomes those who discover the castle's best secret: the ▨**Museum of Childhood,** a veritable Antiques Roadshow of 18th-century dollhouses and toys. This charity trust can't afford to advertise, so few are aware of the world's oldest known dollhouse, finished in 1700. Beyond the main drag of clothing and craft boutiques, you'll find Malahide beach. Closer to neighboring Portmarnock (2km) is the even more luxurious 2mi. stretch of beach known as the **Velvet Strand.** (*DART serves Malahide station; 20min., 2 per hr, roundtrip €3.40. From the DART station, turn right on Main St. and over the bridge, 15min., to get to the castle entrance gate. Castle ☎846 2184; www.malahidecastle.com. Open Jan.-Dec. M-Sa 10am-12:45pm and 2-5pm, Apr.-Sept. Su and bank holidays 10am-12:45pm and 2-6pm, Oct.-Mar. Su and bank holidays 11am-12:45pm and 2-5pm. Admission only by 35min. tour. €7, students €6. Museum open M-Sa 10am-1pm and 2-5pm, Su 2-6pm. €2. Gardens open May-Sept. 2-5pm. €4.*)

SOUTHEASTERN IRELAND

Ireland's southeastern region is famous for its strawberries and oysters. Round towers, built by monks to defend against Viking attacks, litter the countryside from the medieval city of Kilkenny to the Rock of Cashel. The grassy fields and stunning mountain views provide a brilliant contrast to the trad and rock pumping through the pubs of Waterford, Kilkenny, and Wexford.

▣ TRANSPORTATION

Rosslare Harbour is a useful departure point for ferries to Wales or France. **Stena Line** (☎01 204 7777; www.stenaline.ie) and **Irish Ferries** (☎01 850 366 222; www.irishferries.com) bring passengers from Rosslare Harbour to Pembroke, BRI (3¾hr., 2 per day, €29) and to Roscoff and Cherbourg, FRA (18-19½hr., 1 per 2 days, €69-78). From Rosslare Harbour, **trains** run to Dublin and Limerick via Waterford, while **buses** go to: Dublin (3hr., 14 per day, €16); Galway via Waterford (6hr., 4 per day, €26); Limerick (4hr., 3-5 per day, €21); Tralee (2-4 per day, €26).

THE WICKLOW MOUNTAINS ☎0404

Over 600m tall, carpeted in fragrant heather and pleated by sparkling rivers, the Wicklow summits provide a tranquil stop just outside Dublin. The **Wicklow Way,** a 125km hiking trail, winds past grazing sheep, scattered villages, and monastic ruins. The **National Park Information Office,** between the two lakes, is the best source for hiking advice. (☎45425. Open May-Aug. daily 10am-1pm and 2-6pm; Sept.-Apr. Sa-Su 10am-dusk.) When the office is closed, call the **ranger office** (☎45800) in nearby Trooperstown Wood. The valley of **Glendalough** is home to St.

Kevin's sixth-century monastery. A particularly good hike in the area is the **Spinc and Glenealo Valley path** (3hr.), marked by white arrows. The trail ascends to a glorious lookout over Upper Lake, circles the valley where goats and deer wander, and passes old mining ruins before looping back. At the secluded **🏠Glendalough International Hostel (HI) ❷,** 5min. up the road from the Glendalough Visitor Centre, guests won't hear rambunctious travelers, just chirping birds. (☎45342; www.anoige.ie. Breakfast €4-6.50; packed lunches €5.50; request the night before. Laundry €5. Single-sex dorms June-Oct. €23; Nov.-May €18. €2 HI discount. MC/V.) Just 1.5km up the road, tiny **Laragh** has food options and plenty of B&Bs. **St. Kevin's Bus Service** (☎01 281 8119; www.glendaloughbus.com) arrives at the Glendalough Visitor's Centre from the end of Dawson St. nearest to St. Stephen's Green in Dublin. (Buses run M-Sa 2 per day, €18.) Public transportation in the mountains is extremely limited; buses or taxis are your best bet. **Glendalough Cabs** (☎087 972 9452; www.glendaloughcabs.com) offers 24hr. service.

KILKENNY   ☎05677

Eight churches share the streets with 80 pubs in Kilkenny (pop. 30,000), Ireland's best-preserved medieval town. The 13th-century **Kilkenny Castle** housed the Earls of Ormonde until 1932. (☎21450. Open daily June-Aug. 9:30am-7pm; Sept. 10am-6:30pm; Oct.-Mar. 10:30am-12:45pm and 2-5pm; Apr.-May 10:30am-5pm. Required tour €5.30, students €2.10.) Don't miss the chance to grab a free pint at **Smithwicks Brewery,** Parliament St. (☎21014. Tours July-Aug. M-F 3pm. Pick up a free ticket in the morning at the security station on the right past the Watergate Theatre.) Climb the steep steps of the 30m tower of **St. Canice's Cathedral,** up the hill off Dean St., for a panoramic view. (☎64971. Open June-Aug. M-Sa 9am-6pm, Su 2-6pm; Apr.-May and Sept. M-Sa 10am-1pm and 2-5pm, Su 2-5pm; Oct.-Mar. M-Sa 10am-1pm and 2-4pm, Su 2-4pm. €4, students €3. Tower €3/2.50.) Conveniently located near the pubs on High St., the **Kilkenny Tourist Hostel ❶,** 35 Parliament St., offers clean, spacious rooms. (☎63541. Free Wi-Fi. Check-in 9am-11pm. Check-out 10am. Dorms €17; doubles €42; quads €76. Cash only.) **The Two Dames ❶,** 80 John St., serves stuffed baked potatoes (€5.50) that are as good as they smell. (Open M-F 8:30am-5pm, Sa 10am-4:30pm. Cash only.) Make a meal of free samples at the **SuperQuinn** grocery store in the Market Cross shopping center off High St. (☎52444. Open M-Tu 8am-8pm, W-F 8am-9pm, Sa 8am-7pm, Su 10am-7pm.) Start your pub crawl at the end of **Parliament Street,** then work your way to the wilder bars on **John Street,** which stay open later. **Trains** (☎22024) leave from Dublin Rd. for Dublin (2hr., €22-28) and Waterford (45min., €10-13). **Buses** (☎64933) depart from the same station for: Cork (3hr., 5 per day, €17); Dublin (2hr., 6 per day, €11); Galway (5hr., 5 per day, €21); Limerick (2½hr., 4 per day, €17); Rosslare Harbour (2hr., 2 per day, €17); Waterford (1½hr., 2 per day, €9). The **tourist office** is on Rose Inn St. (☎51500; www.southeastireland.com. Open May-Sept. M-F 9am-6:30pm, Sa 10am-6pm, Su 11am-5pm; Oct.-Apr. M-F 9:30am-5:30pm, Sa 10am-6pm.)

WATERFORD   ☎051

Waterford is Ireland's oldest city, founded in AD 914 by the grandson of Viking Ivor the Boneless. The small city, situated on a river, attracts travelers looking to shop, club, and relax on beaches. The city's real highlight, however, is the fully operational **🏠Waterford Crystal Factory,** 3km away on N25. Tours allow you to watch experienced cutters transform grains of sand into molten glass and finally into sparkling crystal. To get there, catch the City bus outside Dunnes on Michael St. (10-15min., M-Sa 3-4 per hr., €1.40) and request to stop at the factory. (☎332 500; www.waterfordvisitorcentre.com. Open daily Mar.-Oct. 8:30am-6pm; Nov.-Feb. 9am-5pm. Free. 1hr. tours 3-4 per hr. in high season. €9, students €6.) **Water-**

ford Treasures at the granary has Viking artifacts. (☎304 500; www.waterfordtreasures.com. Open Apr.-Sept. M-Sa 9:30am-6pm, Su 11am-6pm; Oct.-Mar. M-Sa 10am-5pm, Su 11am-6pm. €7, students €5.) Stellar tour guide Jack Burtchaell keeps audiences entertained on his ◪**Walking Tour of Historic Waterford.** (☎873 711. 1hr. tours depart from Waterford Treasures Mar.-Oct. daily 11:45am and 1:45pm. €7.)

For clean, quiet accommodations, head to **Mayor's Walk B&B ❸.** From the bus station, walk down the quay to the clock tower and turn right. Head up the main street and turn right at the traffic lights. Mayor's Walk is the second road on the left up the hill. (☎855 427; www.mayorswalk.com. Shared bathrooms. Singles €28; doubles €50. Cash only.) **Cafe Sumatra ❷,** 53 John St., is a good option for lunch or dinner. (☎876 404. Sandwiches €7-8. Entrees €10-11. Open M-Th 8:30am-7pm, F-Sa 8:30am-11pm, Su 11am-9pm. MC/V.) **T&H Doolan's,** 31-32 George's St., has been serving drinks for 300 years. (☎841 504. Trad nightly 9:30pm. Open M-Th 10:30am-11:30pm, F-Sa 10:30am-12:30am, Su 12:30-11pm. MC/V.) A younger crowd flocks to the "Golden Mile" of bars at the intersection of **John, Manor,** and **Parnell Streets.** Try **Geoff's,** 8 John St. (☎874 787) or **Ruby Lounge** (☎858 130) on the corner.

Trains (☎873 401; www.irishrail.ie) leave from the quay across the bridge for: Dublin (2½hr., M-F 8 per day, €24); Kilkenny (50min., 3-5 per day, €10); Limerick (2½hr., 5 per day, €30). **Buses** depart for: Cork (2½hr.); Dublin (2¾hr.); Galway (5¾hr.); Limerick (2½hr.). The **tourist office** is across from the bus station. (☎875 823; www.southeastireland.com. Open in summer M-Sa 9am-6pm, Su 10am-6pm.)

CASHEL ☎062

Cashel sits at the foot of the 90m ◪**Rock of Cashel** (also called **St. Patrick's Rock** or **Cashel of the Kings**), a limestone outcropping topped by medieval buildings. (☎61437. Open daily mid-June to mid-Sept. 9am-7pm; mid-Mar. to mid-June and mid-Sept. to mid-Oct. 9am-5:30pm; mid.-Oct. to mid-Mar. 9am-4:30pm. Tours 1 per hr. €5.30, students €2.10.) Head down the cow path from the Rock to see the ruins of **Hore Abbey,** built by Cistercian monks and relatively free of tourist hordes. (Open 24hr. Free.). The internationally acclaimed **Brú Ború Heritage Centre,** at the base of the Rock, stages traditional music and dance performances. (☎61122; www.comhaltas.com. Mid-June to mid-Sept. Tu-Sa 9pm. €18, students €10.) The **Bolton Library,** on John St., houses rare manuscripts and what's reputed to be the world's smallest book. (☎61944. Open M-Th 10am-2:30pm.) Enjoy a view of the Rock from the homey rooms and campsite at ◪**O'Brien's Holiday Lodge ❷,** a 10min. walk out of town on Dundrum Rd. From the tourist office, walk down Main St. and turn right at the end. (☎61003; www.cashel-lodge.com. Laundry €12. Camping €9 per person. Dorms €18; doubles €65. MC/V.) **Spearman's ❶,** near the Friary St. end of Main St., has *panini* (€3.50-6) made from freshly baked bread. (☎61143. Open M-F 9am-5:45pm, Sa 9am-5pm. MC/V.) **Buses** (☎061 313 333) leave from Main St. near the tourist office for Cork (1½hr., 6 per day, €11) and Dublin (3hr., 6 per day, €10). Buy tickets in the SPAR grocery store. The **tourist office** is in City Hall on Main St. (☎62511; www.casheltouristoffice.com. Open daily 9:30am-5:30pm.)

SOUTHWESTERN IRELAND

The dramatic landscape of Southwestern Ireland ranges from lakes and mountains to stark, ocean-battered cliffs. Rebels once hid among the coves and glens, but the region is now dominated by tourists taking in the stunning scenery of the Ring of Kerry and Cork's southern coast.

CORK   ☎ 021

Cork (pop. 150,000) hosts most of the cultural activities in the southwest. The county gained the nickname "Rebel Cork" from its residents' early opposition to the British Crown and 20th-century support for Irish independence. Today, Cork's river quays and pub-lined streets reveal architecture both grand and grimy, evidence of the city's legacy of resistance and reconstruction.

⌐ TRANSPORTATION

Trains: Kent Station, Lower Glanmire Rd. (☎450 6766; www.irishrail.ie), across the North Channel from the city center. Open M-Sa 6am-8pm, Su 8am-8:50pm. To: **Dublin** (3hr., 10-15 per day, €55) via **Limerick** (1½hr., 9 per day, €23); **Killarney** (2hr., 6-9 per day, €23); **Tralee** (2½hr., 6-9 per day, €30).

Buses: Parnell Pl. (☎450 8188), on Merchant's Quay. Info desk open daily 9am-5:30pm. **Bus Éireann** to: **Dublin** (4½hr., M-Su 6 per day, €10); **Galway** (4hr., 12 per day, €15); **Killarney** (2hr., 11-14 per day, €14); **Limerick** (2hr., 14 per day, €11); **Rosslare Harbour** (4hr., 2-3 per day, €19); **Sligo** (7hr., 3 per day, €23); **Tralee** (2½hr., 11-14 per day, €16); **Waterford** (2¼hr., 2-3 per day, €15).

Ferries: Brittany Ferries, 42 Grand Parade, sails from Cork to Roscoff, FRA. (☎021 427 7801. 12hr., Sa only, from €108.)

Public Transportation: Downtown **buses** run 2-6 per hr. M-Sa 7:30am-11:15pm, with reduced service Su 10am-11:15pm. Fares from €1.30. Catch buses and pick up schedules along St. Patrick's St., across from the Father Matthew statue.

✦ ⁊ ORIENTATION AND PRACTICAL INFORMATION

The center of Cork is compact and pedestrian-friendly, framed by the North and South Channels of the River Lee. From the bus station along the North Channel, **Merchant's Quay** leads west to **St. Patrick's Street,** which curves through the center of the city and becomes **Grand Parade.** On the other side of the North Channel, across St. Patrick's Bridge, **MacCurtain Street** runs east to **Lower Glanmire Road** and passes the train station before becoming the N8 to Dublin. Downtown shopping and nightlife concentrates on **Washington, Oliver Plunkett,** and St. Patrick's Streets.

Tourist Office: Tourist House, Grand Parade (☎425 5100; www.corkkerry.ie), near the corner of South Mall, books accommodations (€4) and provides a free city guide and map. Open June and Aug.-Sept. M-F 9am-6pm, Sa 9am-5pm; July M-F 9am-6pm, Sa 9am-5pm, Su 10am-5pm; Sept.-May M-Sa 9:15am-5pm.

Police (Garda): Anglesea St. (☎452 2000).

Pharmacies: Regional Late-Night Pharmacy, Wilton Rd. (☎434 4575), opposite the hospital. Bus #8. Open M-F 9am-10pm, Sa-Su 10am-10pm. **Late Night,** 9 St. Patrick's St. (☎427 2511). Open M-F 8:30am-10pm, Sa 9am-10pm, Su 10am-10pm.

Hospital: Cork University Hospital, Wilton Rd. (☎454 6400). Bus #8.

Internet Access: ▓ **Wired To The World Internet Cafe,** 6 Thompson House, MacCurtain St., north of River Lee (www.wiredtotheworld.ie). Gaming, phone booths, and Wi-Fi. Internet €1 per hr. Open daily 8am-midnight.

Post Office: Oliver Plunkett St. (☎485 1032). Open M-Sa 9am-5:30pm.

⌂ ACCOMMODATIONS

Cork's fine array of busy hostels should put a smile on any budget traveler's face, but rooms go fast, so call ahead. For a full Irish breakfast and a little more privacy, head to one of the many B&Bs on **Western Road,** near the University.

▨ **Sheila's Budget Accommodation Centre (IHH),** 4 Belgrave Pl. (☎450 5562; www.sheilashostel.ie). Breakfast €3. Laundry €6.50. Free Wi-Fi. Reception 24hr. Check-out 10:30am. Dorms €15-20; doubles €44-52. MC/V. ❷

Brú Bar and Hostel, 57 MacCurtain St. (☎455 9667; www.bruhostel.com), north of the river. A lively place to stay up late and hang out at the attached bar (open 4pm-4am). Continental breakfast included. Towels €2. Laundry €5. Free Internet. Check-in 1pm. Check-out 10:30am. 6-bed dorms €17; 4-bed dorms €21-23; doubles €50. MC/V. ❷

Roman House, 3 St. John's Terr. (☎450 3606; www.romanhouse.info), across from Kinlay House. Colorful Roman House markets itself as a welcoming place for GLBT travelers. Full Irish breakfast included. Singles from €55; doubles from €75. ❹

Cork International Hostel (An Óige/HI), 1-2 Redclyffe, Western Rd. (☎454 3289), near University College and a 20min. walk from Grand Parade. Offers clean, spacious rooms, all with bath. Continental breakfast €4; Irish breakfast €6.50. Luggage storage available. Internet €1 per 15min. Reception 8am-midnight. Check-in 1pm. Check-out 10:30am. Dorms €17-19; doubles €42. €2 HI discount. ❶

◳ FOOD

Inside the Shopping Centre on Paul St., **Tesco** is the biggest grocery store in town. (☎427 0791. Open M-Sa 8am-10pm, Su 10am-8pm.)

▨ **Eastern Tandoori,** 1-2 Emmett Pl., across from Opera House (☎427 2232). Delicious, authentic Indian fare served in a spacious, elegant dining room overlooking the water. 3-course early-bird special M-Th 5pm-7pm, F-Sa 5pm-6pm, Su 5pm-6:30pm, €15. Entrees €12-19. Open daily 5pm-11:30pm. AmEx/MC/V. ❹

Tribes, 8 Tuckey St. (☎427 4446), off Oliver Plunkett St. Late-night, low-light java shop serves sandwiches, full meals and tea into the wee hours. Food served until 30min. before closing. Open Tu-Th 10:30am-midnight, F-Sa 10:30am-4am, Su 12pm-11pm. ❶

Amicus, St. Paul St., (☎427 6455), across from Tesco. Artistically presented dishes taste as good as they look. Lunch €8-12. Dinner €12-25. Open M-Sa 8am-10:30pm, Su 11:30am-10pm. MC/V. ❸

◉ SIGHTS

Cork's sights are concentrated in the old town, the Shandon neighborhood to the north, and the university to the west; you can reach all sights by foot. In the old city, looming over Proby's Quay, **St. Finbarr's Cathedral** is a testament to the Victorian obsession with the neo-Gothic. The cathedral houses art exhibits in the summer. *(Bishop St. ☎963 387. Open M-F 10am-12:45pm and 2-5pm. €3, students €1.50.)* In Shandon, the steeple of **St. Anne's Church** houses the **Bells of Shandon,** which you can ring before climbing to the top. Its four clock faces are notoriously out of sync, earning the church its nickname, "the four-faced liar." *(Walk up John Redmond St. and take a right at the Craft Centre; St. Anne's is on the right. ☎450 5906. Open M-Sa 10am-5:30pm. €6, students €5.)* In Western Cork, ▨**University College Cork's** campus, built in 1845, has brooding Gothic buildings, manicured lawns, and sculpture-studded grounds. *(Main gate on Western Rd. ☎490 3000; www.ucc.ie.)* ▨**Fitzgerald Park** has rose gardens, a pond, and art exhibits courtesy of the **Cork Public Museum.** *(From the front gate of UCC, follow the signs across the street. ☎427 0679. Open M-F 11am-1pm and 2:15-5pm, Su 3-5pm. Free.)* Don't miss the **Cork City Gaol** across the river from the park. Furnished cells, sound effects, and videos illustrate the experience of inmates at the 19th-century prison. *(☎430 5022; www.corkcitygaol.com. Open daily Mar.-Oct. 9:30am-6pm; Nov.-Feb. 10am-5pm. €6, students €5. 1hr. audio tour.)*

▐ NIGHTLIFE

Try **Oliver Plunkett Street, Washington Street,** and **South Main Street** for pubs and clubs. Check out the *WhazOn? Cork* pamphlet, free at local shops, or the Thursday "Downtown" section in the *Evening Echo* newspaper. ▐**The Old Oak,** 113 Oliver Plunkett St., is great for the 20- and 30-something crowd. (☎427 6165. Pints €4. Open M-Sa noon-1:45am, Su noon-1am.) **An Spailpín Fánac** (on spal-PEEN FAW-nuhk), 28 South Main St., is one of Cork's oldest (est. 1779) and favorite pubs. (☎427 7949. Live trad every night. Storytelling last Tu of every month.)

▐ DAYTRIP FROM CORK

BLARNEY. Those impressed by the Irish way of speaking should head to **Blarney Castle** and its legendary Blarney Stone. The legend goes that the Earl of Blarney cooed and cajoled his way out of giving up his abode to Queen Elizabeth I, and his smooth-talking skills were imparted to the stone, which when kissed passes on the "gift of Irish gab." After stealing a smooch, enjoy the views from the top and take a walk around the dreamlike **rock close** garden, and see what kind of phrases your newfound ability can come up with. *(Buses run from Cork to Blarney. 10-16 per day, round-trip €4.80. Open May-Aug. M-Sa 9am-7pm, Su 9:30am-5:30pm; Sept. M-Sa 9am-6:30pm, Su 9:30am-sunset; Oct.-Apr. M-Sa 9am-6pm, Su 9:30am-5:30pm. Last entry 30min. before closing. Castle and grounds €8, students €6.)*

SCHULL AND THE MIZEN HEAD PENINSULA ☎028

The seaside hamlet of Schull (SKULL) is an ideal base for exploring Ireland's southwestern tip. Although the town has only 700 residents in winter, its population increases to over 3000 in summer, offering numerous activites for warm weather. Sail with the ▐**Fastnet Marine Outdoor Education Centre,** or stargaze at the **Planetarium,** on Colla Rd. (Fastnet ☎28515; www.schullsailing.ie. Reserve ahead. 5-day sailing course €275. Planetarium ☎28552. 45min. shows June M, Th 8pm; July-Aug. M, Th 8pm, W, Sa 4pm.) The coastal road winds past **Barley Coast Beach** and continues on to **Mizen Head.** The Mizen becomes more scenic and less populated to the west of Schull, but it's mobbed in summer. **Betty Johnson's Bus Hire** offers 3hr. tours of the area. (☎28410, mobile 086 265 6078. Call ahead. €10 per person.) The quaint **Galley Cove House ❹**, a few kilometers before town on the Goleen Rd., is perfect for extended stays on the village's sandy shores. (☎35137; www.galleycovehouse.com. All rooms with bath and TV. Singles €45-55; doubles €76-90 per person.) Many chippers claim to be Ireland's best, but **The Fish Shop ❷**, on the pier, may be right. (☎28599. Fish and chips €8. Wine €2. Open daily in summer noon-10pm.) For a pint-sized pub crawl, head to Main St. for **Hackett's Bar** (☎28625), **Bunratty Inn** (☎28341), and **The Black Sheep** (☎28022). **Back in Schull** (☎28278) runs **ferries** to Cape Clear Island (June-Sept. 2-3 per day, round-trip €13). **Buses** (☎021 450 8188; www.buseireann.ie) arrive in Schull from Cork (2-3 per day, €15) and Goleen (1-2 per day, €3.80). There is no other public transportation on the peninsula, though confident bicyclists can daytrip to Mizen Head (29km from Schull).

IRELAND

CAPE CLEAR ISLAND (OILEÁN CHLÉIRE) ☎028

The beautiful island of Cape Clear is worth a daytrip from Schull or Baltimore. Its staggering cliffs make for steep walks, but once conquered, the heights reveal the land and sea's stunning scenery. The island provides asylum for gulls, petrels, and their attendant flocks of ornithologists at the **Cape Clear Bird Observatory** (☎39181) on North Harbour. The **Cape Clear Heritage Centre** has everything from a family tree of the ubiquitous O'Driscolls to a well-preserved chair from the *Lusitania*. (Open June-Aug. M-Sa noon-5pm, Su 2-5pm. €4, students €2.) On the road to the Heritage Centre, **Cléire Goats** (☎39126) sells popular goat's milk ice cream (€2.50). **Cape Clear Island Youth Hostel (HI)** ❶ has simple but clean rooms. It's a 10min. walk from the pier; turn right onto the main road past the pottery shop and stay to the left. (☎41968; www.anoige.fenlon.net. Internet €2 per 15min. Dorms €15.) To reach **Cuas an Uisce Campsite** ❶, follow the directions to the hostel but bear right before Ciarán Danny Mike's; it's 400m up on the left. (☎39119. Open June-Sept. Tent sites €7 per person.) **Ciarán Danny Mike's Pub** ❸ has the distinction of being Ireland's southernmost pub and serves food all day. (☎39153. Open noon-10pm.) Groceries and Wi-Fi are available at pier-side **An Siopa Beag.** (☎39099. Open June-Aug. daily 10am-8pm; Sept.-May M-Sa 11am-4pm.) **Ferries** go to Schull (☎28138; 45min., 3-4 per day, round-trip €14) and Baltimore (☎086 346 5110; www.islandtripper.com. 45min., 3-5 per day; €8, round-trip €14.) There is an **information office** in the pottery shop at the end of the pier. (☎39100. Open June-Sept. daily 11am-1pm and 3-6pm.)

KILLARNEY AND KILLARNEY NATIONAL PARK ☎064

Killarney is just minutes from some of Ireland's most beautiful scenery. Outside of town, mountains rise from the three **Lakes of Killarney** in the 95 sq. km national park. The ◪**Muckross House,** 5km south of Killarney on Kenmare Rd., is a 19th-century manor. A path leads to the 20m **Torc Waterfall,** the starting point for several short trails along beautiful **Torc Mountain.** To get to the 14th-century **Ross Castle,** the last stronghold in Munster to fall to Cromwell's army, take a right on Ross Rd. off Muckross Rd. when leaving town. The castle is 3km from Killarney. (☎35851. Open daily June-Aug. 9am-6:30pm; May and Sept. 10am-6pm; mid-Mar. to Apr. and Oct. 10am-5pm. €5.30, students €2.10.) The nicest outdoor activity in the area is the biking around the **Gap of Dunloe,** which borders **Macgillycuddy's Reeks,** Ireland's highest mountain range. From **Lord Brandon's Cottage,** on the Gap trail, head left over the stone bridge, continue 3km to the church, and then turn right onto a winding road. Climb 2km and enjoy an 11km stroll downhill with gorgeous views. The 13km trip back to Killarney passes the ruins of **Dunloe Castle.** Bear right after Kate Kearney's Cottage, turn left on the road to Fossa, and turn right on Killorglin Rd.

◪**Neptune's Hostel (IHH)** ❶, on Bishop's Ln. off New St., has a central location and clean dorms. (☎35255; www.neptuneshostel.com. Breakfast €2.50. Free bike storage. Free Internet and Wi-Fi. Check-in 1-3pm. Dorms €13-16; doubles €37-42. MC/V.) The renovated **Fairview Guest House** ❸, College St., near the bus station, pampers guests with sparkling suites and whirlpool tubs. (☎34164; www.fairviewkillarney.com. €53-105 per person; €35-54 for *Let's Go* readers.) For delectable dishes, try **The Stonechat** ❸, 8 Fleming's Ln. (☎34295. Lunch €7-10. Dinner €13-20. Early-bird special 6-7:30pm, 4 courses for €22. Open M 6:30-10pm and Tu-Sa 12:30-3pm and 6:30-10pm.) A young, trendy crowd gets down in the loungelike ◪**McSorley's,** on College St., which starts the night with the usual trad, but switches it up first with rock and again with a late-night DJ. (☎39770. Pints €4. Cover F €7, Sa €10. Open M-Sa noon-2:30am, Su noon-1:30am. Nightclub upstairs open 11:30pm-2:30am.) **Scott's Bar,** also on College St., keeps it simple with trad. (☎31060. Pub food served daily noon-9pm.)

Trains (☎31067) leave from Killarney station, off E. Avenue Rd., for Cork (2hr., 7 per day, €20), Dublin (3½hr., 7 per day, €59), and Limerick (3hr., 7 per day, €22). Book ahead online for the best rates. **Buses** (☎30011) leave from Park Rd. for: Belfast, BRI (4 per day, €33); Cork (2hr., 10 per day, €15); Dublin (6hr., 6 per day, €22). **O'Sullivan's,** on Lower New St., rents **bikes.** (☎31282. Open daily 8:30am-6:30pm. €12 per day, €70 per week.) The **tourist office** is on Beech Rd. (☎31633; www.corkkerry.ie. Open July-Aug. M-Sa 9am-8pm, Su 10am-5:45pm; June and Sept. M-Sa 9am-6pm, Su 10am-5:45pm; Oct.-May M-Sa 9:15am-5pm.)

RING OF KERRY

The Southwest's most celebrated peninsula offers picturesque villages, ancient forts, and rugged mountains. You'll have to brave congested roads hogged by tour buses, but rewards await those who take the time to explore on foot or by bike.

▞ TRANSPORTATION

The term "Ring of Kerry" usually describes the entire **Iveragh Peninsula,** though it technically refers to the ring of roads circumnavigating it. Hop on the circuit run by **Bus Éireann** (☎064 30011), based in Killarney (mid-June to Aug., 1 per day, departs 1:15pm, returns 5:30pm; entire ring in 1 day €21). Stops include Cahersiveen (2½hr. from Killarney, €12) and Caherdaniel (1hr. from Cahersiveen, €7.50). Or, book a bus tour with a private company; offices are scattered across town, and many accommodations will book a tour for you.

CAHERSIVEEN   ☎066

Although best known as the birthplace of patriot Daniel O'Connell, Cahersiveen (CAH-her-sah-veen) also serves as a useful base for jaunts to Valentia Island, the Skelligs, and local archaeological sites. To see the ruins of **Ballycarbery Castle,** head past the barracks on Bridge St., turn left over the bridge, then left off the main road. Enjoy views of the countryside and castle from the second-floor balcony at **Sive Hostel (IHH) ❶,** 15 East End, Church St. (☎947 2717. Laundry €8. Dorms €15; doubles €44. Camping €7 per person.) **O'Shea's B&B ❸,** next to the post office on Main St., has comfortable rooms and impressive views. (☎947 2402. Singles €35-40; doubles €66-70.) The pubs on **Main Street** still retain the authentic feel of their former proprietors' main businesses, including a general store, a smithy, and a leather shop. **The Harp** nightclub caters to local youth on weekend nights. (☎947 2436. 18+. Cover €7-9. Open F-Sa midnight-3am.) The Ring of Kerry **bus** stops in front of Banks Store on Main St. (mid-June to Aug., 2 per day) and continues on to Killarney (2½hr., €12) and Caherdaniel (1hr., €7.50). The **tourist office** is across from the bus stop. (☎947 2589. Open June to mid-Sept. M, W, F 9:15am-1pm and 2-5:15pm, Tu and Th 9:15am-1pm.)

SNEEM   ☎064

Sneem is usually a quick stop for tour buses on the Ring of Kerry, but this tiny spot is worth more than a 20min. visit; in years past, it has won awards for being Ireland's tidiest and prettiest town. Its unique **Sculpture Park** provides just a taste of the town's charm. The two sides are connected by a stone bridge. The cheerful **Bank House B&B ❸,** in North Sq., has delicious breakfast options. (☎45226; the_bank_house@yahoo.ie. Singles €45; doubles €64-70.) **The Village Kitchen ❷,** in the center of town, serves fresh seafood and sandwiches made on homemade brown bread. (☎45281. Entrees €8-10. Open daily 9:30am-8:30pm.)

DINGLE PENINSULA

For decades, the Ring of Kerry's undertouristed counterpart, the Dingle Peninsula, has maintained a healthy ancient-site-to-tour-bus ratio. Only recently has the Ring's tourist blitz begun to encroach upon the spectacular cliffs and sweeping beaches of this Irish-speaking peninsula.

▄ TRANSPORTATION

Dingle Town is most easily reached by **Bus Éireann** from Tralee (1¼hr., 2-6 per day, €9). The bus stop is behind the big SuperValu. There is no public transportation on the peninsula; many visitors chose to explore the area by **bike.**

DINGLE TOWN   ☎066

Dingle Town is the adopted home of **Fungi the Dolphin,** who has lived in the harbor for over two decades and is now a focus of the tourism industry. **Boat tours** leave from the pier daily 11am-6pm in summer; call ahead Sept.-June. (☎915 2626. 1hr. €16, 2-12 €8; free if Fungi gets the jitters and doesn't show.) **Sciúird Archaeology Tours** leave from the Dingle pier for bus tours of the area's ancient sites. (☎915 1606. 2½hr., 2 per day, €20.) **Moran's Tours** runs trips to Slea Head, passing through majestic scenery and stopping at historic sites. (☎915 1155. 2 per day, €20.) ▓**Ballintaggart Hostel (IHH) ❶,** a 25min. walk east of town on Tralee Rd. (N86), is supposedly haunted by the Earl of Cork's murdered wife. According to local legend, the Earl tried to kill her with poisonous mushrooms, but when that failed, he strangled her instead. (☎915 1454; info@dingleaccommodation.com. Quiet hours after 11pm. Laundry €8. Towels €1.50. Open Apr.-Oct. Dorms €13-19; doubles €55-70. Tent sites €8. MC/V.) The busy **Homely House Cafe ❷,** Green St., has a varied menu. (☎915 2431; www.homelyhouse.com. Entrees €4.50-11. Open July-Aug. M-Tu 11am-5pm, W-Sa 11am-5pm and 6-10pm; Sept.-June M-Sa 11am-5pm.) The **tourist office** is on Strand St. (☎915 1188. Open mid-June to mid-Sept. M-Sa 9am-7pm, Su 10am-1pm and 2:15-5pm; mid-Sept. to mid-June daily 9am-1pm and 2:15-5pm.)

SLEA HEAD, VENTRY, AND DUNQUIN   ☎066

The most rewarding way to see the cliffs and crashing waves of Dunquin and Slea Head is to **bike** along **Slea Head Drive.** Past Dingle Town toward Slea Head, the village of **Ventry** (*Ceann Trá*) is home to a **beach** and the **Celtic and Prehistoric Museum,** a collection that includes the largest intact woolly mammoth skull in the world. (☎915 9191; www.celticmuseum.com. Open Mar.-Nov. daily 10am-5:30pm; call ahead Dec.-Feb. €4.) Hop on one of seven free daily shuttles from Dingle Town to reach the **Ballybeag Hostel ❶** in Ventry. Its secluded yet convenient location makes it an ideal base for exploring the western end of the peninsula. (☎915 9876; www.iol.ie/~balybeag. Laundry €4. Dorms €17; doubles €48. Cash only.)

North of Slea Head and Ventry, the settlement of Dunquin (*Dún Chaoin*) consists of stone houses and little else. Past Dunquin on the road to Ballyferriter, the **Great Blasket Centre** has exhibits about the now-abandoned Blasket Islands. (☎915 6444. Open daily July-Aug. 10am-7pm; Easter-June and Sept.-Oct. 10am-6pm. Last entry 45min. before closing. €3.70, students €1.30.) At the **Dun Chaoin An Óige Hostel (HI) ❶** in Ballyferriter, on Dingle Way across from the turn-off to the Blasket Centre, each bunk has a panoramic ocean view. (☎915 6121; mailbox@anoige.ie. Breakfast €4. Reception 9-10am and 5-10pm. Lockout 10am-5pm. Open Feb.-Nov. Dorms €16-19; doubles €37. €2 HI discount. MC/V.) **Kruger's,** Europe's westernmost pub, has great views. (☎915 6127. Live music Tu, Th, Sa 9:30pm, Su 7:30pm. Open M-Th 11am-11:30pm, F-Sa 11am-12:30pm, Su 11am-11pm.)

TRALEE   ☎066

The economic and residential capital of Co. Kerry, Tralee (pop. 20,000) is a good base for exploring the Ring of Kerry or the Dingle Peninsula. The **Kerry County Museum,** in Ashe Memorial Hall on Denny St., colorfully illustrates the history of Ireland and Co. Kerry and takes visitors to an impressive lifelike reproduction of medieval Tralee. (☎712 7777; www.kerrymuseum.ie. Open June-Aug. daily 9:30am-5:30pm; Sept.-Dec. Tu-Sa 9:30am-5pm; Jan.-Mar. Tu-F 10am-4:30pm; Apr.-May Tu-Sa 9:30am-5:30pm. €8, students €6.50.) During the last week of August, Tralee hosts the nationally known **Rose of Tralee Festival,** at which lovely Irish lasses compete for the title of "Rose of Tralee." Gaze at the rose garden from rooms named after great Irish authors at convenient **Finnegan's Hostel ❷,** on Denny St., 100m from the museum. (☎712 7610; www.finneganshostel.com. Breakfast included. Dorms €17; singles €30; doubles €40.) **Brat's Place ❷,** 18 Milk Market Ln., across the Mall from the eastern side of the square, serves organic vegetarian and vegan dishes. (Soup €3.50. Entrees €7-10. Open M-Sa 12:30-3pm.) **Trains** depart from the station on Oakpark Rd. for: Cork (2½hr., 3-5 per day, €23); Dublin (4hr., 3-6 per day, €31); Galway (5-6hr., 3 per day, €59); Killarney (40min., 4 per day, €8.20). **Buses** leave from the train station for: Cork (2½hr., 8 per day, €15); Galway (9 per day, €18); Killarney (40min., 10-14 per day, €5.90); Limerick (2¼hr., 10 per day, €14). To get from the station to the **tourist office** in Ashe Memorial Hall, head down Edward St., turn right on Castle St., and left on Denny St. (☎712 1288. Open July-Aug. M-Sa 9am-7pm, Su 10am-6pm; Sept.-May M-Sa 9am-6pm.)

WESTERN IRELAND

Even Dubliners will say that the west is the "most Irish" part of Ireland; in remote areas you may hear Irish being spoken almost as often as English. The potato famine was most devastating in the west—entire villages emigrated or died—and the current population is still less than half of what it was in 1841.

LIMERICK   ☎061

Although the city's 18th-century Georgian streets and parks are regal and elegant, 20th-century industrial and commercial development cursed Limerick (pop. 80,000) with a featureless urban feel. The city gained a reputation for violence, and Frank McCourt's celebrated memoir *Angela's Ashes* revealed its squalor. But now, with help from the EU and a strong student presence, Limerick is on the rise. The **Hunt Museum,** in the Custom House on Rutland St., holds a gold crucifix that Mary, Queen of Scots gave to her executioner, as well as a coin reputed to be one of the infamous 30 pieces of silver paid to Judas by the Romans. (☎312 833; www.huntmuseum.com. Open M-Sa 10am-5pm, Su 2-5pm. €7.50, students €6.)

A number of B&Bs can be found on **O'Connell Street** or **Ennis Road.** Sunny singles and a well-equipped kitchen make up for the distant location of **Courtbrack Accommodation ❸,** Dock Rd., 20min. from town. (☎302 500. Laundry €5. Free Wi-Fi. Singles €30; doubles €52. MC/V.) **O'Grady's Cellar Restaurant ❷,** 118 O'Connell St., serves traditional favorites in a cozy underground spot. (☎418 286; www.ogradyscellarrestaurant.com. Entrees €8.50-14. Open daily 9am-10:30pm. MC/V.) The area where **Denmark Street** and **Cornmarket Row** intersect is a good place to quench your thirst or listen to live music. **Dolan's,** 3-4 Dock Rd., is a bit of a walk from the center of town, but hosts rambunctious local patrons and nightly trad in its dark interior. (☎314 483. Entrees €6-10. Lunch menu €3.50-8; served noon-7pm. Music nightly 9:30pm-close. Open M 7:30am-11:30pm, Tu-Th 9am-11:30pm, F-Sa 7:30am-2am, Su 10am-11pm. MC/V.)

IRELAND

WILLY-NILLY LOVE

An interview with Willie Daly, the Lis-doonvarna matchmaker

LG: How did the September matchmaking begin?

A: It started just before the turn of the century, and it started because Lisdoonvarna was a small market town. There was a doctor who lived there named Dr. Foster who found out there were sulphur and iron waters in the town, and he developed a health spa. The matchmaking started almost accidentally. The people who would come to the spa would be the more wealthy farmers. And they'd start matchmaking their children in conversation over breakfast, saying "now I have a John who is 28..." In the 30s and 40s the festival became popular, and they started having big bands and dances.

LG: What does it take to be a successful matchmaker these days?

A: Being a successful matchmaker is getting people together...there has to be an element of magic there, and today there has to be an element of love there, quickly. Irish men want a partner, someone to share their home, their life, to share their world with. There's a huge number of men in Ireland. In the past, most of the properties—restaurants, hotels, pubs, farms—would be left to a son. This would be done so that the family name would continue. And in hindsight,

Trains (☎315 555) leave for Cork (2½hr., 7-9 per day, €23) and Dublin (2½hr., 12-14 per day, €43). **Buses** (☎313 333; www.buseireann.ie) leave Colbert Station, off Parnell St., for Cork (2hr., 14 per day, €15), Dublin (3½hr., 1 per hr., €13), and Galway (2½hr., 1 per hr., €15). The **tourist office** is on Arthurs Quay. From the station, walk down Davis St., turn right on O'Connell St., and take a left at Arthurs Quay Mall. (☎317 522. Open June-Sept. M-Sa 9am-6pm, Su 9:30am-1pm and 2-5:30pm; Oct.-May M-F 9:30am-5:30pm, Sa 9:30am-1:30pm.)

◪ LET'S GO TO THE WEST: ENNIS ☎065

Ennis's proximity to Shannon Airport and the Burren makes it a common stopover for tourists, though there is little to do in the town itself. **Trains** (☎684 0444; www.irishrail.ie) leave from Station Rd. for Dublin (7 per day, €43). **Buses** (☎682 4177) also leave from Station Rd. 1 per hr. for: Cork (3hr., €14); Dublin (4hr., €17); Galway (1hr., €11); Limerick (40min., €8); Shannon Airport (40min., €6).

If you do care to explore Ennis, the friendly owners of **St. Jude's B&B ❸**, Greine Rd., are happy to provide info on the town. From the bus station, head down Station Rd. and make a left on Greine Rd. (☎684 2383. Doubles €60. Cash only.) The French chef serves up creative sandwiches (€5) and salads (€12-15) at **The Gourmet Store ❷**, 1 Barrack St. (☎684 3314. Open M-W 9:30am-7:30pm, Th-Sa 9:30am-9pm, Su noon-6pm. MC/V.) The **tourist office** is on Arthur's Row, off O'Connell square. (☎682 8366; www.shannonregiontourism.ie. Open June-Aug. M-F 9:30am-5:30pm, Sa-Su 9:30am-1pm and 2-5:30pm; mid-Mar. to June and Sept.-Dec. M-Sa 9:30am-1pm and 2-5:30pm; Jan. to mid-Mar. M-F 9:30am-1pm and 2-5:30pm.)

THE CLIFFS OF MOHER AND THE BURREN ☎065

Plunging 213m straight down to the sea, the ◪**Cliffs of Moher** provide incredible views of the Kerry Mountains, the Twelve Bens mountains, and the Aran Islands. Be careful of extremely strong winds; they blow a few tourists off every year, though new barriers make it difficult to wander into danger. Let's Go strongly discourages straying from the established paths. The new **Visitors Centre** and **Atlantic Edge Exhibition** educate tourists on the cliffs. (☎708 6141; www.cliffsofmoher.ie. Open daily mid-July to mid-Aug. 9am-7:30pm; mid-Aug. to mid-July 9:30am-5:30pm. €4, students €3.50.) To reach the cliffs, head 5km south of Doolin on R478, or hop on the Galway-Cork **bus** (in summer 2-3 per day). From Liscannor, **Cliffs of Moher**

Cruises (☎ 708 6060; www.mohercruises.com) sails under the cliffs (1¾hr., 1 per day, €20). **Ferries** also run to the cliffs from Doolin (1hr., 2-3 per day, €20.)

The nearby **Burren** resembles an enchanted fairyland, with coves, wildflowers, and 28 species of butterflies. The town of **Lisdoonvarna** is known for its **Matchmaking Festival**, a six-week-long *craic*-and-snogging celebration that attracts over 10,000 singles each September. **Sleepzone Burren ❶**, past the smokehouse on Doolin Rd., is an elegant hotel-turned-hostel perfect for launching into the Burren wild. (☎ 707 4036. Breakfast included. Free Wi-Fi. Dorms €15-22; singles €30-45.) In the town of **Ballyvaughan**, guests at **O'Brien B&B ❸**, on Main St., enjoy the huge rooms and the fireplaces in the adjacent pub. The bus from Galway arrives in front of the B&B. (☎ 707 7003. Doubles from €60-70. MC/V.) Locals and tourists flock to **Monk's Pub and Restaurant ❷**, on the pier, for its trad. (☎ 707 7059. Famous seafood chowder €6. Music 2 nights per week, usually Th and Sa.) There are **no ATMs** in Ballyvaughan. A **bus** (☎ 091 562 000) connects Galway to towns in the Burren a few times a day in summer but infrequently in winter.

GALWAY ☎091

With its youthful, exuberant spirit, Galway (pop. 70,000) is one of the fastest growing cities in Europe. Performers dazzle crowds on the appropriately named Shop St., locals and tourists lounge in outdoor cafes, and hip crowds pack the pubs and clubs at night. In addition to its peaceful quay-side walks, Galway is only a short drive away from beautiful Connemara.

█ ▨ TRANSPORTATION AND PRACTICAL INFORMATION. Trains leave from Eyre Sq. (☎ 561 444) for Dublin (3hr., 5-6 per day, €30) via Portarlington (€24); transfer at Portarlington for all other lines. **Buses** also leave from Eyre Sq. (☎ 562 000) for: Belfast, BRI (7½hr., 3 per day, €30); Donegal (4hr., 5 per day, €19); and Dublin (4hr., 1 per hr., €14). The **tourist office**, on Forster St., is near the train and bus stations. (☎ 537 700. Open May-Sept. daily 9am-5:45pm; Oct.-June M-Sa 9am-5:45pm.) For **Internet**, head to **Runner Internet Cafe**, 4 Eyre Sq. (☎ 539 966. Noon-10pm €4 per hr., 9am-noon and 10pm-midnight €2 per hr. Open daily 9am-midnight.) The **post office** is at 3 Eglinton St. (☎ 534 720. Open M-Sa 9am-5:30pm.)

▐ ▯ ACCOMMODATIONS AND FOOD. The number of accommodations in Galway has recently skyrocketed, but reservations are necessary in summer. **▨ Barnacle's Quay Street House (IHH) ❶**, 10 Quay St., offers bright, spacious rooms. (☎ 568 644; www.barna-

it's not good, because there are too many men, and all the women have gone to Dublin, London, and New York. Irish men—the thing that they have that's so very rare in the world—they have a marvelous sense of humor, and a great aptitude for music, singing, dancing, and drinking, and a very relaxed lifestyle. It's this lifestyle that gives them so much time to make a woman feel cherished and loved. When a man from the West of Ireland finds a woman, he really adores her. He might look a bit rough and rugged, but he'll have a heart full of love, and his mind won't be confused, like so many people in towns and cities.

LG: What advice do you give your potential matches?

A: To someone from another country, I would say that some of the finest men in the world live in Ireland, and especially in the West of Ireland. They're so close to nature themselves; they are unspoiled, and that's important. A lot of women find themselves secure and okay in life, but not in love—I think in one life you owe it to yourself to try to find love, and to find happiness. If you die without that, you have lived life a little bit in vain.

Willie and his daughter, Marie, can be found in the Matchmaker Bar on Th-Sa nights during the festival. They can also be contacted at: ☎ 707 1385 or williedaly@tinet.ie.

cles.ie. Breakfast included. Laundry €7. Free Wi-Fi. Single-sex dorms available. 4- to 12-bed dorms €17-24; doubles €56. Low season reduced rates. MC/V.) The friendly owner of **St. Martin's B&B ❸**, 2 Nun's Island Rd., on the west bank of the river at the end of O'Brien's Bridge, greets every guest with coffee and homemade brown bread. (☎568 286; stmartins@gmail.com. Singles €35; doubles €70. Cash only.) **Sleepzone ❷**, Bóthar na mBán, Woodquay, up Prospect Hill, has large rooms and top-notch facilities. (☎566 999; www.sleepzone.ie. Breakfast included. Laundry €7. Free Wi-Fi. Single-sex dorms available. Dorms €20-25; singles €30-50; doubles €50-76. Weekend and low-season rates vary. MC/V.)

The cafes and pubs around Quay, High, and Shop Streets are good options for budget dining. On Saturdays, an **open-air market** on Market St. sells fruit and ethnic foods. (Open 8am-4pm.) At ▧**The Home Plate ❷**, on Mary St., diners enjoy large sandwiches and entrees (€6-10) on tiny wooden tables. (☎561 475. Open M-Th noon-8pm, F-Sa noon-9pm, Su noon-7pm. Cash only.) Cross Wolfe Tone Bridge and walk 3min. up Father Griffin Rd. to reach **Anton's ❷** and its homemade fare. The walls feature the work of local artists. (☎582 067; www.antonscafe.com. Sandwiches €5.50. Open M-F 8am-6pm. Cash only.)

▧▨ **SIGHTS AND ENTERTAINMENT.** At the **Church of St. Nicholas** on Market St., a stone marks the spot where Columbus supposedly stopped to pray to the patron saint of travelers before sailing the ocean blue. (Open May-Sept. daily 8:30am-6:30pm. Free.) From Quay St., head across Wolfe Tone Bridge to the **Claddagh**, an area that was an Irish-speaking, thatch-roofed fishing village until the 1930s. The **Nora Barnacle House,** 8 Bowling Green, off Market St., has hardly changed since James Joyce's future wife Nora lived there with her family at the turn of the 20th century. (www.norabarnacle.com. Open mid-May to mid-Sept. M-Sa 10am-1pm and 2-5pm, or by appointment. €2.50, students €2.) Satiate your aquatic cravings at the **National Aquarium of Ireland,** on the Salt Hill Promenade. (☎585 100; www.nationalaquarium.ie. Open Apr.-Sept. daily 9am-6pm; Oct.-Mar. M-F 9am-5pm, Sa-Su 9am-6pm. €9, students €6.50.) Event listings are published in the free *Galway Advertiser,* available at the tourist office and most accommodations. In mid-July, the **Galway Arts Festival** (☎566 577) attracts droves of filmmakers, rock groups, theater troupes, and trad musicians.

Fantastic trad fills two floors at ▧**The Crane,** 2 Sea Rd. (☎587 419. Open M-Th 3-11:30pm, F-Sa 1pm-12:30am, Su 1-11pm. Cash only.) Nearby, at the **Roisín Dubh (The Black Rose),** on Dominick St., an intimate, bookshelved front hides some of Galway's hottest live music. (☎586 540; www.roisindubh.net. Pints €3.50. W stand-up comedy 9pm. Cover €5-25 most nights for music in the back room; front room and upstairs bar free. Open M-Tu 3-11:30pm, W-Su 3pm-2am.) The crowd usually ends up at ▧**Central Park,** 36 Upper Abbeygate St. With five bars and a huge dance floor, this is the place to be in Galway. (☎565 976; www.centralparkclub.com. Pints €4. Cover €5-10. Open Su-F 11pm-2am, Sa 10:45pm-2:30am.)

ARAN ISLANDS (OILEÁIN ÁRANN)   ☎099

The spectacular Aran Islands lie on the westernmost edge of Co. Galway. Churches, forts, ruins, and holy wells rise from the stony terrain of **Inishmore** (Inis Mór; pop. 900), the largest of the three islands. At the **Dún Aonghasa** ring fort, stones circle a sheer 100m drop. The **Inis Mór Way** is a mostly paved route that passes most of the island's sights. There are similar paths on **Inisheer** (Inis Oírr; pop. 260), the smallest island, and windswept **Inishmaan** (Inis Meáin; pop. 200). On Inishmore, the **Kilronan Hostel ❷**, next to the pier, offers free Internet and a TV room with DVD collection. (☎61255. Breakfast included. Single-sex dorms available. Dorms €20.) The **SPAR** supermarket in Kilronan has the island's only **ATM** (☎61203). **Aran Island Ferries** (☎091 561 767; www.aranisland-ferries.com) go from Rossaveal, west of Galway, to Inishmore (45min., 2-4 per day, round-trip €25) and Inisheer (2 per day). **Aran Direct** (☎566 535) also leaves from Rossaveal for Inishmore (45min., 3 per day, round-trip €25) and runs island-hopping ferries. Both companies run **buses** to Rossaveal (€6), which leave from Kinlay House, on Merchant St. in Galway, 1½hr. before ferry departure. The **tourist office** on Inishmore stores luggage (€1) and helps find accommodations. (☎61263. Open daily June-Aug. 10am-7pm; Sept.-May 10am-5pm.)

CONNEMARA

The Connemara region in northwest Co. Galway is an outdoorsman's dream, comprised of a lacy net of inlets and islands that provide stunning views of two major mountain ranges: the Twelve Bens and the Maumturks.

CLIFDEN AND CONNEMARA NATIONAL PARK   ☎095

For the best scenery in **Clifden**, bike along **Sky Road**, a 20km loop that overlooks the coastline. **Bike** rental is available at **Mannion's**, on Bridge St. (☎21160. June-Aug. €15 per day, €70 per week; Sept.-May €10 per day. €10 deposit. Open daily 9:30am-7pm.) Near the pubs, **Clifden Town Hostel (IHH) ❶**, Market St., has a helpful owner and good facilities. (☎21076; www.clifdentownhostel.com. Dorms €15; doubles €36; triples €52; quads €65.) **Shanaheever Campsite ❶** is 1.5km outside Clifden on Westport Rd. (☎22150; www.clifdencamping.com. Laundry €8. Tent or trailer sites €9 per person. Electricity €4. Free showers.) **Cullen's Bistro and Coffee Shop ❸**, Market St., cooks up hearty meals. (☎21983. Irish stew €16. Open Apr.-Nov. daily noon-10pm.) **O'Connor's SuperValu**, on the square, sells groceries. (☎21182. Open M-Sa 8:30am-10pm, Su 9am-7pm.) Bus Éireann runs **buses** from the library on Market St. to Galway via Oughterard (1½hr.; 2-6 per day; €10, students €7.70) and to Westport via Leenane (1½hr., late June-Aug. M-Sa 1 per day, €11/9). The **tourist office** is on Galway Rd. (☎21163; www.irelandwest.ie. Open July-Aug. daily 10am-6pm; Mar.-June and Sept.-Oct. M-Sa 10am-5pm.)

Connemara National Park occupies 12.5 sq. km of mountainous countryside. Bogs, often covered by a thin screen of grass and flowers, constitute much of the park's terrain. The **Sruffaunboy Nature** and **Ellis Wood** trails are easy 20min. hikes. The newly constructed pathway up ▣**Diamond Hill** is a more difficult journey, but it rewards climbers with views of the harbor and the spectacular Bens. Experienced hikers head for the **Twelve Bens** (Na Beanna Beola; also called the Twelve Pins), a rugged mountain range that reaches heights of 2200m. A tour of six peaks takes a full day. Trails are scarce, so consult the Clifden tourist office before jumping into the bog. **Biking** the 65km circle through Clifden, Letterfrack, and the Inagh Valley is truly captivating, but only appropriate for fit bikers. The **Visitors Centre** provides minimal help in planning hikes. (☎41054. Open daily June-Aug. 9:30am-6:30pm; Mar.-May and Sept. 10am-5:30pm.) Turn off from N59, 13km east of Clifden near Letterfrack, to reach the park.

WESTPORT   ☎098

Natural attractions await just outside Westport's busy streets. Rising 650m over Clew Bay, **Croagh Patrick** has been revered as a holy site for thousands of years. According to legend, St. Patrick prayed on the mountain for 40 days and nights in AD 441 to banish all snakes from Ireland. Climbers start their journey up Croagh Patrick from the 15th-century **Murrisk Abbey**, west of town on R335 toward Louisburgh. **Buses** go to Murrisk via Louisburgh (2-3 per day); ask to be dropped off in Murrisk. Sheep rule **Clare Island**, a beautiful speck of land in the Atlantic. Hop on a bus to Roonagh Pier, 29km from Westport, and then take a ferry to the island. (Bus departs from Westport's tourist office July-Aug. 10am, returns by 6pm; €25 for bus and ferry combined.) The extensive breakfast options and warm hospitality at ◪**The Altamont B&B ❸**, Altamont St., have kept travelers coming back for 44 years. (☎25226. Rooms €35-40.) Dine on **Bridge Street,** home to most of the town's restaurants, or grab groceries at the **SuperValu** market on Shop St. (☎27000. Open M-Sa 8am-10pm, Su 9am-9pm.) **Matt Molloy's,** owned by the flutist of the Chieftains, has nightly trad at 9:30pm. (☎26655. Pints €3.50. Open Su-Th 1pm-1am, F-Sa 1pm-2am.) **Trains** (☎25253) leave from the Altamont St. Station, a 10min. walk up the North Mall, to Dublin (3-4 per day, €32) via Athlone. **Buses** (☎71800) leave from Mill St. to Galway (2hr., 8 per day, €13). The **tourist office** is on James St. (☎25711. Open M-Sa 9am-5:45pm.)

SLIGO ☎071

Since the beginning of the 20th century, William Butler Yeats devotees have made literary pilgrimages to Sligo; the poet spent summers in town as a child. ◪**Model Arts and Niland Gallery,** on the Mall, houses one of the country's finest collections of modern Irish art. (☎914 1405; www.modelart.ie. Open June-Oct. Tu-Sa 10am-5:30pm, Su 11am-4pm. Free.) The well-preserved former Dominican friary, **Sligo Abbey,** is on Abbey St. (Open Apr.-Dec. daily 10am-6pm, last entry 5:15pm; Jan.-Mar. reduced hours. €2.10, students €1.10.) Yeats is buried in **Drumcliffe Churchyard,** on the N15, 6.5km northwest of Sligo. To get there, catch a bus from Sligo to the Derry stop at Drumcliffe (10min., 7 per day, €5.50).

Eden Hill Holiday Hostel (IHH) ❶, off Pearse Rd., offers respite from the clamor of town. Follow Pearse Rd., go right at the Marymount sign and right again after one block. (☎914 3204; www.edenhillhostel.com. Bike rental €15 per day. Laundry €8. Dorms €11-15; doubles €40. 2-person tents €18. MC/V.) **Pepper Alley ❶,** Rockwood Parade, serves cheap sandwiches. (☎917 0720. Entrees €3.50-8. Open M-Sa 8am-5:30pm, Su 10am-4pm.) A **Tesco** supermarket is on O'Connell St. (☎916 2788. Open 24hr.) Have a laugh with the locals in a comfortable atmosphere at **Foley's,** 14/15 Castle St. (☎914 2381. Pints €3.40. Open M-Sa 9:30am-11:30pm, Su 11am-11pm.) **Trains** (☎1850 836 6222; www.irishrail.ie) leave from Lord Edward St. to Dublin (3hr., 6 per day, round-trip €25) via Carrick-on-Shannon and Mullingar. From the same station, **buses** (☎916 0066; www.buseireann.ie) head to: Belfast (4hr.; 3-4 per day; €24, students €18); Derry/Londonderry (3hr., 8-10 per day, €16/13); Donegal (1hr., 7-9 per day, €11/9); Dublin (3-4hr., 7 per day, €16/13); Galway (2½hr., 7 per day, €13/11). Turn left on Lord Edward St., then right on to Adelaide St., and head around the corner to Temple St. to reach the **tourist office.** (☎916 1201; www.irelandnorthwest.ie. Open July-Aug. M-F 9am-5pm, Sa 11am-3pm.)

NORTHWESTERN IRELAND

A sliver of land connects the mountains, lakes, and ancient monuments of Co. Sligo to Co. Donegal. Among Ireland's counties, Donegal (DUN-ee-gahl) is second only to Cork in size. Its *gaeltacht* is the largest sanctuary of the living Irish language, and its geographic isolation and natural beauty embrace travelers sick of the tourist hordes farther south.

DONEGAL TOWN (DÚN NA NGALL) ☎074 97

A gateway for travelers heading to more isolated destinations in the north and northwest, the compact Donegal Town erupts with live music in pubs on weekends. The triangular center of town is called **the Diamond.** Six craftsmen open their studios to the public around the pleasant courtyard of the ⊠**Donegal Craft Village,** 2km south of town on the Ballyshannon Rd. (☎22225. Open 10am-5pm, daily in summer, M-Sa spring and autumn, Tu-Sa winter.) The **Waterbus** shuttle provides aquatic tours of Donegal Bay, departing from the quay next to the tourist office. (☎23666. Departure times depend on tides; call ahead. €10.) For two weeks in July, the **Earagail Arts Festival** celebrates the county's art scene, while the **Donegal Bluestacks Festival** features theater, arts, poetry, and music from late September to early October. (☎074 91 29186; www.donegalculture.com. Tickets range from free to €25.)

A 10min. walk from town, ⊠**Donegal Town Independent Hostel (IHH/IHO) ❶,** Killybegs Rd., welcomes backpackers with a dog named Scooby. (☎22805. Dorms €16; doubles €36, with bath €40. Tent sites €9 per person. MC/V.) Patrons enjoy breakfast (€6) and daily specials (€10) at **The Blueberry Tea Room ❷,** Castle St. (☎22933. Internet €2 for 30min. Open M-Sa 8:30am-7:30pm.) For groceries, head to **SuperValu,** 2min. from the Diamond down Ballyshannon Rd. (☎22977. Open M-Sa 8:30am-9pm, Su 10am-7pm.) **The Reveller,** in the Diamond, caters to a young crowd. (☎21201. Th-Su live music 10:30pm-close. Open M-Th 10:30am-11:30pm, F-Sa 10:30am-12:30am, Su noon-11pm.) **Bus Eireann** (☎21101) leaves from the Abbey Hotel on the Diamond for Derry/Londonderry (1½hr., 3-7 per day, €13) via Letterkenny (€6.40), Dublin (3½hr., 6-7 per day, €17), and Galway (4hr., 4-6 per day, €12). To reach the **tourist office,** face away from the Abbey Hotel and turn right; the office is on the Ballyshannon/Sligo Rd. (☎21148; www.donegaltown.ie. Open June-Aug. M-F 9am-6pm, Sa 10am-6pm, Su 11am-3pm; Sept.-May, M-F 9am-5pm.)

LETTERKENNY   ☎074 91

Letterkenny is difficult to navigate, but it is a useful stop for making bus connections to the rest of Ireland and to Northern Ireland. Cool green rooms with bath await guests at the **Pearse Road Guesthouse ❸.** Walk down Pearse Rd. from the bus depot (7min.) and look for a large white house. (☎23002. Singles €40; doubles €70.) The town's only hostel is **The International Port Hostel (IHO) ❶,** Covehill Port Rd., behind the theater. (☎25315; www.porthostel.ie. Free Wi-Fi. Dorms Su-F €16, Sa €20; doubles Su-F €40, Sa €50. Reduced rates online and in winter. MC/V.) A **Tesco supermarket** is in the shopping center behind the bus station. (Open 24hr.) **Buses** leave from the station at the junction of Port (Derry) and Pearse Rd., in front of the shopping center. Bus Éireann (☎21309) runs to: Derry/Londonderry (35min., 3-8 per day, €7.50); Donegal Town (1hr., 4-6 per day, €8.40); Dublin (4½hr., 9 per day, €18); Galway (4½hr., 3-4 per day, €19); Sligo (2hr., 3-4 per day, €13). Lough Swilly (☎22863) buses run to Derry/Londonderry (M-F 9 per day, Sa 4 per day) and the Inishowen Peninsula (M-Sa 2-3 per day). The **tourist office** (☎21160) is off the second roundabout at the intersection of Port (Derry) and Blaney Rd., 1.2km from town past the bus station.

NORTHERN IRELAND

The calm tenor of everyday life in Northern Ireland has long been overshadowed by headlines about riots and bombs. While the violence has subdued, the divisions in civil society continue. Protestants and Catholics usually live in separate neighborhoods, attend separate schools, and patronize different stores and pubs. The 1998 Good Friday Accord began a slow march to peace, and all sides have renewed their efforts to make their country as peaceful as it is beautiful.

BELFAST (BÉAL FEIRSTE)   ☎028

The second-largest city on the island of Ireland, Belfast (pop. 270,000) is the focus of Northern Ireland's cultural, commercial, and political activity. The city's pub scene ranks among the best in the world, combining the historical appeal of old-fashioned watering holes with more modern bars and clubs. While Belfast has suffered from the stigma of its violent past, it has rebuilt itself and now surprises most visitors with its neighborly, urbane feel.

⌐ TRANSPORTATION

Flights: Belfast is served by 2 airports. **Belfast International Airport (BFS;** ☎9442 2448; www.belfastairport.com) in Aldergrove. **Aer Lingus** (☎0845 084 4444; www.aer-lingus.com), **British Airways** (☎0845 850 9850; www.ba.com), **EasyJet** (☎0870 567 6676; www.easyjet.com), and many other airlines arrive from London and other European cities. **Translink Bus 300** (☎9066 6630; www.translink.co.uk) has 24hr. service from the airport to Europa bus station in the city center (1-6 per hr.; £6, round-trip £9). **Taxis** (☎9448 4353) make the trip for £25-30. **Belfast City Airport (BHD;** ☎9093 9093; www.belfastcityairport.com), at the harbor, has arrivals from regional carriers. To get from City Airport to Europa bus station, take **Translink Bus 600** (1-3 per hr.).

Trains: For train and bus info, contact **Translink.** (☎9066 6630; www.translink.co.uk. Inquiries daily 7am-8pm.) Trains leave Belfast's **Central Station,** E. Bridge St. to **Derry/Londonderry** (2hr.; M-F 10 per day, Sa 9 per day, Su 5 per day; £10) and **Dublin** (2hr.; M-Sa 8 per day, Su 5 per day; £24). The **Metro** buses are free with rail tickets.

Buses: Europa Bus Terminal, off Great Victoria St., behind the Europa Hotel (☎9066 6630; ticket office open M-Sa 7:30am-6:30pm, Su 12:30-5:30pm). Buses to **Derry/Londonderry** (1¾hr., 11-34 per day, £9) and **Dublin** (3hr.; M-Sa 17 per day, Su 1 per day, leaving from Glengall St. rather than Europa; £9.70). The Centrelink bus connects the station with the city center.

Ferries: Norfolk Ferries (www.norfolkline-ferries.co.uk) operates out of the SeaCat terminal and runs to **Liverpool, BRI** (8hr.; from £20, book online to avoid a £10 booking fee.) **Stena Line** (☎0870 570 7070; www.stenaline.com) has the quickest service to Scotland, docking in **Stranraer** (1¾hr.; fares seasonal, book online).

Public Transportation: Belfast has 2 bus services. Many local bus routes connect through Laganside Bus Station, Queen's Sq. Transport cards and tickets are available at the pink kiosks in Donegall Sq. W (open M-F 8am-6pm, Sa 9am-5:20pm) and around the city. **Metro buses** (☎9066 6630; www.translink.co.uk) gather in Donegall Sq. 12 main routes cover Belfast. **Nightlink Buses** travel from Donegall Sq. W. to towns outside Belfast. Sa 1 and 2am. £3.50.

Taxis: 24hr. metered cabs abound. **Value Cabs** (☎9080 9080); **City Cab** (☎9024 2000); **Fon a Cab** (☎9033 3333).

Bike Rental: Life Cycles, 36-37 Smithfield Market (☎9043 9959; www.lifecycles.co.uk). £9 per day. Offers **bicycle city tours.**

✈ ORIENTATION

Buses arrive at the Europa Bus Station on **Great Victoria Street.** To the northeast is **City Hall** in **Donegall Square.** Donegall Pl. turns into **Royal Avenue** and runs from Donegall Sq. through the shopping area. To the east, in **Cornmarket,** pubs in narrow alleyways offer an escape. The stretch of Great Victoria St. between the bus station and Shaftesbury Sq. is known as the **Golden Mile** for its high-brow establishments and Victorian architecture. **Botanic Avenue** and **Bradbury Place** (which becomes **University Road**) extend south from Shaftesbury Sq. into **Queen's University** turf. While central Belfast is safer for tourists than most European cities, locals advise caution in the

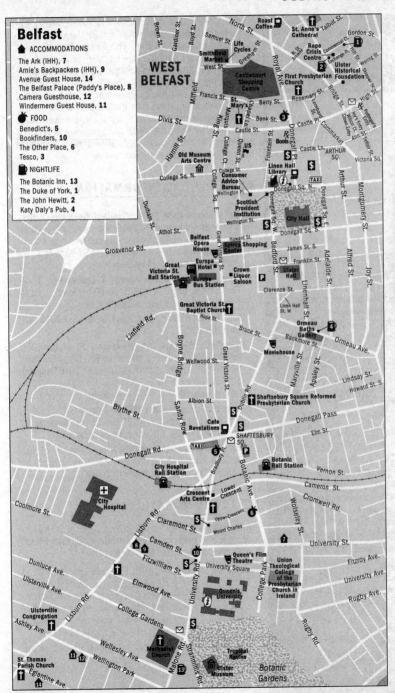

Belfast

♦ ACCOMMODATIONS

The Ark (IHH), **7**
Arnie's Backpackers (IHH), **9**
Avenue Guest House, **14**
The Belfast Palace (Paddy's Place), **8**
Camera Guesthouse, **12**
Windermere Guest House, **11**

♦ FOOD

Benedict's, **5**
Bookfinders, **10**
The Other Place, **6**
Tesco, **3**

♦ NIGHTLIFE

The Botanic Inn, **13**
The Duke of York, **1**
The John Hewitt, **2**
Katy Daly's Pub, **4**

IRELAND

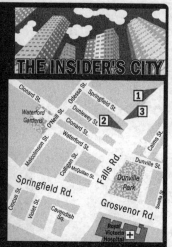

THE INSIDER'S CITY

THE CATHOLIC MURALS

The murals of West Belfast are a powerful testament to the volatile past and fierce loyalties of the divided neighborhoods. Many of the most famous Catholic murals are on Falls Rd., an area that saw some of the worst of the Troubles.

1 Illustrations of protestors during the **Hunger Strikes of 1981,** during which they fasted for the right to be considered political prisoners.

2 Portrayal of **Bobby Sands,** the first hunger-striker to die, is located on the side of the Sinn Féin Office, Sevastopol St. Sands was elected as a member of the British Parliament under a "political prisoner" ticket during this time and is remembered as the North's most famous martyr.

3 Formerly operating as Northern Ireland's National RUC Headquarters, the most bombed of any police station in England, the Republic, or the North. Its fortified, barbed wire facade is on Springfield St.

east and west. Westlink Motorway divides working-class **West Belfast,** more volatile than the city center, from the rest of Belfast. The Protestant district stretches along Shankill Rd., just north of the Catholic neighborhood, centered around Falls Rd. The **River Lagan** splits industrial **East Belfast** from Belfast proper. The shipyards and docks extend north on both sides of the river as it grows into **Belfast Lough.** During the week, the area north of City Hall is essentially deserted after 6pm. Although muggings are infrequent in Belfast, it's wise to use taxis after dark, particularly near clubs and pubs in the northeast.

🛈 PRACTICAL INFORMATION

Tourist Information Centre: Belfast Welcome Centre, 47 Donegall Pl. (☎9024 6609; www.gotobelfast.com). Offers helpful free booklet on Belfast and info on surrounding areas. Open June-Sept. M-Sa 9am-7pm, Su noon-5pm; Oct.-May M-Sa 9am-5pm.

Laundromat: Globe Drycleaners & Launderers, 37-39 Botanic Ave. (☎9024 3956). £6.80 per load. Open M-F 8am-9pm, Sa 8am-6pm, Su noon-6pm.

Police: 6-18 Donegall Pass and 65 Knock Rd. (☎9065 0222).

Hospitals: Belfast City Hospital, 91 Lisburn Rd. (☎9032 9241). From Shaftesbury Sq., follow Bradbury Pl. and take a right at the fork. **Royal Victoria Hospital,** 12 Grosvenor Rd. (☎9024 0503). From Donegall Sq., take Howard St. west to Grosvenor Rd.

Internet Access: Belfast Welcome Centre, 47 Donegall Pl., is the most central. £1.25 per 15min., students £1 per hr. Open M-Sa 9:30am-7pm, Su noon-5pm.

Post Office: Central Post Office, on the corner of High St. and Bridge St. (☎08457 223 344). Open M-Sa 10am-5:30pm. **Postal Code:** BT2 7FD.

🏠 ACCOMMODATIONS

Almost all accommodations are near Queen's University, close to pubs and restaurants. Lodgings fill up fast in summer, so reserve ahead.

Arnie's Backpackers (IHH), 63 Fitzwilliam St. (☎9024 2867). Look for a cutout sign of a backpacker. Bunked beds in bright, clean rooms. Library of travel info includes bus and train timetables. Kitchen often has a small stack of free food. If you're looking to find work, check the bulletin board in the entryway. 8-bed dorms £9; 4-bed £11. ❶

The Belfast Palace (Paddy's Palace), 68 Lisburn Rd. (☎9033 3367; www.paddyspalace.com), use the entrance at 70 Fitzwilliam St. Sociable new hostel offers free Internet (daily 8am-10:30pm), satellite TV, and videos in the lounge. Breakfast included. Reception M-Th and Su 8am-8pm, F-Sa 8am-10pm. Dorms from £10-17. ❶

Windermere Guest House, 60 Wellington Park (☎9066 2693; www.windermereguesthouse.co.uk). Relatively cheap for a B&B. Leather couches provide comfy seating in the living room. Singles £28, with bath £40; doubles £52/55. Cash only. ❸

Camera Guesthouse, 44 Wellington Park (☎9066 0026; malonedrumm@hotmail.com). Quiet, pristine Victorian house. Breakfast offers a selection of organic foods and herbal teas. Singles £34, with bath £48; doubles £56/62. AmEx/MC/V. ❹

The Ark (IHH), 44 University St. (☎9032 9626). 10min. walk from Europa bus station. Spacious dorms and a well-stocked kitchen with free tea and coffee. Staff provides info on finding work and books tours of Belfast (£8) and Giant's Causeway (£16). Internet £1 per 20min. Laundry £5. Curfew 2am. Co-ed 4- to 6-bed dorms £11; doubles £36; long-term housing from £60 per week. ❶

Avenue Guest House, 23 Eglantine Ave. (☎9066 5904; www.avenueguesthouse.com). 4 large, airy rooms equipped with TV and Wi-Fi. Comfortable living room has DVDs and books. £25 per person. ❸

🍴 FOOD

Dublin Rd., Botanic Ave., and the Golden Mile around **Shaftesbury Square,** have the highest concentration of restaurants. The huge **Tesco Supermarket** is at 2 Royal Ave. (☎9032 3270. Open M-W and Sa 8am-7pm, Th 8am-9pm, F 8am-8pm, Su 1-5pm.)

The Other Place, 79 Botanic Ave. (☎9020 7200). Popular eatery serves fried breakfasts until 5pm (from £3), hearty specials, and ethnic entrees. Try the "bang bang chicken," with spicy soy, sweet chili, and crunchy peanut sauce. Open daily 8am-10pm. ❷

Bookfinders, 47 University Rd. (☎9032 8269). 1 block from the University, on the corner of Camden St. and University Rd. Cluttered bookshelves and mismatched dishes. Soup and bread £2.50. Sandwiches £2.20. Open M-Sa 10am-5:30pm. ❶

Benedict's, 7-21 Bradbury Pl. (☎9059 1999; www.benedictshotel.co.uk). Swanky hotel restaurant providing an upscale break from sandwiches and pizza. "Beat the Clock" meal deal offers fine meals daily 5-7:30pm for £7.50-10. Lunch £7.50-12. Dinner £12-16. Open M-Sa noon-2:30pm and 5:30-10:30pm, Su noon-3:30pm and 5:30-9pm. ❸

THE INSIDER'S CITY

THE PROTESTANT MURALS

Many of the Protestant murals, in the Shankill area of West Belfast, are overtly militant. Most are found near Hopewell St. and Hopewell Cr., to the north of Shankill Rd., or down Shankill Parade, and are accessed by traveling south from Crumlin Rd.

1 Commemoration of the **Red Hand Commando,** a militant Loyalist group.

2 Painting of a **Loyalist martyr,** killed in prison in 1997.

3 Depiction of the **Grim Reaper,** with gun and British flag.

4 A collage of Loyalist militant groups including the **UVF, UDU,** and **UDA.**

5 Mural of the **Battle of the Boyne,** commemorating William of Orange's 1690 victory over James II.

6 The **Marksman's** gun seems to follow you as you pass by.

7 Portrait of the infamous **Top Gun,** a man responsible for the deaths of many high-ranking Republicans.

IRELAND

👁 SIGHTS

DONEGALL SQUARE. The most impressive piece of architecture in Belfast is also its administrative and geographic center. Dominating the grassy square that serves as the locus of downtown, **City Hall's** green copper dome (52m) is visible from nearly any point in the city. Inside, a grand staircase ascends to the second floor, where portraits of the city's Lord Mayors line the halls. The interior is only accessible by guided tour. *(☎9027 0456. 1hr. tours M-F 11am, 2, 3pm; Sa 2 and 3pm. Free.)*

THE DOCKS AND EAST BELFAST. The poster child of Belfast's riverfront revival, **Odyssey** packs big attractions into one huge entertainment center. The best feature is the **W5 Discovery Centre** (short for "whowhatwherewhywhen?"), a playground for curious minds and hyperactive schoolchildren. *(☎9046 7700; www.w5online.co.uk. Workshops run throughout summer. Wheelchair-accessible. Open M-Sa 10am-6pm, closes at 5pm when school is in session; Su noon-6pm. Last entry 1hr. before closing. £6.50, children £4.50. Family discounts available.)* **Sinclair Seamen's Church** is sure to please nautical enthusiasts. The minister delivers his sermons from a pulpit carved in the shape of a prow, collections are taken in miniature lifeboats, and an organ from a Guinness barge—with port and starboard lights—carries the tune. *(Corporation St., down from the SeaCat terminal. ☎9071 5997. Open W 2-5pm; Su service at 11:30am and 7pm.)*

CORNMARKET AND ST. ANNE'S. North of the city center, this shopping district envelops eight blocks around **Castle Street** and **Royal Avenue.** Relics of the old city remain in **entries,** or tiny alleys. Construction on St. Anne's Cathedral, also known as the **Belfast Cathedral,** was begun in 1899, but to keep from disturbing regular worship, it was built around a smaller church already on the site. Upon completion of the new exterior, builders extracted the earlier church brick by brick. *(Donegall St. Open M-Sa 10am-4pm, Su before and after services at 10, 11am, 3:30pm.)*

GRAND OPERA HOUSE. The opera house was repeatedly bombed by the IRA, restored to its original splendor at enormous cost, and bombed again. Visitors today enjoy the calm in high fashion, and tours offer a look behind the ornate facade. *(☎9024 1919; www.goh.co.uk. Open M-F 8:30am-9pm. Tours W-Sa 11am. £3.)*

WEST BELFAST. West Belfast is not a tourist "sight" in the traditional sense. The buildings display political **murals.** Visitors should definitely take a ⬛black cab tour of the murals, easily booked at most hostels. **Black Taxi Tours** offer witty, objective presentations. *(☎0800 032 2003. 1½hr. tour from £8 per person.)* The Catholic neighborhood is centered on **Falls Road,** where the **Sinn Féin** office is easily spotted: one side of it is covered with an advertisement for the Sinn Féin newspaper, *An Phoblacht.* On **Divis Street,** Divis Tower was formerly an IRA stronghold. Farther north is **Shankill Road** and the Protestant neighborhood. Between the Falls and Shankill is the **Peace Line.** The side streets on the right guide you to the **Shankill Estate** and more murals. **Crumlin Road,** through the estate, has the oldest Loyalist murals.

It's best to visit the Falls and Shankill during the day, when the neighborhoods are full of locals and, more importantly, the murals are visible. Do not visit the area during **Marching Season** (the weeks around July 12) when the parades are underscored by mutual antagonism that can lead to violence.

🎵🎭 ENTERTAINMENT AND NIGHTLIFE

Belfast's cultural events and performances are covered in the *Arts Council Artslink,* free at the Tourist Information Centre, while the *Arts Listings* covers entertainment throughout Northern Ireland. **Fenderesky Gallery,** 2 University Rd., in the Crescent Arts building, hosts shows and sells local work. (☎9023 5245. Open Tu-Sa 11:30am-5pm.) The **Old Museum Arts Centre**, 7 College Sq. N, is the largest venue for contemporary work. (☎9023 5053; www.oldmuseumartscentre.org. Open M-Sa 9:30am-5:30pm.) For more entertainment options, grab a free copy of *The Big List* or *Fate*, available in tourist centers, hostels, and certain and pubs.

▓ **The Duke of York**, 7-11 Commercial Ct. (☎9024 1062). Old boxing venue turned Communist printing press, rebuilt after it was bombed by IRA in the 60s; now home to the city's largest selection of Irish whiskeys. Kitchen serves sandwiches and toasties daily until 2:30pm. Th trad 10pm, F acoustic guitar, Sa disco with £5 cover. 18+. Open M 11:30am-11pm, Tu-F 11:30am-1am, Su 11:30am-2am.

▓ **Katy Daly's Pub**, 17 Ormeau Ave. (☎9032 5942; www.the-limelight.co.uk). Go straight behind City Hall toward Queen's and make a left on Ormeau Ave. High-ceilinged, wood-paneled, antique pub is a true stalwart of the Belfast music scene. Lunch served M-F noon-2:30pm. Bar open M-Sa until 1am, Su until midnight.

The Botanic Inn, 23 Malone Rd. (☎9050 9740). Standing in as the unofficial student union, the hugely popular "Bot" is packed nightly. 20+. Kitchen serves pub grub daily noon-8pm. Open M-Sa 11:30am-1am, Su noon-midnight.

The John Hewitt, 51 Lower Donegall St. (☎9023 3768; www.thejohnhewitt.com), around the corner from the Duke. Named after the late Ulster poet and run by the Unemployment Resource Centre. Half the profits go to the center, so drink up. 18+. Open M-F 11:30am-1am, Sa noon-1am, Su 6pm-1am.

DERRY/LONDONDERRY ☎028

Modern Derry/Londonderry is trying to cast off the legacy of its political Troubles with much success. Although the landscape was razed by years of bombings, recent years have been relatively peaceful. Today's rebuilt city is beautiful and intimate with a cosmopolitan vibe.

> **WHAT'S IN A NAME?** Originally christened *Diore*, meaning "oak grove," the city's name was anglicized to Derry and finally to Londonderry. The city's label remains a source of contention, as the minority Protestant population uses the official title while many Republican Northerners and informal Protestants refer to the city as Derry. Even in the city center, some signs refer to Derry and Londonderry without any consistency.

▓▓ **TRANSPORTATION AND PRACTICAL INFORMATION. Trains** (☎7134 2228) arrive on Duke St., from Belfast (2hr., 4-9 per day, £9.80). A free Rail-Link bus connects the **train station** and the **bus station**, on Foyle St., between the walled city and the river; it leaves the bus station 15min. before each train is due to depart. Ulsterbus (☎7126 2261) **buses** go to Belfast (1½-3hr., 10-36 per day, £8.70). The **Tourist Information Centre**, 44 Foyle St., has free copies of the *Visitor's Guide to Derry*. (☎7126 7284; www.derryvisitor.com. Open July-Sept. M-F 9am-7pm, Sa 10am-6pm, Su 10am-5pm; low season reduced hours.) **Postal Code:** BT48 6AT.

 ACCOMMODATIONS AND FOOD. Go down Strand Rd. and turn left up Great James St. to reach the social ▓**Derry City Independent Hostel ❶**, 44 Great James St. (☎7137 7989; www.derryhostel.com. Breakfast included. Free Internet. Dorms £10; doubles £28. MC/V.) **The Saddler's House (No. 36) ❸**, 36 Great James St., offers elegant rooms in a lovely Victorian home. (☎7126 9691; www.thesaddlershouse.com. TV and tea/coffee facilities in all rooms. Breakfast included. Singles £25-35; doubles £45-50. MC/V.) **The Ice Wharf/Lloyd's No. 1 Bar ❷**, 22-24 Strand Rd., has every type of food imaginable at low prices. Get two meals for the price of one all day long. (☎7127 6610; www.lloydsno1.co.uk. Open M-W, Su 10am-midnight, Th-Sa 10am-1am.) **The Sandwich Co. ❶,** The Diamond, is perfect for cheap sandwiches. (☎7137 2500. Sandwiches £2.60-4. Open M-F 8am-5pm, Sa 9am-5pm.)

◼◼ SIGHTS AND NIGHTLIFE. The **city walls,** 5.5m high and 6m thick, erected between 1614 and 1619, have never been breached—hence Derry's nickname "the Maiden City." The tower topping Derry's southeast wall past New Gate was built to protect **St. Columb's Cathedral,** on London St., the symbolic focus of the city's Protestant defenders. (☎7126 7313. Open M-Sa Easter-Oct. 9am-5pm; Nov.-Easter 9am-4pm. Tours £2.) The **Museum of Free Derry, 55 Glenfada Pk.,** covers the Catholic civil rights struggle in Northern Ireland up until Bloody Sunday. (☎7136 0880; www.museumoffreederry.org. Open June-Sept. M-F 9:30am-4:30pm, Sa-Su 1-4pm; Mar.-Sept. M-F 9:30am-4:30pm, Sa 1-4pm. £3, students £1.50.) West of the city walls, Derry's residential neighborhoods—both the Protestant **Waterside** and **Fountain Estate,** as well as the Catholic **Bogside**—display murals.

After dark, check out ◼**The Gweedore** or ◼**Peadar O'Donnell's,** 53-60 Waterloo St., where live music bangs at night. Peadar O'Donnell's has trad every night at 11pm, while The Gweedore has younger rock bands. The pubs are connected and owned by the same person, although they cater to different crowds. (☎7137 2318; www.peaderodonnells.com. Open daily 11am-1am.) **Sandino's Cafe Bar,** 1 Water St., is a good option for poetry readngs or live music by local bands and international musicians. (☎7130 9297. M-Sa 11:30am-1am, Su 1pm-midnight.)

◣ DAYTRIP FROM DERRY/LONDONDERRY

◼ THE GIANT'S CAUSEWAY

To get to the Giant's Causeway from Derry, take the free shuttle from the city bus station across the river to the train station (it leaves 15min. before the train departs), and catch a train to Coleraine. From Coleraine, catch bus #172 or 252 to the Causeway. Ulsterbuses #172, 252 (the Antrim Coaster), the Causeway Rambler, and the Bushmills Bus (you must catch the last 2 from Bushmills Distillery) drop visitors at the Giant's Causeway Visitors Centre. From the Centre, there is a minibus that runs to the most popular part of the Giant's Causeway (2min., 4 per hr., £1). ☎2073 1855; www.northantrim.com. Centre open daily July-Aug. 10am-6pm; Sept.-June 10am-5pm. The Causeway is free and always open.

Comprising over 40,000 symmetrical hexagonal basalt columns, ◼**The Giant's Causeway** resembles a descending staircase leading from the cliffs to the ocean's floor. Several other formations stand within the Causeway: **the Giant's Organ, the Granny, the Camel,** and **the Giant's Boot.** Advertised as the 8th natural wonder of the world, the Giant's Causeway is Northern Ireland's most famous natural sight, so expect large crowds, or visit early in the morning or after the center closes.

Once travelers reach the Visitors Centre, they have two trail options: the more popular low road, which directly swoops down to the Causeway (20min.), or the more rewarding high road, which takes visitors 4½ mi. up a sea cliff to the romantic Iron Age ruins of Dunseverick Castle. The trail is well-marked and easy to follow, but you can also consult the free map available at the Visitors Centre. The center also offers a 12min. film about the legend of Finn McCool and posits on the geological explanation for the formations.

ITALY (ITALIA)

Innovation, elegance, and culture distinguish Italy and its beloved art, fashion, and food. Steep Alpine peaks in the north; hills, lush with olive trees, in the interior; and the aquamarine waters of the Riviera provide only a few of the country's breathtaking vistas. Civilizations evolved piecemeal throughout the country, bequeathing a culture whose people and traditions retain distinct regional characteristics. Ruins of the Roman empire contextualize the imposing sculptures and paintings of Renaissance masters and the couture creations of today's fashion designers. Indulging in daily siestas and frequently hosting leisurely feasts, Italians seem to possess a knowledge of and appreciation for life's pleasures, while their openness lets travelers ease into Italy's relaxed lifestyle.

 DISCOVER ITALY: SUGGESTED ITINERARIES

THREE DAYS. Spend it all in the Eternal City of **Rome** (p. 578). Go back in time at the **Ancient City**: be a gladiator in the **Colosseum,** explore the **Roman Forum,** and stand in the well-preserved **Pantheon.** Spend the next day admiring the fine art in the **Capitoline Museums** and the **Galleria Borghese,** then satiate your other senses in a disco. The next morning, redeem your debauched soul in **Vatican City,** gazing at the ceiling of the **Sistine Chapel,** gaping at **St. Peter's Cathedral,** and enjoying the **Vatican Museums.**

ONE WEEK. Spend 3 days taking in the sights in **Rome** before heading north to **Florence** (2 days; p. 635) to immerse yourself in Italy's amazing Renaissance art at the Uffizi Gallery. Move to **Venice** (2 days; p. 619) to float through the canals.

BEST OF ITALY, 3 WEEKS. Begin by immersing yourself in the sights and history of **Rome** (3 days), seek out the medieval houses of **Siena** (1 day; p. 646), then move to **Florence** (3 days). Head up the coast to **Camogli** (1 day; p. 612), and the beautiful **Cinque Terre** (2 days; p. 613). Visit cosmopolitan **Milan** (2 days; p. 601) for shopping and **Lake Como** for hiking (1 day; p. 608). Find your Romeo or Juliet in **Verona** (1 day; p. 632). Be paddled through the winding canals in **Venice** (2 days) before flying south to **Naples** (2 days; p. 652), being sure to visit preserved, ancient **Pompeii** (1 day; p. 657). Then hike and swim along the **Amalfi Coast** (1 day; p. 659), and see the Grotto Azzura on the island of **Capri** (1 day; p. 658).

ESSENTIALS

FACTS AND FIGURES

Official Name: Italian Republic.
Capital: Rome.
Major Cities: Florence, Milan, Naples, Venice.
Population: 58,148,000.
Time Zone: GMT +1.

Language: Italian; some German, French, and Slovene.
Religion: Roman Catholic (90%).
Longest Salami: Made by Rino Parenti in Zibello, displayed on Nov. 23, 2003; 486.8m in length.

WHEN TO GO

Traveling to Italy in late May or early September, when the temperature averages a comfortable 77°F (25°C), will ensure a calmer, cooler vacation. When

planning, keep in mind festival schedules and weather patterns in northern and southern areas. Tourism goes into overdrive in June, July, and August: hotels are booked solid and prices know no limits. In August, Italians flock to the coast for vacationing, but northern cities are infested with tourists.

DOCUMENTS AND FORMALITIES

EMBASSIES AND CONSULATES. Foreign embassies in Italy are in Rome (p. 578). Italian embassies abroad include: **Australia,** 12 Grey St., Deakin, Canberra ACT 2600 (☎612 62 73 33 33; www.ambcanberra.esteri.it); **Canada,** 275 Slater St., 21st fl., Ottawa, ON K1P 5H9 (☎613-232-2401; www.ambottawa.esteri.it); **Ireland,** 63/65 Northumberland Rd., Dublin 4 (☎353 16 60 17 44; www.ambdublino.esteri.it); **New Zealand,** 34-38 Grant Rd., Wellington (☎644 473 5339; www.ambwellington.esteri.it); **UK,** 14 Three Kings Yard, London, W1K 4EH (☎020 73 12 22 00;

www.embitaly.org.uk); **US,** 3000 Whitehaven St., Washington, D.C., 20008 (☎202-612-4400; www.ambwashingtondc.esteri.it).

VISA AND ENTRY INFORMATION. EU citizens do not need a visa. Citizens of Australia, Canada, New Zealand, and the US do not need a visa for stays of up to 90 days, beginning upon entry into any of the countries within the EU's freedom-of-movement zone. For more info, see p. 14. For stays longer than 90 days, all non-EU citizens need visas (around €60), available at Italian consulates. For more info on obtaining a visa visit http://www.esteri.it/visti/home_eng.asp.

TOURIST SERVICES AND MONEY

EMERGENCY	Ambulance: ☎118. Fire: ☎115. Police: ☎112. General Emergency: ☎113.

TOURIST OFFICES. The **Italian State Tourist Board** (ENIT; www.enit.it) provides useful info about many aspects of the country, including the arts, history, nature, and leisure activities. The main office in Rome (☎06 49 71 11; sedecentrale@cert.enit.it) can help locate any local office that is not listed online.

MONEY. The **euro (€)** has replaced the **lira** as the unit of currency in Italy. For more info, see p. 17. At many Italian restaurants, a **service charge** (*servizio*) or **cover** (*coperto*) is included in the bill. Most locals do not tip, but it is appropriate for foreign visitors to leave an additional €1-2 at restaurants. Taxi drivers expect about a 10-15% tip. Bargaining is common in Italy, but use discretion. It is appropriate at markets, with vendors, and unmetered taxi fares (settle the price before getting in). Haggling over prices elsewhere is usually inappropriate.

Italy has a 20% **value added tax** (**VAT,** or **IVA** in Italy), a sales tax applied to most goods and services. The prices given in *Let's Go* include VAT. In the airport upon exiting the EU, non-EU citizens can claim a refund on the tax paid for goods purchased at participating stores. In order to qualify for a refund in a store, you must spend at least €150; make sure to ask for a refund form when you pay. For more info on qualifying for a VAT refund, see p. 19.

BUSINESS HOURS. Nearly everything closes around 1-3 or 4pm for *siesta.* Most museums are open 9am-1pm and 3-6pm; some are open through lunch, however. Monday is often a *giorno di chiusura* (day of closure).

TRANSPORTATION

BY PLANE. Most international flights land at Rome's international airport, known as both **Fiumicino** and **Leonardo da Vinci** (FCO; ☎06 65 951; www.adr.it). Other hubs are Florence's **Amerigo Vespucci** airport (FLR) and Milan's **Malpensa** (MXP) and **Linate** (LIN) airports. **Alitalia** (☎800-223-5730; www.alitalia.com) is Italy's national airline. Budget airlines **Ryanair** (☎353 12 49 77 91; www.ryanair.com) and **EasyJet** (☎0871 244 2366; www.easyjet.com) offer inexpensive fares to cities throughout the country; reserve ahead, as the best deals are available weeks in advance.

BY FERRY. Sicily, Sardinia, Corsica, and smaller islands along the coast are connected to the mainland by **ferries** (*traghetti*) and **hydrofoils** (*aliscafi*). Italy's largest private ferry service, **Tirrenia** (www.gruppotirrenia.it), runs ferries to Sardinia, Sicily, and Tunisia. Other lines, such as the **SNAV** (www.aferry.to/snav-ferry.htm), have hydrofoil services from major ports such as Ancona, Bari, Brindisi, Genoa, La Spezia, Livorno, Naples, and Trapani. Ferry service is also prevalent in the Lake Country. Reserve well ahead, especially in July and August.

BY TRAIN. The Italian State Railway **Ferrovie dello Stato**, or **FS** (national info line ☎848 88 80 88; www.trenitalia.com), offers inexpensive, efficient service and Trenitalia passes, the domestic equivalent of the Eurail Pass. There are several types of trains: the *locale* stops at every station on a line, the *diretto* makes fewer stops than the *locale*, and the *espresso* stops only at major stations. The air-conditioned *rapido*, an **InterCity (IC)** train, zips along but costs more. Tickets for the fast, pricey **Eurostar** trains require reservations. **Eurail Passes** are valid without a supplement on all trains except Eurostar. **Always validate** your ticket in the orange or yellow machine before boarding to avoid a €120 fine.

BY BUS. Intercity buses serve points inaccessible by train. For city buses, buy tickets in *tabaccherie* or kiosks. Validate your ticket immediately after boarding to avoid a €120 fine. Websites www.bus.it and www.italybus.it are helpful resources for trip planning.

BY CAR. To drive in Italy, you must be 18 or older and hold an **International Driving Permit (IDP)** or an EU license. There are four kinds of roads: *autostrada* (superhighways; mostly tollroads; usually 130km per hr. speed limit); *strade statali* (state roads); *strade provinciali* (provincial); and *strade communali* (local). **Driving in Italy is frightening;** congested traffic is common in large cities and in the north. On three-lane roads, the center lane is for passing. **Mopeds** (€30-40 per day) can be a great way to see the more scenic areas but can be disastrous in the rain and on rough roads. Always exercise caution. Practice in empty streets and learn to keep up with traffic. Drivers in Italy—especially in the south—are notorious for ignoring traffic laws.

BY BIKE AND BY THUMB. While bicycling is a popular sport in Italy, bike trails are rare. Rent bikes where you see a *noleggio* sign. Let's Go does not recommend hitchhiking, which can be particularly unsafe in Italy, especially in the south.

KEEPING IN TOUCH

PHONE CODES	**Country code: 39. International dialing prefix: 00.** All 10-digit numbers listed in this chapter are mobile phones and do not require a city code. When calling within a city, dial 0 + city code + local number. For more info on how to place international calls, see **Inside Back Cover.**

EMAIL AND THE INTERNET. Internet cafes in large cities swell with patrons, and rural areas and cities in the south are catching up. A new Italian law requires a passport or driver's license to use an Internet cafe. Rates are €1.50-6 per hr. For free Internet access, try local universities and libraries. While Italy initially lagged behind in jumping on the information superhighway, it's now playing catch-up impressively; however, easy laptop connection is still rare.

TELEPHONE. Almost all public phones require a prepaid card *(scheda)*, sold at *tabaccherie*, Internet cafes, and post offices. Italy has no area codes, only regional prefixes that are incorporated into the number. Mobile phones are widely used in Italy; buying a prepaid SIM card for a GSM phone can be a good, inexpensive option. Of the service providers, **TIM** and **Vodafone** have the best networks. International direct dial numbers include: **AT&T Direct** (☎800 17 24 44); **British Telecom** (☎0800 17 24 41); **Canada Direct** (☎800 17 22 13); **Telecom New Zealand Direct** (☎800 17 26 41); **Telstra Australia** (☎800 17 26 10).

MAIL. Airmail letters sent from Australia, North America, or the UK to Italy take anywhere from four to 15 days to arrive. Since Italian mail is notoriously unreliable, it is usually safer and quicker to send mail priority *(prioritaria)* or registered *(raccomandata)*. It costs €0.85 to send a letter worldwide. To receive mail in Italy, have mail delivered **Poste Restante**. Mail will go to the main post office unless you specify a subsidiary by street address. Address mail to be held according to the following example: First name LAST NAME, *Fermo Posta*, City, Italy. Bring a passport to pick up your mail; there may be a small fee.

ACCOMMODATIONS AND CAMPING

ITALY	❶	❷	❸	❹	❺
ACCOMMODATIONS	under €16	€16-25	€26-40	€41-60	over €60

Associazione Italiana Alberghi per la Gioventù (AIG), the Italian hostel federation, is a **Hostelling International (HI)** affiliate. A full list of AIG hostels is available online at www.ostellionline.org. Prices in Italy start at €8 per night for **dorms.** Hostels are the best option for solo travelers (single rooms are relatively scarce in hotels in the country), but curfews, lockouts, distant locations, and less-than-perfect security can detract from their appeal. Italian **hotel** rates are set by the state. A single room in a hotel *(camera singola)* usually starts at €25-50 per night, and a double *(camera doppia)* starts at €40-82 per room. A room with a private bath *(con bagno)* usually costs 30-50% more. Smaller **pensioni** are often cheaper than hotels. Be sure to confirm charges before checking in; Italian hotels are notorious for tacking on additional costs at check-out time. **Affittacamere** (rooms for rent in private houses) are an inexpensive option for longer stays. For more info, inquire at local tourist offices. There are over 1700 **campgrounds** in Italy; tent sites average €4.20. The **Federazione Italiana del Campeggio e del Caravaning** (www.federcampeggio.it) has a complete list of sites. The **Touring Club Italiano** (www.touringclub.it) publishes books and pamphlets on the outdoors.

FOOD AND DRINK

ITALY	❶	❷	❸	❹	❺
FOOD	under €7	€7-15	€16-20	€21-25	over €25

Breakfast is the simplest meal in Italy: at most, *colazione* consists of coffee and a *cornetto* or *brioche* (croissant). For *pranzo* (lunch), people grab *panini* (sandwiches) or salads at bars, or dine more calmly at an inexpensive *tavola calda* (cafeteria-style snack bar), *rosticceria* (grill), or *gastronomia* (snack bar with hot dishes for takeout). *Cena* (dinner) usually begins at 8pm or later. In Naples, it's not unusual to go for a midnight **pizza**. Traditionally, dinner is the longest meal of the day, usually lasting much of the evening and consisting of an *antipasto* (appetizer), a *primo piatto* (starch-based first course like pasta or risotto), a *secondo piatto* (meat or fish), and a *contorno* (vegetable side dish). Finally comes the *dolce* (dessert or fruit), then *caffè* **(espresso),** and often an after-dinner liqueur.

However, lunch is usually the most important meal of the day in rural regions where daily work comes in two shifts and is separated by a long lunch and **siesta.** Many restaurants offer a fixed-price *menù turistico* including *primo, secondo,* bread, water, and wine. While food varies regionally—seafood in the South and on the coast, heartier selections in the North, pesto in Liguria, gnocchi in Trentino-Alto Adige, parmesan and balsamic vinegar in Emilia-Romagna, and rustic stews in Tuscany—the importance of relaxing and having an extended meal does not. The after-dinner **passeggiata** (walk) is as much a tradition as the meal itself. Dense **gelato** is a snack, a dessert, and even a budget meal in itself. **Coffee** and **wine** are their own institutions, each with their own devoted followers.

ITALY

TIP **THE UGLY DUCKLING.** Before shelling out the euro for a *piccolo cono* (small cone), assess the quality of an establishment by looking at the banana *gelato:* if it's bright yellow, it's been made from a mix. If it's slightly gray, real bananas were used. *Gelati* in metal bins also tend to be homemade, whereas plastic tubs indicate mass-production.

HOLIDAYS AND FESTIVALS

Holidays: New Year's Day (Jan. 1); Epiphany (Jan. 6); Easter Sunday and Monday (Mar. 23-24); Liberation Day (Apr. 25); Labor Day (May 1); Ascension (May 1); Feast of the Assumption (Aug. 15); All Saints' Day (Nov. 1); Immaculate Conception (Dec. 8); Christmas (Dec. 25); Santo Stefano (Dec. 26).

Festivals: The most common reason for a local festival in Italy is the celebration of a religious event—everything from a patron saint's holy day to the commemoration of a special miracle counts. Carnevale, a country-wide celebration, is held during the 10 days leading up to Lent (Jan. 25-Feb. 5). In Venice, costumed Carnevale revelers fill the streets and canals. During Scoppio del Carro, held in Florence's P. del Duomo on Easter Sunday, Florentines set off a cart of explosives, remembering Pazziano dei Pazzi, who returned from the Crusades with a few splinters from the holy sepulcher, which he used to light a simple fireworks display. The Spoleto Festival (known as the Festival dei Due Mondi, or Festival of Two Worlds) is one of the world's most prestigious international arts events. Each June and July it features concerts, operas, ballets, film screenings, and modern art shows (www.spoletofestival.it). For more info on festivals in Italy, visit http://www.hostetler.net/italy/italy.cfm.

BEYOND TOURISM

From harvesting grapes on vineyards in Siena to restoring and protecting marine life in the Mediterranean, there are diverse options for working for a cause. Those in search of a more lucrative experience might consider working as an intern for the Italian press or teaching English in Italian schools. For more info on opportunities across Europe, see **Beyond Tourism,** p. 56.

Associazione Culturale Linguista Educational (ACLE), V. Roma 54, 18038 San Remo, Imperio (☎0184 50 60 70; www.acle.org). Non-profit association that works to bring theater, arts, and English language instruction to Italian children. Employees create theater programs in schools, teach English at summer camps, and have converted a medieval house in the village of Baiardio into a student art center.

Carmelita's Cook Italy (☎34 90 07 82 98; www.cookitaly.com). Region- or dish-specific cooking classes. Venues in Bologna, Lucca, and Sicily, among others. Courses run 3 days to 2 weeks. Program fee from €990 (including housing, meals, and recipes).

Gruppi Archeologici d'Italia, V. Baldo degli Ubaldi 168, 00165 Rome (☎06 638 5256; www.gruppiarcheologici.org). Organizes 2-week-long volunteer programs at archaeological digs throughout Italy. Offers links to various programs hoping to promote cultural awareness about archaeological preservation. Program fee €195-400.

ROME (ROMA) ☎06

Rome (pop. 2.8 million), *La Città Eterna*, is a concentrated expression of Italian spirit. Whether flaunting the Italian 2006 World Cup victory or retelling the mythical story of the city's founding, Romans exude a fierce pride for the Rome that was and the Rome that will be. Crumbling pagan ruins form the backdrop for the center of Christianity's largest denomination, and hip clubs and bars border grand cathedrals. The aroma of homemade pasta, pop of opening wine bottles, and rumble of city buses will greet you at every turn on Rome's cobblestone streets.

∎ INTERCITY TRANSPORTATION

Flights: Da Vinci International Airport (FCO; ☎65 21 01), known as **Fiumicino**, handles most flights. The **Termini** line runs nonstop to Rome's main station, **Stazione Termini** (30min., 2 per hr., €11). After hours, take the blue COTRAL **bus** (☎80 01 50 008) to Tiburtina from outside the main doors after customs (4 per day, €5). From Tiburtina, take bus #175 or 492, or metro B to Termini. A few domestic and budget flights, including Ryanair, arrive at **Ciampino (CIA; ☎79 49 41)**. To get to Rome, take the COTRAL bus (2 per hr., €1) to **Anagnina** station, or the **Terravision Shuttle** (www.terravision.it) to V. Marsala at the Hotel Royal Santina (40min., €8).

Trains: Trains leave Stazione Termini for: **Bologna** (2½-3½hr., €33-42); **Florence** (1½-3¾hr., €15-33); **Milan** (4½-8hr., €30-50); **Naples** (1¾-2½hr., €10-25); **Venice** (4½-5½hr., €33-50). Trains arriving in Rome between midnight and 5am arrive at **Stazione Tiburtina** or **Stazione Ostiense**, which are connected to Termini by the #175 bus.

∎ ORIENTATION

Because Rome's narrow, winding streets are difficult to navigate, it's helpful to orient yourself to major landmarks and main streets. The **Tiber River**, which snakes north-south through the city, is also a useful reference point. Most trains arrive at Stazione Termini east of Rome's historical center. **Termini** and neighboring **San Lorenzo** to the east are home to the city's largest university and most of its budget accommodations. **Via Nazionale** originates two blocks northwest of Termini Station in **Piazza della Repubblica** and leads to **Piazza Venezia**, the focal point of the city, recognizable by the white **Vittorio Emanuele II monument**. From P. Venezia, **Via dei Fori Imperiali** runs southeast to the Ancient City, where the **Colosseum** and the **Roman Forum** attest to former glory. **Via del Corso** stretches north from P. Venezia to **Piazza del Popolo**, which has an obelisk in its center. The **Trevi Fountain, Piazza Barberini,** and the fashionable streets around **Piazza di Spagna** lie to the east of V. del Corso. **Villa Borghese**, with its impressive gardens and museums, is northeast of the Spanish Steps. West of V. del Corso is the **centro storico**, the tangle of streets around the **Pantheon, Piazza Navona, Campo dei Fiori,** and the old **Jewish Ghetto**. West of P. Venezia, **Largo Argentina** marks the start of **Corso Vittorio Emanuele II**, which runs through the *centro storico* to the Tiber River. Across the river to the northwest is **Vatican City** and the **Borgo-Prati** neighborhood. South of the Vatican is **Trastevere** and residential **Testaccio**. Be sure to pick up a free color map at the tourist office.

∎ LOCAL TRANSPORTATION

Public Transportation: The A and B **Metropolitana subway** lines (www.metroroma.it) meet at Termini and run 5:30am-11:30pm. **ATAC buses** (www.atac.roma.it) run 5am-midnight (with limited late-night routes); validate your ticket in the machine when you board. Buy tickets (€1) at *tabaccherie*, newsstands, and station machines; they're valid for 1 metro ride or unlimited bus travel within 1¼hr. of validation. **BIG daily tickets** (€4), 3-day tourist passes (€11), and **CIS weekly tickets** (€16) allow for unlimited public transport. Beware: **pickpocketing** is rampant on buses and trains.

Taxis: Radiotaxi (☎06 35 70). Taxis are expensive. Ride only in yellow or white taxis, and make sure your taxi has a meter (if not, negotiate the price before riding). **Surcharges** apply at night (€2.60), on Su (€1), and when heading to or from Fiumicino

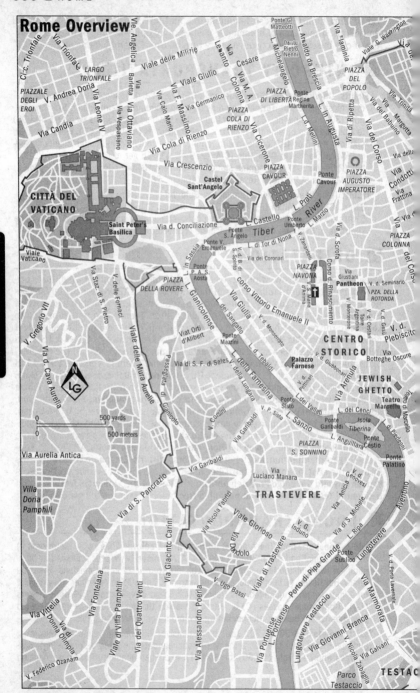

Rome Overview

Crc. Trionfale
Via Trionfale
Vle. Angelica
Viale delle Milizie
Via Leonina
Cesare
Via M. A. Colonna
Ponte G. Matteotti
Dante Pietro Nenni
L. Araldo da Brescia
Via Flaminia
Via G. Washington
Via de

LARGO TRIONFALE
V. Andrea Doria
Via Barletta
Via Giulio
Via F. Massimo
Via Germanico
PIAZZA DI LIBERTA
Ponte Regina Margherita
Via in Arenula
PIAZZA DEL POPOLO
Via Trinit
Via Margutta

PIAZZALE DEGLI EROI
Via Leone IV
Via Vespasiano
Via Ottaviano
Via Caio Mario
PIAZZA COLA DI RIENZO
Via Cicerone
L. Michelangelo
L. d. Mellini
L. in Augusta
Via del Babuino
Via del Corso

Via Candia
Via Cola di Rienzo
Via Crescenzio
PIAZZA CAVOUR
L. di Ripetta
Via della
Via Condotti

CITTÀ DEL VATICANO
Castel Sant'Angelo
Ponte Cavour
PIAZZA AUGUSTO IMPERATORE
Via Frattina

Saint Peter's Basilica
Via d. Conciliazione
Castello
L. Prati
River
L. Marzio
Via d.
PIAZZA COLONNA

Viale Vaticano
L. in Sassia
Ponte S. Angelo
Ponte Umberto I
Tiber
L. di Tor di Nona
Via di Tomacelli
Via d. Scrofa
del Corso

V. delle Fornaci
Ponte P.A.S. Aosta
Ponte V. Emanuele II
S. G. B. di S. Spirito
Via dei Coronari
Via Giustiani
V. d. Seminario
PIAZZA COLONNA

V. Gregorio VII
PIAZZA DELLA ROVERE
L. Gianicolense
Corso Vittorio Emanuele II
PIAZZA NAVONA
S. Maria d'Anima
Pantheon
PZA. DELLA ROTONDA

V. d. Cava Aurelia
Via Star. di S. Pietro
Via Giulia
di Sangallo
V. d. Monserrato
Corso d. Rinascimento
V. S. Marco
Torre Argentina
V. d. Cestari
V. d. Gesù

Viat Orti d'Alibert
L. d. Tebaldi
V. de Monterone
V. d. Plebiscito

Ponte Mazzini
L. della Farnesina
Palazzo Farnese
V. d. Giubbonari
CENTRO STORICO
Via Botteghe Oscure

Viale delle Mura Aurelie
Via di S. F. di Sales
L. della Lungara
Via d. Pettinari
JEWISH GHETTO
Teatro Marcello

Passeggiata di Gianicolo
V. Corsini
Ponte Sisto
L. dei Vallati
L. dei Cenci
Isola Tiberina
Ponte di Marcello

Via Aurelia Antica
Via Garibaldi
Ponte Garibaldi
Ponte Cestio
di Pierleoni

Villa Doria Pamphili
Via Garibaldi
L. Sanzio
V. P. Sisto
L. Anguillara
PIAZZA S. SONNINO
Ponte Palatino

Via di S. Pancrazio
Via Luciano Manara
V. d. Genovesi
Aventino

Via Giacinto Carini
Via Nicola Fabrizi
TRASTEVERE
Via Anicia
Via di S. Michele

Via Fonteiana
V. G. Induno
Viale Glorioso
Via di Trastevere
L. Ripa
Lungotevere

Viale di Villa Pamphili
Via Dandolo
Ponte Sublicio
v. d. Porta Lavernale

Via Vitellia
Via di Donna Olimpia
Via dei Quattro Venti
Via Alessandro Poeria
V. Ugo Bassi
Porto di Pipa Grande
L. Portuense
Via Portuense
Lungotevere Testaccio
Via Marmorata

V. Federico Ozanam
Parco Testaccio
Via Giovanni Branca
V. Nicola Zabaglia
Via Galvani
TESTAC

N LG
0   500 yards
0   500 meters

ITALY

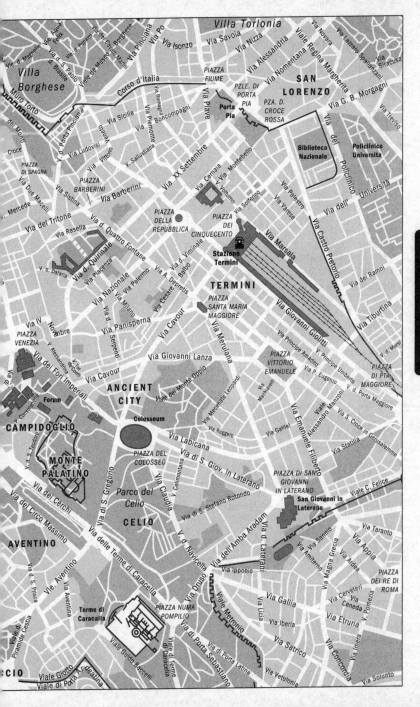

ITALY

(€7.25) or Ciampino (€5.50). Fares run about €11 from Termini to Vatican City, around €35 between the city center and Fiumicino.

Bike and Moped Rental: Bikes generally cost €5 per hr. or €10 per day while scooters cost €35-55 per day. Try **Bici & Baci,** V. del Viminale 5 (☎48 28 443; www.bici-baci.com). 16+. Open daily 8am-7pm. AmEx/MC/V.

🔁 PRACTICAL INFORMATION

Tourist Office: ■**Enjoy Rome,** V. Marghera 8/A (☎44 56 890; www.enjoyrome.com). From the middle concourse of Termini, exit right, with the trains behind you; cross V. Marsala and follow V. Marghera for 3 blocks. Open Apr.-Oct. M-F 8:30am-7pm, Sa 8:30am-2pm; Nov.-Mar. M-F 9am-6pm, Sa 9am-2pm.

Embassies: Australia, V. Antonio Bosio 5 (☎85 27 21; www.italy.embassy.gov.au). Open M-F 9am-5pm. **Canada,** V. Zara 30 (☎85 44 41; www.canada.it). Open M-F 9am-5pm. **Ireland,** P. di Campitelli 3 (☎69 79 121). **New Zealand,** V. Zara 28 (☎44 17 171). Open M-F 8:30am-12:45pm and 1:45-5pm. **UK,** V. XX Settembre 80a (☎42 20 00 01). Consular section open M-F 9:15am-1:30pm. **US,** V. Vittorio Veneto 119/A (☎46 741; www.usembassy.it/mission). Open M-F 8:30am-5:30pm.

American Express: P. di Spagna 38 (☎67 641, lost cards 800 87 20 00). Open M-F 9am-5:30pm, Sa 9am-12:30pm.

Luggage Storage: In Termini, underneath track #24.

GLBT Resources: ARCI-GAY, V. Goito 35/B (☎64 50 11 02; www.arcigayroma.it). Open M-F 4-8pm. **Circolo Mario Mieli di Cultura Omosessuale,** V. Efeso 2/A (☎54 13 985; www.mariomieli.org).

Laundromat: BollaBlu, V. Milazzo 20/B. (☎44 70 30 96). Laundry about €10. Open daily 8am-midnight. **OndaBlu** (info ☎800 86 13 46). 17 locations throughout the city.

Pharmacies: Farmacia Piram, V. Nazionale 228 (☎488 07 54). Open 24hr. MC/V.

Hospitals: International Medical Center, V. Firenze 47 (☎48 82 371; www.imc84.com). Call ahead. Referral service to English-speaking doctors. General visit €100. Open M-Sa 9am-8pm; on-call 24hr.

Internet Access: Splashnet, V. Varese 33 (☎49 38 04 50), near Termini. €1.50 per hr. Open daily in summer 8:30am-1am; in winter 8:30am-11pm.

Post Office: Main Post Office (Posta Centrale), P. San Silvestro 19. Open M-F 8am-7pm, Sa 8am-1:15pm. Branch at V. d. Terme di Diocleziano 30, near Termini.

🔁 ACCOMMODATIONS

Rome swells with tourists around Easter, May through July, and in September. Prices vary with the seasons, and proprietors' willingness to negotiate depends on length of stays and group size. Termini swarms with hotel scouts. Many are legitimate and have IDs issued by tourist offices; however, be wary as some impostors with fake badges direct travelers to run-down locations charging exorbitant rates.

CENTRO STORICO AND ANCIENT CITY

If being a bit closer to the sights is important to you, then choosing Rome's medieval center over the area near Termini may be worth the higher prices.

Pensione Rosetta, V. Cavour 295 (☎47 82 30 69; www.rosettahotel.com), a few blocks past the Fori Imperiali. 18 tidy rooms with bath, TV, and phone. A/C €10. Reserve 2 months ahead. Singles €60; doubles €85; triples €95; quads €110. AmEx/MC/V. ❹

Albergo del Sole, V. d. Biscione 76 (☎68 80 68 73; www.solealbiscione.it), off Campo dei Fiori. Comfortable, modern rooms with phone, TV, and antique furniture. Reception 24hr. Check-in and check-out 11am. Reserve 2 months ahead in high season. Singles €65, with bath €90; doubles €95-€150; triples €185; quads €220. Cash only. ❺

Hotel Navona, V. d. Sediari 8, 1st fl. (☎68 64 203; www.hotelnavona.com). Bus #64 to Corso Vittorio Emmanuele II or #70 to Corso Rinascimento. Outdoor marking is very small. English-speaking owners have a nearby *residenza*, with apartments to rent for longer stays. Breakfast, TV, A/C, and bath included. Luggage storage. 24hr. reception. Check-out 10:30am. Singles €100-120; doubles €135-145; triples €180-210. Reservations with credit card and 1st-night deposit. 5% *Let's Go* discount. D/MC/V. ❺

PIAZZA DI SPAGNA AND ENVIRONS

Though prices near P. di Spagna can be very steep, accommodations are often newer and closer to the metro than in the *centro storico*.

▨ **Pensione Panda,** V. della Croce 35, 2nd fl. (☎67 80 179; www.hotelpanda.it). M: A-Spagna, between P. di Spagna and V. del Corso. 28 renovated rooms with faux marble statues and frescoed ceilings. English spoken. A/C €6. Free Wi-Fi. Reserve ahead. Singles €68, with bath €80; doubles €78/108; triples €140; quads €180. 5% *Let's Go* discount on cash payments. AmEx/MC/V. ❹

Hotel Boccaccio, V. del Boccaccio 25, 1st fl. (☎48 85 962; www.hotelboccaccio.com). M: A-Barberini, near P. Barberini. 8 cozy, simply furnished rooms and a terrace. Singles €45; doubles €80, with bath €100; triples €108/135. AmEx/MC/V. ❸

BORGO AND PRATI (NEAR VATICAN CITY)

Pensioni near the Vatican offer some of the best deals in Rome and the sobriety one would expect from a neighborhood with this kind of nun-to-tourist ratio.

▨ **Colors,** V. Boezio 31 (☎68 74 030; www.colorshotel.com). M: A-Ottaviano. This 3-fl. complex has 2 hostel areas and 1 hotel. Breakfast included. Communal terraces and kitchen. Internet €2 per hr. Call by 9pm the night before to reserve dorms. Hostel dorms €27; singles €90, with bath €105; doubles €100/130; triples €120. Hotel singles €90; doubles €120; triples €140; quads €150. Cash only. ❸

▨ **Hotel San Pietrino,** V. G. Bettolo 43, 3rd fl. (☎37 00 132; www.sanpietrino.it). M: A-Ottaviano. Spacious rooms are simple and clean with free A/C, DVD, and TV. Internet and communal fridge access. Bikes €5 per day. Laundry €6-8. Reserve 2-3 months ahead in high season. Singles €35-45; doubles €70-93; triples €120; family suite €135. 10% *Let's Go* discount. AmEx/MC/V. ❸

Hotel Lady, V. Germanico 198, 4th fl. (☎32 42 112; www.hoteladyroma.it). This cozy hotel's dimly lit hallways accentuate the ceiling's rich wooden beams. Rooms have antique furniture, sinks, desks, phones, and fans, but no A/C. High season singles €80; doubles €100, with bath €145; triples €130. Low-season rates vary. AmEx/MC/V. ❺

Ostello Per La Gioventù Foro Italico (HI), V. delle Olimpiadi 61 (☎32 36 267; bookingrome@tiscali.it). M: A-Ottaviano, then bus #32 from P. di Risorgimento to the 2nd "LGT Cadorna Ostello Gioventù" stop (10-15min.). The hostel is the white building behind the bushes across the street. A barrack-style marble building holds massive dorm rooms, bathrooms, a cafeteria, and a common area. Breakfast, showers, and linens included. Luggage storage €1 per day. Internet access with phone card. Reception 7am-11pm. Curfew 1-1:30am. Dorms €23. €5 HI discount. AmEx/MC/V. ❷

SAN LORENZO AND EAST OF TERMINI

Welcome to budget traveler and backpacker central. While Termini is chock-full of traveler's services, use caution when walking in the area, especially at night, and keep a close eye on your pockets and/or purse.

▨ **Hotel and Hostel Des Artistes,** V. Villafranca 20, 5th fl. (☎44 54 365; www.hoteldesartistes.com). Des Artistes houses a hotel and a renovated hostel with large, pastel-colored rooms. Hostel towels €1, plus €10 deposit. 15min. free Internet. Reception 24hr. Check-out 10:30am. 4- to 10-bed dorms €20-26. Hostel cash only. Hotel AmEx/MC/V. ❷

Pensione Fawlty Towers, V. Magenta 39, 5th fl. (☎44 50 374; www.fawltytowers.org). Common room with DVD, library, and TV. A/C in rooms. Kitchen and lockers available.

Linens included; towels included in private rooms. Call to reserve private rooms; no reservations for dorms. Dorms €18-25; singles €58, with shower €63; doubles €80/89; triples with shower €93, with full bath €99; quads €100. Cash only. ❷

VIA XX SETTEMBRE AND NORTH OF TERMINI

Dominated by government ministries and private apartments, this area is less noisy and touristy than nearby Termini.

Hotel Papa Germano, V. Calatafimi 14/A (☎48 69 19; www.hotelpapagermano.com). Clean rooms with hair dryer, sink, and TV. Mini fridge in rooms with bath. A/C €5. Breakfast, linens, and towels included. Internet €2 per hr. Dorms €23-30; singles €35-45; doubles €60-100; triples €75-120; quads €100-140. AmEx/MC/V. ❷

Hotel Bolognese, V. Palestro 15, 2nd fl. (☎/fax 49 00 45; hbolognese@tiscalinet.it). The artist-owner's impressive paintings and private bath in every room set this otherwise standard hotel apart. Breakfast included. Check-out 11am. Singles €30-60; doubles €50-90; triples €90-120. AmEx/MC/V. ❸

ESQUILINO AND WEST OF TERMINI

Esquilino, south of Termini, has tons of cheap hotels close to major sights. The area west of Termini is more inviting than Esquilino, with busy, shop-lined streets.

▨ **Alessandro Palace,** V. Vicenza 42 (☎44 61 958; www.hostelalessandropalace.com). Exit Termini from track #1. Turn left on V. Marsala, then right on V. Vicenza. Renovated dorms, all with bath and A/C. Fun guests-only bar. Nightly pizza party at 8:30pm free with purchase of any drink. Breakfast and linens included. Towels €2 in dorms. Internet €2 per hr. Dorms €25-30; doubles €90; triples €120; quads €140. AmEx/MC/V. ❷

Alessandro Downtown, V. C. Cattaneo 23 (☎44 34 01 47; www.hostelalessandrodowntown.com). Exit Termini by track #22, make a left on V. Giolitti, then a right onto V. C. Cattaneo. Fun, knowledgeable, English-speaking staff. Slightly quieter than the Palace, though guests can go to its bar. Kitchen, 2 common rooms, TV, and fans. Breakfast and pasta party (M-F 7pm) included. Towels €2. Internet €2 per hr. Dorms €24-25; doubles €70, with bath €90; quads €120/140. AmEx/MC/V. ❷

Hotel Scott House, V. Gioberti 30 (☎44 65 379; www.scotthouse.com). Colorful, modern rooms have A/C, bath, phone, and satellite TV. Breakfast included. Check-out 11am. Singles €35-68; doubles €68-98; triples €75-114; quads €88-129. AmEx/MC/V. €5 discount per night if paid in cash. ❸

ALTERNATIVE HOUSING

RELIGIOUS HOUSING

Don't automatically think "Catholic" or even "inexpensive;" most are open to people of all religions, and single rooms can run to €155. Don't expect quaint rooms in cloisters: the rooms in religious housing have amenities similar to hotel rooms. Do, however, think sober: early curfews and/or chores are standard.

Domus Nova Bethlehem, V. Cavour 85/A (☎47 82 44 14). Take V. Cavour from Termini, past P. d. Esquilino. Religious icons abound. Rooms with A/C, bath, and TV. Huge terrace. Breakfast included. Internet with phonecard. Summer curfew 2am, winter 1am. Singles €78; doubles €114; triples €140; quads €150; quints €170. AmEx/MC/V. ❺

Santa Maria Alle Fornaci, P. S. Maria alle Fornaci 27 (☎39 36 76 32; www.trinitaridematha.it). Facing St. Peter's, turn left through a gate in the basilica onto P. del Uffizio. Take 3rd right onto V. d. Gasperi, which leads to P. S. Maria alle Fornaci. Go down the steps just to the church's left. Rooms have bath. Common room with Internet. Breakfast included. Reception 24hr. Singles €60; doubles €90; triples €125. AmEx/MC/V. ❹

◘ FOOD

Traditional Roman cuisine includes *spaghetti alla carbonara* (egg and cream sauce with bacon), *spaghetti all'amatriciana* (thin tomato sauce with chiles and bacon), *carciofi alla giudia* (deep-fried artichokes, common in the Jewish Ghetto), and *fiori di zucca* (stuffed, fried zucchini flowers). Pizza is often a good and inexpensive option; like elsewhere in Italy, it is eaten with a fork and knife. Instead of the usually bland bread, try *pizza romana*, which is more like foccaccia: a flat bread with olive oil, sea salt, rosemary, and sometimes more toppings. Lunch is typically the main meal, though some Romans now enjoy *panini* on the go during the week. Restaurants tend to close between 3 and 6:30pm.

RESTAURANTS

ANCIENT CITY AND CENTRO STORICO

The restaurants in the *centro storico* can be expensive and generic, especially those near famous landmarks. Head to **Via del Governo Vecchio** and its tiny cross streets for more authentic fare.

▨ **I Buoni Amici**, V. Aleardo 4 (☎70 49 19 93). M: B-Colosseo. The owner's exceptional service complements the popular *linguine alle vongole* (with clams in the shell; €8) and the self-serve *antipasto* bar. *Primi* €7-8. *Secondi* €8-12. Wine €8-15. Homemade *dolci* €4. Cover €1. Open M-Sa 12:30-3pm and 7-11pm. AmEx/MC/V. ❷

▨ **Luzzi**, V. S. Giovanni in Laterano 88 (☎70 96 332), 3 blocks past the Colosseum coming from V. dei Fori Imperiali, yet always packed with locals. Cheap, traditional fare and house wine. The *penne con salmone* (€7) will leave you wanting more. *Primi* €5-7. *Secondi* €7-11. Open M-Tu and Th-Su noon-3pm and 7pm-midnight. AmEx/MC/V. ❷

Miscellanea, V. della Paste 110A (☎67 80 983; www.miscellaneapub.it). A favorite of students and locals, just around the corner from the Pantheon. Priding itself on fresh food, gigantic portions, and low prices, Miscellanea exemplifies what a true *ristorante* should be. Salads (€6), *antipasti* (€6-7), and *panini* (€3) are the best values in town. Drinks (€2-4). Delicious desserts €2-3. Open daily 11am-2am. AmEx. ❶

Pizza Art, V. Arenula 76 (☎68 73 378). This place looks like a typical pizzeria but serves thick slices of foccaccia, priced per kg. Toppings include tomato, mozzarella, nutella, and goat cheese. Average slice €2.40. Open daily 12:30-11pm. Cash only. ❶

JEWISH GHETTO

A 10min. walk south of the Campo, restaurants serve Roman specialties alongside traditional Jewish and kosher dishes. Many close on Saturdays.

▨ **Bar Da Benito**, V. d. Falegnami 14 (☎68 61 508). A rare combination—*secondi* for less than €5 and a place to sit and enjoy your food. Speedy service. *Primi* €4.50. *Secondi* €4.50-7.50. *Dolci* €2-3.50. Open Sept.-July M-Sa 6:30am-7pm. Cash only. ❷

Trattoria da Giggetto, V. d. Portico d'Ottavia 21-22 (☎68 61 105; www.giggettoalportico.com). Dark, large restaurant right next to the ruins of the Portico d'Ottavia. No animal parts go to waste here. In the Roman tradition, *fritto di cervello d'abbacchio* (brains with vegetables; €12) are served alongside delicacies like fried artichokes (€6). *Primi* €8.50-14. *Secondi* €9-20. Cover €1.50. Open Tu-Su 12:30-3:30pm and 7:30-11pm. Closed the last 2 weeks of July. Reserve ahead for dinner. AmEx/MC/V. ❸

PIAZZA DI SPAGNA

The P. di Spagna and Trevi Fountain area, though busy at night and closer to tourist destinations, offers few high quality options at low prices. Head off the main drags (V. del Corso and V. dei Condotti) for worthy eateries.

Trattoria da Settimio all'Arancio, V. dell'Arancio 50-52 (☎68 76 119). Take V. dei Condotti from P. di Spagna; bear right on V. Tomacelli after V. del Corso, then take the 1st left. It's the 2nd restaurant on the left (not the pizzeria). Portions are generous and dishes decadent. *Primi* from €8-15. *Secondi* from €8-20. Open M-Sa 12:30-3pm and 7:30-midnight. Reserve ahead. AmEx/MC/V. ❹

Vini e Buffet, V. della Torretta 60 (☎68 71 445), near P. di Spagna. A favorite of Romans with a penchant for regional wine, *pâtés* (€4-4.50), *crostini*, or *scamorze* (smoked mozzarella; €8-9). Salads €7.50-11. Wine €10-24. Open M-Sa 12:30-3pm and 7:30-11pm. Reservations recommended. Cash only. ❷

Il Brillo Parlante, V. della Fontanella 12 (☎32 43 334; www.ilbrilloparlante.com). The wood-burning oven turns out pizza (€7-10); handmade pasta and small plates, including *pecorino* cheese with honey and walnuts (€8.50), set this place apart. Open M 5pm-1am, Tu-Su 12:30-3:30pm lunch, 3:30-5pm pizza only, 5-7:30pm bar only, 7:30pm-1am dinner. Reserve ahead. MC/V. ❷

BORGO AND PRATI (NEAR VATICAN CITY)

The streets near the Vatican are paved with bars and pizzerias that serve mediocre sandwiches at inflated prices. For better, much cheaper food, venture down **Via Cola di Rienzo** several blocks toward P. Cavour and explore the side streets.

Paninoteca da Guido e Patrizia, Borgo Pio 13 (☎68 75 491), near Castel Sant'Angelo. Casual environment and homey decor make this place popular with lunching locals. Guido holds court behind a well-stocked *tavola calda* (snack bar). Full meal (*primo, secondo*, and beverage) runs around €11. Open M-Sa 8am-6pm. Cash only. ❷

Franchi, V. Cola di Rienzo 200/204 (☎68 74 651; www.franchi.it). Especially delicious *fritti misti* (deep-fried zucchini flowers, artichoke hearts, and zucchini). 2 people can stuff themselves for around €15. Open M-Sa 9am-8:30pm. AmEx/MC/V. ❷

Cacio e Pepe, V. Giuseppe Avezzana 11 (☎32 17 268). From P. Mazzini, turn right on V. Settembrini, at P. dei Martiri di Belfiore, and again on V. G. Avezzana (a 20min. walk from P. di Risorgimento). Dine outside and enjoy the namesake pasta, piled high with olive oil, grated cheese, and freshly ground pepper (€6). Full lunch €5-10. Open M-F 12:30-3pm and 7:30-11pm, Sa 12:30-3pm. Cash only. ❷

TRASTEVERE

The waits are long and the street-side tables are cramped, but you can't get more Roman than Trastevere. The tiny cobblestone side streets winding in and out of the *piazze* are crowded with locals sitting at the cafes, stands, and restaurants.

▨ **Pizzeria San Callisto,** P. S. Callisto 9/A (☎581 82 56), off P. S. Maria. Simply the best pizza (€4-8) in Rome. Thin-crust pizzas so large they hang off the plates. Order takeout to avoid waits. Open Tu-Su 6:30pm-midnight. AmEx/MC/V. ❷

Augusto, P. de' Renzi 15 (☎58 03 798). Pastas (€5) appear almost immediately. Open Sept.-July M-F 12:30-3pm and 8-11pm, Sa 12:30-3pm. Cash only. ❶

La Piazzetta, V. Cardinale Merry del Val, 16B (☎58 06 241). Take V. Trastevere away from the Tiber and turn right on V. Cardinale Merry del Val. Eat outside under shady trees or inside under the discerning eyes of the dead fish on ice. Cover €2. *Primi* €7-12. Salads €7-8. Pizzas €5-9. Open daily noon-midnight. AmEx/MC/V. ❷

SAN LORENZO AND TERMINI

Tourist traps proliferate in the Termini area. There is a well-stocked **CONAD** supermarket on the lower floor of the Termini Station, just inside the V. Marsala entrance. (☎87 40 60 55. Open daily 8am-midnight.) In San Lorenzo, inexpensive food options with local character cater to budget-conscious students with discriminating palates. At night, map a route first and avoid walking alone.

▨ **Hostaria Romana da Dino,** V. dei Mille, 10 (☎49 14 25). Exit Termini near track 1, take a left on V. Marsala, a right on V. Vicenza, and a left on V. dei Mille. Look for the vertical, blue Pizzeria sign. Delectable pizzas (€5-7) and pastas (€4.50-5). Try the house wine for a mere €1.10 per 0.25L. Su-Tu and Th-Sa noon-3pm and 6:30-10:30pm. MC/V. ❶

Africa, V. Gaeta 26-28 (☎49 41 077), near P. Indipendenza. Africa has been serving Eritrean and Ethiopian food for 32 years. The meat-filled *sambusas* (€3) are a flavorful starter. Vegetarian *secondi* €8-11. Cover €1. Open Tu-Su 8am-2am. MC/V. ❷

Arancia Blu, V. d. Latini 65 (☎44 54 105), off V. Tiburtina. This elegant and popular vegetarian restaurant has an inspired menu, affordable in spite of its fine ingredients and upscale style. Phenomenal warm pesto salad (€7.50). Extensive wine list €12-130 per bottle. Chocolate tasting *menù* (€15). Open daily 8:30pm-midnight. Cash only. ❷

TESTACCIO

▨ **Il Volpetti Più,** V. Alessandro Volta 8 (☎57 44 306; www.volpetti.com). Turn left on V. A. Volta off V. Marmorata. This *tavola calda* serves lunch in large portions. Choose your food cafeteria-style, and battle the locals for a seat. Fresh salad, pasta, and pizza from €4. *Antipasti* €3-5. Open M-Sa 10:30am-3:30pm and 5:30-9:30pm. AmEx/MC/V. ❶

Il Cantinone, P. Testaccio 31/32 (☎57 46 253). M: B-Piramide. Go up V. Marmorata and turn left on V. G. B. Bodoni; P. Testaccio is after V. Luca della Robbia. Serves huge portions of pasta (*pappardelle* with boar sauce €8) and terrific house wine (€6 per L). Open M and W-Su noon-3pm and 7pm-midnight. AmEx/D/MC/V. ❸

DESSERT AND COFFEE

While gelato is everywhere in Rome, good gelato is not. Look for the signs of quality (See **The Ugly Duckling,** p. 578). Bakeries sell all kinds of cookies, pastries, and cakes, all priced by the *etto* (100g). Coffee is taken either standing up at the bar or sitting down at a table, with higher prices for the latter.

▨ **Gelato di San Crispino,** V. della Panetteria 42, (☎67 93 924), 2nd left off V. del Lavatore. Forget Prince Charming—a scoop from San Crispino's is worth wishing for at the Trevi fountain. Open Su-M and W-Th noon-12:30am, F-Sa noon-1:30am. Cash only.

▨ **Biscottificio Artigiano Innocenti,** V. della Luce 21, Travestevere (☎57 03 926). From P. Sonnino, take V. Giulio Cesare Santina and turn left on V. della Luce. The shop sells divine cookies and biscuits at a counter in its no-nonsense stockroom. Try the hazelnut, chocolate, and jam cookies (€2.50 for 10 cookies).

The Lion Bookshop and Café, V. dei Greci 33/36, P. di Spagna (☎326 54 007). This English-language bookstore has a cafe for thumbing through books while you sip espresso (€1.50-2.50). Open M 3:30-7:30pm, Tu-Su 10am-7:30pm. AmEx/MC/V.

Pasticceria Ebraico Boccione, V. del Portico d'Ottavia 1, Jewish Ghetto (☎68 78 637), on the corner of P. Costaguti under the white awning. This family-run bakery has a limited selection, including delicious challah twisted into croissants and filled with custard (€0.60). Su-Th 8am-7:30pm, F 8am-3:30pm. In summer closed Su 2-4pm.

Bar Giulia (a.k.a. Cafe Peru), V. Giulia 84, Ancient City (☎68 61 310), near P. V. Emanuele II. Serves possibly the cheapest, most *squisito* coffee in Rome (€0.60, at table €0.70) and adds your favorite liqueur free. Open M-Sa 5am-9:30pm. Cash only.

ENOTECHE (WINE BARS)

The tinkling of crystal in intimate settings differentiates *enoteche* from more rough-and-tumble pubs. These wine bars usually serve small dishes, like cheese selections, smoked meats, *antipasti*, and salads, which make light, budget meals. Romans eat dinner around 9pm, so they either go to *enoteche* before dinner or sip and nibble their way through the entire night.

▨ **Enoteca Trastevere,** V. della Lungaretta, 86, Trastevere (☎58 85 659). A block off P. S. Maria. Staff helps pick a bottle from the high-caliber wine list. Make a meal of cured meats and cheeses (€9-12). Arrive after 10pm, as things pick up around midnight. Wine €3.50-5 per glass. Open M-Sa 6pm-2:30am, Su 6pm-1am.

Trimani Wine Bar, V. Cernaia 37/B (☎44 69 630), near Termini, perpendicular to V. Volturno. Look to the menu for suggested wines to complement mixed meat plates (€9-13.50). Wines from €3-15 a glass. Happy hour 11:30am-12:30pm and 5:30-7pm. Open M-Sa 11:30am-3pm and 5:30pm-12:30am. AmEx/MC/V.

◉ SIGHTS

From ancient temples, medieval churches, and Renaissance basilicas to Baroque fountains and modern museums, *La Città Eterna* bursts with masterpieces. Dress modestly at churches and the Vatican. Travelers planning to visit many Roman monuments should consider the **Archeologica Card** (☎39 96 77 00; 7-day €22), valid at the Colosseum, Palantine Hill, and Baths of Caracalla, among others.

ANCIENT CITY

COLOSSEUM. This enduring symbol of the Eternal City—a hollowed-out marble structure that dwarfs every other ruin in Rome—once held as many as 50,000 spectators. Within 100 days of its AD 80 opening, some 5000 wild beasts perished in the arena. The floor once covered a labyrinth of brick cells, ramps, and elevators used to transport wild animals from cages up to arena level. Not only animals were killed for sport: men were also pitted against each other. *(M: B-Colosseo. Open daily late Mar.-Aug. 8:30am-7:15pm; Sept. 9am-7pm; Oct. 9am-6:30pm; Nov. to mid-Feb. 9am-4:30pm; mid-Feb. to Mar. 9am-5pm. Combined ticket with Palatine Hill €11. English-language tours with archaeologist daily 1-2 per hr. 9:45am-1:45pm and 3-5:15pm. €3.50.)*

PALATINE HILL. Legend has it that the Palatine Hill was home to the she-wolf who suckled brothers Romulus and Remus, mythical founders of Rome. The best way to attack the Palatine is from the stairs near the Forum's **Arch of Titus** (where ticket lines are shorter than at the Colosseum), which lead to gardens and lookouts. On the southwest side of the hill is an ancient village with the **Casa di Romulo,** alleged home of Romulus, and the podium of the **Temple of Cybele.** The stairs to the left lead to the **Casa di Livia,** home of Augustus's wife, which once connected to the **Casa Augusto** next door. Around the corner, the spooky **Cryptoporticus** tunnel ties Tiberius's palace to nearby buildings. **Domus Augustana** was once the emperors' private space; sprawling **Domus Flavia,** to its right, once held a gigantic octagonal fountain. Between them stands the **Stadium Palatinum,** or hippodrome, a sunken space once used as a riding school and now a museum with artifacts excavated from the hill. *(South of the Forum. Same hours and prices as Colosseum. Guided English-language tour daily 12:15pm. €3.50.)*

ROMAN FORUM. Etruscans and Greeks used the Forum as a marketplace, then early Romans founded a thatched-hut shanty town here in 753 BC. Enter through **Via Sacra,** Rome's oldest street, which leads to the **Arch of Titus.** In front of the **Curia** (Senate House), off V. Sacra to the right, was the **Comitium,** where male citizens came to vote and representatives gathered for public discussion. Bordering the Comitium is the large brick **Rostra** (speaker's platform), erected by Julius Caesar in 44 BC. The **market square** holds a number of shrines and sacred precincts, including the *Lapis Niger* (Black Stone), where Romulus was supposedly murdered by Republican senators; below are the underground ruins of a 6th-century BC altar and the oldest known Latin inscription in Rome. In the square, the **Three Sacred Trees of Rome**—olive, fig, and grape—have been replanted. The **Lower Forum** holds the eight-columned, 5th-century BC **Temple of Saturn,** next to the *Rostra*, which achieved mythological status during Rome's Golden Age, when it hosted Saturnalia, a raucous, anything-goes Roman winter party. At the end of Vicus Tuscus stands the **Temple of Castor and Pollux,** built to celebrate the 499 BC Roman defeat of the Etruscans. The **Temple of Vesta,** where Vestal Virgins kept the city's sacred fire lit for more than 1000 years, is next to the **House of the Vestal Virgins,** where they lived for 30 secluded years beginning at the ripe old age of seven. V.

Sacra continues out of the Forum proper to the Velia and the gargantuan **Basilica of Maxentius,** which once contained a gigantic bronze and marble statue of Constantine. *(M: B-Colosseo, or bus to P. Venezia. Main entrance is on V. dei Fori Imperiali, at Largo C. Ricci. Open daily in summer 8:30am-7:15pm, last entry 6:15pm; in winter 9am-4:15pm, last entry 3:30pm. English-language guided tour 12:30pm. Audio tour €3.50.)*

FORI IMPERIALI. Closed indefinitely for excavations, the **Fori Imperiali,** across the street from the Ancient Forum, is a complex of temples, basilicas, and public squares constructed in the first and second centuries, still visible from the railing at V. dei Fori Imperiali. Built between AD 107 and 113, the **Forum of Trajan** included a colossal equestrian statue of Trajan and an immense triumphal arch. At one end of the now-destroyed Forum, 2500 carved legionnaires march their way up the almost perfectly preserved ▓**Trajan's Column,** one of the greatest specimens of Roman relief-sculpture. The crowning statue is St. Peter, who replaced Trajan in 1588. The gray rock wall of the **Forum of Augustus** commemorates Augustus's victory over Caesar's murderers in 42 BC. The only remnant of **Vespasian's Forum** is the mosaic-filled **Chiesa della Santi Cosma e Damiano** across V. Cavour, near the Roman Forum. *(Visitors Center open daily 9am-6:30pm. Free.)*

CAPITOLINE HILL. Home to the original capitol, the **Monte Capitolino** still serves as the seat of the city government. Michelangelo designed its **Piazza di Campidoglio,** now home to the **Capitoline Museums** (p. 597). Stairs lead up to the rear of the 7th-century **Chiesa di Santa Maria in Aracoeli.** *(Santa Maria open daily 9am-12:30pm and 3-6:30pm. Donation requested.)* The gloomy **Mamertine Prison,** consecrated as the **Chiesa di San Pietro in Carcere,** lies down the hill from the back stairs of the Aracoeli. Imprisoned here, St. Peter baptized his captors with the waters that flooded his cell. *(Prison open daily in summer 9am-7pm; in winter 9am-12:30pm and 2-5pm. Donation requested.)* At the far end of the *piazza*, opposite the stairs, lies the turreted **Palazzo dei Senatori,** the home of Rome's mayor. *(Take any bus to P. Venezia. From P. Venezia, walk around to P. d'Aracoeli and take the stairs up the hill.)*

VELABRUM. The Velabrum area is in a Tiber flood plain, south of the Jewish Ghetto. At the bend of V. del Portico d'Ottavia, a shattered pediment and a few ivy-covered columns are all that remain of the once magnificent **Portico d'Ottavia.** The **Teatro di Marcello** next door was the model for the Colosseum's facade. One block south along V. Luigi Petroselli, the **Chiesa di Santa Maria in Cosmedin,** currently undergoing renovations, harbors the **Bocca della Verità,** a drain cover made famous by the film *Roman Holiday.* The river god's face on it will supposedly chomp any liar's hand. *(Chiesa open daily 9:30am-5:50pm.)*

DOMUS AUREA. Take a break from the relentless sun and enjoy the cacophony of birds chirping in the shady trees. Joggers, wild flowers, and ruins of a palatial estate now occupy Oppian Hill. This park houses a portion of Nero's "Golden House," which once covered a huge chunk of Rome. After deciding that he was a god, Nero had architects build a house worthy of his divinity. The Forum was reduced to a vestibule of the palace; Nero crowned it with the 35m *Colossus,* a huge statue of himself as the sun. *(Open daily 6:30am-9pm. Free.)*

CENTRO STORICO

VIA DEL CORSO AND PIAZZA VENEZIA. Shopping street **Via del Corso,** between P. del Popolo and busy P. Venezia, takes its name from its days as Rome's premier race course. **Palazzo Venezia** was one of the first Renaissance *palazzi* in the city. Mussolini used it as an office and delivered orations from its balcony, but today it's little more than a glorified roundabout dominated by the **Vittorio Emanuele II monument.**

THE PANTHEON. Architects still wonder how this 2000-year-old temple was erected. Its dome—a perfect half-sphere made of poured concrete without the support of vaults, arches, or ribs—is the largest of its kind. The light that enters

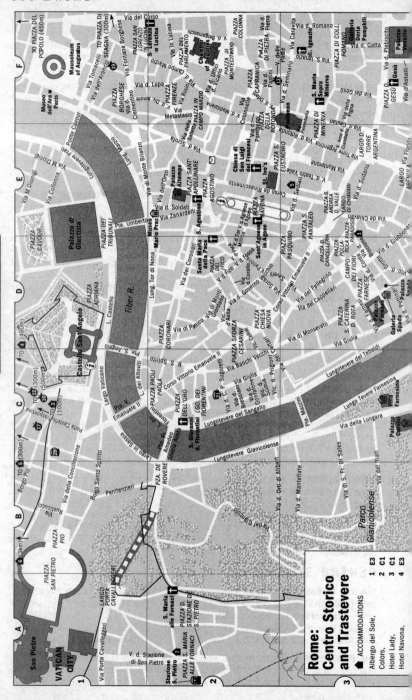

Rome: Centro Storico and Trastevere

▲ ACCOMMODATIONS

Albergo del Sole,	1 E3
Colors,	2 C1
Hotel Lady,	3 C1
Hotel Navona,	4 E3

ITALY

Hotel San Pietrino,	5	B1
Ostello par la Gioventù, Foro Italico (HI),	6	B1
Santa Maria Alle Fornaci,	7	A2
● FOOD		
Augusto,	8	C4
Bar da Benito,	9	E4
Cacio e Pepe,	10	C1
Il Cantinone,	11	C6
Franchi,	12	C1
Miscellanea,	13	F2
La Piazzetta,	14	D5
Pizza Art,	15	E4
Pizzeria San Callisto, Paninoteca da Guido e Patrizia,	16	C4
Trattoria da Gigetto,	17	C1
Trattoria da Settimio all'Arancio,	18	E4
Il Volpetti Più,	19	F1
	20	C6
● CAFES		
Bar Giulia,	21	C2
Biscottificio Artigiano Innocenti,	22	D5
Pasticceria Ebraico Boccione,	23	E4
■ NIGHTLIFE		
Artu Café,	24	C4
Caffè della Scala,	25	C4
Distilleria Clandestine,	26	D6
Jungle,	27	C6
The Proud Lion,	28	C1

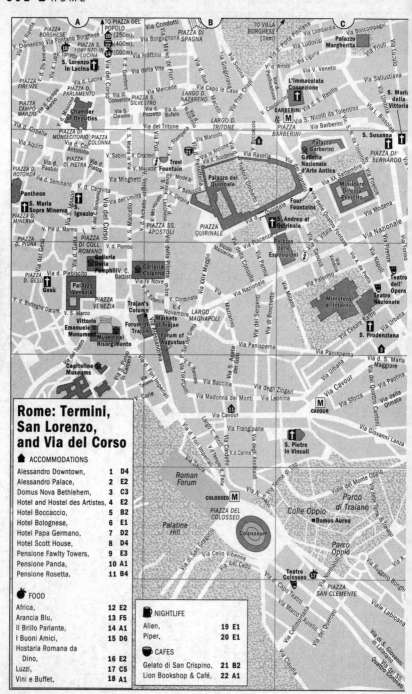

ITALY

Rome: Termini, San Lorenzo, and Via del Corso

🏠 ACCOMMODATIONS

Alessandro Downtown,	1	D4
Alessandro Palace,	2	E2
Domus Nova Bethlehem,	3	C3
Hotel and Hostel des Artistes,	4	E2
Hotel Boccaccio,	5	B2
Hotel Bolognese,	6	E1
Hotel Papa Germano,	7	D2
Hotel Scott House,	8	D4
Pensione Fawlty Towers,	9	E3
Pensione Panda,	10	A1
Pensione Rosetta,	11	B4

🍎 FOOD

Africa,	12	E2
Arancia Blu,	13	F5
Il Brillo Parlante,	14	A1
I Buoni Amici,	15	D6
Hostaria Romana da Dino,	16	E2
Luzzi,	17	C5
Vini e Buffet,	18	A1

🍷 NIGHTLIFE

Alien,	19	E1
Piper,	20	E1

☕ CAFES

Gelato di San Crispino,	21	B2
Lion Bookshop & Café,	22	A1

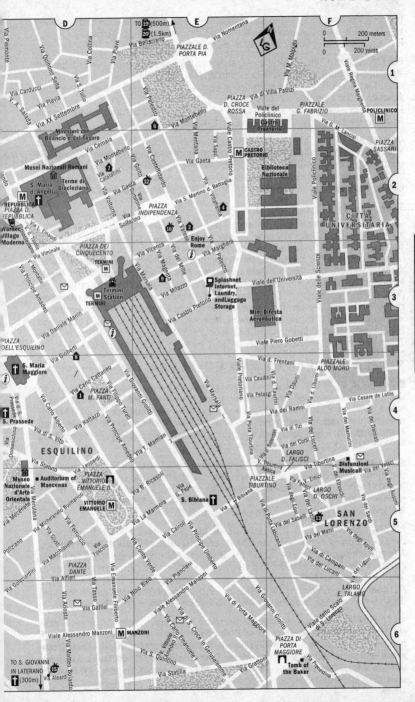

the roof was used as a sundial and to indicate the dates of equinoxes and solstices. In AD 606, it was consecrated as the **Chiesa di Santa Maria ad Martyres.** *(In P. della Rotonda. Open M-Sa 8:30am-7:30pm, Su 9am 6pm. Free.)*

PIAZZA NAVONA. Originally an AD first-century stadium, the *piazza* hosted wrestling matches, track and field events, and mock naval battles in which the stadium was flooded and filled with fleets. Each of the river god statues in Bernini's **Fountain of the Four Rivers** represents one of the four continents of the globe (as known then): Ganges for Asia, Danube for Europe, Nile for Africa, and Río de la Plata for the Americas. *(Open daily 6:45am-12:45pm and 4-7:45pm.)*

CAMPO DEI FIORI. Across C. Vittorio Emanuele II from P. Navona, Campo dei Fiori is one of the last authentically Roman areas of the *centro storico*. Home to a bustling market Monday through Saturday mornings, it becomes a hot spot at night. The Renaissance **Palazzo Farnese,** built by Alessandro Farnese, the first Counter-Reformation pope, dominates P. Farnese, south of the Campo.

THE JEWISH GHETTO

Rome's Jewish community is the oldest in Europe—Israelites came in 161 BC as ambassadors from Judas Maccabei, asking for help against invaders. The Ghetto, a tiny area to which Pope Paul IV confined the Jews in 1555, was dissolved in 1870 but is still the center of Rome's Jewish population. In the center are **Piazza Mattei** and the 16th-century **Fontana delle Tartarughe.** Nearby is the **Chiesa di Sant'Angelo in Pescheria** where Jews, forced to attend mass, resisted by stuffing wax in their ears. *(V. de Funari, after P. Campitelli. Church under restoration indefinitely.)* The **Sinagoga Ashkenazita,** on the Tiber near the Theater of Marcellus, was bombed in 1982; guards now search all visitors. Inside is the **Jewish Museum,** which has ancient Torahs and Holocaust artifacts. *(Synagogue open for services only. Museum open Oct.-May Su-Th 10am-10pm, F 10am-4pm; June-Sept. Su-Th 10am-7pm, F 9am-4pm. €7.50, students €3.)*

PIAZZA DI SPAGNA AND ENVIRONS

■**FONTANA DI TREVI.** The bombastic **Fontana di Trevi** has enough presence to turn even the most jaded visitor into a romantic mush. Legend has it that a traveler who throws a coin into the fountain is ensured a speedy return to Rome; one who tosses two will fall in love there. Opposite is the Baroque **Chiesa dei Santi Vincenzo e Anastasio.** The crypt preserves the hearts and lungs of popes who served from 1590 to 1903. *(Open daily 7am-noon and 4-7pm.)*

SCALINATA DI SPAGNA. Designed by an Italian, paid for by the French, named for the Spaniards, occupied by the British, and currently featuring American greats like Ronald McDonald, the **Spanish Steps** exude worldliness. The pink house to the right is where John Keats died; it's now the **Keats-Shelley Memorial Museum.** *(Open M-F 9am-1pm and 3-6pm, Su 11am-2pm and 3-6pm. €3.50.)*

PIAZZA DEL POPOLO. In the center of the "people's square," once the venue for the execution of heretics, is the 3200-year-old **Obelisk of Pharaoh Ramses II** that Augustus brought back from Egypt in AD 10. The **Church of Santa Maria del Popolo** contains Renaissance and Baroque masterpieces. *(Open M-Sa 7am-noon and 4-7pm, Su 8am-1:30pm and 4:30-7:30pm.)* Two exquisite Caravaggios, *The Conversion of St. Paul* and *Crucifixion of St. Peter,* are in the **Cappella Cerasi,** which Raphael designed. *(Open M-Sa 7am-noon and 4-7pm, Su 7:30am-1:30pm and 4:30-7:30pm.)*

VILLA BORGHESE. To celebrate his purchase of a cardinalship, Scipione Borghese built the **Villa Borghese** north of P. di Spagna and V. V. Veneto. Its huge park houses three art museums: world-renowned **Galleria Borghese,** stark **Galleria Nazionale d'Arte Moderna,** and intriguing **Museo Nazionale Etrusco di Villa Giulia.** North are the **Santa Priscilla catacombs** and the **Villa Ada** gardens. *(M: A-Spagna and follow the signs. Open M-F 9:30am-6pm, Sa-Su 9:30am-7pm. €8.50.)*

VATICAN CITY

Once the mightiest power in Europe, the foothold of the Roman Catholic Church now lies on 108½ autonomous acres within Rome. The Vatican has symbolically preserved its independence by minting coins (euro with the Pope's face), running a separate press and postal system, maintaining an army of Swiss Guards, and hoarding art in the **Musei Vaticani.** (M: A-Ottaviano. Or catch bus #64, 271, or 492 from Termini or Largo Argentina, #62 from P. Barberini, or #23 from Testaccio.)

BASILICA DI SAN PIETRO (ST. PETER'S). A colonnade by Bernini leads from **Piazza San Pietro** to the church. The **obelisk** in the *piazza*'s center is framed by two fountains; stand on the round discs set in the pavement and the quadruple rows of the colonnade will visually resolve into one perfectly aligned row. Above the colonnade are 140 statues of saints; those on the basilica represent Christ, John the Baptist, and the Apostles (except for Peter). The pope opens the **Porta Sancta** (Holy Door) every 25 years by knocking in the bricks with a silver hammer; on warm Wednesday mornings, he holds papal audiences on a platform in the *piazza*. The basilica itself rests on the reputed site of St. Peter's tomb. Inside, metal lines mark the lengths of other major world churches. To the right, Michelangelo's *Pietà* has been protected by bullet-proof glass since 1972, when an axe-wielding fiend smashed Christ's nose and broke Mary's hand. The climb to the top of the **dome** might very well be worth the heart attack it could cause. An elevator will take you up about 300 of the 350 stairs. (Modest dress required. Multilingual confession available. Church: Open daily Apr.-Sept. 7am-7pm; Oct.-Mar. 7am-6pm. Mass M-Sa 8:30, 10, 11am, noon, 5pm; Su 9, 10:30, 11:30am, 12:15, 1, 4, 5:30pm. Free. Dome: From inside the basilica, exit the building and re-enter the door to the far left. Open daily Apr.-Sept. 8am-5pm; Oct.-Mar. 8am-4pm. Stairs €4, elevator €7.)

SISTINE SIGHTSEEING. The Sistine Chapel is at the end of the standard route through the Vatican Museums (p. 597), and it's extremely crowded. Go straight to the Sistine Chapel to enjoy Michelangelo's masterpiece, and then backtrack. It's relatively empty early in the morning.

SISTINE CHAPEL. Since its completion in the 16th century, the Sistine Chapel (named for its founder, Pope Sixtus IV) has served as the chamber in which the College of Cardinals elects new popes. Michelangelo's ceiling, at the pinnacle of artistic creation, gleams post-restoration. The meticulous compositions hover above, each section depicting a story from Genesis, each scene framed by *ignudi* (young nude males). Michelangelo did not in fact paint flat on his back, but standing up craning backward, a position that irreparably strained his neck and eyes. *The Last Judgment* fills the altar wall; the figure of Christ, as judge, sits in the upper center surrounded by saints and Mary. Michelangelo painted himself as a flayed human skin hanging between heaven and hell. The cycle was completed by 1483 by artists under Perugino, including Botticelli, Ghirlandaio, Roselli, Pinturicchio, Signorelli, and della Gatta. The frescoes on the side walls predate Michelangelo's ceiling; on the right, scenes from the life of Moses parallel scenes of Christ's life on the left. (Admission included with Vatican Museums, p. 597.)

CASTEL SANT'ANGELO. Built by Hadrian (AD 117-138) as a mausoleum for himself and his family, this mass of brick and stone has been a fortress, prison, and palace. When the plague struck Rome, Pope Gregory the Great saw an angel at its top; the plague soon abated, and the edifice was rededicated to the angel. The fortress offers an incomparable view of Rome. (Walk along the river from St. Peter's toward Trastevere. Open in summer Tu-Su 9am-7:30pm; in winter daily 9am-7pm. €5. Audio tour €4.)

TRASTEVERE

On V. di Santa Cecilia, through the gate and the courtyard is the **Basilica di Santa Cecilia in Trastevere.** Carlo Maderno's statue of Santa Cecilia is under the altar.

(Open daily 9:30am-12:30pm and 4-6:30pm. Donation requested. Cloisters open M-F 10:15am-12:15pm, Sa-Su 11:15am-12:15pm. Cloisters €2.50. Crypt €2.50.) From P. Sonnino, V. della Lungaretta leads west to P. S. Maria in Trastevere, home to the 4th-century **Chiesa di Santa Maria in Trastevere.** *(Open M-Sa 9am-5:30pm, Su 8:30-10:30am and noon-5:30pm.)* North of the *piazza* are the Rococo **Galleria Corsini,** V. della Lungara 10, and the **Villa Farnesina** (see p. 598), once home to Europe's wealthiest man. Atop the Gianicolo Hill is the **Chiesa di San Pietro in Montorio,** built on the spot believed to be that of St. Peter's upside-down crucifixion. Inside is del Piombo's *Flagellation,* which uses Michelangelo's designs. Next door is Bramante's ◼**Tempietto,** which commemorates Peter's martyrdom. Rome's **botanical gardens** have a rose garden with the bush from which all the world's roses are said to descend. *(Church and Tempietto open Tu-Su May-Oct. 9:30am-12:30pm and 4-6pm; Nov.-Apr. 9:30am-12:30pm and 2-4pm. Gardens open M-Sa Oct.-Mar. 9:30am-5:30pm; Apr.-Oct. 9:30am-6:30pm.)*

NEAR TERMINI

◼**PIAZZA DEL QUIRINALE.** At the southeast end of V. del Quirinale, this *piazza* occupies the summit of one of Ancient Rome's seven hills. In its center, statues of Castor and Pollux stand on either side of an obelisk from the Mausoleum of Augustus. The President of the Republic resides in the **Palazzo del Quirinale,** its Baroque architecture by Bernini, Maderno, and Fontana. Bernini's ◼**Four Fountains** are built into the intersection of V. delle Quattro Fontane and V. del Quirinale. *(Palazzo closed to the public. San Carlo open M-F 10am-1pm and 3-6pm, Sa 10am-1pm.)*

BASILICA OF SANTA MARIA MAGGIORE. Crowning the Esquiline Hill, this is officially part of Vatican City. To the right of the altar, a marble slab marks **Bernini's tomb.** The 14th-century mosaics in the **loggia** *(open daily with guided tour at 1pm; €3)* depict the August snowfall that showed the pope where to build the church; the snowstorm is re-enacted each August with white flower petals. *(Modest dress required. Open daily 7am-7pm. Audio tour €4.)*

SOUTHERN ROME

The area south of the center is home to the city's best nightlife as well as some of its grandest churches. Residential area EUR has strangely square architecture and a beautiful, artificial lake. Take bus #714 or M: B-EUR Palasport.

◼**APPIAN WAY.** The Appian Way was the most important thoroughfare of Ancient Rome. Early Christians secretly constructed maze-like catacombs under the ashes of their persecutors. Sundays, when the street is closed to traffic, take a break from the city to bike through the countryside. *(M: B-S. Giovanni to P. Appio; take bus #218 from P. di S. Giovanni to V. Appia Antica; get off at the info office.)* **San Callisto** is the largest catacomb in Rome. Its four levels once held 16 popes, St. Cecilia, and 500,000 other Christians. *(V. Appia Antica 126, entrance on road parallel to V. Appia. Open M-Tu and Th-Su 9am-noon and 2-5pm. €5.)* Catacomb **Santa Domitilla** houses an intact 3rd-century portrait of Christ and the Apostles. *(V. delle Sette Chiese 282. Facing V. Ardeatina from San Callisto exit, cross the street and walk right up V. Sette Chiese. Open Feb.-Dec. M and W-Su 9am-noon and 2-5pm. €5. Cash only.)*

CAELIAN HILL. Southeast of the Colosseum, the Caelian was the hill where elite Romans made their home in ancient times. The ◼**Chiesa di San Giovanni in Laterano** was the seat of the papacy until the 14th century; founded by Constantine in AD 314, it is Rome's oldest Christian basilica. The two golden reliquaries over the altar contain the skulls of St. Peter and St. Paul. Outside to the left, **Scala Santa** has what are believed to be the 28 steps used by Jesus outside Pontius Pilate's home. *(Modest dress required. M: A-S. Giovanni or bus #16. Through the archway of the wall. Open daily 7am-6:30pm. €2, students €1.)* The **Chiesa di San Clemente** is split into three levels, each from a different era. A fresco cycle by Masolino dating from the 1420s graces its

Chapel of Santa Caterina. *(M: B-Colosseo. Turn left down V. Labicana away from the Forum. Open M-Sa 9am-12:30pm and 3-6pm, Su 10am-12:30pm and 3-6pm. €5, students €3.50.)*

AVENTINE HILL. The **Roseto Comunale,** a public rose garden, is host to the annual Premio Roma, the worldwide competition for the best blossom. *(V. d. Valle Murcia, across the Circus Maximus from the Palatine Hill. Open May-June daily 8am-7:30pm.)* Just before the crest of the hill, stroll among orange trees at **Giardini degli Aranci.** *(Open daily dawn-dusk.)* The top left-hand panel of the wooden front doors at nearby **Chiesa di Santa Sabina** is one of the earliest-known representations of the Crucifixion. V. S. Sabina runs along the crest of the hill to **Piazza dei Cavalieri di Malta,** home of the crusading order of the Knights of Malta. Through the ▓**keyhole** in the cream-colored, arched gate is a perfectly framed view of the dome of St. Peter's Cathedral.

🏛 MUSEUMS

Etruscans, emperors, and popes have been busily stuffing Rome with artwork for several millennia, leaving behind a city teeming with collections. Museums are generally closed on Mondays, Sunday afternoons, and holidays.

▓ GALLERIA BORGHESE. Upon entering, don't miss Mark Antonio's **ceiling,** depicting the Roman conquest of Gaul. **Room I,** on the right, houses Canova's sexy statue of **Paolina Borghese** portrayed as Venus triumphant with Paris's golden apple. The next rooms display the most famous sculptures by Bernini: a striking **David,** crouching with his slingshot; **Apollo and Daphne;** the weightless body in **Rape of Proserpina;** and weary-looking Aeneas in **Eneo e Anchise.** Paintings in the **Caravaggio Room** include *Self Portrait as Bacchus* and *David and Goliath.* The collection continues in the **pinacoteca** upstairs, accessible from the gardens around the back by a winding staircase. **Room IX** holds Raphael's ▓**Deposition** while Sodoma's *Pietà* graces **Room XII.** Look for Bernini's self portraits, del Conte's *Cleopatra and Lucrezia,* Rubens's *Pianto sul Cristo Morto,* and Titian's *Amor Sacro e Amor Profano.* *(Vle. del Museo Borghese. M: A-Spagna; take the Villa Borghese exit. Open Tu-Su 9am-7:30pm. Entrance every 2hr. Reserve ahead. Tickets €8.50. Audio tour €5.)*

VATICAN MUSEUMS. The Vatican Museums constitute one of the world's greatest art collections. Ancient, Renaissance, and modern statues and paintings are rounded out with papal odds and ends. The **Museo Pio-Clementino** has the world's greatest collection of antique sculpture. Two Molossian hounds guard the **Stanza degli Animali,** a marble menagerie. Among other gems is the ▓**Apollo Belvedere.** From the last room, the Simonetti Stairway climbs to the **Museo Etrusco,** filled with artifacts from Tuscany and northern Lazio. Its landing is where the long trudge to the Sistine Chapel begins, passing through the **Galleria degli Arazzi** (tapestries), the **Galleria delle Mappe** (maps), the **Apartamento di Pio V** (where there is a sneaky shortcut to *la Sistina*), the **Stanza Sobieski,** and the **Stanza della Immaculata Concezione.** A door leads into the first of the four ▓**Stanze di Rafaele,** apartments built for Pope Julius II. One *stanza* features Raphael's **School of Athens,** painted as a trial piece for Julius, who fired his other painters and commissioned Raphael to decorate the entire suite. Take a staircase to the frescoed Borgia Apartments, which house the **Museum of Modern Religious Art,** or go to the Sistine Chapel (p. 595). On the way out of the Sistine Chapel, take a look at the **Room of the Aldobrandini Marriage,** which contains ancient Roman frescoes. The Vatican's painting collection, the **pinacoteca,** spans eight centuries and is one of the best in Rome. *(Walk north from P.S. Pietro along the wall of the Vatican City for 10 blocks. ☎ 69 88 49 47; www.vatican.va. Open Mar.-Oct. M-F 10am-4:45pm, Sa 10am-2:45pm; Nov.-Feb. M-Sa 10am-1:45pm. Last entrance 1¼hr. before closing. €13, with ISIC €8. Open last Su of the month 9am-1:45pm. Free.)*

MUSEI CAPITOLINI. This collection of ancient sculpture is the world's first public museum of ancient art. The original statue of **Marcus Aurelius,** Bernini's **Head of Medusa,** and the famous **Capitoline Wolf**—a statue that has symbolized the city of

Rome since antiquity—occupy the first floor. The **pinacoteca's** masterpieces include Bellini's *Portrait of a Young Man*, Caravaggio's *St. John the Baptist* and *Gypsy Fortune-Teller*, Rubens's *Romulus and Remus Fed by the Wolf*, and Titian's *Baptism of Christ*. (On Capitoline Hill behind the Vittorio Emanuele II monument. ☎82 05 91 27. Open Tu-Su 9am-8pm. €6.50-8, students with ISIC €4.50-6.)

OTHER COLLECTIONS. The **Villa Farnesina** was the sumptuous home of the one-time wealthiest man in Europe, Agostino "il Magnifico" Chigi, and now displays decadent artwork. The **Stanza delle Nozze** (Marriage Room), is particularly noteworthy. (V. della Lungara 230. Across from Palazzo Corsini on Lungotevere della Farnesina. ☎68 02 72 67. Open M-Sa 9am-1pm; 1st Su of the month 9am-1pm. Last entrance 12:40pm. €5.) The **Museo Nazionale D'Arte Antica's** collection of 12th- through 18th-century art is split between Palazzo Barberini and Palazzo Corsini, in different parts of the city. **Palazzo Barberini** contains paintings from the medieval through Baroque periods, while the **Galleria Corsini** holds works by 17th- and 18th-century painters from Rubens to Caravaggio. (Palazzo: V. Barberini 18. Open Tu-Su 9am-7:30pm. €5. Galleria Corsini: V. della Lungara 10. Opposite Villa Farnesina in Trastevere. Open Tu-Su; entrance from 9:30-9:45am, 11-11:15am, and 12:30-12:45pm. €4.) The fascinating **Museo Nazionale Romano Palazzo Massimo alle Terme** covers the art of the Roman Empire, including the *Lancellotti Discus Thrower*. (Largo di V. Peretti 1, in P. dei Cinquecento. Open Tu-Su 9am-7:45pm. €5.) Differently themed *Museo Nazionale* are located around the city.

♫ ENTERTAINMENT

The weekly *Roma C'è* (with a section in English) and *Time Out*, both available at newsstands, have comprehensive and up-to-date club, movie, and event listings.

THEATER AND CINEMA

The **Festival Roma-Europa** (www.romaeuropa.net) in late summer brings a number of world-class acts to Rome. For year-round performances of classic Italian theater, **Teatro Argentina**, Largo di Torre Argentina 52, is the matriarch of all Italian venues. (☎684 00 01 11. Box office open M-F 10am-2pm and 3-7pm, Sa 10am-2pm. Tickets €14-26, students €12-21. AmEx/D/MC/V.) **Teatro Colosseo**, V. Capo d'Africa 5/A, usually features work by foreign playwrights translated into Italian, but also hosts an English-language theater night. (☎70 04 932. M: B-Colosseo. Box office open Sept.-Apr. Tu-Sa 6-9:30pm. Tickets €10-20, students €8.)

Most English-language films are dubbed into Italian; for films in their original languages, check newspapers for listings with a **v.o.** or **l.o.** The theater of

Italian director Nanni Moretti, **Nuovo Sacher,** Largo Ascianghi 1, shows independent films. (☎58 18 116. Films in the original language M-Tu. €7, matinee €4.50.)

MUSIC

Founded by Palestrina in the 16th century, the **Accademia Nazionale di Santa Cecilia,** V. Vittoria 6, off V. del Corso (☎36 11 064 or 800 90 70 80; www.santacecilia.it) remains the best in classical music performance. Concerts are held at the **Parco della Musica,** V. Pietro di Coubertin 30, near P. del Popolo. (www.musicaperroma.it. Tickets at Parco della Musica. Regular season runs Sept.-June. €15, students €8.) Known as one of Europe's best jazz clubs, ▨**Alexanderplatz Jazz Club,** V. Ostia 9, is decorated with messages left on its walls by old greats. The club moves outside to the Villa Celimontana during summer. (☎39 74 21 71; www.alexanderplatz.it. M: A-Ottaviano. Required membership €10. Open daily Sept.-May 9pm-2am. Shows start at 10pm.) The **Cornetto Free Music Festival Roma Live** (www.cornettoalgida.it) has attracted the likes of Pink Floyd and the Black Eyed Peas; it takes place at various venues throughout the city during summer.

SPECTATOR SPORTS

Though May brings tennis and equestrian events, sports revolve around *calcio*, or football. Rome has two teams in *Serie A*, Italy's prestigious league: **S.S. Lazio** and **A.S. Roma.** Matches are held at the **Stadio Olimpico**, in Foro Italico, almost every Sunday from September to June. If possible, check out the two Roma-Lazio games, which often prove decisive in the race for the championship. Single-game tickets (from €16) can be bought at team stores like **A.S. Roma**, P. Colonna 360 (☎67 86 514; www.asroma.it. Tickets sold daily 10am-6:30pm. AmEx/MC/V), and **Lazio Point,** V. Farini 34/36, near Termini. (☎48 26 688. Open daily 9am-7pm. AmEx/MC/V.) Tickets can also be obtained at the stadium before games, but beware of long lines and the possibility of tickets running out. If you're buying last minute, watch out for overpriced or fake tickets.

▢ SHOPPING

No trip to Italy is complete without a bit of shopping. There are four kinds of clothing shops in Rome. International chain stores like **Motivi, Mango, Stefanel, Intimissimi, Zara,** and the ubiquitous **United Colors of Benetton,** are supplemented by techno-blasting teen stores in the city center, boutiques like **Ethic** and **Havana** in the *centro storico* and throughout the city, and designer shrines like **Cavalli, Dolce & Gabbana,** and **Prada,** with their cardiac-arrest-inducing prices.

Via del Corso, the main street connecting P. del Popolo and P. Venezia, offers high- and low-end, Euro-chic leather goods, men's suits, and silk ties, but beware of tourist traps. Across the river from V. d. Corso, **Via Cola di Rienzo** offers a more leisurely shopping approach with stores like **Mandarina Duck,** Stefanel, and Benetton. Unique boutiques and designer stores cluster around the Spanish Steps and V. dei Condotti. Most of the fancy-schmancy stores—**Armani, Bruno Magli, Dolce & Gabbana, Gianni Versace, Gucci, Prada, Salvatore Ferragamo**—can be found on **V. dei Condotti.** Italian favorite The **General Store,** V. della Scala 62a (☎58 17 675), sells discounted Diesel, Adidas, and Nike. Authentic Euro-chic clothing stores on **Via dei Giubbonari,** off Campo dei Fiori, will have you dressed to the nines before eight.

OUTDOOR MARKETS

▨ **Porta Portese,** in Trastevere. Tram #8 from Largo d. Torre Argentina. This gigantic flea market is a surreal experience, with booths selling lots of items you never knew you needed. Keep your friends close and your money closer. Open Su 5am-1:30pm.

Campo dei Fiori, in the *centro storico*. Tram #8 or bus #64. Transformed daily by stalls of fruit, vegetables, meat, poultry, and fish. Also find dried fruit, nuts, spices, fresh flowers, and the usual basic cotton tops, skirts, socks, and knock-off designer bags. Open M-Sa 7am until vendors decide their wares have run out (usually 1:30pm).

◪ NIGHTLIFE

Though *enoteche* tend to be the primary destination for many locals, pubs are still a fun way to knock a few back without covers. Many are of the Irish variety, and the best are in Campo dei Fiori. Italian discos are flashy and fun, and may have spoken or unspoken dress codes. Clubs in many areas of the city close in the summer in favor areas such as Fregene or Frascati, where clubs stay open until 5am and club-goers party on the beach until the first trains depart for Rome.

◪ Caffé della Scala, P. della Scala 4 (☎58 03 610), on V. della Scala before P. San Egidio. In nice weather the tables at this cafe-bar line the neighboring street of V. della Scala day and night. Drinks have unusual ingredients, like whiskey, creme of cocoa, and cardamom pods in "Christian Alexander;" Open daily 5:30pm-2am. Cash only.

The Proud Lion Pub, Borgo Pio 36 (☎68 32 841). A tiny pub in the Vatican area whose Roman location belies its Scottish atmosphere. Beer €4. Open daily noon-2am.

Artu Café, Largo Fumasoni Biondi 5 (☎58 80 398), in P. San Egidio, behind Santa Maria. Patrons swear this bar is the best in Trastevere. Beer €4.50. Wine €3-5.50 per glass. Martinis €6-7. Free snack buffet 7:30-9pm. Open Tu-Su 6pm-2am. MC/V.

Distillerie Clandestine, V. Libetta 13 (☎57 30 51 02). Hosts a restaurant with live music and DJ. Cover F-Sa €20. Open Sept. to mid-June W-Sa 8:30pm-3am.

Jungle, V. di Monte Testaccio 95 (☎33 37 20 86 94; www.jungleclubroma.com). A rock feel pervades on F; it becomes a smoky bar full of Italian goths on Sa. Extravagant yet disorienting light effects. Cover €10. Open F-Sa midnight-4am.

Gilda-Alien-Piper, (www.gildabar.it). With steep covers and exclusive guest lists, this nightclub empire caters to the hipsters of Roman nightlife. In the summer, Piper and Alien move to Gilda on the Beach, located in Fregene near Fiumicino, 30km from Rome.

Alien, V. Velletri 13-19 (☎84 12 212). One of the biggest discos in Rome. Attracts a well-dressed crowd. Cover €15, includes 1 drink; Sa €20. Open Tu-Su midnight-4:30am.

Piper, V. Tagliamento 9 (☎85 55 398). North of Termini. From V. XX Settembre, take V. Piave (V. Salaria). Turn right on V. Po (V. Tagliamento). Or take bus #319 from Termini to Tagliamento. Caters to a more exclusive crowd, with international DJs spinning 70s, disco, house, rock, and underground. Cover €15-20, includes 1 drink. Open F-Sa 11pm-4:30am.

Gilda on the Beach, Lungomare di Ponente 11 (☎66 56 06 49). Ultra-cool clientele make the pilgrimage to Gilda for 4 dance floors, a private beach, a pool, and a restaurant. Cover €20. Disco open daily 11pm-4am. Dinner served from 8:30pm. Open May-Sept. AmEx/MC/V.

▣ DAYTRIP FROM ROME: TIVOLI

From M: B-Rebibbia, exit the station, turn right, and follow signs for Tivoli through an underpass to reach the other side of V. Tiburtina. Take the blue COTRAL bus to Tivoli. Tickets (€1.60) are sold in the metro station or in the bar next door. Once the bus reaches Tivoli (35-45min.), get off at Ple. delle Nazioni Unite. The return bus to Rome stops across the street from the tourist office, which offers maps and bus schedules. (☎0774 31 12 49. Open Tu-Su 10am-6pm.) There is also an information kiosk in Ple. delle Nazioni Unite with free maps.

Tivoli is a beautifully preserved medieval town whose villas once owned by Latin poets Horace, Catullus, and Propertius, are the major attraction. The tourist office provides a **map** with walking tours to temple ruins, a 15th-century castle, and Gothic-style houses. **Villa d'Este,** a castle with a fountain-filled garden, was intended to recreate an ancient Roman *nymphaea* and pleasure palace. (☎0774 31 20 70; www.villadestetivoli.info. Open Tu-Su May-Aug. 8:30am-6:45pm; Sept. 8:30am-6:15pm; Oct. 8:30am-5:30pm; Nov.-Jan. 8:30am-4pm; Feb. 8:30am-4:30pm; Mar. 8:30am-5:15pm; Apr. 8:30am-6:30pm. €9. Audio tour €4.) **◪ Villa Gregoriana,** at the other end of town, is a park with hiking trails and views of the well-preserved **Temple of Vesta.** (☎ 0639 96 77 61. Open Apr. to mid-Oct. 10am-6:30pm; mid-Oct. to Nov. and Mar. 10am-2:30pm; Dec.-Feb. by reservation only. €4. Audio tour €4.)

LOMBARDY (LOMBARDIA)

Part of the industrial triangle that drives Italy's economy, home to fashion mecca Milan, and producer of rice fields as lush as China's, Lombardy is one of the most prosperous regions of Italy. The Lombards who ruled the area after the fall of the Romans had close relations with the Franks and the Bavarians, and the region's modern culture has much in common with the traditions of its northern neighbors.

MILAN (MILANO)   ☎ 02

Unlike Rome, Venice, or Florence, which wrap themselves in veils of historic allure, Milan (pop. 1,400,000), once the capital of the western half of the Roman Empire, presents itself simply as it is: rushed, refined, and cosmopolitan. Home to Da Vinci's *Last Supper*, Milan owes much of its artistic heritage to the medieval Visconti and Sforza families, and its culture to Austrian, French, and Spanish occupiers. Now that Italians run the show, the city flourishes as the country's producer of cutting-edge style, hearty risotto, and die-hard soccer fans.

▐ TRANSPORTATION

Flights: Malpensa Airport (MXP), 48km from the city, handles intercontinental flights. **Malpensa Express** leaves from Stazione Nord for the airport. Accessible via Cadorna metro station (40min., €5). **Linate Airport (LIN),** 7km away, covers domestic and European flights. From there, take **Starfly buses** (20min., €2.50) to Stazione Centrale, which is quicker than bus #73 (€1) to San Babila Metro Station. Some budget airlines fly into **Orio al Serio Airport (BGY)** in Bergamo (p. 607).

Trains: Stazione Centrale (☎ 89 20 21; www.trenitalia.com), in P. Duca d'Aosta on M2. Trains run 1 per hr. to: **Bergamo** (1hr., €4.10); **Florence** (3½hr., €15-33); **Rome** (7hr., €52-73); **Turin** (2hr., €8.20); **Venice** (3hr., €27).

Buses: Stazione Centrale. Intercity buses tend to be less convenient and more expensive than trains. **Autostradale, SAL, SIA,** and other carriers leave from P. Castello (M1: Cairoli) and Porta Garibaldi for **Bergamo,** the **Lake Country, Trieste,** and **Turin.**

Public Transportation: The **Metro** (Metropolitana Milanese, or **M**) runs 6am-midnight. Line #1 (red) stretches from the *pensioni* district east of Stazione Centrale, through the center of town, and west to the youth hostel. Line #2 (green) connects Milan's 3 train stations. Use the **bus** system for trips outside the city proper. Metro tickets can be purchased at *tabaccherie,* ticket booths, and station machines. Single-fare tickets €1, 1-day pass €3, 2-day €5.50, 10 trips €9.20. White **taxis** are omnipresent.

▐ ORIENTATION AND PRACTICAL INFORMATION

Milan resembles a giant bull's-eye, defined by its ancient concentric city walls. In the outer rings lie suburbs built during the 50s and 60s to house southern immigrants. In the inner circle are four squares: **Piazza del Duomo,** where **Via Orefici, Via Mazzini,** and **Corso Vittorio Emanuele II** meet; **Piazza Castello** and the attached **Largo Cairoli,** near the Castello Sforzesco; **Piazza Cordusio,** connected to Largo Cairoli by

ITALY

Milan

▲ ACCOMMODATIONS
Camping Città di Milano, 4
La Cordata, 8
Hotel Amo, 16
Hotel Aurora, 18
Hotel Cà Grande, 13
Hotel Eva, 15
Hotel Malta, 14
Hotel San Tomaso, 17

◆ FOOD
Big Pizza: Da Noi 2, 9
Caffè Vecchia Brera, 2
Il Forno dei Navigli, 11
Il Panino Giusto, 19
Peck, 5
Princi il Bread B&B, 3

★ NIGHTLIFE
L'elephant, 20
Flying Circus, 6
Old Fashion Café, 1
Scimmie, 12
Le Trottoir, 10
Yguana Cafe
Restaurant, 7

Around Stazione Centrale

Via Dante; and Piazza San Babila, the entrance to the business and fashion district. The duomo and Galleria Vittorio Emanuele are roughly at the center of the circles. The Giardini Pubblici and the Parco Sempione radiate from the center. From the colossal Stazione Centrale, northeast of the city, take M3 to the *duomo*.

Tourist Office: IAT, P. Duomo 19A, Underground. (☎72 52 43 01; www.milanoinfotourist.com), in P. del Duomo. Pick up helpful *Hello Milano*. Open M-Sa 8:45am-1pm and 2-6pm, Su 9am-1pm and 2-5pm. Branch in Stazione Centrale (☎77 40 43 18) has shorter lines. Open M-Sa 9am-6pm, Su 9am-1pm and 2-5pm.

American Express: V. Larga 4 (☎72 10 41), on the corner of V. Larga and S. Clemente. Exchanges currency, handles wire transfers, and holds mail for up to 1 month for AmEx cardholders. Open M-F 9am-5:30pm.

Hospital: Ospedale Maggiore di Milano, V. Francesco Sforza 35 (☎55 031).

24hr. Pharmacy: (☎66 90 735). In Stazione Centrale's 2nd fl. *galleria.*

Internet Access: Internet Enjoy, Vle. Tunisia 11 (☎36 55 58 05). M1: Porta Venezia. €2-3 per hr. Open M-Sa 9am-midnight, Su 2pm-midnight.

Post Office: P. Cordusio 4 (☎72 48 21 26), near P. del Duomo. Currency exchange and ATM. Open M-F 8am-7pm, Sa 8:30am-noon. Postal Code: 20100.

▌ ACCOMMODATIONS

Every season is high season in expensive, fashionable Milan—except August, when many hotels close. Prices rise in September, November, March, and April due to theater season and business conventions. For the best deals, try the hostels on the city periphery or in the areas east of Stazione Centrale. Reserve well ahead.

▨ La Cordata, V. Burigozzo 11 (☎58 31 46 75; www.ostellimilano.it. M3: Missori. From P. Missori, take tram #15 2 stops to Italia San Luca; then walk in the same direction for 1 block and turn right on V. Burigozzo. Entrance around the corner on V. Aurispa. Ideal for female and solo travelers. Kitchen access. Laundry €3. Free Internet. Max. 7-night stay. Check-in 2-10pm. No curfew. Closed Aug. 10-20 and Dec. 23-Jan. 2. Single-sex dorms €21; doubles €70-100; triples €90-110; quads €100-120. Cash only. ❷

▨ Hotel San Tomaso, Vle. Tunisia 6, 3rd fl. (☎29 51 47 47; www.hotelsantomaso.com). M1: Porta Venezia. Sparkling rooms with fan, phone, and TV. Singles €35-65; doubles €45-95, with bath €50-120; triples €75-135. AmEx/MC/V. ❸

Hotel Malta, V. Ricordi 20 (☎20 49 615; www.hotelmalta.it). Offers a respite from busy Milan. The 15 bright, quiet rooms have bath, fan, hair dryer, and TV; some have balconies over the rose garden. Reserve ahead. Singles €30-75; doubles €50-120. MC/V. ❹

Hotel Cà Grande, V. Porpora 87 (☎/fax 26 14 40 01; www.hotelcagrande.it). 7 blocks from P. Loreto, in a pleasant yellow house on the right. English-speaking owners will have you feeling right at home. All rooms have phone, sink, and TV. Breakfast included. Singles €40-60, with bath €45-85; doubles €55-85/60-110. AmEx/D/MC/V. ❹

Hotel Aurora, C. Buenos Aires 18 (☎20 47 960; www.hotelaurorasrl.com). M1: Porta Venezia. On the right side of C. Buenos Aires after V. F. Casati. Rooms with A/C and TV. Reserve ahead. Singles €50-80; doubles €80-125; triples €85-150. AmEx/MC/V. ❹

Hotel Eva and Hotel Arno, both at V. Lazzaretto 17, 4th fl. (☎67 06 093; www.hotelevamilano.com and www.hotelarno.com). M1: Porta Venezia. 18 large rooms with phone and TV. Ring bell to enter. Clean shared bathroom. Free luggage storage. 30min. free Internet. Singles €30-45; doubles €50-100; triples €65-90. AmEx/MC/V. ❸

Campeggio Città di Milano, V. G. Airaghi 61 (☎48 20 01 34; www.parcoaquatica.com). M1: De Angeli, then bus #72 to S. Romanello Togni. Backtrack 10m and turn right on V. Togni. Campsite is a 10min. walk straight ahead. Enter at Aquatica waterpark. Modern facilities. Laundry €5. Reserve ahead. Closed Dec.-Jan. €11 per person, €6.50-8.50 per tent, €6.50 per car. 2- to 6-person cabins €37-88; bungalows with bath and A/C €80-120. Electricity included. MC/V. ❶

⬛ FOOD

Trattorie still adhere to Milanese traditions by preparing *risotto alla Milanese* (rice with saffron), *cotoletta alla Milanese* (breaded veal cutlet with lemon), and *osso buco* (shank of lamb, beef, or veal). The Navigli district is home to cheap grub and the Saturday **Fiera di Sinigallia,** a bargaining extravaganza (on Darsena Banks, a canal near V. d'Annunzio). The area's bars include Happy hour buffets of foccaccia, pasta, and risotto with drinks.

⬛ **Princi Il Bread & Breakfast,** V. Speronari 6, off P. del Duomo. Busy deli welcomes a lunch crowd that comes for its cheap takeout *primi* and *secondi* (€5). Fresh bread and pastries €1-4. *Panini* and pizza €3.50-5. Open M-Sa 7am-8pm. Cash only. ❶

⬛ **Il Forno dei Navigli,** V. A. Naviglio Pavese 2. At the corner of Ripa di Porta Ticinese. Out of "the oven of Navigli" come the most elaborate pastries in the city. The *cestini,* pear tarts with Nutella, define decadence (€3). Pastries and breads €0.50-6. Open M-Sa 7am-2pm and 6pm-1am, Su 6pm-1am. Cash only. ❶

Big Pizza: Da Noi 2, V. G. Borsi 1 (☎83 96 77), takes its name seriously. Epic pizzas (€4-9) emerge from the stone oven, and beer flows liberally. The house pizza has pasta on top (€8.50). Cover €1. Open M-Sa 10am-2:30pm and 7pm-midnight. **Branches:** Ple. XXIV Maggio 7 (M2: Porta Genova) and V. Buonarroti 16 (M1: Buonarroti). ❷

Il Panino Giusto, V. Malpighi 3. M1: Porta Venezia. (☎29 40 92 97) If you believe sandwiches should contain goat cheese, truffled olive oil, veal *pâté,* or lard with honey and walnuts for under €8, welcome home. *Panini* €5-8. Beer €4-5. Open daily noon-1am. Branch on P. Beccaria near P. del Duomo. AmEx/MC/V. ❷

Peck, V. Spadari 9 (☎02 80 23 161; www.peck.it). Aromas from the ground floor spread throughout the wine cellar in the basement and the bar/restaurant above. *Primi* €9-18. *Secondi* €9-20. Open M 3-7:30pm, Tu-Sa 8:45am-7:30pm. AmEx/MC/V. ❷

Caffè Vecchia Brera, V. Dell'Orso 20 (☎86 46 16 95; www.vecchiabrera.it). M1: Cairoli. Take V. Cusani out of piazza Cairoli for 2 blocks. Sugar-topped, meat-filled, or liqueur-soaked crepes (€3.50-7). *Primi* €7.50-9. *Secondi* €12-14. Cover €1. Service 10%. Open daily 7am-2am. Happy hour 5-8:30pm; mixed drinks €5. AmEx/MC/V. ❸

👁 SIGHTS

⬛ **DUOMO.** The geographical and spiritual center of Milan and a good starting point for any walking tour of the city, the *duomo*—the third-largest church in the world—was begun in 1386 by **Gian Galeazzo Visconti,** who hoped to persuade the Virgin Mary to grant him a male heir. Work proceeded over the next centuries and was completed in 1809 at Napoleon's command. Climb (or ride) to the ⬛**roof walkway** for prime views of the city and the Alps. *(M1/3: Duomo. Cathedral open daily 7am-7pm. Modest dress required. Free. Roof open daily mid-Feb. to mid-Nov. 9am-5:45pm; mid-Nov. to mid-Feb. 9am-4:15pm. €4, elevator €6.)* The **Museo del Duomo** displays artifacts relating to the cathedral's construction. *(P. del Duomo 14, to the right of the duomo. Open daily 10am-1:15pm and 3-6pm. €5, students €3.)*

⬛ **PINACOTECA AMBROSIANA.** The 23 palatial rooms of the Ambrosiana display exquisite works from the 14th through 19th centuries, including Botticelli's circular *Madonna of the Canopy,* Caravaggio's *Basket of Fruit* (the first Italian still-life), Raphael's wall-sized *School of Athens,* Titian's *Adoration of the Magi,* and da Vinci's *Portrait of a Musician.* The statue-filled courtyard is enchanting. *(P. Pio XI 2. M1/3: Duomo. Open Tu-Su 10am-5:30pm. €7.50, under 18 or over 65 €4.50.)*

CASTELLO SFORZESCO. The Castello Sforzesco was constructed in 1368 as a defense against Venice. Later, it was used as an army barrack, a horse stall, and a storage house before da Vinci converted it into a studio. Restored after WWII bomb damage, the complex houses 10 **Musei Civici** (Civic Museums). The **Museum**

of Ancient Art contains Michelangelo's unfinished *Pietà Rondanini* (1564), his last work, and the **Museum of Decorative Art** has ornate furnishings and Murano glass. The underground level has a small Egyptian collection. *(M1: Cairoli or M2: Lanza. Open Tu-Su 9am-5:30pm. Combined admission €3, students €1.50, F 2-5:30pm free.)*

TEATRO ALLA SCALA. Founded in 1778, La Scala has established Milan as the opera capital of the world. Its understated Neoclassical facade and lavish interior set the stage for premieres of works by Mascagni, Puccini, Rossini, and Verdi, performed by virtuosos like Maria Callas and Enrico Caruso. Visitors can soak up La Scala's historical glow at the **Museo Teatrale alla Scala.** *(Access through the Galleria Vittorio Emanuele from P. del Duomo. www.teatroallascala.org. Museum on left side of building. Open daily 9am-12:30pm and 1:30-5:30pm. €5, students €4.)*

BASILICA DI SANT'AMBROGIO. A prototype for Lombard-Romanesque churches throughout Italy, Sant'Ambrogio is the most influential medieval building in Milan. St. Ambrose presided over this church from AD 379 to 386, and his skeletal remains rest beside martyr St. Protasio. The 4th-century Cappella di San Vittore in Ciel D'oro, with exquisite mosaics adorning its cupola, lies through the seventh chapel on the right. *(M2: S. Ambrogio. Walk up V. G. Carducci, and the church is on the right. Church open M-Sa 7:15am-noon and 2:30-7pm, Su 7:15am-1pm and 3-8pm. Free. Chapel open Tu-Su 9:30-11:45am and 2:30-6pm. €2, students €1.)*

CHIESA DI SANTA MARIA DELLA GRAZIE. The church's Gothic nave is dark and patterned with frescoes, in contrast to the airy Renaissance tribune Bramante added in 1497. To the left of the church entrance is the **Cenacolo Vinciano** (Vinciano Refectory), home to Leonardo da Vinci's ■**Last Supper.** Following a 20-year restoration effort, the painting was put back on display in 1999. Reserve ahead or risk missing it. *(P. di S. Maria della Grazie 2. M1: Conciliazione. From P. Conciliazione, take V. Boccaccio and then go right onto V. Ruffini for about 2 blocks. Church open M-Sa 7am-noon and 3-7pm, Su 7:30am-12:15pm and 3:30-9pm. Modest dress required. Refectory open Tu-Su 8:15am-6:45pm. €6.50. Reservations ☎89 42 11 46. Reservation fee €1.50.)*

BASILICA DI SANT'EUSTORGIO. Founded in the 4th century to house the bones of the Magi, the church lost its original function when the dead sages were spirited off to Cologne in 1164. A great masterpiece of early Renaissance art is the **Portinari Chapel,** to the left of the entrance. Frescoes below the rainbow dome illustrate the life of St. Peter. The chapel stands on a **Paleochristian cemetery;** pagan and early Christian tombs are down the steps before the chapel entrance. *(P. S. Eustorgio 3. M2: S. Ambrogio. Basilica open M and W-Su 8:30am-noon and 3:30-6pm. Cappella open Tu-Su 10am-6:30pm. Basilica free. Cappella €6, students and seniors €3.)*

GALLERIA D'ARTE MODERNA. Napoleon lived here with Josephine when Milan was the capital of the Napoleonic Kingdom of Italy (1805-1814). The gallery displays modern Lombard art and Impressionist works. Of note are Klee's *Wald Bau,* Modigliani's *Beatrice Hastings,* Morandi's *Natura Morta con Bottiglia,* and Picasso's *Testa. (V. Palestro 16, in the Villa Reale. M1/2: Palestro. Open Tu-Su 9am-1pm and 2-5:30pm. Free.)* The adjacent **Padiglione D'Arte Contemporanea (PAC)** is an extravaganza of photographs, multimedia, and painting. *(Open Tu-W and F 9:30am-5:30pm, Th 9:30am-9pm, Sa-Su 9:30am-7pm. Free)*

MUSEO NAZIONALE DELLA SCIENZA E DELLA TECNOLOGIA "DA VINCI". This hands-on museum traces technological advances from da Vinci to today. The hall of computers features a piano converted to a typewriter. *(V. San Vittore 21, off V. G. Carducci. M2: S. Ambrogio. Open Tu-F 9:30am-5pm, Sa-Su 9:30am-6:30pm. €8, students €6.)*

🗖 🎵 SHOPPING AND ENTERTAINMENT

In a city where clothes really do make the man (or woman), fashionistas arrive in spring and summer to watch models dressed in the newest styles glide down the runway. When the music has faded and the designers have bowed, world-famous

saldi (sales) in July and January usher the garb into the real world. The **Quadrilatero della Moda** (fashion district) has become a sanctuary in its own right. This posh land is the block formed by Via Monte Napoleone, Borgospresso, Via della Spiga, and Via Gesu. Designer creations are available to mere mortals at the trendy boutiques along **Corso di Porta Ticinese.** Small shops and affordable staples from brand names can be found on **Via Torino** near the *duomo* and on **Corso Buenos Aires** near M1: Porta Venezia. Those who don't mind being a season behind can purchase famous designer wear from *blochisti* (stocks or wholesale clothing outlets), such as the well-known **Il Salvagente,** V. Bronzetti 16, off C. XXII Marzo (M1: S. Babila), or **Gruppo Italia Grandi Firme,** V. Montegani #7/A (M2: Famagosta), which offers designer duds at 70% off. True bargain hunters cull the bazaars on **Via Faucé** (M2: Garibaldi; Tu and Sa) and **Viale Papinian** (M2: Agnostino; Sa mornings).

La Scala (see p. 605) is one of the best places in the world to see an opera. La Scala also sponsors a **ballet** season run primarily out of **Teatro degli Arcimboldi,** north of the city. (Infotel Scala ☎72 00 37 44; www.teatroallascala.org. Opera season runs Jan.-July and Sept.-Nov. Tickets €10-105.) The **Milan Symphony Orchestra** plays from September to May at the **Auditorium di Milano.** (☎83 38 92 01; www.orchestrasinfonica.milano.it) The football clubs **Inter Milan** and **AC Milan** face off at their shared stadium. **Ticket One,** located in FNAC stores, sells tickets for both teams as well as for other events (☎39 22 61; www.ticketone.it). There are tours of the **stadium,** V. Piccolomini 5, on non-game days. (☎40 42 432. M2: Lotto. Entrance at Gate 21. Tours M-Sa 10am-6pm. €13, under 18 or over 65 €10.)

▮ NIGHTLIFE

The nightlife in **Navigli** is popular with students and centers around V. Sforza. The **Brera** district invites tourists and Milanese to test their singing skills while sipping mixed drinks at one of its piano bars. **Corso di Porta Ticinese** is the sleek land of the all-night Happy-hour buffet, where the price of an mixed drink (€6-8) also buys dinner. A single block of **Corso Como** near **Stazione Garibaldi** is home to the most exclusive clubs. Bars and clubs cluster around **Largo Cairoli,** where summer brings Milan's hottest outdoor dance venues. Southeast of **Stazione Centrale** is home to an eclectic mix of bars and much of Milan's gay and lesbian scene.

▨ **Le Trottoir,** P. XXIV Maggio 1 (☎/fax 02 83 78 166; www.letrottoir.it) may be the loudest, most crowded bar and club in the Navagli. A young crowd comes nightly for underground music downstairs and jazz or a DJ upstairs. Pizza and sandwiches €8, available until 2am. Mixed drinks €6-9. Happy hour daily 6-8pm; beer €4, mixed drinks €6. Open daily 3pm-3am. Cover €8, includes 1 drink. AmEx/MC/V.

▨ **Old Fashion Café,** Vle. Alemagna 6 (☎80 56 231; www.oldfashion.it). M1/2: Cadorna F. N. Summer brings stylish clubgoers to couches encircling an outdoor dance floor with live music and DJ. Tu is the most popular night, with live music. F R&B. Cover M-Sa €20; W €10, students free. Open 11pm-4:30am.

Scimmie, V. A. Sforza 49 (☎89 40 28 74; www.scimmie.it). Legendary nightclub offers nightly performances. Talented underground musicians play blues, fusion, jazz, Italian swing, and reggae. Mixed drinks €4-9. Concerts 7:30-9:30pm and 10:30pm-1:30am. Schedule posted online. Open daily 7pm-2am. MC/V.

Flying Circus, P. Vetra 21 (☎58 31 35 77). A pair of cacti welcomes you to this glass-encased lounge. Mixed drinks and wine €6-8. Weekly themed calendar includes Tu "Re-Wine" (2nd wine free), W "Kill Beer" (€3 beer), Th "Chupa Chupitos" (€1 shots), and Sa "Try Flying" (3 cocktails for €15). Themes change in winter. Happy hour buffet daily 6:30-9:30pm. Open M-F 10am-2am, Sa 6:30pm-2am. AmEx/MC/V.

Yguana Café Restaurant, V. P. Gregorio XIV 16 (☎89 40 41 95), just off P. Vetra. Lounge outside or groove to DJs spinning house and hip hop. Mixed drinks €8-10. Happy hour buffet M-Sa 5:30-9:30pm, Su 5:30-10pm. Lunch M-F 12:30-3pm. Su brunch noon-4pm. Open for drinks daily 5:30pm-2am, F-Sa 5:30pm-3am. AmEx/MC/V.

▒ LET'S GO TO MILAN: BERGAMO   ☎ 035

Home to the **Orio al Serio International Airport** (**BGY;** ☎ 32 63 23; www.sacbo.it), Bergamo (pop. 120,000) is a hub for budget airlines **Ryanair, SkyEurope,** and **Wizz Air. Trains** (☎ 24 79 50) run from Ple. Marconi to Milan (1hr., 1 per hr., €3.50). **Buses** run from the left of the train station to Como (6 per day, €4.40) and Milan (2 per hr., €4.40). **Airport buses** go to the train station in Bergamo (10min., €1.60) and Milan (1hr., 2 per hr., €6).

For overnight layovers or missed flights, head to the cheap rooms of **Ostello Città di Bergamo (HI) ❷,** V. G. Ferraris 1. From the airport, take bus 1C to Porta Nuova and change to bus #6; the hostel is at the next-to-last stop. (☎ 36 17 24; www.ostellodibergamo.it. 6- and 8-bed dorms €17; singles €27; doubles €40; 3-6 person rooms €18 per person. €3 HI discount.) Another option is the B&B **La Torretta Citta Alta ❹,** Via Rocca 2, in the high city. (☎ 23 17 71; www.latorrettabergamoalta.com. Singles €50-70; doubles €70-90; triples €90-110.) Dine at ▓**Trattoria Casa Mia ❷,** V. S. Bernardino 20, which makes up for its out-of-the-way location with local flavor. From the station, walk along V. P. Giovanni to Largo Porta Nuova. Turn left on V. G. Tiraboschi, which becomes V. Zambonate, then turn left at the last intersection, onto V. S. Bernardino. (☎ 22 06 76. Lunch *menù* €9. Dinner *menù* €15. Open M-Sa noon-2pm and 7-10pm. Cash only.) Supermarket **Pellicano** is at Vle. V. Emanuele II 17; walk from the station past Ple. Repubblica. (Open M 8:30am-1:30pm, Tu-F 8:30am-1:30pm and 3:30-8pm, Sa 8:30am-8pm. MC/V.) **Postal Code:** 24122.

MANTUA (MANTOVA)   ☎ 0376

Though Mantua (pop. 47,000) did not become a dynamic cultural haven until the Renaissance, art and culture have shaped the city's history since the birth of the poet Virgil in 70 BC. Today, the **Festivaletteratura** brings writers from John Grisham to Salman Rushdie to the city in early September. Mantua's grand *palazzi*, including the opulent **Palazzo Ducale,** P. Sordello 40, were built by the powerful Gonzaga family, who ascended to power in 1328, ruled for 400 years, and brought well-known artists to leave their marks on the town's mansions and churches. The **New Gallery** houses dozens of locally produced altarpieces from the 16th-18th centuries, removed from monasteries during the Habsburg and Napoleonic eras. (Open Tu-Su 8:45am-7:15pm. €6.50.) Music lovers first filled the balconies of the ▓**Teatro Bibiena,** V. Accademia 4, when 14-year-old Mozart inaugurated the building in 1769. Inside, the rose and gray stone balconies create the illusion of a fairy-tale castle. (Open Tu-Su 9:30am-12:30pm and 3-6pm. €2.50, under 18 €1.20.) In the south of the city, down V. P. Amedeo, which becomes V. Acrebi, through P. Veneto, and down Largo Parri, lies the **Palazzo del Te,** built by Giulio Romano in 1534 as a suburban retreat for Federico II Gonzaga. It is widely considered the finest building in the Mannerist style. The entirely frescoed ▓ **Room of Giants** depicts the demise of the rebellious titans at the hands of Jupiter. Don't miss the hidden garden and grotto at the far end. (Open M 1-6pm, Tu-Su 9am-6pm. €8, students €2.50.)

Accommodations in Mantua are costly. **Hotel ABC ❹,** P. D. Leoni 25, across from the train station, is a modern hotel with comfortable rooms. (☎ 32 23 29; www.hotelabcmantova.it. Breakfast included. Reserve ahead. Singles €44-88; doubles €66-121; triples €77-160; quads €88-180.) **Ostello del Mincio ❷,** V. Porto 23/25, 10km from Mantua, is the only youth hostel in the area. (☎ 65 39 24; www.ostellodelmincio.org. Dorms €15-22.) **Antica Osteria ai Ranari ❸,** V. Trieste 11, south of the canal, offers regional dishes. Try the *tortelli di zucca* or mint pesto. (☎ 32 84 31. *Primi* €6-7. *Secondi* €9-13. Cover €1. Open Tu-Su noon-3pm and 8pm-2am. Closed for 3 weeks in summer; call ahead. AmEx/MC/V.) A **market** is held every Thursday morning in P. d'Erbe. **Supermarket Sma,** V. Giustiziati 11, is behind the Rotonda di San Lorenzo on P. d'Erbe. (Open M-Sa 8:30am-7:30pm. AmEx/MC/V.) **Trains** go from P. D. Leoni to Milan (2¼hr., 9 per day, €8.40) and Verona (40min., 21 per hr., €2.30). From the train station, turn left on V. Solferino,

ITALY

then right on Via Bonomi to the main street, **Corso Vittorio Emanuele II.** Follow it to P. Cavallotti, across the river to C. Umberto I, which leads to P. Marconi, P. Mantegna, and the main *piazze*, **Piazza dell'Erbe** and **Piazza Sordello.** The **tourist office** is at P. Mantegna 6; follow V. Solferino until it becomes V. Fratelli Bandiera, then go right on V. Verdi. (☎ 32 82 53; www.aptmantova.it. Open daily 9am-7pm.) **Internet** access is available at **Bit and Phone,** V. Bertinelli 21. **Postal Code:** 46100.

THE LAKE COUNTRY

When Italy's monuments start blurring together, escape to the clear waters and mountains of the northern Lake Country, partly in Piedmont, partly in Lombardy. Artistic visionaries like Liszt, Longfellow, and Wordsworth sought rest among the shores of the northern lakes. The mansion-spotted coast of Lake Como welcomes the rich and famous, palatial hotels dot Lake Maggiore's sleepy shores, and a young crowd descends upon Lake Garda for its watersports and bars.

LAKE COMO (LAGO DI COMO)

As the numerous luxurious villas on the lake's shores attest, the well-to-do have been using Lake Como as a refuge since before the Roman Empire. Three lakes form the forked Lake Como, joined at the three central towns: Bellagio, Menaggio, and Varenna. These smaller towns offer a more relaxing stay than Como. For a taste of the Lake's true beauty, hop on a bus or ferry, and step off whenever a castle, villa, vineyard, or small town beckons.

☐ TRANSPORTATION. The only town on the lake accessible by **train** is Como. Trains go from Stazione San Giovanni (☎ 031 89 20 21) to Milan (1hr., 1-2 per hr., €4.90) and Zürich, SWI (4hr., 5 per day, €43). From P. Matteotti, **bus** C46 goes to Bergamo (2hr., 5 per day, €4.40), and C10 goes to Menaggio (1hr., 1 per hr., €3). From the train station, bus C30 goes to Bellagio (1hr., 16 per day, €2.60). Spend the day zipping between the boutiques, gardens, villas, and wineries of the lake by **ferry** (day pass €20), leaving from the piers at P. Cavour.

COMO. Situated on the southwestern tip of the lake, semi-industrial Como (pop. 86,000) is the lake's largest town. **Ostello Villa Olmo (HI) ❷,** V. Bellinzona 2, offers clean rooms and a friendly staff. From the train station, walk 20min. down V. Borgo Vico to V. Bellinzona. (☎ 031 57 38 00; ostellocomo@tin.it. Breakfast included. Reception 7-10am and 4pm-midnight. Lockout 10am-4pm. Strict curfew midnight. Open Mar.-Nov. Reserve ahead. Dorms €18. €3 HI discount. Cash only.) A **Gran Mercato** supermarket is at P. Matteotti 3. (Open Su-M 8:30am-1pm, Tu-F 8:30am-1:30pm and 3:30-7:30pm, Sa 8am-7:30pm.) The **tourist office** is at P. Cavour 17. From the station, go left on V. Fratelli Ricchi and right on Vle. Fratelli Rosselli, which turns into Lungo Lario Trento and leads to the *piazza*. (☎ 031 26 97 12. Open M-Sa 9am-1pm and 2:30-6pm, Su 9:30am-1pm.) **Postal Code:** 22100.

MENAGGIO. Halfway up Lake Como's western shore are the terra-cotta rooftops of Menaggio (pop. 3200). The town's beauty and excellent ferry connections make it the perfect base for exploring the lake. Daytrips by ferry to the gardens and villas of **Bellagio** and **Varenna** (both: 10-15min., 1-2 per hr., €3.40) are extremely popular. The **Rifugio Menaggio** mountain station is the starting point for a 2½hr. round-trip hike to **Monte Grona** (1736m) that offers views of the pre-Alps and the lakes; or a 2¼hr. hike to **Chiesa di San Amate** (1623m) that takes you over a mountain ridge to sneak a peak at alpine pasture. A number of shorter hikes start in Menaggio. To get to the laid-back ⬛**Ostello La Prinula (HI) ❶,** V. IV Novembre 86, head uphill from the ferry dock and turn left onto the main thoroughfare. The expert staff arranges outdoor activities. (☎ 034 43 23 56; www.menaggiohostel.com. Breakfast included. Reception 8-10am and 4pm-midnight. Lockout 10am-4pm. Curfew midnight.

THE LAKE COUNTRY ■ 609

Reserve ahead. Open Mar.-Nov. Dorms €16; 4- to 6-bed suites with bath €18 per person. €3 HI discount. Cash only.) Just up the street from the ferry dock, **Super Cappa Market,** V. IV Novembre 107, stocks groceries and hiking supplies. (Open M 8-12:30pm, Tu-Sa 8am-12:30pm and 3-7pm.) In the *centro* at P. Garibaldi 4, the helpful **tourist office** has info and maps on lake excursions. **Postal Code:** 22017.

LAKE MAGGIORE (LAGO MAGGIORE)

A translation of Stendhal reads: "If it should befall that you possess a heart and shirt, then sell the shirt and visit the shores of Lake Maggiore." Though writers have always been seduced by the lake's beauty, Lake Maggiore remains less touristed than its neighbors. **Stresa** is a perfect stepping-stone to the gorgeous **Borromean Islands.** Stay at the **Albergo Luina ❸,** V. Garibaldi 21, to the right past the ferry dock. (☎032 33 02 85. Breakfast €3.50. Reserve ahead in summer. Singles €35-52; doubles €55-80; triples €56-80. MC/V.) Daily excursion tickets allow you to travel between Stresa and the three islands. **Trains** run from Stresa to Milan (1¼hr., 2 per hr., €4.30). To reach the *centro* and the **IAT Tourist Office,** P. Marconi 16, from the ferry dock, exit the train station, turn right on V. P. d. Piemonte, take a left on Vle. D. d. Genova, and walk toward the water.

🎏 THE BORROMEAN ISLANDS. On **Isola Bella,** the **Palazzo e Giardini Borromeo** showcases priceless tapestries and paintings. (Open Mar. 21-Oct. 21 daily 9am-5:30pm. €11.) From Isola Bella, ferries go to **Isola Superiore dei Pescatori,** which has a quaint fishing village with a rocky beach and ice-cold water. **Isola Madre** is the greenest island, most favored by the locals. The 16th-century **Villa Taranto** contains several puppet theaters, and its gardens hold exotic flowers. (Open daily 8:30am-6:30pm. €8.50. Combined ticket with the Palazzo e Giardini Borromeo €16.)

LAKE GARDA (LAGO DI GARDA)

Garda has staggering mountains and breezy summers. **Desenzano,** the lake's southern transport hub, is 1hr. from Milan and 2hr. from Venice. Sirmione and Limone are best explored as daytrips. **Riva del Garda,** at the lake's northern tip, has an affordable hostel to use as a base. Exploring **Sirmione's** 13th-century castle and Roman ruins can fill a leisurely day or busy afternoon. In **Limone,** windsurfing, swimming, and eating all revolve around the view of the lake as it winds through the mountains. Uphill from the center near the water, **La Limonaia del Castèl,** V. IV Novembre 25, transports tourists into the world of a functioning 18th-century citrus house that grows clementines, grapefruits, lemons, and limes. (☎0365 95 40 08; www.limone-sulgarda.it. €1.) Riva del Garda's pebble beaches are Lake Garda's restitution for budget travelers put off by

TOP TEN MOST COMMON STREET NAMES IN ITALY

After only a day or two in Italy, it's apparent that just a few big names run Italy's streets.

1. In 1849 **Vittorio Emanuele II** became unified Italy's 1st king.

2. Giuseppe Garibaldi, a 19th-century military hero, is credited with making the unification of Italy possible.

3. Count Camillo Benso di Cavour designed the constitutional structure of the "Kingdom of Italy" in the 19th century.

4. Guglielmo Marconi sent three short beeps to Canada in 1901—the first transatlantic telegraph signals.

5. XX Settembre (1870) is the date of Italy's final unification.

6. Socialist **Giacomo Matteoti** wrote a book critical of fascism in 1924, but was murdered in response.

7. Cesare Battisti, a native of Trent, was a WWI martyr.

8. Giuseppe Mazzini tried to instigate popular uprisings to unify Italy, but failed time and again.

9. Solferino was a battle fought on June 24, 1859 for the the unification of Italy in the region between Milan and Verona. Italy along with French ally Napolean III defeated Austria.

10. Umberto I, reigned as King of Italy from 1878 until 1900 when he became and remains the only modern Italian head of state to be assassinated.

sleep local prices. Visitors swim, windsurf, and hike near the most stunning portion of the lake. Sleep at the **Ostello Benacus (HI) ❶**, P. Cavour 10. (☎0464 55 49 11. Breakfast included. Laundry €4. Internet €2 per hr. Reception 7-9am and 3-11pm. Reserve ahead. Dorms €14; private rooms €17 per person. AmEx/MC/V.) Sirmione's **tourist office** is at V. Guglilmo Marconi 6. (☎030 91 61 14; www.commune.sirmione.bs.it. Open Apr.-Oct. daily 9am-8pm; Nov.-Mar. M-F 9am-12:30pm and 3-6pm, Sa 9am-12:30pm.) Limone's tourist office, V. IV Novembre 29, is across from the bus stop. (☎0365 91 89 87. Open daily 8:30am-9pm.) Riva del Garda's tourist office is at Largo Medaglie d'Oro 5. (☎0464 55 44 44; www.gardatrentino.it. Open M-Sa 9am-noon and 3-6:30pm, Su 9am-noon and 3:30-6:30pm.) **Buses** run from Sirmione and Riva del Garde to Verona (1-2hr., 1 per hr., €3.90-5.20). **Ferries** (☎030 91 49 511; www.navigazionelaghi.it) run from Limone to Desenzano (4 per day, €10-13), Riva (17 per day, €3.30-5.10), and Sirmione (8 per day, €10-13); check schedule at ferry docks. **Postal Codes:** 25019 (Sirmione), 25087 (Limone), 38066 (Riva del Garda).

ITALIAN RIVIERA (LIGURIA)

The Italian Riviera stretches 350km along the Mediterranean between France and Tuscany, forming the most touristed area of the Italian coastline. Genoa anchors the Ligurian coastal strip between the **Riviera di Levante** (rising sun) to the east and the **Riviera di Ponente** (setting sun) to the west. Riviera glamor mixes with seaside relaxation, as its lemon trees, almond blossoms, and turquoise seas greet visitors. The **Cinque Terre** area (p. 613) is especially worth the journey.

GENOA (GENOVA)   ☎010

Genoa (pop. 640,000), city of grit and grandeur, has little in common with its resort neighbors. As a Ligurian will tell you, *"si deve conoscerla per amarla"* (you have to know her to love her). Once home to Liguria's most noble families, Genoa's main streets are lined with *palazzi* and *piazze;* wander through medieval churches and maze-like pathways scented with pesto to discover this port city.

▐ TRANSPORTATION. Colombo Internazionale Airport (GOA; ☎60 15 461), in Sesti Ponente, services European destinations. Volabus #100 runs to Stazione Brignole from the airport (3 per hr. 5:30am-10:30pm, €3). Most visitors arrive at one of Genoa's two train stations: **Stazione Principe**, in P. Acquaverde, or **Stazione Brignole**, in P. Verdi. **Trains** go to Rome (5-6hr., 12 per day, €33), Turin (2hr., 2-3 per hr., €8-12), and points along the Italian Riviera. AMT **buses** (☎55 82 414) run through the city (€1.20; day pass €3.50). **Ferries** to Olbia, Sardinia, and Palermo, Sicily depart from Terminal Traghetti in the Ponte Assereto section of the port.

▟▐ ORIENTATION AND PRACTICAL INFORMATION. From Stazione Principe, take V. Balbi to V. Cairoli, which becomes V. Garibaldi. Turn right on V. XXV Aprile at P. delle Fontane Marose to get to **Piazza de Ferrari** in the center of town. From Stazione Brignole, turn right out of the station, left on V. Fiume, and right onto V. XX Settembre. Or, take bus #18, 19, or 30 from Stazione Principe, or bus #19 or 40 from Stazione Brignole. The **tourist office**, GenovaInforma, has several locations, including a kiosk in P. Matteotti and one near the aquarium on Portico Antico. (☎86 87 452. Open daily 9am-1pm and 2-6pm.) **Postal Code:** 16121.

 The shadowy streets of the *centro storico* are riddled with drug dealers and prostitutes, especially the area around Stazione Principe, as well as those around V. della Maddalena, V. Sottoripa, and V. di Prè. Avoid them when shops are closed and streets are empty.

▐▊ ACCOMMODATIONS AND FOOD. Delight in views of the city at **Ostello per la Gioventù (HI) ❶**, V. Costanzi 120. From Stazione Principe, take bus #35 to V. Napoli and transfer to #40. From Stazione Brignole, take bus #40 (last bus 12:50am) all the way up the hill. (☎24 22 457; www.geocities.com/hostelge. Breakfast included. Dorms €16. HI members only.) The rooms at **Albergo Carola ❸**, V. Gropallo 4/12, are meticulously decorated. (☎83 91 340; albergocarola@libero.it. Singles €30; doubles €50, with bath €60; triples €80; quads €90. Cash only.) For camping, try **Genova Est ❶**, on V. Marcon Loc Cassa. Take the train from Stazione Brignole to Bogliasco (10min., 6 per day, €1). A van (5min., 1 per 2hr. 8:10am-6pm, free) runs from there to the campground. (☎34 72 053; www.camping-genova-est.it. Laundry €3.50. €5.90 per person, €5.60-8.60 per tent. Electricity €2.20.) **▉Trattoria da Maria ❷**, V. Testa d'Oro 14R, off V. XXV Aprile, has authentic daily specials. (☎58 10 80. 2-course *menù* €9. Open M-Sa 11:45am-3pm. MC/V.)

◉▐ SIGHTS AND ENTERTAINMENT. Genoa's multitude of *palazzi* were built by its famous merchant families. Follow V. Balbi through P. della Nunziata and continue to L. Zecca, where V. Cairoli leads to **▉Via Garibaldi**, called "Via Aurea" (Golden Street) after the wealthy families who inhabited it. Rococo rooms bathed in gold and upholstered in red velvet fill the 17th-century **▉Palazzo Reale**, V. Balbi 10, west of V. Garibaldi. (Open Tu-W 9am-1:30pm, Th-Su 9am-7pm. €4, 18-25 €2.). The **Villetta Di Negro**, V. Garibaldi, contains grottoes, terraced gardens, and waterfalls. From P. delle Fontane Marose, take Salita di S. Caterina to P. Corvetto. (Open daily 8am-dusk.) From P. de Ferrari, take V. Boetto to P. Matteotti for a glimpse of the ornate interior and Rubens paintings in **Chiesa di Gesù**. (Church open M-Sa 7am-4pm, Su 8am-5pm. Closed to tourists during Su Mass. Free.) Head past the church down V. di Porta Soprana to V. Ravecca to reach the twin-towered **Porta Soprana**, one of the four gates into the city, near the boyhood home of **Christopher Columbus**. (Porta and Columbus' home open daily 10am-6pm. Combo ticket €7.) **Centro storico**, the eerie and beautiful historical center bordered by Porto Antico, V. Garibaldi, and P. Ferrari, is a mass of winding streets. The area contains some of Genoa's most memorable sights, including the asymmetrical **San Lorenzo Duomo**, down V. San Lorenzo from P. Matteotti (open daily 9am-noon and 3-6pm; free), and the medieval **Torre Embriaci**. Go down V. S. Lorenzo toward the water, turn left on V. Chiabrera, and left on V. di Mascherona to reach the **Chiesa Santa Maria di Castello**, in P. Caricamento, a labyrinth of chapels, courtyards, and crucifixes. (Open daily 9am-noon and 3:30-6:30pm. Closed to tourists during Su Mass. Free.) The **▉aquarium** on Porto Antico is Europe's largest. (Open July-Aug. daily 9am-11pm; Mar.-June and Sept.-Oct. M-W and F 9am-7:30pm, Th 9am-10pm, Sa-Su 9am-8:30pm; Nov.-Feb. daily 9:30am-7:30pm. Last entry 1½hr. before closing. €15.)

Corso Italia, an upscale promenade, is home to much of Genoa's nightlife. Most people drive to get to clubs, as they are difficult to reach on foot and the city streets can be dangerous. Italians flock to bars in **Piazza Erbe** and along **Via San Bernardo**. The swanky bar **Al Parador**, P. della Vittoria 49R, is in the northeast corner of P. Vittoria, near the intersection of V. Cadorna and V. B. Liguria. (☎58 17 71. Mixed drinks €4.50. Open M-Sa 24hr. Cash only.)

FINALE LIGURE   ☎019

A beachside plaque proclaims Finale Ligure (pop. 12,000) the place for *"il riposo del popolo"* ("the people's rest"). From bodysurfing in choppy waves to scaling the 15th-century ruins of **Castello di San Giovanni**, *riposo* takes many forms. The nearby towns **Borgio** and **Verezzi** are also worth exploring. Walk east along V. Aurelia to find a free **beach**, less populated than those closer to town. Enclosed by ancient walls, **Finalborgo**, Finale Ligure's historic center, is a 1km walk or 2min. ACTS bus ride up V. Brunenghi from the station. With clean rooms and incomparable views, **▉Castello Wuillerman (HI) ❶**, V. Generale Caviglia, is well worth the hike

ITALY

up its daunting steps. From the train station, cross the street and turn left onto V. Raimondo Pertica. After passing a church on the left, turn left onto V. Alonzo and climb the stairs to the *castello*. (☎69 06 15, www.hostelfinaleligure.com. Breakfast included. Reception 7-10am and 5-10pm. Curfew midnight. Dorms €14. HI members only. Cash only.) **Camping Del Mulino ❶**, on V. Castelli, has a restaurant and mini-market. Take the Calvisio bus from the station to the Boncardo Hotel, turn left at Piazza Oberdan, turn right on V. Porro, and follow the signs up the hill. (☎60 16 69; www.campingmulino.it. Reception 8am-8pm. Open Apr.-Sept. Tent sites €9.50-14. MC/V.) Cheap restaurants lie along **Via Rossi, Via Roma,** and **Via Garibaldi.** Fill up on huge portions of pasta at **Spaghetteria Il Posto ❷**, V. Porro 21. (☎60 00 95. Entrees €7. Cover €1. Open Tu-Su 7-10:30pm. Closed for 2 weeks in Mar. Cash only.) Cafe and night spot **Pilade ❶**, V. Garibaldi 67, has live jazz on Fridays. (Beer from €3. Open daily 10am-2am. MC/V.) **Di per Di Express** supermarket is at V. Alonzo 10. (Open M-Sa 8:15am-1pm and 4:30-7:30pm, Su 9am-1pm. MC/V.)

   Trains leave from P. V. Veneto for Genoa (1hr., 2 per hr., €4). SAR **buses** run from the train station to Borgo Verezzi (10min., 4 per hr., €1). The city is divided into **Finalpia** to the east, **Finalmarina** in the center, and **Finalborgo,** farther inland. The station and most sights are in Finalmarina. The IAT **tourist office** is at V.S. Pietro 14. (☎68 10 19; www.inforiviera.it. Open M-Sa 9am-1pm and 3:30-6:30pm, Su 9am-noon; low season M-Sa 9am-1pm and 3:30-6:30pm.) **Postal Code:** 17024.

CAMOGLI   ☎0185

Postcard-perfect Camogli shimmers with color. Sun-faded peach houses crowd the hilltop, and red and turquoise boats bob in the water. Turn right out of the train station and keep walking until V. Repubblica turns into V. P. Schaffino to reach the handsomely furnished **Hotel Augusta ❸**, V.P. Schaffino 100. (☎77 05 92; www.htlaugusta.com. Breakfast €10 per room. 15min. free Internet. Singles €35-65; doubles €68-98; triples €90-135. AmEx/MC/V.) The *gelato* from **Gelato e Dintorni ❶**, V. Garibaldi 104/105, puts nationally ranked rivals to shame. (2 scoops €1.40. Open daily 11:30am-11pm. Cash only.) **Trains** run line to Genoa (40min., 38 per day, €1.60). Golfo Paradiso **ferries**, V. Scalo 3 (☎77 20 91; www.golfoparadiso.it), near P. Colombo, go to Cinque Terre (round-trip €20) and Portofino (round-trip €13). Buy tickets on the dock; call ahead for the schedule. Turn right from the station to find the **tourist office**, V. XX Settembre 33. (☎77 10 66. Open M-Sa 9am-12:30pm and 3:30-7pm, Su 9am-12:30pm; low season reduced hours.) **Postal Code:** 16032.

SANTA MARGHERITA LIGURE   ☎0185

Santa Margherita Ligure was a calm fishing village until the early 20th century, when it fell into favor with Hollywood stars. Today, glitz and glamor paint the shore, but the serenity of the town's early days still lingers. If you find gardens more enticing than beaches, take the paths off V. della Vittoria uphill to the pink-and-white **Villa Durazzo.** (Gardens open daily July-Aug. 9am-8pm; May-June and Sept. 9am-7pm; Apr. and Oct. 9am-6pm; Nov.-Dec. 9am-5pm. *Villa* open 9am-1pm and 2:30-6pm.) **Hotel Conte Verde ❹**, V. Zara 1, offers cozy beds and private showers. From the train station, turn right on V. Trieste, which becomes V. Roma. (☎28 71 39; www.hotelconteverde.it. Breakfast included. Singles €40-120; doubles €65-150; triples €90-210; quads €100-230. AmEx/MC/V.) **Trattoria Da Pezzi ❷**, V. Cavour 21, is popular with the locals for its homestyle cuisine. (☎28 53 03. *Primi* €3.80-6.70. *Secondi* €4.80-15. Cover €0.80. Open Su-F 10am-2:15pm and 5-9:15pm. MC/V.) **Trains** along the Pisa-Genoa line go from P. Federico Raoul Nobili, at the top of V. Roma, to Genoa (50min., 2-4 per hr., €2.10). Tigullio **buses** (☎28 88 34) go from P. V. Veneto to Camogli (30min., 1-2 per hr., €1.10) and Portofino (20min., 3 per hr., €1). Tigullio **ferries,** V. Palestro 8/1B (☎28 46 70), run tours to Cinque Terre (early May-late Sept. 1 per day, round-trip €22) and Portofino (Sa-Su 1 per hr., €4.50). Turn right out of the train station, go right on C. Rainusso and left on V. Gimelli to find the **tourist office,** V. XXV Aprile 2/B. (☎28 74 85;

iat.santamargheritaligure@provincia.genova.it. Open M-Sa 9:30am-12:30pm and 3-7:30pm, Su 9:30am-12:30pm and 4:30-7:30pm.) **Postal Code:** 16032.

CINQUE TERRE   ☎0187

Cinque Terre is an outdoorsman's paradise: strong hikers can cover all five villages—Corniglia, Manarola, Monterosso, Riomaggiore, and Vernazza—in about 5hr., and there are numerous opportunities for kayaking, cliff jumping, and horseback riding along the way. Rather than rushing, take the time to wander through the villages' tiny clusters of rainbow-colored houses amid hilly stretches of olive groves and vineyards. Though Cinque Terre was formerly a hidden treasure, increased publicity has made the towns fodder for a booming tourism industry.

⊟⊿ TRANSPORTATION AND PRACTICAL INFORMATION. Trains run along the Genoa-La Spezia (Pisa) line. A **Cinque Terre Card** (1-day €8, 3-day €19, 7-day €34) allows for unlimited train, bus, and path access among the five villages, La Spezia, and Levanto; it can be purchased at the train stations and Cinque Terre National Park. Monterosso is the most accessible village by train. From the station on V. Fegina, in the northern end of town, trains run to: Florence (3½hr., 1 per hr., €7.90); Genoa (1½hr., 1 per hr., €4.50); La Spezia (20min., 2 per hr., €1.60); Pisa (2½hr., 1 per hr., €4.70); Rome (7hr., 1 per 2hr., €17-27). **Ferries** run from La Spezia to Monterosso (2hr., 4 per day, €18). The five villages stretch along the shore between Levanto and La Spezia, connected by trains (5-20min., 1 per hr., €1.10), roads (although cars are not allowed inside the towns), and footpaths. **Monterosso** is the easternmost town and the largest, containing most of the services for the area, followed by higher-end **Vernazza,** cliffside **Corniglia,** swimming-cove-dotted **Manarola,** and affordable **Riomaggiore.** The Monterosso **park office** is at P. Garibaldi 20. (☎81 78 38. Open daily 8am-8pm.) The Pro Loco **tourist office,** V. Fegina 38, Monterosso, is below the train station. (☎/fax 81 75 06. Open daily 9:30am-6:30pm.) **Postal Codes:** 19016 (Monterosso); 19017 (Manarola and Riomaggiore); 19018 (Corniglia and Vernazza).

⌐⌂ ACCOMMODATIONS AND FOOD. Most hotels are in Monterosso, and they fill quickly in summer. For help in Riomaggiore, call **Edi,** V. Colombo 111. (☎92 03 25; edi-vesigna@iol.it.) Popular with students, **⊠Hotel Souvenir ❷,** V. Gioberti 30, Monterosso, has 47 beds and a friendly staff. (☎/fax 81 75 95. Doubles €50-80; triples €75-120. Cash only.) Modern **⊠Ostello Cinque Terre ❷,** V. B. Riccobaldi 21, in Manarola, has a sweeping roof terrace. (☎92 02 15; www.hostel5terre.com. Bike, kayak, and snorkeling equipment rental. Laun-

THE BEATEN PATH

Cinque Terre is doubtless a paradise for hikers, with trails connecting cliff-hugging towns along the mountainous shore of the Ligurian coast. Its beauty has even earned it inclusion on the UNESCO World Heritage List. The uniqueness of this land, however, is far from undiscovered, and the tourist stands that line the main streets of the towns offer proof of just that.

Even the picturesque trails, far into the brush, have been unable to escape tourism's impact. The shoes that have packed down the dirt trails have caused deterioration to the landscape, causing it to go (literally) downhill. In response, Cinque Terre was placed on the "World Monument Fund's List of 100 Sites at Risk," and workers at the Parco Nazionale delle Cinque Terre are committed to its restoration.

The Park's Landscape University organizes work camps to rebuild stone walls and stabilize trails. In exchange for your able hands, you will gain knowledge of the region's geography, customs, and specialized work techniques (hopefully perching on precarious cliffs doesn't faze you) and contribute to an effort that will ultimately enhance and preserve this vibrant patch of earth.

For more info, contact the Parco Nazionale delle Cinque Terre (☎0187 76 00 00; info@parconazionale5terre.it).

dry €6. Curfew 1am, midnight in winter. Dorms €22. MC/V.) All 23 rooms at **Hotel Gianni Franzi ❹**, P. Marconi 1, in Vernazza, have lovely antiques. (☎82 10 03; www.giannifranzi.it. Singles €42-65; doubles €60-85; triples €105. AmEx/MC/V.)

Meals at ▨**Il Ciliegio ❷**, Località Beo, in Monterosso, near P. Garibaldi, feature ingredients from the owner's garden. (☎81 78 29. *Primi* €6-10. *Secondi* €7-13. Open Tu-Su 12:30-2:30pm and 7:30-10:30pm. AmEx/MC/V.) **Focacceria Il Frantoio ❶**, V. Gioberti 1, in Monterosso, bakes mouth-watering foccaccia (€1-3) stuffed with olives, herbs, and more. (☎81 83 33. Open M-W and F-Su 9am-2pm and 3:30-8pm. Cash only.) Vernazza's oldest *trattoria*, **Trattoria Gianni Franzi ❷**, P. Marconi 1, offers local specialties and is famed for its pesto. (☎82 10 03. *Primi* €4-12. *Secondi* €6-20. Open M-Tu and Th-Su noon-3pm and 7:30-9:30pm. AmEx/MC/V.) **Ripa del Sole ❸**, V. de Gasperi 282, in Riomaggiore, serves some of the area's best seafood. (☎92 07 43. *Primi* €9.50. *Secondi* €9-21. Open Tu-Su noon-2pm and 7-10pm. AmEx/MC/V.) Get groceries at **SuperCONAD Margherita**, P. Matteotti 9, Monterosso. (Open June-Sept. M-Sa 8am-1pm and 5-8pm, Su 8am-1pm. MC/V.)

▨▨ **OUTDOOR ACTIVITIES AND NIGHTLIFE.** The best sights in Cinque Terre are the five villages themselves, and the gorgeous paths that connect them. Monterosso has Cinque Terre's largest free **beach**, in front of the historic center, sheltered by a cliff cove. The hike between Monterosso and Vernazza (1½hr.) is considered the most difficult, with steep climbs winding past terraced vineyards and hillside cottages. From there, the trip to Corniglia (1½hr.) offers breathtaking views of the sea and olive groves, with scents of rosemary, lemon, and lavender. Near Corniglia, the secluded **Guvano Beach**, accessed through a tunnel, is popular with students and adventurous types willing to make the trek down the mountain. Take the stairs down to the station from V. della Stazione in Corniglia and turn left, following the path along the railroad tracks to the public beach; the hike to youthful Manarola (1hr.) begins just past the beach, and is easier, though less picturesque. The most famous Cinque Terre hike, the **Via dell'Amore,** from Manarola to Riomaggiore, the smallest of the five towns, is a 20min. slate-paved walk that features a stone tunnel of love decorated in graffiti with romantic scenes.

At night, the liveliest towns are Monterosso and Riomaggiore. In Monterosso, **Il Casello,** V. Lungo Fessario 70, lures backpackers with its beachside location. (Wine from €3. Mixed drinks from €6. Open daily noon-midnight. Cash only.) **Bar Centrale,** V. C. Colombo 144, Riomaggiore, caters to a young, international crowd. (Beer €2-4. Mixed drinks €4-6. Open daily 7:30am-1am. Cash only.)

EMILIA-ROMAGNA

Go to Florence, Venice, and Rome to sightsee. Come to Emilia-Romagna to eat. Italy's wealthy wheat- and dairy-producing region covers the fertile plains of the Po River Valley, whose harvest weighs tables with some of the finest culinary traditions on the peninsula, freeing visitors from the binds of the elsewhere omnipresent *menù turistico*. But Emilia-Romagna deserves more than just a quick stop-over for some *Bolognese;* combining a rich history with modern cities, it's an essential destination for any Italian traveler.

BOLOGNA ☎**051**

Affectionately referred to as the *grassa* (fat) and *dotta* (learned) city, Bologna (pop. 369,955) has a legacy of excellent food, education, and art. Bologna's museums and churches house priceless artistic treasures and its university is Europe's oldest. After experiencing the city's many free sights and student-friendly nightlife, visitors leave Bologna satisfied, having tasted the Italian good life. Be as cautious in Bologna as in a big city; guard your wallet, and don't travel solo at night.

📞 TRANSPORTATION AND PRACTICAL INFORMATION. Trains leave the northern tip of Bologna's walled city for: Florence (1½hr., 39 per day, €4.80); Milan (3hr., 46 per day, €19); Rome (3hr., 36 per day, €32); Venice (2hr., 29 per day, €8.20). **Buses** #25 and 30 run between the train station and the center at **Piazza Maggiore** (€1). Alternatively, head through P. XX Settembre to V. dell'Indipendenza, which leads to P. del Nettuno and the nearby P. Maggiore. The **tourist office,** P. Maggiore 1, is in Palazzo del Podestà. (☎24 65 41; www.iperbole.bologna.it/bolognaturismo. Open daily 9:30am-7:30pm.) **Postal Code:** 40100.

🏠🍴 ACCOMMODATIONS AND FOOD. Bologna's hotels, mostly located around V. Ugo Bassi and V. Marconi, are pricey; reserve ahead, especially in summer. Take V. Ugo Bassi from P. del Nettuno, then take the third left to reach **Albergo Panorama ❹,** V. Livraghi 1, 4th fl., where sunny rooms look out over V. Ugo Bassi. Three sparkling bathrooms serve all 10 rooms, which have sink and TV. (☎22 18 02; www.hotelpanoramabologna.it. Curfew 3am. Singles €50; doubles €60-70; triples €75-85; quads €85-95; quints €100. AmEx/MC/V.) Six kilometers northeast of the *centro,* **Ostello due Torre San Sisto (HI) ❷,** V. Viadagola 5, has a basketball court and a reading room with satellite TV. Take bus #93 (301 on Su) from V. Marconi 69 (M-Sa 2 per hr.); ask the driver for the San Sisto stop. The hostel is the yellow building on the right. (☎/fax 50 18 10. Lockout 10am-3:30pm. Dorms €18; doubles €36. €3 HI discount. AmEx/MC/V.)

Scout **Via Augusto Righi, Via Piella,** and **Via Saragozza** for traditional *trattorie* with *spaghetti alla Bolognese.* **Nuova Pizzeria Gianna ❶,** V. S. Stefano 76A, serves pizzas made fresh in front of you. (☎22 25 16. Pizzas from €3.20, slices from €2. Open M-Sa 8:30am-11pm. Cash only.) **Osteria dell'Orsa ❶,** V. Mentana 1/F has communal tables where students eat before hitting nearby nightlife. (☎23 15 76. Open daily noon-4pm and 7pm-midnight. Cash only.) Some of the best gelato in Italy is churned at **Ill Gelatauro,** V. S. Vitale 98B. (☎23 00 49. 2 scoops €2.60. Open M 8am-7pm, Tu-Su 8am-11pm. Cash only.) A **PAM** supermarket, V. Marconi 26, is by the intersection with V. Riva di Reno. (Open M-Sa 7:45am-8pm. AmEx/MC/V.)

👁🎆 SIGHTS AND NIGHTLIFE. The ancient *palazzi* and expensive boutiques in **Piazza Maggiore** are dwarfed by the Romanesque **Palazzo del Podestà** and the nearby **Basilica di San Petronio,** P. Maggiore 3. The basilica hosted the Council of Trent (when not in Trent) and the 1530 ceremony in which Pope Clement VII gave Italy to Germany. (Open daily 9:30am-12:30pm and 2:30-5:30pm. Free.) The **Palazzo Archiginnasio,** behind S. Petronio, was the first home of Bolo-

gna's modern university. (V. Archiginnasio 1. Open M-F 9am-1pm. Free.) **Piazza del Nettuno** contains Giambologna's 16th-century fountain, **Neptune and Attendants.** Two towers rise from P. Porta Ravegana, at the end of V. Rizzoli; the **Torre degli Garisenda** leans to one side, but the nearly 98m **Torre degli Asinelli** is climbable. (Open daily 9am-6pm. €3.) From V. Rizzoli, follow V. S. Stefano to P. S. Stefano, where the Romanesque ■**Chiesa Santo Stefano** contains the basin where Pontius Pilate absolved himself of responsibility for Christ's death. (☎22 32 56. Modest dress required. Open M-Sa 9am-noon and 3:30-6:45pm, Su 9am-12:45pm and 3:30-7pm. Free.) The **Pinacoteca Nazionale,** V. delle Belle Arti 56, off V. Zamboni, traces the history of Bolognese art. (☎42 09 411. Open Tu-Su 9am-7pm. €4.)

Bologna's hip students ensure raucous nighttime fun, especially around V. Zamboni. **Cluricaune,** V. Zamboni 18/B, a multi-level Irish pub, ropes in students with its beer selection. (☎26 34 19. Pints €3.10-4.20. Happy hour W 7-10:30pm; pints €2.50. Open daily noon-3am.) **Cassero,** located in a 17th-century salt warehouse in the Porta Saragozza, is popular with the gay community, but all are welcome. (☎64 94 416. Drinks €3-6. ARCI-GAY card, available at ARCI-GAY, V. Don Minzoni 18, required. Open M-F 10pm-2am, Sa-Su 10pm-5am.) Every year from mid-June to mid-September, the city commune sponsors a ■**festival** of art, cinema, dance, music, and theater. Many events are free, and few cost much more than €5.

PARMA   ☎0521

Though famous for its *parmigiano* cheese and *prosciutto,* Parma's (pop. 172,000) artistic excellence is not confined to the kitchen. Giuseppe Verdi composed some of his greatest works here, and native artists Parmigianino and Correggio cultivated Mannerist painting in the 16th century. The town centers around the 11th-century **duomo** where Correggio's *Virgin* ascends to a golden heaven, and the pink-and-white marble **baptistry** displays early Medieval frescoes of enthroned saints and apostles. From P. Garibaldi, follow Str. Cavour and take the third right on Str. al Duomo. (*Duomo* open daily 9am-12:30pm and 3-6:30pm. Baptistry open daily 9am-12:30pm and 3-6:30pm. Duomo free. Baptistry €4, students €3.) Built in 1521 to house a miraculous picture of the Virgin Mary, the **Chiesa Magistrale di Santa Maria della Steccata,** up V. Garibaldi from P. Garibaldi, features frescoes by Parmigianino. (Open daily 7:30am-noon and 3-6:30pm. Free.) From P. del Duomo, follow Str. al Duomo across Str. Cavour, walk one block down Str. Piscane, and cross P. della Pace to reach the 17th-century **Palazzo della Pilotta,** with the **Galleria Nazionale** and the wooden **Teatro Farnese.** (Both open Tu-Su 8:30am-1:45pm. Ticket office closes 1pm. Theater €2, students €1. Gallery €6, students €4.)

Take bus #2, 2N, or 13 from the bus station to the beautiful, brand new ■**Ostello della Gioventu (HI) ❷,** Via San Leonardo 86, and its young, English-speaking staff. (☎19 17 547; www.ostelloparma.it. Reception 24hr. Dorms €18; singles €21; doubles €40; triples €59; quads €76.) **Albergo Leon d'Oro ❸,** V. Fratti 4a, after intersection with Str. Garibaldi, has clean, basic rooms with shared bath. (☎77 31 82; www.leondoroparma.com. Singles €35-55; doubles €60-80. AmEx/MC/V.) Resist the urge to dine outside on one of Parma's many patios, and eat downstairs in the 14th-century stone building of **Ristorante Gallo d'Oro ❷,** Borgo della Salina 3. From P. Garibaldi, take Str. Farini and turn left. (☎20 88 46. *Primi* €6.50-9. *Secondi* €6.50-9.50. Cover €2. Open M-Sa noon-2:30pm and 7:30-11pm. AmEx/MC/V.) **K2,** Str. Cairoli 23, next to the Chiesa di San Giovanni Evangelista, tops each cone with creamy *gelato* in a flower shape. (*Gelato* from €1.50. Open M-Tu and Th-Su 11am-midnight. Cash only.) An **open-air market** comes to P. Ghiaia, off V. Marcotti near the intersection with Str. Mazzini, every Wednesday and Saturday morning 8am-1pm and Wednesday and Friday nights in summer. **Dimeglio** supermarket is at Str. Ventidue Luglio 27/c. (Open daily 8:30am-1:30pm and 4:30-8pm.) **Trains** go from P. Carlo Alberto della Chiesa to: Bologna (1hr., 3 per hr., €4.90); Florence (2hr., 3 per day, €9.20); Milan (1½hr., 3-5 per hr., €7.10). Walk left on V. Bottego from the station, turn right on Str. Garibaldi, then left on Str. Melloni to reach the **tourist office,** Str. Melloni 1/A. (☎21 88 89; www.turismo.comune.parma.it. Open M 9am-1pm and 3-7pm, Tu-Sa 9am-7pm, Su 9am-1pm.) **Postal Code:** 43100.

RAVENNA ☎0544

Ravenna (pop. 150,000) enjoyed its 15 minutes of fame 14 centuries ago, when Justinian and Theodora, rulers of the Byzantine Empire, made it the headquarters of their western campaign. Take V. Argentario from V. Cavour to reach the 6th-century ◪**Basilica di San Vitale,** V. S. Vitale 17, whose windows let in enough light to make its mosaics glow. Across the courtyard is the brick **Mausoleo di Galla Placidia,** where a single lamp illuminates 570 gold stars against a night sky. (☎21 62 92. Open daily Apr.-Sept. 9am-7pm; Mar. and Oct. 9am-5:30pm; Nov.-Feb. 10am-5pm.) To see the pastoral mosaics in the **Basilica di Sant'Apollinare,** take bus #4 or 44 across from the train station (€0.80) to Classe. (Basilica open M-Sa 8:30am-7:30pm, Su 9am-7pm. €3, under 18 free.) Ravenna's most popular monument is the **Tomb of Dante Alighieri,** who was exiled from Florence in 1301 and died in Ravenna in 1321. The adjoining **Dante Museum** contains the fir chest that held Dante's bones and 18,000 scholarly volumes on his works. From P. del Popolo, cut through P. Garibaldi to V. D. Alighieri. (☎33 667. Tomb open daily 9am-7pm. Free. Museum open Tu-Su Apr.-Sept. 9am-noon and 3:30-6pm; Oct.-Mar. 9am-noon. €2.)

From P. Farini, walk down Vle. Farini and make a left on V. Roma to get to the luxurious ◪**Ostello Galletti Abbiosi ❹,** V. Roma 140. (☎/fax 31 313; www.galletti.ra.it. Breakfast included. Free Wi-Fi. Reception M-F 8am-6:30pm, Sa-Su 8am-6pm. Singles €55-60; doubles €80-100; triples €100-110; quads €120-130. AmEx/MC/V.) Take bus #70 or 80 from the train station (3-6 per hr., €1) to reach **Ostello Dante (HI) ❷,** V. Nicolodi 12. (☎42 11 64. Breakfast included. Laundry €2.50. Internet 1st 10min. free, €3 per hr. thereafter. Lockout 10am-3:30pm. Curfew 11:30pm; €1 key deposit. Dorms €17; family rooms €16 per person. €3 HI discount. MC/V.) Feast on pizzas (€2-8) and local specialties outside at **Babaleus ❷,** Vicolo Gabbani 7. (☎21 64 64. *Primi* €6.50. *Secondi* €7-13. Open M-Tu, Th-Su noon-2:30pm and 7pm-midnight. AmEx/MC/V.) **Trains** run from P. Farini to Bologna (1hr., 1 per hr., €5) and Ferrara (1hr., 1 per hr., €4.50), with connections to Florence and Venice. Follow V. Farini from the station to V. Diaz and the central P. del Popolo to find the **tourist office,** V. Salara 8. (☎35 404; www.turismo.ravenna.it. Open Apr.-Sept. M-Sa 8:30am-7pm, Su 10am-6pm; Oct.-Mar. M-Sa 8:30am-6pm.) **Postal Code:** 48100.

RIMINI ☎0541

The Ibiza of the Adriatic, Rimini is the party town of choice for young European fashionistas. Beaches, nightclubs, and boardwalks crammed with boutiques, fortune tellers, and artists characterize a city where it is perfectly acceptable—and admirable—to collapse into bed and bid the rising sun good night. Rimini's most treasured attraction is its remarkable **beach** with fine sand and mild Adriatic waves. Rimini's nightlife heats up around the **lungomare** in southern Rimini and near the port. Bus #11 fills with rowdy partygoers as it traverses the strip of clubs. At ◪**Coconuts,** Lungomare Tintorin 5, a diverse crowd gathers until the wee hours for the tropical decor and two outdoor dance floors. (☎52 35; www.coconuts.it. Drinks €4-8. Open daily 6pm-5am.) From Coconuts, continue walking north along the *lungomare* to find **Rock Island by Black Jack,** at the farthest point from shore, on a pier. In the evening, the restaurant offers seafood specialties and classy beachside ambience. Later on, the lights of Rimini sparkle from the outdoor bar and dance floor. (☎50 178; www.rockislandrimini.com. Open Tu-Su. Dinner served 7:30pm-midnight; dancing until late. Reserve ahead for dinner.)

Hotel Jammin (HI) ❷, Vle. Derna 22, is at stop 13 of bus #11. Seconds from the beach, the brand-new hostel accommodates the Rimini partying lifestyle with a social bar, no lockout, and breakfast until 10:30am. (Breakfast and linens included. Open Feb.-Dec. Dorms €19. AmEx/MC/V.) After overspending on drinks, get groceries at the **STANDA** supermarket, V. Vespucci 13. (Open daily 8am-9pm. AmEx/MC/V.) **Trains** (☎89 20 21) run to Bologna (1½hr., 2 per hr., €6.70), Milan (3hr., 1 per hr., €28), and Ravenna (1hr., 1 per hr., €3). The **IAT tourist office** is at P. Fellini 3, stop 10 on bus #11. (Open in summer M-Sa 8:30am-7:30pm, Su 8:30am-2:30pm; winter M-Sa 9am-12:30pm and 3:30-6pm.) **Postal Code:** 47900.

FERRARA   ☎0532

Rome has mopeds, Venice has gondolas, and Ferrara has *biciclette* (bicycles). In a city with 160,000 bicycles for 130,000 residents, bikers are a more common sight than pedestrians. The **medieval wall** supports a 9km path with views of the city. The 14th-century **Castello Estense** is surrounded by a fairy-tale moat. Inside, themed rooms, gardens, and dungeon tunnels wind through this former fortress. (☎29 92 33. Open Tu-Su 9:30am-5:30pm. €6, under 18 and over 65 €5. Audio tour €3.) From the *castello*, take C. Martiri della Libertà to P. Cattedrale and the **Duomo San Romano**, across V. S. Romano from the **Museo della Cattedrale,** home to the church's precious works. (*Duomo* open M-Sa 7:30am-noon and 3-6:30pm, Su 7:30am-12:30pm and 3:30-7:30pm. Museum open Tu-Su 9am-1pm and 3-6pm. €5, students €3.) From the *castello*, cross Largo Castello to C. Ercole I d'Este and walk to its intersection with C. Rossetti to reach the **Palazzo Diamanti,** whose facade is covered by white pyramid-shaped studs. Within, the **Pinacoteca Nazionale** holds works from the Ferrarese school and panels by El Greco. (Open Tu-W and F-Sa 9am-2pm, Th 9am-7pm, Su 9am-1pm. €4, students €2.) Follow C. Ercole I d'Este behind the *castello* to find the **Palazzo Massari**, C. Porta Mare 9, home to **Padiglione d'Arte Contemporanea, Museo d'Arte Moderna e Contemporanea Filippo de Pisis,** and tapestry-walled **Museo Ferrarese dell'Ottocentro/Museo Giovanni Boldini,** dedicated to the artist of its title. (All open Tu-Su 9am-1pm and 3-6pm. Filippo de Pisis €3, students €2. Ottocentro/Boldini €5/3. Combination ticket €8/3.)

   Pensione Artisti ❷, V. Vittoria 66, near P. Lampronti, offers free bike use. From C. Martiri d. Libertà, turn left at the cathedral, right on V. S. Romano, left on V. Ragno, then immediately left. (☎76 10 38. Singles €25; doubles €48, with bath €60. Cash only.) **Osteria Degli Angeli ❸**, V. delle Volte 4, offers regional fare in its 16th-century dining room. From the *basilica*, take C. Porta Reno and turn left under the arch. (*Primi* €7-8. *Secondi* €7-15. Open daily 6-11pm; kitchen open 7-10pm. MC/V.) Italy's oldest *osteria*, **Osteria Al Brindisi ❸**, V. G. degli Adelardi 11, has wined and dined the likes of Titian and Pope John Paul II since 1435. (☎20 91 42. Cover €2. Open Tu-Su 9am-1am. MC/V.) For groceries, stop by **Supermercato Conad**, V. Garibaldi 53. (Open M-Sa 8:30am-8pm, Su 9:15am-1:15pm. MC/V.) **Trains** go to: Bologna (30min., 3 per hr., €3); Padua (1hr., 2 per hr., €4.40); Ravenna (1hr., 1 per hr., €4.40); Rome (3-4hr., 12 per day, €23); Venice (1½hr., 1-2 per hr., €6.10). ACFT (☎59 94 92) and GGFP **buses** run from the train station to local beaches (1½hr., 12 per day, €4.30) and Bologna (1½hr., 15 per day, €3.40). Rent **bikes** at **Pirani e Bagni**, P. Stazione 2. (☎77 21 90. €2 per hr., €7 per day. Open M-F 7am-8pm, Sa 6am-2pm. Cash only.) The **tourist office** is in Castello Estense. (☎20 93 70. Open M-Sa 9am-1pm and 2-6pm, Su 9:30am-1pm and 2-5:30pm.) **Postal Code:** 44100

TRENTINO-ALTO ADIGE

With its steep mountain trails and small towns largely free of tourist mobs, Trentino-Alto Adige appeals to outdoor enthusiasts. The near-impenetrable dolomitic rock has slowed major industrialization, preserving the jagged pink-purple cliffs of the Dolomites and evergreen forests that Le Corbusier once called "the most beautiful natural architecture in the world."

TRENT (TRENTO)   ☎ 0461

Between the Dolomites and the Veneto, Trent (pop. 105,000) offers a taste of northern Italian life with festivals, delicious food, and spectacular scenery. The **Piazza del Duomo,** Trent's epicenter, is anchored by the massive **Fontana del Nettuno** in the center of the *piazza*. Nearby is the **Cattedrale di San Vigilio,** where the Council of Trent first called for the Counter-Reformation. (Open daily 7am-noon and 2:30-6pm. Free.) Walk down V. Belenzani and head right on V. Roma to reach the historic **Castello del Buonconsiglio,** home to the execution site of famed Trentino martyrs Cesare Battisti, Damiano Chiesa, and Fabio Filzi. During WWI, the three men joined the Italian army, but because Trent was then a part of Austria-Hungry, they were identified as Austrian subjects and executed as traitors. (www.buonconsiglio.it. Open Tu-Su 9:30am-5pm. €6, students €3.) From the station, turn right on V. Pozzo, then right on V. Torre Vanga to get to the tidy rooms of **Ostello Giovane Europa (HI) ❶,** V. Torre Vanga 11. (☎26 34 84. Breakfast included. Reception 7:30am-11pm. Ask for door code if returning after 11:30pm. Dorms €14; singles €25; doubles €40. AmEx/MC/V.) **Hotel Venezia ❹,** P. Duomo 45, offers rooms across from the *duomo*. (☎23 41 14. Singles €49; doubles €69. MC/V.) Head to ▨**Alla Grotta ❷,** Vico S. Marco 6, for huge pizzas piled high with toppings. (☎98 71 97. Pizza €4.10-7.20. *Primi* €5.60-7.20. Open noon-2:30pm and 6:30pm-midnight. MC/V.) The **tourist office,** V. Manci 2, offers advice on local trails, festivals, and guided tours. Turn right from the train station and left on V. Roma, which becomes V. Manci. (☎21 60 00; www.apt.trento.it. Open daily 9am-7pm.) **Postal Code:** 38100.

BOLZANO (BOZEN)   ☎ 0471

German street names in Bolzano (pop. 100,000) alert visitors to the town's Italian-Austrian cultural fusion. Gothic spires rise skyward from the Romanesque **duomo,** in P. Walther. (Open M-F 9:45am-noon and 2-5pm, Sa 9:45am-noon. Free.) The **South Tyrol Museum of Archaeology,** V. Museo 43, near Ponte Talvera, lets tourists file by **Ötzi,** a 5000-year-old frozen Neanderthal. (Open Tu-W and F-Su 10am-5pm, Th 10am-7pm. €8, students €6.) Take a right from the train station and walk 5min. to reach the ▨**Youth Hostel Bolzano ❷,** V. Renon 22, where guests enjoy clean rooms and lots of amenities. (☎30 08 65. Breakfast included. Internet €2 per hr. Reception 8am-9pm. Dorms €21. €2 discount for longer stays. AmEx/MC/V.) The markets of **Piazza delle Erbe** and the **wurst stand** at the intersection of V. Museo and P. delle Erbe allow visitors to sample Bolzano's Austrian-influenced fare. (Market open M-F 7am-7pm, Sa 8am-1pm; wurst stand open M-Sa 8am-7pm). The **tourist office,** P. Walther 8, is near the *duomo*. (☎30 70 00; www.bolzano-bozen.it. Open M-F 9am-1pm and 2-7pm, Sa 9am-2pm.) **Postal Code:** 39100.

THE VENETO

From the rocky foothills of the Dolomites to the fertile valleys of the Po River, the Veneto's geography is as diverse as its history. Once loosely united under the Venetian Empire, its towns have retained their cultural independence; in fact, visitors are more likely to hear regional dialects than standard Italian during neighborly exchanges. The tenacity of local culture and customs will come as a pleasant surprise for those expecting only mandolins and gondolas.

VENICE (VENEZIA)   ☎ 041

In Venice (pop. 60,000), palaces stand tall on a steadily sinking network of wood, and the waters of age-old canals creep up the mossy steps of abandoned homes.

People flock year-round to peer into delicate blown-glass and gaze at the master-works of Tintoretto and Titian. Though hordes of tourists and pigeons are inescapable, the city proves to be a unique source of wonder.

▢ TRANSPORTATION

The **train station** is on the northwest edge of the city; be sure to get off at **Santa Lucia,** not at Mestre on the mainland. Buses and boats arrive at **Piazzale Roma,** just across the Canal Grande from the train station. To get from either station to **Piazza San Marco,** take *vaporetto* (water bus) #82 or follow signs for a 40min. walk.

Flights: Aeroporto Marco Polo (VCE; ☎26 09 260; www.veniceairport.it), 10km north of the city. Take the **ATVO shuttlebus** (☎042 13 83 671) from the airport to Ple. Roma on the main island (30min., 1 per hr. 8am-midnight, €3).

Trains: Stazione Santa Lucia. Ticket windows open M-F 8:30am-7:30pm, Sa-Su 9am-1:30pm and 2-5:30pm. **Information office** (☎89 20 21) to the left as you exit the platforms. Open daily 7am-9pm. Trains go to: **Bologna** (2hr., 30 per day, €8.20); **Florence** (3hr., 8 per day, €30); **Milan** (3hr., 19 per day, €13); **Rome** (4½hr., 7 per day, €57). **Luggage storage** by track #14.

Buses: Local **ACTV** buses (☎24 24; www.hellovenezia.it), in Ple. Roma. Open daily 7:30am-8pm. **ACTV long-distance carrier** runs buses to **Padua** (1hr., 2 per hr., €4).

Public Transportation: The **Canal Grande** can be crossed on foot only at the Scalzi, Rialto, and Accademia *ponti* (bridges). **Traghetti** (gondola ferry boats) traverse the canals at 7 locations, including Ferrovia, San Marculola, Cà d'Oro, and Rialto (€0.50). **Vaporetti** (V; water buses) provide 24hr. service around the city, with reduced service midnight-5am (single-ride €3.50, the Canal Grande €5; 24hr. *biglietto turistico* pass €12, 3-day €25). Buy tickets at *vaporetti* stops. Stock up on tickets by asking for a pass *non timbrato* (unvalidated), then validate before boarding by inserting tickets into one of the yellow boxes at each stop. **Lines #1** (slow) and **82** (fast) run from the station down Canal Grande and Canale della Giudecca; lines **#41** and **51** circumnavigate Venice from the station to Lido; **#42** and **52** do the reverse; line **LN** runs from F. Nuove to Burano, Murano, and Lido, and connects to Torcello.

ISLAND HOPPING. *Vaporetto* ticket prices border on extortion. Buy the 24hr. *vaporetto* pass for €12, then leap from 1 island to the next in 1 day.

▣ ORIENTATION

Venice is composed of 118 islands in a lagoon, connected to the mainland by a thin causeway. The city is a veritable labyrinth and can confuse even natives, most of whom simply set off in a general direction and patiently weave their way. If you unglue your eyes from your map and go with the flow, you'll discover some of the unexpected surprises that make Venice spectacular. Yellow signs all over the city point toward the following landmarks: **Ponte di Rialto** (in the center), **Piazza San Marco** (central south), **Ponte Accademia** (southwest), **Ferrovia** (or the train station, in the northwest), and **Piazzale Roma** (south of the station). The **Canal Grande** winds through the city, creating six nebulous *sestieri* (sections): **Cannaregio** is in the north and includes the train station, Jewish ghetto, and Cà d'Oro; **Castello** extends east toward the Arsenale; **Dorsoduro,** across the bridge from S. Marco, stretches the length of Canale della Giudecca and up to Campo S. Pantalon; **Santa Croce** lies west of S. Polo, across the Canal Grande from the train station; **San Marco** fills in the area between the Ponte di Rialto and Ponte Accademia; and **San Polo** runs north from Chiesa S. Maria dei Frari to the Ponte di Rialto. Within each *sestiere,* addresses are not specific to a particular street—every building is given a number, and jumps between address numbers are unpredictable. If *sestiere* boundaries prove too vague, Venice's **parrochie** (parishes) provide a more defined idea of where you are; *parrochia* signs, like *sestiere* signs, are on the sides of buildings.

◪ PRACTICAL INFORMATION

Tourist Office: APT, Cal. della Ascensione, S. Marco 71/F (☎52 98 740; www.doge.it), directly opposite the basilica. Open daily 9am-3:30pm. Avoid the mobbed branches at the train and bus stations. The **Rolling Venice Card** (€4) offers discounts on transportation and at over 200 restaurants, cafes, hotels, museums, and shops for ages 14-29. Cards are valid for 1 year from date of purchase and can be purchased at APT, which provides a list of participating vendors, or at the **ACTV VeLa** office (☎27 47 650) in Ple. Roma. Open daily 7am-8pm. **VeneziaSi** (☎800 84 30 06), next to the tourist office in the train station, books rooms for a €2 fee. Open daily 8am-9pm. Branches in Ple. Roma (☎52 28 640) and the airport (☎54 15 133).

Hospital: Ospedale Civile, Campo S. S. Giovanni e Paolo, Castello (☎52 94 111).

Internet Access: ABColor, Lista di Spagna, Cannaregio 220 (☎52 44 380). Look for the "@" symbol on a yellow sign, left off the main street heading from the train station. €6 per hr., students €4. Printing €0.15 per page. Open M-Sa 10am-8pm.

Post Office: Poste Venezia Centrale, Salizzada Fontego dei Tedeschi, S. Marco 5554 (☎27 17 111), off Campo S. Bartolomeo. Open M-Sa 8:30am-6:30pm. **Postal Codes:** 30121 (Cannaregio); 30122 (Castello); 30123 (Dorsoduro); 30135 (S. Croce); 30124 (S. Marco); 30125 (S. Polo).

⌂⌂ ACCOMMODATIONS AND CAMPING

Hotels in Venice are often more expensive than those elsewhere in Italy, but savvy travelers can find cheap rooms if they sniff out options early in summer. Agree on a price before booking, and reserve one month ahead. **VeneziaSi** (see **Tourist Offices,** p. 621) finds rooms on the same day, but not cheap ones. If you're looking for a miracle, try religious institutions, which often offer rooms in summer for €25-110. Options include: **Casa Murialdo,** F. Madonna dell'Orto, Cannaregio 3512 (☎71 99 33); **Domus Cavanis,** Dorsoduro 896 (☎52 87 374), near the Ponte Accademia; **Istituto Canossiano,** F. delle Romite, Dorsoduro 1323 (☎24 09 713); **Istituto Ciliota,** Cal. Muneghe S. Stefano, San Marco 2976 (☎52 04 888); **Patronato Salesiano Leone XIII,** Cal. S. Domenico, Castello 1281 (☎52 87 299). For camping, plan on a 20min. boat ride from Venice. In addition to camping options listed here, Litorale del Cavallino, on the Lido's Adriatic side, has multiple beach campgrounds.

▨ **Alloggi Gerotto Calderan,** Campo S. Geremia 283 (☎71 55 62; www.casagerottocalderan.com). Half hostel, half hotel, all good. Location makes it the best deal in Venice. Check-in 2pm. Check-out 10am. Curfew 12:30am. Reserve at least 15 days ahead. Dorms €25; singles €40-50; doubles €50-90; triples €75-105. 10% Rolling Venice discount; reduced prices for extended stays. Cash only. ❷

▨ **Hotel Bernardi-Semenzato,** Cal. dell'Oca, Cannaregio 4366 (☎52 27 257; www.hotelbernardi.com). Squeaky clean, elegantly furnished rooms, all with A/C and TV. Check-out 11am. Singles €30-40; doubles €70-75, with bath €60-90; triples €95; quads €120-130. 10% Rolling Venice discount on larger rooms. AmEx/MC/V. ❸

Albergo Casa Petrarca, Cal. Schiavine, San Marco 4386 (☎52 00 430). Cheerful proprietors run a tiny hotel with 7 rooms, most with bath and A/C. Breakfast included. Singles €80-90; doubles €125, with canal view €155. Extra bed €35. Cash only. ❺

ITALY

Venice

🏠🏠 ACCOMMODATIONS

Albergo Casa Petrarca, **20**
Albergo Doni, **14**
Albergo San Samuele, **21**
Alloggi Gerotto Calderan, **4**
Camping Fusina, **1**
Camping Miramare, **10**
Domus Civica (ACISJF), **8**
Foresteria Valdese, **9**
Hotel Bernardi-Semenzato, **5**
Ostello di Venezia (HI), **31**
Ostello Santa Fosca, **3**

🍔 FOOD

Antica Birraria la Corte, **18**
Le Bistro de Venise, **19**
Cantinone Gia Schiavi, **23**
Gelateria Nico, **15**
Osteria al Portego, **13**
Pizzeria La Perla, **7**
Trattoria da Bepi, **6**

🍷 NIGHTLIFE

Café Blue, **11**
Bistrot ai Do Draghi, **12**
Naranzaria, **17**
Paradiso Perduto, **2**
Piccolo Mondo, **22**

Ⓥ Vaporetti Stops

TO MURANO (1.5km),
TORCELLO (4km), BURANO (7km),
AEROPORTO MARCO POLO ✈ (10km).

CIMITERO **V**

V **ORTO**

Canale delle Fondamente Nuove

Isola di San Michele

✝ **Chiesa della Madonna dell'Orto**

Madonna dell'Orto

Sacca della Misericordia

2 🇮🇹 **S. Maria Valverde** ✝

C. Lunga Santa Caterina

FONDAMENTA NUOVE V

3 Canal

"CAMPO SANTA 'OSCA" **S. Fosca** ✝

Rio di Noale

Rio S. Girolamo

Chiesa dei Gesuiti ✝ CAMPO DEL GESUITI

Calle Larga dei Botteri

Fondamenta Nuove

Isola di San Michele

200 meters

200 yards

N LG

Billa Supermarket

Strada Nuova

Calle Racchetta
Calle delle Viale
Ruga Due Pozzi

Calle dell Fumo

Calle del Squero

V OSPEDALE

Cà d'Oro

V CA D'ORO

5 🇮🇹 **6** 🇮🇹 **7** ✝ CAMPO S.S. APOSTOLI

Calle del Pistor

Rio dei Mendicanti

✝ Ospedale Civile

S.S. Giovanni e Paolo ✝

Rio di San Marina

Barbaria delle Tole

C. d. Cappuccine

CELESTIA V

17 Ponte di Rialto

SAN POLO

✉

Riva del Vin

CAMPO S. BARTOLOMEO

Sal. di S. Lio

CAMPO S. MARIA FORMOSA

Ruga Giuffa

Ponte Rosso Fanosa

9 Calle del Cappello

S. Francesco della Vigna ✝ CAMPO D. CELESTIA

TO **10** (10km)

SAN SILVESTRO V

RIALTO V

Riva del Carbon

Canal

Rio di S. Salvador

Rio di S. Luca

✝ **S. Maria Formosa**

B. Lorenzo
C. Castello

C. di Mezzo

C. S. Giorgio

Fondamenta

CAMPO SAN LORENZO

Scuola Dalmata San Giorgio degli Schiavoni

CASTELLO

Calle Lion
C. d. Furlani

CAMPO MANIN

Calle del Fabbri

19

20

Rio del Palazzo

C. Corona
Fond. Osmarin
13 🇮🇹
S. Provolo
S. Zaccaria ✝

C. d. Madonna

CAMPO BANDIERA E MORO

Rio d. Greci

Calle d. Mandola

CAMPO SANT'ANGELO

SAN MARCO

Frezzeria

Rio di San Mois

✝ **San Marco**

14

C. del Vin

Palazzo Ducale

PIAZZA SAN MARCO

CAMPO S. ZACCARIA

Calle della Pietà

C. Pietà

C. del Dose

C. Crosera

C. del Forno

TO ARSENALE (150m)

Rio dell'Arsenale

Rio della Ostreghe

ℹ

ℹ V **SAN MARCO**

Riva degli Schiavoni

V **S. ZACCARIA**

ARSENALE V

V **GIGLIO**

ione eggenheim

V **GIGLIO**

V **SALUTE**

🇮🇹 **S. Maria della Salute** ✝

SEE CENTRAL VENICE MAP, P. 624-625

Canale di San Marco

TO GIARDINI PUBLICI (250m)

Rio di Fornace

Fond. Zattere al Saloni

SAN GIORGIO V

S. Giorgio Maggiore ✝

Isola di S. Giorgio Maggiore

Fond. delle Zitelle

ZITELLE V
To **16** (100m)

TO LIDO (2km)

ITALY

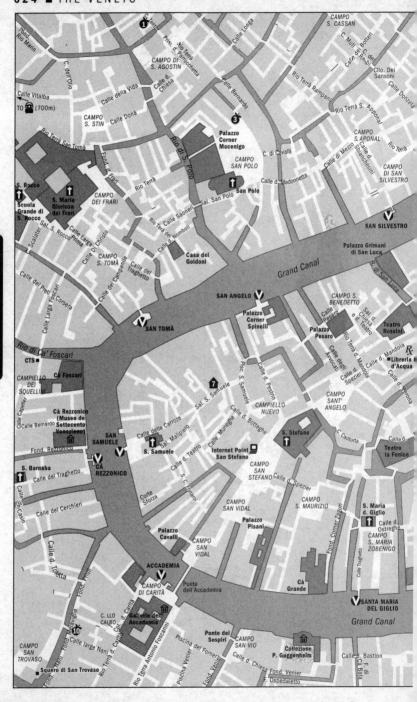

ITALY

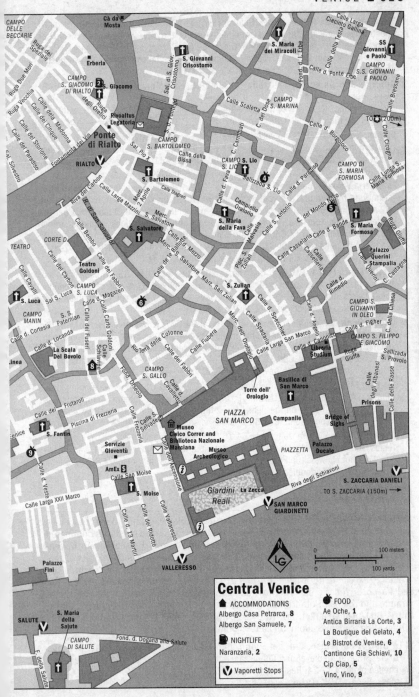

ITALY

Central Venice

🏠 **ACCOMMODATIONS**
Albergo Casa Petrarca, **8**
Albergo San Samuele, **7**

🍸 **NIGHTLIFE**
Naranzaria, **2**

V Vaporetti Stops

🍅 FOOD
Ae Oche, **1**
Antica Birraria La Corte, **3**
La Boutique del Gelato, **4**
Le Bistrot de Venise, **6**
Cantinone Gia Schiavi, **10**
Cip Ciap, **5**
Vino, Vino, **9**

Ostello di Venezia (HI), F. Zitelle, Giudecca 87 (☎52 38 211). This efficiently managed hostel has sparkling baths and sweeping views of the city. 250 beds on single-sex floors. Breakfast and linens included. Dinner €9.50. Reception 7-9:30am and 1:30pm-midnight. Lock-out 9:30am-1:30pm. Curfew 11:30pm. Reserve online at www.hostel-booking.com. Dorms €20. HI discount €3. MC/V. ❷

Albergo San Samuele, Salizzada S. Samuele, San Marco 3358 (☎52 28 045; www.albergosansamuele.it). Small but well-kept rooms, with welcoming staff and great location. Reserve 1-2 months ahead. Singles €55; doubles €75-90, with bath €100-120; triples €110-130. Cash only. ❹

Domus Civica (ACISJF), Campiello Chiovere Frari, San Polo 3082 (☎72 11 03). Spartan white rooms with shared TV, piano, and bath. Free Internet. Reception 7am-12:30am. Strict curfew 12:30am. Open June-Sept. 25. Singles €31; doubles €54; triples €81. 15% Rolling Venice discount; 20% ISIC discount. AmEx/MC/V. ❸

Foresteria Valdese, Castello 5170 (☎52 86 797; www.diaconiavaldese.org/venezia). A crumbling but grand 18th-century guest house run by Venice's largest Protestant church, 2min. from major sights. Breakfast and linens included. Internet €5 per hr. Reception 9am-1pm and 6-8pm. Lockout 10am-1pm. Reservations required. Dorms €21-23; doubles with TV €60-64, with bath and TV €76-80; quads with bath and TV €110-118; quints with bath €127-137; apartments (no breakfast) €104. Min. 2-night stay for private rooms. €1 Rolling Venice discount. MC/V. ❷

Ostello Santa Fosca, F. Canal, Cannaregio 2372 (☎/fax 71 57 33). A brick-enclosed walkway leads to this social hostel in a series of crumbling courtyards of questionable romanticism. Internet available. Curfew July-Sept. 12:30am. Dorms €19; doubles €44. €2 ISIC or Rolling Venice discount. MC/V. ❷

Albergo Doni, Cal. del Vin, Castello 4656 (☎52 24 267; www.albergodoni.it). Friendly staff and proximity to P. San Marco make this hotel an amazing deal. Rooms with phone, TV, and fan or A/C. Breakfast included. Reception 24hr. Singles €40-65; doubles €60-95, with bath €80-120; triples €80-125, with bath 120-160; quads €140-200. €5 discount with cash payment. MC/V. ❸

Camping Miramare, Lungomare Dante Alighieri 29 (☎96 61 50; www.camping-mira-mare.it). A 1hr. ride on V #LN from P. S. Marco to Punta Sabbioni. Campground is 700m along the beach on the right. Min. 2-night stay in high season. Open Apr.-Oct. €4.70-7 per person; cabins €27-60 plus per-person charge. MC/V. ❶

Camping Fusina, V. Moranzani 93 (☎54 70 055; www.camping-fusina.com), in Malcontenta. From Mestre, take bus #11. ATM, Internet, laundromat, restaurant, and TV on-site. Free hot showers. Call ahead to reserve cabins. €8-9 per person, €8.50 per tent. Cabin singles €25; doubles €30. AmEx/MC/V. ❷

◖ FOOD

With few exceptions, the best restaurants lie in alleyways, not along the canals around San Marco that advertise a *menù turistico*. Venetian cuisine is dominated by fish, like *sarde in saor* (sardines in vinegar and onions), available only in Venice and sampled cheaply at most bars with other types of *cicchetti* (tidbits of seafood, rice, and meat; €1-3). **Wines** of the Veneto and Friuli regions include the whites *Prosecco della Marca*, *bianco di Custoza*, and dry *Tocai*, as well as the red *Valpolicella*. Venice's renowned Rialto **markets** spread between the Canal Grande and the San Polo foot of the Rialto every Monday through Saturday morning. A **BILLA supermarket,** Str. Nuova, Cannaregio 5660, is near Campo S. Fosca. (Open M-Sa 8:30am-8:30pm, Su 9am-8:30pm. AmEx/MC/V.)

▧ **Le Bistrot de Venise,** Cal. dei Fabbri, San Marco 4685 (☎52 36 651). Delicous dishes, true to medieval and Renaissance recipes. *Enoteca: cichetti* €3-4, meat and cheese plates €12-24. Restaurant: *primi* €12-22, *secondi* €29-32. Wine from €5 per glass. Service 12%. Open daily 10am-1am. MC/V. ❺

Cantinone Gia Schiavi, F. Meraviglie, Dorsoduro 992 (☎52 30 034). Take your pick from hundreds of bottles (from €3.50), or enjoy a glass canal-side with some tasty *cichetti* (€1-4). Open M-Sa 8:30am-2:30pm and 3:15-8:30pm. Cash only. ❶

Gelateria Nico, F. Zattere, Dorsoduro 922 (☎52 25 293). Try the Venetian *gianduiotto de passeggio,* a brick of dense chocolate-hazelnut ice cream dropped into a cup of whipped cream (€2.50). Gelato €1, 2 scoops €1.70. Prices higher for sit-down. Open M-W and F-Su 6:45am-10pm. Cash only. ❶

Antica Birraria La Corte, Campo S. Polo, San Polo 2168 (☎27 50 570). Large restaurant and bar with outside tables. Pizza €5-9. *Primi* €9-11. *Secondi* €11-19. Cover €2. Open mid-Aug. to mid-July daily 12:30-3pm and 7-10:30pm; mid-July to mid-Aug. M-F 12:30-3pm and 7-10:30pm, Sa-Su 12:30-3pm. AmEx/MC/V. ❸

Cip Ciap, Cal. del Mondo Novo 5799/A (☎52 36 621). Pizzeria uses fresh ingredients and sells pizza by the gram (€2-2.50 per kg). Filling calzones (€2.50). There's no seating, so find a bench in the nearby *campo.* Open M and W-Su 9am-9pm. Cash only. ❶

Trattoria da Bepi, Cannaregio 4550. This Venetian *trattoria* attracts tourists and locals who come for the expertly prepared cuisine. *Primi* €7-11. *Secondi* from €10. Cover €1.50. Reserve ahead. Open M-W and F-Su noon-3pm and 7-10pm. MC/V. ❸

Osteria al Portego, Cal. Malvasia 6015. Heading south on Salizzada S. Lio, turn left onto Cal. Malvasia, and left again toward Cte. Perina. This hidden *osteria,* filled with barrels of wine, is a favorite of students and locals. Dizzying array of *cicchetti* and wine. Open M-Sa 10:30am-3pm and 5:30-10pm. Cash only. ❶

La Boutique del Gelato, Salizzada S. Lio, Castello 5727 (☎52 23 283). Doles out big portions of gelato. 1 scoop €1, 2 scoops €1.70. Open daily July-Aug. 10:30am-10:30pm; Sept.-June 10:30am-8:30pm. Cash only. ❶

Ae Oche, Santa Croce 1552A/B (☎52 41 161). American advertisements from the 60s and a duck logo create a charming effect. Pizza €4.50-9. *Primi* €5.50-7. *Secondi* €8-15. Cover €1.50. Service 12%. Open daily noon-3:30pm and 7-11:30pm. MC/V. ❷

Pizzeria La Perla, Rio Terra dei Franceschi, Cannaregio 4615. Satisfied diners savor over 40 varieties of pizza. Pizza €4.70-9. Pasta €6.10-8.20. Cover €1.10. Service 10%. Open M-Tu and Th-Su noon-3pm and 6:30-10:30pm; daily in Aug. AmEx/MC/V. ❷

Vino, Vino, Ponte delle Veste, San Marco 2007/A. From Cal. Larga XXII Marzo, turn on Cal. delle Veste. Jazz plays quietly in this bar, which offers over 350 kinds of wine, plus traditional *sarde in saor* and pasta from a daily *menù. Primi* €9-10. *Secondi* €10-17. Cover €2. Open daily 11:30am-11:30pm. 10% Rolling Venice discount. Cash only. ❸

◉ SIGHTS

Venice's layout makes sightseeing a disorienting affair. Most sights center around the **Piazza San Marco,** but getting lost can be better than being found in its tourist crowds. Museum passes (€18, students €12), sold at participating museums, grant one-time admission to each of 10 museums over the course of three months. The Foundation for the Churches of Venice sells the **Chorus Pass** (☎27 50 462; www.chorusvenezia.org), which provides admission to all of Venice's churches. A yearly pass (€8, students €5) is available at most participating churches.

AROUND PIAZZA SAN MARCO

Venice's only official *piazza,* **Piazza San Marco,** is an un-Venetian expanse of light, space, and architectural harmony. The 96m brick **campanile** (bell tower; open daily 9am-9pm, €6), built on a Roman base, provides one of the best views of the city; on clear days, the panorama spans Croatia and Slovenia.

■BASILICA DI SAN MARCO. The symmetrical arches and incomparable mosaics of Venice's crown jewel grace Piazza San Marco. The city's premier tourist attraction, the Basilica di San Marco also has the longest lines. Late afternoon visits profit from the best natural light but are the most crowded. Built to house the remains of St. Mark, 13th-century Byzantine and 16th-century Renaissance mosaics now make the interior sparkle. Behind the altar, the **Pala d'Oro** relief frames a parade of saints in gem-encrusted gold. Steep stairs in the atrium lead to the **Galleria della Basilica**, whose view is of tiny golden tiles in the basilica's vast ceiling mosaics and the original bronze **Cavalli di San Marco** (Horses of St. Mark). A balcony overlooks the *piazza*. *(Basilica open M-Sa 9:45am-5pm, Su 2-4pm. Modest dress required. Free. Pala d'Oro open M-Sa 9:45am-5:30pm, Su 2-4pm. €1.50. Treasury open M-Sa 9:45am-7pm, Su 2-4:30pm; €2. Galleria open M-F 9:45am-4:15pm, Sa-Su 9:45am-4:45pm. €3.)*

■ **PALAZZO DUCALE (DOGE'S PALACE).** Once the home of Venice's *doge* (mayor), the Palazzo Ducale is now a museum. Veronese's *Rape of Europa* is among its spectacular works of art. In the courtyard, Sansovino's enormous sculptures, *Mars* and *Neptune*, flank the **Scala dei Giganti** (Stairs of the Giants), upon which new *doges* were crowned. The Council of Ten, the *doge*'s administrators, would drop the names of suspected criminals into the **Bocca di Leone** (Lion's Mouth), on the balcony. Climb the **Scala d'Oro** (Golden Staircase) to the **Sala delle Quattro Porte** (Room of the Four Doors), whose ceiling depicts biblical judgements, and the **Sala dell'Anticollegio** (Antechamber of the Senate), whose decorations are myths about Venice. Courtrooms of the Council of Ten and the Council of Three lead to the **Sala del Maggior Consiglio** (Great Council Room), dominated by Tintoretto's *Paradise*, the largest oil painting in the world. Near the end, thick stone lattices line the **Ponte dei Sospiri** (Bridge of Sighs), named after the mournful groans of prisoners who walked it on their way to the prison's damp cells. *(Wheelchair-accessible. Open daily Apr.-Oct. 9am-7pm; Nov.-Mar. 9am-5pm. €12, students €6.50.)*

■ **CHIESA DI SAN ZACCARIA.** Designed in the late 1400s by Coducci and others, and dedicated to John the Baptist's father, this Gothic-Renaissance church holds S. Zaccaria's corpse in an elevated sarcophagus along the nave's right wall. Nearby is Bellini's *Virgin and Child Enthroned with Four Saints*, a Renaissance masterpiece. *(S. Marco. V: S. Zaccaria. Open daily 10am-noon and 4-6pm. Free.)*

AROUND THE PONTE RIALTO

■ **THE GRAND CANAL.** The Grand Canal is Venice's "main street." Over 3km long and nearly 50m wide, it loops through the city and passes under three bridges: the **Ponte Scalzi, Rialto,** and **Accademia.** The *bricole*, candy-cane posts used for mooring boats on the canal, are painted with the colors of the family whose *palazzo* adjoins them. *(For great facade views, ride V. #1, 4 or 82 from the train station to P. S. Marco. The facades are lit at night and produce dazzling reflections.)*

■ **RIVOALTUS LEGATORIA.** Step into the book-lined Rivoaltus shop on any given day and hear Wanda Scarpa greet you from the attic, where she has been sewing leatherbound, antique-style ■journals for an international cadre of customers and faithful locals for more than three decades. Though Venice is now littered with shops selling journals, Rivoaltus was the first and remains the best. *(Ponte di Rialto 11. Notebooks €18-31. Photo albums €31-78. Open daily 10am-7:30pm.)*

SAN POLO

The second-largest *campo* in Venice, **Campo San Polo** once hosted bloody bull-baiting matches during *Carnevale*. Today, blood is no longer spilled—only gelato.

BASILICA DI SANTA MARIA GLORIOSA DEI FRARI. Titian's corpse and two of his paintings reside within this Gothic church, known as *I Frari* and begun by Franciscans in 1340. ■**Assumption** (1516-18), on the high altar, marks the height of the Venetian Renaissance. The golden Florentine chapel, to the right of the high altar, frames Donatello's gaunt wooden sculpture, **St. John the Baptist.** Titian's tomb is an elaborate lion-topped triumphal arch with bas-relief scenes of Paradise. *(S. Polo. V: S. Tomà. Open M-Sa 9am-6pm, Su 1-6pm. €2.50.)*

CHIESA DI SAN GIACOMO DI RIALTO. Between the Rialto and nearby markets stands Venice's first church, diminutively called "San Giacometto." An ornate clock-face adorns its *campanile*. Across the *piazza*, a statue called *Il Gobbo* (The Hunchback) supports the steps, once used for announcements. At the foot of the statue, convicted thieves would collapse after being forced to run naked from P. S. Marco. *(V: Rialto. Cross bridge and turn right. Church open daily 9:30am-noon and 4-6pm. Free.)*

SCUOLA GRANDE DI SAN ROCCO. The most illustrious of Venice's *scuole* (schools) commemorates Jacopo Tintoretto, who left Venice only once in his 76 years, and who sought to combine "the color of Titian with the drawing of Michelangelo." The school commissioned Tintoretto to complete all the paintings in the building, which took 23 years. The *Crucifixion* in the last room upstairs is the collection's crowning glory. *(Behind Basilica dei Frari in Campo S. Rocco. Open daily Mar. 28-Nov. 2 9am-5:30pm; Nov. 3-Mar. 27 10am-4pm. €7, students and Rolling Venice €5.)*

DORSODURO

■ **COLLEZIONE PEGGY GUGGENHEIM.** Guggenheim's Palazzo Venier dei Leoni displays works by Dalí, Duchamp, Ernst, Kandinsky, Klee, Magritte, Picasso, and Pollock. The Marini sculpture *Angel in the City*, in front of the palazzo, was designed with a detachable penis so that Ms. Guggenheim could avoid offending her more prudish guests. *(F. Venier dei Leoni, Dorsoduro 701. V: Accademia. Turn left and follow the yellow signs. Open M and W-Su 10am-6pm. €10; students and Rolling Venice €5.)*

■ **GALLERIE DELL'ACCADEMIA.** The Accademia houses the world's most extensive collection of Venetian art. Among the enormous altarpieces in **Room II,** Giovanni Bellini's *Madonna Enthroned with Child, Saints, and Angels* stands out with its soothing serenity. **Rooms IV** and **V** have more Bellinis plus Giorgione's enigmatic *La Tempesta*. In **Room VI,** three paintings by Tintoretto, *The Creation of the Animals*, *The Temptation of Adam and Eve*, and *Cain and Abel*, grow progressively darker. **Room X** displays Titian's last painting, a *Pietà* intended for his tomb. In **Room XX,** works by Bellini and Carpaccio depict Venetian processions and cityscapes so accurately that scholars use them as "photos" of Venice's past. *(V: Accademia. Open M 8:15am-2pm, Tu-Su 8:15am-7:15pm. €6.50. English tours Tu-Su 11am €7.)*

CHIESA DI SANTA MARIA DELLA SALUTE. The *salute* (Italian for "health") is a hallmark of the Venetian skyline: perched on Dorsoduro's peninsula just southwest of San Marco, the church and its domes are visible from everywhere in the city. In 1631, the city had **Baldassarre Longhena** build the church for the Virgin, who they believed would end the current plague. Next to the *salute* stands the *dogana*, the customs house, where ships sailing into Venice were required to pay duties. *(Dorsoduro. V: Salute. ☎522 55 58. Open daily 9am-noon and 2:30-5:30pm. Free. Entrance to sacristy with donation. The inside of the dogana is closed to the public.)*

CHIESA DI SAN SEBASTIANO. This church is devoted to Renaissance painter **Veronese,** who took refuge in this white-marble and brown-stucco, 16th-century church when he fled Verona in 1555 after allegedly killing a man. By 1565 he had filled the church with a series of paintings and frescoes. His breathtaking *Stories of Queen Esther* covers the ceiling, while the artist's body rests by the organ. *(Dorsoduro. V: S. Basilio. Open M-Sa 10am-5pm, Su 1-5pm. €2.50.)*

CASTELLO

SCUOLA DALMATA SAN GIORGIO DEGLI SCHIAVONI. Carpaccio's finest artwork, visual tales of St. George, Jerome, and Tryfon, hang in the early 16th-century building. *(Castello 3259/A. V: S. Zaccaria. Modest dress required. Open Tu-Sa 9:15am-1pm, 2:45-6pm, M, Su 9:15am-1pm. €3, Rolling Venice €2.)*

ITALY

CANNAREGIO

JEWISH GHETTO. In 1516 the *doge* forced Venice's Jewish population into the old cannon-foundry area, creating the first Jewish ghetto in Europe and coining the word "ghetto," the Venetian word for foundry. In the Campo del Ghetto Nuovo, the **Schola Grande Tedesca** (German Synagogue), the area's oldest synagogue, and the **Museo Ebraica di Venezia** (Hebrew Museum of Venice) now share a building. *(Cannaregio 2899/B. V: S. Marcuola. Museum open Su-F June-Sept. 10am-7pm; Oct.-May 10am-4:30pm. Enter synagogue by 40min. tour every hr. daily June-Sept. 10:30am-5:30pm; Oct.-May 10:30am-4:30pm. Museum €3, students €2. Museum and tour €8.50/7.)*

CÀ D'ORO. Delicate spires and interlocking arches make the Cà d'Oro's facade the most spectacular on the Canal Grande. Built between 1425 and 1440, it now houses the **Galleria Giorgio Franchetti.** For the best view of the palace, take a *traghetto* (ferry) across the canal to the Rialto Markets. *(V: Cà d'Oro. Open M 8:15am-2pm, Tu-Su 8:15am-7:15pm. €5, EU students and under 35 €2.50. Audio tour €4.)*

🐟 ISLANDS OF THE LAGOON

🐚 LIDO. The breezy resort island of Lido provided the setting for Thomas Mann's haunting novella, *Death in Venice.* Visonti's film version was also shot here at the Hotel des Bains. Today, people flock to Lido to enjoy the surf at the popular public beach. A casino, horseback riding, and the Alberoni Golf Club add to the island's charm. *(V #1 and 82: Lido. Beach open daily 9am-8pm. Free.)*

🐚 MURANO. Famous since 1292 for its glass, the six-island cluster of Murano affords visitors the opportunity to witness resident artisans blow and spin glass free of charge. For demonstrations, look for signs directing to the *fornace.* Quiet streets are lined with tiny shops and glass boutiques. The collection at the **Museo Vetrario** (Glass Museum) ranges from first-century funereal urns to a cartoonish, sea-green octopus. *(V #DM, LN, 5, 13, 41, 42: Faro from either S. Zaccaria or F. Nuove. Museo Vetrario, F. Giustian 8. Open M-Tu and Th-Su Apr.-Oct. 10am-5pm; Nov.-Mar. 10am-4pm. €4, students and Rolling Venice €2.50. Combined ticket with Burano Lace Museum €6, students and Rolling Venice €4. Basilica open daily 8am-7pm. Modest dress required. Free.)*

🎜 ENTERTAINMENT

Admire Venetian houses and *palazzi* via their original canal pathways on **gondola** rides, most romantic about 50min. before sunset and most affordable if shared by six people. The most price-flexible gondoliers are those standing by themselves rather than those in groups at the "taxi-stands" throughout the city. The rate that a gondolier quotes is negotiable, but expect to pay €80-100 for a 40min. ride.

Teatro Goldoni, Cal. del Teatro, S. Marco 4650/B (☎24 02 011), near the Ponte di Rialto, showcases various types of live productions, often with seasonal themes. The **Mostra Internazionale di Cinema** (Venice International Film Festival), held annually from late August to early September, draws established names and rising phenoms from around the world. Movies are shown in their original language. (☎52 18 878. Tickets sold throughout the city, €20. Some late-night outdoor showings free.) The famed **Biennale di Venezia** (☎52 11 898; www.labiennale.org) is a contemporary exhibit of provocative art and architecture. The weekly publication *A Guest in Venice,* offered for free at hotels, tourist offices, or online (www.unospitedivenezia.it), lists current festivals, concerts, and gallery exhibits.

Long banned, Venice's famous **Carnevale** was reinstated in the early 1970s, and the 10 days before Ash Wednesday see masked figures in the streets and outdoor performances. For **Mardi Gras** (Feb. 5, 2008), the population doubles; make arrangements well ahead. Venice's second-most colorful festival is the **Festa del Redentore** (3rd Su in July), originally held to celebrate the end of a 16th-century plague, which kicks off with fireworks at 11:30pm the Saturday before.

▶ NIGHTLIFE

Most residents would rather spend an evening sipping wine or beer in a *piazza* than bumping and grinding in a disco. Establishments come and go with some regularity, though student nightlife is consistently concentrated around **Campo Santa Margherita**, in Dorsoduro, while that of tourists centers around the **Lista di Spagna.**

■ **Café Blue,** Dorsoduro 3778 (☎71 02 27). Grab a glass of wine (from €1.50) and a stool to watch the daytime coffee crowd turn into a chill and laid-back set as night falls. Free Wi-Fi. DJ W, live music in winter F. Open daily 8am-2am. MC/V.

Naranzaria, Sottoportego del Banco, San Polo 130 (☎72 41 035). At the canal-side corner of C. S. Giacomo. Up-close views of the Grand Canal and Rialto complement the wine, *cicchetti* (including sushi), and trendy vibe. Open Tu-Su noon-2am. MC/V.

Bistrot ai Do Draghi, Campo S. Margherita 3665 (☎52 89 731). The crowd at this tiny bistro is not as fierce as the name ("dragon") implies. Its wine selection has won accolades. Wine from €1.20 per glass. Open daily 7am-1am.

Paradiso Perduto, F. della Misericordia, Cannaregio 2540 (☎09 94 540). Students flood this unassuming bar, which also serves *cicchetti* (mixed plate €11-15). Live jazz F. Open daily 11am-3pm and 6pm-1am.

Piccolo Mondo, Accademia, Dorsoduro 1056/A (☎52 00 371). Facing toward the Accademia, turn right. Ring bell to enter. Disco, hip hop, and vodka with Red Bull (€10) keep a full house at this small, popular *discoteca*, which heats up late behind its heavy, locked doors. Drinks from €7. Open daily 11pm-4am. AmEx/MC/V.

PADUA (PADOVA)   ☎049

The oldest institutions in Padua (pop. 210,000) are the ones that still draw visitors: St. Anthony's tomb, the looping Prato della Valle, and the university, founded in 1222. The starry blue ceiling of the ■**Cappella degli Scrovegni,** P. Eremitani 8, overlooks Giotto's epic 38-panel fresco cycle depicting Mary, Jesus, St. Anne, and St. Joachim in *Last Judgment.* Buy tickets at the attached **Musei Civici Eremitani,** whose art collection includes Giotto's beautiful crucifix, which once adorned the Scrovegni Chapel. (☎20 10 020; www.cappelladegliscrovegni.it. Entrance to chapel only with museum. Open daily Feb.-Oct. 9am-7pm; Nov.-Jan. 9am-6pm. Reserve ahead. Museum €10, with chapel €12, students €8. AmEx/MC/V.) Pilgrims flock to see St. Anthony's jawbone, tongue, and tomb displayed at the **Basilica di Sant'Antonio,** in P. del Santo. (☎82 42 811. Modest dress required. Open daily Apr.-Sept. 6:15am-7:45pm; Nov.-Mar. 6:15am-7pm. Free.) The university centers around the two interior coutyards of **Palazzo Bò,** as does the student-heavy nightlife. The chair of Galileo is preserved in the **Sala dei Quaranta,** where he once lectured. Across the street, **Caffè Pedrocchi** served as the headquarters for 19th-century liberals who supported Risogimento leader Giuseppe Mazzini. Next to the **duomo,** in P. Duomo, sits the tiny **Battistero,** with a domed interior coated with New Testament frescoes. (*Duomo* open M-Sa 7:20am-noon and 4-7:30pm, Su 8am-1pm and 4-8:30pm. Free. *Battistero* open daily 10am-6pm. €2.50, students €1.50.)

The stone artwork in the lobby of **Hotel Al Santo ❹,** V. del Santo 147, near the basilica, leads to large, wood-floored rooms. (☎87 52 131. Breakfast included. Reception 24hr. Singles €65; doubles €80-100; triples €120. AmEx/MC/V.) Go to V. Aleardi and turn left; walk to the end of the block and **Ostello Città di Padova (HI) ❷,** V. Aleardi 30, will be on your left. (☎87 52 219; pdyhtl@tin.it. Internet €5 per hr. Lockout 9:30am-3:30pm. Curfew midnight. Reserve ahead. Dorms €17. MC/V.) The place to go for Paduan cuisine is **Antica Trattoria Paccagnella ❷,** V. del Santo 113. (☎/fax 87 50 549. *Primi* €7-11. *Secondi* €7-15. Cover €2.50. Open M-Sa 8am-4pm and 6:30pm-midnight. AmEx/MC/V.) Morning **markets** are held in P. delle Erbe and P. della Frutta. **Fly,** Galleria Tito Livio 4/6, between V. Roma and Riviera Tito Livio, is a pedestrian cafe by day and a swinging hot spot by night. (☎87 52 892. Wine €2-

3.50; mixed drinks €3.50-4.50. Open M-Sa 9am-midnight.) **Trains** run from P. Stazione to: Bologna (1½hr., 34 per day, €6); Milan (2½hr., 25 per day, €12); Venice (30min., 82 per day, €2.70); Verona (1hr., 44 per day, €4.80). **SITA Buses** (☎82 06 834) leave from P. Boschetti for Venice (45min., 32 per day, €3.05). The **tourist office** is in the train station. (☎87 52 077. Open M-Sa 9am-7pm, Su 9am-12:30pm.) To reach the *centro* from the station, take Corso del Popolo south from the train station, continuing as it becomes Corso Garibaldi. **Postal Code:** 35100.

VERONA   ☎045

In Verona (pop. 245,000), bright gardens and life-like sculptures delight the hopeless romantics who wander into its walls, seeking Romeo or Juliet, whose drama Shakespeare set here. But there's more to Verona: its rich wines, authentic cuisine, and renowned opera are affordable even for students.

▛▞ TRANSPORTATION AND PRACTICAL INFORMATION. Trains (☎89 20 21) go from P. XXV Aprile to: **Bologna** (2hr., 22 per day, €6); **Milan** (2hr., 34 per day, €7); **Trent** (1hr., 25 per day, €4.70); **Venice** (1½hr., 41 per day, €8). From the station walk 20min. up **Corso Porta Nuova** or take bus #11, 12, 13, 51, 72, or 73 (Sa-Su take #91, 92, or 93) to Verona's center, the **Arena** in **Piazza Brà**. The **tourist office** is next to the *piazza* at V. d. Alpini 9. (☎806 86 80. Open M-Sa 9am-7pm, Su 9am-3pm.) Check email at **Internet Train**, V. Roma 17/A. (☎801 33 94. €5 per hr. Open M-F 10am-10pm, Sa-Su 2-8pm. MC/V.) **Postal Code:** 37100.

▛▞ ACCOMMODATIONS AND FOOD. Reserve hotel rooms ahead, especially during opera season (June-Sept.). The **Ostello della Gioventù (HI) ❶**, Villa Francescatti, Salita Fontana del Ferro 15, is in a renovated 16th-century villa with handsome gardens and antique frescoes. From the station, take bus #73 or night bus #90 to P. Isolo, turn right, and follow the yellow signs uphill. (☎59 03 60. Breakfast included; dinner €8. Lockout 9am-5pm. Curfew 11:30pm; flexible for opera-goers. Dorms €15; family rooms €19. HI members only. Cash only.) To get to the romantic, central **Bed and Breakfast Anfiteatro ❹**, V. Alberto Mario 5, follow V. Mazzini toward P. Brà until it branches to the right to become V. Alberto Mario. (☎347 24 88 462; www.anfiteatro-bedandbreakfast.com. TV and private bath. Breakfast included. Singles €60-90; Doubles €80-130.) ◪**Osteria al Duomo ❷**, V. Duomo 7/a, on the way to the *duomo*, offers a small menu, but serves authentic, simple cuisine like *tagliatelle* with shrimp and zucchini. (☎80 04 505. *Primi* €6-6.30; *secondi* €8-12. Cover €1. Open Tu-Sa noon-2:30pm and 7-10pm. Cash only.) A **PAM** supermarket is at V. dei Mutilati 3. (Open M-Sa 8am-8:30pm, Su 9am-8pm.)

▨▟ SIGHTS AND ENTERTAINMENT. The heart of Verona is the tiered first-century **Arena** in P. Brà. (☎80 03 204. Open M 1:30-7:30pm, Tu-Su 8:30am-7:30pm. Closes 4:30pm on opera night. Ticket office closes 1hr. before Arena. €4, students €3. Cash only.) From late June to early September, tourists and singers from around the world descend on the Arena for the city's annual ◪**Opera Festival.** *Aida*, *Nabucco*, and *Carmen* are among the 2008 highlights. (☎80 05 151; www.arena.it. Box office open on opera night 10am-9pm, non-performance days 10am-5:45pm. General admission Su-Th €17-25, F-Sa €19-27. AmEx/MC/V.) From P. Brà, V. Mazzini leads to the markets and stunning medieval architecture of **Piazza delle Erbe.** The 83m ◪**Torre dei Lamberti**, in P. dei Signori, offers a perfect view of Verona. (Open Su-Th 9:30am-8:30pm, F-Sa 9:30am-10pm. Elevator €4, students €3; stairs €3. Cash only.) The **Giardino Giusti**, V. Giardino Giusti 2, is a 16th-century garden with a floral labyrinth, whose cypress-lined avenue gradually winds up to porticoes and curving balconies with stunning views of Verona. (☎80 34 029. Open daily Apr.-Sept. 9am-8pm; Oct.-Mar. 9am-7pm. €4.50.) The della Scala family fortress, **Castelvecchio**, down V. Roma from P. Brà, now has an art collection that includes Pisanello's *Madonna della Quaglia*. (☎80 62 611. Open M 1:30-7:30pm,

Tu-Su 8:30am-7:30pm. €4, students €3. Cash only.) The balcony at **Casa di Giulietta** (Juliet's House), V. Cappello 23, overlooks a courtyard of tourists waiting to rub the statue of Juliet and lovers adding their vows to graffitied walls. The Capulets never lived here, so save your money for another scoop of *gelato*. (☎80 34 303. Open M 1:30-7:30pm, Tu-Su 8:30am-7:30pm. €4, students €3. Courtyard free.)

FRIULI-VENEZIA GIULIA

Bounded by the Veneto to the west and Slovenia to the east is the kaleidoscope that is Friuli-Venezia Giulia. Regional control has changed hands multiple times, resulting in a potpourri of cuisines, styles, and architecture.

TRIESTE (TRIEST) ☎040

After being volleyed among Italian, Austrian, and Slavic powers for hundreds of years, Trieste (pop. 241,000) celebrated its 50th anniversary as an Italian city in 2004. Subtle reminders of Trieste's Eastern European past are manifest in its churches, cuisine, and portraits of smirking Habsburg rulers in museums. The gridded streets of the Città Nuova, all lined with majestic Neoclassical palaces, center around the Canale Grande. Facing the canal from the south is the blue-domed Serbian Orthodox **Chiesa di San Spiridione.** (Open Tu-Sa 9am-noon and 5-8pm, Su 9am-noon. Modest dress required.) The ornate **Municipio** (Town Hall) is in the **P. dell'Unità d'Italia,** the largest waterfront *piazza* in Italy. P. della Cattedrale overlooks the town center. In the mid-19th century, Archduke Maximilian of Austria commissioned the lavish **⬛Castello Miramare,** where each room is carefully preserved. Legend holds that visitors can still hear the wailing of Carlotta, Maximilian's wife, who went crazy after his murder. Take bus #36 (15min.; €0.90) to Ostello Tergeste and walk along the water for 15min. (Open M-Sa 9am-7pm, Su 8:30am-7pm. Ticket office open daily 9am-6:30pm. €4, 18-25 €2.)

Centrally located **⬛Nuovo Albergo Centro ❸,** V. Roma 13, has spacious rooms. (☎34 78 790; www.hotelcentrotrieste.it. Breakfast included. Internet €4 per hr. Singles €35, with bath €48; doubles €50/68. 10% *Let's Go* discount. AmEx/MC/V.) On a shaded *piazza*, **⬛Buffet da Siora Rosa ❷,** P. Hortis 3, serves Triestini favorites, like bread *gnocchi* (€6.20) and *prosciutto panini* (€1.20-4) doused in mustard and horseradish. (☎30 14 60. *Primi* €4-7. *Secondi* €5-10. Cover €1. Reserve ahead. Open daily 8am-4pm and 6:30-9:30pm. MC/V.) The covered market at V. Carducci 36/D has tables piled high with fruits and cheese. (Open M 8am-2pm, Tu-Sa 8am-5pm.) At night, head to **Via Roma Quattro,** whose name is also its address. (☎634 633. Open M-Sa 7:30am-11:30pm.) **Trains** leave P. della Libertà 8, down C. Cavour from the quay for Udine (1½hr., 28 per day, €6.60) and Venice (2hr., 20 per day, €8). The APT **tourist office** is at P. dell'Unità d'Italia 4/E, near the harbor. (☎34 78 312. Open daily 9:30am-7pm.) **Postal Code:** 34100.

PIEDMONT (PIEMONTE)

More than just the source of the Po River, Piedmont rose to prominence when the Savoys briefly named Turin capital of their reunited Italy in 1861. Today, European tourists escape Turin's whirlwind pace on the banks of Lake Maggiore, while hikers and skiers conquer Alpine mountaintops.

TURIN (TORINO) ☎011

A century and a half before Turin (pop. 910,000) was selected to host the 2006 Winter Olympics, it served as the first capital of a unified Italy. Renowned for chocolate and its cafe culture, Turin also lays claim to numerous parks and contemporary art

EAT. SHOP. LEARN.

In January 2007, a new restaurant opened in Turin. Actually, 10 of them did, all under one roof. More than just a food court, Eataly is a culinary amusement park.

Each of Eataly's restaurants specialize in a different food group and prepare your meal in front of you. Including the €1 cover, dishes generally cost €8-15 at each station, a bargain for their high quality. Splitting meals is highly recommended in order to taste from more stations. The daily menus of cheese, meat, pasta, pizza, seafood, and vegetables are only the beginning. A coffee shop and *gelato* stand are also on the ground floor, while the basement showcases meat and cheese cellars. The basement also has two more restaurants, one dedicated to wine and one to beer. The bottled wine selection is overwhelming but, if you are the mood for something simple, you can fill up your own liter from the tap for €1.30-4 per L.

You can take the cooking into your own hands at the expansive organic food store or at the learning center, which offers varied and valuable cooking lessons from world-famous guest chefs (€20-100). While the calendar of classes is in Italian, many of the cooking lessons are also available in English for groups. *(V. Nizza 224. Take bus #1, 18, or 35 to the Biglieri stop. Reservations ☎011 19 50 68; www.eataly.com.)*

pieces, as well as some of the country's best social and nightlife offerings, all while avoiding the pollution and crime problems of a big city.

☎⚑ TRANSPORTATION AND PRACTICAL INFORMATION. Trains (☎66 53 098) run from **Porta Nuova**, in the center of the city, on C. V. Emanuele II to: Genoa (2hr., 1 per hr., €8.20); Milan (2hr., 1 per hr., €8.20); Rome (6-7hr., 26 per day, from €44); Venice (5hr., 20 per day, €35). A new **metro line** was recently installed and Turin's transportation system will continue to change in the next few years. Eventually, Porta Susa will be the main train station; for now, it is a departure point for trains to Paris via Lyon, FRA (5-6hr., 4 per day). Contact the **Turismo Torino,** P. Solferino, for brochures with art, literary, and walking tours. (☎53 51 81; www.turismo-torino.org. Open M-Sa 9:30am-7pm, Su 9:30am-3pm.) Unlike in other Italian cities, streets in Turin meet at right angles, so it's relatively easy to navigate. V. Roma is the major north-south thoroughfare. It runs to P. Castello, from which V. Pietro Micca extends southwest to the Olympic Atrium. **Postal Code:** 10100.

☎⚑ ACCOMMODATIONS AND FOOD. Turin's budget accommodations are scattered around the city, though a few cluster near Stazione Porta Nuova. Family-run bed and breakfasts offer some of the city's best deals, though many close in summer. The new **⚐Open 011 ❷**, C. Venezia 11, is near the V. Chiesa della Salute stop on bus #11 and has a bar, library, restaurant, terrace, TV, and Wi-Fi. (☎51 62 038; www.openzero11.it. Dorms €17; singles €30; doubles €42.) To get to the comfortable **Ostello Torino (HI) ❶**, V. Alby 1, take bus #52 (#64 on Su) from Porta Nuova. After crossing the river, get off at the Lanza stop at V. Crimea and follow the "Ostello" signs to C. G. Lanza, before turning left at V. L. Gatti. (☎66 02 939; www.ostellotorino.it. Breakfast and linens included. Laundry €4. Reception M-Sa 7am-12:30pm and 3-11pm, Su 7-10am and 3-11pm. Lockout 10am-3pm. Curfew 11pm; ask for key if going out. Closed Dec. 21-Jan. 14. 3- to 8-bed dorms €15; doubles €31-38; triples €51; quads €68. MC/V.) The **Albergo Azalea ❸**, V. Mercanti 16, 3th floor, has cozy rooms. Exit Porta Nuova on the right and take #58 or 72 to V. Garibaldi. Turn left on V. Garibaldi, then left on V. Mercanti. (☎53 81 15; albergo.azalea@virgilio.it. Singles €35, with bath €45; doubles €55-65. MC/V.)

⚐Eataly, via Nizza 224, is Turin's new 10,000 sq. ft. culinary amusement park. Tastings of wine and beer are just the beginning: classrooms feature cooking classes by famous chefs, meat and cheese lockers are on display, and museum-quality exhibits demonstrate food preparation techniques. Take bus #1, 18 or 35 to the Biglieri stop, near the Lingotto Expo Center. (☎19 50 68 11;

www.eataly.it. Reserve ahead for classes and wine tasting. Open daily 10am-10:30pm.) Chocolate has been the city's glory ever since Turin nobles began taking an evening cup of it in 1678. *Gianduiotto* (hazelnut chocolate) turns up in candies and *gelato*. Sample *bicerin* (Turin's hot coffee-chocolate-cream drink; €4), craved by Nietzsche and Dumas, at **Caffè Cioccolateria al Bicerin ❶**, Piazza della Consolata, 5. (☎43 69 325. Open M-Tu and Th-F 8:30am-7:30pm, Sa-Su 8:30am-1pm and 3:30-7:30pm.)

🔲🔳 **SIGHTS AND NIGHTLIFE.** The **Torino Card** (48hr. €18; 72hr. €20) is the best deal in the city: it provides entrance to more than 140 castles, monuments, museums, and royal residences in Turin. Once the largest structure in the world built using traditional masonry, the 🔲**Mole Antonelliana**, V. Montebello 20, a few blocks east of P. Castello, was originally a synagogue. It's home to the eccentric **Museo Nazionale del Cinema.** (Museum open Tu-F and Su 9am-8pm, Sa 9am-11pm. €5.20, students €4.20.) The **Holy Shroud of Turin,** said to be Jesus' burial cloth, is housed in the **Cattedrale di San Giovanni,** behind the **Palazzo Reale.** With rare exception, a photograph of the shroud is as close as visitors will get. (Open daily 8am-noon and 3-6pm. Free.) The **Museo Egizio,** in the **Palazzo dell'Accademia delle Scienze,** V. dell'Accademia delle Scienze 6, has a world-class collection of Egyptian artifacts. (Open Tu-Su 8:30am-7:30pm. €6.50, ages 18-25 €3.)

🔲**I Murazzi** is the center of Turin's social scene and consists of two stretches of boardwalk, one between Ponte V. Emanuele I and Ponte Umberto, and another smaller stretch downstream. Most people show up between 7:30-9:30pm and spend the next 5hr. sipping drinks, maneuvering among crowds at the waterfront, or dancing in the clubs. **The Beach,** V. Murazzi del Po 18-22, has the best dance floor in Turin. By 1am, this large, modern club fills with the young and the trendy, dancing to electronica music. (☎88 87 77. Mixed drinks €6. Open Tu-W 10pm-2am and Th-Sa noon-4am.) **Quadrilatero Romano,** the recently renovated buildings between P. della Repubblica and V. Garibaldi, attracts those who would rather sit, drink, and chat until 4am than dance to techno music. **Arancia di Mezzanotte,** P. E. Filiberto 11/I, is a popular place for an *aperitivo.* (Open daily 6pm-4am. MC/V.)

TUSCANY (TOSCANA)

Recently, popular culture has glorified Tuscany as a sun-soaked sanctuary of art, nature, and civilization, and this time pop culture has gotten it right. Every town claims a Renaissance master, every highway offers scenic vistas, every celebration culminates in parades and festivals, and every year brings more tourists.

FLORENCE (FIRENZE) ☎055

Florence (pop. 400,000) is the city of the Renaissance. By the 14th century, it had already become one of the most influential cities in Europe. In the 15th century, Florence overflowed with artistic excellence as the Medici family amassed a peerless collection, supporting masters like Botticelli, Brunelleschi, Donatello, and Michelangelo. These days, the tourists who flood the streets are captivated by Florence's distinctive character, creative spirit, and timeless beauty.

🔲 TRANSPORTATION

Flights: Amerigo Vespucci Airport (FLR; ☎30 61 300), in Peretola. **SITA** runs buses connecting the airport to the train station (€4.50).

Trains: Stazione Santa Maria Novella, across from S. Maria Novella. Trains run 1 per hr. to: **Bologna** (1hr., €4.70-6.80); **Milan** (3½hr., €29); **Pisa** (1hr., €5.20); **Rome** (3½hr., €30); **Siena** (1½hr., €5.70); **Venice** (3hr., €16). For more info visit www.trenitalia.it.

Buses: SITA, V. S. Caterina da Siena 17 (☎800 37 37 60; www.sita-on-line.it), runs buses to **San Gimignano** (1½hr., 14 per day, €5.90) and **Siena** (1½hr., 2 per day, €6.50). **LAZZI,** P. Adua 1-4R (☎35 10 61; www.lazzi.it), runs to **Pisa** (1 per hr., €6.10). Both offices are near S. Maria Novella.

Public Transportation: ATAF (☎800 42 45 00; www.ataf.net), outside the train station, runs orange city buses 6am-1am. Tickets 70min. €1.20; 24hr. €5; 3-day €12. Buy them at any newsstand, *tabaccheria,* or ticket dispenser before boarding. Validate your ticket using the orange machine on board or risk a €50 fine.

Taxis: ☎43 90, 47 98, or 42 42. Outside the train station.

Bike/Moped Rental: Alinari Noleggi, V. San Zanobi, 38r (☎28 05 00; www.alinarirental.com). Bikes €12-16 per day. Scooters €30 per day. Open M-Sa 9:30am-1:30pm and 2:45-7:30pm, Su and holidays 10am-1pm and 3-6pm. MC/V.

✦ ORIENTATION

From the train station, a short walk on V. Panzani and a left on V. dei Cerretani leads to the **duomo,** in the center of Florence. The bustling walkway **Via dei Calzaiuoli** runs south from the *duomo* to **Piazza della Signoria.** V. Roma leads from the *duomo* through **Piazza della Repubblica** to the **Ponte Vecchio** (Old Bridge), which crosses from central Florence to **Oltrarno,** the district south of the **Arno River.** Note that most streets change names unpredictably. Street numbers are either in red (commercial establishments) or black, and occasionally blue (residences.) If you reach an address and it's not what you expected, you may have the wrong color.

🛈 PRACTICAL INFORMATION

Tourist Office: Informazione Turistica, P. della Stazione 4 (☎21 22 45). Info on cultural events. Free maps with street index. Open M-Sa 8:30am-7pm, Su 8:30am-2pm.

Consulates: UK, Lungarno Corsini 2 (☎28 41 33). Open M-F 9am-1pm and 2-5pm. **US,** Lungarno Amerigo Vespucci 38 (☎26 69 51), near the station. Open M-F 9am-12:30pm.

Currency Exchange: Local banks have the best rates; beware of independent exchange services with high fees. Most banks are open M-F 8:20am-1:20pm and 2:45-3:45pm.

American Express: V. Dante Alighieri 22R (☎50 98). From the *duomo,* walk down V. dei Calzaiuoli and turn left on V. dei Tavolini. Mail held free for AmEx customers, otherwise €1.55. Open M-F 9am-5:30pm.

24hr. Pharmacies: Farmacia Comunale (☎28 94 35), at the train station by track #16. **Molteni,** V. dei Calzaiuoli 7R (☎28 94 90). AmEx/MC/V.

Internet Access: Walk down almost any busy street and you'll find an Internet cafe. **Internet Train,** V. Guelfa 54/56R, has 15 locations in the city listed on www.internettrain.it. €4.30 per hr., students €3.20. Most branches open M-F 9am-midnight, Sa 10am-8pm, Su noon-9pm. AmEx/MC/V.

Post Office: V. Pellicceria (☎27 36 480), off P. della Repubblica. Poste Restante available. Open M-Sa 8:15am-7pm. **Postal Code:** 50100.

🏠 🏕 ACCOMMODATIONS AND CAMPING

Lodging in Florence doesn't come cheap. **Consorzio ITA,** in the train station by track #16, can find rooms for a €3-8.50 fee. (☎066 99 10 00. Open M-Sa 8am-8pm, Su 10am-7pm.) It is best to make *prenotazioni* (reservations) ahead, especially if you plan to visit during Easter or summer.

HOSTELS AND CAMPING

▨ **Ostello Archi Rossi,** V. Faenza 94R (☎29 08 04; www.hostelarchirossi.com), near S. Maria Novella station. Outdoor patio is packed with students after dark. Home-cooked

ITALY

Florence

▲ ACCOMMODATIONS

Albergo Sampaoli,	1	D1
Campeggio Michelangelo,	2	E4
Hotel Abaco,	3	C2
Hotel Elite,	4	B2
Hotel Il Perseo,	5	C2
Hotel Nazionale,	6	C1
Hotel Tina,	7	E1
Istituto Gould,	8	B4
Katti House,	9	C2
Locanda Orchidea,	10	E3
Ostello Archi Rossi,	11	C1
Ostello della Gioventù Europa Villa Camerata (HI),	12	G3
Albergo Armonia,	13	C1
Hotel Anna's,	14	C1
Locanda Paola,	15	C1
Pensione Azzi,	16	C1
Ostello Santa Monaca,	17	C4
Pensionato Pio X,	18	C4
Relais Cavalcanti,	19	C4
Soggiorno Luna Rossa,	20	C1
Villa Camerata,	21	G3

● FOOD

Acqua al 2,	22	E3
all' Antico Ristoro Di Cambi,	23	A3
Il Borgo Antico,	24	B4
Gelateria dei Neri,	25	E4
Grom,	26	D3
Il Latini,	27	B3
La Loggia degli Albizi,	28	E3
Osteria de' Benci,	29	E4
Trattoria Anita,	30	E4
Trattoria Contadino,	31	B2
Trattoria da Zà-Zà,	32	D1
Trattoria Mario,	33	D1
Tre Merli,	34	B3
Vivoli,	35	E4

NIGHTLIFE

Central Park,	36	B3
Enoteca Alessi,	37	D3
Enoteca Fuori Porta,	38	E4
May Day Lounge,	39	D3
Moyo,	40	E4
Noir,	41	B3
Tabasco Gay Club,	42	D4

breakfast included. Laundry €6. Free Internet. Lockout 11am-2:30pm. Curfew 2am. Reserve online 1 week ahead, especially in summer. Dorms €21-26. MC/V. ❷

Istituto Gould, V. dei Serragli 49 (☎21 25 76; www.istitutogould.it), in the Oltrarno. Take bus #36 or 37 from the train station to the 2nd stop across the river. Spotless rooms. Reception M-F 8:45am-1pm and 3-7:30pm, Sa 9am-1:30pm. Dorms €21; singles €36, with bath €42; doubles €52-62. MC/V. ❷

Ostello Santa Monaca, V. S. Monaca 6 (☎26 83 38; www.ostello.it). Follow the directions to the Istituto Gould, but turn left off V. dei Serragli onto V. S. Monaca. Breakfast €2.70-3.80. Laundry €6.50 per 5kg. Internet €3 per hr. June-Sept. max. stay 7 nights. Curfew 1am. Reserve ahead. 10-bed dorms €18. AmEx/MC/V. ❷

Ostello della Gioventù Europa Villa Camerata (HI), V. Augusto Righi 2-4 (☎60 14 51), northeast of town. Take bus #17 from the train station (near track #5); ask for Salviatino. From the entrance, walk 10min. up a driveway past a vineyard. Tidy and crowded, in a beautiful villa. Breakfast included. Laundry €5.20. Max. stay 3 nights. Lockout 10am-2pm. Strict midnight curfew. Dorms €21. €3 HI discount. MC/V. ❷

Pensionato Pio X, V. dei Serragli 106 (☎/fax 22 50 44). Rooms, while not fancy, are clean and quiet. Check-out 9am. Curfew 1am. Dorms €17. Cash only. ❷

Campeggio Michelangelo, V. Michelangelo 80 (☎68 11 977; www.ecvacanze.it), beneath P. Michelangelo. Bus #13 from the bus station (15min.; last bus 11:25pm). Reception 7am-11pm. €11 per person, €16 per tent site. MC/V; min. €100. ❶

Villa Camerata, V. A. Righi 2-4 (☎60 03 15; fax 61 03 00). Take bus #17 outside the train station (near track #5); ask for Salviatino stop. Walk down driveway. Same entrance and reception as HI hostel (p. 638). Breakfast €2. Reception 7am-12:30pm and 1pm-midnight. Max. stay 6 nights. €8 per person, €7 per tent site. MC/V. ❶

HOTELS

🏨 **Locanda Orchidea,** Borgo degli Albizi 11 (☎24 80 346; hotelorchidea@yahoo.it). Dante's wife was born in this 12th-century *palazzo*, built around a still-intact tower. Carefully decorated rooms with marble floors; some open onto a garden. Singles €55; doubles €75; triples with shower €100; quads with shower €120. Cash only. ❹

🏨 **Soggiorno Luna Rossa,** V. Nazionale 7 (☎23 02 185). 3rd fl. Airy rooms have TV, fan, and colorful stained-glass windows. Small shared baths. Breakfast included. Dorms €22. Singles €35; doubles €85; triples €100; quads €140. Cash only. ❷

🏨 **Katti House/Soggiorno Annamaria,** V. Faenza 21/24 (☎21 34 10). Lovingly kept lodgings with 400-year-old antiques and an attentive staff. Large, recently renovated rooms with A/C, bath, and TV. Singles €60-75; doubles €75-120; triples €90; quads €120. Nov.-Mar. reduced rates. MC/V. ❹

Albergo Sampaoli, V. S. Gallo 14 (☎28 48 34; www.hotelsampaoli.it). Helpful staff and a large common area with fridge access. All rooms with fans, some with balcony. Singles €30-40, with bath €60-65; doubles €65/75; triples €70/80. MC/V. ❹

Hotel Il Perseo, V. de Cerretani 1 (☎21 25 04; www.hotelperseo.it). 20 spotless rooms with fans, satellite TVs, and free Internet. Breakfast included. Singles €85-95; doubles €110-140; triples €135-170; quads €160-210. AmEx/MC/V; min. 2 nights. ❺

Relais Cavalcanti, V. Pellicceria 2 (☎21 09 62). Unbeatable location just steps from P. della Repubblica. Ring bell to enter. Beautiful gold-trimmed rooms with antique wardrobes. Singles €100; doubles €125; triples €155. 10% *Let's Go* discount. MC/V. ❺

Hotel Tina, V. S. Gallo 31 (☎48 35 19; www.hoteltina.it). *Pensione* with new furniture, and amiable owners. Singles €30-50; doubles €46-65; extra bed €25. MC/V. ❹

Hotel Abaco, V. dei Banchi 1 (☎23 81 919; www.abaco-hotel.it). Extravagant rooms, each one named after a Renaissance master. Breakfast and A/C included when paying in cash. Laundry €7. Limited Internet access free at reception. Doubles €75, with bath €90; triples €110; quads €135. 10% *Let's Go* discount Nov.-Mar. MC/V. ❺

Hotel Elite, V. della Scala 12 (☎21 53 95). Brass bedposts shine in lovely rooms. Breakfast €6. Singles €50; doubles €75-90; triples €110; quads €130. MC/V. ❹

Hotel Nazionale, V. Nazionale 22 (☎23 82 203; www.nazionalehotel.it). 9 sunny rooms with comfy beds and A/C. Breakfast brought to your room 8-9:30am (€6). Singles €60-70; doubles €85-115; triples €115-145. MC/V. ❺

Via Faenza 56 houses 4 *pensioni* that are among the best deals in the area. From the train station, exit left onto V. Nazionale, walk 1 block, and turn left on V. Faenza.

> **Pensione Azzi** (☎21 38 06; www.hotelazzi.com) has large rooms and a terrace. Styled as an artists' inn. Breakfast included. Singles €55-70; doubles €80-110. AmEx/MC/V. ❹
>
> **Hotel Anna's** (☎23 02 714; www.hotelannas.com), on the 2nd fl. Rooms with TV, bath, phone, and A/C. Breakfast €5. Singles €60-80; doubles €80-100; triples €75-130. AmEx/MC/V. ❹
>
> **Locanda Paola** (☎21 36 82) has doubles with views of the surrounding hills. Breakfast included. Internet access. Flexible 2am curfew. Dorms €25. MC/V. ❸
>
> **Albergo Armonia** (☎21 11 46). Rooms have high ceilings. Singles €42; doubles €65; triples €75. Extra bed €25. Low season reduced rates. Cash only. ❸

◗ FOOD

Florentine specialties include *bruschetta* (grilled bread soaked in oil and garlic and topped with tomatoes, basil, and anchovy or liver paste) and *bistecca alla Fiorentina* (thick sirloin). The best local cheese is pecorino, made from sheep's milk. A liter of house wine usually costs €3.50-6 in a *trattoria*, but stores sell bottles of chianti for as little as €2.50. The local dessert is *cantuccini di prato* (almond cookies) dipped in *vinsanto* (a rich dessert wine). Florence's own Buontalenti family supposedly invented gelato; extensive sampling is a must. For lunch, visit a *rosticceria gastronomia*, peruse the city's pushcarts, or pick up fresh produce and meats at the **Mercato Centrale,** between V. Nazionale and S. Lorenzo. (Open June-Sept. M-Sa 7:30am-2pm; Oct.-May M-F 7am-2pm, Sa 7am-2pm and 4-8pm.) To get to **STANDA** supermarket, V. Pietrapiana 1R, turn right on V. del Proconsolo, take the first left on Borgo degli Albizi, and continue straight through P. G. Salvemini. (Open M-Sa 8am-9pm, Su 9am-9pm. MC/V.)

RESTAURANTS

▨ Osteria de' Benci, V. de' Benci 13R (☎23 44 923), on the corner of V. dei Neri. Join locals for classics like *carpaccio* (thinly sliced beef; €14). *Primi* €9. *Secondi* €9-14. Cover €3.30. Reserve ahead. Open M-Sa 1-2:45pm and 7:30-11:45pm. AmEx/MC/V. ❹

▨ Acqua al 2, V. Vigna Vecchia 40R (☎28 41 70), behind the Bargello. Popular with young Italians and tourists. Serves Florentine specialties, including an excellent *filetto al mirtillo* (steak in a blueberry sauce; €15). *Primi* €7. *Secondi* €8-19. Cover €1. Service 10%. Reserve ahead. Open daily 7pm-1am. AmEx/MC/V. ❸

▨ Il Latini, V. dei Palchetti 6R (☎21 09 16). Crowds line up nightly; prepare to wait for your *arrosto misto* (platter of roast meats). Waiters keep the wine flowing. *Primi* €6-8. *Secondi* €10-18. Reserve ahead. Open Tu-Su 12:30-2:30pm and 7:30-10:30pm. Closed 2 weeks in Aug. AmEx/MC/V. ❸

all'Antico Ristoro Di' Cambi, V. S. Onofrio 1R (☎21 71 34). Near Ponte Vespucci. Prosciutto hangs from the restored 5th-century ceiling. 3rd-generation owner Stefano serves up Florentine speciality *bistecca alla Fiorentina* (€4 per 100g). The *sorbetto limone* (€4) is the ideal finish. *Primi* €6-8. *Secondi* €7-16. Cover €1. Open M-Sa noon-3pm and 7:30pm-midnight. Closed 2 weeks in mid-Aug. AmEx/MC/V. ❹

Trattoria Zà-Zà, P. del Mercato Centrale 26R (☎21 54 11). Wooden-beam ceilings and brick archways inside, lively patio outside. Try the *tris* (mixed bean and vegetable soup; €7) or the *tagliata di manzo* (cut of beef; €14-19). Cover €2. Reserve ahead. Open daily 11am-11pm. AmEx/MC/V. ❸

Trattoria Anita, V. del Parlascio 2R (☎21 86 98), behind the Bargello. Dine by candle-light, surrounded by shelves of expensive wine. Traditional Tuscan fare, including pasta, roast chicken, and steak. *Primi* €5. *Secondi* from €6. Lunch *menù* €6. Cover €1. Open M-Sa noon-2:30pm and 7-10pm. AmEx/MC/V. ❷

La Loggia degli Albizi, Borgo degli Albizi 39R (☎24 79 574). From behind the *duomo*, go right on V. del Proconsolo and take the 1st left onto Borgo degli Albizi. Head 2 blocks down and look right. A hidden treasure, this bakery/cafe offers an escape from the tour-ist hordes. Pastries and coffee from €0.80, more at tables. Open M-Sa 7am-8pm. ❶

Trattoria Contadino, V. Palazzuolo 71R (☎23 82 673). Filling, homestyle, fixed-price *menù* (€10-11) includes *primo, secondo*, bread, water, and 0.25L of wine. Open Sept.-May daily 11am-2:30pm and 6-9:30pm. June-July closed Sa-Su. AmEx/MC/V. ❷

Tre Merli, entrances on V. del Moro 11R and V. dei Fossi 12R (☎28 70 62). Sumptuous dishes like *spaghettino all'Imperiale* (with mussels, clams, and shrimp; €14). *Primi* €7.50-14. *Secondi* €12-19. Lunch *menù* €12. Cover €2. Open daily 11am-11pm. 10% discount and free glass of wine with *Let's Go*. AmEx/MC/V. ❹

Trattoria Mario, V. Rosina 2R (☎21 85 50), around the corner from P. del Mercato Cen-trale. Informal lunch establishment with incredible pasta, a stellar rendition of *bistecca alla Fiorentina*, and a loyal local following. *Secondi* €3.10-11. Cover €0.50. Open M-Sa noon-3:30pm. Closed Aug. Cash only. ❷

Il Borgo Antico, P. S. Spirito 6R (☎21 04 37). Trendy spot with young staff and stu-dent-heavy clientele. Memorable pastas, pizzas, and salads (€7). *Primi* €7. *Secondi* €10-20. Cover €2. Reserve ahead. Open daily June-Sept. 11am-midnight; Oct.-May 12:45-2:30pm and 7:45pm-1am. AmEx/MC/V. ❸

GELATERIE

Florence's *gelaterie* get crowded, and to avoid making salespeople cranky, fol-low protocol when ordering: first, pay at the register for the size you request, then—receipt in hand—choose a flavor. Most gelaterie also serve *granite*, fla-vored ices that are easier on the waistline.

▓ **Grom,** Via del Campanile (☎21 61 58). The kind of gelato you'll be talking about in 50 years. As fresh as it gets. Sublimely balanced texture. Cups start at €2. Open daily Apr.-Sept. 10:30am-midnight; Oct.-Mar. 10:30am-11pm.

▓ **Vivoli,** V. Isole della Stinche 7 (☎29 23 34), behind the Bargello. A renowned *gelateria* and long-time contender for the distinction of the best ice cream in Florence. Cups from €1.60. Open Tu-Sa 7:30am-1am, Su 9:30am-1am.

Gelateria dei Neri, V. dei Neri 20-22R (☎21 00 34). Stand outside and watch through the window as dozens of delicious flavors are mixed right before your eyes. Try *crema giotto* (coconut, almond, and hazelnut). Cones and cups from €1.40.

ENOTECHE (WINE BARS)

Check out an *enoteca* to sample Italy's fine wines. A meal can often be made out of complementary side dishes (cheeses, olives, toast and spreads, and salami).

Enoteca Alessi, V. della Oche 27/29R (☎21 49 66), 1 block from the *duomo*. Among Florence's finest wine bars, with a cavernous interior that stocks over 1000 wines. Dou-bles as a candy store. Open M-F 9am-1pm and 3:30-7:30pm. AmEx/MC/V.

Enoteca Fuori Porta, V. Monte alle Croci 10R (☎23 42 483), near S. Miniato. This casual *enoteca* serves an extensive selection of *bruschetta* (€1-2.50) and *crostini* (€5-8). Cover €1.50. Open daily noon-4pm and 7-10pm. Closed Su in Aug. MC/V.

◩ SIGHTS

For a full list of museum openings, check out www.firenzeturismo.it. For museum reservations, call **Firenze Musei** (☎29 48 83; www.firenzemusei.it). There are **no stu-**

dent discounts at museums and admission can be expensive. Choose destinations carefully and plan to spend a few hours at each landmark.

PIAZZA DEL DUOMO

■**DUOMO (CATTEDRALE DI SANTA MARIA DEL FIORE).** In 1296, the city fathers commissioned Arnolfo di Cambio to erect a cathedral so magnificent that it would be "impossible to make it either better or more beautiful with the industry and power of man." Di Cambio succeeded, designing a massive nave with the confidence that by the time it was completed (1418), technology would have advanced enough to provide a solution to erect a dome. **Filippo Brunelleschi** was called in to add a dome: after studying long-neglected classical methods, he came up with his double-shelled, interlocking-brick construction. The *duomo* claims the world's third longest nave, trailing only St. Peter's in Rome and St. Paul's in London. *(Open M-W and F 10am-5pm, Th 10am-4:30pm, Sa 10am-4:45pm, Su 1:30-4:45pm. Mass daily 7am, 12:30, 5-7pm. Free.)* Climb the 463 steps inside the dome to **Michelangelo's lantern,** which offers an expansive view of the city from the 100m high external gallery. *(Open M-F 8:30am-7pm, Sa 8:30am-5:40pm. €6.)* The climb up the 82m **campanile** next to the duomo, also called "Giotto's Tower," reveals views of the city and the **battistero** (baptistry), whose bronze doors are known as the ■**Gates of Paradise.** Mosaics inside the baptistry inspired details of the *Inferno* by Dante, who was christened here. *(Campanile open daily 8:30am-7:30pm. €6. Baptistry open M-Sa noon-7pm, Su 8:30am-2pm. €3.)* Most of the *duomo*'s art resides behind the cathedral in the **Museo dell'Opera del Duomo.** Up the first flight of stairs is a late *Pietà* by Michelangelo; according to legend, he broke Christ's left arm in a fit of frustration. *(P. del Duomo 9, behind the duomo. ☎ 23 02 885. Open M-Sa 9am-7:30pm, Su 9am-1:40pm. €6.)*

■**ORSANMICHELE.** Built in 1337 as a granary, the Orsanmichele became a church after a fire convinced officials to move grain operations outside the city. The ancient grain chutes are still visible outside. Within, tenacious visitors will discover Ghiberti's *St. John the Baptist* and *St. Stephen*, Donatello's *St. Peter* and *St. Mark*, and Giambologna's *St. Luke*. *(V. Arte della Lana, between the duomo and P. della Signoria. Open Tu-Su 10am-5pm. Free.)*

PIAZZA DELLA SIGNORIA AND ENVIRONS

From P. del Duomo, **Via dei Calzaiuoli,** one of the city's oldest streets, runs south past crowds, street vendors, *gelaterie*, and chic shops to **Piazza della Signoria,** the 13th-century *piazza* bordered by the Palazzo Vecchio and the Uffizi. With the construction of the Palazzo Vecchio in 1299, the square became Florence's civic and political center. In 1497, religious zealot Girolamo Savonarola lit the **Bonfire of the Vanities** here, barbecuing some of Florence's best art. Today P. della Signoria fills daily with photo-snapping tourists who later return for drinks and dessert in its upscale cafes. Monumental sculptures bunch in front of the *palazzo* and inside the 14th-century **Loggia dei Lanzi.** *(Free.)* From the Uffizi, follow V. Georgofili left and turn right along the river to reach the **Ponte Vecchio** (old bridge), the oldest bridge in Florence. Don't miss the **sunset view** from neighboring **Ponte alle Grazie.**

■**THE UFFIZI.** Giorgio Vasari designed this palace in 1554 for the offices *(uffizi)* of Duke Cosimo's administration; today, the gallery holds one of the world's finest art collections. Beautiful statues overlook the walkway from niches in the columns; play "spot the Renaissance man" and try to find Leonardo, Machiavelli, Petrarch, and Vespucci among them. Botticelli, Caravaggio, Cimabue, Fra Angelico, della Francesca, Giotto, Michelangelo, Raphael, del Sarto, Titian, da Vinci, even Dürer, Rembrandt, Rubens—you name it, it's here. Be sure to visit the **Cabinet of Drawings and Prints** on the first floor before confining yourself to the U-shaped corridor of the second floor. A few rooms are usually closed each day, and some works may be on loan. A sign at the ticket office lists the rooms that are closed; ask when they will reopen. *(From P. B. S. Giovanni, take V. Roma past P. della Repubblica, where the street turns into V. Calimala. Continue until V. Vaccereccia and turn left.* ☎ *23 88 651. Open Tu-Su 8:15am-6:50pm. €6.50. Reserve ahead for €3 fee. Audio tour €4.70.)*

◨PALAZZO VECCHIO. Arnolfo del Cambio designed this fortress-like *palazzo* in the late 13th century to be the seat of government. It included apartments which served as living quarters for members of the city council while they served two-month terms. After the *palazzo* became the Medici's home in 1470, Michelozzo decorated the courtyard. The **Monumental Apartments,** which house the *palazzo's* extensive art collections, are now an art and history museum. The worthwhile **Activities Tour** includes the "Secret Routes," which reveal hidden stairwells and chambers tucked behind exquisite oil paintings. The ceiling of the **Salone del Cinquecento,** where the Grand Council of the Republic met, is so elaborately decorated that the walls can hardly support its weight. The tiny **Studio di Francesco I** is a treasure trove of Mannerist art. *(☎ 27 68 224. Open M-W and F-Sa 9am-7pm, Su 9am-1pm. Palazzo and Monumental Apartments each €6, ages 18-25 €4.50. Activities tour €8/5.50. Courtyard free. Reserve ahead for tours.)*

THE BARGELLO AND ENVIRONS

◨BARGELLO. The heart of medieval Florence is in this 13th-century fortress, once the residence of the chief magistrate and later a brutal prison with public executions in its courtyard. It was restored in the 19th century and now houses the sculpture-filled, largely untouristed **Museo Nazionale.** Donatello's bronze *David,* the first free-standing nude since antiquity, stands opposite the two bronze panels of the *Sacrifice of Isaac,* submitted by Ghiberti and Brunelleschi in the baptistry door competition. Michelangelo's early works, including *Bacchus, Brutus,* and *Apollo,* are on the ground floor. *(V. del Proconsolo 4, between the duomo and P. della Signoria. ☎ 23 88 606. Open daily 8:15am-6pm. Closed 2nd and 4th M of each month. €4.)*

BADIA. The site of medieval Florence's richest monastery, the Badia church is now buried in the interior of a residential block. Filippino Lippi's *Apparition of the Virgin to St. Bernard,* one of the most famous paintings of the 15th century, hangs in eerie gloom to the left of the church. Be sure to glance up at the intricately carved dark wood ceiling. Some say Dante may have first glimpsed his beloved Beatrice here. Visitors are asked to walk silently among the prostrate, white-robed worshippers. *(Entrance on V. Dante Alighieri, off V. Proconsolo. ☎ 26 44 02. Open to tourists M 3-6pm, but respectful visitors can walk through at any time.)*

PIAZZA DELLA REPUBBLICA AND FARTHER WEST

The largest open space in Florence, the P. della Repubblica teems with crowds, overpriced cafes, restaurants, and *gelaterie.* In 1890, it replaced the Mercato Vecchio as the site of the city market, but has since traded stalls for more fashionable vendors. The inscription *"antico centro della città, da secolare squalore, a vita nuova restituito"* ("ancient center of the city, squalid for centuries, restored to new life") makes a derogatory reference to the *piazza's* location in the old Jewish ghetto. The area around Mercato Nuovo and V. Tornabuoni was Florence's financial capital in the 1400s. Now it's residential, but still touristy.

◨CHIESA DI SANTA MARIA NOVELLA. This church houses the chapels of the wealthiest 13th- and 14th-century merchants. Santa Maria Novella was home to an order of Dominicans, or *Domini canes* (Hounds of the Lord), who took a bite out of sin and corruption. The facade of the *chiesa* is made of Florentine marble and is considered one of the great masterpieces of early Renaissance architecture. The Medicis commissioned Vasari to paint new frescoes over the 13th-century ones on the walls, but the painter spared Masaccio's **◨Trinity,** the first painting to use geometric perspective. In the **Gondi Chapel** is Brunelleschi's *Crucifix,* designed in response to Donatello's, in Santa Croce, which Brunelleschi found too full of "vigorous naturalism." Donatello was supposedly so impressed by his rival's creation that he dropped the bag of eggs he was carrying. *(Open M-Th and Sa 9am-5pm. €2.70.)*

CHIESA DI SANTA TRINITÀ. Hoping to spend eternity in elite company, the most fashionable *palazzo* owners commissioned family chapels in this church. The facade, designed by Bernardo Buontalenti in the 16th century, is almost Baroque in its elaborate ornamentation. Scenes from Ghirlandaio's *Life of St. Francis* decorate the **Sassetti Chapel** in the right arm of the transept. The famous altarpiece, Ghirlandaio's *Adoration of the Shepherds*, resides in the Uffizi—this one is a copy. *(In P. S. Trinità. Open M-Sa 7am-noon and 4-7pm, Su 7-noon. Free.)*

MERCATO NUOVO. The *loggie* (guilds) of the New Market have housed gold and silk traders since 1547. Today, imitation designer gear dominates vendors' wares. Rubbing the snout of Pietro Tacca's plump statue, *Il Porcellino* (The Little Pig) is reputed to bring luck, but don't wait for that purse you covet to become real leather. *(Off V. Calimala, between P. della Repubblica and the Ponte Vecchio. Open dawn-dusk.)*

SAN LORENZO AND FARTHER NORTH

■**ACCADEMIA.** It doesn't matter how many pictures of him you've seen—when you come around the corner to see Michelangelo's triumphant ▨**David** towering in self-assured perfection under the rotunda designed just for him, you will be blown away. The statue's base was struck by lightning in 1512, the figure was damaged by anti-Medici riots in 1527, and David's left wrist was broken by a stone, after which he was moved here from P. della Signoria in 1873. In the hallway leading to *David* are Michelangelo's four **Slaves** and a *Pietà*. The master purposely left these statues unfinished, staying true to his theory of "releasing" figures from the living stone. *(V. Ricasoli 60, between the churches of S. Marco and S. S. Annunziata. ☎ 23 88 609. Open Tu-Su 8:15am-6:50pm. Reserve ahead. May-Sept. €10; Oct.-Apr. €7.)*

BASILICA DI SAN LORENZO. Because the Medicis lent the funds to build this church, they retained artistic control over its construction and decided to add Cosimo dei Medici's grave to Brunelleschi's spacious basilica, placing it in front of the high altar to make the entire church his personal mausoleum. Michelangelo began the exterior, but, disgusted by Florentine politics, he abandoned the project, which accounts for the plain facade. *(Open M-Sa 10am-5pm. Mar.-Oct. open M-Sa 10am-5pm, Su 1:30-5pm. €2.50.)* While the **Cappelle dei Medici** (Medici Chapels) offer a rare glimpse of the Baroque in Florence, the **Cappella dei Principi** (Princes' Chapel) emulates the baptistry in P. del Duomo. Michelangelo sculpted the **Sacrestia Nuova** (New Sacristy) to hold two Medici tombs. On the tomb of Lorenzo he placed the female Night and the muscular male Day; on Giuliano's sit the more androgynous Dawn and Dusk. *(Walk around to the back entrance in P. Madonna degli Aldobrandini. Open daily 8:15am-5pm. Closed 1st and 3rd M and 2nd and 4th Su. €6.)* The adjacent **Laurentian Library** houses one of the world's most valuable manuscript collections. Michelangelo's *pietra serena* sandstone staircase at its entrance is one of his most innovative architectural designs. *(Open daily 8:30am-1:30pm. Free with entrance to San Lorenzo.)*

MUSEO DELLA CHIESA DI SAN MARCO. Remarkable works by Fra Angelico adorn this museum, once part of a convent complex and one of the most peaceful places in Florence. A large room to the right of the courtyard houses some of the painter's major works, including the church's altarpiece. The second floor displays Angelico's *Annunciation*. Every cell in the convent has its own Angelico fresco. To the right of the stairwell, Michelozzo's library, modeled on Michelangelo's work in S. Lorenzo, is designed for reflection. In cells 17 and 22, underground artwork, excavated from the medieval period, peeks through a glass floor. Toward the exit, the two rooms of the **Museo di Firenze Antica** show Florence's ancient roots. Be sure to peek into the church itself, next to the museum, to admire the elaborate altar and vaulted ceiling. *(Enter at P.S. Marco 3. Open M-F 8:15am-1:50pm, Sa 8:15am-6:50pm, Su 8:15am-7pm. Closed 2nd and 4th M and 1st and 3rd Su of each month. €4.)*

PIAZZA SANTA CROCE AND ENVIRONS

■ **CHIESA DI SANTA CROCE.** The Franciscans built this church as far as possible from their Dominican rivals at S. Maria Novella. Ironically, the ascetic Franciscans produced what is arguably the most splendid church in the city. Luminaries buried here include Galileo, Machiavelli, Michelangelo (whose tomb was designed by Vasari), and Leonardo Bruni, shown holding his beloved *History of Florence*, all lie here. Check out Donatello's *Crucifix*, so irksome to Brunelleschi, in the Vernio Chapel, and his gilded *Annunciation*, by Bruni's tomb. At the end of the cloister next to the church is the ■**Cappella Pazzi,** whose proportions are perfect and whose decorations include Luca della Robbia's *tondi* of the apostles and Brunelleschi's moldings of the evangelists. *(Open M-Sa 9:30am-5:30pm, Su 1-5:30pm. €5.)*

SYNAGOGUE OF FLORENCE. This synagogue, also known as the **Museo del Tempio Israelitico,** is resplendent with Sephardic domes, arches, and patterns. David Levi, a wealthy Florentine Jewish businessman, donated his fortune in 1870 to build "a monumental temple worthy of Florence," recognizing the Jews' new freedom to live and worship outside the old Jewish ghetto. *(V. Farini 4, at V. Pilastri. ☎ 24 52 52. Free tours 1 per hr.; reserve ahead. Open Su-Th 10am-6pm, F 10am-2pm. €4.)*

THE OLTRARNO

Historically disdained by downtown Florentines, the far side of the Arno remains an animated and unpretentious quarter, filled with students and, thankfully, not too many tourists. Head back over Ponte S. Trinità after dallying in P. S. Spirito.

■ **PALAZZO PITTI.** Luca Pitti, a 15th-century banker, built his *palazzo* east of P. S. Spirito against the Boboli hill. The Medicis acquired the *palazzo* and the hill in 1550 and expanded it in every way possible. Today, it houses six museums, including the **Galleria Palatina.** Florence's most important art collection after the Uffizi, the gallery has works by Caravaggio, Raphael, Rubens, and Titian. Other museums display Medici family costumes, porcelain, carriages, and **Royal Apartments**—lavish reminders of the time when the *palazzo* was the living quarters of the royal House of Savoy. The **Galleria d'Arte Moderna** hides one of Italian art history's big surprises, the proto-Impressionist works of the Macchiaioli group. *(Open Tu-Su 8:15am-6:50pm. Ticket for Palatine Gallery, Royal Apartments, and Modern Art Gallery €8.50.)* An elaborately designed park, the ■**Boboli Gardens,** with geometrically sculpted hedges, contrasting groves of holly and cypress trees, and bubbling fountains, are an exquisite example of stylized Renaissance landscaping. A large oval lawn is just up the hill from the back of the *Palazzo Pitti*, with an Egyptian obelisk in the middle and marble statues in portals dotting the perimeter. *(Open daily June-Aug. 8:15am-7:30pm; Apr.-May and Sept.-Oct. 8:15am-6:30pm; Nov.-Mar. reduced hours. €6.)*

SAN MINIATO AL MONTE AND ENVIRONS

■ **SAN MINIATO AL MONTE.** An inlaid marble facade and 13th-century mosaics provide a prelude to the floor inside, patterned with doves, lions, and astrological signs. Visit at 5:40pm to hear the monks chanting. *(Take bus #13 from the station or climb the stairs from Piazzale Michelangelo. ☎ 23 42 731. Open daily Mar.-Nov. 8am-7pm; Dec.-Feb. 8am-1pm and 2:30-6pm. Free.)*

PIAZZALE MICHELANGELO. A visit to Piazzale Michelangelo is a must. At sunset, waning light casts a warm glow over the city. Views from here are even better (and certainly cheaper) than those from the top of the *duomo*. Make the challenging uphill trek at around 8:30pm during the summer to arrive at the *piazza* in time for sunset. Unfortunately, the *piazza* doubles as a large parking lot, and is home to hordes of tour buses during summer days. *(Cross the Ponte Vecchio to the Oltrarno and turn left, walk through the piazza, and turn right up V. de Bardi. Follow it uphill as it becomes V. del Monte alle Croci, where a staircase to the left heads to the piazza.)*

🎵 ENTERTAINMENT

May starts the summer music festival season with the classical **Maggio Musicale.** The **Festa del Grillo** (Festival of the Cricket) is held on the first Sunday after Ascension Day, when crickets in tiny wooden cages are sold in the Cascine park to be released into the grass—Florentines believe the song of a cricket is good luck. In June, the *quartieri* of Florence turn out in costume to play their own medieval version of football, known as **calcio storico,** in which two teams face off over a wooden ball in one of the city's *piazze,* their games so often ending in riots that the festival was actually cancelled in 2007. The **Festival of San Giovanni Battista,** on June 24, features a tremendous fireworks display visible all along the Arno, beginning around 10pm. The **Estate Fiesolana** (June-Aug.) fills the Roman theater in nearby Fiesole with concerts, opera, theater, ballet, and film events (☎800 41 42 40; www.estatefiesolana.com). In summer, the **Europa dei Sensi** program hosts **Rime Rampanti** (☎348 58 04 812; www.firenzenotte.it), nightly cultural shows with music, poetry, and food from a chosen European country.

🛍 SHOPPING

For both the budget shopper and the big spender who's looking to make the splurge of a lifetime, Florence offers too many options and temptations. *Saldi* (sales) take over in January and July, even in V. Tornabuoni's swanky boutiques. The city's artisanal traditions thrive at its open markets. **San Lorenzo,** the largest, cheapest, and most touristed, sprawls for several blocks around P. S. Lorenzo. In front of the leather shops, vendors sell all kinds of goods—bags, clothes, food, toys, and flags. High prices are rare, but so are quality and honesty. (Open daily 9am-twilight.) For everything from pot-holders to parakeets, shop at the market in **Parco delle Cascine,** which begins four bridges west of the Ponte Vecchio at P. V. Veneto and stretches along the Arno River each Tuesday morning. *Carta fiorentina,* paper covered in intricate floral designs, adorns books, journals, and paper goods, at **Alinari,** L. Alinari 15. (☎23 951. Open M 2:30-6:30pm, Tu-F 9am-1pm and 2:30-6:30pm, Sa 9am-1pm and 3-7pm. Closed 2 weeks in Aug. AmEx/MC/V.) Florentine **leatherwork** is affordable and renowned for its quality. Some of the best leather artisans in the city work around P. S. Croce and V. Porta S. Maria. The **Santa Croce Leather School,** in Chiesa di Santa Croce, offers first-rate products at reasonable prices. (☎24 45 34; www.leatherschool.it. Open Mar. 15-Nov. 15 daily 9:30am-6pm; Nov. 16-Mar. 14 M-Sa 10am-12:30pm and 3-6pm. AmEx/MC/V.)

🎭 NIGHTLIFE

For reliable info, consult the city's entertainment monthly, *Firenze Spettacolo* (€2) or www.informacittafirenze.it. **Piazza Santo Spirito** in Oltrarno has live music in the summer. To go to clubs or bars that run late and are far from the *centro,* keep in mind that the last bus may leave before the fun winds down, and taxis are rare in the area with the most popular discos.

Moyo, V. dei Banchi 23R (☎24 79 738), near P. Santa Croce. Thriving lunch spot by day, hip bar by night, always crowded with young Italians. Lunch options from €7. Evening cocktails include free, self-serve snacks. Open daily 8am-3am. AmEx/MC/V.

ITALY

Noir, Lungarno Corsini 12R (☎21 07 51). This bar mixes mojitos (€7) and other refreshing cocktails for locals. After paying, take your drink outside by the Arno. Mixed drinks €5-6.50. Beer from €3.50. Open 11am-1am. Closed 2 weeks in Aug. MC/V.

Central Park, in Parco della Cascinè (☎35 35 05). Open-air dance floor pulses with hiphop, reggae, and rock. Favored by Florentine and foreign teens and college students. Mixed drinks €8. Cover €20; no cover for foreign students before 12:30am. Open M-Tu and Th-Sa 11pm-late, W 9pm-late. AmEx/MC/V.

May Day Lounge, V. Dante Alighieri 16R. Aspiring artists display their work on the walls of this eclectic lounge that fills with offbeat Italians. Play Pong on the early 80s gaming system or sip mixed drinks (€4.50-6.50) to the beat of the background funk. Beer €4.50. Happy hour 8-10pm. Open daily 8pm-2am. Closed most of Aug. AmEx/MC/V.

Tabasco Gay Club, P. S. Cecilia 3R, near Palazzo Vecchio. Smoke machines and strobe lights on the dance floor. Florence's most popular and classiest gay disco caters primarily to men. 18+. Cover €13, includes 1 drink. Open Tu-Su 10pm-4am. AmEx/MC/V.

SIENA ☎0577

Many travelers rush from Rome to Florence, ignoring medieval Siena (pop. 50,000) despite its rich artistic, political, and economic history. *Il Palio*, Siena's intoxicating series of bareback horse races, is a party and a spectacle.

⌨🔊 TRANSPORTATION AND PRACTICAL INFORMATION. Trains run from P. Rosselli to Florence (1¾hr., 16 per day, €5.70) and Rome (3hr., 20 per day, €13) via Chiusi. TRA-IN/SITA **buses** (☎20 42 46) run from P. Gramsci and the train station to Florence (1 per hr., €6.50) and San Gimignano (31 per day, €5.20). Across from the train station, take TRA-IN buses #3, 4, 7-10, 17, or 77 (€0.90) to **Piazza del Sale** or **Piazza Gramsci,** then follow signs to **Piazza del Campo,** Siena's *centro storico,* also known as **Il Campo.** The central APT **tourist office** is at P. del Campo 56. (☎28 05; www.terresiena.it. Open mid-Mar. to mid-Nov. daily 9:30am-1pm and 2:30-6pm; mid-Nov. to mid-Mar. M-Sa 8:30am-1pm and 3-7pm, Su 9am-1pm.) Check email at **Cafe Internet,** Galleria Cecco Angiolieri 16. (€1.80 per hr. Open M-Sa 8:30am-11pm, Su 9am-11pm.) **Postal Code:** 53100.

⌨🛏 ACCOMMODATIONS AND FOOD. Finding rooms in Siena can be difficult between Easter and October. Reserve a month ahead for *Il Palio.* **Prenotazioni Alberghi e Ristoranti,** in P. S. Domenico, finds rooms for a €2 fee. (☎94 08 09. Open M-Sa 9am-7pm, Su 9am-noon.) 🏠**Casa Laura ❸,** V. Roma 3, is in the university area; ring the doorbell labeled "Bencini Valentini." (☎22 60 61; fax 22 52 40. Kitchen available. Doubles €65-67; triples €70; quads €75. MC/V.) Bus #10 and 15 from P. Gramsci stop at the spotless **Ostello della Gioventù "Guidoriccio" (HI) ❶,** V. Fiorentina 89, in Località Lo Stellino. (☎52 212. Curfew midnight. Dorms €14. Cash only.) To **camp** at **Colleverde ❶,** Str. di Scacciapensieri 47, take bus #3 or 8 from P. del Sale; confirm destination with driver. (☎28 00 44; www.terresiena.it. Open late Mar. to mid-Nov. €7.80 per person, €3.50 per tent site. MC/V.)

Sienese bakeries prepare *panforte,* a confection of honey, almonds, and citron, sold at **Bar/Pasticceria Nannini ❶,** V. Banchi di Sopra 22-24 (€2.10 per 100g). *Tagliatelle al ragù di coniglio* (pasta with rabbit sauce; €6.50) is a classic served at **Il Cantiere del Gusto ❸,** V. Calzoleria 12, behind the curve of P. del Campo off V. Banchi d. Sotto. (☎28 90 10. *Primi* €5-6. *Secondi* €8-20. Cover €1. Service 10%. Open M 12:30-2:30pm, Tu-Sa 12:30-2:30pm and 7-10pm. MC/V.) **Osteria La Chiacchera ❷,** Costa di S. Antonio 4, has delicious pasta. (☎28 06 31. *Primi* €5-6. *Secondi* €8-12. Open M and W-Su noon-3:30pm and 7pm-midnight. AmEx/MC/V.) A **CONAD** supermarket is in P. Matteoti. (Open M-Sa 8:30am-8:30pm, Su 9am-1pm and 4-8pm.)

📷🎭 SIGHTS AND ENTERTAINMENT. Siena radiates from 🏛**Piazza del Campo (Il Campo),** a shell-shaped brick square designed for civic events. At the top of the slope by Il Campo is the **Fonte Gaia,** a marble fountain that has refreshed Siena since the

1300s. At the bottom, the **Torre del Mangia** bell tower looms over the graceful **Palazzo Pubblico**. Inside the *palazzo* is the **Museo Civico**. (*Palazzo*, museum, and tower open daily Mar.-Oct. 10am-6:15pm; Nov.-Feb. 10am-5:30pm. Museum €7, students €4.50. Tower €6. Combo €10.) From the *palazzo* facing Il Campo, take the left stairs and cross V. di Città to get to Siena's hilltop **☒duomo**. To prevent the apse from being left hanging in mid-air, the lavish **baptistry** was constructed below. (Open June-Aug. M-Sa 10:30am-8pm, Su 1:30-6pm; Mar.-May and Sept.-Oct. M-Sa 10:30am-7:30pm, Su 1:30-6pm; Nov.-Feb. M-Sa 10:30am-6:30pm, Su 1:30-5:30pm. €3-5.50.) The decorated underground rooms of the **cripta** (crypt) were used by pilgrims about to enter the *duomo*. (Check hours at the *duomo*. €6, students €5.) The **Museo dell'Opera della Metropolitana**, to the right of the *duomo*, houses its overflow art. (Open mid-Mar. to Sept. daily 9am-7:30pm; Oct. to mid-Mar. reduced hours. €6.) Every year on July 2 and August 16, **☒Il Palio** morphs the mellow Campo into a chaotic arena as horses speed around its edge. Arrive three days early to watch the trial runs and to pick a favorite *contrada* (team).

⚡ DAYTRIP FROM SIENA: SAN GIMIGNANO.
The hilltop village of San Gimignano (pop. 7000) looks like an illustration from a medieval manuscript with prototypical churches, palaces, and tower looming above the city walls. San Gimignano's 14 famous towers, all that remain of the original 72, attract many daytrippers due to their massive presence in the tiny town. The **Museo Civico**, on the second floor of **Palazzo Comunale**, has a collection of Sienese and Florentine artwork. Within the museum is the entrance to the **☒Torre Grossa**, the *palazzo*'s tallest remaining tower; climb its 218 steps for a view of Tuscany's harmonious hills. *(Open daily Mar.-Oct. 9:30am-7pm; Nov.-Feb. 10am-5:30pm. €5, students €4.)* **Piazza della Cisterna** is the center of life in San Gimignano and adjoins **Piazza del Duomo**, site of the impressive tower of the **Palazzo del Podestà**. The famous **Vernaccia di San Gimignano**, a light, sweet white wine, is sold at **La Buca**, V. S. Giovanni 16, as are sausages and meats from the store's own farm. *(Open daily Apr.-Oct. 9am-8pm; Nov.-Mar. 10am-6pm. AmEx/MC/V.)* **Buses** leave P. Montemaggio for Florence (1½hr., 1 per hr., €6) via Poggibonsi, and Siena (1½hr., 1 per 1-2hr., €5.20). To reach the *centro*, pass through Pta. San Matteo and follow V. San Giovanni to P. della Cisterna, which merges with P. del Duomo on the left. **Postal Code:** 53037.

LUCCA ☎ 0583

Lucca ("LOO-ka"; pop. 9000) dabbles successfully in every area of tourist enjoyment: bikers rattle along the tree-lined promenade atop the town's medieval walls, fashionistas shop at trendy boutiques, and art

LUCCAN LORE

The Luccan tale of Lucida Mansi breathes serious morals into Italian primping practices. Lucida was a drop-dead gorgeous woman who knew exactly how to seduce men and get what she wanted. An active lover, she even killed her husband to indulge in such revelry. In vanity, she covered the rooms of her *palazzo* (Palazzo Mansi, still in Lucca today) with mirrors.

Eventually Lucida began to age—wrinkles won out on her flawless skin. To thwart these unsightly signs of age, Lucida did the only thing she could think of: she contacted the Devil. The Devil gave her 30 years of youth in exchange for her soul.

Lucida continued her hedonistic life of fashion, passion, and great wine. At the end of her 30 years, the punctual Devil returned, and the two fell into an abyss. In the *palazzo*'s Camera degli Sposi, there is a ring believed to have been their entrance to Hell.

Though there is no evidence of her existence, Lucida is one of Tuscany's most famous ghosts. Luccans say that along the town's walls, and over the pond in the Botanical Gardens, her seductive ghost appears at night, riding wild and nude on a blazing chariot. Some even say you can see the reflection of her face in the pond's water.

lovers admire the architecture of the *centro*. No tour of the city is complete without seeing the perfectly intact city walls, or ▓**baluardi** (battlements). The **Duomo di San Martino** was begun in the 6th century and finished in the 15th century. Nearby, the **Museo della Cattedrale** houses religious objects from the *duomo*. (*Duomo* open M-F 9:30am-5:45pm, Sa 9:30am-6:45pm, Su between masses. Free. *Museo* open Apr.-Oct. daily 10am-6pm; Nov.-Mar. M-F 10am-2pm, Sa-Su 10am-5pm. €4.) Climb the 227 stairs of the **Torre Guinigi**, V. Sant'Andrea 41, for a view of the city and the hills beyond. (☎31 68 46. Open daily June-Sept. 9am-11pm; Oct.-Jan. 9am-7pm; Feb.-May 9am-5pm. €5, students €3.) In the evening, *Lucchese* pack the **Piazza Anfiteatro and the Piazza Napoleone**.

▓**Bed and Breakfast La Torre ❸**, V. del Carmine 11, offers large, bright rooms. (☎/fax 95 70 44; www.roomslatorre.com. Breakfast included. Free Internet. Singles €35, with bath €50; doubles €50/80. MC/V.) From P. Napoleone, take V. Beccheria, then turn right on V. Roma and left on V. Fillungo. After six blocks, turn left into P. San Frediano and right on V. della Cavallerizza to reach the **Ostello per la Gioventù San Frediano (HI) ❶**, V. della Cavallerizza 12. (☎46 99 57; www.ostellolucca.it. Breakfast €2.50. Reception 7:30-10am and 3:30pm-midnight. Lockout 10am-3:30pm. Dorms €18; 2- to 6-person rooms with bath €48-138. €3 HI discount. Cash only.) **Ristorante da Francesco ❷**, Corte Portici 13, off V. Calderia between P. San Salvatore and P. San Michele, offers well-prepared dishes. (☎41 80 49. *Primi* €6. *Secondi* €8-12. 1L wine €7.20. Cover €1.50. Open Tu-Su noon-2:30pm and 8-10:30pm. MC/V.) Offering interesting *gelato* flavors and swanky seating, **Gelateria Veneta**, V. V. Veneto 74, is the place to see and be seen on Saturday nights. (☎46 70 37. Cones €1.80-3.50. Open M-F and Su 10am-1am, Sa 10am-2am.)

Trains (☎89 20 21) run hourly from Ple. Ricasoli to Florence (1½hr., €4.80), Pisa (30min., €2.20), and Viareggio (20min., €2.20). **Buses** (☎46 49 63) leave hourly from Ple. Verdi, next to the tourist office, for Florence (1½hr., €4.70) and Pisa (50min., €2.50). The **tourist office** is in Ple. San Donato. (☎58 31 50. Open daily 9am-7pm.) Rent bikes at **Cicli Bizzari**, P. Santa Maria 32. (☎49 60 31. €2.50 per hr., €13 per day. Open daily 9am-7:30pm. Cash only.) **Postal Code:** 55100.

PISA   ☎050

Millions of tourists arrive in Pisa (pop. 95,000) each year to marvel at the famous "Leaning Tower," forming a gelato-slurping, photo-snapping mire. Commanding a beautiful stretch of the Arno, Pisa has a diverse array of cultural diversions, as well as a top-notch university. The **Piazza del Duomo**, also known as the **Campo dei Miracoli** (Field of Miracles), is a grassy expanse that contrasts with the white stone of the tower, *duomo*, baptistry, and surrounding museums. Begun in 1173, the famous ▓**Leaning Tower** began to tilt when the soil beneath it suddenly shifted. The tilt intensified after WWII, and thanks to the tourists who climb its steps daily, the tower slips 1-2m each year, though it's now considered stable. Tours of 30 visitors can ascend the 294 steps once every 30min. (Tours depart daily June-Aug. 8:30am-11pm; Sept.-May 8:30am-7:30pm. Assemble next to info office 10min. before tour. €15.) Also on the Campo, the dazzling **duomo** has a collection of splendid art and is considered one of the finest Romanesque cathedrals in the world. (Open Apr.-Sept. M-Sa 10am-8pm; Mar. and Oct. M-Sa 10am-7pm, Su 1-5:45pm; Nov.-Feb. M-F 10am-5pm. €2.) Next door is the ▓**Battistero** (Baptistry), whose precise acoustics allow an unamplified choir to be heard 2km away; demonstrations occur every 30min. (Open daily Apr.-Sept. 8am-7:30pm; Mar. and Oct. 9am-5:30pm; Nov.-Feb. 9am-4:30pm. €6, includes admission to one other monument on the combined ticket list.) An **all-inclusive ticket** to the Campo's sights—excluding the tower—costs €10 and is available at the two *biglietterie* (ticket booths) on the Campo.

Near the *duomo*, the **Albergo Helvetia ❸**, V. Don Gaefano Boschi 31, off P. Archivescovado, has clean rooms and a multilingual staff. (☎55 30 84. Reception 8am-midnight. Reserve ahead. Singles €35, with bath €50; doubles €45-62. Cash only.) **Centro Turistico Madonna dell'Acqua ❶,** V. Pietrasantina 15, is 2km from the tower. Take bus marked LAM ROSSA (red line) from the station (4 per hr., last bus 9:45pm); ask the driver to stop at the *ostello*. (☎89 06 22. Linens €1. Reception 6-9pm. Dorms €15. MC/V.) To dine, head for the river, where restaurants are authentic and of higher quality. Try the risotto at ▨**Il Paiolo ❶,** V. Curtatone e Montanara 9, near the university. (*Menù* €5-8. Open M-F 12:30-3pm and 8pm-1am, Sa-Su 8pm-2am. MC/V.) **Trains** (☎89 20 21) run from P. della Stazione, in the southern end of town, to Florence (1hr., 1 per hr., €5.20), Genoa (2½hr., 1 per hr., €7.90), and Rome (3hr., 12 per day, €23-29). To reach the **tourist office,** walk straight out of the train station and go left to P. Vittorio Emanuele. (☎422 91; www.turismo.toscana.it. Open M-F 9am-7pm, Sa 9am-1:30pm.) Take bus marked LAM ROSSA (€0.85) from the station to the Campo. **Postal Code:** 56100.

UMBRIA

Umbria is known as the "green heart of Italy" due to its wild woods, fertile plains, and gentle hills. Cobblestone streets and active international universities give the region a lively character rooted in tradition and history. Umbria holds Giotto's greatest masterpieces and was home to painters Perugino and Pinturicchio.

PERUGIA   ☎075

In Perugia (pop. 160,000), visitors can experience the city's renowned jazz festival, digest its decadent chocolate, and meander through its two universities. The city's most popular sights frame **Piazza IV Novembre,** the heart of Perugia's social life. At its center, the **Fontana Maggiore** is adorned with sculptures and bas-reliefs by Nicolà and Giovanni Pisano. At the end of the *piazza* is the rugged, unfinished exterior of the Gothic **Cattedrale di San Lorenzo,** also known as the *duomo,* which houses the purported wedding ring of the Virgin Mary. (Open M-Sa 8am-12:45pm and 4-5:15pm, Su 4-5:45pm. Free.) The 13th-century **Palazzo dei Priori,** on the left when looking at the fountain, contains the impressive **Galleria Nazionale dell'Umbria,** C. Vannucci 19, which displays 13th- and 14th-century religious works. (Open Tu-Su 8:30am-7:30pm. €6.50.) ▨**Ostello della Gioventù/Centro Internazionale di Accoglienza per la Gioventù ❶,** V. Bontempi 13, is a welcoming and well-located hostel, with frescoed ceilings in the lobby, kitchen access, and a terrace. From P. IV Novembre, keep to the right past the *duomo* and P. Danti into P. Piccinino, and onto V. Bontempi. (☎57 22 880; www.ostello.perugia.it. Linens €2. Lockout 9:30am-4pm. Curfew 1am, midnight in winter. Closed mid-Dec. to mid-Jan. Dorms €15. AmEx/MC/V.) On the corner of P. B. Ferri and C. Vannucci, **Albergo Anna ❸,** V. dei Priori 48, has antique furnishings in large rooms. (☎57 36 304. Breakfast €2. Singles €30; doubles €58. AmEx/MC/V.) Head to ▨**Trattoria Dal Mi Cocco ❷,** C. Garibaldi 12, for its generous *menù* which includes an appetizer, two courses, and dessert. (*Menù* €13. Reserve ahead. Open Tu-Su 1-2pm and 8:30-10pm. MC/V.) No trip to Perugia would be complete without a visit to its famous chocolate store, **Perugina,** C. Vannucci 101. (Open M 2:30-8pm, Tu-Sa 9:30am-7:45pm, Su 10:30am-1:30pm and 3-8pm.) Be sure to visit the city in mid-July, during the **Umbria Jazz Festival** (www.umbriajazz.com) or in mid-October for **Eurochocolate,** a festival that pays tribute to the cacoa bean (☎50 25 880; www.eurochocolate.com).

    Trains leave Perugia FS in P. Vittorio Veneto, Fontiveggio, for: Assisi (25min., 1 per hr., €1.80); Florence (2hr., 6 per day, from €8); Orvieto (1¾hr., 11 per day, €11); Rome (2½hr., 7 per day, €11). From the station, take **bus** #6, 7, 9, 11, 13D, or 15 to the central P. Italia (€1); then walk down C. Vannucci, the main shopping street, to P. IV Novembre and the *duomo.* V. Baglioni is one block east of P. IV Novembre and leads to P. Matteotti and the **tourist office,** P. Matteotti 18. (☎57 36 458. Open M-Sa 8:30am-1:30pm and 3:30-6:30pm, Su 9am-1pm.) **Postal Code:** 06100.

ON THE MENU

SLOW FOOD SPREADS FAST

The Slow Food movement sprung in 1986 when Carlo Petrini of Bra, Italy decided enough was enough with grab-n-go fast-food chains. In a mere 22 years, his movement has grown to 80,000 members from all points of the globe, who are attempting to counteract consumers' dwindling interest in the food they eat. Where is it from? What does it taste like? Sometimes we eat too fast to even remember.

Slow Food's requirements are three fold: the food must be good, clean, and fair. In other words, it must taste good, not harm the environment, and food producers must receive fair compensation for their work. Ultimately, their view is that when you lift your fork to swirl that first bite of *linguine*, you are not a consumer, but an informed co-producer.

Keep an eye out for Slow Food's snail symbol on the doors of many restaurants in Italy for assured quality. They've even opened a University of Gastronomical Sciences in 2004, offering Bachelor's and Master's degrees, along with many cultural seminars.

So before you grab that *panini* *"da portare via"* ("to go"), take a moment to step back and remember where your food is coming from. Even a little acknowledgment is a start.

For more info, visit www.slow-food.com.

## ASSISI 	☎ 075

Assisi (pop. 25,000) emanates tranquility, owing its character to the legacy of St. Francis, patron saint of Italy. The jewel of the town is the 13th-century ▧**Basilica di San Francesco.** The subdued art of the lower church celebrates St. Francis's modest lifestyle and houses his tomb, while Giotto's renowned fresco cycle, the *Life of St. Francis*, adorns the walls of the upper church. (Lower basilica open daily 6am-6:45pm. Upper basilica open daily 8:30am-6:45pm. Modest dress required. Free.) Hike up to the looming fortress **Rocca Maggiore** for views of the countryside. From P. del Comune, follow V. S. Rufino to P. S. Rufino. Continue up V. Pta. Perlici and take the first left up a narrow staircase. (Open daily 9am-8pm. €3.50, students €2.50.) The pink-and-white **Basilica di Santa Chiara** houses the crucifix that is said to have spoken to St. Francis. (Open daily 6:30am-noon and 2-7pm.) ▧**Camere Martini ❷,** V. S. Gregorio 6, has sunny rooms surrounding a central courtyard and a familial atmosphere. (☎81 35 36; cameremartini@libero.it. Singles €25-27; doubles €40; triples €55; quads €65. Cash only.) **Ostello della Pace (HI) ❶,** V. d. Valecchi 177, offers bright rooms with two or three bunk beds and shared baths. From the train station, take the bus to P. Unità d'Italia; then walk downhill on V. Marconi, turn left at the sign, and walk for 500m. (☎81 67 67; www.assisihostel.com. Breakfast included. Dinner €9.50. Laundry €3.50. Reception 7-9:30am and 3:30-11:30pm. Lockout 9:30am-3:30pm. Curfew 11pm. Reserve ahead. Dorms €15, with bath €17. HI card required; buy at hostel. MC/V.) Grab a personal pizza (€5-7) at **Pizzeria Otello ❶,** V. San Antonio 1. (Open daily noon-3pm and 7-10:30pm. AmEx/MC/V.) From the station near the Basilica Santa Maria degli Angeli, **trains** go to Florence (2½hr., 7 per day, €9), Perugia (30min., 1-2 per hr., €1.80), and Rome (2½hr., 7 per day, €9). From P. Matteotti, follow V. del Torrione to P. S. Rufino, where the downhill left leads to V. S. Rufino, **Piazza del Comune,** the city center, and the **tourist office.** (☎81 25 34. Open M-Sa 8am-2pm and 3-6pm, Su 9am-1pm.) **Postal Code:** 06081.

## ORVIETO 	☎ 0763

A city upon a city, Orvieto (pop. 21,000) was built in layers: medieval structures stand over ancient subterranean tunnels that Etruscans began burrowing into the hillside in the 7th century BC. **Underground City Excursions** offers the most complete tour of the city's dark, twisted bowels. (☎34 48 91. English-language tours leave the tourist office daily 11:15am and 4:15pm. €5.50, students €3.50.) It took 600 years, 152 sculptors, 68 painters, 90 mosaic artisans, and 33

architects to construct Orvieto's ∎**duomo**. The **Capella della Madonna di San Brizio**, off the right transept, houses the dramatic apocalypse frescoes of Luca Signorelli. Opposite it, the ∎**Cappella Corporale** holds the gold-encrusted chalice-cloth, soaked with the blood of Christ. (Open M-Sa 7:30am-12:45pm and 2:30-7pm, Su 2:30-6:45pm. Modest dress required. *Duomo* free. *Capella* €5.) Two blocks down from the *duomo*, V. della Piazza del Popolo leads to the luxurious **Grand Hotel Reale ❸**, P. del Popolo 25. The deal is unparalleled. (Breakfast €8. Singles €35, with bath €66; doubles €55/88. V.) **Nonnamella ❸**, V. del Duomo 25, cooks fresh ingredients into creative dishes. (☎34 24 02. *Primi* €5.50-10. *Secondi* €7.50-13. Open daily noon-3pm and 7-11pm. Cash only.) For a free tasting of Orvieto Classico and other wines, try **Cantina Freddano**, C. Cavour 5. (☎30 82 48. Bottles from €3.50. Open M-F 9:30am-1pm and 3-8pm, Sa-Su 10am-8pm.) **Trains** run hourly to Florence (2½hr., €11) and Rome (1½hr., €7.10). The funicular travels up the hill from the train station to the center, **Piazza Cahen**, and a shuttle goes to the **tourist office**, P. del Duomo 24. (☎34 17 72. Open M-F 8:15am-1:50pm and 4-7pm, Sa-Su 10am-1pm and 3-6pm.) **Postal Code:** 05018.

THE MARCHES (LE MARCHE)

In the Marches, green foothills separate the gray shores of the Adriatic from Apennine peaks, and umbrella-dotted beaches from traditional hill towns. Inland villages, easily accessible by train, rely on agriculture and preserve the region's historical legacy in the architectural remains of the Gauls and Romans.

URBINO ☎0722

The birthplace of Raphael, Urbino (pop. 15,500) charms visitors with stone dwellings scattered along its steep streets. Most remarkable is the Renaissance **Palazzo Ducale**, in P. Rinascimento, a turreted palace that ornaments the skyline. Inside, a stairway leads to the **Galleria Nazionale delle Marche**, in the former residence of Duke Frederico da Montefeltro. Watch for Raphael's *Portrait of a Lady*, and don't miss the subterranean servants' tunnels. (☎32 26 25. Open M 8:30am-2pm, Tu-Su 8:30am-7:15pm. Ticket office closes 1hr. before museum. €4, students 18-25 €2.) Walk back across P. della Repubblica onto V. Raffaello to the site of Raphael's 1483 birth, the **Casa Natale di Raffaello**, V. Raffaello 57, now a museum of period furniture, works by local masters, and the *Madonna col Bambino*, attributed to Raphael himself. (☎32 01 05. Open Mar.-Oct. M-Sa 9am-1pm and 3-7pm, Su 10am-1pm; Nov.-Feb. M-Sa 9am-2pm, Su 10am-1pm. €3. Cash only.)

Just doors down from Raphael's home, **Pensione Fosca ❷**, V. Raffaello 67, is a great value. (☎32 96 22. Call ahead to arrange a check-in time. Singles €21; doubles €35; triples €45. Cash only.) At **Pizzeria Le Tre Piante ❷**, V. Voltaccia della Vecchia 1, a cheery staff serves pizzas (€2.50-8) on a terrace overlooking the Apennines. (☎48 63. *Primi* from €6.30. *Secondi* from €8. Reserve ahead F-Sa. Open Tu-Su noon-3pm and 7-11:30pm. Cash only.) **Supermarket Margherita** is on V. Raffaello 37. (Open M-Sa 7:30am-2pm and 4:30-8pm. MC/V.) Bucci **buses** (☎0721 32 401) run from Borgo Mercatale to Rome (4½hr., 2 per day, €25). V. Mazzini leads from Borgo Mercatale to P. della Repubblica, the city's hub. From there, V. Vittorio Veneto leads to P. Rinascimento, the *palazzo*, and the **tourist office**, V. Puccinotti 35. (☎26 13. Open M and Sa 9am-1pm, Tu-F 9am-1pm and 3-6pm.)

ANCONA ☎071

Ancona (pop. 102,000) is the center of transportation for those heading to Croatia, Greece, and Slovenia. The P. del Duomo, atop Monte Guasco offers a view of the red rooftops and sapphire port below. Across the *piazza* is the **Cattedrale di San Ciriaco,** a Romanesque church with its namesake saint shrouded in velvet in the crypt. (☎ 52 688. Open in summer M-Sa 8am-noon and 3-7pm; winter M-Sa 8am-noon and 3-6pm. Free.) **Pasetto Beach** seems far from the port's industrial clutter, though its "beach" is concrete. From the train station, cross the *piazza*, turn left, take the first right, then make a sharp right behind the newsstand to reach the **Ostello della Gioventù (HI) ❶**, V. Lamaticci 7, (☎ 42 257. Lockout 11am-4:30pm. Dorms €16. AmEx/MC/V.) **La Cantineta ❷**, V. Gramsci, offers specialties like *stoccafisso* (stockfish) at reasonable prices. (☎ 20 11 07. *Primi* €4-12. *Secondi* €5-15. Cover €1.50. Open Tu-Su noon-2:45pm and 7:30-10:45pm. AmEx/MC/V.) **Di per Di** supermarket is at V. Matteotti 115. (Open M-W and F 8:15am-1:30pm and 5-7:35pm, Th 8:15am-1:30pm, Sa 8:15am-1pm and 5-7:40pm. Cash only.) **Ferries** leave Stazione Marittima for Croatia, Greece, and northern Italy. Jadrolinija (☎ 20 43 05; www.jadrolinija.hr) runs to Split, CRO (9hr., €37-47). ANEK (☎ 20 72 346; www.anekitalia.com) ferries go to Patras, GCE (22hr., €50-70). Schedules and tickets are available at the Stazione Marittima. Get up-to-date info at www.doricaportservices.it. **Trains** leave P. Rosselli for: Bologna (2½hr., 1-2 per hr., €11); Milan (4-5hr., 16 per day, €34); Rome (3-4hr., 11 per day, €14); Venice (5hr., 1 per hr., €28). The train station is a 25min. walk from Stazione Marittima. **Buses** #1, 1/3, and 1/4 (€0.90) head up C. Stamira to P. Cavour, the city center. The **tourist office** is across from Stazione Marittima. (☎ 20 79 029. Open daily Apr.-Sept. 9:30am-2pm and 3-7:30pm; Oct.-Dec. 10am-1:30pm and 2:30-6pm.) **Postal Code:** 60100.

CAMPANIA

Sprung from the shadow of Mt. Vesuvius, Campania thrives in defiance of natural disasters. The submerged city at Baia, the relics at Pompeii, and the ruins at Cumae all attest to a land resigned to harsh natural outbursts. While the vibrant city of Naples and the emerald waters of the Amalfi Coast reel in tourists, Campania is one of Italy's poorest regions, often overshadowed by the prosperous North.

NAPLES (NAPOLI) ☎ 081

Italy's third largest city, Naples (pop. 1 million), is also its most chaotic. Neapolitans spend their waking moments out on the town, eating, drinking, shouting, and pausing in the middle of busy streets to finish conversations. The birthplace of pizza and the modern-day home of tantalizing seafood, Neapolitan cuisine is unbeatable. Once you submit to the city's rapid pulse, everywhere else will just seem slow.

▶ TRANSPORTATION

Flights: Aeroporto Capodichino, V. Umberto Maddalena **(NAP;** ☎ 78 96 259; www.gesac.it), northeast of the city. Connects to major Italian and European cities. **Alibus** (☎ 53 11 706) goes to P. Municipio and P. Garibaldi (20min., 6am-11:30pm, €3).

Trains: Trenitalia (www.trenitalia.it) goes from Stazione Centrale in P. Garibaldi to **Milan** (9hr., 13 per day, €50) and **Rome** (2hr., 40 per day, €11). **Circumvesuviana** (☎ 800 05 39 39) runs to **Herculaneum** (€1.70) and **Pompeii** (€2.30).

Ferries: Depart from **Stazione Marittima,** on Molo Angioino, and **Molo Beverello,** at the base of P. Municipio. From P. Garibaldi, take the R2, 152, 3S, or the Alibus to P. Municipio. **Caremar,** Molo Beverello (☎ 199 12 31 99), runs frequently to **Capri** and **Ischia** (both 1½hr., €4.80). **Tirrenia Lines,** Molo Angioino (☎ 199 12 31 199), goes to **Cagliari** (16hr.) and **Palermo** (11hr.). Hydrofoils are generally faster and more expensive. The daily newspaper *Il Mattino* (€0.90) lists up-to-date ferry schedules.

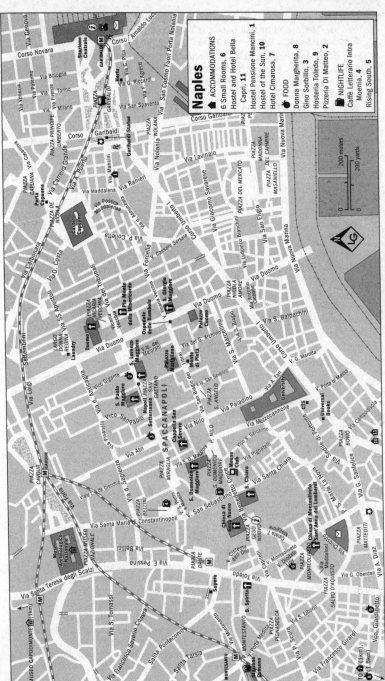

ITALY

Naples

▲ ACCOMMODATIONS
6 Small Rooms, 6
Hostel and Hotel Bella
Capri, 11
Hostel Pensione Mancini, 1
Hostel of the Sun, 10
Hotel Cimarosa, 7

◆ FOOD
Donna Margherita, 8
Gino Sorbillo, 3
Hosteria Toledo, 9
Pizzeria Di Matteo, 2

■ NIGHTLIFE
Caffè Letterario Intra
Moenia, 4
Rising South, 5

Public Transportation: One **UnicoNapoli** (www.napolipass.it) ticket is valid on buses, funicular, Metro, and train in Naples (€1 per 1½hr., full-day €3). Route info for the Metro and funiculars is at www.metro.na.it.

Taxis: Consortaxi (☎55 25 252); **Radio** (☎55 15 151); **Napoli** (☎55 64 444). Only take metered taxis, and always ask about prices up front. Meter starts at €2.60; €0.05 per 70m thereafter. €2.10 surcharge added from 10pm-7am.

⭐ 🎇 ORIENTATION AND PRACTICAL INFORMATION

The main train and bus terminals are in the immense **Piazza Garibaldi** on the east side of Naples. From P. Garibaldi, a left on **Corso Garibaldi** leads to the waterfront district; **Piazza Guglielmo Pepe** is at the end of C. Garibaldi. **Piazza Plebiscito,** home to upscale little restaurants and shops, is accessible by walking down **Via Nuova Marina** with the water on your left. **Via Toledo,** a chic pedestrian shopping street, links the waterfront to the Plebiscito district, where the well-to-do hang out, and the maze-like **Spanish Quarter.** Along V. Toledo, **Piazza Dante** lies on the western extreme of the **Spaccanapoli** *(centro storico)* neighborhood. Walking away from the waterfront, a right at any of the streets will lead to the historic district. While violent crime is rare in Naples, theft is fairly common, so exercise caution.

Tourist Offices: EPT (☎26 87 79; www.eptnapoli.info), at Stazione Centrale. Free maps. Grab 📓 **Qui Napoli,** a bimonthly publication full of listings and events. Open M-Sa 9am-7pm, Su 9am-1pm. **Branch** at P. Gesù Nuovo (☎55 12 701).

Consulates: Canada, V. Carducci 29 (☎40 13 38). **UK,** V. dei Mille 40 (☎42 38 911). **US,** P. della Repubblica (☎58 38 111, 24hr. emergency 033 79 45 083).

Currency Exchange: Thomas Cook, at the airport and in P. Municipio 70 (☎55 18 399). Open M-F 9:30am-1pm and 3-7pm. **Branch:** P. Municipio 70 (☎55 18 399).

Police: ☎79 41 111. **Ambulance:** ☎75 28 282.

Hospital: Cardarelli (☎74 72 859), on the R4 or OF line.

Post Office: P. Matteotti (☎552 42 33), at V. Diaz on the R2 line. Unreliable *fermo-posta.* Open M-F 8:15am-6pm, Sa 8:15am-noon. **Postal Code:** 80100.

🏠 ACCOMMODATIONS

Although Naples has some fantastic bargain accommodations, especially near **Piazza Garibaldi,** be cautious when choosing a room. Avoid hotels that solicit customers at the station, never give your passport until you've seen the room, agree on the price before unpacking, and be alert for hidden costs.

📓 **Hostel Pensione Mancini,** V. P. S. Mancini, 33 (☎55 36 731; www.hostelpensioneman-cini.com), off the far end of P. Garibaldi from station, 2nd fl.; not to be confused with more distant V. Mancini. Bright, spacious rooms, with common room and kitchen. Breakfast and Internet included. Free luggage storage and lockers. Reception 24hr. Reserve 1 week ahead. Dorms €20; singles €35, with bath €45; doubles €55/60; triples €75/80; quads €90/100. 10% *Let's Go* discount. Cash only. ❷

📓 **Hostel and Hotel Bella Capri,** V. Melisurgo 4 (☎55 29 494; www.bellacapri.it). Take the R2 bus from station, exit at V. De Pretis. Top-notch hostel offers kitchen and clean rooms with A/C and TV. Breakfast included. Free luggage storage, lockers, and Internet. Reception 24hr. Dorms €20; singles €45-50, with bath €60-70; doubles €55-60/70; triples €80-84/90-100; quads €90-100/100-110. 10% *Let's Go* discount. AmEx/MC/V. ❸

Hostel of the Sun, V. Melisurgo 15 (☎42 06 393; www.hostelnapoli.com). Take the R2 bus from station, exit at V. De Pretis. Buzz #51. Take the elevator (€0.05) during business hours. Large, colorful common room has satellite TV, DVDs, and small library. Dorms and private rooms are spacious, clean, and equipped with free lockers. Kitchen available. Breakfast included. Laundry €3, free load with 3-day stay. Free Internet. Reserve ahead in summer. Dorms €20; singles €45, with bath €50; doubles €55/70; triples €80/90; quads €90/100. 10% *Let's Go* discount. MC/V. ❷

Hotel Cimarosa, V. D. Cimarosa 29, 5th fl. (☎55 67 044; www.hotelcimarosa.it). Take the funicular from near P. Plebiscito, exit at the station. Go around the corner to the right. Over 30 beautiful rooms share spotless baths. A bit out of the way, it feels far from the bustle of Naples. Great views of the harbor. Check-out 11am. Curfew 1am. Singles €40; doubles €70; triples €95. With private bath, prices nearly double. MC/V. ❹

6 Small Rooms, V. Diodato Lioy 18 (☎79 01 378; www.6smallrooms.com). No sign; look for the call button. Larger rooms than the name suggests. Kitchen available. Free lockers. Key (€5 deposit) for returning after midnight curfew. Dorms €18; singles with bath €35; doubles €55, with bath €65. Cash only. ❷

🍴 FOOD

If you ever doubted that Neapolitans invented pizza, Naples's *pizzerie* will take that doubt, knead it into a ball, throw it in the air, spin it on their collective finger, punch it down, cover it with sauce and mozzarella, and serve it *alla margherita*. For a culinary change of pace from the plethora of pizza, the **waterfront** offers traditional Neapolitan seafood. Some of the cheapest, most authentic options lie along **Via dei Tribunali** in the heart of Spaccanapoli.

▨ **Gino Sorbillo,** V. dei Tribunali 32 (☎44 66 43; www.accademiadellapizza.it). The pizzeria's owners claim links to a forbearer who invented the *ripieno al forno* (calzone) and has 21 pizza-makers in this generation. The kitchen has the original brick oven. *Margherita* €3. Service 10%. Open M-Sa noon-3:30pm and 7-11:30pm. MC/V. ❶

Pizzeria Di Matteo, V. dei Tribunali 94 (☎45 52 62), near V. Duomo. Former President Clinton ate here during the G-7 Conference in 1994. Pies, like the *marinara* (€2), burst with flavor, while the building bursts with pizza aficionados—put your name on the list and expect a short wait. Pizza €2.50-6. Open M-Sa 9am-midnight. Cash only. ❶

Hosteria Toledo, Vicolo Giardinetto 78A (☎42 12 57), in the Spanish Quarter. Prepare yourself for courses of Neapolitan comfort food. The *gnocchi* (€6) is hearty enough to be a meal on its own. If you're feeling adventurous or indecisive, try the chef's surprise. *Primi* €6-12. *Secondi* €5-10. Open daily 8pm-midnight. MC/V. ❷

IN RECENT NEWS

TRASH TALK

The beautiful *centro storico* in Naples is being overshadowed by a new kind of monument: 10ft. trash piles.

Over 3000 tons of uncollected trash—along with rats and other pests attracted to the filth—started piling up on the streets when safety violations caused the government to close all four city dumps in May 2007. As a city whose trash collection is largely controlled by Camorra (the Neapolitan mafia), Naples is no stranger to garbage problems.

In 2004, internal problems in Camorra—whose waste-removal profits are an estimated €22 million per year—caused collectors to stop collecting. It is rumored that the mafia is also involved in the 2007 garbage crisis, and that the organizations is pocketing a lot of the money that would otherwise go towards waste collection. When the trash started piling up, citizens began setting fire to uncollected heaps of waste—up to 150 fires a day—and wearing masks to avoid toxic fumes. With schools closures due to rat infestations, a threat of infectious diseases, and a suspected link between the chronic waste problem and increases in cancer and genetic defects, Naples knows it must act quickly to avoid a smellier version of Pompeii's destruction by burial.

Donna Margherita, Vico II Alabardieri 4/5/6 (☎40 01 29). This place offers high quality food in a location close to city nightlife. Beautiful decoration inside displays the elegance and simplicity of the Neapolitan lifestyle. Pizzas €3.50-7. *Primi* €6-15. Open daily noon-3pm and 7pm-midnight. ❷

🔍 SIGHTS

▨ MUSEO ARCHEOLOGICO NAZIONALE. Situated in a 16th-century *palazzo* and former barracks, the archaeological museum houses treasures from Pompeii and Herculaneum. Unreliable labeling makes the audio tour a good investment. The mezzanine has a mosaic room, with one design featuring a fearless Alexander the Great routing the Persian army. Check out the Farnese Bull, the largest extant ancient statue. The *Gabinetto Segreto* (secret cabinet) of Aphrodite grants glimpses into the goddess's life. *(M: P. Cavour. Turn right from the station and walk 2 blocks.* ☎44 01 66. Open M and W-Su 9am-7:30pm. €6.50. Audio tour in English, French, or Italian €4.)

▨ MUSEO AND GALLERIE DI CAPODIMONTE. Housed in another 16th-century *palazzo*, the museum resides inside a park often filled with locals. A plush royal apartment and the Italian National Picture Gallery are within the palace. Among its impressive works are Bellini's *Transfiguration*, Masaccio's *Crucifixion*, and Titian's *Danae*. *(Take bus #24, 110, M4, or M5 from the Archaeological Museum and exit at the gate to the park, on the right. 2 entrances: Pta. Piccola and Pta. Grande.* ☎74 99 111. Open M-Tu and Th-Su 8:30am-7:30pm. €7.50, after 2pm €3.80.)

PALAZZO REALE AND MASCHIO ANGIONO. The 17th-century Palazzo Reale has opulent royal apartments, the **Museo di Palazzo Reale,** and a view from the terrace of the **Royal Chapel.** *(P. Plebescito 1. Take the R2 bus from P. Garibaldi to P. Trieste e Trento and walk around the palazzo to the entrance on P. Plebiscito.* ☎40 05 47; www.pierreci.it. Open M-Tu and Th-Su 9am-7pm. €4, EU students and under 18 free.) The **Biblioteca Nazionale** stores 1.5 million volumes, including the scrolls from the **Villa dei Papiri** in Herculaneum. *(*☎78 19 231. Open M-F 10am-1pm with reservation.) The **Teatro San Carlo's** acoustics are reputed to top those of Milan's La Scala. *(Theater entrance on P. Trieste e Trento.* ☎66 45 45; www.teatrosancarlo.it. Open daily 9am-7pm.) **Maschio Angiono's** five turrets' shadow the bay. Built in 1286 by Charles II of Anjou as his royal residence, the fortress's best feature is its entrance, with reliefs of Alphonse I of Aragon. *(P. Municipio. Take the R2 bus from P. Garibaldi.* ☎42 01 241. Open M-Sa 9am-7pm. €5.)

VIRGIL'S TOMB. The celebrated Latin poet's resting place is at V. Salita della Grotta. Below the tomb is the entrance to the closed Crypta Neapolitana, built during the reign of Augustus, which connected ancient Neapolis to Pozzuoli and Baia. Call ahead for a translator to explain the inscriptions, or just come for the view. *(M: Mergellina. From the station, take 2 quick rights. Entrance between overpass and tunnel.* ☎66 93 90. Guided tours upon request. Open daily 9am-1hr. before sunset. Free.)

NAPOLI SOTTERRANEA (CATACOMBS AND THE UNDERGROUND). The catacombs of S. Gennaro, S. Gaudioso, and S. Severo all date back to the early centuries AD. Tours of the subterranean alleys beneath the city are fascinating: they involve crawling through narrow underground passageways, spotting Mussolini-era graffiti, and exploring Roman aqueducts. Napoli Sotterranea runs below the historic center. *(P. S. Gaetano 68. Take V. dei Tribunali and turn left right before S. Paolo Maggiore.* ☎29 69 44. Tours 1 per 2hr. M-F noon-4pm, Sa-Su 10am-6pm. €9.30, students €8.)

DUOMO. The *duomo's* main attraction is the **Capella del Tesoro di San Gennaro.** A bronze grille protects the altar, home to the saint's head and two vials of his blood. *(Walk 3 blocks up V. Duomo from C. Umberto I or take bus #42 from P. Garibaldi.* ☎44 90 97. Open M-Sa 8:30am-noon and 4:30-6pm. Free. Excavation site €3.)

NIGHTLIFE

Piazza Vanvitelli in Vomero draws young people. Take the funicular from V. Toledo or bus C28 from P. Vittoria. **Via Santa Maria La Nova** is another hot spot. Outdoor bars and cafes are a popular choice in **Piazza Bellini**, near P. Dante. ◪**Rising South,** V.S. Sebastiano 19, nearby P. Gesu Nuovo, does it all: *enoteca*, bar, cultural association, cinema. (Drinks €3-6. Bar open daily Sept.-May 10pm-3am, with special events in summer.) **Caffè Letterario Intra Moenia,** P. Bellini 70, appeals to intellectuals by keeping books amid the wicker furniture. (Open daily 10am-2am. Cash only.) **ARCI-GAY/Lesbica** (☎55 28 815) has info on gay and lesbian club nights.

DAYTRIPS FROM NAPLES

■**HERCULANEUM.** Buried deeper than Pompeii, Herculaneum is less excavated than its neighbor, and a modern city sits on its remains. Don't miss the **House of Deer.** *(Open daily 8:30am-7:30pm. €10.)* As its name suggests, the **House of the Mosaic of Neptune and Amphitrite** is famous for its mosaics. The city is 500m downhill from the Ercolano Scavi stop on the Circumvesuviana train from Naples (dir.: Sorrento; 20min.). The **tourist office** (☎78 81 243) is at V. IV Novembre 84 .

POMPEII. On the morning of August 24, AD 79, a deadly cloud of volcanic ash from Mt. Vesuvius settled over the Roman city of Pompeii, catching the 12,000 prosperous residents by surprise and engulfing the city in suffocating black clouds. Mere hours after the eruption, stately buildings, works of art, and human bodies were sealed in hardened casts of ash. These natural tombs would remain undisturbed until 1748, when excavations began to unearth a stunningly well-preserved picture of daily Roman life. Walk down V. della Marina to reach the colonnaded **Forum,** which was once the civic and religious center of the city. Continue on V. della Fortuna and turn left on V. dei Vettii to reach the **House of the Vettii** and the most vivid frescoes in Pompeii. Backtrack on V. dei Vettii, cross V. della Fortuna to V. Storto, turn left on V. degli Augustali, and take a quick right to reach a small frescoed **brothel** (the *Lupenare*). V. dei Teatri, across the street, leads to the oldest standing **amphitheater** in the world (80 BC), which once held up to 20,000 spectators. To get to the ◪**Villa of the Mysteries,** the ancient city's best-preserved villa, head west on V. della Fortuna, right on V. Consolare, and all the way up Porta Ercolano and V. della Tombe. *(Archaeological site open daily Apr.-Oct. 8:30am-7:30pm; Nov.-Mar. 8:30am-5pm. €10.)* The **tourist office** is at V. Sacra 1. *(Open M-F 8am-3:30pm, Sa 8am-2pm.)* Take the Circumvesuviana **train** (☎77 22 444) from Naples to the Pompeii Scavi stop (dir.: Sorrento; 40min., 2 per hr., round-trip €2.30.)

MOUNT VESUVIUS. Peer into the only active volcano in mainland Europe at Mt. Vesuvius. It hasn't erupted since March 31, 1944 (scientists estimate the volcano becomes active, on average, every 30 years), and experts claim the trip up the mountain is relatively safe. Great views of the **Bay of Naples** can be enjoyed from the top. Vesuvio Express **buses** (☎73 93 666) run from Herculaneum to the crater of Vesuvius (3 per hr. or as soon as the van is filled, round-trip €10).

BAY OF NAPLES

SORRENTO   ☎807

Cliffside Sorrento makes a convenient base for daytrips around the Bay of Naples. **Ostello Le Sirene ❷,** V. degli Aranci 160, is located near the train station. (☎80 72 925. Dorms €18-25; doubles €60.) Campground **Santa Fortunata Campogaio ❶,** V.

del Capo 39, has a private beach. (☎80 73 579. Tent sites €16-25. Dorms €19.) Try the *gnocchi* (€5) or the *linguini al cartoccio* (linguini with mixed seafood; €7) at **Ristorante e Pizzeria Giardiniello ❷**, V. dell'Accademia 7. (☎87 84 616. Cover €1. Open Apr.-Nov. daily 11am-midnight; Dec.-Mar. M-W and F-Su 11am-midnight. AmEx/MC/V.) **Ferries** and **hydrofoils** depart for the Bay of Naples islands. **Linee Marittime Partenopee** (☎80 71 812) runs ferries (40min., 5 per day, €7.50) and hydrofoils (20min., 19 per day, €11) to Capri. The **tourist office**, L. de Maio 35, is off P. Tasso, in the C. dei Forestieri compound. (☎80 74 033. Open M-Sa Apr.-Sept. 8:30am-6:30pm; Oct.-Mar. 8:30am-2pm and 4-6:15pm.) **Postal Code:** 80067.

▓CAPRI   ☎081

Augustus fell in love with Capri in 29 BC, and since then, the "pearl of the Mediterranean" has been a hot spot for the rich and famous. There are two towns on the island—**Capri** proper, near the ports, and **Anacapri**, high on the hills. The best times to visit are in late spring and early fall, as crowds and prices increase in summer. Visitors flock to the **Blue Grotto**, a sea cave where the water shimmers a vivid neon blue. (Short boat ride from Marina Grande €10. Tickets at Grotta Azzurra Travel Office, V. Roma 53. Tours until 5pm.) Buses departing from V. Roma make the trip up the mountain to Anacapri every 15min. until 1:40am; buses leave Anacapri for most tourist attractions. Away from the throngs of pricey Capri, Anacapri is home to less expensive hotels, lovely vistas, and quiet mountain paths. Upstairs from P. Vittoria in Anacapri, **Villa San Michele** has lush gardens, ancient sculptures, and summer concerts. (Open daily 9am-6pm. €6.) Take the chairlift up ▓**Monte Solaro** from P. Vittoria for great views. (Chairlift open Mar.-Oct. daily 9:30am-4:45pm. Round-trip €7.) For those who prefer cliff to coastline, the **Faraglioni**, three massive rocks, are accessible by a 1hr. walk, and there's a steep 1½hr. hike to the ruins of Emperor Tiberius's **Villa Jovis**. The view from the **Cappella di Santa Maria del Soccorso,** built onto the villa, is unrivaled. (Open daily 9am-6pm. €2.)

▓**Bussola di Hermes ❸**, V. Traversa La Vigna 14, in Anacapri, has the best deals on the island. Call from P. Vittoria in Anacapri for pickup. (☎83 82 010; www.bussolahermes.com. Reserve ahead. Dorms €27-30; doubles €70-110. MC/V.) For convenient access to the beach, stay at **Vuotto Antonio ❹**, V. Campo di Teste 2. Take V. V. Emanuele out of P. Umberto, a left onto V. Camerelle, a right onto V. Cerio, and left onto V. Campo di Teste. Housed in "Villa Margherita," simple, elegant rooms are nicely decorated. (☎83 70 230. Doubles €55-95. Cash only.) ▓**Ristorante Il Cucciolo ❷**, V. La Fabbrica 52, in Anacapri, has fresh food at low prices. (☎83 71 917. *Primi* and *secondi* €6-9 with *Let's Go* discount.) The **supermarket,** V.G. Orlandi 299, in Anacapri, is well-stocked. (Open M-Sa 8:30am-1:30pm and 5-8:30pm, Su 8:30am-noon.) At night, Italians dressed to kill come out for Capri's bars near **Piazza Umberto,** open late; younger crowds head to Anacapri.

Caremar (☎83 70 700) **ferries** run from Marina Grande to Naples (1¼hr., 3 per day, €7). LineaJet (☎83 70 819) runs **hydrofoils** to Naples (40-50min., 11 per day, €12) and Sorrento (25min., 15 per day, €10). Boats to other destinations run less frequently; check at Marina Grande for info. The Capri **tourist office** sits at the end of Marina Grande. (☎83 70 634; www.capritourism.com. Open June-Sept. daily 9am-1pm and 3:30-6:45pm; Oct.-May reduced hours.) In Anacapri, it's at V. Orlandi 59; turn right when leaving the bus stop. (☎83 71 524. Open M-Sa 9am-3pm; Oct.-May reduced hours.) **Postal Codes:** 80073 (Capri); 80021 (Anacapri).

▓ISCHIA   ☎081

Travelers have sought out Ischia since ancient times; both *The Iliad* and *The Aeneid* mention the island. Ischia (pop. 60,000) was once an active volcano, but now lemon groves, hot springs, and ruins keep travelers coming back. SEPSA

buses CS, CD, and #1, and 2 (2-4 per hr.) depart from the intersection on V. Iasolino and V. B. Cossa, stopping at: **Ischia Porto**, the major port town and site of the island's most active nightlife, **Casamicciola Terme** and **Lacco Ameno**, homes of legendary thermal waters, and **Forio**, the island's largest town. The **Ring Hostel ❷**, V. Gaetano Morgera 66, in Forio, is in a 19th-century convent. (☎98 75 46; www.ringhostel.com. 12-bed dorms €17; singles €30). Take bus #13 from Ischia Porto to reach **Eurocamping dei Pini ❶**, V. delle Ginestre, 34. Ideal for budget travelers, this campsite offers clean areas, friendly services, and a restaurant. (☎98 20 69. €7-10 per person, €6-10 per tent. Bungalows €13-25 per person.) **Castillo de Aragona ❷**, Ischia Ponte (☎98 31 53), right next to the entrance of the Castello Aragonese, offers amazing views and inexpensive cuisine. (*Primi* €7-10. Open daily 10am-3am.) Caremar **ferries** (☎98 48 18; www.caremar.it) head to Naples (1½hr., 8 per day, €11). Alilauro (☎99 18 88) runs **hydrofoils** to Capri (1 per day, €13) and Sorrento (1 per day, €15). The **tourist office** is on V. Iasolino. (☎50 74 231. Open M-Sa 9am-2pm and 3-8pm.) **Postal Code:** 80077.

THE AMALFI COAST   ☎089

It happens almost imperceptibly: after the exhausting tumult of Naples and the compact grit of Sorrento, the highway narrows to a two-lane, coastal road, and the horizon becomes illuminated with lemon groves and bright village pastels. Though the coastal towns combine simplicity and sophistication, the region's ultimate appeal rests in the tenuous balance it strikes between man and nature.

▐ **TRANSPORTATION. Trains** run to Salerno from Naples (45min., 40 per day, €5-10) and Rome (2½-3hr., 22 per day, €21-33). **SITA buses** (☎26 66 04) connect Salerno to Amalfi (1¼hr., 20 per day, €1.80). From Amalfi, buses also go to Positano (40min., 25 per day, €1.30) and Sorrento (1¼hr., 1 per hr., €2.40). Travelmar (☎87 29 50) runs **hydrofoils** from Amalfi to Positano (25min., 7 per day, €5) and Salerno (35min., 6 per day, €4), and from Salerno to Positano (1¼hr., 6 per day, €6).

AMALFI AND ATRANI. Jagged rocks of the Sorrentine Peninsula, azure waters of the Tyrrhenian, and bright lemons define Amalfi. Visitors crowd P. del Duomo to admire the elegant 9th-century **Duomo di Sant'Andrea** and the nearby **Fontana di Sant'Andrea.** The hostel **A'Scalinatella ❶**, P. Umberto 6, runs dorms, private rooms, and camping all over Amalfi and Atrani. (☎87 19 30; www.hostelscalinatella.com. Tent sites €5 per person. Dorms €21; doubles €50-60, with bath €73-83. Cash only.) The **AAST Tourist Office** is at C. Repubbliche Marinare 27. On the same street, a tunnel leads to beach town Atrani, 750m down the coast. The 4hr. **Path of the Gods** follows the coast from **Bomerano** to **Positano**, with great views along the way. The hike from **Atrani** to **Ravello** (1½-2hr.) runs through gently bending lemon groves, up secluded stairways, and down into green valleys. **Postal Code:** 84011.

RAVELLO. Perched atop cliffs, Ravello has been claimed by artists and intellectuals, its natural beauty seeping into their works. The Moorish cloister and gardens of **Villa Rufolo**, off P. del Duomo, inspired Boccaccio's *Decameron* and Wagner's *Parsifal*. (Open daily 9am-8pm. €5.) The villa puts on a **summer concert series** in the gardens; tickets are sold at the Ravello Festival box office, V. Roma 10-12 (☎85 84 22; www.ravellofestival.com). Don't miss Ravello's **duomo** and its bronze doors; follow V. S. Francesco out of P. Duomo to the impressive **Villa Cimbrone**, whose floral walkways and gardens hide temples, grottoes, and magnificent views. (Open daily 9am-sunset. €5.) **Palazzo della Marra ❸**, V. della Marra 3, offers immaculate rooms with terraces and kitchen access. (☎85 83 02. Breakfast included. Reserve ahead. Doubles €60-80. MC/V.) **Postal Code:** 84010.

POSITANO. Today, Positano's most frequent visitors are the wealthy few who can afford its high prices, but the town still has its charms for the budget traveler. To see the large *pertusione* (hole) in the mountain **Montepertuso,** hike 45min. uphill or take the bus from P. dei Mulini. The three **Isole dei Galli,** islands off Positano's coast, were allegedly home to Homer's mythical Sirens. The beach at **Fornillo** is a serene alternative to **Spiaggia Grande,** the area's main beach. **Ostello Brikette ❷,** V. Marconi 358, with two large terraces and free Wi-Fi, is accessible by the orange Interno bus or SITA bus; exit at the Chiesa Nuova stop and walk 100m to the left of Bar Internazionale. (☎87 58 57. Dorms €22-25; doubles €65-100. MC/V.) The *pasta alla norma* (pasta in tomato sauce with eggplant; €8) at ◪**Da Gabrisa ❷,** Vle. Pasitea 219, is a treat. (☎81 14 98. *Primi* and *secondi* €6-15. Open daily 6-11pm. MC/V.) The four small bars on the beach at Fornillo serve simple, fresh food. The **tourist office,** V. del Saraceno 4, is below the *duomo.* (☎87 50 67. Open M-Sa 8am-2pm and 3-8pm; low season reduced hours.) **Postal Code:** 84017.

SICILY (SICILIA)

An island of contradictions, Sicily owes its cultural complexity to Phoenicians, Greeks, Romans, Arabs, and Normans, all of whom invaded and left their mark. Ancient Greeks lauded the golden island as the second home of the gods. Now, tourists seek it as the home of *The Godfather.* While the Mafia's presence lingers in Sicily, its power is waning. Active volcano Mt. Etna ominously shadows chic resorts, archaeological treasures, and fast-paced cities.

▣ TRANSPORTATION

From southern Italy, take a train to Reggio di Calabria, then a Trenitalia **hydrofoil** (25min., 7-14 per day, €2.80) to Messina, Sicily's transport hub. **Buses** (☎090 77 19 14) serve destinations throughout the island and also make the long trek to mainland cities. **Trains** head to Messina directly (via ferry) from Rome (9hr., 6 per day, €43), then connect to Palermo (3½hr., 22 per day, €11), Syracuse (3½hr., 16 per day, €8.75), and Taormina (40min., 27 per day, €15).

PALERMO   ☎091

In gritty Palermo (pop. 680,000), the shrinking shadow of organized crime hovers over the twisting streets lined with ancient ruins. While poverty, bombings, and centuries of neglect have taken their toll on much of the city, Palermo is experiencing a revival. Operas and ballets are performed year-round at the Neoclassical ◪**Teatro Massimo,** where the climactic opera scene of *The Godfather: Part III* was filmed. Walk up V. Maqueda from Quattro Canti; it's on P. Verdi. (Tu-Su 10am-3pm. Tours 25min., 2 per hr., €3.) From Quattro Canti, take a left on V. Vittorio Emanuele and another one just before P. Indipendenza to get to the ◪**Cappella Palatina,** full of golden mosaics, in **Palazzo dei Normanni.** (Open M-Sa 8:30am-5pm, Su 8:30am-12:30pm. Tu-Th €4; M and F-Su €6.) At the haunting **Cappuccini Catacombs,** P. Cappuccini 1, 8000 corpses in various states of decay line the underground tunnels. Take bus #109 from Stazione Centrale to P. Indipendenza, then transfer to bus #327. (Open daily 9am-noon and 3-5:30pm. €1.50.) For the sake of comfort, and more importantly, safety, plan to spend a bit more on accommodations in Palermo. Homey **Hotel Regina ❷,** C. Vittorio Emanuele 316, is near the intersection of V. Maqueda and C. V. Emanuele. (☎61 14 216. Reserve ahead. Singles €25; doubles €44, with bath €54; triples €66/75.

AmEx/MC/V.) The best restaurants in town are between Teatro Massimo and the Politeama. **Trains** leave Stazione Centrale in P. Giulio Cesare at the southern end of V. Roma and V. Maqueda, for Rome (12hr.; 6 per day; €45, with bunk €70). All **bus** lines run from V. Balsamo, next to the train station. After purchasing tickets, ask the ticket agent for the exact departure point. Pick up a combined metro and bus map from an **AMAT** or **metro** information booth. Buses #101 and 102 (€1 for 2hr.) circle the large downtown area. To reach the **tourist office**, P. Castelnuovo 34, at the west end of the *piazza*, take a bus from the station to P. Politeama, at the end of V. Maqueda. (☎60 58 351; www.palermotourism.com. Open M-F 8:30am-2pm and 2:30-6pm.) **Postal Code:** 90100.

SYRACUSE (SIRACUSA)   ☎0931

With the glory of its Grecian golden days behind it, the modern city of Syracuse (pop. 125,000) takes pride in its ruins and the beauty of its offshore island, Ortigia. Syracuse's role as a Mediterranean superpower is still evident in the **Archaeological Park.** Aeschylus premiered his *Persians* before 15,000 spectators in the park's enormous **Greek theater.** (Open daily 9am until 2hr. before sunset; low season 9am-3pm. €6.) Across from the tourist office on V. S. Giovanni is the ▨**Catacomba di San Giovanni,** 20,000 now-empty tombs carved into the remains of a Greek aqueduct. (Open Tu-Su 9:30am-12:30pm and 2:30-5:30pm. Mandatory guided tour 3-4 per hr. €5.) More ruins lie over the Ponte Umbertino on **Ortigia,** the serene island on which the attacking Greeks first landed. The **Temple of Apollo** has a few columns still standing, but those at the **Temple of Diana** are much more impressive. For those who prefer tans to temples, take bus #21 or 22 to **Fontane Bianche,** a glitzy beach with plenty of discos. Recently opened **lolhostel ❷,** V. Francesco Crispi 92/96, is the city's first youth hostel. (☎46 50 88; www.lolhostel.com. A/C. Internet €3 per hr. Dorms €17-20; singles €33-40; doubles €50-65. Cash only.) Get the best deals around the station and Archaeological Park, or at Ortigia's **open-air market,** V. Trento, off P. Pancali. (Open M-Sa 8am-1pm.) On the mainland, C. Umberto links Ponte Umbertino to the train station, passing through P. Marconi, from which C. Gelone extends through town to the Archaeological Park. **Trains** leave V. Francesco Crispi for Messina (3hr., 1 per hr., €8.75) and Rome (10-13hr., 6 per day, €38). To get from the train station to the **tourist office,** V. S. Sebastiano 45, take V. F. Crispi to C. Gelone, turn right on V. Teocrito, then left on V. S. Sebastiano. (☎48 12 32. Open M-F 8:30am-1:30pm and 3:30-6:30pm, Sa 9am-1pm and 3:30-6:30pm, Su 9am-1pm; low season reduced hours.) **Postal Code:** 96100.

TAORMINA   ☎0942

Legend has it that Neptune wrecked a Greek boat off the eastern coast of Sicily in the 8th century BC, and the sole survivor, inspired by the scenery on shore, founded Taormina. As historians tell it, the Carthaginians founded Tauromenium at the turn of the 4th century BC only to have it wrested away by the Greek tyrant Dionysius. Taormina's Greek roots are apparent in its best-preserved treasure, the **Greek theater.** (Open daily 9am until 1hr. before sunset. €6.) The 5000-seat theater offers unrivaled views of Mt. Etna and hosts the annual ▨**Taormina Arte** summer concert, theater, and dance series. (www.taormina-arte.com. Box office in P. V. Emanuele.) ▨**Taormina's Odyssey Youth Hostel ❷,** Traversa A. d. V. G. Martino 2, offers clean rooms and a social environment that make it worth the hike. Take V. C. Patrizio to V. Cappuccini; when it forks, turn right onto V. Fontana Vecchia and follow signs to the hostel. (☎24 533. Breakfast included. Dorms €18; doubles €60. Cash only.) Off C. Umberto, **La Cisterna del Moro ❶,** V. Bonifacio 1, serves pizza on its terrace. (☎23 001. Pizza €5-8.50. Open daily noon-3pm and 7pm-midnight. AmEx/MC/V.) An **SMA** supermarket is at V. Apollo Arcageta

21, at the end of C. Umberto, near the post office. (Open M-Sa 8:30am-9:30pm, Su 8:30am-12:30pm.) **Trains** run to Messina (1hr., 1 per hr., €3) and Syracuse (2hr., 11 per day, €10). The **tourist office** is in the courtyard of Palazzo Corvaja, off C. Umberto across from P. V. Emanuele. (☎23 243; www.gate2taormina.com. Open daily 9am-2pm and 4-7pm.) **Postal Code:** 98039.

AEOLIAN ISLANDS (ISOLE EOLIE) ☎090

Homer believed these islands to be a home of the gods, while residents consider them *Le Perle del Mare* (Pearls of the Sea). The rugged shores, pristine landscapes, ruins, volcanoes, and mud baths might as well be divinely inspired. However, living among the gods isn't cheap and prices rise steeply in summer.

TRANSPORTATION. The archipelago lies off the Sicilian coast, north of **Milazzo**, the principal and least expensive departure point. Trains run from Milazzo to Messina (30min., 1 per hr., €3) and Palermo (3hr., 13 per day, €10). An orange AST **bus** runs from Milazzo's train station to the port (10min., 2 per hr., €0.90). Ustica (☎92 87 821), Siremar (☎92 83 242), and Navigazione Generale Italiana (NGI; ☎92 84 091) **ferries** depart for Lipari (2hr., 3 per day, €6.60) and Vulcano (1½hr., 3 per day, €6.30). **Hydrofoils** run twice as fast as ferries and more frequently, but for twice the price. Ticket offices are on V. dei Mille in Milazzo.

LIPARI. Lipari is renowned for its beaches, which summer visitors ravage just as pirates did centuries ago. To reach the beaches of the **Spiaggia Bianca** and **Porticello**, take the Lipari-Cavedi **bus** to **Canneto**. Lipari's best sights—aside from its beaches—are all in the hilltop *castello*, where a **fortress** with ancient Greek foundations dwarfs the surrounding town. Nearby is the ■**Museo Archeological Eoliano**, whose collection includes Greek and Sicilian pottery. (Open daily May-Oct. 9am-1pm and 3-7pm; Nov.-Apr. reduced hours. €4.) *Affittacamere* (private rooms) may be the best deals, but ask to see the room before accepting and get a price in writing. Relax on your private terrace away from the bustle of the main drag in one of the eight rooms with bath and A/C at **Villa Rosa ❷**, V. Francesco Crispi 134. To reach it from the port, turn right away from the city center and walk until you reach a gas station. (☎98 80 280; www.liparivillarosa.it. Doubles €30-90.) Camp at **Baia Unci ❶**, V. Marina Garibaldi 2, at the entrance to the hamlet of Canneto, 2km from Lipari. (☎98 11 909. Open mid-Mar. to mid-Oct. Tent sites €8-14. Cash only.) ■**Da Gilberto e Vera ❶**, V. Marina Garibaldi 22-24, is renowned for its sandwiches. (☎98 12 756. *Panini* €4.50. Open daily Mar.-Oct. 7am-4am; Nov.-Feb. 7am-2am. AmEx/MC/V.) The **tourist office**, C. V. Emanuele 202, is near the dock. (☎98 80 095; www.aasteolie.191.it. Open July-Aug. M-F 8am-2pm and 4:30-9:30pm, Sa 8am-2pm and 4-9pm; Sept.-June M-F 8am-2pm and 4:30-9:30pm.) **Postal Code:** 98050.

VULCANO. Black beaches, bubbling seas, and sulfuric mud spas attract visitors from around the world. A steep 1hr. **hike** (€3) to the inactive ■**Gran Cratere** (Grand Crater), the summit of Fossa di Volcane, snakes among the volcano's *fumaroli* (noxious emissions). The therapeutic **Laghetto di Fanghi** (mud pool) is up V. Provinciale from the port. Step into the waters of the **acquacalda**, where volcanic outlets make the shoreline bubble, or tan on the black sands of **Sabbie Nere** (follow signs off V. Ponente). To get to Vulcano, take the **hydrofoil** from Lipari (10min., 17 per day, €5.50). Ferries and hydrofoils dock at **Porto di Levante**, on the east side of **Vulcanello**, the youngest volcano. V. Provinciale heads to Fossa di Vulcane from the port. The **tourist office** is at V. Provinciale 41 (☎98 52 028. Open Aug. daily 8am-1:30pm and 3-5pm) or get info at the Lipari office. **Postal Code:** 98050.

STROMBOLI. If you find hot springs a bit tame, a visit to Stromboli's active **volcano,** which spews cascades of orange lava and molten rock about every 10min., might quench your thirst for adventure. Hiking the volcano on your own is illegal and dangerous, but **Magmatrek,** on V. V. Emanuele, offers **tours,** which also should be taken at your own risk. Don't wear contact lenses, as the wind sweeps ash and dust everywhere. (☎/fax 98 65 768. Helmets provided. Reserve 2-3 days ahead. €25.) From the main road, walk uphill to P. S. Vincenzo and then follow the small side street next to the church to reach **Casa del Sole ①,** on V. Cincotta. The large rooms face a shared terrace. (☎/fax 98 60 17. Open Mar.-Oct. Dorms €13-27; doubles €30-70. Cash only.) From July to September, you won't find a room without a reservation; your best bet may be an *affittacamera*. Siremar (☎98 60 16) and Ustica (☎98 60 03) run **ferries** and **hydrofoils** between Stromboli and the other Aeolian Islands, Milazzo, and mainland Reggio Calabria. **Postal Code:** 98050.

SARDINIA (SARDEGNA)

An old Sardinian legend says that when God finished making the world, He had a handful of dirt left over, which He took, threw into the Mediterranean, stepped on, and—behold—created the island of Sardinia. African, Spanish, and Italian influences have shaped its architecture, language, and cuisine.

TRANSPORTATION

Alitalia **flights** link Alghero, Cagliari, and Olbia to major Italian cities, and recently Ryanair and easyJet have started to serve Sardinia's airports as well. Tirrenia **ferries** (☎89 21 23; www.tirrenia.it) run to Olbia from Civitavecchia, just north of Rome (5-7hr., 2 per day, €22-91), and Genoa (13hr., 6 per week, from €23-50), and to Cagliari from Civitavecchia (14½hr., 1 per day, €29-44), Naples (16hr., 1 per week, €29-44), and Palermo (13½hr., 1 per week, €28-42). **Trains** run from Cagliari to Olbia (4hr., 1 per day, €15), Oristano (1hr., 17 per day, €5.20), and Sassari (4hr., 4 per day, €14). From Sassari, trains run to Alghero (35min., 11 per day, €2.20). **Buses** connect Cagliari to Oristano (1½hr., 2 per day, €6.50) and run from Olbia to Palau (12 per day, €2.50), where ferries access the beaches of La Maddalena.

CAGLIARI ☎070

Cagliari's Roman ruins and cobblestones contrast with the sweeping beaches just minutes away. The **Roman amphitheater** comes alive for the **arts festival** in July and August. Take bus P, PF, or PQ to the crystal-clear waters of **Il Poetto** beach (20min., €1). Cross V. Roma from the train station or ARST station and turn right to get to the spacious rooms of **B&B Vittoria ③,** V. Roma 75. (☎64 04 026; www.bbvittoria.com. Singles €48; doubles €78. 10% *Let's Go* discount. Cash only.) The B&B's owners also run **Hotel aer Bundes Jack ④,** in the same building. (☎/fax 66 79 70; hotel.aerbundesjack@libero.it. Breakfast €6. Check-in on 2nd fl. Reserve ahead. Singles €54; doubles €82-86; triples €114. Cash only.) The **tourist office** is in P. Matteotti. (☎66 92 55. Open M-F 8:30am-1:30pm and 2-8pm; Sa-Su 8am-8pm; low season reduced hours.) **Postal Code:** 09100.

ALGHERO ☎079

Vineyards, ruins, and horseback rides are just a short trip away from Alghero. Between massive white cliffs, 654 steps plunge downward at **Grotte di Nettuno,** 70-million-year-old, stalactite-filled caverns in Capo Caccia. Take the bus (50min.,

3 per day, round-trip €3.50) or a boat (1¼hr.; 3-8 per day; round-trip €13, includes tour but not cave entrance. Cave open daily Apr.-Sept. 9am-7pm; Oct. 9am-5pm; Nov.-Mar. 9am-4pm. €10.) **Hostal de l'Alguer ❶**, V. Parenzo 79, is the cheapest option in the area. From the port, take bus AF to Fertilia; turn right, and walk down the street. (☎/fax 93 20 39. Breakfast included. Dorms €17-20; doubles €21-25. €3 HI discount.) Toward Fertilia, 2km from Alghero, **La Mariposa ❶** campground, V. Lido 22, has a bar, beach access, and a restaurant. (☎95 03 60; www.lamariposa.it. Mar.-Oct. €8-11 per person, €4-13 per tent; 4-person bungalows €45-75. Apr.-June no charge for tents and cars. AmEx/MC/V.) The **tourist office,** P. Porta Terra 9, is to the right of the bus stop. (☎97 90 5. Open Apr.-Oct. M-Sa 8am-8pm, Su 10am-1pm; Nov.-Mar. M-Sa 8am-8pm.) **Postal Code:** 07041.

▓ LA MADDALENA ARCHIPELAGO ☎078

La Maddalena, now a national park, was once part of a land bridge connecting Corsica and Sardinia. The nearby island of **Razzoli** has magnificent swimming holes and is the gateway to the other islands. **▨Marinella IV** (☎33 92 30 28 42; www.marinellagite.it) runs boat tours from Palau, on Sardinia's northern coast. They make two or three 2hr. stops at beaches and normally serve lunch on the way. (€35; boats leave at 10 or 11am and return 5-6pm. Purchase tickets 1 day ahead.) **Panoramica Dei Comi** is a paved road circling the island, lined with beaches for sunbathing. **Hotel Arcipelago ❹,** V. Indipendenza 2, is a good deal but a 20min. walk from the *centro*. From P. Umberto, follow V. Mirabello along the water until the intersection with the stoplight, turn left, then take your first right on V. Indipendenza. Take the first left on a branch of the main road; the hotel is around the corner from the grocery store. (☎72 73 28. Breakfast included. Reservation required July-Aug. Singles €45-55; doubles €60-85. V.) EneRmaR and Saremar run **ferries** from Palau (15min., 2 per hr., round-trip €10). A **map** of La Maddelena is on the Palau map; pick it up before boarding the ferry. **Postal Code:** 07024.

LATVIA (LATVIJA)

The serenity and easy charm of Latvia belie centuries of suffering. The country has been conquered and reconquered so many times that the year 2007 was only the 38th year of Latvian independence—ever. These days, Latvia's vibrant capital, Rīga, is under siege by a new force: tourism. Cheap flights have brought so many Western visitors that the Rīga Old Town can feel like one big British bachelor party on summer weekends. You don't have to wander far from the beaten path, however, to discover the allure of Rīga's art nouveau elegance and student nightlife, its stunning seacoast, and the wild beauty of its Gaujas Valley National Park.

 DISCOVER LATVIA: SUGGESTED ITINERARIES

THREE DAYS. Settle into **Rīga** (2 days; p. 669) to enjoy stunning **Art Nouveau** architecture, **cafe culture,** and the best **music and performing arts** scene in the Baltics.

ONE WEEK. Begin your tour in seaside **Ventspils** (2 days; p. 674). After three days in **Rīga** (p. 669), head to **Cēsis** (2 days; p. 674) to enjoy **Cēsis Castle** and the wilds of **Gaujas Valley National Park.**

ESSENTIALS

FACTS AND FIGURES

Official Name: Republic of Latvia.

Capital: Rīga.

Major Cities: Daugavpils, Rēzekne.

Population: 2,253,000.

Time Zone: GMT +2.

Language: Latvian.

Religions: Lutheran 55%, Roman Catholic 24%, Russian Orthodox 9%.

National bird: White Wagtail.

Years of compulsory education: 9.

WHEN TO GO

Latvia is wet year-round, with cold, snowy winters and short, rainy summers. Tourism peaks in July and August; if you'd prefer not to experience central Rīga in the company of throngs of British stag parties, late spring or early fall is the best time to visit. Still, much of the seacoast stays untouristed even in summer.

DOCUMENTS AND FORMALITIES

EMBASSIES AND CONSULATES. Foreign embassies and consulates to Latvia are in **Rīga** (p. 670). Latvian embassies and consulates abroad include: **Australia,** Honorary Consul, 2 Mackennel St., East Ivanhoe, VIC 3079(☎613 94 99 69 20; latcon@ozemail.com.au); **Canada,** 350 Sparks St., Ste. 1200, Ottawa, ON K1R 7S8 (☎613-238-6014; embassy.canada@mfa.gov.lv); **Ireland,** 92 St. Stephen's Green, Dublin, 2 (☎353 14 28 33 20; http://www.am.gov.lv/en/ireland/); **New Zealand,** Honorary Consul, 161 Kilmore St., Amsterdam House, Level 3, Christchurch (☎640 33 65 35 05; lrconsulate@ebox.lv); **UK,** 45 Nottingham Place, London, W1U 5LY (☎442 073 120 040; www.london.am.gov.lv).

VISA AND ENTRY INFORMATION. Those wishing to stay for a longer period must submit an Aim of Residence form to the Visas Divison, Office of Citizenship and

ENTRANCE REQUIREMENTS.
Passport: Required of all travelers.
Visa: Not required of citizens of Australia, Canada, Ireland, New Zealand, the UK, and the US for stays up to 90 days.
Letter of Invitation: Not required for countries listed above.
Inoculations: Recommended up-to-date on DTaP (diphtheria, tetanus, and pertussis), hepatitis A, hepatitis B, MMR, polio booster, and typhoid.
Work Permit: Required of all foreigners planning to work in Latvia.
Driving Permit: Required of all those planning to drive in Latvia.

Migration Affairs, Aluna-na iela- 1, Rīga, LV-1050 (☎ 67 21 96 51; www.ocma.gov.lv) to receive a visa for either temporary or permanent residence. All travelers must display a passport valid for three months beyond the duration of their planned stay in Latvia, and must also be able to give proof of a valid insurance policy to cover potential health service needs while in Latvia. The best way to enter Latvia is by plane, train, or bus to Rīga.

TOURIST SERVICES AND MONEY

EMERGENCY	Ambulance: ☎ 03. Fire: ☎ 01. Police: ☎ 02. General Emergency: ☎ 112.

TOURIST OFFICES. Offices of the state-run **tourist bureau**, distinguished by a green "i" are not particularly numerous. In Rīga, employees of such establishments will speak fluent English, but elsewhere, they may not. Private tourist offices are more helpful.

MONEY. The Latvian unit of c-urrency is the **lat** (Ls), plural *latu*, each of which is divided into 100 **santīmu** (singular *santīms*). Although Latvia has been a member of the EU since 2004, persistent inflation has rendered it unlikely that it will switch to the Euro until 2012 at the earliest. The **inflation** rate in 2007 was 3.7%, representing a significant decrease over the past 3 years. Most banks **exchange currency** for

1% commission, except for Hansabanka, which does not charge fees. **ATMs** are common in Rīga and may also be found in larger towns. Some businesses, restaurants, and hotels accept **MasterCard** and **Visa**. **Traveler's checks** are harder to use, but both AmEx and Thomas Cook checks can be converted in Rīga. It's often difficult to exchange non-Baltic currencies other than US dollars or euro.

LATVIAN LATI		
AUS$1 = 0.41LS		1LS = AUS$2.40
CDN$1 = 0.50LS		1LS = CDN$2.01
EUR€1 = 0.70LS		1LS = EUR€1.42
NZ$1 = 0.35LS		1LS = NZ$2.86
UK£1 = 1.03LS		1LS = UK£0.97
US$1 = 0.55LS		1LS = US$1.82

HEALTH AND SAFETY

Although some private clinics provide adequate medical supplies and services, Latvian medical facilities generally fall below Western standards. Latvia has been hotlisted by the World Health Organization for its periodic outbreaks of incurable varieties of **tuberculosis,** though none have been reported since 2000. As a precaution, drink **bottled water** (available at grocery stores and kiosks and often carbonated) or boil tap water before drinking. **Pharmacies** *(aptieka)* in Latvia are generally privately-owned and fairly well-stocked with antibiotics and prescription medication produced in Latvia or other Eastern European countries. Although violent **crime** in Latvia is rare, travelers should be on their guard for pickpockets and scam artists. A common scam is to dupe foreigners into ordering outrageously expensive drinks in bars; travelers should always verify the price of drinks in advance. Both men and women should avoid walking alone at night. If you feel threatened, say *"Ej prom"* (EY prawm), which means "go away"; *"Liec man miera"* (LEEtz mahn MEE-rah; "leave me alone") says it more forcefully, and *"Ej bekot"* (EY bek-oht; "go pick mushrooms"), is even ruder. **Women** travelers may be verbally hassled at any hour, especially if traveling alone, but usually such harassment is unaccompanied by physical action. **Minorities** in Latvia are rare; incidents of verbal and physical harassment have been known to occur, although generally there is little discrimination. Although **homosexuality** is legal in Latvia, public displays of affection may result in violence. Women walk down the street holding hands, but this is strictly an indication of friendship and does not render Latvia gay-friendly. Safe options for GLBT travelers include **gay and lesbian clubs,** which advertise themselves freely in Rīga. Expect less tolerance outside the capital.

TRANSPORTATION

BY PLANE. Airlines flying to Latvia use the Rīga international airport. **Air Baltic, Finnair, Lufthansa, SAS,** and others make the hop to Rīga from their hubs. Round-trip fares typically run to US$900-1000 during the summer months.

BY TRAIN AND BUS. Trains link Latvia to Berlin, Germany; Lviv, Ukraine; Moscow, Russia; Odessa, Ukraine; St. Petersburg, Russia; Tallinn, Estonia; and Vilnius, Lithuania. Trains are cheap and efficient, and stations are clearly marked. Latvia is not covered by **Eurail.** The Rīga **commuter rail** is very good and provides extensive service. For daytrips from Rīga, it's best to take the **electric train.** The Latvian word for "departures" is *atiet;* "arrivals" is *pienāk.* Buses, often adorned with the driver's collection of icons and stuffed animals, are faster, cheaper, and more comfortable than trains for travel within Latvia. The major bus company servicing Latvia is Eurolines (www.eurolines.lv). Some crowded trips may leave you standing for long hours without a seat.

BY CAR. Road conditions in Latvia are improving after years of deterioration. For more info, consult the **Latvian State Roads** (www.lad.lv). Taxi stands in front of hotels charge higher rates. Let's Go does not recommend hitchhiking, but it is common. Drivers may ask for a fee comparable to bus fares.

KEEPING IN TOUCH

PHONE CODES	**Country code: 371. International dialing prefix: 011.** From outside Latvia, dial international dialing prefix (see inside back cover) + 371 + city code + local number. Inside Latvia, dial city code + local number, even when calling from within the city. For more info on how to place international calls, see **Inside Back Cover.**

EMAIL AND INTERNET. Internet is readily available in Rīga but rarer elsewhere and averages 1Ls per hour at Internet cafes (outside of Rīga service is somewhat cheaper, but not by much); many libraries and cafes offer free service. Internet cafes, however, are more prevalent, and typically offer a range of services inclyding printing, laminating, and CD burning.

TELEPHONE. To make local or international calls, you must purchase a **phone card,** which are come in 3, 5, and 10Ls denominations from post offices, telephone offices, kiosks, and state stores and have instructions in English. To operate a phone, dial 0, then press 1 or 2 for English and follow the instructions. For international calls, **Tele 2** has the best rates. For domestic calls, if a number is six digits, dial a 2 before it; if it's seven, you needn't dial anything before it.

MAIL. Latvia's postal system is reliable; it generally takes mail 10-12 days to reach the US or Canada from Latvia. All post offices have information desks where English is spoken. The standard rate for a letter to the US or Canada is 0.50Ls. Mail can be received through **Poste Restante,** though this is not especially prevalent. Envelopes should be addressed as follows: First name LAST NAME, POSTE RESTANTE, post office address, Postal Code, city, LATVIA.

LANGUAGE. Heavily influenced by German, Russian, Estonian, and Swedish, Latvian is one of two languages (the other is Lithuanian) in the Baltic language group. Many young Latvians study English; the older set knows some German.

ACCOMMODATIONS AND CAMPING

LATVIA	❶	❷	❸	❹	❺
ACCOMMODATIONS	under 9Ls	9-14Ls	15-19Ls	20-24Ls	over 24Ls

Hostels are common in Latvia, as are hotel chains, bed and breakfasts, and family-run guesthouses. Hostels are prone to being overrun by large and raucous British stag parties, especially on summer weekends. The **Latvian Youth Hostel Association,** Aldaru 8, Rīga LV-1050 (☎921 8560; www.hostellinglatvia.com), is a useful resource for info on hostels in Rīga and elsewhere. **College dormitories** are often the cheapest option, but are open to travelers only in the summer. Most small towns outside the capital have at most one hotel in the budget range; expect to pay 3-15Ls per night. **Campgrounds** are in the countryside. Camping outside marked areas is illegal.

FOOD AND DRINK

LATVIA	❶	❷	❸	❹	❺
FOOD	under 2Ls	2-3Ls	4-5Ls	6-7Ls2	over 7Ls

Latvian food is heavy and starchy—and therefore delicious. Dark rye bread is a staple. Try *speķa rauši*, a warm pastry, or *biezpienmaize*, bread with sweet curds. Dark-colored *kaņepju sviests* (hemp butter) is good but too diluted for "medicinal" purposes. A particularly good Latvian beer is *Porteris*, from the Aldaris brewery. Cities offer foreign, **kosher**, and **vegetarian** cuisine.

HOLIDAYS AND FESTIVALS

Holidays: New Year's Day (Jan. 1); Good Friday (Mar. 21, 2008); Easter Monday (Mar. 24, 2008; Apr. 12, 2009); Labor Day (May 1); Ligo Day (June 23); St. John's Day (June 24); Independence Day (Nov. 18); Christmas (Dec. 25).

Festivals: Midsummer's Eve is celebrated across the Baltic states every June 23-24. An updated calendar of cultural events is available at http://latviatourism.lv. Dziesmu Svē-tki, a song festival will pack the streets of Rīga (summer 2008). Check out their website for updated dates and other details: www.dziesmusvetki2008.lv.

BEYOND TOURISM

For more info on opportunities across Europe, see **Beyond Tourism**, p. 56.

American Field Service (AFS), 71 W. 23rd St., 17th fl., New York, NY 10010, USA (☎1-212-807-8686; www.afs.org). Offers summer-, semester-, and year-long homestay exchange programs and community service programs also offered for young adults 18+. Teaching programs available for current and retired teachers. Financial aid available.

RĪGA ☎7

Rīga (pop. 750,000) is the center of Latvia's cultural and economic life, fusing a fascinating mix of Russian and Latvian influences. Medieval church spires domi-nate the Old Town, founded in 1201 by the German Bishop Albert, while early 20th-century Art Nouveau masterpieces line the city's newer streets. The recent boom in tourism has transformed large sections of the city, particularly the Old Town, but it's not hard to find unspoiled sections off the main drags. The city's cal-endar is filled with music, opera, and theater festivals, while bright costumes and colors dominate the streets during holidays and celebrations.

◩ TRANSPORTATION

Flights: Lidosta Rīga (RIX; ☎720 7009; www.riga-airport.com), 8km southwest of *Vecrīga*. Take bus #22 from Janvara iela 13 (30min., 2-6 per hr., 0.30Ls) to the south side of Old Town. **Air Baltic** (☎720 7777; www.airbaltic.com) flies cheaply to many European cities.

Trains: Centrālā Stacija (Central Station), Stacijas laukums (☎723 3113; www.ldz.lv), next to the bus station south of the Old Town. International tickets are sold at counters 1-6; destinations include **Moscow, RUS** (17hr., 1 per day, 16Ls), **St. Petersburg, RUS** (14hr., 2 per day, 9Ls), and **Vilnius, LIT** (5hr., 1 per day, 10-17Ls).

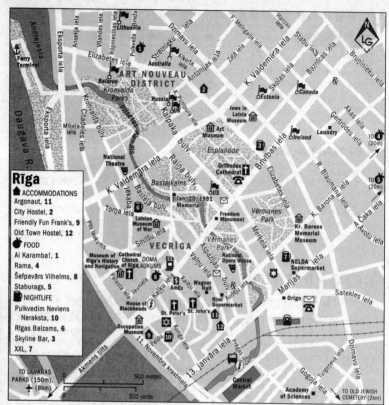

Rīga

🔺 **ACCOMMODATIONS**
Argonaut, **11**
City Hostel, **2**
Friendly Fun Frank's, **9**
Old Town Hostel, **12**
🍎 **FOOD**
Ai Karambal, **1**
Rama, **4**
Šefpavārs Vilhelms, **8**
Staburags, **5**
🌙 **NIGHTLIFE**
Pulkvedim Neviens
  Neraksta, **10**
Rīgas Balzams, **6**
Skyline Bar, **3**
XXL, **7**

Buses: Autoosta, Prāgas 1 (☎900 0009; www.autoosta.lv), 100m from the train station, across the canal from the Central Market. To: **Kaunas, LIT** (4½-5½hr., 2 per day, 7-8.30Ls); **Minsk, BLR** (10-12hr., 1 per day, 14-15Ls); **Tallinn, EST** (4-6hr., 11 per day, 7-10Ls); **Vilnius, LIT** (5-6hr., 4-6 per day, 7-9Ls).

✦ 🛈 ORIENTATION AND PRACTICAL INFORMATION

The city is divided in half by **Brīvības bulvāris,** which leads from the outskirts of town to the **Freedom Monument** in the center, becomes **Kaļķu iela,** and passes through **Vecrīga** (Old Rīga). To reach *Vecrīga* from the train station, turn left on **Marijas iela** and then right on any of the small streets beyond the canal.

Tourist Office: Rātslaukums 6 (☎703 4377; www.rigatourism.com), in the town square, next to the House of the Blackheads. Gives out **free maps,** arranges walking and bus tours (6-9Ls), books accommodation for 10% fee, and provides advice and brochures, including *Rīga in Your Pocket* (1.20Ls). Open daily in summer 9am-7pm; in low season 10am-7pm. AmEx/MC/V.

Embassies and Consulates: Australia, Alberta iela 13 (☎733 6383; acr@latnet.lv). Open Tu 10am-noon, Th 3-5pm. **Canada,** Baznīcas 20/22 (☎781 3945; riga@dfait-maeci.gc.ca). Open M-F 9am-5:30pm. **Ireland,** Brīvības bul. 54 (☎67 03 52 86; fax 702 5223). Entrance on Blaumana. Open M-Tu and Th-F 10am-noon. **UK,** Alunāna iela

5 (☎777 4700; www.britain.lv). Open M-F 9am-5pm. **US,** Raiņa bul. 7 (☎703 6200; www.usembassy.lv). Open M-Tu and Th 9-11:30am.

Currency Exchange: At any of the **Valutos Maiņa** kiosks. **Unibanka,** Pils iela 23, gives MC/V **cash advances** and cashes both AmEx and Thomas Cook **traveler's checks** without commission. Open M-F 9am-5pm.

24hr. Pharmacy: Vecpilsētas Aptieka, Audeju 20 (☎721 3340).

Internet Access: Elik, Kaļķu iela 11 (☎722 7079; www.elikkafe.lv), in the center of *Vecrīga;* branch at Merķeļa iela 1 (☎722 1175). 3Ls per day. Open 24hr. Cash only. **Lattlecom**'s Wi-Fi networks blanket the Old Town. Look for establishments with the Lattlecom logo in the window and purchase an access card inside (0.94Ls per hr.).

Post Office: Stacijas laukumā 1 (☎701 8804; www.pasts.lv/en), near the train station. **Poste Restante** at window #9. Open M-F 7am-8pm, Sa 8am-6pm, Su 8am-4pm. Another branch at Brīvības bul. 19. **Postal Code:** LV-1050.

▮ ACCOMMODATIONS

Make reservations well ahead during the high season. **Patricia,** Elizabetes iela 22 (☎728 4868; room@findroom.net), arranges homestays from 22Ls and apartments for 40-60Ls. (Open M-F 8:30am-6pm, Sa-Su 11am-3pm. MC/V.)

Old Town Hostel, Vaļņu iela 43 (☎722 3406; www.rigaoldtownhostel.lv). A friendly hostel equipped with a pub downstairs. The bright, freshly painted dorms are home to the cleanest beds in Rīga. Kitchen, free Internet, and Wi-Fi. English spoken. Safes in rooms. Check-in noon. 12-bed dorms from 8Ls; 6-bed 10Ls. MC/V. ❷

Friendly Fun Frank's, 11 Novembra krastmala 29 (☎599 0612; www.franks.lv). Walk toward the river and turn right on Novembra krastmala. Peach building with koala plaque beside buzzer. This party hostel offers nightly outings (cover waived) to pubs and clubs in Rīga, as well as a free beer when you arrive. Spacious dorms and common room. Free Internet and Wi-Fi. Dorms from 9Ls, online booking discount. Cash only. ❷

City Hostel, Elizabetes iela 101 (☎670 5476; www.cityhostel.lv). From the station, turn right and walk along Marijas; turn right on Elizabetes. Wooden bunks in a converted town house make for a quiet, comfy stay. Kitchen, common room, and free Internet. 10-bed dorm 8Ls; 6-bed 11Ls. Low season discount. Cash only. ❶

Argonaut, Kalēju 50 (☎614 7214; www.argonauthostel.com). Key-card door access and gigantic lockers ensure security. Dorms are slightly crowded, but staff is friendly. Basic kitchen, free Internet, and Wi-Fi. 10-bed dorms 8Ls; 4-bed dorms 12Ls. MC/V. ❷

▮ FOOD

Twenty-four hour food and liquor stores are at Marijas 5 (Nelda) and Brīvības bul. 68. **Centrālais Tirgus** (Central Market), in Zeppelin hangars behind the bus station, is one of the largest markets in Europe. (Open M and Su 8am-4pm, Tu-Sa 8am-5pm.) One fabulous Russian import that has stuck around is tea: tearooms dot the city and are perfect for an afternoon or evening snack.

Rama, K. Barona iela 56 (☎727 2490). Between Gertrudes and Stabu iela. Eat well for about 2Ls at this Hare-Krishna-run cafeteria, which dishes out hearty Indian-style vegetarian fare and donates profits to feed the poor. Open M-Sa 10am-7pm. Cash only. ❶

Šefpavārs Vilhelms, Škuņu iela 6. Look for the large chef statue outside this pancake house that offers meat, sweet, salty, and vegetarian pancakes. Slather on jam or sour cream, grab a glass of milk or yogurt, and you'll be well fed for under 2Ls. Open M-Th 9am-10pm, F-Sa 10am-11pm, Su 10am-10pm. Cash only. ❶

LATVIA

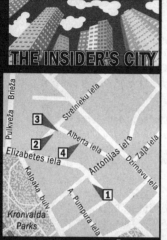

THE INSIDER'S CITY

ART NOUVEAU RĪGA

Rīga's remarkable architecture makes its Old Town a sight in itself. About 40% of the downtown is built in the unique Art Nouveau style, characterized by stylized, curvilinear designs and floral motifs. To see the most impressive buildings, most of which were designed by Russian architect **Mikhail Eisenstein** in the early 20th century, take this walk:

1 From K. Valdemara iela, turn left on Elizabetes iela to reach 10b, on your left. Admire the work from across the street.

2 Turn right on Strelnieku for blue-and-white 1905 student hostel at 4b, now the Stockholm School of Economics.

3 Next door is the massive, cream-colored corner edifice at Alberta iela 13, with fine details and pointed turrets.

4 Turn on Alberta iela. Numbers 8, 6, 4, 2, and 2a, in various states of repair, showcase a colorful and impressive catalogue of Art Nouveau balconies and intricate brickwork.

Staburags, A. Čaka iela 55 (☎729 9787). Follow A. Čaka iela away from Vecrīga until it intersects Stabu iela. Enormous portions of authentic Latvian cuisine served amid rustic decor. Try the unfiltered house beer (1.50Ls per 0.5L). Entrees 3-6Ls. Open daily noon-midnight. Cash only. ❷

Ai Karamba!, Pulkveza Brieza 2 (☎733 4672). American-themed diner with a Baltic twist. All-day breakfast includes omelettes (1.60-3Ls), as well as lunch and dinner. Try the mint leaf tea (0.65Ls) after a night out. Entrees 2-4Ls. Open M-Th 8am-midnight, F-Sa 8am-1am, Su 10am-midnight. AmEx/MC/V. ❷

🅖 SIGHTS

FREEDOM MONUMENT AND ENVIRONS. In the center of Vecrīga is the Freedom Monument (Brīvības Piemineklis), known as "Milda." (At Raina bul. and Brīvības bul.) Continuing along Kaļķu iela to the river, you'll see one of the few remaining Soviet monuments: the **Latvian Riflemen Monument** (Latviešu Strēlnieku Laukums) in the town square, honoring Lenin's famous bodyguards. Rising behind the statue is the 🅼**Occupation Museum** (Okupācijas muzejs), Strēlnieku laukums 1, where displays vividly depict the Soviet and Nazi occupations. (Open M-F 9am-7pm, Sa-Su 10am-7pm. Donations accepted.) Next to the museum stands the **House of the Blackheads** (Melngalvju nams), Rātslaukums 7. Built in 1344 by a guild of unmarried merchants and destroyed by the Nazis and Soviets, the unusual but magnificent building was reconstructed in honor of Rīga's 800th birthday. The structure houses a museum and an assembly hall, and occasionally hosts concerts. (Open Tu-Sa May-Sept. 10am-5pm, Tu-Su Oct.-Apr. 11am-5pm. 1.50Ls, students 0.70Ls. Cash only.)

ELSEWHERE IN VECRĪGA. Follow Kaļķu iela from the Freedom Monument and turn right on Šķūņu iela to reach **Dome Square** (Doma laukums) and the **Cathedral Church of Rīga** (Doma baznīca). The organ boasts over 6700 pipes. (Open May-Sept. M-Tu, Th, Sa-Su 9am-6:30pm, W and F 9am-5:30pm; Oct.-May M-Th and Sa-Su 10am-6:30pm, F 10am-5:30pm. Concerts Oct.-Dec. Th-F 7pm ,3-7Ls, and occasionally in summer (5-20Ls). Gallery open May-Oct. Tu-F 11am-4pm, Sa 10am-2pm. Cathedral 1Ls, students 0.50Ls. Cash only.) Next to the cathedral is the 🅼**Museum of Rīga's History and Navigation** (Rīgas Vēstures un Kugnie-cības Muzejs), Palasta iela 4. Established in 1773, this museum helped rekindle Latvia's cultural heritage after Soviet efforts to suppress it. (Open W-Su May-Sept. 10am-5pm; Oct.-Apr. 11am-5pm. 1.20Ls, students 0.40Ls. Tours in English, German, and Russian, 3Ls.) From the top of the 123m spire of **St. Peter's Church** (Sv. Pētera baznīca), you can see the Baltic Sea. (On Skāmu iela, off Kaļķu iela. Open Tu-Su in *summer 10am-6pm; low season 10am-5pm. Ticket office closes for lunch. Church 0.50Ls. Tower 2Ls, under 18 1Ls. Cash only.)* The magnificent Neoclassical **State Museum of Art** (Latvjas nacionalais), Kr. Valdemāra iela 10A, has 18th- to 20th-century Latvian art and occasional concerts. *(www.vmm.lv; open Apr.-Oct. M and W-Su 11am-5pm, Th 11am-7pm; Oct.-Apr. M and W-Su 11am-5pm. 0.70Ls, students 0.30Ls.)* The newer areas of Rīga display **Art Nouveau** Jugendstil architecture; the style is most visible on Alberta iela, Elizabetes iela, and Strēlnieku laukums.

BASTEJKALNS. Rīga's central park, surrounded by the Old City moat (Pīlsētas kanāls), has ruins of the old city walls. Across and around the canal, five red slabs of stone stand as **memorials** to the events of January 20, 1991, when Soviet special forces stormed the Interior Ministry on Raiņa bul. At the northern end of Baste-jkalns, on K. Valdemāra iela, sits the **National Theater**, where Latvia first declared its independence on November 18, 1918. *(Open daily 10am-7pm.)*

NIGHTLIFE

The nightlife scene is centered in *Vecrīga*, but **Skyline Bar**, Elizabetes iela 55, on the 26th floor of the Reval Hotel Latvija, has the best view in the city. (Beer 2-3Ls. Mixed drinks 3-5Ls. F-Sa DJ from 9pm. 21+ after 11pm. Open Su-Th 3pm-2am, F-Sa 3pm-3am. AmEx/MC/V.) If you prefer a more relaxed, alternative scene, spend the evening with great DJs at **Pulkvedim Neviens Neraksta,** Peldu 26/28. The dark upstairs bar and dance floor contrast with the colorful basement lounge. (www.pulkvedis.lv. Beer 1.30-3Ls. F-Sa 3Ls. Open M-Th 8pm-3am, F-Sa 8pm-5am. AmEx/MC/V.) Try *balzams*, Latvia's national liquor—a mysterious and heady herb and berry brew—in one of the dozen creative cocktails at **Rīgas Balzams,** Torņa iela 4, in *Vecrīga*, 100m east of Rīga Castle's Powder Tower. *(Balzams* drinks 3-5Ls. Open Su-Th 11am-midnight, F-Sa 11am-1am. AmEx/MC/V.) The gay bar, club, and sauna **XXL**, A. Kalniņa iela 4, is off K. Barona iela; buzz to be let in. (☎ 728 2276; www.xxl.lv. Mixed men and women F-Sa. Cover Tu-Sa 1-3Ls. Open daily 6pm-7am. Club open F-Sa 10pm-7am. MC/V.)

DAYTRIPS FROM RĪGA

JŪRMALA. Boardwalks and sun-bleached sand cover the narrow spit of Jūr-mala. Visitors, especially the Soviet elite, have come to this set of 13 small towns since the 19th century. The coastal towns between **Bulduri** and **Dubulti** are popular for sunning and swimming, but Jūrmala's social center is **Majori,** where masses flock to crowded beaches or wander **Jomas iela,** a pedestrian street lined with cafes and shops. **Bicycles** are a popular mode of transport; rent one along the beach. *(2Ls per hr., 6Ls per day.)* **Sue's Asia ❸**, Jomas iela 74, offers Chinese, Indian, and Thai cuisine, serving the same fine fare that scored Rīga's branch a spot on Condé Nast's list of the world's 100 best restaurants. *(☎ 775 5900. Entrees 4-11Ls. Open daily noon-midnight. MC/V.)* Head to **Dukats ❶**, Dubulti, Baznicas 12/14, for homemade soups and entrees under 2Ls. Don't forget to grab a delicious pastry on your way out. *(☎ 776 4267.)* The **commuter rail** runs from Rīga to Jūr-mala (30min., 2 per hr., 0.50Ls). **Public buses** (0.30Ls) and **microbuses** (0.50Ls) also string together Jūrmala's towns. There are two **tourist offices** in Majori. The first, Lienes iela 5, by the train station, has free maps. *(☎ 714 7900; www.jurmala.lv. Open M-F 9am-7pm, Sa 10am-5pm, Su 10am-3pm.)* The other, Jomas iela 42, arranges accommodations for a 1Ls fee. *(☎ 776 4276; jurmalainfo@bkc.lv. Open in summer M-F 9am-7pm, Sa-Su 1-7pm; winter M-F 9am-7pm. Cash only.)* **Postal Code:** LV-2105.

SIGULDA. The Knights of the Sword, Germanic crusaders who Christianized much of Latvia in the 13th century, made Segewald—modern-day Sigulda (pop. 10,000)—their base of operations. Now the Gauja National Park Administration has planted its head-

LATVIA

quarters in this cutesy town 50km from Rīga. The area offers biking, bobsledding, bungee-jumping, horseback riding, hot-air ballooning, and skiing. **Makars Tourism Agency,** Peldu 1, arranges excursions and rents bikes, boats, and camping equipment. *(☎924 4948; www.makars.lv.)* The main sights of the area lie along a 4km stretch of road. Farthest from town are the restored brick fortifications of the **Turaida Castle Complex** (Turaidas Muzejrezervats), Turaidas iela 10, visible throughout the Gauja Valley; climb the staircase in the main tower for a view of the region. *(Tower open daily 8am-9pm. Admission free with ticket from Turaidas Museum Reserve. Cash only.)* Take Turaidas iela back down the hill to reach the famous **caves** of Sigulda. Inscriptions and coats of arms from as early as the 16th century cover the chiseled mouth of **Gutman's Cave** (Gūtmaņa ala), whose spring has any number of legends attached to it. On a ridge to the right of Gaujas iela, on the same side of the river as town, is the **Sigulda Dome** palace, behind which lie the ruins of **Sigulda Castle** (Siguldas pilsdrupas).

For a cheap bite, head to **Elvi ➊,** Vidus iela 1, which shares a building with a supermarket of the same name. Food is sold by weight, and you can easily fill up on 1Ls. *(Open daily 7am-11pm.)* **Trains** run from Rīga on the Rīga-Lugaži commuter rail line (1hr., 9 per day, 0.80Ls). From the station, walk up Raiņa iela, passing the bus station, to the town center. **Buses** run from Rīga hourly (1Ls). Continue on from the station as Raiņa iela turns into Gaujas iela, which, after the bridge, turns into the steep Turaidas iela and passes Turaida Castle. A bus labeled "Turaida" runs directly to Turaida Castle (7 per day, 0.20Ls). From the station, 1km along Raiņa iela is the **Gauja National Park Visitor Centre,** Baznicas 3. *(☎780 0388; www.gnp.gov.lv. Open M 9am-5:30pm, Tu-Su 9am-7pm.)* **Postal Code:** LV-2150.

CĒSIS. Sprawling medieval ruins and Cēsu, the local brew, make Cēsis (TSEY-sis; pop. 18,400) the classic Latvian town. Crusading Germans came in 1209 and built the famous ▧**Cēsis Castle.** The new castle's **tower** offers stunning views of the Gauja Valley. Explore the old castle's **ruins** with a hard-hat and lantern, or check out the fallen Lenin statue, complete with a wooden coffin, at the garden entrance. *(☎412 1815. Open mid-May to Sept. Tu-Su 10am-6pm; Nov. to mid-May W-Su 10am-5pm. 2Ls, students 1Ls. Ruins open mid-May-Sept. M 10am-6pm; tickets at the garden entrance, same price as castle. Cash only.)* Cēsis is served by infrequent **trains** from Rīga via Sigulda (1½-2hr., 2 per day, 1.30Ls). **Buses** are more convenient (2hr., 1-2 per hr., 1.70Ls). The **tourist office,** Pils laukums 1, across from the castle, offers free maps, has Internet access (1Ls per hr.), and arranges **private rooms** for a 1Ls fee. *(☎412 1815; www.tourism.cesis.lv. Open mid-May to mid-Sept. M-F 9am-6pm, Sa 9am-5pm, Su 10am-3pm; mid-Sept. to mid-May M-F 9am-5pm. AmEx/MC/V.)* **Postal Code:** LV-4101.

VENTSPILS. The colorful, cobblestone streets and perfectly manicured gardens of Ventspils (pop. 43,800) hardly convey the city's industrial past. This wealthy port city, once a base for Russian oil exports, is now home to the cleanest, most beautiful coastlines in Latvia. Bask in the sunset on the west shore at the ▧**Blue Flag Beach,** internationally recognized for high water safety and cleanliness. Nearby, the **Seaside Open Air Museum,** Rinka iela 2, showcases the history of fishing in Ventspils, including an extensive exhibition of boats, cabins, and a forest path dotted with the largest anchor collection in the world. *(☎362 4467. Open May-Oct. 10am-6pm; Nov.-Apr. M-F 11am-5pm. 0.60Ls, students 0.30Ls.)* The **Livonian Order Castle,** Jana iela 17, is one of the oldest standing medieval fortresses. In the summer, knights duel in the courtyard. *(☎362 2031; www.ventspilsmuzejs.lv. 1Ls, students 0.50Ls.)* The **Guesthouse at Meza Street ➋,** Mezu iela 13, is a family-run guesthouse with clean rooms surrounded by beautiful private gardens. *(☎29 42 24 07. Shared baths. Breakfast 2Ls. Laundry 8Ls. Singles 8Ls; doubles 12Ls.)* ▧**Krodzins Don Basil ➋,** Annas iela 5, has enormous pasta plates (2-4Lt), salads, and excellent coffee. *(☎26 56 32 09. Open 11am-11pm.)* **Buses** go to Kuldiga (7 per day, 1.40 Ls), Leipaja (6 per day, 2-4Ls), and Rīga (17 per day, 4Ls). The **TIC** is at Tirgus iela 7. *(☎362 2263; www.tourism.ventspils.lv. Open M-F 8am-7pm, Sa 10am-5pm, Su 10am-3pm.)* The **post office** is at Platā iela 8. *(Open M-F 8am-6pm, Sa 8am-4pm.)* **Postal Code:** LV-3601.

LIECHTENSTEIN

Every year on Assumption Day (Aug. 15), Prince Hans-Adam II invites all of Liechtenstein's citizens to celebrate with him at his Vaduz palace. Lucky for his chefs and his wallet, only 35,000 people reside in the 160 sq. km nation. But despite its miniscule size and population, Europe's only absolute monarchy boasts unspoiled mountains with great biking, hiking, and skiing.

 DISCOVER LIECHTENSTEIN: SUGGESTED ITINERARY

8AM. Wake-up. Shower.

8:15AM. Breakfast. Brush your teeth!

9AM. Spy on the royal family outside **Schloß Vaduz** (p. 676).

9:25AM. Debate the best hiking routes (p. 676) with the tourist office staff.

9:55AM. 5min. bathroom break.

10AM. Stampede the **Postmuseum.**

11AM. Lose track of time at the **Liechtensteinisches Landesmuseum** (p. 676).

NOON. Devour a pizza at **Brasserie Burg.**

12:30PM. Leave for Malbun.

1PM. Arrive in Malbun.

1:15PM. Ride the chairlift and marvel at views of the **Silberhorn** and **Sareiserjoch.**

2PM. Become king of two mountains; trek the **Fürstin-Gina-Weg.**

3:22PM. 10min. hiking break. Eat trail mix and have a drink—water, preferably.

6:45PM. Shed your clothes (but don a swimsuit) for a refreshing dip in the **Alpenhotel** pool (p. 677).

7:45PM. If hiking smell persists, shower.

8PM. Dinner and bed. You're done!

ESSENTIALS

FACTS AND FIGURES

Official Name: Principality of Liechtenstein.

Capital: Vaduz.

Major Towns: Schaan, Triesen.

Population: 35,000.

Land Area: 160 sq. km.

Coastline: 0km. One of only two doubly landlocked countries (the other being Uzbekistan).

Time Zone: GMT +1

Language: German (see p. 1060).

Religions: Roman Catholic (76%), Protestant (7%).

Form of Government: Constitutional hereditary monarchy.

Major Exports: Machinery, Dental Products, Stamps.

DOCUMENTS AND FORMALITIES. Citizens of Australia, Canada, New Zealand, the UK, and the US do not need a visa for stays of up to 90 days.

TRANSPORTATION. Catch a **bus** from Feldkirch in Austria (30min., 1 per hr., 3.80CHF), or from Buchs (25min., 4-5 per hr., 3.60CHF) or Sargans (30-40min. 4 per hr., 5.80CHF), across the border in Switzerland. Liechtenstein has no rail system. Its cheap, efficient **PostBus** (www.sbb.ch) system links all 11 towns. A **one-week bus ticket** (19CHF) covers the entire principality and buses to Swiss and Austrian border towns. You can buy all tickets and passes on board. The SwissPass and Swiss Youth Pass are valid in Liechtenstein (p. 997).

EMERGENCY	Ambulance, Fire, and Police: ☎ 112.

MONEY. The Liechtenstein unit of currency is the **Swiss franc (CHF)**, plural Swiss francs. One Swiss franc is equal to 100 centimes, with standard denominations of 5, 10, 20, and 50 centimes and 1, 2, and 5CHF in coins, and 10, 20, 50, 100, 200, 500, and 1000CHF in notes. AmEx/MC/V are widely accepted. As restaurant checks generally include a small service charge, most patrons round up their bill rather than leave an additional tip. Go to Switzerland to exchange currency at reasonable rates. Conversion rates for the Swiss franc are listed on p. 997.

Liechtenstein has a 7.6% **value added tax (VAT)**, a sales tax applied to national deliveries and services made in return for payments, in-house consumption, and importing services and objects. The prices given in *Let's Go* include VAT. In the airport upon exiting Liechtenstein and the EU, non-EU citizens can claim a refund on VAT paid for goods purchased at participating stores. In order to qualify for a refund, you must spend at least 400CHF; make sure to ask for a refund form when you pay. For more info on qualifying for a VAT refund, see p. 19.

BEYOND TOURISM. European Voluntary Service programs (http://europa.eu.int/comm/youth/program/guide/action2_en.html) enable EU citizens to spend a fully funded year doing service in another European nation. Non-EU residents may visit local tourist offices to see about regional positions available. The **Special Olympics** (www.specialolympics.li) also provides travelers with volunteer opportunities. For more info on opportunities across Europe, see p. 56.

VADUZ AND LOWER LIECHTENSTEIN ☎ 00423

As the national capital, **Vaduz** (pop. 5000) attracts the most visitors of any village in Liechtenstein. The 12th-century **Schloß Vaduz** (Vaduz Castle) is the principality's most recognizable icon and home to the ruling Prince. Its interior is off-limits, but visitors can hike to the castle for a closer look. Diagonally across from the tourist office at Städtle 32 is the cube-shaped **Kunstmuseum Liechtenstein.** Its collection is split between Neoclassical art owned by the royal family and rotating exhibits of contemporary art. (☎ 235 0300; www.kunstmuseum.li. Open Tu-W and F-Su 10am-5pm, Th 10am-8pm. 8CHF, students 5CHF.) Above the tourist office, the **Postmuseum** showcases almost every stamp the country has printed. (☎ 239 6846. Open daily 10am-noon and 1-5pm. Free.) The **Liechtensteinisches Landesmuseum,**

Städtle 43, chronicles the principality's history, beginning with its first inhabitants 8000 years ago. (☎239 6820; www.landesmuseum.li. Open Tu and Th-Su 10am-5pm, W 10am-8pm.)In between Vaduz and the village of **Schaan** is Liechtenstein's sole **Jugendherberge (HI)** ❷, Untere Rüttig. 6. From Vaduz, take bus #11, 12, or 14 to Mühleholz, walk to the intersection, turn left on Marianumstr., and follow the signs. (☎232 5022; www.youthhostel.ch/schaan. Breakfast included. Laundry 6CHF. Internet 1CHF per 5min. Reception 7:30-10am and 5-10pm. Open Mar.-Oct. Dorms 37CHF; singles 62CHF; doubles 94CHF. 6CHF HI discount. AmEx/MC/V.) Finding cheap food in Liechtenstein may turn into a neverending quest. Cut your losses and head to **Brasserie Burg** ❸, Städtle 15, in the center of Vaduz, for sandwiches and burgers for 10-15CHF. (☎232 2131. Salad buffet 18 CHF. Pizza 16-23CHF. Open M-F 8:30am-11pm, Sa 9am-midnight, Su 9:30am-11pm. AmEx/MC/V.) There is a **Coop** supermarket at Aulestr. 20. (Open M-F 8am-7pm, Sa-Su 8am-5pm. MC/V.) Pick up a **hiking map** (16CHF) and route suggestions at Liechtenstein's **tourist office,** Städtle 37, up the hill from the Vaduz bus stop. (☎239 6300; www.tourismus.li. Open M-F 9am-noon and 1:30-5pm.)

UPPER LIECHTENSTEIN ☎00423

 A CLIFFHANGER. Be careful on the ridges above Malbun: the paths are narrow and often edge very close to cliffs.

Full of winding roads and hiking trails, the villages in Upper Liechtenstein are where the country's real beauty lies. In the principality's southeastern corner, **Malbun** sits in an alpine valley accessible by bus #21 (30min., 1 per hr.). A popular hiking trail (4-5hr.) starts at the **chairlift** base at the Malbun Zentrum bus stop and follows **Fürstin-Gina-Weg** along two mountain crests. (Chairlift open July to mid-Oct. daily 8am-12:15pm and 1:15-4:50pm. 9CHF, students 7CHF; round-trip 13/10CHF.) In winter, skiers take to the slopes on the **Sareiserjoch** and the **Silberhorn.** (Chairlift open mid-Dec. to mid-Apr. 9am-4pm. ½-day passes 46CHF, students 35CHF; 1 day 68/55CHF; 2 days 123/98CHF.) **Hotel Steg** ❶, in the village of Steg, has the country's cheapest lodging. Take bus #21 to Steg Hotel. (☎263 2146. Breakfast included. Linens included for private rooms. 10-bed dorms 25CHF; singles 45CHF; doubles 80CHF. MC/V.) **Alpenhotel Malbun** ❸, opposite the Malbun Jörabaoda bus stop, has an indoor pool. (☎263 1181; www.alpenhotel.li. Reception 8am-10pm. Open mid-May to Oct. and mid-Dec. to Apr. Singles 40-70CHF, with bath 70-110CHF; doubles 80-130/120-180CHF. AmEx/MC/V.) The **Schädler-Shop,** between the chairlift and the tourist office, has groceries. (Open M-F 8am-12:30pm and 1:30-5pm, Sa-Su 8am-6pm.) The **tourist office** is down the street from the Malbun Zentrum bus stop. (☎263 6577; www.malbun.li. Open June-Oct. and mid-Dec. to mid-Apr. M-F 8am-6pm, Sa 9am-5pm, Su 8am-5pm.)

LITHUANIA (LIETUVA)

Lithuania has always been an offbeat place. Once the last pagan holdout in Christian Europe, today the tiny country continues to forge an eccentric path, from the breakaway artists' republic and Frank Zappa statue in its capital, to the drifting sand dunes, the quirky folk art, and even a decaying Soviet missile base in the countryside. More conventional treats include the wild beauty of the coast and the Baroque architecture of Vilnius. Lithuania became the first Baltic nation to declare independence from the USSR in 1990. Having gained EU membership in 2004, it continues to push ahead with optimism.

 DISCOVER LITHUANIA: SUGGESTED ITINERARIES

THREE DAYS. Head to the **Baltic Coast** to enjoy the stunning sands of the **Drifting Dunes of Parnidis** (p. 688), then leave the **Curonian Spit** and go inland to the flourishing capital of **Vilnius** (p. 682).

ONE WEEK. After 4 days on the **Baltic Coast,** visit **Vilnius** (3 days), where you can explore the **Old Town,** wander through offbeat **Užupis,** and take a day-trip to **Trakai Castle,** the ancient capital.

ESSENTIALS

FACTS AND FIGURES

Official Name: Republic of Lithuania.
Capital: Vilnius.
Major Cities: Kaunas, Klaipėda.
Population: 3,575,000.

Time Zone: GMT +2.
Language: Lithuanian.
Number of Tractors: 101,300.
Vehicle Density: 18.5 per sq. km.

WHEN TO GO

Summer is brief but glorious in Lithuania, while winter is long and cold. Tourist season peaks betweeen June and September, especially along the coast, where temperatures reach 22°C (72°F). A winter visit has its charms, especially if you're headed for Vilnius, but be aware that the coast all but closes in the low season.

DOCUMENTS AND FORMALITIES

 ENTRANCE REQUIREMENTS.
Passport: Required for all travelers.
Visa: Not required for stays under 90 days for citizens of Australia, Canada, Ireland, New Zealand, the UK, and the US.
Letter of Invitation: Not required for citizens of Australia, Canada, Ireland, New Zealand, the UK, and the US.
Inoculations: Recommended up-to-date on DTaP (diphtheria, tetanus, and pertussis), Hepatitis A, Hepatitis B, MMR (measles, mumps, and rubella), polio booster, and typhoid.
Work Permit: Required of all foreigners planning to work in Lithuania.
International Driving Permit: Required for all those planning to drive in Lithuania for periods of under 90 days except citizens of the United States.

EMBASSIES AND CONSULATES. Foreign embassies to Lithuania are in Vilnius (p. 684). Lithuanian embassies and consulates abroad include: **Australia,** 40B Fiddens Wharf Rd., Killara, NSW 2071 (☎02 94 98 25 71); **Canada,** 130 Albert St., Ste. 204, Ottowa, ON K1P 5G4 (☎613-567-5458; amb.ca@urm.lt). **Ireland,** 90 Merrion Rd., Ballsbridge, Dublin 4 (☎1 668 8292); **New Zealand,** 17 Koraha St., Remuera, Auckland 1005 (☎9 524 9463; jurgispec@hotmail.com); **UK,** 84 Gloucester Pl., London, W1U 6AU (☎20 74 86 64 01; amb.uk@urm.lt); **US,** 4590 MacArthur Blvd., Ste. 200, NW, Washington, D.C. 20007 (☎202-234-5860; amb.us@urm.lt). Check www.lithuania.embassyhomepage.com for more embassy info.

VISA AND ENTRY INFORMATION. Citizens of the EU do not need visas to travel to Lithuania. Citizens of Australia, Canada, New Zealand, the UK, and the US do not need a visa for stays of up to 90 days. Long-term visas for temporary residence (€60) can be purchased from the nearest embassy or consulate. Avoid crossing through Belarus to enter or exit Lithuania: not only do you need to obtain a transit visa (US$50) for Belarus in advance, but guards may hassle you at the border.

TOURIST SERVICES AND MONEY

TOURIST OFFICES. Major cities have official **tourist offices. Litinterp** (www.litinterp.lt) reserves accommodations and rents cars, usually without a surcharge. Most cities have have an edition of the *In Your Pocket* series, available at kiosks and some hotels. Employees at tourist stations often speak English.

EMERGENCY	Ambulance: ☎033. Fire: ☎011. Police: ☎022. General Emergency: ☎112.

MONEY. The unit of currency is the **Lita** (Lt), plural Litai or Litų. One Lita is equal to 100 Centų. The Lita is fixed to the euro at €1 to 3.45Lt until the euro replaces the Lita altogether after 2010. The rapidly expanding economy (growing at over 7% anually) has created **inflation** of over 3% in recent years. Exchange bureaus near the train station usually have poorer rates than **banks.** Most banks cash **traveler's checks** for 2-3% commission. **Vilniaus Bankas,** with outlets in major cities, accepts major credit cards and traveler's checks for a small commission. Most places catering to locals don't take credit cards. Additionally, some establishments that claim to take MasterCard or Visa may not actually be able to do so.

LITHUANIAN LITAI (LT)		
AUS$1 = 2.14LT		1LT = AUS$0.47
CDN$1 = 2.32LT		1LT = CDN$0.43
EUR€1 = 3.45LT		1LT = EUR€0.30
NZ$1 = 1.97LT		1LT = NZ$0.51
UK£1 = 5.08LT		1LT = UK£0.20
US$1 = 2.81LT		1LT = US$0.36

HEALTH AND SAFETY

Lithuania's medical facilities are quickly catching up to Western standards. However, while most hospitals are stocked in basic medical supplies, there is a shortage of doctors. Many doctors, too, expect immediate payment in cash. Drink bottled mineral water, and **boil tap water** for 10min. before drinking. Many bathrooms are nothing but a hole in the ground; carry toilet paper. Lithuania's **crime rate** is low, especially when it comes to violent crime towards tourists, though cab drivers will think nothing of ripping you off and petty crime is rampant. Nevertheless, Vilnius is one of the safer capitals in Europe. Lithuanian **police** are helpful but understaffed, so your best bet for assistance in English is your **consulate.**

Women traveling alone will be noticed but shouldn't encounter too much difficulty. Skirts, blouses, and heels are far more common than jeans, shorts, tank tops, or sneakers, but showing skin is acceptable in the club scene. **Minorities** traveling to Lithuania may encounter unwanted attention or discrimination, though most is directed toward Roma (gypsies). Lithuania has made little effort to accommodate **disabled** travelers. **Homosexuality** is legal but not always tolerated.

BY PLANE. AirBaltic, Delta, Finnair, LOT, Lufthansa, SAS, and other airlines fly into Vilnius, and Ryanair flies into Kaunas. However, if you're already near the Baltic, buses and trains are unbeatable.

BY TRAIN. Trains are more popular for international and long-distance travel. Two major lines cross Lithuania: one runs north-south from Latvia through Šiauliai and Kaunas to Poland; the other runs east-west from Belarus through Vilnius and Kaunas to Kaliningrad, branching out around Vilnius and Klaipėda.

BY BUS AND FERRY. Domestic **buses** are faster, more common, less crowded, and only a bit more expensive than trains. Whenever possible, try to catch an express bus; such buses are normally marked with an asterisk or an "E" on the timetable. They are typically direct and can be up to twice as fast. Vilnius, Kaunas, and Klaipėda are easily reached by train or bus from Estonia, Latvia, Poland, and Russia. **Ferries** connect Klaipėda with Arhus and Aabenraa, DEN; Kiel, Zasnicas, and Mukran, GER; Baltijskas, RUS; and Ahus and Karlshamn, SWE.

BY CAR AND BY TAXI. All travelers planning to **drive** in Lithuania must purchase a Liability Insurance Policy at the Lithuanian border (79Lt for the min. 15-day). These policies may only be purchased with Litas, so make sure to convert some cash before reaching the border. There are inexpensive **taxis** in most cities. Agree on a price before getting in, or make sure that the meter is running. **Hitchhiking** is common; locals line up along major roads leaving large cities. Many drivers charge a fee comparable to local bus fares. Let's Go does not recommend hitchhiking.

KEEPING IN TOUCH

PHONE CODES	**Country code: 370. International dialing prefix: 810.** For more info on how to place international calls, see **Inside Back Cover.**

EMAIL AND INTERNET. Internet is widely available in Lithuania, though rarely for free. Most well-located Internet cafes charge 3-6Lt per hr.

TELEPHONE. There are two kinds of public **phones:** rectangular ones take magnetic strip cards, and rounded ones take chip cards. Phone cards (8-30Lt) are sold at phone offices and kiosks. Calls to Estonia and Latvia cost 1.65Lt per min.; Europe 5.80Lt; and the US 7.32Lt. Major cell phone operators include **Bite, Omnitel,** and **Tele2.** International access numbers include: **AT&T Direct** (☎8 800 900 28); **Canada Direct** (☎8 800 900 04); and **Sprint** (☎8 800 958 77).

MAIL. Airmail *(oro pastu)* **letters** abroad cost 1.70Lt (postcards 1.20Lt) and take about one week to reach the US. **Poste Restante** is available in Vilnius but hard to find elsewhere. Address the envelope as follows: first name LAST NAME, POSTE RESTANTE, post office address, Postal Code, city, LITHUANIA.

LANGUAGE. Lithuanian is one of only two Baltic languages (Latvian is the other). All "r"s are trilled. **Polish** is helpful in the south and **German** on the coast. **Russian** is understood in most places. Most Lithuanians understand basic English phrases. If someone seems to sneeze at you, he might be saying *ačiu* (ah-choo; thank you). For a phrasebook and glossary, see **Appendix: Lithuanian,** p. 1064.

ACCOMMODATIONS AND CAMPING

LITHUANIA	❶	❷	❸	❹	❺
ACCOMMODATIONS	under 30Lt	31-80Lt	81-130Lt	131-180Lt	over 180Lt

Lithuania has many youth **hostels,** particularly in Vilnius and Klaipėda. HI membership is nominally required, but an LJNN guest card (10.50Lt at any of the hostels) will suffice. Their *Hostel Guide* has maps and info on bike and car rentals and hotel reservations. **Hotels** across the price spectrum abound in Vilnius and most major towns. **Litinterp,** with offices in Vilnius, Kaunas, and Klaipėda, assists in finding homestays or apartments for rent. **Camping** is restricted by law to marked campgrounds; the law is well enforced, particularly along the Curonian Spit.

FOOD AND DRINK

LITHUANIA	❶	❷	❸	❹	❺
FOOD	under 8Lt	8-17Lt	18-30Lt	31-40Lt	over 40Lt

Lithuanian cuisine is heavy and sometimes greasy. Keeping a **vegetarian** or **kosher** diet is difficult. Restaurants serve various types of *blynai* (pancakes) with *mėsa* (meat) or *varske* (cheese). *Cepelinai* ("zeppelins") are potato-dough missiles of meat, cheese, and mushrooms; *saltibarščiai* is a beet-and-cucumber soup prevalent in the east; *karbonadas* is breaded pork fillet; and *koldunai* are meat dumplings. Lithuanian **beer** flows freely. *Kalnapis* is popular in Vilnius and most of Lithuania, *Baltijos* reigns supreme around Klaipėda, and the award-winning *Utenos* is everywhere. Lithuanian **vodka** *(degtinė)* is also popular.

HOLIDAYS AND FESTIVALS

Holidays: New Year's Day and Flag Day (Jan. 1); Independence Day (Feb. 16); Restoration of Independence (Mar. 11); Easter (Mar. 23-24, 2008; April 12-13, 2009); Labor Day (May 1); Statehood Day (July 6); Assumption (Aug. 15); All Saints' Day (Nov. 1).

Festivals: Since the 19th century, regional craftsmen have gathered to display their wares each March in Vilnius at the Kaziukas Fair.

BEYOND TOURISM

For more info on opportunities across Europe, see **Beyond Tourism**, p. 56.

Lithuanian Academy of Theater and Music, Gedimino pr. 42, LT-01110 Vilnius, Lithuania (☎37 05 21 24 96; www.lmta.lt). Classes in music, art, and theater in Lithuania. Offers some music and multimedia arts classes in English.

VILNIUS   ☎ 5

In 1323 an iron wolf on the top of Gediminas's Hill is said to have appeared to the Grand Duke in a dream and inspired him to found the city. It remains a good vantage point to take in the extraordinary breadth of Lithuania's capital, which has turned its gaze resolutely toward modernity. The decades of decaying ruins in the city are steadily giving way to stucco facades, Prada storefronts, and refurbished Baroque, Gothic, and Neoclassical architecture—reminders that Vilnius flourished for centuries before WWII and the iron grip of Soviet rule. Vilnius was chosen as one of the European Union's 2009 European Capitals of Culture.

▐ TRANSPORTATION

Flights: Vilnius International Airport (VNO; Vilniaus oro uostas), Rodūnės Kelias 10a (info ☎230 6666; www.vilnius-airport.lt), 5km south of town. Buy a bus ticket (1.10Lt) from the Lietuvos Spauda kiosk on your right as you exit the hall. Take Bus #1 to the Geležinkelio Stotis train station to reach the Old Town.

Trains: Geležinkelio Stotis, Geležinkelio 16 (☎233 0086, reservations in English 269 3722). Domestic tickets are sold in the hall to the left of the main entrance; international ticketing is directly to the left of the main doors. Open daily 6-11am and noon-6pm. Trains run to: **Berlin, GER** (22hr., 1 per day, 305Lt); **Kaliningrad, RUS** (7hr., 14 per day, 48Lt); **Minsk, BLR** (6hr., 2 per day, 20-60Lt); **Moscow, RUS** (17hr., 3 per day, 110Lt); **St. Petersburg, RUS** (18hr., 3 per day, 90Lt); **Rīga, LAT** (8hr., 1 per day, 118Lt); **Warsaw, POL** (8hr., 2 per day, 85Lt).

Buses: Autobusų Stotis, Sodų 22 (☎290 1661, reservations 216 2977; www.toks.lt). **Eurolines Baltic International (EBI;** ☎215 1377; www.eurolines.lt) offers routes to **Berlin, GER** (17hr., 1 per day, 187Lt); **Rīga, LAT** (5hr., 4 per day, 45Lt); **St. Petersburg, RUS** (18hr., 4 per day, 129Lt); **Tallinn, EST** (9hr., 2 per day, 81Lt); **Warsaw, POL** (9-10hr., 3 per day, 105Lt); and other points west. Tickets in EBI kiosks to the right of the entrance to the bus station. English spoken. ISIC discount. Open daily 6am-10pm.

Public Transportation: Buses and **trolleys** run daily 4am-midnight. Buy tickets at any **Lietuvos Spauda** kiosk (1.10Lt) or from the driver (1.40Lt). Tickets are checked frequently; punch them on board to avoid the 10Lt fine.

Taxis: Martono (☎240 0004). Cabbies are notorious for overcharging foreigners; get a local to hail one for you if at all possible. Make sure the meter is running or agree on a price before getting in.

J. Lelevelio g.   Vilniaus g.   Tilto g.   Radvilų g.   Žygimantų g.   Neris R.

Arsenalo g.

TO ANTAKALNIS
CEMETERY (300m)
AND CHURCH OF ST.
PETER AND PAUL (2km)

UK

Kalnų
Park

TO R (200m), MUSEUM OF
GENOCIDE VICTIMS (400m),
PARLIAMENT (1km)

Lithuanian
National
Museum

Gediminas, Tower,
and Higher Castle

Vilnia R.

T. Vrublevskio g.   Z. Liauksmino g.   K. Šyrvido g.   Tilto g.

Supermarket

Gedimino pr.

Canada

Australia

24-hour ATM/Bank

Lithuanian National
Drama Theater

Arkikatedra
Bazilika

Clock
Tower

Gedimino
Hill

TO HILL OF
THREE CROSSES
(600m)

TO VILNA GAON
JEWISH STATE
MUSEUM OF
LITHUANIA (50m)

Totoriu g.   Jogailos g.   Vilniaus g.

Labdarių g.

Odminiu g.

Restoration of
the Royal Palace

ARKIKATEDROS
AIKŠTĖ

Gediminas
Statue

Islandijos g.

Pamenkalnio g.

Sventaragio g.

OLD
TOWN

B. Radvilaitės g.

Maironio g.

Sereikiškių
Park

K. Kalinausko g.

Palangos g.

Liejyklos g.   Benediktinų g.

Totoriu g.   Sv. Ignoto g.   Vilniaus g.

DAUKANTO
SQUARE

VILNIUS
UNIVERSITY

S. Skapo g.

Pilies g.   Bernardinų g.

Mickiewicz
Memorial
Apartment

St. Anne's and
Bernadine's Monstery

TO FRANK ZAPPA
MONUMENT (50m), US (400m)

Klaipėdos g.

President's
Palace

St. John's

Collegium

Sv. Mykolo g.

St. Michael's and
Architecture
Museum

St. Catherine's

Church of the
Holy Spirit

Universiteto g.   Sv. Jono g.

Literatų g.

Rusų g.

Lithuanian National
Museum of Theater,
Music and Cinema Art

Dominikonu g.

Stikliu g.   Žydų g.

Svarco g.

France

Latako g.

Išganytojo

Maironio g.

Vilnia R.

TO (1km)

Incubator

Užupio g.   Paupio

AmEx

M. Antokolskio   Vokiečių g.

Vilnius
Picture
Gallery

Bokšto g.

J. Basanavičiaus g.

TO OTHER
EMBASSIES (1.2km)

Traku g.   Kėdainių g.

TAXI

Savičiaus g.

Aukštaičių g.

Vingriu g.

Naugarduko g.

Lydos g.

Žemaitijos g.

Sv. Mikalojaus g.

St. Nicholas'

Ašmenos g.

Rudninku g.

St. Nicholas'

Town Hall and
Lithuanian
Artists' Center

Supermarket

Didžioji g.

Sv. Kazimiero g.

Bokšto g.

Kūdrų g.   Maironio g.

Ligoninės g.

Šiaulių g.   Mėsiniu g.

St. Casimir's

Artillery
Bastion

Aguonu g.

Šaltiniu

Pylimo g.   Ploščiu g.

Vilnius Choral
Synagogue

Kaменitu g.   Arklių g.   Visu Šventuju g.

Etmonu g.

Pasažo g.

National
Philharmonic

Aušros Vartu g.

Orthodox Church
of the Holy Spirit

A. Strazdelio

Subačiaus g.

M. Daukšos g.

K. Vanagelio g.

Juodoji

Kruopu g.   Kuopu g.

St. Theresa's

Sv. Dvasios g.

Raugyklos g.   Sv. Stepono g.

TAXI

Geliu g.   Pylimo g.

Bazilijonu g.

Gates of Dawn

Prie
Hales
Market

Aušros Vartu g.

Lapu g.

F. Šopeno g.

Sodu g.   Stoties g.

Seinu g.

Geležinkelio g.

Peleso g.

TO (5km)

LITHUANIA

Vilnius

🏠 ACCOMMODATIONS
Arts Academy Hostel, **3**
Filaretai Youth
   Hostel (HI), **4**
LITINTERP, **1**

🍴 FOOD
Čili Pica, **5**
Cozy, **2**

🎵 NIGHTLIFE
Broadway, **7**
Helios, **6**
ŠMC, **8**

Autobusu
Stotis

TO PANERIAI
MEMORIAL
(8km)

Gelezinkelio
Stotis

Peleso g.   Liepkalnio g.

0   150 meters
0   150 yards

✦🛈 ORIENTATION AND PRACTICAL INFORMATION

Geležinkelio runs east from the train and bus stations to **Aušros Vartų**, which leads downhill through the **Gates of Dawn** (Aušros Vartai) and into the **Old Town** (Senamiestis). Heading north, Aušros Vartų becomes **Didžioji** and then **Pilies** before reaching the base of Gediminas Hill. On the hill, the **Gediminas Tower** of the Higher Castle presides over **Cathedral Square** (Katedros Aikštė) and the banks of the River Neris. **Gedimino,** the main commercial artery, runs west from Katedros Aikštė.

Tourist Office: Vilniaus 22 (☎262 9660; www.vilnius.lt). Open M-F 9am-6pm, Sa 10am-4pm. Branches in the train station (☎269 2091) and town hall (☎262 6470). Open M-F 9am-6pm, Sa-Su 10am-4pm. **Laisvalaikis** discount card (100Lt) offers good deals for long-term visitors; the card is available at Respublika offices (☎852 123 344).

Embassies: Australia, Vilniaus 23 (☎212 3369; www.lithuania.embassy.gov.au/lt.html). Open Tu 10am-1pm, Th 2-5pm. **Canada,** Jogailos 4 (☎249 0950; www.canada.lt). Open daily 8:30am-5pm; consular section M, W, F 9am-noon. Open daily 8:30am-5pm. **UK,** Antakalnio 2 (☎246 2900, emergency 869 837 097; www.britain.lt). Open M-Th 8:30am-5:45pm, F 8:30am-3:30pm; consular services M-F 8:30am-11:30am. Open M-Th 8:30am-5pm, F 8:30am-4pm. **US,** Akmenų 6 (☎266 5600; www.usembassy.lt). Open M-F 8am-4pm; consular services M-Th 8:30am-11:30am. Closed last W of each month.

Currency Exchange: Vilniaus Bankas, Vokiečių 9, cashes traveler's checks. Open M-Th 9am-6pm, F 9am-5pm. **Parex Bankas,** Geležinkelio 6, to the left of the train station. Open 24hr.

24hr. Pharmacy: Gedimino Vaistinė, Gedimino pr. 27 (☎261 0135). Only essential items available at night.

Hospital: Baltic-American Medical and Surgical Clinic, Nemenčinės 54A (☎234 2020 or 698 526 55; www.bak.lt). Accepts major American, British, and international insurance plans. Doctors on call 24hr.

Internet Access: Collegium, Pilies 22 (☎261 8334). 6Lt per hr. Open M-F 8am-10pm, Sa-Su 11am-10pm.

Post Office: Lietuvos Paštas, Gedimino 7 (☎261 6759; www.post.lt), west of Katedros Aikštė. Poste Restante at the window labeled "iki pareikalavimo"; 0.50Lt fee. Open M-F 7am-7pm, Sa 9am-4pm. **Postal Code:** 01001.

🏠🍴 ACCOMMODATIONS AND FOOD

Young travelers flock to the clean, friendly ▓**Filaretai Youth Hostel (HI) ❷**, Filaretų 17, in Užupis, 1km east of the Old Town. Walk east on Užupio across the Vilnia River. At the fork, bear left onto Krivių, then bear right onto Filaretų. (☎215 4627; www.filaretaihostel.lt. Laundry 10Lt. Free Internet. Reserve ahead June-Sept. and weekends. Dorms 35Lt first night, 32Lt every night thereafter; triples and quads 42-52Lt. 4Lt HI discount. MC/V.) **Arts Academy Hostel ❶**, Latako 2, provides basic, centrally located rooms at unbeatable prices. (☎212 0102. Dorms only in summer. Dorms 18Lt; singles 43Lt; doubles 76Lt; triples 72-76Lt. Cash only.) **LITINTERP ❷**, Bernardinv 7/2, places guests in B&Bs in the Old Town or in its own beautiful, spacious rooms. (☎212 3850; www.litinterp.lt. Reception M-F 8:30am-5:30pm, Sa 9am-3pm. Reserve ahead. Singles 80-140Lt, with bath 100Lt; doubles 140-160Lt; triples 180-210Lt. 5% ISIC discount. MC/V.) Ultra-70s art deco decor make **Cozy ❶**, Dominikonų 10, strangely cozy. Choose from a wide variety of coffees and teas. (☎261 1137; www.cozy.lt. Free Wi-Fi. English menu. Open M-W 9am-2am, Th 9am-4am, Sa 10am-4am, Su 10am-2am.) **Čili Pica ❶**, Didžioji 5, dishes out pizza until 3am. For the cheapest eats, join women in babushka scarves at **Halés Market,** sandwiched between Pylimo and Bazilijonv near the Gates of Dawn. (Large loaves of bread 0.50-2Lt. Open M-F 7am-7pm, Sa-Su 7am-3pm.) **Iki** supermarkets stock local and Western brands. (Branch at Sodu 22. Open daily 8am-10pm.)

🌀 SIGHTS

SENAMIESTIS. Facing the northern side of the **Gates of Dawn** (Aušros Vartai), enter the first door on the left to ascend to the 17th-century **Gates of Dawn Chapel** (Aušros Vartai Koplyčia). A few steps down Aušros Vartų, a gateway leads to the **Orthodox Church of the Holy Spirit** (Šv. Dvasios bažnyčia), home to the remains of Saints Anthony, John, and Eustachio, beloved martyrs of Lithuania. The preserved bodies of Saints Antonius, Eustachius, and Ivan, martyred in 1347 by pagan militants, are clothed in black during Lent, white during Christmas, and red during the remainder of the year—except on June 26, when they're displayed naked. Heading north, the street merges with Pilies and leads to **Vilnius University** (Vilniaus Universitetas), at Pilies and Šv. Jono. Founded in 1579, the university is the oldest in Eastern Europe. North on Pilies is **Cathedral Square** (Katedros Aikštė); its **cathedral** contains the ornate **Chapel of St. Casimir** (v. Kazimiero koplyčia) and the royal mausoleum. Walk up the hill to **Gediminas Tower** for a great view. Europe's most unexpected monument stands 50km west of the Old Town: a 4m steel shaft topped with a bust of the late freak rock legend 📷**Frank Zappa** against a backdrop of spectacular wall graffiti. Zappa had no connection to Lithuania, but apparently he had fans there. *(Off Pylimo, between Kalinausko 1 and 3, on the right side of a parking lot.)*

OLD JEWISH QUARTER AND PANERIAI MEMORIAL. At the start of WWII, Vilnius had a thriving Jewish community of 100,000 (in a city of 230,000). Nazis left just 6000 survivors, and the **synagogue** at Pylimo 39 is the only of the former 105 synagogues still standing. The **Vilna Gaon Jewish State Museum of Lithuania** commemorates the city's Jewish heritage, providing an honest account of Lithuanians' persecution of their Jewish neighbors on the eve of the war. *(Pylimo 4. ☎212 7912; www.jmuseum.lt. Open M-Th 10am-5pm, F 10am-4pm. Donations requested.)* For a kosher meal or info on locating ancestors, visit the **Chabad Lubavitch Center.** *(Šaltiniv 12. ☎215 0387. Open daily 9am-6pm.)* The **Paneriai Memorial,** Agrastų 15, southwest of the city, marks the spot in a forest where Nazis butchered 100,000 Lithuanians—70,000 of them Jews. The memorials are near pits that served as mass graves. *(Take the train to Paneriai from Platforms 5 and 7. 10min., 0.90Lt. From the station, take a right and follow Agrastų. Open M and W-F 11am-5pm. Free.)*

REPUBLIC OF UŽUPIS

Cross over the Vilnia River, and you'll find residents of an off-beat artists' community that declared itself the independent Rebublic of Užupis in 1997, with its own president, flag, constitution, and army of 12 men. Although many of its eccentric citizens are fleeing rising prices, the remaining studios and landmarks make its winding streets still worth a visit.

Greet the **Užupis Angel (1)** in the town square. This massive statue, unveiled in 2002 on April Fool's Day, the Republic's national holiday, symbolizes the rebirth of artistic freedom. The offbeat **constitution (2)** is just around the corner, engraved in English, French, and Lithuanian. You might catch a local goldsmith working at the **Užupis Galerija (3)**, or chat up some young artists at the **Incubator (4)**, a graffitied artist's workshop and hangout by the river. Finally, rest your feet and enjoy thin-crust pizzas at **Prie Angelo (5)**, Užupio 9. Entrees 10-28Lt. Open M-Th and Su 10am-11pm, F-Sa 10am-midnight. MC/V.

MUSEUM OF GENOCIDE VICTIMS. The horrors of the Soviet regime are on full display at this former KGB headquarters, which served as a Gestapo outpost during WWII. The basement has isolation rooms, torture chambers, and an execution cell open to the public. *(Guided tours in Lithuanian 15Lt, in English or Russian 30Lt. Aukv 2a. Turn left after Gedimino 40, the building inscribed with names of KGB victims. ☎ 249 6264. English captions. Open Tu-Sa 10am-5pm, Su 10am-3pm. Museum 2-4Lt; W free. 50% discount for students June-Sept. English-language audio tour 8Lt.)*

▨ TRAKAI CASTLE. Built in the 14th century, Trakai Castle lies on an island 28km west of Vilnius and once served as a residence for the Grand Dukes of Lithuania. Consisting of a wonderfully preserved palace, dungeon, and four defense towers, the castle currently displays priceless collections of porcelain, weaponry, and artifacts (including hundreds of smoking pipes). Highlights include the coin gallery and the fascinating ethnography exhibit about the Dzūkija, Tartar, and Karaimai minority groups. *(Buses leave for Trakai from Vilnius about 2hr. from platforms 8 and 9. 3Lt; pay. From Trakai station, head toward the water and bear left on the lakeside path. Continue for approx. 3km to reach the castle. Open daily 10am-7pm. 10Lt, 5Lt ISIC discount.)*

🎵 🎭 ENTERTAINMENT AND NIGHTLIFE

The National Philharmonic's **Vilniaus Festivalis** starts in late May or early June (www.filharmonija.lt). Check *Vilnius in Your Pocket* and *Exploring Vilnius*, distributed at hotels, or the Lithuanian-language morning paper *Lietuvos Rytas* for event or festival listings. English-language movies are shown at **Lietuva Cinema,** Pylimo 17 (☎ 262 3422), which has the biggest screen in Lithuania. Look for postcards announcing events and offering club discounts. For info on **GLBT nightlife,** check www.gayline.lt. **Broadway** (Brodvėjus), Mėsinių 4, is an enormously popular club. (Cover 10Lt, includes 2 drinks. Open M noon-3am, Tu noon-4am, W-Sa noon-5am, Su noon-2am. MC/V.) Ultra-modern style and an all-night sushi bar make **Helios,** Didžioji 28, the latest craze in Vilnius. (Dress code enforced. 21+. Cover 15Lt. Open Tu-Sa 10pm-5am.) The chrome-and-black outdoor patio at **ŠMC** (Contemporary Art Center), Vokiečiv 2, fills with a young and hip clientele. (Beer 6Lt. Open Su-Th 11am-midnight, F 11am-3am, Sa noon-3am. MC/V.)

KAUNAS ☎ 37

Kaunas (pop. 381,300) marked the Russian border in the late 17th century and served as the capital of Lithuania between WWI and WWII. Today, it is the nation's second-largest city. At the eastern end of **Laisvfs,** the main pedestrian boulevard, the silver domes of the **Church of St. Michael the Archangel** sparkle over the city. (Open M-F 9am-3pm, Sa-Su 8:30am-2pm. Free.) Nearby, the **Devil Museum,** V. Putvinskio 64, exhibits more than 2000 depictions of the devil, who was revered as a guardian in Lithuanian folklore until Christianity rained on the Satanic parade. (Open Tu-Su 11am-5pm. 5Lt, students 2.50Lt.) The western end of Laisvfs merges with Vilniaus and leads to the well-preserved **Old Town.** Walk west from Old Town Square to reach the meeting of the Neris and Nemunas rivers and the beautiful **Santakos Park.** Take a bus to the **Ninth Fort,** where the Nazis killed 50,000 prisoners, 30,000 of them Jews. It now holds an exhibit on Lithuanians sent to Siberia during Stalin's purges. Telsai-bound buses (20min., 1.70Lt) from the main station stop in front of the fort. Return on the same bus, which stops every 10 to 30min. on the highway in front of the new museum. (☎ 37 77 15. Open M and W-Su 10am-6pm. Each museum 2Lt, students 1Lt.) Stumble through the pitch-black catacombs of St. Michael the Archangel at the **Museum for the Blind,** guided only by smells and sounds. (Open W 11am-3:30pm, Sa 11am-1:30pm. 3Lt.) At the **Museum of the History**

of **Lithuanian Medicine and Pharmacy,** Rotuses 28, visitors can catch a glimpse of 19th-
and 20th-century medical history through grotesque medical samples and funky recipes for love potions. (☎20 15 69. Open W-Su 10am-6pm. 3Lt.)

🏠**Kaunas Archdiocese GuestHouse ❷**, Rotuses 21, offers pristine rooms with private baths, making it the best find in Kaunas. (☎32 25 97; sveciunamai@kn.lcn.lt.
Singles 50Lt; doubles 80Lt; triples 110Lt; quads 130Lt. Cash only.) **Litinterp ❸**, Gedimino 28, arranges private rooms. (☎22 87 18; www.litinterp.lt. Open M-F 8:30am-
5:30pm, Sa 9:30am-3pm. Singles 80-120Lt; doubles 140-160Lt. MC/V.) Just off Laisvfs, **Metropolis ❷**, S. Daukanto 21, is popular with backpackers. (☎20 59 92. Singles
90Lt; doubles 100Lt-120Lt; triples 170Lt. MC/V.) Tables quake and chairs levitate
without warning at the wacky **Crazy House ❷**, Vilniaus 16, in the basement. It's
one of only two restaurants in the world where diners have to contend with moving furniture. (☎22 11 82. Entrees 6-26Lt. Open Su-Th 11am-midnight, F-Sa 11am-
2am. MC/V.) **Dviese ❶**, Vilniaus 8, is a small and bright restaurant whose hearty
lunch special (main course, soup, and tea; 6.50Lt) is a steal. (☎20 36 38. Open M-Sa
10am-midnight, Su 10am-11pm. Cash only.) The brewery **Avilys,** Vilniaus 34, features a hops- and honey-tinged menu, as well as an award-winning house brew.
(☎52 12 19 00; www.avilys.lt. Beer 4Lt. Open Tu-Th 9pm-4am, F-Sa 9pm-6am, Su
1pm-5pm. MC/V.) **Club Los Patrankos,** Savanoriv 124 (☎33 82 28; www.lospatran-
kos.lt), is a nighttime hotspot for techno, pop, and dancing.)Live DJ on weekends.
Open Tu-Th 9pm-4am, F-Sa 9pm-6am, Su 1-5pm. MC/V.)

To reach Kaunas from Vilnius, take a **bus** (1½hr., 2-3 per hr., 11-16Lt). The **tourist office** is at Laisvės 36. (☎32 34 36; http://visit.kaunas.lt. Open M-F 9am-6pm,
Sa-Su 9am-1pm and 2-6pm.) **Postal Code:** 3000.

KLAIPÉDA   ☎46

Strategically located on the tip of the Neringa peninsula, Klaipéda (pop. 192,500)
was briefly the capital of Prussia in the 19th century. As the northernmost Baltic
harbor that doesn't freeze, Klaipéda's port still serves as a major shipping hub, and
the city has a growing reputation as a jazz center. Follow Liepų eastward from the
intersection with H. Manto to reach the **Clock Museum** (Laikrodžių Muziejus),
Liepų 12, which displays everything from Egyptian sundials to Chinese candle
clocks. (English-language pamphlet in each room. Open Tu-Sa noon-5:30pm, Su
noon-4:30pm. 4Lt, students 2Lt.) The top of the 46m **Mary Queen of Peace Church
Tower,** Rumpiškės 6A, offers a panoramic view. (2Lt, tickets available from the
tourist office.) **Smiltynė,** across the lagoon, has gorgeous beaches. Would-be
pirates will enjoy roaming the decks of the three Old Fishing Vessels on the road
leading toward the **Sea Museum** (Lietuvos Jūrų Muziejus) in Smiltynė. To reach the
museum, purchase a ticket at the kiosk at the ferry terminal (2Lt) and ride a small
yellow tram. (www.juru.muziejus.lt. Open June-Aug. Tu-Su 10:30am-6:30pm; May
and Sept. W-Su 10:30am-6:30pm; Oct.-Apr. Sa-Su 10:30am-5pm. Tickets 4-8Lt.)

Klaipéda Traveler's Guesthouse (HI) ❷, Butkų Juzés 7-4, near the bus station, has
large, spotless dorms. (☎21 18 79; guestplace@yahoo.com. Dorms June-Sept.
42Lt; Oct.-May 32Lt. HI nonmembers 2Lt extra. Cash only.) When it comes to
food, head to **Péda ❷**, Targaus 10. Admire the works of Lithuanian metal sculptor Vytautas Karčiauskas while sipping coffee (2Lt), or enjoy a delicious entree
(10-18Lt) at an alcove table. Upstairs and around the corner, find the full gallery.
(☎41 07 10. Open M-Th and Su 11am-11pm, F-Sa 11am-midnight. MC/V.) **Kebab
stands** near the ferry terminal in Smiltynė sell cheap and satisfying fare (4Lt).
The **central market** in Klaipéda is on Turgaus aikštė. (Open daily 8am-6pm.) The
best bars line H. Manto on the mainland. 🏠**Kurpiai,** Kurpių 1A, is a popular restaurant and jazz club. (☎41 05 55; www.jazz.lt. Beer 7Lt. Live jazz nightly 9:30pm.
Cover F-Sa 10Lt. Open Su-M noon-midnight, Tu-Sa noon-2am. MC/V.)

Buses (☎41 15 47, reservations 41 15 40) go from Butkų Juzės 9 to Kaunas (3hr., 12 per day, 38Lt), Palanga (30-40min., 2 per hour, 4Lt), and Vilnius (4-5hr., 10-14 per day, 49Lt). **Ferries** (☎31 42 17, info 31 11 17) run from Old Port Ferry Terminal, Žvejų 8, to Smiltynė (7min., 2 per hr., 2Lt), with connections to Nida (1½hr., 7Lt). From the International Ferry Terminal, take microbus 8A to the city center (3Lt). The **tourist office**, offering **Internet** access (2Lt per hr.), is at Turgaus 7. (☎41 21 86; www.klaipedainfo.lt. Open M-F 9am-7pm, Sa-Su 10am-4pm.) **Postal Code:** 91247.

NIDA   ☎469

Windswept sand dunes and quiet hiking trails have long drawn vacationers to the former fishing village of **Nida** (pop. 1500). One of four municipalities that make up the town of Neringa, Nida is the largest settlement on the **Curonian Spit,** one of the longest sea spits in the world. From the center, turn onto Naglių and head south to the ▓**Drifting Dunes of Parnidis.** The remains of an immense sundial sit atop the tallest dune (69m), marking a spot where beachgoers have the unique opportunity to look down on both the Curonian Lagoon and the Baltic Sea at once. Along Naglių on the way to the dunes, the **Fisherman's Ethnography Museum** provides a snapshot of one local fisherman's life (☎523 72). The **Neringa Museum of History** (Neringos Istorijos Muziejus), Pamario 53, presents a thought-provoking exhibit on Neringa's history and fishing community (☎511 62. Open June-Aug. M-Su 10am-6pm; 2Lt, students 0.50Lt.) The regional specialty is *rūkyta žuvis* (smoked fish), served with bread. Stop by **Fischbrotchen ❶,** a yellow hut next to the bus station, for a 7Lt herring sandwich. (Open daily 11am-8pm.) From Naglių 18E, **buses** (☎524 72) run to Klaipėda/Smiltynė (1hr., 1 per hr., 7Lt). The **tourist office,** Taikos 4, opposite the bus station, arranges private rooms for a 5Lt fee. (☎523 45; www.visitneringa.com. Rooms 30-50Lt. Open June-Aug. M-Sa 10am-6pm, Su 10am-3pm; Sept.-May M-F 10am-1pm and 2-6pm, Sa 10am-3pm.) **Postal Code:** 93121.

PALANGA   ☎460

The country's largest botanical park, over 20km of shoreline, and an exuberant nightlife make Palanga (pop. 20,000) the hottest summer spot in Lithuania. The beach and the Pier are the main attractions, but Palanga's pride and joy is the Amber Museum (Gintaro Muziejus), housed in a mansion in the tranquil ▓**Botanical Gardens.** The collection includes 15,000 pieces of the fossilized resin—known as "Baltic Gold"—with primeval flora and fauna trapped inside. (☎513 19; www.pgm.lt. Open daily June-Aug. 10am-12:30pm and 1:30-7pm; Sept.-May 11am-4:30pm. 5Lt, students 2.50Lt.) **Mėguva ❷,** Valančiaus 1, just west of the Church of the Assumption, has plain and slightly musty rooms with private baths and TVs. (☎488 39. June singles 50Lt; doubles 80Lt. July-Aug. 60/120Lt. Sept.-May 40/60Lt. Cash only.) Cafes and restaurants line **Vytauto,** which runs parallel to the shore and passes the bus station, as well as the tourist-ridden pedestrian thoroughfare **J. Basanavičiaus,** perpendicular to Vytauto. Travelers hit the dance floor at **Honolulu Night Club,** S. Neriės 39, north of J. Basanavičiaus. (☎356 41. Open 10pm-2am). Buses (☎533 33) or microbuses from Klaipėda (30min., 2 per hr., 4Lt) arrive at Kretinjos 1. The **tourist office** to the right of the station books private rooms by email. (☎488 11; palangaturinfo@is.lt. Open daily 9am-2pm and 3-6pm.)

LUXEMBOURG

Tiny Luxembourg is often overlooked by travelers smitten with Dutch windmills or hungry for Belgian waffles. However, its castles rival those of the Rhineland, its villages are uncrowded and perfect for easy hikes, and Luxembourg City is a European financial powerhouse. It might be a stretch to call Luxembourg the "lux" of the Benelux countries, but the world's last grand duchy has considerable draw.

DISCOVER LUXEMBOURG: SUGGESTED ITINERARY

Budget two days for **Luxembourg City** (p. 692), where you can explore the capital's well-fortified tunnels by day and its lively nightlife after hours. The towns of **Echternach** (p. 696) and **Vianden** (p. 697) are notable stops, the former for its historic basilica and the latter for its hilltop château. From there, proceed west to the village of **Esch-sur-Sûre** (p. 697) for scenic hiking through wooded river valleys.

ESSENTIALS

FACTS AND FIGURES

Official Name: Grand Duchy of Luxembourg.

Capital: Luxembourg City.

Population: 480,000.

Land Area: 2,600 sq. km.

Time Zone: GMT+1.

Languages: Luxembourgish, French, and German. English is widely spoken.

Religion: Roman Catholic 87%.

No. of Cars per 1000 People: Approx. 650, one of the highest rates in the world.

WHEN TO GO

The sea winds that routinely douse Belgium with rain have usually shed their moisture by the time they reach Luxembourg; good weather prevails from May through October, although travelers leery of crowds may want to avoid July and August. Temperatures average 17°C (64°F) in summer, and 1°C (34°F) in winter.

DOCUMENTS AND FORMALITIES

EMBASSIES AND CONSULATES. Foreign embassies and consulates are in Luxembourg City. Luxembourgian embassies and consulates abroad include: **Australia,** Level 4, Quay West, 111 Harrington St., Sydney, NSW, 2000 (☎02 9253 4708); **UK,** 27 Wilton Cres., London, SW1X 8SD (☎020 72 35 69 61); **US,** 2200 Massachusetts Ave., NW, Washington, D.C., 20008 (☎202-265-4171; www.luxembourg-usa.org). **Canadians** should visit the Luxembourg embassy in Washington, D.C.; **Irish** citizens should go to the embassy in London.

VISA AND ENTRY INFORMATION. EU citizens do not need a visa. Citizens of Australia, Canada, New Zealand, and the US do not need a visa for stays of up to 90 days, beginning upon entry into any of the countries in the EU's freedom-of-movement zone. For more info, see p. 14.

TOURIST SERVICES AND MONEY

EMERGENCY	Ambulance: ☎ 112
	Fire: ☎ 112.
	Police: ☎ 113.

TOURIST OFFICES. Contact the **Luxembourg National Tourist Office**, Gare Centrale, P.O. Box 1001, L-1010 Luxembourg (☎ 42 82 821; www.visitluxembourg.lu).

MONEY. The **euro (€)** has replaced the **Luxembourg franc** as the unit of currency in Austria. For more info, see p. 16. The cost of living in Luxembourg City is quite high, although the countryside is more reasonable. Restaurant bills usually include a service charge, although an extra 5-10% tip can be a classy gesture. Tip taxi drivers 10%. Luxembourg has a 15% **value added tax (VAT)**, a sales tax applied to most purchased goods. The prices given in *Let's Go* include VAT. In an airport upon exiting the EU, non-EU citizens can claim a refund on the tax paid for goods purchased at participating stores. In order to qualify for a refund in a store, you must spend at least €100; make sure to ask for a refund form when you pay. For more info on qualifying for a VAT refund, see p. 19.

TRANSPORTATION

BY PLANE. The national airline, **Luxair** (☎ 2456 4242; www.luxair.lu), and a slew of other European airlines fly to the Luxembourg City airport (LUX). Cheap last-minute flights on Luxair are available online.

BY TRAIN AND BUS. A **Benelux Tourrail Pass** (€94 second class, under 26 €71) allows five days of unlimited train travel in a one-month period in Belgium, Luxembourg, and the Netherlands. Within Luxembourg, the **Billet Réseau** (€5, book of 5 €20) is good for one day of unlimited bus and train travel. The **Luxembourg Card** (€10-24) includes one to three days of unlimited transportation along with free or discounted admission to 50+ sights around the country.

BY BIKE AND THUMB. A 575km network of **cycling paths** already snakes its way through Luxembourg, and plans are in place to add another 325km to the network in the near future. Bikes aren't permitted on buses, but domestic trains will transport them for a small fee (€1.20). While Let's Go does not recommend hitchhiking as a safe means of transport, service areas in Luxembourg are popular places to hitch rides into Belgium, France, and the Netherlands, as many motorists stop to take advantage of relatively low fuel prices.

KEEPING IN TOUCH

PHONE CODES	Country code: 352. International dialing prefix: 00. Luxembourg has no city codes. For more info on how to place international calls, see **Inside Back Cover**.

TELEPHONES. There are no city codes in Luxembourg; from outside the country, dial 352 plus the local number. Public phones can only be operated with a phone card, available at post offices, train stations, and newspaper stands. Internet cafes are not abundant. **Mobile phones** are an increasingly popular and economical alternative (p. 29). International direct dial numbers include: **AT&T** (☎8002 0111); **British Telecom** (☎08002 0044); **Canada Direct** (☎8002 0119); **MCI** (☎8002 0112); **Sprint** (☎8002 0115); **Telecom New Zealand** (☎8002 0064); **Telstra Australia** (☎8002 0061).

LANGUAGE. The three official languages of Luxembourg are Luxembourgish, French, and German. While Luxembourgish, a West Germanic language, is used primarily in daily conversation, official documents are written in French, and the press is in German. English is often spoken as a second, third, or fourth language.

ACCOMMODATIONS AND CAMPING

LUXEMBOURG	❶	❷	❸	❹	❺
ACCOMMODATIONS	under €18	€18-24	€25-34	€35-55	over €55

Luxembourg's nine **HI youth hostels** (*Auberges de Jeunesse*) are often booked solid during the summer, and it's wise to reserve ahead. Many of the hostels close for several weeks in December. Beds are approximately €17-20. Contact **Centrale des Auberges de Jeunesse Luxembourgeoises** (☎26 27 66 40; www.youthhostels.lu) for more info. **Hotels** are typically expensive, costing upwards of €40 per night in the capital. Luxembourg is a camper's paradise, and most towns have nearby campsites. Contact **Camprilux** (www.camping.lu/gb/gbstart.htm) for more info.

FOOD AND DRINK

LUXEMBOURG	❶	❷	❸	❹	❺
FOOD AND DRINK	under €5	€5-9	€10-14	€15-22	over €22

Luxembourgish cuisine combines elements of French and German cooking. Specialties include *Judd mat Gaardenbou'nen* (smoked pork with beans), *Friture de la Moselle* (fried fish), and *Quetscheflued* (plum tart). Riesling wines, which show up most Chardonnays, are produced in the Moselle Valley.

HOLIDAYS AND FESTIVALS

Holidays: New Year's Day (Jan. 1); Maundy Thursday (Mar. 20); Easter (Mar. 23-24); Labor Day (May 1); Ascension (May 1); May Day (May 1); Whit Sunday and Monday (May 11-12); Corpus Christi (May 22); National Day (June 23); Assumption (Aug. 15); All Saints' Day (Nov. 1); Christmas (Dec. 25); St. Stephen's Day (Dec. 26).

Festivals: The weeks leading up to Lent bring parades and masked balls under the guise of Carnival. Echternach hosts the International Music Festival in May and June, while Riesling Open wine festivals kick off in Wormeldange, Ahn, and Ehnen during the 3rd weekend of September.

LUXEMBOURG

LUXEMBOURG CITY

As an international banking hot spot, Luxembourg City (pop. 76,000) has become one of the wealthiest cities in the world. Though small, the metropolis has a lot to offer, from the relics of its military history to the boons of its thriving economy.

▐ TRANSPORTATION

Flights: Findel International Airport (LUX; www.aeroport.public.lu), 6km from the city. Bus #16 (€2, 2-4 per hr.) runs to the train station. Taxis are €17-25 to the city center.

Trains: Gare CFL, pl. de la Gare (☎24 89 24 89; www.cfl.lu), a 15min. walk south of the city center. To: **Amsterdam, NTH** (6hr.; 1 per hr.; €52, under 26 €36); **Brussels, BEL** (2¾hr., 1 per hr., €30/16); **Ettelbrück** (25min., 3 per hr., €5); **Frankfurt, GER** (3½hr., 1 per hr., €52); **Paris, FRA** (2½-4hr., 1 per 2hr., €25-84).

Buses: For travel within the city, buy a **billet courte distance** (short-distance ticket; €1.50, book of 10 €10), valid for 1hr. A **billet réseau** (network pass; €5, book of 5 €20), also accepted on trains, allows for unlimited travel throughout the entire country for 1 day and is the most economical option for intercity travel. Most buses run until midnight. The **free night bus** (☎47 96 29 75) runs F-Sa 10pm-3:30am.

Taxis: €2.40 per km. 10% more 10pm-6am; 25% more on Su. **Colux Taxis:** ☎48 22 33.

Bikes: Rent from **Vélo en Ville,** 8 r. Bisserwé (☎47 96 23 83), in the Grund. Open Apr.-Oct. M-Sa 10am-noon and 1-8pm. €5 per hr., €13 per ½-day, €20 per day, €38 per weekend, €75 per week. Under 26 20% discount for full day and longer. MC/V.

✦ ❷ ORIENTATION AND PRACTICAL INFORMATION

Five minutes by bus and 15min. by foot from the train station, Luxembourg City's historic center revolves around the **Place d'Armes.** From the train station, follow av. de la Gare or av. de la Liberté, then watch for signs with directions to the city's main sights. From the pl. d'Armes, walk down r. de Chimay; you will see the **Pétrusse Valley** in front of you, the **Place de la Constitution** on your right, and the **Pétrusse Casemates** to your left. Once there, the city's lower areas, the **Grund** and the **Clausen,** will be located diagonally to your right and left, 10min. and 15min. on foot, respectively. Halfway between these areas are the **Bock Casemates.**

Tourist Offices: Grand Duchy National Tourist Office (☎42 82 82 20; www.ont.lu), in the train station. Open daily June-Sept. 8:30am-6:30pm; Oct.-May 9:15am-12:30pm and 1:45-6pm. **Luxembourg City Tourist Office,** pl. Guillaume II (☎22 28 09; www.lcto.lu). Open Oct.-Mar. M-Sa 9am-6pm, Su 10am-6pm; Apr.-Sept. M-Sa 9am-7pm, Su 10am-6pm. In summer, look for the helpful **"Ask Me"** representatives around the city. **Centre Information Jeunes,** 26 pl. de la Gare (☎26 29 32 00; www.visitlux-embourg.lu), across from the station inside Galerie Kons, provides young travelers with everything from tourist info to help on finding jobs in the area. Open M-F 10am-6pm.

Embassies: Ireland, 28 rte. d'Arlon (☎45 06 10). Open M-F 9:30am-12:30pm. **UK,** 5 bd. Joseph II (☎22 98 64; www.britain.lu). Open M-F 9:30am-12:30pm. **US,** 22 bd. Emmanuel Servais (☎46 01 23; luxembourg.usembassy.gov). Open M-F 8:30am-5:30pm. **Australians, Canadians,** and **New Zealanders** should contact their embassies in France or Belgium.

Currency Exchange: Banks are the only option for changing money or cashing traveler's checks. Most are open M-F 8:30am-4 or 4:30pm. Only the banks at the airport and at the train station are opened on weekends. Expect to pay commissions of €5 for cash and €8 for traveler's checks.

Luggage Storage: (☎49 90 55 74), in the train station. €3 per bag. 1-day storage during opening hours. Open daily 6am-9:30pm.

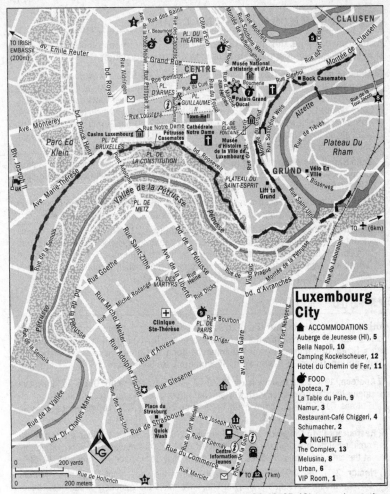

Laundromat: Quick Wash, 31 pl. de Strasbourg (☎26 19 65 42), near the station. Wash and dry €10. Open M-F 8:30am-6:30pm, Sa 8am-6pm.

Pharmacy: Pharmacies are marked by green crosses. Call ☎90 07 12 34 32 for a list of 24hr. pharmacies.

Hospital: Clinique St-Thérèse, 36 r. Ste-Zithe (☎49 77 61 or 49 77 65; www.zitha.lu). Call ☎90 07 12 34 32 for a schedule of 24hr. hospitals.

Internet Access: Centre Information Jeunes (see above) has limited free Internet for students. **Cyberbeach**, 3 r. du Curé, (☎26 47 80 70; www.cyber-beach.lu), by pl. d'Armes. From €1 per hr. Open M-F 10am-10pm, Sa 2-8pm.

Post Office: 38 pl. de la Gare, across the street and to the left of the station. Open M-F 6am-7pm, Sa 6am-noon. Address mail to be held according to the following example: First name LAST NAME, *Poste Restante*, L-1009 Luxembourg G-I Gare, LUXEMBOURG. Branch at 25 r. Aldringen, near pl. d'Armes. Open M-Sa 7am-7pm, Su 7am-5pm.

🏠🏕 ACCOMMODATIONS AND CAMPING

Aside from camping, the city hostel is the only budget option in Luxembourg City. Hotels are cheaper near the train station than in the city center.

Auberge de Jeunesse (HI), 2 r. du Fort Olisy (☎22 68 89 20; www.youthhostels.lu). Take bus #9 (dir.: Neudorf) and ask to get off at the hostel. From bus stop, take the steep pathway down alongside bridge. This new hostel has river views and a restaurant. Bike rentals €8 per half-day, €15 per day. Breakfast and linens included. In-room lockers; bring or rent a lock. Laundry €7.50. Internet €2.50 per 30min. Reception 24hr. Call ahead to reserve shuttles straight from airport (€3) or train station (€2), M-F 9am-5pm. Dorms €23; singles €35; doubles €55. €3 HI discount. AmEx/MC/V. ❷

Bella Napoli, 4 r. de Strasbourg (☎49 33 67). Hotel located above a pizza joint. Simple rooms with hardwood floors and full bath. Breakfast included. Reception 8am-midnight. Singles €41; doubles €48; triples €60. AmEx/MC/V. ❹

Hotel Du Chemin De Fer, 4 r. Joseph Junck (☎49 35 28). Ordinary, clean rooms right across from the train station. Singles €45; doubles €65; triples €80. MC/V. ❸

Camping Kockelscheuer, 22 rte. de Bettembourg (☎47 18 15), 5km outside Luxembourg City. Take bus #5 from the station or city center to Kockelscheuer-Camping. Tennis courts, mini golf, hot water. Showers included. Laundry €5. Open Easter-Oct. Reception 7am-noon and 2-10:30pm; cars must arrive when reception is open. Tent sites €4.50, each additional adult €3.75. Cash only. ❶

🍴 FOOD

Although the area around the pl. d'Armes teems with a strange mix of fast-food joints and upscale restaurants, there are a few affordable and appealing alternatives. Stock up on groceries at **Supermarché Boon**, in Galerie Kons across from the train station. (Open M-F 8am-8pm, Sa 8am-6pm, Su 8am-noon.)

Apoteca, 12 r. de la Boucherie (☎26 73 77 77; www.apoteca.lu). Offers an innovative menu that changes weekly. Downstairs bar offers a less expensive, but limited menu. Entrees €16-29. Restaurant open Tu-Sa noon-2pm and 7:30-10pm; bar open Tu-Sa 5pm-1am. AmEx/MC/V. ❹

Restaurant-Café Chiggeri, 15 r. du Nord (☎22 82 36). Serves traditional French food amid shimmering, night-sky decor. Wine list offers 2300 vintages. Dine more affordably at the cafe downstairs. Entrees €17-24. Open daily 11am-midnight. AmEx/MC/V. ❹

Namur, 27 r. des Capucins (☎22 34 08), down the street from pl. d'Armes. Marble floors, outdoor seating, and elegant ambience make the selection of pastries, chocolates, and sundaes (€5-6) even sweeter. Open M 2-6pm, Tu-Sa 8:30am-6pm. MC/V. ❷

La Table du Pain, 37 av. de la Liberté (☎29 56 63). Serves sandwiches (€5-7), salads (€10-14), and baked goods on wooden tables. Open M-F 7am-6pm. Cash only. ❷

Schumacher, 18 av. de la Porte-Neuve (☎22 90 09). Get takeout for picnics in the Pétrusse Valley. Sandwiches €3-5. Open M-Sa 7am-6pm. AmEx/MC/V. ❶

👁 SIGHTS

Luxembourg City is compact enough to be explored on foot. The most spectacular views of the city are from **Place de la Constitution** and from the bridge closest to the **Bock Casemates.** For guidance on your stroll, follow the signs pointing out the **Wenzel Walk.** It leads visitors through 1000 years of history as it winds around the old city, from the **Chemin de la Corniche** down into the casemates.

FORTRESSES AND THE OLD CITY. The city's first fortress, built in AD 963, saw its network of fortifications expand so far over the years that the city earned the nickname "Gibraltar of the North." The fortress contains the ▧**casemates,** an intricate 17km network of tunnels through the fortress walls. First built to fortify the city's defenses, the casemates were partially dismantled when Luxembourg was declared a neutral state in 1867. Start at the **Bock Casemates** fortress, part of Luxembourg's original castle; the fortress looms over the Alzette River Valley and offers a fantastic view of the **Grund** and the **Clausen.** *(Entrance on r. Sigefroi, just past the bridge leading to the hostel. ☎ 22 28 09 or 22 67 53. Open Mar.-Oct. daily 10am-5pm. €1.75, students €1.50.)* A visit to the ▧**Pétrusse Casemates,** built by the Spanish in the 1600s, takes explorers down 250 steps into historic chambers while providing views of the Pétrusse Valley. A tour is required, but it's interesting, short (30min.), and cheap. *(Pl. de la Constitution. English-language tours 1 per hr., July-Aug. 11am-4pm; intermittently in June. €1.75, students €1.50.)* The peaceful paths of the green **Pétrusse Valley** beckon for a stroll or an afternoon picnic in the shadow of the fortress walls. More sedentary visitors can catch one of the **Pétrusse Express tourist trains** that depart from pl. de la Constitution and meander through the city and into the valley. *(Mid-Mar. to Oct. 2 per hr. 10am-12:30pm and 1:30-6pm. Trip lasts 50-60min. €8. Purchase tickets at pl. de la Constitution.)* Double-decker **tourist buses** allow you to "hop on" and "hop off" at will; recordings play commentary in multiple languages. *(Info for train and buses ☎ 26 65 11; www.sightseeing.lu. 3 per hr. 9:40am-5:20 or 6:20pm from marked stops throughout the city. €12, students €10. Ticket valid for 24hr. Wheelchair-accessible.)*

MUSEUMS. The **Luxembourg Card** covers entrance to 55 museums and tourist attractions throughout the country. *(www.luxembourgcard.lu. Available at tourist offices and youth hostels. 1-day card €10, 2-day €17, 3-day €24.)* The collection at the ▧**Musée National d'Histoire et d'Art** includes both modern and ancient art and a chronicle of the conquering powers' influences on Luxembourg's art. *(Marché-aux-Poissons, at r. Boucherie and Sigefroi. ☎ 47 93 30 214; www.mnha.lu. Open Tu-Su 10am-5pm. €5, students free.)* There's no gambling at **Casino Luxembourg,** only contemporary art exhibits. *(41 r. Notre Dame, near pl. de la Constitution. ☎ 22 50 45; www.casino-luxembourg.lu. Open M, W, F 11am-7pm, Th 11am-8pm, Sa-Su 11am-6pm. €4, under 26 €3, under 18 free.)* The **Musée d'Histoire de la Ville de Luxembourg** narrates the history of the city with interactive displays. Most exhibits are in French and German. *(14 r. du St-Esprit, near pl. de Clairefontaine. ☎ 47 96 45 00. Open Tu-W and F-Su 10am-6pm, Th 10am-8pm. €5, students €3.70.)*

NO WORK, ALL PLAY

MAKE A WISH, YOUR HIGHNESS

Luxembourg's diminutive size doesn't stop it from throwing one hell of a royal birthday party. The circumstances of the June 23 bash are a little puzzling, since Grand Duke Henri, the head of Luxembourg's constitutional monarchy, was born on April 16, 1955. Henri inherited the date-changing from his grandmother, Grand Duchess Charlotte, born on January 23, 1896. When her court realized that mid-winter doesn't lend itself to open-air bashes, they pushed celebrations back five months. Reluctant to further confuse their subjects, both Henri and his father Jean took June 23 as their own.

A procession through the old city starts things off on the evening of June 22. At 11pm, fireworks rip through the air, putting the city's bridges into sharp relief. In a flash, the narrow streets are transformed into impromptu all-ages bars and dance floors; alcohol flows like water, spirits are high, and it takes the rising sun to finally break up the party. The disheveled partygoers pour into the Place d'Armes for breakfast before staggering home to sleep. June 23 is a public holiday, so once the city wakes around noon, everyone heads downtown to see Henri strolling through the streets. With his aged parents in tow and royal security out of sight, the duke restores calm and a sense of routine to a city unaccustomed to such glorious commotion.

🎵 🎭 ENTERTAINMENT AND NIGHTLIFE

There is no central location for nightlife in Luxembourg City, so an evening of bar-hopping also involves hopping on and off the city's night bus. In summer, the **Place d'Armes** comes to life with free concerts (www.summerinthecity.lu) and stand-up comedy. Pick up a copy of *UP FRONT* at the tourist office for nightlife options.

Melusina, 145 r. de la Tour Jacob (☎43 59 22). Eat at the classy restaurant or dance all night on weekends. Cover €8. 1 free drink 11pm-midnight. Restaurant open M-Sa noon-2pm and 7-11pm. Club open F-Sa 11pm-3am. Restaurant MC/V; club cash only.

Urban, at the corner of r. de la Boucherie and r. du Marché-aux-Herbes (☎26 47 85 78). A friendly, crowded bar in the heart of downtown. Beer €2-4. Mixed drinks €6. Open daily noon-1am. AmEx/MC/V.

The Complex, 42-44 r. de Hollerich, is a cluster of bars in the south of the city. Take bus #1 or 22, or walk on av. de la Gare away from the center. **Marx** caters to the 25+ crowd. DJs W and F-Sa. (☎48 84 26. Beer €2.20. Mixed drinks €6.50. Open M-F and Su 5pm-1am, Sa 6pm-1am. MC/V.) Next door, **Chocolate Elvis** features party music and beer (€2.20), the **Bronx** high decibels. (☎29 79 46. Mixed drinks €6-6.50. Open M-F 5pm-1am, Sa-Su 6pm-1am.)

VIP Room, 19 r. des Bains (☎26 18 78 67), near pl. du Théatre. Glitzy and exclusive, this club has an atmosphere modeled after VIP clubs in Paris and St-Tropez. Open before 7pm for dinner. Club open Tu 7pm-midnight, W-Sa 7pm-late. AmEx/MC/V.

THE ARDENNES

In 1944, one of the bloodiest battles of World War II, the Battle of the Bulge, took place in these hills. Now quiet towns, imposing castles, and stunning scenery make the Ardennes an ideal tourist attraction. Carry raingear, as the humidity here often breaks into short storms. Check transportation schedules thoroughly and budget extra time for waiting; the system is geared towards locals, not tourists.

ETTELBRÜCK. The main railway linking Luxembourg City to Liège, BEL, runs through Ettelbrück (pop. 7500), making the town the transportation hub for the Ardennes. Little else draws tourists to Ettelbrück, although history buffs waiting out a layover might check out the **General Patton Memorial Museum,** 5 r. Dr. Klein, which commemorates Luxembourg's liberation during WWII. (☎81 03 22. Open June-Sept. 15 daily 10am-5pm; Sept. 16-May 30 Su 2-5pm. €2.50.) Stay in the modest rooms of **Hotel Herckmans ❹,** 3 pl. de la Résistance. (☎81 74 28. Breakfast included. Singles €35-40; doubles €45-60; triples €80. AmEx/MC/V.) Grab a quick meal at **Bakes ❷,** 55 Grande Rue. (☎81 13 33. Sandwiches €2.65-4.20. Pastas €8.65. Open daily 7am-5:30pm. AmEx/MC/V.) **Trains** go to Clervaux (30min., 1 per hr., €5) and Luxembourg City (25min., 3 per hr., €4.50). Buy the €5 day pass for unlimited bus and train use for one day; validate the pass at the orange booth on the platform. To reach the **tourist office,** walk to the end of Grande Rue and turn right onto r. de Bastogne. (☎81 20 68; www.sit-e.lu. Open Tu-Sa 9am-noon and 1:30-5pm.)

ECHTERNACH. In the heart of the Little Switzerland region, Echternach (pop. 5200) is a paradise for **hikers** and **bikers.** The turrets of the 15th-century **town hall** share the skyline with the **Basilica of St. Willibrord,** less interesting inside than out. To get there, go down r. de la Gare and take a left at pl. du Marché. (Open M-Sa 9am-6pm, Su noon-6pm. Free.) The basilica and the intimate Église Saints Pierre-et-Paul host Echternach's renowned **International Music Festival** from May to July. (☎72 83 47; www.echternachfestival.lu. Tickets free to €47.) The remains of a **Roman villa,** 47a r. des Romains, can be found near the lake, a 25min. walk from the station; take r. de la Gare and make a right from pl. du Marché onto rte. de Luxembourg, then a left on r. C.M. Spoo, which will become r. des Romains. The museum and open-air exhibit cast light on the area's 2000-year history. (☎26 72 09 74; www.villa-echternach.lu. Open Tu-Sa from the Su before Easter-June 30 11am-1pm and 2-5pm; July-Aug. 11am-6pm; Oct.-Nov. 1 11am-1pm and 2-5pm. €3.)

The lakeside ▓Auberge de Jeunesse (HI) ❷, 1 chemin vert Roudenhaff, is a 30min. walk from the station and is equipped with a sports hall and an indoor climbing wall. Walk past the Roman villa to get there. (☎72 01 58; www.youthhostels.lu. Breakfast and linens included. Reception 8am-10pm. Check-in 2-10pm. Bike rental €2.50 per hr., €8 per half day, €16 per day. Reserve ahead in summer. Dorms €21; singles €33; doubles €26. €3 HI discount. MC/V.) Camping Officiel ❶, 5 rte. de Diekirch, is a 5min. walk from the bus station. (☎72 02 72; www.camping-echternach.lu. Laundry €2.50. Open 9am-7pm. Tent sites €5, extra person €5.00. AmEx/MC/V.) Pick up groceries at Match, near pl. du Marché. (Open M-F 8am-7pm, Sa 8am-1pm.) Buses run to Ettelbrück (#500; 50min., 1 per hr.) and Luxembourg City (#111 or 110; 45min.-1hr., 2 per hr.). Rent bikes at Trisport, 31 rte. de Luxembourg. (☎72 00 86. €2.50 per hr., €15 per day. Open Tu-Sa 9am-noon and 2-6pm.) The tourist office, 9 parvis de la Basilique, is in front of the Basilica. (☎72 02 30; www.echternach-tourist.lu. Open July-Aug. daily 9:30am-5:30pm; June and Sept. M-Sa 10am-noon and 2-5pm; Oct.-May M-F 9am-noon and 2-4pm.)

VIANDEN. The village of Vianden (pop. 2000) is home to one of the most impressive castles in Europe, the ▓Château de Vianden, which holds displays of armor, furniture, and tapestries. (☎84 92 91; www.castle-vianden.lu. Open daily Apr.-Sept. 10am-6pm; Oct. and Mar. 10am-5pm; Nov.-Feb. 10am-4pm. €5.50, students €4.50.) Take the Chairlift from 3 r. du Sanatorium up the mountain for thrilling views. (☎83 43 23. €3, round-trip €4.50. Open Easter-Oct. M-Sa 10am-5pm, Su 10am-6pm.) To get to the modern ▓Auberge de Jeunesse (HI) ❷, 3 Montée du Château, climb Grande Rue up the hill and toward the castle. The road will change to Montée du Château, and the hostel is behind Hotel Oranienburg. (☎83 41 77. Breakfast included. Reception 8-10am and 5-9pm. Dorms €19; singles €31. €3 HI discount.) Cozy Hotel Petry's Restaurant ❸, 15 r. de la Gare, serves filling dishes. (☎83 41 22. Meat entrees €6-19. Open May-Aug. daily 8am-9:30pm.) Buses head to Ettelbrück (#570; 30min., 2 per hr.) and Clervaux (#663; 40min., 2-4 per day). Rent bikes at the bus station. (Open mid-July to Aug. M-Sa 8am-noon and 1-5pm. €10 per half-day, €14 per day.) From the bus station, take r. de la Gare to the center of town; the tourist office, 1 r. du Vieux Marché, is over the bridge on the right. (☎83 42 571; www.tourist-info-vianden.lu. Internet €2 per hr. Open mid-July to Aug. M-F 8am-6pm, Sa-Su 10am-2pm; Sept.-June M-F 8am-noon and 1-5pm, Sa-Su 10am-2pm.)

ESCH-SUR-SÛRE. Cradled by the green Ardennes mountains and encircled by the ruins of Luxembourg's oldest castle, this village (pop. 320) is an ideal base for exploring the Haute-Sûre Nature Reserve, 15 rte. de Lultzhausen (☎89 93 311), or the area's 700km of nature trails. (Reserve open Mar.-Oct. M-Tu and Th-F 10am-noon and 2-6pm, Sa-Su 2-6pm; Nov.-Apr. closes 5pm.) Hotel de la Sûre ❸, 1 r. du Pont, the village's unofficial tourist office and best bet for lodgings, has a slew of activities and amenities. From the bus stop, walk up r. de l'Église (the street on the right closest to the tunnel) past the church. (☎83 91 10; www.hotel-de-la-sure.lu. Bike rental €5 per hr., €12-13 per half-day, €19-22 per day. Breakfast included. Free Internet. Reception 7am-midnight. Singles M-Th €27-70, F-Su €30-77. Discounts for longer stays. AmEx/MC/V.) Buses to Ettelbrück leave every hour, except on Sundays when they leave every two to four hours (#535; 25min.).

THE NETHERLANDS (NEDERLAND)

The Dutch take great pride in their country, in part because they created vast stretches of it, claiming land from the ocean using dikes and canals. With most of the country's land area below sea level, the task of keeping iconic tulips and windmills on dry ground has become something of a national pastime. Over the centuries, planners built dikes higher and higher to hold back the sea, culminating in a new "flexible coast" policy that depends on spillways and reservoirs to contain potentially disastrous flood waters. For a people whose land constantly threatens to become ocean, the staunch Dutch have a deeply grounded culture and down-to-earth friendliness. Time-tested art, ambitious architecture, and dynamic nightlife make the Netherlands one of the most popular destinations in Europe.

DISCOVER THE NETHERLANDS: SUGGESTED ITINERARIES

THREE DAYS. Go no farther than the canals and coffee shops of **Amsterdam** (p. 703). **Museumplein** is home to some of the finest art collections in Europe, while the houses of ill repute in the **Red Light District** are shockingly lurid.

ONE WEEK. Begin in the capital city of **Amsterdam** (4 days). Take time to recover among the stately monuments of **The Hague** (2 days; p. 723). End the week in youthful, hyper-modern **Rotterdam** (1 day; p. 725).

TWO WEEKS. You can't go wrong starting off in **Amsterdam** (5 days), especially if you detour to buy flowers in **Aalsmeer** (1 day; p. 720) and visit .the beaches of **Texel** (1 day; p. 729). The history of **Haarlem** (1 day; p. 721) is next, then on to **The Hague** (2 days) and **Rotterdam** (1 day). Explore museums in the college town of **Utrecht** (1 day; p. 726). The paths and galleries of **De Hoge Veluwe National Park** (1 day; p. 727) and **Maastricht** (1 day; p. 728) mark the end of the trail.

ESSENTIALS

FACTS AND FIGURES

Official Name: Kingdom of the Netherlands.

Capital: Amsterdam; The Hague is the seat of government.

Major Cities: The Hague, Rotterdam, Utrecht.

Population: 16,571,000.

Land Area: 41,500 sq. km.

Time Zone: GMT +1.

Language: Dutch; English is spoken almost universally.

Religions: Catholic (31%), Protestant (20%), Muslim (6%).

Land below sea level: One third of the country, kept dry by an extensive network of dikes 1500 miles (2400km) long.

WHEN TO GO

July and August are lovely for travel in the Netherlands, as the crowded hostels and lengthy lines during those months will confirm. If you fancy a bit more elbow

The Netherlands

THE NETHERLANDS

room, you may prefer April, May, and early June, as tulips and fruit trees furiously bloom and temperatures hover around 12-20°C (53-68°F). The Netherlands is famously drizzly year-round, so travelers should bring raingear.

DOCUMENTS AND FORMALITIES

EMBASSIES AND CONSULATES. Foreign embassies and most consulates in the Netherlands are in The Hague (p. 723). Both the UK and the US have consulates in Amsterdam (p. 703). Dutch embassies abroad include: **Australia,** 120 Empire Circuit, Yarralumla Canberra, ACT, 2600 (☎262 20 94 00; www.netherlands.org.au); **Canada,** 350 Albert St., Ste. 2020, Ottawa, ON, K1R 1A4 (☎613-237-5030; www.netherland-sembassy.ca); **Ireland,** 160 Merrion Rd., Dublin, 4 (☎12 69 34 44; www.netherland-sembassy.ie); **New Zealand,** P.O. Box 840, at Ballance and Featherston St., Wellington (☎044 71 63 90; www.netherlandsembassy.co.nz); **UK,** 38 Hyde Park Gate, London, SW7 5DP (☎20 75 90 32 00; www.netherlands-embassy.org.uk); **US,** 4200 Linnean Ave., NW, Washington, D.C., 20008 (☎202-244-5300; www.netherlands-embassy.org).

VISA AND ENTRY INFORMATION. EU citizens do not need a visa. Citizens of Australia, Canada, New Zealand, and the US do not need a visa for stays of up to 90 days, beginning upon entry into any of the countries in the EU's freedom of movement zone. For more info, see p. 14. For stays longer than 90 days, all non-EU citizens need visas (around US$80), available at Dutch embassies and consulates or online at www.minbuza.nl/en/home, the website for the Dutch Ministry of Foreign Affairs. It will take about two weeksafter application submission to receive a visa.

TOURIST SERVICES AND MONEY

EMERGENCY	Ambulance, Fire, and Police: ☎112.

TOURIST OFFICES. VVV (vay-vay-vay) tourist offices are marked by triangular blue signs. The website www.visitholland.com is also a useful resource. The **Holland Pass** (www.hollandpass.com, €25) grants free admission to five museums or sites of your choice and also provides discounts at restaurants and attractions.

MONEY. The **euro (€)** has replaced the **guilder** as the unit of currency in the Netherlands. For more info, see p. 14. As a general rule, it's cheaper to exchange money in the Netherlands than at home. A bare-bones day in the Netherlands will cost €35-40; a slightly more comfortable day will run €50-60. Hotels and restaurants include a service charge in the bill; additional tips are appreciated but not necessary. Taxi drivers are generally tipped 10% of the fare.

The Netherlands has a 19% **value added tax (VAT)**, a sales tax applied to retail goods. The prices given in *Let's Go* include VAT. In the airport upon exiting the EU, non-EU citizens who have stayed in the EU fewer than 180 days can claim a refund on the tax paid for purchases at participating stores. In order to qualify for a refund in a store, you must spend at least €130; make sure to ask for a refund form when you pay. For more info on qualifying for a VAT refund, see p. 15.

TRANSPORTATION

BY PLANE. Most flights land at Amsterdam's **Schiphol Airport** (**AMS;** ☎800 72 44 74 65, flight info 900 724 47 46; www.schiphol.nl). Budget airlines, like **Ryanair** and **easyJet,** fly out of **Eindhoven Airport** (**EIN;** ☎314 02 91 98 18; www.eindhovenairport.com), 10min. away from Eindhoven, and Amsterdam's Schiphol Airport, to locations around Europe. The Dutch national airline, **KLM** (☎020 474 7747, US ☎800-447-4747, UK ☎08705 074 074; www.klm.com), offers student discounts. For more info on traveling by plane around Europe, see p. 46.

BY TRAIN. The national rail company is **Nederlandse Spoorwegen** (**NS;** Netherlands Railways; www.ns.nl). **Sneltreinen** are the fastest, while **stoptreinen** make many local stops. One-way tickets are called *enkele reis*. Same-day, round-trip tickets (*dagretour*) are valid only on the day of purchase, but are roughly 15% cheaper than normal round-trip tickets. **Weekendretour** tickets are not quite as cheap, but are valid from 7pm Friday through 4pm Monday. A *dagkaart* (day pass) allows unlimited travel for one day, for the price of the most expensive one-way fare across the country. **Eurail** and **InterRail** passes are valid. The **Holland Railpass** is good for three or five travel days in any one-month period. Although available in the US, the Holland Railpass is cheaper in the Netherlands at DER Travel Service or RailEurope offices. Overall, train service tends to be faster than bus service. For more info on traveling by train around Europe, see p. 46.

ALL ABOARD. Nederlandse Spoorwegen is the Dutch national rail company, operating the country's intercity train service. Their website, www.ns.nl, has a user-friendly English-language section with train times, prices, and door-to-door directions for all stops in the Netherlands.

BY BUS. With transportation largely covered by the extensive rail system, bus lines are limited to short trips and travel to areas without rail lines. A nationalized fare system covers city buses, trams, and long-distance buses. The country is divided into zones: a trip between destinations in the same zone costs two strips on a *strippenkaart* (strip card); a trip in two zones will set you back three strips. On buses, tell the driver your destination and he or she will cancel the correct number of strips; on trams and subways, stamp your own in either a yellow box at the back of the tram or in the subway station. Drivers sell cards with two, three, and eight strips, but it's cheaper to buy 15-strip or 45-strip cards at tourist offices, post offices, and some newsstands. Day passes *(dagkaarten)* are valid for travel throughout the country and are discounted as special summer tickets *(zomerzwerfkaarten)* June through August. Riding without a ticket can result in a fine.

BY CAR. Normally, tourists with a driver's license valid in their home country can drive in the Netherlands for fewer than 185 days. The country has well-maintained roadways, although drivers may cringe at high fuel prices, traffic, and scarce parking near Amsterdam, The Hague, and Rotterdam. The yellow cars of the **Royal Dutch Touring Club** (**ANWB**; ☎ 08 00 08 88) patrol many major roads, and will offer prompt roadside assistance, in case of a breakdown.

BY BIKE AND BY THUMB. Cycling is the way to go in the Netherlands—distances between cities are short, the countryside is absolutely flat, and most streets have separate bike lanes. Bike rentals run €6-7 per day and €25-40 per week. For a database of bike rental shops and other cycling tips and info, visit www.holland.com/global/discover/active/cycling. **Hitchhiking** is illegal on motorways but common elsewhere. Droves of hitchhikers can be found along roads leading out of Amsterdam. Those choosing this mode of transport often try their luck close to a town. Let's Go does not recommend hitchhiking.

KEEPING IN TOUCH

EMAIL AND THE INTERNET. Email is easily accessible within the Netherlands. In small towns where Internet access is not listed, try the public library. Cities have an increasing number of hot spots, which offer Wi-Fi for free or for a small fee. Websites like www.jiwire.com, www.wi-fihotspotlist.com, and www.locfinder.net can help locate hot spots.

PHONE CODES	**Country code:** 31. **International dialing prefix:** 00. For more info on how to place international calls, see **Inside Back Cover.**

TELEPHONE. Some pay phones still accept coins, but phone cards are the rule. KPT and Telfort are the most widely accepted varieties, the former available at post offices and the latter at train stations (from €5). Whenever possible, use a calling card for international phone calls, as long-distance rates for national phone services are often very high. Mobile phones are an increasingly popular and economical option. Major mobile carriers include **Vodafone, KPN, T-Mobile,** and **Telfort.** For directory assistance, dial ☎ 09 00 80 08, for collect calls ☎ 08 00 01 01. Direct-dial access numbers for calling out of the Netherlands include: **AT&T Direct** (☎ 0800 022 91 11); **British Telecom** (☎ 0800 022 0444); **Canada Direct** (☎ 0800 022 91 16); **Telecom New Zealand** (☎ 0800 022 44 64); **Telstra Australia** (☎ 0800 022 00 61). For more info on calling home from Europe, see p. 28.

MAIL. Post offices are generally open Monday through Friday 9am-5pm, Thursday or Friday nights, and Saturday mornings in some larger towns. Amsterdam and

Rotterdam have 24hr. post offices. Mailing a postcard or letter within the EU costs €0.69 and up to €0.85 outside of Europe. To receive mail in the Netherlands, have mail delivered **Poste Restante.** Mail will go to the main post office unless you specify a subsidiary by street address. Address mail to be held according to the following example: First Name, Last Name, Poste Restante, followed by the address of the post office. Bring a passport to pick up your mail; there may be a small fee.

ACCOMMODATIONS AND CAMPING

NETHERLANDS	❶	❷	❸	❹	❺
ACCOMMODATIONS	under €36	€36-55	€56-77	€78-100	over €100

VVV offices around the country supply travelers with accommodation listings and can almost always reserve rooms for a €2-5 fee. **Private rooms** cost about two-thirds the price of a hotel, but are harder to find; check with the VVV. During July and August, many cities add a tourist tax (€1-2) to the price of all rooms. The country's 30 **Hostelling International (HI)** youth hostels are run by **Stayokay** (www.stayokay.com) and are dependably clean and modern. There is **camping** across the country, although sites tend to be crowded during the summer months; **CityCamps Holland** has a network of 17 well-maintained sites. The website www.strandheem.nl has camping info.

FOOD AND DRINK

NETHERLANDS	❶	❷	❸	❹	❺
FOOD	under €8	€8-12	€13-17	€18-22	over €22

Traditional Dutch cuisine is hearty, heavy, and meaty. Expect bread for breakfast and lunch, topped with melting **hagelslag** (flaked chocolate topping) in the morning and cheese later in the day. Generous portions of meat and fish make up dinner, traditionally the only hot meal of the day. **Seafood,** from various grilled fish and shellfish to fish stews and raw herring, is popular. For a truly authentic Dutch meal (most commonly available in May and June), ask for **spargel** (white asparagus), served with potatoes, ham, and eggs. Light snacks include **tostis** (hot grilled-cheese sandwiches, sometimes with ham) and **broodjes** (light, cold sandwiches). The Dutch colonial legacy has brought Surinamese and Indonesian cuisine to the Netherlands, bestowing cheaper and lighter dining options and a wealth of falafel stands in cities. Wash down meals with brimming glasses of Heineken or Amstel.

HOLIDAYS AND FESTIVALS

Holidays: New Year's Day (Jan. 1); Epiphany (Jan. 6); Good Friday (Mar. 21); Easter (Mar. 23-24); Queen's Day (Apr. 30); Ascension (May 1); WWII Remembrance Day (May 4); Liberation Day (May 5); Pentecost (May 11-12); Corpus Christi (May 22); Assumption (Aug. 15); All Saints' Day (Nov. 1); Saint Nicholas' Eve (December 5); Christmas (Dec. 25); Boxing Day (Dec. 26).

Festivals: Koninginnedag (Queen's Day; Apr. 30) turns the country into a huge carnival. The Holland Festival (June; www.hollandfestival.nl) has been celebrating performing arts in Amsterdam since 1948. In the Bloemencorso (Flower Parade; early Sept.), flower-covered floats crawl from Aalsmeer to Amsterdam. Historic canal houses and windmills are open to the public for National Monument Day (Sept. 13-14). The High Times Cannabis Cup (late Nov.) celebrates pot.

BEYOND TOURISM

Volunteer and work opportunities often revolve around international politics or programs resulting from liberal social attitudes. Studying in the Netherlands can entail in-depth looks at sex and drugs. For more info on opportunties across Europe, see **Beyond Tourism**, p. 56.

COC Amsterdam, Rozenstr. 14, Amsterdam (☎626 3087; www.cocamsterdam.nl). The world's oldest organization dedicated to the support of homosexuals and their families. Contact for involvement in support groups, gay pride activities, and publications.

University of Amsterdam, Spui 21, Amsterdam (☎525 8080 or 525 3333; www.uva.nl/english). Amsterdam's largest university offers a full range of degree programs in Dutch. Open to college and graduate students. The Summer Institute on Sexuality, Culture, and Society (www.ishss.uva.nl/summerinstitute), set in one of the world's most tolerant cities, examines sexuality in various cultures. Tuition €1445-10,000 per year.

AMSTERDAM ☎020

Amsterdam's reputation precedes it—and what a reputation it is. Born out of a murky bog and cobbled together over eight centuries, the "Dam on the River Amstel" (pop. 743,000) coaxes visitors with an alluring blend of grandeur and decadence. Thick clouds of marijuana smoke waft from subdued coffee shops, and countless bicycles zip past blooming tulip markets. Against the legacy of Vincent van Gogh's thick swirls and Johannes Vermeer's luminous figures, gritty street artists spray graffiti in protest. Squatters sharpen the city's defiant edge, while professional politicians push the boundaries of progressive reform.

▐ TRANSPORTATION

Flights: Schiphol Airport (AMS; ☎0800 72 44 74 65, flight info 0900 724 4746). **Sneltrainen** connect the airport to Centraal Station (15-20min., €3.60).

Trains: Centraal Station, Stationspl. 1 (☎0900 9292, €0.50 per min.; www.ns.nl). To: **Brussels, BEL** (2½-3hr.; 5 per day; €32, under 26 €24); **Groningen** (2½hr., with an additional 30min. between trains; 2 per hr.; €27); **Haarlem** (20min., 6 per hr., €3.60); **The Hague** (50min., 1-6 per hr., €9.60); **Leiden** (35min., 8 per hr., €7.60); **Rotterdam** (1¼hr., 1-5 per hr., €13); **Utrecht** (30min., 3-6 per hr., €6.40).

Public Transportation: GVB (☎460 6060; www.gvb.nl), on Stationspl. in front of Centraal Station. Open M-F 7am-9pm, Sa-Su 10am-6pm. **Tram, metro,** and **bus** lines radiate from Centraal Station. Trams are most convenient for center-city travel; the metro leads to farther-out neighborhoods. Normal public transportation runs daily 6am-12:15am. **Night buses** traverse the city 12:30-7am; pick up a schedule and map at the GVB (€3 per trip). *Strippenkaarten* (p. 701) are used on all public transportation in Amsterdam; 2 strips (€1.60) get you to almost all sights within the city center and include unlimited transfers for 1hr.

Bike Rental: **Frédéric Rent a Bike,** Brouwersgr. 78 (☎624 5509; www.frederic.nl), in the Scheepvaartbuurt. Bikes €10 per day, €40 per week. Lock and theft insurance included. Maps and advice liberally dispensed. Open daily 9am-6pm. Cash only.

⬡TIP
BIKE THE DIKES. The best way to get around Amsterdam is by bike. Get a single-speed bike that has lights in the front and back—you can be ticketed for not using both at night. Get two locks—one for each wheel—and secure your bike to something sturdy. You'll inevitably see people biking down the wrong side of a street, running red lights, and playing chicken with trucks, but that doesn't mean you should join in the fun. Always bike perpendicular to tram rails (so your wheels don't get caught in them) and, finally, use hand signals.

⚓ ORIENTATION

Let the canals guide you through Amsterdam's confusing neighborhoods. In the center, water runs in concentric half-circles, beginning at Centraal Station. The **Singel** runs around the **Centrum,** which includes the **Oude Zijd** (Old Side), the infamous **Red Light District,** and the **Nieuwe Zijd** (New Side), which, oddly enough, is older than the Oude Zijd. Barely a kilometer in diameter, the Centrum overflows with brothels, bars, clubs, and tourists wading through wafts of marijuana smoke. The next three canals—the **Herengracht,** the **Keizersgracht,** and the **Prinsengracht**—constitute the **Canal Ring.** Nearby **Rembrandtplein** and **Leidseplein** sport classy nightlife that spans flashy bars and *bruin cafes.* **Museumplein** is just over the **Singelgracht.** Farther out lie the more residential Amsterdam neighborhoods: to the north and west, the **Scheepvaartbuurt, Jordaan, Westerpark,** and **Oud-West;** to the south and east, **Jodenbuurt, Plantage, De Pijp,** and far-flung **Greater Amsterdam.**

🛈 PRACTICAL INFORMATION

Tourist Office: VVV, Stationspl. 10 (☎0900 400 4040, €0.40 per min.; www.amsterdamtourist.nl), opposite Centraal Station. Books rooms and sells maps for €2. Open daily 9am-5pm. Branches at Stadhouderskade 1, Schiphol Airport, and inside Centraal.

Consulates: All foreign embassies are in **The Hague** (p. 723). **UK Consulate,** Koningslaan 44 (☎676 4343). Open M-F 8:30am-1:30pm. **US Consulate,** Museumpl. 19 (☎575 5309; http://amsterdam.usconsulate.gov). Open M-F 8:30-11:30am. Closed last W of every month.

Currency Exchange: American Express, Damrak 66 (☎504 8777), offers the best rates, no commission on American Express Travelers Cheques, and a €4 flat fee for all non-euro cash and non-AmEx traveler's checks. Open M-F 9am-5pm, Sa 9am-noon.

Library: Openbare Bibliotheek Amsterdam, Prinsengr. 587 (☎523 0900). Reserve free Internet access for 30min. at the info desk. Adequate English selection. Open M 1-9pm, Tu-Th 10am-9pm, F-Sa 10am-5pm; Oct.-Mar. also Su 1-5pm.

GLBT Resources: Pink Point (☎428 1070; www.pinkpoint.org), a kiosk in front of the Westerkerk, provides info on GLBT life in Amsterdam. Open daily noon-6pm. The **Gay and Lesbian Switchboard** (☎623 6565; www.switchboard.nl) takes calls M-F noon-10pm, Sa-Su 4pm-8pm.

Police: Headquarters at Elandsgr. 117 (☎559 9111). The national non-emergency line, ☎0900 8844, connects you to the nearest station or the rape crisis department.

Crisis Lines: General counseling at Telephone Helpline (☎675 7575). Open 24hr. Rape crisis hotline (☎612 0245) staffed M-F 10:30am-11pm, Sa-Su 3:30-11pm. Drug counseling at the Jellinek Clinic (☎570 2378). Open M-F 9am-5pm.

24hr. Pharmacy: A hotline (☎694 8709) will direct you to the nearest 24hr. pharmacy.

Medical Services: For hospital care, **Academisch Medisch Centrum,** Meibergdreef 9 (☎566 9111), is easily accessible on subway #50 or 54 (dir.: Gein; stop: Holendrecht). **Tourist Medical Service** (☎592 3355) offers 24hr. referrals for visitors.

Amsterdam	
🏠 ACCOMMODATIONS	Stayokay Amsterdam
Aivergo Youth Hostel, **4**	Stadsdoelen, **19**
Bicycle Hotel, **34**	Stayokay Amsterdam
City Hotel, **21**	Vondelpark, **27**
Flying Pig Downtown, **6**	🍴 BEST OF FOOD
Flying Pig Palace, **39**	Cafe-Restaurant Amsterdam, **3**
Frédéric Rent a Bike, **2**	Cafe De Pijp, **33**
Freeland, **22**	Cafe Latei, **17**
The Golden Bear, **5**	Eat at Jo's, **23**
Hemp Hotel, **30**	In de Waag, **15**
Hotel Abba, **24**	Lanskroon, **18**
Hotel Asterisk, **31**	
Hotel Bema, **35**	🍵 BEST OF COFFEE SHOPS
Hotel Brouwer, **7**	Amnesia, **10**
Hotel The Crown, **8**	Kadinsky, **11**
Hotel de Filosoof, **28**	
Hotel Fantasia, **12**	⭐ BEST OF NIGHTLIFE
Hotel Royal Taste, **14**	Alto, **26**
Hotel Van Onna, **9**	Café de Jaren, **20**
Luckytravellers	Café Zool, **13**
Fantasia Hotel, **25**	Dulac, **1**
Nadia Hotel, **16**	Kingfisher, **32**

THE NETHERLANDS

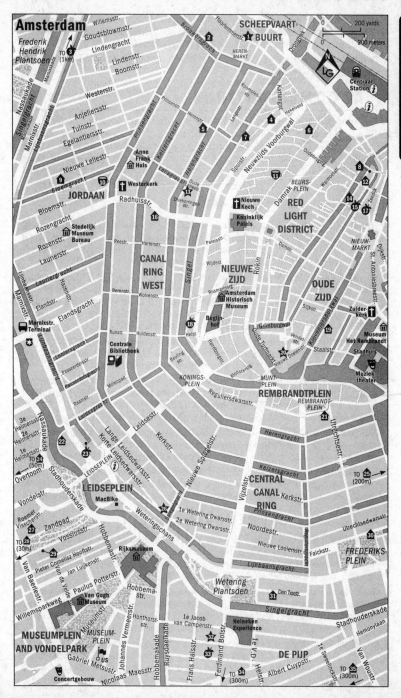

Internet Access: Many coffee shops and hostels offer Internet access for customers and guests. ▓ **easyInternetcafé,** Damrak 33 (☎ 320 8082), charges €1 per 22min., €6 for 24hr., €10 for 1 week, €22 for 20 days. Open daily 9am-10pm.

Post Office: Main post office, Singel 250, at Raadhuisstr. Open M-W and F 9am-6pm, Th 9am-8pm, Sa 10am-1:30pm.

ACCOMMODATIONS

Accommodations in the **Red Light District** are often bars with beds over them. Before signing up for a bunk, consider just how much noise and drug use you can tolerate from your neighbors. Amsterdam's canal-side hotels and hostels offer affordable accommodations highlighted by beautiful views, although they are often criticized for their tight quarters. Prices vary dramatically by season and amenities desired, and if you pay with plastic, there is often a 3-6.5% surcharge.

CENTRUM

▓ **Flying Pig Downtown,** Nieuwendijk 100 (☎ 420 6822; www.flyingpig.nl). A perennial favorite among party-hardy backpackers. Breakfast included. Key deposit, including a locker, €10. Linens included. Free Internet access. 16- to 22-bed dorms €21; 8- to 10-bed dorms €24; 4- to 6-bed dorms €27; singles and twins €76. AmEx/MC/V. ❶

Stayokay Amsterdam Stadsdoelen, Kloveniersburgwal 97 (☎ 624 6832; www.stay-okay.com/stadsdoelen). This branch of the chain sleeps 158 and provides clean, drug-free lodgings in (relatively) quiet environs. Breakfast, lockers, and linens included. Locker deposit €20 or passport. Internet access €5 per hr. Reception 24hr. Co-ed or single-sex 8- to 20-bed dorms €25-27. €2.50 HI discount. MC/V. ❶

Hotel Brouwer, Singel 83 (☎ 624 6358; www.hotelbrouwer.nl). Restored rooms have private bath, canal view, and Dutch painter theme. Breakfast included. Rooms for 1 person €55; for 2 €90; for 3 €115. Cash and traveler's checks only. ❷

Hotel Royal Taste, Oudezijds Achterburgwal 47 (☎ 623 2478; www.hotelroyaltaste.nl). Clean, comfortable, almost fancy accommodations at reasonable prices. Breakfast €7.50. Singles with sink €50, with full bath €60; doubles with bath €100-110, with canal view €120; triples €150-165; quads €190. Cash only. ❷

Aivergo Youth Hostel, Spuistr. 6 (☎ 421 3670). Huge, perfectly clean dorm rooms decorated with gauzy purple curtains. Linens and towels included in women-only dorms; €1 in co-ed. Free lockers and Internet access. Dorms €25-40; double €60. Cash only. ❶

Hotel The Crown, Oudezijds Voorburgwal 21 (☎ 626 9664; www.hotelthecrown.com). Handsome digs in a fun, rowdy environment. Loads of British tourists. Beds €40-55 per person in rooms that sleep 1-3; rooms with hall showers €10 less. AmEx/MC/V. ❷

CANAL RING AND REMBRANDTPLEIN

▓ **Hemp Hotel,** Frederikspl. 15 (☎ 625 4425; www.hemp-hotel.com). Revel amid all things hemp. Each room designed and decorated according to a different cultural theme. Breakfast—featuring yummy hemp bread—included and served from 11am-noon. 1 single €50; doubles €65-80. MC/V; 5% surcharge. ❷

Nadia Hotel, Raadhuisstr. 51 (☎ 620 1550; www.nadia.nl). Elegantly decorated with an attentive staff. Each well-kept, cozy room includes fridge, safe, and TV. Breakfast and Wi-Fi included. Weekday high-season singles €75; doubles €115; triples €150. Higher prices for balcony or rooms with canal views and on weekends. AmEx/MC/V. ❸

City Hotel, Utrechtsestr. 2 (☎ 627 2323; www.city-hotel.nl). Classy, spacious accommodations above a pub on Rembrandtpl. Popular with young travelers. Rooms and baths all immaculately kept. Breakfast included in a spacious dining room with great views. Reception 24hr. 2- to 8-bed rooms €45 per person. AmEx/MC/V. ❷

Hotel Asterisk, Den Texstr. 16 (☎626 2396 or 624 1768; www.asteriskhotel.nl). Beautiful hotel with friendly, professional staff. Spacious and pristine rooms with TV, phone, and safe. High-season singles €45-59, with shower or toilet €49-64; doubles €59-79, with bath €84-129; triples €99-144; quads €119-165. MC/V; 4% surcharge. ❷

The Golden Bear, Kerkstr. 37 (☎624 4785; www.goldenbear.nl). Amsterdam's oldest openly gay hotel. Welcoming and informed staff. All rooms with brightly painted walls, phone, safe, TV, VCR, and DVD player. Continental breakfast included, served 8:30am-noon. Singles from €60, with bath €105; doubles €62-132; twins €71-94. ❸

WEST OF TOWN

🏠 **Frédéric Rent a Bike,** Brouwersgr. 78 (☎624 5509; www.frederic.nl). 3 lived-in, homey, and cheerful rooms in the back of a bike shop or 2 at Frédéric's parents' home. Reception 9am-6pm. *Chez* Frédéric's parents €35; singles €40-50; doubles €60-100; houseboats for 2-4 people €100-160. Cash only; AmEx/MC/V required for reservation. ❶

Hotel Abba, Overtoom 122 (☎618 3058; www.abbabudgethotel.com). Budget hotel with a clean, welcoming feel close to Leidsepl. and the museums. Breakfast included 8-9:30am. Reception until 11pm. Credit card needed for reservation. Singles €35-50; twins €65-80; special family-style quints €175. Cash only. ❶

Hotel de Filosoof, Anna Vondelstr. 6 (☎683 3013; www.hotelfilosoof.nl). Each room in this lovely hotel is dedicated to a different philosopher. All rooms with cable TV and bath. Breakfast included. Singles €125; small doubles €108, larger doubles €175. ❺

Hotel Van Onna, Bloemgr. 104 (☎626 5801; www.vanonna.nl). Cozy rooms all have private bath. Breakfast included. Reception 8am-11pm. Singles €45; doubles €90; triples €135; quads €180. Cash only. ❷

LEIDSEPLEIN AND MUSEUMPLEIN

🏠 **Stayokay Amsterdam Vondelpark,** Zandpad 5 (☎589 8996; www.stayokay.com/vondelpark). Palatial, spotless hostel. Breakfast and linens included; towels €3. Internet €0.50 per min. Reception 7:30am-midnight. 12- to 14-bed dorms in high season €24; 6- or 8-bed dorms €26; doubles €80; quads €116. €2.50 HI discount. MC/V. ❶

Freeland, Marnixstr. 386 (☎622 7511; www.hotelfreeland.com). Happy, fresh, and well-run establishment. All rooms with DVD player and private bath; most with A/C. Breakfast included. Free Internet in lobby; Wi-Fi throughout the hotel. Singles €65-80; doubles €90-110; triples €115-130. Book early. AmEx/MC/V. ❸

Hotel Bema, Concertgebouw 19B (☎679 1396; www.bemahotel.com). Winning 7-room hotel with airy accommodations, and a funky style. Breakfast included. Reception 8am-midnight. Singles €35-45; doubles and twins €65, with shower €90; triples €85/100; quads with shower €100-115. AmEx/MC/V; 5% surcharge. ❶

Flying Pig Palace, Vossiusstr. 46-47 (☎400 4187; www.flyingpig.nl). Friendly community in a tranquil setting. Breakfast included. Free Internet access. Reception 8:30am-9:30pm; 24hr. check-in possible. High-season 14-bed dorms €24; 10-bed dorms €27; 8-bed dorms €29; 4-bed dorms €32; double with bath €36. AmEx/MC/V. ❶

DE PIJP, JODENBUURT, AND PLANTAGE

🏠 **Bicycle Hotel,** Van Ostadestr. 123 (☎679 3452; www.bicyclehotel.com). Clean digs and spotless bathrooms, plus a large common room and leafy garden. Free bike maps and bike parking. Bike rental €7.50 per day. Sink and TV in all rooms. Breakfast included 8-10am. Free Internet and safe. Min. 3-night weekend stay. Singles €65, with bath €95; doubles €80-115; triples €95-130. AmEx/MC/V; 4% surcharge. ❸

Luckytravellers Fantasia Hotel, Nieuwe Keizersgr. 16 (☎623 8259; www.fantasia-hotel.com). Younger feel than most hotels around. Facilities include coffeemakers, phones, radios, and safe. Breakfast included. Singles €65-75; doubles €85-95; triples €120-130; quads and family rooms €150. AmEx/MC/V; 3% surcharge. ❸

🔾 MUNCHIES

The sheer number of options—from shawarma to Argentine barbecue to pan-Asian noodles—can be dizzying. Cheap restaurants cluster around **Leidseplein**, **Rembrandtplein**, and **De Pijp**. Food and flowers are sold at markets on **Albert Cuypstraat** in De Pijp. (Open M-Sa 9am-5pm.) **Albert Heijn** supermarkets are plentiful.

CENTRUM

🔳 **Cafe Latei**, Zeedijk 143 (☎625 7485; www.latei.net). At this unique cafe and curiosity shop, nearly everything is for sale—even your plate. Sandwiches around €3. All-day continental breakfast €6.40. Fresh juices €2-4. Th couscous nights; call for other special events. Open M-F 8am-6pm, Sa 9am-6pm, Su 11am-6pm. ❶

🔳 **In de Waag**, Nieuwmarkt 4 (☎452 7772; www.indewaag.nl). A high-class restaurant with stone walls and long wood tables in a weigh-house from 1488. Lunch sandwiches €5-10. Dinner entrees around €20. Open daily 10am-midnight. ❹

Pannenkoekenhuis Upstairs, Grimburgwal 2 (☎626 5603). Adorned with vintage photos of Dutch royalty and only 4 tables. Traditional pancakes said to be among the best in Amsterdam (€9). Open M and F noon-7pm, Sa noon-6pm, Su noon-5pm. ❷

Ristorante Caprese, Spuistr. 259-261 (☎620 0059). Authentic Italian food and relaxed jazz by comforting candlelight. Main pasta dishes €10-11. Meat and fish dishes €18-22. Open daily 5pm-1am. Kitchen closes at 11:45pm. ❸

Aneka Rasa, Warmoesstr. 25-29 (☎626 1560). Clean, relaxed Indonesian joint with very friendly staff. Popular *rijsttafel* €17-18 per person. Other main dishes €12-13. Vegetarian plates €7.50-8.40. Open daily 5-10:30pm. AmEx/MC/V. ❷

CANAL RING AND REMBRANDTPLEIN

🔳 **Lanskroon**, Singel 385 (☎623 7743). Traditional Dutch pastries like *stroopwafels* (honey-filled cookies; €1.50), fresh fruit pies (€2.50), and exotically flavored sorbets, made on-site. Open Tu-F 8am-5:30pm, Sa 9am-6pm, Su 10am-6pm. Cash only. ❶

NOA, Leidsegr. 84 (☎626 0802; www.withnoa.com). Artsy, elegant restaurant that serves up a diverse menu of pan-Asian dishes. Everything on the menu €6-17. Mixed drinks €7-9. Open Tu-Th and Su noon-midnight; F-Sa noon-1am. AmEx/MC/V. ❸

Ristorante Pizzeria Firenze, Halvemaanstg. 9-11 (☎627 3360). Delightful little Italian spot with murals of the Italian countryside, friendly service, and simply unbeatable prices. 25 types of pizza (€4.60-8) and pasta (€5.30-8). Open daily 1-11pm. MC/V. ❶

Foodism, Oude Leliestr. 8 (☎427 5103). Bright green walls, red tables, and a cozy, alternative staff serving vegetarian and pasta platters (€10-13). Breakfast all day (€9.50). Open M-Sa 11:30am-10pm, Su 1-10pm. Cash only. ❷

Hein, Berenstr. 20 (☎623 1048). Watch fresh food prepared in the open kitchen from of the seating area. The menu changes daily, subject to the owner's tastes. Entrees average €10. Open M-Sa 8:30am-4pm, Su 9am-4pm. Reservations accepted. Cash only. ❷

WEST OF TOWN

🔳 **Cafe-Restaurant Amsterdam**, Watertorenpl. 6 (☎682 2667; www.cradam.nl). Surprisingly casual and child-friendly, with a continental menu of meat, fish, and vegetable choices (€10-20) that changes seasonally. Open M-Th 10:30am-midnight, F-Sa 10:30am-1am. Kitchen open M-Th until 10:30pm, F-Sa until 11:30pm. AmEx/MC/V. ❸

Harlem: Drinks and Soulfood, Haarlemmerstr. 77 (☎330 1498). American Southern soul food, like catfish and macaroni and cheese, infused with Cajun and Caribbean flavors. Dinner entrees €11-17. Lunch includes club sandwiches (€4.40-7.50). Open M-Th 10am-1am, F-Sa 10am-3am, Su 11am-1am. Kitchen closes 10pm. MC/V. ❸

De Vliegende Schotel, Nieuwe Leliestr. 162-168 (☎625 2041; www.vliegendeschotel.com). Simple, organic, delicious vegetarian food. Soups and starters from €2.50. Entrees from €9.40. Open daily 5-11:30pm. Kitchen closes 10:15pm. AmEx/MC/V. ❷

Peperwortel, Overtoom 140 (☎685 1053; www.peperwortel.nl). Deli-slash-restaurant and a foodie's paradise. Rotating menu of entrees (around €9.50) like Indonesian beef or couscous and ratatouille. Open M-F 4-9pm, Sa-Su 3-9pm. Cash only. ❷

LEIDSEPLEIN AND MUSEUMPLEIN

▨ **Eat at Jo's,** Marnixstr. 409 (☎624 1777; www.melkweg.nl). Multi-ethnic, freshly prepared menu that changes daily earns rave reviews. Bands often grab a bite to eat after a performance at Melkweg. Open W-Su noon-9pm. Cash only. ❸

Bombay Inn, Lange Leidsedwarsstr. 46 (☎624 1784). Generous "tourist menu" includes 3 courses of delicately spiced dishes (chicken menu €8.50; lamb menu €9.50). Veggie sides €5.50. Extras like rice (€2.30) not included. Open daily 5-11pm. AmEx/MC/V. ❷

Cafe Vertigo, Vondelpark 3 (☎612 3021; www.vertigo.nl). Filling lunch sandwiches (BLTC—C is for chicken—€5.50) and tasty snacks (spring rolls €3.50). You'd have to be psycho to skip Vertigo. Sept.-Mar. Sa disco nights. Lunch until 5pm, soups and salads available 5-6pm, and dinner 6-10pm. Open daily 10am-1am. MC/V. ❶

DE PIJP, JODENBUURT, AND PLANTAGE

▨ **Cafe De Pijp,** Ferdinand Bolstr. 17-19 (☎670 4161). Good Mediterranean food complimented by even better company. Tapas for 2 €15. Entrees €13-15. Mixed drinks €5. Open M-Th 3:30pm-1am, F 3:30pm-3am, Sa noon-2am, Su noon-1am. Cash only. ❸

Abe Veneto, Plantage Kerklaan 2 (☎639 2364). Friendly entourage of proprietors and absolutely terrific food. Over 45 freshly made pizzas (€5-9.50), pastas (€7-9.50), and salads (under €5). Wine by the bottle or the carafe. Takeout and delivery available to nearby hotels or for eating in a nearby park. Open daily noon-midnight. Cash only. ❷

Bazar, Albert Cuypstr. 182 (☎664 7173). In the open space of a former church. Cuisine from North Africa, Lebanon, and Turkey. Lunch special €10 per person (min. 2 people). Breakfast and lunch start at €3.50. Dinner entrees around €10. Reserve ahead for dinner. Open M-Th 9am-1am, F-Sa 9am-2am, Su 9am-midnight. ❷

◪ SIGHTS

This city—as a collection of nearly 100 interlocking islands—is a sight in itself. Amsterdam is fairly compact, so tourists can easily explore the city on foot; otherwise, the tram system will get you to any of the city's major sights within minutes. For a peaceful view of the city from the water, the Saint Nicolaas Boat Club (www.amsterdamboatclub.com) organizes canal tours.

CENTRUM

▨ **NIEUWMARKT.** Nieuwmarkt is one of Amsterdam's most beloved squares. Stop and to take a look at the **Waag,** Amsterdam's largest surviving medieval building. Dating from the 15th century, the Waag was originally one of Amsterdam's fortified city gates. As Amsterdam expanded, it was converted into a house for public weights and measures. At the end of the 17th century, the Surgeon's Guild built an amphitheater at the top of the central tower to house public dissections as well as private anatomy lessons—famously depicted by **Rembrandt van Rijn's** The Anat-

omy Lesson of Dr. Tulp (p. 723). The Waag has also housed a number of other sites, including the Jewish Historical Museum and the Amsterdam Historical Museum. Today, it is home to 🎭**In de Waag** (p. 708). *(Metro to Nieuwmarkt.)*

🎭**BEGIJNHOF.** You don't have to take vows to enter this secluded courtyard in the 14th-century home of the Beguines—a sect of free-thinking and religiously devoted laywomen. The peaceful Begijnhof's rosy gardens, beautifully manicured lawns, gabled houses, and tree-lined walkways afford a much-needed respite from the excesses of the Nieuwe Zijd. While there, visit the court's two churches, the **Engelsekerk** and the **Begijnhofkapel.** *(From Dam, take Nieuwezijds Voorburgwal south 5min. to Spui, turn left, and then go left again on Gedempte Begijnensloot; the gardens are on the left. Alternatively, follow signs to Begijnhof from Spui. No guided tours, bikes, or pets. Open daily 9am-5pm. Free.)* One of the oldest houses in Amsterdam, **Het Houten Huys** (The Wooden House), is located on the premises. *(☎623 5554. Open M-F 10am-4pm.)*

RED LIGHT DISTRICT. No trip to Amsterdam would be complete without witnessing the notorious spectacle that is the Red Light District. After dark, the area actually glows red—sex theaters throw open their doors, and the streets are thick with people gawking at lingerie-clad prostitutes pressing themselves against windows. Wall-to-wall brothels crowd **Warmoesstraat** and **Oudezijds Achterburgwal.** There are also **sex shows,** in which actors perform strictly choreographed fantasies on stage; the most famous takes place at **Casa Rosso.** *(Oudezijds Achterburgwal 106-108. ☎627 8954; www.janot.com. Open M-Th 8pm-2am, F-Sa 8pm-3am. €35, with 4 drinks €45.)*

> ⚡**TIP** **FLESH PHOTOGRAPHY.** As tempting as it may be, do not take pictures in the Red Light District, especially of prostitutes. Taking pictures is incredibly rude and can land the photographer in trouble.

OUDE KERK. The Old Church may be the only church in the world completely bounded by prostitution sites. Erected in 1306, it was the earliest parish church built in Amsterdam, but it is now a center for cultural activities, hosting photography and modern art exhibits. At the head of the church is the massive **Vater-Müller organ,** still played for public concerts. The Gothic church has seen hard times, having been stripped of its artwork and religious artifacts during the Alteration. The Protestant church has since served a number of functions: a home for vagrants, a theater, a market, and a space for fishermen to mend broken sails. Today, the church is one of the most impressive and prominent structures in the city. *(Oudekerkspl. 23. ☎625 8284; www.oudekerk.nl. Open M-Sa 11am-5pm, Su 1-5pm. €4.50, students and over 65 €3.50, under 12 free. Additional charge for exhibits.)*

SINT NICOLAASKERK. A burst of color emanates from the stained-glass windows over the impressive columned altar of this relatively new Roman Catholic church. The Neo-Renaissance structure humbles visitors with stern black marble columns, a domed ceiling, and wooden vaults that make for a grand interior. The walls of the church are art themselves, lined with magnificent murals depicting the life and story of St. Nicolaas. Take time to admire the church's massive 2300-pipe organ. *(Prins Hendrikkade 73. ☎624 8749. Daily service 12:30pm; Su mass 10:30am Dutch, 1pm Spanish. Organ festival July-Sept. Sa 8:15pm. Contemporary and classical organ concerts occasionally Sa 3pm—call ahead. Open M 1-4pm, Tu-F 11am-4pm, Sa noon-3pm. Organ festival €6.)*

DAM SQUARE AND KONINKLIJK PALEIS. Next to the Nieuwe Kerk on Dam Sq. is the Koninklijk Paleis, one of Amsterdam's most impressive architectural feats. The palace is closed for renovations until 2009, but even its exterior bursts with history. Across Dam Sq. is the Dutch **Nationaal Monument,** honoring Dutch victims of WWII. Inside the 22m white stone obelisk is soil from all 12 of the Netherlands's provinces and the Dutch East Indies. *(Tram #5, 13, 17, or 20 to Dam.)*

CANAL RING AND REMBRANDTPLEIN

■ **WESTERKERK.** This stunning Protestant church was designed by Hendrick de Keyser and completed in 1631. The blue and yellow imperial crown of Maximilian of Austria rests atop the 85m tower, which has become a patriotic symbol for the citizens of Amsterdam. Rembrandt is believed to be buried here, but no one knows exactly where. In contrast to the decorative exterior, the church remains sober and plain inside; it is still used by a Presbyterian congregation. Make sure to climb the **Westerkerkstoren** as part of a 30min. guided tour for an awe-inspiring view of the city. *(Prinsengr. 281. ☎624 7766. Open Apr.-Sept. M-F 11am-3pm; July-Aug. M-Sa 11am-3pm. Tower closed Oct.-Mar. Tower tours Apr.-Sept. every 30min. 10am-5:30pm. €5.)*

HOMOMONUMENT. Since 1987, the Homomonument has marked Amsterdam as a testament to the strength and resilience of the homosexual community. Its pale pink granite triangles allude to the symbols homosexuals were required to wear in Nazi concentration camps. The raised triangle points to the **COC** (p. 703); the ground-level triangle to the **Anne Frank Huis;** and the last triangle to the **Nationaal Monument** on the Dam, a reminder that homosexuals were among those sent to concentration camps. On Queen's Day (Apr. 30) and Liberation Day (May 5), massive celebrations surround the monument. *(Next to Westerkerk.)*

CENTRAL CANAL RING. You haven't seen Amsterdam until you've spent some time wandering in the Central Canal Ring, the city's highest rent district and arguably its most beautiful. In the 17th century, residents of Amsterdam were taxed according to the width of their homes, and houses could not be more than a few meters wide. To encourage investment in construction, the city government allowed its elite to build homes that were twice as wide on a stretch now known as the **Golden Bend,** on Herengr. between Leidsegr. and Vijzelstr. Across the Amstel is the **Magere Brug** (Skinny Bridge), the oldest of the city's many pedestrian drawbridges and the only one still operated by hand.

LEIDSEPLEIN AND MUSEUMPLEIN

■ **VONDELPARK.** With meandering walkways, green meadows, and several ponds, this leafy park—the largest within the city center—is a lovely meeting place. Vondelpark has an open-air theater where visi-

THE RED LIGHT SPECIAL

Prostitution has always been legal in the Netherlands, yet brothels were illegal for most of the 20th century. Since October 2000, it has been legal for a business to employ men or women as prostitues as long as they are over the legal age of consent (16) and work voluntarily. The owner of a brothel must have a license from the government and adhere to specific regulations, set by local authorities. These require the payment of a tax by both prostitutes and employers, mandate the upkeep of a certain sized work space, and suggest that prostitues get medical checkups four times per year.

There are thought to be 25,000 men and women of the night in the Netherlands; about 12,000 of them work at any given time, in about 6000 locations. The Netherlands has 12 red-light districts with window prostitution. The majority of prostitutes work in brothels and sex clubs; many also work as escorts. While statistics vary, research has reported that a majority of the prostitutes are foreigners.

Windows are generally rented to prostitutes for 8hr. shifts which cost them €60-150; they make back the payment by charging €40-50 for 15-20min. of sex. Negotiations occur between prostitute and potential customer, through a propped-open door. Prostitutes have the final say about who gets admitted.

THE INSIDER'S CITY

BICYCLE BUILT
FOR YOU

Even if you've experienced the Red Light District or clouded yourself in smoke at all of Amsterdam's coffeeshops, you can't say you've truly done this city unless you've ridden a bike here. The red bike lanes and special bike lights, as well as the multitude of cheap and convenient rental companies, permit tourists to whiz around as if they were locals. If you're bent on remaining a tourist, you can pay for a guided bike tour or a map with one laid out, but if you're keen on blending in, you can simply pedal your way to destinations you'd planned on seeing anyway. A horseshoe-shaped path along any of the canals of the Central Canal Ring—Prinsengracht is prettiest—passes near the Anne Frank Huis, the Rijksmuseum, the van Gogh Museum, and the Heineken Brewery.

Of course you might as well take advantage of your increased mobility to explore places your tootsies wouldn't take you. Leave Amsterdam to ride along the Amstel River, glimpsing windmills, houseboats, and quintessentially Dutch rolling hills. Cycle east along green trails to the seaside town of Spaarndam (20-25km). Or, use the canals as racetracks, leaving mellow locals in the dust.

MacBike (p. 703), Weteringsschans 2 (☎528 76 88; www.macbike.nl), in Leidseplein, rents bikes and sells reliable bike-tour maps.

tors can enjoy free music and dance concerts Thursday through Sunday during the summer. Every Friday, you can meet up with about 350-600 in-line skaters at 8pm by the Filmmuseum for a group skate through Amsterdam. For the less daring, wander around the hexagonally shaped, beautifully maintained rose gardens. *(In the southwest corner of the city, outside the Singelgr. www.vondelpark.org. Theater ☎673 1499; www.openluchttheater.nl.)*

LEIDSEPLEIN. Leidsepl. is a crush of cacophonous street musicians, blaring neon lights, and clanging trams. A slight respite from the hordes is available just east of Leidsepl. along Weteringschans at **Max Euweplein,** with its enormous chess board and oversized pieces. One of Amsterdam's more bizarre public spaces, it is notable both for the tiny park across the street (where bronze iguanas provide amusement) and for the Latin motto inscribed above its pillars.

DE PIJP, JODENBUURT, AND PLANTAGE

■ **HORTUS BOTANICUS.** With over 4000 species of plants, this outstanding botanical garden is a terrific place to get lost. Visitors can wander past lush palms, flowering cacti, and working beehives or stroll through simulated ecosystems, a three-climate greenhouse, and a butterfly room. Many of its more exceptional specimens were gathered during the 17th and 18th centuries by members of the Dutch East India Company. *(Plantage Middenlaan 2A. ☎638 1670; www.dehortus.nl. Open Feb.-June and Sept.-Nov. M-F 9am-5pm, Sa-Su 10am-5pm; July-Aug. M-F 9am-9pm, Sa-Su 10am-9pm; Dec.-Jan. M-F 9am-4pm, Sa-Su 10am-4pm. Guided tours in English Su 2pm €1. €6, ages 5-14 and seniors €3. Cafe open M-F 10am-5pm, Sa-Su 11am-5pm; in summer also daily 6-9pm.)*

HEINEKEN EXPERIENCE. Heineken stopped producing here in 1988 and has turned the place into a corporate altar devoted to their green-bottled beer. Visitors guide themselves past holograms, virtual reality machines, and other multimedia that inform you of more than you ever needed to know about the Heineken corporation and beer production. A visit includes three beers or soft drinks and a souvenir, all of which is alone worth the price of admission. To avoid the crowds, come before 11am and take your alcohol before noon like the real fans do. *(☎523 9666; www.heinekenexperience.com. Open in summer daily 10am-7pm, last entry at 5:45pm; otherwise Tu-Su 10am-6pm, last entry at 5pm. Under 18 must be accompanied by a parent. €11. MC/V.)*

HOLLANDSCHE SCHOUWBURG. Now a poignant memorial to Amsterdam's Holocaust victims, Hollandsche Schouwburg opened at the end of the 19th century as a Dutch theater on the edge of the old Jewish quarter. A stone monument now occupies the space where the theater's stage used to be. *(Plantage Middenlaan 24. ☎531 0430; www.hollandscheschouwburg.nl. Open daily 11am-4pm; closed on Yom Kippur. Free.)*

ARTIS ZOO. Artis is the oldest zoo and park in the Netherlands; it is also a zoological museum, a museum of geology, an aquarium, and a planetarium. A day of good weather is enough to make the Artis complex worth a visit. The zoo's got all the big guns: a polar bear, elephants, giraffes, and hundreds of free-roaming schoolchildren—be careful not to trip over any as you stroll the grounds. *(Plantage Kerklaan 38-40. ☎523 3400; www.artis.nl. Open daily 9am-5pm, during daylight saving time 9am-6pm. €18, ages 3-9 €14, seniors €17, under 3 free. Guidebooks €2.50. AmEx/MC/V.)*

PORTUGEES-ISRAELIETISCHE SYNAGOGE. Amsterdam's early Sephardic Jewish community, mainly refugees fleeing religious persecution in Spain, founded this large synagogue, known as the Esnoga, in 1675. It is one of the few tangible remnants of Amsterdam's once-thriving Jewish community. The large worship hall is free to walk through and features massive brass candelabras and an architectural style similar to the arches of Amsterdam's canal houses. Just after you leave, take a look at **The Dockworker,** a statue just behind the synagogue. *(Mr. Visserpl. 1-3. ☎624 5351; www.esnoga.com. Open Apr.-Oct. M-F and Su 10am-4pm; Nov.-Mar. M-Th and Su 10am-4pm, F 10am-3pm. €6.50, students, seniors, and Museumjaarkaart holders €5, under 17 €4.)*

🏛 MUSEUMS

Whether you crave Rembrandts and van Goghs, cutting-edge photography, WWII history, or sexual oddities, Amsterdam has a museum for you. The useful www.amsterdammuseums.nl has info for easy planning.

> **⬛TIP** **MORE MUSEUMS FOR LESS.** Visitors planning to see even a handful of museums may want to invest in a **Museumjaarkaart.** The pass (€35, under 25 €20) entitles the holder to admission at most of the major museums in the Netherlands. To buy the pass, bring a passport photo to a participating museum. For more info, check the Dutch-only www.museumjaarkaart.nl.

CENTRUM

■**NIEUWE KERK.** The New Church, the extravagant 15th-century brick-red cathedral at the heart of the Nieuwe Zijd, now serves a triple role as a religious edifice, historical monument, and art museum. **Commemorative windows** are given to the church to honor royal inaugurations and other events. The church, which has been rebuilt several times after several fires, is still used for royal inaugurations and weddings. Check the website before you go; the church closes for two weeks between art exhibits. *(Adjacent to Dam Sq., beside Koninklijk Paleis. ☎638 6909; www.nieuwekerk.nl. Open daily 10am-5pm. Organ recitals June-Sept. Th 12:30pm, Su 8pm. Call ahead for exact times. €8, ages 6-15 and seniors €6.)*

■**AMSTERDAMS HISTORISCH MUSEUM.** This archival museum offers an eclectic introduction to Amsterdam's development by way of ancient archaeological findings, medieval manuscripts, Baroque paintings, and multimedia displays. The section of the museum that features artistic accounts of gory Golden Age anatomy lessons is particularly interesting. Catch one of the Historical Museum's hidden surprises: in the covered passageway between the museum and the Begijnhof, there is an extensive collection of large 17th-century paintings of Amsterdam's civic guards. *(Kalverstr. 92 and Nieuwezijds Voorburgwal 357. ☎523 1822; www.ahm.nl. Open M-F 10am-5pm, Sa-Su 11am-5pm; closed Queen's Day. €7, ages 6-16 €3.50, seniors €5.30.)*

■**STEDELIJK MUSEUM FOR MODERN AND CONTEMPORARY ART.** As the Stedelijk's building on Museumpl. undergoes extensive renovations, its home until 2009 is a drab 11-story building to the east of Centraal Station. The museum has filled two cavernous floors with exhibits that rotate every three months. These pieces, none of which predate 1968, are sometimes interspersed with masterpieces from the museum's extensive permanent collection of avant-garde art. *(Oosterdokskade 5. ☎573 2745, recorded info 573 2911; www.stedelijk.nl. Open daily 11am-6pm. €9; 7-16, over 65, and groups of 15 or more €4.50; under 7 free; families €23.)*

■**MUSEUM AMSTELKRING "ONS' LIEVE HEER OP SOLDER".** The continued persecution of Catholics after the Alteration led Jan Hartmann, a wealthy Dutch merchant, to build this secret church in 1663. The chapel is housed in the attics of three separate canal houses and includes a fantastic 18th-century Baroque altar. The large antique organ is equally impressive. Period rooms re-create life during the Dutch Reformation, embellished by Dutch paintings and antique silver. The church is still active, holding mass six times per year; check the website for info on either. *(Oudezijds Voorburgwal 40, at Heintje Hoeksstg. ☎624 6604; www.opsolder.nl. Open M-Sa 10am-5pm, Su and holidays 1-5pm. €7, students €5, 5-18 €1, under 5 free.)*

■**CANNABIS COLLEGE.** This info center is your best bet for marijuana matters. The staff of volunteers is unbelievably friendly, knowledgeable, and eager to answer any questions. If you think you're enough of an expert and want to spread your reefer know-how, don't be afraid to ask about lending a hand. *(Oudezijds Achterburgwal 124. ☎423 4420; www.cannabiscollege.com. Open daily 11am-7pm. Free.)*

AMSTERDAM SEX MUSEUM. This almost requisite museum will disappoint only those looking for a sophisticated examination of sexuality. The museum features such ancient artifacts as a stone phallus from the Roman age, but the exhibits are hardly informative; the majority is composed of mannequins and photographs of sexual acts. The gallery of fetishes is not for the weak of stomach. *(Damrak 18. ☎622 8376; www.sexmuseumamsterdam.nl. Open daily 10am-11:30pm. €3.)*

CANAL RING

■**ANNE FRANK HUIS.** In 1942, the Nazis began deporting all Jews to ghettos and concentration camps, forcing Anne Frank's family and four other Dutch Jews to hide in the *achterhuis*, or annex, of this warehouse on the Prinsengracht. All eight refugees lived in this secret annex for two years, during which time Anne penned her diary. Displays of various household objects, text panels mounted with pages from the diary, and video footage of the rooms as they looked during WWII give some sense of life in that tumultuous time. The original bookcase used to hide the entrance to the secret annex remains, cracked open for visitors to pass through. The endless line stretching around the corner attests to the popularity of the Anne Frank Huis, but it is not as long before 10am and after 7pm. *(Prinsengr. 267. ☎556 7100; www.annefrank.nl. Open daily Apr.-Aug. 9am-9pm; Sept.-Mar. 9am-7pm; closed on Yom Kippur. Last entry 30min. before closing. €6.50, ages 10-17 €3, under 10 free.)*

■**MUSEUM VAN LOON.** Built in 1672, this house eventually fell into the hands of the Van Loon family. Their portraits, along with the family crest commemorating their connection with the East Indies, adorn the walls of this exquisite residence. Numerous other heirlooms and antique furniture decorate each room. *(Keizersgr. 672, between Vijzelstr. and Reguliersgr. ☎624 5255; www.museumvanloon.nl. Open Sept.-June F-M 11am-5pm; July-Aug. daily 11am-5pm. €5, students €4, under 12 free.)*

■**FOAM PHOTOGRAPHY MUSEUM.** Housed in a traditional canal house, the Foam Photography Museum fearlessly explores every aspect of modern photography. All genres of the photographed image are welcome here, regardless of message or content. The museum hosts as many as 20 exhibits per year. *(Keizersgr. 609.* ☎ *551 6500; www.foam.nl. Open daily 10am-5pm. €6, students with ID €5.)*

BIJBELS MUSEUM. Inside two canal houses, this museum presents info on both the contents and history of the Bible and the cultural context in which it was written. It includes the first Bible ever printed in the Netherlands. The house is a monument in itself, containing artistic designs that demonstrate the Bible's influence on culture and society. *(Herengr. 366-368.* ☎ *624 2436; www.bijbelsmuseum.nl. Open M-Sa 10am-5pm, Su 11am-5pm. €6, students and children 13-18 €3, under 13 free.)*

MUSEUMPLEIN

🖼 **VAN GOGH MUSEUM.** For better or for worse, the Van Gogh Museum is one of Amsterdam's biggest cultural tourist attractions. The shortest wait are around 10:30am or after 4pm. You'll find the permanent collection, including the meat of the museum, the van Gogh masterpieces, on the first floor. The second floor is home to a study area with web consoles and a small library, while the third floor houses a substantial collection of important 19th-century art. The partially subterranean exhibition wing is the venue for the museum's top-notch traveling exhibitions. *(Paulus Potterstr. 7.* ☎ *570 5252; www.vangoghmuseum.nl. Open Sa-Th 10am-6pm, F 10am-10pm. €10, 13-17 €2.50, under 12 free. Audio tour €4. AmEx/MC/V; min. €25.)*

🖼 **RIJKSMUSEUM AMSTERDAM.** Even though the main building of the museum is closed for renovations, the Rijksmuseum is still a mandatory Amsterdam excursion. Originally opened in 1800, the Rijks—or "state"—museum settled into its current monumental quarters, designed by the architect of Centraal Station, in 1885. As the national museum of art and history, it houses masterpieces by Rembrandt van Rijn, Johannes Vermeer, Frans Hals, and Jan Steen. Of this tour-de-force collection, **Rembrandt's** gargantuan militia portrait *Night Watch* is a crowning, and deservedly famous, achievement. Equally astounding is the museum's collection of paintings by **Vermeer,** including *The Milkmaid. (Stadhouderskade 42. Visitors must enter through the Philips Wing, around the corner at the intersection of Hobbemastr. and Jan Luijkenstr.* ☎ *674 7000; www.rijksmuseum.nl. Open Sa-Th 10am-5pm, F 10am-10pm. Maps available at the ticket counters. €10, under 18 free. Audio tours €4.)*

ELSEWHERE

JOODS HISTORISCH MUSEUM. In the heart of Amsterdam's traditional Jewish neighborhood, the Jewish Historical Museum links four different 17th- and 18th-century Ashkenazi synagogues with glass and steel connections. Through exhibits by Jewish artists and galleries of historically significant Judaica, the museum presents the Netherlands's most comprehensive picture of Jewish life. *(Jonas Daniel Meijerpl. 2-4.* ☎ *531 0310; www.jhm.nl. Open F-W 11am-5pm, Th 11am-9pm; closed on Yom Kippur. Free audio tour. €7.50, seniors and ISIC holders €4.50, ages 13-17 €3, under 13 free.)*

MUSEUM HET REMBRANDT. Dutch master Rembrandt van Rijn's house at Waterloopl. has become the happy home of the artist's impressive collection of 250 etchings. In the upstairs studio, Rembrandt produced some of his most important works. On display are some of his tools and plates, including an original pot he used to mix paint. *(Jodenbreestr. 4, at the corner of Oude Schans.* ☎ *520 0400; www.rembrandthuis.nl. Open daily 10am-5pm. €8, students €5.50, ages 6-15 €1.50, under 6 free.)*

VERZETSMUSEUM. The Resistance Museum uses a wide variety of media and presentations to illustrate life under the Nazi occupation and the steps the Dutch took to oppose the German forces. Displays allow visitors to track the occupation and resistance chronologically, ending with an enlightening exhibit on post-war Dutch regeneration. *(Plantage Kerklaan 61.* ☎ *620 2535; www.verzetsmuseum.org. Open Sa-M noon-5pm, Tu-F 10am-5pm, public holidays noon-5pm. €5.50, ages 7-15 €3, under 7 free.)*

■ **COBRA MUSEUM.** This museum pays tribute to the 20th-century CoBrA art movement: the name is an abbreviation of the capital cities of the group's founding members (Copenhagen, Brussels, and Amsterdam). The beautiful, modern museum effectively presents a range of the movement's work from Karel Appel's experimentation with sculpture to Corneille's developing interest in color and non-Western worlds. *(Sandbergpl. 1-3, south of Amsterdam in Amstelveen. Tram #5 or bus #170, 171, or 172. The tram stop is a 10min. walk from the museum; after a 15min. ride, the bus will drop you off across the street. ☎547 5050, tour reservations 547 5045; www.cobra-museum.nl. Open Tu-Su 11am-5pm. €7, students and seniors €4, ages 6-18 €3. AmEx/MC/V.)*

■ COFFEE SHOPS AND SMART SHOPS

Soft drugs, including marijuana and mushrooms, are tolerated in the Netherlands. **Let's Go does not recommend drug use in any form.** Those who decide to partake should use common sense and remember that any experience with drugs can be dangerous. If you do choose to indulge in drug tourism, you must follow basic ground rules and take careful safety precautions. Never buy drugs from street dealers. If a friend is tripping, it is important never to leave his or her side. If there is a medical emergency, call ☎**112 for an ambulance.**

> **KNOW THE LAW.** On July 1, 2008, Amsterdam will ban smoking indoors. At coffee shops, this means that you can only puff your stuff in designated smoking rooms. Add that to the list of already-mandated regulations: no advertising that a shop sells marijuana; no one under age 18 permitted; no hard drugs; no alcohol; and no aggression or disruptive behavior. Shops cannot store more than 500g of cannabis and cannot sell more than 5g to a person per day. Tokers should also know that they are personally allowed to possess up to 30g.

COFFEE SHOPS

Places calling themselves coffee shops sell hashish, marijuana, and "space" goodies. As a general rule, the farther you travel from touristed spots, the better value and higher quality the establishments you'll find. Look for the green-and-white **BCD** sticker that certifies a shop's credibility. When you move from one coffee shop to another, it is obligatory to buy a drink in the next shop. While it's all right to smoke on the outdoor patio of a coffee shop, don't go walking down the street smoking a joint: it's simply not done. Not only is this an easy way for pickpockets and con artists to pick out a tourist, but locals also consider it offensive.

Hashish comes in three varieties: blonde (Moroccan), black (Indian), and Dutch (Ice-o-Lator), all of which can cost €4-35 per g. Typically, cost is proportional to quality and strength. Black hash hits harder than blonde, and Ice-o-Lator can send even a seasoned smoker off his or her head. Hash is the marijuana flower's extracted resin crystals, which give a different kind of high. **Marijuana** is a dried, cured flower whose Dutch variety is incredibly strong. Take it easy so you don't pass out. The Dutch tend to mix tobacco with their pot, so joints are harsher on your lungs and throat. Pre-rolled joints are always rolled with tobacco; most coffee shops also offer pure joints. A coffee shop's staff is accustomed to explaining the different kinds of pot on the menu to tourists. It is recommended that you buy only a gram at a time. Most places will supply rolling papers and filter tips—Europeans smoke only joints. When pipes or bongs are provided, they are usually for tourists. Another popular way of getting high in Amsterdam is to use a vaporizer. These devices heat up cannabis products until the hallucinogenic substances like THC become gaseous, extracting more out of the product than regular burning via cigarettes. Beware that vaporizers are very strong, and those with copper piping may release nasty (and potentially carcinogenic) copper particles.

Space cakes, brownies, and all members of the baked-goods family are made with hash or weed, but the drugs take longer to affect a person, producing a "body stone" that can take up to two hours or longer to start. Start off with half a serving and see how you feel after an hour or two. It's always easier to eat more later than to wait out a higher dose than you can handle. It is impossible to know what grade of drugs is in space goods, making this form of ingestion much more dangerous than smoking, with which you can monitor your intake more closely.

■ **Amnesia,** Herengr. 133 (☎ 638 3003). Larger and more elegant than other coffee shops. Wide selection of drinks, shakes, or snacks. Buy 5 joints (€3-5 each) and get 1 free. Amnesia Haze, a 2004 Cannabis Cup winner, €11 per g. Open daily 9:30am-1am.

■ **Kadinsky,** Rosmarijnstg. 9 (☎ 624 7023). One of the city's friendliest, hippest, and most comfortable stoneries. Joints €3.40-4. Weed €7-11 per g. Open daily 9:30am-1am.

Dampkring, Handboogstr. 29 (☎ 638 0705). Scenes from the film *Ocean's Twelve* were shot in this shop. Extremely detailed cannabis menu with 10 choices of pre-rolled joints €3.50-8. Salad Bowl weed €5 per g. NYC Diesel €8.50 per g. Open M-F 10am-1am.

Yo Yo, 2e Jan van der Heijdenstr. 79 (☎ 664 7173). One of the few coffee shops where neighborhood non-smokers can relax. Apple pie (€1.80), *tostis*, soup, and (normal) brownies served. All weed is organic and sold in bags for €5 or €10, with a monthly €3.50 special. Joints €2.50. Open M-Sa noon-7pm.

Rusland, Rusland 16 (☎ 627 9468). More than just a drug store: over 40 varieties of herbal tea or yogurt shakes. Pre-rolled joints €2.50-4.50. Especially tasty Afghan bud €7 per g. Space muffins €5. Open Su-Th 10am-midnight, F-Sa 10am-1am. Cash only.

Grey Area, Oude Leliestr. 2 (☎ 420 4301; www.greyarea.nl). Borrow a glass bong to smoke, or hit one of Amsterdam's cheapest pure marijuana joints (€3.50). Juice (€1.50) is also available. Open Tu-Su noon-8pm.

Siberië, Brouwersgr. 11 (☎ 623 5909; www.siberie.nl). Extensive menu of snacks, including *tostis*, different types of yogurt (€2-2.50), and an assortment of teas. Pre-rolled joints (€4) are especially popular. Experienced smokers can try the strong White Widow Mighty Whitey (€6.50 per g). Open M-F 11am-11pm, Sa-Su 11am-midnight.

Bluebird, Sint Antoniesbreestr. 71 (☎ 622 5232, www.coffeeshopbluebird.nl). At this companionable spot, the vast menu is presented in 2 thick scrapbooks that include real samples of each variety of hash and marijuana for inspection. High-quality house blend 1.4g for €13. Volcano vaporizer and bongs available. Open daily 9:30am-1am.

Hill Street Blues, Warmoesstr. 52 (www.hill-street-blues.nl). It's all about leisurely comfort at this busy but mellow coffee shop. Space cakes and cookies €3-5. Pot and hash €4.50-12 per g. Pre-rolled joints €3. Open Su-Th 9am-1am, F-Sa 9am-3am.

SMART SHOPS

Smart shops are scattered throughout Amsterdam and peddle a variety of "herbal enhancers" and hallucinogens like **magic mushrooms ('shrooms). Mexican** and **Thai** mushrooms are generally used by beginners: they are the least potent and give a laughy, colorful, speedy high with some visual hallucination. **Philosophers' stones** and **Hawaiians** are significantly more intense and should be taken only by experienced users. A mild high is a dose of about 10-15g of fresh 'shrooms; a weak trip has 15-30g; a strong trip has 30-50g. Be sure to ask the salesperson exactly how many grams there are in your purchase. 'Shrooms will start to work around 30-50min. after ingestion, and the effects will last anywhere from three to eight hours, depending on the amount of the dose. Do not take more than one dose at a time—many first-time users take too much because they don't feel anything immediately. A bad trip will occur if you mix hallucinogens with each other, marijuana, or alcohol. Be sure that you take 'shrooms in a safe environment with people you know, preferably outside and during daytime hours. Don't be ashamed to tell someone if you have a bad trip. You won't be arrested, and locals have seen it all before.

■ **Conscious Dreams,** Kerkstr. 119 (☎626 6907; www.consciousdreams.nl). Variety of mushrooms, herbs, vitamins, "dream extracts," and herbal ecstasies. Don't hesitate to ask the staff for help. Mushrooms €12-15. Herbal ecstasy €12 for 2 servings. Open daily 11am-10pm. AmEx/MC/V for purchases over €25.

Conscious Dreams Kokopelli, Warmoesstr. 12 (☎421 7000). Perhaps the best place to begin with psychedelic experimentation. Books, gifts, pipes, and lava lamps available with an overwhelming selection of 'shrooms, oxygen drinks, fertility elixirs, vitamins, and herbs. A staff with background in neurobiology and botany. Herbal XTC €12-14. Mushrooms €13-18 for a colorful variety of effects. Open daily 11am-10pm.

Magic Valley, Spuistr. 60 (☎320 3001). Small, colorful shop also vends sex stimulants. Potent Hawaiian 'shrooms €18. Mexican (€13) and Thai (€14) less potent but still pack a punch. Ask for help from the well-versed staff. Small back section that sells bongs and souvenirs. Open Su-Th 11am-10pm, F-Sa 10am-10pm. AmEx/MC/V.

♫ ENTERTAINMENT

The **Amsterdams Uit Buro (AUB),** Leidsepl. 26, is stuffed with free magazines, pamphlets, and tips to help you sift through seasonal offerings. It also sells tickets and makes reservations for just about any cultural event in the city for a commission. Visit its **Last Minute Ticket Shop** for a list of same-day performances at 50% off. (☎0900 0191; www.amsterdamsuitburo.nl or www.lastminueticketshop.nl. AUB open M-Sa 10am-7:30pm, Su noon-7:30pm. Last Minute Ticket Shop begins selling tickets daily at noon.) The theater desk at the **VVV,** Stationspl. 10, can also make reservations for cultural events. (☎0900 400 4040, €0.40 per min.; www.amsterdamtourist.nl. Open F-Sa 9am-8pm.)

■ **Filmmuseum,** Vondelpark 3 (☎589 1400; www.filmmuseum.nl). At least 4 daily screenings, many of them older classics or organized around a special theme. Also houses an extensive info center, with 1900 periodicals and over 30,000 books on film theory, history, and screenplays. Box office open 9am-10:15pm.

■ **Boom Chicago,** Leidsepl. 12 (☎423 0101; www.boomchicago.nl). English improv comedy show Su-Th 8:15pm (€20) and 2 shows per day F-Sa (€24) after a 2-course meal (appetizers from €5, entrees around €15). Open Su-Th 10am-1am, F-Sa 10am-3am.

Concertgebouw, Concertgebouwpl. 2-6 (☎671 8345; www.concertgebouw.nl). Gorgeous concert hall and home to the **Royal Concertgebouw Orchestra.** Hosts 650 events per year. Rush tickets for 26 and under from €7.50. Free lunchtime concerts during fall, winter and spring W 12:30pm. Ticket office open daily 10am-7pm; until 8:15pm for same-day ticketing. phone reservations until 5pm. AmEx/MC/V.

Stadhuis-Het Muziektheater, Waterloopl. (☎625 5455; www.hetmuziektheater.nl). Also known as the "Stopera," this gargantuan complex is home to the Dutch National Ballet (☎551 8225; www.het-nationale-ballet.nl), the Holland Symfonia (☎551 8823; www.hollandsymfonia.com), and the Netherlands Opera (☎625 5455; www.dno.nl). Box office open M-Sa 10am-6pm, Su and holidays 11:30am-2:30pm, or until curtain on performance days. Opera tickets from €20; ballet tickets from €15. AmEx/MC/V.

▨ NIGHTLIFE

Leidseplein and **Rembrandtplein** remain the liveliest areas for nightlife, with coffeeshops, loud bars, and tacky clubs galore. Amsterdam's most traditional joints are the old, dark, wood-paneled *bruin cafes* (brown cafes). The concept of a completely "straight" versus "gay" nightlife does not really apply; most establishments are gay-friendly and attract a mixed crowd. Rembrandtpl. is the hub for gay bars almost exclusively for men.

THE NETHERLANDS

CENTRUM

Café de Jaren, Nieuwe Doelenstr. 20-22 (☎625 5771). This fabulous 2-floor cafe's air of sophistication doesn't quite mesh with its budget-friendly prices. Popular with students and staff from the nearby University of Amsterdam. 2 impressive bars serve mixed drinks and beer (€1.80-3.10). Open Su-Th 10am-1am, F-Sa 10am-2am. MC/V.

Club NL, Nieuwezijds Voorburgwal 169 (☎622 7510; www.clubnl.nl). The beautiful flock to sip designer mixed drinks and groove to the house tunes of nightly DJs. Cover F-Su €5. Mandatory €1 coat check. Open Su-Th 10pm-3am, F-Sa 10pm-4am. AmEx/MC/V.

Absinthe, Nieuwezijds Voorburgwal 171 (☎320 6780). Whitewashed stone walls and cushioned niches are bathed in light from several disco balls. 17 varieties of absinthe available (€5-18). Open Su-Th 10pm-3am, F-Sa 10pm-4am. Cash only.

Club Winston, Warmoesstr. 129 (☎625 3912; www.winston.nl). Eclectic little club with a packed crowd and deceptively large dance floor. Cover varies nightly, but usually €3-7. Opening time varies, but usually daily 9pm-3am.

Cockring, Warmoesstr. 96 (☎623 9604; www.clubcockring.com). "Amsterdam's Premier Gay Disco." Straddles the line between a dance venue and a sex club. Live strip shows Th-Su from 1am. Special "SafeSex" parties 1st and 3rd Su of the month (€7.50, with free condoms; dress code "shoes only" or naked; 3-7pm). Men only. Cover M-W €2.50, Th-F and Su €3.50, Sa €5. Open Su-Th 11pm-4am, F-Sa 11pm-5am.

HARD SELL. In the Red Light District, it is not uncommon to be approached by drug pushers selling hard drugs such as cocaine and ecstasy. Remember, however, that **all hard drugs are illegal** in the Netherlands.

CANAL RING AND REMBRANDTPLEIN

Café Zool, Oude Leliestr. 9 (☎065 131 8542; www.cafezool.nl). Neighborhood bar with a friendly clientele and a wonderful feel. Ask for Tim or Bas, great sources for info about Amsterdam. Open Su-Th 4pm-1am, F 4pm-3am, Sa noon-3am. Cash only.

Arc Bar, Reguliersdwarsstr. 44 (☎689 7070; www.bararc.com). A perfect match for the young, trendy crowd that overtakes the bar weekend nights. 600-800 mixed drinks €7.50-9. DJs spin every night. Open Su-Th 4pm-1am, F-Sa 4pm-3am. AmEx/MC/V.

Montmartre, Halvemaanstg. 17 (☎620 7622). Voted best gay bar by local gay mag *Gay Krant* 7 years in a row, but definitely straight-friendly. Popular with transgendered folks. Open Su-Th 5pm-1am, F-Sa 5pm-3am. Cash only.

Escape, Rembrandtpl. 11 (☎622 1111; www.escape.nl). One of Amsterdam's hottest clubs, with 6 bars, a breezy upstairs lounge, and a cafe on the 1st fl. Lines grow long through 2am. Beer €2.30. Mixed drinks €7.50. Cover Th-Sa €10-16, students Th €6. Club open Th 11pm-4am, F-Sa 11pm-5am, Su 11pm-4:30am. Cash only.

WEST OF TOWN

Dulac, Haarlemmerstr. 118 (☎624 4265). Attracts Amsterdammers and university students with its pool table and ample nooks and booths. Entrees (€7.50-17) are half-price for students. Pint €3.50. Mixed drinks €7. DJ spins F-Sa 10pm-3am. Open Su-Th 4pm-1am, F-Sa 4pm-3am. Kitchen open daily until 10:30pm. AmEx/MC/V.

OT301, Overtoom 301 (www.squat.net/ot301). Frequent weekend club nights fill the basement with young, open-minded people ready to dance and have fun. Cover never more than €5. Beer €2. Check the website in advance for events and opening hours.

Festina Lente, Looiersgr. 40 (☎638 1412; www.cafefestinalente.nl). Super-charming bar and cafe that attracts a young, fashionable crowd. Multi-level indoor space filled with books. Wine and beer from €2.50. Open M 2pm-1am, Tu-Th 10:30am-1am, F 10:30am-3am, Sa 11am-3am, Su noon-1am. Cash only.

Café 't Smalle, Egelantiersgr. 12 (☎623 9617). A bar rich with its own history. A good place in the afternoon as well as in the evening. Rightfully one of the west's most popular cafes. Wieckse Witte beer €2.50. Open Su-Th 10am-1am, F-Sa 10am-2am.

LEIDSEPLEIN

▨ **Alto,** Korte Leidsedwarsstr. 115. Vibe is subdued but the jazz is sizzling. Show up early to get a table up front or listen from the bar. Free nightly jazz (and occasionally blues) Su-Th 10pm-2am, F-Sa 10pm-3am. Open Su-Th 9pm-3am, F-Sa 9pm-4am. Cash only.

The Waterhole, Korte Leidsedwarsstr. 49 (☎620 8904; www.waterhole.nl). Shoot a round of pool with the locals over a lager (€4.20) in this eclectic live-music bar. Music varies by night. Su-W are jam nights, and Th-Sa mostly feature local bands. Music starts nightly around 8:30pm. Open Su-Th 4pm-3am, F-Sa 4pm-4am.

Bourbon Street Jazz & Blues Club, Leidsekruisstr. 6-8 (☎623 3440; www.bourbonstreet.nl). A slightly older tourist crowd dances with abandon to blues, soul, funk, and rock bands. Beer €2.50. Cover Th and Su €3, F-Sa €5. Music Su-Th 10:30pm-3am, F-Sa 11pm-4am. Open Su-Th 10pm-4am, F-Sa 10pm-5am. AmEx/MC/V.

Paradiso, Weteringschans 6-8 (☎626 4521; www.paradiso.nl). After summer concerts, becomes a club with multiple dance halls for a variety of music styles. Concert tickets €5-25; additional mandatory membership fee €2.50. M-Th cover €6, F-Su €13. Open until 2am. Hours vary depending on performances; check the website for showtimes.

DE PIJP, JODENBUURT, AND PLANTAGE

▨ **Kingfisher,** Ferdinand Bolstr. 24 (☎671 2395). Low-key and unpretentious but hipper than its neighbors. Global beer selections €2-4. Mixed drinks €6. Fruit smoothies €2. Sandwiches €4.50. Open M-Th 11am-1am, F-Sa 11am-3am, Su noon-1am. Cash only.

Chocolate Bar, 1e Van Der Helststr. 62A (☎675 7672). 20-somethings lounge on sofas on the terrace, heading indoors for relaxed lounge music on the weekends. 12-15 mixed drinks roughly €6.50. Open Su-Th 10am-1am, F-Sa 10am-3am. MC/V.

Arena, 's-Gravesandestr. 51-53 (☎850 2400). Club bizarrely housed in the chapel of a former Catholic orphanage. More than enough enthusiasm for someone looking for a big night out. Different theme parties every night. Cover €10-25. Open F-Su 11pm-4am.

🎇 **DAYTRIP FROM AMSTERDAM: AALSMEER.** Really the only reason to visit Aalsmeer is the ▨**Bloemenveiling Aalsmeer** (Aalsmeer flower auction), Legmeerdijk 313. This massive warehouse and trading floor hosts thousands of flower traders every day. Nineteen million flowers and over two million plants are bought and sold daily, with an annual turnover of almost US$2 billion. All of the flowers, often flown overnight from across the globe, go through Aalsmeer's massive trading floor, the largest commercial trading space in the world. Almost all the trading is finished by 11am; the most action is between 7 and 9am. The trading floor is visible to tourists via a large catwalk along the ceiling. The self-guided tour takes approximately an hour to complete. (☎739 2185; www.aalsmeer.com. Open M-F 7-11am. €5, 6-11 €3, €4 per person for groups of 15+. Guides available to hire for €75.) Take **bus** #172 across from the Victoria Hotel near Centraal Station to the flower auction (Bloe-

THE NETHERLANDS

menveiling Aalsmeer) and then on to the town of Aalsmeer. The first bus leaves at 5:12am. (45min.; 4 per hr.; 6 strips to the flower auction, 2 more to the town.)

HAARLEM   ☎023

Haarlem's (pop. 150,000) narrow cobblestone streets, rippling canals, and fields of tulips in spring make for a great escape from the urban frenzy of Amsterdam, but the city also beats with a relaxed energy that befits its size.

⬛▪ TRANSPORTATION AND PRACTICAL INFORMATION. Trains depart for Amsterdam every few minutes (20min., €3.60). The **VVV,** Stationspl. 1, sells maps (€2) and finds accommodations for a €5 fee. It also vends discounted passes to museums. (☎0900 616 1600, €0.50 per min.; www.vvvzk.nl. Open Oct.-Mar. M-F 9:30am-5pm, Sa 10am-3pm; Apr.-Sept. M-F 9am-5:30pm, Sa 10am-4pm.)

▪▪ ACCOMMODATIONS AND FOOD. The best place to stay in Haarlem is the **Stayokay Haarlem ❶,** Jan Gijzenpad 3, three kilometers from Haarlem's train station. Rooms are spare but cheery and clean with bath. (☎537 3793; www.stayokay.com/haarlem. Breakfast included. High-season dorms €29; doubles €102. €2.50 HI discount. AmEx/MC/V.) Right in the town square is **Hotel Carillon ❷,** Grote Markt 27. (☎531 0591; www.hotelcarillon.com. Breakfast included. Reception and bar open daily in summer 7:30am-1am; in winter 7:30am-midnight. Singles €40, with bath €60; doubles €65/80; triples €102; quads €110. MC/V.) The Indonesian **Toko Nina ❷,** Koningstr. 48, has delicious prepared foods behind the deli counter. (☎531 7819; www.tokonina.nl. Combo meals €6-9. Open M 11am-7pm, Tu-F 9:30am-7pm, Sa 9:30am-6pm, Su 1-6pm. Cash only.) **Fortuyn ❸,** Grote Markt 23, is one of the Grote Markt's smaller *grandcafes*. (☎542 1899; www.grandcafe-fortuyn.nl. Open Su-W 10am-midnight, Th-Sa 10am-1am. Cash only.)

◰ SIGHTS. The action in Haarlem centers on Grote Markt, its vibrant main square. Its main attraction is the **Grote Kerk,** whose interior glows with light from the enormous stained-glass windows and houses the splendid, mammoth Müller organ, once played by both Handel and Mozart. Also known as St. Bavo's, it holds many historical artifacts and the graves of Jacob van Ruisdael, Pieter Saenredam, and Frans Hals. (☎553 2040; www.bavo.nl. Open Nov.-Feb. M-Sa 10am-4pm, Mar.-Oct. Tu-Sa 10am-4pm. €2, children €1.30. Guided tours by appointment €0.50. Organ concerts Tu 8:15pm, June-Sept. also Th 3pm; www.organfestival.nl. €2.50.) These painters' masterpieces can be found in the **Frans Hals Museum,** Groot Heiligland 62. Spread through recreated period rooms, the paintings are displayed as they might have been in the Golden Age. (☎511 5775; www.franshalsmuseum.com. Wheelchair-accessible. Open Tu-Sa 11am-5pm, Su noon-5pm. €7, under 19 free, groups €5.30 per person.) The **Corrie ten Boomhuis,** Barteljorisstr. 19, served as a headquarters for the Dutch Resistance in WWII. It is estimated that Corrie ten Boom saved the lives of over 800 people by arranging to have them hidden in houses, including her own. The mandatory 1hr. tour through the house provides a glance at her moving life, but the most extraordinary sight is undoubtedly the famed hiding spot. (☎531 0823; www.corrietenboom.com. Open daily Apr.-Oct. 10am-4pm; Nov.-Mar. 11am-3pm. Last tour 30min. before closing. Dutch- and English-language tours 1 per hr. Free; donations accepted.)

▪ DAYTRIP FROM HAARLEM: ZANDVOORT AND BLOEMENDAAL AAN ZEE. A mere 11km from Haarlem, the seaside town of **Zandvoort aan Zee** draws sun-starved Dutch and Germans to its miles of sandy beaches. You can stake out a spot on the sand for free, but most locals catch their rays through the comfort of **beach clubs,** wood pavilions that run along the shore with enclosed restaurants and outdoor patios. These clubs open early each morning, close at midnight, and are only in service during the summer. Nearby **Bloemendaal aan Zee** is a purely hedonistic collection of fashionable and fabulous beach clubs. **Woodstock 69** has a distinct hippie feel. *(☎573 8084.)* **Bloomingdale** tends to be the favorite of most locals. *(☎573 7580; www.bloomingdaleaanzee.com. Open daily 10am-midnight.)* From Zandvoort, take a **train** to Amsterdam (30min., 3 per hr., €4.70) or Haarlem (10min., round-trip €3.20). Bloemendaal is a 30min. walk north of Zandvoort. You can also take **bus** #81 to Haarlem from either. Zandvoort's **VVV** is on Schoolpl. 1. *(☎571 7947; www.vvvzk.nl. Open Oct.-Mar. M-F 9am-12:30pm and 1:30-4:30pm, Sa 10am-2pm; Apr.-Sept. M-F 9am-12:30pm and 1:30-4:30pm, Sa 10am-4pm.)*

LEIDEN   ☎070

Home to one of the oldest and most prestigious universities in Europe, Leiden (pop. 120,000) brims with bookstores, canals, windmills, gated gardens, antique churches, hidden walkways, and some truly outstanding museums. The **⌧Rijksmuseum voor Volkenkunde,** Steenstr. 1, displays Incan sculptures, Chinese paintings, African bronzes, and Indonesian artifacts. In all, the collection holds more than 200,000 artifacts depicting the dress, customs, and artwork of myriad indigenous cultures. (☎516 8800; www.volkenkunde.nl. Open Tu-Su 10am-5pm. €7.50, ages 4-12 and over 65 €4.) The prize **⌧Museum Naturalis,** Darwinweg 2, brings natural history to life through stunning exhibits of animals, plants, minerals, rocks, and fossils—all brilliantly explained on English and Dutch panels. (☎568 7600; www.naturalis.nl. Open July-Aug. daily 10am-6pm; Sept.-June Tu-F 10am-5pm, Sa-Su 10am-6pm. €9, ages 4-17 €5, under 3 free.) The **Rijksmuseum van Oudheden,** Rapenburg 28, focuses on the cultures of Ancient Egypt, Greece, and Rome as well as the ancient beginnings of the Netherlands, showcasing everything from mummies and sarcophagi from North Africa and Europe to Dutch artifacts from the Roman Empire. (☎516 3163; www.rmo.nl. Open Tu-F 10am-5pm, Sa-Su noon-5pm. €8.50, ages 4-17 €5.50, over 65 €7.50.) **Stedelijk Museum "De Lakenhal" Leiden,** Oude Singel 28-32, is housed in the former cloth hall that was vital to Leiden's economic development. It provides a glimpse into the history and development of the city through Dutch masterpieces. (☎516 5360. Open Tu-F 10am-5pm, Sa-Su noon-5pm. €4, under 18 free.) Scale steep staircases to inspect a functioning windmill at the **Molenmuseum De Valk,** 2e Binnenvestgr. 1. The living quarters on the mill's ground floor have been preserved to depict the life of a 19th-century miller. A climb to the top grants visitors a sweeping view of Leiden's green expanses. (☎516 5353; http://home.wanadoo.nl/molenmuseum. Open Tu-Sa 10am-5pm, Su 1-5pm. €2.50.)

The seven-room guesthouse the owners of **⌧Hotel Pension Witte Singel ❷,** Witte Singel 80, share with their guests is elegant and clean. A series of large, well-appointed, and immaculate rooms have excellent views over Leiden's gorgeous gardens and canals. (☎512 4592; www.pension-ws.demon.nl. Breakfast included. Free Wi-Fi. Singles €44-50; doubles €64-85. MC/V; 2% surcharge.) The restaurant and cafe **Annie's Verjaardag ❷,** Hoogstr. 1A, is a favorite with locals and students. (☎512 5737. Open Su-Th noon-1am, F noon-2am, Sa 11am-2am. MC/V.)

Trains haul out of Leiden's slick, translucent Centraal Station from Amsterdam (35min., 8 per hr., €7.60) and The Hague (20min., 4 per hr., €3.10). To get to the **VVV,** Stationsweg 2D, walk 5min. on Stationsweg from the train station's south exit toward the city center. (☎516 1211; www.hollandrijnland.nl. Open M 11am-5:30pm, Tu-F 9:30am-5:30pm, Sa 10am-4:30pm; Apr.-Aug. also Su 11am-3pm.)

THE HAGUE (DEN HAAG) ☎070

Whereas Amsterdam is the cultural and commercial center of the Netherlands, The Hague (pop. 480,000) is the political nucleus. The Hague is best known as the epicenter for international law. World-class art museums, a happening center, high-class shopping, and more parks per sq. km than almost any other Dutch city combine to make the Netherlands's political hub anything but boring.

🖂🖪 TRANSPORTATION AND PRACTICAL INFORMATION.

Trains run to Amsterdam (50min., 1-6 per hr., €9.60) and Rotterdam (30min., 1-6 per hr., €4.20) to both of The Hague's major stations, Den Haag Centraal and Holland Spoor. The **VVV**, Hofweg 1, has lots of city guides, bicycle maps, and guidebooks for sale in their shop, and the desk can arrange canal, carriage, and city tours. (☎361 8888; www.denhaag.com. Open M-F 10am-6pm, Sa 10am-5pm, Su noon-5pm.)

🖪🖸 ACCOMMODATIONS AND FOOD.

One of the best hostels in the Netherlands, **◪Stayokay City Hostel Den Haag ❶**, Scheepmakerstr. 27, near Holland Spoor, has spacious, sparkling rooms with private baths, a remarkably helpful staff, and lots of space in which to lounge around. (☎315 7888; www.stayokay.com/denhaag. Breakfast buffet included 7:30-9:30am. Locker rental €2 for 24hr. Internet access €5 per hr. Reception 7:30am-10:30pm. Special night keycard (and deposit) required to stay out later than 1am. 4- to 8-bed dorms €26; singles €56; doubles €61-66; triples €94; quads €113. €2.50 HI discount. €2.50 weekend surcharge. MC/V.) **Hotel 't Centrum ❶**, Veenkade 5-6, has lovely rooms. (☎346 3657. Breakfast €10. Singles €35, with bath €60; doubles with bath €70; singles €70; doubles €85; triples €100. AmEx/MC/V.) **◪HNM Café ❶**, Molenstr. 21A, has floor-to-ceiling windows, brightly colored chairs and walls, and a big bowl of Thai noodle soup (€7) on the menu. (☎365 6553. Open M-W noon-midnight, Th-Sa noon-1am, Su noon-6pm. Cash only.) **Tapaskeuken Sally ❷**, Oude Molstr. 61, is one of The Hague's best-kept dining secrets, with delicious tapas (€2.50-7) accompanied on Monday nights by live music. (☎345 1623. Open W-Sa 5:30-10:30pm. Cash only.)

🖾🎜 SIGHTS AND ENTERTAINMENT.

The opulent home of the International Court of Justice and the Permanent Court of Arbitration, the **◪Peace Palace**, Carnegiepl. 2, has served as the site of international arbitrations, peace-treaty negotiations, and high-profile conflict resolutions. Although the Permanent Court of Arbitration is closed to the public, hearings of the International Court of Jus-

IN RECENT NEWS

TRIALS AND TRIBULATIONS

Charles Taylor, warlord and former president of Liberia, is set to go on trial in The Hague. He is accused of supporting rebels who committed atrocities in neighboring Sierra Leone and of trafficking in guns and diamonds. The judges who will preside over Taylor's trial wished for the trial to occur in a more neutral place than Sierra Leone, where it could instigate instability; in The Hague, his supporters would be unable to disrupt decorum.

The Hague is the rational choice for the trial, since it has an established practice for hosting infamous war-crimes suspects, gaining visas for involved parties, and consolidating international agencies as it is in the former president's case: Taylor will be tried under the auspices of the Special Court of Sierra Leone, held in the Netherlands, and jailed, if found guilty, in Britain.

The International Court of Justice is housed in the neo-Baroque Peace Palace, which was endowed by Andrew Carnegie in the 1900s, mostly designed by French architect Louis Cordonnier, and completed in 1913. The city itself was put on the map in 1899, when the young Nicholas II, czar of Russia, planned a disarmament conference here. Since then, The Hague has held international courts and weapons conferences, and has ushered in a tradition of world leaders assembling in support of peace.

tice are free to attend. (☎302 4242, guided tours 302 4137; www.vredespaleis.nl. Tours M-F 10, 11am, 2, 3pm. Book 1 week in advance. No tours when the court is in session. €5, under 13 €3. Cash only.) With only two modest stories, the ◼**Mauritshuis,** Korte Vijverberg 8, is one of the most beautiful small museums anywhere, with a near-perfect collection of Dutch Golden Age art. Not counting the precious selection of paintings by Peter Paul Rubens, Jacob van Ruisdael, and Jan Steen, the museum has several excellent Rembrandts, including his famous *The Anatomy Lesson of Dr. Tulp.* The showstopping pieces are, without hesitation, *Girl with a Pearl Earring* and *View of Delft*, both by Johannes Vermeer. (☎302 3435; www.mauritshuis.nl. Open Tu-Sa 10am-5pm, Su 11am-5pm. Free audio tour. €9.50, under 18 free.) Show up at the **Binnenhof,** Binnenhof 8A, for a guided tour that covers both the historic **Ridderzaal** (Hall of Knights) and the **Second Chamber of the States-General,** the Netherlands's main legislative body. Tours don't run when Parliament is in session, but if you show up early you can sit in on the proceedings. The Binnenhof's courtyard is one of The Hague's most photogenic sights. (☎364 6144; www.eerstekamer.nl or www.tweedekamer.nl. Open M-Sa 10am-4pm. Last tour 3:45pm. You can enter the Second Chamber only with a passport or driver's license. Courtyard free. Tours €5, seniors and children €4.30. Cash only.) The best reason to visit the **Gemeentemuseum,** Stadhouderslaan 41, is for the world's collection of 280 Piet Mondrian paintings. (☎338 1111; www.gemeentemuseum.nl. Open Tu-Su 11am-5pm. €8.50, seniors €6.50, Museumjaarkaart holders free.)

In late June, The Hague hosts what the largest free public pop concert in Europe, **Parkpop,** on 3 big stages in Zuiderpark. (☎523 9064; www.parkpop.nl.) At other times, experimental theater, opera, jazz and blues, world-class classical ensembles, indie music, and modern dance all find a home at the **Theater aan het Spui,** Spui 187. (Ticket office ☎880 0333, main office 880 0300; www.theateraanhetspui.nl. Closed late June-Aug. Ticket office open Tu-Sa 11am-6pm.) For a cozy, pleasant bar, ◼**De Paas,** Dunne Bierkade 16A, has 11 unusually good beers on tap, 170 more in bottles, and as many friendly faces. (☎360 0019; www.depaas.nl. Beer from €1.70. Open Su-Th 3pm-1am; F-Sa 3pm-1:30am. Cash only.)

◪ **DAYTRIP FROM THE HAGUE: DELFT.** Lilied canals and stone footbridges still line the streets of picturesque Delft (pop. 100,000). Delft is famously the birthplace of the 17th-century Dutch painter **Johannes Vermeer** and the home of the famous blue-and-white ceramic pottery known as ◼**Delftware.** The best of the three factories that produce it is **De Candelaer,** Kerkstr. 13, which makes the stuff from scratch. Visitors can listen to a free explanation of the process. *(☎213 1848; www.candelaer.nl. Open daily 9am-6pm. Will ship to the US. AmEx/MC/V.)* William of Orange, father of the Netherlands, used ◼**Het Prinsenhof,** St. Agathapl. 1, as his headquarters during the Dutch resistance to Spain in the 16th century. The gorgeous old building now houses a museum chronicling his life and death as well as a collection of paintings, Delftware, and other artifacts from the Dutch Golden Age. *(☎260 2358; www.prinsenhof-delft.nl. Open Tu-Sa 10am-5pm, Su 1-5pm. €5, ages 12-16 €4, under 12 free.)* Admire the 27 stained-glass windows and three antique organs at the ◼**Oude Kerk,** Heilige Geestkerkhof 25. The church is also Vermeer's final resting place. Its tower is approximately 75m high and leans an unnerving 1.96m out of line. *(☎212 3015; www.oudekerk-delft.nl. Open Apr.-Oct. M-Sa 9am-6pm; Nov.-Mar. M-F 11am-4pm, Sa 10am-5pm. Entrance to both Nieuwe Kerk and Oude Kerk €3, ages 3-12 €1.50, seniors €2.)* You can catch the **train** to either of the two train stations in The Hague (8min., €2) or to Amsterdam (1hr., €9). The **Tourist Information Point,** Hippolytusbuurt 4, has free **Internet.** *(☎215 4015; www.delft.nl. Open Su-M 10am-4pm, Tu-F 9am-6pm, Sa 9am-5pm.)*

ROTTERDAM ☎ 010

Marked by a razor-sharp skyline, countless steamships, and darting high-speed trains, Rotterdam (pop. 590,000) is the busiest port in Europe. Festivals, art galleries, and extremely dynamic nightlife make Rotterdam a busy center of cultural activity and the hippest, most up-and-coming city in the Netherlands.

⌐ ▯ TRANSPORTATION AND PRACTICAL INFORMATION. Trains roll out of Rotterdam Centraal to Amsterdam (1¼hr., 1-5 per hr., €13) and The Hague (30min., 1-4 per hr., €4.20). Rotterdam has a network of buses, trams, and two Metro lines (**Calandlijn** and **Erasmuslijn**) that intersect in the center of the city at Beurs station. Metro tickets are equivalent to two strips and are valid for two hours. The **VVV**, Coolsingel 5, has free maps of public transportation as well as maps of the city. (☎0900 271 0120, €0.40 per min.; from abroad 414 0000; www.vvvrotterdam.nl. Open M-Th 9:30am-6pm, F 9:30am-9pm, Sa 9:30am-5pm.) Also stop by the student-oriented ▧**Use-it Rotterdam,** Conradstr. 2. (☎240 9158; www.use-it.nl.)

▮ ▯ ACCOMMODATIONS AND FOOD. Friendly, knowledgeable staff and clean, comfortable rooms help create a pleasant and relaxed air at the **Stayokay Rotterdam ❶,** Rochussenstr. 107-109. In April 2008, this location will shut its doors but will reopen in a series of the famed cube houses, at Overblaak 85-87, taking its comfort and convenience into the trendiest of Rotterdam's architectural attractions. (☎436 5763; www.stayokay.com/rotterdam. Internet access €5 per hr. Reception 24hr. Dorms €23; singles €40-45; doubles €56-65. €2.50 HI discount. AmEx/MC/V.) If you're tired of Europe, you can escape to the Middle East, Africa, or South America at the **Hotel Bazar ❸,** Witte de Withstr. 16. (☎206 5151; www.hotelbazar.nl. Rooms with bath and TV. Breakfast included. Singles €60-100; doubles €75-120. Extra bed €30. AmEx/MC/V.) Its restaurant, ▧**Bazar ❷,** attracts nightly crowds with satisfying Middle Eastern cuisine. (Sandwiches €4. Daily special entree €8. Breakfast and lunch served all day. Open M-Th 8am-1am, F 8am-2am, Sa 10am-2am, Su 10am-midnight. AmEx/MC/V.) For inexpensive grub, head to Witte de Withstr., where you can grab Chinese or Shawarma for under €5.

◎ ▯ SIGHTS AND ENTERTAINMENT. Only the extremely ambitious should attempt to see the ▧**Museum Boijmans van Beuningen,** Museumpark 18-20, in one day. On the ground floor, you'll find post-war work by artists like Andy Warhol. The second floor is home to a large selection of Surrealist and Expressionist pieces, plus an impressive collection of Dutch and Flemish art. (☎441 9400; www.boijmans.nl. Open Tu-Sa 10am-5pm, Su 11am-5pm. €9, seniors €3.50, under 18 and Museumjaarkaart holders free. Library open M-F 10am-4pm; free with entrance ticket.) The **Nederlands Architectuurinstituut (NAI),** Museumpark 25, boasts one of the most extraordinary designs in all of Rotterdam. The multi-leveled glass and steel construction is home to several exhibition spaces, a world-class archive, and 39,500 books. Entrance to the museum grants free access to the **Sonnenveld House,** a former private mansion restored to the way it would have looked in 1933. (☎440 1200; www.nai.nl. Open Tu-Sa 10am-5pm, Su 11am-5pm. €8, students and seniors €5, 4-12 €1, under 15 and Museumjaarkaart holders free.) The tallest structure in the Netherlands, the popular **Euromast,** Parkhaven 20, is the best way to take in a panoramic view of Rotterdam's jagged skyline. From the 112m viewing deck, you can take an elevator to the 185m mark to see all the way to Delft and The Hague. (☎436 4811; www.euromast.nl. Open daily Apr.-Sept. 9:30am-11pm; Oct.-Mar. 10am-11pm. €8, ages 4-11 €5.20.) The yellow **Cube Houses,** Overblaak 70, are on one corner on tall concrete columns and are designed to resemble a forest. Though they've been inhabited as private homes for over 20 years, a **Show Cube**

(Kijk-Kubus) is open to the public. (☎ 414 2285; www.cubehouse.nl. Open Mar.-Dec. daily 11am-5pm; Jan.-Feb. Sa-Su 11am-5pm. €2, 4-12 and seniors €1.50.)

 LEARNED DRINKING. Student travelers: don't forget to ask bartenders if there is a student discount. It's almost always worth a shot.

The **Rotterdamse Schouwburg,** Schouwburgpl. 25, is Rotterdam's main theater venue, with over 200 performances of opera, musical theater, modern dance, classical ballet, theater, and family performances. (☎ 411 8110; www.rotterdamse-schouwburg.nl.) **De Doelen,** Doelen Schouwburgpl. 50, the biggest concert hall in the Netherlands, is home to the **Rotterdam Philharmonic Orchestra.** (☎ 217 1717; www.dedoelen.nl. Philharmonic ☎ 217 1707; www.rpho.nl.) ■**Dizzy,** 's-Gravendijk-wal 127, Rotterdam's premier jazz cafe for 25 years, Dizzy hosts frequent jam sessions. (☎ 477 3014; www.dizzy.nl. Beer €1.80. Whiskey €5.20. Open M-Th noon-1am, F-Sa noon-2am, Su noon-midnight. AmEx/MC/V.)

UTRECHT   ☎ 030

The swarms of fraternity boys that fill Utrecht's (pop. 290,000) outdoor cafes are a visible testament to its status as the Netherlands's largest university town. Utrecht is also a cultural hub: visitors come here for action-packed festivals, museums, nightlife, and winding, tree-lined canals. Utrecht's **Domtoren,** Achter de Dom 1, the city's most beloved landmark, is the highest church tower in the Netherlands at 112m. The brick-red **Domkerk** was attached to the tower until an errant tornado blew away the nave in 1674. The church has 26,000kg of bells. (☎ 231 0403. Open Oct.-Apr. M-F 11am-4pm, Sa 11am-3:30pm, Su 2-4pm; May-Sept. M-F 10am-5pm, Sa 10am-3:30pm, Su 2-4pm. Domtoren accessible only through 1hr. tours daily Oct.-Mar. M-F noon, 2, 4pm, Sa 1 per hr. 10am-5pm, Su 1 per hr. noon-5pm. Apr.-Sept. M-Sa 1 per hr. 10am-5pm, Su 1 per hr. noon-5pm. Domkerk free. Domtoren €7.50, 4-12 €4.50.) At the **Centraal Museum,** Nicolaaskerkhof 10, visitors enter a labyrinth of pavilions to experience Dutch art from Roman and medieval archaeological finds to old masterpieces to modern art. The museum oversees the world's largest collection of work by Gerrit Rietveld, but many have been moved to the **Rietveld Schroderhuis,** accessible only by guided tour through the Centraal Museum. (☎ 236 2362 or 236 2310; www.centraalmuseum.nl. Open Tu-Th and Sa-Su noon-5pm, F noon-9pm. Audio tour free. €8, students €3, under 12 free.) The Netherlands's largest college town has nightlife to match. At ■**'t Oude Pothuys,** Oudegr. 279, uninhibited patrons have been known to jump off the bar's terrace into the canal after a long night. (☎ 231 8970. Live music nightly 11pm. Beer €2. Open Su-W 3pm-2am, Th-Sa 3pm-3am. AmEx/MC.) A former squat, **ACU Politiek Cultureel Centrum,** Voorstr. 71, hosts live music (W and F; cover €5-6), a political discussion group (M 8pm-2am), and a Sunday movie night. (☎ 231 4590; www.acu.nl. Beer €1.70. Open Su-M 8pm-2am, Tu-W 6pm-2am, Th 6pm-3am, F-Sa 9pm-4am. Cash only.) ■**Strowis Hostel ❶,** Boothstr. 8, has a laid-back staff, convenient location, and unbeatable prices. This former squat feels more like a homey country villa. Rooms and bathrooms are very clean. (☎ 238 0280; www.strowis.nl. Breakfast €5. Linens €1.30. Free Internet access and lockers. Max. 2-week stay. Curfew M-F 2am, Sa-Su 3am. 14-bed dorms €15; 8-bed dorms €16; 6-bed €17; 4-bed €18; doubles €58; triples €69.) Utrecht's few cheap eats, in the form of pizzerias, pubs, and sandwich shops, line **Nobelstraat.** A flashy clientele crowds the canal-side terrace until late at **Het Nachtrestaurant ❷,** Oudegr. 158. (☎ 230 3036. Tapas €3-6. Open M-Sa 6-11pm or later. Becomes a nightclub Sa 11pm. AmEx/MC/V.)

Take the **train** to Amsterdam (30min., 3-6 per hr., €6.40). The **VVV,** Dompl. 9, dispenses free maps of the city and complete listings of museums and sights. (☎ 0900 128 8732, €0.50 per min.; www.utrechtyourway.nl. Open Apr.-Sept. M-Sa 10am-5pm, Su noon-5pm; Oct.-Mar. Su-F noon-5pm, Sa 10am-5pm.)

DE HOGE VELUWE NATIONAL PARK ☎ 0318

At 13,565 acres, De Hoge Veluwe is the largest nature reserve in the Netherlands. Exploration through the park reveals wooded areas, moors, grassy plains, diverse wildlife, and—extraordinarily—sand dunes. The park's 36km of biking trails are its main attraction, and 1700 white bikes are available free of charge at five convenient spots in the park. (Grounds open daily Apr. 8am-8pm; May and Aug. 8am-9pm; June-July 8am-10pm; Sept. 9am-8pm; Oct. 9am-7pm; Nov.-Mar. 9am-6pm. €7, ages 6-12 €3; 50% discount May-Sept. after 5pm. Cars €6. V.) Begin by picking up a map (€2.50) at any of the park entrances or at the De Hoge Veluwe Visitors Center, known as the **Bezoekerscentrum.** (☎59 16 27; www.hogeveluwe.nl. Open daily Apr.-Oct. 9:30am-6pm, Nov.-Mar. 9:30am-5pm.) The world-class **◼Kröller-Müller Museum** is tucked deep within the park's expanses, boasting an astounding 87 paintings and 180 drawings by **Vincent van Gogh.** The sprawling, modern complex is also home to work by other early Modernists. (☎59 12 41; www.kmm.nl. Open Tu-Su 10am-5pm; sculpture garden closes 4:30pm. €7, ages 6-12 €3.50, under 6 free.)

Arnhem is a good base for exploring the park. From its rail station, trains go to Amsterdam (1¼hr., every 15min., €14). From Arnhem, take bus #105 to Otterloo and transfer to bus #106 into De Hoge Veluwe. (M-F 10 per day 8:03am-4:02pm, Sa 9 per day 8:03am-4:02pm, Su 7 per day 10:03am-4:02pm; €4.80 or 6 strips). Your best bet for accommodations is the **Stayokay Arnhem ❶,** Diepenbrocklaan 27, whose exceptionally clean rooms appeal to a slightly older crowd. (☎442 0114; www.stayokay.com/arnhem. Breakfast included. Laundry €3.50; dryer €2. Reception 8am-11pm. 6-bed dorms €23-32; 4-bed dorms €25-35; doubles €63-90. €2.50 HI discount. AmEx/MC/V.) For food, the elegant and inviting **◼Zilli & Zilli ❸,** Marienburgstr. 1, is one of the most popular spots in Arnhem. (☎442 0288; www.zillizilli.nl. Sandwiches €4.50-8.50; salads €7-12. Pasta entrees €7.50-14. Meat entrees €16-22. Lunch served 11:30am-4:30pm. Dinner served after 5pm. Open Su-Th 11:30am-1am, F-Sa 11:30am-2am. AmEx/MC/V.)

GRONINGEN ☎ 050

Groningen (pop. 185,000), easily the most happening city in the northern Netherlands, pulses with rejuvenated spirit. Heavily bombed in WWII, Groningen rebuilt itself completely yet managed to retain its Old World feel. More than half of the city's inhabitants are under 35, due in no small part to its universities. As a result, Groningen is known throughout the Netherlands as a party city. **Vera,** Oosterstr. 44, bills itself as the "club for the international pop underground." This center for live music and cinema of all stripes is a not-to-be-missed party nearly every night. (☎313 4681; www.vera-groningen.nl. Events from €4-11. Open daily 10pm-3am, sometimes later.) The intimate, candlelit **Jazzcafe de Spieghel,** Peperstr. 11, has two bars and a large stage for live jazz, funk, or blues nightly at 11pm or later. The Monday open jazz session (10:30pm) is a tradition. (☎312 6300. Wine €2.20 per glass. Open daily 8pm-4am.) **Dee's Cafe,** Papengang 3, has rock music, and foosball and pool tables (both €0.50). Its weed and hash are grown and cut without additives. (www.cafedees.nl. Weed sold in €5 and €12 denominations. Space cakes €2.70. Internet access €1 per 30min. Open M-W 11am-midnight, Th 11am-1am, F-Sa noon-3am.) The **◼Groninger Museum,** Museumeiland 1, presents modern art, traditional paintings, and ancient artifacts in steel-trimmed pavilions. (☎366 6555; www.groninger-museum.nl. Open Sept.-June Tu-Su 10am-5pm; July-Aug. M 1-5pm, Tu-Su 10am-5pm. €8, seniors €7, children €4.)

◼Simplon Jongerenhotel ❶, Boterdiep 73-2, pulls in young residents with its clean lodgings, rock-bottom prices and homey feel. (☎313 5221; www.simplon-jongerenhotel.nl. Breakfast and linens included with private rooms. Lockers with €10 deposit. Laundry €4. Reception 24hr. Lockout noon-3pm. Bike rental €6. Large dorm €13; small dorm €18; singles €33-39; doubles €50-55; triples €70; quads €100; quints €120; 6-person room €132. Cash only.) **Ben'z ❸,** Peperstr. 17, has dishes from North Africa, Europe, and the Middle East. (☎313 7917; www.restaurantbenz.nl. Entrees €10-17. 5-course menu €33. Open daily 4:30pm-midnight. Kitchen closes at 9pm. Cash only.) **Trains** run to Amsterdam transfer in Amersfoort (3hr., 2 per hr., €27). The **VVV,** Grote Markt 25, gives guided walking tours through out the year; reserve in advance. (☎900 202 3050, €0.50 per min.; www.vvvgroningen.nl. Open M-W 9am-6pm, Sa 10am-5pm; July-Aug. also Su 11am-3pm.)

MAASTRICHT   ☎043

In a little pocket of land surrounded by Belgium and Germany, Maastricht's (pop. 120,000) strategic location has made it a hotbed of military conquest and given it a pleasingly sedate, Old World feel. The manmade **■Caves of Mt. St. Pieter** has been expanded into the world's second largest underground complex with more than 20,000 passages totaling 200km. Capable of sheltering up to 40,000 people at a time, this enormous labyrinth was used as a defensive hideaway during the many sieges of Maastricht. Graffiti, carvings, and charcoal drawings from as early as Roman times cover the miles and miles of limestone. Wear a coat or sweater. There are two entrances to the vast system of caves; the most convenient starting point is Grotten Noord, Luikerweg 71. (☎325 2121; www.pietersberg.nl. €4.30, under 12 €3.30; combination with entrance to Fort St. Pieter €5.50/3.50. 1hr. English tours, Apr.-June and Sept.-Oct. Sa-Su 2pm, depending on demand.) The Zonneberg Caves, Slavante 1, are more difficult to reach. (English tours June-Aug. daily 1:55pm—plan to arrive at the docks at 1pm. Prices same as Grotten Noord; combination boat trip and visit €11, children €7.20. V.) The official seat of government for the Dutch province of Limburg, the sleek **Province House,** Limburglaan 10, has an impressive collection of modern artwork mostly by local artists. Most famously, on February 7, 1992, the leaders of 12 European nations met to sign the **Maastricht Treaty** at the small table in the center of the Council Chamber. There is a small plaque on the table commemorating the mammoth event. (☎389 9999; www.limburg.nl. Open M-F 8am-5pm.) A steady stream of visitors from nearby Belgium, Germany, and France endow Maastricht with a relatively high number of coffee shops. **■Heaven 69,** Brusselsestr. 146, doubles as a serious restaurant. (☎325 3493; www.heaven69.nl. 3 types of marijuana and 4 types of hash €7-10 per g. Pre-rolled joints €4-5. Open daily 9am-midnight. Kitchen closes at 10pm.)

The brand-new **Stayokay Maastricht ❶,** Maasblvd. 101, is your best bet for a bed. It boasts a waterside terrace, clean rooms with bath, a small bar, and a restaurant. (☎750 1790; www.stayokay.com/maastricht. Breakfast and linens included. Towels €1.30. Internet access €5 per hr. Bike rental €11.50 per day. 6-bed dorms €21-30; 4-bed dorms €23-33; 2-bed €28-40. €2.50 HI discount. AmEx/MC/V.) Find Indonesian and Chinese dishes at **■New City ❶,** Hoenderstr. 11. (☎326 1031. All-you-can-eat buffet €7. Open daily noon-10pm. Cash only.) **Cool Runnings,** Brusselsestr. 35, has a cheery upstairs, but the basement is darker, with loud music and graffiti covering literally every surface. Happy Brother weed (€13 per g), the house specialty, is some of the strongest pot in town. (Pizza and hot dogs €2. Open M-Th 10am-midnight, F-Sa 10am-2am, Su 2pm-midnight. Cash only.) The best bars in town are run by fraternities at the University of Maastricht: **■De Uni,** Brusselsestr. 31, has evolved into an unbeatable spot for imbibing with locals. (www.deuni.nl. Beer €1. Shots €1-1.50. Mixed drinks €2. €5 or €10 cards buy 5 or 10 beers. Open W-Th 9:30pm-2am, F-Sa 9:30pm-3am. Closed mid-July to mid-Aug. Cash only.)

Trains to Amsterdam (2½hr., 2 per hr., €27) leave from the station on the quiet east side of Maastricht. The **VVV,** Kleine Staat 1, sells maps (€1.30) of the city center and hefty €2.20 tourist booklets. (☎325 2121; www.vvvmaastricht.nl. Open May-Oct. M-Sa 9am-6pm, Su 11am-3pm; Nov.-Apr. M-Th 9am-6pm, Sa 9am-5pm.)

TEXEL

☎ 0222

Tucked away off the northwestern coast of the Netherlands, the Wadden Islands are an unassuming vacation destination. Texel is the most touristed island, offering all the amenities of the mainland in a remote-feeling setting. The diversity of landscape here is dazzling, and entirely bikeable. The isle's stretch of sand runs up the western coast and is divided into *paals*. The most popular strands lie near De Koog, including **paal 20.** All beaches are open to the public, and the water becomes friendly to swimmers when it warms in July and August. The **Ecomare Museum and Aquarium,** Ruijslaan 92, aims to spread the word about Texel's ecology. A seal refuge at the center houses around 30 seals per year. (☎31 77 41; www.ecomare.nl. Seal feedings 11am, 3pm. Open daily 9am-5pm. €8, 4-13 €5, under 4 free.) The **Schipbreuk- en Juttersmuseum Flora,** Pontweg 141, is a wonderful showcase of almost 70 years of beachcombing. (☎32 12 30. €4, under 16 €2.50. Open M-Sa 10am-5pm. Cash only.) On the other side of the island, a windmill marks the site of the **Maritiem en Jutters Museum,** Barentzstr. 21. Visitors can climb into the windmill or stroll across a constructed canal to peer into life-size replicas of smiths' and fishermen's houses. Indoor displays include hundreds of letters found in bottles washed up on the Texel shores. (☎31 49 56; www.texels-maritiem.nl. Open Sept.-June Tu-Sa 10am-5pm; July-Aug. M-Sa 10am-5pm. €5, under 14 €3.50.) **Le Berry,** Dorpsstr. 3, has the air of a pub and caters to a slightly older crowd. There is dancing most nights, though, especially on weekends in the summer. (☎31 71 14; www.leberry.nl. DJ W-Su nights. Open noon-4am. Dancing from 11pm.)

The massive **Stayokay Texel ❶,** Haffelderweg 29, is the island's cheapest and most reliable accommodations option. (☎31 54 41. Breakfast and linens included. Internet access €1 per 30min. Reception 8am-8pm. Bar open 5pm-midnight. 4- to 6-bed dorms €30; 2-bed dorms from €35.) Fresh seafood is served in most restaurants in Den Burg. The pub **De 12 Balcken Tavern ❶,** Weverstr. 20, has a cozy *bruin cafe* feel. Sample a shot of '*t Juttertje* (€2.20), the island's popular licorice-flavored schnapps. (☎31 26 81. Open M-Sa 10am-3am.) In De Koog, venture down Dorpsstr. for all manner of beach bars, cafes, Shawarma huts, and ice cream stands.Take the **train** to Amsterdam from Den Helder (1½hr., €11), but first you must take a **Teso ferry** there from Het Horntje, the southernmost town on Texel (20min.; 1 per hr. 6:30am-9:30pm; round-trip €3, under 12 €1.50, additional €2.50 for bikes). **Buses** depart from the ferry dock to various locales on the island; buy a **Texel Ticket,** which allows unlimited one-day travel on the island-wide bus system (mid-June to mid-Sept., €4.50). The **VVV,** Emmalaan 66, is outside Den Burg, 300m south of the main bus stop. (☎31 47 41; www.texel.net. Open M-F 9am-5:30pm, Sa 9am-5pm.)

NORWAY (NORGE)

Norway's rugged countryside and remote mountain farms gave birth to one of the most feared seafaring civilizations of pre-medieval Europe: the Vikings. Modern-day Norwegians have inherited their ancestors' independent streak, voting against joining the EU in 1994 and drawing the ire of environmental groups for their refusal to ban commercial whaling. Because of high revenues from petroleum exports, Norway enjoys one of the highest standards of living in the world. Its stunning fjords and miles of undisturbed coastline make the country a truly worthwhile destination—but sky-high prices and limited public transportation in rural areas may challenge even the best-prepared budget traveler.

🧭 DISCOVER NORWAY: SUGGESTED ITINERARY

Oslo (p. 735) is the best jumping-off point. Tear yourself away from the museums and ethnic restaurants for a daytrip to seaside **Stavanger** (p. 744). Back in Oslo, catch a westbound train for the scenic ride to **Bergen** (p. 746). En route, get sidetracked on the **Flåm Railway** (p. 752), or hike on the Hardangervidda plateau near **Eidfjord** (p. 752). Plan a few days in Bergen, then head north to the postcard-perfect **Geirangerfjord** (p. 755) and less-trafficked **Sognefjord** (p. 752). Visit the Art Nouveau architecture in **Ålesund** (p. 757) and the Nidaros Cathedral in **Trondheim** (p. 758). Then venture beyond the Arctic Circle to the fishing villages and scenery of the **Lofoten Islands** (p. 762), **Tromsø** (p. 760), happening despite its remote location, and the windswept Arctic desert of **Svalbard** (p. 764).

ESSENTIALS

FACTS AND FIGURES

Official Name: Kingdom of Norway.

Capital: Oslo.

Major Cities: Bergen, Stavanger, Tromsø, Trondheim.

Population: 4,628,000.

Land Area: 307,500 sq. km.

Time Zone: GMT +1.

Languages: Bokmål and Nynorsk Norwegian; Sámi; Swedish and English are both widely spoken.

Winter Olympic Medals won since the first games in 1924: 280; more than any other nation.

WHEN TO GO

Oslo averages 18°C (63°F) in July and -4°C (24°F) in January. The north is the coldest and wettest region, though Bergen and the surrounding mountains to the south are also rainy. For a few weeks around the summer solstice (June 21), the area north of Bodø basks in the midnight sun. The **Northern Lights,** spectacular nighttime displays formed when solar flares produce plasma clouds that run into atmospheric gases, peak from November to February. Skiing is best just before Easter.

DOCUMENTS AND FORMALITIES

EMBASSIES AND CONSULATES. Foreign embassies in Norway are in Oslo. Norwegian embassies abroad include: **Australia,** 17 Hunter St., Yarralumla, ACT, 2600

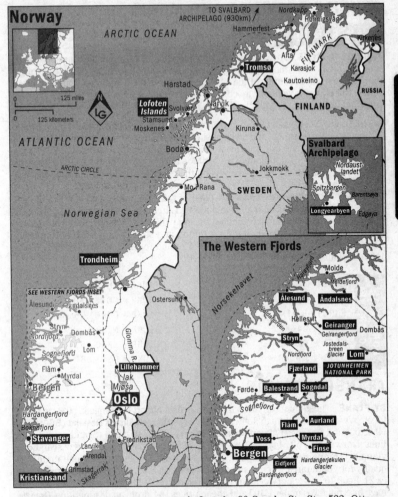

Norway

TO SVALBARD
ARCHIPELAGO (930km)

ARCTIC OCEAN

Nordkapp
Honningsvåg
Hammerfest
Vardø
Vadsø
Alta
Karasjok
Tromsø
Kautokeino
Harstad
Lofoten Islands
Svolvær
Narvik
Stamsund
Kiruna
Moskenes
Westfjord
Bodø
Jokkmokk
ARCTIC CIRCLE
Mo i Rana
SWEDEN
Norwegian Sea
RUSSIA
FINLAND
FINNMARK

125 miles
125 kilometers
ATLANTIC OCEAN

Svalbard Archipelago
Nordaust-landet
Spitzbergen
Barentsøya
Longyearbyen
Edgøya

Trondheim
SEE WESTERN FJORDS INSET
Ålesund
Åndalsnes
Ostersund
Stryn
Nordfjord
Dombås
Lom
Sognefjord
Glomma R.
Flåm
Myrdal
Bergen
Lillehammer
Jak
Mjøsa
Oslo
Hardangerfjord
Boknafjord
Stavanger
Larvik
Fredrikstad
Arendal
Grimstad
Skagerrak
Kristiansand

The Western Fjords
Molde
Moldefjord
Norsekehavet
Ålesund
Åndalsnes
Hellesylt
Geiranger
Geirangerfjord
Dombås
Stryn
Nordfjord
Jostedals-breen glacier
Lom
Fjærland
JOTUNHEIMEN NATIONAL PARK
Førde
Balestrand
Sogndal
Sognefjord
Flåm
Aurland
Voss
Myrdal
Finse
Bergen
Eidfjord
Hardangerjøkulen Glacier
Hardangerfjord

NORWAY

(☎ 262 73 34 44; www.norway.org.au); **Canada,** 90 Sparks St., Ste. 532, Ottawa, ON, K1P 5B4 (☎ 613-238-6571; www.emb-norway.ca); **Ireland,** 34 Molesworth St., Dublin 2 (☎ 16 62 18 00; www.norway.ie); **UK,** 25 Belgrave Sq., London, SW1X 8QD (☎ 20 75 91 55 00; www.norway.org.uk); **US,** 2720 34th St., NW, Washington, D.C., 20008 (☎ 202-333-6000; www.norway.org).

VISA AND ENTRY INFORMATION. EU citizens do not need a visa. Citizens of Australia, Canada, New Zealand, and the US do not need a visa for stays of up to 90 days, beginning upon entry into any of the countries within the EU's freedom of movement zone. For more info, see p. 14. For stays longer than 90 days, all non-EU citizens need visas (around US$80; fee is waived for students and teachers traveling for educational purposes), available at Norwegian consulates. For more info on obtaining a visa go to www.norway.org/visas.

TOURIST SERVICES AND MONEY

EMERGENCY	Ambulance: ☎113. Fire: ☎110. Police: ☎112.

TOURIST OFFICES. Virtually every town and village has a **Turistinformasjon** office; look for a white "i" on a square green sign. From the latter half of June through early August, most tourist offices are open daily; expect reduced hours at other times. Check www.visitnorway.com for a directory of local offices. More info on traveling in Norway is available at www.norway.no.

MONEY. The Norwegian unit of currency is the **krone (kr)**, plural **kroner.** One krone is equal to 100 **øre.** Banks and large post offices change money, usually for a small commission. It's generally cheaper to exchange money in Norway than at home. **Tipping** is not expected, but an extra 5-10% is always welcome for good restaurant service. It is customary to leave coins on the counter or table rather than putting the tip on a credit card. Hotel bills often include a 15% service charge.

Norway has a 25% **value added tax (VAT)**, a sales tax applied to goods and services. The prices given in *Let's Go* include VAT. In the airport upon exiting the EU, non-EU citizens can claim a refund on the tax paid for goods purchased at participating stores. In order to qualify for a refund in a store, you must spend at least 315kr in a single store; be sure to ask for a refund form when you pay. For more info on qualifying for a VAT refund, see p. 19.

NORWEGIAN KRONER (KR)		
AUS$1 = 4.74KR	10KR = AUS$2.11	
CDN$1 = 5.61KR	10KR = CDN$1.78	
EUR€1 = 8.01KR	10KR = EUR€1.25	
NZ$1 = 4.14KR	10KR = NZ$2.41	
UK£1 = 11.78KR	10KR = UK£0.85	
US$1 = 5.95KR	10KR = US$1.68	

TRANSPORTATION

BY PLANE. The main international airport is **Oslo Airport Gardermoen (OSL; ☎81 55 02 50; www.osl.no)**, though some flights land at **Bergen Airport Flesland (BGO; ☎55 99 80 00)** and **Trondheim Airport Værnes (TRD; ☎74 84 30 00)**. **SAS** (Scandinavian Airlines; Norway ☎91 50 54 00, UK 08 70 60 72 77 27, US 800-221-2350; www.scandinavian.net), Finnair, and Icelandair, fly to Norway. Students and those under 25 qualify for youth fares when flying domestically on SAS. Budget airlines **Norwegian** (☎21 49 00 15; www.norwegian.no) and **Widerøe** (☎75 11 11 11; www.wideroe.no) have internal fares under €100 and cheap prices to European destinations. **Ryanair** (☎353 12 49 77 91; www.ryanair.com) flies to Sandefjord Airport Torp (p. 743), near Oslo, and Haugesund, near Bergen. Book early for the best fares on all airlines, or try your luck with SAS domestic standby tickets *(sjanse billetter)*, purchased at the airport on the day of travel for around 400kr.

BY TRAIN. Norway's train system includes a commuter network around Oslo and long-distance lines running from Oslo to Bergen and to Stavanger via Kristiansand. Contact **Norwegian State Railways (NSB)** for timetables and tickets (☎81 50 08 88; www.nsb.no). The unguided **Norway in a Nutshell** tour combines a ride along the **Flåm Railway**, a **cruise** through Aurlandsfjord and Nærøyfjord to the port of Gudvangen, and a **bus ride** over the mountains to Voss. Tickets can be purchased from tourist offices or train stations in Bergen and Oslo. (☎81 56 82 22; www.norwaynutshell.com. Round-trip from Voss 530kr, from Bergen 820kr, from Oslo

1650kr.) Overnight trains may be the best option for travel as far north as Bodø and Trondheim; from there, you'll need buses or ferries to get farther north. **Eurail Passes** are valid in Norway. The **Norway Railpass**, available only outside Norway, allows three to five days of unlimited travel in a one-month period (from US$183). The **Scanrail pass**, valid in Norway, Denmark, Finland, and Sweden, allows five travel days in a two-month period (US$214, under 26 US$161) or 21 consecutive days (US$332/249) of unlimited rail travel, as well as discounted fares on many ferries and buses. However, only three of those travel days can be used in the country of purchase, so a Scanrail pass purchased at home (p. 49) may be more economical. Neither pass includes trips on the Flåm Railway.

RAIL SAVINGS. For rail travel within Norway, the **Minipris** offered by NSB is a great deal. A limited number of seats are made available on regional trains for 199kr and 299kr, including on expensive routes. Go to www.nsb.no to purchase tickets; when asked to choose the type of ticket, select Minipris. (If it is not on the menu, tickets are sold out.) Minipris tickets purchased outside Norway are 50kr cheaper than those purchased in the country.

BY BUS. Buses can be quite expensive but are the only land travel option north of Bodø and in the fjords. **Nor-way Bussekspress** (☎81 54 44 44; www.nor-way.no) operates most of the domestic bus routes and publishes a timetable *(Rutehefte)* with schedules and prices, available at bus stations and on buses. Scanrail pass holders are entitled to a 50% discount on most routes, and students with ISIC are eligible for a 25-50% discount—be insistent, and follow the rules listed in the *Norway Bussekspress* booklet. Bus passes, valid for 10 or 21 consecutive travel days (1300/2400kr), are good deals for those exploring the fjords or the north.

BY FERRY. Car ferries *(ferjer)* are usually cheaper (and slower) than the passenger express boats *(hurtigbat or ekspressbat)* cruising the coasts and fjords; both often have student, Scanrail, and InterRail discounts. The **Hurtigruten** (☎81 03 00 00; www.hurtigruten.com) takes six to 11 days for the incredible cruise from Bergen to Kirkenes on the Russian border (from 6000kr in high season, 3500kr in low season). Discounts for rail pass holders are limited to 50% off the Bergen-Stavanger route, but some lines also offer a 50% student discount. The common ports for international ferries are Oslo, Bergen, Kristiansand, and Stavanger. **DFDS Seaways** (☎21 62 13 40; www.dfdsseaways.com) sails from Oslo and Kristiansand to Copenhagen, DEN and Gothenburg, SWE. **Color Line** (☎81 00 08 11; www.colorline.com) runs ferries between Norway and Denmark, plus several domestic routes.

BY CAR. Citizens of Australia, Canada, the EU, New Zealand, and the US can drive in Norway for up to one year with a valid driver's license from their home country. Vehicles are required to keep headlights on at all times. Roads in Norway are in good condition, although blind curves are common and roads are narrow in some places. Drivers should be cautious, especially on mountain roads and in tunnels, as reindeer and sheep can make unexpected appearances. Driving around the fjords can be frustrating, as only Nordfjord has a road completely circumnavigating it. Insurance is required and usually included in the price of rental. Though expensive, renting a car can be more affordable than trains and buses when traveling in a group. There are numerous car ferries, so check schedules in advance. For more info on driving in Europe, see p. 50.

BY BIKE AND BY THUMB. The beautiful scenery around Norway is rewarding for cyclists, but the hilly terrain can be rough on bikes. Contact **Syklistenes Landsforening** (☎22 47 30 30; www.slf.no) for maps, suggested routes, and other info. **Hitchhiking** is difficult in mainland Norway, but easier on the Lofoten and Svalbard Islands.

Some travelers successfully hitchhike beyond the rail lines in northern Norway and the fjord areas of the west, while many others try for hours without success. Hitchhikers suggest bringing several layers of clothing, rain gear, and a warm sleeping bag. Let's Go does not recommend hitchhiking.

KEEPING IN TOUCH

PHONE CODES	**Country code: 47. International dialing prefix:** 095. For more info on how to place international calls, see **Inside Back Cover.**

EMAIL AND THE INTERNET. Oslo and Bergen have many Internet cafes. Expect to pay about 1kr per min. Smaller cities might have one or two Internet cafes, and most have a public library open on weekdays that offers 15-30min. of free Internet access. Free Wi-Fi connections for travelers with laptops are also readily available. For more info on Internet access in Europe see p. 27.

TELEPHONE. There are three types of **public phones:** black and gray phones accept 1, 5, 10, and 20kr coins; green phones accept only phone cards; red phones accept coins, phone cards, and major credit cards. **Phone cards** (*telekort;* 40, 90, or 140kr at post offices and Narvesen kiosks) are the most economical option, especially when prices drop between 5pm and 8am. Mobile phones are increasingly popular and cheap in Norway; buying a prepaid SIM card for a GSM phone can be a good, inexpensive option. Of the service providers, Netcom and Telenor have the best networks. For help with domestic calls, dial ☎117. International direct access numbers include: **AT&T Direct** (☎80 01 90 11); **British Telecom** (☎80 01 99 44); **Canada Direct** (☎80 01 91 11); **MCI WorldPhone** (☎80 01 99 12); **Telecom New Zealand** (☎80 01 99 64); **Telstra Australia** (☎80 01 99 61).

MAIL. Mailing a first-class postcard or letter (under 20g) within Norway costs 6.50kr; outside Norway costs 9.50-11kr. To receive mail in Norway, have mail delivered **Poste Restante.** Mail will go to the main post office unless you specify a subsidiary by street address. Address mail to be held according to the following example: First name LAST NAME, *Poste Restante*, City, Norway. Bring a passport to pick up your mail; there may be a small fee.

LANGUAGE. Norwegian is universal, and many also speak English and Swedish. The indigenous people of northern Norway speak different dialects of Sámi. For basic Norwegian words and phrases, see **Phrasebook: Norwegian** (p. 1064).

ACCOMMODATIONS AND CAMPING

NORWAY	❶	❷	❸	❹	❺
ACCOMMODATIONS	under 160kr	160-260kr	261-400kr	401-550kr	over 550kr

Norske Vandrerhjem (☎23 12 45 10; www.vandrerhjem.no) operates **HI youth hostels** (*vandrerhjem*). Beds run 100-300kr, and HI members receive a 15% discount. Linens typically cost 45-60kr per stay, and sleeping bags are forbidden. Few hostels have curfews. Most hostels open in mid- to late June and close after the third week in August. Many tourist offices book **private rooms** and hotels for a fee (usually 30kr). Norwegian **right of public access** allows camping anywhere on public land for fewer than three nights, as long as you keep 150m from buildings and leave no trace. **Den Norske Turistforening** (DNT; Norwegian Mountain Touring Association) sells maps (60-70kr), offers guided hiking trips, and maintains more than 350 **mountain huts** (*hytter*) throughout Norway. A one-year membership (465kr, under 26 265kr) entitles the holder to discounts on DNT lodgings (☎40 00 18 68;

www.dntoslo.no). The 42 staffed huts are open in summer; most have showers and serve dinner. Unstaffed huts are open mid-February to mid-October; a sizable minority have basic provisions for sale on the honor system. Members can leave a 100kr deposit at any tourist office to borrow a key. Prices vary according to age, season and membership; official campgrounds ask 25-140kr for tent sites, 300-600kr for cabins. For more info on camping in Norway, visit www.camping.no.

FOOD AND DRINK

NORWAY	❶	❷	❸	❹	❺
FOOD	under 60kr	60-100kr	101-150kr	151-250kr	over 250kr

Many restaurants have inexpensive *dagens ret* (dish of the day; 70-80kr). Otherwise, you'll rarely spend less than 150kr for a full meal. Fish—cod, herring, and salmon—is fresh and relatively inexpensive. Non-fish specialties include cheese *(ost)*, Jarlsberg being the most popular; pork-and-veal meatballs *(kjøttkaker)* with boiled potatoes; and, for more adventurous carnivores, reindeer, ptarmigan, and whale meat *(hval)*. Christmas brings a meal of dried fish soaked in water and lye *(lutefisk)*. Beer is expensive in bars (45-60kr for ½L), though 0.33L bottles can be found for 10-13kr in supermarkets. Try the local favorite, *Frydenlund*, or go rock-bottom with Danish *Tuborg*. You must be 18 to buy beer and wine, and 20 to buy liquor at the aptly named **Vinmonopolet** (wine monopoly) stores.

HOLIDAYS AND FESTIVALS

Holidays: New Year's Day (Jan. 1); Maundy Thursday (Mar. 20); Good Friday (Mar. 21); Easter (Mar. 23-24); Labor Day (May 1); Ascension (May 1); Pentecost (May 11-12); Constitution Day (May 17); Christmas (Dec. 25); Boxing Day (Dec. 26).

Festivals: Norway throws festivals virtually year-round, from the Tromsø International Film Festival (Jan. 15-20; www.tiff.no) to Bergen's operatic Festpillene (May 21-June 4; www.fib.no). The Norwegian Wood Festival in Frognerbadet (mid-June; www.norwegian-wood.no) features pop, folk, and classic rock. Heavy metal enthusiasts flock to Inferno, held in Oslo on Easter weekend (Mar. 23-24; www.infernofestival.net). For more info, check www.norwayfestivals.com.

BEYOND TOURISM

Citizens of the 40 signatory countries of the **Svalbard Treaty,** including Australia, Canada, New Zealand, the UK, and the US, can work on the Svalbard archipelago (p. 764). For more info on opportunities across Europe, see **Beyond Tourism,** p. 56.

The American-Scandinavian Foundation (AMSCAN), 58 Park Ave., New York, NY, 10016, USA (☎212-879-9779; www.amscan.org/jobs/index.html). Volunteer and job opportunities throughout Scandinavia. Limited number of fellowships for study in Norway available to Americans.

Study in Norway (www.studyinnorway.no). Education and research opportunities throughout the country for summer and term-time study. Scholarships available.

OSLO   ☎ 21, 22, 23

Scandinavian capitals consent to being urban without renouncing the landscape around them, and Oslo (pop. 550,000) is no exception. The Nordmarka forest to the north and Oslofjord to the south bracket the city's cultural institutions, busy cafes, and expensive boutiques. While most of Norway remains homogeneous, Oslo has a small multi-ethnic immigrant community in its eastern and northern sections. Even with globalization, Norwegian history and folk traditions still shape Oslo, a somewhat pricey city but an essential stop on any trip to Scandinavia.

TRANSPORTATION

Flights: Oslo Airport Gardermoen (OSL; ☎81 55 02 50; www.osl.no), 45km north of the center. The high-speed **FlyToget train** (☎815 0777; www.flytoget.no) runs between the airport and downtown (20min.; 3-6 per hr.; 160kr, students 80kr). White SAS **Flybussen** run a similar route. (☎22 80 49 71; www.flybussen.no. 40min.; 2-3 per hr.; 120kr, students 60kr; round-trip 220/110kr.) Some budget airlines fly into Sandefjord Airport Torp, south of Oslo (p. 743).

Trains: Oslo Sentralstasjon (Oslo S), Jernbanetorget 1 (☎81 50 08 88). To: **Bergen** (6-8hr., 4-5 per day, 716kr); **Trondheim** (6-8hr., 2-5 per day, 797kr); **Copenhagen, DEN** via **Gothenburg, SWE** (7-8hr., 2 per day, from 717kr); **Stockholm, SWE** (4¾hr., 3 per day, from 650kr). Mandatory seat reservations for domestic trains 41-71kr.

Buses: Nor-way Bussekspress, Schweigårds gt. 8 (☎81 54 44 44; www.nor-way.no). Follow the signs from the train station through the Oslo Galleri Mall to the Bussterminalen Galleriet. Schedules available at the info office. 25-50% ISIC discount.

Ferries: Color Line (☎81 00 08 11; www.colorline.com). To **Frederikshavn, DEN** (12½hr.; 7:30pm; 250-490kr, in winter students 95kr-230kr) and **Kiel, GER** (19½hr.; 2pm; 780-3690kr/390-1845kr). **DFDS Seaways** (☎21 62 13 40; www.dfdsseaways.com). To **Copenhagen, DEN** (16hr.) and **Helsingborg, SWE** (14½hr.) daily at 5pm (both 810-1010kr). For more info on ferries in Scandinavia, see p. 53.

Public Transportation: Buses, ferries, subways, and **trams** cost 30kr per ride or 20kr in advance. Tickets include 1hr. of unlimited transfers. If you are caught traveling without a valid ticket, you can be fined 700-900kr. **Trafikanten** (☎177; www.trafikanten.no), in front of Oslo S, sells the **Dagskort** (day pass; 60kr), **Flexicard** (8 trips; 160kr), and **7-day Card** (210kr). Open M-F 7am-8pm, Sa-Su 8am-6pm. Tickets also at Narvesen kiosks and Automat machines in the metro.

Bike Rental: The city's bike-share system allows visitors to borrow one of the 1000+ bikes available at racks throughout the city center. Both the main tourist office and the Oslo S branch sell system enrollment cards (70kr per day). Note that bikes must be returned to a rack every 3hr., a means of keeping track of them.

Hitchhiking: Hitchhiking is not common in this area of Norway because of the extensive transportation network. Some travelers report hitching rides to major cities at truck terminals. Let's Go does not recommend hitchhiking.

ORIENTATION AND PRACTICAL INFORMATION

In Oslo center, the garden plaza **Slottsparken (Castle Park)** lies beside **Oslo University** and the **Nationaltheatret (National Theater)** and surrounds the **Royal Palace.** The city's main street, **Karl Johans gate,** runs through the heart of town from Slottsparken to the train station **Oslo Sentralstasjon (Oslo S)** at the eastern end. Ferries depart from the harbor, southwest of Oslo S near Akershus Castle. Many museums and beaches are southwest on the **Bygdøy** peninsula. Ferries to Bygdøy depart from the dock behind **Rådhus (City Hall).** Massive construction projects are currently reshaping the harbor, a project marked by a new opera house. Parks are scattered throughout Oslo, especially north of the Nationaltheatret. Of note is **Saint Hanshaugen,** a hilly park north of the city center up **Akersgata** as it becomes **Ullevålsveien.** A network of public trams, buses, and subways makes transit through the outskirts quick and easy. **Grünerløkka** to the north and **Grønland** to the east, largely home to Oslo's immigrant population, are often cheaper than the city's other neighborhoods, and their boutiques, cafes, and parks showcase the latest urban trends. While some believe this area is less safe, crime is generally low.

NORWAY

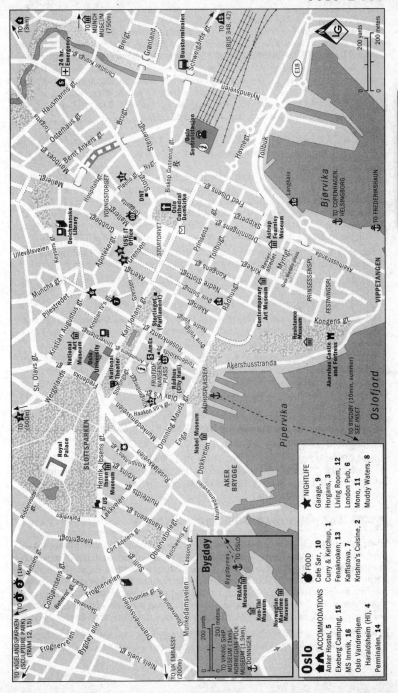

Oslo

ACCOMMODATIONS
Anker Hostel, **5**
Ekeberg Camping, **15**
MS Innvik, **16**
Oslo Vandrerhjem
Haraldsheim (HI), **4**
Perminalen, **14**

FOOD
Cafe Sør, **10**
Curry & Ketchup, **1**
Fenaknoken, **13**
Kaffistova, **7**
Krishna's Cuisine, **2**
Garage, **9**
Horgans, **3**
Living Room, **12**
London Pub, **6**
Mono, **11**
Muddy Waters, **8**

NIGHTLIFE
Garage, **9**
Horgans, **3**
Living Room, **12**
London Pub, **6**
Mono, **11**
Muddy Waters, **8**

Tourist Offices: Fridtjof Nansenspl. 5 (☎81 53 05 55; www.visitoslo.com). Sells the **Oslo Pass,** offering unlimited public transport and admission to most museums. 1-day pass 250kr, 2-day 300kr, 3-day 390kr. Open June-Aug. daily 9am-7pm; Sept. and Apr.-May M-Sa 9am-5pm; Oct.-Mar. M-F 9am-4pm. **Oslo Central Station Tourist Info,** Jernbanetorget 1, outside Oslo S. Open M-F 7am-8pm, Sa-Su 8am-8pm. ▨ **Use-It,** Møllergt. 3 (☎24 14 98 20; www.unginfo.oslo.no/useit), targets students and backpackers but welcomes all travelers. Helps find beds for no fee, offers free Internet and baggage storage, and publishes the invaluable *Streetwise Budget Guide to Oslo.* Open July-Aug. M-F 9am-6pm; Sept.-June M-F 11am-5pm.

TIP

A HAPPENING PLACE. Use-It organizes summer events and "happenings" for youth and foreign travelers in Oslo. Check at the office for details.

Embassies and Consulates: Australia: contact the embassy in Denmark (p. 255). **Canada,** Wergelandsv. 7, 4th fl. (☎22 99 53 00; www.canada.no). Open June-Aug. M-F 8am-4pm; Sept.-May M-F 8:30am-4:30pm. **Ireland,** Haakon VII's gt. 1 (☎22 01 72 00; osloembassy@dfa.ie). Open M-F 8:30am-4:30pm. **UK,** Thomas Heftyes gt. 8 (☎23 13 27 00; www.britian.no). Open in summer M-F 8:30am-4pm; in winter M-F 9am-4pm. **US,** Henrik Ibsens gt. 48 (☎22 44 85 50; www.usa.no). Open M-F 7:30am-5pm.

Currency Exchange: At any major bank: **Christiania, Den Norske, Landsbanker** and **Forebu Oslo. Forex,** Fridtjof Nansens pl. 6 (☎22 41 30 60), offers the best rates.

Luggage Storage: Lockers at Oslo S and at the Nationaltheatret station. 20-45kr per 24hr. Max. 7 days. Available 4:30am-1:10am. Office open M-F 9am-3pm. You can leave bags in the Use-It office (see above) for an afternoon or night.

Library and Internet Access: Free terminals at the **Deichmanske Library,** Arne Garborgs pl. 4. Sign up for 1hr. drop in for 15-30min. Open Sept.-May M-F 10am-7pm, Sa 11am-2pm; June-Aug. M-F 10am-6pm, Sa 11am-2pm.

GLBT Resources: Landsforeningen for Lesbisk og Homofil fri gjøring (LLH), Kongensgt. 12 (☎23 10 39 39; www.llh.no). Tourist office also has GLBT resources.

Laundromat: Look for the word *"myntvaskeri."* **Selva AS,** Ullevålsveien 15 (☎41 64 08 33). Wash 40kr, dry 30kr. Open M-F 8am-9pm, Sa 10am-3pm.

Police: ☎02800 to bypass dispatch and connect directly.

24hr. Pharmacy: Jernbanetorvets Apotek (☎23 35 81 00), opposite Oslo S.

Hospital: Oslo Kommunale Legevakt, Storgt. 40 (☎22 93 22 93).

Post Office: Main branch at Kirkegt. 20 (☎23 35 86 90). Address mail to be held in the following format: First name, LAST NAME, *Poste Restante,* Oslo Central Post Office, N-0101 Oslo, NORWAY. Open M-F 9am-6pm, Sa 10am-3pm. The post office at Oslo S is open M-F 9am-8pm.

ACCOMMODATIONS AND CAMPING

Hostels in Oslo fill up in summer. Reservations are essential. The **private rooms** available through **Use-It** (see tourist offices) are good deals, starting from 140kr. **Pensjonater** (pensions) are centrally located but can be more expensive. Check with the tourist office for last-minute accommodation deals. Travelers can **camp** for free in the forest north of town; try the end of the Sognsvann line #3. Young Norwegians often drink at home before heading out because of high bar prices, but most hostels, including HI, prohibit alcohol consumption on their premises.

▨ **Perminalen,** Øvre Slottsgt. 2 (☎23 09 30 81; www.perminalen.no). 15min. walk from Oslo S or tram #12 to Christianian Torv. Backpackers looking for the full package head to this central hotel/hostel. Spacious rooms equipped with A/C and cable TV. Breakfast included. Internet 15kr per 15min. Reception 24hr. Dorms 335kr; singles 499kr; doubles 720kr. AmEx/D/MC/V. ❸

Anker Hostel, Storgt. 55 (☎22 99 72 00, booking 22 99 72 10; www.ankerhostel.no). Walk 10min. north from Oslo S or take tram #11, 12, 13, or 17 to Hausmanns gt. Renovated rooms with kitchenettes and bath. Breakfast 75kr. Linens 50kr. Internet 10kr per 15min. Reception in summer 24hr. Dorms 200kr; doubles 500kr. AmEx/D/MC/V. ❷

Oslo Vandrerhjem Haraldsheim (HI), Haraldsheimvn. 4 (☎22 22 29 65; www.haraldsheim.oslo.no). Take tram #17 from Stortorvet for 15min. to Sinsenkrysset and walk up the hill through the park. Standard bunk dorms in a quiet, residential neighborhood. Breakfast included. Linens 50kr. Reception 24hr. Dorms 220kr, with bath 245kr; singles 320/425kr; doubles 495/575kr. 15% HI discount. MC/V. ❷

MS Innvik, Langkaia 49 (☎22 41 95 00; www.msinnvik.no). From Oslo S, cross the highway E18 overpass and head right along the harbor. This artsy, boat-borne B&B is on Bjørvika Bay. Don't worry—the boat is very stable and seasickness is a non-issue. Compact cabins come with bath. Breakfast included. Reception 24hr. Check-in 5pm. Check-out noon. Singles 425kr; doubles 750kr. MC/V. ❹

Ekeberg Camping, Ekebergveien 65 (☎22 19 85 68; www.ekebergcamping.no), 3km from town. Bus #34A or 46. 24hr. security. Grocery store open daily 8am-10pm. Showers 10kr per 6min. Laundry 40kr. Reception 7:30am-11pm. Open June-Aug. 2-person tent sites 150kr, 4-person 245kr; 55kr per extra person. AmEx/D/MC/V. ❶

FOOD

Visitors can choose between hearty, often bland Norwegian fare and a variety of ethnic dishes. Either way, they usually feel robbed blind once the check arrives. Smart backpackers stock up at the city's grocery stores. Look for the chains **ICA, Kiwi,** and **Rema 1000** (generally open M-F 9am-9pm, Sa-Su 9am-6pm), or pick up fresh produce at the Youngstorget **open-air market** (M-Sa 7am-2pm). In the budget-friendly **Grønland** district, east of Oslo S, vendors hawk **kebabs** and **falafel** (around 40kr), while *halal* butchers can provide travelers with cooking meat.

DINING FOR POCKET CHANGE. Oslo's sky-high food prices can bring travelers to tears. For a bite on the cheap, head east beyond Karl Johans gate to the Grønland neighborhood, home to low cost ethnic eateries.

Cafe Sør, Torggata 11 (☎41 46 30 47). This artsy, relaxing cafe attracts a young crowd with an array of teas and coffees (26-31kr) and free Wi-Fi. Sandwiches 87kr. Beer 36-53kr. Open M-Th 11am-1:30am, F-Sa 11am-3am, Su 2pm-1:30am. MC/V. ❷

Kaffistova, Rosenkrantz gt. 8 (☎23 21 41 00). Posh, airy eatery with modest portions of Norwegian fish, meat, and porridges. Vegetarian options. Lunch from 64kr. Dinner 150-169kr. Open M-F 10am-9pm, Sa-Su 11am-7pm. AmEx/D/MC/V. ❸

Krishna's Cuisine, Kirkeveien 59B (☎22 60 62 50), on the 2nd fl. Large plates of inexpensive Indian food. Exclusively vegetarian fare prepared with fresh seasonal ingredients. Lunch served all day 65kr. Entrees 60-90kr. Open M-F noon-8pm. Cash only. ❷

Curry and Ketchup, Kirkeveien 51 (☎22 69 05 22). A neighbor of Krishna's, this restaurant has a relaxed, sit-down feel. Generous helpings of Indian mainstays. Entrees 69-99kr. Open daily 2-10:30pm. Cash only. ❷

Fenaknoken, Matkultur i Tordenskidsgt. 7 (☎22 42 34 57). Gourmet Norwegian food store with seafood and free samples of delicacies like smoked elk or reindeer sausage. Fresh snack rolls 25kr. Open M-F 10am-5pm, Sa 10am-2pm. AmEx/MC/V. ❷

👁 SIGHTS

◼ **VIGELANDSPARKEN.** Sculptor Gustav Vigeland (1860-1943) designed this 80-acre expanse west of the city center. The park is home to over 200 of his mammoth works, each depicting a stage of the human life cycle. His controversial, puzzling art is worth deciphering. *Monolith* is a towering granite column of intertwining bodies in the middle of the park. *(Entrance on Kirkeveien. Take bus #20 or tram #12 or 15 to Vigelandsparken. Open 24hr. Free.)* While wandering through the park, stop at the **Oslo Bymuseum** (Oslo City Museum) for art and photography collections, displays on the city's history, and restored pavilions. *(☎23 28 41 70; www.oslobymuseum.no. Open June-Aug. Tu-Su 11am-5pm; Sept.-May Tu-Su noon-4pm. Free.)* Next to the park, the **Vigelandmuseet** (Vigeland Museum) traces the artist's development from his early works to the monumental pieces of his later years. The museum is housed in the building Vigeland used as his apartment and studio. *(Nobelsgt. 32. ☎23 49 37 00. Open June-Aug. Tu-Su 10am-5pm; Sept.-May Tu-Su noon-4pm. 45kr, students 25kr. Oct.-Mar free. MC/V.)*

ART MUSEUMS. Recent renovations at **Munchmuseet** (Munch Museum) improved its security system after a 2004 theft of two paintings, including a version of *The Scream*, Munch's most famous work. The paintings have been recovered, albeit with some damage. The museum has a collection of Munch's other abstract works along with temporary Impressionist exhibits. *(Tøyengt. 53. Take the subway to Tøyen or bus #20 to Munchmuseet. ☎23 49 35 00; www.munch.museum.no. Open June-Aug. daily 10am-6pm; Sept.-May Tu-F 10am-4pm, Sa-Su 11am-5pm. 65kr, students 35kr; free with Oslo Pass. AmEx/D/MC/V.)* The definitive version of *The Scream* is at the **Nasjonalmuseet** (National Art Museum), which also has a collection of works by Cézanne, Gauguin, van Gogh, Matisse, Picasso, and Sohlberg. *(Universitetsgt. 13. ☎21 98 20 00; www.nasjonalmuseet.no. Open Tu-W and F 10am-6pm, Th 10am-8pm, Sa-Su 10am-5pm. Free.)* Next door at Oslo University's **Aulaen** (Assembly Hall), several of Munch's dreamy, idealistic murals show his interest in bringing art to the masses. *(Enter through the door by the ionic columns off Karl Johans gt. Open June 27-Aug 3 M-F 10am-4pm. Free.)*

The **Museet for Samtidskunst** (Contemporary Art Museum) displays works by Norwegian artists and rotates its collection frequently. If you can find it, check out *Inner Space V*, a steel staircase leading to a mysterious corridor with a true "light at the end of the tunnel." *(Bankplassen 4. Take bus #60 or tram #10, 12, 13, or 19 to Kongens gt. ☎22 86 22 10. Open Tu-W and F 10am-6pm, Th 10am-8pm, Sa-Su 10am-5pm. Free.)* Nearby, the private **Astrup Fearnly Museum of Modern Art** has a more international collection, with some striking installations and video pieces. *(Dronningens gt. 4. ☎22 93 60 60; www.afmuseet.no. Open Tu-W and F 11am-5pm, Th 11am-7pm, Sa-Su noon-5pm. Free.)*

AKERSHUS CASTLE AND FORTRESS. Originally constructed in 1299, this waterfront complex was rebuilt as a Renaissance palace after Oslo burned in 1624. Norway's infamous traitor, Vidkun Quisling, was imprisoned here prior to his execution for aiding the 1940 Nazi invasion. *(Tram #10 or 12 to Rådhusplassen. ☎23 09 39 17. Complex open daily 6am-9pm. Castle open May-Aug. M-Sa 10am-4pm, Su 12:30-4pm. Sept.-Oct. admission for guided tours only. English- and Norwegian-language guided tours mid-June to early Aug. M-Sa 11am, 1, 2, 3pm; Su 1, 3pm; in winter English-language Th 1pm. Grounds free. Castle 50kr, students 35kr; free with Oslo Pass. Cash only.)* The castle grounds include the powerful **Resistance Museum**, which documents Norway's campaign against the Nazi occupation. *(☎23 09 31 38. Open June-Aug. M-Sa 10am-5pm, Su 11am-5pm; Sept.-Apr. Tu-F 11am-4pm, Sa-Su 11am-5pm. 30kr, students 15kr. Cash only.)*

BYGDØY. Bygdøy peninsula, across the inlet from central Oslo, is mainly residential, but its beaches and museums are worth a visit. In summer, a public **ferry** leaves from Pier 3, Råhusbrygges, in front of City Hall. *(☎23 35 68 90; www.boatsightseeing.com.*

10min.; Apr.-Sept. and late May to mid-Aug. 2-3 per hr.; 20kr, 30kr on board. Or take bus #30 from Oslo S to Folkemuseet or Bygdøynes.) The open-air **Norsk Folkemuseum,** near the ferry's first stop at Dronningen, recreates the lifestyle of medieval Norway with restored thatch huts, actors in period costume, and performances. *(Walk uphill from the dock and follow signs to the right for 10min., or take bus #30 from Nationaltheatret.* ☎*22 12 37 00; www.norskfolke-museum.no. Open mid-May to mid-Sept. daily 10am-6pm; mid-Sept. to mid-May M-F 11am-3pm, Sa-Su 11am-4pm. In summer 90kr, students 60kr; in winter 70/45kr. MC/V.)* Down the road (5min.), the **Vikingskipshuset** (Viking Ship Museum) showcases the stunning remains of three well-preserved burial vessels. *(*☎*22 13 52 80; www.khm.uio.no. Open daily May-Sept. 9am-6pm; Oct.-Apr. 11am-4pm. 50kr, students 25kr; free with Oslo Pass. MC/V.)* At Bygdøynes, the ferry's second stop, the **Kon-Tiki Museet,** named after a displayed balsa wood raft used on a journey from Lima, Peru to the Polynesian Islands, depicts Oscar-winning documentarian Thor Heyerdahl's globe-trotting adventures. *(Bygdøynesveien 36.* ☎*23 08 67 67; www.kon-tiki.no. Open daily June-Aug. 9:30am-5:30pm; Apr.-May and Sept. 10am-5pm; Oct.-Mar. 10:30am-4pm. 45kr, students 30kr; free with Oslo Pass. Guidebook 50kr. D/MC/V.)* Next door, the **Norsk Sjøfarts-museum** (Norwegian Maritime Museum) is home to Norway's oldest boat. Learn about the nation's seafaring history, from log canoes to cruise ships, and enjoy the view of Oslofjord. *(Bygdøynesveien 37.* ☎*24 11 41 50. Open mid-May to Aug. daily 10am-6pm; Sept. to mid-May M-W and Sa-Su 10:30am-4pm, Th 10:30am-6pm. 40kr, students 25kr. Audio tour 30kr. D/MC/V.)* The Arctic exploration vessel **FRAM,** adjacent to the museum, was used on three expeditions in the early 20th century and has advanced farther north and south than any other vessel in history. Visitors can roam through the well-preserved interior. *(Bygdøynesveien 36.* ☎*23 28 29 50. Open daily mid-June to Aug. 9am-6:45pm; May to mid-June 10am-5:45pm; Sept. 10am-4:45pm; Oct.-Apr. 10am-3:45pm. 40kr, students 20kr. MC/V.)* The southwestern side of Bygdøy is home to two popular beaches: **Huk** appeals to a younger crowd, while **Paradisbukta** is more family-oriented. The shore between them is a nude beach. *(Take bus #30 or walk south for 25min. left along the shore from the Bygdøynes ferry stop.)*

OTHER SIGHTS. The **Royal Palace,** in Slottsparken, is open for guided tours, although tickets sell out well ahead. Watch the daily changing of the guard for free at 1:30pm in front of the palace. *(Tram #12, 15, 19, or bus #30-32 or 45 to Slottsparken. Open late June to mid-Aug. English-language tours M, Th, Sa noon, 2, 2:20pm; F and Su 2 and 2:20pm. Buy tickets at post and tourist offices. 80kr, students 70kr.)* The nearby **Ibsenmuseet** (Henrik Ibsen

THE LOCAL STORY

UP FOR SOME KUBB?

A funny thing might happen walking through Oslo's parks. Out of nowhere, you may stumble upon people throwing wooden sticks at figurines. What's going on here? Are they vandalizing those poor, defenseless figurines?

Closer inspection reveals a whole world of fun you never knew existed—Kubb. No, not the obscure British band of the same name. Kubb is a game, nicknamed "Viking Chess," that combines bowling, chess, and horseshoes. The objective is to knock down your opponent's ten kubbs, rectangular wooden blocks. After taking these down, you move on to eliminate the king kubb, marked by a carved crown design, for the win.

Kubb dates back to AD 1000 and was likely played by Vikings. It spread throughout Europe during the Norman conquests. Morbidly, some maintain that the Vikings played with the skulls and bones of their victims rather than wooden blocks. When rampant plundering and using your victims for games went out of fashion, the transition to wooden blocks began. Others believe that wooden blocks have always been used. They are common in Scandinavia, after all, and it would be unfortunate to postpone a game of kubb due to lack of skulls. Talk about a gathering gone wrong.

The game involves a surprising amount of strategy. Try your luck, but don't bet your life savings.

Museum) documents the notoriously private playwright's life with a dramatic exhibition space and guided tours of his apartment. *(Henrik Ibsens gt. 26. ☎22 12 35 50; www.ibsen.net/ibsen-museum. Open mid-May to mid-Sept. Tu-Su 11am-6pm; mid-Sept. to mid-May Tu-Su 11am-3pm. English- and Norwegian-language tours 7 per day; in winter 3 per day. 35kr; with tour 70kr, students 45kr. AmEx/D/MC/V.)* The **Domkirke**, next to Stortorvet in the city center, is hard to miss. The Lutheran cathedral has a colorful ceiling with biblical motifs. *(Karl Johans gt. 11. ☎23 31 46 00; www.oslodomkirke.no. Open M-Th 10am-4pm, F 10am-4pm and 10pm-midnight, Sa 10am-4pm and 9-11pm. Free.)* The **Nobel Museum,** by the harbor, features profiles on all 112 laureates. *(Brynjulf Bulls Plass 1. Tram #12 to Aker Brygge. ☎23 31 46 00; www.nobelpeace.org. Open June-Aug. daily 10am-6pm; Jan.-May and Sept.-Dec. W and F 10am-4pm, Th 10am-6pm, Sa-Su 11am-5pm; 80kr, students 55kr.)* Climb the Holmenkollen ski jump, after an elevator ride halfway up, for views of the city and an exploration of 4000 years of skiing history at the world's oldest **Ski Museum,** founded in 1923. A simulator recreates a leap off a ski jump and a blisteringly swift downhill run. *(Kongeveien 5. Take subway #1 on the Frognerseteren line to Holmenkollen and follow the signs 10min. ☎22 92 32 64; www.skiforeningen.no. Open daily June-Aug. 9am-8pm; Sept. and May 10am-5pm; Oct.-Apr. 10am-4pm. Museum 70kr, students 60kr; free with Oslo Pass. Simulator 50kr, with Oslo Pass 40kr. AmEx/D/MC/V.)*

🎵 🎭 ENTERTAINMENT AND NIGHTLIFE

The monthly *What's On in Oslo,* free at tourist offices, follows the latest in opera, symphony, and theater. **Filmens Hus,** Dronningens gt. 16, is the center of Oslo's indie film scene. (☎22 47 45 00. Open Tu-W and F noon-5pm, Th noon-7pm, Sa noon-4pm. 70kr per movie, members 45kr; registration 100kr.) Jazz enthusiasts head to town for the **Oslo Jazz Festival** in mid-August. (☎22 42 91 20; www.oslojazz.no). Countless bars along **Karl Johans gate** and in the **Aker Brygge** harbor complex attract a hard-partying crowd, while a mellow mood prevails at the cafe-by-day, bar-by-night lounges along **Thorvald Meyers gate** in Grüner Løkka. Alcohol tends to be expensive out on the town, so young Norwegians have taken to the custom of the *Vorspiel*—gathering at private homes to sip comparatively cheap, store-bought liquor before staggering out to the streets.

   Mono, Pløens gt. 4 (☎22 41 41 66). Jam to classic rock at this popular, funky club. Backyard area for drinks during the day. Beer 52kr. Su-Th 20+, F-Sa 22+. Cover for concerts 50-70kr. Open M-Sa 3pm-3:30am, Su 6pm-3:30am. MC/V.

   Garage, Grensen 9 (☎22 42 37 44; www.garageoslo.no). A venue M-Th for live music from across the globe. A bouncing club F-Su with rock beats. Beer 52kr at night, 42kr during the day. Su-Th 20+, F-Sa 22+. Cover for concerts 50-180kr. Open M-Sa 2pm-3:30am, Su 6pm-3:30am. MC/V.

   Muddy Waters, Grensen 13 (☎22 40 33 70; www.muddywaters.no). Lives up to its billing as one of Europe's top blues clubs. Attracts an older crowd. Beer 56kr. 20+. Cover F-Sa around 90kr. Open daily 2pm-3am. AmEx/D/MC/V.

   Living Room, Olav V's gt. 1 (☎22 83 63 54; www.living-room.no). Popular lounge morphs into dance floor on weekends. Fairly strict dress code. Beer 61kr. 24+. Cover F-Sa 100kr. Open W-Su 11pm-3am. AmEx/D/MC/V.

   Horgans, Hegdehaugsv. 24 (☎22 60 87 87). Boisterous sports bar with plenty of TVs showing the latest games, especially football matches. Also a club on weekends. Beer 54kr. Th student night. F-Sa club. 22+. Cover Sa 50kr. Open M-Tu 5pm-midnight, W-Th and Su 5pm-1:30am, F-Sa 5pm-3am. AmEx/D/MC/V.

   London Pub, C.J. Hambros pl. (☎22 70 87 00; www.londonpub.no). Entrance on Rosenkrantz gt. Oslo's "gay headquarters" since 1979. Large upstairs dance floor plays a mix of beats. Basement pool tables and bars. Beer 36-52kr. 21+. Cover F-Sa 40kr. Open daily 3pm-4am. AmEx/D/MC/V.

🇳 LET'S GO TO OSLO: SANDEFJORD ☎ 33

Sandefjord Airport Torp (TRF; ☎ 42 70 00; www.torp.no), 120km south of Oslo, is a budget airline hub for **Ryanair, Widerøe,** and **Wizz Air. Trains** (☎ 81 50 08 88) run to Oslo (1¾hr.; 1 per hr.; 222kr, students 167kr). Buses (2 per hr.) and taxis shuttle between the train station and airport. **Buses** also go to Oslo (1-2 per hr., 140kr) and coordinate with Ryanair arrivals and departures.

🇳 DAYTRIPS FROM OSLO: AROUND THE CITY. Harbor cruises visit the nearby islands of inner **Oslofjord.** The ruins of a **Cistercian Abbey,** as well as a picnic-friendly southern shore, lie on the island of **Hovedøya,** while **Langøyene** has Oslo's best **beach** and a free campground. *(Take bus #60 for 22kr from City Hall to Vippetangen to catch ferry #92 or 93 to Hovedøya or ferry #94 to Langøyene.)* The well-preserved fortress town of **Fredrikstad** is less than 2hr. south of Oslo. The 28km **Glommastien** path winds through abandoned brickyards and timber mills along the Glomma River. Ferries travel to seaside resorts on the **Hvaler Islands.** The **info office** on the harbor, Toyhusgt. 98, has **ferry** schedules. *(☎ 69 30 46 00. Open M-F 9am-5pm, Sa-Su noon-5pm. Train to Fredrikstad 1hr.; 1 per 2hr.; 170kr, students 153kr.)*

LILLEHAMMER ☎ 61

Lillehammer (pop. 27,000) cherishes the laurels it earned as host of the 1994 Winter Olympics. The **Norwegian Olympic Museum** in Olympic Park traces the history of the Games. It's a 20min. walk from the train station; head two blocks uphill, turn left on Storgt., right on Tomtegt., go up the stairs, and follow the road uphill to the left. Or take bus #5 to Sigrid Undsetsveg (5min., 20kr). The museum is in the far dome, the 1994 hockey rink. (☎ 25 21 00; www.ol.museum.no. Open June-Aug. daily 10am-5pm; Sept.-May Tu-Su 11am-4pm. 75kr, students 60kr. AmEx/D/MC/V.) Climb the steps of the **ski jump** in Olympic Park for a view of **Lake Mjøsa,** Norway's largest lake. Give your spine a jolt on the **bobsled simulator** at the bottom of the hill. (☎ 05 42 00; www.olympiaparken.no. Open mid-June to late Aug. daily 9am-8pm; May to mid-June Sa-Su 9am-8pm. Ski jump tower 15kr. Chairlift 40kr. Simulator 45kr. Combination ticket including chairlift 65kr.) The open-air museum **Maihaugen** chronicles rural Norwegian life over the past 300 years. From the train station, head up Jernbanegt., turn right onto Gågt., and continue down the street until it becomes Storgt. Turn left on Søndre gt., follow it to the end, and make a right on Sykenes. Travel uphill and make a left on Maihaugvegan. (☎ 28 89 00; www.maihaugen.no. Open June-Aug. daily 10am-5pm; Oct.-May Tu-Su 11am-4pm. Summer 100kr, students 80kr; low season 80/70kr. AmEx/D/MC/V.) The town is, of course, also home to excellent sports facilities. To the north, **Hafjell,** Aaslettvegen 1, is home to some of the best skiing slopes in the country. In summer, the trails are used for mountain biking. Buses to the complex leave from the tourist office. (☎ 27 47 00; www.hafjell.no. Skis 180-300kr per day. Bikes 750kr per day.)

Lillehammer Vandrerhjem Stasjon ❸, Jernbanetorget 2, a hostel attached to the train station, features clean rooms with bath and TV. (☎ 26 00 24; www.stasjonen.no. Breakfast, linens, and laundry included. Free Wi-Fi. Reception 7am-11pm. Dorms 325kr; singles 590kr; doubles 790kr. 15% HI discount.) The basic accommodations at **Gjeste Bu ❷,** Gamleveien 110, come with a dose of mountainside charm. (☎ 25 43 21; gjestebu@lillehammer.online.no. Breakfast 55kr. Linens 60kr. Reception M-Sa 9am-11pm, Su 11am-11pm. Dorms 200kr; singles 275-300kr; doubles 400-450kr. Cash only.) Pizzerias and candy shops line Gågt., which runs north-south through the town center, changing names to Storgt. at both ends. Buy groceries at **Spar,** up the hill north of Storgt. on Lilletorget 1. (☎ 22 16 40. Open M-F 8am-9pm, Sa 8am-8pm.) **Trains** run to Oslo (2¼hr.; 10-19 per day, 304kr) and Trondheim (4½-5½hr., 4 per day, 596kr). The **tourist office** is in the station. (☎28 98 00; www.lillehammerturist.no. Open June and Aug. M-Sa 9am-6pm, Su noon-5pm; July M-F 9am-8pm, Su 11am-6pm; Sept.-June M-F 9am-4pm, Sa 10am-2pm.)

SOUTHERN NORWAY

Norway's southern coastline is a premier summer holiday destination. Its towns feature red-tiled bungalows and jetties full of powerboats. The nearby rocky archipelagos *(skjærgarden)* can be explored on the cheap by hopping on a local ferry.

KRISTIANSAND
☎38

Vacationers ferrying their way from Denmark to Oslo often stop in Kristiansand (pop. 77,000), Norway's fifth largest city and home to some of the country's best beaches. **Hamresandsen,** accessible by the yellow city buses (#35 or 36), is an especially popular beach to the north, where temperatures often reach a sizzling 20°C (68°F). The white wooden houses in the old town of **Posebyen,** northeast of the city center, quartered soldiers over the centuries and sheltered Jewish refugees during WWII. **Dyreparken,** a zoo 11km east of the city, is Kristiansand's main attraction. Catch bus #1 (dir.: Sørlandsparken; 33kr) right around the corner from the tourist office. (☎04 97 00; www.dyreparken.com. Open June-late Aug. daily 10am-7pm; late Aug.-May M-F 10am-3pm, Sa-Su 10am-5pm. 290kr, low season from 90kr.) The first week in July, music fans take over the island of **Odderøya** for the ▓**Quart Festival,** which features acts such as Death Cab for Cutie, Kanye West, and The Who. (☎14 69 69; www.quart.no.) Farther south, take in the view of the **skerries,** a string of small islands and coves, on a boat trip with the **M/S Patricia.** (☎90 76 14 53; www.pollen.as. 2½hr.; July-Aug. 20 daily 10:30am, 12:30, 3:30pm; 150kr.) The **Midt-Agder Friluftsråd,** on Tollbodgt., offers free walking tours of the city (daily June 18 to Aug. 11). Walk down the center road Festningsgt. to **Banehela** park for an easy, 1.6km hike to another lush nature preserve in neighboring **Ravnedalen.**

The harborside **Kristiansand Youth Hostel (HI) ❷,** Skansen 8, a 25min. walk from the center, offers fantastic views of the water and cliffs. From the harbor, head northeast along Østre Strandgt. until you reach Elvegt., turn right, then turn left onto Skansen. Reserve ahead for the festival. (☎02 83 10. Breakfast included. Linens 60kr. Internet 2kr per 15min. Reception mid-June to Aug. 3-11pm; Sept. to mid-June 5-9pm. Dorms 220kr; private rooms 490kr per person. 25kr HI discount. D/MC/V.) For cheap fare, head to the harbor **Fiskebrygga** (fish market), on Gravane near the intersection of Vestre Strandgt. and Østre Strandgt., between 11am and 4pm, when fishermen's families sell part of the morning's catch. **Rimi,** on the corner of Festningsgt. and Gyldenløvesgt., sells groceries. (☎02 95 16. Open M-F 8am-9pm, Sa 9am-6pm. Cash only.) **Trains** run to Oslo (4½-5½hr., 4 per day, 580kr), and Stavanger (3hr., 6 per day, 390kr). Color Line **ferries** (☎81 00 08 11; www.color-line.no) sail to Hirsthals, DEN (2½-4hr.; 1-5 per day; in summer 440kr-480kr, low season 280-320kr; 50% student discount in low season). The **tourist office,** Vestre Strandgt. 32, opposite the train station at the junction of Henrik Wegerlandsgt. and Vestre Strandgt., books rooms for a 50kr fee and offers **Internet** access. (☎12 13 14. Internet 1kr per min. Open mid-June to mid-Aug. M-F 8:30am-6pm, Sa 10am-6pm, Su noon-6pm; mid-Aug. to mid-June M-F 8:30am-3:30pm.) **Postal Code:** 4601.

STAVANGER
☎51

The harbor town of Stavanger (pop. 117,000) will serve as a **2008 European Capital of Culture,** along with Liverpool, BRI (p. 158), as decided by the EU. Throughout the year, the city will host a series of festivals and cultural events, making the area a tourist magnet. Book ahead for accommodations. For a schedule, visit www.stavanger2008.no or call the tourist office. Shedding the perception that it is merely a port city and a hub for the oil industry, Stavanger boasts a number of attractions, including the stunning **Lysefjord** to the east. On the western side of the harbor is **Gamle Stavanger** (Old Town), where lamp-lit, pedestrian walkways wind past well-preserved cottages. The 12th-century **Stavanger Domkirke** is one of Norway's oldest cathedrals. (☎65 33 60; www.kirken.stavanger.no. Open June-Aug. daily 11am-7pm; Sept.-May Tu-Th and Sa 11am-4pm. Free tours daily noon-5pm.) The sleek **Norwegian Petroleum Museum** (Norsk Oljemuseum), down Kirkegt. from the church, explains drilling, refining, and life on oil platforms with high-tech, if somewhat romanticized, displays. (☎93 93 00; www.norskolje.museum.no. Open June-Aug. daily 10am-7pm; Sept.-May M-Sa 10am-4pm, Su 10am-6pm. 80kr, students 40kr. AmEx/D/MC/V.) A popular attraction, **☒Pulpit Rock** (Preikestolen) offers magnificent views from an altitude of 600m. If the crowds and your sense of vertigo permit, lie flat and look into the abyss below. Take the ferry to Tau from Fiskepiren dock, catch a bus, and hike up the well-marked trail (1½-2hr.).

The best budget accommodations are around **Lake Mosvatnet,** south of the city, and near the airport (bus #5a or 5b, 2-4 per hr., 25kr). **Stavanger Hostel ❷,** Henrik Ibsens gt. 19, on the south shore of the lake, is a small red bungalow with quiet dorms. (☎54 36 36; www.vandrerhjem.no. Open June 12 to Aug. 8. Dorms 240kr; singles 420kr; doubles 720kr. 15% HI discount. MC/V.) Bring your own tent and settle down at **Stavanger Camping ❶,** next door to the hostel. It offers stunning lake views. (☎53 29 71; www.stavangercamping.no. 110-120kr per tent site, 350-600kr per cabin. Showers 10kr. Electricity 30kr.) Sample native strawberries (15-25kr per bushel) at the **market** opposite the cathedral in the main square (open M-F 8am-5pm). **Trains** run to Kristiansand (4hr., 1 per 3hr., 390kr) and Oslo (8hr., 4 per day, 846kr). **Buses** to Bergen (5-6hr.; 2 per hr.; 400kr, students 300kr) leave from Stavanger Byterminal. The Flaggruten **express boat** (4hr., 200-620kr) sails past fjords to Bergen. (☎055 05; www.hsd.no. 1-4 per day. 50% Eurail and Scanrail discount. 40% student discount.) The **tourist office,** Domkirkeplassen 3, books rooms for a 30kr fee. (☎85 92 00; www.regionstavanger.com. Open June-Aug. daily 9am-8pm; Sept.-May M-F 9am-4pm, Sa 9am-2pm.) **Postal Code:** 4001.

THE FJORDS AND WEST NORWAY

No trip to Norway is complete without seeing the Western Fjords. The region boasts a dramatic grandeur, from the depths of Sognefjord to the peaks of Jotunheimen National Park. Tourists come to Sogndal and Stryn to walk on the Jostedalsbreen glacier, continental Europe's largest, and visit fjord towns like Balestrand and Geiranger. On the Atlantic coast, Bergen is the region's major port city.

WHAT THE FJUCK IS A FJORD? Fjords are long, narrow, U-shaped valleys flooded by the sea. Norway's formed from deep grooves cut into the ground by glacial erosion during the last Ice Age.

▐ TRANSPORTATION

Transportation around the Western Fjords can be tricky and often involves lengthy rides, but scenery-gazing is half the fun. Trains go to **Åndalsnes** in the north and **Bergen** in the south. Buses and boats run to locales in between these cities, including the main fjords and national parks. From Strandkaiterminalen in Bergen, **HSD express boats** (☎55 23 87 80; www.hsd.no) run to Stavanger and points south of the city, while **Fylkesbaatane** (☎55 90 70 710; www.fjord1.no/fylkesbaatane) sails north into Nordfjord, Sognefjord, and Sunnfjord. Almost all destinations connect via **bus** to Bergen; check www.nor-way.no for schedules and fares. **Fjord1** (www.fjord1.no), a consortium of boat, bus, and ferry, companies, is an invaluable resource for planning regional trips. Schedules vary daily; call ☎177 for transportation info. Tourist offices, boat terminals, and bus stations can also help with itineraries. Plan your trip at least 2-3 days ahead.

BERGEN ☎55

Situated in a narrow valley between steep mountains and the waters of the Puddefjorden, Bergen (pop. 235,000) bills itself as the "Gateway to the Fjords." Norway's second-largest city has a pedestrian-friendly downtown, meticulously preserved medieval district, and a thriving late-night music scene.

⌐ TRANSPORTATION

Trains: The **station** is on Strømgtn. (☎96 69 00), 10min. southeast of the harbor. Trains run to **Myrdal** (2¼hr., 6-8 per day, 232kr), **Oslo** (6½-7½hr., 4-5 per day, 728kr), and **Voss** (1¼hr., 1 per 1-2hr., 153kr).

Buses: Busstasjon, Strømgtn. 8 (☎177, outside Bergen 55 90 70), in the Bergen Storsenter mall next to the library. Buses run to **Ålesund** (9-10hr., 2 per day, 585kr), **Balestrand** (4½hr., 1-2 per day), **Oslo** (9-11hr., 4 per day, 467kr), **Sogndal** (4½-5hr., 3-4 per day, 389kr), **Stryn** (6hr., 4 per day, 405kr), and **Trondheim** (14½hr., 2 per day, 751kr). 25% student discount.

Domestic Ferries: The **Hurtigruten** steamer (☎81 03 00 00; www.hurtigruten.com) begins its coastal journey in **Bergen** and stops in **Ålesund**, the **Lofoten Islands**, **Tromsø,** and **Trondheim.** (Mid-Apr. to mid-Sept. daily 8pm, 1058-3622kr; mid-Sept. to mid-Apr. 10:30pm. 50% student discount.) **Flaggruten** express boats (☎055 05; www.flaggruten.no) head south to **Stavanger** (4hr., 2-4 per day, 640kr).

International Ferries: Depart from **Skoltegrunnskaien,** a 10-15min. walk past Bryggen along the right side of the harbor. **Fjord Line** (☎81 53 35 00; www.fjordline.co.uk) runs to **Hanstholm, DEN** (16hr.; 3-4 per week; mid-June to mid-Aug. from 500kr, mid-Aug. to mid-June from 300kr) and **Newcastle, BRI** (25hr.; 2-3 per week; mid-May to early Sept. from 800kr, mid-Sept. to mid-May from 500kr). **Smyril Line** (☎59 65 20; www.smyril-line.no) goes to the **Faroe Islands** (24hr.; 1240kr, students 560kr, low season from 875/400kr) and **Seyðisfjörður, ICE** (41hr.; 2050kr, students 1430kr, low season 900/620kr), both departing June-Aug. Tu 3pm; check website for Sept.-May hours.

Public Transportation: Buses are 23kr within the city center, 31-38kr outside. The **Bergen Card** (1-day 170kr, 2-day 250kr), available at the train station and tourist office, includes unlimited rides on city buses, free admission to most of the city's museums, and discounts at select shops and restaurants.

◢❷ ORIENTATION AND PRACTICAL INFORMATION

The harborside **Torget** (fish market) is a central landmark. North of the *Torget*, **Bryggen** curves around the harbor to the old city. **Torgalmenningen,** the main pedestrian street, runs southwest from the *Torget*. Locals tend to stay farther down Torgalmenningen, near **Håkons gaten** and **Nygårds gaten.** South of the *Torget* is **Lille Lungegårdsvann,** a park-lined lake. The train and bus stations are beyond the lake.

Tourist Office: Vågsalmenningen 1 (☎55 20 00; www.visitbergen.com), past the *Torget* in the Fresco Hall. Crowded in summer, often with 1hr. waits; visit early and pick up a copy of the city guide. The staff books private rooms for a 30kr fee and helps visitors

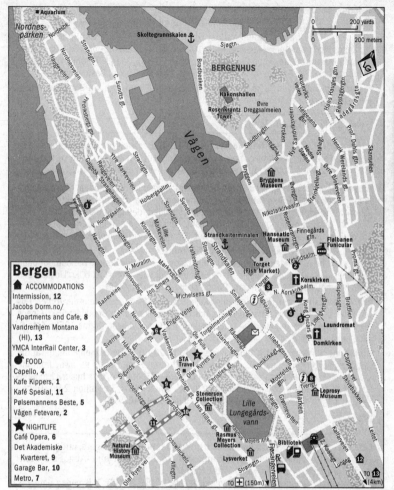

Bergen

🏠 ACCOMMODATIONS
Intermission, **12**
Jacobs Dorm.no/
  Apartments and Cafe, **8**
Vandrerhjem Montana
  (HI), **13**
YMCA InterRail Center, **3**

🍎 FOOD
Capello, **4**
Kafe Kippers, **1**
Kafé Spesial, **11**
Pølsemannens Beste, **5**
Vågen Fetevare, **2**

⭐ NIGHTLIFE
Café Opera, **6**
Det Akademiske
  Kvarteret, **9**
Garage Bar, **10**
Metro, **7**

plan fjord travel. Open June-Aug. daily 8:30am-10pm; May and Sept. daily 9am-8pm; Oct.-Apr. M-Sa 9am-4pm. **DNT** (Norwegian Mountain Touring Association), Tverrgt. 4-6 (☎33 58 10), off Marken, sells maps (94-119kr) and provides hiking info. Open M-W and F 10am-4pm, Th 10am-6pm, Sa 10am-2pm.

Budget Travel: STA Travel, Vaskerelven 32 (☎55 99 05; bergen@statravel.no). Sells student airline tickets and books accommodations. Open M-F 10am-5pm. D/MC/V.

Currency Exchange: At banks near the harbor and at the post office. Usually open M-W and F 9am-3pm, Th 9am-4:30pm; low season reduced hours. Tourist office changes currency without commission.

Luggage Storage: At train and bus stations. 20-40kr per day, depending on locker size.

Laundromat: Jarlens Vaskoteque, Lille Øvregt. 17 (☎32 55 04; www.jarlens.no). Wash and dry 70kr. Open M-Tu and F 10am-6pm, W-Th 10am-8pm, Sa 10am-3pm.

Hospital: 24-Hour Clinic, Vestre Strømkai 19 (☎56 87 00).

Internet Access: The public **library,** Strømgt. 6 (☎55 56 85), between the train and bus stations, offers free 15-30min. slots. Open Sept.-Apr. M-Th 10am-8pm, F 10am-4:30pm, Sa 10am-4pm; May-Aug. M-Th 10am-6pm, F 10am-4:30pm, Sa 10am-4pm. **Bergen Internet C@fe,** Kong Oscars gt. 2B (☎96 08 36). Open M-F 9am-11pm, Sa-Su 10am-10pm. 1kr per min., min. 15kr. Students 25kr per 30min. Cash only.

Post Office: Småstrandgt. (☎81 00 07 10). Open M-F 9am-8pm, Sa 9am-6pm. Poste Restante office open 9am-3pm.

▐ ACCOMMODATIONS

The tourist office books **private rooms** for a 30kr fee; travelers can sometimes nab doubles for as little as 300kr. You can **camp** for free on the far side of the hills above the city; walk 30min. up the slopes of Mount Fløyen or take the funicular.

▨ Intermission, Kalfarveien 8 (☎30 04 00), near the train station. Students from a Christian college in the US staff this hostel with a homey vibe. Free waffle night M and Th. Breakfast 20kr. Linens deposit 20kr. Laundry included; detergent 5kr. Reception Su-Th 7-11am and 3pm-midnight, F-Sa until 1am. Lockout 11am-3pm. Curfew Su-Th midnight, F-Sa 1am. Open mid-June to mid-Aug. Dorms 135kr. Cash only. ❶

Jacobs Dorm.no/Apartments and Cafe, Kong Oscars gt. 44 (☎98 23 86 00; www.dorm.no or www.apartments.no). Bright, social, and tidy dorms. The outdoor patio becomes busy at night as guests get acquainted over beer. Breakfast 60kr. Linens 55kr. Free Internet. Lockout 11am-1pm. Dorms 165kr. AmEx/MC/V. ❷

YMCA InterRail Center (HI), Nedre Korskirkealm. 4 (☎60 60 55), near the *Torget*. This lively hostel, popular with backpackers, has barracks-like dorms. Breakfast 55kr. Linens 45kr. Free Internet. Reception 7-10:30am and 3:30pm-midnight. Dorms 155kr; 4- to 6-bed rooms 210-230kr per person. 15% HI discount. MC/V. ❶

Vandrerhjem Montana (HI), Johan Blyttsvei 30 (☎20 80 70; www.montana.no), at the base of Mt. Ulriken, 5km outside Bergen. Head down Kong Oscars gt. away from the center until you see a bus shelter next to a cemetery. From there, take bus #31 to Montana and follow the signs. Breakfast included. Linens 65kr. Reception 24hr. Dorms 180kr; singles 460kr; doubles 600kr. 15% HI discount. MC/V. ❷

▐ FOOD

Bergen's *Torget* panders to tourists with colorful tents, fishmongers, and free samples of caviar, reindeer, salmon, shrimp, and whale. (Open June-Aug. Su-F 7am-5pm, Sa 7am-4pm; Sept.-May M-Sa 7am-4pm.)

Kafé Spesial, Christiesgt. 13, off Nygårdsgtn. (☎92 81 27 36). This cheap eatery is popular with students. Pizza from 15kr. Heaping sandwiches 22-72kr. Open M-F 11am-10pm, Sa 11am-1am, Su noon-10pm. MC/V. ❶

Capello, Skosteredet 14 (☎96 12 11; www.capello.no). Take in the 60s Americana while eating pancakes stuffed with fresh ingredients (44-62kr). Open M-W noon-midnight, Th-Sa noon-1am. Kitchen open M-W noon-6pm, Th-Sa noon-10pm. D/MC/V. ❶

Vågen Fetevare, Kong Oscars gt. 10 (☎31 65 13). The plush chairs, wall trinkets, and colorful interior make this place a relaxing alternative to bustling *Torget*. For lunch, locals crave the open-faced sandwich (43kr) made with seasonal ingredients. Open M-Th 8am-11pm, F 8am-9pm, Sa 9am-7pm, Su 11am-11pm. Cash only. ❶

Kafe Kippers, Georgernes Verft. 12 (☎31 00 60). In USF Verftet, a large warehouse with a cinema, studios, and a theater, all with striking views of the fjord. Specialties include Caribbean prawn curry (128kr) and Iranian beef stew (112kr). Open M-F 11am-midnight, Sa-Su noon-midnight. 10% discount with Bergen Card. AmEx/D/MC/V. ❸

Pølsemannens Beste, Kong Oscars gt. 16 (☎31 73 33). This meal-on-the-go kiosk has many options, from pork hot dogs (12kr) to gourmet reindeer sausages infused with cheese and chili (40kr), Santa's least favorite selection. Open Su-Th 11am-4am, F-Sa 11am-6am. Cash only. ❶

👁 SIGHTS

BRYGGEN AND BERGENHUS. The signature pointed gables of **Bryggen** line the right side of the harbor from the *Torget*. This row of medieval buildings—Bergen's most touristed area—serves as a reminder of the city's past status as the Hanseatic trading league's major Nordic port. The narrow alleys and crooked balconies have survived many fires and the explosion of a Nazi munitions ship. Today, Bryggen is home to galleries, restaurants, and shops striving to maintain a traditional Norwegian feel. **Bryggens Museum** displays archaeological artifacts from the area and a 12min. film on the city's history. *(Dreggsalm. 3, behind a small park at the end of the Bryggen houses. ☎58 80 10. Open May-Aug. daily 10am-5pm; Sept.-Apr. M-F 11am-3pm, Sa noon-3pm, Su noon-4pm. 40kr, students 20kr. AmEx/D/MC/V.)* From the museum, a walking tour (80kr) of the city grants free admission to the **Hanseatic Museum,** in an old trading house near the Fløibanen funicular station. *(Finnegaardsgt. 1A. ☎54 46 90; www.hanseatisk.museum.no. Open June-Aug. daily 9am-5pm; Sept.-May Tu-Su 11am-2pm. May to mid-Sept. 45kr, mid-Sept. to Apr. 25kr. MC/V.)* **Bergenhus,** the city's harborside fortress, is home to 16th-century **Rosenkrantz Tower,** which has splendid views of the city. The **Håkonshallen** contains the restored grand hall where Norwegian kings held court in the Middle Ages. *(Walk down Bryggen away from the Torget. ☎31 43 80. Hall and tower open mid-May to mid-Sept. daily 10am-4pm; Sept. to mid-May hall open M-W and F-Su noon-3pm, Th 3-6pm; tower open Su noon-3pm only. In summer includes guided tour 1 per hr. 40kr, students 20kr. Separate admission for each building. Cash only.)*

MUSEUMS. Branches of the **Bergen Art Museum** are on the western side of Lille Lungegårdsvann. **Lysverket** has 13th-century Russian icons and works of 15th-century Dutch Masters, while the **Rasmus Meyers Collection** displays the canvases of Norwegians painters such as Dahl and Munch. The **Stenersen Collection** specializes in temporary exhibits and has an extensive collection of modernist works, including pieces by Klee and Picasso. *(Rasmus Meyers allé 3, 7, and 9. ☎56 80 00; www.bergenartmuseum.no. Open mid-May to mid-Sept. daily 11am-5pm; mid-Sept. to mid-May Tu-Su 11am-5pm. All 3 museums 50kr, students 35kr, temporary exhibits 15kr. AmEx/D/MC/V.)* The **Leprosy Museum,** Kong Oscars gt. 59, east of Lille Lungegårdsvann in St. Jørgens Hospital, is part of the Bergen City Museum system. Wondering why Bergen has a museum dedicated to leprosy? The bacteria that causes the disease was first identified in the 19th century by physician Gerhard Armauer Hansenin, a native of Bergen. *(☎96 11 55; www.lepra.no. Open June-Aug. daily 11am-3pm. 40kr, students 20kr.)*

🏔 HIKING

Seven fjords and **seven mountains** surround Bergen, a popular base for outdoor excursions. Visits to the waterways require careful planning and guided tours, but the peaks are easily accessible from the city center and have well-kept, marked **hiking trails.** Locals are keen to inform visitors that they have not seen Bergen until they have seen it from above. Free **maps** are at the tourist and DNT offices, but if you plan to spend the night in the mountains, or if the weather is poor, invest in a detailed map. The four eastern mountains are the most popular, due to their proximity and relative ease. **Mount Fløyen** can be reached by the **Fløibanen funicular** or by hiking up a steep, paved road (45min.). Board the funicular 150m from the *Torget*. The road up the mountain begins nearby. (☎33 68 00. Funicular open May-Aug. M-F

7:30am-midnight, Sa 8am-midnight, Su 9am-midnight; Sept.-May M-F 7:30am-11pm, Sa 8am-11pm, Su 9am-11pm. 35kr.) At the summit, several relatively easy trails head into a forest with secluded ponds and stunning vistas (30min.-4hr.).

 Even though the mountains are close to Bergen, they can still be dangerous, especially in inclement weather or thick fog. Always check with the tourist office or the DNT for up-to-date weather and safety info before departing for a hike.

A bus and cable car combination also runs from the city center to the top of 🏔**Mount Ulriken,** the highest of the eastern peaks. At 650m, the mountain provides a stellar panoramic view of the city, fjords, islands, and mountains. Take bus #31 to Haukeland Sykehus and walk up Haukelandsbakken until you reach the cable car. (☎20 20 20. Cable car daily May-Sept. 9am-9pm; Oct.-Apr. 10am-5pm. 50kr. Cash only.) A 7hr. hike on fairly flat terrain between Floyen and Ulriken is possible. For the easiest trip, start at taller Ulriken.

🎵 🍸 ENTERTAINMENT AND NIGHTLIFE

Bergen hosts two festivals in late May and early June. **Festspillene** (☎21 06 30; www.festspillene.no), a two week international festival, explores all genres of art—from visual to theater to dance. Since 1973, **Nattjazz** has attracted jazz acts big and small. (☎30 72 50; www.nattjazz.no. Day pass 360kr, students 310kr.) October brings the up-and-coming **Bergen International Film Festival.** (☎30 08 40; www.biff.no). The city has an excellent live music scene, but nightlife rarely picks up until around 11:30pm on weekends; many locals throw back a round or two at home to avoid costly drinks at bars and clubs. Steer clear of pricey harborside tourist traps and head to the cafes and pubs on **Nygårds gaten.**

Det Akademiske Kvarteret, Olav Kyrres gt. 49-53 (☎58 99 10). This large complex, run by student volunteers from the University of Bergen, is home to the happening **Grøhndals** bar and sells some of the cheapest beer in town (Su-W 43kr, Th-Sa 39kr). **Teglverket** hosts summer jazz and rock concerts (usually 10pm; tickets 30-100kr). 18+; low season 20+. Open Su-W 7pm-1am, Th 7pm-2am, F-Sa 7pm-3am.

Café Opera, Engen 18 (☎23 03 15). Draws an eclectic clientele of artists and students. DJs after 11pm. Beer 48-59kr. F-Sa club nights pound a mix of styles. No cover. Open M 11am-12:30am, Tu-Sa noon-3:30am, Su noon-12:30am. AmEx/D/MC/V.

Garage Bar, at the corner of Nygårdsgtn. and Christiesgt. (☎32 02 10), is an alt-rock pub. 20+. Cover 30kr after 1am. Open M-Sa 1pm-3:30am, Su 3pm-3:30am. MC/V.

Metro, Ole Bulls pl. 4 (☎57 30 37; www.sincoas.no). This lounge/nightclub with hip-hop beats attracts posh, well-dressed patrons. Beer 56kr. Su-Th 20+, F-Sa 24+. Cover 90kr. Open daily 10pm-3am. AmEx/D/MC/V.

THE OSLO-BERGEN RAIL LINE

The 7hr. train journey from Oslo to Bergen is one of the world's most scenic rides, regardless of season. From Oslo, trains climb 1222m to remote Finse, stop in Myrdal for transfers to the Flåm railway, and then pass through Voss en route to Bergen. Purchase advance tickets at www.nsb.no. Note that you cannot buy a ticket that allows you to get off at all stops and hop back on. You must plan each leg of the trip separately and choose your destinations ahead.

FINSE. Outdoor enthusiasts head to Finse, the highest point on the line, and hike north through the Aurlandsdalen Valley to **Aurland,** 53km from Flåm. Before setting out, ask about trail conditions at Finse's train station or at DNT offices in Oslo or Bergen; between early June and late September the trails are usually snow-free and accessible. You can sleep in DNT *hytte* (mountain huts), spaced one day's walk apart on the Aurland trails. **Bikers** can head down the rutted **Rallarvegen** trail, which parallels the Oslo-Bergen train and extends 81km west to Voss. Most of the ride is downhill; exercise extreme caution on the steep curves in the **Flåmdalen Valley.** Stay in a *hytte* in Hallingskeid (21km from Finse) or forge onward to Flåm (57km). Rent bikes at **Finsehytta.** (☎56 52 67 32. Open July-Aug. daily 8am-11pm. Bike rental M-F 390kr, Sa-Su 495kr for 2 days.) Sci-Fi nerds will appreciate the nearby **Hardangerjøkulen** glacier (p. 752), which was a shooting location for ice planet scenes from *Star Wars: The Empire Strikes Back*. **Postal Code:** 5719

FLÅM AND THE FLÅM RAILWAY. The railway connecting Myrdal, a stop on the Oslo-Bergen line, with the tiny Sognefjord (p. 752) town of Flåm (pop. 500) is one of Norway's most celebrated attractions. An incredible feat of engineering, it has the steepest descent of any railway in the world and ducks through hand-excavated tunnels. The highlight of the 55min. ride is a view of the thunderous **Kjosfossen** waterfall, where the train stops to allow photography. The scenic trip is heavily touristed. Guided tours often book up the majority of the train—plan ahead and brace yourself for limited leg room. (☎57 63 14 00; www.flaamsbana.no or www.nsb.no. 55min.; 8-10 per day; 190kr. 30% ScanRail or Eurail discount.) A 20km **hike** (4-5hr.) on the well-tended paths between Myrdal and Flåm more or less follows the train route and passes by smaller cascades and knoll campsites. The easiest route is downhill from Myrdal to Flåm, while the reverse makes for a more strenuous climb. You can also take the train uphill from Flåm to Myrdal and **bike** back down; check your brakes beforehand and be ready to dismount on the steepest sections. The **Flåm Vandrerhjem (HI) ❶**, a half-hostel, half-campground, is the best bet for cheap overnight stays. (☎57 63 21 21. Showers 10kr per 5min. Linens 65kr. Laundry 50kr. Dorms 170kr; singles 300kr; doubles 450-540kr. Tent sites 70kr per person; cabins 525-825kr. 15% HI discount. MC/V.) Fylkesbaatane **express boats** run daily to Aurland (10min.), Balestrand (1½hr.), and Bergen (5hr.); check www.fjord1.no/fylkesbaatane for schedules. A popular sightseeing **ferry** route runs west through Sognefjord branches to Gudvangen (2hr., 5 per day, 180-220kr). From Gudvangen, you can take a **bus** south to Voss (see below) and get back on the train (1hr., 5 per day, 70-90kr). Flåm's **tourist office** is next to the train station. (☎57 63 21 06; www.visitflam.com. Open daily June-Aug. 8:30am-8pm; Sept. 8:45am-4pm; May 8:30am-4pm.) Between October and April, direct questions about Flåm to the tourist office in nearby Aurland, 9km north. (☎57 63 33 13; www.alr.no. Bike rental 30kr per hr., 175kr per day. Open June-Aug. M-F 8:30am-7pm, Sa-Su 10am-5pm; Sept.-May M-F 8:30am-3:30pm.) **Postal Code:** 5742.

VOSS. Along a glassy lake, Voss (pop. 14,000) is an adventurer's dream. Deep powder and 40km of marked trails attract skiers in winter, while kayaking, paragliding, and parabungeeing (jumping from a flying parasail) draw summer thrillseekers. **Extreme Sports Week** (late June; www.ekstremsportveko.com) draws sports fanatics with a variety of daredevil feats. The safety-conscious staff at **Nordic Ventures,** behind the Park Hotel in a mini-mall, runs adventure expeditions. A new office is in the works at Voss Camping. The **kayaking** trips to nearby Nærøyfjord allow beginners to visit otherwise inaccessible areas. Rental kayaks (1-day 495kr, 2-days 795kr, 3-days 1050kr, 250kr per day thereafter) are also available. (☎56 51 00 17; www.nordicventures.com. Open daily May to mid-Oct. 9am-9pm; mid-Oct. to Apr. 10am-5pm. Kayaking daytrips 895kr; 2 days 1895kr; 3 days including hiking 2595kr. All trips fully catered. MC/V.) **Voss Rafting Center,** Nedkvitnevegen 25, 3½km from Voss in Skulestadmo, leads rafting trips at 10am and 3pm daily (from 500kr). Pickup from Voss can be arranged. (☎56 51 05 25; www.vossrafting.no. Open in summer daily 9am-5pm, phone bookings until 10pm; winter M-F 9am-4pm. MC/V.) If you'd rather stay dry, take the 30min. **hike** from Voss to **Bordal Gorge.** From the tourist office, turn on the path marked Prestegardsalleen by the lake. Make the trek between July and August, when the path is safest.

Turn right as you exit the train station and walk along E16 away from town for **Voss Vandrerhjem (HI) ❷.** If money is short, sleep on a foam mattress in the attic for 180kr. (☎56 51 20 17; www.vosshostel.com. Bike, canoe, and kayak rental. Breakfast included. Linens 45kr. Internet 1kr per min. Reception 24hr. Dorms 250kr; singles 535kr; doubles 700kr. 15% HI discount. MC/V.) To reach lakeside **Voss Camping ❶,** behind the tourist office, head left from the train station, stick to the lake shore, and turn right onto the gravel path at the church. (☎56 51 15 97; www.vosscamping.no. Reception May-Sept. 8am-10pm. Reserve ahead. 100kr per tent site; 5-person cabin 500kr. Showers 10kr for 6min. MC/V.) Pick up groceries at **Kiwi,** on the main street past the post office. (☎56 51 27 35. Open M-F 9am-9pm, Sa 9am-8pm.) **Trains** leave for Bergen (1¼hr., 1 per 1-2hr., 153kr) and Oslo (5½-6hr., 4-5 per day, 699kr). To get to the **tourist office,** Uttrågt. 9, turn left as you exit the train station, follow the main road and bear right at the fork by the church. (☎56 52 08 00; www.visitvoss.no. Open June-Aug. M-F 8am-7pm, Sa 9am-7pm, Su noon-7pm; Sept.-May M-F 8am-3:30pm. MC/V.) **Postal Code:** 5700.

EIDFJORD. In an eastern arm of Hardangerfjord accessible only by bus or car, Eidfjord (pop. 950) allows visitors to explore beyond the touristed Oslo-Bergen Line. The town draws hikers bound for the nearby **Hardangervidda** mountain plateau, the largest of its kind in Europe. Inexperienced hikers should stick to the plateau's eastern half, while more seasoned adventurers can tackle the **Hardangerjøkulen** glacier in the north or, with a guide, its pristine southern tip. A 2hr. walk on a trail from the harbor leads to a **Viking burial ground** on top of a plateau in **Hereid.** Pick up a trail map from the tourist office and then head out along Simadalvegen. After passing the bridge, turn right and walk along the river; follow the path as it goes by the lake and winds uphill. A **mini-tour** from Voss whisks a mixed-age crowd to **Hardangervidda Nature Center,** which features interactive displays on the region's botany and zoology. (☎53 66 59 00; www.hardangervidda.org. Open daily June-Aug. 10am-8pm; Apr.-May and Sept.-Oct. 10am-6pm. Nature center 80kr. MC/V.) From there, the tour continues to the roaring **Vøringfossen Waterfall,** which plummets 182m into a serrated glacial valley. Be careful; the stones are slippery, and safety rails are few and far between. (Mini-tour daily mid-June to mid-Aug. Departs from the harbor after ferry arrival. 195kr, students 110kr.) **Sæbø Camping ❶,** 7km from town near the Nature Center, has a spectacular lakeside location and a service building with most amenities. (☎53 66 59 27; www.saebocamping.com. Kitchen available. Breakfast included. 105kr per tent site, 10-15kr per person; 4- to 8-bed cabins 350-800kr. Electricity 30kr. Showers included.) Eidfjord is best reached from Voss via Ulvik. **Buses** leave Voss at 8:45am (1 per day; 69kr, students 57kr) and arrive in Ulvik at 11:10am. From there, the **ferry** travels to Eidfjord, returning at 2:40pm (June-Aug.). The **tourist office,** in the town center, finds accommodations for a 60kr fee. (☎53 67 34 00. Open mid-June to mid-Aug. M-F 9am-6pm, Sa-Su noon-6pm; May to mid-June and mid-Aug. to Sept. M-F 8:30am-4pm; Oct.-Apr. M, W, and every other F 10am-4pm.) **Postal Code:** 5783.

SOGNEFJORD

The slender fingers of Sognefjord, Europe's longest fjord and the world's second longest, reach the foot of the Jotunheimen Mountains in central Norway. **Jostedalsbreen** glacier, the largest in mainland Europe, lies just north of the region. The town of Sogndal is the main gateway for glacier trips, while Balestrand and Fjærland are more charming villages ideal for sightseeing and exploring the fjord. Due to uncertain road conditions and limited bus routes, regional overland transportation is often more confusing than it's worth. For an alternative way to explore the area, try Fylkesbaatane **boats** (☎55 90 70 70; www.fylkesbaatane.no), which leave from Bergen on tours of Sognefjord and the Flåm valley.

BALESTRAND. Balestrand (pop. 1400) is known as a community for artists, who first flocked to the area in the 1800s, lured by the scenery. This legacy continues with the town's many free galleries. ◪**Golden House,** in the same building as the tourist office, features a town history museum, Scandinavian art displays, and works and greeting cards by local artists. (☎91 56 28 42. Open May-Sept. daily 10am-10pm. Free.) In front of Balestrand's docks, **Sognefjord Akvarium** showcases the rarely seen marine life of the fjords. The aquarium also has **Cafe Fløyfisken ❷.** Try some fish soup (70kr) or the grilled ham and cheese (35kr) while enjoying the dockside views. (☎57 69 13 03. Open daily late June to mid-Aug. 9am-11:30pm; May-late June and mid-Aug. to early Sept. 10am-6pm. 70kr. 50% discount for Kringsjå Hostel guests. AmEx/D/MC/V.) To reach the well-marked **hiking trails** from the harbor, head uphill to the right, take the second left, and walk along the main road next to the youth hostel for 10min.; turn right on Sygna and follow the signs. **Moreld** leads 3hr. **kayak** tours (390kr) and day excursions (600kr, with lunch 700kr) on Sognefjord. They also rent kayaks. (☎40 46 71 00; www.moreld.net. Single kayaks 350kr per day, double 525kr per day. Branch in Sogndal.) Walk up the hill past the tourist office, follow the curve right and take the next left to reach ◪**Kringsjå Hotel and Youth Hostel (HI) ❷.** The top-floor dorms have excellent fjord views. (☎57 69 13 03; www.kringsja.no. Breakfast included. Linens 60kr. Laundry 30kr. Open July to mid-Aug. Dorms 210kr; singles 450kr; doubles 620kr; triples 750kr. 15% HI discount. MC/V.) **Sjøtun Camping ❶** is past the brown church on the coastal road. (☎57 69 12 23; www.sjotun.com. Showers free. Reception 9-9:30am, 6-6:30pm, and 9-9:30pm; call for other arrival times. Open June-early Sept. Tent sites 60kr. 4- to 6-person cabins 235-330kr. Cash only.) **Buses** run to: Bergen (4½hr., 1-2 per day), Oslo (8-8½hr., 3-4 per day), and Sogndal (1¼hr., 2-3 per day). Fylkesbaatane **express boats** run to Balestrand (4hr.; M-Sa 2 per day; 433kr, students 215kr) and Flåm (1½hr.). The **tourist office,** across from the aquarium and just off the ship landing, rents **scooters** (300kr per day) and **bikes.** (☎57 69 12 55; www.sognefjord.no. Bikes 75kr per 6hr., 140kr per day. Internet 15kr per 15min. Open mid-June to mid-Aug. M-Sa 7:30am-6pm, Sa-Su 10am-5pm; May to mid-June and mid-Aug. to Sept. M-F 10am-5pm, Sa-Su 10am-3pm; Oct.-Apr. M-F 8:30am-3:30pm.)

FJÆRLAND AND FJÆRLANDSFJORD. ◪**Fjærlandsfjord** branches off Sognefjord in a thin northward line past Balestrand to Fjærland (pop. 300) at the base of Jostedalsbreen glacier. The town's preserved houses have largely been converted into secondhand bookstores set against stellar scenery. ◪**Norwegian Book Town,** a network of 15 secondhand shops, holds over 250,000 volumes and sells novels for as little as 10kr. (☎57 69 22 10; www.bokbyen.no. Open May-Sept. daily 10am-6pm. MC/V.) The **Norsk Bremuseum** (Glacier Museum), 3km outside town on the only road, is famous for its eccentric geometric architecture. (☎57 69 32 88; www.bre.museum.no. Open daily June-Aug. 9am-7pm; Apr.-May and Sept.-Oct. 10am-4pm. 85kr, students 40kr. AmEx/D/MC/V.) Fjærland does not offer many winter activities because of inadequate bus transportation, but summer thaws out a dozen well-marked **trails.** One of the longer hikes runs up **Flatbreen** (2-3hr.), an arm of Jostedalsbreen glacier, to the Flatbrehytta self-service **cabin.** The hike begins 5km northeast from the Norsk Bremuseum at the Øygard parking lot. (☎57 69 32 29. Limited availability June-Aug. Reserve ahead and bring a sleeping bag.) **Ferries** run to Balestrand (1¼hr.; 2 per day; 175kr, students 84kr). The **Glacier Bus**

provides a guided **tour** of the area and shuttles passengers from Mundal (Fjær-land's ferry dock) to the Norsk Bremuseum, two Jostedalsbreen outcroppings, and then back to the harbor. (2 per day; 124-135kr; transportation back from glacier museum to Mundal 24kı). From behind the Norsk Bremuseum, **buses** run to Ålesund (6hr.; 4 per day; 349kr, students 277kr); Sogndal (30min.; M-Sa 2-5 per day; 99kr, students 65kr); and Stryn (2¼hr., 1 per day, 250kr). Pick up groceries at the **Joker** across from the tourist office (open M-F 9am-5pm). The **tourist office,** near the harbor, rents **bikes** (30kr per hr., 140kr per day) and provides hiking info. (☎57 69 32 33; www.fjaerland.org. Open May-Sept. daily 10am-6pm.)

SOGNDAL. East of Balestrand along the fjord, Sogndal (pop. 6700) is less charming than its neighbor but is an essential stop for trips to Jostedalsbreen glacier and a key transportation hub. Adventure companies like **Jostedalen Breførarlag** (☎57 68 31 11; www.bfl.no) run easy glacier walks (from 150kr) and offer courses in rock climbing (from 2050kr, not including equipment). **Icetroll** (☎57 68 32 50; www.icetroll.com) runs kayaking trips on Jostedalsbreen's glacial lakes, some combined with hiking (from 750kr). Most adventure tours depart from Gaupne or Jostedal, two small towns north of Sogndal. **Buses** run to Gaupne (45min.) and Jostedal (2-2½hr.) fairly often; visit the tourist office for more info or check www.fjord1.no and www.nor-way.no. **Sogndal Vandrerhjem (HI) ❷**, Helgheimsvegen 9, has some of the town's more affordable rooms. (☎57 62 75 75. Breakfast included. Linens 105kr. Open mid-June to mid-Aug. Dorms 200kr; singles 280kr; doubles 450-610kr. 15% HI discount.) **Buses** run from the west end of Gravensteinsgata in the town center to: Balestrand (1¼hr., 2-3 per day); Bergen (4½-5hr., 3-4 per day, 389kr); Fjærland (30min.; M-Sa 2-5 per day; 99kr, students 65kr); Oslo (7hr., 3-4 per day, 505kr); Stryn via Skei (2¾hr., 1 per day, 270kr). Fylkesbaatane **express boats** run to Bergen (4½hr.; M-Sa 2 per day; 500kr, students 250kr) and stop at several destinations along Sognefjord. The **tourist office,** Hovevegen 2, is near the bus station. (☎57 67 30 83; www.sognefjord.no. Open late June to late Aug. M-F 9am-8pm, Sa 9am-5pm, Su 3-8pm; Sept. to late June M-F 9am-4pm.)

NORDFJORD

Nordfjord runs north of the ice-blue expanse of **Jostedalsbreen** glacier. The region was formerly less popular than Geirangerfjord and Sognefjord, but Jostedalsbreen National Park has attracted many visitors to the area in recent years. Although solo trips onto the glacier are tempting, it has dangerous soft spots and crevasses. Guided tours are essential, with Stryn serving as a major hub for such excursions.

STRYN. Stryn municipality has three ideal base towns for exploring the area: **Stryn, Olden** and **Loen.** The least flashy of the three, **Stryn** (pop. 3000) is a departure point for trips on **Briksdalsbreen,** a branch of Jostedalsbreen glacier. A **bus** (76kr) runs from Stryn's bus terminal to the base of Briksdalsbreen, via **Olden** (daily June-Aug. 9:30am, returning 1:40pm). **Olden Aktiv** (☎57 87 38 88; www.oldenaktiv.no) runs a variety of glacier tours and hikes (6-7hr., 2½hr. on the glacier, 600kr) and rafting trips around icebergs (300kr). The tours depart from **Melkevoll Bretun ❶**, a campground and tourist office 45min. from Stryn. In addition to huts and cabins, Melkevoll Bretun also has **stone age** cave lodgings, where guests sleep on wooden slabs swaddled in reindeer skins. Bring an insulated sleeping bag. (☎57 87 38 64; www.melkevoll.no. Showers 10kr per 5min. Firewood 50kr. Huts from 290kr. Cabins 590-750kr. Cave dorms 110kr per person; min. 4 people to reserve. Call ahead for availability. MC/V.) Glacier walks (500kr) on **Bødalsbreen,** another arm of Jostedalsbreen, leave from **Loen.** To reach the family-friendly **Stryn Vandrerhjem (HI) ❷**, Geilevegen 14, from the bus station, turn left on Setrevegen, head uphill, and look for signs. If you arrive late, call for a pickup. (☎57 87 11 06. Breakfast included. Linens 55kr. Laundry 40kr. Internet 15kr per 15min. Reception 4-11pm. Lockout 11am-4pm. Open June-Aug. Dorms 245kr; singles 400kr; doubles 530kr. 15% HI discount. D/MC/V.) **Buses** run to Ålesund (3½hr., 4-5 per day, 244kr); Bergen (6hr., 4 per day, 405kr); Fjærland (2¼hr., 1 per day, 250kr); Stryn via Skei (2¾hr., 1 per day, 270kr); Trondheim (7½hr., 1 per day 3pm, 412kr) via Lom (2hr., 213kr). Stryn's **tourist office**, Tinggata 3, is across the street and down a block from the Esso station near the bus stop. (☎57 87 40 40; www.nordfjord.no. Internet 15kr per 15min. Open July M-F 8:30am-8pm, Sa-Su 9:30am-9pm; June and Aug. M-F 8:30am-6pm, Sa 9:30am-5pm; Sept.-May M-F 8:30am-3:30pm.)

GEIRANGERFJORD

The 16km long Geirangerfjord, a UNESCO World Heritage Site, is lined with cliffs and waterfalls that make it one of Norway's most spectacular—and heavily touristed—destinations. While cruising through the icy blue water, watch for the Seven Sisters waterfalls and, across from them, the wooing Suitor waterfall. The suitor was soundly rejected by all seven sisters and took to the bottle, explaining why the shape of a beer bottle is visible through the roaring water. So the story goes. Geirangerfjord can be reached from the north via the Trollstigen road from Åndalsnes, or by bus from Ålesund or Stryn via ferry from Hellesylt.

GEIRANGER. Geiranger (pop. 300), at the eastern end of Geirangerfjord, is a tourist mecca at the final point of the Trollstigen road. In summer, thousands overrun the town to take in the stunning views of the fjord. The surrounding, well-marked **trails** offer stunning views and some escape from the crowds. Nearby natural attractions include **Flydalsjuvet Cliff** (round-trip 2hr.), **Storseter Waterfall** (2½hr.), and views of the Seven Sisters waterfalls from **Skageflå Farm** (5hr.). At **Lanfvaten**, hikers can climb into cloud cover that shrouds the top of **Dalsnibba Mountain Plateau** (1476m). To get there, take a bus from opposite the ferry docks (1hr., 2 per day, 160kr). The **Geiranger Fjordsenter**, a 15min. walk from the tourist office on Rte. 63, explores the history of the region. Concerts and traditional Norwegian music and folklore performances are held throughout summer. (☎70 26 30 07; www.geirangerfjord.no. Open daily July 9am-10pm; June and Aug. 9am-6pm; May and Sept. 9am-4pm; 85kr. Concerts M and Th 9pm, 50kr.) For free summer **concerts,** check out the white **Geiranger Kyrkje** church overlooking the town (W 9pm). ◪**Geiranger Camping ❶**, 100m from the town center by the water, is set at the mouth of the fjord. **Kayak** rentals (150kr per hr., 225kr per 2hr., 1000kr per 2 days) are also available. (☎70 26 31 20. Showers 5kr per 5min. Laundry 80kr. Reception 8am-10pm. Open mid-May to early Sept. 20kr per person, 85kr per tent site. MC/V.) For the tentless, **Villa Utsikten Hotel & Restaurant ❸**, 3.5km from the town center, has affordable rooms. (☎70 26 96 60; www.villautsikten.no. Open May-Sept. Rooms from 300kr.) **Buses** run to Ålesund (3hr., 2-4 per day, 182kr). There is no bus station; buy tickets on board. **Ferries** depart for Hellesylt (1hr., 4-6 per day, 100kr). For info on hiking and rental **bikes** (50kr per hr., 150kr per day), visit the **tourist office,** up the path from the ferry landing. (☎70 26 30 99; www.visitgeirangerfjorden.com. Open daily mid-June to Aug. 9am-7pm; mid-May to mid-June and Sept. 9am-5pm.)

HELLESYLT. West of Geiranger at the intersection of Geirangerfjord and **Sunnylvsfjord,** Hellesylt (pop. 600), a base for seven well-marked **hikes,** is quieter than Geiranger. **Skaret** (2-3hr.) has a mountainside outlook with views of the town and fjord. From there, you can continue to **Steimnebba,** a nearby peak that adds an extra uphill climb to the trip (4-6hr.). The **Peer Gynt Gallery,** behind the tourist office, features 10 life-size wood carvings depicting the epic story of Norwegian playwright Henrik Ibsen's famous protagonist. (☎70 26 38 80. Open June-Aug. daily 11am-7pm; Sept. Sa-Su 11am-7pm. 50kr.) The **Stadheimfossen Campground ❶** has tent sites and cabins for groups. (☎70 26 50 79; www.stadheimfossen.no. Open Jan.-Sept. 50kr per tent site, 350kr per 4-person cabin.) **Hellesylt Vandrerhjem (HI) ❷**, in a white building above **Hellesyltfossen waterfall**, is a funky, 60s-style lodge. (☎70 26 51 28. Breakfast 55kr. Linens and towels 30kr. Free Internet. Open June-early Sept. Dorms 160kr; singles 290kr; doubles 400kr. 15% HI discount.) When hunger strikes after mountain excursions, head to one of two grocery stores in town, **Spar** and **Coop**. They also offer sporting equipment if you're missing gear. **Buses** go to Ålesund (3 per day, 350kr) and Styrn (2-3 per day, 150kr). **Ferries** depart for Geiranger (1hr., 4-6 per day, 100kr). The **tourist office,** by the docks, stores luggage for free. (☎70 26 50 52. Open June-Aug. daily 9am-5:30pm.)

LOM, JOTUNHEIMEN, AND REINHEIMEN

Near the last tributaries of the Western Fjords and the remote towns of the interior lies the pristine landscape of Jotunheimen ("home of the giants") National Park. In 2007, Reinheimen ("home of the reindeer") National Park was established north of Jotunheimen. These enormous parks flank the village of Lom, with Breheimen to the west, a glacier area that will soon attain park status. Hunters chased wild reindeer here for thousands of years. Norwegian writers and painters discovered it anew in the 19th century, channeling its rugged beauty into a National Romantic artistic movement. Today, it is Scandinavia's top summer hiking destination.

LOM. Lom's (pop. 2500) sights are not entirely budget-friendly, but a trip is well worth the nearby parks. Hiking season usually runs from July to mid-Aug. In Jotunheimen, a popular trek leads to the summit of 2469m **Galhøpiggen**, northern Europe's tallest mountain. Ask at the tourist office for the best departure points, which vary according to skill level and weather conditions. The 6hr. trail from **Juvashytta** is the most popular route, but can only be completed with the help of paid guides (150kr) who navigate the perilous soft spots of the Jostedalsbreen glacier. Before guides were mandatory, several inexperienced tourists fell through crevasses and died. A bus leaves from Lom for Juvashytta (mid-June to mid-Aug. daily 8:40am, 60kr). From **Krossbu**, hikers can take a 4-6hr. glacier walk. Less experienced travelers looking to reach the summit without a guide should catch the bus to **Spiterstulen** (1 per day 8:45am, 60kr). From there, plan to hike 8-9hr., although not on the glacier. Also consider the **Memurubu-Gjendesheim** trail mentioned in Henrik Ibsen's *Peer Gynt*. To explore Reinheimen, visit **Aursjøen**, off Rte. 15, which has several trails. **Billingen,** also off Rte. 15, has hikes (4hr.) up to a **DNT** (Norwegian Mountain Touring Association) cabin. **Nordal Turistsenter ❷,** in the city center, has affordable cabin accommodations. Walk left as you exit the tourist office and cross the bridge to the main roundabout, take a left and follow the road until you see the signs and cabins on your left. (☎61 21 93 00; www.nordalturist-senter.no. Laundry 25kr. Reception July-Aug. 8am-11pm; Sept.-May reduced hours. Open Apr.-Dec. Tent sites 50kr per person, 200kr per car; 2- to 4-person cabins 380-430kr. Showers free.) Pick up groceries at **Kiwi,** off the main roundabout. (Open M-F 9am-9pm, Sa 9am-6pm. Cash only.) **Buses** run to: Bergen (8½hr., 2 per day, 450kr); Oslo (6-6½hr., 5 per day, 465kr); Sogndal (3½hr., mid-June to mid-Sept. 2 per day, 220kr); Trondheim (5½hr., 2 per day, 429kr). The **tourist office** is in the Fjellmuseum. From the bus station, turn left and cross the bridge. (☎61 21 29 90; www.visitjotunheimen.com. Open mid-June to mid-Aug. M-F 9am-7pm, Sa-Su 10am-7pm; mid-Aug. to mid-June reduced hours.)

ROMSDAL AND TRØNDELAG

Between the Western Fjords and the sparsely inhabited stretches of northern Norway, a group of small coastal cities forms the third point of a triangle with Oslo and Bergen. Travelers are only beginning to discover this Norwegian heartland, hemmed in by the spiny Trollstigen range and the valleys along Trondheimsfjord.

ÅLESUND ☎ 70

Seaside Ålesund (OH-less-oont; pop. 40,000) welcomes fjord-weary travelers with Art Nouveau architecture. Climb up 418 steps to the **Aksla** outlook for views of the city and distant mountains. Head through the park across from Ålesund Vandrerhjem hostel and walk 25min. to the top. At the ◪**Art Nouveau Center,** Apotekergt. 16, a time machine exhibit transports visitors back to Ålesund's devastating 1904 fire and explains how the city got its artistic flair. (☎ 10 49 70. Open June-Aug. M-F 10am-7pm, Sa-Su noon-5pm; Sept.-May Tu-Sa 11am-4pm, Su noon-4pm. 50kr, students 40kr. AmEx/MC/V.) For a glimpse of another time, visit the **Sunnmøre Museum,** which has reconstructed farmhouses and the excavated remains of an 11th-century trading post. On Wednesday afternoons, locals demonstrate traditional handicrafts, and a replica Viking ship takes visitors for a short cruise. Take bus #618 (10min., 24kr) to Sunnmøre. (☎ 17 40 00; www.sunnmore.museum.no. Open late June-late Aug. M-Sa 11am-5pm, Su noon-5pm; late Aug.-late June M-Tu and F 11am-3pm, Su noon-3pm. Cruise 30kr. Museum 65kr, students 45kr. MC/V.) The ◪**62° Fjord Sightseeing Center,** just down the harbor from the tourist office, runs guided tours of **Hjørundfjord** and **Geirangerfjord** (p. 755). The prices may not seem budget-friendly, but tickets on their circular tours are good for a week of fjord sightseeing—well worth the fee. (☎ 11 44 30; www.62nord.net. Open late-May to Aug. 7:30am-8pm. Tours 600-1200kr; ask about cheaper one-way fares.) **Cruise Service AS,** Brunholmgt. 10, offers evening excursions to boat-access only **Trandal.** The town is home to the raging **Christian Gaard** pub, which has live music and parties nightly. (☎ 10 28 01; www.cruiseservice.no. Tours 150-500kr.)

Ålesund Vandrerhjem (HI) ❷, Parkgt. 14, has Ålesund's most affordable rooms. From the bus station, walk east down Keiser Wilhelmsgt., turn left on Storgt., and then right on Parkgt. (☎ 11 58 30. Breakfast, linens, and laundry included. Reception May-Sept. 8:30-11am and 3:30pm-midnight; Sept.-May 4-6pm. Dorms 235kr; singles 490kr; doubles 690kr. 15% HI discount. D/MC/V.) American-inspired food meets Norwegian flair at **Let's Eat Deli ❶,** Keiser Wilhelmsgt. 37, half a block from Storgt. (☎ 13 13 07. Sandwiches 55-68kr. Open M-F 10:30am-5pm, Sa 10:30am-4pm. V.) Across the street, **Rema 1000** stocks groceries. (☎ 12 42 57. Open M-F 9am-10pm. Cash only.) **Buses** go to Stryn (3½hr., 4 per day, 244kr) and Trondheim (8hr., 2 per day, 511kr). You can also bus to Åndalsnes (2½hr., 3 per day, 183kr) and catch a train to Trondheim (4-5hr., 500kr). Hurtigruten **boats** to Trondheim are costly, but trips include one night of lodging on the boat; beware that "dormitory accommodations" can mean a space on the floor. (13½hr.; 1 per day; 974kr, students 487kr.) The exceptional **tourist office,** at the Skateflukaia dock, helps plan regional travel. (☎ 15 76 00; www.visitalesund.com. Walking tours depart daily June 20-Aug. 20 at noon, 75kr. Internet 10kr per 10min. Open June-Aug. M-F 8:30am-7pm, Sa 9am-5pm, Su 11am-5pm; Sept.-May M-F 8:30am-4pm.)

ÅNDALSNES ☎ 71

Åndalsnes (pop. 4000), on Romsdalsfjord, is a port on the edge of fjord country. Twenty kilometers out of town, accessible by bus or bike, **hikes** along the **Trollstigen** (Troll's Road) climb to over 1000m. The **Frokostplassen** path is suitable for both expert and casual hikers. The trail passes the 180m **Stigfossen** waterfall and approaches the sheer **Trollveggen** (Troll's Wall). The lip of the wall lured base jumpers for years, until helicopter rescues drove the town into debt and the activity was outlawed. Thrill-seeking scofflaws continue to make jumps on the sly. Let's Go does not recommend illegal activities. Head back to Åndalsnes on the **Kløvstien path** (5hr.), which was recently smoothed over for walkers but is still steep enough to require a handrail in some places. If you're feeling sedentary, the **Raumabanen** train tour (45min., 108kr) south to the town of **Bjorli** offers magnificent views of the natural sights. (☎22 16 22; www.raumabanen.net.) Bjorli is a hub for **skiing** in winter, especially at the end of January during the **Romsdalsvinter** festivals, with ski trips throughout the region. In mid-July, the paths between Åndalsnes and Bjorli fill for the **Norwegian Mountain Festival** (www.norsk-fjellfestival.no). During the first weekend of August, Åndalsnes hosts the **RaumaRock Festival** (www.rauma-rock.com; 2-day pass 700kr), which highlights Scandinavian artists. An outdoor theater across the fjord in **Klungnes** is the site of the **Sinclairfestivalen** (Aug. 5-10), an open-air re-enactment of a 1612 battle between Scottish mercenaries and Norwegian farmers. (www.sinclairfestivalen.com. 250kr, students 150kr.) After the battle, an annual rowboat **regatta** from the theater back to the town center provides entertainment beyond the traditional fjord scenery. Just 2km from town, **Åndalsnes Vandrerhjem (HI) ❷**, Setnes, resembles a farmhouse with its grass roof and homey dorms. The Ålesund bus will stop at the hostel upon request. (☎22 13 82. Breakfast included. Linens and towels 60kr. Internet 15kr per 15min. Reception 4pm-10am. Dorms 230kr; singles 395kr; doubles 600kr. 15% HI discount. MC/V.) **Trains** run to Oslo (5½hr., 2-4 per day, 705kr). **Buses** depart outside the train station for Ålesund (2½hr., 1-2 per day, 183kr) and Geiranger (3hr., 1-2 per day, 200kr). The **tourist office** is in the train station. (☎22 16 22; www.visitandalsnes.com. Internet 20kr per 15min. Open mid-May to mid-Sept. M-Sa 9am-6pm, Su noon-6pm.)

TRONDHEIM   ☎73

A thousand years have passed since Vikings made Trondheim (pop. 162,000) Norway's seat of power. Today, the city is a gateway to the north, and nearly 30,000 university students give its canals and restored townhouses youthful energy.

🖪🖬 TRANSPORTATION AND PRACTICAL INFORMATION. Trains go to Bodø (11hr., 2 per day, 937kr) and Oslo (6½hr., 3 per day, 810kr). **Buses** leave the train station for Ålesund (8hr.; 4 per day; 500kr, students 375kr) and Bergen (14½hr.; 2 per day; 735kr, students 536kr). The Hurtigruten **boat** departs daily at noon for Stamsund, in the Lofoten Islands (31½hr.; 1938kr, 50% student discount). To get to the **tourist office**, Munkegt. 19, from the train station, cross the bridge, walk six blocks down Søndregt., turn right on Kongensgt., and look to your left as you approach the roundabout. (☎80 76 60; www.visit-trondheim.com. Open July-early Aug. M-F 8:30am-8pm, Sa-Su 10am-6pm; low season reduced hours.) **DNT** (Norwegian Mountain Touring Association), Sandgt. 30, has maps and hiking info and offers keys for cabins on nearby trails. (☎92 42 00; www.turistforeningen.no. Open May-Sept. M-W and F 8am-4pm, Th 8am-6pm.)

🖪🖸 ACCOMMODATIONS AND FOOD. Trondheim InterRail Center ❶, Elgesetergt. 1, in the Studentersamfundet (p. 759), has a fun-loving mood. Cross the bridge from the train station, walk south along Søndregt., and go right on Kongensgt. Turn left on Prinsensgt.; the hostel is on the left after the bridge. The walk is about 35min. (☎89 95 38; www.tirc.no. Breakfast included. Linens 60kr deposit. Free Internet. Open July 5 to Aug. 19. Dorms 150kr. Cash only.) For a tidy budget option, take Lillegårdsbakken, off Øvre Bakklandet, uphill to **Singsaker Sommerho-**

tell ❷, Rogertsgt. 1. (☎89 31 00; http://sommerhotell.singsaker.no. Breakfast and linens included. Open mid-June to mid-Aug. Dorms 200kr; singles 410kr; doubles 620kr; triples 940kr. MC/V.) Gluttony may be one of the seven deadly sins, but that doesn't detract from the appeal of the all-you-can-eat ▨**cake buffet** (Su 1-7pm; 59kr) at **Mormors Stue** ❷, Nedre Enkeltskillingsveita 2. (☎52 20 22. Open M-Sa 10am-11:30pm, Su 1-11:30pm. MC/V.) The early-bird dinner crowd snaps up fresh fish platters (125kr) and beer at the riverside **Den Gode Nabo** ❸, Øvre Bakklandet 66, just over the Old Town Bridge in a basement to the right. (☎87 42 40; www.dengodenabo.com. Dinner special daily 4-7pm. Beer 42-52kr. Open daily 1pm-1:30am. D/MC/V.) Try **Ramp** ❷, Strandv. 25A, for scrumptious vegetarian cuisine. (☎51 80 20; www.lamoramp.net. Entrees 67-100kr. Beer 43kr. Open M-W 10am-midnight, Th-F 10am-1am, Sa noon-1am, Su noon-midnight. MC/V.)

◪ **SIGHTS.** Start in the north near the train station and head down Fjordgt. to the *Ravnkloa* (fish market), where you can catch a ferry (June-Aug. daily 10am-6pm. 50kr round-trip) to **Munkholmen** (The Monks' Island). Home to an 11th-century monastery, the island is now popular for its pristine beaches. ▨**Nidaros Cathedral,** in the southern end of the city, tops the list of churches to visit in Norway. Built in the 11th century, the cathedral sits on King Olof's (Norway's patron saint) tomb and is home to royal coronations. (☎53 91 60; www.nidarosdomen.no. Open mid-June to mid-Aug. M-F 9am-6pm, Sa 9am-2pm, Su 1-4pm; mid-Aug. to mid-June reduced hours. Organ concerts mid-June to mid-Aug M-F 1 and 5:40pm, Sa 1pm; mid-Aug. to mid-June Sa 1pm. 50kr admission includes the nearby Museum at Archbishop's Palace. Low season free/50kr. AmEx/D/MC/V.) The same complex also has a museum for the **Crown Jewels and Regalia.** (☎53 91 60. Open June-Aug. M-F 10am-4pm, Sa 10am-2pm, Su noon-4pm; low season reduced hours. 70kr, combination ticket for cathedral, museum, and jewels 100kr. AmEx/D/MC/V.) Across the scenic **Gamle Bybro** (Old Town Bridge) to the east, the weather-worn fishing houses of the **old district** are now chic galleries and cafes. On the hill opposite Gamle Bybro is the world's first **bicycle elevator,** built in 1993 to encourage cycling in hilly Trondheim. Test your balance as you are shoved up the steep hill by an automated pulley with a stirrup for your foot. The reward is a speedy ride down. (Access card available at the tourist office for 100kr deposit.) **Bike** racks, at the tourist office and throughout the city, offer rentals. (☎81 50 02 50. 200kr deposit, 70kr per 2-3 days.) **Kristiansten Festning** (Kristiansten Fortress), overlooking Trondheim and the fjords, is one of the city's best picnic spots. Built in 1681 after a fire destroyed Trondheim, the fortress saved the city from Swedish invaders in 1781 and served as the Nazi execution grounds for members of the Norwegian resistance. (☎98 80 66 23; www.kristiansten-festning.no. Grounds open daily 8am-midnight. Interior open June-Aug. daily 11am-4pm. Museum 50kr.)

▣▨ **ENTERTAINMENT AND NIGHTLIFE.** The **Olavsfestdagene Medieval Festival** (late July to early Aug.) fills the city with pop bands and pilgrims. (☎84 14 50; www.olavsfestdagene.no.) The **Studentersamfundet,** the student society's headquarters, houses a cafe with cheap food and beer next to the InterRail Center. You may discover one of the 18 private bars in the maze-like building. (☎89 95 00; www.samfundet.no. Beer 25-48kr. Open daily Sept.-June until 2am.) The **Solsiden** (Sunny Side) district is a waterfront promenade home to popular restaurants and lounges. The standout ▨**Club Blæst,** TMV kaia 17, has three bars and a theater that hosts rock acts, DJs most weekends, and an improv comedy troupe on Saturdays. (☎60 01 00; www.blaest.no. Beer 58kr. Concerts from 50kr. 20+ after 8pm. Open daily noon-3:30am. AmEx/D/MC/V.) Nearby, **Cafe and Bar Bare Blåbær,** Innherredsveien 16, serves burgers and pizza (99-129kr) until midnight and then becomes a lounge and bar. (☎53 30 33. Beer 56kr. 20+ after 6pm. Open M-Th 11am-1:30am, F-

Sa 11am-3:30am, Su 3pm-1:30am. AmEx/D/MC/V.) When school is in session, the clubs and bars along **Brattorgata,** in the north near the train station, offer everything from tapas to fine malt whiskey. In summer, a stroll along **Carl Johans gate** or **Nordre gate** is the best bet for nightlife beyond Solsiden.

NORTHERN NORWAY

Beyond the Arctic Circle, Norway's northern stretches are home to a mix of cultures and sights. Norwegians live side by side with the indigenous Sámi people, from the city center of Tromsø to the natural wonders of the Lofoten Islands. Even farther north, the remote Svalbard Archipelago sits on top of the world.

TROMSØ ☎ 77

Dubbed the "Paris of the Arctic" by explorers in awe of its cosmopolitan flair, Tromsø (pop. 60,000) exudes a worldly sensibility that belies its location north of the Arctic Circle. The town is a base for exploring Norway's northern mountains and lakes. However, a few days wandering the pedestrian-friendly center or pub-crawling will satiate travelers longing for an urban scene.

🖪🗷 TRANSPORTATION AND PRACTICAL INFORMATION. The Hurtigruten **boat** arrives in Tromsø from Stamsund, in the Lofoten Islands (19hr.; departs 7:30pm; 1043kr, students 521kr; sleeping cabins 1578/1074kr). **Buses** go to Narvik (4½hr.; 2-4 per day; 340kr, students and Scanrail holders 180kr), a transportation hub for Finnish and Swedish destinations. The **tourist office,** Kirkegt. 2, books dogsled, glacier, rafting, snowmobile, and whale watching trips. (☎61 00 00; www.destinasjontromso.no. Open May 22-Aug. M-F 8:30am-6pm, Sa-Su 10am-5pm; Sept.-May 21 reduced hours.) The cheapest tour (475kr) goes by bus from behind the tourist office, through the **Lyngen Alps** to the island of **Skjervøy,** where a costal steamer then sails back to Tromsø. For hiking advice, visit **DNT** (Norwegian Mountain Touring Association), Kirkegt. 2, in the same building as the tourist office on the second floor. (☎68 51 75; www.turistforeningen.no/tromsturlag. Open June-Aug. noon-4pm.) Local city **buses** stop 2-3 times per day at each stop (23kr, 100kr day pass; purchase at the bus station behind the tourist office). **Postal Code:** 9253.

🖪 🗗 ACCOMMODATIONS AND FOOD. The ▨**Fjellheim Sommerhotell ❶,** Mellomvegen 96, 15min. from town, has the area's best accommodations. The dorms are basic, but the hostel offers an included breakfast and 24hr. make-your-own waffles. Take bus #28 to Bjerkely or walk along Mellomvegen. (☎75 55 60; fjellheim@nlm.no. Linens included. Internet 30kr per hr. Laundry 25kr. Reception 24hr. Open mid-June to mid-Aug. Dorms 200kr; singles 500kr; doubles 700kr. AmEx/D/MC/V.) To reach the oceanside views at **Tromsø Vandrerhjem (HI) ❷,** Åsgårdv. 9, from the tourist office, turn right and walk two blocks down Storgt., take a right on Fr. Langes gt., and catch bus #26. (☎65 76 28; www.tromsohostel.no. Linens 50kr. Reception 8-10:30am and 4-10pm; call ahead if arriving after 8pm. Open mid-June to mid-Aug. Dorms 200kr; singles 350kr; doubles 460kr. 15% HI discount. MC/V.) For **Tromsø Camping ❶,** take bus #20 or 24 to Kraftforsyninga, walk back across the red bridge, turn left, and follow the road 400m. (☎63 80 37; www.tromsocamping.no. Linens 60kr. Towels 20kr. Reception 7am-11pm. Tent sites 125kr. 2- to 5-person cabins 450-1250kr. Free showers. Electricity 50kr. MC/V.) **Jimmis ❶,** Amtmannsgata 3 off of Grønnegt., serves cheap, huge baguette sandwiches (54kr); try a smoothie (50kr) to wash it down. (☎65 52 27; www.jimmis.no. Open daily 10am-5pm.) For ham or seal sandwiches (49kr), head to **Skarven ❷,** Strandtorget 1, by the harbor.

(☎60 07 20; www.skarven.no. Beer 60kr. Open Su-Th 11am-12:30am, F-Sa 11am-1am. AmEx/D/MC/V.) Stock up on groceries at **Spar**, Storgt. 63. (☎68 21 40. Open M-F 9am-8pm, Sa 9am-7pm.)

🔲🔳 **SIGHTS AND HIKING.** The tour at the 🔳**Mack Brewery**, Storgt. 4-13, introduces visitors to beer-making with samples of beverages made on-site. After the tour, have another drink in the 80-year-old daytime pub and sample over 8 brews (52-63kr). Stave off drunkenness with traditional *lapskaus*—a cabbage, pork, and potato stew. (☎62 45 80; www.mack.no. 1hr. English-language tours leave from Øllhallen at Storgt. 4 June-Aug. M-Th 1 and 3:30pm; Sept.-May M-Th 1pm. 130kr; includes 1 beer.) In the same building, but down a side street off Storgt., **Blåst**, Peder Hansens gt. 4, is a glassblowing factory that gives free demonstrations. (☎68 34 60; www.blaast.no. Open M-F 9am-5pm, Sa 9am-3pm.) The **Tromsø University Museum** delves into geology, meteorology, and the indigenous Sámi culture. Visitors can request to view a 10min. slideshow with dazzling images of the Northern Lights. Take bus #37 from the city center or walk south along Mellomvegen for 30min. (☎64 50 00; www.tmu.uit.no. Open daily June-Aug. 9am-6pm; Sept.-May reduced hours. 30kr, students 15kr. MC/V.) **Polaria**, Hjalmar Johansens gt. 12, right off Strandv. Storgt. transition, is a small, interactive museum and aquarium focused on Arctic ecosystems. (☎75 01 00; www.polaria.no. Open daily mid-May to mid-Aug. 10am-7pm; mid-Aug. to Apr. noon-5pm. Seal feedings 12:30 and 3:30pm. 90kr, students 60kr. AmEx/D/MC/V.) **Polarmuseet**, Søndre Tollbodgt. 11, has detailed exhibits on polar exploration over the past century. Pick up an English-language guide at the ticket desk. (☎68 43 73; www.polarmuseum.no. Open daily Mar. to mid-June and mid-Aug. to Sept. 11am-5pm; mid-June to mid-Aug. 10am-7pm; Oct.-Feb. 11am-4pm. 50kr, students 45kr.) At the Tromsdalen end of the Tromsøbua Bridge, the **Arctic Cathedral** resembles a glacier—metallic plates covering its surface reflect natural light in long streaks. Eleven tons of glass make up the stained-glass window behind the altar. In summer, the cathedral hosts performances of Norwegian folk songs and hymns (80kr) at 11:30pm. (Open June to mid-Aug. M-Sa 9am-7pm, Su 1-7pm; mid-Aug. to May daily 4-6pm. 25kr. Mass Su 11am.)

To see the midnight sun in June and early July, take the **Fjellheisen** cable car, Solliveien 12, a 10min. walk from the Arctic Cathedral, 420m to the top of Mt. Storsteinen. (☎63 87 37; www.fjellheisen.no. Daily 2 per hr. 90kr.) Students take the lift at night for an introspective evening at the **Fjellstua** cafe. (☎63 86 55; www.utelivsbyen.no. Beer 58kr. Open daily mid-

The Chronicle

IN RECENT NEWS

SUCCESS FOR THE SÁMI

For centuries, the Sámi people have herded reindeer, hunted, and farmed in some of Norway's most remote and inhospitable regions. One of the largest indigenous groups in Europe, the Sámi live in northern Finland, Norway, Sweden, and part of Russia. Their current population is estimated to be around 85,000.

Because they occupy such rugged territory, the Sámi largely escaped outside influence until the 20th century. They were poorly understood by their neighbors. Lappland—the European name for the Sámi homeland—was considered the mythical home of Santa Claus in many European cultures. In the early 20th century, the Norwegian government made aggressive attempts to wipe out Sámi culture, including banning the use of their languages in schools.

Norway has since reversed its policy, taking steps today to protect the livelihood of the Sámi. The Sámediggi, the representative assembly for the Sámi in Norway, held its first session in 1989. Among other responsibilities, the parliament is charged with ensuring that the rights of the Sámi are upheld. In Norway, Finland, and Sweden, festivals celebrate Sámi music, a newspaper is published in the Sámi language, and each year February 6 is observed as Sámi National Day.

May to mid-Aug. 10am-1am; Apr. to mid-May and mid-Aug. to Sept. 10am-5pm. AmEx/D/MC/V.) Manageable **hikes** near Tromsø include the 6-8hr. climb up **Tromsdalstinden** (1283m). Hikers looking for a challenge can trek to **Treriksrøysa**, southeast of the city, and stand in Finland, Norway, and Sweden all at once—the ■budget-friendly way to say "I toured all of Scandinavia."

■■ **FESTIVALS AND NIGHTLIFE.** The **Tromsø International Film Festival** is Norway's largest, attracting over 47,000 visitors annually (Jan. 15-20, 2008; ☎75 30 90; www.tiff.no). The following week, the **Northern Lights Festival** showcases classic music under the *aurora borealis*. **Sámi National Day** (Feb. 6) culminates in a reindeer race through the city center. Tromsø is a university town famous for its nightlife, which centers on **Storgata** and the side streets **Strandskillet** and **Grønnegata**. Drop in for tapas or a cappuccino at **Åpen Bar** (Open Bar), Grønnegt. 81, a relaxed, candlelit lounge and bar. (☎68 49 06. Beer 59kr; F 38kr. Sept.-May F-Sa DJ. 20+. Cover F-Sa 60kr. Restaurant open Tu-F 3-10pm, Sa noon-10pm. Nightclub open F-Sa 10pm-3:30am. D/MC/V.) At **Kaos,** Strangt. 22, students hang out in a subterranean bar. Monday nights bring out the DJ in everyone with ■**Free-Jay:** spin your own tunes for 30min. on the club's stereo system and get two free beers. The pros take over on weekends, with some of Norway's best spinning for a young crowd. (☎63 59 99. M 6pm-2am beer 56kr, F-Sa 8pm-midnight 35kr. Cover 30kr. 18+. Concerts W-Th 30-100kr. Open Su-Th 6pm-2am, F-Sa 6pm-3:30am. Cash only.)

LOFOTEN ISLANDS   ☎76

A jumble of emerald mountains, glassy waters, and colorful villages, the Lofoten Islands prove there is more to Norwegian beauty than fjords. The chain extends from Moskenesøya island in the south to Vestvågøy and several other islands in the north. Aside from tourism, Lofoten's major industry is fishing. *Rorbuer*, red fishing shacks, are rented to those on village forays above the Arctic Circle.

■**TRANSPORTATION.** The Hurtigruten **express boat** runs from Trondheim to Stamsund (31hr.; departs daily at noon, arrives at 7pm the next day; 1873kr). Another option is to take a **train** to Bodø (11hr., 2 per day, 940kr). From there, catch a **ferry,** departing from behind the train station, to Moskenes (3-4hr., 4-7 per day, 150kr) or take the Hurtigruten to Svolvær (6hr., 3pm, 398kr) via Stamsund (4hr.; 9:30pm; 331kr, students 167kr). **Flights** go from Bodø to **Leknes Airport,** Lufthavnveien 30 (**LKN;** ☎05 55 80), on Vestvågøy (45min., 5-6 per day, 783kr). Check www.wideroe.no for more info and discounts. Bodø's **tourist office** is down Sjogt. from the train station. (☎75 54 80 00; www.visitbodo.com. Open June-Aug. M-F 9am-8pm, Sa 10am-6pm, Su noon-8pm; Sept.-May M-F 9am-4pm, Sa 10am-2pm.) Within the islands, **local buses** (☎11 11 11; www.nordtrafikk.no) are the main form of transport; pick up schedules at tourist offices. Renting a **car** is the easiest way to see the island chain and visit locales off E10, the main highway. Agencies at Leknes Airport include: **Avis** (☎08 01 04) and **Hertz** (☎08 18 44). **Berres Bil & Båt** (☎09 32 40) is in Ramberg, southwest of Leknes on Flakstadøya. Some visitors hitchhike by boat or car. Let's Go does not recommend hitchhiking.

■**MOSKENESØYA.** At the southern tip of the scenic E10 highway, the quiet island of Moskenesøya (pop. 1200) accommodates 19th-century fishing communities and eco-adventure tourism. Frequent ferries from Bodø make **Moskenes,** a small collection of fishing lodges in southern Moskenesøya, a crossroads for tourists. **Moskenes Harbour Tourist Office,** in the red building at the ferry landing, helps with local tour reservations. (☎76 09 15 99; www.lofoten-info.no. and www.lofoten.info. Internet 15kr per 15min. Open late June-early Aug. daily 10am-7pm; early May-late June and late Aug. M-F 10am-5pm.) Getting a spot on the area's adventure **boat tours** (☎90 77 07 41; 400-900kr), **guided hikes** (☎08 13 61 or 09 34 20; 250kr), or

fishing trips with locals (☎91 34 55 99; 400-500kr) requires booking at least a few days ahead. A thrilling ⬛**boat safari** (6hr.; 800kr) is well worth the expense. The trip takes 12 passengers through the **Maelstrom**, one of the world's most dangerous ocean currents, past the fishing hamlet of **Hell** (the one place where Hell can actually freeze over), and hiking into the ancient **Refsvikhula caves** to view 3000-year-old drawings. The trip ends with a fireside dinner of fish burgers, smoked salmon, and sausage. (☎90 77 07 41; visit www.lofoten-info.no.) Challenging, mountainous **hikes** are the primary attraction in the region, although trails are often sparsely marked; make sure you have the proper gear and pick up a map (105kr) at the tourist office. A 3hr. trek heads to the **DNT**'s (Norwegian Mountain Touring Association) **Munkebu cabin**, a good place to spend the night. DNT membership (p. 734) and a 300kr deposit are required for key rental. Nonmembers may accompany members. (200kr per night, under 25 100kr. Members 100/50kr.) Keys are available at the Sørvågen Handel (☎09 12 15) and KIN Trykk, Ramberg (☎09 34 20).

South of Moskenes, the fishing village of **Å** ("OH") takes great pride in being first alphabetically among world cities. Experienced hikers can tackle the 8hr. **Stokkvikka hike.** Head down the southern bank of Lake Ågvatnet and up 400m to cross the Stokkvikskaret Pass; bring a map. To relax on the region's sandy **beaches,** take the bus from Moskenesøya to **Reine** and catch a ferry (100kr) to **Vinstad.** An easy, well-marked trail follows the fjord to the water. The trip takes about 5hr. The **Norsk Fiskeværsmuseum** has displays on the island's maritime mainstay—cod fishing—in six village buildings. If something smells fishy, it's probably a spoonful of homemade cod-liver oil that the locals may offer. For a more conventional snack, try fresh cinnamon rolls (10kr) from the 160-year-old bakery. (☎09 14 88. Open mid-June to mid-Aug. daily 10:30am-5:30pm; mid-Aug. to mid-June M-F 11am-3:30pm. 50kr, students 25kr. MC/V.) Visitors can rent rooms in the private fishing lodges by the dock. **Å Hamna Rorbuer As ❶** has small *rorbuer* cabins for groups of four or more. (☎09 12 11. Reception June-Sept. 10am-10pm; call ahead at other times. Cabins 450-1000kr. AmEx/D/MC/V.) **Å Lofoten Vandrerhjem (HI) ❷** provides simple, homey accommodations in an attic above the Fiskeværsmuseum bakery. Cabins are also available. (☎09 11 21; www.lofoten-rorbu.com. Rowboat rental 150kr. Linens 60kr. Laundry 60kr. Reception daily 9am-10:30pm. Dorms 180kr; doubles 360kr. 30kr HI discount. MC/V.) **Å Dagligvarer A/S** sells groceries. (☎09 24 66. Open M-F 9am-7pm, Sa 9am-5pm, Su 4-7pm. Cash only.) **Buses** depart from behind the tourist office for Moskenes center (15min., 2-4 per day, 26kr).

🔲**VESTVÅGØY.** Northeast of Moskenesøya, the island of Vestvågøy (pop. 11,000) is home to some of the chain's most striking scenery. Flights from Bodø and most buses arrive in **Leknes,** a town with less charm than Vestvågøy's coastal villages. Local favorite **Surprise Cafe ❶**, Idrettgaten 27, a mix of American and Scandinavian cuisine, serves beer (50kr) and the mainstay hot sandwich (37kr) stuffed with ham, cheese, and toppings. (☎08 15 10. Open June-Aug. M-W 10am-6pm, Th-F 10am-10pm, Sa 11am-4pm, Su 1-6pm; Sept.-May reduced hours. Cash only.) The sparsely populated town of **Stamsund** is a port for the Hurtigruten steamer. **Stein Tinden** (500m) and **Justad Tinden** (732m), nearby peaks, are both 6hr. round-trip hikes and provide panoramic views. In June and early July, visitors can tan into the wee hours under the **midnight sun,** while clear nights in late autumn or early spring may reveal the **Northern Lights.** The comfy common rooms at ⬛**Stamsund Vandrerhjem (HI) ❶** have kindled enough friendships between travelers to earn the hostel a national reputation. (☎08 93 34. Wheelchair-accessible. Fishing gear 100kr deposit. Free use of rowboats. Bike rental 100kr per day. Showers 5kr per 5min. Laundry 30kr. Open mid-Dec. to mid-Oct. Dorms 120kr; doubles 400kr; triples 500kr; cabins 400-700kr. 25kr HI discount. Cash only.) Given the sporadic bus schedules, a rental **car** may be the way to go. Rent a used car for cheap from a local or an agency at **Stamsund Hotel,** Postboks 89 (☎08 93 00; 300-800kr per day).

SVALBARD ARCHIPELAGO ☎ 79

Only 1000km south of the North Pole, the Svalbard Archipelago is home to a breathtaking Arctic desert. The research and mining community of Longyearbyen (pop. 1800), the world's northernmost town, lies on the island of Spitsbergen, the center of the archipelago. Although temperatures may be bone-chilling and polar bears outnumber humans, many visitors still arrive each year to see the vast, fragile Arctic wilderness and mingle with the locals.

> **!** Svalbard is dangerous. We mean it. If you don't know what you're doing, do not venture beyond Longyearbyen without a well-trained guide. In recent years, several tourists have been killed by polar bears and glacier accidents.

TRANSPORTATION AND PRACTICAL INFORMATION. Planes arrive at **Svalbard Airport** (**LYR**; ☎02 38 00), outside Longyearbyen, from Oslo (3hr., 1-3 per day in summer, from 1465kr) and Tromsø (1½hr., 1-3 per day in summer, from 1310kr). The **Flybus** (40kr) will take you from the airport directly to your hotel or hostel. In early 2008, **Norwegian** (☎21 49 00 15; www.norwegian.no) will join **SAS Braathens** (www.sasbraathens.no) as the only airlines flying to Longyearbyen. Expect prices as low as 1000kr round-trip. Tourist season peaks in late spring (Apr.-May), when the midnight sun starts to appear and winter activities are still possible. The last week of July and first week of August are when temperatures climb to a scorching 6°C (43°F). During the remaining months—the dark season—minimal sunlight and ice-cold temperatures keep most tourists away. Regardless of the time of year, bring cold-weather gear to guard against the temperamental weather. The **tourist office,** in the UNIS building complex shared with the museum (see below), is 500m north of Longyearbyen center. It's the first stop for navigating address-less Longyearbyen and the rest of Svalbard. (☎02 55 50; www.svalbard.net. Open M-F 8am-6pm, Sa 9am-4pm, Su noon-4pm. Town maps free. Hiking maps 75-85kr.) The **library,** at the Lompensenteret in the city center, provides 30min. of free **Internet**; visitors are encouraged to reserve ahead. (☎02 23 70. Open July to mid-Aug. M-Th 10am-5pm, F 10am-4pm.) **Taxis** are an attractive option given the weather conditions, and often offer guided city tours. (Longyearbyen Taxi ☎02 13 75. Svalbard Maxi Taxi 02 13 05.) Renting a **car** (from 300kr per day) is the easiest way to navigate the wilderness along 35km of road around Longyearbyen. Visitors in rental cars do not need to carry a rifle (p. 766), but must remain close to their vehicles in case a polar bear wanders by. Several agencies rent in town, including **Hertz** (☎02 11 88). **Bikes** are also a popular way to navigate the city. Visit **Basecamp Spitsbergen** in the town center for rentals. (☎02 46 00). **Hitchhiking** around Longyearbyen is common. Let's Go does not recommend hitchhiking.

> **COOL JOB.** Svalbard, though technically a part of Norway, is governed by a special treaty that allows many foreigners to **work** without a permit. The **University Center in Svalbard (UNIS)** is an option for students interested in the hard sciences (☎02 33 00; www.unis.no).

ACCOMMODATIONS AND FOOD. Accommodations on Svalbard are limited; book well ahead. Budget lodgings cluster in **Nybyen,** 25min. north of Longyearbyen center. **Gjestehuset 102 ❸,** part of the **Svalbard Wildlife Service** (p. 766), has basic dorms with sinks. (☎02 56 60; info@wildlife.no. Breakfast, linens, and towels included. Dorms 300kr; singles Mar.-Sept. 495kr, Oct.-Feb. 350kr; doubles 550kr.

AmEx/D/MC/V.) The centrally located **Mary-Ann's Polarrigg** ❺ has accommodations and a charming greenhouse cafe serving Norwegian and Thai food for 200-300kr. (☎02 37 42; info@polarriggen.com. Breakfast 95kr. Beer 41kr. Singles Mar.-Sept. 595kr, Oct.-Feb. 495kr; doubles 825/775kr. AmEx/D/MC/V.) Since camping on public land is strictly prohibited, try **Longyearbyen Campground** ❶, 4.5km out of town next to the airport. Late arrivals can pay the next morning. (☎02 14 44; info@longyearbyen-camping.no. Open late June-early Sept. Reception 8-10am and 8-10pm. Tent sites 90kr. Tent rental 120kr per night. Mattress rental 20kr per night. Shower 10kr per 6min. Cash only. Free winter camping when shower and kitchen facilities are down.) Food is expensive in Svalbard, but other goods (including alcohol) are often cheaper due to the archipelago's tax-free status. **Kroa** ❷, in Basecamp Spitsbergen, serves hearty fare at long tables with seal-skin seats. In the evenings, it's a popular bar where patrons enjoy drinks beneath the gaze of a huge bust of Lenin. (☎02 13 00. Beer 38kr. Open daily 11:30am-2am. AmEx/D/MC/V.) **Svalbard Butikken** stocks groceries and duty-free goods. (☎02 25 20; www.svalbardbutikken.no. Open M-F 10am-8pm, Sa 10am-6pm. AmEx/D/MC/V.)

🔊 📷 **SIGHTS AND NIGHTLIFE.** Stop by the newly expanded **Svalbard Museum** at the University Center in Svalbard (UNIS) to learn about the flora and fauna of the islands along with a history of their settlements. (☎02 13 84; www.svalbardmuseum.no. Open M-F 8am-6pm, Sa 9am-4pm, Su noon-4pm. 50kr, students 30kr. AmEx/MC/V.) **Galleri Svalbard**, near Nybyen, displays wilderness paintings, maps of the Arctic from as late as 1570 (before Svalbard was even discovered in 1596), and Svalbard's official currency, used until the Norwegian krona took hold in 1979. (☎02 23 40; galleri.svalbard@ssd.no. Open daily 11am-5pm. 50kr, students 35kr.) Since 20-somethings arrive in Svalbard from around the world to study by day and party by night, Longyearbyen's social scene is surprisingly happening, especially from April to May. The **Karls-Bergers Pub** stocks 1020 liquors (a blessing during rough winters) and is a great place to hear miners' drunken coal stories. (☎02 25 11; www.karlsbergerpub.com. Beer 35kr. Mixed drinks 48kr. Open M-F 5pm-2am, Sa-Su 3pm-2am. MC/V.) The fancier **Barents Pub,** in the lobby of the Radisson, is popular among younger crowds, drawing tourists and locals with its cheap beer. (☎02 34 66. Beer 41kr. Open daily 4pm-2am. AmEx/D/MC/V.) The legendary **Huset** nightclub has been the stomping grounds for generations of miners, naturalists, and geology students since the 1950s.

IN RECENT NEWS

PEAR-MAGEDDON

We're a pessimistic bunch. Humans have envisioned many ways in which our species could be wiped out. Perhaps it will be a meteorite impact, or a worldwide nuclear war. Maybe super-intelligent machines will take over and enslave us. Whatever happens, let's just hope there's an underground shelter somewhere we can hide in to ride things out, playing endless games of Monopoly and subsisting on canned soup until things on the surface improve.

Protection like this may not exist, but we can at least take solace knowing that there's a cave for the seeds. In 2008, construction is expected to finish on the **Svalbard Global Seed Vault,** a subterranean shelter built into a mountainside near Longyearbyen. The vault will hold seeds for our most important crops, protecting them in the event of catastrophe so they can be reintroduced in the post-apocalyptic world. Remote Svalbard is an ideal location for the project. The thick rock above the vault and the bitter cold permafrost will keep the seeds frozen, preserving them indefinitely. There is the concern of how people will get to Svalbard (a.k.a. the middle of nowhere) after the world ends, but that's a problem for another day.

Who knows what will happen to the world and humanity. Whatever lies ahead, at least there will be apples and bananas waiting for us somewhere off the coast of mainland Norway.

Today, it is still the premier nightlife destination for UNIS students when they aren't hosting underground parties in abandoned mines. (☎02 25 00. Beer 39kr. Restaurant open daily 4-11pm. Nightclub open F-Sa 9pm-4am. AmEx/D/MC/V.)

⚠ OUTDOOR ACTIVITIES

No activity in Svalbard is totally safe. The glacial cover and roaming polar bears make any trip outside Longyearbyen potentially hazardous. Visit the Governor's Office website for **safety information** (www.sysselmannen.svalbard.no). Even experienced hikers often travel with guides. Those who venture beyond Longyearbyen without a guide must first register with the Governor. Registration requires proof of outdoor experience and insurance to cover potential rescue operations. Never leave Longyearbyen alone; always travel with at least one companion.

GUIDED TOURS. For most travelers, tours are the safest, most practical option; unfortunately, they are also expensive. Winter activities include ice caving, skiing, and snowmobiling. In summer, visitors can take boat trips, cross glaciers, hunt for fossils, and hike. Tours of abandoned mines, dogsledding, and visits to the Wilderness Center are possible year-round. For a listing of tours, visit www.svalbard.net. Book online or at accommodations. A boat trip to the ghost-like abandoned mining town of ■**Pyramiden,** surrounded by pristine blue glaciers, or the Russian mining settlement of **Barentsburg** should be in every itinerary. Book ahead—tours are not daily. The energetic guides at **Svalbard Wildlife Service,** in Longyearbyen center, lead trips to both destinations. (☎02 56 60; info@wildlife.no. Office open in summer M-F 8am-6pm, Sa 10am-1pm; winter M-F 10am-4pm. 1100-1200kr; includes hot lunch.) Join the huskies of **Svalbard Villmarksenter** for a 6-7hr. tour of Foxfonna, a region outside Longyearbyen that is a "no-go" zone for snowmobiles. Hikers and skiers arrive year-round to spot Svalbard reindeer. (☎02 19 85; www.svalbard-adventure.com. Foxfonna hike 550kr; includes lunch.) **Spitsbergen Travel,** Svalbard's biggest tour provider, organizes trips up the **Trollsteinen** mountain, visible to the northwest from the town center, crossing a glacier on the way. (☎02 61 00; www.spitsbergentravel.no. 550kr; includes sandwiches and hot drinks.) For safe **polar bear** spotting, book a multi-day boat tour with Spitsbergen Travel or Svalbard Wildlife Service. If you have money to burn, a cool 25,000kr will whisk you by helicopter to the North Pole.

INDEPENDENT TRAVEL. Only experienced hikers should venture into the Svalbardean wilderness without a guide. Quick-flaring foul weather makes even brief hikes from Longyearbyen surprisingly challenging; roaming polar bears ensure that overnight trips include emergency beacons, trip-wires, and a rifle. If you do not know how to use a rifle, you cannot travel on your own. Those experienced with rifles can rent equipment at several stores throughout the city center, including **Sportscenteret** in the Lompensenteret Mall. (☎02 15 35; sports.centeret@longyearbyen.net. Rifle rental 100kr per day. 1000kr cash only deposit for rifle plus 200kr for ammunition. AmEx/D/MC/V.) Permits are not required by law in Svalbard, but some stores may ask for one. Travelers should spend several days in Longyearbyen to plan routes and arrive having already created a hiking group. Relatively few visitors come alone; most groups have planned their trips well ahead. A popular route is the three-day hike from Longyearbyen to Barentsburg. Several companies (see above) run boat trips between the two destinations; arrange to travel at least part of the way with them.

POLAND (POLSKA)

Poland is a sprawling country in which history casts a long shadow. Plains that stretch from the Tatras Mountains in the south to the Baltic Sea in the north have seen foreign invaders time and time again. Meanwhile, the contrast between Western cities like Wrocław and Eastern outposts like Białystok is a remnant of Poland's subjection to competing empires. Ravaged during WWII and later viciously suppressed by the USSR, Poland is finally self-governed, and the change is marked. And although prices are rising now that Poland has joined the EU, all of it still comes cheap by Western standards.

 DISCOVER POLAND: SUGGESTED ITINERARIES

THREE DAYS. In **Kraków** (p. 780), enjoy the stunning **Wawel Castle,** medieval **Stare Miasto,** and the bohemian nightlife of **the Kazimierz area.** Take a daytrip to **Auschwitz-Birkenau** concentration camp (p. 786).

ONE WEEK. After three days in **Kraków,** go to **Warsaw** (2 days; p. 772), where the **Uprising Museum** and **Russian Market** shouldn't be missed; then head north to **Gdańsk** (2 days; p. 793) and soak up the sun on the beach of **Sopot.**

BEST OF POLAND, THREE WEEKS. Begin with five days in **Kraków,** including a daytrip to **Auschwitz-Birkenau** or the **Wieliczka** salt mines. Spend two days in lovely **Wrocław** (p. 789), then enjoy the mountain air of **Zakopane** (1 day; p. 788). After a night at the edgy bars and clubs of **Poznań** (p. 790), head east to dynamic **Warsaw** (6 days), then take a break in scenic **Toruń** (2 days; p. 791). In **Gdańsk** (4 days), don't miss the resort town of **Sopot** or **Malbork Castle.**

ESSENTIALS

FACTS AND FIGURES

Official Name: Republic of Poland.
Capital: Warsaw.
Major Cities: Katowice, Kraków, Łódź.
Population: 38,518,000.

Time Zone: GMT +1.
Language: Polish.
Annual Pork Consumption Per Capita: 83.2 lbs.

WHEN TO GO

Poland has snowy winters and warm summers, though summer weather can be unpredictable and rain is frequent in July. Tourist season runs from late May to early September, except in mountain areas, which also have a winter high season (Dec.-Mar.). Though rain is a risk in the late spring and early autumn, these months are mild, so travelers may want to consider visiting in late April, September, or early October. Many attractions are closed from mid-autumn to mid-spring.

DOCUMENTS AND FORMALITIES

EMBASSIES AND CONSULATES. Foreign embassies to Poland are in Warsaw and Kraków. For Polish embassies and consulates abroad, contact: **Australia,** 7 Turrana St., Yarralumla, Canberra, ACT 2600 (☎02 62 73 12 08; www.poland.org.au); **Canada,** 443 Daly Ave., Ottawa, ON K1N 6H3 (☎613-789-

0468; www.polishembassy.ca); **Ireland,** 5 Ailesbury Rd., Ballbridge, Dublin 4 (☎01 283 0855; www.polishheritage.co.nz); **New Zealand,** 51 Granger Rd., Howick, Auckland 1705 (☎09 534 4670); **UK,** 47 Portland Pl., London, W1B 1JH (☎020 75 80 43 24; www.polishembassy.org.uk); **US,** 2040 10th St., NW, Washington, D.C. 20009 (☎202-234-3800; www.polandembassy.org).

VISA AND ENTRY INFORMATION. Citizens of Australia, Canada, and the US need a visa for stays of over 90 days. EU citizens do not require a visa but will need to apply for temporary residence after 90 days. Visas for US citizens are free. Processing may take up to two weeks, but express visas can be processed within 24hr. You must be ready to present ample documentation concerning your stay, including verification of accommodation reservations, sufficient funds for the duration of your stay, and confirmation of health insurance coverage.

ENTRANCE REQUIREMENTS.

Passport: Required for all travelers.

Visa: Not required for stays of under 90 days for citizens of Australia, Canada, New Zealand, and the US; not required for stays of under 180 days for citizens of the UK.

Letter of Invitation: Not required for most travelers.

Inoculations: Recommended up-to-date on DTaP (diphtheria, tetanus, and pertussis), Hepatitis A, Hepatitis B, MMR, rabies, polio booster, and typhoid.

Work Permit: Required for all non-EU citizens planning to work in Poland.

International Driving Permit: Required for all non-EU citizens planning to drive.

TOURIST SERVICES AND MONEY

EMERGENCY	**Ambulance:** ☎999. **Fire:** ☎150. **Police:** ☎158. **Cell Phone Emergency Number** ☎112.

TOURIST OFFICES. City-specific tourist offices are the most helpful. Almost all provide free info in English. Most have reliable free maps and sell more detailed ones. Orbis, the state-sponsored travel bureau, operates hotels in most cities and sells transportation tickets. Almatur, a student travel organization with offices in 15 major cities, offers ISICs. The state-sponsored PTTK and IT bureaus, in nearly every city, are helpful for basic traveling needs. Try Polish Pages, a free guide available at hotels and tourist agencies

MONEY. The Polish currency is the **złotych** (zł), plural is złoty (zwah-tee). Inflation is around 2%, so prices should be reasonably stable. **ATMs** *(bankomaty)* are common, and generally offer the best rates; MasterCard and Visa are widely accepted at ATMs. Budget accommodations rarely accept credit cards, but some restaurants and upscale hotels do. Normal business hours in Poland are 8am-4pm. **Tipping** varies, but is generally a few additional złoty.

POLISH ZŁOTYCH (ZŁ)		
AUS$1 = 2.29zł		1zł = AUS$0.44
CDN$1 = 2.77zł		1zł = CDN$0.36
EUR€1 = 3.96zł		1zł = EUR€0.25
NZ$1 = 1.94zł		1zł = NZ$0.52
UK£1 = 5.74zł		1zł = UK£0.17
US$1 = 3.09zł		1zł = US$0.32

Poland

HEALTH AND SAFETY

Medical clinics in major cities have private, **English-speaking doctors.** Expect to pay at least 50zł per visit. **Pharmacies** are well stocked, and some stay open 24hr. Tap water is theoretically drinkable, but bottled mineral water will spare you from some unpleasant metals and chemicals. **Crime** rates are low, but tourists are sometimes targeted. Watch for muggings and pickpockets, especially on trains and in lower-priced hostels. Cab drivers may attempt to cheat those who do not speak Polish, and "friendly locals" looking to assist tourists are sometimes merely setting them up for scams. **Women** traveling alone should take usual precautions and avoid dangerous places at night or being open that they are traveling without a companion. Those with darker skin may encounter discrimination due to long-standing prejudice against the **Roma** people (gypsies). There may be lingering prejudice against Jews despite governmental efforts; casual anti-Semitic remarks are heard frequently. Like many Eastern European nations, Poland is not widely **wheelchair-accessible** but special-interest groups, newly armed with EU funds, are working to change that. **Warsaw** in particular, with its multitude of steep, winding steps, is known to be difficult to access. **Homosexuality** is not widely accepted; discretion is advised. GLBT travelers might find www.gay.pl a useful resource.

TRANSPORTATION

BY PLANE. Warsaw's modern **Okęcie Airport (WAW)** is the hub for international flights. **LOT,** the national airline, flies to major cities in Poland.

BY TRAIN AND BUS. It's usually better to take a train than a bus, as buses are slow and uncomfortable. For a timetable, see www.pkp.pl. *Odjazdy* (departures) are in yellow, *przyjazdy* (arrivals) in white. *InterCity* and *ekspresowy* (express) trains are listed in red with an "IC" or "Ex" in front of the train number. *Pośpieszny* (direct; in red) are almost as fast and a bit cheaper. Low-priced *osobowy* (in black) are the slowest and have no restrooms. If you see a boxed "R" on the schedule, ask the clerk for a *miejscówka* (reservation). Students and seniors buy *ulgowy* (half-price) tickets instead of *normalny* tickets. Beware: foreign travelers are not eligible for discounts on domestic buses and trains. Eurail is not valid in Poland. Look for Wasteels tickets and Eurotrain passes, sold at Almatur and Orbis for discounts. Stations are not announced and are often poorly marked. Theft frequently occurs on overnight trains; avoid night trains, especially Kraków-Warsaw and Prague-Kraków. In the countryside, PKS markers (yellow steering wheels that look like upside-down Mercedes-Benz symbols) indicate stops. Buses have no luggage compartments. **Polski Express,** a private company, offers more luxurious service, but does not run to all cities.

BY CAR, TAXI, AND THUMB. Rental cars are readily available in Warsaw and Kraków. For taxis, either arrange the price before getting in (in Polish, if possible) or be sure the driver turns on the meter. Arrange cabs by phone if possible. Though legal, **hitchhiking** is rare and dangerous for foreigners. Hand-waving is the accepted sign. Let's Go does not recommend hitchhiking.

KEEPING IN TOUCH

PHONE CODES	**Country code:** 48. **International dialing prefix:** 00. For more information on how to place international calls, see **Inside Back Cover.**

EMAIL AND INTERNET. Internet access is readily available in most of Poland, costing from 5-15zł per hr.

TELEPHONE. You can purchase a long distance card at many places, including grocery stores. To operate the phone, start dialing the numbers you're given or insert the magnetic card inside. International access numbers include: **ATT Direct** (☎00 800 111 111); **Australia Direct** (☎00 800 641); **Canada Direct** (☎0 800 111 4118); **MCI** (☎00 800 111 2122); **Sprint** (☎00 800 11 3115).

MAIL. Mail in Poland is admirably efficient. Airmail *(lotnicza)* takes two to five days to Western Europe and seven to 10 days to Australia, New Zealand, and the US. Mail can be received via **Poste Restante.** Address mail as follows: First name, LAST NAME, POSTE RESTANTE, post office address, Postal Code, city, POLAND. Letters cost about 2.20zł. To pick up mail, show a passport.

LANGUAGE. Polish is a West Slavic language written in the Latin alphabet, and is closely related to **Czech** and **Slovak.** The language varies little across the country. The two exceptions are in the region of **Kaszuby,** where the distinctive Germanized dialect is sometimes classified as a separate language, and in **Karpaty,** known for highlander accents. In western Poland and Mazury, **German** is the most common foreign language, although many Poles in big cities, especially young people, speak **English.** One more thing: the English word "no" means "yes" in Polish. For a phrasebook and glossary, see **Appendix: Polish,** p. 1065.

ACCOMMODATIONS AND CAMPING

POLAND	❶	❷	❸	❹	❺
ACCOMMODATIONS	under 45zł	45-65zł	66-80zł	81-120zł	over 120zł

Hostels *(schroniska młodzieżowe)* abound and cost 30-60zł per night. They are often booked solid by tour groups; call at least a week ahead. **PTSM** is the national hostel organization. **University dorms** become budget housing in July and August; these are an especially good option in Kraków. The **Almatur** office in Warsaw arranges stays throughout Poland. **PTTK** runs **hotels** called Dom Turysty, which have multi-bed rooms and budget singles and doubles. These hotels generally cost 80-180zł. **Pensions** are often the best deal: the owner's service more than makes up for the small sacrifice in privacy. **Private rooms** *(wolne pokoje)* are available most places, but be careful what you agree to; they should only cost 20-60zł. **Homestays** can be a great way to meet locals; inquire at the tourist office. **Campsites** average 10-15zł per person or 20zł with a car. Campgrounds may also rent out **bungalows;** a bed costs 20-30zł. *Polska Mapa Campingów,* available at tourist offices, lists campsites. Almatur runs a number of sites in summer; ask them for a list. Camp only in official campsites or risk a night in jail.

FOOD AND DRINK

POLAND	❶	❷	❸	❹	❺
FOOD	under 8zł	8-17zł	18-30zł	31-45zł	over 45zł

Polish cuisine derives from French, Italian, and Slavic traditions. Meals begin with **soup,** usually *barszcz* (beet or rye), *chłodnik* (cold beets with buttermilk and eggs), *ogórkowa* (sour cucumbers), *kapuśniak* (cabbage), or *rosół* (chicken). **Main courses** include *gołąbki* (cabbage rolls with meat and rice), *kotlet schabowy* (pork cutlet), *naleśniki* (crepes), and *pierogi* (dumplings). **Kosher** eating is next to impossible, as most Jewish restaurants are not actually kosher. Poland offers a wealth of **beer, vodka,** and **spiced liquor.** *Żywiec* is the most popular beer. Even those who dislike beer will enjoy sweet ▓**piwo z sokiem,** beer with raspberry syrup. *Wyborowa, Żytnia,* and *Polonez* are popular *wódka* (vodka) brands, while *Belweder* (Belvedere) is a major alcoholic export. *Żubrówka* vodka, also known as "Bison grass vodka," comes packaged with a strand of grass from the Białowieża forest. It's often mixed with apple juice *(z sokem jabłkowym).* *Miód* (beer made with honey) and *krupnik* (mead) are old-fashioned favorites; as is *nalewka na porzeczce* (black currant vodka).

HOLIDAYS AND FESTIVALS

Holidays: Easter Holiday (Mar. 24, 2008); May Day (May 1); Constitution Day (May 3); Pentecost (May 11, 2008); Corpus Christi (May 22, 2008); Assumption Day (Aug. 15); All Saints' Day (Nov. 1); Independence Day (Nov. 11); Christmas (Dec. 25-26).

Festivals: Unsurprisingly, many of the festivals revolve around Catholic holidays. Uniquely Polish festivals include all-night bonfire merrymaking before St. John's Day in June, as well as an annual August folk festival in Kraków.

BEYOND TOURISM

Auschwitz Jewish Center, Auschwitz Jewish Center Foundation, 36 Battery Place, New York, NY 10280, USA (☎212-575-1050; www.ajcf.org). Offers fully paid 6-week programs for college graduates and graduate students in Oswiecim. Focuses on cultural exchange and the study of pre-war Jewish life in Poland, with visits to the Auschwitz-Birkenau State Museum and other sites.

Jagiellonian University, Centre for European Studies, ul. Garbarska 7a, 31-131 Kraków, Poland (☎481 24 29 62 U7; www.coc.uj edu.pl). University founded in 1364 offers undergraduates summer- and semester-long programs in Central European studies and Polish language. Semester tuition US$5000. Scholarships available.

WARSAW (WARSZAWA)   ☎022

Massive rebuilding is nothing new for Warsaw (pop. 1,700,000). At the end of World War II, two-thirds of its population had been killed and 83% of the city was destroyed by the Nazis in revenge for the 1944 Warsaw Uprising. Having weathered the further blow of a half-century of communist rule, Warsaw has now sprung back to life as a dynamic center of business, politics, and culture, as evidenced by the gleaming new glass skyscrapers popping up next to crumbling concrete from the communist era. With Poland's recent accession into the European Union, the city is transforming its culture and landscape at an even faster pace. Now is the time to visit this compelling and grossly underrated city.

▐ TRANSPORTATION

Flights: Port Lotniczy Warszawa-Okęcie ("Terminal 1"), Żwirki i Wigury (info desk ☎650 4100, reservations 0 801 300 952). Take bus #175 to the city center (after 10:40pm, bus #611); buy tickets at the *Ruch* kiosk at the top of the escalator in the arrivals hall. (Open M-F 5:30am-10:30pm.) If you arrive past 10:30pm, it is possible to buy tickets from the bus driver for a 3zł surcharge (students 1.50zł). The **IT** (Informacja Turystyczna) office is at the top of the escalator in the arrivals hall (see **Tourist Offices,** p. 774). Open M-F 8am-8pm.

Trains: Warszawa Centralna, al. Jerozolimskie 54 (☎94 36; www.intercity.pkp.pl), is the most convenient of Warsaw's 3 major train stations. Most trains also stop at **Warszawa Zachodnia (Western Station),** Towarowa 1, and **Warszawa Wschodnia (Eastern Station),** Lubelska 1, in Praga. Yellow signs list departures *(odjazdy);* white signs list arrivals *(przyjazdy).* English is rarely understood; write down when and where you want to go, then ask *"Który peron?"* ("Which platform?"). Prices listed are for IC (intercity) trains and *normale* (2nd class) fares. To: **Gdańsk** (4hr., 20 per day, 47-90zł); **Kraków** (2½-5hr., 30 per day, 47-89zł); **Łódź** (1½-2hr., 11 per day, 31zł); **Lublin** (2½hr., 17 per day, 35zł); **Poznań** (2½-3hr., 20 per day, 46-89zł); **Wrocław** (4½-6hr., 11 per day, 50-96zł); **Berlin, GER** (6hr., 6 per day, €29-45); **Budapest, HUN** (10-13hr., 1 per day, 280zł); **Prague, CZR** (9-12hr., 2 per day, 270-310zł).

Buses: Both Polski Express and PKS buses run out of Warsaw.

Polski Express, al. Jana Pawła II (☎854 0285), in a kiosk next to Warszawa Centralna. Faster than PKS. Kiosk open daily 6:30am-10pm. To: **Gdańsk** (6hr., 2 per day, 60zł); **Kraków** (8hr., 2 per day, 69zł); **Łódź** (2½hr., 7 per day, 25zł); **Lublin** (3hr., 7 per day, 41zł).

PKS Warszawa Zachodnia, al. Jerozolimskie 144 (☎822 4811, domestic info 03 00 30 01 30, from cell phones ☎720 8383; www.pks.warszawa.pl), connected by tunnels to the Warszawa Zachodnia train station. Cross to far side al. Jerozolimskie and take bus #127, 130, 508, or E5 to the center. To: **Gdańsk** (5-7hr., 16 per day, 35-51zł); **Kraków** (5½-7hr., 8 per day, 40zł); **Lublin** (3hr., 9 per day, 22-30zł); **Toruń** (4hr., 10 per day, 32zł); **Wrocław** (6½-8½hr., 3 per day, 43zł); **Kyiv, UKR** (14½hr., 1 per day, 155zł); **Vilnius, LIT** (9½hr., 3 per day, 115zł).

Centrum Podróży AURA, al. Jerozolimskie 144 (☎ 659 4785; www.aura.pl), at the Zachodnia station, left of the entrance. Books international buses to: **Amsterdam, NTH** (23hr., 2 per day, 209-279zł); **Geneva, SWI** (27hr., 2 per day, 269-320zł); **London, GBR** (27hr., 3 per day, 280-450zł); **Paris, FRA** (25hr., 1-3 per day, 220-334zł); **Prague, CZR** (28hr.; 3 per week; 115-145zł); **Rome, ITA** (28hr., 1 per day, 249-418zł).

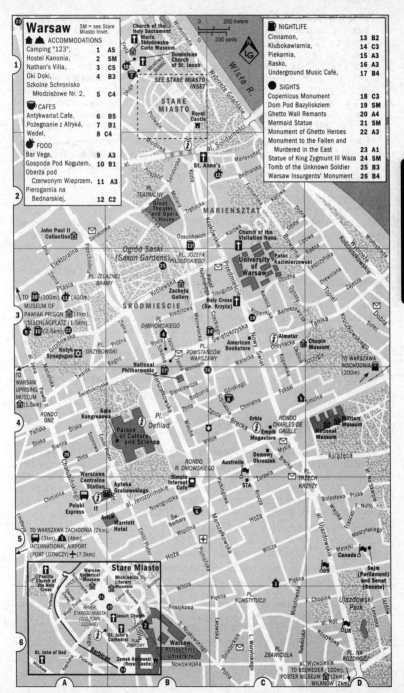

Warsaw

SM = see Stare Miasto Inset

ACCOMMODATIONS

Camping "123",	1	A5
Hostel Kanonia,	2	SM
Nathan's Villa,	3	C5
Oki Doki,	4	B3
Szkolne Schronisko Młodzieżowe Nr. 2,	5	C4

CAFES

Antykwariat Cafe,	6	B5
Pożegnanie z Afryką,	7	B1
Wedel,	8	C4

FOOD

Bar Vega,	9	A3
Gospoda Pod Kogutem,	10	B1
Oberża pod Czerwonym Wieprzem,	11	A3
Pierogarnia na Bednarskiej,	12	C2

NIGHTLIFE

Cinnamon,	13	B2
Klubokawiarnia,	14	C3
Piekarnia,	15	A3
Rasko,	16	A3
Underground Music Cafe,	17	B4

SIGHTS

Copernicus Monument	18	C3
Dom Pod Bazyliszkiem	19	SM
Ghetto Wall Remants	20	A4
Mermaid Statue	21	SM
Monument of Ghetto Heroes	22	A3
Monument to the Fallen and Murdered in the East	23	A1
Statue of King Zygmunt III Waza	24	SM
Tomb of the Unknown Soldier	25	SM
Warsaw Insurgents' Monument	26	B4

Public Transportation: (info line ☎94 84; www.ztm.waw.pl). Warsaw's public transit is excellent. Daytime **trams** and **buses** 2.40zł, with ISIC 1.25zł; day pass 7.20/3.70zł; weekly pass 26/12zł. Punch the ticket in the yellow machines on board or face a 120zł fine. If you find that you're the only one validating your ticket, remember that many locals carry 90-day passes. Bus, tram, and subway lines share the same tickets, passes, and prices. There are also 2 **sightseeing bus routes:** #180 (M-F) and #100 (Sa-Su). Purchase an all-day ticket and you can hop on and off the bus. Night buses cost double, have "N" prefixes, and run 11:30pm-5:30am. If you need to use one, ask at a tourist bureau or accommodation to explain the system for ordering them; without an order, they won't stop. Warsaw's **Metro** is not particularly convenient for tourists.

Taxis: The government sets cab fare at 2zł per km; with privately run cabs, stated prices may be lower but the risk of overcharging is greater. State-run: **ME.RC. Taxi** (☎677 7777), **Wawa Taxi** (☎96 44). Privately run: **Euro Taxi** (☎96 62), **Halo Taxi** (☎96 23).

✦ ORIENTATION

The most prominent section of Warsaw lies west of the **Wisła River.** The city's grid layout and efficient public transportation make it very accessible. **Aleje Jerozolimskie** is the main east-west thoroughfare. **Warszawa Centralna,** the main train station, is at the intersection of al. Jerozolimskie and **aleje Jana Pawła II,** the north-south street one block west of Marsza kowska. The northern boundary of pl. Defilad is **Świętokrzyska,** another east-west thoroughfare. Intersecting al. Jerozolimskie one city block east of Marsza kowska and the city center, the **Trakt Królewski** (Royal Way) takes different names as it runs north-south. Going north it first becomes **Nowy Świat** and then **Krakowskie Przedmieście** as it leads into **Stare Miasto** (Old Town; just north of al. Solidarności overlooking the Wisła). Going south, the road becomes **aleje Ujazdowskie** as it runs past embassy row, palaces, and **Łazienki Park,** all to the south the city center. **Praga,** the part of the city on the east bank of the Wisła, is accessible by tram via **aleje Jerozolimskie** and **aleje Solidarności.** In Praga, and the two most trafficked north-south thoroughfares are **Targowa,** near the zoo, and **Francuska,** south of al. Jerozolimskie.

🛈 PRACTICAL INFORMATION

Tourist Offices: Informacji Turystyczna (IT), al. Jerozolimskie 54 (☎94 31; www.warsawtour.pl), inside Centralna train station. Provides **maps** and arranges accommodations (no fee). Their free booklets list popular restaurants and special events. Open daily May-Sept. 8am-8pm; Oct.-Apr. 8am-6pm. **Branches:** Krakowskie Przedmieście 39. Open daily, same hours. In the airport, open daily, same hours. Pl. Zamkowy 1/13 (outside the Stare Miasto. Open M-F 9am-6pm, Sa 10am-6pm, Su 11am-6pm.

Budget Travel: Almatur, Kopernika 23 (☎826 3512). ISIC 69zł. Open M-F 9am-7pm, Sa 10am-3pm. AmEx/MC/V. **Orbis,** Bracka 16 (☎827 3857), entrance on al. Jerozolimskie. Open M-F 8am-6pm, Sa 9am-3pm. MC/V.

Embassies: Most are near al. Ujazdowskie. **Australia,** Nowogrodzka 11 (☎521 3444; fax 627 3500; ambasada@australia.pl). Open M-F 9am-1pm and 2-5pm. **Canada,** al. Matejki 1/5 (☎584 3100, fax 584 3192; wsaw@international.gc.ca). Open M-F 8:30am-4:30pm. Open M-F 8:30am-4:30pm. **Ireland,** Mysia 5 (☎849 6633, fax 849 8431; ambasada@irlandial.pl). Open M-F 9am-1pm. **UK,** al. Róż (☎311 0000). Open M-F 8:30am-4:30pm. **US,** ul. Piękna 12 (☎625 1401 or 504 2784, fax 504 2122). Open M, W, F 9am-noon, Tu, Th 9am-3pm.

Currency Exchange: Except at tourist sights, *kantory* (exchange booths) have the best rates for exchanging currency and traveler's checks. 24hr. at Warszawa Centralna or at al. Jerozolimskie 61. Many 24hr. *kantory* offer worse rates at night.

Luggage Storage (Kasa Bagażowa): At Warszawa Centralna train station. 5zł per item per day, plus 2.25zł per 50zł of declared value if you want insurance. To sidestep the language barrier and retain more control over your bag, choose a locker. Open 24hr.

GLBT Resources: Lambda, (☎628 5222; www.lambda.org.pl), in English and Polish. Open Tu-W 6-9pm, F 4-10pm. Info at the English-language site warsaw.gayguide.net. The GLBT scene in Warsaw is discrete and lacks widespread political support.

24hr. Pharmacy: Apteka Grabowskiego "21" (☎825 6986), upstairs at Warszawa Centralna train station. AmEx/MC/V.

Medical Services: Centrum Medyczyne LIM, al. Jerozolimskie 65/79, 9th fl. (24hr. **emergency line** ☎458 7000, 24hr. **ambulance** 430 3030; www.cm-lim.com.pl), at the Marriott. English-speaking doctors. Open M-F 7am-9pm, Sa 8am-4pm, Su 9am-6pm, Holidays 9am-1pm. **Branch** at Domaniewski 41 (☎458 7000). Open M-F 7am-9pm, Sa 8am-8pm. **Central Emergency Station,** Hoża 56 (☎999) has a 24hr. ambulance.

Telephones: Directory assistance ☎118 913.

Internet Access: Simple Internet Cafe, Marszałkowska 99/101 (☎628 3190), at the corner of al. Jerozolimskie, has English-speaking staff and good hourly rates. The largest and orangest Internet cafe in Warsaw. Open 24hr. Rates vary from 1zł per hr. late-night to 4zł per hr. midday. 24hr. Internet cafes line the bowels of Centralna train station.

Post Office: Main branch, Świętokrzyska 31/33 (☎827 00 52). Take a number at the entrance. For stamps and letters push "D"; packages "F." For **Poste Restante,** inquire at window #42. Open 24hr. *Kantor* open daily 7am-10pm. Most other branches open 8am-8pm. **Postal Code:** 00001.

ACCOMMODATIONS

Although accommodation options are rapidly improving, demand still outpaces supply, so reserve ahead, especially in summer. **Informacji Turystyczna** (IT; p. 774) maintains a list of accommodations in the city, including **private rooms,** and also arranges stays in **university dorms** (25-30zł) July through September.

Oki Doki, pl. Dąbrowskiego 3 (☎826 5112; www.okidoki.pl). From pl. Defilad, head 1 block east on Świętokrzyska and take a left; the sign will point you to the hostel. Each room of this chic hostel was designed by a different Warsaw artist and has a unique theme, be it geographical ("Santorini") or artistic ("House of Photography"). Beer (5zł) and breakfast (10zł) in the dining room/bar (open until 1am or later). Bike rental 30zł per day, 6zł per hr. Laundry 10zł. Free Internet. 24hr. reception. Check-in 3pm. Check-out 11am. Reserve ahead. May-Aug. dorms 45-60zł; singles 110zł; doubles 135zł, with baths 185zł. Sept.-Apr. prices tend to increase by around 5zł. MC/V. ❷

Nathan's Villa, Piękna 24/26 (☎05 09 35 84 87; www.nathansvilla.com). From pl. Defilad, take any tram south on Marszałkowska to pl. Konstytucji. Go left on Piękna; the hostel is on the left. Nathan's matches a convenient location with unparalleled facilities and services. Though guests have been known to pass out on the lawn of this relentlessly hard-partying hostel, the rooms gleam with bright colors and brand-new furniture. Young staff will be happy to point you to clubs and cheap places to eat (many of which offer discounts for Nathan's customers). Breakfast included. Free laundry. Free Internet. Reception 24hr. Dorms 45-60zł; private rooms 120-140zł. MC/V. ❷

Szkolne Schronisko Młodzieżowe nr. 2, Smolna 30 (☎827 8952), 2 blocks up Smolna from Nowy Świat. From Centralna Station, take any tram east on al. Jerozolimskie and get off at Rondo Charles de Gaulle. The well-kept rooms of this sunny hostel exude

MILK IT FOR ALL IT'S WORTH

During the Soviet era, locals flocked to Warsaw's subsidized cafeteria-style milk bars out of pure necessity, and they remain the cheapest meal in town. Named because of their dairy-heavy offerings, these establishments still receive large subsidies, making it cheaper to buy homestyle cooking here than to cook for yourself. Patrons range from the homeless or elderly to students and young professionals looking for a quick, cheap meal. There are between 10 and 20 milk bars in Warsaw, and the number will continue to fall along with subsidy-levels.

Milk bars can be a challenge to those who don't speak Polish. First, choose your meal from the big board: some form of kotlet, or meat cutlet, is a safe bet, with zemniaki (potatoes) and perhaps a surówka (salad). Then tell the cashier what you want, pay, and get a receipt. Give the receipt to the cooks at the next window and they'll get you what you want.

Bar Uniwersytet, Krakowskie Przedmiescie 20/22, has an authentic camp-like interior, long lines, and extremely traditional dishes. Bar Mleczny Familijny, ul. Nowy Swiat 39, allows you to enjoy beautiful Nowy Swiat for cheap. Bar Kubus, Ordynacka 13, serves great soups and has a friendly staff. Zlota Kurka, Marszalkowska 55/73, is a student favorite at Polytechnic.

respectability, and the central location can't be beat. The several flights of stairs can be a bit daunting and the curfew and lockout are not conducive to partying, but the atmosphere is safe and friendly. Large kitchen. A/C. Free lockers and linen. Reception 24hr., but front doors locked midnight-6am. Lockout 10am-4pm. Curfew midnight. Dorms 36zł; singles 65zł. Cash only. ❶

Hostel Kanonia, ul. Jezuicka 2 (☎635 0676; www.kanonia.pl). Tucked into an alley right in the thick of Stare Miasto, this hostel's cheery yellow paint and gleaming wood trim soften the no-frills, spartan rooms. Kitchen available. Breakfast 10zł. Free Internet. Check-in noon. Check-out 10am. Dorms 45-60zł; doubles 150zł. ISIC discount. ❷

Camping "123," Bitwy Warszawskiej 15/17 (☎822 9121). From Warszawa Centralna, take bus #127, 130, 508, or 517 to Zachodnia bus station. Cross to the far side of al. Jerozolimskie and take the pedestrian path west to Bitwy Warszawskiej; turn left. The campground is on the right. This tranquil campground is close to the center and provides reliable service but few amenities. Guarded 24hr. Open May-Sept. 12zł per person, 14zł per tent, 55-65zł for campsites with electricity (labeled "stream," a literal translation of the Polish word for electricity). Singles 40zł; doubles 70zł; triples 100zł; quads 120zł. AmEx/MC/V. ❶

▸ FOOD

At roadside stands, the food of choice is the *kebab turecki,* a pita with spicy meat, cabbage, and pickles (5-10zł). The stand **Kebab Bar,** ul. Nowy Świat 31, serves up an excellent version. **MarcPol,** on ul. Marszałkowska, is a 24hr. grocery store.

RESTAURANTS

▨ **Gospoda Pod Kogutem,** Freta 48 (☎635 8282; www.gospodapodkogutem.pl). A rare find in touristy Stare Miasto: generous portions of delectable local food. Enjoy the barn-themed interior or sit outside on Freta. The place to try something shamelessly traditional, like Polish-style *golonka* (pig's knuckle; 21zł) or *smalec,* surprisingly tasty fried bits of lard. Entrees 15-40zł. Open M noon-midnight, Tu-Su 11am-midnight. MC/V. ❷

Oberża pod Czerwonym Wieprzem, Żelazna 68 (☎850 3144; www.czerwonywieprz.pl). Waitresses in bright red ties welcome you to this beautifully capitalist exploitation of Poland's communist past, with a gigantic mural of Lenin along one wall and Soviet flags all around. Each part of the menu is split into sections "for the proletariat" (with cheaper items) and "for dignitaries and the bourgeoisie" (with more expensive ones). Other touches include dishes such as Mao's Chicken (24zł) and Fidel's

Cigar (rolls of ground meat in "Cuban" sauce; 23zł). Entrees 13-22zł for the proletariat, 26-44zł for dignitaries and the bourgeoisie. M-Su 11am-midnight. MC/V. ❸

Pierogarnia na Bednarskiej, ul. Bednarka 28/30 (☎828 0392), on a side street west of ul. Krakówscie Przedmiescie. Locals get their pierogi fix at this tiny, pleasant, and deliciously fragrant shop; you don't even have to wait—they keep new pierogi boiling constantly. 3 pierogi 6zł. Open daily 11am-9pm. Cash only. ❶

Bar Vega, al. Jana Pawła II 36c (☎652 2754), near the former Ghetto. Secluded from the bustle of al. Jana Pawła II street vendors, Bar Vega serves a full vegetarian Indian meal for about the price of a coffee on Nowy Świat (small or big plate; 8 or 12zł, respectively). The inexplicably cheap cafeteria-style offerings allow you to sample a variety of *pakoras* and *koftas.* Bar Vega funds a nonprofit to feed Warsaw's homeless children. Open daily noon-8pm. Cash only. ❶

CAFES

▨ **Pożegnanie z Afryką (Out of Africa),** Freta 4/6. This Polish chain of cafes brews consistently incredible coffee (8-15zł). Worth the wait for 1 of 4 tables in the candlelit interior. In warm weather, enjoy the Stare Miasto sidewalk seating and the iced coffee (8zł). Branches throughout the city. Open daily 11am-9pm. Cash only.

▨ **Antykwariat Cafe,** Żurawia 45 (☎629 9929). Antykwariat ("Antiquarian") recalls an inviting old personal library with sloppily shelved books, an antique piano, and engravings of pre-war Warsaw. Delicate cups of coffee (5-17zł) and many varieties of tea (5zł) served with a wrapped chocolate. Also serves beer, wine, and desserts. Plush wicker chairs and outdoor seating. Open M-F 11am-11pm, Sa-Su 1-11pm. Cash only.

Wedel, Szpitalna 17 (☎827 2916). The Emil Wedel house, built in 1893 for the Polish chocolate tycoon, was one of the few buildings in Warsaw to survive WWII. Its 1st fl. now houses an elegant dessert cafe. The glass chandeliers and dark marble columns of this chocolate-themed cafe offer a rare glimpse of pre-war Warsaw. Enjoy the suspicion that you've traveled back in time, along with miraculously good hot chocolate (8zł). The adjacent **Wedel Chocolate** company store has a whimsical diorama of elves making chocolate. Open M-Sa 10am-10pm, Su noon-5pm. AmEx/MC/V.

ⓖ SIGHTS

The tourist bus routes #100 and 180 are convenient; they begin at pl. Zamkowy and run along pl. Teatralny, Marszałkowska, al. Ujazdowskie, Łazienki Park, and back up the Royal Way, then loop through Praga before returning to pl. Zamkowy.

STARE AND NOWE MIASTO. Warsaw's postwar reconstruction shows its finest face in *Stare Miasto* (Old Town), which features cobblestoned streets and colorful facades. *(Take bus #175 or E3 from the city center to Miodowa.)* The landmark **Statue of King Zygmunt III Waza,** constructed in 1644 to honor the king who moved the capital from Kraków to Warsaw, towers over the entrance to *Stare Miasto*. To its right stands the impressive **Royal Castle** (Zamek Królewski), the royal residence from the 16th to 19th centuries. When the Nazis plundered and burned the castle in 1939, many Varsovians risked their lives hiding its priceless works. Today, the ▨**Royal Castle Museum** houses these rescued treasures. It also has artifacts, paintings, and the stunning Royal Apartments. *(Pl. Zamkowy 4. ☎657 21 70; www.zamek-krolewski.art.pl. Tickets and guides inside the courtyard. Open Su-M 11am-6pm, Tu-Sa 10am-6pm. 20zł, students 13zł. Free highlights tour Su 11am-6pm. English-language tour M-Sa, 85zł per group. AmEx/MC/V.)* Across Świętojańska sits Warsaw's oldest church, **St. John's Cathedral** (Katedra św. Jana), which was destroyed in the 1944 Uprising but rebuilt after the war. *(Open daily 10am-1pm and 3-5:30pm. Crypts 1zł.)*

POLAND

Świętojańska leads to the restored Renaissance and Baroque **Rynek Starego Miasta** (Old Town Square); the statue of the **Warsaw Mermaid** (Warszawa Syrenka) marks the center. According to legend, a greedy merchant kidnapped the mermaid from the Wisła River, but local fishermen rescued her. In return, she swore to defend the city, protecting it with a shield and raised sword. Ul. Krzywe Koło runs from the northeast corner of the Rynek to the restored **Barbican** *(barbakan)*, a rare example of 16th-century Polish fortification and a popular spot to relax. The Barbican opens onto Freta, the edge of **Nowe Miasto** (New Town). Nobel Prize-winning physicist and chemist **Marie Curie** was born at Freta 16 in 1867. The house is now a museum. *(☎831 8092. Open Tu-Sa 10am-4pm, Su 10am-2pm. 6zl, students 3zl.)*

TRAKT KRÓLEWSKI. The Trakt Królewski (Royal Way) begins at the entrance to Stare Miasto on pl. Zamkowy and stretches 4km south toward Kraków, the former capital. On the left after pl. Zamkowy, the 15th-century **St. Anne's Church** (Kościół św. Anny) features a striking gilded interior. *(Open daily dawn-dusk.)* Frederick Chopin grew up near Krakówskie Przedmieście and gave his first public concert in **Pałac Radziwiłłów,** now the Polish presidential mansion guarded by four stone lions and the military police. A block down the road, set back from the street behind a grove of trees, the **Church of the Visitation Nuns** (Kościół Wizytówek) once rang with Chopin's Romantic chords. *(Open daily dawn-1pm and 3pm-dusk.)* Though the composer died abroad at 39, his heart belongs to Poland; it now rests in an urn in **Holy Cross Church.** *(Kościół sw. Krzyża. Krakówskie Przedmiescie 3. Open daily dawn-dusk.)* The **Frédéric Chopin Museum** (Muzeum Fryderyka Chopina) displays original letters, keepsakes, and scores, including the composer's last piano and part of his first *polonaise*, penned at age seven. *(Okólnik 1, in Ostrogski Castle. Enter from Tamka. ☎827 5475. Open Tu-Su 10am-6pm. Last entry at 5:30pm. 8zl, students 4zl. English-language guides 100zl. Concerts 15zl, students 10zl. Cash only.)*

The Royal Way continues down fashionable **Nowy Świat.** Turn left at Rondo Charles de Gaulle to reach Poland's largest museum, the **National Museum** (Muzeum Narodowe), which holds 16th- to 20th-century paintings. *(Al. Jerozolimskie 3. ☎629 3093, English-language tours 629 5060; www.mnw.art.pl. Open Tu-Su 10am-5pm. Permanent exhibits 12zl, students 7zl. Special exhibits 17/10zl. English-language tours 50zl; call 1 week ahead. AmEx/MC/V.)* Farther down, the Royal Way turns into al. Ujazdowskie and runs alongside **Łazienki Park** (Pałac Łazienkowski), which houses the striking Neoclassical **Palace on Water** (Pałac na Wodzie). Buildings in the park feature rotating art exhibits. *(Bus #116, 180, or 195 from Nowy Świat or #119 from pl. Defilad to Bagatela. Park open daily dawn-dusk. Palace open Tu-Su 8:30am-3:30pm. 12zl, students 9zl.)* Just north of the park, off ul. Agrykola, the **Center of Contemporary Art** (Centrum Sztuki Współczesnej), al. Ujazdowskie 6, hosts installations in the reconstructed 17th-century Ujazdowskie Castle. *(☎62 81 27 13; www.csw.art.pl. Open Tu-Th and Sa-Su 11am-7pm, F 11am-9pm. 12zl, students 6zl. Cash only.)*

FORMER GHETTO AND SYNAGOGUE. Walled **Muranów,** Warsaw's former ghetto, north of the city center, holds few traces of the nearly 400,000 Jews who made up one-third of the city's pre-war population. Built in the 1830s, the **Museum of Pawiak Prison** (Muzeum Więzienia Pawiaka) exhibits former inmates' photography and poetry. Over 100,000 Polish Jews were imprisoned here from 1939 to 1944. A dead tree outside bears the names of over 30,000 prisoners killed during WWII. *(Dzielna 24/26. ☎831 13 17. Open W 9am-5pm, Th and Sa 9am-4pm, F 10am-5pm, Su 10am-4pm. Donation requested.)* Follow al. Jana Pawła II, take a left on Anielewicza, and walk five blocks to reach the **Jewish Cemetery** (Cmentarz Żydowski). The thickly wooded cemetery holds the remains of socialist Ferdinand Lasalle, the families of physicist Max Born and chemist Fritz Haber, and writer Thomas Mann's wife. *(Ślężna 37/39. Tram #9 to Ślężna. ☎791 5904. Open Apr.-Oct. daily 9am-6pm. 5zl, students 3zl. Free English- and Polish-language tours Su noon.)* The restored **Nożyk Synagogue** (Synagoga Nożyka) was the city's only synagogue to survive WWII, and now serves as the spiritual home for the 500 observant Jews remaining in Warsaw. *(Twarda 6. From the center, take any tram along al. Jana Pawła II to Rondo Onz. Turn right on Twarda and left at Teatr Żydowski, the Jewish Theater. ☎ 620 1037. Open Su-F Apr.-Oct. 10am-5pm; Nov.-Feb. 10am-3pm. Closed Jewish holidays. Morning and evening prayer daily. 5zł.)*

ELSEWHERE IN WARSAW. Warsaw's commercial district, southwest of Stare Miasto, is dominated by the 52-story Stalinist **Palace of Culture and Science** (Pałac Kultury i Nauki, PKiN) on Marszałkowska, which contains shops and offices. Locals claim the view from the top is the best in Warsaw—largely because you can't see the building itself. *(☎ 656 6000. Open daily 9am-8pm. Observation deck on 33rd fl. 20zł, students15zł.)* Though a bit far from the city center, the new ⬛**Warsaw Uprising Museum** is a must-see. Educational without being pedantic and somber without being heavy-handed, it recounts the tragic 1944 Uprising with full-scale replica bunkers and ruins haunted by the sound of approaching bombs. *(Grzybowska 79, enter on Przyokopowa. From the center, take tram #12, 20, or 22 to Grzybowska; the museum is on the left. ☎ 539 79 01; www.1944.pl. Multimedia presentations have English-language subtitles. Open W and F-Su 10am-6pm, Th 10am-8pm. 4zł, students 2zł; Su free. Cash only.)*

PRAGA. Across the Wisła River from central Warsaw, the formerly run-down district of Praga is undergoing a renaissance, though visitors should still exercise caution, especially after dark. The onion domes of the **St. Mary Magdalene Cathedral** hint at the pre-Soviet Russian presence in Warsaw. *(Al. Solidarnosci 52. From Russian Market, take tram #2, 8, 12, or 25 to the intersection of Targowa and al. Solidarności; church is across the street on the left. ☎ 619 8467. Open Su-M 1-4pm, Tu-Sa 11am-3pm.)* With two tall spires, pointed arches, and a long nave reconstructed in 1972, the **St. Michael and St. Florian Cathedral** is less restrained than Stare Miasto's churches. *(Floriańska 3, 1 block from St. Mary Magdalene. ☎ 619 0960; www.katedra-floriana.wpraga.opoka.org.pl.)* Across the street, **Praski Park** spans 45 acres and contains the **Island of Bears,** a manmade island on which bears have been kept since 1949. *(Free.)*

WILANÓW. In 1677, King Jan III Sobieski bought the sleepy village of Milanowo and rebuilt the existing mansion into a Baroque palace. Since 1805, **Pałac Wilanowski,** south of Warsaw, has served as a public museum and a residence for the Polish state's highest-ranking guests. Surrounded by elegant gardens, the palace is filled with frescoed rooms, portraits, and extravagant royal apartments. *(Take bus #180 from Krakówskie Przedmiesce, #516 or 519 from Marszałkowska south to Wilanów. From the bus stop, cross the highway and follow signs. ☎ 842 0795; www.wilanow-palac.art.pl. Open mid-May to mid-Sept. M and W-Su 9:30am-4:30pm; mid-Sept. to mid-May M and Th-Sa 9:30am-4pm, W 9:30am-6pm, Su 9:30am-7pm. Last entry 1½hr. before closing. Gardens open M and W-F 9:30am-dusk. Wilanów 20zł, students 10zł; Th free. Gardens 4.50/2.50zł. Cash only.)*

🎵 🎭 ENTERTAINMENT AND NIGHTLIFE

Warsaw offers a variety of live music options, and free outdoor concerts abound in summer. Classical music performances rarely sell out; standby tickets cost as little as 10zł. Inquire at the **Warsaw Music Society** (Warszawskie Towarzystwo Muzyczne), ul. Morskie Oko 2 (☎ 849 5651). Take tram #4, 18, 19, 35, or 36 to Morskie Oko from ul. Marszałkowska. Nearby Łazienki Park has free Sunday performances at the **Chopin Monument** (Pomnik Chopina; concerts mid-May to Sept. Su noon, 4pm). **Jazz Klub Tygmont** (☎ 828 3409; www.tygmont.com.pl), ul. Mazowiecka 6/8, hosts free concerts on weekday evenings. From July through September, the Old Market Square of Stare Miasto swings with free jazz nightly at 7pm.

Teatr Dramatyczny, in the Pałac Kultury, has a stage for big productions and a studio theater playing avant-garde works. *(☎ 656 6865; www.teatrdramatyczny.pl. 18-*

40zł; standby tickets 11-17zł.) **Teatr Żydowski, pl.** Grzybowski 12/16 (☎620 6281), is a Jewish theater with primarily Yiddish-language shows. **Kinoteka** (☎826 1961), in the Pałac Kultury, shows Hollywood blockbusters. **Kino Lab,** ul. Ujazdowskie 6 (☎628 1271), features independent films. See **Center for Contemporary Art,** p. 778.

Warsaw is full of energy in the evenings. *Kawiarnie* (cafes) around Stare Miasto and ul. Nowy Świat are open late, and pubs with live music attract crowds. In summer, outdoor beer gardens complement the pub scene. Several publications, including *Gazeta Wyborcza*, list gay nightlife.

■ **Piekarnia,** Młocińska 11 (☎636 4979). Take the #22 tram to Rondo Babka and backtrack on Okopowa. Make a right on Powiązkowska, a right on Burakowa, and a right on Młocińska. The unmarked club will be down the road on your left. Boasting a host of resident DJs and a constant stream of partiers, Piekarnia was one of the first modern clubs in Poland. These days the so-hip-it-hurts scene really picks up around 4am. The selective bouncer, packed dance floor, and progressive house music make this a local institution. Cover F 20zł, Sa 25zł. Open F-Sa 10pm-late.

Klubokawiarnia, Czeckiego 3 (www.klubo.pl). An authentic communist-era sign advertising "coffee, tea, and cold beverages" hangs over the bar, while portraits of Lenin gaze down from the bright red walls in this ironic imitation of the bad old days. Despite the nostalgic decor, Klubokawiarnia's DJs spin the hottest new tracks for a stylish young crowd. Special events on occasion, such as a "Caribbean Night" with imported sand. Cover varies. Open daily 10pm-late. Cash only.

Underground Music Cafe, Marszałkowska 126/134 (☎826 7048; www.under.pl). Walk down the steps behind the large McDonald's. This 2-level dance club is a guaranteed weeknight party. Casual, young student crowd keeps the smoky dance floor completely packed until 4am. M-Tu and Su old-school house; W and Sa hip-hop; Th 70s and 80s. Beer 5zł 11pm-midnight. Cover W and F 10zł, students 5zł; Sa 20/10zł; Th 10zł. No cover M-Tu and Su. Open M-Sa 1pm-late, Su 4pm-late.

Cinnamon, Piłsudskiego 1 (☎323 7600), in the Metropolitan Building across pl. Piłsudskiego from the National Opera. At this bar with attitude, one of Warsaw's strictest door policies ensures that Cinnamon is favored only by the hottest locals and expats. The lunar-themed interior and pink accents complement suave and impeccably dressed staff who keep the martinis flowing all night long. Don't be surprised if you pop in for an elegant lunch and emerge at dawn the next day. Open daily 9am-late. MC/V.

Rasko, Krochmalna 32A (☎890 0299; www.rasko.pl). 1 block north of Grzybowska, turn left on Krochmalna; the bar is 2 blocks down on your right near a small sign and blue unmarked door. Rasko is a small, secluded, and artsy establishment that serves Warsaw's largely underground GLBT scene. Laid-back but cautious bouncer ensures that Warsaw's less tolerant elements stay out. The close-knit and friendly staff will be happy to direct you to other GLBT establishments. Beer 7zł. Open daily 5pm-3am. Cash only.

KRAKÓW ☎012

Although Kraków (KRAH-koof; pop 758,000) only recently emerged as a trendy international capital, it has long been Poland's darling. The regal architecture, rich cafe culture, and palpable sense of history that now bewitch throngs of foreign visitors have drawn Polish kings, artists, and scholars for centuries. Unlike most Polish cities, Kraków emerged from WWII and years of socialist planning unscathed. The maze-like Old Town and the old Jewish quarter of Kazimierz hide scores of museums, galleries, cellar pubs, and clubs; 130,000 students add to the spirited nightlife. Still, the city's gloss and glamor can't completely hide the scars of the 20th century: the nearby Auschwitz-Birkenau Nazi death camps provide a sobering reminder of the atrocities committed in the not-so-distant past.

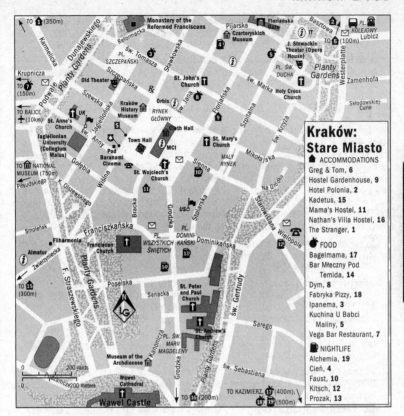

**Kraków:
Stare Miasto**

▲ ACCOMMODATIONS
Greg & Tom, 6
Hostel Gardenhouse, 9
Hotel Polonia, 2
Kadetus, 15
Mama's Hostel, 11
Nathan's Villa Hostel, 16
The Stranger, 1

🍴 FOOD
Bagelmama, 17
Bar Mleczny Pod
  Temida, 14
Dym, 8
Fabryka Pizzy, 18
Ipanema, 3
Kuchina U Babci
  Maliny, 5
Vega Bar Restaurant, 7

🎵 NIGHTLIFE
Alchemia, 19
Cień, 4
Faust, 10
Kitsch, 12
Prozak, 13

POLAND

⊏ TRANSPORTATION

Flights: Balice Airport (John Paul II International Airport; Port Lotniczy im. Jana Pawła), Kapitana Medweckiego 1 (☎411 19 55; airport@lotnisko-balice.pl), 18km from the center. Connect to the main train station by bus #192 (40min.) or 208 (1hr.). Or take the airport train that leaves from the train platform #1 on W and F-Sa, at least once per hour. A taxi to the center costs 50-60zł. Carriers include **British Airways, Central Wings, German Wings, LOT, Lufthansa,** and **Sky Europe.** Open 24hr.

Trains: Kraków Główny, pl. Kolejowy 1 (☎393 5409 info, 1580; www.pkp.pl). Ticket office open 5am-11pm. Go to Kasa Krajowej for domestic trains and Kasa Międzynardowa for international trains. You can reserve spaces on the train ahead of time. AmEx/MC/V. To: **Gdańsk** ("Gdynia"; 7-10hr., 10 per day, 60-100zł); **Warsaw** (3hr., 15 per day, 81-127zł); **Zakopane** (3-5hr., 17 per day, 30-50zł); **Bratislava, SLK** (8hr., 1 per day, 188zł); **Budapest, HUN** (11hr., 1 per day, 159-208zł); **Kyiv, UKR** (22hr., 2 per day, 240zł); **Odessa, UKR** (21hr., 1 per day, 240zł); **Prague, CZR** (9hr., 2 per day, 128-165zł); **Vienna, AUT** (8½hr., 2 per day, 157-194zł). Let's Go does not recommend traveling on night trains.

Buses: Bosacka 18 (☎300 300 150). Open daily 5am-11pm. To: **Łódź** (5hr., 5 per day, 50zł); **Warsaw** (6hr., 3 per day, 50zł); **Wrocław** (5hr., 2 per day, 43zł). AmEx/MC/V.

Public Transportation: Buy **bus** and **tram** tickets at Ruch kiosks (2.50zł) or from the driver (3zł) and punch them on board. Large packs need their own tickets. Night buses after 11pm 5zł; day pass 11zł; 100zł fine if you or your bag are caught ticketless.

Taxis: Reliable taxi companies include: **Barbakan Taxi** (☎96 61, toll-free 08 00 00 40 04 00); **Euro Taxi** (☎96 64); **Radio Taxi** (☎919, toll-free 08 00 50 09 19); **Wawel Taxi** (☎96 66). It is up to 30% cheaper to call a taxi than to hail one.

◆ 🔼 ORIENTATION AND PRACTICAL INFORMATION

The heart of the city is the huge **Rynek Główny** (Main Marketplace), in the center of **Stare Miasto** (Old Town). *Stare Miasto* is encircled by the **Planty** gardens and, a bit farther out, a broad ring road, which is confusingly divided into sections with different names: **Basztowa, Dunajewskiego, Podwale,** and **Westerplatte.** South of Rynek Główny looms the celebrated **Wawel Castle.** The **Wisła River** snakes past the castle and borders the old Jewish district of **Kazimierz.** The train station sits northeast of Stare Miasto. A large, well-marked underpass cuts beneath the ring road and into the Planty gardens; from there a number of paths lead into the Rynek (10min.). Turn left from the train station to reach the underpass.

Tourist Office: City Tourist Information, Szpitalna 25 (☎432 0110; www.krakow.pl/en). The official tourist office arranges accommodations and guided tours, and sells maps and guides (7-12zł). English spoken. Private tourist offices throughout town.

Budget Travel: Orbis, Rynek Główny 41 (☎619 2449; www.orbis.krakow.pl). Sells train tickets and arranges trips to Wieliczka and Auschwitz (each 120zł, both 238zł; up to 50% ISIC discount). Also cashes **traveler's checks** and **exchanges currency.** Open M-F 9am-7pm, Sa 9am-3pm. There are many travel agencies in Stare Miasto.

Consulates: UK, św. Anny 9 (☎421 5656 or 421 7030; ukconsul@bci.krakow.pl). Open M-F 9am-4pm. **US,** Stolarska 9 (☎424 5100; krakow.usconsulate.gov). Open M-F 8:30am-4:40pm; citizen services until 3pm.

Currency Exchange and Banks: ATMs, found all over the city, offer the best rates. **Bank BPH,** Rynek Główny 4, has **Western Union Services.** Many banks require those receiving money from abroad to change it into *złotych* at a bad rate. Open M-F 8am-6pm.

Bike Rental: Rentabike (☎501 745 986; www.rentabike.pl) will deliver a bike anywhere in Kraków's center. Bikes 15zł per 3hr., 35zł per day, students 30zł per day. Open M-Sa 9am-8pm.

Luggage Storage: At the train station. 1% of value per day plus 5zł for the 1st day and 3zł for each additional day. Lockers near the exit. Open 5am-11pm. Lockers also available at bus station. Small bag 4zł, large bag 8zł. Open 24hr.

English-Language Bookstore: Massolit, Felicjanek 4 (☎432 4150. www.massolit.com). Cozy atmosphere. Open mic night 3rd Su each month at 7pm. Open Su-Th 10am-8pm; F-Sa 10am-9pm.

Laundromat: Piastowska 47 (☎622 31 81), in the basement of **Hotel Piast.** Take tram #4, 13, or 14 to WKS Wawel and turn left on Piastowska. Wash 15zł, dry 15zł, detergent 3zł. Open Tu and Th 11am-4pm, Sa 11am-2pm.

Pharmacy: Apteka Pod Żółtym Tygrysem, Szczepańska 1 (☎422 9293), just off Rynek Główny. Posts a list of 24hr. pharmacies. Open M-F 8am-8pm, Sa 8am-3pm. MC/V.

Medical Services: Medicover, Krótka 1 (☎616 1000). Ambulance services available. English spoken. Open M-F 7am-9pm, Sa 9am-2pm.

Telephones: At the post office and throughout the city.

Internet: Koffeina Internet Cafe, Rynek Główny 23. 2zł per 30min., 3zł per hr. Open 24hr. **Klub Garinet,** Floriańska 18 (☎423 2233, ext 23). 4zł per hr. Open daily 9am-midnight. **Telekomunikacja Polska** offers free Internet, but has standing room only.

Post Office: Westerplatte 20 (☎422 24 97). **Poste Restante** at counter #1. Open M-F 7:30am-8:30pm, Sa 8am-2pm. **Postal Code:** 31075.

ACCOMMODATIONS

New hostels frequently open in Kraków to meet the growing demand, but budget accommodations fill up quickly in summer. Travelers should call ahead. University dorms open up in July and August; *Kraków in Your Pocket* has a list.

Nathan's Villa Hostel, ul. św. Agnieszki 1 (☎422 3545; www.nathansvilla.com), south of Stare Miasto. Famous for its social atmosphere, the hostel has spacious rooms and a lively cellar pub. Breakfast, laundry, and Wi-Fi included. Reception 24hr. Dorms 50-60zł. MC/V; 3% surcharge. ❷

The Stranger, ul. Kochanowskiego 1 (☎634 2516; www.thestrangerhostel.com), northwest of Stare Miasto. A laid-back hostel with mellow, retro-lit dorms. Common room has a mammoth couch, and a fantastic entertainment system. Breakfast included. Free Internet. Reception 24hr. Dorms 55-60zł. Cash only. ❷

Mama's Hostel, ul. Bracka 4 (☎429 5940; www.mamashostel.com.pl), off Rynek Główny. Popular hostel with bright, clean facilities. The central, party-friendly location means it can get noisy. Breakfast and laundry included. Reception 24hr. Flexible check-in and check-out. 10-bed dorms 45zł; 6-bed dorms 60zł. MC/V; 3% surcharge. ❶

Hostel Gardenhouse, ul. Floriańska 5 (☎431 2824; www.gardenhousehostel.com), in a courtyard off Rynek Główny. Spotless, quiet dorms with floral motif. Breakfast, laundry, and Internet included. Reception 24hr. Dorms 55-65zł; doubles 160zł. MC/V. ❷

Hotel Polonia, Basztowa 25 (☎422 1233; www.hotel-polonia.com.pl), across from the train station. Neoclassical exterior, modern rooms, and see-through bathtubs in suites. Breakfast 18zł, included for rooms with bath. Reception 24hr. Check-out noon. Singles 100zł, with bath 295zł; doubles 119/303zł; triples 139/429zł; suites 526zł. MC/V. ❹

Greg and Tom, ul. Pawia 12/15 (☎422 4100; www.gregtomhostel.com). Look past the climb to the 4th fl. of a weary Soviet-era building: this small hostel is clean, attractive, and next to the train and bus stations. Breakfast, laundry, and Internet included. Reception 24hr. Dorms 50zł; doubles 60zł. AmEx/MC/V. ❷

Kadetus, ul. Zwierzyniecka 25 (☎422 3617; www.kadetus.com), southwest of Rynek Główny. Simple, colorful dorms with modern furnishings. Laundry and Internet included. Reception 24hr. Dorms 40zł; doubles 60zł. Cash only. ❷

FOOD

Many restaurants, cafes, and grocery stores are located on and around Rynek Główny. More grocery stores surround the bus and train stations.

Bagelmama, ul. Podbrzezie 2 (☎431 1942), in Kazimierz, facing the Tempel Synagogue. Poland is the mother of the bagel; here the blessed food returns home in triumph (2.50zł, with cream cheese or hummus 5-8.50zł). Strangely, has Kraków's best burritos (12-15zł). Open Tu-Th and Su 10am-9pm, F-Sa 10am-10pm. Cash only. ❶

Kuchina U Babci Maliny, ul. Szpitalna 38 (☎421 4818). Hearty Polish food served in quarters resembling a wooden stable upstairs and, incongruously, a Victorian drawing room below. Soup 3zł. Pierogi 6-12zł. Open daily 11am-10pm. ❶

Ipanema, św. Tomasza 28 (☎422 5323). Toucan figurines, bright paint, and hanging plants create a rainforest vibe to go along with the superb Brazilian cuisine. Entrees 17-40zł. Open Su-Th 1-11pm, F-Sa 1pm-midnight. AmEX/MC/V. ❸

Dym, św. Tomasza 13 (☎429 6661). A hub for sophisticated locals, Dym (meaning "smoke") earns high praise for its coffee (4.50zł), though many prefer to enjoy the relaxed vibe over beer (5.50zł). Open M-F 10am-midnight. Cash only. ❶

Fabryka Pizzy, Józefa 34 (☎433 8080). This wildly popular Kazimierz pizza place lives up to its hype, preparing unusual, delicious pizzas. Pizzas 17.50-25zł. Open M-Th and Su 11am-11pm, F-Sa noon-midnight. MC/V. ❷

POLAND

Vega Bar Restaurant, Krupnicza 22 (☎430 0846), also at św. Gertrudy 7 (☎422 3494). Fresh flowers set the mood for delightful veggie cuisine (3-10zł). 32 varieties of tea (2.50zł). Open daily 9am-9pm. MC/V. ❶

Bar Mleczny Pod Temida, ul. Grodzka 43. Conveniently located between Rynok Główny and Wawel Castle, this milk bar is a crowd-pleasing lunch spot. Entrees 2.50-10zł. Open daily 9am-8pm. ❶

⊙ SIGHTS

STARE MIASTO. At the center of *Stare Miasto* is the *Rynek Główny*, the largest market square in Europe, and at the heart of the *Rynek* stands the **Sukiennice** (Cloth Hall). Surrounded by multicolored row houses and cafes, it's a convenient center for exploring the nearby sights. The **Royal Road** (Droga Królewska), traversed by medieval royals on the way to coronations in Wawel, starts at St. Florian's Church (Kościół św. Floriana), crosses pl. Matejki, passes the **Academy of Fine Arts** (Akademia Sztuk Pięknych), and crosses Basztowa to the Barbakan. The Gothic-style **Barbakan,** built in 1499, is the best preserved of the three such defensive fortifications surviving in Europe. *(Open daily 10:30am-6pm. 6zl, students 4zl.)* The royal road continues through Floriańska Gate, the old city entrance and the only remnant of the city's medieval walls. Inside *Stare Miasto*, the road runs down Floriańska, past the *Rynek* and along Grodzka, which ends with Wawel in sight. A map marking all the points can be found in front of Floriańska Gate. Every hour at ▣**St. Mary's Church** (Kościół Mariacki), the blaring Hejnał trumpet calls from the taller of St. Mary's two towers and cuts off abruptly to recall the near-destruction of Kraków in 1241, when invading Tatars shot down the trumpeter as he attempted to warn the city. A stunning interior encases the world's oldest **Gothic altarpiece,** a 500-year-old treasure dismantled, but not destroyed, by the Nazis. *(At the corner of the Rynek closest to the train station. Cover shoulders and knees. Church open daily 11:30am-6pm. Tower open Tu, Th, and Sa 9-11:30am and 1-5:30pm. Tower 5zł, students 3zł. Altar 4/2zł.)*

Collegium Maius of Kraków's **Jagiellonian University** (Uniwersytet Jagielloński) is the third oldest university in Europe, established in 1364. Alumni include astronomer **Mikołaj Kopernik (Copernicus)** and painter Jan Matejko. The Collegium became a museum in 1964 and now boasts an extensive collection of historical scientific instruments. *(ul. Jagiellońska 15. ☎633 1521; www.uj.edu.pl/muzeum. Open M-W and F 10am-2:20pm, Th 10am-5:20pm, Sa 10am-1:20pm. Guided visits only; tours 3 per hr. English-language tour daily 1pm. 12zł, students 6zł, Sa free.)* **Ulica Floriańska** runs from the Rynek to the **Barbakan** and the **Floriańska Gate,** which formed the entrance to the old city and are now the only remnants of the medieval fortifications. The **Czartoryskich Museum** has letters by Copernicus and paintings by Matejko, da Vinci, and Rembrandt. *(św. Jana 19. ☎422 5566. Open Tu, Th 10am-4pm; W, F 11am-7pm; Sa-Su 10am-3pm; closed last Su of each month. 10zł, students 5zł, Th free.)* From the Rynek, walk down Grodzka and turn right to reach the brightly colored **Franciscan Church** *(Kościół Franciscańska),* decorated with vibrant colors and Stanisław Wyspiański's amazing stained-glass window *God the Father. (Pl. Wszystkich Świętych 5. ☎422 5376. Open daily until 7:30pm. English-language tours free; donations requested.)*

WAWEL CASTLE AND SURROUNDINGS. ▣**Wawel Castle** (Zamek Wawelski), one of Poland's top attractions, is an architectural masterpiece. Begun in the 10th century and remodeled in the 16th, the castle contains 71 chambers, including the **Komnaty** (state rooms) and the **Apartamenty** (royal chambers). Among the treasures are a magnificent sequence of 16th-century tapestries commissioned by the royal family and a cache of armor, swords, spears, and ancient guns.The **Lost Wawel** exhibit traces Wawel Hill's evolution from the Stone Age, displaying archaeological fragments of ancient Wawel. You can also visit the **Oriental Collection** of Turkish military regalia, the spoils of Polish military victories, and Asian porcelain. *(Open*

Apr.-Oct. M 9:30am-1pm, Tu, W and Sa 9:30am-3pm, Th-F 9:30am-4pm, Su 10am-4pm. Nov.-Mar. Tu-Sa 9:30am-4pm, Su 10am-4pm. Royal Private Apartments and Oriental Collection closed M. Wawel Castle 15zł, students 8zł, M free. Lost Wawel and Oriental Collection 7/4zł each. Royal Apartments and Treasury and Armory 20/15zł each.) Next door is **Wawel Cathedral** (Katedra Wawelska), which once hosted the coronations and funerals of Polish monarchs. Famed poet Adam Mikiewicz lies entombed here, and Kraków native Karol Wojtyła served as archbishop before becoming Pope John Paul II. Steep stairs from the church lead to **Sigismund's Bell** (Dwon Zygmunta); the view of the city is worth the climb. *(Cathedral open M-Sa 9am-2:45pm, Su and holy days 12:15-2:45pm. Buy tickets at the kasa across from the entrance. 10zł, students 5zł.)* In the complex's southwest corner is the entrance to the **⛏Dragon's Den** (Smocza Jama), a small cavern. The real treat is down to the path that borders the castle walls: a wonderfully ugly metal statue of the fire-breathing dragon. *(Open daily May-Oct. 10am-5pm. 3zł.)*

KAZIMIERZ. South of *Stare Miasto* lies Kazimierz, Kraków's 600-year-old **Jewish quarter.** On the eve of WWII, 68,000 Jews lived in the Kraków area, most of them in Kazimierz, but the occupying Nazis forced many out. The 15,000 remaining were deported to death camps by March 1943. Only about 100 practicing Jews now live here, but Kazimierz is a favorite haunt of Kraków's artists and intellectuals and the center of a resurgence of Central European Jewish culture. *(From the Rynek, go down ul. Sienna, which turns into Starowiślana. After 1km, turn right onto Miodowa, then left onto Szeroka.)* The **Galicia Jewish Museum** documents the past and present of Galicia, a region in southern Poland that was once the heart of Ashkenazi Jewish culture. *(Dajwór 18. ☎ 421 6842; www.galiciajewishmuseum.org. Open daily 9am-7pm. 7zł, students 5zł.)* The tiny **Remuh Synagogue** is surrounded by **Remuh's Cemetery,** which has graves dating to the plague of 1551-1552 and a wall constructed from tombstones recovered after WWII. For centuries, the cemetery was covered with sand, protecting it from 19th-century Austrian invaders and from the Nazis, who used the area as a garbage dump. *(Szeroka 40. Open M-F and Su 9am-6pm. Services F at sundown and Sa morning. 5zł, students 2zł.)* Also on Szeroka, the **Old Synagogue** is Poland's earliest example of Jewish religious architecture and now houses a museum. *(Szeroka 24. ☎ 422 0962. Open Apr.-Oct. M 10am-2pm, Tu-Su 9am-5pm; Nov.-Mar. M 10am-2pm, W-Th and Sa-Su 9am-4pm, F 10am-5pm. 7zł, students 5zł, M free.)* The **Center for Jewish Culture** organizes cultural events and arranges heritage tours. *(Meiselsa 17. ☎ 430 6449; www.judaica.pl. Open M-F 10am-6pm, Sa-Su 10am-2pm.)*

🎵 ENTERTAINMENT

The **Cultural Information Center,** św. Jana 2, sells the monthly guide *Karnet* (4zł) and directs visitors to box offices. (☎ 421 7787. Open daily 10am-6pm.) The city jumps with jazz; check out **U Muniaka,** Floriańska 3 (☎ 423 1205; open daily 6:30pm-2am) and **Harris Piano Jazz Bar,** Rynek Główny 28 (☎ 421 5741; shows 9pm-midnight; open daily 1pm-2am except M.) Classical music-lovers will relish the **Sala Filharmonia** (Philharmonic Hall), Zwierzyniecka 1. (☎ 422 9477, ext. 31; www.filharmonia.krakow.pl. Box office open Tu-F noon-7pm, Sa-Su 1hr. before curtain; closed June 9-Sept. 20.) The **opera** performs at the **Słowacki Theater,** św. Ducha 1. (☎ 424 4525. Box office open M-Sa 9am-7pm, Su 4hr. before curtain. 30-50zł, students 25-35zł.) The **Stary Teatr** (Old Theater) has a few stages that host films, plays, and exhibits. (☎ 422 4040. Open Tu-Sa 10am-1pm and 5-7pm, Su 5-7pm. 30-60zł, students 20-35zł.)

🎭 NIGHTLIFE

Kraków in Your Pocket has up-to-date info on the hottest club and pub scenes, while the free monthly English-language *KrakOut* magazine has day-by-day listings of events. Most dance clubs are in *Stare Miasto*, while bohemian pubs and cafes cluster in Kazimierz. For tips on Kraków's **GLBT nightlife,** see http://gayeuro.com/krakow or www.cracow.gayguide.net.

Alchemia, Estery 5 (☎421 2200). Candles twinkle in this pleasantly disheveled bar, which includes bizarre and fascinating decor—one of the many rooms is decorated to look like a 1950s kitchen. Frequented by artists, Brits and students downing beer (Żywiec; 6.5zł) until dawn. During the day, this Kazimierz bar masquerades as a smoky cafe. Occasional live music and film screenings. Open daily 9am-4am.

Prozak, Dominikańska 6 (☎429 1128; www.prozak.pl). With a shisha bar, and more dance floors, bars, and intimate nooks than you'll be able to count, Prozak is one of the top clubs in town. Hipster students, porn star look-alikes, and large groups of foreigners lounge on low-slung couches. Pass on the undersized mixed drinks (5-20zł) for pints of beer (7-10zł). No sneakers or sandals. Cover F-Sa 10zł. Open daily 7pm-late.

Kitsch, ul. Wielopole 15 (☎698 613 790), located between the Rynek and Kazimierz. This gay-friendly establishment offers a great dancing atmosphere and proximity to the 3 other clubs in the building. 6-7zł beer, mixed drinks from 8zł. W Boys' night, Th student Night, with beer at 5zł for men and students, respectively. Open 5pm-late.

Cień, św. Jana 15 (☎422 2177). The vaults of the "Shadow" fill with Kraków's beautiful people. The club plays house techno and can be selective at the door. Mixed drinks 10-20zł. No sneakers or sandals. Open Tu-Th 8pm-5am, F-Sa 8pm-6am. MC/V.

Faust, Rynek Główny 6, entrance off of Sienna St. (☎423 8300). Sell your soul in this underground labyrinth, where a raucous, friendly crowd sits at massive wooden tables or dances unabashedly to pop and techno hits. Beer 4-8zł. Disco W-Sa. Cover F-Sa 5zł. Open M-Th and Su noon-1am, F-Sa noon-4am. Cash only.

DAYTRIPS FROM KRAKÓW

AUSCHWITZ-BIRKENAU. An estimated 1.5 million people, mostly Jews, were murdered and thousands more suffered unthinkable horrors in the Nazi concentration camps at **Auschwitz** (in Oświęcim) and **Birkenau** (in Brzezinka). The gates over the smaller **Konzentrationslager Auschwitz I** are inscribed with the ironic dictum *"Arbeit Macht Frei"* (Work Will Set You Free). Tours begin at the **museum** at Auschwitz. As you walk past the remainders of thousands of lives—suitcases, shoes, glasses, kilos upon kilos of women's hair—the enormity of the atrocity begins to come into focus. A 15min. English-language film, with footage shot by the Soviet Army that liberated the camp on January 27, 1945, is shown at 11am and 1pm. Children under 14 are strongly advised not to visit the museum. (☎843 20 22. *Open daily June-Aug. 8am-7pm; Sept. and May 8am-6pm; Oct. and Apr. 8am-5pm; Nov. and Mar. 8am-4pm; Dec.-Feb. 8am-3pm. English-language tour 4 per day. Museum free. Film 3.50zł. Guided 3½hr. tour 26zł; film and bus included. English-language guidebook 3zł.*)

The larger, starker **Konzentrationslager Auschwitz II-Birkenau** is in the countryside 3km from the original camp, a 30min. walk along a well-marked route or a short **shuttle** ride from the Auschwitz museum parking lot (1 per hr., free). Birkenau was built later in the war, when the Nazis developed a brutal, efficient means of killing. Little is left of the camp today; most was destroyed by retreating Nazis to conceal the genocide. Reconstructed train tracks lead to the ruins of the crematoria and gas chambers. Near the monument lies a pond still gray from the ashes deposited there over 60 years ago. (*Open mid-Apr. to Oct. 8am-dusk. Free.*) **Auschwitz Jewish Center and Synagogue** features exhibits on pre-war Jewish life in the town of Oświęcim, films based on survivors' testimonies, genealogy resources, and a reading room. Take a **taxi** for about 17zł, or take **bus** #1, 3-6, or 8 from the train station in the town center, get off at the first stop after the bridge, and backtrack. (*Pl. Ks. Jana Skarbka 3-5.* ☎844 70 02; *www.ajcf.pl. Open Su-F Apr.-Sept. 8:30am-8pm; Oct.-Mar. 8:30am-6pm.*)

Buses from Kraków's central station go to Oświęcim (1½-2hr., 5 per day, 7-10zł). Return buses and minibuses leave frequently from the stop on the other side of the parking lot; turn right out of the museum. PKS buses also depart from the stop outside the premises. Less convenient **trains** leave from Kraków Plaszów, south of the town center (10zł). Buses #2-5, 8-9, and 24-29 connect the Oświęcim train station to the Muzeum Oświęcim stop; alternatively, walk a block to the right out of the station, turn left onto ul. Więźniów Oświęcimia, and continue 1.6km.

WIELICZKA. The tiny town of Wieliczka, 13km southeast of Kraków, is home to a 700-year-old **salt mine.** Pious Poles carved the immense underground complex of chambers out of salt; in 1978, UNESCO declared the mine one of the world's 12 most priceless monuments. The most spectacular cavern is **St. Kinga's Chapel,** complete with an altar, relief works, and salt chandeliers. Most travel companies, including **Orbis** (p. 774), organize trips to the mines, but it's cheapest to take a private **minibus,** like "Contrabus," that departs near the train and bus stations (30min., 4 per hr., 2.50zł). Look for "Wieliczka" marked on the door. In Wieliczka, head along the path of the former tracks, then follow signs marked *"do kopalni."* The only way to see the mines is by taking a lengthy guided tour, so allot at least 3½hr. for the daytrip. *(ul. Daniłowicza 10. ☎278 73 02; www.kopalnia.pl. Wheelchair-accessible. Open daily Apr.-Oct. 7:30am-7:30pm; Nov.-Mar. 8am-5pm; closed holidays. Polish-language tours 45zł, students 30zł. English-language tours June and Sept. 8 per day, July and Aug. every 35 people. 8:30am-6pm. 50zł, students under 25 40zł; Nov.-Feb. 40/32zł. MC/V.)*

LUBLIN   ☎081

Unlike most Polish cities, Lublin (LOO-blin; pop. 400,000) survived WWII with cobblestones and medieval buildings intact. Its medieval Old Town is not a Disneyfied reconstruction like Warsaw's, but a slice of romantically crumbling reality. The **Rynek** (main square) of the **Stare Miasto** (Old Town) contains many of the city's historic sights. The 14th-century **Lublin Castle** (Zamek Lubelski) was used as a Gestapo jail during the Nazi occupation. The adjacent **Holy Trinity Chapel** has stunning Russo-Byzantine frescoes from 1418. (☎532 5001, ext. 35; www.zamek-lublin.pl. Open M-Sa 10am-5pm, Su 10am-6pm. Museum and chapel each 6.50zł, students 4.50zł; both 11zł/9zł.) Great views and seriously old art make the ■**Archdiocesan Museum of Sacred Art** (Muzeum Archidiecezjalne Sztuki Sakralnej), in the 17th-century **Trinitarska Tower,** worth a visit. (☎444 7450. Open Mar. 25-Nov. 15 daily 10am-5pm. 5zł, students 3zł.) Take eastbound bus #28 from the train station or trolley #153 or 156 from al. Racławickie to reach **Majdanek,** the second largest Nazi concentration camp. The Nazis did not have time to destroy the camp as they retreated, so the original structures still stand. Visitors can walk from Lublin along Droga Męczenników Majdanka (Road of the Martyrs of Majdanek; 30min.) to Zamość. (☎744 2648; www.majdanek.pl. Open Apr.-Oct. Tu-Su 8am-6pm; Nov.-March 8am-3pm. Closed national holidays. Children under 14 not permitted. Free.)

From the bus station, bear left around pl. Zamkowy and head past the castle to reach ■**Domu Rekolekcyjnym ❶,** ul. Podwale 15, a rectory with simple rooms, friendly nuns, and an unbeatable location. (☎532 4138. Dorms 20-40zł. Cash only) **Szkolne Schroniско Młodziezowe ❶,** ul. Długosza 6, is a quiet youth hostel located in a residential area. (☎533 0628. Lockout 10am-5pm. Flexible curfew 10pm. 10-bed dorms 24zł, students 16zł; triples 84/69zł. Cash only.) Lublin's eateries cluster near **ulica Krakówskie Przedmieście;** a dozen beer gardens can be found in *Stare Miasto.* **Naleśnikarnia Zadora ❷,** ul. Rynek 8, tucked in an alley on the northeast of the square, adds a creative touch to its savory and dessert crepes. (☎534 5534. Polish crepes 9-19zł. AmEx/MC/V.) Menorahs, stars of David, and pictures of Israel cover the walls of **Mandragora,** Rynek 9, a self-proclaimed "Jewish Pub," which offers traditional Jewish dishes alongside Israeli favorites (☎536 2020. Gefilte fish 15zł. Falafel 18zł. Kosher. Special Shabbat menu F-Sa. Open daily 1-11pm.) **Trains** (☎94 36) run from pl. Dworcowy 1 to Kraków (4hr., 2 per day, 47zł), Warsaw (3hr., 9per day, 34zł), and Wrocław (9½hr., 2 per day, 54zł). From the train station, take bus #1 to *Stare Miasto* and the bus station. The **tourist office**, ul. Jezuica 1/3, is near the Kraków Gate. (☎532 4412; itlublin@onet.pl. Open M-Sa 9am-6pm, Su 10am-3pm.)

ZAKOPANE
☎018

The year-round resort of Zakopane (zah-ko-PAH-neh; pop. 28,000) lies in a valley surrounded by jagged Tatran peaks and alpine meadows. During prime vacation season (Jan.-Feb. and June-Sept.), the town fills with skiers or hikers headed for the magnificent **Tatra National Park** (Tatrzański Park Narodowy; 5zł, students 2.50zł). To find accommodations, look for signs marked *"pokój"* and *"noclegi"* that indicate private rooms; owners may greet you at the station. **Schronisko PISM "Szarotka" ❷**, ul. Notowarska 45G, has small, clean rooms with private baths. (☎201 3618; schroniskoptsm@pn.onet.pl. Linens 6zł. Lockout 11pm. Reserve ahead. Dorms 35-50zł, low season 26-30zł. Cash only.) **Schronisko Morskie Oko ❶**, by the **Morskie Oko** lake, is in an ideal hiking location. Take a bus (45min., 11 per day, 4zł) to Palenice Białczańska or a direct minibus (20min., 5zł) from opposite the bus station, and then hike (1-2hr., 9km) up the paved road. (☎207 7609. Linens 7zł. Reserve ahead. June-Oct. space on floor 34zł; 3- to 6-bed dorms 44zł. Nov.-June 24/34zł. Cash only.) Most restaurants and shops can be found along **ul. Krupówki**. The live music and regional fare at the kitschy **Gazdowo Kuźnia ❸**, ul. Krupówki 1, always draw a crowd. (☎206 4111; www.gazdowokuznia.pl. Entrees 7-28zł. Open daily 2-10pm.) Next door, **Bar Młeczny ❶** serves the cheapest eats around. (Entrees 6-12zł. Open daily 8am-8pm. Cash only.)

The bus station (☎201 4603) is located on the corner of ul. Kościuszki and ul. Jagiellońska, facing the train station (☎201 4504). **Buses** run to Kraków (2-2½hr., 2 per day, 10zł) and Warsaw (8½hr., 4 per day, 55zł). A private express line runs between Zakopane and Kraków (2hr., 15 per day, 13zł), leaving from a stop on ul. Kościuszki, 50m toward the center from the station. **Trains** go to Kraków (3-4hr., 18 per day, 19zł) and Warsaw (8hr., 9 per day, 50zł). To reach the center from the station, walk down ul. Kościuszki, which intersects ul. Krupówki (15min.). The **tourist office**, ul. Kościuszki 17, provides info on hiking, sells maps (5-9zł), helps locate rooms, and books English-language rafting trips (70-80zł) on the Dunajec. (☎201 2211. Open daily July-Sept. 8am-8pm; Oct.-June 9am-6pm.) **Postal Code:** 34500.

🏃 **HIKING NEAR ZAKOPANE. Kuźnice,** south of Zakopane, is a popular place to begin hikes. To get there, head uphill on ul. Krupówki to ul. Zamoyskiego; follow this road as it becomes ul. Chałubińskiego, which turns into ul. Przewodników Tatrzańskich and continues to the trailheads (1hr. from Zakopane center). You can also take a "mikro-bus" (2zł) from the stop in front of the bus station. From Kuźnice, the Kasprowy Wierch **cable car** takes passengers to the top of **Kasprowy Mountain,** 1987m above sea level, where Poland borders Slovakia.

Trails from Kuźnice are well marked. The Tatrzański Park Narodowy map (7zł), available at kiosks or bookstores, is a useful guide. The 🏔**Valley of the Five Polish Tarns** (Dolina Pięciu Stawów Polskich; 1 day) is an intense, beautiful hike. It starts at Kuźnice and follows the yellow trail through **Dolina Jaworzynka** (Jaworzynka Valley) to the steep blue trail, which leads to **Hala Gasienicowa** (2½hr.). Crowds tend to gather on the steep final ascent to the peak of **Mount Giewont** (1894m; 6½hr.). The mountain's silhouette resembles a man lying down; you'll envy him after the climb. From Kuźnice, the moderately difficult blue trail (7km) to the peak has a view of Zakopane, the Tatras, and Slovakia.

Morskie Oko (1406m) is a dazzling glacial lake. Take a bus from Zakopane (45min., 11 per day, 5zł) or a private minibus from opposite the station (30min., 6zł) to **Palenice Białczańska** or **Polona Palenica.** Hike the popular paved 18km loop (5-6hr.) or take the green trail to the blue trail (4hr.) for a majestic view. Donkey carts also take passengers to the lake (30min.; 30zł up, 20zł down).

WROCŁAW
☎071

Wrocław (VROTS-wahv), the capital of Lower Silesia (Dolny Śląsk), is a graceful city of Gothic spires and stone bridges. The tranquil main square was the last Nazi stronghold on the retreat to Berlin. Today, investment has rejuvenated the city, which enjoys one of the fastest development rates in Poland as tourist numbers are rising and cheap airlines turn it into a prime stag party destination.

TRANSPORTATION AND PRACTICAL INFORMATION. Trains run from Wrocław Główny, ul. Piłsudskiego 105 (☎367 5882), to: Kraków (4½hr., 13 per day, 45-85zł); Poznań (3¼hr., 25 per day, 25-55zł); Warsaw (4¼-6hr., 8 per day, 50-90zł); Berlin, GER (5½-6¼hr., 2 per day, 185zł). **Buses** leave from behind the train station. From the station, turn left on ul. Piłsudskiego, take a right on ul. Świdnicka, and go past Kościuszki pl. over the Fosa River to reach the **Rynek** (main square). The **tourist office,** Rynek 14, offers **maps** (6-16zł), **bike** rentals (10zł for 1st hr., 5zł per hr. thereafter, 50zł per day; 400zł deposit) and free **Internet.** (☎344 3111; www.itwroclaw.pl. Open daily 9am-9pm.) **Postal Code:** 50-900.

ACCOMMODATIONS AND FOOD. Rooms are plentiful in Wrocław, but reserve ahead for rooms near the center. Check with the tourist office to make reservations in student dorms, which rent rooms July through August (20-50zł). ■**The Stranger Hostel ❷,** ul. Kołłątaja 16/3, is opposite the train station on a road perpendicular to ul. Piłsudskiego, on the third floor of an unmarked building (ring buzzer #3). Quirky touches—from decorated glass toilet seats to a raised platform in the common room—fill the hostel. (☎634 1206. Free laundry and Internet. Reception 24hr. Dorms 50zł. AmEx/MC/V.) Across the street from The Stranger Hostel, the **Youth Hostel Mlodziezowy Dom Kultury Kopernika (HI) ❶,** ul. Kołłątaja 20, has basic dorms. (☎343 8856. Lockout 10am-5pm. Curfew 10pm. Reserve ahead. Dorms 22zł; doubles 58zł. Discount for stays over 1 night. Cash only.)

The tongue-in-cheek presentation of Cuban communism at ■**La Havana ❷,** Kuźnicza 12, has made it wildly popular with the locals, where students feast on Cuban-influenced Polish dishes surrounded by images of Che and Castro. (☎343 2072. Large tropical mixed drinks 12-18zł. Open Su-Th 11am-11:30pm, F-Sa noon-1am. Reservations recommended on weekends. MC/V.) With its sleek, modern decor, **Bazylia ❶,** ul. Kuźnicza 42, is more posh than traditional milk bars, but still serves reliably inexpensive fare. Order at the counter from the long list of milk bar classics, but prepare for a language barrier if you don't speak Polish. (Open M-F 7am-8pm, Sa-Su 7:30am-8pm. Entrees 3-7zł. Open M-F 7am-7pm, Sa 8am-5pm. Cash only.) Etruscan-style frescoes and comfortable sidewalk seating on the *Rynek* set the tone at **Kaliteros ❸,** one of a surprising number of local "Mediterranean" restaurants. (☎343 5617. Greek entrees 20-60zł. Open M-Th 11am-11pm, F-Su 11am-midnight.) The new cafe-bistro **French Connection ❷,** ul. Kuźnicza 10, right off the market square, offers a bewildering variety of both sweet and savory *naleśniki* (6-12zł; extra toppings 0.50-2zł) stuffed with fillings in a sparse but elegant French-themed setting. (Open daily 10am-10pm. MC/V.)

SIGHTS AND NIGHTLIFE. The Gothic **Ratusz** (Town Hall) towers over the *Rynek* in the heart of the city. The beautiful central street **ulica Świdnicka** runs past the *Rynek*. The rotunda containing the 120-by-5m ■**Racławice Panorama,** ul. Purkyniego 11, was the site of an 18th-century peasant insurrection against the Russian occupation. To reach it, face away from the *Ratusz*, bear left onto ul. Kuźnicza, then turn right onto ul. Kotlarska, which becomes ul. Purkyniego. (☎344 2344. Shows 2 per hr. 9:30am-5pm. Open Tu-Su 9am-4pm. 20zł, students 15zł.) A ticket to the panorama includes admission to the **National Museum** (Muzeum Narodowe), pl. Powstańców Warszawy 5, across the street, whose exhibits range from medieval sculpture to modern art. (Open W, F, Su 10am-4pm; Th 9am-4pm, Sa

POLAND

10am-6pm. 15zł, students 10zł; Sa free.) The impressive Gothic buildings and winding roads of **Uniwersytet Wrocławski** (Wrocław University) form the cultural center of the city. **Aula Leopoldina**, an 18th-century frescoed lecture hall, is perhaps its most impressive sight, though the **Mathematical Tower**, pl. Uniwcrcoytecka 1, offers a sweeping view of Wrocław. (Pl. Uniwersytecka 1, 2nd fl. ☎ 375 2618. Open M-Tu and Th-Su 10am-3pm. All the university sights 8zł, students 6zł.) Across the Oder River lies the serene **Plac Katedralny** (Cathedral Square) and the 13th-century **Katedra św. Jana Chrzciciela** (Cathedral of St. John the Baptist) with its impressive spires. (Open M-Sa 10am-5:30pm, Su 2-4pm. 4zł, students 3zł.)

For nightlife, head to ▧**Bezenność** (Insomnia), where a mannequin dressed as a grey-haired woman gazes eerily down onto patrons in upholstered chairs. A raucous mix of dance, hip-hop, and rock heat up the loft-like hall split down the middle by the bar. (Cover F-Sa 5zł. Beer 6zł. Open Su-Th 6pm-1am, F-Sa 6pm-4am. Cash only.) Stop by **Niebo Cafe**, ul. Ruska 51, a boisterous alt-rock hideout, for an unpretentious drink. (☎ 342 9867. Beer 6zł. Open 1pm-last customer.) For a more laidback crowd, the bar-cafe **Kawiarnia "Pod Kalamburem,"** ul. Kuźnicza 29A, founded by an experimental theater group, hosts readings and film screenings. (Beer 3-15zł. Open M-Th 1pm-midnight, F-Sa 1pm-late, Su 4pm-midnight. Cash only.)

POZNAŃ
☎ 061

International trade fairs throughout the year bring business travelers to industrial Poznań (pop. 59,000), the capital of Wielkopolska (Greater Poland). The sprawling city has inefficient public transportation and few tourist attractions outside of the cobblestone **Stary Rynek** (Old Square). Opulent 15th-century merchants' residences surround the Renaissance **Ratusz** (Town Hall), now a history museum. (☎ 852 5613. Open M-Tu 10am-4pm, W 11am-6pm, F 9am-4pm, Sa-Su 10am-3pm. 5.50zł, students 3.50zł, Sa free.) The ▧**Museum of Musical Instruments** (Muzeum Instrumentów Muzycznych), Stary Rynek 45, exhibits an eclectic assortment of antique music-makers, including one of Chopin's pianos. (☎ 852 0857. Open Tu-Sa 11am-5pm, Su 11am-3pm. 5.50zł, students 3.50zł, Sa free.) The first Polish cathedral, the **Cathedral of St. Peter and St. Paul** (Katedra Piotra i Pawła), is on the outskirts of town. Its ▧**Golden Chapel** (Kaplica Złota) contains the tombs of Prince Mieszko I and his son Bolesław Chrobry, the first king of Poland. (Cathedral open M-Sa 9am-6pm, Su 1:15-6:30pm.)

▧**Frolic Goats Hostel ❸**, is by far the best value in the city, with state-of-the-art facilities, comfortable beds, clean baths, and a laid-back staff. (☎ 501 144 704. Dorms 50-60zł, private rooms 70-100zł per person. Free Internet. Breakfast included. Reception 24hr. MC/V.) **Przemysław ❶**, ul. Głogowska 16, books private rooms near the main square. (☎ 866 3560; www.przemyslaw.com.pl. Singles 42zł, during fairs 70zł; doubles 65/100zł. Open M-F 8am-6pm, Sa 10am-2pm; open 2hr. later during fairs; July-Aug. closed some Sa.) Reasonably priced beds are elusive; book in advance. The new **Green Way Bar Wegetariański ❶**, offers generous servings from a rotating menu of lasagnas, salads, and soy dishes. (☎ 843 4027. Entrees 5-9zł. Open M-F 11am-7pm, Sa noon-7pm, Su noon-5pm. Cash only.)

Trains run from **Poznań Główny**, ul. Dworcowa 1 (☎ 866 1212), to Kraków (5hr., 9 per day, 50-80zł), Warsaw (3-4½hr., 12 per day, 50-90zł), and Berlin, GER (3½hr., 6 per day, 95-125zł). To get to the center, exit the train station, climb the stairs, turn left on the bridge and then right on Roosevelta. After several blocks, turn right on Śweti Marci and catch any **tram** going to the right along Św. Marcin from the end of Dworcowa. From Roosevelta, trams #5 and 8 run to *Stare Miasto*. The **tourist office**, Stary Rynek 59/60, has free maps and books rooms. (☎ 852 6156; fax 855 3379. Open June-Aug. M-F 9am-8pm, Sa 10am-6pm.) **Postal Code:** 61890.

TORUŃ
☎ 056

Long known as "beautiful red Toruń" (pop. 210,000) for its impressive brick-and-stone architecture, this university town is the birthplace of Mikołaj Kopernik, better known as Copernicus. Five-hundred-year-old churches and the ruins of the local Teutonic castle are fascinating stops for a walk down the city's cobblestone streets, or take a stroll down the riverwalk on the banks of the Wisła.

▐▌▐ TRANSPORTATION AND PRACTICAL INFORMATION. Trains leave from **Torun Głowny,** Kujawska 1 (☎94 36. Open M-F 7am-5pm, Sa-Su 7am-2pm) for: Gdańsk (3¼hr., 7 per day, 38zł); Łódź (3hr., 9 per day, 21-34zł); Poznań (2¼hr., 7 per day, 20-33zł); Warsaw (2¾hr., 6 per day, 40zł). Buses leave from **Dworzec PKS,** Dąbrowskiego 26 (☎655 5333; open 4am-midnight) for Gdańsk (3½hr., 2 per day, 34zł), Łódź (3¼hr., 13 per day, 27zł) and Warsaw (4hr., 6 per day, 32zł). **Polski Express** (☎228 445 555) runs buses from the Ruch kiosk north of pl. Teatralny to Łódź (3hr., 1 per day, 37/22zł) and Warsaw (3½hr., 9 per day, 55/30zł). The **tourist office** and most sights are in and around **Rynek Staromiejski** (Old Town Square). To get to the *Rynek* from the train station, take bus #22 or 27 across the **Wisła River** to **plac Rapackiego.** Head through the park, with the river on your right, to find the square. (☎621 0931; www.it.torun.pl. Open May-Aug. M and Sa 9am-4pm, Tu-F 9am-6pm, Su 9am-1pm; Sept.-Apr. M and Sa 9am-4pm, Tu-F 9am-6pm. Maps free-7zł.) **Postal Code:** 87100.

▐▐ ACCOMMODATIONS AND FOOD. There are a number of reasonably priced accommodations in the center, but they fill up fast, so call ahead. Inexpensive hotels are often the best-situated budget option, but deal-seekers can check the tourist office for far-flung rooms in university dorms in July and August. (Singles 45zł; doubles 60zł.) Toruń's first true backpacker hostel, ▓**Orange Hostel ❶,** ul. Prosta 19, gets everything right, from a location in the middle of the Old Town to laundry facilities that even include—amazingly—a dryer. (☎652 0033; www.hostelorange.pl. Kitchen. Breakfast included 7am-noon. Free laundry. Free Internet. Reception 24hr. Dorms 30zł; singles 50zł; doubles 80zł; triples 120zł.) **Attic Hostel ❶,** ul. gen. Chłopickiego 4, across the tracks from the Toruń Miasto train station, offers basic beds in large, bright rooms. Breakfast included. Free Internet. Reception 7am-10pm. (☎659 8517. May-Aug. large dorms 30zł; singles 50zł; singles 70zł; doubles 100zł; triples 120zł; quads 160zł. Sept.-Apr. 25/50/80/105/140zł. MC/V.) Although a trek from town, **PTTK Dom Turystyczny ❶,** Legionów 24, offers friendly service and fresh linens. (☎/fax 622 3855. Check-in 2pm. Check-out noon. Reserve ahead. Dorms 28zł; singles 60zł; doubles 76zł; triples 94zł; quads 112zł; quints 140zł. Cash only.) The **Kopernik Factory Store ❷,** Żeglarska 25, sells the most collectible dessert in town: gingerbread effigies of Polish kings, saints, and astronomers from 0.70zł for a small taste to 26zł for top-of-the-line historical figures. (☎621 0561. Open M-F 9am-7pm, Sa-Su 10am-2pm. MC/V.) The popular **Manekin ❶,** Rynek Staromiejski 16, serves massive yet artful sweet and savory *naleśniki* for 3-11zł. The curry chicken and cheese (8.50zł) is a favorite. (☎652 2885. Open Su-Th 10am-10pm, F-Sa 10am-11pm. Cash only.)

▐▐ SIGHTS AND NIGHTLIFE. Stare Miasto (Old Town), on the right bank of the Wisła River, was constructed by the Teutonic Knights in the 13th century. **Dom Kopernika,** the probable birthplace of Copernicus, has been restored and showcases artifacts pertaining to the astronomer. A sound-and-light show centered on a miniature model of the medieval city (c. 1550) plays every 30min. and features an excellent video about the town's early history. Choose from eight lan-

THE LOCAL STORY

ŁÓDŹ KALISKA

Chances are, most of the bars you frequent don't have manifestos. In Łódź, however, the line between a bar and an art movement can be blurry. Not just any drink-tank, Łódź Kaliska is named for the art movement founded in Łódz in 1979 and has a seasoned cult following: if you're here on the weekend, you may run into some of Poland's most acclaimed actors and artists taking a flaming shot off the club's tilted bar. Łódź Kaliska, the group, was originally created as an anti-Communist art group. Under martial law in the 80s the group printed a secret art magazine, Tango, and screened films in a hidden location.

Once a perennial object of criticism for both the political and the artistic establishment, today the group enjoys respect from scholars and bargoers alike. The walls and furniture of Łódź Kaliska—the bar—are adorned with the group's influential work, and the unusual toilets, along with the Bartender's Special Shot, are among the artistic touches tucked into this playful local institution. Spend a night here to understand why people drive all the way from Warsaw to drink at Kaliska—and why many locals consider this the best bar in Poland.

Łódź Kaliska, Piotrkowska 102 (Group ☎63 06 95 51; www.lodz-kaliska.pl. Club: www.klub.lodz-kaliska.pl). Disco F-Sa. Open M-Sa noon-3am, Su 4pm-3am.

guages, including English. (Kopernika 15/17. ☎622 7038, ext.13. Open W, F, Su 10am-4pm; Tu, Th, Sa noon-6pm. 10zł students, 6zł. English-language captions available. Sound-and-light show 10/6zł. Both 18/11zł.) The 14th-century **Ratusz** (Town Hall) that dominates *Rynek Staromiejski* is a fine example of monumental burgher architecture. (☎622 7038. Museum open May-Aug. Tu-W and Sa noon-6pm, Th and Su 10am-4pm; Sept.-Apr. Tu-Su 10am-4pm. 10zł, students 6zł, Su free. Tower open May-Sept. Tu-Su 10am-8pm. 10/6zł.) A revolt in 1454 led to the destruction of the **Teutonic Knights' Castle,** but its ruins, on ul. Przedzamcze, are still impressive. (☎622 7039. Open daily 9am-8pm. Free). The 15m **Krzywą Wieżą** (Leaning Tower), ul. Krzywą Wieżą 17, was built in 1271 by a Teutonic Knight as punishment for breaking his order's rule of celibacy. The **Cathedral of St. John the Baptist and St. John the Evangelist** (Bazylika Katedralna pw. św. Janów), at the corner of ul. Żeglarska and św. Jana, is the most impressive of the many Gothic churches in the area. (At the corner of Żeglarska and Sw. Jana. Open Apr.-Oct. M-Sa 8:30am-5:30pm, Su 2-5:30pm. 2zł, students 1zł. Tower 6/4zł.) Just across the *Rynek Staromiejski* are the stained-glass windows and intricate altars of the **Church of the Virgin Mary** (Kosciól sw. Marii), on ul. Panny Marii. (Open M-Sa 8am-5pm. Audio tour 2zł.)

◼**Niebo,** Rynek Staromiejski 1, whose name translates to "heaven," is a Gothic cellar beneath the *Ratusz* boasting live jazz and cabaret. (☎621 0327. Open Su-Th noon-midnight, F-Sa noon-2am. Check out the folk art at the adjacent pub **Piwnica pod Aniolami** (Cellar Beneath the Angels; ☎658 5482. Beer 4-5zł. Open M-F 10am-1am, Sa-Su 10am-4am. Cash only.) **Club Jazz God,** Rabianska 17, lives up to its name with free live jazz Su 10pm; the rest of the week, students fill scattered seats for lively conversation and thunderous reggae, rock, and Polish pop starting around 8:30pm. (☎65 22 13 08; www.jazz-god.torun.com.pl. Open Su-Th 5pm-2am, F-Sa 5pm-4am.) On the second and third floors of the Leaning Tower is the **Galeria "Krzywą Wieżą,"** Pod Krzywą Wieżą 1/3, a gathering point for students and professors. (Beer 4.50-6zł. Open M-F 1pm-1am, Sa-Su 10am-2am.)

ŁÓDŹ   ☎042

Poland's second largest city, Łódź (WOODGE; pop. 813,000) has few postcard-worthy attractions, but it is home to some of the country's most interesting and least known sights and tastes. Łódź once housed the largest Jewish ghetto in Europe; today, residents are putting this plucky working-class city back on the map by hosting extraordinary art festivals and Jewish heritage exhibits. The eerily beautiful **Jewish Cem-**

etery (Cmentarz Żydowski), on ul. Zmienna, has over 200,000 graves. Near the entrance is a memorial to the Jews killed in the ghetto; signs lead to the **Ghetto Fields** (Pole Ghettowe), which are lined with faintly marked graves. Take tram #1 from ul. Kilinskiego or #6 from ul. Kościuszki or Zachodnia north to the end of the line (20min.); continue up the street, turn left on ul. Zmienna, and enter through the small gate on the right. (☎656 7019. Open May-Sept. Su-Th 9am-5pm, F 9am-3pm; Oct.-Apr. Su-F 8am-3pm. Closed Jewish holidays. 4zł, free for those visiting relatives' graves.) The **Jewish Community Center** (Gmina Wyznaniowa Żydowska), ul. Pomorska 18, in the town center, has information on those buried in the cemetery. (☎633 5156. Open M-F 10am-2pm. English spoken.)

The convenient **PTSM Youth Hostel (HI) ❶**, ul. Legionów 27, has quiet rooms with spacious bath and TV. Take tram #4 toward Helenówek from Fabryczna station to pl. Wolnosci; walk on Legionów past Zachodnia. (☎630 6680; www.yhlodz.pl. Curfew 10pm. Singles 65zł; doubles 80zł; triples 120zł. MC/V.) 🍴**Anatewka ❸**, ul. 6 Sierpnia 2/4, serves phenomenal Jewish cuisine with flair. (Entrees 15-45zł. Open daily 11am-11pm.) **Green Way Bar Wegetarianski ❶**, Piotrkowska 80, serves healthy vegetarian meals with fresh and seasonal ingredients. (☎632 0852. Entrees 7.50zł. Open daily 10am-9pm. Cash only.) Łódź's main thoroughfare, **ulica Piotrkowska**, is a bustling pedestrian shopping drag by day and a lively pub strip by night. Designed by an arts collective, the legendary bar and club 🍴**Łódź Kaliska**, ul. Piotrkowska 102, draws famous Polish actors and artists to its fun dance floor. (☎630 6955; www.klub.lodzkaliska.pl. Beer 8zł. Open M-Sa noon-3am, Su 4pm-3am.)

Trains run from **Łódź Kaliska**, al. Unii Lubelskiej 1 (☎41 02), to: **Kraków** (3¼hr., 1 per day, 46zł); **Gdańsk** (7½hr., 5 per day, 49zł); **Warsaw** (2hr., 3 per day, 31zł); **Wrocław** (3¾hr., 3 per day, 42zł). **Polski Express buses** (☎02 28 54 02 85; www.polskiexpress.org) depart from Łódź Fabryczna, pl. B. Sałacińskiego 1, to **Gdańsk** (4hr., 1 per day, 57zł) and **Warsaw** (2½hr., 7 per day, 36zł). The IT **tourist office**, ul. Piotrkowska 87, books rooms, including university dorms in summer. (☎638 5955; www.cityoflodz.pl. Open M-F 9am-7pm, Sa-Su 10am-3pm.) **Postal Code:** 90-001.

GDAŃSK   ☎058

At the mouth of the Wisła and Motława Rivers, Gdańsk (gh-DA-insk; pop. 458,000) has flourished for more than a millennium as a crossroads of art and commerce. This onetime Hanseatic trade city was treasured as the "gateway to the sea" during Poland's foreign occupation in the 18th and 19th centuries. Gdańsk has faced its challenges admirably—WWII left the ancient city center in ruins, yet today much of it been restored. The rise of Lech Wałęsa's Solidarity movement, before its brutal suppression by martial law in 1981, brought months of hope to the now-famous shipyards and to the Eastern Bloc. Now, with its amber-filled beaches, cobblestone alleys, and sprawling construction, Gdańsk displays both beauty and brawn.

█ TRANSPORTATION

Planes: Gdańsk Lech Wałesa Airport, 12km west of the city center. ZKMS buses run Gdańsk Główny train station (30-40min., around 8zł). Budget airlines (p. 44) that fly to the city include **easyJet, Ryanair,** and **Wizz Air.**

Trains: Gdańsk Główny, Podwale Grodzkie 1 (☎94 36). To: **Kraków** (7-11hr., 15 per day, 59-105zł); **Łódź** (8hr., 6 per day, 49zł); **Lublin** (7hr., 3 per day, 54-98zł); **Malbork** (50min., 40 per day, 10-32zł); **Poznań** (4-5hr., 7 per day, 46zł); **Toruń** (3¼hr., 6 per day, 38zł); **Warsaw** (4hr., 22 per day, 50-82zł); **Wrocław** (6-7hr., 4 per day, 52zł). **SKM** (Fast City Trains; ☎628 5778) run to **Gdynia** (35min.; 4zł, students 2zł) and **Sopot**

(20min.; 2.80/1.40zł) 6 per hr. during the day and less frequently at night. Buy tickets downstairs. Punch ticket in a *kasownik* machine before boarding.

Buses: 3 Maja 12 (☎302 1532), behind the train station, connected by an underground passageway. To: **Malbork** (1hr., 8 per day, 10-13zł); **Toruń** (2½hr., 2 per day, 32zł); **Warsaw** (5¾hr., 9 per day, 45zł); **Kaliningrad, RUS** (6-7hr., 2 per day, 28zł). **Polski Express** buses run to **Warsaw** (4½hr., 2 per day, 45zł).

Public Transportation: Gdańsk has an extensive **bus** and **tram** system. Buses run 6am-10pm. Tickets priced by the min. 10min. 1.40zł; 30min. 2.80zł; 1hr. 4.20zł; day pass 9zł. **Night buses,** marked "n," 10pm-6am. 3.30zł; night pass 5.50zł. Students ½-price.

Taxis: To avoid paying inflated tourist rates for taxis, book a cab by phone or over the Internet at the state-run **MPT** (☎96 33; www.artusmpt.gda.pl).

◢▪▮ ORIENTATION AND PRACTICAL INFORMATION

Although Gdańsk sits on the Baltic Coast, its commercial center is 5km inland. From the train and bus stations, the center is just a few blocks southeast, bordered by **Wały Jagiellońskie** and by the **Motława River**. Take the underpass in front of the station, go right, and turn left on Heweliusza. Turn right on Rajska and follow the signs to **Główne Miasto** (Main Town), turning left on Długa, also called **Trakt Królewski** (Royal Way). Długa becomes Długi Targ. Piwna and Sw. Ducha are Główne Miasto's other main thoroughfare and parallel to Długa just to the north.

Tourist Offices: PTTK Gdańsk, Długa 45 (☎301 9151; www.pttk-gdansk.com.pl), in Główne Miasto, has **free maps.** Tours May-Sept. for groups of 3-10, 80zł per person. Open May-Sept. M-F 9am-5pm, Sa-Su 9am-3pm; Oct.-Apr. M-F 9am-6pm.

Budget Travel: Almatur, Długi Targ 11, 2nd fl. (☎301 2403; www.almatur.gda.pl). Sells **ISIC** (59zł), and books air and ferry tickets. Open M-F 10am-6pm, Sa 10am-2pm.

Currency Exchange: Bank Pekao SA, Garncarska 31 (☎801 365 365). **Cashes traveler's checks** for 1% commission and provides MC/V **cash advances** for no commission. Open M-F 8am-6pm, first and last Sa of each month 10am-2pm.

English-Language Bookstore: Empik, Podwale Grodzkie 8 (☎301 6288, ext. 115). Sells maps. Open M-Sa 9am-9pm, Su 11am-8pm.

24hr. Pharmacy: Apteka Plus (☎763 1074), at the train station. Ring bell at night.

Medical Services: For **emergency care,** go to **Szpital Specjalistyczny im. M. Kopernika,** Nowe Ogrody 5 (☎302 3031).

Internet: Jazz'n'Java, Tkacka 17/18 (☎305 3616; www.cafe.jnj.pl), in the Old Town. 3zł per 30min., 5zł per hr. Open daily 10am-10pm.

Post Office: Długa 23/28 (☎301 88 53). For **Poste Restante,** use the entrance on Pocztowa. **Telephones** inside. Open M-F 8am-8pm, Sa 9am-3pm. **Postal Code:** 80-801.

▮ ACCOMMODATIONS

With Gdańsk's limited tourist infrastructure and increasing popularity among travelers, it's best to make accommodation arrangements ahead, especially in summer. **University dorms** are open to travelers in July and August; for further info consult the **PTTK** tourist office (p. 794). Private rooms (20-80zł) can be arranged through either PTTK or **Grand-Tourist ❷** (Biuro Podróży i Zakwaterowania), ul. Podwale Grodzkie 8, across from Empik. (☎301 2634; www.grand-tourist.pl. Open daily July-Aug. 8am-8pm; Sept.-June M-Sa 10am-6pm. Singles from 50-60zł; doubles 80-100zł; apartments 180-280zł. Cash only.)

▨ **Hostel Przy Targu Rybnym,** ul. Grodzka 21 (☎301 5627; www.gdanskhostel.com), off Targ Rybny, across from the *baszta* (tower). Bright, well-appointed hostel has a hilari-

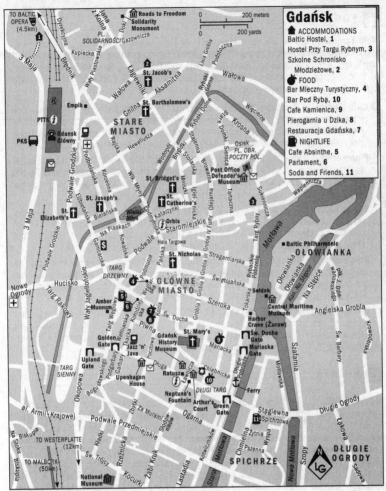

Gdańsk

🏠 **ACCOMMODATIONS**
Baltic Hostel, **1**
Hostel Przy Targu Rybnym, **3**
Szkolne Schronisko
  Młodzieżowe, **2**
🍴 **FOOD**
Bar Mleczny Turystyczny, **4**
Bar Pod Rybą, **10**
Cafe Kamienica, **9**
Pierogarnia u Dzika, **8**
Restauracja Gdańska, **7**
🌙 **NIGHTLIFE**
Cafe Absinthe, **5**
Parlament, **6**
Soda and Friends, **11**

ously bitchy staff. Breakfast included. Free Internet. Reception 24hr. Dorms 50zł; doubles 200-250zł; quads and quints 240-350zł. Cash only. ❶

Baltic Hostel, 3 Maja 25 (☎721 9657; www.baltichostel.com), 3min. from the station. From the train station, take the KFC underpass to bus station, then go right on 3 Maja and take the pedestrian path on the right. The renovated Baltic has excellent rooms full of backpackers. Crowded bathroom leaves little privacy, and the main hostel doors are often left unlocked. Breakfast and linens included. Free Internet. Free bike and kayak use. Reception 24hr. Dorms 35-40zł; doubles 50zł. Cash only. ❷

Szkolne Schronisko Młodzieżowe, Wałowa 21 (☎301 2313). From the train station, follow Karmelicka from City Forum; go left on Rajska and right on Wałowa. Dorms feature new furnishings. Full kitchen and common room set the facilities a cut above most HI hostels, but the living is as clean as the rooms: there's a midnight curfew and no smoking or drinking. Reception 8am-10pm. Dorms 13-20zł; singles 23-30zł. Cash only. ❶

◧ FOOD

Hala Targowa, on Pańska, in the shadow of Kościół św. Katarzyny, just off Podwale Staromiejskie has rows of stands selling everything from raw meat and
dried fruits to shoe soles. (Open May-Aug. M-F 9am-7pm, Sa 9am-5pm; Sept-Apr.
M-F 9am-6pm, Sa 9am-3pm.) An **Esta** supermarket is at Podwale Staromiejskie
109/112, in Targ Drzewny. (Open M-Sa 10am-10pm, Su noon-10pm.)

■ **Cafe Kamienica,** Mariacka 37/39 (☎301 1230), in St. Mary's shadow. Enjoy fresh, delicate entrees, such as salad with grilled chicken (14zł), next to antique couches and an
elegant stone patio. Tea 5zł. Superb coffee drinks 6-11zł. Light entrees 7-30zł. Open
daily June-Sept. 9am-midnight; Oct.-May 10am-10pm. AmEx/MC/V. ❷

Pierogarnia u Dzika (Wild Boar Pierogi Bar), Piwna 59/60 (☎305 2676). Locals swear
by these *pierogi* (12-18zł) stuffed with everything from caviar to strawberries. Try the
rich *pierogi farmerski* with chicken, nuts, and raisins (14zł). The 35-piece mixed platter
(50zł) is terrific for large groups. Open daily 11am-11pm. MC/V. ❸

Bar Pod Rybą (Bar Under the Fish), Długi Targ 35/38/1 (☎305 1307). An unusual take
on a Polish staple—huge baked potatoes with fillings (6-20zł) that run the gamut from
chicken *shawarma* to chili (4-7.50zł). The Hungarian sausage topping is top-notch.
Open daily July-Aug. 11am-10pm; Sept.-June 11am-7pm. AmEx/MC/V. ❶

Restaurancja Gdańska, ul. Sw. Ducha 16/24. Crowded walls covered in clocks, oil
paintings, and figurines add a sense of Baroque topsy-turvy to crystal elegance. A favorite of local celebrities, including former president Lech Wałesa (try his "favorite ribs," a
restaurant specialty; 25zł). Entrees 18-60zł. Open daily 11am-midnight. ❷

Bar Mleczny Turystyczny, Szeroka 8/10 (☎301 60 13). The brightly painted walls and
gleaming new wood tables of this renovated milk bar complement truly delicious Polish
staples. *Gołąbki* (stuffed cabbage, 4.20zł), are among the meaty specialties (3-6zł).
Open M-F 7:30am-6pm, Sa-Su 9am-4pm. Cash only. ❶

◉ SIGHTS

DŁUGI TARG. Długi Targ (Long Market) is the handsome square at the heart of
Główne Miasto (Main Town). The stone Upland Gate and the elegant blue-gray
Golden Gate, emblazoned with gold leaf moldings and the shields of Poland, Prus-
sia, and Germany, mark the western entrance to ul. Długa. In the square, **Neptune's
Fountain** (Fontanna Neptuna) faces the 16th-century facade of **Arthur's Court** (Dwór
Artusa), a palace with a Renaissance interior and wood-carved spiral staircase
that was restored in 1997. At the intersection of ul. Długa and Długi Targ, the 14th-
century **Ratusz** (Town Hall) houses a branch of the **Gdańsk History Museum**
(Muzeum Historii Gdańska), which covers the city's past from its first historical
mention to the rubble left behind by WWII. *(Ratusz open June-Sept. M 11am-3pm, Tu-
Sa 10am-6pm, Su 11am-6pm; Oct.-May Tu-Sa 10am-4pm, Su 11am-4pm. Arthur's Court
open Tu-Su 10am-3pm. Each 8zł, students 5zł; combined ticket 15/7zł; W free.)* A block
north, the brick **St. Mary's Church** (Kościół Najświętszej Marii Panny) has an intricate 15th-century astronomical clock and a panoramic view of the city. *(Open June-
Aug. M-Sa 9am-5:30pm, Su 1-5:30pm; low-season hours vary. 3zł, students 1.50zł.)*

ELSEWHERE IN GŁÓWNE MIASTO. In the vaults of a former Franciscan monastery, the ■**National Museum** (Muzeum Narodowe) has a large collection of 16th- to
20th-century art and furniture, including Hans Memling's *Last Judgment*. *(Toruń-
ska 1. ☎301 70 61; www.muzeum.narodowe.gda.pl. Open June to mid-Sept. Tu-F 9am-4pm, Sa-
Su 10am-5pm; mid-Sept. to May Tu-Su 9am-4pm. 10zł, students 6zł; Sa free.)* The **Memorial to
the Defenders of the Post Office Square** (Obrońców Poczty) honors the postal work-

ers' courageous stand against the invading Germans at the start of WWII. *(From Pod-wale Staromiejskie, go north on Tartaczna and turn right onto Obrońców Polskiej Poczty 1-2.* ☎ *301 7611. Open Tu-F 10am-4pm, Sa-Su 10:30am-4pm. 3zł, students 2zł; Tu free.)* Row houses line the cobblestoned ul. św. Ducha, ul. Mariacka, and ul. Chlebnicka, north of Długi Targ. Ul. Mariacka, with its stone porches and gaping dragon-head gutter spouts, leads to riverside ul. Długie Pobrzeże. To the left is the huge Gothic **Harbor Crane** (Żuraw) from the 13th century, part of the **Central Maritime Museum** (Centralne Muzeum Morskie). Two more branches of the museum lie across the river: one on land, the other on the ship **Sołdek**. *(☎ 301 8611. Open June-Aug. daily 10am-6pm; Sept.-May Tu-Su 9:30am-4pm. Crane 6zł, students 4zł. Museum 6/4zł. Sołdek 6/4zł. Shuttle boat round-trip 3/1.50zł.)* The flags of the Soviet bloc's first trade union, Lech Wałęsa's Solidarity (Solidarność), fly again at the **Solidarity Monument,** pl. Solidarności, north of the city center at the end of ul. Wały Piastowskie. At the ■**Roads to Freedom** (Drogi do wolniści) in the Gdańsk Shipyard (Stocznia Gdańska) where the movement was born, powerful multimedia depict the rise of the movement. *(Doki 1, in the Shipyard. ☎ 308 4280. Open Tu-Su 10am-5pm. 6zł, students 4zł; W free.)*

WESTERPLATTE. When Germany attacked Poland, the little island fort guarding the entrance to Gdańsk's harbor gained unfortunate distinction as the first target of WWII. Outnumbered 20 to one, the Polish troops held out for a week until a lack of food and munitions forced them to surrender. **Guardhouse #1** has been turned into a museum. *(☎ 343 69 72. Open daily May-Sept. 9am-7pm. 3zł, students 2zł. English booklet 6zł.)* The main attraction lies down the path leading beyond the exhibit past the bunker ruins to the massive **Memorial to the Defenders of the Coast.** The words *Nigdy Więcej Wojny* (Never More War) are inscribed at the base of the monument, on a tall hill overlooking the city. *(From the train station, take bus #106 or 606 south to the last stop. The bus stop is to the right of the station entrance in front of the KFC. Żegluga Gdańska also runs a 50min. ferry; 1 per hr. 10am-6pm; round-trip 34zł, students 18zł. ☎ 301 4926. Board by the Green Gate, Zielona Brama, at the end of Długi Targ.)*

■ NIGHTLIFE

When the sun sets, crowds turn to the party spots of **Długi Targ.** *City* lists events in the Tri-City Area, and *Gdańsk in Your Pocket* offers updated club listings. **Cafe Absinthe,** ul. św. Ducha 2, next to Teatr Wybrzeże, attracts ruminating intellectuals by day and a rambunctious, absinthe-imbibing set by night. *(☎ 320 3784. Open daily 10am-4am.)* Restaurant and nightclub **Soda and Friends,** ul. Chmielna 103/104, pulsates with energy and enthusiasm. *(☎ 346 3861; www.sodacafe.pl. Open Su-W 11am-2am, Th-Sa noon-5am. Kitchen closes midnight.)* The popular club **Parlament,** sw. Ducha 2, entices a young crowd with its mile-long bar, fog machine, and maze of voyeuristic balconies overlooking the dance floor. *(☎ 302 1365. Beer 5zl. 18+. Cover Th after 10pm 5zl; F-Sa before 10pm 5zl, 10zl after. Purchase drinks with non-refundable "prepaid cards," which are available at the entrance. Open Tu-Sa 8pm-late. Dance floor open Th-Sa 10pm-late.)*

■ DAYTRIP FROM GDAŃSK

MALBORK. Malbork (pop. 40,000) is home to the **world's largest brick castle,** built by the Teutonic Knights in the 14th century. To get there, turn right out of the station on ul. Dworcowa, then left at the fork. Go around the corner to the roundabout and cross to ul. Kościuszki, then veer right on ul. Piasłowska and follow the signs for the castle. *(Trains 40min.-1hr.; 40 per day; 9.30zł, express 32zł. Buses 1hr., 8 per day, 9.40-13zł. Both run from Gdańsk to Malbork. ☎ 647 0800; www.zamek.malbork.com.pl. Castle open May-Sept. Tu-Su 9am-7pm; Oct.-Apr. Tu-Su 9am-3pm. Courtyards, terraces, and* *moats stay open 1hr. later. Kasa open 8:30am-7:30pm. Castle 30zł, students 17.50zł; 3hr. Polish tour included. English-language tours 3 per day; 5zł. Tour required to enter the castle, but you can wander off on your own once inside. M free; with Polish tour 5zł, English-speaking guide 150zł. Sound-and-light show May 15-Oct. 15 10pm; 5zł. AmEx/MC/V.*

SOPOT
☎058

Poland's premier resort town, Sopot (pop. 50,000) draws visitors to its sandy beaches and renowned nightlife. Restaurants, shops, and musicians dot the pedestrian promenade **ulica Bohaterów Monte Cassino**. Europe's longest **molo** (wooden pier; 512m) provides sweeping views of the Baltic. (Open M-F. 2.50zł, Sa-Su 3.50zł.) In summer, the beachside, wooden **Copacabana** becomes Poland's choice party spot, shedding its by-day restaurant and yacht club veneer. (www.copaca-banasopot.pl. Cover after 10pm. Open 24hr.) **Soho clubogaleria,** ul. Monte Cassino 61, spins electropop, house, and lounge with attitude. (☎551 6527. Beer 7zł. Open daily noon-5am.) **Mandarynka,** ul. Bema 6, off ul. Monte Cassino, offers three tangerine-splashed floors of partying. (☎550 4563. Beer 7zł. Open daily noon-5am.)

Affordable university **dorms,** which can be arranged through the tourist office, are available in summer. Adorned with fishing nets and hanging blowfish, █**Bar Przystań ❶,** al. Wojska Polskiego 11, along the beach, serves fresh seafood. (☎550 0241; www.barprzystan.pl. Fresh fish 4.20-7zł per 100g. Fish salads from 3.20zł per 100g. Open daily 11am-11pm. Cash only.) For dirt-cheap Polish food served in simple elegance try **Bar Elita ❷,** ul. Podjazd 3, across the tracks from ul. Dworcowa. (☎551 0620. Pierogi 8-12zł. Open 11am-last customer. Cash only.) The **SKM commuter rail** connects Sopot to Gdańsk (20min.; 1-6 per hr.; 2.80zł, students 1.40zł). Ulica Dworcowa begins at the station and leads to ul. Monte Cassino, which runs along the sea to the pier. **Ferries** (*tramwaj wodny;* ☎604 837 793) head from the end of the pier to Gdańsk (1hr.; 4 per day; 8zł, students 4zł) and Hel (1½hr., 3 per day, 12/6zł). The IT **tourist office,** ul. Dworcowa 4, by the train station, sells maps (4-5zł) and arranges rooms. (☎550 3783. Open daily June to mid-Sept. 9am-8pm; mid-Sept. to May M-F 10am-6pm.)

PORTUGAL

While Portugal is small, its imposing forests and mountains, scenic vineyards, and almost 2000km of coastline rival the attractions of Spain. Portugal's capital, Lisbon, offers marvelous museums, castles, and churches. The country experienced international glory and fabulous wealth 400 hundred years ago during the Golden Age of Vasco da Gama. Despite suffering under the dictatorship of Salazar for 30 years in the 20th century, Portugal has reemerged as a European cultural center with a growing economy. Extremes of fortune have contributed to the unique Portuguese concept of *saudade*, a yearning for the glories of the past and a dignified resignation to the fact that the future can never compete. Visitors may experience *saudade* through a *fado* singer's song or over a glass of port, but Portugal's attractions are more likely to inspire delight than nostalgia.

 DISCOVER PORTUGAL: SUGGESTED ITINERARIES

THREE DAYS. Make your way through **Lisbon** (1 day; p. 804); venture through its famous Moorish district, the Alfama, Castelo de São Jorge, and the Parque das Nações. By night, listen to *fado* and hit the clubs in Barrio Alto. Daytrip to **Sintra's** fairytale castles (1 day; p. 813), then sip wine in **Porto** (1 day; p. 814).

ONE WEEK. After wandering the streets of **Lisbon** (2 days) and **Sintra** (1 day), lounge on the beaches of **Lagos** (1 day; p. 819) and admire the cliffs of **Sagres** (1 day; p. 820). Move on to the university town of **Coimbra** (1 day; p. 816) before

ending your week in **Porto** (1 day).

BEST OF PORTUGAL, TWO WEEKS. After taking in the sights of **Lisbon** (4 days), daytrip to enchanting **Sintra** (1 day). Head down to the infamous beaches and bars of **Lagos** (2 days), where hordes of visitors dance the night away. Take an afternoon in **Sagres** (1 day), once considered the edge of the world. Check out the macabre bone chapel in **Évora** (1 day; p. 817) and the impressive monastery in **Batalha** (1 day; p. 818). Head north to the vibrant cities of **Coimbra** (2 days) and **Porto** (2 days).

ESSENTIALS

FACTS AND FIGURES

Official Name: The Portuguese Republic.
Capital: Lisbon.
Major Cities: Coimbra, Porto.
Population: 10,463,000.
Land Area: 92,000 sq. km.

Time Zone: GMT.
Languages: Portuguese, Mirandese.
Religion: Roman Catholic (85%).
Number of Grape Varietals Authorized for Making Port: 48.

WHEN TO GO

Summer is high season, but the southern coast draws tourists between March and November. In the low season, many hostels slash their prices, and reservations are seldom necessary. While Lisbon and some of the larger towns (especially the university town of Coimbra) burst with vitality year-round, many smaller towns virtually shut down in winter, and sights reduce their hours.

DOCUMENTS AND FORMALITIES

EMBASSIES AND CONSULATES. Foreign embassies in Portugal are in Lisbon. Portuguese embassies abroad include: **Australia,** 23 Culgoa Circuit, O'Malley, Canberra, ACT 2606 (☎612 6290 1733); **Canada,** 645 Island Park Dr., Ottawa, ON K1Y 0B8 (☎613-729-2270); **Ireland,** Knocksinna Mews, 7 Willow Park, Foxrock, Dublin, 18 (☎353 289 4416); **UK,** 11 Belgrave Sq., London, SW1X 8PP (☎020 7235 5331); **US,** 2012 Massachusetts Ave. NW, Washington, D.C., 20036 (☎202-350-5400). **New Zealand** citizens should contact the embassy in Australia.

VISA AND ENTRY INFORMATION. EU citizens do not need a visa. Citizens of Australia, Canada, New Zealand, the UK, and the US do not need a visa for stays up to 90 days, beginning upon entry into any of the countries within the EU's freedom-of-movement zone. For more info, see p. 14. For stays longer than 90 days, all non-EU citizens need visas (around $100), available at Portuguese consulates.

TOURIST SERVICES AND MONEY

EMERGENCY	General Emergency: ☎112.

TOURIST OFFICES. For general info, contact the **Portuguese Tourism Board,** Av. Antonio Augusto de Aguiar, 86, 1004 Lisbon (☎808 78 12 12; www.portugal.org/index.shtml). When in Portugal, stop by municipal and provincial tourist offices, listed in the **Practical Information** section of each city and town.

MONEY. The **euro (€)** has replaced the **escudo** as the unit of currency in Portu-

gal. For more info on the euro, see p. 16. Generally, it's cheaper to exchange money in Portugal than at home. **ATMs** have the best exchange rates. Credit cards also offer good rates and may sometimes be required to reserve hotel rooms or rental cars; **MasterCard** (known in Portugal as **Eurocard**) and **Visa** are the most frequently accepted. **Tips** of 5-10% are customary only in fancy restaurants or hotels. Some cheaper restaurants include a 10% service charge; if they don't and you'd like to leave a tip, round up to the nearest euro and leave the change. Taxi drivers do not expect tips except for especially long trips. **Bargaining** is not customary in shops, but you can give it a shot at the local market *(mercado)* or when looking for a private room *(quarto)*. Portugal has a 21% **value added tax (VAT),** a sales tax applied to retail goods. The prices given in *Let's Go* include VAT. In the airport upon exiting the EU, non-EU citizens can claim a refund on the tax paid for goods purchased at participating stores. In order to qualify for a refund in a store, you must spend at least €50-100, depending on the shopkeeper; make sure to ask for a refund form when you pay. For more info on qualifying for a VAT refund, see p. 19.

BUSINESS HOURS. Shops are open M-F from 9am to 6pm, although many close for a few hours in the afternoon. Restaurants serve lunch from noon to 3pm and dinner from 7 to 10pm—or later. Museums are often closed on Monday, and many shops are closed over the weekend. Banks usually open around 9am M-F and close in the afternoon.

TRANSPORTATION

BY PLANE. Most international flights land at **Portela Airport** in Lisbon (**LIS**; ☎218 41 35 00); some also land at **Faro** (**FAO**; ☎289 80 08 00) or **Porto** (**OPO**; ☎229 43 24 00). **TAP Air Portugal** (Canada and the US ☎800-221-7370, Portugal ☎707 20 57 00, UK ☎845 601 0932; www.tap.pt) is Portugal's national airline, serving domestic and international locations. **Portugália** (☎218 938 070; www.flypga.pt) is smaller and flies between Faro, Lisbon, Porto, major Spanish cities, and other Western European destinations. For more information on European air travel, see p. 46.

BY TRAIN. Caminhos de Ferro Portugueses (☎213 18 59 90; www.cp.pt) is Portugal's national railway. Lines run to domestic destinations, Madrid, and Paris. For travel outside of the Braga-Porto-Coimbra-Lisbon line, buses are better. Lisbon, where local trains are fast and efficient, is the exception. Trains often leave at irregular hours, and posted schedules *(horários)* aren't always accurate; check ticket booths upon arrival. Fines for riding without a ticket *(sem bilhete)* are high. Those under 12 or over 65 get half-price tickets. **Youth discounts** are only available to Portuguese citizens. Train passes are usually not worth buying, as tickets are inexpensive. For more information on getting to Portugal, see p. 46.

BY BUS. Buses are cheap, frequent, and connect to just about every town in Portugal. **Rodoviária** (☎212 94 71 00), formerly the national bus company, has recently been privatized. Each company name corresponds to a particular region of the country, such as Rodoviária Alentejo or Minho e Douro, with a few exceptions such as **EVA** in the Algarve. Private regional companies, including **AVIC, Cabanelas,** and **Mafrense,** also operate buses. Beware of non-express buses in small regions like Estremadura and Alentejo, which stop every few minutes. Express service *(expressos)* between major cities is good, and inexpensive city buses often run to nearby villages. Portugal's main **Euroline** (p. 50) affiliates are Internorte, Intercentro, and Intersul. **Busabout** coaches stop in Portugal at Lisbon, Lagos, and Porto. Every coach has a guide onboard to answer questions and to make travel arrangements en route.

BY CAR. A **driver's license** from one's home country is required to rent a car; no International Driving Permit is necessary. Portugal has the **highest automobile accident rate** per capita in Western Europe. The highway system *(itinerarios principais)* is easily accessible, but off the main arteries, the narrow roads are difficult to negotiate. Speed limits are ignored, recklessness is common, and lighting and road surfaces are often inadequate. Parking space in cities is nonexistent. In short, buses are safer. The national automobile association, the **Automóvel Clube de Portugal (ACP),** (☎800 502 502; www.acp.pt), has breakdown and towing service, as well as first aid.

BY THUMB. In Portugal, **hitchhiking** is rare. Beach-bound locals occasionally hitchhike in summer, but more commonly stick to the inexpensive bus system. Rides are easiest to come by between smaller towns and at gas stations near highways and rest stops. Let's Go does not recommend hitchhiking.

KEEPING IN TOUCH

PHONE CODES	**Country code:** 351. **International dialing prefix:** 00. Within Portugal, dial city code + local number. For more info on placing international calls, see **Inside Back Cover.**

EMAIL AND THE INTERNET. Internet cafes in cities and most towns charge around €1.20-4 per hr. for Internet access. When in doubt, try the library, where there is often at least one computer equipped for Internet access.

TELEPHONE. Whenever possible, use a calling card for international phone calls, as long-distance rates for national phone services are often high. Mobile phones are an increasingly popular and economical option. Major mobile carriers include: **TMN, Optimus Telecom SA,** and **Vodafone.** Direct-dial access numbers for calling out of Portugal include: **AT&T Direct** (☎800 80 01 28); **British Telecom** (☎800 80 04 40); **Canada Direct** (☎800 80 01 22); **Telecom New Zealand Direct** (☎800 80 06 40); **Telstra Australia** (☎800 80 06 10). For more info on calling home from Europe, see p. 28.

MAIL. Mail in Portugal is somewhat inefficient. **Airmail** *(via aerea)* takes one to two weeks to reach Canada or the US, and more to get to Australia and New Zealand. **Surface mail** *(superficie)*, for packages only, takes up to two months. **Registered** or **blue mail** takes five to eight business days for roughly three times the price of airmail. **EMS** or **Express Mail** will most likely arrive overseas in three to four days, though it costs more than double the blue mail price. To receive mail in Portugal, have mail delivered **Poste Restante.** Mail will go to the main post office unless you specify a subsidiary by street address. Address mail to be held according to the following example: Last Name, First Name, Posta Restante, Postal code City, PORTUGAL; AIRMAIL.

ACCOMMODATIONS AND CAMPING

PORTUGAL	❶	❷	❸	❹	❺
ACCOMMODATIONS	under €16	€16-20	€21-30	€31-40	over €40

Movijovem, R. Lúcio de Azevedo 27, 1600-146 Lisbon (☎707 20 30 30; www.pousa-dasjuventude.pt), the Portuguese Hostelling International affiliate, oversees the country's **HI hostels.** All bookings can be made through them. A bed in a *pousada da juventude* costs €9-15 per night, including breakfast and linens, slightly less in the low season. Though often the cheapest option, hostels may lie far from the town center. To reserve rooms in the high season, get an **International Booking Voucher** from Movijovem (or your country's HI affiliate) and send it to the desired hostel four to eight weeks in advance. In the low season (Oct.-Apr.), double-check to see if the hostel is open. **Hotels** in Portugal tend to be pricey. Rates typically include breakfast and showers, and most rooms without bath or shower have a sink. When business is slow, try bargaining in advance—the "official price" is just the maximum. **Pensões,** also called **residencias,** are a budget traveler's mainstay, cheaper than hotels and only slightly more expensive (and much more common) than crowded youth hostels. Like hostels, *pensões* generally provide sheets and towels. Many do not take reservations in high season; for those that do, book a week ahead. **Quartos** are rooms in private residences, similar to Spain's *casas particulares.* These may be the cheapest option in cities and the only option in town; tourist offices can help find one. Prices are flexible and bargaining expected. Portugal has 150 **official campgrounds** *(parques de campismo)*, often beach-accessible and equipped with grocery stores and cafes. Urban and coastal parks may require reservations. Police are cracking down on illegal camping, so don't try it. Tourist offices stock *Portugal: Camping and Caravan Sites,* a free guide to official campgrounds.

FOOD AND DRINK

PORTUGAL	❶	❷	❸	❹	❺
FOOD	under €6	€6-10	€11-15	€16-20	over €20

Portuguese dishes are seasoned with olive oil, garlic, herbs, and sea salt, but few spices. The fish selection includes *choco grelhado* (grilled cuttlefish), *linguado grelhado* (grilled sole), and *peixe espada* (swordfish). Portugal's renowned *queijos* (cheeses) are made from cow, goat, and sheep milk. For dessert, try *pudim flan* (egg custard). A hearty *almoço* (lunch) is eaten between noon and 2pm; *jantar* (dinner) is served between 8pm and midnight. *Meia dose* (half-portions) cost more than half-price but are often more than adequate. The *prato do dia* (special of the day) and the set *menú* of appetizer, bread, entree, and dessert, are also filling choices. Cheap, high-quality Portuguese *vinho* (wine) is astounding. Its delicious relative, *vinho do porto* (port), is a dessert in itself. Coffees include *bica* (black espresso), *galão* (with milk, in a glass), and *café com leite* (with milk, in a cup). **Mini-Preço** and **Pingo Doce** have cheap groceries.

NO SUCH THING AS A FREE LUNCH. Waiters in Portugal will put an assortment of snacks, ranging from simple bread and butter to sardine paste, cured ham, or herbed olives, on your table before the appetizer is served. But check the menu for the prices before you dig in: you nibble it, you buy it.

HOLIDAYS AND FESTIVALS

Holidays: New Year's Day (Jan. 1); Epiphany (Jan. 6); Good Friday (Mar. 21); Easter (Mar. 23-24); Liberation Day (Apr. 25); Ascension (May 1); Labor Day (May 1); Corpus Christi (May 22); Portugal Day (June 10); Assumption (Aug. 15); Republic Day (Oct. 5); All Saints' Day (Nov. 1); Restoration of Independence Day (Dec. 1); Immaculate Conception (Dec. 8); Christmas (Dec. 25); New Year's Eve (Dec. 31).

Festivals: All of Portugal celebrates *Carnaval* (Feb. 5) and Holy Week (Apr. 1-8). Coimbra holds the *Queima das Fitas* (Burning of the Ribbons) festival in early May, celebrating the end of the university school year. In June, Batalha holds a *Feira International* celebrating the food, wine, and traditional handicrafts of the region, and Lisbon hosts the *Festas da Cidade,* honoring the birth of St. Anthony with music, games, parades, and street fairs. For more information on Portuguese festivals, see www.portugal.org.

BEYOND TOURISM

As a **volunteer** in Portugal, you can contribute to efforts concerning environmental protection, social welfare, or political activism. While not many students think of **studying** abroad in Portugal, most Portuguese universities open their gates to foreign students. Being an au pair and teaching English are popular options for long-term **work,** though many people choose to seek more casual—and often illegal—jobs in resort areas. Let's Go does not recommend any type of illegal employment. For more info on opportunities across Europe, see **Beyond Tourism,** p. 56.

Canadian Alliance for Development Initiatives and Projects (www.cadip.org/volunteer-in-portugal.htm). Posts opportunities to volunteer for development projects in Granja do Ulmeiro, Coimbra.

Teach Abroad (www.teachabroad.com). Brings you to listings around the world for paid or stipend positions teaching English.

Universidade de Lisboa, Rectorate Al. da Universidade, Cidade Universitária, 1649-004 Lisbon, POR (☎217 96 76 24; www.ul.pt). Allows foreign students to enroll directly.

Volunteer Abroad (www.volunteer-abroad.com/Portugal.cfm). Offers opportunities to volunteer with conservation efforts around Portugal.

LISBON (LISBOA) ☎21

In 1755, a terrible earthquake destroyed much of Lisbon a tragedy kept fresh by the nostalgic ballads of *fado* singers. But today, Portugal's seaside capital thrives as a center of architecture, art, and nightlife. Romans and Arabs once called Lisbon home, and the city remains one of the most multicultural in Europe.

▐ TRANSPORTATION

Flights: Aeroporto de Lisboa (LIS; ☎841 3500). From the terminal, turn right and follow the path to the bus stop. Take the express **AeroBus** #91 (15min., 3 per hr., €1.50) to Pr. dos Restauradores, in front of the tourist office, or take bus #44 or 45 to the same location (15-20min., every 12-15min., €1.50). A **taxi** from downtown costs about €10 plus a €1.60 baggage fee. Ask at the tourist office (☎845 0660) inside the airport about buying prepaid vouchers for taxi rides from the airport. (M-F €15, Sa-Su €18. Open daily 7am-midnight.) Major airlines have offices at Pr. Marquês do Pombal and along Av. da Liberdade.

Trains: Caminhos de Ferro Portugueses (☎808 20 82 08; www.cp.pt). 5 main stations, each serving different destinations. Trains in Portugal—slow, inconsistent, and confusing—are the bane of every traveler's existence; buses, though more expensive and lacking toilets, are faster and more comfortable.

Estação do Barreiro (☎347 2930), across the Rio Tejo. Travels south. Accessible by ferry from the Terreiro do Paço dock off Pr. do Comércio (30min., 2 per hr., €2). To get to **Évora** and **Lagos,** take a train to **Pinhal Novo** station and transfer. From Pinhal Novo, trains go to: **Lagos** (3½hr., 5 per day 9:04am-8:04pm, €12-17) and **Évora** (1½hr., 2 per day, €7).

Estação Cais do Sodré (☎347 0181), just beyond R. do Alecrim, near Baixa. M: Cais do Sodré. Take the metro or bus #36, 45, or 91 from Pr. dos Restauradores or tram #28 from Estação Santa Apolónia. To: the monastery in **Belém** (10min., 4 per hr., €1.20), **Cascais** and **Estoril** (30min., 2 per hr., €1.60), and the youth hostel in **Oeiras** (20min., 2 per hr., €1.30).

Estação Rossio (☎346 5022). M: Rossio or Restauradores. Travels west.

Estação Santa Apolónia (☎888 4025), Av. Infante Dom Henrique, runs the international, northern, and eastern lines. All trains to Santa Apolónia also stop at **Estação Oriente** (M: Oriente) by the Parque das Nações. The international terminal has currency exchange and an info desk. To reach downtown, take bus #9, 46, or 59 to Pr. dos Restauradores. To: **Braga** (5hr., 3 per day, €2-30); **Coimbra** (2½hr., 24 per day, €16-23); **Madrid, SPA** (10hr., 10:05pm, €60); **Porto** (3-4½hr., 20 per day, €19-30).

Buses: M: Jardim Zoológico. In the metro station, follow exit signs to Av. C. Bordalo Pinheiro, cross the street, and follow the path up the stairs. Look for *autocarros* signs. **Rede Expressos** buses (☎707 22 33 44; www.rede-expressos.pt) go to: **Braga** (5hr., 13 per day, €17); **Coimbra** (2½hr., 25 per day, €12); **Évora** (2hr., 20 per day, €11); **Faro** (4hr., 16 per day, €17); **Lagos** (4-5hr., 16 per day, €17); **Porto** (3½-4hr., 19 per day, €16) via **Leiria** (2hr., €9).

Public Transportation: CARRIS (☎361 3000; www.carris.pt) runs **buses, trams,** and **funiculars.** If you plan to stay in Lisbon for any length of time, consider a *passe turístico,* good for unlimited travel on all CARRIS transports. 1- and 5-day passes are sold in CARRIS booths in most train stations and busier metro stations. (€3.40/13.50.) The 4 lines of the **metro** (☎350 0100; www.metrolisboa.pt) cover downtown and the modern business district. Single ride €0.80; unlimited daily-use ticket €3.40; book of 10 tickets €11. Trains run daily 6:30am-1am; some stations close earlier.

Taxis: Rádio Táxis de Lisboa (☎811 9000), **Autocoope** (☎793 2756), and **Teletáxis** (☎811 1100). Along Av. da Liberdade and Rossio. Luggage €1.60.

▐ ORIENTATION

The city center is made up of three neighborhoods: **Baixa** (low district), **Bairro Alto** (high district), and hilly **Alfama.** The suburbs extending in both directions along the river represent some of the fastest-growing sections of the city. Sev-

PORTUGAL

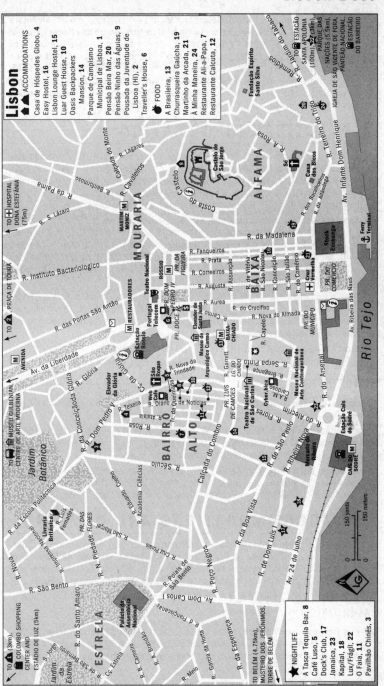

Lisbon

▲▲ ACCOMMODATIONS
Casa de Hóspedes Globo, **4**
Easy Hostel, **16**
Lisbon Lounge Hostel, **15**
Luar Guest House, **10**
Oasis Backpackers
Mansion, **14**
Parque de Campismo
Municipal de Lisboa, **1**
Pensão Beira Mar, **20**
Pensão Ninho das Águias, **9**
Pousada da Juventude de
Lisboa (HI), **2**
Traveller's House, **6**

◆ FOOD
A Brasileira, **13**
Churrasqueira Gaúcha, **19**
Martinho da Arcada, **21**
À Minha Maneira, **24**
Restaurante Ali-a-Papa, **7**
Restaurante Calcuta, **12**

★ NIGHTLIFE
A Tasca Tequila Bar, **8**
Café Luso, **5**
Dock's Club, **17**
Jamaica, **23**
Kapital, **18**
Lux/Frágil, **22**
O Faia, **11**
Pavilhão Chinês, **3**

eral kilometers from downtown, **Belém** is a walk into Portugal's past. **Alcântara** is home to much of Lisbon's party scene as well as the **Parque das Nações**, site of the 1998 World Expo. Baixa's grid of mostly pedestrian streets is bordered to the north by **Rossio** (a.k.a. Praça Dom Pedro IV) and to the south by **Praça do Comércio**, on the Rio Tejo (River Tagus). East of Baixa is Alfama, Lisbon's oldest, labyrinthine district, and west of Baixa is Bairro Alto. Bairro Alto's upscale shopping district, the **Chiado,** is crossed by R. do Carmo and R. Garrett. **Avenida da Liberdade** runs north, uphill from Pr. dos Restauradores.

▨ PRACTICAL INFORMATION

Tourist Office: Palácio da Foz, Pr. dos Restauradores (☎346 3314). M: Restauradores. Open daily 9am-8pm. The **Welcome Center,** Pr. do Comércio (☎031 2810), the city's main office, sells the Lisbon Card, which includes transportation and entrance to most sights (1-day €15, 2-day €26, 3-day €31). English spoken. Open daily 9am-8pm. Kiosks at Santa Apolónia, Belém, and other locations provide tourist info.

Embassies and Consulates: Australia, Av. da Liberdade 200 (☎310 1500; www.portugal.embassy.gov.au); **Canada,** Av. Liberdade 196 (☎444 3301; geo.international.gc.ca/canada-europa/portugal); **Ireland,** R. da Imprensa a Estrela 1-4 (☎392 9440). **New Zealand,** R. da Vista Alegre 10 (☎370 5787); **UK,** R. de São Bernardo 33 (☎392 4000; www.britishembassy.gov.uk/portugal); **US,** Av. das Forças Armadas (☎727-3300; www.american-embassy.pt).

Currency Exchange: Banks are open M-F 8:30am-3pm. **Cota Câmbios,** Pr. Dom Pedro IV 41 (☎322 0480), exchanges currency. Open daily 9am-8pm. The main post office, most banks, and travel agencies also change money. Exchanges line the streets of Baixa, but fees can be high.

Police: R. Capelo 13 (☎346 6141 or 342 1634). English spoken.

Late-Night Pharmacy: ☎118 (directory assistance). Look for the green cross at intersections, or try **Farmácia Azevedos,** Pr. Dom Pedro IV 31 (☎343 0482), at the base of Rossio in front of the metro.

Hospital: Hospital de Saint Louis, R. Luz Soriano 182 (☎321 6500), Bairro Alto. Open daily 9am-6pm.

Internet Access: Web C@fé, R. Diário de Notícias 126 (☎342 1181). €0.75 per 15min. Open daily 4pm-2am. **Cyber.bica,** R. Duques de Bragança 7 (☎322 5004), in Bairro Alto. €0.75 per 15min. Open M-Sa 11am-midnight.

Post Office: Main office, Ctt. Correios, Pr. dos Restauradores (☎323 8700). Open M-F 8am-10pm, Sa-Su 9am-7pm. Often crowded. Branch at Pr. do Comércio (☎322 0920). Open M-F 8:30am-6:30pm. Cash only. Central Lisbon **Postal Code:** 1100.

▐ ▞ ACCOMMODATIONS AND CAMPING

Hotels cluster on **Avenida da Liberdade,** while many convenient hostels are in Baixa along the Rossio and on **Rua da Prata, Rua dos Correeiros,** and **Rua do Ouro.** Most youth hostels are in Bairro Alto and around Santa Catarina. Lodgings near the Castelo de São Jorge are quiet and close to the sights. At night, be careful in Baixa, Bairro Alto, and especially Graça—many streets are isolated and poorly lit.

BAIRRO ALTO

▨ **Oasis Backpackers Mansion,** R. de Santa Catarina 24 (☎347 8044; www.oasislisboa.com). M: Baixa-Chiado, exit Largo do Chiado. The Oasis is a backpacker's dream, located in a gorgeous building with a spacious living room. Enjoy an incredible dinner

M-Sa for €5 and complimentary Portuguese lessons. Breakfast included. Laundry €6. Free Internet. Co-ed dorms €20. Cash only. ❷

Luar Guest House, R. das Gáveas 101 (☎346 0949; www.pensaoluar.com). Follow the beautiful *azulejo* and wood staircase to brightly decorated rooms. Laundry €10 per 6kg. Singles €15, with shower €20; doubles €30; triples €45; quads €60. Cash only. ❷

Casa de Hóspedes Globo, R. Teixeira 37 (☎346 2279; www.pensaoglobo.com). Popular for its location near nightlife. Rooms with phone, TV, and often bath. English spoken. Laundry €10 per 6kg. Internet €2 per hr. Singles €35; doubles €40; triples with bath €45; quads with bath €60. Low season €10-15 discount. Cash only. ❷

BAIXA

🗺 **Lisbon Lounge Hostel,** R. de São Nicolau 41, 2nd fl. (☎346 2061). M: Rossio or Baixa-Chiado. The hostel with the look of a sleek resort features a living room, in addition to a lounge area on each floor. Perks include free Internet, Wi-Fi, and lockers. Breakfast included; dinner €6. Dorms €20; doubles with bath €54. Cash only. ❸

🗺 **Easy Hostel,** R. de São Nicolau 13, 4th fl. (☎886 4280). This recently opened hostel in the middle of Baixa offers spacious rooms, Internet, and free breakfast with fresh-baked bread. Laundry is cheap, and there is a living room for hanging out with fellow travelers. An elevator makes life at Easy so much easier. Dorms €18. Cash only. ❷

Traveller's House, R. Augusta 89 (☎210 11 59 22) M: Baixa-Chiado. Wooden bunk beds and 4 common areas give this well-located hostel a warm and inviting feel. Free Internet, Wi-Fi, and breakfast. Lunch or dinner €5-6. Co-ed dorms €20. Cash only.

ALFAMA

🗺 **Pensão Ninho das Águias,** Costa do Castelo 74 (☎885 4070). Climb the spiral stair-case on the terrace to reach the reception desk. Among the best views Lisbon has to offer, especially from rooms 5, 6, and 12-14. English and French spoken. Reserve ahead in summer. May-Aug. singles €30; doubles €45, with bath €50; triples €60. Sept.-Apr. prices €5 lower. Cash only. ❸

Pensão Beira Mar, Lg. Terreiro do Trigo 16 (☎886 9933; beira@iol.pt), near the Sta. Apolonia train station. Close to the water, the Beira Mar is a calm getaway for budget travelers. Brightly decorated rooms include a shower, television, and sink. Breakfast included. Free Internet and snacks. Living room and kitchen available. Reservations by email only. June-Aug. singles €20-35; doubles €30-40; triples €45; quads €60. Oct.-May prices €5 lower. Cash only. ❷

OTHER AREAS

Pousada de Juventude de Lisboa (HI), R. Andrade Corvo 46 (☎353 2696). M: Picoas. Spacious, recently renovated rooms with a bar and reading room. Breakfast included. Reserve ahead. Dorms €16; doubles with bath €43. HI members only. MC/V. ❶

Parque de Campismo Municipal de Lisboa (☎762 3100), on the road to Benfica. Take bus #14 to Parque Florestal Monsanto; campsite is at entrance to park. Pool and super-market nearby. €5 per person, €5-6 per tent, €3.50 per car. Low season discounts. ❶

🖸 FOOD

Lisbon offers some of Europe's best wine and cheapest restaurants. Dinner costs €7-12 per person; the *prato do dia* (daily special) is often only €5. Head to **Rua dos Bacalhoeiros** and **Rua dos Correeiros** to find smaller and usually less expensive restaurants. The city's culinary specialties include *creme de mariscos* (seafood chowder with tomatoes) and *bacalhau cozido com grão e* *batatas* (cod with chickpeas and boiled potatoes). For cheap groceries, look for any **Mini-Preço** or **Pingo Doce** supermarket. (Most open M-Sa 8:30am-9pm.)

BAIRRO ALTO

A Brasileira, R. Garrett 120-122 (☎346 9541). M: Baixa-Chiado. A former stomping ground of early 20th-century poets and intellectuals. Sandwiches and croissants €2-5. Entrees €6-13. Open daily 8am-2am. AmEx/MC/V. ❷

Restaurante Calcuta, R. do Norte 17 (☎342 8295; www.calcuta1.com), near Lg. Camões. Listen to soothing Indian music while you enjoy Calcuta favorites like the prawn masala (€9.50). Offers a wide selection of vegetarian options (€6.50-7.50). Open M-F noon-3pm and 6-11pm, Sa-Su 6-11pm. AmEx/MC/V. ❷

Restaurante Ali-a-Papa, R. da Atalaia 95 (☎347 4143). Serves generous helpings of Moroccan food in a peaceful space; dishes include couscous and tangine. Vegetarian-friendly. Entrees €9-15. Open M and W-Sa 7pm-12:30am. AmEx/MC/V. ❸

BAIXA AND ALFAMA

▨ **À Minha Maneira,** Lg. do Terreiro do Trigo 1 (☎886 1112; www.a-minha-maneira.pt). A former bank vault has been revamped as a wine closet. Menu consists of various meat and fish dishes. Entrees €8-15. Open daily 11am-11pm. Cash only. ❷

Churrasqueira Gaúcha, R. dos Bacalhoeiros, 26C-D (☎887 0609). Affordable Portuguese food cooked to perfection in a comfortable, cavernous setting. Fresh meat, poultry, and fish. Open M-Sa 10am-midnight. AmEx/MC/V. ❷

Martinho da Arcada, Pr. do Comércio 3 (☎887 9259). Founded in 1782, this is the oldest restaurant in Lisbon and a former haunt of poet Fernando Pessoa. The entrees (€17-35) are somewhat overpriced, but the ambience is one of a kind. Outdoor seating available. Open M-Sa noon-3pm and 7-10:30pm. AmEx/MC/V. ❸

◎ SIGHTS

BAIXA

Though Baixa has few historic sights, the neighborhood's happening feel and dramatic history make it a monument in its own right.

AROUND THE ROSSIO. The **Rossio** (Pr. Dom Pedro IV) was once a cattle market, the site of public executions, a bullring, and carnival ground. Now, the *praça* is the domain of ruthless local motorists who circle a statue of Dom Pedro IV. A statue of Gil Vicente, Portugal's first great dramatist, sits at the top of the **Teatro Nacional de Dona Maria II** at one end of the *praça*.

AROUND PRAÇA DOS RESTAURADORES. Just past the Rossio train station, an obelisk and a bronze sculpture of the "Spirit of Independence" commemorate Portugal's break from Spain in 1640. Numerous shops line the *praça* and C. da Glória, the hill that leads to Bairro Alto. Pr. dos Restauradores also begins **Avenida da Liberdade,** Lisbon's most elegant promenade. Modeled after the wide boulevards of 19th-century Paris, this shady thoroughfare ends at **Praça do Marquês de Pombal,** where an 18th-century statue of the Marquês himself overlooks the city.

BAIRRO ALTO

Intellectuals mix with teens and university students in the Bairro Alto. **Praça Luís de Camões,** in the neighborhood's center, is a good place to rest while sightseeing.

▨ **MUSEU ARQUEOLÓGICO DO CARMO.** Located under the skeletal arches of an old church destroyed in the 1755 earthquake, this partially outdoor museum allows visitors to get very close to historical relics like mummies and a coat of arms. *(Lg. do Carmo. Open M-Sa 10am-8pm. €2.50, students €1.50, under 14 free.)*

BASÍLICA DA ESTRELA. Directly across from the Jardim da Estrela, the Basílica da Estrela dates back to 1796. Its dome, poised behind a pair of tall belfries, towers over surrounding buildings in the Lisbon skyline. Half-mad Dona Maria I promised God anything for a son. When she finally gave birth to a baby boy, she built this church in thanks. Ask to see the 10th-century nativity. *(Pr. da Estrela. Accessible by metro or tram #28 from Pr. do Comércio. ☎396 0915. Open daily 7:45am-8pm. Free.)*

ALFAMA

Alfama, Lisbon's medieval quarter, was the only neighborhood to survive the infamous 1755 earthquake. The area descends in tiers from the **Castelo de São Jorge** facing the Rio Tejo. Between Alfama and Baixa is the **Mouraria** (Moorish quarter), ironically established following the expulsion of the Moors in 1147. This labyrinth of *becos* (alleys), *escandinhas* (small stairways), and unmarked streets is a challenge to navigate, so be careful after nightfall.

■**CASTELO DE SÃO JORGE.** Built in the 5th century by the Visigoths and enlarged 400 years later by the Moors, this castle was again improved and converted into the royal family's playground between the 14th and 16th centuries. Today the Castelo consists of little more than stone ramparts, but the towers provide spectacular views of Lisbon. Wander around the ruins, explore the ponds, or gawk at exotic birds in the gardens. *(☎880 0620; www.egeac.pt. Open daily Mar.-Oct. 9am-9pm; Nov.-Feb. 9am-6pm. €5, students €2.50, under 10 and over 65 free.)*

LOWER ALFAMA. The small **Igreja de Santo António** was built in 1812 over the beloved saint's alleged birthplace. The construction was funded with money collected by the city's children, who fashioned miniature altars bearing saintly images to place on doorsteps—a custom reenacted annually on June 13, the saint's feast day and Lisbon's biggest holiday. *(Veer right when you see Igreja da Madalena in Lg. da Madalena on the right. Take R. de Santo António da Sé and follow the tram tracks. ☎886 9145. Open daily 8am-7pm. Mass daily 11am, 5, 7pm.)* In the square beyond the church is the 12th-century ■**Sé de Lisboa.** Although the cathedral's interior lacks the ornamentation of the city's other churches, its age and treasury make for an intriguing visit. The cloister includes an archaeological dig with ruins from the Iron Age, the Roman Empire, and the Muslim and Medieval Ages in Lisbon. *(☎886 6752. Open daily 9am-7pm except during Mass, held Tu-Sa 6:30pm and Su 11:30am and 7pm. Free. Treasury open M-Sa 10am-5pm. €2.50, students €1.50. Cloister open daily May-Sept. 2-7pm; Oct.-Apr. M-Sa 10am-6pm, Su 2-6pm. €2.50, students €1.30.)*

GRAÇA

Graça is one of Lisbon's oldest neighborhoods. In addition to views of the city and river, it offers impressive historical sights that keep tourists trekking up its hilly streets. Graça is mainly a residential area, accessible by tram (#28; €1.30).

■**PANTEÃO NACIONAL.** The massive building that is now the Panteão Nacional (National Pantheon) was originally meant to be the Igreja da Santa Engrácia. The citizens of Graça started building the church in 1680 to honor their patron saint, but their ambitions soon outstripped their finances. Salazar's military regime eventually took over construction, completing the project and dedicating it in 1966 as a burial ground for important statesmen. When democracy was restored in 1975, the new government relocated the remains of prominent anti-fascist opponents to this building. The building also houses the honorary tombs of explorers like Vasco da Gama and Pedro Cabral, as well as the remains of Portuguese artists. *(Take tram #28 from R. do Loreto or R. Garrett. ☎885 4820. Open Tu-Su 10am-5pm. €2, seniors €1.)*

PORTUGAL

IGREJA DE SÃO VICENTE DE FORA. The church, built between 1582 and 1692, is dedicated to Lisbon's patron saint. Ask to see the *sacristia* (chapel) with its inlaid walls of Sintra marble. *(Open daily 10am-6pm except for Mass, Tu and F-Sa 9:30am, Su 10:00am. Free. Chapel open Tu-Su 10am-5pm. €2.)*

SÃO SEBASTIÃO

Located north of Baixa, São Sebastião features busy avenues, department stores, and scores of strip malls. The area also houses two of the finest art museums in Portugal, legacies of oil tycoon Calouste Gulbenkian.

■ **MUSEU CALOUSTE GULBENKIAN.** When British citizen Calouste Gulbenkian died in 1955, he left his extensive art collection to Portugal, the country he chose to call home. The formidable collection includes Egyptian, European, Greek, Islamic, Mesopotamian, Oriental and Roman art from the 15th to 20th centuries. Highlights include works by Dégas, Manet, Monet, Rembrandt, Renoir, and Rodin. *(Av. Berna 45. M: São Sebastião. ☎ 782 3000; www.gulbenkian.pt. Open Tu-Su 10am-5:45pm. €3; students, teachers, and seniors free; Su free.)*

CENTRO DE ARTE MODERNO. The Centro de Arte Moderno showcases Portuguese talent from the late 19th century to the present. The museum also has art from Portugal's former colonies. *(R. Dr. Nicolau Bettencourt. M: São Sebastião. ☎ 782 3474. Open Tu-Su 10am-5:45pm. €3; students, teachers, and seniors free; Su free.)*

BELÉM

The concentration of monuments and museums in Belém, a suburb of Lisbon, makes it a crucial stop on any tour of the capital. To reach Belém, take tram #15 from Pr. do Comércio (15min.) and get off at the Mosteiro dos Jerónimos stop, one stop beyond the regular Belém stop. Alternatively, take the train from Estação Cais do Sodré. Exit the station by the overpass near the Padrão dos Descobrimentos. To reach the Mosteiro dos Jerónimos, exit the overpass to the right, then go through the public gardens to R. de Belém.

■ **MOSTEIRO DOS JERÓNIMOS.** Established in 1502 to commemorate Vasco da Gama's expedition to India, the Mosteiro dos Jerónimos was granted UNESCO World Heritage status in the 1980s. The country's most refined celebration of the Age of Discovery, the monastery showcases Portugal's native Manueline style, combining Gothic forms with minute Renaissance detail. Note the anachronism on the main church door: Prince Henry the Navigator mingles with the Twelve Apostles on both sides of the central column. The symbolic tombs of Luís de Camões and navigator Vasco da Gama lie in opposing transepts. *(☎ 362 0034. Open Tu-Su May-Sept. 10am-6:30pm; Oct.-Apr. 10am-5:30pm. Church free. Cloister €4.50.)*

TORRE DE BELÉM. The best-known tower in Portugal and a UNESCO World Heritage site, the Torre de Belém rises from the north bank of the Rio Tejo and is surrounded by the ocean on three sides. This icon of Portuguese grandeur offers panoramic views of Belém and the Atlantic. Built under Manuel I from 1515 to 1520 as a military stronghold, the Torre has since served several functions, including a stint as Portugal's most famous political prison. *(Open Tu-Su May-Sept. 10am-6:30pm; Oct.-Apr. 10am-5:30pm. €3, under 25 and seniors €1.50.)*

■ PARQUE DAS NAÇÕES

The Parque das Nações (Park of Nations) inhabits the former Expo '98 grounds. Until the mid-1990s, the area was a muddy wasteland with a few run-down factories and warehouses along the banks of the Tejo. However, the government transformed it to prepare for the World Exposition and afterward spent millions

row for three weeks in the outdoor **Feira do Livro** in the Parque Eduardo VII behind Pr. Marquês do Pombal. The **Feira Internacional de Lisboa** occurs every few months in the Parque das Nações, while in July and August the **Feira de Mar de Cascais** and the **Feira de Artesania de Estoril,** celebrating famous Portuguese pottery, take place near the casino. Year-round *feiras* include the **Feira de Oeiras** (antiques), on the fourth Sunday of every month, and the **Feira de Carcanelos** (clothes) in Rato (Th 8am-2pm). Packrats will enjoy the **Feira da Ladra** (flea market; literally "thieves' fair"), held behind the Igreja de São Vicente de Fora in Graça (Tu 7am-1pm, Sa 7am-3pm). To get there, take tram #28 (€1.30).

▐ NIGHTLIFE

Bairro Alto, where small bars and clubs fill side streets, is the premier destination for nightlife in Lisbon. **Rua do Norte, Rua do Diário Notícias,** and **Rua da Atalaia** have many small clubs packed into three short blocks. Several gay and lesbian clubs are between **Praça de Camões** and **Travessa da Queimada,** as well as in the **Rato** area near the edge of Bairro Alto. The **Docas de Santo Amaro** hosts waterfront clubs and bars, while **Avenida 24 de Julho** and **Rua das Janelas Verdes** in the Santos area have the most popular clubs and discos. Another hot spot is the area along the river opposite the **Santa Apolónia** train station. Jeans, sandals, and sneakers are generally not allowed. At clubs, beer runs €3-5. Crowds flow in around 2am and stay until dawn. The easiest option to reach most clubs is to take a taxi.

▐ **A Tasca Tequila Bar,** Tr. da Queimada 13-15 (☎ 919 40 79 14). This always-full Mexican bar is a great place to go on a slow week night. Bartenders at the T-shaped counter serve potent beverages. Mixed drinks €5. Open M-Sa 6pm-2am.

Pavilhão Chinês, Dom Pedro V 89 (☎ 342 4729). Despite the thousands of collection pieces hanging from the ceiling and covering the walls, this famous bar manages to look classy. Open daily 6pm-2am.

Dock's Club, R. da Cintura do Porto de Lisboa 226 (☎395 0856). This huge club plays hip hop, Latin, and house music and has an outdoor bar where you can cool down (or dry off). Famous Tu ladies nights, where the women get in free and receive 4 free drinks. Open Tu-Sa 11pm-6am.

Jamaica, R. Nova do Carvalho 6 (☎342 1859). M: Cais do Sodre. This small club is famous for playing 80s music. Packed until the early morning. Women get in free, but men pay a €6 cover (includes 3 beers). Be careful when leaving the club; it's not the safest neighborhood late at night. Open Tu-Sa 10:30pm-6am.

Lux/Frágil, Av. Infante D. Henrique A, Cais da Pedra a Sta. Apolonia (☎882 0890). Described by many of its fans as the perfect nightclub, Lux has a high-tech lighting system and an amazing view of the water from its roof. Min. consumption is usually €15. Open Tu-Sa 10pm-6am. AmEx/MC/V.

Kapital, Av. 24 de Julho 68 (☎395 7101). The classiest club in Lisbon has a ruthless door policy that makes admission a competitive sport. 3 floors, with a terrace on top level. Mixed drinks €5-8. Cover €10-20. Open M-Sa 11pm-6am. AmEx/MC/V.

▐ DAYTRIPS FROM LISBON

CASCAIS

Trains from Lisbon's Estação Cais do Sodré (☎213 42 48 93; M: Cais do Sodré) head to Cascais (30min., 3 per hr., €1.60). Take the "SAAP"; it has fewer stops. ScottURB has a bus terminal in downtown Cascais, underground next to the blue glass tower of the shopping center by the train station. Buses #417 (40min., 1 per hr.) and the more scenic #403 (1½hr., 1 per hr.) go from Cascais to Sintra for €3.20.

converting the grounds into a park. The entrance leads through the Centro
da Gama **shopping mall** (open daily 10am-midnight) to the center of the gr
where kiosks provide maps. *(M: Oriente. Park ☎891 9393; www.parquedasnac*
The park's biggest attraction, the ◼**Uceanario** has interactive sections rec
the four major oceans down to their sounds, smells, and climates. A mai
has over 470 different species of fish, sharks, and other sea creatures. \
can get within arm's length of playful sea otters and penguins. *(☎89.*
www.oceanario.pt. Open daily Apr.-Oct. 10am-7pm; Nov.-Mar. 10am-6pm. €11, over 6£
under 12 €5.30, families €25.) Pavilions scattered around the park appeal to
ety of interests. The **Pavilhão do Conhecimento** (Pavilion of Knowledge
interactive science museum. *(☎891 7100; www.pavconhecimento.pt. Open Tu-*
6pm, Sa-Su 11am-7pm. €6, under 17 and over 65 €3.) The rides of the **Virtual**
Pavilion challenge the senses. The **Atlantic Pavilion** hosts many of Lisbon
certs, and the **International Fairgrounds** accommodate rotating exhibits.

🎵 ENTERTAINMENT

Agenda Cultural and *Follow Me Lisboa*, free at the tourist office and at ki
the Rossio on R. Portas de Santo Antão, have information on concerts, *fad*
ies, plays, and bullfights. They also have lists of museums, gardens, and lib

FADO

Lisbon's trademark is **fado**, an art combining singing and narrative poet
expresses *saudade* (nostalgia). Numerous *fado* houses lie in the small st
Bairro Alto and near R. de São João da Praça in **Alfama**. Some also offer fol
ing performances. Popular *fado* houses have high minimum consur
requirements (€10-20). To avoid breaking the bank, explore nearby
where various bars and small venues offer free shows with less notab
formers. Arrive early if you don't have a reservation.

- ◼ **Café Luso,** Tv. da Queimada 10 (☎342 2281; www.cafeluso.pt). Pass below th
  yellow sign to reach *fado* nirvana. Lisbon's premier *fado* club combines the bes
  tuguese music, cuisine, and atmosphere. Folk dance and 5 *fado* singers per r
  menu €25. Entrees €22-29. Min. consumption €20, for late night show €15.
  10:30pm and 11pm-2am. Open M-Sa 8pm-2am. F-Su reserve ahead. AmEx/M

- **O Faia,** R. Barroca 56 (☎342 6742). Performances by famous *fadistas* like Ani
  reiro and Lenita Gentil and some of the finest Portuguese cuisine available mak
  worth your time and money. 4 singers. Entrees €23-30. Min. consumptio
  includes 2 drinks. *Fado* 9:30, 11:30pm. Open M-Sa 8pm-2am. AmEx/MC/V. ◼

BULLFIGHTING

Portuguese bullfighting differs from its Spanish counterpart in that the bu
killed in the ring, a tradition that dates back to the 18th century. These spe
take place most Thursdays from late June to late September at ◼**Praça de Tc**
Lisboa, Campo Pequeno. (☎793 2143. Open daily 10pm-2am.) The newly rer
praça is a shopping center during the day and a venue for the distinctly
guese *toureio equestre* (horseback bullfighting) at night.

🌸 FESTIVALS

In June, the people of Lisbon spill into the city for a summer's worth of r
Open-air *feiras* (fairs)—smorgasbords of food, drink, live music, and d
fill the streets. On the night of June 12, the streets explode in song and
during the **Festa de Santo António.** From late May to early June, bookwor

Cascais *("CASH-kise")* is a beautiful beach town, serene during the low season but full of vacationers in summer. **Praia da Ribeira, Praia da Rainha,** and **Praia da Conceição** are especially popular with sunbathers. To reach Praia da Ribeira, take a right upon leaving the tourist office and walk down Av. dos Combatantes de Grande Guerra until you see the water. Facing the water, Praia da Rainha and Praia da Conceição are to your left. Those in search of less crowded beaches should take advantage of the **free bike rentals** offered at two kiosks in Cascais. One is in front of the train station; the other is in the parking lot of the Cidadela fortress, up Av. dos Carlos I. Bring your passport or driver's license and hotel information to use the bikes from 8am to 6:30pm. Ride along the coast (to your right when facing the water) to reach the **Boca de Inferno** (Mouth of Hell), so named because the cleft carved in the rock by the Atlantic surf creates a haunting sound as waves pummel the cliffs. This natural wonder is 1km outside Cascais.

When the sun sets, nightlife picks up on **Largo Luís de Camões,** a pedestrian square. There are several good restaurants on Av. dos Combatantes de Grande Guerra, between the tourist office and the ocean. The best is **Restaurante Dom Manolo ❷,** which serves big portions of chicken, mussels, and salmon. (☎214 83 11 26. Entrees €5-11. Open daily 10am-midnight.) The **tourist office** is at Av. dos Combatantes de Grande Guerra 25. (☎214 86 82 04. Open in summer M-Sa 9am-8pm, Su 10am-6pm; in winter M-Sa 9am-7pm, Su 10am-6pm.)

SINTRA ☎219

Trains (☎219 23 26 05) arrive at Av. Dr. Miguel Bombarda from Lisbon's Estação Sete Rios (35min., 6 per hr., €1.50). ScottURB buses (☎214 69 91 00; www.scotturb.com) leave from Av. Dr. Miguel Bombarda for Cascais (#417 or 403; 40min., 1 per hr., €3.25) and Estoril (#418; 40min., 1 per hr., €3.25).

For centuries, monarchs and noblemen were drawn by the hypnotic beauty of Sintra (pop. 20,000). They left a trail of opulence and grandeur behind them. The town's must-see is the UNESCO World Heritage Site **Quinta da Regaleira,** a stunning palace whose backyard was turned into a fantasy land by its eccentric millionaire owner at the turn of the 20th century. The *Poço Iniciático* (Initiatory Well) was inspired by secret Knights Templar rituals; bring a flashlight for exploring the caves lurking beneath the main sights. To get to the palace, turn right out of the tourist office and follow R. Consiglieri Pedroso out of town as it turns into R.M.E.F. Navarro. (☎10 66 50. Open daily Apr.-Sept. 10am-8pm; Oct. and Feb.-Apr. 10am-6:30pm; Nov.-Jan. 10am-5:30pm. €5, students €4. Tours €10; 10:30am, 11am, noon, 2:30, 3:30pm.) Equally embellished is the **Palácio de Pena,** a Bavarian palace resting atop a dark green mountain. (ScottURB bus #434 goes to the palace; €4. ☎10 53 40; www.parquesdesintra.pt. Open Tu-Su June-Sept. 10am-5:30pm; Oct.-May 10am-4pm. €8, children and seniors €4. Tours €4.50.) Other Sintra highlights include the **Palácio Nacional de Sintra,** a sprawling palace built in many architectural styles in the center of town, and the 8th-century **Castelo dos Mouros,** down the hill from the Palácio de Pena. Restaurants crowd the end of **Rua João de Deus** and **Avenida Heliodoro Salgado. Tourist offices** are located in Pr. da República 23 (☎23 11 57) and in the train station (☎24 16 23. Both open daily June-Sept. 9am-8pm; Oct.-May 9am-7pm.)

NORTHERN PORTUGAL

The unspoiled Costa da Prata (Silver Coast), plush greenery of the interior, and rugged peaks of the Serra Estrela compose the Three Beiras region. To the north, port flows freely and *azulejo*-lined houses grace charming streets.

I EAT MY FEELINGS

You've probably found yourself ogling the glass display case of Portugal's many *pastelarias* wondering which tempting treat to pick. Wonder no more—here's a guide to heaven:

Altreia. A sweet and simple treat from Northern Portugal made of pasta cooked with eggs and sugar topped with cinnamon.

Arroz-doce. Sweet rice. There are many variations of this rice pudding, so try it in different places.

Bolinhos. Little balls of cake filled with cream and/or dried fruit .

Bolinhos de Jerimu. Pumpkin, egg, and Port fried to sweet perfection. Yum.

Dolce de Ovos. Aveiro's small sweets made of egg yolks and sugar.

Pão-de-ló. The Portuguese version of sponge cake.

Pastel de Natas. Petit pastries filled with cinnamon cream, also known as *pastel de Belém*.

Pastel de Santa Clara. Star shaped puffs filled with almond flavored cream from the North east.

Rabanadas. Thick slices of bread soaked in milk or wine, tossed in sugar, and fried.

Pão de Deus. Sweet bread topped with a pineapple and coconut concoction. Add butter and the bread melts in your mouth while the shredded coconut gives a slight crunch. God's bread indeed.

PORTO (OPORTO)   ☎22

Porto (pop. 263,000) is famous for its namesake product—a strong, sugary wine developed by English merchants in the early 18th century. The port industry is at the root of the city's successful economy, but Porto has more to offer than fine alcohol. The city retains traditional charm with granite church towers, orange-tiled houses, and graceful bridges.

TRANSPORTATION AND PRACTICAL INFORMATION. Airlines including **TAP Air Portugal** (☎608 0231) fly to major European cities from **Aeroporto Francisco de Sá Carneiro (OPO; ☎943 2400)**, 13km from downtown. The recently completed metro E (violet line) goes to the airport (25min., €1.35). The **aerobus** (☎225 07 10 54) runs from Av. dos Aliados near Pr. da Liberdade to OPO (40min., 2 per hr., €4). **Taxis** to Lisbon are €18-20 (15-20min.). Most **trains** (☎808 20 82 08; www.cp.pt) pass through Porto's main station, **Estação de Campanhã**, on R. da Estação. Trains run to: Braga (1hr., 26 per day, €2-13); Coimbra (1½-2hr., 24 per day, €12-16); Lisbon (3½-4½hr., 18 per day, €16-29); Madrid, SPA via Entroncamento (11-12hr., 1 per day, €64). **Estação São Bento**, Pr. Almeida Garrett, has local and regional trains. Internorte (☎605 2420), Pr. Galiza 96, sends **buses** to Madrid, SPA (10hr., 1-2 per day, €43) and other international hubs. Rede Expressos buses (☎200 6954; www.redexpresso.pt), R. Alexandre Herculano 366, travel to Braga (1¼hr., 10 per day, €5), Coimbra (1½hr., 11 per day, €10), and Lisbon (4hr., 11 per day, €16). Renex (☎200 3395), Campo Mártires da Pátria, has express service to Lagos (8½hr., 6 per day, €23) via Lisbon (3½hr., 12 per day, €16). Buy tickets for local buses and **trams** at kiosks or at the **STCP** office, Pr. Almeida Garrett 27, across from Estação São Bento (€1.60 for 2 trips, day-pass €4). The city's main **tourist office**, R. Clube dos Fenianos 25, is off Pr. da Liberdade. (☎339 3470; www.portoturismo.pt. Open M-F 9am-6:30pm, Sa-Su 9:30am-6:30pm.) **OnWeb**, Pr. Gen. Humberto Delgado 291, has **Internet** access. (Open M-Sa 10am-2am, Su 3pm-2am. Min. 1hr. €1.20 per hr., Wi-Fi €0.60 per hr.) The **post office** is in Pr. Gen. Humberto Delgado. (☎340 0200. Open M-F 8:30am-7:30pm, Sa 9:30am-3pm.) **Postal Code:** 4000.

ACCOMMODATIONS AND FOOD. For good deals, look on **Praça Filipa de Lancastre** or near the *mercado* on **Rua Fernandes Tomás** and **Rua Formosa**. The ◆**Pensão Duas Nações ❶**, Pr. Guilherme Gomes Fernandes 59, has the best combination of low price and high comfort. (☎208 1616. Reserve ahead or arrive well before noon. Laundry €7. Internet €1 per 30min. Singles €14, with bath €23-25; doubles €23-25; triples €36; quads €46. Cash only.) Budget meals can be found near Pr. da Batalha on **Rua Cimo de Vila** and **Rua do Cativo**. Places selling *bifanas* (small pork sandwiches) line R. Bomjardim. **Ribeira** is the place to go for a high-quality, affordable dinner. The **Café Majestic ❷**, R. de Santa Catarina 112, is a snapshot of 19th-century bourgeois opulence. (☎200 3887. Entrees €9-16. Open M-Sa 9:30am-midnight. AmEx/MC/V.) The sprawling 🄼**Mercado de Bolhão** has a wide range of fresh food. (Open M-F 8am-5pm, Sa 7am-1pm.)

🄿 **WINERIES.** No visit to Porto is complete without one of the city's famous **wine tasting tours.** They are cheap (€1-3) if not free, and take about 30min. Wine tasting is most prevalent across the river, in Vila Nova de Gaia.

THE REAL DEAL. To find the cheapest prices on port, avoid retail stores and check out the wineries and non-profit stores scattered around the city. If you are looking for a particular label, be sure to call before heading out.

🄾 🄹 **SIGHTS AND ENTERTAINMENT.** From the train station, follow signs downhill on R. Mouzinho da Silveira to R. Ferreira Borges and the 🄼**Palácio da Bolsa** (Stock Exchange), the epitome of 19th-century Portuguese elegance. The most striking room of the *Palácio* is the extravagant **Sala Árabe** (Arabian Hall). Its gold and silver walls are covered with the juxtaposed inscriptions "Glory to Allah" and "Glory to Doña Maria II." (☎339 9000. Open daily Apr.-Oct. 9am-7pm; Nov.-Mar. 9am-1pm and 2-6pm. €5, students €3. Multilingual tours 2 per hr.) Nearby on R. Infante Dom Henrique, the Gothic **Igreja de São Francisco** glitters with an elaborately gilded wood interior. The museum has religious art and artifacts; in the basement is a labyrinth of catacombs. (☎206 2100. Open daily in summer 9am-8pm; winter 9am-5pm. €3, students €2.50.) On R. dos Clérigos rises the **Torre dos Clérigos** (Tower of Clerics), adjacent to the 18th-century **Igreja dos Clérigos**. (☎200 1729. Tower open daily Apr.-Oct. 9:30am-1pm and 2:30-7pm; Nov.-Mar. 10am-noon and 2-5pm. Church open M-Sa 8:45am-12:30pm and 3:30-7:30pm, Su 10am-1pm and 8:30-10:30pm. Tower €2, church free.) After hours, most people congregate around the bar-restaurants of Ribeira, where Brazilian music plays until 2am.

BRAGA
☎253

The beautiful gardens, plazas, museums, and markets of Braga (pop. 166,000) have earned it the nickname "Portuguese Rome." A showcase of the archdiocese's most precious paintings and relics, including a collection of *cofres cranianos* (brain boxes), is in the treasury of the **Sé,** Portugal's oldest cathedral. (☎26 33 17. Open Tu-Su 9am-noon and 2-5:30pm. Mass daily 5:30pm. Cathedral free. Treasury and chapels €2.) Braga's most famous landmark, **Igreja do Bom Jesús,** is 5km outside of town. This 18th-century church was built in an effort to recreate Jerusalem in Braga. Take the bus labeled "#02 Bom Jesús" at 10- or 40min. past the hour in front of Farmácia Cristal, Av. da Liberdade 571 (€1.30). At the site, either go on a 285m ride on the funicular (8am-8pm, 2 per hr., €1) or walk up the granite-paved pathway that leads to a 326-step zig-zagging staircase (20-25min.).

Take a taxi (€5) to 🄼**Pousada da Juventude de Braga (HI) ❶**, R. Santa Margarida 6, which has a friendly vibe and a convenient location. (☎61 61 63. Reception 8am-noon and 6pm-midnight. Lockout noon-6pm. Dorms €9; doubles with bath €22.) Braga's speciality is *pudim do Abade de Priscos*, a pudding flavored with caramel and port wine. The **market** is in Pr. do Comércio. (Open M-Sa 7am-3pm.) A supermarket, **Pingo Doce,** is in the basement of the Braga shopping mall. (Open daily 10am-11pm.) **Trains** (☎808 20 82 08) depart from Estação da Braga, 1km from Pr. da República, for Lisbon (4-5½hr., 3 per day, €22-30) via Porto (1hr., 26 per day, €2-13). **Buses** leave Central de Camionagem (☎20 94 00) for: Coimbra (3hr., 6 per day, €12); Faro (12-15hr., 3-6 per day, €25); Lisbon (5¼hr., 10-11 per day, €17); Porto (1¼hr., 25 per day, €5).The **tourist office** is at Av. da Liberdade 1. (☎26 25 50. Open June-Sept. M-F 9am-7pm, Sa-Su 9am-12:30pm and 2-5:30pm; Oct.-May M-Sa 9am-12:30pm and 2-6:30pm.) **Postal Code:** 4700.

COIMBRA ☎239

For centuries, the Universidade de Coimbra was the only institute of higher education in Portugal, attracting young men from the country's elite. Today, tourists of all ages are drawn to see the historic university district, but it is the many students who dominate youthful Coimbra (pop. 200,000).

⛐❷ TRANSPORTATION AND PRACTICAL INFORMATION. Regional **trains** (☎808 20 82 08; www.cp.pt) stop at both Estação Coimbra-B (Velha) and Estação Coimbra-A (Nova), just two short blocks from the town center of Coimbra, while long-distance trains stop only at Coimbra-B station. A local train connects the two stations, departing after regional trains arrive (4min.; €1, free if transferring from another train). Trains run to Lisbon (2-3hr., 17 per day, €12-30) and Porto (1-2hr., 28 per day, €7-20). **Buses** (☎23 87 69) go from the end of Av. Fernão de Magalhães, 15min. past Coimbra-A, to Lisbon (2½hr., 18 per day, €12) and Porto (1-2hr., 14 per day, €11). From the bus station, turn right, follow the avenue to Coimbra-A, then walk to Lg. da Portagem to reach the **tourist office.** (☎85 59 30; www.turismo-centro.pt. Open June 16-Sept. 14 daily 9am-7pm, Sept. 15-June 15 M-F 9:30am-5:30pm, Sa-Su 10am-1pm and 2:30-5:30pm.) **Espaço Internet,** Pr. 8 de Maio, has free **Internet,** but you may have to wait in line. (Passport or driver's license required. Open M-Sa 10am-midnight, Su 2pm-midnight.) **Postal Code:** 3000.

⛐❑ ACCOMMODATIONS AND FOOD. Residencial Vitória ❷, R. da Sota 11-19, has spacious, newly renovated rooms with bath, phone, cable TV, and A/C. Older rooms are cheaper, and still roomy and quiet. (☎82 40 49. Breakfast €2.50. In summer, singles €15-30; doubles €25-45; triples €60. Winter €15-25/25-40/50. AmEx/MC/V.) ▨**Restaurante Adega Paço do Conde ❶,** R. do Paço do Conde, is a local favorite. A budget oasis surrounded by tourist traps, the restaurant offers a variety of fish and meat options for only €5 and has outdoor seating. (☎82 56 05. Open M-Sa 11:30am-3pm and 7-10:30pm. MC/V.) Even cheaper fare can be found at the **UC Cantinas ❶,** the university student cafeterias, where full meals run under €2. One is on the right side of R. Oliveiro Matos, and the other is up the stairs in Lg. Dom Dinis. (ISIC required. Open daily for lunch at noon, dinner at 7pm.) The supermarket **Pingo Doce,** R. João de Ruão 14, is 3min. up R. da Sofia from Pr. 8 de Maio. (☎85 29 30. Open daily 8:30am-9pm.)

◱◪ SIGHTS AND ENTERTAINMENT. Take in the sights of the **cidade velha** (Old Town) by following the narrow stone steps from the river up to the university. Begin your ascent at the **Arco de Almedina,** a remnant of the Moorish town wall, one block uphill from Lg. da Portagem. The looming 12th-century Romanesque **Sé Velha** (Old Cathedral) is at the top. (Open M-Th and Sa 10am-6pm, F 10am-1pm. Cloister €1, students €0.80.) Follow signs to the Jesuit-built **Sé Nova** (New Cathedral), with its blinding gold altar. (Open Tu-Sa 9am-noon and 2-6:30pm. Free.) Just a few blocks uphill is the 16th-century **Universidade de Coimbra.** Enter through the **Porta Férrea** (Iron Gate), off R. São Pedro, to the **Pátio das Escolas,** through which an excellent view of the rural outskirts of Coimbra stretches out to the horizon. The stairs to the right lead to the **Sala dos Capelos** (Graduates' Hall), which houses portraits of Portugal's kings, six of whom were born in Coimbra. The **Capela de São Miguel,** the university chapel, is adorned with magnificent *talha dourada* (gilded wood) carvings. The 18th-century **Biblioteca Joanina** (university library) lies past the Baroque clock tower. (☎85 98 00. Open daily Mar. 13-Oct. 9am-7:20pm; Nov.-Mar. 12 10am-5:30pm. Chapel and library €3.50, students and seniors €2.50; combined ticket €6/4.20.)

Coimbra's nightlife is best from October to July, when students are in town. **A Capela,** R. Corpo de Deus, a former chapel converted into a small late-night cafe, is the best place to hear Coimbra-style *fado*, which is performed by both students and professionals. (☎83 39 85. Mixed drinks €4-5. *Fado* at 9:30, 10:30, 11:30pm. Cover €10; includes 1 drink. Open daily 1pm-3am.) **Quebra Club,** Parque Verde do Mondego, blasts jazz and funk by the river. (☎83 60 36. Beer €1-3. Mixed drinks €4-5. Open Su-Th noon-2am, F-Sa noon-4am. AmEx/MC/V.) Graduates burn the narrow ribbons they got as first-years and receive wide ribbons in return during the **Queima das Fitas** (Burning of the Ribbons), Coimbra's week-long festival in the second week of May.

CENTRAL PORTUGAL

Jagged cliffs and whitewashed fishing villages line the Costa de Prata of Estremadura, which has beaches that rival even those of the Algarve. Lush greenery surrounds historic sights in the fertile region on the banks of the Rio Tejo.

ÉVORA ☎266

Évora (pop. 55,000) is the capital and largest city of the Alentejo region. Moorish arches line the streets of its historic center, which boasts a Roman temple, an imposing cathedral, and a 16th-century university. Attached to the **Igreja Real de São Francisco** in Pr. 1 de Mayo, the eerie **Capela dos Ossos** (Chapel of Bones) was built by three Franciscan monks out of the bones of 5000 people as a hallowed space to reflect on the profundity of life and death. From Pr. do Giraldo, follow R. República; the church is on the right and the chapel is to the right of the main entrance. (☎70 45 21. Open daily May-Sept. 9am-12:50pm and 2:30-5:45pm; Oct.-Apr. 9am-1pm and 2:30-5:15pm. €1.50; photos €0.50.) The 2nd-century **Templo Romano,** on Lg. Conde do Vila Flor, was built for the goddess Diana. Facing the temple is the **Convento dos Loíos,** whose chapel interior is covered with dazzling *azulejos*. The actual monastery is now a luxury hotel. (Open Tu-Su 10am-12:30pm and 2-6pm.

LOCAL LEGEND

THE REAL CORPSE BRIDE

When Prince Dom Pedro took one look at his wife's lady-in-waiting, Inês de Castro, it was (forbidden) love at first sight. Upon discovering this illicit *amor*, Dom Pedro's father, King Alfonso, condemned the affair and had Inês exiled to a convent in Coimbra. The prince's wife soon died in childbirth, however, and Pedro and Inês continued their affair for the next decade. The prince's plans for a wedding were cut short: his father had Inês killed for fear that her and Pedro's children would eventually claim the throne. Dom Pedro, in retaliation, waged war against the king until his mother convinced him to put the civil strife to an end.

Two years later, Dom Pedro took the throne; he had his lover's assassins tracked down and brought to the public courtyard. There, he watched as their hearts were torn from their living bodies. He then set about making his children rightful heirs to the throne. In a shocking announcement, Dom Pedro ordered a posthumous matrimonial ceremony to take place. Five years after her death, Inês was removed from her grave and dressed like a queen. Dom Pedro forced the court to kneel before her corpse and kiss her rotting hand. He had his own tomb built opposite hers, and on it reads *"Até ao fim do mundo"* (until the end of the world).

€3.) Around the corner is the 12th-century **Basílica Catedral;** the 12 apostles on the doorway are masterpieces of medieval Portuguese sculpture. (Open daily in summer 9am-4:45pm; in winter 9am-12:30pm and 2-4:30pm. €1.)

Pensões cluster around **Praça do Giraldo.** From the tourist office, turn right onto R. Bernardo Matos to get to cozy **Casa Palma ❷,** R. Bernardo Matos 29A. (☎70 35 60. Singles €15-25; doubles €30-35. Cash only.) Budget restaurants can be found near the streets off Pr. do Giraldo, particularly **Rua Mercadores.** Intimate ▧**Restaurante Burgo Velho ❷,** R. de Burgos 10, serves *alentejano* cuisine. (☎22 58 58. Entrees €5-9. Open M-Sa noon-3pm and 7-10pm. AmEx/MC/V.) After sunset, head to **Praxis,** R. Valdevinos, the only club in town. From Pr. do Giraldo, take R. 5 de Outubro; the club will be on the right. (☎933 35 57 82. Beer €1.50. Mixed drinks €4-6. Min. consumption for men €7, for women €5. Open daily 11pm-4am.) **Trains** (☎70 21 25; www.cp.pt) run from Av. dos Combatentes de Grande Guerra to Faro (5hr., 2 per day, €13-20) and Lisbon (2½hr., 4-6 per day, €11). **Buses** (☎76 94 10; www.rede-expressos.pt) go from Av. São Sebastião to: Braga (8-10hr., 8 per day, €20) via Porto (6-8½hr., 10 per day, €19); Faro (4hr., 3 per day, €14); Lisbon (2hr., 20 per day, €11). The **tourist office** is at Pr. do Giraldo 73. (☎77 70 71. Open daily May-Oct. 9am-7pm; Nov.-Apr. 9am-6pm.) **Postal Code:** 7999.

BATALHA
☎244

The centerpiece of Batalha (pop. 75,000) is the gigantic ▧**Mosteiro de Santa Maria da Vitória.** Built in 1386, the Gothic and Manueline monastery remains one of Portugal's greatest monuments. (Open daily Apr.-Sept. 9am-6pm; Oct.-Mar. 9am-5pm. €4.50, 15-25 and seniors €2.30, under 14 and Su before 2pm free.) Take a taxi (€30-40 round-trip) outside town to a series of spectacular underground *grutas* (caves) in Estremadura's natural park. The **Grutas de Mira de Aire,** with a river 110m below ground level, are the deepest and largest caves in Portugal. Travelers to Batalha should stay in the nearby city of **Leiria.** The **Pousada da Juventude de Leiria (HI) ❶,** Cândido dos Reis 7, has an elegant courtyard and small book-swap. (☎83 18 68. Lockout noon-6pm. Dorms €11; doubles €26-28. HI card required. AmEx/MC/V.) **Residencial Dom Dinis ❷,** Tr. Tomar 2, offers 25 neatly decorated rooms with phone, TV, and private baths. (July-Aug. singles €25; doubles €38; triples €50. Sept.-June €23/34/45. AmEx/MC/V.) Leaving across from the monastery, **buses** run to Leiria (20min., 16 per day, €1.60) and Lisbon (2hr. 5 per day, €6.60). For more info on the caves, check with the **tourist office,** Pr. Mouzinho de Albuquerque. (☎76 51 80. Open daily May-Sept. 10am-1pm and 3-7pm; Oct.-Apr. 10am-1pm and 2-6pm.) **Postal Code:** 2440.

ALGARVE

The Algarve, a desert on the sea, is a popular vacation spot, largely due to the nearly 3000 hours of sunshine it receives every year. In July and August, tourists mob the resorts and beaches, packing bars and clubs from sunset until long after sunrise. In low season, the resorts become pleasantly depopulated.

FARO
☎289

Many Europeans begin their holidays in Faro (pop. 58,000), the Algarve's capital city. The **Vila Adentro** (Old Town) begins at the **Arco da Vila,** a stone passageway. On Lg. do Carmo stands the **Igreja de Nossa Senhora do Carmo** and its chilling ▧**Capela dos Ossos** (Chapel of Bones), built from the remains of monks buried in the church's cemetery. (☎82 44 90. Open May-Sept. M-F 10am-1pm and 3-6pm; Oct.-Apr. M-F 10am-1pm and 3-5pm, Sa 10am-1pm. Su Mass 8:30am. Church free. Chapel €1.) To get to the sunny beach **Praia de Faro,** take bus #16 from the bus station or from the front of the tourist office (5-10min.; 5 per day, return 9 per day; €1). **Pousada da Juventude (HI)** ❶, R. Polícia de Segurança Pública, is a bargain. (☎82 65 21; faro@movijovem.pt. Breakfast included. July-Aug. dorms €13; doubles €28, with bath €36. Sept.-June €9/22/25. AmEx/MC/V.) Enjoy coffee and local marzipan at cafes along **Rua Conselheiro Bívar** and **Praça Dom Francisco Gomes. Trains** (☎82 64 72) run from Lg. da Estação to Évora (4½-6hr., 3-4 per day, €13) and Lagos (1½hr., 9 per day, €17). **EVA buses** (☎89 97 00) go from Av. da República to Lagos (2hr., 8 per day, €4.30). Renex (☎81 29 80), across the street, sends buses to Porto (7½hr., 6-13 per day, €22) via Lisbon (4hr., 9 per day, €15). The **tourist office** is at R. da Misericórdia 8. (☎80 36 04. Open daily May-Sept. 9:30am-12:30pm and 2-7pm; Oct.-Apr. 9:30am-12:30pm and 2-5:30pm.) **Postal Code:** 8000.

LAGOS ☎282

Lagos resembles an exotic fraternity at night, swarming with surfers and college-aged students spilling out of bars into the stone streets. The waterfront and marina offer jet ski rentals, scuba diving lessons, sailboat and dolphin-sighting trips, and motorboat tours of the ▨**coastal rocks and grottoes.** For a lazier day, head to one of Lagos's many beaches. A 4km blanket of sand marks **Meia Praia,** across the river from town. Take a 20min. walk over the footbridge or hop on the quick ferry near Pr. Infante Dom Henrique (€0.50). For less crowded beaches, follow Av. dos Descobrimentos toward Sagres to **Praia de Pinhão** and **Praia Dona Ana.** Lagos offers water sports from scuba diving to surfing to (booze) cruising. Companies that offer tours of the grottoes line Av. dos Descobrimentos and the marina. **Algarve Dolphins,** Marina de Lagos 10, organizes 1½hr. dolphin-watching tours in high-speed rescue boats. (☎08 75 87; www.algarve-dolphins.com. €30.)

In summer, budget accommodations fill up quickly; reserve at least two weeks ahead. ▨**Pousada da Juventude de Lagos (HI)** ❶, R. Lançarote de Freitas 50, has a personable staff and social lodgers. (☎76 19 70. In summer, book through the central Movijovem office ☎217 23 21 00. Breakfast included. Mid-June to mid-Sept. dorms €16; doubles with bath €43. Mid-Sept. to mid-June €11/30. Cash only.) The ▨**Rising Cock** ❷, Tv. do Forno 14, is a short walk from most of Lagos's bars and keeps up the city's famous party-town reputation. (☎969 41 11 31; www.risingcock.com. Free Internet. High season dorms €20, low season €15; prices may vary. Cash only.) Peruse multilingual tourist menus around **Praça Gil Eanes** and **Rua 25 de Abril.** A dedicated following goes to **Casa Rosa** ❶, R. do Fer-

GIVING BACK

STATELY STORKS

A hollow clatter fills the air. Guarding your eyes from Faro's afternoon sun, you see a winged silhouette sporting what appears to be a beard. Meet the white stork, a migratory bird native to Europe, the Middle East, South Africa, and west-central Asia.

Year after year, the storks come to Faro to construct enormous nests, sometimes more than 2m in diameter. Some nests, built on medieval structures, have been used for centuries.

But increased pollution, pesticide use, and wetland drainage have endangered the storks' eating and breeding grounds, leading to population decline, especially in Western Europe. Catch-and-release efforts have yielded semi-domesticated storks that forgo migration in order to to feast on the abundant fish and shellfish in Faro's marina and beaches. Locals welcome these prehistoric-looking neighbors, but the birds' habit of nesting on power lines led to the electrocution of a stork and the subsequent blackout of all of southern Portugal in 2000. **The Sociedade Portuguesa para o Estudo das Aves (SPEA)** has initiated volunteer groups to monitor and help move nests located on or near power lines.

E-mail spea@spea.pt or call ☎213 22 04 30 to get involved.

rador 22, which offers diners many vegetarian options and provides free Internet. (☎18 02 38. All-you-can-eat spaghetti or vegetarian bolognaise €7. Open daily 5-11pm.) The indoor **market**, outside Pr. Gil Eanes on Av. dos Descobrimentos, has cheap, fresh food on Saturday. **Supermercado São Roque** is on R. da Porta de Portugal 61. (☎76 28 55. Open July-Sept. M-F 9am-8pm, Sa 9am-7pm; Oct.-June M-F 9am-7:30pm, Sa 9am-7pm. AmEx/MC/V.)

As the sun sets, beachgoers head to bars and cafes between **Praça Gil Eanes** and **Praça Luis de Camões**. For late-night establishments, try **Rua Cândido dos Reis** and **Rua do Ferrador**, as well as the intersection of **Rua 25 de Abril, Rua Silva Lopes**, and **Rua Soeiro da Costa**. Around midnight, Brits and Aussies flood **The Red Eye**, R. Cândido dos Reis 63, in search of classic rock, cheap liquor, and games of pool. (Beer €2-3. Mixed drinks €3.50-5. Shots €2.50. Free shot with 1st drink. Happy hour 8-10pm. Open daily 8pm-2am.) **Inside Out Bar**, R. Cândido dos Reis 119, serves a house specialty—the Fishbowl, made with an entire bottle of vodka. (Beer €3. Shots €1-3. Fishbowl €25. Open daily 8pm-4am. **Trains** (☎76 29 87) run from behind the marina to Évora (5-5½hr., €15-€22) and Lisbon (4hr., 7 per day, €16). The bus station (☎76 29 44), off **Avenida dos Descobrimentos**, is across the channel from the train station and marina. **Buses** run to Faro (2½hr., 6 per day 7am-5:15pm, €4), Lisbon (5hr., 6 per day, €15), and Sagres (1hr., 16 per day, €3.05). From the train station, walk through the marina and cross the pedestrian suspension bridge, then turn left onto Av. dos Descobrimentos. From the bus station, walk straight until you reach Av. dos Descobrimentos and turn right; after 15min., take another right onto R. Porta de Portugal to reach **Praça Gil Eanes**, the center of the Old Town. Praça Gil Eanes extends into Lg. Marquéz de Pombal, where the **tourist office** is located. (☎76 41 11. Open M-Sa 10am-6pm.) **Postal Code:** 8600.

▶ **DAYTRIP FROM LAGOS: SAGRES.** Marooned atop a windy plateau at the southwesternmost point in Europe, desolate Sagres (pop. 2500) and its cape were once believed to be the edge of the world. Near the town stands the ▨**Fortaleza de Sagres**, former home to Prince Henry the Navigator and his school of navigation. The pentagonal 15th-century fortress yields striking views of the cliffs and sea. *(Open daily May-Sept. 9:30am-8pm; Oct.-Apr. 9:30am-5:30pm. €3, under 25 €1.50.)* Six kilometers west lies the dramatic **Cabo de São Vicente**, where the second most powerful lighthouse in Europe shines over 100km out to sea. To get there on weekdays, take the bus from R. Comandante Matoso (10min., 2 per day, €1). **EVA buses** (☎76 29 44) run to Lagos (1hr., 14 per day, €3.10). From July to September, buses also run to Lisbon (1 per day, €15). The **tourist office** is on R. Comandante Matoso. *(☎62 48 73; www.visitalgarve.pt. Open Tu-Sa 9:30am-12:30pm and 1:30-5:30pm.)*

ROMANIA (ROMÂNIA)

Devastated by the lengthy and oppressive reign of Nicolae Ceauşescu (in office 1965-1989), modern Romania remains in the midst of economic and political transition. This condition of flux, combined with a reputation for poverty and crime, sometimes discourages foreign visitors. But travelers who dismiss Romania do themselves a disservice—it is a budget traveler's paradise, rich in history, rustic beauty, and hospitality. Romania's fascinating legacy draws visitors to Dracula's dark castle and to the famous frescoes of the Bucovina monasteries. Meanwhile, modern Romania is embodied by Bucharest, where visitors can explore the imposing remnants of Ceauşescu's rule, as well as by the heavily touristed Black Sea Coast, where resorts entice throngs of vacationers each summer

---

 DISCOVER ROMANIA: SUGGESTED ITINERARIES

THREE DAYS. Head for **Transylvania** (3 days; p. 831), a budget traveler's haven, to relax in the Gothic towns of **Sighişoara** (p. 832), **Sinaia** (p. 831), and the ruins of **Râşnov** castle (p. 834).

ONE WEEK. After three days in **Transylvania,** head to medieval **Bran** (1 day; p. 834) and stylish **Braşov** (1 day; p. 833), before ending in **Bucharest** (2 days; p. 826), the enigmatic capital.

ESSENTIALS

FACTS AND FIGURES

Official Name: Romania.
Capital: Bucharest.
Major Cities: Iaşi, Timişoara, Constanţa.
Population: 22,276,000.
Land Area: 237,500 sq. km.

Time Zone: GMT + 2.
Language: Romanian.
Religions: Eastern Orthodox (87%).
First European City with Electric Streetlamps: Timişoara.

WHEN TO GO

Romania's varied climate makes it a year-round destination. The south has hot summers and mild winters, while in the northern mountains, winters are harsher and summers are cooler. Tourist season peaks sharply in July and August only along the Black Sea Coast; elsewhere, travelers will find a refreshing lack of crowds even in mid-summer. Travelers would do well to remember, however, that summer can be brutally hot in much of Romania.

DOCUMENTS AND FORMALITIES

EMBASSIES AND CONSULATES. Foreign embassies are in Bucharest (p. 828). Romanian embassies abroad include: **Australia,** 4 Dalman Crescent, O'Malley, Canberra, ACT 2606 (☎262 862 343; www.canberra.mae.ro); **Canada,** 655 Rideau St., Ottawa, ON K1N 6A3 (☎613-789-3709; www.ottawa.mae.ro); **Ireland,** 26 Waterloo Rd., Ballsbridge, Dublin 4 (☎016 681 085; www.dublin.mae.ro); **UK,** 4 Palace Green, London W8 4QD (☎020 79 37 96 66; www.london.mae.ro); **US,** 1607 23rd St., NW, Washington, D.C. 20008 (☎202-332-4848; www.roembus.org).

ENTRANCE REQUIREMENTS.
Passport: Required for all travelers.
Visa: Not required for stays under 90 days for citizens of Australia, Canada, the EU, Ireland, New Zealand, the UK, and the US.
Letter of Invitation: Not required for citizens of Australia, Canada, Ireland, New Zealand, the UK, and the US.
Inoculations: Recommended up-to-date on DTaP (diphtheria, tetanus, and pertussis), Hepatitis A, Hepatitis B, MMR (measles, mumps, and rubella), polio booster, rabies, and typhoid.
Work Permit: Required of all foreigners planning to work in Romania.
International Driving Permit: For stays longer than 90 days, all foreigners must obtain an International Driving Permit or a Romanian driver's license.

VISA AND ENTRY INFORMATION. Romanian **visa** regulations change frequently; check with your embassy or consulate for the most current information. Citizens of Australia, Canada, Ireland, New Zealand, the UK, and the US can visit Romania for up to 90 days without visas. In all cases, passports are required and must be valid for six months after the date of departure. Travelers should consult the Romanian embassy in their country of origin to apply for a long-term visa. For citizens of the US, a single-entry visa costs US$40; multiple-entry US$75. Visas are not available at the border. Romanian embassies estimate—but do not guarantee—a five-day processing time for most visas. Apply early to allow the bureaucratic process to run its slow, frustrating course. **Visa extensions** and related services are available at police headquarters in large cities or at Bucharest's **Visas for Foreigners Office** (☎01 650 3050), Str. Luigi Cazzavillan 11. Long lines are common at the border for customs. Bags are rarely searched, but customs officials are strict about visa laws. In order to avoid being scammed, travelers should be aware that there is no entry tax for Romania. For additional information on visas and a list of Romanian embassies and consulates abroad, check out www.mae.ro.

TOURIST SERVICES AND MONEY

EMERGENCY | Ambulance: ☎961. Fire: ☎981. Police: ☎955. General Emergency: ☎112.

TOURIST OFFICES. Romania has limited resources for tourists, but the **National Tourist Office** (www.romaniatourism.com) is useful. Large hotels, however, can be excellent resources in smaller towns, even for those not staying in them.

MONEY. The Romanian **currency** is the **leu** (L), plural lei (pronounced "lay"), which was revalued in 2005. One leu is equal to 100 bani (singular ban), with standard denominations in 1, 5, 10, and 50 bani in coins and L1, L5, L10, L50, L100, and L500 in notes. Romania joined the EU in 2007, and Romanian officials are currently aiming to adopt the **euro** by 2014. As the leu strengthens, **inflation** rates continue to drop dramatically and now hover around 5%, though this statistic is liable to fluctuate. Romania has a 19% **value added tax (VAT),** a sales tax on goods and services. The prices given in *Let's Go* include VAT. **ATMs** generally accept MasterCard and Visa, and are the best way to withdraw money. **Private exchange bureaus,** which often offer better rates than **banks,** are everywhere. Many banks will cash traveler's checks in US dollars, then exchange them for lei, with high fees. Changing money on the street is both illegal and a surefire way to get cheated.

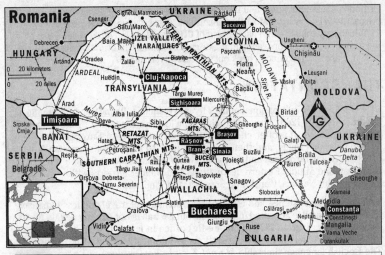

ROMANIAN LEI (L)	
AUS$1 = L2.05	1L = AUS$0.49
CDN$1 = L2.48	1L = CDN$0.40
EUR€1 = L3.53	1L = EUR€0.28
NZ$1 = L1.72	1L = NZ$0.58
UK£1 = L5.14	1L = UK£0.19
US$1 = L2.73	1L = US$0.37

HEALTH AND SAFETY

If possible, avoid Romanian **hospitals,** as most are not up to Western standards. Embassies can recommend good private doctors for emergencies. Some **European medical clinics** in Bucharest have English-speaking doctors and will require **cash payments.** *Farmacii* (pharmacies) stock basic medical supplies. **Public restrooms** are relatively uncommon in Romania and often lack soap, towels, and toilet paper. Though water in Romania is less contaminated than it once was, avoid untreated **tap water** and do not use **ice cubes;** boil water before drinking it or drink imported **bottled water.** Beware of contaminated vendor food.

Violent **crime** is not a major concern, but petty **crime** against tourists is common. Be especially careful on public transport and night trains. Pickpocketing, money exchange, and taxi scams are prevalent in Romania. Beware of distracting children and con artists dressed as policemen who ask for your passport or wallet. If someone shows a badge and claims to be a plainclothes policeman, he may be lying and trying to scam you. No police officer would ask to see credit cards or cash. When in doubt, ask the officer to escort you to the nearest police station. The **drinking age,** which is 18, is reportedly not strictly enforced, but if you smoke marijuana, be prepared to spend the next seven years in a Romanian prison. Solo **female travelers** shouldn't go out alone after dark, should say they are traveling with a male, and should dress conservatively. Sexual harassment is a problem in Bucharest. **Minorities,** and especially those with dark skin, may encounter unwanted attention, as they may be mistaken for Roma (gypsies), who face discrimination in Romania. Practitioners of **religions** other than

Orthodox Christianity may feel uncomfortable in the province of Moldavia. Though **homosexuality** is now legal, Most Romanians hold conservative attitudes toward sexuality, which may translate into harassment of **GLBT** travelers and often manifests itself in the form of anti-gay propaganda in major cities. For more information about gay and lesbian clubs and resources, check out **www.accept-romania.ro.**

TRANSPORTATION

BY PLANE. Many international **airlines** fly into **Bucharest Henri Coanda International Airport** (☎021 204 1200), although flights from locations outside of Europe tend to be very expensive. It is often cheaper to fly into another major European city, such as Budapest or Prague, and then to catch a train to Bucharest. **Romanian Airlines** (TAROM; www.tarom.ro) and **CarpatAir** (www.carpatair.com) fly to a number of European and Middle Eastern destinations and smaller airports within Romania, including Cluj-Napoca, Constanţa, Suceava, and Timişoara.

BY TRAIN. Trains are fast and efficient for international travel and less expensive than flights. **Eurail** is accepted in Romania, but **Eastrail** is not. To buy tickets for the national railway, go to **CFR** (Che-Fe-Re) office in larger towns. You must buy international tickets ahead. Train stations sell domestic tickets 1hr. in advance. The English-language timetable *Mersul Trenurilor* (hardcopy L12; www.cfr.ro) is very useful. There are four types of trains: *InterCity* (indicated by an "IC"); *rapid* (in green); *accelerat* (red); and *personal* (black). International trains (blue) are indicated with an "i." *InterCity* trains stop only at major cities. *Rapid* trains are the next fastest; *accelerat* trains are slower and dirtier. The sluggish and decrepit *personal* trains stop at every station. The difference between **first class** (*clasa întâi;* 6 people per compartment) and **2nd class** (*clasa doua;* 8 people) is small, except on *personal* trains. In an **overnight train,** shell out for a *vagon de dormit* (sleeper car) and buy both compartment tickets if you don't want to share.

BY BUS. Traveling to Romania by **bus** is often cheaper than entering by plane or train, but not as fast. Tourist agencies may sell tickets, but buying tickets from the carrier saves commission and is often cheaper. Use the slow **local bus system** only when trains are unavailable. Local buses can be cheaper than trains but are packed and poorly ventilated. Minibuses are a good option for short distances, as they are often cheaper, faster, and cleaner than trains. Rates are posted inside.

BY FERRY AND BY TAXI. In the Danube Delta, boats are the best mode of transport. A ferry runs down the new European riverway from Rotterdam, NTH to Constanţa, and in the Black Sea between İstanbul, TUR and Constanţa. Taxis should be avoided if possible, as scams are very, very common. If it is necessary to take a taxi, particularly an intercity taxi, it is advisable to call for a taxi, verify that the meter is operational, and agree on a price beforehand. Your ride should cost no more than L6 per km plus a L7 flat fee.

BY THUMB. Some travelers report that **hitchhiking** is very common in rural Romania and, in some places, is the only way to get around without a car. Hitchhikers stand on the side of the road and put out their palm, as if waving. Drivers generally expect a **payment** similar to the price of a train or bus ticket for the distance traveled; L1 for every 10km is a fair price. Let's Go does not recommend hitchhiking.

KEEPING IN TOUCH

PHONE CODES	**Country code: 40. International dialing prefix: 00.** For more information on how to place international calls, see **Inside Back Cover.**

INTERNET AND TELEPHONE. Internet cafes are relatively common—though not always easy to find—in cities and larger towns and cost L3 per hr. They are typically open late and sometimes 24hr. Most public phones are orange and only accept **phone cards**, sold at telephone offices, Metro stops, and some post offices and kiosks. These cards are only accepted at telephones of the same brand; the most prevalent is **Romtelecom**. Rates run around L1.20 per min. to neighboring countries, L1.60 per min. to most of Europe, and L2 per min. to the US. Phones operate in English if you press "i." At an analog phone, dial ☎971 for international calls. People with European cell phones can avoid roaming charges by buying a **SIM card** at **Connex, Dialog,** or **CosmoRom**. International access codes include: **AT&T** (☎02 18 00 42 88); **British Telecom** (☎02 18 00 44 44); **Canada Direct** (☎02 18 00 50 00); **MCI WorldPhone** (☎02 18 00 18 00).

MAIL. At the post office, request *par avion* for **airmail**, which takes two weeks for delivery. For postcards or letters, it costs L3 to mail within Europe and L5 to mail to the rest of the world. **Mail** can be received through **Poste Restante,** though you may run into problems picking up your package. Address envelopes as follows: LAST NAME, first name, Oficiul Postal nr. 1 (post office address), city-POSTE RESTANTE, Romania, Postal Code. Major cities have **UPS** and **Federal Express.**

LANGUAGE. Romanian is a Romance language, but differs from other Romance tongues in its Slavic-influenced vocabulary. **German** and **Hungarian** are widely spoken in Transylvania. **French** is a common second language for the older generation, while **English** is common among the younger. Avoid **Russian,** which is often understood but disliked. For a phrasebook and glossary, see **Appendix: Romanian,** p. 1066.

ACCOMMODATIONS AND CAMPING

ROMANIA	❶	❷	❸	❹	❺
ACCOMMODATIONS	under L40	L40-70	L71-100	L101-200	over L200

Many **hostels** are fairly pleasant, and some have perks like breakfast and free beer. While some **hotels** charge foreigners 50-100% more, lodging is still inexpensive (US$7-20). **Guesthouses** and **pensions** are simple and comfortable but rare. In summer, many towns rent low-priced rooms in **university dorms.** Consult the tourist office. **Private rooms** and **homestays** are a great option, but hosts rarely speak English. Rooms run L50-80. Look at the room and fix a price before accepting. **Bungalows** are often full in summer; reserve far ahead. Hotels and hostels often provide the best info for tourists.

FOOD AND DRINK

ROMANIA	❶	❷	❸	❹	❺
FOOD	under L7	L7-11	L12-15	L16-20	over L20

A complete **Romanian meal** includes an appetizer, soup, fish, an entree, and dessert. Lunch includes **soup,** called *supă* or *ciorbă* (the former has noodles or dumplings, the latter is saltier and with vegetables), an entree, and dessert. *Clătite* (crepes), *papanaşi* (doughnuts with jam and sour cream), and *torts* (creamy cakes) are all delicious. In the west, you'll find as much **Hungarian food** as Romanian. Some restaurants **charge by weight** rather than by portion; although prices may be listed per 50 or 100 grams, the actual serving can be up to 300 grams. Some servers will attempt to charge unsuspecting tourists extra. If the menu is not specific, always ask. *Garnituri,* the extras that come with a meal, are usually charged separately. This means you're paying for everything, even a bit of butter or a dollop of mustard. **Pork** rules in Romania, so keeping **kosher** is difficult. Local **drinks** include *ţuică,* a brandy made from plums and apples, and double-distilled *palincă,* which approaches 70% alcohol. *Vişinată* liqueur is made from wild cherries. Always verify that the server brings the exact vintage that was ordered; some will attempt to substitute a more expensive wine and claim that they ran out of the other.

HOLIDAYS AND FESTIVALS

Holidays: New Year's (Jan. 1-2); Epiphany (Jan. 6); *Mărţişor* (Mar. 1); Orthodox Easter Holiday (Apr. 27-28, 2008; Apr. 19-20, 2009); Labor Day (May 1); National Unity Day/ Romania Day (Dec. 1); Christmas (Dec. 25-26).

Festivals: *Dragobete* (Feb. 24), known as "the day when the birds are getting engaged," is a traditional Romanian fertility festival. For *Mărţişor* (Mar. 1), locals wear *porteboneurs* (good-luck charms) and give flowers to friends and lovers. Romania Day (Dec. 1), commemorates the day in 1918 that Transylvania became a part of Romania.

BEYOND TOURISM

Central European Teaching Program, 3800 NE 72nd Ave., Portland, OR 97213, USA (☎ 1-503-287-4977; www.ticon.net/~cetp). Places English teachers in state schools in Hungary and Romania for one semester (US$1700) or a full school year (US$2250).

University of Bucharest, 36-46, M. Kogălniceanu Bd., Sector 5, 70709 Bucharest, Romania (☎ 402 13 07 73 00; www.unibuc.ro). Accepts international students.

BUCHAREST (BUCUREŞTI) ☎ 021

Once a storied stop on the Orient Express, Bucharest (booh-kooh-RESHT; pop. 2,100,000) is now infamous for its heavy-handed transformation under dictator Nicolae Ceauşescu. During his 25-year reign, he nearly ruined the city's splendor by replacing historic neighborhoods, boulevards, and Ottoman ruins with concrete blocks, highways, and communist monuments. Adults remember and may have participated in the 1989 revolution, but all have since endured a mix of communist nostalgia and break-neck capitalism. Though it retains only glimmers of the sophisticated city it once was, life here is now as fascinating as it is frustrating.

▐ TRANSPORTATION

Flights: Henri Coanda (Otopeni) Airport (☎ 204 1200; www.otp-airport.ro). Avoid taxis outside the terminal; the FlyTaxi company has exclusive rights to the space and charges several times the normal rate. Call a cab or buy a bus ticket (L5 per 2 trips) from the corner kiosk at the exit from the airport. Bus #783 runs from the airport to Pţa. Unirii (45min., every 30min. 5:23am-11:53pm). Flying into Bucharest can be expensive; often, a better idea is to fly into Budapest or Zagreb and enter Romania via train or bus.

Trains: Gara de Nord (☎ 223 0880, info 95 21). M1: Gara de Nord. To: **Braşov** (2½-4hr., 26 per day, L26); **Constanţa** (5hr., 9 per day, L41); **Sighişoara** (4-5hr., 10 per day, L49); **Budapest, HUN** (14hr., 3 per day, L172); **Kraków, POL** (27hr., 1 per day, L299); **Prague, CZR** (36hr., 1 per day, L336); **Sofia, BUL** (11hr., 2 per day, L95). **CFR,** Str. Domniţa Anastasia 10-14 (☎ 313 2643; www.cfr.ro), books domestic and international tickets. Open M-F 7am-8pm, Sa 9am-1:30pm. Cash only. **Wasteels** (☎ 317 0369; www.wasteels.ro), inside Gara de Nord, books international tickets. English spoken. Open M-F 8am-7pm, Sa 8am-2pm. AmEx/MC/V.

Buses: The profusion of bus services, both private and public, in Bucharest makes taking a bus notoriously difficult; trains are preferable for domestic travel. There are 6 official bus stations in Bucharest, each serving different directions. Internationally, however,

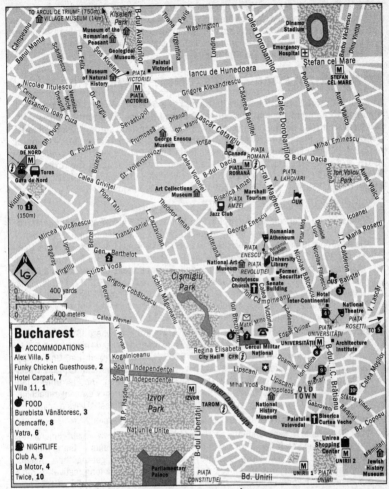

TO ARCUL DE TRIUMF (750m),
VILLAGE MUSEUM (1km)

Kiseleff Park

Câmpeanu

Banul Manta

Scărlătescu

Dr. Felix

Șos Kiseleff

B-dul Aviatorilor

Tirana Paris

Washington

Londra

Argentina

Dinamo Stadium

Emergency Hospital

Ștefan cel Mare

ȘTEFAN CEL MARE

Museum of the Romanian Peasant

Geological Museum

Palatul Victoriei

PIAȚA VICTORIEI

Iancu de Hunedoara

Polonă

Banu Văcărescu

Radu Vintu

Aurel Vlaicu

Tunari

Nicolae Titulescu

Dr. Sergiu

Museum of Natural History

Veronica Micle

Dreaptă

PIAȚA VICTORIEI

Grigore Alexandrescu

Cădera Basiliei

Calea Dorobanților

Mihai Eminescu

Cenat

Alexandru Ioan Cuza

Gh. Duca

Sevastopol

Orlando

Gh. Manu

Lascăr Catargiu

PIAȚA ROMANĂ

B-dul. Dacia

PIAȚA A. LAHOVARI

Polonă

Ion Voicu Park

Frumoasă

George Enescu Museum

Iorga

Canada

PIAȚA ROMANĂ

Gt. Volovdzievozi

Aurel Vlaicu

GARA DE NORD

G. Polizu

Buzești

Calea Griviței

Calea Victoriei

B-dul. Dacia

G-ral. Magheru

Marshall Tourism

OUK

Icoanei

Toros

Gara de Nord

Popa Tatu

Art Collections Museum

Biserica Amzei

PIAȚA AMZEI

Maria Rosetti

TO (150m)

Witting

Theodor Aman

Jazz Club

George Enescu

Sos. Ștefan

Dionisie Lupu

Nicolae Filipescu

J.L. Calderon

Mircea Vulcănescu

L. Cazzavilan

Transilvaniei

Romanian Athenaeum

Bus Batiste

Lipova

Berzei

Fâgâras

Virgiliu

Gen. Berthelot

Știrbei Vodă

Grigore Cobălcescu

Schitu Măgureanu

Luterană

PIAȚA ENESCU

National Art Museum

PIAȚA REVOLUȚIEI

St. Benjamin Franklin

University Library

Former Securitate

Nicolae Bălcescu

3

National Theatre

PIAȚA ROSETTI

Cișmigiu Park

Cretzulescu Church

Senate Building

Hotel Inter-Continental

V. Lascăr

400 yards

Berzei

V. Pârvan

Calea Plevnei

Ion Câmpineanu

Academiei

Edgar Quinet

Matei Millo

PIAȚA UNIVERSITĂȚII

UNIVERSITĂȚII

Doamnei

National Theatre

PIAȚA ROSETTI

5

400 meters

Kogalniceanu

Spaiul Independenței

Regina Elisabeta
City Hall

Cercul Militar National

CFR

6

7

Architecture Institute

Ion Ghica

Doamnei

Calea Moșilor

Bucharest

ACCOMMODATIONS
Alex Villa, 5
Funky Chicken Guesthouse, 2
Hotel Carpati, 7
Villa 11, 1

FOOD
Burebista Vânătoresc, 3
Cremcaffe, 8
Vatra, 6

NIGHTLIFE
Club A, 9
La Motor, 4
Twice, 10

Spaiul Independenței

B.P. Hasdeu

Izvor Park

IZVOR

Lipscani

Mihai Vodă

Stavropoleos

OLD TOWN

Gabrovei

Sfânta Vineri

B-dul. I.C. Brătianu

9

Bănari

10

River Dambovița

TAROM

National History Museum

Palatul Voievodal

Biserica Curtea Veche

Bd. Coposu

Națiunile Unite

B-dul Libertății

Unirea Shopping Center

Mămulari

Jewish History Museum

Parliament Palace

PIAȚA CONSTITUȚIEI

Bd. Unirii

UNIRII 2

PIAȚA UNIRII

UNIRII 1

ROMANIA

buses are the best way to reach **Athens, GCE** and **İstanbul, TUR.** Multiple companies near the train station sell tickets to most of Europe. **Toros,** Calea Griviței 134 (☎223 1918), outside the station, sends buses to İstanbul (2 per day, L125). Open daily 7am-5pm. Cash only. Next door at Calea Griviței 136-138, **Transcontinental** (☎202 9030; www.tci.ro) goes to Athens (2 per week, €73). They also sell **Eurolines** bus tickets, which cover most of Western Europe. English spoken. Open daily 9am-5pm. Cash only.

Public Transportation: Buses, trolleys, and **trams** cost L1.10 and run daily 5:30am-11:30pm. Validate tickets by sliding them into the small boxes to avoid a L30 fine. The transportation system is invaluable, but figuring out how it works is a chore. **Express buses** take only magnetic cards (L5 per 2 trips, L20 per 10 trips). Tickets and magnetic cards are sold at RATB kiosks, often near bus stops. Pickpocketing is a problem during peak hours. The **Metro** offers reliable, less-crowded service (L2 per 2 trips, L7 per 10). Runs 5am-11:30pm. Maps of the public transportation system, which include a detailed city map, can be purchased from kiosks.

Taxis: Taxi drivers will cheerfully rip off foreigners. Drivers rarely speak English. Normal rates should be around L1 base fee and L1.4 per km. The base fee is often posted; look for the "tarif." Fake taxis are a problem, avoid taxis that post the number "9403," as this is a commonly used fake number. Reliable companies include **Meridien** (☎94 44), **ChrisTaxi** (☎94 61), and **Taxi2000** (☎94 94).

ORIENTATION AND PRACTICAL INFORMATION

Bucharest's main street changes its name from **Şosea Kiseleff** to **Bulevard Lascăr Catargiu** to **Bulevard General Magheru** to **Bulevard Nicolae Bălcescu** to **Bulevard I.C. Brătianu** as it runs north-south through the city's four main squares: **Piaţa Victoriei, Piaţa Română, Piaţa Universităţii,** and **Piaţa Unirii.** Another thoroughfare, running parallel, is **Calea Victoriei,** which crosses **Piaţa Revoluţiei.** To reach the center from Gara de Nord, take M1 to Pţa. Victoriei, then change to M2 in the direction of Depoul IMGB. Go one stop to Pţa. Română, two stops to Pţa. Universităţii, or three stops to Pţa. Unirii. It's a 15min. walk between each of squares.

Tourist Office: No municipal office. Hotels are a good resource.

Embassies and Consulates: Australia, Pţa. Montreal 10, World Trade Center, entrance F, 1st fl. (☎316 7553; www.austrade.gov.au). M4: 1 Mai. Open M-Th 9am-5:30pm, F 9am-2:30pm. **Canada,** Str. Tuberozelor 1-3 (☎307 5000). M1 or 2: Pţa. Victoriei. Open M-Th 8:30am-5pm, F 8:30am-2pm. **Ireland,** Str. Buzeşti 50-52, 3rd fl. (☎310 2131). M2: Pţa. Victoriei. Open M-F 10am-noon and 2-4pm. Citizens of **New Zealand** should contact the UK embassy. **UK,** Str. Jules Michelet 24 (☎201 7279). M2: Pţa. Romană. Open M-Th 9am-noon and 2-6pm, F 9am-noon. **US,** Str. Nicolae Filipescu 26 (☎200 3300, after hours 200 3433; www.bucharest.usembassy.gov). M2: Pţa. Universităţii. A block behind Hotel Intercontinental. Open M-Th 9-11am and 1-3pm, F 9-11am.

Currency Exchange: Exchange agencies and **ATMs** are everywhere. Stock up before heading to remote areas, but don't exchange more than you'll need—many won't buy *lei* back. **Banca Comercială Română** (☎312 6185; www.bcr.com), in Pţa. Universităţii and on Ştefan cel Mare, exchanges currency for no fee and **American Express Travellers Cheques** for 1.5% commission. Open M-F 8:30am-5:30pm. The Pţa. Universităţii location, Bd. Regina Elisabeta 5, has both an **ATM** and a currency exchange machine, available 24hr. Changing money on the street is illegal and almost always a scam.

Luggage Storage: Gara de Nord. L3 per bag, L6 per large bag. Open 24hr.

GLBT Resources: Accept Romania, Str. Lirei 10 (☎252 5620; www.accept-romania.ro). English-speaking staff has a wealth of information on GLBT events in the center and organizes counseling services, support groups, and informal get-togethers. Accept Romania is also responsible for the annual **Gay-Fest,** a week-long festival to raise awareness of minority issues, the 1st and 2nd weeks of June. Open M-F 9:30am-5pm.

Medical Services: Spitalul de Urgenţă (Emergency Hospital), Calea Floreasca 8 (☎317 0121). M1: Ştefan cel Mare. Open 24hr.

Telephones and Internet: Phone cards (L10 or L15) are necessary for all calls. Internet cafes are everywhere. Free Wi-Fi available at all KFC and Pizza Hut locations in the city.

Post Office: Central Post Office, Str. Matei Millo 10 (☎315 8793). M2: Pţa. Universităţii. Like most branches, this one has **Poste Restante.** Open M-F 7:30am-1pm and 1:30-8pm. **Postal Code:** 014700.

ACCOMMODATIONS

Renting private rooms is uncommon, and hotels here are more expensive than in other Romanian cities. Travelers should avoid "representatives" who greet them at Gara de Nord, sticking with established hostels and hotels instead.

Alex Villa, Str. Avram Iancu 5 (☎312 1653). M2: Pţa. Universităţii. From Gara de Nord, take trolley #85 to Calea Moşilor. Follow Bd. Carol I to Pţa. Pache Protopopescu, then go right on Str. Sf. Ştefan. At the playground, take a left on Avram Iancu. In a quiet, historic neighborhood. Diverse international clientele. Breakfast, laundry, and Internet included. 4-bed dorms €10. Cash only. ❶

Funky Chicken Guesthouse, Str. General Berthelot 63 (☎312 1425). Bucharest's most centrally located hostel, near Cişmigiu Park and Pţa.Revoluţiei. The cheapest prices in town draw diverse patrons. Small kitchen available. Laundry included. 4- to 8-bed dorms €8. Call ahead in summer. Cash only. ❶

Hotel Carpati, Str. Matei Millo 6 (☎315 0140). M2: Universităţii. A short walk down Bd. Regina Elizabeta to Str. I. Brezoianu from Pţa. Universităţii. Turn right; hotel is at the 2nd corner. Meticulously clean hotel with balconies, central location, and English-speaking staff. Breakfast included. Check-in 2pm. Check-out noon. Singles with shared bath L118; doubles L160, with bath L220. Reserve ahead. MC/V. ❸

Villa 11, Str. Institut Medico Militar 11 (☎07 22 49 59 00). M1 or M4: Gara de Nord. From the train station, take a right on Bd. Dinicu Golescu and left on Str. Vespasian. Quiet hostel offering home-cooked breakfast daily. English spoken. Shared baths. 3- to 8-bed dorms L45; singles L80; doubles L100. Cash only. ❷

🍴 FOOD

The open-air **market** at Pţa. Amzei, near Pţa. Romană has cheese, meat, and produce. (Open M-F 6am-9pm, Sa 6am-7pm, Su 6am-3pm. Cash only.) A large **La Fourmi Supermarket** is in the basement of the Unirea Shopping Center on Pţa. Unirii. (Open M-F 8am-9:30pm, Sa 8:30am-9pm, Su 10am-6pm. MC/V.)

▨ Burebista Vânătoresc, Str. Batistei 14, off B-dul. Nicolae Bălcescu (☎211 8929; www.restaurantburebista.ro). M2: Pţa. Universităţii. Complete with a stuffed bear, hunting trophies, and a live folk band daily after 8pm. Menu features game, including wild boar. English-language menu. Entrees L13-70. Open daily noon-midnight. MC/V. ❸

Cremcaffe, Str. Toma Caragiu 3 (☎313 9740; www.cremcaffe.ro). M2: Pţa. Universităţii. Off B-dul. Regina Elisabeta, find Str. Toma Caragiu behind the statues, 1 block from Pţa. Universităţii. Established in 1950, this elegant Italian coffeehouse features delicious *foccaccia* and *ciabatta* sandwiches (from L14), along with a good vegetarian selection. Coffee and liqueur blends L11-19. Ice cream L10-15. English-language menu. Open M-F 7:30am-midnight, Sa-Su 9am-midnight. Cash only. ❷

Vatra, Str. Brezoianu 23-25 (☎315 8375; www.vatra.ro). M2: Pţa. Universităţii. From Pţa. Universităţii, head down B-dul. Regina Elisabeta. A block before Cişmigiu Park, turn right down Brezoianu. Traditionally attired waitstaff serves relatively cheap, authentic Romanian cuisine in a lively dining room with rough-hewn wooden tables. English-language menu. Beer L4-6. Entrees L9-24. Open daily noon-midnight. Cash only. ❷

🄢 SIGHTS

CIVIC CENTER. To create his ideal Socialist capital, Ceauşescu destroyed five sq. km of Bucharest's historical center, demolishing over 9000 19th-century houses and displacing more than 40,000 people. The Civic Center (Centru Civic) that he built lies at the end of the 6km B-dul. Unirii, built 1m wider than its inspiration, the Champs-Elysées. Its centerpiece, the 1000-room ▨**Parliamentary Palace** (Palatul Parlamentului), is the world's second-largest building after the Pentagon in Washington, D.C. As much as 80% of Romania's GDP was consumed by the project during its construction. *(M1 or 3: Izvor. M2: Unirii. Visitors' entrance on the north side of the building by the river. Open daily 10am-4pm. 40min. English-language tours L15. Cash only.)*

CIŞMIGIU PARK. One of Bucharest's oldest parks, Cişmigiu Park (Parcul Cişmigiu) is the peaceful, tree-filled eye of central Bucharest's storm of gray modernity. Stroll among carefully tended flower gardens, statues, cobblestone pathways, and fountains that surround the small lake. (M2: Pţa. Universităţii. Bus #61 or 336. Open 24hr. Rowboats and paddleboats L10 per hr. Open M-Th 11am-9pm, F 11am-midnight, Sa 10am-midnight, Su 10am-9pm. Cash only.)

SIGHTS OF THE REVOLUTION. Crosses and plaques throughout the city commemorate the *eroii revoluţiei Române*, "heroes of the revolution," and the year 1989. The first shots of the Revolution were fired at Piaţa Revoluţiei on December 21, 1989. In the square are the University Library, the National Art Museum, and the Senate Building (former Communist Party Headquarters) where Ceauşescu delivered his final speech. Afterward, he fled the roof by helicopter, but didn't get very far; shortly thereafter, he was captured by his pursuers and executed on national television. A white marble triangle with the inscription *Glorie martirilor noştri* ("glory to our martyrs") commemorates the rioters who overthrew the dictator. (M2: Pţa. Universitatii. Turn right on Bd. Regina Elisabeta and then right on Calea Victoriei.) Piaţa Universităţii overlooks memorials to victims of the revolution and the 1990 protests against the corrupt government that replaced Ceauşescu. Crosses line Bd. Nicolae Bălcescu—the black cross lies where the first victim died.

MUSEUMS. The ▇**Village Museum** (Muzeul Satului), Şos. Kiseleff 28-30, is an excellently designed open-air replica of traditional rural village life in different Romanian regions. (M2: Aviatorilor. ☎ 222 9068; www.muzeulsatului.ro. English-lang. captions. Open M 10am-5pm, Tu-Su 9am-7pm. L5, students L2.50. Cash only.) The massive **National Art Museum** (Muzeul Naţional de Artă al României) has works by famous Westerners, but the highlight is the Romanian section. (Calea Victoriei 49-53, in Pţa. Revolutiei. M2: Pţa. Universitatii. ☎ 313 3030. Open W-Su May-Sept. 11am-7pm; Oct.-Apr. 10am-6pm. Each wing L10, students L5; both wings L15/7.50; free 1st W of each month. Cash only.) The **Museum of the Romanian Peasant** (Muzeul Ţăranului Român) captures Romanian rural life. Don't miss the small, fascinating collection of Communist memorabilia, tucked downstairs near the restrooms, with one of the few remaining publicly exhibited portraits of Nicolae Ceauşescu. (Şos. Kiseleff 3. M2 or 3: Pţa. Victoriei or bus #300. ☎ 317 9661; www.muzeultaranului.ro. Some English captions. Open Tu-Su 10am-6pm. L6, students L2. Cash only.) The **National History Museum** (Muzeul Naţional de Istorie al României), has extensive jewel collections. (Calea Victoriei 12. M1 or 2: Pţa. Unirii. www.mnir.ro. Open W-Su 10am-6pm. L7, students L2. Cash only.)

OTHER SIGHTS. Several of modern Bucharest's most fashionable streets, including **Calea Victoriei, Şoseauna Kiseleff, Bulevardul Aviatorilor,** and **Bulevardul Magheru,** are sights in themselves. Side streets just off Pţa. Victoriei and Pţa. Dorobanţilor are lined with villas and houses typical of beautiful 19th-century Bucharest. **Herăstrău Park,** bordering Şos. Kiseleff, is a popular place for people of all ages to stroll; it also contains rides for people of all ages. At the head of Şos. Kiseleff is Romania's **Arcul de Triumf,** commemorating Romania's WWI casualties. The **old center** lies west of B-dul. Brătianu and south of B-dul. Regina Elisabeta. On Str. Lipscani, cafes, art galleries, and quaint cobblestone streets abound. The ruins of one of Dracula's actual palaces, **Curtea Veche** (Old Court), can be seen on Str. Franceza.

▇▇ ENTERTAINMENT AND NIGHTLIFE

For the best deals on already cheap **opera, symphony,** and **theater** tickets, stop by the box office about a week before a show. There are no summer performances. (Opera at B-dul. Mihail Kogălniceanu 70-72; ☎ 313 18 57; www.operanb.ro.) At night, pack a map and cab fare—many streets are poorly lit and public transportation stops at midnight. ■**Twice,** Str. Sfânta Vineri 4, has multi-level dance floors. (☎313 5592. M2: Pţa. Universităţii. Beer L3-10. Mixed drinks L10-18. Cover men W L5; F-Sa L10. Open Th-Su 9pm-5am. Cash only.) **Club A,** Str. Blănari 14, is Bucharest's most famous hot spot, with cheap drinks and loud music. (☎315 5592; www.cluba.ro. M2: Pţa. Universităţii. Beer from L2.40. Cover M-W and Su men L3, Th men L4, F-Sa men L5 and women L2. Open M-Th 10am-5am, F 10am-6am, Sa 9pm-6am, Su 9pm-5am. Cash only.) **La Motor/Lăptăria,** B-dul. Bălcescu 1-3, atop the National Theater, is a student bar with a huge terrace. (M2: Pţa. Universităţii. Beer L3-5. Open M-Th and Su noon-2am, F-Sa noon-4am. Cash only.)

SINAIA   ☎0244

Sinaia (sih-NYE-uh; pop. 15,000) first made its mark in the late 1880s as an alpine getaway for Romania's royal family. Carol I, king of the newly independent country, oversaw construction of the fantastically opulent ■**Peleş Castle** (Castelul Peleş), completed in 1914. The more modest, nearby **Pelişor Castle,** built in 1902, was furnished in the Art Nouveau style. (☎31 09 18; www.peles.ro. Both castles open Tu 11am-5pm, W-Su 9am-5pm; low season closed Tu. Tours required at Peleş L12, students L5. Pelişor L9/3.) The nearby **Bucegi Mountains** are good for hiking in summer and skiing in winter. A **telecabină** (cable car) to the mountains leaves from B-dul. Carol I 26; to reach it, turn up the hill across from the tourist office on Str. Cuza Vodă. There are two stops, one at 1400m and the other at 2000m. (☎31 19 39. Cable cars run Tu-Su 8:30am-5pm; Dec.-Feb. and June-Aug. also M 10:30am-5pm. L12 to 1400m, L21 to 2000m; round-trip L20/40. Cash only.)

The **Cabana Mioriţa ❶,** at the Cota 2000 station, with a bar and restaurant, is the queen of the mountain cabin system. (☎31 22 99. 12-bed dorms L20; 7-bed dorms L30; private rooms L40-50. Cash only.) For traditional fare, head to **Restaurant Bucegi ❶,** on Sinaia's main street, Bd. Carol I, near Hotel New Montana. (Entrees L5.50-27. Open daily 9am-10pm. MC/V.) After a long day of hiking, grab a beer and some pizza with the locals at **Old Nick's Pub ❶,** B-dul. Carol I 8, by Hotel Sinaia. (☎31 24 91; www.oldnickpub.ro. Beer L5-12. Entrees L10-18. Open daily 9am-2am. Cash only.) **Trains** (☎31 00 40) run to Braşov (1hr., 33 per day, L15), Bucharest (1½-2½hr., 27 per day, L30), and Cluj-Napoca (6hr., 6 per day, L60). To get to the center of town from the train station, climb the set of stone steps across from the station, and at the top go left on Bd. Carol I. The at the **tourist office,** B-dul. Carol I 47, speaks English. (☎31 56 56; www.infosinaia.ro. Open M-F 8:30am-4:30pm, occasionally Sa-Su 10am-12:30pm.) The Bancpost **ATM, telephone office,** and **post office** are in the same building at B-dul. Carol I 33. (Post office open M-F 7am-8pm, Sa 8am-1pm.) **Postal Code:** 106100.

TRANSYLVANIA (TRANSILVANIA)

The name evokes images of a evil land of black magic and vampires, but Transylvania (also known as Ardeal)—with a history of Saxon settlement dating back to the 12th century—is a relatively Westernized region. It sees the lion's share of tourists in Romania. The vampire legends do, however, resonate with the region's architecture: Transylvanian buildings are tilted, jagged, and more sternly Gothic than anywhere else in Europe. Medieval cities make this a travelers' favorite, while hikers revel in the untamed wilderness of the misty Făgăraş Mountains.

CLUJ-NAPOCA   ☎0264

Cluj-Napoca (KLOOZH nah-POH-kah; pop. 298,006) is Transylvania's student center and unofficial capital. The 80m Gothic steeple of the 14th-century Catholic

Church of St. Michael (Biserica Sf. Mihail) rises from **Piaţa Unirii**. Take Str. Regele Ferdinand across the river, turn left on Str. Drăgălina, and climb the stairs to your right for a dazzling city view from atop ◼**Cetătuie Hill**. Over 12,000 plant species grow in the **Botanical Garden** (Grădina Botanica), Str. Republicii 42, off Str. Napoca. (Gardens open daily summer 9am-8pm, fall-spring 9am-6pm; green-houses daily 9am-6pm; museum Tu-Th 10am-1pm. L4, students L2.) Hotels distribute the free pamphlet *Zile si Nopţi? (Days and Nights?)*, which lists the latest nightlife. The **National History Museum of Transylvania**, on the corner of Str. Constantin Daicoviciu and Str. Roosevelt, has over 400,000 displays. (☎004 0264. Open Tu-Su 10am-4pm. L6, students L3; photography L5. Cash only.) **Opera Naţională Română,** located in the **National Theater** at Ştefan cel Mare 24, has shows many evenings at 7pm. (Theater ☎59 71 75; www.operanationalacluj.ro. Ticket office Ştefan cel Mare 14; ☎59 53 63; open Tu-Su 11am-5pm and 30min. before shows. Cash only.) The **Transylvanian International Film Festival** takes place in early June; most films are subtitled or in English. There is live music in town every night during the festival. (Films L5-10; student discounts available.) ◼**Retro Youth Hostel ❷**, Str. Potaissa 13, has clean dorm rooms and arranges excursions for groups to nearby ice caves and salt mines. (☎45 04 52; www.retro.ro. Breakfast L14. Laundry L10. Dorms L44. HI and ISIC discount 5%. MC/V.) ◼**Roata ❷**, Str. Alexandru Ciura 6A, off Str. Emil Isac, is a traditional Romanian restaurant that serves excellent food in big portions. (☎19 20 22. Appetizers L4-10. Entrees L11-30. Open Su-M 1pm-midnight, Tu-Sa noon-midnight. Cash only.) **Diesel,** Piaţa Unirii 17, is a busy cafe whose stylish club and cellar lounge attract beautiful people on weekends. (☎43 90 43. Dress code at club and lounge. Cafe open daily 8am-late. Club open daily 9pm-late. Lounge open Th-Sa. Parties with live music or DJs Th-Sa. Beer L7-15. Mixed drinks L7-20. Cash only.)

Trains go to: Bucharest (8-12hr., 6 per day, L56) via Braşov (5-7hr., L36); Sibiu (4hr., 1 per day, L38); Timişoara (5-7hr., 6 per day, L37); Budapest, HUN (6½-7hr., 2 per day, L114). Local **buses** and **trams** run 5am-10pm; tickets (L1.30) are sold at **RATUC** kiosks (open 5am). Validate your ticket on board. **ATMs** line B-dul. Ferdinand. Internet cafe **Total Net Soft,** is at Str. Emil Isac 2. (7am-11pm L1.50 per hr., 11pm-7am L1 per hour. Open 24hr. Cash only.) **Postal Code:** 400110.

SIGHIŞOARA ☎0265

Vlad Ţepeş, the inspiration for Bram Stoker's *Dracula* (see **Bran,** p. 834), was born in this hillside town (pop. 32,000). Its gilded steeples and old clock tower have survived centuries of assault, fires, and floods. The **Cetatea** (Citadel), built by the Saxons in 1191, is now a medieval city within a city. Enter through the **turnul cu ceas** (clock tower), off Str. O. Goga, passing the **History Museum** on the way up. To the left as you leave the clock tower, the **Colecţia de Arme Medievale** (Museum of Medieval Armory) offers a modest, English-captioned exhibit on Vlad Ţepeş. (Open M 10am-4:30pm, Tu-F 9am-6:30pm, Sa-Su 9am-4:30pm. Clock tower and museum L5, students L2.50; armory L4/2; both L10. Cash only.) Central **Piaţa Cetăţii** was historically used for markets, executions, and impalings. The nearby church, **Biserica Mănăstirii,** holds organ concerts Fridays at 6pm. (Open Tu-Sa 10am-5pm, Su 11:15am-3pm. L2, students L1. Concert L4. Cash only.) Turn right from the station to reach ◼**Nathan's Villa Hostel ❶**, Str. Libertăţii 8. The staff organizes daytrips. (☎77 25 46; www.nathansvilla.com. Breakfast included. Free laundry. Kitchen available. Reception 24hr. 12-bed dorms L35; doubles L80. Cash only.) **Casa Vlad Dracul ❷**, where Vlad Ţepeş was born, is now a restaurant and bar. (☎77 15 96. Beer from L4. Entrees L11-41. Vegetarian options available. Open 24hr. Cash only.)

Trains go to Bucharest (4½hr., 10 per day, L48) via Braşov (1½-2½hr., 19 per day, L29) and Cluj-Napoca (3hr., 7 per day, L40). To reach the city center from the station, turn right on Str. Libertății and left on Str. Gării, veer left at the Russian cemetery, right on the footbridge over Târana Mare, and walk down Str. Morii. The **Associatia Turistică Sighișoara** (tourist office) is at Str. Octavian Goga 8. (☎77 04 15. Open M-Sa 10am-5pm.) **Culture Cafe** in the citadel, attached to Burg Hostel, has **Internet.** (☎77 84 89. Open daily 7am-late. L3.50 per hr. MC/V.) **Postal Code:** 545400.

BRAȘOV ☎0268

Brașov (pop. 284,000) is an ideal departure point for mountain trips. A **telecabină** goes up **Muntele Tâmpa;** to reach it from the main square, **Piața Sfatului,** walk down Apollonia Hirscher, make a left on Str. Castelui, a right on Suișul Castelui, and climb the stairs to the beige building on the right. (*Cable car runs M noon-5:45pm, Tu-F 9:30am-5:45pm, Sa-Su 9:30am-6:45pm. L5, round-trip L7. Cash only.*) Alternatively, follow the red triangle markings to hike to the top (1-1½hr.). Brașov is a picturesque town with a lively German heritage. **Strada Republicii** is the city's main pedestrian avenue, while beyond the square and along Str. Gh. Barițiu is Romania's most celebrated Gothic edifice, the Lutheran **Black Church** (Biserica Neagră). Built in 1383, it received its name after being charred by a 1689 fire. (*Open M-Sa 10am-5pm. Organ concerts June and Sept. Tu 6pm; July-Aug. Tu, Th, Sa 6pm. L5. Cash only.*) Tickets to the **opera** (Str. Bisericii Române 51; ☎41 59 90; www.opera-brasov.ro) and **orchestra** (Str. Apollonia Hirscher 10; ☎47 30 58) may be purchased at the Agencia Teatrală de Bilete, Str. Gh. Barițiu 20. (☎47 18 89. Open Tu-F 10am-5pm, Sa 10am-2pm. Opera tickets L8-10, students L3. Orchestra L10/5. Cash only.*) August through September, Pța. Sfatului hosts the **Golden Stag Festival** (Cerbul de Aur), which attracts international musicians. The **International Chamber Music Festival** is in September.

Locals offer **private rooms** at the train station; expect to pay €15 per night. **Kismet Dao Villa Hostel ❷,** at Str. Democrației 2B, has a great common room, great views of the hills from the balconies, and lots of free perks, like breakfast, Internet, Wi-Fi, one free drink per day, and laundry. From Pța. Unirii, walk up Str. Bâlea and turn right on Str. Democrației. (☎51 42 96. Check-out noon. 8- to 10-bed dorms L40; 6-bed dorms L42-45; doubles L110. MC/V; 4% surcharge.) Romantic, candlelit **Bella Muzica ❷,** downstairs at Str. G. Barițiu 2, has an eclectic Mexican-Romanian menu, as well as free tortilla chips and free shots of *pălincă*. (☎47 69 46. English menu. Beer L4-8. Appetizers L6-22. Entrees L9-45. Open daily noon-midnight. MC/V.) **Trains** run to Bucharest (2½-3hr., over 26 per day, L33), Cluj-Napoca (5hr., 8 per day, L52), and Sibiu

(2½-3½hr., 10 per day, L30). Buy tickets at **CFR**, B-dul. 15 Noiembrie 43. (☎47 06 96. Open M-F 7am-8pm. Cash only.) From the station, either take bus #4 to Pţa. Sfatului (10min.) and get off in front of Black Church, or take bus #51 to Pţa. Unirii. The **tourist office**, located inside the museum in Pţa. Sfatului, has an English-speaking staff. (☎41 90 78; www.brasovcity.ro. Open daily 9am-5pm.) Get **Internet** at **Non-stop Internet Cafe**, G. Baritsiu 8. (☎41 01 85. L2 per hr. Open 24hr.) **Postal Code:** 500001.

▶ DAYTRIPS FROM BRAŞOV

BRAN CASTLE. Vlad Ţepeş, the model for the hero-villain of Bram Stoker's novel *Dracula*, probably never actually lived in Bran, the inspiration for his fictional castle, though he may have been a prisoner here. Nor, in fact, did Stoker, an Irishman, ever visit Romania. But Dracula's fictional exploits pale in comparison with Ţepeş's actual ones: as a local prince of the Wallachia region, he protected the area from the encroaching Turks of the Ottoman Empire, garnering infamy for impaling not only his enemies, but even some of his own people. The ticket to the castle also includes a visit to the **Bran Village Museum,** which re-creates a traditional village. *(Open M noon-6pm, Tu-Su 9am-6pm. L12, students L6.)* To reach Bran from Braşov, take a taxi or city bus #12 to Autogară 2 (45min., 2 per hr., L3.50). Get off at the souvenir market or at the sign marked "Cabana Bran Castle—500m." Backtrack toward Braşov; the castle is on the right. **Postal Code:** 507025.

RÂŞNOV FORTRESS. On a windswept hill near **Râşnov** sits a ▨**ruined fortress** topped by an immense wooden crucifix. Much of the castle has been renovated recently, but work continues on the topmost portion, which shows every one of its nearly 800 years. Drop a coin down the spectacularly deep well (146m), dug in 17 years by two Turkish prisoners in exchange for their freedom. The small museum houses a collection of the weapons used to protect the fortress over the ages. The fortress is less touristy than Bran, and the 360° panoramic view from the top is breathtaking. *(☎23 02 55. English-language captions. Open daily 9am-7pm. L10. Cash only.)* Most buses to Bran stop in **Râşnov** (25min.), and direct buses to Râşnov depart from the *Autogara* (4 per hr., L2.50). From the bus stop, follow Str. Republicii past an open-air market. Following the signs for Muzeu Cetate, go right and then left through an arch; if all else fails, keep watch for the archway.

TIMIŞOARA   ☎0256

In addition to holding an important place in national history, Timişoara (pop. 307,000), Romania's westernmost city, has earned the name of Little Vienna for its grand boulevards, magnificent town squares, riverside cafes, and wellgroomed parks and gardens. In 1989, an anti-Ceauşescu rally in **Piaţa Victoriei** ignited the revolution that overthrew the communist dictators. At one end of the square stands the imposing ▨**Metropolitan Cathedral,** with a brightly tiled roof in the Byzantine and Moldavian folk style. (Open daily 6:30am-8pm. Free.) In nearby Huniade Castle, the **Muzeul Banatului** (Banat Museum) traces Timişoara's history. (Open Tu-Su 10am-4:30pm. L2 per fl., students L1.) Across the square is the **National Theater and Opera.** (Box office Str. Mărăşeşti 2. Open daily Sept.-June 10am-1pm and 5-7pm. Theater up to L15; opera up to L20. Cash only.)

    Hotel Nord ❷, Str. Gen. Ion Dragalina 47, by the train station, has comfy rooms with fridge and TV. (☎49 75 04. Breakfast included. Singles €20-32; doubles €29-37; apartments €50. MC/V.) **Beciul Sârbesc ❸**, Str. G. Ungureanu 14, near the Serbian Orthodox Church, serves Serbian food. (☎07 24 27 73 70. English menu. Entrees L10-40. Live music daily 7pm. Open daily 10am-late. Cash only.) **Trains** run from Timişoara Nord to Braşov (9hr., 1 per day, L47), Bucharest (8-11hr., 8 per day, L73), and Cluj-Napoca (5-7hr., 6 per day, L38). From the station, take city bus #11 or 14 to the center of town (L2.50 for 2 trips; buy tickets at RATT kiosks). The **Tourist Information Center** (Info Centrul Turistic Timişoara), Str. Alba Iulia 2, is in the Opera building, to the left of the main entrance. (☎43 79 73. English spoken. Open June-Aug. M-F 9am-8pm, Sa 9am-5pm; Sept.-May M-F 9am-6pm, Sa 10am-3pm.) **Postal Code:** 300005.

MOLDAVIA (MOLDOVA)

Northeastern Romania, known as Moldavia, extends from the Carpathian Mountains to the Prut River. Starker than Transylvania but more developed than Maramureş, Moldavia is home to the painted monasteries of Bucovina, which combine Moldavian and Byzantine architecture with Romanian Orthodox Christian images. Dress modestly; avoid wearing shorts or sleeveless tops.

Moldavia and Moldova are not the same place. While Moldavia is the northeastern part of Romania, Moldova is a separate country between Russia and Romania. The distinction is further confused because the region of Moldavia is known as "Moldova" in Romanian. Although as of 2007, US citizens no longer need a visa to enter Moldova, Australians and New Zealanders still do. Make sure you don't accidentally book a bus that passes through Moldova unless you have proper documentation.

SUCEAVA   ☎0230

Once Moldavia's capital, Suceava is home to the grand 1388 **Citadel of the Throne** (Cetatea de Scaun). Climb up and walk along the ramparts for a spectacular view of the city and surrounding park. Taxis (5min., L4) can be arranged from the main square, Pţa. 22 Decembrie, but the 10min. hike uphill following the forest path is pleasant. (Open daily 8am-8pm; low season 10am-6pm. L2, students L1; photography L5.) The nearby **Village Museum of Bucovina** immortalizes traditional life. (Open M-F 10am-6pm, Sa-Su 10am-8pm. L2, students L1.) From Str. Ana Ipătescu, walk past the bus shelter and turn left to find the **Biserica St. Dumitru,** built in 1535 and decorated inside with frescoes. It is a functioning church, so visiting hours vary.

The delightful █ **High Class Hostel ❷**, Str. Aurel Vlaicu 195, is 7km from town (bus #5, L1), but the exceptional service is worth the travel time. As of late 2007, the hostel will move to a new location near the city center at Str. Mihai Eminescu 19. (☎515 213; www.classhostel.ro. Breakfast L10. Dinner L25. Laundry L10 per 3kg. Free Internet. 2- to 4- bed dorms L50. MC/V.) **Pub Chagall ❷,** in a courtyard off the pedestrian part of Str. Ştefan cel Mare, serves thin-crust pizzas and filling pub food in a red brick cellar. (☎53 06 21. Entrees L8-19. Open M-Sa 10am-midnight, Su 11am-midnight. Cash only.) **Trains** run to: Braşov (8hr., 1 per day, L43); Bucharest (6-7hr., 6 per day, L35); Cluj-Napoca (6-7hr., 6 per day, L36); Gura Humorului (1hr., 6 per day, L7.80). Buy tickets at **CFR,** Str. N. Bălcescu 4. (☎21 43 35. Open M-F 7:30am-8:30pm. Cash only.) Turn right off Str. N. Bălcescu for **buses** (☎52 43 40) that run from the station on Str. V. Alecsandri (open 5am-9pm) to Bucharest (8hr., 5 per day, L25), Cluj-Napoca (6½hr., 2 per day, L37), and Gura Humorului (1hr., 12 per day, L4.50). **Taxis** around town charge about L1.50 per km. **Bilco Agenţia de Turism,** Str. N. Bălcescu 2, organizes car tours to the monasteries and sells maps of

Bucovina (L8), but not Suceava. (☎52 24 60. €60-100 per car. Private guides available. Open in summer M-Sa 8:30am-7pm; in winter M-F 9:30am-5pm, Sa 9:30am-3pm. MC/V.) **Librăria Lidana,** on Str. C. Porumbescu behind the theater in the main square, sells maps of Suceava. (☎37 73 24. Open M-F 9am-6pm, Sa 9am-3pm.) **Postal Code:** 720290.

☒ DAYTRIP FROM SUCEAVA: BUCOVINA MONASTERIES. Hidden in rural Romania, Bucovina's painted monasteries are a source of national pride. Forty-seven of them were built 500 years ago by Ștefan cel Mare—rumor has it that he built one after every victory over the Turks—and they offer perfect examples of Moldavian architecture, a unique mix of Byzantine, Roman, and Gothic styles. Suceava can serve as an ideal base for monastery tours. A half-day trip from Suceava leads to ☒**Moldovița,** which houses a small, vibrant community of 40 nuns and some of the best-preserved frescoes in Romania. *(Open in summer daily 8am-7pm; in winter 8am-5pm. L4, students L2.)* Take a **train** from Suceava to Vama (1hr., 8 per day, L4) and continue to Vatra Moldoviței (40min., 3 per day, L2.30).☒**Sucevița,** for its part, is as much a fortress as a convent. After passing four-meter- thick walls and a watchtower, visitors enter through a tiny door meant to hinder mounted attackers. The frescoes that cover the church's outside walls are in fantastic—some might say miraculous—condition. Public transportation to Sucevița is unavailable, but many car tours run out of Suceava. *(Open daily 7am-8pm. L4, students L2.)* Ștefan cel Mare built **Voroneț** in 1488 in three months, three weeks, and three days. Almost 40 years later, in 1524, his illegitimate son Petru Rareș added its famous frescoes. The monastery is accessible by foot from Gura Humorului. Walk left from the train station on Ștefan cel Mare, turn left on Cartierul Voroneț, and follow the signs for a scenic 5km. *(Open daily in summer 8am-7pm; in winter 8am-5pm. L4, students L2.)*

THE BLACK SEA COAST

CONSTANȚA ☎0241

Constanța (pop. 308,000) straddles the line between industrial city and beach resort, while a more singular purpose unites Mamaia and other resort towns—the beach. The **Museum of Art,** B-dul. Tomis 84, highlights 19th- and 20th-century Romanian art. (☎61 80 19. Open in high season daily 9am-8pm; low season

W-Su 9am-5pm. L9, students L4.50.) The site of the Forum from the 4th to the 6th century, the ▨**Museum of National History and Archaeology,** Pţa. Ovidiu 12, celebrates Constanţa's Roman heritage. (☎90 60 40. Open in high season daily 8am-8pm; low season W-Su 9am-5pm. L10, students L5.) The impressive **Great Mosque** stands at Str. Arhiepiscopiei 5. The 47m minaret has the best view of the city. (Open daily 9:30am-9:30pm. L4, students L2.) Visit Constanţa's **Modern Beach.** Or, stay cool by careening down the waterslides at **Aqua Magic,** the waterpark inside the southern entrance to the Mamaia resort. (☎83 31 83; www.aquamagic.ro. Open June 15th-Sept. 1 daily 10am-7pm daily. L30-40.) Get an overview of the resort by taking the **Telegondola** next to Aqua Magic. (Open 10am-10pm. L8.)

Hotel Tineretului ❸, B-dul. Tomis 20-26, is a two-star hotel with TVs in all rooms and a disco downstairs. (☎61 35 90. English-speaking reception. Breakfast included. Wi-Fi L2 per 2hr. Singles L84; doubles L94. Cash only.) **Restaurant Nur ❸,** B-dul. Tomis 48, offers quality Turkish food with great music and hookahs to match. (☎91 21 21. Appetizers L5. Beer L6. Entrees L15-26. Open daily 8am-midnight. Cash only.) When the sun sets, **Oscar,** Str. Sarmisegetusa 15, rocks out to older tunes, or dance into the wee hours at **Club "No Problem,"** Complex Dacia on B-dul. Tomis. (☎51 33 77. Cover L10 for live music. Open Th-Sa 10pm-5am.) The **tourist information center** (☎55 50 00; www.infolitoral.ro) has an English-speaking staff that books accommodations for a commission. Don't be fooled by the signs pointing you to a non-existent "official" office on Str. Traian. Instead try the Litoral s.a. **tourist office,** B-dul. Tomis 133. (☎83 11 63; www.litoral.info.ro. Open M-F 9am-5pm.) The **post office** is at B-dul. Tomis 79-81. (☎66 46 34. Open M-F 7am-8pm, Sa 8am-1pm.) **Taxis** (☎55 55 55) are easily waved down. Public transit (L1 per ride) consists of buses, trams, and trolleys and runs 5am-11:30pm. **Trains** run to Bucharest, HUN (4-6hr., 7 per day, L38). Buy tickets at **CFR,** Vasile Canarache 4. (☎61 49 50. Open M-F 7:30am-7:30pm, Sa 8am-2pm. International booth open M-F 9am-4pm. Cash only.) Condor, Niş-Tur, and Ozlem (☎63 83 43), run **buses** to İstanbul, TUR (L100) via Varna, BUL (L40). The bus station is open daily 5am-11pm.

RUSSIA (РОССИЯ)

Over a decade after the fall of the USSR, mammoth Russia still struggles to redefine itself. Between fierce, worldly Moscow and graceful, majestic St. Petersburg lies a gulf as wide as any in Europe—and a swath of provincial towns that seem frozen in time. Mysterious and inexpensive, with good public transportation and scores of breathtaking sights, Russia is in many ways ideal for the adventurous budget traveler. While the legacy of Communism endures in bureaucratic headaches and the situation in Chechnya raises tensions, Russia remains the epitome of Eastern European grandeur.

 DISCOVER RUSSIA: SUGGESTED ITINERARIES

BEST OF MOSCOW, ONE WEEK. Queue up for the **Lenin Mausoleum** (p. 851) in the morning, then visit Russia's most recognizable landmark, **St. Basil's Cathedral** (p. 851). Check out the minarets and armory inside the **Kremlin** (p. 850) and play spy on a private tour through the old **KGB Building** (p. 853). Don't miss the collections of Russian art at the **State** and **New Tretyakov Galleries** (p. 853), or the shrines to literary success at museums for **Pushkin, Gorky, Tolstoy,** and **Mayakovsky** (p. 853).

BEST OF ST. PETERSBURG, ONE WEEK. Begin with a stroll down **Nevskiy prospekt** (p. 854), St. Petersburg's main drag, then stop at the city's most famous church, the **Church of Our Savior on Spilled Blood** (p. 862). Head to the bell tower of **St. Isaac's Cathedral** (p. 861) for an incomparable view of the city. Visit that attic of aristocracy, the **Hermitage** (p. 861), where the riches are displayed in unthinkable abundance. Then wander the canals for which St. Petersburg is nicknamed "the Venice of the North."

ESSENTIALS

FACTS AND FIGURES

Official Name: Russian Federation.

Capital: Moscow.

Major Cities: St. Petersburg, Nizhniy Novgorod, Novosibirsk, Yekaterinburg.

Population: 141,378,000.

Time Zone (Western Russia): GMT +3.

Language: Russian.

Chess Grandmasters: 156.

Oil Refining Ability: 6,600,000 barrels per day.

WHEN TO GO

It may be wise to plan around the high season (June-Aug.). Fall and spring (Sept.-Oct. and Apr.-May) are more appealing times to visit; the weather is mild and flights are cheaper. If you intend to visit the large cities and linger indoors at museums and theaters, the bitter winter (Nov.-Mar.) is most economical. Keep in mind, however, that some sights and accommodations close or run reduced hours. Another factor to consider is hours of daylight—in St. Petersburg, summer light lasts almost to midnight, but in winter the sun sets at around 3:45pm.

DOCUMENTS AND FORMALITIES

EMBASSIES AND CONSULATES. Foreign embassies are in Moscow (p. 846); consulates are in St. Petersburg (p. 859). Russian embassies abroad include: **Australia,**

78 Canberra Ave., Griffith, ACT 2603 (☎662 959 033; www.australia.mid.ru); **Canada,** 285 Charlotte St., Ottawa, ON K1N 8L5 (☎613-235-4341; www.rusembcanada.mid.ru); **Ireland,** 184-186 Orwell Rd., Rathgar, Dublin 14 (☎14 92 20 48; www.ireland.mid.ru); **New Zealand,** 57 Messines Rd., Karori, Wellington (☎44 76 61 13, visas 476 9548; www.rus.co.nz); **UK,** 13 Kensington Palace Gardens, London W8 4QX (☎20 72 29 36 28, visa 229 8027; www.great-britain.mid.ru); **US,** 2650 Wisconsin Ave., NW, Washington, D.C. 20007 (☎202-298-5700; www.russianembassy.org).

VISA AND ENTRY INFORMATION. Almost every visitor to Russia needs a visa. The standard tourist visa is valid for 30 days, while a business visa is valid for up to three months. Both come in single-entry and double-entry varieties. All applications for Russian visas require an **invitation** stating dates of travel.If you have an invitation from an authorized travel agency or Russian organization and want to get a visa on your own, apply for the visa in person or by mail at a Russian

ENTRANCE REQUIREMENTS.

Passport: Required for all travelers.

Visa: Required for all travelers.

Letter of Invitation: Required for all travelers.

Inoculations: Recommended up-to-date on DTaP (diphtheria, tetanus, and pertussis), Hepatitis A, Hepatitis B, MMR (measles, mumps, and rubella), polio booster, rabies, and typhoid.

Work Permit: Required of all foreigners planning to work in Russia.

International Driving Permit: Required of all those planning to drive in Russia.

embassy or consulate; for same-day processing, however, you must apply in person. (Download an application form at www.ruscon.org. Single-entry visas US$100-300; double-entry US$150-350, except on 10-day processing; multiple-entry US$100-450. Prices change constantly, so check with the embassy.) **Visa services** and **travel agencies** can also provide visa invitations (US$30-80), as well as secure visas in a matter of days (from US$160). Some agencies may even be able to get a visa overnight (up to US$450-700). **Host Families Association (HOFA),** 3 Linia 6, V.O., St. Petersburg 199053, Russia (☎91 19 14 27 62 or 81 22 75 19 92; www.hofa.us), arranges homestays, meals, and transport. Visa invitations for Russia, Ukraine, and Belarus cost US$30-40. **Red Bear Tours/Russian Passport,** 401 St. Kilda Rd., Ste. 11A, Melbourne 3004, Australia (☎03 98 67 38 88; www.travelcentre.com.au), provides invitations to Russia, sells rail tickets, and arranges tours. **VISAtoRUSSIA.com,** 309A Peters St., Atlanta, GA 30313, USA (☎800-339-2118, in Europe 749 59 56 44 22; www.visatorussia.com), provides Russian visa invitations from US$30. Students and employees may be able to obtain student visas from their school or host organization.

The best way to cross the **border** is to fly directly into Moscow or St. Petersburg. Another option is to take a train or bus into one of the major cities. Expect delays and red tape. Upon arrival, travelers must fill out an **immigration card,** part of which must be kept until departure from Russia, and to **register** their visa within three working days. Registration can be done at your hostel or hotel, or for a fee at a travel agency. As a last resort, head to the central **OVIR** (ОВИР) office to register. Though many travelers skip this nuisance, taking care of it will leave one less thing for bribe-seeking authorities to hassle you about—fines for visa non-registration run about US$150. When in Russia, carry your passport at all times; never, ever give it to anyone, except to hotel or OVIR staff during registration.

TOURIST SERVICES AND MONEY

EMERGENCY	Ambulance: ☎03. Fire: ☎01 Police: ☎02.

TOURIST OFFICES. There are two types of Russian tourist offices—those that only arrange tours and those that offer general travel assistance. Offices of the former type are often unhelpful with general questions, but those of the latter are usually eager to assist, particularly with visa registration. Big hotels often house tourist agencies with English-speaking staff. The most accurate maps are sold by street kiosks. A great online resource is www.waytorussia.net.

MONEY. The Russian unit of currency is the **рубль** (ruble; R), plural рубли (ru-BLEE). One ruble is equal to 100 **копейки** (kopecks; k), singular копейка, which comes in denominations of 1, 5, 10 and 50. Rubles have banknote denominations of 5, 10, 50, 100, 500, and 1000 and in coin denominations of 1, 2, and 5. Govern-

RUSSIAN RUBLES (R)	AUS$1 = 21.72R	10R = AUS$0.46
	CDN$1 = 24.07R	10R = CDN$0.42
	EUR€1 = 34.85R	10R = EUR€0.29
	NZ$1 = 19.27R	10R = NZ$0.52
	UK£1 = 51.57R	10R = UK£0.19
	US$1 = 25.45R	10R = US$0.39

ment regulations require that you show your passport when you exchange money. Find an **Обмен Валюта** (Obmen Valyuta), hand over your currency—most will only exchange US dollars and euro—and receive your rubles. **Inflation** runs around 9%. Do not exchange money on the street. **Banks** offer the best combination of good rates and security. **ATMs** (банкоматы; bankomaty) linked to major networks can be found in most cities. Banks, large restaurants, and currency exchanges often accept major **credit cards,** especially Visa. Main branches of banks will usually accept **traveler's checks** and give **cash advances** on credit cards. It's wise to keep a small amount of money (US$20 or less) on hand. Most establishments don't accept torn, written-on, or crumpled bills, and Russians are wary of old US money; bring new bills. Keep in mind, however, that establishments that display prices in dollars or euro also tend to be much more expensive.

HEALTH AND SAFETY

In a **medical emergency,** either leave the country or go to the American or European Medical Centers in Moscow or St. Petersburg; these clinics have English-speaking, Western doctors. Water is drinkable in much of Russia, but not in Moscow or St. Petersburg; buy **bottled water.** The 0.5-5R charge for **public toilets** generally gets you a hole in the ground and maybe a piece of toilet paper.

Crimes against foreigners are on the rise, particularly in Moscow and St. Petersburg. Although it is often difficult to blend in, try not to flaunt your nationality. Seeming Russian may increase your chances of police attention, but keeps you safer among the citizenry. It is unwise to take pictures of anything related to the military or to act in a way that might attract the attention of a man in uniform. Avoid interaction with the police unless an emergency necessitates it. It is legal for police to stop anyone on the street, including foreigners, to ask for documentation; **carry your passport and visa with you at all times.** If you do not (and sometimes even if you do), expect to be taken to a police station and/or to be asked to pay a fine. Let's Go does not endorse bribery, but some travelers report that such "fines" are negotiable and, for minor infractions, should not amount to more than 500-1000R. Do not let officials go through your possessions; travelers have reported incidences of police theft. If police try to detain you, threaten to call your embassy ("*ya pozvonyu svoyu posolstvu*"). It may be simpler and safer to go ahead and pay.

The concept of **sexual harassment** hasn't yet reached Russia. Local men will try to pick up lone **women** and will get away with offensive language and actions. The routine starts with an innocent-sounding "*Devushka...*" (young lady); say "*Nyet*" (No) or simply walk away. Women in Russia tend to dress quite formally. Those who do not speak Russian will also find themselves the target of unwanted attention. The authorities on the Metro and police on the street will frequently stop and question dark-skinned individuals, who may also receive rude treatment in shops and restaurants. Although **violent crime** against foreigners is generally rare, anti-Semitic and racist hate crimes—including murder—are on the rise. **Homosexuality** is still taboo even in the larger cities; it is best to be discreet.

RUSSIA

TRANSPORTATION

BY PLANE. Most major international carriers fly into **Sheremetyevo-2** in Moscow or **Pulkovo-2** in St. Petersburg. **Aeroflot,** Leningradskiy Prospect 37, Building 9, Moscow 125167 (☎49 52 23 55 55; www.aeroflot.org) is the most popular domestic carrier. The majority of domestic routes are served by Soviet-model planes, many of which are in disrepair and have poor safety records. These routes should be avoided. From London, BRI, Aeroflot offers cheap flights into Russia. A number of European budget airlines land in Tallinn, EST; Rīga, LAT; or Helsinki, FIN, from which you can reach Russia by bus or train.

BY TRAIN AND BY BUS. In a perfect world, all travelers would fly into St. Petersburg or Moscow, skipping customs officials who tear packs apart and demand bribes, and avoiding Belarus entirely. Nevertheless, many travelers find themselves headed to Russia on an eastbound train. If that train is passing through Belarus, you will need a US$100 transit visa to pass through the country. If you wait until you reach the Belarusian border to get one, you'll likely pay more and risk a forced no-expense-paid weekend getaway in Minsk. Trains, however, are a cheap and relatively comfortable way to travel to Russia from Tallinn, EST; Rīga LAT; and Vilnius, LIT. Domestically, trains are generally the best option. Weekend or holiday trains between St. Petersburg and Moscow sometimes sell out a week in advance. The best class is *lyuks*, with two beds, while the 2nd-class *kupeyny* has four bunks. The next class down is *platskartny*, an open car with 52 shorter, harder bunks. Aim for places 1-33; they're farthest from the bathroom. Day trains sometimes have a very cheap fourth class, "*opshiya*," which typically only provides hard wooden benches. Hotels and tourist offices are invaluable resources for those who don't speak Russian; almost no train station officials speak English, and train schedules are impossibly complicated. **Women** traveling alone can try to buy out a *lyuks* compartment or can travel *platskartny* and depend on the crowds to shame would-be harassers. *Platskartny* is a better idea on the theft-ridden St. Petersburg-Moscow line, as you are less likely to be targeted in that class. Try to board trains on time; changing your ticket carries a fee of up to 25%.

BY BUS. Buses, less expensive than trains, are better for very short distances. Russian roads are in poor condition; by bus, long-distance trips can be bumpy. Buses are often crowded and overbooked; oust people who try to sit in your seat.

BY BOAT. Cruise ships stop in the main Russian ports: St. Petersburg, Murmansk, and Vladivostok. However, they usually allow travelers less than 48hr. in the city. In December 2002, a regular ferry route opened between Kaliningrad and St. Petersburg (1-2 per week; for schedules and fares see www.balticline.ru/eng/translubeca.htm). Kaliningrad ferries also operate to **Poland** and **Germany.** A river cruise runs between Moscow and St. Petersburg.

BY CAR AND BY TAXI. Although it is sometimes necessary to reach Russia's more remote regions, renting a car is both expensive and difficult, and poor road conditions, the necessity of bribing traffic inspectors, dangerous driving practices, and the frequency of automobile crime make the experience particularly stressful. If you must drive, however, remember to bring your **International Driving Permit. Avis, Budget,** and **Hertz** rent cars in Russia. Hailing a taxi is indistinguishable from **hitchhiking,** and should be treated with equal caution. Though it is technically illegal, most drivers who stop will be private citizens trying to make a little extra cash;

even cars labeled taxis may not be official. Those seeking a ride should stand off the curb and hold out a hand into the street, palm down; when a car stops, riders tell the driver the destination before getting in; he will either refuse altogether or ask "*Сколько?*" (Skolko?; How much?), leading to negotiations. Non-Russian speakers will get ripped off unless they manage a firm agreement and are well-aware of the fair price—if the driver agrees without asking for a price, you must ask "*skolko?*" yourself (sign language works too). Never get into a car that has more than one person in it. Let's Go does not recommend hitchhiking.

KEEPING IN TOUCH

PHONE CODES	**Country code: 7. International dialing prefix: 8**, await a second tone, then 10. For more information on placing international calls, see **Inside Back Cover.**

EMAIL AND INTERNET. Internet cafes are prevalent throughout St. Petersburg and Moscow, but aren't as popular elsewhere, where connections are less reliable. Internet typically costs 35-70R per hr. Many Internet cafes are open 24hr.

TELEPHONE. Most public telephones take phonecards, which are sold at central telephone offices, Metro stations, and newspaper kiosks. When you are purchasing phonecards from a telephone office or Metro station, the attendant will often ask, "На улицу?" (*Na ulitsu?;* On the street?) to find out whether you want a card for the phones in the station or for outdoor public phones. Be careful: phone cards in Russia are very specific, and it is easy to purchase the wrong kind. For five-digit numbers, insert a "2" between the dialing code and the phone number. Make direct **international** calls from telephone offices in St. Petersburg and Moscow: calls to Europe run US$1-1.50 per min., to the US and Australia about US$1.50-2. Mobile phones have become a popular accessory among Russians and a comforting safety blanket for visitors. Most new phones are compatible with Russian networks and cell phone shops are common, but service can be costly. On average, a minute costs US$0.20 and users are charged for incoming calls. Major providers Megafon, BeeLine GSM, and MTS have stores throughout the cities, as do rental chains like Euroset and Svyaznoy. **International access codes** include: AT&T, which varies by region: see www.consumer.att.com/global/english/access_codes.html for specific info; British Telecom (☎08 00 89 07 00); Canada Direct (☎810 800 110 1012); Sprint (in Moscow ☎747 3324).

MAIL. Mail service is more reliable leaving the country than coming in. Letters to the US arrive one to two weeks after mailing; letters to other destinations take two to three weeks. **Airmail** is "авиа" (*aviya*). Send mail "заказное" (*zakaznoye;* certified; 40R) to reduce the chance of it being lost. Most post office employees do not speak English; it can be helpful to say "*banderoley,*" which signifies international mail, and to know the Russian name of the country of destination. **Poste Restante** is *Pismo Do Vostrebovaniya.* Address envelopes: LAST NAME, first name, Postal Code, city, Письмо До Востребования, Россия.

LANGUAGE. Russian is an East Slavic language written in the Cyrillic alphabet. Once you get the hang of the Cyrillic alphabet, you can pronounce just about any Russian word, even if you think you sound like an idiot. Although **English** is increasingly common among young people, come equipped with at least a few helpful Russian phrases. For a phrasebook, see **Appendix: Russian**, p. 1067.

ACCOMMODATIONS AND CAMPING

RUSSIA	❶	❷	❸	❹	❺
ACCOMMODATIONS	under 400R	400-700R	701-1200R	1201-2000R	over 2000R

The **hostel** scene in Russia is limited mostly to St. Petersburg and Moscow and averages US$18-25 per night. Some hostels, particularly those in smaller towns, will only accept Russian guests. Reserve in advance. **Hotels** offer several classes of rooms. "Люкс" *(Lyux)*, usually two-room doubles with TV, phone, fridge, and bath, are the most expensive. "Поли-люкс" *(Polu-lyux)* rooms are singles or doubles with TV, phone, and bath. The lowest-priced rooms are "без удобств" *(bez udobstv)*, which means one room with a sink. Expect to pay 300-450R for a single in a budget hotel. As a rule, only cash is accepted as payment. In many hotels, **hot water**—and sometimes all water—is only turned on for a few hours each day.

University dorms offer cheap rooms; some accept foreign students for about US$5-10 per night. The rooms are livable, but don't expect sparkling bathrooms or reliable hot water. Make arrangements through an educational institute from home. In the larger cities, **private rooms** and **apartments** can often be found for very reasonable prices (about 200R per night). Outside major train stations, there are usually women offering private rooms to rent—bargain with them and ask to see the room before agreeing. **Camping** is very rare in Russia.

FOOD AND DRINK

RUSSIA	❶	❷	❸	❹	❺
FOOD	under 70R	70-150R	1510-300R	301-500R	over 500R

Russian cuisine is a medley of dishes both delectable and unpleasant; tasty *borshch* (борщ; beet soup) can come in the same meal as *salo* (сало; pig fat). The largest meal of the day, *obed* (обед; lunch), includes: *salat* (салат; salad), usually cucumbers and tomatoes or beets and potatoes with mayonnaise or sour cream; *sup* (суп; soup); and *kuritsa* (курица; chicken) or *myaso* (мясо; meat), often called *kotlety* (котлеты; cutlets). Other common foods include *shchi* (щи; cabbage soup) and *bliny* (блины; potato pancakes). **Vegetarians** and **kosher** diners traveling in Russia will probably find it easiest to stick to the cuisine in large cities and to eat in foreign restaurants. On the streets, you'll see a lot of *shashliki* (шашлики; barbecued meat on a stick) and *kvas* (квас), a slightly alcoholic dark-brown drink. Beware of any meat products hawked by sidewalk vendors; they may be several days old. Kiosks often carry **alcohol;** imported cans of beer are warm but safe, but be wary of Russian labels—you have no way of knowing what's really in the bottle. *Russkiy Standart* (Русский Стандарт) and *Flagman* (Флагман) are the best **vodkas;** the much-touted *Stolichnaya* is made mostly for export. Among local **beers**, *Baltika* (Ѣалтика; numbered 1-7 according to brew and alcohol content) is the most popular and arguably the best. *Baltika 1* is the weakest (5%), *Baltika 7* the strongest (7%). *Baltikas 4* and *6* are dark; the rest are lagers.

HOLIDAYS AND FESTIVALS

Holidays: New Year's (Jan. 1-2); Orthodox Christmas (Jan. 7); Orthodox New Year (Jan. 14); Defenders of the Motherland Day (Feb. 23); Orthodox Easter Holiday (Apr. 27, 2008; Apr. 19th, 2009); Labor Day (May 1); Victory Day (May 9); Independence Day (June Accord and Reconciliation Day; Nov. 7); Constitution Day (Dec. 12).

Festivals: The country that perfected the "workers' rally" may have lost Communism but still knows how to Party. Come April, St. Petersburg celebrates Music Spring, an international classical music festival, with a twin festival in Moscow. In June, the city stays up late to celebrate the sunlight of White Nights (*Beliye Nochi;* mid-June to early July). The Russian Winter Festival is celebrated in major cities from late Dec. to early Jan. with folklore exhibitions and vodka. People eat pancakes covered in honey, caviar, fresh cream, and butter during *Maslyanitsa* (Butter Festival; end of Feb.).

BEYOND TOURISM

Kitezh Children's Community (http://atschool.eduweb.co.uk/ecoliza/files/kitezh.html). Teach English to Russian orphans in a rural setting. Young people taking a "gap year" between high school and college are especially common as volunteers.

The School of Russian and Asian Studies, 175 E. 74th, Ste. 21B, New York, NY 10021 (☎ 1-800-557-8774; www.sras.org). Provides study-abroad opportunities at language schools and degree programs at universities. Also arranges work, internship, and volunteer programs throughout Russia.

MOSCOW (МОСКВА) ☎ (8)495

On the 16th-century sidestreets of Moscow (pop. 12,600,000), it's still possible to glimpse centuries-old golden domes squeezed between drab Soviet housing complexes and countless Lenin statues. Visiting Europe's largest city is a thrilling, intense experience, flashier and costlier than Petersburg, and undeniably rougher too. Slowly—very slowly—Moscow is re-creating itself as one of the world's most urbane capitals, embracing innovation with the same sense of enterprise that helped it command and then survive history's most ambitious social experiment.

◪ TRANSPORTATION

Flights: International flights arrive at **Sheremetyevo-2** (Шереметыево-2; ☎ 956 4666). Take the van under the "автолайн" sign in front of the station to M2: Rechnoy Vokzal (Речной Вокзал), or take bus #851 to M2: Rechnoy Vokzal or bus #517 to M8: **Taxis** to the center of town tend to be overpriced; bargain down to at most 750R. **Yellow Taxi** (☎ 940 8888) has fixed prices (base fare usually 400R). Cars outside the departures level charge 350-500R; agree on a price before getting in.

Trains: Moscow has 8 train stations arranged around the M5 (circle) line. Tickets for longer trips can be bought at the **Moskovskoye Zheleznodorozhnoye Agenstvo** (Московскоые Железнодорожноые Агенство; Moscow Train Agency; Russian destinations ☎ 266 9333, international 262 0604; www.mza.ru; MC/V), on the far side of Yaroslavskiy Vokzal from the Metro station. Train Schedules and station names are posted in Cyrillic on both sides of the hall. (*Kassa* open M-F 8am-1pm and 2-7pm, Sa 8am-1pm and 2-6pm. 24hr. service is available at the stations.

Belorusskiy Vokzal (Белорусский), pl. Tverskoy Zastavy 7 (Тверской Заставы; ☎ 266 0300). M2: Belorusskaya (Белорусская). To: **Berlin, GER** (27hr., 1 per day, 3820R); **Prague, CZR** (32hr., 1 per day, 3800R); **Vilnius, LIT** (14½hr., 1 per day, 1360-1700R); **Warsaw, POL** (21hr., 2 per day, 2200R).

Kazanskiy Vokzal (Казанский), Komsomolskaya pl. 2 (Комсомольская; ☎ 266 2300). M5: Komsomolskaya. Opposite Leningradskiy Vokzal. To **Kazan** (10-12hr., 2 per day, 660-1550R).

Leningradskiy Vokzal (Ленинградский), Komsomolskaya pl. 3 (☎ 262 9143). M1 or 5: Komsomolskaya. To **St. Petersburg** (8hr., 10-15 per day, 500-2100R); **Helsinki, FIN** (14hr., 1 per day, 3500R); and **Tallinn, EST** (16hr., 1 per day, 1300-2300R).

Rizhskiy Vokzal (Рижский), pr. Mira 79/3 (пр. Мира; ☎631 1588). M6: Rizhskaya (Рижская). To **Rīga, LAT** (16hr., 2 per day, 800-4000R) and destinations in **Estonia.**

Yaroslavskiy Vokzal (Ярославский), Komsomolskaya pl. 5a (☎921 5914). M1 or 5: Komsomol-skaya. The starting point for the legendary **Trans-Siberian Railroad.** To **Novosibirsk** (48hr., every other day, 1900-4900R), **Yaroslavl** (4hr., 1-2 per day, 220-500R), **Siberia,** and the **Far East.**

Public Transportation: The **Metro** (Метро) is fast, clean, and efficient. Metro trains and buses run daily 6am-1am. A station serving multiple lines may have multiple names. Buy token-cards fare cards (17R; 5 trips 75R, 10 trips 140R) from the *kassy* in stations. Buy **bus** and **trolley** tickets from kiosks labeled "проездные билеты" (15R) or from the driver (25R). Punch your ticket when you get on, or risk a fine.

METRO MADNESS. *Let's Go* has tried to simplify navigation by number-ing each Metro line; for a key, see this guide's color map of the Moscow Metro. When speaking with Russians, use the color or name, not our given number.

Taxis: Most taxis do not use meters and tend to overcharge Agree on a price before get-ting in (100-200R across town). **Yellow Taxis** (☎940 8888) have fixed rates (base fare 400R). It is common and cheaper to hail a private car (called gypsy cabs; частники; chastniki), done by holding one's arm out horizontally. To be safe, never get into a taxi or car with more than 1 person already in it. Let's Go does not recommend hitchhiking.

✈🔁 ORIENTATION AND PRACTICAL INFORMATION

A series of concentric rings spread outward from the **Kremlin** (Кремль; Kreml) and **Red Square** (Красная Площадь; Krasnaya Ploshchad). The outermost **Moscow Ring Road** marks the city limits, but most sights lie within the **Garden Ring** (Садовое Кольцо; Sadovoe Koltso). Main streets include **Tverskaya Ulitsa** (Тверская), which extends north along the Metro's green line, as well as **Arbat** (Арбат) and **Novyy Arbat** (Новый Арбат), which run west parallel to the blue lines. Some kiosks sell English-language and Cyrillic maps; hostels and hotels also have English tourist maps. Be careful when crossing streets, as drivers are oblivious to pedestrians; for safety's sake, most major intersections have an underpass (переход; perekhod).

Tours: Tourist Information Centre, Ilyinka 4 (☎232 5657; www.moscow-city.ru). M: Gostiny Dvor. Open daily 10am-7pm.

Tours: Capital Tours, ul. Ilyinka 4 (☎232 2442; www.capitaltours.ru), in Gostinyy Dvor. Offers 3hr. English-language bus tours of the city. Tours daily 11am and 2:30pm; 750R. 3hr. tours of the Kremlin and armory M-W and F-Su 10:30am and 3pm (1400R). **Patri-arshy Dom Tours,** Vspolny per. 6 (Вспольный; from the US ☎65 06 78 70 76, in Rus-sia 49 57 95 09 27; www.russiatravel-pdtours.netfirms.com). M5 or 7: Barrikadnaya (Баррикадная). Wide range of English-language tours (510-2380R) including "Stalin's Moscow" and "Bulgakov in Moscow." Open M-F 9am-6pm.

Budget Travel: Student Travel Agency Russia (STAR), Baltiyskaya 9, 3rd fl. (Балтийская; ☎797 9557; www.startravel.ru). M2: Sokol (Сокол). Discount plane tick-ets, ISICs, and worldwide hostel booking. Branch at Mokhovaya 9 (Моховая), near the Kremlin. Open M-F 10am-7pm, Sa 11am-4pm; June-Aug. also Su 11am-4pm.

Embassies: Australia, Podkolokolnyy per. 10/2 (Подколокольный; ☎956 6070; www.australianembassy.ru). M6: Kitai Gorod (Китай Город). Open M-F 9am-12:30pm and 1:10-5pm. **Canada,** Starokonyushennyy per. 23 (Староконюшенный; ☎105 6000; www.canadianembassy.ru). M1: Kropotkinskaya (Кропоткинская) or M4: Arbatskaya (Арбатская). Open 9am-3pm. **Ireland,** Grokholskiy per. 5 (Грохольский; ☎937 5911). M5 or 6: Prospekt Mira (Проспект Мира). Open M-F 9:30am-5:30pm. **New Zealand,** Povarskaya 44 (Поварская; ☎956 3579). M7: Bar-ikadnaya (Барикадная). Open M-F 9am-12:30pm and 1:30-5:30pm. **UK,** Smolen-skaya nab. 10 (Смоленская; ☎956 7200; www.britemb.msk.ru). M3: Smolenskaya.

■ FOOD
Art Cafe "SAD," 12
Guria, 11
Korchma Taras Bulba, 3
Lyudi Kak Lyudi, 8
Matryoshka, 13
Moo-Moo, 9

■ NIGHTLIFE
Art-Garbage, 7
B2, 1
FAQ Art Club, 6
Karma Bar, 4
Propaganda, 5

Moscow
▲ ACCOMMODATIONS
G&R Hostel Asia (HI), 14
Godzilla's Hostel (HI), 2
Gostinitsa Moskovsko-
  Uzbekskiy, 15
Sweet Moscow, 10

RUSSIA

Open M-F 9am-1pm and 2-5pm. **US,** Novinskiy 21 (Новинский; ☎728 5000; www.usembassy.ru). M5: Krasnopresnenskaya (Краснопресненская). Open M-F 9am-6pm. **American Citizen Services** (☎728 5577, after hours 728 5000) lists English-speaking establishments. Open M-F 9am-noon and 2-4pm.

Currency Exchange: Banks are everywhere. Typically only main branches cash **traveler's checks** or issue **cash advances.** Many banks and hotels have **ATMs.** Avoid withdrawing cash from machines on busy streets, as it make you a target for muggers.

American Express: ul. Usacheva 33 (☎933 8400). M1: Sportivnaya. Exit at the front of the train, turn right, and then right again on Usacheva. Open M-F 9am-5pm.

English-Language Bookstore: Anglia British Bookshop, Vorotnikovskiy per. 6 (Воротниковский; ☎299 7766; www.anglophile.ru). M2: Mayakovskaya. Open M-F 10am-7pm, Sa 10am-6pm; Sept.-May also Su 11am-5pm. AmEx/MC/V.

24hr. Pharmacies: Look for signs marked "круглосуточно" (kruglosutochno; always open). Locations include: Tverskaya 17 (Тверская; ☎629 6333), M2: Tverskaya and Zemlyanoy Val 1/4 (Земляной Вал; ☎917 0434), M5: Kurskaya (Курская).

Medical Services: American Clinic, Grokholskiy per. 31 (☎937 57 57; www.americanclinic.ru). M5 or 6: Prospekt Mira (Проспект Мира). American board-certified doctors that practice family and internal medicine. Consultations US\$120. Open 24hr., including house calls. AmEx/MC/V. **European Medical Center,** Spiridonievsky per. 5 (☎933 66 55; www.emcmos.ru). M3: Smolenskaya. Consultations 4320R.

Telephones: Local calls require phone cards, sold at kiosks and some Metro stops.

Internet Access: Timeonline (☎223 9687), on the bottom level of the Okhotnyy Ryad (Охотный Ряд) underground mall. M1: Okhotnyy Ryad. At night, enter through the Metro underpass. Wi-Fi 50-90R per hr. Open 24hr. Cash only. **Cafemax** (www.cafemax.ru) has 4 locations: Pyatnitskaya 25/1 (Пятницкая; M2: Novokuznetskaya); Akademika Khokhlova 3 (Академика Хохлова; M1: Universitet), on the territory of MGU; Volokolamskoye shosse 10 (Волоколамское шоссе; M2: Sokol); and Novoslobodskaya 3 (Новослободская; M9: Novoslobodskaya). 24-100R per hr. Open 24hr. MC/V.

Post Offices: Moscow Central Telegraph, Tverskaya ul. 7 (Тверская), uphill from the Kremlin. M1: Okhotnyy Ryad (Охотный Ряд). **International mail** at window #23. **Faxes** at #11. Bring packages unwrapped; they will be wrapped and mailed for you. Open M-F 8am-2pm and 3-8pm, Sa-Su 7am-2pm and 3-7pm. **Postal Code:** 125009.

▌ ACCOMMODATIONS

Older women standing outside major rail stations often offer private rooms (сдаю комнату) or apartments (сдаю квартиру) to rent—be sure to haggle.

▨ Godzilla's Hostel (HI), Bolshoy Karetniy 6/5 (Большой Каретний; ☎699 4223; www.godzillashostel.com). M9: Tsvetnoy Bulvar (Цветной Бульвар). Fun, social hostel with great location, 7min. from Pushkin Square and 20min. from the Kremlin. English spoken. Single-sex dorms available. Kitchen available. Free Internet. Reception 24hr. Check-out noon. Dorms 725R; doubles 1740R. ❷

Sweet Moscow, Stariy Arbat ul. 51, 8th fl. #31 (☎241 1446; www.sweetmoscow.com). M4: Smolenskaya. Turn right on Smolenskaya pl. out of Metro, then left at the McDonald's onto Stariy Arbat. The hostel is located across from Hard Rock Cafe; no signs are displayed, so ring the buzzer. In the middle of the city's most famous pedestrian street. Laundry 150R. Free Internet. Extremely helpful English-speaking reception 24hr. 6-, 8-, and 10-bed dorms US\$25. Cash only. ❷

G&R Hostel Asia (HI), Zelenodolskaya 3/2 (Зеленодольская; ☎378 0001; hostel-asia@mtu-net.ru). M7: Ryazanskiy Prospekt (Рязанский). On the 5th fl. of the Gostinitsa Moskovsko-Uzbekskiy (see below). Clean rooms with TV and fridge. Staff helps with rail, theater, and tour reservations. Free luggage storage and safe. Visa invitations €30. Airport transport €25-45. Internet 40R per hr. English spoken. Reception 9am-10pm. Singles €35-60; doubles €50-60; triples €80. €1 HI discount. 10th day free. MC/V. ❸

Gostinitsa Moskovsko-Uzbekskiy, Zelenodolskaya 3/2 (Зеленодольская; ☎378 3392 or 77 03 01). M7: Ryazanskiy Prospekt (Рязанский). Exit the Metro near the back car of the outbound train. A "Гостиница" sign will be visible on top of the hotel to your left. A wide range of rooms; non-renovated ones are clean and ultra-cheap. English spoken. Singles 1050-2350R; doubles 1450-2400R. V. ❷

🍴 FOOD

Many restaurants offer "business lunch" specials (бизнес ланч; typically noon-4pm; US$5-10). For fresh produce, head to a **market.** Some of the best are by the **Turgenevskaya** and **Kuznetskiy Most** Metro stations. (Open daily 10am-8pm.) To find grocery stores, look for "продукты" (produkty) signs.

🔲 **Lyudi Kak Lyudi** (Люди как Люди; "People like People"), Solyanskiy Tupik 1/4 (☎921 1201). Enter from Solyanka. Fun, dimly lit cafe is a favorite of young Russians. Business lunch 130R. Smoothies 100R. Sandwiches 90-100R. English-language menu. Open M-Th 8am-11pm, F 8am-6am, Sa 11am-6am, Su 11am-10pm. Cash only. ❶

🔲 **Korchma Taras Bulba** (Корчма Тарас Бульба), Sadovaya-Samotechnaya 13 (Садовая-Самотечная; ☎694 0056, 24hr. 778 3430; www.tarasbulba.ru). M9: Tsvetnoy Bulvar (Цветной Бульвар). From the Metro, turn left and walk up Tsvetnoy bul. Delicious Ukrainian specialities served by waitresses in folk dress. English-language menu. Entrees 75-550R. Open 24hr. 12 locations. MC/V. ❸

Matryoshka (Матрёшка), Klimentovskiy per. 10 (Климентовский; ☎953 9400), off bul. Ordynka. M6: Tretyakovskaya (Третьяковская). Inexpensive traditional Russian entrees (from 135R) in a winter setting. Business lunch 220R. Open noon-midnight. Branch at Triumfalnaya 1 (Триумфальная; ☎49 99 78 16 60). V. ❷

Guria (Гурия), Komsomolskiy pr. 7/3 (Комсомольский; ☎246 0378), opposite St. Nicholas of the Weavers. M1 or 5: Park Kultury (Парк Культуры). Walk behind 7/

A NEW SORT OF CHEMISTRY CLASS

If you have an extra several thousand rubles handy, you also have the chance to try the newest and perhaps strangest gastronomic experience to hit Moscow since the creation of *okroshka*, a soup flavored with *kvas* (a weakly alcoholic drink). These days, chef Anatoly Komm has introduced to Russians—the people of hearty meals—tiny creations of the newest fad: molecular cuisine.

With four high-class restaurants in Moscow, Komm holds tasting events with such suggestive titles as "The Alchemy of Taste" and "Frost and Sea Molecular Spectacle." Diners are asked to turn off their cell phones, not to smoke, and to keep their minds open before being presented with between 10 and 20 courses of visionary taste treasures.

Komm's kitchen is better likened to a scientific laboratory. The basic principle behind these meals is purely scientific: by breaking food down into its smallest components, one can later put these particles back together in combinations that will excite the tastebuds in new ways. For the small price of some 6000R, you can try a *Russkaya Zakuska* (Russian Appetizer), a tequila glass of liquid combining the tastes of every traditional Russian appetizer—a thought that is at once disturbing and intriguing.

Check out www.anatolykomm.ru.

3 until you reach the restaurant. Near Gorky Park and art galleries. Classy and traditional restaurant serves authentic Georgian fare at some of the city's lowest prices. Locals prefer the private, green-roofed gazebo tables in the garden. English-language menu. Entrees 200-500R. Open daily noon-midnight. MC/V. ❸

Artcafe "SAD" (Арткафе "САД"), Bul. Tolmachevskiy per. 3 (Толмачевский; ☎239 9115), near the Tretyakov Gallery. M2, 6 or 8: Tretyakovskaya. Hip Muscovites dine in a setting to match. English-language menu. Weekday business lunch 160-330R. Sushi rolls 70-290R. Entrees 160-600R. Open 10am-midnight. AmEx/MC/V. ❸

Moo-Moo (My-My), Koroviy Val 1 (Коровый Вал; ☎237 2900), M5: Dobryninskaya (Добрынинская); and Arbat 45/42 (Арбат; ☎241 1364), M4: Smolenskaya (Смоленская). Look for the signature cow statue outside. Moo-Moo's many locations offer cheap continental and Russian home cooking, served cafeteria-style. English-language menu. Salads 30-60R. Entrees 40-100R. Open daily 10am-11pm. Cash only. ❶

◙ SIGHTS

Moscow's sights reflect the city's interrupted history: because St. Petersburg was the seat of the tsardom for 200 years, there are 16th-century churches and Soviet-era museums, but little in between. Though Moscow has no grand palaces and 80% of its pre-revolutionary splendor was demolished by the Soviet regime, the city's museums house the very best of Russian art and history.

■ THE KREMLIN

The Kremlin (Кнтмль; Kreml) is the geographical and historical center of Moscow, its origins dating back to the 12th century. In the Kremlin's Armory and in its magnificent churches, the glory and the riches of the Russian Empire are on display. Besides the sights listed below, the only other place in the triangular complex visitors may enter is the **Kremlin Palace of Congresses,** the white marble behemoth built by Khrushchev in 1961 for the Communist Party, and since converted into a theater. Tourists were banned from entering the Kremlin until the 1960s; now English-speaking guides offer **tours** of the complex at steep prices. Haggle away or consider a prearranged tour through Capital Tours (see **Tours,** p. 846). *(☎202 3776; www.kremlin.museum.ru. M1, 3, 4, or 9: Aleksandrovskiy Sad (Александровский Сад). Open M-W and F-Su 10am-5pm. Buy tickets at the kassa in the Alexander Gardens 9:30am-4:30pm. No large bags. 300R, students 150R. Audio tour 220R. MC/V.)*

■ ARMORY MUSEUM AND DIAMOND FUND.
At the southwest corner of the Kremlin, the Armory Museum (Онужтйнfя Палата; Oruzheynaya Palata) shows the opulence of the Russian court and includes coronation gowns, crowns, and the best collection of carriages in the world. Each of the **Fabergé Eggs** in Room 2 reveals an intricate jeweled miniature. The **Diamond Fund** (Выстfвкf Алмfзнjгj Аонда; Vystavka Almaznovo Fonda) has even more glitter, including the world's largest chunks of platinum. Consider hiring a guide, as most exhibits are in Russian. *(☎202 4631. Open M-W and F-Su. Armory lets in groups for 1½hr. visits at 10am, noon, 2:30, 4:30pm. 350R, students 70R. Diamond Fund lets in groups every 20min. 10am-1pm and 2-6pm. 350R, students 250R. Bags and cameras must be checked.)*

CATHEDRAL SQUARE.
Russia's famous golden domes can be seen in Cathedral Square. Nine cathedrals in all were constructed to display the might of the tsars. The church closest to the Armory is the **Annunciation Cathedral** (Благовещенский Собор; Blagoveshchenskiy Sobor), the former private church of the tsars, which guards luminous icons by Andrei Rublev and Theophanes the Greek. The square

Archangel Michael Cathedral (Архíнгтльский **Собор;** Arkhangelskiy Sobor), which gleams with metallic coffins, is the final resting place for many tsars who ruled before Peter the Great, including Ivans III (the Great) and IV (the Terrible), and Mikhail Romanov. The colorful 15th-century **Assumption Cathedral** (Успінский **Собор;** Uspenskiy Sobor), located in the center of the square, was used to host tsars' coronations and weddings and housed Napoleon's cavalry in 1812. To the right lies the **Ivan the Great Bell Tower** (Кíлјкíльнíя Ивíнг Втликíгј; Kolokolnaya Ivana Velikovo), once the highest point in Moscow; the tower is currently under renovation. Directly behind it is the 200-ton **Tsar Bell** (Царь-колокол; Tsar-kolokol), the world's largest bell. It has never rung and probably never will—a 1737 fire caused an 11½-ton piece to break off.

RED SQUARE

The 700m-long Red Square (Красная Площадь; Krasnaya Ploshchad) has hosted everything from farmer's markets to public hangings, from Communist parades to renegade Cessna landings. Across Red Square, northeast of the Kremlin, is **GUM**, once the world's largest purveyor of Soviet "consumer goods," now an upscale shopping mall. Also flanking the square are the **Lenin Mausoleum, St. Basil's Cathedral,** the **State Historical Museum,** and the pink-and-green **Kazan Cathedral.** *(Combo ticket for St. Basil's and Historical museum available at either location. 230R, students 115R.)*

■ **LENIN'S MAUSOLEUM.** Lenin's likeness can be seen in bronze all over the city, but he appears in the eerily luminescent flesh in Lenin's Mausoleum (Мíвзјлтй В/И/Лтнинf; Mavzoley V.I. Lenina). In the Soviet era, this squat red structure was guarded fiercely, and the wait to get in took three hours. Today's line is still long, and the guards remain stone-faced, but the atmosphere is more curious than reverent. Exit along the **Kremlin wall,** where Stalin, Brezhnev, and John Reed, founder of the American Communist Party, are buried. The line to see Lenin forms between the Historical Museum and the Kremlin wall; arrive at least by noon to have a chance of making it through. *(Open Tu-Th and Sa-Su 10am-1pm. Free. No cameras or cell phones; check them at the bag check in the Alexander Gardens.)*

■ **ST. BASIL'S CATHEDRAL.** Moscow has no more familiar symbol than the colorful onion-shaped domes of St. Basil's Cathedral (Cјбјн Вíсилия <лíжтннјгј; Sobor Vasiliya Blazhennovo). Ivan the Terrible commissioned it to celebrate his victory over the Tatars in Kazan in 1552, and it was completed in 1561. "Basil" is the English equivalent of Vasily, the name of a holy fool who correctly predicted that Ivan would murder his own son. St. Basil's labyrinthine interior is filled with decorative and religious frescoes. *(M3: Ploshchad Revolyutsii (Площадь Революции). ☎ 698 3304. Open daily 11am-6pm; kassa closes 5:30pm. 100R, students 50R. English-language audio tour 120R. Tours 1000R; call 2 weeks ahead. Photo 100R, video 130R.)*

NORTH OF RED SQUARE

Just outside the main gate to Red Square is an elaborate gold circle marking **Kilometer 0,** the spot from which all distances from Moscow are measured. Don't be fooled by this tourist attraction—the real Kilometer 0 lies underneath the Lenin Mausoleum. Just a few steps away, the **Alexander Gardens** (Алтксíндíјвский Сíд; Aleksandrovskiy Sad) are a respite from the pollution of central Moscow. At the northern end of the gardens is the **Tomb of the Unknown Soldier** (Могила Неизвестноио Солдата; Mogila Neizvestnovo Soldata), where an **eternal flame** burns in memory of the losses suffered in the Great Patriotic War (WWII). Soldiers still regularly perform ceremonies here. To the west is **Manezh Square** (Манежная Глощадь; Manezhnaya Ploshchad), a recently converted pedestrian area; nearby lies the smaller **Revolution Square** (Площадь Нтвјлюции; Ploshchad Revolyutsii). Both squares are connected in the north by **Okhotnyy Ryad** (Охотный Ряд; Hunters' Row), once a market for wild game, now an underground mall. Across Okhotnyy Ryad is the **Duma,** the lower house of Parliament. Opposite Revolution Square is **Theater Square** (Театральная Глощадь; Teatralnaya Ploshchad), home of the **Bolshoi Theatre** (see **Entertainment,** p. 854). More posh hotels, chic stores, and government buildings line **Tverskaya Ulitsa,** Moscow's main thoroughfare.

CHURCHES, MONASTERIES, AND SYNAGOGUES

CATHEDRAL OF CHRIST THE SAVIOR. Moscow's most controversial landmark is the enormous gold-domed Cathedral of Christ the Savior (Храм Христа Спасителя; Khram Khrista Spasitelya). Stalin demolished Nicholas I's original cathedral on this site to make way for a gigantic Palace of the Soviets, but Khrushchev abandoned the project and built a heated outdoor pool instead. In 1995, after the pool's water vapors damaged paintings in the nearby Pushkin Museum, Mayor Yury Luzhkov and the Orthodox Church won a renewed battle for the site and built the US$250 million cathedral in only five years. *(Volkhonka 15 (Волхонка), near the Moscow River. M1: Kropotkinskaya (Кропоткинская). Open M 1-6pm, Tu-Sa 10am-6pm, Su 8:30am-6pm. Cathedral and museum free. No cameras, shorts, or hats.)*

NOVODEVICHY MONASTERY AND CEMETERY. Moscow's most famous monastery (Новодевичий Монастырь; Novodevichiy Monastyr) is hard to miss thanks to its high brick walls, golden domes, and tourist buses. In the center, the **Smolensk Cathedral** (Смоленский Собор; Smolenskiy Sobor) displays icons and frescoes. The cemetery (кладбище; kladbishche) is a pilgrimage site that holds the graves of such famous figures as Khrushchev, Chekhov, and Shostakovich. *(M1: Sportivnaya (Спортивная). ☎ 246 5607. Open M and W-Su 10am-5:30pm; kassa closes 4:45pm; closed 1st M of month. Cathedral closed on rainy and humid days. Cemetery ☎ 246 0832. Open daily 9am-5pm. Cathedral and special exhibits each 150R, students 55R. Photo 80R, video 170R.)*

MOSCOW CHORAL SYNAGOGUE. Over 100 years old, the synagogue provides a break from the city's ubiquitous onion domes. Though the synagogue remained open during Soviet rule, all but the bravest Jews were deterred by KGB agents who photographed anyone who entered. More than 200,000 Jews now live in Moscow, and services are increasingly well attended, but the occasional graffiti is a sad reminder that anti-Semitism is not dead in Russia. *(M6 or 7: Kitai-Gorod (Китай-Город). Go north on Solyanskiy Proyezd (Солянский Проезд) and take the first left. Open M-F 7am-11pm, Sa-Su 7am-1am. Services M-F 8:30am, Sa-Su 9am; evening services daily at sunset.)*

AREAS TO EXPLORE

▨**MOSCOW METRO.** Most cities put their marble above ground and their cement below, but Moscow is not most cities. The Metro (Московское Метро) is worth a tour of its own. See the Baroque elegance of **Komsomolskaya** (Косомолская), the stained glass of **Novoslobodskaya** (Новослободская), and the bronze statues of revolutionary archetypes from farmer to factory worker in **Ploshchad Revolyutsii** (Площадь Революции), all for the price of a Metro ticket.

THE ARBAT. Now a pedestrian shopping arcade, the Arbat (Арбат) was once a showpiece of *glasnost* and a haven for political radicals, Hare Krishnas, street poets, and *metallisty* (heavy metal rockers). Some of that eccentric flavor remains thanks to street performers and guitar-playing teenagers. Nearby runs the bigger, newer, and uglier **Novyy Arbat,** lined with gray high-rises and massive modern stores. *(M3: Arbatskaya; Арбатская.)*

VICTORY PARK. On the left past the **Triumphal Arch,** which celebrates the 1812 defeat of Napoleon, lies Victory Park (Парк Победы; Park Pobedy), a monument to WWII. It includes the **Museum of the Great Patriotic War** (Музей Отечественной Войны; Muzey Otechestvennoy Voyny; open Tu-Su 10am-7pm, closed last Th of each month), the **Victory Monument,** and the gold-domed **Church of St. George the Victorious** (Храм Георгия Победаносного; Khram Georgiya Pobedonosnovo), which honors the 27 million Russians who died in battle during WWII. *(M3: Park Pobedy.)*

🏛 MUSEUMS

Moscow's museums are by far the most patriotic part of the city. Government museums and small galleries alike proudly display Russian art, and dozens of historical and literary museums are devoted to the nation's past.

■ STATE TRETYAKOV GALLERY. A treasury of 11th- to early 20th-century Russian art, the Tretyakov Gallery (Государственная Третьяковская Галерея; Gosudarstvennaya Tretyakovskaya Galereya) also has a superb collection of icons, including works by Andrei Rublev and Theophanes the Greek. *(Lavrushinskiy per. 10 (Лаврушинский).* ☎ *951 1362; www.tretyakov.ru. M8: Tretyakovskaya. Turn left out of the Metro, left again, then take a right on Bolshoy Tolmachevskiy per.; turn right after 2 blocks onto Lavrushinskiy per. Open Tu-Su 10am-7:30pm; kassa closes 6:30pm. 250R, students 150R.)*

■ NEW TRETYAKOV GALLERY. Where the first Tretyakov chronologically leaves off, this new gallery (Новая Третьяковская Галерея; Novaya Tretyakovskaya Galereya) begins. The collection starts on the third floor with early 20th-century art and moves through the neo-Primitivist, Futurist, Suprematist, Cubist, and Social Realist schools. The second floor holds temporary exhibits; go on weekday mornings. Leaving the front door, turn left to find a statue gallery; it is a real gem. The dumping ground for decapitated Lenins and Stalins and other Soviet-era statues, it now also contains sculptures of Gandhi, Einstein, Niels Bohr, and Dzerzhinsky, the founder of the Soviet secret police. *(Krymskiy Val 10 (Крымский Вал).* ☎ *283 1378; www.tretyakov.ru. M5: Oktyabraskaya (Октябрьская). Open Tu-Su 10am-7:30pm; kassa closes at 6:30pm. 250R, students 150R. Sculpture garden open daily 9am-10pm. 100R.)*

PUSHKIN MUSEUM OF FINE ARTS. Moscow's most important collection of non-Russian art, the Pushkin Museum (Музей Изобразительных Искусств им. А.С. Пушкина; Muzey Izobrazitelnykh Iskusstv im. A.S. Pushkina) contains major Classical, Egyptian, and Renaissance works. As of August 2007, the second floor is closed for renovations. *(Volkhonka 12 (Волхонка).* ☎ *203 9578; www.gmii.com. M1: Kropotkinskaya (Кропоткинская). Open Tu-Su 10am-7pm; kassa closes 6pm. 60R, students 30R.)* The building to the right of the entrance houses the **Museum of Private Collections** (Музей Личныч Коллеций; Muzey Lichnych Kolletsiy), with artwork by Kandinsky, Rodchenko, and Stepanov. *(Open W-Su noon-7pm; kassa closes 6pm. 100R, students 50R.)*

STATE HISTORICAL MUSEUM. This English-language exhibit (Государственный Исторический Музей; Gosudarstvennyy Istoricheskiy Muzey) on Russian history runs from the Neanderthals through Kiyvan Rus to modern Russia. *(Krasnaya pl. 1/ 2. M1: Okhotnyy Ryad (Охотный Ряд).* ☎ *692 3731; www.shm.ru. Open M and W-Sa 10am-6pm, Su 11am-8pm; kassa closes 1hr. earlier; closed 1st M of month. 150R, students 60R.)*

KGB MUSEUM. Documenting the history and strategies of Russian secret intelligence from Ivan the Terrible to Putin, the KGB Museum (Музей КГ<; Muzey KGB) gives a chance to quiz a current FSB agent. As of August 2007, the museum is closed for restoration. *(Bul. Lubyanka 12 (Лубянка). M1: Lubyanka. By tour only. Patriarshy Dom Tours, p. 846, leads 2hr. group tours; US$18 per person.)*

HOMES OF THE LITERARY AND FAMOUS. The Mayakovsky Museum (Музей им. D. D. Маяковского; Muzey im. V. V. Mayakovskovo) is a walk-through work of Futurist art, created as a biography of the Revolution's greatest poet. Mayakovsky lived and died in a communal apartment on the fourth floor of this building. *(Lubyanskiy pr. 3/6 (Лубянский). M1: Lubyanka. Open M-Tu and F-Su 10am-6pm; Th 1-9pm; kassa closes 1hr. earlier; closed last F of month. 90R, students 50R.)* If you've never seen Pushkin-worship first-hand, the **Pushkin Literary Museum** (Литературный Музей Пушкина; Literaturnyy Muzey Pushkina) with its large collection of Pushkin memorabilia, will either convert or frighten you. *(Prechistenka 12/2 (Пречистенка). Entrance on Khrushchevskiy per (Хрущевский). M1: Kropotkinskaya (Кропоткинская). Open Tu-Su 10am-6pm; kassa closes 5:30pm; closed last F of month. 60R.)* The **Tolstoy Museum** (Музей Толстого; Muzey Tolstovo), in the neighborhood of the author's first Moscow residence, displays original texts, paintings, and letters related to his masterpieces. *(Prechistenka 11 (Пречистенка). M1: Kropotkinskaya (Кропоткинская). ☎637 7410; www.tolstoymuseum.ru. Open Tu-Su 10am-6pm; kassa closes 30min. earlier; closed last F of month. 150R, students 50R.)*

🎵 ENTERTAINMENT

From September through June, Moscow boasts some of the world's best **ballet, opera,** and **theater** performances. Tickets are often cheap (from 130R) if purchased ahead and can be purchased from the theater *kassa* or from kiosks in town. **Bolshoi Theater** (Большой Театр), Teatralnaya pl. 1, is home to the opera and the ballet company. Though the main stage is under renovation until at least 2008, performances continue on the secondary stage. (Театральная; ☎250 7317; www.bolshoi.ru. M2: Teatralnaya. *Kassa* on Petrovska ul. open daily 11am-3pm and 4-8pm. Performances Sept.-June daily 7pm, occasional matinees. 50-5000R. AmEx/MC/V.) The **Moscow Operetta Theater,** Bolshaya Dmitrovka 6, stages operettas. (Большая Дмитровка; ☎692 1237; www.mosoperetta.ru. *Kassa* open daily 11am-3pm and 4-7:30pm. Performances daily 6 or 7pm. 300-1500R.)

🌃 NIGHTLIFE

Moscow's nightlife is the most varied, expensive, and debaucherous in Eastern Europe. Many clubs flaunt their exclusivity. Check the weekend editions of *The Moscow Times* or *The Moscow Tribune* for club reviews and music listings.

🎭 **Propaganda** (Пропаганда), Bolshoy Zlatoustinskiy per. 7 (Большой Златоустинский; ☎624 5732; www.propogandamoscow.com). M6 or 7: Kitai Gorod (Китай-Город). Exiting the Metro, walk down Maroseyka and take a left on Bolshoy Zlatoustinsky per. Get down to house music at this Moscow hot spot without feeling like you're in a meat market. Go early to eat (and avoid strict face control). Dancing after midnight. Th DJ night. Su gay night. Beer from 100R, after 11pm from 60R. Open daily noon-6am.

> **SAVE FACE.** When navigating the hostile, exclusive world of Moscow nightlife, our researchers have found that there is only one proven technique to ensure that "face control" (bouncer) doesn't ruin the night before it starts: become a wealthy, tall, waifish, blonde model in high Russian style. More realistically, try to find friends with connections, dress up, go early, and get ready to have your face controlled.

FAQ Art Club, Gozetniy per. 9/2 (☎629 0827; www.faqclub.ru). M2: Teatralnaya. Chill with Moscow's young, alternative crowd on the tented patio or in house-themed rooms—drawings for the "children's room" are accepted and appreciated. Jazz concerts Su

8pm, 300R. Call ahead to reserve a table. Entrees 115-420R. Beer from 115R. Mixed drinks from 130R. Hookahs from 500R. Open daily 7pm-6am.

Karma Bar, Pushechnaya 3 (Пушечная; ☎624 5633; www.karmabar.ru). M1 or 7: Kuznetzkiy Most (Кузнетский Мост). With your back to the Metro, walk through the arch on your left and turn right on Pushechnaya. Crowd-pleasing dance music keeps the party alive. English spoken. Beer 110-170R. Vodka 150-160R. Mixed drinks 260-320R. Latin dance lessons 9pm-midnight. Su hip-hop. Cover F-Sa after 11pm men 300R, women 200R. Open Th-Sa 9pm-6am, Su 11pm-6am.

Art-Garbage, Starosadskiy per. 5 (Старосадский; ☎628 8745; www.art-garbage.ru). M6 or 7: Kitai Gorod (Китай-Город). Art gallery, club, and restaurant, Art-Garbage is refreshingly more laid-back than many of the chic and trendy Moscow establishments. Better for drinking on the inviting patio than for dancing. Hard alcohol from 60R. Beer from 70R. Cover F-Sa 150-500R. Open noon-6am.

B2, Bolshaya Sadovaya 8 (Большая Садовая; ☎650 9918; www.b2club.ru). M5: Mayakovskaya. This multi-story complex has it all, and without the face control: a quiet beer garden, billiard room, several dance floors, jazz club, karaoke, restaurant, sushi bar, and weekend disco. Beer 80-180R. Hard alcohol from 100R. F-Sa Concerts from 300R; some free with ISIC; check website. Open noon-6am. MC/V.

▓ DAYTRIP FROM MOSCOW: SERGIYEV POSAD. Russia's most famous pilgrimage site, Sergiyev Posad (Сергиев Посад; pop. 200,000) attracts visitors to several churches huddled around its centerpiece: the fully operational **St. Sergius's Trinity Monastery** (Свят-Троицкфя Сергиева Лавра; Svyato-Troitskaya Sergiyeva Lavra). After decades of state-propagated atheism, the stunning monastery, founded around 1340, is once again a thriving religious center. **Assumption Cathedral** (Успенский Собор; Uspenskiy Sobor) was modeled after its Moscow namesake. The frescoes of the **Refectory** (Нрапезная; Trapeznaya) and Andrei Rublev's gilded icons at **Trinity Cathedral** (Нроицкий Собор; Troitskiy Sobor) are captivating. *(Monastery open daily 5am-9pm.)* **Elektrichki** (commuter trains) run to Sergiyev Posad from Moscow's Yaroslavskiy Vokzal (1½-2hr., 2-3 per hr., round-trip 168R). From the station, turn right, cross the street, and walk down the road until you see the city. *(☎49 65 40 57 21; www.stsl.ru. Open daily 10am-5pm. 160R, students 60R.)*

ST. PETERSBURG (САНКТ-ПЕТЕРБУРГ) ☎8812

St. Petersburg's wide boulevards, spacious squares, and bright facades are exactly what Peter the Great envisioned when he turned a mosquito-infested swamp into his "window on the West." The Bolsheviks drew the curtains when St. Petersburg (pop. 4,600,000) became the birthplace of the 1917 February Revolution, turning Russia into a Communist state; the city's name became Petrograd and then Leningrad. Since the fall of Communism and its subsequent reversion to its original name, the city has rediscovered the genius of former residents like Dostoevsky, Gogol, Tchaikovsky, and Stravinsky, whose legacies (and statues) mingle with the centuries-old buildings, streets, and canals of this remarkable city.

▚ TRANSPORTATION

Flights: The main airport, **Pulkovo** (Пулково), 18/4 Pilotov str. (www.pulkovo.ru) has 2 terminals: Pulkovo-1 (☎704 3822) for domestic flights and Pulkovo-2 (☎704 3444) for international flights. From M2: Moskovskaya (Московская), take bus #13 to Pulkovo-1 (20min.) or bus #39 to Pulkovo-2 (25min.). Hostels can arrange taxis (usually US$30-35).

RUSSIA

0 — 300 meters
0 — 300 yards

PETROGRAD SIDE

Kropotkina

Malaya Posadskaya
Malaya Monetnaya

Bolshaya Zelenina

Voskova
Markina
Sytninskaya

GORKOVSKAYA M

Mosque

Museum of Russian Political History

Kurbysheva

Lizy Chaikinoy

Vvedenskaya

Bolshaya Pashkarskaya

Bolshoy pr.

Alexandrovskiy Park

Peter's Cabin Museum

Sezzhinskaya

Tatarsky per.

Military History Museum

Zverinskaya

Petrovskaya nab.

Blokhina

Zoo

SPORTIVNAYA M

Tuchkov most

Dobrolyubova

Yablochkova

Peter and Paul Cathedral

Nevskiy Gate

Fortress of Peter and Paul

Mytninskaya nab.

Trubetskoy Bastion

Birzhevoy most

Malaya Neva

The Marble Palace

Troitskiy most

Tuchkov Volkhovskiy Pr.

Birzhevoy Pr.

Birzheva I.

nab. Makarova

Rostral Column

Central Naval Museum

Apteksrskiy per.

1-ya Linii

Repina

2-3-ya Linii

Mendeleyevskaya

Filologichestry Pr.

VASILEVSKIY ISLAND

Zoological Museum

Rostral Column

Dvortsovaya nab.

Millionnaya

Pushkin Museum

Akademicheskaya Kapella

nab. Kan Griboyedova

Kunstkamera Anthropological and Ethnographic Museum

Dvortsovy most

Hermitage

Winter Palace

DVORTSOVAYA PLOSHCHAD

Alexander Column

Finnair

St. Petersburg State University

BA

Menshikov Palace

Bolshaya Konyushennaya

Malaya Konyushennaya

Academy of Arts

Universitetskaya nab.

The Admiralty

Bolshaya Neva

Admiralteyskaya nab.

Admiralty Proezd

Nevskiy Prospekt

Dom Knigi

Lufthansa

most Leytenanta Shmidta

Bronze Horseman

Air France

AmEx

SAS

Stroyanar Palace

Austrian

Au Ali

Angliyskaya nab.

Manezh

Malaya Morskaya

Bolshaya Morskaya

Kazansky Cathedral

St. Isaac's Cathedral

KLM Dutch Airlines

Delta Airlines

Central Railroad Ticket Office

Galernaya

Trudd

Konnogvardeyskiy bul.

Yakubovicha

Pochtamtskiy per.

CSA Czech Airlines

nab. Reki Moyki

nab. Reki Moyki

Grivtsova Pr.

Griboyedov Canal

Bankovsky per.

Pochtamtskaya

Moyka River

American Medical Center

Voznesenskiy Pr.

Kazanskaya

Sadovaya Pr.

Apraksin Pr.

Gorokhovaya

New Holland

ul. Pisareva

Dekabristov

Stolyarny Pr.

SENNAYA

SADOVAYA

SENNAYA PL.

Kirov Opera and Ballet/ Marlinskiy Theater

Conservatory

Sadovaya ul.

Great Choral Synagogue

Central St. Petersburg
(also see St. Petersburg color map)

ACCOMMODATIONS
Hostel Zimmer Freie, 6
Hotel LokoSphinx, 15
Hotel Vera, 9
Nord Hostel, 7
Sleep Cheap, 2

FOOD
Al Shark, 3
Cafe Zoom, 11
Chillout Cafe TRIZET, 4
Literaturnoye Kafe, 10
The Stray Dog, 8
Traktir Shury Mury, 5

NIGHTLIFE AND CAFES
Che, 13
Fish Fabrique, 12
JFC Jazz Club, 1
Ob'ekt, 14

VYBORG SIDE

PLOSHCHAD LENINA
Finlyandskiy Vokzal
ul. Komsomola
Pl. Lenina
Arsenalnaya nab.
Akademika Lebedeva
Mikhailova ul.

Bolshaya Nevka
Cruiser Aurora

Liteynyy most

Neva

nab. Kutuzova
Robespyera
Shpalernaya
Zakharevskaya
Chaikovskogo
Furshtatskaya
Kirochnaya
Ryleeva
Pestelya
Kovenskiy Pr.
Nekrasova
Ozernyy p.

Peter the Great's Summer Palace
Summer Gardens
Mars Field
Monument to the Heroes of the Revolution

Church of Our Savior on Spilled Blood
Russian Museum
Russian Ethnographic Museum
Tsirk
Mussorgsky Theater
Shostakovich Philharmonic Hall
NEVSKIY PROSPEKT
Merchant's Yard
GOSTINNY DVOR
Gostinny Dvor
Russian National Library
Marionette Theater
Statue of Catherine the Great
PL. OSTROVSKOGO
Aleksandrinskiy Theater
Theater and Music Museum
PRAKSIN DVOR
Maly Theater

CHERNYSHEVSKAYA
Tavricheskiy Gardens

Gagarinskaya
Mokhovaya
Solyanoy Pr.
Gangutskaya ul.
Sadovaya
Ksenofya
Karavannaya
Italyanskaya
Liteynyy Pr.
Korolenko
Chekhova
Zhukovskogo
Mayakovskovo
Radishcheva
Vosstaniya
Pr. Chernyshevskogo

Nahodka Supermarket
Transaero Airlines
Anna Akhmatova Museum
Sheremetev Palace
Angliya
LOT Polish Airlines
Knizhnaya Lavka Pisteliey
Quo Vadis
Aeroflot Russian International Airlines
Cafemax
il. Belinskogo

24hr. Supermarket
Maltsevskiy Rynok

PLOSHCHAD VOSSTANIYA
Nevskiy Prospekt
UPRISING SQUARE
MAYAKOVSKAYA
International Clinic MEDEM
PLOSHCHAD VOSSTANIYA
Moskovskiy Vokzal
Sindbad

Vladimirskiy pr.
Stremyannaya
Marata
Pushkinskaya
Ligovskiy Pr.
Kolokolnaya
Rubinshteyna
DOSTOYEVSKAYA
Kuznechniy per.
VLADIMIRSKAYA
Dostoevsky Museum
Covered Market
Arctic and Antarctic Museum

8-ya Sovetskaya
7-ya Sovetskaya
6-ya Sovetskaya
5-ya Sovetskaya
Paradnaya
4-ya Sovetskaya
3-ya Sovetskaya
2-ya Sovetskaya
1-ya Sovetskaya
Suvorovskiy Pr.
Nevskiy Prospekt
TO 9 (1km)
Poltavskaya
Mirgorodskaya

Lomonosova
Fontanka
nab. Reki Fontanki
Leshtukov Pr.
Berodinskaya
Zagorodnyy Pr.
Razyezzhaya
Dostoevskogo
Svechnoy per.

TO VITEBSKIY VOKZAL (650m)
(1.5km)

RUSSIA

Trains: Tsentralnye Zheleznodorozhny Kassy (Центральные Железнодорожные Кассы; Central Railroad Ticket Offices), Canal Griboyedova 24 (Грибоедова; ☎067). Buy tickets at *kassy* on the left.

Finlyandskiy Vokzal (Финляндский; Finland Station; ☎768 7539). M1: Pl. Lenina. Sells tickets to destinations in the suburbs of St. Petersburg, as well as to **Helsinki, FIN** (6hr., 2 per day, 2000-3600R). Also sells airline tickets to destinations within Russia.

Moskovskiy Vokzal (Московский; Moscow Station; ☎768 4428*).* M1: Pl. Vosstaniya. 24hr. luggage storage; look for signs. From 50R. To: **Moscow** (5-9hr., 15-20 per day, 515-2500R); **Novgorod** (*electrichka* 3-4hr., 1 per day, 320R); and **Sevastopol, UKR** (35hr., 1 per day, 1520-2700R).

Vitebskiy Vokzal (Витебский; Vitebskiy Station; ☎168 5939 or 168 3918). M1: Pushkinskaya. To: **Kyiv, UKR** (24hr., 1 per day, 990-1450R); **Odessa, UKR** (36hr.; June-Sept 1 per day, Oct.-May 4 per week; 1100-2330R); **Riga, LAT** (13hr., 1 per day, 1700-2600R); **Tallinn, EST** (8hr., 1 per day, 640-1600R); **Vilnius, LIT** (14hr., 1 every other day, 1070-1790R). Luggage storage 51R per day.

Buses: Автовокзал (Bus Station), nab. Obvodnogo Kanala 36 (Обводного Канала; ☎766 3644; www.avokzal.ru). M4: Ligovsky Prospekt. Take bus #3, 34, 74 or trolley-bus #42 to the canal. Facing the canal, turn right and walk 2 long blocks. The station will be on your right. 10R surcharge for advance tickets. Open daily 8am-8pm.

Local Transportation: St. Petersburg's **Metro** (Метро) runs daily 5:45am-12:15am. **Zheton** (жетон; tokens) cost 14R. Passes available for 7, 15, 30, or 90 days. 4 lines cover much of the city. **Buses, trams,** and **trolleys** (14R) run fairly frequently 6am-midnight. Licensed private **minibuses** (маршрутки; *marshrutki;* 15-17R) move more quickly and stop on request (routes and prices are displayed on windows in Cyrillic).

Taxis: Both marked and private cabs operate in St. Petersburg. **St. Petersburg Taxi** is the city's umbrella service. (☎068 from a land line, ☎324 7777 from a mobile phone; 20R per km.) Marked cabs have a metered rate of 15-20R per km but most cabs want to set prices without the meter. Because taxis are notorious for overcharging tourists, always confirm the price before your trip. Instead of taking a taxi, many locals hail private cars, which is usually cheaper but unsafe for travelers new to the area. Never get in a car with more than 1 person in it. Let's Go does not recommend hitchhiking.

✦ ⏱ ORIENTATION AND PRACTICAL INFORMATION

St. Petersburg sits at the mouth of the **Neva River** (Нева) on 44 islands among 50 canals. The heart of the city lies on the mainland, between the south bank of the Neva and the **Fontanka River.** Many of St. Petersburg's major sights—including the Hermitage—are on or near **Nevskiy Prospekt** (Невский Проспект), the city's main street, which extends from the **Admiralty** to the **Alexander Nevskiy Monastery; Moscow Train Station** is near the midpoint. Trolleys #1, 5, 7, 10, 17, and 22 run along Nevskiy pr. Northwest of the center and across the Neva lies **Vasilevskiy Island** (Василев-ский Остров; Vasilevskiy Ostrov), the city's largest island. On the north side of the Neva is the **Petrograd Side** archipelago, where the **Peter and Paul Fortress** stands.

Tourist Office: City Tourist Information Center, ul. Sadovaya 14 (Садовая; ☎310 2822; www.visit-petersburg.com). M3: Gostinyy Dvor. English-language advice, brochures, and guidebooks. Open M-Sa 10am-7pm, Sa noon-8pm. *Where* and *St. Petersburg Times* (www.sptimes.ru), free in tourist offices, hotels, and hostels, provide culture, entertainment, and nightlife listings.

Tours: Peter's Walking Tours, 3-ya Sovyetskaya 28 (3-я Советская; www.peterswalk.com), in the International Youth Hostel. Tours, including the ever-popular "Friday Night Pub Crawl," 430-800R. Specialty tours (4-6hr.) available on request.

Budget Travel: Sindbad Travel (FIYTO), 2-ya Sovetskaya 12 (2-я Советская; ☎332 2020; www.sindbad.ru). M1: pl. Vostanniya. Books plane, train, and bus tickets. Student discounts on flights, partnered with STA Travel. English spoken. Open M-F 10am-10pm, Sa-Su 10am-6pm.

Consulates: Australia, Italyanskaya 1 (Итальянская; ☎/fax 325 7333; www.australianembassy.ru). M2: Nevskiy Prospekt. Open M-F 9am-6pm. In an emergency, citizens of **Ireland** and **New Zealand** can call the UK consulate. **UK,** Pl. Proletarskoy Diktatury 5 (Пролетарской Диктатуры; ☎320 3200; www.britain.spb.ru). M1: Chernyshevskaya. Open M-F 9am-1pm, 2-5pm. **US,** Furshtatskaya 15 (Фурштатская; ☎331 2600, emergency ☎331 2888; www.stpetersburg-usconsulate.ru). M1: Chernyshevskaya. Open M-Tu, Th-F 2-5pm, W 10am-1pm. Phone inquiries M-Tu, Th-F 10am-1pm, W 3-5pm.

Currency Exchange: ATMs are ubiquitous downtown and occasionally dispense dollars or euros. It's cheaper to take out rubles than other currencies, and many establishments accept only rubles. Look for "обмен валюты" (obmen valyuti) signs everywhere, and don't forget your passport.

English-Language Bookstore: Angliya British Bookshop (Англия), nab. Reki Fontanka 38 (Реки Фонтанки; ☎579 8284). M2: Nevskiy Prospekt. Open daily 10am-8pm. MC/V. **Dom Knigi** (Дом Книги; House of Books), Nevskiy pr. 28 (☎570 6438; www.spbdk.ru). M2: Nevskiy Prospekt. Open daily 9am-midnight. MC/V.

Emergency: Police: ☎02. **Ambulance:** ☎03. **Fire:** ☎01.

Police Services for Foreigners: ☎702 2177.

24hr. Pharmacy: PetroFarm, Nevskiy pr. 22 (☎314 5401), stocks Western medicines and toiletries. Pharmacist daily 9am-10pm. MC/V.

Medical Services: American Medical Center, nab. Reki Moyki 78 (Реки Мойки; ☎740 2090; www.amclinic.com). M2: Sennaya Pl. English-speaking doctors provide comprehensive services, including house calls. Insurance billing available. Consultation $75. Open 24hr. AmEx/MC/V.

 St. Petersburg lacks an effective water purification system, making exposure to **giardia** (p. 25) very likely, so boil tap water, buy bottled water, or use iodine.

Internet Access: Quo Vadis, Nevskiy pr. 76 (☎333 0708; www.quovadis.ru). Enter from Liteynyy pr. and go to the 2nd fl.; it's the door on the left. Internet and Wi-Fi 70R per 30min., with ISIC 50R; 130R per hr., with ISIC 90R. Open 9am-11pm. MC/V. **Cafe-Max,** Nevsky pr. 90 (☎273 6655), 2nd fl. Internet 65-150R per hr. Open 24hr.

Post Office: Почта России (Pochta Rossii). Main branch at Pochtamtskaya 9 (Почтамтская; ☎312 3954). From Nevskiy pr., turn onto Malaya Morskaya (Малая Морская), which becomes Pochtamtskaya. **Currency exchange** at window 1, information at window 2. **Telephone** service. Internet 50R per 30 min. International mail at windows 8 & 9. Open 24hr. **Postal Code:** 190 000.

ACCOMMODATIONS

Travelers can choose from a variety of hostels, hotels, and private apartments, though hotels tend to be outrageously expensive. Hotels and hostels will register your visa upon arrival and in most cases can provide you with the necessary invitation for a fee, usually about 1000-2000R (see p. 839).

■ **Nord Hostel,** Bolshaya Morskaya 10 (Большая Морская; ☎571 0342; www.nordhostel.com). M2: Nevskiy Prospekt. Centrally located in a beautiful building, Nord Hostel has much to offer: kitchen, lounge, TV, and even a piano. Staff and many of the guests speak English. Some small but airy dorms, usually co-ed. Breakfast included. Free luggage storage. Laundry 175R per 8kg. Free Internet access. Check-out 11am. 6- or 10-bed dorms Apr.-Jan. €24; Feb.-Mar. €18. Cash only. ❸

■ **Hotel LokoSphinx** (Локосфинкс), Canal Griboyedova 101 (Грибоедова; ☎314 8890; www.lokosphinxhotel.ru). Overlooking the canal and regally furnished, this hotel provides fantastic prices for its location and services. All rooms equipped with phone and TV. English spoken. Sauna additional charge. Breakfast included. Laundry US$1-2 per item. Free Wi-Fi. Check-in 2pm. Check-out noon. Singles 2000-3900R; doubles 2500-4450R; apartments 4700-5200R. MC/V. ❹

Sleep Cheap, Mokhovaya 18, apt. 32 (Моховая; ☎115 1304; www.sleepcheap.spb.ru). M1: Chernyshevskaya. When you reach Mokhovaya 18, head into the courtyard; the hostel is the first black door on your right. The welcoming, familial setting complements its full-size dorm beds and private baths. The English-speaking staff is more than happy to help you book tickets. Airport and train transfer available. Breakfast included. Laundry 150R. 8-bed dorms 700R. Cash only. ❷

Hostel Zimmer Freie, Liteynyy pr. 46 (Литейный; ☎973 3757; www.zimmer.ru). Walk through the archway and bear left; enter at the sign "Fast Link." Clean rooms laid out apartment-style include kitchen, refrigerator, showers, and TV. Laundry 100R per 4kg. Internet 50R per hr. Check-out noon. Mid-May to Aug. dorms US$28, singles US$56; Sept. to mid-May US$20/40. 5% YIHA and ISIC discount. Cash only. ❶

Hotel Vera (Вера), Suvorovsky pr. 25, 5th fl. (Суворовский; ☎/fax 702 7206; www.hotelvera.ru). In a renovated Art Nouveau building, Hotel Vera is both centrally located and warmly decorated. Professional, English-speaking staff help arrange tours, reserve theater seats, and provide transfer services. All rooms equipped with broadband Internet, phone, and TV. Small library and DVD collection. Security cameras and guard. Breakfast included. Laundry 150R. May-Sept. singles 2700-3900R; doubles 4900R. Oct.-Apr. 1900-2700/3500R. AmEx/MC/V. ❺

🍴 FOOD

The **covered market,** Kuznechnyy per. 3, just around the corner from M1: Vladimirskaya (Repytxysq; open M-Sa 8am-8pm, Su 8am-7pm) and the **Maltsevskiy Rynok** (Vfkmwtdcrbq Hsyjr), Nekrasova 52 (Некрасова), at the top of Ligovskiy pr. (Kbujdcrbq; M1: Pl. Vosstaniya; open daily 9am-8pm), are St. Petersburg's largest outdoor markets. The cheapest supermarkets are **Dixie,** indicated by orange and yellow square signs with white lettering, but **Nakhodka** (Находка) supermarkets, nab. Reki Fontanki 5 (Реки Фонтанки), are considered the best. There are **24-hour supermarkets** on the side streets off Nevskiy pr. Look for "24 Часа" signs.

■ **Cafe Zoom,** Gorokhovaya 22 (Гороховая; ☎448 5001; www.cafezoom.ru). With menus detailing world history and geography and golden theater masks on its walls, this eatery attracts a intelligent clientele. English-language menu. Vegetarian options. Entrees 100-240R. Open M-Sa 11am-midnight, Su 1pm-midnight. Kitchen open M-Sa 11am-10:30pm, Su 1-10:30pm. 20% lunch discount until 4pm. Cash only. ❷

The Stray Dog (Подвалъ Бродячей Собаки), pl. Iskusstv 5/4 (Искусств; ☎312 8047), to the left of the Russian Museum. The favorite hangout of early 20th-century artists, including Anna Akhmatova's circle. Serves fantastic food and remains artistic despite the ragged stuffed dogs and messages scrawled on its walls. Occassional poetry readings (200-600R). English-language menu. Open daily 11:30am-11:30pm. AmEx/MC/V. ❹

Literaturnoye Kafe (Литературное Кафе), 18 Nevskiy pr. (☎312 6057). M2: Gostinyy Dvor. In its former incarnation as a confectioner's shop, this cafe boasted a clientele of luminaries from Dostoevsky to Pushkin, who came here the night before his fatal duel. Now caters to tourists. English-language menu. Entrees 100-600R. Pushkin's favorite dishes 70-220R. Open daily 11am-11pm. MC/V. ❸

Chillout Cafe TRIZET (Чилайт Кафе ТРИЗЕТ), ul. Vosstaniya 30/7 (Восстания; ☎579 9315). M1: Cherne-shevskaya. Perfect for a relaxing lunch, a good evening spent with friends, or a nighttime party spot. Helpful staff serve European and Middle Eastern food to patrons loung-ing on the wall-to-wall couches. Business lunch noon-6pm 120R. Entrees 140-350R. Beer and liquor from 60R. Hoo-kah 300-500R. DJ Th 9pm-2am, F-Su 9pm-5am. Open M-Th 11am-2am, F-Su 11am-5am. ❸

Traktir Shury Mury (Трактир Шуры Муры), ul. Belin-skogo 8 (Белинского; ☎279 8550). M2: Gostinyy Dvor. Russian and European cuisine served to locals in a traditional *dacha* (Russian countryhouse) by tradi-tionally costumed waitresses. English-language menu. Entrees 110-280R. Open 11am-6am. MC/V. ❷

◉ SIGHTS

Museums and sights often charge foreigners several times more than Russians. Avoid paying the higher price by handing the cashier the exact amount for a Russian ticket and saying "adeen" (one). Walk as if you know where you are going, and do not keep your map, camera, or *Let's Go* in plain sight.

▨ THE HERMITAGE. Originally a collection of 255 paintings bought by Catherine the Great in 1764, the State Hermitage Museum (Эhvbnf;; Ermitazh) houses the world's largest art collection; it rivals the Louvre and the Prado in architectural, historical, and artistic significance. The collection is housed in the **Winter Palace** (Зимний Дворец; Zimniy Dvorets), commis-sioned in 1762. Tsars lived in the complex until 1917, when the museum was nationalized. Only 5% of the three million-piece collection is on display at a time; even so, a full tour would cover a distance of 24 mi. English-language floor plans are available at the info desk. *(Nab. Dvortsovaya 36 (Дворцовая). ☎571 3420; www.hermitagemuseum.org. M2: Nevskiy pr. Open Tu-Sa 10:30am-6pm, Su 10:30am-5pm. Long lines; arrive early. 350R, students free. English-language tours 200R. Audio tour 300R. Photography 100R. Free entrance 1st Th of month.)*

▨ ST. ISAAC'S CATHEDRAL. Intricately carved masterpieces of iconography are housed under the awesome 19th-century dome of St. Isaac's Cathedral

THE CATS THAT SAVED ART HISTORY

While cats have historically served as popular pets for Rus-sians, during the 900-day siege of Leningrad in World War II, they served as something else also. As food supplies dwindled and grow-ing numbers of citizens died of starvation, cats suffered the bru-tal indignity of being added to the menus of the desperate.

The obliteration of cats led to a revitalization of the city's rodent population. Any naturalist will tell you that such an upset of balance can only have disastrous results. Having no plans to starve, the colossal vermin population infil-trated the Hermitage and began to nosh on the paintings that had been stored in its basement as protection from the relentless Ger-man bombing. When the siege finally ended, hundreds of furry felines were purchased by the state and set free in the Hermit-age to help eliminate the rats. The program was successful, and it is said that today there are still 150 cats on staff at the Hermitage patrolling the storage areas.

This accounts in part for cats' ubiquitous presence in the city. In fact, the pedestrian stretch of Mikhailovskaya ul. beside Eli-seevskiy is lined with small cat statues paying tribute to the rodent-hunters. For good luck, throw a coin up on these figu-rines, many of which are located on platforms one story above street-level.

(Bcffrbtdcrbq Cj,jh; Isaakievskiy Sobor). On a sunny day, the 100kg of gold that coats the dome is visible for miles. The 360° view of the city from atop the **colonnade** is worth the 260-step climb. *(☎315 9732. M2: Nevskiy pr. Turn left on Nevskiy pr., then left on ul. Malaya Morskaya. Cathedral open M-Tu and Th-Su in summer 10am-8pm; in winter 11am-7pm. Colonnade open in summer M-Tu and Th-Su 10am-7pm; in winter 11am-3pm. Cathedral 300R, students 170R; colonnade 150/100R. Photography 50R museum, 25R colonnade.)*

■**CHURCH OF OUR SAVIOR ON SPILLED BLOOD.** This church's colorful forest of elaborate "Russian style" domes was built between 1883 and 1907 over the site of Tsar Alexander II's 1881 assassination. Also known as the Church of Christ's Resurrection and the Church of the Bleeding Savior, the cathedral (Спас На Крови; Spas Na Krovi) took 27 years to restore after it was used as a vegetable warehouse and morgue during the Communist crackdown on religion. It is equally impressive on the inside, housing the largest display of tile mosaic in the world. *(☎315 1636. Open M-Tu and Th-Su in summer 10am-8pm; in winter 11am-7pm. Kassa closes 1hr. earlier. 300R, students 170R. Photography 50R.)*

PALACE SQUARE. (Дворцовая Площадь; Dvortsovaya Ploshchad) This huge, wind-swept expanse in front of the Winter Palace has witnessed many turning points in Russia's history. Catherine took the crown here after overthrowing her husband, Tsar Peter III. Much later, Nicholas II's guards fired into a crowd of protestors on "Bloody Sunday," precipitating the 1905 revolution. Finally, Lenin's Bolsheviks seized power from the provisional government during the storming of the Winter Palace in October 1917. The 700-ton **Alexander Column**—which took two years to cut from a cliff and, at 47m, is the largest freestanding monument in the world—commemorates Russia's defeat of Napoleon in 1812.

PETER AND PAUL FORTRESS. Across the river from the Hermitage stand the walls and golden spire of the Peter and Paul Fortress (Gtnhjgfdkjdcrfz Rhtgjcnm; Petropavlovskaya Krepost). Originally built as a defense against the Swedes in 1703, the fortress was later used as a prison for political dissidents. Inside, the **Peter and Paul Cathedral** (Gtnhjgfdkjdcrbq Cj,jh; Petropavlovskiy Sobor) glows with rosy marble walls and a Baroque partition covered with intricate iconography. The cathedral holds the remains of Peter the Great and his successors. Turn right upon entering to view the **Chapel of St. Catherine the Martyr.** The remains of the last Romanovs—Tsar Nicholas II and his family—were moved here from the Artists' Necropolis on July 17, 1998, the 80th anniversary of their murder by the Bolsheviks. Condemned prisoners awaited their fate at **Trubetskoy Bastion** (Nhe6twrjq <fcnjy), where Peter the Great tortured his son, Aleksei. Dostoevsky and Trotsky served time here. *(M2: Gorkovskaya. ☎230 6431. Fortress open M and W-Su 11am-6pm, Tu 11am-4pm. Cathedral open daily 10am-8pm. A single ticket covers most sights. Purchase at the central kassa or in the smaller one inside the main entrance. 250R, students 130R.)*

ALEXANDER NEVSKIY MONASTERY. Alexander Nevskiy Monastery (Fktrcfylhj-Htdcrfz Kfdhf; Aleksandro-Nevskaya Lavra) is a major pilgrimage site and peaceful strolling ground. The **Artists' Necropolis** (Ytrhfgjk Vfcnthjd Bcreccnd; Nekropol Masterov Iskusstv) is the resting place of Fyodor Dostoevsky and composers Mussorgsky, Rimsky-Korsakov, and Tchaikovsky. The **Church of the Annunciation** (<kfujdtotycrfz Wthrjd; Blagoveshchenskaya Tserkov), along the stone path on the left, holds the remains of war heroes. At the end of the path is the **Holy Trinity Cathedral** (Cdznj-Nhjqncrbq Cj,jh; Svyato-Troytskiy Sobor), teeming with devout *babushki* kissing Orthodox icons. This is an active monastery, so there is a strict dress code in the Cathedral: no shorts, and women must cover their shoulders and heads. *(M3/4: Pl. Aleksandra Nevskovo. ☎274 1112. Grounds open daily*

6am-11pm. Artists' Necropolis open daily 10am-8pm. Cathedral open daily 6am-9pm. Kassa closes 5pm. Cemetery 100R, students 50R; cathedral grounds 100/50R.)

ALONG NEVSKIY PROSPEKT. Many sights are clustered around the western end of bustling Nevskiy pr., the city's 4.5km main thoroughfare. Unfortunately, there is no metro station immediately nearby; one was built, but after the station was completed, construction of an entrance or exit connecting it to the surface was not approved due to concerns about crime and vagrancy. The **Admiralty** (Гдминҟкпейство; Admiralteystvo), across the street from the Winter Palace, towers over the surrounding gardens and most of Nevskiy pr. Originally intended for shipbuilding by Peter the Great, it was a naval headquarters until recently, when it became a naval college. In the park to the left of the Admiralty stands the **Bronze Horseman** statue of Peter the Great, one of the most widely recognized symbols of the city. *(M2: Nevskiy pr.)* Walking east on Nevskiy pr., the enormous, Roman-style **Kazansky Cathedral** (Казанский Собор; Kazanskiy Sobor) looms to the right. It houses the remains of General Kutuzov, commander of the Russian army in the war against Napoleon. *(☎314 4663. M2: Nevskiy pr. Open daily 8:30am-7:30pm. Free.)* The 220-year-old **Merchants' Yard** (Гҏстиный Двјһ; Gostinyy Dvor), one of the world's oldest indoor shopping malls, is to the right. *(M3: Gostinyy Dvor. Open M-Sa 10am-10pm, Su 10am-9pm.)* Nearby **Ostrovskovo Square** (Островского) houses the Aleksandrinskiy Theater (see **Festivals and Entertainment,** p. 844), a massive statue of Catherine the Great, and the **public library,** which contains Voltaire's private library, purchased in its entirety by Catherine the Great. *(Foreigners can obtain a library card for free; bring passport, visa, and 2 photographs. Library open daily 9am-9pm.)* Turn left before the Fontanka canal on nab. Reki Fontanka and look down before crossing the bridge at ul. Pestelya to find the **Smallest Monument in the World.** According to lore, landing a coin on the platform of the tiny bird statue brings good luck.

SUMMER GARDENS AND PALACE. The long, shady paths of the Summer Gardens and Palace (Летний Сад и Дворец; Letniy Sad i Dvorets) are a lovely place to rest and cool off. Peter's modest **Summer Palace,** in the northeast corner, reflects his diverse taste in everything from Spanish and Portuguese chairs to Dutch tile and German clocks. **Mars Field** (Марсово Поле; Marsovo Pole), a memorial to the victims of the Revolution and Civil War (1917-1919), extends out from the Summer Gardens. *(M2: Nevskiy pr. Turn right on nab. Kanala Griboyedova (Канала Грибоедова), cross the Moyka, and turn right on ul. Pestelya (Пестеля). ☎314 0374. Garden open daily May-Oct. 10am-10pm; Nov.-Apr. 10am-8pm. Free. Palace open M 10am-4pm, Tu-Su 10am-6pm; closed last M of the month; kassa closes 5pm. Palace 300R, students 150R.)*

OTHER MUSEUMS. The ▨**State Russian Museum** (Русский Музей; Russkiy Muzey) boasts the world's second-largest collection of Russian art. Exhibits are displayed in three other locations throughout the city. *(M3: Gostinyy Dvor. ☎595 4248; www.rusmuseum.ru. Open M 10am-5pm, W-Su 10am-6pm. 300R, students 150R. Tickets to all museum sites 600R/300R. Photography 100R.)* **Dostoevsky's House** (Дом Достоевского; Dom Dostoevskovo) is where the author penned *The Brothers Karamazov.* *(Kuznechnyy per. 5/2 (Ёȯçįȃ÷íûé). M1: Vladimirskaya. On the corner of ul. Dostoevskovo. ☎311 4031. Open daily 11am-6pm; kassa closes 5pm. 120R, students 60R.)* The **Museum of Russian Political History** (Музей Политической Истории России; Muzey Politicheskoy Istorii Rossii) showcases WWII artifacts and Soviet propaganda portraying the "ideal reality" of the Communist ethos. *(Kuybysheva 2 (Куйбышева). M2: Gorkovskaya. Go down Kamennoostrovskiy (Каменноостровский) and turn left on Kuybysheva. ☎233 7052. Open M-W and F-Su 10am-6pm. 150R, students 70R.)*

🌴 🎵 FESTIVALS AND ENTERTAINMENT

From mid-May to mid-July, the city holds a series of outdoor concerts as part of the **White Nights Festival.** Bridges over the Neva River go up at 1:30am and don't come back down until 4:30 or 5:30am. The home of Tchaikovsky, Prokofiev, and Stravinsky still lives up to its reputation as a mecca for the performing arts. The **🎭Mariinskiy Teatr** (Мариинский, or Kirov), Teatralnaya pl. 1 (Театральная), M4: Sadovaya, is perhaps the world's most famous ballet hall. Tchaikovsky's *Nutcracker* and *The Sleeping Beauty*, along with works by Baryshnikov and Nijinsky premiered here. Tickets can be purchased in Gostinyy Dvor. (☎326 4141. Tickets 320-4800R. *Kassa* open Tu-Su 10am-7pm.) **Aleksandrinskiy Teatr** (Александринский Театр), pl. Ostrovskovo 6, M3: Gostinyy Dvor, attracts famous Russian actors and companies. (☎312 1546. Tickets 100-2500R.) **Mussorgsky Opera and Ballet Theater** (Театр Имени Муссоргского; Teatr Imeni Mussorgskovo), pl. Iskusstv, is open all summer, whereas the Mariynskiy closes for several weeks. (☎595 4284; www.mikhailovsky.ru. Bring your passport. Tickets 300-1500R. *Kassa* open 11am-3pm, 4-7pm.) **Shostakovich Philharmonic Hall,** ul. Mikhailovskaya 2, M3: Gostinyy Dvor, opposite the Russian Museum, has classical and modern concerts. (☎710 4290; www.philharmonia.spb.ru. Tickets 750-2000R. *Kassa* open daily 11am-3pm and 4-7pm.) The Mussorgsky and Shostakovich Theaters both lie around the **Square of the Arts.** The Friday issue of the *St. Petersburg Times* has comprehensive listings of entertainment and nightlife. Book tickets to various performances online in English at **www.kassir.ru.**

🎷 NIGHTLIFE

🎵 JFC Jazz Club, Shpalernaya 33 (Шпалерная; ☎272 9850; www.jfc.sp.ru). M1: Chernyshevskaya. This friendly club offers a wide variety of quality jazz and holds occasional classical, folk, and funk concerts. Beer from 100R. Hard liquor from 50R. Live music nightly 8-10pm. Cover 150-300R. Reserve table ahead. Open daily 7-11pm.

🎵 Fish Fabrique, Ligovskiy 53 (Лиговский; ☎264 4857; www.fishfabrique.spb.ru). M1: pl. Vosstaniya. Walk in through the courtyard, into the black door directly in front, and follow the corridor and stairs to the bar. An almost hidden location and a tight-knit, young clientele make this bar the perfect chill hangout. Th-Sa rock concerts 11pm. Beer 50-90R. Hard liquor 40-130R. Cover 100-150R. Open 6pm-6am. Cash only.

Che, Poltavskaya 3 (Полтавская; ☎277 7600). M1: Vosstaniya. Named for the fiery revolutionary, Che is a comfortable place to relax among the young, trendy, and well-to-do while listening to Latin or jazz. Drinks 130-550R. Hookah 500R. Live music 10pm-2am. English-language menu. Open 24hr. MC/V.

Ob'ekt, nab. Reki Moyki 82 (наб. Реки Мойки; ☎312 1134). This basement bar and club is perfect for after dinner drinks, smoking a hookah (250R) with friends, or alternative dancing on the weekends. Young, vivacious crowd any day of the week, but especially during Drum&Bass (Th 6pm) and Retro (F-Sa 11pm; don't forget your in-line skates) nights. Beer from 70R. Open 24hr.

🔃 DAYTRIP FROM ST. PETERSBURG

PETERHOF (Петергоф). Now the largest and the best-restored of the Russian palaces, Peterhof was burned to the ground during the Nazi retreat. Today, the gates open onto the **Lower Gardens,** a perfect place for a picnic along the shores of the Gulf of Finland. *(Open daily 10:30am-5pm.)* Bent on creating his own Versailles, Peter started building the **Grand Palace** (<ольшой Дворец; Bolshoy Dvorets) in 1714. Catherine the Great later expanded and remodeled it. *(☎420 0073. Open Tu-Su 10:30am-5pm; closed last Tu of month. 430R, students 215R.)* The 64 fountains of the **Grand Cascade** shoot into the Grand Canal. *(Fountains operate May-Oct. M-F 10:30am-5pm, Sa-Su 10:30am-6pm. 300R, students 150R.)* There are 17 museums on the grounds. You can roam the nearby **Upper Gardens** for free. *(Take the train from Baltiyskiy station (Балтийский; M1: Baltiyskaya; 35min., 1-6 per hr., 36R). Tickets are sold at the courtyard office (пригородная касса; prigorodnaya kassa). Get off at Novyy Peterhof (Новый Петергоф). From the station, take any minivan (5min.; 10R) or bus (10min.; 7R) to Petrodvorets (Петродворец; Peter's Palace). On the way back, take a minivan to the Metro (30R). Alternatively, in summer, take the hydrofoil from the quay on nab. Dvortsovaya (Дворцовая) in front of the Hermitage 40min.; 1-2 per hr. 9:30am-6pm; 450R, round-trip 800R.)*

SLOVAKIA (SLOVENSKO)

Slovakia is a nation of split personalities. Known for its beautiful mountain ranges, vibrant folk culture, and generous hospitality, Slovakia appeals especially to hikers and lovers of rural life. But the country also enjoys rapid industrialization and one of the fastest-growing economies in the former Eastern Bloc. Many scenic villages await only hours away from the sophisticated, up-and-coming capital.

 DISCOVER SLOVAKIA: SUGGESTED ITINERARIES

THREE DAYS. Devote your stay to a leisurely exploration of **Bratislava**. Make sure to check out **Primate's Palace** (no monkeys, unfortunately; p. 873). Also stop by the **UFO**, atop New Bridge, to see if there's a party going on (p. 873).

ONE WEEK. From **Bratislava** (2 days), head to **Starý Smokovec** (5 days, p. 875). There you can mountain bike, hike, or ski the grand **High Tatras**. Leave time for a daytrip to **Štrbské Pleso** (p. 876), with its waterfalls and rigorous hikes.

ESSENTIALS

FACTS AND FIGURES

Official Name: Slovak Republic.

Major Cities: Bratislava.

Population: 5,448,000.

Time Zone: GMT +2.

Languages: Slovak (84%), Hungarian (11%).

Religions: Roman Catholic (69%), Protestant (11%), Greek Catholic (4%).

Known Mammal Species: 85.

WHEN TO GO

Slovakia is blissfully free of massive crowds during any season. The Tatras draw the most tourists during peak season from July to August, and for good reason: the summer is a much more pleasant (and safe) time for hiking the beautiful mountain range than the cold winter weather. To avoid any crowds, explore the Tatras in the two months before or after high season.

DOCUMENTS AND FORMALITIES

EMBASSIES AND CONSULATES. Foreign embassies to Slovakia are in Bratislava (p. 872). Slovak embassies abroad include: **Australia,** 47 Culgoa Circuit, O'Malley, Canberra, ACT 2606 (☎262 901 516; www.slovakemb-aust.org); **Canada,** 50 Rideau Ter., Ottawa, ON K1M 2A1 (☎613-749-4442; www.ottawa.mfa.sk); **Ireland,** 20 Clyde Rd., Ballsbridge, Dublin 4 (☎33 56 66 00 12; fax 660 0014); **UK,** 25 Kensington Palace Gardens, London W8 4QY (☎020 73 1364 70; www.slovakembassy.co.uk); **US,** 3523 International Ct., NW, Washington, D.C. 20008 (☎202-237-1054; www.slovakembassy-us.org).

VISA AND ENTRY INFORMATION. Citizens of Australia, Canada, Ireland, New Zealand, the UK, and the US can travel to Slovakia without a visa for up to 90 days. Those traveling for business, employment, or study must obtain a temporary residence permit. There are many kinds of visas, including single- and multiple-entry, as well as long term. The visas range in price from US$37-154.

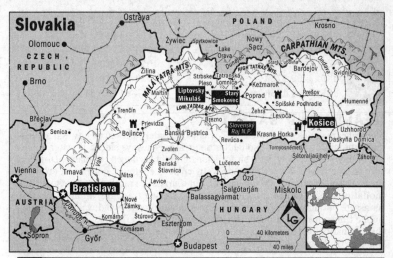

 ENTRANCE REQUIREMENTS.
Passport: Required for all travelers.
Letter of Invitation: Not required for citizens of Australia, Canada, Ireland, New Zealand, the UK, and the US.
Inoculations: Recommended up-to-date on DTap (Diphtheria, tetanus, and petussi) Hepatitis A, Hepatitis B, MMR, polio booster, rabies, and typhoid.
Work Permit: Required for foreigners planning to work in Slovakia.
International Driving Permit: Required for all those planning to drive in Slovakia except for UK citizens, who only need an IDP to rent cars.

TOURIST SERVICES AND MONEY

EMERGENCY	Ambulance and General Emergency: ☎ 112. Fire: ☎ 150. Police: ☎ 158.

TOURIST OFFICES. The **Slovak Tourist Board** (☎ 484 136 146; www.sacr.sk) provides useful information. Public tourist offices are marked by a white "i" inside a green square. English is often spoken at tourist offices, which usually provide maps and information about transportation. If booking accommodations at an office, be wary of handing over cash on the spot.

MONEY. Although Slovakia is now a member state of the EU, the **Slovak koruna** (Sk), plural koruny, remains the main unit of currency and comes in denominations of 20, 50, 100, 200, 500, 1000 and 5000 koruny. Slovakia's changeover to the euro is slated for early 2009. The koruna is divided into 100 halier, issued in standard denominations of 50 halier. Bear in mind that smaller establishments may not be able to break 5000Sk bills. **Credit cards** are not accepted in many Slovak establishments, but MasterCard and Visa are the most useful, followed by American Express. Inflation is down to about 4.5%, which means prices are relatively stable. ATMs are plentiful and give the best exchange rates, but also tend to charge a flat service fee; it is most economical to withdraw large amounts at once. Banks **Slovenská-Sporiteľňa** and **Unibank** handle MC/V cash advances. Banks require that you present your passport for most transactions.

AUS$1 = 22.26SK	10SK = AUS$0.45
CDN$1 = 27.00SK	10SK = CDN$0.37
EUR€1 = 38.07SK	10SK = EUR€0.26
NZ$1 = 18.73SK	10SK = NZ$0.53
UK£1 = 55.77SK	10SK = UK£0.18
US$1 = 30.15SK	10SK = US$0.33

SLOVAKIAN KORUNY (SK)

HEALTH AND SAFETY

Medical care varies a great deal in Slovakia. **Tap water** varies in quality and appearance but is probably safe, though bottled water is always safest. If water comes out of the faucet cloudy, let it sit for 5min; air bubbles may be to blame. *Drogerii* (drugstores) stock Western brands. **Petty crime** is common; be wary in crowded areas. **Violent crimes** are not unheard of, but tourists are rarely the targets. Accommodations for **disabled** travelers are rare. **Women** traveling alone are rarely harassed, but may encounter stares. Dress modestly and avoid walking or riding public transportation at night. **Minority** travelers with darker skin may encounter discrimination and should exercise caution. **Homosexuality** is not accepted by all Slovaks; GLBT couples may experience stares or insults.

TRANSPORTATION

BY PLANE AND TRAIN. Bratislava is a large hub for budget airlines. Many travelers fly to Bratislava and then take a shuttle to Vienna, AUT. For more info on budget airlines, see p. 47. If you are flying from outside Europe, it's best to fly to another budget hub and then connect to Bratislava. For train info, check the national company's website (**ŽSR;** www.zsr.sk). **EastPass** is valid in Slovakia, but **Eurail** is not. *InterCity* or *EuroCity* trains are faster but cost more. A boxed R on the timetable means that a *miestenka* (reservation; 7Sk) is required. Reservations are often required for *expresný* (express) trains and first-class seats, but are not necessary for *rychlík* (fast), *spešný* (semi-fast), or *osobný* (local) trains. Both first and second class are relatively comfortable and considered safe. Buy tickets before boarding the train, except in small towns. Master schedules *(cestovný poriadok)* are sold at info desks and are posted in most stations.

BY BUS. In hilly regions, **ČSAD** or **Slovak Lines buses** are the best and sometimes the only option. Except for very long trips, buy tickets on board. You can probably ignore most footnotes on schedules, but the following are important: **x** (crossed hammers) means weekdays only; **a** is Saturday and Sunday; **b** means Monday through Saturday; **n** is Sunday; and **r** and **k** mean excluding holidays. *"Premava"* means "including"; *"nepremava"* is "except"; following those words are often lists of dates. Check www.slovaklines.sk for updated schedules.

BY BIKE AND BY THUMB. Rambling wilds and ruined castles inspire great bike tours, and renting a bike in Bratislava is becoming easier. Biking is very popular, especially in the Tatras. Let's Go does not recommend hitchhiking, but it is common and considered somewhat safe in Slovakia.

KEEPING IN TOUCH

PHONE CODES	**Country code: 421. International dialing prefix: 00.** For more info on placing international calls, see **Inside Back Cover.**

EMAIL AND INTERNET. Internet access is common in Slovakia, even in smaller towns. **Internet** cafes usually offer cheap (1Sk per min.), fast access.

TELEPHONE. Recent modernization of the Slovak **phone** system has required many businesses and individuals to switch phone numbers. The phone system is still somewhat unreliable; try multiple times if you don't get through. International and national phones exist in each city, but there is no good way to distinguish between them. **Card phones** are common and are usually much better than the coin-operated variety. Purchase cards (100-500Sk) at the post office. Be sure to buy the "Global Phone" card if you plan to make international calls.

MAIL. Mail service is generally efficient. Letters abroad take two to three weeks to arrive. Letters to Europe cost 11-14Sk; letters to the US cost 21S. Almost every **pošta** (post office) provides express mail services. To send a package abroad, go to a **colnice** (customs office). Address **Poste Restante** as follows: First name LAST NAME, POSTE RESTANTE, post office address, Postal Code, city, Slovakia.

LANGUAGE. Slovak is a West Slavic language written in the Latin alphabet. It is closely related to the other languages in this group—**Czech** and **Polish**—and speakers of one will understand the others. Attempts to speak Slovak will be appreciated. Older people will speak a little Polish. English is common among Bratislava's youth, but German is more prevalent outside the capital. **Russian** is occasionally understood but unwelcome. The golden rules of speaking Slovak are to pronounce every letter and stress the first syllable. Accents over vowels lengthen them.

ACCOMMODATIONS AND CAMPING

SLOVAKIA	❶	❷	❸	❹	❺
ACCOMMODATIONS	under 250Sk	250-500Sk	501-800Sk	801-1000Sk	over 1000Sk

Foreigners are often charged much more than Slovaks for accommodation. Finding cheap rooms in Bratislava before student dorms open in July is very difficult, especially in Slovenský Raj and the Tatras. In other regions, finding a bed is relatively easy if you call ahead. The tourist office, **SlovakoTourist,** and other tourist agencies usually can help. Slovakia has few hostels, most of which are found in and around Bratislava. These usually provide towels and a bar of soap. **Juniorhotels (HI)** tend to be a bit nicer than hostels. **Hotel** prices are dramatically lower outside Bratislava and the Tatras, with budget hotels running 300-600Sk. **Pensions** (pen-zióny) are smaller and less expensive than hotels. **Campgrounds** are on the outskirts of most towns and usually rent bungalows to travelers. Camping in national parks is illegal. In the mountains, *chaty* (mountain huts) range from plush quarters around 600Sk to bunks with outhouses (about 200Sk).

FOOD AND DRINK

SLOVAKIA	❶	❷	❸	❹	❺
FOOD	under 120Sk	120-190Sk	191-270Sk	271-330Sk	over 330Sk

The national dish, *bryndzové halušky* (small dumplings in sauce), is a godsend for **vegetarians** and those sticking to a **kosher** diet. Pork products, however, are central to many traditional meals. *Knedliky* (dumplings) or *zemiaky* (potatoes) frequently accompany entrees. Enjoy *koláčky* (pastry), baked with cheese, jam or poppy seeds, and honey, for dessert. White **wines** are produced northeast of Bratislava, while *Tokaj* wines (distinct from Hungarian *Tokaji Aszú*) are produced around Košice. Enjoy them at a *vináreň* (wine hall). *Pivo* (beer) is served at a *pivnica* or *piváreň* (tavern). The favorite Slovak beer is the slightly bitter *Spis*. Another popular alcohol is *Slivovica*, a plum brandy with an alcoholic content of well over 50%; it is rumored not to cause hangovers when taken in moderation because it is so concentrated.

SLOVAKIA

HOLIDAYS AND FESTIVALS

Holidays: Independence Day of Slovakia (Jan. 1); Epiphany (Jan. 6); Good Friday (Mar. 21 in 2008; Apr. 10 in 2009); Easter Holiday (Mar. 24, 2008; Apr. 13, 2009); May Day (May 1); Sts. Cyril and Methodius Day (July 5); Anniversary of Slovak National Uprising (Aug. 29); Constitution Day (Sept. 1); Our Lady of the 7 Sorrows (Sept. 15); All Saints' Day (Nov. 1); Day of Freedom and Democracy (Nov. 17); Christmas (Dec. 24-26).

Festivals: Bojnice's Festival of Ghosts and Spirits, in late spring, is a celebration of the dead and the ghosts that are said to haunt the castle. Bratislava hosts Junifest, a 10-day beer festival that includes hundreds of performances by artists, in early June. Near Poprad, the Vychod Folk Festival occurs in mid-summer.

BEYOND TOURISM

For more info on opportunities across Europe, see **Beyond Tourism,** p. 56.

Brethren Volunteer Service, 1451 Dundee Ave., Elgin, IL 60120 USA (☎1-800-323-8039, ext. 410; www.brethrenvolunteerservice.org). Christian organization places volunteers with civic and environmental groups in Slovakia.

The British Trust for Conservation Volunteers (BTCV), 163 Balby Rd., Balby, Doncaster DN4 0RH, UK (☎440 13 02 57 22 24; http://www2.btcv.org.uk). Works in concert with the Slovak Wildlife Society (www.slovakwildlife.org) to give volunteers the opportunity to assist in monitoring bear and wolf populations in the Tatras Mountains.

BRATISLAVA ☎02

Often eclipsed by its famous neighboring capitals, sophisticated Bratislava (pop. 450,000) is finally stepping into the limelight. Each night of the week, the city's artfully lit streets buzz with activity. During the day, both locals and visitors can be found sipping coffee at the hundreds of chic cafes dotting the cobblestone *Staré Mesto* (Old Town), sauntering along the Danube River, or exploring the well-kept castle that shines over the city.

▛ TRANSPORTATION

Flights: M.R. Štefánik International Airport (**BTS;** ☎48 57 11 11; www.letiskobratislava.sk), 9km northeast of town. Often used as a hub to reach Vienna, AUT (see **Let's Go to Vienna,** p. 78). To reach the center of Bratislava, take bus #61 (1hr.) to the train station and then take tram #1 to Poštová on nám. SNP.

Trains: Bratislava Hlavná Stanica, at the end of Predstaničné nám., off Šancová. **Železnice Slovenskej republiky** (☎20 29 11 11; www.zsr.sk) posts schedules on its website. To **Košice** (5-6hr., 10 per day, 518Sk); **Prague, CZR** (4½-5½hr., 3 per day, 400Sk); and **Vienna, AUT** (1hr., 1 per hr., round-trip 283Sk). Make sure to get off at **Hlavná Stanica,** the main train station. To reach the center from the **train station,** take tram #2 to the 6th stop or walk downhill, take a right, then an immediate left, and walk down Stefanikova (15-20min).

Buses: Mlynské nivy 31 (☎55 42 16 67, info 09 84 22 22 22). Bus #210 runs between the train and bus stations. Check your ticket for the bus number (č. aut.), as several depart from the same stand. **Eurolines** has a 10% discount for those under 26. To: **Banská Bystrica** (3-4½hr., 2-3 per hr., 290-450Sk); **Budapest, HUN** (4hr., 2 per day, 610Sk); **Prague, CZR** (4¾hr., 5 per day, 520Sk); **Vienna, AUT** (1½hr., 1 per hr., 400Sk). From the station, take trolley #202, or turn right on Mlynské nivy and walk to Dunajská, which leads to **Kamenné námestie** (Stone Sq.) and the center of town (15-20min).

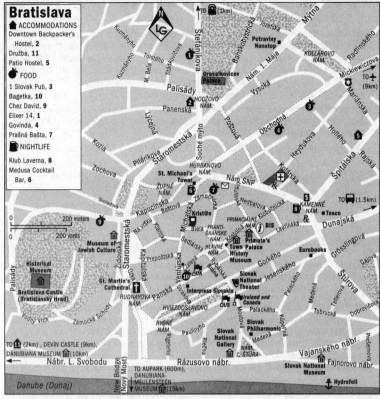

Bratislava

▲ ACCOMMODATIONS
Downtown Backpacker's
   Hostel, **2**
Družba, **11**
Patio Hostel, **5**

🍎 FOOD
1 Slovak Pub, **3**
Bagetka, **10**
Chez David, **9**
Elixer 14, **1**
Govinda, **4**
Prašná Bašta, **7**

🎵 NIGHTLIFE
Klub Laverna, **8**
Medusa Cocktail
   Bar, **6**

Local Transportation: Tram and **bus** tickets (10min. 14Sk, 30min. 18Sk, 1hr. 22Sk) are sold at kiosks and at the orange *automaty* in bus stations. Use an *automat* only if its light is on. Stamp your ticket when you board; the fine for riding ticketless is 1200Sk. Trams and buses run 4am-11pm. **Night buses,** marked with blue-and-yellow numbers with an "N" in front of them, run midnight-4am. Some kiosks and ticket machines sell **passes** (1-day 90Sk, 2-day 170Sk, 3-day 210Sk).

Taxis: BP (☎ 169 99); **FunTaxi** (☎ 167 77); **Profi Taxi** (☎ 162 22).

✈️🛈 ORIENTATION AND PRACTICAL INFORMATION

The **Dunaj** (Danube) flows eastward across Bratislava. Four bridges span the river; the main **Nový Most** (New Bridge) connects Bratislava's center, **Staromestská** (Old Town) in the north, to the commercial and entertainment district on the river's southern bank. **Bratislavský Hrad** (Bratislava Castle) towers on a hill to the west, while the city center sits between the river and **námestie Slovenského Národného Povstania** (nám. SNP; Slovak National Uprising Sq.).

Tourist Office: Bratislava Culture and Information Center (BKIS), Klobúčnicka 2 (☎ 161 86; www.bkis.sk). Books **private rooms** and hotels (800-3000Sk plus 50Sk fee); sells **maps** (free-80Sk) and books **tours** (1200Sk per hr.; max. 19 people). Open June-Oct. 15 M-F 8:30am-7pm, Sa 9am-6pm, Su 9:30am-6pm; May M-F 8am-6pm, Sa

9am-4pm, Su 10am-3pm. **Branch** in train station annex open M-F 8am-2pm and 2:30-7pm, Sa-Su 8am-2pm and 2:30-5pm.

Embassies: Citizens of **Australia** and **New Zealand** should contact the UK embassy in an emergency. **Canada,** Mostová 2 (☎59 20 40 31). Open M-F 8:30am-noon and 1:30pm-4:30pm. **Ireland,** Mostová 2 (☎59 30 96 11; bratislava@dfa.ie). Open M-F 9am-12:30pm. **UK,** Panská 16 (☎59 98 20 00; www.britishembassy.sk). Open M-F 8:30-11am. **US,** Hviezdoslavovo nám. 5 (☎54 43 08 61, emergency 09 03 70 36 66; www.usembassy.sk). Open M-F 8am-noon and 2-3:30pm.

Currency Exchange: Ľudová Banka, nám. SNP 15 (☎59 21 17 63, ext. 760; www.luba.sk) cashes American Express **traveller's cheques** for 1% commission and offers MC/V **cash advances.** Open M-F 8am-8pm.

Luggage Storage: At the train station. 30-40Sk. Open daily 5:30am-midnight.

Internet: There are Internet cafes all over central Bratislava, especially along Michalská and Obchodná. **Megainet,** Šancová 25. 1Sk per min. Open daily 9am-10pm.

Post Office: Nám. SNP 34 (☎59 39 31 11). Offers **fax** service. **Poste Restante** and phone cards at counters #2-4. Poste restante M-F 7am-8pm, Sa 7am-2pm. Open M-F 7am-8pm, Sa 7am-6pm, Su 9am-2pm. **Postal Code:** 81000 Bratislava 1.

ACCOMMODATIONS

In July and August, several **university dorms** open as hostels (from 150Sk). Pensions and private rooms are inexpensive and comfy alternatives. Most places add a 30Sk tourist tax. BKIS (see **Orientation and Practical Information,** p. 871) has more info.

Patio Hostel, Špitálska 35 (☎529 257 97; www.patiohostel.com), near the bus station. From the train station, take tram #13 to the arch. The entrance is tucked behind a dimly lit, run-down archway, but the hostel itself is clean and comfortable, with sunny rooms, a friendly staff, and a colorful common area. Free Internet. Check-in 1pm. Check-out 10pm. 2- to 12-bed dorms 600-800Sk. MC/V. ❸

Downtown Backpacker's Hostel, Panenská 31 (☎546 411 91; www.backpackers.sk). From the train station, turn left on Stefánikova and right on Panenská, or take bus #81, 91, or 93 for 2 stops. Swanky, centrally located 19th-century building, with backpackers relaxing under a bust of Lenin and enjoying beers from the downstairs bar. Laundry 200Sk. Reception 24hr. Reserve ahead. Check-out noon. Dorms 500-600Sk; doubles 1000Sk. 60-100Sk HI discount. 30Sk Tourist tax. MC/V. ❸

Družba, Botanická 25 (☎654 200 65; www.hotel-druzba.sk). Take bus #32 (dir.: Pri Kríži) or tram #1 or 5 to Botanická Záhrada. Cross the pedestrian overpass and go to the 2nd of the 2 concrete buildings. The university dorm/hotel is far from the Old Town, but its dorms are brightly painted and remarkably cheap. Dorms open early July-late Aug. Reception 24hr. Dorms 170Sk. Hotel open year-round. Reception M-Th 7am-3:30pm, F 7am-1pm. Singles 790Sk; doubles 1966Sk. MC/V. ❶

FOOD

Buy groceries at **Tesco Potraviny,** Kamenné nám. 1. (Open M-F 8am-10pm, Sa 8am-8pm, Su 9am-8pm.) Or, try the nearby indoor **fruit market** at Stará Trznícá, Kamenné nám. (Open M-F 7am-6pm, Sa 7am-1pm.)

1 Slovak Pub, Obchodná 62 (☎905 35 32 30; www.slovakpub.sk). Join the student crowd at one of Bratislava's largest and cheapest traditional Slovak restaurants. Each of the rooms has a theme, including "country cottage" and "Room of Poets." Lunch until 5pm; 35-89Sk. Dinner entrees 79-250Sk. 10% discount for Patio Hostel guests. Open M-Th 10am-midnight, F-Sa 10am-2pm, Su noon-midnight. Cash only. ❷

Govinda, Obchodná 30 (☎529 623 66). The veggie fare is heavenly. Combination plate 95/150Sk. Open M-F 11am-8pm, Sa 11:30am-7:30pm. Cash only. ❶

Elixir 14, Stefánikova 14 (☎524 998 49; www.elixir.sk). The menu is a treasure trove of creative vegetarian dishes. Vegan and meat options available. Daily lunch special 99Sk. Entrees 115-235Sk. Open M-W 10am-10pm, Th-F 10am-midnight, Sa 11am-midnight, Su 11am-10pm. MC/V. ❷

Prašná Bašta, Zámočnícka 11 (☎544 349 57; www.prasnabasta.sk). Hidden away from the Old Town bustle, this eatery's counter-culture vibe draws 20-somethings for generous portions of Slovak cuisine. Sit outside on the leafy terrace or downstairs amid sculptures and artful decor. Entrees 85-325Sk. Open daily 11am-11pm. MC/V. ❸

Bagetka, Zelená 8 (☎544 194 36). This sandwich bar is a fast, cheap, and satisfying option. Entrees 50-90Sk. Open M-Sa 9:30am-9pm, Su 2-9pm. Cash only. ❶

Chez David, Zámocká 13 (☎544 138 24). Located in a quarter steeped in Jewish culture. Elegant, excellent dishes (57-397Sk). Open daily 7am-10pm. AmEx/MC/V. ❸

⬛ SIGHTS

NÁMESTIE SNP AND ENVIRONS. Most of the city's major attractions are in the Staré Mesto (Old Town). From Nám. SNP, which commemorates the bloody 1944 Slovak National Uprising, walk down Uršulínska to the pink-and-gold ■**Primate's Palace** (Primaciálný Palác), built in the 1700s for Hungary's religious leaders and now home to Bratislava's mayor. In the Hall of Mirrors (Zrkadlová Sieň), Napoleon and Austrian Emperor Franz I signed the 1805 Peace of Pressburg. *(Primaciálné nám. 1. Buy tickets on 2nd fl. Open Tu-Su 10am-5pm. 40Sk, students free.)* Established in September 2000, the contemporary ■**Danubiana-Meulensteen Art Museum** is a piece of modern art in itself. On a small peninsula near the Hungarian border, the museum is surrounded by a small sculpture park. The remote location prevents crowding, so you can admire cutting-edge exhibits at your leisure. *(Take bus #91 from beneath Nový Most to the last stop, Cunovo; 35min., 20Sk. Follow the signs 3.5km to the museum. ☎09 03 60 55 05; www.danubiana.sk. Open Tu-Su May-Sept. 10am-8pm; Oct.-Apr. 10am-6pm. 80Sk, students 40Sk. MC/V.)* Hviezdoslavovo námestie is home to the gorgeous 1886 **Slovak National Theater** (Slovenské Národné Divadlo). With the Danube on your left, walk along the waterfront to the gaudy, neon-lit **Nový Most** (New Bridge), designed by the Communist government in the 70s. *(☎62 53 03 00; www.u-f-o.sk. Deck open daily 10am-10pm. 50Sk, free with restaurant reservations. Restaurant open Su-F 10am-1am, Sa 10am-10pm.)* The **Museum of Jewish Culture** preserves artifacts from Slovak Jews. *(Židovská 17. ☎54 41 85 07; www.slovak-jewish-heritage.org. Open Su-F 11am-5pm; last admission 4:30pm. 200Sk, students 60Sk.)*

CASTLES. On an imposing cliff 9km west of the center, the stunning **Devín Castle** (Hrad Devín) ruins overlook the confluence of the mighty Danube and Morava rivers. With the advent of communism, Devín became a functioning symbol of totalitarianism: sharpshooters hid in the ruins with orders to open fire on anyone who tried to scale the barbed-wire fence beside the Morava. Today, visitors can walk along the rocks and ruins. A museum details the castle's history. *(Bus #29 from Nový Most to the last stop. ☎65 73 01 05. English-language info 35Sk. Open July-Aug. Tu-F 10am-5pm, Sa-Su 10am-7pm; May-June and Sept.-Oct. Tu-Su 10am-5pm; last entry 30min. before closing. Museum 90Sk, students 40Sk.)* Visible from Danube Banks, the four-towered **Bratislava Castle** (Bratislavský Hrad) is Bratislava's defining landmark. The spectacular view from the **Crown Tower** (Korunná Veža) is a highlight. *(Castle open daily Apr.-Sept. 9am-8pm; Oct.-Mar. 9am-6pm. Free. Museum ☎54 41 14 44; www.snm-hm.sk. Open Tu-Su 9am-5pm; last entry 4:15pm. 100Sk, students 70Sk.)*

🎵 🎭 ENTERTAINMENT AND NIGHTLIFE

The weekly English newspaper, *Slovak Spectator*, also has current events info. **Slovenské Národné Divadlo** (Slovak National Theater), Hviezdoslavovo nám. 1, puts on ballets and operas. (☎54 43 30 83; www.snd.sk. Box office open M-F 8am-5:30pm, Sa 9am-1pm. Closed July-Aug. 100-200Sk.) The **Slovenská Filharmónia** (Slovak Philharmonic), Medená 3, has two to three performances per week in fall and winter. The box office, Palackého 2, is around the corner. (☎54 43 33 51; www.filharm.sk. Open M-Tu and Th-F 1-7pm, W 8am-2pm. 100-200Sk.)

By night, The Old Town is filled with young people priming for a night out. Nightlife in Bratislava is relatively subdued, but there is no shortage of places to party. At the packed hot spot ◼**Klub Laverna,** Laurinská 19, a slide transports drunken clubbers from the upper level to the floor. (☎54 43 31 65; www.laverna.sk, entrance on SNP street. Mixed drinks 75-230Sk. Cover F-Sa 100Sk. Open daily 9pm-6am.) For a less crazed evening, head to **Medusa Cocktail Bar,** Michalská 33, which defines chic with its posh decor and huge selection of mixed drinks. (Open M-Th 11am-1am, Sa 11am-3am, Su 11am-midnight. AmEx/MC/V.) For info on **GLBT nightlife,** pick up a copy of *Atribut* at any kiosk.

THE TATRA MOUNTAINS (TATRY)

The mesmerizing Tatras, spanning the border between Slovakia and Poland, form the highest part of the Carpathian mountain range. The High Tatras feature sky-scraping hikes, glacial lakes, and deep snows. Sadly, many of the lower slopes on the Slovak side of the High Tatras were devastated by freak storms and mudslides in the fall of 2004, and vast swaths of the formerly lush pine forest are now brown fields of broken trees. Recent forest fires further scarred the landscape, though the upper regions escaped largely unscathed. To the south, the separate Low Tatras have ski resorts and tree-covered mountains.

> **!** The Tatras are a great place to hike, but many of the hikes require experience and are extremely demanding, even in summer. In winter, a guide is almost always necessary. For current conditions, check **www.tanap.sk**.

LIPTOVSKÝ MIKULÁŠ   ☎044

Liptovský Mikuláš (pop. 33,000) is a springboard for hikes in the **Low Tatras** (Nízke Tatry). To scale **Mount Ďumbier** (2043m), the region's tallest peak, catch an early bus to Liptovský Ján (25-30min., 1-2 per 2hr., 16-20Sk), then follow the blue trail up the Štiavnica River toward the **Svidovské Sedlo.** Go right at the red trail (2hr.), then begin the 1½hr. climb up Sedlo Javorie. Head left on the yellow trail to the summit of Mt. Ďumbier (2½hr.). Descend the ridge and follow the red sign to **Chopok** (2024m), the second-highest peak in the range. From Chopok, it's a winding walk down the blue trail to the bus stop behind the Hotel Grand at Otupné (1¾hr.).

An extremely worthwhile visit from Liptovský Mikuláš is the **Demänovská Jaskyňa Slobody** (Demänov Cave of Liberty). To get to the cave, take the **bus** from platform #3 in Liptovský Mikuláš to Demänovská Dolina, get off at Demänovská Jaskyňa Slobody (20-35min., 1 per hr., 20Sk), and walk to the cave on the blue trail toward Pusté Sedlo Machnate (1½hr.). Tours are mandatory, with two lengths offered. The short tour covers 1.5km and passes through amazing underground chambers, lakes, and a magnificent waterfall, all carved out of rock by water falling at a rate of one drop per day. The longer tour includes 2km of additional corridors. Bring a sweater. (☎559 1673; www.ssj.sk. Open June-Aug. Tu-Su 9am-4pm, entrance every hr.; Sept. to mid-Nov. and mid-Dec. to May 9:30am-2pm, entrance 1 per 2hr. 45min. tour 180Sk, with ISIC 160Sk. 2hr. tour 390/340Sk.)

Hotel Kriváň ❷, Štúrova 5, opposite the tourist office, has basic, centrally located rooms. (☎552 2414. Singles 350Sk, with bath 450Sk; doubles 570/770Sk. Cash only.) The local favorite **Liptovská Izba Reštaurácia ❶,** nám. Osloboditeľov 22, serves delicious Slovak dishes. (☎551 4853. Entrees 35-135Sk. Open M-Sa 10am-10pm, Su noon-10pm. Cash only.) Buy groceries at **Coop Supermarket,** ul. 1 Maja 54, in the Prior Building. (Open M-F 7am-8pm, Sa 7am-7pm, Su 8am-5pm. MC/V.) For fresh fruits and vegetables, check out the **open-air market** to the right of the tourist office. (Open M-F 8am-4pm, Sa 8am-noon.) **Trains** from Liptovský Mikuláš to Bratislava (4hr., 12 per day, 364Sk) are cheaper than buses. To reach the town center from the station, follow Štefánikova toward the gas station at the far end of the lot, go right on Hodžu, and take a left on Štúrova. The **tourist office,** nám. Mieru 1, in the Dom Služieb complex, books private rooms (245-400Sk) and sells hiking maps. (☎552 2418; www.mikulas.sk. Open mid-June to mid-Sept. M-F 9am-6pm, Sa 8am-noon, Su 11am-4pm; low season reduced hours.)

STARÝ SMOKOVEC ☎052

Spectacular trails begin at Starý Smokovec, the central resort in the **High Tatras.** A **funicular** picks up passengers behind the train station and takes them to **Hrebienok** (1285m), the starting point for many hikes. (Open daily 7:30am-7pm. Ascent July-Aug. 130Sk, Sept.-June 90Sk; descent 40/30Sk; round-trip 150/100Sk.) Alternatively, from the funicular station, hike 55min. up the green trail to Hrebienok. The green trail then continues 20min. north to the foaming **Cold Stream Waterfalls** (Volopáday studeného potoka). From the falls, take the red trail, which connects with the eastward blue trail to **Tatranská Lomnica** (1¾-2hr.). The hike to **Little Cold Valley** (Malá studená dolina) is fairly relaxed.

Many chalets along the trails provide lodging for travelers. **Zamkovského chata ❷** (☎442 2636) is on the red trail (40min.) from Hrebienok. The green trail (2hr.) climbs above the treeline to a high lake and another chalet, **Téryho chata ❷.** (☎442 5245. Dorms 280Sk.) Inexpensive accommodations in town are scarce; inquire at the tourist office. *Penzión* runners greeting backpackers at the station often offer the cheapest beds (500-600Sk per person). The conveniently located, newly refurbished **Penzión Tatra ❸**

THE LOCAL STORY

THE BLOODY COUNTESS

Four hundred years ago in Slovakia, status and wealth meant you could get away with murder. Or at least it did for Elizabeth Bathory, one of the most infamous criminals in Slovakian history. As a Hungarian countess, Bathory is said to have terrorized as many as 650 young women between 1580 to 1610. Her husband was often away and Bathory grew bored; teaming up with her two maids, one of whom became her lover, she found entertainment by torturing peasant girls, whom she seduced into the castle by hiring them for work.

It wasn't until she made the mistake of kidnapping girls from the lower gentry that a local count launched an investigation. As the investigators moved throughout the castle, they found evidence of Bathory's brutality everywhere in the form of various girls, some dead and some half-dead, drained of their blood, their bodies marked up from Bathory's beatings and piercings.

Put on trial in 1610, Bathory's nobility prevented her from execution, unlike her accomplices. Instead, she was kept under house arrest in her castle, where she died a natural death at the age of 54.

Bathory's former castle is in modern-day Slovakia at Čachtice near the town of Trenčín and a short bus ride from Bratislava

offers tidy rooms. Turn right out of the train station; the pension is on the right just before the bus station. (☎903 650 802; www.tatraski.sk. Rooms 650-750Sk.) More budget options are located two TEŽ stops away in **Horný Smokovec.** Worthwhile restaurants cluster above the bus and train stations in Starý Smokovec. **Supermarket Sintra** is in the shopping complex opposite the bus station. (Open M-F 8am-8pm, Sa 8am-8:45pm, Su noon-8:45pm. MC/V.)

TEŽ **trains** run to Poprad (30min., 1 per hr., 20Sk). **Buses** run to Bratislava (6hr., 2 per day, 440Sk) and Levoča (20-50min., 2-4 per day, 60Sk). The **Tatranská Informačná Kancelária (TIK),** in the strip mall above the train station, provides weather forecasts, sells maps, including the essential VKÚ map #113 (110Sk), and books private rooms. (☎442 3440; www.zcrvt.szm.sk. Rooms 250-300Sk; pensions 500Sk; hotels 650Sk. Open daily June-Sept. 8am-8pm; Oct.-May 8am-5pm.)

Ⓚ HIKING NEAR STARÝ SMOKOVEC. The town of **Štrbské Pleso** is the base for many beautiful hikes. From the tourist office, pass the souvenir lot and go left at the junction. Head uphill to reach the lift that goes 1840m up to **Chata pod Soliskom,** a chalet overlooking the lakes and valleys. (☎905 652 036. Dorms 230Sk. Lift open daily late May-Sept. and Dec.-Mar. 8:30am-4pm. Last lift up 3:30pm. 150Sk, students 90Sk; round-trip 230/120Sk.) Or, continue on the challenging yellow trail and along **Mlynická dolina** past several mountain lakes and the dramatic **Vodopády Skok** waterfalls. The path (6-7hr.) involves strenuous ascents on **Bystré Sedlo** (2314m) and **Veľké Solisko** (2412m). At the end of the yellow trail, turn left onto the red trail to complete the loop and return to Štrbské Pleso (30min.). The **grocery store** is opposite the train station (open 7am-10pm). TEŽ **trains** run to Štrbské Pleso from Starý Smokovec (30min., 1-2 per hr., 20Sk). The **tourist office** is across from the station. (Open M-Sa 8-11:30am and noon-4pm; low season reduced hours.)

SLOVENSKÝ RAJ. Southeast of the Low Tatras, the less-touristed Slovenský Raj (Slovak Paradise) National Park is filled with forested hills, deep ravines, and fast-flowing streams. The excellent **trail guide,** VKÚ map #4, is available at many hotels. The Ⓚ**Dobšinská Ice Caves** (Dobšinská ľadová jaskyňa) are composed of 110,000 cubic meters of water still frozen from the last Ice Age. Tours cover 475m, passing halls of frozen columns, gigantic ice wells, and waterfalls that don't fall. Dress warmly. (☎788 1470; www.ssj.sk. Open Tu-Su July-Aug. 9am-4pm, entrance every hr.; mid-May to June and early to mid-Sept. 9:30am-2pm, entrance every 1½hr. Mandatory guided tour; in English, min. 40 people. 180Sk, with ISIC 160Sk.) **Buses** run directly to the caves from Poprad (2hr., 8 per day, 47Sk) and Spišská Nová Ves (3-3½hr., 6 per day, 73-146Sk). To get to the caves from **Dedinky** (pop. 400), on the park's southern border, take the train two stops toward Červana Skala (15min., 3 per day, 15Sk). Head 100m to the main road, turn left, and continue to the parking lot, where the steep blue trail (20min.) leads up to the caves.

KOŠICE ☎055

Established nearly 900 years ago, Košice (KO-shih-tseh; pop. 236,000) is Slovakia's second-largest city. Every October, athletes from around the world converge at the Košice Peace Marathon, Europe's oldest marathon. The city's enchanting **Staré Mešto** (Old Town) is home to peaceful fountains, shady parks, and Slovakia's largest church, the magnificent Cathedral of St. Elizabeth. Outside the center, towering concrete housing blocks surround the city for miles, providing a stark reminder of Košice's Communist past.

⊡Ⓝ TRANSPORTATION AND PRACTICAL INFORMATION. Trains (☎181 88) run from the station on Predstaničné nám. to: Bratislava (6hr., 13 per day, 518Sk);

Budapest, HUN (4hr., 3 per day, 662Sk); Kraków, POL (6-7hr., 3 per day, 756Sk). **Buses** (☎625 1445), slightly cheaper and slower, depart to the left of the train station. To reach the city center, exit the train station and follow the "Centrum" signs across the park. Walk down **Mlynská** to reach **Hlavná námestie,** the main square, or take tram #6 to nám. Osloboditeľov and turn right to find the **tourist office,** Hlavná nám. 59. (☎625 8888; www.kosice.sk/icmk. Open M-F 9am-6pm, Sa 9am-1pm, Su 1pm-5pm.) Check email at **Internet Cafe,** Hlavná nám. 9. (50Sk per hr. Open daily 9am-10pm.) Košice's **post office,** Poštová 20, has Poste Restante at window #16. (☎617 1401. Open M-F 7am-7pm, Sa 8am-noon.) **Postal Code:** 04001.

🏠🍴 ACCOMMODATIONS AND FOOD. Hotels and pensions add a 20Sk tax per person per night. **K2 Tourist Hotel ❷,** Štúrova 32, a bargain near Staré Mešto, provides travelers with info. From Hlavná nám., turn right on Štúrova. (☎625 5948. Reception 24hr. Check-in and check-out noon. 3- to 4-bed dorms 375Sk. MC/V; 50sk surcharge.) The friendly staff at central **Gazdovská Pension ❸,** Cajkovského 4, helps visitors navigate the city. (☎622 8894. Reserve ahead. Singles 810Sk; doubles 810Sk. Cash only.) 🍴 **Reštaurácia Ajvega ❶,** Orlia 10, offers organic Slovak and Mexican food, including vegetarian options. (☎622 0452. Soups 30-40Sk. Entrees 89-155Sk. Open M-F 8am-10pm, Sa-Su 11am-10pm. Cash only.) The popular **Reštaurácia Veverička** (Squirrel Restaurant) ❷, Hlavná nám. 95, serves local dishes on its sun-drenched patio. (☎622 3360. English menu. Entrees 65-290Sk. Open daily 9am-10pm. Cash only.) A **Tesco** supermarket is located at Hlavná nám. 109. (☎670 4810. Open M-F 7am-10pm, Sa-7am-6pm, Su 8am-6pm. MC/V.)

🎭🏛 SIGHTS AND NIGHTLIFE. The 🏛**Cathedral of St. Elizabeth** (Dom sv. Alžbety), in Hlavná nám., was constructed in high Gothic style in 1378 but has been renovated repeatedly since. Climb the north tower for a view of Staré Mešto and the intricate cathedral roof. (Tower open M-F 9am-5pm, Sa 9am-1pm. Cathedral €30Sk, students 15Sk. Tower 35/20Sk. Both 70/15Sk.) The **East Slovak Museum** (Východnoslovenské Múzeum), Hrnčiarska 7, includes **Ferenc Rakóczi's House,** an exhibit on a rebellion leader, and **Mikluš's Prison,** an exposé on jail life from the 17th to 19th centuries. From Hlavná nám., take a right at the State Theatre onto Univerzitná. (Open Tu-Sa 9am-5pm, Su 9am-1pm. Mandatory Slovak-language tours 30Sk, students 15Sk. Prison exhibit 30/15Sk.)

The stylish **Jazz Club,** Kováčska 39, houses a disco and pub. (☎622 4237. Beer 27-55Sk. Tu and Th-Sa disco nights; cover 50Sk. Open M,W, Su 4pm-2am, Tu and Th-Sa 8pm-4am. Cash only.) Party-goers are off to the races at the Formula 1-themed **Monopost,** Hlavná nám. 54. (☎091 548 18 87. Tu and F-Sa disco nights. Open M and W-Th 11am-midnight, Tu 11am-3am, F 11am-4am, Sa 2pm-4am, Su 3pm-midnight.)

🚩 DAYTRIP FROM KOŠICE: 🕳JASKYŇA DOMICA. Jaskyňa Domica, a challenge to reach, has breathtaking caverns. Stalactites and stalagmites jut from three-million-year-old UNESCO-protected walls. The largest cave measures 48 million L. When underground water levels permit, the longer tour includes a boat ride covering 1.5km of the cave. The shorter tour covers a mere 780m. Only 5km of the 23km cave lie on the Slovak side—the rest is accessible from Hungary. To see more, travel 1km (10min. on foot above ground) to the border and find the **Hungarian** entrance. Buses from Košice go to Plešivec (1½hr., 7-10 per day, 128Sk) where a connecting bus (1 per 1-2hr., 3Sk) leaves for Jaskyňa Domica. Check the timetable across from the cave entrance or at the TIC for bus schedules. (☎788 2010; www.domica.sk. Mandatory tours June-Aug. Tu-Su 1 per hr.; Sept.-Dec. and Feb.-May 4 per day. 45min. tour 140Sk, students 120Sk; 1½hr. tour 180/160Sk. Cash only.)

SLOVENIA (SLOVENIJA)

The first and most prosperous of Yugoslavia's breakaway republics, tiny Slovenia revels in republicanism, peace, and independence. With a historically westward gaze, Slovenia's liberal politics and high GDP helped it gain early entry into the European Union, further eroding its weak relationship with Eastern Europe. Fortunately, modernization has not adversely affected the tiny country's natural beauty and diversity: it is still possible to go skiing, explore Slovenia's stunning caves, bathe under the Mediterranean sun, and catch an opera—all in a single day.

 DISCOVER SLOVENIA: SUGGESTED ITINERARIES

THREE DAYS. In **Ljubljana** (p. 881), the charming cafe culture and nightlife—especially in eclectic, Soviet-chic Metelkova—is worth at least two days. Then relax in tranquil, fairytale **Bled** (1 day; p. 885).

ONE WEEK. After 3 days in the capital city **Ljubljana,** enjoy **Bled** (1 day) and its cousin **Bohinj** (1 day; p. 886). Head down the coast to the mini-Venice of **Piran** (2 days; p. 884).

ESSENTIALS

FACTS AND FIGURES

Official Name: Republic of Slovenia.
Capital: Ljubljana.
Major Cities: Maribor, Celje, Kranj.
Population: 2,009,000.

Time Zone: GMT + 1.
Language: Slovenian.
Religion: Roman Catholic (58%).
Tractors per 100 People: 6.

WHEN TO GO

July and August are the peak months in Slovenia; tourists flood the coast, and prices for accommodations rise. Go in spring or early autumn, and you will be blessed with a dearth of crowds and great weather for hiking and exploring the countryside. Skiing is popular from December to March.

DOCUMENTS AND FORMALITIES

EMBASSIES AND CONSULATES. Foreign embassies to Slovenia are in Ljubljana (p. 882). Embassies and consulates abroad include: **Australia,** Level 6, 60 Marcus Clarke St., Canberra, ACT 2601 (☎262 434 830; vca@gov.si); **Canada,** 150 Metcalfe St., Ste. 2101, Ottawa, ON K2P 1P1 (☎613-565-5781; www.gov.si/mzz-dkp/veleposlanistva/eng/ottawa/embassy.shtml); **Ireland,** Morrison Chambers, 2nd fl., 32 Nassau St., Dublin 2 (☎1 670 5240; vdb@mzz-dkp.gov.si); **UK,** 10 Little College St., London SW1P 3SJ (☎020 72 22 57 00; www.gov.si/mzz-dkp/veleposlanistva/eng/london/events.shtml); **US,** 1525 New Hampshire Ave., NW, Washington, D.C. 20036 (☎202-667-5363; www.gov.si/mzz-dkp/veleposlanistva/eng/washington). Citizens of **New Zealand** should contact the embassy in Australia.

VISA AND ENTRY INFORMATION. Citizens of Australia, Canada, Ireland, New Zealand, the UK, and the US do not need **visas** for stays of up to 90 days. Visas take four to seven business days to process (US$45 for all types). Visas are not available at the border.

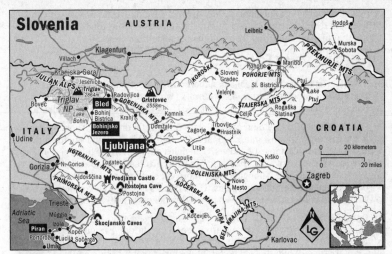

 ENTRANCE REQUIREMENTS.

Passport: Required for all travelers.

Visa: Not required for stays of under 90 days for citizens of Australia, Canada, Ireland, New Zealand, the UK, and the US.

Letter of Invitation: Not required.

Inoculations: Recommended up-to-date on DTaP (diphtheria, tetanus, and pertussis), Hepatitis A, Hepatitis B, MMR (measles, mumps, and rubella), polio booster, and typhoid.

Work Permit: Required of all foreigners planning to work in Slovenia.

International Driving Permit: Required of those planning to drive in Slovenia.

TOURIST SERVICES AND MONEY

EMERGENCY   Ambulance and **Fire:** ☎ 112. **Police:** ☎ 113.

There are **tourist offices** in most major cities and tourist destinations. Staff members generally speak English or German and, on the coast, perfect Italian. They can usually find accommodations for a small fee and generally give advice and maps for free. **Kompas** is the main tourist organization.

The **euro** (€) has replaced the tolar in Slovenia. SKB Banka, Ljubljanska Banka and Gorenjska Banka are common **banks.** American Express Travelers Cheques and Eurocheques are accepted almost everywhere, but major credit cards are not consistently accepted. MasterCard and Visa **ATMs** are everywhere.

HEALTH AND SAFETY

Medical facilities are of high quality, and most have English-speaking doctors. EU citizens receive free medical care with a valid passport; other foreigners must pay cash. **Pharmacies** are stocked according to Western standards; ask for *obliž* (band-aids), *tamponi* (tampons), and *vložki* (sanitary pads). **Tap water** is safe to drink. **Crime** is rare in Slovenia. **Women** should, as always, exercise caution and avoid being out alone after dark. There are few **minorities** in Slovenia, but minorities gen-

SLOVENIA

erally just receive curious glances. Navigating Slovenia with a **wheelchair** can be difficult and requires patience and caution on slippery cobblestones. **Homosexuality** is legal, but may elicit unfriendly reactions outside urban areas.

TRANSPORTATION

BY PLANE. Flights arrive at **Ljubljana Airport** (LJU). Most major airlines offer connections to the national carrier, **Adria Airways** (www.adria-airways.com). To enter inexpensively, consider flying into Vienna, AUT and taking a train to Ljubljana.

BY TRAIN AND BUS. First and second class differ little on **trains.** Those under 26 get a 20% discount on most international fares. ISIC-holders should ask for the 30% *popust* (discount) off domestic tickets. Schedules often list trains by direction. *Prihodi vlakov* means arrivals; *odhodi vlakov* is departures; *dnevno* is daily. **Eurail** is not accepted in Slovenia. Though usually more expensive than trains, **buses** may be the only option in mountainous regions. The bus is also a better choice than the train to Bled, as the train station is far from town. Buy tickets at stations or on board.

BY CAR, FERRY, BIKE, AND THUMB. Car rental agencies in Ljubljana offer reasonable rates, and Slovenia's roads are in good condition. A regular **ferry** service connects Portorož to Venice, ITA in summer.   Nearly every town in Slovenia has a bike rental office. While those who hitchhike insist that it is safe and widespread in the countryside, hitchhiking is not recommended by Let's Go.

KEEPING IN TOUCH

PHONE CODES	**Country code: 386. International dialing prefix: 00.** For more info on placing international calls, see **Inside Back Cover.**

EMAIL AND INTERNET. Internet access is fast and common. Though free Internet is hard to find anywhere but in the biggest cities, there are Internet cafes in most major tourist destinations. Expect to pay approximately €2-4 per hour.

TELEPHONE. All phones take **phonecards,** sold at post offices, kiosks, and gas stations. Dial ☎ 115 for collect calls and ☎ 1180 for the international operator. Calling abroad is expensive without a phonecard (over US$6 per min. to the US). Use the phones at the post office and pay when you're finished. **British Telecom** (☎ 080 080 832) offers one of the only international access codes in Slovenia.

MAIL. Airmail *(letalsko)* takes one to two weeks to reach Australia, New Zealand, and the US. Address **Poste Restante** as follows: first name, LAST NAME, Poste Restante, post office address, Postal Code, city, SLOVENIA.

LANGUAGE. Slovenian is a South Slavic language written in the Latin alphabet. Most young Slovenes speak at least some English, but the older generations are more likely to understand German or Italian. The tourist industry is generally geared toward Germans, but most tourist office employees speak English.

ACCOMMODATIONS AND CAMPING

SLOVENIA	❶	❷	❸	❹	❺
ACCOMMODATIONS	under €15	€15-21	€22-27	€28-33	over €33

All establishments charge a nightly **tourist tax. Youth hostels** and **student dormitories** are cheap (€15-20), but generally open only in summer (June 25-Aug. 30). **Hotels** fall into five categories (L, deluxe; A; B; C; and D) and are expensive. **Pensions** are the most common form of accommodation; usually they have private singles as well as inexpensive dorms. **Private rooms** are the only cheap option on the coast and at Lake Bohinj. Prices vary, but rarely exceed US$30. Inquire at the tourist office or look for *Zimmer frei* or *Sobe* signs. **Campgrounds** can be crowded, but most are in excellent condition. Camp in designated areas to avoid fines.

FOOD AND DRINK

SLOVENIA	❶	❷	❸	❹	❺
FOOD	under €3	€3-5	€6-8	€9-10	over €10

For home-style cooking, try a *gostilna* or *gostišče* (country-style inn or restaurant). Traditional meals begin with *jota*, a soup with potatoes, beans, and sauerkraut. Pork is the basis for many dishes, such as *Svinjska pečenka* (roast pork). **Kosher** and **vegetarian** eating is therefore very difficult within the confines of Slovenian cuisine. Those with such dietary restrictions might find pizza and bakery items their best options. Slovenia's **winemaking** tradition dates from antiquity. Renski, Rizling, and Šipon are popular whites, while Cviček and Teran are favorite reds. Brewing is also centuries old; Laško and Union are good beers. For something stronger, try *žganje*, a fruit brandy, or Viljamovka, distilled by monks who closely guard the secret of getting a whole pear inside the bottle.

HOLIDAYS AND FESTIVALS

Holidays: New Year's Day (Jan. 1); Culture Day (Prešeren Day; Feb. 8); Easter Holiday (Mar. 23-34, 2008; April 12-13, 2009); National Resistance Day (WWII; Apr. 27); Labor Day (May 1-2); Independence Day (National Statehood; June 25); Reformation Day (Oct. 31); Christmas Day (Dec. 25).

Festivals: Slovenia embraces its alternative artistic culture as much as its folk heritage. Hitting Ljubljana in July and August, the International Summer Festival is the nation's most famous. The Peasant's Wedding Day *(Kmecka ohcet)*, a presentation of ancient wedding customs held in Bohinj at the end of July, and the Cow's Ball *(Kravji Bal)* in mid-September, which celebrates the return of the cows to the valleys from higher pastures, are a couple of the country's many summertime folk exhibitions.

LJUBLJANA   ☎ 01

The average traveler only stops in Ljubljana (loob-lee-AH-na; pop. 280,000) for an hour en route from Venice to Zagreb, but those who stay longer become enchanted by this lively town full of folklore. ◗**Dragons** protect one of the many bridges, while street performances liven up summer nights. Baroque monuments, Art Nouveau facades, and modern high-rises tell of the city's richly layered history.

▐ TRANSPORTATION

Trains: Trg OF 6 (☎291 3332). To: **Bled** (1hr., 14 per day, €4); **Koper** (2¼hr., 10 per day, €7.50); **Budapest, HUN** (9hr., 3 per day, €50); **Sarajevo, BOS** (11hr., 3 per day, €840) via **Zagreb, CRO** (2hr., 9 per day, €12); **Venice, ITA** (6hr., 3 per day, €25).

Buses: Trg OF 4 (☎090 4230; www.ap-ljubljana.si). To: **Bled** (1½hr., 1 per hr. until 9pm, €6.40); **Koper** (2½hr., 5-10 per day, €12); **Maribor** (3hr., 10 per day, €12); **Zagreb, CRO** (3hr., 1 per day, €15).

Public Transportation: Buses run until 10:30pm. Drop €1.30 in the box beside the driver or buy cheaper €0.80 *žetoni* (tickets) at post offices, kiosks, or the main bus terminal. Day passes (€3.80) sold at **Ljubljanski Potniški Promet,** Celovška c. 160 (☎582 2426 or 205 6045). Open M-F 6:45am-7pm, Sa 6:45am-1pm. Pick up a bus map at the **Tourist Information Center (TIC).**

✈ 🛈 ORIENTATION AND PRACTICAL INFORMATION

The train and bus stations are side-by-side on **Trg Osvobodilne Fronte** (Trg OF or OF Sq.). To reach the center from the stations, turn right on Masarykova and left on Miklošičeva c.; continue to **Prešernov trg,** the main square. After crossing the Tromostovje (Triple Bridge), you'll see Stare Miasto at the base of Castle Hill. The tourist office is on the left at the corner of Stritarjeva and Adamič-Lundrovo nab.

Tourist Office: Tourist Information Center (TIC), Stritarjeva 1 (☎306 1215, 24hr. English-language info 090 939 881; www.ljubljana.si). Helpful staff speak excellent English. Pick up **free maps** and the useful, free *Ljubljana from A to Z.* Open daily June-Sept. 8am-10pm; Oct.-May 10am-7pm. Box office in TIC open M-F 9am-6pm, Sa-Su 9am-1pm. AmEx/MC/V.

Embassies: Australia, Trg Republike 3 (☎425 4252). Open M-F 9am-1pm. **Canada,** Miklošičeva c. 19 (☎430 3570). Open M-F 9am-1pm. **Ireland,** Poljanski nasip 6 (☎300 8970). Open M-F 9am-noon. **UK,** Trg Republike 3 (☎200 3910). Open M-F 9am-noon. **US,** Prešernova 31 (☎200 5500). Open M-F 9am-noon and 2-4pm.

Currency Exchange: Menjalnice (private exchange) booths abound. **Ljubljanska banka** branches throughout town exchange currency for no commission and cash **traveler's checks** for a 1.5% commission. Open M-F 9am-noon and 2-7pm, Sa 9am-noon.

Luggage Storage: *Garderoba* (lockers) at train station. €2 per day. Open 24hr.

24hr. Pharmacy: Lekarna Miklošič, Miklošičeva 24 (☎231 4558).

Internet: Most hostels in town offer free Internet. **Cyber Cafe Xplorer,** Petkovško nab. 23 (☎430 1991; www.sisky.com), has fast connections and Wi-Fi. €2.30 per 30min., students €2. 20% discount 10am-noon. Open M-F 10am-10pm, Sa-Su 2-10pm.

Post Office: Trg OF 5 (☎433 0605). Open M-F 7am-midnight, Sa 7am-6pm, Su 9am-noon. **Poste Restante,** Slovenska 32 (☎426 4668), at *izročitev pošiljk* (outgoing mail) counter. Open M-F 7am-8pm, Sa 7am-1pm. **Postal Code:** 1000.

🏠 ACCOMMODATIONS

Finding cheap accommodations in Ljubljana is easy in July and August. **Hostelling International Slovenia** (PZS; ☎231 2156) provides info on youth hostels in Slovenia. The **TIC** finds private rooms (singles €27-45; doubles €40-75). There is a daily **tourist tax** (€0.62-1.25) at all establishments.

■ **Celica,** Metelkova 8 (☎430 1890; www.hostelcelica.com). With your back to the train station, walk left down Masarykova, then right on Metelkova; blue signs will lead the way. Local and foreign artists transformed this former prison into a modern work of art. Bar, cafe, free Internet, and cultural arts programs. Breakfast included. Reception 24hr. Reserve ahead. Dorms €17-20; cells €25. Cash-only deposit €10 per person. MC/V. ❷

Fluxus, Tomšičeva 4 (☎251 5760; www.fluxus-hostel.com). The elegant decor and host of services complement its main square location. 1 bath for 15 beds. Kitchen. Free Internet. Reception 24hr. Reserve ahead. Dorms €20; doubles €55. Cash only. ❷

Autocamp Ježica, Dunajska 270 (☎568 3913; ac.jezica@gpl.si). Take bus #6 or 8 to Ježica. Both wooded campground and spacious, impeccable rooms with TVs and showers are available. Reception 24hr. Flexible check-out 1pm. Reservations recommended. June 20-Aug. 20 camping €10 per person; Aug. 21-June 19 €7.50. Electricity €2. Singles €45; doubles €65. Tourist tax €0.70. MC/V. ❶

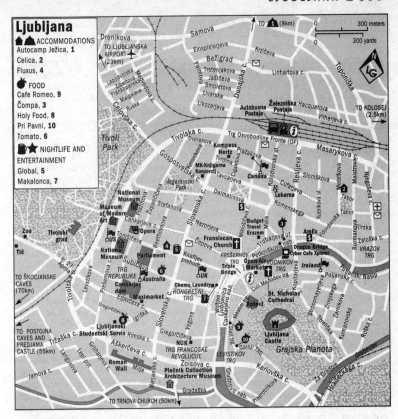

Ljubljana

▲▲ ACCOMMODATIONS
Autocamp Ježica, **1**
Celica, **2**
Fluxus, **4**

🍴 FOOD
Cafe Romeo, **9**
Čompa, **3**
Holy Food, **8**
Pri Pavni, **10**
Tomato, **6**

**■★ NIGHTLIFE AND
ENTERTAINMENT**
Global, **5**
Makalonca, **7**

🍴 FOOD

Maximarket, Trg Republike 1, has a **Mercator** grocery store in its basement. (Open M-Th 9am-8pm, F 9am-10pm, Sa 8am-3pm.) There is a large **open-air market** next to St. Nicholas's Cathedral. (Open June-Aug. M-Sa 6am-6pm; Sept.-May 6am-4pm.) Fast-food stands feature Slovenian favorites such as *burek*, fried dough filled with *mesni* (meat) or *sirov* (cheese), that usually cost €2.

Cafe Romeo, Stari trg 6. Popular with local hipsters, this is one of the few places in town that serves food on Su. Riverside outdoor seating supplements a fashionable black-and-red leather interior. Snack-oriented menu features burritos (€4.50), nachos (€3.50), and dessert crepes (€3.50). Open daily 10am-1am. Kitchen open M-Sa 11am-midnight, Su 11am-11pm. Cash only. ❷

Čompa, Trubarjeva ul. 40. This small family-run restaurant serves delicious, light Slovenian cuisine. Try the potato-and-goulash *čompa* cheese (€6.50). Complementary after-dinner drink is highly potent. ❸

Pri Pavni, Stari trg 21. Commended by the "Society for the Recognition of Sauteed Potato and Onions as an Independent Dish," according to a plaque on the wall, Pri Pavni has heavy, flavorful Slovenian dishes. Try the "smoked meat with turnips and hard-boiled corn mush" (€6.50) with a side of roasted potatoes (€1.50). Cash only. ❸

Holy Food, Ponedeljek petek. Vegetarian fast-food haven with flavorful pizzas and *burek* in the heart of the university scene. With Ganesha and Buddha lining the walls, you can feel enlightened and sated all at once. Entrees €1-6. Open M-Sa 9:30-6pm. ❶

Tomato, Šubičeva 1 (☎252 7555). Slovenian fast food that predates (and tastes better than) McDonald's. Specializes in an assortment of burgers (€3.30-6.70), although salads (€5.40) are also available. Good if you're on the run, but if you're looking for a meal, skip the formica tables for a restaurant with more flavor. Open M-Sa 7am-9pm. ❷

🔍 SIGHTS

A good way to see the sights is a 2hr. walking tour, in English and Slovenian, which departs from the *rotovž* (city hall), Mestni trg 1. (July-Aug. M-F 10am, Su 11am; May-Sept. daily 10am; Oct.-Apr. F-Su 11am. €6, students €3.50. Buy tickets at the tour or at the TIC.) Close to city hall, down Stritarjeva and across the Tromostovje (Triple Bridge), is Prešernov trg with its pink 17th-century **Franciscan Church** (Frančiškanska cerkev). Cross back to Old Town and take a left to reach the dazzling ▨**St. Nicholas's Cathedral.** (Stolnica Sv. Nikolaia; open daily 6am-noon and 3-7pm. Free.) Continue along the river to Vodnikov trg, where ▨**Dragon Bridge** (Zmajski Most) stretches across the Ljubljanica. On the far side of Vodnikov trg, the narrow Studentovska leads uphill to **Ljubljana Castle** (Ljubljanski Grad), which has a breathtaking view. (Open daily May-Oct. 10am-9pm; Nov.-Apr. 10am-7pm. English tours €4.50, students €3.50; min. 3 people) Cross the Dragon Bridge to Resljeva c., turn left on Tubarjeva c., and continue to Prešernov trg; take a left on Wolfova (which becomes Gosposka), then take a right on Zoisova c. and a left onto Emonska ul. Across the bridge is the **Plečnik Collection** (Plečnikova Zbrika), Karunova 5, which exhibits the works of Ljubljana's best-known architect. (Open Tu-Th 10am-6pm, Sa 10am-3pm. €4.50, students €2. Mandatory 30min. tour available in English.) Walking back from the museum, take a left on Zoisova c. and a right onto Slovenska c.; after the Ursuline Church, take a left to find **Trg Republike,** home to the National Parliament and Cankarjev Dom, the city's cultural center. Two blocks past the square, the ▨**National Museum** (Narodni Musei) contains exhibits on archaeology, culture, and local history from the prehistoric era to the present. Upstairs, the **Natural History Museum** features an impressive taxidermy collection. (Open Su-W, and F 10am-6pm, Th 10am-8pm. National Museum and National History Museum each €3, students €2. Both €4/3. 1st Su of month free.)

🎵🎭 ENTERTAINMENT AND NIGHTLIFE

Ljubljana International Summer Festival hosts music, opera, and theater from mid-June to mid-September. The neighborhood surrounding the former military compound in **Metelkova Mesto,** behind the Celica hostel from Trg Osvobodilne Fronte to the Ethnographic Museum, is now a graffiti-covered artists' colony with plenty of bars and clubs. On a terrace below the waterfront, the cavernous bar ▨**Makalonca,** Hribarjevo nab., just past the Triple Bridge, has gorgeous views of the river, fewer crowds, and more attitude than its neighbors. (Sangria €1.60. Mixed drinks €2.50-4.50. Open M-Sa 10am-1am, Su 10am-3pm.) With castle views, eclectic music, and a disco-era ambience, rooftop ▨**Global,** Tomšičeva 2, is the city's top dance club. (Mixed drinks €4-6. Cover for men after 11pm €4.50. Free Wi-Fi. Bar open M-Sa 8am-10pm. Club open Th-Sa 10pm-5am.)

PIRAN ☎05

Unlike more modern towns on the Istrian Peninsula, Piran has retained its Venetian charm, with beautiful churches, winding cobblestone streets, and dilapidated medieval architecture. A short walk uphill from behind the red building at **Tartinijev trg,** the town's central square, leads to the Gothic **Church of Saint George** (Cerkev sv. Jurija) and the 17th-century **Saint George's Tower**, with a view of Piran and the Adriatic. (Open daily mid-June to Sept. 10am-1pm and 4-7pm; Oct. to mid-June 11am-5pm. Free.) From the tower, head away from the church and continue uphill to the medieval **city walls** for the best views of the surrounding area. (Open Apr.-Oct. 8am-8pm; Nov.-Mar. 9am-5pm. Free.) Piran's real attraction, however, is the sea. While the closest sand beach is in the neighboring town of Portorož, it's possible to go swimming off Piran's own rocky shores, and excellent **scuba diving** can be arranged through **Sub-net**, Prešemovo nab. 24, which runs certification classes and guided dives. (☎673 2218; www.sub-net.si. €30 guided dive, €40 to explore a wreck. €60 per rental piece. €220 beginner's open-water dive. Open Tu-Su 9am-7pm. Cash only.) The **Maritime Museum** (Pomorski Muzej), off Tartinijev trg on Cankarjevo nab., has three stories of exhibits on marine archaeology and seamanship, and an impressive collection of ship replicas. (☎671 0040. English captions. Open in the summer Tu-Su 9am-noon and 6-9pm, in the winter 3-6pm. €3.50, students €2.50.) July welcomes the **Primorska Summer Festival**, featuring outdoor plays, ballets, and concerts. (Inquire at the tourist office for schedules.)

🛏 **Youth Hostel Val (HI) ❸**, Gregorčičeva 38A, has spotless two- to four-bed suites. From the bus station, follow the coast past Tartinijev trg as it curves away from the harbor; the hostel is three blocks up. (☎673 2555; www.hostel-val.com. Breakfast included. Reception 8am-10pm. Dorms mid-May to mid-Sept. €24; mid-Sept. to mid-May €20.) Waterfront cafes line Prešemovo nab., but **Tri Vdove ❷** stands out for its seafood dishes. (☎673 0290. Entrees 1300-5200Sit. Open daily 10am-midnight.) A **Mercator** supermarket, Levstikova 5, is behind the tourist office. (Open M-F 7am-8pm, Sa 7am-1pm, Su 8am-noon. AmEx/MC/V.) **Buses** go to Ljubljana (7-8 per day; €12). A **minibus** runs the length of Obala, from Lucija through Portorož and on to Piran (2 per hr. 5:30am-midnight, €1). Alternatively, a 25min. walk takes you from Piran to Portorož; facing the sea, head left. The friendly, English-speaking staff at the **tourist office**, Tartinijev trg 2. in the central square, provides bus schedules. (☎673 0220. 10am-5pm; later in summer.) **Postal Code:** 6330.

BLED ☎ 04

Alpine hills, snow-covered peaks, a turquoise lake, and a stately castle make Bled (pop. 11,000) one of Slovenia's most striking, popular destinations. The **Church of the Assumption** (Cerkev Marijinega Vnebovzetja) rises from the only Slovenian island in

IN RECENT NEWS

POLITICAL HORSEPLAY

Shortly after Slovenia became the first Eastern bloc country to switch over to the Euro in 2007, national pride manifested itself in the unexpected form of dancing horses—specifically the two leaping Lipizzaners the Slovenian government chose to engrave on its new 20-euro-cent coin.

This might seem strange, given that the Lipizzaner breed is most famously associated with the Spanish Riding School in Vienna, Austria, but the Slovenians steadfastly point to their small town of Lipica as the breed's birthplace and source of its name. And even though the town has spent time under Italian, Austrian, and Yugoslavian rule, making the claim to the horses anyone's game, possession, they seem to argue, is nine tenths the law.

For the time being, the Austrians are refusing to enter the fray, contenting themselves with their recent purchase of the breed's genealogical Book of Origins, previously held by Italy.

Despite these setbacks, the Slovenian government, however, remains undaunted and has publicly declared its intention to secure the return of the book of origins, thereby ensuring that the dancing horse sticks to a Slovenian tune.

the center of the lake. To get there, either rent a boat (1st hr. €10-11, €6.30 per hr. thereafter), hop on a gondola (round-trip €10), or just swim (500m from the west side of the lake, next to the campground). At the edge of a rock face rising above the lake's shores is **Bled Castle** (Blejski grad), built in 1004. It contains a museum detailing the archaeological history of the region and has an amazing view of Bled and the mountains surrounding it. (☎578 0525. Open daily May-Oct. 8am-8pm; Nov.-Apr. 8am-5pm. €5, students €4.50. MC.) ⬛**Soteska Vintgar,** a 1.6km gorge carved by the waterfalls and rapids of the Radovna River, winds through the rocks of the **Triglav National Park** (Triglavski Narodni Park) and culminates with the 16m **Šum Waterfall** (down the stairs behind the second ticket booth). Walk the 4km instead of taking the bus to the trailhead, and you'll pass small towns and open fields. Bring food; a picnic bench tucked neatly into a nook lies halfway along the hike. The park info office is at Kidričeva c. 2. (☎574 1188. €2.50, students €2.) To get there, go over the hill on Grajska c., away from the town center, and right at the bottom of the hill. Turn left after 100m and follow signs for Vintgar. Alternatively, hop on one of the frequent buses to Podhom (10min., M-Sa 10 per day, €1.30) and follow the 1.5km route. From mid-June through September, **Alpetour** (☎532 0440) runs a bus to the trailhead (15min., 10am; one-way €2.50, round-trip €4.50).

Agency Kompas, Ljubljanska c. 4, rents **bikes** (€3.50 per hr., €8 per ½-day, €11 per day) and offers **whitewater rafting** trips. (☎572 7500; www.kompas-bled.si. Rafting €23 per day. Open 8am-7pm, Su 8am-noon and 4-7pm. AmEx/MC/V.) The comfortable dorm beds, spotless private baths, and filling breakfast at **Bledec Youth Hostel (HI)** ❸, Grajska c. 17, make it feel more like a pension. Turn left from the bus station and follow the street to the top, bearing left at the fork. (☎574 5250; bledec@mlino.si. Breakfast included. Laundry €8.50. Internet €2 per 30min. Reception 24hr. Check-out 10am. Restaurant and common room available. Reserve ahead. Dorms €20, members €19; doubles €25; tourist tax €0.10. AmEx/MC/V.) To reach lakeside **Camping Bled** ❶, Kidričeva 10C, from the Bled Jezero train station, walk down the steep footpath across from the station and then bear right along the lake for 5min. From the bus station, walk downhill on c. Svobode, turn right, and walk along the lake for about 3km. (☎575 2000; www.camping.bled.si. Laundry €4. Internet €7.50 per hr. Reception 24hr. Check-out 3pm. €6.80-10 per person. Electricity €3. Tourist tax €0.50.) Big portions, high-quality food, and excellent service distinguish **Gostilna pri Planincu** ❸, Grajska c. 8, near the bus station. (☎574 1613. Crepes €2.50-3.50. Pizza €4.60-10.50. Open daily 9am-11pm.) **Trains** leave from the Lesce-Bled station, about 4km from Bled, for Ljubljana (1hr., 7 per day, €4). **Buses** from Bled go to Bohinjsko Jezero (35min., 1 per hr. 7:20am-8:20pm, €3.60), Ljubljana (1½hr., 1 per hr. 5am-9:30pm, €6.30), and Vintgar (1 per day June 14-Sept. 30; €2.50.) The lakeside **tourist office** is on the corner of the c. Svobode 10 building. The staff give out free maps of Bled and sell hiking maps (€4-10) of the entire region. (☎574 1122; www.bled.si. Open June-Sept. M-Sa 8am-7pm; Mar.-May 9am-7pm; Nov.-Feb. 9am-5pm.) **Postal Code:** 4260.

LAKE BOHINJ (BOHINJSKO JEZERO)   ☎04

Although it is only 26km southwest of Bled, Bohinjsko Jezero (BOH-heen-sko YEH-zeh-roh) surpasses its famous neighbor in its largely untouched natural beauty. Protected by the borders of Triglav National Park, the larger glacial lake draws aquatic adventurers with its pristine navy waters. But it is the towering mountains rising right out of the lake that attract most travelers who yearn to scale or ski these local summits. Trails are marked with a white circle inside a red circle; trail maps are available at the **tourist bureau,** Ribčev Laz 48, in Bohinjska Bistrica, a bigger town 6km east of the lake. The most popular hike, **Savica Waterfall** (Slap Savica), at the Ukanc end of the lake, is often crowded; strike out on your own. If the hiking spirit compels you, head to the stunning **Black Lake** (Črno Jezero) at the base of the Julian Alps' highest peaks (1½hr.). Although this is a fun climb, be aware that the hike is extremely steep; avoid going alone or carrying a pack. Facing the small lake's shore, a trail to the right (Dol Pod Stadorjem) leads to **Mt. Viševnik,** a grassy hillside that overlooks the small peaks.

The cheapest accommodation options around the lake are private rooms (€10-15; tourist tax €1) and campgrounds. To reach **Camping Danica ●,** Bohinjska Bistrica 4264, take the bus to town and backtrack about 75m; the site is on the right. (☎572 1055; www.bohinj.si/camping-danica. July 1-Aug. 18 €10; Aug. 19-Sept. 1 and June 10-30 €8.35; Sept. 2-30 and May 1-June 9. Electricity €2.50. 10% off stays longer than 1 week. Tourist tax €0.50. AmEx/MC/V.) Take the bus to Hotel Zlatorog and backtrack 300m to reach the lakeside **AvtoCamp Zlatorog ●,** Ukanc 2. Reception July-Aug. 24hr.; Sept.-May daily 8am-noon and 4-8pm. Check-out noon. July-Aug. €7-8 per day; Sept. and May-June €8.90-11.50. Tourist tax €0.50. Cash only.) Open M-F 7am-8pm, Sa 7am-8pm, Su 7am-5pm. Buses run to **Bohinjska Bistrica,** the largest town in the area, 6km from the lake; from there, **trains** head to Ljubljana (2½hr., 8 per day, €5.30) via Jesenice. **Buses,** the more convenient option, run from Hotel Zlatorog in Ukanc to Ribčev Laz (10min., 1 per hr., €1.30) and from Ribčev Laz to: Bled (35min., 11-16 per day, €3.60); Bohinjska Bistrica (15min., 1 per hr., €1.60); Ljubljana (2hr., 1 per hr., €8.30). Buses going to Bohinjsko Jezero (Lake Bohinj) stop at Hotel Jezero in Ribčev Laz or at Hotel Zlatorog in Ukanc. Ribčev Laz, where most buses bring the lake's visitors, contains numerous private tourist bureaus that help to books rooms and arrange transportation to the lake. The lake is also surrounded by two other villages, Stara Fužina and Ukanc. The **tourist bureau,** Ribčev Laz 48, provides maps and transportation info, issues fishing permits; books private rooms, and arranges guided excursions. (☎574 6010; www.bohinj.si. Open July-Aug. M-Sa 8am-8pm, Su 8am-7pm; Sept.-June M-Sa 8am-6pm, Su 9am-3pm.) **Postal Code:** 4265.

SPAIN (ESPAÑA)

The fiery spirit of flamenco; the energy of artistic genius; the explosive merging of urban style and archaic tradition—this is Spain. Here, dry golden plains give way to rugged coastline, and modern architectural feats rise from ancient plazas. Explore winding medieval alleyways that lead to bustling city centers, or watch from a sidewalk cafe as curiously hair-styled youth pass by. In Spain, there is always a reason to stay up late, and there is always time for an afternoon *siesta*.

 DISCOVER SPAIN: SUGGESTED ITINERARIES

THREE DAYS. Soak in **Madrid's** (p. 894) art and culture as you walk through the **Retiro's** gardens and peruse the halls of the **Prado, Thyssen-Bornemisza,** and **Nacional Centro de Arte Reina Sofía.** By night, move from the tapas bars of Santa Ana to Malasaña and Chueca. Daytrip to **Segovia** (p. 908) or **El Escorial** (p. 905).

ONE WEEK. Begin in southern Spain, exploring the Alhambra's Moorish palaces in **Granada** (1 day; p. 922) and the mosque in **Córdoba** (1 day; p. 912). After two days in **Madrid,** travel northeast to **Barcelona** (2 days) and the beaches of **Costa Brava** (1 day; p. 946).

THREE WEEKS. See the beautiful cathedral of **León** (1 day; p. 910), then head to **Madrid** (3 days), with daytrips to **El Escorial** (1 day) and **Segovia** (1 day). Take the train to **Córdoba** (2 days), and on to **Seville** (2 days; p. 915). Catch the bus to the magnificent gorge near **Ronda** (1 day; p. 922) before heading south to charming **Málaga**, on the **Costa del Sol** (1 day p. 926). Head inland to **Granada** (2 days), then seaward again to **Valencia** (1 day; p. 930) before traveling up the coast to **Barcelona** (3 days). Daytrip to the **Costa Brava** (1 day), taking in the Teatre-Museu Dalí and the Casa-Museu Salvador Dalí. From Barcelona, head to the beaches and tapas bars of **San Sebastián** (1 day; p. 950) and **Bilbao** (1 day; p. 952), home of the world-famous Guggenheim Museum.

ESSENTIALS

FACTS AND FIGURES

Official Name: Kingdom of Spain.
Capital: Madrid.
Government: Parliamentary monarchy.
Major Cities: Barcelona, Granada, Valencia.
Population: 40,448,000.
Land Area: 500,500 sq. km.

Time Zone: GMT +1.
Languages: Spanish (Castilian), Basque, Catalan, Galician.
Religion: Roman Catholic (94%).
Largest Paella Ever Made: 20m in diameter, this paella fed 100,000 people in 1992.

WHEN TO GO

Summer is high season in Spain, though in many parts of the country, *Semana Santa* and other festival days are particularly busy. Tourism peaks in August, when the coastal regions overflow while inland cities empty out. Winter travel has the advantage of lighter crowds and lower prices, but sights reduce their hours.

DOCUMENTS AND FORMALITIES

EMBASSIES. Foreign embassies in Spain are in Madrid. Spanish embassies abroad include: **Australia** and **New Zealand,** 15 Arkana St., Yarralumla, ACT, 2600 (☎6273 35 55; www.mae.es/embajadas/canberra/es/home); **Canada,** 74 Stanley Ave., Ottawa, ON, K1M 1P4 (☎613-747-2252; www.embaspain.ca); **Ireland,** 17 Merlyn Park, Ballsbridge, Dublin, 4 (☎353 126 08 066; www.mae.es/embajadas/dublin); **UK,** 39 Chesham Pl., London, SW1X 8SB (☎020 72 35 55 55); **US,** 2375 Pennsylvania Ave., NW, Washington, D.C., 20037 (☎202-728-2340; www.mae.es/embajadas/washington/es/home). All countries listed have consulates in Barcelona. Australia, the UK, and the US also have consulates in Seville.

VISA AND ENTRY INFORMATION. EU citizens do not need a visa. Citizens of Australia, Canada, New Zealand, the US, and many Latin American countries do not need a visa for stays of up to 90 days, beginning upon entry into the EU's freedom-of-movement zone. For more info, see p. 14. For stays longer than 90 days, all non-EU citizens need visas, available at Spanish consulates (€100).

TOURIST SERVICES AND MONEY

TOURIST OFFICES. For general info, contact the **Instituto de Turismo de España,** Jose Lazaro Galdiano 6, 28071 Madrid (☎913 433 500; www.tourspain.es).

EMERGENCY	**Ambulance:** ☎061. **Fire:** ☎080. **Local Police:** ☎092. **National Police:** ☎091. **General Emergency:** ☎112.

MONEY. The **euro (€)** has replaced the **peseta** as the unit of currency in Spain. For more info, see p. 16. As a general rule, it's cheaper to exchange money in Spain than at home. **ATMs** usually have good exchange rates. In restaurants, all prices include a service charge. Satisfied customers occasionally toss in some spare change—usually no more than 5%—and while it is purely optional, **tipping** is becoming increasingly widespread in restaurants and other places that cater to tourists. Many people give train, airport, and hotel porters €1 per bag, while taxi drivers sometimes get 5-10%. **Bargaining** is only common at flea markets and with street vendors.

Spain has a 7% **value added tax (VAT;** in Spain, **IVA)** on restaurant meals and accommodations and a 16% VAT on retail goods. The prices listed in *Let's Go* include VAT. In an airport upon exiting the EU, non-EU citizens can claim a refund on the tax paid for goods purchased at participating stores. In order to qualify for a refund in a store, you must spend at least €50-100, depending on the shop; make sure to ask for a refund form when you pay. For more info on qualifying for a VAT refund, see p. 19.

BUSINESS HOURS. Almost all museums, shops, and churches close from 2-4pm or longer for an afternoon **siesta**. Most Spaniards eat lunch during their *siesta* (as well as nap), so restaurants open in the late afternoon. Shops and sights reopen at 3pm, and some may stay open until 8pm. Most restaurants will start serving dinner by 9pm, although eating close to midnight is very common in Spain. After midnight, the clubhopping commences. Increasingly, some large chains and offices are open all day, in large part due to an effort by the Spanish government to encourage a stronger economy and more "normal" business hours. It's still a safe bet that nearly every store will be closed on Sundays.

TRANSPORTATION

BY PLANE. Flights land mainly at **Barajas Airport** in Madrid (**MAD;** ☎913 93 60 00) and the **Barcelona International Airport** (BCN; ☎932 98 39 25). Contact AENA (☎902 40 47 04; www.aena.es) for info on flight times at most airports. See p. 43 for info on flying to Spain.

BY FERRY. Spain's islands are accessible by ferry; see the **Balearic Islands** (p. 956). Ferries are the least expensive way of traveling between Spain and **Tangier** or the Spanish enclave of **Ceuta** in Morocco. See p. 53.

BY TRAIN. Direct trains are available to Madrid and Barcelona from several European cities, including Geneva, SWI; Lisbon, POR; and Paris, FRA. Spanish trains are clean, relatively punctual, and reasonably priced. However, most train routes do tend to bypass small towns. Spain's national railway is **RENFE** (☎902 24 02 02; www.renfe.es). When possible, avoid *transvía, semidirecto,* or *correo* trains, as they are very slow. *Estrellas* are slow night trains with bunks and showers. *Cercanías* (commuter trains) go from cities to suburbs and nearby towns. There is no reason to buy a Eurail Pass if you plan to travel only within Spain. Trains are cheap, so a pass saves little money; moreover, buses are the most efficient means of traveling around Spain. Several Rail Europe passes cover travel within Spain. See www.raileurope.com for more information on the following passes. The **Spain Flexipass** ($155) offers three days of unlimited travel in a two-month period. The **Spain Rail 'n' Drive Pass** ($307) is good for three days of unlimited first-class train travel and two days of unlimited mileage in a rental car. The **Spain-Portugal Pass** offers three days or more of unlimited first-class travel in Spain and Portugal over a two-month period (from $289). For more info, see p. 48.

JUST SAY NO. If you are planning on traveling only within Spain (and Portugal), do not buy a **Eurail Pass.** Bus travel is usually the best option, and trains are less expensive than in the rest of Europe. A Eurail Pass makes sense only for those planning to travel in other European countries as well.

BY BUS. In Spain, buses are cheaper and have far more comprehensive routes than trains. Buses provide the only public transportation to many isolated areas. For those traveling primarily within one region, **buses are the best method of transportation.** Spain has numerous private companies and the lack of a centralized bus company may make itinerary planning difficult. Companies' routes rarely overlap, so it is unlikely that more than one will serve your intended destination. **Alsa/Enatcar** (☎913 27 05 40; www.alsa.es) serves Asturias, Castilla and León, Galicia, and Madrid, as well as international destinations including France, Germany, Italy, and Portugal. **Auto-Res/Cunisa, S.A.** (☎902 02 09 99; www.auto-res.net) serves Castilla and León, Extremadura, Galicia, Valencia, and Portugal.

BY CAR. Spain's highway system connects major cities by four-lane *autopistas*. **Speeders beware:** police can "photograph" the speed and license plate of your car and issue a ticket without pulling you over. If you are pulled over, fines must be paid on the spot. **Gas** prices, €0.80-1.10 per liter, are lower than in many European countries but high by North American standards. **Renting** a car is cheaper than elsewhere in Europe. Spain accepts Canadian, EU, and US driver's licenses; otherwise, an International Driving Permit (IDP) is required. Try **Atesa** (Spain ☎902 10 01 01, elsewhere 10 05 15; www.atesa.es), Spain's largest rental agency. The automobile association is **Real Automóvil Club de España** (**RACE;** ☎902 40 45 45; www.race.es). For more on renting and driving a car, see p. 50.

BY THUMB. Hitchhikers report that Castilla and Andalucía are long, hot waits, and hitchhiking out of Madrid is virtually impossible. The Mediterranean coast and the islands are more promising; remote areas in the Balearics, Catalonia, or Galicia may be best accessible by hitchhiking. Although approaching people for rides at gas stations near highways and rest stops purportedly gets results, Let's Go does not recommend hitchhiking.

KEEPING IN TOUCH

PHONE CODES	**Country code: 34. International dialing prefix:** 00. Within Spain, dial city code + local number, even when dialing inside the city. For more information on how to place international calls, see **Inside Back Cover.**

EMAIL AND THE INTERNET. Email is easily accessible within Spain. Internet cafes are listed in most towns and all cities, and generally charge as little as €2 per hr. In small towns, if Internet is not listed, check the library or the tourist office, which may have public Internet access. For a list of internet cafes in Spain, consult www.cybercafes.com.

TELEPHONE. Whenever possible, use a prepaid phone card for international phone calls, as long-distance rates for national phone service are often very high. Find them at tobacconists. However, some public phones will only accept change. Mobile phones are an increasingly popular and economical option, costing as little as €30 (not including minutes). Major mobile carriers include **Movistar** and **Vodafone.** Direct-dial access numbers for calling out of Spain include: **AT&T Direct** (☎900 990 011); **British Telecom** (☎900 990 044); **Canada Direct** (☎900 990 015); **Telecom New Zealand Direct** (☎900 990 064); **Telstra Australia** (☎900 990 061).

MAIL. Airmail *(por avión)* takes five to eight business days to reach Canada or the US; service is faster to the UK and Ireland and slower to Australia and New Zealand. Standard postage is €0.78 to North America. Surface mail *(por barco)* can take over a month, and packages take two to three months. Certified mail *(certificado)* is the most reliable way to send a letter or parcel and takes four to seven business days. Spain's overnight mail is not actually overnight, and is thus not worth the expense. To receive mail in Spain, have it delivered **Poste Restante.** Mail will go to the main post office unless you specify a subsidiary by street address. Address mail to be held according to the following example: Last Name, First Name; *Lista de Correos;* City; Postal Code; SPAIN; AIRMAIL.

ACCOMMODATIONS AND CAMPING

SPAIN	❶	❷	❸	❹	❺
ACCOMMODATIONS	under €15	€15-24	€25-34	€35-40	over €40

The cheapest and most basic options are *refugios, casas de huéspedes,* and *hospedajes,* while *pensiones* and *fondas* tend to be a bit nicer. All are essentially boarding houses with basic rooms, shared bath, and no A/C. Higher up the ladder but not necessarily more expensive, *hostales* generally have sinks in bedrooms and provide linens and lockers, while *hostal-residencias* are similar to hotels in overall quality. The government rates *hostales* on a two-star system; even establishments receiving one star are typically quite comfortable. The system also fixes *hostal* prices, posted in the lounge or main entrance. Prices invariably dip below the official rates in the low season (Sept.-May), so bargain away. **Red Española de Albergues Juveniles** (REAJ), the Spanish **Hostelling International** (HI) affiliate (Madrid ☎915 22 70 07; www.reaj.com), runs more than 200 hostels year-round. Prices depend on season, location, and services offered, but are generally €9-15 for guests under 26 and higher for those 26 and over. Breakfast is usually included; lunch and dinner are occasionally offered at an additional charge. Hostels usually have lockouts around 11am and have curfews between midnight and 3am. As a rule, don't expect much privacy—rooms typically have 4-20 beds in them. To reserve a bed in the high season (July-Aug. and during festivals), call at least a few weeks in advance. **Campgrounds** are generally the cheapest choice for two or more people. Most charge separate fees per person, per tent, and per car; others charge for a *parcela* (a small plot of land), plus per-person fees. Tourist offices can provide more info, including the *Guía de Campings.*

FOOD AND DRINK

SPAIN	❶	❷	❸	❹	❺
FOOD AND DRINK	under €6	€6-10	€11-15	€16-20	over €20

Fresh, local ingredients are still an integral part of Spanish cuisine, varying according to each region's climate, geography, and history. The old Spanish saying holds true: *"Que comer es muy importante, porque de la panza, ¡nace la danza!"* (Eating is very important, because from the belly, dance is born!)

Spaniards start the day with a light breakfast *(desayuno)* of coffee or thick, hot chocolate, and a pastry. The main meal of the day *(comida)* consists of several courses and is typically eaten around 2 or 3pm. Dinner at home *(cena)* tends to be light. Dining out begins anywhere between 8pm and midnight. Bar-hopping for tapas is an integral part of the Spanish lifestyle. Some restaurants are "open" from 8am until 1 or 2am, but most serve meals only from 1 or 2 to 4pm and 8pm to midnight. Many restaurants offer a *plato combinado* (main course, side dish, bread, and sometimes a beverage) or a *menú del día* (two or three set dishes, bread, beverage, and dessert) for roughly €5-9. If you ask for a *menú,* this is what you may receive; *carta* is the word for menu.

Tapas (small dishes of savory meats and vegetables cooked according to local recipes) are quite tasty, and in most regions they are paired with beer or wine. *Raciones* are large tapas served as entrees; *bocadillos* are sandwiches. Spanish specialties include *tortilla de patata* (potato omelet), *jamón serrano* (smoked ham), *calamares fritos* (fried squid), *arroz* (rice), *chorizo* (spicy sausage), *gambas* (shrimp), *lomo de cerdo* (pork loin), *paella* (steamed saffron rice with seafood, chicken, and vegetables), and *gazpacho* (cold tomato-based soup). Vegetarians should learn the phrase *"yo soy vegetariano"* (I am a vegetarian) and specify this means no *jamón* (ham) or *atún* (tuna). A normal-sized draft beer is a *caña de cerveza;* a *tubo* is a little bigger. A *calimocho* is a mix of Coca-Cola and red wine, while *sangria* is a drink of red wine, sugar, brandy, and fruit. *Tinto de verano* is a lighter version of sangria: red wine and Fanta. *Café solo* means black coffee; add a touch of milk for a *nube;* a little more and it's a *café cortado;* half milk and half coffee makes a *café con leche.*

HOLIDAYS AND FESTIVALS

Holidays: New Year's Day (Jan. 1); Epiphany (Jan. 6); Maundy Thursday (Mar. 20); Good Friday (Mar. 21); Easter (Mar. 23-24); Labor Day (May 1); Assumption (Aug. 15); National Day (Oct. 12); All Saints' Day (Nov. 1); Constitution Day (Dec. 6); Feast of the Immaculate Conception (Dec. 8); Christmas (Dec. 25); New Year's Eve (Dec. 31).

Festivals: Almost every town in Spain has several festivals. In total, there are more than 3000. Nearly everything closes during festivals. All of Spain celebrates *Carnaval* the week before Ash Wednesday (Feb. 6); the biggest parties are in Catalonia and Cádiz. During the annual festival of *Las Fallas* in mid-Mar., Valencia honors St. Joseph with parades, fireworks, and the burning of effigies. The entire country honors the Holy Week, or *Semana Santa* (Mar. 16-22). Seville's *Feria de Abril* has events showcasing many different Andalusian traditions, including bullfighting and flamenco (Apr. 8-13). *San Fermín* (The Running of the Bulls) takes over Pamplona July 6-14 (see p. 949). For more information, see www.tourspain.es or www.gospain.org/fiestas.

BEYOND TOURISM

Spain offers volunteer opportunities from protecting dolphins on the Costa del Sol to fighting for immigrants' rights. Universities in major cities host thousands of foreign students every year, and language schools are a good alternative to university **study** if you desire a deeper focus on language or a slightly less rigorous courseload. Those seeking **long-term work** in Spain should consider teaching English. Short-term jobs are widely available in the restaurant, hotel, and tourism industries, and are typically held by those without permits. For more info on opportunities across Europe, see **Beyond Tourism**, p. 56.

Don Quijote, Placentinos 2, 37008 Salamanca (☎923 26 88 60; www.don-quijote.org). A nationwide language school offering Spanish courses for all levels throughout the country. Very social atmosphere. 2-week intensive courses start at €338. €95 enrollment fee. Discounts for longer sessions.

Ecoforest, Apdo, Correos 29, 29100 Coin, Málaga (☎661 07 99 50; www.ecoforest.org). Fruit farm and vegan community in southern Spain that uses ecoforest education to help participants develop a sustainable lifestyle.

Escuela de Cocina Luis Irizar, C. Mari 5 Bajo, 20003 San Sebastián (☎943 43 15 40; www.escuelairizar.com). Learn how to cook Basque cuisine at this culinary institute. Programs range from week-long summer courses to comprehensive 2-year apprenticeships. Some summer courses may be taught in English.

MADRID
☎ 91

After Franco's death in 1975, young *Madrileños* celebrated their liberation from totalitarian repression with raging all-night parties across the city. This revelry became so widespread that it defined an era, and *la Movida* (the Movement) is now recognized as a world-famous nightlife renaissance. The newest generation has kept the spirit of *la Movida* alive—other claimants aside, Madrid is truly the city that never sleeps. While neither as funky as Barcelona nor as charming as Seville, Madrid is the political, intellectual, and cultural capital of Spain.

SPAIN

▐ TRANSPORTATION

Flights: All flights land at **Aeropuerto Internacional de Barajas** (**MAD;** ☎902 40 47 04), 20min. northeast of Madrid. The **Barajas metro line** connects the airport to all of Madrid (€1). Another option is the **Bus-Aeropuerto #200** (look for "EMT" signs), which runs to the city center. (☎902 50 78 50. 4-6 per hr., €1.) The bus stops in the metro station **Avenida de América.**

Trains: 2 *largo recorrido* (long distance) **RENFE** stations, **Atocha** and **Chamartín,** connect Madrid to the rest of Europe. Call RENFE (☎902 24 02 02; www.renfe.es) for info.

Estación de Atocha (☎506 6137). M: Atocha Renfe. Domestic service only. AVE (☎506 6137) has high-speed service to southern Spain, including **Seville** (2½hr., 22 per day, €63-70) via **Córdoba** (1¾hr., €40-52). Grandes Líneas trains leave for **Barcelona** (4½-5hr., 9 per day, €36-63).

Estación Chamartín (☎300 6969). M: Chamartín. Bus #5 runs to and from Puerta del Sol (45min.). Alternatively, take a red Cercanías train (15min., 6 per hr., €1) from M: Atocha Renfe. Chamartín services both international and domestic destinations in the northeast and south. Major destinations include: **Barcelona** (9hr., 2 per day, €35-42); **Bilbao** (6½hr., 2 per day, €32-40); **Lisbon, POR** (9¼hr., 10:45pm, €54); **Paris, FRA** (13½hr., 7pm, €112-129). Chamartín offers services, including a **tourist office,** Vestíbulo, Puerta 14 (☎315 9976; open M-Sa 8am-8pm, Su 8am-2pm), **accommodations service, car rental, currency exchange, luggage storage** (*consignas;* €2.40-4.50; open daily 7am-11pm), **police,** and **post office.**

Buses: Many private companies, each with its own station and set of destinations, serve Madrid. Most pass through the Estación Sur de Autobuses and Estación Auto-Res.

Estación Auto-Res: C. Fernández Shaw 1 (☎902 02 09 99; www.auto-res.net). M: Conde de Casal. Info booth open daily 6:30am-1am. To **Cuenca** (2½hr., 6-10 per day, €10-14), **Salamanca** (3hr., 9 per day, €11-16), and **Valencia** (5hr., 10-11 per day, €29).

Estación La Sepulvedana: C. Palos de la Frontera 16 (☎559 5955; www.lasepulvedana.es). M: Príncipe Pío (via extension from M: Ópera). To **Segovia** (1½hr., 2 per hr., €6).

Estación Sur de Autobuses: C. Méndez Álvaro (☎468 4200; www.estaciondeautobuses.com). M: Méndez Álvaro. Info booth open daily 6am-1am. **ATMs** and **luggage storage** (€1.25 per bag per day) available. Destinations include **Alicante, Santiago de Compostela,** and **Toledo.**

Local Transportation: Madrid's **metro** is safe, speedy, and spotless (☎902 44 44 03; www.metromadrid.es). Metro tickets cost €1; a *metrobus* (ticket of 10 rides valid for the metro and bus) is €6.40. Also available are 1-, 2-, 3-, 5-, and 7-day unlimited ride tickets (*abono turístico;* €4-40). Hold onto your ticket until you leave the metro or face a fine. Spanish-language **bus** info ☎406 8810. Buses run 6am-11pm. Bus fares are the same as metro fares and tickets are interchangeable. *Búho* (owl), the **night bus** service, runs 2 buses per hr. midnight-3am, 1 per hr. 3-6am. Look for buses N1-N24.

Taxis: Call **Radio Taxi** (☎405 5500), **Radio-Taxi Independiente** (☎405 1213), or **Teletaxi** (☎371 3711). A *libre* sign in the window or a green light indicates availability. Base fare is €1.85 (€2.90 after 10pm), plus €0.87-1 per km from 6am-10pm and €1-1.10 from 10pm-6am. **Teletaxi** charges a flat rate of €1 per km.

⚡ ORIENTATION

Marking the epicenter of both Madrid and Spain, **Kilómetro 0** in **Puerta del Sol** ("Sol" for short) is within walking distance of most sights. To the west are the **Plaza Mayor,** the **Palacio Real,** and the **Ópera** district. East of Sol lies **Huertas,** the heart of cafe, museum, and theater life. The area north of Sol is bordered by **Gran Vía,** which runs northwest to **Plaza de España.** North of Gran Vía are three club- and bar-hopping districts, linked by Calle de Fuencarral: **Malasaña, Bilbao,** and **Chueca.** Modern Madrid is beyond Gran Vía and east of Malasaña and Chueca. East of Sol, the tree-lined thoroughfares **Paseo de la Castellana, Paseo de Recoletos,** and **Paseo del Prado** split Madrid in two, running from **Atocha** in the south to **Plaza Castilla** in the north, passing the Prado, the fountains of **Plaza de Cibeles,** and **Plaza de Colón.** Madrid is safer than many European cities, but Sol, Pl. de España, Pl. Chueca, and Pl. Dos de Mayo are still intimidating at night.

🛈 PRACTICAL INFORMATION

Tourist Offices: Madrid Tourism Centre, Pl. Mayor 27 (☎588 1636; www.esmadrid.com). M: Sol. **Branches** at Estación Chamartín, Estación de Atocha, and the airport. English and French usually spoken. All open daily 9:30am-8pm. Regional Office of the **Comunidad de Madrid,** C. del Duque de Medinaceli 2 (☎429 4951; www.madrid.org). M: Banco de España. Open M-Sa 8am-8pm, Su 9am-2pm. Pick up the *Guia del Ocio* (€1) or *In Madrid* for info on city events and establishments.

General Information Line: ☎901 30 06 00 or 010. Info on anything about Madrid, from police locations to zoo hours. Ask for *inglés* for an English-speaking operator.

Embassies: Australia, Pl. del Descubridor Diego de Ordás 3, 2nd fl. (☎353 6600; www.spain.embassy.gov.au). **Canada,** Núñez de Balboa 35 (☎423 3250; www.canada-es.org). **Ireland,** Po. Castellana 46, 4th fl. (☎436 4093). **New Zealand,** Pl. de la Lealtad 2, 3rd fl. (☎523 0226). **UK,** Po. de Recoletos 7-9 (☎524 9700; www.ukinspain.com). **US,** C. Serrano 75 (☎587 2200; www.embusa.es).

Currency Exchange: In general, credit and ATM cards offer the best exchange rates. Avoid changing money at airport and train station counters. **Banco Santander Central Hispano** charges no commission on AmEx **Travellers Cheques** up to €300. Main branch, Po. Castellana 7 (☎558 1111). M: Sol. Open Apr.-Sept. M-F 8:30am-2pm; Oct.-Mar. M-F 8:30am-2pm, Sa 8:30am-1pm. **Banks** usually charge 1-2% commission. Booths in Sol and Gran Vía are not a good deal.

Luggage Storage: At the airport and bus and train stations (€2.75 per bag per day).

GLBT Resources: Most establishments in Chueca carry a free guide to gay nightlife in Spain called **Shanguide.** The **Colectivo de Gais y Lesbianas de Madrid (COGAM),** C. de las Infantas 40, 1st fl. (☎522 4517; www.cogam.org), M: Gran Vía, provides a wide range of services and activities. Reception M-Sa 5-10pm.

Laundromat: Lavandería Ondablu, C. León, 3 (☎913 69 50 71). M: Antón Martín, Sol, or Sevilla. Wash €3.50, dry €1. Open M-F 9:30am-10pm, Sa 10:30am-7pm. Also at C. Hortaleza 84 (☎915 31 28 73). M: Chueca. Same hours and prices.

Police: C. de los Madrazos 9 (☎322 1160). M: Sevilla. From C. de Alcalá, take a right on C. Cedacneros and a left on C. de los Madrazos. Open daily 9am-2pm. To report crimes committed in the **metro,** go to the office in the Sol station.

Medical Services: In a medical emergency, dial ☎061 or 112. **Hospital de Madrid,** Pl. del Conde del Valle Suchil 16 (☎447 6600; www.hospitaldemadrid.com). **Hospital Ramón y Cajal,** Ctra. Colmenar Viejo, km 9100 (☎336 8000). Bus #135 from Pl. de

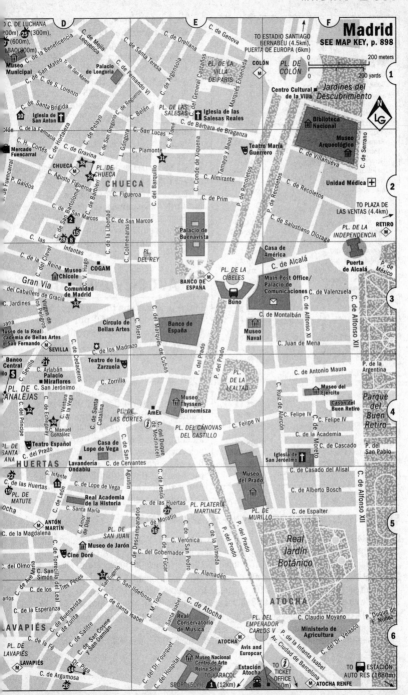

SPAIN

Madrid
SEE MAP KEY, p. 898

SPAIN

Madrid
SEE MAP, pp. 896-897

🏠 ACCOMMODATIONS

Camping Alpha,	1	E6
Casa Chueca,	2	D2
Cat's Hostel,	3	C5
Hostal Esparteros,	4	C4
Hostal Oriente,	5	B3
Hostal Paz,	6	B3
Hostal Plaza D'Ort,	7	C5
Hostal Rio Miño,	8	D2
Hostal Santillan,	9	B2
Hostal-Residencia Domínguez,	10	D1
La Posada de Huertas,	11	D5
Hostal-Residencia Luz,	12	B4
Mad Hostel,	13	C5

🍎 FOOD

Achuri,	14	D6
Al-Jaima,	15	D2
Arrocería Gala,	16	E5
Café Commercial,	17	D1
Café de Oriente,	18	A3
Casa Alberto,	19	D5
El Estragón Vegetariano,	20	A5
La Finca de Susana,	21	D4
Heladería Giuseppe Ricci,	22	D5
Inshala,	23	A4
Restaurante Casa Granada,	24	C5
Rey de Tallarines,	25	D1
Taberna "Er 77,"	26	D6
Taberna Maceira,	27	E5
El Tigre,	28	D2

⭐ NIGHTLIFE

Acuarela,	29	D2
Cardamomo,	30	D4
El Clandestino,	31	E2
Cuevas de Sésamo,	32	D4
De Las Letras Restaurante,	33	D3
La Ida,	34	C1
Ocho y Medio Club,	35	C3
Palacio Gaviria,	36	B4
Taberna Vinocola Mentridana,	37	D5
El Truco,	38	D2

Castilla. For non-emergencies, go to **Unidad Médica,** C. del Conde de Aranda 1, 1st fl. (☎435 1823; www.unidadmedica.com). M: Serrano or Retiro. Regular personnel on duty M-F 9am-8pm, Sa 10am-1pm. Initial visit €110, students €75. AmEx/MC/V. Embassies and consulates keep lists of English-speaking doctors.

Internet Access: ▨**SATS XXI,** C. San Jerónimo (☎/fax 532 0970), has fast connections, printing, fax, disks, and CDs. €1.85 per hr. Open daily 10am-midnight.

Post Office: Palacio de Comunicaciones, C. Alcalá 51, on Pl. de Cibeles (☎902 19 71 97; www.correos.es). M: Banco de España. Fax and **Lista de Correos.** Windows open M-Sa 8:30am-9:30pm, Su 8:30am-2pm for stamp purchases. **Postal Code:** 28080.

🏨 ACCOMMODATIONS

Make reservations for summer visits. Expect to pay €15-50 per person, depending on location, amenities, and season. While prices are high in El Centro, the triangle between Puerta del Sol, Ópera, and Pl. Mayor, the location is as good as it gets, especially for those planning to brave the legendary nightlife. The cultural hotbed of **Huertas,** framed by Ctra. de San Jerónimo, C. de las Huertas, and C. de Atocha, is almost as central and more fun. Trendy and eclectic Malasaña and Chueca, bisected by C. Fuencarral, boast cheap rooms in the heart of the action. *Hostales,* like temptations, are everywhere among Gran Vía's sex shops and scam artists.

EL CENTRO: SOL, ÓPERA, AND PLAZA MAYOR

▨ **Hostal-Residencia Luz,** C. de las Fuentes 10, 3rd fl. (☎542 0759; www.hostalluz.com). M: Ópera. Redecorated rooms are clean and comfortable. A/C and TV. Free Wi-Fi. Laundry €5. Singles €36; doubles €72; triples €108. Discounts for longer stays. MC/V. ❷

▨ **Hostal Paz,** C. Flora 4, 1st and 4th fl. (☎547 3047). M: Ópera. Spotless rooms with A/C and satellite TV. Laundry €10. Singles €30; doubles €36-38, with shower €42; triples with shower €54; quad €68. Monthly rentals available; reserve ahead. MC/V. ❸

Hostal Esparteros, C. de Esparteros 12, 4th fl. (☎521 0903). M: Sol. Unbeatable location and sparkling rooms with balconies or large windows; some have private bath, fans, and TV. Laundry €9-10. Singles €25; doubles €35; triples €45. Cash only. ❷

Hostal Oriente, C. Arenal 23, 1st fl. (☎548 0314; www.hostaloriente.com). M: Ópera. Classy, hotel-quality hostel with chandeliers, tiled floors, and friendly owners. 17 rooms with A/C, bath, phone, and TV. Singles €40; doubles €60; triples €80. MC/V. ●

HUERTAS

La Posada de Huertas, C. Huertas, 21 (☎429 5526; www.posadadehuertas.com). M: Antón Martín or Sol. Small rooms of 4 or 8 are clean, well-kept, and equipped with comfortable beds. Bathrooms are spotless. Breakfast, kitchen, and Wi-Fi included. Laundry €5. Luggage storage available. Beds fom €18. MC/V. ❷

Cat's Hostel, C. Cañizares 6 (☎369 2807; www.catshostel.com). M: Antón Martín. This renovated 18th-century palace features dorms with up to 16 beds, small doubles with private baths, an authentic *mudéjar* patio area, a bar, and a cafe. Cheap beer (€2-3). Bathrooms are not the cleanest. Breakfast, luggage storage, and Internet included. Laundry €5. Dorms €20; doubles €22. MC/V. ❷

Hostal Plaza D'Ort, Pl. del Angel 13 (☎429 9041; www.plazadort.com). M: Antón Martín. Conveniently located outside Pl. Santa Ana. Beautiful rooms are comfortable and a good deal. All have A/C, phone and TV. Internet and in-room movies €11. Singles €30, with bath €40; doubles €50/60; triples €75-85; suite €110. MC/V. ●

Mad Hostel, C. Cabeza 24 (☎506 4840; www.madhostel.com) M: Tirso de Molina. A relaxed and brand-new hostel with high-tech flair. Dorms are sparking. A bar area with pool table, gym, kitchen, and rooftop terrace. Breakfast included. Free Wi-Fi. Laundry €5. Reserve ahead. Dorms €20-22. MC/V. ❷

MALASAÑA AND CHUECA

Hostal-Residencia Domínguez, C. de Santa Brígida 1. (☎532 1547). M: Tribunal. A modern look and low prices. Brand new, immaculate doubles on the 2nd and 3rd fl. Hospitable young owner provides tips on local nightlife. Singles €39; doubles with A/C and bath €49; triples €59. Cash only. ●

Casa Chueca, C. de San Bartolomé 4, 2nd fl. (☎523 8127; www.casachueca.com). M: Chueca. Rooms have A/C, free Internet, and satellite TV. "Mini-breakfast" included. Reservations required. Singles €40; doubles €55; triples €70. MC/V. ●

Hostal Río Miño, C. de Barbieri 3, 1st fl. (☎522 1417). M: Chueca. Simple rooms are cheap and of decent quality. All have A/C. Common baths are very clean. Reserve 2 weeks ahead. Singles €20; doubles €28, €40 with bath; triples €54. Cash only. ❷

GRAN VÍA AND CAMPING

Hostal Santillan, Gran Vía 64, 8th fl. (☎548 2328; www.hostalsantillan.com). M: Pl. de España. Take the elevator to the top of this gorgeous building. Leaf-patterned curtains and wooden furniture give rooms a homey feel. All with fan, shower, sink, and TV. Doubles €50-55; triples €66. MC/V. ●

Camping Alpha (☎695 8069; www.campingalpha.com), on a tree-lined site 12.4km down Ctra. de Andalucía in Getafe. M: Legazpi. From the metro, walk down Vado Santa Catalina, cross the bridge, and bear right. Take the green bus #447, which stops across from the Museo de Jamón (10min., 1-2 per hr., €1.25). Ask for the Camp Alpha stop. Cross the footbridge and walk 1.5km back toward Madrid along the busy highway; signs lead the way. Amenities include laundry, paved roads, pool, tennis courts, and showers. €6.50 per person, €6.70 per tent or per car. Singles €36; doubles €45; bungalows 1-2 people €62, 3-4 people €92. IVA not included. ●

SPAIN

◘ FOOD

Many small eateries cluster on **Calles Echegaray, Ventura de la Vega,** and **Manuel Fernández González** in Huertas. Chueca is filled with bars *de cañas* (small beer from the tap), which serve complimentary tapas. The streets west of **Calle Fuencarral** in Gran Vía are lined with cheap restaurants, while **Bilbao** has affordable ethnic cuisine. Keep in mind the following words for quick, cheap *madrileño* fare: *bocadillo* (a baguette sandwich; €2-3); *ración* (a large tapa served with bread; €3-6); and *empanada* (a puff pastry with meat fillings; €1.30-2). The *Guía del Ocio* has a complete listing of Madrid's vegetarian options under the section *"Otras Cocinas."* **%Día** and **Champion** are the cheapest supermarket chains; smaller markets are open later but are more expensive.

▓ **La Finca de Susana,** C. Arlabán 4 (☎369 3557). M: Sevilla. Of the lesser-known restauranteur philosophy that quality should not come with a high price, this fine-dining establishment is packed every day for lunch—come early to avoid the ever-present line. *Menú* M-F €8.40. Open daily 1-3:45pm and 8:30-11:45pm. AmEx/MC/V. ❷

▓ **El Estragón Vegetariano,** Pl. de la Paja 10 (☎365 8982; www.guiadelocio.com/estragonvegetariano). M: La Latina. Among the best medium-priced restaurants in Madrid, with vegetarian delights that tempt even die-hard carnivores. *Menú* (M-F €10, Sa-Su and evenings €25). Open daily 1:30-4pm and 8pm-midnight. AmEx/MC/V. ❸

Taberna "Er 77", C. Argumosa 8. M: Lavapiés. The small kitchen of this local find produces some of the area's most creative dishes. Try the asparagus with raw salmon (€7). Entrees €5-11. Open Tu-Th 6pm-midnight, F-Sa 1pm-1am, Su 1pm-6pm. Cash only. ❷

Heladería Giuseppe Ricci (Gelato & Cafe), C. de las Huertas 9 (☎687 98 96 12; www.heladeriaricci.com). M: Antón Martín. Forget tapas and *jamón*—this *gelato* provides the best relief from a hot Madrid day. Small cones €2, large €3. Open M-Th and Su 10am-10pm, F-Sa 10am-10:30pm. ❶

Al-Jaima, Cocina del Desierto, C. de Barbieri 1 (☎523 1142). M: Gran Vía or Chueca. Egyptian, Lebanese, and Moroccan food served to patrons seated on pillows on the floor. Specialties include kebabs and *tajine* (appetizer €4, main courses €8). Try *pollo con higos y miel* (chicken with figs and honey; €6.10). Open daily 1:30-4pm and 9pm-midnight. Reserve ahead. MC/V. ❷

Taberna Maceira, C. de Jesús 7 (☎914 29 15 84). M: Antón Martín. Branch at C. Huertas 66 (☎429 5818). This funky tavern has fantastic seafood and great prices. 2 people can feast for under €25. Open M 8pm-12:45am, Tu-F 1-4:15pm and 8:30pm-12:45am, Sa-Su 1-4:45pm and 8:30pm-1:30am. Cash only. ❸

Inshala, C. de la Amnistía 10 (☎548 2632). M: Ópera. Eclectic selection of delicious Italian, Japanese, Mexican, Moroccan, and Spanish dishes. Weekday lunch *menú* €9. Dinner €10-26. Reserve ahead. Open in summer M-Th noon-5pm and 8pm-1am, F-Sa noon-5pm and 8pm-2am; in winter M-Sa noon-2am. MC/V. ❸

Arrocería Gala, C. de Moratín 22 (☎429 2562; www.paellas-gala.com). M: Antón Martín. Decor is as colorful as the specialty, paella. *Menú* (€14) includes dessert, paella, salad, and wine. Excellent sangria. Lush, vine-covered interior garden. Reserve ahead F-Sa. Open Tu-Su 1-5pm and 9pm-1:30am. Cash only. ❸

Rey de Tallarines, C. Cardenal Cisneros 33 (☎447 6828). Huge portions of Beijing cuisine and tiny prices. *Menú* €8.30. Noodle dishes €3-8. Open daily noon-midnight. ❷

Achuri, C. Argumosa 21 (☎468 7856). M: Lavapiés. A cheap, mostly vegetarian restaurant with a young clientele. *Bocadillos* €2.70. *Raciones* €4.80. Wine €0.80-2.20 per glass. Open Su-Th 1:30pm-2am, F-Sa 1:30pm-2:30am. Cash only. ❶

Café de Oriente, Pl. del Oriente 2 (☎547 9831). M: Ópera. A traditional cafe catering to a ritzy, older crowd and hungry tourists strolling by the Palacio. Specialty coffees (€4-

7). Open Su-Th 8:30am-1:30am, F-Sa 8:30am-12:30am. AmEx/D/MC/V. ●

Café Comercial, Glorieta de Bilbao 7 (☎521 5655). M: Bilbao. Founded in 1887, Madrid's oldest cafe boasts cushioned chairs, high ceilings, and huge mirrors perfect for people-watching. Coffee at the bar €1.20, at a table €1.90. Internet €1 per 50min. Open M-Th 7:30am-1am, F 7:30am-2am, Sa 8:30am-2am, Su 10am-1am. ●

TAPAS

Not long ago, bartenders in Madrid covered *(tapar)* drinks with saucers to keep away the flies. Later, servers began putting little sandwiches on top of the saucers, which became known as "tapas." Many tapas bars *(tascas or tabernas)* are on **Plaza Santa Ana** and **Plaza Mayor** as well as north of Gran Vía in **Chueca.**

🦐 **Restaurante Casa Granada,** C. Doctor Cortezo 17, 6th fl. (☎420 0825). Enter in an unmarked door on the left side of C. Doctor Cortezo. Place your name on the outdoor seating list when you arrive. *Cañas* of beer (small glass; €2.20) come with tapas. *Raciones* €5.50-8. Open M-Sa noon-midnight, Su noon-9pm. MC/V. ●

El Tigre, C. Infantas 30 (☎532 0072), is the most happening *cañas* spot in Chueca. Tapas free with drink. Young and inviting crowd. Beer €1.50. *Raciones* €4-7. Open M-F 12:30pm-1:30am, Sa-Su 1pm-2am. Cash only. ●

Casa Alberto, C. de las Huertas 18 (☎429 9356; www.casaalberto.es). M: Antón Martín. A classic tapas bar founded in 1827. Sweet vermouth (€1.50) is served with original house tapas. Try the delicious *gambas al ajillo* (shrimp with garlic; €10.50) or the *canapés* (€2.25-3). Open Tu-Sa noon-5:30pm and 8pm-1:30am. MC/V. ❷

🗺 SIGHTS

Madrid, large as it may seem, is a walking city. Its public transportation should only be used for longer distances or between the day's starting and ending points; you don't want to miss the sights above ground. Madrid also has many shaded sidewalk cafe and romantic parks perfect for relaxation.

EL CENTRO

The area known as El Centro, spreading out from Puerta del Sol (Gate of the Sun), is the gateway to historical Madrid. Although several rulers carved the winding streets, the Habsburgs and the Bourbons built El Centro's most celebrated monuments. Unless otherwise specified, Habsburg directions are given from Puerta del Sol and Bourbon directions from Ópera. Kilómetro 0, the origin of six national highways, marks the center of the city. *(M: Sol).*

TAPAS A TO Z

Food on toothpicks and in small bowls? The restaurant isn't being stingy, and your food isn't shrinking; you're merely experiencing an integral part of the Spanish lifestyle. The tapas tradition is one of the oldest in Spain. These tasty little dishes are Spain's answer to hors d'oeuvres, but have more taste, less pretension, and are eaten instead of meals.

To the untrained tourist, tapas menus are often indecipherable, if the bar has even bothered to print any. In order to avoid awkward encounters with tentacles or parts of the horse you rode in on, keep the following things in mind before *tapeando* (eating tapas).

Servings come in three sizes: *pinchos* (eaten with toothpicks), *tapas* (small plate), and *raciónes* (meal portion). On any basic menu you'll find: *Aceitunas* (olives), *albóndigas* (meatballs), *callos* (tripe), *chorizo* (sausage), *gambas* (shrimp), *jamón* (ham), *patatas bravas* (fried potatoes with spicy sauce), *pimientos* (peppers), *pulpo* (octopus), and *tortilla española* (onion and potato omelette). The more adventurous should try *morcilla* (blood sausage), or *sesos* (cow's brains). Often, bartenders will offer tastes of tapas with your drink and strike up a conversation. Ask for a *caña* (glass) of the house *cerveza* (beer) to guarantee the full respect of the establishment.

SPAIN

HABSBURG MADRID

PLAZA MAYOR. Juan de Herrera, the architect of El Escorial (p. 905), also designed this plaza. Its elegant arcades, spindly towers, and open verandas, built for Felipe III in 1620, are defining elements of the "Madrid-style," which inspired architects nationwide. Toward evening, Pl. Mayor awakens as *Madrileños* resurface, tourists multiply, and cafes reopen. Live flamenco performances are a common treat. While the cafes are a nice spot for a drink, food is overpriced. *(M: Sol.)*

CATEDRAL DE SAN ISIDRO. Though Isidro, patron saint of crops, farmers, and Madrid, was humble, his final resting place is anything but. Designed in the Jesuit Baroque style at the beginning of the 17th century, the cathedral received San Isidro's remains in 1769. During the Spanish Civil War, rioters damaged much of the cathedral, burning its exterior—the main chapel, a 17th-century banner, and the mummified remains of San Isidro were all that survived. *(M: Latina. Open daily in summer 7:30am-1:30pm and 5:30-9pm; in winter 7:30am-1pm and 5:30-8:30pm. Free.)*

PLAZA DE LA VILLA. Plaza de la Villa marks the heart of what was once Old Madrid. The horseshoe-shaped door on C. Codo is one of the few examples of the Gothic-*mudéjar* style left in Madrid, and the 15th-century *Torre de los Lujanes* was once the prison of French king Francisco I. Across the plaza is the 17th-century **Ayuntamiento,** designed as both the mayor's home and the city jail. Inside is Goya's *Allegory of the City of Madrid. (M: Sol.)*

BOURBON MADRID

PALACIO REAL. Palacio Real sits at the western tip of central Madrid, overlooking the Río Manzanares. Felipe V commissioned Giovanni Sachetti to replace the Alcázar, which burned down in 1734, with a palace that would dwarf all others. Today, the palace is used by King Juan Carlos and Queen Sofía only on special occasions. The **Salón del Trono** (Throne Room) contains a ceiling fresco outlining the qualities of the ideal ruler, and the **Salón de Gasparini** houses Goya's portrait of Carlos IV. Perhaps the most beautiful is the **Chinese Room,** whose walls swirl with green tendrils. The **Real Oficina de Farmacia** (Royal Pharmacy) has crystal and china receptacles used to hold royal medicine. Also open to the public is the **Real Armería** (Armory), which has an entire floor devoted to knights' armor. *(M: Ópera. ☎454 8788. Open Apr.-Sept. M-Sa 9am-6pm, Su 9am-3pm; Oct.-Mar. M-Sa 9:30am-5pm, Su 9am-2pm. €8, students €3.50; with tour €6/10. Under 5 free. W EU citizens free.)*

PLAZA DE ORIENTE. Royal paranoia was responsible for this sculpture park. Because of the queen's nightmare about the roof collapsing under new weight, the statues designed for *Palacio Real* were placed in this shady plaza. *(M: Ópera.)*

ARGÜELLES

Argüelles and the zone surrounding C. de San Bernardo form a mix of elegant homes, student apartments, and bohemian hangouts. Unlike most of Madrid, it is easily navigable. By day, families and joggers roam the city's largest park, **Casa del Campo.** The park is unsafe by night. The **Parque de la Montaña** is home to the ◪**Templo de Debod,** built by King Adijalamani in the 2nd century BC; it is the only Egyptian temple in Spain. *(M: Pl. de España or Ventura Rodríguez. ☎366 7415; www.munimadrid.es/templodebod. Guided tours available. Open Apr.-Sept. Tu-F 10am-2pm and 6-8pm, Sa-Su 10am-2pm; Oct.-Mar. Tu-F 9:45am-1:45pm and 4:15-6:15pm, Sa-Su 10am-2pm. Free.)*

OTHER SIGHTS

◪**PARQUE DEL BUEN RETIRO.** Join vendors, palm-readers, soccer players, and sunbathers in the area Felipe IV converted from a hunting ground into a *buen* *retiro* (nice retreat). The 300-acre park is centered around a magnificent monument to King Alfonso XII and a rectangular lake, the **Estanque Grande.** Rowboats for four people are available for €5 per 45min. Sundays from 5pm to midnight, over 100 percussionists gather for an intense ◙**drum circle** by the monument on the Estanque; hypnotic rhythms and hash smoke fill the air.

▥ MUSEUMS

Considered individually to be among the world's best art galleries, the Museo del Prado, Museo de Thyssen-Bornemisza, and the Museo Nacional Centro de Arte Reina Sofía together form the impressive "Avenida del Arte."

■**MUSEO DEL PRADO.** One of Europe's finest centers for 12th- to 17th-century art, the Prado is Spain's most prestigious museum and home to the world's greatest collection of Spanish paintings. Its 7000 pieces from the 12th to the 17th centuries are the result of hundreds of years of Habsburg and Bourbon art-collecting. The museum provides a free guide for each room. On the first floor, keep an eye out for the unforgiving realism of **Diego Velázquez** (1599-1660). His technique of "illusionism" is on display in ◙**Las Meninas.** Court portraitist **Francisco de Goya y Lucientes** (1746-1828) created the stark *2 de Mayo* and *Fusilamientas de 3 de Mayo*, which depict the terrors of the 1808 Napoleonic invasion. Deaf and alone, Goya painted the *Pinturas Negras (Black Paintings)*, so named for the darkness of both their color and their subject matter. The Prado also displays many of **El Greco's** religious paintings along with a formidable collection of Italian works, including pieces by **Botticelli, Raphael, Rubens, Tintoretto,** and **Titian.** As a result of the Spanish Habsburgs' control of the Netherlands, Flemish holdings are top-notch. Works by **van Dyck** and **Albrecht Durer** are here, as well as **Peter Bruegel the Elder's** *The Triumph of Death.* **Hieronymus Bosch's** moralistic *The Garden of Earthly Delights* depicts hedonists and the destiny awaiting them. *(Po. del Prado at Pl. Cánovas del Castillo. M: Banco de España or Atocha. ☎330 2800; www.museoprado.es. Open Tu-Su 9am-8pm. €6, students €3, under 18 and over 65 free, Su free.)*

■**MUSEO NACIONAL CENTRO DE ARTE REINA SOFÍA.** Since Juan Carlos I decreed this renovated hospital a national museum in 1988, the Reina Sofía's collection of **twentieth-century art** has grown steadily. The building itself is a work of art, and is much easier to navigate than the Prado. Rooms dedicated to **Dalí, Gris,** and **Miró** display Spain's contributions to Surrealism. Picasso's masterpiece, ◙**Guernica,** is the highlight of the Reina Sofía's permanent collection. *(Pl. Santa Isabel 52. ☎774 1000; www.museoreinasofia.es. M: Atocha. Open M and W-Sa 10am-9pm, Su 10am-2:30pm. €3, students €1.50. Sa after 2:30pm, Su, holidays, under 18, over 65 free.)*

■**MUSEO THYSSEN-BORNEMISZA.** The Thyssen-Bornemisza exhibits works ranging from 14th-century paintings to 20th-century sculptures. The museum's 775 pieces constitute the world's most extensive private showcase. The top floor is dedicated to the **Old Masters** collection, which includes such notables as Hans Holbein's austere *Portrait of Henry VIII* and El Greco's *Annunciation.* The Thyssen-Bornemisza's **Baroque** collection, with pieces by Caravaggio, Claude Lorraine, and Ribera, rivals the Prado's. Look for works by Cézanne, Degas, van Gogh, Manet, Matisse, Monet, and Renoir in the **Impressionist** and **Post-Impressionist** collections. The highlight of the museum is the **twentieth-century** collection on the first floor. The showcased artists include Chagall, Dalí, Hopper, O'Keeffe, Picasso, Pollock, and Rothko. *(On the corner of Po. del Prado and C. Manuel González. M: Banco de España or Atocha. ☎369 0151; www.museothyssen.org. Open Tu-Su 10am-7pm. Last entry 6:30pm. €6, students with ISIC and seniors €4, under 12 free. Audio guides €3.)*

♫ ENTERTAINMENT

▓ EL RASTRO (FLEA MARKET)

The market begins in La Latina at Pl. Cascorro off C. de Toledo and ends at the bottom of C. Ribera de Curtidores. The main street is a labyrinth of clothing, cheap jewelry, leather goods, incense, and sunglasses, branching out into side streets, each with its own concert of vendors and wares. Antique-sellers contribute their peculiar mustiness to C. del Prado, and in their own shops in small plazas off C. Ribera de Cortidores. Fantastic collections of old books and LPs are sold in Pl. del Campillo del Mundo, at the bottom of C. de Carlos Arnides. The flea market is a pickpocket's paradise, so leave the camera in your room, bust out the money belt, and turn that backpack into a frontpack. *(Open Su and holidays 9am-3pm.)*

MUSIC AND FLAMENCO

Madrid's principal performance venue is the prestigious **Teatro Real**, Pl. de Oriente, which features the city's best ballet and opera. (☎516 0606. M: Ópera. Tickets sold M-Sa 10am-1:30pm and 5:30-8pm.) Check the *Guía del Ocio* for info on city-sponsored concerts, movies, and plays. Flamenco in Madrid is tourist-oriented and expensive. A few nightlife spots are authentic, but pricey. **Las Tablas,** Pl. de España 9, on the corner of C. Bailén and Cuesta San Vicente, has lower prices than most other flamenco clubs (€22). Shows start nightly at 10:30pm. *(M: Pl. de España.* ☎542 0520; www.lastablasmadrid.com.)* **Casa Patas,** C. Cañizares 10, has excellent shows and offers intensive courses in flamenco. *(M: Antón Martín.* ☎369 0496; www.casapatas.com. Shows €25-30; M-Th 10:30pm, F-Sa 8pm and midnight. Course €65.)*

FÚTBOL

Spanish sports fans go ballistic for *fútbol* (football). Every Sunday and some Saturdays from September to June, one of the two local teams plays at home. **Real Madrid** plays at Estadio Santiago Bernabéu. *(Av. Cochina Espina 1. M: Santiago Bernabéu.* ☎457 1112.)* **Atlético de Madrid** plays at Estadio Vicente Calderón. *(Po. de la Virgen del Puerto 67. M: Pirámides or Marqués de Vadillos.* ☎364 2234. Tickets €22-50.)*

BULLFIGHTS

Hemingway-toting Americans and true fans of the contorted struggle between man and beast clog Pl. de las Ventas for the heart-pounding, albeit gruesome, events. From early May to early June, the **Fiestas de San Isidro** stage a daily *corrida* (bullfight) with the top *matadores* and the fiercest bulls. Advance tickets are recommended; those without a seat crowd into bars to watch the televised festival. There are bullfights every Sunday from March to October and less frequently during the rest of the year. Look for posters in bars and cafes for upcoming *corridas* (especially on C. Victoria, off C. San Jerónimo). **Plaza de las Ventas,** C. de Alcalá 237, is the biggest ring in Spain. *(M: Ventas.* ☎356 2200; www.las-ventas.com. Seats €2-115. Tickets available at booth F-Su.)* **Plaza de Toros Palacio de Vistalegre** also hosts bullfights and cultural events. *(M: Vista Alegre.* ☎422 0780.)* To watch amateurs, head to the **bullfighting school,** which has its own *corridas*. *(M: Batán.* ☎470 1990. Tickets €7, children €3.50. Open M-F 10am-2pm.)*

♞ NIGHTLIFE

Madrileños start the night in the tapas bars of **Huertas,** move to the youthful scene in **Malasaña,** and end at the wild parties of **Chueca** or late-night clubs of **Gran Vía.** Students fill the streets of **Bilbao** and **Moncloa.** Madrid's superb gay scene centers on **Plaza Chueca.** Chueca establishments carry *Shanguide,* a free guide to gay nightlife. Most clubs don't heat up until 2am; don't be surprised to see lines at 5:30am. Dress to impress to avoid being overcharged or denied by bouncers.

■ **Taberna Vinocola Mentridana,** C. San Eugenio 9 (☎527 8760), 1 block from M: Antón Martín off C. Atocha. A popular local tapas bar by day, this place revs up at night when locals get thirsty for a glass of wine or a vermouth (€2.50-7). The crowd is sophisticated and somewhat philosophical, so don't forget your thinking cap. MC/V.

■ **Palacio Gaviria,** C. Arenal 9 (☎526 6069; www.palaciogaviria.com). M: Sol or Ópera. Party like royalty in 3 ballrooms of this palace-turned-disco, but don't spill Red Bull and vodka on the high art. Mixed drinks €10. Cover €15; includes 1 drink. Open Tu-W and Su 11pm-3:30am, Th 10:30pm-4:30am, F-Sa 11pm-6am.

■ **Cuevas de Sésamo,** C. del Príncipe 7 (☎429 6524). M: Antón Martín. "Descend into these caves like Dante!" (Antonio Machado) is the first of many literary tidbits that welcome you to this underground gem. Cheap pitchers of sangria (small €6.50, large €10) and live jazz piano draw hipsters of all ages. Open daily 7pm-2am.

La Ida, C. Colón 11 (☎522 9107), a few blocks from Pl. Chueca toward Malasaña. Young locals fill this colorful bar. Bartenders make tourists feel at home. Mojitos €6. Open daily 1pm-2am. MC/V.

De Las Letras Restaurante, C. Gran Vía 11 (☎523 7980; www.hoteldelasletras.com). Situated on the border between El Centro, Chueca, and Gran Vía, this beautiful terrace atop the hotel of the same name is a great place to start the night. Drinks are pricey but the view is impressive. Open Su-Th 7:30pm-midnight, Fri-Sa 7:30pm-12:30am. MC/V.

Cardamomo, C. de Echegaray, 15 (☎913 69 07 57; www.cardamomo.net). M: Sevilla. Flamenco and Latin music spin all night. Those who prefer to relax retreat to the lounge area. Beer €4. W live music midnight-late. Open daily 9pm-3:30am.

Ocho y Medio Club, C. Mesonero Romanos 13 (☎541 3500; www.tripfamily.com). Where cool kids go for their late-night *discoteca* fix; the line will probably be long, but the wait is worth it. F DJ or live performance. Sa "Dark Hole," a gothic extravaganza. Check website for schedule. Drinks €7. Cover €8; includes 1 drink. Open F-Sa 1-6am.

Acuarela, C. de Gravina 10 (☎522 2143). M: Chueca. A welcome alternative to the club scene. Candles surround antique furniture and conversation flows. Coffees and teas €1.80-4.50. Liquors €3.20-5. Open daily 11pm-2am.

El Clandestino, C. del Barquillo 34 (☎521 5563). M: Chueca. A chill 20-something crowd drinks and debates at the bar upstairs, then heads down to the caves to dance to funk, fusion, and acid jazz. Beer €3. Mixed drinks €6. Live music most Th-Sa at 11:30pm. Open M-Sa 6:30pm-3am.

El Truco, C. de Gravina 10 (☎532 8921). M: Chueca. This gay- and lesbian-friendly club blasts pop far into the night. The line gets very long and the club gets very packed; luckily, there is outdoor seating. Same owners also run the popular **Escape,** nearby on the plaza. Cover €1. Open Th 10pm-late, F-Sa midnight-late.

▶ **DAYTRIP FROM MADRID: EL ESCORIAL.** This enormous complex was described by Felipe II as "majesty without ostentation." The **Monasterio de San Lorenzo del Escorial** was a gift from Felipe II to God, the people, and himself, commemorating his victory over the French at the battle of San Quintín in 1557. Near the town of San Lorenzo, El Escorial is filled with artistic treasures, a church, a magnificent library, two palaces, and two pantheons. The adjacent **Museo de Arquitectura y Pintura** has an exhibit comparing El Escorial's construction to that of similar structures. The **Palacio Real,** lined with 16th-century *azulejo* tiles, includes the majestic **Salón del Trono** (Throne Room), Felipe II's spartan 16th-century apartments, and the luxurious 18th-century rooms of Carlos III and Carlos IV. (*Autocares Herranz buses run between El Escorial and Moncloa Metro.; 50min., 2-6 per hr., €3.20. Complex ☎918 90 59 03. Open Tu-Su Apr.-Sept. 10am-7pm; Oct.-Mar. 10am-6pm. Last entry 1hr. before closing. Monastery €7, with guide €9; students and seniors €3.50.*)

CENTRAL SPAIN

Medieval cities and olive groves fill Castilla La Mancha, the land south and east of Madrid. Castilla y León's dramatic cathedrals are testaments to its storied history. Farther west, bordering Portugal, stark Extremadura was the birthplace of world-famous explorers such as Hernán Cortés and Francisco Pizarro.

CASTILLA LA MANCHA

Land of austere plains and miles of empty landscapes, Castilla La Mancha has played host to bloody conflicts and epic heroes both real and imaginary. The region is one of Spain's least developed and provokes the imagination with its solitary crags, gloomy medieval fortresses, and whirling windmills.

TOLEDO
☎925

Cervantes called Toledo (pop. 66,000) "the glory of Spain and light of her cities." The city is a former capital of the Holy Roman, Visigoth, and Muslim Empires, and its churches, synagogues, and mosques share twisting alleyways. Toledo is known as the "City of Three Cultures," a symbol of a time when Spain's three religions coexisted peacefully, although locals will tell you the history is a bit romanticized.

▐▌ TRANSPORTATION AND PRACTICAL INFORMATION. From the station on Po. de la Rosa, just over Puente de Azarquiel, **trains** (RENFE info ☎ 902 24 02 02) run to Madrid (30min., 9-11 per day, €9). **Buses** run from Av. Castilla La Mancha (☎21 58 50), 5min. from **Puerta de Bisagra** (the city gate), to Madrid (1½hr., 2 per hr., €4.40) and Valencia (5½hr., 1 per day, €24). Within the city, buses #5 and 6 serve the bus and train stations and the central **Plaza de Zocodóver.** Buses (€1; at night €1.30) stop to the right of the train station, underneath and across the street from the bus station. The **tourist office** is at Pta. de Bisagra. (☎22 08 43. Open July-Sept. M-F 9am-7pm, Sa 10am-6pm, Su 10am-2pm; Oct.-June M-F 9am-6pm, Sa 10am-6pm, Su 10am-2pm.) **Postal Code:** 45070.

▐▌ ACCOMMODATIONS AND FOOD. Toledo is full of accommodations, but finding a bed in summer can be a hassle, especially on weekends. Reservations are strongly recommended. **Hostal La Campana ❶**, C. de la Campana 10-12, has monuments at its doorstep and quintessential Toledo hospitality. Quaint, clean rooms all have A/C, bath, phone, TV, and Wi-Fi. (☎22 16 59 or 22 16 62; www.hostalcampana.com. Breakfast included. Singles €36; doubles €60. MC/V.) Spacious rooms among suits of armor await at the **Residencia Juvenil San Servando (HI) ❶**, Castillo San Servando, uphill on Subida del Hospital from the train station, in a 14th-century castle with a pool, TV room, and Internet. (☎22 45 54. Dorms €11, with breakfast €15; under 30 €9.20/11. MC/V.) *Pastelería* windows beckon with *mazapán* (marzipan) of every shape and size. For the widest array, stop by the **market** in Pl. Mayor, behind the cathedral. (Open M-Sa 9am-8pm.) To reach **La Abadía ❶**, Pl. de San Nicolás 3, bear left when C. de la Sillería splits; Pl. de San Nicolás is on the right. Dine on the regional lunch *menú* (€10) in a maze of underground rooms. (☎25 11 40. Open daily 8am-midnight. AmEx/MC/V.)

▐▌ SIGHTS AND NIGHTLIFE. Within the fortified walls, Toledo's attractions form a belt around its middle. At Arco de Palacio, up C. del Comercio from Pl. de Zocodóver, Toledo's ■**cathedral** boasts five naves, delicate stained glass, and

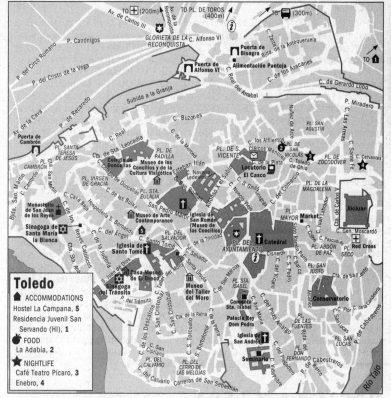

Toledo

🏠 ACCOMMODATIONS
Hostel La Campana, **5**
Residencia Juvenil San
   Servando (HI), **1**
🍴 FOOD
La Adabía, **2**
★ NIGHTLIFE
Café Teatro Pícaro, **3**
Enebro, **4**

unapologetic ostentation. Beneath the dome is the **Capilla Mozárabe,** the only place where the ancient ⬛**Visigoth mass** (in Mozarabic) is still held. The **sacristía** holds 18 El Grecos (including *El Espolio*), as well as paintings by other notable Spanish and European masters. (☎22 22 41. Open M-Sa 10am-6:30pm, Su 2-6:30pm. €8, students €6. Audio tour €3. Dress modestly.) Greek painter Doménikos Theotokópoulos, better known as El Greco, spent most of his life in Toledo. Though the majority of his masterpieces have been carted off to the Prado (p. 903), some are still displayed throughout town. The best place to start is the **Casa Museo de El Greco,** on C. Samuel Leví 2, which contains 19 of his works. (☎22 44 05. Open in summer Tu-Sa 10am-2pm and 4-9pm, Su 10am-2pm; in winter Tu-Sa 10am-2pm and 4-6pm, Su 10am-2pm. €2.40; students, under 18, Sa afternoon, and Su free. Closed for renovations until mid-2008.) On the same street as the Museo El Greco is the **Sinagoga del Tránsito,** one of two remaining synagogues in Toledo's *judería* (Jewish quarter).

For nightlife, head to **Calle Santa Fé,** through the arch from Pl. de Zocodóver. **Enebro,** Pl. Santiago de los Caballeros 4, off C. Cervantes, serves free tapas with drinks in the evenings. (Beer €1.50. Open daily 10am-1am.) For more upscale bars and clubs, try **Calle de la Sillería** and **Calle los Alfileritos,** west of Pl. de Zocodóver. Check out the chill **Café Teatro Pícaro,** C. Cadenas 6, where it's just as cool to be sipping on a *batido* (milkshake; €3) as a beer. (☎22 13 01; www.picarocafeteatro.com. Beer €1.50-2.50. Mixed drinks €4. Open M-F 4pm-3am, Sa-Su 4pm-5am.)

CUENCA ☎969

Cuenca (pop. 50,000) is a quiet hilltop retreat that owes its fame to the geological foundations upon which it stands. The city is flanked by two rivers and the stunning rock formations they have carved. The enchanting **Old Town** includes the famed ▨**casas colgadas** (hanging houses), which sit precariously on cliffs above the Río Huécar. The **Museo de Arte Abstracto Español**, in Pl. Ciudad de Ronda, is in the only *casa* open to the public. (☎21 29 83. Open July-Sept. Tu-F 11am-2pm and 5-7pm, Sa 11am-2pm and 4-9pm, Su 11am-2:30pm; Oct.-June Tu-F 11am-2pm and 4-6pm, Sa 11am-2pm and 4-8pm, Su 11am-2:30pm.) The **Catedral de Cuenca** is the centerpiece of the **Plaza Major.** A perfect square, it is the only Anglo-Norman Gothic cathedral in Spain. (Open July-Sept. M-F 10am-2pm and 4-7pm, Sa 10am-7pm, Su 10am-6:30pm; Oct.-Apr. daily 10:30am-1:30pm and 4-6pm; May-June Sa 10:30am-2pm and 4-6pm, Su 10:30am-2pm and 4-6:30pm. €2.80.)

It's worth spending a little extra to stay in the quaint Old Town with its stunning views of the gorge. ▨**Posada de San José ❷**, C. Julián Romero 4, a block from the cathedral, has bright rooms with gorgeous vistas and a **restaurant** on its terrace. (☎21 13 00. Breakfast €8. Entrees €7-11. Restaurant open Tu-Su 8-11am and 6-10:30pm. Singles €25, with bath €50; doubles €38/75; triples with bath €83; quads with bath €128. *Semana Santa* increased prices; Su-Th and low season reduced prices. AmEx/MC/V.) Budget dining spots line **Calle Cervantes** and **Avenida de la República Argentina;** the cafes off **Calle Fray Luis de León** are even cheaper. **Trains** (☎902 24 02 02) run from C. Mariano Catalina 10 to Madrid (2½-3hr., 5-6 per day, €11) and Valencia (3-4hr., 3-4 per day, €12). **Buses** (☎22 70 87) depart from C. Fermín Caballero 20 to Barcelona (9hr., 1 per day, €35), Madrid (2½hr., 8-9 per day, €10-11), and Toledo (2¼hr., 1-2 per day, €11-13). To get to Pl. Mayor from either station, turn left onto C. Fermín Caballero, following it as it becomes C. Cervantes and C. José Cobo, and then bearing left through Pl. Hispanidad as the street becomes C. Carretería. The **tourist office** is at Pl. Mayor 1. (☎24 10 51; www.cuenca.org. Open daily July-Sept. 9am-9pm; Oct.-June M-Sa 9am-2pm and 4-6:30pm, Su 9am-2pm.) **Postal Code:** 16002.

CASTILLA Y LEÓN

Well before Fernando of Aragón and Isabel of Castilla were joined in world-shaking matrimony, Castilla was the political and military powerhouse of Spain. *Castellano* became the dominant language of the nation in the High Middle Ages. The aqueduct of Segovia, the Gothic cathedrals of León, and the sandstone of Salamanca continue to stand out as national images. Castilla's comrade in arms, León, though chagrined to be lumped with Castilla in a 1970s provincial reorganization, shares many cultural similarities with its co-province.

SEGOVIA ☎921

Legend has it that the devil built Segovia's (pop. 56,000) famed aqueduct in an effort to win the soul of a Segovian water-seller named Juanilla. With or without Lucifer's help, Segovia's attractions draw their share of eager tourists.

◪▨ TRANSPORTATION AND PRACTICAL INFORMATION. Trains (RENFE ☎902 24 02 02) run from Po. Obispo Quesada, rather far from town, to Madrid (2hr., 7-9 per day, €5.60). La Sepulvedana **buses** (☎42 77 07) run from Estación Municipal de Autobuses, Po. Ezequiel González 12, to Madrid (1½hr., 2 per hr., €6.30) and Salamanca (3hr., 2 per day, €9.30). From the train station, bus #8 stops near the **Plaza Mayor,** the city's historical center and site of the regional **tourist office.** Segovia is impossible to navigate without a map, so pick one up. (☎46 03 34. Open July-Sept. 15 Su-Th 9am-8pm, F-Sa 9am-9pm; Sept. 16-June 9am-2pm and 5-8pm.) Access the **Internet** for free at the **public library,** C. Juan Bravo 11. (☎46 35 33. Passport required. Limit 30min. Open Sept.-June M-F 9am-9pm, Sa 9am-2pm; July-Aug. M-F 9am-3pm, Sa 9am-2pm.) **Postal Code:** 40001.

ACCOMMODATIONS AND FOOD. Reservations are a must for any of Segovia's hotels, especially those near major plazas. **Hospedaje El Gato ❷,** Pl. del Salvador 10, offers a bar as well as rooms with A/C, comfortable beds, private baths, and satellite TV. To reach El Gato, follow the aqueduct up the hill, turning left on C. Ochoa Ondategui; it meets San Alfonso Rodríguez, which leads into Pl. del Salvador. (☎42 32 44. Singles €23; doubles €38; triples €52. MC/V.) Sample Segovia's famed lamb, *cochinillo asado* (roast suckling pig), or *sopa castellana* (soup with bread, eggs, and garlic), but steer clear of expensive Pl. Mayor and Pl. del Azoguejo. For eclectic, scrumptious dishes (€4-11), try ◼**Restaurante La Almuzara ❷,** C. Marqués del Arco 3, past the cathedral. (☎46 06 22. Soups €6.50-9. Lunch *menú* €10. Open Tu 8-11:30pm, W-Su 12:45-4pm and 8-11:30pm. MC/V.) Buy groceries at **Día%,** C. Gobernador Fernández Jiménez, 3, off Av. de Fernández Ladreda. (Open M-Th 9:30am-2pm and 5:30-8:30pm, F-Sa 9am-9pm.)

SIGHTS AND ENTERTAINMENT. The serpentine ◼**Roman aqueduct,** built in 50 BC and spanning 813m, commands the entrance to the Old Town. Some 20,000 blocks of granite were used in the construction—without a drop of mortar. This spectacular feat of engineering, restored by the monarchy in the 15th century, can transport 30L of water per second and was used until the late 1940s. Segovia's ◼**Alcázar,** a late-medieval castle and site of Isabel's coronation in 1474, would be at home in a fairy tale—it was reportedly a model for the castle in Disney's *Cinderella*. In the **Sala de Solio** (throne room), an inscription reads: *Tanto monta, monta tanto* ("she mounts, as does he"). Get your mind out of the gutter—it signifies that Fernando and Isabel had equal authority as sovereigns. The **Torre de Juan II** (80m), 140 steps up a nausea-inducing spiral staircase, provides a marvelous view of Segovia. (Pl. de la Reina Victoria Eugenia. ☎46 07 59. *Alcázar* open daily Apr.-Sept. 10am-7pm; Oct.-Mar. 10am-6pm. Tower closed Tu. Palace €4, seniors and students €2.50. Tower €2. English-language audio tour €3.) The 23 chapels of the **cathedral,** towering over Pl. Mayor, earned it the nickname "The Lady of all Cathedrals." The interior may look less impressive than the facade, but its enormity will make you feel truly small. (☎46 22 05. Open daily Apr.-Oct. 9am-6:30pm; Nov.-Mar. 9:30am-5:30pm. Mass M-Sa 10am, Su 11am and 12:30pm. €3, under 14 free.)

Packed with bars and cafes, the **Plaza Mayor** is the center of Segovia's nightlife. Head for **Calle Infanta Isabel,** appropriately nicknamed *calle de los bares* (street of the bars). Find drinks and plastic tchotchkes in the fun techno club **Toys,** C. Infanta Isabel 13. (☎609 65 41 42. Beer €1. Mixed drinks €4.50-5.50. Open daily 10pm-4am.) From June 23 to 29, Segovia holds a **fiesta** in honor of San Juan and San Pedro, with concerts on Pl. del Azoguejo and dances and fireworks on June 29.

SALAMANCA   ☎923

Salamanca *"la blanca"* (pop. 363,000), city of royals, saints, and scholars, glows with the yellow stones of Spanish Plateresque architecture by day and a vivacious club scene by night. The prestigious Universidad de Salamanca, grouped in medieval times with Bologna, Oxford, and Paris as one of the "four leading lights of the world," continues to add the energy of thousands of students to the city.

█▉ TRANSPORTATION AND PRACTICAL INFORMATION. Trains go from Po. de la Estación (☎ 12 02 02) to Madrid (2½hr., 6-7 per day, €15) and Lisbon, POR (6hr., 1 per day, €47). **Buses** leave from the station (☎ 23 67 17) on Av. Filiberto Villalobos 71-85 for: Barcelona (11hr., 2 per day, €45); León (2½hr., 4-6 per day, €13); Madrid (2½hr., 16 per day, €12-17); Segovia (2¾hr., 2 per day, €10). Majestic **Plaza Mayor** is the center of Salamanca. From the train station, catch bus #1 (€0.80) to Gran Vía and ask to be let off at Pl. San Julián, a block from Pl. Mayor. The **tourist office** is at Pl. Mayor 32. (☎ 21 83 42. Open June-Sept. M-F 9am-2pm and 4:30-8pm, Sa 10am-8pm, Su 10am-2pm; Oct.-May M-F 9am-2pm and 4:30-6:30pm, Sa 10am-6:30pm, Su 10am-2pm.) *DGratis*, a free weekly newspaper about events in Salamanca, is available from newsstands, tourist offices, and around Pl. Mayor. Free **Internet** is available at the **public library,** C. Compañía 2, in Casa de las Conchas. (☎ 26 93 17. Limit 30min. Open July to mid-Sept. M-F 9am-3pm, Sa 9am-2pm; mid-Sept. to June M-F 9am-9pm, Sa 9am-2pm.) **Postal Code:** 37080.

█▉ ACCOMMODATIONS AND FOOD. Reasonably priced *hostales* and *pensiones* cater to student visitors. **Hostal Las Vegas Centro ❷,** C. Meléndez 13, 1st fl., has spotless rooms with terrace and TV. (☎ 21 87 49; www.lasvegascentro.com. Singles €20, with bath €24; doubles €30/36. MC/V.) At nearby **Pensión Barez ❶,** C. Meléndez 19, 1st fl., clean rooms overlook the street. (☎ 21 74 95. Rooms €13. Cash only.) Many cafes and restaurants are in Pl. Mayor. Pork is the city's speciality, with dishes ranging from *chorizo* (spicy sausage) to *cochinillo* (suckling pig). Funky **Restaurante Delicatessen Café ❷,** C. Meléndez 25, serves a wide variety of *platos combinados* (€9.50-10) and a lunch *menú* (€11) in a colorful solarium. (☎ 28 03 09. Open daily 1:30-4pm and 9pm-midnight. MC/V.) **Champion,** C. Toro 82, is a central supermarket. (☎ 21 22 08. Open M-Sa 9am-9:30pm.)

█▉ SIGHTS AND NIGHTLIFE. From Pl. Mayor, follow R. Mayor, veer right onto T. Antigua, and left onto C. Libreros to reach █**La Universidad de Salamanca** (est. 1218), the city's focal point. The 15th-century classroom **Aula Fray Luis de León** has been left in more or less its original state. Located on the second floor atop a Plateresque staircase is the **Biblioteca Antigua,** one of Europe's oldest libraries. Across the street and through the hall on the left corner of the patio is the **University Museum.** (University ☎ 29 44 00, museum ☎ 29 12 25. University open M-F 9:30am-1:30pm and 4-7:30pm, Sa 9:30am-1:30pm and 4-7pm, Su 10am-1:30pm. €4, students and seniors €2. Museum open Tu-Sa noon-2pm and 6-9pm, Su 10am-2pm.) It's not surprising it took 220 years to build the stunning **Catedral Nueva,** in Pl. de Anaya. Be sure to climb the tower to get a spectacular █**view** from above. (Open daily Apr.-Sept. 9am-8pm; Oct.-Mar. 9am-1pm and 4-6pm. Tower open daily 10am-8pm, last entry 7:45pm. Cathedral free. Tower €3.)

According to *salamantinos*, Salamanca is the best place in Spain to party. It is said that there is one bar for every 100 people living in the city. Nightlife centers on **Plaza Mayor** and spreads out to **Gran Vía, Calle Bordadores,** and side streets. **Calle Prior** and **Rúa Mayor** are also full of bars, while intense partying occurs off **Calle Varillas.** After a few shots (€1-2) at █**Bar La Chupitería,** Pl. de Monterrey, wander from club to club on C. Prior and C. Compañía, where tipsy Americans mingle with tireless *salamantinos*. Once you get past the bouncers, **Niebla,** C. Bordadores 14 (☎ 26 86 04), **Gatsby,** C. Bordadores 16 (☎ 21 73 62), **Camelot,** C. Bordadores 3 (☎ 21 21 82), and **Cum Laude,** C. Prior 5-7 (☎ 26 75 77) all offer a party that doesn't peak until 2:30-3:30am and stays strong for another 2hr. (Dress to impress. All clubs have no cover and are cash only.)

LEÓN ☎ 987

Formerly the center of Christian Spain, León (pop. 165,000) is best known today for its 13th-century Gothic █**cathedral, in** Pl. Regla, arguably the most beautiful in Spain. Its spectacular 1800 meters of stained glass have earned León the nickname

SPAIN

"La Ciudad Azul" (The Blue City). The cathedral's **museum** displays gruesome wonders, including a sculpture depicting the skinning of a saint. (☎87 57 70; www.catedraldeleon.org. Cathedral open July-Sept. M-Sa 8:30am-1:30pm and 4-8pm; Oct.-June 8:30am-1:30pm and 4-7pm. Museum open June-Sept. M-F 9:30am-1:30pm and 4-6:30pm, Sa 9:30am-1pm; Oct.-May M-F 9:30am-1pm and 4-6pm. Cathedral free. Museum €4, cloisters €1. Required tour of museum in Spanish.)

🗺**Hostal Bayón ❶**, C. Alcázar de Toledo 6, 2nd fl., has peaceful, sun-drenched rooms with hardwood floors. (☎23 14 46. Singles €15, with shower €25; doubles €28/35. Cash only.) Inexpensive eateries fill the area near the cathedral and the small streets off C. Ancha; also check **Plaza de San Martín**, near Plaza Mayor. For bars, head to the *barrio húmedo* (drinker's neighborhood) around **Plaza de San Martín** and **Plaza Mayor**. RENFE trains (☎902 24 02 02) run from Av. de Astorga 2 to Barcelona (9½hr., 2-3 per day, €44-57), Bilbao (5½hr., 1 per day, €23), and Madrid (4½hr., 7 per day, €21-37). **Buses** (☎21 00 00) leave from Po. del Ingeniero Sáenz de Miera for Madrid (4½hr., 9-13 per day, €20-30) and Salamanca (2½hr., 3-6 per day, €12). The **tourist office** is at Pl. Regla 3. (☎23 70 82; www.turismocastillayleon.com. Open M-F 9am-2pm and 5-7pm, Sa-Su 10am-2pm and 5-8pm. July and Aug. open M-F 9am-7pm and Sa-Su 10am-8pm.) **Postal Code:** 24004.

EXTREMADURA

Arid plains bake under the intense summer sun, relieved only by scattered patches of golden sunflowers. This land of harsh beauty and cruel extremes hardened New World conquistadors such as Hernán Cortés and Francisco Pizarro. The region is only now beginning to draw tourists looking for the "classic" Spanish countryside.

CÁCERES ☎927

Built between the 14th and 16th centuries by rival noble families in an architectural war for prestige, Cáceres's **ciudad monumental** (Old Town) is comprised of miniature palaces once used to show off each family's wealth. From the bus or train station, the best way to get to the center of Cáceres (pop. 90,000) is via bus #1 (€0.75 per ride, 10 rides for €5.50). The main attraction is the neighborhood itself, since most buildings don't let tourists in beyond a peek into the patio from an open door. From Pl. Mayor, take the stairs from the left of the tourist office to the Arco de la Estrella, the entrance to the walled city. The 16th-century **Casa del Sol** is the most famous of Cáceres's numerous mansions; its crest is the city's emblem. The **Palacio Y Torre de Carvajal**, on the corner of C. Amargura, is one of the few *palacios* in the city open to the public. (Open M-F 8am-8pm, Sa-Su 10am-2pm. Free.) Inside the Casa de los Caballos, the **Museo de Cáceres** houses a tiny but brilliant Who's Who of Spanish art. The neighboring **Casa de las Veletas** (House of Weathervanes), on Pl. de las Veletas, displays an astonishing 🗺**Muslim cistern.** (☎01 08 77. Open Apr.-Sept. Tu-Sa 9am-2:30pm and 5-8:15pm, Su 10:15am-2:30pm. Oct.-Apr. Tu-Sa 9am-2:30pm and 4-7:15pm, Su 10:15am-2:30pm. €1.20; students, seniors, and EU citizens free.)

Hostels are scattered throughout the new city and line Pl. Mayor in the Old Town. Reserve ahead on summer weekends. **Pensión Carretero ❷**, Pl. Mayor 22, has spacious rooms with painted tile floors. (☎24 74 82; pens_carretero@yahoo.es). June-Aug. singles €25; doubles €30; triples €40; Sept.-May €15/20/35. AmEx/MC/V. **Plaza Mayor** overflows with restaurants and cafes serving up *bocadillos*, *raciones*, and *extremeño* specialties. Take in the stork-covered walls of the *ciudad monumental* at **Cafetería El Pato ❸**, in the Pl. Mayor, which dishes out ewe's milk cheese sandwiches. (☎24 67 36. Entrees €6.60-15. *Menú* €10-13. Open Tu-Sa noon-4pm and 8pm-midnight. AmEx/MC/V.) A **Hiper Tambo** market is on C. Alfonso IX 25 (☎21 17 71. Open M-Sa 9:30am-9pm. AmEx/MC/V.)

Nightlife centers in Pl. Mayor and along **Calle Pizarro**, which is lined with bars showcasing live music. Later, the party migrates to **La Madrila**, an area near Pl. del

Albatros in the new city. RENFE **trains** (☎23 37 61), run from on Av. de Alemania, 3km from the Old Town, to Lisbon, POR (6hr., 2 per day, €35), Madrid (4hr., 6 per day, €16-35), and Seville (4hr., 1 per day, €15). **Buses** (☎23 25 50) go from Av. de la Hispanidad to Madrid (4-5hr., 7-9 per day, €19), Salamanca (4hr., 7-28 per day, €13), and Seville (4hr., 8-14 per day, €16). The **tourist office** is on Pl. Mayor 9-10 (☎01 08 34; otcaceres@eco.juntaex.es), in the outer wall of the *ciudad monumental.* (Open July-Sept. M-F 8am-3pm, Sa-Su 10am-2pm; Oct.-June M-F 9am-2pm, Sa-Su 9:45am-2pm.) The **post office** is on Av. Miguel Primo de Rivera. (☎62 66 81. Open M-F 8:30am-8:30pm, Sa 9:30am-2pm.) **Postal Code:** 10071.

▶ DAYTRIP FROM CÁCERES: TRUJILLO. Hilltop Trujillo (pop. 9200) is often called the "Cradle of Conquistadors" because the city produced over 600 explorers of the New World. Crowning the hill are the ruins of a 10th-century **Moorish castle.** *(Open daily June-Sept. 10am-2pm and 5-8:30pm; Oct.-May 9:30am-2pm and 4:30-8:30pm. €1.40.)* Trujillo's **Plaza Mayor** was the inspiration for the Plaza de Armas in Cuzco, Perú. To reach the Gothic **Iglesia de Santa María la Mayor,** take C. de las Cambroneras from the plaza in front of the Iglesia de San Martín and turn right on C. de Sta. María. The steps leading to the top of the Romanesque church tower are exhausting, but the 🔲**view** is spectacular. *(Open daily May-Oct. 10am-2pm and 4:30-8:30pm; Nov.-Apr. 10am-2pm and 4-6:30pm. €1.25. Su mass 11am.)* **Buses** (☎927 32 12 02) run from the corner of C. de las Cruces and C. del M. de Albayada to Cáceres (45min., 1-4 per day, €3). The **tourist office** is in Pl. Mayor, on the left when facing Pizarro's statue. Tours (€6.75) leave from the front of the office at 11am and 5pm. *(☎32 26 77. Open daily June-Sept. 10am-2pm and 4:30-7:30pm; Oct.-May 9:30am-2pm and 4-7pm.)*

SOUTHERN SPAIN

Southern Spain (Andalucía) is all that you expect of Spanish culture—flamenco, bullfighting, tall pitchers of sangria, and streets lined with orange trees. The Moors arrived in AD 711 and bequeathed to the region far more than flamenco music and gypsy ballads. The cities of Seville and Granada reached the pinnacle of Islamic arts, while Córdoba matured into the most culturally influential city in medieval Islam. Despite (or perhaps because of) modern-day poverty and high unemployment, Andalusians maintain a passionate dedication to living the good life. Their *festivales, ferias,* and *carnavales* are world-famous for their extravagance.

CÓRDOBA ☎957

Córdoba (pop. 310,000), located on the bank of the Río Guadalquivir, was Western Europe's largest city in the 10th century. Remnants of the city's heyday survive in its well-preserved Roman, Jewish, Islamic, and Catholic monuments. Today, lively festivals and nightlife make Córdoba one of Spain's most beloved cities.

◧ TRANSPORTATION. RENFE **trains** (☎40 02 02; www.renfe.es) run from Pl. de las Tres Culturas, off Av. de América, to: Barcelona (10-11hr., 4 per day, €50-76); Cádiz (2½hr., 5 per day, €24); Madrid (2-4hr., 21-33 per day, €47); Málaga (2-3hr., 5 per day, €12-22); Seville (45min., 4-8 per day, €8-15). **Buses** (☎40 40 40) leave from Estación de Autobuses, on Glorieta de las Tres Culturas across from the train station. Alsina Graells Sur (☎27 81 00) sends buses to Cádiz (4-5hr., 1-2 per day, €20), Granada (3-4hr., 9-11 per day, €12), and Málaga (3-3½hr., 5 per day, €12). Bacoma (☎902 42 22 42) runs to Barcelona (10hr., 3 per day, €63). Secorbus (☎902 22 92 92) has cheap buses to Madrid (4½hr., 3-6 per day, €14).

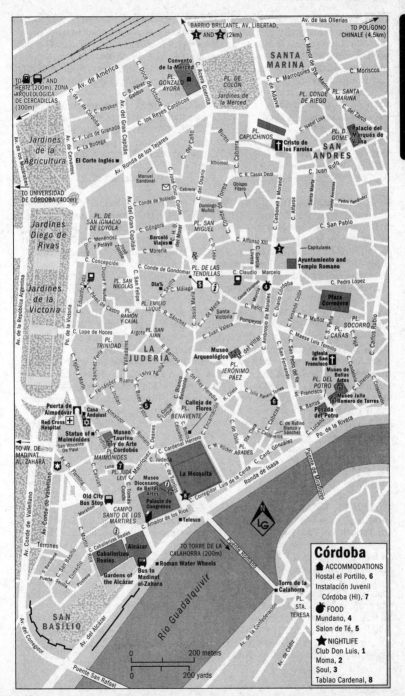

Córdoba

🏠 ACCOMMODATIONS
Hostal el Portillo, 6
Instalación Juvenil
  Córdoba (HI), 7

🍴 FOOD
Mundano, 4
Salon de Té, 5

★ NIGHTLIFE
Club Don Luis, 1
Moma, 2
Soul, 3
Tablao Cardenal, 8

SPAIN

■■⚎ ORIENTATION AND PRACTICAL INFORMATION. Córdoba is split into the old city and new city. The modern and commercial northern half extends from the train station on Av. de América to **Plaza de las Tendillas,** the city center. The old section in the south includes a medieval maze known as the **Judería** (Jewish quarter). The easiest way to reach the old city from the train station is to walk (20min.). Exit left from the station, cross the parking plaza and take a right onto Av. de los Mozárabes. Walk through the **Jardines de la Victoria.**

To get to the **tourist office,** C. Torrijos 10, from the train station, take bus #3 along the river to the Puente Romano. Walk under the stone arch and the office will be on your left. (☎35 51 79. Open July-Aug. M-F 9:30am-7:30pm, Sa 10am-7:30pm, Su 10am-2pm; Sept.-June M-Sa 9am-7:30pm, Su 10am-2pm.) **Tele-Click,** C. Eduardo Dato 9, has **Internet.** (☎94 06 15. €1.80 per hr. Open M-F 10am-3pm and 5:30-10:30pm, Sa-Su noon-11pm.) The **post office** is at C. José Cruz Conde 15. (☎47 97 96. Open M-F 8:30am-8:30pm, Sa-Su 9:30am-2pm.) **Postal Code:** 14070.

⬛⬜ ACCOMMODATIONS AND FOOD. Most accommodations can be found around the whitewashed walls of the Judería and in Old Córdoba, a more residential area between the Mezquita and C. de San Fernando. Reserve ahead during *Semana Santa* and May through June. Popular **⬛Instalación Juvenil Córdoba (HI) ❷,** Pl. Judá Leví, is a former mental asylum converted into a backpacker's paradise. The large rooms all have A/C and bath. (☎29 01 66. Wheelchair-accessible. Breakfast included; dinner €5.50. Linens €1.20. Laundry €4. Reception 24hr. Private rooms available. Mar.-Oct. dorms €20, under 26 €19; Nov.-Feb. €18/17. €3.50 HI discount. MC/V.) **Hostal el Portillo ❷,** C. Cabezas 2, is a traditional yet unexpectedly decorated Andalusian house in the quiet area. Rooms are spacious and equipped with baths and A/C. (☎47 20 91. Singles €18-20; doubles €30-35. MC/V.)

Cordobeses converge on the outdoor *terrazas* between **Calle Doctor Severo Ochoa** and **Calle Doctor Jiménez Díaz** for drinks and tapas before dinner. Cheap restaurants are farther away from the Judería in **Barrio Cruz Conde** and around **Avenida Menéndez Pidal** and **Plaza de las Tendillas.** Regional specialties include *salmorejo* (cream soup) and *rabo de toro* (bull's tail simmered in tomato sauce). **⬛Mundano ❶,** C. Conde de Cárdenas 3, combines delicious home-style food—including many vegetarian options—with a funky style and art shows. (☎47 37 85. Entrees €3-5. Tapas €1-3. Open M-F 10am-5pm and 10pm-2am, Sa noon-6pm and 10pm-2am. Cash only.) For a taste of the old Moorish Córdoba, head to **Salon de Té ❶,** C. Buen Pastor 13, a recreated 12th-century teahouse with a huge variety of Arab pastries, juices, and teas. (☎48 79 84. Beverages €2-4. Pastries €1.50-3. Open daily 11am-10:30pm. Cash only.) Find groceries at **El Corte Inglés,** Av. Ronda de los Tejares 30. (Open M-Sa 10am-10pm. AmEx/MC/V.)

◩ SIGHTS. Built in AD 784, Córdoba's **⬛La Mezquita** mosque is considered the most important Islamic monument in the Western world. Visitors enter through the **Patio de los Naranjos,** a courtyard featuring orange trees and fountains. Inside, 850 granite and marble columns support hundreds of striped arches. At the far end of the Mezquita lies the **Capilla Villaviciosa,** the first Christian chapel to be built in the mosque. In the center, intricate pink-and-blue marble Byzantine mosaics shimmer across the arches of the **Mihrab** (prayer niche), which is covered in Kufic inscriptions of the 99 names of Allah. Although the town rallied violently against the proposed construction of a **cathedral** in the center of the mosque, after the Crusaders conquered Córdoba in 1236, the towering *crucero* (transept) and *coro* (choir dome) were built. (☎47 91 70. Strict silence enforced. Wheelchair-accessible. Open Mar.-Oct. M-Sa 8:30am-7pm, Su 8:30-10:30am and 2-7pm. €8, 10-14 €4, under 10 free. Admission free during mass M-Sa 8:30-10am, Su 11am and 1pm.)

Along the river on the left of the Mezquita is the ▩**Alcázar,** built for Catholic monarchs in 1328 during the *Reconquista.* Fernando and Isabel bade Columbus *adiós* here; the building later served as Inquisition headquarters. The gardens have ponds and beautiful greenery. (☎42 01 51. Open Tu-Sa 8:30am-2:30pm and 4:30-6:30pm, Su and holidays 9:30am-2:30pm. Gardens open summer 8pm-midnight. Alcázar €4, gardens €2; F free.) The **Judería** is the historic area northwest of the Mezquita. Just past the statue of Maimonides, the small **Sinagoga,** C. Judíos 20, is one of very few Spanish synagogues to survive the Inquisition; it is a solemn reminder of the 1492 expulsion of the Jews. (☎20 29 28. Open Tu-Sa 9:30am-2pm and 3:30-5:30pm, Su 9:30am-1:30pm. €0.30, EU citizens free.)

▣▨ **ENTERTAINMENT AND NIGHTLIFE.** Flamenco is not cheap in Córdoba, but the shows are a bargain compared to similar shows in Seville and Madrid. Hordes of tourists flock to see the prize-winning dancers at the **Tablao Cardenal,** C. Torrijos 10. (☎48 33 20. €18, includes 1 drink. Shows M-Sa 10:30pm.) **Soul,** C. Alfonso XIII 3, is a hip bar with an older crowd and deafening bass. (☎49 15 80; www.bar-soul.com. Beer €2.10. Mixed drinks €4.50. Open Sept.-June daily 9am-4am.) Starting in June, the **Barrio Brillante,** uphill from Av. de América, is packed with young *córdobeses* hopping between dance clubs and outdoor bars. Bus #10 goes to Brillante from the train station until about 11pm, but the bars don't pick up until around 1am (most are open until 4am); a lift from **Radio Taxi** (☎76 44 44) costs €4-6. To walk, head up Av. Brillante; it is a 45min. uphill hike from the Judería. A string of popular nightclubs runs along **Avenida Brillante,** such as **Club Don Luis** (open Th-Sa midnight-4:30am; cash only). Pubs with crowded *terrazas* line ▩**Avenida Libertad,** including African-influenced **Moma.** (☎76 84 77. Beer €2-2.50. Mixed drinks from €5. Open Su-W 9am-3am, Th-Sa 9am-5am; AmEx/MC/V.)

Of Córdoba's festivals, floats, and parades, **Semana Santa** (Holy Week; Mar. 16-22, 2008) is the most extravagant. The first few days of May are dedicated to the **Festival de las Cruces,** during which residents make crosses decorated with flowers. In the first two weeks of May during the **Festival de los Patios,** the city erupts with classical music concerts, flamenco, and a city-wide patio-decorating contest. Late May brings the **Feria de Nuestra Señora de Salud** (*La Feria de Córdoba*), a week of colorful garb, dancing, music, and wine-drinking. Every July, Córdoba hosts a **guitar festival,** attracting talented strummers from all over the world.

SEVILLE (SEVILLA)   ☎954

Site of a Roman acropolis, capital of the Moorish empire, focal point of the Spanish Renaissance, and guardian of traditional Andalusian culture, romantic Seville (pop. 700,000) is a conglomeration of cultures. Bullfighting, flamenco, and tapas are at their best here, and Seville's cathedral is among the most impressive in Spain. The city offers more than historical sights: its *Semana Santa* and *Feria de Abril* celebrations are among the most elaborate in Europe.

▐ TRANSPORTATION

Flights: All flights arrive at **Aeropuerto San Pablo (SVQ;** ☎44 90 00), 12km out of town on Ctra. de Madrid. A taxi ride to the town center costs about €25. **Los Amarillos** (☎98 91 84) buses run to the airport from outside Hotel Alfonso XIII at the Pta. de Jerez (1-2 per hr., €2.40). **Iberia,** C. Guadaira 8 (☎22 89 01), flies to **Barcelona** (1hr., 6 per day) and **Madrid** (45min., 6 per day).

Trains: Estación Santa Justa, on Av. de Kansas City (☎902 24 02 02). Near Pl. Nueva is the **RENFE** office, C. Zaragoza 29. (☎54 02 02. Open M-F 9am-1:15pm and 4-7pm.)

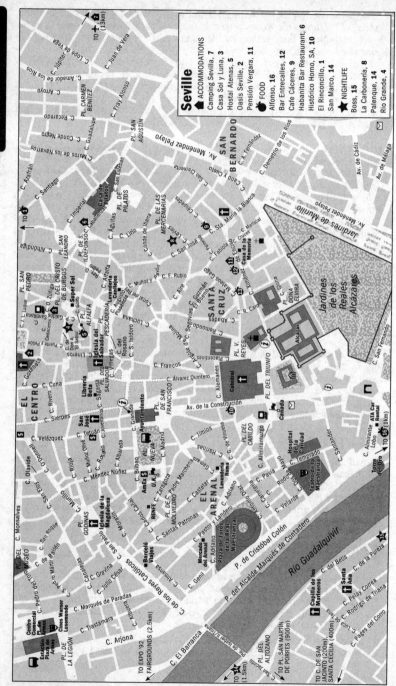

Seville

■ ACCOMMODATIONS
Camping Sevilla, 7
Casa Sol y Luna, 3
Hostal Atenas, 5
Oasis Seville, 2
Pensión Vergara, 11
● FOOD
Alfonso, 16
Bar Entrecalles, 12
Café Cáceres, 9
Habanita Bar Restaurant, 6
Histórico Horno, SA, 10
El Rinconcillo, 1
San Marco, 14
★ NIGHTLIFE
Boss, 15
La Carbonería, 8
Palenque, 14
Rio Grande, 4

Altaria and Talgo trains run to: **Barcelona** (9-13hr., 3 per day, €54-88); **Córdoba** (1hr., 6 per day, €13); **Madrid** (3½hr., 2 per day, €53); **Valencia** (9hr., 1 per day, €44). AVE trains go to **Córdoba** (45min., 15-20 per day, €22) and **Madrid** (2½hr., 15-21 per day, €64-70). *Regionales* trains run to: **Cádiz** (2hr., 7-12 per day, €9.10); **Córdoba** (1½hr., 6 per day, €7.60); **Granada** (3hr., 4 per day, €20); **Málaga** (2½hr., 5-6 per day, €16).

Buses: The station at **Prado de San Sebastián**, C. Manuel Vázquez Sagastizabal, serves most of Andalucía. (☎41 71 11. Open daily 5:30am-1am.) **Estación Plaza de Armas** (☎90 80 40) mainly serves areas outside of Andalucía. To: **Córdoba** (2hr., 7-9 per day, €9.50); **Granada** (3½hr., 10 per day, €18); **Lagos, POR** (7hr., 4 per day, €18); **León** (11hr., 3 per day, €38)); **Lisbon, POR** (6¼hr., 3 per day, €29); **Madrid** (6hr., 14 per day, €19); **Málaga** (2½hr., 10-12 per day, €14); **Ronda** (2½hr., 3-5 per day, €10); **Salamanca** (8hr., 5 per day, €27); **Valencia** (9-11hr., 4 per day, €44-51).

Public Transportation: TUSSAM (☎900 71 01 71; www.tussam.es) is the city bus network. Most lines run daily 6 per hr. (6am-11:15pm) and converge on Pl. Nueva, Pl. de la Encarnación, and in front of the cathedral. C-3 and C-4 circle the city center, and #34 hits the youth hostel, university, cathedral, and Pl. Nueva. **Night service** departs from Pl. Nueva (Su-Th 1 per hr. midnight-2am, F-Sa 1 per hr. all night). Fare €1, 10-ride *bonobús* ticket €4.50, 30-day pass €26.

Taxis: Radio Taxi (☎58 00 00). Base rate €1, €0.40 per km, Su 25% surcharge. Extra charge for luggage and night taxis.

➍➐ ORIENTATION AND PRACTICAL INFORMATION

The **Río Guadalquivir** flows roughly north to south through the city. Most of the touristed areas of Seville, including **Santa Cruz** and **El Arenal**, are on the east bank. The *barrios* of **Triana, Santa Cecilia,** and **Los Remedios,** as well as the **Expo '92 fairgrounds,** occupy the west bank. The cathedral, next to Santa Cruz, is Seville's centerpiece. **Avenida de la Constitución** runs alongside it. **El Centro,** a commercial pedestrian zone, lies north of the cathedral, starting where Av. Constitución hits **Plaza Nueva** and **Plaza de San Francisco,** site of the *Ayuntamiento*. **Calle Tetuán,** a popular shopping street, runs north from Pl. Nueva through El Centro.

Tourist Offices: Centro de Información de Sevilla Laredo, Pl. de San Francisco 19 (☎59 52 88; www.turismo.sevilla.org). Free Internet M-F 10am-2pm and 5-8pm; max. 1hr. Open M-F 8am-3pm. **Turismo Andaluz,** Av. de la Constitución 21B (☎22 14 04; fax 22 97 53). Open M-F 9am-7pm, Sa 10am-2pm and 3-7pm, Su 10am-2pm.

Luggage Storage: Estación Prado de San Sebastián (€1 per bag per day; open 6:30am-10pm), Estación Plaza de Armas (€3 per day), and the train station (€3 per day).

Laundromat: Lavandería y Tintorería Roma, C. Castelar 2C (☎21 05 35). Wash, dry, and fold €6 per load. Open M-F 9:30am-2pm and 5:30-8:30pm, Sa 9am-2pm.

24hr. Pharmacy: Check list posted at any pharmacy for those open 24hr.

Medical Services: Red Cross (☎913 35 45 45). **Ambulatorio Esperanza Macarena** (☎42 01 05). **Hospital Virgen Macarena,** Av. Dr. Fedriani 56 (☎955 00 80 00).

Internet Access: Post Office, Av. de la Constitución 32. €1.50 per hr. Open M-F 8:30am-10pm, Sa 9:30am-10pm, Su noon-10pm.

Post Office: Av. de la Constitución 32 (☎21 64 76), opposite the cathedral. **Lista de Correos** and fax. Open M-F 8:30am-8:30pm, Sa 9:30am-2pm. **Postal Code:** 41080.

▌ ACCOMMODATIONS

Rooms vanish and prices soar during *Semana Santa* and the *Feria de Abril;* reserve several months ahead. In Santa Cruz, the streets around **Calle Santa María la Blanca** are full of cheap, centrally located hostels. Hostels by the **Plaza de Armas** bus station are convenient for visits to **El Centro** and **Calle del Betis** across the river.

SPAIN

■ **Hostal Atenas,** C. Caballerizas 1 (☎21 80 47), near Pl. Pilatos. Slightly pricier than other options but with good reason—everything about this hostel is appealing, from ivy arches leading to an old-fashioned indoor patio to cheerful rooms. All rooms with A/C and bath. Singles €35; doubles €58; triples €70. MC/V. ❸

Casa Sol y Luna, C. Pérez Galdós 1A (☎21 06 82). Beautiful hostel with marble staircase, antique mirrors, and themed rooms. Laundry €10. Min. 2-night stay. Singles €22; doubles €38, with bath €45; triples €60; quads €80. Cash only. ❷

Oasis Sevilla, reception at Pl. Encarnación, 29 1/2, rooms above reception and at C. Alonso el Sabio 1A (☎429 3777; www.hostelsoasis.com). The place to be for travelers looking for hotel amenities such as a pool. Dorms on Pl. Encarnación are crowded but centrally located; doubles and 4-person dorms on C. Alonso are more quiet. Breakfast included. Free Internet. Reserve ahead. Dorms €18; doubles €40. MC/V. ❷

Pensión Vergara, C. Ximénez de Enciso 11, 2nd fl. (☎21 56 68), above the souvenir shop at C. Mesón del Moro. Quirky, antique decor and perfect location. Most rooms have fans and a few have A/C. Towels provided upon request. Singles €20; doubles €40; triples €60; quads €80. Cash only. ❷

Camping Sevilla, Ctra. Madrid-Cádiz km 534 (☎51 43 79), near the airport. From Pr. San Sebastián, take bus #70 (stops 800m away at Parque Alcosa). Hot showers, supermarket, and pool. €3.80 per tent, €3.30 per car. MC/V. ❶

◘ FOOD

Seville, which claims to be the birthplace of tapas, keeps its cuisine light. Tapas bars cluster around **Plaza San Martín** and along **Calle San Jacinto.** Popular venues for *el tapeo* (tapas barhopping) include **Barrio de Santa Cruz** and **El Arenal.** Find produce at **Mercado de la Encarnación,** near the bullring in Pl. de la Encarnación. (Open M-Sa 9am-2pm.) There is a supermarket in the basement of **El Corte Inglés,** in Pl. del Duque de la Victoria. (☎27 93 97. Open M-Sa 9am-10pm. AmEx/MC/V.)

■ **Habanita Bar Restaurant,** C. Golfo 3 (☎606 71 64 56; www.andalunet.com/habanita), on a tiny street off C. Pérez Galdós, next to Pl. Alfalfa. Exquisite Cuban fare, including *yucca* (yam) and *ropa vieja* ("old clothes"; shredded beef and rice). Entrees €7-15. Open M-Sa 12:30-4:30pm and 8pm-12:30am, Su 12:30-4:30pm. MC/V. ❷

Bar Entrecalles, C. Ximenez de Enciso 14 (☎617 86 77 52). Situated at the center of the tourist buzz, but retains a local following. Tapas €2. Generous portions of delicious gazpacho (€2). Open daily 1pm-2am. Cash only. ❶

San Marco, C. Mesón del Moro 6 (☎56 43 90), in Santa Cruz's *casco antiguo.* Pizza, pasta, and dessert in an 18th-century house with 17th-century Arab baths. Other San Marco locations around town are equally impressive settings. Entrees €5-10; salads €4-9. Open daily 1:15-4:30pm and 8:15pm-12:30am. AmEx/MC/V. ❷

El Rinconcillo, C. Gerona 40 (☎22 31 83). This hangout teems with gray-haired men deep in conversation and locals coming in for a quick glass of wine. Tapas €1.70-2.50. *Raciones* (small dishes) €5-14.50. Open daily 1:30pm-1:30pm. AmEx/MC/V. ❷

Café Cáceres, C. San José 24 (☎21 54 26). Choose from a huge spread of cheeses, cereals, jams, yogurts, fresh orange juice, and omelettes. *Desayuno de la casa* (€6) includes coffee, ham, eggs, and toast. Open in summer M-F 7:30am-5pm, Sa 8am-2pm; in winter Sa and Su 7:30am-7:30pm. MC/V. ❶

Histórico Horno, SA, Av. de la Constitución 16 (☎22 18 19). Renowned for its delicious desserts as well as its gourmet *jamón* (ham). Enjoy your delicacy inside or have it *para llevar* (to go). Open M-Sa 8am-11pm, Su 9am-11pm. AmEx/D/MC/V. ❷

◉ SIGHTS

■**CATEDRAL.** Legend has it that 15th-century *reconquistadores* wished to demonstrate their religious fervor by constructing a church so great that "those who come after us will take us for madmen." With 44 chapels, the cathedral of Seville is the third largest in the world (after St. Peter's Basilica in Rome and St. Paul's Cathedral in London) and the biggest Gothic edifice ever constructed. In the center, the **Capilla Real** stands opposite **choir stalls** made of mahogany recycled from a 19th-century Austrian railway. The ■**retablo mayor** is a golden wall of intricately wrought saints and disciples. Nearby is the **Sepulcro de Cristóbal Colón** (Columbus's tomb), which supposedly holds the explorer's remains. The black-and-gold pallbearers represent the monarchs of Castilla, León, Aragón, and Navarra. Farther on stands the **Sacristía Mayor** (treasury), which holds Juan de Arefe's gilded panels of Alfonso X el Sabio, works by Ribera and Murillo, and a glittering Corpus Christi icon, **La Custodia Processional.** In 1401, a 12th-century Almohad mosque was destroyed to clear space for the massive cathedral. All that remains of it is the **Patio de Los Naranjos,** where the faithful would wash before prayer, the **Puerta del Perdón** entryway on C. Alemanes, and **La Giralda,** a minaret with 35 ramps leading to the top. (☎21 49 71. Entrance by the Pl. de la Virgen de los Reyes. Open M-Sa 9:30am-4pm, Su 2:30-6pm. €7.50, seniors and students €2, under 16 free. Audio tour €3. Mass in the Capilla Real M-Sa 8:30, 10am, noon, 5pm; Su 8:30, 10, 11am, noon, 1, 5, 6pm.)

■**ALCÁZAR.** The oldest European palace still used as a private residence for royals, Seville's Alcázar epitomizes extravagance. Built by the Moors in the 7th century, the palace was embellished greatly during the 17th century. It now displays a mix of Moorish, Gothic, Renaissance, and Baroque architecture, most prominently on display in the *mudéjar* style of many of the arches, tiles, and ceilings. Catholic monarchs Fernando and Isabel are the palace's most well-known former residents. Visitors enter through the **Patio de la Montería,** across from the Almohad facade of the Moorish palace. Through the archway lie the Arabic residences, including the **Patio del Yeso** (Patio of Mortar) and the **Patio de las Muñecas** (Patio of the Dolls), so named because of the miniature faces carved into the bottom of one of the room's pillars. Of the Christian additions, the most notable is the **Patio de las Doncellas** (Patio of the Maids). The golden-domed **Salón de los Embajadores** (Ambassadors' Room) is allegedly the site where Fernando and Isabel welcomed Columbus back from the New World. The **private residences,** the official home of the king and queen of Spain, have been renovated and redecorated throughout the centuries; most of the furniture dates from the 18th and 19th centuries. These residences are accessible only by 25min. tours. (Pl. del Triunfo 7. ☎50 23 23. Open Tu-Sa 9:30am-7pm, Su 9:30am-5pm. Tours of the upper palace living quarters 2 per hr. Aug.-May 10am-1:30pm and 3:30-5:30pm; June-July 10am-1:30pm; max. 15 people per tour. Buy tickets in advance. €7; disabled, students, under 16, and over 65 free. Tours €4. Audio tours €3.)

CASA DE PILATOS. Inhabited continuously by Spanish aristocrats since the 15th century, this large private residence combines all the virtues of Andalusian architecture and art. On the ground floor, Roman artifacts and tropical gardens coexist in *mudéjar* patios. The second floor features rooms decorated with oil portraits, sculptures, and tapestries. (Pl. de Pilatos 1. ☎22 52 98. Open daily 9am-7pm. Tours 2 per hr. Ground level only €5, with 2nd fl. €8; EU citizens free Tu 1-5pm.)

MUSEO PROVINCIAL DE BELLAS ARTES. This museum contains Spain's finest collection of works by painters of the *Sevillana* School, notably Murillo, Valdés

Leal, and Zurbarán, as well as El Greco and Dutch master Jan Brueghel. The art is heavily biased toward religious themes, but later works include landscape paintings and portraits of Seville, its environs, and its residents. *(Pl. del Museo 9.* ☎*78 65 00; www.museosdeandalucia.es. Open Tu 2:30-8:30pm, W-Sa 9am-8:30pm, Su 9am-2:30pm. €1.50, students and EU citizens free.)*

PLAZA DE TOROS DE LA REAL MAESTRANZA. Home to one of the two great bullfighting schools (the other is in **Ronda,** p. 922), Plaza de Toros de la Real Maestranza fills to capacity (13,800) for weekly fights and the 13 *corridas* of the *Feria de Abril*. Visitors must follow the multilingual tours through the small **Museo Taurino de la Real Maestranza.** *(☎22 45 77; www.realmaestranza.com. Open May-Oct. 9:30am-8pm; Nov-Apr. 9:30am-7pm. Tours 3 per hr. €5; seniors 20% discount.)*

🎵 ENTERTAINMENT

The tourist office distributes *El Giraldillo* (also online, www.elgiraldillo.es), a free magazine with listings of music, art exhibits, theater, dance, fairs, and film.

FLAMENCO. Flamenco—traditionally consisting of dance, guitar, and song, and originally brought to Spain by gypsies—is at its best in Seville. Rhythmic clapping, intricate fretwork on the guitar, throaty wailing, and rapid foot-tapping form a mesmerizing backdrop for the swirling dancers. Flamenco can be seen either in highly touristed *tablaos*, where skilled professional dancers perform, or in *tabernas*, bars where locals merrily dance *sevillanas*. Both have merit, but the *tabernas* tend to be free. The tourist office has a complete list of *tablaos* and *tabernas*. **Los Gallos,** Pl. de Santa Cruz 11, is arguably the best tourist show in Seville. Buy tickets ahead and arrive early. (☎21 69 81; www.tablaolosgallos.com. Shows nightly 8 and 10:30pm. €27, includes 1 drink.) A less expensive alternative is the impressive 1hr. show at the cultural center ▧**Casa de la Memoria Al-Andalus,** C. Ximénez de Enciso 28, in the middle of Santa Cruz. Ask at their ticket office for a schedule of performances. (☎/fax 56 06 70. Shows daily in summer 9 and 10:30pm. Limited seating; buy tickets ahead. €13, students €11, under 10 €6.)

BULLFIGHTING. Seville's bullring, one of the most beautiful in Spain, hosts bullfights from *Semana Santa* through October. The cheapest place to buy tickets is at the ring on Po. Alcalde Marqués de Contadero. When there's a good *cartel* (line-up), the booths on C. Sierpes, C. Velázquez, and Pl. de Toros might be the only source of advance tickets. Ticket prices can run from €20 for a *grada de sol* (nosebleed seat in the sun) to €75 for a *barrera de sombra* (front-row seat in the shade); scalpers usually add 20%. *Corridas de toros* (bullfights) and *novilladas* (fights with apprentice bullfighters and younger bulls) are held on the 13 days around the *Feria de Abril* and into May, on Sundays April through June and September through October, more often during Corpus Cristi in June and early July, and during the *Feria de San Miguel* near the end of September. During July and August, *corridas* occur on Thursday at 9pm; check posters around town. For current info and ticket sales, call the Plaza de Toros ticket office at ☎50 13 82.

❋ FESTIVALS

Seville swells with tourists during its fiestas, and with good reason. If you're in Spain during any of the major festivals, head straight to Seville. Reserve a room a few months in advance, and expect to pay two or three times the normal rate. Seville's world-famous ▧**Semana Santa** lasts from Palm Sunday to Easter Sunday (Mar. 16-22, 2008). Thousands of penitents in hooded cassocks guide *pasos* (lavishly decorated floats) through the streets, illuminated by hundreds of candles. On

Good Friday, the entire city turns out for the procession along the bridges and through the oldest neighborhoods. The city rewards itself for its Lenten piety with the ▒Feria de Abril (Apr. 12-17, 2008). Begun as part of a 19th-century revolt against foreign influence, the *Feria* has grown into a massive celebration of all things Andalusian, with circuses, bullfights, and flamenco shows. At the fairgrounds on the southern end of Los Remedios, an array of flowers and lanterns decorates over 1000 kiosks, tents, and pavilions, collectively called *casetas*.

◙ NIGHTLIFE

Seville's reputation for hoopla is tried and true—most clubs don't get going until well after midnight or even 3am. Popular bars can be found around **Calle Mateos Gago** near the cathedral, **Calle Adriano** by the bullring, and **Calle del Betis** across the river in Triana. Many gay clubs are around **Plaza de Armas**.

- ▒ **La Carbonería,** C. Levies 18 (☎22 99 45), off C. Santa María La Blanca. Guitar-strumming Romeos abound on the massive outdoor stage and the sea of picnic tables. Tapas €1.50-2. Beer €1.50. *Agua de Sevilla* (champage, cream, 4 liquors, and pineapples) €15-20. Sangria pitchers €8. Th free live flamenco. Open daily 8pm-3am. Cash only.

- ▒ **Boss,** C. del Betis, knows how to get a crowd fired up. Irresistible beats and a hip atmosphere make this a wildly popular destination. Beer €3.50. Mixed drinks €6. Open fall-spring daily 9pm-5am. MC/V.

- **Palenque,** Av. Blas Pascal (☎46 74 08). Cross Pte. de la Barqueta, turn left, and follow C. Materático Rey Pastor to the first big intersection. Turn left again and look for the entrance on the right. Gigantic dance club, complete with 2 dance floors and a small ice skating rink (€3; includes skate rental; closes at 4am). During the summer, the crowd consists largely of teenagers. Beer €3. Mixed drinks €5. Cover Th free, F-Sa €7. Dress to impress. Open June-Sept. Th-Sa midnight-7am. MC/V.

- **Alfonso,** Av. la Palmera (☎23 37 35), adjacent to Po. de las Delicias. Avoid the longer lines elsewhere and shake it to the DJ's crazy beats in this spacious outdoor club. Palm trees and mini-bars are scattered around the dance floor. Beer €1.50-2.50. Mixed drinks €4.50-6. Open Su-Th 10pm-5am, F-Sa 10pm-7am. AmEx/MC/V.

- **Rio Grande: Puerto de Cuba,** on the right as you cross into Triana on the San Telmo bridge. Wicker couches and pillow-strewn dingies provide a unique and intimate club setting on the riverbank. Drinks from €6. Open in summer daily 11pm-4:30am.

◤ DAYTRIPS FROM SEVILLE

ARCOS DE LA FRONTERA

Los Amarillos buses (☎956 32 93 47) run from C. Corregidores to Seville (2hr., 2 per day, €6.30). Transportes Generales buses go to Cádiz (1½hr., 6 per day, €4.80), Costa del Sol (3-4hr., 1 per day, €10-13), and Ronda (1¾hr., 4 per day, €6).

Peaceful and romantic, Arcos (pop. 33,000) is the best of Spain's *pueblos blancos* (white towns). In the town square is the **Basílica de Santa María de la Asunción,** a hodgepodge of Baroque, Gothic, and Renaissance styles under renovations through 2008. (Open M-F 10am-1pm and 3:30-6:30pm, Sa 10am-2pm. €1.50.) Wander through the **cuarto viejo** (Old Quarter) and marvel at the view from ▒Plaza del Cabildo. The Gothic **Iglesia de San Pedro** stands on the site of an Arab fortress. (Open daily 10am-1:30pm. €1.) To reach the *cuarto viejo* from the bus station, exit left, follow the road, turn left again, and continue uphill on C. Josefa Moreno Seguro. Take a right on C. Muñoz Vásquez; upon reaching Pl. de España, veer left onto C. Debajo del Coral, which becomes C. Corredera. **Buses** run every 30min. from the bus station to C. Corredera (€1). Cheap cafes and restaurants cluster at the bottom end of **Calle Corredera**, while tapas nirvana can be achieved in the *cuarto viejo*. The **tourist office** is on Pl. del Cabildo. (☎956 70 22 64. Open mid-Mar. to mid-Oct. M-Sa 10am-2pm and 4-8pm, Su 10am-2pm; mid-Oct. to mid-Mar. M-Sa 10am-2pm and 3:30-7:30pm, Su 10am-2pm.)

RONDA

Trains (☎952 87 16 73) depart from Av. Alferez Provisional for Granada (3hr., 3 per day, €12), Madrid (4½hr., 2 per day, €62), and Málaga (2hr., 1 per day, €8). Buses (☎952 18 70 61) go from Pl. Concepción García Redondo 2 to Cádiz (4hr., 2-3 per day, €13), Málaga (2½hr., 8-11 per day, €9), and Seville (2½hr., 3-5 per day, €10).

Ancient bridges, old dungeons, and a famed bullring attract many visitors to picturesque Ronda (pop. 350,000), which has all the charm of a small, medieval town with the amenities and culture of a thriving city. A precipitous 100m gorge, carved by the Río Guadalevín, drops below the **Puente Nuevo**, opposite Pl. España. The ◪**views** from the **Puente Nuevo, Puente Viejo,** and **Puente San Miguel** are unparalleled. Take the first left after crossing the Puente Nuevo to Cuesta de Santo Domingo, and descend the stairs of the **Casa Del Rey Moro** into the 14th-century water mine for an otherworldly view of the ravine. (☎952 18 72 00. Open daily 10am-7pm. €4, children €2.) Ronda's **Plaza de Toros** is Spain's oldest bullring (est. 1785) as well as the cradle of the modern *corrida*. In early September, the Pl. de Toros hosts *corridas goyescas* (bullfights in traditional costumes) as part of the **Feria de Ronda**. The **tourist office** is at Po. Blas Infante, across from the bullring. (☎952 18 71 19. English spoken. Open June-Aug. M-F 9:30am-7:30pm, Sa-Su 10am-2pm and 3:30-6:30pm; Sept.-May M-F 9:30am-6:30pm, Sa-Su 10am-2pm and 3:30-6:30pm.)

GRANADA   ☎958

The splendors of the Alhambra, the magnificent palace which crowns the highest point of Granada (pop. 238,000), have fascinated both prince and pauper for centuries. Legend has it that in 1492, when the Moorish ruler Boabdil fled the city, the last Muslim stronghold in Spain, his mother berated him for casting a longing look back at the Alhambra. "You do well to weep as a woman," she told him, "for what you could not defend as a man." The Albaicín, an enchanting maze of Moorish houses, is Spain's best-preserved Arab quarter. Granada has grown into a university city infused with the energy of students, backpackers, and Andalusian youth.

▆ TRANSPORTATION

Trains: RENFE Station, Av. Andaluces (☎902 24 02 02; www.renfe.es). To **Barcelona** (12-13hr., 2 per day, €54), **Madrid** (5-6hr., 2 per day, €32-36), and **Seville** (4-5hr., 4 per day, €21).

Buses: The bus station (☎18 54 80) is on the outskirts of Granada on Ctra. de Madrid, near C. Arzobispo Pedro de Castro. **ALSA** (☎15 75 57) goes to **Alicante** (6hr., 11 per day, €26), **Barcelona** (14hr., 6 per day, €62), and **Valencia** (9hr., 9 per day, €38). **Alsina Graells** (☎18 54 80) runs to: **Cádiz** (5½hr., 4 per day, €26); **Córdoba** (3hr., 9-10 per day, €11); **Madrid** (5-6hr., 18 per day, €15); **Málaga** (2hr., 17-18 per day, €8.30); **Marbella** (2hr., 6 per day, €14); **Seville** (3hr., 10 per day, €17).

Public Transportation: Pick up a free bus map at the tourist office. Important buses include: Alhambra bus **#30** from Gran Vía de Cólon or Pl. Nueva; **#31** from Gran Vía or Pl. Nueva to the Albaicín; **#10** from the bus station to C. de Ronda, C. Recogidas, and C. Acera de Darro; **#3** from the bus station to Av. de la Constitución, Gran Vía, and Pl. Isabel la Católica. Rides €1, *bonobus* (10 rides) €5.20.

S P A I N

Granada

ACCOMMODATIONS
Funky Backpacker's, 9
Hospedaje Almohada, 12
Hostal Venecia, 6
Oasis Granada, 3
Pensión Viena, 2

FOOD
Bocadillería Baraka, 4
Hicuri, 11
Los Italianos, 10
La Riviera, 8
Samarcanda, 5

NIGHTLIFE
Camborio, 1
Granada 10, 7
Salsero Mayor, 13

SPAIN

⊕ 🔢 ORIENTATION AND PRACTICAL INFORMATION

The center of Granada is the small **Plaza Isabel la Católica,** at the intersection of the city's two main arteries, **Calle de los Reyes Católicos** and **Gran Vía de Colón.** The **cathedral** is on Gran Vía. Two blocks uphill on C. de los Reyes Católicos sits **Plaza Nueva.** Downhill on C. de los Reyes Católicos lies **Plaza Carmen,** site of the **Ayuntamiento** and **Puerta Real.** The **Alhambra** commands the steep hill above **Plaza Nueva.**

Tourist Offices: Junta de Andalucía, C. Santa Ana 2 (☎22 59 90). Open M-F 9am-8pm, Sa 10am-8pm, Su 10am-2pm. **Oficina Provincial,** Pl. Mariana Pineda 10 (☎24 71 28). Open M-F 9am-8pm, Sa 10am-7pm, Su 10am-4pm.

American Express: C. de los Reyes Católicos 31 (☎22 45 12), between Pl. Isabel la Católica and Pta. Real. Open M-F 9am-10pm, Sa 11am-3pm, Su 4-9pm.

Luggage Storage: 24hr. storage at the train station (€3).

Laundromat: C. de la Paz 19. Wash €6, dry €1 per 10min. Detergent included. Open M-F 10am-2pm and 5-8pm.

Medical Services: Clínica de San Cecilio, C. Dr. Olóriz 16 (☎28 02 00), toward Jaén.

Internet Access: Net, Pl. de los Girones 3 (☎22 69 19). €1 per hr. With *Bono* card €8 per 10hr. Open M-F 10am-2:30pm and 5-10pm, Sa-Su 5-10pm.

Post Office: Pta. Real (☎22 48 35). **Lista de Correos** and **fax** service. Open M-F 8:30am-8:30pm, Sa 9:30am-2pm. **Postal Code:** 18009.

🛏 ACCOMMODATIONS

Hostels line **Cuesta de Gomérez, Plaza Trinidad,** and **Gran Vía.** Be sure to call ahead during *Semana Santa* (Mar. 16-22, 2008).

Funky Backpacker's, Cuesta de Rodrigo del Campo 13 (☎22 14 62). Take in an incredible view of the Alhambra while drinking a cold one at the bar. The friendly staff hangs out with travelers. Dorms are unusually large with A/C and lockers. Breakfast included. Laundry €7. Free Internet. Dorms €17; doubles €38. MC/V. ❶

Hostal Venecia, Cuesta de Gomérez 2, 3rd fl. (☎22 39 87). Eccentrically decorated, this small hostel has the most character per square foot of any in Granada. Complimentary tea. Dorms and singles €18; doubles €32; triples €45; quads €60. MC/V. ❷

Hospedaje Almohada, C. Postigo de Zarate 4 (☎20 74 46). Red doors with hand-shaped knockers open to a staircase lined with boldly-colored rooms. Lounge in the TV area, listen to the stereo, use the fridge, and cook your own pasta. Laundry €5 per 8kg. Dorms €15; singles €19; doubles €35; triples €50. Cash only. ❶

Oasis Granada, Placeta Correo Viejo 3 (☎21 58 48; free from inside Spain 900 162 747; www.hostelsoasis.com). Weekly parties and daily activities like tapas tours and pub crawls around Granada. 3-course dinner €3.50. Breakfast included. Free Internet. Reserve ahead or arrive early. Dorms €15; doubles €36. MC/V. ❶

Pensión Viena, C. Hospital Santa Ana 2 (☎/fax 22 18 59; www.hostalviena.com). Bare rooms with A/C and a view of Pl. Nueva. Singles €25, with bath €35; doubles €37/45; triples €50/60; quads €57/70; quints €60/90. MC/V. ❷

🍴 FOOD

Cheap North African cuisine can be found around the Albaicín, while more typical *menús* await in Pl. Nueva and Pl. Trinidad. Picnickers can gather fresh fruit, vegetables, and meat at the indoor **market** on Pl. San Agustín. (Open M-Sa 9am-3pm.)

⬚ **Bocadillería Baraka,** C. Elvira 20 (☎22 97 60). The cheapest and tastiest of Granada's Middle Eastern eateries, Baraka serves delicious pitas (€2.50-3) and homemade lemonade infused with *hierbabuena* (€1). Open daily 1pm-2am. Cash only. ❶

⬚ **Hicuri,** C. Santa Escolástica 12 (☎22 12 82), on the corner of Pl. de los Girones. This popular restaurant has a huge selection of vegetarian and vegan dishes that will satisfy any tofu craving. Entrees €5-6. Menú €11. Open daily 8:30am-4:30pm. ❷

La Riviera, C. Cetti Meriem 7 (☎22 79 69). Serves traditional, generously-sized tapas. Drinks €1.50-2. Open daily 12:30-4pm and 8pm-midnight.

Los Italianos, Gran Vía 4 (☎22 40 34). Great ice cream at extremely low prices. Cups and cones from €0.50. Open daily 9am-2am. Cash only. ❶

Samarcanda, C. Calderería Vieja 3 (☎21 00 04). Delicious Lebanese food. Entrees €6-10. Open M-Tu and Th-Su 1-4:30pm and 7:30pm-midnight. MC/V. ❷

◉ SIGHTS

⬛ **THE ALHAMBRA.** From the streets of Granada, the Alhambra appears blocky and practical. But up close, the Alhambra is an elaborate and detailed work of architecture, one that unites water, light, wood, stucco, and ceramics to create a fortress-palace of aesthetic grandeur. The age-old saying holds true: *"Si mueres sin ver la Alhambra, no has vivido."* (If you die without seeing the Alhambra, you have not lived.) Follow signs for the *Palacio Nazaries* to see the ⬛**Alcázar,** a 14th-century royal palace full of stalactite archways and sculpted fountains. The walls of the **Patio del Cuarto Dorado** are topped by the shielded windows of the harem. Off the far side of the patio, archways open onto the **Cuarto Dorado,** whose carved wooden ceiling is inlaid with ivory and mother-of-pearl. From the top of the patio, glimpse the 14th-century **Fachada de Serallo,** the palace's intricately carved facade. In the **Sala de los Abencerrajes,** Boabdil had the throats of 16 sons of the Abencerrajes family slit after one of them allegedly had amorous encounters with the sultana. Rust-colored stains in the basin are said to be traces of the massacre.

Over a bridge, across the **Callejón de los Cipreses** and the **Callejón de las Adelfas,** are the vibrant blossoms, towering cypresses, and streaming waterways of El Generalife, vacation retreat of the sultans. Over the centuries, the estate passed through private hands until it was finally repatriated in 1931. The two buildings of El Generalife, the **Palacio** and the **Sala Regia,** connect across the **Patio de la Acequia,** embellished with a pool fed by fountains whose falling water forms an archway.

When the Christians drove the first Nasrid King Alhamar from the Albaicín to this more strategic hill, he built the series of rust-colored brick towers which form the **Alcazaba** (fortress). A dark, spiraling staircase leads to the **Torre de la Vela** (watchtower), where visitors have a 360° view of Granada and the surrounding mountains. After the *Reconquista* drove the Moors from Spain, Fernando and Isabel restored the *Alcázar.* Only two generations later, Emperor Carlos V demolished part of it to make way for his *Palacio,* a Renaissance masterpiece by Pedro Machuca, a disciple of Michelangelo. While incongruous with the surrounding Moorish splendor, is considered one of the most beautiful Renaissance buildings in Spain. (☎57 51 26, *reservations 902 22 44 60; online reservations www.alhambratickets.com. Open daily Apr.-Sept. 8:30am-8pm; Oct.-Mar. M-Sa 8:30am-6pm. Nighttime visits June-Sept. Tu-Sa 10-11:30pm; Oct.-May Sa 8-9:30pm. €10. Worthwhile English-language audio tour €3. Admission is limited, so arrive early or reserve tickets in advance online.)*

⬛ **THE ALBAICÍN.** A labyrinth of steep, narrow alleys, the Albaicín was the only Moorish neighborhood to escape the torches of the *Reconquista.* After the fall of the Alhambra, a small Muslim population remained here until their expulsion in the 17th century. Today, with North African cuisine, outdoor bazaars blasting Arabic music, teahouses, and the mosque near Pl. San Nicolás, the Albaicín attests to the persistence of Islamic culture in Andalucía. The best way to explore this maze is to proceed along Carrera del Darro off Pl. Santa Ana, climb the Cuesta del Chapiz on the left, then wander through the Muslim ramparts, cisterns, and gates. On Pl. Santa Ana, the 16th-century **Real Cancillería**, with its arcaded patio and stalactite ceiling, was the Christians' *Ayuntamiento* (city hall). Farther uphill are the 11th-century **Arab baths.** *(Carrera del Darro 31. ☎02 78 00. Open Tu-Sa 10am-2pm. Free.)* The ■mirador adjacent to **Iglesia de San Nicolás** affords the city's best view of the Alhambra, especially in winter when snow adorns the Sierra Nevada behind it.

CAPILLA REAL AND CATHEDRAL. Downhill from the Alhambra, the **Capilla Real** (Royal Chapel), Fernando and Isabel's private chapel, exemplifies Christian Granada. Gothic masonry and meticulously rendered figurines, as well as **La Reja,** the gilded iron grille of Maestro Bartolomé, grace the couple's resting place. The **Sacristía** houses Isabel's private **art collection** and the **royal jewels.** *(The Capilla is on C. Oficios through the Pta. Real off Gran Vía. ☎22 92 39. Capilla and Sacristía open M-Sa 10:30am-1pm and 4-7pm, Su 11am-1pm and 4-7pm. Both sights €3.)* Behind the Capilla Real and the Sacristía is Granada's **cathedral.** After the *Reconquista,* construction of the cathedral began upon the smoldering embers of Granada's largest mosque. *(☎22 29 59. Open Apr.-Sept. M-Sa 10:45am-1:30pm and 4-8pm, Su 4-8pm; Oct.-Mar. M-Sa 10:30am-1:30pm and 3:30-6:30pm, Su 11am-1:30pm and 3:30-6:30pm. €3.)*

⬛ NIGHTLIFE

Granada's policy of "free tapas with a drink" lures students and tourists to its many pubs and bars. Great tapas bars can be found off the side streets near Pl. Nueva. The most boisterous nightspots belong to **Calle Pedro Antonio de Alarcón,** between Pl. Albert Einstein and Ancha de Gracia, while hip new bars and clubs line **Calle Elvira** from Cárcel to C. Cedrán. Gay bars are around **Carrera del Darro.**

Camborio, Camino del Sacromonte 48 (☎22 12 15), a 20min. walk uphill from Pl. Nueva. Night bus #31 runs until 2am. Pop music spun by DJs echoes through dance floors to the rooftop patio. Striking view of the Alhambra. Beer €1.80-3. Mixed drinks €5-6. Cover F-Sa €7. Open Tu-Sa 11pm-dawn. Cash only.

Salsero Mayor, C. la Paz 20 (www.salseromayorgranada.com). Locals and tourists flock here for crowded nights of *bachata,* merengue, and salsa. Beer €2-3. Mixed drinks €5. Open Su-Th 10pm-3am, F and Sa 1pm-4am. Cash only.

Granada 10, C. Cárcel Baja 3 (☎22 40 01). Movie theater by evening (shows Sept.-June at 8 and 10pm), raging dance club by night. Flashy and opulent. Strict dress code. Open Su-Th 12:30am-4am, F-Sa 12:30am-5am. MC/V.

COSTA DEL SOL

The Costa del Sol combines rocky beaches with chic promenades and swank hotels. While some spots are over-developed and can be hard on the wallet, elsewhere the coast's stunning landscape has been left untouched.

MÁLAGA   ☎952

Málaga (pop. 550,000) is the transportation hub of the coast, and while its beaches are known more for bars than for natural beauty, the city has much to offer. At the east end of Po. del Parque, the **Alcazaba** was originally a military fortress and royal palace for Moorish kings. (Open June-Aug. Tu-Su 9:30am-8pm; Sept.-May Tu-Sa 8:30am-7pm. €2, students and seniors €0.60. Free Su after 2pm.) Málaga's **cathe-**

dral, C. Molina Lario 4, is nicknamed *La Manquita* (One-Armed Lady) because one of its two towers was never completed. (☎22 03 45. Open M-F 10am-6pm, Sa 10am-5pm. Mass daily 9am. €3.50, includes audio tour.) Picasso's birthplace, Pl. de la Merced 15, is now home to the **Casa Natal y Fundación Picasso,** which organizes concerts, exhibits, and lectures. Upstairs is a permanent collection of Picasso's drawings, photographs, and pottery. (☎06 02 15; www.fundacionpicasso.es. Open daily 9:30am-8pm. €1; students, seniors, and under 17 free.)

One of few spots in Málaga just for backpackers, friendly ▧**Picasso's Corner ❷,** C. San Juan de Letrán 9, off Pl. de la Merced, offers free Internet and top-notch bathrooms. (☎21 22 87; www.picassoscorner.com. Dorms €18-19; doubles €45. MC/V.) Sit outside and indulge in a mojito (€2.50 glass, €6 pitcher) and any of the couscous or combo dishes (€1.80-8.20) at ▧**Mediterráneo ❶,** C. Santiago 4, offering Arabic cuisine with a Greek spin. (☎21 64 38. Open Tu-Su 8pm-12am.) RENFE **trains** (☎902 24 02 02) leave from Explanada de la Estación for: Barcelona (13hr., 2 per day, €55); Córdoba (2hr., 9 per day, €16); Madrid (5hr., 7 per day, €35); Seville (3hr., 5-6 per day, €17). **Buses** run from Po. de los Tilos (☎35 00 61), one block from the RENFE station along C. Roger de Flor, to: Cádiz (5hr., 3-6 per day, €21); Córdoba (3hr., 7 per day, €12); Granada (2hr., 17-19 per day, €9); Madrid (7hr., 8-12 per day, €20); Marbella (1½hr., 1 per hr., €5); Ronda (3hr., 4-12 per day, €10); Seville (3hr., 11-12 per day, €14). To get to the city center from the bus station, take bus #3, 4, or 21 (€1) or exit right onto Callejones del Perchel, walk through the intersection with Av. de la Aurora, turn right on Av. de Andalucía, and cross Puente de Tetuán. Alameda Principal leads into Pl. de la Marina and the **tourist office.** (☎12 20 20. Open M-F 9am-7pm.) **Postal Code:** 29080.

TARIFA
☎**956**

Prepare for wind-blown hair—when the breezes pick up in the southernmost city of continental Europe, it becomes clear why Tarifa (pop. 15,000) is known as the Hawaii of Spain. World-renowned winds combined with kilometers of white beaches attracts some of the best kite and windsurfers from around the world to Tarifa, while the tropical, relaxed environment beckons to the less adventurous. Directly across the Strait of Gibraltar from Tangier, Morocco, Tarifa boasts incomparable views of Africa, the Atlantic, and the Mediterranean. **Playa de los Lances** has 5km of the finest sand on the Atlantic coast. Bathers should be aware of the occasional high winds and strong undertow. Adjacent to Playa de los Lances is **Playa Chica,** which is tiny but sheltered from the winds. **Tarifa Spin Out Surfbase,** 9km up the road toward Cádiz, rents **windsurfing** and **kitesurfing** boards and instructs all levels. (☎23 63 52; www.tarifaspinout.com. Book ahead. Windsurf rental €25 per hr., €56 per day; 2hr. lesson including equipment €50. Kite and board rental €28 per hr., €58 per day; 1½hr. lesson with all equipment €99.)

The cheapest accommodations line **Calle Batalla del Salado** and its side streets. Prices rise significantly in summer; those visiting in August and on weekends from June to September should call ahead and arrive early. Comfortable **Hostal Villanueva ❷,** Av. de Andalucía, 11, has a restaurant and rooftop terrace with an ocean view. Spotless rooms all have bath and TV. (☎68 41 49. Breakfast €2.25. Singles €20-25; doubles €35-45. Cash only.) **Hostal Facundo I and II ❶,** C. Batalla del Salado, 47, with its "Welcome backpackers" slogan, draws a young, budget crowd. (☎68 42 98; www.hostalfacundo.com. Dorms €10-22; singles €25; doubles €22-45, with bath €26-55. Cash only.) For cheap sandwiches (€1.50-3), try any one of the many *bagueterías* around C. Sancho IV el Bravo. Alternatively, C. San Francisco offers a variety of affordable, appetizing options. Take off your shoes and lounge on eclectic, pillow-covered couches in the open-air seating area of ▧**Bamboo ❷,** across from the castle. The lounge becomes a bar at night. (☎62 73 04. Teas €1.60-

2. Fresh juices €2.50-3. Panini €2.80-3.50. Full breakfast €4. F-Sa Live DJ. Open Su-Th 10am-2pm, F-Sa 10am-3am. MC/V.)

At night, sunburnt travelers mellow out in the Old Town's many bars, which range from jazz to psychedelic to Irish. **Moskito,** C. San Francisco 11, is a combination bar-club with a Caribbean motif, dance music, and tropical cocktails. (Free salsa lessons W night 10:30pm. Beer €2.50. Mixed drinks €4.50-6. Open in summer daily 11pm-3am; in winter Th-Sa 11pm-late.) **La Tribu,** C. Nuestra Señora de la Luz 7, a favorite among kite surfers, makes some of the most creative mixed drinks in town (€4-7). (Beer €2-3. Shots €1.50. Open daily 8pm-2am.)

From the bus station on C. Batalla del Salado 19 (☎68 40 38), **buses** run to Cádiz (2¼hr., 7 per day, €7.50) and Seville (3hr., 4 per day, €15). FRS **ferries** (☎68 18 30; www.frs.com) run to Tangier, MOR (35min., 1 per 2hr., €29). For a **taxi,** call **Parada Taxi** (☎68 42 41). The **tourist office,** in Parque de la Alameda, has info on adventure sports. (☎68 09 93; www.tarifaweb.com. Open in summer M-F 10:30am-2pm and 6-8pm, Sa-Su 9am-2pm; in winter M-F 10am-2pm and 4-6pm, Sa-Su 9:30am-3pm.) The **post office,** C. Coronel Moscardó, 9, is near Pl. San Matéo. (☎68 42 37. Open M-F 8:30am-2:30pm, Sa 9:30am-1pm.) **Postal Code:** 11380.

GIBRALTAR   UK/US ☎350; SPAIN ☎9567

Among history's most contested plots of land, Gibraltar today is officially a self-governing British colony, though Spain continues to campaign for its sovereignty. Gibraltar has a culture all its own—a curious mixture of not-quite-British, definitely-not-Spanish that makes it a sight worth visiting, despite the fact that it is something of a tourist trap. The craggy face of the ■**Rock of Gibraltar** emerges imposingly from the mist. Ancient seafarers called "Gib" one of the Pillars of Hercules, believing that it marked the end of the world. About halfway up the Rock is the **Apes' Den,** where Barbary Macaques cavort on the sides of rocks, the tops of taxis, and the heads of tourists. At the northern tip of the Rock, facing Spain, are the **Great Siege Tunnels.** Originally used to fend off a Franco-Spanish siege in the 18th century, the underground tunnels were expanded during WWII to span 53km. Thousands of years of water erosion formed the eerie chambers of **St. Michael's Cave,** 500m from the siege tunnels. At the southern tip of Gibraltar, **Europa Point** commands a view of the straits; its lighthouse can be seen from 27km away at sea. (Cable car 6 per hr. Round-trip £8/€13.50. Combined ticket to all sights, including one-way cable car ride, £16/€21.50.)

Most establishments accept the euro, although the British pound is preferred. Gibraltar is best done as a daytrip: the few accommodations in the area are relatively pricey and often full, and camping is illegal. Spending the night across the border in the Spanish town of **La Línea** is the cheapest option. Sample the treats of Gibraltar's Hindu community at **Mumtaz ❶,** 20 Cornwalls Ln., where authentic tastes come at low prices. (☎442 57. Entrees £2.50-6.75, with ample vegetarian selection. Takeout available. Open daily 11am-3pm and 6pm-12:30am. Cash only.)

Buses run from La Línea to: Cádiz (3hr., 4 per day, €13); Granada (5hr., 2 per day, €20); Madrid (7hr., 2 per day, €26); Seville (6hr., 4 per day, €20). Turner & Co., 65/67 Irish Town St. (☎783 05; fax 720 06), runs **ferries** to Tangier, MOR (1¼hr.; 1 per day; £18/€32, under 12 £9/€17). British Airways (☎793 00) **flights** leave from **Gibraltar Airport (GIB; ☎**730 26) for London, BRI (2½hr., 2 per day, £168/€233). You must have a valid passport to enter Gibraltar or you'll be turned away at the border. From the bus station in La Línea, walk toward the Rock; the border is 5min. away. Once through customs and passport control, catch bus #9 or 10 or walk across the airport tarmac into town (20min.). Stay left on Av. Winston Churchill when the road forks. The **tourist office** is at Duke of Kent House, Cathedral Sq. (☎450 00. Open M-F 9am-4:30pm, Sa 10am-1pm.)

EASTERN SPAIN

Its rich soil and famous orange groves, fed by Moorish irrigation systems, have earned Eastern Spain the nickname *Huerta de España* (Spain's Orchard). Dunes, jagged promontories, and lagoons mark the coastline, while fountains and pools grace landscaped public gardens in Valencian cities. The region has made a rapid transition from traditional to commercial, and continues to modernize.

ALICANTE (ALICANT) ☎965

Alicante (pop. 320,000) is a city with verve. Though its wild bars, crowded beaches, and busy streets seem decidedly modern, the castle-topped crag, 14th-century churches, and marble esplanades declare otherwise. Alicante is also home to the remains of a 5th-century Iberian settlement.

🖃🖬 TRANSPORTATION AND PRACTICAL INFORMATION. RENFE **trains** (☎902 24 02 02) run from Estación Término on Av. Salamanca to Barcelona (4½-6hr., 5-6 per day, €45), Madrid (4hr., 4-9 per day, €42-73), and Valencia (1½hr., 10 per day, €10-24). **Buses** (☎13 07 00) leave C. Portugal 17 for: Barcelona (9hr., 2 per day, €38); Granada (6hr., 10 per day, €26-32); Madrid (5hr., 15 per day, €24-32); Málaga (8hr., 6 per day, €35-43); Seville (10hr., daily, €45); Valencia (3hr., 14-21 per day, €16-18). The **tourist office** is by the bus station. (☎92 98 02; www.alicante-turismo.com. Open M-F 9am-2pm and 5-8pm, Sa 10am-2pm.) **Internet** is available at **Fundación BanCaja,** Rbla. Méndez Nuñez 4, 2nd fl. (1hr. free with ISIC. Open M-F 9am-2pm and 4-9pm, Sa 9am-2pm.) **Postal Code:** 03002.

🖿🗎 ACCOMMODATIONS AND FOOD. Hostels in the **casco antigua** must be booked in advance. For simple rooms with A/C and views of the town's oldest church, try 🖾**Hostal-Pension La Milagrosa ❶,** C. Villa Vieja. (☎21 69 18. Laundry €2. Internet €1 per hr. Dorms €15. MC/V.) 🖾**Kebap ❶,** Av. Dr. Gadea 5, has the best Middle Eastern food in Alicante. (☎22 92 35. Entrees €6-7. Open Su-Th 1-4pm and 8pm-midnight, F-Sa 1pm-midnight. MC/V.) For a more local taste, try the family-run restaurants in the *casco antiguo.* Buy groceries at **Supermarket Mercadona,** C. Alvarez Sereix 5, off Av. Federico Soto. (☎21 58 94. Open M-Sa 9am-9pm.)

🖾🖾 SIGHTS AND NIGHTLIFE. The **Castell de Santa Barbara** keeps imposing guard over Alicante's shores. The 166m high Carthaginian monument exhibits 9th- to 17th-century artifacts and offers a spectacular panorama of the city. (☎26 31 31. Open daily Apr.-Sept. 10am-7:30pm; Oct.-Mar. 9am-6:30pm. Elevator €2.40 on C. Jovellanos near the beach.) The **Museu Arqueológico Provincial de Alicante,** Pl. Dr. Gomez Ulls, imaginatively showcases artifacts from a variety of periods, including an entire hall dedicated to historical Alicante. (☎14 90 00; www.marqalicante.com. Open Tu-Sa 10am-7pm, Su 10am-2pm. €3, students €1.50.) Alicante's **Playa del Postiguet** attracts beach-lovers, as do nearby **Playa de San Juan** (TAM bus #21, 22, or 31) and **Playa del Mutxavista** (TAM bus #21). Buses (€0.95) depart every 15-25min.

Nightlife in Alicante is unrelenting and unpredictable. Delightfully bizarre bars in the *casco antiguo* are the best place to start the night. The bars that overlook the water in the **main port** and the discos on **Puerto Nuevo** tend to fill up after 2:30am. **Astrónomo,** C. Virgen de Belén, at C. Padre Maltés (☎965 14 35 22), plays traditional and modern Spanish tunes. (Beer €3. Mixed drinks from €5. Happy hour midnight-2am. Open Th-Sa 11pm-4am.) The **Fogueres de Sant Joan** (Bonfire of Saint John; June 19-24, 2008) sets Alicante aflame for a week, celebrating the summer solstice with revelry from morning until night. *Fogueras* (giant papier-mâché struc-

SEEING RED

On the last Wednesday of every August, tens of thousands of tourists descend upon the small town of Buñol, a town in Valencia, to participate in the world's largest food fight: La Tomatina. A tradition since 1944, this tomato battle serves as the culmination of a week-long festival. Although the sloppy free-for-all is followed by a celebration of the town's patron saints, the tomato fight has no significance beyond the primal desire to get dirty and throw food.

Festivities begin when an overgrown ham is placed on a greased pole in the center of town. Locals and tourists scramble up the slippery pole, climbing on top of one another to be the captor of the prized ham. Once a winner is announced, a cannon starts the marinara blood bath.

Throngs of tourists wearing clothes destined for the dumpster crowd around the open-bed trucks that haul 240,000 lb. of tomatoes into the plaza. Over the next 2hr., Buñol becomes an every-man-for-himself battle of oozy carnage. Revelers pelt one another with tomatoes until the entire crowd is covered in tomato guts.

The origins of this food fight are unclear: some say it began as a fight between friends, while others say the original tomatoes were directed at unsatisfactory civil dignitaries. Today, no one is safe from the wrath of tomatoes hurled at friends and foreigners alike.

tures) are erected and then burned in the street during *la Cremà*. Afterward, firefighters soak everyone during *la Banyà* and the party continues until dawn.

VALENCIA ☎963

Valencia's white beaches, palm-lined avenues, and architectural treasures are noticeably less crowded than those of Spain's other major cities. Yet Valencia possesses the stamina of Alicante, the off-beat sophistication of Barcelona, and the warmth of Seville.

▛▟ TRANSPORTATION AND PRACTICAL INFORMATION. Trains arrive at Estación del Norte, C. Xàtiva 24 (☎52 02 02) and a slick new metro line runs from the **Airport of Valencia** to C. Colon. **RENFE** (☎902 24 02 02) runs to: Alicante (2-3hr., 12 per day, €10-24); Barcelona (3hr., 8-16 per day, €29-37); Madrid (3½hr., 12 per day, €20-39); (8½hr., 11:20am, €44). **Buses** (☎46 62 66) go from Av. Menéndez Pidal 13 to: Alicante via the Costa Blanca (4½hr., 10-30 per day, €16-18); Barcelona (4½hr., 19 per day, €21); Granada (8hr., 9 per day, €36-43); Madrid (4hr., 13 per day, €21-26); Málaga (11hr., 9 per day, €44-53); (11hr., 3-4 per day, €43-50). Trasmediterránea **ferries,** Muelle de Poniente (☎902 45 46 45; www.trasmediterranea.es), sail to the Balearic Islands (p. 956). Take bus #1 or 2 from the bus station. The huge **tourist office,** C. de la Paz 48, has branches at the train station and at Pl. de la Reina. (☎98 64 22; www.valencia.es. Open M-F 9am-2:30pm and 4:30-8pm.) **Ono,** C. San Vicente Mártir 22, provides daily **Internet** until 1am. (☎28 19 02. €1-4 per hr.) The **post office** is at Pl. del Ajuntament 24. (☎51 23 70. Open M-F 8:30am-8:30pm, Sa 9:30am-2pm.) **Postal Code:** divided into zones, 46000-46025.

▛▙ ACCOMMODATIONS AND FOOD. For the best deals and location, try hostels around **Plaça del Ajuntament, Plaça del Mercat,** and **Plaça de la Reina.** From Pl. de la Reina, turn right on C. de la Paz to reach the hopping ■**Red Nest Youth Hostel ❷,** C. de la Paz 36. The hostel is spotless and smoothly operated, with an avant-garde decor. (☎42 71 68; www.nesthostelsvalencia.net. Kitchen, dining area, and vending machines. Free luggage storage. Linens included. Internet €1 per hr. 4-12 person dorms €18-20; doubles €41/47. AmEx/MC/V.) The **Home Youth Hostel ❶,** C. Lonja 4, is across from the Mercado Central on a side street off Pl. Dr. Collado. A couch-laden lounge makes this funky 20-room complex the area's most social hostel. (☎91 62 29; www.likeathome.net. Fully equipped kitchen. Linens included. Internet €0.50 per 15min. Singles €23; doubles €40. MC/V.)

Valencia is renowned for its paella, served in mammoth skillets all over town. Stuff yourself with huge portions of *paella valenciana* in the courtyard outside **El Rall ❸**, by the old Gothic silk exchange monument on C. Tundidores 2. (☎92 20 90. Paella €10-21 per person, min. 2 people. Open daily 1:30-4pm and 9-11:30pm. Reserve ahead. MC/V.) **Zumeria Naturalia ❶**, C. Del Mar 12, by the Pl. de la Reina, is a sherbert-hued gem offering fruit drinks and crepes. (Open M-W 5pm-midnight, Th 5pm-1am, F-Sa 5pm-2am, Su 5-10:30pm.) For groceries, stop by the **Mercado Central**, where fresh fish, meat, and fruit (including Valencia's famous oranges) are sold.

◙ SIGHTS. Most sights line the Río Turia or cluster near Pl. de la Reina, Pl. del Mercado, and Pl. de la Virgin. EMT bus #5 is the only public bus that passes by most of Valencia's historical sites; for a guided tour, try the **Bus Turistico** from Pl. de la Reina (☎15 85 15; €12). The 13th-century **◙Catedral de Santa María** in Pl. de la Reina, which holds a chalice said to be the Holy Grail, is an impressive mix of Romanesque, Gothic, and Baroque architecture. (☎91 01 89. Open daily 7:30am-1pm and 4:30-8:30pm. Closes earlier in winter. Free.) Take bus #35 from Pl. del Ajuntament to reach the mini-city that is the **◙Ciutat de les Arts i de les Ciències.** The complex is divided into five large spaces, including the eye-shaped **L'Hemisfèric** (with an IMAX theater and planetarium) and the **Museu de les Ciències Príncipe Felipe**, an interactive science playground. The **Palau de les Arts** houses performances and **L'Oceanogràfic**, an enormous aquarium, recreates nine aquatic environments. (☎902 10 00 31; www.cac.es. Hourly shows at L'Hemisfèric IMAX and planetarium. Open M-Th 11am-7pm, F-Sa 11am-9pm. Museum open mid-June to mid-Sept daily 10am-8pm; Mar. to mid-June and mid-Sept. to Jan. Su-F 10am-6pm and Sa 10am-8pm. L'Oceanogràfic open Aug. daily 10am-midnight; mid-June to Aug. daily 10am-8pm; Sept. to mid-June Su-F 10am-6pm, Sa 10am-8pm. Combination tickets for the entire complex €30.50.) Across the river, the blue-domed **Museu Provincial de Belles Artes**, C. Sant Pío V, displays stunning 14th- to 16th-century Valencian art. (☎60 57 93. Open Tu-Sa 10am-8pm. Free.)

◙◙ ENTERTAINMENT AND NIGHTLIFE. To reach Valencia's two most popular beaches, **Las Arenas** and **Malvarrosa**, bike along Av. de la Puerta or take bus #20, 21, 22, or 23. Discos dominate the university area, while the gay and lesbian scene centers further along C. Caballeros on **Calle Quart**. Sip *agua de Valencia* (orange juice, champagne, and vodka) in Pl. Tossal, where you will find **◙Bolsería Café**, C. Bolsería 41, a cafe-style club packed every night with the very chic. (☎91 89 03. Beer €3. Mixed drinks €6. Funk W, house music Sa-Su. Open daily 7:30pm-3:30am. Cash only.) **Radio City**, C. Sta. Teresa 19, along C. Caballeros past Bolseria, offers a relaxed bar and wild dance floor. (☎91 41 51; www.radiocityvalencia.com. Beer €3.50. Mixed drinks from €6. Flamenco Tu 11pm. Open daily 7:30pm-3:30am. Cash only.) For more info, consult the entertainment supplement *La Cartelera* (€0.50), or the free *24/7 Valencia*, available at hostels and cafes. During the famous festival of **Las Fallas** (Mar. 12-19), hundreds of colossal papier-mâché puppets are paraded, then burned, in celebration of spring. The nearby town of **Buñol** hosts the world's largest food fight (Aug. 27, 2008; see p. 930).

NORTHERN SPAIN

Northern Spain encompasses the country's most fiercely regionalistic areas. From rocky Costa Brava to chic Barcelona, prosperous Catalonia *(Cataluña)* is graced with the nation's richest resources. However, Catalonia isn't the only reason to head northeast. The area is also home to the parties of the Balearic Islands, the coasts of the Basque Country, and the beauty of Galicia and the Pyrenees.

BARCELONA ☎93

Home to expats from the US, South America, and a host of other countries, Barcelona is a city in which there are no outsiders. In the 16 years since it hosted the Olympics, travelers have been drawn to its beaches, clubs, and first-rate restaurants. The city has a strong art scene, which continues the tradition of the whimsical and daring *Modernisme* architectural movement and Barcelonese painter Pablo Picasso. Barcelona is a gateway, not only to Catalan art and culture, but also to the Mediterranean and the Pyrenees.

■ INTERCITY TRANSPORTATION

Flights: Aeroport El Prat de Llobregat (BCN; ☎902 40 47 04; www.aena.es and choose Airport: Barcelona from the dropdown on the left), 13km southwest of Barcelona. To get to Pl. Catalunya, take **RENFE train** L10 (20-25min., 2 per hr., €2.40) or the **Aerobus** (☎415 6020; 30min., 4-10 per hr., €4).

Trains: Barcelona has 2 main train stations. **Estació Barcelona-Sants,** in Pl. Països Catalans (M: Sants-Estació), is the main terminal for domestic and international traffic. **Estació de França,** on Av. Marquès de l'Argentera (M: Barceloneta), serves regional destinations and some international arrivals. RENFE (Spain ☎902 24 02 02, international 902 24 34 02; www.renfe.es) **trains** go to: **Bilbao** (9-10hr., 12:30 and 10pm, €38-50); **Madrid** (5-9hr., 10 per day, €37-66); **Seville** (10-12hr., 3 per day, €33-85); **Valencia** (3-5hr., 12-15 per day, €21-38). 20% discount on round-trip tickets.

Buses: Most buses arrive at the **Barcelona Nord Estació d'Autobusos,** C. Alí-bei 80 (☎902 26 06 06; www.barcelonanord.com). M: Arc de Triomf or #54 bus. Buses also depart from Estació Barcelona-Sants and the airport. **Sarfa** (☎902 30 20 25; www.sarfa.es) goes to **Cadaqués** (2½hr., 3 per day, €19). **Eurolines** (☎367 4400; www.eurolines.es) travels to **Paris, FRA** (15hr., M-Sa 8:30pm, €84) and **Naples, ITA** (24hr; M, W, F 5:30pm; €120). **ALSA/Enatcar** (☎902 42 22 42; www.alsa.es) goes to: **Alicante** (8-9hr., 11 per day, €37-42); **Madrid** (8hr., 3 per day, €26-34); **Seville** (14-16hr., 2 per day, €71-83); **Valencia** (4-5hr., 14 per day, €23-28).

Ferries: Trasmediterránea (☎902 45 46 45; www.transmediterranea.es), in Terminal Drassanes, Moll Sant Bertran. Ferries go to **Ibiza** (5-9hr., 1 per day, €50), **Mahón** (3½-9hr., 1 per day, €50), and **Palma** (3½-7hr., 2-3 per day, €70).

■ ORIENTATION

Imagine yourself perched on Columbus's head at the **Monument a Colom** (on Passeig de Colom, along the shore), viewing the city with the sea at your back. From the harbor, the city slopes upward to the mountains. From the Monument a Colom, **La Rambla,** a pedestrian thoroughfare, runs from the harbor to **Plaça de Catalunya** (M: Catalunya), the city center. *Let's Go* uses "Las Ramblas" to refer to the general area and "La Rambla" in address listings. The **Ciutat Vella** (Old City) centers around Las Ramblas and includes the neighborhoods of Barri Gòtic, La Ribera, and El Raval. The **Barri Gòtic** is east of Las Ramblas, enclosed on the other side by **Vía Laietana.** East of V. Laietana lies the maze-like **La Ribera,** bordered by Parc de la Ciutadella and Estació de França. Beyond La Ribera—farther east, outside the Ciutat Vella—are **Poble Nou** and **Port Olímpic.** To the west of Las Ramblas is **El Raval.** Farther west rises **Montjuïc,** with sprawling gardens, museums, the 1992 Olympic grounds, and a fortress. Directly behind the Monument a Colom is the **Port Vell** (old port) development, where a wavy bridge leads across to the ultramodern shopping and entertainment complexes **Moll d'Espanya** and **Maremàgnum.**

North of the Ciutat Vella is **l'Eixample,** a gridded neighborhood created during the expansion of the 1860s, which sprawls from Pl. Catalunya toward the mountains. **Gran Vía de les Corts Catalanes** defines its lower edge, and the **Passeig de Gràcia,** l'Eixample's main avenue, bisects the neighborhood. **Avinguda Diagonal** marks the border between l'Eixample and the **Zona Alta** (uptown), which includes **Pedralbes, Gràcia,** and other older neighborhoods in the foothills. The peak of **Tibidabo,** the northwest border of the city, offers the most comprehensive view of Barcelona.

▣ LOCAL TRANSPORTATION

Public Transportation: ☎010. Passes *(abonos)* work for the Metro, bus, urban lines of FGC commuter trains, RENFE *cercanías,* Trams, and Nitbus. A *sencillo* ticket (one ride) costs €1.20. A **T-10 pass** (€6.90) is valid for 10 rides; a **T-Día pass** entitles you to unlimited bus and Metro travel for 1 day (€5.25) and the **T-mes** (€45) for 1 month.

Metro: ☎298 70 00; www.tmb.net. Vending machines and ticket windows sell passes. Hold on to your ticket until you exit or risk a €40 fine. Trains run M-Th 5am-midnight, F-Sa 5am-2am, Su and holidays 6am-midnight. €1.25.

Ferrocarrils de la Generalitat de Catalunya (FGC): ☎205 1515; www.fgc.es. Commuter trains to local destinations; main stations at Pl. de Catalunya and Pl. d'Espanya. After Tibidabo, rates increase by zone. Info office at the Pl. de Catalunya station open M-F 7am-9pm. €1.25.

Buses: Go just about anywhere, usually 5am-10pm. Most stops have maps posted. Buses run 4-6 per hr. in central locations. €1.25.

Nitbus: ☎901 511 151. 18 different lines run every 20-30min. 10:30pm-4:30am. Buses depart from Pl. de Catalunya, stop by most club complexes, and go through Ciutat Vella and Zona Alta.

Taxis: Try **RadioTaxi033** (☎303 3033; www.radiotaxi033.com; AmEx/MC/V) or **Servi-Taxi** (☎330 0300).

Car Rental: Avis, C. Corcega 293-295 (☎237 5680; www.avis.com). Also at airport (☎298 3600. Open M-Sa 7am-12:30am, Su 7am-midnight) and Estació Barcelona-Sants, Pl. dels Països Catalans. (☎330 4193. Open M-F 7:30am-10:30pm, Sa 8am-7pm, Su 9am-7pm.)

◪ PRACTICAL INFORMATION

Tourist Offices: ☎907 30 12 82; www.barcelonaturisme.com. In addition to several tourist offices, Barcelona has numerous mobile information kiosks.

Aeroport El Prat de Llobregat, terminals A and B (☎478 0565). Info and last-minute accommodation booking. Open daily 9am-9pm.

Estació Barcelona-Sants, Pl. Països Catalans. M: Sants-Estació. Info and last-minute accommodation booking. Open in summer daily 8am-8pm; winter M-F 8am-8pm, Sa-Su 8am-2pm.

Oficina de Turisme de Catalunya, Pg. de Gràcia 107 (☎238 4000; www.gencat.es/probert). M: Diagonal. Open M-Sa 10am-7pm, Su 10am-2pm.

Plaça de Catalunya, Pl. de Catalunya 17S. M: Catalunya. The biggest, best, and busiest tourist office. Free maps, brochures on sights and public transportation, booking service for last-minute accommodations, gift shop, currency exchange, and box office. Open daily 9am-9pm.

Plaça de Sant Jaume, C. Ciutat 2. M: Jaume I. Open M-F 9am-8pm, Sa 10am-8pm, Su and holidays 10am-2pm.

Currency Exchange: ATMs give the best rates; the next-best rates are available at banks. General banking hours are M-F 8:30am-2pm.

Luggage Storage: Estació Barcelona-Sants. €3-4.50 per day. Open daily 5:30am-11pm. **Estació de França.** €3 per day. Open daily 7am-10pm.

Library: Biblioteca Sant Pau, C. de l'Hospital 56 (☎302 0797). M: Liceu. Walk to the far end of the courtyard; the library is on the left. Do not confuse it with the Catalan library,

SPAIN

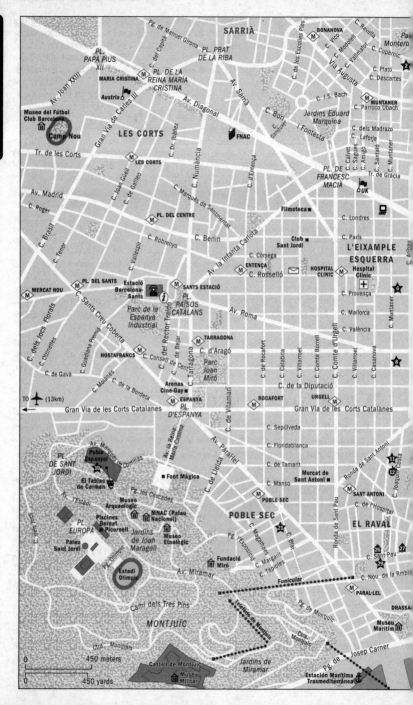

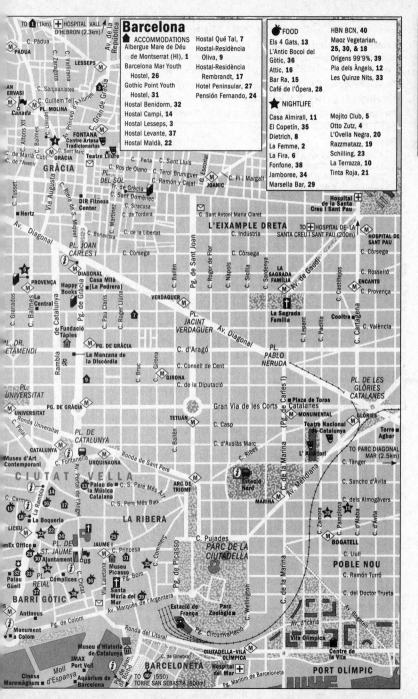

Barcelona

▲ **ACCOMMODATIONS**
Albergue Mare de Déu
  de Montserrat (HI), **1**
Barcelona Mar Youth
  Hostel, **26**
Gothic Point Youth
  Hostel, **31**
Hostal Benidorm, **32**
Hostal Campi, **14**
Hostal Lesseps, **3**
Hostal Levante, **37**
Hostal Maldà, **22**

Hostal Qué Tal, **7**
Hostal-Residència
  Oliva, **9**
Hostal-Residència
  Rembrandt, **17**
Hotel Peninsular, **27**
Pensión Fernando, **24**

🍎 **FOOD**
Els 4 Gats, **13**
L'Antic Bocoi del
  Gòtic, **36**
Attic, **16**
Bar Ra, **15**
Café de l'Òpera, **28**

★ **NIGHTLIFE**
Casa Almirall, **11**
El Copetín, **35**
Dietrich, **8**
La Femme, **2**
La Fira, **6**
Fonfone, **38**
Jamboree, **34**
Marsella Bar, **29**

HBN BCN, **40**
Maoz Vegetarian,
  25, 30, & 18
Orígens 99'9%, **39**
Pla dels Àngels, **12**
Les Quinze Nits, **33**

Mojito Club, **5**
Otto Zutz, **4**
L'Ovella Negra, **20**
Razzmatazz, **19**
Schilling, **23**
La Terrazza, **10**
Tinta Roja, **21**

SPAIN

which you'll see first and requires permission to enter. Free Internet. Open mid-Sept. to June M-Tu and F 3:30-8:30pm, W-Th and Sa 10am-2pm.

Laundromat: Tintorería Ferrán, C. Ferran 11 (☎301 8730). M: Liceu. Wash, dry, and fold €15. Open M-F 9am-2pm and 4-8pm. **Lavomatic,** Pl. Joaquim Xirau (☎268 4768). Wash €4.75, dry €0.85 per 5min. Both open M-Sa 9am-9pm

Tourist Police: La Rambla 43 (☎344 1300). M: Liceu. Multilingual officers. Open 24hr.

Late-Night Pharmacy: Rotates; check any pharmacy window for the nearest on duty.

Medical Services: Medical Emergency: ☎061. **Hospital Clìnic i Provincal,** C. Villarroel 170 (☎227 5400). M: Hospital Clìnic.

Internet Access:

> ▨ **Easy Internet Café,** La Rambla 31 (☎301 7507). M: Liceu. Reasonable prices and over 200 terminals in a bright, modern center make this Internet heaven. Digital camera, CD burning, faxing, copying, and scanning services. €2.20 per hr., 1-day pass €7, 1-week €15, 1-month €30. Open daily 8am-2:30am. **Branch** at Ronda Universitat 35. M: Catalunya. €2 per hr., 1-day pass €3, 1-week €7, 1-month €15. Open daily 8am-2am.
>
> **Navegaweb,** La Rambla 88-94 (☎317 9026). M: Liceu. Good rates on international calls. Internet €1.60 per hr. Open Su-Th 9am-midnight, F 9am-1am, Sa 9am-2am.

Post Office: Pl. d'Antoni López (☎902 19 71 97). M: Jaume I or Barceloneta. Fax and **Lista de Correos.** Open M-F 8:30am-10pm, Su noon-10pm. **Postal Code:** 08003.

⚑ ACCOMMODATIONS

Finding an affordable room in Barcelona can be difficult. To crash in touristy **Barri Gòtic** or **Las Ramblas** during the busier months (June-Sept. and Dec.), make reservations weeks, even months, in advance. Consider staying outside of touristy Ciutat Vella; many nice hostels in **l'Eixample** and **Gràcia** tend to have more vacancies. For camping info, contact the **Associació de Càmpings i C.V. de Barcelona,** Gran Via de les Corts Catalanes 608 (☎412 5955; www.campingsbcn.com).

BARRI GÒTIC

Backpackers flock to these hostels to be close to happening Las Ramblas.

> ▨ **Hostal Levante,** Baixada de San Miquel 2 (☎317 9565; www.hostallevante.com). M: Liceu. This hostel has a TV lounge and large, tastefully decorated rooms with light wood furnishings and fans. 4- to 8-person apartments have kitchen, living room, and laundry machine. Singles €33-43; doubles €56-65; apartments €30 per person. MC/V. ❸
>
> ▨ **Hostal-Residència Rembrandt,** C. de la Portaferrissa 23 (☎318 1011; www.hostalrembrandt.com). M: Liceu. This fantastic hostel has rooms superior to others in the area; all are unique, some with large bath, patio, sitting area, and TV. Restaurant-quality dining area for breakfast (€5). Fans available. Reception 9am-11pm. Reservations require credit card. Singles €28; doubles €45/55; triples €70-80. MC/V. ❸
>
> **Pensión Fernando,** C. Ferran 31 (☎301 7993; www.hfernando.com). M: Liceu. This clean hostel is conveniently located. Dorms with A/C and lockers. Common kitchen with dining room and TV on 3rd fl. Towels €2. Dorms €16-21; singles €30-36, with bath €40-45; doubles with bath €52-64; triples with bath €58-70. MC/V. ❷
>
> **Hostal Maldà,** C. Pi 5 (☎317 3002). M: Liceu. Enter inside the shopping center. The friendly owner keeps this hostel's great, affordable rooms occupied. No reservations; claim your space 9-11am. Doubles €30; triples with shower €45. Cash only. ❸
>
> **Hostal Benidorm,** La Rambla 37 (☎302 2054; www.hostalbenidorm.com). M: Drassanes or Liceu. Phone, bath, A/C, and balconies overlooking the street. Internet €1 per 15min. Singles €36; doubles €56; triples €76; quads €90; quints €105. MC/V. ❸

LA RIBERA AND EL RAVAL
Be careful in the areas near the port and farther from Las Ramblas at night.

■ **Gothic Point Youth Hostel,** C. Vigatans 5 (☎268 7808; www.gothicpoint.com). M: Jaume I. Hostel offers colorfully painted lounge area with TV, rooftop terrace, weekly craft fair, and jungle-gym rooms with A/C. Breakfast included. Free Wi-Fi. Lockers €1.50 per day. Linens €2, towels €2. Refrigerator access. High season dorms €22; mid-season €19; low season €17. AmEx/MC/V; €2 fee. ❷

Hotel Peninsular, C. de Sant Pau 34 (☎302 3138; www.hotelpeninsular.net). M: Liceu. 80 beautiful rooms with phone and A/C around a 4-story interior courtyard. Breakfast included. Singles €30, with bath €52; doubles with bath €75. MC/V. ❸

Barcelona Mar Youth Hostel, C. de Sant Pau 80 (☎324 8530; www.barcelonamar.es). M: Parallel. This hostel squeezes 120 dorm-style beds into rooms with A/C. Breakfast included. Free Internet. All beds come with locker. Linens €2.50, towels €2.50, both €3.50. Self-serve laundry €4.50; laundry service available. Dorms in summer €22-23; in winter €16-19. Double beds Su-Tu €5, F-Sa €6.50 AmEx/MC/V. ❷

L'EIXAMPLE
Accommodations in this area tend to be nicer than those in Ciutat Vella.

■ **Hostal Residència Oliva,** Pg. de Gràcia 32, 4th fl. (☎488 0162; www.lasguias.com/ hostaloliva). M: Pg. de Gràcia. Elegant bureaus, mirrors, ceilings, and a light marble floor give this hostel a classy character. Rooms have high ceilings, TVs, and fans. Singles €36; doubles €60, with bath €75; triples with bath €84. Cash only. ❸

Hostal Qué Tal, C. Mallorca 290 (☎459 2366; www.quetalbarcelona.com), near C. Bruc. M: Pg. de Gràcia or Verdaguer. This high-quality gay- and lesbian-friendly hostel has one of the best interiors in the city, with murals, a plant-filled terrace, and snazzy decor in all 13 rooms. Singles €45; doubles €65, with bath €84. Cash only. ❹

ZONA ALTA: GRÀCIA AND OUTER BARRIS
Gràcia is Barcelona's "undiscovered" quarter, so last-minute arrivals may find vacancies here, even though options are few.

■ **Albergue Mare de Déu de Montserrat (HI),** Pg. Mare de Déu del Coll, 41-45 (☎210 5151; www.xanascat.net). M: Vallcarca. Take the #92 or 28 bus from the station. Palacial building was once home to a wealthy Catalan family. Breakfast included. Max. stay 5 days. Dorms €20-24, under 25 €16-20. MC/V. ❷

Hostal Lesseps, C. Gran de Gràcia, 239 (☎218 4434; www.hostallesseps.com). M: Lesseps. The 16 spacious rooms have TV and bath; 4 have A/C (€5 extra). Rooms facing the street are a bit noisy. Cats and dogs allowed. Free Internet access and Wi-Fi. Singles €45; doubles €75; triples €80; quads €90. MC/V. ❹

◘ FOOD

The restaurants on **Carrer Aragó** by Pg. de Gràcia have lunchtime *menús*, and the **Passeig de Gràcia** has outdoor dining. Gràcia's **Plaça Sol** and La Ribera's **Santa Maria del Mar** are the best tapas spots. For fruit, cheese, and wine, head to ■**La Boqueria (Mercat de Sant Josep),** off La Rambla outside M: Liceu. (Open M-Sa 6am-8pm.) Buy groceries at **Champion,** La Rambla 13. (M: Liceu. Open M-Sa 9am-10pm.)

SPAIN

BARRI GÒTIC

■ **Les Quinze Nits,** Pl. Reial 6 (☎317 3075). M: Liceu. Popular restaurant with nightly lines halfway through the plaza; arrive early to have dinner in this beautiful setting. Catalan entrees at shockingly low prices. Pasta and rice €4-7. Fish €7-9. Meat €6-10. Open daily 1-3:45pm and 8:30-11:30pm. MC/V. ❶

■ **L'Antic Bocoi del Gòtic,** Baixada de Viladecols 3 (☎310 5067). M: Jaume I. Bounded by an ancient Roman wall, this restaurant is tiny and romantic. Excellent salads (€6.50-7.50), exquisite pâtés (€9-12), and fine cheese platters (€11.50-16) feature *jamón iberico* (ham). Reserve early. Open M-Sa 8:30pm-midnight. AmEx/V. ❷

Els 4 Gats, C. Montsió 3 (☎302 4140; www.4gats.com). M: Catalunya. Picasso's old *Modernista* hangout with plenty of bohemian character. Cuisine includes Mediterranean salad (€9.50) and Iberian pork with apples (€18). Entrees €12-26. The M-F lunch *menú* (€12) is the best deal and comes with epic desserts; try the *crema catalana*. Live piano 9pm-1am. Open daily 1pm-1am. AmEx/MC/V. ❹

Attic, La Rambla 120 (☎302 4866; www.angrup.com). M: Liceu. This chic, modern restaurant has surprisingly reasonable prices for touristy La Rambla. Mediterranean fusion cuisine, including fish (€9-13), meat (€6-14), and rice (€6-9) dishes. Open daily 1-4:30pm and 7pm-midnight. AmEx/MC/V. ❸

Maoz Vegetarian, 3 locations: at C. Ferran 13; La Rambla 95; and C. Jaume I 7 (www.maozvegetarian.com). A vegetarian chain and city institution with only 1 menu option—falafel, with or without hummus—and an array of fresh vegetable toppings. Falafel €2.90-4.70. Open M-Th and Su 11am-2:30am, F-Sa 11am-3am. MC/V. ❶

Café de l'Òpera, La Rambla 74 (☎317 7585; www.cafeoperabcn.com). M: Liceu. This antique mirror-covered cafe was once a post-opera tradition of the bourgeoisie; now, it's beloved for its breakfast. The hot chocolate (€1.80) is as thick as a melted candy bar. *Churros* €1.30. Tapas €3-6. Salads €3-8. Open daily 8am. Cash only. ❶

ELSEWHERE IN BARCELONA

■ **Orígens 99'9%,** C. Enric Granados 9 (☎453 1120; www.origen99.com), C. Vidrieria 6-8 (☎310 7531), Pg. de Born 4 (☎295 6690), and C. Ramón y Cajal 12 (☎213 6031). Delectable entrees such as the beef-stuffed onion (€4.85) and the rabbit with almonds (€5) are made with 99.9% local ingredients. Small soups and vegetarian and meat dishes €5-6. Open 12:30pm-1am. AmEx/MC/V. ❶

■ **Bar Ra,** Pl. de la Garduña (☎615 95 98 32; www.ratown.com). M: Liceu. Lots of vegetarian options. Enjoy creative cuisine like grilled tuna with avocado (€12) on the shady terrace with a view of La Boqueria. Entrees €9-15. Obligatory lunch *menú* €11. Dinner *menú* €12.50. Reservations required. Open daily 9:30am-1:30am. Kitchen open 1:30-4pm and 9:30pm-midnight. AmEx/MC/V. ❷

HBN BCN, C. Escar 1 (☎225 0263; www.habanabarcelona.com), right on Platja San Sebastián in Barceloneta, at the end of Pg. Joan de Borbó on the right. M: Barceloneta. Try the combined plate of Cuban tapas (plantains, yucca, avocado, shredded beef, rice, and beans; €8). Lunch *menú* €9. Dinner reservations recommended. Kitchen open 1pm-midnight. Th Salsa lessons; €30. MC/V. ❸

Pla dels Àngels, C. Ferlandina 23 (☎349 4047). M: Universitat. Healthy dishes, including a large vegetarian selection, are served on a terrace. Entrees €7-15. Open M-Sa 1:30-4pm and 9-11:30pm. MC/V. ❷

◙ SIGHTS

The **Ruta del Modernisme** pass is the cheapest and most flexible option for those with an interest in seeing Barcelona's major sights. Passes (free with the purchase of a €12 guidebook, €5 per additional adult, under 18 free) give holders a 25-30%

discount on attractions including Palau de la Música Catalana, the Museu de Zoología, tours of Hospital de la Santa Creu i Sant Pau, and the facades of La Manzana de la Discòrdia. Purchase passes at the Pl. Catalunya tourist office or at the Modernisme Centre at Hospital Santa Creu i Sant Pau, C. Sant Antoni Maria Claret 167. (☎933 17 76 52; www.rutadelmodernisme.com.)

LAS RAMBLAS

This pedestrian-only strip (roughly 1km long) is a cornucopia of street performers, fortune-tellers, human statues, pet and flower stands, and artists. The wide, tree-lined street, known in Catalan as *Les Rambles*, is actually six *ramblas* (promenades) that form one boulevard from the Pl. de Catalunya and the **Font de Canaletes.** According to legend, visitors who sample the water will return to Barcelona.

■ **GRAN TEATRE DEL LICEU.** After burning down for the second time in 1994, the Liceu was rebuilt and expanded; a tour of the building includes not just the original 1847 Sala de Espejos (Hall of Mirrors), but also the 1999 Foyer (a curvatious bar/lecture hall/small theater). The five-level, 2292-seat theater is considered one of Europe's top stages, adorned with palatial ornamentation, gold facades, and sculptures. *(La Rambla 51-59, by C. Sant Pau. M: Liceu. ☎485 9913, tours 85 99 14; www.liceubarcelona.com. Box office open M-F 2-8:30pm, Sa 1hr. before show. Short 20min. guided visits daily 10am-1pm; €4. 1¼hr. tours 10am by reservation only, call 9am-2pm; €8.50.)*

CENTRE D'ART DE SANTA MÓNICA. One can only imagine what the nuns of this former convent would have thought of the edgy art installations that now rotate through this large modern gallery. *(La Rambla 7. M: Drassanes. ☎316 2810. Open Tu-Sa 11am-8pm, Su 11am-3pm. Free.)*

LA BOQUERIA (MERCAT DE SANT JOSEP). Just the place to pick up that hard-to-find animal part you've been looking for, La Boqueria is a traditional Catalan market located in a giant, all-steel *Modernista* structure. Specialized vendors sell produce, fish, and meat from a seemingly infinite number of independent stands. *(La Rambla 89. M: Liceu. Open M-Sa 6am-8pm.)*

BARRI GÒTIC

Brimming with cathedrals, palaces, and tourism, Barcelona's oldest zone and political center masks its old age with unflagging energy.

■ **MUSEU D'HISTÒRIA DE LA CIUTAT.** Buried some 20m below a seemingly innocuous old plaza lies one of the two components to the Museu d'Història de la Ciutat: the subterranean excavations of the Roman city of Barcino. This 4000-square-meter **archaeological exhibit** displays incredibly well-preserved 1st- to 6th-century ruins. Built on top of those 4th-century walls, the second part, **Palau Reial Major,** served as the residence of the Catalan-Aragonese monarchs. *(Pl. del Rei. M: Jaume I. ☎315 1111; www.museuhistoria.bcn.es. Wheelchair-accessible. Open June-Sept. Tu-Sa 10am-8pm, Su 10am-3pm; Oct.-May Tu-Sa 10am-2pm and 4-8pm, Su 10am-3pm. Palace €4, students €2.50. Archaeological exhibit €1.50/1. Combination ticket €4.50/3.50.)*

ESGLÉSIA CATEDRAL DE LA SANTA CREU. This cathedral is one of Barcelona's most recognizable monuments. The altar holds a cross designed by Frederic Marès in 1976 and beneath lies the Crypt of Santa Eulàlia. The museum in La Sala Capitular holds Bartolomé Bermejo's *Pietà*. *(M: Jaume I. In Pl. Seu, up C. Bisbe from Pl. St. Jaume. Cathedral open daily 8am-12:45pm and 5:15-7:30pm. Cloister open daily 9am-12:30pm and 5:15-7pm. Elevator to the roof open M-Sa 10:30am-6pm; €2. Choir area open M-F 9am-12:30pm and 5:15-7pm, Sa-Su 9am-12:30pm; €1. Guided tours daily 1-5pm; €4.)*

LA RIBERA

This neighborhood has recently evolved into a bohemian nucleus, with art galleries, chic eateries, and exclusive bars.

■ **PALAU DE LA MÚSICA CATALANA.** By day, the must-see concert venue is illuminated by tall stained-glass windows and an ornate stained-glass skylight, which gleam again after dark by electric light. Sculptures of wild horses and busts of the muses are on the walls flanking the stage. (*C. Sant Francese de Paula 2. ☎ 295 7200; www.palaumusica.org. M: Jaume I. Mandatory 50min. tours in English almost every hr. Open daily July-Sept. 10am-7pm; Oct.-June 10am-3:30pm. €9, students and seniors €8, with Barcelona Card €6.40. Check the Guía del Ocio for concert listings. Concert tickets €6-330. MC/V.*)

MUSEU PICASSO. Barcelona's most-visited museum traces Picasso's artistic development with the world's most comprehensive collection of work from his formative Barcelona period. (*C. Montcada 15-23. ☎ 319 6310; www.museupicasso.bcn.es. M: Jaume I. Open Tu-Su 10am-8pm. Last entrance 30min. before closing. €6, students and seniors €4, temporary exhibits €2.50/1. Under 16 and 1st Su of the month free.*)

PARC DE LA CIUTADELLA. Host of the 1888 World's Fair, the park harbors several museums, well-labeled horticulture, the Cascada fountains, a pond, and a zoo. Buildings of note include Domènech i Montaner's *Modernista* **Castell dels Tres Dracs** (now the **Museu de Zoología**) and Josep Amergós's **Hivernacle.** The **Parc Zoològic** is home to threatened and endangered species, including the Iberian wolf and the Sumatran tiger. (*M: Ciutadella or Marina. Park open daily 8am-9pm. Zoo open daily June-Sept. 10am-7pm; low season 10am-5pm. Park €15, children 3-12 €9, over 65 €8.*)

MUSEU DE LA XOCOLATA (CHOCOLATE MUSEUM). The museum presents gobs of information about the history, production, and ingestion of this sensuous sweet. Chocolate sculptures include La Sagrada Família and soccer star Ronaldo. The cafe offers tasting and baking workshops. (*Pl. Pons i Clerch, by C. Comerç. ☎ 268 7878; www.museudelaxocolata.com. M: Jaume I. Open M and W-Sa 10am-7pm, Su 10am-3pm. Workshops for kids from €6.50; reservations required. €4, students and seniors €3.50, under 7 free.*)

EL RAVAL

Where over-crowding once led to crime, prostitution, and drug use, revitalization efforts, especially since the '92 Olympic Games, have worked wonders. New museums and cultural centers in Raval have paved the way for hip restaurants and bars.

■ **PALAU GÜELL.** Gaudí's 1886 Palau Güell, the Modernist residence built for patron Eusebi Güell, has one of Barcelona's most spectacular interiors. Güell spared no expense on this house, considered to be the first example of Gaudí's revolutionary style. The *palau* is closed for renovations until an undetermined date. (*C. Nou de La Rambla 3-5. M: Liceu. ☎ 317 3974. Mandatory tour every 15min. Open Mar.-Oct. M-Sa 10am-8pm, Su 10am-2pm; Nov.-Dec. M-Sa 10am-6pm. €3, students €1.50.*)

MUSEU D'ART CONTEMPORANI (MACBA). The MACBA has received worldwide acclaim for its focus on post-avant-garde art and contemporary works. Its main attractions are its innovative three-month rotating exhibitions and the "Nits MACBA," which keep the museum open until midnight—and let you in cheap. (*Pl. dels Àngels, 1. M: Catalunya. ☎ 412 0810; www.macba.es. Open M, W 11am-7:30pm, Th-F 11am-midnight, Sa 10am-8pm, Su 10am-3pm. English language tours M 6pm. €7.50, students €6, under 14 free; exhibits €4/3. W €3.50 for everything. Nits MACBA Th-F, €3 after 8pm.*)

L'EIXAMPLE

The Catalan Renaissance during the 19th century pushed the city into modernity. Though Ildefons Cerdà drew up a plan for a new neighborhood where people of all classes could live side by side, l'Eixample (luh-SHOMP-luh) did not thrive as a uto-pian community; it emerged instead as a playground for the bourgeoisie. Today, L'Eixample remains a pretty neighborhood full of *Modernista* oddities.

■ **LA SAGRADA FAMÍLIA.** Antoni Gaudí's masterpiece is far from finished, which makes La Sagrada Família the world's most visited construction site. Only 8 of the 18 planned towers have been completed and the church still lacks an "interior," yet millions of people make the touristic pilgrimage to witness its work-in-progress majesty. Of the three facades, only the **Nativity Facade** was finished under Gaudí. A new team of architects led by Jordi Bonet hopes to lay the last stone by 2026. The affiliated museum displays plans and computer models of the fully realized struc-ture. (*C. Mallorca 401. ☎ 207 3031; www.sagradafamilia.org. M: Sagrada Família. Open daily Apr.-Sept. 9am-8pm; Oct.-Mar. 9am-5:45pm. Elevator open Apr.-Sept. 9am-7:45pm; Oct.-Mar. 9am-5:45pm. Entrance €8, with ISIC €5. Combined ticket with Casa-Museu Gaudí €9. Elevator €2. English-language tours in summer 11am, 1pm, 3pm, 5pm; winter 11am and 1pm. €3.*)

■ **LA MANZANA DE LA DISCÒRDIA.** A short walk from Pl. de Catalunya, the odd-numbered side of Pg. de Gràcia between C. Aragó and C. Consell de Cent has been leaving passersby scratching their heads for a century. The Spanish nickname, which translates to the "block of discord," comes from the stylistic clashing of its three most extravagant buildings. Sprouting flowers, stained glass, and legendary doorway sculp-tures adorn **Casa Lleó i Morera**, #35, by Domènech i Montaner, on the far left corner of the block. Two buildings down is Puig i Cadafalch's geometric, Moorish-influenced facade makes **Casa Amatller** #41, perhaps the most beautiful building on the block. The real discord comes next door at **Casa Batlló**, #43, popularly believed to represent Cata-lonia's patron Sant Jordi (St. Jordi) slaying a dragon. The chimney plays the lance, the scaly roof is the dragon's back, and the bony balconies are the remains of his victims. The house was built using shapes from nature, especially from the ocean—the balco-nies ripple like the ocean. (*☎ 488 0666; www.casabatllo.es. Open daily 9am-8pm. €16.50, students €13.20. Call for group discounts. Free multilingual audio tour.*)

CASA MILÀ (LA PEDRERA). From the outside, this Gaudí creation looks like the sea—the undulating walls seem like waves and the iron balconies are remi-niscent of seaweed. Chimneys resembling armored soldiers have views of every corner of Barcelona. The entrance fee entitles visitors to tour one well-equipped apartment, the roof, and the winding brick attic, now functioning as the **Espai Gaudí**, a multimedia presentation of Gaudí's life and works. (*Pg. de Grà-cia 92. ☎ 902 40 09 73. Open daily in summer 9am-8pm, last admission 7:30pm, Nov.-Feb. 9am-6:30pm. €8, €4.50 students and seniors. Free audio tour.*)

HOSPITAL DE LA SANTA CREU I SANT PAU. Designated a UNESCO monument in 1997, this is Europe's second-oldest functioning hospital and Domènech i Mon-taner's lifetime *Modernista* masterpiece. The entire complex covers nine l'Eixam-ple blocks with whimsically decorated pavilions resembling gingerbread houses and Taj Mahals. (*Sant Antoni M. Claret 167. ☎ 291 9000; www.santpau.es. M: Hospital de St. Pau, L5. Open 24hr. Guided tours 10:15am-1:15pm; €5. Info desk open daily 10am-2pm.*)

MONTJUÏC

Historically, whoever controlled Montjuïc (mon-joo-EEK; "Hill of the Jews") con-trolled the city. Dozens of rulers have occupied and modified the **Castell de Mont-juïc,** a fortress built atop an ancient Jewish cemetery. Franco made it one of his "interrogation" headquarters. Today, the area is a peaceful park by day and a debaucherous playground by night.

■ **FUNDACIÓ MIRÓ.** An large collection of sculptures, drawings, and paintings from Miró's career, ranging from sketches to wall-sized canvases, engages visitors with the work of this Barcelona-born artist. His best-known pieces here include *El Carnival de Arlequín*, *La Masia*, and *L'or de l'Azuz*. The gallery also displays experimental work by young artists and a few other famous contributors, including Alexander Calder. (☎ 443 9470; www.bcn.fjmiro.es. *Funicular from M: Parallel or Park Montjuïc bus from Pl. Espanya. Open July-Sept. Tu-W and F-Sa 10am-8pm; Oct.-June Tu-W and F-Sa 10am-7pm; all year Th 10am-9:30pm, Su and holidays 10am-2:30pm. Last entry 15min. before closing. €7.50, students and seniors €5, under 14 free. Temporary exhibitions €4/3.)*

MUSEU NACIONAL D'ART DE CATALUNYA (PALAU NACIONAL). Designed by Enric Catá and Pedro Cendoya, the Palau Nacional has housed the Museu Nacional d'Art de Catalunya (MNAC) since 1934. Its main hall is an event space, while the wings house the world's finest collection of Catalan Romanesque art and a variety of Gothic pieces. (☎ 622 0376; www.mnac.es. *Open Tu-Sa 10am-7pm, Su and holidays 10am-2:30pm. Temporary exhibits €3-5; 2 temporary exhibits €6; all exhibits €8.50. 30% discount for students and seniors; under 14 and first Su of the month free. Audio tour included.)*

CASTELL DE MONTJUÏC. This historic fortress and its **Museu Militar** sit high on the hill, and from the scenic outlook, guests can enjoy a multitude of panoramic jaw-droppers. The *telefèric* (funicular) to and from the castle is usually half the fun. (☎ 329 8613. *From M: Parallel, take the funicular to Av. Miramar and then the cable car to the castle; €5.50, round-trip €7.50. Parc de Montjuïc bus runs up the slope from in front of the telefèric. Open daily 9am-10pm. Museum open Tu-Sa Mar.-Nov. 9:30am-8pm; Dec.-Feb. 9:30am-5pm. €3 for museum, fortress, Plaza de Armas, and outlook; €1 without museum.)*

WATERFRONT

■ **MUSEU D'HISTÒRIA DE CATALUNYA.** The Museu provides a patriotic introduction to Catalan history, politics, and culture. Recreations of a 1930s Spanish bar and an 8th-century Islamic prayer tent make the museum a full sensory experience. (*Pl. Pau Vila 3.* ☎ 225 4700; mhc.cultura@gencat.net. *Open Tu and Th-Sa 10am-7pm, W 10am-8pm, Su 10am-2:30pm. €3; students €2.10, EU students free; under 7 and over 65 free.)*

TORRE SAN SEBASTIÀ. One of the easiest and best ways to view the city is from the cable cars, which span the Port Vell, connecting beachy Barceloneta with mountainous Montjuïc. (*Pg. Joan de Borbó. M: Barceloneta. Open daily 11am-8pm. Elevator to the cable cars €4. To Montjuïc €9, round-trip €12.50.)*

L'AQUÀRIUM DE BARCELONA. This kid-friendly aquarium features sharks, exhibits on marine creatures, and a cafeteria. Its highlight is a life-size model of a sperm whale. (*Moll d'Espanya. M: Drassanes or Barceloneta.* ☎ 221 7474; www.aquarium-bcn.com. *Open daily July-Aug. 9:30am-10pm; Oct.-May 9:30am-9:30pm; June and Sept. 9:30am-9pm. €16, students with ISIC €14, under 12 and seniors €12.50. AmEx/MC/V.)*

ZONA ALTA

The most visited part of Zona Alta is Gràcia, which was incorporated into Barcelona in 1897 despite the protests of its residents. The area has always had a political streak, and calls for Gràcian independence crop up sporadically. Gràcia packs a surprising number of *Modernista* buildings and parks, international cuisine, and chic shops into a relatively small area.

■ **PARK GÜELL.** This fantastical park was designed entirely by Gaudí but, in typical Gaudí fashion, was not completed until after his death. Gaudí intended Parc Güell to be a garden city, and its buildings and ceramic-mosaic stairways were designed to house the city's elite. However, only one house, now know as the **Casa-Museu Gaudí,** was built. The longest park bench in the world, a multicolored serpentine wonder made of tile shards, decorates the top of the pavilion. (*Bus #24 from*

Pl. Catalunya stops at the upper entrance. Park open daily 10am-dusk. Museum open daily Apr.-Sept. 10am-8pm; Oct.-Mar. 10am-6pm. Park free. Museum €4, with ISIC €3.)

MUSEU DEL FÚTBOL CLUB BARCELONA. A close second to the Picasso Museum as Barcelona's most-visited museum, the FCB merits all the attention it gets from football fanatics. Fans will appreciate the storied history of the team. The high point is entering the stadium and taking in the 100,000-seat **Camp Nou.** *(Next to the stadium. ☎ 496 3608. M: Collblanc. Enter through access gate 7 or 9. Open M-Sa 10am-6:15pm, Su and holidays 10am-2pm. €7, students and seniors €5.60. Museum and tour €11/8.80.)*

🎵🌺 ENTERTAINMENT AND FESTIVALS

For tips on entertainment, nightlife, and food, pick up the *Guía del Ocio* (www.guiadelociobcn.es; €1) at any newsstand. The best shopping in the city is in the **Barri Gòtic,** but if you feel like dropping some extra cash, check out the posh **Passeig de Gràcia** in l'Eixample. Grab face paint to join fans of **F.C. Barcelona (Barça)** at the Camp Nou stadium for **fútbol.** (Box office C. Arístedes Maillol 12-18. ☎ 902 18 99 00. Tickets €30-60.) **Barceloneta** and **Poble Nou** feature sand for topless tanning and many places to rent sailboats and water-sports equipment. Head up to Montjuïc to take advantage of the **Olympic Facilities,** which are now open for public use, including **Piscines Bernat Picornell,** a gorgeous pool complex. (Av. de l'Estadi 30-40. ☎ 423 4041. Open M-F 6:45am-midnight, Sa 7am-9pm, Su 6am-4pm.)

Check sight and museum hours during festival times, as well as during the Christmas season and *Semana Santa* (Holy Week). The **Festa de Sant Jordi** (St. George; Apr. 23, 2008) celebrates Catalonia's patron saint with a feast. In the last two weeks of August, city folk jam at Gràcia's **Festa Mayor;** lights blaze in *plaças* and music plays all night. The three-day **Sónar** music festival comes to town in mid-June, attracting renowned DJs and electronica enthusiasts from all over the world. The **Festa Nacional de Catalunya** (Sept. 11) brings traditional costumes and dancing. **Festa de Sant Joan** takes place the night of June 23; ceaseless fireworks will prevent any attempts to sleep. The largest celebration in Barcelona is the **Festa de Mercè,** the weeks before and after September 24. To honor the patron saint of the city, *Barceloneses* revel with fireworks, *sardana* dancing, and concerts.

🎵 NIGHTLIFE

Barcelona's wild, varied nightlife treads the line between slick and kitschy. In many ways, the city is clubbing heaven—things don't get going until late (don't bother showing up at a club before 1am), and they continue until dawn. Yet for every full-blown dance club, there are 100 more relaxed bars, from Irish pubs to absinthe dens. Check the *Guía del Ocio* (www.guiadelocio.com) for the address and phone number of that place your hip Barcelonese friend just told you about.

 DON'T FEAR FLYERS. Many clubs hand out flyers, particularly in La Ribera. They are far from a tourist trap–travelers can save lots of money with free admission and drink passes.

CIUTAT VELLA

Main streets such as C. Ferran have cookie-cutter *cervecerías* and *bar-restaurantes* every five steps. C. Escudellers is the location for post-bar dancing, while Pl. Reial remains packed until the early morning. Las Ramblas, while lively, becomes a bit questionable late at night. In recent years, La Ribera has evolved into a hip, artsy district, attracting a young crowd of tourists and locals. The streets of El Raval are densely packed with a place for every variety of bar-hopper.

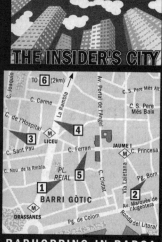

THE INSIDER'S CITY

BARHOPPING IN BARÇA

To aid you on your late-night adventures, here are our favorite places to bar-hop in Barcelona:

1 Plaça Reial. The center of the Barri Gòtic, you can begin your evening here with dinner and stay until the clubs get out the next morning.

2 Passeig del Born. The Ribera's main drag is a relaxed good time from dusk to dawn. Every kind of bar draws a young crowd.

3 C. Gran de Gràcia. From this short stretch in L'Eixample, turn off onto a sidestreet and enjoy the best dancing in Barcelona.

4 Rambla del Raval. This neighborhood offers terraces and tea during the day and laid-back bars at night.

5 La Boqueria. Once the pesky market crowd has gone home, you'll find colorful bars that serve elaborate mixed drinks.

6 C. Ferran. This often gritty off-shoot of La Rambla features Irish bars, late-night falafel, and everything in between.

El Copetín, Pg. del Born 19. (607 2021 76) M: Jaume I. Cuban rhythm pervades this casual, dimly lit nightspot with a crowd of variable age. Copetín's headstart on many other bars (it's full before some places open) makes it a good place to start the night. Awe-inspiring mojitos €7. Open M-Th and Su 7pm-2:30am, F-Sa 7pm-3am. Cash only.

Marsella Bar, C. de Sant Pau 65. M: Liceu. Religious figurines grace the walls of Barcelona's oldest bar, first opened in 1820; perhaps they're praying for the *absenta* (absinthe; €3.30) drinkers. Beer €3.20. Mixed drinks €4-6. Open M-Sa 10pm-2am.

Jamboree, Pl. Reial 17 (☎319 1789; www.masimas.com). M: Liceu. A maze of stone arches and lights thumps with hip-hop; 2nd fl. plays 80s and 90s music. Cover M €3, Tu-Su €10; look for flyers with discounts. Drinks €8-10. Open daily 8pm-5am. Jazz 9-11pm, €3-10. Upstairs, **Tarantos** hosts flamenco shows (€5). Open M-Sa 8-11pm.

Fonfone, C. Escudellers 24 (☎317 1424; www.fonfone.com). M: Liceu or Drassanes. Trippy orange and red bubbles protruding from the wall combined with funky music draw crowds 1-3am. Beer €3. Mixed drinks €6-8. Open daily 10pm-2:30 or 3am.

Schilling, C. Ferran 23 (☎317 6787). M: Liceu. Excellent sangria (pitcher €17). Wine €2-3, bottle from €13. Serves breakfast and sandwiches (€3-6) during the day. Though officially affiliated with neither group, Schilling often attracts British and gay crowds. Open M-W 10am-2:30am, Th-Sa 10am-3am, Su noon-3am.

Casa Almirall, C. Joaquín Costa 33. M: Universitat. Cavernous space with weathered couches and dim lights. It's house policy to stop you after your 3rd absinthe (€5-8), but the staff is fond of saying that you won't make it there anyway. Beer €2-4. Mixed drinks €5-7. Open M-Th and Su 5pm-2:30am, F-Sa 7pm-3am, Su 7pm-2am. Cash only.

L'EIXAMPLE

L'Eixample has upscale bars and some of the best gay nightlife in Europe.

Mojito Club, C. Rosselló 217 (☎237 6528; www.mojito-bcn.com). M: Diagonal. This club lures a fun-loving crowd with Latin beats. W free samba lessons 11pm; F-Sa salsa 11pm-1:30am. W Brazilian party with live salsa. Th and Su free drink with entry. F-Sa cover €10 cash after 2:30am; includes 1 drink. Open daily 11pm-4:30am. V.

Dietrich, C. Consell de Cent 255 (☎451 7707; www.dietrichcafe.com). M: Pg. de Gràcia. A caricature of a semi-nude Marlene Dietrich greets patrons at this inclusive gay bar. Beer €5. Mixed drinks €6-8. Nightly trapeze show 1:30am, drag shows some weekends. Open M-Sa 11pm-2:30am. MC/V.

La Fira, C. Provença 171 (☎650 85 53 84). M: Hospital Clínic or FGC: Provença. A hip crowd is surrounded by carousel swings, mirrors, and a fortune teller. F dance show and class 2, 3, 4am. Open W-Th 11pm-2:30am, F-Sa 11pm-5am. Cash only.

MONTJUÏC

Lower Montjuïc is home to **Poble Espanyol,** Av. Marqués de Comillas, a re-creation of famous buildings and sights from all regions of Spain. At night the complex becomes a disco theme park that offers the craziest clubbing experience in all of Barcelona. (☎508 6300; www.poble-espanyol.com. M: Espanya.)

■ **Tinta Roja,** C. Creus dels Molers 17 (☎443 3243; www.tintaroja.net), is the best combination bar and dance floor in the city. It often has tango music after midnight. Open Th 9pm-1:30am, F-Sa 9pm-2:30am, Su 7pm-midnight. Cash only.

La Terrazza, Avda. Marquès de Comillas, s/n (☎934 23 12 85). An outdoor madhouse and the undisputed king of Poble Espanyol nightlife. Cover €10; €3 with flyer. Open June-Oct. Th-Sa midnight-6am.

WATERFRONT

Poble Nou and **Port Olímpic** are home to a long strip of nightclubs. The entire waterfront area, which stretches from **Maremàgnum** to **Port Vell,** may be as hedonistic and touristy as Barcelona gets. Come nightfall, Maremàgnum, the city's biggest mall, turns into a tri-level maze of clubs packed with crowds even on weeknights. There is no cover; clubs make their money by charging exorbitant drink prices (beer €5; mixed drinks €8-10). Catching a cab home can be difficult.

L'Ovella Negra (Megataverna del Poble Nou), C. Zamora 78 (☎309 5938; www.ovellanegra.net). M: Bogatell or Marina. On the corner with C. Pallars. What was once a warehouse is now the place to come for the first few beers of the night. Large beers €2, 2L pitchers €8.50. Mixed drinks €4-5. Open Th 10pm-2:30am, F-Sa 5pm-3am, Su 7pm-1am. Kitchen open all night. Cash only.

Razzmatazz, C. Pamplona 88 and Almogàvers 122, around the corner (☎272 0910; www.salarazzmatazz.com). M: Marina. A huge warehouse houses 5 clubs: Pop, The Loft, Razz Club, Lo*Li*Ta, and Rex Room, each with its own live music specialty. Concert prices vary; call ahead or check website. Beer €3.50. Mixed drinks €7. Cover €12-15; includes access to all 5 clubs. Open F-Sa and holidays 1-5am. AmEx/MC/V.

ZONA ALTA

The area around C. de Marià Cubí has great nightlife undiscovered by tourists. Take a taxi or the NitBus. For more accessible fun in Gràcia, head to **Plaça del Sol.**

■ **Otto Zutz,** C. Lincoln 15 (☎238 0722). FGC: Pl. Molina or M: Fontana. One of Barcelona's most famous clubs, with three dance floors. Beer €6. Mixed drinks €6-12. Cover €10-15, includes 1 drink. Open Tu-Sa midnight-6am. AmEx/MC/V.

La Femme, C. Plató 13 (☎201 6207), on the corner with Muntaner. FCG: Muntaner. Caters to lesbians of all ages. Beer €5. Mixed drinks €7. Open F 11pm-3am, Sa 11:30pm-last customer. Cash only.

◤ LET'S GO TO BARCELONA: GIRONA   ☎972

Girona (pop. 92,000) is home to the **Aeropuerto de Girona-Costa Brava (GRO;** ☎18 66 00), served by budget airline **Ryanair** (☎47 36 50; www.ryanair.com). While Girona is not without worthwhile sights—it was once the the home of the *cabalistas de Girona,* who spread the teachings of Kabbalah (mystical Judaism)—many tourists simply fly into GRO and head straight out to Barcelona or other cities. **Barcelona Bus** (☎902 36 15 50; www.barcelonabus.com) runs express shuttles from GRO to Barcelona (1¼hr., 23-28 per day, €11) and Figueres (1hr., 3-6 per day, €4-5). RENFE **trains** (☎902 24 02 02) run from Pl. de Espanya in Girona to Barcelona (1½hr., 25 per day, €6-7) and Madrid (10½hr., 1 per day, €42).

Those interested in sightseeing should head to the *barrio antiguo*, across the **Riu Onyar** from the train station. The remnants of the Middle Ages Jewish community **El Call** are around the corner from the imposing Gothic **Cathedral de Girona**. A must for movie buffs, the ▨**Museu del Cinema**, C. Sèquia 1, chronicles the rise of cinema from the mid-17th to 20th centuries. (☎41 27 77; www.museudelcinema.org. Open May-Sept. Tu-Su 10am-8pm; Oct.-Apr. Tu-F 10am-6pm, Sa 10am-8pm, Su 11am-3pm. €4, students and seniors €2, under 16 free. AmEx/MC/V.)

Quality budget accommodations can be found in the *barrio antiguo*. Plain **Alberg de Joventut Cerverí de Girona (HI)** ❶, C. dels Ciutadans 9, is affordable and well-located. Sitting rooms have board games, ping-pong, TV, and videos. (☎21 80 03; www.xanascat.net. Breakfast included. Lockers available. Linens included. Wash €2, dry €1.50. Internet €1 per day. Reception 8:30am-2:30pm, 3:30-9:30pm, 10-11pm. Check-in 24hr. Dorms July-Sept. €24, under 25 €21; Oct.-June €20/17. €2 HI discount. AmEx/MC/V.) **Carrer Cort-Reial** is the best place to find good, cheap food, while cafes on **Plaza de la Independencia** offer outdoor seating. Girona's major nightlife destination in summer is **Las Carpas**, an outdoor circus of dance floors, bars, and lights in the middle of the Parc de la Devesa. (Drinks from €3. Open Apr.-Sept. 15 M-Th and Su 11pm-3:30am, F-Sa 11pm-4am.) The **tourist office**, Rbla. de la Libertat 1, is by Pont de Pedra on the old bank. (☎22 65 75; www.ajuntament.gi. Open M-Sa 8am-8pm, Su 9am-2pm.) **Postal Code:** 17007.

◪ DAYTRIP FROM BARCELONA: THE COSTA BRAVA.

The Costa Brava's jagged cliffs cut into the Mediterranean Sea from Barcelona to France. Its visitors are demanding super-vacationers, which keeps the food world-class and the beaches pristine. In 1974, Salvador Dalí chose his native, beachless **Figueres** (pop. 35,000) as the site for a museum to house his works, catapulting the city to international fame. The ▨**Teatre-Museu Dalí** is at Pl. Gala i Salvador Dalí 5. From La Rambla, take C. Girona, which becomes C. Jonquera. The museum contains the artist's nightmarish landscapes and bizarre installations, as well as his tomb. (☎972 67 75 00; www.salvador-dali.org. Open daily Aug. 9am-7:15pm and 10pm-12:30am; July and Sept. 9am-7:45pm; Oct.-June Tu-Su 10:30am-5:45pm. Aug. €11, Sept.-July €10, students and seniors €7.) The **tourist office** is in Pl. Sol. (☎972 50 31 55; www.figueresciutat.com. Open July-Sept. M-Sa 8am-8pm, Su 10am-3pm; Apr.-June and Oct. M-F 8:30am-3pm and 4:30-8pm, Sa 9:30am-1:30pm and 3:30-6:30pm; Nov.-Mar. M-F 8am-3pm.) **Postal Code:** 17600.

The whitewashed houses and small bay of **Cadaqués** (pop. 2900) have attracted artists, writers, and musicians ever since Dalí built his summer home in nearby Port Lligat. Take C. Miranda away from the ocean and follow the signs to Port Lligat and the Casa de Dalí (20min.), or take a trolley to Port Lligat (1hr., 6 per day, €7) from Pl. Frederic Rahola. ▨**Casa-Museu Salvador Dalí** was the home of Dalí and his wife until her death in 1982. Though two of Dalí's unfinished original paintings remain in the house, the wild decorations—including a lip-shaped sofa and a Pop-Art miniature Alhambra—are the best part. (☎972 25 10 15. Open mid-June to mid-Sept. daily 10:30am-9pm; mid-Sept. to Jan. and mid-Mar. to mid-June Tu-Su 10:30am-6pm. Tour required; make reservations 5 days ahead. €10, students, seniors, and children €8.)

From Figueres, **trains** (☎902 24 02 02) leave Pl. de l'Estació for Barcelona (2hr., 14-22 per day, €8-10) and Girona (30min., 14-22 per day, €3). **Buses** (☎972 67 33 54) run from Pl. de l'Estació to Barcelona (2¼hr., 2-5 per day, €15), Cadaqués (1hr., 6-7 per day, €4.30), and Girona (1hr., 2-5 per day, €4.10). Buses from Cadaqués go to Barcelona (2½hr., 3-5 per day, €19), Figueres (1hr., 3-7 per day, €4.30), and Girona (2hr., 1-2 per day, €8.30). The **tourist office**, C. Cotxe 2, is to the right of the *plaça*. (☎972 25 83 15. Open July-Aug. M-Sa 9am-2pm and 3-9pm, Su 10:30am-1pm; Sept.-June M-Sa 9am-2pm and 4-7pm.) **Postal Code:** 17488.

THE PYRENEES

The dramatic mountain scenery, Romanesque architecture, and cultural diversity of Spain's Pyrenees mountain range draw numerous explorers, hikers, and skiers searching for outdoor adventure. The Pyrenees are best reached by car, as public transportation is as common as the area's endangered bears.

VAL D'ARAN ☎973

Some of the most dazzling peaks of the Catalan Pyrenees cluster around the Val d'Aran, in the northwest corner of Catalonia, best known for its chic ski resorts. The Spanish royal family's favorite slopes are those of **Baquiera-Beret.** Nearby, Salardú's 13th-century **Església de Sant Andreu** houses beautifully restored 16th-century murals. For skiing info and reservations, contact the **Oficeria de Baquiera-Beret.** (☎63 90 00; www.baqueira.es. €39 for day pass.) The **Auberja Era Garona (HI) ❶,** Ctra. de Vielha, is a five-minute walk up the highway from Salardú towards Baqueira. The enormous Auberja has plenty of dorm rooms. Front door locked at midnight, and only opened every hour on the hour. (☎64 52 71; www.eragarona.com. Breakfast included; lunch and dinner available for additional price. Private bath €3. Bike and ski rentals available. Linens €3. Laundry €3.70. Internet €3.50 per hr. Reception 8am-11:30pm. Dorms €20-24, under 25 €16-20. MC/V.)

The capital of the valley, **Vielha** (pop. 4,500) welcomes hikers and skiers and offers services for the adventure-seeker. **Pensión Casa Vicenta ❷,** C. Reiau 3, is a good value with quiet rooms (some with skylights), private baths, and a common area. (☎64 08 19; casavincenta@teleline.es. Closed parts of May, June, Oct.-Nov. Singles €20; doubles €27. Cash only.) **Eth Breç ❶,** Av. Castièro 5, beneath Hotel d'Aran along the main road, serves delicious pastries (€1-3), teas, and has free Internet access. (☎64 00 50. Open daily 8:30am-1:30pm and 4-8:30pm. MC/V.) Alsina Graells (☎27 14 70) runs **buses** from Vielha to Barcelona (6hr., 2-3 per day, €28-33). Consult the **tourist office,** C. Sarriulèra 10, for an updated schedule of buses within Val D'Aran. For a **taxi,** call ☎64 01 95. **Postal Code:** 25530.

NAVARRA

From the unfathomable mayhem of Pamplona and the Running of the Bulls to the many hiking trails that wind up the peaks of the Pyrenees, there is seldom a dull moment in Navarra. Bordered by Basque Country and Aragón, the region is a mix of overlapping cultures and traditions.

PAMPLONA (IRUÑA) ☎948

El encierro, la Fiesta de San Fermín, the Running of the Bulls, utter debauchery: call it what you will, the outrageous festival of the city's patron saint is the principal reason tourists come to Pamplona (pop. 200,000). Since the city's immortalization in Ernest Hemingway's *The Sun Also Rises,* hordes of travelers have flocked to Pamplona for a week each July to witness the daily *corridas* and ensuing chaos. The city's monuments, museums, and parks merit exploration as well.

> **!** Although Pamplona is usually safe, crime skyrockets during *San Fermín.* Beware of assaults and muggings and do not walk alone at night during the festival.

 TRANSPORTATION AND PRACTICAL INFORMATION. Trains (☎902 24 02 02) run from Estación RENFE, Av. de San Jorge, to Barcelona (6-8hr., 3 per day, from €33), Madrid (3¾hr., 4 per day, €50), and San Sebastián (1½hr., 2-3 per day, €19). **Buses** leave from the corner of C. Conde Oliveto and C. Yangüas y Miranda for

SAN FERMÍN EXPOSED

A mass of flesh running through the streets of Pamplona may sound like old news, but for the past five years, the bare hides have not belonged only to the bulls. Since 2002, the international organization People for the Ethical Treatment of Animals, or PETA, has annually held the "Running of the Nudes," a clothes-free march through the streets of Pamplona to protest the treatment of the bulls throughout San Fermín.

Exactly 24hr. before the official San Fermín festivities start, the marchers gather near the lower corrals where the bulls are kept. Due to controversy, the authorities in Pamplona have permitted the mock run to proceed only under the condition that the marchers are not fully exposed. These are no meek tree-huggers, however; the participants have since made an art form of stripping down as much as possible.

Carrying anti-bullfighting signs in multiple languages and shouting slogans such as "*Fiesta Si! Corrida no!*" (Yes to the party! No to Bullfights!) or "*La cultura no es tortura*" (Culture isn't torture), the participants walk through the center of Pamplona, passing by masses of curious spectators. The march quickly becomes an all-out party in the spirit of the *fiesta*.

Full video highlights, complete with a sexiest runner spotlight and details about PETA's campaign can be found at www.runningofthenudes.com.

Barcelona (6-8hr., 4 per day, €24), Bilbao (2hr., 5-6 per day, €13), and Madrid (5hr., 6-10 per day, €26). From Pl. del Castillo, take C. San Nicolás, turn right on C. San Miguel, and walk through Pl. San Francisco to reach the **tourist office**, C. Hilarión Eslava. (☎42 04 20; www.turismo.navarra.es. Open during *San Fermín* daily 8am-8pm; July-Aug. M-Sa 9am-8pm, Su 10am-2pm; Sept.-June M-Sa 10am-2pm and 4-7pm, Su 10am-2pm.) **Luggage storage** is at the Escuelas de San Francisco in Pl. San Francisco during *San Fermín*. (€2 per day. Open from July 4 at 8am to July 16 at 2pm.) The **biblioteca** has free **Internet**. (Open Sept.-June M-F 8:30am-8:45pm, Sa 8:30am-1:45pm, July-Aug. M-F 8:30am-2:45pm.) **Postal Code:** 31001.

[icons] ACCOMMODATIONS AND FOOD. Book rooms up to a year ahead for *San Fermín*, and expect to pay up to four times the normal price. Check the newspaper *Diario de Navarra* for *casas particulares* (private homes that rent rooms). Be aware, though, that some owners prefer Spanish guests. Roomless backpackers are forced to fluff up their sweatshirts and sleep outside. Stay in large groups, and if you can't store your backpack, sleep on top of it. Budget accommodations line **Calle San Gregorio** and **Calle San Nicolás** off Pl. del Castillo. Deep within the *casco antiguo* (Old Town), **Pensión Eslava ❶**, C. Hilarión Eslava 13, 2nd fl., is quieter and less crowded than other *pensiones*. Older rooms have a balcony and shared bath. (☎22 15 58. Singles €10-15; doubles €20-30, during *San Fermín* €100. Cash only.) To get to **Camping Ezcaba ❶**, 7km from the city in Eusa, take city bus line 4-V (4 per day, 26 per day during *San Fermín*) from Pl. de las Merindades. (☎33 03 15. €4.50 per person, €4.80 per tent, €4.30 per car. *San Fermín* €9 per person, €8 per tent. MC/V.) **Calle Navarrería** and **Paseo de Sarasate** are home to good *bocadillo* bars. **Café-Bar Iruña ❸**, Pl. del Castillo, is the former casino made famous in Hemingway's *The Sun Also Rises*. The *menú* (€12) is required if eating at a table, but you can have drinks at the bar or terrace. (☎22 20 64. Open M-Th 8am-11pm, F 8am-2am, Sa 9am-2am, Su 9am-11pm. MC/V.) Get groceries at **Vendi Supermarket,** C. Hilarión Eslava and C. Mayor. (☎948 22 15 55. Open M-F 9am-2pm and 5:30-7:30pm, Sa 9am-2pm; *San Fermín* M-Sa 9am-2pm. MC/V.)

[icons] SIGHTS AND NIGHTLIFE. Pamplona's rich architectural legacy is reason enough to visit during the 51 other weeks of the year. The restored 14th-century Gothic **Catedral de Santa María,** at the end of C. Navarrería, is one of only four cathedrals of its kind in Europe. (☎22 29 90. Open M-F 10am-2pm and 4-7pm, Sa 10am-2pm. Free.) The walls of the pentagonal ■Ciudadela enclose free art exhibits, various summer concerts, and an amazing *San Fermín* fireworks display. Follow Po. de Sarasate to its end and go right on C. Navas de Tolosa, then take the next left onto C. Chinchilla and follow it to its end. (☎22 82 37. Open M-Sa 7:30am-9:30pm, Su 9am-9:30pm. Closed for *San Fermín*. Free.) At night, a young crowd boozes up in the *casco antiguo*, particularly along **Calle San Nicolás, Calle Jarauta,** and **Calle San Gregorio,** before hitting the **Travesía de Bayona,** a plaza of bars and *discotecas*.

■**FIESTA DE SAN FERMÍN (JULY 6-14, 2008).** Visitors overcrowd the city as it delivers an eight-day frenzy of bullfights, concerts, dancing, fireworks, parades, parties, and wine in what is perhaps Europe's premier party. Pamplonese, clad in white with red sashes and bandanas, throw themselves into the merry-making, displaying obscene levels of both physical stamina and alcohol tolerance. *El encierro,* or "The Running of the Bulls," is the highlight of *San Fermines;* the first *encierro* takes place on July 7 at 8am and is repeated at 8am every day for the next seven days. Hundreds of bleary-eyed, hungover, hyper-adrenalized runners flee from large bulls as bystanders cheer from balconies, barricades, doorways, and windows. Both the bulls and the mob are dangerous; terrified runners react without concern for those around them. To participate in the bullring excitement without the risk of the *encierro*, onlookers should arrive at 6:45am. Tickets for the *grada* section of the ring are available at 7am in the bullring box office (July 7, 8 and 14 €5.50, July 9-13 €4.50). You can watch for free, but the free section is overcrowded, making it hard to see and breathe. To watch a **bullfight,** wait in the line that forms at the bullring around 7:30pm. As one fight ends, the next day's tickets go on sale. (Tickets from €10; check www.feriadeltoro.com for details.) Tickets are incredibly hard to get at face value, as over 90% belong to season holders. Once the running ends, insanity spills into the streets and builds until nightfall, when it explodes with singing in bars, dancing in alleyways, spontaneous parades, and a no-holds-barred party in **Plaza del Castillo.**

RUNNING SCARED. So, you're going to run, and nobody's going to stop you. Because nobody—except the angry, angry bulls—wants to see you get seriously injured, here are a few words of *San Fermín* wisdom:

1. Research the *encierro* before you run; the tourist office has a pamphlet that outlines the route and offers tips for the inexperienced. Running the entire 850m course is highly inadvisable; it would mean 2-8min. of evading 6 bulls moving at 24kph (15mph). Instead, pick a 50m stretch.

2. Don't stay up all night drinking and carousing. Experienced runners get lots of sleep the night before and arrive at the course around 6:30am.

3. Take a fashion tip from the locals: wear the traditonal white-and-red outfit with closed-toe shoes. Ditch the baggy clothes, backpacks, and cameras.

4. Give up on getting near the bulls and concentrate on getting to the bullring in one piece. Though some whack the bulls with rolled newspapers, runners should never distract or touch the animals.

5. Never stop in doorways, alleys, or corners; you can be trapped and killed.

6. Run in a straight line; if you cut someone off, they can easily fall.

7. Be particularly wary of isolated bulls—they seek company in the crowds. In 2007, 13 runners were seriously injured by a bull who separated from the pack.

8. If you fall, stay down. Curl up into a fetal position, lock your hands behind your head, and do not get up until the clatter of hooves has passed.

SPAIN

BASQUE COUNTRY (PAÍS VASCO)

The varied landscape of Spain's Basque Country combines energetic cities, lush hills, industrial wastelands, and fishing villages. Many believe that the strongly nationalistic Basques are the native people of Iberia, as their culture and language cannot be traced to any known source.

SAN SEBASTIÁN (DONOSTIA)   ☎943

Glittering on the shores of the Cantabrian Sea, coolly elegant San Sebastián (pop. 185,000) is known for its world-famous bars, beaches, and scenery. Locals and travelers consume *pintxos* (tapas) and drinks in the *parte vieja* (Old Town), which claims the most bars per square meter in the world. Residents and posters provide a constant reminder: you're not in Spain, you're in Basque Country.

TRANSPORTATION. RENFE trains (☎902 24 02 02) run from Estación del Norte, Po. de Francia, to Barcelona (8½hr., 1-2 per day, €37-47), Madrid (8hr., 2 per day, €37-48), and Salamanca (6½hr., 2 per day, €31). Estación de Amara runs *cercanías* to Bilbao (2½hr., 1 per hr., €6). San Sebastián has no **bus** station, only a platform and ticket windows at Av. de Sancho el Sabio 31-33 and Po. de Vizcaya 16. Buses run to: Barcelona (7hr., 3 per day, €28); Bilbao (1¼hr., 1-2 per hr., €9); Madrid (6hr., 7-9 per day, €29); Pamplona (1hr., 6-10 per day, €6.20).

ORIENTATION AND PRACTICAL INFORMATION. The **Río Urumea** splits San Sebastián down the middle, with the **parte vieja** (Old Town) to the east and **El Centro** (the new downtown) to the west, separated by the wide walkway **Alameda del Boulevard.** The city center, most monuments, and the popular beaches **Playa de la Concha** and **Playa de Ondarreta** also line the peninsula on the western side of the river. At the tip of the peninsula rises **Monte Urgull.** The **bus platform** is south of the city center on Pl. Pío XII. To get to the *parte vieja* from the train station, cross the Puente María Cristina and turn right at the fountain. Continue four blocks north to Av. de la Libertad, then turn left and follow it to the port; the *parte vieja* fans out to the right and Playa de la Concha sits to the left.

The **tourist office** is at C. Reina Regente 3, on the edge of the *parte vieja.* (☎48 11 66; www.sansebastianturismo.com. Open July-Aug. M-Sa 9am-8pm, Su 10am-2pm and 3:30-7pm; June 15-Aug. M-Sa 9am-8pm, Su 10am-2pm; Oct.-May M-Sa 9am-1:30pm and 3:30-7pm, Su 10am-2pm.) **Luggage storage** is available at Estación del Norte. (€3 per day. Open daily 7am-11pm.) Free **Internet** is at **Biblioteca Central,** Pl. Ajuntamiento. (45min. max. Open M-F 10am–8:30pm, Sa 10am-2pm and 4:30-8pm.) The **post office** is behind the cathedral on C. Urdaneta. (☎902 19 71 97. Open M-F 10am-8:30pm, Sa 10am-2pm.) **Postal Code: 20006.**

ACCOMMODATIONS AND FOOD. *Pensiones* are scattered throughout the streets of the noisy *parte vieja.* For a more restful night's sleep, look for hostels and *pensiones* on the outskirts of El Centro. **Pensión Amaiur ❷**, C. 31 de Agosto 44, 2nd fl., offers lovely rooms in an historic house. (☎42 96 54; www.pensionamaiur.com. Internet €1 per 18min. Singles €24-42; doubles €36-60; triples €54-80; quads €65-96. AmEx/MC/V.) **Pensión San Lorenzo ❷**, C. San Lorenzo 2, off C. San Juani, has sunny rooms with fridge and private bath. (☎42 55 16; www.pensionsanlorenzo.com. Internet €1.50 per hr.; free Wi-Fi. Singles available Oct.-May €20; doubles year-round €28-50.) **Pensión La Perla ❸**, C. Loiola 10, 2nd fl., has balconies, private baths, and hardwood floors in each room. (☎42 81 23; www.pensionlaperla.com. Singles €25-35; doubles €35-55. Cash only.)

Pintxos (tapas), washed down with the fizzy regional white wine *txakoli*, are a religion in San Sebastián. Choose from a selection of *bocadillos* (€3-3.50), *pintxos* (€1.20-2), and *raciones* (small dishes; €3-5) at **Juantxo ❶**, C. Esterlines.

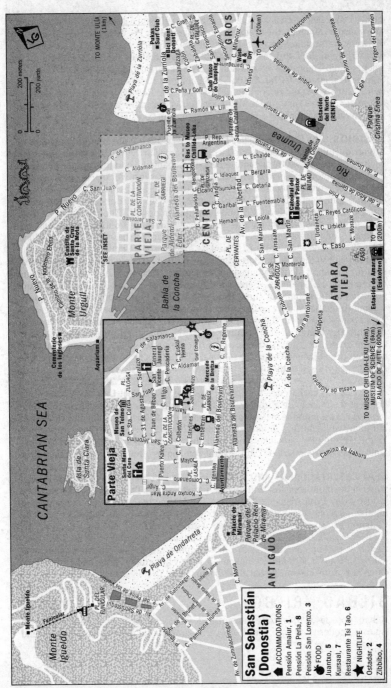

San Sebastián (Donostia)

ACCOMMODATIONS
Pensión Amaiur, 1
Pensión La Perla, 8
Pensión San Lorenzo, 3

FOOD
Juantxo, 5
Kursaal, 7
Restaurante Tsi Tao, 6

NIGHTLIFE
Ostadar, 2
Zibbibo, 4

Parte Vieja

(☎ 42 74 05. Open M-Th 9am-11:30pm, F-Su 9am-1:45am. Cash only.) Treat yourself to a gourmet lunch on the breezy patio of **Kursaal ❹**, Po. de la Zurriola 1. (☎ 00 31 62; www.restaurantekursaal.com. M-F lunch cafeteria *menú* from €19. Entrees €20-30. Open Sept.-July W-Sa 1:30-3:30pm and 8:30-10:30pm, Tu and Su 1:30-3:30pm; Aug. Tu-Sa 1:30-3:30pm and 8:30-10:30pm, Su 1:30-3:30pm. AmEx/MC/V.) Stylish **Restaurante Tsi Tao ❸**, Po. de Salamanca 1, serves filling Asian cuisine. (☎ 42 42 05; www.tsitao.com. Lunch *menú* €13. Reserve ahead. Open daily 1-3:30pm and 8:30-11pm. AmEx/MC/V. Find groceries at the **Mercado de la Bretxa**, in an underground shopping center. (Open M-Sa 8am-9pm.)

◙ SIGHTS. The ▓**Museo Chillida-Leku** houses a large collection of the works of Eduardo Chillida, San Sebastián's contemporary art guru. His stone and steel sculptures are spread throughout a peaceful, spacious outdoor garden. The 16th-century farmhouse displays some of the artist's earliest works. (Bo. Jauregui 66. ☎ 33 60 06; www.museochillidaleku.com. Open July-Aug. M-Sa 10:30am-8pm, Su 10:30am-3pm; Sept.-June M, W-Su 10:30am-3pm. Walking tours and 45min. audio tours included in admission. €8, under 12 and seniors €6.) Though the views from both of San Sebastián's mountains are spectacular, those from ▓**Monte Igueldo** are superior. The sidewalk from the city ends just before the base of Monte Igueldo at Eduardo Chillida's sculpture *El Peine de los Vientos* (Comb of the Winds). The road leading to the top, bordered by a low cliffside stone wall, is a favorite local spot for romantic picnics at sunset. A **funicular** (€1.20, 4 per hr.) runs to the summit. (☎ 21 02 11. Open June-Sept. daily 10am-10pm; Oct. and Jan.-May M-F 11am-6pm, Sa-Su 11am-8pm; Apr.-June M-F 11am-8pm, Sa 11am-10pm, Su 10am-10pm.)

Fancy buildings sprang up like wildflowers after Queen Isabel II began vacationing in San Sebastián in the mid-19th century. The **Palacio de Miramar** has passed through the hands of the Spanish court, Napoleon III, and Bismarck; it is now managed by the *Ayuntamiento* (local municipality), but you can stroll through the adjacent **Parque de Miramar.** The other royal residence, **Palacio de Aiete,** is also closed to the public, but its garden is not. (Head up Cta. de Aldapeta or take bus #19 or 31. Grounds open daily June-Sept. 8am-9pm, Oct.-May 8am-7pm. Free.)

Playa de la Concha curves from the port to the **Pico del Loro,** the promontory home of the Palacio de Miramar. The flat beach disappears during high tide. Sunbathers crowd onto the smaller and steeper **Playa de Ondarreta,** beyond Palacio de Miramar, while surfers flock to **Playa de la Zurriola,** across the river from Monte Urgull. In summer, picnickers head for the **Isla de Santa Clara.** (Motorboat ferry 5min., 2 per hr., round-trip €3.30.) Several companies offer sporting activities.

◪◩ ENTERTAINMENT AND NIGHTLIFE. The *parte vieja* pulls out all the stops in the months of July and August, particularly on **Calle Fermín Calbetón,** three blocks away from Alameda del Boulevard. During the year, when students outnumber backpackers, nightlife moves beyond the *parte vieja*. **Ostadar,** C. Fermín Calbetón 13, attracts locals and tourists with its cheap beer and hip decor. (☎ 42 62 78. Beer €2. Mixed drinks €5. Open daily 5pm-3am. Cash only.) **Zibbibo,** Pl. de Sarriegi 8, is perhaps San Sebastián's most popular dance club among young backpackers. (☎ 42 53 34. 2-pint Heineken €5. Happy hour daily 7-9pm and 10-11:30pm. Open M-W 4pm-2:30am, Th-Sa 4pm-3:30am. MC/V.)

BILBAO (BILBO)   ☎ 944

Bilbao (pop. 354,000) is a city transformed. What was once a gritty industrial town is now a modern city with wide boulevards, grand buildings, expansive parks, and an efficient subway system. The shining Guggenheim Museum has been the most visible contribution to Bilbao's rise to international prominence, but there is more to Bilbao than its oddly shaped claim to fame.

▐▋ TRANSPORTATION AND PRACTICAL INFORMATION. To reach the **airport (BIO; ☎86 96 64)**, 25km from Bilbao, take the Bizkai bus (☎902 22 22 65) marked *Aeropuerto* from the Termibús terminal or Pl. Moyúa (line A-3247; 25min., 2 per hr., €1.10). RENFE **trains** (☎902 24 02 02) leave from Estación de Abando, Pl. Circular 2, for Barcelona (9-10hr., 2 per day, €38-49), Madrid (6hr., 2 per day, €37-42), and Salamanca (5hr., 2pm, €27). Trains run between Bilboa's Estación de Atxuri and San Sebastián (2¾hr., 17-18 per day) via Guernica. Most **bus** companies leave from Termibús, C. Gurtubay 1 (☎39 52 05; M: San Mamés), for: Barcelona (7¼hr., 4 per day, €39); Madrid (4-5hr., 10-18 per day, €25); Pamplona (2hr., 4-6 per day, €12); San Sebastián (1¼hr., 1-2 per hr., €8.70).

The city's major thoroughfare, **Gran Vía de Don Diego López de Haro** connects three of Bilbao's main plazas. Heading east from Pl. de Sagrado Corazón, Gran Vía continues through the central Pl. Moyúa and ends at Pl. Circular. Past Pl. Circular, cross the Río de Bilbao on **Puente del Arenal** to arrive in **Plaza de Arriaga,** the entrance to the *casco viejo* and **Plaza Nueva.** The **tourist office** is at Pl. Ensanche 11. (☎79 57 60; www.bilbao.net/bilbaoturismo. Open M-F 9am-2pm and 4-7:30pm.) **Net House,** C. Villariás 6, has **Internet.** (☎23 71 53. €1.50 per 1st 30min., €0.05 per min. thereafter. Open daily 9am-11pm.) **Postal Code:** 48008.

▐▐ ACCOMMODATIONS AND FOOD. Plaza Arriaga and **Calle Arenal** have many budget accommodations, while upscale hotels are in the new city off **Gran Vía.** Rates climb during *Semana Grande.* **Iturrienea Ostatua ❸,** C. Santa Maria 14 (☎16 15 00; www.iturrieneaostatua.com) is in the heart of the *casco viejo.* (All rooms with private bath and TV, some with balcony. Breakfast €8. Singles €50; doubles €60-66; triples €80. MC/V.) **Pensión Méndez ❷,** C. Sta. María 13, 4th fl., offers cheery rooms with balconies. (☎16 03 64. Singles €25; doubles €35; triples €50. MC/V.) Restaurants and bars in the *casco viejo* offer a wide selection of local dishes, *pintxos* (tapas), and *bocadillos.* The new city has even more variety. **▊Restaurante Peruano Ají Colorado ❸,** C. Barrenkale 5, specializes in traditional Andean *ceviche* (marinated raw fish; €10-13). (☎15 22 09. M-F lunch *menú* €12. Open Tu-Sa 1:30-4pm and 9-11pm, Su 1:30-4pm. MC/V.) **Agape ❷,** C. Hernani 13, has creative modern Spanish cuisine. (☎16 05 06. Daily lunchtime *menú* €9.50. Open W-Sa 1-4pm and 8-11pm, Tue 1-4pm. MC/V.) **Mercado de la Ribera,** by the river on C. Pelota, is the biggest indoor market in Spain. (Open M-Th and Sa 8am-2pm, F 8am-2:30pm and 4:30-7:30pm.) Get groceries at **Champion,** Pl. Santos Juanes, past Mercado de la Ribera. (Open M-Sa 9am-9:30pm. AmEx/MC/V.)

▐ SIGHTS. Frank Gehry's **▊Museo Guggenheim Bilbao,** Av. Abandoibarra 2, is awe-inspiring and has catapulted Bilbao straight into cultural stardom. Sheathed in titanium, limestone, and fluid glass, the €95 million building is said to resemble either an iridescent fish or a blossoming flower. The museum hosts rotating exhibits drawn from the Guggenheim Foundation's often eccentric collection; don't be surprised if you are asked to take your shoes off, lie on the floor, or even sing throughout your visit. (☎35 90 80; www.guggenheim-bilbao.es. Wheelchair-accessible. Admission includes English-language guided tours Tu-Su 11am, 12:30, 4:30, 6:30pm; sign up 30min. before tour at the info desk. Open July-Aug. daily 10am-8pm; Sept.-June Tu-Su 10am-8pm. €13, students €7.50, under 12 free.) Although the **▊Museo de Bellas Artes,** Pl. del Museo 2, can't boast the name recognition of the

THE TRAGEDY OF GUERNICA

Billing itself today as a "City of Peace," Guernica was once the site of one of the most horrifying displays of absolute warfare. The historic Basque town was almost entirely wiped out on April 26, 1937, as bomb after bomb was dropped on the town for more than 3hr., until over 100,000 lb. of explosives had been unloaded on the battered buildings.

The bombardment was carried out at the behest of Generalissimo Francisco Franco by the German Condor Legion, eager to test out its new strategy of carpet-bombing civilian populations to achieve quick military victories. The Spanish leader-to-be wanted to make an example of Guernica and to nip any potential Basque uprising in the bud. While the town itself had no real strategic military significance, both Franco and the Germans had something to gain from the utterly demoralizing blow it delivered.

Survivors from that Monday, a market day, recall being chased in the fields and forced into their homes by machine-gun fire, only to have the buildings above them torn apart by the bombs moments later. One woman recalled fires burning in the town for three days after the bombardment. When it was all over, over three-quarters of the town had been destroyed, leaving only the *Casa de Juntas* (the Biscayan assembly chamber), the church of Santa Maria, and the symbolic oak tree of Guer-

Guggenheim, it wins the favor of locals. The museum has an impressive collection of 12th- to 20th-century art, including excellent 15th- to 17th-century Flemish paintings, canvases by Basque artists, and works by Mary Cassatt, El Greco, Gauguin, Goya, and Velázquez. Take C. Elcano to Pl. del Museo or bus #10 from Pte. del Arenal. (☎39 60 60, guided tours 39 61 37. Open Tu-Sa 10am-8pm, Su 10am-2pm. €5, students and seniors €4, under 12 and W free.)

🎭 ENTERTAINMENT AND NIGHTLIFE. In the *casco viejo*, locals spill out into the streets to sip their *txikitos* (chee-KEE-tos; small glasses of wine), especially on **Calle Barrenkale**, one of Bilbao's seven original streets. A young crowd fill **Calle Licenciado Poza** on the west side of town, especially between C. General Concha and Alameda de Recalde. Mellow **Alambique**, Alda. Urquijo 37, provides elegant seating and a chance for conversation under chandeliers and photos of old Bilbao. (☎43 41 88. Beer €2-3. Open M-Th 8am-2am, F-Sa 8am-3am, Su 5pm-3am.) The massive *fiesta* in honor of *Nuestra Señora de Begoña* (Our Lady of Begoña)—complete with bullfighting, concerts, fireworks, and theater—occurs during **Semana Grande** (Aug. 17-25, 2008).

🗺 DAYTRIP FROM BILBAO: GUERNICA. Founded in 1366, Guernica (Gernika; pop. 16,000) long served as the ceremonial seat of the Basque Country. On April 26, 1937, at the behest of General Franco, the Nazi "Condor Legion" dropped 29,000kg of explosives on Guernica, obliterating 70% of the city in three hours. The atrocity, which killed nearly 2000 people, is immortalized in Pablo Picasso's masterpiece, **Guernica** (p. 903). The thought-provoking **Guernica Peace Museum**, Pl. Foru 1, features a variety of multimedia exhibits. From the train station, walk two blocks up C. Adolfo Urioste and turn right on C. Artekalea. (☎946 27 02 13. *Open July-Aug. Tu-Sa 10am-8pm, Su 10am-2pm; Sept.-June Tu-Sa 10am-2pm and 4-7pm, Su 10am-2pm. English-language tours noon and 5pm. €4, students and seniors €2.)* **El Árbol**, a 300-year-old oak trunk encased in stone columns, marks the former political center of the *País Vasco*. **Trains** (☎902 54 32 10; www.euskotren.es) head to Bilbao (45min., 1-2 per hr., €2.25). Bizkai Bus (☎902 22 22 65) runs frequent, convenient **buses** between Guernica and Bilbao's Estación Abando; buses leave from Hdo. Amezaga in front of the Bilbao RENFE station. (Lines A-3514 and A-3515; 45min., 2-4 per hr., €2.20.) To reach the **tourist office**, C. Artekale 8, from the train station, walk three blocks up C. Adolfo Urioste, turn right on C. Barrenkale, go left at the alleyway, and look for the signs. (☎946 25 58 92; www.gernika-lumo.net. Open July-Aug. M-Sa 10am-7pm, Su 10am-2pm; Sept.-June M-Sa 10am-2pm and 4-7pm, Su 10am-2pm.)

GALICIA (GALIZA)

If, as the Galician saying goes, "rain is art," then there is no gallery more beautiful than the Northwest's misty skies. Often veiled in silvery drizzle, it is a province of fern-laden eucalyptus woods, slate-roofed fishing villages, and endless white beaches. Locals speak *Gallego*, a linguistic hybrid of Castilian and Portuguese.

SANTIAGO DE COMPOSTELA ☎981

Santiago (pop. 94,000) is a city of song; its plazas are filled with roving *guita* players and outdoor operas. However, as the terminus of the ancient **Camino de Santiago** (Way of St. James), Santiago is also a city of pilgrimage. Each of the four facades of Santiago's ▧**cathedral** is a masterpiece of a different era, with entrances opening to four different plazas: Inmaculada, Obradoiro, Praterías, and Quintana. The **Obradoiro** is considered one of the most beautiful squares in the world. (☎58 35 48. Open daily 7am-9pm. Free.) Entrance to the cathedral **museums** includes a visit to the archaeology rooms, archives, chapter house, cloister, library, relics, tapestry room, and treasury. (☎58 11 55. Open June-Sept. M-Sa 10am-2pm and 4-8pm, Su and holidays 10am-2pm; Oct.-May M-Sa 10am-1:30pm and 4-6:30pm, Su and holidays 10am-1:30pm. €5, students €3.)

Nearly every street in the *ciudad vieja* (Old Town) has at least one *pensión*. ▧**Hospedaje Ramos ❷**, R. da Raíña 18, 2nd fl., has well-lit rooms with shining floors and private baths. Reserve two weeks ahead in summer. (☎58 18 59. Singles €22; doubles €35. Cash only.) Most restaurants are on R. do Vilar, R. do Franco, R. Nova, and R. da Raíña. **A Tulla ❷**, R. de Entrerúas 1, is a small family restaurant serving fresh seafood, accessible only through an alley between R. do Vilar and R. Nova. (☎58 08 89. Entrees €6.50-8.50. Open M-Sa 1-4pm and 8:30pm-midnight. MC/V.) Santiago's **mercado** (market) is located between Pl. San Felix and Convento de Santo Agustín. (Open M-Sa 8am-2pm.) At night, take R. Montero Ríos to the bars and clubs off **Praza Roxa** to party with local students. The witchcraft-themed ▧**Casa das Crechas,** Vía Sacra 3, is renowned for live jazz and Galician folk concerts. (☎56 07 51. Beer €2. Open daily in summer noon-4am; winter 4pm-3am.)

Trains (☎902 24 02 02) run from R. do Hórreo to Bilbao (10¾hr., 1 per day, €41) (6½hr., €29) and

nica untouched. Hundreds had been killed in the attack and many thousands more injured. In just a few hours, Guernica had been transformed into a smoldering shell of its former self.

Guernica was rebuilt over the following five years, but it has remained a symbol of the atrocities of warfare and indiscriminate killing. Many pictures, sketches, and paintings have attempted to capture this nightmarish day. In a painting now at the Guernica Peace Museum (p. 954), Sofia Gandarias depicted women holding dead children underneath the words "*y del cielo llovía sangre*" (and from the sky rained blood). Picasso's famous masterpiece, Guernica, which now hangs in Madrid's Reina Sofia (p. 903), captured the horror of that day, and brought Guernica's tragedy lasting widespread international recognition. When asked by a German ambassador, "Did you do this?" Picasso answered simply, "No, you did."

Today, however, Guernica is looking to move beyond its devastating past and become a herald of peace and reconciliation throughout the world. In 1989, the town received a public apology from the president of Germany for his country's role in the attack, and it has since adopted the motto "*renunciar a olvidar, renunciar a la venganza*" (renounce forgetfulness, renounce vengeance). Once the setting for some of humanity's darkest moments, Guernica is now looking to light the way for the rest of the world.

THE LOCAL STORY

SHELLS BY THE SEASHORE

If you're anywhere on the Camino de Santiago, you're likely to find scallop shells on roadways, doorways to lodgings, and backpacks. The scallop shell is a symbol of the ancient pilgrimage, but its use dates back to pre-Christian times.

Long before the Romans and Christianity settled in what today is Spain and Portugal, the Iberian Peninsula was populated by various tribes, including the Celts (known in Spain as the Castros). Before the route became a Christian pilgrimage to St. James's remains in the Cathedral of Santiago de Compostela, it was a pagan route. One theory claims that the route was part of a fertility ritual and the scallop shell the symbol of fertility. Another suggests that the shell, symbolic of the setting sun which it resembles, was part of a Celtic death pilgrimage through northern Spain, westwards with the setting sun to Cabo Fisterra and the Costa de Morta—the End of the World and the Coast of Death.

During the Middle Ages, when the route became popular among devout Christians, pilgrims would bring back Galician scallop shells as proof that they completed their journey. Today, the scallop shell continues to point the way towards Santiago.

Madrid (8hr., 2 per day, €43-67). To reach the city, take bus #6 to Pr. de Galicia. **Buses** (☎54 24 16) run from R. de Rodríguez to Madrid (8-9hr.; 4-6 per day; €39-56) and San Sebastián (13½hr., 2 per day, €54-102). To get to the Old Town from the bus station, take bus #5 or 10. The **tourist office** is at R. do Vilar 63. (☎55 51 29; www.santiagoturismo.com. Open daily June-Sept. 9am-9pm; Oct.-May 9am-2pm and 4-7pm.) **Postal Code:** 15703.

BALEARIC ISLANDS ☎971

While all of the *Islas Baleares* are famous for their beautiful beaches and landscapes, each island has its own character. Mallorca absorbs the bulk of moneyed, package-tour invaders, Ibiza has perhaps the best nightlife in Europe, and quieter Menorca offers tranquil white beaches, hidden coves, and Bronze Age megaliths.

🧭 TRANSPORTATION

Flying is the easiest way to reach the islands. Students with an ISIC can often get discounts from **Iberia** (☎902 40 05 00; www.iberia.com), which flies to Ibiza and Palma de Mallorca from Barcelona (40min., €80) and Madrid (1hr., €50). **Air Europa** (☎902 40 15 01; www.air-europa.com), **Spanair** (☎902 92 91 91; www.spanair.com), and **Vueling** (☎902 33 39 33; www.vueling.com) offer budget flights to and between the islands (€20-50). Another option is a **charter flight,** which may include a week's stay in a hotel; some companies, called *mayoristas,* sell left-over spots on package-tour flights as "seat-only" (find them through travel agencies).

Ferries to the islands are less popular and take longer. **Trasmediterránea** (☎902 45 46 45; www.tras-mediterranea.com) departs from Barcelona's Estació Marítima Moll and Valencia's Estació Marítima for Ibiza, Mallorca, and Menorca (€69-110). Fares between the islands run €28-82. **Buquebus** (☎902 41 42 42) has fast catamaran service between Barcelona and Palma de Mallorca (4hr., 2 per day, €11-150). The three major islands have extensive **bus** systems with fares ranging €1.20-7, though transportation comes to a halt on Sundays in most locations; check schedules. **Car** rental costs about €40 per day, **mopeds** €30, and **bikes** €6-15.

🏖 MALLORCA

A favorite of Spain's royal family, Mallorca has long attracted the rich and famous. Lemon groves and olive trees adorn the jagged cliffs of the northern coast, while lazy beaches sink into calm bays to the east. The capital of the Balearics, **Palma** (pop. 375,000) is filled with Brits and Germans, but still retains genuine local flavor. In many of its cafes and traditional tapas bars, the native dialect of *mallorquí* is the only language heard. The tourist office distributes a list of over 40 nearby **beaches.** Popular choices are **El Arenal** (bus #15), 11km southeast of town toward the airport, **Cala Major** (bus #3), and **Illetes** (bus #3).

Budget accommodations are scarce and must be reserved weeks ahead. **Hostal Ritzi ❸,** C. Apuntadors 6, stands a block away from Pl. de la Reina. Located in the culinary heart of the *casco antiguo,* this hostel with old-fashioned rooms is flanked by the area's best bars and eateries. (☎71 46 10. Breakfast included. Laundry €7. Singles €30; doubles €45, with shower €48, with bath €52. Cash only.) Palma's many round-the-clock ethnic restaurants are paradise for those sick of tapas. Budget travelers head to the crooked streets between Pl. de la Reina and Pl. Llotja. Try the *frito mallorquín* (fried lamb liver with potato, peppers, and herbs) at ▓**Sa Premsa ❶,** Pl. Obispo, a cavernous restaurant that serves local cuisine. (☎72 35 29; www.cellersapremsa.com. ½-portions €3.70-6.40. Entrees €3.75-8.50. Open M-Sa noon-4pm and 7:30-11:30pm. MC/V.)

A law requiring downtown bars to close by 1am during the week and 3am on weekends has shifted the late-night action to the waterfront. ▓**The Soho,** Av. Argentina 5, is a hip bar that plays rock and techno. (Beer €1-2.50. Open daily 8pm-2am. MC/V, min. €5.) Palma's clubbers start their night in the *bares-musicales* lining the **Passeig Marítim** strip, then move on to *discotecas* around 3am. **Tito's,** in a gorgeous Art Deco palace on Pg. Marítim, is the city's coolest club, sporting fountains, a glass elevator, a view of the water, and beautiful people. (Beer €3. Mixed drinks €5. Cover €15-18, includes 1 drink. Open daily 11pm-6:30am. MC/V.) The **tourist office** is in Pl. d'Espanya (bus #1; 15min. 3 per hr. €1.10. ☎22 59 00; www.a-palma.es. Open daily 9am-8pm.) **Postal Code:** 07003.

▓ IBIZA

Nowhere on Earth are decadence, opulence, and hedonism celebrated as religiously as on the glamorous island of Ibiza (pop. 84,000). Disco-goers, fashion gurus, movie stars, and party-hungry backpackers arrive to immerse themselves in the island's outrageous clubs and gorgeous beaches. Only one of Ibiza's beaches, **Figueretes,** is within walking distance of **Eivissa** (Ibiza City), but most, including bar-lined **Platja d'en Bossa,** are a bike or bus ride away. The best beach near the city is ▓**Playa de ses Salinas.** (Bus #11 runs to Salinas from Av. d'Isidor Macabich.)

THE LOCAL STORY

ROCKCREATION

Mallorca's terrain is a dramatic mosaic of azure coastline, smooth limestone, vaulting hillsides, and sharp cliffs. While sun-seeking tourists flock to the island's beaches during the summer, packs of gung-ho daredevils come in cooler seasons for an island adventure beyond the disco strips of Palma: a chance to conquer the world-famous rock climbing routes of Mallorca.

Mallorca's efficient bus routes and network of cliffsides make climbing an easy getaway. The island's climbing terrain includes more than 900 routes and over 20 crags. Difficulty ranges from grades 4 to 8c, accommodating everyone from family groups to intrepid individual climbers.

The eastern part of the island has the easiest routes. Many travelers looking for routes with a range of difficulty take the vintage train to Soller, where many climbs and hikes are available.

One of the most popular climbing areas is Sa Gubia, a gorge with more routes and variation than anywhere else on the island. Cala Magraner is also a popular destination for climbers with children. Its beachside locale, caves, and long walls are well-suited for neophytes.

For more information on rock climbing on Mallorca, check out www.rockandsun.com, www.mondaventura.com, or www.tramuntana-pursuits.com.

Cheap *hostales* in town are rare, especially in summer; reserve well ahead. Rooms to rent (*casa de huéspedes;* look for the letters "CH" in doorways) are a much better deal. **CH La Peña ❷,** C. La Virgen 76, is in an alley right beside the port. This house offers great, clean rooms at low prices. (☎ 19 02 40. Open June-Sept. Singles €23; doubles €32; triples €48. MC/V.) **La Bodeguita Del Medio ❶,** C. St. Cruz 15, has outdoor tables ideal for consuming beer (€3) and plates of paellas, *tortillas* (€6.40), and tapas. (☎ 39 92 90. Cash only.) The **Mercat Vell,** at the end of the bridge leading to D'alt Villa, sells meat and produce. (Open M-Sa 7am-7pm.)

The crowds return from the beaches by nightfall. The bar scene centers around **Carrer de Barcelona,** while **Carrer de la Verge** is the nexus of gay nightlife. The island's giant ■**discos** are world-famous—and outrageously expensive. Always be on the lookout for publicity flyers, which list the week or night's events and often double as a coupon for a discounts. The **Discobus** runs to major hot spots (leaves Eivissa from Av. d'Isidor Macabich; 1 per hr. 12:30-6:30am, €1.75). ■**Amnesia,** on the road to the city of San Antoni, has a phenomenal sound system and psychedelic lights. (☎ 19 80 41. W drag performances. Cover €20-50. Open daily midnight-8am.) World-famous **Pachá,** on Pg. Perimitral, is a 15min. walk or a 2min. cab ride from the port. (☎ 31 36 00; www.pacha.com. M "Release Yourself" night with up-and-coming DJs. Cover €45-60. Open daily midnight-7:30am.) Cap off your night in **Space,** on Platja d'en Bossa, which starts hopping around 8am, peaks mid-afternoon, and doesn't wind down until 5pm. (☎ 39 67 93; www.space-ibiza.es. Cover €30-60.) The **tourist office,** Pl. d'Antoni Riquer 2, is across from the Estació Marítima. (☎ 30 19 00. Open June-Nov. M-F 9am-9pm, Sa 9:30am-7:30pm; Dec.-May M-F 8:30am-3pm, Sa 10:30am-1pm.) **Postal Code:** 07800.

■ MENORCA

Menorca's (pop. 75,000) fantastic 200km of coastline, rustic landscapes, and picturesque towns draw ecologists, photographers, and sun-worshippers. Atop a steep bluff, **Mahón** (Maó; pop. 21,000) is the gateway to the island. The popular **beaches** outside Mahón are accessible by **bus.** Transportes Menorca buses leave from the bus station, up C. Vasallo at the far end of Pl. de s'Esplanada, for **Platges de Son Bou** (30min., 7 per day, €1.90), the island's largest beach, which spreads out into 4km of gorgeous but jam-packed sand on the southern shore. Autobuses Fornells **buses** leave Mahón for the breathtaking **Arenal d'en Castell** (30min., 2-5 per day, €1.90), while TMSA buses go to the heavily touristed **Cala'n Porter** (7 per day, €1.20). While there, don't miss the ■**Covas d'en Xoroi,** an amazing network of caves in the cliffs high above the sea. Naturally air-conditioned, the caves house several bars during the day (cover €3.50-9, includes 1 drink; open Apr.-Oct. daily 11am-11pm) and a crowded ambient disco at night. (☎ 37 72 36. Beer €3. Mixed drinks €5-8. Th foam parties. Cover €17-21. Open Apr.-Oct. daily 11pm-late.)

To get to the splashy rooms of **Posada Orsi ❷,** C. de la Infanta 19, from Pl. de s'Esplanada, take C. Moreres, which becomes C. Hannover; turn right at Pl. Constitució and follow C. Nou through Pl. Real. (☎ 36 47 51. Fans available on request. Singles €20-25; doubles €30-40, with shower €40-50. Cash only.) ■**Elefant ❷,** Moll. de Llevant 106, has sunset views and deliciously creative lunches. (☎ 676 89 24 23. Tapas €3.80-5. Entrees €8-14. Open M and W-Su noon-4pm and 7pm-midnight. Cash only.) The Mahón **tourist office** is at Moll. de Llevant 2. (☎ 35 59 52; www.e-menorca.org. Open M-F 8am-8:30pm, Sa 8am-1pm.) **Postal Code:** 07700.

SWEDEN (SVERIGE)

With the design world cooing over bright, blocky Swedish furniture and college students donning faux-designer wear from H&M, Scandinavia's largest nation has earned a reputation abroad for its chic, mass-marketable style. At home, Sweden's struggle to balance a market economy with its generous social welfare system stems from its belief that all citizens should have access to education and affordable health care. This neutral nation's zest for spending money on butter instead of guns has also shored up a strong sense of national unity, from Sámi reindeer herders in the Lappland wilderness to bankers in bustling Stockholm.

 DISCOVER SWEDEN: SUGGESTED ITINERARY

Plan three days in the capital city of **Stockholm** (p. 964), including one sunny afternoon out on the towns and beaches of the **Skärgård Archipelago** (p. 975). Daytrip north to the university town of **Uppsala** (p. 980), or take an eastbound ferry out to the island of **Gotland** (p. 977), where serene bike paths and medieval towns overlook the Baltic Sea. **Malmö** (p. 979) and **Lund** (p. 980) are not known for their serenity,

with clamorous ethnic markets in the former and booming student nightlife in the latter. Soak up some high culture in the museums of elegant **Gothenburg** (p. 983), then get ready to rough it on hikes out of **Åre** (p. 990) and **Örnsköldsvik** (p. 991). **Kiruna** (p. 993) is the end of the line up in mountainous Lappland, where ore miners and the indigenous Sami share vast stretches of Arctic wilderness.

ESSENTIALS

FACTS AND FIGURES

Official Name: Kingdom of Sweden.

Capital: Stockholm.

Major Cities: Gothenburg, Malmö.

Population: 9,067,000.

Land Area: 450,000 sq. km.

Time Zone: GMT +1.

Language: Swedish.

Religion: Lutheran (87%).

Income Tax: As high as 60% for top wage-earners. Ouch.

WHEN TO GO

The most popular months to visit Sweden are July and August, when temperatures average 20°C (68°F) in the south and 16°C (61°F) in the north. Travelers who arrive in May and early June can take advantage of low season prices and enjoy the spring wildflowers, but some attractions don't open until late June. The 24 hours of daylight known as the **midnight sun** are best experienced between early June and mid-July. In winter, keep an eye out for the **Northern Lights** and bring heavy cold-weather gear; temperatures hover around -5°C (23°F).

DOCUMENTS AND FORMALITIES

EMBASSIES AND CONSULATES. Foreign embassies are in Stockholm (p. 967). Swedish embassies abroad: **Australia,** 5 Turrana St., Yarralumla, Canberra, ACT, 2600 (☎2 62 70 27 00; www.swedenabroad.com/canberra); **Canada,** 377 Dalhousie St., Ottawa, ON, K1N 9N8 (☎613-241-8553; www.swedenabroad.com/ottawa); **Ireland,** 13-17 Dawson St., Dublin 2 (☎1 474 44 00; www.swedenabroad.com/dublin);

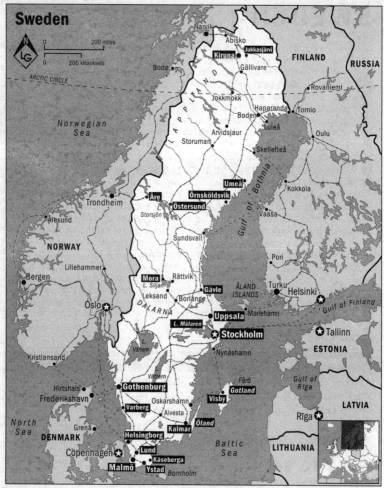

New Zealand, Vogel Building, Level 13, Aitken St., Wellington (☎4 499 9895; www.swedenabroad.com/canberra); **UK**, 11 Montagu Pl., London, W1H 2AL (☎020 79 17 64 00; www.swedenabroad.com/london); **US**, 901 30th St., NW, Washington, D.C., 20007 (☎202-467-2600; www.swedenabroad.com/washington).

VISA AND ENTRY INFORMATION. EU citizens do not need a visa. Citizens of Australia, Canada, New Zealand, and the US do not need a visa for stays of up to 90 days, beginning upon entry into any of the countries in the EU's freedom-of-movement zone. For more info, see p. 14. For stays longer than 90 days, all non-EU citizens need visas (around US$75), available at Swedish consulates or online at www.swedenabroad.com. For US citizens, visas are usually issued a few weeks after application submission.

TOURIST SERVICES AND MONEY

EMERGENCY | Ambulance, Fire, and **Police:** ☎112.

TOURIST OFFICES. There are two types of tourist offices in Sweden: those marked with a yellow and blue "i" have both local and national information, while those marked with a green "i" have information only on the town they serve. The Swedish Tourist Board can be found online at www.visitsweden.com.

MONEY. Swedish voters rejected the adoption of the euro as the country's currency in September 2003. The Swedish unit of currency remains the **krona (kr)**, plural kronor. One krona is equal to 100 öre, with standard denominations of 50 öre, 1kr, 5kr, and 10kr in coins, and 20kr, 50kr, 100kr, 500kr, and 1000kr in notes. Many **ATMs** do not accept non-Swedish debit cards. Banks and post offices exchange currency; expect a 20-35kr commission for cash, and 5-15kr for traveler's checks. **Forex** generally offers the best exchange rates, and has ATMs that accept foreign debit cards. Note that many Swedish ATMs do not accept PINs longer than four digits; if your PIN is longer than this, entering the first four digits of your PIN should work. Although a service charge is usually added to the bill at restaurants, **tipping** is becoming more common and a 7-10% tip is now considered standard. Tip taxi drivers 5-10%. For more info on money in Europe, see p. 16.

Sweden has a whopping 25% **value added tax (VAT)**, a sales tax applied to most goods and services. The prices given in *Let's Go* include VAT. In the airport upon exiting the EU, non-EU citizens can claim a refund on the tax paid for goods purchased at participating stores. Some stores may have minimum expenditure requirements for refunds; make sure to ask for a refund form when you pay. For more info on qualifying for a VAT refund, see p. 19.

SWEDISH KRONOR (KR)		
AUS$1 = 5.53KR	10KR = AUS$1.81
CDN$1 = 6.53KR	10KR = CDN$1.53
EUR€1 = 9.35KR	10KR = EUR€1.07
NZ$1 = 4.82KR	10KR = NZ$2.07
UK£1= 13.74KR	10KR = UK£0.73
US$1 = 6.93KR	10KR = US$1.44

TRANSPORTATION

BY PLANE. Most international flights land at **Arlanda Airport** in Stockholm (**ARN;** ☎797 6000; www.arlanda.com). Budget airlines, like **Ryanair**, fly out of **Västerås Airport (VST;** ☎21 805 600; www.stockholmvasteras.se) and Skavsta Airport (see p. 974 for more info), each located 1hr. from Stockholm. Other destinations in Sweden include **Gothenburg Airport (GSE)** and **Malmö-Sturup Airport (MMX)**. The main carrier in Sweden, **SAS** (☎08 797 4000, UK 0870 6072 7727, US 800-221-2350; www.scandinavian.net), offers youth fares for those under 26 on some regional flights. For more info on traveling by plane around Europe, see p. 43.

BY TRAIN. Statens Järnväger (SJ), the state railway company, runs trains throughout southern Sweden, and offers a 30% discount for travelers under 26 (☎0771 75 75 75; www.sj.se/english). Seat reservations (28-55kr) are required on **InterCity** and high-speed **X2000** trains; they are included in the ticket price but not in rail passes. On other routes, check to see how full the train is; don't bother with reservations on empty trains. In northern Sweden, **Connex** runs trains from Stockholm through

Umeå and Kiruna to Narvik, NOR (☎0771 26 00 00; https://bokning.connex.se/con-nexp/index_en.html). The 35min. trip over **Öresund Bridge** connecting Malmö to Copenhagen, DEN (70kr) is the fastest way to travel from continental Europe; reserve ahead. Timetables for all SJ and Connex trains are at www.resplus.se. **Eurail Passes** are valid on all of these trains. In the south, purple **Pågatågen** trains service local traffic between Helsingborg, Lund, Malmö, and Ystad; **ScanRail** and **Eurail Passes** are valid. You can also purchase tickets from special vending machines. The **ScanRail Pass** (www.scanrail.com) is good for rail travel through Denmark, Finland, Norway, and Sweden, and for many discounted ferry and bus fares. The pass is best purchased outside Scandinavia. Although they are available in Scandinavia, in this case passholders can only use three travel days in the country of purchase. For more info on traveling by train around Europe, see p. 46.

 THE RAIL DEAL. ScanRail passes purchased outside Scandinavia are much more flexible than ScanRail passes purchased once you arrive, and may be less expensive depending on the exchange rate. Check www.scanrail.com for more info on where to purchase passes at home.

BY BUS. In the north, buses may be a better option than trains. **Swebus** (☎08 546 300 00; www.swebus.se) is the main carrier nationwide. **Swebus Express** (☎7712 182 18, international 46 36 290 80 00; www.swebusexpress.se) serves the region around Stockholm and Gothenburg. **Biljettservice** (p. 966), inside Stockholm's City-terminalen, will reserve tickets for longer routes. Students and travelers under 26 get a 20% discount on express buses. Bicycles are not allowed on board.

BY FERRY. Ferries run from Stockholm (p. 966) to the Åland Islands, Gotland, Finland, and the Baltic states. Ystad (p. 982) sends several ferries a day to Born-holm, DEN. Ferries from Gothenburg (p. 983) serve Frederikshavn, DEN and Kiel, GER. Popular lines include **Tallinksilja**, Kungsg. 2 (☎08 22 21 40, US 800-533-3755 ext. 114; www.tallinksilja.com), and the **Viking Line** (☎08 452 40 00, US 800-843-0602; www.vikingline.fi). On Tallinksilja, both Scan- and Eurail Pass holders ride for free or at reduced rates. On Viking ferries, ScanRail holders get 50% off, and a Eurail Pass plus a train ticket entitles holders to a free passenger fare. (Mention this discount when booking.) Additionally, Viking offers "early bird" discounts of 15-50% for those who book at least 30 days in advance within Finland or Sweden.

BY CAR. Sweden honors foreign drivers' licenses for up to one year for visitors over 18. **Speed limits** are 110kph on expressways, 50kph in densely populated areas, and 70-90kph elsewhere. Headlights must be used at all times. Swedish roads are uncrowded and in good condition, but take extra care in winter weather and be wary of reindeer or elk in the road. Many gas stations are open until 10pm; after hours, look for cash-operated pumps marked *sedel automat*. For more info on car rental and driving in Europe, see p. 50.

BY BIKE AND THUMB. Bicycling is popular in Sweden. Paths are common, and both the **Sverigeleden** (National Route) and **Cykelspåret** (Bike Path) traverse the country. **Hitchhiking** is uncommon. Let's Go does not recommend hitchhiking.

KEEPING IN TOUCH

EMAIL AND THE INTERNET. There are a limited number of cybercafes in Stock-holm and other big cities. Expect to pay about 20kr per hr. In smaller towns, Inter-net is available for free at most tourist offices marked with the yellow and blue "i" (p. 961), as well as for a small fee at most public libraries.

TELEPHONE. Pay phones take credit cards and often accept phone cards (*Telefonkort*); buy them at newsstands or other shops (60kr and 100kr). Whenever possible, use a calling card for international phone calls, as long-distance rates for national phone services are often very high. Mobile phones are an increasingly popular and economical option. Major mobile carriers include **Telia, Tele2, Vodafone,** and **3.** Direct-dial access numbers for calling out of Sweden include: **AT&T Direct** (☎ 020 79 91 11); **British Telecom** (☎ 020 799 144); **Canada Direct** (☎ 020 79 90 15); **Telecom New Zealand** (☎ 020 799 064); **Telstra Australia** (☎ 020 799 061). For more info on calling home from Europe, see p. 28.

PHONE CODES	Country code: 46. International dialing prefix: 00. For more info on how to place international calls, see **Inside Back Cover.**

MAIL. From Sweden, it costs approximately 5kr to send a postcard or letter (up to 20g in mass) domestically, 10kr within Europe, and 10.20kr to the rest of the world. For more info, visit www.posten.se. To receive mail in Sweden, have mail delivered **Poste Restante.** Mail will go to the main post office unless you specify a subsidiary by street address. Address mail to be held according to the following example: First name, Last Name, Poste Restante, Postal Code, City, SWEDEN. Bring a passport to pick up your mail; there may be a small fee.

LANGUAGE. Although Sweden has no official language, Swedish is universally spoken. The region around Kiruna is home to a small minority of Finnish speakers, as well as 7000 speakers of the Sámi languages. Almost all Swedes speak English fluently. For basic Swedish words and phrases, see **Phrasebook: Swedish,** p. 1068.

ACCOMMODATIONS AND CAMPING

SWEDEN	❶	❷	❸	❹	❺
ACCOMMODATIONS	under 160kr	160-230kr	231-350kr	351-500kr	over 500kr

Youth hostels (*vandrarhem*) cost 120-200kr per night. The hostels run by the **Svenska Turistföreningen (STF)** and affiliated with HI are uniformly top-notch. nonmembers should expect to pay 200-240kr per night; HI members receive a 45kr discount (☎ 08 463 21 00; www.svenskaturistforeningen.se). STF also manages **mountain huts** in the northern wilds (150-350kr). Many **campgrounds** (tent sites 80-110kr; www.camping.se) offer **cottages** (*stugor*) for 100-300kr per person. International Camping Cards aren't valid in Sweden; **Swedish Camping Cards,** available at all SCR campgrounds, are mandatory (one-year pass 90kr). The Swedish **right of public access** (*allemansrätten*) means travelers can camp for free in the countryside, as long as they are roughly 150m away from private homes. Tents may be pitched in one location usually for no more than one or two days. Guidelines vary depending on the community. Visit www.allemansratten.se for more info.

FOOD AND DRINK

SWEDEN	❶	❷	❸	❹	❺
FOOD	under 50kr	50-75kr	76-100kr	101-160kr	over 160kr

Restaurant fare is usually expensive in Sweden, but **food halls** (*saluhallen*), open-air markets, and **hot dog stands** (*varmkorv*) make budget eating easy enough. Many restaurants offer affordable **daily lunch specials** (*dagens rätt*) for 60-75kr. The Swedish palate has long been attuned to simple, hearty meat-and-potatoes fare, but immigrant communities in Malmö and Stockholm have spiced things up for budget travelers. A league of five-star chefs in Gothenburg are tossing off increasingly imaginative riffs on herring and salmon. The Swedish love **drip coffee** (as opposed to espresso) and have institutionalized coffee breaks as a near-sacred rite of the workday. Aside from light beer containing less than 3.5% alcohol, alcohol can be purchased only at state-run **Systembolaget** liquor stores and in licensed bars and restaurants. You can buy light beer at 18, but it's 20+ otherwise. Carding is common. Some classier bars and clubs have age restrictions as high as 25.

HOLIDAYS AND FESTIVALS

Holidays: New Year's Day (Jan. 1); Epiphany (Jan. 6); Good Friday (Mar. 21); Easter (Mar. 23-24); Ascension (May 1); May Day (May 1); Pentecost (May 11-12); Corpus Christi (May 22); National Day (June 6); Assumption (Aug. 15); All Saints' Day (Nov. 1); Christmas (Dec. 25); Boxing Day (Dec. 26).

Festivals: Valborgsmässoafton (Walpurgis Eve; Apr. 30) celebrates the arrival of spring with roaring bonfires in Dalarna and choral singing in Lund and Uppsala. Dalarna erects flowery maypoles in time for Midsummer (June 24), as young people flock to the islands of Gotland, Öland, and the Skärgård archipelago for all-night parties. Mid-July welcomes the Stockholm Jazz Festival (www.stockholmjazz.com) to the capital, while crayfish parties in Aug. and eel parties in Sept. leave the timid swimming for sanctuary.

BEYOND TOURISM

Summer employment is often easier to find than long-term work, since Sweden has fairly strict regulations governing the employment of foreigners. For more info on opportunities across Europe, see **Beyond Tourism**, p. 56.

The American-Scandinavian Foundation (AMSCAN), 58 Park Ave., New York, NY 10016, USA (☎212 8799 779; www.amscan.org/jobs/index.html). Volunteer and job opportunities throughout Scandinavia. Fellowships for study in Sweden for Americans.

Council of International Fellowship (CIF), Karlbergsvägen 80 nb. ög, 113 35 Stockholm (☎04 68 32 31 21; www.cif-sweden.org). Funds exchange programs for service professionals, including homestays in various Swedish cities. Must have at least 3 years professional experience.

Internationella Arbetslag, Tegelviksgatan 40, 116 41 Stockholm, SWE (☎08 643 08 89; www.ial.nu). Branch of Service Civil International (SCI; www.sciint.org) organizes a broad range of workcamps. 700-900kr camp fee. 150kr SCI membership fee.

STOCKHOLM ☎08

The largest city in Scandinavia's biggest country, Stockholm (pop. 1,250,000) is aptly self-titled the "capital of the north" and a focal point for culture, design, and cuisine. Built on an archipelago, the elegant city exists by virtue of a latticework of bridges connecting its islands and peninsulas, bringing together individual neighborhoods, each with a distinct character.

▐ TRANSPORTATION

Flights: Arlanda Airport (ARN; ☎797 6000; www.arlanda.com), 42km north of the city. **Flygbussarna** shuttles (☎600 1000; www.flygbussarna.se) run between Arlanda and Centralstationen in Stockholm (40min.; every 15min. Station to airport 4am-10pm, airport to station 4:50am-12:30am; 95kr, students, children, and seniors 65kr; MC/V), as do **Arlanda Express** trains (☎0202 222 24; www.arlandaexpress.com. 20min.; every 15min. 5am-midnight; 200kr, students 100kr). **Bus** #583 runs to the T-bana stop Märsta (10min., 20kr); take the T-bana to T-Centralen in downtown Stockholm (40min., 20kr). Flygbussarna also operates shuttles to **Västerås Airport (VST;** ☎218 056 00)

SWEDEN

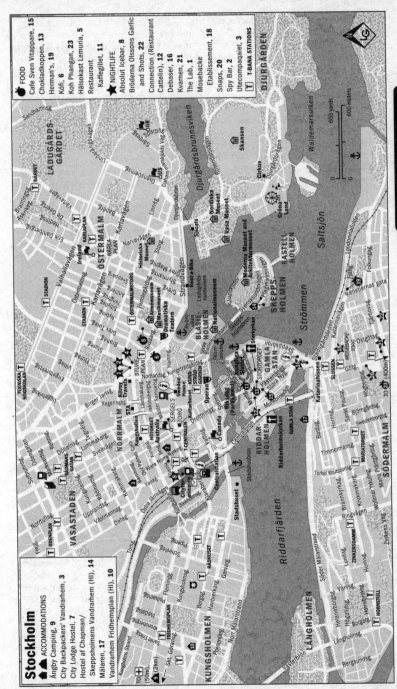

Stockholm

▲ ACCOMMODATIONS
Ängby Camping, **9**
City Backpackers' Vandrarhem, **3**
City Lodge Hostel, **7**
Hostel at Chapman/
Skeppsholmens Vandrarhem (HI), **14**
Mälaren, **17**
Vandrarhem Fridhemsplan (HI), **10**

❖ FOOD
Cafe Sven Vitappare, **15**
Chokladkoppen, **13**
Herman's, **19**
Köfi, **6**
Koh Phangan, **23**
Hälsokost Lemuria, **5**
Restaurant
Kaffegillet, **11**

★ NIGHTLIFE
Absolut Icebar, **8**
Bröderna Olssons Garlic
and Shots, **22**
Connection (Restaurant
Cattelin), **12**
Debaser, **16**
Kvarnen, **21**
The Lab, **1**
Mosebacke
Etablissement, **18**
Snaps, **20**
Spy Bar, **2**
Utecompaqaiet, **3**
Ⓣ T-BANA STATIONS

coordinating with Ryanair departures (1½hr., 100kr). Skavsta Airport is a major budget airline hub for the region. See p. 974 for more info.

Trains: Centralstationen (☎762 2580). T-bana: T-Centralen. To: **Copenhagen, DEN** (5½hr.; 7-14 per day; 1099kr, under 26 948kr); **Gothenburg** (3-5hr.; every 1-2hr.; 512-1110kr, under 26 437-955kr); and **Oslo, NOR** (6-8hr.; 1-5 per day; 672kr, under 26 572kr). Book up to 90 days In advance for lower fares. Fewer trains on Sa.

Buses: Cityterminalen, upstairs on the north end of Centralstationen. **Terminal Service** (☎762 5997) goes to the airport (95kr, 65kr students) and Gotland ferries (70kr). **Biljettservice** (☎762 5979) makes reservations with Sweden's bus companies for longer routes. **Swebus** (☎7712 182 18; www.swebusexpress.se), one of the largest, runs to: **Copenhagen, DEN** (9hr., 2per day, 400-500kr); **Gothenburg** (7hr., 7 per day, 250-300kr); and **Malmö** (8½hr., 3 per day, 400-500kr).

Ferries: Tallinksilja, Kungsg. 2 (☎22 21 40; www.tallinksilja.com), sails to: **Helsinki, FIN** (17hr., 1 per day at 5pm, from 75kr); **Turku, FIN** (12hr., 2 per day, from 150kr); **Tallinn, EST** (16hr., 1 per day, from 470kr, low season 260kr). T-bana: Gärdet, follow signs to Värtahamnen, or take the Tallinksilja bus (20kr) from Cityterminalen. 50% ScanRail discount on select fares. **Viking Line** (☎452 4000; www.vikingline.fi) sails to: **Helsinki, FIN** (17hr.; 1 per day; mid-June to mid-Aug. from 430kr, low season 300kr); **Turku, FIN** (12hr.; 2 per day; mid-June to mid-Aug. from 230kr, low season 130kr). Office in Cityterminalen (open M-Th 8am-7pm, F 7:30am-6:30pm, Sa 8am-5pm). For more info on traveling by ferry in Scandinavia, see p. 53.

Public Transportation: T-bana (Tunnelbana, Stockholm's subway; stations marked with white circular sign with blue "T") runs Su-Th 5am-12:30am, F-Sa 5am-3am. **Night buses** run 12:30am-5:30am. Tickets 20kr; 10 rides 180kr, sold at Pressbyrån news agents; 1hr. unlimited transfer. The **SL Tourist Card** (Turistkort) is valid on all public transportation. 1-day 90kr; 3-day 190kr. Office in Centralstationen (☎600 1000). T-bana: T-Centralen. Open M-Sa 6:30am-11:15pm, Su 7am-11:15pm. MC/V.

Taxis: Many cabs have fixed prices to certain destinations; ask when you enter the cab. Expect to pay 440-475kr from Arlanda to Centralstationen. Major companies include **Taxi 020** (☎33 66 99), **Taxi Kurir** (☎30 00 00; www.taxikurir.se), and **Taxi Stockholm** (☎15 00 00; www.taxistockholm.com).

Bike Rental: Rent-a-Bike, Strandvägen, Kajplats 24 (☎0762 26 76 83). From 200kr per day. Open May-Sept. daily 10am-6pm. MC/V. **Djurgårdsbrons Sjöcafé,** Galärvarvsvägen 2 (☎660 5757). Bikes 250kr per day, canoes 300kr per day, in-line skates 200kr per day, kayaks 500kr per day. Open June-Aug. daily 9am-9pm. AmEx/MC/V.

✈ 🛈 ORIENTATION AND PRACTICAL INFORMATION

Stockholm spans a number of small islands (linked by bridges and the T-bana) at the junction of **Lake Mälaren** to the west and the **Baltic Sea** to the east. The large northern island is divided into two sections: **Norrmalm,** home to Centralstationen and the crowded shopping district around Drottningg., and **Östermalm,** which boasts the **Strandvägen** waterfront and upscale nightlife fanning out from **Stureplan.** The mainly residential western island, **Kungsholmen,** features beaches, waterside promenades, and the *Stadhuset* (city hall) on its eastern tip. The southern island of **Södermalm** retains a traditional feel in the midst of a budding cafe culture and club scene. Nearby **Långholmen** houses a nature preserve and a prison-turned-hotel and museum, while the similarly woodsy eastern island **Djurgården** exhibits several popular museums on its western side. At the center of these five islands is **Gamla Stan** (Old Town). Gamla Stan's less-trafficked neighbor (via Norrmalm) is **Skeppsholmen.** Each of Stockholm's streets begins with number "1" at the end closest to the Kungliga Slottet (p. 969) in Gamla Stan; the lower the numbers, the closer you are to Old Town. Street signs also contain that block's address numbers.

Tourist Offices: Sweden House (Sverigehuset), Hamng. 27 (☎508 285 08; www.stockholmtown.com), entrance off Kungsträdsgården. From Centralstationen, walk up Klarabergsg. to Sergels Torg (look for the glass obelisk), bear right on Hamng., and turn right at the park. Agents sell the **SL card** and **Stockholm Card** (Stockholmskortet), which includes public transportation and admission to 75 museums and attractions. 1-day 290kr; 2-day 420kr; 3-day 540kr. Internet 1kr per min. Open M-F 9am-7pm, Sa 10am-5pm, Su 10am-4pm. AmEx/MC/V.

Budget Travel: Kilroy Travels, Kungsg. 4 (☎0771 54 57 69; www.kilroytravels.se). Open M-F 10am-6pm. **STA Travel,** Kungsg. 30 (☎0771 61 10 10; www.statravel.se). Open M-F 10am-6pm. AmEx/MC/V.

Embassies: Australia, Sergels Torg 12, 11th fl. (☎613 2900; www.sweden.embassy.gov.au). Open M-F 8:30am-4:30pm. **Canada,** Tegelbacken 4, 7th fl. (☎453 3000; www.canadaemb.se). Open 8:30am-noon and 1-5pm. **Ireland,** Östermalmsg. 97 (☎661 8005). Open M-F 10am-noon and 2:30-4pm. **UK,** Skarpög. 6-8 (☎671 3000; www.britishembassy.se). Open M-F 9am-5pm. **US,** Daghammarskjölds väg 31 (☎783 5300; www.usemb.se). Open M-Th 9-11am and 1-3pm, F 9-11am.

Currency Exchange: Forex, Centralstationen (☎411 6734; open daily 7am-9pm) and Cityterminalen (☎21 42 80; open M-F 7am-8pm, Sa 8am-5pm). 25kr commission.

Luggage Storage: Lockers at Centralstationen and Cityterminalen (30-80kr per day). Cash only.

GLBT Resources: The Queer Extra (QX) and the QueerMap give info about Stockholm's GLBT hot spots. Swedish-language version available at the Sweden House tourist office or online at www.qx.se. For an English-language version, visit www.qx.se/english.

24hr. Pharmacy: Look for green-and-white Apoteket signs. **Apoteket C. W. Scheele,** Klarabergsg. 64 (☎454 8130), at the overpass over Vasag. T-bana: T-Centralen.

Hospitals: Karolinska (☎517 740 93), north of Norrmalm near Solnavägen. T-Bana: Skt. Eriksplan. **Sankt Göran** (☎587 010 00), on Kungsholmen. T-Bana: Fridhemsplan.

Medical Services: 24hr. hotline ☎32 01 00.

Telephones: Almost all public phones require **Telia** phone cards; buy them at Pressbyrån newsstands in increments of 50 (50kr) or 120 (100kr) units.

Internet Access: Stadsbiblioteket (library), Odeng. 53, in the annex. T-bana: Odenplan. Sign up for 2 free 30min. slots daily or drop in for 15min., but bring your passport. Open M-Th 9am-9pm, F 9am-7pm, Sa-Su noon-4pm. **Dome House,** Sveavg. 108, has almost 80 terminals. 19kr per hr. Open 24hr. **Sidewalk Express** Internet stations are located inside malls and 7-Elevens throughout the city. 19kr per hr., 149kr monthly pass. Open 24hr. MC/V.

Post Office: 84 Klarabergsg. (☎23 22 20). Open M-F 7am-7pm. Stamps also available at press stands and souvenir shops.

ACCOMMODATIONS AND CAMPING

Reservations are indispensable in summer. In high season, many HI hostels limit stays to five nights. If you haven't booked ahead, arrive around 8am. Some non-HI hostels are hotel-hostel combinations. Specify that you want to stay in a dorm-style hostel, or risk paying hotel rates. Stockholm's **botels** (boat-hotels) often make for camaraderie, but they can be cramped—request a room with harbor views. There are also various **B&B booking services,** including the **Bed and Breakfast Agency.** (☎643 8028; www.bba.nu. Open M 10am-noon and 1-5pm, Tu-W 9am-noon and 1-5pm.) The **Sweden House** tourist office can also help book rooms (5kr hostel booking fee, 75kr hotel booking fee). An SL or Stockholm Card is the cheapest way for campers to reach some of the more remote **campgrounds.** The right of public access (p. 963) does not apply within the city limits, although camping is allowed on most of the Skärgård archipelago (p. 975).

■ **Hostel af Chapman/Skeppsholmens Vandrarhem (HI),** Flaggmansväg. 8 (☎463 2266; www.stfchapman.com). T-bana: Kungsträdgården. Bus #65 from Centralstation. This modern, roomy hostel is accompanied by a newly renovated 19th-century schooner botel. Breakfast 70kr. Linens 65kr. Laundry 35kr. Internet 1kr per min. Reception 24hr, Lockout 11am-3pm. Dorms 215kr; 3- to 6-person dorm 260kr; doubles 590kr. 5-10kr HI discount for meals, linens, and laundry. 50kr HI discount for rooms. AmEx/MC/V. ❷

City Backpackers' Vandrarhem, Upplandsg. 2A (☎20 69 20; www.citybackpackers.se). T-bana: T-centralen. Just north of the city center, this hostel features friendly service, free pasta, coffee, and tea. Linens 50kr. Laundry 50kr. Sauna 20kr, late-afternoon free. Free Internet and Wi-Fi. Reception 8am-2pm. Low season dorms from 190kr, 210kr high season; doubles 560kr. MC/V. ❷

City Lodge Hostel, Klara Norra Kyrkog. 15 (☎22 66 30; www.citylodge.se). T-bana: T-centralen. Newly renovated, tidy rooms, and a can't-beat location make this a great place to rest. Breakfast 50kr. Linens 50kr. Towels 10kr. Laundry 50kr. Free Internet. Reception June-Aug. 8:30am-11pm, Sept.-May 8:30am-10pm. 16-bed dorms 185kr, 6-person 250kr; doubles from 590kr. MC/V. ❷

Mälaren, Södermälarstrand, Kajplats 6 (☎644 4385; www.theredboat.com). T-bana: Gamla Stan. This bright red steamer botel has a great location just south of Gamla Stan. Breakfast 60kr. Towels 20kr. Reception 8am-11pm. Internet 10kr per 15min. Dorms 210kr; singles 430kr; doubles 530kr; triples 720kr; quads 960kr. MC/V. ❷

Vandrarhem Fridhemsplan (HI), S:t Eriksg. 20 (☎653 8800; www.fridhemsplan.se). T-bana: Fridhemsplan. The city's largest hostel has spacious rooms. Wheelchair-accessible. Breakfast 60kr. Lockers 20kr. Linens 50kr. Laundry 50kr. Free Internet. Reception 24hr. Dorms 250kr; singles 450kr; doubles 600kr. 50kr HI discount. AmEx/MC/V. ❸

Ängby Camping, Blackebergsv. 24 (☎37 04 20; www.angbycamping.se), on Lake Mälaren. T-bana: Ängbyplan. Wooded campsite with swimming area. Cable TV 10kr. Stockholm Card vendor. Reception June-Aug. 8am-10pm; Sept.-May 5-8pm. 2-person tent sites 135kr; cabins 475-725kr. Electricity from 35kr. AmEx/MC/V. ❶

⬛ FOOD

Götgatan and **Folkunggatan** in Södermalm offer affordable cuisine from around the world, while pizza and kebabs are plentiful on Vasastaden's **Odengatan**. The **SoFo** (south of Folkunggatan) neighborhood offers many trendy cafe options. Grocery stores are easy to find around any T-bana station. Head to the outdoor fruit market at **Hötorget** for your Vitamin C fix (open M-Sa 7am-6pm), or to the **Kungshallen** food hall, Kungsg. 44, for a meal from one of the international food stands. (www.kungshallen.com. Open M-F 9am-11pm, Sa 11am-11pm, Su noon-11pm.) The **Östermalms Saluhall,** Nybrog. 31 (T-bana: Östermalmstorg), is a more traditional indoor market with fish, meat, cheese, fruit, and pastry stands, as well as more expensive restaurants serving Swedish dishes. (www.ostermalmshallen.se. Open M-Th 9:30am-6pm, F 9:30am-6:30pm, Sa 9:30am-4pm.) Take advantage of low lunch prices and track down *dagens rätt* (lunch specials; 50-80kr) to save money.

■ **Herman's,** Fjällg. 23A (☎643 9480). T-bana: Slussen. Hearty, well-seasoned vegetarian fare, served buffet-style with a view of the water. Lunch (78-118kr) and dinner (118-168kr) include dessert and drink combos. Open daily June-Aug. 11am-11pm, arrive by 9:30pm for full buffet; Sept.-May 11am-10pm. MC/V. ❹

Restaurant Kaffegillet, Trangsund 4 (☎21 39 95). T-bana: Gamla Stan. An excellent place to try classic Swedish cuisine. The reindeer roast (215kr) and the marinated herring with sour cream (135kr) are popular choices. Small dishes 95-105kr. Swedish Kitchen 135-345kr. Desserts 65-95kr. Salad and bread included. Open daily May-Sept. 9am-11pm; Oct.-Apr. 9am-6pm. AmEx/MC/V. ❹

Koh Phangan, Skåneg. 57 (☎642 5040). T-Bana: Skanstull. Dine on Thai food in this stellar restaurant made to look like a jungle treehouse, a welcoming sight in winter. Vegetarian entrees 135-155kr. Meat entrees 150-200kr. Seafood 180-265kr. Open M-Th 11am-11pm, F 11am-11:45pm, Sa 2-11:45pm, Su 2-11pm. AmEx/MC/V. ❺

Chokladkoppen, Stortorg. 18 (☎20 31 70). T-bana: Gamla Stan. Serves light meals (39-80kr) and generous desserts (23-48kr). The outdoor seating is a top people-watching spot on Stortorget. Open in summer Su-Th 9am-11pm, F-Sa 9am-midnight; low season Su-Th 9am-10pm, F 9am-midnight. Cash only. ❷

Hälsokust Lemuria, Nybrog. 26 (☎660 0221). T-bana: Östermalmstorg. Near the Östermalms Saluhall. Serves nicely balanced gluten- and lactose-free vegetarian and vegan lunches (55kr). Open M-F 11am-3pm. AmEx/MC/V. ❶

Cafe Sven Vitappare, Sven Vintappares Gränd 3 (☎22 26 40). T-bana: Gamla Stan. This intimate cafe resembles a 17th-century shop. Serves savory pastries (15kr) and a selection of sandwiches (20-30kr). Open daily 8am-5pm. MC/V. ❶

Kófi, Birger Jarlsg. 11 (☎611 3335). T-bana: Östermalmstorg. Stylish affordability in an upscale neighborhood, Kófi serves sandwiches (25-49kr) and pastries (20-35kr) ideal for a light lunch. Open M-F 7am-last customer, Sa 8am-1am, Su 9am-around midnight. MC/V. Branch at Dottningg. 42. ❶

◐ SIGHTS

With over 75 museums, visitors to Stockholm never lack places to see. Break up your walking tour (p. 970) of the city's inner neighborhoods with T-bana rides to more remote locations to get a sense of the capital's scope. The T-bana, spanning 110km, has been called the world's longest art exhibit—over the past 50 years, the city has commissioned more than 140 artists to decorate its stations. The blue line's art is particularly notable, while the murals and sculptures of T-Centralen remain the best-recognized example of T-bana artistry.

GAMLA STAN (OLD TOWN). Stockholm was once confined to the small island of Staden. Today, the island is the center of the city. The main pedestrian street is **Västerlånggatan,** but its maze of small side streets preserves the area's historic feel. *(Tours of the island are available June-Aug. M and W-Th 7:30pm. Meet at the obelisk in front of Storkyrkan. 60kr. Cash only.)* Gamla Stan is dominated by the magnificent 1754 ▧**Kungliga Slottet** (Royal Palace), one of the largest palaces in Europe and the winter home of the Swedish royal family. The **Royal Apartments** and the adjacent **Rikssalen** (State Hall) and **Slottskyrkan** (Royal Chapel, open W-F) are all lavishly decorated in blue and gold, the colors of the Swedish flag. The **Skattkammaren** (Royal Treasury) houses a collection of jewel-encrusted crowns and other regal accoutrements. The statues in the **Gustav III Antikmuseum** are forgettable, while the **Museum Tre Konor** offers an interesting look at the foundation of a 13th-century castle that once stood on the same site. Expect lines in summer. *(Main ticket office and info area at the rear of the complex, near the Storkyrkan. ☎402 6130; www.royalcourt.se. Open Feb. to mid-May Tu-Su noon-4pm; mid-May to June 1st daily 10am-4pm; June 1st-Aug. daily 10am-5pm; Sept. 1st to mid-Sept. daily 10am-4pm; mid-Sept. to mid-May Tu-Su noon-3pm. Each attraction 90kr, students 35kr. Combination ticket 130/65kr. Guided tours 1 per hr. AmEx/MC/V.)* The **Livrustkammaren** (Armory) presents an extensive collection of royal clothes and weapons along with the coaches of Swedish kings and queens. *(Slottsbacken 3. ☎519 555 44; www.livrustkammaren.se. Open June-Aug. daily 10am-5pm; Sept.-May Tu-W and F-Su 11am-5pm, Th 11am-8pm. 50kr, under 20 free. AmEx/MC/V.)*

SWEDEN

TIME: 4hr., 5-6hr. with visits to the Stadhuset, Moderna Museet, or Kungliga Slottet.

DISTANCE: About 6km.

SEASON: Mid-Apr. to late Oct.

A WALKING TOUR OF STOCKHOLM

A walking tour of a city spread out over a dozen islands sounds unlikely, but both goods and people have streamed across Stockholm's bridges since it emerged as a 13th-century trading port. These bridges string their way across the city's waterways and are at least half the reason why Stockholm is such a walkable city. Factor in a network of parks and thoroughly continental boulevards and it's not hard to see why residents of Stockholm happily hoof it during the summer months—even though comfortable mass transit options are never very far away. This tour starts at **Sweden House** (p. 967), Stockholm's main tourist office, and ends in the old town of **Gamla Stan.**

1 SERGELS TORG. Begin by walking west on Hamngatan past the exclusive **NK** department store. Make for the 37m glass obelisk at the center of Sergels Torg, the plaza that was carved out of Lower Norrmalm after WWII in what the Swedes called "the great demolition wave." Modernist city planners were convinced that they could arbitrarily designate a new city center and have civic life revolve around it, but they got more than they bargained for with the covey of drug dealers who flocked to the western side of Sergels Torg. Known as the **Plattan,** this sunken plaza should be avoided at night. The glassy **Kulturhuset** (p. 973), on the southern side of the square, is a more savory point of interest. Check the schedule of events posted inside **Lava,** a hangout popular with Stockholm's university students.

2 STADHUSET. Turn left onto Drottninggatan, Norrmalm's main pedestrian thoroughfare, and then turn right just before the bridge onto Strömgatan. Take the steps down to the quay just before the Centralbron overpass, and go under two bridges and over one to the majestic Stadshuset (p. 966). Guided tours (45min.; 50kr) leave on the hour. If time or money is short, make a point of walking around the manicured waterside grounds before continuing on your way.

3 RIDDARHOLMEN. Head back to Centralbron by crossing back over the bridge, take the steps up, and then turn right on the second bridge, Vasabron, onto Gamla Stan. Turn right onto Riddarhuskajen and stay on the waterfront. Peek into the lawns of Riddarhuset on your left, built in the 17th century for Parliament and now occasionally used by Swedish nobility. Take a right on the first bridge you come to, Riddarhbron, into the plaza on Riddarholmen (The Knight's Island). Stockholm's 17th-century elite built private palaces around the **Riddarholmskyrkan** church. Parts of the church date back to the 13th century, when it was used as a Franciscan monastery. Lutherans booted out the Franciscans after the Protestant Reformation and then set aside the church as the burial place for Swedish monarchs in 1807. Almost every Swedish king from 1290 to 1950 has been buried there.

4 SKEPPSHOLMEN. Head straight out of the plaza, cross Centralbron, and make a right onto charming Stora Nygatan. Turn left down any of the side streets and then left onto Västerlånggatan, lined with shops and confectionaries. Cross two bridges, cutting through the back of the Riksdag (Parliament), then turn right onto Strömgatan and right again back across the water, this time past the Riksdag's long east-facing facade. Turn left onto Slottskajen alongside the royal palace of Kungliga Slottet (p. 969), and left onto the bridge toward the Grand Hotel. Bear right onto Södra Blasieholmshamnen and then cross the scenic Skeppsholmbron bridge onto the island of Skeppsholmen. The main attraction here is the **Moderna Museet** (p. 972), home to the works of many celebrated artists from the 20th century. Admission is ▓ **free.**

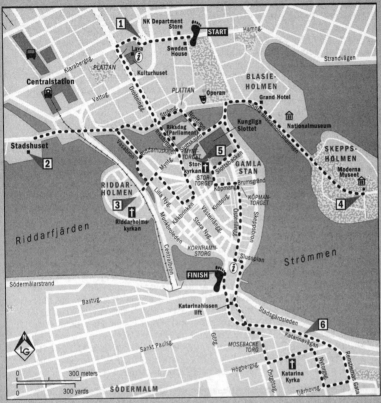

5 KUNGLIGA SLOTTET. Retrace your steps and turn right back onto Gamla Stan, flanking the palace on Skappsbron this time. You could spend a full day wandering through the palace's museums and courtyards, but for the sake of time confine your visit to the **Royal Apartments.** Turn into the plaza leading up to Storkyrkan; the ticket office is on the right.

6 SÖDERMALM. From the palace, walk straight into Stortorget, the main square of the island. Take a left and walk along its east end, and then another left onto Köpmangatan, with its array of antique shops. At the St. George and Dragon statue, make a right along Österlånggatan. When it ends, take a left on Slussplan, then a right on the bridge connecting Gamla Stan to the southern island of Södermalm. Keep to the left as you cross the bridge, hop the **Katarinahissen lift** (10kr), and cross the bridge to the north-facing cliffs for one of the best views of the city. You can also get the view for free by walking up the steps on the opposite side of Katarinavägen. Head straight to intimate Mosebacke Torg and continue south down Östgötagatan. Take your first left onto Högbergsgatan, passing by the octagonal tower of the **Katarina kyrka,** devastated by fire in 1990 but rebuilt to its former Baroque splendor. At the end of Högbergsgatan, turn right onto Nytorgsgatan, left onto Tjärhovsgatan, and then left onto Renstiernas gata. As the street begins curving to the west, a beautiful view of Stockholm's spires spreads out before you. Finish by heading down to Slussen and crossing back onto Gamla Stan to rest your weary legs.

Across the street from the palace ticket office is the gilded **Storkyrkan** church, where recipients of the Nobel Peace Prize speak after accepting their awards. Don't miss the statue of St. George slaying the dragon. (☎ 723 3016. Open M-Sa June-Aug. 9am-6pm; Sept.-May 9am-4pm. Church 25kr. 3 tower tours per day in summer. Cash only.) Around the corner on **Stortorget,** the main square, the small **Nobelmuseet** traces the story of the Nobel Prize and its laureates. (☎ 534 818 00; www.nobelprize.org/nobelmuseum. Open mid-May to mid-Sept. Tu 10am-8pm, M and W-Su 10am-5pm; mid-Sept. to mid-May Tu 11am-8pm, W-Su 11am-5pm. 60kr, students 40kr. Guided English-language tours: M-F 11:15am and 3pm, Sa-Su 11:15am and 4pm. AmEx/MC/V.)

KUNGSHOLMEN. The **Stadshuset** (City Hall) has been the seat of local government since the early 20th century. The required tour of the interior takes you through the council room and the enormous Blue Hall, where a 10,000-pipe organ greets Nobel Prize banquet attendees. In the stunning **Gold Room,** 18 million shimmering tiles make up a gold Art Deco mosaic. The **tower** provides the best panoramic view of the city center. (Hantverkarg. 1. T-bana: T-Centralen. ☎ 508 290 58; www.stockholm.se/stadshuset. Open daily May-Sept. 9am-4pm. Call the day of your visit to make sure the building will not be closed for a banquet or reception. 20kr. Tours daily June-Aug. 1 per hr. 10am-4pm; Sept. 10am, noon, 2pm; Oct.-May 10am, noon. 60kr, students 50kr. AmEx/MC/V.)

SKEPPSHOLMEN AND BLASIEHOLMEN. The collection of ◼Moderna Museet, on the island of Skeppsholmen (SHEPS-hole-men), contains canvases by Dalí, Matisse, Munch, Picasso, Pollock, and Warhol. (T-Bana: Kungsträdgården. Bus #65. ☎ 519 552 00; www.modernamuseet.se. 80kr, students 60kr, under 19 free. Open Tu 10am-8pm, W-Su 10am-6pm. MC/V.) In the same building, the **Arkitekturmuseet** displays the history of Swedish architecture and design using 3D models. (T-Bana: Kungsträdgården. Bus #65. ☎ 587 270 00. Open Tu 10am-8pm, W-Su 10am-6pm. 50kr, F free. Combination ticket for both museums 110kr, students 90kr. MC/V.) Across the bridge on Blasieholmen peninsula, the **Nationalmuseum,** Sweden's largest art museum, features pieces by Cézanne, El Greco, Monet, and Rembrandt. (T-bana: Kungsträdgården. Bus #65. ☎ 519 544 10; www.nationalmuseum.se. Open Sept.-May Tu and Th 11am-8pm, W and F-Su 11am-5pm; June-Aug. Tu 11am-8pm, W-Su 11am-5pm. 80kr, students 60kr, under 19 free. AmEx/MC/V.)

ÖSTERMALM. Among the houses of this quiet area are a number of small, quirky museums—the **Musikmuseet** is both. Try an array of instruments or visit the room dedicated to 1970s Swedish pop group ABBA. (Sibylleg. 2. T-bana: Östermalmstorg, exit Sibylleg. ☎ 519 554 90; www.stockholm.music.museum. Open Tu-Su July-Aug. 10am-5pm; Sept.-June noon-5pm. 40kr, students 20kr, under 19 free.) Less than a block away, the **Armémuseum** chronicles Swedish military history. All signs are in Swedish, so be sure to pick up a language guide at the ticket desk. (Riddarg. 13. T-bana: Östermalmstorg, exit Sibylleg. ☎ 519 563 00; www.armemuseum.se. Open late June to Aug. Tu 10am-8pm, M and W-Su 10am-5pm; Sept.-June W-Sa 11am-5pm. 40kr, under 20 free.) For a more complete account of Swedish history, head to the **Historiska Museet,** which plays host to famous collections of both Viking and ecclesiastical memorabilia. (Narvav. 13-17. T-bana: Karlaplan. ☎ 519 556 00; www.historiska.se. Open May-Sept. daily 10am-5pm; Oct.-Apr. Tu-W and F-Su 11am-5pm, Th 11am-8pm. 50kr, students and seniors 40kr, under 19 free.)

DJURGÅRDEN. This national park is a perfect summer picnic spot. The main attraction is the haunting ◼Vasa Museet, home to a massive warship that sank in Stockholm's harbor during its maiden voyage in 1628 and was salvaged, fantastically preserved, three centuries later. (From the Galärvarvet bus stop, take bus #44, 47, or 69. ☎ 519 548 00; www.vasamuseet.se. Open June-Aug. daily 8:30am-6pm; Sept.-May W 10am-8pm, M-Tu and Th-Su 10am-5pm. 80kr, students 40kr. AmEx/MC/V.) Next door, the **Nordiska Museet** explores Swedish cultural history from the 1500s to the present day, highlighting Swedish holidays. (☎ 519 546 00; www.nordiskamuseet.se. Open

June-Aug. daily 10am-5pm; Sept.-Aug. M-F 10am-4pm, Sa-Su 11am-5pm. 60kr, special exhibits 60kr. AmEx/MC/V.) The **Gröna Lund** amusement park features a handful of exciting rides, including roller coasters. (☎ *587 502 00; www.gronalund.se. Open daily late Apr. to late Aug., usually 11am-11pm; check website for detailed schedule. 60kr, rides 20-60kr each.)* A large portion of Djurgården is home to **Skansen,** an open-air museum the size of Gamla Stan that features 150 historical buildings, handicrafts, a small zoo, and an aquarium. Many festivals and events are held throughout the year—of note is a Christmas market in early December. If its scope seems intimidating, limit your visit to the Old Town, a scattering of 17th-century buildings. Costumed actors inhabit the homes, and their attention to period authenticity somehow redeems the project from kitschiness. *(Take bus #44 or 47.* ☎ *442 8000; www.skansen.se. Park and zoo open daily June-Aug. 10am-10pm; Sept.-May 10am-5pm. Most homes open daily June-Aug. 11am-7pm; Sept.-May 11am-5pm. June-Aug. M and W-Su 90kr, Tu 110kr for popular concerts; Sept. 80kr; Oct.-May 60kr. AmEx/MC/V.)*

🎵 🌺 ENTERTAINMENT AND FESTIVALS

Stockholm's smaller performance venues are featured in the *What's On* pamphlet, available at the Sweden House tourist office. There are also a number of larger, more widely known performance spots. The stages of the national theater, **Dramatiska Teatern,** Nybroplan (☎ 667 0680; www.dramaten.se), feature performances of works by August Strindberg and others (60-300kr). Arrive an hour early to snatch up a 35% discount on last-minute tickets. A smaller stage behind the theater focuses on experimental material. The **Kulturhuset at Sergels Torg** (☎ 508 315 08; www.kulturhuset.se) houses art galleries, performance spaces, and cultural venues often free to the public. It also hosts **Lava** (☎ 508 314 44; www.lavaland.se; closed in July), a popular hangout with a stage, library, and cafe that lend themselves to poetry readings and other events geared toward a younger set. The **Operan,** Jakobs Torg 2, stages operas and ballets from late August through mid-June. (☎ 791 4400. Tickets 265-590kr. Student rush tickets available. AmEx/MC/V.) The imposing **Konserthuset,** Hötorg. 8, hosts the Stockholm Philharmonic and the Nobel Prize ceremony. (☎ 10 21 10; www.konserthuset.se. 100-270kr. AmEx/MC/V.) Culture buffs on a budget should sample Stockholm's **Parkteatern** (☎ 506 202 99; www.stadsteatern.stockholm.se), a summer-long program of free outdoor theater, dance, and music in city parks. Call **BiljettDirect** (☎ 0771 707 070; www.ticnet.se) for tickets. The world-class **◘Stockholm Jazz Festival** (☎ 556 924 40; www.stockholmjazz.com) arrives in mid- to late July. Other festivals include GLBT **Stockholm Pride** (early Aug.; ☎ 33 59 55; www.stockholmpride.org), the November **Stockholm Film Festival,** (☎ 677 5000; www.filmfestival.se), and late August's **Strindberg Festival,** a celebration of Sweden's most famous morose playwright.

◙ NIGHTLIFE

For a city with lasting summer sunlight, Stockholm knows a thing or two about nightlife. The scene varies by neighborhood, with particular social codes prevailing in different areas. The posh **Stureplan** area in Östermalm (T-bana: Östermalmtorg) and **Kungsgatan** (T-bana: Hötorget) are where beautiful people party until 5am. Expect long lines and note that many clubs honor strict guest lists. Across the river, **Södermalm's** (T-bana: Mariatorget) nightlife is less glitzy but more accessible and just as popular, with a diverse mix of bars and clubs along Götg. and around Medborgarpl. In the northern part of town, nightlife options line **Sveavägen** and the **Vasastaden** area (T-bana: Odenplan or Rådmansg.). Many bars and clubs set age limits as high as 25 to avoid crowds of drunk teenagers, but showing up early may get you in. Stockholm is compact enough to walk among all the islands, although night buses cover most of the city. The T-bana is generally safe until closing. Pick up *Queer Extra (QX)* and the *QueerMap* for gay nightlife tips.

Absolut Icebar, Vasaplan 2-4 (☎505 631 24; www.absoluticebar.com), in the Nordic Sea Hotel. T-bana: T-Centralen. Provided jacket and gloves keep you warm in the -5°C temperature of this bar, made completely out of natural ice. Make reservations at least 3 days ahead. Drop-in usually requires waiting. Cover 105-160kr with drink; under 18 60kr. Refills 85kr. Open June-Aug. M-W 12:45pm-midnight, Th-Sa 12:45pm-1am, Su 12:45pm-10pm; check website for details on Sept.-May hours. AmEx/MC/V.

Mosebacke Etablissement, Mosebacke Torg 3 (☎556 098 90). T-bana: Slussen. Take the Katarina lift (10kr) to Söder Heights. Usually a large crowd inside at the bar and on the dance floor. Outside terrace is more relaxed with 3 bars, a great view, and ample seating. Beer 46kr. Mixed drinks 74kr. 20+. Cover 50-150kr. Open F-Sa 5pm-2am, Su-Th 5pm-1am. Terrace open in summer daily 11am-1am. AmEx/MC/V.

Kvarnen, Tjärhovsg. 4 (☎643 0380; www.kvarnen.com). T-bana: Medborgarpl. Look for the red windmill. The mod cocktail lounge **H2O,** the energetic **Eld** dance club, and a 200-year-old beer hall coexist under the same roof. Beer 29-42kr. Su-Th 21+, F-Sa 23+. Open M-F 11am-3am, Sa noon-3am, Su 5pm-3am. MC/V.

Connection, Storkyrkobrinken 9 (☎20 18 18; www.clubconnection.nu). Inside Restaurant Cattelin. T-bana: Gamla Stan, or bus #3 or 53. This spacious gay bar fills up quickly with a diverse clientele that drinks and dances to disco and Madonna. Beer 48kr, mixed drinks 86-108kr. Mixed crowd W and Sa, mostly men F. W 18+, F-Sa 23+. Open W and F-Sa 10pm-3am. AmEx/MC/V.

Debaser, Karl Johans Torg 1 (☎462 9860; www.debaser.nu). T-bana: Slussen. This popular rock club draws crowds with live music. 18+. Cover 60-100kr. Bar open daily 5pm-3am. Club open daily June-Aug. 10pm-3am; Sept.-May 8pm-3am. AmEx/MC/V.

Snaps, Götg. 48 (☎640 2868). T-bana: Medborgarpl. On the corner of Medborgarpl. Rock upstairs, house music outside, and an intimate basement dance floor that becomes more mainstream around midnight. Beer 51kr. Wine 61kr. Mixed drinks from 60kr. 23+. Cover F-Sa 60kr. Open M-W 5pm-1am, Th-Sa 5pm-3am. AmEx/MC/V.

Utecompaqalet, Stureplan Sq. (www.stureplan.se). Nicknamed the "mushroom" for its proximity to a large mushroom-roofed phone booth stand, this outdoor bar is a casual, hip place to grab a drink and relax. DJ W-Sa. Drinks 96-106kr. 21+. Cover 80kr. Open daily late Apr. to late Sept. noon-3am.

Bröderna Olssons Garlic and Shots, Folkungag. 84 (☎640 8446; www.garlicand-shots.com). T-bana: Medborgarpl. Follow your nose 3 blocks up Folkungag. This laid-back, 2-floor rocker-style locale serves garlic beer (39kr) and a repertoire of 130 shots (39kr). 23+. Open daily 5pm-1am. AmEx/MC/V.

Spy Bar, Birjer Jarlsg. 20 (☎545 037 01). T-bana: Östermalmtorg. Straight out of Moulin Rouge, Spy Bar is one of the city's hottest, and most exclusive, nightspots. Beer 54kr. Mixed drinks 92-142kr. 23+. Cover 100-120kr. Open W-Sa 10pm-5am. AmEx/MC/V.

◪ LET'S GO TO STOCKHOLM: NYKÖPING ☎155

Stockholm Skavsta Airport (NYO; ☎28 04 00; www.skavsta.se) is 100km south of Stockholm in the town of Nyköping. Skavsta is a budget airline hub for Ryanair and Wizz Air. Flygbussarna (☎08 600 1000; www.flygbussarna.se) operates frequent **buses** from Stockholm (1¼hr., 100-200kr) coordinated with Ryanair arrivals and departures. SJ **trains** (☎0771 75 75 75; www.sj.se/english) also run from Stockholm (1hr., 1-2 per hr., 90-160kr). Taxis (200kr) and local buses (20kr) run to the airport from Nyköping station.

❖ DAYTRIPS FROM STOCKHOLM

Stockholm is situated in the center of an archipelago, where the mainland gradually crumbles into the Baltic. The islands in either direction—east toward the Baltic or west toward Lake Mälaren—are a lovely escape from the city. **Ferries** to the archipelago leave from in front of the Grand Hotel on the **Stromkajen** docks between Gamla Stan and Skeppsholmen or the **Nybrohamnen** docks (T-bana: Kungsträdgården). Visit the **Excursion Shop** in Sweden House (p. 967) for more info.

STOCKHOLM ARCHIPELAGO (SKÄRGÅRD). The wooded islands of the Stockholm archipelago become less developed as the chain of 24,000 islands coils out into the Baltic Sea. **Vaxholm** is the de facto capital of the archipelago and its most touristed island. Its pristine **beaches**, Eriksö and Tenö in particular, and 16th-century **fortress** have spawned pricey waterside cafes, but the rest of the streets still maintain their charm. Vaxholm is accessible by ferry (1hr., late June to late Aug. 2 per hr., 65kr) or bus #670 from T-bana: Tekniska Hogskolan (45min., 1-4 per hr., 20kr). The **tourist office** is at Torget 1. (☎541 708 00; www.vaxholm.se.) Three hours from Stockholm, **Sandhamn** is quieter, although the white sands of Trouville Beach have many devotees. The island, with its active nightlife scene, is especially popular among a younger crowd. Hikers can escape from the masses by exploring coastal trails on the **Finnhamn** group and **Tjockö** to the north. Ask at Sweden House about **hostels**. They are usually booked up months in advance, but there are alternatives—the islands are a promising place to exercise the right of public access (p. 963). Waxholmsbolaget runs **ferries** to even the tiniest islands year-round. All ferries depart from Vaxholm. (☎679 5830; www.waxholmsbolaget.se. June-Aug. 1 per hr.; Sept.-May 1 per 2hr. 65kr, ages 7-19 40kr, under 7 free. AmEx/MC/V.) Sweden House sells the **Båtluffarkort card**, good for unlimited Waxholmsbolaget rides. The pass pays for itself after a few long trips. (5-day 300kr; 30-day 700kr.)

LAKE MÄLAREN. Drottningholms Slott (☎402 6280; www.royalcourt.se) was built for the queens of Sweden in the late 17th century and has served as the royal family's residence since 1981, when they left Kungliga Slottet (p. 969). The interior and formal Baroque gardens are impressive, but the highlight is the 1766 **Court Theater,** where the artistic director uses 18th-century sets and stage equipment to mount provocative ballets, operas, and pantomime shows. The colorful **Chinese Pavillion** was built by King Adolf Fredrick as a surprise birthday present for his queen; how the large pavillion was kept secret enough to maintain the surprise remains a mystery. (Drottningholms Slott open daily May-Aug. 10am-4:30pm; Sept. noon-3:30pm; Sa-Su Oct.-Apr. noon-3:30pm. Palace 70kr, students 35kr; palace and pavillion 110/55kr. Court Theater tickets start at 165kr. Drottningholms Slott English tours daily June-Aug. 1 per 2hr.; Sa-Su Oct.-May noon and 2pm. Court Theater 30min. guided tours 60/40kr. AmEx/MC/V.) The island of **Björkö** on Lake Mälaren is home to **Birka**, Sweden's largest Viking-era settlement, dated to AD 750. All that remains are some burial mounds and a hill fort. In July and August, amateur excavations and modern Vikings bring the island to life. Strömma Kanalbolaget **ferries** (☎587 140 00; www.strommakanalbolaget.com) depart Stockholm from the Stadshusbron docks next to the Stadshuset for Drottningholms Slott (45min.; 1-2 per hr.; round-trip 130kr, plus admission 210kr), and Björkö. (July-Aug. 9:30am and 1pm, return 2:45 and 6:15pm; May and Sept. 9:30am, return 2:45pm. 195kr. Guided tour, museum admission, and round-trip ferry 265kr. MC/V.)

UPPSALA ☎018

The footbridges and side streets of Uppsala (pop. 127,000) teem with almost 40,000 undergraduates. Archbishop Jakob Ulvsson founded **Uppsala University** in 1477, but the Reformation wrested control away from the Catholic Church and set the stage for the secular inquiry that dominates the town today. Academics aside, the city is home to **Domkyrka,** Domkyrkoplan 5-7, the largest cathedral in Scandinavia. Its red-brick facade houses a bright interior, with artwork spanning eight centuries. Many famous Swedes, ranging from scientist Carolus Linnaeus to Saint Erik, the patron saint of Stockholm, are buried within. (☎18 71 73; www.uppsala-domkyrka.se. Open daily 8am-6pm. Free.) Just across Akademig. from the church, the **Gustavianum,** Akademig. 3, takes you through the university's scientific past with physicians' tools and a reconstructed Anatomical Theater, where public dissections were conducted in the late 17th century. (☎471 7571. Open Tu-Su late June to Aug. 10am-4pm; Jan. to late June 11am-4pm. Tours Sa-Su 1pm. 40kr, students 30kr. AmEx/MC/V.) A walk through the center of town along the Fyrisån River is an excellent way to sample the city's gardens and cafes. Up the hill on Övre Slottsgatan lies the light pink castle, **Uppsala Slott.** Inside is the **Uppsala Konstmuseum,** with art exhibits from the university's collection. (☎727 2482; www.uppsala.se/konstmuseum. Museum open Tu-F noon-4pm, Sa-Su 11am-5pm. Guided tours of the castle June-Aug. 1 and 3pm. Museum 30kr, with tour 60kr, under 21 free. AmEx/MC/V.) On the other side of the river, the **Linnéträdgården,** Svartbäcksg. 27, reconstructs Sweden's first botanical gardens, tended by Carolus Linnaeus, using his 1745 sketch. The grounds include a small museum in Linnaeus's former home. (☎471 2576; www.linnaeus.uu.se. Museum and garden open daily May-Sept. 11am-5pm. Museum and garden 50kr, under 16 free, garden free 5pm-8pm. AmEx/MC/V.) The MS *Kung Carl Justaf* sails south of Uppsala to **Skoklosters Slott,** a 17th-century castle with an impressive armory. (☎38 60 77; www.lsh.se/skokloster. Open Tu-Su June-Aug. 10:30am-5pm; Sept.-May 11:30am-4pm. 30kr, under 19 free. Guided tour 1 per hr. 11:15am-4:15pm 50kr. Boat departs daily mid-May to mid-Aug. 11am from Islandsbron on Östra Åg. and Munkg.; returns 4:15pm. Roundtrip 200kr. Purchase tickets on board or by phone ☎0702 938 161. AmEx/MC/V.)

STF Uppsala City Hostel (HI) ❷, S:t Persgatan 16, is the most affordable city center accommodation. (☎10 00 08; www.uppsalavandrarhem.se. Linens 60kr. Free Internet. Reception 8am-10pm. Pets allowed in some rooms. 8-bed dorms 220kr; singles 380kr; doubles 500kr. 50kr HI discount. AmEx/MC/V.) The university is home to student organizations known as **nations.** Each nation owns a house, most with their own restaurants or bars, which have lower prices than other establishments in town. However, only students are allowed in; non-Uppsalan students can pick up a guest pass at **Ubbo,** Övre Slottsg. 7. (☎480 3151; www.kuratorskonventet.se. Open Tu-F 5-7pm, Sa 1-3pm. 1-week pass 50kr; 2-week 70kr; 4-week 90kr; summer 200kr. Valid student ID and photo ID required. MC/V.) One nation restaurant serves non-students June to August: **Västamanlands-Dale's Taken ❷,** S:t Larsgatan 13 (entrance on Sysslomangs.), offers a sizable 50-80kr dinner. (☎13 48 59; www.taket06.se. Open daily 5pm-2am. AmEx/MC/V.) Retro **Hugo's Kaffe ❶,** Svartbacksg. 21, has a massage chair (20kr per 15min.) and popular lunch deals. (☎13 00 83. Entrees 20-55kr. Open daily 10am-8pm. AmEx/MC/V.) Pick up groceries at **Hemköp,** Kungsg. 95 (open daily 8am-10pm). Bars cluster around **Stortorget,** especially on **Sysslomansgatan, Västra Ågatan,** and the pedestrian areas of **Svartbäcksgatan** and **Kungsgatan.** During the academic year, nightlife in Uppsala revolves around the nations.

Trains go to Stockholm (40min.; 1-6 per hr.; 64kr, students 61kr). From the station, walk right on Kungsg., left on S:t Persg., and cross the bridge for the **tourist office,** Fyristorg 8. The office sells the **Uppsalakortet** (125kr), providing up to 50% off sight admission. (☎727 4800; www.uppland.nu. Open in summer M-F 10am-6pm, Sa 10am-3pm, Su 10am-3pm only in July.) The library, **Stadbiblioteket,** Svartbäcksg. 17, has 30min. slots of free **Internet** and 15min. drop-in. (☎727 1700. Open M-Tu 9am-8pm, W-Th 9am-7pm, F 9am-6pm, Sa 11am-3pm.) **Postal Code:** 75320.

GOTLAND ☎0498

Along the shores of Gotland, Sweden's largest island, families head to sandy beaches in the east before returning to Visby, a town that recalls the Middle Ages with its winding alleyways and historic city wall. Each May, 30 species of orchids come into bloom, transforming the island. Even though summer is busy, visitors can still leave the crowds behind to stroll along the island's cliffs and coast.

⌦ TRANSPORTATION. Destination Gotland **ferries** (☎771 22 33 00; www.destinationgotland.se) sail from Visby to Nynäshamn and Oskarshamn. (3-3¼hr.; June-Aug. 2-6 per day, Oct.-May 1-4 per day. 231-519kr, students 177-390kr. Online booking discounts. AmEx/MC/V.) To get to Nynäshamn from Stockholm, take the Båtbussen bus from Cityterminalen (1hr.; 2-4 per day; leaves 1¾hr. before ferry departures; 80kr, 110kr on bus) or the Pendeltåg train from Centralstationen (1hr., 90kr, SL passes valid). To get to Oskarshamn from Kalmar, hop on a KLT bus (1½hr., every 1-2hr., 73kr). **Gotland City**, Kungsg. 57A, books ferries from Stockholm. (☎08 406 1500. Open June-Aug. M-F 9:30am-6pm, Sa 10am-2pm; Sept.-May M-F 9:30am-5pm. AmEx/MC/V.) Pick up a bus timetable at the ferry terminal or at the Visby **bus station**, Kung Magnusväg 1, outside the wall east of the city. (☎21 41 12; www.gotland.se/kollektivtrafiken. Cash only on buses; AmEx/MC/V at station.) Buses on the island are fairly expensive (59kr) and only three or four cover the routes each day, making daytrips almost impossible. **Cycling** is a better way to explore Gotland's terrain. Extensive paths and bike-friendly motorways can be supplemented by strategic bus rides, as buses will carry bikes for an extra 40kr. Bike **rental shops** can be found in Visby and in most towns across the island.

VISBY. Passing through the medieval **Ringmuren** (Ring Wall) of Visby (pop. 22,500) is like stepping into another time. The wall encloses the ruins of churches, the most intricate of which, **S:ta Karin** (or S:ta Katarina), is open for exploration. (☎29 27 00. Open in summer M-F and Su 8am-9pm, Sa 8am-7pm.) Stairs behind the **Domkyrka** lead to a scenic terrace. Follow the path along the cliff for a view of the town and sea, then walk left along the northern perimeter of the wall to visit the **botanical gardens.** Visby attracts thousands in the first week of August for **Medieval Week** (☎29 10 70; www.medeltidsveckan.se.), a festival with theater and dancing performances, a jousting tournament, and wandering minstrels strumming lutes. **Vandrarhem Visby (HI) ❷**, Fältg. 30, is 2km from the docks at the Alléskolan and within walking distance of the wall. (☎26 98 42. Linens 55kr. Laundry 30kr. Reception 8-10am and 5-7:30pm. Open late June to mid-Aug. Dorms 165kr; doubles 470kr. 50kr HI discount. Cash only.) You'll recognize **Visby Fängelse Vandrarhem ❷**, Skeppsbron 1, by the barbed wire atop its walls, remnants of the prison that preceded it. (☎20 60 50. Breakfast 50kr for dorms. Laundry 30kr. Reception in summer 9-11am and 5-7pm; low season 11am-2pm. Dorms 230-310kr; 6-person apartment with kitchen and bath 1950kr. AmEx/MC/V.) Bars and cafes line **Stora Torget, Adelsgatan,** and the harbor. Take advantage of lunch specials (60-90kr), or pick up groceries at **ICA** on Stora Torg. (Open daily 8am-10pm.) From the ferry terminal, walk left down Färjeleden, then right down Skeppsbron. to the **tourist office,** Skeppsbron 4-6. (☎20 17 00; www.gotland.info. Internet 2kr per min. Open mid-June to mid-Aug. daily 8am-7pm; low season reduced hours.) **Gotlandsresor,** Färjeleden 3, near the ferry terminal, books ferries, finds private rooms, and rents bikes. (☎20 12 60; www.gotlandsresor.se. Open daily June-Aug. 6am-10pm; Sept.-May 8am-6pm.) **Bike rental** shops surround the terminal; prices start at 70kr per day. **Internet** is available at the **Gotlands Bibliotek** (library), Cramerg. 5. (☎29 90 00. Sept.-June free; July-Aug. 20kr per hr. Open Sept.-June M-F 10am-7pm, Sa noon-4pm; July-Aug. M-F 10am-7pm, Sa noon-4pm. Cash only.) **Postal Code:** 62101.

ELSEWHERE ON GOTLAND. Use Visby as a launchpad for visiting **Tofta** beach at the village of **Klintehamn** (bus #10, 40min.), or the cliffs of **Hoburgen,** at the island's southernmost tip (bus #11, 2hr.). Bus #20 runs from Visby to Fårösund (1½hr.), taking passengers to a free 10min. ferry ride past **Fårö,** a small island off Gotland's northern tip. Take the earliest bus to Hoburgen and Fårösund unless you plan to stay overnight. Visit Gotlandsresor (see above) for help booking hostels and campgrounds outside of Visby, or you can take advantage of the right of public access (p. 963) and **camp** by the brackish waters of the Baltic Sea.

SOUTHERN SWEDEN (SKÅNE)

A fiercely contested no-man's-land during 17th-century wars between Sweden and Denmark, this region bears the marks of its martial past with well-preserved castles and forts. Today, the only invaders are the cranes and cormorants that nest alongside marshes and lakes, and the flocks of vacationers who savor the region's immaculate beaches and supremely polished cities of Malmö and Gothenburg.

KALMAR AND ÖLAND ☎0480

An important border city when southern Sweden was part of Denmark, Kalmar (pop. 60,000) is no longer at the center of Scandinavian politics, but retains the dignity of its glory days. Across from downtown, the medieval ▓**Kalmar Slott** is the town's top attraction. In 1397, the castle witnessed the birth of the Union of Kalmar, a short-lived union of Denmark, Norway, and Sweden. King Johann III gave the castle a Renaissance makeover in the 1580s, and, today, it houses lavish furnishings and exhibits. (☎45 14 90; www.kalmarslott.kalmar.se. Open daily July 10am-6pm; June and Aug. 10am-5pm; May and Sept. 10am-4pm; Oct.-Apr. reduced hours. 75kr, students 50kr. Free tours mid-June to mid-Aug. AmEx/MC/V.) Adjoining the castle's moat are the majority of the town's other sights: the cobblestoned **Gamla Stan** (Old Town), the tree-lined **Kyrkogarden** cemetery, the lush **Stadspark,** and a handful of small museums. In the center of town, Kalmar's luminous **Domkyrkan,** the first Baroque church in Sweden, exemplifies 17th-century architecture.

If you have an extra day, cross Kalmar Sound by bridge to the long, thin island of Öland. The white-sand beaches of **Böda** line the northeast shore, while the orchid-dotted steppe of Stora lies to the south. **Solliden Palace,** a summer residence for the royal family since 1906, is 40km north of Öland Bridge. (☎51 53 56; www.sollidensslott.se. Park and exhibits open mid-May to mid-Sept. 11am-6pm. 55kr, students 45kr. MC/V.) The ruins of **Borgholms Slott** reflect eight centuries of Swedish history. (☎51 23 33; www.borgholmsslott.se. Open daily May-Aug. 10am-6pm; Apr. and Sept. 10am-4pm. 50kr, under 18 20kr.) **Biking** is the best way to explore the island. The Träffpunkt Öland **tourist office** has a list of shops that rent bikes; follow signs from the first bus stop after the Öland Bridge. (☎556 0600; www.olandsturist.se. Open May-June M-F 9am-6pm, Sa 9am-5pm, Su 9am-3pm; July-Aug. 5 M-F 9am-7pm, Sa 9am-6pm, Su 9am-6pm; Aug. 6-19 M-F 9am-6pm, Sa 9am-5pm, Su 9am-3pm; low season reduced hours.) Buses #103 and 106 run from Kalmar's train station to Borgholm, on the island (50min., 46kr).

To reach **Vandrarhem Svanen (SVIF) and Hotel ❷,** Rappeg. 1, 2km from the Kalmar tourist office, on the island of Ängö, take bus #402 from the train station (13kr). To get there by foot, turn left on Larmg., right on Södra Kanalg., continue to the end, and turn left across the bridge onto Ängöleden. (☎129 28; www.hotellsvanen.se. Breakfast 60kr. Linens 50kr. Laundry 30kr. Internet 1kr per min. Reception late June to mid-Aug. 7:30am-10pm; mid-Aug. to May 7:30am-9pm. Dorms 195kr; doubles 410kr; triples 615kr.) **Söderportshotellet ❹,** Slottsväg. 1, across from Kalmar Slott, rents spacious student apartments in summer. (☎125 01; www.soderportsgarden.se. Breakfast included. Live music W-Su 9pm-1am in the cafe. Open mid-June to mid-Aug. Reception 7:30am-1am. Singles 495kr; doubles from 595kr. MC/V.) Seaside **Stensö Camping ❶** is 3km south of Kalmar. Take bus #121 to Lanssjukhuset, turn right on Stensbergsv., and right on Stensöv. (☎888 03; www.stenso-camping.se. Water included. Open Apr.-Sept. Tent sites 130-170kr; cabins from 400kr. Electricity 35kr. MC/V.) Hunt for cheap eats along **Larmtorget, Larmgata,** and **Storgata,** or pick up groceries at **ICA** in Baronen pl. near the station. (Open M-F 8am-8pm, Sa 8am-6pm, Su 11am-6pm.) **Trains** and **buses** arrive in Kalmar south of the center. Trains go to Gothenburg (4hr.; 1 per 2hr.; 400kr, under 26 300kr), Malmö (3hr., 1 per 2hr., 346/242kr), and Stockholm (4½hr., 1 per 2hr., 1044/883kr). Buses run directly to Stockholm (6hr.; 3 per day; 263kr, students 210kr). The **tourist office,** Ölandskajen 9, offers **Internet** (10kr per 15min.). From the train station, turn right onto Stationsg. and then right onto Ölandskajen. (☎41 77 00; www.kalmar.se. Open July to mid-Aug. M-F 9am-9pm, Sa-Su 10am-5pm; June and late Aug. M-F 9am-7pm, Sa-Su 10am-4pm; Sept.-May M-F 9am-5pm.) **Postal Code:** 39120.

MALMÖ   ☎040

A vigorous stone's throw from Copenhagen, Malmö (pop. 276,000), Sweden's third-largest city, boasts a cultural diversity unmatched elsewhere in the country. The city's proximity to the rest of Europe makes it a gateway for the thousands of immigrants who flock to the country each year. Intimate and full of outdoor cafes, Lilla Torg is a mecca for people-watching, especially as outdoor patios light up under the glow of evening lamps.

▐▌ TRANSPORTATION AND PRACTICAL INFORMATION. The train station and harbor are north of the old town. **Trains** go to Copenhagen (35min., 3 per hr., 90kr), Gothenburg (3hr., 1 per hr., 500kr), and Stockholm (4½hr.; 1 per hr.; 1065kr, under 26 300kr). **Bus** rides within most of the city are 15kr with 1hr. transfer, and many buses pass by the train station. The **tourist office** is in the station and offers the **Malmö Card** (1-day 130kr, 2-day 160kr, 3-day 190kr.), which provides free public transportation, parking, sightseeing bus tours, and museum admission. (☎34 12 00; www.malmo.se/tourist. Open June-Aug. M-F 9am-7pm, Sa-Su 10am-5pm; Sept.-May reduced hours. AmEx/MC/V.) **Internet** is available in the train station (19kr per hr.; MC/V), or **Cafe ZeZe,** Engelbrektsg. 13, between Lilla Torg and Gustav Adolfs Torg. (☎23 81 28. 30kr per hr. Open M-F 11am-11pm, Sa 1pm-midnight, Su 1-11pm. 10% student discount. Cash only.) **Postal Code:** 20110.

▐▌ ACCOMMODATIONS AND FOOD. STF Vandrarhem Malmö City ❷, 3. Rönngatan 1, is near the center of town. Take bus #2 toward Lindängen to the Davidshall stop and turn right on Holmg. (☎611 6220; www.stfturist.se/malmocity. Breakfast 50kr. Linens 50kr. Towels 20kr. Free Internet. Reception 24hr. Dorms 230kr; singles 380kr; doubles 270kr; triples 240kr; quads 210kr. 50kr HI discount. AmEx/MC/V.) **Vandrarhemmet Villa Hilleröd ❷,** Ängdalav. 38, fills up quickly, but a stay in this cozy house is worth the extra planning. Take bus #3 from the train station to Mellanheden, turn left on Piläkersv., then left on Ängdalav. (☎26 56 26; www.villahillerod.se. Kitchen available. Breakfast 50kr. Linens 50kr. Towels 25kr. Free Internet. Reception 8-10:30am and 4-8pm. Check-in 6pm. Check-out before 11am. 6-bed dorms 190kr; doubles and quads 240-280kr. MC/V.) **Vandrarhem Malmö (HI) ❶,** Backav. 18, is the cheapest option, but brace yourself for communal showers. Take bus #2 from the train station to the Vandrarhemmet stop. (☎822 20; www.malmohostel.se. Breakfast 50kr. Linens 50kr. Towels 20kr. Reception mid-May to Aug. 8-10am and 4-10pm; Sept. to mid-May 8-10am and 4-8pm. Dorms 200kr; singles 350kr; doubles 480kr; triples 600kr. 50kr HI discount. AmEx/MC/V.)

SWEDEN

Möllevångstorget, south of the city center, has a spirited open-air market, folksy local bars, and affordable ethnic eateries. For food, you can't go wrong with any of Malmö's international offerings. Restaurants with low-cost lunches (50-75kr) line **Lilla Torg,** the best square in the city for a good meal, and **Södra Förstadsg.** For Moorish cuisine, stop at **Gök Boct ❶,** Lilla Torg 3, an intimate restaurant by day and popular bar by night. (☎611 21. Open M-Th 11am-midnight, F-Sa 11am-2am, Su noon-11pm. AmEx/MC/V.) Next door, the **Saluhallen** is a massive food court with inexpensive restaurants ranging from Greek to Japanese. (Open M-F 10am-6pm, Sa 10am-4pm.) Ten minutes down Stora Nyg. is **Vegegården ❸,** Rörsjög. 23, which features all-vegetarian Chinese dishes (75-85kr) and a buffet (M-F 63kr, Sa-Su 108kr) for the thrifty herbivore. (☎611 3888. Open M-W 11am-5pm, Th 11am-9pm, F 11am-11pm, Sa noon-11pm, Su noon-9pm. Buffet M-F 11am-3pm, Sa-Su 4-8pm. AmEx/MC/V.) Cap off a meal by sampling one of the 48 homemade flavors of ice cream at ▨**Lilla Glassfabriken ❶,** Holmg. 9, across from STF Vandrarhem Malmö City. (☎611 9760. 1-6 scoops 16-60kr. Open in summer M-F 11am-6:30pm, Sa-Su noon-7pm; low season M-F 11am-6:30pm, Sa-Su noon-6pm. MC/V.)

🎫🎭 SIGHTS AND ENTERTAINMENT. Malmö's most famous sight is **Malmöhus Castle,** a Renaissance stronghold dating to the 15th century that today holds five museums. The **Stadsmuseet** documents the city's history. The **Konstmuseum** offers a large collection of Scandinavian art and a small **Aquarium** and **Tropicarium.** Across the moat, the **Kommendanthuset** hosts pop culture exhibits. The **Teknikens och Sjöfartens Hus** (Technology and Maritime Museum) down the road lets you ogle airplanes, cars, and ships, and submarines. Most exhibit labels in the museums are in Swedish, although the castle exhibits have English translations. (☎34 44 37; www.malmo.se/museer. Open daily June-Aug. 10am-4pm; Sept.-May noon-4pm. Combination ticket 40kr, students 20kr. MC/V.) **Turning Torso,** Vastra Varvsg. 44, the tallest building in Sweden, is also one of the world's unique structures—the 54-stories twist 90 degrees from bottom to top. A film in the neighboring **Turning Torso Gallery** gives a virtual tour. (☎17 45 39; www.turningtorso.com. Open daily noon-6pm.) The **Form/Design Center,** Lilla Torg 9, shows off cutting-edge Swedish design for the Ikea generation. (☎664 5150; www.formdesigncenter.com. Open Tu-W and F 11am-5pm, Th 11am-6pm, Sa-Su 11am-4pm. Free.) The stark **Malmö Konsthall,** St. Johannesg. 7, hosts modern art exhibits and has a playground that resembles a Dr. Seuss world. (☎34 12 93; www.konsthall.malmo.se. Open M-Tu and Th-Su 11am-5pm, W 11am-9pm. Tours daily 2pm. Free.) After strolling through the museums, kick back at the **bars** on Lilla Torg and Möllevångstorget, or case the **club** scene around Stortorg; some venues were once run by "Pleasureman Günther" Mats Söderlund, best known for the "Ding Dong Song."

LUND
☎046

With vibrant student life and proximity to Malmö and Copenhagen, Lund (pop. 100,400) makes a fine base for exploring Skåne. The Romanesque **Lunds Domkyrka** (cathedral) is a massive 900-year-old reminder of the city's former reign as Scandinavia's religious center. Its floor-to-ceiling, 15th-century astronomical clock rings at noon and 3pm, and the 7074-pipe organ is Sweden's largest. The popular Giant Finn column at the crypt entrance has a Rumpelstiltskin-like tale behind it. (☎35 88 80; www.lundsdomkyrka.org. Open M-F 8am-6pm, Sa 9:30am-5pm, Su 9:30am-6pm. Free 30min. tours mid-June to mid-Aug. daily 2:50pm.) **Lund University's** antagonism toward its scholarly northern neighbor in Uppsala has inspired countless pranks, in addition to the drag shows and drinkfests that already grace the city's busy streets. The **campus** is across the park from the cathedral. **Student Info,** Sandg. 2, in the Akademiska Föreningen building, has details on upcoming events. (☎38

49 49; www.af.lu.se. Open late Aug. to June M-W and F 9am-5pm, Th 9am-6pm.)
Continuing north on Sandg. will bring you to the ◼Skissernas Museum (The
Museum of Sketches), adorned from floor to ceiling with paper and sculpture
studies of art from around the world. (☎222 7283; www.skissernasmuseum.se.
Open Tu-Su noon-5pm, W noon-9pm. 50kr, students free. MC/V.) Kulturen, an open-
air museum behind the Student Union at the end of Sankt Anneg. on Tegnerplas-
tén, chronicles Lund's history since the Middle Ages through a series of reconstructed houses. (☎35 04 00; www.kulturen.com. Open mid-Apr. to Sept. daily
11am-5pm; Oct. to mid-Apr. Tu-Su noon-4pm. 50kr, students free. MC/V.)

The cramped Vandrarhem Tåget (HI) ❷, Vävareg. 22, is in the sleeping compart-
ments of a 1940s train. Take the overpass to the park side of the train station. (☎14
28 20; www.trainhostel.com. Located in a potentially unsafe area. Breakfast 55kr.
Linens 60kr. Hot water 1kr per 2min. Reception Apr.-Oct. 8-10am and 5-8pm; Nov.-
Mar. 8-10am and 5-7pm. Dorms 190kr. 50kr HI discount. Cash only.) To get to
Källby Camping ❶, next to the Källby Bad outdoor swimming pool, take bus #1 (dir.:
Klostergården; 18kr) 2km south of the city center. (☎35 51 88. Laundry 40kr.
Reception M-F 7am-9pm, Sa-Su 9am-7pm. Open mid-June to Aug. 55kr per person.
Electricity 25kr. MC/V.) Decorated with caricatures of professors, Conditori Lun-
dagård ❶, Kyrkog. 17, serves sandwiches (30-45kr) and pastries. (☎211 1358. Open
mid-June to mid-Aug. daily 10am-6pm; Sept. to mid-June M-F 7:30am-8pm, Sa
8:30am-6pm, Su 10am-6pm. MC/V.) The open-air market at Mårtenstorg. (open daily
7am-2pm) and the adjoining turn-of-the-century Saluhallen (open M-F 9:30am-6pm,
Sa 9am-3pm) are the best bet for budget food. Cafes around Stortorg. and the
cathedral are pricier. As in Uppsala (p. 976), Lund's nightlife revolves around
nations, student clubs that throw parties and serve as social centers. Stop by Student Info, Sandg. 2, for tips on snagging a 50kr guest pass. Another popular option
is Kulturmejeriet, Stora Söderg. 64, an arthouse cinema, concert venue, and bar.
(☎211 0023; www.kulturmejeriet.se. Films Th 7pm, free. Concerts free-300kr. MC/
V.) Stortorget/Herkules Bar, Stortorg. 1, a former bank, is now a low-key restaurant,
bar, and club with theme nights and a patio. (☎13 92 90; www.stortorget.net. Beer
52kr. Wine 66kr. Mixed drinks from 86kr. 22+. Cover 50kr. Bar open M-Tu 11am-
11pm, W 11am-1am, Th-Sa 11am-3am. Club open Th-Sa 11pm-3am. AmEx/MC/V.)

SJ trains (43kr) and local Pågatågen trains (10-20min., 1-5 per hr., 36kr) run from
Malmö to Lund. Trains run from Lund to Gothenburg (3½hr., 1 per hr., 580kr), Kalmar (3hr., 1 per 2hr., 346kr), and Stockholm (4-5hr.; 1 per 2hr.; 1040kr, under 26
879kr). The tourist office, Kyrkog. 11, across from the cathedral, sells maps (50-
120kr) of the nearby Skåneleden trail. (☎35 50 40; www.lund.se. Open June-Aug. M-
F 10am-6pm, Sa-Su 10am-3pm; May and Sept. M-F 10am-5pm, Sa 10am-2pm; Oct.-
Apr. M-F 10am-5pm. MC/V.) Internet is available 24hr. in the 7-Eleven across from
the station. (19kr per hr. MC/V.) Postal Code: 22100.

KÅSEBERGA   ☎0411

Most travelers would pass by Kåseberga's (pop. 150) quiet valley without giving it
much notice, were it not for what lies on its coast. The riddle of Ales Stenar is Sweden's answer to the enigma of Stonehenge. Its 59 stones are set in the shape of a
ship, with the bow and stern aligned to the position of the sun at the solstices. The
stones are a popular picnic spot as well as the starting point of several trails along
the surrounding windswept hills. The closest hostels are in Ystad, but there are a
number of B&Bs in Kåseberga, including Ales Smedja ❸, Ales väg. 24, which also
offers cabins. (☎52 74 87. Breakfast 65kr. Linens 50kr. Reception 7am-6pm. Singles 350kr; doubles 600kr; cabins 800kr. MC/V.) Cafe Solständet, Kaseväg. 13, in the
village's small marina, is home to Kåseberga Fisk Ab ❶, a well-known fish smokery.
Resist the temptation to buy a raw flounder filet (239kr) and sample the *sil-*

lamacka (fried herring served on bread with tartar sauce, 35kr) instead. (☎52 71 80; www.kaseberga-fisk.se. Fresh fish available June-Aug. Open daily 9am-6pm. MC/V.) Bus #322 from Ystad (30min., 3 per day, 24kr) is the only public transportation that serves Kåseberga from June 17 to Aug. 20. For the rest of the year, visitors must book at least 1hr. ahead for a bus that leaves daily at 1:30pm (☎24 98 98) It is also possible to bike the 18km between the towns.

YSTAD   ☎0411

Best known as a ferry port for trips to Bornholm, DEN (p. 264), Ystad (EE-stad; pop. 27,000) is better known by Swedes as the home of fictional detective Kurt Wallander. Ystad has one of Sweden's best-preserved downtowns, a tight network of streets just inland of the terminal. A few of the town's half-timbered houses date back to the 15th century; Scandinavia's oldest is at Pilgr. and Stora Österg. The **Klostret** (Monastery), on Klosterg., showcases church and town history. From the tourist office, turn left onto Lingsg., left onto Stora Österg., and right out of Stortorg. onto Klosterg. (☎57 72 86; www.klostret.ystad.se. Open June-Aug. Tu-F 10am-5pm, Sa-Su noon-4pm; Sept.-May reduced hours. 30kr. MC/V.) Next to the tourist office, the **Konstmuseum** features work by Swedish and Danish artists. (☎57 72 85. Open high season M 10am-6pm, Tu-F 10am-5pm, Sa-Su noon-4pm; low season Tu-F noon-5pm, Sa-Su noon-4pm. 30kr. AmEx/MC/V.) ◙**Vandrarhemmet Stationen ❷** hostel is in the train station. (☎0708 57 79 95. Breakfast 55kr. Linens 60kr. Reception June-Aug. daily 9-10am and 5-7pm; Oct.-May call ahead. Dorms 200kr; singles 300kr; doubles 400kr. Cash only.) **Stora Östergatan,** a pedestrian street lined with cafes and shops, passes through the main square. The **Saluhallen** market is just off Stortorg. (Open daily 8am-9pm. MC/V.) Bornholms Trafikken (☎55 87 00) **ferries** go to Bornholm, DEN (1¼hr., up to 4 per day, 216kr). **Trains** run to Malmö (45min., 1 per hr., 72kr). The **tourist office** is across from the station. (☎57 76 81; www.ystad.se. Free Internet. Open mid-June to mid-Aug. M-F 9am-7pm, Sa-Su 10am-6pm; mid-Aug. to mid-June reduced hours.) **Postal Code:** 27101.

HELSINGBORG   ☎042

Warring Swedish and Danish armies passed Helsingborg (pop. 122,500) back and forth 12 times in the 17th century. By the time Magnus Stenbock captured the town for the Swedes once and for all in 1710, most of it lay in shambles. It wasn't until the 19th century that Helsingborg regained affluence. More recently, it has transformed into an elegant cultural center. The city's showpiece, **Knutpunkten,** houses transit terminals, restaurants, and shops under one glass roof. Exit Knutpunkten and make a left on Järnvägsg. to reach **Stortorget,** a long, wide main square that branches out into shopping streets like swanky **Kullagatan.** Stortorget ends at the **Terrassen,** a series of steps leading up to the 34m high **Kärnan,** a 700 year-old remnant of the fortress that once guarded the city. The tower offers a view across the water to Copenhagen on a clear day. (☎10 59 91. Open June-Aug. daily 11am-7pm; low season reduced hours. 20kr. Cash only.) Closer to sea level, the harborside **Dunkers Kulturhus,** Kungsg. 11, is the city's newest venue, with a concert hall and theater, unusual contemporary art exhibits, and a multimedia installation on city history. From the tourist office, turn right onto Drottningg. and then left onto Sundstorg. (☎10 74 00; www.dunkerskulturhus.se. Open Tu-W and F-Su 10am-5pm, Th 10am-8pm. 70kr, students 35kr. MC/V.) North of Helsingborg, the former royal retreat of ◙**Sofiero Slott,** built in 1864, sits on a hill overlooking the sound. The surrounding nature is worth exploring, especially from late May to early June when the rhododendrons bloom. Take bus #219 (18kr) from Knutpunkten to Sofiero Huvudentréen. (☎13 74 00; www.sofiero.helsingborg.se. Open daily late Apr. to early May and late Aug. to early Sept. 11am-5pm; early May to late Aug. 10am-6pm. Grounds 70kr, with castle 90kr, students 60/80kr. MC/V.)

To reach the well-kept **Helsingborgs Vandrarhem ❷**, Järnvägsg. 39, from Knutpunkten, cross Järnvägsg., turn right, and walk three blocks. (☎14 58 50; www.hbgturist.com. Linens 40kr. Laundry 25kr. Reception 3-6pm. Dorms 185kr; singles 275kr; doubles 395kr. MC/V.) Affordable cafes line **Södra Storgatan,** the last right off Stortorg. before Terrassen. The Knutpunkten **food court** has a wide selection. Pick up groceries at **ICA,** Drottningg. 48, past the Rådhuset. (☎13 15 70. Open M-Sa 8am-9pm, Su 10am-9pm. MC/V.) The harbor area has a handful of late-night bars and clubs, although the restaurants on board the Helsingør ferries (see below) can be more fun than terrestrial options during summer—stay at sea as long as you like while the ferry shuttles continuously between Denmark and Sweden.

Trains depart from Järnvägsgt. for Gothenburg (2½hr.; 1 per hr.; 294kr, under 26 252kr*)*, Malmö (1hr., 1 per hr. 84kr), and Stockholm (4-6hr.; 2-4 per day; 1066kr, under 26 912kr). **Ferries** go to Helsingør, DEN (p. 262), near Copenhagen; popular **Scandlines boats** depart every 20min. (☎18 61 00. 20min.; 26kr, round-trip 48kr. AmEx/MC/V.) Most **city buses** (15-20kr) pass Knutpunkten and include 1hr. of free transfers. For the **tourist office,** exit the station in the direction of the towering Rådhuset; head through the doors next to the closest turret. (☎10 43 50; www.helsingborg.se. Open mid-June to mid-Aug. M-F 9am-8pm, Sa 9am-5pm, Su 10am-3pm; mid-Aug. to mid-June M-F 10am-6pm, Sa 10am-2pm.) **Internet** is available in the **7-Eleven** across from the train station. (29kr per 90min. MC/V.) **Postal Code:** 25189.

GOTHENBURG (GÖTEBORG)　　　☎031

Wrongly dismissed as Sweden's industrial center, Gothenburg (YO-teh-bor-ee; pop. 770,000), the country's second largest city, is a sprawling, active metropolis threaded with parks, strewn with museums and theaters, and intersected by the glitzy Avenyn thoroughfare that cuts through the heart of the city. While Gothenburg is often overlooked on whirlwind tours of northern Europe, it has the cultural attractions of a Scandinavian capital, but with an unapologetically youthful twist.

▐ TRANSPORTATION

Trains run from Central Station to Malmö (2¾-3¾hr.; 1 per 1-2hr.; 362kr, under 26 307kr); Oslo, NOR (4hr., 2-3 per day, 444/332kr); and Stockholm (3-5hr., every 1-2hr., 538/460kr). Stena Line **ferries** (☎704 0000; www.stenaline.com) sail to Frederikshavn, DEN (2-3¼hr.; 6-10 per day; 160-200kr, 50% ScanRail or Eurail discount) and Kiel, GER (13½hr., daily 7:30pm, 340-810kr). Gothenburg has an extensive **tram** and **bus** system; rides are 20kr, and most trams and buses pass by the train station or through Brunnsparken, south of the Nordstan mall. A **day pass** (50kr), valid on both trams and buses, is available at kiosks throughout the city.

◀▶ ✷ ⁊ ORIENTATION AND PRACTICAL INFORMATION

Central Gothenburg is on the southern bank of the Göta River. The city's transportation hub is in **Nordstaden,** the northernmost part of the center. Across the Stora Hamn canal lies the busy central district of **Inom Vallgraven.** The main street, **Kungsportsavenyn** (a.k.a. "Avenyn"), begins just north of the Vallgraven canal at Kungsportsplatsen and continues south 1km to **Götaplatsen,** the main square in the Lorensberg district, where theaters and museums cluster. Vasagatan leads west through Vasastaden to the city's newly trendy but oldest suburb, the **Haga** district.

The **tourist office** has a branch in the Nordstan mall near the train and bus stations. (Open M-Sa 10am-6pm, Su noon-5pm.) The main branch, Kungsportspl. 2, sells the **Göteborg pass** (1-day 225kr, 2-day 310kr), which includes unlimited public transit, admission to many attractions, and free accommodations booking. The

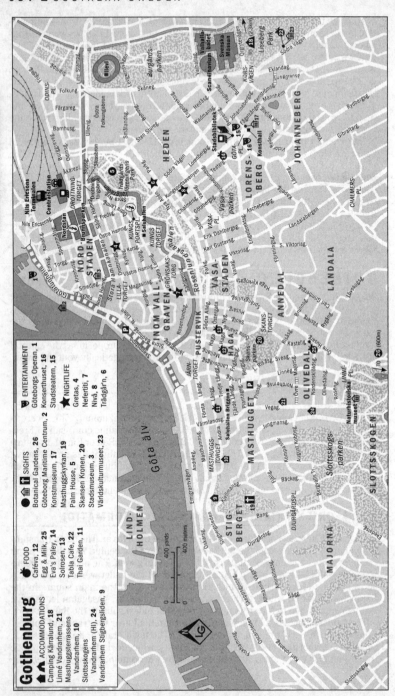

Gothenburg

ACCOMMODATIONS
Camping Kärralund, **18**
Linné Vandrarhem, **21**
Masthuggsterrassens
  Vandrarhem, **10**
Slottsskogens
  Vandrarhem (HI), **24**
Vandrarhem Stigbergsliden, **9**

FOOD
Cafèva, **12**
Egg & Milk, **25**
Eva's Paley, **14**
Solrosen, **13**
Tabla Cafe, **22**
Thai Garden, **11**

SIGHTS
Botanical Gardens, **26**
Göteborg Maritime Centrum, **2**
Konstmuseum, **17**
Masthuggskyrkan, **19**
Palm House, **5**
Skansen Kronen, **20**
Stadsmuseum, **3**
Världskulturmuseet, **23**

ENTERTAINMENT
Göteborgs Operan, **1**
Konserthuset, **16**
Stadsteatern, **15**

NIGHTLIFE
Gretas, **4**
Nefertiti, **7**
Nivå, **8**
Trädgår'n, **6**

pass is only worthwhile for city tours or if you plan to see at least four sights. (☎61 25 00; www.goteborg.com. Open late June to early Aug. daily 9:30am-8:15pm; low season M-F 9:30am-5pm, Sa 10am-2pm. AmEx/MC/V.) The **Stadsbibliotek** (public library), off Götapl., has 15min. of free **Internet.** Reserve at the desk and be prepared to wait in line. (Open M-F 10am-8pm, Sa 11am-5pm.) There are **Sidewalk Express Internet** kiosks in the train and bus stations. **Postal Code:** 40401.

◪ ◪ ACCOMMODATIONS AND CAMPING

Most of the city's hostels are in the West End, in and around **Masthugget;** trams and buses make it an easy ride to the city center. Reserve ahead, especially in July.

Slottsskogens Vandrarhem (HI), Vegag. 21 (☎42 65 20; www.sov.nu). Bus #60 (dir.: Masthugget) to Vegag. Spacious dorms and common areas with a kitchen and sauna (40kr). Bike rental 90kr per day. Breakfast 55kr. Linens 50kr. Laundry 40kr. Free Internet. Reception 8am-noon and 2pm-6am. 12- to 14-bed dorms 175kr; 3- to 6-bed dorms 195kr; singles 330kr; doubles 450kr. 50kr HI discount. MC/V. ❷

Masthuggsterrassens Vandrarhem, Masthuggsterr. 10H (☎42 48 20; www.mastenvandrarhem.com). Tram #3, 9, or 11 to Masthuggstorget. Cross the square diagonally, walk up the stairs, then follow the signs. Classic movie posters and long hallways give this tidy hostel a college-dorm feel. Breakfast 55kr. Linens 55kr. Laundry 45kr. Free Wi-Fi. TV in all private rooms. Reception 8-10am and 5-8pm. Dorms 170kr; doubles 440kr; triples 520kr; quads 620kr. MC/V. ❷

Vandrarhem Stigbergsliden (HI), Stigbergsl. 10 (☎24 16 20). Tram #3, 9, or 11 to Stigbergstorget. Walk downhill in the direction of the tram. Cozy rooms organized around a courtyard. Breakfast 50kr. Linens 50kr. Internet 1kr per min.; free Wi-Fi. Bike rental 50kr per day. Reception 8am-noon and 4-10pm. Dorms 190kr; singles 315kr; doubles 430kr. 50kr HI discount. AmEx/MC/V. ❷

Linné Vandrarhem, Vegag. 22 (☎12 10 60; www.vandrarhemmet-linne.com). Take bus #60 (dir.: Masthugget) to Vegag. Dorms turn into bright, private rooms when space is available. Breakfast 45kr, summer only. Linens 45kr. Reception 9am-1pm and 3-7pm. Dorms 190kr; doubles 400kr; triples 570kr; quads 760kr. AmEx/MC/V. ❷

Camping Kärralund, Olbersg. 9 (☎84 02 00; www.liseberg.se). Take tram #5 to Welanderg. and turn right onto Olbersg. Conveniently located in Liseberg Park, but slightly pricey. Breakfast 55kr. Laundry 55kr. Reception May-Aug. 7am-11pm; low season reduced hours. July-Aug. tent sites 235kr, electricity and water included; Sept.-June 100-165kr, electricity 45kr. AmEx/MC/V. ❷

◪ FOOD

The Avenyn is a great place for a stroll, but steer clear of its pricey eats in favor of the affordable options on **Vasagatan, Linnégatan,** and near the **Haga** neighborhood. **Saluhallen,** a food hall in Kungstorg., has the iron arches and the glass ceiling of a huge train station. (Open M-Th 9am-6pm, F 8am-6pm, Sa 8am-3pm.) **Saluhallen Briggen,** Nordhemsg. 28, is in an old fire station. (Open M-F 9am-6pm, Sa 9am-2pm.) **Hemköp** grocery stores are throughout the city, with branches on Andra Långgatan, Nordensklöldsg, and Vasag. (Open M-F 7am-10pm, Sa-Su 9am-8pm.)

▩ **Caféva,** Haga Nyg. 5E (☎711 6364). Locals flock to this homey cafe for traditional fare with some quirky twists. You can't go wrong with fresh-baked bread and cakes, hearty soups with coffee or tea (55kr), and filling sandwiches (38kr). Open June-Aug. M-F 10am-6pm, Sa 10am-4pm; Sept.-May M-F 9am-6pm, Sa 11am-4pm. MC/V. ❶

Solrosen, Kaponjärg. 4 (☎711 6697). Even carnivores can chow down at this cozy, flower-themed vegetarian haven in Haga. Soup 50kr. Entrees 70kr including salad bar. Open M-Th 11:30am-11:30pm, F 11:30am-12:30am, Sa 1pm-12:30am, Su 2pm-8:30pm. Kitchen closes M-Th 10pm, F-Sa 10:30pm, Su 7:30pm. AmEx/MC/V. ❷

Thai Garden, Andra Långg. 18 (☎ 12 76 60). Fill up on the delicious buffet (M-F 11am-3pm, 69kr) at this stand-out restaurant on a street lined with Thai eateries. Popular Mongolian barbecue Th-Su and take-out menu. Open M-Th 11am-10pm, F 11am-11pm, Sa noon-11pm, Su noon-10pm. AmEx/MC/V. ❷

Tabla Cafe, Södra Vägen 54 (☎ 63 27 20). Upstairs in the Världskulturmuseet. Enjoy lavish creations for reasonable prices. Try the bread (35-40kr) or the exquisite salads (45-65kr). Open Tu and Sa-Su noon-5pm, W-F noon-9pm. AmEx/MC/V. ❷

Egg & Milk, Ovre Husarg. 23 (☎ 701 0350). This hip 50s-style diner has an English-language menu and serves generous portions of all things breakfast (pancakes 50-54kr, omelettes 54-58kr, bagel platters 43-45kr). Open daily 7am-3pm. MC/V. ❷

Eva's Paley, Avenyn 39 (☎ 16 30 70), at the Götapl. end. Cheap, delicious food at a great location. Sandwiches 19-45kr. M-F 11am-3pm salad buffet 52kr. Free Wi-Fi. Open M-Th 8am-11pm, F 8am-midnight, Sa-Su 10am-11pm. AmEx/MC/V. ❷

ⒼSIGHTS

CITY CENTER. ◪**Göteborg Maritime Centrum,** a flotilla of 19 ships open for exploration, features a 1962 submarine and a WWII destroyer, with effects that bring the dormant vessels to life. *(☎ 10 59 60; www.maritima.se. Open May-Aug. daily 10am-6pm; Sept.-Oct. and Mar.-Apr. daily 10am-4pm; Nov. F-Sa 10am-4pm. 75kr, students 50kr. English-language tours in summer noon and 2pm. MC/V.)* **Nordstan,** Scandinavia's largest shopping center, is across from the train station. *(Open M-F 10am-7pm, Sa 10am-6pm, Su 11am-5pm.)* The **Stadsmuseum,** Norra Hamng. 12, contains the remains of the Äskekärr ship, the only preserved Viking ship exhibited in Sweden, and uses large-scale re-creations to recall the city's history. *(☎ 61 27 70; www.stadsmuseum.goteborg.se. Open May-Aug. daily 10am-5pm; Sept.-Apr. Tu-Su 10am-5pm, W 10am-8pm. 40kr, under 20 free; entrance fee, valid for 1 year, provides entrance to the Stadsmuseum, the Röhsska fashion, design and decorative arts museum, the Maritime museum, and the Konstmuseum. AmEx/MC/V.)* **Trädgårdsföreningens Park** is to the left as you cross the Avenyn bridge. Wind your way through the rosarium to the **Palm House.** *(☎ 365 5858; www.tradgardsforeningen.se. Park open daily Apr.-Sept. 7am-9pm; Oct.-Mar. 7am-7:30pm. Apr.-Sept. 15kr, free before 9am and after 8pm; Oct.-Mar. free. Palm House open daily 10am-5pm. Free.)* Avenyn ends at the **Götaplatsen** city square, built for the 1923 World Expo—the square is also the site of Carl Milles's famous **Poseidon fountain.** Even the sea god is dwarfed by the imposing ◪**Konstmuseum,** which holds a spectacular sculpture and photography collection. Works by Gaugin, Monet, Picasso, Rembrandt, and van Gogh are also displayed. *(☎ 61 29 80; www.konstmuseum.goteborg.se. Open Tu and Th 11am-6pm, W 11am-9pm, F-Su 11am-5pm. 40kr, temporary exhibits 20-40kr, under 20 free. AmEx/MC/V.)* Adjacent to the Konstmuseum, the **Konsthall** showcases contemporary art. *(☎ 61 50 40; www.konsthallen.goteborg.se. Open Tu and Th 11am-6pm, W 11am-8pm, F-Su 11am-5pm. Free.)*

HAGA. Westward, the Haga district offers art galleries, bookstores, and cafes, especially along the main thoroughfare, **Haga Nygata.** The flight of steps at the southern end of Kaponjärg. leads to **Skansen Kronen,** the most impressive of the hilltop towers that surround Gothenburg; the climb may be strenuous, but the view of the city from the tower's base is stellar. For a bird's-eye view of Gothenburg's harbor, head out to the **Masthuggskyrkan,** Storebackeg. 1, a 1914 brick church with a timber ceiling that suggests the inside of a Viking ship. Take tram #3, 9, or 11 to Masthuggstorg—it's the second church up the hill. *(☎ 731 9230. Open in summer daily 9am-6pm; low season usually M-F 11am-4pm.)* South of the church, the vast **Slottsskogsparken** invites you to wander among its aviaries, meadows, and ponds. Take tram #1 or 6 to Linnépl. Across the highway lies Sweden's largest **Botanical**

Gardens, Carl Skottsbergs G. 22A, home to orchid greenhouses, herb gardens, a bamboo grove, and 20,000 different flower, shrub, and tree species from across the globe. Take tram #1, 7, 8, or 13 to Botaniska Trädgården. (☎741 1100; www.gotbot.se. Open daily 9am-sunset. 20kr. Greenhouses 20kr. MC/V.)

NEAR LISEBERG PARK. In the southeastern part of the city, near the Svenska Mässan, the **Världskulturmuseet** (Museum of World Culture), Södra Vägen 54, challenges visitors with bold exhibits addressing culture's role in an increasingly globalized society. (☎63 27 00; www.varldskulturmuseet.se. Open Tu and Sa-Su noon-5pm, W-F noon-9pm. 40kr; entrance fee valid for 1 year. 19 and under free.) The muffled screams near the museum originate at **Liseberg,** Scandinavia's largest amusement park. Strap yourself in tight for a ride on Balder, the park's bone-rattling wooden rollercoaster. Take tram #4, 5, 6, 8, or 14 to Korsvägen. (☎40 01 00. Open mid-May to late Aug. daily; early Sept. Th-Su; mid- to late Sept. F-Su. Hours vary; check www.liseberg.se for schedule. Entry 60kr; rides 15-60kr each, 1-day ride pass 280kr. AmEx/MC/V.)

GÖTEBORGS SKÄRGÅRD. Beachgoers should head to **Göteborgs Skärgård,** a string of islands in Kattegat Bay. **Brännö** and **Styrsö** have shops and resort amenities, while the cliffs and beaches of **Vargö** are wilder and more secluded. (Take tram #11 to Saltholmen, 30min., and make a free transfer to the ferry, 30-45min.)

🎵 🎭 ENTERTAINMENT AND NIGHTLIFE

The enormous **Göteborgs Operan,** at Lilla Bommen, hosts concerts, musical theater, and opera from August through May. (☎13 13 00; www.opera.se. Tickets from 95-540kr, students 25% off Su-Th. Box office open daily noon-6pm. AmEx/MC/V.) Gothenburg's **Stadsteatern** (☎61 50 50) and **Konserthuset** (☎726 5300) round out the theater and music scene. The event calendar at www.goteborg.com has details on performances. Gothenburg's annual **film festival** (www.filmfestival.org) draws more than 110,000 to the city for 400 films (Jan. 25-Feb. 4, 2008). Mid-August brings the **Göteborg Kulturkalas,** an annual party that transforms the city with culinary masterpieces, entertainment, and music.

The chic but affordable bars that line **Linnégatan** are a good place to start or end an evening. Gothenburg's club scene is one of Scandinavia's most exclusive. Expect lines, steep covers, and strict dress codes. Many restaurants on Avenyn become posh clubs after nightfall. **Nivå,** Kungsportsavenyn 9, is the scene's standard-bearer, with four floors and an outside terrace. (☎701 8090. W "Soul Train" night. W 25+, F-Sa 27+. Cover F 70kr, Sa 100kr. Open W 8pm-3am, F 4:30pm-4am, Sa 8pm-4am. AmEx/MC/V.) For a little less attitude, head for **⛵Trädgår'n,** Nya Allén 11. Behind the unassuming, ivy-clad exterior is a stylish restaurant, concert venue, club, and bar. (☎10 20 80. 20+. Cover from 100kr. Club open F-Sa 9pm-5am. AmEx/MC/V.) On a low-tempo evening, head to **Nefertiti,** Hvitfeldtspl. 6, an intimate jazz bar that reinvents itself as a dance club after 12:30am. (☎711 4076; www.nefertiti.se. 20+. Club cover 80kr. Tickets 80-280kr. Concerts in summer Tu-W and F-Sa 8:30 or 9pm. MC/V.) The biggest gay club in Sweden, **Gretas,** Drottningg. 35, has plenty of room to party in its bar and on the dance floor. (☎13 69 49; www.gretas.nu. 20+. Cover F 60kr, Sa 100kr. Open F-Sa 11pm-4am. MC/V.)

🔲 DAYTRIP FROM GOTHENBURG: VARBERG

This summer paradise, a classic seaside town with beaches and bath houses, lies between Gothenburg and Helsingborg. Varberg's grand **fortress** is home to a number of attractions. The **Länsmuseet Varberg** displays **Bocksten Man,** an eerily well-preserved bog corpse from 1360. To reach the fortress, turn right out of the station and right onto S. Hamnv. *(☎0340 828 30; www.lansmuseet.varberg.se. Museum open June to mid-Aug. daily 10am-5pm; mid-Aug. to May M-F 10am-4pm, Sa-Su noon-4pm. June-Aug. 50kr; Sept.-May 30kr. MC/V.)* Follow the boardwalk 2km south of town for the shallow **Apelviken Bay,** which has some of the best **surfing** and **windsurfing** in Northern Europe. **Surfers Paradise,** Söderg. 22 *(☎0340 67 70 55)*, rents gear and gives lessons and tips. The boardwalk also passes several **nude beaches: Kärringhålan** for women and Goda Hopp for men. The **Getterön Peninsula,** 5km north, is a popular spot for camping and raucous parties. The peninsula is also accessible by the 15min. **Getteröbåtarna** boat taxi from the harbor. *(☎0703 10 13 24; www.getterobatarna.se. 1 per hr.; 30kr, bikes 10kr. Runs late June-Aug. daily 10am-midnight. Cash only.)* Live like a jailbird on the fortress grounds in the former prison cells of **Fästningens Vandrarhem ❷,** Varbergs Fästning. This penitentiary-turned-hostel, built during the 1850s, was once one of Sweden's largest prisons. *(☎0340 868 28; www.turist.varberg.se/vandrarhem. Reception 9-11am and 4-7pm. Rooms from 205kr. MC/V.)* **Trains** leave for Gothenburg (1hr.; 93kr, under 26 76kr) and Helsingborg (1½hr., 198/166kr). To reach the **tourist office,** in Brunnsparken, turn right out of the train station and walk two blocks. *(☎0340 868 00; www.turist.varberg.se. Open July M-Sa 9:30am-7pm, Su 1-6pm; May-June and Aug. M-F 10am-6pm, Sa 10am-3pm; Sept.-Apr. M-F 10am-5pm.)* **Postal Code:** 43201.

CENTRAL SWEDEN

Central Sweden extends from foothills along the Norwegian border to lakeside villages in the heart of the country. Many of the region's counties are known for the handicraft industry, with stylized religious paintings and colorful wooden horses from the area filling homes throughout Sweden. Central Sweden is also home to some of the country's best skiing in winter and popular hiking trails in summer.

MORA. The quiet town of Mora (pop. 22,000) sits in Europe's largest meteorite impact site: a 75km wide, 400m deep crater formed 360 million years ago. Lake Orsa borders the town to the north with Lake Siljan to the south and east. On the first Sunday in March, Mora marks the finish of the **Vasaloppet,** the world's oldest and longest cross-country ski race at 90km. The town hosts a week-long **festival** (www.vasaloppet.se; Feb. 22 to Mar. 2, 2008) during the race. The **◧Vasaloppet Museum** documents the history of the race with a film and serves samples of the warm blueberry soup participants drink during the competition. *(☎0250 392 25. Open mid-June to mid-Aug. daily 10am-5pm; mid-Aug. to mid-June M-F 10am-5pm; closed Th at 3pm year-round. 30kr, including film and soup. MC/V.)* Tucked away behind the city's church, **◧Zorngården,** Vasag. 37, was the 19th-century home of Anders Zorn, a renowned Swedish painter best remembered for his folk portrayals, nude paintings, and portraits. The house interior is only accessible by a 45min. tour. (Open mid-May to mid-Sept M-Sa 10am-4pm, Su 11am-4pm. Tours daily at noon, 1, 2, 3pm; call ahead for English-language tour availability. 60kr, students 50kr. AmEx/MC/V.) The **Zornmuseet** showcases a collection of Zorn's work. *(☎0250 59 23 10; www.zorn.se. Open mid-May to mid-Sept. M-Sa 9am-5pm, Su 11am-5pm; mid-Sept. to mid-May daily noon-4pm. 50kr, students 40kr. AmEx/MC/V.)* Hikers of any skill level can tackle the **Siljansleden** network of trails that circles the two lakes, including a well-marked 310km **bike trail.** In winter, a ploughed track across Lake Orsa draws **ice skaters** *(☎0250 172 30; www.frilufts.se/mora/is).*

For comfy, yet slightly cramped dorm rooms in a convenient location, head to **Vandrarhem Mora (HI) ❸,** Fredsg. 6. Turn left on the main road and right on Fredsg. Pleasant common areas make up for the communal showers. *(☎0250 381 96; www.maalkullann.se. Breakfast 65kr. Linens 80kr. Reception M-F 5-7pm, Sa-Su 5-6pm. Dorms 240kr; singles 370kr; doubles 600kr. 50kr HI discount on dorms and singles, 100kr on doubles. AmEx/MC/V.) **Mora Parken Camping ❶** sits on the Vasaloppet track. (☎0250 276 00; www.moraparken.se. Free showers. Breakfast 65kr. Linens 100kr. Laundry 10kr. Reception in the Mora Parken Hotel. Mid-June to mid-Aug. tent sites 150kr, with electricity 195kr; 2-person cabins 330kr, 4-person 480kr; low season reduced rates. AmEx/MC/V.) Restaurants in Mora tend to come in two varieties: overpriced and pizzeria-kebaberies. A departure from both is **VI På Kajen (Glassbar) ❶**, across from the tourist office on the water, which serves light meals for 35-65kr. (☎0250 177 07. Open June-Aug. daily 10am-9pm. AmEx/MC/V.) Pick up groceries at **ICA** on Kyrkog. (☎0250 103 28. Open daily 9am-9pm. MC/V.)

Trains go to Östersund (7hr., mid-June to early Aug. 1 per day, 876kr) and Stockholm (4hr., 7 per day, 351kr). **Bus** #45 (5hr., 2 per day, 182kr) runs to Östersund year-round. The **tourist office** is on Strandg., Turn left out of the station and follow Vasag. for about 15min. (☎0250 59 20 20; www.siljan.se. Open mid-June to mid-Aug. and during the ski race M-F 10am-7pm, Sa-Su 10am-5pm; mid-Aug. to mid-June M-F 10am-5pm. AmEx/MC/V.) **Internet** access is at the library, Köpmang. 4, off Kyrkog., 1 block from the bus station. (☎0250 267 79. 10kr per 30min. Open M-F 10am-7pm, Sa 10am-2pm; closed Sa June-Aug. Cash only.) **Postal Code:** 79230.

ÖSTERSUND. Travelers heading to Lappland often stop for a few days in Östersund (pop. 58,000). Deep, reedy **Lake Storsjön** lines the town's western shore. Many residents believe the lake is home to the **Storsjöodjuret monster.** In 1894, the town called in Norwegian whalers to flush out the creature, but appeals by local Quakers and the tourist office resulted in a 1986 ban (revoked in 2005) on any monster harassment. The SS *Thomée* runs cruises and monster-spotting tours. (2-3 per day; 80-110kr.) Rent a **bike** at the Badhusparken, near the *Thomée* dock, and pedal 8km over the footbridge to **Frösön Island,** a getaway aptly named for the Norse god of crops and fertility. (☎0730 62 99 72. Open June-Aug. M-F 8am-5pm. Bikes 50kr per ½-day. Cash only.) Swedish couples have taken the hint by making the island's 12th-century **Frösö kyrka** (church) one of Sweden's most popular wedding chapels. Bus #3 (20kr) from the town center also runs to the island. (☎063 16 11 50. Open daily 8am-8pm.) On the edge of the island closer to town, at the top of Frösön's highest point (468m), stands the **Frösötornet** (Frösö Tower) and the Frösötornets Vandrarhem (see below). Norwegian mountains can be seen from the top on a clear day. (☎063 12 81 69. Open daily late June to mid-Aug. 9am-9pm; mid-Aug. to Sept. and mid-May to late June 11am-5pm. 10kr. Cash only.) Östersund will host the **2008 Biathlon World Championships,** a combination of cross-country skiing and rifle shooting. (Feb. 8-17; visit www.ostersund2008.se.)

Reserve ahead for hostels in high season. The homey **Hostel Rallaren ❶** is at Bangårdsg. 6. Turn right out of the train station, take the right fork in the road, and continue straight for 150m. (☎063 13 22 32; sventa_rallaren@hotmail.com. Linens 50kr. Reception M-F 9:30am-2:30pm, Sa-Su reduced hours. Dorms 160kr; singles 210kr; doubles 360kr. Cash only.) Wild strawberries grow on the 257-year-old lofthouse at **Frösötornets Vandrarhem ❶**, Utsiktv. 10, Frösön. Bus #5 runs from the city center (11am-10:20pm) and stops at the bottom of a steep hill. The hostel is a tiring climb away. (☎063 51 57 67; vandrarhem@froson.com. Linens 50kr. Call for reception. Dorms 150kr; singles 190kr; doubles 300kr. Cash only.) Pick up groceries at **Hemköp,** Kyrkg. 56. (Open M-Sa 8am-10pm, Su 10am-10pm. MC/V.)

Trains run to Stockholm (6hr.; 6 per day; 554kr, under 26 461kr) and Trondheim, NOR (4hr., 2 per day, 289/202kr). From mid-June to early August, an Inlandsbanan train (☎0771 53 53 53; www.grandnordic.se) runs to Gällivare (14hr., 1 per day, from 762kr) and Mora (6hr., 1-2 per day, 379kr). The **tourist office,** Rådhusg. 44, offers bike rentals (100kr per day, 300kr per week) and no fee room booking. (☎063 14 40 01; www.turist.ostersund.se. Open July M-F 9am-8pm, Sa-Su 10am-7pm; early to mid-June M-Th 9am-7pm, F-Su 10am-3pm; mid-June to mid-Aug. M-F

SWEDEN

9am-5pm, Sa-Su 10am-3pm; Sept.-May M-F 9am-5pm. AmEx/MC/V.) **Internet** is at the tourist office (20kr per 10min.) or train station (open M-F and Su 7am-9:15pm, Sa 7am-5pm. 29kr per 1½hr., 57kr per 3hr., 149kr per month). **Postal Code:** 83100.

ÅRE. The village of Åre (pop. 1200) is one of Sweden's top skiing destinations. The **Åre Ski Star Resort** (☎0771 84 00 00; www.skistar.com/are/english) has beginner and intermediate cross-country and downhill trails along with a ski school. When the snow melts, the town becomes a base for outdoor activities on and around **Åreskutan,** the region's highest peak. Serious cyclists can take their chances with **downhill mountain biking,** a sport extreme enough to justify sky-high bike rental prices (300-800kr per day). **Rental shops** are around the base of the mountain. The **chairlift** brings you halfway up the mountain to a number of trailheads. (Lift runs daily late June-Aug. 10am-4pm. Round-trip 60kr.) For ambitious hikers, the 7km **Åreskutan trail** runs from the town square to a 1420m peak. The Kabinbanan **cable car** shortens the trip to under 1km. (Cable car runs late June-Aug. 10am-4pm. Round-trip 100kr.) The **Åre Ski Lodge ❸,** Trondheimsleden 44, is one of the cheaper accommodations in an expensive town. (☎0647 510 29. Breakfast and linens included. Laundry and lockers available. Free Wi-Fi. Reception 24hr. Reserve ahead during ski season. Summer doubles 580kr; quads 1180kr, 4760 per week Winter doubles 5000-9000kr per week; quads 20,000-32,000kr per week MC/V.) Pick up groceries at the train station's **ICA.** (Open M-Sa 8am-8pm, Su 10am-8pm. MC/V.) **Trains** run from Åre to Östersund (1¼hr.; 2 per day; 140kr, students 118kr) and Trondheim, NOR (2¾hr., 2 per day, 179kr). Nabotåget (☎0771 26 00 00; www.nabotaget.nu) has the best fares to Trondheim and destinations along the way. The **tourist office,** in the station, sells essential hiking maps (99kr), helps organize outdoor activities, and provides free **Internet.** (☎0647 177 20; www.visitare.se. Open late June-Aug. and mid-Dec. to Apr. daily 9am-6pm; Sept. to mid-Dec. and May-late June M-F 9am-5pm, Sa-Su 10am-3pm. AmEx/MC/V.) **Postal Code:** 83013.

GULF OF BOTHNIA

Sweden's Gulf of Bothnia region is well-known for its deep pine forests, stark ravines, and pristine coastline. Its quiet cities contrast with Sweden's glittery metropolitan centers to the south and serve as bases for wilderness excursions.

GÄVLE. Two hours north of Stockholm, Gävle (YEV-leh; pop. 90,000) is a gateway to Lappland. **Gamle Gefle** (Old Town), the only part of Gävle that survived a 19th-century fire, lies just across the canal. **Länsmuseet Gävleborg,** Södra Strandg. 20, displays contemporary art with traditional museum fare. (☎0266 556 00; www.lansmuseetgavleborg.se. Open late-June to mid-Aug. M-F 11am-5pm, Sa-Su noon-4pm; Sept.-May Tu and Th-F 10am-4pm, W 10am-9pm, Sa-Su noon-4pm. 50kr, students free. W free. MC/V.) Farther inland, the **Gävle Konstcentrum,** Kungsbäcksv. 32, displays Swedish and international contemporary art. (☎0261 794 24; www.gavle.se/konstcentrum. Open June to mid-Aug. Tu-Su noon-4pm; mid-Aug. to May Tu-F noon-5pm, Sa-Su noon-4pm. Free.) On the opposite bank, stroll through the city park's **sculpture garden.** The **Gävle Goat** is a giant straw Yule Goat built in Slottstorget every year since 1966. The display is famously the target of arson attacks and vandalism. As protection for the goat has amped up over the years, finding a way to destroy it has become a pastime that draws tourists to the region. Since the tradition started, fewer than 50% of the goats have survived unscathed. 🗷**Vandrarhem Gävle (HI) ❶,** Södra Rådmansg. 1, has rooms around an Old Town courtyard. From the train station, turn left, cross the canal, and make your first right on Södra Strandg. After the library, make a left, go through the square, up

the stairs, and past the parking lot. (☎0266 217 45.
Breakfast 55kr. Linens 80kr. Laundry 30kr. Reception 8-10am and 4:30-7pm. Dorms 205kr; singles
340kr; doubles 480kr. 50kr HI discount. MC/V.) For
a delectable lunch (16-68kr; daily special 60kr) in a
traditional Swedish setting, head to ▨Mamsell ❷,
Kyrkog. 14, in the Berggrenska Gårdens. From the
market square, walk one block on N. Stottsg. toward
the canal. (☎0261 234 10. Pastries 6-30kr. Sandwiches 16-58kr. Salads 54-68kr. Open M-F 11am-
5pm, Sa 11am-3pm. MC/V.) Pick up groceries at ICA,
across the street from the train station. (Open M-Sa
8am-8pm, Su 11am-8pm. MC/V.) Trains run to Östersund (4-6hr., 2-4 per day, 624kr) and Stockholm
(1½hr., 1 per hr., 236kr). To get to the tourist office,
Drottningg. 9, head straight out of the train station
down Drottningg. to the market square; it's in the
center of the Gallerian Nian shopping center.
(☎0261 474 30; www.gastrikland.com. Open M-F
10am-7pm, Sa 10am-4pm, Su noon-4pm. AmEx/MC/
V.) Free Internet is available at the library, Stadsbiblioteket, Slottstorget 1, for 15min. slots, usually with
a short wait. (☎0261 794 29. Open M-Th 10am-7pm,
F 10am-5pm, Sa-Su 10am-2pm.) Postal Code: 80250.

ÖRNSKÖLDSVIK. Although drab concrete dominates the center of Örnsköldsvik (urn-SHULDS-vik;
"Ö-vik" to locals; pop. 29,000), the city is forgiven its
architectural missteps thanks to popular nearby
hikes. The 127km Höga Kusten Leden (High Coast
Trail) winds south through Skuleskogen National Park
as far as Veda, just north of the High Coast Bridge.
Flanked by cliffs that drop into the Gulf of Bothnia,
the trail is divided into 13 segments with free mountain
huts at the end of each leg. Bring an insulated sleeping
bag and arrive early to cut firewood. Day hikes
include the 6km Yellow Trail loop. You'll find the trailhead on Hantverkareg. From the tourist office, walk
up Centralespl., turn left on Storg., and then left again.
A lift runs to the top of the mountain. (☎0660 156 92.
Open M 2-4pm, Tu-Th and Sa-Su 11am-4pm, F 11am-
4pm and 5:30-7pm. Round-trip 50kr. Cash only. Tickets also available at the tourist office. AmEx/MC/V.)
▨Örnsköldsviks Vandrarhem ❷, Viktoriaespl. 32, is a
cozy converted family manor. From the bus station,
turn left onto Lasarettsg., walk four blocks, make a
right onto Bergsg., then a left onto Viktoriaespl.
(☎0660 29 61 11. Wheelchair-accessible. Breakfast
50kr. Linens 50kr. Free Wi-Fi. Call for reception.
Dorms 200kr; doubles 400kr. MC/V.) Lundberg Bröd o
Cafe ❷, Nygatan 35, serves large meals (50kr). The
chicken pasta salad is especially popular. (☎0660 12
51 25. Open in summer M-F 7am-5pm; winter M-F

7am-5pm, Sa 10am-2pm. AmEx/MC/V.) Pick up groceries at **Hemköp**, Stora Torg. 3. (Open M-F 8am-8pm, Sa-Su 8am-10pm. MC/V.) **Buses** run to Östersund (4½hr.; M-F 2-3 per day, Sa-Su 1 per day; 275kr) and Umeå (1½hr., 14 per day, 216kr). The **tourist office**, Strandg. 24, next to the station, has free **Internet**. (☎0660 881 00; www.ornskoldsvik.se. Open late June to mid-Aug. M-F 9am-6pm, Sa-Su 10am-2pm; mid-Aug. to late June M-F 10am-6pm, Sa 10am-2pm. AmEx/MC/V.) **Postal Code:** 89133.

UMEÅ. In the 1970s, leftist students in Umeå (OOM-eh-oh; pop. 111,000) earned their school the nickname "red university." Today, northern Sweden's largest city is better known for its birch-lined boulevards than its Marxist leanings, although echoes of its egalitarian past live on in a slew of free attractions. At the **Gammlia** open-air museum, a 20min. walk east of the city center, visitors get a crack at 19th-century crafts they've been itching to try, like churning butter, while munching on *tunnbröd* (20kr), a Swedish flatbread. (Open daily 10am-5pm. Free.) In the same complex, the **Västerbottens Museum** houses the world's oldest ski, dating back to 3200 BC, and the modern **forUm** exhibit, where visitors can learn about the town. (☎090 17 18 00; www.vasterbottensmuseum.se. Open mid-June to mid-Aug. daily 10am-5pm; low season reduced hours. Free.) The **BildMuseet**, at Umeå University, displays Swedish and international contemporary art. (☎090 786 5227; www.bild-museet.umu.se. Open Tu-Sa noon-4pm, Su noon-5pm. Free.) Umeå is also 5km away from the celebrated **Umedalen Sculpture Park,** featuring 25 pieces by leading Swedish and international artists. Take bus #1 or 61 from Vasaplan (20kr, 1hr. transfer) to Umedalen. (☎090 903 64; www.gsa.se. Free.) West of the city, the 30km **Umeleden** bike and car trail snakes past 5000-year-old rock carvings, an arbo-retum, and **Baggböle Herrgård,** a cafe in a 19th-century manor. (☎090 321 51. Open June-Aug. Tu-Su 11am-6pm. Cash only.) Pick up the trail at the **Gamla Bron** (Old Bridge) and veer across the Norvarpsbron to cut the route in half. Hikers can fol-low the **Tavelsjöleden** trail (30km) along a boulder ridge, or brave the **Isälvsleden** trail (60km), 80km from Umeå and carved out of the stone by melting pack ice.

    YMCA Hostel (SVIF) ❷, Järvägsallen 22, offers spacious common areas and plain rooms that get the job done. (☎090 18 57 00; www.hostel.kfum.nu. Breakfast 50kr. Linens 65kr. Towels 25kr. Laundry 6kr. Internet 30kr per hr., 200kr per stay. Reception M-F 8am-noon and 1-6pm, Sa-Su 8-10am and 4-6pm. Dorms 160kr; sin-gles from 330kr; doubles from 420kr. MC/V.) The city center has many cafes and *pâtisseries* (32-48kr). **Taj Mahal ❷**, Vasag. 10, serves a vegetarian-friendly lunch buffet for 75kr. (☎090 12 12 52; www.tajmahalumea.com. Open M-Th 11am-2:30pm and 4-9pm, F 11am-3pm and 4-11pm, Sa noon-11pm, Su 2-8pm. MC/V.) Pick up gro-ceries at **ICA**, across from the bus station. (Open M-F 8am-10pm, Sa-Su 9am-10pm. MC/V.) Mingle with students at the bars in **Renmarkstorget Square** or on **Västra Strandgatan** along the river. **Trains** run to Gothenburg (11-15hr., 5-6 per day, 632kr). Ybuss **buses** (☎090 70 65 00) run to Stockholm (10hr., 1-3 per day, 385kr, students 300kr). The bus terminal is across from the train station on the right. The **tourist office,** Renmarkstorg. 15, gives free English-language tours of the city in summer and has free **Internet.** From the stations, walk to the right down Rådhusespl. and turn right on Skolg. (☎090 16 16 16; www.visitumea.se. Tours W 4pm, Su 4pm. Open mid-June to mid-Aug. M-F 8:30am-7pm, Sa 10am-4pm, Su noon-4pm; mid-Aug. to mid-June M-F 10am-5pm.) **Cykel och Mopedhandlaren,** Kungsg. 101, rents **bikes.** (☎090 14 01 70. Open M-F 9:30am-5:30pm, Sa 10am-1pm. 90kr for 1st day, 30kr per day thereafter, 250kr per week MC/V.) **Postal Code:** 90326.

LAPPLAND (SÁPMI)

Mountains and alpine dales sprawl across Lappland, known as "Europe's last wil-derness," a frontier that extends through northern Finland, Norway, Russia, and Sweden. Today, the region's indigenous Sámi people use helicopters and snowmobiles to tend their reindeer herds while continuing to wrangle with Stockholm over the hunting and grazing rights their ancestors enjoyed for centuries.

 BUG CONTROL. While locals swear by a concoction of diluted vinegar—imbibed every morning—to ward off mosquitoes, most travelers will want to carry a large supply of old-fashioned bug spray when heading into forests up north.

⊟ TRANSPORTATION

Connex runs **trains** along the coastal route from Stockholm through Umeå, Boden, and Kiruna to Narvik, NOR, along the iron ore railway. From late June to early August, Inlandsbanan trains run north from Mora (p. 988) through the country. (☎063 19 44 12; www.inlandsbanan.se.) **Buses** are the only way to reach smaller towns; call ☎020 47 00 47 or stop by Kiruna's tourist office for schedules.

KIRUNA   ☎0980

The only large settlement in Lappland, Kiruna (pop. 23,000), 250km north of the Arctic Circle, retains the rough edges of a mining town, despite its proximity to the chic **Riksgänsen** ski resort. The midnight sun shines for 100 days from May 31st to July 11th. The *aurora borealis* can be seen as darkness returns in August. While Kiruna's main appeal is its proximity to other sights, the town also has some surprisingly innovative architecture. **Kiruna Church,** Kyrkog. 8, resembles a Sámi *goahti*, a tent-like dwelling. (☎101 40. Open daily 9am-6pm. Free.) **City Hall,** designed by architect Arthur von Schmalensee, houses a modern art collection. (☎700 00. Open M-F June-Aug. 7am-5pm; Sept.-May 8am-5pm. Free.) The state-owned mining company, **LKAB,** hauls 20 million tons of iron ore out of the ground each year. The deposits stretch underneath the city, prompting the decision to move Kiruna's buildings farther north to counter subsidence, the downward movement of the Earth's surface. Don't worry about showing up and finding that Kiruna has vanished—the moving process is expected to take 30 years. LKAB offers 3hr. 🔳**InfoMine** tours, which descend 540m to a museum with exhibits on the history of the mine. Every morning at 1:15 and 1:30am, **dynamite blasts** loosen the mine's iron ore—back on the surface, stay awake for a very light earthquake. (2-4 tours per day. Tickets available at the tourist office. 240kr, students 140kr. AmEx/MC/V.) **Esrange,** 40km outside Kiruna, is Europe's only non-military space station. Scientists here launch short-range rockets and conduct ozone layer research. A current proposal calls for building a spaceport at the complex for suborbital spaceflight and space tourism, which sadly will not be budget-friendly. (☎04 02 70. 4hr. tours leave Kiruna late June to mid-Aug. Tu and Th 9:15am. Reserve at the tourist office at least 24hr. ahead. 390kr. AmEx/MC/V.) Hikers take bus #92 from Kiruna to Nikkaluokta (1¼hr., 1-3 per day, 73kr) and pick up the well-marked 440km **Kungsleden** trail at Fjällstation, near the base of **Kebnekaise** (2104m), Sweden's highest peak. A week's trek north brings travelers into **Abisko National Park.** The STF runs cabins 10-20km apart on the trail. (☎084 63 22 00; www.stfturist.se. Cabins mid-July to mid-Sept. 255-355kr; late Feb. to mid-July 190-235kr. 100kr HI discount. MC/V.) Day hikers can journey directly from Kiruna to Abisko on bus #91 (1¼hr., 1-3 per day, 73kr) and choose from any number of trails.

The **Yellow House Hostel ❶,** Hantverkareg. 25, has bright, spacious rooms. Turn left from the tourist office entrance, walk uphill and turn left again on Vänortsg., which turns into Hantverkareg. (☎137 50; www.yellowhouse.nu. Breakfast 50kr. Linens 50kr. Reception 2-11pm. Reserve ahead. Dorms 150-160kr; singles 300kr; doubles 400kr. MC/V.) **STF Vandrarhem (HI) ❷,** Bergmästareg. 7, offers standard rooms in the town center. From the tourist office, walk across the plaza, along the path next to the ICA supermarket, past the pharmacy, then make a left onto Bergmästareg. (☎171 95; www.kirunahostel.com. Breakfast 60kr. Luggage storage

50kr. Linens 50kr. Towels 15kr. Sauna 50kr. Free Wi-Fi. Reception M-F 7am-10pm, Sa-Su 8am-noon and 4-8pm. Dorms 160kr; singles 300kr; doubles 400kr. AmEx/MC/V.) For a two-course lunch special (9am-1:30pm, 68kr), head to the cafeteria-style **Svarta Björn ❷**, Hj. Lundbohmsv. 42, across the street from the bus station. (☎157 90. Open July-Aug. M-F 8am-7pm, Sa-Su 11am-5pm; Sept.-June M-F 6:30am-3pm, occasionally extended to 7pm, Sa-Su 11am-1pm. Cash only.) Warm and cozy **Kaffekoppen ❶**, Föreningsg. 13B, serves light meals and *souvas* (wraps) from 39kr, along with huge mugs of hot chocolate from 25kr. (☎180 61. Open M 9am-6pm, Tu-Sa 9am-10pm, Su 10am-10pm. MC/V.) Get groceries at **ICA** in the central square. (Open M-F 9am-7pm, Sa 10am-4pm, Su 11am-4pm. MC/V.)

Connex **trains** run to Narvik, NOR (3hr., 3 per day, 235kr) and Stockholm (17hr., 2 per day, from 460kr). **Flights** to Stockholm (3-4 per day; from 500kr, students from 350kr) depart from **Kiruna Flygplats** (**KRN;** ☎680 00). The **tourist office,** L. Jans-sonsgat. 17, is in the Folkets Hus. Walk from the train station, follow the footpath through the tunnel, and go up the stairs through the park to the top of the hill. The office helps arrange dogsled excursions (www.kirunanature.com) and year-round moose safaris. (☎188 80; www.lappland.se. Luggage storage 20kr per bag 1st day, 10kr per day thereafter. Internet 25kr per 20min. Open mid-June to mid-Aug. M-F 8:30am-8pm, Sa-Su 8:30am-6pm; mid-Aug. to mid-June M-F 8:30am-5pm, Sa 8:30am-2pm. AmEx/MC/V.) The town library, Biblioteksg. 4, offers free **Internet.** Expect lines in winter. (☎707 50. Open June-Aug. M-Th 1-6pm, F 1-5pm; Sept.-May M-Th 10am-7pm, F 2:30-6pm, Sa-Su 11am-3pm.) **Postal Code:** 98122.

⧉ DAYTRIP FROM KIRUNA: JUKKASJÄRVI. Nestled on the shores of the Torne River, quiet Jukkasjärvi (pop. 800; sled dog pop. 1000) transforms into one of the country's hottest tourist spots in winter. The main reason for the sudden acclaim is the ⧉**Icehotel,** which crystallizes anew each November only to melt back into the river in May. The hotel is open for tours in winter (Jan.-Apr.). Summertime vis-itors get to see more than just a giant puddle—get a taste of the cold by visiting the ice exhibit in the **Art Center** and sipping drinks (45-105kr) from ice glasses at the Art Center's **Absolut Icebar.** (☎668 00; www.icehotel.com. Icehotel open mid-June to Aug. daily 10am-6pm; Dec.-Apr. M-F 10am-5pm. 150kr, students 120kr. AmEx/MC/V.) The hotel's affiliated museum, **The Homestead,** is a short boat ride or 10min. walk away, and features a 19th-century family home and small Sámi exhibit. (☎668 00. Open daily 10am-6pm. 40kr. Tours daily 10am-5pm. MC/V.) Across the street is the open-air ⧉**Sámi Siida Kulturcenter,** where Sámi guides mix discussions of their cultural identity with reindeer lassoing lessons. (☎0980 213 29; www.nutti.se. Open daily early June to mid-Aug. 10am-6pm. 90kr. Tours daily 11am, 12:30, 2, 3:30, 5pm. Cash only.)

Budget lodgings do not exist in Jukkasjärvi, save for finding a good spot to pitch your tent. The only restaurants are in the Icehotel and museums. In summer, **Sámi Siida ❷** has traditional Sámi dishes and sandwiches (25-35kr) inside a cozy rein-deer skin tent. The **Homestead Restaurant ❸,** at the museum, has a 95kr lunch buf-fet 11:30am-2pm. (☎668 07. Open daily M-Th 11:30am-9pm, F-Su 11:30am-10pm. AmEx/MC/V.) **Bus** #501 goes to the Kiruna (30min., 2-4 per day, round-trip 51kr). **Wi-Fi** is available at the Icehotel reception for those with laptops. **Postal Code:** 98191.

SWITZERLAND

(SCHWEIZ, SUISSE, SVIZZERA)

While the stereotype of Switzerland as a country of bankers, chocolatiers, and watchmakers still holds partly true, an energetic youth culture and a growing adventure sports industry belies its staid reputation. The country's gorgeous lakes and formidable peaks entice outdoor enthusiasts from around the globe. Mountains dominate three-fifths of the country: the Jura cover the northwest region, the Alps stretch across the lower half, and the eastern Rhaetian Alps border Austria. Only in Switzerland can you indulge in chocolate and in three cultures at once.

DISCOVER SWITZERLAND: SUGGESTED ITINERARIES

THREE DAYS. Experience the great outdoors at **Interlaken** (1 day; p. 1003). Head to **Luzern** (1 day; p. 1011) for the perfect combination of city culture and natural splendor before jetting to international **Geneva** (1 day; p. 1019).

ONE WEEK. Begin in Luzern (1 day), which will fulfill your visions of a charming Swiss city. Then head to the capital, Bern (1 day; p. 1000), before getting your adventure thrills in Interlaken (1 day). Get a taste of Italian Switzerland in Locarno (1 day; p. 1026), then traverse northern Italy to reach Zermatt and the **Matterhorn**

(1 day; p. 1017). End your trip in cosmopolitan **Geneva** (2 days).

TWO WEEKS. Start in Geneva (2 days), then check out **Lausanne** (1 day; p. 1023) and **Montreux** (1 day; p. 1024). Tackle the Matterhorn in **Zermatt** (1 day) and keep hiking above **Interlaken** (1 day). Bask in **Locarno's** sun (1 day), then explore the **Swiss National Park** (1 day; p. 1016). Head to **Luzern** (1 day) and **Zürich** (2 days; p. 1006). Unwind in tiny **Stein am Rhein** (1 day; p. 1011) and visit the abbey of **St. Gallen** (1 day; p. 1012). Return to civilization via the capital, **Bern** (1 day).

ESSENTIALS

FACTS AND FIGURES

Official Name: Swiss Confederation.

Capital: Bern.

Major Cities: Basel, Geneva, Zürich.

Population: 7,555,000.

Land Area: 41,300 sq. km.

Time Zone: GMT+1.

Languages: German (64%), French (19%), Italian (8%), Romansch (1%).

Religions: Roman Catholic (48%), Protestant (44%), other (8%).

Avg. Chocolate Consumed: 23 lbs. per person annually (twice as much as an American citizen).

WHEN TO GO

During ski season (Nov.-Mar.) prices double in eastern Switzerland and travelers must make reservations months ahead. The situation reverses in the summer, especially July and August, when the flatter, western half of Switzerland fills with

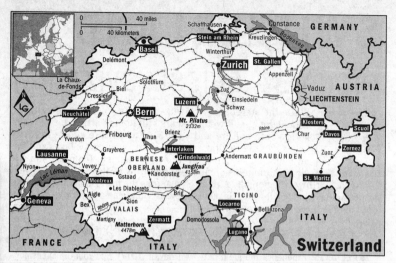

Switzerland

vacationers and hikers enjoying low humidity and temperatures rarely exceeding 26°C (80°F). A good budget option is to travel during the shoulder season: May-June and September-October, when tourism lulls and the daytime temperature ranges from -2-7°C (46-59°F). Many mountain towns throughout Switzerland shut down completely in May and June, however, so call ahead.

DOCUMENTS AND FORMALITIES

EMBASSIES. Most foreign embassies in Switzerland are in Bern (p. 1000). Swiss embassies abroad include: **Australia,** 7 Melbourne Ave., Forrest, Canberra, ACT, 2603 (☎02 6162 8400; www.eda.admin.ch/australia); **Canada,** 5 Marlborough Ave., Ottawa, ON, K1N 8E6 (☎613-235-1837; www.eda.admin.ch/canada); **Ireland,** 6 Ailesbury Rd., Ballsbridge, Dublin, 4 (☎353 12 18 63 82; www.eda.admin.ch/dublin); **New Zealand,** 22 Panama St., Wellington (☎04 472 15 93; www.eda.admin.ch/wellington); **UK,** 16-18 Montagu Pl., London, W1H 2BQ (☎020 76 16 60 00; www.eda.admin.ch/london); **US,** 2900 Cathedral Ave., NW, Washington, D.C., 20008 (☎202-745-7900; www.eda.admin.ch/washington).

VISA AND ENTRY INFORMATION. EU citizens do not need a visa. Citizens of Australia, Canada, New Zealand, and the US do not need a visa for stays of up to 90 days. For stays longer than 90 days, all visitors need visas (around US$44), available at Swiss consulates. Travelers should anticipate a processing time of about six to eight weeks.

TOURIST SERVICES AND MONEY

EMERGENCY	Ambulance: ☎144. Fire: ☎118. Police: ☎117.

TOURIST OFFICES. Branches of the **Swiss National Tourist Office,** marked by a standard blue "i" sign, are present in nearly every town in Switzerland; most agents speak English. The official tourism website for Switzerland is www.myswitzerland.com.

MONEY. The Swiss unit of currency is the **Swiss franc (CHF),** plural Swiss francs. One Swiss franc is equal to 100 centimes (called *Rappen* in German Switzer-

THE REAL DEAL. If you're planning on spending a long time in Switzerland, consider the **Museum Pass** (30CHF). Available at some tourist offices and participating venues, it lets you into most major Swiss museums.

land), with standard denominations of 5, 10, 20, and 50 centimes and 1, 2, and 5CHF in coins, and 10, 20, 50, 100, 200, 500, and 1000CHF in notes. Widely accepted credit cards include American Express, MasterCard, and Visa. **Euro** (€) are also accepted at many museums and restaurants. Switzerland is not cheap; if you stay in hostels and prepare most of your own food, expect to spend 55-80CHF per day. Generally, it's less expensive to exchange money at home than in Switzerland. **ATMs** offer the best exchange rates. Although restaurant bills already include a 15% service charge, an additional **tip** of 1-2CHF for a modest meal or 5-10CHF for a more upscale dinner is expected. Give hotel porter and doormen about 1CHF per bag and airport porters 5CHF per bag.

Switzerland has a 7.6% **value added tax (VAT)**, a sales tax applied to goods and services. The prices given in *Let's Go* include VAT. In the airport upon exiting Switzerland, non-Swiss citizens can claim a refund on the tax paid for goods purchased at participating stores. In order to qualify for a refund in a store, you must spend at least 500CHF; make sure to ask for a refund form when you pay. For more info on qualifying for a VAT refund, see p. 19.

SWISS FRANC (CHF)		
AUS$1 = 0.99CHF		1CHF = AUS$1.01
CDN$1 = 1.15CHF		1CHF = CDN$0.87
EUR€1 = 1.64CHF		1CHF = EUR€0.61
NZ$1 = 0.86CHF		1CHF = NZ$1.16
UK£1 = 2.42CHF		1CHF = UK£0.41
US$1 = 1.21CHF		1CHF = US$0.83

TRANSPORTATION

BY PLANE. Major international airports are in **Bern** (**BRN;** ☎031 960 21 11; www.alpar.ch), **Geneva** (**GVA;** ☎022 717 71 11; www.gva.ch), and **Zürich** (**ZRH;** ☎043 816 86 00; www.zurich-airport.com). From London, **easyJet** (☎0871 244 23 66; www.easyjet.com) has flights to Geneva and Zürich. **Aer Lingus** (Ireland ☎0818 365 000, Switzerland 422 86 99 33, UK 0870 876 5000; www.aerlingus.com) sells tickets from Dublin, IRE to Geneva. For more information on flying to Switzerland from other locations, see p. 46.

BY TRAIN. Federal (**SBB, CFF**) and private railways connect most towns with frequent trains. For times and prices, check online (www.sbb.ch). **Eurail, Europass,** and **Inter Rail** are all valid on federal trains. The **Swiss Pass,** sold worldwide, offers four, eight, 15, 22, or 30 consecutive days of unlimited rail travel. It also doubles as a **Swiss Museum Pass,** allowing free entry to 400 museums. (2nd-class 4-day pass US$194, 8-day US$276, 15-day US$336, 21-day US$390, 1mo. US$434.)

BY BUS. PTT Post Buses, a barrage of government-run yellow coaches, connect rural villages and towns that trains don't service. **Swiss Passes** are valid on many buses; **Eurail** passes are not. Even with the SwissPass, you might have to pay 5-10CHF extra if you're riding certain buses.

BY CAR. Roads, generally in good condition, may become dangerous at higher altitudes in the winter. The speed limit is 50kph in cities, 80kph on open roads, and 120kph on highways. Many small towns forbid cars; some require special permits or restrict driving hours. US and British citizens 18 and older with a

SWITZERLAND

valid driver's license may drive in Switzerland for up to one year following their arrival; for stays longer than one year, drivers should contact the **Service des automobiles et de la navigation** (SAN; ☎ 022 388 30 30; www.geneve.ch/san) about acquiring a Swiss permit. Custom posts sell windshield stickers (US$33) required for driving on Swiss roads. Call ☎ 140 for roadside assistance.

BY BIKE. Cycling is a splendid way to see the country. Find bikes to rent at large train stations. The **Touring Club Suisse,** with locations throughout Switzerland (☎ 022 417 22 20; www.tcs.ch), is a good source for maps and route descriptions.

KEEPING IN TOUCH

PHONE CODES	**Country code: 41. International dialing prefix:** 00. For more info on how to place international calls, see **Inside Back Cover.**

EMAIL AND THE INTERNET. Most Swiss cities, as well as a number of smaller towns, have at least one Internet cafe with web access available for about 12-24CHF per hour. Hostels and restaurants frequently offer Internet access as well, but it seldom comes for free: rates can climb as high as 12CHF per hour.

TELEPHONE. Whenever possible, use a calling card for international phone calls, as long-distance rates are often exorbitant for national phone services. For info about using mobile phones abroad, see p. 29. Most pay phones in Switzerland accept only prepaid taxcards, which are available at kiosks, post offices, and train stations. Direct access numbers include: **AT&T Direct** (☎ 800 89 00 11); **Canada Direct** (☎ 800 55 83 30); **MCI WorldPhone** (☎ 800 444 41 41); **Sprint** (☎ 800 877 46 46); **Telecom New Zealand** (☎ 800 55 64 11).

MAIL. Airmail from Switzerland averages three to 15 days to North America, although times are unpredictable from smaller towns. Domestic letters take one to three days. Bright yellow logos outside buildings mark Swiss national post offices, referred to as **Die Post** in German or **La Poste** in French. Letters from Switzerland weighing less than 20g cost 1.40CHF to mail to the US, 1.30CHF to mail to the UK, and 0.85CHF mailed nationally. To receive mail in Switzerland, have mail delivered **Poste Restante.** Mail will go to the main post office unless you specify a subsidiary by street address. Address mail to be held according to the following example: LAST NAME, First Name, *Postlagernde Briefe*, Postal Code, City, SWITZERLAND. Bring a passport to pick up your mail; there may be a small fee.

ACCOMMODATIONS AND CAMPING

SWITZERLAND ACCOMMODATIONS	❶ under 30CHF	❷ 30-42CHF	❸ 43-65CHF	❹ 66-125CHF	❺ over 125CHF

There are **hostels** (*Jugendherbergen* in German, *auberges de jeunesse* in French, *ostelli* in Italian) in all cities in Switzerland as well as in most towns. **Schweizer Jugendherbergen** (SJH; www.youthhostel.ch) runs HI hostels throughout Switzerland. Non-HI members can stay in any HI hostel, where beds are usually 30-44CHF; members typically receive a 6CHF discount. The more informal **Swiss Backpackers (SB)** organization (☎ 062 892 2675; www.backpacker.ch) lists over 25 hostels aimed at young, foreign travelers interested in socializing. Most Swiss **campgrounds** are not idyllic refuges but large plots glutted with RVs. Prices average 12-20CHF per tent site and 6-9CHF per extra person. **Hotels** and **pen-**

sions tend to charge at least 65-80CHF for a single room and 80-120CHF for a double. The cheapest have *Gasthof*, *Gästehaus*, or *Hotel-Garni* in the name. **Privatzimmer** (rooms in a family home) run about 30-60CHF per person. Breakfast is included at most hotels, pensions, and *Privatzimmer*.

HIKING AND SKIING. Nearly every town has **hiking trails:** Interlaken (p. 1003), Grindelwald (p. 1005), Luzern (p. 1011), and Zermatt (p. 1017) offer particularly good hiking opportunities. Trails are marked with either red-white-red markers (only sturdy boots and hiking poles needed) or blue-white-blue markers (mountaineering equipment needed). **Skiing** in Switzerland is less expensive than in North America, provided you avoid pricey resorts. **Ski passes** run 40-70CHF per day, 100-300CHF per week; a week of lift tickets, equipment rental, lessons, lodging, and *demi-pension* (breakfast plus one other meal) averages 475CHF. **Summer skiing** is available in a few towns such as Zermatt.

FOOD AND DRINK

SWITZERLAND	❶	❷	❸	❹	❺
FOOD	under 9CHF	9-23CHF	24-32CHF	33-52CHF	over 52CHF

Switzerland is not for the lactose intolerant. The Swiss are serious about dairy products, from rich and varied **cheeses** to decadent **milk chocolate**—even the major Swiss soft drink, **Rivella,** contains dairy. Swiss dishes vary from region to region. Bernese **röstl,** a plateful of hash-brown potatoes (sometimes flavored with bacon or cheese), is prevalent in the German regions; cheese or meat **fondue** is popular in the French regions. Try Valaisian **raclette,** made by melting cheese over a fire, scraping it onto a baked potato, and garnishing it with meat or vegetables. Supermarkets **Migros** and **Co-op** double as cafeterias; stop in for a cheap meal and groceries. Water from the fountains that adorn cities and large towns is usually safe; filling your bottle with it will save you money. *Kein Trinkwasser* or *Eau non potable* signs indicate unclean water. Each canton has its own local beer, which is often cheaper than soda.

HOLIDAYS AND FESTIVALS

Holidays: New Year's Day (Jan. 1); Epiphany (Jan. 6); Good Friday (Mar. 21); Easter (Mar. 23-24); Ascension (May 1); Labor Day (May 1); Pentecost (May 12); Whit Monday (May 13); Corpus Christi (May 22); Swiss National Day (Aug. 1); All Saints' Day (Nov. 1); Christmas (Dec. 25-26).

Festivals: Two raucous festivals are the *Fasnacht* (Feb. 11-13, 2008; www.fasnacht.ch.) in Basel and the *Escalade*, celebrating the invading Duke of Savoy's 1602 defeat by Geneva (Dec. 12-14, 2008; www.compagniede1602.ch/home_page.htm). Music festivals occur throughout the summer, including Open-Air St. Gallen (Late June; ☎0900 500 700; www.openairsg.ch) and the Montreux Jazz Festival (July; ☎963 8282; www.montreux.ch/mjf).

BEYOND TOURISM

Although Switzerland's volunteer opportunities are limited, a number of ecotourism and rural development organizations allow you to give back to the country. Your best bet is to go through a placement service. Look for opportunities for short-term work on websites like www.emploi.ch. For more info on opportunities across Europe, see **Beyond Tourism,** p. 56.

Bergwald Projekt/Mountain Forest Project, Hauptstr. 24, 7014 Trin (☎081 630 41 45; www.bergwaldprojekt.ch). Organizes week-long conservation projects in Austria, Germany, and Switzerland.

Workcamp Switzerland, Komturei Tobel, Postfach 7, 9555 Tobel (☎071 917 24 86; www.workcamp.ch). Offers 2-3 week sessions during which volunteers live in a group environment and work on a common community service project.

GERMAN SWITZERLAND

German Switzerland encompasses 65% of the country. While the region's intoxicating brews and industrious cities will remind visitors of Germany, the natural beauty at every turn is uniquely Swiss. Different forms of Swiss German, a dialect distinct from High German, are spoken.

BERNESE OBERLAND

The peaks of the Bernese Oberland shelter a pristine wilderness best seen on hikes up the mountains and around the twin lakes, the Thunersee and Brienzersee. Not surprisingly, the area's opportunities for paragliding, mountaineering, and whitewater rafting are unparalleled. North of the mountains lies the relaxed city of Bern, Switzerland's capital and the heartbeat of the region.

BERN   ☎031

Bern (pop. 127,000) has been Switzerland's capital since 1848, but don't expect power politics or men in suits—the Bernese prefer to focus on the more leisurely things in life, strolling through the arcades of the *Altstadt* (Old Town) or along the banks of the serpentine Aare River.

█▐ TRANSPORTATION AND PRACTICAL INFORMATION. Bern's small **airport** (BRN; ☎960 2111) is 20min. from the city. A **bus** runs from the train station 50min. before each flight (10min., 14CHF). **Trains** run from the station at Bahnhofpl. to: Geneva (2hr., 2 per hr., 45CHF); Luzern (1½hr., 2 per hr., 34CHF); St. Gallen (2¼hr., 1 per hr., 63CHF); Zürich (1¼hr., 4 per day, 45CHF); Berlin, GER (12hr., 1-2 per hr., 95CHF); Paris, FRA (6hr., 4-5 per day, 115CHF). Local Bernmobil **buses** (departing from the left of the train station) and **trams** (departing from the front of the station) run 5:45am-midnight. (☎321 86 41; www.bernmobil.ch. Single ride 3.20CHF, day pass 12CHF.) **Buses** depart from the back of the station and post office. **Free bikes** are available from **Bern Rollt** at two locations, on Hirscheng. near the train station and on Zeugausg. near Waisenhauspl. (☎079 277 2857; www.bernrollt.ch. Passport and 20CHF deposit. Open May-Oct. daily 7:30am-9:30pm.)

Most of old Bern lies to your left as you leave the train station, along the Aare River. Take extra caution in the parks around the Parliament (Bundeshaus). The **tourist office** is in the station. (☎328 1212; www.berninfo.ch. Open June-Sept. daily 9am-8:30pm; Oct.-May M-Sa 9am-6:30pm, Su 10am-5pm.) The **post office,** Schanzenpost 1, is one block to the right from the train station. (Open M-F 7:30am-9pm, Sa 8am-4pm, Su 4-9pm.) **Postal Codes:** CH-3000 to CH-3030.

Embassies in Bern include: **Canada,** Kirchenfeldstr. 88 (☎357 3200; www.geo.international.gc.ca/canada-europa/switzerland); **Ireland,** Kirchenfeldstr. 68 (☎352 1442); **UK,** Thunstraße 50 (☎359 7700; www.britishembassy.gov.uk/switzerland); **US,** Jubilaumsstr. 93 (☎357 7011; bern.usembassy.gov). The **Australian** consulate is in Geneva (p. 1021). **New Zealanders** should contact their embassy in Berlin, GER (p. 393).

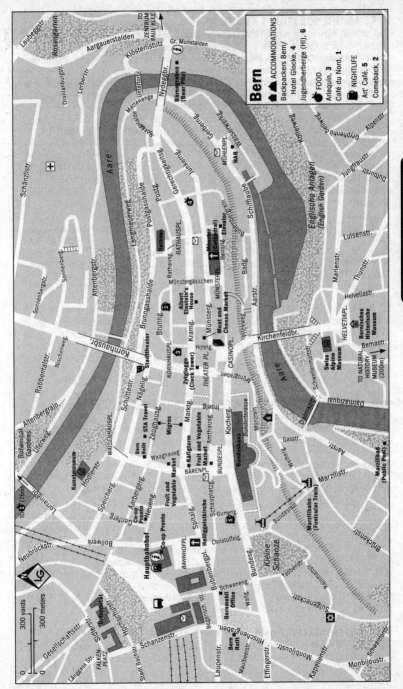

SWITZERLAND

Bern

▲▲ ACCOMMODATIONS
Backpackers Bern/
Hotel Glocke, 4
Jugendherberge (HI), 6

🍴 FOOD
Arlequin, 3
Café du Nord, 1

◼ NIGHTLIFE
Art' Café, 5
Comeback, 2

▌▐ ACCOMMODATIONS AND FOOD. If Bern's cheaper hostels are full, check the tourist office for a list of private rooms. **Backpackers Bern/Hotel Glocke ❷**, Rathausg. 75, in the middle of the *Altstadt*, has friendly owners and a large common room. From the train station, cross the tram lines and turn left on Spitalg., continuing onto Marktg. Turn left at Kornhauspl., then right on Rathausg. (☎311 3771; www.bern-backpackers.ch. Internet 1CHF per 10min. Reception 8am-11am and 3-10pm. Dorms 31CHF; singles 65CHF; doubles 78-140CHF, with bath 160CHF; quads 114CHF. AmEx/MC/V.) At **Jugendherberge (HI) ❷**, Weiherg. 4 near the river, guests receive free access to a public swimming pool. From the station, go down Christoffelg.; take the stairs to the left of the park gates, go down the slope, and turn left on Weiherg. (☎311 6316; www.youthhostel.ch/bern. Breakfast included. Internet 6CHF per hr. Reception June to mid-Sept. 7-10am and 2pm-midnight; mid-Sept. to May 7-10am and 5pm-midnight. Closed 2nd and 3rd weeks of Jan. Dorms 34CHF; singles 55CHF; doubles 84-98CHF.; quads 148CHF. 1.30CHF visitor's fee per person; 6CHF HI discount. AmEx/MC/V.)

Markets sell produce daily at Weinhauspl. and every Tuesday and Saturday on Bundespl. from May through October. A friendly couple owns **Arlequin ❷**, Gerechtigkeitsg. 51, an 80s-inspired restaurant. (☎311 3946. Sandwiches 6-12CHF. Meat fondue 35CHF. Open Tu-W 11am-11:30pm, Th-F 11am-1:30am, Sa 11am-11pm. AmEx/MC/V; min. 20CHF). A diverse crowd gathers on the terrace at **Café du Nord ❸**, Lorrainestr. 2. (☎332 2328. Pasta 18-25CHF. Meat entrees 22-32CHF. Open M-W 8am-11:30pm, Th-F 8am-1:30am, Sa 9am-1:30am, Su 4pm-11:30pm. Kitchen open M-Sa 11:30am-2pm and 6:30-10pm, Su 4:30-11:30pm. MC/V.) **Migros**, Marktg. 46, has groceries. (Open M 9am-6:30pm, Tu 8am-6:30pm, W-F 8am-9pm, Sa 7am-4pm.)

◪ SIGHTS. Bern's historic center (*Altstadt*), one of the best-preserved in Switzerland, is a UNESCO World Heritage sight. The Swiss national parliament meets in the massive **Bundeshaus,** which rises high over the Aare; water tumbles from fountains in front of the entrance. (www.parlament.ch. Under renovation; no tours until mid-2008. 1 45min. tour per hr. M-Sa 9-11am and 2-4pm. English-language tour usually 2pm. Free.) From the Bundeshaus, Kocherg. and Herreng. lead to the 15th-century Protestant **Münster** (Cathedral); above the main entrance, a golden sculpture depicts the torments of hell. For a fantastic view of the city, climb the Münster's 100m spire. (Cathedral open Easter-Oct. Tu-Sa 10am-5pm, Su. 11:30am-5pm; Nov.-Easter Tu-Sa 10am-noon, Su 11:30am-2pm. Free. Tower open Easter-Oct. M-Sa 10am-4:30pm, Su 11:30am-4:30pm; Nov.-Mar. M-F 2pm-3pm, Sa 2pm-5pm, Su 11:30am-1pm. 4CHF.) Down the road is **Albert Einstein's house,** Kramg. 49, where he conceived the theory of general relativity in 1915. His home is now filled with photos, letters, and video exhibits. (☎312 0091; www.einstein-bern.ch. Open Apr.-Sept. daily 10am-5pm; Feb.-Mar. Tu-F 10am-5pm, Sa 10am-4pm. 6CHF, students 4.50CHF.) Several steep walkways lead down from the Bundeshaus to the **Aare River.**

A recent addition to Bern's many museums is the ◪**Zentrum Paul Klee,** Monument im Fruchtland 3, which houses the world's largest Klee collection in a ripple-shaped building built into a hillside. (☎359 0101; www.zpk.org. Take bus #12 to Zentrum Paul Klee. Open Tu-Su 10am-5pm, Th 10am-9pm. 16CHF, students 14CHF.) Near Lorrainebrücke, the **Kunstmuseum,** Hodlerstr. 8-12, has paintings from the Middle Ages to the contemporary era and features a smattering of big 20th-century names. (☎328 0944; www.kunstmuseumbern.ch. Open Tu 10am-9pm, W-Su 10am-5pm. 7CHF, students 5CHF. Special exhibits up to 18CHF.) At the east side of the river, across the Nydeggbrücke, is the ◪**Rosengarten** (Rose Garden), which provides visitors with a memorable view of Bern's *Altstadt.*

▌▐ ENTERTAINMENT AND NIGHTLIFE. Check out *Bewegungsmelder*, available at the tourist office, for events. July's **Gurten Festival** (www.gurtenfestival.ch) draws young and energetic crowds and has attracted such luminaries as Bob Dylan and Elvis Costello while jazz-lovers arrive in early May for the **International Jazz Festival** (www.jazzfestival-bern.ch). Bern's traditional folk festival is the **Onion Market**, which brings 50 tons of onions to the city (Nov. 24, 2008). The orange grove at **Stadtgärtnerei Elfenau** (tram #19, dir.: Elfenau, to Luternauweg) has free Sunday concerts in summer. From mid-July to mid-August, **OrangeCinema** (☎0800 07 80 78; www.orange-cinema.ch) screens recent films outdoors; tickets are available from the tourist office in the train station.

The fashionable folk linger in the *Altstadt*'s bars and cafes, while a leftist crowd gathers under the gargoyles of the Lorrainebrücke. Find new DJs at **▨Art' Café**, Gurteng. 6, a cafe and club with huge windows overlooking the street. (☎318 20 70; www.artcafe.ch. Open M-W 7am-1:30am, Th-F 7am-3:30am, Sa 8am-3:30am, Su 10am-3:30am. Cash only.) **Comeback**, Rathausg. 42, a gay and lesbian basement bar, caters to 30-somethings. (☎311 7713. Beer 5CHF. Open Su-M 6pm-12:30am, Tu-Th 6pm-2:30am, F-Sa 6pm-3:30am. AmEx/MC/V.)

JUNGFRAU REGION

The most famous region of the Bernese Oberland, Jungfrau draws tourists with its splendid hiking trails, glacier lakes, and snow-capped peaks. From Interlaken, the valley splits at the foot of the Jungfrau Mountain. The eastern valley contains Grindelwald, with easy access to two glaciers, while the western valley harbors many smaller towns. The two valleys are divided by an easily hikeable ridge.

INTERLAKEN   ☎033

Interlaken (pop. 21,000) lies between the Thunersee and the Brienzersee at the foot of the largest mountains in Switzerland. Countless hiking trails, raging rivers, and peaceful lakes have turned the town into one of Switzerland's prime tourist attractions and its top adventure-sport destination.

▬▤ **TRANSPORTATION AND PRACTICAL INFORMATION.** Westbahnhof (☎826 4750) and Ostbahnhof (☎828 7319) have **trains** to: Basel (2-3hr., 1-2 per hr., 53CHF); Bern (1hr., 1-2 per hr., 25CHF); Geneva (3hr., 1-2 per hr., 61CHF); Zürich (2hr., 1 per 2hr., 61CHF). Ostbahnhof also sends trains to Grindelwald (1-2 per hr.,10CHF) and Luzern (2hr., 1-2 per hr., 30CHF). The **tourist office** is at Höheweg 37 in Hotel Metropole. (☎826 5300; www.interlaken.ch. Open May-Oct. M-F 8am-7pm, Sa 8am-5pm, Su 10am-noon and 5pm-7pm; Nov.-Apr. M-F 8am-noon and 1:30-6pm,

THE LOCAL STORY

A SAINTLY BREED

In AD 1050, the Archdeacon Bernard de Menthon founded a hospice in a mountain pass in the Jungfrau region and brought with him a breed of large, furry dogs of Gallic origin. In addition to providing shelter for passing merchants, Bernard and the monks working under him would venture into blizzards in search of stranded travelers. Though it is uncertain whether the dogs accompanied the monks on their rescue missions—early accounts relate that dogs were used to run an exercise wheel that turned a cooking spit—by the time of Bernard's canonization, dogs bearing his name had become famous and regularly patrolled the pass (now also named after Bernard).

Gifted with a fine sense of smell, a thick coat, an amiable manner, and a neck just made to tie a barrel of brandy to, the St. Bernards made a name for themselves by saving over 2000 lives over several hundred years. In the 1810s, a single dog named Barry saved 40 lost travelers. Today, few St. Bernards still work as rescue dogs—smaller, lighter breeds less liable to sink in the snow have taken their place. The St. Bernard is now a popular household pet, as well as the star of popular films like Cujo and the Beethoven movies. But it will always have dignity as the Alpine fixture it once was.

Sa 9am-noon.) Both train stations rent **bikes.** (31CHF per day. Open M-F 6am-8pm, Sa-Su 8am-8pm.) For **weather info,** call ☎828 7931. The **post office** is at Marktg. 1. (Open M-F 8am-noon and 1:45-6:30pm, Sa 8:30am-4pm.) **Postal Code:** CH-3800.

⌐⌐ ACCOMMODATIONS AND FOOD. Interlaken is a backpacking hot spot, so hostels tend to fill up quickly; reserve more than a month ahead. Diagonally across the Höhenmatte from the tourist office, the friendly, low-key ◪**Backpackers Villa Sonnenhof ❷,** Alpenstr. 16, includes admission to a nearby spa for the duration of your stay, minigolf, and free use of local buses. (☎826 7171; www.villa.ch. Breakfast included. Laundry 10CHF. Internet 1CHF per 8min. Free Wi-Fi. Reception 7:30-11am and 4-10pm. Mid-Apr. to mid-Sept. and mid-Dec. to mid-Jan. dorms 35CHF; doubles 98CHF; triples 135CHF; quads 156CHF. Mid-Sept. to mid.-Dec. and mid-Jan. to mid-Apr. dorms 33-37CHF; doubles 90CHF; triples 123CHF. AmEx/ MC/V.) Lively **Balmer's Herberge ❶,** Hauptstr. 23, Switzerland's oldest private hostel (est. 1945), is a place to party, not to relax. Services include mountain bike rental (35CHF per day), nightly movies, free sleds, and a popular bar. (☎822 1961. Breakfast included. Laundry 4CHF. Internet 10CHF per hr. Reception in summer 7am-9pm, in winter 6:30-10am and 4:30-10pm. Dorms 27-29CHF; doubles 74-78CHF; triples 99-105CHF; quads 99-105CHF. AmEx/MC/V.)

My Little Thai ❷, Hauptstr. 19 (right next to Balmer's Herberge), fills with hungry backpackers in the evening. (☎821 1017. Pad thai 14-21CHF. Vegetarian options available. Internet 8CHF per hr. Open daily 11:30am-10pm. AmEx/MC/V.) **El Azteca ❷,** Jungfraustr. 30, serves cactus salad (16CHF), fajitas (28-38CHF), and other Mexican fare. (☎822 7131. Open daily 7:30am-2pm and 6:30pm-11:30pm. AmEx/ MC/V.) There are **Migros** and **Coop** supermarkets by both train stations. (Open M-Th 8am-6:30pm, F 8am-9pm, Sa 7:30am-5pm.)

⚠ OUTDOOR ACTIVITIES. With the incredible surrounding Alpine scenery, it's no wonder that many of Interlaken's tourists seem compelled to try otherwise unthinkable adventure sports. ◪**Alpin Raft,** Hauptstr. 7 (☎823 4100; www.alpin-raft.ch), the most established company in Interlaken, has qualified, entertaining guides and offers a wide range of activities, including paragliding (150CHF), river rafting (99-110CHF), skydiving (380CHF), and hang-gliding (185CHF). They also offer two different types of **bungee jumping.** One of the most popular adventure activities at Alpin Raft is **canyoning** (110-175CHF), which involves rappelling down a series of gorge faces, jumping off cliffs into pools of churning water, and swinging, Tarzan-style, from ropes and zip cords through the canyon. All prices include transportation to and from any hostel in Interlaken, and usually a beer upon completion. ◪**Skywings Adventures** has witty professionals and a wide range of activities from paragliding (150-220CHF) to river rafting (99CHF); their booth is across the street from the tourist office (☎079 266 8282; www.skywings.ch). **Outdoor Interlaken,** Hauptstr. 15 (☎826 7719; www.outdoor-interlaken.ch), offers many of the same activities as Alpin Raft at similar prices, as well as rock-climbing lessons (½-day 89CHF) and whitewater **kayaking** tours (½-day 155CHF). At **Skydive Xdream,** skydivers can make their ascent in a glass-walled helicopter, then jump from a standing position. (☎079 759 3483; www.justjump.ch. 380CHF per tandem plane jump; 430CHF per tandem helicopter jump. Open Apr.-Oct. Pick-ups 9am and 1pm, Sa-Su also 4pm. Call for winter availability.) **Swiss Alpine Guide** offers **ice climbing,** running full-day trips to a nearby glacier and providing all the equipment needed to scale vertical glacier walls and rappel into icy crevasses. (☎822 6000; www.swissalpineguides.ch. Trips May-Nov. daily, weather permitting. 160CHF.)

Interlaken's adventure sports industry is thrilling, but **accidents do happen.** On July 27, 1999, 21 tourists were killed by a sudden flash flood while canyoning. Be aware that you participate in all adventure sports at your own risk.

Interlaken's most traversed trail climbs **Harder Kulm** (1310m). From the Ostbahnhof, head toward town, take the first road bridge right across the river, and follow the yellow signs that give way to white-red-white rock markings. From the top, signs lead back down to the Westbahnhof. The hike is be about 2½hr. up and 1½hr. down. In summer, the **Harderbahn funicular** runs from the trailhead to the top. (Open daily May to Oct. 15CHF, round-trip 25CHF. 25% Eurail and 50% Swiss-Pass discount.) For a flatter trail, turn left from the train station and left before the bridge, then follow the canal over to the nature reserve on the shore of the Thunersee. The 3hr. trail winds along the Lombach River and back toward town.

GRINDELWALD ☎033

Interlaken is frenetic center for adventure sports; Grindelwald (pop. 4500) is its more serene counterpart, with more opportunities for hiking and skiing. Tucked between the Eiger and the Jungfraujoch, the village is the launching point for the only glaciers accessible by foot in the Bernese Oberland. The **Bergführerbüro** (Mountain Guide's Office), in the sports center near the tourist office, sells hiking maps and coordinates glacier walks, ice climbing, and mountaineering. (☎853 1200. Open June-Oct. M-F 9am-noon and 2-5pm.) The **Untere Grindelwaldgletscher** (Lower Glacier) hike is moderately steep (5hr.). To reach the trailhead, walk away from the station on the main street and follow the signs downhill to Pfinstegg. Hikers can either walk the first forested section of the trail (1hr.) or take a funicular (July to mid-Sept. 8am-7pm; mid-Sept. to June 9am-5:30pm; 12CHF, SwissPass 9CHF). Pet goats greet guests at the ▨**Jugendherberge (HI) ❷**, whose rooms have terraces that offer spectacular views. To reach the lodge, head left out of the train station for 400m, then cut uphill to the right and follow the steep trail all the way up the hill for 20 minutes. (☎853 1009; www.youthhostel.ch/grindelwald. Breakfast included. Reception 7:30-10am and 3-10pm. Summer dorms 29-37CHF; doubles 76-106CHF. Winter dorms 31-38CHF; doubles 78-106CHF. 6CHF HI discount. AmEx/MC/V.) **Downtown Lodge ❶** is conveniently located 200m past the tourist office, to the right of the train station. It offers free entrance to the public swimming pool. (☎853 0825; www.downtown-lodge.ch. Breakfast included. Dorms 25-35CHF; doubles 70-90CHF. AmEx/MC/V.) **Hotel Eiger,** on Hauptstr. near the tourist office, houses a bar and two restaurants, **Memory ❷** and the more upscale **Barry's ❸**. (☎854 3131. Memory open daily 8:30am-midnight, meals 10-30CHF; Barry's open daily 6pm-midnight, meals 12-40CHF; bar open daily 5pm-1am. AmEx/MC/V.) The **Jungfraubahn train** runs to Grindelwald from Interlaken's Ostbahnhof (35min., 2 per hr., 10CHF). A **Coop** supermarket is across from the tourist office. (Open M-F 8am-6:30pm, Sa 8am-6pm.) The **tourist office,** in the Sport-Zentrum 200m to the right of the station, provides chairlift information and a list of free guided excursions. (☎854 1212. Open July-Aug. M-F 8am-noon and 1:30-6pm, Sa 8am-noon and 1:30-5pm; Sept.-June M-F 9am-noon and 2-5pm, Sa 2-5pm.) **Postal Code:** CH-3818.

CENTRAL SWITZERLAND

In contrast to the unspoiled scenic vistas of the mountainous southern cantons, Central Switzerland seems to overflow with people and culture. Unique museums, majestic cathedrals, and lovely *Altstädte* (Old Towns) in Zürich and other cities are the main attractions of this vibrant region.

ZÜRICH ☎ 044

Battalions of briefcase-toting executives charge daily through Zürich, Switzerland's largest city (pop. 360,000) and the world's fourth-largest stock exchange—bringing with them enough money to keep upper-crust boutiques thriving. But only footsteps away from flashy shopping is the city's student quarter, home to an counter-culture that has inspired generations of Swiss philosophers and artists.

▙ TRANSPORTATION

Flights: Zürich-Kloten Airport (ZRH; ☎816 2211; www.zurich-airport.com) is a major hub for Swiss International Airlines (☎084 885 2000; www.swiss.com). Daily connections to: **Frankfurt, GER; London, BRI; Paris, FRA.** Trains connect the airport to the Hauptbahnhof in the city center. 3-6 per hr., 6CHF. Eurail and SwissPass valid.)

Trains: Run to: **Basel** (1¼hr., 2-3 per hr., 30CHF); **Bern** (1¼hr., 3-4 per hr., 45CHF); **Geneva** (3hr., 1-2 per hr., 77CHF); **Luzern** (1hr., 1-2 per hr., 22CHF); **St. Gallen** (½hr.; 2-3 per hr.; 27CHF); **Locarno** (2hr.; 1 per 2hr.; 55CHF); **Milan, ITA** (4hr., 1 per 2hr., 72-87CHF); **Munich, GER** (5hr., 4-5 per day, 90CHF); **Paris, FRA** (5hr., 4 per day, 112-140CHF, under 26 86CHF).

Public Transportation: Trams criss-cross the city, originating at the Hauptbahnhof. Tickets valid for 1hr. cost 4CHF (press the blue button on automatic ticket machines); tickets for shorter rides (valid for 30min.) cost 2.40CHF (yellow button). Police fine riders without tickets 60CHF. If you plan to ride several times, buy a 24hr. **Tageskarte** (7.60CHF; green button), valid on trams, buses, and ferries. **Night buses** (5CHF ticket valid all night) run from the city center to outlying areas (F-Su).

Car Rental: The tourist office offers a 20% discount and free upgrade deal with **Europcar** (☎804 4646; www.europcar.ch). Prices from 155CHF per day for 1-2 days with unlimited mileage. 20+. Branches at the airport (☎043 255 5656), Josefstr. 53 (☎271 5656), and Lindenstr. 33 (☎383 1747). Rent in the city; a 40% tax is added at the airport.

Bike Rental: Bike loans from **Züri Rollt** (☎043 288 3400; www.zuerirollt.ch) are free for 6hr. during business hours, otherwise 5CHF per day, 20CHF per night. Pick up a bike from **Globus City,** the green hut on the edge of the garden between Bahnhofstr. and Löwenstr.; **Opernhaus,** by the opera house past Bellevuepl.; **Velogate,** across from Hauptbahnhof's tracks next to the Landesmuseum castle. Bikes must be returned to original rental station. Passport and 20CHF deposit. Open May-Oct. 7:30am-9:30pm.

✦ ▐ ORIENTATION AND PRACTICAL INFORMATION

Zürich is in north-central Switzerland, close to the German border and on some of the lowest land in the country. The **Limmat River** splits the city down the middle on its way to the **Zürichsee** (Lake Zürich). The **Hauptbahnhof** (train station) lies on the western bank and marks the beginning of **Bahnhofstraße,** the city's main shopping street. Two-thirds of the way down Bahnhofstr. lies **Paradeplatz,** the banking center of Zürich, which marks the beginning of the last stretch of the shopping street. The eastern bank of the river is dominated by the university district, which stretches above the narrow **Niederdorfstraße.**

Tourist Office: In the **Hauptbahnhof** (☎215 40 00; www.zuerich.com). Sells the **ZürichCARD,** which is good for unlimited public transportation, free museum admission, and discounts on sights (1-day pass 17CHF, 3-day 34CHF). Open May-Oct. M-Sa 8am-8:30pm, Su 8:30am-6:30pm; Nov.-Apr. M-Sa 8:30am-7pm, Su 9am-6:30pm.

Currency Exchange: On the main floor of the train station. Cash advances for MC/V with photo ID; min. 200CHF, max. 1000CHF. Open daily 6:30am-9:30pm. **Crédit Suisse,** at Paradepl. 5CHF commission. Open M-F 8:15am-5pm.

Luggage Storage: Middle level of Hauptbahnhof. 5-8CHF. Open daily 4:15am-1:30am.

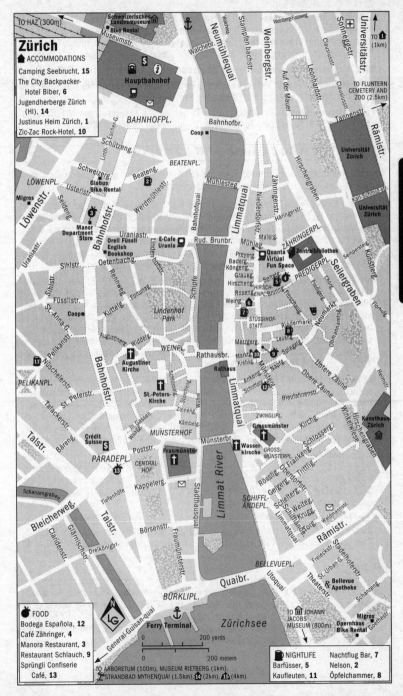

TO HAZ (300m)

Schweizerisches
Landesmuseum
Bike Rental
Museumstr.

Zürich
■ ACCOMMODATIONS

Camping Seebrucht, **15**
The City Backpacker-
Hotel Biber, **6**
Jugendherberge Zürich
(HI), **14**
Justinus Heim Zürich, **1**
Zic-Zac Rock-Hotel, **10**

Hauptbahnhof

TO FLUNTERN
CEMETERY AND
ZOO (2.5km)

TO
(1km)

Universität
Zürich

Universität
Zürich

BAHNHOFPL.

Bahnhofbr.

Coop

BEATENPL.

LÖWENPL.

Schweizerg.
Globus
Bike Rental

Beateng.

Mühlesteg

ZÄHRINGERPL.

Migros

Löwenstr.

Manor
Department
Store

Bahnhofstr.

Werdmühlestr.

Bahnhofquai

Uraniastr.

Orell Füssli
English
Bookshop

Oetenbachg.

E-Cafe
Urania

Rud. Brunbr.

Mühleg.

Preyerg.

Baderg.

Köngeng.

Grauer

Hirscheng.

Rosengg.

Weing.

Quanta
Virtual
Fun Space

Zentralbibliothek

PREDIGERPL.

Seilergraben

Sihlstr.

Füsslistr.

St.-Anna-G.

Coop

Rennweg

Fortunag.

Lindenhof
Park

Augustinerg. Widderg.

HIRSCH-
ENGPL.-Brunn

STÜSSIHOF-
STATT.

Rindermarkt

Neumarkt

Pelikanstr.

St. Peterstr.

Talackerstr.

PELIKANPL.

WEINPL.

Augustiner
Kirche

St.-Peters-
Kirche

Rathausbr.

Rathaus

Metzgerg.

Markt

Krebs.

Ankeng.

Schofferg.

Spiegelg.

Untere Zäune

Obere Zäune

Bleufahnstr.

ZWINGLIPL.

Grossmünster

Kirchg.

Schlosserg.

Winkelwiese

Kunsthaus
Zürich

Bahnhofstr.

In Gassen

Bäreng.

Crédit
Suisse

PARADEPL.

MÜNSTERHOF

Fraumünster

CENTRAL-
HOF

Poststr.

Kappelerg.

Münsterbr.

Wasser-
kirche

GROSS-
MÜNSTERPL.

Rösslig.

Oberdorfstr.

Geigerg.

Schelteng.

Trittlig.

Frankeng.

Limmat River

SCHIFFL-
ÄNDEPL.

Schifflände

Limmatquai

Krug.

Rämistr.

Talstr.

Bleicherweg

Claridenstr.

Glärnischstr.

Dreikönigstr.

Börsenstr.

Tiefenhöfe

Stadthausquai

Fraumünsterstr.

BELLEVUEPL.

Utoquai

Bellevue
Apotheke

Theaterstr.

Stadelhoferstr.

Schanzeng.

Schanzengraben

BÜRKLIPL.

Quaibr.

Zürichsee

TO JOHANN
JACOBS
MUSEUM (800m)

Migros
Opernhaus
Bike Rental

Ferry Terminal

General-Guisan-quai

0   200 yards
0   200 meters

■ FOOD
Bodega Española, **12**
Café Zähringer, **4**
Manora Restaurant, **3**
Restaurant Schlauch, **9**
Sprüngli Confiserie
Café, **13**

TO ARBORETUM (100m), MUSEUM RIETBERG (1km),
STRANDBAD MYTHENQUAI (1.5km), **14** (2km), **15** (4km)

■ NIGHTLIFE
Barfüsser, **5**
Kaufleuten, **11**

Nachtflug Bar, **7**
Nelson, **2**
Öpfelchammer, **8**

GLBT Resources: Homosexuelle Arbeitsgruppe Zürich (HAZ), on the 3rd fl. of Sihlquai 67 (☎271 22 50; www.haz.ch), has a library, meetings, and the newsletter *InfoSchwül.* Open W 2-6pm. **Frauenzentrum Zürich,** Matteng. 27 (☎272 0504; http://frauenzentrum.fembit.ch), provides resources for lesbians. Open Tu and Th 6-8pm.

24hr. Pharmacy: Bellevue Apotheke, Theaterstr. 14, on Bellevuepl. (☎266 6222).

Internet Access: Quanta Virtual Fun Space (☎260 7266), at the corner of Mühleg. and Niederdorfstr. 3CHF per 15min. Open daily 9am-midnight.

Post Office: Sihlpost, Kasernestr. 95-97, behind the station. Open M-F 6:30am-10:30pm, Sa 6:30am-8pm, Su 10am-10:30pm. **Postal Code: CH-8021.**

ACCOMMODATIONS AND CAMPING

Zürich's few budget accommodations are easily accessible by foot or public transportation. Reserve ahead, especially in summer.

Justinus Heim Zürich, Freudenbergstr. 146 (☎362 2980; justinuszh@bluewin.ch). Take tram #9 or 10 (dir.: Bahnhof Oerlikon) to Seilbahn Rigiblick, then take the funicular to the top (open daily 5:20am-12:40am). This hillside stay-in is removed from the downtown bustle but is easily accessible. Private rooms with a beautiful view of the city. Breakfast included. Reception 8am-noon and 5-9pm. Singles 50CHF, with shower 65CHF; doubles 90-110CHF. Rates higher in July and August. V. ❸

The City Backpacker-Hotel Biber, Niederdorfstr. 5 (☎251 9015; www.city-backpacker.ch). From the *Hauptbanhof,* cross the bridge and Limmatquai, turn right onto Niederdorfst., and walk for 5min. The beds are somewhat uncomfortable and the street noise constant—but with Niederdorfstr. nightlife right outside, you may not need your bunk bed. Kitchens and showers on each floor. Linens and towels each 3CHF, blanket provided. Next-day laundry service 10CHF. Internet 6CHF per hr. Reception 8-11am and 3-10pm. Check-out 10am. Dorms 33CHF; singles 69CHF; doubles 98CHF; triples 135CHF; quads 176CHF. MC/V. ❷

Jugendherberge Zürich (HI), Mutschellenstr. 114 (☎399 7800; www.youthhostel.ch/zuerich). From the station, take tram #7 (dir.: Wollishofen) to Morgental, then backtrack 20m and head down Mutschellenstr. 24hr. snack bar with beer on tap. Breakfast included. Internet 1CHF per 4min. Reception 24hr. Dorms 44CHF; singles with shower 105CHF; doubles with shower 123CHF; triples 141CHF, with shower 156CHF; quads178CHF; quints 194CHF. Rates rise July-Aug. HI discount 6CHF. MC/V. ❸

Zic-Zac Rock-Hotel, Marktg. 17 (☎261 2181; www.ziczac.ch). Hotel is 1min. down the road past City Backpacker. Each room is named after a band and decorated with funky paintings. Rooms have TV, phone, and sink. Internet 1CHF per 4min. Reception 24hr. Singles 83CHF, with shower 94CHF; doubles 133/147CHF; triples 173CHF/180CHF; quads with shower 280CHF. AmEx/MC/V. ❹

Camping Seebrucht, Seestr. 559 (☎482 1612), by the lake. Take tram #11 to Bürklipl., then bus #161 or 165 to Stadtgrenze. Reception 8am-noon and 3-9pm. Check-out 11:30am. 20CHF per tent, 8CHF per extra person. Showers 2CHF. MC/V. ❶

FOOD

Zürich's more than 1300 restaurants offer a bite of everything. The cheapest meals are available at *Würstli* (sausage) stands for 5CHF. The **farmer's markets** at Bürklipl. (Tu and F 6-11am) and Rosenhof (Th 10am-8pm, Sa 10am-5pm) sell produce and flowers. Head to **Niederdorfstraße** for a variety of snack bars and cheaper restaurants interspersed among fancier establishments.

Café Zähringer, Zähringerpl. 11 (☎252 0500; www.cafe-zaehringer.ch). Enjoy mainly vegetarian and vegan fare in this student-friendly cafe. Stir-fries 16-27CHF. Open M 6pm-midnight, Tu-Th, Su 8am-midnight, F-Sa 8am-12:30am. Cash only. ❷

Restaurant Schlauch, Münstergasse 20. Enjoy the billiard tables at this affordable downtown eatery. Soups 5-8.50CHF. Salads 7-17CHF. Entrees 8-20CHF. Open Tu-Sa 11:30am-2pm and 6-9pm. AmEx/MC/V. ❷

Bodega Española, Münsterg. 15 (☎251 2310). Has been serving Catalán delights since 1874. Egg-and-potato tortilla dishes 16-18CHF. Tapas 4.80CHF. Open daily 10am-midnight. Kitchen open noon-2pm and 6-10pm. AmEx/MC/V. ❷

Sprüngli Confiserie Café, Paradepl. (☎224 4711), a Zürich landmark, was founded by one of the original Lindt chocolate makers. Pick up a handful of the bite-size *Luxemburgerli* (8.40CHF per 100g) or eat a full meal (19-28CHF). Open M-F 7am-8pm, Sa 8am-7pm, Su 10am-6pm. AmEx/MC/V. ❷

Manora Restaurant, Banhofst. 75. Mingle with bankers at this fast-paced self-serve restaurant on the 5th fl. of the Manor department store. Sandwiches 3-6CHF. Salads 4-11CHF. Entrees 6-15CHF. Open M-F 9am-8pm, Sa 9am-5pm. AmEx/MC/V. ❶

SIGHTS

Bahnhofstraße leads into the city from the train station. The street is filled with shoppers during the day but falls dead quiet after 6pm and on weekends. At the Zürichsee end of Bahnhofstr., **Bürkliplatz** is a good place to begin walking along the lake shore. The *platz* itself hosts a Saturday **flea market** *(May-Oct. 6am-3pm)*. On the other side of the Limmat River, the pedestrian zone continues on Niederdorfstr. and Münsterg. Off Niederdorfstr., **Spiegelgasse** was once home to Goethe and Lenin. **Fraumünster, Grossmünster,** and **St. Peters Kirche** straddle the Limmat River. For a view of Zürich from the water, as well as a chance to see some of the towns on the banks of the Zürichsee, **boat tours** costing a fraction of those in other Swiss cities leave from the ferry terminal at Bürklipl. The shortest tour, **A Kleine Rundfahrten,** lasts 1½hr. *(May-Sept. daily 11am-6:30pm., 7.80CHF.)*

FRAUMÜNSTER. Marc Chagall's stained glass windows depicting Biblical scenes add vibrancy to this otherwise austere 13th-century Gothic cathedral. A mural decorating the courtyard's archway depicts Felix and Regula (the decapitated patron saints of Zürich) with their heads in their hands. *(Off Paradepl. Open May-Nov. M-Sa 10am-6pm, Su 11:30am-6pm; Dec.-Apr. M-Sa 10am-4pm, Su 11:30am-4pm. Free.)*

GROSSMÜNSTER. Ulrich Zwingli kickstarted the Swiss German Reformation at Grossmünster in the 16th century. Today, the cathedral is Zürich's main landmark. Its defining twin towers are best viewed on the bridge near the Fraumünster. *(Towers open daily Mar.-Oct. 9:15am-5pm; Nov.-Feb. 10:15am-4:30pm. 2CHF.)* One of Zwingli's Bibles lies in a case near his pulpit. Downstairs in the cavernous 12th-century crypt is a menacing statue of Charlemagne and his 2m sword. *(Church open daily mid-Mar. to Oct. 9am-6pm; Nov. to mid-Mar. 10am-5pm. Free.)*

BEACHES. The convenient and popular **Arboretum** is about 100m down from the Quaibrücke. *(Tram #5 to Rentenanstalt and head to the water.)* Across the lake, **Zürichhorn** draws crowds with its peaceful gardens and a famous statue by Jean Tinguely. *(Tram #2 or 4 to Frolichst., then walk towards the lake.)* **Strandbad Mythenquai,** along the western shore, offers diving towers and a water trampoline. *(Tram #7 to Brunaustr. ☎201 0000. Open daily May to early Sept. 9am-8pm. 6CHF, 16-20 4.50CHF.)*

🏛 MUSEUMS

█MUSEUM RIETBERG. Rietberg presents an outstanding collection of Asian, African, and other non-European art, housed in three structures spread around the Rieter-Park. The basement of the new **Emerald building** houses masterpieces from Asia and Africa. **Villa Wesendonck** (where Wagner wrote Tristan and Isolde) holds works from South Asia, Central America, and Oceania, while **Park-Villa Rieter** includes collection of Near Eastern art. *(Gablerstr. 15. Tram #7 to Museum Rietberg. ☎206 3131; www.rietberg.ch. All buildings open Apr.-Sept. Tu, F-Su 10am-5pm, W-Th 10am-8pm. 12CHF, students 10CHF, under 16 free. MC/V; buy tickets in the Emerald building.)*

KUNSTHAUS ZÜRICH. The Kunsthaus, Europe's largest privately funded museum, houses a vast collection including works by Chagall, Dalí, Gauguin, van Gogh, Munch, Picasso, Rembrandt, Renoir, and Rubens *(Heimpl. 1. Take tram #3, 5, 8, or 9 to Kunsthaus. ☎253 8484; www.kunsthaus.ch. English-language audio tour and brochure. Open Tu-Th 10am-9pm, F-Su 10am-5pm. 16CHF, students 10CHF. AmEx/MC/V.)*

🍸 NIGHTLIFE

For information on after-dark happenings, check **ZüriTipp** (www.zueritipp.ch) or pick up a free copy of *ZürichGuide* or *ZürichEvents* from the tourist office. On **Niederdorfstraße,** the epicenter of Zürich's *Altstadt* nightlife, bars are packed to the brim almost every night. **Kreis 5,** once the industrial area of Zürich, has recently developed into party central, with ubiquitous clubs, bars, and lounges taking over former factories. Kreis 5 lies northwest of the Hauptbahnhof. To get there, take tram #4 (dir.: Werdholzi) or #13 (dir.: Albisgütli) to Escher-Wyss-Pl. and follow the crowds. Closer to the Old Town, **Langstraße,** reached by walking away from the river on the city's western side, is the reputed red-light district. Beer in Zürich is pricey (from 6CHF), but a number of cheap bars have established themselves on Niederdorfstr. near Mühleg.

> **📏TIP** **THAT EXPLAINS THE TASSELS.** Beware the deceptive and common title of "night club"—it's really just a euphemism for "strip club."

█ Kaufleuten, Pelikanstr. 18 (☎225 3322; www.kaufleuten.ch). A former theater, this trendy club—still decked out in red velvet—attracts the who's who of Zürich by throwing nightly themed parties. Madonna and Prince have both paid visits. Cover 10-30CHF. Hours vary, but generally open Su-Th 11pm-2am, F-Sa 11pm-4am. MC/V.

Nelson, Beateng. 11 (☎212 6016). Locals, backpackers, and businessmen chug beer (9CHF per pint) at this large Irish pub. 20+. Open M-W 11:30am-2am, Th 11:30am-3am, F 11:30am-4:30am, Sa 3pm-4:30am, Su 3pm-2am. MC/V.

Barfüsser, Spitalg. 14 (☎251 4064), off Zähringerpl. Freely flowing mixed drinks (14-17CHF) and wine (6-9CHF) accompany delicious sushi at this gay bar. Open M-Th noon-1am, F-Sa noon-2am, Su 5pm-1am. AmEx/MC/V.

Nachtflug Bar, Café, and Lounge, Stüssihofstatt 4 (☎261 9966; www.n8flug.ch). Sleek bar with outdoor seating. Wine from 6CHF. Beer from 4.90CHF. Open M-Th 9am-midnight, F 9am-1:30am, Sa 11am-1:30am, Su 11am-midnight. Outdoor bar open M-W 9am-midnight, Th-F 9am-10pm, Sa-Su 11am-10pm. AmEx/MC/V.

Öpfelchammer, Rindermarkt 12 (☎251 2336). This wine chamber (8-10CHF per glass) has low ceilings and wooden crossbeams covered with initials and messages from 200 years of merry-making. Those who can hang upside from the beams while drinking a complimentary glass of wine get to engrave their names on the wall. It's harder than it looks. Open mid-Aug. to mid-July Tu-Sa 11am-12:30am. AmEx/MC/V.

⚡ DAYTRIP FROM ZÜRICH: STEIN AM RHEIN.

The tiny, medieval *Altstadt* of Stein am Rhein (pop. 3190) is postcard-perfect, with traditional Swiss architecture framed by hills and the Rhine River. The buildings on the main square, the **Rathausplatz,** date back to the 15th century and feature remarkable facade paintings depicting the animal or scene for which each house is named. The stately **Rathaus** (town council building) is to the right upon reaching the square. Heading away from the Rathauspl., the **Understadt,** the main road running through the village, leads to the **Museum Lindwurm,** a 19th-century house restored to its bourgeois glory, roosters and all. *(Open Mar.-Oct. M and W-Su 10am-5pm. 5CHF, students 3CHF.)* For a look at a completely different facet of village life, visit Stein am Rhein's oldest claim to fame, the 12th-century **Kloster St. Georgen.** You can reach the tucked-away entrance to this Benedictine monastery by going through the arch across from the tourist office, behind and to the left of the Rathaus. Explore monks' dormitories, a scriptorium, preserved wall drawings, and the gorgeous **Festsaal.** *(☎052 741 2142. Open Apr.-Oct. Tu-Su 10am-5pm. 4CHF, students 3CHF.)* **Trains** connect Stein am Rhein to Zürich via Winterthur or Schaffhausen (1hr., 1-2 per hr., 21CHF). The **tourist office** is at Oberstadt. 3. *(☎052 42 20 90; www.steinamrhein.ch. Open July-Aug. M-Sa 9:30am-noon and 1:30-4pm; Sept.-June M-F 9:30am-noon and 1:30-4pm.)*

LUZERN (LUCERNE) ☎041

Luzern (pop. 60,000) welcomes busloads of tourists each day in the summer, and with good reason. The streets of the *Altstadt* lead down to the placid Vierwaldstättersee (Lake Lucerne), the covered bridges over the river are among the most photographed sights in Switzerland, and the sunrise over the famous Mt. Pilatus has hypnotized artists—including Goethe, Twain, and Wagner—for centuries.

☎⚡ TRANSPORTATION AND PRACTICAL INFORMATION. **Trains** leave the large Bahnhof for: Bern via Olten (1½hr., 2 per hr., 34CHF); Geneva (3½hr., 1-2 per hr., 70CHF); Zürich (1hr., 2 per hr., 22CHF). VBL **buses** depart in front of the train station and provide extensive coverage of Luzern. **Boats** leave from across the road to destinations all over Lake Luzern; some offer themed cruises (☎612 9090; www.lakelucerne.ch. Cruises 15-60CHF). Route maps are available at the station **tourist office,** Banhofstraße 3, holds daily guided tours at 9:45 am. (☎227 1717; www.luzern.org. Open May-Oct. M-F

LOCAL LEGEND

HI-YO, SWISS INDEPENDENCE!

Everyone knows some element of the William Tell story, whether it be the famous apple-shooting scene or the ubiquitous overture from Rossini's opera (later appropriated, of course, as the theme song of *The Lone Ranger*). But few would guess that this tale of martial defiance originated in neutral Switzerland.

According to legend, Wilhelm Tell lived in the 14th century in the canton of Uri, just south of Zürich. The Hapsburg emperors installed an Austrian "protector," Hermann Gessler, to further their attempts to dominate the region. Gessler demanded that all citizens of Altdorf bow before a pole with his hat on it, but the stubborn Tell refused. The protector ordered Tell to shoot an apple off his son's head, or else both would be executed.

Tell, an expert marksman, had no problem with his crossbow. He then declared that if he had hit his son, he would have immediately attacked Gessler. None too happy, Gessler ordered Tell brought to his castle on the Vierwaldstättersee. Tell escaped his captors in a storm, waited for the Austrian in the castle, and promptly dispatched him at first sight—with a crossbow, of course. The act sparked a wave of defiance that led to the formation of the Swiss Confederation.

8:30am-6:30pm, Sa 9am-6:30pm; Nov.-Apr. M-F 8:30am-5:30pm, Sa 9am-1pm.) There are two **post offices** by the train station.

ACCOMMODATIONS AND FOOD. Inexpensive beds are limited, so call ahead. To reach **Backpackers Lucerne ❷**, Alpenquai 42, turn right from the station onto Inseliquai and follow it for 20min. until it turns into Alpenquai. The hostel's distance from the center of town may be inconvenient, but it has a fun, communal vibe. (☎360 0420; www.backpackerslucerne.ch. Laundry 9CHF. Internet 10CHF per hr. Reception 7:30-10am and 4-11pm. Dorms 29CHF; doubles 66-70CHF. Bike rental 18CHF per day. Cash only.) Overlooking the river from the *Altstadt* is the **Tourist Hotel ❷**, St. Karliquai 12, which offers plain rooms and a prime location. From the station, walk along Bahnhofstr., cross the river at the second covered bridge, and make a left onto St. Karliquai. (☎410 2474; www.touristhotel.ch. Breakfast included. Summer dorms 38-43CHF; doubles 98-112CHF; triples 129-138CHF; quads 172-180CHF. Winter dorms 38-40CHF; doubles 88-98CHF; triples 111-129CHF; quads 152-172CHF. AmEx/MC/V.) **Erdem Kebab ❶**, down Zentralstr. from the *Banhof*, has delicious Middle Eastern fare. (Falafel 8CHF. Kebab 8-12CHF. Open M-Th 10am-midnight, F-Sa 11am-8pm. Cash only.) **Markets** along the river sell cheap, fresh food on Tuesday and Saturday mornings. There's also a **Coop** supermarket at the train station. (Open M-Sa 6:30am-9pm, Su 8am-9pm.)

SIGHTS AND ENTERTAINMENT. The *Altstadt*, across the river from the station, is famous for its frescoed houses. The 14th-century **Kapellbrücke**, a wooden-roofed bridge, runs from left of the train station to the *Altstadt* and is decorated with Swiss historical scenes. Farther down the river, the **Spreuerbrücke** is adorned by Kaspar Meglinger's eerie *Totentanz* (Dance of Death) paintings. On the hills above the river, the **Museggmauer** and its towers are all that remain of the medieval city's ramparts. Three of the towers are accessible to visitors and provide panoramic views of the city. From Mühlenpl., walk up Brugglig., then head uphill to the right on Museggstr. and follow the castle signs. (Open in summer daily 8am-7pm.) To the east is the magnificent **Löwendenkmal,** the dying lion of Luzern, carved into a cliff on Denkmalstr. to honor the Swiss soldiers who died defending King Louis XVI of France during the invasion of the Tuileries in 1792.

Europe's largest transportation museum, the **Verkehrshaus der Schweiz** (Swiss Transport Museum), Lidostr. 5, has interactive displays on everything from early flying machines to cars, but the highlight is its train warehouse. Take bus #6, 8, or 24 to Verkehrshaus. (☎370 4444; www.verkehrshaus.ch. Open daily Apr.-Oct. 10am-6pm; Nov.-Mar. 10am-5pm. 24CHF, students 22CHF, with Eurail Pass 14CHF.) The **Picasso Museum,** Am Rhyn Haus, Furreng. 21, displays a some of Picasso's sketches and a large collection of photographs from the artist's later years. From Schwanenpl., take Rathausquai to Furreng. (☎410 3533. Open daily Apr.-Oct. 10am-6pm; Nov.-Mar. 11am-1pm and 2pm-4pm. 8CHF, students 5CHF.)

Although Luzern's nightlife is more about chilling than club-hopping, there are still many options. **The Loft,** Haldenstr. 21, hosts special DJs and theme nights. (Beer 9-11CHF. Open W 9pm-2am, Th-Su 10am-4am.) The mellow **Jazzkantine** club, Grabenstr. 8, is affiliated with the renowned **Lucerne School of Music.** (Sandwiches 6-8CHF. Open mid-Aug. to mid-July M-Sa 7am-1:30am, Su 4pm-1:30am. MC/V.) Luzern attracts big names for its two jazz festivals: **Blue Balls Festival** (last week of July) and **Blues Festival** (2nd week of Nov.)

ST. GALLEN   ☎071

Founded as a religious center by the Irish monk Gallus in the 7th century, St. Gallen (pop. 75,000)has retained an intimate feel—especially in the historic center, where you can get enjoyably lost in a maze of narrow, winding streets. The ▨**Abbey Precinct** is a grouping of remarkable Benedictine structures—some dating back to the 1400s—with UNESCO World Heritage Landmark status. The soaring towers of the Baroque **cathedral,** constructed from 1755 to 1767, dominate the scene; the ornate interior, with its majestic painted ceiling, is no less dramatic. (Open M-Tu and Th-F 9am-6pm, W 10am-6pm, Sa 9am-3:45pm, Su 12:15am-5:30pm.) The **Abbey Library** has a world-famous collection of over 140,000 valuable books and manuscripts, all housed in a fittingly grand Rococo hall. (Open Jan. 2-Feb. 25; Mar. 3-Nov. 11; Dec. 3-Dec. 31; M-Sa 10am-5pm, Su 10 am-4pm. 7CHF.) The **Lapidarium** holds ancient artifacts from the 8th century onwards (Open M-Sa 10am-5pm, Su 10am-4pm. 3CHF). Religious egalitarians shouldn't miss the neighboring **Church of St. Laurence,** once the hotbed of Reformation in St. Gallen; visitors who make the long trek up to the church's viewing platform (mind those immense, oft-ringing bells) will find divine views of the city and surrounding countryside. (Church open M 9:30-11:30am and 2-4pm, Tu-F 9:30am-6pm, Sa 9:30am-4pm. Viewing platform open M-Sa 9:30-11:30am and 2-4pm. 2CHF.)

Jugendherberge (HI) ❷, 25 Jüchstr., has clean rooms and scenic views of the hillside; take the orange Trogenerbahn tram (dir: Trogen) from the right of the train station to the Schuleraus stop, then walk up the hill for 5min. and turn left. (☎245 4777. Breakfast included. Reception 7:30-10am, 5-10:30pm. Laundry 6CHF. Internet 12CHF per hr. Dorms 30-36CHF; singles 50-52CHF; doubles 39-42CHF.) There's no shortage of restaurants. for low prices and friendly surroundings seek out **Isabel's Imbisshöck ❷,** tucked away in a quiet corner at the end of Engelgaße. (Meals 6-14CHF. Mixed drinks 3-9CHF. Wines 20-22CHF. Open M-Th 11am-2pm and 5-10pm, F-Sa 11am-2pm and 5pm-12:30am. Cash only.) If pious St. Gallen moves you to gluttony, indulge with two floors of Swiss cocoa at the **Chocolaterie Maestrani ❶,** next to the Abbey Precinct. (Open Tu-W 9am-9pm, Th-F 9am-6:30pm, Sa 9am-5pm, Su 9:30am-4pm.) **Trains** run to: Luzern (2hr., 2 per hr., 45CHF); Zürich (1¼hr., 1-2 per hr., 25CHF); Bern (1½hr., 1 per hr., 63CHF); Geneva (4hr., 1 per hr., 95CHF); Lausanne (3½hr., 2 per hr., 81CHF). The **tourist office** is in the plaza in front of the station. (May-Oct. M-F 9am-6pm, Sa 10am-3pm; Nov.-Apr. M-F 9am-3pm, Sa 10am-1pm). The **post office** is opposite the station. **Postal Code:** CH-9000.

NORTHWESTERN SWITZERLAND

Though at the junction of the French and German borders, this peaceful region remains defiantly Swiss; locals speak Swiss-German and welcome visitors with distinctive hospitality. The best part of Northwestern Switzerland is youthful Basel, Switzerland's preeminent university town.

BASEL (BÂLE)   ☎061

Basel bills itself as Switzerland's "cultural capital," and though nearby Zürich might beg to differ, it's hard to argue with the city's lively medieval quarter and many museums. Basel is home to one of the oldest universities in Europe—former professors include Erasmus and Nietzsche.

🖪🔁 **TRANSPORTATION AND PRACTICAL INFORMATION.** Basel has three train stations: the **French (SNCF)** and **Swiss (SBB)** stations on Centralbahnpl., near the *Altstadt,* and the **German (DB)** station across the Rhine (take tram #2 from the other train stations or connect directly from the SBB). **Trains** leave from the SBB to: Bern (1¼hr., 1-2 per hr., 36CHF); Geneva (3hr., 1 per hr., 67CHF); Lausanne (2½hr., 1 per hr., 57CHF); Zürich (1hr., every 15-30min., 30CHF). The main **tourist** office is on Steinenbergstr. in the Stadt Casino building (from the SBB station, take #6, 8, 14, 16, or 17 to Barfüsserpl.). There is also a branch in the SBB station. (Both offices: ☎ 268 6868; www.baseltourismus.ch. Open M-F 8:30am-6:30pm, Sa 9am-5pm, Su 10am-4pm.) For info on **GLBT** establishments, stop by the bookstore **Arcados,** Rheing. 69. (☎ 681 3132; www.arcados.com. Open Tu-F 1-7pm, Sa noon-4pm.) To reach the **post office,** Rüdeng. 1, take tram #1 or 8 to Marktpl. (Open M-F 7:30am-9pm, Sa 8am-5pm, Su 2-7pm.)

⌐⌐ ACCOMMODATIONS AND FOOD. The **Jugendherberge (HI) ❷,** St. Alban-Kirchrain 10, is located near the Rhine in a beautiful 19th-century building. To get there, take tram #2 or 15 to Kunstmuseum, turn right on St. Alban-Vorstadt, then follow the signs. (☎ 272 0572; www.youthhostel.ch/basel. Breakfast included. Laundry 7CHF. Internet 6CHF per hr. Reception Mar.-Oct. 7-10am and 2pm-midnight; Nov.-Feb. 7-10am and 2-11pm. Dorms 37-39CHF; doubles 112CHF; quads 168CHF. HI discount 6CHF. AmEx/MC/V.) **Basel Back Pack ❷,** Dornacherstr. 192, is far from the *Altstadt*, but the hostel provides free tickets for all trams and buses. To reach it, walk out the back entrance of the SBB station, turn left on Güterst., then turn right onto Brudenholzst. at Tellpl. The hostel is in the complex on your left after a block. (☎ 333 0037; www.baselbackpack.ch. Breakfast 7CHF. Laundry 6CHF. Internet 1CHF per 5min. Reception 8-11:30am, 2-6pm, and 8-10:30pm. Dorms 31CHF; singles 80CHF; doubles 96CHF; triples 123CHF; quads 144CHF; quints 180CHF. AmEx/MC/V; min. 60CHF.)

Barfüsserplatz and Marktplatz are full of satisfying restaurants. ⬛**Restaurant Hirscheneck ❷,** Lindenberg 23 in Klein-Basel, is popular with students, vegetarians, and Basel's alternative crowd. (Take tram #2 or 15 to Wettsteinpl., then walk back towards the river and turn right on Kartausg. ☎ 692 7333; www.hirscheneck.ch. Daily menu 12-24CHF. Smaller portions 9-15CHF. Su brunch 10am-4pm. Open M 2pm-midnight, Tu-Th 11am-midnight, F 11am-1am, Sa 2pm-1am, Su 10am-midnight. Cash only.) On the other bank of the Rhine off Barfüsserpl., **Café Barfi ❸,** Leonhardsberg 4, belies its name with tasty, affordable Italian meals. (☎ 261 7038. Pizza 18-21CHF. Pasta 15-20CHF. Open M-Sa 11am-11pm). Groceries are available at **Migros,** in the SBB station. (Open M-F 6am-10pm, Sa-Su 7:30am-10pm.)

> **EURO CUP 2008.** The **2008 European Football Championship** (June 7-29) will be held in Austria and Switzerland. Basel, Bern, Geneva, and Zürich will host matches. Expect crowds and unrestrained merrymaking. Visit www.uefa.com for more info. For venues in Austria, see p. 77.

◉⌐ SIGHTS AND ENTERTAINMENT. The Rhine separates Groß-Basel (Greater Basel) and the SBB/SNCF train stations from the Klein-Basel (Lesser Basel). Behind the Marktpl., the nearly 800-year-old **Mittlere Rheinbrücke** (Middle Rhine Bridge) connects the two halves of the city. To get to the Old Town from the train station, take tram #16. The very red **Rathaus** (City Hall) brightens the **Marktplatz.** Behind Marktpl. stands the red sandstone **Münster** (Cathedral), where you can see the tomb of Erasmus or climb the tower for a view of the city. (Church open Easter to mid-Oct. M-F 10am-5pm, Sa 10am-4pm, Su 11:30am-5pm; mid-Oct. to Easter M-Sa 11am-4pm, Su 11:30am-4pm. Tower closes 30min. before the church. Church free. Tower 3CHF.) Get off at the Theater stop to see the spectacular ⬛**Jean Tinguely Fountain,** also known as the **Fasnachtsbrunnen.** Basel has over 30 museums; pick up a comprehensive guide at the tourist office. The **Basel Card,** also available at the tourist office, provides admission to most museums and free sightseeing tours. (1-day pass 20CHF, 2-day 27CHF, 3-day 35CHF.) The must-see ⬛**Kunstmuseum** (Museum of Fine Arts), St. Alban-Graben 16, houses what may be Switzerland's greatest collections of new and old masters. Admission also gives access to the **Museum für Gegenwartskunst** (Museum of Modern Art), St. Alban-Rheinweg 60, which has changing exhibits of contemporary work. (Kunstmuseum open Tu and Th-Su 10am-5pm, W 10am-7pm. Gegenwartskunst open Tu-Su 11am-5pm. Each museum 12CHF, students 5CHF. Free daily 4-5pm and 1st Su of each month.)

Basel's **Fasnacht** (Feb. 11-13, 2008) commences the week after Lent with the *Morgestraich*, a three-day parade with a centuries-old goal—to scare away winter. Head to **Barfüsserplatz** and **Steinenvorstadt** for an evening of bar-hopping. **Atlantis,** Klosterberg 13, is a multi-level, sophisticated bar that plays reggae, jazz, and funk. (☎228 9696. Summer drink special 12CHF. Cover 10-15CHF; students with ID 5CHF discount; July-Sept. no cover F. Open M 11:30am-2pm, Tu-Th 11:30am-2pm and 6pm-midnight, F 11:30am-2pm and 6pm-4am, Sa 6pm-4am. AmEx/MC/V.)

GRAUBÜNDEN

Graubünden's rugged gorges, fir forests, and eddying rivers give the region a wildness seldom found in comfortably settled Switzerland. Visitors should plan their trips carefully, especially during ski season when reservations are absolutely required, and in May and June, when nearly everything shuts down.

DAVOS ☎081

Davos (pop. 13,000) sprawls along the valley floor under mountains criss-crossed with chairlifts and cable cars. Originally a health resort, the city catered to such *fin-de-siècle* giants as Robert Louis Stevenson and Thomas Mann. The influx of tourists and political conferences has given the city a somewhat artificial feel, but the thrill of carving down the famed, wickedly steep ski slopes or exploring the 700km of hiking paths may make up for it. Davos provides direct access to two mountains—**Parsenn** and **Jakobshorn**—and four skiing areas. Parsenn, with long runs and fearsome vertical drops, is the mountain around which Davos built its reputation. (Day pass 60CHF.) Jakobshorn has found a niche with the younger crowd since opening a snowboarding park with two half-pipes (day pass 55CHF). Cross-country trails cover 75km, and one is lit at night. In the summer, ski lifts (½-price after 3pm) connect to **hiking trails**, such as the **Panoramaweg** (2hr.). Europe's largest natural **ice rink** (18,000 sq. m) allows for curling, figure skating, hockey, ice dancing, and speed skating. (☎41 53 04. Open July-Aug. and Dec. 15-Feb., 10am-4:30pm. 5CHF; M and Th evening free evening skating. Skate rental 6.50CHF.)

Davos has high prices; staying in nearby Klosters is more economical. Davos is accessible by **train** from Klosters (25min., 2 per hr., 9.20CHF). The town is divided into two areas, Davos-Platz and Davos-Dorf, each with a train station. Platz has the post office and the main **tourist office,** Promenade 67, which is up the hill and to the right on Promenade from the station. (☎415 2121; www.davos.ch. Free Internet. Open Dec. to mid-Apr. and mid-June to mid-Oct. M-F 8:30am-6:30pm, Sa 9am-5pm, Su 10am-noon and 3-5:30pm; mid-Oct. to Nov. and mid-Apr. to mid-June M-F 8:30am-noon and 1:45pm-6pm, Sa 9am-noon.) **Postal Code:** CH-7260.

KLOSTERS ☎081

Though Klosters (pop. 3000) is not far from Davos, it's a world away in atmosphere. Davos aspires to be cosmopolitan, while Klosters, despite receiving international attention as the favorite ski resort of Prince Charles Windsor, capitalizes on its natural serenity and cozy chalets. **Ski passes** for the Klosters-Davos region run 121CHF per two days and 282CHF per six days, including public transportation. The **Grotschnabahn,** right behind the train station, gives access to Parsenn and Strela in Davos and Madrisa in Klosters. (1-day pass 60CHF; 6-day pass 324CHF.) The **Madrisabahn** leaves from Klosters-Dorf on the other side of town (1-day pass;

47CHF). **Ski rental** is also available at **Sport Gotschna,** Alte Bahnhofstr. 5, across from the tourist office. (☎422 11 97. Skis and snowboards 28-50CHF per day plus 10% insurance. Open mid-June to late April M-F 8am-6:30pm, Sa-Su 8am-6pm. AmEx/MC/V.) In summer, Klosters has access to fantastic hiking trails. On the lush, green valley floor, hikers can make a large loop from Klosters's Protestant church on Monbielstr. to Monbiel, returning to Klosters via Pardels after climbing to an elevation of 1634m. There are fourteen other local routes available, from the genteel to the exhausting. Several adventure companies offer **river rafting, canoeing, horseback riding, paragliding,** and **glacier trekking.** Summer cable car passes (valid on Grotschnabahn and Madrisabahn) are also available (4-day pass 80CHF).

> **THE REAL DEAL.** Staying in Klosters but skiing in both Klosters and Davos is the most affordable and pleasant option for the budget traveler. Many ski packages include mountains from both towns, and Kloster's main lift, the **Grotschnabahn,** leads to a mountain pass accessing both.

To get to **Jugendherberge Soldanella (HI)** ❷, Talstr. 73, from the station, go left uphill past Hotel Alpina to the church, then cross the street and head up the alleyway to the right of the Kirchpl. bus station sign. Walk 10min. along the path. This massive chalet has a reading room and a flagstone terrace. (☎422 1316; www.youthhostel.ch/klosters. Breakfast included. Reception 8-10am and 5-9pm. Open mid-Dec. to mid-Apr. and late June to mid-Oct. Dorms 35CHF; singles 46CHF; doubles 88CHF; family rooms 44CHF per person. 6CHF HI discount. AmEx/MC/V.) Turn right from the train station to reach the **Coop** supermarket, Bahnhofstr. 10. (Open M-F 8am-12:30pm and 2-6:30pm. Sa 8am-5pm.) Trains run to Davos (25min., 2 per hr., 9.20CHF) and Zürich via Landquart (2hr., 1 per hr., 45CHF). Pick up biking and hiking maps at the main **tourist office,** reached by turning right from the station and taking another right on Alte Banhofstr. (☎410 2020; www.klosters.ch. Open May-Nov. M-F 9am-5pm; Dec.-Apr. M-F 8:30am-6pm, Sat-Su 8:30am-5pm.) **Postal code:** CH-7250.

SWISS NATIONAL PARK   ☎081

One of the world's best-kept nature preserves, the Swiss National Park showcases some of the Graubünden region's abundant wildlife and most stunning views. A network of 20 hiking trails, mostly concentrated in the center, runs throughout the park. Few trails are level; most involve a lot of climbing, often into snow-covered areas. All trails are clearly marked, and it is against park rules to wander off the designated trails. Trails that require no mountaineering gear are marked with white-red-white markers. Keep in mind that every route can be tricky.

Zernez is the main gateway to the park and home to its headquarters, the **National Parkhouse.** The staff provides helpful trail maps as well as information on which trails are navigable. (☎856 1378; www.nationalpark.ch. Open June-Oct. daily 8:30am-6pm.) To reach the park itself, take a Post **bus** (1 per hr., 4.60CHF) from the front of the train station to one of several destinations within the wilderness. Trains and buses also run to other towns in the area, including **Scuol, Samedan,** and **S-chanf.** Despite its location in ski-happy Graubünden, the park, closed November through May, is not a site for winter sports. It is one of the most strictly regulated nature reserves in the world; camping and campfires are prohibited, as is collecting flowers and plants. Wardens patrol the park at all times, so it's better not to test the rules. Nearby towns have campgrounds outside the park boundaries.

ST. MORITZ   ☎081

The savvy promoters of St. Moritz were the first to bring their British guests to the "top of the world," giving birth to Alpine winter tourism. The average 322 days of sunshine per year still fall mostly upon the chic in this luxury-obsessed resort town. Yet St. Moritz remains a top destination for year-round sports—you don't have to stay at a world-famous hotel to enjoy the ski slopes that have hosted the Olympic Games and Alpine skiing world championships. Ski and snowboard rentals (38CHF per day, 139CHF per 6 days) and ski lifts are no more expensive than at other resort towns in the region. In summer, **St. Moritz Experience** (☎ 833 7714) organizes adventures such as canyoning and glacial hiking. The cheapest beds in town are at the cozy **Central Hostel ❸**, V. Dal Bagn 17; take bus #3 (2-3 per hr., 2.80CHF) from the train station to Via Salet, then walk back up the hill. Buzz at the door. (☎ 869 3692. Breakfast included. Reception 5-8pm. Dorms 36CHF; doubles 110CHF; triples 135CHF. Cash only.) To reach **Camping Olypiaschanze ❶**, take bus #1 or 4 from the train station. (☎ 833 4090. Tent sites 18CHF, extra person 5.60CHF. MC/V.) **Coop** supermarket has a self-serve restaurant. (Open M-Th 8am-6:30pm, F 8am-8pm, Sa 8am-5pm.) **Trains** run to Davos (1½hr., 1 per hr., 28CHF) via Filisur, Zernez via Samedan (45min., 1 per hr., 17CHF), and Zürich via Chur (3½hr., 1 per hr., 67CHF). The **tourist office**, V. Maista 12, is uphill from the train station. (☎ 837 3333. Open mid-June to mid-Sept. and mid-Dec. to mid-Apr. M-F 9am-6:30pm, Sa 9am-6pm, Su 4-6pm; mid-Apr. to mid-June and mid-Sept. to mid-Dec. M-F 9am-noon and 4-6pm, Sa 9am-noon.) **Postal Code:** CH-7500.

VALAIS

The Valais occupies the deep glacial gorge traced by the Rhône River. The clefts of the valley divide the land linguistically: in the west, French predominates, and in the east, Swiss German is used. Though its mountain resorts can be over-touristed, the region's spectacular peaks make fighting the traffic worthwhile.

ZERMATT AND THE MATTERHORN   ☎ 027

Year-round, tourists pack the trains to Zermatt (pop. 3500) where the monolithic **Matterhorn** (4478m) rises above the endless hotels and lodges in town. To many foreigners, the mountain is the symbol of Switzerland, and you can't turn around in this resort town without glimpsing a poster or logo featuring the famously sharp peak. The area has attained mecca status with Europe's longest ski run, the 13km

> **HEY, WHERE DID THE MOUNTAIN GO?** The Matterhorn is a wondrous sight—when you can see it. Be sure to check the weather forecast before heading to Zermatt, even in summer. No amount of Matterhorn merchandise will cheer you up when the peak is covered with clouds.

trail from Klein Matterhorn to Zermatt, and more **summer ski trails** than any other Alpine resort. The **Zermatt Alpin Center,** Bahnhofstr. 58, just past the post office, houses both the **Bergführerbüro** (Mountain Guide's Office; ☎ 966 2460) and the **Skischulbüro** (Ski School Office; ☎ 966 2466). The center provides ski passes (½-day 52CHF, 1-day 68CHF), four-day weather forecasts, and info on guided climbing. (www.alpincenter-zermatt.ch. Open daily July-Sept. 8:30am-noon and 3-7pm; late Dec. to mid-May 4-7pm.) The Bergführerbüro is also the only company to lead formal expeditions above Zermatt. Groups scale Breithorn (4164m, 2hr., 155CHF), Castor (4228m, 5-6hr., 319CHF), and Pollux (4091m, 5-6hr., 302CHF) daily in summer. Prices do not include equipment, insurance, sleeping huts, or lifts to departure points. **Rental prices** for skis and snowboards are standard in Zermatt (28-50CHF per day). For a new perspective on the Matterhorn, try a tandem flight with

THE SCRAPED DISH

Though fondue is Switzerland's main culinary claim to fame, visitors to the western, French-speaking part of the country will notice another item popping up on menus: *raclette*. Not surprisingly, it also involves cheese.

Raclette dates from the medieval era, when peasants would heat cheese made from their cows' milk next to evening fires. When the cheese had reached the right consistency and softness, the farmers would scrape it off the plate onto some bread—hence the name (the French *racler* means "to scrape"). The German equivalent was termed *Bratchas*, or "roasted cheese."

Today, the dish has left the Alpine pastures and advanced into the resorts that dot the region, especially the Valais (home of the Matterhorn). The cheese is still heated and scraped, though in many cases fires have given way to stovetops. Traditional embellishments include bell peppers, tomatoes, pickles, and potatoes. *Raclette* is accompanied by warm beverages or white wine; the combination of a chilled drink and hot cheese is thought to cause indigestion.

So do your best to ignore the parade of expensive lodges and tourists around you; enjoy some roasted, scraped cheese in the tradition of Swiss mountain herders. Partaking on steep Alpine slopes may lend a certain authenticity to the experience—just don't forget the wine.

Paraglide Zermatt (☎967 6744; www.paragliding-zermatt.ch. 150-190CHF.) For those who prefer to stay connected to the ground, the Gornergrat Bahn rack railway, departing from just across the train station, brings spectators 3089m above sea level to a viewing platform and to Europe's highest hotel (☎921 4711; www.gornergrat.ch; 36CHF, 72CHF round trip).

Hotel Bahnhof ❷, on Bahnhofpl. 54, to the left of the station, provides hotel housing at hostel rates. Though small, it has a central location and mountain views. (☎967 2406; www.hotelbahnhof.com. Open mid-June to Oct. and mid-Dec. to mid-May. Reception 8am-8pm. Dorms 35CHF; singles 68CHF, with shower 78CHF; doubles 92-108CHF; quads 184CHF. MC/V.) A wide variety of traditional Swiss fare is available at **Walliserkanne ❷**, Bahnhofstr. 32, next to the post office. (☎966 4610. *Raclette* 8CHF. Pasta 17-25CHF. Cheese fondues 23-25CHF. Open daily 8am-midnight. Kitchen closes 11pm. AmEx/MC/V.) Get groceries at the **Coop Center,** opposite the station. (Open M-Sa 8:15am-6:30pm.) **The Pipe Surfer's Cantina ❸**, on Kirchstr., specializes in Mexican-Thai-Indian fusion cuisine and caramel vodka (6CHF), and by night throws the craziest "beach parties" in the Alps. (☎079 213 3807; www.gozermatt.com/thepipe. Salads 23-27CHF. Entrees 28-32CHF. Happy hour 6-7pm, in winter 4-5pm. Open daily 4pm-midnight. MC/V.)

To preserve the Alpine air, cars and buses are banned in Zermatt; the only way in is the hourly **BVZ** (Brig-Visp-Zermatt) rail line, which connects to Lausanne (3hr., 71CHF) and Bern (3hr., 78CHF) via Brig. Buy hiking maps (26CHF) at the **tourist office,** in the station. (☎966 8100; www.zermatt.ch. Open mid-June to Sept. M-Sa 8:30am-6pm, Su 8:30am-noon and 1:30-6pm; Oct. to mid-June M-Sa 8:30am-noon and 1:30-6pm; Su 9:30am-noon and 4-6pm. **Postal Code:** CH-3920.

FRENCH SWITZERLAND

The picturesque scenery and refined cities of French Switzerland have attracted herds of tourists for centuries, and there's no denying that the area's charm often comes at a steep price. But the best experiences in French Switzerland are free: strolling down tree-lined avenues, soaking up endearing *vieilles villes* (Old Towns), and taking in the mountain vistas from across Lac Léman (Lake Geneva) and Lac Neuchâtel.

GENEVA (GENÈVE)   ☎ 022

Geneva (pop. 183,000) began with a tomb, blossomed into a religious center, became the "Protestant Rome," and ultimately emerged as a center for world diplomacy. Today, thanks to the presence of dozens of multinational organizations, including the United Nations and the Red Cross, the city is easily the most worldly in Switzerland. But Geneva's heritage lingers; you can sense it in the street names paying homage to Genevese patriots of old and the ubiquitous presence of the cherished cuckoo clock.

▛ TRANSPORTATION

Flights: Cointrin Airport (GVA; ☎ 717 7111, flight info 799 3111 or 717 7105) is a hub for **Swiss International Airlines** (☎ 0848 85 20 00) and also serves **Air France** (☎ 827 8787) and **British Airways** (☎ 0848 80 10 10). Several direct flights per day to **Amsterdam, NTH; London, BRI; New York, USA; Paris, FRA;** and **Rome, ITA.** Bus #10 runs to the Gare Cornavin (15min., 6-12 per hr., 3CHF), but the train trip is shorter (6min., 6 per hr., 3CHF).

Trains: Trains run 4:30am-1am. **Gare Cornavin,** pl. Cornavin, is the main station. To: **Basel** (2¾hr., 1 per 2 hr., 67CHF); **Bern** (2hr., 2 per hr., 45CHF); **Lausanne** (40min., 3-4 per hr., 20CHF); **Zürich** (3½hr., 1-2 per hr., 77CHF); **St. Gallen** (4 hr., 1-2 per hr., 95CHF). Ticket counter open M-F 5:15am-9:30pm, Sa-Su 5:30am-9:30pm. **Gare des Eaux-Vives** (☎ 736 1620), on av. de la Gare des Eaux-Vives (tram #12 to Amandoliers SNCF), connects to France's regional rail through **Annecy, FRA** (1½hr., 6 per day, 15CHF) or **Chamonix, FRA** (2½hr., 4 per day, 25CHF).

Public Transportation: Geneva has an efficient bus and tram network (www.tpg.ch). Single tickets valid for 1hr. within the "orange" city zone, which includes the airport, are 3CHF, rides of 3 stops or less 2CHF. **Day passes** (10CHF) and a **9hr. pass** (7CHF) are available for the canton of Geneva. Day passes for the whole region 18CHF. Stamp multi-use tickets before boarding at machines in the station. Buses run 5am-12:30am; **Noctambus** (F-Sa 12:30-3:45am, 3CHF) offers night service.

Taxis: Taxi-Phone (☎ 331 4133). 6.80CHF plus 2.90CHF per km. 30CHF from airport.

Bike Rental: Geneva has well-marked bike paths and special traffic signals. Behind the station, **Genève Roule,** pl. Montbrillant 17 (☎ 740 1343), has ▉ **free bikes** (passport and 50CHF deposit; fines run upward of 300CHF if bike is lost or stolen). Other locations at Bains des Pâquis and pl. du Rhône. Arrive before 9am, as bikes go quickly. Open daily May-Oct. 7:30am-9:30pm; Nov.-Apr. 8am-6pm. Cash only.

Hitchhiking: Let's Go does not recommend hitchhiking. Those headed to Germany or northern Switzerland take bus #4 to Jardin Botanique, where they try to catch a ride. Those headed to France take bus #4 to Palettes, then line D to St. Julien.

◆▌ ORIENTATION AND PRACTICAL INFORMATION

The twisting, cobbled streets and quiet squares of the historic *vieille ville* (Old Town), centered on **Cathédrale de St-Pierre,** make up the heart of Geneva. Across the **Rhône River** to the north, five-star hotels give way to lakeside promenades, **International Hill,** and rolling parks. Across the **Arve River** to the south lies the village of **Carouge,** home to student bars and clubs (take tram #12 or 13 to pl. du Marché).

Tourist Office: r. du Mont-Blanc 18 (☎ 909 7000; www.geneva-tourism.ch), in the Central Post Office Building. From Cornavin, walk 5min. toward the Pont du Mont-Blanc. Staff books hotel rooms for 5CHF, leads English-language walking tours, and offers free city maps. Open M 10am-6pm, Tu-Su 9am-6pm.

SWITZERLAND

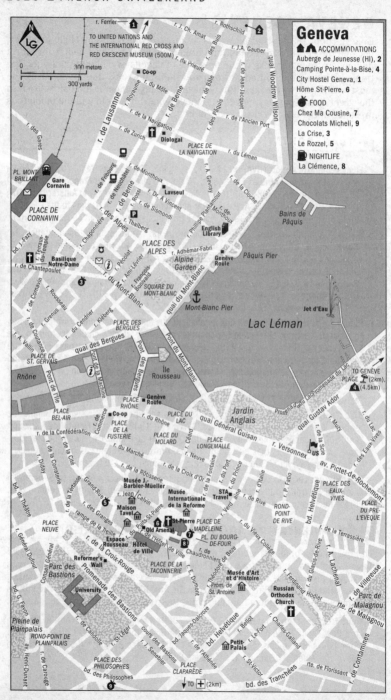

Geneva

■▲▲ ACCOMMODATIONS
Auberge de Jeunesse (HI), **2**
Camping Pointe-à-la-Bise, **4**
City Hostel Geneva, **1**
Hôme St-Pierre, **6**

🍎 FOOD
Chez Ma Cousine, **7**
Chocolats Micheli, **9**
La Crise, **3**
Le Rozzel, **5**

🍷 NIGHTLIFE
La Clémence, **8**

Consulates: Australia, chemin des Fins 2 (☎799 9100). **Canada,** av. de l'Ariana 5 (☎919 9200). **New Zealand,** chemin des Fins 2 (☎929 0350). **UK,** r. de Vermont 37 (☎918 2400). **US,** r. Versonnex 7 (☎840 5160, recorded info 840 5161).

Currency Exchange: ATMs have the best rates. The currency exchange inside the **Gare Cornavin** has good rates with no commission on traveler's checks, makes cash advances on credit cards (min. 200CHF), and arranges **Western Union** transfers. Open M-Sa 7am-8pm, Su 8am-5:50pm.

GLBT Resources: Dialogai, r. de la Navigation 11-13, entrance Rue d. Levant 5 (☎906 4040). From Gare Cornavin, turn left, walk 5min. down r. de Lausanne, and turn right onto r. de la Navigation. Offers brochures and maps on GBLT nightlife; doubles as a cafe and nighttime hot spot. Mostly male, but women welcome. Open M 9am-10pm, Tu-Th 9am-6pm, F 9am-5pm.

Laundromat: Lavseul, r. de Monthoux 29 (☎735 9051). Wash 5CHF, dry 1CHF per 9min. Open daily 7am-midnight.

Police: R. de Berne 6 (☎117). Open M-F 9am-noon and 3-6:30pm, Sa 9am-noon.

Hospital: Hôpital Cantonal, r. Micheli-du-Crest 24 (☎372 3311; www.hug-ge.ch). Bus #1 or 5 or tram #12. Door #2 is for emergency care; door #3 is for consultations. For info on walk-in clinics, contact the **Association des Médecins** (☎320 8420).

Internet Access: Charly's Multimedia Check Point, r. de Fribourg 7 (☎901 1313; www.charlys.com). 1CHF per 10min., 6CHF per hr. Open M-Sa 9am-midnight, Su 1-11pm. **12Mix,** r. de-Monthoux 58 (☎731 6747; www.12mix.com). 3CHF per 30min., 5CHF per hr. Open daily 10am-midnight.

Post Office: Poste Centrale, r. du Mont-Blanc 18, 1 block from Gare Cornavin. Open M-F 7:30am-6pm, Sa 9am-4pm. **Postal Code:** CH-1200.

🏠 🏨 ACCOMMODATIONS AND CAMPING

The indispensable *Info Jeunes* lists about 30 budget options, and the tourist office publishes *Budget Hotels*, which stretches the definition of budget to 120CHF per person. Cheap beds are relatively scarce, so be sure to reserve ahead.

Hôme St-Pierre, Cour St-Pierre 4 (☎310 3707; info@homestpierre.ch). Take bus #5 to pl. Neuve, then walk up Rampe de la Treille, turn left onto R. Puits-St-Pierre, then right on R. du Soleil Levant. The hostel will be on your left. Comfortable beds and a great location beside the cathedral. The hostel acts primarily as a dorm for women, though, so backpackers (especially men) may be cramped. Church bells ring frequently at all hours of the night. Breakfast M-Sa 7CHF. Wi-Fi available. Reception M-Sa 9am-noon and 4-8pm, Su 9am-noon. Dorms 27CHF; singles 40CHF; doubles 60CHF. MC/V. ❶

City Hostel Geneva, r. Ferrier 2 (☎901 1500; www.cityhostel.ch). From the train station, head down r. de Lausanne. Take the 1st left on r. du Prieuré, which becomes r. Ferrier. Spotless, cozy rooms. Kitchens on each floor. Linens 3.50CHF. Internet 5CHF per hr. Reception 7:30am-noon and 1pm-midnight. Single-sex dorms (3-4 beds) 31CHF; singles 59-63CHF; doubles 72-86CHF. Reserve ahead in summer. MC/V. ❷

Auberge de Jeunesse (HI), r. Rothschild 30 (☎732 6260; www.youthhostel.ch/geneva). Standard rooms, some of which have lakeviews. Breakfast included. Laundry 8CHF. Internet 4CHF per hr. Max. stay 6 nights. Reception 6:30-10am and 2pm-midnight. Dorms 34CHF; doubles 92CHF, with shower 102CHF; quads 154CHF. 6CHF HI discount. AmEx/MC/V. ❷

Camping Pointe-à-la-Bise, chemin de la Bise (☎752 1296). Take bus #8 or tram #16 to Rive, then bus E north to Bise. Reception July-Aug. 8am-noon and 2-9pm; Apr.-June and Sept. 8am-noon and 4-8pm. Open Apr.-Sept. Reserve ahead. 7CHF per person, 18 CHF per tent, 4-person bungalows 98CHF. AmEx/MC/V. ❶

SWITZERLAND

🍴 FOOD

Geneva has it all, from sushi to paella, but you may need a banker's salary to foot the bill. Pick up basics at *boulangeries*, *pâtisseries*, or supermarkets, which often have attached cafeterias. Try the **Coop** on the corner of r. du Commerce and r. du Rhône, in the Centre Rhône Fusterie, or the **Migros** in the basement of the Places des Cygnes shopping center on r. de Lausanne, down the street from the station. A variety of relatively cheap ethnic eateries center in the **Les Pâquis** area, bordered by r. de Lausanne and Gare Cornavin on one side and the quais Mont-Blanc and Wilson on the other. Around **place du Cirque** and **plaine de Plainpalais** are student-oriented tea rooms. To the south, the neighborhood of **Carouge** is known for its cozy pizzerias and funky *brasseries*.

Le Rozzel, Grand-Rue 18 (☎312 4272). Take bus #5 to pl. Neuve, then walk up the hill on r. Jean-Calvin to Grand-Rue. Pleasant outdoor seating on a winding street in the *vieille ville*. Sweet crepes 7-12CHF; savory crepes 14-18CHF. Open M, W, F 7:30am-8:30pm, Tu and Th 7:30am-7pm, Sa 7:30am-6pm. MC/V. ❷

La Crise, r. de Chantepoulet 13 (☎738 0264). Every morning, the vegetables for the soup of the day (3.50CHF) are prepared in front of customers at this small but popular snack bar. *Plat du jour* 15CHF; 11CHF for a smaller portion. Open M-F 6am-3pm and 6-8pm, Sa 6am-3pm. Lunch served after noon. Cash only. ❷

Chocolats Micheli, r. Micheli-du-Crest 1 (☎329 9006). Take tram #13 to Plainpalais and walk up bd. des Philosophes until it intersects with r. Micheli-du-Crest. Confectionery masterpieces (1-3CHF) abound in this Victorian cafe. Purists should try the "100% chocolate." Coffee 3.40CHF. Open M-F 8am-6:45pm, Sa 8am-5pm. MC/V. ❶

Chez Ma Cousine, pl. du Bourg-de-Four 6 (☎310 9696), down the stairs behind the cathedral. This cheery cafe has perfected *poulet*, offering only 3 chicken dishes (all 14CHF), as well as chicken salads (14-15CHF). Open M-Sa 11am-11:30pm, Su 11am-10:30pm. AmEx/MC/V. ❷

🎬 SIGHTS

The most interesting sites are in a dense, easily walkable area. The tourist office offers 2hr. English-language walking tours. (Mid-June to Sept. M, W, F-Sa 10am, Tu and Th at 6:30pm; Oct. to mid-June Sa 10am. 15CHF, students 10CHF.)

VIEILLE VILLE. From 1536 to 1564, Calvin preached at the **Cathédrale de St-Pierre.** Climb the **north tower** if the stairs around the cathedral aren't enough of a workout. *(Cathedral open June-Sept. daily 9am-7pm; Oct.-May M-Sa 10am-12pm and 2-5pm, Su 11am-12:30pm and 1:30-5pm. Tower open June-Sept. M-F 9am-6pm, Sa 9am-4:30pm. Cathedral free; tower 4CHF.)* Ruins, including a Roman sanctuary and an AD 4th-century basilica, rest in an ▧**archaeological site** below the cathedral. *(Open Tu-Su 10am-5pm; Oct.-May Tu-F 2-5pm, Sa-Su 1:30-5:30pm. 8CHF, students 4CHF.)* For a dense presentation of Reformation 101 and an informative look at Geneva's history, visit the **Musée International de la Réforme,** 4 r. du Cloître. *(☎310 2431; www.musee-reforme.ch. Open Tu-Su 10am-5pm. 10CHF, students 7CHF.)* At the western end of the *vieille ville* sits the 12th-century **Maison Tavel,** which now houses a museum showcasing Geneva's history. *(Open Tu-Su 10am-5pm. Free.)* Across the street is the **Hôtel de Ville** (Town Hall). The **Grand-Rue,** beginning at the Hôtel de Ville, is lined with medieval workshops and 18th-century mansions. Plaques commemorate famous residents like Jean-Jacques Rousseau, who was born at #40. Visit the ▧**Espace Rousseau** there for an presentation of his life and work. *(☎310 1028; www.espace-rousseau.ch. Open Tu.-Su. 11am-5:30pm. 5CHF, students 3CHF.)* Below the cathedral, along r. de la Croix-Rouge, the **Parc des Bastions** stretches from pl. Neuve to pl. des Philosophes and includes **Le Mur des Réformateurs** (The Reformers' Wall), a collection of bas-relief figures depicting Protestant Reformers. The hulking **Musée d'Art et d'Histoire,** R. Charles-Galland 2, offers everything from prehistoric relics to contemporary art. (☎418 2600, mah.ville-ge.ch. Open Tu-Sun 10am-5pm. Free.)

WATERFRONT. Down quai Gustave Ardor, the **Jet d'Eau,** Europe's highest fountain and Geneva's city symbol, spews a seven-ton plume of water 134m into the air. The **floral clock** in the **Jardin Anglais** pays homage to Geneva's watch industry. Possibly the city's most overrated attraction, it was once its most hazardous—the clock had to be cut back because tourists, intent on taking photographs, repeatedly backed into oncoming traffic. For a water slide and an enormous pool, head up the south shore of the lake to **Genève Plage.** (☎ 736 2482; www.geneve-plage.ch. Open mid-May to mid-Sept. daily 10am-8pm. 7CHF, students 4.50CHF.)

INTERNATIONAL HILL. The International Red Cross building contains the impressive ▧**International Red Cross and Red Crescent Museum,** av. de la Paix 17. (Bus #8, F, V or Z to Appia ☎748 9511. www.micr.org. Open M and W-Su 10am-5pm. 10CHF, students 5CHF. English-language audio tour 3CHF.) Across the street, the European headquarters of the **United Nations,** av. de la Paix 14, is in the same building that once held the League of Nations. The constant traffic of international diplomats is entertainment in itself. (☎917 4896. Open July-Aug. daily 10am-5pm; Apr.-June and Sept.-Oct. daily 10am-noon and 2-4pm; Nov.-Mar. M-F 10am-noon and 2-4pm. 10CHF, students 8CHF.)

♫▧ ENTERTAINMENT AND NIGHTLIFE

Genève Agenda, available at the tourist office, features event listings from festivals to movies. In late June, the **Fête de la Musique** fills the city with nearly 500 free concerts. Parc de la Grange has free **jazz concerts.** Geneva hosts the biggest celebration of **American Independence Day** outside the US (July 4), and the **Fêtes de Genève** in early August fill the city with music and fireworks. **L'Escalade** (Dec. 12-14, 2008) commemorates the repulsion of invading Savoyard troops. Nightlife in Geneva is divided by neighborhood. **Place Bourg-de-Four,** below the cathedral in the *vieille ville*, attracts students to its charming terraces. **Place du Molard** has loud, somewhat upscale bars and clubs. For something more frenetic, head to **Les Pâquis,** near Gare Cornavin and pl. de la Navigation. The city's red-light district, it has a wide array of rowdy, low-lit bars and some nightclubs. This neighborhood is also home to many of the city's gay bars. **Carouge,** across the Arve River, is a student-friendly locus of nightlife activity. In the *vieille ville*, generations of students have had their share of drinks at the intimate bar of **La Clémence,** pl. du Bourg-de-Four 20. Try the local Calvinus beer (7CHF) to do your part for Protestantism. (Open M-Th 7am-12:30am, F-Sa 7am-1:30am.)

LAUSANNE   ☎021

The unique museums, medieval *vieille ville*, and lazy Lac Léman waterfront of Lausanne (pop. 125,000) make it well worth a visit. The centerpiece of the *vieille ville* is the Gothic **Cathédrale.** (Open May to mid-Sept. M-F 7am-7pm, Sa-Su 8am-7pm; mid-Sept. to Apr. M-F 7am-5:30pm, Sa-Su 8am-5:30pm.) Below the cathedral is the city hall, **Hôtel de Ville,** on pl. de la Palud, the meeting point for **guided tours** of the town. (☎321 7766; www.lausanne.ch/visites. Tours May-Sept. M-Sa 10am and 3pm. 10CHF, students free.) The ▧**Musée Olympique,** quai d'Ouchy 1, is a high-tech shrine to modern Olympians. Take bus #2 to Ouchy, bus #8 to Musée Olympique, or bus #4 to Montchoisi. (☎621 6511; www.olympic.org. Open Apr.-Oct. daily 9am-6pm; Nov.-Mar. Tu-Su 9am-6pm. 15CHF, students 10CHF.) The fascinating **Collection de l'Art Brut,** av. Bergières 11, is filled with unusual sculptures, drawings, and paintings by fringe artists—schizophrenics, peasants, and criminals. Take bus #2 to Jomini or 3 to Beaulieu. (☎315 2570; www.artbrut.ch. Open July-Aug. daily 11am-6pm; Sept.-June Tu-Su 11am-10pm. 8CHF, students 5CHF.) In Ouchy, Lausanne's port, several booths along quai de Belgique rent **pedal boats** (13CHF per 30min., 20CHF per hr.) and offer **water skiing** or **wake boarding** (35CHF per 15min.) on Lac Léman. **Lausanne Roule** loans **free bikes** beside pl. de la Riponne on R. du Tennel (☎076 441 8378. www.lausanneroule.ch. ID and 20CHF deposit. Open late Apr. to late Oct. daily 7:30am-9:30pm.)

🛏**Lausanne Guesthouse and Backpacker ❷,** chemin des Epinettes 4, at the train tracks, keeps the noise out and makes the most of its lakeviews. Head left out of the station on W. Fraisse; take the first right on chemin des Epinettes. (☎601 8000; www.lausanne-guesthouse.ch. Bike rental 20CHF per day. Linens 5CHF. Laundry 5CHF. Internet 8CHF per hr. Reception daily 7:30am-noon and 3-10pm. Dorms 32CHF; singles 85CHF, with bath 94CHF; doubles 90/110CHF. 5% ISIC discount. MC/V.) Restaurants center around **Place St-François** and the *vieille ville*, and *boulangeries* sell sandwiches on practically every street. **Le Barbare ❶,** Escaliers du Marché 27, near the cathedral, has sandwiches (5.50CHF) and omelettes (7.50-16CHF) for cheap. (☎312 2132. Open M-Sa 8:30am-midnight. AmEx/MC/V.) **Trains** leave for: Basel (2½hr., 1 per 2 hr., 57CHF); Geneva (50min., 3-4 per hr., 20CHF); Montreux (20min., 3-4 per hr., 10CHF); Zürich (2½hr., 1-2 per hr., 65CHF); Paris, FRA (4hr., 4 per day, 104CHF). **Tourist offices** are in the train station and by the Ouchy lakefront. (☎613 7373. Open daily 9am-7pm.) **Postal Code:** CH-1000.

MONTREUX
☎021

Although Montreux (pop. 23,000) is a gaudy resort at heart, its views of snow-capped peaks and Lac Léman are free. Though long past its Jazz Age heyday, the city still swings during the annual 🎵**Montreux Jazz Festival,** which erupts for 15 days starting the first Friday in July (July 4, 2008). World-famous for discovering and drawing exceptional talent, the festival has hosted icons like Bob Dylan and and Miles Davis. (www.montreuxjazz.com. Tickets 59-189CHF.) If you can't get tickets, come anyway for **Montreux Jazz Under the Sky,** 500 hours of free, open-air concerts on three stages. The 🏰**Château de Chillon,** a medieval fortress on a nearby island, features all the comforts of home: prison cells, a torture chamber, and a weapons room. Don't miss Lord Byron's etched autograph in Bonivard's cell. Take bus #1 (3CHF) to Chillon. (☎966 8910; www.chillon.ch. Open daily Apr.-Sept. 9am-6pm; Mar. and Oct. 9:30am-5pm; Nov.-Feb. 10am-4pm. 12CHF, students 10CHF. Tours in summer daily 11:30am and 3:30pm. 6CHF.)

Cheap rooms in Montreux are scarce year-round and nonexistent during the Jazz Festival, so reserve ahead. 🛏**Riviera Lodge ❷,** pl. du Marché 5, in the neighboring town of Vevey, is worth the commute for its friendly staff and water views. Guests receive a pass including free bus transportation and discounts on museums and attractions. Take the train or bus #1 to Vevey (15min., 6 per hr., 2.80CHF). Head to the left away from the train station on the main road and follow the brown signs to the lodge, located in the main square on the water. (☎923 8040; www.rivieralodge.ch. Breakfast 8CHF. Linens 5CHF. Laundry 6CHF. Internet 7CHF per hr. Reception 8am-noon and 4-8pm. Call ahead if arriving late. Dorms 32CHF; doubles 88CHF. Prices 4-7CHF higher during festival. MC/V.) **Babette's ❷,** Grand-Rue 60, downstairs from the station and to the left, serves crepes (6-15CHF) for lunch and dessert. (☎963 7796. Open daily 7am-7pm. MC/V.) Grand-Rue and av. de Casino have inexpensive markets. **Trains** leave for Geneva (1hr., 2-3 per hr.,

27CHF), and Lausanne (20min., 4-6 per hr., 9.80CHF). The **tourist office** is on Grand-Rue, downstairs and left from the station. (☎962 8484; www.montreux-vevey.com. Open May to mid-Sept. M-F 9am-6pm, Sa-Su 9:30am-5pm; mid-Sept. to Apr. M-F 9am-noon and 1-5:30pm, Sa-Su 10am-2pm.) **Postal Code:** CH-1820.

NEUCHÂTEL   ☎032

Alexandre Dumas once said that the town of Neuchâtel (pop. 30,000) appeared to be carved out of butter; visitors gazing down street after street filled with yellow stone architecture will immediately see why. The *vieille ville* centers around **place des Halles**, a block from **place Pury**, the hub of every bus line. From pl. des Halles, turn left on r. de Château and climb the stairs on the right to reach the **Collégiale Church** and the **château** that gives the town its name. (Church open daily Apr.-Sept. 9am-8pm; Oct.-Mar. 9am-6:30pm.) Entrance to the château is available only through a free tour. (1 per hr. Apr.-Sept. M 2-4pm, Tu-F 10am-4pm, Sa-Su 2-4pm.) The **Tour des Prisons** (Prison Tower), on r. Jeanne-Hochberg, has old prison cells, models of the town in centuries past, and prime views. (Open Apr.-Sept. daily 8am-6pm. 1CHF.) The **Musée d'Histoire Naturelle**, Av. Léopold-Robert 63, has a great collection of stuffed creatures. Turn right from pl. des Halles onto Croix du Marché, which becomes r. de l'Hôpital, then turn left onto R. des Terraux. (☎967 6071. Open Tu-Su 10am-6pm. 6CHF, students 4CHF. W free.) At the edge of the waterside square by the tourist office, **Neuchâtel Roule** lends free bikes. (☎717 5091; www.neuchatelroule.ch. Passport and 20CHF deposit. Open Apr.-Sept. daily 7:30am-9:30pm.; Oct. 8:30am-8:30pm.) For the best views, ride your bike or take bus #7 to La Coudre, where you can hop on the **funicular** that rises up through the forest to the village of Chaumont. (1 per hr. 9am-7pm. 4.60CHF.)

The ⬛**Auberg'inn,** Rue Fleury 1, offers themed rooms in the middle of the *vieille ville.* From Place des Halles, walk up R. du Trésor until you reach Croix-du-Marché; the hostel is in the small square on your left. (☎078 615 8421; www.auberginn.com. Reception open M 7:30am-9pm, Tu-W 7:30am-10pm, Th 7:30am-1pm, F-Sa 7:30am-2pm, Su 7:30am-9pm. Dorms 35CHF; singles 80CHF; doubles 120CHF; triples 135CHF; quads 160CHF; quints 175CHF. MC/V.) **Wodey-Suchard ❶,** r. de Trésor 5, serves omelettes (6-8CHF) and salads (4-13CHF)—don't miss the *chocolaterie* in back, which has been going strong ever since Philippe Suchard first brought chocolate to Neuchâtel in 1825. (Open M 11am-6:30pm, Tu-F 6:30am-6:30pm, Sa 6:30am-5pm. Cash only.) **Migros,** r. de l'Hôpital 12, sells groceries. (Open M-W 8am-6:30pm, Th 8am-10pm, F 7:30am-6:30pm, Sa 7:30am-7pm.) **Trains** run to: Basel (1¾hr., 1 per hr., 34CHF); Bern (45min., 1 per hr., 18CHF); Zürich (1½hr., 1 per hr., 44CHF); Geneva (1½hr., 1 per hr., 37CHF). A **tram** (1CHF) runs from the station to the shore. Head to the right after disembarking and walk 5min. along the lake to the **tourist office.** (☎889 6890; www.neuchateltourisme.ch. Open July-Aug. M-F 9am-6:30pm, Sa 9am-4pm, Su 10am-2pm; Sept.-June M-F 9am-noon and 1:30-5:30pm, Sa 9am-noon.) **Postal Code:** CH-2001.

ITALIAN SWITZERLAND

Ever since Switzerland won Ticino, the only Italian-speaking Swiss canton, from Italy in 1512, the region has been renowned for its mix of Swiss efficiency and Italian *dolce vita.* It's no wonder the rest of Switzerland vacations here among jasmine-laced villas painted in the muted pastels of gelato.

SWITZERLAND

LUGANO   ☎091

Set in a valley between sloping green mountains, Lugano (pop. 52,000) draws plenty of visitors with its mix of artistic flair and historical religious sites. The frescoes inside the 16th-century **Cattedrale San Lorenzo**, just down the ramp from the train station, are still vivid. The most spectacular fresco in town is the gargantuan crucifix in the **Chiesa Santa Maria degli Angiuli**, 200m to the right as you leave the tourist office. Hikers can tackle the rewarding 5hr. **hike** to the top of **Monte Boglia** (1516m). Tamer souls can turn around after 2hr. at the peak of **Monte Bré** (923m), which is also accessible by **funicular**. (V. Ceresio 36; take bus #1,11, or 12 to the Cassarate M. Bré stop, then walk forward for several minutes and turn left on Via Pico. ☎971 3171; www.montebre.ch. Open Apr.-Oct. daily 9am-7pm. 14CHF, round-trip 20CHF. Cash only.) In early July, the **Estival Jazz** fills Lugano's colorful, crowded streets and main *piazza* with free jazz performances.

Surrounded by palm trees, the pink 19th-century villa of **Hotel and Hostel Montarina ❶**, V. Montarina 1, has a swimming pool, a terrace, and a convenient location next to the train station, though backpackers will find themselves in cramped ground floor rooms. At the end of the station parking lot, cross the tracks, and walk up the hill to the right until you reach the gate on your left. (☎966 7272; www.montarina.ch. Breakfast 12CHF. Linens 4CHF. Laundry 5CHF. Reception 8am-10:30pm. Open Mar.-Oct. Dorms 25CHF; singles 70CHF, with bath 80CHF; doubles 100/120CHF. AmEx/MC/V.) The **Coop City** supermarket, V. Nassa 22, has a food court on the top floor. (Open M-W and F 8am-6:30pm, Th 8am-9pm, Sa 8am-5pm.) **Trains** leave P. della Stazione on the hill above the city for Locarno via Giubiasco (1hr., 2 per hr., 16.20CHF), Milan, ITA (1½hr., 1 per hr., 25CHF), and Zürich (3hr., 11 per day, 57CHF). The **tourist office** is across from the ferry station at the corner of P. Rezzonico. Free guided walks of the city are on Monday at 9am. (☎913 3232; www.lugano-tourism.ch. Open Apr.-Oct. M-F 9am-7pm, Sa 9am-6pm, Su 10am-6pm; Nov.-Mar. M-F 9am-noon and 2-5pm.) **Postal Code:** CH-6900.

LOCARNO   ☎091

A Swiss vacation spot on the shores of Lago Maggiore, Locarno (pop. 30,000) gets over 2200 hours of sunlight per year—more than anywhere else in Switzerland. For centuries, visitors have journeyed here to see the orange-yellow church of **Madonna del Sasso** (Madonna of the Rock), founded in 1487. Take the funicular (4 per hr., round-trip 6.60CHF), or walk for 20min. up the smooth stones of the Via Crucis (open 6:30am-6pm) to the top, passing reliefs depicting the Stations of the Cross. Hundreds of heart-shaped medallions on the interior church walls commemorate acts of Mary's intervention in the lives of worshippers who have journeyed here. (Grounds open daily 6:30am-6:45pm.) For ten days at the beginning of August, Locarno swells with pilgrims of a different sort and prices soar when its world-famous open-air **film festival** draws over 150,000 to the Piazza Grande.

For **Pensione Città Vecchia ❷**, V. Toretta 15, turn right onto V. Toretta from P. Grande. (☎751 4554. Breakfast included. Dorms 37CHF; doubles 120CHF; triples 150CHF. Cash only.) **Ristorante Manora ❶**, V. della Stazione 1, offers self-service dining. (Salad bar 4.50-11CHF. Pasta buffet 6-13CHF. Entrees 11-19CHF. Open Apr.-Oct. M-Sa 7:30am-10pm, Su 8am-10pm; Nov.-Mar. M-Sa 7:30am-9pm, Su 8am-9pm.) **Trains** run from P. Stazione to Lugano (1hr., 2 per hr., 16CHF) via Giubiasco, Luzern (2½hr., 1 per 2hr., 51CHF), and Milan, ITA (2hr., 2 per hr., 37CHF). The **tourist office** is on P. Grande in the *Kursaal* (casino). From the station, go left down V. della Stazione until you reach P. Grande. (☎791 0091; www.maggiore.ch. Open Apr.-Oct. M-F 9am-6pm, Sa 10am-6pm, Su 10am-1:30pm and 2:30-5pm; Nov.-Mar. M-F 9am-6pm, Sa 10am-6pm.) **Postal Code:** CH-6600.

TURKEY (TÜRKİYE)

Turkey is a land rich with history and beauty. Home to some of the world's greatest civilizations—the Hellenes, Hittites, Macedonians, Romans, Byzantines, and Ottomans—Turkey is at the intersection of two very different continents. İstanbul, on the land bridge that connects Europe and Asia, is the infinitely intricate and surprisingly seductive progeny of three thousand years of migrant history. Though resolutely secular by government decree, every facet of Turkish life is graced by the religious traditions of its 99% Muslim population. Tourists cram İstanbul and the glittering western coast, while Anatolia (the Asian portion of Turkey) remains a purist backpacker's paradise of alpine meadows, cliffside monasteries, and a truly hospitable people.

ESSENTIALS

FACTS AND FIGURES

Official Name: Republic of Turkey.

Form of Government: Republican parliamentary democracy.

Capital: Ankara.

Major Cities: Adana, Bursa, Gaziantep, İstanbul, İzmir.

Population: 70,414,000.

Time Zone: GMT +2 or +3.

Language: Turkish.

Religion: Muslim (99.8%).

Number of Roller Coasters: 4.

Largest Skewer of Kebab Meat: Created by the Melike Döner Co. in Osmangazi-Bursa, Turkey on Nov. 6, 2005. Weighed in at 2698kg (5948 lb.).

Number of Army Battle Tanks: 2317.

WHEN TO GO

With mild winters and hot summers, there's no wrong time to travel to Turkey. While most tourists go in July and August, visiting between April and June or September and October brings temperate days, smaller crowds, and lower prices. November to February is the rainy season, so bring appropriate gear.

DOCUMENTS AND FORMALITIES

ENTRANCE REQUIREMENTS.

Passport: Required for all travelers.

Visa: Required for citizens of Australia, Canada, some EU countries, the UK, and the US. Citizens of New Zealand do not need a visa to enter. Multiple-entry visas (€10-20) are available at the border and are valid for up to 90 days.

Letter of Invitation: Not required.

Inoculations: Not required. Recommended up-to-date on DTaP (diphtheria, tetanus, and pertussis), hepatitis A, hepatitis B, MMR (measles, mumps, and rubella), polio booster, and typhoid.

Work Permit: Required for all foreigners planning to work in Turkey.

Driving Permit: Required for all those planning to drive.

EMBASSIES AND CONSULATES. Foreign embassies to Turkey are in Ankara, though many nations also have consulates in İstanbul. Turkish embassies and consulates abroad include: **Australia,** 6 Moonah Pl., Yarralumla, Canberra, ACT 2600

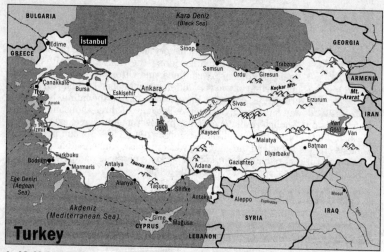

Turkey

(☎02 62 34 00 00; www.turkishembassy.org.au); **Canada,** 197 Wurtemburg St., Ottawa, ON, K1N 8L9 (☎613-789-4044; www.turkishembassy.com); **Ireland,** 11 Clyde Rd., Ballsbridge, Dublin 4 (☎668 52 40); **New Zealand,** 15-17 Murphy St., Level 8, Wellington 6011 (☎044 721 290; turkem@xtra.co.nz); **UK,** 43 Belgrave Sq., London SW1X 8PA (☎020 73 93 02 02; www.turkishembassylondon.org); **US,** 2525 Massachusetts Ave., NW, Washington, D.C. 20008 (☎202-612-6700; www.turkishembassy.org).

VISA AND ENTRY INFORMATION. Citizens of Canada and the US may obtain visas at entry points into Turkey for stays of less than three months (paid in cash). For longer stays, study, or work visas, and for citizens of Australia, New Zealand, and countries of the EU, it is necessary to obtain visas in advance (about US$20; Canadians, about US$60), available at Turkish consulates abroad. Travelers must apply at least one month in advance. For more info, check out www.mfa.gov.tr/mfa. If arriving by ferry, expect to pay a port tax of at least €10.

TOURIST SERVICES

In big cities like İstanbul, many establishments that claim to be tourist offices are actually travel agencies. That said, **travel agencies** can often be more helpful for finding accommodations or booking transportation than the official Turkish **tourist offices.** Although it's best to shop around from agency to agency for a deal on tickets, be wary of exceptionally low prices—offices may tack on exorbitant hidden charges. The official tourism website (www.tourismturkey.org) has a list of visa info, helpful links, and office locations.

MONEY

In response to rampant inflation and ever-confusing prices, Turkey revalued its currency in 2005, dropping 6 zeroes. One million Turkish Lira became 1 **Yeni Türk Lirası** (New Turkish Lira; YTL). One New Turkish Lira equals 100 **New Kuruş,** with standard denominations of 5, 10, 25, and 50. 1YTL are available as both coins and bills, while denominations of 1, 5, 10, 20, 50 and 100YTL come only as banknotes. While Old Turkish Lira are no longer accepted as currency, Turkish Lira banknotes (bills) can be redeemed until 2016 by the Central Bank of the Republic of

NEW TURKISH LIRA (YTL)	AUS\$1 = 1.11YTL	1YTL = AUS\$0.90
	CDN\$1 = 1.22YTL	1YTL = CDN\$0.82
	EUR€1 = 1.77YTL	1YTL = EUR€0.57
	NZ\$1 = 0.97YTL	1YTL = NZ\$1.03
	UK£1 = 2.62YTL	1YTL = UK£0.38
	US\$1 = 1.29YTL	1YTL = US\$0.77

Turkey (CBRT) and T.C. Ziraat Bank branches. Old Lira coins are no longer redeemable. **Banks** are generally open 8:30am-noon and 1:30-5:30pm. **Inflation** has decreased dramatically in recent years, dropping from 45% in 2003 to an all-time low of 7.7% in 2005 before rising again slightly. The best currency exchange rates can be found at state-run post and telephone offices (PTT). Many places in İstanbul and other major cities accept euro. Turkey has a **value added tax (VAT)** of 18% on general purchases and 8% on food. The prices in *Let's Go* include VAT. Spending more than 118YTL in one store entitles travelers to a tax refund upon leaving Turkey; look for "Tax-Free Shopping" stickers in shop windows or ask for a form inside. For more info on VAT refunds, see p. 15.

HEALTH AND SAFETY

EMERGENCY   **Ambulance:** ☎112. **Fire:** ☎110. **Police:** ☎155.

Medical facilities in Turkey vary greatly. In İstanbul and Ankara, high-quality hospitals for foreigners and expats provide care for all but the most serious of conditions, and most have adequate medical supplies. Outside the cities, though, it is a different story; try to avoid rural hospitals. **Pharmacies** are easy to find in major cities and are generally well stocked and have at least one professional pharmacist, as they're mandated by the government. Don't drink **water** that hasn't been boiled or filtered, and watch out for ice in drinks. Most local dairy products are safe to eat, but make sure that perishable products are still good before eating them.

Petty crime is common in urban centers, especially in crowded squares, the Grand Bazaar, and on public transportation. Common schemes include distracting travelers with a staged fight while they are being robbed; drugging travelers with tea, juice, or other drinks and then robbing them; or simply presenting travelers with outrageously expensive bills. Pay attention to your valuables, never accept drinks from a stranger, and always ask in advance for prices at bars and restaurants. Though **pirated goods** are sold on the street, it is illegal to buy them, and doing so can result in fines. **Drug trafficking** leads to severe jail time. It is also illegal to show disrespect to Atatürk or to insult the state.

Foreign **women,** especially those traveling alone, attract significant attention in Turkey. Unwanted catcalls and other forms of verbal harassment are common, although physical harassment is rare. Regardless of the signals a foreign woman intends to send, her foreignness alone may suggest a liberal openness to amorous advances. Smiling, regarded in the West as a sign of confidence and friendliness, is sometimes associated in Turkey with sexual attraction. As long as women expect plenty of attention and take common-sense precautions, however, even single travelers need not feel anxious. Although **homosexuality** is legal in Turkey, religious and social norms keep most homosexual activity discreet. Homophobia can be a problem, especially in remote areas; expect authorities to be unsympathetic. Despite the close contact that Turks maintain with same-sex friends, public displays of affection between gay and lesbian travelers should be avoided. Turkey's urban centers have bars and informal cruising areas for men only, though they may not be very overt. **Lambda İstanbul**, a GLBT support group, lists guides to gay-friendly establishments on its website (www.qrd.org/www/world/europe/turkey).

KEEPING IN TOUCH

PHONE CODES	**Country code:** 90. **International dialing prefix:** 00. From outside Turkey, dial int'l dialing prefix (see inside back cover) + 90 + city code + local number. Within Turkey, dial city code + local number, even when dialing inside the city.

EMAIL AND THE INTERNET. Like everything in Turkey, the availability of Internet services depends on where in the country you are. In İstanbul, Internet cafes are everywhere; out east, they can be tough to find. Free Wi-Fi is available at hostels and cafes across the city.

TELEPHONES. Whenever possible, use a calling card for international phone calls, as long-distance rates for national phone services are often very high. Mobile phones are an increasingly popular and economical option. Major mobile carriers include **Turkcell, Telsim,** and **Avea.** Direct-dial access numbers for calling out of Turkey include: **AT&T Direct** (☎80 01 22 77); **British Telecom** (☎80 044 1177); **Canada Direct** (☎80 01 66 77); and **Telstra Australia** (☎80 061 1177). For more info on calling home from Europe, see p. 28.

MAIL. The postal system is quick and expensive in Turkey. Airmail should be marked *par avion*, and Poste Restante is available in most major cities.

ACCOMMODATIONS AND CAMPING

TURKEY	❶	❷	❸	❹	❺
ACCOMMODATIONS	under 20YTL	20-39YTL	40-59YTL	60-80YTL	over 80YTL

When it comes to lodging, Turkey is a budget traveler's paradise. **Hostels** are available in nearly every major city. **Pensions**—a step above hostels in both quality and price—are also generally available, as are **hotels** in every price range. **Camping** is very common throughout Turkey, and especially on the Aegean coast; campgrounds are generally inexpensive (US$3-10) or free.

FOOD AND DRINK

TURKEY	❶	❷	❸	❹	❺
FOOD	under 8YTL	8-15YTL	16-20YTL	21-30YTL	over 30YTL

Turkish cuisine is as varied as Turkish culture. Strategically located on the land bridge between Europe and Asia, İstanbul is the culinary epicenter of the region, drawing from the dietary practices of many different cultures. Fish is a staple in Turkey, especially along the coast, where it is prepared with local spices according to traditional recipes. When it comes to meat, lamb and chicken are Turkish favorites, and are typically prepared as ▨kebap—a term which means far more in Turkey than the dry meat cubes on a stick found in most Western restaurants. Despite its strong Muslim majority, Turkey produces good wines. More interesting, however, is the unofficial national drink: rakı. Translated as "lion's milk," rakı is Turkey's answer to French pastis, Italian sambuca, and Greek ouzo. An anise-flavored liquor, it turns milky white when mixed with water. The strong drink has inspired a Turkish saying: "you must drink the rakı, and not let the rakı drink you."

PEOPLE AND CULTURE

LANGUAGE. Turkish *(Türkçe)*, the official language of Turkey, is spoken by approximately 65 million people domestically and a few million more abroad. It is the most prominent member of the Turkic language family, which also includes Azerbaijani, Kazakh, Kyrgyz, Uighur, and Uzbek. Turkish was originally written in Arabic script and exhibited strong Arabic and Persian influences. In 1928, however, Atatürk reformed the language, purging foreign influences (despite using a Romanized alphabet). This linguistic standardization was not absolute, and common Arabic and Persian words such as *merhaba* (hello) remain.

Visitors who speak little or no Turkish should not be intimidated. Though Turks appreciate attempts at conversing in their language, English is widely spoken wherever tourism is big business—mainly in the major coastal towns. Especially in İstanbul, a small phrasebook will help greatly. For more in-depth study, consult *Teach Yourself Turkish* by Pollard and Pollard (New York, 2004; $17).

DEMOGRAPHICS. Over 99% of the Turkish population is **Muslim.** Jews and Orthodox Christians of Armenian, Greek, and Syrian backgrounds comprise the remainder. While Turkey does not have an official state religion, every Turkish citizen's national identification card states his or her faith. Although Atatürk's reforms aimed to secularize the nation, Islam continues to play a key role in the country's politics and culture.

CUSTOMS AND ETIQUETTE. Turks value **hospitality** and will frequently go out of their way to welcome travelers, commonly offering to buy visitors a meal or a cup of *çay* (tea). Try not to refuse tea unless you have very strong objections; accepting the offer provides a friendly, easy way to converse with locals. If you are invited to a Turkish house as a guest, it is customary to bring a small gift, often pastries or chocolates, and to remove your shoes before entering. A pair of slippers will usually be provided. Always treat elders with special respect. When chatting with Turks, do not speak with any disrespect or skepticism about **Atatürk**, as this is illegal, and avoid other sensitive subjects. In particular, it may be best not to discuss the Kurdish issue, the PKK (the Kurdistan Workers' Party), Northern Cyprus, or Turkey's human rights record.

Many of Turkey's greatest architectural monuments, including **tombs** and **mosques**, have religious significance. Visitors are welcome but should show respect by dressing and acting appropriately. Shorts and skimpy clothing are forbidden inside mosques. Women must cover their arms, heads, and legs, and both sexes should take off their shoes and carry them inside. There are usually shoe racks in the back of the mosques; otherwise, caretakers will provide plastic bags for carrying shoes. Do not take flash photos, never photograph people in prayer, and avoid visits on Fridays (Islam's holy day). Also forgo visiting during prayer times, which are announced by the *müezzin*'s call to prayer from the mosque's minarets. Donations are sometimes expected.

If **bargaining** is a fine art, then İstanbul has lots and lots of that art. In most places, bargaining is expected. Never pay full price at the Grand Bazaar; start out by offering less than 50% of the asking price. For that matter, bargain just about everywhere—even when stores list prices, they'll usually take around 60-70%. If you're not asked to pay a service charge when paying by credit card, you're probably paying too much for your purchase. Tipping isn't required in Turkey: at bathhouses, hairdressers, hotels, and restaurants, a tip of 5-15% is common, but taxis and *dolmuş* drivers do not expect tips—just try to round up to the nearest YTL.

BODY VIBES. In Turkey, **body language** often matters as much as the spoken word. When a Turk raises his chin and clicks his tongue, he means *hayır* (no); this gesture is sometimes accompanied by a shutting of the eyes or the raising of eyebrows. A sideways shake of the head means *anlamadım* (I don't under-stand), and *evet* (yes) may be signaled by a sharp downward nod. If a Turk waves a hand up and down at you, palm toward the ground, he is signaling you to come, not bidding you farewell. In Turkey, the idle habit of snapping the fingers of one hand and then slapping the top of the other fist is considered obscene; so too is the hand gesture made by bringing thumb and forefinger together (the Western sign for "OK"). However, bringing all fingers toward the thumb is a compliment, generally meaning that something is "good." It is also considered rude to point your finger or the sole of your shoe toward someone. Though public displays of affection are considered inappropriate, Turks of both sexes greet each other with a kiss on both cheeks, and often touch or hug one another during conversation. Turks also tend to stand close to one another while talking.

DRESS. Wearing shorts will single you out as a tourist, as most Turks—particu-larly women—prefer pants or skirts. Women will probably find a **head scarf** or a bandana handy, perhaps essential, in more conservative regions. Even in İstanbul and the resort towns of the Aegean and Mediterranean coasts where casual, beachy dress is more widely accepted, revealing clothing sends a flirtatious signal. Knee-length skirts and lightweight pants, more acceptable, are also comfortable and practical, especially in summer. T-shirts are generally acceptable, though you should always cover your arms when entering mosques or traveling in the more religious parts of the country. Topless bathing is common in some areas along the Aegean and Mediterranean coasts but unacceptable in other regions.

BEYOND TOURISM

Finding work in Turkey is tough, as the government tries to restrict employment to Turkish citizens. Foreigners seeking jobs must obtain a **work visa,** which in turn requires a **permit** issued by the Ministry of the Interior. An excellent idea for work-ing in Turkey is **teaching English.** Because English is the language of instruction at many Turkish universities, it's also possible to enroll directly as a special student, which might be less expensive than enrolling in an American university program. For more info on opportunities across Europe, see **Beyond Tourism,** p. 56.

Buğday Ekolojik Yaşam Kapısı İletişim Bilgileri, Kemankeş Cad. Akçe Sok. 14, Kar-aköy, İstanbul (☎212 252 5255; www.bugday.org/eng). Support sustainable agricul-ture by living or working on an *Ekolojik TaTuTa* (organic farm), or volunteer at the national organic farm association.

Gençtur Turizm ve Seyahat Ac. Ltd., İstiklal Cad. 212, Aznavur Pasajı, Kat: 5, Galatasa-ray, İstanbul 80080 (☎212 244 62 30; www.genctur.com). A tourism and travel agency that sets up various workshops, nannying jobs, volunteer camps, and year-round study tours in Turkey.

Volunteers for Peace, 1034 Tiffany Rd., Belmont, VT 05730, USA (☎802-259-2759; www.vfp.org). Arranges placement in volunteer camps. Registration fee US$250.

İSTANBUL

İstanbul is Turkey's heart. In this giant city that straddles Europe and Asia on two intercontinental bridges, the "East meets West" refrain of fusion restaurants, trendy boutiques, and yoga studios returns to its semantic roots. The huge, West-ern-style suburbs on the Asian side are evidence of rampant modernization, while across the Bosphorus the sprawling ancient city of mosques and bazaars—Old İstanbul—brims with cafes, bars, and people, day or night. As taxis rush by at mind-boggling speeds, shop owners sip tea with potential customers and tourists mingle with devout Muslims at the entrances to magnificent mosques in Sultanahmet. İstanbul is a turbulent city, full of history yet charged with a dynamism and energy that makes it one of the most exciting cities in Europe—or Asia.

⬛ INTERCITY TRANSPORTATION

Flights: İstanbul's airport, **Atatürk Havaalanı (IST;** ☎663 6400), is 30km from the city. Buses (3 per hr. 6am-11pm) connect domestic and international terminals. To get to Sultanahmet from the airport, catch the HAVAS bus or the metro to the Aksaray stop at the end of the line. From there catch a tram to Sultanahmet. A direct taxi to Sultanahmet costs 25YTL. Most hostels and hotels in Sultanahmet arrange convenient airport shuttles several times a day.

Trains: Haydarpaşa Garı (☎21 63 36 04 75 or 336 2063), on the Asian side, sends trains to Anatolia. To get to the station, take the ferry from Karaköy pier #7 (every 20min. 6am-midnight), halfway between Galata Bridge and the Karaköy tourist office. Rail tickets for Anatolia can be bought in advance at the TCDD office upstairs or at any of the travel agencies in Sultanahmet; many of these offices also offer free transportation to the station. Trains go to **Ankara** (6½-9½hr., 6 per day, from 22YTL) and **Kars** (11-13½hr., 1 per day, from 35YTL). Sirkeci Garı (☎527 0050 or 527 0051), in Eminönü, sends trains to Europe via **Athens, GCE** (24hr., 1 per day, 110YTL); **Bucharest, ROM** (17½hr., 1 per day, 65YTL); and **Budapest, HUN** (40hr., 1 per day, 185YTL).

Buses: Modern, comfortable buses run to all major destinations in Turkey and are the cheapest and most convenient way to get around. If you arrange your tickets with any travel agency in Sultanahmet, a free ride is included from there to the bus station. To reach **Esenler Otobüs Terminal** (☎658 0036), take the tram to Yusufpaşa (1.30YTL); then, walk to the Aksaray Metro, and take it to the *otogar* (bus station; 15min., 1.30YTL). Most companies have courtesy buses, called *servis*, that run to the *otogar* from Eminönü, Taksim, and other city points (free with bus ticket purchase). From İstanbul, buses travel to every city in Turkey. Buses run to: **Ankara** (8hr., 6-8 per day, 30YTL); **Antalya** (11hr., 2 per day, 40YTL); **Bodrum** (15hr., 2 per day, 45YTL); **İzmir** (10hr., 4 per day, 35YTL); **Kappadokia** (8hr., 2 per day, 30YTL). International buses run to: **Amman, JOR** (28hr., daily noon, 100YTL); **Athens, GCE** (19hr., daily 10am, 130YTL, students 135YTL); **Damascus, SYR** (25hr., daily 1:30pm and 7:30pm, 50YTL); **Sofia, BUL** (15hr., daily 10am and 9pm, 65YTL); **Tehran, IRAN** (40hr., M-Sa 1:30pm, 70YTL). To get to Sultanahmet from the *otogar*, catch the metro to the Aksaray stop at the end of the line. From there, catch a tram to Sultanahmet.

 Be wary of bus companies offering ludicrously low prices. Unlicensed companies have been known to offer discounts to Western European destinations and then ditch passengers somewhere en route. To make sure you're on a legitimate bus, reserve your tickets with a travel agency in advance.

Ferries: Turkish Maritime Lines (reservations ☎252 1700, info 21 22 49 92 22), near pier #7 at Karaköy, to the left of the Haydarpaşa ferry terminal (blue awning marked Denizcilik İşletmeleri). To **İzmir** (16hr., every 2 days, 65YTL) and other destinations on the coast. Many travel agencies don't know much about ferry connections, so you're better off going to the pier by the Galata Bridge, where you can pick up a free schedule. For more info, call ☎444 4436 or visit www.ido.com.tr. **To and from Greece:** One of the most popular routes into Turkey is from the Greek Dodecanese and Northern Aegean islands, whose proximity to the Turkish coast makes for an easy and inexpensive way into Asia. There are 5 main crossing points from Greece to Turkey: Rhodes to Marmaris, Kos to Bodrum, Samos to Kusadasi, Chios to Çeşme, and Lesvos to Ayvalik. Ferries run

Tram and Cable Car Ⓣ
Metro and Tünel Ⓜ

HALİÇ
(GOLDEN HORN)

DALAT

FENER

St. Stephen
of the Bulgars

Orthodox
Patriarchate

Karlye Camii
(Chora Church)

Fethiye
Museum

KARAGÜMRÜK

Selimiye
Camii

ÇARŞAMBA

Tabak Yunus
Sok.

ZEYREK

Fatih Camii

FATİH

KÜÇÜKPAZAR

Hacıkadın Cad.

SÜLEYMANİYE

ÇAPA

Guraba Hastanesi Cad.

EMNİYET Ⓜ

SARAÇHANE

ÇAPA Ⓣ

Millet Cad.

FINDIKZADE Ⓣ

Ahmet Vekif Paşa Cad.

Gökalp Ziya Sok.

HASEKİ Ⓣ

YUSUFPAŞA Ⓣ

AKSARAY Ⓜ

AKSARAY

Belediye
(City Hall)

LALELİ

Ordu Cad. ÜNİVERSİTE

Yeniçeriler

Haseki Cad.

Cerrahpaşa Cad.

Hekimoğlu Alipaşa Cad.

Koca Mustafa
Paşa Cad.

İnkilap Cad.

Tir. Hasan P. Sok.

Küçük Langa Cad.

Langabastoni Sok.

Mesih i Paşa Cad.

Namık Kemal Cad.

Bostani Sok.

Küçük Langa Cad.

TÜRKeli Cad.

YENİKAPI

Kennedy Cad.

Yenikapı
Seabus Pier

İstanbul

🍴 **FOOD**
Haci Abdullah, **1**
Koska Helvacisi, **6**

🎵 **NIGHTLIFE**
Araf, **3**
Jazz Stop, **4**
Nayah Music Club, **2**
Sinerji Bar, **5**

TURKEY

1-2 times per day in summer, the ride takes under 2hr., and the tickets are usually €25-34, plus €10 port tax when entering Turkey and a €10-20 visa (see p. 1027). If you are visiting a Greek island as a daytrip from Turkey, port taxes are usually waived.

✦ ORIENTATION

Waterways divide İstanbul into three sections. The **Bosphorus Strait** (Boğaz) separates **Asya** (Asia) from **Avrupa** (Europe). The **Golden Horn,** a sizeable river originating just outside the city, splits Avrupa into northern and southern parts. Directions in İstanbul are usually further specified by neighborhood. On the European side, **Sultanahmet,** home to the major sights, is packed with tourists and has plenty of parks and benches and many monuments, shops, and cafes. In Sultanahmet, backpackers congregate in **Akbıyık Cad.,** while **Divan Yolu** is the main street. Walk away from **Aya Sofya** and the **Blue Mosque** to reach the **Grand Bazaar.** As you walk out of the covered Bazaar on the northern side, you'll reach more streets of outdoor markets that lead uphill to the massive **Suleymaniye Mosque** and the gardens of İstanbul's **University.** To the right, descend through the **Spice Bazaar** to reach the well-lit **Galata Bridge,** where street vendors and seafood restaurants keep the night lively. Across the two-level bridge, narrow, warehouse-filled streets lead to the panoramic **Galata Tower.** Past the tower is the broad main shopping drag **İstiklâl Cad.,** which takes you directly to **Taksim Square,** modern İstanbul's pulsing center. Sultanahmet and Taksim (on the European side), and **Kadıköy** (on the Asian side) are the most relevant for sightseers. Asya is primarily residential.

⌐ TRANSPORTATION

PUBLIC TRANSPORTATION. AKBİL is an electronic ticket system that saves you 15-50% on fares for municipal ferries, buses, trams, water taxis, and subway (but not *dolmuş*). Cards (6YTL) are sold at tram stations or ticket offices, and can be recharged it in 1YTL increments at the white IETT public bus booths, marked **AKBİL satılır.**

Buses: Run 6am-midnight, arriving every 10min. to most stops, less frequently after 10:30pm. 1-2YTL. Hubs are Eminönü, Aksaray (Yusuf Paşa tram stop), Beyazıt, Taksim, Beşiktaş, and Üsküdar. Signs on the front of buses indicate destination, and signs on the right side list major stops. **Dolmuş** (shared taxi vans) are more comfortable but less frequent than buses. Most *dolmuş* gather on the side streets north of Taksim Sq.

Tram: The *Tramvay* runs from Eminönü to Zeytinburnu every 5min. Make sure to be on the right side of the street, as the carriage follows the traffic. Get tokens at any station and toss them in at the turnstile to board (1.30YTL). The old-fashioned carriages of the **historical tram** run 1km uphill from Tunel (by the Galata Bridge) through İstiklâl Cad. and up to Taksim Sq. They're the same ones that made the trip in the early 20th century.

Metro: İstanbul operates two metro lines (☎568 9970): one from Aksaray to the Esenler Bus Terminal and the other from Taksim Sq. to 4th Levent. A funicular connects the tram stop Cabatas to Taksim Sq. The metro runs daily every 5min. 5:40am-11:15pm.

Commuter Rail: A slow commuter rail *(tren)* runs 6am-11pm between Sirkeci Gar and the far western suburbs, as well as the Asian side. The stop in Bostanci is near the ferry to the Princes Islands. Keep your ticket until the end of the journey.

Taxis: Taxi drivers are even more reckless and speed-crazed than other İstanbul drivers, but the city's more than 20,000 taxis offer an undoubtedly quick way to get around. Don't ask the driver to fix a price before getting in; instead, make sure he restarts the meter. Night fares, usually starting at midnight, are double. Rides from Sultanahmet to Taksim Sq. should be around 15YTL, and to the airport around 25YTL.

GETTING A FARE PRICE. While most İstanbul taxis are metered, some cabdrivers have an annoying tendency to drive circles around the city before bringing you to your destination. Watch the roads and look out for signs pointing to where you're going. To avoid the risk altogether, take taxis only as far as the Galata Bridge, and walk from there to Sultanahmet or Taksim.

⁊ PRACTICAL INFORMATION

Tourist Office: 3 Divan Yolu (☎/fax 518 8754), at the north end of the Hippodrome in Sultanahmet. Open daily 9am-5pm. Branches in Taksim's Hilton Hotel Arcade on Cumhuriyet Cad., Sirkeci train station, Atatürk Airport, and Karaköy Maritime Station.

Budget Travel: İstanbul has many travel agencies, almost all speak English, and most hostels and hotels have started running their own travel services as well. Though most are trustworthy, there are some scams. Always check that the agency is licensed. If anything happens, make sure you have your agent's info and report it to the tourist police.

Fez Travel, 15 Akbıyık Cad. (☎516 9024; www.feztravel.com). İstanbul's most efficient and well informed, Fez's English-speaking staff organizes anything from accommodations to ferries, flights, and buses, as well as their own backpacker-tailored tours of Turkey and Greece. STA-affiliated. Open daily 9am-7pm. MC/V.

Hassle Free, 10 Akbıyık Cad. (☎458 9500; www.anzacgouse.com), right next to New Backpackers. The name is self-explanatory and the young, friendly staff provides great deals and tips. Books local buses or boat cruises of southern Turkey. Open daily 9am-11pm.

Barefoot Travel, 1 Cetinkaya Sok. (☎517 0269; www.barefoot-travel.com), just off Akbıyık Cad. The English-speaking staff is helpful and offers good deals on airfare, as well as free maps of İstanbul and Turkey. Open daily in summer 8am-8pm; in winter 8am-6pm. AmEx/MC/V.

Consulates: Australia, 15 Asker Ocaği Cad., Elmadag Sisli (☎257 7050; fax 243 1332). **Canada,** 373/5 İstiklâl Cad. (☎251 9838; fax 251 9888). **Ireland,** 26 Cumhuriyet Cad., Mobil Altı, Elmadağ (☎246 6025). **UK,** 34 Meşrutiyet Cad., Beyoğlu/Tepebaşı (☎252 6436). **US,** 2 Kaplıcalar Mevkii Sok., Istinye (☎335 9000).

Currency Exchange: *Bureaux de change* around the city are open M-F 8:30am-noon and 1:30-5pm. Most don't charge commission. **ATMs** generally accept all international cards. Most banks exchange **traveler's checks.** Exchanges in Sultanahmet have poor rates, but are open late and on weekends. There is a yellow **PTT** kiosk between the Aya Sofya and the Blue Mosque that changes currency for no commission. **Western Union** offices are in banks throughout Sultanahmet and Taksim; they operate M-F 8:30am-noon and 1:30-5pm.

English-Language Bookstores: English-language books are all over the city. In Sultanahmet, *köşk* (kiosks) at the Blue Mosque, on Aya Sofya Meydanı, and on Divan Yolu sell international papers. **Galeri Kayseri,** 58 Divan Yolu (☎512 0456), caters to tourists with informational books on Turkish and Islamic history and literature, as well as a host of guidebooks. Open daily 9am-9pm. D/MC/V.

Laundromat: Star Laundry, 18 Akbıyık Cad., between New Backpackers and Hassle Free. Wash, dry, and iron 4YTL per kg. Min. 2kg. Ready in 3hr. Open daily 9am-8pm.

Tourist Police: In Sultanahmet, at the beginning of Yerebatan Cad. (24hr. hotline ☎527 4503 or 528 5369). Tourist police speak excellent English, and their mere presence causes hawkers to scatter. In an **emergency,** call from any phone.

Hospitals: American Hospital, Admiral Bristol Hastanesi, 20 Güzelbahçe Sok., Nişantaşı (☎231 4050), is applauded by locals and tourists. Has many English-speaking doctors. **German Hospital,** 119 Sıraselviler Cad., Taksim (☎293 2150), also has a multilingual staff and is conveniently located for Sultanahmet hostelers. **International Hospital,** 82 İstanbul Cad., Yesilköy (☎663 3000).

Internet Access: Internet in İstanbul is everywhere from hotels to barber shops, and connections are usually cheap and decently fast—notwithstanding the frequent power cuts.

Most hostels have free Internet, though many impose a 15min. limit. Some hostels now offer Wi-Fi, as do more upscale hotels and eateries; signs are usually posted on the door. Rates at travel agencies are usually 1YTL per 15min., 3YTL per hr.

Post and Telephone Offices: Known as **PTTs.** All accept packages. **Main branch** in Sirkeci, 25 Büyük Postane Sok. Stamp and currency exchange services open daily 8:30am-midnight. 24hr. phones. Phone cards available for 5-10YIL. There is a yellow PTT kiosk in Sultanahmet between the Aya Sofya and the Blue Mosque, which exchanges currency and sells stamps. Open daily 9am-5pm.

PHONE CODES. The code is **212** on the European side and **216** on the Asian side. All numbers listed here begin with 212 unless otherwise specified. For more on how to place international calls, see **Inside Back Cover.**

ACCOMMODATIONS

Budget accommodations are concentrated in **Sultanahmet** (a.k.a. Türist Şeğntral). In the past couple of years, as Turkey has become a backpacker's must, there has been an explosion of cheap places to stay, turning Akbıyık Cad. into a virtually uninterrupted line of hostels. All offer similar quality and prices. The side streets around **Sirkeci** railway station and **Aksaray** have dozens of dirt-cheap, run-down hotels, while more expensive options are in more touristy districts. All accommodations listed below are in Sultanahmet and, despite their number, they fill up quickly in high season. Though you will always find a bed somewhere, reserve ahead to get the hostel of your choice. Hotels in **Lâleli** are in İstanbul's center of prostitution and should be avoided. Rates can rise by up to 20% in July and August.

Big Apple Hostel, 12 Bayram Fırını Sok. (☎517 7931; www.hostelbigapple.com), down the road from Akbıyık Cad., next to Barefoot Travel. On a quieter side street off of Akbıyık Cad., this hostel offers one of the most fun and relaxing atmospheres in İstanbul for both individuals and groups. Has a large downstairs common room and an upstairs terrace with beanbag chairs, beach loungers, and a swing, not to mention some of the friendliest staff around. Breakfast (8:30-10:30am), towels, and linens included. Internet. Dorms US$12. MC/V. ❷

Metropolis, 24 Terbıyık Sok. (☎212 518 1822; www.metropolishostel.com), removed from the hustle of Akbıyık, in a quieter though still central back street. This beautifully kept hostel has comfortable, stylish rooms, friendly staff, and a peaceful location. Guests get a 10% discount at the Metropolis Restaurant and Downunder bar around the corner. Breakfast included. Free Internet. Single-sex dorms 23YTL; doubles 60YTL. ❷

Bahaus Guesthouse, 11-13 Akbıyık Cad. (☎638 6534; www.travelinistanbul.com), across the street from Big Apple. Though its dorm rooms are simple, Bahaus' cozy Anatolian-themed closed terrace and couch-filled open terrace are comfortable and lively. Travelers rave about this place, and the rooms are usually full. Book in advance. Airport pickup available. Free Internet. Breakfast included. Dorms €9; doubles €44. ❶

İstanbul Hostel, 35 Kutlugün Sok. (☎516 9380; www.istanbulhostel.net). In business well before Sultanahmet was invaded by backpackers, this hostel has all the usual amenities, as well as a welcoming family feel and an extremely helpful staff. Bar, travel agency, rooftop lounge, and board games also available. The fireplace near the bar makes this a great place for a cozy winter visit. Breakfast included. Free Internet. Beds on the roof 12YTL; dorms 20YTL; doubles 55YTL. ❷

Sultan Hostel, 21 Akbiyik Cad. (516 9260; www.sultanhostel.com). Right in the middle of backpacker land, this happening hostel is İstanbul's most famous. With a streetside, rooftop restaurant and comfortable, clean dorms, Sultan's is a great place to meet fellow travelers. Breakfast included. Free safes. Free Internet. Reserve ahead. Dorms €12; singles €30; doubles €30, with bathroom €34; quads €52/56. ❷

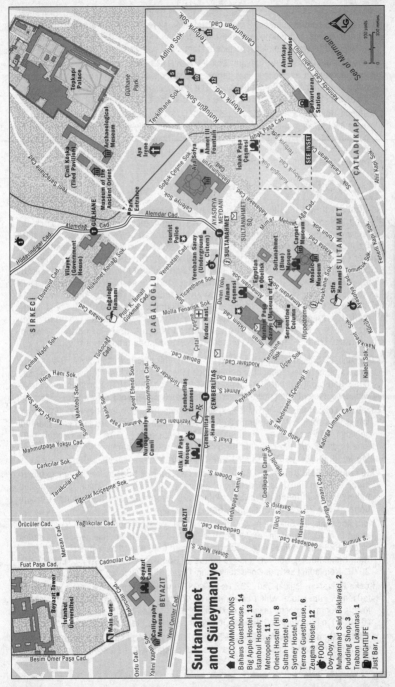

TURKEY

Sultanahmet and Süleymaniye

▲ **ACCOMMODATIONS**
Bahaus Guesthouse, **14**
Big Apple Hostel, **13**
Istanbul Hostel, **5**
Metropolis, **11**
Orient Hostel (HI), **8**
Sultan Hostel, **8**
Sydney Hostel, **10**
Terrace Guesthouse, **6**
Zeugma Hostel, **12**

♦ **FOOD**
Doy-Doy, **4**
Muhammad Said Baklavaci, **2**
Pudding Shop, **3**
Trabzon Lokantasi, **1**

■ **NIGHTLIFE**
Just Bar, **7**

Sydney Hostel, 42 Akbıyık Cad. (☎518 6671; fax 518 6672), in the middle of Akbıyık. Despite its central location, Sydney Hostel remains calm, with cheerful sky-blue walls, modern rooms and bathrooms, and much-coveted in-room A/C. Rooftop terrace. Free safes. Free Internet. Breakfast included. Dorms €10; singles and doubles €35. ❶

Terrace Guesthouse, 39 Kutlugün Sok. (☎638 9733; www.terracehotelistanbul.com), behind Akbıyık Cad. Housed in a narrow carpet shop, this elegant hotel has beautifully decorated rooms for affordable prices. The 2 upstairs terraces have spectacular views. Breakfast included. Free Wi-Fi. Singles €50; doubles €60; triples €70. ❺

Zeugma Hostel, 35 Akbıyık Cad. (☎517 4040; www.zeugmahostel.com). This clean, 1-room hostel has a huge basement dorm with comfortable wooden bunks separated by colorful curtains, giving it a bedouin camp feel. Though there is no common space, the dorm has A/C and a quiet, relaxed vibe. Airport pick-up available. Linens included. Free Internet. Reception 24hr. Dorms 15YTL. ❶

🍴 FOOD

İstanbul's restaurants, like its clubs and bars, often demonstrate the golden rule: if it's well advertised or easy to find, it's not worth a visit. Sultanahmet's "Turkish" restaurants are convenient, but much better meals can be found across the **Galata Bridge** and around **Taksim Square.** Small Bosphorus suburbs such as **Arnavutköy** and **Sarıyer** (on the European side) and **Çengelköy** (on the Asian side) are the best places for fresh fish. For a cheaper meal, **İstiklâl Caddesi** has all the major Western chains, as well as quick and tasty Turkish fast food. Vendors in Ottoman dress sell *Vişne suyu* (sour cherry juice), and on any street you'll find dried fruit and nuts for sale, as well as the omnipresent stalls of sesame bagels (1YTL). The best open-air **market** is open daily in **Beşiktaş,** near Barbaros Cad., while at the Egyptian Spice Bazaar *(Mısır Çarşısı)* you can find almonds, fruit, and—of course—**kebap,** which range from shawarma-type meat to Western-style meat-on-a-stick.

🍴 **Doy-Doy,** 13 Şifa Hammamı Sok. (☎517 1588). The best in Sultanahmet, 3-story Doy-Doy's rooftop tables are right under the Blue Mosque. On the lower levels are cushioned floors and plenty of *nargilas* (hookahs). Try the *kebap* (5-10YTL) or shepherd salads with *cacik* (yogurt and cucumber; 4YTL). Open daily 8am-11pm. MC/V. ❷

🍴 **Trabzon Lokantasi,** 10 Dervisler Sok, near Sirkeci. Tucked in an alleyway off the tram tracks, this small cafe-restaurant features real Turkish homecooking in cheap, plentiful servings, with several vegetarian options. The lentil soup (1.50YTL) is exceptional. Be sure to check out the colorful guestbook, filled with notes from visitors from around the world. Entrees 3-6YTL. Open 11am-11pm. ❶

Muhammed Said Baklavaci, 88 Divan Yolu Cad. (☎526 9666). Specializing in home-made baklava and Turkish delight of almost every flavor, this small, locally-owned bakery is a wonderland of sweets. Prices are reasonable and the quality is excep-tional. 1 kilo 20-29YTL. Open daily 9am-10pm. ❸

Hacı Abdullah, 17 Sakizağacı Cad. (☎293 8561; www.haciabdullah.com.tr), down the street from Ağa Camii, in Taksim Sq. This family-style restaurant has been going strong since 1888 and features huge vases of preserved fruit, as well as high-tech bathrooms. Their homemade grapefruit juice is fantastic. Soups and salads 3-7YTL. Entrees 10-20YTL. No alcohol served. Open daily noon-11pm. Kitchen closes 10:30pm. MC/V. ❷

Koska Helvacısı, İstiklâl Cad. 238 (☎244 0877; www.koskahelvacisi.com.tr). This con-fectionery superstore, which celebrated its 100th anniversary in 2007, is any sugar-lover's dream. Fantastic take-out baklava trays (3YTL) and boxed assortments of sweets (6-20YTL) in all colors and flavors. Open daily 9am-11:30pm. ❷

Pudding Shop, 6 Divan Yolu Cad. (☎522 2970). A major pit stop on the Hippie Trail to the Far and Middle East during the 70s. Young travelers en route to Goa and Kathmandu left messages on a board that's still here. Today, the former setting for the drug deal scene in *Midnight Express* (1978) is a clean and tasty fast-food joint, more nostalgic than exciting. A/C upstairs. Kebap 5-12YTL. Open daily 7am-11pm. ❷

SIGHTS

İstanbul's incomparable array of churches, mosques, palaces, and museums can keep an ardent tourist busy for weeks. Most first time travelers to İstanbul spend a lot of time in Sultanahmet, the area around the Aya Sofya, south of and uphill from Sirkeci. Merchants crowd the district between the enormous Grand Bazaar, east of the university, and the less touristy Egyptian Spice Bazaar, just southeast of Eminönü. To soak in the city's sights the easy way, hop on one of the small boats on either side of the Galata Bridge and go for a relaxing and panoramic ▓ **Bosphorus tour.** Most tours last about 2hr. and return to their starting point.

> **▓TIP▓ BARGAINING FOR BEGINNERS.** Though the Grand Bazaar is haggling at its finest, bargaining doesn't end at carpets. It's acceptable to bargain for almost anything in İstanbul, including tours. For the best deals on boat trips, bargain with boat owners at the port. Trips shouldn't be more than 20YTL per person for a few hours of floating down the Bosphorus.

▓ **AYA SOFYA** (HAGIA SOPHIA). When Aya Sofya (Divine Wisdom) was built in AD 537, it was the biggest building in the world. Built as a church, it fell to the Ottomans in 1453 and was converted into a mosque; it remained such until 1932, when Atatürk declared it a museum. The nave is overshadowed by the gold-leaf mosaic dome lined with hundreds of circular windows that make it seem as though the dome is floating on a bed of luminescent pearls. Throughout the building, Qur'anic inscriptions and mosaics of Mary and the angels intertwine in a fascinating symmetry. The gallery contains Byzantine mosaics uncovered from beneath a thick layer of Ottoman plaster, as well as the famed **sweating pillar,** sheathed in bronze. The pillar has a hole big enough to stick a finger in and collect the odd drop of water, believed to possess healing powers. The column is often disappointingly dry. *(Open daily 9am-7:30pm. Upper gallery open 9:30am-6:45pm. 10YTL.)*

▓ **BLUE MOSQUE** (SULTANAHMET CAMİİ). Named for the beautiful blue İznik tiles covering the interior, the extravagant Blue Mosque and its six **minarets** were Sultan Ahmet's 1617 claim to fame. At the time of construction, only the mosque at Mecca had as many minarets, and the thought of rivaling that sacred edifice was considered heretical. The crafty Sultan circumvented this difficulty by financing the construction of a seventh minaret at Mecca. The interior was originally lit with candles, the chandelier structure intended to create the illusion of tiny starlights floating freely in the air. The small, square, single-domed structure in front of the Blue Mosque is **Sultanahmet'in Türbesi,** or Sultan Ahmet's Tomb, which contains the sultan's remains. The reliquary in the back contains strands of the Prophet Muhammad's beard. *(Open Su-Th and Sa 9am-12:30pm, 1:45-4:40pm, and 5:40-6:30pm, F noon-2:20pm. The Blue Mosque is a working religious facility, and closes to the public for prayer 5 times a day. Scarves are provided at the entrance; women should cover their knees, hair, and shoulders. Inside the mosque, behave respectfully and don't cross into the sections limited to prayer. Donations are welcome on the way out. See p. 1031 for more on mosque etiquette.)*

TOPKAPI PALACE (TOPKAPI SARAYI). Towering from the high ground at the tip of the old city and hidden behind walls up to 12m high, Topkapı was the nerve center of the Ottoman Empire. Built by Mehmet the Conqueror in 1458-1465, the palace became an imperial residence during the reign of Süleyman the Magnificent.

BUMPER CARS, TURKEY STYLE

It happens every year for one glorious week. In early January, the city of Selçuk, Turkey, hosts the country's Camel Wrestling Championship.

Maybe "wrestling" isn't quite the appropriate word here. Camels aren't exactly the most vicious of creatures, and their fighting tactics resemble a childhood game of bumper cars more than an all-out war. And while Spain's bulls ultimately reach the sword at the hands of bullfighters, PETA protestors can sleep easy over the fate of Turkey's camels. Perhaps as a testament to their true character, the game ends not with death, but when one of the camels runs away, barrelling into the audience and scattering the lounging spectators.

Despite the seeming absurdity of camel-wrestling, the sport has many wealthy supporters, and continues to draw crowds despite Turkey's dwindling camel population. Tickets to the festival's competitions can be bought at the gate, and it's common to gamble on the competitions. Spectators should watch out for flying camel spittle and, um, urine.

Selçuk is on the Aegean Sea and is accessible by bus from İstanbul or İzmir. Check with travel agencies in İstanbul for tickets and information about the festival, which usually takes place in late January.

The palace is divided into a series of courtyards. The **first courtyard** was the popular center of the palace, where the general public could enter to watch executions and other displays of imperial might. The **second courtyard** leads to displays of wealth, including collections of porcelain, silver, gold, and torture instruments—not to mention crystal staircases. The Gate of Felicity leads to the **third courtyard,** which houses imperial clothing and the awesome ■**Palace Treasury.** The **fourth courtyard** is the pleasure center of the palace—it was among these pavilions, gardens, and fountains that the Ottomans really got their mojo working. The most interesting part of Topkapı is the 400-plus-room ■**harem.** Tours begin at the Black Eunuchs' Dormitory and continue into the chambers of the Valide Sultan, the sultan's mother and the harem's most powerful woman. Surrounding the room of the queen mum are the chambers of the concubines. If a particular woman attracted the sultan's affections or if the sultan spent a night with her, she would be promoted to "odalisque" status, which meant that she had to stay in İstanbul forever, but got nicer quarters in exchange for her undying ministrations. *(Palace open M and W-Su 9am-7pm. 10YTL. Harem open 10am-5pm. 10YTL. Audio tour of palace 5YTL. Harem can only be visited on guided tours, which leave every 30min. Lines for tours can be long; arrive early.)*

UNDERGROUND CISTERN (YEREBATAN SARAYI). This underground "palace" is actually a vast cavern whose shallow water eerily reflects the images of its 336 supporting columns. The columns are all illuminated by colored ambient lighting, making the cistern slightly resemble a horror-movie set. Underground walkways originally linked the cistern to Topkapı Palace, but were blocked to curb rampant trafficking in stolen goods and abducted women. At the far end of the cistern, two huge Medusa heads lie upside down in the water. Legend has it that looking at them directly turns people to stone. The cistern's overpriced **cafe,** in a dark corner, is a cross between creepy and romantic. *(The entrance lies 175m from the Aya Sofya in the small stone kiosk on the left side of Yerebatan Cad. Open daily 9am-6:30pm. 10YTL.)*

ARCHAEOLOGICAL MUSEUM COMPLEX. The Archaeological Museum Complex is made of four distinct museums. The **Tiled Pavilion** explains more than you ever wanted to know about the omnipresent İznik tiles. The smaller, adjacent building is the ■**Ancient Orient Museum.** It houses an excellent collection of 3000-year-old stone artifacts from the ancient Middle East and the Treaty of Kadesh, the world's oldest known written treaty, drafted after a battle between Ramses II of Egypt and the Hittite

King Muvatellish. The immense **Archaeology Museum** has one of the world's greatest collections of Classical and Hellenistic art, but is surprisingly bereft of visitors. The highlight is the famous Alexander Sarcophagus, covered with intricate carvings depicting the king in battle. The superb **Museum of Turkish and Islamic Art** features a large collection of Islamic art, organized by period. *(150m downhill from the Topkapı Palace's 1st courtyard. All museums open Tu-Su 8:30am-5pm. 5YTL.)*

GRAND BAZAAR. Through banter, barter, and haggle, **Kapalı Çarşısı** (Grand Bazaar) operates on a scale unmatched by even the most frenetic of markets elsewhere in the Europe. The largest, oldest covered bazaar in the world, the Grand Bazaar began in 1461 as a modest affair during the reign of Mehmet the Conqueror. Today, the enormous Kapalı Çarşısı combines the best and worst of shopping in Turkey to form the massive mercantile sprawl that starts at Çemberlitaş and covers the hill down to Eminönü, ending at the more authentic and less claustrophobic **Mısır Çarşısı** (Egyptian Spice Bazaar) and the Golden Horn waterfront. Rule number one in bargaining: never settle for more than half the first price asked; the place is touristy and shop owners know their tricks. Most wares in the grand bazaar are available for less in the Spice Bazaar or in shopss. And don't worry about getting lost—there are directional arrows from virtually any spot, so relax and enjoy the ride. *(From Sultanahmet, follow the tram tracks toward Aksaray until you see the Nuruosmaniye Camii on the right. Walk down Vezirhanı Cad. for one block, keeping the mosque on your left. Otherwise, follow the crowds. www.grandbazaar.com. Open M-Sa 9am-7pm.)*

SÜLEYMANİYE COMPLEX. To the north of İstanbul University stands the elegant **Süleymaniye Camii,** one of Ottoman architect Sinan's great masterpieces. This mosque is part of a larger **külliye** (complex), which includes **tombs,** an **imaret** (soup kitchen), and several **madrasas** (Islamic schools). After walking through the cemetery to see the **royal tombs** of Süleyman I and his wife, proceed inside the vast and perfectly proportioned mosque—the height of the dome (53m) is exactly twice the measurement of each side of the square base. The **stained-glass windows** are the sobering work of the master Sarhoş İbrahim (İbrahim the Drunkard). The İznik tile İnzanity all started here: the area around the **mihrab** showcases Sinan's first experiment in blue tiles. *(From Sultanahmet, take the tramvay to the Üniversite stop, walk across the square, and take Besim Ömer Paşa Cad. past the walls of the university to Süleymaniye Cad. Open daily except during prayer. Leave your shoes at the entrance. Women need to cover their shoulders, men and women should cover their heads. Scarves are available at the entrance.)*

HAMMAMS (TURKISH BATHS)

In the past a man found in a women's bath was sentenced to death, but today customs have relaxed and it's not rare to find co-ed baths where both genders strip beyond their skivvies. Most baths have separate women's sections or hours, but only some have designated female attendants. If you'd rather have a masseuse of your same sex, make sure to ask at the entrance.

Cağaloğlu Hamami, on Yerebatan Cad. at Babiali Cad. (☎522 2424; www.cagaloglu-hamami.com.tr), near Cağaloğlu Sq. in Sultanahmet. Donated to İstanbul in 1741 by Sultan Mehmet I, this luxurious white-marble bath is one of the city's most illustrious. Self-service bath 20YTL, bath with scrub 30YTL, complete bath and massage 40YTL, luxury treatment with hand-knit Oriental washcloth 60YTL. Slippers, soap, and towels included. Open daily for women 8am-8pm, for men 8am-10pm.

Çemberlitaş Hamami, 8 Vezirhan Cad. (☎522 7974; www.cemberlitashamami.com.tr). Just a soap-slide away from the Çemberlitaş tram stop. Built in 1584, the marble interiors make this place downright regal. Vigorous "towel service" after the bath; guests are welcome to hang around the hot marble rooms afterward. Open daily 6am-midnight.

▓ NIGHTLIFE

After the hot afternoons, İstanbul lights up its mosques. Locals and travelers alike pour into the streets to savor intense nightlife, which falls into three categories. The first includes male-only *çay* (tea) houses, backgammon parlors, and dancing shows. Women are not prohibited but are unwelcome and should avoid these places, which are often unsafe for male travelers as well. Let's Go does not endorse patronage of these establishments. The second category includes the local youth **cafe-bars, rock bars,** and many **backpacker bars.** In **Sultanahmet,** pubs are crammed within 10m of one another, usually on the rooftop or front tables of the hostels. They have standardized beer prices (5YTL) and are usually Australian-dominated; **Orient,** the most popular hostel bar, is open to all. **Clubs** and **discos** comprise the third nightlife category. Even taxi drivers can't keep up with the ever-fluctuating club scene. The Beşiktaş end of **Ortaköy** is a maze of upscale hangouts. The cheerful **Nevizade** is a virtually uninterrupted row of wine shops and tapas bars, parallel to İstiklâl Cad. İstanbul's local specialty is *balyoz* (sledgehammer/wrecking ball). Getting wrecked won't be difficult: *balyoz* consists of *rakı*, whiskey, vodka, and gin with orange juice. Bottoms up.

▓ **Just Bar,** 18 Akbıyık Cad. (☎01 23 45 67 89). This bar has become almost as much of a must-see as the Aya Sofya. Outdoor wooden pub tables, rock/funk/R&B music, and free-flowing beer make for a typical backpacker's night, every night. Beer 5YTL. Mixed drinks 7-10YTL. Open daily 11am-4am. It's hard to tell where Just Bar stops and **Cheers,** next door, begins. Cheers is equally popular, friendly, and laid-back. Beer 4-5YTL. Mixed drinks and shots 7-10YTL. Open daily noon-late.

Jazz Stop, at the end of Büyük Parmakkapı Sok., in Taksim. A mixed group of music lovers sit in this large underground tavern while live bands lay the funk, blues, and jazz on thick. The owner, the drummer from one of Turkey's oldest and most respected rock groups, occasionally takes part in the jams. A late-night hangout where the crowds don't build until 2 or 3am. Beer 5YTL. Mixed drinks 7-20YTL. Live music daily 2am. Cover F-Sa 10YTL; includes 1 drink. Open daily 7pm-6am.

Araf, İstiklâl Cad. and 32 Balo Sok. (☎244 8301), across from the entrance to Nevizade. Take the elevator to the 4th fl., then walk upstairs to reach this funky rooftop veranda with international music and freestyle dancing in a birthday-party atmosphere. No cover. Beer 4YTL. Mixed drinks 7-20YTL. Open daily 5pm-2am.

Sinerji Bar, İpek Sok. 14 (☎249 8426), off Küçük Parmakkapı Sok. Fascinated with Spanish surrealist paintings and Turkish indie rock, the understated Sinerji is popular with students and young foreigners looking for one of the cheapest pints in Taksim. Beer 4YTL, with occasional 1.50YTL specials. Mixed drinks 5-10YTL. Open daily 2pm-2am.

Nayah Music Club, Kurabiye Sok. 23 (☎244 1183; www.nayah.org), in Beyoglu. From İstiklâl Cad., take a right onto Mis Sok.; Nayah is one block down, on the corner with Kurabiye Sok. This reggae bar is small and relaxed, with rasta bartenders. Customers don't really dance, but instead sit and accompany the music with subtle head bobs. Beer 4YTL. Mixed drinks 7-14YTL. Open M-Th 6pm-2am, F-Sa 6pm-4am.

UKRAINE (УКРАЇНА)

In late 2004, Ukraine's Orange Revolution won international fame for the country. President Viktor Yushchenko and his administration have since enacted important reforms, however, as reforms have slowed down, Ukrainian politics have become more muddled. Today, Ukrainians are divided over their own identity: this internal struggle to reinvent and yet retain traditions can make Ukrainian culture confusing to navigate. Don't be surprised if a desk clerk and a website provide two different prices for a room, and don't expect anyone outside Kyiv to speak much English. Despite these inconveniences, Ukraine is captivating. Whole cities are under renovation, and the energy of development spills over into the streets. If you can get past the almost complete lack of tourist infrastructure, Ukraine can be a beautiful, delicious, and adventurous place to travel.

 DISCOVER UKRAINE: SUGGESTED ITINERARIES

THREE DAYS. Stick to **Kyiv,** the epicenter of the Orange Revolution. Check out **Independence Square,** stop by **Shevchenko Park** to enjoy real Ukrainian fare at **O'Panas,** and ponder your mortality among the mummified monks of the **Kyiv-Cave Monastery** (p. 1053).

ONE WEEK. After three days in **Kyiv,** take a train to **Lviv** (2 days; p. 1054), the cultural capital of Ukraine. Spend your last two days in **Odessa** (p. 1055) soaking up the sun on the beach and experiencing high culture for cheap at the **Theater of Opera and Ballet.**

ESSENTIALS

FACTS AND FIGURES

Official Name: Ukraine.

Capital: Kyiv.

Major Cities: Lviv, Odessa, Sevastopol, Simferopol, Yalta.

Population: 46,300,000.

Land Area: 603,700 sq. km.

Time Zone: GMT + 2.

Language: Ukrainian.

Religions: Ukrainian Orthodox (29%), Orthodox (16%), other (55%).

The Heart of it All: Some measurements have placed the geographic center of Europe in Dilove, UKR.

WHEN TO GO

Ukraine is a huge country with a diverse climate. Things heat up from June to August in Odessa and Crimea, which are just barely subtropical. It is best to reserve in advance at these times. Kyiv enjoys a moderate climate, while the more mountainous west remains cool even in summer. Winter tourism is popular in the Carpathians, but unless you're skiing, spring and summer are probably the best times to visit the country. Book accommodations early around the May 1 holiday.

DOCUMENTS AND FORMALITIES

EMBASSIES AND CONSULATES. Foreign embassies to Ukraine are in Kyiv (p. 1051). Ukrainian embassies and consulates abroad include: **Australia,** Level 12, St. George Centre, 60 Marcus Clarke St., Canberra, ACT 2601 (☎02 62 30 57 89; www.ukremb.info); **Canada,** 310 Somerset St., West Ottawa, ON K2P 0J9 (☎613-

UKRAINE

ENTRANCE REQUIREMENTS.

Passport: Required for all travelers.

Visa: Not required for citizens of Canada, the EU, or the US, but mandatory for citizens of Australia and New Zealand.

Letter of Invitation: Required for citizens of Australia and New Zealand.

Inoculations: Recommended up-to-date on DTaP (diphtheria, tetanus, and pertussis), Hepatitis A, Hepatitis B, MMR (measles, mumps, and rubella), polio booster, rabies (if you'll be in rural areas for long periods of time), and typhoid.

Work Permit: Required of all foreigners planning to work in Ukraine.

International Driving Permit: Required for all those planning to drive.

230-2400; www.mfa.gov.ua/canada); **UK,** 60 Holland Park, London, W11 3SJ (☎020 77 27 63 12, visas ☎020 72 43 89 23; www.ukremb.org.uk); **US,** 3350 M St., NW, Washington, D.C. 20007 (☎202-333-0606; www.mfa.gov.ua/usa).

VISA AND ENTRY INFORMATION. Ukraine's visa requirements have changed rapidly since 2005 as the new government works to encourage tourism. **Visas** are no longer required for American or Canadian citizens or citizens of the EU for stays of up to 90 days. All visas are valid for 90 days. Citizens of Australia and New Zealand require a letter of invitation, but citizens of Canada, the EU, and the US do not.

Allow plenty of time for processing. You can extend your visa in Ukraine, at the Ministry of Foreign Affairs, 2 Zhytomyska Str., Kyiv, or at the local **Office of Visas and Registration** (ОВИР; OVYR), often located at the police station. **Do not lose the paper given to you when entering the country to supplement your visa.** Make sure to carry your passport and visa at all times.

TOURIST SERVICES AND MONEY

EMERGENCY	Ambulance: ☎03. Fire: ☎01. Police: ☎02.

TOURIST OFFICES. Lviv's tourist office is helpful, but is the only official tourist office in Ukraine. The remains of the Soviet giant **Intourist** have offices in hotels, but staff often doesn't speak English. The official tourist website, **www.travel-toukraine.org,** has a list of "reliable travel agents." While local travel agencies can be sometimes helpful, they are always delighted to help you lighten your wallet.

UKRANHIAN HRYVNIA (HV)		
AUS$1 = 3.85HV	1HV = AUS$0.26
CDN$1 = 4.58HV	1HV = CDN$0.22
EUR€1 = 6.47HV	1HV = EUR€0.15
NZ$1 = 3.23HV	1HV = NZ$0.31
UK£1 = 9.45HV	1HV = UK£0.11
US$1 = 5.05HV	1HV = US$0.20

MONEY. The Ukrainian unit of currency is the **hryvnya** (hv), and *Obmin Valyut* (Обмін Валют) kiosks in most cities offer the best rates for **currency exchange. Traveler's checks** can be changed for a small commission in many cities. **ATMs** are everywhere. Most banks will give MasterCard and Visa **cash advances** for a high commission. The lobbies of upscale hotels usually exchange US dollars at lousy rates. **Private money changers** lurk near kiosks, ready with brilliant schemes for scamming you, but **exchanging money with them is illegal.**

HEALTH AND SAFETY

Hospital facilities in Ukraine are limited and do not meet American or Western European standards. Patients may be required to bring their own medical supplies (e.g., bandages). When in doubt, it is advisable to seek aid from your local embassy. Medical evacuations to Western Europe cost US$25,000 and upwards of US$50,000 to the US. **Pharmacies** (Аптеки; Apteky) are quite common and carry basic Western products. **Boil all water** or learn to love brushing your teeth with soda water. Peel or wash **fruits and vegetables** from open markets. Meat purchased at public markets should be checked carefully and cooked thoroughly; refrigeration is infrequent and insects run rampant. Avoid the tasty-looking hunks of meat for sale out of buckets on the Kyiv metro. Embassy officials declare that Chernobyl-related **radiation** poses minimal risk to short-term travelers. Public restrooms range from disgusting to frightening. **Pay toilets** (платні; platni) are cleaner and might provide toilet paper, but bring your own anyway.

While Ukraine is politically stable, it is poor. Pickpocketing and wallet scams are the most common **crimes** against tourists; instances of armed robbery and assault, however, have been reported. Do not accept drinks from strangers, as this could result in your being drugged and robbed. Credit card and ATM fraud are rampant; only use ATMs inside of banks and hotels, and avoid using credit cards whenever possible. Also use caution when crossing the street—drivers do not stop for pedestrians. It's wise to **register** with your embassy once you get to Ukraine.

UKRAINE

Women traveling alone may receive catcalls by men pretty much anywhere they go, but usually will be safe otherwise. Ukrainian women rarely go to restaurants alone, so expect to feel conspicuous if you do. Women may request to ride in female-only compartments during long train rides, though most do not. Although non-Caucasians may experience **discrimination,** the biggest problems stem from the militia, who frequently stop people who appear non-Slavic. **Homosexuality** is not yet accepted in Ukraine; it's best to be discreet.

TRANSPORTATION

BY PLANE. It is expensive to travel to Ukraine by plane, and few budget airlines fly in or out of the country. Ground transportation tends to be safer and more pleasant, but it can take a long time to traverse the great distances between cities. **Air Ukraine** flies to Kyiv, Lviv, and Odessa from many European capitals. **Aerosvit, Air France, ČSA, Delta, Lufthansa, LOT,** and **Malév** fly to Kyiv.

BY TRAIN. Trains run frequently and are the best way to travel. While *Let's Go* discourages the use of night trains, Ukraine's system is generally safe. When coming from a non-ex-Soviet country, expect a 2hr. stop at the border. To purchase tickets, you must present a passport or student ID. Once on board, you must present both your ticket and ID to the *konduktor.* On most Ukrainian trains, there are three classes: плацкарт, or *platskart*, where you'll be crammed in with *babushki* and baskets of strawberries; купе, or *kupe*, a clean, more private, four-person compartment; and first class, referred to as CB, or SV (for *Spalny Wagon*), which is twice as roomy and expensive as *kupe*. Unless you're determined to live like a local, pay the extra two dollars for *kupe*. Then again, women traveling alone may want to avoid the smaller, enclosed compartments of *kupe;* in that case, *platskart* may be the safer option. The *kasa* will sell you a *kupe* seat unless you say otherwise. Except in larger cities, where platform numbers are posted on the electronic board, the only way to figure out which platform your train leaves from is by listening to the distorted announcement. In large cities, trains arrive well before they are scheduled to depart, so you'll have a few minutes to show your ticket to cashiers or fellow passengers and ask "plaht-FORM-ah?"

DON'T MESS WITH TRANSINISTRA. If you're planning a trip from Western Ukraine to the Crimea, make sure that your train or bus route doesn't pass through Moldova on the way. Most of northern Moldova is part of the unrecognized breakaway territory of Transinistra; border guards in Transinistra have been known to demand bribes, confiscate expensive items like laptops and cameras, or simply throw unlucky travelers off of the train. To make sure this doesn't happen to you, check at the ticket counter before buying to make sure your ticket won't take you for an unpleasant ride.

BY BUS, TAXI, AND THUMB. Buses cost about the same as trains, but are often much shabbier. For long distances, the train is usually more comfortable. One exception is AutoLux (АвтоЛюкс), which runs buses with A/C, snacks, and movies. Bus schedules are generally reliable, but low demand can cause cancellations. Buy tickets at the *kasa;* if they're sold out, try going directly to the driver, who might just magically find you a seat and pocket the money. Navigating the bus system can be tough for those who do not speak Ukrainian or Russian. **Taxi** drivers love to rip off foreigners, so negotiate the price beforehand. Few Ukrainians **hitch-hike,** but those who do hold a sign with their desired destination or just wave an outstretched hand. Let's Go does not recommend hitchhiking.

KEEPING IN TOUCH

PHONE CODES	**Country code: 380. International dialing prefix:** 8, await a second tone, then 10. For more info on placing international calls, see **Inside Back Cover.**

TELEPHONE AND INTERNET. Telephone services are stumbling toward modernity. The easiest way to make international calls is with **Utel.** Buy an Utel phonecard (sold at most Utel phone locations) and dial the number of your international operator (counted as a local call). International access codes include: **AT&T Direct** (☎8 100 11); **Canada Direct** (☎8 100 17); and **MCI WorldPhone** (☎8 100 13). Alternatively, call at the central telephone office; estimate the length of your call and pay at the counter, and they'll direct you to a booth. Calling can be expensive, but you can purchase a 30min. international calling card for 15hv. Local calls from gray payphones generally cost 10-30hv. For an English-speaking operator, dial ☎8192. Cell phones are everywhere; to get one, stop at any kiosk or corner store. **Internet cafes** can be found in every major city and typically charge 4-12hv per hour of use. Major cities typically have 24hr. Internet cafes.

MAIL. Mail is cheap, reliable, and extremely user-friendly, taking about 8-10 days to reach North America. Sending a postcard or a letter of less than 20g internationally costs 0.66hv. Address **Poste Restante** (до запитання; do zapytannya) as follows: First name LAST NAME, post office address, Postal Code, city, UKRAINE.

LANGUAGE. Traveling in Ukraine is much easier if you know some **Ukrainian** or **Russian.** Ukrainian is an East Slavic language written in the Cyrillic alphabet. In Kyiv, Odessa, and Crimea, Russian is more commonly spoken than Ukrainian (although all official signs are in Ukrainian). If you're trying to get by with Russian in western Ukraine, you may run into some difficulty: everyone understands Russian, but some people will answer in Ukrainian out of habit or nationalist sentiment. *Let's Go* provides city names in Ukrainian for Kyiv and western Ukraine, while Russian names are used for Crimea and Odessa.

ACCOMMODATIONS AND CAMPING

UKRAINE	❶	❷	❸	❹	❺
ACCOMMODATIONS	under 75hv	75-150hv	151-250hv	251-350hv	over 350hv

The hostel scene in Ukraine is quickly establishing itself. Though youth **hostels** aren't prevalent in Ukraine, some can be found in Lviv, Kyiv, and Odessa; budget accommodations are often in unrenovated Soviet-era buildings, though they're being renovated at an incredible pace. More expensive lodgings aren't necessarily nicer. Not all **hotels** accept foreigners, and those that do often overcharge them. Though room prices in Kyiv are astronomical, singles run anywhere from 65-110hv in the rest of the country. Standard hotel rooms include TVs, phones, and refrigerators. You will be given a *vizitka* (hotel card) to show to the hall monitor *(dezhurnaya)* to get a key; return it upon leaving. **Hot water** doesn't necessarily come with a bath—ask before checking in. **Private rooms** are the best bargain and run 20-50hv. These can be arranged through overseas agencies or bargained for at the train station. Big cities have **camping** facilities—usually a remote spot with trailers. Camping outside designated areas is illegal, and enforcement is strict.

UKRAINE

FOOD AND DRINK

UKRAINE	❶	❷	❸	❹	❺
FOOD	under 15hv	15-35hv	36-55hv	56-75hv	over 75hv

New, fancy restaurants accommodate tourists and the few Ukrainians who can afford them, while *stolovayas* (cafeterias)—remnants of ⊠Soviet times—serve cheap, hot food. Pierogi-like dumplings called *vavenyky* are ubiquitous and delicious. **Vegetarians** beware: meat has a tendency to show up in so-called "vegetarian" dishes. Finding **kosher** foods can be daunting, but it helps to eat non-meat items. Fruits and veggies are sold at **markets;** bring your own bag. **State food stores** are classified by content: *hastronom* (packaged goods); *moloko* (milk products); *ovochi-frukty* (fruits and vegetables); *myaso* (meat); *khlib* (bread); *kolbasy* (sausage); and *ryba* (fish). *Kvas* is a popular, barely-alcoholic, fermented-bread drink. Grocery stores are often simply labeled *mahazyn* (store). Beer can be drunk on the streets, but hard liquor can't. The distinction is telling—"I drink beer," goes one Ukrainian saying, "and I also drink alcohol."

HOLIDAYS AND FESTIVALS

Holidays: Orthodox Christmas (Jan. 7); Orthodox New Year (Jan. 14); International Women's Day (Mar. 8); Easter (Apr. 27); Labor Day (May 1-2); Victory Day (May 9); Holy Trinity Day (June 16); Constitution Day (June 28); Independence Day (Aug. 24).

Festivals: One of the most widely celebrated festivals is the Donetsk Jazz Festival, usually held in March. The Chervona Ruta Festival, which occurs in different Ukrainian cities each year, celebrating both modern Ukrainian pop and traditional music. The Molodist Kyiv International Film Festival, held in the last week of October, sets the stage for student films and film debuts.

BEYOND TOURISM

For more info on opportunities across Europe, see **Beyond Tourism,** p. 56.

Jewish Volunteer Corps, American Jewish World Service, 45 W. 36th St., New York, NY 10018, USA (☎800-889-7146). Places volunteers at summer camps and Jewish community centers in Russia Ukraine.

Odessa Language Center (☎380 482 345 058; www.studyrus.com). Spend a year or a summer in **Ukraine** learning Russian and taking courses on history and culture.

KYIV (КИЇВ)   ☎8044

Since its position as the capital of the Kyivan Rus empire over a millennium ago, Kyiv (pop. 2,700,000) has stood as a social and economic center for the region. No stranger to foreign control, the city was razed by the Nazi army only to be rebuilt with extravagant Stalinist pomp by the Soviets. Since Ukraine gained its independence from the USSR in 1991, Kyiv has reemerged as a proud capital and cultural center. The streets buzz with energy, even as the cost of living rises and the new government, elected beneath the international spotlight during the 2004 Orange Revolution, struggles to institute promised reforms.

▮ TRANSPORTATION

Flights: Boryspil International Airport (Бориспіль; ☎490 4777), 30km southeast of the capital. **Polit** (Політ; ☎296 7367), just right of the main entrance, sends buses to

Ploshcha Peremohi, the train station, and Boryspilska, the metro stop. Buy tickets on board (1-2 per hr., 17-22hv). A taxi to the center costs 70-100hv. Negotiate with drivers near the Polit bus stop; those stationed outside customs will take you for a ride.

Trains: Kyiv-Pasazhyrskyy (Київ-Пасажирський), Vokzalna pl. (☎005 or 465 4895). MR: Vokzalna (Вокзальна). Purchase tickets for domestic trains in the main hall. For international tickets, go to window #40 or 41 in the newest section of the train station, across the tracks. For the *elektrychka* commuter rail (електричка), go to the *Prymiskyy Vokzal* (Приміский Вокзал; Suburban Station), next to the Metro station. A passport is required for the purchase of any train ticket. Information (довідка; *dovidka*) windows are located in each section of the train station; some stay open 24hr. However, assistance is entirely in Ukrainian or Russian; expect no help in English. There is an **Advance Ticket Office** next to Hotel Express at Shevchenka 38. Trains to: **Lviv** (10hr., 5-6 per day, 65-100hv); **Odessa** (10hr., 4-5 per day, 60-85hv); **Sevastopol** (20hr., 3 per day, 70-115hv); **Bratislava, SLK** (21hr., 1 per day, 480hv); **Budapest, HUN** (24hr., 1 per day, 595hv); **Moscow, RUS** (14-17hr., 12-15 per day, 280hv); **Prague, CZR** (35hr., 1 per day, 600hv); **Warsaw, POL** (19hr., 2 per day, 370hv).

Buses: Tsentralny Avtovokzal (Центральний Автовокзал), Moskovska pl. 3 (Московська; ☎525 5774). Take trolley #1 or 11 from the Libidska metro station. Open 5am-10pm. Buses to: **Lviv** (7-12hr., 4 per day, 70hv); **Odessa** (8-10hr., 9 per day, 75hv); **Moscow, RUS** (18hr., 1 per day, 150hv); **Prague, CZR** (28hr., 1 per day Tu and Th-F; 380hv).

Public Transportation: 3 **metro** lines—blue (MB), green (MG), and red (MR)—cover the city center. Purchase tokens (житон; *zhyton*; 0.50hv) at the *kasa* (каса). "Вхід" (*vkhid*) indicates an entrance, "перехід" (*perekhid*) a walkway to another station, and "вихід у місто" (*vykhid u misto*) an exit onto the street. **Trolleys, buses,** and **marshrutki** (private vans) go where the metro doesn't. Bus tickets are sold at kiosks or can be purchased from the driver; punch your ticket using the manual lever on board or face a fine. Marshrutki tickets (1-3hv) are sold on board; pay attention and request stops from the driver. Public transport runs approx. 5:45am-12:15am. The *elektrychka* (електричка) commuter rail leaves from Prymiskyy Vokzal (Приміський Вокзал), MR: Vokzalna.

Taxis: Taxis are everywhere. A ride to the center of town should cost about 10hv. Always agree on the price before getting in.

✦ 🛈 ORIENTATION AND PRACTICAL INFORMATION

Most attractions and services lie on the west bank of the Dniper River. Three metro stops from the train station is the main avenue, **vulitsa Khreshchatyk** (Хрещатик; MR line). The center of Kyiv is vul. Khreshchatyk's fountained **Independence Square** (Майдан Незалежності; Maidan Nezalezhnosti; MB line).

Tourist Offices: Kyiv lacks official tourist services. Representatives of various agencies at the airport offer vouchers, excursion packages, hotel arrangements, and other services. Travel agencies also organize tours. **Carlson Wagonlit Travel,** Khnoelnistkiy 33/34, 2nd fl. (☎238 6156). Open daily 9am-9pm. Also has branch at the US Embassy. **Yana Travel Group,** Saksahanskoho 42 (Саксаганського; ☎490 7373; www.yana.kiev.ua). Open M-F 10am-7pm, Sa 10am-5pm. Students should check out **STI Ukraine,** Proreznaya 18/1 #6, on the 2nd fl. (Прорезная; ☎490 5960). Open M-F 9am-9pm, Sa-Su 10am-4pm.

Embassies: Australia, Kominternu 18/137 (Комінтерну; ☎225 7586; fax 244 3597). Open M-Th 10am-1pm. **Canada,** Yaroslaviv Val. 31 (Ярославів; ☎270 7144; fax 270 6598). Open M-F 8:30am-1pm and 2-5pm; visa section open M-Th. **Russia,** Povitroflotskyy pr. 27 (Повітрофлотський; ☎244 0963). Open M-Tu and Th 9am-1:30pm and 3-5pm, W 10am-1:30pm, F 10am-1:30pm and 3-4pm. Visa section at Kutuzova 8 (Кутузова; ☎294 6701; fax 294 6816). Open M-F 10am-1pm, 3-5pm. **UK,** Desyatynna 9 (Десятинна; ☎490 3660; fax 490 3662). Consular section at Glybo-

CHERNOBYL REMEMBERED?

April 2006 marked the 20th anniversary of the world's worst nuclear accident. Controversy still exists about the overall effect of the explosion at Chernobyl: a recent Greenpeace study contests the UN's estimate of 4000-9000 cancer deaths, suggesting a staggering figure of 93,000 casualties.

Today, however, a new trade is beginning in the ghost-towns of Chernobyl: tourism. Although radiation levels remain extremely high in the "Dead Zone," several travel agencies have begun leading tours, which cost US$100-400, to look at fateful reactor 4, visit towns in the Dead Zone, and check out radiation-filled tanks.

Despite the influx of tourism, though, Chernobyl is by no means considered safe. Geiger counters find over 50 times normal radiation. And to make matters worse, the ruins of reactor 4—still filled with nuclear material—are showing signs of breaking down, prompting Ukraine to propose the building of a new steel facility in 2008. Tour agencies press ahead, leading over 500 tourists every year, insising that the danger lies in long-term radiation, not a one-day encounter. Others feel that the name of the Dead Zone speaks for itself.

For info on tours, visit www.tourkiev.com/chernobyl.php, or call ☎ *405 35 00. Solo East Tours is located at Travneva St. 12.*

chytska 4 (Глибочицька; ☎494 3400; fax 494 3418). Open M-Th 9am-1pm and 2-5:30pm, F 9am-1pm and 2-4pm. **US,** Yu. Kotsyubynskoho 10 (Коцюбинського; ☎490 4000; www.usembassy.kiev.ua). Consular sec tion at Pymonenka 6 (Пимоненка; ☎490 4422 or 490 4445; fax 490 4040). From the corner of Maidan Nezalezhnosti and Sofievska (Софієвска), take trolley #16 or 18 for 4 stops. Continue on Artema (Артема) until it curves to the right, then take the 1st right, Pymonenka. Open M-F 9am-noon.

Medical Services: American Medical Center, Berdychivska 1 (Бердичерска; ☎490 7600; www.amcenters.com). English-speaking doctors will take patients without documents or insurance. Open 24hr. MC/V.

Telephones: English operator ☎81 92. **Telephone-Telegraph** (Телефон-Телеграф; *telefon-telehraf*) around the corner of the post office (enter on Khreshchatyk). Open daily 8am-10pm. Buy cards for **public telephones** (таксофон; taksofon) at any post office. Less widespread than Taksofon phones, **Utel phones** and cards are in the post office, train station, hotels, and nice restaurants.

Internet Access: C-Club, Bessarabskaye pl. 1 (Бесарабскае; ☎247 5647), in the underground mall between Bessarabsky market and the Lenin statue. Over 100 computers. 8hv per hr. 9am-8am.

Post Office: Khreshchatyk 22 (☎278 1167; www.poshta.kiev.ua). Spotless and well organized office; though the signs are in Cyrillic, the helpful staff should point you in the right direction. Some English is spoken at information desk #18. **Poste Restante** at counters #28 and 30. For packages, enter on Maidan Nezalezhnosti. Copy, fax, and photo services available. Open M-Sa 8am-9pm, Su 9am-7pm. **Postal Code:** 01001.

🦄🗝 ACCOMMODATIONS AND FOOD

Hotels in Kyiv tend to be expensive; the *Kyiv Post* (www.kyivpost.com) lists short-term apartment rentals, as do most English-language publications and websites about Kyiv. People at train stations offer even cheaper rooms (from US$5), though English speakers are rare and quality of rooms varies. Another way to find lodging is through the commission-free telephone service **Okean-9.** (☎443 6167. Open M-F 9am-5pm, Sa 9am-3pm.) Backpackers flock to 🏠**International Youth Hostel Yaroslav ❸** (Ярослав), vul. Yaroslavska 10 (Ярославська), in the historic Podil district. This 11-bed hostel with an English-speaking staff fills up quickly. (☎417 3189. MB: Kontraktova Ploshcha. Internet next door 9hv per hr. Doubles 250hv; 4- to 5-bed dorms 125hv. Cash only.) Down vul. Kominternu from the train station, **Hotel Express ❸** (Експрес), bul. Shevchenka 38/40, has rooms with TV, A/C, and balconies. (☎503 3045; www.expresskiev.com.ua. Internet 4hv per 30min. Singles with shower 350-430hv; doubles 480-600/540-660hv.)

Located in the Taras Shevchenko Park, ▨**O'Panas ❸** (О'Панас), Tereshchenkivska vul. 10 (Терещенківська), serves local dishes amid traditional Ukrainian decor. (☎235 2132. Entrees 35-100hv. Open M-F 8am-1am, Sa-Su 10am-1am. MC/V.) **Antresol ❸** (Антресоль), bul. T. Shevchenka 2, has a hip bookstore-cafe downstairs and a restaurant upstairs. (☎235 8347. English-language menu. Salads 19-45hv. Entrees 29-110hv. Tu and Su live piano 8-10pm. Open daily 10am-late. MC/V.) **King David's ❹,** Esplanadna 24 (Еспланадна), is a kosher restaurant with menus in English, Hebrew, and Ukrainian. (☎235 7436. MG: Palats Sportu; Палац Спорту. Entrees 35-95hv. Open Su-Th 10am-11pm, F 10am-10pm. Cash only.) Hit up Besarabsky Market at Besarabska Ploscha for 24hr. fresh produce. (MR: Teatralna.)

ⓖ SIGHTS

The ▨**Kyiv-Cave Monastery** (Києво-Печерська Лавра; Kyivo-Pecherska Lavra), Kyiv's oldest holy site, houses the Refectory Church, the 12th-century Holy Trinity Gate Church, and caves where monks lie mummified. The **Great Lavra Bell Tower** (closed for renovations) offers views of the domes. (MR: Arsenalna; Арсенальна. Turn left out of the metro and walk down vul. Sichnevoho Povstaniya. Open daily May-Aug. 9am-7pm; Sept.-Apr. 9:30am-6pm. Monastery 10hv, students 5hv. Photography 12hv.) Once the religious center of Kyivan Rus, the **St. Sophia Cathedral,** with its ornamented facades and Byzantine mosaics, offers an original look into the religious history of Ukraine. (vul. Volodymyrska. MG: Zoloti Vorota or trolley #16 from Maidan Nezalezhnosti. Grounds open daily 9am-7pm. Museums open M-Tu and F-Su 10am-6pm, W 10am-5pm. Grounds 2hv. Museums 20hv, students 8hv. Bell tower 5/3hv.) Kyiv's central road, **vul. Khreshchatyk** (Хрещатик), is where locals go to see and be seen. It begins at bul. T. Shevchenka and extends to **Independence Square** (Майдан Незалежності; Maidan Nezalezhnosti), which hosted a massive tent city during the Orange Revolution. **Khreshchatyk Park,** past the Friendship of the Peoples Arch, contains a monument to Prince Volodymyr, who converted the Kyivan Rus to Christianity. (MR: Khreshchatyk; Хрещатик.) Full of cafes and galleries, the cobblestone distict of **Andrew's Rise** (Андріївский Узвіз; Andriyivskyy uzviz) can be reached by walking down Desyatynna from Mikhaylivska Sq. (MB: Poshtova Ploshcha; Поштова Площа.) The **Museum of One Street,** Andriyivskyy uzviz 2B, recounts the street's colorful history. (Open Tu-Su noon-6pm. 10hv. 45min. English-language tour 100hv.) At the corner of Volodymyrska and Andriyivskyy uzviz is **St. Andrew's Church.** (Open 10am-5pm.) One block down from Andriyivskyy uzviz, steep wooden stairs lead to a great view of the **Podil District,** Kyiv's oldest district. The **Chernobyl Museum,** Provulok Khoryva 1, showcases artifacts and testimonies from the nuclear disaster's aftermath, as well as a poster exhibit commemorating its 20th anniversary. (Open M-Sa 10am-6pm. Closed last M of each month. 5hv, with ISIC 1hv.)

♫ ⓡ ENTERTAINMENT AND NIGHTLIFE

The last weekend in May brings the **Kyiv Days,** attracting thousands of spectators with art and music performances all over the city. During the rest of the year, the **National Philharmonic,** Volodymyrska 2, holds concerts most nights at 7pm. (☎278 1697; www.filharmonia.com.ua. Kasa open Tu-Su noon-2pm and 3-7pm. 5-30hv.) **Shevchenko Opera and Ballet Theater,** vul. Volodymyrska 50, has several performances each week. (MR: Teatralna; Театральна. ☎279 1169. *Kasa* open M 3-7:30pm, Tu-Su 11am-3pm and 4-7:30pm. 5-100hv.) If you're in town in the summer, don't miss **Dynamo Kyiv,** one of Europe's top football teams. (*Kasa* in front of stadium.) On hot days, head to **Hydropark** (Гідропарк), an **amusement park, sports complex,** and **nightclub.** (MR: Hidropark.)

Check out *What's On* magazine (www.whatson-kiev.com) and the *Kyiv Post* (www.kyivpost.com) for nightlife listings. Kyiv's popular jazz club, ▓**Artclub 44,** vul. Khreshchatyk 44, has live music nightly starting at 10pm. (☎279 4137. Cover 10-20hv. Open daily 11am-last customer.) **Cyber Cafe** (Сибер Кафе), Prorizna 21 (Прорізна), is a small club with drag shows on the weekends. (MG: Zoloty Vorota toward Khreshchatyk. Disco daily 10pm-6am, drag shows F-Sa 2am. Cover free-30hv men, 10-40hv women. Open daily 11am-last customer.)

LVIV (ЛЬВІВ)   ☎80322

Lviv's star is rising. While Kyiv is the political and economic capital of Ukraine, many consider Lviv (pop. 1,000,000) to be the cultural and patriotic center of the country. Lviv's cobblestone streets and picturesque churches, packed with architecture of every imaginable style, still manage to feel lived-in rather than on display. The modern city, which stretches beyond the historic center, is bustling, chock-full of cafes, and close to the beautiful Carpathian mountains

🖿🔃 TRANSPORTATION AND PRACTICAL INFORMATION. Trains go from pl. Vokzalna (Вокзальна) to: Kyiv (9hr., 3 per day, 50-100hv); Odessa (12hr., 1 per day, 60-110hv); Budapest, HUN (13hr., 1 per day, 400hv); Kraków, POL (8hr., 1 per day, 250hv); Moscow, RUS (25hr., 3 per day, 250hv); Prague, CZR (32hr., 1 per day, 400hv); Warsaw, POL (14hr., every other day, 400hv). Tickets can be bought at the railway *kasa* at Hnatyuka 20. (Гнатюка; ☎226 1176. Open M-Sa 8am-2pm and 3-8pm, Su 8am-2pm and 3-6pm.) **Taxis** from the train station into town cost about 20hv. **Buses** run from the main station, vul. Stryyska 189 (Стрийська; ☎294 9817) to Kraków, POL (10hr., 1 per day, 103hv) and Warsaw, POL (10hr., 3 per day, 150hv). **Trolleys** in town cost 0.50hv. The **Lviv Tourist Info Center,** vul. Pidvalna 3, has an English-speaking staff. (☎297 5751; www.tourism.lviv.ua. Open M-F 10am-6pm.) ▓**Internet Club,** vul. Dudaeva 12, offers Internet and international calling. (☎72 27 38; www.ic.lviv.ua. Open 24hr. Internet 4hv per hr.) **Postal Code:** 79000.

For local phone calls from a landline, dial "2" before numbers that begin with "9."

🖿🔂 ACCOMMODATIONS AND FOOD. Two new hostels welcome visitors to town. **Lviv Backpackers' Hostel,** Kolyaretskoho 37 (Лщтлязуцькщго), offers more amenities than most backpackers will ever need, among them a hot tub, free Wi-Fi, a patio, satellite TV, and a DVD collection. (☎237 2053. English spoken. Dorms US$16-22; special offers available. AmEx/D/MC/V.) **Kosmonaut Hostel ❷,** Sichovykh Striltsiv 8, has a more rustic, relaxed feel, with airy rooms and a friendly staff that makes up for ongoing renovations. (Dorms 75-120hv. Cash only.) **Caverna Blue Bottle** (Kavarna Pid Synoyu Flyazhkoyu), Ruska 4, offers sandwiches (6-8hv) and mixed drinks (4-20hv) from different parts of the Austro-Hungarian empire in its five-table dining room lit only by candles. (☎294 9152. Cash only.) ▓**Veronika ❶** (Вероніка), pr. Shevchenko 21, serves pastries (5hv) and cakes (10-24hv) in its upstairs cafe, as well as classic European dishes (30-166hv) in the small, dark restaurant downstairs. (☎297 8128. Open daily 10am-11pm. MC/V.)

🖿🔂 SIGHTS AND ENTERTAINMENT. Climb up the ▓**High Castle Hill** (Високий Замок; Vysokyy Zamok), the former site of the Galician King's Palace, for a stunning panoramic view of Lviv. **Ploshcha Rynok,** the historic market square, is surrounded by richly decorated homes and numerous Baroque churches. The **History Museum** (Історичний Музей; Istorichnyy Muzey) complex is at pl. Rynok #4, 6, and 24. Exhibits at #4 recount the history of Ukraine's struggle for liberation during WWI and WWII; some are accompanied by English translations. (☎ 72 06 71. Open M-Tu and Th-Su 10am-5pm. Each museum 2-7hv, some student discounts.) Walk up to the end of vul. Staroyevreiska (Old Jewish St.), and on your left at Arsenalna Square you'll see the ruins of the 16th-century **Golden Rose Synagogue,** a center of Jewish culture before its destruction by the Nazis. **Ivano-Franko Opera and Ballet Theater,** Prospekt Svobody 28, holds performances at fantastic prices in a turn-of-the-century hall. (☎ 74 20 80. Performances several times per week at noon and 6pm. 10-75hv.) The party at **Millennium,** vul. Chornovola 2, is spread across three levels of dance floors. (☎ 40 35 91; www.favorite-club.com. Beer 5hv. Cover up to 50hv. Open Tu-Su 9pm-4am.)

ODESSA (ОДЕСА)   ☎ 80482

Odessa (pop. 1,000,000) has been blessed with prosperity and cursed with corruption since its founding by Catherine the Great in 1794. This port town has been kept dynamic by local hipsters and intellectuals, and has inspired writers from Alexander Pushkin to Isaac Babel. The **Odessa Art Museum** (Художний Музей; Khudozhniy Muzey), ul. Sofiyevskaya 5A, houses a diverse collection of 19th-century art, as well as an underground grotto of secret passageways. (☎ 23 84 62. Open M and W-Su 10:30am-5:30pm. 2hv for each of the 3 exhibits.) The crowds on **ul. Deribasovskaya** guarantee an animated scene at any time of day, and the fashion stores and cafes provide entertainment for all. The **Pushkin Museum and Memorial** (Литературно-мемориальный Узей Пушкина; Literaturno-memorialniy Muzey Pushkina) at #13 was the hotel where Pushkin lived during his 1823-1824 exile from St. Petersburg. (Open M-Sa 10am-5pm. 5hv, students 2hv.) Beneath the city lies the world's longest series of ▓catacombs; the tunnels were the base of resistance during the Nazi occupation. The labyrinth is only legally accessible with a private guide. FGT and Eugenia travel agencies, as well as most hotels, organize excursions. The city's crowded **beaches** are easily accessible, though quality varies. To reach nearby **Lanzheron** (Ланжерон) beach, walk through Shevchenko park or take *marshrutki* 253 or 233. Tram #5 goes to **Arkadiya** (Аркадия), the city's most popular beach. At the end of ul. Rishelyevskaya, the **Opera and Ballet Theater** (Театр Оперы и <алетf; Teatr Opery i Baleta) presents classic ballet and opera in a beautiful, recently renovated theater. (*Kasa* ul. Preobrazhenskaya 28. ☎ 22 02 45. Open daily 10am-6pm.)

Private rooms (from 30hv) are the cheapest accommodation options; hosts solicit customers at the train station. Hostels, however, rival private rooms in price and often trump them in confort. **Black Sea Backpackers' Hostel ❸,** Yekaterinskaya 25, 2nd fl., has a bar, computer access, jacuzzi, kitchen, and Wi-Fi, along with a great location. (☎ 25 22 00 or 24 55 67; www.blackseahostels.com. US$25 per night.) ▓**Tavriya** (Ефврша), Ploshcha Grechevskaya, in the basement of Galeria Afena, has a huge selection of cheap Ukrainian food, pizzas, crepes, and desserts, with live music. (Drinks 3-8hv. Soups 3-5hv. Entrees 6-20hv. Desserts 3-5hv. Open daily 8am-11pm. Cash only.) Another cafeteria, **Zharu Paru ❶** (Жару Пару), ul. Grechevskaya 45 (Гречевская), also serves classic Ukrainian fare. (☎ 22 44 30. Meals 10-15hv. Open daily 8am-10pm. Cash only.) Summer nights, the crowds head to **Arkadiya,** where a strip of nightclubs blasts everything from electronic to hip hop with an emphasis on Russian pop. Tram #5 goes to Arkadiya but stops running around 11:30pm; taxis back from the clubs cost 25-40hv.

Trains run from pl. Privokzalnaya 2 (Привокзальная; tickets ☎ 005), at the northern end of ul. Pushkinskaya, to: Kyiv (8hr., 5 per day, 60-80hv); Lviv (12hr., 2 per day, 60-80hv); Moscow, RUS (23-27hr., 2-4 per day, 173-287hv); Simferopol (12hr., 70-90hv); Warsaw, POL (24hr., 1 per 2 days, 400hv). To reach the bus station, take tram #5 to the last stop. **Buses** run from ul. Kolontayevskaya 58 (Колонтаевская) to Kyiv (8-10hr., 8 per day, 66-88hv). **FGT Travel,** ul. Deribasovskaya 13, in Hotel

Frapolli, provides info. (☎37 52 01; www.odessapassage.com. Open daily 8:30am-8pm.) **Eugenia Travel**, ul. Rishelievskaya 23, can help with hotel bookings. (☎22 03 31; www.eugeniatours.com.ua.) For **Internet**, go to **Internet Kiev**, ul. Deribasovskaya 8. (☎37 70 44. 6hv per hr. Open 24hr.) **Postal Code:** 65001.

YALTA (ЯЛТА) ☎80654

One of the most popular vacation spots for the Russian and Ukrainian elite, Yalta (pop. 81,000) sheltered Chekhov and Tolstoy, as well as many of Europe's finest architects. Some of Yalta's best sights are, however, located outside town. The **Great Livadiya Palace,** built in 1911, hosted the 1945 Yalta Conference that shaped the face of the postwar world. (☎31 55 79. Open M-Tu and Th-Su 10am-5pm. 20hv.) The **Massandra Winery** offers tastings of its over one million bottles. (Vinodela Egorova 9. ☎23 26 62 or 35 27 95. From Yalta, take *marshrutka* #40 from the downtown station to Vinzavod. 1hr. tours 1 per 2hr. daily May-Oct. 11am-7pm; Nov.-Apr. 11am-5pm. Tour 25hv, with tasting 55hv.) At ul. Kirova 12, explore the ◪white **dacha** built by Anton Chekhov in 1899. Take *marshrutka* #8 from Kinoteatr Spartak on ul. Pushkinskaya. (☎39 49 47. Open June-Sept. Tu-Su 10am-5:15pm; Oct.-May W-Su 10am-4pm. 20hv.) Catch a gondola up the mountain for an impressive view of the city. (Enter to the right of the Gastronom on Nab. Lenina. Open daily 10am-8pm. 14hv.) Follow the shore away from the harbor to reach Yalta's **beaches** (2-5hv).

The best time to visit Yalta is early summer or fall. Reserve at least two months ahead for July and August. When tourists flood Yalta's streets, hotels are booked, and prices double. If you arrive in summer without prior arrangements, negotiate with locals offering **private rooms** (20-100hv); most will approach you at the bus station. A good mid-range accommodation for two or more travelers is **Hotel Otdizh ❶**, vul. Drazhynskoho 14. (☎35 30 79. Breakfast included. Doubles with bath 300hv; suites 400hv. Cash only.) **Pension T.M.M. ❸**, ul. Lesi Ukrayinki 16, has views of the sea and rooms with bath, balcony, and TV. The hotel also has a private swimming pool, outdoor bar, and Russian sauna. (☎23 09 50; www.firmatmm.ua. Take trolleybus #1 to the Sadovaya stop, and backtrack a few steps to the Pensionat sign. Turn left and go up the hill, taking the 1st left. Follow to the end of the road and turn right, entering through an unmarked black gate on the left. Little English spoken. 3 meals included. Doubles 350-570hv.) Several **stolovaya** (столовая; cafeterias) in the center of town serve good inexpensive fare (10-20hv). **Stolovaya Rabotaet ❶**, on vul. Ihnatenko, stands out. (Entrees 10-15hv. Open daily 8am-8pm.) **Cafe Voschod ❷**, ul. Ignatenko 2, near pl. Sovetskaya, serves Turkish and Russian cuisine and has an English-language menu. (☎23 39 43. Entrees 15-45hv. Open May-Sept. 24hr.; Oct.-Apr. daily 9am-midnight.) At night, walk along **naberezhnaya Lenina**, or try one of its many cafes. Overlooking the waterfront is the glitzy nightclub **Tornado,** nab. Lenina 11. (☎32 20 36. Beer 12hv. Cover 50-100hv. Open July-Sept. daily 10pm-5am; Oct.-Nov. Th-Sa 10pm-5am; Dec.-May F-Sa 10pm-5am.)

Yalta is not accessible by train. **Buses** run from ul. Moskovskaya to Kyiv (17½hr., 2 per day, 110-150hv) and Odessa (14hr., 2 per day, 70-100hv). Transportation to Yalta usually departs from Simferopol; there are *marshrutki*, buses, and a trolley to Yalta that leaves the Simferopol train station parking lot. Once in Yalta, take a trolley (under 1hv) or taxi (10-15hv) into the center of town. **Postal Code:** 98600.

APPENDIX

LANGUAGE PHRASEBOOK

CYRILLIC ALPHABET

Bulgaria and **Ukraine** use variations of the Russian Cyrillic alphabet.

CYRILLIC	ENGLISH	PRONOUNCE	CYRILLIC	ENGLISH	PRONOUNCE
А а	a	*ah* as in Pr**a**gue	Р р	r	*r* as in **r**evolution
Б б	b	*b* as in **B**osnia	С с	s	*s* as in **S**erbia
В в	v	*v* as in **V**olga	Т т	t	*t* as in **t**ank
Г г	g	*g* as in **G**lasnost	У у	u	*oo* as in B**u**dapest
Д д	d	*d* as in **d**ictatorship	Ф ф	f	*f* as in **f**ormer USSR
Е е	e	*yeh* as in **Y**eltsin	Х х	kh	*kh* as in Ba**ch**
Ё ё	yo	*yo* as in **yo**!	Ц ц	ts	*ts* as in **ts**ar
Ж ж	zh	*zh* as in mira**g**e	Ч ч	ch	*ch* as in Gorba**ch**ev
З з	z	*z* as in communi**sm**	Ш ш	sh	*sh* as in Bol**sh**evik
И и	i	*ee* as in Gr**ee**k	Щ щ	shch	*shch* in Khru**shch**ev
Й й	y	*y* as in bo**y** or ke**y**	Ъ ъ	(hard sign)	(not pronounced)
К к	k	*k* as in **K**remlin	Ы ы	i	*i* as in s**i**lver
Л л	l	*l* as in **L**enin	Ь ь	(soft sign)	(not pronounced)
М м	m	*m* as in **M**oscow	Э э	e	*eh* as in **E**stonia
Н н	n	*n* as in **n**uclear	Ю ю	yu	*yoo* as in **U**kraine
О о	o	*o* as in Cr**o**atia	Я я	ya	*yah* as in **Y**alta
П п	p	*p* as in **P**oland			

GREEK ALPHABET

SYMBOL	NAME	PRONOUNCE	SYMBOL	NAME	PRONOUNCE
α A	alpha	*a* as in f**a**ther	ν N	nu	*n* as in **n**et
β B	beta	*v* as in **v**elvet	ξ Ξ	xi	*x* as in mi**x**
γ Γ	gamma	*y* as in **y**o/*g* as in **g**o	ο O	omicron	*o* as in r**o**w
δ Δ	delta	*th* as in **th**ere	π Π	pi	*p* as in **p**eace
ε E	epsilon	*e* as in j**e**t	ρ P	rho	*r* as in **r**oll
ζ Z	zeta	*z* as in **z**ebra	σ Σ	sigma	*s* as in **s**ense
η H	eta	*ee* as in qu**ee**n	τ T	tau	*t* as in **t**ent
θ Θ	theta	*th* as in **th**ree	υ Y	upsilon	*ee* as in gr**ee**n
ι I	iota	*ee* as in tr**ee**	φ Φ	phi	*f* as in **f**og
κ K	kappa	*k* as in **k**ite	χ X	chi	*h* as in **h**orse
λ Λ	lambda	*l* as in **l**and	ψ Ψ	psi	*ps* as in oo**ps**
μ M	mu	*m* as in **m**oose	ω Ω	omega	*o* as in Let's G**o**

CROATIAN

ENGLISH	CROATIAN	PRONOUNCE	ENGLISH	CROATIAN	PRONOUNCE
Yes/No	Da/Ne	dah/neh	Train/Bus	Vlak/Autobus	vlahk/OW-toh-bus
Please	Molim	MOH-leem	Station	Kolodvor	KOH-loh-dvor
Thank you	Hvala lijepa	HVAH-la lee-yee-pah	Airport	Zračna Luka	ZRA-chna LU-kah
Good morning	Dobro jutro	DOH-broh YOO-tro	Ticket	Karta	KAHR-tah
Goodbye	Bog	Bog	Taxi	Taksi	TAH-ksee
Sorry/Excuse me	Oprostite	oh-PROH-stee-teh	Hotel	Hotel	HOH-tel
Help!	U pomoć!	OO poh-mohch	Bathroom	zahod	ZAH-hod
I'm lost.	Izgubljen sam.	eez-GUB-lye-n sahm	Open/Closed	Otvoreno/Zatvoreno	OHT-voh-reh-noh/ZAHT-voh-reh-noh
Police	Policija	po-LEE-tsee-ya	Left/Right	Lijevo/Desno	lee-YEH-voh/DEHS-noh
Embassy	Ambasada	ahm-bah-SAH-da	Bank	Banka	BAHN-kah
Passport	Putovnica	POO-toh-vnee-tsah	Exchange	Mjenjačnica	myehn-YAHCH-nee-tsah
Doctor/Hospital	Liječnik/Bolnica	lee-YECH-neek/BOHL-neet-sa	Grocery/Market	Trgovina	TER-goh-vee-nah
Pharmacy	Ljekarna	lye-KHAR-na	Post Office	Pošta	POSH-tah

ENGLISH	CROATIAN	PRONOUNCE
Where is...?	Gdje je...?	GDYE yeh
How much does this cost?	Koliko to košta?	KOH-lee-koh toh KOH-shtah
When is the next...?	Kada polazi sljedeći...?	ka-DA po-LA-zee SLYE-de-tchee
Do you have (a vacant room)?	Imate li (slobodne sobe)?	ee-MAH-teh lee (SLOH-boh-dneh SOH-beh)
I would like...	Želim...	ZHE-leem
I don't eat...	Ne jedem...	ne YEH-dem
Do you speak English?	Govorite li engleski?	GO-vohr-ee-teh lee ehn-GLEH-skee
I don't speak Croatian.	Ne govorim hrvatski.	neh goh-VOH-reem KHR-va-tskee

CZECH

ENGLISH	CZECH	PRONOUNCE	ENGLISH	CZECH	PRONOUNCE
Yes/No	Ano/Ne	AH-no/neh	Train/Bus	Vlak/Autobus	vlahk/OW-toh-boos
Please	Prosím	PROH-seem	Station	Nádraží	NA-drah-zhee
Thank you	Děkuji	DYEH-koo-yee	Airport	Letiště	LEH-teesh-tyeh
Hello	Dobrý den	DOH-bree den	Ticket	Lístek	LIS-tek
Goodbye	Nashledanou	NAS-kleh-dah-noh	Taxi	Taxi	TEHK-see
Sorry/Excuse me	Promiňte	PROH-meen-teh	Hotel	Hotel	HOH-tel
Help!	Pomoc!	POH-mots	Bathroom	WC	VEE-TSEE
I'm lost.	Zabloudil jsem.	ZAH-bloh-dyeel-sem	Open/Closed	Otevřeno/Zavřeno	O-te-zheno/ZAV-rzhen-o
Police	Policie	POH-leets-ee-yeh	Left/Right	Vlevo/Vpravo	VLE-voh/VPRAH-voh

ENGLISH	CZECH	PRONOUNCE	ENGLISH	CZECH	PRONOUNCE
Embassy	Velvyslanectví	VEHL-vee-slah-nehts-vee	Bank	Banka	BAN-ka
Passport	Cestovní pas	TSEH-stohv-nee pahs	Exchange	Směnárna	smyeh-NAR-na
Doctor	Lékař	LEK-arzh	Grocery	Potraviny	PO-tra-vee-nee
Pharmacy	Lékárna	LEE-khaar-nah	Post Office	Pošta	POSH-tah

ENGLISH	CZECH	PRONOUNCE
Where is...?	Kde je...?	gdeh yeh
How much does this cost?	Kolik to stojí?	KOH-lihk STOH-yee
When is the next...?	Kdy jede příští...?	gdi YEH-deh przh-EESH-tyee
Do you have (a vacant room)?	Máte (volný pokoj)?	MAA-teh (VOHL-nee POH-koy)
I would like...	Prosím...	PROH-seem
I do not eat...	Nejím maso...	NEH-yeem MAH-soh
Do you speak English?	Mluvíte anglicky?	MLOO-vit-eh ahng-GLEET-skee
I don't speak Czech.	Nemluvim Česky.	NEH-mloo-veem CHESS-kee

FINNISH

ENGLISH	FINNISH	PRONOUNCE	ENGLISH	FINNISH	PRONOUNCE
Yes/No	Kyllä/Ei	KEW-la/ay	Ticket	Lippu	LIP-ooh
Please	Olkaa hyvä	OHL-ka HEW-va	Train/Bus	Juna/Bussi	YU-nuh/BUS-see
Thank you	Kiitos	KEE-tohss	Boat	Vene	VEH-nay
Hello	Hei	hey	Departures	Lähtevät	lah-teh-VAHT
Goodbye	Näkemiin	NA-keh-meen	Market	Tori	TOH-ree
Sorry/Excuse me	Anteeksi	ON-take-see	Hotel	Hotelli	HO-tehl-lee
Help!	Apua!	AH-poo-ah	Hostel	Retkeilymaja	reht-kayl-oo-MAH-yuh
Police	Poliisi	POH-lee-see	Bathroom	Vessa	VEHS-sah
Embassy	Suurlähetystö	SOOHR-la-heh-toos-ter	Telephone	Puhelin	POO-heh-leen
I'm lost!	Olen kadoksissa!	OH-lehn cou-doc-sissa	Open/Closed	Avoinna/Suljettu	a-VOH-een-ah/sool-JET-too
Railway station	Rautatieasema	ROW-tah-tiah-ah-seh-ma	Hospital	Sairaala	SAIH-raah-lah
Bank	Pankki	PAHNK-kih	Left/Right	Vasen/Oikea	VAH-sen/OY-kay-uh
Currency exchange	Rahanvaihto-piste	RAA-han-vyeh-tow-pees-teh	Post Office	Posti	PAUS-teeh
Airport	lentokenttä	LEH-toh-kehnt-tah	Pharmacy	Apteekki	UHP-take-kee

ENGLISH	FINNISH	PRONOUNCE
Where is...?	Missä on...?	MEE-sah ohn
How do I get to...?	Miten pääsen...?	MEE-ten PA-sen
How much does this cost?	Paljonko se maksaa?	PAHL-yon-ko seh MOCK-sah
I'd like to buy...	Haluaisin ostaa...	HUH-loo-ay-sihn OS-tuh
Do you speak English?	Puhutteko englantia?	POO-hoot-teh-kaw ENG-lan-tee-ah
When is the next...?	Milloin on seuraava...?	MEEHL-loyhn OHN SEUH-raah-vah
I don't speak Finnish.	En puhu suomea.	ehn POO-hoo SUA-meh-ah
I'm allergic to/I cannot eat...	En voi syödä...	ehn voy SEW-dah

FRENCH

ENGLISH	FRENCH	PRONOUNCE	ENGLISH	FRENCH	PRONOUNCE
Hello	Bonjour	bohn-zhoor	Exchange	L'échange	lay-shanzh
Please	S'il vous plaît	see voo pley	Grocery	L'épicerie	lay-pees-ree
Thank you	Merci	mehr-see	Market	Le marché	leuh marzh-chay
Excuse me	Excusez-moi	ex-ku-zey mwah	Police	La police	la poh-lees
Yes/No	Oui/Non	wee/nohn	Embassy	L'ambassade	lahm-ba-sahd
Goodbye	Au revoir	oh ruh-vwahr	Passport	Le passeport	leuh pass-por
Help!	Au secours!	oh seh-coor	Post Office	La poste	la pohst
I'm lost.	Je suis perdu.	zhe swee pehr-doo	One-way	Le billet simple	leuh bee-ay samp
Train/Bus	Le train/Le bus	leuh tran/leuh boos	Round-trip	Le billet aller-retour	leuh bee-ay a-lay-re-toor
Station	La gare	la gahr	Ticket	Le billet	leuh bee-ay
Airport	L'aéroport	la-ehr-o-por	Single room	Une chambre simple	oon shahm-br samp
Hotel	L'hôtel	lo-tel	Double room	Une chambre pour deux	oon shahm-br poor duh
Hostel	L'auberge	lo-berzhe	With shower	Avec une douche	ah-vec une doosh
Bathroom	La salle de bain	la sal de bahn	Taxi	Le taxi	leuh tax-ee
Open/Closed	Ouvert/Fermé	oo-ver/fer-may	Ferry	Le bac	leuh bak
Doctor	Le médecin	leuh mehd-sen	Tourist office	Le bureau de tourisme	leuh byur-oh de toor-eesm
Hospital	L'hôpital	loh-pee-tal	Town hall	L'hôtel de ville	lo-tel de veel
Pharmacy	La pharmacie	la far-ma-see	Vegetarian	Végétarien	vay-jay-ta-ree-ehn
Left/Right	À gauche/À droite	a gohsh/a dwat	Kosher/Halal	Kascher/Halal	ka-shey/ha-lal
Straight	Tout droit	too dwa	Newsstand	Le tabac	leuh ta-bac
Turn	Tournez	toor-neh	Cigarette	La cigarette	la see-ga-ret

ENGLISH	FRENCH	PRONOUNCE
Do you speak English?	Parlez-vous anglais?	par-leh voo ahn-gleh
Where is...?	Où se trouve...?	oo seh-trhoov
When is the next...?	À quelle heure part le prochain...?	ah kel ur par leuh pro-chan
How much does this cost?	Ça fait combien?	sah f com-bee-en?
Do you have rooms available?	Avez-vous des chambres disponibles?	av-eh voo deh shahm-br dees-pon-eeb-bl?
I would like ...	Je voudrais...	zhe voo-dreh
I don't speak French.	Je ne parle pas Français.	zhe neuh parl pah frawn-seh
I'm allergic to...	Je suis allergique à...	zhe swee al-ehr-zheek a
I love you.	Je t'aime.	zhe tem

GERMAN

ENGLISH	GERMAN	PRONOUNCE	ENGLISH	GERMAN	PRONOUNCE
Yes/No	Ja/Nein	yah/nein	Train/Bus	Zug/Bus	tsoog/boos
Please	Bitte	BIH-tuh	Station	Bahnhof	BAHN-hohf
Thank you	Danke	DAHNG-kuh	Airport	Flughafen	FLOOG-hah-fen
Hello	Hallo	HAH-lo	Taxi	Taxi	TAHK-see
Goodbye	Auf Wiedersehen	owf VEE-der-zehn	Ticket	Fahrkarte	FAR-kar-tuh

ENGLISH	GERMAN	PRONOUNCE	ENGLISH	GERMAN	PRONOUNCE
Excuse me	Entschuldigung	ent-SHOOL-dih-gung	Departure	Abfahrt	AHB-fart
Help!	Hilfe!	HIL-fuh	One-way	Einfache	AYHN-fah-kuh
I'm lost.	Ich habe mich verlaufen.	eesh HAH-buh meesh fer-LAU-fun	Round-trip	Hin und zurück	hin oond tsuh-RYOOK
Police	Polizei	poh-lee-TSAI	Reservation	Reservierung	reh-zer-VEER-ung
Embassy	Botschaft	BOAT-shahft	Ferry	Fährschiff	FAYHR-shiff
Passport	Reisepass	RYE-zeh-pahss	Bank	Bank	bahnk
Doctor/Hospital	Arzt/Kranken-haus	ahrtst/KRANK-en-house	Exchange	Wechseln	VEHK-zeln
Pharmacy	Apotheke	AH-po-TAY-kuh	Grocery	Lebensmittelge-schäft	LAY-bens-miht-tel-guh-SHEFT
Hotel/Hostel	Hotel/Jugendherberge	ho-TEL/YOO-gend-air-BAIR-guh	Tourist office	Touristbüro	TU-reest-byur-oh
Single room	Einzelzimmer	EIN-tsel-tsihm-meh	Post Office	Postamt	POST-ahmt
Double room	Doppelzimmer	DOP-pel-tsihm-meh	Old Town/City Center	Altstadt	AHLT-shtat
Dorm	Schlafsaal	SHLAF-zahl	Vegetarian	Vegetarier	Feh-geh-TAYR-ee-er
With shower	Mit dusche	mitt DOO-shuh	Vegan	Veganer	FEH-gan-er
Bathroom	Badezimmer	BAH-deh-tsihm-meh	Kosher/Halal	Koscher/Halaal	KOH-shehr/hah-LAAL
Open/Closed	Geöffnet/Geschlossen	geh-UHF-net/geh-SHLOS-sen	Nuts/Milk	Nüsse/Milch	NYOO-seh/mihlsh
Left/Right	Links/Rechts	lihnks/rekhts	Bridge	Brücke	BRUKE-eh
Straight	Geradeaus	geh-RAH-de-OWS	Castle	Schloß	shloss
(To) Turn	Drehen	DREH-ehn	Square	Platz	plahtz

ENGLISH	GERMAN	PRONOUNCE
Where is...?	Wo ist...?	vo ihst
How do I get to...?	Wie komme ich nach...?	vee KOM-muh eesh NAHKH
How much does that cost?	Wieviel kostet das?	VEE-feel KOS-tet das
Do you have...?	Haben Sie...?	HOB-en zee
I would like...	Ich möchte...	eesh MERSH-teh
I'm allergic to...	Ich bin zu...allergisch.	eesh bihn tsoo...ah-LEHR-gish
Do you speak English?	Sprechen sie Englisch?	SHPREK-en zee EHNG-lish
I do not speak German.	Ich spreche kein Deutsch.	eesh-SHPREK-eh kyne DOYCH
I'm waiting for my boyfriend/husband.	Ich warte auf meinen Freund/Mann.	eesh VAHR-tuh owf MYN-en froynd/mahn

GREEK

ENGLISH	GREEK	PRONOUNCE	ENGLISH	GREEK	PRONOUNCE
Yes/No	Ναι/Όχι	neh/OH-hee	Train/Bus	Τραίνο/Λεωφορείο	TREH-no/leh-o-fo-REE-o
Please	Παρακαλώ	pah-rah-kah-LO	Ferry	Πλοίο	PLEE-o
Thank you	Ευχαριστώ	ef-hah-ree-STO	Station	Σταθμός	stath-MOS
Hello/Goodbye	Γειά σας	YAH-sas	Airport	Αεροδρόμιο	ah-e-ro-DHRO-mee-o
Sorry/Excuse me	Συγνόμη	sig-NO-mee	Taxi	Ταξί	tah-XEE
Help!	Βοήθειά!	vo-EE-thee-ah	Hotel/Hostel	Ξενοδοχείο	kse-no-dho-HEE-o

ENGLISH	GREEK	PRONOUNCE	ENGLISH	GREEK	PRONOUNCE
I'm lost.	Έχω χαθεί.	EH-o ha-THEE	Rooms to let	Δωμάτια	do-MA-tee-ah
Police	Αστυνομία	as-tee-no-MEE-a	Bathroom	Τουαλέττα	tou-ah-LET-ta
Embassy	Πρεσβεία	prez-VEE-ah	Open/Closed	Ανοικτό/ Κλειστό	ah-nee-KTO/ klee-STO
Passport	Διαβατήριο	dhee-ah-vah-TEE-ree-o	Left/Right	Αριστερα/ Δεξία	aiis-te-RA/ de-XIA
Doctor	Γιατρός	yah-TROSE	Bank	Τράπεζα	TRAH-peh-zah
Pharmacy	Φαρμακείο	fahr-mah-KEE-o	Exchange	Ανταλλάσσω	an-da-LAS-so
Post Office	Ταχυδρομείο	ta-hi-dhro-MEE-o	Market	Αγορά	ah-go-RAH

ENGLISH	GREEK	PRONOUNCE
Where is...?	Που είναι...?	poo-EE-neh
How much does this cost?	Πόσο κάνει?	PO-so KAH-nee
Do you have (a vacant room)?	Μηπώς έχετε (ελέυθερα δωμάτια)?	mee-POSE EK-he-teh (e-LEF-the-ra dho-MA-tee-a)
I would like...	Θα ήθελα...	thah EE-the-lah
Do you speak English?	Μιλατε αγγλικά?	mee-LAH-teh ahn-glee-KAH
I don't speak Greek.	Δεν μιλαώ ελληνικά.	dthen mee-LOW el-lee-nee-KAH

HUNGARIAN

ENGLISH	HUNGARIAN	PRONOUNCE	ENGLISH	HUNGARIAN	PRONOUNCE
Yes/No	Igen/Nem	EE-ghen/nehm	Train/Bus	Vonat/Autóbusz	VAW-noht/AU-OO-toh-boos
Please	Kérem	KEH-rehm	Train Station	Pályaudvar	pah-yoh-OOT-vahr
Thank you	Köszönöm	KUH-suh-nuhm	Airport	Repülőtér	rep-oo-loo-TAYR
Hello	Szervusz	SAYHR-voose	Ticket	Jegyet	YEHD-eht
Goodbye	Viszontlátásra	VEE-sohnt-laht-ah-shrah	Bus Station	Buszmegálló	boos-mehg-AH-loh
Excuse me	Elnézést	EHL-neh-zaysht	Hotel	Szálloda	SAH-law-dah
Help!	Segítség!	she-GHEET-sheg	Toilet	WC	VEH-tseh
I'm lost.	Eltévedtem.	el-TEH-ved-tem	Open/Closed	Nyitva/Zárva	NYEET-vah/ ZAHR-vuh
Police	Rendőrség	REN-dur-shayg	Left/Right	Bal/Jobb	bol/yowb
Embassy	Követséget	ker-vet-SHE-get	Bank	Bank	bohnk
Passport	Az útlevelemet	ahz oot-leh-veh-leh-meht	Exchange	Pénzaváltó	pehn-zah-VAHL-toh
Doctor/ Hospital	Orvos/Kórház	OR-vosh/kohr-HAAZ	Grocery	Élelmiszerbolt	EH-lehl-meh-sehr-bawlt
Pharmacy	Gyógyszertár	DYAW-dyser-tar	Post Office	Posta	PAWSH-tuh

ENGLISH	HUNGARIAN	PRONOUNCE
Where is...?	Hol van...?	haul vahn
How much does this cost?	Mennyibe kerül?	MEHN-yee-beh KEH-rool
When is the next...?	Mikor indul a következő...?	mee-KOR in-DUL ah ker-VET-ke-zoer
Do you have (a vacant room)?	Van üres (szoba)?	vahn ew-REHSH (SAH-bah)
Can I have...?	Kaphatok...?	KAH-foht-tohk
I do not eat...	Nem eszem...	nem EH-sem
Do you speak English?	Beszél angolul?	BESS-ayl AHN-gawl-ool
I don't speak Hungarian.	Nem tudok magyarul.	nehm TOO-dawk MAW-jyah-rool

APPENDIX

ITALIAN

ENGLISH	ITALIAN	PRONOUNCE	ENGLISH	ITALIAN	PRONOUNCE
Hello (informal/formal)	Ciao/Buongiorno	chow/bwohn-JOHR-noh	Bank	La banca	lah bahn-KAH
Please	Per favore/Per piacere	pehr fah-VOH-reh/pehr pyah-CHEH-reh	Supermarket	Il Supermercato	eel soo-pair-mehr-CAHT-oh
Thank you	Grazie	GRAHT-see-yeh	Exchange	Il cambio	eel CAHM-bee-oh
Sorry/Excuse me	Mi dispiace/Scusi	mee dees-PYAH-cheh/SKOO-zee	Police	La Polizia	lah po-LEET-ZEE-ah
Yes/No	Sì/No	see/no	Embassy	L'Ambasciata	lahm-bah-SHAH-tah
Help!	Aiuto!	ah-YOO-toh	Goodbye	Arrivederci/Arrivederla	ah-ree-veh-DAIR-chee/ah-ree-veh-DAIR-lah
I'm lost.	Sono perso.	SO-noh PERH-so	One-way	Solo andata	SO-lo ahn-DAH-tah
Train/Bus	Il treno/l'autobus	eel TREH-no/laow-toh-BOOS	Round-trip	Andata e ritorno	ahn-DAH-tah eh ree-TOHR-noh
Station	La stazione	lah staht-see-YOH-neh	Ticket	Il biglietto	eel beel-YEHT-toh
Airport	L'aeroporto	LAYR-o-PORT-o	Single room	Una camera singola	OO-nah CAH-meh-rah SEEN-goh-lah
Hotel/Hostel	L'albergo/L'ostello	lal-BEHR-go/los-TEHL-loh	Left/Right	Sinistra/destra	see-NEE-strah/DEH-strah
Bathroom	Un gabinetto/Un bagno	oon gah-bee-NEHT-toh/oon BAHN-yoh	Double room	Una camera doppia	OO-nah CAH-meh-rah DOH-pee-yah
Open/Closed	Aperto/Chiuso	ah-PAIR-toh/KYOO-zoh	Tourist office	L'Ufficio Turistico	loof-FEETCH-o tur-EES-tee-koh
Doctor	Il medico	eel MEH-dee-koh	Ferry	Il traghetto	eel tra-GHEHT-toh
Hospital	L'ospedale	lohs-sped-DAL-e	Tip	La mancia	lah MAHN-cha
Vegetarian	Vegetariano	veh-jeh-tar-ee-AN-oh	Kosher/Halal	Kasher/Halal	KA-sher/HA-lal
Turn	Gira a	JEE-rah ah	Bill	Il conto	eel COHN-toh

ENGLISH	ITALIAN	PRONOUNCE
Do you speak English?	Parla inglese?	PAHR-lah een-GLAY-zeh
Where is...?	Dov'è...?	doh-VEH
When is the next...?	A che ora è il prossimo...?	AH keh OH-rah eh eel pross-EE-moh
How much does this cost?	Quanto costa?	KWAN-toh CO-stah
Do you have rooms available?	Ha camere libere?	ah CAH-mer-reh LEE-ber-eh
I would like...	Vorrei...	VOH-reh
I don't speak Italian.	Non parlo italiano.	nohn PARL-loh ee-tahl-YAH-noh
Not even if you were the last man on Earth!	Neanche se tu fossi l'unico uomo sulla terra!	neh-AHN-keh seh too FOH-see LOO-nee-koh WOH-moh soo-LAH TEH-rah!

LITHUANIAN

ENGLISH	LITHUANIAN	PRONOUNCE	ENGLISH	LITHUANIAN	PRONOUNCE
Yes/no	Taip/ne	tayp/neh	Train/Bus	Traukinys/auto-busas	TROW-kihn-ees/ow-to-BOO-sahs
Please	Prašau	prah-SHAU	Station	Stotis	STOH-tees
Thank you	Ačiū	AH-chyoo	Airport	Oro uostas	OH-roh oo-OH-stahs
Hello	Labas	LAH-bahss	Ticket	Bilietas	BEE-lee-tahs
Goodbye	Viso gero	VEE-soh GEH-roh	Hotel	Viešbutis	vee-esh-BOO-tihs
Sorry/Excuse me	Atsiprašau	aht-sih-prah-SHAU	Bathroom	Tualetas	too-ah-LEH-tas
Help!	Gelbėkite!	GYEL-behk-ite	Open/Closed	Atidarytas/uždarytas	ah-tee-DAH-ree-tas/ oozh-DAH-ree-tas
Police	Policija	po-LEET-siya	Exchange	Valiutos keiti-mas	va-lee-OOT-os keh-TEE-mahs
Market	Turgus	TOORG-us	Post Office	Paštas	PAHSH-tahs

ENGLISH	LITHUANIAN	PRONOUNCE
Where is...?	Kur yra...?	koor ee-RAH
How much does this cost?	Kiek kainuoja?	KEE-yek KYE-new-oh-yah
Do you speak English?	Ar Jūs kalbate angliškai?	ahr yoos KAHL-bah-teh AHNG-leesh-kai
I do not speak Lithuanian.	Aš nekalbu lietuviškai	ash ne-KAL-boo lut-VEESH-kee

NORWEGIAN

ENGLISH	NORWEGIAN	PRONOUNCE	ENGLISH	NORWEGIAN	PRONOUNCE
Yes/No	Ja/Nei	yah/neh	Ticket	Billett	bee-LEHT
Please	Vær så snill	vah sho SNEEL	Train/Bus	Toget/Buss	TOR-guh/buhs
Thank you	Takk	tahk	Airport	Lufthavn	LUFT-hahn
Hello	Goddag	gud-DAHG	Departures	Avgang	AHV-gahng
Goodbye	Ha det bra	HAH deh BRAH	Market	Torget	TOHR-geh
Sorry/Excuse me	Unnskyld	UHRN-shuhrl (UHN-shuhl)	Hotel/Hostel	Hotell/Van-drerhjem	hoo-TEHL/VAN-drair-yaim
Help!	Hjelp!	yehlp	Pharmacy	Apotek	ah-pu-TAYK
Police	politiet	poh-lih-TEE-eh	Toilets	Toalettene	tuah-LEHT-tuh-nuh
Embassy	Ambassade	ahm-bah-SAH-duh	City center	Sentrum	SEHN-trum
I'm lost.	Jeg har gått meg bort	yai har goht mai boort	Open/Closed	Åpen/Stengt	OH-pen/Stengt
Railway sta-tion	Jernbanestas-jon	YEH'N-baa-ne-stah-shuh-nen	Hospital	Sykehus	SHUCK-hoos
Bank	Bank	banhk	Left/Right	Venstre/Høyre	VEHN-stre/HUHR-uh
Currency exchange	Vekslingskontor	VEHK-shlings-koon-toohr	Post Office	Postkontor	POST-koon-toohr

ENGLISH	NORWEGIAN	PRONOUNCE
Where is...?	Hvor er...?	VORR ahr
How do I get to...?	Hvordan kommer jeg til...?	VOOR-dan KOH-mer yai teel
How much is...?	Hvor mye koster...?	voor MEE-uh KOH-ster

ENGLISH	NORWEGIAN	PRONOUNCE
Do you speak English?	Snakker du engelsk?	SNA-koh dü EHNG-olsk
When is the...?	Når går...?	nohr gohr
I don't speak Norwegian.	Jeg snakker ikke norsk.	yeh SNAH-kerr IK-ker noshk
Do you have any vacancies?	Har dere noen ledige rom?	har DEH-reh NOO-en LAY-dee-yuh room

POLISH

ENGLISH	POLISH	PRONOUNCE	ENGLISH	POLISH	PRONOUNCE
Yes/No	Tak/Nie	tahk/nyeh	Train/Bus	Pociąg/Autobus	POH-chawnk/ow-TOH-booss
Please	Proszę	PROH-sheh	Train Station	Dworzec	DVOH-zhets
Thank you	Dziękuję	jen-KOO-yeh	Airport	Lotnisko	loht-NEE-skoh
Hello	Cześć	cheshch	Ticket	Bilet	BEE-leht
Goodbye	Do widzenia	doh veed-ZEHN-yah	Hostel	Schronisko młodzieżowe	sroh-NEE-skoh mwo-jeh-ZHO-veh
Sorry/Excuse me	Przepraszam	psheh-PRAH-shahm	Bathroom	Toaleta	toh-ah-LEH-tah
Help!	Pomocy!	poh-MOH-tsih	Open/Closed	Otwarty/Zamknięty	ot-FAHR-tih/zahmk-NYENT-ih
I'm lost.	Zgubiłem się.	zgoo-BEE-wem sheh	Left/Right	Lewo/Prawo	LEH-voh/PRAH-voh
Police	Policja	poh-LEETS-yah	Bank	Bank	bahnk
Embassy	Ambasada	am-ba-SA-da	Exchange	Kantor	KAHN-tor
Doctor/Hospital	Lekarz/Szpital	LEH-kazh/SHPEE-tal	Grocery/Market	Sklep spożywczy	sklehp spoh-ZHIV-chih
Pharmacy	Apteka	ahp-TEH-ka	Post Office	Poczta	POHCH-tah

ENGLISH	POLISH	PRONOUNCE
Where is...?	Gdzie jest...?	g-JEH yest...?
How much does this cost?	Ile to kosztuje?	EE-leh toh kohsh-TOO-yeh
When is the next...?	O której jest następny...?	o KTOO-rey yest nas-TEMP-nee
Do you have (a vacant room)?	Czy są (jakieś wolne pokoje)?	chih SAWN (yah-kyesh VOHL-neh poh-KOY-eh)
I'd like to order...	Chciałbym zamówić...	kh-CHOW-bihm za-MOOV-eech
I do not eat...	Nie jadam...	nyeh JAH-dahm
Do you (m/f) speak English?	Czy pan(i) mówi po angielsku?	chih PAHN(-ee) MOO-vee poh ahn-GYEL-skoo
I don't speak Polish.	Nie mowię po polsku.	nyeh MOO-vyeh poh POHL-skoo

PORTUGUESE

ENGLISH	PORTUGUESE	PRONOUNCE	ENGLISH	PORTUGUESE	PRONOUNCE
Hello	Olá/Oi	oh-LAH/oy	Hotel	Pousada	poh-ZAH-dah
Please	Por favor	pohr fah-VOHR	Bathroom	Banheiro	bahn-YEH-roo
Thank you (m/f)	Obrigado/Obrigada	oh-bree-GAH-doo/dah	Open/Closed	Aberto/Fechado	ah-BEHR-toh/feh-CHAH-do
Sorry/Excuse me	Desculpe	dish-KOOLP-eh	Doctor	Médico	MEH-dee-koo
Yes/No	Sim/Não	seem/now	Pharmacy	Farmácia	far-MAH-see-ah

ENGLISH	PORTUGUESE	PRONOUNCE	ENGLISH	PORTUGUESE	PRONOUNCE
Goodbye	Adeus	ah-DEH-oosh	Left/Right	Esquerda/ Direita	esh-KER-dah/ dee-REH-tah
Help!	Socorro!	soh-KOO-roh	Bank	Banco	BAHN-koh
I'm lost.	Estou perdido	ish-TOW per-DEE-doo	Exchange	Câmbio	CAHM-bee-yoo
Ticket	Bilhete	beel-YEHT	Market	Mercado	mer-KAH-doo
Train/Bus	Comboio/ Autocarro	kom-BOY-yoo/ OW-to-KAH-roo	Police	Polícia	po-LEE-see-ah
Station	Estação	eh-stah-SAO	Embassy	Embaixada	ehm-bai-SHAH-dah
Airport	Aeroporto	aye-ro-POR-too	Post Office	Correio	coh-REH-yoh

ENGLISH	PORTUGUESE	PRONOUNCE
Do you speak English?	Fala inglês?	FAH-lah een-GLAYSH
Where is...?	Onde é...?	OHN-deh eh
How much does this cost?	Quanto custa?	KWAHN-too KOOSH-tah
Do you have rooms available?	Tem quartos disponíveis?	teng KWAHR-toosh dish-po-NEE-veysh
I want/would like...	Eu quero/gostaria de...	eh-oo KER-oh/gost-ar-EE-ah deh
I don't speak Portuguese.	Não falo Português	now FAH-loo por-too-GEZH
I cannot eat...	Não posso comer...	now POH-soo coh-MEHR
Another round, please.	Mais uma rodada, por favor.	maish OO-mah roh-DAH-dah pohr fah-VOHR

ROMANIAN

ENGLISH	ROMANIAN	PRONOUNCE	ENGLISH	ROMANIAN	PRONOUNCE
Yes/No	Da/Nu	dah/noo	Train/Bus	Trenul/Autobuz	TREH-nuhl/au-toh-BOOZ
Please/ Thank you	Vă rog/ Mulţumesc	vuh rohg/ mool-tsoo-MESK	Station	Gară	GAH-ruh
Hello	Bună ziua	BOO-nuh ZEE-wah	Airport	Aeroportul	ai-roh-POHR-tool
Goodbye	La revedere	lah reh-veh-DEH-reh	Ticket	Bilet	bee-LEHT
Sorry	Îmi pare rău	uhm PAH-reh ruh-oo	Taxi	Taxi	tak-SEE
Excuse me	Scuzaţi-mă	skoo-ZAH-tsee muh	Hotel	Hotel	ho-TEHL
Help!	Ajutor!	ah-zhoo-TOHR	Bathroom	Toaletă	toh-ah-LEH-tah
I'm lost.	Sînt pierdut.	sunt PYER-dut	Open/Closed	Deschis/închis	DESS-kees/un-KEES
Police	Poliţie	poh-LEE-tsee-eh	Left/Right	Stânga/ Dreapta	STUHN-gah/ drahp-TAH
Embassy	Ambasada	ahm-bah-SAH-da	Bank	Banca	BAHN-cah
Passport	Paşaport	pah-shah-PORT	Exchange	Birou de schimb	bee-ROW deh skeemb
Doctor/ Hospital	Doctorul/ spitalul	DOK-toh-rul/ SPEE-ta-lul	Grocery	Alimentară	a-lee-men-TAH-ruh
Pharmacy	Farmacie	fahr-ma-CHEE-eh	Post Office	Poşta	POH-shta

ENGLISH	ROMANIAN	PRONOUNCE
Where is...?	Unde e...?	OON-deh YEH
How much does this cost?	Cât costă?	kuht KOH-stuh
When is the next...?	Cînd este următorul...?	kuhnd es-te ur-muh-TOH-rul
Do you have (a vacant room)?	Aveţi (camere libere)?	a-VETS (KAH-meh-reh LEE-beh-reh)
I would like...	Aş vrea...	ahsh vreh-AH
I do not eat...	Eu nu mănînc...	yau noo muh-NUHNK
Do you speak English?	Vorbiţi englezeşte?	vohr-BEETS ehng-leh-ZEHSH-teh
I don't speak Romanian.	Nu vorbesc Românеşte.	noo vohr-BEHSK roh-muh-NEHSH-teh

RUSSIAN

ENGLISH	RUSSIAN	PRONOUNCE	ENGLISH	RUSSIAN	PRONOUNCE
Yes/No	Да/нет	dah/nyet	Train/Bus	Поезд/автобус	POH-yihzt/av-TOH-boos
Please	Пожалуйста	pah-ZHAHL-uy-stah	Station	вокзал	vak-ZAL
Thank you	Спасибо	spa-SEE-bah	Airport	аэропорт	ai-roh-PORT
Hello	Здравствуйте	ZDRAHV-zvuht-yeh	Ticket	билет	bil-YET
Goodbye	До свидания	da svee-DAHN-yah	Hotel	гостиница	gahs-TEE-nee-tsah
Sorry/Excuse me	Извините	eez-vee-NEET-yeh	Dorm/Hostel	общежитие	ob-sheh-ZHEE-tee-yeh
Help!	Помогите!	pah-mah-GEE-tyeh	Bathroom	туалет	TOO-ah-lyet
I'm lost.	Я потерен.	ya po-TYE-ren	Open/Closed	открыт/закрыт	ot-KRIHT/za-KRIHT
Police	милиция	mee-LEE-tsee-ya	Left/Right	налево/направо	nah-LYEH-vah/nah-PRAH-vah
Embassy	посольство	pah-SOHL-stva	Bank	банк	bahnk
Passport	паспорт	PAS-pahrt	Exchange	обмен валюты	ab-MYEHN val-ee-YU-tee
Doctor/Hospital	Врач/больница	vrach/bol-NEE-tsa	Grocery/Market	гастроном/рынок	gah-stroh-NOM/REE-nohk
Pharmacy	аптека	ahp-TYE-kah	Post Office	Почта	POCH-ta

ENGLISH	RUSSIAN	PRONOUNCE
Where is...?	Где...?	gdyeh
How much does this cost?	Сколько это стоит?	SKOHL-ka EH-ta STOY-iht
When is the next...?	Когда будет следущий...?	kog-DAH BOOD-yet SLYED-ooshee
Do you have a vacancy?	У вас есть свободный номер?	oo vahs yehst svah-BOHD-neey NOH-myehr
I'd like (m/f)...	Я хотел(а) бы...	ya khah-TYEL(a) bwee
I do not eat...	Я не ем...	ya nye yem
Do you speak English?	Вы говорите по-английски?	vy gah-vah-REE-tyeh pah ahn-GLEE-skee
I don't speak Russian.	Я не говорю по-русски.	yah neh gah-vah-RYOO pah ROO-skee

SPANISH

ENGLISH	SPANISH	PRONOUNCE	ENGLISH	SPANISH	PRONOUNCE
Hello	Hola	O-lah	Hotel/Hostel	Hotel/Hostal	oh-TEL/ohs-TAHL
Please	Por favor	pohr fah-VOHR	Bathroom	Baño	BAHN-yoh
Thank you	Gracias	GRAH-see-ahs	Open/Closed	Abierto(a)/Cerrado(a)	ah-bee-EHR-toh/ sehr-RAH-doh
Sorry/ Excuse me	Perdón	pehr-DOHN	Doctor	Médico	MEH-dee-koh
Yes/No	Sí/No	see/no	Pharmacy	Farmacia	far-MAH-see-ah
Goodbye	Adiós	ah-dee-OHS	Left/Right	Izquierda/ Derecha	ihz-kee-EHR-da/ deh-REH-chah
Help!	¡Ayuda!	ay-YOOH-dah	Bank	Banco	BAHN-koh
I'm lost.	Estoy perdido (a).	ess-TOY pehr-DEE-doh (dah)	Exchange	Cambio	CAHM-bee-oh
Ticket	Boleto	boh-LEH-toh	Grocery	Supermercado	soo-pehr-mer-KAH-doh
Train/Bus	Tren/ Autobús	trehn/ ow-toh-BOOS	Police	Policía	poh-lee-SEE-ah
Station	Estación	es-tah-see-OHN	Embassy	Embajada	em-bah-HA-dah
Airport	Aeropuerto	ay-roh-PWER-toh	Post Office	Oficina de correos	oh-fee-SEE-nah deh coh-REH-ohs

ENGLISH	SPANISH	PRONOUNCE
Do you speak English?	¿Habla inglés?	AH-blah een-GLEHS?
Where is...?	¿Dónde está...?	DOHN-deh eh-STA?
How much does this cost?	¿Cuánto cuesta...?	KWAN-toh KWEHS-tah...?
Do you have rooms available?	¿Tiene habitaciones libres?	tee-YEH-neh ah-bee-tah-see-YOH-nehs LEE-brehs?
I want/ would like...	Quiero/Me gustaría...	kee-YEH-roh/may goos-tah-REE-ah
I don't speak Spanish.	No hablo español.	no AH-bloh ehs-pahn-YOHL
I cannot eat...	No puedo comer...	no PWEH-doh coh-MEHR...

SWEDISH

ENGLISH	SWEDISH	PRONOUNCE	ENGLISH	SWEDISH	PRONOUNCE
Yes/No	Ja/Nej	yah/nay	Ticket	Biljett	bihl-YEHT
Please	Va så snäll	VAH sahw snel	Train/Bus	Tåget/Buss	TOH-get/boos
Thank you	Tack	tahk	Ferry	Färjan	FAR-yuhn
Hello	Hej	hay	Departure	Avgångar	uhv-GONG-er
Goodbye	Hejdå	HAY-doh	Market	Torget	TOHR-yet
Excuse me	Ursäkta mig	oor-SHEHK-tuh MAY	Hotel/Hostel	Hotell/Vandrarhem	hoo-TEHL/vun-DRAR-huhm
Help!	Hjälp!	yehlp	Pharmacy	Apotek	uh-poo-TEEK
Police	Polisen	poo-LEE-sehn	Toilets	Toaletten	too-uh-LEHT-en
Embassy	Ambassad	uhm-bah-SAHD	Post Office	Posten	POHS-tehn
I'm lost.	Jag har kommit bort.	yuh hahr KUM-met borht	Open/Closed	Öppen/Stängd	UH-pen/staingd
Railway station	Järnvägsstationen	yairn-vas-guesstah-SHO-nen	Hospital	Sjukhus	SHUHK-huhs
Currency exchange	Växel kontor	vai-xil KOON-toohr	Left/Right	Vänster/Höger	VAIN-ster/ HUH-ger

ENGLISH	SWEDISH	PRONOUNCE
Where is...?	Var finns...?	vahr FIHNS
How much does this cost?	Hur mycket kostar det?	hurr MUEK-keh KOS-tuhr deh
I'd like to buy...	Jag skulle vilja köpa...	yuh SKOO-leh vihl-yuh CHEU-pah
Do you speak English?	Talar du engelska?	TAH-luhr du EHNG-ehl-skuh
I don't speak Swedish.	Jag talar inte svenska.	yuh tahlahr ihntuh svenskah
I'm allergic to/I cannot eat...	Jag är allergisk mot/Jag kan inte ata...	yuh air ALLEHR-ghihsk moot/yuh kahn intuh aitah
Do you have rooms available?	Har Ni fria rum?	harh nih freeah ruhm

WEATHER

City	JANUARY			APRIL			JULY			OCTOBER		
	High (F/C)	Low (F/C)	Rain (in.)	High (F/C)	Low (F/C)	Rain (in.)	High (F/C)	Low (F/C)	Rain (in.)	High (F/C)	Low (F/C)	Rain (in.)
Amsterdam	40/4	31/-1	2.7	55/13	38/3	2.1	71/22	53/12	3	58/14	44/7	2.9
Athens	56/13	44/7	1.8	66/19	53/12	1.0	88/31	73/23	0.2	73/22	59/15	1.9
Berlin	35/2	26/-3	1.7	55/13	39/4	1.7	73/23	55/13	2.1	55/13	42/6	1.4
Copenhagen	37/2	30/-1	1.7	49/9	36/2	1.6	69/20	55/12	2.6	53/11	44/6	2.1
Dublin	46/8	37/3	2.7	53/12	40/4	2.0	66/19	53/12	2.0	57/14	46/8	2.8
London	44/7	32/0	3.1	54/12	38/3	2.1	71/22	52/11	1.8	59/15	43/6	2.9
Madrid	51/10	32/0	1.8	63/17	42/5	1.8	90/32	61/16	0.4	68/20	47/8	1.8
Paris	43/6	34/1	2.2	57/13	42/5	1.7	75/23	58/14	2.3	59/15	46/7	2.0
Rome	55/13	38/3	3.2	64/18	46/8	2.2	83/28	64/18	0.6	71/22	53/12	3.7
Vienna	36/2	27/-3	1.5	57/14	41/5	2.0	77/25	59/15	2.5	57/14	43/6	1.6

APPENDIX

INDEX

INDEX

INDEX

INDEX

GET CONNECTED & SAVE WITH THE HI CARD

An HI card gives you access to friendly and affordable accommodations at over 4,000 hostels in over 60 countries, including across Europe. Members also receive complementary travel insurance, members-only airfare deals, and thousands of discounts on everything from tours and dining to shopping, communications and transportation.

Join millions of HI members worldwide who save money and have more fun every time they travel.

 Hostelling International USA

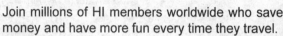

MAP INDEX

MAP LEGEND

■ Sight/Service	✈ Airport
🏠 Accommodation	⌂ Arch/Gate
▲ Camping	$ Bank
🍴 Food	🏖 Beach
☕ Cafe	🚌 Bus Station
🏛 Museum	⊙ Capital City
● Sight	🏰 Castle
🍺 Bar/Pub	⊤ Church
★ Nightlife	⚑ Consulate/Embassy
Park	Water	Beach

⚏ Convent/Monastery	℞ Pharmacy
⚓ Ferry Landing	✚ Police
(347) Highway Sign	✉ Post Office
✚ Hospital	⛷ Skiing
💻 Internet Cafe	✡ Synagogue
Library	☎ Telephone Office
M Ⓜ Metro Station	⛉ Theater
▲ Mountain	ⓘ Tourist Office
🕌 Mosque	🚆 Train Station
Pedestrian Zone	
Stairs	🧭 The Let's Go compass always points NORTH